TheStreet Ratings' Guide to Bond and Money Market Mutual Funds

TheStreet Ratings' Guide to Bond and Money Market Mutual Funds

A Quarterly Compilation of Investment Ratings and Analyses Covering Fixed Income Funds

Spring 2016

GREY HOUSE PUBLISHING

TheStreet, Inc.
14 Wall Street, 15th Floor
New York, NY 10005
800-706-2501

TheStreet Ratings

Published by Grey House Publishing, Inc. located at 4919 Route 22, Amenia, NY, 12501; telephone 518-789-8700. Grey House Publishing neither guarantees the accuracy of the data contained herein nor assumes any responsibility for errors, omissions or discrepancies. Grey House Publishing accepts no payment for listing; inclusion in the publication of any organization agency, institution, publication, service or individual does not imply endorsement of the publisher.

Grey House Publishing
4919 Route 22
PO Box 56
Amenia, NY 12501-0056

Edition No. 66, Spring 2016

ISBN: 978-1-61925-994-2
ISSN: 2158-5997

Contents

Terms and Conditions

This Document is prepared strictly for the confidential use of our customer(s). It has been provided to you at your specific request. It is not directed to, or intended for distribution to or use by, any person or entity who is a citizen or resident of or located in any locality, state, country or other jurisdiction where such distribution, publication, availability or use would be contrary to law or regulation or which would subject TheStreet Ratings or its affiliates to any registration or licensing requirement within such jurisdiction.

No part of the analysts' compensation was, is, or will be, directly or indirectly, related to the specific recommendations or views expressed in this research report.

This Document is not intended for the direct or indirect solicitation of business. TheStreet, Inc. and its affiliates disclaims any and all liability to any person or entity for any loss or damage caused, in whole or in part, by any error (negligent or otherwise) or other circumstances involved in, resulting from or relating to the procurement, compilation, analysis, interpretation, editing, transcribing, publishing and/or dissemination or transmittal of any information contained herein.

TheStreet has not taken any steps to ensure that the securities or investment vehicle referred to in this report are suitable for any particular investor. The investment or services contained or referred to in this report may not be suitable for you and it is recommended that you consult an independent investment advisor if you are in doubt about such investments or investment services. Nothing in this report constitutes investment, legal, accounting or tax advice or a representation that any investment or strategy is suitable or appropriate to your individual circumstances or otherwise constitutes a personal recommendation to you.

The ratings and other opinions contained in this Document must be construed solely as statements of opinion from TheStreet, Inc., and not statements of fact. Each rating or opinion must be weighed solely as a factor in your choice of an institution and should not be construed as a recommendation to buy, sell or otherwise act with respect to the particular product or company involved.

Past performance should not be taken as an indication or guarantee of future performance, and no representation or warranty, expressed or implied, is made regarding future performance. Information, opinions and estimates contained in this report reflect a judgment at its original date of publication and are subject to change without notice. TheStreet Ratings offers a notification service for rating changes on companies you specify. For more information call 1-800-706-2501 or visit www.thestreet.com/ratings. The price, value and income from any of the securities or financial instruments mentioned in this report can fall as well as rise.

Welcome to TheStreet Ratings
Guide to Bond and Money Market Mutual Funds

With the growing popularity of mutual fund investing, consumers need a reliable source to help them track and evaluate the performance of their mutual fund holdings. Plus, they need a way of identifying and monitoring other funds as potential new investments. Unfortunately, the hundreds of performance and risk measures available – multiplied by the vast number of mutual fund investments on the market today – can make this a daunting task for even the most sophisticated investor.

TheStreet Investment Ratings simplify the evaluation process. We condense all of the available mutual fund data into a single composite opinion of each fund's risk-adjusted performance. This allows you to instantly identify those funds that have historically done well and those that have underperformed the market. While there is no guarantee of future performance, TheStreet Investment Ratings provide a solid framework for making informed investment decisions.

TheStreet Ratings' Mission Statement

TheStreet Ratings' mission is to empower consumers, professionals, and institutions with high quality advisory information for selecting or monitoring a financial investments.

In doing so, TheStreet Ratings will adhere to the highest ethical standards by maintaining our independent, unbiased outlook and approach to advising our customers.

Why rely on TheStreet Ratings?

Our mission is to provide fair, objective information to help professionals and consumers alike make educated purchasing decisions.

At TheStreet Ratings, objectivity and total independence are never compromised. We never take a penny from rated companies for issuing our ratings, and we publish them without regard for the companies' preferences. TheStreet's ratings are more frequently reviewed and updated than any other ratings, so you can be sure that the information you receive is accurate and current.

Our rating scale, from A to E, is easy to understand as follows:

	Rating	Description
Top 10% of mutual funds	A	Excellent
Next 20% of mutual funds	B	Good
Middle 40% of mutual funds	C	Fair
Next 20% of mutual funds	D	Weak
Bottom 10% of mutual funds	E	Very Weak

In addition, a plus or minus sign designates that a fund is in the top third or bottom third of funds with the same letter grade.

Thank you for your trust and purchase of this Guide. If you have any comments, or wish to review other products from TheStreet Ratings, please call 1-800-706-2501 or visit www.thestreetratings.com. We look forward to hearing from you.

How to Use This Guide

The purpose of the *Guide to Bond and Money Market Mutual Funds* is to provide investors with a reliable source of investment ratings and analyses on a timely basis. We realize that past performance is an important factor to consider when making the decision to purchase shares in a mutual fund. The ratings and analyses in this Guide can make that evaluation easier when you are considering:

- corporate bond funds
- municipal bond funds
- government bond funds
- money market funds

However, this Guide does not include funds with significant investments in equity securities since they are not comparable investments to funds invested primarily in fixed income securities. The rating for a particular fund indicates our opinion regarding that fund's past risk-adjusted performance.

When evaluating a specific mutual fund, we recommend you follow these steps:

Step 1 **Confirm the fund name and ticker symbol.** To ensure you evaluate the correct mutual fund, verify the fund's exact name and ticker symbol as it was given to you in its prospectus or appears on your account statement. Many funds have similar names, so you want to make sure the fund you look up is really the one you are interested in evaluating. For a definition of the most commonly used share classes see page 531.

Step 2 **Check the fund's Investment Rating.** Turn to Section I, the Index of Bond and Money Market Mutual Funds, and locate the fund you are evaluating. This section contains all bond and money market mutual funds analyzed by TheStreet Ratings including those that did not receive an Investment Rating. All funds are listed in alphabetical order by the name of the fund with the ticker symbol following the name for additional verification. Once you have located your specific fund, the first column after the ticker symbol shows its Investment Rating. Turn to *About TheStreet Investment Ratings* on page 7 for information about what this rating means.

Step 3 **Analyze the supporting data.** Following TheStreet Investment Rating are some of the various measures we have used in rating the fund. Refer to the Section I introduction (beginning on page 17) to see what each of these factors measures. In most cases, lower rated funds will have a low performance rating and/or a low risk rating (i.e., high volatility). Bear in mind, however, that TheStreet Investment Rating is the result of a complex computer-generated analysis which cannot be reproduced using only the data provided here.

When looking to identify a mutual fund that achieves your specific investing goals, we recommend the following:

Step 4 **Take our Investor Profile Quiz.** Turn to page 523 of the Appendix and take our Investor Profile Quiz to help determine your level of risk tolerance. After you have scored yourself, the last page of the quiz will refer you to the risk category in Section VII (Top-Rated Bond Mutual Funds by Risk Category) that is best for you. There you can choose a fund that has historically provided top notch returns while keeping the risk at a level that is suited to your investment style.

Step 5 **View the 100 top performing funds.** If your priority is to achieve the highest return, regardless of the amount of risk, turn to Section V which lists the top 100 bond mutual funds with the best financial performance. Keep in mind that past performance alone is not always a true indicator of the future since these funds have already experienced a run up in price and could be due for a correction.

Step 6 **View the 100 funds with the lowest risk.** On the other hand, if capital preservation is your top priority, turn to Section VI which lists the top 100 bond mutual funds with the lowest risk. These funds will have lower performance ratings than most other funds, but can provide a safe harbor for your savings.

Step 7 **View the top-rated funds by fund type.** If you are looking to invest in a particular type of mutual fund (e.g., corporate high yield or a U.S. Government agency fund), turn to Section VIII, Top-Rated Bond Mutual Funds by Fund Type. There you will find the top 100 bond mutual funds with the highest performance rating in each category. Please be careful to also consider the risk component when selecting a fund from one of these lists.

Step 8 **Refer back to Section I.** Once you have identified a particular fund that interests you, refer back to Section I, the Index of Bond and Money Market Mutual Funds, for a more thorough analysis.

Always remember:

Step 9 **Read our warnings and cautions.** In order to use TheStreet Investment Ratings most effectively, we strongly recommend you consult the Important Warnings and Cautions listed on page 13. These are more than just "standard disclaimers." They are very important factors you should be aware of before using this Guide.

Step 10 **Stay up to date.** Periodically review the latest TheStreet Investment Ratings for the funds that you own to make sure they are still in line with your investment goals and level of risk tolerance. For information on how to acquire follow-up reports on a particular mutual fund, call 1-800-706-2501 or visit www.thestreetratings.com.

Data Source: Thomson Wealth Management
1455 Research Boulevard
Rockville, MD 20850

Date of data analyzed: March 31, 2016

About TheStreet Investment Ratings

TheStreet Investment Ratings represent a completely independent, unbiased opinion of a mutual fund's historical risk-adjusted performance. Each fund's rating is based on two primary components:

Primary Component #1

A fund's **Performance Rating** is based on its total return to shareholders over the last trailing three years, including share price appreciation and distributions to shareholders. This total return figure is stated net of the expenses and fees charged by the fund, and we also make additional adjustments for any front-end or deferred sales loads. In the case of funds investing in municipal or other tax-free securities, the tax-free return is adjusted to its taxable equivalent based on the maximum marginal U.S. tax rate (35%).

This adjusted return is then weighted to give more recent performance a slightly greater emphasis. Thus, two mutual funds may have provided identical returns to their shareholders over the last three years, but the one with the better performance in the last 12 months will receive a slightly higher performance rating.

Primary Component #2

The **Risk Rating** is based on the level of volatility in the fund's monthly returns, also over the last trailing three years. We use a statistical measure – standard deviation from the mean – as our barometer of volatility. Funds with more volatility relative to other mutual funds are considered riskier, and thus receive a lower risk rating. By contrast, funds with a very stable returns are considered less risky and receive a higher risk rating.

In addition to past volatility, the risk rating component also takes into consideration the credit risk of the fund's underlying investments and its relative exposure to interest rate risk.

Rarely will you ever find a mutual fund that has both a very high Performance Rating and, at the same time, a very high Risk Rating. Therefore, the funds that receive the highest overall Investment Ratings are those that combine the ideal combination of both primary components. There is always a tradeoff between risk and reward. That is why we suggest you assess your own personal risk tolerance using the quiz on page 513 as a part of your decision-making process.

Keep in mind that while TheStreet Investment Ratings use the same rating scale as TheStreet Financial Strength Ratings of financial institutions, the two ratings have totally independent meanings. The Financial Strength Ratings assess the *future* financial stability of an insurer or bank as a way of helping investors place their money with a financially sound company and minimize the risk of loss. These ratings are derived without regard to the performance of the individual investments offered by the insurance companies, banks, or thrifts.

On the other hand, the Investment Ratings employ a ranking system to evaluate both safety and performance. Based on these measures, funds are divided into points, and an individual performance rating and a risk rating are assigned to each fund. Then these measures are combined to derive a fund's composite point ranking. Finally, TheStreet Investment Ratings are assigned to their corresponding point rankings as shown on page 3.

How Our Ratings Differ From Those of Other Services

Balanced approach: TheStreet Investment Ratings are designed to meet the needs of aggressive *as well as* conservative investors. We realize that your investment goals can be different from those of other investors based upon your age, income, and tolerance for risk. Therefore, our ratings balance a fund's performance against the amount of risk it poses to identify those funds that have achieved the optimum mix of both factors. Some of these top funds have achieved excellent returns with only average risk. Others have achieved average returns with only moderate risk. Whatever your personal preferences, we can help you identify a top-notch fund that meets your investing style.

Other investment rating firms give a far greater weight to performance and insufficient consideration to risk. In effect, they are betting too heavily on a continuation of the prevailing economic climate and not giving enough consideration to the risk of a decline. While performance is obviously a very important factor to consider, we believe that the riskiness of a fund is also very important. Therefore, we weigh these two components more equally when assigning TheStreet Investment Ratings.

But we don't stop there. We also assign a separate performance rating and risk rating to each fund so you can focus on the component that is most important to you. In fact, Sections V, VI, and VII are designed specifically to help you select the best mutual funds based on these two factors. No other source gives you the cream of the crop in this manner.

Easy to use: Unlike those of other services, TheStreet Investment Ratings are extremely intuitive and easy to use. Our rating scale (A to E) is easily understood by members of the general public based on their familiarity with school grades. So, there are no stars to count and no numbering systems to interpret.

More funds: *TheStreet Ratings Guide to Bond and Money Market Mutual Funds* tracks more mutual funds than any other publication – with updates that come out more frequently than those of other rating agencies. We've included almost 7,100 funds in this edition, all of which are updated every three months. Compare that to other investment rating agencies, such as Morningstar, where coverage stops after the top 1,500 funds and it takes five months for a fund to cycle through their publication's update process.

Recency: Recognizing that every fund's performance is going to have its peaks and valleys, superior long-term performance is a major consideration in TheStreet Investment Ratings. Even so, we do not give a fund a top rating solely because it did well 10 or 15 years ago. Times change and the top performing funds in the current economic environment are often very different from those of a decade ago. Thus, our ratings are designed to keep you abreast of the best funds available *today* and in the *near future,* not the distant past.

No bias toward load funds: In keeping with our conservative, consumer-oriented nature, we adjust the performance for so-called "load" funds differently from other rating agencies. We spread the impact to you of front-end loads and back-end loads (a.k.a. deferred sales charges) over a much shorter period in our evaluation of a fund. Thus our performance rating, as well as the overall TheStreet Investment Rating, more fully reflects the actual returns the typical investor experiences when placing money in a load fund.

Peer Comparison of Mutual Fund Investment Ratings		
TheStreet Ratings	**Morningstar**	**Lipper / Barra**
A+, A, A-	Five stars	√
B+, B, B-	Four stars	2
C+, C, C-	Three stars	3
D+, D, D-	Two stars	4
E+, E, E-	One star	5

What Our Ratings Mean

A **Excellent.** The mutual fund has an excellent track record for maximizing performance while minimizing risk, thus delivering the best possible combination of total return on investment and reduced volatility. It has made the most of the recent economic environment to maximize risk-adjusted returns compared to other mutual funds. While past performance is just an indication – not a guarantee – we believe this fund is among the most likely to deliver superior performance relative to risk in the future.

B **Good.** The mutual fund has a good track record for balancing performance with risk. Compared to other mutual funds, it has achieved above-average returns given the level of risk in its underlying investments. While the risk-adjusted performance of any mutual fund is subject to change, we believe that this fund has proven to be a good investment in the recent past.

C **Fair.** In the trade-off between performance and risk, the mutual fund has a track record which is about average. It is neither significantly better nor significantly worse than most other mutual funds. With some funds in this category, the total return may be better than average, but this can be misleading since the higher return was achieved with higher than average risk. With other funds, the risk may be lower than average, but the returns are also lower. In short, based on recent history, there is no particular advantage to investing in this fund.

D **Weak.** The mutual fund has underperformed the universe of other funds given the level of risk in its underlying investments, resulting in a weak risk-adjusted performance. Thus, its investment strategy and/or management has not been attuned to capitalize on the recent economic environment. While the risk-adjusted performance of any mutual fund is subject to change, we believe that this fund has proven to be a bad investment over the recent past.

E **Very Weak.** The mutual fund has significantly underperformed most other funds given the level of risk in its underlying investments, resulting in a very weak risk-adjusted performance. Thus, its investment strategy and/or management has done just the opposite of what was needed to maximize returns in the recent economic environment. While the risk-adjusted performance of any mutual fund is subject to change, we believe this fund has proven to be a very bad investment in the recent past.

\+ **The plus sign** is an indication that the fund is in the top third of its letter grade.

\- **The minus sign** is an indication that the fund is in the bottom third of its letter grade.

U **Unrated.** The mutual fund is unrated because it is too new to make a reliable assessment of its risk-adjusted performance. Typically, a fund must be established for at least three years before it is eligible to receive a TheStreet Investment Rating.

Important Warnings And Cautions

1. **A rating alone cannot tell the whole story.** Please read the explanatory information contained here, in the section introductions and in the appendix. It is provided in order to give you an understanding of our rating methodology as well as to paint a more complete picture of a mutual fund's strengths and weaknesses.

2. **Investment ratings shown in this directory were current as of the publication date.** In the meantime, the rating may have been updated based on more recent data. TheStreet Ratings offers a notification service for ratings changes on companies that you specify. For more information call 1-800-706-2501 or visit www.thestreet.com/ratings.

3. **When deciding to buy or sell shares in a specific mutual fund, your decision must be based on a wide variety of factors in addition to TheStreet Investment Rating**. These include any charges you may incur from switching funds, to what degree it meets your long-term planning needs, and what other choices are available to you.

4. **TheStreet Investment Ratings represent our opinion of a mutual fund's past risk-adjusted performance.** As such, a high rating means we feel that the mutual fund has performed very well for its shareholders compared to other mutual funds. A high rating is not a guarantee that a fund will continue to perform well, nor is a low rating a prediction of continued weak performance. TheStreet Investment Ratings are not deemed to be a recommendation concerning the purchase or sale of any mutual fund.

5. **A mutual fund's individual performance is not the only factor in determining its rating.** Since TheStreet Investment Ratings are based on performance relative to other funds, it is possible for a fund's rating to be upgraded or downgraded based strictly on the improved or deteriorated performance of other funds.

6. **All funds that have the same TheStreet Investment Rating should be considered to be essentially equal from a risk/reward perspective.** This is true regardless of any differences in the underlying numbers which might appear to indicate greater strengths.

7. **Our rating standards are more consumer-oriented than those used by other rating agencies.** We make more conservative assumptions about the amortization of loads and other fees as we attempt to identify those funds that have historically provided superior returns with only little or moderate risk.

8. **We are an independent rating agency and do not depend on the cooperation of the managers operating the mutual funds we rate**. Our data are derived, for the most part, from price quotes obtained and documented on the open market. This is supplemented by information collected from the mutual fund prospectuses and regulatory filings. Although we seek to maintain an open line of communication with the mutual fund managers, we do not grant them the right to stop or influence publication of the ratings. This policy stems from the fact that this Guide is designed for the information of the consumer.

9. **This Guide does not cover stock funds.** Because stock funds represent a whole separate class of investments with unique risk profiles and performance expectations, they are excluded from this publication.

Section I

Index of Bond and Money Market Mutual Funds

An analysis of all rated and unrated

Fixed Income Mutual Funds

Funds are listed in alphabetical order.

Section I Contents

Left Pages

1. Fund Type

The mutual fund's peer category based on its investment objective as stated in its prospectus.

COH	Corporate - High Yield	MMT	Money Market - Tax Free
COI	Corporate - Inv. Grade	MTG	Mortgage
EM	Emerging Market	MUH	Municipal - High Yield
GEN	General	MUI	Municipal - Insured
GEI	General - Inv. Grade	MUN	Municipal - National
GEL	General - Long Term	MUS	Municipal - Single State
GES	General - Short & Interm.	USL	U.S. Gov.- Long Term
GL	Global	USS	U.S. Gov. - Short & Interm
LP	Loan Participation	USA	U.S. Gov. - Agency
MM	Money Market	US	U.S. Gov. - Treasury

A blank fund type means that the mutual fund has not yet been categorized.

2. Fund Name

The name of the mutual fund as stated in its prospectus, which can sometimes differ slightly from the name that the company uses for advertising. If you cannot find the particular mutual fund you are interested in, or if you have any doubts regarding the precise name, verify the information with your broker or on your account statement. Also, use the fund's ticker symbol for confirmation. (See column 3.)

3. Ticker Symbol

The unique alphabetic symbol used for identifying and trading a specific mutual fund. No two funds can have the same ticker symbol, and the ticker symbol for mutual funds always ends with an "X".

A handful of funds currently show no associated ticker symbol. This means that the fund is either small or new since the NASD assigns a ticker symbol only to funds with at least $25 million in assets or 1,000 shareholders.

4. Overall Investment Rating

Our overall rating is measured on a scale from A to E based on each fund's risk-adjusted performance. Please see page 11 for specific descriptions of each letter grade. Also, refer to page 7 for information on how our ratings are derived. Most important, when using this rating, please be sure to consider the warnings beginning on page 13 regarding the ratings' limitations and the underlying assumptions.

5. Phone

The telephone number of the company managing the fund. Call this number to receive a prospectus or other information about the fund.

6. Performance Rating/Points

A letter grade rating based solely on the mutual fund's financial performance over the trailing three years, without any consideration for the amount of risk the fund poses. Like the overall Investment Rating, the Performance Rating is measured on a scale from A to E for ease of interpretation. The points score indicates where the Performance Rating falls on a scale of 0 to 10.

In the case of funds investing in municipal or other tax-free securities, this rating is based on the taxable equivalent return of the fund assuming the maximum marginal U.S. tax rate (35%).

7. 3-Month Total Return

The total return the fund has provided to investors over the preceding three months. This total return figure is computed based on the fund's dividend distributions and share price appreciation/depreciation during the period, net of the expenses and fees it imposes on its shareholders. Although the total return figure does not reflect an adjustment for any loads the fund may carry, such adjustments have been made in deriving TheStreet Investment Ratings. The 3-Month Total Return shown here is not annualized.

8. 6-Month Total Return

The total return the fund has provided investors over the preceding six months, not annualized.

9. 1-Year Total Return

The total return the fund has provided investors over the preceding twelve months.

10. 1-Year Total Return Percentile

The fund's percentile rank based on its one-year performance compared to that of all other fixed income funds in existence for at least one year. A score of 99 is the best possible, indicating that the fund outperformed 99% of the other mutual funds. Zero is the worst possible percentile score.

In the case of funds investing in municipal or other tax-free securities, this percentile rank is based on the taxable equivalent return of the fund assuming the maximum marginal U.S. tax rate (35%).

11. 3-Year Total Return

The total annual return the fund has provided investors over the preceding three years.

12. 3-Year Total Return Percentile

The fund's percentile rank based on its three-year performance compared to that of all other fixed income funds in existence for at least three years. A score of 99 is the best possible, indicating that the fund outperformed 99% of the other mutual funds. Zero is the worst possible percentile score.

In the case of funds investing in municipal or other tax-free securities, this percentile rank is based on the taxable equivalent return of the fund assuming the maximum marginal U.S. tax rate (35%).

13. 5-Year Total Return

The total annual return the fund has provided investors over the preceding five years.

14. 5-Year Total Return Percentile

The fund's percentile rank based on its five-year performance compared to that of all other fixed income funds in existence for at least five years. A score of 99 is the best possible, indicating that the fund outperformed 99% of the other mutual funds. Zero is the worst possible percentile score.

In the case of funds investing in municipal or other tax-free securities, this percentile rank is based on the taxable equivalent return of the fund assuming the maximum marginal U.S. tax rate (35%).

15. Dividend Yield

Distributions provided to fund investors over the preceding 12 months, expressed as a percent of the fund's current share price. The dividend yield of a fund may have little correlation to the amount of dividends the fund has received from its underlying investments. Rather, dividend distributions are based on a fund's need to pass earnings from both dividends and gains on the sale of investments along to shareholders. Thus, these dividend distributions are included as a part of the fund's total return.

Keep in mind that a higher dividend yield means more current income, as opposed to capital appreciation, which in turn means a higher tax liability in the year of the distribution.

16. Expense Ratio

The expense ratio is taken directly from each fund's annual report with no further calculation. It indicates the percentage of the fund's assets that are deducted each fiscal year to cover its expenses, although for practical purposes, it is actually accrued daily. Typical fund expenses include 12b-1 fees, management fees, administrative fees, operating costs, and all other asset-based costs incurred by the fund. Brokerage costs incurred by the fund to buy or sell the underlying securities, as well as any sales loads levied on investors, are not included in the expense ratio.

If a mutual fund's net assets are small, its expense ratio can be quite high because the fund must cover its expenses from a smaller asset base. Conversely, as the net assets of the fund grow, the expense percentage ideally should diminish since the expenses are being spread across a larger asset base.

Funds with higher expense ratios are generally less attractive since the expense ratio represents a hurdle that must be met before the investment becomes profitable to its shareholders. Since a fund's expenses affect its total return though, they are already factored into its Investment Rating.

Right Pages

1. **Risk Rating/Points** A letter grade rating based solely on the mutual fund's risk as determined by its monthly performance volatility over the trailing three years and the underlying credit risk and interest rate risk of its investment portfolio. The risk rating does not take into consideration the overall financial performance the fund has achieved or the total return it has provided to its shareholders. Like the overall Investment Rating, the Risk Rating is measured on a scale from A to E for ease of interpretation. The points score indicates where the Risk Rating falls on a scale of 0 to 10.

2. **Standard Deviation** A statistical measure of the amount of volatility in a fund's monthly performance over the last trailing 36 months. In absolute terms, standard deviation provides a historical measure of a fund's deviation from its mean, or average, monthly total return over the period.

   A high standard deviation indicates a high degree of volatility in the past, which usually means you should expect to see a high degree of volatility in the future as well. This translates into higher risk since a large negative swing could easily become a sizable loss in the event you need to liquidate your shares.

3. **Average Duration** Expressed in years, duration is a measure of a fund's sensitivity to interest rate fluctuations, or its level of interest rate risk.

   The longer a fund's duration, the more sensitive the fund is to shifts in interest rates. For example, a fund with a duration of eight years is twice as sensitive to a change in rates as a fund with a four year duration.

4. **Net Asset Value (NAV)** The fund's share price as of the date indicated. A fund's NAV is computed by dividing the value of the fund's asset holdings, less accrued fees and expenses, by the number of its shares outstanding.

5. **Net Assets** The total value (stated in millions of dollars) of all of the fund's asset holdings including stocks, bonds, cash, and other financial instruments, less accrued expenses and fees.

   Larger funds have the advantage of being able to spread their expenses over a greater asset base so that the effect per share is lessened. On the other hand, if a fund becomes too large, it can be more difficult for the fund manager to buy and sell investments for the benefit of shareholders.

6. **Cash %** The percentage of the fund's assets held in cash and cash equivalent assets as of the last reporting period. Investments in this area will tend to hamper the fund's returns while adding to its stability during market swings.

7. **Government Bonds %** The percentage of the fund's assets invested in U.S. government and U.S. government agency bonds as of the last reporting period. These investments carry little or no credit risk, but also tend to offer lower than average yields.

8. Municipal Bonds %

The percentage of the fund's assets invested as of the last reporting period in bonds issued by state and local governments. The quality of municipal bonds can vary greatly, so it is important to check TheStreet Risk Rating for funds with a high concentration of assets in this category.

9. Corporate Bonds %

The percentage of the fund's assets invested as of the last reporting period in bonds issued by corporations. This includes both high yield corporate bonds (i.e. junk bonds) and investment grade corporate bonds, so it is important to check TheStreet Risk Rating for funds with a high concentration of assets in this category.

10. Other %

The percentage of the fund's assets invested as of the last reporting period in other types of financial instruments such as convertible or equity securities.

11. Portfolio Turnover Ratio

The average annual portion of the fund's holdings that have been moved from one specific investment to another over the past three years. This indicates the amount of buying and selling the fund manager engages in. A portfolio turnover ratio of 100% signifies that on average, the entire value of the fund's assets is turned over once during the course of a year.

A high portfolio turnover ratio has implications for shareholders since the fund is required to pass all realized earnings along to shareholders each year. Thus a high portfolio turnover ratio will result in higher annual distributions for shareholders, effectively increasing their annual taxable income. In contrast, a low turnover ratio means a higher level of unrealized gains that will not be taxable until you sell your shares in the fund.

12. Average Coupon Rate

The average overall interest rate being received on the fund's fixed income investments based on a weighted average of each individual bond's stated interest rate, or coupon rate.

Interest payments are only one factor contributing to a fund's overall performance. However, the higher the average coupon rate, the higher the level of realized gains that the fund will have to distribute to its shareholders in the form of a taxable dividend distribution.

13. Manager Quality Percentile

The manager quality percentile is based on a ranking of the fund's alpha, a statistical measure representing the difference between a fund's actual returns and its expected performance given its level of risk. Fund managers who have been able to exceed the fund's statistically expected performance receive a high percentile rank with 99 representing the best possible score. At the other end of the spectrum, fund managers who actually have detracted from the fund's expected performance receive a low percentile rank with 0 representing the worst possible score.

14. Manager Tenure

The number of years the current manager has been managing the fund. Since fund managers who deliver substandard returns are usually replaced, a long tenure is usually a good sign that shareholders are satisfied that the fund is achieving its stated objectives.

15. Initial Purchase Minimum

The minimum investment amount, stated in dollars, that the fund management company requires in order for you to initially purchase shares in the fund. In theory, funds with high purchase minimums are able to keep expenses down because they have fewer accounts to administer. Don't be misled, however, by the misconception that a fund with a high purchase minimum will deliver superior results simply because it is designed for "high rollers."

Additional Purchase Minimum

The minimum subsequent fund purchase, stated in dollars, that you could make once you have opened an existing account. This minimum may be lowered or waived if you participate in an electronic transfer plan where shares of the fund are automatically purchased at regularly scheduled intervals.

17. Front-End Load

A fee charged on all new investments in the fund, stated as a percentage of the initial investment. Thus a fund with a 4% front-end load means that only 96% of your initial investment is working for you while the other 4% is immediately sacrificed to the fund company. It is generally best to avoid funds that charge a front-end load since there is usually a comparable no-load fund available to serve as an alternative.

While a fund's total return does not reflect the expense to shareholders of a front-end load, we have factored this fee into our evaluation when deriving its Investment Rating.

18. Back-End Load

Also known as a deferred sales charge, this fee is levied when you sell the fund, and is stated as a percentage of your total sales price. For instance, investing in a fund with a 5% back-end load means that you will only receive 95% of your total investment when you sell the fund. The remaining 5% goes to the fund company. As with front-end loads, it is generally best to avoid funds that charge a back-end load since there is usually a comparable no-load fund available to serve as an alternative.

While a fund's total return does not reflect the expense to shareholders of a back-end load, we have factored this fee into our evaluation when deriving its Investment Rating.

Fund Type	Fund Name (99 Pct = Best, 0 Pct = Worst)	Ticker Symbol	Overall Investment Rating	Phone	PERFORMANCE: Performance Rating/Pts	Total Return % through 3/31/16: 3 Mo	6 Mo	1Yr / Pct	Annualized: 3Yr / Pct	Annualized: 5Yr / Pct	Incl. in Returns: Dividend Yield	Expense Ratio
COH	1290 High Yield Bond A	TNHAX	**U**	(888) 310-0416	**U** /	2.35	-0.60	-5.44 / 4	--	--	7.77	1.99
COH	1290 High Yield Bond C	TNHCX	**U**	(888) 310-0416	**U** /	2.41	-0.47	-5.20 / 5	--	--	8.41	2.74
COH	1290 High Yield Bond I	TNHIX	**U**	(888) 310-0416	**U** /	2.41	-0.47	-5.20 / 5	--	--	8.41	1.74
COH	1290 High Yield Bond R	TNHRX	**U**	(888) 310-0416	**U** /	2.29	-0.72	-5.68 / 4	--	--	7.87	2.24
MUS	1919 Maryland Tax-Free Income A	LMMDX	**C+**	(844) 828-1919	**C / 5.3**	1.05	1.74	2.10 /78	1.90 /75	4.17 /79	3.53	0.91
MUS	1919 Maryland Tax-Free Income C	LMMCX	**B+**	(844) 828-1919	**C+ / 6.6**	0.92	1.47	1.55 /74	1.33 /62	3.57 /74	3.14	1.48
MUS	1919 Maryland Tax-Free Income I	LMMIX	**A+**	(844) 828-1919	**B / 8.0**	1.09	1.82	2.31 /79	2.06 /78	4.35 /80	3.83	0.83
COI	AAM Select Income A	CPUAX	**U**	(888) 966-9661	**U** /	3.27	2.60	-0.12 /30	--	--	2.99	1.94
COI	AAM Select Income C	CPUCX	**U**	(888) 966-9661	**U** /	3.17	2.41	-0.69 /24	--	--	2.41	2.69
COI	AAM Select Income I	CPUIX	**U**	(888) 966-9661	**U** /	3.33	2.93	0.30 /46	--	--	3.30	1.69
COI	AAM/HIMCO Short Duration A	ASDAX	**U**	(888) 966-9661	**U** /	0.80	0.89	1.12 /61	--	--	1.98	1.46
COI	AAM/HIMCO Short Duration C	ASDCX	**U**	(888) 966-9661	**U** /	0.54	0.37	0.33 /46	--	--	1.45	2.21
COI	AAM/HIMCO Short Duration I	ASDIX	**U**	(888) 966-9661	**U** /	0.76	0.91	1.36 /64	--	--	2.26	1.21
GES	AB All Mkt Real Return 1	AMTOX	**E-**	(800) 221-5672	**E- / 0.0**	2.74	0.32	-14.49 / 0	-10.66 / 0	-7.53 / 0	2.02	1.16
GES	AB All Mkt Real Return 2	AMTTX	**E-**	(800) 221-5672	**E- / 0.0**	2.69	0.33	-14.30 / 0	-10.45 / 0	-7.31 / 0	2.26	0.92
GES	AB All Mkt Real Return A	AMTAX	**E-**	(800) 221-5672	**E- / 0.0**	2.56	0.20	-14.66 / 0	-10.78 / 0	-7.62 / 0	1.30	1.42
GES	AB All Mkt Real Return Adv	AMTYX	**E-**	(800) 221-5672	**E- / 0.0**	2.71	0.42	-14.37 / 0	-10.51 / 0	-7.33 / 0	1.83	1.17
GES	AB All Mkt Real Return C	ACMTX	**E-**	(800) 221-5672	**E- / 0.0**	2.43	-0.20	-15.22 / 0	-11.39 / 0	-8.27 / 0	0.32	2.16
GES	AB All Mkt Real Return I	AMTIX	**E-**	(800) 221-5672	**E- / 0.0**	2.59	0.28	-14.43 / 0	-10.49 / 0	-7.34 / 0	2.23	0.96
GES	AB All Mkt Real Return K	AMTKX	**E-**	(800) 221-5672	**E- / 0.0**	2.59	0.20	-14.64 / 0	-10.72 / 0	-7.57 / 0	1.76	1.34
GES	AB All Mkt Real Return R	AMTRX	**E-**	(800) 221-5672	**E- / 0.0**	2.45	0.08	-14.87 / 0	-10.97 / 0	-7.82 / 0	1.38	1.64
COI	AB Bond Inflation Strat 1	ABNOX	**D**	(800) 221-5672	**D+ / 2.6**	4.13	3.40	1.36 /64	-0.80 / 9	2.04 /32	1.50	0.87
COI	AB Bond Inflation Strat 2	ABNTX	**D**	(800) 221-5672	**D+ / 2.8**	4.13	3.41	1.45 /65	-0.69 /10	2.13 /33	1.59	0.77
COI	AB Bond Inflation Strat A	ABNAX	**D-**	(800) 221-5672	**E+ / 0.8**	3.99	3.30	1.18 /61	-1.00 / 8	1.75 /28	1.01	1.31
COI	AB Bond Inflation Strat Adv	ABNYX	**D**	(800) 221-5672	**D+ / 2.8**	4.08	3.44	1.47 /66	-0.70 /10	2.11 /32	1.33	1.06
COI	AB Bond Inflation Strat C	ABNCX	**D-**	(800) 221-5672	**D- / 1.0**	3.86	2.84	0.37 /47	-1.71 / 5	1.10 /21	0.73	2.07
COI	AB Bond Inflation Strat I	ANBIX	**D**	(800) 221-5672	**D+ / 2.8**	4.11	3.39	1.50 /66	-0.70 /10	2.15 /33	1.55	0.69
COI	AB Bond Inflation Strat K	ABNKX	**D-**	(800) 221-5672	**D / 1.7**	4.10	3.32	1.22 /62	-0.97 / 9	1.88 /30	1.19	1.07
COI	AB Bond Inflation Strat R	ABNRX	**D-**	(800) 221-5672	**D- / 1.4**	3.99	3.19	0.99 /58	-1.20 / 7	1.62 /27	0.87	1.40
GL	AB Bond Inflation Strat Z	ABNZX	**U**	(800) 221-5672	**U** /	4.12	3.41	1.45 /65	--	--	1.59	0.68
COI	AB Corporate Income	ACISX	**C**	(800) 221-5672	**B / 8.0**	3.78	2.83	0.33 /46	3.35 /79	5.28 /73	3.60	N/A
MM	AB Exchange Reserve A	AEAXX	**C**	(800) 221-5672	**D+ / 2.6**	0.09	0.13	0.17 /43	0.09 /27	0.10 /14	0.17	0.62
MM	● AB Exchange Reserve B	AEBXX	**C**	(800) 221-5672	**D+ / 2.6**	0.09	0.13	0.17 /43	0.08 /26	0.09 /14	0.17	1.33
MM	AB Exchange Reserve C	AECXX	**C**	(800) 221-5672	**D+ / 2.6**	0.09	0.13	0.17 /43	0.08 /26	0.10 /14	0.17	1.08
MM	AB Exchange Reserve I	AIEXX	**C**	(800) 221-5672	**D+ / 2.7**	0.09	0.13	0.17 /43	0.11 /27	0.12 /15	0.17	0.28
MM	AB Exchange Reserve K	AEKXX	**C**	(800) 221-5672	**D+ / 2.6**	0.09	0.13	0.17 /43	0.08 /26	0.09 /14	0.17	0.60
MM	AB Exchange Reserve R	AREXX	**C**	(800) 221-5672	**D+ / 2.6**	0.09	0.13	0.17 /43	0.07 /26	0.09 /14	0.17	0.84
* GL	AB Global Bond A	ANAGX	**C**	(800) 221-5672	**C / 5.4**	2.97	2.93	1.70 /69	2.37 /69	3.85 /59	3.45	0.85
GL	AB Global Bond Adv	ANAYX	**B**	(800) 221-5672	**B / 7.6**	3.04	3.07	1.87 /71	2.67 /73	4.14 /63	3.90	0.60
GL	● AB Global Bond B	ANABX	**C+**	(800) 221-5672	**C+ / 5.9**	2.77	2.54	0.82 /56	1.63 /54	3.11 /47	2.86	1.63
GL	AB Global Bond C	ANACX	**C**	(800) 221-5672	**C+ / 6.0**	2.90	2.67	0.97 /58	1.64 /55	3.12 /47	2.88	1.60
GL	AB Global Bond I	ANAIX	**B+**	(800) 221-5672	**B / 7.6**	3.04	3.07	1.87 /71	2.70 /73	4.17 /64	3.90	0.59
GL	AB Global Bond K	ANAKX	**B-**	(800) 221-5672	**B- / 7.1**	2.96	2.90	1.52 /67	2.33 /68	3.84 /59	3.55	0.95
GL	AB Global Bond R	ANARX	**C+**	(800) 221-5672	**C+ / 6.6**	2.86	2.73	1.19 /61	2.01 /61	3.48 /53	3.22	1.27
GL	AB Global Bond Z	ANAZX	**B**	(800) 221-5672	**B / 7.6**	3.05	3.10	1.93 /71	2.68 /73	4.04 /62	3.95	0.53
MM	AB Govt Reserves 1	AGRXX	**U**	(800) 221-5672	**U** /	--	--	--	--	--	0.02	0.41
* GL	AB High Income A	AGDAX	**D**	(800) 221-5672	**C- / 3.7**	3.44	1.91	-2.23 /15	1.92 /60	5.07 /72	7.22	0.85
GL	AB High Income Adv	AGDYX	**D+**	(800) 221-5672	**C+ / 6.2**	3.50	2.05	-1.94 /16	2.22 /66	5.38 /74	7.84	0.60
GL	● AB High Income B	AGDBX	**D**	(800) 221-5672	**C- / 4.2**	3.21	1.38	-3.05 /11	1.13 /45	4.28 /65	6.70	1.63
GL	AB High Income C	AGDCX	**D**	(800) 221-5672	**C / 4.3**	3.34	1.53	-2.89 /12	1.15 /45	4.27 /65	6.71	1.60
GL	AB High Income I	AGDIX	**D+**	(800) 221-5672	**C+ / 6.3**	3.52	2.08	-1.89 /16	2.27 /67	5.43 /74	7.89	0.54
GL	AB High Income K	AGDKX	**D+**	(800) 221-5672	**C+ / 5.7**	3.44	1.92	-2.24 /15	1.92 /60	5.07 /72	7.53	0.94

● Denotes fund is closed to new investors
* Denotes fund is included in Section II

RISK			NET ASSETS		ASSET							FUND MANAGER		MINIMUM		LOADS	
Risk Rating/Pts	3 Yr Avg Standard Deviation	Avg Duration	NAV As of 3/31/16	Total $(Mil)	Cash %	Gov. Bond %	Muni. Bond %	Corp. Bond %	Other %	Portfolio Turnover Ratio	Avg Coupon Rate	Manager Quality Pct	Manager Tenure (Years)	Initial Purch. $	Additional Purch. $	Front End Load	Back End Load
U /	N/A	3.4	8.54	8	1	0	0	0	99	57	0.0	N/A	N/A	2,000	100	4.5	0.0
U /	N/A	3.4	8.54	3	1	0	0	0	99	57	0.0	N/A	N/A	2,000	100	0.0	0.0
U /	N/A	3.4	8.54	8	1	0	0	0	99	57	0.0	N/A	N/A	1,000,000	0	0.0	0.0
U /	N/A	3.4	8.54	8	1	0	0	0	99	57	0.0	N/A	N/A	0	0	0.0	0.0
B- / 7.3	2.8	5.4	16.18	92	1	0	98	0	1	1	4.9	33	9	1,000	50	4.3	0.0
B- / 7.3	2.8	5.4	16.18	22	1	0	98	0	1	1	4.9	19	9	1,000	50	0.0	0.0
B- / 7.3	2.8	5.4	16.19	17	1	0	98	0	1	1	4.9	38	9	1,000,000	0	0.0	0.0
U /	N/A	N/A	9.80	1	4	13	2	66	15	38	0.0	N/A	3	2,500	500	3.0	2.0
U /	N/A	N/A	9.81	1	4	13	2	66	15	38	0.0	N/A	3	2,500	500	0.0	2.0
U /	N/A	N/A	9.81	30	4	13	2	66	15	38	0.0	N/A	3	25,000	5,000	0.0	2.0
U /	N/A	N/A	9.87	3	3	0	0	62	35	29	0.0	N/A	2	2,500	500	2.5	1.0
U /	N/A	N/A	9.85	1	3	0	0	62	35	29	0.0	N/A	2	2,500	500	0.0	1.0
U /	N/A	N/A	9.87	60	3	0	0	62	35	29	0.0	N/A	2	25,000	5,000	0.0	1.0
E- / 0.0	13.2	N/A	7.49	469	14	23	0	0	63	53	0.0	0	1	5,000	0	0.0	0.0
E- / 0.0	13.2	N/A	7.64	N/A	14	23	0	0	63	53	0.0	0	1	0	0	0.0	0.0
E- / 0.0	13.2	N/A	7.61	13	14	23	0	0	63	53	0.0	0	1	2,500	50	4.3	0.0
E- / 0.0	13.2	N/A	7.59	26	14	23	0	0	63	53	0.0	0	1	0	0	0.0	0.0
E- / 0.0	13.2	N/A	7.58	3	14	23	0	0	63	53	0.0	0	1	2,500	50	0.0	0.0
E- / 0.0	13.1	N/A	7.53	14	14	23	0	0	63	53	0.0	0	1	0	0	0.0	0.0
E- / 0.0	13.2	N/A	7.53	2	14	23	0	0	63	53	0.0	0	1	0	0	0.0	0.0
E- / 0.0	13.2	N/A	7.53	N/A	14	23	0	0	63	53	0.0	0	1	0	0	0.0	0.0
C- / 3.3	4.5	3.7	10.60	238	0	63	0	18	19	51	1.3	6	6	5,000	0	0.0	0.0
C- / 3.3	4.5	3.7	10.60	44	0	63	0	18	19	51	1.3	7	6	0	0	0.0	0.0
C- / 3.2	4.5	3.7	10.68	12	0	63	0	18	19	51	1.3	6	6	2,500	50	4.3	0.0
C- / 3.3	4.4	3.7	10.71	19	0	63	0	18	19	51	1.3	7	6	0	0	0.0	0.0
C- / 3.3	4.4	3.7	10.49	3	0	63	0	18	19	51	1.3	5	6	2,500	50	0.0	0.0
C- / 3.3	4.4	3.7	10.63	N/A	0	63	0	18	19	51	1.3	7	6	0	0	0.0	0.0
C- / 3.3	4.4	3.7	10.67	2	0	63	0	18	19	51	1.3	6	6	0	0	0.0	0.0
C- / 3.3	4.5	3.7	10.68	N/A	0	63	0	18	19	51	1.3	6	6	0	0	0.0	0.0
U /	N/A	3.7	10.62	10	0	63	0	18	19	51	1.3	N/A	6	0	0	0.0	0.0
C- / 3.1	4.6	N/A	11.08	63	1	5	0	92	2	42	0.0	77	10	0	0	0.0	0.0
A+ / 9.9	N/A	N/A	1.00	147	100	0	0	0	0	0	0.2	69	N/A	2,500	50	0.0	0.0
A+ / 9.9	N/A	N/A	1.00	4	100	0	0	0	0	0	0.2	68	N/A	2,500	50	0.0	0.0
A+ / 9.9	N/A	N/A	1.00	18	100	0	0	0	0	0	0.2	68	N/A	2,500	50	0.0	0.0
A+ / 9.9	N/A	N/A	1.00	1,584	100	0	0	0	0	0	0.2	70	N/A	0	0	0.0	0.0
A+ / 9.9	N/A	N/A	1.00	29	100	0	0	0	0	0	0.2	68	N/A	0	0	0.0	0.0
A+ / 9.9	N/A	N/A	1.00	5	100	0	0	0	0	0	0.2	66	N/A	0	0	0.0	0.0
C+ / 6.0	3.1	5.5	8.36	1,077	0	54	2	29	15	167	3.4	97	24	2,500	50	4.3	0.0
C+ / 5.8	3.2	5.5	8.35	2,678	0	54	2	29	15	167	3.4	98	24	0	0	0.0	0.0
C+ / 5.9	3.2	5.5	8.36	2	0	54	2	29	15	167	3.4	94	24	2,500	50	0.0	0.0
C+ / 5.8	3.2	5.5	8.39	346	0	54	2	29	15	167	3.4	94	24	2,500	50	0.0	0.0
C+ / 5.9	3.2	5.5	8.35	640	0	54	2	29	15	167	3.4	98	24	0	0	0.0	0.0
C+ / 5.7	3.2	5.5	8.35	26	0	54	2	29	15	167	3.4	97	24	0	0	0.0	0.0
C+ / 5.7	3.2	5.5	8.35	71	0	54	2	29	15	167	3.4	96	24	0	0	0.0	0.0
C+ / 5.8	3.2	5.5	8.35	198	0	54	2	29	15	167	3.4	98	24	0	0	0.0	0.0
U /	N/A	N/A	1.00	689	100	0	0	0	0	0	0.0	N/A	N/A	100,000	0	0.0	0.0
D / 2.2	5.5	4.8	8.15	1,882	6	8	0	66	20	53	6.8	96	14	2,500	50	4.3	0.0
D+ / 2.3	5.4	4.8	8.16	2,592	6	8	0	66	20	53	6.8	97	14	0	0	0.0	0.0
D+ / 2.3	5.4	4.8	8.22	3	6	8	0	66	20	53	6.8	91	14	2,500	50	0.0	0.0
D+ / 2.3	5.4	4.8	8.25	1,171	6	8	0	66	20	53	6.8	91	14	2,500	50	0.0	0.0
D+ / 2.3	5.4	4.8	8.16	293	6	8	0	66	20	53	6.8	97	14	0	0	0.0	0.0
D+ / 2.3	5.4	4.8	8.15	96	6	8	0	66	20	53	6.8	96	14	0	0	0.0	0.0

99 Pct = Best 0 Pct = Worst Fund Type	Fund Name	Ticker Symbol	Overall Investment Rating	Phone	PERFORMANCE Performance Rating/Pts	Total Return % through 3/31/16 3 Mo	6 Mo	1Yr / Pct	Annualized 3Yr / Pct	5Yr / Pct	Incl. in Returns Dividend Yield	Expense Ratio
* MUH	AB High Income Municipal A	ABTHX	**C**	(800) 221-5672	**A+ / 9.7**	2.26	5.35	5.78 /99	4.78 /98	9.05 /99	4.18	0.87
MUH	AB High Income Municipal Adv	ABTYX	**C**	(800) 221-5672	**A+ / 9.9**	2.33	5.48	6.04 /99	5.08 /99	9.37 /99	4.56	0.62
MUH	AB High Income Municipal C	ABTFX	**C**	(800) 221-5672	**A+ / 9.7**	2.08	4.96	4.90 /98	4.04 /96	8.26 /99	3.58	1.62
GL	AB High Income R	AGDRX	**D+**	(800) 221-5672	**C / 5.1**	3.36	1.74	-2.57 /13	1.58 /54	4.76 /70	7.17	1.27
GL	AB High Income Z	AGDZX	**D+**	(800) 221-5672	**C+ / 6.2**	3.53	2.09	-1.88 /16	2.19 /65	5.23 /73	7.90	0.53
GL	AB High Yield A	HIYAX	**U**	(800) 221-5672	**U /**	3.24	1.52	-3.98 / 8	--	--	5.44	6.57
GL	AB High Yield Adv	HIYYX	**U**	(800) 221-5672	**U /**	3.30	1.65	-3.74 / 9	--	--	5.95	7.35
GL	AB High Yield C	HIYCX	**U**	(800) 221-5672	**U /**	3.05	1.15	-4.69 / 6	--	--	4.92	7.85
GL	AB High Yield I	HIYIX	**U**	(800) 221-5672	**U /**	3.30	1.65	-3.74 / 9	--	--	5.96	3.86
GL	AB High Yield K	HIYKX	**U**	(800) 221-5672	**U /**	3.24	1.55	-3.95 / 8	--	--	5.72	4.13
GL	AB High Yield R	HIYRX	**U**	(800) 221-5672	**U /**	3.18	1.40	-4.21 / 7	--	--	5.44	4.39
GL	AB High Yield Z	HIYZX	**U**	(800) 221-5672	**U /**	3.30	1.65	-3.73 / 9	--	--	5.96	3.86
MUS	AB Interm CA Muni A	AICAX	**B**	(800) 221-5672	**C+ / 5.7**	1.24	2.03	2.41 /80	1.59 /70	2.90 /67	1.90	0.81
MUS ●	AB Interm CA Muni B	ACLBX	**C+**	(800) 221-5672	**C / 5.0**	1.07	1.51	1.41 /73	0.63 /42	2.03 /47	0.98	1.88
MUS	AB Interm CA Muni C	ACMCX	**B**	(800) 221-5672	**C+ / 5.6**	0.98	1.58	1.58 /74	0.84 /48	2.16 /50	1.22	1.57
MUN	AB Interm Diversif Muni A	AIDAX	**B**	(800) 221-5672	**C+ / 5.7**	1.16	1.91	2.27 /79	1.62 /70	2.83 /66	1.63	0.81
MUN	AB Interm Diversif Muni Adv	AIDYX	**U**	(800) 221-5672	**U /**	1.27	2.16	--	--	--	0.00	0.57
MUN ●	AB Interm Diversif Muni B	AIDBX	**B**	(800) 221-5672	**C+ / 5.6**	0.94	1.48	1.46 /73	0.86 /49	2.08 /48	0.89	1.59
MUN	AB Interm Diversif Muni C	AIMCX	**B**	(800) 221-5672	**C+ / 5.7**	0.97	1.53	1.50 /74	0.90 /50	2.11 /49	0.94	1.57
MUS	AB Interm NY Muni A	ANIAX	**B+**	(800) 221-5672	**C+ / 5.9**	1.20	2.17	2.73 /82	1.65 /71	2.81 /66	2.05	0.80
MUS ●	AB Interm NY Muni B	ANYBX	**B+**	(800) 221-5672	**C+ / 5.9**	0.97	1.77	1.87 /76	0.91 /50	2.06 /48	1.35	1.57
MUS	AB Interm NY Muni C	ANMCX	**B+**	(800) 221-5672	**C+ / 6.0**	1.02	1.79	1.96 /77	0.92 /50	2.08 /48	1.37	1.55
GEI	AB Intermediate Bond A	ABQUX	**C-**	(800) 221-5672	**C / 5.0**	2.62	1.92	0.81 /55	2.41 /69	3.67 /56	3.25	1.03
GEI	AB Intermediate Bond Adv	ABQYX	**B**	(800) 221-5672	**B- / 7.3**	2.69	2.03	0.98 /58	2.67 /73	3.97 /61	3.65	0.77
GEI ●	AB Intermediate Bond B	ABQBX	**C**	(800) 221-5672	**C+ / 5.6**	2.43	1.52	-0.03 /31	1.65 /55	2.95 /44	2.65	1.80
GEI	AB Intermediate Bond C	ABQCX	**C**	(800) 221-5672	**C+ / 5.7**	2.44	1.53	0.07 /40	1.69 /56	2.95 /44	2.66	1.78
GEI	AB Intermediate Bond I	ABQIX	**B**	(800) 221-5672	**B- / 7.3**	2.68	2.03	0.97 /58	2.67 /73	3.97 /61	3.65	0.75
GEI	AB Intermediate Bond K	ABQKX	**C+**	(800) 221-5672	**B- / 7.0**	2.62	1.90	0.81 /55	2.44 /70	3.73 /57	3.40	1.08
GEI	AB Intermediate Bond R	ABQRX	**C+**	(800) 221-5672	**C+ / 6.5**	2.56	1.78	0.57 /51	2.19 /65	3.46 /52	3.15	1.38
COI	AB Intermediate Bond Z	ABQZX	**B-**	(800) 221-5672	**B- / 7.2**	2.68	2.03	0.98 /58	2.59 /72	3.78 /58	3.65	0.71
COH	AB Limited Dur High Inc A	ALHAX	**D+**	(800) 221-5672	**C- / 4.0**	2.29	1.65	0.13 /42	1.91 /60	--	3.67	1.08
COH	AB Limited Dur High Inc Adv	ALHYX	**C-**	(800) 221-5672	**C+ / 6.5**	2.36	1.90	0.42 /48	2.22 /66	--	4.13	0.84
COH	AB Limited Dur High Inc C	ALHCX	**D+**	(800) 221-5672	**C / 4.6**	2.00	1.29	-0.67 /24	1.20 /46	--	3.12	1.84
COH	AB Limited Dur High Inc I	ALIHX	**C-**	(800) 221-5672	**C+ / 6.6**	2.36	1.80	0.45 /49	2.26 /67	--	4.15	1.38
COH	AB Limited Dur High Inc K	ALHKX	**C-**	(800) 221-5672	**C+ / 6.1**	2.29	1.66	0.16 /43	1.95 /60	--	3.86	1.71
COH	AB Limited Dur High Inc R	ALHRX	**C-**	(800) 221-5672	**C+ / 5.6**	2.23	1.64	-0.13 /30	1.69 /56	--	3.57	2.02
MUN	AB Muni Bond Inf Str 1	AUNOX	**C-**	(800) 221-5672	**C- / 4.0**	1.25	2.99	2.02 /77	-0.05 /15	1.98 /46	1.89	0.67
MUN	AB Muni Bond Inf Str 2	AUNTX	**C-**	(800) 221-5672	**C / 4.3**	1.27	3.14	2.13 /78	0.05 /26	2.08 /48	1.98	0.57
MUN	AB Muni Bond Inf Str A	AUNAX	**D**	(800) 221-5672	**D- / 1.3**	1.20	2.98	1.82 /76	-0.25 /13	1.76 /40	1.64	0.87
MUN	AB Muni Bond Inf Str Adv	AUNYX	**C-**	(800) 221-5672	**C / 4.4**	1.36	3.11	2.17 /78	0.07 /27	2.08 /48	1.93	0.61
MUN	AB Muni Bond Inf Str C	AUNCX	**D**	(800) 221-5672	**D- / 1.4**	1.02	2.60	1.05 /68	-0.94 / 9	1.04 /26	0.93	1.61
* MUH	AB Municipal Income	MISHX	**C**	(800) 221-5672	**A+ / 9.9**	2.75	5.87	6.83 /99	5.93 /99	10.11 /99	4.29	0.01
MUS	AB Municipal Income CA A	ALCAX	**B+**	(800) 221-5672	**A- / 9.0**	1.61	3.28	3.96 /94	3.79 /95	6.01 /92	3.23	0.81
MUS	AB Municipal Income CA Adv	ALCVX	**A**	(800) 221-5672	**A+ / 9.6**	1.68	3.41	4.22 /95	4.08 /96	6.31 /94	3.57	0.55
MUS ●	AB Municipal Income CA B	ALCBX	**B+**	(800) 221-5672	**A- / 9.0**	1.43	2.90	3.19 /87	3.05 /88	5.26 /87	2.59	1.57
MUS	AB Municipal Income CA C	ACACX	**B+**	(800) 221-5672	**A- / 9.1**	1.43	2.99	3.19 /87	3.08 /89	5.26 /87	2.59	1.55
MUS	AB Municipal Income II AZ A	AAZAX	**A**	(800) 221-5672	**B+ / 8.9**	1.92	3.85	4.67 /97	3.45 /92	5.25 /87	3.08	0.97
MUS ●	AB Municipal Income II AZ B	AAZBX	**A-**	(800) 221-5672	**A- / 9.0**	1.83	3.47	3.90 /93	2.72 /85	4.53 /82	2.45	1.72
MUS	AB Municipal Income II AZ C	AAZCX	**A-**	(800) 221-5672	**A- / 9.0**	1.83	3.47	3.90 /93	2.72 /85	4.53 /82	2.45	1.72
MUS	AB Municipal Income II MA A	AMAAX	**B-**	(800) 221-5672	**B+ / 8.3**	1.56	2.90	3.68 /92	3.02 /88	5.21 /87	3.06	0.87
MUS ●	AB Municipal Income II MA B	AMABX	**B-**	(800) 221-5672	**B+ / 8.4**	1.38	2.53	2.92 /84	2.30 /80	4.48 /81	2.42	1.63
MUS	AB Municipal Income II MA C	AMACX	**B-**	(800) 221-5672	**B+ / 8.4**	1.38	2.53	2.92 /84	2.30 /80	4.48 /81	2.42	1.63

● Denotes fund is closed to new investors
* Denotes fund is included in Section II

RISK			NET ASSETS		ASSET							FUND MANAGER		MINIMUM		LOADS	
Risk Rating/Pts	3 Yr Avg Standard Deviation	Avg Dura- tion	NAV As of 3/31/16	Total $(Mil)	Cash %	Gov. Bond %	Muni. Bond %	Corp. Bond %	Other %	Portfolio Turnover Ratio	Avg Coupon Rate	Manager Quality Pct	Manager Tenure (Years)	Initial Purch. $	Additional Purch. $	Front End Load	Back End Load
E+ / 0.8	6.3	6.3	11.51	805	0	0	100	0	0	9	0.0	18	6	2,500	50	3.0	0.0
E+ / 0.8	6.4	6.3	11.50	1,202	0	0	100	0	0	9	0.0	22	6	0	0	0.0	0.0
E+ / 0.8	6.4	6.3	11.50	330	0	0	100	0	0	9	0.0	10	6	2,500	50	0.0	0.0
D+ / 2.3	5.5	4.8	8.15	84	6	8	0	66	20	53	6.8	94	14	0	0	0.0	0.0
D+ / 2.3	5.5	4.8	8.16	89	6	8	0	66	20	53	6.8	97	14	0	0	0.0	0.0
U /	N/A	4.7	8.83	1	13	3	0	77	7	56	6.0	N/A	2	2,500	50	4.3	0.0
U /	N/A	4.7	8.83	N/A	13	3	0	77	7	56	6.0	N/A	2	0	0	0.0	0.0
U /	N/A	4.7	8.83	N/A	13	3	0	77	7	56	6.0	N/A	2	2,500	50	0.0	0.0
U /	N/A	4.7	8.83	16	13	3	0	77	7	56	6.0	N/A	2	0	0	0.0	0.0
U /	N/A	4.7	8.83	N/A	13	3	0	77	7	56	6.0	N/A	2	0	0	0.0	0.0
U /	N/A	4.7	8.83	N/A	13	3	0	77	7	56	6.0	N/A	2	0	0	0.0	0.0
U /	N/A	4.7	8.83	N/A	13	3	0	77	7	56	6.0	N/A	2	0	0	0.0	0.0
B / 7.9	2.4	4.1	14.55	91	1	0	97	1	1	16	5.0	32	26	2,500	50	3.0	0.0
B / 8.0	2.4	4.1	14.54	N/A	1	0	97	1	1	16	5.0	14	26	2,500	50	0.0	0.0
B / 7.9	2.5	4.1	14.54	22	1	0	97	1	1	16	5.0	16	26	2,500	50	0.0	0.0
B / 8.2	2.3	4.1	14.64	471	0	0	97	1	2	15	5.0	38	27	2,500	50	3.0	0.0
U /	N/A	4.1	14.63	1,094	0	0	97	1	2	15	5.0	N/A	27	0	0	0.0	0.0
B / 8.2	2.3	4.1	14.64	N/A	0	0	97	1	2	15	5.0	19	27	2,500	50	0.0	0.0
B / 8.2	2.3	4.1	14.64	114	0	0	97	1	2	15	5.0	20	27	2,500	50	0.0	0.0
B / 8.1	2.3	4.2	14.26	179	2	0	96	0	2	17	5.0	38	27	2,500	50	3.0	0.0
B / 8.0	2.4	4.2	14.25	N/A	2	0	96	0	2	17	5.0	18	27	2,500	50	0.0	0.0
B / 8.1	2.3	4.2	14.26	59	2	0	96	0	2	17	5.0	19	27	2,500	50	0.0	0.0
C+ / 5.7	3.2	4.9	11.04	251	0	17	0	32	51	198	3.5	56	11	2,500	50	4.3	0.0
C+ / 5.9	3.2	4.9	11.04	38	0	17	0	32	51	198	3.5	72	11	0	0	0.0	0.0
C+ / 5.8	3.2	4.9	11.04	1	0	17	0	32	51	198	3.5	32	11	2,500	50	0.0	0.0
C+ / 5.6	3.2	4.9	11.02	42	0	17	0	32	51	198	3.5	31	11	2,500	50	0.0	0.0
C+ / 6.0	3.1	4.9	11.05	1	0	17	0	32	51	198	3.5	73	11	0	0	0.0	0.0
C+ / 5.7	3.2	4.9	11.05	5	0	17	0	32	51	198	3.5	57	11	0	0	0.0	0.0
C+ / 5.6	3.2	4.9	11.04	3	0	17	0	32	51	198	3.5	48	11	0	0	0.0	0.0
C+ / 5.8	3.2	4.9	11.06	13	0	17	0	32	51	198	3.5	83	11	0	0	0.0	0.0
C- / 4.2	3.4	2.8	9.95	34	11	1	0	81	7	40	5.6	89	5	2,500	50	4.3	0.0
C- / 4.2	3.4	2.8	9.94	232	11	1	0	81	7	40	5.6	91	5	0	0	0.0	0.0
C- / 4.1	3.4	2.8	9.94	31	11	1	0	81	7	40	5.6	74	5	2,500	50	0.0	0.0
C- / 4.1	3.4	2.8	9.95	N/A	11	1	0	81	7	40	5.6	92	5	0	0	0.0	0.0
C- / 4.2	3.4	2.8	9.95	N/A	11	1	0	81	7	40	5.6	89	5	0	0	0.0	0.0
C- / 4.1	3.4	2.8	9.95	N/A	11	1	0	81	7	40	5.6	86	5	0	0	0.0	0.0
C+ / 6.4	3.0	2.5	10.22	358	0	1	95	3	1	17	0.0	9	6	5,000	0	0.0	0.0
C+ / 6.5	3.0	2.5	10.23	165	0	1	95	3	1	17	0.0	9	6	0	0	0.0	0.0
C+ / 6.5	3.0	2.5	10.25	37	0	1	95	3	1	17	0.0	8	6	2,500	50	3.0	0.0
C+ / 6.3	3.1	2.5	10.26	165	0	1	95	3	1	17	0.0	9	6	0	0	0.0	0.0
C+ / 6.6	3.0	2.5	10.23	12	0	1	95	3	1	17	0.0	6	6	2,500	50	0.0	0.0
E+ / 0.7	6.5	N/A	11.48	1,031	0	0	98	0	2	10	0.0	38	6	0	0	0.0	0.0
C / 4.8	3.6	4.6	11.50	475	0	0	100	0	0	12	4.5	64	21	2,500	50	3.0	0.0
C / 4.8	3.6	4.6	11.50	91	0	0	100	0	0	12	4.5	77	21	0	0	0.0	0.0
C / 4.7	3.6	4.6	11.50	N/A	0	0	100	0	0	12	4.5	36	21	2,500	50	0.0	0.0
C / 4.7	3.6	4.6	11.50	88	0	0	100	0	0	12	4.5	38	21	2,500	50	0.0	0.0
C / 5.3	3.3	4.6	11.30	105	2	0	97	0	1	21	5.4	62	21	2,500	50	3.0	0.0
C / 5.2	3.4	4.6	11.29	N/A	2	0	97	0	1	21	5.4	35	21	2,500	50	0.0	0.0
C / 5.2	3.4	4.6	11.29	26	2	0	97	0	1	21	5.4	36	21	2,500	50	0.0	0.0
C / 4.5	3.7	4.9	11.58	182	1	0	98	0	1	12	5.2	34	21	2,500	50	3.0	0.0
C / 4.5	3.7	4.9	11.56	N/A	1	0	98	0	1	12	5.2	17	21	2,500	50	0.0	0.0
C / 4.5	3.7	4.9	11.56	55	1	0	98	0	1	12	5.2	18	21	2,500	50	0.0	0.0

Fund Type	Fund Name (99 Pct = Best, 0 Pct = Worst)	Ticker Symbol	Overall Investment Rating	Phone	PERFORMANCE: Performance Rating/Pts	Total Return % through 3/31/16: 3 Mo	6 Mo	1Yr / Pct	Annualized: 3Yr / Pct	Annualized: 5Yr / Pct	Incl. in Returns: Dividend Yield	Incl. in Returns: Expense Ratio
MUS	AB Municipal Income II MI A	AMIAX	**C+**	(800) 221-5672	**B+ / 8.6**	1.92	4.04	4.96 /98	2.95 /88	4.13 /79	3.08	1.22
MUS ●	AB Municipal Income II MI B	AMIBX	**B-**	(800) 221-5672	**B+ / 8.6**	1.74	3.66	4.29 /96	2.22 /79	3.41 /73	2.44	1.99
MUS	AB Municipal Income II MI C	AMICX	**C+**	(800) 221-5672	**B+ / 8.6**	1.83	3.76	4.29 /96	2.22 /79	3.40 /73	2.44	1.98
MUS	AB Municipal Income II MN A	AMNAX	**A-**	(800) 221-5672	**B+ / 8.4**	1.82	2.92	3.56 /91	3.11 /89	4.75 /83	2.99	1.05
MUS ●	AB Municipal Income II MN B	AMNBX	**A-**	(800) 221-5672	**B+ / 8.4**	1.63	2.53	2.88 /84	2.37 /81	4.01 /77	2.34	1.82
MUS	AB Municipal Income II MN C	AMNCX	**A-**	(800) 221-5672	**B+ / 8.4**	1.63	2.54	2.78 /83	2.37 /81	4.01 /78	2.34	1.81
MUS	AB Municipal Income II NJ A	ANJAX	**B**	(800) 221-5672	**B+ / 8.3**	1.86	3.70	4.15 /95	2.82 /86	5.02 /85	3.31	0.97
MUS ●	AB Municipal Income II NJ B	ANJBX	**B**	(800) 221-5672	**B+ / 8.4**	1.78	3.42	3.48 /90	2.12 /78	4.31 /80	2.67	1.73
MUS	AB Municipal Income II NJ C	ANJCX	**B**	(800) 221-5672	**B+ / 8.3**	1.68	3.31	3.37 /89	2.08 /78	4.28 /80	2.67	1.72
MUS	AB Municipal Income II OH A	AOHAX	**B**	(800) 221-5672	**B / 8.2**	2.03	3.95	4.66 /97	2.59 /83	4.26 /79	2.93	0.98
MUS ●	AB Municipal Income II OH B	AOHBX	**B**	(800) 221-5672	**B / 8.2**	1.74	3.47	3.79 /92	1.83 /75	3.53 /74	2.29	1.75
MUS	AB Municipal Income II OH C	AOHCX	**B**	(800) 221-5672	**B / 8.2**	1.74	3.57	3.89 /93	1.86 /75	3.53 /74	2.29	1.74
MUS	AB Municipal Income II PA A	APAAX	**B+**	(800) 221-5672	**B+ / 8.8**	1.89	3.54	4.16 /95	3.33 /91	5.10 /86	2.91	1.01
MUS ●	AB Municipal Income II PA B	APABX	**B+**	(800) 221-5672	**B+ / 8.8**	1.61	3.06	3.39 /89	2.60 /84	4.36 /80	2.26	1.79
MUS	AB Municipal Income II PA C	APACX	**B+**	(800) 221-5672	**B+ / 8.7**	1.59	3.14	3.38 /89	2.59 /83	4.35 /80	2.25	1.77
MUS	AB Municipal Income II VA A	AVAAX	**B-**	(800) 221-5672	**B+ / 8.5**	1.84	3.11	3.92 /93	3.13 /89	5.11 /86	3.01	0.87
MUS ●	AB Municipal Income II VA B	AVABX	**B-**	(800) 221-5672	**B+ / 8.5**	1.56	2.73	3.15 /86	2.40 /82	4.38 /80	2.37	1.63
MUS	AB Municipal Income II VA C	AVACX	**B-**	(800) 221-5672	**B+ / 8.5**	1.66	2.74	3.16 /86	2.40 /82	4.38 /80	2.37	1.63
* MUN	AB Municipal Income Natl A	ALTHX	**B**	(800) 221-5672	**B+ / 8.7**	1.75	3.61	4.07 /94	3.23 /90	5.67 /90	3.17	0.80
MUN	AB Municipal Income Natl Adv	ALTVX	**B+**	(800) 221-5672	**A / 9.4**	1.81	3.74	4.32 /96	3.52 /93	5.98 /92	3.51	0.55
MUN ●	AB Municipal Income Natl B	ALTBX	**B**	(800) 221-5672	**B+ / 8.8**	1.67	3.44	3.40 /89	2.57 /83	4.96 /85	2.64	1.57
MUN	AB Municipal Income Natl C	ALNCX	**B**	(800) 221-5672	**B+ / 8.7**	1.56	3.23	3.30 /88	2.53 /83	4.93 /85	2.53	1.56
MUS	AB Municipal Income NY A	ALNYX	**B**	(800) 221-5672	**B / 8.2**	1.72	3.44	3.96 /94	2.76 /86	4.66 /83	2.96	0.83
MUS	AB Municipal Income NY Adv	ALNVX	**A-**	(800) 221-5672	**A- / 9.2**	1.78	3.67	4.32 /96	3.08 /89	4.98 /85	3.29	0.57
MUS ●	AB Municipal Income NY B	ALNBX	**B**	(800) 221-5672	**B / 8.2**	1.54	3.16	3.30 /88	2.04 /77	3.95 /77	2.32	1.59
MUS	AB Municipal Income NY C	ANYCX	**B**	(800) 221-5672	**B+ / 8.3**	1.54	3.16	3.29 /88	2.07 /78	3.94 /77	2.32	1.58
GEI	AB Short Duration A	ADPAX	**C-**	(800) 221-5672	**D- / 1.0**	0.62	0.14	0.26 /45	0.17 /28	0.28 /16	0.50	0.96
GEI ●	AB Short Duration B	ADPBX	**C-**	(800) 221-5672	**D / 1.7**	0.54	-0.10	-0.17 /29	-0.09 /15	-0.07 / 3	0.17	1.72
GEI	AB Short Duration C	ADPCX	**C-**	(800) 221-5672	**D / 1.8**	0.57	0.02	-0.12 /30	-0.06 /15	-0.01 / 3	0.22	1.72
MUN	AB Tax Aware Fxd Inc A	ATTAX	**U**	(800) 221-5672	**U /**	1.79	3.55	4.19 /95	--	--	1.77	2.18
MUN	AB Tax Aware Fxd Inc Adv	ATTYX	**U**	(800) 221-5672	**U /**	1.85	3.59	4.45 /96	--	--	2.07	1.92
MUN	AB Tax Aware Fxd Inc C	ATCCX	**U**	(800) 221-5672	**U /**	1.60	3.07	3.41 /89	--	--	1.09	2.85
GEN	AB Taxable MS Income	CSHTX	**B+**	(800) 221-5672	**C / 4.9**	1.21	0.98	1.15 /61	1.21 /46	2.36 /36	1.85	N/A
GL	AB Unconstrained Bond A	AGSAX	**D**	(800) 221-5672	**E+ / 0.8**	0.18	-0.22	-2.04 /15	0.20 /29	2.29 /35	2.33	1.01
GL	AB Unconstrained Bond Adv	AGSIX	**C-**	(800) 221-5672	**D+ / 2.8**	0.25	-0.08	-1.86 /16	0.50 /33	2.57 /39	2.74	0.76
GL ●	AB Unconstrained Bond B	AGSBX	**D+**	(800) 221-5672	**D- / 1.0**	-0.02	-0.59	-2.75 /12	-0.50 /11	1.60 /27	1.69	1.76
GL	AB Unconstrained Bond C	AGCCX	**D+**	(800) 221-5672	**D- / 1.0**	-0.01	-0.58	-2.73 /12	-0.48 /12	1.61 /27	1.72	1.77
GL	AB Unconstrained Bond I	AGLIX	**C-**	(800) 221-5672	**D+ / 2.8**	0.14	-0.17	-1.84 /16	0.50 /33	2.61 /39	2.77	0.78
GL	AB Unconstrained Bond K	AGSKX	**D+**	(800) 221-5672	**D / 1.8**	0.27	-0.14	-1.99 /16	0.26 /29	2.35 /36	2.35	1.12
GL	AB Unconstrained Bond R	AGSRX	**D+**	(800) 221-5672	**D- / 1.4**	0.08	-0.41	-2.30 /14	0.02 /18	2.11 /32	2.04	1.46
GL	Aberdeen Asia Bond A	AEEAX	**E+**	(866) 667-9231	**E+ / 0.8**	4.18	6.79	0.20 /44	-1.22 / 7	--	0.92	1.05
GL	Aberdeen Asia Bond C	AEECX	**E+**	(866) 667-9231	**E+ / 0.9**	3.92	6.31	-0.63 /25	-2.00 / 4	--	0.86	1.80
GL	Aberdeen Asia Bond Inst Service	ABISX	**E+**	(866) 667-9231	**D / 1.6**	4.19	6.69	0.10 /41	-1.23 / 7	1.16 /22	0.96	1.04
GL	Aberdeen Asia Bond Instituitonal	CSABX	**D-**	(866) 667-9231	**D+ / 2.6**	4.18	6.83	0.34 /47	-1.00 / 8	1.41 /25	1.00	0.80
GL	Aberdeen Asia Bond R	AEERX	**E+**	(866) 667-9231	**D- / 1.4**	4.09	6.67	-0.04 /31	-1.52 / 6	--	0.93	1.30
GL	Aberdeen Em Mkts Debt Loc Curr A	ADLAX	**E-**	(866) 667-9231	**E- / 0.0**	9.37	9.85	-5.08 / 5	-8.92 / 0	--	1.19	1.66
GL	Aberdeen Em Mkts Debt Loc Curr C	ADLCX	**E-**	(866) 667-9231	**E- / 0.0**	9.20	9.39	-5.66 / 4	-9.52 / 0	--	1.01	2.37
GL	Aberdeen Em Mkts Debt Loc Curr	AEDSX	**E-**	(866) 667-9231	**E- / 0.1**	9.45	10.00	-4.47 / 6	-8.61 / 0	--	1.30	1.37
GL	Aberdeen Em Mkts Debt Loc Curr IS	AEDIX	**E-**	(866) 667-9231	**E- / 0.1**	9.45	10.01	-4.59 / 6	-8.61 / 0	--	1.30	1.37
GL	Aberdeen Em Mkts Debt Loc Curr R	AECRX	**E-**	(866) 667-9231	**E- / 0.0**	9.15	9.57	-5.43 / 4	-9.31 / 0	--	1.20	2.12
EM	Aberdeen Emerging Markets Debt A	AKFAX	**E**	(866) 667-9231	**E+ / 0.8**	4.80	6.33	-0.24 /29	-1.20 / 7	--	3.79	1.85
EM	Aberdeen Emerging Markets Debt C	AKFCX	**E**	(866) 667-9231	**D- / 1.0**	4.68	5.98	-0.98 /22	-1.87 / 5	--	3.45	2.60

● Denotes fund is closed to new investors
* Denotes fund is included in Section II

RISK			NET ASSETS		ASSET							FUND MANAGER		MINIMUM		LOADS	
Risk Rating/Pts	3 Yr Avg Standard Deviation	Avg Duration	NAV As of 3/31/16	Total $(Mil)	Cash %	Gov. Bond %	Muni. Bond %	Corp. Bond %	Other %	Portfolio Turnover Ratio	Avg Coupon Rate	Manager Quality Pct	Manager Tenure (Years)	Initial Purch. $	Additional Purch. $	Front End Load	Back End Load
C- / 3.8	4.1	4.9	10.63	38	0	0	99	0	1	5	5.4	24	21	2,500	50	3.0	0.0
C- / 3.8	4.1	4.9	10.61	N/A	0	0	99	0	1	5	5.4	13	21	2,500	50	0.0	0.0
C- / 3.7	4.2	4.9	10.62	19	0	0	99	0	1	5	5.4	12	21	2,500	50	0.0	0.0
C+ / 5.7	3.2	4.9	10.52	67	0	0	99	0	1	11	5.2	52	21	2,500	50	3.0	0.0
C+ / 5.7	3.2	4.9	10.52	N/A	0	0	99	0	1	11	5.2	29	21	2,500	50	0.0	0.0
C+ / 5.7	3.2	4.9	10.53	16	0	0	99	0	1	11	5.2	29	21	2,500	50	0.0	0.0
C / 4.8	3.6	4.8	9.87	86	0	0	99	0	1	2	4.9	32	21	2,500	50	3.0	0.0
C / 4.8	3.5	4.8	9.88	N/A	0	0	99	0	1	2	4.9	17	21	2,500	50	0.0	0.0
C / 4.9	3.5	4.8	9.88	30	0	0	99	0	1	2	4.9	17	21	2,500	50	0.0	0.0
C / 5.1	3.4	5.0	10.16	87	2	0	97	0	1	14	5.2	32	23	2,500	50	3.0	0.0
C / 5.1	3.4	5.0	10.14	N/A	2	0	97	0	1	14	5.2	16	23	2,500	50	0.0	0.0
C / 5.1	3.4	5.0	10.15	27	2	0	97	0	1	14	5.2	16	23	2,500	50	0.0	0.0
C / 4.6	3.7	5.0	10.67	75	2	0	98	0	0	2	5.1	44	21	2,500	50	3.0	0.0
C / 4.5	3.7	5.0	10.67	N/A	2	0	98	0	0	2	5.1	24	21	2,500	50	0.0	0.0
C / 4.5	3.7	5.0	10.67	22	2	0	98	0	0	2	5.1	24	21	2,500	50	0.0	0.0
C / 4.3	3.8	4.7	11.33	187	1	0	98	0	1	5	5.1	33	21	2,500	50	3.0	0.0
C / 4.3	3.8	4.7	11.31	N/A	1	0	98	0	1	5	5.1	17	21	2,500	50	0.0	0.0
C- / 4.2	3.8	4.7	11.30	55	1	0	98	0	1	5	5.1	17	21	2,500	50	0.0	0.0
C / 4.3	3.8	4.8	10.43	635	2	0	97	0	1	6	5.4	35	21	2,500	50	3.0	0.0
C- / 4.2	3.9	4.8	10.43	429	2	0	97	0	1	6	5.4	42	21	0	0	0.0	0.0
C- / 4.2	3.8	4.8	10.42	1	2	0	97	0	1	6	5.4	19	21	2,500	50	0.0	0.0
C- / 4.2	3.8	4.8	10.42	142	2	0	97	0	1	6	5.4	18	21	2,500	50	0.0	0.0
C / 4.9	3.5	4.7	10.13	449	3	0	96	0	1	12	5.0	33	21	2,500	50	3.0	0.0
C / 4.9	3.5	4.7	10.14	47	3	0	96	0	1	12	5.0	41	21	0	0	0.0	0.0
C / 5.0	3.5	4.7	10.12	1	3	0	96	0	1	12	5.0	17	21	2,500	50	0.0	0.0
C / 5.0	3.5	4.7	10.13	79	3	0	96	0	1	12	5.0	17	21	2,500	50	0.0	0.0
A+ / 9.7	0.6	1.8	11.74	27	9	19	0	26	46	86	1.6	52	11	2,500	50	4.3	0.0
A+ / 9.7	0.6	1.8	11.71	N/A	9	19	0	26	46	86	1.6	42	11	2,500	50	0.0	0.0
A+ / 9.7	0.6	1.8	11.71	13	9	19	0	26	46	86	1.6	43	11	2,500	50	0.0	0.0
U /	N/A	6.0	10.82	7	4	0	92	2	2	35	0.0	N/A	3	2,500	50	3.0	0.0
U /	N/A	6.0	10.82	31	4	0	92	2	2	35	0.0	N/A	3	0	0	0.0	0.0
U /	N/A	6.0	10.82	2	4	0	92	2	2	35	0.0	N/A	3	2,500	50	0.0	0.0
A / 9.4	0.9	N/A	9.90	267	0	4	0	71	25	109	0.0	83	6	0	0	0.0	0.0
B- / 7.3	2.8	4.6	8.35	44	15	51	0	19	15	149	2.3	74	20	2,500	50	4.3	0.0
B- / 7.4	2.7	4.6	8.34	210	15	51	0	19	15	149	2.3	82	20	0	0	0.0	0.0
B- / 7.3	2.8	4.6	8.36	N/A	15	51	0	19	15	149	2.3	43	20	2,500	50	0.0	0.0
B- / 7.5	2.7	4.6	8.35	24	15	51	0	19	15	149	2.3	43	20	2,500	50	0.0	0.0
B- / 7.4	2.7	4.6	8.33	44	15	51	0	19	15	149	2.3	83	20	0	0	0.0	0.0
B- / 7.3	2.8	4.6	8.38	N/A	15	51	0	19	15	149	2.3	76	20	0	0	0.0	0.0
B- / 7.4	2.7	4.6	8.35	1	15	51	0	19	15	149	2.3	64	20	0	0	0.0	0.0
D- / 1.5	6.1	3.2	9.97	1	6	38	0	53	3	93	5.0	24	7	1,000	50	4.3	0.0
D- / 1.5	6.1	3.2	9.81	N/A	6	38	0	53	3	93	5.0	12	7	1,000	50	0.0	0.0
D / 1.6	6.1	3.2	9.95	10	6	38	0	53	3	93	5.0	24	7	1,000,000	0	0.0	0.0
D / 1.6	6.1	3.2	9.98	23	6	38	0	53	3	93	5.0	30	7	1,000,000	0	0.0	0.0
D- / 1.5	6.1	3.2	9.92	N/A	6	38	0	53	3	93	5.0	18	7	0	0	0.0	0.0
E- / 0.1	12.7	5.0	7.24	N/A	2	85	0	11	2	58	0.0	0	5	1,000	50	4.3	0.0
E- / 0.1	12.6	5.0	7.12	N/A	2	85	0	11	2	58	0.0	0	5	1,000	50	0.0	0.0
E- / 0.0	12.7	5.0	7.30	9	2	85	0	11	2	58	0.0	0	5	1,000,000	0	0.0	0.0
E- / 0.1	12.6	5.0	7.30	N/A	2	85	0	11	2	58	0.0	0	5	1,000,000	0	0.0	0.0
E- / 0.1	12.6	5.0	7.16	1	2	85	0	11	2	58	0.0	0	5	0	0	0.0	0.0
E / 0.5	7.8	6.5	8.73	N/A	3	75	1	15	6	65	0.0	25	4	1,000	50	4.3	0.0
E / 0.5	7.8	6.5	8.72	1	3	75	1	15	6	65	0.0	14	4	1,000	50	0.0	0.0

99 Pct = Best 0 Pct = Worst Fund Type	Fund Name	Ticker Symbol	Overall Investment Rating	Phone	PERFORMANCE Performance Rating/Pts	Total Return % through 3/31/16 3 Mo	6 Mo	1Yr / Pct	Annualized 3Yr / Pct	5Yr / Pct	Incl. in Returns Dividend Yield	Expense Ratio
EM	Aberdeen Emerging Markets Debt	AKFIX	**E+**	(866) 667-9231	**D+ / 2.3**	4.93	6.52	0.01 /31	-1.04 / 8	--	4.20	1.60
EM	Aberdeen Emerging Markets Debt IS	AKFSX	**D-**	(866) 667-9231	**D+ / 2.7**	4.92	6.51	0.12 /42	-0.94 / 9	--	4.20	1.60
EM	Aberdeen Emerging Markets Debt R	AKFRX	**E+**	(866) 667-9231	**D- / 1.4**	4.80	6.22	-0.51 /26	-1.41 / 6	--	3.80	2.10
GL	Aberdeen Global Fixed Income A	CUGAX	**D-**	(866) 667-9231	**D- / 1.1**	5.31	4.20	2.23 /73	-0.80 / 9	0.31 /16	0.31	1.71
GL	Aberdeen Global Fixed Income C	CGBCX	**D-**	(866) 667-9231	**D- / 1.3**	5.04	3.79	1.38 /64	-1.56 / 6	-0.42 / 2	0.21	2.46
GL	Aberdeen Global Fixed Income Inst	AGCIX	**D**	(866) 667-9231	**C- / 3.6**	5.39	4.33	2.48 /74	-0.54 /11	0.59 /18	0.36	1.46
GL	Aberdeen Global Fixed Income IS	CGFIX	**D**	(866) 667-9231	**C- / 3.1**	5.19	4.20	2.13 /73	-0.75 /10	0.42 /17	0.33	1.62
GL	Aberdeen Global High Income A	BJBHX	**E+**	(866) 667-9231	**E / 0.3**	-0.16	-3.76	-10.69 / 1	-1.10 / 8	2.01 /31	5.25	1.01
GL	Aberdeen Global High Income I	JHYIX	**E+**	(866) 667-9231	**E / 0.4**	-0.10	-3.60	-10.49 / 1	-0.84 / 9	2.27 /34	5.89	0.75
MUN	Aberdeen Tax-Free Income A	NTFAX	**C+**	(866) 667-9231	**C+ / 6.2**	1.15	1.74	2.04 /77	2.31 /80	4.47 /81	2.96	1.00
MUN	Aberdeen Tax-Free Income C	GTICX	**B**	(866) 667-9231	**B- / 7.0**	0.97	1.37	1.30 /72	1.56 /69	3.70 /75	2.37	1.75
MUN	Aberdeen Tax-Free Income Inst	ABEIX	**A**	(866) 667-9231	**B+ / 8.4**	1.21	1.87	2.31 /79	2.57 /83	4.73 /83	3.35	0.75
MUN	Aberdeen Tax-Free Income IS	ABESX	**A**	(866) 667-9231	**B+ / 8.4**	1.22	1.88	2.22 /79	2.58 /83	--	3.36	0.75
MUN	Aberdeen Tax-Free Income R	ABERX	**A-**	(866) 667-9231	**B / 7.9**	1.09	1.63	1.82 /76	2.07 /78	--	2.87	1.25
GL	Aberdeen Total Return Bond A	BJBGX	**C**	(866) 667-9231	**C+ / 5.9**	2.92	2.50	0.95 /58	1.56 /53	3.47 /52	1.44	0.71
GL	Aberdeen Total Return Bond I	JBGIX	**C**	(866) 667-9231	**C+ / 6.3**	2.95	2.59	1.24 /62	1.83 /58	3.73 /57	1.73	0.43
GEI	Aberdeen Ultra-Short Dur Bond A	AUDAX	**C-**	(866) 667-9231	**D- / 1.0**	0.31	0.22	0.22 /44	0.17 /28	--	0.40	1.38
GEI	Aberdeen Ultra-Short Dur Bond Inst	AUDIX	**C+**	(866) 667-9231	**C- / 3.1**	0.27	0.34	0.47 /49	0.35 /31	0.66 /18	0.67	1.13
GEI	Aberdeen Ultra-Short Dur Bond IS	AUSIX	**C+**	(866) 667-9231	**C- / 3.1**	0.27	0.34	0.37 /47	0.35 /31	--	0.67	1.13
USS	Access Cap Community Invs A	ACASX	**C+**	(800) 422-2766	**C / 4.3**	1.77	1.36	1.49 /66	1.79 /57	2.70 /40	2.67	1.06
USS	Access Cap Community Invs I	ACCSX	**A**	(800) 422-2766	**C+ / 6.7**	1.86	1.65	1.97 /72	2.18 /65	3.02 /45	3.14	0.63
COH	Access Flex Bear High Yield Inv	AFBIX	**E-**	(888) 776-3637	**E- / 0.0**	-6.06	-8.05	-7.66 / 2	-9.52 / 0	-12.00 / 0	0.00	2.60
COH	Access Flex Bear High Yield Svc	AFBSX	**E-**	(888) 776-3637	**E- / 0.0**	-6.23	-8.54	-8.54 / 1	-10.45 / 0	-12.91 / 0	0.00	3.60
COH	Access Flex High Yield Inv	FYAIX	**C-**	(888) 776-3637	**B+ / 8.5**	4.41	5.14	2.25 /73	3.76 /82	5.71 /75	8.44	1.77
COH	Access Flex High Yield Svc	FYASX	**C-**	(888) 776-3637	**B / 7.8**	4.25	4.69	1.31 /63	2.73 /74	4.68 /69	7.83	2.77
MM	Active Assets Inst Govt Sec Trust	AISXX	**C**	(800) 869-6397	**D / 2.2**	0.05	0.06	0.07 /40	0.03 /22	0.02 / 7	0.07	0.18
MM	Active Assets Inst Money Trust	AVIXX	**C**	(800) 869-6397	**D+ / 2.5**	0.08	0.11	0.14 /42	0.06 /25	0.07 /14	0.14	0.18
MM	Active Assets Money Trust	AAMXX	**C**	(800) 869-6397	**D / 2.0**	0.03	0.04	0.04 /37	0.02 /18	0.02 / 7	0.05	0.42
COH	Advance Capital I Ret Inc Inst	ADRNX	**C+**	(800) 345-4783	**B / 7.6**	3.09	2.83	1.46 /66	2.77 /74	4.28 /65	3.13	0.66
COH	Advance Capital I Ret Inc Retail	ADRIX	**C+**	(800) 345-4783	**B- / 7.3**	3.09	2.71	1.07 /60	2.51 /71	4.02 /62	2.74	0.90
COI	Advantus Short Duration Bond Inst	VBSIX	**U**	(800) 665-6005	**U /**	0.55	-0.22	-0.01 /31	--	--	1.81	0.74
COI	Advantus Short Duration Bond Inv	ABSNX	**U**	(800) 665-6005	**U /**	0.49	-0.34	--	--	--	0.00	0.99
GES	AdvisorOne CLS Flexible Income N	CLFLX	**C**	(866) 811-0225	**C / 4.5**	2.26	2.08	0.08 /40	0.90 /41	2.45 /37	2.33	1.22
GL	AdvisorOne Horizon Active Income N	AIMNX	**U**	(866) 811-0225	**U /**	1.64	1.30	-1.62 /18	--	--	1.44	1.50
MTG	Advisors Series Trust PIA MBS Bond	PMTGX	**A**	(800) 251-1970	**B- / 7.2**	1.88	1.50	1.85 /70	2.58 /72	3.05 /46	2.85	0.30
GEN	Advisory Research Strategic Income	ADVNX	**C-**	(888) 665-1414	**C+ / 6.3**	0.56	1.83	0.64 /52	2.80 /74	--	4.63	1.14
GEI	AI Boyd Watterson Core+ A	IBFSX	**C-**	(866) 410-2006	**C- / 4.1**	2.42	1.58	0.28 /45	1.91 /60	3.12 /47	1.85	1.06
GEI	AI Boyd Watterson Core+ I	IIISX	**B**	(866) 410-2006	**C+ / 6.7**	2.61	1.82	0.68 /53	2.28 /67	3.49 /53	2.24	0.71
MUS	AI KS Tax-Exempt Bond A	IKSTX	**A**	(866) 410-2006	**B- / 7.5**	1.16	1.94	2.40 /80	2.89 /87	3.95 /77	2.52	0.97
MUS	AI KS Tax-Exempt Bond C	IKTEX	**A+**	(866) 410-2006	**B / 8.1**	1.02	1.67	1.82 /76	2.28 /80	3.33 /73	2.06	1.58
MUS	AI KS Tax-Exempt Bond I	SEKSX	**A+**	(866) 410-2006	**A- / 9.1**	1.25	2.09	2.75 /83	3.27 /91	4.35 /80	2.97	0.58
USS	AI US Infl Protected A	FNIHX	**E+**	(866) 410-2006	**E+ / 0.6**	4.40	3.62	1.07 /60	-1.43 / 6	2.39 /36	0.11	1.14
GEI	AI US Infl Protected C	FCIHX	**E+**	(866) 410-2006	**E+ / 0.9**	4.20	3.30	0.41 /48	-1.98 / 4	--	0.12	1.69
USS	AI US Infl Protected Inst	FFIHX	**D-**	(866) 410-2006	**D / 1.8**	4.48	3.80	1.35 /64	-1.01 / 8	2.83 /42	0.12	0.69
GEI	AI US Infl Protected Prm	AIIPX	**D-**	(866) 410-2006	**D / 1.6**	4.50	3.82	1.26 /63	-1.15 / 8	2.74 /41	0.12	0.84
MUS	Alabama Tax Free Bond	ALABX	**B+**	(866) 738-1125	**C / 5.4**	0.67	0.70	1.27 /71	0.89 /50	1.66 /38	1.26	0.79
GEI	AllianceBern CBF Bond IS A		**U**	(800) 221-5672	**U /**	4.07	3.23	1.19 /61	--	--	0.00	N/A
GEI	AllianceBern CBF Bond IS C		**U**	(800) 221-5672	**U /**	3.92	2.86	0.40 /48	--	--	0.00	N/A
GEI	AllianceBern CBF Bond IS R		**U**	(800) 221-5672	**U /**	4.16	3.43	1.48 /66	--	--	0.00	N/A
GEI	AllianceBern CBF Bond IS RI		**U**	(800) 221-5672	**U /**	4.16	3.42	1.48 /66	--	--	0.00	N/A
GEI	AllianceBern CBF Global Bond A		**U**	(800) 221-5672	**U /**	2.94	2.94	1.59 /67	--	--	0.00	N/A
GEI	AllianceBern CBF Global Bond B		**U**	(800) 221-5672	**U /**	2.79	2.59	0.95 /58	--	--	0.00	N/A

● Denotes fund is closed to new investors
* Denotes fund is included in Section II

RISK			NET ASSETS		ASSET							FUND MANAGER		MINIMUM		LOADS	
Risk Rating/Pts	3 Yr Avg Standard Deviation	Avg Duration	NAV As of 3/31/16	Total $(Mil)	Cash %	Gov. Bond %	Muni. Bond %	Corp. Bond %	Other %	Portfolio Turnover Ratio	Avg Coupon Rate	Manager Quality Pct	Manager Tenure (Years)	Initial Purch. $	Additional Purch. $	Front End Load	Back End Load
E / 0.5	7.8	6.5	8.73	28	3	75	1	15	6	65	0.0	30	4	1,000,000	0	0.0	0.0
E / 0.5	7.8	6.5	8.74	N/A	3	75	1	15	6	65	0.0	33	4	1,000,000	0	0.0	0.0
E / 0.5	7.8	6.5	8.73	N/A	3	75	1	15	6	65	0.0	21	4	0	0	0.0	0.0
D+ / 2.7	5.1	6.7	9.72	1	2	49	0	32	17	174	5.7	37	7	1,000	50	4.3	0.0
D+ / 2.8	5.0	6.7	9.59	N/A	2	49	0	32	17	174	5.7	18	7	1,000	50	0.0	0.0
D+ / 2.7	5.0	6.7	9.78	2	2	49	0	32	17	174	5.7	45	7	1,000,000	0	0.0	0.0
D+ / 2.8	5.0	6.7	9.73	11	2	49	0	32	17	174	5.7	39	7	1,000,000	0	0.0	0.0
D / 2.0	5.6	N/A	8.33	336	6	3	0	79	12	79	0.0	26	14	1,000	50	0.0	0.0
D / 2.0	5.6	N/A	7.85	532	6	3	0	79	12	79	0.0	33	14	1,000,000	0	0.0	0.0
C+ / 6.4	3.0	4.4	10.21	10	0	0	100	0	0	5	4.8	33	3	1,000	50	4.3	0.0
C+ / 6.4	3.0	4.4	10.20	1	0	0	100	0	0	5	4.8	17	3	1,000	50	0.0	0.0
C+ / 6.5	3.0	4.4	10.22	83	0	0	100	0	0	5	4.8	41	3	1,000,000	0	0.0	0.0
C+ / 6.4	3.0	4.4	10.22	N/A	0	0	100	0	0	5	4.8	41	3	1,000,000	0	0.0	0.0
C+ / 6.5	3.0	4.4	10.22	N/A	0	0	100	0	0	5	4.8	27	3	0	0	0.0	0.0
C / 5.2	3.4	4.7	13.51	73	3	13	4	38	42	102	0.0	94	15	1,000	50	0.0	0.0
C / 5.3	3.4	4.7	13.33	889	3	13	4	38	42	102	0.0	95	15	1,000,000	0	0.0	0.0
A+ / 9.9	0.3	0.7	9.92	1	1	21	0	76	2	59	0.9	64	6	1,000	50	4.3	0.0
A+ / 9.9	0.3	0.7	9.89	7	1	21	0	76	2	59	0.9	74	6	100,000	0	0.0	0.0
A+ / 9.9	0.3	0.7	9.89	N/A	1	21	0	76	2	59	0.9	74	6	100,000	0	0.0	0.0
B / 8.2	2.3	N/A	9.25	21	0	0	3	0	97	23	0.0	79	10	2,500	100	3.8	0.0
B+ / 8.3	2.2	N/A	9.25	532	0	0	3	0	97	23	0.0	87	10	1,000,000	10,000	0.0	0.0
E+ / 0.7	6.5	N/A	8.68	1	100	0	0	0	0	0	0.0	0	11	15,000	0	0.0	0.0
E+ / 0.7	6.5	N/A	7.82	N/A	100	0	0	0	0	0	0.0	0	11	15,000	0	0.0	0.0
D- / 1.2	5.9	N/A	32.19	26	48	51	0	0	1	2,247	0.0	97	12	15,000	0	0.0	0.0
D- / 1.2	5.9	N/A	31.41	10	48	51	0	0	1	2,247	0.0	92	12	15,000	0	0.0	0.0
A+ / 9.9	N/A	N/A	1.00	2,753	100	0	0	0	0	0	0.1	64	N/A	2,000,000	0	0.0	0.0
A+ / 9.9	N/A	N/A	1.00	1,453	100	0	0	0	0	0	0.1	66	N/A	2,000,000	0	0.0	0.0
A+ / 9.9	N/A	N/A	1.00	5,240	100	0	0	0	0	0	0.1	64	N/A	5,000	0	0.0	0.0
C / 4.5	3.2	5.7	8.78	1	5	16	2	52	25	37	4.0	96	21	250,000	0	0.0	0.0
C / 4.4	3.2	5.7	8.79	128	5	16	2	52	25	37	4.0	95	21	10,000	0	0.0	0.0
U /	N/A	N/A	9.86	25	3	13	0	46	38	119	0.0	N/A	2	100,000	1,000	0.0	0.0
U /	N/A	N/A	9.86	N/A	3	13	0	46	38	119	0.0	N/A	2	1,000	100	0.0	0.0
B- / 7.4	2.7	N/A	10.11	196	0	29	4	45	22	5	0.0	34	2	2,500	250	0.0	0.0
U /	N/A	N/A	9.92	182	0	0	0	0	100	324	0.0	N/A	3	2,500	250	0.0	0.0
B / 8.0	2.4	4.3	9.76	90	0	0	0	0	100	161	0.0	62	10	1,000	50	0.0	0.0
C / 4.3	3.8	N/A	9.36	14	6	0	0	46	48	26	0.0	86	13	2,500	500	0.0	2.0
C+ / 6.7	3.0	4.9	11.00	2	3	21	0	39	37	68	0.0	42	10	5,000	250	4.3	0.0
C+ / 6.6	3.0	4.9	10.93	92	3	21	0	39	37	68	0.0	55	10	3,000,000	5,000	0.0	0.0
B- / 7.2	2.8	4.9	11.18	11	7	0	92	0	1	13	0.0	60	16	5,000	250	4.3	0.0
B- / 7.2	2.8	4.9	11.18	1	7	0	92	0	1	13	0.0	39	16	5,000	250	0.0	0.0
B- / 7.2	2.8	4.9	11.18	176	7	0	92	0	1	13	0.0	78	16	3,000,000	5,000	0.0	0.0
D / 2.2	5.2	8.1	10.67	10	1	98	0	0	1	200	0.0	5	10	5,000	250	4.3	0.0
D+ / 2.3	5.2	8.1	10.42	9	1	98	0	0	1	200	0.0	2	10	5,000	250	0.0	0.0
D+ / 2.3	5.1	8.1	10.72	235	1	98	0	0	1	200	0.0	6	10	20,000,000	5,000	0.0	0.0
D+ / 2.3	5.1	8.1	10.68	2	1	98	0	0	1	200	0.0	4	10	250,000	5,000	0.0	0.0
B+ / 8.9	1.5	2.7	10.49	29	4	0	95	0	1	6	0.0	46	23	5,000	0	0.0	0.0
U /	N/A	N/A	10.22	1	0	0	0	0	100	0	0.0	N/A	N/A	1,000	50	4.3	0.0
U /	N/A	N/A	10.08	N/A	0	0	0	0	100	0	0.0	N/A	N/A	1,000	50	0.0	0.0
U /	N/A	N/A	10.26	N/A	0	0	0	0	100	0	0.0	N/A	N/A	250	50	0.0	0.0
U /	N/A	N/A	10.27	N/A	0	0	0	0	100	0	0.0	N/A	N/A	250	50	0.0	0.0
U /	N/A	N/A	10.84	23	0	0	0	0	100	0	0.0	N/A	N/A	1,000	50	4.3	0.0
U /	N/A	N/A	10.68	2	0	0	0	0	100	0	0.0	N/A	N/A	1,000	50	0.0	0.0

Fund Type	Fund Name (99 Pct = Best, 0 Pct = Worst)	Ticker Symbol	Overall Investment Rating	Phone	PERFORMANCE: Performance Rating/Pts	Total Return % through 3/31/16: 3 Mo	6 Mo	1Yr / Pct	Annualized: 3Yr / Pct	5Yr / Pct	Incl. in Returns: Dividend Yield	Expense Ratio
GEI	AllianceBern CBF Global Bond C		**U**	(800) 221-5672	**U** /	2.79	2.59	0.95 /58	--	--	0.00	N/A
GEI	AllianceBern CBF Global Bond R		**U**	(800) 221-5672	**U** /	3.02	3.12	1.96 /71	--	--	0.00	0.59
GEI	AllianceBern CBF Global Bond RA		**U**	(800) 221-5672	**U** /	2.94	2.94	1.69 /69	--	--	0.00	0.84
GEI	AllianceBern CBF Global Bond RI		**U**	(800) 221-5672	**U** /	3.02	3.12	1.96 /71	--	--	0.00	N/A
GEI	AllianceBern CBF Global Bond RZ		**U**	(800) 221-5672	**U** /	3.02	3.12	1.96 /71	--	--	0.00	N/A
GEI	AllianceBern CBF PrincPro Income A		**B-**	(800) 221-5672	**C- / 3.9**	0.43	0.89	1.85 /70	1.83 /58	2.20 /34	0.00	1.15
GEI	AllianceBern CBF PrincPro Income B		**B+**	(800) 221-5672	**C / 4.5**	0.25	0.51	1.09 /60	1.07 /44	1.43 /25	0.00	1.90
GEI	AllianceBern CBF PrincPro Income C		**B+**	(800) 221-5672	**C / 4.5**	0.25	0.51	1.09 /60	1.07 /44	1.43 /25	0.00	1.90
GEI	AllianceBern CBF PrincPro Income R		**A+**	(800) 221-5672	**C+ / 6.7**	0.55	1.12	2.31 /74	2.29 /67	2.66 /40	0.00	0.70
GEI	AllianceBern CBF PrincPro Income		**A+**	(800) 221-5672	**C+ / 6.2**	0.48	0.99	2.05 /72	2.03 /62	2.40 /36	0.00	0.95
EM	AllianzGI Emerging Markets Dbt Inst	AGMIX	**U**	(800) 988-8380	**U** /	4.63	5.29	0.12 /42	--	--	4.05	1.84
EM	AllianzGI Emerging Markets Debt A	AGMAX	**U**	(800) 988-8380	**U** /	4.67	5.20	-0.09 /30	--	--	3.63	2.10
EM	AllianzGI Emerging Markets Debt C	AGMCX	**U**	(800) 988-8380	**U** /	4.50	4.83	-0.82 /23	--	--	2.54	2.84
EM	AllianzGI Emerging Markets Debt P	AGMPX	**U**	(800) 988-8380	**U** /	4.65	5.27	0.05 /38	--	--	3.83	1.87
COH	AllianzGI High Yield Bond A	AYBAX	**E**	(800) 988-8380	**E+ / 0.6**	1.50	-0.67	-6.05 / 3	0.23 /29	3.45 /52	6.32	0.94
COH	AllianzGI High Yield Bond Admn	AYBVX	**E+**	(800) 988-8380	**D- / 1.1**	1.61	-0.57	-6.59 / 3	0.05 /24	3.37 /51	7.16	0.97
COH	AllianzGI High Yield Bond C	AYBCX	**E**	(800) 988-8380	**E+ / 0.7**	1.27	-0.97	-6.73 / 2	-0.49 /12	2.71 /40	5.82	1.67
COH	AllianzGI High Yield Bond Inst	AYBIX	**E+**	(800) 988-8380	**D / 1.7**	1.61	-0.42	-5.65 / 4	0.60 /35	3.83 /59	7.20	0.64
COH	AllianzGI High Yield Bond P	AYBPX	**E+**	(800) 988-8380	**D / 1.6**	1.50	-0.54	-5.68 / 4	0.54 /34	3.71 /57	7.21	0.71
COH	AllianzGI High Yield Bond R	AYBRX	**E+**	(800) 988-8380	**E+ / 0.9**	1.49	-0.91	-6.71 / 2	-0.24 /14	3.05 /46	6.17	1.45
COH	AllianzGI Short Dur High Inc A	ASHAX	**C-**	(800) 988-8380	**C / 4.8**	1.90	0.38	-0.76 /24	2.10 /63	--	5.68	0.88
COH	AllianzGI Short Dur High Inc C	ASHCX	**C-**	(800) 988-8380	**C / 5.4**	1.86	0.29	-1.06 /21	1.83 /58	--	5.44	1.13
COH	AllianzGI Short Dur High Inc Inst	ASHIX	**C**	(800) 988-8380	**C+ / 6.3**	2.01	0.50	-0.50 /26	2.35 /68	--	6.37	0.60
COH	AllianzGI Short Dur High Inc P	ASHPX	**C**	(800) 988-8380	**C+ / 6.2**	2.00	0.53	-0.51 /26	2.29 /67	--	6.21	0.68
GEI	AlphaCentric Bond Rotation A	BDRAX	**U**	(844) 223-8637	**U** /	1.84	0.26	--	--	--	0.00	2.00
GEI	AlphaCentric Bond Rotation C	BDRCX	**U**	(844) 223-8637	**U** /	1.72	-0.11	--	--	--	0.00	2.75
GEI	AlphaCentric Bond Rotation I	BDRIX	**U**	(844) 223-8637	**U** /	1.99	0.37	--	--	--	0.00	1.75
GEN	AlphaCentric Income Opportunities A	IOFAX	**U**	(844) 223-8637	**U** /	0.28	2.33	--	--	--	0.00	2.15
GEN	AlphaCentric Income Opportunities C	IOFCX	**U**	(844) 223-8637	**U** /	0.10	1.90	--	--	--	0.00	2.90
GEN	AlphaCentric Income Opportunities I	IOFIX	**U**	(844) 223-8637	**U** /	0.33	2.35	--	--	--	0.00	1.90
MUH	Alpine HY Managed Duration Muni A	AAHMX	**U**	(888) 785-5578	**U** /	1.64	2.03	2.80 /83	--	--	2.97	1.37
MUH	Alpine HY Managed Duration Muni	AHYMX	**U**	(888) 785-5578	**U** /	1.70	2.15	3.04 /85	--	--	3.28	1.12
MUN	Alpine Ultra Short Muni Inc A	ATOAX	**C**	(888) 785-5578	**D+ / 2.3**	-0.03	0.03	0.19 /46	0.24 /31	0.52 /19	0.29	1.18
MUN	Alpine Ultra Short Muni Inc Inst	ATOIX	**B-**	(888) 785-5578	**C- / 3.7**	0.13	0.26	0.54 /56	0.52 /39	0.79 /22	0.54	0.93
GL	Altegris Fixed Income Long Short A	FXDAX	**E+**	(877) 772-5838	**E- / 0.0**	-8.11	-11.62	-14.75 / 0	-2.09 / 4	--	6.45	2.61
GL	Altegris Fixed Income Long Short C	FXDCX	**U**	(877) 772-5838	**U** /	-8.29	-11.98	-15.49 / 0	--	--	5.84	3.45
GL	Altegris Fixed Income Long Short I	FXDIX	**E+**	(877) 772-5838	**E- / 0.1**	-8.04	-11.49	-14.59 / 0	-1.87 / 5	--	7.07	2.39
GL	Altegris Fixed Income Long Short N	FXDNX	**E+**	(877) 772-5838	**E- / 0.1**	-8.01	-11.53	-14.76 / 0	-2.12 / 4	--	6.75	2.64
GL	Altegris Futures Evolution Strat A	EVOAX	**C-**	(877) 772-5838	**A+ / 9.6**	3.31	3.46	-1.18 /20	9.46 /99	--	7.56	1.98
GL	Altegris Futures Evolution Strat I	EVOIX	**C-**	(877) 772-5838	**A+ / 9.9**	3.42	3.59	-0.88 /23	9.75 /99	--	8.71	1.74
GL	Altegris Futures Evolution Strat N	EVONX	**C-**	(877) 772-5838	**A+ / 9.9**	3.31	3.44	-1.21 /20	9.47 /99	--	8.00	1.99
GEN	Amana Participation Institutional	AMIPX	**U**	(800) 732-6262	**U** /	0.86	0.25	--	--	--	0.00	N/A
GEN	Amana Participation Investor	AMAPX	**U**	(800) 732-6262	**U** /	0.80	0.10	--	--	--	0.00	N/A
COH	American Beacon Crescent SD HI A	ACHAX	**U**	(800) 658-5811	**U** /	1.71	0.98	-2.15 /15	--	--	4.38	1.96
COH	American Beacon Crescent SD HI C	ACHCX	**U**	(800) 658-5811	**U** /	1.55	0.63	-2.83 /12	--	--	3.76	2.71
COH	American Beacon Crescent SD HI	ACHIX	**U**	(800) 658-5811	**U** /	1.76	1.13	-1.79 /17	--	--	4.86	1.56
COH	American Beacon Crescent SD HI Inv	ACHPX	**U**	(800) 658-5811	**U** /	1.71	0.99	-2.11 /15	--	--	4.52	1.94
COH	American Beacon Crescent SD HI Y	ACHYX	**U**	(800) 658-5811	**U** /	1.90	1.24	-1.83 /16	--	--	4.81	1.66
GL	American Beacon Flexible Bond A	AFXAX	**D**	(800) 658-5811	**E / 0.3**	0.56	0.55	-2.94 /12	-1.42 / 6	--	3.75	1.67
GL	American Beacon Flexible Bond C	AFXCX	**D**	(800) 658-5811	**E / 0.4**	0.37	0.22	-3.69 / 9	-2.15 / 4	--	2.94	2.41
GL	American Beacon Flexible Bond Inst	AFXIX	**D**	(800) 658-5811	**E+ / 0.8**	0.57	0.71	-2.58 /13	-1.01 / 8	--	4.39	1.28
GL	American Beacon Flexible Bond Inv	AFXPX	**D**	(800) 658-5811	**E+ / 0.6**	0.55	0.52	-2.94 /12	-1.36 / 7	--	3.91	1.52

● Denotes fund is closed to new investors
* Denotes fund is included in Section II

RISK			NET ASSETS		ASSET							FUND MANAGER		MINIMUM		LOADS	
Risk Rating/Pts	3 Yr Avg Standard Deviation	Avg Duration	NAV As of 3/31/16	Total $(Mil)	Cash %	Gov. Bond %	Muni. Bond %	Corp. Bond %	Other %	Portfolio Turnover Ratio	Avg Coupon Rate	Manager Quality Pct	Manager Tenure (Years)	Initial Purch. $	Additional Purch. $	Front End Load	Back End Load
U /	N/A	N/A	10.68	10	0	0	0	0	100	0	0.0	N/A	N/A	1,000	50	0.0	0.0
U /	N/A	N/A	10.90	12	0	0	0	0	100	0	0.0	N/A	N/A	250	50	0.0	0.0
U /	N/A	N/A	10.84	1	0	0	0	0	100	0	0.0	N/A	N/A	250	50	0.0	0.0
U /	N/A	N/A	10.90	1	0	0	0	0	100	0	0.0	N/A	N/A	250	50	0.0	0.0
U /	N/A	N/A	10.90	N/A	0	0	0	0	100	0	0.0	N/A	N/A	250	50	4.0	0.0
A+ / 9.9	0.1	4.0	15.09	331	0	0	0	0	100	0	0.0	95	14	1,000	50	4.3	0.0
A+ / 9.9	0.1	4.0	13.57	41	0	0	0	0	100	0	0.0	90	14	1,000	50	0.0	0.0
A+ / 9.9	0.1	4.0	13.57	158	0	0	0	0	100	0	0.0	90	14	1,000	50	0.0	0.0
A+ / 9.9	0.1	4.0	16.07	47	0	0	0	0	100	0	0.0	97	14	250	50	0.0	0.0
A+ / 9.9	0.1	4.0	15.50	15	0	0	0	0	100	0	0.0	96	14	250	50	0.0	0.0
U /	N/A	N/A	13.87	43	9	41	0	48	2	125	0.0	N/A	2	1,000,000	0	0.0	0.0
U /	N/A	N/A	13.88	N/A	9	41	0	48	2	125	0.0	N/A	2	1,000	50	3.8	0.0
U /	N/A	N/A	13.95	N/A	9	41	0	48	2	125	0.0	N/A	2	1,000	50	0.0	0.0
U /	N/A	N/A	13.89	N/A	9	41	0	48	2	125	0.0	N/A	2	1,000,000	0	0.0	0.0
D- / 1.2	5.8	N/A	8.57	57	2	0	0	96	2	47	0.0	18	20	1,000	50	3.8	0.0
D- / 1.0	6.0	N/A	8.18	2	2	0	0	96	2	47	0.0	15	20	1,000,000	0	0.0	0.0
D- / 1.2	5.8	N/A	8.56	14	2	0	0	96	2	47	0.0	10	20	1,000	50	0.0	0.0
D- / 1.2	5.8	N/A	8.30	185	2	0	0	96	2	47	0.0	26	20	1,000,000	0	0.0	0.0
D- / 1.3	5.8	N/A	8.27	51	2	0	0	96	2	47	0.0	25	20	1,000,000	0	0.0	0.0
D- / 1.3	5.8	N/A	8.26	1	2	0	0	96	2	47	0.0	13	20	0	0	0.0	0.0
C / 4.8	3.1	N/A	14.60	174	4	0	0	94	2	65	0.0	91	5	1,000	50	2.3	0.0
C / 4.8	3.1	N/A	14.58	107	4	0	0	94	2	65	0.0	89	5	1,000	50	0.0	0.0
C / 4.8	3.1	N/A	14.57	344	4	0	0	94	2	65	0.0	93	5	1,000,000	0	0.0	0.0
C / 4.7	3.1	N/A	14.57	283	4	0	0	94	2	65	0.0	92	5	1,000,000	0	0.0	0.0
U /	N/A	N/A	9.58	10	2	49	48	0	1	0	0.0	N/A	1	2,500	50	4.8	0.0
U /	N/A	N/A	9.56	N/A	2	49	48	0	1	0	0.0	N/A	1	2,500	50	0.0	0.0
U /	N/A	N/A	9.59	N/A	2	49	48	0	1	0	0.0	N/A	1	2,500	50	0.0	0.0
U /	N/A	N/A	10.72	28	4	0	0	0	96	0	0.0	N/A	1	2,500	50	4.8	0.0
U /	N/A	N/A	10.71	1	4	0	0	0	96	0	0.0	N/A	1	2,500	50	0.0	0.0
U /	N/A	N/A	10.72	73	4	0	0	0	96	0	0.0	N/A	1	2,500	50	0.0	0.0
U /	N/A	N/A	10.32	21	1	0	98	0	1	58	0.0	N/A	N/A	2,500	0	2.5	0.8
U /	N/A	N/A	10.32	72	1	0	98	0	1	58	0.0	N/A	N/A	250,000	0	0.0	0.8
A+ / 9.9	0.2	N/A	10.09	190	0	0	100	0	0	155	0.0	73	14	2,500	0	0.5	0.3
A+ / 9.9	0.1	N/A	10.04	820	0	0	100	0	0	155	0.0	82	14	250,000	0	0.0	0.3
D+ / 2.5	5.2	N/A	8.41	11	6	0	0	32	62	74	0.0	11	3	2,500	250	4.8	1.0
U /	N/A	N/A	8.39	6	6	0	0	32	62	74	0.0	N/A	3	5,000	250	0.0	0.0
D+ / 2.5	5.2	N/A	8.42	53	6	0	0	32	62	74	0.0	13	3	1,000,000	250	0.0	1.0
D+ / 2.5	5.2	N/A	8.41	9	6	0	0	32	62	74	0.0	10	3	2,500	250	0.0	1.0
E- / 0.1	12.3	N/A	10.76	96	32	6	1	16	45	68	0.0	99	5	2,500	250	5.8	1.0
E- / 0.1	12.2	N/A	10.74	342	32	6	1	16	45	68	0.0	99	5	1,000,000	500	0.0	1.0
E- / 0.1	12.3	N/A	10.75	96	32	6	1	16	45	68	0.0	99	5	2,500	250	0.0	1.0
U /	N/A	N/A	10.00	12	73	0	0	26	1	0	0.0	N/A	1	100,000	25	0.0	2.0
U /	N/A	N/A	9.98	2	73	0	0	26	1	0	0.0	N/A	1	5,000	25	0.0	2.0
U /	N/A	2.8	9.17	1	5	0	0	62	33	0	0.0	N/A	N/A	2,500	50	2.5	0.0
U /	N/A	2.8	9.18	N/A	5	0	0	62	33	0	0.0	N/A	N/A	1,000	50	0.0	0.0
U /	N/A	2.8	9.18	36	5	0	0	62	33	0	0.0	N/A	N/A	250,000	50	0.0	0.0
U /	N/A	2.8	9.18	4	5	0	0	62	33	0	0.0	N/A	N/A	2,500	50	0.0	0.0
U /	N/A	2.8	9.18	6	5	0	0	62	33	0	0.0	N/A	N/A	100,000	50	0.0	0.0
C+ / 6.5	3.0	1.4	9.32	10	2	48	0	30	20	492	0.0	19	5	2,500	50	4.8	0.0
C+ / 6.4	3.0	1.4	9.31	4	2	48	0	30	20	492	0.0	10	5	1,000	50	0.0	0.0
C+ / 6.6	3.0	1.4	9.36	113	2	48	0	30	20	492	0.0	28	5	250,000	50	0.0	0.0
C+ / 6.5	3.0	1.4	9.36	4	2	48	0	30	20	492	0.0	20	5	2,500	50	0.0	0.0

99 Pct = Best
0 Pct = Worst

					PERFORMANCE							
						Total Return % through 3/31/16					Incl. in Returns	
									Annualized			
Fund Type	Fund Name	Ticker Symbol	Overall Investment Rating	Phone	Performance Rating/Pts	3 Mo	6 Mo	1Yr / Pct	3Yr / Pct	5Yr / Pct	Dividend Yield	Expense Ratio
GL	American Beacon Flexible Bond Y	AFXYX	**D**	(800) 658-5811	**E+ / 0.8**	0.52	0.63	-2.69 /12	-1.11 / 8	--	4.28	1.35
MM	American Beacon MM Select Fd	ASRXX	**U**	(800) 658-5811	**U /**	--	--	--	--	--	0.13	0.13
COH	American Beacon SiM Hi Yld Opps A	SHOAX	**D-**	(800) 658-5811	**D+ / 2.7**	3.54	0.20	-2.88 /12	2.31 /67	5.46 /74	5.53	1.23
COH	American Beacon SiM Hi Yld Opps C	SHOCX	**D**	(800) 658-5811	**C- / 3.6**	3.24	-0.15	-3.66 / 9	1.62 /54	4.72 /70	5.04	1.98
COH	American Beacon SiM Hi Yld Opps	SHOIX	**D+**	(800) 658-5811	**C+ / 5.7**	3.53	0.39	-2.61 /13	2.68 /73	5.90 /76	6.22	0.89
COH	American Beacon SiM Hi Yld Opps	SHYPX	**D**	(800) 658-5811	**C / 5.1**	3.46	0.21	-2.86 /12	2.38 /69	5.55 /75	5.87	1.20
COH	American Beacon SiM Hi Yld Opps Y	SHOYX	**D**	(800) 658-5811	**C / 5.5**	3.51	0.35	-2.69 /12	2.59 /72	5.78 /76	6.14	0.92
LP	American Beacon Sound Pt FR Inc I	SPFLX	**U**	(800) 658-5811	**U /**	0.40	-0.07	2.37 /74	--	--	4.40	1.90
LP	American Beacon Sound Pt FR Inc	SPFRX	**U**	(800) 658-5811	**U /**	0.40	-0.16	2.14 /73	--	--	4.36	2.28
MUH	American Century CA Hi-Yld Muni A	CAYAX	**B-**	(800) 345-6488	**A+ / 9.7**	2.34	4.80	5.74 /99	5.23 /99	7.75 /98	3.18	0.75
MUH	American Century CA Hi-Yld Muni C	CAYCX	**B**	(800) 345-6488	**A+ / 9.8**	2.15	4.42	4.85 /97	4.41 /97	6.95 /96	2.59	1.50
MUH	American Century CA Hi-Yld Muni Ins	BCHIX	**B**	(800) 345-6488	**A+ / 9.9**	2.55	5.14	6.21 /99	5.70 /99	8.23 /98	3.76	0.30
MUH	American Century CA Hi-Yld Muni Inv	BCHYX	**B**	(800) 345-6488	**A+ / 9.9**	2.40	5.04	6.00 /99	5.49 /99	8.02 /98	3.57	0.50
MUS	American Century CA IT TxFr Bd A	BCIAX	**A-**	(800) 345-6488	**B- / 7.1**	1.44	2.49	3.17 /87	2.54 /83	4.55 /82	2.01	0.72
MUS	American Century CA IT TxFr Bd C	BCIYX	**A**	(800) 345-6488	**B / 7.8**	1.26	2.20	2.40 /80	1.80 /74	3.79 /76	1.36	1.47
MUS	American Century CA IT TxFr Bd Inst	BCTIX	**A+**	(800) 345-6488	**A- / 9.0**	1.56	2.72	3.64 /91	3.00 /88	5.02 /85	2.54	0.27
MUS	American Century CA IT TxFr Bd Inv	BCITX	**A+**	(800) 345-6488	**B+ / 8.9**	1.51	2.62	3.43 /89	2.79 /86	4.81 /84	2.35	0.47
MUS	American Century CA Lg Term T/F A	ALTAX	**B**	(800) 345-6488	**B+ / 8.6**	1.62	3.37	3.78 /92	3.70 /94	6.30 /94	2.95	0.72
MUS	American Century CA Lg Term T/F C	ALTCX	**B+**	(800) 345-6488	**B+ / 8.9**	1.35	2.98	3.01 /85	2.93 /87	5.51 /89	2.35	1.47
MUS	American Century CA Lg Term T/F	BCLIX	**A**	(800) 345-6488	**A+ / 9.7**	1.64	3.60	4.25 /95	4.13 /96	6.77 /96	3.53	0.27
MUS	American Century CA Lg Term T/F	BCLTX	**A**	(800) 345-6488	**A+ / 9.6**	1.59	3.50	4.04 /94	3.96 /95	6.56 /95	3.33	0.47
GEI	American Century Core Plus Fd A	ACCQX	**C-**	(800) 345-6488	**C- / 4.0**	2.84	2.33	0.76 /54	1.77 /57	3.45 /52	2.46	0.90
GEI	American Century Core Plus Fd C	ACCKX	**C-**	(800) 345-6488	**C / 4.8**	2.75	1.95	0.10 /41	1.01 /43	2.68 /40	1.83	1.65
GEI	American Century Core Plus Fd Inst	ACCUX	**B-**	(800) 345-6488	**C+ / 6.9**	3.05	2.56	1.22 /62	2.23 /66	3.92 /60	3.02	0.45
GEI	American Century Core Plus Fd Inv	ACCNX	**B-**	(800) 345-6488	**C+ / 6.5**	3.00	2.46	1.01 /59	2.02 /62	3.69 /56	2.83	0.65
GEI	American Century Core Plus Fd R	ACCPX	**C+**	(800) 345-6488	**C+ / 5.7**	2.88	2.21	0.60 /51	1.52 /52	3.20 /48	2.33	1.15
GEI	American Century Diversified Bd A	ADFAX	**C-**	(800) 345-6488	**C / 4.4**	2.86	2.31	1.23 /62	1.92 /60	3.43 /52	2.28	0.85
GEI	American Century Diversified Bd C	CDBCX	**C**	(800) 345-6488	**C / 5.1**	2.68	1.93	0.57 /51	1.16 /45	2.68 /40	1.64	1.60
GEI	American Century Diversified Bd I	ACBPX	**B+**	(800) 345-6488	**B- / 7.1**	2.88	2.44	1.68 /68	2.37 /69	3.89 /60	2.83	0.40
GEI	American Century Diversified Bd Inv	ADFIX	**B**	(800) 345-6488	**C+ / 6.8**	2.83	2.34	1.48 /66	2.17 /65	3.69 /56	2.64	0.60
GEI	American Century Diversified Bd R	ADVRX	**C+**	(800) 345-6488	**C+ / 6.0**	2.80	2.18	0.98 /58	1.66 /55	3.17 /48	2.14	1.10
COI	American Century Diversified Bd R6	ADDVX	**U**	(800) 345-6488	**U /**	2.99	2.56	1.83 /70	--	--	2.88	0.35
EM	American Century Em Mkts Debt A	AEDQX	**U**	(800) 345-6488	**U /**	4.41	4.98	3.44 /79	--	--	3.09	1.22
EM	American Century Em Mkts Debt C	AEDHX	**U**	(800) 345-6488	**U /**	4.23	4.60	2.66 /75	--	--	2.50	1.97
EM	American Century Em Mkts Debt Inst	AEDJX	**U**	(800) 345-6488	**U /**	4.42	5.10	3.90 /81	--	--	3.68	0.77
EM	American Century Em Mkts Debt Inv	AEDVX	**U**	(800) 345-6488	**U /**	4.48	5.00	3.69 /80	--	--	3.49	0.97
EM	American Century Em Mkts Debt R	AEDWX	**U**	(800) 345-6488	**U /**	4.35	4.85	3.18 /78	--	--	2.99	1.47
EM	American Century Em Mkts Debt R6	AEXDX	**U**	(800) 345-6488	**U /**	4.54	5.24	3.95 /81	--	--	3.73	0.72
USA	American Century Ginnie Mae A	BGNAX	**C-**	(800) 345-6488	**C- / 3.0**	1.56	1.35	1.27 /63	1.32 /49	2.53 /38	2.00	0.80
USA	American Century Ginnie Mae C	BGNCX	**C**	(800) 345-6488	**C- / 3.7**	1.28	0.88	0.52 /50	0.56 /34	1.76 /28	1.34	1.55
USA	American Century Ginnie Mae I	AGMNX	**B+**	(800) 345-6488	**C+ / 6.1**	1.67	1.58	1.73 /69	1.77 /57	3.01 /45	2.54	0.35
USA	American Century Ginnie Mae Inv	BGNMX	**B**	(800) 345-6488	**C+ / 5.7**	1.62	1.48	1.52 /67	1.57 /53	2.78 /41	2.34	0.55
USA	American Century Ginnie Mae R	AGMWX	**C+**	(800) 345-6488	**C / 4.8**	1.50	1.23	1.02 /59	1.10 /44	2.29 /35	1.84	1.05
GL	American Century Global Bond A	AGBAX	**C+**	(800) 345-6488	**C / 5.3**	2.98	3.14	1.07 /60	2.47 /70	--	0.34	1.21
GL	American Century Global Bond C	AGBTX	**B-**	(800) 345-6488	**C+ / 6.0**	2.79	2.71	0.33 /46	1.72 /56	--	0.12	1.96
GL	American Century Global Bond Inst	AGBNX	**A**	(800) 345-6488	**B / 7.8**	3.17	3.37	1.48 /66	2.91 /75	--	0.56	0.76
GL	American Century Global Bond Inv	AGBVX	**A**	(800) 345-6488	**B- / 7.5**	3.07	3.21	1.24 /62	2.71 /73	--	0.43	0.96
GL	American Century Global Bond R	AGBRX	**B+**	(800) 345-6488	**C+ / 6.8**	2.99	2.96	0.79 /55	2.20 /65	--	0.28	1.46
GL	American Century Global Bond R6	AGBDX	**U**	(800) 345-6488	**U /**	3.17	3.39	1.52 /67	--	--	0.59	0.71
USS	American Century Govt Bond A	ABTAX	**C-**	(800) 345-6488	**C- / 3.3**	2.53	1.70	1.64 /68	1.30 /48	2.57 /39	1.37	0.72
USS	American Century Govt Bond C	ABTCX	**C**	(800) 345-6488	**C- / 4.1**	2.35	1.32	0.88 /57	0.58 /35	1.80 /29	0.69	1.47
USS	American Century Govt Bond Inst	ABTIX	**B+**	(800) 345-6488	**C+ / 6.4**	2.65	1.93	2.09 /72	1.79 /57	3.03 /46	1.88	0.27

• Denotes fund is closed to new investors
* Denotes fund is included in Section II

RISK			NET ASSETS		ASSET							FUND MANAGER		MINIMUM		LOADS	
Risk Rating/Pts	3 Yr Avg Standard Deviation	Avg Duration	NAV As of 3/31/16	Total $(Mil)	Cash %	Gov. Bond %	Muni. Bond %	Corp. Bond %	Other %	Portfolio Turnover Ratio	Avg Coupon Rate	Manager Quality Pct	Manager Tenure (Years)	Initial Purch. $	Additional Purch. $	Front End Load	Back End Load
C+ / 6.5	3.0	1.4	9.36	38	2	48	0	30	20	492	0.0	26	5	100,000	50	0.0	0.0
U /	N/A	N/A	1.00	159	100	0	0	0	0	0	0.1	71	16	1,000,000	0	0.0	0.0
D / 1.6	5.5	4.2	8.97	67	3	1	0	88	8	43	0.0	86	5	2,500	50	4.8	2.0
D / 1.6	5.5	4.2	9.00	66	3	1	0	88	8	43	0.0	66	5	1,000	50	0.0	2.0
D / 1.6	5.6	4.2	8.96	271	3	1	0	88	8	43	0.0	90	5	250,000	50	0.0	2.0
D / 1.6	5.6	4.2	8.93	87	3	1	0	88	8	43	0.0	87	5	2,500	50	0.0	2.0
D / 1.6	5.5	4.2	8.95	276	3	1	0	88	8	43	0.0	90	5	100,000	50	0.0	2.0
U /	N/A	0.3	10.10	50	0	0	0	0	100	196	0.0	N/A	2	250,000	0	0.0	0.0
U /	N/A	0.3	10.09	10	0	0	0	0	100	196	0.0	N/A	2	2,500	0	0.0	0.0
D+ / 2.7	4.5	6.2	10.68	128	2	0	97	0	1	41	4.9	83	29	5,000	50	4.5	0.0
D+ / 2.8	4.5	6.2	10.68	31	2	0	97	0	1	41	4.9	52	29	5,000	50	0.0	0.0
D+ / 2.8	4.5	6.2	10.68	107	2	0	97	0	1	41	4.9	90	29	5,000,000	0	0.0	0.0
D+ / 2.8	4.5	6.2	10.68	741	2	0	97	0	1	41	4.9	87	29	5,000	50	0.0	0.0
B- / 7.2	2.8	4.5	12.08	39	1	0	98	0	1	30	4.4	47	14	5,000	50	4.5	0.0
B- / 7.1	2.8	4.5	12.09	18	1	0	98	0	1	30	4.4	25	14	5,000	50	0.0	0.0
B- / 7.2	2.8	4.5	12.08	265	1	0	98	0	1	30	4.4	69	14	5,000,000	0	0.0	0.0
B- / 7.1	2.8	4.5	12.08	1,242	1	0	98	0	1	30	4.4	55	14	5,000	50	0.0	0.0
C / 4.7	3.6	5.2	11.95	7	3	0	96	0	1	31	4.7	59	19	5,000	50	4.5	0.0
C / 4.6	3.7	5.2	11.95	7	3	0	96	0	1	31	4.7	31	19	5,000	50	0.0	0.0
C / 4.5	3.7	5.2	11.95	N/A	3	0	96	0	1	31	4.7	77	19	5,000,000	0	0.0	0.0
C / 4.6	3.6	5.2	11.95	331	3	0	96	0	1	31	4.7	72	19	5,000	50	0.0	0.0
C+ / 6.4	3.0	5.7	10.82	28	0	17	1	40	42	119	4.2	40	10	2,500	50	4.5	0.0
C+ / 6.1	3.1	5.7	10.82	9	0	17	1	40	42	119	4.2	19	10	2,500	50	0.0	0.0
C+ / 6.2	3.1	5.7	10.82	1	0	17	1	40	42	119	4.2	54	10	5,000,000	50	0.0	0.0
C+ / 6.4	3.0	5.7	10.82	90	0	17	1	40	42	119	4.2	48	10	2,500	50	0.0	0.0
C+ / 6.3	3.1	5.7	10.82	3	0	17	1	40	42	119	4.2	31	10	2,500	50	0.0	0.0
C+ / 6.6	3.0	5.7	10.89	455	0	31	1	32	36	153	3.7	42	15	2,500	50	4.5	0.0
C+ / 6.5	3.0	5.7	10.89	81	0	31	1	32	36	153	3.7	22	15	2,500	50	0.0	0.0
C+ / 6.5	3.0	5.7	10.88	2,247	0	31	1	32	36	153	3.7	58	15	5,000,000	50	0.0	0.0
C+ / 6.4	3.0	5.7	10.88	2,117	0	31	1	32	36	153	3.7	50	15	2,500	50	0.0	0.0
C+ / 6.6	3.0	5.7	10.89	20	0	31	1	32	36	153	3.7	35	15	2,500	50	0.0	0.0
U /	N/A	5.7	10.89	94	0	31	1	32	36	153	3.7	N/A	15	0	0	0.0	0.0
U /	N/A	4.6	9.89	6	19	11	0	69	1	46	4.7	N/A	2	2,500	50	4.5	0.0
U /	N/A	4.6	9.87	1	19	11	0	69	1	46	4.7	N/A	2	2,500	50	0.0	0.0
U /	N/A	4.6	9.89	5	19	11	0	69	1	46	4.7	N/A	2	5,000,000	50	0.0	0.0
U /	N/A	4.6	9.89	2	19	11	0	69	1	46	4.7	N/A	2	2,500	50	0.0	0.0
U /	N/A	4.6	9.88	1	19	11	0	69	1	46	4.7	N/A	2	2,500	50	0.0	0.0
U /	N/A	4.6	9.90	13	19	11	0	69	1	46	4.7	N/A	2	0	0	0.0	0.0
B / 7.9	2.5	4.1	10.80	76	0	0	0	0	100	306	4.2	59	10	2,500	50	4.5	0.0
B / 7.9	2.5	4.1	10.80	12	0	0	0	0	100	306	4.2	33	12	2,500	50	0.0	0.0
B / 7.9	2.5	4.1	10.80	71	0	0	0	0	100	306	4.2	80	10	5,000,000	50	0.0	0.0
B / 7.9	2.5	4.1	10.80	1,035	0	0	0	0	100	306	4.2	74	10	2,500	50	0.0	0.0
B / 7.8	2.6	4.1	10.80	7	0	0	0	0	100	306	4.2	48	10	2,500	50	0.0	0.0
B- / 7.1	2.9	6.4	10.03	8	0	49	1	24	26	114	3.3	97	4	2,500	50	4.5	0.0
B- / 7.1	2.9	6.4	9.94	3	0	49	1	24	26	114	3.3	95	4	2,500	50	0.0	0.0
B- / 7.1	2.8	6.4	10.08	744	0	49	1	24	26	114	3.3	98	4	5,000,000	50	0.0	0.0
B- / 7.2	2.8	6.4	10.06	241	0	49	1	24	26	114	3.3	98	4	2,500	50	0.0	0.0
B- / 7.0	2.9	6.4	10.00	N/A	0	49	1	24	26	114	3.3	97	4	2,500	50	0.0	0.0
U /	N/A	6.4	10.08	70	0	49	1	24	26	114	3.3	N/A	4	0	0	0.0	0.0
B / 7.6	2.7	5.2	11.31	112	0	47	0	0	53	270	3.5	43	14	2,500	50	4.5	0.0
B / 7.6	2.7	5.2	11.31	5	0	47	0	0	53	270	3.5	22	14	2,500	50	0.0	0.0
B / 7.6	2.7	5.2	11.31	315	0	47	0	0	53	270	3.5	60	14	5,000,000	50	0.0	0.0

99 Pct = Best
0 Pct = Worst

Fund Type	Fund Name	Ticker Symbol	Overall Investment Rating	Phone	PERFORMANCE Performance Rating/Pts	Total Return % through 3/31/16 3 Mo	6 Mo	1Yr / Pct	Annualized 3Yr / Pct	Annualized 5Yr / Pct	Incl. in Returns Dividend Yield	Expense Ratio
USS	American Century Govt Bond Inv	CPTNX	**B**	(800) 345-6488	**C+ / 6.0**	2.59	1.92	1.89 /71	1.58 /54	2.84 /42	1.68	0.47
USS	American Century Govt Bond R	ABTRX	**C+**	(800) 345-6488	**C / 5.1**	2.47	1.58	1.38 /64	1.08 /44	2.31 /35	1.18	0.97
MUH	American Century High Yld Muni A	AYMAX	**C+**	(800) 345-6488	**A- / 9.1**	1.99	4.44	5.18 /98	3.99 /96	7.30 /97	3.36	0.85
MUH	American Century High Yld Muni C	AYMCX	**C+**	(800) 345-6488	**A / 9.4**	1.91	4.05	4.51 /97	3.25 /90	6.52 /94	2.78	1.60
MUH	American Century High Yld Muni Inst	AYMIX	**B**	(800) 345-6488	**A+ / 9.8**	2.11	4.68	5.65 /99	4.46 /97	7.78 /98	3.95	0.40
MUH	American Century High Yld Muni Inv	ABHYX	**B**	(800) 345-6488	**A+ / 9.8**	2.06	4.57	5.44 /98	4.25 /97	7.56 /97	3.76	0.60
COH	American Century High-Yield A	AHYVX	**E+**	(800) 345-6488	**D- / 1.0**	3.10	1.07	-4.55 / 6	0.57 /34	3.64 /55	5.21	1.10
COH	American Century High-Yield C	AHDCX	**E+**	(800) 345-6488	**D- / 1.3**	2.91	0.70	-5.27 / 4	-0.18 /14	2.87 /43	4.68	1.85
COH	American Century High-Yield Inst	ACYIX	**D-**	(800) 345-6488	**C- / 3.7**	3.21	1.30	-4.12 / 7	1.03 /43	4.11 /63	5.93	0.65
COH	American Century High-Yield Inv	ABHIX	**D-**	(800) 345-6488	**C- / 3.4**	3.36	1.20	-4.32 / 7	0.82 /39	3.90 /60	5.72	0.85
COH	American Century High-Yield R	AHYRX	**E+**	(800) 345-6488	**D / 1.8**	3.04	0.95	-4.79 / 5	0.32 /30	3.39 /51	5.20	1.35
COH	American Century High-Yield R6	AHYDX	**U**	(800) 345-6488	**U /**	3.42	1.51	-4.08 / 7	--	--	5.97	0.60
GEI	American Century Infl Adj Bd A	AIAVX	**E+**	(800) 345-6488	**E / 0.5**	4.36	3.64	0.73 /54	-1.69 / 5	2.21 /34	0.67	0.72
GEI	American Century Infl Adj Bd C	AINOX	**E+**	(800) 345-6488	**E+ / 0.6**	4.17	3.29	-0.05 /31	-2.41 / 3	1.45 /25	0.12	1.47
GEI	American Century Infl Adj Bd Inst	AIANX	**D-**	(800) 345-6488	**D / 1.6**	4.53	3.89	1.19 /61	-1.21 / 7	2.68 /40	1.14	0.27
GEI	American Century Infl Adj Bd Inv	ACITX	**D-**	(800) 345-6488	**D- / 1.3**	4.44	3.68	0.98 /58	-1.45 / 6	2.46 /37	0.95	0.47
GEI	American Century Infl Adj Bd R	AIARX	**E+**	(800) 345-6488	**E+ / 0.9**	4.25	3.48	0.48 /49	-1.93 / 5	1.95 /31	0.46	0.97
MUN	American Century Int Tax-Fr Bd A	TWWOX	**B-**	(800) 345-6488	**C+ / 5.9**	1.36	2.57	2.88 /84	2.03 /77	3.95 /77	2.20	0.72
MUN	American Century Int Tax-Fr Bd C	TWTCX	**B+**	(800) 345-6488	**C+ / 6.9**	1.17	2.10	2.12 /78	1.27 /60	3.18 /71	1.56	1.47
MUN	American Century Int Tax-Fr Bd Inst	AXBIX	**A+**	(800) 345-6488	**B+ / 8.6**	1.47	2.80	3.35 /89	2.49 /82	4.42 /81	2.74	0.27
MUN	American Century Int Tax-Fr Bd Inv	TWTIX	**A+**	(800) 345-6488	**B+ / 8.4**	1.42	2.70	3.14 /86	2.29 /80	4.21 /79	2.55	0.47
GL	American Century Intl Bond A	AIBDX	**E+**	(800) 345-6488	**D- / 1.1**	7.65	6.22	5.03 /88	-1.47 / 6	-0.39 / 2	0.00	1.06
GL	American Century Intl Bond C	AIQCX	**E+**	(800) 345-6488	**D- / 1.5**	7.48	5.86	4.24 /83	-2.21 / 4	-1.13 / 1	0.00	1.81
GL	American Century Intl Bond Inst	AIDIX	**D**	(800) 345-6488	**C / 4.3**	7.87	6.54	5.60 /91	-1.01 / 8	0.06 /13	0.23	0.61
GL	American Century Intl Bond Inv	BEGBX	**D-**	(800) 345-6488	**C- / 3.9**	7.78	6.41	5.39 /90	-1.21 / 7	-0.14 / 3	0.05	0.81
GL	American Century Intl Bond R	AIBRX	**D-**	(800) 345-6488	**D+ / 2.9**	7.67	6.14	4.78 /86	-1.69 / 5	-0.63 / 2	0.00	1.31
GL	American Century Intl Bond R6	AIDDX	**U**	(800) 345-6488	**U /**	7.79	6.51	5.57 /91	--	--	0.28	0.56
MUN	American Century Lg-Term T/F A	MMBAX	**C+**	(800) 345-6488	**B- / 7.4**	1.55	3.32	3.33 /88	2.60 /84	5.11 /86	2.94	0.72
MUN	American Century Lg-Term T/F C	ACTCX	**C+**	(800) 345-6488	**B / 8.0**	1.45	3.03	2.65 /82	1.87 /75	4.35 /80	2.33	1.47
MUN	American Century Lg-Term T/F Inst	ACLSX	**B+**	(800) 345-6488	**A- / 9.2**	1.67	3.55	3.89 /93	3.09 /89	5.60 /90	3.52	0.27
MUN	American Century Lg-Term T/F Inv	ACLVX	**B+**	(800) 345-6488	**A- / 9.0**	1.70	3.54	3.68 /92	2.89 /87	5.39 /88	3.32	0.47
GEN	American Century NT Diver Bd Inst	ACLDX	**B**	(800) 345-6488	**B- / 7.0**	2.92	2.47	1.57 /67	2.28 /67	3.86 /59	2.08	0.40
COI	American Century NT Diver Bd R6	ACDDX	**U**	(800) 345-6488	**U /**	2.83	2.40	1.62 /68	--	--	2.13	0.35
MM	American Century Prime MM A	ACAXX	**U**	(800) 345-6488	**U /**	--	--	--	--	--	0.01	0.83
MM	American Century Prime MM C	ARCXX	**U**	(800) 345-6488	**U /**	--	--	--	--	--	0.01	1.33
MM	American Century Prime MM Inv	BPRXX	**U**	(800) 345-6488	**U /**	--	--	--	--	--	0.01	0.58
GEI	American Century SD Inf Prot Bd A	APOAX	**D+**	(800) 345-6488	**E+ / 0.7**	1.93	1.31	0.60 /51	-1.25 / 7	1.24 /23	0.00	0.82
GEI	American Century SD Inf Prot Bd C	APOCX	**D+**	(800) 345-6488	**E+ / 0.6**	1.77	0.93	-0.20 /29	-2.01 / 4	0.48 /17	0.00	1.57
GEI	American Century SD Inf Prot Bd Ins	APISX	**D+**	(800) 345-6488	**D- / 1.5**	2.10	1.60	1.10 /60	-0.80 / 9	1.71 /28	0.01	0.37
GEI	American Century SD Inf Prot Bd Inv	APOIX	**D+**	(800) 345-6488	**D- / 1.3**	2.01	1.50	0.80 /55	-1.01 / 8	1.50 /26	0.00	0.57
GEI	American Century SD Inf Prot Bd R	APORX	**D+**	(800) 345-6488	**D- / 1.0**	1.99	1.28	0.39 /48	-1.46 / 6	1.01 /20	0.00	1.07
GEI	American Century SD Inf Prot Bd R6	APODX	**D+**	(800) 345-6488	**D / 1.6**	2.10	1.65	1.15 /61	-0.76 /10	1.65 /27	0.06	0.32
GL	American Century Sh Dur St Inc A	ASADX	**U**	(800) 345-6488	**U /**	0.54	0.28	-1.50 /18	--	--	3.10	1.05
GL	American Century Sh Dur St Inc C	ASCDX	**U**	(800) 345-6488	**U /**	0.36	-0.10	-2.25 /14	--	--	2.39	1.80
GL	American Century Sh Dur St Inc Inst	ASDJX	**U**	(800) 345-6488	**U /**	0.65	0.49	-1.07 /21	--	--	3.61	0.60
GL	American Century Sh Dur St Inc Inv	ASDVX	**U**	(800) 345-6488	**U /**	0.61	0.39	-1.27 /20	--	--	3.41	0.80
GL	American Century Sh Dur St Inc R	ASDRX	**U**	(800) 345-6488	**U /**	0.48	0.15	-1.76 /17	--	--	2.90	1.30
GL	American Century Sh Dur St Inc R6	ASXDX	**U**	(800) 345-6488	**U /**	0.67	0.52	-1.02 /21	--	--	3.67	0.55
GEI	American Century Sh Duration A	ACSQX	**C-**	(800) 345-6488	**D / 1.8**	0.74	0.51	0.62 /52	0.47 /32	1.00 /20	1.36	0.85
GEI	American Century Sh Duration C	ACSKX	**C-**	(800) 345-6488	**D / 1.6**	0.66	0.23	-0.13 /30	-0.26 /13	0.27 /16	0.64	1.60
GEI	American Century Sh Duration Inst	ACSUX	**B**	(800) 345-6488	**C / 4.4**	0.85	0.73	1.07 /60	0.92 /41	1.46 /25	1.84	0.40
GEI	American Century Sh Duration Inv	ACSNX	**C+**	(800) 345-6488	**C- / 4.0**	0.81	0.63	0.87 /56	0.72 /37	1.25 /23	1.64	0.60

● Denotes fund is closed to new investors
* Denotes fund is included in Section II

RISK			NET ASSETS		ASSET							FUND MANAGER		MINIMUM		LOADS	
Risk Rating/Pts	3 Yr Avg Standard Deviation	Avg Duration	NAV As of 3/31/16	Total $(Mil)	Cash %	Gov. Bond %	Muni. Bond %	Corp. Bond %	Other %	Portfolio Turnover Ratio	Avg Coupon Rate	Manager Quality Pct	Manager Tenure (Years)	Initial Purch. $	Additional Purch. $	Front End Load	Back End Load
B / 7.7	2.6	5.2	11.32	668	0	47	0	0	53	270	3.5	54	14	2,500	50	0.0	0.0
B- / 7.5	2.7	5.2	11.31	3	0	47	0	0	53	270	3.5	35	14	2,500	50	0.0	0.0
D+ / 2.8	4.5	5.8	9.61	87	1	0	98	0	1	48	5.1	42	18	5,000	50	4.5	0.0
D+ / 2.8	4.5	5.8	9.61	26	1	0	98	0	1	48	5.1	23	18	5,000	50	0.0	0.0
D+ / 2.8	4.5	5.8	9.61	29	1	0	98	0	1	48	5.1	58	18	5,000,000	0	0.0	0.0
D+ / 2.8	4.5	5.8	9.61	341	1	0	98	0	1	48	5.1	51	18	5,000	50	0.0	0.0
D- / 1.1	6.0	4.0	5.36	25	2	0	0	96	2	34	6.0	24	8	2,500	50	4.5	0.0
D- / 1.1	6.0	4.0	5.36	10	2	0	0	96	2	34	6.0	13	8	2,500	50	0.0	0.0
D- / 1.1	6.0	4.0	5.36	471	2	0	0	96	2	34	6.0	36	8	5,000,000	50	0.0	0.0
D- / 1.1	6.0	4.0	5.36	343	2	0	0	96	2	34	6.0	31	8	2,500	50	0.0	0.0
D- / 1.1	6.0	4.0	5.36	2	2	0	0	96	2	34	6.0	19	8	2,500	50	0.0	0.0
U /	N/A	4.0	5.36	55	2	0	0	96	2	34	6.0	N/A	8	0	0	0.0	0.0
D / 2.2	5.5	6.1	11.73	194	0	85	0	5	10	18	1.5	2	10	2,500	50	4.5	0.0
D+ / 2.3	5.5	6.1	11.74	17	0	85	0	5	10	18	1.5	1	10	2,500	50	0.0	0.0
D / 2.2	5.5	6.1	11.76	1,144	0	85	0	5	10	18	1.5	3	10	5,000,000	50	0.0	0.0
D / 2.2	5.5	6.1	11.76	1,498	0	85	0	5	10	18	1.5	3	10	2,500	50	0.0	0.0
D / 2.2	5.5	6.1	11.78	18	0	85	0	5	10	18	1.5	2	10	2,500	50	0.0	0.0
B- / 7.3	2.8	4.5	11.53	69	1	0	98	0	1	34	4.8	33	10	5,000	50	4.5	0.0
B- / 7.3	2.8	4.5	11.52	17	1	0	98	0	1	34	4.8	16	10	5,000	50	0.0	0.0
B- / 7.3	2.8	4.5	11.53	1,732	1	0	98	0	1	34	4.8	48	10	5,000,000	0	0.0	0.0
B- / 7.3	2.8	4.5	11.53	1,611	1	0	98	0	1	34	4.8	41	10	5,000	50	0.0	0.0
D- / 1.0	6.4	7.2	12.80	20	6	74	2	15	3	67	3.0	21	7	2,500	50	4.5	0.0
D- / 1.0	6.4	7.2	12.64	1	6	74	2	15	3	67	3.0	11	7	2,500	50	0.0	0.0
D- / 1.0	6.4	7.2	12.88	353	6	74	2	15	3	67	3.0	33	7	5,000,000	50	0.0	0.0
D- / 1.0	6.4	7.2	12.88	459	6	74	2	15	3	67	3.0	27	7	2,500	50	0.0	0.0
D- / 1.0	6.4	7.2	12.78	N/A	6	74	2	15	3	67	3.0	17	7	2,500	50	0.0	0.0
U /	N/A	7.2	12.87	38	6	74	2	15	3	67	3.0	N/A	7	0	0	0.0	0.0
C / 4.4	3.7	4.9	11.65	11	1	0	98	0	1	27	5.0	23	10	5,000	50	4.5	0.0
C / 4.4	3.7	4.9	11.66	2	1	0	98	0	1	27	5.0	12	10	5,000	50	0.0	0.0
C / 4.4	3.7	4.9	11.66	2	1	0	98	0	1	27	5.0	34	10	5,000,000	0	0.0	0.0
C / 4.4	3.7	4.9	11.66	42	1	0	98	0	1	27	5.0	28	10	5,000	50	0.0	0.0
C+ / 6.3	3.1	5.0	10.85	2,403	0	33	1	31	35	248	4.2	54	10	0	0	0.0	0.0
U /	N/A	5.0	10.85	174	0	33	1	31	35	248	4.2	N/A	10	0	0	0.0	0.0
U /	N/A	N/A	1.00	209	100	0	0	0	0	0	0.0	N/A	N/A	2,500	50	0.0	0.0
U /	N/A	N/A	1.00	9	100	0	0	0	0	0	0.0	N/A	N/A	2,500	50	0.0	0.0
U /	N/A	N/A	1.00	1,562	100	0	0	0	0	0	0.0	N/A	N/A	2,500	50	0.0	0.0
B+ / 8.3	2.2	2.2	10.04	54	0	86	0	5	9	56	1.3	9	10	2,500	50	2.3	0.0
B+ / 8.3	2.2	2.2	9.78	32	0	86	0	5	9	56	1.3	7	10	2,500	50	0.0	0.0
B / 8.2	2.3	2.2	10.22	575	0	86	0	5	9	56	1.3	11	10	5,000,000	50	0.0	0.0
B / 8.2	2.2	2.2	10.14	508	0	86	0	5	9	56	1.3	10	10	2,500	50	0.0	0.0
B / 8.2	2.2	2.2	10.25	14	0	86	0	5	9	56	1.3	8	10	2,500	50	0.0	0.0
B / 8.2	2.3	2.2	10.22	167	0	86	0	5	9	56	1.3	12	10	0	0	0.0	0.0
U /	N/A	1.0	9.31	10	7	0	0	67	26	18	4.2	N/A	N/A	2,500	50	2.3	0.0
U /	N/A	1.0	9.31	1	7	0	0	67	26	18	4.2	N/A	N/A	2,500	50	0.0	0.0
U /	N/A	1.0	9.31	7	7	0	0	67	26	18	4.2	N/A	N/A	5,000,000	50	0.0	0.0
U /	N/A	1.0	9.31	5	7	0	0	67	26	18	4.2	N/A	N/A	2,500	50	0.0	0.0
U /	N/A	1.0	9.31	1	7	0	0	67	26	18	4.2	N/A	N/A	2,500	50	0.0	0.0
U /	N/A	1.0	9.31	1	7	0	0	67	26	18	4.2	N/A	N/A	0	0	0.0	0.0
A / 9.5	0.8	1.9	10.25	61	0	21	0	53	26	56	2.9	62	N/A	2,500	50	2.3	0.0
A / 9.4	0.8	1.9	10.26	19	0	21	0	53	26	56	2.9	35	N/A	2,500	50	0.0	0.0
A / 9.5	0.8	1.9	10.25	65	0	21	0	53	26	56	2.9	81	N/A	5,000,000	50	0.0	0.0
A / 9.5	0.8	1.9	10.25	225	0	21	0	53	26	56	2.9	75	N/A	2,500	50	0.0	0.0

Fund Type	Fund Name (99 Pct = Best, 0 Pct = Worst)	Ticker Symbol	Overall Investment Rating	Phone	PERFORMANCE: Performance Rating/Pts	Total Return % through 3/31/16: 3 Mo	6 Mo	1Yr / Pct	Annualized: 3Yr / Pct	Annualized: 5Yr / Pct	Incl. in Returns: Dividend Yield	Expense Ratio
GEI	American Century Sh Duration R	ACSPX	C	(800) 345-6488	C- / 3.0	0.78	0.48	0.37 /47	0.22 /29	0.75 /19	1.14	1.10
USS	American Century Sh-Term Govt A	TWAVX	C-	(800) 345-6488	D- / 1.3	0.71	0.05	0.19 /44	-0.01 /15	0.29 /16	0.28	0.80
USS	American Century Sh-Term Govt C	TWACX	C-	(800) 345-6488	D- / 1.1	0.54	-0.32	-0.63 /25	-0.77 / 9	-0.46 / 2	0.00	1.55
USS	American Century Sh-Term Govt Inst	TWUOX	C+	(800) 345-6488	C- / 3.4	0.82	0.27	0.64 /52	0.43 /32	0.74 /19	0.74	0.35
USS	American Century Sh-Term Govt Inv	TWUSX	C+	(800) 345-6488	C- / 3.0	0.77	0.27	0.44 /48	0.26 /29	0.54 /17	0.54	0.55
USS	American Century Sh-Term Govt R	TWARX	C-	(800) 345-6488	D / 1.6	0.63	0.00	-0.10 /30	-0.24 /14	0.06 /13	0.00	1.05
US	American Century Str Inf Opp Fd A	ASIDX	E+	(800) 345-6488	E- / 0.1	3.27	1.21	-4.78 / 5	-3.94 / 2	-2.91 / 1	0.00	1.42
US	American Century Str Inf Opp Fd C	ASIZX	E+	(800) 345-6488	E- / 0.2	3.01	0.79	-5.52 / 4	-4.66 / 2	-3.65 / 0	0.00	2.17
US	American Century Str Inf Opp Fd Ins	ASINX	E+	(800) 345-6488	E / 0.3	3.36	1.43	-4.35 / 7	-3.51 / 2	-2.47 / 1	0.00	0.97
US	American Century Str Inf Opp Fd Inv	ASIOX	E+	(800) 345-6488	E- / 0.2	3.36	1.32	-4.55 / 6	-3.71 / 2	-2.67 / 1	0.00	1.17
US	American Century Str Inf Opp Fd R	ASIUX	E+	(800) 345-6488	E- / 0.2	3.18	1.11	-5.02 / 5	-4.17 / 2	-3.15 / 1	0.00	1.67
GEL	American Century Strategic Inc A	ASIQX	U	(800) 345-6488	U /	2.35	2.38	0.18 /43	--	--	3.77	1.09
GEL	American Century Strategic Inc C	ASIHX	U	(800) 345-6488	U /	2.16	2.11	-0.57 /25	--	--	3.19	1.84
GEL	American Century Strategic Inc Inst	ASIJX	U	(800) 345-6488	U /	2.46	2.72	0.63 /52	--	--	4.40	0.64
GEL	American Century Strategic Inc Inv	ASIEX	U	(800) 345-6488	U /	2.40	2.50	0.42 /48	--	--	4.19	0.84
GEL	American Century Strategic Inc R	ASIWX	U	(800) 345-6488	U /	2.29	2.25	-0.07 /31	--	--	3.69	1.34
GEL	American Century Strategic Inc R6	ASIPX	U	(800) 345-6488	U /	2.47	2.63	0.68 /53	--	--	4.45	0.59
USL	American Century VP Infl Prot I	APTIX	D-	(800) 345-6488	D- / 1.3	3.69	3.28	0.11 /41	-1.20 / 7	2.69 /40	1.69	0.47
USL	American Century VP Infl Prot II	AIPTX	D-	(800) 345-6488	D- / 1.1	3.68	3.26	-0.04 /31	-1.43 / 6	2.45 /37	1.44	0.72
US	American Century Zero Cpn 2020	ACTEX	D+	(800) 345-6488	C / 5.4	2.93	1.76	2.32 /74	1.10 /44	5.37 /74	2.94	0.80
US	American Century Zero Cpn 2020 Inv	BTTTX	D+	(800) 345-6488	C+ / 5.7	2.99	1.64	2.31 /74	1.27 /48	5.58 /75	2.92	0.55
GEI	American Century Zero Cpn 2025	ACTVX	C-	(800) 345-6488	B+ / 8.3	5.56	3.54	3.12 /77	3.41 /79	8.56 /89	2.45	0.80
GEI	American Century Zero Cpn 2025 Inv	BTTRX	C-	(800) 345-6488	B+ / 8.5	5.63	3.67	3.38 /78	3.67 /81	8.84 /91	2.59	0.55
COI	American Fds College Enroll 529A	CENAX	C+	(800) 421-0180	C- / 3.6	1.52	1.01	1.42 /65	1.05 /44	--	0.97	0.78
COI	American Fds College Enroll 529B	CENBX	C	(800) 421-0180	C- / 3.4	1.32	0.71	0.71 /53	0.33 /30	--	0.40	1.52
COI	American Fds College Enroll 529C	CENCX	C	(800) 421-0180	C- / 3.3	1.22	0.65	0.65 /52	0.30 /30	--	0.55	1.53
COI	American Fds College Enroll 529E	CENEX	C+	(800) 421-0180	C / 4.3	1.32	0.88	1.18 /61	0.83 /39	--	0.87	1.00
COI	American Fds College Enroll 529F1	CENFX	B+	(800) 421-0180	C / 5.3	1.52	1.19	1.69 /69	1.30 /48	--	1.17	0.53
MUS	American Fds Tax-Exempt Fd of NY	NYAAX	C+	(800) 421-0180	B / 8.2	1.61	3.32	3.30 /88	3.11 /89	5.56 /89	2.47	0.72
MUS ●	American Fds Tax-Exempt Fd of NY	NYABX	B-	(800) 421-0180	B+ / 8.5	1.54	3.15	2.83 /83	2.40 /82	4.77 /83	2.12	1.49
MUS	American Fds Tax-Exempt Fd of NY	NYACX	C+	(800) 421-0180	B+ / 8.3	1.41	2.92	2.49 /80	2.24 /80	4.65 /82	1.79	1.56
MUS	American Fds Tax-Exempt Fd of NY	NYAEX	B+	(800) 421-0180	A- / 9.1	1.63	3.36	3.35 /89	3.06 /89	5.46 /89	2.62	0.80
MUS	American Fds Tax-Exempt Fd of NY	NYAFX	B+	(800) 421-0180	A- / 9.2	1.65	3.40	3.45 /89	3.20 /90	5.64 /90	2.71	0.61
MUN	American Fds TxEx Preservation C	TEPCX	B+	(800) 421-0180	C+ / 6.4	0.81	1.38	1.32 /72	1.27 /60	--	1.61	1.46
GEI	American Funds Bd Fd of Amer 529A	CFAAX	C-	(800) 421-0180	C / 5.0	2.89	2.23	1.43 /65	2.09 /63	3.53 /53	1.80	0.70
GEI ●	American Funds Bd Fd of Amer 529B	CFABX	C	(800) 421-0180	C / 5.3	2.69	1.82	0.64 /52	1.30 /48	2.72 /41	1.09	1.47
GEI	American Funds Bd Fd of Amer 529C	CFACX	C	(800) 421-0180	C / 5.3	2.70	1.84	0.66 /52	1.32 /49	2.73 /41	1.11	1.46
GEI	American Funds Bd Fd of Amer 529E	CFAEX	C+	(800) 421-0180	C+ / 6.3	2.84	2.13	1.22 /62	1.87 /59	3.29 /50	1.66	0.91
GEI	American Funds Bd Fd of Amer	CFAFX	B-	(800) 421-0180	B- / 7.1	2.95	2.35	1.66 /68	2.32 /68	3.76 /58	2.09	0.47
* GEI	American Funds Bd Fd of Amer A	ABNDX	C-	(800) 421-0180	C / 5.2	2.92	2.28	1.54 /67	2.19 /65	3.62 /55	1.89	0.60
GEI ●	American Funds Bd Fd of Amer B	BFABX	C	(800) 421-0180	C+ / 5.6	2.72	1.90	0.78 /55	1.43 /51	2.85 /43	1.23	1.34
GEI	American Funds Bd Fd of Amer C	BFACX	C	(800) 421-0180	C / 5.5	2.71	1.88	0.73 /54	1.39 /50	2.80 /42	1.18	1.40
GEI	American Funds Bd Fd of Amer F1	BFAFX	C+	(800) 421-0180	C+ / 6.8	2.91	2.27	1.50 /66	2.17 /65	3.60 /55	1.93	0.63
GEI	American Funds Bd Fd of Amer F2	ABNFX	B-	(800) 421-0180	B- / 7.2	2.98	2.41	1.77 /69	2.44 /70	3.87 /60	2.20	0.37
GEI	American Funds Bd Fd of Amer R1	RBFAX	C	(800) 421-0180	C+ / 5.6	2.72	1.89	0.76 /54	1.43 /51	2.84 /43	1.21	1.36
GEI	American Funds Bd Fd of Amer R2	RBFBX	C	(800) 421-0180	C+ / 5.6	2.72	1.89	0.77 /54	1.43 /51	2.84 /43	1.22	1.36
COI	American Funds Bd Fd of Amer R2E	RBEBX	C+	(800) 421-0180	C+ / 6.2	2.83	2.10	1.25 /62	1.78 /57	3.12 /47	1.69	0.98
GEI	American Funds Bd Fd of Amer R3	RBFCX	C+	(800) 421-0180	C+ / 6.3	2.83	2.12	1.21 /62	1.87 /59	3.29 /50	1.65	0.91
GEI	American Funds Bd Fd of Amer R4	RBFEX	C+	(800) 421-0180	C+ / 6.9	2.92	2.29	1.54 /67	2.20 /65	3.62 /55	1.97	0.59
GEI	American Funds Bd Fd of Amer R5	RBFFX	B	(800) 421-0180	B- / 7.4	2.99	2.44	1.84 /70	2.50 /71	3.93 /60	2.26	0.30
COI	American Funds Bd Fd of Amer R5E	RBFHX	C+	(800) 421-0180	C+ / 6.9	2.95	2.35	1.60 /68	2.21 /66	3.63 /55	2.02	0.40
GEI	American Funds Bd Fd of Amer R6	RBFGX	B	(800) 421-0180	B- / 7.4	3.00	2.46	1.89 /71	2.55 /71	3.98 /61	2.31	0.25

● Denotes fund is closed to new investors
* Denotes fund is included in Section II

RISK			NET ASSETS		ASSET							FUND MANAGER		MINIMUM		LOADS	
Risk Rating/Pts	3 Yr Avg Standard Deviation	Avg Duration	NAV As of 3/31/16	Total $(Mil)	Cash %	Gov. Bond %	Muni. Bond %	Corp. Bond %	Other %	Portfolio Turnover Ratio	Avg Coupon Rate	Manager Quality Pct	Manager Tenure (Years)	Initial Purch. $	Additional Purch. $	Front End Load	Back End Load
A / 9.5	0.8	1.9	10.26	1	0	21	0	53	26	56	2.9	51	N/A	2,500	50	0.0	0.0
A+ / 9.6	0.7	1.8	9.66	15	0	66	0	0	34	76	1.2	44	14	2,500	50	2.3	0.0
A / 9.5	0.8	1.8	9.39	1	0	66	0	0	34	76	1.2	22	14	2,500	50	0.0	0.0
A+ / 9.6	0.7	1.8	9.66	42	0	66	0	0	34	76	1.2	60	14	5,000,000	50	0.0	0.0
A+ / 9.7	0.7	1.8	9.66	237	0	66	0	0	34	76	1.2	54	14	2,500	50	0.0	0.0
A+ / 9.7	0.7	1.8	9.62	1	0	66	0	0	34	76	1.2	37	14	2,500	50	0.0	0.0
D+ / 2.6	5.1	1.5	9.17	5	10	43	0	20	27	93	1.8	4	6	2,500	50	5.8	0.0
D+ / 2.7	5.0	1.5	8.90	2	10	43	0	20	27	93	1.8	3	6	2,500	50	0.0	0.0
D+ / 2.7	5.1	1.5	9.24	1	10	43	0	20	27	93	1.8	5	6	5,000,000	0	0.0	0.0
D+ / 2.6	5.1	1.5	9.22	14	10	43	0	20	27	93	1.8	5	6	2,500	50	0.0	0.0
D+ / 2.6	5.1	1.5	9.09	N/A	10	43	0	20	27	93	1.8	4	6	2,500	50	0.0	0.0
U /	N/A	3.7	9.45	1	3	2	0	64	31	9	4.8	N/A	N/A	2,500	50	4.5	0.0
U /	N/A	3.7	9.45	1	3	2	0	64	31	9	4.8	N/A	N/A	2,500	50	0.0	0.0
U /	N/A	3.7	9.45	1	3	2	0	64	31	9	4.8	N/A	N/A	5,000,000	50	0.0	0.0
U /	N/A	3.7	9.45	2	3	2	0	64	31	9	4.8	N/A	N/A	2,500	50	0.0	0.0
U /	N/A	3.7	9.45	1	3	2	0	64	31	9	4.8	N/A	N/A	2,500	50	0.0	0.0
U /	N/A	3.7	9.45	1	3	2	0	64	31	9	4.8	N/A	N/A	0	0	0.0	0.0
D+ / 2.6	5.1	6.4	10.12	52	0	69	0	17	14	23	2.0	7	9	0	0	0.0	0.0
D+ / 2.6	5.1	6.4	10.11	530	0	69	0	17	14	23	2.0	6	9	0	0	0.0	0.0
C- / 3.1	4.6	4.8	99.56	6	0	100	0	0	0	39	0.0	14	10	2,500	50	0.0	0.0
C- / 3.1	4.6	4.8	103.91	211	0	100	0	0	0	39	0.0	16	10	2,500	50	0.0	0.0
E / 0.4	8.1	9.9	94.67	7	0	99	0	0	1	33	0.0	7	10	2,500	50	0.0	0.0
E / 0.4	8.1	9.9	98.92	194	0	99	0	0	1	33	0.0	8	10	2,500	50	0.0	0.0
B+ / 8.8	1.6	N/A	10.01	242	0	41	0	19	40	15	0.0	72	4	250	50	2.5	0.0
B+ / 8.8	1.7	N/A	9.97	1	0	41	0	19	40	15	0.0	40	4	250	50	0.0	0.0
B+ / 8.8	1.7	N/A	9.94	115	0	41	0	19	40	15	0.0	39	4	250	50	0.0	0.0
B+ / 8.8	1.6	N/A	9.98	17	0	41	0	19	40	15	0.0	59	4	250	50	0.0	0.0
B+ / 8.8	1.7	N/A	10.03	43	0	41	0	19	40	15	0.0	79	4	250	50	0.0	0.0
C- / 4.1	3.9	5.7	10.91	146	2	0	97	0	1	42	4.2	30	6	1,000	50	3.8	0.0
C- / 4.1	3.9	5.7	10.91	N/A	2	0	97	0	1	42	4.2	15	6	1,000	50	0.0	0.0
C- / 4.1	3.9	5.7	10.91	14	2	0	97	0	1	42	4.2	14	6	1,000	50	0.0	0.0
C- / 4.1	3.9	5.7	10.91	2	2	0	97	0	1	42	4.2	28	6	1,000	50	0.0	0.0
C- / 4.1	3.9	5.7	10.91	29	2	0	97	0	1	42	4.2	32	6	1,000	50	0.0	0.0
B / 8.0	2.4	4.3	9.94	58	0	0	99	0	1	8	4.7	24	4	250	50	0.0	0.0
C+ / 5.9	3.2	5.4	12.90	927	0	38	2	30	30	401	3.0	44	27	250	50	3.8	0.0
C+ / 5.9	3.2	5.4	12.90	6	0	38	2	30	30	401	3.0	22	27	250	50	0.0	0.0
C+ / 5.9	3.2	5.4	12.90	342	0	38	2	30	30	401	3.0	22	27	250	50	0.0	0.0
C+ / 5.9	3.2	5.4	12.90	49	0	38	2	30	30	401	3.0	36	27	250	50	0.0	0.0
C+ / 5.8	3.2	5.4	12.90	75	0	38	2	30	30	401	3.0	52	27	250	50	0.0	0.0
C+ / 5.8	3.2	5.4	12.90	19,401	0	38	2	30	30	401	3.0	47	27	250	50	3.8	0.0
C+ / 5.8	3.2	5.4	12.90	66	0	38	2	30	30	401	3.0	25	27	250	50	0.0	0.0
C+ / 5.9	3.2	5.4	12.90	1,387	0	38	2	30	30	401	3.0	24	27	250	50	0.0	0.0
C+ / 5.8	3.2	5.4	12.90	724	0	38	2	30	30	401	3.0	46	27	250	50	0.0	0.0
C+ / 5.8	3.2	5.4	12.90	1,686	0	38	2	30	30	401	3.0	56	27	250	50	0.0	0.0
C+ / 5.9	3.2	5.4	12.90	47	0	38	2	30	30	401	3.0	25	27	250	50	0.0	0.0
C+ / 5.9	3.2	5.4	12.90	558	0	38	2	30	30	401	3.0	25	27	250	50	0.0	0.0
C+ / 5.8	3.2	5.4	12.90	4	0	38	2	30	30	401	3.0	53	27	250	50	0.0	0.0
C+ / 5.9	3.2	5.4	12.90	682	0	38	2	30	30	401	3.0	37	27	250	50	0.0	0.0
C+ / 5.8	3.2	5.4	12.90	540	0	38	2	30	30	401	3.0	47	27	250	50	0.0	0.0
C+ / 5.8	3.2	5.4	12.90	220	0	38	2	30	30	401	3.0	58	27	250	50	0.0	0.0
C+ / 5.9	3.2	5.4	12.90	N/A	0	38	2	30	30	401	3.0	74	27	250	50	0.0	0.0
C+ / 5.8	3.2	5.4	12.90	2,994	0	38	2	30	30	401	3.0	60	27	250	50	0.0	0.0

Fund Type	Fund Name (99 Pct = Best, 0 Pct = Worst)	Ticker Symbol	Overall Investment Rating	Phone	PERFORMANCE: Performance Rating/Pts	Total Return % through 3/31/16: 3 Mo	6 Mo	1Yr / Pct	Annualized: 3Yr / Pct	Annualized: 5Yr / Pct	Incl. in Returns: Dividend Yield	Expense Ratio
GL	American Funds Cap World Bond	CCWAX	D	(800) 421-0180	D+ / 2.9	5.41	4.10	1.49 /66	0.36 /31	1.72 /28	0.73	1.02
GL	● American Funds Cap World Bond	CCWBX	D	(800) 421-0180	C- / 3.2	5.15	3.61	0.66 /52	-0.44 /12	0.91 /20	0.15	1.80
GL	American Funds Cap World Bond	CCWCX	D	(800) 421-0180	C- / 3.2	5.12	3.66	0.70 /53	-0.42 /12	0.92 /20	0.23	1.79
GL	American Funds Cap World Bond	CCWEX	D	(800) 421-0180	C / 4.4	5.29	3.94	1.27 /63	0.15 /28	1.50 /26	0.59	1.21
GL	American Funds Cap World Bond	CCWFX	D+	(800) 421-0180	C / 5.2	5.44	4.19	1.73 /69	0.58 /35	1.94 /30	0.99	0.79
* GL	American Funds Cap World Bond A	CWBFX	D	(800) 421-0180	C- / 3.1	5.40	4.13	1.60 /68	0.44 /32	1.80 /29	0.82	0.93
GL	● American Funds Cap World Bond B	WBFBX	D	(800) 421-0180	C- / 3.5	5.19	3.75	0.83 /56	-0.30 /13	1.04 /21	0.22	1.68
GL	American Funds Cap World Bond C	CWBCX	D	(800) 421-0180	C- / 3.3	5.17	3.67	0.74 /54	-0.36 /13	1.00 /20	0.27	1.73
GL	American Funds Cap World Bond F1	WBFFX	D+	(800) 421-0180	C / 4.9	5.38	4.13	1.59 /67	0.45 /32	1.80 /29	0.49	0.91
GL	American Funds Cap World Bond F2	BFWFX	D+	(800) 421-0180	C / 5.5	5.50	4.29	1.92 /71	0.74 /38	2.09 /32	1.16	0.65
GL	American Funds Cap World Bond R1	RCWAX	D	(800) 421-0180	C- / 3.5	5.21	3.73	0.86 /56	-0.29 /13	1.05 /21	0.29	1.66
GL	American Funds Cap World Bond R2	RCWBX	D	(800) 421-0180	C- / 3.4	5.19	3.70	0.79 /55	-0.33 /13	1.01 /20	0.27	1.75
GL	American Funds Cap World Bond	RCEBX	D+	(800) 421-0180	C / 4.5	5.32	4.04	1.55 /67	0.17 /28	1.39 /24	0.86	1.38
GL	American Funds Cap World Bond R3	RCWCX	D	(800) 421-0180	C / 4.3	5.27	3.96	1.24 /62	0.14 /28	1.49 /25	0.56	1.24
GL	American Funds Cap World Bond R4	RCWEX	D+	(800) 421-0180	C / 5.0	5.41	4.13	1.65 /68	0.48 /33	1.84 /29	0.90	0.88
GL	American Funds Cap World Bond R5	RCWFX	D+	(800) 421-0180	C+ / 5.6	5.48	4.30	1.90 /71	0.79 /39	2.13 /33	1.19	0.58
GL	American Funds Cap World Bond	RCWHX	D+	(800) 421-0180	C / 5.0	5.46	4.24	1.70 /69	0.47 /32	1.83 /29	1.01	0.70
GL	American Funds Cap World Bond R6	RCWGX	D+	(800) 421-0180	C+ / 5.7	5.50	4.29	1.95 /71	0.84 /40	2.19 /33	1.25	0.53
* MUH	American Funds High Inc Muni Bnd A	AMHIX	C+	(800) 421-0180	A+ / 9.7	2.20	4.36	5.09 /98	4.95 /99	8.15 /98	3.80	0.68
MUH	● American Funds High Inc Muni Bnd B	ABHMX	B-	(800) 421-0180	A+ / 9.7	2.02	4.00	4.35 /96	4.19 /97	7.37 /97	3.25	1.39
MUH	American Funds High Inc Muni Bnd C	AHICX	B-	(800) 421-0180	A+ / 9.7	2.01	3.97	4.30 /96	4.14 /96	7.32 /97	3.20	1.44
MUH	American Funds High Inc Muni Bnd	ABHFX	B-	(800) 421-0180	A+ / 9.9	2.18	4.33	5.01 /98	4.87 /98	8.05 /98	3.88	0.75
MUH	American Funds High Inc Muni Bnd	AHMFX	B-	(800) 421-0180	A+ / 9.9	2.24	4.46	5.27 /98	5.12 /99	8.34 /99	4.12	0.49
COH	American Funds High Income Tr	CITAX	E	(800) 421-0180	E / 0.5	2.75	-0.54	-7.28 / 2	-0.31 /13	2.66 /40	6.33	0.76
COH	● American Funds High Income Tr	CITBX	E	(800) 421-0180	E / 0.5	2.54	-0.94	-8.02 / 1	-1.09 / 8	1.85 /29	5.73	1.55
COH	American Funds High Income Tr	CITCX	E	(800) 421-0180	E / 0.5	2.55	-0.92	-8.00 / 1	-1.08 / 8	1.87 /30	5.76	1.53
COH	American Funds High Income Tr	CITEX	E	(800) 421-0180	E+ / 0.8	2.70	-0.63	-7.47 / 2	-0.52 /11	2.43 /37	6.36	0.97
COH	American Funds High Income Tr	CITFX	E+	(800) 421-0180	D- / 1.1	2.80	-0.43	-7.08 / 2	-0.09 /15	2.88 /43	6.81	0.54
* COH	American Funds High Income Tr A	AHITX	E	(800) 421-0180	E / 0.5	2.77	-0.49	-7.19 / 2	-0.21 /14	2.76 /41	6.43	0.67
COH	● American Funds High Income Tr B	AHTBX	E	(800) 421-0180	E+ / 0.6	2.58	-0.86	-7.89 / 1	-0.96 / 9	1.99 /31	5.88	1.42
COH	American Funds High Income Tr C	AHTCX	E	(800) 421-0180	E+ / 0.6	2.57	-0.88	-7.93 / 1	-1.01 / 8	1.94 /30	5.83	1.47
COH	American Funds High Income Tr F1	AHTFX	E	(800) 421-0180	E+ / 0.9	2.76	-0.50	-7.23 / 2	-0.26 /13	2.71 /40	6.64	0.70
COH	American Funds High Income Tr F2	AHIFX	U	(800) 421-0180	U /	2.83	-0.37	-6.98 / 2	--	2.98 /45	6.92	0.45
COH	American Funds High Income Tr R1	RITAX	E	(800) 421-0180	E+ / 0.6	2.57	-0.88	-7.93 / 1	-1.00 / 8	1.94 /30	5.84	1.46
COH	American Funds High Income Tr R2	RITBX	E	(800) 421-0180	E / 0.5	2.55	-0.91	-7.97 / 1	-1.04 / 8	1.91 /30	5.79	1.53
COH	American Funds High Income Tr R2E	RTEHX	E	(800) 421-0180	E+ / 0.8	2.69	-0.64	-7.47 / 2	-0.46 /12	2.35 /36	6.37	1.26
COH	American Funds High Income Tr R3	RITCX	E	(800) 421-0180	E+ / 0.7	2.68	-0.66	-7.52 / 2	-0.56 /11	2.40 /36	6.31	1.04
COH	American Funds High Income Tr R4	RITEX	E	(800) 421-0180	D- / 1.0	2.77	-0.49	-7.21 / 2	-0.24 /14	2.73 /41	6.66	0.69
COH	American Funds High Income Tr R5	RITFX	E+	(800) 421-0180	D- / 1.2	2.84	-0.34	-6.93 / 2	0.06 /25	3.03 /46	6.98	0.39
COH	American Funds High Income Tr R5E	RITHX	E+	(800) 421-0180	D- / 1.0	2.80	-0.43	-7.14 / 2	-0.20 /14	2.77 /41	6.71	0.50
COH	American Funds High Income Tr R6	RITGX	E+	(800) 421-0180	D- / 1.2	2.86	-0.31	-6.88 / 2	0.11 /27	3.08 /46	7.03	0.34
GEI	American Funds Infl Lnk Bond 529A	CNLAX	D-	(800) 421-0180	D- / 1.5	3.89	3.47	1.11 /60	-0.45 /12	--	0.45	0.93
GEI	American Funds Infl Lnk Bond 529B	CNLBX	D-	(800) 421-0180	D / 1.7	3.78	3.19	0.52 /50	-0.91 / 9	--	0.00	1.65
GEI	American Funds Infl Lnk Bond 529C	CNLCX	D-	(800) 421-0180	D- / 1.4	3.68	2.99	0.21 /44	-1.08 / 8	--	0.00	1.64
GEI	American Funds Infl Lnk Bond 529E	CNLEX	D-	(800) 421-0180	D+ / 2.4	3.78	3.33	0.76 /54	-0.72 /10	--	0.23	1.09
GEI	American Funds Infl Lnk Bond 529F1	CNLFX	D	(800) 421-0180	C- / 3.1	3.88	3.46	1.10 /60	-0.42 /12	--	0.46	0.64
GEI	American Funds Infl Lnk Bond A	BFIAX	D-	(800) 421-0180	D / 1.7	3.89	3.52	1.05 /59	-0.18 /14	--	0.40	0.80
GEI	American Funds Infl Lnk Bond B	BFIBX	D-	(800) 421-0180	D / 1.6	3.78	3.19	0.52 /50	-0.95 / 9	--	0.00	1.52
GEI	American Funds Infl Lnk Bond C	BFICX	D-	(800) 421-0180	D- / 1.4	3.68	3.05	0.27 /45	-1.06 / 8	--	0.06	1.55
GEI	American Funds Infl Lnk Bond F1	BFIFX	D	(800) 421-0180	C- / 3.0	3.89	3.51	1.04 /59	-0.47 /12	--	0.40	0.82
GEI	American Funds Infl Lnk Bond F2	BFIGX	D	(800) 421-0180	C- / 3.6	3.88	3.52	1.16 /61	-0.11 /15	--	0.52	0.55
GEI	American Funds Infl Lnk Bond R1	RILAX	D-	(800) 421-0180	D- / 1.5	3.67	3.09	0.31 /46	-0.98 / 8	--	0.00	1.59

● Denotes fund is closed to new investors
* Denotes fund is included in Section II

RISK			NET ASSETS		ASSET							FUND MANAGER		MINIMUM		LOADS	
Risk Rating/Pts	3 Yr Avg Standard Deviation	Avg Duration	NAV As of 3/31/16	Total $(Mil)	Cash %	Gov. Bond %	Muni. Bond %	Corp. Bond %	Other %	Portfolio Turnover Ratio	Avg Coupon Rate	Manager Quality Pct	Manager Tenure (Years)	Initial Purch. $	Additional Purch. $	Front End Load	Back End Load
D+ / 2.9	4.8	6.4	19.91	315	0	65	0	27	8	185	3.7	82	17	250	50	3.8	0.0
C- / 3.0	4.7	6.4	19.76	2	0	65	0	27	8	185	3.7	49	17	250	50	0.0	0.0
C- / 3.0	4.7	6.4	19.65	125	0	65	0	27	8	185	3.7	49	17	250	50	0.0	0.0
C- / 3.0	4.7	6.4	19.78	17	0	65	0	27	8	185	3.7	76	17	250	50	0.0	0.0
C- / 3.0	4.8	6.4	19.79	40	0	65	0	27	8	185	3.7	86	17	250	50	0.0	0.0
C- / 3.0	4.7	6.4	19.85	6,381	0	65	0	27	8	185	3.7	83	17	250	50	3.8	0.0
D+ / 2.9	4.8	6.4	19.71	23	0	65	0	27	8	185	3.7	54	17	250	50	0.0	0.0
D+ / 2.9	4.8	6.4	19.52	405	0	65	0	27	8	185	3.7	52	17	250	50	0.0	0.0
C- / 3.0	4.8	6.4	19.80	2,149	0	65	0	27	8	185	3.7	83	17	250	50	0.0	0.0
C- / 3.0	4.8	6.4	19.82	793	0	65	0	27	8	185	3.7	88	17	250	50	0.0	0.0
D+ / 2.9	4.8	6.4	19.66	13	0	65	0	27	8	185	3.7	54	17	250	50	0.0	0.0
D+ / 2.9	4.8	6.4	19.65	147	0	65	0	27	8	185	3.7	53	17	250	50	0.0	0.0
C- / 3.0	4.7	6.4	19.83	1	0	65	0	27	8	185	3.7	77	17	250	50	0.0	0.0
D+ / 2.9	4.8	6.4	19.82	147	0	65	0	27	8	185	3.7	75	17	250	50	0.0	0.0
C- / 3.0	4.8	6.4	19.84	102	0	65	0	27	8	185	3.7	84	17	250	50	0.0	0.0
D+ / 2.9	4.8	6.4	19.86	153	0	65	0	27	8	185	3.7	88	17	250	50	0.0	0.0
C- / 3.0	4.8	6.4	19.84	N/A	0	65	0	27	8	185	3.7	84	17	250	50	0.0	0.0
C- / 3.0	4.7	6.4	19.85	1,999	0	65	0	27	8	185	3.7	89	17	250	50	0.0	0.0
D+ / 2.5	4.5	7.0	15.81	3,159	1	0	98	0	1	23	5.3	78	22	250	50	3.8	0.0
D+ / 2.5	4.5	7.0	15.81	2	1	0	98	0	1	23	5.3	46	22	250	50	0.0	0.0
D+ / 2.5	4.5	7.0	15.81	215	1	0	98	0	1	23	5.3	44	22	250	50	0.0	0.0
D+ / 2.5	4.5	7.0	15.81	251	1	0	98	0	1	23	5.3	75	22	250	50	0.0	0.0
D+ / 2.5	4.5	7.0	15.81	474	1	0	98	0	1	23	5.3	82	22	250	50	0.0	0.0
D- / 1.0	6.0	3.5	9.46	292	1	5	0	87	7	49	6.6	11	27	250	50	3.8	0.0
D- / 1.0	6.0	3.5	9.46	2	1	5	0	87	7	49	6.6	8	27	250	50	0.0	0.0
D- / 1.0	6.0	3.5	9.46	99	1	5	0	87	7	49	6.6	8	27	250	50	0.0	0.0
D- / 1.0	6.0	3.5	9.46	16	1	5	0	87	7	49	6.6	10	27	250	50	0.0	0.0
D- / 1.0	6.0	3.5	9.46	22	1	5	0	87	7	49	6.6	13	27	250	50	0.0	0.0
D- / 1.0	6.0	3.5	9.46	11,033	1	5	0	87	7	49	6.6	12	27	250	50	3.8	0.0
D- / 1.0	6.0	3.5	9.46	26	1	5	0	87	7	49	6.6	8	27	250	50	0.0	0.0
D- / 1.0	6.0	3.5	9.46	841	1	5	0	87	7	49	6.6	8	27	250	50	0.0	0.0
D- / 1.0	6.0	3.5	9.46	639	1	5	0	87	7	49	6.6	12	27	250	50	0.0	0.0
U /	6.0	3.5	9.46	1,271	1	5	0	87	7	49	6.6	N/A	27	250	50	0.0	0.0
D- / 1.0	6.0	3.5	9.46	16	1	5	0	87	7	49	6.6	8	27	250	50	0.0	0.0
D- / 1.0	6.0	3.5	9.46	173	1	5	0	87	7	49	6.6	8	27	250	50	0.0	0.0
D- / 1.0	6.1	3.5	9.46	2	1	5	0	87	7	49	6.6	10	27	250	50	0.0	0.0
D- / 1.0	6.0	3.5	9.46	188	1	5	0	87	7	49	6.6	9	27	250	50	0.0	0.0
D- / 1.0	6.0	3.5	9.46	162	1	5	0	87	7	49	6.6	12	27	250	50	0.0	0.0
D- / 1.0	6.0	3.5	9.46	82	1	5	0	87	7	49	6.6	15	27	250	50	0.0	0.0
D- / 1.0	6.0	3.5	9.46	N/A	1	5	0	87	7	49	6.6	12	27	250	50	0.0	0.0
D- / 1.0	6.0	3.5	9.46	980	1	5	0	87	7	49	6.6	16	27	250	50	0.0	0.0
D+ / 2.3	5.5	4.9	9.62	3	0	96	0	1	3	801	0.9	5	4	250	50	2.5	0.0
D / 2.2	5.5	4.9	9.62	N/A	0	96	0	1	3	801	0.9	4	4	250	50	0.0	0.0
D / 2.2	5.5	4.9	9.57	1	0	96	0	1	3	801	0.9	3	4	250	50	0.0	0.0
D+ / 2.3	5.5	4.9	9.61	N/A	0	96	0	1	3	801	0.9	4	4	250	50	0.0	0.0
D+ / 2.3	5.5	4.9	9.63	N/A	0	96	0	1	3	801	0.9	5	4	250	50	0.0	0.0
D+ / 2.3	5.5	4.9	9.62	101	0	96	0	1	3	801	0.9	5	4	250	50	2.5	0.0
D / 2.2	5.5	4.9	9.61	N/A	0	96	0	1	3	801	0.9	4	4	250	50	0.0	0.0
D / 2.2	5.5	4.9	9.57	4	0	96	0	1	3	801	0.9	3	4	250	50	0.0	0.0
D / 2.2	5.5	4.9	9.62	3	0	96	0	1	3	801	0.9	5	4	250	50	0.0	0.0
D+ / 2.3	5.5	4.9	9.63	35	0	96	0	1	3	801	0.9	5	4	250	50	0.0	0.0
D / 2.2	5.5	4.9	9.60	N/A	0	96	0	1	3	801	0.9	4	4	250	50	0.0	0.0

Fund Type	Fund Name (99 Pct = Best, 0 Pct = Worst)	Ticker Symbol	Overall Investment Rating	Phone	PERFORMANCE: Performance Rating/Pts	Total Return % through 3/31/16: 3 Mo	6 Mo	1Yr / Pct	Annualized: 3Yr / Pct	5Yr / Pct	Incl. in Returns: Dividend Yield	Expense Ratio
GEI	American Funds Infl Lnk Bond R2	RILBX	**D-**	(800) 421-0180	**D- / 1.4**	3.58	2.91	0.24 /45	-1.04 / 8	--	0.33	1.72
GEI	American Funds Infl Lnk Bond R2E	RILGX	**D-**	(800) 421-0180	**D+ / 2.7**	3.88	3.46	0.99 /58	-0.67 /10	--	0.35	1.35
GEI	American Funds Infl Lnk Bond R3	RILCX	**D-**	(800) 421-0180	**D / 2.2**	3.79	3.27	0.60 /51	-0.73 /10	--	0.38	1.31
GEI	American Funds Infl Lnk Bond R4	RILDX	**D**	(800) 421-0180	**C- / 3.0**	3.89	3.46	0.99 /58	-0.45 /12	--	0.46	0.83
GEI	American Funds Infl Lnk Bond R5	RILEX	**D**	(800) 421-0180	**C- / 3.7**	4.00	3.58	1.22 /62	-0.09 /15	--	0.57	0.53
GEI	American Funds Infl Lnk Bond R5E	RILHX	**D**	(800) 421-0180	**C- / 3.6**	4.00	3.63	1.16 /61	-0.14 /14	--	0.62	0.62
GEI	American Funds Infl Lnk Bond R6	RILFX	**D**	(800) 421-0180	**C- / 3.7**	4.00	3.59	1.33 /64	-0.09 /15	--	0.58	0.48
COI	American Funds Ins Ser Bond 4		**C+**	(800) 421-0180	**C+ / 6.5**	3.11	2.55	1.46 /66	1.90 /59	--	1.58	0.89
GL	American Funds Ins Ser Glb Bond 4		**D+**	(800) 421-0180	**C / 5.0**	5.42	3.80	1.44 /65	0.56 /34	--	0.03	1.07
MTG	American Funds Ins Ser Mtge 4		**A**	(800) 421-0180	**B- / 7.1**	2.09	1.62	2.40 /74	2.37 /69	--	1.52	0.95
USL	American Funds Ins Ser USGAAA		**B+**	(800) 421-0180	**C+ / 6.7**	2.78	2.05	2.61 /75	1.99 /61	--	1.37	0.85
GEI	American Funds Intm Bd Fd Amr	CBOAX	**C**	(800) 421-0180	**C- / 3.6**	1.72	1.03	1.41 /65	1.04 /43	1.80 /29	1.13	0.70
GEI ●	American Funds Intm Bd Fd Amr	CBOBX	**C**	(800) 421-0180	**C- / 3.2**	1.45	0.57	0.57 /51	0.24 /29	1.00 /20	0.40	1.46
GEI	American Funds Intm Bd Fd Amr	CBOCX	**C**	(800) 421-0180	**C- / 3.2**	1.46	0.58	0.58 /51	0.25 /29	1.01 /20	0.42	1.46
GEI	American Funds Intm Bd Fd Amr	CBOEX	**C+**	(800) 421-0180	**C / 4.4**	1.67	0.93	1.20 /62	0.82 /39	1.57 /26	0.96	0.91
GEI	American Funds Intm Bd Fd Amr	CBOFX	**B**	(800) 421-0180	**C / 5.2**	1.77	1.14	1.64 /68	1.27 /48	2.03 /31	1.39	0.47
* GEI	American Funds Intm Bd Fd Amr A	AIBAX	**C+**	(800) 421-0180	**C- / 3.7**	1.74	1.07	1.50 /66	1.13 /45	1.89 /30	1.22	0.61
GEI ●	American Funds Intm Bd Fd Amr B	IBFBX	**C**	(800) 421-0180	**C- / 3.5**	1.56	0.70	0.77 /55	0.39 /31	1.14 /22	0.53	1.34
GEI	American Funds Intm Bd Fd Amr C	IBFCX	**C**	(800) 421-0180	**C- / 3.4**	1.55	0.69	0.72 /53	0.34 /30	1.09 /21	0.48	1.39
GEI	American Funds Intm Bd Fd Amr F1	IBFFX	**B-**	(800) 421-0180	**C / 4.9**	1.73	1.05	1.45 /65	1.08 /44	1.84 /29	1.20	0.66
GEI	American Funds Intm Bd Fd Amr F2	IBAFX	**B+**	(800) 421-0180	**C / 5.4**	1.80	1.19	1.73 /69	1.36 /49	2.13 /33	1.48	0.39
GEI	American Funds Intm Bd Fd Amr R1	RBOAX	**C**	(800) 421-0180	**C- / 3.4**	1.55	0.69	0.73 /54	0.35 /31	1.10 /21	0.49	1.38
GEI	American Funds Intm Bd Fd Amr R2	RBOBX	**C**	(800) 421-0180	**C- / 3.3**	1.47	0.67	0.63 /52	0.31 /30	1.08 /21	0.47	1.45
COI	American Funds Intm Bd Fd Amr R2E	REBBX	**C+**	(800) 421-0180	**C / 4.5**	1.66	0.96	1.36 /64	0.83 /39	1.46 /25	1.19	1.15
GEI	American Funds Intm Bd Fd Amr R3	RBOCX	**C+**	(800) 421-0180	**C / 4.3**	1.66	0.91	1.18 /61	0.80 /39	1.55 /26	0.93	0.95
GEI	American Funds Intm Bd Fd Amr R4	RBOEX	**B-**	(800) 421-0180	**C / 4.9**	1.74	1.07	1.49 /66	1.12 /45	1.87 /30	1.24	0.61
GEI	American Funds Intm Bd Fd Amr R5	RBOFX	**B+**	(800) 421-0180	**C / 5.5**	1.81	1.22	1.79 /70	1.42 /50	2.17 /33	1.53	0.32
COI	American Funds Intm Bd Fd Amr R5E	RBOHX	**B**	(800) 421-0180	**C / 5.0**	1.78	1.13	1.57 /67	1.15 /45	1.90 /30	1.31	0.43
GEI	American Funds Intm Bd Fd Amr R6	RBOGX	**B+**	(800) 421-0180	**C+ / 5.6**	1.82	1.24	1.84 /70	1.47 /51	2.23 /34	1.58	0.27
* MUN	American Funds Ltd Term T/E Bond	LTEBX	**B+**	(800) 421-0180	**C / 5.5**	0.91	1.35	1.73 /75	1.57 /69	3.27 /72	2.22	0.57
MUN ●	American Funds Ltd Term T/E Bond	LTXBX	**B**	(800) 421-0180	**C / 5.3**	0.73	1.00	1.01 /67	0.86 /49	2.56 /60	1.57	1.28
MUN	American Funds Ltd Term T/E Bond	LTXCX	**B**	(800) 421-0180	**C / 5.1**	0.72	0.97	0.96 /66	0.81 /47	2.51 /59	1.51	1.33
MUN	American Funds Ltd Term T/E Bond	LTXFX	**A+**	(800) 421-0180	**C+ / 6.9**	0.89	1.31	1.63 /75	1.48 /67	3.20 /71	2.18	0.67
MUN	American Funds Ltd Term T/E Bond	LTEFX	**A+**	(800) 421-0180	**B- / 7.5**	0.95	1.44	1.88 /76	1.74 /73	3.46 /74	2.42	0.41
MTG	American Funds Mortgage Fund	CMFAX	**C+**	(800) 421-0180	**C / 5.3**	1.96	1.71	2.78 /76	2.23 /66	3.12 /47	1.16	0.79
MTG ●	American Funds Mortgage Fund	CMFBX	**B-**	(800) 421-0180	**C+ / 5.6**	1.77	1.24	1.93 /71	1.43 /51	2.30 /35	0.48	1.56
MTG	American Funds Mortgage Fund	CMFCX	**B-**	(800) 421-0180	**C / 5.5**	1.68	1.22	1.88 /71	1.39 /50	2.27 /34	0.42	1.57
MTG	American Funds Mortgage Fund	CMFEX	**B+**	(800) 421-0180	**C+ / 6.5**	1.90	1.57	2.48 /74	1.96 /61	2.83 /42	0.92	1.04
MTG	American Funds Mortgage Fund	CMFFX	**A**	(800) 421-0180	**B- / 7.3**	2.02	1.81	2.97 /77	2.44 /70	3.32 /50	1.38	0.57
MTG	American Funds Mortgage Fund A	MFAAX	**B-**	(800) 421-0180	**C / 5.5**	1.99	1.75	2.85 /76	2.32 /68	3.21 /48	1.22	0.70
MTG ●	American Funds Mortgage Fund B	MFABX	**B**	(800) 421-0180	**C+ / 5.8**	1.80	1.37	1.98 /72	1.53 /53	2.40 /36	0.53	1.45
MTG	American Funds Mortgage Fund C	MFACX	**B-**	(800) 421-0180	**C+ / 5.6**	1.69	1.26	1.94 /71	1.46 /51	2.35 /36	0.49	1.50
MTG	American Funds Mortgage Fund F1	MFAEX	**A**	(800) 421-0180	**B- / 7.0**	1.98	1.74	2.73 /75	2.30 /67	3.18 /48	1.25	0.71
MTG	American Funds Mortgage Fund F2	MFAFX	**A+**	(800) 421-0180	**B- / 7.4**	2.06	1.89	3.01 /77	2.58 /72	3.44 /52	1.52	0.42
MTG	American Funds Mortgage Fund R1	RMAAX	**A-**	(800) 421-0180	**C+ / 6.7**	1.69	1.32	2.21 /73	2.19 /65	2.88 /43	0.75	1.45
MTG	American Funds Mortgage Fund R2	RMABX	**B-**	(800) 421-0180	**C+ / 5.6**	1.77	1.20	1.83 /70	1.48 /52	2.45 /37	0.38	1.68
MTG	American Funds Mortgage Fund R2E	RMBEX	**A-**	(800) 421-0180	**C+ / 6.8**	2.04	1.83	2.90 /76	2.09 /63	2.80 /42	1.41	1.17
MTG	American Funds Mortgage Fund R3	RMACX	**B+**	(800) 421-0180	**C+ / 6.6**	1.90	1.57	2.40 /74	2.03 /62	2.94 /44	0.93	1.04
MTG	American Funds Mortgage Fund R4	RMAEX	**A**	(800) 421-0180	**B- / 7.2**	1.98	1.76	2.89 /76	2.38 /69	3.25 /49	1.31	0.67
MTG	American Funds Mortgage Fund R5	RMAFX	**A**	(800) 421-0180	**B- / 7.5**	2.06	1.89	3.03 /77	2.62 /72	3.49 /53	1.54	0.38
USS	American Funds Mortgage Fund R5E	RMAHX	**A**	(800) 421-0180	**B- / 7.2**	2.03	1.81	2.91 /76	2.34 /68	3.22 /48	1.33	0.48
MTG	American Funds Mortgage Fund R6	RMAGX	**A+**	(800) 421-0180	**B / 7.6**	2.08	1.93	3.11 /77	2.68 /73	3.54 /54	1.62	0.32

● Denotes fund is closed to new investors
* Denotes fund is included in Section II

RISK			NET ASSETS		ASSET							FUND MANAGER		MINIMUM		LOADS	
Risk Rating/Pts	3 Yr Avg Standard Deviation	Avg Dura-tion	NAV As of 3/31/16	Total $(Mil)	Cash %	Gov. Bond %	Muni. Bond %	Corp. Bond %	Other %	Portfolio Turnover Ratio	Avg Coupon Rate	Manager Quality Pct	Manager Tenure (Years)	Initial Purch. $	Additional Purch. $	Front End Load	Back End Load
D / 2.2	5.5	4.9	9.55	N/A	0	96	0	1	3	801	0.9	4	4	250	50	0.0	0.0
D / 2.2	5.5	4.9	9.63	N/A	0	96	0	1	3	801	0.9	4	4	250	50	0.0	0.0
D+ / 2.3	5.5	4.9	9.59	1	0	96	0	1	3	801	0.9	4	4	250	50	0.0	0.0
D+ / 2.3	5.5	4.9	9.62	N/A	0	96	0	1	3	801	0.9	5	4	250	50	0.0	0.0
D+ / 2.3	5.5	4.9	9.63	N/A	0	96	0	1	3	801	0.9	5	4	250	50	0.0	0.0
D / 2.2	5.5	4.9	9.61	N/A	0	96	0	1	3	801	0.9	5	4	250	50	0.0	0.0
D+ / 2.3	5.5	4.9	9.63	1,135	0	96	0	1	3	801	0.9	5	4	250	50	0.0	0.0
C+ / 6.0	3.1	5.7	10.94	68	0	0	0	0	100	434	3.1	58	N/A	0	0	0.0	0.0
C- / 3.1	4.7	6.5	11.48	7	0	0	0	0	100	200	3.8	86	3	0	0	0.0	0.0
B / 7.7	2.6	4.4	10.74	17	0	0	0	0	100	1,103	3.0	49	6	0	0	0.0	0.0
B- / 7.0	2.9	4.9	12.56	66	0	0	0	0	100	901	2.5	83	6	0	0	0.0	0.0
B+ / 8.6	1.8	2.9	13.63	371	0	57	0	21	22	192	2.1	46	25	250	50	2.5	0.0
B+ / 8.6	1.9	2.9	13.62	1	0	57	0	21	22	192	2.1	23	25	250	50	0.0	0.0
B+ / 8.7	1.8	2.9	13.62	67	0	57	0	21	22	192	2.1	24	25	250	50	0.0	0.0
B+ / 8.6	1.8	2.9	13.63	19	0	57	0	21	22	192	2.1	39	25	250	50	0.0	0.0
B+ / 8.6	1.8	2.9	13.63	83	0	57	0	21	22	192	2.1	55	25	250	50	0.0	0.0
B+ / 8.6	1.8	2.9	13.63	7,095	0	57	0	21	22	192	2.1	50	25	250	50	2.5	0.0
B+ / 8.6	1.8	2.9	13.63	7	0	57	0	21	22	192	2.1	27	25	250	50	0.0	0.0
B+ / 8.6	1.8	2.9	13.63	113	0	57	0	21	22	192	2.1	26	25	250	50	0.0	0.0
B+ / 8.6	1.8	2.9	13.63	255	0	57	0	21	22	192	2.1	48	25	250	50	0.0	0.0
B+ / 8.6	1.8	2.9	13.63	402	0	57	0	21	22	192	2.1	58	25	250	50	0.0	0.0
B+ / 8.6	1.8	2.9	13.63	10	0	57	0	21	22	192	2.1	26	25	250	50	0.0	0.0
B+ / 8.7	1.8	2.9	13.62	120	0	57	0	21	22	192	2.1	25	25	250	50	0.0	0.0
B+ / 8.6	1.9	2.9	13.62	2	0	57	0	21	22	192	2.1	52	25	250	50	0.0	0.0
B+ / 8.6	1.8	2.9	13.63	149	0	57	0	21	22	192	2.1	38	25	250	50	0.0	0.0
B+ / 8.6	1.8	2.9	13.63	115	0	57	0	21	22	192	2.1	49	25	250	50	0.0	0.0
B+ / 8.6	1.8	2.9	13.63	32	0	57	0	21	22	192	2.1	60	25	250	50	0.0	0.0
B+ / 8.6	1.8	2.9	13.63	N/A	0	57	0	21	22	192	2.1	69	25	250	50	0.0	0.0
B+ / 8.6	1.8	2.9	13.63	3,072	0	57	0	21	22	192	2.1	64	25	250	50	0.0	0.0
B+ / 8.5	1.9	3.0	15.97	2,850	0	0	99	0	1	19	4.4	49	23	250	50	2.5	0.0
B+ / 8.5	1.9	3.0	15.97	1	0	0	99	0	1	19	4.4	27	23	250	50	0.0	0.0
B+ / 8.5	1.9	3.0	15.97	30	0	0	99	0	1	19	4.4	26	23	250	50	0.0	0.0
B+ / 8.5	1.9	3.0	15.97	87	0	0	99	0	1	19	4.4	45	23	250	50	0.0	0.0
B+ / 8.5	1.9	3.0	15.97	236	0	0	99	0	1	19	4.4	55	23	250	50	0.0	0.0
B / 7.7	2.6	4.6	10.28	17	0	27	0	12	61	1,205	3.1	44	6	250	50	3.8	0.0
B / 7.8	2.6	4.6	10.23	N/A	0	27	0	12	61	1,205	3.1	22	6	250	50	0.0	0.0
B / 7.7	2.6	4.6	10.23	7	0	27	0	12	61	1,205	3.1	21	6	250	50	0.0	0.0
B / 7.7	2.6	4.6	10.28	1	0	27	0	12	61	1,205	3.1	36	6	250	50	0.0	0.0
B / 7.8	2.6	4.6	10.28	6	0	27	0	12	61	1,205	3.1	53	6	250	50	0.0	0.0
B / 7.8	2.5	4.6	10.28	221	0	27	0	12	61	1,205	3.1	49	6	250	50	3.8	0.0
B / 7.8	2.6	4.6	10.25	N/A	0	27	0	12	61	1,205	3.1	25	6	250	50	0.0	0.0
B / 7.8	2.5	4.6	10.24	27	0	27	0	12	61	1,205	3.1	24	6	250	50	0.0	0.0
B / 7.8	2.5	4.6	10.28	22	0	27	0	12	61	1,205	3.1	49	6	250	50	0.0	0.0
B / 7.8	2.6	4.6	10.28	39	0	27	0	12	61	1,205	3.1	58	6	250	50	0.0	0.0
B / 7.9	2.5	4.6	10.25	N/A	0	27	0	12	61	1,205	3.1	47	6	250	50	0.0	0.0
B / 7.7	2.6	4.6	10.23	3	0	27	0	12	61	1,205	3.1	23	6	250	50	0.0	0.0
B / 7.8	2.6	4.6	10.28	N/A	0	27	0	12	61	1,205	3.1	40	6	250	50	0.0	0.0
B / 7.8	2.6	4.6	10.27	3	0	27	0	12	61	1,205	3.1	39	6	250	50	0.0	0.0
B / 7.8	2.6	4.6	10.28	3	0	27	0	12	61	1,205	3.1	50	6	250	50	0.0	0.0
B / 7.6	2.7	4.6	10.28	N/A	0	27	0	12	61	1,205	3.1	57	6	250	50	0.0	0.0
B / 7.8	2.5	4.6	10.28	N/A	0	27	0	12	61	1,205	3.1	86	6	250	50	0.0	0.0
B / 7.8	2.6	4.6	10.28	1,785	0	27	0	12	61	1,205	3.1	62	6	250	50	0.0	0.0

99 Pct = Best
0 Pct = Worst

Fund Type	Fund Name	Ticker Symbol	Overall Investment Rating	Phone	PERFORMANCE: Performance Rating/Pts	Total Return % through 3/31/16: 3 Mo	6 Mo	1Yr / Pct	Annualized: 3Yr / Pct	5Yr / Pct	Incl. in Returns: Dividend Yield	Expense Ratio
GEI	American Funds Preservation 529A	CPPAX	C	(800) 421-0180	C- / 3.3	1.64	1.05	1.03 /59	0.92 /41	--	1.09	0.77
GEI	American Funds Preservation 529B	CPPBX	C	(800) 421-0180	C- / 3.0	1.42	0.71	0.31 /46	0.12 /27	--	0.31	1.53
GEI	American Funds Preservation 529C	CPPCX	C	(800) 421-0180	D+ / 2.9	1.34	0.65	0.25 /45	0.12 /27	--	0.35	1.52
GEI	American Funds Preservation 529E	CPPEX	C+	(800) 421-0180	C- / 4.1	1.61	0.98	0.84 /56	0.69 /37	--	0.93	0.99
GEI	American Funds Preservation 529F1	CPPFX	B	(800) 421-0180	C / 4.9	1.66	1.16	1.27 /63	1.15 /45	--	1.35	0.52
* GEI	American Funds Preservation A	PPVAX	C	(800) 421-0180	C- / 3.4	1.53	1.08	1.10 /60	0.98 /42	--	1.16	0.71
GEI	American Funds Preservation B	PPVBX	C	(800) 421-0180	C- / 3.2	1.44	0.77	0.42 /48	0.24 /29	--	0.42	1.44
GEI	American Funds Preservation C	PPVCX	C	(800) 421-0180	C- / 3.2	1.46	0.71	0.36 /47	0.25 /29	--	0.46	1.43
GEI	American Funds Preservation F1	PPVFX	B-	(800) 421-0180	C / 4.7	1.64	1.20	1.22 /62	1.00 /43	--	1.20	0.70
GEI	American Funds Preservation F2	PPEFX	B	(800) 421-0180	C / 5.2	1.67	1.30	1.43 /65	1.25 /47	--	1.42	0.45
GEI	American Funds Preservation R1	RPPVX	C	(800) 421-0180	C- / 3.1	1.47	0.70	0.35 /47	0.23 /29	--	0.45	1.44
GEI	American Funds Preservation R2	RPPBX	C	(800) 421-0180	C- / 3.0	1.35	0.68	0.31 /46	0.18 /28	--	0.41	1.48
COI	American Funds Preservation R2E	RPBEX	C+	(800) 421-0180	C- / 4.2	1.50	1.04	1.12 /61	0.74 /38	--	1.20	1.18
GEI	American Funds Preservation R3	RPPCX	C+	(800) 421-0180	C- / 4.0	1.55	0.91	0.78 /55	0.67 /36	--	0.88	1.01
GEI	American Funds Preservation R4	RPPEX	B-	(800) 421-0180	C / 4.7	1.64	1.10	1.23 /62	1.03 /43	--	1.21	0.68
GEI	American Funds Preservation R5	RPPFX	B	(800) 421-0180	C / 5.2	1.68	1.22	1.39 /65	1.29 /48	--	1.47	0.40
COI	American Funds Preservation R5E	RGMFX	B-	(800) 421-0180	C / 4.8	1.75	1.26	1.28 /63	1.04 /43	--	1.17	0.51
GEI	American Funds Preservation R6	RPPGX	B+	(800) 421-0180	C / 5.3	1.68	1.24	1.43 /65	1.32 /49	--	1.51	0.35
GES	American Funds Sh-T Bd of Amr	CAAFX	C-	(800) 421-0180	D / 1.7	0.86	0.56	0.65 /52	0.37 /31	0.59 /18	0.73	0.66
GES ●	American Funds Sh-T Bd of Amr	CBAMX	C-	(800) 421-0180	D- / 1.5	0.72	0.20	-0.05 /31	-0.38 /12	-0.18 / 3	0.17	1.42
GES ●	American Funds Sh-T Bd of Amr	CCAMX	C-	(800) 421-0180	D- / 1.4	0.61	0.10	-0.17 /29	-0.49 /12	-0.27 / 2	0.14	1.52
GES	American Funds Sh-T Bd of Amr	CEAMX	C	(800) 421-0180	D+ / 2.7	0.68	0.31	0.33 /46	0.04 /23	0.24 /16	0.44	1.00
GES	American Funds Sh-T Bd of Amr	CFAMX	C+	(800) 421-0180	C- / 3.6	0.89	0.63	0.79 /55	0.51 /33	0.72 /19	0.89	0.53
* GES	American Funds Sh-T Bd of Amr A	ASBAX	C-	(800) 421-0180	D / 1.7	0.87	0.59	0.71 /53	0.44 /32	0.65 /18	0.80	0.60
GES ●	American Funds Sh-T Bd of Amr B	AMSBX	C-	(800) 421-0180	D / 1.7	0.72	0.21	0.10 /41	-0.26 /13	-0.04 / 3	0.21	1.28
GES ●	American Funds Sh-T Bd of Amr C	ASBCX	C-	(800) 421-0180	D- / 1.5	0.72	0.20	0.05 /38	-0.38 /12	-0.18 / 3	0.16	1.44
GES	American Funds Sh-T Bd of Amr F1	ASBFX	C+	(800) 421-0180	C- / 3.2	0.84	0.54	0.59 /51	0.31 /30	0.53 /17	0.70	0.73
GES	American Funds Sh-T Bd of Amr F2	SBFFX	C+	(800) 421-0180	C- / 3.7	0.91	0.67	0.86 /56	0.59 /35	0.81 /19	0.97	0.45
GES	American Funds Sh-T Bd of Amr R1	RAMAX	C-	(800) 421-0180	D- / 1.4	0.61	0.20	-0.06 /31	-0.42 /12	-0.21 / 3	0.15	1.47
GES	American Funds Sh-T Bd of Amr R2	RAMBX	C-	(800) 421-0180	D- / 1.5	0.72	0.20	-0.05 /31	-0.42 /12	-0.20 / 3	0.16	1.51
COI	American Funds Sh-T Bd of Amr R2E	RAAEX	C	(800) 421-0180	D+ / 2.9	0.82	0.51	0.66 /52	0.08 /26	0.17 /16	0.76	1.19
GES	American Funds Sh-T Bd of Amr R3	RAMCX	C	(800) 421-0180	D+ / 2.7	0.77	0.40	0.31 /46	0.03 /21	0.23 /16	0.42	1.03
GES	American Funds Sh-T Bd of Amr R4	RAMEX	C+	(800) 421-0180	C- / 3.3	0.85	0.55	0.61 /51	0.33 /30	0.55 /17	0.72	0.70
GES	American Funds Sh-T Bd of Amr R5	RAMFX	C+	(800) 421-0180	C- / 3.9	0.92	0.70	1.01 /59	0.66 /36	0.86 /19	1.01	0.40
USS	American Funds Sh-T Bd of Amr R5E	RAAGX	C+	(800) 421-0180	C- / 3.6	0.89	0.73	0.85 /56	0.48 /33	0.67 /18	0.85	0.52
GES	American Funds Sh-T Bd of Amr R6	RMMGX	C+	(800) 421-0180	C- / 4.0	0.93	0.72	0.96 /58	0.69 /37	0.89 /19	1.06	0.35
* MUN	American Funds ST T/E Bnd Fd A	ASTEX	C-	(800) 421-0180	D / 1.8	0.44	0.49	0.62 /58	0.58 /41	1.23 /30	0.99	0.58
MUN	American Funds ST T/E Bnd Fd F1	FSTTX	C+	(800) 421-0180	C- / 3.6	0.39	0.38	0.40 /52	0.36 /34	1.01 /26	0.80	0.80
MUN	American Funds ST T/E Bnd Fd F2	ASTFX	B-	(800) 421-0180	C / 4.4	0.45	0.51	0.66 /59	0.61 /41	1.27 /31	1.05	0.55
* MUN	American Funds T/E Bd of America A	AFTEX	B+	(800) 421-0180	B+ / 8.6	1.54	3.07	3.64 /91	3.52 /93	6.00 /92	3.05	0.54
MUN ●	American Funds T/E Bd of America B	TEBFX	B+	(800) 421-0180	B+ / 8.8	1.35	2.69	2.88 /84	2.76 /86	5.22 /87	2.43	1.28
MUN	American Funds T/E Bd of America C	TEBCX	B+	(800) 421-0180	B+ / 8.7	1.34	2.66	2.83 /83	2.71 /85	5.17 /87	2.39	1.33
MUN	American Funds T/E Bd of America	AFTFX	A	(800) 421-0180	A / 9.3	1.51	3.00	3.51 /90	3.40 /92	5.87 /91	3.04	0.67
MUN	American Funds T/E Bd of America	TEAFX	A	(800) 421-0180	A / 9.4	1.57	3.14	3.78 /92	3.66 /94	6.15 /93	3.29	0.41
* MUS	American Funds Tax-Exempt of CA A	TAFTX	B+	(800) 421-0180	A- / 9.1	1.67	3.20	3.96 /94	4.06 /96	6.96 /96	3.11	0.62
MUS ●	American Funds Tax-Exempt of CA B	TECBX	B+	(800) 421-0180	A- / 9.2	1.48	2.82	3.20 /87	3.29 /91	6.18 /93	2.50	1.35
MUS	American Funds Tax-Exempt of CA C	TECCX	B+	(800) 421-0180	A- / 9.1	1.47	2.80	3.14 /86	3.24 /90	6.12 /93	2.45	1.40
MUS	American Funds Tax-Exempt of CA	TECFX	A-	(800) 421-0180	A+ / 9.6	1.64	3.14	3.83 /93	3.93 /95	6.83 /96	3.11	0.74
MUS	American Funds Tax-Exempt of CA	TEFEX	A	(800) 421-0180	A+ / 9.7	1.70	3.27	4.08 /94	4.18 /97	7.10 /97	3.35	0.49
MUS	American Funds Tax-Exempt of MD A	TMMDX	B	(800) 421-0180	C+ / 6.8	1.33	2.33	2.83 /83	2.23 /79	4.51 /81	2.97	0.69
MUS ●	American Funds Tax-Exempt of MD B	TEMBX	B+	(800) 421-0180	B- / 7.2	1.15	1.96	2.07 /78	1.48 /67	3.74 /76	2.35	1.42
MUS	American Funds Tax-Exempt of MD	TEMCX	B+	(800) 421-0180	B- / 7.1	1.14	1.93	2.03 /77	1.43 /65	3.69 /75	2.31	1.47

● Denotes fund is closed to new investors
* Denotes fund is included in Section II

RISK			NET ASSETS		ASSET							FUND MANAGER		MINIMUM		LOADS	
Risk Rating/Pts	3 Yr Avg Standard Deviation	Avg Duration	NAV As of 3/31/16	Total $(Mil)	Cash %	Gov. Bond %	Muni. Bond %	Corp. Bond %	Other %	Portfolio Turnover Ratio	Avg Coupon Rate	Manager Quality Pct	Manager Tenure (Years)	Initial Purch. $	Additional Purch. $	Front End Load	Back End Load
B+ / 8.8	1.7	3.3	10.00	64	0	46	1	25	28	2	2.7	46	4	250	50	2.5	0.0
B+ / 8.8	1.6	3.3	10.01	N/A	0	46	1	25	28	2	2.7	24	4	250	50	0.0	0.0
B+ / 8.8	1.7	3.3	9.99	28	0	46	1	25	28	2	2.7	24	4	250	50	0.0	0.0
B+ / 8.8	1.7	3.3	10.00	3	0	46	1	25	28	2	2.7	40	4	250	50	0.0	0.0
B+ / 8.8	1.7	3.3	10.00	12	0	46	1	25	28	2	2.7	55	4	250	50	0.0	0.0
B+ / 8.8	1.7	3.3	10.00	678	0	46	1	25	28	2	2.7	47	4	250	50	2.5	0.0
B+ / 8.8	1.7	3.3	10.01	1	0	46	1	25	28	2	2.7	26	4	250	50	0.0	0.0
B+ / 8.8	1.7	3.3	9.99	157	0	46	1	25	28	2	2.7	25	4	250	50	0.0	0.0
B+ / 8.8	1.7	3.3	10.01	28	0	46	1	25	28	2	2.7	N/A	4	250	50	0.0	0.0
B+ / 8.8	1.7	3.3	10.01	30	0	46	1	25	28	2	2.7	59	4	250	50	0.0	0.0
B+ / 8.8	1.7	3.3	10.00	2	0	46	1	25	28	2	2.7	26	4	250	50	0.0	0.0
B+ / 8.8	1.6	3.3	9.98	17	0	46	1	25	28	2	2.7	26	4	250	50	0.0	0.0
B+ / 8.8	1.7	3.3	10.00	N/A	0	46	1	25	28	2	2.7	51	4	250	50	0.0	0.0
B+ / 8.8	1.6	3.3	10.00	14	0	46	1	25	28	2	2.7	40	4	250	50	0.0	0.0
B+ / 8.8	1.7	3.3	10.01	7	0	46	1	25	28	2	2.7	51	4	250	50	0.0	0.0
B+ / 8.8	1.7	3.3	10.01	1	0	46	1	25	28	2	2.7	60	4	250	50	0.0	0.0
B+ / 8.8	1.7	3.3	10.02	N/A	0	46	1	25	28	2	2.7	61	4	250	50	0.0	0.0
B+ / 8.8	1.6	3.3	10.01	8	0	46	1	25	28	2	2.7	64	4	250	50	0.0	0.0
A / 9.5	0.8	1.5	9.99	297	3	38	2	26	31	452	1.6	54	5	250	50	2.5	0.0
A / 9.5	0.8	1.5	9.89	1	3	38	2	26	31	452	1.6	30	5	250	50	0.0	0.0
A / 9.5	0.8	1.5	9.86	69	3	38	2	26	31	452	1.6	26	5	250	50	0.0	0.0
A / 9.5	0.8	1.5	9.98	17	3	38	2	26	31	452	1.6	43	5	250	50	0.0	0.0
A / 9.5	0.8	1.5	9.99	56	3	38	2	26	31	452	1.6	60	5	250	50	0.0	0.0
A / 9.5	0.8	1.5	9.99	3,082	3	38	2	26	31	452	1.6	57	5	250	50	2.5	0.0
A / 9.4	0.9	1.5	9.93	4	3	38	2	26	31	452	1.6	32	5	250	50	0.0	0.0
A / 9.4	0.9	1.5	9.89	104	3	38	2	26	31	452	1.6	28	5	250	50	0.0	0.0
A / 9.5	0.8	1.5	9.99	141	3	38	2	26	31	452	1.6	51	5	250	50	0.0	0.0
A / 9.5	0.8	1.5	9.99	342	3	38	2	26	31	452	1.6	62	5	250	50	0.0	0.0
A / 9.4	0.9	1.5	9.88	5	3	38	2	26	31	452	1.6	28	5	250	50	0.0	0.0
A / 9.4	0.9	1.5	9.88	47	3	38	2	26	31	452	1.6	27	5	250	50	0.0	0.0
A / 9.4	0.8	1.5	9.99	N/A	3	38	2	26	31	452	1.6	49	5	250	50	0.0	0.0
A / 9.5	0.8	1.5	9.98	57	3	38	2	26	31	452	1.6	42	5	250	50	0.0	0.0
A / 9.5	0.8	1.5	9.99	26	3	38	2	26	31	452	1.6	52	5	250	50	0.0	0.0
A / 9.5	0.8	1.5	10.00	8	3	38	2	26	31	452	1.6	70	5	250	50	0.0	0.0
A / 9.5	0.8	1.5	10.00	N/A	3	38	2	26	31	452	1.6	61	5	250	50	0.0	0.0
A / 9.5	0.8	1.5	9.99	895	3	38	2	26	31	452	1.6	71	5	250	50	0.0	0.0
A / 9.4	0.9	1.9	10.17	673	1	0	98	0	1	38	3.5	54	7	250	50	2.5	0.0
A / 9.4	0.9	1.9	10.17	13	1	0	98	0	1	38	3.5	45	7	250	50	0.0	0.0
A / 9.4	0.9	1.9	10.17	72	1	0	98	0	1	38	3.5	54	7	250	50	0.0	0.0
C / 4.9	3.5	5.5	13.19	8,142	0	0	99	0	1	14	4.8	56	37	250	50	3.8	0.0
C / 4.9	3.5	5.5	13.19	5	0	0	99	0	1	14	4.8	31	37	250	50	0.0	0.0
C / 4.9	3.5	5.5	13.19	396	0	0	99	0	1	14	4.8	30	37	250	50	0.0	0.0
C / 4.9	3.5	5.5	13.19	1,678	0	0	99	0	1	14	4.8	51	37	250	50	0.0	0.0
C / 4.9	3.5	5.5	13.19	1,243	0	0	99	0	1	14	4.8	61	37	250	50	0.0	0.0
C / 4.5	3.7	5.4	17.97	1,535	2	0	97	0	1	17	4.8	74	30	1,000	50	3.8	0.0
C / 4.4	3.7	5.4	17.97	1	2	0	97	0	1	17	4.8	41	30	1,000	50	0.0	0.0
C / 4.4	3.7	5.4	17.97	85	2	0	97	0	1	17	4.8	40	30	1,000	50	0.0	0.0
C / 4.5	3.7	5.4	17.97	73	2	0	97	0	1	17	4.8	68	30	1,000	50	0.0	0.0
C / 4.5	3.7	5.4	17.97	173	2	0	97	0	1	17	4.8	77	30	1,000	50	0.0	0.0
C+ / 6.8	2.9	4.8	15.97	243	0	0	100	0	0	27	4.8	34	N/A	1,000	50	3.8	0.0
C+ / 6.8	2.9	4.8	15.97	N/A	0	0	100	0	0	27	4.8	17	N/A	1,000	50	0.0	0.0
C+ / 6.8	2.9	4.8	15.97	29	0	0	100	0	0	27	4.8	16	N/A	1,000	50	0.0	0.0

Fund Type	Fund Name (99 Pct = Best, 0 Pct = Worst)	Ticker Symbol	Overall Investment Rating	Phone	PERFORMANCE: Performance Rating/Pts	Total Return % through 3/31/16: 3 Mo	6 Mo	1Yr / Pct	Annualized: 3Yr / Pct	Annualized: 5Yr / Pct	Incl. in Returns: Dividend Yield	Expense Ratio
MUS	American Funds Tax-Exempt of MD	TMDFX	A	(800) 421-0180	B / 8.1	1.30	2.27	2.71 /82	2.10 /78	4.38 /80	2.97	0.80
MUS	American Funds Tax-Exempt of MD	TMMFX	A+	(800) 421-0180	B+ / 8.4	1.37	2.40	2.96 /85	2.36 /81	4.66 /83	3.22	0.56
MUS	American Funds Tax-Exempt of VA A	TFVAX	B-	(800) 421-0180	B- / 7.2	1.36	2.41	2.85 /83	2.41 /82	4.47 /81	2.80	0.66
MUS ●	American Funds Tax-Exempt of VA B	TEVBX	B	(800) 421-0180	B / 7.6	1.19	2.05	2.12 /78	1.67 /72	3.70 /75	2.20	1.39
MUS	American Funds Tax-Exempt of VA C	TEVCX	B	(800) 421-0180	B- / 7.5	1.16	2.01	2.04 /77	1.61 /70	3.65 /75	2.13	1.45
MUS	American Funds Tax-Exempt of VA	TEVFX	A-	(800) 421-0180	B+ / 8.3	1.33	2.35	2.73 /82	2.29 /80	4.34 /80	2.79	0.77
MUS	American Funds Tax-Exempt of VA	TEFFX	A	(800) 421-0180	B+ / 8.6	1.39	2.47	2.98 /85	2.54 /83	4.61 /82	3.03	0.53
MUN	American Funds TxEx Preservation A	TEPAX	A-	(800) 421-0180	C+ / 6.7	1.10	1.88	2.17 /78	1.98 /77	--	2.27	0.76
MUN	American Funds TxEx Preservation B	TEPBX	B+	(800) 421-0180	C+ / 6.4	0.79	1.37	1.35 /72	1.26 /60	--	1.54	1.47
MUN	American Funds TxEx Preservation	TEPFX	A+	(800) 421-0180	B / 7.9	1.11	1.79	2.20 /78	2.00 /77	--	2.37	0.73
MUN	American Funds TxEx Preservation	TXEFX	A+	(800) 421-0180	B / 8.2	1.14	2.00	2.43 /80	2.29 /80	--	2.59	0.48
USS	American Funds U.S. Govt Sec 529A	CGTAX	C	(800) 421-0180	C / 4.9	2.55	1.93	2.53 /75	1.89 /59	3.00 /45	1.12	0.72
USS ●	American Funds U.S. Govt Sec 529B	CGTBX	C	(800) 421-0180	C / 5.2	2.40	1.51	1.79 /70	1.12 /45	2.20 /34	0.45	1.48
USS	American Funds U.S. Govt Sec 529C	CGTCX	C+	(800) 421-0180	C / 5.1	2.33	1.52	1.73 /69	1.10 /44	2.21 /34	0.46	1.47
USS	American Funds U.S. Govt Sec 529E	CGTEX	B-	(800) 421-0180	C+ / 6.1	2.49	1.82	2.30 /74	1.66 /55	2.75 /41	0.94	0.95
USS	American Funds U.S. Govt Sec	CGTFX	B+	(800) 421-0180	C+ / 6.9	2.61	1.97	2.76 /76	2.12 /64	3.23 /49	1.38	0.49
* USS	American Funds US Govt Sec A	AMUSX	C+	(800) 421-0180	C / 5.0	2.57	1.90	2.61 /75	1.98 /61	3.08 /46	1.20	0.65
USS ●	American Funds US Govt Sec B	UGSBX	C+	(800) 421-0180	C / 5.4	2.41	1.55	1.89 /71	1.22 /46	2.33 /35	0.55	1.37
USS	American Funds US Govt Sec C	UGSCX	C+	(800) 421-0180	C / 5.2	2.33	1.54	1.78 /70	1.16 /45	2.27 /35	0.51	1.42
USS	American Funds US Govt Sec F1	UGSFX	B+	(800) 421-0180	C+ / 6.7	2.57	1.90	2.62 /75	1.99 /61	3.09 /47	1.25	0.62
USS	American Funds US Govt Sec F2	GVTFX	B+	(800) 421-0180	B- / 7.1	2.64	2.03	2.87 /76	2.24 /66	3.34 /50	1.49	0.38
USS	American Funds US Govt Sec R1	RGVAX	C+	(800) 421-0180	C / 5.3	2.41	1.54	1.86 /70	1.20 /46	2.30 /35	0.52	1.39
USS	American Funds US Govt Sec R2	RGVBX	C+	(800) 421-0180	C / 5.3	2.33	1.47	1.80 /70	1.18 /46	2.29 /35	0.53	1.42
USL	American Funds US Govt Sec R2E	RGEVX	B-	(800) 421-0180	C+ / 6.3	2.50	1.81	2.53 /75	1.69 /56	2.66 /40	1.23	1.11
USS	American Funds US Govt Sec R3	RGVCX	B-	(800) 421-0180	C+ / 6.2	2.49	1.81	2.29 /74	1.66 /55	2.75 /41	0.93	0.95
USS	American Funds US Govt Sec R4	RGVEX	B+	(800) 421-0180	C+ / 6.7	2.57	1.91	2.63 /75	1.99 /61	3.09 /47	1.26	0.61
USS	American Funds US Govt Sec R5	RGVFX	B+	(800) 421-0180	B- / 7.2	2.65	2.06	2.93 /76	2.30 /67	3.40 /51	1.55	0.32
USL	American Funds US Govt Sec R5E	RGVJX	B+	(800) 421-0180	C+ / 6.7	2.68	1.97	2.68 /75	2.00 /61	3.10 /47	1.30	0.43
USS	American Funds US Govt Sec R6	RGVGX	A-	(800) 421-0180	B- / 7.3	2.66	2.16	2.98 /77	2.35 /68	3.45 /52	1.60	0.27
USS	AMF Short-US Government	ASITX	C+	(800) 527-3713	C- / 3.8	0.71	0.44	0.57 /51	0.70 /37	1.11 /21	1.57	0.86
MTG	AMF Ultra Short Mortgage Fund	ASARX	C+	(800) 527-3713	C- / 3.9	0.07	-0.51	-0.42 /27	1.06 /44	1.16 /22	1.38	1.16
COI	AMG GW&K Core Bond Inst	MBDLX	U	(800) 835-3879	U /	3.24	2.86	--	--	--	0.00	0.59
COI	AMG GW&K Core Bond Inv	MBGVX	U	(800) 835-3879	U /	3.14	2.65	--	--	--	0.00	0.99
GEI	AMG GW&K Core Bond Svc	MBDFX	C	(800) 835-3879	C+ / 6.4	3.32	2.83	1.20 /62	1.83 /58	3.52 /53	1.87	0.67
GEI	AMG GW&K Enhanced Core Bd C	MFDCX	D+	(800) 835-3879	C- / 3.7	2.90	1.32	-2.59 /13	0.79 /39	2.73 /41	1.97	1.85
GEI	AMG GW&K Enhanced Core Bd Inst	MFDYX	C-	(800) 835-3879	C / 5.5	3.04	1.72	-1.69 /17	1.76 /57	3.76 /58	2.98	0.85
GEI	AMG GW&K Enhanced Core Bd Inv	MFDAX	C-	(800) 835-3879	C / 5.0	2.98	1.60	-1.94 /16	1.51 /52	3.48 /53	2.73	1.10
COI	AMG GW&K Enhanced Core Bd Svc	MFDSX	C-	(800) 835-3879	C / 5.4	3.12	1.79	-1.74 /17	1.69 /56	3.72 /57	2.92	0.91
MUN	AMG GW&K Municipal Bond Inst	GWMIX	B+	(800) 835-3879	A / 9.4	1.64	3.31	4.32 /96	3.57 /93	5.69 /90	1.65	0.66
MUN	AMG GW&K Municipal Bond Inv	GWMTX	B+	(800) 835-3879	A- / 9.2	1.61	3.15	3.91 /93	3.09 /89	5.18 /87	1.17	1.12
MUN	AMG GW&K Municipal Bond Svc	GWMSX	B+	(800) 835-3879	A / 9.3	1.60	3.23	4.15 /95	3.39 /92	5.49 /89	1.48	0.84
MUH	AMG GW&K Municipal Enhcd Yld Inst	GWMEX	C	(800) 835-3879	A+ / 9.9	2.78	5.97	5.36 /98	4.82 /98	8.80 /99	3.32	0.83
MUH	AMG GW&K Municipal Enhcd Yld Inv	GWMNX	C	(800) 835-3879	A+ / 9.8	2.66	5.71	4.86 /98	4.36 /97	8.33 /99	2.86	1.19
MUH	AMG GW&K Municipal Enhcd Yld	GWMRX	C	(800) 835-3879	A+ / 9.9	2.76	5.94	5.28 /98	4.77 /98	8.66 /99	3.25	0.91
COI	AMG Mgrs Bond Inst	MGBIX	C	(800) 835-3879	C+ / 6.5	2.95	2.53	0.25 /45	2.08 /63	4.62 /69	2.78	0.93
* GEL	AMG Mgrs Bond Svc	MGFIX	C-	(800) 835-3879	C+ / 6.3	2.89	2.47	0.11 /41	1.98 /61	4.56 /68	2.68	1.03
GL	AMG Mgrs Global Income Oppty	MGGBX	D	(800) 835-3879	C- / 3.1	5.56	3.90	0.83 /56	-0.26 /13	2.21 /34	1.44	1.26
COH	AMG Mgrs High Yield Inst	MHHYX	D-	(800) 835-3879	C- / 3.0	2.66	0.19	-4.09 / 7	1.31 /48	4.52 /68	6.19	1.43
COH	AMG Mgrs High Yield Inv	MHHAX	E+	(800) 835-3879	D / 1.8	2.46	0.03	-4.43 / 6	1.02 /43	4.24 /65	5.94	1.68
USS	AMG Mgrs Intmd Duration Govt	MGIDX	A-	(800) 835-3879	B- / 7.3	1.62	1.27	1.69 /69	2.71 /73	3.27 /49	1.01	1.00
USS	AMG Mgrs Short Duration Govt	MGSDX	C	(800) 835-3879	D+ / 2.8	0.20	0.12	-0.08 /30	0.27 /30	0.58 /18	0.23	0.81
COI	Amundi Smith Breeden Tot Rtn B Inst	ATRBX	U		U /	2.73	2.41	--	--	--	0.00	2.34

● Denotes fund is closed to new investors
* Denotes fund is included in Section II

RISK			NET ASSETS		ASSET							FUND MANAGER		MINIMUM		LOADS	
Risk Rating/Pts	3 Yr Avg Standard Deviation	Avg Duration	NAV As of 3/31/16	Total $(Mil)	Cash %	Gov. Bond %	Muni. Bond %	Corp. Bond %	Other %	Portfolio Turnover Ratio	Avg Coupon Rate	Manager Quality Pct	Manager Tenure (Years)	Initial Purch. $	Additional Purch. $	Front End Load	Back End Load
C+ / 6.8	2.9	4.8	15.97	17	0	0	100	0	0	27	4.8	30	N/A	1,000	50	0.0	0.0
C+ / 6.8	2.9	4.8	15.97	29	0	0	100	0	0	27	4.8	37	N/A	1,000	50	0.0	0.0
C+ / 5.9	3.2	5.1	16.95	378	0	0	99	0	1	14	4.6	31	N/A	1,000	50	3.8	0.0
C+ / 5.9	3.2	5.1	16.95	N/A	0	0	99	0	1	14	4.6	16	N/A	1,000	50	0.0	0.0
C+ / 5.9	3.2	5.1	16.95	35	0	0	99	0	1	14	4.6	15	N/A	1,000	50	0.0	0.0
C+ / 5.9	3.2	5.1	16.95	22	0	0	99	0	1	14	4.6	28	N/A	1,000	50	0.0	0.0
C+ / 5.9	3.2	5.1	16.95	56	0	0	99	0	1	14	4.6	35	N/A	1,000	50	0.0	0.0
B / 8.0	2.4	4.3	9.96	259	0	0	99	0	1	8	4.7	44	4	250	50	2.5	0.0
B / 8.1	2.4	4.3	9.97	N/A	0	0	99	0	1	8	4.7	24	4	250	50	0.0	0.0
B / 8.1	2.3	4.3	9.96	8	0	0	99	0	1	8	4.7	47	4	250	50	0.0	0.0
B / 8.0	2.4	4.3	9.96	31	0	0	99	0	1	8	4.7	55	4	250	50	0.0	0.0
B- / 7.1	2.9	5.0	14.18	139	0	56	0	2	42	771	2.3	60	6	250	50	3.8	0.0
C+ / 6.8	2.9	5.0	14.14	1	0	56	0	2	42	771	2.3	33	6	250	50	0.0	0.0
B- / 7.0	2.9	5.0	14.14	56	0	56	0	2	42	771	2.3	33	6	250	50	0.0	0.0
C+ / 6.9	2.9	5.0	14.18	10	0	56	0	2	42	771	2.3	50	6	250	50	0.0	0.0
B- / 7.0	2.9	5.0	14.18	12	0	56	0	2	42	771	2.3	74	6	250	50	0.0	0.0
B- / 7.0	2.9	5.0	14.18	2,929	0	56	0	2	42	771	2.3	66	6	250	50	3.8	0.0
C+ / 6.8	2.9	5.0	14.16	17	0	56	0	2	42	771	2.3	36	6	250	50	0.0	0.0
C+ / 6.9	2.9	5.0	14.15	297	0	56	0	2	42	771	2.3	34	6	250	50	0.0	0.0
B- / 7.0	2.9	5.0	14.18	241	0	56	0	2	42	771	2.3	67	6	250	50	0.0	0.0
B- / 7.0	2.9	5.0	14.18	219	0	56	0	2	42	771	2.3	77	6	250	50	0.0	0.0
C+ / 6.8	2.9	5.0	14.16	11	0	56	0	2	42	771	2.3	35	6	250	50	0.0	0.0
C+ / 6.9	2.9	5.0	14.15	141	0	56	0	2	42	771	2.3	35	6	250	50	0.0	0.0
C+ / 6.9	2.9	5.0	14.18	1	0	56	0	2	42	771	2.3	75	6	250	50	0.0	0.0
C+ / 6.9	2.9	5.0	14.18	151	0	56	0	2	42	771	2.3	51	6	250	50	0.0	0.0
B- / 7.0	2.9	5.0	14.18	155	0	56	0	2	42	771	2.3	67	6	250	50	0.0	0.0
B- / 7.0	2.9	5.0	14.18	157	0	56	0	2	42	771	2.3	78	6	250	50	0.0	0.0
B- / 7.0	2.9	5.0	14.18	N/A	0	56	0	2	42	771	2.3	83	6	250	50	0.0	0.0
B- / 7.0	2.9	5.0	14.18	3,199	0	56	0	2	42	771	2.3	80	6	250	50	0.0	0.0
A- / 9.2	1.1	1.6	9.02	9	3	1	0	0	96	28	3.7	N/A	7	10,000	0	0.0	0.0
A- / 9.2	1.1	1.2	7.22	145	2	2	0	0	96	22	3.2	86	7	10,000	0	0.0	0.0
U /	N/A	5.7	10.17	5	4	15	3	42	36	175	4.8	N/A	N/A	1,000,000	1,000	0.0	0.0
U /	N/A	5.7	10.17	N/A	4	15	3	42	36	175	4.8	N/A	N/A	2,000	100	0.0	0.0
C / 4.6	3.6	5.7	10.18	466	4	15	3	42	36	175	4.8	26	N/A	100,000	100	0.0	0.0
C / 4.8	3.6	6.0	9.81	10	3	11	5	52	29	22	5.4	16	4	2,000	100	0.0	0.0
C / 4.9	3.5	6.0	9.85	54	3	11	5	52	29	22	5.4	39	4	1,000,000	1,000	0.0	0.0
C / 5.0	3.5	6.0	9.82	19	3	11	5	52	29	22	5.4	33	4	2,000	100	0.0	0.0
C / 4.9	3.5	6.0	9.86	8	3	11	5	52	29	22	5.4	46	4	100,000	100	0.0	0.0
C- / 4.2	3.9	6.6	11.92	731	0	0	99	0	1	31	5.0	49	7	1,000,000	1,000	0.0	0.0
C- / 4.2	3.8	6.6	11.86	30	0	0	99	0	1	31	5.0	34	7	2,000	100	0.0	0.0
C- / 4.2	3.8	6.6	11.88	152	0	0	99	0	1	31	5.0	43	7	100,000	100	0.0	0.0
E+ / 0.6	6.6	13.9	10.27	222	2	0	97	0	1	83	5.3	14	11	1,000,000	1,000	0.0	0.0
E+ / 0.6	6.7	13.9	10.28	6	2	0	97	0	1	83	5.3	10	11	2,000	100	0.0	0.0
E+ / 0.6	6.6	13.9	10.29	13	2	0	97	0	1	83	5.3	13	11	100,000	100	0.0	0.0
C / 4.5	3.7	4.4	26.76	911	1	34	1	53	11	26	4.3	58	22	1,000,000	1,000	0.0	0.0
C / 4.5	3.7	4.4	26.76	1,542	1	34	1	53	11	26	4.3	52	22	2,000	100	0.0	0.0
D / 2.1	5.6	5.4	19.19	31	3	40	0	53	4	56	5.0	56	14	2,000	100	0.0	1.0
D- / 1.4	5.7	4.7	7.21	3	2	0	0	93	5	40	6.6	49	15	1,000,000	1,000	0.0	2.0
D- / 1.4	5.7	4.7	7.13	26	2	0	0	93	5	40	6.6	39	15	2,000	100	0.0	2.0
B- / 7.1	2.3	395.0	10.95	204	0	0	0	0	100	11	4.6	92	24	2,000	100	0.0	0.0
A / 9.3	0.5	25.0	9.63	356	0	16	0	0	84	41	3.4	76	24	2,000	100	0.0	0.0
U /	N/A	N/A	10.16	30	0	0	0	0	100	0	0.0	N/A	1	500,000	0	0.0	2.0

Fund Type	Fund Name (99 Pct = Best, 0 Pct = Worst)	Ticker Symbol	Overall Investment Rating	Phone	PERFORMANCE: Performance Rating/Pts	Total Return % through 3/31/16: 3 Mo	6 Mo	1Yr / Pct	Annualized: 3Yr / Pct	Annualized: 5Yr / Pct	Incl. in Returns: Dividend Yield	Expense Ratio
COI	Amundi Smith Breeden Tot Rtn B Svc	ATRSX	U		U /	2.73	2.46	--	--	--	0.00	2.54
COI	Anfield Universal Fixed Income A	AFLEX	U	(866) 851-2525	U /	0.72	0.84	1.32 /64	--	--	2.78	2.10
COI	Anfield Universal Fixed Income C	AFLKX	U	(866) 851-2525	U /	0.56	0.48	0.55 /50	--	--	2.17	2.85
COI	Anfield Universal Fixed Income I	AFLIX	U	(866) 851-2525	U /	0.87	1.05	1.67 /68	--	--	3.19	1.85
GEN	Angel Oak Flexible Income A	ANFLX	U	(877) 625-3042	U /	-7.10	-7.39	-6.63 / 2	--	--	5.39	1.62
GEL	Angel Oak Flexible Income C	AFLCX	U	(877) 625-3042	U /	-7.23	-7.73	--	--	--	0.00	2.37
GEN	Angel Oak Flexible Income Inst	ANFIX	U	(877) 625-3042	U /	-7.11	-7.43	-6.48 / 3	--	--	5.81	1.37
GL	Angel Oak Multi Strategy Income C	ANGCX	U	(877) 625-3042	U /	-2.76	-3.29	--	--	--	0.00	N/A
GL	Angel Oak Multi Strategy Income I	ANGIX	D+	(877) 625-3042	C / 4.4	-2.54	-2.79	-2.38 /14	2.13 /64	--	7.44	1.20
GEI	API Efficient Frontier Income Fd A	APIUX	E-	(800) 544-6060	E / 0.3	2.72	4.09	-5.80 / 3	-1.63 / 5	2.31 /35	7.91	2.59
GEI	API Efficient Frontier Income L	AFFIX	E-	(800) 544-6060	E / 0.4	2.55	3.74	-6.29 / 3	-2.12 / 4	1.86 /29	8.34	3.09
COI ●	AQR Multi-Strategy Alternative I	ASAIX	B-	(866) 290-2688	A / 9.5	-0.92	1.19	5.96 /93	6.69 /97	--	7.58	3.68
COI ●	AQR Multi-Strategy Alternative N	ASANX	C+	(866) 290-2688	A / 9.4	-1.03	1.05	5.62 /91	6.42 /97	--	7.34	3.97
MUS	Aquila Churchill Tax-Free of KY A	CHTFX	A	(800) 437-1020	B / 7.6	1.29	2.04	2.75 /83	2.83 /86	4.43 /81	2.85	0.78
MUS	Aquila Churchill Tax-Free of KY C	CHKCX	A+	(800) 437-1020	B / 7.8	0.98	1.61	1.88 /76	1.96 /76	3.55 /74	2.13	1.63
MUS	Aquila Churchill Tax-Free of KY I	CHKIX	A+	(800) 437-1020	B+ / 8.5	1.16	1.97	2.60 /81	2.65 /84	4.27 /80	2.84	0.92
MUS	Aquila Churchill Tax-Free of KY Y	CHKYX	A+	(800) 437-1020	B+ / 8.9	1.23	2.12	2.91 /84	2.96 /88	4.59 /82	3.13	0.63
* MUN	Aquila Hawaiian Tax Free Trust A	HULAX	B+	(800) 437-1020	C+ / 6.4	1.48	2.29	2.92 /84	2.12 /78	3.42 /73	2.08	0.81
MUN	Aquila Hawaiian Tax Free Trust C	HULCX	A-	(800) 437-1020	C+ / 6.9	1.19	1.89	2.12 /78	1.31 /62	2.60 /61	1.39	1.61
MUN	Aquila Hawaiian Tax Free Trust Y	HULYX	A+	(800) 437-1020	B+ / 8.4	1.53	2.39	3.13 /86	2.33 /81	3.62 /75	2.37	0.61
MUI	Aquila Narragansett TxFr Income A	NITFX	B	(800) 437-1020	B+ / 8.5	1.77	3.14	3.84 /93	3.51 /93	4.28 /80	2.61	0.88
MUI	Aquila Narragansett TxFr Income C	NITCX	B+	(800) 437-1020	B+ / 8.7	1.56	2.71	2.97 /85	2.63 /84	3.41 /73	1.89	1.73
MUI	Aquila Narragansett TxFr Income I	NITIX	A-	(800) 437-1020	A / 9.3	1.83	3.16	3.79 /92	3.39 /92	4.15 /79	2.58	1.02
MUI	Aquila Narragansett TxFr Income Y	NITYX	A	(800) 437-1020	A / 9.5	1.81	3.22	4.00 /94	3.66 /94	4.44 /81	2.88	0.73
MUS	Aquila Tax-Free Fd for Utah A	UTAHX	A	(800) 437-1020	B+ / 8.8	1.60	2.72	3.41 /89	3.87 /95	5.60 /90	2.59	0.91
MUS	Aquila Tax-Free Fd for Utah C	UTACX	A+	(800) 437-1020	B+ / 8.9	1.40	2.36	2.55 /81	3.03 /88	4.75 /83	1.96	1.71
MUS	Aquila Tax-Free Fd for Utah Y	UTAYX	A+	(800) 437-1020	A+ / 9.6	1.64	2.81	3.60 /91	4.04 /96	5.80 /91	2.88	0.70
MUS	Aquila Tax-Free Fd of Colorado A	COTFX	B+	(800) 437-1020	B / 8.1	1.52	2.36	3.20 /87	3.13 /89	4.61 /82	2.74	0.75
MUS	Aquila Tax-Free Fd of Colorado C	COTCX	B+	(800) 437-1020	B / 8.1	1.19	1.78	2.18 /78	2.15 /79	3.61 /75	1.96	1.70
MUS	Aquila Tax-Free Fd of Colorado Y	COTYX	A	(800) 437-1020	A- / 9.1	1.53	2.37	3.23 /87	3.18 /90	4.65 /82	2.88	0.70
MUS	Aquila Tax-Free Tr of Arizona A	AZTFX	A-	(800) 437-1020	B+ / 8.4	1.38	2.52	3.20 /87	3.50 /93	5.19 /87	3.08	0.73
MUS	Aquila Tax-Free Tr of Arizona C	AZTCX	A-	(800) 437-1020	B+ / 8.5	1.27	2.09	2.34 /79	2.63 /84	4.30 /80	2.36	1.58
MUS	Aquila Tax-Free Tr of Arizona Y	AZTYX	A+	(800) 437-1020	A / 9.4	1.51	2.59	3.37 /89	3.66 /94	5.34 /88	3.36	0.58
MUS	Aquila Tax-Free Trust of Oregon A	ORTFX	A-	(800) 437-1020	B / 7.7	1.34	2.11	2.91 /84	2.86 /87	4.61 /82	2.57	0.74
MUS	Aquila Tax-Free Trust of Oregon C	ORTCX	A-	(800) 437-1020	B / 7.9	1.13	1.68	2.05 /77	2.00 /77	3.73 /76	1.84	1.59
MUS	Aquila Tax-Free Trust of Oregon Y	ORTYX	A+	(800) 437-1020	A- / 9.0	1.38	2.19	3.07 /86	3.02 /88	4.77 /83	2.83	0.59
COH	Aquila Three Peaks High Inc A	ATPAX	C	(800) 437-1020	C+ / 6.5	1.39	2.68	2.81 /76	3.41 /79	4.45 /67	3.47	1.29
COH	Aquila Three Peaks High Inc C	ATPCX	C+	(800) 437-1020	B- / 7.3	1.32	2.39	2.10 /72	2.62 /72	3.64 /55	2.79	2.09
COH	Aquila Three Peaks High Inc I	ATIPX	C+	(800) 437-1020	B / 7.8	1.50	2.77	2.85 /76	3.36 /79	4.44 /67	3.52	1.33
COH	Aquila Three Peaks High Inc Y	ATPYX	B-	(800) 437-1020	B / 8.1	1.57	2.78	3.13 /77	3.61 /81	4.68 /69	3.80	1.09
COI	AR 529 Gift College Inv Inc		C-	(800) 662-7447	C- / 3.5	2.00	1.55	0.51 /50	0.29 /30	1.89 /30	0.00	0.75
GEL	Arbitrage Credit Opportunities A	AGCAX	U	(800) 295-4485	U /	1.23	0.99	-0.70 /24	--	--	2.62	2.30
GEN	Arbitrage Credit Opportunities C	ARCCX	C+	(800) 295-4485	C- / 4.1	1.15	0.69	-1.34 /19	1.09 /44	--	2.17	3.05
GEN	Arbitrage Credit Opportunities I	ACFIX	B-	(800) 295-4485	C / 4.9	1.36	1.09	-0.43 /27	2.04 /62	--	2.99	2.05
GEN	Arbitrage Credit Opportunities R	ARCFX	C+	(800) 295-4485	C / 4.6	1.30	1.06	-0.63 /25	1.82 /58	--	2.78	2.30
GEN	Archer Income Fund	ARINX	D+	(800) 494-2755	C- / 3.9	2.35	1.42	0.15 /43	0.74 /38	2.89 /43	2.77	1.77
COH	Artisan High Income Advisor	APDFX	U	(800) 344-1770	U /	1.10	0.34	-0.78 /23	--	--	7.04	0.93
COH	Artisan High Income Investor	ARTFX	U	(800) 344-1770	U /	1.18	0.36	-0.85 /23	--	--	6.84	1.09
GL	Ashmore Em Mkts Hard Curr Debt A	ESDAX	D	(866) 876-8294	C+ / 5.9	4.95	6.54	5.85 /93	1.51 /52	--	6.39	3.81
GL	Ashmore Em Mkts Hard Curr Debt C	ESDCX	D+	(866) 876-8294	C+ / 6.5	3.94	6.91	5.72 /92	0.81 /39	--	6.67	4.49
GL	Ashmore Em Mkts Hard Curr Debt	ESDIX	D+	(866) 876-8294	B- / 7.2	4.16	5.94	5.36 /90	1.39 /50	4.59 /68	6.20	3.49
GL	Ashmore Emerg Mkts Corp Dbt A	ECDAX	E-	(866) 876-8294	E / 0.3	2.71	1.70	-0.93 /22	-2.41 / 3	--	9.82	1.55

● Denotes fund is closed to new investors
* Denotes fund is included in Section II

RISK			NET ASSETS		ASSET							FUND MANAGER		MINIMUM		LOADS	
Risk Rating/Pts	3 Yr Avg Standard Deviation	Avg Duration	NAV As of 3/31/16	Total $(Mil)	Cash %	Gov. Bond %	Muni. Bond %	Corp. Bond %	Other %	Portfolio Turnover Ratio	Avg Coupon Rate	Manager Quality Pct	Manager Tenure (Years)	Initial Purch. $	Additional Purch. $	Front End Load	Back End Load
U /	N/A	N/A	10.16	1	0	0	0	0	100	0	0.0	N/A	1	500,000	0	0.0	2.0
U /	N/A	2.1	9.89	11	1	0	1	63	35	26	0.0	N/A	3	2,500	500	5.8	0.0
U /	N/A	2.1	9.90	N/A	1	0	1	63	35	26	0.0	N/A	3	2,500	500	0.0	0.0
U /	N/A	2.1	9.90	76	1	0	1	63	35	26	0.0	N/A	3	100,000	1,000	0.0	0.0
U /	N/A	N/A	9.08	12	0	0	0	22	78	0	0.0	N/A	2	1,000	100	2.3	0.0
U /	N/A	N/A	9.07	1	0	0	0	22	78	0	0.0	N/A	2	1,000	100	0.0	0.0
U /	N/A	N/A	9.07	192	0	0	0	22	78	0	0.0	N/A	2	1,000,000	100	0.0	0.0
U /	N/A	N/A	11.02	20	0	0	0	8	92	54	0.0	N/A	5	1,000	100	0.0	0.0
C / 4.8	3.6	N/A	11.03	3,884	0	0	0	8	92	54	0.0	96	5	1,000,000	100	0.0	0.0
E / 0.3	8.9	8.4	9.51	146	0	0	0	38	62	50	5.3	6	19	1,000	100	5.8	0.0
E / 0.3	8.9	8.4	9.06	347	0	0	0	38	62	50	5.3	5	19	1,000	100	0.0	0.0
D+ / 2.8	5.0	4.7	9.67	2,664	61	0	0	0	39	204	0.0	99	5	5,000,000	0	0.0	0.0
D+ / 2.7	5.0	4.7	9.64	342	61	0	0	0	39	204	0.0	99	5	1,000,000	0	0.0	0.0
B- / 7.5	2.7	4.4	10.88	189	0	0	98	0	2	14	0.0	62	7	1,000	0	4.0	0.0
B- / 7.5	2.7	4.4	10.87	10	0	0	98	0	2	14	0.0	33	7	1,000	0	0.0	0.0
B- / 7.5	2.7	4.4	10.87	9	0	0	98	0	2	14	0.0	56	7	0	0	0.0	0.0
B- / 7.5	2.7	4.4	10.88	47	0	0	98	0	2	14	0.0	72	7	0	0	0.0	0.0
B- / 7.5	2.7	4.5	11.61	672	0	0	99	0	1	14	5.3	38	31	1,000	0	4.0	0.0
B / 7.6	2.7	4.5	11.60	55	0	0	99	0	1	14	5.3	18	31	1,000	0	0.0	0.0
B- / 7.4	2.7	4.5	11.63	46	0	0	99	0	1	14	5.3	44	31	0	0	0.0	0.0
C / 4.7	3.6	5.3	10.92	133	0	0	99	0	1	8	0.0	52	24	1,000	0	4.0	0.0
C / 4.7	3.6	5.3	10.92	14	0	0	99	0	1	8	0.0	25	24	1,000	0	0.0	0.0
C / 4.5	3.7	5.3	10.92	N/A	0	0	99	0	1	8	0.0	46	24	0	0	0.0	0.0
C / 4.7	3.6	5.3	10.92	101	0	0	99	0	1	8	0.0	59	24	0	0	0.0	0.0
C+ / 6.0	3.1	5.9	10.56	221	1	0	98	0	1	16	0.0	84	7	1,000	0	4.0	0.0
C+ / 6.1	3.1	5.9	10.55	75	1	0	98	0	1	16	0.0	54	7	1,000	0	0.0	0.0
C+ / 6.0	3.1	5.9	10.59	111	1	0	98	0	1	16	0.0	87	7	0	0	0.0	0.0
C+ / 5.6	3.2	4.9	10.83	220	1	0	98	0	1	8	0.0	53	29	1,000	0	4.0	0.0
C+ / 5.6	3.2	4.9	10.80	24	1	0	98	0	1	8	0.0	24	29	1,000	0	0.0	0.0
C+ / 5.6	3.2	4.9	10.86	79	1	0	98	0	1	8	0.0	55	29	0	0	0.0	0.0
C+ / 5.7	3.2	5.8	10.95	242	0	0	99	0	1	14	0.0	71	30	1,000	0	4.0	0.0
C+ / 5.7	3.2	5.8	10.95	18	0	0	99	0	1	14	0.0	36	30	1,000	0	0.0	0.0
C+ / 5.7	3.2	5.8	10.97	41	0	0	99	0	1	14	0.0	77	30	0	0	0.0	0.0
C+ / 6.5	3.0	5.0	11.33	419	1	0	98	0	1	5	0.0	52	30	1,000	0	4.0	0.0
C+ / 6.5	3.0	5.0	11.32	36	1	0	98	0	1	5	0.0	26	30	1,000	0	0.0	0.0
C+ / 6.4	3.0	5.0	11.32	180	1	0	98	0	1	5	0.0	56	30	0	0	0.0	0.0
C / 4.8	3.1	4.2	8.41	72	6	0	0	93	1	115	0.0	98	10	1,000	0	4.0	1.0
C / 4.8	3.1	4.2	8.42	18	6	0	0	93	1	115	0.0	95	10	1,000	0	0.0	0.0
C / 4.5	3.2	4.2	8.42	2	6	0	0	93	1	115	0.0	97	10	0	0	0.0	1.0
C / 4.5	3.2	4.2	8.42	155	6	0	0	93	1	115	0.0	98	10	0	0	0.0	1.0
B- / 7.1	2.8	N/A	13.75	46	25	48	0	12	15	0	0.0	19	11	25	10	0.0	0.0
U /	N/A	N/A	9.59	N/A	26	0	0	54	20	191	0.0	N/A	6	2,000	0	3.3	2.0
B+ / 8.7	1.8	N/A	9.55	1	26	0	0	54	20	191	0.0	86	6	2,000	0	0.0	0.0
B+ / 8.7	1.8	N/A	9.59	43	26	0	0	54	20	191	0.0	94	6	100,000	0	0.0	2.0
B+ / 8.7	1.8	N/A	9.61	13	26	0	0	54	20	191	0.0	93	6	2,000	0	0.0	2.0
C / 4.8	3.6	N/A	19.25	11	11	1	22	57	9	17	0.0	15	5	2,500	100	0.0	0.5
U /	N/A	N/A	9.15	709	0	0	0	83	17	91	0.0	N/A	2	250,000	0	0.0	2.0
U /	N/A	N/A	9.16	445	0	0	0	83	17	91	0.0	N/A	2	1,000	0	0.0	2.0
E / 0.4	8.2	5.2	8.13	N/A	9	63	0	24	4	35	0.0	94	6	1,000	50	4.0	0.0
E / 0.4	8.2	5.2	8.08	N/A	9	63	0	24	4	35	0.0	88	6	1,000	50	0.0	0.0
E / 0.5	8.1	5.2	8.07	6	9	63	0	24	4	35	0.0	93	6	1,000,000	5,000	0.0	0.0
E / 0.3	9.3	3.4	7.21	8	4	4	0	82	10	90	0.0	9	6	1,000	50	4.0	0.0

					PERFORMANCE							
99 Pct = Best 0 Pct = Worst						Total Return % through 3/31/16					Incl. in Returns	
									Annualized			
Fund Type	Fund Name	Ticker Symbol	Overall Investment Rating	Phone	Performance Rating/Pts	3 Mo	6 Mo	1Yr / Pct	3Yr / Pct	5Yr / Pct	Dividend Yield	Expense Ratio
GL	Ashmore Emerg Mkts Corp Dbt C	ECDCX	**E-**	(866) 876-8294	**E / 0.3**	2.52	1.46	-1.65 /17	-3.12 / 2	--	9.43	2.30
GL	Ashmore Emerg Mkts Corp Dbt Inst	EMCIX	**E-**	(866) 876-8294	**E+ / 0.6**	2.75	1.81	-0.63 /25	-2.14 / 4	1.72 /28	10.36	1.30
GL	Ashmore Emerg Mkts Loc Cur Bd A	ELBAX	**E-**	(866) 876-8294	**E- / 0.0**	11.29	10.53	-3.60 / 9	-8.19 / 1	--	3.81	1.51
GL	Ashmore Emerg Mkts Loc Cur Bd C	ELBCX	**E-**	(866) 876-8294	**E- / 0.1**	11.11	10.13	-4.33 / 7	-8.91 / 0	--	3.22	2.26
GL	Ashmore Emerg Mkts Loc Cur Bd Inst	ELBIX	**E-**	(866) 876-8294	**E- / 0.1**	11.32	10.52	-3.37 /10	-7.93 / 1	-2.73 / 1	4.21	1.26
EM	Ashmore Emerg Mkts Sht Dur Inst	ESFIX	**U**	(866) 876-8294	**U /**	4.73	6.95	8.80 /99	--	--	8.51	1.41
GL	Ashmore Emerg Mkts Total Rtn A	EMKAX	**E-**	(866) 876-8294	**E / 0.3**	7.44	7.08	1.26 /63	-3.36 / 2	--	7.10	1.37
GL	Ashmore Emerg Mkts Total Rtn C	EMKCX	**E-**	(866) 876-8294	**E / 0.4**	7.26	6.70	0.52 /50	-4.08 / 2	--	6.66	2.12
GL	Ashmore Emerg Mkts Total Rtn Inst	EMKIX	**E**	(866) 876-8294	**E+ / 0.8**	7.42	7.17	1.47 /66	-3.09 / 2	0.59 /18	7.65	1.12
MUN	Aspiriant Risk Managed Municipal Bd	RMMBX	**U**	(877) 997-9971	**U /**	1.43	2.87	--	--	--	0.00	0.61
GEN	ASTON/DoubleLine Core Plus Fixed I	ADLIX	**C+**	(800) 992-8151	**B- / 7.0**	2.45	1.73	0.92 /57	2.51 /71	--	3.55	0.85
GEN	ASTON/DoubleLine Core Plus Fixed	ADBLX	**C+**	(800) 992-8151	**C+ / 6.7**	2.49	1.61	0.68 /53	2.29 /67	--	3.30	1.10
GEI	ASTON/TCH Fixed Income I	CTBIX	**D+**	(800) 992-8151	**C / 4.8**	3.05	1.77	-1.77 /17	1.33 /49	3.94 /60	3.46	0.93
GEI	ASTON/TCH Fixed Income N	CHTBX	**D+**	(800) 992-8151	**C / 4.3**	2.89	1.55	-2.11 /15	1.10 /44	3.70 /56	3.21	1.18
GEI	Ave Maria Bond	AVEFX	**A+**	(866) 283-6274	**B / 8.0**	2.61	3.54	2.51 /75	3.08 /77	3.70 /56	1.32	0.55
GEN	Avenue Credit Strategies Inst	ACSBX	**E-**	(877) 525-7445	**E- / 0.0**	-5.37	-15.42	-18.10 / 0	-4.78 / 2	--	7.84	1.79
GEN	Avenue Credit Strategies Inv	ACSAX	**E-**	(877) 525-7445	**E- / 0.0**	-5.44	-15.59	-18.41 / 0	-5.07 / 1	--	7.43	2.03
COI	Babson Active Short Duration Bd A	BXDAX	**U**		**U /**	1.16	0.50	--	--	--	0.00	1.15
COI	Babson Active Short Duration Bd C	BXDCX	**U**		**U /**	0.98	0.14	--	--	--	0.00	1.40
COI	Babson Active Short Duration Bd I	BXDIX	**U**		**U /**	1.23	0.64	--	--	--	0.00	0.90
COI	Babson Active Short Duration Bd Y	BXDYX	**U**		**U /**	1.23	0.64	--	--	--	0.00	0.90
GL	Babson Global Cr Inc Opty A	BXIAX	**U**		**U /**	0.77	-2.06	-3.13 /11	--	--	6.80	1.98
GL	Babson Global Cr Inc Opty C	BXICX	**U**		**U /**	0.58	-2.42	-3.87 / 8	--	--	6.27	4.09
GL	Babson Global Cr Inc Opty I	BXITX	**U**		**U /**	0.83	-1.94	-2.89 /12	--	--	7.33	1.58
GL	Babson Global Cr Inc Opty Y	BXIYX	**U**		**U /**	0.83	-1.94	-2.89 /12	--	--	7.33	1.58
GL	Babson Global Floating Rate A	BXFAX	**U**		**U /**	1.08	-0.83	-1.96 /16	--	--	4.67	1.74
GL	Babson Global Floating Rate C	BXFCX	**U**		**U /**	0.89	-1.21	-2.61 /13	--	--	4.05	3.12
GL	Babson Global Floating Rate I	BXFIX	**U**		**U /**	1.15	-0.67	-1.54 /18	--	--	5.14	1.31
GL	Babson Global Floating Rate Y	BXFYX	**U**		**U /**	1.04	-0.78	-1.65 /17	--	--	5.14	1.25
COI	Babson Total Return Bond A	BXTAX	**U**		**U /**	2.63	1.67	--	--	--	0.00	1.25
COI	Babson Total Return Bond C	BXTCX	**U**		**U /**	2.44	1.29	--	--	--	0.00	2.00
COI	Babson Total Return Bond I	BXTIX	**U**		**U /**	2.69	1.79	--	--	--	0.00	1.00
COI	Babson Total Return Bond Y	BXTYX	**U**		**U /**	2.69	1.79	--	--	--	0.00	1.00
COI	Baird Aggregate Bond Inst	BAGIX	**B+**	(866) 442-2473	**B / 7.7**	3.03	2.37	1.78 /70	2.87 /75	4.69 /69	2.38	0.30
COI	Baird Aggregate Bond Inv	BAGSX	**B**	(866) 442-2473	**B- / 7.4**	2.97	2.17	1.47 /66	2.60 /72	4.44 /67	2.06	0.55
MUN	Baird Core Interm Muni Bd Inst	BMNIX	**U**	(866) 442-2473	**U /**	1.51	2.91	--	--	--	0.00	0.30
MUN	Baird Core Interm Muni Bd Inv	BMNSX	**U**	(866) 442-2473	**U /**	1.45	2.80	--	--	--	0.00	0.55
GEI	Baird Core Plus Bond Inst	BCOIX	**B-**	(866) 442-2473	**B- / 7.4**	3.06	2.21	1.38 /64	2.66 /73	4.49 /67	2.78	0.30
* GEI	Baird Core Plus Bond Inv	BCOSX	**C+**	(866) 442-2473	**B- / 7.1**	3.07	2.18	1.16 /61	2.43 /69	4.23 /64	2.43	0.55
GEI	Baird Interm Bond Inst	BIMIX	**A**	(866) 442-2473	**C+ / 6.7**	2.55	1.71	1.93 /71	2.09 /63	3.67 /56	2.21	0.30
GEI	Baird Interm Bond Inv	BIMSX	**B+**	(866) 442-2473	**C+ / 6.3**	2.48	1.60	1.69 /69	1.84 /58	3.42 /52	1.88	0.55
GEI	Baird Quality Interm Muni Bd Inst	BMBIX	**A-**	(866) 442-2473	**C+ / 6.7**	1.18	1.81	2.72 /75	2.14 /64	3.45 /52	2.41	0.30
GEI	Baird Quality Interm Muni Bd Inv	BMBSX	**B+**	(866) 442-2473	**C+ / 6.4**	1.18	1.73	2.49 /75	1.90 /59	3.19 /48	2.11	0.55
GES	Baird Short-Term Bond Inst	BSBIX	**A-**	(866) 442-2473	**C / 5.4**	1.21	0.96	1.30 /63	1.46 /51	2.09 /32	1.56	0.30
COI	Baird Short-Term Bond Inv	BSBSX	**B+**	(866) 442-2473	**C / 4.9**	1.15	0.84	1.06 /59	1.22 /47	--	1.31	0.55
MUN	Baird Short-Term Municipal Bd Inst	BTMIX	**U**	(866) 442-2473	**U /**	0.89	1.47	--	--	--	0.00	0.30
MUN	Baird Short-Term Municipal Bd Inv	BTMSX	**U**	(866) 442-2473	**U /**	0.74	1.26	--	--	--	0.00	0.55
GEI	Baird Ultra Short Bond Inst	BUBIX	**U**	(866) 442-2473	**U /**	0.35	0.31	0.38 /47	--	--	0.88	0.30
GEI	Baird Ultra Short Bond Investor	BUBSX	**U**	(866) 442-2473	**U /**	0.29	0.19	0.14 /42	--	--	0.64	0.55
MUN	BBH Intermediate Municipal Bond I	BBIIX	**U**	(800) 625-5759	**U /**	1.56	3.51	3.68 /92	--	--	1.73	0.88
MUN	BBH Intermediate Municipal Bond N	BBINX	**U**	(800) 625-5759	**U /**	1.53	3.43	3.53 /90	--	--	1.58	8.78
GL	BBH Limited Duration Class I	BBBIX	**C+**	(800) 625-5759	**C- / 3.8**	0.27	0.44	0.22 /44	0.81 /39	1.33 /23	2.21	0.29

● Denotes fund is closed to new investors
* Denotes fund is included in Section II

RISK			NET ASSETS		ASSET							FUND MANAGER		MINIMUM		LOADS	
Risk Rating/Pts	3 Yr Avg Standard Deviation	Avg Duration	NAV As of 3/31/16	Total $(Mil)	Cash %	Gov. Bond %	Muni. Bond %	Corp. Bond %	Other %	Portfolio Turnover Ratio	Avg Coupon Rate	Manager Quality Pct	Manager Tenure (Years)	Initial Purch. $	Additional Purch. $	Front End Load	Back End Load
E / 0.3	9.4	3.4	7.21	4	4	4	0	82	10	90	0.0	7	6	1,000	50	0.0	0.0
E / 0.3	9.3	3.4	7.51	201	4	4	0	82	10	90	0.0	11	6	1,000,000	5,000	0.0	0.0
E- / 0.0	12.8	N/A	6.86	1	30	66	0	0	4	83	0.0	1	6	1,000	50	4.0	0.0
E- / 0.0	12.8	N/A	6.85	N/A	30	66	0	0	4	83	0.0	0	6	1,000	50	0.0	0.0
E- / 0.0	12.9	N/A	7.10	77	30	66	0	0	4	83	0.0	1	6	1,000,000	5,000	0.0	0.0
U /	N/A	1.9	9.34	27	0	0	0	0	100	38	0.0	N/A	N/A	1,000,000	5,000	0.0	0.0
E / 0.3	9.5	5.1	7.48	3	6	60	0	29	5	101	0.0	7	6	1,000	50	4.0	0.0
E / 0.3	9.5	5.1	7.47	1	6	60	0	29	5	101	0.0	5	6	1,000	50	0.0	0.0
E / 0.3	9.4	5.1	7.59	546	6	60	0	29	5	101	0.0	7	6	1,000,000	5,000	0.0	0.0
U /	N/A	N/A	10.20	701	3	0	96	0	1	0	0.0	N/A	1	0	0	0.0	0.0
C / 5.2	3.4	4.9	10.59	366	4	14	0	41	41	59	4.7	71	5	100,000	50	0.0	0.0
C / 5.2	3.4	4.9	10.60	305	4	14	0	41	41	59	4.7	58	5	2,500	50	0.0	0.0
C / 4.3	3.8	5.2	10.28	12	7	19	0	45	29	29	4.1	23	10	1,000,000	50	0.0	0.0
C / 4.3	3.8	5.2	10.27	33	7	19	0	45	29	29	4.1	19	10	2,500	50	0.0	0.0
B / 8.1	2.3	3.2	11.27	232	6	27	0	47	20	21	3.5	97	13	2,500	0	0.0	0.0
E / 0.5	8.0	N/A	8.17	735	23	0	0	51	26	51	0.0	2	4	1,000,000	0	0.0	2.0
E / 0.5	7.9	N/A	8.16	341	23	0	0	51	26	51	0.0	2	4	5,000	0	0.0	2.0
U /	N/A	N/A	9.92	21	0	0	0	0	100	0	0.0	N/A	1	1,000	250	0.0	0.0
U /	N/A	N/A	9.91	N/A	0	0	0	0	100	0	0.0	N/A	1	1,000	250	0.0	0.0
U /	N/A	N/A	9.91	22	0	0	0	0	100	0	0.0	N/A	1	500,000	250	0.0	0.0
U /	N/A	N/A	9.91	112	0	0	0	0	100	0	0.0	N/A	1	100,000	250	0.0	0.0
U /	N/A	2.2	8.63	11	6	0	0	62	32	85	0.0	N/A	N/A	1,000	250	3.8	1.0
U /	N/A	2.2	8.62	3	6	0	0	62	32	85	0.0	N/A	N/A	1,000	250	0.0	1.0
U /	N/A	2.2	8.63	24	6	0	0	62	32	85	0.0	N/A	N/A	500,000	250	0.0	1.0
U /	N/A	2.2	8.63	48	6	0	0	62	32	85	0.0	N/A	N/A	100,000	250	0.0	1.0
U /	N/A	N/A	9.01	6	8	0	0	54	38	63	0.0	N/A	N/A	1,000	250	3.0	1.0
U /	N/A	N/A	8.98	6	8	0	0	54	38	63	0.0	N/A	N/A	1,000	250	0.0	1.0
U /	N/A	N/A	9.03	22	8	0	0	54	38	63	0.0	N/A	N/A	500,000	250	0.0	1.0
U /	N/A	N/A	9.02	128	8	0	0	54	38	63	0.0	N/A	N/A	100,000	250	0.0	1.0
U /	N/A	N/A	9.96	N/A	0	0	0	0	100	0	0.0	N/A	1	1,000	250	4.0	0.0
U /	N/A	N/A	9.96	N/A	0	0	0	0	100	0	0.0	N/A	1	1,000	250	0.0	0.0
U /	N/A	N/A	9.96	12	0	0	0	0	100	0	0.0	N/A	1	500,000	250	0.0	0.0
U /	N/A	N/A	9.96	12	0	0	0	0	100	0	0.0	N/A	1	100,000	250	0.0	0.0
C+ / 6.1	3.1	5.7	10.87	7,255	2	17	1	41	39	32	0.0	88	16	25,000	0	0.0	0.0
C+ / 6.0	3.1	5.7	11.21	480	2	17	1	41	39	32	0.0	84	16	2,500	100	0.0	0.0
U /	N/A	4.6	10.24	60	7	0	90	0	3	0	0.0	N/A	1	25,000	0	0.0	0.0
U /	N/A	4.6	10.24	N/A	7	0	90	0	3	0	0.0	N/A	1	2,500	100	0.0	0.0
C+ / 5.6	3.2	5.5	11.11	7,947	2	14	1	48	35	35	0.0	68	16	25,000	0	0.0	0.0
C+ / 5.6	3.3	5.5	11.54	2,291	2	14	1	48	35	35	0.0	54	16	2,500	100	0.0	0.0
B / 8.1	2.3	4.0	11.15	1,869	3	31	2	47	17	29	0.0	75	16	25,000	0	0.0	0.0
B / 8.1	2.4	4.0	11.62	105	3	31	2	47	17	29	0.0	60	16	2,500	100	0.0	0.0
B / 7.7	2.6	4.4	11.81	1,041	2	0	97	0	1	5	0.0	75	15	25,000	0	0.0	0.0
B / 7.6	2.6	4.4	12.08	160	2	0	97	0	1	5	0.0	61	15	2,500	100	0.0	0.0
A / 9.4	0.9	1.9	9.68	3,307	3	10	3	65	19	51	0.0	88	12	25,000	0	0.0	0.0
A / 9.4	0.9	1.9	9.68	48	3	10	3	65	19	51	0.0	86	12	2,500	100	0.0	0.0
U /	N/A	2.3	10.10	19	4	0	94	0	2	0	0.0	N/A	1	25,000	0	0.0	0.0
U /	N/A	2.3	10.09	N/A	4	0	94	0	2	0	0.0	N/A	1	2,500	100	0.0	0.0
U /	N/A	0.4	9.99	211	2	14	2	67	15	58	0.0	N/A	3	25,000	0	0.0	0.0
U /	N/A	0.4	9.99	1	2	14	2	67	15	58	0.0	N/A	3	2,500	100	0.0	0.0
U /	N/A	N/A	10.44	68	1	0	98	0	1	83	0.0	N/A	2	5,000,000	25,000	0.0	1.0
U /	N/A	N/A	10.45	25	1	0	98	0	1	83	0.0	N/A	2	5,000	500	0.0	1.0
A+ / 9.6	0.7	4.4	10.06	4,930	0	14	5	35	46	46	0.0	87	5	5,000,000	25,000	0.0	0.0

Fund Type	Fund Name (99 Pct = Best, 0 Pct = Worst)	Ticker Symbol	Overall Investment Rating	Phone	PERFORMANCE: Performance Rating/Pts	Total Return % through 3/31/16: 3 Mo	6 Mo	1Yr / Pct	Annualized: 3Yr / Pct	Annualized: 5Yr / Pct	Incl. in Returns: Dividend Yield	Expense Ratio
GL	BBH Limited Duration Class N	BBBMX	C+	(800) 625-5759	C- / 3.3	0.19	0.21	-0.01 /31	0.57 /34	1.13 /22	1.98	0.48
MM	BBH US Government Money Market	BBSXX	U	(800) 625-5759	U /	0.01	0.01	0.01 /32	0.01 /16	0.01 / 3	0.01	0.26
* GES	Berwyn Income Fund	BERIX	C+	(800) 992-6757	B+ / 8.7	3.08	3.15	-0.83 /23	5.11 /91	5.45 /74	2.26	0.64
MMT	BIF Connecticut Municipal Money	MCOXX	U	(800) 441-7762	U /	--	--	--	--	--	0.01	0.74
MMT	BIF New Jersey Municipal Money	CMJXX	U	(800) 441-7762	U /	--	--	--	--	--	0.01	0.68
MMT	BIF New York Municipal Money	CMYXX	C-	(800) 441-7762	D / 1.9	0.00	0.01	0.01 /33	0.01 /18	0.01 / 7	0.01	0.66
MUS	Bishop Street HI Muni Bond A	BHIAX	A-	(800) 262-9565	B- / 7.3	1.20	2.26	2.88 /84	2.26 /80	3.90 /77	2.24	1.24
MUS	Bishop Street HI Muni Bond Inst	BSHIX	A+	(800) 262-9565	B+ / 8.5	1.26	2.38	3.13 /86	2.51 /83	4.16 /79	2.56	0.99
GEI	Bishop Street High Grade Inc Inst	BSHGX	C+	(800) 262-9565	B- / 7.0	3.19	2.57	1.96 /71	2.19 /65	3.63 /55	2.22	1.20
GEI	BlackRock Alloc Target Srs C	BRACX	C+	(800) 441-7762	B / 8.1	3.87	3.19	0.70 /53	3.45 /80	5.78 /76	3.59	0.14
MUN	BlackRock Alloc Target Srs E	BATEX	U	(800) 441-7762	U /	2.51	6.44	7.14 /99	--	--	4.00	0.94
* GEI	BlackRock Alloc Target Srs M	BRAMX	B+	(800) 441-7762	B / 7.7	2.15	1.94	2.43 /74	2.93 /76	5.63 /75	2.92	0.14
GL	BlackRock Alloc Target Srs P	BATPX	E+	(800) 441-7762	E- / 0.2	-4.48	-3.03	-4.48 / 6	-3.53 / 2	--	0.00	0.16
GEI	BlackRock Alloc Target Srs S	BRASX	B+	(800) 441-7762	C / 5.3	0.74	0.60	1.17 /61	1.54 /53	2.62 /39	3.48	0.16
MTG	BlackRock Bd Alloc Target Srs A	BATAX	U	(800) 441-7762	U /	-0.84	1.74	--	--	--	0.00	0.35
MUS	BlackRock CA Muni Opptys A	MECMX	C	(800) 441-7762	B+ / 8.5	0.73	3.39	4.18 /95	3.60 /93	7.23 /97	2.89	0.95
MUS ●	BlackRock CA Muni Opptys A1	MDCMX	C+	(800) 441-7762	A / 9.5	0.75	3.45	4.30 /96	3.73 /94	7.37 /97	3.14	0.81
MUS	BlackRock CA Muni Opptys C	MFCMX	C+	(800) 441-7762	B+ / 8.8	0.54	3.00	3.40 /89	2.82 /86	6.42 /94	2.27	1.72
MUS	BlackRock CA Muni Opptys Inst	MACMX	C+	(800) 441-7762	A / 9.5	0.78	3.51	4.41 /96	3.80 /95	7.45 /97	3.24	0.73
MUS ●	BlackRock CA Muni Opptys Inv C1	MCCMX	C+	(800) 441-7762	A- / 9.2	0.71	3.28	3.78 /92	3.24 /90	6.85 /96	2.64	1.32
MM	BlackRock Cash:Inst Sel	BGLXX	C	(800) 441-7762	D+ / 2.6	0.09	0.13	0.16 /43	0.09 /27	0.10 /14	0.16	0.25
MM	BlackRock Cash:Prime Cap	BCPXX	C+	(800) 441-7762	D+ / 2.7	0.10	0.15	0.21 /44	0.13 /28	0.14 /15	0.21	N/A
MM	BlackRock Cash:Prime Premium	BPSXX	C	(800) 441-7762	D+ / 2.6	0.10	0.14	0.18 /44	0.10 /27	0.11 /15	0.18	0.20
GEI	BlackRock Core Bond Inst	BFMCX	B	(800) 441-7762	B- / 7.4	2.79	2.19	1.29 /63	2.69 /73	4.17 /64	2.33	0.58
GEI	BlackRock Core Bond Inv A	BCBAX	C	(800) 441-7762	C / 5.2	2.70	2.02	0.95 /58	2.39 /69	3.85 /59	1.91	0.87
GEI	BlackRock Core Bond Inv C	BCBCX	C	(800) 441-7762	C+ / 5.7	2.53	1.65	0.31 /46	1.64 /55	3.09 /47	1.26	1.60
GEI	BlackRock Core Bond K	CCBBX	B	(800) 441-7762	B- / 7.5	2.79	2.21	1.34 /64	2.81 /74	4.26 /65	2.37	0.45
GEI	BlackRock Core Bond R	BCBRX	C+	(800) 441-7762	C+ / 6.5	2.64	1.90	0.70 /53	2.11 /64	3.55 /54	1.75	1.15
GEI	BlackRock Core Bond Svc	CMCBX	B-	(800) 441-7762	B- / 7.0	2.70	2.02	0.96 /58	2.43 /69	3.85 /59	2.00	0.88
GEI	BlackRock CoreAlpha Bond Inst	BCRIX	B-	(800) 441-7762	B- / 7.3	3.01	2.61	1.77 /69	2.47 /70	3.97 /61	2.70	0.36
COI	BlackRock CoreAlpha Bond Inv A	BCRAX	C-	(800) 441-7762	C / 4.9	2.92	2.43	1.33 /64	2.11 /64	--	2.26	0.71
COI	BlackRock CoreAlpha Bond Inv C	BCRCX	C	(800) 441-7762	C / 5.5	2.73	2.05	0.66 /52	1.38 /50	--	1.61	1.46
COI	BlackRock CoRI 2015 Inst	BCVIX	U	(800) 441-7762	U /	6.97	5.88	3.63 /80	--	--	2.72	1.69
COI	BlackRock CoRI 2015 Inv A	BCVAX	U	(800) 441-7762	U /	6.88	5.71	3.37 /78	--	--	2.46	2.06
COI	BlackRock CoRI 2017 Inst	BCWIX	U	(800) 441-7762	U /	7.06	5.86	2.30 /74	--	--	2.82	1.65
COI	BlackRock CoRI 2017 Inv A	BCWAX	U	(800) 441-7762	U /	6.98	5.76	2.02 /72	--	--	2.54	2.03
COI	BlackRock CoRI 2019 Inst	BCXIX	U	(800) 441-7762	U /	7.66	6.48	2.14 /73	--	--	2.88	1.58
COI	BlackRock CoRI 2019 Inv A	BCXAX	U	(800) 441-7762	U /	7.57	6.23	1.82 /70	--	--	2.64	1.92
COI	BlackRock CoRI 2021 Inst	BCYIX	U	(800) 441-7762	U /	8.43	7.36	1.05 /59	--	--	3.03	1.58
COI	BlackRock CoRI 2021 Inv A	BCYAX	U	(800) 441-7762	U /	8.45	7.32	0.81 /55	--	--	2.78	1.88
COI	BlackRock CoRI 2023 Inst	BCZIX	U	(800) 441-7762	U /	8.96	7.55	-0.32 /28	--	--	3.14	1.45
COI	BlackRock CoRI 2023 Inv A	BCZAX	U	(800) 441-7762	U /	8.89	7.42	-0.63 /25	--	--	2.82	1.55
EM	BlackRock Emg Mkts Flex Dyn Bd	BEDIX	E	(800) 441-7762	D- / 1.3	1.47	7.06	2.69 /75	-1.76 / 5	3.83 /59	3.17	1.31
EM	BlackRock Emg Mkts Flex Dyn Bd	BAEDX	E-	(800) 441-7762	E / 0.5	1.28	6.79	2.27 /73	-2.09 / 4	3.51 /53	2.76	1.66
EM	BlackRock Emg Mkts Flex Dyn Bd	BCEDX	E-	(800) 441-7762	E+ / 0.6	1.09	6.51	1.54 /67	-2.81 / 3	2.75 /41	2.16	2.46
EM	BlackRock Emg Mkts Flex Dyn Bd K	BREDX	E	(800) 441-7762	D- / 1.4	1.38	6.99	2.67 /75	-1.70 / 5	3.92 /60	3.26	1.24
LP	BlackRock Floating Rate Inc Inst	BFRIX	A-	(800) 441-7762	C+ / 6.2	1.14	0.05	0.02 /33	2.34 /68	3.58 /54	4.25	0.70
* LP	BlackRock Floating Rate Inc Inv A	BFRAX	C+	(800) 441-7762	C / 4.5	1.16	-0.12	-0.29 /28	2.03 /62	3.27 /49	3.84	0.99
LP	BlackRock Floating Rate Inc Inv C	BFRCX	C+	(800) 441-7762	C / 4.3	0.98	-0.46	-1.01 /22	1.28 /48	2.51 /38	3.20	1.73
LP ●	BlackRock Floating Rate Inc Inv C1	BFRPX	C+	(800) 441-7762	C / 4.8	1.05	-0.33	-0.75 /24	1.55 /53	2.78 /41	3.46	1.46
* GL	BlackRock Glbl Long/Short Crd Iv A	BGCAX	D+	(800) 441-7762	E+ / 0.7	-0.82	-1.46	-3.61 / 9	0.38 /31	--	4.73	1.99
GL	BlackRock Glbl Long/Short Crd Iv C	BGCCX	D+	(800) 441-7762	E+ / 0.8	-1.03	-1.76	-4.30 / 7	-0.36 /13	--	4.47	2.73

● Denotes fund is closed to new investors
* Denotes fund is included in Section II

RISK			NET ASSETS		ASSET							FUND MANAGER		MINIMUM		LOADS	
Risk Rating/Pts	3 Yr Avg Standard Deviation	Avg Duration	NAV As of 3/31/16	Total $(Mil)	Cash %	Gov. Bond %	Muni. Bond %	Corp. Bond %	Other %	Portfolio Turnover Ratio	Avg Coupon Rate	Manager Quality Pct	Manager Tenure (Years)	Initial Purch. $	Additional Purch. $	Front End Load	Back End Load
A+ / 9.7	0.7	4.4	10.06	36	0	14	5	35	46	46	0.0	84	5	25,000	25,000	0.0	0.0
U /	N/A	N/A	1.00	2,097	100	0	0	0	0	0	0.0	N/A	N/A	5,000,000	0	0.0	0.0
C- / 3.1	4.7	3.3	13.19	1,694	14	0	0	54	32	45	0.0	99	11	1,000	250	0.0	1.0
U /	N/A	N/A	1.00	103	100	0	0	0	0	0	0.0	N/A	N/A	5,000	1,000	0.0	0.0
U /	N/A	N/A	1.00	316	100	0	0	0	0	0	0.0	N/A	N/A	5,000	1,000	0.0	0.0
A+ / 9.9	N/A	N/A	1.00	546	100	0	0	0	0	0	0.0	64	N/A	5,000	1,000	0.0	0.0
B- / 7.0	2.9	5.3	10.87	23	1	0	95	0	4	28	0.0	36	9	1,000	0	3.0	0.0
B- / 7.1	2.9	5.3	10.87	128	1	0	95	0	4	28	0.0	44	9	1,000	0	0.0	0.0
C+ / 5.6	3.2	5.7	10.06	71	1	24	9	58	8	28	0.0	44	10	1,000	0	0.0	0.0
C- / 3.9	4.1	N/A	10.37	353	2	9	2	84	3	44	0.0	78	7	0	0	0.0	0.0
U /	N/A	N/A	10.75	110	0	0	99	0	1	30	0.0	N/A	2	0	0	0.0	0.0
C+ / 6.2	3.1	N/A	9.93	553	0	0	0	0	100	2,258	0.0	86	5	0	0	0.0	0.0
D+ / 2.3	5.4	N/A	8.95	223	56	0	0	14	30	6	0.0	6	7	0	0	0.0	0.0
A- / 9.1	1.1	N/A	9.54	240	0	0	0	33	67	318	0.0	87	8	0	0	0.0	0.0
U /	N/A	N/A	9.82	39	0	0	0	0	100	0	0.0	N/A	1	0	0	0.0	0.0
D+ / 2.5	5.2	N/A	12.58	317	3	0	96	0	1	70	0.0	17	23	1,000	50	4.3	0.0
D+ / 2.5	5.2	N/A	12.59	139	3	0	96	0	1	70	0.0	19	23	0	0	0.0	0.0
D+ / 2.5	5.3	N/A	12.59	93	3	0	96	0	1	70	0.0	9	23	1,000	50	0.0	0.0
D+ / 2.5	5.2	N/A	12.59	462	3	0	96	0	1	70	0.0	20	23	2,000,000	0	0.0	0.0
D+ / 2.5	5.3	N/A	12.60	15	3	0	96	0	1	70	0.0	12	23	0	0	0.0	0.0
A+ / 9.9	N/A	N/A	1.00	N/A	100	0	0	0	0	0	0.2	68	N/A	1,000,000	0	0.0	0.0
A+ / 9.9	N/A	N/A	1.00	1,805	100	0	0	0	0	0	0.2	71	N/A	25,000,000	0	0.0	0.0
A+ / 9.9	N/A	N/A	1.00	2,731	100	0	0	0	0	0	0.2	69	N/A	10,000,000	0	0.0	0.0
C+ / 5.9	3.0	7.1	9.73	1,825	0	38	1	23	38	863	3.4	76	6	2,000,000	0	0.0	0.0
C+ / 6.1	2.9	7.1	9.75	495	0	38	1	23	38	863	3.4	61	6	1,000	50	4.0	0.0
C+ / 6.0	2.9	7.1	9.71	109	0	38	1	23	38	863	3.4	35	6	1,000	50	0.0	0.0
C+ / 5.9	3.0	7.1	9.76	690	0	38	1	23	38	863	3.4	79	6	5,000,000	0	0.0	0.0
C+ / 5.8	3.0	7.1	9.75	4	0	38	1	23	38	863	3.4	50	6	100	0	0.0	0.0
C+ / 5.9	3.0	7.1	9.74	48	0	38	1	23	38	863	3.4	62	6	5,000	0	0.0	0.0
C+ / 5.7	3.2	N/A	10.56	266	0	10	0	33	57	686	0.0	56	N/A	2,000,000	0	0.0	0.0
C+ / 5.7	3.2	N/A	10.56	4	0	10	0	33	57	686	0.0	69	N/A	1,000	50	4.0	0.0
C+ / 5.8	3.2	N/A	10.56	N/A	0	10	0	33	57	686	0.0	40	N/A	1,000	50	0.0	0.0
U /	N/A	12.0	11.21	11	1	60	0	38	1	36	0.0	N/A	2	2,000,000	0	0.0	0.0
U /	N/A	12.0	11.18	N/A	1	60	0	38	1	36	0.0	N/A	2	1,000	50	4.0	0.0
U /	N/A	13.1	11.22	11	1	61	0	36	2	27	0.0	N/A	2	2,000,000	0	0.0	0.0
U /	N/A	13.1	11.19	N/A	1	61	0	36	2	27	0.0	N/A	2	1,000	50	4.0	0.0
U /	N/A	15.0	11.38	12	1	63	0	35	1	31	0.0	N/A	N/A	2,000,000	0	0.0	0.0
U /	N/A	15.0	11.37	1	1	63	0	35	1	31	0.0	N/A	N/A	1,000	50	4.0	0.0
U /	N/A	17.0	11.45	11	1	60	0	37	2	37	0.0	N/A	2	2,000,000	0	0.0	0.0
U /	N/A	17.0	11.42	1	1	60	0	37	2	37	0.0	N/A	2	1,000	50	4.0	0.0
U /	N/A	19.0	11.79	12	1	56	0	41	2	43	0.0	N/A	2	2,000,000	0	0.0	0.0
U /	N/A	19.0	11.76	1	1	56	0	41	2	43	0.0	N/A	2	1,000	50	4.0	0.0
E / 0.4	8.6	0.8	8.84	21	12	61	0	24	3	449	0.0	15	8	2,000,000	0	0.0	0.0
E / 0.4	8.6	0.8	8.82	12	12	61	0	24	3	449	0.0	12	8	1,000	50	4.0	0.0
E / 0.4	8.6	0.8	8.83	6	12	61	0	24	3	449	0.0	8	8	1,000	50	0.0	0.0
E / 0.4	8.6	0.8	8.83	13	12	61	0	24	3	449	0.0	16	8	5,000,000	0	0.0	0.0
B+ / 8.3	2.2	0.2	9.91	2,098	3	0	0	12	85	78	5.2	96	7	2,000,000	0	0.0	0.0
B / 8.2	2.2	0.2	9.91	541	3	0	0	12	85	78	5.2	95	7	1,000	50	2.5	0.0
B / 8.2	2.2	0.2	9.91	125	3	0	0	12	85	78	5.2	89	7	1,000	50	0.0	0.0
B / 8.2	2.2	0.2	9.91	49	3	0	0	12	85	78	5.2	92	7	0	0	0.0	0.0
B+ / 8.3	2.2	N/A	9.68	552	6	0	0	48	46	211	0.0	79	5	1,000	50	4.0	0.0
B+ / 8.3	2.2	N/A	9.58	259	6	0	0	48	46	211	0.0	48	5	1,000	50	0.0	0.0

	99 Pct = Best 0 Pct = Worst				PERFORMANCE							
						Total Return % through 3/31/16					Incl. in Returns	
									Annualized			
Fund Type	Fund Name	Ticker Symbol	Overall Investment Rating	Phone	Perfor-mance Rating/Pts	3 Mo	6 Mo	1Yr / Pct	3Yr / Pct	5Yr / Pct	Dividend Yield	Expense Ratio
GL	BlackRock Glbl Long/Short Cred Inst	BGCIX	**C-**	(800) 441-7762	**D / 1.7**	-0.72	-1.24	-3.39 /10	0.63 /35	--	5.15	1.74
MTG	BlackRock GNMA Port Inst	BGNIX	**B**	(800) 441-7762	**C+ / 6.6**	1.61	1.86	2.17 /73	2.09 /63	3.40 /51	2.64	0.70
MTG	BlackRock GNMA Port Inv A	BGPAX	**C-**	(800) 441-7762	**C- / 4.1**	1.53	1.69	1.72 /69	1.73 /56	3.01 /45	2.21	0.95
MTG	BlackRock GNMA Port Inv C	BGPCX	**C**	(800) 441-7762	**C / 4.6**	1.45	1.31	1.06 /59	0.97 /42	2.26 /34	1.56	1.70
MTG	BlackRock GNMA Port K	BBGPX	**B**	(800) 441-7762	**C+ / 6.7**	1.73	1.88	2.19 /73	2.12 /64	3.41 /52	2.67	0.58
MTG	BlackRock GNMA Port Svc	BGPSX	**C+**	(800) 441-7762	**C+ / 6.0**	1.64	1.69	1.82 /70	1.74 /56	3.04 /46	2.30	1.04
COH	BlackRock High Yield Bond Inst	BHYIX	**D**	(800) 441-7762	**C / 5.1**	1.63	-0.39	-4.39 / 7	2.20 /65	5.12 /73	5.59	0.60
*COH	BlackRock High Yield Bond Inv A	BHYAX	**D-**	(800) 441-7762	**D+ / 2.4**	1.56	-0.41	-4.67 / 6	1.88 /59	4.78 /70	5.06	0.94
COH ●	BlackRock High Yield Bond Inv B	BHYBX	**D-**	(800) 441-7762	**D+ / 2.6**	1.30	-1.06	-5.68 / 4	0.95 /42	3.88 /60	4.30	1.81
COH ●	BlackRock High Yield Bond Inv B1	BHYDX	**D-**	(800) 441-7762	**C- / 3.4**	1.43	-0.81	-5.18 / 5	1.35 /49	4.22 /64	4.71	1.76
COH	BlackRock High Yield Bond Inv C	BHYCX	**D-**	(800) 441-7762	**D+ / 2.9**	1.37	-0.91	-5.39 / 4	1.11 /45	3.99 /61	4.46	1.68
COH ●	BlackRock High Yield Bond Inv C1	BHYEX	**D-**	(800) 441-7762	**C- / 3.3**	1.42	-0.82	-5.33 / 4	1.30 /48	4.16 /64	4.66	1.50
COH	BlackRock High Yield Bond K	BRHYX	**D**	(800) 441-7762	**C / 5.3**	1.80	-0.20	-4.29 / 7	2.32 /68	5.19 /73	5.68	0.54
COH	BlackRock High Yield Bond R	BHYRX	**D**	(800) 441-7762	**C- / 3.8**	1.48	-0.69	-4.97 / 5	1.56 /53	4.45 /67	4.94	1.24
COH	BlackRock High Yield Bond Svc	BHYSX	**D**	(800) 441-7762	**C / 4.5**	1.56	-0.54	-4.80 / 5	1.88 /59	4.75 /70	5.27	0.91
MUH	BlackRock High Yld Muni Inst	MAYHX	**C**	(800) 441-7762	**A+ / 9.9**	2.41	5.56	6.44 /99	5.09 /99	8.93 /99	4.24	0.70
MUH	BlackRock High Yld Muni Inv A	MDYHX	**C**	(800) 441-7762	**A+ / 9.6**	2.35	5.43	6.17 /99	4.82 /98	8.66 /99	3.82	0.97
MUH	BlackRock High Yld Muni Inv C	MCYHX	**C**	(800) 441-7762	**A+ / 9.7**	2.16	5.03	5.27 /98	4.03 /96	7.83 /98	3.26	1.72
GES	BlackRock Inflation Prot Bond Inst	BPRIX	**D-**	(800) 441-7762	**D- / 1.2**	3.68	3.05	0.02 /33	-1.28 / 7	2.33 /35	0.17	0.53
GES	BlackRock Inflation Prot Bond Inv A	BPRAX	**E+**	(800) 441-7762	**E / 0.5**	3.56	2.82	-0.37 /27	-1.63 / 5	1.99 /31	0.15	0.88
GES	BlackRock Inflation Prot Bond Inv C	BPRCX	**E+**	(800) 441-7762	**E+ / 0.6**	3.44	2.49	-1.08 /21	-2.32 / 3	1.27 /23	0.13	1.56
GES	BlackRock Inflation Prot Bond K	BPLBX	**D-**	(800) 441-7762	**D- / 1.4**	3.75	3.11	0.11 /41	-1.17 / 7	2.44 /37	0.17	0.43
GES	BlackRock Inflation Prot Bond Svc	BPRSX	**D-**	(800) 441-7762	**D- / 1.0**	3.52	2.79	-0.37 /27	-1.61 / 6	2.00 /31	0.16	0.84
GEI	BlackRock Investment Grade Bd Inst	BLDIX	**D+**	(800) 441-7762	**C+ / 6.4**	3.97	3.08	0.68 /53	1.77 /57	7.03 /82	2.77	0.85
GEI	BlackRock Investment Grade Bd Inv	BLADX	**D**	(800) 441-7762	**C- / 3.8**	3.90	2.93	0.36 /47	1.40 /50	6.63 /80	2.36	1.17
GEI	BlackRock Investment Grade Bd K	BLDRX	**D+**	(800) 441-7762	**C+ / 6.5**	3.98	3.11	0.76 /54	1.85 /58	7.11 /82	2.84	0.75
MMT	BlackRock Liqdty CA Mny Admin	BLCXX	**U**	(800) 441-7762	**U /**	--	--	--	--	--	0.01	0.55
MMT	BlackRock Liqdty CA Mny Inst	MUCXX	**C-**	(800) 441-7762	**D / 1.9**	0.01	0.01	0.01 /33	0.01 /18	0.05 /14	0.01	0.45
MM	BlackRock Liqdty FedFd Admin	BLFXX	**C-**	(800) 441-7762	**D / 1.9**	0.02	0.03	0.03 /36	0.02 /19	0.02 / 7	0.03	0.31
MM	BlackRock Liqdty FedFd Cash Mgmt		**U**	(800) 441-7762	**U /**	--	--	--	--	--	0.01	0.71
MM	BlackRock Liqdty FedFd Cash Rsv	BFRXX	**U**	(800) 441-7762	**U /**	--	--	--	--	--	0.01	0.61
MM	BlackRock Liqdty FedFd Dlr	TDDXX	**U**	(800) 441-7762	**U /**	--	--	--	--	--	0.01	0.46
MM	BlackRock Liqdty FedFd Inst	TFDXX	**C**	(800) 441-7762	**D / 2.2**	0.05	0.06	0.06 /39	0.03 /22	0.02 / 7	0.06	0.21
MM	BlackRock Liqdty FedFd Prem	BUPXX	**U**	(800) 441-7762	**U /**	--	--	--	--	--	0.01	0.81
MM	BlackRock Liqdty FedFd Prvte Client	BRPXX	**U**	(800) 441-7762	**U /**	--	--	--	--	--	0.01	1.06
MM	BlackRock Liqdty FedFd Select	BFBXX	**U**	(800) 441-7762	**U /**	--	--	--	--	--	0.01	1.06
MMT	BlackRock Liqdty MuniCash Port D	MCDXX	**U**		**U /**	0.00	0.01	0.02 /36	0.01 /19	0.01 / 7	0.02	0.67
MMT	BlackRock Liqdty MuniCash Port Inst	MCSXX	**C**	(800) 441-7762	**D / 2.0**	0.01	0.01	0.02 /36	0.02 /22	0.04 /13	0.02	0.42
MMT	BlackRock Liqdty MuniFd Cash Mgmt	BCMXX	**C**	(800) 441-7762	**D+ / 2.3**	0.00	0.02	0.03 /38	0.03 /24	0.02 / 9	0.03	0.85
MMT	BlackRock Liqdty MuniFd Premier	BLSXX	**C**	(800) 441-7762	**D+ / 2.3**	0.00	0.02	0.03 /38	0.03 /24	0.02 / 9	0.03	0.95
MMT	BlackRock Liqdty MuniFund Select	BMBXX	**C**	(800) 441-7762	**D+ / 2.3**	0.00	0.02	0.03 /38	0.03 /24	0.02 / 9	0.03	1.20
MMT	BlackRock Liqdty NY Money Admin	BLNXX	**U**	(800) 441-7762	**U /**	0.00	0.01	0.01 /33	0.01 /19	0.07 /15	0.01	0.56
MMT	BlackRock Liqdty NY Money CshMgt	BLYXX	**U**	(800) 441-7762	**U /**	0.00	0.01	0.01 /33	0.01 /19	0.07 /15	0.01	0.96
MMT	BlackRock Liqdty NY Money Inst	MUNXX	**U**	(800) 441-7762	**U /**	0.00	0.01	0.02 /36	0.01 /19	0.08 /15	0.02	0.46
MMT	BlackRock Liqdty NY Money Prv Cl	BYPXX	**U**	(800) 441-7762	**U /**	0.00	0.01	0.01 /33	0.01 /19	0.07 /15	0.01	1.31
MMT	BlackRock Liqdty NY Money Select	BIBXX	**U**	(800) 441-7762	**U /**	0.00	0.01	0.01 /34	0.01 /19	0.07 /15	0.01	1.31
MM	BlackRock Liqdty TempFd Admin	BTMXX	**C**	(800) 441-7762	**D+ / 2.3**	0.06	0.08	0.09 /41	0.04 /24	0.04 /11	0.09	0.29
MM	BlackRock Liqdty TempFd Dollar	TDOXX	**C**	(800) 441-7762	**D / 2.0**	0.03	0.03	0.04 /37	0.03 /22	0.02 / 7	0.04	0.44
MM	BlackRock Liqdty TempFd Inst	TMPXX	**C**	(800) 441-7762	**D+ / 2.6**	0.09	0.13	0.17 /43	0.09 /27	0.10 /15	0.17	0.19
MM	BlackRock Liqdty T-Fund Ptf Admin	BTAXX	**U**	(800) 441-7762	**U /**	--	--	--	--	--	0.02	0.31
MM	BlackRock Liqdty T-Fund Ptf Csh Mgt	BPTXX	**U**	(800) 441-7762	**U /**	--	--	--	--	--	0.01	0.71
MM	BlackRock Liqdty Treas Tr Fd Admin	BITXX	**U**	(800) 441-7762	**U /**	0.01	0.01	0.01 /32	0.01 /16	0.01 / 3	0.01	0.32

● Denotes fund is closed to new investors
* Denotes fund is included in Section II

RISK			NET ASSETS		ASSET							FUND MANAGER		MINIMUM		LOADS	
Risk Rating/Pts	3 Yr Avg Standard Deviation	Avg Duration	NAV As of 3/31/16	Total $(Mil)	Cash %	Gov. Bond %	Muni. Bond %	Corp. Bond %	Other %	Portfolio Turnover Ratio	Avg Coupon Rate	Manager Quality Pct	Manager Tenure (Years)	Initial Purch. $	Additional Purch. $	Front End Load	Back End Load
B+ / 8.3	2.2	N/A	9.70	4,022	6	0	0	48	46	211	0.0	85	5	2,000,000	0	0.0	0.0
B- / 7.1	2.9	3.9	9.87	453	0	3	0	0	97	1,164	0.0	32	7	2,000,000	0	0.0	0.0
B- / 7.1	2.8	3.9	9.91	242	0	3	0	0	97	1,164	0.0	24	7	1,000	50	4.0	0.0
C+ / 6.9	2.9	3.9	9.87	102	0	3	0	0	97	1,164	0.0	12	7	1,000	50	0.0	0.0
C+ / 6.8	2.9	3.9	9.84	18	0	3	0	0	97	1,164	0.0	31	7	5,000,000	0	0.0	0.0
C+ / 6.9	2.9	3.9	9.86	24	0	3	0	0	97	1,164	0.0	22	7	5,000	0	0.0	0.0
D- / 1.5	5.6	4.1	7.15	9,084	1	0	0	82	17	70	0.7	84	9	2,000,000	0	0.0	0.0
D- / 1.5	5.6	4.1	7.15	2,893	1	0	0	82	17	70	0.7	77	9	1,000	50	4.0	0.0
D- / 1.5	5.6	4.1	7.15	1	1	0	0	82	17	70	0.7	38	9	0	0	0.0	0.0
D- / 1.5	5.6	4.1	7.15	1	1	0	0	82	17	70	0.7	52	9	0	0	0.0	0.0
D- / 1.5	5.6	4.1	7.16	523	1	0	0	82	17	70	0.7	44	9	1,000	50	0.0	0.0
D- / 1.5	5.6	4.1	7.16	54	1	0	0	82	17	70	0.7	50	9	0	0	0.0	0.0
D- / 1.4	5.7	4.1	7.16	4,265	1	0	0	82	17	70	0.7	86	9	5,000,000	0	0.0	0.0
D- / 1.5	5.6	4.1	7.15	95	1	0	0	82	17	70	0.7	61	9	100	0	0.0	0.0
D- / 1.5	5.6	4.1	7.15	312	1	0	0	82	17	70	0.7	76	9	5,000	0	0.0	0.0
E+ / 0.6	6.5	8.8	9.66	464	3	0	96	0	1	41	4.8	21	10	2,000,000	0	0.0	0.0
E+ / 0.6	6.5	8.8	9.64	195	3	0	96	0	1	41	4.8	16	10	1,000	50	4.3	0.0
E+ / 0.6	6.5	8.8	9.66	64	3	0	96	0	1	41	4.8	9	10	1,000	50	0.0	0.0
D+ / 2.4	5.1	7.1	10.70	1,526	0	99	0	0	1	61	0.3	4	6	2,000,000	0	0.0	0.0
D+ / 2.5	5.1	7.1	10.47	458	0	99	0	0	1	61	0.3	3	6	1,000	50	4.0	0.0
D+ / 2.4	5.1	7.1	10.21	211	0	99	0	0	1	61	0.3	2	6	1,000	50	0.0	0.0
D+ / 2.4	5.1	7.1	10.52	359	0	99	0	0	1	61	0.3	4	6	5,000,000	0	0.0	0.0
D+ / 2.4	5.1	7.1	10.58	44	0	99	0	0	1	61	0.3	3	6	5,000	0	0.0	0.0
D / 1.9	5.8	6.5	9.77	11	4	15	1	74	6	74	4.4	9	7	2,000,000	0	0.0	0.0
D / 1.9	5.8	6.5	9.77	23	4	15	1	74	6	74	4.4	8	7	1,000	50	4.0	0.0
D / 1.9	5.8	6.5	9.79	52	4	15	1	74	6	74	4.4	10	7	5,000,000	0	0.0	0.0
U /	N/A	N/A	1.00	2	100	0	0	0	0	0	0.0	N/A	N/A	5,000	0	0.0	0.0
A+ / 9.9	N/A	N/A	1.00	266	100	0	0	0	0	0	0.0	N/A	N/A	3,000,000	0	0.0	0.0
A+ / 9.9	N/A	N/A	1.00	316	100	0	0	0	0	0	0.0	N/A	N/A	5,000	0	0.0	0.0
U /	N/A	N/A	1.00	191	100	0	0	0	0	0	0.0	N/A	N/A	5,000	0	0.0	0.0
U /	N/A	N/A	1.00	5	100	0	0	0	0	0	0.0	N/A	N/A	5,000	0	0.0	0.0
U /	N/A	N/A	1.00	1,310	100	0	0	0	0	0	0.0	N/A	N/A	5,000	0	0.0	0.0
A+ / 9.9	N/A	N/A	1.00	11,336	100	0	0	0	0	0	0.1	64	N/A	3,000,000	0	0.0	0.0
U /	N/A	N/A	1.00	N/A	100	0	0	0	0	0	0.0	N/A	N/A	0	0	0.0	0.0
U /	N/A	N/A	1.00	4	100	0	0	0	0	0	0.0	N/A	N/A	0	0	0.0	0.0
U /	N/A	N/A	1.00	168	100	0	0	0	0	0	0.0	N/A	N/A	0	0	0.0	0.0
U /	N/A	N/A	1.00	2	100	0	0	0	0	0	0.0	N/A	N/A	5,000	0	0.0	0.0
A+ / 9.9	N/A	N/A	1.00	1,432	100	0	0	0	0	0	0.0	N/A	N/A	3,000,000	0	0.0	0.0
A+ / 9.9	N/A	N/A	1.00	2	100	0	0	0	0	0	0.0	66	N/A	5,000	0	0.0	0.0
A+ / 9.9	N/A	N/A	1.00	1	100	0	0	0	0	0	0.0	66	N/A	0	0	0.0	0.0
A+ / 9.9	N/A	N/A	1.00	11	100	0	0	0	0	0	0.0	67	N/A	0	0	0.0	0.0
U /	N/A	N/A	1.00	5	100	0	0	0	0	0	0.0	N/A	N/A	5,000	0	0.0	0.0
U /	N/A	N/A	1.00	7	100	0	0	0	0	0	0.0	N/A	N/A	5,000	0	0.0	0.0
U /	N/A	N/A	1.00	86	100	0	0	0	0	0	0.0	N/A	N/A	3,000,000	0	0.0	0.0
U /	N/A	N/A	1.00	1	100	0	0	0	0	0	0.0	N/A	N/A	0	0	0.0	0.0
U /	N/A	N/A	1.00	3	100	0	0	0	0	0	0.0	N/A	N/A	0	0	0.0	0.0
A+ / 9.9	N/A	N/A	1.00	3,614	100	0	0	0	0	0	0.1	N/A	N/A	5,000	0	0.0	0.0
A+ / 9.9	N/A	N/A	1.00	1,843	100	0	0	0	0	0	0.0	N/A	N/A	5,000	0	0.0	0.0
A+ / 9.9	N/A	N/A	1.00	54,912	100	0	0	0	0	0	0.2	69	N/A	3,000,000	0	0.0	0.0
U /	N/A	N/A	1.00	N/A	100	0	0	0	0	0	0.0	N/A	N/A	5,000	0	0.0	0.0
U /	N/A	N/A	1.00	912	100	0	0	0	0	0	0.0	N/A	N/A	5,000	0	0.0	0.0
U /	N/A	N/A	1.00	656	100	0	0	0	0	0	0.0	N/A	N/A	5,000	0	0.0	0.0

99 Pct = Best
0 Pct = Worst

Fund Type	Fund Name	Ticker Symbol	Overall Investment Rating	Phone	PERFORMANCE: Performance Rating/Pts	Total Return % through 3/31/16: 3 Mo	6 Mo	1Yr / Pct	Annualized: 3Yr / Pct	Annualized: 5Yr / Pct	Incl. in Returns: Dividend Yield	Incl. in Returns: Expense Ratio
MM	BlackRock Liqdty Treas Tr Fd Inst	TTTXX	C-	(800) 221-8120	D / 1.9	0.02	0.03	0.03 /36	0.01 /16	0.01 / 3	0.03	0.22
GEI	BlackRock Low Duration Bond Inst	BFMSX	B	(800) 441-7762	C / 4.6	0.63	0.34	0.66 /52	1.24 /47	2.19 /33	1.68	0.50
* GEI	BlackRock Low Duration Bond Inv A	BLDAX	C	(800) 441-7762	D+ / 2.9	0.65	0.28	0.43 /48	0.90 /41	1.84 /29	1.32	0.84
GEI ●	BlackRock Low Duration Bond Inv A1	CMGAX	C+	(800) 441-7762	C- / 3.9	0.70	0.37	0.61 /51	1.07 /44	2.01 /31	1.52	0.67
GEI	BlackRock Low Duration Bond Inv C	BLDCX	C	(800) 441-7762	D+ / 2.6	0.48	-0.08	-0.31 /28	0.16 /28	1.10 /21	0.61	1.57
GEI ●	BlackRock Low Duration Bond Inv C2	CLDCX	C+	(800) 441-7762	C- / 3.7	0.62	0.20	0.28 /45	0.74 /38	1.69 /27	1.20	0.97
COI ●	BlackRock Low Duration Bond Inv C3	BLDFX	C	(800) 441-7762	D+ / 2.7	0.49	-0.06	-0.26 /28	0.18 /28	--	0.66	1.55
GEI	BlackRock Low Duration Bond K	CLDBX	B	(800) 441-7762	C / 4.8	0.74	0.47	0.81 /55	1.28 /48	2.25 /34	1.73	0.42
COI	BlackRock Low Duration Bond R	BLDPX	C+	(800) 441-7762	C- / 3.5	0.61	0.17	0.19 /44	0.59 /35	--	1.12	1.14
GEI	BlackRock Low Duration Bond Svc	CMGBX	C+	(800) 441-7762	C- / 4.1	0.65	0.28	0.46 /49	0.90 /41	1.84 /29	1.38	0.86
MUN ●	BlackRock Natl Muni BR	BNMLX	A-	(800) 441-7762	A / 9.4	1.14	2.83	3.42 /89	3.71 /94	--	3.33	0.56
MUN	BlackRock Natl Muni Inst	MANLX	B+	(800) 441-7762	A / 9.3	1.11	2.77	3.31 /88	3.60 /93	6.54 /95	3.23	0.59
* MUN	BlackRock Natl Muni Inv A	MDNLX	B-	(800) 441-7762	B / 8.2	1.07	2.69	3.15 /86	3.44 /92	6.36 /94	2.94	0.85
MUN ●	BlackRock Natl Muni Inv B	MBNLX	B	(800) 441-7762	B+ / 8.8	0.95	2.53	2.63 /81	2.92 /87	5.85 /91	2.57	1.35
MUN	BlackRock Natl Muni Inv C	MFNLX	B	(800) 441-7762	B+ / 8.5	0.89	2.31	2.38 /80	2.67 /84	5.57 /89	2.33	1.54
MUN ●	BlackRock Natl Muni Inv C1	MCNLX	B	(800) 441-7762	B+ / 8.8	0.85	2.41	2.58 /81	2.86 /87	5.78 /91	2.52	1.37
MUN	BlackRock Natl Muni Svc	BNMSX	B+	(800) 441-7762	A- / 9.2	1.06	2.67	3.11 /86	3.39 /92	--	3.04	0.85
MUS	BlackRock NJ Muni Bond Inst	MANJX	B-	(800) 441-7762	A / 9.5	1.59	4.30	3.56 /91	3.78 /94	6.78 /96	3.52	0.84
MUS	BlackRock NJ Muni Bond Inv A	MENJX	C+	(800) 441-7762	B+ / 8.7	1.56	4.33	3.45 /90	3.67 /94	6.64 /95	3.26	0.98
MUS ●	BlackRock NJ Muni Bond Inv A1	MDNJX	B-	(800) 441-7762	A / 9.5	1.50	4.30	3.57 /91	3.78 /94	6.79 /96	3.52	0.83
MUS	BlackRock NJ Muni Bond Inv C	MFNJX	C+	(800) 441-7762	A- / 9.0	1.37	3.94	2.75 /83	2.88 /87	5.85 /91	2.65	1.73
MUS ●	BlackRock NJ Muni Bond Inv C1	MCNJX	C+	(800) 441-7762	A- / 9.2	1.46	4.04	3.05 /85	3.29 /91	6.25 /93	3.02	1.33
MUS	BlackRock NJ Muni Bond Svc	MSNJX	B-	(800) 441-7762	A / 9.5	1.56	4.24	3.45 /90	3.67 /94	6.65 /95	3.40	1.04
MUS	BlackRock NY Muni Oppty Inst	MANKX	B-	(800) 441-7762	A+ / 9.7	0.98	4.07	5.01 /98	4.19 /97	6.50 /94	3.40	0.78
MUS	BlackRock NY Muni Oppty Inv A	MENKX	C+	(800) 441-7762	B+ / 8.9	0.92	3.85	4.67 /97	3.91 /95	6.22 /93	3.03	1.04
MUS ●	BlackRock NY Muni Oppty Inv A1	MDNKX	C+	(800) 441-7762	A- / 9.1	0.95	3.91	4.78 /97	4.04 /96	6.39 /94	3.14	0.88
MUS	BlackRock NY Muni Oppty Inv C	MFNKX	C+	(800) 441-7762	A- / 9.2	0.74	3.47	3.98 /94	3.17 /90	5.46 /89	2.43	1.78
MUS ●	BlackRock NY Muni Oppty Inv C1	MCNKX	C+	(800) 441-7762	A / 9.4	0.83	3.65	4.26 /95	3.57 /93	5.87 /91	2.78	1.37
MUS	BlackRock PA Muni Bond Inst	MAPYX	B-	(800) 441-7762	A+ / 9.6	1.62	3.58	4.10 /94	3.85 /95	6.89 /96	3.98	0.87
MUS	BlackRock PA Muni Bond Inv A	MEPYX	C+	(800) 441-7762	B+ / 8.7	1.67	3.58	4.01 /94	3.69 /94	6.70 /95	3.64	1.02
MUS ●	BlackRock PA Muni Bond Inv A1	MDPYX	B-	(800) 441-7762	A+ / 9.6	1.62	3.66	4.17 /95	3.83 /95	6.87 /96	3.96	0.86
MUS	BlackRock PA Muni Bond Inv C	MFPYX	C+	(800) 441-7762	B+ / 8.9	1.38	3.09	3.10 /86	2.85 /86	5.85 /91	3.02	1.75
MUS ●	BlackRock PA Muni Bond Inv C1	MCPYX	C+	(800) 441-7762	A- / 9.2	1.49	3.30	3.53 /90	3.28 /91	6.29 /94	3.44	1.35
MUS	BlackRock PA Muni Bond Svc	MSPYX	B-	(800) 441-7762	A / 9.5	1.67	3.58	4.10 /94	3.69 /94	6.72 /95	3.80	1.04
MMT ●	BlackRock PA Municipal MM Inst	PPIXX	U	(800) 441-7762	U /	--	--	--	--	--	0.01	0.75
MMT ●	BlackRock PA Municipal MM Inv A	PENXX	U	(800) 441-7762	U /	--	--	--	--	--	0.01	1.53
MMT ●	BlackRock PA Municipal MM Svc	PNSXX	U	(800) 441-7762	U /	--	--	--	--	--	0.01	0.99
GES	BlackRock Secured Credit Inst	BMSIX	B+	(800) 441-7762	B- / 7.1	1.90	0.88	0.08 /40	2.82 /75	4.64 /69	4.23	0.81
GES	BlackRock Secured Credit Inv A	BMSAX	C+	(800) 441-7762	C+ / 5.7	1.94	0.76	-0.17 /29	2.60 /72	4.38 /66	3.88	1.11
GES	BlackRock Secured Credit Inv C	BMSCX	C+	(800) 441-7762	C / 5.5	1.76	0.49	-0.82 /23	1.83 /58	3.61 /55	3.21	1.84
MM	BlackRock Select Government Inst	MLSXX	C	(800) 441-7762	D+ / 2.5	0.04	0.06	0.10 /41	0.07 /26	0.09 /14	0.10	0.20
GEI	BlackRock Short Obligations Inst	BISOX	C+	(800) 441-7762	C- / 3.6	0.41	0.48	0.78 /55	0.59 /35	--	0.68	1.02
COI	BlackRock Short Obligations K	BBSOX	B-	(800) 441-7762	C- / 3.7	0.42	0.49	0.80 /55	0.61 /35	--	0.70	0.99
MUN	BlackRock Short Term Muni Inst	MALMX	B-	(800) 441-7762	C- / 3.7	0.41	0.23	0.62 /58	0.40 /35	0.67 /21	0.41	0.51
MUN	BlackRock Short Term Muni Inv A	MELMX	C-	(800) 441-7762	D- / 1.2	0.34	0.09	0.34 /50	0.12 /28	0.41 /18	0.13	0.70
MUN ●	BlackRock Short Term Muni Inv A1	MDLMX	C+	(800) 441-7762	C- / 3.4	0.38	0.17	0.50 /55	0.28 /32	0.55 /19	0.30	0.54
MUN	BlackRock Short Term Muni Inv C	MFLMX	C-	(800) 441-7762	D- / 1.2	0.20	-0.19	-0.39 /27	-0.66 /10	-0.37 / 2	0.00	1.47
MUN	BlackRock Short-Term Muni K	MPLMX	C+	(800) 441-7762	C- / 3.7	0.41	0.22	0.61 /57	0.40 /35	0.67 /21	0.40	0.39
MUN	BlackRock Strat Muni Opps Instl	MAMTX	B+	(800) 441-7762	A / 9.5	1.43	4.39	4.66 /97	3.58 /93	6.06 /92	2.76	0.70
* MUN	BlackRock Strat Muni Opps Inv A	MEMTX	B-	(800) 441-7762	B+ / 8.4	1.29	4.19	4.34 /96	3.31 /91	5.81 /91	2.44	0.93
MUN ●	BlackRock Strat Muni Opps Inv A1	MDMTX	B+	(800) 441-7762	A / 9.4	1.33	4.26	4.49 /97	3.46 /92	5.96 /92	2.68	0.79
MUN	BlackRock Strat Muni Opps Inv C	MFMTX	B	(800) 441-7762	B+ / 8.7	1.10	3.80	3.54 /90	2.53 /83	5.01 /85	1.80	1.70

● Denotes fund is closed to new investors
* Denotes fund is included in Section II

RISK			NET ASSETS		ASSET							FUND MANAGER		MINIMUM		LOADS	
Risk Rating/Pts	3 Yr Avg Standard Deviation	Avg Duration	NAV As of 3/31/16	Total $(Mil)	Cash %	Gov. Bond %	Muni. Bond %	Corp. Bond %	Other %	Portfolio Turnover Ratio	Avg Coupon Rate	Manager Quality Pct	Manager Tenure (Years)	Initial Purch. $	Additional Purch. $	Front End Load	Back End Load
A+ / 9.9	N/A	N/A	1.00	14,391	100	0	0	0	0	0	0.0	63	N/A	3,000,000	0	0.0	0.0
A- / 9.2	1.1	1.8	9.61	2,897	0	19	0	36	45	289	4.3	83	8	2,000,000	0	0.0	0.0
A- / 9.2	1.1	1.8	9.61	830	0	19	0	36	45	289	4.3	75	8	1,000	50	2.3	0.0
A- / 9.1	1.1	1.8	9.62	14	0	19	0	36	45	289	4.3	79	8	0	0	1.0	0.0
A- / 9.2	1.1	1.8	9.61	382	0	19	0	36	45	289	4.3	42	8	1,000	50	0.0	0.0
A- / 9.2	1.1	1.8	9.61	7	0	19	0	36	45	289	4.3	68	8	0	0	0.0	0.0
A- / 9.2	1.1	1.8	9.61	20	0	19	0	36	45	289	4.3	45	8	0	0	0.0	0.0
A- / 9.2	1.1	1.8	9.61	750	0	19	0	36	45	289	4.3	85	8	5,000,000	0	0.0	0.0
A- / 9.2	1.1	1.8	9.61	5	0	19	0	36	45	289	4.3	62	8	100	0	0.0	0.0
A- / 9.2	1.1	1.8	9.61	60	0	19	0	36	45	289	4.3	75	8	5,000	0	0.0	0.0
C / 4.4	3.7	N/A	11.04	330	9	0	90	0	1	28	0.0	56	20	5,000,000	0	0.0	0.0
C / 4.4	3.7	N/A	11.04	2,953	9	0	90	0	1	28	0.0	53	20	2,000,000	0	0.0	0.0
C / 4.4	3.7	N/A	11.05	2,615	9	0	90	0	1	28	0.0	46	20	1,000	50	4.3	0.0
C / 4.4	3.8	N/A	11.04	2	9	0	90	0	1	28	0.0	30	20	0	0	0.0	0.0
C / 4.4	3.7	N/A	11.05	449	9	0	90	0	1	28	0.0	25	20	1,000	50	0.0	0.0
C / 4.4	3.7	N/A	11.04	61	9	0	90	0	1	28	0.0	30	20	0	0	0.0	0.0
C / 4.4	3.7	N/A	11.03	2	9	0	90	0	1	28	0.0	45	20	5,000	0	0.0	0.0
D+ / 2.8	4.9	N/A	11.26	132	0	0	99	0	1	14	3.7	23	10	2,000,000	0	0.0	0.0
D+ / 2.8	4.9	N/A	11.27	79	0	0	99	0	1	14	3.7	21	10	1,000	50	4.3	0.0
D+ / 2.9	4.8	N/A	11.27	26	0	0	99	0	1	14	3.7	24	10	0	0	0.0	0.0
D+ / 2.9	4.8	N/A	11.26	30	0	0	99	0	1	14	3.7	11	10	1,000	50	0.0	0.0
D+ / 2.8	4.9	N/A	11.26	8	0	0	99	0	1	14	3.7	15	10	0	0	0.0	0.0
D+ / 2.8	4.9	N/A	11.26	10	0	0	99	0	1	14	3.7	21	10	5,000	0	0.0	0.0
D+ / 2.6	5.1	6.4	11.21	149	3	0	96	0	1	22	4.8	29	10	2,000,000	0	0.0	0.0
D+ / 2.6	5.1	6.4	11.21	156	3	0	96	0	1	22	4.8	22	10	1,000	50	4.3	0.0
D+ / 2.5	5.2	6.4	11.21	123	3	0	96	0	1	22	4.8	23	10	0	0	4.0	0.0
D+ / 2.6	5.2	6.4	11.21	62	3	0	96	0	1	22	4.8	12	10	1,000	50	0.0	0.0
D+ / 2.5	5.2	6.4	11.21	8	3	0	96	0	1	22	4.8	15	10	0	0	0.0	0.0
D+ / 2.8	5.0	N/A	11.49	320	0	0	100	0	0	18	5.1	22	10	2,000,000	0	0.0	0.0
D+ / 2.7	5.0	N/A	11.51	82	0	0	100	0	0	18	5.1	19	10	1,000	50	4.3	0.0
D+ / 2.8	5.0	N/A	11.51	16	0	0	100	0	0	18	5.1	22	10	0	0	0.0	0.0
D+ / 2.7	5.0	N/A	11.50	33	0	0	100	0	0	18	5.1	10	10	1,000	50	0.0	0.0
D+ / 2.8	5.0	N/A	11.49	5	0	0	100	0	0	18	5.1	14	10	0	0	0.0	0.0
D+ / 2.7	5.0	N/A	11.51	1	0	0	100	0	0	18	5.1	19	10	5,000	0	0.0	0.0
U /	N/A	N/A	1.00	427	100	0	0	0	0	0	0.0	N/A	N/A	2,000,000	0	0.0	0.0
U /	N/A	N/A	1.00	N/A	100	0	0	0	0	0	0.0	N/A	N/A	1,000	50	0.0	0.0
U /	N/A	N/A	1.00	11	100	0	0	0	0	0	0.0	N/A	N/A	5,000	0	0.0	0.0
C+ / 6.8	2.9	1.1	9.86	228	3	0	0	25	72	65	5.3	95	6	2,000,000	0	0.0	0.0
B- / 7.0	2.9	1.1	9.86	111	3	0	0	25	72	65	5.3	95	6	1,000	50	2.5	0.0
C+ / 6.7	3.0	1.1	9.87	24	3	0	0	25	72	65	5.3	89	6	1,000	50	0.0	0.0
A+ / 9.9	N/A	N/A	1.00	1,104	100	0	0	0	0	0	0.1	69	N/A	10,000,000	1,000	0.0	0.0
A+ / 9.9	0.2	N/A	10.01	13	26	0	0	49	25	68	0.0	82	N/A	2,000,000	0	0.0	0.0
A+ / 9.9	0.2	N/A	10.02	47	26	0	0	49	25	68	0.0	83	N/A	5,000,000	0	0.0	0.0
A+ / 9.8	0.6	1.7	10.15	467	3	0	96	0	1	72	4.4	68	20	2,000,000	0	0.0	0.0
A+ / 9.7	0.6	1.7	10.16	91	3	0	96	0	1	72	4.4	52	20	1,000	50	3.0	0.0
A+ / 9.7	0.6	1.7	10.16	31	3	0	96	0	1	72	4.4	59	20	0	0	0.0	0.0
A+ / 9.8	0.6	1.7	9.95	33	3	0	96	0	1	72	4.4	29	20	1,000	50	0.0	0.0
A+ / 9.8	0.6	1.7	10.15	3	3	0	96	0	1	72	4.4	67	20	5,000,000	0	0.0	0.0
C- / 4.2	3.9	N/A	11.62	2,880	5	0	93	0	2	185	4.4	53	10	2,000,000	0	0.0	0.0
C- / 4.2	3.9	N/A	11.61	1,025	5	0	93	0	2	185	4.4	43	10	1,000	50	4.3	0.0
C- / 4.1	3.9	N/A	11.61	33	5	0	93	0	2	185	4.4	47	10	0	0	0.0	0.0
C- / 4.1	3.9	N/A	11.61	248	5	0	93	0	2	185	4.4	21	10	1,000	50	0.0	0.0

Fund Type	Fund Name	Ticker Symbol	Overall Investment Rating	Phone	PERFORMANCE: Performance Rating/Pts	Total Return % through 3/31/16: 3 Mo	6 Mo	1Yr / Pct	Annualized: 3Yr / Pct	5Yr / Pct	Incl. in Returns: Dividend Yield	Expense Ratio
99 Pct = Best, 0 Pct = Worst												
GL	BlackRock Strategic Global Bd Inst	MAWIX	**C**	(800) 441-7762	**C+ / 6.4**	5.34	4.65	1.91 /71	1.31 /48	2.90 /44	1.48	0.99
GL	BlackRock Strategic Global Bd Inv A	MDWIX	**D+**	(800) 441-7762	**C- / 4.1**	5.46	4.52	1.67 /68	1.08 /44	2.68 /40	1.21	1.22
GL	BlackRock Strategic Global Bd Inv C	MHWIX	**C-**	(800) 441-7762	**C / 4.4**	5.10	3.96	0.74 /54	0.26 /29	1.86 /29	0.54	2.02
GL	● BlackRock Strategic Global Bond C1	MCWIX	**C-**	(800) 441-7762	**C / 4.8**	5.15	4.25	1.06 /59	0.43 /32	2.04 /32	0.68	1.77
GEI	BlackRock Total Return Inst	MAHQX	**B**	(800) 441-7762	**B / 7.8**	2.52	1.95	0.62 /52	3.29 /79	4.94 /71	2.89	0.55
* GEI	BlackRock Total Return Inv A	MDHQX	**C**	(800) 441-7762	**C+ / 6.0**	2.52	1.88	0.38 /47	3.01 /76	4.62 /69	2.46	0.86
GEI	● BlackRock Total Return Inv A1	MEHQX	**B**	(800) 441-7762	**B / 7.7**	2.57	1.97	0.48 /49	3.20 /78	4.82 /70	2.74	0.66
GEI	● BlackRock Total Return Inv B	MBHQX	**C+**	(800) 441-7762	**C+ / 6.6**	2.40	1.63	-0.20 /29	2.38 /69	3.93 /60	2.07	1.54
GEI	BlackRock Total Return Inv C	MFHQX	**C+**	(800) 441-7762	**C+ / 6.5**	2.36	1.54	-0.29 /28	2.34 /68	3.96 /61	1.89	1.59
GEI	● BlackRock Total Return Inv C1	MCHQX	**C+**	(800) 441-7762	**C+ / 6.6**	2.29	1.49	-0.29 /28	2.39 /69	4.02 /62	1.98	1.43
GEI	● BlackRock Total Return Inv C2	MHHQX	**C+**	(800) 441-7762	**B- / 7.1**	2.37	1.66	0.03 /35	2.69 /73	4.29 /65	2.31	1.15
GEI	BlackRock Total Return K	MPHQX	**B+**	(800) 441-7762	**B / 7.9**	2.53	1.98	0.68 /53	3.39 /79	5.05 /72	2.95	0.45
GEI	BlackRock Total Return R	MRCBX	**C+**	(800) 441-7762	**B- / 7.2**	2.46	1.75	0.13 /42	2.75 /74	4.36 /66	2.31	1.13
GEI	BlackRock Total Return Service	MSHQX	**B**	(800) 441-7762	**B / 7.6**	2.44	1.81	0.37 /47	3.05 /77	4.68 /69	2.63	0.79
USS	BlackRock US Govt Bond Inst	PNIGX	**B+**	(800) 441-7762	**C+ / 6.6**	2.51	1.97	1.61 /68	2.10 /63	3.21 /48	2.13	0.92
USS	BlackRock US Govt Bond Inv A	CIGAX	**C**	(800) 441-7762	**C / 4.3**	2.42	1.71	1.21 /62	1.81 /58	2.88 /43	1.76	1.10
USS	BlackRock US Govt Bond Inv B1	BIGEX	**C+**	(800) 441-7762	**C / 5.2**	2.42	1.58	0.81 /55	1.28 /48	--	1.35	2.00
USS	BlackRock US Govt Bond Inv C	BIGCX	**C**	(800) 441-7762	**C / 4.6**	2.24	1.43	0.51 /50	1.00 /43	2.07 /32	1.05	1.91
USS	● BlackRock US Govt Bond Inv C1	BIGHX	**C+**	(800) 441-7762	**C / 5.1**	2.40	1.54	0.72 /54	1.19 /46	--	1.25	1.74
USS	BlackRock US Govt Bond R	BGBRX	**C+**	(800) 441-7762	**C+ / 5.6**	2.38	1.60	1.04 /59	1.51 /52	--	1.57	1.41
USS	BlackRock US Govt Bond Svc	PIGSX	**B**	(800) 441-7762	**C+ / 6.3**	2.46	1.78	1.42 /65	1.91 /60	2.99 /45	1.94	1.14
GEI	BlackRock US Total Bond Index Fund	WFBIX	**B**	(800) 441-7762	**B- / 7.2**	3.05	2.36	1.77 /69	2.37 /69	3.58 /54	2.22	0.10
GEI	BlackRock US Total Bond Index Inst	BMOIX	**B**	(800) 441-7762	**B- / 7.1**	3.04	2.33	1.72 /69	2.32 /68	3.53 /53	2.17	0.15
GEI	BlackRock US Total Bond Index Inv A	BMOAX	**B-**	(800) 441-7762	**C+ / 6.7**	2.98	2.31	1.47 /66	2.07 /63	3.29 /50	1.93	0.40
MM	BlackRock-Lq Federal Tr Admin	BFTXX	**U**	(800) 441-7762	**U /**	--	--	--	--	--	0.01	0.42
MM	BlackRock-Lq Federal Tr Instl	TFFXX	**C**	(800) 441-7762	**D / 2.0**	0.03	0.04	0.04 /37	0.02 /19	0.02 / 7	0.04	0.32
MM	BlackRock-Lq TempCash Dollar	TCDXX	**U**	(800) 441-7762	**U /**	--	--	--	--	--	0.02	0.56
MM	BlackRock-Lq TempCash Instl	TMCXX	**C**	(800) 441-7762	**D+ / 2.6**	0.06	0.08	0.12 /42	0.09 /27	0.11 /15	0.12	0.31
MM	BlackRock-Lq T-Fund Instl	TSTXX	**C**	(800) 441-7762	**D / 2.2**	0.04	0.04	0.05 /38	0.03 /22	0.02 / 7	0.05	0.21
MM	BlackRock-Money Market Prtf Instl	PNIXX	**C**	(800) 441-7762	**D+ / 2.3**	0.08	0.12	0.13 /42	0.04 /24	0.03 /10	0.13	0.69
MM	BlackRock-Money Market Prtf Inv A	PINXX	**C**	(800) 441-7762	**D / 2.2**	0.06	0.07	0.07 /40	0.03 /22	0.02 / 7	0.07	0.91
MM	● BlackRock-Money Market Prtf Inv B	CIBXX	**C**	(800) 441-7762	**D / 2.0**	0.05	0.06	0.06 /39	0.02 /19	0.01 / 3	0.06	1.73
MM	● BlackRock-Money Market Prtf Inv C	BMCXX	**C**	(800) 441-7762	**D+ / 2.3**	0.07	0.10	0.10 /41	0.04 /24	0.02 / 7	0.10	1.58
MM	BlackRock-Money Market Prtf Svc	PNPXX	**C**	(800) 441-7762	**D+ / 2.3**	0.07	0.08	0.08 /40	0.03 /22	0.02 / 7	0.08	0.96
MUN	BMO Intermediate Tax Free A	BITAX	**A**	(800) 236-3863	**B / 8.0**	1.40	2.47	3.02 /85	2.94 /87	4.75 /83	2.01	0.59
MUN	BMO Intermediate Tax Free I	MIITX	**A+**	(800) 236-3863	**A- / 9.2**	1.45	2.67	3.25 /87	3.26 /90	5.09 /86	2.31	0.34
MUN	BMO Intermediate Tax Free Y	MITFX	**A+**	(800) 236-3863	**A- / 9.0**	1.40	2.47	3.02 /85	3.04 /88	4.91 /84	2.09	0.59
COH	BMO Monegy High Yield Bond A	BMHAX	**D**	(800) 236-3863	**D+ / 2.8**	2.69	1.45	-2.25 /14	1.28 /48	--	5.11	1.26
GL	BMO Monegy High Yield Bond I	MHBNX	**D+**	(800) 236-3863	**C / 5.3**	2.87	1.57	-2.01 /16	1.66 /55	--	5.54	1.01
MTG	BMO Mortgage Income A	BMTAX	**C+**	(800) 236-3863	**C / 4.8**	1.76	1.49	1.87 /71	1.96 /61	2.75 /41	2.71	0.85
USS	BMO Mortgage Income I	MGIIX	**A-**	(800) 236-3863	**C+ / 6.8**	1.71	1.62	2.01 /72	2.27 /67	3.17 /48	3.06	0.60
USS	BMO Mortgage Income Y	MRGIX	**B+**	(800) 236-3863	**C+ / 6.5**	1.76	1.49	1.87 /71	2.06 /63	2.91 /44	2.81	0.85
MM	BMO Prime Money Market Premier	MAIXX	**C**	(800) 236-3863	**D+ / 2.3**	0.07	0.09	0.10 /41	0.04 /24	0.09 /14	0.10	0.21
MM	BMO Prime Money Market Y	MARXX	**U**	(800) 236-3863	**U /**	0.01	0.01	0.02 /33	0.01 /16	0.01 / 3	0.02	0.46
MUN	BMO Short Tax Free Y	MTFYX	**A+**	(800) 236-3863	**C+ / 6.7**	0.41	0.75	1.14 /69	1.56 /69	--	1.09	0.85
MUN	BMO Short Term Tax Free A	BASFX	**B+**	(800) 236-3863	**C / 5.3**	0.41	0.75	1.14 /69	1.50 /67	--	1.07	0.85
MUN	BMO Short Term Tax Free I	MTFIX	**A+**	(800) 236-3863	**B- / 7.2**	0.55	0.92	1.29 /72	1.75 /73	--	1.24	0.60
COI	BMO Short-Term Income A	BTMAX	**C**	(800) 236-3863	**D+ / 2.9**	0.90	0.61	0.94 /57	0.66 /36	1.36 /24	1.02	0.74
GEI	BMO Short-Term Income I	MSIFX	**B**	(800) 236-3863	**C / 4.6**	0.95	0.73	1.18 /61	1.04 /43	1.79 /29	1.28	0.49
GEI	BMO Short-Term Income Y	MSINX	**B-**	(800) 236-3863	**C- / 4.0**	0.90	0.61	0.93 /57	0.75 /38	1.52 /26	1.03	0.74
MMT	BMO T/F Money Market Premier	MFIXX	**C**	(800) 236-3863	**D+ / 2.4**	0.03	0.04	0.06 /41	0.04 /25	0.12 /16	0.06	0.28
COI	BMO TCH Core Plus Bond A	BATCX	**D+**	(800) 236-3863	**C- / 3.7**	3.19	1.92	-0.98 /22	1.58 /54	4.13 /63	2.85	0.58

● Denotes fund is closed to new investors
* Denotes fund is included in Section II

RISK			NET ASSETS		ASSET							FUND MANAGER		MINIMUM		LOADS	
Risk Rating/Pts	3 Yr Avg Standard Deviation	Avg Duration	NAV As of 3/31/16	Total $(Mil)	Cash %	Gov. Bond %	Muni. Bond %	Corp. Bond %	Other %	Portfolio Turnover Ratio	Avg Coupon Rate	Manager Quality Pct	Manager Tenure (Years)	Initial Purch. $	Additional Purch. $	Front End Load	Back End Load
C / 5.0	3.5	3.2	5.92	40	1	60	1	23	15	147	4.3	92	5	2,000,000	0	0.0	0.0
C / 4.9	3.5	3.2	5.92	61	1	60	1	23	15	147	4.3	91	5	1,000	50	4.0	0.0
C / 5.0	3.5	3.2	5.91	14	1	60	1	23	15	147	4.3	77	5	1,000	50	0.0	0.0
C / 4.9	3.5	3.2	5.91	4	1	60	1	23	15	147	4.3	82	5	0	0	0.0	0.0
C+ / 5.6	3.2	5.2	11.72	2,376	0	28	2	28	42	1,015	8.0	86	6	2,000,000	0	0.0	0.0
C / 5.4	3.3	5.2	11.73	2,538	0	28	2	28	42	1,015	8.0	79	6	1,000	50	4.0	0.0
C / 5.4	3.3	5.2	11.72	36	0	28	2	28	42	1,015	8.0	83	6	0	0	0.0	0.0
C / 5.4	3.3	5.2	11.72	3	0	28	2	28	42	1,015	8.0	52	6	0	0	0.0	0.0
C / 5.4	3.3	5.2	11.72	458	0	28	2	28	42	1,015	8.0	51	6	1,000	50	0.0	0.0
C+ / 5.6	3.2	5.2	11.72	77	0	28	2	28	42	1,015	8.0	54	6	0	0	0.0	0.0
C / 5.5	3.3	5.2	11.71	4	0	28	2	28	42	1,015	8.0	69	6	0	0	0.0	0.0
C+ / 5.6	3.3	5.2	11.72	2,722	0	28	2	28	42	1,015	8.0	87	6	5,000,000	0	0.0	0.0
C / 5.4	3.3	5.2	11.73	73	0	28	2	28	42	1,015	8.0	70	6	100	0	0.0	0.0
C / 5.5	3.3	5.2	11.72	61	0	28	2	28	42	1,015	8.0	81	6	5,000	0	0.0	0.0
B- / 7.4	2.7	4.9	10.68	177	0	47	0	8	45	1,090	12.1	77	7	2,000,000	0	0.0	0.0
B- / 7.4	2.8	4.9	10.70	480	0	47	0	8	45	1,090	12.1	62	7	1,000	50	4.0	0.0
B- / 7.4	2.7	4.9	10.67	N/A	0	47	0	8	45	1,090	12.1	42	7	0	0	0.0	0.0
B- / 7.4	2.7	4.9	10.69	52	0	47	0	8	45	1,090	12.1	34	7	1,000	50	0.0	0.0
B- / 7.4	2.7	4.9	10.69	58	0	47	0	8	45	1,090	12.1	39	7	0	0	0.0	0.0
B- / 7.4	2.7	4.9	10.70	25	0	47	0	8	45	1,090	12.1	51	7	100	0	0.0	0.0
B- / 7.4	2.7	4.9	10.67	4	0	47	0	8	45	1,090	12.1	71	7	5,000	0	0.0	0.0
C+ / 6.4	3.0	N/A	10.24	278	0	43	1	24	32	476	0.0	56	7	1	1	0.0	0.0
C+ / 6.4	3.0	N/A	10.24	81	0	43	1	24	32	476	0.0	54	7	2,000,000	0	0.0	0.0
C+ / 6.4	3.0	N/A	10.24	30	0	43	1	24	32	476	0.0	45	7	1,000	50	0.0	0.0
U /	N/A	N/A	1.00	N/A	100	0	0	0	0	0	0.0	N/A	N/A	5,000	0	0.0	0.0
A+ / 9.9	N/A	N/A	1.00	314	100	0	0	0	0	0	0.0	64	N/A	3,000,000	0	0.0	0.0
U /	N/A	N/A	1.00	90	100	0	0	0	0	0	0.0	67	N/A	5,000	0	0.0	0.0
A+ / 9.9	N/A	N/A	1.00	880	100	0	0	0	0	0	0.1	70	N/A	3,000,000	0	0.0	0.0
A+ / 9.9	N/A	N/A	1.00	20,214	100	0	0	0	0	0	0.1	64	N/A	3,000,000	0	0.0	0.0
A+ / 9.9	N/A	N/A	1.00	605	100	0	0	0	0	0	0.1	63	8	2,000,000	0	0.0	0.0
A+ / 9.9	N/A	N/A	1.00	177	100	0	0	0	0	0	0.1	63	8	1,000	50	0.0	0.0
A+ / 9.9	N/A	N/A	1.00	N/A	100	0	0	0	0	0	0.1	63	8	1,000	50	0.0	0.0
A+ / 9.9	N/A	N/A	1.00	38	100	0	0	0	0	0	0.1	63	8	1,000	50	0.0	0.0
A+ / 9.9	N/A	N/A	1.00	520	100	0	0	0	0	0	0.1	62	8	5,000	0	0.0	0.0
B- / 7.0	2.9	3.9	11.45	2	1	0	98	0	1	26	3.9	59	22	1,000	50	3.5	0.0
B- / 7.0	2.9	3.9	11.45	534	1	0	98	0	1	26	3.9	75	22	2,000,000	0	0.0	0.0
B- / 7.0	2.9	3.9	11.45	1,232	1	0	98	0	1	26	3.9	N/A	22	1,000	50	0.0	0.0
D+ / 2.6	4.7	4.3	9.08	43	5	0	0	94	1	46	6.4	59	5	1,000	50	3.5	0.0
C- / 3.1	4.7	4.3	9.08	28	5	0	0	94	1	46	6.4	95	5	2,000,000	0	0.0	0.0
B / 7.8	2.6	3.8	9.36	N/A	5	0	0	0	95	44	3.9	36	4	1,000	50	3.5	0.0
B / 7.8	2.5	3.8	9.35	25	5	0	0	0	95	44	3.9	86	4	2,000,000	0	0.0	0.0
B / 7.8	2.5	3.8	9.36	88	5	0	0	0	95	44	3.9	81	4	1,000	50	0.0	0.0
A+ / 9.9	N/A	N/A	1.00	2,276	100	0	0	0	0	0	0.1	64	4	10,000,000	0	0.0	0.0
U /	N/A	N/A	1.00	1,179	100	0	0	0	0	0	0.0	N/A	4	1,000	50	0.0	0.0
A- / 9.2	1.1	1.6	10.21	15	1	0	98	0	1	50	2.8	82	4	1,000	50	0.0	0.0
A- / 9.1	1.1	1.6	10.21	1	1	0	98	0	1	50	2.8	80	4	1,000	50	2.0	0.0
A- / 9.1	1.1	1.6	10.22	181	1	0	98	0	1	50	2.8	85	4	2,000,000	0	0.0	0.0
A / 9.5	0.8	1.9	9.36	N/A	2	26	0	45	27	29	1.8	74	4	1,000	50	2.0	0.0
A / 9.5	0.8	1.9	9.38	285	2	26	0	45	27	29	1.8	81	4	2,000,000	0	0.0	0.0
A / 9.5	0.8	1.9	9.36	60	2	26	0	45	27	29	1.8	73	4	1,000	50	0.0	0.0
A+ / 9.9	N/A	N/A	1.00	511	100	0	0	0	0	0	0.1	66	12	10,000,000	0	0.0	0.0
C / 4.3	3.8	5.3	11.37	1	4	16	0	49	31	25	3.7	35	8	1,000	50	3.5	0.0

Fund Type	Fund Name (99 Pct = Best, 0 Pct = Worst)	Ticker Symbol	Overall Investment Rating	Phone	PERFORMANCE: Performance Rating/Pts	Total Return % through 3/31/16: 3 Mo	6 Mo	1Yr / Pct	Annualized: 3Yr / Pct	5Yr / Pct	Incl. in Returns: Dividend Yield	Expense Ratio
GEI	BMO TCH Core Plus Bond I	MCBIX	**C-**	(800) 236-3863	**C+ / 6.0**	3.25	2.14	-0.74 /24	1.91 /60	4.53 /68	3.20	0.33
GEI	BMO TCH Core Plus Bond Y	MCYBX	**C-**	(800) 236-3863	**C+ / 5.6**	3.19	1.92	-0.98 /22	1.67 /55	4.29 /65	2.96	0.58
COI	BMO TCH Corporate Income A	BATIX	**D**	(800) 236-3863	**C / 4.3**	3.98	2.47	-2.20 /15	1.93 /60	4.56 /68	3.25	0.71
COI	BMO TCH Corporate Income I	MCIIX	**C-**	(800) 236-3863	**C+ / 6.3**	4.10	2.62	-2.00 /16	2.14 /64	4.90 /71	3.50	0.46
COI	BMO TCH Corporate Income Y	MCIYX	**C-**	(800) 236-3863	**C+ / 6.1**	3.98	2.47	-2.20 /15	2.03 /62	4.73 /70	3.37	0.71
EM	BMO TCH Emerging Markets Bond A	BAMEX	**U**	(800) 236-3863	**U /**	6.12	3.75	-1.78 /17	--	--	4.80	3.22
EM	BMO TCH Emerging Markets Bond I	MEBIX	**U**	(800) 236-3863	**U /**	6.12	3.80	-1.72 /17	--	--	5.13	2.97
COI	BMO TCH Intermediate Income A	BAIIX	**D+**	(800) 236-3863	**D+ / 2.3**	2.06	1.24	-0.74 /24	0.93 /41	2.51 /38	2.15	0.83
GEI	BMO TCH Intermediate Income I	MIBIX	**C**	(800) 236-3863	**C / 4.8**	2.12	1.37	-0.50 /26	1.27 /48	2.91 /44	2.48	0.58
MUN	BMO Ultra Sht Tax-Free A	BAUSX	**C-**	(800) 236-3863	**D / 1.6**	0.09	0.15	0.11 /43	0.34 /33	0.62 /20	0.31	0.63
MUN	BMO Ultra Sht Tax-Free I	MUISX	**B**	(800) 236-3863	**C / 4.3**	0.14	0.18	0.36 /50	0.69 /44	1.03 /26	0.56	0.38
MUN	BMO Ultra Sht Tax-Free Y	MUYSX	**C+**	(800) 236-3863	**C- / 3.5**	0.09	0.15	0.11 /43	0.44 /36	0.78 /22	0.31	0.63
GEI	BNY Mellon Bond Inv	MIBDX	**C+**	(800) 645-6561	**C+ / 6.2**	2.86	2.44	1.75 /69	1.64 /55	3.07 /46	2.56	0.80
* GEI	BNY Mellon Bond M	MPBFX	**B**	(800) 645-6561	**C+ / 6.6**	2.91	2.57	2.01 /72	1.92 /60	3.34 /50	2.81	0.55
GEI	BNY Mellon Corporate Bond Inv	BYMIX	**C+**	(800) 645-6561	**C+ / 6.7**	3.14	2.34	0.84 /56	2.17 /65	--	3.17	0.81
GEI	BNY Mellon Corporate Bond M	BYMMX	**B-**	(800) 645-6561	**B- / 7.2**	3.28	2.55	1.18 /61	2.44 /70	--	3.42	0.56
GEI	BNY Mellon Inter Bond Inv	MIIDX	**C+**	(800) 645-6561	**C / 4.3**	1.90	1.44	1.11 /60	0.70 /37	1.93 /30	1.80	0.80
* GEI	BNY Mellon Inter Bond M	MPIBX	**B-**	(800) 645-6561	**C / 4.8**	1.97	1.56	1.36 /64	0.99 /42	2.19 /33	2.04	0.55
MUS	BNY Mellon MA Inter Mun Bd Inv	MMBIX	**A+**	(800) 645-6561	**B / 8.0**	1.22	2.67	2.86 /84	1.86 /75	3.55 /74	2.26	0.78
MUS	BNY Mellon MA Inter Mun Bd M	MMBMX	**A+**	(800) 645-6561	**B+ / 8.3**	1.36	2.88	3.11 /86	2.14 /79	3.83 /76	2.50	0.53
MM	BNY Mellon Money Market Fund M	MLMXX	**C-**	(800) 645-6561	**D / 1.9**	0.03	0.03	0.03 /36	0.01 /16	0.01 / 3	0.03	0.31
GL	● BNY Mellon Muni Opptys Fd Inv	MOTIX	**C+**	(800) 645-6561	**B / 8.1**	0.37	3.17	2.52 /75	3.47 /80	6.42 /79	3.31	0.96
GL	● BNY Mellon Muni Opptys Fd M	MOTMX	**C+**	(800) 645-6561	**B / 8.2**	0.35	3.22	2.71 /75	3.69 /82	6.69 /80	3.56	0.69
MUI	BNY Mellon National ST Muni Bd Inv	MINSX	**C+**	(800) 645-6561	**C- / 3.0**	0.14	0.19	0.20 /46	0.20 /30	0.66 /20	0.62	0.76
* MUI	BNY Mellon National ST Muni Bd M	MPSTX	**C+**	(800) 645-6561	**C- / 3.6**	0.20	0.23	0.37 /51	0.42 /36	0.88 /24	0.86	0.50
MUN	BNY Mellon Natl Int Muni Inv	MINMX	**A+**	(800) 645-6561	**B+ / 8.4**	1.15	2.68	2.89 /84	2.39 /81	4.15 /79	2.38	0.75
* MUN	BNY Mellon Natl Int Muni M	MPNIX	**A+**	(800) 645-6561	**B+ / 8.7**	1.28	2.80	3.22 /87	2.64 /84	4.42 /81	2.62	0.50
MUN	BNY Mellon NY Int TxEx Inv	MNYIX	**A+**	(800) 645-6561	**B+ / 8.4**	1.18	2.98	3.13 /86	2.26 /80	4.02 /78	2.34	0.96
MUS	BNY Mellon NY Int TxEx M	MNYMX	**A+**	(800) 645-6561	**B+ / 8.7**	1.24	3.11	3.38 /89	2.52 /83	4.28 /80	2.58	0.71
MUI	BNY Mellon PA Inter Muni Bond Inv	MIPAX	**A**	(800) 645-6561	**B / 7.7**	1.27	2.79	2.30 /79	1.69 /72	3.50 /74	2.34	0.93
MUI	BNY Mellon PA Inter Muni Bond M	MPPIX	**A+**	(800) 645-6561	**B / 8.1**	1.33	2.83	2.55 /81	1.95 /76	3.73 /76	2.58	0.68
USS	BNY Mellon ST US Gov Sec Inv	MISTX	**C**	(800) 645-6561	**D+ / 2.8**	0.71	0.21	0.25 /45	0.09 /27	0.10 /14	0.85	0.79
USS	BNY Mellon ST US Gov Sec M	MPSUX	**C+**	(800) 645-6561	**C- / 3.2**	0.77	0.35	0.59 /51	0.34 /30	0.37 /16	1.10	0.54
MM	BofA Cash Reserves Adviser	NCRXX	**C-**	(888) 331-0904	**D / 1.8**	0.02	0.02	0.02 /34	0.01 /16	0.01 / 3	0.02	0.52
MM	BofA Cash Reserves Cptl	CPMXX	**C**	(888) 331-0904	**D+ / 2.5**	0.08	0.11	0.14 /42	0.07 /26	0.09 /14	0.14	0.27
MM	BofA Cash Reserves Inst	NCIXX	**C**	(888) 331-0904	**D+ / 2.4**	0.07	0.09	0.10 /41	0.04 /24	0.06 /13	0.10	0.31
MM	BofA Cash Reserves Inst Cap	BOIXX	**C**	(888) 331-0904	**D+ / 2.5**	0.08	0.11	0.14 /42	0.07 /26	--	0.14	0.27
MM	BofA Cash Reserves Liqdty	NCLXX	**C**	(888) 331-0904	**D / 2.0**	0.05	0.05	0.05 /38	0.02 /19	0.02 / 7	0.05	0.52
MM	BofA Cash Reserves Trust	NRSXX	**C**	(888) 331-0904	**D / 2.0**	0.06	0.06	0.06 /39	0.02 /19	0.03 /10	0.06	0.37
MM	BofA Government Plus Rsv Adviser	GGCXX	**U**	(888) 331-0904	**U /**	--	--	--	--	--	0.04	0.59
MM	BofA Government Plus Rsv Cap	GIGXX	**C**	(888) 331-0904	**D+ / 2.4**	0.04	0.05	0.07 /40	0.05 /24	0.03 /10	0.07	0.34
MM	BofA Government Plus Rsv Daily	BOTXX	**U**	(888) 331-0904	**U /**	--	--	--	--	--	0.04	0.94
MM	BofA Government Plus Rsv Inst	CVIXX	**C**	(888) 331-0904	**D+ / 2.3**	0.03	0.04	0.06 /39	0.04 /24	0.03 /10	0.06	0.38
MM	BofA Government Plus Rsv Inst Cap	CVTXX	**C**	(888) 331-0904	**D+ / 2.4**	0.04	0.05	0.07 /40	0.05 /24	0.03 /10	0.07	0.34
MM	BofA Government Plus Rsv Investor	BOPXX	**U**	(888) 331-0904	**U /**	--	--	--	--	--	0.04	0.69
MM	BofA Government Plus Rsv Liqdty	CLQXX	**U**	(888) 331-0904	**U /**	--	--	--	--	--	0.04	0.59
MM	BofA Government Plus Rsv Trust	CGPXX	**U**	(888) 331-0904	**U /**	--	--	--	--	--	0.04	0.44
MM	BofA Government Plus Rsvs Inv II	BOGXX	**U**	(888) 331-0904	**U /**	--	--	--	--	--	0.04	0.79
MM	BofA Government Reserves Cap	CGCXX	**C**	(888) 331-0904	**D / 2.0**	0.03	0.03	0.04 /37	0.02 /19	0.01 / 4	0.04	0.27
MM	BofA Government Reserves Inst Cap	CGGXX	**C**	(888) 331-0904	**D / 2.0**	0.03	0.03	0.04 /37	0.02 /19	0.01 / 4	0.04	0.27
MM	BofA Government Reserves Instl	NVIXX	**C-**	(888) 331-0904	**D / 1.9**	0.02	0.02	0.03 /36	0.02 /19	0.01 / 4	0.03	0.31
MM	BofA Government Reserves Liqdty	NGLXX	**U**	(888) 331-0904	**U /**	--	--	--	--	--	0.01	0.52

● Denotes fund is closed to new investors
* Denotes fund is included in Section II

RISK			NET ASSETS		ASSET							FUND MANAGER		MINIMUM		LOADS	
Risk Rating/Pts	3 Yr Avg Standard Deviation	Avg Duration	NAV As of 3/31/16	Total $(Mil)	Cash %	Gov. Bond %	Muni. Bond %	Corp. Bond %	Other %	Portfolio Turnover Ratio	Avg Coupon Rate	Manager Quality Pct	Manager Tenure (Years)	Initial Purch. $	Additional Purch. $	Front End Load	Back End Load
C / 4.3	3.8	5.3	11.37	439	4	16	0	49	31	25	3.7	37	8	2,000,000	0	0.0	0.0
C / 4.3	3.8	5.3	11.37	523	4	16	0	49	31	25	3.7	29	8	1,000	50	0.0	0.0
D+ / 2.9	4.8	5.6	12.18	N/A	4	8	0	86	2	26	3.9	35	8	1,000	50	3.5	0.0
D+ / 2.9	4.8	5.6	12.17	118	4	8	0	86	2	26	3.9	40	8	2,000,000	0	0.0	0.0
D+ / 2.9	4.8	5.6	12.18	77	4	8	0	86	2	26	3.9	38	8	1,000	50	0.0	0.0
U /	N/A	3.7	9.37	4	3	39	0	56	2	60	3.3	N/A	3	1,000	50	3.5	2.0
U /	N/A	3.7	9.37	4	3	39	0	56	2	60	3.3	N/A	3	2,000,000	0	0.0	2.0
B- / 7.3	2.8	6.5	10.30	25	2	13	0	55	30	58	5.7	39	3	1,000	50	3.5	0.0
B- / 7.2	2.8	6.5	10.29	59	2	13	0	55	30	58	5.7	47	3	2,000,000	0	0.0	0.0
A+ / 9.9	0.3	0.4	10.07	N/A	0	0	99	0	1	57	1.6	72	1	1,000	50	2.0	0.0
A+ / 9.9	0.3	0.4	10.06	544	0	0	99	0	1	57	1.6	82	1	2,000,000	0	0.0	0.0
A+ / 9.9	0.3	0.4	10.07	57	0	0	99	0	1	57	1.6	75	1	1,000	50	0.0	0.0
C+ / 6.6	3.0	5.2	12.91	9	0	19	8	40	33	60	0.0	35	11	10,000	100	0.0	0.0
C+ / 6.7	3.0	5.2	12.94	1,007	0	19	8	40	33	60	0.0	44	11	10,000	100	0.0	0.0
C+ / 5.6	3.3	4.9	12.67	1	2	3	7	86	2	35	0.0	51	4	10,000	100	0.0	0.0
C+ / 5.6	3.3	4.9	12.68	772	2	3	7	86	2	35	0.0	61	4	10,000	100	0.0	0.0
B+ / 8.5	2.0	3.1	12.67	6	1	38	6	49	6	51	0.0	32	10	10,000	100	0.0	0.0
B+ / 8.5	2.0	3.1	12.67	861	1	38	6	49	6	51	0.0	41	10	10,000	100	0.0	0.0
B- / 7.4	2.7	4.3	12.99	9	0	0	99	0	1	42	0.0	30	10	10,000	100	0.0	0.0
B- / 7.3	2.8	4.3	13.00	339	0	0	99	0	1	42	0.0	37	10	10,000	100	0.0	0.0
A+ / 9.9	N/A	N/A	1.00	344	100	0	0	0	0	0	0.0	63	N/A	10,000	100	0.0	0.0
C / 4.3	3.8	3.6	13.19	17	0	0	100	0	0	42	0.0	99	8	10,000	100	0.0	0.0
C / 4.3	3.8	3.6	13.18	1,101	0	0	100	0	0	42	0.0	99	8	10,000	100	0.0	0.0
A+ / 9.6	0.7	1.5	12.81	6	2	0	97	0	1	34	0.0	46	1	10,000	100	0.0	0.0
A / 9.5	0.8	1.5	12.81	1,009	2	0	97	0	1	34	0.0	53	1	10,000	100	0.0	0.0
B- / 7.4	2.7	4.3	13.81	52	0	0	99	0	1	36	0.0	45	16	10,000	100	0.0	0.0
B- / 7.4	2.8	4.3	13.83	2,108	0	0	99	0	1	36	0.0	54	16	10,000	100	0.0	0.0
B- / 7.2	2.8	4.3	11.46	15	0	0	99	0	1	53	0.0	39	9	10,000	100	0.0	0.0
B- / 7.2	2.8	4.3	11.45	170	0	0	99	0	1	53	0.0	47	9	10,000	100	0.0	0.0
B- / 7.1	2.8	4.3	12.50	6	1	0	98	0	1	36	0.0	24	16	10,000	100	0.0	0.0
B- / 7.1	2.9	4.3	12.51	265	1	0	98	0	1	36	0.0	30	16	10,000	100	0.0	0.0
A+ / 9.6	0.7	1.9	11.82	2	1	62	4	0	33	105	0.0	47	16	10,000	100	0.0	0.0
A+ / 9.6	0.7	1.9	11.84	192	1	62	4	0	33	105	0.0	56	16	10,000	100	0.0	0.0
A+ / 9.9	N/A	N/A	1.00	1,043	100	0	0	0	0	0	0.0	63	N/A	100,000	0	0.0	0.0
A+ / 9.9	N/A	N/A	1.00	5,392	100	0	0	0	0	0	0.1	67	N/A	1,000,000	0	0.0	0.0
A+ / 9.9	N/A	N/A	1.00	143	100	0	0	0	0	0	0.1	63	N/A	750,000	0	0.0	0.0
A+ / 9.9	N/A	N/A	1.00	90	100	0	0	0	0	0	0.1	67	N/A	100,000	0	0.0	0.0
A+ / 9.9	N/A	N/A	1.00	21	100	0	0	0	0	0	0.1	63	N/A	500,000	0	0.0	0.0
A+ / 9.9	N/A	N/A	1.00	625	100	0	0	0	0	0	0.1	63	N/A	250,000	0	0.0	0.0
U /	N/A	N/A	1.00	2	100	0	0	0	0	0	0.0	N/A	N/A	100,000	0	0.0	0.0
A+ / 9.9	N/A	N/A	1.00	1,661	100	0	0	0	0	0	0.1	68	N/A	1,000,000	0	0.0	0.0
U /	N/A	N/A	1.00	N/A	100	0	0	0	0	0	0.0	N/A	N/A	2,500	0	0.0	0.0
A+ / 9.9	N/A	N/A	1.00	3	100	0	0	0	0	0	0.1	68	N/A	750,000	0	0.0	0.0
A+ / 9.9	N/A	N/A	1.00	1	100	0	0	0	0	0	0.1	68	N/A	100,000	0	0.0	0.0
U /	N/A	N/A	1.00	23	100	0	0	0	0	0	0.0	N/A	N/A	5,000	0	0.0	0.0
U /	N/A	N/A	1.00	N/A	100	0	0	0	0	0	0.0	N/A	N/A	500,000	0	0.0	0.0
U /	N/A	N/A	1.00	35	100	0	0	0	0	0	0.0	N/A	N/A	250,000	0	0.0	0.0
U /	N/A	N/A	1.00	6	100	0	0	0	0	0	0.0	N/A	N/A	2,500	0	0.0	0.0
A+ / 9.9	N/A	N/A	1.00	2,961	100	0	0	0	0	0	0.0	64	N/A	1,000,000	0	0.0	0.0
A+ / 9.9	N/A	N/A	1.00	38	100	0	0	0	0	0	0.0	64	N/A	100,000	0	0.0	0.0
A+ / 9.9	N/A	N/A	1.00	80	100	0	0	0	0	0	0.0	64	N/A	750,000	0	0.0	0.0
U /	N/A	N/A	1.00	23	100	0	0	0	0	0	0.0	N/A	N/A	500,000	0	0.0	0.0

Fund Type	Fund Name (99 Pct = Best; 0 Pct = Worst)	Ticker Symbol	Overall Investment Rating	Phone	PERFORMANCE: Performance Rating/Pts	Total Return % through 3/31/16: 3 Mo	6 Mo	1Yr / Pct	Annualized: 3Yr / Pct	5Yr / Pct	Incl. in Returns: Dividend Yield	Expense Ratio
MM	BofA Government Reserves Trust	NGOXX	**U**	(888) 331-0904	**U /**	0.01	0.01	0.02 /34	0.01 /16	0.01 / 4	0.01	0.37
MM	BofA Money Market Reserves	NRAXX	**C-**	(888) 331-0904	**D / 1.9**	0.03	0.03	0.03 /36	0.01 /16	0.01 / 4	0.03	0.51
MM	BofA Money Market Reserves Cap	NMCXX	**C**	(888) 331-0904	**D+ / 2.6**	0.09	0.13	0.17 /43	0.09 /27	0.10 /15	0.17	0.26
MM	BofA Money Market Reserves Inst	NRIXX	**C**	(888) 331-0904	**D+ / 2.4**	0.08	0.11	0.13 /42	0.05 /24	0.06 /13	0.13	0.30
MM	BofA Money Market Reserves Inst	CVGXX	**C**	(888) 331-0904	**D+ / 2.6**	0.09	0.13	0.17 /43	0.09 /27	0.10 /15	0.17	0.26
MM	BofA Money Market Reserves Liqdty	NRLXX	**C**	(888) 331-0904	**D / 2.0**	0.06	0.06	0.06 /39	0.02 /19	0.01 / 4	0.06	0.51
MM	BofA Money Market Reserves Trust	NRTXX	**C**	(888) 331-0904	**D+ / 2.3**	0.07	0.08	0.08 /40	0.03 /22	0.02 / 7	0.08	0.36
MM	BofA Treasury Reserves Cap	CPLXX	**C**	(888) 331-0904	**D / 2.0**	0.03	0.03	0.04 /37	0.02 /19	0.01 / 4	0.04	0.26
MM	BofA Treasury Reserves Daily	NDLXX	**U**	(888) 331-0904	**U /**	--	--	--	--	--	0.01	0.86
MM	BofA Treasury Reserves Inst	NTIXX	**U**	(888) 331-0904	**U /**	0.02	0.02	0.03 /36	0.02 /19	0.01 / 4	0.03	0.30
MM	BofA Treasury Reserves Inst Cap	BOUXX	**C**	(888) 331-0904	**D / 2.0**	0.03	0.03	0.04 /37	0.02 /19	--	0.04	0.26
MM	BofA Treasury Reserves Trust	NTTXX	**U**	(888) 331-0904	**U /**	--	--	--	--	--	0.01	0.36
EM	Bradesco LA Hard Curr Bd Inst	BHCIX	**U**	(888) 739-1390	**U /**	6.15	4.63	-5.88 / 3	--	--	3.40	2.84
EM	Bradesco LA Hard Curr Bd Retail	BHCRX	**U**	(888) 739-1390	**U /**	6.08	4.49	-6.09 / 3	--	--	3.16	3.09
GL	Brandes Core Plus Fixed Inc A	BCPAX	**C-**	(800) 237-7119	**C- / 4.0**	3.24	1.12	0.31 /46	1.66 /55	--	2.19	1.39
GL	● Brandes Core Plus Fixed Inc E	BCPEX	**C+**	(800) 237-7119	**C+ / 6.0**	3.34	1.13	0.34 /47	1.79 /57	3.62 /55	2.29	1.39
GL	Brandes Core Plus Fixed Inc I	BCPIX	**B**	(800) 237-7119	**C+ / 6.3**	3.28	1.12	0.53 /50	1.99 /61	3.78 /58	2.49	1.19
GL	Brandes Credit Focus Yield A	BCFAX	**D+**	(800) 237-7119	**D- / 1.4**	3.16	0.28	-1.49 /18	0.57 /34	2.94 /44	2.57	1.51
GL	Brandes Credit Focus Yield I	BCFIX	**C-**	(800) 237-7119	**C- / 4.0**	3.12	0.30	-1.34 /19	0.87 /40	3.18 /48	2.92	1.31
COH	Brandes Separately Mgd Acct Res	SMARX	**C-**	(800) 237-7119	**C+ / 6.5**	3.79	0.14	-1.94 /16	2.57 /72	5.00 /72	5.21	0.77
GEN	Bridge Builder Core Bond	BBTBX	**U**	(855) 823-3611	**U /**	3.10	2.38	2.15 /73	--	--	2.42	0.39
COI	Bridge Builder Core Plus Bond	BBCPX	**U**	(855) 823-3611	**U /**	2.02	0.75	--	--	--	0.00	0.44
MUN	Bridge Builder Municipal Bond	BBMUX	**U**	(855) 823-3611	**U /**	0.89	1.75	--	--	--	0.00	0.48
GEI	Brown Advisory Interm Income Adv	BAIAX	**C+**	(800) 540-6807	**C / 4.8**	1.91	1.55	1.19 /61	1.01 /43	2.30 /35	1.77	0.84
GEI	Brown Advisory Interm Income Inv	BIAIX	**B-**	(800) 540-6807	**C / 5.3**	2.03	1.64	1.42 /65	1.24 /47	2.54 /38	1.98	0.59
MUS	Brown Advisory Maryland Bond Inv	BIAMX	**A+**	(800) 540-6807	**B / 7.8**	1.39	2.32	2.66 /82	1.70 /72	2.72 /64	1.94	0.50
MTG	Brown Advisory Mortgage Sec Ins	BAFZX	**U**	(800) 540-6807	**U /**	2.14	1.73	2.26 /73	--	--	2.53	0.47
MTG	Brown Advisory Mortgage Sec Inv	BIAZX	**U**	(800) 540-6807	**U /**	2.12	1.67	2.18 /73	--	--	2.45	0.52
GEL	Brown Advisory Strategic Bond Adv	BATBX	**D**	(800) 540-6807	**D- / 1.2**	0.31	-0.04	-2.31 /14	-0.35 /13	--	3.97	1.00
MUN	Brown Advisory Tax Exempt Bd Inv	BIAEX	**A+**	(800) 540-6807	**B / 8.0**	1.38	2.52	2.48 /80	1.94 /76	--	2.23	0.51
GL	Brown Advisory Total Return Instl	BAFTX	**U**	(800) 540-6807	**U /**	2.47	2.10	1.15 /61	--	--	2.72	0.56
GL	Brown Advisory Total Return Inv	BIATX	**U**	(800) 540-6807	**U /**	2.46	2.07	1.09 /60	--	--	2.67	0.61
GEN	BTS Tactical Fixed Income A	BTFAX	**U**	(877) 287-9820	**U /**	8.12	4.92	4.50 /84	--	--	0.77	2.08
GEN	BTS Tactical Fixed Income C	BTFCX	**U**	(877) 287-9820	**U /**	7.89	4.42	3.68 /80	--	--	0.22	2.83
COH	Buffalo High Yield Fund	BUFHX	**C-**	(800) 492-8332	**C+ / 6.7**	0.50	0.67	-0.43 /27	3.38 /79	4.82 /70	4.04	1.03
MUS	CA Tax-Free Income Direct	CFNTX	**A+**	(800) 955-9988	**B+ / 8.7**	1.23	2.09	2.67 /82	2.73 /85	4.71 /83	2.37	0.71
COH	Calamos High Income A	CHYDX	**E**	(800) 582-6959	**E+ / 0.6**	1.15	-0.62	-5.75 / 3	0.23 /29	2.91 /44	5.09	1.29
COH	● Calamos High Income B	CAHBX	**E**	(800) 582-6959	**E+ / 0.8**	1.00	-0.98	-6.40 / 3	-0.52 /11	2.14 /33	4.21	2.03
COH	Calamos High Income C	CCHYX	**E**	(800) 582-6959	**E+ / 0.8**	1.02	-0.97	-6.33 / 3	-0.50 /11	2.16 /33	4.29	2.04
COH	Calamos High Income I	CIHYX	**E+**	(800) 582-6959	**D- / 1.5**	1.21	-0.50	-5.51 / 4	0.45 /32	3.17 /48	5.61	1.04
COH	Calamos High Income R	CHYRX	**E+**	(800) 582-6959	**D- / 1.1**	1.08	-0.75	-5.88 / 3	-0.02 /15	2.66 /40	5.09	1.54
GEI	Calamos Total Return Bond A	CTRAX	**B**	(800) 582-6959	**C+ / 6.1**	2.82	2.82	1.93 /71	2.65 /73	2.81 /42	2.66	1.12
GEI	● Calamos Total Return Bond B	CTXBX	**B+**	(800) 582-6959	**C+ / 6.4**	2.64	2.45	1.27 /63	1.89 /59	2.05 /32	2.03	1.87
GEI	Calamos Total Return Bond C	CTRCX	**B+**	(800) 582-6959	**C+ / 6.4**	2.64	2.45	1.27 /63	1.89 /59	2.05 /32	2.03	1.87
GEI	Calamos Total Return Bond I	CTRIX	**A+**	(800) 582-6959	**B / 7.8**	2.88	2.95	2.28 /74	2.91 /75	3.06 /46	3.01	0.87
GEI	Calamos Total Return Bond R	CTRRX	**A**	(800) 582-6959	**B- / 7.2**	2.76	2.70	1.78 /70	2.39 /69	2.55 /38	2.52	1.37
GEI	Calvert Bond Portfolio A	CSIBX	**D+**	(800) 368-2745	**C- / 3.1**	2.20	2.00	0.02 /33	1.81 /58	3.51 /53	2.40	1.12
GEI	Calvert Bond Portfolio C	CSBCX	**D+**	(800) 368-2745	**C- / 3.3**	1.99	1.57	-0.85 /23	0.98 /42	2.67 /40	1.64	1.92
GEI	Calvert Bond Portfolio I	CBDIX	**C**	(800) 368-2745	**C+ / 6.8**	2.29	2.15	0.49 /49	2.37 /69	4.09 /63	2.96	0.50
GEI	Calvert Bond Portfolio Y	CSIYX	**C-**	(800) 368-2745	**C / 5.5**	2.25	2.13	0.26 /45	2.10 /63	3.80 /58	2.71	0.85
COI	Calvert Green Bond A	CGAFX	**U**	(800) 368-2745	**U /**	2.64	1.99	0.68 /53	--	--	1.45	1.99
COI	Calvert Green Bond I	CGBIX	**U**	(800) 368-2745	**U /**	2.74	2.25	1.20 /62	--	--	1.89	1.17

● Denotes fund is closed to new investors
* Denotes fund is included in Section II

RISK			NET ASSETS		ASSET							FUND MANAGER		MINIMUM		LOADS	
Risk Rating/Pts	3 Yr Avg Standard Deviation	Avg Duration	NAV As of 3/31/16	Total $(Mil)	Cash %	Gov. Bond %	Muni. Bond %	Corp. Bond %	Other %	Portfolio Turnover Ratio	Avg Coupon Rate	Manager Quality Pct	Manager Tenure (Years)	Initial Purch. $	Additional Purch. $	Front End Load	Back End Load
U /	N/A	N/A	1.00	1,654	100	0	0	0	0	0	0.0	N/A	N/A	250,000	0	0.0	0.0
A+ / 9.9	N/A	N/A	1.00	310	100	0	0	0	0	0	0.0	63	N/A	100,000	0	0.0	0.0
A+ / 9.9	N/A	N/A	1.00	16,710	100	0	0	0	0	0	0.2	69	N/A	1,000,000	0	0.0	0.0
A+ / 9.9	N/A	N/A	1.00	276	100	0	0	0	0	0	0.1	64	N/A	750,000	0	0.0	0.0
A+ / 9.9	N/A	N/A	1.00	784	100	0	0	0	0	0	0.2	69	N/A	100,000	0	0.0	0.0
A+ / 9.9	N/A	N/A	1.00	6	100	0	0	0	0	0	0.1	62	N/A	500,000	0	0.0	0.0
A+ / 9.9	N/A	N/A	1.00	318	100	0	0	0	0	0	0.1	62	N/A	250,000	0	0.0	0.0
A+ / 9.9	N/A	N/A	1.00	5,823	100	0	0	0	0	0	0.0	64	N/A	1,000,000	0	0.0	0.0
U /	N/A	N/A	1.00	226	100	0	0	0	0	0	0.0	N/A	N/A	2,500	0	0.0	0.0
U /	N/A	N/A	1.00	290	100	0	0	0	0	0	0.0	N/A	N/A	750,000	0	0.0	0.0
A+ / 9.9	N/A	N/A	1.00	405	100	0	0	0	0	0	0.0	64	N/A	100,000	0	0.0	0.0
U /	N/A	N/A	1.00	658	100	0	0	0	0	0	0.0	N/A	N/A	250,000	0	0.0	0.0
U /	N/A	N/A	8.98	14	0	0	0	0	100	109	0.0	N/A	3	1,000,000	0	0.0	2.0
U /	N/A	N/A	9.00	N/A	0	0	0	0	100	109	0.0	N/A	3	1,000	250	0.0	2.0
B- / 7.0	2.9	N/A	9.12	3	3	63	0	27	7	11	0.0	94	9	2,500	500	3.8	0.0
C+ / 6.9	2.9	N/A	9.20	N/A	3	63	0	27	7	11	0.0	95	9	2,500	500	0.0	0.0
B- / 7.1	2.8	N/A	9.17	75	3	63	0	27	7	11	0.0	96	9	100,000	500	0.0	0.0
B- / 7.2	2.8	N/A	9.90	2	4	36	0	53	7	26	0.0	84	16	2,500	500	3.8	0.0
B- / 7.2	2.8	N/A	9.89	27	4	36	0	53	7	26	0.0	88	16	100,000	500	0.0	0.0
C- / 3.8	3.6	N/A	8.47	158	2	31	0	54	13	33	0.0	95	11	0	0	0.0	0.0
U /	N/A	5.3	10.28	10,093	1	23	0	30	46	115	0.0	N/A	3	0	0	0.0	0.0
U /	N/A	5.5	10.09	2,228	1	30	0	32	37	0	0.0	N/A	1	0	0	0.0	0.0
U /	N/A	N/A	10.21	1,322	0	0	0	0	100	0	0.0	N/A	1	0	0	0.0	0.0
B / 8.2	2.3	3.7	10.46	9	4	14	19	26	37	130	5.0	34	24	2,000	100	0.0	0.0
B / 8.2	2.3	3.7	10.67	145	4	14	19	26	37	130	5.0	40	24	5,000	100	0.0	0.0
B+ / 8.4	2.1	3.8	10.80	184	2	0	97	0	1	61	4.7	46	2	5,000	100	0.0	0.0
U /	N/A	N/A	10.15	367	0	0	1	0	99	147	0.0	N/A	3	1,000,000	100	0.0	0.0
U /	N/A	N/A	10.15	2	0	0	1	0	99	147	0.0	N/A	3	5,000	100	0.0	0.0
C+ / 5.7	3.2	2.2	9.34	1	3	0	5	32	60	317	0.0	12	5	2,000	100	0.0	0.0
B / 8.0	2.4	N/A	10.10	222	1	0	98	0	1	109	0.0	42	4	5,000	100	0.0	0.0
U /	N/A	N/A	9.94	79	0	5	2	28	65	235	0.0	N/A	1	1,000,000	100	0.0	0.0
U /	N/A	N/A	9.94	2	0	5	2	28	65	235	0.0	N/A	1	5,000	100	0.0	0.0
U /	N/A	N/A	10.27	139	33	0	0	65	2	190	0.0	N/A	3	1,000	100	5.0	1.0
U /	N/A	N/A	10.18	42	33	0	0	65	2	190	0.0	N/A	3	1,000	100	0.0	1.0
C- / 3.9	3.5	N/A	11.04	283	10	0	0	66	24	25	0.0	97	13	2,500	100	0.0	2.0
B / 7.6	2.6	4.4	11.82	89	0	0	99	0	1	12	4.3	61	13	1,000	100	0.0	0.0
D- / 1.3	5.8	4.9	8.16	59	1	0	0	96	3	65	6.1	19	17	2,500	50	4.8	0.0
D- / 1.3	5.8	4.9	8.64	1	1	0	0	96	3	65	6.1	10	17	2,500	50	0.0	0.0
D- / 1.2	5.8	4.9	8.55	18	1	0	0	96	3	65	6.1	10	17	2,500	50	0.0	0.0
D- / 1.3	5.8	4.9	8.16	15	1	0	0	96	3	65	6.1	23	17	1,000,000	0	0.0	0.0
D- / 1.3	5.8	4.9	8.15	N/A	1	0	0	96	3	65	6.1	15	17	0	0	0.0	0.0
B / 7.8	2.6	4.8	10.43	59	3	10	0	86	1	80	3.5	87	9	2,500	50	3.8	0.0
B / 7.8	2.5	4.8	10.43	1	3	10	0	86	1	80	3.5	67	9	2,500	50	0.0	0.0
B / 7.8	2.5	4.8	10.43	17	3	10	0	86	1	80	3.5	69	9	2,500	50	0.0	0.0
B / 7.8	2.5	4.8	10.43	19	3	10	0	86	1	80	3.5	90	9	1,000,000	0	0.0	0.0
B / 7.8	2.6	4.8	10.43	N/A	3	10	0	86	1	80	3.5	83	9	0	0	0.0	0.0
C / 4.6	3.6	5.4	15.94	395	3	6	3	61	27	241	3.9	27	5	2,000	250	3.8	2.0
C / 4.6	3.6	5.4	15.84	33	3	6	3	61	27	241	3.9	13	5	2,000	250	0.0	2.0
C / 4.7	3.6	5.4	15.95	309	3	6	3	61	27	241	3.9	43	5	1,000,000	0	0.0	0.0
C / 4.6	3.7	5.4	16.05	89	3	6	3	61	27	241	3.9	34	5	2,000	250	0.0	2.0
U /	N/A	5.3	15.29	27	15	28	6	36	15	444	3.0	N/A	3	2,000	250	3.8	2.0
U /	N/A	5.3	15.29	25	15	28	6	36	15	444	3.0	N/A	3	1,000,000	0	0.0	0.0

Fund Type	Fund Name (99 Pct = Best, 0 Pct = Worst)	Ticker Symbol	Overall Investment Rating	Phone	PERFORMANCE: Performance Rating/Pts	Total Return % through 3/31/16: 3 Mo	6 Mo	1Yr / Pct	Annualized: 3Yr / Pct	Annualized: 5Yr / Pct	Incl. in Returns: Dividend Yield	Expense Ratio
COI	Calvert Green Bond Y	CGYFX	**U**	(800) 368-2745	**U /**	2.70	2.12	0.87 /56	--	--	1.75	14.21
COH	Calvert High Yield Bond A	CYBAX	**D-**	(800) 368-2745	**D- / 1.5**	2.56	1.44	-1.65 /17	1.32 /49	4.45 /67	5.04	1.37
COH	Calvert High Yield Bond C	CHBCX	**D-**	(800) 368-2745	**D- / 1.5**	2.35	0.95	-2.59 /13	0.33 /30	--	4.18	2.15
COH	Calvert High Yield Bond I	CYBIX	**D+**	(800) 368-2745	**C / 5.3**	2.64	1.60	-1.34 /19	1.64 /55	4.91 /71	5.64	0.89
COH	Calvert High Yield Bond Y	CYBYX	**D**	(800) 368-2745	**C- / 4.2**	2.59	1.54	-1.41 /19	1.57 /53	4.70 /70	5.26	1.04
GEI	Calvert Income A	CFICX	**D**	(800) 368-2745	**C- / 3.0**	3.04	2.53	-0.33 /28	1.64 /55	3.06 /46	2.80	1.25
GEI	Calvert Income C	CIFCX	**D+**	(800) 368-2745	**C- / 3.4**	2.85	2.15	-1.06 /21	0.92 /41	2.33 /35	2.17	1.94
GEI	Calvert Income I	CINCX	**C**	(800) 368-2745	**C+ / 6.8**	3.14	2.78	0.27 /45	2.27 /67	3.69 /56	3.44	0.62
GEI	Calvert Income R	CICRX	**C-**	(800) 368-2745	**C / 5.1**	2.91	2.33	-0.64 /25	1.32 /49	2.80 /42	2.57	1.69
GEI	Calvert Income Y	CIFYX	**C-**	(800) 368-2745	**C / 5.3**	3.08	2.66	-0.04 /31	1.89 /59	3.36 /51	3.16	0.89
GEI	Calvert Long Term Income A	CLDAX	**D+**	(800) 368-2745	**B- / 7.1**	6.07	5.26	-1.07 /21	3.88 /83	5.91 /76	2.68	1.27
COI	Calvert Long Term Income I	CLDIX	**C-**	(800) 368-2745	**B+ / 8.6**	6.22	5.66	-0.25 /28	4.14 /85	6.06 /77	3.54	N/A
* COI	Calvert Short Duration Income A	CSDAX	**C-**	(800) 368-2745	**D- / 1.4**	1.25	0.78	0.41 /48	0.73 /37	1.68 /27	1.86	1.14
COI	Calvert Short Duration Income C	CDICX	**C-**	(800) 368-2745	**D- / 1.3**	1.06	0.34	-0.33 /28	-0.02 /15	0.95 /20	1.18	1.80
COI	Calvert Short Duration Income I	CDSIX	**B**	(800) 368-2745	**C / 5.1**	1.34	1.01	0.94 /57	1.31 /48	2.25 /34	2.44	0.48
COI	Calvert Short Duration Income Y	CSDYX	**C+**	(800) 368-2745	**C- / 3.5**	1.31	0.91	0.68 /53	1.02 /43	2.00 /31	2.16	0.76
MUN	Calvert TF Responsible Impact Bd A	CTTLX	**C**	(800) 368-2745	**B- / 7.3**	1.10	3.07	3.58 /91	2.33 /81	4.65 /82	2.51	0.94
MUN	Calvert TF Responsible Impact Bd C	CTTCX	**C**	(800) 368-2745	**B- / 7.5**	0.90	2.78	2.79 /83	1.45 /66	3.73 /76	1.83	N/A
MUN	Calvert TF Responsible Impact Bd I	CTTIX	**B-**	(800) 368-2745	**B+ / 8.6**	1.13	3.25	3.82 /93	2.41 /82	4.70 /83	2.72	N/A
MUN	Calvert TF Responsible Impact Bd Y	CTTYX	**B-**	(800) 368-2745	**B+ / 8.6**	1.17	3.20	3.76 /92	2.39 /81	4.68 /83	2.66	N/A
GEI	Calvert Ultra-Short Inc A	CULAX	**C**	(800) 368-2745	**D+ / 2.7**	0.19	0.32	0.17 /43	0.49 /33	0.78 /19	0.81	1.04
GEI	Calvert Ultra-Short Inc I	CULIX	**B-**	(800) 368-2745	**C- / 3.8**	0.29	0.53	0.55 /50	0.73 /37	0.93 /20	1.20	N/A
GEI	Calvert Ultra-Short Inc Y	CULYX	**C+**	(800) 368-2745	**C- / 3.6**	0.21	0.40	0.34 /47	0.67 /36	0.99 /20	1.04	0.67
MUS	Capital Group California Core Muni	CCCMX	**A+**	(800) 421-0180	**B+ / 8.4**	1.52	2.29	2.82 /83	2.33 /81	3.60 /75	1.92	0.42
MUN	Capital Group California Sh-Tm Muni	CCSTX	**B+**	(800) 421-0180	**C / 5.0**	0.55	0.52	0.96 /66	0.84 /48	1.47 /34	1.05	0.46
GES	Capital Group Core Bond	CCBPX	**B**	(800) 421-0180	**C+ / 5.6**	2.35	1.74	1.65 /68	1.39 /50	2.57 /39	1.63	0.42
MUN	Capital Group Core Municipal	CCMPX	**A+**	(800) 421-0180	**B / 7.6**	1.07	1.65	2.08 /78	1.71 /72	3.16 /71	1.97	0.42
MUN	Capital Group Short-Term Municipal	CSTMX	**B+**	(800) 421-0180	**C / 5.2**	0.65	0.75	1.05 /68	0.84 /48	1.54 /36	1.13	0.46
MM	Cash Reserve Prime Inst Shares	ABPXX	**C**	(800) 728-3337	**D / 2.2**	0.05	0.05	0.06 /39	0.03 /22	0.02 / 7	0.06	0.30
MM	Cash Reserve Prime Shares	ABRXX	**U**	(800) 728-3337	**U /**	0.00	0.01	0.01 /32	0.01 /16	0.01 / 4	0.01	0.68
COI	Catalyst Insider Income A	IIXAX	**U**	(866) 447-4228	**U /**	1.61	-2.61	-2.13 /15	--	--	2.24	14.21
COI	Catalyst Insider Income C	IIXCX	**U**	(866) 447-4228	**U /**	1.29	-2.98	-2.73 /12	--	--	1.61	14.96
COI	Catalyst Insider Income I	IIXIX	**U**	(866) 447-4228	**U /**	1.67	-2.49	-1.78 /17	--	--	2.60	13.96
GEN	Catalyst Princeton Hedged Income A	HIFAX	**U**	(866) 447-4228	**U /**	0.51	-4.49	-8.03 / 1	--	--	4.57	19.02
GEN	Catalyst Princeton Hedged Income C	HIFCX	**U**	(866) 447-4228	**U /**	0.32	-4.76	-8.66 / 1	--	--	3.95	19.77
GEN	Catalyst Princeton Hedged Income I	HIFIX	**U**	(866) 447-4228	**U /**	0.70	-4.26	-7.70 / 2	--	--	5.06	18.77
LP	Catalyst/Princeton Float Rate Inc A	CFRAX	**D-**	(866) 447-4228	**E- / 0.2**	-1.82	-7.45	-8.90 / 1	-0.70 /10	--	6.32	1.60
LP	Catalyst/Princeton Float Rate Inc C	CFRCX	**D-**	(866) 447-4228	**E- / 0.2**	-1.99	-7.82	-9.61 / 1	-1.45 / 6	--	5.81	2.35
LP	Catalyst/Princeton Float Rate Inc I	CFRIX	**D-**	(866) 447-4228	**E / 0.4**	-1.75	-7.32	-8.66 / 1	-0.46 /12	--	6.93	1.35
COH	Catalyst/SMH High Income A	HIIFX	**E-**	(866) 447-4228	**E- / 0.0**	7.99	0.51	-25.42 / 0	-13.08 / 0	-6.60 / 0	10.98	1.57
COH	Catalyst/SMH High Income C	HIICX	**E-**	(866) 447-4228	**E- / 0.0**	7.44	0.14	-26.15 / 0	-13.73 / 0	-7.30 / 0	10.65	2.32
COH	Catalyst/SMH High Income I	HIIIX	**U**	(866) 447-4228	**U /**	7.69	0.64	-25.38 / 0	--	--	11.83	1.32
MTG	Catalyst/Stone Beach Income Oppty	IOXAX	**U**	(866) 447-4228	**U /**	0.96	0.46	-0.90 /22	--	--	3.26	6.59
MTG	Catalyst/Stone Beach Income Oppty	IOXCX	**U**	(866) 447-4228	**U /**	0.79	0.08	-1.66 /17	--	--	2.78	7.34
MTG	Catalyst/Stone Beach Income Oppty I	IOXIX	**U**	(866) 447-4228	**U /**	1.02	0.69	-0.72 /24	--	--	3.74	6.34
GL	Cavalier Hedged High Income Adv	CAHIX	**D+**	(877) 773-3863	**C / 5.2**	1.42	-0.37	-0.56 /25	1.73 /56	--	2.56	2.55
GL	Cavalier Hedged High Income Inst	CHIIX	**C-**	(877) 773-3863	**B- / 7.4**	1.64	0.12	0.44 /48	3.07 /77	--	3.15	1.55
GEI	Cavalier Stable Income Adv	CADAX	**C-**	(877) 773-3863	**D+ / 2.7**	2.99	1.42	0.09 /41	-0.24 /14	0.76 /19	0.40	3.27
GEI	Cavalier Stable Income Inst	CADTX	**C+**	(877) 773-3863	**C / 4.6**	3.28	1.88	1.08 /60	0.76 /38	1.78 /28	1.16	2.27
COI	Cavanal Hill Bond A	AABOX	**B**	(800) 762-7085	**C+ / 5.9**	2.58	1.67	1.73 /69	2.17 /65	--	1.87	1.16
GEI	Cavanal Hill Bond Inst	AIBNX	**A**	(800) 762-7085	**B- / 7.2**	2.64	1.79	1.98 /72	2.42 /69	4.17 /64	2.15	1.06
GEI	Cavanal Hill Bond NL Inv	APBDX	**A-**	(800) 762-7085	**C+ / 6.8**	2.58	1.88	1.91 /71	2.19 /65	3.94 /60	1.87	1.31

● Denotes fund is closed to new investors
* Denotes fund is included in Section II

RISK			NET ASSETS		ASSET							FUND MANAGER		MINIMUM		LOADS	
Risk Rating/Pts	3 Yr Avg Standard Deviation	Avg Duration	NAV As of 3/31/16	Total $(Mil)	Cash %	Gov. Bond %	Muni. Bond %	Corp. Bond %	Other %	Portfolio Turnover Ratio	Avg Coupon Rate	Manager Quality Pct	Manager Tenure (Years)	Initial Purch. $	Additional Purch. $	Front End Load	Back End Load
U /	N/A	5.3	15.32	13	15	28	6	36	15	444	3.0	N/A	3	2,000	250	0.0	2.0
D+ / 2.3	4.9	2.7	26.00	65	3	0	0	89	8	198	7.1	60	6	2,000	250	3.8	2.0
D+ / 2.3	4.9	2.7	26.35	5	3	0	0	89	8	198	7.1	27	6	2,000	250	0.0	2.0
D+ / 2.4	4.9	2.7	25.65	68	3	0	0	89	8	198	7.1	77	6	1,000,000	0	0.0	0.0
D+ / 2.4	4.9	2.7	27.17	16	3	0	0	89	8	198	7.1	74	6	2,000	250	0.0	2.0
C / 4.4	3.8	6.7	16.05	441	3	7	0	64	26	236	4.3	24	3	2,000	250	3.8	2.0
C / 4.4	3.7	6.7	16.05	84	3	7	0	64	26	236	4.3	13	3	2,000	250	0.0	2.0
C / 4.4	3.7	6.7	16.07	30	3	7	0	64	26	236	4.3	42	3	1,000,000	0	0.0	0.0
C / 4.4	3.7	6.7	16.18	4	3	7	0	64	26	236	4.3	18	3	0	0	0.0	0.0
C / 4.4	3.7	6.7	16.23	57	3	7	0	64	26	236	4.3	30	3	2,000	250	0.0	2.0
E / 0.5	7.5	12.7	17.21	71	1	22	1	63	13	290	4.2	13	3	2,000	250	3.8	2.0
E / 0.5	7.5	12.7	17.22	N/A	1	22	1	63	13	290	4.2	40	3	1,000,000	0	0.0	0.0
B+ / 8.9	1.5	2.5	15.92	669	3	6	0	57	34	206	3.4	56	7	2,000	250	2.8	2.0
B+ / 8.9	1.5	2.5	15.86	139	3	6	0	57	34	206	3.4	31	7	2,000	250	0.0	2.0
B+ / 8.9	1.4	2.5	16.01	226	3	6	0	57	34	206	3.4	82	7	1,000,000	0	0.0	0.0
B+ / 8.9	1.5	2.5	16.05	337	3	6	0	57	34	206	3.4	72	7	2,000	250	0.0	2.0
C- / 3.9	4.0	4.4	16.10	142	0	0	98	0	2	79	4.5	14	12	2,000	250	3.8	0.0
C- / 3.9	4.0	4.4	16.11	1	0	0	98	0	2	79	4.5	8	12	2,000	250	0.0	0.0
C- / 3.9	4.0	4.4	16.12	4	0	0	98	0	2	79	4.5	16	12	1,000,000	0	0.0	0.0
C- / 3.9	4.0	4.4	16.12	2	0	0	98	0	2	79	4.5	15	12	2,000	250	0.0	0.0
A+ / 9.8	0.5	0.2	15.47	468	12	0	3	49	36	66	2.3	81	4	2,000	250	1.3	0.0
A+ / 9.8	0.4	0.2	15.48	37	12	0	3	49	36	66	2.3	85	4	1,000,000	0	0.0	0.0
A+ / 9.8	0.4	0.2	15.51	207	12	0	3	49	36	66	2.3	85	4	2,000	250	0.0	0.0
B / 8.0	2.4	N/A	10.71	320	1	0	95	0	4	13	0.0	59	6	25,000	0	0.0	0.0
A- / 9.1	1.2	N/A	10.26	111	6	0	93	0	1	23	0.0	55	6	25,000	0	0.0	0.0
B+ / 8.3	2.2	N/A	10.28	336	0	49	2	26	23	126	0.0	47	6	25,000	0	0.0	0.0
B+ / 8.5	1.9	N/A	10.53	389	0	0	99	0	1	16	0.0	54	6	25,000	0	0.0	0.0
A / 9.4	0.9	N/A	10.13	164	1	0	90	0	9	27	0.0	72	6	25,000	0	0.0	0.0
A+ / 9.9	N/A	N/A	1.00	233	100	0	0	0	0	0	0.1	64	N/A	1,000,000	0	0.0	0.0
U /	N/A	N/A	1.00	634	100	0	0	0	0	0	0.0	N/A	N/A	1,500	0	0.0	0.0
U /	N/A	N/A	9.01	1	8	0	0	67	25	58	0.0	N/A	2	2,500	50	4.8	0.0
U /	N/A	N/A	9.01	N/A	8	0	0	67	25	58	0.0	N/A	2	2,500	50	0.0	0.0
U /	N/A	N/A	9.01	N/A	8	0	0	67	25	58	0.0	N/A	2	2,500	50	0.0	0.0
U /	N/A	N/A	8.28	N/A	8	3	0	83	6	460	0.0	N/A	2	2,500	50	4.8	0.0
U /	N/A	N/A	8.28	N/A	8	3	0	83	6	460	0.0	N/A	2	2,500	50	0.0	0.0
U /	N/A	N/A	8.28	N/A	8	3	0	83	6	460	0.0	N/A	2	2,500	50	0.0	0.0
C- / 3.4	4.3	N/A	8.69	8	0	0	0	22	78	102	0.0	28	4	2,500	50	4.8	0.0
C- / 3.5	4.3	N/A	8.67	5	0	0	0	22	78	102	0.0	14	4	2,500	50	0.0	0.0
C- / 3.4	4.4	N/A	8.69	5	0	0	0	22	78	102	0.0	33	4	2,500	50	0.0	0.0
E- / 0.0	14.0	N/A	3.12	11	9	0	0	84	7	42	0.0	0	8	2,500	50	4.8	0.0
E- / 0.0	13.9	N/A	3.12	12	9	0	0	84	7	42	0.0	0	8	2,500	50	0.0	0.0
U /	N/A	N/A	3.12	3	9	0	0	84	7	42	0.0	N/A	8	2,500	50	0.0	0.0
U /	N/A	N/A	9.78	N/A	11	0	0	0	89	19	0.0	N/A	N/A	2,500	50	5.8	0.0
U /	N/A	N/A	9.77	N/A	11	0	0	0	89	19	0.0	N/A	N/A	2,500	50	0.0	0.0
U /	N/A	N/A	9.78	4	11	0	0	0	89	19	0.0	N/A	N/A	2,500	50	0.0	0.0
D+ / 2.6	5.1	N/A	9.26	1	4	61	0	33	2	65	0.0	95	4	250	50	0.0	0.0
D+ / 2.7	5.0	N/A	9.27	8	4	61	0	33	2	65	0.0	98	4	250	50	0.0	0.0
B+ / 8.4	2.1	N/A	9.66	1	27	36	0	23	14	106	0.0	21	7	250	50	0.0	0.0
B+ / 8.4	2.1	N/A	9.96	7	27	36	0	23	14	106	0.0	48	7	250	50	0.0	0.0
B / 7.8	2.6	5.5	9.66	2	4	48	0	2	46	83	2.6	86	23	0	0	2.0	0.0
B / 7.8	2.6	5.5	9.65	146	4	48	0	2	46	83	2.6	80	23	100,000	100	0.0	0.0
B / 7.8	2.6	5.5	9.67	11	4	48	0	2	46	83	2.6	72	23	1,000	0	0.0	0.0

Fund Type	Fund Name	Ticker Symbol	Overall Investment Rating	Phone	Performance Rating/Pts	Total Return % through 3/31/16 3 Mo	6 Mo	1Yr / Pct	Annualized 3Yr / Pct	Annualized 5Yr / Pct	Incl. in Returns Dividend Yield	Expense Ratio
MM	Cavanal Hill Cash Mgt Instl	APHXX	**U**	(800) 762-7085	**U** /	0.02	0.02	0.02 /34	0.01 /16	0.01 / 4	0.02	0.61
MM	Cavanal Hill Cash Mgt Prem	APPXX	**C-**	(800) 762-7085	**D / 1.9**	0.02	0.03	0.03 /36	0.02 /19	--	0.03	1.11
COI	Cavanal Hill Intmdt Bond A	AAIBX	**B+**	(800) 762-7085	**C+ / 5.7**	1.81	0.92	1.05 /59	2.27 /67	--	1.30	1.28
GEI	Cavanal Hill Intmdt Bond Instl	AIFBX	**A+**	(800) 762-7085	**C+ / 6.9**	1.78	0.95	1.30 /63	2.49 /70	4.36 /66	1.57	1.18
GEI	Cavanal Hill Intmdt Bond NL Inv	APFBX	**A**	(800) 762-7085	**C+ / 6.5**	1.71	0.90	1.09 /60	2.24 /66	4.10 /63	1.27	1.43
MUN	Cavanal Hill Intmdt TxFr Bd A	AATFX	**B+**	(800) 762-7085	**C+ / 6.1**	1.12	1.52	1.80 /76	1.64 /71	--	2.18	1.25
MUN	Cavanal Hill Intmdt TxFr Bd Instl	AITEX	**A+**	(800) 762-7085	**B / 7.8**	1.19	1.67	2.16 /78	1.90 /76	3.65 /75	2.49	1.15
MUN	Cavanal Hill Intmdt TxFr Bd NL Inv	APTFX	**A+**	(800) 762-7085	**B- / 7.4**	1.13	1.63	1.89 /76	1.63 /71	3.39 /73	2.22	1.40
GEI	Cavanal Hill Sht-Tm Inc A	AASTX	**C+**	(800) 762-7085	**C- / 3.2**	0.63	0.42	0.50 /49	0.96 /42	--	1.10	1.15
GEI	Cavanal Hill Sht-Tm Inc Instl	AISTX	**B**	(800) 762-7085	**C / 4.7**	0.69	0.44	0.75 /54	1.21 /46	2.22 /34	1.38	1.05
GEI	Cavanal Hill Sht-Tm Inc NL Inv	APSTX	**B-**	(800) 762-7085	**C- / 4.2**	0.62	0.40	0.58 /51	0.94 /41	1.99 /31	1.10	1.30
MM	Cavanal Hill US Treasury Instl	APKXX	**U**	(800) 762-7085	**U** /	--	--	--	--	--	0.01	0.61
MUN	Centre Active US Tax Exempt Inst	DHBIX	**B**	(800) 955-7175	**B / 7.9**	1.85	2.43	3.48 /90	1.68 /72	3.47 /74	2.37	0.84
MUN	Centre Active US Tax Exempt Inv	DHBRX	**C**	(800) 955-7175	**C+ / 6.2**	1.77	2.29	3.30 /88	1.63 /71	3.32 /72	2.04	1.09
US	Centre Active US Treasury Inst	DHTUX	**U**	(855) 298-4236	**U** /	4.07	2.44	3.87 /81	--	--	0.00	1.02
US	Centre Active US Treasury Inv	DHTRX	**U**	(855) 298-4236	**U** /	3.89	2.26	3.48 /79	--	--	0.00	0.95
* GEI	CGCM Core Fixed Inc Invest	TIIUX	**B-**	(800) 444-4273	**C+ / 6.8**	2.61	2.33	1.42 /65	2.22 /66	4.03 /62	2.66	0.54
COH	CGCM High Yield Invest	THYUX	**E**	(800) 444-4273	**E+ / 0.6**	1.59	-2.04	-7.92 / 1	-0.59 /11	2.71 /40	7.09	0.90
GL	CGCM Intl Fixed Inc Invest	TIFUX	**C+**	(800) 444-4273	**B- / 7.5**	3.19	4.08	0.28 /45	2.67 /73	4.66 /69	6.83	0.87
MUN	CGCM Municipal Bd Invest	TMUUX	**B+**	(800) 444-4273	**A- / 9.1**	1.49	2.79	3.32 /88	3.15 /90	4.84 /84	2.81	0.66
GES	Changing Parameters	CPMPX	**B**	(866) 618-3456	**B / 7.6**	4.30	2.68	1.83 /70	2.60 /72	3.02 /45	1.45	2.50
COH	Chartwell Short Duration Hi Yld I	CWFIX	**U**	(866) 585-6552	**U** /	1.39	0.05	-2.36 /14	--	--	3.27	2.16
GL	Chou Income	CHOIX	**E-**	(877) 682-6352	**E- / 0.0**	-4.37	-7.24	-11.61 / 0	-4.50 / 2	2.33 /35	12.82	2.11
MM	CitizensSelect Treasury MM Hamilton	CEAXX	**C-**	(800) 645-6561	**D / 1.8**	0.02	0.02	0.02 /34	0.01 /16	--	0.02	0.23
MUN	Clearwater Tax-Exempt Bond	QWVQX	**B**	(888) 228-0935	**A+ / 9.9**	1.92	4.51	5.48 /98	5.50 /99	7.80 /98	4.09	0.67
GEI	CM Advisors Fixed Income	CMFIX	**C+**	(800) 664-4888	**C- / 3.7**	2.03	0.46	-0.04 /31	0.61 /35	2.00 /31	2.18	0.80
COH	CMG Tactical Bond A	CHYAX	**U**	(866) 264-9456	**U** /	2.04	0.73	--	--	--	0.00	2.22
MUI	CNR CA Tax-Exempt Bond N	CCTEX	**A+**	(888) 889-0799	**B- / 7.3**	0.84	1.27	1.73 /75	1.64 /71	2.70 /64	1.12	1.00
MUI	CNR CA Tax-Exempt Bond Servicing	CNTIX	**A+**	(888) 889-0799	**B / 7.7**	0.89	1.39	1.99 /77	1.90 /75	2.97 /68	1.36	0.75
COI	CNR Corporate Bond N	CCBAX	**C+**	(888) 889-0799	**C- / 3.7**	1.07	0.67	0.03 /35	0.65 /36	1.85 /29	1.51	1.09
COI	CNR Corporate Bond Servicing	CNCIX	**C+**	(888) 889-0799	**C- / 4.1**	1.14	0.70	0.28 /45	0.87 /40	2.08 /32	1.77	0.84
* GEI	CNR Fixed Income Opportunities N	RIMOX	**D+**	(888) 889-0799	**C / 4.3**	-0.74	-0.99	-0.86 /23	1.49 /52	3.42 /52	6.10	1.12
USS	CNR Government Bond Institutional	CNIGX	**C+**	(888) 889-0799	**C- / 3.7**	1.35	0.59	1.12 /61	0.51 /33	--	0.73	0.57
USS	CNR Government Bond N	CGBAX	**C**	(888) 889-0799	**D+ / 2.8**	1.13	0.34	0.52 /50	0.01 /16	0.93 /20	0.24	1.07
USS	CNR Government Bond Servicing	CNBIX	**C**	(888) 889-0799	**C- / 3.2**	1.19	0.47	0.77 /55	0.26 /29	1.18 /22	0.49	0.82
MM	CNR Government MM N	CNGXX	**U**	(888) 889-0799	**U** /	--	--	--	--	--	0.01	0.88
MM	CNR Government MM S	CNFXX	**U**	(888) 889-0799	**U** /	--	--	--	--	--	0.01	1.08
MM	CNR Government MM Servicing	CNIXX	**U**	(888) 889-0799	**U** /	--	--	--	--	--	0.01	0.58
COH	CNR High Yield Bond Institutional	CNIHX	**D-**	(888) 889-0799	**D+ / 2.4**	1.38	-1.72	-5.73 / 4	0.96 /42	--	6.75	0.83
COH	CNR High Yield Bond N	CHBAX	**E+**	(888) 889-0799	**D- / 1.2**	1.12	-2.09	-6.32 / 3	0.41 /31	3.80 /58	6.23	1.33
COH	CNR High Yield Bond Servicing	CHYIX	**E+**	(888) 889-0799	**D- / 1.5**	1.18	-1.97	-6.09 / 3	0.70 /37	4.07 /62	6.49	1.08
COI	CNR Intermediate Fixed Income Inst	CNRIX	**U**	(888) 889-0799	**U** /	1.31	1.07	0.85 /56	--	--	1.83	0.53
GEI	CNR Intermediate Fixed Income N	RIMCX	**C+**	(888) 889-0799	**C / 4.7**	1.28	0.94	0.47 /49	1.18 /46	2.84 /43	1.45	1.03
MUH	CNR Municipal High Income N	CNRNX	**U**	(888) 889-0799	**U** /	1.62	3.80	3.88 /93	--	--	3.75	1.04
MUH	CNR Municipal High Income	CNRMX	**U**	(888) 889-0799	**U** /	1.77	3.92	4.14 /95	--	--	3.99	0.80
MM	CNR Prime Money Market Instl	CNRXX	**U**	(888) 889-0799	**U** /	--	--	--	--	--	0.02	0.32
MM	CNR Prime Money Market N	CNPXX	**U**	(888) 889-0799	**U** /	--	--	--	--	--	0.01	0.87
MM	CNR Prime Money Market S	CNSXX	**U**	(888) 889-0799	**U** /	--	--	--	--	--	0.01	1.07
MM	CNR Prime Money Market Servicing	CNMXX	**U**	(888) 889-0799	**U** /	--	--	--	--	--	0.01	0.57
GEI	CO 529 CollegeInvest Bond Index		**B-**	(800) 662-7447	**C+ / 6.6**	3.00	2.32	1.51 /66	2.04 /62	3.34 /51	0.00	0.52
GEI	CO 529 CollegeInvest Income Port		**C**	(800) 662-7447	**C / 4.5**	2.07	1.71	0.78 /55	0.83 /39	2.34 /35	0.00	0.52
GL	Cohen and Steers Pref Sec and Inc Z	CPXZX	**U**	(800) 330-7348	**U** /	0.17	3.03	2.59 /75	--	--	6.00	0.84

99 Pct = Best
0 Pct = Worst

● Denotes fund is closed to new investors
* Denotes fund is included in Section II

RISK			NET ASSETS		ASSET							FUND MANAGER		MINIMUM		LOADS	
Risk Rating/Pts	3 Yr Avg Standard Deviation	Avg Duration	NAV As of 3/31/16	Total $(Mil)	Cash %	Gov. Bond %	Muni. Bond %	Corp. Bond %	Other %	Portfolio Turnover Ratio	Avg Coupon Rate	Manager Quality Pct	Manager Tenure (Years)	Initial Purch. $	Additional Purch. $	Front End Load	Back End Load
U /	N/A	N/A	1.00	726	100	0	0	0	0	0	0.0	N/A	N/A	100,000	0	0.0	0.0
A+ / 9.9	N/A	N/A	1.00	6	100	0	0	0	0	0	0.0	64	N/A	1,000	0	0.0	0.0
B+ / 8.6	1.9	3.7	10.57	23	5	45	0	5	45	57	2.2	92	23	0	0	2.0	0.0
B+ / 8.7	1.8	3.7	10.57	29	5	45	0	5	45	57	2.2	91	23	100,000	100	0.0	0.0
B+ / 8.6	1.8	3.7	10.57	17	5	45	0	5	45	57	2.2	89	23	1,000	0	0.0	0.0
B / 8.1	2.4	3.5	11.25	2	11	0	88	0	1	6	4.4	35	23	0	0	2.0	0.0
B / 8.0	2.4	3.5	11.26	33	11	0	88	0	1	6	4.4	41	23	100,000	100	0.0	0.0
B / 8.1	2.3	3.5	11.25	5	11	0	88	0	1	6	4.4	35	23	1,000	0	0.0	0.0
A / 9.4	0.9	1.7	9.59	3	4	41	0	10	45	39	2.1	77	22	0	0	2.0	0.0
A / 9.5	0.8	1.7	9.58	94	4	41	0	10	45	39	2.1	84	22	100,000	100	0.0	0.0
A / 9.4	0.9	1.7	9.59	41	4	41	0	10	45	39	2.1	77	22	1,000	0	0.0	0.0
U /	N/A	N/A	1.00	156	100	0	0	0	0	0	0.0	N/A	N/A	100,000	0	0.0	0.0
C / 5.2	3.4	4.2	10.49	7	8	0	91	0	1	32	4.6	15	1	100,000	100	0.0	0.0
C / 5.3	3.3	4.2	10.55	37	8	0	91	0	1	32	4.6	15	1	5,000	100	3.0	0.0
U /	N/A	N/A	10.48	23	8	91	0	0	1	70	0.0	N/A	2	1,000,000	10,000	0.0	0.0
U /	N/A	N/A	10.42	70	8	91	0	0	1	70	0.0	N/A	2	5,000	1,000	0.0	0.0
C+ / 6.1	3.1	4.0	8.24	661	28	20	0	23	29	326	0.0	51	2	100	0	0.0	0.0
D- / 1.1	5.9	N/A	3.55	213	11	0	0	86	3	42	0.0	10	10	100	0	0.0	0.0
C / 4.5	3.7	N/A	7.43	194	0	46	3	20	31	416	0.0	98	2	100	0	0.0	0.0
C- / 4.1	3.4	11.2	9.78	68	4	0	95	0	1	8	0.0	46	11	100	0	0.0	0.0
C+ / 5.6	3.3	N/A	9.71	83	76	0	12	9	3	734	0.0	94	9	2,500	100	0.0	0.0
U /	N/A	N/A	9.31	21	3	0	0	96	1	40	0.0	N/A	2	1,000,000	0	0.0	2.0
E- / 0.1	12.3	N/A	7.23	15	31	0	0	28	41	17	0.0	4	6	5,000	500	0.0	2.0
A+ / 9.9	N/A	N/A	1.00	137	100	0	0	0	0	0	0.0	63	N/A	1,000,000,00	0	0.0	0.0
C- / 3.0	4.8	N/A	10.25	519	1	0	97	0	2	22	0.0	84	16	1,000	1,000	0.0	0.0
B+ / 8.7	1.8	2.9	11.21	63	11	60	0	28	1	1	0.0	47	5	2,500	0	0.0	0.0
U /	N/A	N/A	9.49	N/A	3	0	0	90	7	442	0.0	N/A	2	25,000	1,000	5.8	0.0
B+ / 8.5	2.0	4.4	10.78	14	5	0	89	0	6	10	4.9	51	7	0	0	0.0	0.0
B+ / 8.5	2.0	4.4	10.75	85	5	0	89	0	6	10	4.9	61	7	0	0	0.0	0.0
B+ / 8.9	1.5	2.6	10.41	4	2	1	5	85	7	32	0.0	52	15	0	0	0.0	0.0
B+ / 8.9	1.5	2.6	10.39	126	2	1	5	85	7	32	0.0	60	15	0	0	0.0	0.0
C- / 4.0	4.0	N/A	24.29	1,678	8	1	0	52	39	73	0.0	90	5	0	0	0.0	0.0
A- / 9.0	1.3	2.4	10.61	62	1	37	0	0	62	37	0.0	48	13	1,000,000	0	0.0	0.0
A- / 9.0	1.3	2.4	10.62	2	1	37	0	0	62	37	0.0	31	13	0	0	0.0	0.0
A- / 9.0	1.3	2.4	10.60	86	1	37	0	0	62	37	0.0	39	13	0	0	0.0	0.0
U /	N/A	N/A	1.00	2,927	100	0	0	0	0	0	0.0	N/A	N/A	0	0	0.0	0.0
U /	N/A	N/A	1.00	804	100	0	0	0	0	0	0.0	N/A	N/A	0	0	0.0	0.0
U /	N/A	N/A	1.00	318	100	0	0	0	0	0	0.0	N/A	N/A	0	0	0.0	0.0
D / 1.6	5.5	4.8	7.20	36	2	0	0	83	15	77	0.0	39	5	1,000,000	0	0.0	0.0
D / 1.7	5.5	4.8	7.19	18	2	0	0	83	15	77	0.0	25	5	0	0	0.0	0.0
D / 1.7	5.5	4.8	7.19	22	2	0	0	83	15	77	0.0	32	5	0	0	0.0	0.0
U /	N/A	N/A	26.22	12	5	3	5	77	10	21	0.0	N/A	3	1,000,000	0	0.0	0.0
B / 8.2	2.3	N/A	26.21	258	5	3	5	77	10	21	0.0	42	3	0	0	0.0	0.0
U /	N/A	N/A	10.87	447	0	0	0	0	100	2	0.0	N/A	3	0	0	0.0	0.0
U /	N/A	N/A	10.88	371	0	0	0	0	100	2	0.0	N/A	3	0	0	0.0	0.0
U /	N/A	N/A	1.00	110	100	0	0	0	0	0	0.0	N/A	N/A	1,000,000	0	0.0	0.0
U /	N/A	N/A	1.00	274	100	0	0	0	0	0	0.0	N/A	N/A	0	0	0.0	0.0
U /	N/A	N/A	1.00	263	100	0	0	0	0	0	0.0	N/A	N/A	0	0	0.0	0.0
U /	N/A	N/A	1.00	420	100	0	0	0	0	0	0.0	N/A	N/A	0	0	0.0	0.0
C+ / 6.3	3.1	N/A	15.46	37	0	46	1	25	28	0	0.0	43	12	25	15	0.0	0.0
B- / 7.5	2.7	N/A	14.27	247	25	51	0	12	12	0	0.0	20	12	25	15	0.0	0.0
U /	N/A	N/A	13.41	N/A	3	0	0	55	42	41	0.0	N/A	6	0	0	0.0	0.0

Fund Type	Fund Name (99 Pct = Best, 0 Pct = Worst)	Ticker Symbol	Overall Investment Rating	Phone	Performance Rating/Pts	3 Mo	6 Mo	1Yr / Pct	3Yr / Pct (Annualized)	5Yr / Pct (Annualized)	Dividend Yield	Expense Ratio
* GEI	Cohen and Steers Pref Sec&Inc A	CPXAX	B-	(800) 330-7348	A- / 9.1	0.08	2.86	2.24 /73	5.55 /93	8.01 /87	5.40	1.19
GEI	Cohen and Steers Pref Sec&Inc C	CPXCX	C+	(800) 330-7348	B+ / 8.7	-0.07	2.47	1.58 /67	4.86 /90	7.31 /83	5.02	1.84
GEI	Cohen and Steers Pref Sec&Inc I	CPXIX	B-	(800) 330-7348	A / 9.3	0.17	3.03	2.59 /75	5.94 /95	8.41 /89	5.99	0.94
GL	Cohen and Steers Pref Sec&Inc R	CPRRX	U	(800) 330-7348	U /	-0.06	2.66	2.04 /72	--	--	5.54	1.34
* MUS	Colorado Bond Shares Tax-Exempt	HICOX	A+	(800) 572-0069	B+ / 8.8	1.27	2.29	4.61 /97	4.05 /96	4.80 /84	4.03	0.58
GEI	Columbia Abs Rtn Currency & Inc A	RARAX	C-	(800) 345-6611	A / 9.3	0.00	11.35	5.54 /91	5.66 /94	3.85 /59	4.33	1.75
GEI ●	Columbia Abs Rtn Currency & Inc B	CARBX	C-	(800) 345-6611	A- / 9.2	-0.20	10.94	4.75 /86	4.85 /90	3.08 /46	3.93	2.50
GEI	Columbia Abs Rtn Currency & Inc C	RARCX	C-	(800) 345-6611	A- / 9.2	-0.20	10.95	4.76 /86	4.85 /90	3.08 /46	3.94	2.50
GEI	Columbia Abs Rtn Currency & Inc I	RVAIX	C-	(800) 345-6611	A+ / 9.7	0.19	11.66	6.01 /93	6.06 /95	4.35 /66	4.66	1.34
GEI	Columbia Abs Rtn Currency & Inc W	RACWX	C-	(800) 345-6611	A / 9.5	0.00	11.40	5.57 /91	5.65 /94	3.81 /58	4.47	1.75
GEI	Columbia Abs Rtn Currency & Inc Z	CACZX	C-	(800) 345-6611	A+ / 9.6	0.00	11.49	5.73 /92	5.92 /95	4.18 /64	4.57	1.50
* COI	Columbia Act Ptf MMrg Core Pl Bd A	CMCPX	B-	(800) 345-6611	C+ / 6.0	2.59	1.79	0.70 /53	1.76 /57	--	1.80	0.81
MUS	Columbia AMT Fr NY Intm Muni Bd A	LNYAX	A	(800) 345-6611	B / 7.7	1.34	2.42	3.17 /87	2.51 /83	4.02 /78	2.77	0.97
MUS ●	Columbia AMT Fr NY Intm Muni Bd B	LNYBX	A	(800) 345-6611	B / 7.7	1.16	2.04	2.41 /80	1.74 /73	3.24 /72	2.12	1.72
MUS	Columbia AMT Fr NY Intm Muni Bd C	LNYCX	A+	(800) 345-6611	B / 8.1	1.23	2.19	2.79 /83	2.06 /78	3.58 /75	2.41	1.72
MUN	Columbia AMT Fr NY Intm Muni Bd	CNYIX	A+	(800) 345-6611	B+ / 8.8	1.40	2.55	3.51 /90	2.76 /86	4.28 /80	3.10	0.72
MUS ●	Columbia AMT Fr NY Intm Muni Bd T	GANYX	A-	(800) 345-6611	B- / 7.0	1.36	2.47	3.27 /88	2.58 /83	4.11 /78	2.82	0.87
MUS	Columbia AMT Fr NY Intm Muni Bd Z	GNYTX	A+	(800) 345-6611	B+ / 8.8	1.40	2.55	3.43 /89	2.73 /85	4.26 /79	3.10	0.72
MUS	Columbia AMT-Fr CA Intm Muni Bd A	NACMX	B+	(800) 345-6611	B+ / 8.5	1.76	3.00	3.58 /91	3.19 /90	5.08 /86	2.47	0.95
MUS ●	Columbia AMT-Fr CA Intm Muni Bd B	CCIBX	B+	(800) 345-6611	B+ / 8.5	1.58	2.63	2.82 /83	2.42 /82	4.30 /80	1.82	1.70
MUS	Columbia AMT-Fr CA Intm Muni Bd C	CCICX	B+	(800) 345-6611	B+ / 8.4	1.48	2.53	2.82 /83	2.39 /81	4.29 /80	1.81	1.70
MUN	Columbia AMT-Fr CA Intm Muni Bd	CCMRX	A+	(800) 345-6611	A / 9.4	1.82	3.13	3.94 /94	3.45 /92	5.34 /88	2.79	0.70
MUN	Columbia AMT-Fr CA Intm Muni Bd	CNBRX	A	(800) 345-6611	A / 9.4	1.75	3.09	3.94 /94	3.51 /93	5.39 /88	2.88	0.55
MUS	Columbia AMT-Fr CA Intm Muni Bd Z	NCMAX	A	(800) 345-6611	A / 9.3	1.73	3.03	3.84 /93	3.41 /92	5.32 /88	2.79	0.70
MUS	Columbia AMT-Fr CT Intm Muni Bd A	LCTAX	B+	(800) 345-6611	B- / 7.1	1.49	2.20	2.59 /81	2.21 /79	3.70 /75	2.63	0.99
MUS ●	Columbia AMT-Fr CT Intm Muni Bd B	LCTBX	B+	(800) 345-6611	B- / 7.1	1.31	1.82	1.82 /76	1.45 /66	2.92 /67	1.97	1.74
MUS	Columbia AMT-Fr CT Intm Muni Bd C	LCTCX	A	(800) 345-6611	B / 7.7	1.29	1.88	2.03 /77	1.74 /73	3.24 /72	2.26	1.74
MUN	Columbia AMT-Fr CT Intm Muni Bd	CCTMX	A+	(800) 345-6611	B+ / 8.4	1.46	2.33	2.84 /83	2.45 /82	3.94 /77	2.95	0.74
MUS	Columbia AMT-Fr CT Intm Muni Bd T	GCBAX	B-	(800) 345-6611	C+ / 6.2	1.42	2.16	2.69 /82	2.29 /80	3.79 /76	2.67	0.89
MUS	Columbia AMT-Fr CT Intm Muni Bd Z	SCTEX	A+	(800) 345-6611	B+ / 8.4	1.46	2.23	2.75 /83	2.44 /82	3.94 /77	2.96	0.74
MUS	Columbia AMT-Fr GA Intm Muni Bd A	NGIMX	A	(800) 345-6611	B- / 7.5	1.49	2.34	3.02 /85	2.36 /81	3.83 /76	2.62	1.07
MUS ●	Columbia AMT-Fr GA Intm Muni Bd B	NGITX	A	(800) 345-6611	B- / 7.4	1.31	1.96	2.16 /78	1.57 /69	3.05 /69	1.97	1.82
MUS	Columbia AMT-Fr GA Intm Muni Bd C	NGINX	A	(800) 345-6611	B- / 7.5	1.31	1.96	2.16 /78	1.60 /70	3.05 /70	1.97	1.82
MUN	Columbia AMT-Fr GA Intm Muni Bd	CGIMX	A+	(800) 345-6611	B+ / 8.7	1.56	2.47	3.18 /87	2.59 /83	4.07 /78	2.96	0.82
MUS	Columbia AMT-Fr GA Intm Muni Bd Z	NGAMX	A+	(800) 345-6611	B+ / 8.7	1.56	2.47	3.27 /88	2.62 /84	4.08 /78	2.95	0.82
MUH	Columbia AMT-Fr Intm Muni Bond A	LITAX	B	(800) 345-6611	B / 8.1	1.46	2.84	3.33 /88	2.85 /86	4.56 /82	2.97	0.87
MUH ●	Columbia AMT-Fr Intm Muni Bond B	LITBX	B	(800) 345-6611	B / 8.2	1.21	2.42	2.67 /82	2.16 /79	3.86 /77	2.42	1.52
MUH	Columbia AMT-Fr Intm Muni Bond C	LITCX	B	(800) 345-6611	B+ / 8.3	1.30	2.51	2.67 /82	2.33 /81	4.16 /79	2.42	1.52
MUN	Columbia AMT-Fr Intm Muni Bond R4	CIMRX	A+	(800) 345-6611	A- / 9.1	1.51	2.94	3.54 /90	3.04 /88	4.75 /83	3.26	0.67
MUN	Columbia AMT-Fr Intm Muni Bond R5	CTMRX	A+	(800) 345-6611	A- / 9.1	1.53	3.00	3.64 /91	3.12 /89	4.81 /84	3.36	0.53
MUH ●	Columbia AMT-Fr Intm Muni Bond T	GIMAX	B-	(800) 345-6611	B / 7.7	1.47	2.87	3.38 /89	2.91 /87	4.61 /82	2.97	0.82
MUH	Columbia AMT-Fr Intm Muni Bond Z	SETMX	A-	(800) 345-6611	A- / 9.1	1.51	2.95	3.54 /90	3.03 /88	4.76 /83	3.26	0.67
MUS	Columbia AMT-Fr MA Intm Muni Bd A	LMIAX	A-	(800) 345-6611	B / 7.6	1.43	2.36	3.02 /85	2.39 /81	3.85 /77	2.78	0.96
MUS ●	Columbia AMT-Fr MA Intm Muni Bd B	LMIBX	A-	(800) 345-6611	B- / 7.5	1.25	1.98	2.26 /79	1.60 /70	3.06 /70	2.12	1.71
MUS	Columbia AMT-Fr MA Intm Muni Bd C	LMICX	A	(800) 345-6611	B / 8.0	1.32	2.13	2.56 /81	1.94 /76	3.41 /73	2.42	1.71
MUN	Columbia AMT-Fr MA Intm Muni Bd	CMANX	A+	(800) 345-6611	B+ / 8.7	1.49	2.39	3.28 /88	2.64 /84	4.10 /78	3.11	0.71
MUS ●	Columbia AMT-Fr MA Intm Muni Bd T	GMBAX	B	(800) 345-6611	C+ / 6.8	1.45	2.41	3.12 /86	2.49 /82	3.95 /77	2.82	0.86
MUS	Columbia AMT-Fr MA Intm Muni Bd Z	SEMAX	A+	(800) 345-6611	B+ / 8.7	1.49	2.48	3.28 /88	2.64 /84	4.10 /78	3.11	0.71
MUS	Columbia AMT-Fr MD Intm Muni Bd A	NMDMX	A-	(800) 345-6611	B- / 7.3	1.66	2.36	2.75 /83	2.26 /80	3.79 /76	2.62	1.05
MUS ●	Columbia AMT-Fr MD Intm Muni Bd B	NMITX	A	(800) 345-6611	B- / 7.3	1.48	2.08	1.99 /77	1.49 /67	3.01 /69	1.96	1.80
MUS	Columbia AMT-Fr MD Intm Muni Bd	NMINX	A-	(800) 345-6611	B- / 7.3	1.48	1.98	1.99 /77	1.49 /67	3.02 /69	1.96	1.80
MUN	Columbia AMT-Fr MD Intm Muni Bd	CMDMX	A+	(800) 345-6611	B+ / 8.6	1.73	2.58	3.01 /85	2.54 /83	3.94 /77	2.94	0.80

Performance: Total Return % through 3/31/16; Dividend Yield and Expense Ratio: Incl. in Returns.

● Denotes fund is closed to new investors
* Denotes fund is included in Section II

RISK			NET ASSETS		ASSET							FUND MANAGER		MINIMUM		LOADS	
Risk Rating/Pts	3 Yr Avg Standard Deviation	Avg Duration	NAV As of 3/31/16	Total $(Mil)	Cash %	Gov. Bond %	Muni. Bond %	Corp. Bond %	Other %	Portfolio Turnover Ratio	Avg Coupon Rate	Manager Quality Pct	Manager Tenure (Years)	Initial Purch. $	Additional Purch. $	Front End Load	Back End Load
C- / 3.4	4.4	N/A	13.39	821	3	0	0	55	42	41	0.0	99	6	1,000	250	0.0	0.0
C- / 3.5	4.3	N/A	13.32	703	3	0	0	55	42	41	0.0	98	6	1,000	250	0.0	0.0
C- / 3.4	4.4	N/A	13.42	3,197	3	0	0	55	42	41	0.0	99	6	100,000	0	0.0	0.0
U /	N/A	N/A	13.40	1	3	0	0	55	42	41	0.0	N/A	6	0	0	0.0	0.0
A- / 9.1	1.2	6.1	9.14	984	33	0	63	0	4	19	5.3	98	26	500	0	4.8	0.0
E- / 0.1	11.9	0.1	10.41	24	98	0	1	0	1	0	0.6	96	10	10,000	0	3.0	0.0
E- / 0.1	11.9	0.1	9.83	N/A	98	0	1	0	1	0	0.6	91	10	10,000	0	0.0	0.0
E- / 0.1	11.9	0.1	9.82	3	98	0	1	0	1	0	0.6	91	10	10,000	0	0.0	0.0
E- / 0.1	11.9	0.1	10.79	26	98	0	1	0	1	0	0.6	97	10	0	0	0.0	0.0
E- / 0.1	11.9	0.1	10.37	N/A	98	0	1	0	1	0	0.6	96	10	500	0	0.0	0.0
E- / 0.1	11.9	0.1	10.72	16	98	0	1	0	1	0	0.6	97	10	2,000	0	0.0	0.0
B- / 7.1	2.9	4.9	10.13	5,507	4	21	0	30	45	269	3.1	59	4	500	0	0.0	0.0
B- / 7.3	2.8	4.6	12.23	29	0	0	99	0	1	12	4.7	48	18	2,000	0	3.0	0.0
B- / 7.3	2.8	4.6	12.23	N/A	0	0	99	0	1	12	4.7	25	18	2,000	0	0.0	0.0
B- / 7.3	2.8	4.6	12.23	22	0	0	99	0	1	12	4.7	34	18	2,000	0	0.0	0.0
B- / 7.4	2.8	4.6	12.22	1	0	0	99	0	1	12	4.7	58	18	0	0	0.0	0.0
B- / 7.5	2.7	4.6	12.22	7	0	0	99	0	1	12	4.7	53	18	2,000	0	4.8	0.0
B- / 7.5	2.7	4.6	12.22	226	0	0	99	0	1	12	4.7	59	18	2,000	0	0.0	0.0
C / 5.4	3.3	5.1	10.68	51	0	0	100	0	0	6	4.3	53	5	2,000	0	3.0	0.0
C / 5.4	3.3	5.1	10.68	N/A	0	0	100	0	0	6	4.3	28	5	2,000	0	0.0	0.0
C / 5.5	3.3	5.1	10.67	15	0	0	100	0	0	6	4.3	29	5	2,000	0	0.0	0.0
C / 5.5	3.3	5.1	10.65	2	0	0	100	0	0	6	4.3	N/A	5	0	0	0.0	0.0
C / 5.3	3.3	5.1	10.62	3	0	0	100	0	0	6	4.3	68	5	0	0	0.0	0.0
C / 5.5	3.3	5.1	10.65	372	0	0	100	0	0	6	4.3	61	5	2,000	0	0.0	0.0
C+ / 6.9	2.9	4.4	10.98	10	1	0	98	0	1	6	4.8	35	14	2,000	0	3.0	0.0
C+ / 6.9	2.9	4.4	10.98	N/A	1	0	98	0	1	6	4.8	17	14	2,000	0	0.0	0.0
C+ / 6.9	2.9	4.4	10.97	6	1	0	98	0	1	6	4.8	22	14	2,000	0	0.0	0.0
C+ / 6.9	2.9	4.4	10.96	1	1	0	98	0	1	6	4.8	42	14	0	0	0.0	0.0
C+ / 6.9	2.9	4.4	10.96	12	1	0	98	0	1	6	4.8	37	14	2,000	0	4.8	0.0
C+ / 6.9	2.9	4.4	10.97	129	1	0	98	0	1	6	4.8	41	14	2,000	0	0.0	0.0
B- / 7.5	2.7	4.6	10.85	20	0	0	100	0	0	19	4.9	47	5	2,000	0	3.0	0.0
B- / 7.5	2.7	4.6	10.85	N/A	0	0	100	0	0	19	4.9	24	5	2,000	0	0.0	0.0
B- / 7.4	2.7	4.6	10.85	5	0	0	100	0	0	19	4.9	24	5	2,000	0	0.0	0.0
B- / 7.4	2.7	4.6	10.83	N/A	0	0	100	0	0	19	4.9	54	5	0	0	0.0	0.0
B- / 7.5	2.7	4.6	10.85	51	0	0	100	0	0	19	4.9	56	5	2,000	0	0.0	0.0
C / 5.0	3.0	5.0	10.81	244	0	0	99	0	1	15	4.6	51	7	2,000	0	3.0	0.0
C / 4.9	3.0	5.0	10.80	N/A	0	0	99	0	1	15	4.6	29	7	2,000	0	0.0	0.0
C / 4.9	3.0	5.0	10.81	59	0	0	99	0	1	15	4.6	35	7	2,000	0	0.0	0.0
C+ / 6.4	3.0	5.0	10.80	4	0	0	99	0	1	15	4.6	57	7	0	0	0.0	0.0
C+ / 6.4	3.0	5.0	10.79	13	0	0	99	0	1	15	4.6	60	7	0	0	0.0	0.0
C / 5.0	3.0	5.0	10.81	14	0	0	99	0	1	15	4.6	54	7	2,000	0	4.8	0.0
C / 4.9	3.0	5.0	10.81	2,017	0	0	99	0	1	15	4.6	57	7	2,000	0	0.0	0.0
C+ / 6.8	2.9	4.7	11.02	25	0	0	99	0	1	8	5.0	39	7	2,000	0	3.0	0.0
C+ / 6.8	2.9	4.7	11.02	N/A	0	0	99	0	1	8	5.0	19	7	2,000	0	0.0	0.0
C+ / 6.7	3.0	4.7	11.02	10	0	0	99	0	1	8	5.0	26	7	2,000	0	0.0	0.0
C+ / 6.9	2.9	4.7	11.01	3	0	0	99	0	1	8	5.0	49	7	0	0	0.0	0.0
C+ / 6.8	2.9	4.7	11.02	19	0	0	99	0	1	8	5.0	42	7	2,000	0	4.8	0.0
C+ / 6.8	2.9	4.7	11.02	239	0	0	99	0	1	8	5.0	47	7	2,000	0	0.0	0.0
B- / 7.2	2.8	4.7	10.87	18	0	0	100	0	0	10	4.7	39	5	2,000	0	3.0	0.0
B- / 7.3	2.8	4.7	10.88	N/A	0	0	100	0	0	10	4.7	20	5	2,000	0	0.0	0.0
B- / 7.2	2.8	4.7	10.87	3	0	0	100	0	0	10	4.7	20	5	2,000	0	0.0	0.0
B- / 7.3	2.8	4.7	10.87	N/A	0	0	100	0	0	10	4.7	50	5	0	0	0.0	0.0

99 Pct = Best
0 Pct = Worst

Fund Type	Fund Name	Ticker Symbol	Overall Investment Rating	Phone	PERFORMANCE Performance Rating/Pts	Total Return % through 3/31/16 3 Mo	6 Mo	1Yr / Pct	Annualized 3Yr / Pct	5Yr / Pct	Incl. in Returns Dividend Yield	Expense Ratio
MUS	Columbia AMT-Fr MD Intm Muni Bd Z	NMDBX	**A+**	(800) 345-6611	**B+ / 8.6**	1.73	2.49	3.01 / 85	2.51 / 83	4.05 / 78	2.94	0.80
MUS	Columbia AMT-Fr NC Intm Muni Bd A	NNCIX	**A-**	(800) 345-6611	**B- / 7.0**	1.34	2.28	2.81 / 83	2.10 / 78	3.78 / 76	2.49	0.99
MUS •	Columbia AMT-Fr NC Intm Muni Bd B	NNITX	**A-**	(800) 345-6611	**C+ / 6.9**	1.15	1.80	2.05 / 77	1.34 / 63	2.98 / 68	1.83	1.74
MUS	Columbia AMT-Fr NC Intm Muni Bd C	NNINX	**A-**	(800) 345-6611	**B- / 7.0**	1.25	1.90	2.05 / 77	1.34 / 63	3.01 / 69	1.82	1.74
MUN	Columbia AMT-Fr NC Intm Muni Bd	CNCEX	**A+**	(800) 345-6611	**B+ / 8.4**	1.40	2.41	3.06 / 86	2.35 / 81	4.04 / 78	2.81	0.74
MUS	Columbia AMT-Fr NC Intm Muni Bd Z	NNIBX	**A+**	(800) 345-6611	**B+ / 8.4**	1.40	2.41	3.07 / 86	2.35 / 81	4.04 / 78	2.81	0.74
MUS	Columbia AMT-Fr OR Inter Muni Bd A	COEAX	**A-**	(800) 345-6611	**B- / 7.4**	1.27	2.10	2.99 / 85	2.34 / 81	3.96 / 77	2.54	0.86
MUS •	Columbia AMT-Fr OR Inter Muni Bd B	COEBX	**A-**	(800) 345-6611	**B- / 7.5**	1.16	1.81	2.23 / 79	1.60 / 70	3.20 / 71	1.87	1.61
MUS	Columbia AMT-Fr OR Inter Muni Bd	CORCX	**A**	(800) 345-6611	**B / 7.9**	1.16	1.88	2.45 / 80	1.91 / 76	3.53 / 74	2.17	1.61
MUN	Columbia AMT-Fr OR Inter Muni Bd	CORMX	**A+**	(800) 345-6611	**B+ / 8.7**	1.33	2.23	3.25 / 87	2.61 / 84	4.22 / 79	2.86	0.61
MUN	Columbia AMT-Fr OR Inter Muni Bd	CODRX	**A+**	(800) 345-6611	**B+ / 8.7**	1.34	2.34	3.30 / 88	2.66 / 84	4.25 / 79	2.91	0.55
MUS	Columbia AMT-Fr OR Inter Muni Bd Z	CMBFX	**A+**	(800) 345-6611	**B+ / 8.6**	1.33	2.23	3.17 / 87	2.60 / 84	4.22 / 79	2.86	0.61
MUS	Columbia AMT-Fr SC Intm Muni Bd A	NSCIX	**A**	(800) 345-6611	**B / 7.7**	1.64	2.68	3.30 / 88	2.36 / 81	4.08 / 78	2.74	1.00
MUS •	Columbia AMT-Fr SC Intm Muni Bd B	NISCX	**A**	(800) 345-6611	**B / 7.6**	1.45	2.30	2.54 / 81	1.60 / 70	3.32 / 72	2.09	1.75
MUS	Columbia AMT-Fr SC Intm Muni Bd C	NSICX	**A**	(800) 345-6611	**B / 7.6**	1.36	2.30	2.54 / 81	1.57 / 69	3.30 / 72	2.09	1.75
MUN	Columbia AMT-Fr SC Intm Muni Bd	CSICX	**A+**	(800) 345-6611	**B+ / 8.7**	1.60	2.81	3.56 / 91	2.59 / 84	4.34 / 80	3.08	0.75
MUS	Columbia AMT-Fr SC Intm Muni Bd Z	NSCMX	**A+**	(800) 345-6611	**B+ / 8.8**	1.60	2.81	3.56 / 91	2.62 / 84	4.34 / 80	3.08	0.75
MUS	Columbia AMT-Fr VA Intm Muni Bd A	NVAFX	**B+**	(800) 345-6611	**B- / 7.2**	1.44	2.11	2.70 / 82	2.24 / 80	3.60 / 75	2.71	0.97
MUS •	Columbia AMT-Fr VA Intm Muni Bd B	NVANX	**A-**	(800) 345-6611	**B- / 7.2**	1.35	1.83	2.04 / 77	1.47 / 67	2.85 / 66	2.05	1.72
MUS	Columbia AMT-Fr VA Intm Muni Bd C	NVRCX	**A-**	(800) 345-6611	**B- / 7.2**	1.35	1.83	2.03 / 77	1.48 / 67	2.85 / 66	2.05	1.72
MUN	Columbia AMT-Fr VA Intm Muni Bd	CAIVX	**A+**	(800) 345-6611	**B+ / 8.6**	1.59	2.33	3.05 / 85	2.52 / 83	3.89 / 77	3.04	0.72
MUS	Columbia AMT-Fr VA Intm Muni Bd Z	NVABX	**A+**	(800) 345-6611	**B+ / 8.5**	1.50	2.24	2.96 / 85	2.49 / 83	3.88 / 77	3.04	0.72
MUN	Columbia AMT-Free Tax-Exempt Bd	CATRX	**B+**	(800) 345-6611	**A+ / 9.8**	1.51	3.72	4.42 / 96	4.58 / 98	7.23 / 97	4.22	0.58
MUN	Columbia AMT-Free Tax-Exempt Bd	CADNX	**B+**	(800) 345-6611	**A+ / 9.8**	1.26	3.71	4.16 / 95	4.52 / 98	7.19 / 97	4.22	0.57
* MUN	Columbia AMT-Free Tax-Exempt	INTAX	**B**	(800) 345-6611	**A / 9.4**	1.45	3.59	4.17 / 95	4.32 / 97	7.07 / 97	3.86	0.83
MUN •	Columbia AMT-Free Tax-Exempt	ITEBX	**B**	(800) 345-6611	**A / 9.3**	1.26	3.20	3.39 / 89	3.54 / 93	6.27 / 93	3.24	1.58
MUN	Columbia AMT-Free Tax-Exempt	RTCEX	**B**	(800) 345-6611	**A / 9.3**	1.27	3.21	3.40 / 89	3.54 / 93	6.27 / 94	3.24	1.58
MUN	Columbia AMT-Free Tax-Exempt	CATZX	**B+**	(800) 345-6611	**A+ / 9.8**	1.51	3.72	4.42 / 96	4.58 / 98	7.35 / 97	4.22	0.58
COI	Columbia Bond A	CNDAX	**C-**	(800) 345-6611	**C- / 4.1**	3.21	2.61	1.56 / 67	1.72 / 56	3.33 / 50	2.23	1.01
COI •	Columbia Bond B	CNDBX	**C**	(800) 345-6611	**C / 4.9**	3.02	2.23	0.80 / 55	0.96 / 42	2.56 / 38	1.61	1.76
COI	Columbia Bond C	CNDCX	**C**	(800) 345-6611	**C / 5.0**	3.03	2.23	0.80 / 55	1.03 / 43	2.67 / 40	1.61	1.76
COI	Columbia Bond I	CBNIX	**B-**	(800) 345-6611	**B- / 7.0**	3.31	2.81	1.97 / 72	2.18 / 65	3.75 / 57	2.74	0.54
COI	Columbia Bond R	CBFRX	**C+**	(800) 345-6611	**C+ / 5.9**	3.15	2.49	1.31 / 63	1.47 / 51	3.08 / 46	2.10	1.26
COI	Columbia Bond R4	CNDRX	**B**	(800) 345-6611	**C+ / 6.8**	3.27	2.73	1.93 / 71	2.01 / 61	3.61 / 55	2.59	0.76
COI	Columbia Bond R5	CNFRX	**B**	(800) 345-6611	**C+ / 6.9**	3.31	2.79	1.92 / 71	2.08 / 63	3.67 / 56	2.69	0.59
COI •	Columbia Bond T	CNDTX	**C-**	(800) 345-6611	**C / 4.3**	3.24	2.66	1.77 / 69	1.82 / 58	3.44 / 52	2.32	0.91
COI	Columbia Bond W	CBDWX	**C+**	(800) 345-6611	**C+ / 6.3**	3.21	2.49	1.56 / 67	1.73 / 56	3.36 / 51	2.34	1.01
COI	Columbia Bond Y	CBFYX	**B**	(800) 345-6611	**B- / 7.0**	3.31	2.69	1.97 / 72	2.14 / 64	3.72 / 57	2.74	0.54
COI	Columbia Bond Z	UMMGX	**B-**	(800) 345-6611	**C+ / 6.7**	3.27	2.73	1.81 / 70	1.97 / 61	3.59 / 54	2.58	0.76
MUS	Columbia CA Tax Exempt A	CLMPX	**B+**	(800) 345-6611	**A / 9.5**	1.68	3.61	4.14 / 95	4.66 / 98	7.62 / 98	3.59	0.88
MUS •	Columbia CA Tax Exempt B	CCABX	**B+**	(800) 345-6611	**A / 9.5**	1.50	3.22	3.36 / 89	3.88 / 95	6.82 / 96	2.97	1.63
MUS	Columbia CA Tax Exempt C	CCAOX	**B+**	(800) 345-6611	**A+ / 9.7**	1.70	3.51	3.81 / 93	4.19 / 97	7.17 / 97	3.26	1.63
MUN	Columbia CA Tax Exempt R4	CCARX	**B+**	(800) 345-6611	**A+ / 9.8**	1.74	3.60	4.40 / 96	4.92 / 98	7.78 / 98	3.95	0.63
MUS	Columbia CA Tax Exempt Z	CCAZX	**B+**	(800) 345-6611	**A+ / 9.8**	1.87	3.73	4.53 / 97	4.92 / 98	7.91 / 98	3.95	0.63
* GEI	Columbia CMG Ultra Short Term	CMGUX	**C+**	(800) 345-6611	**C- / 3.3**	0.41	0.33	0.48 / 49	0.46 / 32	0.64 / 18	0.48	0.26
USS	Columbia Corporate Income A	LIIAX	**D**	(800) 345-6611	**C- / 3.0**	3.56	2.80	-1.88 / 16	1.52 / 53	4.31 / 65	2.95	0.98
USS •	Columbia Corporate Income B	CIOBX	**D**	(800) 345-6611	**C- / 3.9**	3.38	2.42	-2.61 / 13	0.77 / 38	3.54 / 54	2.34	1.73
USS	Columbia Corporate Income C	CIOCX	**D**	(800) 345-6611	**C- / 4.2**	3.41	2.50	-2.46 / 13	0.92 / 41	3.69 / 56	2.50	1.73
COI	Columbia Corporate Income I	CPTIX	**C-**	(800) 345-6611	**C+ / 6.1**	3.67	3.01	-1.47 / 19	1.96 / 61	4.75 / 70	3.51	0.52
COI	Columbia Corporate Income R4	CIFRX	**C-**	(800) 345-6611	**C+ / 5.9**	3.63	2.93	-1.54 / 18	1.81 / 58	4.59 / 68	3.34	0.73
COI	Columbia Corporate Income R5	CPIRX	**C-**	(800) 345-6611	**C+ / 6.0**	3.55	2.88	-1.52 / 18	1.91 / 60	4.66 / 69	3.46	0.57
COI	Columbia Corporate Income W	CPIWX	**D+**	(800) 345-6611	**C / 5.4**	3.56	2.80	-1.88 / 16	1.52 / 53	4.31 / 65	3.09	0.98

• Denotes fund is closed to new investors
* Denotes fund is included in Section II

RISK			NET ASSETS		ASSET							FUND MANAGER		MINIMUM		LOADS	
Risk Rating/Pts	3 Yr Avg Standard Deviation	Avg Duration	NAV As of 3/31/16	Total $(Mil)	Cash %	Gov. Bond %	Muni. Bond %	Corp. Bond %	Other %	Portfolio Turnover Ratio	Avg Coupon Rate	Manager Quality Pct	Manager Tenure (Years)	Initial Purch. $	Additional Purch. $	Front End Load	Back End Load
B- / 7.2	2.8	4.7	10.87	71	0	0	100	0	0	10	4.7	48	5	2,000	0	0.0	0.0
B / 7.6	2.7	4.5	10.66	27	0	0	100	0	0	6	4.6	38	5	2,000	0	3.0	0.0
B- / 7.5	2.7	4.5	10.66	N/A	0	0	100	0	0	6	4.6	19	5	2,000	0	0.0	0.0
B- / 7.4	2.7	4.5	10.66	8	0	0	100	0	0	6	4.6	18	5	2,000	0	0.0	0.0
B- / 7.5	2.7	4.5	10.65	3	0	0	100	0	0	6	4.6	45	5	0	0	0.0	0.0
B / 7.6	2.7	4.5	10.65	184	0	0	100	0	0	6	4.6	46	5	2,000	0	0.0	0.0
C+ / 6.9	2.9	4.8	12.70	46	0	0	99	0	1	11	4.2	38	13	2,000	0	3.0	0.0
B- / 7.0	2.9	4.8	12.70	N/A	0	0	99	0	1	11	4.2	20	13	2,000	0	0.0	0.0
B- / 7.0	2.9	4.8	12.70	28	0	0	99	0	1	11	4.2	26	13	2,000	0	0.0	0.0
C+ / 6.9	2.9	4.8	12.70	N/A	0	0	99	0	1	11	4.2	46	13	0	0	0.0	0.0
C+ / 6.9	2.9	4.8	12.69	23	0	0	99	0	1	11	4.2	49	13	0	0	0.0	0.0
B- / 7.0	2.9	4.8	12.70	367	0	0	99	0	1	11	4.2	47	13	2,000	0	0.0	0.0
B- / 7.1	2.9	5.0	10.52	21	0	0	100	0	0	16	4.7	40	5	2,000	0	3.0	0.0
B- / 7.1	2.8	5.0	10.53	N/A	0	0	100	0	0	16	4.7	21	5	2,000	0	0.0	0.0
B- / 7.1	2.8	5.0	10.52	15	0	0	100	0	0	16	4.7	20	5	2,000	0	0.0	0.0
B- / 7.1	2.8	5.0	10.51	1	0	0	100	0	0	16	4.7	49	5	0	0	0.0	0.0
B- / 7.1	2.9	5.0	10.52	103	0	0	100	0	0	16	4.7	50	5	2,000	0	0.0	0.0
B- / 7.0	2.9	4.8	11.14	42	0	0	100	0	0	9	4.6	36	5	2,000	0	3.0	0.0
B- / 7.1	2.8	4.8	11.15	N/A	0	0	100	0	0	9	4.6	19	5	2,000	0	0.0	0.0
B- / 7.1	2.8	4.8	11.15	5	0	0	100	0	0	9	4.6	19	5	2,000	0	0.0	0.0
B- / 7.1	2.8	4.8	11.14	1	0	0	100	0	0	9	4.6	46	5	0	0	0.0	0.0
B- / 7.0	2.9	4.8	11.14	170	0	0	100	0	0	9	4.6	44	5	2,000	0	0.0	0.0
C- / 3.5	4.1	7.4	4.08	2	0	0	100	0	0	16	5.2	78	9	0	0	0.0	0.0
C- / 3.3	4.2	7.4	4.08	5	0	0	100	0	0	16	5.2	73	9	100,000	0	0.0	0.0
C- / 3.5	4.1	7.4	4.09	611	0	0	100	0	0	16	5.2	70	9	2,000	0	3.0	0.0
C- / 3.5	4.1	7.4	4.09	N/A	0	0	100	0	0	16	5.2	37	9	2,000	0	0.0	0.0
C- / 3.5	4.1	7.4	4.09	21	0	0	100	0	0	16	5.2	38	9	2,000	0	0.0	0.0
C- / 3.5	4.1	7.4	4.08	61	0	0	100	0	0	16	5.2	78	9	2,000	0	0.0	0.0
C+ / 6.3	3.1	5.4	8.67	54	0	22	1	25	52	350	3.1	54	11	2,000	0	4.8	0.0
C+ / 6.3	3.1	5.4	8.67	N/A	0	22	1	25	52	350	3.1	30	11	2,000	0	0.0	0.0
C+ / 6.3	3.1	5.4	8.66	11	0	22	1	25	52	350	3.1	31	11	2,000	0	0.0	0.0
C+ / 6.1	3.1	5.4	8.69	N/A	0	22	1	25	52	350	3.1	74	11	0	0	0.0	0.0
C+ / 6.3	3.1	5.4	8.67	2	0	22	1	25	52	350	3.1	44	11	0	0	0.0	0.0
C+ / 6.5	3.0	5.4	8.67	N/A	0	22	1	25	52	350	3.1	71	11	0	0	0.0	0.0
C+ / 6.3	3.1	5.4	8.65	N/A	0	22	1	25	52	350	3.1	72	11	0	0	0.0	0.0
C+ / 6.4	3.0	5.4	8.66	11	0	22	1	25	52	350	3.1	59	11	2,000	0	4.8	0.0
C+ / 6.4	3.0	5.4	8.68	N/A	0	22	1	25	52	350	3.1	54	11	500	0	0.0	0.0
C+ / 6.4	3.0	5.4	8.68	32	0	22	1	25	52	350	3.1	75	11	0	0	0.0	0.0
C+ / 6.2	3.1	5.4	8.67	437	0	22	1	25	52	350	3.1	N/A	11	2,000	0	0.0	0.0
C- / 3.7	4.2	6.9	7.98	387	0	0	99	0	1	12	4.8	77	6	2,000	0	3.0	0.0
C- / 3.7	4.2	6.9	7.98	N/A	0	0	99	0	1	12	4.8	44	6	2,000	0	0.0	0.0
C- / 3.7	4.2	6.9	7.99	47	0	0	99	0	1	12	4.8	57	6	2,000	0	0.0	0.0
C- / 3.7	4.2	6.9	7.98	N/A	0	0	99	0	1	12	4.8	84	6	0	0	0.0	0.0
C- / 3.7	4.2	6.9	7.99	110	0	0	99	0	1	12	4.8	83	6	2,000	0	0.0	0.0
A+ / 9.9	0.3	0.5	9.00	1,463	6	13	1	57	23	62	1.6	77	4	3,000,000	2,500	0.0	0.0
C- / 3.2	4.6	5.4	9.75	96	0	0	0	99	1	78	4.4	75	6	2,000	0	4.8	0.0
C- / 3.1	4.6	5.4	9.75	N/A	0	0	0	99	1	78	4.4	42	6	2,000	0	0.0	0.0
C- / 3.1	4.6	5.4	9.75	12	0	0	0	99	1	78	4.4	48	6	2,000	0	0.0	0.0
C- / 3.2	4.6	5.4	9.75	562	0	0	0	99	1	78	4.4	38	6	0	0	0.0	0.0
C- / 3.2	4.5	5.4	9.74	16	0	0	0	99	1	78	4.4	34	6	0	0	0.0	0.0
C- / 3.2	4.5	5.4	9.73	1	0	0	0	99	1	78	4.4	38	6	0	0	0.0	0.0
C- / 3.2	4.6	5.4	9.75	41	0	0	0	99	1	78	4.4	26	6	500	0	0.0	0.0

99 Pct = Best 0 Pct = Worst					PERFORMANCE							
						Total Return % through 3/31/16					Incl. in Returns	
									Annualized			
Fund Type	Fund Name	Ticker Symbol	Overall Investment Rating	Phone	Perfor-mance Rating/Pts	3 Mo	6 Mo	1Yr / Pct	3Yr / Pct	5Yr / Pct	Dividend Yield	Expense Ratio
COI	Columbia Corporate Income Y	CRIYX	**C-**	(800) 345-6611	**C+ / 6.2**	3.67	3.01	-1.47 /19	1.99 /61	4.72 /70	3.51	0.52
USS	Columbia Corporate Income Z	SRINX	**D+**	(800) 345-6611	**C+ / 5.8**	3.63	2.93	-1.64 /18	1.78 /57	4.57 /68	3.34	0.73
GEI	Columbia Diversified Real Return A	CDRAX	**U**	(800) 345-6611	**U /**	3.93	1.32	-2.64 /13	--	--	2.14	3.20
GEI	Columbia Diversified Real Return C	CDRCX	**U**	(800) 345-6611	**U /**	3.62	0.94	-3.37 /10	--	--	1.49	3.95
GEI	Columbia Diversified Real Return R4	CDRRX	**U**	(800) 345-6611	**U /**	3.88	1.45	-2.39 /14	--	--	2.51	2.95
GEI	Columbia Diversified Real Return R5	CDRFX	**U**	(800) 345-6611	**U /**	3.87	1.42	-2.44 /13	--	--	2.46	2.85
GEI	Columbia Diversified Real Return W	CDTWX	**U**	(800) 345-6611	**U /**	3.94	1.43	-2.64 /13	--	--	2.26	3.20
GEI	Columbia Diversified Real Return Z	CDRZX	**U**	(800) 345-6611	**U /**	3.88	1.44	-2.39 /14	--	--	2.50	2.95
EM	Columbia Emerging Markets Bond A	REBAX	**E**	(800) 345-6611	**D- / 1.0**	4.60	6.60	1.49 /66	-0.90 / 9	3.92 /60	2.61	1.14
EM	● Columbia Emerging Markets Bond B	CMBBX	**E**	(800) 345-6611	**D- / 1.3**	4.38	6.14	0.72 /54	-1.67 / 5	3.11 /47	2.09	1.89
EM	Columbia Emerging Markets Bond C	REBCX	**E**	(800) 345-6611	**D- / 1.4**	4.50	6.16	0.82 /56	-1.65 / 5	3.13 /47	2.10	1.89
EM	Columbia Emerging Markets Bond I	RSMIX	**D-**	(800) 345-6611	**C- / 3.9**	4.68	6.78	1.96 /71	-0.44 /12	4.42 /67	3.11	0.66
EM	● Columbia Emerging Markets Bond K	CMKRX	**D-**	(800) 345-6611	**C- / 3.5**	4.74	6.78	1.74 /69	-0.69 /10	4.13 /63	2.89	0.96
EM	Columbia Emerging Markets Bond R	CMBRX	**D-**	(800) 345-6611	**D+ / 2.6**	4.66	6.51	1.39 /65	-1.13 / 8	3.69 /56	2.55	1.39
EM	Columbia Emerging Markets Bond R4	CEBSX	**D-**	(800) 345-6611	**C- / 3.6**	4.74	6.78	1.78 /70	-0.64 /11	4.09 /63	2.93	0.89
EM	Columbia Emerging Markets Bond R5	CEBRX	**D-**	(800) 345-6611	**C- / 3.9**	4.78	6.86	2.02 /72	-0.46 /12	4.23 /64	3.07	0.71
EM	Columbia Emerging Markets Bond W	REMWX	**D-**	(800) 345-6611	**C- / 3.1**	4.71	6.61	1.58 /67	-0.90 / 9	3.92 /60	2.74	1.14
EM	Columbia Emerging Markets Bond Y	CEBYX	**D-**	(800) 345-6611	**C- / 4.0**	4.68	6.77	1.96 /72	-0.42 /12	4.26 /65	3.11	0.66
EM	Columbia Emerging Markets Bond Z	CMBZX	**D-**	(800) 345-6611	**C- / 3.5**	4.74	6.79	1.77 /69	-0.67 /10	4.20 /64	2.92	0.89
LP	Columbia Floating Rate A	RFRAX	**C**	(800) 345-6611	**C- / 3.8**	1.60	-0.15	-0.96 /22	1.82 /58	3.22 /48	3.97	1.07
LP	● Columbia Floating Rate B	RSFBX	**C**	(800) 345-6611	**C- / 3.8**	1.41	-0.41	-1.70 /17	1.06 /44	2.45 /37	3.32	1.82
LP	Columbia Floating Rate C	RFRCX	**C**	(800) 345-6611	**C- / 3.8**	1.30	-0.52	-1.70 /17	1.06 /44	2.45 /37	3.33	1.82
LP	Columbia Floating Rate I	RFRIX	**B**	(800) 345-6611	**C+ / 6.0**	1.69	0.13	-0.61 /25	2.19 /65	3.60 /55	4.45	0.70
LP	● Columbia Floating Rate K	CFERX	**B-**	(800) 345-6611	**C / 5.5**	1.61	-0.01	-0.90 /22	1.92 /60	3.29 /50	4.14	1.00
LP	Columbia Floating Rate R	CFRRX	**C+**	(800) 345-6611	**C / 4.8**	1.54	-0.16	-1.20 /20	1.57 /53	2.97 /44	3.83	1.32
LP	Columbia Floating Rate R4	CFLRX	**B**	(800) 345-6611	**C+ / 5.8**	1.66	0.08	-0.61 /25	2.11 /64	3.38 /51	4.34	0.82
LP	Columbia Floating Rate R5	RFRFX	**B**	(800) 345-6611	**C+ / 5.8**	1.55	0.00	-0.65 /25	2.14 /64	3.56 /54	4.40	0.75
LP	Columbia Floating Rate W	RFRWX	**C+**	(800) 345-6611	**C / 5.3**	1.49	-0.17	-1.00 /22	1.83 /58	3.24 /49	4.04	1.07
LP	Columbia Floating Rate Y	CFRYX	**B-**	(800) 345-6611	**C / 5.5**	1.57	0.02	-0.69 /24	1.91 /60	3.28 /49	4.36	0.70
LP	Columbia Floating Rate Z	CFRZX	**B**	(800) 345-6611	**C+ / 5.8**	1.66	0.08	-0.72 /24	2.07 /63	3.48 /53	4.34	0.82
GL	Columbia Global Bond A	IGBFX	**E+**	(800) 345-6611	**E- / 0.2**	4.32	1.05	-3.65 / 9	-2.90 / 3	-0.32 / 2	0.00	1.35
GL	● Columbia Global Bond B	IGLOX	**E+**	(800) 345-6611	**E- / 0.2**	4.14	0.70	-4.46 / 6	-3.64 / 2	-1.07 / 2	0.00	2.10
GL	Columbia Global Bond C	AGBCX	**E+**	(800) 345-6611	**E- / 0.2**	4.01	0.53	-4.52 / 6	-3.69 / 2	-1.09 / 2	0.00	2.10
GL	Columbia Global Bond I	AGBIX	**E+**	(800) 345-6611	**E / 0.4**	4.32	1.05	-3.34 /10	-2.54 / 3	0.08 /14	0.00	0.88
GL	● Columbia Global Bond K	RGBRX	**E+**	(800) 345-6611	**E / 0.4**	4.31	1.04	-3.65 / 9	-2.81 / 3	-0.20 / 3	0.00	1.18
GL	Columbia Global Bond R	RBGRX	**E+**	(800) 345-6611	**E / 0.3**	4.15	0.87	-3.99 / 8	-3.17 / 2	-0.57 / 2	0.00	1.60
GL	Columbia Global Bond W	RGBWX	**E+**	(800) 345-6611	**E / 0.3**	4.32	1.05	-3.65 / 9	-2.91 / 3	-0.33 / 2	0.00	1.35
GL	Columbia Global Bond Y	CGBYX	**E+**	(800) 345-6611	**E / 0.4**	4.51	1.22	-3.18 /11	-2.49 / 3	-0.02 / 3	0.00	0.88
GL	Columbia Global Bond Z	CGBZX	**E+**	(800) 345-6611	**E / 0.4**	4.30	1.22	-3.48 /10	-2.69 / 3	-0.05 / 3	0.00	1.10
*COH	Columbia High Yield Bond A	INEAX	**D**	(800) 345-6611	**C / 5.0**	2.75	2.57	-1.32 /19	2.77 /74	5.42 /74	4.77	1.07
COH	● Columbia High Yield Bond B	IEIBX	**D+**	(800) 345-6611	**C+ / 5.8**	2.57	2.19	-2.05 /15	2.00 /61	4.62 /69	4.24	1.82
COH	Columbia High Yield Bond C	APECX	**D+**	(800) 345-6611	**C+ / 5.7**	2.58	2.19	-2.10 /15	1.95 /60	4.67 /69	4.24	1.82
COH	Columbia High Yield Bond I	RSHIX	**C-**	(800) 345-6611	**B / 7.7**	2.85	2.77	-0.91 /22	3.19 /78	5.84 /76	5.42	0.65
COH	● Columbia High Yield Bond K	RSHYX	**D+**	(800) 345-6611	**B- / 7.0**	2.78	2.26	-1.54 /18	2.77 /74	5.53 /75	5.13	0.95
COH	Columbia High Yield Bond R	CHBRX	**D+**	(800) 345-6611	**C+ / 6.7**	2.69	2.44	-1.54 /18	2.52 /71	5.16 /73	4.75	1.32
COH	Columbia High Yield Bond R4	CYLRX	**C-**	(800) 345-6611	**B- / 7.5**	3.17	2.69	-1.03 /21	3.04 /77	5.54 /75	5.25	0.82
COH	Columbia High Yield Bond R5	RSHRX	**C-**	(800) 345-6611	**B- / 7.5**	2.85	2.75	-0.98 /22	3.02 /77	5.71 /75	5.38	0.70
COH	Columbia High Yield Bond W	RHYWX	**D+**	(800) 345-6611	**C+ / 6.9**	2.55	2.35	-1.56 /18	2.68 /73	5.37 /74	5.18	1.07
COH	Columbia High Yield Bond Y	CHYYX	**C-**	(800) 345-6611	**B- / 7.4**	2.86	2.40	-1.27 /20	3.07 /77	5.69 /75	5.43	0.65
COH	Columbia High Yield Bond Z	CHYZX	**C-**	(800) 345-6611	**B- / 7.5**	2.81	2.69	-1.08 /21	3.03 /77	5.75 /76	5.25	0.82
MUH	Columbia High Yield Municipal A	LHIAX	**C+**	(800) 345-6611	**A / 9.5**	1.21	3.10	4.24 /95	4.70 /98	7.86 /98	4.18	0.97
MUH	● Columbia High Yield Municipal B	CHMBX	**C+**	(800) 345-6611	**A / 9.5**	1.03	2.72	3.47 /90	3.93 /95	7.06 /96	3.57	1.72

● Denotes fund is closed to new investors
* Denotes fund is included in Section II

RISK			NET ASSETS		ASSET							FUND MANAGER		MINIMUM		LOADS	
Risk Rating/Pts	3 Yr Avg Standard Deviation	Avg Duration	NAV As of 3/31/16	Total $(Mil)	Cash %	Gov. Bond %	Muni. Bond %	Corp. Bond %	Other %	Portfolio Turnover Ratio	Avg Coupon Rate	Manager Quality Pct	Manager Tenure (Years)	Initial Purch. $	Additional Purch. $	Front End Load	Back End Load
C- / 3.2	4.6	5.4	9.75	18	0	0	0	99	1	78	4.4	39	6	0	0	0.0	0.0
C- / 3.1	4.6	5.4	9.75	472	0	0	0	99	1	78	4.4	82	6	2,000	0	0.0	0.0
U /	N/A	N/A	8.96	N/A	17	27	0	21	35	17	0.0	N/A	2	2,000	0	4.8	0.0
U /	N/A	N/A	8.96	N/A	17	27	0	21	35	17	0.0	N/A	2	2,000	0	0.0	0.0
U /	N/A	N/A	8.96	N/A	17	27	0	21	35	17	0.0	N/A	2	0	0	0.0	0.0
U /	N/A	N/A	8.95	N/A	17	27	0	21	35	17	0.0	N/A	2	100,000	0	0.0	0.0
U /	N/A	N/A	8.95	N/A	17	27	0	21	35	17	0.0	N/A	2	500	0	0.0	0.0
U /	N/A	N/A	8.96	4	17	27	0	21	35	17	0.0	N/A	2	2,000	0	0.0	0.0
E / 0.4	8.5	6.1	10.65	130	3	60	0	34	3	32	6.8	34	5	2,000	0	4.8	0.0
E / 0.4	8.5	6.1	10.63	N/A	3	60	0	34	3	32	6.8	16	5	2,000	0	0.0	0.0
E / 0.4	8.5	6.1	10.59	27	3	60	0	34	3	32	6.8	17	5	2,000	0	0.0	0.0
E / 0.4	8.5	6.1	10.66	163	3	60	0	34	3	32	6.8	49	5	0	0	0.0	0.0
E / 0.4	8.4	6.1	10.65	N/A	3	60	0	34	3	32	6.8	40	5	0	0	0.0	0.0
E / 0.4	8.5	6.1	10.65	15	3	60	0	34	3	32	6.8	27	5	0	0	0.0	0.0
E / 0.4	8.5	6.1	10.67	2	3	60	0	34	3	32	6.8	42	5	0	0	0.0	0.0
E / 0.4	8.4	6.1	10.66	11	3	60	0	34	3	32	6.8	49	5	0	0	0.0	0.0
E / 0.4	8.4	6.1	10.64	8	3	60	0	34	3	32	6.8	34	5	500	0	0.0	0.0
E / 0.4	8.5	6.1	10.66	1	3	60	0	34	3	32	6.8	50	5	0	0	0.0	0.0
E / 0.4	8.4	6.1	10.66	81	3	60	0	34	3	32	6.8	41	5	2,000	0	0.0	0.0
B / 7.8	2.6	0.2	8.64	458	2	0	0	33	65	36	4.7	92	10	5,000	0	3.0	0.0
B / 7.6	2.7	0.2	8.65	1	2	0	0	33	65	36	4.7	83	10	5,000	0	0.0	0.0
B / 7.7	2.6	0.2	8.64	91	2	0	0	33	65	36	4.7	83	10	5,000	0	0.0	0.0
B / 7.6	2.7	0.2	8.64	95	2	0	0	33	65	36	4.7	94	10	0	0	0.0	0.0
B / 7.6	2.7	0.2	8.66	N/A	2	0	0	33	65	36	4.7	92	10	0	0	0.0	0.0
B / 7.6	2.7	0.2	8.65	6	2	0	0	33	65	36	4.7	90	10	0	0	0.0	0.0
B / 7.6	2.7	0.2	8.63	15	2	0	0	33	65	36	4.7	94	10	0	0	0.0	0.0
B / 7.7	2.6	0.2	8.67	15	2	0	0	33	65	36	4.7	94	10	0	0	0.0	0.0
B / 7.8	2.6	0.2	8.65	N/A	2	0	0	33	65	36	4.7	92	10	500	0	0.0	0.0
B / 7.8	2.6	0.2	8.64	N/A	2	0	0	33	65	36	4.7	92	10	0	0	0.0	0.0
B / 7.7	2.6	0.2	8.63	91	2	0	0	33	65	36	4.7	94	10	2,000	0	0.0	0.0
D / 2.2	5.5	5.5	5.80	82	15	32	0	41	12	90	5.2	8	3	2,000	0	4.8	0.0
D / 2.1	5.6	5.5	5.79	1	15	32	0	41	12	90	5.2	6	3	2,000	0	0.0	0.0
D+ / 2.3	5.5	5.5	5.71	3	15	32	0	41	12	90	5.2	6	3	2,000	0	0.0	0.0
D+ / 2.3	5.5	5.5	5.79	N/A	15	32	0	41	12	90	5.2	9	3	0	0	0.0	0.0
D+ / 2.3	5.5	5.5	5.81	N/A	15	32	0	41	12	90	5.2	8	3	0	0	0.0	0.0
D / 2.2	5.5	5.5	5.77	N/A	15	32	0	41	12	90	5.2	7	3	0	0	0.0	0.0
D / 2.2	5.5	5.5	5.80	N/A	15	32	0	41	12	90	5.2	8	3	500	0	0.0	0.0
D / 2.2	5.5	5.5	5.79	N/A	15	32	0	41	12	90	5.2	9	3	0	0	0.0	0.0
D / 2.2	5.5	5.5	5.82	2	15	32	0	41	12	90	5.2	8	3	2,000	0	0.0	0.0
D / 1.8	5.4	4.2	2.80	1,151	4	0	0	94	2	64	6.2	92	6	2,000	0	4.8	0.0
D / 1.7	5.4	4.2	2.80	5	4	0	0	94	2	64	6.2	82	6	2,000	0	0.0	0.0
D / 1.8	5.3	4.2	2.78	77	4	0	0	94	2	64	6.2	81	6	2,000	0	0.0	0.0
D / 1.7	5.4	4.2	2.80	339	4	0	0	94	2	64	6.2	94	6	0	0	0.0	0.0
D / 1.7	5.4	4.2	2.80	36	4	0	0	94	2	64	6.2	92	6	0	0	0.0	0.0
D / 1.7	5.4	4.2	2.81	21	4	0	0	94	2	64	6.2	89	6	0	0	0.0	0.0
D / 1.7	5.5	4.2	2.82	30	4	0	0	94	2	64	6.2	93	6	0	0	0.0	0.0
D / 1.7	5.5	4.2	2.79	26	4	0	0	94	2	64	6.2	93	6	0	0	0.0	0.0
D / 1.7	5.4	4.2	2.77	N/A	4	0	0	94	2	64	6.2	91	6	500	0	0.0	0.0
D / 1.7	5.4	4.2	2.79	17	4	0	0	94	2	64	6.2	93	6	0	0	0.0	0.0
D / 1.7	5.5	4.2	2.80	193	4	0	0	94	2	64	6.2	93	6	2,000	0	0.0	0.0
D+ / 2.6	4.5	7.1	10.80	184	0	0	99	0	1	7	4.9	74	7	2,000	0	3.0	0.0
D+ / 2.6	4.5	7.1	10.80	N/A	0	0	99	0	1	7	4.9	41	7	2,000	0	0.0	0.0

99 Pct = Best
0 Pct = Worst

Fund Type	Fund Name	Ticker Symbol	Overall Investment Rating	Phone	PERFORMANCE Performance Rating/Pts	Total Return % through 3/31/16 3 Mo	6 Mo	1Yr / Pct	Annualized 3Yr / Pct	5Yr / Pct	Incl. in Returns Dividend Yield	Expense Ratio
MUH	Columbia High Yield Municipal C	CHMCX	C+	(800) 345-6611	A / 9.5	1.05	2.77	3.57 /91	4.05 /96	7.20 /97	3.67	1.72
MUH	Columbia High Yield Municipal R4	CHIYX	B-	(800) 345-6611	A+ / 9.8	1.17	3.20	4.45 /96	4.93 /99	8.08 /98	4.51	0.77
MUH	Columbia High Yield Municipal R5	CHMYX	B-	(800) 345-6611	A+ / 9.8	1.19	3.25	4.53 /97	5.03 /99	8.14 /98	4.59	0.63
MUH	Columbia High Yield Municipal Z	SRHMX	B-	(800) 345-6611	A+ / 9.8	1.26	3.20	4.45 /96	4.91 /98	8.07 /98	4.51	0.77
*COH	Columbia Income Opportunities A	AIOAX	D	(800) 345-6611	C / 4.8	2.53	2.75	-1.43 /19	2.64 /72	5.18 /73	4.46	1.11
COH ●	Columbia Income Opportunities B	AIOBX	D+	(800) 345-6611	C+ / 5.6	2.45	2.37	-2.07 /15	1.88 /59	4.40 /66	3.92	1.86
COH	Columbia Income Opportunities C	RIOCX	D+	(800) 345-6611	C+ / 5.7	2.45	2.37	-2.07 /15	1.95 /60	4.49 /67	3.92	1.86
COH	Columbia Income Opportunities I	AOPIX	C-	(800) 345-6611	B / 7.6	2.74	2.96	-0.90 /22	3.13 /77	5.62 /75	5.11	0.64
COH ●	Columbia Income Opportunities K	COPRX	C-	(800) 345-6611	B- / 7.1	2.55	2.81	-1.29 /20	2.79 /74	5.29 /73	4.81	0.94
COH	Columbia Income Opportunities R	CIORX	D+	(800) 345-6611	C+ / 6.5	2.58	2.62	-1.57 /18	2.39 /69	4.93 /71	4.43	1.36
COH	Columbia Income Opportunities R4	CPPRX	C-	(800) 345-6611	B- / 7.4	2.70	2.87	-1.06 /21	2.94 /76	5.38 /74	4.93	0.86
COH	Columbia Income Opportunities R5	CEPRX	C-	(800) 345-6611	B- / 7.5	2.62	2.93	-1.04 /21	3.04 /77	5.45 /74	5.06	0.69
COH	Columbia Income Opportunities W	CIOWX	D+	(800) 345-6611	B- / 7.0	2.64	2.75	-1.33 /19	2.68 /73	5.19 /73	4.68	1.11
COH	Columbia Income Opportunities Y	CIOYX	C-	(800) 345-6611	B / 7.6	2.74	2.96	-0.90 /22	3.09 /77	5.62 /75	5.11	0.64
COH	Columbia Income Opportunities Z	CIOZX	C-	(800) 345-6611	B- / 7.3	2.70	2.87	-1.07 /21	2.90 /75	5.45 /74	4.93	0.86
GEI	Columbia Inflation Protected Sec A	APSAX	E	(800) 345-6611	E / 0.4	5.20	5.08	-1.55 /18	-2.67 / 3	1.65 /27	0.00	1.20
GEI ●	Columbia Inflation Protected Sec B	APSBX	E	(800) 345-6611	E / 0.4	4.90	4.65	-2.34 /14	-3.35 / 2	0.91 /20	0.00	1.95
GEI	Columbia Inflation Protected Sec C	RIPCX	E	(800) 345-6611	E / 0.4	4.92	4.67	-2.34 /14	-3.36 / 2	0.91 /20	0.00	1.95
GEI	Columbia Inflation Protected Sec I	AIPIX	E+	(800) 345-6611	E+ / 0.8	5.16	5.29	-1.21 /20	-2.26 / 4	2.08 /32	0.00	0.63
GEI ●	Columbia Inflation Protected Sec K	CISRX	E	(800) 345-6611	E+ / 0.6	5.19	5.07	-1.44 /19	-2.54 / 3	1.78 /28	0.00	0.93
GEI	Columbia Inflation Protected Sec R	RIPRX	E	(800) 345-6611	E / 0.5	5.11	4.99	-1.89 /16	-2.90 / 3	1.39 /24	0.00	1.45
GEI	Columbia Inflation Protected Sec R5	CFSRX	E	(800) 345-6611	E+ / 0.7	5.08	5.20	-1.33 /19	-2.33 / 3	1.88 /30	0.00	0.68
GEI	Columbia Inflation Protected Sec W	RIPWX	E	(800) 345-6611	E+ / 0.6	5.07	5.07	-1.66 /17	-2.67 / 3	1.65 /27	0.00	1.20
GEI	Columbia Inflation Protected Sec Z	CIPZX	E	(800) 345-6611	E+ / 0.7	5.31	5.31	-1.33 /19	-2.42 / 3	1.91 /30	0.00	0.95
GEI	Columbia Limited Duration Credit A	ALDAX	D+	(800) 345-6611	D- / 1.5	2.01	1.05	-0.92 /22	0.44 /32	1.71 /28	2.22	0.85
GEI ●	Columbia Limited Duration Credit B	ALDBX	D+	(800) 345-6611	D- / 1.4	1.71	0.57	-1.67 /17	-0.35 /13	0.93 /20	1.53	1.60
GEI	Columbia Limited Duration Credit C	RDCLX	D+	(800) 345-6611	D- / 1.4	1.71	0.68	-1.66 /17	-0.35 /13	0.93 /20	1.53	1.60
GEI	Columbia Limited Duration Credit I	ALDIX	C-	(800) 345-6611	C- / 4.0	2.10	1.24	-0.56 /25	0.78 /38	2.07 /32	2.66	0.46
GEI ●	Columbia Limited Duration Credit K	CLDRX	C-	(800) 345-6611	C- / 3.4	2.02	1.09	-0.85 /23	0.48 /33	1.77 /28	2.36	0.76
COI	Columbia Limited Duration Credit R4	CDLRX	C-	(800) 345-6611	C- / 3.8	2.07	1.18	-0.67 /24	0.69 /37	1.87 /30	2.54	0.60
COI	Columbia Limited Duration Credit R5	CTLRX	C-	(800) 345-6611	C- / 3.9	1.98	1.21	-0.61 /25	0.73 /37	1.93 /30	2.61	0.51
GEI	Columbia Limited Duration Credit W	RLDWX	C-	(800) 345-6611	C- / 3.3	2.01	1.05	-0.92 /22	0.40 /31	1.70 /28	2.29	0.85
COI	Columbia Limited Duration Credit Y	CLDYX	C-	(800) 345-6611	C- / 4.0	1.99	1.24	-0.56 /25	0.78 /38	1.94 /30	2.66	0.46
COI	Columbia Limited Duration Credit Z	CLDZX	C-	(800) 345-6611	C- / 3.8	2.07	1.18	-0.67 /24	0.66 /36	1.95 /31	2.54	0.60
MUS	Columbia Minnesota Tax-Exempt A	IMNTX	A-	(800) 345-6611	A- / 9.0	1.35	2.97	3.86 /93	3.73 /94	5.92 /91	3.30	0.81
MUS ●	Columbia Minnesota Tax-Exempt B	IDSMX	A-	(800) 345-6611	B+ / 8.9	1.35	2.58	3.09 /86	2.95 /88	5.16 /86	2.66	1.56
MUS	Columbia Minnesota Tax-Exempt C	RMTCX	A-	(800) 345-6611	B+ / 8.9	1.17	2.59	3.09 /86	2.96 /88	5.13 /86	2.66	1.56
MUN	Columbia Minnesota Tax-Exempt R4	CLONX	A+	(800) 345-6611	A+ / 9.6	1.59	3.09	4.31 /96	4.06 /96	6.12 /93	3.65	0.56
MUN	Columbia Minnesota Tax-Exempt R5	CADOX	A+	(800) 345-6611	A+ / 9.6	1.60	3.10	4.32 /96	4.00 /96	6.08 /92	3.66	0.55
MUS	Columbia Minnesota Tax-Exempt Z	CMNZX	A+	(800) 345-6611	A+ / 9.6	1.59	3.09	4.31 /96	4.05 /96	6.18 /93	3.65	0.56
MM	Columbia Money Market C	RCCXX	U	(800) 345-6611	U /	--	--	--	--	--	0.01	1.44
MUS	Columbia NY Tax-Exempt A	COLNX	B+	(800) 345-6611	A- / 9.1	1.74	3.44	4.32 /96	3.83 /95	6.26 /93	3.30	0.91
MUS ●	Columbia NY Tax-Exempt B	CNYBX	B	(800) 345-6611	A- / 9.0	1.42	3.06	3.40 /89	3.01 /88	5.43 /88	2.67	1.66
MUS	Columbia NY Tax-Exempt C	CNYCX	B+	(800) 345-6611	A / 9.3	1.50	3.21	3.71 /92	3.32 /91	5.76 /91	2.96	1.66
MUN	Columbia NY Tax-Exempt R4	CNYEX	A-	(800) 345-6611	A+ / 9.6	1.67	3.43	4.44 /96	4.04 /96	6.39 /94	3.65	0.66
MUN	Columbia NY Tax-Exempt R5	CNYRX	A-	(800) 345-6611	A+ / 9.7	1.68	3.59	4.48 /97	4.08 /96	6.43 /94	3.69	0.59
MUN	Columbia NY Tax-Exempt Z	CNYZX	A-	(800) 345-6611	A+ / 9.7	1.67	3.57	4.44 /96	4.04 /96	6.47 /94	3.65	0.66
GEI	Columbia Short Term Bond A	NSTRX	C	(800) 345-6611	D+ / 2.9	0.91	0.41	0.40 /48	0.48 /33	1.00 /20	0.50	0.89
GEI ●	Columbia Short Term Bond B	NSTFX	C+	(800) 345-6611	D+ / 2.8	0.83	0.16	0.10 /41	0.18 /28	0.53 /17	0.20	1.64
GEI	Columbia Short Term Bond C	NSTIX	C	(800) 345-6611	D+ / 2.3	0.81	0.10	-0.19 /29	0.01 /16	0.59 /18	0.01	1.64
GEI	Columbia Short Term Bond I	CTMIX	B	(800) 345-6611	C- / 4.2	1.01	0.51	0.81 /55	0.89 /41	1.36 /24	0.91	0.44
GEI ●	Columbia Short Term Bond K	CBRFX	C+	(800) 345-6611	C- / 3.6	0.93	0.46	0.51 /50	0.58 /35	1.09 /21	0.61	0.74

● Denotes fund is closed to new investors
* Denotes fund is included in Section II

RISK			NET ASSETS		ASSET							FUND MANAGER		MINIMUM		LOADS	
Risk Rating/Pts	3 Yr Avg Standard Deviation	Avg Duration	NAV As of 3/31/16	Total $(Mil)	Cash %	Gov. Bond %	Muni. Bond %	Corp. Bond %	Other %	Portfolio Turnover Ratio	Avg Coupon Rate	Manager Quality Pct	Manager Tenure (Years)	Initial Purch. $	Additional Purch. $	Front End Load	Back End Load
D+ / 2.6	4.5	7.1	10.80	54	0	0	99	0	1	7	4.9	45	7	2,000	0	0.0	0.0
D+ / 2.6	4.4	7.1	10.81	5	0	0	99	0	1	7	4.9	81	7	0	0	0.0	0.0
D+ / 2.6	4.5	7.1	10.79	8	0	0	99	0	1	7	4.9	83	7	0	0	0.0	0.0
D+ / 2.6	4.5	7.1	10.80	663	0	0	99	0	1	7	4.9	80	7	2,000	0	0.0	0.0
D / 1.6	5.5	4.6	9.41	1,482	6	0	0	93	1	61	6.0	90	13	2,000	0	4.8	0.0
D / 1.7	5.5	4.6	9.41	5	6	0	0	93	1	61	6.0	79	13	2,000	0	0.0	0.0
D / 1.6	5.5	4.6	9.41	94	6	0	0	93	1	61	6.0	80	13	2,000	0	0.0	0.0
D / 1.6	5.5	4.6	9.43	466	6	0	0	93	1	61	6.0	94	13	0	0	0.0	0.0
D / 1.6	5.5	4.6	9.44	N/A	6	0	0	93	1	61	6.0	91	13	0	0	0.0	0.0
D / 1.7	5.4	4.6	9.42	1	6	0	0	93	1	61	6.0	88	13	0	0	0.0	0.0
D / 1.7	5.5	4.6	9.45	6	6	0	0	93	1	61	6.0	92	13	0	0	0.0	0.0
D / 1.6	5.5	4.6	9.44	27	6	0	0	93	1	61	6.0	93	13	0	0	0.0	0.0
D / 1.7	5.4	4.6	9.42	6	6	0	0	93	1	61	6.0	91	13	500	0	0.0	0.0
D / 1.7	5.4	4.6	9.43	10	6	0	0	93	1	61	6.0	93	13	1,000,000	0	0.0	0.0
D / 1.7	5.4	4.6	9.44	649	6	0	0	93	1	61	6.0	92	13	2,000	0	0.0	0.0
D- / 1.3	6.3	5.5	8.90	58	0	81	0	13	6	88	2.6	2	4	5,000	0	3.0	0.0
D- / 1.3	6.2	5.5	8.77	N/A	0	81	0	13	6	88	2.6	1	4	5,000	0	0.0	0.0
D- / 1.4	6.2	5.5	8.75	7	0	81	0	13	6	88	2.6	1	4	5,000	0	0.0	0.0
D- / 1.3	6.2	5.5	8.96	86	0	81	0	13	6	88	2.6	2	4	0	0	0.0	0.0
D- / 1.3	6.2	5.5	8.91	N/A	0	81	0	13	6	88	2.6	2	4	0	0	0.0	0.0
D- / 1.3	6.3	5.5	8.84	6	0	81	0	13	6	88	2.6	1	4	0	0	0.0	0.0
D- / 1.3	6.2	5.5	8.90	N/A	0	81	0	13	6	88	2.6	2	4	0	0	0.0	0.0
D- / 1.4	6.2	5.5	8.91	N/A	0	81	0	13	6	88	2.6	2	4	500	0	0.0	0.0
D- / 1.3	6.3	5.5	8.93	9	0	81	0	13	6	88	2.6	2	4	2,000	0	0.0	0.0
B- / 7.1	2.8	2.0	9.53	418	3	0	0	96	1	68	3.9	53	13	2,000	0	3.0	0.0
B- / 7.3	2.8	2.0	9.52	1	3	0	0	96	1	68	3.9	29	13	2,000	0	0.0	0.0
B- / 7.2	2.8	2.0	9.52	54	3	0	0	96	1	68	3.9	29	13	2,000	0	0.0	0.0
B- / 7.2	2.8	2.0	9.53	133	3	0	0	96	1	68	3.9	72	13	0	0	0.0	0.0
B- / 7.2	2.8	2.0	9.55	N/A	3	0	0	96	1	68	3.9	56	13	0	0	0.0	0.0
B- / 7.2	2.8	2.0	9.53	45	3	0	0	96	1	68	3.9	50	13	0	0	0.0	0.0
B- / 7.3	2.8	2.0	9.53	47	3	0	0	96	1	68	3.9	52	13	0	0	0.0	0.0
B- / 7.2	2.8	2.0	9.54	46	3	0	0	96	1	68	3.9	52	13	500	0	0.0	0.0
B- / 7.1	2.8	2.0	9.53	3	3	0	0	96	1	68	3.9	53	13	0	0	0.0	0.0
B- / 7.2	2.8	2.0	9.53	78	3	0	0	96	1	68	3.9	49	13	2,000	0	0.0	0.0
C / 5.2	3.4	6.4	5.60	442	0	0	100	0	0	9	4.9	73	9	2,000	0	3.0	0.0
C / 5.1	3.4	6.4	5.61	N/A	0	0	100	0	0	9	4.9	39	9	2,000	0	0.0	0.0
C / 5.2	3.4	6.4	5.60	59	0	0	100	0	0	9	4.9	40	9	2,000	0	0.0	0.0
C / 5.4	3.3	6.4	5.60	4	0	0	100	0	0	9	4.9	84	9	0	0	0.0	0.0
C / 5.3	3.4	6.4	5.60	N/A	0	0	100	0	0	9	4.9	82	9	100,000	0	0.0	0.0
C / 5.1	3.4	6.4	5.60	18	0	0	100	0	0	9	4.9	82	9	2,000	0	0.0	0.0
U /	N/A	N/A	1.00	25	100	0	0	0	0	0	0.0	N/A	N/A	2,000	0	0.0	0.0
C- / 4.1	3.9	6.5	7.61	164	0	0	99	0	1	11	5.0	51	6	2,000	0	3.0	0.0
C- / 4.1	3.9	6.5	7.60	N/A	0	0	99	0	1	11	5.0	27	6	2,000	0	0.0	0.0
C- / 4.1	3.9	6.5	7.60	24	0	0	99	0	1	11	5.0	35	6	2,000	0	0.0	0.0
C- / 4.1	3.9	6.5	7.59	N/A	0	0	99	0	1	11	5.0	61	6	0	0	0.0	0.0
C- / 4.2	3.9	6.5	7.58	N/A	0	0	99	0	1	11	5.0	N/A	6	0	0	0.0	0.0
C- / 4.1	3.9	6.5	7.60	20	0	0	99	0	1	11	5.0	60	6	2,000	0	0.0	0.0
A / 9.5	0.8	1.6	9.97	372	1	19	1	39	40	60	2.4	60	12	2,000	0	1.0	0.0
A+ / 9.7	0.7	1.6	9.96	1	1	19	1	39	40	60	2.4	52	12	2,000	0	0.0	0.0
A+ / 9.6	0.8	1.6	9.95	73	1	19	1	39	40	60	2.4	43	12	2,000	0	0.0	0.0
A+ / 9.7	0.7	1.6	9.95	335	1	19	1	39	40	60	2.4	81	12	0	0	0.0	0.0
A+ / 9.6	0.8	1.6	9.95	4	1	19	1	39	40	60	2.4	69	12	0	0	0.0	0.0

Fund Type	Fund Name (99 Pct = Best, 0 Pct = Worst)	Ticker Symbol	Overall Investment Rating	Phone	PERFORMANCE: Performance Rating/Pts	Total Return % through 3/31/16: 3 Mo	6 Mo	1Yr / Pct	Annualized: 3Yr / Pct	5Yr / Pct	Incl. in Returns: Dividend Yield	Expense Ratio
GEI	Columbia Short Term Bond R	CSBRX	C+	(800) 345-6611	D+ / 2.9	0.84	0.19	0.15 /43	0.23 /29	0.74 /19	0.25	1.14
COI	Columbia Short Term Bond R4	CMDRX	B-	(800) 345-6611	C- / 4.0	1.07	0.53	0.66 /53	0.77 /38	1.27 /23	0.75	0.64
COI	Columbia Short Term Bond R5	CCBRX	B	(800) 345-6611	C- / 4.2	1.00	0.59	0.76 /54	0.84 /40	1.32 /23	0.86	0.49
GEI	Columbia Short Term Bond W	CSBWX	C+	(800) 345-6611	C- / 3.4	0.91	0.31	0.40 /48	0.48 /33	1.00 /20	0.50	0.89
GEI	Columbia Short Term Bond Y	CSBYX	B	(800) 345-6611	C- / 4.2	1.01	0.51	0.81 /55	0.89 /41	1.38 /24	0.91	0.44
GEI	Columbia Short Term Bond Z	NSTMX	B-	(800) 345-6611	C- / 3.9	0.97	0.43	0.65 /52	0.73 /37	1.25 /23	0.75	0.64
MUN	Columbia Sh-Term Muni Bd A	NSMMX	C+	(800) 345-6611	C- / 3.0	0.43	0.37	0.54 /56	0.42 /36	0.88 /24	0.63	0.90
MUN ●	Columbia Sh-Term Muni Bd B	NSMNX	C-	(800) 345-6611	D- / 1.5	0.19	0.00	-0.19 /29	-0.33 /13	0.13 /16	0.00	1.65
MUN	Columbia Sh-Term Muni Bd C	NSMUX	C-	(800) 345-6611	D- / 1.5	0.19	0.00	-0.19 /29	-0.33 /13	0.13 /16	0.00	1.65
MUN	Columbia Sh-Term Muni Bd R4	CSMTX	B+	(800) 345-6611	C / 4.6	0.49	0.49	0.80 /62	0.67 /43	1.14 /28	0.89	0.65
MUN	Columbia Sh-Term Muni Bd R5	CNNRX	B+	(800) 345-6611	C / 4.9	0.51	0.54	0.90 /64	0.78 /46	1.21 /29	0.99	0.49
MUN	Columbia Sh-Term Muni Bd Z	NSMIX	B+	(800) 345-6611	C / 4.5	0.39	0.49	0.79 /62	0.67 /43	1.14 /28	0.89	0.65
* GES	Columbia Strategic Income A	COSIX	D	(800) 345-6611	C- / 3.7	2.22	2.49	0.17 /43	1.82 /58	4.21 /64	3.95	1.05
GES ●	Columbia Strategic Income B	CLSBX	D+	(800) 345-6611	C / 4.6	2.09	1.99	-0.52 /26	1.08 /44	3.41 /52	3.27	1.80
GES	Columbia Strategic Income C	CLSCX	D+	(800) 345-6611	C / 4.6	1.91	1.99	-0.69 /24	1.10 /44	3.52 /53	3.27	1.80
GES ●	Columbia Strategic Income K	CSIVX	C-	(800) 345-6611	C+ / 6.2	2.27	2.39	0.28 /45	1.96 /61	4.31 /66	4.32	0.92
GES	Columbia Strategic Income R	CSNRX	D+	(800) 345-6611	C / 5.5	2.16	2.19	-0.06 /31	1.56 /53	4.01 /62	3.71	1.30
GL	Columbia Strategic Income R4	CMNRX	C-	(800) 345-6611	C+ / 6.5	2.30	2.64	0.58 /51	2.10 /63	4.38 /66	4.45	0.80
GES	Columbia Strategic Income R5	CTIVX	C-	(800) 345-6611	C+ / 6.8	2.49	2.68	0.68 /53	2.26 /67	4.60 /69	4.54	0.67
GES	Columbia Strategic Income W	CTTWX	C-	(800) 345-6611	C+ / 6.2	2.40	2.49	0.34 /47	1.90 /59	4.25 /65	4.15	1.05
GL	Columbia Strategic Income Y	CPHUX	C-	(800) 345-6611	C+ / 6.6	2.33	2.52	0.55 /50	2.20 /65	4.44 /67	4.61	0.62
GES	Columbia Strategic Income Z	LSIZX	C-	(800) 345-6611	C+ / 6.4	2.29	2.45	0.40 /48	2.10 /63	4.45 /67	4.45	0.80
* MUN	Columbia Tax-Exempt A	COLTX	B+	(800) 345-6611	B+ / 8.9	1.05	2.91	3.29 /88	3.75 /94	6.45 /94	3.95	0.76
MUN ●	Columbia Tax-Exempt B	CTEBX	B	(800) 345-6611	B+ / 8.8	0.87	2.45	2.52 /81	2.95 /88	5.64 /90	3.33	1.51
MUN	Columbia Tax-Exempt C	COLCX	B+	(800) 345-6611	A- / 9.0	0.90	2.50	2.62 /81	3.16 /90	5.85 /91	3.43	1.51
MUN	Columbia Tax-Exempt R4	CTERX	A-	(800) 345-6611	A / 9.5	1.10	2.94	3.49 /90	3.93 /95	6.58 /95	4.27	0.56
MUN	Columbia Tax-Exempt R5	CADMX	A-	(800) 345-6611	A / 9.5	1.05	2.97	3.56 /91	3.93 /95	6.56 /95	4.34	0.50
MUN	Columbia Tax-Exempt Z	CTEZX	A-	(800) 345-6611	A / 9.5	1.10	2.94	3.49 /90	3.95 /95	6.65 /95	4.27	0.56
* COI	Columbia Total Return Bond A	LIBAX	C-	(800) 345-6611	C / 4.6	2.70	1.75	0.96 /58	1.74 /56	3.48 /53	1.76	0.91
COI ●	Columbia Total Return Bond B	LIBBX	C	(800) 345-6611	C / 4.6	2.52	1.38	0.21 /44	0.98 /42	2.71 /40	1.07	1.66
COI	Columbia Total Return Bond C	LIBCX	C	(800) 345-6611	C / 4.7	2.52	1.38	0.21 /44	1.07 /44	2.83 /42	1.07	1.66
COI	Columbia Total Return Bond I	CIMIX	B-	(800) 345-6611	C+ / 6.6	2.91	1.94	1.33 /64	2.10 /63	3.87 /60	2.18	0.50
COI ●	Columbia Total Return Bond K	CIBKX	C+	(800) 345-6611	C+ / 6.1	2.72	1.79	1.03 /59	1.81 /58	3.62 /55	1.88	0.80
COI	Columbia Total Return Bond R	CIBRX	C+	(800) 345-6611	C+ / 5.6	2.64	1.63	0.71 /53	1.48 /52	3.22 /48	1.57	1.16
COI	Columbia Total Return Bond R4	CBNRX	B-	(800) 345-6611	C+ / 6.4	2.77	1.77	1.10 /60	1.95 /60	3.71 /57	2.06	0.66
COI	Columbia Total Return Bond R5	CTBRX	B-	(800) 345-6611	C+ / 6.6	2.78	1.91	1.28 /63	2.07 /63	3.79 /58	2.13	0.55
COI	Columbia Total Return Bond W	CIBWX	C+	(800) 345-6611	C+ / 6.1	2.70	1.75	0.96 /58	1.77 /57	3.50 /53	1.81	0.91
COI	Columbia Total Return Bond Y	CTBYX	B-	(800) 345-6611	C+ / 6.6	2.80	1.94	1.22 /62	2.10 /63	3.81 /58	2.18	0.50
COI	Columbia Total Return Bond Z	SRBFX	B-	(800) 345-6611	C+ / 6.4	2.77	1.88	1.21 /62	1.99 /61	3.74 /57	2.06	0.66
* USS	Columbia US Government Mortgage	AUGAX	B-	(800) 345-6611	C / 4.7	1.28	0.74	1.17 /61	1.99 /61	3.92 /60	2.43	0.97
USS ●	Columbia US Government Mortgage	AUGBX	B-	(800) 345-6611	C / 4.8	1.28	0.55	0.42 /48	1.29 /48	3.18 /48	1.75	1.72
USS	Columbia US Government Mortgage	AUGCX	B-	(800) 345-6611	C / 4.7	1.09	0.37	0.42 /48	1.23 /47	3.14 /47	1.76	1.72
USS	Columbia US Government Mortgage I	RVGIX	A	(800) 345-6611	C+ / 6.8	1.38	1.13	1.56 /67	2.38 /69	4.30 /65	2.90	0.51
USS ●	Columbia US Government Mortgage	RSGYX	A-	(800) 345-6611	C+ / 6.2	1.31	0.79	1.26 /63	2.07 /63	3.96 /61	2.60	0.81
MTG	Columbia US Government Mortgage	CUVRX	A	(800) 345-6611	C+ / 6.5	1.34	1.05	1.42 /65	2.25 /66	4.09 /63	2.75	0.72
MTG	Columbia US Government Mortgage	CGVRX	A	(800) 345-6611	C+ / 6.7	1.37	1.10	1.51 /66	2.33 /68	4.15 /64	2.85	0.56
MTG	Columbia US Government Mortgage	CGMWX	A	(800) 345-6611	C+ / 6.3	1.47	0.93	1.36 /64	2.06 /63	3.99 /61	2.51	0.97
MTG	Columbia US Government Mortgage	CUGYX	A	(800) 345-6611	C+ / 6.6	1.57	1.13	1.56 /67	2.27 /67	4.09 /63	2.90	0.51
MUN	Columbia US Social Bond A	CONAX	U	(800) 345-6611	U /	1.57	2.58	3.24 /87	--	--	1.16	1.24
MUN	Columbia US Social Bond C	CONCX	U	(800) 345-6611	U /	1.38	2.20	2.57 /81	--	--	0.55	1.99
MUN	Columbia US Social Bond R4	CONFX	U	(800) 345-6611	U /	1.73	2.81	3.61 /91	--	--	1.45	0.99
MUN	Columbia US Social Bond R5	COVNX	U	(800) 345-6611	U /	1.71	2.78	3.56 /91	--	--	1.40	0.84

● Denotes fund is closed to new investors
* Denotes fund is included in Section II

RISK			NET ASSETS		ASSET							FUND MANAGER		MINIMUM		LOADS	
Risk Rating/Pts	3 Yr Avg Standard Deviation	Avg Duration	NAV As of 3/31/16	Total $(Mil)	Cash %	Gov. Bond %	Muni. Bond %	Corp. Bond %	Other %	Portfolio Turnover Ratio	Avg Coupon Rate	Manager Quality Pct	Manager Tenure (Years)	Initial Purch. $	Additional Purch. $	Front End Load	Back End Load
A+ / 9.7	0.7	1.6	9.97	3	1	19	1	39	40	60	2.4	54	12	0	0	0.0	0.0
A / 9.5	0.8	1.6	9.96	11	1	19	1	39	40	60	2.4	78	12	0	0	0.0	0.0
A+ / 9.6	0.7	1.6	9.95	14	1	19	1	39	40	60	2.4	81	12	0	0	0.0	0.0
A+ / 9.6	0.7	1.6	9.97	7	1	19	1	39	40	60	2.4	62	12	500	0	0.0	0.0
A+ / 9.6	0.7	1.6	9.95	7	1	19	1	39	40	60	2.4	80	12	0	0	0.0	0.0
A+ / 9.7	0.7	1.6	9.95	1,095	1	19	1	39	40	60	2.4	77	12	2,000	0	0.0	0.0
A+ / 9.7	0.7	1.7	10.42	131	0	0	99	0	1	28	3.8	59	4	2,000	0	1.0	0.0
A+ / 9.6	0.7	1.7	10.41	N/A	0	0	99	0	1	28	3.8	33	4	2,000	0	0.0	0.0
A+ / 9.7	0.6	1.7	10.41	19	0	0	99	0	1	28	3.8	34	4	2,000	0	0.0	0.0
A+ / 9.7	0.7	1.7	10.42	1	0	0	99	0	1	28	3.8	73	4	0	0	0.0	0.0
A+ / 9.7	0.7	1.7	10.42	22	0	0	99	0	1	28	3.8	77	4	0	0	0.0	0.0
A+ / 9.7	0.7	1.7	10.42	1,658	0	0	99	0	1	28	3.8	74	4	2,000	0	0.0	0.0
C- / 3.3	4.5	2.6	5.73	1,546	6	12	0	54	28	169	5.1	77	6	2,000	0	4.8	0.0
C- / 3.4	4.3	2.6	5.73	7	6	12	0	54	28	169	5.1	48	6	2,000	0	0.0	0.0
C- / 3.2	4.5	2.6	5.73	248	6	12	0	54	28	169	5.1	47	6	2,000	0	0.0	0.0
C- / 3.3	4.5	2.6	5.64	N/A	6	12	0	54	28	169	5.1	80	6	0	0	0.0	0.0
C- / 3.4	4.4	2.6	5.77	4	6	12	0	54	28	169	5.1	62	6	0	0	0.0	0.0
C- / 3.2	4.5	2.6	5.64	26	6	12	0	54	28	169	5.1	96	6	0	0	0.0	0.0
C- / 3.2	4.5	2.6	5.65	31	6	12	0	54	28	169	5.1	86	6	0	0	0.0	0.0
C- / 3.4	4.4	2.6	5.73	N/A	6	12	0	54	28	169	5.1	80	6	500	0	0.0	0.0
C- / 3.3	4.4	2.6	5.63	13	6	12	0	54	28	169	5.1	97	6	0	0	0.0	0.0
C- / 3.3	4.4	2.6	5.64	599	6	12	0	54	28	169	5.1	84	6	2,000	0	0.0	0.0
C / 4.3	3.8	6.9	14.00	3,274	0	0	99	0	1	13	5.2	56	14	2,000	0	3.0	0.0
C / 4.4	3.8	6.9	13.98	1	0	0	99	0	1	13	5.2	30	14	2,000	0	0.0	0.0
C / 4.4	3.7	6.9	13.99	111	0	0	99	0	1	13	5.2	37	14	2,000	0	0.0	0.0
C / 4.4	3.7	6.9	13.99	2	0	0	99	0	1	13	5.2	68	14	0	0	0.0	0.0
C / 4.3	3.8	6.9	13.99	1	0	0	99	0	1	13	5.2	62	14	100,000	0	0.0	0.0
C / 4.3	3.8	6.9	14.00	797	0	0	99	0	1	13	5.2	N/A	14	2,000	0	0.0	0.0
C+ / 6.6	3.0	5.5	9.11	1,107	0	17	1	31	51	316	3.5	55	11	2,000	0	3.0	0.0
C+ / 6.7	3.0	5.5	9.11	6	0	17	1	31	51	316	3.5	31	11	2,000	0	0.0	0.0
C+ / 6.6	3.0	5.5	9.11	56	0	17	1	31	51	316	3.5	33	11	2,000	0	0.0	0.0
C+ / 6.6	3.0	5.5	9.12	369	0	17	1	31	51	316	3.5	74	11	0	0	0.0	0.0
C+ / 6.7	3.0	5.5	9.10	12	0	17	1	31	51	316	3.5	58	11	0	0	0.0	0.0
C+ / 6.7	3.0	5.5	9.11	3	0	17	1	31	51	316	3.5	46	11	0	0	0.0	0.0
C+ / 6.7	3.0	5.5	9.09	8	0	17	1	31	51	316	3.5	66	11	0	0	0.0	0.0
C+ / 6.6	3.0	5.5	9.10	22	0	17	1	31	51	316	3.5	72	11	0	0	0.0	0.0
C+ / 6.6	3.0	5.5	9.12	568	0	17	1	31	51	316	3.5	56	11	500	0	0.0	0.0
C+ / 6.6	3.0	5.5	9.11	18	0	17	1	31	51	316	3.5	74	11	0	0	0.0	0.0
C+ / 6.7	3.0	5.5	9.11	1,081	0	17	1	31	51	316	3.5	70	11	2,000	0	0.0	0.0
B+ / 8.6	1.9	4.6	5.46	667	1	0	0	7	92	358	6.0	90	7	2,000	0	3.0	0.0
B+ / 8.5	2.0	4.6	5.47	1	1	0	0	7	92	358	6.0	76	7	2,000	0	0.0	0.0
B+ / 8.7	1.8	4.6	5.47	46	1	0	0	7	92	358	6.0	79	7	2,000	0	0.0	0.0
B+ / 8.6	1.9	4.6	5.46	729	1	0	0	7	92	358	6.0	93	7	0	0	0.0	0.0
B+ / 8.6	1.9	4.6	5.45	1	1	0	0	7	92	358	6.0	90	7	0	0	0.0	0.0
B+ / 8.6	1.9	4.6	5.46	47	1	0	0	7	92	358	6.0	82	7	0	0	0.0	0.0
B+ / 8.5	2.0	4.6	5.46	21	1	0	0	7	92	358	6.0	83	7	0	0	0.0	0.0
B+ / 8.6	1.9	4.6	5.48	3	1	0	0	7	92	358	6.0	79	7	500	0	0.0	0.0
B+ / 8.5	1.9	4.6	5.44	39	1	0	0	7	92	358	6.0	82	7	0	0	0.0	0.0
U /	N/A	5.5	10.20	1	0	0	90	9	1	0	3.7	N/A	1	2,000	0	3.0	0.0
U /	N/A	5.5	10.20	N/A	0	0	90	9	1	0	3.7	N/A	1	2,000	0	0.0	0.0
U /	N/A	5.5	10.21	N/A	0	0	90	9	1	0	3.7	N/A	1	0	0	0.0	0.0
U /	N/A	5.5	10.21	N/A	0	0	90	9	1	0	3.7	N/A	1	0	0	0.0	0.0

Fund Type	Fund Name (99 Pct = Best, 0 Pct = Worst)	Ticker Symbol	Overall Investment Rating	Phone	PERFORMANCE: Performance Rating/Pts	Total Return % through 3/31/16: 3 Mo	6 Mo	1Yr / Pct	Annualized: 3Yr / Pct	Annualized: 5Yr / Pct	Incl. in Returns: Dividend Yield	Incl. in Returns: Expense Ratio
MUN	Columbia US Social Bond Z	CONZX	**U**	(800) 345-6611	**U /**	1.63	2.71	3.50 /90	--	--	1.45	0.99
US	Columbia US Treasury Index A	LUTAX	**C+**	(800) 345-6611	**C+ / 6.2**	3.12	2.00	1.92 /71	1.68 /55	3.12 /47	1.28	0.66
US	● Columbia US Treasury Index B	LUTBX	**C-**	(800) 345-6611	**C / 4.8**	2.85	1.62	1.17 /61	0.89 /41	2.33 /35	0.55	1.41
US	Columbia US Treasury Index C	LUTCX	**C**	(800) 345-6611	**C / 5.0**	2.95	1.74	1.31 /63	1.02 /43	2.47 /37	0.60	1.41
US	Columbia US Treasury Index I	CUTIX	**B-**	(800) 345-6611	**C+ / 6.6**	3.16	2.17	2.17 /73	1.88 /59	3.34 /51	1.42	0.41
US	Columbia US Treasury Index R5	CUTRX	**C+**	(800) 345-6611	**C+ / 6.5**	3.17	2.08	2.08 /72	1.88 /59	3.34 /51	1.42	0.41
US	Columbia US Treasury Index W	CTIWX	**C+**	(800) 345-6611	**C+ / 6.1**	3.10	1.95	1.91 /71	1.63 /54	3.06 /46	1.18	0.66
US	Columbia US Treasury Index Z	IUTIX	**B-**	(800) 345-6611	**C+ / 6.6**	3.16	2.16	2.17 /73	1.88 /59	3.34 /51	1.42	0.41
* GEI	Commerce Bond	CFBNX	**B+**	(800) 995-6365	**C+ / 6.7**	2.38	1.49	0.95 /58	2.33 /68	4.05 /62	3.38	0.68
MUI	Commerce Kansas T/F Intm Bond	KTXIX	**A**	(800) 995-6365	**B+ / 8.4**	1.25	2.07	2.72 /82	2.47 /82	4.23 /79	2.16	0.85
MUS	Commerce Missouri T/F Intm Bd	CFMOX	**A**	(800) 995-6365	**B+ / 8.3**	1.37	2.26	2.92 /84	2.22 /79	4.05 /78	2.40	0.67
MUN	Commerce National T/F Intm Bd	CFNLX	**B+**	(800) 995-6365	**B+ / 8.3**	1.65	2.82	3.47 /90	2.13 /78	4.98 /85	2.16	0.65
USS	Commerce Short Term Govt	CFSTX	**C+**	(800) 995-6365	**C- / 3.7**	1.02	0.42	0.73 /54	0.60 /35	1.28 /23	1.42	0.83
GEI	Cornerstone Advisors Inc Oppty Inst	CAIOX	**E-**		**E- / 0.2**	1.00	-2.55	-14.39 / 0	-2.77 / 3	--	4.23	0.92
COH	Counterpoint Tactical Income A	CPATX	**U**	(844) 273-8637	**U /**	4.53	2.87	3.74 /80	--	--	0.78	2.40
COH	Counterpoint Tactical Income C	CPCTX	**U**	(844) 273-8637	**U /**	4.25	2.49	3.00 /77	--	--	0.68	3.13
COH	Counterpoint Tactical Income I	CPITX	**U**	(844) 273-8637	**U /**	4.63	2.97	3.99 /81	--	--	0.86	2.29
GEI	CRA Qualified Investment CRA	CRAIX	**B-**	(877) 272-1977	**C+ / 5.8**	1.94	1.32	2.03 /72	1.54 /53	2.91 /44	2.09	0.92
GEI	CRA Qualified Investment Inst	CRANX	**B+**	(877) 272-1977	**C+ / 6.5**	2.05	1.55	2.50 /75	1.99 /61	3.38 /51	2.55	0.47
GEI	CRA Qualified Investment Retail	CRATX	**B**	(877) 272-1977	**C+ / 6.0**	1.97	1.29	2.15 /73	1.65 /55	3.02 /45	2.21	0.82
GEI	Credit Suisse Cmdty Rtn Strat A	CRSAX	**E-**	(877) 927-2874	**E- / 0.0**	0.68	-9.72	-19.78 / 0	-17.07 / 0	-14.54 / 0	0.00	1.11
GEI	Credit Suisse Cmdty Rtn Strat C	CRSCX	**E-**	(877) 927-2874	**E- / 0.0**	0.24	-10.21	-20.38 / 0	-17.70 / 0	-15.18 / 0	0.00	1.86
GEI	Credit Suisse Cmdty Rtn Strat Inst	CRSOX	**E-**	(877) 927-2874	**E- / 0.0**	0.67	-9.74	-19.65 / 0	-16.90 / 0	-14.34 / 0	0.00	0.86
GEI	Credit Suisse Commdty Ret Str	CCRSX	**E-**	(877) 927-2874	**E- / 0.0**	0.77	-9.63	-19.59 / 0	-17.04 / 0	-14.55 / 0	0.00	1.10
COH	Credit Suisse Floating Rate HI A	CHIAX	**D+**	(877) 927-2874	**D+ / 2.9**	0.66	-0.78	-0.38 /27	1.88 /59	--	4.14	1.02
COH	● Credit Suisse Floating Rate HI B	CHOBX	**C-**	(877) 927-2874	**C- / 3.9**	0.34	-1.12	-1.09 /21	1.19 /46	--	3.59	1.77
COH	Credit Suisse Floating Rate HI C	CHICX	**C-**	(877) 927-2874	**C- / 3.8**	0.49	-1.13	-1.24 /20	1.13 /45	--	3.58	1.77
COH	Credit Suisse Floating Rate HI Inst	CSHIX	**C**	(877) 927-2874	**C+ / 5.6**	0.52	-0.71	-0.35 /27	2.06 /63	--	4.56	0.77
GEN	Credit Suisse Strategic Income A	CSOAX	**D-**	(877) 927-2874	**D- / 1.3**	-1.88	-4.24	-4.04 / 7	2.11 /64	--	6.25	1.40
GEN	Credit Suisse Strategic Income C	CSOCX	**D-**	(877) 927-2874	**D / 1.7**	-2.28	-4.71	-4.86 / 5	1.31 /48	--	5.77	2.15
GEN	Credit Suisse Strategic Income I	CSOIX	**D**	(877) 927-2874	**C- / 4.2**	-1.93	-4.23	-3.89 / 8	2.33 /68	--	6.85	1.15
GEI	Croft Income	CLINX	**C-**	(800) 551-0990	**D- / 1.3**	0.87	-0.14	-0.76 /24	0.13 /28	1.27 /23	1.41	1.64
GL	Crow Point Alternative Income	AAIFX	**D**	(855) 282-1100	**E+ / 0.8**	0.61	-0.17	-3.71 / 9	-0.83 / 9	--	2.81	4.16
USS	CT 529 Advisor Mny Mkt 529 Ptf A		**U**	(888) 843-7824	**U /**	--	--	--	--	--	0.00	1.11
USS	CT 529 Advisor Mny Mkt 529 Ptf E		**U**	(888) 843-7824	**U /**	--	--	--	--	--	0.00	0.86
COI	CT 529 Hartford Inf Plus 529 Ptf A		**E+**	(888) 843-7824	**E / 0.4**	3.21	2.63	0.55 /50	-2.41 / 3	1.68 /27	0.00	1.16
COI	CT 529 Hartford Inf Plus 529 Ptf C		**E+**	(888) 843-7824	**E / 0.4**	3.05	2.24	-0.19 /29	-3.13 / 2	0.93 /20	0.00	1.91
COI	CT 529 Hartford Inf Plus 529 Ptf E		**D-**	(888) 843-7824	**E+ / 0.8**	3.36	2.78	0.82 /56	-2.15 / 4	1.94 /30	0.00	0.91
GEL	CT 529 Hartford TR Bond 529 Ptf A		**D+**	(888) 843-7824	**C- / 4.1**	2.61	1.82	0.26 /45	1.52 /52	3.34 /51	0.00	1.15
GEL	CT 529 Hartford TR Bond 529 Ptf C		**D+**	(888) 843-7824	**C- / 4.1**	2.45	1.53	-0.44 /27	0.77 /38	2.57 /39	0.00	1.90
GEL	CT 529 Hartford TR Bond 529 Ptf E		**C**	(888) 843-7824	**C+ / 6.0**	2.67	1.96	0.59 /51	1.79 /57	3.60 /55	0.00	0.90
GEI	Cutler Fixed Income Fund	CALFX	**D**	(888) 288-5374	**C- / 3.7**	2.84	-0.91	-2.37 /14	1.00 /43	1.96 /31	3.86	1.52
COI	Cutwater Invest Grade Bond Inst	CWBIX	**C**	(866) 678-6242	**C+ / 6.4**	2.48	2.11	0.51 /50	2.38 /69	4.20 /64	2.98	1.27
USS	Davis Government Bond A	RFBAX	**C-**	(800) 279-0279	**E+ / 0.9**	0.54	0.16	0.11 /41	0.22 /29	0.55 /17	0.63	0.90
USS	● Davis Government Bond B	VRPFX	**C-**	(800) 279-0279	**D- / 1.1**	0.19	-0.55	-0.91 /22	-0.67 /10	-0.38 / 2	0.01	1.80
USS	Davis Government Bond C	DGVCX	**C-**	(800) 279-0279	**D- / 1.2**	0.37	-0.37	-0.53 /26	-0.54 /11	-0.24 / 2	0.02	1.69
USS	Davis Government Bond Y	DGVYX	**C+**	(800) 279-0279	**C- / 3.6**	0.61	0.15	0.38 /47	0.64 /36	0.89 /19	1.12	0.50
MM	● Davis Government MM B		**C**	(800) 279-0279	**D+ / 2.4**	0.05	0.05	0.09 /41	0.05 /24	0.05 /12	0.09	0.64
MM	Davis Government MM C		**C**	(800) 279-0279	**D+ / 2.4**	0.05	0.05	0.09 /41	0.05 /24	0.05 /12	0.09	0.64
MM	Davis Government MM Y		**C**	(800) 279-0279	**D+ / 2.4**	0.05	0.05	0.09 /41	0.05 /24	0.05 /12	0.09	0.64
COH	DDJ Opportunistic Hi Yld I	DDJCX	**U**	(866) 759-5679	**U /**	2.48	-0.05	--	--	--	0.00	1.88
COH	DDJ Opportunistic Hi Yld II	DDJRX	**U**	(866) 759-5679	**U /**	2.42	-0.17	--	--	--	0.00	2.13

● Denotes fund is closed to new investors
* Denotes fund is included in Section II

RISK			NET ASSETS		ASSET							FUND MANAGER		MINIMUM		LOADS	
Risk Rating/Pts	3 Yr Avg Standard Deviation	Avg Dura-tion	NAV As of 3/31/16	Total $(Mil)	Cash %	Gov. Bond %	Muni. Bond %	Corp. Bond %	Other %	Portfolio Turnover Ratio	Avg Coupon Rate	Manager Quality Pct	Manager Tenure (Years)	Initial Purch. $	Additional Purch. $	Front End Load	Back End Load
U /	N/A	5.5	10.20	26	0	0	90	9	1	0	3.7	N/A	1	2,000	0	0.0	0.0
C+ / 6.2	3.1	5.7	11.37	41	0	99	0	0	1	65	1.9	48	6	2,000	0	0.0	0.0
C+ / 6.2	3.1	5.7	11.36	1	0	99	0	0	1	65	1.9	25	6	2,000	0	0.0	0.0
C+ / 6.2	3.1	5.7	11.37	10	0	99	0	0	1	65	1.9	28	6	2,000	0	0.0	0.0
C+ / 6.3	3.1	5.7	11.37	176	0	99	0	0	1	65	1.9	56	6	0	0	0.0	0.0
C+ / 6.1	3.1	5.7	11.35	4	0	99	0	0	1	65	1.9	54	6	0	0	0.0	0.0
C+ / 6.1	3.1	5.7	11.36	259	0	99	0	0	1	65	1.9	45	6	500	0	0.0	0.0
C+ / 6.3	3.1	5.7	11.37	275	0	99	0	0	1	65	1.9	56	6	2,000	0	0.0	0.0
B- / 7.4	2.7	5.0	19.98	1,062	1	7	10	53	29	21	5.5	73	22	1,000	250	0.0	0.0
C+ / 6.0	3.1	4.4	19.64	131	2	0	97	0	1	13	0.0	34	16	1,000	250	0.0	0.0
C+ / 6.4	3.0	4.9	19.74	335	3	0	96	0	1	17	5.2	33	17	1,000	250	0.0	0.0
C / 5.1	3.4	5.6	19.86	319	0	0	99	0	1	37	0.0	21	17	1,000	250	0.0	0.0
A- / 9.1	1.2	2.3	17.42	97	0	71	0	0	29	68	0.0	55	22	1,000	250	0.0	0.0
E- / 0.2	10.1	N/A	8.26	168	30	16	0	26	28	22	0.0	5	4	2,000	0	0.0	0.0
U /	N/A	N/A	10.38	31	99	0	0	0	1	211	0.0	N/A	2	5,000	250	4.5	1.0
U /	N/A	N/A	10.31	9	99	0	0	0	1	211	0.0	N/A	2	5,000	250	0.0	1.0
U /	N/A	N/A	10.40	84	99	0	0	0	1	211	0.0	N/A	2	100,000	10,000	0.0	1.0
B / 7.6	2.7	6.6	10.86	1,502	0	0	21	0	79	24	0.0	42	7	500,000	0	0.0	0.0
B / 7.6	2.7	6.6	10.85	266	0	0	21	0	79	24	0.0	59	7	500,000	0	0.0	0.0
B- / 7.5	2.7	6.6	10.84	79	0	0	21	0	79	24	0.0	44	7	2,500	1,000	0.0	0.0
E- / 0.0	12.8	N/A	4.46	104	22	76	0	1	1	122	0.0	0	10	2,500	100	4.8	0.0
E- / 0.0	12.8	N/A	4.22	7	22	76	0	1	1	122	0.0	N/A	10	2,500	100	0.0	0.0
E- / 0.0	12.8	N/A	4.54	3,593	22	76	0	1	1	122	0.0	0	10	250,000	100,000	0.0	0.0
E- / 0.0	12.8	N/A	3.94	289	7	76	0	1	16	96	0.0	0	10	0	0	0.0	0.0
C+ / 6.1	2.6	0.5	6.56	253	4	0	0	72	24	46	5.0	92	11	2,500	100	4.8	0.0
C+ / 5.8	2.7	0.5	6.59	2	4	0	0	72	24	46	5.0	83	11	2,500	100	0.0	0.0
C+ / 6.1	2.6	0.5	6.58	118	4	0	0	72	24	46	5.0	82	11	2,500	100	0.0	0.0
C+ / 6.1	2.6	0.5	6.52	2,095	4	0	0	72	24	46	5.0	93	11	250,000	100,000	0.0	0.0
D+ / 2.6	5.1	1.5	9.04	8	2	0	0	32	66	85	6.3	96	4	2,500	100	4.8	0.0
D+ / 2.6	5.1	1.5	9.03	4	2	0	0	32	66	85	6.3	92	4	2,500	100	0.0	0.0
D+ / 2.7	5.1	1.5	9.03	58	2	0	0	32	66	85	6.3	97	4	250,000	100,000	0.0	0.0
A- / 9.1	1.2	1.6	9.59	13	25	29	0	43	3	39	3.3	43	21	2,000	100	0.0	2.0
C / 4.9	3.5	N/A	8.28	7	80	0	0	12	8	999	0.0	33	4	2,500	100	0.0	0.0
U /	N/A	N/A	10.01	4	0	0	0	0	100	0	0.0	64	6	50	25	0.0	0.0
U /	N/A	N/A	10.01	2	0	0	0	0	100	0	0.0	64	6	50	25	0.0	0.0
C- / 3.0	4.7	N/A	10.93	2	0	92	0	0	8	0	0.0	3	6	50	25	3.0	0.0
C- / 3.0	4.7	N/A	10.49	1	0	92	0	0	8	0	0.0	2	6	50	25	0.0	0.0
C- / 3.0	4.7	N/A	11.08	N/A	0	92	0	0	8	0	0.0	4	6	50	25	0.0	0.0
C / 5.1	3.4	N/A	11.78	3	0	20	1	29	50	0	0.0	26	6	50	25	3.0	0.0
C / 5.1	3.4	N/A	11.30	3	0	20	1	29	50	0	0.0	13	6	50	25	0.0	0.0
C / 5.1	3.4	N/A	11.94	1	0	20	1	29	50	0	0.0	33	6	50	25	0.0	0.0
C- / 3.7	4.2	N/A	9.78	17	8	22	0	5	65	85	0.0	21	29	2,500	0	0.0	0.0
C / 5.3	3.4	N/A	9.99	39	3	13	2	49	33	54	0.0	76	6	100,000	0	0.0	1.0
A / 9.3	1.0	1.9	5.42	34	4	0	0	0	96	25	3.0	46	17	1,000	25	4.8	0.0
A- / 9.2	1.1	1.9	5.38	1	4	0	0	0	96	25	3.0	21	17	1,000	25	0.0	0.0
A- / 9.1	1.1	1.9	5.42	11	4	0	0	0	96	25	3.0	23	17	1,000	25	0.0	0.0
A- / 9.1	1.1	1.9	5.46	15	4	0	0	0	96	25	3.0	61	17	5,000,000	25	0.0	0.0
A+ / 9.9	N/A	N/A	1.00	6	100	0	0	0	0	0	0.1	68	17	1,000	25	0.0	0.0
A+ / 9.9	N/A	N/A	1.00	7	100	0	0	0	0	0	0.1	68	17	1,000	25	0.0	0.0
A+ / 9.9	N/A	N/A	1.00	4	100	0	0	0	0	0	0.1	68	17	5,000,000	25	0.0	0.0
U /	N/A	N/A	9.42	1	0	0	0	0	100	0	0.0	N/A	1	1,000,000	50,000	0.0	1.0
U /	N/A	N/A	9.42	N/A	0	0	0	0	100	0	0.0	N/A	1	5,000	2,500	0.0	1.0

Fund Type	Fund Name (99 Pct = Best, 0 Pct = Worst)	Ticker Symbol	Overall Investment Rating	Phone	PERFORMANCE: Performance Rating/Pts	Total Return % through 3/31/16: 3 Mo	6 Mo	1Yr / Pct	Annualized: 3Yr / Pct	5Yr / Pct	Incl. in Returns: Dividend Yield	Expense Ratio
COH	DDJ Opportunistic Hi Yld Inst	DDJIX	**U**	(866) 759-5679	**U /**	2.50	-0.03	--	--	--	0.00	1.78
USS	Delaware Core Plus Bond Fund A	DEGGX	**D+**	(800) 523-1918	**C- / 3.5**	2.22	1.17	-0.20 /29	1.79 /57	3.58 /54	2.39	1.20
USS	Delaware Core Plus Bond Fund C	DUGCX	**C-**	(800) 523-1918	**C / 4.3**	2.04	0.80	-0.93 /22	1.04 /43	2.81 /42	1.77	1.95
USS	Delaware Core Plus Bond Fund I	DUGIX	**C**	(800) 523-1918	**C+ / 6.1**	2.28	1.29	0.04 /37	2.05 /62	3.84 /59	2.75	0.95
USS	Delaware Core Plus Bond Fund R	DUGRX	**C-**	(800) 523-1918	**C / 5.1**	2.03	0.92	-0.56 /25	1.50 /52	3.29 /50	2.26	1.45
COI	Delaware Corporate Bond A	DGCAX	**D**	(800) 523-1918	**C- / 3.6**	2.75	1.74	-1.88 /16	1.97 /61	5.28 /73	3.42	0.95
COI	Delaware Corporate Bond C	DGCCX	**D**	(800) 523-1918	**C / 4.3**	2.57	1.38	-2.60 /13	1.22 /47	4.50 /67	2.84	1.70
COI	Delaware Corporate Bond I	DGCIX	**C-**	(800) 523-1918	**C+ / 6.2**	2.81	1.86	-1.64 /18	2.23 /66	5.54 /75	3.83	0.70
COI	Delaware Corporate Bond R	DGCRX	**D+**	(800) 523-1918	**C / 5.4**	2.69	1.62	-1.95 /16	1.73 /56	5.05 /72	3.33	1.20
LP	Delaware Diverse Floating Rate Fd A	DDFAX	**D+**	(800) 523-1918	**E+ / 0.9**	-0.10	-0.73	-1.66 /17	0.06 /25	1.06 /21	1.91	0.95
LP	Delaware Diverse Floating Rate Fd C	DDFCX	**D+**	(800) 523-1918	**D- / 1.0**	-0.28	-0.97	-2.26 /14	-0.64 /11	0.31 /16	1.22	1.70
LP	Delaware Diverse Floating Rate Fd I	DDFLX	**C-**	(800) 523-1918	**D+ / 2.5**	-0.05	-0.50	-1.30 /19	0.35 /31	1.32 /23	2.22	0.70
LP	Delaware Diverse Floating Rate Fd R	DDFFX	**C-**	(800) 523-1918	**D- / 1.3**	-0.16	-0.74	-1.78 /17	-0.15 /14	0.59 /18	1.72	1.20
*GES	Delaware Diversified Income A	DPDFX	**D**	(800) 523-1918	**D+ / 2.9**	2.30	1.10	-0.75 /24	1.47 /51	3.32 /50	3.08	0.90
GES	Delaware Diversified Income C	DPCFX	**D+**	(800) 523-1918	**C- / 3.6**	2.12	0.73	-1.48 /18	0.72 /37	2.55 /38	2.48	1.65
GES	Delaware Diversified Income I	DPFFX	**C-**	(800) 523-1918	**C+ / 5.7**	2.48	1.34	-0.50 /26	1.76 /57	3.57 /54	3.47	0.65
GES	Delaware Diversified Income R	DPRFX	**C-**	(800) 523-1918	**C / 4.7**	2.36	1.09	-0.99 /22	1.26 /47	3.08 /46	2.97	1.15
EM	Delaware Emerging Markets Debt A	DEDAX	**U**	(800) 523-1918	**U /**	4.38	4.19	1.11 /60	--	--	3.38	2.02
EM	Delaware Emerging Markets Debt C	DEDCX	**U**	(800) 523-1918	**U /**	4.38	4.19	1.11 /60	--	--	3.54	2.77
EM	Delaware Emerging Markets Debt	DEDIX	**U**	(800) 523-1918	**U /**	4.38	4.19	1.11 /60	--	--	3.54	1.77
EM	Delaware Emerging Markets Debt R	DEDRX	**U**	(800) 523-1918	**U /**	4.38	4.19	1.11 /60	--	--	3.54	2.27
COI	Delaware Extended Duration Bd A	DEEAX	**D+**	(800) 523-1918	**C+ / 6.8**	5.31	3.97	-2.85 /12	3.76 /82	8.41 /89	3.62	1.00
COI	Delaware Extended Duration Bd C	DEECX	**D+**	(800) 523-1918	**B- / 7.4**	5.13	3.76	-3.41 /10	3.00 /76	7.61 /85	3.06	1.75
COI	Delaware Extended Duration Bd I	DEEIX	**C-**	(800) 523-1918	**B / 8.2**	5.38	4.09	-2.47 /13	4.02 /84	8.69 /90	4.03	0.75
COI	Delaware Extended Duration Bd R	DEERX	**D+**	(800) 523-1918	**B / 7.9**	5.25	3.84	-3.07 /11	3.51 /80	8.14 /88	3.54	1.25
COH	Delaware High-Yield Bond	DPHYX	**D-**	(800) 523-1918	**C- / 3.5**	2.70	0.55	-4.85 / 5	1.11 /45	4.56 /68	5.12	0.56
COH	Delaware High-Yield Opps A	DHOAX	**E**	(800) 523-1918	**E / 0.5**	2.18	-0.69	-6.76 / 2	-0.10 /15	3.44 /52	5.88	1.12
COH	Delaware High-Yield Opps C	DHOCX	**E**	(800) 523-1918	**E+ / 0.6**	2.00	-1.05	-7.67 / 2	-0.84 / 9	2.69 /40	5.38	1.87
COH	Delaware High-Yield Opps I	DHOIX	**E+**	(800) 523-1918	**D- / 1.2**	2.52	-0.57	-6.53 / 3	0.15 /28	3.72 /57	6.43	0.87
COH	Delaware High-Yield Opps R	DHIRX	**E**	(800) 523-1918	**E+ / 0.8**	2.11	-0.81	-7.19 / 2	-0.33 /13	3.21 /48	5.90	1.37
USS	Delaware Limited-Term Diver Inc A	DTRIX	**C-**	(800) 523-1918	**D+ / 2.4**	1.43	1.13	0.81 /55	0.55 /34	1.32 /23	1.58	0.93
USS	Delaware Limited-Term Diver Inc C	DTICX	**C-**	(800) 523-1918	**D / 1.7**	1.24	0.59	-0.14 /30	-0.30 /13	0.45 /17	0.79	1.68
USS	Delaware Limited-Term Diver Inc I	DTINX	**C+**	(800) 523-1918	**C- / 4.1**	1.35	1.08	0.85 /56	0.69 /37	1.45 /25	1.78	0.68
USS	Delaware Limited-Term Diver Inc R	DLTRX	**C**	(800) 523-1918	**C- / 3.1**	1.35	0.83	0.35 /47	0.19 /29	0.97 /20	1.28	1.18
MUH	Delaware MN HY Muni Bond A	DVMHX	**C+**	(800) 523-1918	**B / 8.2**	1.24	2.49	3.54 /90	3.37 /92	5.80 /91	3.22	0.99
MUH	Delaware MN HY Muni Bond C	DVMMX	**B-**	(800) 523-1918	**B+ / 8.5**	1.06	2.11	2.78 /83	2.60 /84	5.03 /85	2.64	1.74
MUN	Delaware MN HY Muni Bond Inst	DMHIX	**U**	(800) 523-1918	**U /**	1.30	2.61	3.79 /92	--	--	3.61	0.74
MUH	Delaware Natl HY Muni Bd A	CXHYX	**C+**	(800) 523-1918	**A / 9.4**	1.97	4.19	5.06 /98	4.59 /98	8.43 /99	3.53	0.96
MUH	Delaware Natl HY Muni Bd C	DVHCX	**C+**	(800) 523-1918	**A+ / 9.6**	1.79	3.81	4.38 /96	3.81 /95	7.63 /98	2.97	1.71
MUH	Delaware Natl HY Muni Bd Inst	DVHIX	**C+**	(800) 523-1918	**A+ / 9.9**	2.11	4.39	5.40 /98	4.88 /98	8.70 /99	3.93	0.71
GEI	Delaware Pooled Trust Core Plus FI	DCPFX	**C+**	(800) 523-1918	**C+ / 6.4**	2.41	1.54	0.46 /49	2.17 /65	4.02 /62	2.25	0.60
MUS	Delaware Tax Free Arizona Fund A	VAZIX	**C+**	(800) 523-1918	**B / 8.2**	1.71	3.26	3.61 /91	3.32 /91	5.47 /89	3.02	0.96
MUS	Delaware Tax Free Arizona Fund C	DVACX	**C+**	(800) 523-1918	**B+ / 8.6**	1.53	2.89	2.85 /83	2.55 /83	4.68 /83	2.44	1.71
MUN	Delaware Tax Free Arizona Inst	DAZIX	**U**	(800) 523-1918	**U /**	1.77	3.39	3.86 /93	--	--	3.41	0.71
MUS	Delaware Tax Free California A	DVTAX	**C+**	(800) 523-1918	**B+ / 8.9**	1.87	3.71	4.69 /97	3.90 /95	7.29 /97	3.24	1.00
MUS	Delaware Tax Free California C	DVFTX	**B-**	(800) 523-1918	**A- / 9.2**	1.61	3.25	3.91 /93	3.13 /89	6.49 /94	2.67	1.75
MUN	Delaware Tax Free California Inst	DCTIX	**U**	(800) 523-1918	**U /**	1.93	3.84	5.03 /98	--	--	3.63	0.75
MUS	Delaware Tax Free Colorado A	VCTFX	**C+**	(800) 523-1918	**B+ / 8.5**	1.89	3.73	4.14 /95	3.47 /92	5.86 /91	3.33	0.97
MUS	Delaware Tax Free Colorado C	DVCTX	**B-**	(800) 523-1918	**B+ / 8.9**	1.71	3.35	3.37 /89	2.70 /85	5.07 /86	2.76	1.72
MUN	Delaware Tax Free Colorado Inst	DCOIX	**U**	(800) 523-1918	**U /**	1.95	3.86	4.39 /96	--	--	3.73	0.72
MUS	Delaware Tax Free Idaho A	VIDAX	**C**	(800) 523-1918	**B- / 7.1**	1.51	2.78	3.53 /90	2.45 /82	4.23 /79	2.96	0.99
MUS	Delaware Tax Free Idaho C	DVICX	**C+**	(800) 523-1918	**B / 7.8**	1.33	2.41	2.69 /82	1.69 /72	3.45 /74	2.37	1.74

• Denotes fund is closed to new investors
* Denotes fund is included in Section II

RISK			NET ASSETS		ASSET							FUND MANAGER		MINIMUM		LOADS	
Risk Rating/Pts	3 Yr Avg Standard Deviation	Avg Duration	NAV As of 3/31/16	Total $(Mil)	Cash %	Gov. Bond %	Muni. Bond %	Corp. Bond %	Other %	Portfolio Turnover Ratio	Avg Coupon Rate	Manager Quality Pct	Manager Tenure (Years)	Initial Purch. $	Additional Purch. $	Front End Load	Back End Load
U /	N/A	N/A	9.43	8	0	0	0	0	100	0	0.0	N/A	1	5,000,000	0	0.0	1.0
C /5.3	3.4	5.3	8.39	70	3	10	0	32	55	313	3.6	54	19	1,000	100	4.5	0.0
C /5.3	3.4	5.3	8.40	10	3	10	0	32	55	313	3.6	30	19	1,000	100	0.0	0.0
C /5.3	3.3	5.3	8.40	47	3	10	0	32	55	313	3.6	68	19	0	0	0.0	0.0
C /5.1	3.4	5.3	8.41	6	3	10	0	32	55	313	3.6	42	19	0	0	0.0	0.0
C- /3.0	4.5	7.0	5.70	359	2	1	1	90	6	215	4.5	33	9	1,000	100	4.5	0.0
C- /3.1	4.5	7.0	5.70	173	2	1	1	90	6	215	4.5	17	9	1,000	100	0.0	0.0
C- /3.1	4.5	7.0	5.70	604	2	1	1	90	6	215	4.5	40	9	0	0	0.0	0.0
C- /3.0	4.5	7.0	5.71	27	2	1	1	90	6	215	4.5	26	9	0	0	0.0	0.0
A- /9.0	1.4	0.1	8.18	65	7	1	1	48	43	86	2.6	55	6	1,000	100	2.8	0.0
A- /9.0	1.4	0.1	8.18	56	7	1	1	48	43	86	2.6	32	6	1,000	100	0.0	0.0
A- /9.0	1.4	0.1	8.18	181	7	1	1	48	43	86	2.6	72	6	0	0	0.0	0.0
A- /9.0	1.4	0.1	8.18	1	7	1	1	48	43	86	2.6	48	6	0	0	0.0	0.0
C /4.7	3.6	5.3	8.71	1,500	4	12	0	37	47	218	4.0	23	15	1,000	100	4.5	0.0
C /4.8	3.6	5.3	8.71	939	4	12	0	37	47	218	4.0	13	15	1,000	100	0.0	0.0
C /4.8	3.6	5.3	8.72	2,611	4	12	0	37	47	218	4.0	32	15	0	0	0.0	0.0
C /4.7	3.6	5.3	8.71	93	4	12	0	37	47	218	4.0	19	15	0	0	0.0	0.0
U /	N/A	5.3	8.02	N/A	3	26	1	65	5	288	5.2	N/A	3	1,000	100	4.5	0.0
U /	N/A	5.3	8.02	N/A	3	26	1	65	5	288	5.2	N/A	3	1,000	100	0.0	0.0
U /	N/A	5.3	8.02	19	3	26	1	65	5	288	5.2	N/A	3	0	0	0.0	0.0
U /	N/A	5.3	8.02	N/A	3	26	1	65	5	288	5.2	N/A	3	0	0	0.0	0.0
E /0.4	7.7	13.4	6.32	215	3	0	5	88	4	185	4.7	24	9	1,000	100	4.5	0.0
E /0.4	7.8	13.4	6.32	30	3	0	5	88	4	185	4.7	12	9	1,000	100	0.0	0.0
E /0.4	7.7	13.4	6.31	335	3	0	5	88	4	185	4.7	30	9	0	0	0.0	0.0
E /0.4	7.7	13.4	6.33	26	3	0	5	88	4	185	4.7	19	9	0	0	0.0	0.0
D- /1.3	5.8	4.8	7.23	223	13	0	0	80	7	84	6.4	42	9	1,000,000	0	0.0	0.0
E+ /0.9	6.1	4.6	3.58	178	5	0	0	86	9	86	6.5	13	4	1,000	100	4.5	0.0
E+ /0.9	6.2	4.6	3.58	48	5	0	0	86	9	86	6.5	8	4	1,000	100	0.0	0.0
E+ /0.9	6.2	4.6	3.58	102	5	0	0	86	9	86	6.5	16	4	0	0	0.0	0.0
E+ /0.9	6.1	4.6	3.59	9	5	0	0	86	9	86	6.5	11	4	0	0	0.0	0.0
B+ /8.9	1.6	2.7	8.52	439	1	1	0	51	47	80	2.6	47	17	1,000	100	2.8	0.0
B+ /8.9	1.6	2.7	8.51	139	1	1	0	51	47	80	2.6	23	17	1,000	100	0.0	0.0
B+ /8.9	1.5	2.7	8.51	448	1	1	0	51	47	80	2.6	54	17	0	0	0.0	0.0
B+ /8.8	1.6	2.7	8.52	6	1	1	0	51	47	80	2.6	35	17	0	0	0.0	0.0
C- /4.2	3.4	4.1	10.96	120	1	0	98	0	1	16	5.2	58	13	1,000	100	4.5	0.0
C- /4.2	3.3	4.1	10.98	34	1	0	98	0	1	16	5.2	33	13	1,000	100	0.0	0.0
U /	N/A	4.1	10.96	24	1	0	98	0	1	16	5.2	N/A	13	0	0	0.0	0.0
D /1.8	5.4	5.8	11.05	240	2	0	97	0	1	10	5.7	34	13	1,000	100	4.5	0.0
D /1.8	5.4	5.8	11.10	105	2	0	97	0	1	10	5.7	17	13	1,000	100	0.0	0.0
D /1.8	5.4	5.8	11.16	790	2	0	97	0	1	10	5.7	43	13	0	0	0.0	0.0
C /5.4	3.3	5.3	10.19	133	3	12	0	31	54	436	3.5	44	14	1,000,000	0	0.0	0.0
C- /3.4	4.3	4.6	11.66	78	1	0	98	0	1	12	5.2	25	13	1,000	100	4.5	0.0
C- /3.4	4.3	4.6	11.69	7	1	0	98	0	1	12	5.2	13	13	1,000	100	0.0	0.0
U /	N/A	4.6	11.66	1	1	0	98	0	1	12	5.2	N/A	13	0	0	0.0	0.0
C- /3.2	4.6	5.0	12.39	66	2	0	97	0	1	24	5.4	33	13	1,000	100	4.5	0.0
C- /3.1	4.6	5.0	12.41	18	2	0	97	0	1	24	5.4	17	13	1,000	100	0.0	0.0
U /	N/A	5.0	12.39	13	2	0	97	0	1	24	5.4	N/A	13	0	0	0.0	0.0
C- /3.5	4.3	5.1	11.49	180	0	0	99	0	1	10	5.3	29	13	1,000	100	4.5	0.0
C- /3.5	4.3	5.1	11.52	14	0	0	99	0	1	10	5.3	15	13	1,000	100	0.0	0.0
U /	N/A	5.1	11.49	6	0	0	99	0	1	10	5.3	N/A	13	0	0	0.0	0.0
C /4.4	3.7	4.4	11.68	75	1	0	98	0	1	7	5.2	20	13	1,000	100	4.5	0.0
C /4.4	3.7	4.4	11.67	29	1	0	98	0	1	7	5.2	11	13	1,000	100	0.0	0.0

Fund Type	Fund Name (99 Pct = Best, 0 Pct = Worst)	Ticker Symbol	Overall Investment Rating	Phone	PERFORMANCE: Performance Rating/Pts	Total Return % through 3/31/16: 3 Mo	6 Mo	1Yr / Pct	Annualized: 3Yr / Pct	Annualized: 5Yr / Pct	Incl. in Returns: Dividend Yield	Expense Ratio
MUN	Delaware Tax Free Idaho Inst	DTIDX	U	(800) 523-1918	U /	1.57	2.90	3.70 /92	--	--	3.34	0.74
MUS	Delaware Tax Free Minnesota A	DEFFX	B+	(800) 523-1918	B / 8.1	1.32	2.52	3.46 /90	3.30 /91	5.47 /89	3.23	0.95
MUS	Delaware Tax Free Minnesota C	DMOCX	B+	(800) 523-1918	B+ / 8.4	1.14	2.15	2.70 /82	2.51 /83	4.68 /83	2.65	1.70
MUN	Delaware Tax Free Minnesota Inst	DMNIX	U	(800) 523-1918	U /	1.29	2.56	3.63 /91	--	--	3.63	0.70
MUS	Delaware Tax Free MN Intmdt A	DXCCX	A+	(800) 523-1918	B / 7.9	1.13	2.17	2.90 /84	2.65 /84	4.29 /80	2.85	0.97
MUS	Delaware Tax Free MN Intmdt C	DVSCX	A	(800) 523-1918	B / 7.6	0.94	1.66	1.95 /77	1.76 /73	3.41 /73	2.10	1.72
MUN	Delaware Tax Free MN Intmdt Inst	DMIIX	U	(800) 523-1918	U /	1.17	2.15	2.96 /85	--	--	3.08	0.72
MUS	Delaware Tax Free New York A	FTNYX	C+	(800) 523-1918	B+ / 8.6	1.58	3.63	4.12 /95	3.60 /93	6.21 /93	2.92	1.04
MUS	Delaware Tax Free New York C	DVFNX	C+	(800) 523-1918	B+ / 8.9	1.41	3.26	3.36 /89	2.80 /86	5.43 /88	2.33	1.79
MUN	Delaware Tax Free New York Inst	DTNIX	U	(800) 523-1918	U /	1.64	3.75	4.38 /96	--	--	3.30	0.79
MUS	Delaware Tax-Free Pennsylvania A	DELIX	C+	(800) 523-1918	B / 8.2	1.44	2.86	3.57 /91	3.37 /92	5.85 /91	3.33	0.94
MUS	Delaware Tax-Free Pennsylvania C	DPTCX	B-	(800) 523-1918	B+ / 8.6	1.26	2.35	2.68 /82	2.60 /84	5.03 /86	2.75	1.70
MUN	Delaware Tax-Free Pennsylvania Inst	DTPIX	U	(800) 523-1918	U /	1.62	2.97	3.82 /93	--	--	3.72	0.70
MUN	Delaware Tax-Free USA A	DMTFX	C+	(800) 523-1918	B / 8.1	1.50	3.12	3.63 /91	3.18 /90	6.31 /94	3.38	0.96
MUN	Delaware Tax-Free USA C	DUSCX	C+	(800) 523-1918	B+ / 8.4	1.32	2.75	2.87 /84	2.41 /82	5.52 /89	2.80	1.71
MUN	Delaware Tax-Free USA I	DTFIX	B	(800) 523-1918	A / 9.4	1.55	3.32	3.97 /94	3.44 /92	6.57 /95	3.77	0.71
MUN	Delaware Tax-Free USA Intmdt A	DMUSX	A-	(800) 523-1918	B / 7.8	1.40	2.76	3.04 /85	2.47 /82	4.42 /81	2.81	0.92
MUN	Delaware Tax-Free USA Intmdt C	DUICX	B+	(800) 523-1918	B- / 7.5	1.12	2.26	2.18 /78	1.61 /70	3.54 /74	2.06	1.67
MUN	Delaware Tax-Free USA Intmdt Inst	DUSIX	A+	(800) 523-1918	B+ / 8.7	1.43	2.82	3.19 /87	2.63 /84	4.58 /82	3.03	0.67
COI	Delaware VIP Capital Reserves Svc		C+	(800) 523-1918	C- / 4.2	1.35	1.17	0.70 /53	0.78 /38	1.40 /24	1.41	0.86
MMT	DEU Tax Free Money Fund	DTBXX	C	(800) 728-3337	D / 2.2	0.00	0.02	0.02 /36	0.03 /24	0.03 /12	0.02	0.23
MMT	DEU Tax Free Money Fund S	DTCXX	C	(800) 728-3337	D / 2.2	0.00	0.02	0.02 /36	0.03 /24	0.03 /12	0.02	0.26
*MUS	Deutsche CA Tax Free Inc A	KCTAX	B-	(800) 728-3337	B+ / 8.9	1.50	3.13	3.43 /89	3.67 /94	6.69 /95	3.45	0.93
MUS	Deutsche CA Tax Free Inc C	KCTCX	B-	(800) 728-3337	B+ / 8.9	1.32	2.77	2.66 /82	2.91 /87	5.87 /91	2.82	1.70
MUS	Deutsche CA Tax Free Inc S	SDCSX	B	(800) 728-3337	A+ / 9.6	1.69	3.26	3.68 /92	3.93 /95	6.95 /96	3.80	0.79
MM	Deutsche Cash Investment Trust C	DOCXX	U	(800) 728-3337	U /	--	--	--	--	--	0.01	1.50
MM	Deutsche Cash Investment Trust S	DOSXX	U	(800) 728-3337	U /	--	--	--	--	--	0.01	0.54
MM	Deutsche Cash Management Fund	BICXX	C	(800) 728-3337	D / 2.0	0.04	0.05	0.05 /38	0.02 /19	0.02 / 7	0.05	0.33
MM	Deutsche Cash Reserves Instl	BIRXX	C	(800) 728-3337	D+ / 2.4	0.06	0.09	0.10 /41	0.04 /24	0.05 /12	0.10	0.27
MM	Deutsche CAT GASP - Govt Cash	DBBXX	C	(800) 728-3337	D+ / 2.4	0.06	0.07	0.09 /41	0.05 /24	0.04 /11	0.09	0.20
MM	Deutsche CAT GASP - Money	DTGXX	C-	(800) 728-3337	D / 1.9	0.02	0.03	0.03 /36	0.02 /19	0.02 / 7	0.03	0.27
MM	Deutsche CAT Tax-Exempt Port Svc	CHSXX	C	(800) 728-3337	D / 2.0	0.00	0.02	0.02 /34	0.03 /22	0.02 / 7	0.02	1.04
MMT	Deutsche CAT-TEP TF Inv Shs	DTDXX	C	(800) 728-3337	D / 2.2	0.00	0.02	0.02 /36	0.03 /24	0.03 /12	0.02	0.64
GES	Deutsche Core Fixed Income A	SFXAX	C	(800) 728-3337	C / 4.5	2.49	2.33	0.76 /54	2.08 /63	3.83 /59	2.04	1.07
GES	Deutsche Core Fixed Income C	SFXCX	C+	(800) 728-3337	C / 5.1	2.31	1.95	0.01 /31	1.32 /49	3.06 /46	1.40	1.80
GES	Deutsche Core Fixed Income Inst	MFINX	A-	(800) 728-3337	C+ / 6.9	2.66	2.46	1.01 /59	2.34 /68	4.11 /63	2.39	0.75
GES	Deutsche Core Fixed Income R	SFXRX	B	(800) 728-3337	C+ / 6.1	2.52	2.30	0.51 /50	1.86 /59	3.59 /55	1.89	1.48
GES	Deutsche Core Fixed Income S	SFXSX	A-	(800) 728-3337	C+ / 6.8	2.63	2.41	0.90 /57	2.28 /67	4.01 /62	2.28	0.81
GEI	Deutsche Core Plus Income A	SZIAX	D	(800) 728-3337	D+ / 2.3	2.29	1.44	-0.16 /30	1.09 /44	2.91 /44	2.61	1.08
GEI	Deutsche Core Plus Income C	SZICX	D	(800) 728-3337	C- / 3.2	2.00	1.06	-0.91 /22	0.33 /30	2.12 /33	1.97	1.88
GEI	Deutsche Core Plus Income Inst	SZIIX	C-	(800) 728-3337	C / 5.1	2.27	1.47	0.08 /40	1.33 /49	3.16 /48	2.99	0.74
GEI	Deutsche Core Plus Income S	SCSBX	C-	(800) 728-3337	C / 5.1	2.36	1.57	0.09 /41	1.34 /49	3.17 /48	2.98	0.84
MM	Deutsche Daily Assets Capital	DAFXX	C+	(800) 728-3337	D+ / 2.7	0.10	0.15	0.23 /45	0.14 /28	0.16 /15	0.23	0.21
EM	Deutsche Enh Emg Mrkts Fxd Inc A	SZEAX	E-	(800) 728-3337	E- / 0.2	4.45	3.57	-2.95 /12	-2.87 / 3	0.40 /17	4.52	1.29
EM	Deutsche Enh Emg Mrkts Fxd Inc C	SZECX	E-	(800) 728-3337	E / 0.3	4.13	3.06	-3.77 / 8	-3.64 / 2	-0.39 / 2	3.96	2.02
EM	Deutsche Enh Emg Mrkts Fxd Inc Inst	SZEIX	E	(800) 728-3337	E / 0.5	4.43	3.65	-2.70 /12	-2.56 / 3	0.76 /19	5.13	0.85
EM	Deutsche Enh Emg Mrkts Fxd Inc S	SCEMX	E	(800) 728-3337	E / 0.5	4.40	3.71	-2.72 /12	-2.66 / 3	0.63 /18	4.99	1.00
GL	Deutsche Enhanced Global Bond A	SZGAX	E+	(800) 728-3337	E+ / 0.7	2.15	2.06	0.18 /43	-0.59 /11	0.24 /16	2.48	1.31
GL	Deutsche Enhanced Global Bond C	SZGCX	D-	(800) 728-3337	D- / 1.0	1.96	1.68	-0.68 /24	-1.34 / 7	-0.50 / 2	1.85	2.07
GL	Deutsche Enhanced Global Bond S	SSTGX	D	(800) 728-3337	D+ / 2.6	2.22	2.19	0.43 /48	-0.34 /13	0.51 /17	2.85	1.01
LP	Deutsche Floating Rate A	DFRAX	D	(800) 728-3337	E / 0.4	-1.10	-4.00	-5.54 / 4	-0.50 /11	1.55 /26	4.52	1.14
LP	Deutsche Floating Rate C	DFRCX	D	(800) 728-3337	E / 0.4	-1.15	-4.32	-6.20 / 3	-1.22 / 7	0.80 /19	3.84	1.91

● Denotes fund is closed to new investors
* Denotes fund is included in Section II

RISK			NET ASSETS		ASSET							FUND MANAGER		MINIMUM		LOADS	
Risk Rating/Pts	3 Yr Avg Standard Deviation	Avg Duration	NAV As of 3/31/16	Total $(Mil)	Cash %	Gov. Bond %	Muni. Bond %	Corp. Bond %	Other %	Portfolio Turnover Ratio	Avg Coupon Rate	Manager Quality Pct	Manager Tenure (Years)	Initial Purch. $	Additional Purch. $	Front End Load	Back End Load
U /	N/A	4.4	11.68	4	1	0	98	0	1	7	5.2	N/A	13	0	0	0.0	0.0
C / 5.3	3.3	4.2	12.73	487	1	0	98	0	1	11	5.3	55	13	1,000	100	4.5	0.0
C / 5.3	3.3	4.2	12.77	49	1	0	98	0	1	11	5.3	30	13	1,000	100	0.0	0.0
U /	N/A	4.2	12.72	39	1	0	98	0	1	11	5.3	N/A	13	0	0	0.0	0.0
B- / 7.3	2.8	3.9	11.33	82	2	0	97	0	1	14	5.0	52	13	1,000	100	2.8	0.0
B- / 7.1	2.8	3.9	11.35	13	2	0	97	0	1	14	5.0	24	13	1,000	100	0.0	0.0
U /	N/A	3.9	11.33	9	2	0	97	0	1	14	5.0	N/A	13	0	0	0.0	0.0
C- / 3.3	4.4	4.9	11.75	55	1	0	98	0	1	6	5.1	30	13	1,000	100	4.5	0.0
C- / 3.3	4.4	4.9	11.72	19	1	0	98	0	1	6	5.1	14	13	1,000	100	0.0	0.0
U /	N/A	4.9	11.75	15	1	0	98	0	1	6	5.1	N/A	13	0	0	0.0	0.0
C- / 3.9	4.0	4.5	8.25	437	1	0	98	0	1	13	5.4	35	13	1,000	100	4.5	0.0
C- / 3.8	4.1	4.5	8.25	34	1	0	98	0	1	13	5.4	16	13	1,000	100	0.0	0.0
U /	N/A	4.5	8.25	20	1	0	98	0	1	13	5.4	N/A	13	0	0	0.0	0.0
C- / 3.7	4.1	4.6	12.03	495	2	0	97	0	1	16	5.6	26	13	1,000	100	4.5	0.0
C- / 3.7	4.2	4.6	12.03	31	2	0	97	0	1	16	5.6	13	13	1,000	100	0.0	0.0
C- / 3.7	4.2	4.6	12.12	37	2	0	97	0	1	16	5.6	33	13	0	0	0.0	0.0
C+ / 6.4	3.0	4.7	12.24	185	1	0	98	0	1	19	5.3	38	13	1,000	100	2.8	0.0
C+ / 6.6	3.0	4.7	12.23	50	1	0	98	0	1	19	5.3	18	13	1,000	100	0.0	0.0
C+ / 6.6	3.0	4.7	12.36	478	1	0	98	0	1	19	5.3	44	13	0	0	0.0	0.0
B+ / 8.9	1.5	2.7	9.82	1,349	3	1	0	49	47	113	2.3	58	16	0	0	0.0	0.0
A+ / 9.9	N/A	N/A	1.00	167	100	0	0	0	0	0	0.0	67	N/A	1,000	50	0.0	0.0
A+ / 9.9	N/A	N/A	1.00	69	100	0	0	0	0	0	0.0	67	N/A	2,500	50	0.0	0.0
C- / 3.6	4.2	4.8	7.77	546	0	0	100	0	0	26	0.0	36	17	1,000	50	2.8	0.0
C- / 3.6	4.2	4.8	7.72	50	0	0	100	0	0	26	0.0	18	17	1,000	50	0.0	0.0
C- / 3.4	4.3	4.8	7.76	427	0	0	100	0	0	26	0.0	41	17	2,500	50	0.0	0.0
U /	N/A	N/A	1.00	31	100	0	0	0	0	0	0.0	N/A	N/A	1,000	50	0.0	0.0
U /	N/A	N/A	1.00	279	100	0	0	0	0	0	0.0	N/A	N/A	2,500	50	0.0	0.0
A+ / 9.9	N/A	N/A	1.00	2,194	100	0	0	0	0	0	0.1	64	N/A	1,000,000	0	0.0	0.0
A+ / 9.9	N/A	N/A	1.00	913	100	0	0	0	0	0	0.1	64	N/A	10,000,000	0	0.0	0.0
A+ / 9.9	N/A	N/A	1.00	3,465	100	0	0	0	0	0	0.1	67	N/A	1,000,000	0	0.0	0.0
A+ / 9.9	N/A	N/A	1.00	120	100	0	0	0	0	0	0.0	64	N/A	1,000	50	0.0	0.0
A+ / 9.9	N/A	N/A	1.00	54	100	0	0	0	0	0	0.0	67	N/A	1,000	100	0.0	0.0
A+ / 9.9	N/A	N/A	1.00	256	100	0	0	0	0	0	0.0	67	N/A	2,000	0	0.0	0.0
B / 7.6	2.7	5.2	9.93	76	7	5	0	39	49	318	0.0	62	2	1,000	50	4.5	0.0
B- / 7.5	2.7	5.2	9.93	11	7	5	0	39	49	318	0.0	35	2	1,000	50	0.0	0.0
B- / 7.5	2.7	5.2	9.93	71	7	5	0	39	49	318	0.0	75	2	1,000,000	0	0.0	0.0
B- / 7.5	2.7	5.2	9.99	N/A	7	5	0	39	49	318	0.0	53	2	0	0	0.0	0.0
B / 7.6	2.7	5.2	9.93	42	7	5	0	39	49	318	0.0	74	2	2,500	50	0.0	0.0
C- / 4.2	3.9	6.2	10.61	56	0	23	6	31	40	317	0.0	15	4	1,000	50	4.5	0.0
C- / 4.2	3.8	6.2	10.61	3	0	23	6	31	40	317	0.0	9	4	1,000	50	0.0	0.0
C- / 4.2	3.9	6.2	10.56	38	0	23	6	31	40	317	0.0	19	4	1,000,000	0	0.0	0.0
C- / 4.2	3.9	6.2	10.61	133	0	23	6	31	40	317	0.0	18	4	2,500	50	0.0	0.0
A+ / 9.9	N/A	N/A	1.00	3,852	100	0	0	0	0	0	0.2	72	N/A	25,000,000	0	0.0	0.0
E+ / 0.7	7.2	6.1	9.04	5	0	54	0	44	2	132	0.0	8	5	1,000	50	4.5	0.0
E+ / 0.7	7.1	6.1	9.06	3	0	54	0	44	2	132	0.0	6	5	1,000	50	0.0	0.0
E+ / 0.7	7.1	6.1	9.02	49	0	54	0	44	2	132	0.0	9	5	1,000,000	0	0.0	0.0
E+ / 0.7	7.1	6.1	9.03	63	0	54	0	44	2	132	0.0	8	5	2,500	50	0.0	0.0
D+ / 2.7	5.1	6.6	8.98	20	5	44	0	29	22	336	0.0	42	5	1,000	50	4.5	0.0
D+ / 2.7	5.1	6.6	8.98	2	5	44	0	29	22	336	0.0	22	5	1,000	50	0.0	0.0
D+ / 2.7	5.1	6.6	8.97	60	5	44	0	29	22	336	0.0	51	5	2,500	50	0.0	0.0
B- / 7.1	2.8	N/A	8.29	268	0	0	0	17	83	22	0.0	31	9	1,000	50	2.8	0.0
C+ / 6.8	2.9	N/A	8.34	215	0	0	0	17	83	22	0.0	16	9	1,000	50	0.0	0.0

99 Pct = Best
0 Pct = Worst

Fund Type	Fund Name	Ticker Symbol	Overall Investment Rating	Phone	PERFORMANCE: Performance Rating/Pts	Total Return % through 3/31/16: 3 Mo	6 Mo	1Yr / Pct	Annualized: 3Yr / Pct	Annualized: 5Yr / Pct	Incl. in Returns: Dividend Yield	Expense Ratio
LP	Deutsche Floating Rate Inst	DFRTX	**D**	(800) 728-3337	**E+ / 0.8**	-0.92	-3.76	-5.29 / 4	-0.22 /14	1.85 /29	4.91	0.87
LP	Deutsche Floating Rate R6	DFRRX	**U**	(800) 728-3337	**U /**	-0.92	-3.87	-5.38 / 4	--	--	4.94	0.95
LP	Deutsche Floating Rate S	DFRPX	**D**	(800) 728-3337	**E+ / 0.7**	-0.94	-3.81	-5.40 / 4	-0.31 /13	1.74 /28	4.80	1.00
COH	Deutsche Global High Income A	SGHAX	**D-**	(800) 728-3337	**D+ / 2.9**	2.27	2.42	-2.33 /14	2.20 /66	4.74 /70	4.65	1.08
COH	Deutsche Global High Income C	SGHCX	**D**	(800) 728-3337	**C- / 3.5**	1.92	1.89	-3.17 /11	1.39 /50	3.94 /60	4.11	1.83
COH	Deutsche Global High Income Inst	MGHYX	**D+**	(800) 728-3337	**C+ / 5.7**	2.34	2.56	-2.08 /15	2.50 /71	5.07 /72	5.14	0.78
COH	Deutsche Global High Income S	SGHSX	**D+**	(800) 728-3337	**C / 5.5**	2.31	2.52	-2.10 /15	2.40 /69	4.94 /71	5.07	0.88
USL	Deutsche Global Inflation A	TIPAX	**E**	(800) 728-3337	**E / 0.5**	3.38	2.81	-0.25 /29	-1.80 / 5	1.78 /28	1.20	1.07
USL	Deutsche Global Inflation C	TIPCX	**E**	(800) 728-3337	**E / 0.5**	3.15	2.36	-1.03 /21	-2.53 / 3	1.02 /20	0.65	1.79
USL	Deutsche Global Inflation Inst	TIPIX	**E+**	(800) 728-3337	**D- / 1.0**	3.42	2.84	--	-1.54 / 6	2.06 /32	1.48	0.69
USL	Deutsche Global Inflation S	TIPSX	**E+**	(800) 728-3337	**D- / 1.0**	3.31	2.85	--	-1.56 / 6	2.00 /31	1.48	0.84
USA	Deutsche GNMA A	GGGGX	**D+**	(800) 728-3337	**D+ / 2.9**	1.28	0.73	1.02 /59	0.81 /39	2.23 /34	2.84	0.82
USA	Deutsche GNMA C	GCGGX	**D+**	(800) 728-3337	**D+ / 2.8**	1.09	0.35	0.33 /46	0.05 /24	1.45 /25	2.16	1.57
USA	Deutsche GNMA Institutional	GIGGX	**C**	(800) 728-3337	**C / 4.8**	1.34	0.93	1.35 /64	1.12 /45	2.52 /38	3.18	0.57
USA	Deutsche GNMA R	GRGGX	**C-**	(800) 728-3337	**C- / 3.6**	1.13	0.58	0.72 /54	0.48 /33	--	2.62	1.24
USA	Deutsche GNMA R6	GRRGX	**U**	(800) 728-3337	**U /**	1.33	0.86	1.25 /62	--	--	3.22	0.78
USA	Deutsche GNMA S	SGINX	**C**	(800) 728-3337	**C / 4.8**	1.35	0.93	1.36 /64	1.09 /44	2.49 /38	3.19	0.55
*COH	Deutsche High Income A	KHYAX	**E+**	(800) 728-3337	**D- / 1.1**	1.74	0.94	-4.00 / 8	1.42 /50	4.35 /66	5.22	0.94
COH	Deutsche High Income C	KHYCX	**E+**	(800) 728-3337	**D- / 1.3**	1.54	0.33	-4.75 / 5	0.56 /34	3.51 /53	4.66	1.72
COH	Deutsche High Income Institutional	KHYIX	**D**	(800) 728-3337	**C- / 3.5**	1.80	0.84	-3.78 / 8	1.60 /54	4.58 /68	5.71	0.70
COH	Deutsche High Income R	KHYRX	**D-**	(800) 728-3337	**C- / 3.2**	1.41	0.53	-4.37 / 7	0.96 /42	--	5.10	1.38
COH	Deutsche High Income R6	KHYQX	**U**	(800) 728-3337	**U /**	1.77	1.02	-3.84 / 8	--	--	5.65	0.85
COH	Deutsche High Income S	KHYSX	**D**	(800) 728-3337	**C / 4.4**	1.78	0.81	-3.82 / 8	1.55 /53	--	5.67	0.77
MM	Deutsche ICT Treasury Inst	ICTXX	**C**	(800) 728-3337	**D / 2.0**	0.04	0.04	0.05 /38	0.02 /19	0.02 / 7	0.05	0.24
MM	Deutsche ICT Treasury Investment	ITVXX	**U**	(800) 728-3337	**U /**	0.01	0.01	0.02 /34	0.01 /16	0.01 / 4	0.02	0.58
MM	Deutsche ICT Treasury US Treas M	IUSXX	**U**	(800) 728-3337	**U /**	0.01	0.01	0.02 /34	0.01 /16	0.01 / 4	0.02	0.30
MUN	Deutsche Interm Tax/AMT Free A	SZMAX	**B**	(800) 728-3337	**B / 7.7**	1.46	2.56	2.96 /85	2.42 /82	4.33 /80	2.17	0.79
MUN	Deutsche Interm Tax/AMT Free C	SZMCX	**B-**	(800) 728-3337	**B / 7.6**	1.27	2.18	2.20 /78	1.65 /71	3.56 /74	1.49	1.56
MUN	Deutsche Interm Tax/AMT Free Inst	SZMIX	**A-**	(800) 728-3337	**B+ / 8.8**	1.52	2.60	3.21 /87	2.69 /85	4.60 /82	2.47	0.54
MUN	Deutsche Interm Tax/AMT Free S	SCMTX	**A-**	(800) 728-3337	**B+ / 8.7**	1.51	2.59	3.21 /87	2.66 /84	4.55 /82	2.47	0.61
MUS	Deutsche MA Tax Free A	SQMAX	**C+**	(800) 728-3337	**B / 8.2**	1.33	2.67	3.21 /87	2.89 /87	5.32 /88	3.25	1.03
MUS	Deutsche MA Tax Free C	SQMCX	**C+**	(800) 728-3337	**B / 8.1**	1.22	2.30	2.52 /81	2.13 /78	4.54 /82	2.60	1.79
MUS	Deutsche MA Tax Free S	SCMAX	**B-**	(800) 728-3337	**A- / 9.1**	1.39	2.79	3.46 /90	3.15 /90	5.58 /89	3.58	0.82
*MUN	Deutsche Managed Municipal Bd A	SMLAX	**B-**	(800) 728-3337	**B+ / 8.8**	1.41	2.94	3.34 /88	3.51 /93	6.01 /92	3.57	0.81
MUN	Deutsche Managed Municipal Bd C	SMLCX	**B-**	(800) 728-3337	**B+ / 8.7**	1.22	2.66	2.55 /81	2.71 /85	5.21 /87	2.90	1.61
MUN	Deutsche Managed Municipal Bd Inst	SMLIX	**B+**	(800) 728-3337	**A / 9.5**	1.47	3.06	3.58 /91	3.75 /94	6.26 /93	3.90	0.58
MUN	Deutsche Managed Municipal Bd S	SCMBX	**B+**	(800) 728-3337	**A / 9.4**	1.46	3.03	3.55 /90	3.72 /94	6.21 /93	3.88	0.64
MM	Deutsche Money Market	KMMXX	**U**	(800) 728-3337	**U /**	0.01	0.01	0.01 /32	0.01 /16	0.01 / 4	0.01	0.48
MM	Deutsche Money Mkt Ser Inst	ICAXX	**C**	(800) 728-3337	**D+ / 2.6**	0.08	0.12	0.17 /43	0.10 /27	0.10 /15	0.17	0.27
MUS	Deutsche NY Tax Free Inc A	KNTAX	**B-**	(800) 728-3337	**B+ / 8.3**	1.39	3.11	3.42 /89	2.99 /88	5.10 /86	3.39	0.97
MUS	Deutsche NY Tax Free Inc C	KNTCX	**B-**	(800) 728-3337	**B+ / 8.3**	1.22	2.74	2.57 /81	2.23 /79	4.31 /80	2.76	1.77
MUS	Deutsche NY Tax Free Inc S	SNWYX	**B+**	(800) 728-3337	**A- / 9.2**	1.45	3.24	3.59 /91	3.25 /90	5.34 /88	3.74	0.79
GEI	Deutsche Short Duration A	PPIAX	**C-**	(800) 728-3337	**D- / 1.4**	0.30	-0.10	-0.20 /29	0.38 /31	0.91 /20	2.48	0.87
GEI	Deutsche Short Duration C	PPLCX	**C-**	(800) 728-3337	**D- / 1.3**	0.11	-0.47	-0.95 /22	-0.38 /12	0.16 /15	1.79	1.63
GEI	Deutsche Short Duration Institution	PPILX	**C+**	(800) 728-3337	**C- / 3.3**	0.25	-0.08	-0.06 /31	0.60 /35	1.17 /22	2.81	0.61
COI	Deutsche Short Duration R6	PPLZX	**U**	(800) 728-3337	**U /**	0.36	-0.08	-0.05 /31	--	--	2.82	0.76
GEI	Deutsche Short Duration S	DBPIX	**C+**	(800) 728-3337	**C- / 3.4**	0.36	-0.08	-0.06 /31	0.60 /35	1.15 /22	2.81	0.69
MUN	Deutsche Short Term Muni Bond A	SRMAX	**C**	(800) 728-3337	**D+ / 2.8**	0.47	0.64	0.83 /63	0.56 /40	1.23 /30	1.00	0.89
MUN	Deutsche Short Term Muni Bond C	SRMCX	**C-**	(800) 728-3337	**D / 1.7**	0.29	0.37	0.08 /42	-0.15 /14	0.48 /19	0.28	1.67
MUN	Deutsche Short Term Muni Bond Inst	MGSMX	**B+**	(800) 728-3337	**C / 5.1**	0.53	0.76	1.08 /68	0.82 /47	1.49 /35	1.27	0.64
MUN	Deutsche Short Term Muni Bond S	SRMSX	**B**	(800) 728-3337	**C / 4.8**	0.51	0.81	0.98 /66	0.72 /45	1.38 /33	1.17	0.76
MUH	Deutsche Strat High Yield T/F A	NOTAX	**C**	(800) 728-3337	**B+ / 8.7**	1.94	3.74	4.08 /94	3.20 /90	6.60 /95	4.26	1.00

● Denotes fund is closed to new investors
* Denotes fund is included in Section II

RISK			NET ASSETS		ASSET							FUND MANAGER		MINIMUM		LOADS	
Risk Rating/Pts	3 Yr Avg Standard Deviation	Avg Duration	NAV As of 3/31/16	Total $(Mil)	Cash %	Gov. Bond %	Muni. Bond %	Corp. Bond %	Other %	Portfolio Turnover Ratio	Avg Coupon Rate	Manager Quality Pct	Manager Tenure (Years)	Initial Purch. $	Additional Purch. $	Front End Load	Back End Load
B- / 7.1	2.9	N/A	8.30	256	0	0	0	17	83	22	0.0	39	9	1,000,000	0	0.0	0.0
U /	N/A	N/A	8.29	3	0	0	0	17	83	22	0.0	N/A	9	0	0	0.0	0.0
B- / 7.0	2.9	N/A	8.29	406	0	0	0	17	83	22	0.0	36	9	2,500	50	0.0	0.0
D / 1.8	5.3	4.1	6.32	50	7	1	0	90	2	56	0.0	85	10	1,000	50	4.5	2.0
D / 2.0	5.1	4.1	6.34	17	7	1	0	90	2	56	0.0	59	10	1,000	50	0.0	2.0
D / 1.9	5.3	4.1	6.30	42	7	1	0	90	2	56	0.0	89	10	1,000,000	0	0.0	2.0
D / 1.9	5.2	4.1	6.35	233	7	1	0	90	2	56	0.0	88	10	2,500	50	0.0	2.0
D- / 1.3	6.1	7.8	9.98	9	3	95	0	0	2	164	0.0	5	6	1,000	50	2.8	0.0
D- / 1.3	6.0	7.8	10.02	17	3	95	0	0	2	164	0.0	3	6	1,000	50	0.0	0.0
D- / 1.3	6.0	7.8	9.95	121	3	95	0	0	2	164	0.0	5	6	1,000,000	0	0.0	0.0
D- / 1.4	6.0	7.8	9.94	10	3	95	0	0	2	164	0.0	5	6	2,500	50	0.0	0.0
C+ / 6.7	3.0	3.4	14.13	55	17	8	0	0	75	199	0.0	41	14	1,000	50	2.8	0.0
C+ / 6.7	3.0	3.4	14.14	40	17	8	0	0	75	199	0.0	21	14	1,000	50	0.0	0.0
C+ / 6.7	3.0	3.4	14.15	35	17	8	0	0	75	199	0.0	52	14	1,000,000	0	0.0	0.0
C+ / 6.8	2.9	3.4	14.15	1	17	8	0	0	75	199	0.0	32	14	0	0	0.0	0.0
U /	N/A	3.4	14.14	N/A	17	8	0	0	75	199	0.0	N/A	14	0	0	0.0	0.0
C+ / 6.7	3.0	3.4	14.16	1,284	17	8	0	0	75	199	0.0	52	14	2,500	50	0.0	0.0
D / 1.8	5.4	4.2	4.39	802	9	0	0	89	2	45	0.0	57	10	1,000	50	4.5	2.0
D / 2.0	5.2	4.2	4.39	81	9	0	0	89	2	45	0.0	30	10	1,000	50	0.0	2.0
D / 2.0	5.2	4.2	4.39	76	9	0	0	89	2	45	0.0	71	10	1,000,000	0	0.0	2.0
D / 1.8	5.3	4.2	4.38	1	9	0	0	89	2	45	0.0	41	10	0	0	0.0	0.0
U /	N/A	4.2	4.39	N/A	9	0	0	89	2	45	0.0	N/A	10	0	0	0.0	2.0
D / 1.9	5.2	4.2	4.39	25	9	0	0	89	2	45	0.0	68	10	2,500	50	0.0	0.0
A+ / 9.9	N/A	N/A	1.00	2,487	100	0	0	0	0	0	0.1	64	N/A	1,000,000	0	0.0	0.0
U /	N/A	N/A	1.00	538	100	0	0	0	0	0	0.0	N/A	N/A	2,000	0	0.0	0.0
U /	N/A	N/A	1.00	91	100	0	0	0	0	0	0.0	N/A	N/A	2,500	50	0.0	0.0
C+ / 5.6	3.2	4.3	12.10	292	0	0	99	0	1	54	0.0	30	26	1,000	50	2.8	0.0
C / 5.4	3.3	4.3	12.10	63	0	0	99	0	1	54	0.0	14	26	1,000	50	0.0	0.0
C / 5.5	3.3	4.3	12.10	1,019	0	0	99	0	1	54	0.0	36	26	1,000,000	0	0.0	0.0
C / 5.5	3.3	4.3	12.10	675	0	0	99	0	1	54	0.0	36	26	2,500	50	0.0	0.0
C- / 3.4	4.4	4.8	14.75	85	0	0	99	0	1	14	0.0	16	27	1,000	50	2.8	0.0
C- / 3.4	4.4	4.8	14.75	18	0	0	99	0	1	14	0.0	9	27	1,000	50	0.0	0.0
C- / 3.4	4.4	4.8	14.75	402	0	0	99	0	1	14	0.0	20	27	2,500	50	0.0	0.0
C- / 3.7	4.2	4.6	9.37	1,968	0	0	99	0	1	29	0.0	33	28	1,000	50	2.8	0.0
C- / 3.7	4.2	4.6	9.37	280	0	0	99	0	1	29	0.0	16	28	1,000	50	0.0	0.0
C- / 3.7	4.2	4.6	9.37	170	0	0	99	0	1	29	0.0	39	28	1,000,000	0	0.0	0.0
C- / 3.7	4.2	4.6	9.38	2,895	0	0	99	0	1	29	0.0	38	28	2,500	50	0.0	0.0
U /	N/A	N/A	1.00	743	100	0	0	0	0	0	0.0	N/A	N/A	1,000	50	0.0	0.0
A+ / 9.9	N/A	N/A	1.00	9,700	100	0	0	0	0	0	0.2	70	N/A	1,000,000	0	0.0	0.0
C / 4.4	3.7	4.6	10.92	130	0	0	99	0	1	26	0.0	31	17	1,000	50	2.8	0.0
C / 4.3	3.8	4.6	10.91	21	0	0	99	0	1	26	0.0	15	17	1,000	50	0.0	0.0
C / 4.3	3.8	4.6	10.91	200	0	0	99	0	1	26	0.0	37	17	2,500	50	0.0	0.0
A- / 9.2	1.1	0.7	8.70	293	3	19	0	46	32	34	0.0	74	10	1,000	50	2.8	0.0
A- / 9.2	1.1	0.7	8.69	145	3	19	0	46	32	34	0.0	43	10	1,000	50	0.0	0.0
A- / 9.2	1.1	0.7	8.70	52	3	19	0	46	32	34	0.0	82	10	1,000,000	0	0.0	0.0
U /	N/A	0.7	8.71	N/A	3	19	0	46	32	34	0.0	N/A	10	0	0	0.0	0.0
A / 9.3	1.0	0.7	8.72	629	3	19	0	46	32	34	0.0	82	10	2,500	50	0.0	0.0
A / 9.3	1.0	1.8	10.21	170	0	0	99	0	1	26	0.0	47	13	1,000	50	2.0	0.0
A / 9.3	1.0	1.8	10.21	24	0	0	99	0	1	26	0.0	25	13	1,000	50	0.0	0.0
A / 9.3	1.0	1.8	10.21	92	0	0	99	0	1	26	0.0	58	13	1,000,000	0	0.0	0.0
A / 9.3	1.0	1.8	10.20	84	0	0	99	0	1	26	0.0	52	13	2,500	50	0.0	0.0
D+ / 2.5	4.7	4.8	12.50	357	0	0	99	0	1	29	0.0	16	18	1,000	50	2.8	0.0

99 Pct = Best
0 Pct = Worst

Fund Type	Fund Name	Ticker Symbol	Overall Investment Rating	Phone	PERFORMANCE: Performance Rating/Pts	Total Return % through 3/31/16: 3 Mo	6 Mo	1Yr / Pct	Annualized: 3Yr / Pct	5Yr / Pct	Incl. in Returns: Dividend Yield	Expense Ratio
MUH	Deutsche Strat High Yield T/F C	NOTCX	**C**	(800) 728-3337	**B+ / 8.6**	1.76	3.36	3.32 /88	2.43 /82	5.81 /91	3.65	1.76
MUH	Deutsche Strat High Yield T/F Inst	NOTIX	**C+**	(800) 728-3337	**A / 9.4**	1.99	3.93	4.39 /96	3.45 /92	6.88 /96	4.59	0.75
MUH	Deutsche Strat High Yield T/F S	SHYTX	**C+**	(800) 728-3337	**A / 9.4**	2.00	3.86	4.34 /96	3.46 /92	6.87 /96	4.63	0.83
* USS	Deutsche Strategic Govt Sec A	KUSAX	**C-**	(800) 728-3337	**C- / 3.0**	1.38	0.98	1.10 /60	0.88 /40	2.15 /33	2.86	0.81
USS	Deutsche Strategic Govt Sec C	KUSCX	**C-**	(800) 728-3337	**C- / 3.0**	1.17	0.70	0.42 /48	0.14 /28	1.36 /24	2.14	1.60
USS	Deutsche Strategic Govt Sec Inst	KUSIX	**C**	(800) 728-3337	**C / 4.9**	1.44	1.11	1.48 /66	1.13 /45	2.36 /36	3.20	0.56
USS	Deutsche Strategic Govt Sec S	KUSMX	**C**	(800) 728-3337	**C / 4.7**	1.41	1.05	1.25 /62	1.03 /43	2.30 /35	3.09	0.67
GES	Deutsche Ultra-Short Duration A	SDUAX	**D+**	(800) 728-3337	**E / 0.5**	-1.03	-1.40	-2.52 /13	-0.63 /11	0.57 /18	1.95	0.94
GES	Deutsche Ultra-Short Duration C	SDUCX	**D+**	(800) 728-3337	**E / 0.5**	-1.08	-1.74	-3.23 /11	-1.33 / 7	-0.16 / 3	1.26	1.70
GES	Deutsche Ultra-Short Duration Inst	MGSFX	**D+**	(800) 728-3337	**D- / 1.1**	-0.96	-1.26	-2.26 /14	-0.38 /12	0.83 /19	2.28	0.69
GEL	Deutsche Ultra-Short Duration R6	SDURX	**U**	(800) 728-3337	**U /**	-0.86	-1.28	-2.33 /14	--	--	2.20	0.75
GES	Deutsche Ultra-Short Duration S	SDUSX	**D+**	(800) 728-3337	**D- / 1.0**	-0.87	-1.33	-2.37 /14	-0.42 /12	0.78 /19	2.16	0.77
GES	Deutsche Unconstrained Income A	KSTAX	**D-**	(800) 728-3337	**E+ / 0.7**	1.10	-0.29	-2.99 /11	-0.27 /13	2.84 /43	3.40	1.06
GES	Deutsche Unconstrained Income C	KSTCX	**D-**	(800) 728-3337	**E+ / 0.7**	0.68	-0.66	-3.69 / 9	-1.06 / 8	2.03 /31	2.72	1.81
GEL	Deutsche Unconstrained Income Inst	KSTIX	**U**	(800) 728-3337	**U /**	1.12	-0.02	-2.64 /13	--	--	3.63	1.03
GES	Deutsche Unconstrained Income S	KSTSX	**D-**	(800) 728-3337	**D- / 1.4**	1.14	-0.19	-2.79 /12	-0.06 /15	3.04 /46	3.70	0.88
GEI	Deutsche US Bond Index A	BONDX	**C**	(800) 728-3337	**C / 5.4**	2.81	2.01	1.34 /64	2.04 /62	3.32 /50	2.53	0.77
GEI	Deutsche US Bond Index Inst	BTUSX	**B**	(800) 728-3337	**B- / 7.0**	2.87	2.14	1.69 /69	2.31 /68	3.62 /55	2.85	0.53
GEI	Deutsche US Bond Index S	BONSX	**B**	(800) 728-3337	**C+ / 6.9**	2.85	2.19	1.60 /68	2.23 /66	3.50 /53	2.75	0.59
LP	Deutsche Variable NAV Money Cap	VNVXX	**C+**	(800) 728-3337	**D+ / 2.9**	0.13	0.21	0.34 /47	0.25 /29	--	0.34	0.35
MUN	DFA CA Int Trm Muni Bd Inst	DCIBX	**A+**	(800) 984-9472	**B+ / 8.7**	1.10	1.84	2.82 /83	2.78 /86	--	1.63	0.23
* MUS	DFA CA Sht Trm Muni Bd Inst	DFCMX	**A-**	(800) 984-9472	**C / 5.5**	0.64	0.69	1.26 /71	0.95 /51	1.21 /29	0.86	0.22
* GL	DFA Five Year Glbl Fixed Inc Inst	DFGBX	**A-**	(800) 984-9472	**C+ / 6.5**	2.32	1.70	2.39 /74	1.95 /60	3.04 /46	1.76	0.27
* US	DFA Infltn Protected Sec Port Inst	DIPSX	**D-**	(800) 984-9472	**D+ / 2.8**	5.01	3.83	1.88 /71	-0.84 / 9	3.24 /49	0.57	0.12
* USS	DFA Intmdt Govt Fx Inc Inst	DFIGX	**C+**	(800) 984-9472	**B- / 7.5**	3.71	2.66	3.45 /79	2.31 /68	3.98 /61	2.12	0.12
* MUN	DFA Intmdt Term Municipal Bd Inst	DFTIX	**B+**	(800) 984-9472	**B+ / 8.3**	1.19	2.02	2.94 /84	2.32 /81	--	1.50	0.23
* GL	DFA Int-Term Extended Quality Inst	DFTEX	**C**	(800) 984-9472	**B / 8.0**	4.00	3.56	2.28 /74	3.05 /77	5.22 /73	3.55	0.22
* GL	DFA Investment Grade Portfolio	DFAPX	**C+**	(800) 984-9472	**B / 7.7**	3.36	2.75	2.53 /75	2.67 /73	4.24 /65	2.23	0.22
GEI	DFA LTIP Institutional	DRXIX	**E**	(800) 984-9472	**D / 1.7**	10.85	10.72	-1.45 /19	-2.03 / 4	--	0.69	16.11
MUN	DFA Municipal Bond Institutional	DFMPX	**U**	(800) 984-9472	**U /**	1.35	2.14	2.86 /84	--	--	1.23	0.37
GEI	DFA Municipal Real Return Port Inst	DMREX	**U**	(800) 984-9472	**U /**	1.25	2.87	2.08 /72	--	--	1.13	0.35
MUN	DFA NY Municipal Bond Institutional	DNYMX	**U**		**U /**	1.15	1.85	--	--	--	0.00	0.25
* GES	DFA One-Yr Fixed Inc Inst	DFIHX	**C+**	(800) 984-9472	**C- / 3.2**	0.45	0.31	0.51 /50	0.40 /31	0.54 /17	0.52	0.17
* GL	DFA S/T Extended Quality Port Inst	DFEQX	**A-**	(800) 984-9472	**C+ / 5.7**	1.74	1.32	1.80 /70	1.54 /53	2.21 /34	1.81	0.22
* GL	DFA Selectively Hedged Glb FI Ptf	DFSHX	**D**	(800) 984-9472	**D / 1.7**	3.13	3.72	1.11 /60	-0.97 / 9	0.12 /15	1.08	0.17
GEI	DFA Short Dur Real Ret Port Instl	DFAIX	**U**	(800) 984-9472	**U /**	1.76	2.02	1.50 /66	--	--	1.26	0.24
* MUN	DFA Short Term Municipal Bd Inst	DFSMX	**B+**	(800) 984-9472	**C / 5.2**	0.57	0.65	1.28 /72	0.86 /49	1.06 /27	0.98	0.22
* USS	DFA Short-Term Government Inst	DFFGX	**B**	(800) 984-9472	**C / 4.9**	1.67	0.93	1.67 /68	1.11 /45	1.67 /27	0.97	0.19
COI	DFA Targeted Credit Institutional	DTCPX	**U**	(800) 984-9472	**U /**	1.80	1.27	--	--	--	0.00	0.23
* GL	DFA Two Year Glbl Fixed Inc Inst	DFGFX	**C+**	(800) 984-9472	**C- / 3.5**	0.61	0.30	0.63 /52	0.52 /33	0.68 /18	0.33	0.18
* GL	DFA World ex US Govt Fxd Inc Inst	DWFIX	**C+**	(800) 984-9472	**A- / 9.0**	4.43	4.21	2.25 /73	4.77 /89	--	6.95	0.22
COI	Diamond Hill Corporate Credit A	DSIAX	**C**	(614) 255-3333	**C+ / 6.4**	2.44	2.02	0.82 /56	3.11 /77	4.56 /68	5.22	0.94
COI	Diamond Hill Corporate Credit C	DSICX	**C**	(614) 255-3333	**C+ / 6.6**	2.27	1.64	0.07 /40	2.35 /68	3.77 /58	4.65	1.69
COI	Diamond Hill Corporate Credit I	DHSTX	**C+**	(614) 255-3333	**B / 7.9**	2.51	2.17	1.12 /61	3.36 /79	4.83 /70	5.72	0.65
GEL	Diamond Hill Corporate Credit Y	DSIYX	**B-**		**B / 8.1**	2.54	2.23	1.23 /62	3.54 /80	4.91 /71	5.83	0.55
COH	Diamond Hill High Yield A	DHHAX	**U**		**U /**	2.59	1.59	0.13 /42	--	--	1.30	0.99
COH	Diamond Hill High Yield I	DHHIX	**U**		**U /**	2.68	1.67	0.21 /44	--	--	1.42	0.70
COH	Diamond Hill High Yield Y	DHHYX	**U**		**U /**	2.69	1.69	0.22 /44	--	--	1.43	0.60
COH	Direxion Dynamic HY Bond Fd	PDHYX	**E-**	(800) 851-0511	**E / 0.3**	1.68	-0.82	-8.56 / 1	-1.80 / 5	1.37 /24	19.16	1.68
US	Direxion Mo 7-10 Year Tr Bl 2X Inv	DXKLX	**C-**	(800) 851-0511	**B+ / 8.8**	8.75	5.06	4.67 /85	3.44 /79	9.02 /91	0.00	1.38
US	Direxion Mo 7-10 Year Tr Br 2X Inv	DXKSX	**E-**	(800) 851-0511	**E- / 0.0**	-9.55	-7.62	-9.93 / 1	-8.96 / 0	-14.53 / 0	0.00	1.41
EM	● DMS NASDAQ India MidCap Index I	DIIMX	**E-**	(866) 282-6743	**E+ / 0.6**	-13.32	-11.14	-16.75 / 0	2.93 /76	--	0.00	53.12

● Denotes fund is closed to new investors
* Denotes fund is included in Section II

RISK			NET ASSETS		ASSET							FUND MANAGER		MINIMUM		LOADS	
Risk Rating/Pts	3 Yr Avg Standard Deviation	Avg Duration	NAV As of 3/31/16	Total $(Mil)	Cash %	Gov. Bond %	Muni. Bond %	Corp. Bond %	Other %	Portfolio Turnover Ratio	Avg Coupon Rate	Manager Quality Pct	Manager Tenure (Years)	Initial Purch. $	Additional Purch. $	Front End Load	Back End Load
D+ / 2.5	4.8	4.8	12.51	140	0	0	99	0	1	29	0.0	9	18	1,000	50	0.0	0.0
D+ / 2.5	4.7	4.8	12.52	185	0	0	99	0	1	29	0.0	20	18	1,000,000	0	0.0	0.0
D+ / 2.5	4.7	4.8	12.51	819	0	0	99	0	1	29	0.0	21	18	2,500	50	0.0	0.0
B- / 7.0	2.9	3.4	8.10	949	20	8	0	0	72	175	0.0	43	14	1,000	50	2.8	0.0
C+ / 6.9	2.9	3.4	8.12	38	20	8	0	0	72	175	0.0	23	14	1,000	50	0.0	0.0
C+ / 6.9	2.9	3.4	8.08	20	20	8	0	0	72	175	0.0	51	14	1,000,000	0	0.0	0.0
B- / 7.0	2.9	3.4	8.10	57	20	8	0	0	72	175	0.0	50	14	2,500	50	0.0	0.0
B / 8.1	2.3	-0.6	8.27	118	6	6	0	59	29	46	0.0	44	8	1,000	50	2.8	0.0
B / 8.1	2.3	-0.6	8.27	38	6	6	0	59	29	46	0.0	23	8	1,000	50	0.0	0.0
B / 8.1	2.3	-0.6	8.28	47	6	6	0	59	29	46	0.0	52	8	1,000,000	0	0.0	0.0
U /	N/A	-0.6	8.28	N/A	6	6	0	59	29	46	0.0	N/A	8	0	0	0.0	0.0
B / 8.1	2.3	-0.6	8.28	79	6	6	0	59	29	46	0.0	51	8	2,500	50	0.0	0.0
C- / 3.8	4.1	4.1	4.44	304	8	16	5	44	27	168	0.0	10	10	1,000	50	2.8	0.0
C- / 3.8	4.1	4.1	4.47	63	8	16	5	44	27	168	0.0	7	10	1,000	50	0.0	0.0
U /	N/A	4.1	4.45	9	8	16	5	44	27	168	0.0	N/A	10	1,000,000	0	0.0	0.0
C- / 3.8	4.1	4.1	4.45	72	8	16	5	44	27	168	0.0	12	10	2,500	50	0.0	0.0
C+ / 6.4	3.0	5.4	9.73	16	2	40	1	26	31	38	0.0	44	19	1,000	50	2.8	0.0
C+ / 6.4	3.0	5.4	9.73	60	2	40	1	26	31	38	0.0	54	19	1,000,000	0	0.0	0.0
C+ / 6.7	3.0	5.4	9.74	26	2	40	1	26	31	38	0.0	53	19	2,500	50	0.0	0.0
A+ / 9.9	N/A	N/A	10.00	100	0	0	0	0	100	0	0.0	75	N/A	1,000,000	0	0.0	0.0
C+ / 6.6	3.0	4.6	10.63	217	2	0	96	0	2	2	4.6	57	5	0	0	0.0	0.0
A / 9.4	0.9	2.6	10.35	816	1	0	96	0	3	23	4.8	77	9	0	0	0.0	0.0
B / 8.2	2.3	3.7	11.11	11,737	0	28	4	61	7	51	2.1	96	17	0	0	0.0	0.0
D- / 1.3	6.0	7.9	11.95	3,272	0	99	0	0	1	12	1.5	5	10	0	0	0.0	0.0
C / 4.4	3.7	5.7	12.86	3,412	1	94	0	0	5	19	4.6	51	6	0	0	0.0	0.0
C / 5.3	3.4	4.8	10.26	1,086	1	0	97	0	2	1	4.8	29	N/A	0	0	0.0	0.0
D+ / 2.8	4.9	6.9	10.80	1,165	1	6	0	89	4	30	3.8	98	6	0	0	0.0	0.0
C / 4.3	3.8	N/A	10.94	4,807	1	44	0	53	2	52	0.0	98	5	0	0	0.0	0.0
E- / 0.0	14.5	N/A	9.40	35	2	97	0	0	1	88	0.0	0	N/A	0	0	0.0	0.0
U /	N/A	5.0	10.22	152	0	0	0	0	100	2	4.6	N/A	1	0	0	0.0	0.0
U /	N/A	4.8	9.85	331	0	0	0	0	100	0	3.9	N/A	2	0	0	0.0	0.0
U /	N/A	N/A	10.23	37	0	0	0	0	100	0	0.0	N/A	1	0	0	0.0	0.0
A+ / 9.9	0.3	1.0	10.31	7,350	4	50	2	40	4	81	1.2	76	33	0	0	0.0	0.0
B+ / 8.9	1.5	2.8	10.87	4,106	1	9	0	85	5	28	2.6	93	8	0	0	0.0	0.0
C- / 3.8	4.1	2.8	9.56	942	1	14	0	84	1	56	2.8	31	N/A	0	0	0.0	0.0
U /	N/A	N/A	9.82	758	0	0	0	0	100	30	0.0	N/A	3	0	0	0.0	0.0
A / 9.3	1.0	2.6	10.23	2,192	1	0	96	0	3	18	4.7	77	14	0	0	0.0	0.0
B+ / 8.9	1.4	2.8	10.77	2,089	0	91	0	0	9	82	1.9	71	28	0	0	0.0	0.0
U /	N/A	N/A	9.99	261	0	0	0	0	100	0	0.0	N/A	1	0	0	0.0	0.0
A+ / 9.8	0.4	1.5	9.96	4,961	0	68	3	26	3	125	1.4	83	17	0	0	0.0	0.0
C- / 3.1	4.4	8.2	10.14	636	3	87	8	0	2	27	2.7	99	5	0	0	0.0	0.0
C / 4.7	3.6	4.1	10.63	52	9	0	0	90	1	56	0.0	95	10	2,500	100	3.5	0.0
C / 4.6	3.7	4.1	10.61	25	9	0	0	90	1	56	0.0	90	10	2,500	100	0.0	0.0
C / 4.6	3.6	4.1	10.60	285	9	0	0	90	1	56	0.0	96	10	2,500	100	0.0	0.0
C / 4.6	3.6	4.1	10.60	20	9	0	0	90	1	56	0.0	97	10	500,000	100	0.0	0.0
U /	N/A	N/A	10.26	N/A	0	0	0	0	100	0	0.0	N/A	1	2,500	100	3.5	0.0
U /	N/A	N/A	10.26	16	0	0	0	0	100	0	0.0	N/A	1	2,500	100	0.0	0.0
U /	N/A	N/A	10.26	6	0	0	0	0	100	0	0.0	N/A	1	500,000	100	0.0	0.0
E / 0.5	7.4	N/A	10.62	89	31	0	0	68	1	554	0.0	6	6	25,000	500	0.0	0.0
E- / 0.2	11.5	N/A	37.17	52	100	0	0	0	0	1,286	0.0	6	10	25,000	500	0.0	0.0
E- / 0.2	11.6	N/A	29.47	5	100	0	0	0	0	0	0.0	11	12	25,000	500	0.0	0.0
E- / 0.0	16.0	N/A	9.89	1	33	0	0	0	67	120	0.0	98	4	1,500	100	0.0	0.0

Fund Type	Fund Name	Ticker Symbol	Overall Investment Rating	Phone	Performance Rating/Pts	3 Mo	6 Mo	1Yr / Pct	3Yr / Pct	5Yr / Pct	Dividend Yield	Expense Ratio
	99 Pct = Best 0 Pct = Worst				PERFORMANCE	Total Return % through 3/31/16			Annualized		Incl. in Returns	
GL	Dodge & Cox Global Bond	DODLX	D	(800) 621-3979	C- / 3.6	3.41	3.41	-1.96 /16	0.42 /32	--	0.00	2.18
* GEI	Dodge & Cox Income Fund	DODIX	B+	(800) 621-3979	C+ / 6.9	2.37	2.50	0.47 /49	2.42 /69	3.80 /58	3.14	0.44
COI	Domini Social Bond Inst	DSBIX	C+	(800) 498-1351	C / 5.4	3.17	2.62	1.89 /71	1.68 /55	--	2.09	1.07
COI	Domini Social Bond Inv	DSBFX	C+	(800) 498-1351	C / 4.9	3.09	2.56	1.59 /67	1.44 /51	2.48 /38	1.80	1.24
GL	DoubleLine Core Fixed Income I	DBLFX	B+	(877) 354-6311	B- / 7.4	2.65	1.78	1.31 /63	2.78 /74	5.16 /73	3.40	0.50
* GL	DoubleLine Core Fixed Income N	DLFNX	B	(877) 354-6311	B- / 7.0	2.49	1.56	0.97 /58	2.52 /71	4.89 /71	3.16	0.75
EM	DoubleLine Em Mkts Fxd Inc I	DBLEX	D	(877) 354-6311	C / 5.2	4.89	2.54	-0.48 /26	1.11 /45	3.81 /58	5.13	0.90
EM	DoubleLine Em Mkts Fxd Inc N	DLENX	D	(877) 354-6311	C / 4.7	4.83	2.41	-0.73 /24	0.86 /40	3.56 /54	4.87	1.15
GEN	DoubleLine Flexible Income I	DFLEX	U	(877) 354-6311	U /	0.55	-0.28	-0.43 /27	--	--	4.18	1.35
GEN	DoubleLine Flexible Income N	DLINX	U	(877) 354-6311	U /	0.59	-0.40	-0.66 /25	--	--	3.93	1.60
LP	DoubleLine Floating Rate I	DBFRX	B+	(877) 354-6311	C / 5.4	0.86	-0.38	0.02 /33	2.14 /64	--	3.81	0.71
LP	DoubleLine Floating Rate N	DLFRX	B	(877) 354-6311	C / 5.0	0.80	-0.50	-0.23 /29	1.95 /60	--	3.55	0.96
COI	DoubleLine Long Dur Tot Rtn Bd I	DBLDX	U	(877) 354-6311	U /	6.56	4.59	2.76 /76	--	--	2.77	1.33
COI	DoubleLine Long Dur Tot Rtn Bd N	DLLDX	U	(877) 354-6311	U /	6.40	4.47	2.51 /75	--	--	2.53	1.58
EM	DoubleLine Low Dur Em Mkts FI I	DBLLX	U	(877) 354-6311	U /	2.89	2.13	1.06 /59	--	--	3.57	0.91
EM	DoubleLine Low Dur Em Mkts FI N	DELNX	U	(877) 354-6311	U /	2.93	2.00	0.82 /56	--	--	3.32	1.16
COI	DoubleLine Low Duration Bond I	DBLSX	B+	(877) 354-6311	C / 5.1	0.62	0.66	1.00 /58	1.42 /50	--	2.51	0.46
* COI	DoubleLine Low Duration Bond N	DLSNX	B+	(877) 354-6311	C / 4.7	0.66	0.54	0.85 /56	1.21 /46	--	2.26	0.71
GES	DoubleLine Total Return Bond I	DBLTX	A+	(877) 354-6311	B / 7.8	1.75	1.27	2.45 /74	3.15 /77	5.36 /74	3.99	0.47
* GES	DoubleLine Total Return Bond N	DLTNX	A+	(877) 354-6311	B / 7.6	1.69	1.15	2.20 /73	2.93 /76	5.11 /72	3.74	0.72
MUN	Dreyfus AMT Free Muni Bond A	DMUAX	B	(800) 645-6561	B+ / 8.6	1.67	3.51	4.27 /95	3.65 /93	5.97 /92	3.01	0.94
MUN	Dreyfus AMT Free Muni Bond C	DMUCX	B+	(800) 645-6561	A- / 9.0	1.48	3.12	3.49 /90	2.87 /87	5.18 /87	2.42	1.71
MUN	Dreyfus AMT Free Muni Bond I	DMBIX	A-	(800) 645-6561	A+ / 9.6	1.73	3.56	4.46 /96	3.90 /95	6.23 /93	3.40	0.70
MUN	Dreyfus AMT Free Muni Bond Y	DMUYX	U	(800) 645-6561	U /	1.69	3.62	4.53 /97	--	--	3.47	4.19
MUN	Dreyfus AMT Free Muni Bond Z	DRMBX	A-	(800) 645-6561	A+ / 9.6	1.65	3.54	4.42 /96	3.86 /95	6.17 /93	3.37	0.69
MM	Dreyfus Basic Money Market	DBAXX	U	(800) 645-6561	U /	--	--	--	--	--	0.01	0.71
COI	Dreyfus Bond Market Index Basic	DBIRX	B+	(800) 645-6561	B- / 7.0	2.94	2.28	1.68 /68	2.28 /67	3.55 /54	2.39	0.16
* COI	Dreyfus Bond Market Index Inv	DBMIX	B-	(800) 645-6561	C+ / 6.5	2.88	2.15	1.43 /65	2.00 /61	3.29 /50	2.14	0.41
MMT	Dreyfus CA AMT Free Mun Csh	DIIXX	U	(800) 645-6561	U /	0.00	0.01	0.01 /34	--	0.02 /10	0.01	0.24
MUS	Dreyfus CA AMT Free Muni A	DCAAX	C+	(800) 645-6561	B+ / 8.8	1.89	3.68	4.49 /97	3.82 /95	6.32 /94	3.10	0.93
MUS	Dreyfus CA AMT Free Muni C	DCACX	B-	(800) 645-6561	A- / 9.1	1.71	3.29	3.70 /92	3.05 /88	5.54 /89	2.50	1.69
MUS	Dreyfus CA AMT Free Muni I	DCMIX	B+	(800) 645-6561	A+ / 9.7	1.96	3.81	4.68 /97	4.08 /96	6.59 /95	3.49	0.68
MUN	Dreyfus CA AMT Free Muni Y	DCAYX	U	(800) 645-6561	U /	1.96	3.82	4.70 /97	--	--	3.51	0.67
MUS	Dreyfus CA AMT Free Muni Z	DRCAX	B+	(800) 645-6561	A+ / 9.7	1.95	3.79	4.70 /97	4.06 /96	6.54 /95	3.45	0.72
MM	Dreyfus Cash Mgmt Fund Admin	DACXX	C	(800) 645-6561	D / 2.0	0.05	0.05	0.05 /38	0.02 /19	0.01 / 4	0.05	0.31
MM	Dreyfus Cash Mgmt Fund Agency	DMCXX	C	(800) 645-6561	D / 2.2	0.06	0.07	0.07 /40	0.02 /19	0.02 / 7	0.07	0.27
MM	Dreyfus Cash Mgmt Fund Inst	DICXX	C	(800) 645-6561	D+ / 2.5	0.07	0.09	0.12 /42	0.06 /25	0.07 /14	0.12	0.21
MM	Dreyfus Cash Mgmt Fund Inv	DVCXX	U	(800) 645-6561	U /	--	--	--	--	--	0.01	0.46
MUS	Dreyfus CT Muni A	PSCTX	C-	(800) 645-6561	B- / 7.1	1.60	3.27	3.37 /89	2.41 /82	4.80 /84	2.65	0.92
MUS	Dreyfus CT Muni C	PMCCX	C	(800) 645-6561	B / 7.7	1.41	2.80	2.59 /81	1.63 /71	3.99 /77	2.03	1.68
MUS	Dreyfus CT Muni I	DTCIX	B-	(800) 645-6561	B+ / 8.9	1.75	3.39	3.62 /91	2.66 /84	5.07 /86	3.02	0.67
MUN	Dreyfus CT Muni Y	DPMYX	U	(800) 645-6561	U /	1.75	3.41	3.65 /91	--	--	3.05	0.65
MUS ●	Dreyfus CT Muni Z	DPMZX	B-	(800) 645-6561	B+ / 8.8	1.73	3.37	3.58 /91	2.62 /84	5.02 /85	2.98	0.70
EM	Dreyfus Eme Mkts Dbt LC A	DDBAX	E-	(800) 782-6620	E- / 0.0	8.02	7.71	-5.19 / 5	-8.57 / 0	-3.42 / 1	0.50	1.25
EM	Dreyfus Eme Mkts Dbt LC C	DDBCX	E-	(800) 782-6620	E- / 0.0	7.74	7.31	-5.95 / 3	-9.26 / 0	-4.16 / 0	0.30	2.00
EM	Dreyfus Eme Mkts Dbt LC I	DDBIX	E-	(800) 782-6620	E- / 0.0	8.05	7.95	-4.91 / 5	-8.27 / 0	-3.13 / 1	0.61	0.94
EM	Dreyfus Eme Mkts Dbt LC Y	DDBYX	U	(800) 782-6620	U /	8.16	7.85	-4.89 / 5	--	--	0.63	0.88
LP	Dreyfus Floating Rate Income A	DFLAX	U	(800) 782-6620	U /	0.85	-1.13	-1.62 /18	--	--	4.16	1.04
LP	Dreyfus Floating Rate Income C	DFLCX	U	(800) 782-6620	U /	0.65	-1.47	-2.39 /14	--	--	3.56	1.84
LP	Dreyfus Floating Rate Income I	DFLIX	U	(800) 782-6620	U /	0.82	-1.06	-1.37 /19	--	--	4.55	0.77
LP	Dreyfus Floating Rate Income Y	DFLYX	U	(800) 782-6620	U /	0.83	-1.03	-1.38 /19	--	--	4.62	0.75
MM	Dreyfus General Money Market A	GMMXX	U	(800) 645-6561	U /	--	--	--	--	--	0.01	0.73

● Denotes fund is closed to new investors
* Denotes fund is included in Section II

RISK			NET ASSETS		ASSET							FUND MANAGER		MINIMUM		LOADS	
Risk Rating/Pts	3 Yr Avg Standard Deviation	Avg Duration	NAV As of 3/31/16	Total $(Mil)	Cash %	Gov. Bond %	Muni. Bond %	Corp. Bond %	Other %	Portfolio Turnover Ratio	Avg Coupon Rate	Manager Quality Pct	Manager Tenure (Years)	Initial Purch. $	Additional Purch. $	Front End Load	Back End Load
D / 2.1	5.6	3.1	10.00	73	2	18	6	61	13	36	5.2	82	2	2,500	100	0.0	0.0
B- / 7.4	2.8	4.0	13.47	43,341	1	6	4	48	41	27	4.7	85	N/A	2,500	100	0.0	0.0
B- / 7.4	2.8	4.4	11.27	3	0	16	3	26	55	348	2.5	64	11	500,000	0	0.0	2.0
B- / 7.3	2.8	4.4	11.29	133	0	16	3	26	55	348	2.5	53	11	2,500	100	0.0	2.0
C+ / 6.1	3.1	4.7	10.87	5,093	4	19	3	31	43	65	3.8	98	6	100,000	100	0.0	0.0
C+ / 6.1	3.1	4.7	10.86	950	4	19	3	31	43	65	3.8	97	6	2,000	100	0.0	0.0
E+ / 0.7	7.0	5.2	9.68	546	1	11	0	87	1	67	5.8	91	6	100,000	100	0.0	0.0
E+ / 0.7	7.0	5.2	9.68	199	1	11	0	87	1	67	5.8	89	6	2,000	100	0.0	0.0
U /	N/A	2.0	9.55	160	4	9	0	26	61	55	4.6	N/A	2	100,000	100	0.0	0.0
U /	N/A	2.0	9.55	63	4	9	0	26	61	55	4.6	N/A	2	2,000	100	0.0	0.0
B+ / 8.7	1.8	0.2	9.77	229	7	0	0	16	77	84	3.9	95	3	100,000	100	0.0	1.0
B+ / 8.7	1.8	0.2	9.79	72	7	0	0	16	77	84	3.9	94	3	2,000	100	0.0	1.0
U /	N/A	13.4	10.40	57	2	21	0	0	77	0	2.4	N/A	N/A	100,000	100	0.0	0.0
U /	N/A	13.4	10.39	26	2	21	0	0	77	0	2.4	N/A	N/A	2,000	100	0.0	0.0
U /	N/A	2.9	9.59	66	0	20	0	79	1	21	5.0	N/A	2	100,000	100	0.0	0.0
U /	N/A	2.9	9.60	118	0	20	0	79	1	21	5.0	N/A	2	2,000	100	0.0	0.0
A / 9.5	0.8	1.2	9.99	1,722	6	11	0	31	52	61	3.0	90	5	100,000	100	0.0	0.0
A / 9.5	0.8	1.2	9.99	1,160	6	11	0	31	52	61	3.0	88	5	2,000	100	0.0	0.0
B / 7.8	2.6	3.6	10.87	45,913	1	11	0	4	84	13	3.8	91	6	100,000	100	0.0	0.0
B / 7.7	2.6	3.6	10.87	11,714	1	11	0	4	84	13	3.8	88	6	2,000	100	0.0	0.0
C- / 4.2	3.8	4.9	14.34	509	1	0	98	0	1	12	0.0	48	4	1,000	100	4.5	0.0
C- / 4.2	3.8	4.9	14.34	30	1	0	98	0	1	12	0.0	25	4	1,000	100	0.0	0.0
C- / 4.1	3.9	4.9	14.34	164	1	0	98	0	1	12	0.0	55	4	1,000	100	0.0	0.0
U /	N/A	4.9	14.34	N/A	1	0	98	0	1	12	0.0	N/A	4	1,000,000	0	0.0	0.0
C- / 4.2	3.8	4.9	14.34	196	1	0	98	0	1	12	0.0	55	4	1,000	100	0.0	0.0
U /	N/A	N/A	1.00	188	100	0	0	0	0	0	0.0	N/A	N/A	25,000	1,000	0.0	0.0
C+ / 6.6	3.0	5.7	10.54	1,502	1	42	0	24	33	151	0.0	81	6	10,000	1,000	0.0	0.0
C+ / 6.6	3.0	5.7	10.53	1,086	1	42	0	24	33	151	0.0	72	6	2,500	100	0.0	0.0
U /	N/A	N/A	1.00	175	100	0	0	0	0	0	0.0	N/A	N/A	10,000,000	0	0.0	0.0
C- / 3.5	4.3	5.1	15.60	104	2	0	97	0	1	9	0.0	38	7	1,000	100	4.5	0.0
C- / 3.5	4.3	5.1	15.60	14	2	0	97	0	1	9	0.0	19	7	1,000	100	0.0	0.0
C- / 3.5	4.3	5.1	15.59	39	2	0	97	0	1	9	0.0	46	7	1,000	100	0.0	0.0
U /	N/A	5.1	15.59	4	2	0	97	0	1	9	0.0	N/A	7	1,000,000	0	0.0	0.0
C- / 3.5	4.3	5.1	15.60	873	2	0	97	0	1	9	0.0	45	7	1,000	100	0.0	0.0
A+ / 9.9	N/A	N/A	1.00	2,012	100	0	0	0	0	0	0.1	63	25	10,000,000	0	0.0	0.0
A+ / 9.9	N/A	N/A	1.00	155	100	0	0	0	0	0	0.1	62	25	10,000,000	0	0.0	0.0
A+ / 9.9	N/A	N/A	1.00	19,208	100	0	0	0	0	0	0.1	67	25	10,000,000	0	0.0	0.0
U /	N/A	N/A	1.00	1,436	100	0	0	0	0	0	0.0	N/A	25	10,000,000	0	0.0	0.0
C- / 3.5	4.3	5.0	12.04	168	0	0	99	0	1	8	0.0	12	6	1,000	100	4.5	0.0
C- / 3.6	4.2	5.0	12.02	12	0	0	99	0	1	8	0.0	8	6	1,000	100	0.0	0.0
C- / 3.5	4.3	5.0	12.04	9	0	0	99	0	1	8	0.0	14	6	1,000	100	0.0	0.0
U /	N/A	5.0	12.04	2	0	0	99	0	1	8	0.0	N/A	6	1,000,000	0	0.0	0.0
C- / 3.5	4.3	5.0	12.04	94	0	0	99	0	1	8	0.0	14	6	1,000	100	0.0	0.0
E- / 0.1	12.1	5.1	11.18	6	7	78	0	13	2	61	0.0	0	8	1,000	100	4.5	2.0
E- / 0.1	12.1	5.1	10.86	4	7	78	0	13	2	61	0.0	0	8	1,000	100	0.0	2.0
E- / 0.1	12.1	5.1	11.27	135	7	78	0	13	2	61	0.0	1	8	1,000	100	0.0	2.0
U /	N/A	5.1	11.27	11	7	78	0	13	2	61	0.0	N/A	8	1,000,000	0	0.0	2.0
U /	N/A	0.3	11.77	7	5	0	0	20	75	77	0.0	N/A	3	1,000	100	2.5	0.0
U /	N/A	0.3	11.75	2	5	0	0	20	75	77	0.0	N/A	3	1,000	100	0.0	0.0
U /	N/A	0.3	11.75	7	5	0	0	20	75	77	0.0	N/A	3	1,000	100	0.0	0.0
U /	N/A	0.3	11.74	438	5	0	0	20	75	77	0.0	N/A	3	1,000,000	0	0.0	0.0
U /	N/A	N/A	1.00	2,328	100	0	0	0	0	0	0.0	N/A	N/A	2,500	100	0.0	0.0

99 Pct = Best 0 Pct = Worst					PERFORMANCE							
						Total Return % through 3/31/16					Incl. in Returns	
									Annualized			
Fund Type	Fund Name	Ticker Symbol	Overall Investment Rating	Phone	Performance Rating/Pts	3 Mo	6 Mo	1Yr / Pct	3Yr / Pct	5Yr / Pct	Dividend Yield	Expense Ratio
MMT	Dreyfus General NY AMT-Fr Muni	GNMXX	U	(800) 645-6561	U /	0.00	0.01	0.01 /34	--	--	0.01	0.71
MMT	Dreyfus General NY AMT-Fr Muni	GNYXX	U	(800) 645-6561	U /	0.00	0.01	0.01 /34	--	--	0.01	1.10
GL	Dreyfus Global Dynamic Bond A	DGDAX	D+	(800) 782-6620	D- / 1.3	1.09	0.89	-1.25 /20	0.81 /39	2.84 /43	2.25	1.99
GL	Dreyfus Global Dynamic Bond C	DGDCX	C-	(800) 782-6620	D / 1.8	0.93	0.53	-1.90 /16	0.07 /26	2.06 /32	1.71	2.74
GL	Dreyfus Global Dynamic Bond I	DGDIX	C+	(800) 782-6620	C- / 4.1	1.09	0.96	-1.06 /21	1.02 /43	3.06 /46	2.54	1.70
GL	Dreyfus Global Dynamic Bond Y	DGDYX	U	(800) 782-6620	U /	1.17	1.07	-0.95 /22	--	--	2.57	1.31
USA	Dreyfus GNMA Fund A	GPGAX	C-	(800) 782-6620	C- / 3.3	1.62	1.56	1.58 /67	1.42 /50	2.56 /38	1.80	1.03
USA	Dreyfus GNMA Fund C	GPNCX	C	(800) 782-6620	C- / 4.0	1.43	1.19	0.80 /55	0.61 /35	1.77 /28	1.12	1.84
USA	Dreyfus GNMA Fund Y	GPNYX	U	(800) 782-6620	U /	1.74	1.72	--	--	--	0.00	0.71
USA ●	Dreyfus GNMA Fund Z	DRGMX	B	(800) 782-6620	C+ / 5.8	1.64	1.63	1.70 /69	1.56 /53	2.70 /40	2.00	0.90
MM	Dreyfus Govt Cash Mgmt Admin	DAGXX	U	(800) 645-6561	U /	0.02	0.02	0.02 /34	0.01 /16	0.01 / 4	0.02	0.31
MM	Dreyfus Govt Cash Mgmt Agency	DGMXX	C-	(800) 645-6561	D / 1.9	0.03	0.03	0.03 /36	0.02 /19	0.01 / 4	0.03	0.27
MM	Dreyfus Govt Cash Mgmt Inst	DGCXX	C	(800) 645-6561	D / 2.0	0.04	0.05	0.05 /38	0.02 /19	0.02 / 7	0.05	0.21
MM	Dreyfus Govt Cash Mgmt Part	DPGXX	U	(800) 645-6561	U /	--	--	--	--	--	0.01	0.61
MM	Dreyfus Govt Prime Cash Mgmt	DAPXX	U	(800) 645-6561	U /	0.01	0.01	0.01 /32	--	--	0.01	0.33
MM	Dreyfus Govt Prime Cash Mgmt	DRPXX	C-	(800) 645-6561	D / 1.8	0.02	0.02	0.02 /34	0.01 /16	--	0.02	0.28
MM	Dreyfus Govt Prime Cash Mgmt Inst	DIPXX	C-	(800) 645-6561	D / 1.9	0.04	0.04	0.04 /37	0.01 /16	0.01 / 4	0.04	0.21
COH	Dreyfus High Yield A	DPLTX	E+	(800) 782-6620	D- / 1.2	2.05	-0.28	-4.69 / 6	1.26 /47	3.57 /54	6.04	0.96
COH	Dreyfus High Yield C	PTHIX	E+	(800) 782-6620	D / 1.7	1.86	-0.64	-5.39 / 4	0.51 /33	2.80 /42	5.55	1.71
COH	Dreyfus High Yield I	DLHRX	D	(800) 782-6620	C- / 4.2	2.28	0.02	-4.43 / 6	1.57 /53	3.83 /59	6.59	0.71
MUH	Dreyfus High Yld Muni Bd A	DHYAX	C	(800) 645-6561	A- / 9.0	3.00	6.14	6.46 /99	4.07 /96	7.25 /97	4.26	1.03
MUH	Dreyfus High Yld Muni Bd C	DHYCX	C	(800) 645-6561	A / 9.3	2.81	5.74	5.56 /98	3.28 /91	6.44 /94	3.72	1.80
MUH	Dreyfus High Yld Muni Bd I	DYBIX	C+	(800) 645-6561	A+ / 9.8	3.06	6.27	6.64 /99	4.33 /97	7.52 /97	4.70	0.79
MUH	Dreyfus High Yld Muni Bd Y	DHYYX	U	(800) 645-6561	U /	3.08	6.29	6.67 /99	--	--	4.74	0.78
MUH	Dreyfus High Yld Muni Bd Z	DHMBX	C+	(800) 645-6561	A+ / 9.7	3.11	6.19	6.58 /99	4.21 /97	7.36 /97	4.57	0.93
GEI	Dreyfus Infl Adjusted Sec I	DIASX	D-	(800) 645-6561	D- / 1.2	3.51	2.59	1.31 /63	-1.43 / 6	2.41 /36	0.35	0.52
GEI	Dreyfus Infl Adjusted Sec Inv	DIAVX	D-	(800) 645-6561	D- / 1.0	3.52	2.43	1.13 /61	-1.69 / 5	2.10 /32	0.33	0.74
GEI	Dreyfus Infl Adjusted Sec Y	DAIYX	U	(800) 645-6561	U /	3.59	2.67	1.40 /65	--	--	0.36	0.41
MM	Dreyfus Inst Cash Advant Admin	DDTXX	C	(800) 645-6561	D+ / 2.3	0.07	0.09	0.09 /41	0.03 /22	0.04 /11	0.09	0.23
MM	Dreyfus Inst Cash Advant Inst	DADXX	C	(800) 645-6561	D+ / 2.6	0.09	0.12	0.17 /43	0.10 /27	0.11 /15	0.17	0.16
MM	Dreyfus Inst Cash Advant Inv	DIVXX	C-	(800) 645-6561	D / 1.8	0.02	0.02	0.02 /34	0.01 /16	--	0.02	0.41
MM	Dreyfus Inst Pref Govt Mny Mkt Agcy	DRGXX	C-	(800) 426-9363	D / 1.8	0.02	0.02	0.02 /34	0.01 /16	--	0.02	0.29
MM	Dreyfus Inst Pref Govt Mny Mkt Ham	DSHXX	C	(800) 426-9363	D / 2.0	0.04	0.05	0.07 /40	0.02 /19	0.04 /11	0.07	0.19
MM	Dreyfus Inst Pref Govt Mny Mkt Inst	DSVXX	C	(800) 426-9363	D+ / 2.4	0.06	0.07	0.11 /42	0.06 /25	0.08 /14	0.11	0.14
MM	Dreyfus Inst Preferred Plus MM		C	(800) 645-6561	D+ / 2.6	0.08	0.11	0.16 /43	0.11 /27	0.10 /15	0.16	0.10
MM	Dreyfus Inst Resrv Prf MM Hmltn Shs	DRSXX	C	(800) 645-6561	D / 2.2	0.06	0.07	0.08 /40	0.03 /22	0.06 /13	0.08	0.16
MM	Dreyfus Inst Tr Agcy Cash Adv Agcy	DGYXX	U	(800) 426-9363	U /	--	--	--	--	--	0.01	0.29
MM	Dreyfus Inst Tr Agcy Cash Adv Ham	DHLXX	C-	(800) 426-9363	D / 1.9	0.03	0.04	0.04 /37	0.01 /16	0.01 / 4	0.04	0.19
MM	Dreyfus Inst Tr Agcy Cash Adv Inst	DNSXX	C	(800) 426-9363	D / 2.0	0.05	0.05	0.05 /38	0.02 /19	0.01 / 4	0.05	0.14
MM	Dreyfus Inst Trs Prime Csh Adv Hami	DHMXX	C-	(800) 426-9363	D / 1.9	0.02	0.02	0.02 /34	0.01 /16	--	0.02	0.20
MM	Dreyfus Inst Trs Prime Csh Adv Inst	DUPXX	C-	(800) 426-9363	D / 1.9	0.02	0.02	0.02 /34	0.01 /16	--	0.02	0.16
* GEI	Dreyfus Interm Term Inc A	DRITX	D+	(800) 645-6561	D+ / 2.7	2.10	1.13	-0.93 /22	1.37 /50	3.34 /51	2.25	0.91
GEI	Dreyfus Interm Term Inc C	DTECX	D+	(800) 645-6561	C- / 3.4	1.92	0.77	-1.64 /18	0.62 /35	2.60 /39	1.63	1.64
GEI	Dreyfus Interm Term Inc I	DITIX	C	(800) 645-6561	C / 5.5	2.10	1.30	-0.67 /24	1.70 /56	3.63 /55	2.68	0.63
COI	Dreyfus Interm Term Inc Y	DITYX	U	(800) 645-6561	U /	2.19	1.32	-0.55 /25	--	--	2.73	0.53
* MUN	Dreyfus Intermediate Muni Bd	DITEX	A	(800) 645-6561	A- / 9.1	1.48	2.86	3.63 /91	3.04 /88	4.75 /83	2.55	0.73
GL	Dreyfus Intl Bond A	DIBAX	D-	(800) 645-6561	D- / 1.4	5.94	4.26	-1.16 /20	0.13 /28	1.62 /27	4.18	1.08
GL	Dreyfus Intl Bond C	DIBCX	D	(800) 645-6561	D+ / 2.7	5.78	3.95	-1.79 /17	-0.52 /11	0.93 /20	3.74	1.76
GL	Dreyfus Intl Bond I	DIBRX	D+	(800) 645-6561	C / 4.7	6.05	4.51	-0.73 /24	0.51 /33	1.96 /31	4.85	0.75
GL	Dreyfus Intl Bond Y	DIBYX	U	(800) 645-6561	U /	6.05	4.55	-0.64 /25	--	--	4.94	0.68
MUS	Dreyfus MA Muni A	PSMAX	C	(800) 782-6620	B- / 7.4	1.48	3.02	3.53 /90	2.59 /84	4.94 /85	2.48	0.95
MUS	Dreyfus MA Muni C	PCMAX	C+	(800) 782-6620	B / 7.9	1.28	2.62	2.71 /82	1.79 /74	4.14 /79	1.80	1.71

● Denotes fund is closed to new investors
* Denotes fund is included in Section II

RISK			NET ASSETS		ASSET							FUND MANAGER		MINIMUM		LOADS	
Risk Rating/Pts	3 Yr Avg Standard Deviation	Avg Duration	NAV As of 3/31/16	Total $(Mil)	Cash %	Gov. Bond %	Muni. Bond %	Corp. Bond %	Other %	Portfolio Turnover Ratio	Avg Coupon Rate	Manager Quality Pct	Manager Tenure (Years)	Initial Purch. $	Additional Purch. $	Front End Load	Back End Load
U /	N/A	N/A	1.00	148	100	0	0	0	0	0	0.0	N/A	N/A	2,500	100	0.0	0.0
U /	N/A	N/A	1.00	136	100	0	0	0	0	0	0.0	N/A	N/A	2,500	100	0.0	0.0
B+ / 8.5	2.0	2.8	12.05	2	9	45	0	38	8	134	0.0	87	5	1,000	100	4.5	0.0
B+ / 8.4	2.0	2.8	11.96	1	9	45	0	38	8	134	0.0	70	5	1,000	100	0.0	0.0
B+ / 8.5	2.0	2.8	12.06	1	9	45	0	38	8	134	0.0	90	5	1,000	100	0.0	0.0
U /	N/A	2.8	12.07	19	9	45	0	38	8	134	0.0	N/A	5	1,000,000	0	0.0	0.0
B / 7.9	2.5	4.1	15.33	48	0	9	0	0	91	350	0.0	66	1	1,000	100	4.5	0.0
B / 7.9	2.5	4.1	15.33	5	0	9	0	0	91	350	0.0	35	1	1,000	100	0.0	0.0
U /	N/A	4.1	15.34	N/A	0	9	0	0	91	350	0.0	N/A	1	1,000,000	0	0.0	0.0
B / 7.9	2.5	4.1	15.34	403	0	9	0	0	91	350	0.0	73	1	1,000	100	0.0	0.0
U /	N/A	N/A	1.00	298	100	0	0	0	0	0	0.0	N/A	20	10,000,000	0	0.0	0.0
A+ / 9.9	N/A	N/A	1.00	69	100	0	0	0	0	0	0.0	64	20	10,000,000	0	0.0	0.0
A+ / 9.9	N/A	N/A	1.00	15,494	100	0	0	0	0	0	0.1	64	20	10,000,000	0	0.0	0.0
U /	N/A	N/A	1.00	37	100	0	0	0	0	0	0.0	N/A	20	10,000,000	0	0.0	0.0
U /	N/A	N/A	1.00	604	100	0	0	0	0	0	0.0	N/A	N/A	10,000,000	0	0.0	0.0
A+ / 9.9	N/A	N/A	1.00	14	100	0	0	0	0	0	0.0	63	N/A	10,000,000	0	0.0	0.0
A+ / 9.9	N/A	N/A	1.00	2,510	100	0	0	0	0	0	0.0	63	N/A	10,000,000	0	0.0	0.0
D- / 1.2	5.9	4.3	5.85	169	6	0	0	91	3	72	0.0	45	6	1,000	100	4.5	0.0
D- / 1.2	5.9	4.3	5.85	65	6	0	0	91	3	72	0.0	23	6	1,000	100	0.0	0.0
D- / 1.2	5.9	4.3	5.86	801	6	0	0	91	3	72	0.0	56	6	1,000	100	0.0	0.0
D / 1.8	5.3	6.7	12.08	50	5	0	94	0	1	27	0.0	23	5	1,000	100	4.5	2.0
D / 1.8	5.3	6.7	12.09	17	5	0	94	0	1	27	0.0	12	5	1,000	100	0.0	2.0
D / 1.8	5.3	6.7	12.06	18	5	0	94	0	1	27	0.0	30	5	1,000	100	0.0	2.0
U /	N/A	6.7	12.06	6	5	0	94	0	1	27	0.0	N/A	5	1,000,000	0	0.0	2.0
D / 1.8	5.3	6.7	12.09	63	5	0	94	0	1	27	0.0	27	5	1,000	100	0.0	2.0
D+ / 2.9	4.8	5.3	12.69	17	0	99	0	0	1	54	0.0	4	11	1,000	100	0.0	0.0
D+ / 2.9	4.8	5.3	12.66	19	0	99	0	0	1	54	0.0	3	11	10,000	100	0.0	0.0
U /	N/A	5.3	12.70	104	0	99	0	0	1	54	0.0	N/A	11	1,000,000	0	0.0	0.0
A+ / 9.9	N/A	N/A	1.00	421	100	0	0	0	0	0	0.1	63	N/A	250,000,000	0	0.0	0.0
A+ / 9.9	N/A	N/A	1.00	17,595	100	0	0	0	0	0	0.2	69	N/A	250,000,000	0	0.0	0.0
A+ / 9.9	N/A	N/A	1.00	10	100	0	0	0	0	0	0.0	63	N/A	250,000,000	0	0.0	0.0
A+ / 9.9	N/A	N/A	1.00	10	100	0	0	0	0	0	0.0	63	N/A	500,000,000	0	0.0	0.0
A+ / 9.9	N/A	N/A	1.00	1,129	100	0	0	0	0	0	0.1	65	N/A	500,000,000	0	0.0	0.0
A+ / 9.9	N/A	N/A	1.00	887	100	0	0	0	0	0	0.1	68	N/A	500,000,000	0	0.0	0.0
A+ / 9.9	N/A	N/A	1.00	1,392	100	0	0	0	0	0	0.2	71	N/A	1,000,000,00	0	0.0	0.0
A+ / 9.9	N/A	N/A	1.00	184	100	0	0	0	0	0	0.1	65	N/A	1,000,000,00	0	0.0	0.0
U /	N/A	N/A	1.00	4	100	0	0	0	0	0	0.0	N/A	N/A	275,000,000	0	0.0	0.0
A+ / 9.9	N/A	N/A	1.00	155	100	0	0	0	0	0	0.0	63	N/A	275,000,000	0	0.0	0.0
A+ / 9.9	N/A	N/A	1.00	162	100	0	0	0	0	0	0.1	63	N/A	275,000,000	0	0.0	0.0
A+ / 9.9	N/A	N/A	1.00	4	100	0	0	0	0	0	0.0	63	N/A	275,000,000	0	0.0	0.0
A+ / 9.9	N/A	N/A	1.00	371	100	0	0	0	0	0	0.0	63	N/A	275,000,000	0	0.0	0.0
C+ / 6.0	3.1	5.6	13.49	561	0	33	1	31	35	371	0.0	28	8	1,000	100	4.5	0.0
C+ / 6.1	3.1	5.6	13.49	24	0	33	1	31	35	371	0.0	14	8	1,000	100	0.0	0.0
C+ / 6.2	3.1	5.6	13.48	250	0	33	1	31	35	371	0.0	38	8	1,000	100	0.0	0.0
U /	N/A	5.6	13.49	42	0	33	1	31	35	371	0.0	N/A	8	1,000,000	0	0.0	0.0
C+ / 5.8	3.2	4.8	14.09	782	0	0	99	0	1	20	0.0	51	5	2,500	100	0.0	0.0
D+ / 2.8	4.8	7.2	15.34	161	2	64	0	21	13	217	0.0	75	10	1,000	100	4.5	0.0
D+ / 2.8	4.8	7.2	15.01	59	2	64	0	21	13	217	0.0	45	10	1,000	100	0.0	0.0
D+ / 2.8	4.8	7.2	15.43	742	2	64	0	21	13	217	0.0	84	10	1,000	100	0.0	0.0
U /	N/A	7.2	15.43	27	2	64	0	21	13	217	0.0	N/A	10	1,000,000	0	0.0	0.0
C- / 3.8	4.1	5.2	11.88	34	2	0	97	0	1	9	0.0	15	5	1,000	100	4.5	0.0
C- / 3.8	4.1	5.2	11.89	2	2	0	97	0	1	9	0.0	9	5	1,000	100	0.0	0.0

Fund Type	Fund Name	Ticker Symbol	Overall Investment Rating	Phone	PERFORMANCE: Performance Rating/Pts	Total Return % through 3/31/16: 3 Mo	6 Mo	1Yr / Pct	Annualized: 3Yr / Pct	5Yr / Pct	Incl. in Returns: Dividend Yield	Expense Ratio
MUS ●	Dreyfus MA Muni Z	PMAZX	**B**	(800) 782-6620	**A- / 9.0**	1.53	3.13	3.75 /92	2.84 /86	5.17 /87	2.80	0.72
MUN	Dreyfus Muni Bond Opp A	PTEBX	**B-**	(800) 782-6620	**B+ / 8.8**	1.61	3.55	4.16 /95	3.81 /95	6.02 /92	3.06	0.93
MUN	Dreyfus Muni Bond Opp C	DMBCX	**B**	(800) 782-6620	**A- / 9.0**	1.42	3.09	3.41 /89	3.02 /88	5.22 /87	2.48	1.69
MUN ●	Dreyfus Muni Bond Opp Z	DMBZX	**B+**	(800) 782-6620	**A+ / 9.6**	1.62	3.58	4.22 /95	3.86 /95	6.08 /92	3.25	0.87
MMT	Dreyfus Muni Cash Mgmt Plus Admin	DAMXX	**C-**	(800) 645-6561	**D / 1.9**	0.02	0.03	0.03 /38	0.01 /19	0.01 / 7	0.03	0.37
MMT	Dreyfus Muni Cash Mgmt Plus Inst	DIMXX	**C-**	(800) 645-6561	**D / 1.9**	0.02	0.03	0.03 /38	0.01 /19	0.01 / 7	0.03	0.27
MMT	Dreyfus Muni Cash Mgmt Plus Inv	DVMXX	**C-**	(800) 645-6561	**D / 1.9**	0.02	0.03	0.03 /38	0.01 /19	0.01 / 7	0.03	0.52
MMT	Dreyfus Muni Cash Mgmt Plus Part	DMPXX	**C-**	(800) 645-6561	**D / 1.9**	0.02	0.03	0.03 /38	0.01 /19	0.01 / 7	0.03	0.67
* MUN	Dreyfus Municipal Bond	DRTAX	**B+**	(800) 645-6561	**A / 9.5**	1.62	3.58	4.25 /95	3.69 /94	5.85 /91	3.20	0.72
MUS	Dreyfus NJ Muni Bond A	DRNJX	**C+**	(800) 645-6561	**B / 8.2**	1.81	4.04	4.14 /95	3.10 /89	5.49 /89	3.17	0.95
MUS	Dreyfus NJ Muni Bond C	DCNJX	**C+**	(800) 645-6561	**B+ / 8.5**	1.55	3.57	3.29 /88	2.30 /80	4.69 /83	2.58	1.72
MUS	Dreyfus NJ Muni Bond I	DNMIX	**B+**	(800) 645-6561	**A / 9.4**	1.80	4.16	4.31 /96	3.35 /91	5.72 /90	3.56	0.72
MUN	Dreyfus NJ Muni Bond Y	DNJYX	**U**	(800) 645-6561	**U /**	1.88	4.16	4.39 /96	--	--	3.56	0.76
MUS ●	Dreyfus NJ Muni Bond Z	DZNJX	**B+**	(800) 782-6620	**A / 9.4**	1.86	4.13	4.33 /96	3.30 /91	5.65 /90	3.50	0.77
MUS	Dreyfus NY AMT Free Muni Bd A	PSNYX	**B-**	(800) 645-6561	**B / 8.1**	1.65	3.51	4.11 /95	3.09 /89	5.16 /86	2.80	0.92
MUS	Dreyfus NY AMT Free Muni Bd C	PNYCX	**B**	(800) 645-6561	**B+ / 8.5**	1.46	3.12	3.33 /88	2.31 /80	4.36 /80	2.18	1.68
MUS	Dreyfus NY AMT Free Muni Bd I	DNYIX	**A-**	(800) 645-6561	**A / 9.4**	1.71	3.63	4.37 /96	3.35 /91	5.43 /88	3.17	0.66
MUN	Dreyfus NY AMT Free Muni Bd Y	DNYYX	**U**	(800) 645-6561	**U /**	1.71	3.64	4.35 /96	--	--	3.15	0.79
* MUS	Dreyfus NY Tax Exempt Bond	DRNYX	**B+**	(800) 645-6561	**A- / 9.1**	1.58	3.55	4.24 /95	2.92 /87	5.00 /85	3.18	0.72
GEI	Dreyfus Opportunistic Fixed Inc A	DSTAX	**D-**	(800) 782-6620	**E- / 0.1**	-3.59	-4.62	-10.91 / 0	-2.39 / 3	0.61 /18	6.11	0.98
GEI	Dreyfus Opportunistic Fixed Inc C	DSTCX	**D-**	(800) 782-6620	**E- / 0.1**	-3.71	-4.98	-11.55 / 0	-3.11 / 2	-0.13 / 3	5.37	1.72
GEI	Dreyfus Opportunistic Fixed Inc I	DSTRX	**D-**	(800) 782-6620	**E- / 0.2**	-3.47	-4.45	-10.64 / 1	-2.13 / 4	0.88 /19	6.75	0.72
GEL	Dreyfus Opportunistic Fixed Inc Y	DSTYX	**U**	(800) 782-6620	**U /**	-3.45	-4.47	-10.65 / 1	--	--	6.85	0.61
MUS	Dreyfus PA Muni A	PTPAX	**B-**	(800) 782-6620	**B / 8.1**	1.54	3.33	4.13 /95	3.10 /89	5.29 /88	2.91	0.96
MUS	Dreyfus PA Muni C	PPACX	**B**	(800) 782-6620	**B+ / 8.4**	1.41	2.94	3.35 /89	2.32 /81	4.49 /81	2.29	1.71
MUS ●	Dreyfus PA Muni Z	DPENX	**A-**	(800) 782-6620	**A / 9.3**	1.66	3.44	4.36 /96	3.32 /91	5.51 /89	3.26	0.73
MM	Dreyfus Prime Money Market B	CZBXX	**U**	(800) 645-6561	**U /**	0.01	0.01	0.01 /32	--	--	0.01	0.47
MM	Dreyfus Prime Money Market Citizens	CZAXX	**C**	(800) 645-6561	**D / 2.0**	0.05	0.06	0.06 /39	0.02 /19	0.02 / 7	0.06	0.22
MUI	Dreyfus Sh-Intmd Muni Bd A	DMBAX	**C**	(800) 645-6561	**D+ / 2.9**	0.53	0.58	0.95 /66	0.74 /45	1.27 /31	0.58	0.87
MUI	Dreyfus Sh-Intmd Muni Bd D	DSIBX	**B+**	(800) 645-6561	**C / 5.3**	0.57	0.65	1.10 /69	0.90 /50	1.43 /34	0.75	0.72
MUI	Dreyfus Sh-Intmd Muni Bd I	DIMIX	**A-**	(800) 645-6561	**C / 5.5**	0.59	0.70	1.20 /70	0.97 /52	1.52 /35	0.84	0.65
MUN	Dreyfus Sh-Intmd Muni Bd Y	DMYBX	**U**	(800) 645-6561	**U /**	0.59	0.70	1.20 /70	--	--	0.85	0.70
GEI	Dreyfus Short Term Inc D	DSTIX	**C+**	(800) 782-6620	**C- / 3.3**	1.04	0.30	-0.08 /30	0.49 /33	1.30 /23	1.75	0.90
GEI ●	Dreyfus Short Term Inc P	DSHPX	**C**	(800) 782-6620	**C- / 3.2**	0.92	0.26	-0.16 /30	0.42 /32	1.25 /23	1.67	1.04
MMT	Dreyfus T/E Cash Mgmt Admin	DEAXX	**C-**	(800) 645-6561	**D / 1.9**	0.00	0.01	0.01 /34	0.01 /19	--	0.01	0.32
MMT	Dreyfus T/E Cash Mgmt Inst	DEIXX	**C-**	(800) 645-6561	**D / 1.9**	0.00	0.01	0.01 /34	0.01 /19	0.01 / 7	0.01	0.24
MMT	Dreyfus T/E Cash Mgmt Inv	DEVXX	**C-**	(800) 645-6561	**D / 1.9**	0.00	0.01	0.01 /34	0.01 /19	--	0.01	0.47
MMT	Dreyfus T/E Cash Mgmt Part	DEPXX	**C-**	(800) 645-6561	**D / 1.9**	0.00	0.01	0.01 /34	0.01 /19	--	0.01	0.62
MUN	Dreyfus Tax Sensitive Tot Ret Bd A	DSDAX	**A**	(800) 645-6561	**B- / 7.1**	1.46	2.44	2.91 /84	2.59 /84	3.84 /76	2.04	0.89
MUN	Dreyfus Tax Sensitive Tot Ret Bd C	DSDCX	**A+**	(800) 645-6561	**B / 7.8**	1.24	2.06	2.16 /78	1.81 /74	3.07 /70	1.41	1.69
MUN	Dreyfus Tax Sensitive Tot Ret Bd I	SDITX	**A+**	(800) 645-6561	**B+ / 8.9**	1.52	2.56	3.16 /86	2.84 /86	4.14 /79	2.38	0.58
MUN	Dreyfus Tax Sensitive Tot Ret Bd Y	SDYTX	**U**	(800) 645-6561	**U /**	1.48	2.57	3.16 /86	--	--	2.38	0.59
MM	Dreyfus Treas & Agn Cash Mgt Adm	DTAXX	**U**	(800) 645-6561	**U /**	0.01	0.01	0.02 /34	0.01 /16	0.01 / 4	0.02	0.31
MM	Dreyfus Treas & Agn Cash Mgt Agn	DYAXX	**C-**	(800) 645-6561	**D / 1.9**	0.02	0.02	0.03 /36	0.02 /19	0.01 / 4	0.03	0.27
MM	Dreyfus Treas & Agn Cash Mgt Inst	DTRXX	**C**	(800) 645-6561	**D / 2.0**	0.04	0.04	0.05 /38	0.02 /19	0.02 / 7	0.05	0.21
MM	Dreyfus Treas & Agn Cash Mgt Prm	DYPXX	**U**	(800) 645-6561	**U /**	--	--	--	--	--	0.01	0.52
MM	Dreyfus Treas Prime Csh Mgt Admin	DARXX	**U**	(800) 645-6561	**U /**	0.01	0.01	0.01 /32	--	--	0.01	0.31
MM	Dreyfus Treas Prime Csh Mgt Agency	DSAXX	**U**	(800) 645-6561	**U /**	0.01	0.01	0.01 /32	--	--	0.01	0.27
MM	Dreyfus Treas Prime Csh Mgt Inst	DIRXX	**C-**	(800) 645-6561	**D / 1.9**	0.03	0.03	0.03 /36	0.01 /16	0.01 / 4	0.03	0.21
USS	Dreyfus Ultra Short Income D	DSDDX	**U**	(800) 645-6561	**U /**	-0.08	-0.37	-0.89 /23	--	--	1.88	0.71
USS	Dreyfus Ultra Short Income I		**U**	(800) 645-6561	**U /**	-0.01	-0.34	-0.63 /25	--	--	2.14	0.46
USS	Dreyfus Ultra Short Income Instl	DSYDX	**U**	(800) 645-6561	**U /**	-0.11	-0.34	-0.73 /24	--	--	2.14	0.44

99 Pct = Best
0 Pct = Worst

● Denotes fund is closed to new investors
* Denotes fund is included in Section II

RISK			NET ASSETS		ASSET							FUND MANAGER		MINIMUM		LOADS	
Risk Rating/Pts	3 Yr Avg Standard Deviation	Avg Duration	NAV As of 3/31/16	Total $(Mil)	Cash %	Gov. Bond %	Muni. Bond %	Corp. Bond %	Other %	Portfolio Turnover Ratio	Avg Coupon Rate	Manager Quality Pct	Manager Tenure (Years)	Initial Purch. $	Additional Purch. $	Front End Load	Back End Load
C- / 3.8	4.1	5.2	11.88	143	2	0	97	0	1	9	0.0	19	5	1,000	100	0.0	0.0
C- / 3.9	4.0	5.1	13.17	182	0	0	99	0	1	16	0.0	48	4	1,000	100	4.5	0.0
C- / 3.9	4.0	5.1	13.20	10	0	0	99	0	1	16	0.0	25	4	1,000	100	0.0	0.0
C- / 3.9	4.0	5.1	13.17	215	0	0	99	0	1	16	0.0	50	4	1,000	100	0.0	0.0
A+ / 9.9	N/A	N/A	1.00	6	100	0	0	0	0	0	0.0	63	20	10,000,000	0	0.0	0.0
A+ / 9.9	N/A	N/A	1.00	154	100	0	0	0	0	0	0.0	63	20	10,000,000	0	0.0	0.0
A+ / 9.9	N/A	N/A	1.00	88	100	0	0	0	0	0	0.0	63	20	10,000,000	0	0.0	0.0
A+ / 9.9	N/A	N/A	1.00	13	100	0	0	0	0	0	0.0	63	20	10,000,000	0	0.0	0.0
C- / 4.1	3.9	5.0	11.98	1,453	0	0	99	0	1	15	0.0	47	7	2,500	100	0.0	0.0
C- / 3.8	4.1	4.9	13.16	365	1	0	98	0	1	10	0.0	24	7	1,000	100	4.5	0.0
C- / 3.8	4.1	4.9	13.14	10	1	0	98	0	1	10	0.0	12	7	1,000	100	0.0	0.0
C- / 3.8	4.1	4.9	13.16	10	1	0	98	0	1	10	0.0	31	7	1,000	100	0.0	0.0
U /	N/A	4.9	13.16	N/A	1	0	98	0	1	10	0.0	N/A	7	1,000,000	0	0.0	0.0
C- / 3.8	4.1	4.9	13.16	114	1	0	98	0	1	10	0.0	30	7	1,000	100	0.0	0.0
C / 4.5	3.7	5.1	15.17	338	0	0	99	0	1	25	0.0	36	7	1,000	100	4.5	0.0
C / 4.6	3.6	5.1	15.17	30	0	0	99	0	1	25	0.0	18	7	1,000	100	0.0	0.0
C / 4.5	3.7	5.1	15.17	46	0	0	99	0	1	25	0.0	43	7	1,000	100	0.0	0.0
U /	N/A	5.1	15.17	N/A	0	0	99	0	1	25	0.0	N/A	7	1,000,000	0	0.0	0.0
C / 4.5	3.7	5.2	15.14	1,178	2	0	97	0	1	20	0.0	31	7	2,500	100	0.0	0.0
C- / 3.6	4.2	1.6	11.02	127	3	14	1	52	30	182	1.9	8	6	1,000	100	4.5	0.0
C- / 3.6	4.2	1.6	11.01	44	3	14	1	52	30	182	1.9	6	6	1,000	100	0.0	0.0
C- / 3.5	4.3	1.6	11.01	162	3	14	1	52	30	182	1.9	9	6	1,000	100	0.0	0.0
U /	N/A	1.6	11.00	81	3	14	1	52	30	182	1.9	N/A	6	1,000,000	0	0.0	0.0
C / 4.8	3.6	5.0	16.63	107	1	0	98	0	1	30	0.0	42	4	1,000	100	4.5	0.0
C / 4.7	3.6	5.0	16.64	5	1	0	98	0	1	30	0.0	21	4	1,000	100	0.0	0.0
C / 4.7	3.6	5.0	16.63	51	1	0	98	0	1	30	0.0	49	4	1,000	100	0.0	0.0
U /	N/A	N/A	1.00	94	100	0	0	0	0	0	0.0	N/A	N/A	1,000,000,00	0	0.0	0.0
A+ / 9.9	N/A	N/A	1.00	45	100	0	0	0	0	0	0.1	63	N/A	1,000,000,00	0	0.0	0.0
A- / 9.1	1.1	2.5	13.03	68	2	0	97	0	1	33	0.0	57	7	1,000	100	2.5	0.0
A- / 9.2	1.1	2.5	13.03	308	2	0	97	0	1	33	0.0	64	7	2,500	100	0.0	0.0
A- / 9.2	1.1	2.5	13.03	136	2	0	97	0	1	33	0.0	72	7	1,000	100	0.0	0.0
U /	N/A	2.5	13.03	N/A	2	0	97	0	1	33	0.0	N/A	7	1,000,000	0	0.0	0.0
A- / 9.1	1.2	2.3	10.37	200	6	45	0	35	14	95	0.0	52	8	2,500	100	0.0	0.0
A- / 9.1	1.1	2.3	10.38	N/A	6	45	0	35	14	95	0.0	52	8	100,000	100	0.0	0.0
A+ / 9.9	N/A	N/A	1.00	33	100	0	0	0	0	0	0.0	65	N/A	10,000,000	0	0.0	0.0
A+ / 9.9	N/A	N/A	1.00	1,528	100	0	0	0	0	0	0.0	65	N/A	10,000,000	0	0.0	0.0
A+ / 9.9	N/A	N/A	1.00	268	100	0	0	0	0	0	0.0	65	N/A	10,000,000	0	0.0	0.0
A+ / 9.9	N/A	N/A	1.00	41	100	0	0	0	0	0	0.0	65	N/A	10,000,000	0	0.0	0.0
B / 7.7	2.6	4.6	23.22	6	1	0	90	4	5	30	0.0	60	15	1,000	100	4.5	0.0
B / 7.7	2.6	4.6	23.22	1	1	0	90	4	5	30	0.0	34	15	1,000	100	0.0	0.0
B / 7.7	2.6	4.6	23.23	215	1	0	90	4	5	30	0.0	74	15	1,000	100	0.0	0.0
U /	N/A	4.6	23.22	1	1	0	90	4	5	30	0.0	N/A	15	1,000,000	0	0.0	0.0
U /	N/A	N/A	1.00	333	100	0	0	0	0	0	0.0	N/A	20	10,000,000	0	0.0	0.0
A+ / 9.9	N/A	N/A	1.00	11	100	0	0	0	0	0	0.0	65	20	10,000,000	0	0.0	0.0
A+ / 9.9	N/A	N/A	1.00	15,798	100	0	0	0	0	0	0.1	65	20	10,000,000	0	0.0	0.0
U /	N/A	N/A	1.00	24	100	0	0	0	0	0	0.0	N/A	20	10,000,000	0	0.0	0.0
U /	N/A	N/A	1.00	592	100	0	0	0	0	0	0.0	N/A	N/A	10,000,000	0	0.0	0.0
U /	N/A	N/A	1.00	21	100	0	0	0	0	0	0.0	N/A	N/A	10,000,000	0	0.0	0.0
A+ / 9.9	N/A	N/A	1.00	26,845	100	0	0	0	0	0	0.0	63	N/A	10,000,000	0	0.0	0.0
U /	N/A	1.0	10.07	14	1	44	1	39	15	59	0.0	N/A	3	2,500	100	0.0	0.0
U /	N/A	1.0	10.08	11	1	44	1	39	15	59	0.0	N/A	3	1,000	100	0.0	0.0
U /	N/A	1.0	10.06	19	1	44	1	39	15	59	0.0	N/A	3	1,000,000	0	0.0	0.0

					PERFORMANCE							
99 Pct = Best *0 Pct = Worst*						Total Return % through 3/31/16					Incl. in Returns	
									Annualized			
Fund Type	Fund Name	Ticker Symbol	Overall Investment Rating	Phone	Performance Rating/Pts	3 Mo	6 Mo	1Yr / Pct	3Yr / Pct	5Yr / Pct	Dividend Yield	Expense Ratio
USS	Dreyfus Ultra Short Income Z	DSIGX	**C-**	(800) 645-6561	**D / 1.6**	-0.06	-0.29	-0.75 /24	-0.08 /15	0.11 /15	2.02	0.63
US	Dreyfus US Treasury Intermediate	DRGIX	**C+**	(800) 645-6561	**C / 4.4**	2.13	0.88	1.56 /67	0.71 /37	1.85 /29	1.09	0.56
US	Dreyfus US Treasury Long Term	DRGBX	**C-**	(800) 645-6561	**A / 9.3**	7.69	6.05	2.10 /72	5.03 /91	8.77 /90	2.29	0.68
GL	Dreyfus/Standish Global Fixed Inc A	DHGAX	**C-**	(800) 645-6561	**C- / 4.2**	1.62	1.42	-1.56 /18	2.45 /70	4.02 /62	1.48	0.89
GL	Dreyfus/Standish Global Fixed Inc C	DHGCX	**C-**	(800) 645-6561	**C / 4.9**	1.43	1.07	-2.29 /14	1.70 /56	3.25 /49	1.05	1.65
GL	Dreyfus/Standish Global Fixed Inc I	SDGIX	**B-**	(800) 645-6561	**C+ / 6.8**	1.66	1.60	-1.29 /20	2.77 /74	4.33 /66	1.78	0.59
GL	Dreyfus/Standish Global Fixed Inc Y	DSDYX	**U**	(800) 645-6561	**U /**	1.66	1.56	-1.26 /20	--	--	1.80	0.54
LP	Driehaus Select Credit Fund	DRSLX	**E+**	(800) 560-6111	**E- / 0.1**	-2.40	-7.21	-11.39 / 0	-3.93 / 2	-1.45 / 1	4.53	1.32
COI	Dunham Corporate/Government	DACGX	**D**	(888) 338-6426	**D- / 1.5**	1.96	0.75	-0.60 /25	0.90 /41	2.70 /40	2.20	1.31
COI	Dunham Corporate/Government	DCCGX	**D+**	(888) 338-6426	**C- / 3.2**	1.92	0.55	-1.14 /21	0.42 /32	2.21 /34	1.78	1.81
COI	Dunham Corporate/Government	DNCGX	**C-**	(888) 338-6426	**C / 4.6**	2.10	0.85	-0.55 /25	1.19 /46	3.02 /45	2.35	1.06
LP	Dunham Floating Rate Bond A	DAFRX	**U**	(888) 338-6426	**U /**	1.66	-0.26	-0.98 /22	--	--	2.57	1.52
LP	Dunham Floating Rate Bond C	DCFRX	**U**	(888) 338-6426	**U /**	1.54	-0.45	-1.31 /19	--	--	2.35	2.02
LP	Dunham Floating Rate Bond N	DNFRX	**U**	(888) 338-6426	**U /**	1.72	-0.05	-0.54 /26	--	--	3.03	1.27
COH	Dunham High-Yield Bond A	DAHYX	**E+**	(888) 338-6426	**E+ / 0.6**	1.42	-0.29	-3.93 / 8	-0.05 /15	2.47 /37	3.98	1.27
COH	Dunham High-Yield Bond C	DCHYX	**E+**	(888) 338-6426	**D- / 1.0**	1.20	-0.61	-4.20 / 7	-0.46 /12	2.03 /31	4.01	1.77
COH	Dunham High-Yield Bond N	DNHYX	**D-**	(888) 338-6426	**D / 1.8**	1.50	-0.19	-3.51 /10	0.37 /31	2.92 /44	4.59	1.02
GEI	Dunham International Oppty Bd A	DAIOX	**U**	(888) 338-6426	**U /**	7.09	5.93	4.05 /81	--	--	0.04	1.63
GEI	Dunham International Oppty Bd C	DCIOX	**U**	(888) 338-6426	**U /**	6.91	5.70	3.58 /79	--	--	0.01	2.13
GEI	Dunham International Oppty Bd N	DNIOX	**U**	(888) 338-6426	**U /**	7.08	5.96	4.20 /82	--	--	0.08	1.38
EM	DuPont Capital Emerging Mkts Dbt I	DCDEX	**U**	(888) 739-1390	**U /**	4.16	7.22	12.29 /99	--	--	10.42	2.25
MUS	Dupree AL Tax Free Income	DUALX	**A**	(800) 866-0614	**A- / 9.2**	1.26	2.64	3.13 /86	3.41 /92	5.50 /89	3.14	0.79
USL	Dupree Interm Government Bond	DPIGX	**C-**	(800) 866-0614	**B- / 7.4**	3.23	2.09	2.87 /76	2.38 /69	4.44 /67	2.42	0.51
*MUS	Dupree KY Tax Free Income	KYTFX	**A+**	(800) 866-0614	**A- / 9.1**	1.53	2.75	3.24 /87	3.17 /90	4.87 /84	3.14	0.55
MUS	Dupree KY Tax Free Short-to-Med	KYSMX	**A+**	(800) 866-0614	**C+ / 6.8**	1.03	1.53	2.02 /77	1.32 /62	2.63 /62	1.99	0.73
MUS	Dupree MS Tax Free Income	DUMSX	**B+**	(800) 866-0614	**A / 9.5**	1.54	3.21	3.85 /93	3.86 /95	5.63 /90	2.95	0.86
MUS	Dupree NC Tax Free Income	NTFIX	**A**	(800) 866-0614	**A- / 9.2**	1.38	2.75	3.48 /90	3.21 /90	5.42 /88	2.88	0.71
MUS	Dupree NC Tax Free Sh-to-Med	NTSMX	**A-**	(800) 866-0614	**C+ / 5.9**	0.65	0.87	1.42 /73	1.08 /55	2.40 /56	1.59	0.83
MUN	Dupree Taxable Muni Bd Srs	DUTMX	**B**	(800) 866-0614	**A+ / 9.8**	2.97	3.62	3.77 /92	4.54 /98	8.00 /98	4.68	0.83
MUS	Dupree TN Tax-Free Income	TNTIX	**A+**	(800) 866-0614	**A- / 9.2**	1.33	2.70	3.11 /86	3.27 /91	4.95 /85	2.95	0.70
MUS	Dupree TN Tax-Free Sh-to-Med	TTSMX	**A**	(800) 866-0614	**C+ / 6.8**	0.92	1.29	1.97 /77	1.37 /64	2.18 /51	1.49	0.85
COI	Eagle Investment Grade Bond A	EGBAX	**C-**	(800) 421-4184	**C- / 3.0**	2.06	1.32	1.40 /65	1.04 /43	2.40 /36	1.18	1.21
COI	Eagle Investment Grade Bond C	EGBCX	**C**	(800) 421-4184	**C- / 3.3**	1.93	0.93	0.59 /51	0.24 /29	1.59 /26	0.43	1.96
COI	Eagle Investment Grade Bond I	EGBLX	**B**	(800) 421-4184	**C / 5.4**	2.17	1.45	1.66 /68	1.30 /48	2.68 /40	1.47	0.91
COI	Eagle Investment Grade Bond R3	EGBRX	**C+**	(800) 421-4184	**C / 4.4**	2.03	1.19	1.12 /61	0.75 /38	2.11 /32	0.94	1.55
COI	Eagle Investment Grade Bond R5	EGBTX	**B**	(800) 421-4184	**C / 5.5**	2.24	1.52	1.76 /69	1.30 /48	2.64 /39	1.43	0.81
COI	Eagle Investment Grade Bond R6	EGBUX	**U**	(800) 421-4184	**U /**	2.18	1.49	--	--	--	0.00	0.50
MUN	Eaton Vance AMT-Free Muni Income	ETMBX	**C**	(800) 262-1122	**B+ / 8.5**	1.27	3.73	4.24 /95	3.64 /93	7.42 /97	3.71	0.90
MUN •	Eaton Vance AMT-Free Muni Income	EBMBX	**C+**	(800) 262-1122	**A- / 9.0**	1.09	3.36	3.46 /90	2.87 /87	6.62 /95	3.16	1.65
MUN	Eaton Vance AMT-Free Muni Income	ECMBX	**C+**	(800) 262-1122	**A- / 9.0**	1.08	3.36	3.46 /90	2.87 /87	6.64 /95	3.16	1.65
MUN	Eaton Vance AMT-Free Muni Income	EVMBX	**C+**	(800) 262-1122	**A+ / 9.6**	1.30	3.91	4.48 /97	3.92 /95	7.69 /98	4.14	0.65
MUS	Eaton Vance AZ Municipal Income A	ETAZX	**C+**	(800) 262-1122	**B / 8.0**	1.43	3.60	3.27 /88	3.19 /90	5.61 /90	3.42	0.72
MUS •	Eaton Vance AZ Municipal Income B	EVAZX	**C+**	(800) 262-1122	**B+ / 8.4**	1.18	3.12	2.55 /81	2.38 /81	4.81 /84	2.86	1.47
MUS	Eaton Vance AZ Municipal Income C	ECAZX	**C+**	(800) 262-1122	**B+ / 8.4**	1.18	3.21	2.55 /81	2.42 /82	4.81 /84	2.86	1.47
MUS	Eaton Vance AZ Municipal Income I	EIAZX	**B+**	(800) 262-1122	**A / 9.3**	1.48	3.70	3.48 /90	3.39 /92	5.82 /91	3.79	0.52
COI	Eaton Vance Bond A	EVBAX	**E-**	(800) 262-1122	**E / 0.3**	4.35	0.18	-13.27 / 0	-0.76 /10	--	3.40	0.95
GEL	Eaton Vance Bond C	EVBCX	**E-**	(800) 262-1122	**E / 0.3**	4.16	-0.21	-13.96 / 0	-1.51 / 6	--	2.76	1.70
COI	Eaton Vance Bond I	EVBIX	**E-**	(800) 262-1122	**E+ / 0.6**	4.29	0.31	-13.04 / 0	-0.50 /11	--	3.84	0.70
GL •	Eaton Vance Bond II A	EBTAX	**U**	(800) 262-1122	**U /**	2.21	-1.69	-13.58 / 0	--	--	4.95	1.87
GL •	Eaton Vance Bond II C	EBTCX	**U**	(800) 262-1122	**U /**	1.94	-2.02	-14.25 / 0	--	--	4.50	2.62
GL	Eaton Vance Bond II I	EBTIX	**U**	(800) 262-1122	**U /**	2.12	-1.59	-13.38 / 0	--	--	5.45	1.62
GEL	Eaton Vance Bond R	EVBRX	**E-**	(800) 262-1122	**E / 0.4**	4.17	0.09	-13.58 / 0	-1.03 / 8	--	3.28	1.20

• Denotes fund is closed to new investors
* Denotes fund is included in Section II

RISK			NET ASSETS		ASSET							FUND MANAGER		MINIMUM		LOADS	
Risk Rating/Pts	3 Yr Avg Standard Deviation	Avg Duration	NAV As of 3/31/16	Total $(Mil)	Cash %	Gov. Bond %	Muni. Bond %	Corp. Bond %	Other %	Portfolio Turnover Ratio	Avg Coupon Rate	Manager Quality Pct	Manager Tenure (Years)	Initial Purch. $	Additional Purch. $	Front End Load	Back End Load
A+ / 9.6	0.7	1.0	10.07	85	1	44	1	39	15	59	0.0	56	3	2,500	100	0.0	0.0
B+ / 8.4	2.1	3.8	13.46	66	1	97	0	0	2	250	0.0	39	8	2,500	100	0.0	0.0
E- / 0.2	10.3	16.6	20.54	73	0	99	0	0	1	49	0.0	19	8	2,500	100	0.0	0.0
C+ / 6.2	3.1	5.8	21.37	302	9	54	0	20	17	180	0.0	97	10	1,000	100	4.5	0.0
C+ / 6.2	3.1	5.8	21.25	89	9	54	0	20	17	180	0.0	95	10	1,000	100	0.0	0.0
C+ / 6.1	3.1	5.8	21.41	1,873	9	54	0	20	17	180	0.0	98	10	1,000	100	0.0	0.0
U /	N/A	5.8	21.41	102	9	54	0	20	17	180	0.0	N/A	10	1,000,000	0	0.0	0.0
D+ / 2.3	5.4	0.2	7.80	196	25	0	0	41	34	79	0.0	3	6	25,000	5,000	0.0	0.0
C+ / 5.6	3.2	4.5	13.66	6	4	19	6	41	30	54	5.0	29	N/A	5,000	100	4.5	0.0
C / 5.5	3.3	4.5	13.58	4	4	19	6	41	30	54	5.0	18	N/A	5,000	100	0.0	0.0
C+ / 5.7	3.2	4.5	13.68	42	4	19	6	41	30	54	5.0	38	N/A	100,000	0	0.0	0.0
U /	N/A	N/A	9.48	9	1	0	0	16	83	51	0.0	N/A	3	5,000	100	4.5	0.0
U /	N/A	N/A	9.48	4	1	0	0	16	83	51	0.0	N/A	3	5,000	100	0.0	0.0
U /	N/A	N/A	9.49	73	1	0	0	16	83	51	0.0	N/A	3	100,000	0	0.0	0.0
D / 1.8	5.3	N/A	8.61	10	5	0	0	94	1	51	0.0	17	11	5,000	100	4.5	0.0
D / 1.9	5.3	N/A	8.48	8	5	0	0	94	1	51	0.0	12	11	5,000	100	0.0	0.0
D / 1.8	5.4	N/A	8.54	76	5	0	0	94	1	51	0.0	24	11	100,000	0	0.0	0.0
U /	N/A	N/A	9.36	3	5	56	0	34	5	52	0.0	N/A	N/A	5,000	100	4.5	0.0
U /	N/A	N/A	9.28	1	5	56	0	34	5	52	0.0	N/A	N/A	5,000	100	0.0	0.0
U /	N/A	N/A	9.38	29	5	56	0	34	5	52	0.0	N/A	N/A	100,000	0	0.0	0.0
U /	N/A	N/A	9.26	6	0	0	0	0	100	24	0.0	N/A	N/A	1,000,000	100,000	0.0	2.0
C+ / 5.6	3.2	4.1	12.56	27	0	0	100	0	0	10	5.1	68	15	100	0	0.0	0.0
C- / 3.1	4.7	6.2	10.57	17	0	100	0	0	0	2	5.6	64	17	100	0	0.0	0.0
C+ / 6.3	3.1	5.2	7.96	1,001	0	0	100	0	0	8	5.0	61	17	100	0	0.0	0.0
B+ / 8.8	1.6	3.7	5.41	87	0	0	100	0	0	20	4.6	58	17	100	0	0.0	0.0
C- / 4.1	3.9	5.1	12.35	11	0	0	100	0	0	6	5.1	55	16	100	0	0.0	0.0
C / 5.1	3.4	5.4	11.78	141	0	0	100	0	0	5	5.0	49	12	100	0	0.0	0.0
B+ / 8.9	1.6	2.8	10.99	24	0	0	100	0	0	10	4.7	47	12	100	0	0.0	0.0
D+ / 2.8	4.4	10.8	10.78	11	0	0	100	0	0	8	6.8	86	6	100	0	0.0	0.0
C+ / 5.8	3.2	5.4	11.72	114	0	0	100	0	0	7	5.0	61	12	100	0	0.0	0.0
B+ / 8.6	1.9	3.8	10.88	11	0	0	100	0	0	14	4.6	45	12	100	0	0.0	0.0
B+ / 8.4	2.1	5.3	14.97	17	0	26	0	43	31	82	3.0	57	6	1,000	0	3.8	0.0
B+ / 8.4	2.1	5.3	14.94	21	0	26	0	43	31	82	3.0	30	6	1,000	0	0.0	0.0
B+ / 8.4	2.1	5.3	15.00	9	0	26	0	43	31	82	3.0	70	6	2,500,000	0	0.0	0.0
B+ / 8.4	2.1	5.3	14.97	N/A	0	26	0	43	31	82	3.0	44	6	0	0	0.0	0.0
B+ / 8.4	2.1	5.3	14.99	N/A	0	26	0	43	31	82	3.0	71	6	0	0	0.0	0.0
U /	N/A	5.3	15.04	N/A	0	26	0	43	31	82	3.0	N/A	6	0	0	0.0	0.0
D+ / 2.5	5.2	4.7	9.37	196	1	0	98	0	1	17	5.4	15	11	1,000	0	4.8	0.0
D+ / 2.5	5.3	4.7	9.31	1	1	0	98	0	1	17	5.4	9	11	1,000	0	0.0	0.0
D+ / 2.5	5.3	4.7	9.32	44	1	0	98	0	1	17	5.4	9	11	1,000	0	0.0	0.0
D+ / 2.5	5.2	4.7	10.24	125	1	0	98	0	1	17	5.4	20	11	250,000	0	0.0	0.0
C- / 4.0	4.0	4.5	9.72	47	2	0	97	0	1	8	4.8	31	12	1,000	0	4.8	0.0
C- / 4.0	4.0	4.5	10.80	N/A	2	0	97	0	1	8	4.8	15	12	1,000	0	0.0	0.0
C- / 3.9	4.0	4.5	10.81	6	2	0	97	0	1	8	4.8	15	12	1,000	0	0.0	0.0
C- / 3.9	4.1	4.5	9.72	11	2	0	97	0	1	8	4.8	34	12	250,000	0	0.0	0.0
E- / 0.2	10.3	N/A	8.88	169	5	15	0	35	45	45	5.4	6	3	1,000	0	4.8	0.0
E- / 0.2	10.2	N/A	8.86	133	5	15	0	35	45	45	5.4	7	3	1,000	0	0.0	0.0
E- / 0.2	10.3	N/A	8.88	358	5	15	0	35	45	45	5.4	6	3	250,000	0	0.0	0.0
U /	N/A	6.3	7.98	N/A	4	16	0	54	26	30	5.3	N/A	N/A	1,000	0	4.8	0.0
U /	N/A	6.3	7.97	N/A	4	16	0	54	26	30	5.3	N/A	N/A	1,000	0	0.0	0.0
U /	N/A	6.3	7.98	18	4	16	0	54	26	30	5.3	N/A	N/A	250,000	0	0.0	0.0
E- / 0.2	10.3	N/A	8.88	N/A	5	15	0	35	45	45	5.4	8	3	1,000	0	0.0	0.0

Fund Type	Fund Name (99 Pct = Best, 0 Pct = Worst)	Ticker Symbol	Overall Investment Rating	Phone	PERFORMANCE: Performance Rating/Pts	Total Return % through 3/31/16: 3 Mo	6 Mo	1Yr / Pct	Annualized: 3Yr / Pct	Annualized: 5Yr / Pct	Incl. in Returns: Dividend Yield	Expense Ratio
GEL	Eaton Vance Bond R6	EVBSX	**E-**	(800) 262-1122	**E+ / 0.6**	4.43	0.36	-12.95 / 0	-0.43 /12	--	3.93	0.64
MUN	Eaton Vance CA Municipal Opptys A	EACAX	**C+**	(800) 262-1122	**A / 9.3**	2.12	4.38	5.67 /99	4.44 /97	7.44 /97	3.17	0.88
MUN	Eaton Vance CA Municipal Opptys C	ECCAX	**B-**	(800) 262-1122	**A / 9.5**	1.94	4.00	4.95 /98	3.64 /93	6.64 /95	2.59	1.63
MUN	Eaton Vance CA Municipal Opptys I	EICAX	**B**	(800) 262-1122	**A+ / 9.8**	2.18	4.50	5.93 /99	4.69 /98	7.70 /98	3.57	0.63
COI	Eaton Vance Core Bond A	EAGIX	**C**	(800) 262-1122	**C- / 4.2**	2.78	2.08	0.97 /58	1.98 /61	3.38 /51	2.49	0.99
COI	Eaton Vance Core Bond I	EIGIX	**B+**	(800) 262-1122	**C+ / 6.8**	2.84	2.20	1.22 /62	2.24 /66	3.64 /55	2.87	0.74
USS	Eaton Vance Core Plus Bond A	EBABX	**E+**	(800) 262-1122	**E+ / 0.8**	3.73	2.74	-3.99 / 8	0.04 /23	5.87 /76	3.72	1.14
USS	Eaton Vance Core Plus Bond C	ECBAX	**E+**	(800) 262-1122	**D- / 1.1**	3.45	2.27	-4.79 / 5	-0.70 /10	5.09 /72	3.15	1.89
USS	Eaton Vance Core Plus Bond I	EIBAX	**D-**	(800) 262-1122	**D+ / 2.9**	3.80	2.78	-3.83 / 8	0.26 /29	6.12 /77	4.16	0.89
MUN	Eaton Vance CT Municipal Income A	ETCTX	**C+**	(800) 262-1122	**B / 8.1**	1.80	3.37	3.56 /91	3.29 /91	5.25 /87	3.21	0.75
MUN ●	Eaton Vance CT Municipal Income B	EVCTX	**C+**	(800) 262-1122	**B+ / 8.6**	1.62	3.00	2.79 /83	2.52 /83	4.45 /81	2.63	1.50
MUN	Eaton Vance CT Municipal Income C	ECCTX	**C+**	(800) 262-1122	**B+ / 8.6**	1.62	3.00	2.79 /83	2.52 /83	4.45 /81	2.63	1.50
MUN	Eaton Vance CT Municipal Income I	EICTX	**B+**	(800) 262-1122	**A / 9.4**	1.85	3.48	3.77 /92	3.49 /93	5.44 /88	3.57	0.55
GEI	Eaton Vance Currency Income Adv A	ECIAX	**U**	(800) 262-1122	**U /**	2.10	4.17	-3.32 /10	--	--	0.00	8.60
GEI	Eaton Vance Currency Income Adv I	ECIIX	**U**	(800) 262-1122	**U /**	2.09	4.27	-3.09 /11	--	--	0.00	8.30
GL	Eaton Vance Dvsfd Currency Income	EAIIX	**D-**	(800) 262-1122	**E- / 0.2**	1.34	2.58	-1.16 /20	-2.98 / 2	-0.66 / 2	5.49	1.30
GL	Eaton Vance Dvsfd Currency Income	ECIMX	**D-**	(800) 262-1122	**E / 0.3**	1.23	2.24	-1.81 /16	-3.50 / 2	-1.28 / 1	4.87	2.00
GL	Eaton Vance Dvsfd Currency Income	EIIMX	**D-**	(800) 262-1122	**E / 0.4**	1.44	2.67	-0.90 /22	-2.73 / 3	-0.40 / 2	6.16	1.00
EM	Eaton Vance Em Mkts Debt Oppts A	EADOX	**E**	(800) 262-1122	**E+ / 0.6**	3.25	5.40	-0.74 /24	-1.01 / 8	--	1.26	1.58
EM	Eaton Vance Em Mkts Debt Oppts I	EIDOX	**D-**	(800) 262-1122	**D+ / 2.6**	3.61	5.67	-0.38 /27	-0.72 /10	--	1.57	1.33
EM	Eaton Vance Em Mkts Debt Oppts R6	EELDX	**E+**	(800) 262-1122	**D / 1.8**	3.38	5.46	-0.58 /25	-0.79 / 9	--	1.60	1.28
EM	Eaton Vance Emer Market Local Inc	EEIAX	**E-**	(800) 262-1122	**E- / 0.1**	9.38	12.18	-0.87 /23	-7.77 / 1	-3.03 / 1	10.48	1.43
EM	Eaton Vance Emer Market Local Inc	EEICX	**E-**	(800) 262-1122	**E- / 0.1**	9.16	11.80	-1.54 /18	-8.28 / 0	-3.61 / 1	9.80	2.13
EM	Eaton Vance Emer Market Local Inc I	EEIIX	**E-**	(800) 262-1122	**E- / 0.1**	9.52	12.29	-0.66 /25	-7.58 / 1	-2.78 / 1	11.53	1.13
* LP	Eaton Vance Float Rate Advtage A	EAFAX	**D+**	(800) 262-1122	**C- / 3.4**	2.31	-0.38	-1.87 /16	1.42 /51	3.33 /50	4.95	1.36
LP	Eaton Vance Float Rate Advtage	EVFAX	**C-**	(800) 262-1122	**C / 4.6**	2.31	-0.38	-1.87 /16	1.45 /51	3.33 /50	5.06	1.37
LP ●	Eaton Vance Float Rate Advtage B	EBFAX	**D+**	(800) 262-1122	**C- / 3.8**	2.22	-0.54	-2.20 /15	1.07 /44	2.97 /44	4.71	1.71
LP	Eaton Vance Float Rate Advtage C	ECFAX	**D+**	(800) 262-1122	**C- / 3.5**	2.19	-0.63	-2.37 /14	0.91 /41	2.80 /42	4.55	1.86
LP	Eaton Vance Float Rate Advtage I	EIFAX	**C-**	(800) 262-1122	**C / 5.0**	2.38	-0.26	-1.63 /18	1.67 /55	3.58 /54	5.31	1.12
* LP	Eaton Vance Floating Rate A	EVBLX	**C-**	(800) 262-1122	**D+ / 2.5**	1.85	-0.51	-1.86 /16	0.94 /41	2.52 /38	4.00	1.03
LP	Eaton Vance Floating Rate Adv	EABLX	**C-**	(800) 262-1122	**C- / 3.7**	1.88	-0.48	-1.84 /16	0.96 /42	2.52 /38	4.09	1.03
LP ●	Eaton Vance Floating Rate B	EBBLX	**D+**	(800) 262-1122	**D / 1.7**	1.70	-0.86	-2.57 /13	0.20 /29	1.75 /28	3.32	1.78
LP	Eaton Vance Floating Rate C	ECBLX	**D+**	(800) 262-1122	**D / 1.7**	1.70	-0.86	-2.57 /13	0.20 /29	1.75 /28	3.32	1.78
LP	Eaton Vance Floating Rate I	EIBLX	**C**	(800) 262-1122	**C- / 4.2**	1.94	-0.36	-1.58 /18	1.21 /46	2.77 /41	4.34	0.78
MUN	Eaton Vance Floating-Rte Muni Inc A	EXFLX	**D+**	(800) 262-1122	**E+ / 0.6**	0.15	0.09	-0.46 /26	-1.07 / 8	1.99 /46	0.53	0.66
MUN	Eaton Vance Floating-Rte Muni Inc I	EILMX	**D+**	(800) 262-1122	**D- / 1.0**	0.19	0.16	-0.42 /27	-0.95 / 9	2.14 /50	0.69	0.51
LP	Eaton Vance Flt-Rate and Hi Inc A	EVFHX	**C-**	(800) 262-1122	**C- / 3.3**	2.13	0.08	-1.63 /18	1.29 /48	2.97 /44	4.27	1.07
LP	Eaton Vance Flt-Rate and Hi Inc Adv	EAFHX	**C-**	(800) 262-1122	**C / 4.4**	2.20	0.05	-1.68 /17	1.30 /48	2.97 /44	4.33	1.07
LP ●	Eaton Vance Flt-Rate and Hi Inc B	EBFHX	**C-**	(800) 262-1122	**D+ / 2.9**	1.89	-0.32	-2.41 /14	0.53 /34	2.20 /34	3.57	1.82
LP	Eaton Vance Flt-Rate and Hi Inc C	ECFHX	**C-**	(800) 262-1122	**D+ / 2.9**	1.89	-0.33	-2.43 /14	0.54 /34	2.21 /34	3.56	1.82
LP	Eaton Vance Flt-Rate and Hi Inc I	EIFHX	**C**	(800) 262-1122	**C / 4.8**	2.13	0.17	-1.44 /19	1.51 /52	3.23 /49	4.59	0.82
MUN	Eaton Vance GA Municipal Income A	ETGAX	**C+**	(800) 262-1122	**B+ / 8.3**	1.43	3.19	4.18 /95	3.45 /92	5.14 /86	2.99	0.73
MUN ●	Eaton Vance GA Municipal Income B	EVGAX	**B**	(800) 262-1122	**B+ / 8.8**	1.31	2.81	3.46 /90	2.69 /85	4.37 /80	2.40	1.49
MUN	Eaton Vance GA Municipal Income C	ECGAX	**B-**	(800) 262-1122	**B+ / 8.8**	1.31	2.92	3.46 /90	2.69 /85	4.37 /80	2.40	1.48
MUN	Eaton Vance GA Municipal Income I	EIGAX	**B+**	(800) 262-1122	**A / 9.5**	1.60	3.41	4.51 /97	3.65 /94	5.37 /88	3.33	0.53
GL	Eaton Vance Glb Mac Abslut Ret A	EAGMX	**D+**	(800) 262-1122	**D- / 1.3**	0.11	2.47	0.58 /51	0.51 /33	1.09 /21	5.01	1.07
GL	Eaton Vance Glb Mac Abslut Ret C	ECGMX	**C-**	(800) 262-1122	**D+ / 2.4**	-0.09	2.06	-0.10 /30	-0.09 /15	0.45 /17	4.44	1.77
GL	Eaton Vance Glb Mac Abslut Ret I	EIGMX	**C+**	(800) 262-1122	**C / 4.3**	0.19	2.65	0.92 /57	0.79 /39	1.38 /24	5.60	0.77
GL	Eaton Vance Glb Mac Abslut Ret R	ERGMX	**C-**	(800) 262-1122	**C- / 3.4**	0.05	2.35	0.36 /47	0.36 /31	0.92 /20	5.02	1.27
USS	Eaton Vance Govt Obligation A	EVGOX	**C-**	(800) 262-1122	**D- / 1.2**	0.52	-0.01	0.12 /42	0.64 /36	1.40 /24	3.45	1.18
USS ●	Eaton Vance Govt Obligation B	EMGOX	**C-**	(800) 262-1122	**D / 1.7**	0.49	-0.23	-0.48 /26	-0.06 /15	0.67 /18	2.86	1.94
USS	Eaton Vance Govt Obligation C	ECGOX	**C-**	(800) 262-1122	**D / 1.6**	0.34	-0.38	-0.63 /25	-0.12 /15	0.67 /18	2.87	1.93

● Denotes fund is closed to new investors
* Denotes fund is included in Section II

RISK			NET ASSETS		ASSET							FUND MANAGER		MINIMUM		LOADS	
Risk Rating/Pts	3 Yr Avg Standard Deviation	Avg Duration	NAV As of 3/31/16	Total $(Mil)	Cash %	Gov. Bond %	Muni. Bond %	Corp. Bond %	Other %	Portfolio Turnover Ratio	Avg Coupon Rate	Manager Quality Pct	Manager Tenure (Years)	Initial Purch. $	Additional Purch. $	Front End Load	Back End Load
E- / 0.2	10.3	N/A	8.89	5	5	15	0	35	45	45	5.4	11	3	1,000,000	0	0.0	0.0
D+ / 2.7	5.1	5.3	10.53	135	0	0	99	0	1	66	5.0	34	2	1,000	0	4.8	0.0
D+ / 2.7	5.1	5.3	9.74	25	0	0	99	0	1	66	5.0	17	2	1,000	0	0.0	0.0
D+ / 2.7	5.1	5.3	10.54	49	0	0	99	0	1	66	5.0	41	2	250,000	0	0.0	0.0
B / 7.6	2.7	5.3	9.90	36	0	34	0	29	37	134	3.5	77	6	1,000	0	4.8	0.0
B- / 7.5	2.7	5.3	9.89	100	0	34	0	29	37	134	3.5	83	6	250,000	0	0.0	0.0
D / 2.0	5.6	5.4	10.95	15	10	23	0	30	37	119	4.2	21	7	1,000	0	4.8	0.0
D / 2.0	5.6	5.4	10.94	9	10	23	0	30	37	119	4.2	11	7	1,000	0	0.0	0.0
D / 2.0	5.6	5.4	10.94	4	10	23	0	30	37	119	4.2	26	7	250,000	0	0.0	0.0
C- / 3.8	4.1	4.9	10.42	69	1	0	98	0	1	2	5.0	29	2	1,000	0	4.8	0.0
C- / 3.8	4.1	4.9	10.37	1	1	0	98	0	1	2	5.0	14	2	1,000	0	0.0	0.0
C- / 3.7	4.1	4.9	10.38	7	1	0	98	0	1	2	5.0	14	2	1,000	0	0.0	0.0
C- / 3.8	4.1	4.9	10.42	11	1	0	98	0	1	2	5.0	34	2	250,000	0	0.0	0.0
U /	N/A	N/A	8.75	N/A	0	0	0	0	100	59	0.0	N/A	3	1,000	0	4.8	0.0
U /	N/A	N/A	8.79	1	0	0	0	0	100	59	0.0	N/A	3	250,000	0	0.0	0.0
C / 5.0	3.5	1.0	8.95	50	10	88	0	0	2	23	0.0	7	8	1,000	0	4.8	0.0
C / 5.2	3.4	1.0	8.95	24	10	88	0	0	2	23	0.0	6	8	1,000	0	0.0	0.0
C / 5.1	3.4	1.0	8.93	107	10	88	0	0	2	23	0.0	8	8	250,000	0	0.0	0.0
D- / 1.3	6.3	2.3	8.90	N/A	19	73	0	5	3	74	0.0	30	N/A	1,000	0	4.8	0.0
D- / 1.3	6.3	2.3	8.90	N/A	19	73	0	5	3	74	0.0	38	N/A	250,000	0	0.0	0.0
D- / 1.3	6.3	2.3	8.88	58	19	73	0	5	3	74	0.0	36	N/A	1,000,000	0	0.0	0.0
E- / 0.1	12.3	3.9	6.29	70	10	83	0	5	2	47	0.0	1	8	1,000	0	4.8	0.0
E- / 0.1	12.3	3.9	6.34	31	10	83	0	5	2	47	0.0	1	8	1,000	0	0.0	0.0
E- / 0.1	12.3	3.9	6.29	128	10	83	0	5	2	47	0.0	1	8	250,000	0	0.0	0.0
C / 5.4	3.3	0.3	10.20	1,487	0	0	0	82	18	27	4.6	84	20	1,000	0	2.3	0.0
C+ / 5.6	3.3	0.3	10.20	119	0	0	0	82	18	27	4.6	84	20	1,000	0	0.0	0.0
C / 5.5	3.3	0.3	10.22	8	0	0	0	82	18	27	4.6	76	20	1,000	0	0.0	0.0
C / 5.5	3.3	0.3	10.18	1,037	0	0	0	82	18	27	4.6	70	20	1,000	0	0.0	0.0
C / 5.5	3.3	0.3	10.20	1,763	0	0	0	82	18	27	4.6	88	20	250,000	0	0.0	0.0
B- / 7.4	2.7	0.3	8.76	1,069	3	0	0	80	17	19	4.6	76	15	1,000	0	2.3	0.0
B- / 7.5	2.7	0.3	8.47	343	3	0	0	80	17	19	4.6	76	15	1,000	0	0.0	0.0
B- / 7.4	2.8	0.3	8.46	9	3	0	0	80	17	19	4.6	43	15	1,000	0	0.0	0.0
B- / 7.5	2.7	0.3	8.46	701	3	0	0	80	17	19	4.6	43	15	1,000	0	0.0	0.0
B- / 7.4	2.7	0.3	8.48	5,214	3	0	0	80	17	19	4.6	82	15	250,000	0	0.0	0.0
B+ / 8.5	2.0	0.7	9.80	130	1	0	97	0	2	103	1.3	8	12	1,000	0	2.3	0.0
B+ / 8.5	2.0	0.7	9.80	30	1	0	97	0	2	103	1.3	9	12	250,000	0	0.0	0.0
C+ / 6.9	2.9	1.0	8.88	303	4	0	0	81	15	5	5.0	87	16	1,000	0	2.3	0.0
C+ / 6.8	2.9	1.0	8.35	156	4	0	0	81	15	5	5.0	87	16	1,000	0	0.0	0.0
C+ / 6.8	2.9	1.0	8.34	3	4	0	0	81	15	5	5.0	60	16	1,000	0	0.0	0.0
C+ / 6.9	2.9	1.0	8.33	160	4	0	0	81	15	5	5.0	61	16	1,000	0	0.0	0.0
C+ / 6.9	2.9	1.0	8.35	587	4	0	0	81	15	5	5.0	89	16	250,000	0	0.0	0.0
C- / 4.1	3.9	5.0	8.73	41	2	0	97	0	1	14	5.1	43	9	1,000	0	4.8	0.0
C- / 4.1	3.9	5.0	9.33	N/A	2	0	97	0	1	14	5.1	22	9	1,000	0	0.0	0.0
C- / 3.9	4.0	5.0	9.34	7	2	0	97	0	1	14	5.1	22	9	1,000	0	0.0	0.0
C- / 4.0	3.9	5.0	8.76	24	2	0	97	0	1	14	5.1	50	9	250,000	0	0.0	0.0
B / 7.9	2.5	1.2	8.98	522	18	60	0	2	20	66	0.0	82	19	1,000	0	4.8	0.0
B / 7.9	2.5	1.2	9.01	284	18	60	0	2	20	66	0.0	57	19	1,000	0	0.0	0.0
B / 7.9	2.5	1.2	8.97	3,500	18	60	0	2	20	66	0.0	87	19	250,000	0	0.0	0.0
B / 7.9	2.4	1.2	9.00	1	18	60	0	2	20	66	0.0	78	19	1,000	0	0.0	0.0
A- / 9.0	1.4	1.2	6.55	308	8	7	0	0	85	33	5.9	58	2	1,000	0	4.8	0.0
A- / 9.0	1.4	1.2	6.56	7	8	7	0	0	85	33	5.9	33	2	1,000	0	0.0	0.0
A- / 9.0	1.3	1.2	6.54	115	8	7	0	0	85	33	5.9	33	2	1,000	0	0.0	0.0

99 Pct = Best 0 Pct = Worst Fund Type	Fund Name	Ticker Symbol	Overall Investment Rating	Phone	PERFORMANCE Performance Rating/Pts	Total Return % through 3/31/16 3 Mo	6 Mo	1Yr / Pct	Annualized 3Yr / Pct	5Yr / Pct	Incl. in Returns Dividend Yield	Expense Ratio
USS	Eaton Vance Govt Obligation I	EIGOX	**C+**	(800) 262-1122	**C- / 4.1**	0.59	0.12	0.52 /50	0.90 /41	1.69 /27	3.88	0.93
USS	Eaton Vance Govt Obligation R	ERGOX	**C**	(800) 262-1122	**C- / 3.1**	0.46	0.01	0.01 /31	0.43 /32	1.20 /22	3.37	1.43
COH	Eaton Vance High Inc Opp Fund A	ETHIX	**D+**	(800) 262-1122	**C+ / 6.4**	3.17	2.56	-0.77 /23	3.63 /81	5.86 /76	5.84	0.90
COH ●	Eaton Vance High Inc Opp Fund B	EVHIX	**C-**	(800) 262-1122	**B- / 7.3**	3.21	2.40	-1.30 /19	2.87 /75	5.07 /72	5.34	1.65
COH	Eaton Vance High Inc Opp Fund C	ECHIX	**C-**	(800) 262-1122	**B- / 7.1**	2.97	2.16	-1.54 /18	2.85 /75	5.02 /72	5.34	1.65
COH	Eaton Vance High Inc Opp Fund I	EIHIX	**C-**	(800) 262-1122	**B / 8.1**	3.23	2.69	-0.51 /26	3.82 /82	6.07 /77	6.41	0.65
MUN	Eaton Vance High Yield Muni Inc A	ETHYX	**C+**	(800) 262-1122	**A+ / 9.8**	2.03	4.93	5.52 /98	5.67 /99	9.13 /99	3.88	0.89
MUN ●	Eaton Vance High Yield Muni Inc B	EVHYX	**C+**	(800) 262-1122	**A+ / 9.8**	1.84	4.54	4.74 /97	4.84 /98	8.34 /99	3.34	1.64
MUN	Eaton Vance High Yield Muni Inc C	ECHYX	**C+**	(800) 262-1122	**A+ / 9.8**	1.92	4.51	4.72 /97	4.87 /98	8.32 /99	3.34	1.64
MUN	Eaton Vance High Yield Muni Inc I	EIHYX	**C+**	(800) 262-1122	**A+ / 9.9**	1.98	4.94	5.67 /99	5.89 /99	9.40 /99	4.32	0.64
* COH	Eaton Vance Income Fd of Boston A	EVIBX	**D**	(800) 262-1122	**C / 4.9**	3.26	2.07	-1.34 /19	2.72 /73	4.98 /72	6.06	1.00
COH ●	Eaton Vance Income Fd of Boston B	EBIBX	**D+**	(800) 262-1122	**C+ / 5.9**	3.25	1.85	-1.93 /16	2.01 /61	4.21 /64	5.55	1.75
COH	Eaton Vance Income Fd of Boston C	ECIBX	**D+**	(800) 262-1122	**C+ / 5.8**	3.25	1.85	-2.10 /15	1.95 /60	4.20 /64	5.55	1.75
COH	Eaton Vance Income Fd of Boston I	EIBIX	**C-**	(800) 262-1122	**B- / 7.4**	3.32	2.20	-1.09 /21	2.97 /76	5.21 /73	6.63	0.75
COH	Eaton Vance Income Fd of Boston R	ERIBX	**D+**	(800) 262-1122	**C+ / 6.6**	3.19	1.93	-1.60 /18	2.46 /70	4.72 /70	6.10	1.25
COH	Eaton Vance Income Fd of Boston R6	EIBRX	**C-**	(800) 262-1122	**B- / 7.4**	3.54	2.43	-0.83 /23	2.91 /75	5.10 /72	6.71	0.66
MUS	Eaton Vance MA Ltd Mat Muni Inc A	EXMAX	**B**	(800) 262-1122	**B- / 7.4**	1.44	2.41	2.95 /84	2.06 /78	3.32 /73	2.53	0.77
MUS	Eaton Vance MA Ltd Mat Muni Inc C	EZMAX	**B-**	(800) 262-1122	**C+ / 6.9**	1.29	1.97	2.19 /78	1.30 /61	2.57 /61	1.84	1.52
MUS	Eaton Vance MA Ltd Mat Muni Inc I	EMAIX	**A-**	(800) 262-1122	**B+ / 8.3**	1.48	2.49	3.10 /86	2.21 /79	3.47 /74	2.73	0.62
MUN	Eaton Vance MA Municipal Income A	ETMAX	**C**	(800) 262-1122	**B / 8.1**	1.00	3.18	3.62 /91	3.26 /90	6.70 /95	3.36	0.77
MUN	Eaton Vance MA Municipal Income C	ECMMX	**C**	(800) 262-1122	**B+ / 8.5**	0.81	2.80	2.96 /85	2.53 /83	5.93 /91	2.78	1.52
MUN	Eaton Vance MA Municipal Income I	EIMAX	**C+**	(800) 262-1122	**A / 9.3**	1.05	3.28	3.82 /93	3.50 /93	6.94 /96	3.72	0.57
MUN	Eaton Vance MD Municipal Income A	ETMDX	**C**	(800) 262-1122	**C+ / 6.9**	1.14	2.64	3.13 /86	2.53 /83	5.23 /87	3.12	0.75
MUN ●	Eaton Vance MD Municipal Income B	EVMYX	**C+**	(800) 262-1122	**B / 7.7**	1.03	2.28	2.38 /80	1.75 /73	4.45 /81	2.54	1.50
MUN	Eaton Vance MD Municipal Income C	ECMDX	**C+**	(800) 262-1122	**B / 7.7**	0.92	2.28	2.38 /80	1.72 /73	4.43 /81	2.54	1.50
MUN	Eaton Vance MD Municipal Income I	EIMDX	**B+**	(800) 262-1122	**B+ / 8.8**	1.19	2.74	3.33 /88	2.74 /85	5.46 /89	3.48	0.55
MUS	Eaton Vance MN Municipal Income A	ETMNX	**B**	(800) 262-1122	**B / 7.8**	1.13	2.49	3.28 /88	3.07 /89	5.20 /87	2.96	0.71
MUS ●	Eaton Vance MN Municipal Income B	EVMNX	**B+**	(800) 262-1122	**B / 8.2**	0.92	2.14	2.51 /80	2.32 /81	4.43 /81	2.36	1.46
MUS	Eaton Vance MN Municipal Income C	ECMNX	**B+**	(800) 262-1122	**B / 8.2**	0.92	2.04	2.51 /80	2.32 /81	4.41 /81	2.36	1.46
MUS	Eaton Vance MN Municipal Income I	EIMNX	**A**	(800) 262-1122	**A- / 9.2**	1.08	2.59	3.49 /90	3.28 /91	5.41 /88	3.31	0.51
MUS	Eaton Vance MO Municipal Income A	ETMOX	**C+**	(800) 262-1122	**B+ / 8.3**	1.51	3.20	3.67 /92	3.47 /92	5.68 /90	3.41	0.71
MUS ●	Eaton Vance MO Municipal Income B	EVMOX	**C+**	(800) 262-1122	**B+ / 8.7**	1.27	2.78	2.90 /84	2.69 /85	4.88 /84	2.84	1.47
MUS	Eaton Vance MO Municipal Income C	ECMOX	**C+**	(800) 262-1122	**B+ / 8.7**	1.27	2.78	2.90 /84	2.69 /85	4.88 /84	2.84	1.46
MUS	Eaton Vance MO Municipal Income I	EIMOX	**B**	(800) 262-1122	**A / 9.4**	1.56	3.30	3.88 /93	3.64 /93	5.89 /91	3.77	0.51
GES	Eaton Vance Mult-Str Absolute Rtn A	EADDX	**D+**	(800) 262-1122	**D- / 1.0**	1.16	1.41	-0.17 /29	0.16 /28	0.59 /18	1.49	1.24
GES ●	Eaton Vance Mult-Str Absolute Rtn B	EBDDX	**C-**	(800) 262-1122	**D- / 1.4**	0.97	1.01	-0.95 /22	-0.52 /11	-0.13 / 3	0.78	1.99
GES	Eaton Vance Mult-Str Absolute Rtn C	ECDDX	**C-**	(800) 262-1122	**D- / 1.4**	0.97	0.90	-0.93 /22	-0.54 /11	-0.15 / 3	0.80	1.99
GES	Eaton Vance Mult-Str Absolute Rtn I	EIDDX	**C**	(800) 262-1122	**C- / 3.5**	1.34	1.53	0.08 /40	0.39 /31	0.83 /19	1.81	0.99
MUN	Eaton Vance Municipal Opp A	EMOAX	**C+**	(800) 262-1122	**A / 9.4**	2.04	4.08	4.87 /98	4.75 /98	--	1.74	1.06
MUN	Eaton Vance Municipal Opp C	EMOCX	**B-**	(800) 262-1122	**A+ / 9.6**	1.86	3.70	4.09 /94	3.92 /95	--	1.09	1.81
MUN	Eaton Vance Municipal Opp I	EMOIX	**B-**	(800) 262-1122	**A+ / 9.9**	2.19	4.29	5.13 /98	5.04 /99	--	2.07	0.81
MUN	Eaton Vance Nat Ltd Mat Muni Inc A	EXNAX	**B+**	(800) 262-1122	**B / 7.8**	1.31	2.16	2.78 /83	2.43 /82	4.14 /79	2.86	0.69
MUN ●	Eaton Vance Nat Ltd Mat Muni Inc B	ELNAX	**B+**	(800) 262-1122	**B- / 7.5**	1.23	1.89	2.02 /77	1.67 /72	3.37 /73	2.19	1.44
MUN	Eaton Vance Nat Ltd Mat Muni Inc C	EZNAX	**B+**	(800) 262-1122	**B- / 7.5**	1.17	1.84	2.01 /77	1.66 /71	3.36 /73	2.19	1.44
MUN	Eaton Vance Nat Ltd Mat Muni Inc I	EINAX	**A**	(800) 262-1122	**B+ / 8.6**	1.44	2.34	2.93 /84	2.62 /84	4.30 /80	3.07	0.54
* MUN	Eaton Vance National Muni Inc A	EANAX	**C-**	(800) 262-1122	**B+ / 8.6**	1.37	3.93	4.81 /97	3.64 /93	7.80 /98	3.66	0.76
MUN ●	Eaton Vance National Muni Inc B	EVHMX	**C-**	(800) 262-1122	**A- / 9.0**	1.18	3.55	4.03 /94	2.87 /87	7.00 /96	3.11	1.51
MUN	Eaton Vance National Muni Inc C	ECHMX	**C-**	(800) 262-1122	**A- / 9.0**	1.18	3.55	4.03 /94	2.87 /87	7.00 /96	3.11	1.51
MUN	Eaton Vance National Muni Inc I	EIHMX	**C**	(800) 262-1122	**A+ / 9.6**	1.43	4.06	5.07 /98	3.87 /95	8.07 /98	4.09	0.51
MUN	Eaton Vance NC Muni Inc A	ETNCX	**C-**	(800) 262-1122	**B / 8.1**	1.71	3.15	3.35 /89	3.25 /90	6.09 /92	3.21	0.73
MUN ●	Eaton Vance NC Muni Inc B	EVNCX	**C**	(800) 262-1122	**B+ / 8.6**	1.56	2.87	2.69 /82	2.52 /83	5.31 /88	2.63	1.48
MUN	Eaton Vance NC Muni Inc C	ECNCX	**C**	(800) 262-1122	**B+ / 8.5**	1.56	2.87	2.69 /82	2.49 /83	5.31 /88	2.63	1.48

● Denotes fund is closed to new investors
* Denotes fund is included in Section II

RISK			NET ASSETS		ASSET							FUND MANAGER		MINIMUM		LOADS	
Risk Rating/Pts	3 Yr Avg Standard Deviation	Avg Duration	NAV As of 3/31/16	Total $(Mil)	Cash %	Gov. Bond %	Muni. Bond %	Corp. Bond %	Other %	Portfolio Turnover Ratio	Avg Coupon Rate	Manager Quality Pct	Manager Tenure (Years)	Initial Purch. $	Additional Purch. $	Front End Load	Back End Load
A- / 9.0	1.3	1.2	6.55	94	8	7	0	0	85	33	5.9	74	2	250,000	0	0.0	0.0
A- / 9.0	1.4	1.2	6.53	28	8	7	0	0	85	33	5.9	50	2	1,000	0	0.0	0.0
D / 2.1	5.1	3.7	4.29	316	10	0	0	85	5	38	6.6	96	20	1,000	0	4.8	0.0
D / 2.0	5.1	3.7	4.30	8	10	0	0	85	5	38	6.6	92	20	1,000	0	0.0	0.0
D / 2.1	5.1	3.7	4.29	120	10	0	0	85	5	38	6.6	92	20	1,000	0	0.0	0.0
D / 2.1	5.1	3.7	4.29	482	10	0	0	85	5	38	6.6	97	20	250,000	0	0.0	0.0
D / 1.8	5.8	6.0	8.99	437	3	0	95	0	2	16	5.5	49	12	1,000	0	4.8	0.0
D / 1.8	5.8	6.0	8.96	3	3	0	95	0	2	16	5.5	26	12	1,000	0	0.0	0.0
D / 1.9	5.8	6.0	8.32	211	3	0	95	0	2	16	5.5	27	12	1,000	0	0.0	0.0
D / 1.8	5.9	6.0	8.99	465	3	0	95	0	2	16	5.5	57	12	250,000	0	0.0	0.0
D / 2.1	5.0	3.8	5.49	1,351	5	0	0	91	4	36	6.6	91	15	1,000	0	4.8	0.0
D / 2.1	5.0	3.8	5.50	17	5	0	0	91	4	36	6.6	83	15	1,000	0	0.0	0.0
D / 2.2	5.0	3.8	5.50	235	5	0	0	91	4	36	6.6	82	15	1,000	0	0.0	0.0
D / 2.2	5.0	3.8	5.49	3,924	5	0	0	91	4	36	6.6	93	15	250,000	0	0.0	0.0
D / 2.2	5.0	3.8	5.49	46	5	0	0	91	4	36	6.6	90	15	1,000	0	0.0	0.0
D / 2.1	5.0	3.8	5.50	29	5	0	0	91	4	36	6.6	93	15	1,000,000	0	0.0	0.0
C+ / 6.0	3.1	4.7	10.06	35	2	0	97	0	1	4	4.6	25	2	1,000	0	2.3	0.0
C+ / 6.0	3.1	4.7	9.64	10	2	0	97	0	1	4	4.6	13	2	1,000	0	0.0	0.0
C+ / 6.0	3.1	4.7	10.06	16	2	0	97	0	1	4	4.6	29	2	250,000	0	0.0	0.0
D+ / 2.7	5.0	5.0	9.15	110	1	0	98	0	1	10	5.2	14	6	1,000	0	4.8	0.0
D+ / 2.7	5.0	5.0	9.16	22	1	0	98	0	1	10	5.2	8	6	1,000	0	0.0	0.0
D+ / 2.7	5.0	5.0	9.15	39	1	0	98	0	1	10	5.2	16	6	250,000	0	0.0	0.0
C / 4.6	3.6	4.1	9.09	42	1	0	98	0	1	13	5.1	24	12	1,000	0	4.8	0.0
C / 4.6	3.6	4.1	9.91	1	1	0	98	0	1	13	5.1	12	12	1,000	0	0.0	0.0
C / 4.5	3.7	4.1	9.91	15	1	0	98	0	1	13	5.1	12	12	1,000	0	0.0	0.0
C / 4.7	3.6	4.1	9.11	6	1	0	98	0	1	13	5.1	29	12	250,000	0	0.0	0.0
C / 5.4	3.3	3.6	9.66	73	6	0	93	0	1	2	4.6	50	12	1,000	0	4.8	0.0
C / 5.3	3.3	3.6	10.40	N/A	6	0	93	0	1	2	4.6	26	12	1,000	0	0.0	0.0
C / 5.4	3.3	3.6	10.39	13	6	0	93	0	1	2	4.6	27	12	1,000	0	0.0	0.0
C / 5.5	3.3	3.6	9.66	48	6	0	93	0	1	2	4.6	58	12	250,000	0	0.0	0.0
C- / 3.4	4.3	5.1	9.65	60	0	0	99	0	1	7	4.2	28	24	1,000	0	4.8	0.0
C- / 3.5	4.3	5.1	10.66	1	0	0	99	0	1	7	4.2	14	24	1,000	0	0.0	0.0
C- / 3.5	4.3	5.1	10.65	8	0	0	99	0	1	7	4.2	14	24	1,000	0	0.0	0.0
C- / 3.4	4.3	5.1	9.66	3	0	0	99	0	1	7	4.2	34	24	250,000	0	0.0	0.0
B+ / 8.8	1.7	2.5	8.59	77	65	4	0	16	15	42	7.2	34	12	1,000	0	4.8	0.0
B+ / 8.8	1.7	2.5	8.59	2	65	4	0	16	15	42	7.2	18	12	1,000	0	0.0	0.0
B+ / 8.8	1.6	2.5	8.58	25	65	4	0	16	15	42	7.2	18	12	1,000	0	0.0	0.0
B+ / 8.8	1.7	2.5	8.59	26	65	4	0	16	15	42	7.2	41	12	250,000	0	0.0	0.0
D+ / 2.7	5.1	5.9	11.96	133	1	0	98	0	1	79	4.5	43	5	1,000	0	4.8	0.0
D+ / 2.7	5.1	5.9	11.95	35	1	0	98	0	1	79	4.5	21	5	1,000	0	0.0	0.0
D+ / 2.6	5.1	5.9	11.98	395	1	0	98	0	1	79	4.5	51	5	250,000	0	0.0	0.0
C+ / 6.1	3.1	4.2	10.16	275	2	0	97	0	1	7	4.6	35	2	1,000	0	2.3	0.0
C+ / 6.4	3.0	4.2	10.17	1	2	0	97	0	1	7	4.6	18	2	1,000	0	0.0	0.0
C+ / 6.4	3.0	4.2	9.53	119	2	0	97	0	1	7	4.6	18	2	1,000	0	0.0	0.0
C+ / 6.3	3.1	4.2	10.17	297	2	0	97	0	1	7	4.6	42	2	250,000	0	0.0	0.0
E+ / 0.9	6.6	5.9	10.00	1,879	1	0	97	0	2	57	6.0	7	3	1,000	0	4.8	0.0
E+ / 0.9	6.6	5.9	10.00	21	1	0	97	0	2	57	6.0	6	3	1,000	0	0.0	0.0
E+ / 0.9	6.6	5.9	10.00	580	1	0	97	0	2	57	6.0	6	3	1,000	0	0.0	0.0
E+ / 0.9	6.6	5.9	10.00	717	1	0	97	0	2	57	6.0	8	3	250,000	0	0.0	0.0
D / 2.0	5.6	4.5	9.28	82	4	0	95	0	1	2	5.4	9	2	1,000	0	4.8	0.0
D / 2.0	5.6	4.5	9.99	1	4	0	95	0	1	2	5.4	7	2	1,000	0	0.0	0.0
D / 2.0	5.6	4.5	9.99	19	4	0	95	0	1	2	5.4	7	2	1,000	0	0.0	0.0

Fund Type	Fund Name (99 Pct = Best, 0 Pct = Worst)	Ticker Symbol	Overall Investment Rating	Phone	PERFORMANCE: Performance Rating/Pts	Total Return % through 3/31/16: 3 Mo	6 Mo	1Yr / Pct	Annualized: 3Yr / Pct	Annualized: 5Yr / Pct	Incl. in Returns: Dividend Yield	Incl. in Returns: Expense Ratio
MUN	Eaton Vance NC Muni Inc I	EINCX	C+	(800) 262-1122	A / 9.4	1.76	3.36	3.67 /92	3.46 /92	6.32 /94	3.57	0.53
MUN	Eaton Vance NJ Muni Inc A	ETNJX	B-	(800) 262-1122	B / 8.2	1.54	3.46	4.47 /96	3.21 /90	6.12 /93	3.42	0.75
MUN	Eaton Vance NJ Muni Inc C	ECNJX	B	(800) 262-1122	B+ / 8.6	1.33	3.01	3.66 /91	2.46 /82	5.31 /88	2.85	1.50
MUN	Eaton Vance NJ Muni Inc I	EINJX	B+	(800) 262-1122	A / 9.4	1.59	3.45	4.68 /97	3.41 /92	6.31 /94	3.79	0.55
MUS	Eaton Vance NY Ltd Mat Muni Inc A	EXNYX	B+	(800) 262-1122	C+ / 6.7	1.25	1.93	2.53 /81	1.84 /75	3.27 /72	2.63	0.77
MUS	Eaton Vance NY Ltd Mat Muni Inc C	EZNYX	B	(800) 262-1122	C+ / 6.2	0.99	1.59	1.76 /75	1.06 /54	2.49 /59	1.95	1.52
MUS	Eaton Vance NY Ltd Mat Muni Inc I	ENYIX	A+	(800) 262-1122	B / 8.0	1.29	2.01	2.69 /82	1.99 /77	3.44 /73	2.84	0.62
MUN	Eaton Vance NY Muni Inc A	ETNYX	C+	(800) 262-1122	B+ / 8.8	1.68	3.79	4.59 /97	3.89 /95	7.10 /97	3.20	0.76
MUN ●	Eaton Vance NY Muni Inc B	EVNYX	B-	(800) 262-1122	A- / 9.2	1.40	3.40	3.81 /93	3.12 /89	6.30 /94	2.63	1.52
MUN	Eaton Vance NY Muni Inc C	ECNYX	B-	(800) 262-1122	A- / 9.2	1.40	3.40	3.71 /92	3.12 /89	6.30 /94	2.63	1.51
MUN	Eaton Vance NY Muni Inc I	EINYX	B	(800) 262-1122	A+ / 9.7	1.73	3.89	4.80 /97	4.10 /96	7.31 /97	3.56	0.56
MUN	Eaton Vance OH Muni Inc A	ETOHX	C+	(800) 262-1122	B+ / 8.6	1.55	3.73	4.11 /95	3.70 /94	6.31 /94	3.49	0.74
MUN	Eaton Vance OH Muni Inc C	ECOHX	C+	(800) 262-1122	A- / 9.0	1.36	3.34	3.34 /88	2.93 /87	5.55 /89	2.92	1.49
MUN	Eaton Vance OH Muni Inc I	EIOHX	B-	(800) 262-1122	A+ / 9.6	1.59	3.83	4.32 /96	3.90 /95	6.55 /95	3.86	0.54
MUS	Eaton Vance OR Municipal Income A	ETORX	D	(800) 262-1122	C+ / 5.8	2.17	3.26	3.79 /92	1.74 /73	6.07 /92	3.50	0.74
MUS ●	Eaton Vance OR Municipal Income B	EVORX	D+	(800) 262-1122	C+ / 6.9	1.98	2.97	3.01 /85	0.98 /52	5.28 /87	2.94	1.50
MUS	Eaton Vance OR Municipal Income C	ECORX	D+	(800) 262-1122	C+ / 6.9	1.97	2.97	3.01 /85	0.99 /53	5.28 /88	2.94	1.49
MUS	Eaton Vance OR Municipal Income I	EIORX	C-	(800) 262-1122	B+ / 8.3	2.22	3.36	3.87 /93	1.94 /76	6.28 /94	3.87	0.54
MUN	Eaton Vance PA Muni Inc A	ETPAX	B+	(800) 262-1122	B / 8.2	1.17	2.72	4.07 /94	3.41 /92	5.46 /89	3.68	0.78
MUN ●	Eaton Vance PA Muni Inc B	EVPAX	A-	(800) 262-1122	B+ / 8.7	1.08	2.32	3.29 /88	2.66 /84	4.68 /83	3.12	1.53
MUN	Eaton Vance PA Muni Inc C	ECPAX	A-	(800) 262-1122	B+ / 8.7	0.97	2.32	3.29 /88	2.66 /84	4.68 /83	3.12	1.53
MUN	Eaton Vance PA Muni Inc I	EIPAX	A+	(800) 262-1122	A / 9.5	1.33	2.82	4.39 /96	3.66 /94	5.69 /90	4.06	0.58
MUN	Eaton Vance SC Municipal Income A	EASCX	C-	(800) 262-1122	B / 8.1	1.90	3.73	3.86 /93	3.10 /89	6.43 /94	3.36	0.71
MUN ●	Eaton Vance SC Municipal Income B	EVSCX	C-	(800) 262-1122	B+ / 8.5	1.76	3.34	3.18 /87	2.31 /80	5.64 /90	2.79	1.47
MUN	Eaton Vance SC Municipal Income C	ECSCX	C-	(800) 262-1122	B+ / 8.5	1.75	3.44	3.18 /87	2.35 /81	5.64 /90	2.79	1.46
MUN	Eaton Vance SC Municipal Income I	EISCX	C	(800) 262-1122	A / 9.4	1.95	3.83	4.18 /95	3.31 /91	6.64 /95	3.72	0.51
USS	Eaton Vance Sh Duration Gov Inc A	EALDX	C-	(800) 262-1122	D / 1.7	-0.46	-0.21	0.21 /44	0.65 /36	1.28 /23	2.81	0.99
USS ●	Eaton Vance Sh Duration Gov Inc B	EBLDX	C-	(800) 262-1122	D- / 1.5	-0.65	-0.57	-0.53 /26	-0.10 /15	0.50 /17	2.13	1.75
USS	Eaton Vance Sh Duration Gov Inc C	ECLDX	C-	(800) 262-1122	D / 1.7	-0.61	-0.63	-0.39 /27	0.05 /24	0.67 /18	2.27	1.59
USS	Eaton Vance Sh Duration Gov Inc I	EILDX	C+	(800) 262-1122	C- / 3.8	-0.40	-0.21	0.45 /49	0.90 /41	1.51 /26	3.13	0.74
COI	Eaton Vance Short Dur Real Return A	EARRX	D+	(800) 262-1122	D- / 1.2	2.38	1.44	0.60 /51	-0.51 /11	0.81 /19	1.78	1.24
COI	Eaton Vance Short Dur Real Return	ECRRX	D+	(800) 262-1122	D- / 1.0	2.14	1.11	-0.20 /29	-1.26 / 7	0.06 /13	1.23	1.99
COI	Eaton Vance Short Dur Real Return I	EIRRX	C-	(800) 262-1122	D+ / 2.7	2.34	1.52	0.78 /55	-0.29 /13	1.05 /21	2.20	0.99
* GL	Eaton Vance Short Dur Strat Inc A	ETSIX	D	(800) 262-1122	E+ / 0.9	-0.90	-0.14	-3.47 /10	0.08 /26	1.99 /31	4.22	1.06
GL ●	Eaton Vance Short Dur Strat Inc B	EVSGX	D-	(800) 262-1122	E+ / 0.8	-1.21	-0.51	-4.23 / 7	-0.65 /10	1.27 /23	3.54	1.81
GL	Eaton Vance Short Dur Strat Inc C	ECSIX	D-	(800) 262-1122	E+ / 0.7	-1.21	-0.65	-4.37 / 7	-0.65 /10	1.24 /23	3.54	1.81
GL	Eaton Vance Short Dur Strat Inc I	ESIIX	D	(800) 262-1122	D / 1.6	-0.85	-0.02	-3.24 /11	0.32 /30	2.24 /34	4.58	0.81
GL	Eaton Vance Short Dur Strat Inc R	ERSIX	D	(800) 262-1122	D- / 1.1	-0.96	-0.27	-3.83 / 8	-0.15 /14	1.77 /28	4.05	1.31
GL	Eaton Vance Sht Duration High Inc A	ESHAX	B-	(800) 262-1122	C+ / 5.9	2.48	2.02	0.76 /54	2.38 /69	--	3.82	1.84
GL	Eaton Vance Sht Duration High Inc I	ESHIX	A-	(800) 262-1122	B- / 7.2	2.55	2.15	1.02 /59	2.61 /72	--	4.17	1.59
MUN	Eaton Vance TABS 1 to10 Y Ldr MB	EALBX	U	(800) 262-1122	U /	1.37	2.38	--	--	--	0.00	N/A
MUN	Eaton Vance TABS 1 to10 Y Ldr MB	ECLBX	U	(800) 262-1122	U /	1.18	1.92	--	--	--	0.00	N/A
MUN	Eaton Vance TABS 1 to10 Y Ldr MB I	EILBX	U	(800) 262-1122	U /	1.44	2.52	--	--	--	0.00	N/A
MUN	Eaton Vance TABS 10to20 Y Ldr MB	EATTX	U	(800) 262-1122	U /	2.81	5.56	--	--	--	0.00	N/A
MUN	Eaton Vance TABS 10to20 Y Ldr MB	ECTTX	U	(800) 262-1122	U /	2.54	5.14	--	--	--	0.00	N/A
MUN	Eaton Vance TABS 10to20 Y Ldr MB	EITTX	U	(800) 262-1122	U /	2.89	5.71	--	--	--	0.00	N/A
MUN	Eaton Vance TABS 5to15 Yr Ldr MB	EALTX	C+	(800) 262-1122	A+ / 9.8	2.21	4.47	5.10 /98	5.67 /99	8.36 /99	1.76	1.20
MUN	Eaton Vance TABS 5to15 Yr Ldr MB	ECLTX	C+	(800) 262-1122	A+ / 9.8	2.03	4.09	4.31 /96	4.89 /98	7.54 /97	1.12	1.95
MUN	Eaton Vance TABS 5to15 Yr Ldr MB I	EILTX	C+	(800) 262-1122	A+ / 9.9	2.28	4.60	5.28 /98	5.94 /99	8.61 /99	2.10	0.95
MUN	Eaton Vance TABS Int-Term Muni Bd	EITAX	B+	(800) 262-1122	A- / 9.1	1.96	3.76	4.26 /95	3.48 /92	5.30 /88	1.57	1.00
MUN	Eaton Vance TABS Int-Term Muni Bd	EITCX	B+	(800) 262-1122	B+ / 8.9	1.77	3.37	3.56 /91	2.73 /85	4.53 /82	0.88	1.75
MUN	Eaton Vance TABS Int-Term Muni Bd	ETIIX	A	(800) 262-1122	A+ / 9.6	2.02	3.88	4.51 /97	3.74 /94	5.59 /89	1.85	0.75

● Denotes fund is closed to new investors
* Denotes fund is included in Section II

RISK			NET ASSETS		ASSET							FUND MANAGER		MINIMUM		LOADS	
Risk Rating/Pts	3 Yr Avg Standard Deviation	Avg Duration	NAV As of 3/31/16	Total $(Mil)	Cash %	Gov. Bond %	Muni. Bond %	Corp. Bond %	Other %	Portfolio Turnover Ratio	Avg Coupon Rate	Manager Quality Pct	Manager Tenure (Years)	Initial Purch. $	Additional Purch. $	Front End Load	Back End Load
D / 2.0	5.7	4.5	9.31	24	4	0	95	0	1	2	5.4	10	2	250,000	0	0.0	0.0
C / 4.3	3.8	5.3	9.42	116	0	0	99	0	1	8	4.4	43	6	1,000	0	4.8	0.0
C / 4.3	3.8	5.3	9.83	23	0	0	99	0	1	8	4.4	22	6	1,000	0	0.0	0.0
C / 4.3	3.8	5.3	9.42	27	0	0	99	0	1	8	4.4	48	6	250,000	0	0.0	0.0
B- / 7.5	2.7	3.8	10.09	48	4	0	95	0	1	8	5.0	31	2	1,000	0	2.3	0.0
B- / 7.4	2.7	3.8	9.59	26	4	0	95	0	1	8	5.0	15	2	1,000	0	0.0	0.0
B- / 7.5	2.7	3.8	10.09	14	4	0	95	0	1	8	5.0	35	2	250,000	0	0.0	0.0
C- / 3.2	4.5	5.0	10.28	279	3	0	94	0	3	8	5.0	35	21	1,000	0	4.8	0.0
C- / 3.2	4.5	5.0	10.29	2	3	0	94	0	3	8	5.0	18	21	1,000	0	0.0	0.0
C- / 3.2	4.5	5.0	10.28	72	3	0	94	0	3	8	5.0	17	21	1,000	0	0.0	0.0
C- / 3.1	4.6	5.0	10.28	72	3	0	94	0	3	8	5.0	40	21	250,000	0	0.0	0.0
D+ / 2.8	4.9	5.4	9.23	132	6	0	93	0	1	4	2.4	22	N/A	1,000	0	4.8	0.0
D+ / 2.8	4.9	5.4	9.23	23	6	0	93	0	1	4	2.4	11	N/A	1,000	0	0.0	0.0
D+ / 2.8	4.9	5.4	9.24	16	6	0	93	0	1	4	2.4	26	N/A	250,000	0	0.0	0.0
D- / 1.0	6.5	6.1	8.82	90	1	0	98	0	1	4	4.7	4	2	1,000	0	4.8	0.0
D- / 1.0	6.5	6.1	9.65	1	1	0	98	0	1	4	4.7	2	2	1,000	0	0.0	0.0
D- / 1.0	6.5	6.1	9.66	15	1	0	98	0	1	4	4.7	2	2	1,000	0	0.0	0.0
D- / 1.1	6.5	6.1	8.81	14	1	0	98	0	1	4	4.7	4	2	250,000	0	0.0	0.0
C / 5.5	3.3	4.7	9.01	143	2	0	97	0	1	5	4.8	75	9	1,000	0	4.8	0.0
C / 5.5	3.3	4.7	9.33	2	2	0	97	0	1	5	4.8	43	9	1,000	0	0.0	0.0
C / 5.4	3.3	4.7	9.33	36	2	0	97	0	1	5	4.8	42	9	1,000	0	0.0	0.0
C / 5.5	3.3	4.7	9.05	53	2	0	97	0	1	5	4.8	82	9	250,000	0	0.0	0.0
D / 1.6	6.0	5.2	9.44	69	7	0	92	0	1	5	5.4	7	2	1,000	0	4.8	0.0
D / 1.6	6.0	5.2	10.01	1	7	0	92	0	1	5	5.4	6	2	1,000	0	0.0	0.0
D / 1.6	6.0	5.2	10.02	27	7	0	92	0	1	5	5.4	6	2	1,000	0	0.0	0.0
D / 1.6	6.0	5.2	9.45	33	7	0	92	0	1	5	5.4	8	2	250,000	0	0.0	0.0
A- / 9.1	1.2	0.6	8.28	169	2	18	0	3	77	19	3.7	84	2	1,000	0	2.3	0.0
A- / 9.1	1.2	0.6	8.29	1	2	18	0	3	77	19	3.7	55	2	1,000	0	0.0	0.0
A- / 9.1	1.2	0.6	8.29	89	2	18	0	3	77	19	3.7	61	2	1,000	0	0.0	0.0
A- / 9.1	1.2	0.6	8.27	326	2	18	0	3	77	19	3.7	87	2	250,000	0	0.0	0.0
B / 8.1	2.3	2.1	9.70	22	14	56	0	23	7	74	2.4	19	N/A	1,000	0	2.3	0.0
B / 8.0	2.4	2.1	9.65	8	14	56	0	23	7	74	2.4	11	N/A	1,000	0	0.0	0.0
B / 8.1	2.3	2.1	9.68	22	14	56	0	23	7	74	2.4	25	N/A	250,000	0	0.0	0.0
C / 4.9	3.5	0.5	7.13	1,039	11	28	0	31	30	10	0.0	69	26	1,000	0	2.3	0.0
C / 4.8	3.5	0.5	6.72	33	11	28	0	31	30	10	0.0	38	26	1,000	0	0.0	0.0
C / 4.9	3.5	0.5	6.72	674	11	28	0	31	30	10	0.0	38	26	1,000	0	0.0	0.0
C / 4.9	3.5	0.5	7.12	797	11	28	0	31	30	10	0.0	78	26	250,000	0	0.0	0.0
C / 4.9	3.5	0.5	7.14	3	11	28	0	31	30	10	0.0	56	26	1,000	0	0.0	0.0
B- / 7.3	2.8	1.4	9.48	3	0	0	0	0	100	41	5.9	97	3	1,000	0	2.3	0.0
B- / 7.3	2.8	1.4	9.49	23	0	0	0	0	100	41	5.9	98	3	250,000	0	0.0	0.0
U /	N/A	4.0	10.33	2	4	0	95	0	1	0	4.3	N/A	1	1,000	0	4.8	0.0
U /	N/A	4.0	10.33	N/A	4	0	95	0	1	0	4.3	N/A	1	1,000	0	0.0	0.0
U /	N/A	4.0	10.34	28	4	0	95	0	1	0	4.3	N/A	1	250,000	0	0.0	0.0
U /	N/A	7.1	10.67	1	2	0	97	0	1	0	4.4	N/A	1	1,000	0	4.8	0.0
U /	N/A	7.1	10.67	N/A	2	0	97	0	1	0	4.4	N/A	1	1,000	0	0.0	0.0
U /	N/A	7.1	10.67	6	2	0	97	0	1	0	4.4	N/A	1	250,000	0	0.0	0.0
D / 2.1	5.6	6.3	12.26	79	3	0	96	0	1	122	4.6	54	6	1,000	0	4.8	0.0
D / 2.1	5.6	6.3	12.25	29	3	0	96	0	1	122	4.6	30	6	1,000	0	0.0	0.0
D / 2.1	5.5	6.3	12.25	139	3	0	96	0	1	122	4.6	71	6	250,000	0	0.0	0.0
C / 4.5	3.7	5.3	12.46	61	1	0	98	0	1	77	4.4	50	6	1,000	0	2.3	0.0
C / 4.6	3.7	5.3	12.46	39	1	0	98	0	1	77	4.4	27	6	1,000	0	0.0	0.0
C / 4.5	3.7	5.3	12.47	369	1	0	98	0	1	77	4.4	60	6	250,000	0	0.0	0.0

Fund Type	Fund Name (99 Pct = Best, 0 Pct = Worst)	Ticker Symbol	Overall Investment Rating	Phone	PERFORMANCE: Perfor-mance Rating/Pts	Total Return % through 3/31/16: 3 Mo	6 Mo	1Yr / Pct	Annualized: 3Yr / Pct	Annualized: 5Yr / Pct	Incl. in Returns: Dividend Yield	Expense Ratio
MUN	Eaton Vance TABS ST Muni Bond A	EABSX	**B**	(800) 262-1122	**C / 5.4**	1.06	1.43	2.13 /78	1.37 /64	2.33 /54	1.20	0.90
MUN	Eaton Vance TABS ST Muni Bond C	ECBSX	**B-**	(800) 262-1122	**C / 4.9**	0.97	1.15	1.37 /72	0.61 /41	1.57 /37	0.49	1.65
MUN	Eaton Vance TABS ST Muni Bond I	EIBSX	**A+**	(800) 262-1122	**B- / 7.5**	1.21	1.65	2.48 /80	1.62 /71	2.60 /61	1.48	0.65
MUN	Eaton Vance VA Municipal Income A	ETVAX	**C+**	(800) 262-1122	**B- / 7.5**	1.55	3.55	4.01 /94	2.62 /84	4.46 /81	3.60	0.76
MUN ●	Eaton Vance VA Municipal Income B	EVVAX	**B**	(800) 262-1122	**B / 8.1**	1.42	3.24	3.23 /87	1.87 /75	3.69 /75	3.04	1.51
MUN	Eaton Vance VA Municipal Income C	ECVAX	**B**	(800) 262-1122	**B / 8.1**	1.53	3.36	3.34 /88	1.87 /75	3.69 /75	3.04	1.51
MUN	Eaton Vance VA Municipal Income I	EVAIX	**A-**	(800) 262-1122	**A- / 9.1**	1.60	3.65	4.22 /95	2.83 /86	4.67 /83	3.97	0.56
GEI	Elfun Income	EINFX	**B+**	(800) 242-0134	**B- / 7.2**	2.69	2.52	1.14 /61	2.54 /71	4.07 /62	2.82	0.30
* MUN	Elfun Tax Exempt Income	ELFTX	**B+**	(800) 242-0134	**A / 9.3**	1.56	3.19	3.83 /93	3.40 /92	5.55 /89	3.89	0.21
COI	Estabrook Investment Grade Fxd In I	EEFIX	**C**	(888) 739-1390	**C / 4.7**	1.49	1.38	0.67 /53	1.36 /49	3.24 /49	2.33	1.34
EM	EuroPac International Bond A	EPIBX	**E-**	(888) 558-5851	**E- / 0.1**	5.58	5.19	-3.34 /10	-5.75 / 1	-2.60 / 1	1.35	1.48
GL	EuroPac International Bond I	EPBIX	**U**	(888) 558-5851	**U /**	5.72	5.39	-3.14 /11	--	--	1.60	1.23
GEI	Fairholme Focused Income	FOCIX	**D+**	(866) 202-2263	**B- / 7.2**	0.28	-9.41	-5.74 / 4	4.87 /90	4.29 /65	5.18	1.01
GEI	FCI Bond Fund	FCIZX	**B-**	(800) 408-4682	**C / 5.3**	2.41	1.82	1.59 /67	1.51 /52	2.74 /41	1.84	0.84
COI	FDP BlacRock Franklin Temp TR Inst	MAFFX	**C-**	(800) 441-7762	**C / 4.5**	1.79	1.20	-1.51 /18	1.23 /47	3.27 /49	2.20	0.69
COI	FDP BlacRock Franklin Temp TR Inv	MDFFX	**D**	(800) 441-7762	**D- / 1.5**	1.62	0.97	-1.85 /16	0.97 /42	3.02 /45	1.87	0.94
COI	FDP BlacRock Franklin Temp TR Inv	MCFFX	**D+**	(800) 441-7762	**D+ / 2.8**	1.48	0.69	-2.40 /14	0.41 /31	2.45 /37	1.39	1.50
MTG	Federated Adj Rate Sec Inst	FEUGX	**C-**	(800) 341-7400	**D / 1.6**	-0.17	-0.65	-0.62 /25	-0.05 /15	0.41 /17	0.51	1.01
MTG	Federated Adj Rate Secs Svc	FASSX	**C-**	(800) 341-7400	**D- / 1.4**	-0.22	-0.75	-0.84 /23	-0.27 /13	0.18 /16	0.29	1.02
* COI	Federated Bond Fund A	FDBAX	**D+**	(800) 341-7400	**C / 4.6**	3.35	2.21	-0.80 /23	2.31 /68	4.39 /66	4.19	1.21
COI	Federated Bond Fund B	FDBBX	**D+**	(800) 341-7400	**C / 5.1**	3.08	1.74	-1.65 /17	1.45 /51	3.51 /53	3.50	1.95
COI	Federated Bond Fund C	FDBCX	**D+**	(800) 341-7400	**C / 5.2**	3.20	1.74	-1.54 /18	1.49 /52	3.54 /54	3.50	1.95
COI	Federated Bond Fund Class IS	FDBIX	**C-**	(800) 341-7400	**C+ / 6.9**	3.39	2.29	-0.63 /25	2.50 /71	4.56 /68	4.57	0.95
COI	Federated Bond Fund F	ISHIX	**C-**	(800) 341-7400	**C+ / 6.1**	3.32	2.18	-0.84 /23	2.29 /67	4.34 /66	4.28	1.20
MM	Federated CA Muni Cash Cap	CCCXX	**C**	(800) 341-7400	**D+ / 2.4**	0.00	0.07	0.08 /40	0.05 /25	0.04 /11	0.08	0.84
MMT	Federated CA Muni Cash Svc	CACXX	**C**	(800) 341-7400	**D+ / 2.5**	0.00	0.07	0.08 /42	0.05 /26	0.04 /13	0.08	0.85
MM	Federated CA Muni Cash Tr Cash II	CALXX	**C**	(800) 341-7400	**D+ / 2.4**	0.00	0.07	0.08 /40	0.05 /25	0.04 /11	0.08	1.04
MM	Federated CA Muni Cash Tr Cash	CCSXX	**C**	(800) 341-7400	**D+ / 2.4**	0.00	0.07	0.08 /40	0.05 /25	0.04 /11	0.08	1.44
MMT	Federated CA Muni Cash Tr Wealth	CAIXX	**C**	(800) 341-7400	**D+ / 2.5**	0.00	0.07	0.08 /42	0.05 /26	0.05 /14	0.08	0.59
COI	Federated Corporate Bond Strat	FCSPX	**C-**	(800) 341-7400	**B- / 7.4**	4.40	3.76	-0.65 /25	2.67 /73	5.16 /73	4.37	0.35
MMT	Federated CT Muni Cash Svc	FCTXX	**C**	(800) 341-7400	**D+ / 2.4**	0.00	0.06	0.06 /41	0.03 /25	0.03 /12	0.06	0.93
MMT	Federated CT Muni Cash Tr Cash	CTCXX	**C**	(800) 341-7400	**D+ / 2.4**	0.00	0.06	0.06 /41	0.03 /25	0.03 /12	0.06	1.56
MM	Federated Edward Jones MM Inv	JNSXX	**U**	(800) 341-7400	**U /**	--	--	--	--	--	0.01	0.81
MM	Federated Edward Jones MM Retr	JRSXX	**U**	(800) 341-7400	**U /**	--	--	--	--	--	0.01	0.88
COI	Federated Emerging Mkt Debt A	IHIAX	**E-**	(800) 341-7400	**E+ / 0.6**	5.08	8.21	0.26 /45	-1.76 / 5	3.16 /48	3.75	1.81
COI ●	Federated Emerging Mkt Debt B	IHIBX	**E**	(800) 341-7400	**E+ / 0.8**	5.03	7.83	-0.37 /27	-2.46 / 3	2.40 /36	3.18	2.55
COI	Federated Emerging Mkt Debt C	IHICX	**E**	(800) 341-7400	**E+ / 0.8**	4.91	7.85	-0.37 /27	-2.46 / 3	2.40 /36	3.19	2.55
EM	Federated Emerging Mkt Debt Inst	EMDIX	**E+**	(800) 341-7400	**D / 1.8**	5.27	8.33	0.63 /52	-1.48 / 6	3.40 /51	4.17	1.56
MMT	Federated FL Muni Cash Tr Cash Ser	FLSXX	**C**	(800) 341-7400	**D+ / 2.4**	0.00	0.04	0.04 /39	0.04 /25	0.03 /12	0.04	1.52
MMT	Federated FL Muni Cash Tr Wealth	FLMXX	**C**	(800) 341-7400	**D+ / 2.4**	0.00	0.04	0.04 /39	0.04 /25	0.03 /12	0.04	0.92
MMT	Federated FL Muni Cash Tr-Cash II	FLCXX	**C**	(800) 341-7400	**D+ / 2.4**	0.00	0.04	0.04 /39	0.04 /25	0.03 /12	0.04	1.16
LP	Federated Floating Rt Str Inc A	FRSAX	**C+**	(800) 341-7400	**C / 4.6**	1.22	0.07	0.29 /46	1.85 /58	2.79 /42	3.23	1.22
LP	Federated Floating Rt Str Inc C	FRICX	**U**	(800) 341-7400	**U /**	1.07	-0.23	-0.33 /28	--	--	2.66	1.87
GL	Federated Floating Rt Str Inc Inst	FFRSX	**A-**	(800) 341-7400	**C+ / 6.2**	1.30	0.24	0.64 /52	2.20 /66	3.15 /47	3.65	0.87
USS	Federated Fund for US Govt Sec A	FUSGX	**C**	(800) 341-7400	**C- / 3.8**	1.70	1.14	1.30 /63	1.79 /57	2.44 /37	2.37	0.94
USS ●	Federated Fund for US Govt Sec B	FUSBX	**C+**	(800) 341-7400	**C / 4.6**	1.63	0.75	0.66 /53	1.02 /43	1.69 /27	1.71	1.69
USS	Federated Fund for US Govt Sec C	FUSCX	**C+**	(800) 341-7400	**C / 4.5**	1.64	0.75	0.53 /50	1.03 /43	1.70 /28	1.72	1.69
MMT	Federated GA Muni Cash Tr	GAMXX	**C**	(800) 341-7400	**D+ / 2.3**	0.00	0.04	0.05 /40	0.03 /25	0.03 /12	0.05	0.89
USS	Federated Gov Ultrash Dur Inst	FGUSX	**C-**	(800) 341-7400	**D / 1.8**	-0.20	-0.42	-0.31 /28	0.05 /24	0.23 /16	0.30	0.56
USS	Federated Gov Ultrashort Dur A	FGUAX	**C-**	(800) 341-7400	**E+ / 0.9**	-0.31	-0.61	-0.81 /23	-0.40 /12	-0.22 / 2	0.00	1.06
USS	Federated Gov Ultrashort Dur Svc	FEUSX	**C-**	(800) 341-7400	**D / 1.6**	-0.23	-0.47	-0.40 /27	-0.05 /15	0.13 /15	0.20	0.81
USS	Federated Govt Inc Securities A	FGOAX	**C-**	(800) 341-7400	**C- / 3.5**	2.08	1.34	1.25 /62	1.55 /53	2.64 /39	2.13	1.17

● Denotes fund is closed to new investors
* Denotes fund is included in Section II

RISK			NET ASSETS		ASSET							FUND MANAGER		MINIMUM		LOADS	
Risk Rating/Pts	3 Yr Avg Standard Deviation	Avg Duration	NAV As of 3/31/16	Total $(Mil)	Cash %	Gov. Bond %	Muni. Bond %	Corp. Bond %	Other %	Portfolio Turnover Ratio	Avg Coupon Rate	Manager Quality Pct	Manager Tenure (Years)	Initial Purch. $	Additional Purch. $	Front End Load	Back End Load
B+ / 8.4	2.1	3.7	10.67	224	1	0	98	0	1	33	4.5	41	6	1,000	0	2.3	0.0
B+ / 8.5	2.0	3.7	10.65	84	1	0	98	0	1	33	4.5	22	6	1,000	0	0.0	0.0
B+ / 8.4	2.1	3.7	10.68	218	1	0	98	0	1	33	4.5	50	6	250,000	0	0.0	0.0
C / 5.1	3.4	5.3	8.12	58	0	0	99	0	1	6	5.4	39	9	1,000	0	4.8	0.0
C / 5.1	3.4	5.3	8.99	N/A	0	0	99	0	1	6	5.4	20	9	1,000	0	0.0	0.0
C / 5.1	3.4	5.3	9.00	6	0	0	99	0	1	6	5.4	21	9	1,000	0	0.0	0.0
C / 5.1	3.4	5.3	8.14	15	0	0	99	0	1	6	5.4	45	9	250,000	0	0.0	0.0
C+ / 6.9	2.9	5.5	11.48	291	1	18	0	43	38	326	6.2	77	20	500	100	0.0	0.0
C / 4.3	3.8	6.7	11.95	1,583	3	0	96	0	1	34	5.1	42	16	500	100	0.0	0.0
B- / 7.1	2.8	N/A	10.07	33	0	0	0	0	100	90	0.0	48	6	100,000	100	0.0	1.0
E / 0.5	8.1	N/A	8.14	45	3	61	3	29	4	4	0.0	2	6	2,500	250	4.5	2.0
U /	N/A	N/A	8.17	N/A	3	61	3	29	4	4	0.0	N/A	6	15,000	2,500	0.0	2.0
E- / 0.0	13.8	N/A	9.63	196	17	4	0	62	17	67	0.0	99	7	25,000	2,500	0.0	0.0
B / 7.9	2.5	N/A	10.48	43	1	24	0	69	6	33	0.0	44	11	250,000	100	0.0	1.0
C+ / 5.6	3.2	N/A	10.11	8	0	27	2	36	35	283	0.0	36	11	2,000,000	0	0.0	0.0
C+ / 5.7	3.2	N/A	10.11	87	0	27	2	36	35	283	0.0	29	11	1,000	50	4.0	0.0
C+ / 5.7	3.2	N/A	10.11	128	0	27	2	36	35	283	0.0	17	11	1,000	50	0.0	0.0
A+ / 9.9	0.4	0.4	9.69	426	0	0	0	0	100	27	1.6	53	21	1,000,000	0	0.0	0.0
A+ / 9.9	0.4	0.4	9.69	35	0	0	0	0	100	27	1.6	45	21	1,000,000	0	0.0	0.0
C- / 3.5	4.3	5.5	8.93	663	1	1	0	95	3	10	5.5	50	3	1,500	100	4.5	0.0
C- / 3.5	4.3	5.5	8.98	34	1	1	0	95	3	10	5.5	23	3	1,500	100	0.0	0.0
C- / 3.6	4.2	5.5	8.99	110	1	1	0	95	3	10	5.5	25	3	1,500	100	0.0	0.0
C- / 3.5	4.3	5.5	8.93	189	1	1	0	95	3	10	5.5	57	3	1,000,000	0	0.0	0.0
C- / 3.5	4.3	5.5	9.00	170	1	1	0	95	3	10	5.5	49	3	1,500	100	1.0	0.0
A+ / 9.9	N/A	N/A	1.00	126	100	0	0	0	0	0	0.1	67	20	25,000	0	0.0	0.0
A+ / 9.9	N/A	N/A	1.00	229	100	0	0	0	0	0	0.1	67	20	10,000	0	0.0	0.0
A+ / 9.9	N/A	N/A	1.00	24	100	0	0	0	0	0	0.1	67	20	10,000	0	0.0	0.0
A+ / 9.9	N/A	N/A	1.00	96	100	0	0	0	0	0	0.1	67	20	1,000	0	0.0	0.0
A+ / 9.9	N/A	N/A	1.00	177	100	0	0	0	0	0	0.1	67	20	25,000	0	0.0	0.0
D+ / 2.7	5.0	N/A	10.63	77	1	6	0	91	2	11	0.0	42	6	0	0	0.0	0.0
A+ / 9.9	N/A	N/A	1.00	37	100	0	0	0	0	0	0.1	N/A	20	10,000	0	0.0	0.0
A+ / 9.9	N/A	N/A	1.00	75	100	0	0	0	0	0	0.1	N/A	20	1,000	0	0.0	0.0
U /	N/A	N/A	1.00	11,277	100	0	0	0	0	0	0.0	N/A	22	0	0	0.0	0.0
U /	N/A	N/A	1.00	3,197	100	0	0	0	0	0	0.0	N/A	22	0	0	0.0	0.0
E / 0.3	9.3	7.5	8.20	44	5	66	5	23	1	200	0.0	3	3	1,500	100	4.5	0.0
E / 0.3	9.2	7.5	8.18	4	5	66	5	23	1	200	0.0	2	3	1,500	100	0.0	0.0
E / 0.3	9.2	7.5	8.16	14	5	66	5	23	1	200	0.0	2	3	1,500	100	0.0	0.0
E / 0.3	9.3	7.5	8.22	24	5	66	5	23	1	200	0.0	19	3	1,000,000	0	0.0	0.0
A+ / 9.9	N/A	N/A	1.00	84	100	0	0	0	0	0	0.0	68	N/A	10,000	0	0.0	0.0
A+ / 9.9	N/A	N/A	1.00	56	100	0	0	0	0	0	0.0	68	N/A	10,000	0	0.0	0.0
A+ / 9.9	N/A	N/A	1.00	7	100	0	0	0	0	0	0.0	68	N/A	10,000	0	0.0	0.0
B+ / 8.6	1.9	0.1	9.65	274	69	0	0	18	13	26	7.6	94	6	1,500	100	2.0	0.0
U /	N/A	0.1	9.66	29	69	0	0	18	13	26	7.6	N/A	6	1,500	100	0.0	0.0
B+ / 8.6	1.8	0.1	9.65	267	69	0	0	18	13	26	7.6	96	6	1,000,000	0	0.0	0.0
B / 8.2	2.3	4.2	7.54	329	6	0	0	1	93	26	3.9	80	13	1,500	100	4.5	0.0
B / 8.2	2.3	4.2	7.55	8	6	0	0	1	93	26	3.9	47	13	1,500	100	0.0	0.0
B / 8.1	2.3	4.2	7.54	32	6	0	0	1	93	26	3.9	45	13	1,500	100	0.0	0.0
A+ / 9.9	N/A	N/A	1.00	156	100	0	0	0	0	0	0.1	N/A	N/A	10,000	0	0.0	0.0
A+ / 9.9	0.3	0.2	9.85	420	2	13	0	19	66	22	0.7	62	19	1,000,000	0	0.0	0.0
A+ / 9.9	0.3	0.2	9.80	10	2	13	0	19	66	22	0.7	46	19	1,500	100	2.0	0.0
A+ / 9.9	0.3	0.2	9.85	334	2	13	0	19	66	22	0.7	57	19	1,000,000	0	0.0	0.0
B / 7.9	2.5	4.6	9.00	42	3	19	0	1	77	47	3.4	57	13	1,500	100	4.5	0.0

Fund Type	Fund Name (99 Pct = Best, 0 Pct = Worst)	Ticker Symbol	Overall Investment Rating	Phone	PERFORMANCE: Performance Rating/Pts	Total Return % through 3/31/16: 3 Mo	6 Mo	1Yr / Pct	Annualized: 3Yr / Pct	5Yr / Pct	Incl. in Returns: Dividend Yield	Expense Ratio
USS ●	Federated Govt Inc Securities B	FGOBX	C	(800) 341-7400	C / 4.3	2.01	0.95	0.59 /51	0.81 /39	1.89 /30	1.46	1.92
USS	Federated Govt Inc Securities C	FGOCX	C	(800) 341-7400	C / 4.3	2.01	0.96	0.60 /51	0.81 /39	1.89 /30	1.48	1.92
USS	Federated Govt Inc Securities F	FGOIX	C+	(800) 341-7400	C / 5.2	2.09	1.35	1.26 /63	1.55 /53	2.65 /40	2.22	1.17
USS	Federated Govt Income Trust Inst	FICMX	A-	(800) 341-7400	C+ / 6.3	1.68	1.28	1.59 /67	1.99 /61	2.56 /38	2.24	0.84
USS	Federated Govt Income Trust Svc	FITSX	B+	(800) 341-7400	C+ / 5.9	1.64	1.18	1.39 /65	1.79 /57	2.36 /36	2.05	0.84
MM	Federated Govt Obl Cap	GOCXX	C-	(800) 341-7400	D / 1.9	0.02	0.02	0.03 /36	0.02 /19	0.01 / 4	0.03	0.53
MM	Federated Govt Obl Instl	GOIXX	C	(800) 341-7400	D / 2.0	0.04	0.05	0.05 /38	0.02 /19	0.02 / 7	0.05	0.28
MM	Federated Govt Obl Premier	GOFXX	U	(800) 341-7400	U /	0.05	0.06	0.07 /40	--	--	0.07	N/A
MM	Federated Govt Obl Svc	GOSXX	U	(800) 341-7400	U /	--	--	--	--	--	0.01	0.53
MM	Federated Govt Obl Tr	GORXX	U	(800) 341-7400	U /	--	--	--	--	--	0.01	0.78
MM	Federated Govt Obl Tx-Mgd Auto	GOAXX	U	(800) 341-7400	U /	0.00	0.01	--	--	--	0.00	N/A
MM	Federated Govt Obl Tx-Mgd Instl	GOTXX	C	(800) 341-7400	D / 2.2	0.04	0.05	0.05 /38	0.03 /22	0.02 / 7	0.05	0.29
MM	Federated Govt Obl Tx-Mgd Svc	GTSXX	U	(800) 341-7400	U /	--	--	--	--	--	0.01	0.54
*COH	Federated High Income Bond A	FHIIX	D-	(800) 341-7400	D+ / 2.4	3.40	1.21	-2.42 /14	1.97 /61	4.73 /70	5.49	1.25
COH	Federated High Income Bond B	FHBBX	D-	(800) 341-7400	C- / 3.1	3.07	0.83	-3.28 /10	1.16 /46	3.95 /61	5.00	2.00
COH	Federated High Income Bond C	FHICX	D-	(800) 341-7400	C- / 3.2	3.07	0.83	-3.28 /10	1.21 /46	3.95 /61	5.00	2.00
GL	Federated High Yield Strat Port	FHYSX	C-	(800) 341-7400	B / 7.7	3.56	1.84	-1.13 /21	3.31 /79	6.08 /77	6.76	0.51
COH	Federated High Yield Trust A	FHYAX	D	(800) 341-7400	C / 4.4	2.66	1.06	-3.75 / 9	3.42 /79	6.17 /78	4.82	1.18
COH	Federated High Yield Trust C	FHYCX	D	(800) 341-7400	C / 5.0	2.32	0.54	-4.45 / 6	2.63 /72	5.38 /74	4.30	1.93
COH	Federated High Yield Trust Ins	FHTIX	D+	(800) 341-7400	C+ / 6.6	2.56	1.02	-3.54 / 9	3.52 /80	6.25 /78	5.32	0.91
COH	Federated High Yield Trust Svc	FHYTX	D+	(800) 341-7400	C+ / 6.4	2.66	1.06	-3.76 / 8	3.34 /79	6.14 /77	5.05	1.16
MM	Federated Inst Money Mkt Mgt Cap	MMLXX	C	(800) 341-7400	D+ / 2.4	0.07	0.10	0.12 /42	0.05 /25	0.06 /13	0.12	0.55
MM	Federated Inst Money Mkt Mgt Inst	MMPXX	C	(800) 341-7400	D+ / 2.7	0.10	0.15	0.22 /45	0.12 /27	0.14 /15	0.22	0.31
MM	Federated Inst Money Mkt Mgt Svc	MMSXX	C	(800) 341-7400	D / 2.0	0.04	0.04	0.05 /38	0.02 /19	0.02 / 7	0.05	0.56
USA	Federated Inst Prime Obl Automated	PBAXX	U	(800) 341-7400	U /	0.02	0.03	0.03 /35	--	--	0.04	0.64
MM	Federated Inst Prime Obl Capital	POPXX	C	(800) 341-7400	D+ / 2.5	0.08	0.11	0.12 /42	0.05 /25	--	0.12	0.53
MM	Federated Inst Prime Obl Inst	POIXX	C	(800) 341-7400	D+ / 2.6	0.09	0.14	0.17 /43	0.08 /26	0.10 /15	0.17	0.28
MM	Federated Inst Prime Obl Service	PRSXX	C	(800) 341-7400	D / 2.0	0.03	0.05	0.05 /38	0.02 /19	0.02 / 7	0.05	0.53
MM	Federated Inst Prime Obl Trust	POLXX	U	(800) 341-7400	U /	--	--	--	--	--	0.03	0.79
MM	Federated Inst Prime Value Obl Cap	PVCXX	C	(800) 341-7400	D+ / 2.4	0.07	0.09	0.10 /41	0.04 /24	0.06 /13	0.10	0.54
MM	Federated Inst Prime Value Obl Inst	PVOXX	C	(800) 341-7400	D+ / 2.7	0.09	0.14	0.20 /44	0.11 /27	0.14 /15	0.19	0.28
MM	Federated Inst Prime Value Obl Svc	PVSXX	C	(800) 341-7400	D / 2.0	0.03	0.04	0.04 /37	0.02 /19	0.02 / 7	0.04	0.54
MMT	Federated Inst Tx Fr Cash Tr Prmr	FTFXX	C-	(800) 341-7400	D / 1.9	0.00	0.03	0.03 /38	0.01 /19	0.01 / 7	0.03	0.64
*COH	Federated Instl High Yld Bond	FIHBX	D+	(800) 341-7400	C+ / 6.3	3.52	1.89	-1.64 /18	2.83 /75	5.64 /75	6.18	0.57
COI	Federated Interm Corp Bd Instl	FIIFX	B-	(800) 341-7400	C+ / 6.5	2.27	1.66	0.46 /49	2.19 /65	3.72 /57	3.53	0.97
MUN	Federated Interm Muni Trust Inst	FIMTX	A+	(800) 341-7400	A- / 9.0	1.62	3.22	3.64 /91	2.81 /86	4.59 /82	2.29	0.98
MUN	Federated Interm Muni Trust Y	FIMYX	A+	(800) 341-7400	A- / 9.1	1.67	3.31	3.82 /93	2.99 /88	4.78 /83	2.46	0.74
COI	Federated Intermediate Corp Bd Svc	INISX	C+	(800) 341-7400	C+ / 6.1	2.32	1.54	0.32 /46	1.98 /61	3.49 /53	3.28	1.21
GL	Federated International Bond A	FTIIX	D	(800) 341-7400	C- / 4.2	8.18	7.07	7.07 /97	0.01 /16	-0.22 / 2	0.00	2.21
GL ●	Federated International Bond B	FTBBX	D	(800) 341-7400	C / 5.0	8.02	6.77	6.32 /95	-0.72 /10	-0.95 / 2	0.00	2.70
GL	Federated International Bond C	FTIBX	D	(800) 341-7400	C / 5.0	8.10	6.72	6.26 /94	-0.72 /10	-0.96 / 2	0.00	2.71
GL	Federated International Bond Strat	FIBPX	C-	(800) 341-7400	C+ / 6.8	6.05	6.21	3.41 /79	1.21 /46	3.25 /49	0.00	2.04
MMT	Federated MA Muni Cash Svc	MMCXX	C	(800) 341-7400	D+ / 2.4	0.00	0.04	0.04 /39	0.04 /25	0.05 /14	0.04	0.81
MMT	Federated MA Muni Csh Tr Cash Ser	FMCXX	C	(800) 341-7400	D+ / 2.4	0.00	0.04	0.04 /39	0.04 /25	0.05 /14	0.04	1.43
MM	Federated Master Trust	FMTXX	U	(800) 341-7400	U /	0.01	0.01	0.01 /32	--	--	0.01	0.65
MUS	Federated MI Interm Muni Tr	MMIFX	A-	(800) 341-7400	B / 7.7	1.37	2.39	3.05 /85	2.53 /83	4.51 /81	2.35	0.91
MMT	Federated MI Muni Cash Svc	MIMXX	C	(800) 341-7400	D / 2.2	0.00	0.04	0.05 /40	0.02 /22	0.02 /10	0.05	0.87
MMT	Federated MI Muni Cash Tr Wealth	MINXX	C	(800) 341-7400	D / 2.2	0.00	0.04	0.05 /40	0.02 /22	0.03 /12	0.05	0.62
MMT	Federated MN Muni Cash Tr Wealth	FEMXX	U	(800) 341-7400	U /	--	--	--	--	--	0.01	0.60
MTG	Federated Mortgage Fund Inst	FGFIX	A	(800) 341-7400	C+ / 6.5	1.77	1.25	1.76 /69	2.16 /65	2.88 /43	2.88	0.65
MTG	Federated Mortgage Strat	FMBPX	A	(800) 341-7400	B- / 7.2	1.99	1.62	2.35 /74	2.44 /70	3.10 /47	2.81	0.36
MTG	Federated Mortgage Svc	FGFSX	B+	(800) 341-7400	C+ / 5.9	1.60	0.99	1.36 /64	1.82 /58	2.55 /38	2.58	1.15

● Denotes fund is closed to new investors
* Denotes fund is included in Section II

RISK			NET ASSETS		ASSET							FUND MANAGER		MINIMUM		LOADS	
Risk Rating/Pts	3 Yr Avg Standard Deviation	Avg Duration	NAV As of 3/31/16	Total $(Mil)	Cash %	Gov. Bond %	Muni. Bond %	Corp. Bond %	Other %	Portfolio Turnover Ratio	Avg Coupon Rate	Manager Quality Pct	Manager Tenure (Years)	Initial Purch. $	Additional Purch. $	Front End Load	Back End Load
B / 7.9	2.5	4.6	8.98	3	3	19	0	1	77	47	3.4	32	13	1,500	100	0.0	0.0
B / 7.7	2.6	4.6	9.01	13	3	19	0	1	77	47	3.4	30	13	1,500	100	0.0	0.0
B / 7.9	2.5	4.6	8.98	165	3	19	0	1	77	47	3.4	57	13	1,500	100	1.0	0.0
B+ / 8.3	2.2	4.3	10.36	457	2	0	0	0	98	153	3.9	85	16	1,000,000	0	0.0	0.0
B+ / 8.3	2.2	4.3	10.36	58	2	0	0	0	98	153	3.9	80	16	1,000,000	0	0.0	0.0
A+ / 9.9	N/A	N/A	1.00	852	100	0	0	0	0	0	0.0	65	22	500,000	0	0.0	0.0
A+ / 9.9	N/A	N/A	1.00	16,202	100	0	0	0	0	0	0.1	65	22	500,000	0	0.0	0.0
U /	N/A	N/A	1.00	4,336	100	0	0	0	0	0	0.1	N/A	22	5,000,000	0	0.0	0.0
U /	N/A	N/A	1.00	9,021	100	0	0	0	0	0	0.0	N/A	22	500,000	0	0.0	0.0
U /	N/A	N/A	1.00	803	100	0	0	0	0	0	0.0	N/A	22	500,000	0	0.0	0.0
U /	N/A	N/A	1.00	180	100	0	0	0	0	0	0.0	N/A	N/A	25,000	0	0.0	0.0
A+ / 9.9	N/A	N/A	1.00	3,299	100	0	0	0	0	0	0.1	65	N/A	500,000	0	0.0	0.0
U /	N/A	N/A	1.00	2,699	100	0	0	0	0	0	0.0	N/A	N/A	500,000	0	0.0	0.0
D / 1.7	5.4	4.3	7.06	610	1	0	0	98	1	31	6.4	80	29	1,500	100	4.5	2.0
D / 1.7	5.5	4.3	7.04	37	1	0	0	98	1	31	6.4	45	29	1,500	100	0.0	2.0
D / 1.7	5.5	4.3	7.04	150	1	0	0	98	1	31	6.4	48	29	1,500	100	0.0	2.0
D+ / 2.4	5.4	N/A	12.36	35	100	0	0	0	0	24	0.0	99	8	0	0	0.0	0.0
E+ / 0.8	6.4	5.1	6.27	104	5	0	0	85	10	36	6.2	94	32	1,500	100	4.5	2.0
E+ / 0.8	6.4	5.1	6.26	27	5	0	0	85	10	36	6.2	87	32	1,500	100	0.0	2.0
E+ / 0.8	6.4	5.1	6.24	155	5	0	0	85	10	36	6.2	94	32	1,000,000	0	0.0	2.0
E+ / 0.8	6.4	5.1	6.25	562	5	0	0	85	10	36	6.2	93	32	1,000,000	0	0.0	2.0
A+ / 9.9	N/A	N/A	1.00	40	100	0	0	0	0	0	0.1	65	N/A	500,000	0	0.0	0.0
A+ / 9.9	N/A	N/A	1.00	7,442	100	0	0	0	0	0	0.2	71	N/A	500,000	0	0.0	0.0
A+ / 9.9	N/A	N/A	1.00	175	100	0	0	0	0	0	0.1	65	N/A	500,000	0	0.0	0.0
U /	N/A	N/A	1.00	916	0	0	0	0	100	0	0.0	N/A	25	25,000	0	0.0	0.0
A+ / 9.9	N/A	N/A	1.00	627	100	0	0	0	0	0	0.1	65	25	500,000	0	0.0	0.0
A+ / 9.9	N/A	N/A	1.00	32,858	100	0	0	0	0	0	0.2	68	25	500,000	0	0.0	0.0
A+ / 9.9	N/A	N/A	1.00	2,478	100	0	0	0	0	0	0.1	65	25	500,000	0	0.0	0.0
U /	N/A	N/A	1.00	495	100	0	0	0	0	0	0.0	N/A	25	500,000	0	0.0	0.0
A+ / 9.9	N/A	N/A	1.00	654	100	0	0	0	0	0	0.1	65	N/A	500,000	0	0.0	0.0
A+ / 9.9	N/A	N/A	1.00	6,013	100	0	0	0	0	0	0.2	70	N/A	500,000	0	0.0	0.0
A+ / 9.9	N/A	N/A	1.00	1,194	100	0	0	0	0	0	0.0	65	N/A	500,000	0	0.0	0.0
A+ / 9.9	N/A	N/A	1.00	73	100	0	0	0	0	0	0.0	63	20	25,000	0	0.0	0.0
D / 1.6	5.6	N/A	9.27	4,361	0	0	0	0	100	24	0.0	91	14	1,000,000	0	0.0	2.0
C+ / 6.7	3.0	4.0	9.28	218	0	2	0	96	2	16	4.7	79	3	1,000,000	0	0.0	0.0
B- / 7.0	2.9	5.6	10.31	104	1	0	98	0	1	37	0.0	57	21	1,000,000	0	0.0	0.0
B- / 7.0	2.9	5.6	10.31	5	1	0	98	0	1	37	0.0	N/A	21	100,000	0	0.0	0.0
C+ / 6.6	3.0	4.0	9.29	24	0	2	0	96	2	16	4.7	71	3	1,000,000	0	0.0	0.0
D- / 1.3	6.1	7.7	10.45	30	3	86	0	9	2	90	0.0	74	14	1,500	100	4.5	0.0
D- / 1.2	6.2	7.7	10.10	1	3	86	0	9	2	90	0.0	41	14	1,500	100	0.0	0.0
D- / 1.2	6.1	7.7	10.01	3	3	86	0	9	2	90	0.0	41	14	1,500	100	0.0	0.0
D / 2.0	5.6	5.1	14.54	12	49	50	0	0	1	85	0.0	92	8	0	0	0.0	0.0
A+ / 9.9	N/A	N/A	1.00	140	100	0	0	0	0	0	0.0	68	N/A	10,000	0	0.0	0.0
A+ / 9.9	N/A	N/A	1.00	86	100	0	0	0	0	0	0.0	68	N/A	1,000	0	0.0	0.0
U /	N/A	N/A	1.00	82	100	0	0	0	0	0	0.0	N/A	19	25,000	0	0.0	0.0
C+ / 6.8	2.9	4.5	11.46	124	1	0	98	0	1	25	0.0	43	18	1,500	100	3.0	0.0
A+ / 9.9	N/A	N/A	1.00	81	100	0	0	0	0	0	0.1	N/A	21	10,000	0	0.0	0.0
A+ / 9.9	N/A	N/A	1.00	12	100	0	0	0	0	0	0.1	N/A	20	10,000	0	0.0	0.0
U /	N/A	N/A	1.00	112	100	0	0	0	0	0	0.0	67	N/A	25,000	0	0.0	0.0
B / 8.2	2.2	4.1	9.69	150	7	0	0	3	90	71	4.0	57	13	1,000,000	0	0.0	0.0
B / 8.0	2.4	N/A	10.08	80	3	0	0	1	96	16	0.0	57	9	0	0	0.0	0.0
B / 8.2	2.3	4.1	9.68	15	7	0	0	3	90	71	4.0	43	13	1,000,000	0	0.0	0.0

99 Pct = Best
0 Pct = Worst

Fund Type	Fund Name	Ticker Symbol	Overall Investment Rating	Phone	PERFORMANCE: Performance Rating/Pts	Total Return % through 3/31/16: 3 Mo	6 Mo	1Yr / Pct	Annualized: 3Yr / Pct	5Yr / Pct	Incl. in Returns: Dividend Yield	Expense Ratio
* MUH	Federated Muni & Stock Advantage A	FMUAX	**C-**	(800) 341-7400	**B+ / 8.6**	2.32	5.13	1.24 /71	4.15 /96	6.96 /96	2.58	1.09
MUH	Federated Muni & Stock Advantage B	FMNBX	**C**	(800) 341-7400	**A- / 9.2**	2.21	4.74	0.48 /54	3.37 /92	6.18 /93	1.99	1.84
MUH	Federated Muni & Stock Advantage C	FMUCX	**C**	(800) 341-7400	**A- / 9.1**	2.13	4.65	0.48 /54	3.35 /91	6.17 /93	1.99	1.84
MUH	Federated Muni & Stock Advantage F	FMUFX	**C**	(800) 341-7400	**A / 9.5**	2.32	5.13	1.24 /71	4.15 /96	6.96 /96	2.70	1.09
MUH	Federated Muni High Yield Advn A	FMOAX	**C+**	(800) 341-7400	**A / 9.4**	1.95	4.00	5.03 /98	4.74 /98	8.00 /98	4.10	1.04
MUH	Federated Muni High Yield Advn B	FMOBX	**C+**	(800) 341-7400	**A+ / 9.6**	1.76	3.61	4.25 /95	3.96 /95	7.20 /97	3.55	1.79
MUH	Federated Muni High Yield Advn C	FMNCX	**C+**	(800) 341-7400	**A+ / 9.6**	1.76	3.61	4.24 /95	3.96 /96	7.20 /97	3.55	1.79
MUH	Federated Muni High Yield Advn F	FHTFX	**C+**	(800) 341-7400	**A+ / 9.8**	2.06	3.99	5.03 /98	4.78 /98	8.00 /98	4.24	1.04
MUH	Federated Muni High Yield Advn Ins	FMYIX	**C+**	(800) 341-7400	**A+ / 9.9**	2.01	4.13	5.30 /98	4.94 /99	8.13 /98	4.54	0.79
MUN	Federated Muni Securities Fd A	LMSFX	**C+**	(800) 341-7400	**B / 8.0**	1.55	3.11	3.27 /88	3.10 /89	5.72 /90	2.86	0.95
MUN ●	Federated Muni Securities Fd B	LMSBX	**C+**	(800) 341-7400	**B+ / 8.3**	1.35	2.78	2.51 /80	2.28 /80	4.86 /84	2.18	1.70
MUN	Federated Muni Securities Fd C	LMSCX	**C+**	(800) 341-7400	**B+ / 8.3**	1.35	2.78	2.51 /80	2.28 /80	4.86 /84	2.17	1.70
MUN	Federated Muni Securities Fd F	LMFFX	**B**	(800) 341-7400	**A- / 9.1**	1.55	3.21	3.27 /88	3.10 /89	5.72 /90	2.96	0.95
* MUI	Federated Muni Ultrashrt A	FMUUX	**C-**	(800) 341-7400	**D- / 1.1**	-0.14	-0.20	-0.42 /27	-0.08 /15	0.30 /17	0.18	1.03
MUI	Federated Muni Ultrashrt Inst	FMUSX	**C+**	(800) 341-7400	**C- / 3.4**	0.06	0.12	0.12 /43	0.40 /35	0.77 /22	0.62	0.53
MMT	Federated Municipal Obl Cap	MFCXX	**C**	(800) 341-7400	**D+ / 2.4**	0.01	0.06	0.06 /41	0.03 /25	0.04 /13	0.06	0.55
MMT	Federated Municipal Obl Cash II	MODXX	**U**	(800) 341-7400	**U /**	0.00	0.05	--	--	--	0.00	N/A
MMT	Federated Municipal Obl Cash Series	MFSXX	**U**	(800) 341-7400	**U /**	0.00	0.05	--	--	--	0.00	N/A
MMT	Federated Municipal Obl Investment	MOIXX	**U**	(800) 341-7400	**U /**	0.00	0.05	--	--	--	0.00	N/A
MMT	Federated Municipal Obl Svc	MOSXX	**C**	(800) 341-7400	**D+ / 2.4**	0.00	0.05	0.06 /41	0.03 /25	0.03 /12	0.06	0.55
MMT	Federated Municipal Obl Trust	MOTXX	**U**	(800) 341-7400	**U /**	0.00	0.05	--	--	--	0.00	N/A
MMT	Federated Municipal Obl Wealth	MOFXX	**C**	(800) 341-7400	**D+ / 2.5**	0.01	0.06	0.06 /41	0.04 /25	0.07 /15	0.06	0.30
MMT	Federated NJ Muni Cash Svc	NJSXX	**C**	(800) 341-7400	**D / 2.0**	0.00	0.02	0.03 /38	0.02 /22	0.02 /10	0.03	0.98
MMT	Federated NJ Muni Cash Tr Cash Ser	NJCXX	**C**	(800) 341-7400	**D / 2.0**	0.00	0.02	0.03 /38	0.02 /22	0.02 /10	0.03	1.49
MMT	Federated NJ Muni Cash Tr Wealth	NJMXX	**C**	(800) 341-7400	**D / 2.0**	0.00	0.02	0.03 /38	0.02 /22	0.02 /10	0.03	0.64
MMT	Federated NY Muni Cash Svc	FNTXX	**U**	(800) 341-7400	**U /**	0.00	0.01	0.02 /36	0.01 /19	0.02 /10	0.02	1.09
MMT	Federated NY Muni Cash Tr Cash	FNCXX	**U**	(800) 341-7400	**U /**	0.00	0.01	0.02 /36	0.01 /19	0.02 /10	0.02	1.45
MMT	Federated NY Muni Cash Tr Wealth	NISXX	**U**	(800) 341-7400	**U /**	0.00	0.01	0.02 /36	0.02 /22	0.04 /13	0.02	0.59
MMT	Federated NY Muni Cash Tr-Cash II	NYCXX	**U**	(800) 341-7400	**U /**	0.00	0.01	0.02 /36	0.01 /19	0.02 /10	0.02	1.09
MUS	Federated NY Muni Income Fd A	NYIFX	**C+**	(800) 341-7400	**B / 7.7**	1.44	2.90	3.43 /89	2.80 /86	5.18 /87	2.83	1.41
MUS ●	Federated NY Muni Income Fd B	NYIBX	**B-**	(800) 341-7400	**B / 8.1**	1.17	2.53	2.66 /82	2.04 /77	4.39 /81	2.23	2.17
MUH	Federated Ohio Municipal Inc Fund	OMIFX	**B**	(800) 341-7400	**B+ / 8.6**	1.71	2.99	3.30 /88	2.79 /86	4.87 /84	2.83	1.29
MUH	Federated Ohio Municipal Inc Fund A	OMIAX	**C+**	(800) 341-7400	**B / 7.9**	1.74	3.06	3.44 /89	2.94 /88	5.03 /86	2.86	0.89
MMT	Federated PA Muni Cash Svc	FPAXX	**C**	(800) 341-7400	**D+ / 2.4**	0.00	0.05	0.06 /41	0.03 /25	0.03 /12	0.06	0.85
MMT	Federated PA Muni Cash Tr Cash	PACXX	**C**	(800) 341-7400	**D+ / 2.4**	0.00	0.05	0.06 /41	0.03 /25	0.03 /12	0.06	1.25
MMT	Federated PA Muni Cash Tr Wealth	PAMXX	**C**	(800) 341-7400	**D+ / 2.4**	0.00	0.05	0.06 /41	0.03 /25	0.03 /12	0.06	0.61
MUS	Federated PA Muni Income Fund A	PAMFX	**B-**	(800) 341-7400	**B / 8.0**	1.61	2.88	3.35 /89	3.08 /89	5.20 /87	2.95	0.87
MUS ●	Federated PA Muni Income Fund B	FPABX	**B**	(800) 341-7400	**B / 8.2**	1.30	2.35	2.43 /80	2.27 /80	4.38 /80	2.29	1.62
MM	Federated Prime Cash Obl	PTAXX	**U**	(800) 341-7400	**U /**	0.01	0.01	--	--	--	0.00	N/A
MM	Federated Prime Cash Obl Cap	PCCXX	**C**	(800) 341-7400	**D / 2.2**	0.06	0.07	0.08 /40	0.03 /22	0.04 /11	0.08	0.54
MM	Federated Prime Cash Obl Svc	PRCXX	**C-**	(800) 341-7400	**D / 1.9**	0.02	0.03	0.03 /36	0.02 /19	0.01 / 4	0.03	0.54
MM	Federated Prime Cash Obl Wealth	PCOXX	**C**	(800) 341-7400	**D+ / 2.6**	0.08	0.12	0.16 /43	0.08 /26	0.10 /15	0.16	0.29
GL	Federated Prudent DollarBear A	PSAFX	**E+**	(800) 341-7400	**E- / 0.2**	5.10	3.28	3.81 /80	-4.14 / 2	-3.56 / 1	0.00	1.59
GL	Federated Prudent DollarBear C	FPGCX	**E+**	(800) 341-7400	**E / 0.3**	4.98	2.98	3.09 /77	-4.84 / 1	-4.28 / 0	0.00	2.34
GL	Federated Prudent DollarBear IS	FPGIX	**E+**	(800) 341-7400	**E / 0.4**	5.25	3.44	4.07 /82	-3.90 / 2	-3.32 / 1	0.00	1.34
GEI	Federated Real Return Bond A	RRFAX	**D-**	(800) 341-7400	**E / 0.4**	2.61	2.20	-0.10 /30	-1.66 / 5	0.70 /18	0.63	1.61
GEI	Federated Real Return Bond C	RRFCX	**D-**	(800) 341-7400	**E / 0.5**	2.43	1.81	-0.90 /22	-2.41 / 3	-0.06 / 3	0.47	2.36
GEI	Federated Real Return Bond Inst	RRFIX	**D-**	(800) 341-7400	**D- / 1.0**	2.70	2.29	0.06 /39	-1.44 / 6	0.95 /20	0.72	1.36
MUN	Federated Sh Int Dur Muni A	FMTAX	**C**	(800) 341-7400	**C- / 3.2**	0.38	0.39	0.24 /47	0.52 /39	1.62 /38	0.81	1.04
MUN	Federated Sh Int Dur Muni Inst	FSHIX	**B+**	(800) 341-7400	**C / 5.3**	0.40	0.64	0.64 /58	0.99 /53	2.11 /49	1.31	0.79
MUN	Federated Short Int Dur Muni Svc	FSHSX	**B-**	(800) 341-7400	**C / 4.5**	0.34	0.42	0.40 /52	0.74 /45	1.87 /43	1.07	1.04
GES	Federated Short Term Inc A	FTIAX	**C-**	(800) 341-7400	**D / 1.6**	0.43	0.19	-0.11 /30	0.05 /24	0.82 /19	0.70	1.32

● Denotes fund is closed to new investors
* Denotes fund is included in Section II

RISK			NET ASSETS		ASSET							FUND MANAGER		MINIMUM		LOADS	
Risk Rating/Pts	3 Yr Avg Standard Deviation	Avg Duration	NAV As of 3/31/16	Total $(Mil)	Cash %	Gov. Bond %	Muni. Bond %	Corp. Bond %	Other %	Portfolio Turnover Ratio	Avg Coupon Rate	Manager Quality Pct	Manager Tenure (Years)	Initial Purch. $	Additional Purch. $	Front End Load	Back End Load
D- / 1.4	5.5	7.2	12.31	609	0	0	55	0	45	35	0.0	94	13	1,500	100	5.5	0.0
D- / 1.5	5.4	7.2	12.31	24	0	0	55	0	45	35	0.0	88	13	1,500	100	0.0	0.0
D- / 1.5	5.4	7.2	12.30	305	0	0	55	0	45	35	0.0	88	13	1,500	100	0.0	0.0
D- / 1.4	5.5	7.2	12.31	181	0	0	55	0	45	35	0.0	94	13	1,500	100	1.0	0.0
D / 2.1	4.8	8.2	9.06	258	2	0	97	0	1	12	0.0	59	7	1,500	100	4.5	0.0
D / 2.2	4.7	8.2	9.05	12	2	0	97	0	1	12	0.0	35	7	1,500	100	0.0	0.0
D / 2.1	4.8	8.2	9.05	71	2	0	97	0	1	12	0.0	33	7	1,500	100	0.0	0.0
D / 2.0	4.8	8.2	9.06	197	2	0	97	0	1	12	0.0	59	7	1,500	100	1.0	0.0
D / 2.1	4.8	8.2	9.05	84	2	0	97	0	1	12	0.0	70	7	1,000,000	0	0.0	0.0
C- / 3.9	4.0	6.9	10.68	331	1	0	98	0	1	16	0.0	25	20	1,500	100	4.5	0.0
C- / 3.9	4.0	6.9	10.69	6	1	0	98	0	1	16	0.0	13	20	1,500	100	0.0	0.0
C- / 3.9	4.0	6.9	10.69	21	1	0	98	0	1	16	0.0	13	20	1,500	100	0.0	0.0
C- / 3.9	4.0	6.9	10.68	25	1	0	98	0	1	16	0.0	26	20	1,500	100	0.0	0.0
A+ / 9.9	0.3	0.4	9.97	846	0	0	99	0	1	46	0.0	49	16	1,500	100	2.0	0.0
A+ / 9.9	0.3	0.4	9.98	1,581	0	0	99	0	1	46	0.0	72	16	1,000,000	0	0.0	0.0
A+ / 9.9	N/A	N/A	1.00	280	100	0	0	0	0	0	0.1	N/A	N/A	500,000	0	0.0	0.0
U /	N/A	N/A	1.00	141	100	0	0	0	0	0	0.0	N/A	N/A	25,000	0	0.0	0.0
U /	N/A	N/A	1.00	204	100	0	0	0	0	0	0.0	N/A	N/A	10,000	250	0.0	0.0
U /	N/A	N/A	1.00	N/A	100	0	0	0	0	0	0.0	N/A	N/A	1,500	100	0.0	0.0
A+ / 9.9	N/A	N/A	1.00	617	100	0	0	0	0	0	0.1	N/A	N/A	500,000	0	0.0	0.0
U /	N/A	N/A	1.00	N/A	100	0	0	0	0	0	0.0	N/A	N/A	500,000	0	0.0	0.0
A+ / 9.9	N/A	N/A	1.00	905	100	0	0	0	0	0	0.1	N/A	N/A	500,000	0	0.0	0.0
A+ / 9.9	N/A	N/A	1.00	12	100	0	0	0	0	0	0.0	N/A	N/A	25,000	0	0.0	0.0
A+ / 9.9	N/A	N/A	1.00	109	100	0	0	0	0	0	0.0	N/A	N/A	1,000	0	0.0	0.0
A+ / 9.9	N/A	N/A	1.00	48	100	0	0	0	0	0	0.0	N/A	N/A	25,000	0	0.0	0.0
U /	N/A	N/A	1.00	184	100	0	0	0	0	0	0.0	N/A	N/A	10,000	0	0.0	0.0
U /	N/A	N/A	1.00	229	100	0	0	0	0	0	0.0	N/A	N/A	10,000	0	0.0	0.0
U /	N/A	N/A	1.00	168	100	0	0	0	0	0	0.0	N/A	N/A	10,000	0	0.0	0.0
U /	N/A	N/A	1.00	18	100	0	0	0	0	0	0.0	N/A	N/A	10,000	0	0.0	0.0
C / 4.8	3.6	6.3	10.52	30	1	0	98	0	1	17	0.0	30	21	1,500	100	4.5	0.0
C / 4.7	3.6	6.3	10.52	2	1	0	98	0	1	17	0.0	15	21	1,500	100	0.0	0.0
C- / 4.2	3.3	6.5	11.37	107	1	0	98	0	1	25	0.0	37	21	1,500	100	1.0	0.0
C- / 4.2	3.3	6.5	11.37	66	1	0	98	0	1	25	0.0	41	21	1,500	100	4.5	0.0
A+ / 9.9	N/A	N/A	1.00	110	100	0	0	0	0	0	0.1	67	26	10,000	0	0.0	0.0
A+ / 9.9	N/A	N/A	1.00	70	100	0	0	0	0	0	0.1	67	26	10,000	0	0.0	0.0
A+ / 9.9	N/A	N/A	1.00	45	100	0	0	0	0	0	0.1	67	26	10,000	0	0.0	0.0
C / 4.8	3.6	6.8	11.05	195	0	0	99	0	1	29	0.0	39	21	1,500	100	4.5	0.0
C / 4.7	3.6	6.8	11.05	2	0	0	99	0	1	29	0.0	18	21	1,500	100	0.0	0.0
U /	N/A	N/A	1.00	1,106	100	0	0	0	0	0	0.0	N/A	20	25,000	0	0.0	0.0
A+ / 9.9	N/A	N/A	1.00	2,248	100	0	0	0	0	0	0.1	63	20	500,000	0	0.0	0.0
A+ / 9.9	N/A	N/A	1.00	1,910	100	0	0	0	0	0	0.0	65	20	500,000	0	0.0	0.0
A+ / 9.9	N/A	N/A	1.00	11,243	100	0	0	0	0	0	0.2	68	20	500,000	0	0.0	0.0
D / 2.1	5.5	0.1	10.09	57	47	50	0	0	3	75	0.0	5	16	1,500	100	4.5	0.0
D / 2.1	5.5	0.1	9.69	3	47	50	0	0	3	75	0.0	4	16	1,500	100	0.0	0.0
D / 2.2	5.5	0.1	10.23	5	47	50	0	0	3	75	0.0	6	16	1,000,000	0	0.0	0.0
C- / 3.9	4.0	4.6	10.24	13	1	90	0	7	2	36	1.5	6	10	1,500	100	4.5	0.0
C- / 3.9	4.0	4.6	10.10	5	1	90	0	7	2	36	1.5	4	10	1,500	100	0.0	0.0
C- / 3.9	4.0	4.6	10.28	12	1	90	0	7	2	36	1.5	6	10	1,000,000	0	0.0	0.0
A- / 9.1	1.2	1.7	10.33	296	0	0	99	0	1	17	0.0	39	20	1,500	100	1.0	0.0
A- / 9.1	1.2	1.7	10.32	854	0	0	99	0	1	17	0.0	59	20	1,000,000	0	0.0	0.0
A- / 9.1	1.2	1.7	10.32	26	0	0	99	0	1	17	0.0	49	20	1,000,000	0	0.0	0.0
A+ / 9.7	0.7	1.0	8.49	75	7	3	0	37	53	10	1.9	45	21	1,500	100	1.0	0.0

99 Pct = Best
0 Pct = Worst

Fund Type	Fund Name	Ticker Symbol	Overall Investment Rating	Phone	PERFORMANCE: Performance Rating/Pts	Total Return % through 3/31/16: 3 Mo	6 Mo	1Yr / Pct	Annualized: 3Yr / Pct	5Yr / Pct	Incl. in Returns: Dividend Yield	Expense Ratio
GES	Federated Short Term Inc Inst	FSTIX	**C+**	(800) 341-7400	**C- / 3.7**	0.58	0.48	0.47 /49	0.63 /36	1.41 /25	1.29	0.82
GES	Federated Short Term Inc Svc	FSISX	**C+**	(800) 341-7400	**C- / 3.3**	0.53	0.38	0.27 /45	0.44 /32	1.22 /22	1.09	0.97
GES	Federated Short Term Inc Y	FSTYX	**B-**	(800) 341-7400	**C- / 4.1**	0.73	0.68	0.74 /54	0.84 /40	1.60 /27	1.45	0.57
COI	Federated Sht-Interm Tot Ret B A	FGCAX	**U**	(800) 341-7400	**U /**	1.65	1.15	0.76 /54	--	--	2.37	0.77
COI	Federated Sht-Interm Tot Ret B Inst	FGCIX	**B-**	(800) 341-7400	**C / 5.3**	1.81	1.37	1.00 /59	1.35 /49	2.61 /39	2.64	0.56
COI	Federated Sht-Interm Tot Ret B R	SRBRX	**U**	(800) 341-7400	**U /**	1.63	1.01	0.26 /45	--	--	1.90	1.26
COI	Federated Sht-Interm Tot Ret B Svc	FGCSX	**C+**	(800) 341-7400	**C / 4.7**	1.65	1.15	0.76 /54	1.07 /44	2.34 /36	2.39	0.82
GES	Federated Strategic Income Fund A	STIAX	**D-**	(800) 341-7400	**D- / 1.4**	2.57	1.74	-2.45 /13	0.83 /39	3.10 /47	3.66	1.39
GES	Federated Strategic Income Fund B	SINBX	**D-**	(800) 341-7400	**D / 1.8**	2.38	1.36	-3.19 /11	0.07 /26	2.31 /35	3.06	2.14
GES	Federated Strategic Income Fund C	SINCX	**D-**	(800) 341-7400	**D / 1.7**	2.38	1.24	-3.19 /11	0.04 /23	2.31 /35	3.06	2.14
GES	Federated Strategic Income Fund F	STFSX	**D**	(800) 341-7400	**C- / 3.3**	2.58	1.75	-2.46 /13	0.83 /39	3.09 /47	3.81	1.39
GES	Federated Strategic Income Fund IS	STISX	**D**	(800) 341-7400	**C / 4.3**	2.77	1.88	-2.21 /15	1.09 /44	3.35 /51	4.10	1.14
MMT	Federated T/F Oblig Fund Wealth	TBIXX	**C**	(800) 341-7400	**D / 2.0**	0.01	0.02	0.03 /38	0.02 /22	0.03 /12	0.03	0.29
MMT	Federated Tax-Free MM Inv	TFIXX	**C**	(800) 341-7400	**D+ / 2.4**	0.00	0.06	0.07 /42	0.03 /25	0.03 /12	0.07	0.89
MMT	Federated Tax-Free MM Svc	TFSXX	**C**	(800) 341-7400	**D+ / 2.4**	0.00	0.06	0.07 /42	0.03 /25	0.03 /12	0.07	0.85
MMT	Federated Tax-Free Oblig Svc	TBSXX	**C**	(800) 341-7400	**D / 2.0**	0.00	0.02	0.03 /38	0.02 /22	0.02 /10	0.03	0.54
COI	Federated Tot Ret Bd A	TLRAX	**C-**	(800) 341-7400	**C- / 3.6**	2.58	1.84	0.21 /44	1.70 /56	3.21 /48	2.78	0.99
COI	Federated Tot Ret Bd B	TLRBX	**C**	(800) 341-7400	**C / 4.8**	2.45	1.57	-0.33 /28	1.14 /45	2.65 /40	2.37	1.55
COI	Federated Tot Ret Bd C	TLRCX	**C**	(800) 341-7400	**C / 4.8**	2.46	1.59	-0.30 /28	1.17 /46	2.68 /40	2.40	1.51
COI	Federated Tot Ret Bd Inst	FTRBX	**B**	(800) 341-7400	**C+ / 6.7**	2.62	2.11	0.76 /54	2.23 /66	3.76 /58	3.46	0.48
COI	Federated Tot Ret Bd R	FTRKX	**C+**	(800) 341-7400	**C / 5.5**	2.44	1.76	0.05 /38	1.56 /53	3.05 /46	2.76	1.14
COI	Federated Tot Ret Bd R6	FTRLX	**U**	(800) 341-7400	**U /**	2.72	2.21	--	--	--	0.00	0.44
COI	Federated Tot Ret Bond Svc	FTRFX	**B-**	(800) 341-7400	**C+ / 6.2**	2.55	1.97	0.46 /49	1.95 /60	3.47 /52	3.16	0.97
USS	Federated Tot Ret Gov Bd Inst	FTRGX	**B**	(800) 341-7400	**C+ / 6.0**	2.79	1.93	1.88 /71	1.59 /54	3.06 /46	1.79	0.50
USS	Federated Tot Ret Gov Bond Svc	FTGSX	**C+**	(800) 341-7400	**C / 5.4**	2.70	1.76	1.54 /67	1.24 /47	2.70 /40	1.47	0.99
USA	Federated Treas Oblig Automated	TOAXX	**U**	(800) 341-7400	**U /**	--	--	--	--	--	0.01	0.63
MM	Federated Treas Oblig Cap	TOCXX	**U**	(800) 341-7400	**U /**	--	--	--	--	--	0.02	0.53
MM	Federated Treas Oblig Instl	TOIXX	**C**	(800) 341-7400	**D / 2.0**	0.03	0.04	0.05 /38	0.02 /19	0.02 / 7	0.05	0.28
MM	Federated Treas Oblig Svc	TOSXX	**U**	(800) 341-7400	**U /**	--	--	--	--	--	0.01	0.53
MM	Federated Treas Oblig Tr	TOTXX	**U**	(800) 341-7400	**U /**	--	--	--	--	--	0.01	0.78
MM	Federated Trust For US Trs Obl Inst	TTOXX	**C-**	(800) 341-7400	**D / 1.9**	0.04	0.04	0.04 /37	0.01 /17	0.01 / 4	0.04	0.59
GES	Federated Ultra Short Bd A	FULAX	**C-**	(800) 341-7400	**D- / 1.3**	0.27	0.10	-0.19 /29	0.04 /23	0.61 /18	0.57	1.11
GES	Federated Ultra Short Bd Inst	FULIX	**C+**	(800) 341-7400	**C- / 3.6**	0.40	0.36	0.34 /47	0.62 /35	1.16 /22	1.11	0.56
GES	Federated Ultra Short Bond Svc	FULBX	**C**	(800) 341-7400	**D+ / 2.7**	0.29	0.15	-0.10 /30	0.18 /28	0.71 /18	0.67	1.06
USS	Federated US Gvt Sec:1-3yrs Svc	FSGIX	**C-**	(800) 341-7400	**D / 1.6**	0.74	0.26	-0.11 /30	-0.33 /13	-0.09 / 3	0.56	0.98
USS	Federated US Gvt Sec:2-5yrs Svc	FIGIX	**C**	(800) 341-7400	**C- / 3.2**	1.82	0.89	0.66 /53	0.15 /28	1.14 /22	1.01	0.89
MM	Federated US Trs Csh Res Instl	UTIXX	**C-**	(800) 341-7400	**D / 1.9**	0.03	0.03	0.03 /36	0.01 /17	0.01 / 4	0.03	0.29
USS	Federated USG Sec:1-3yrs Inst	FSGVX	**U**	(800) 341-7400	**U /**	0.81	0.42	0.22 /44	--	0.25 /16	0.88	0.73
USS	Federated USG Sec:1-3yrs Y	FSGTX	**C**	(800) 341-7400	**D+ / 2.9**	0.85	0.49	0.36 /47	0.15 /28	0.41 /17	1.03	0.48
USS	Federated USG Sec:2-5yrs Inst	FIGTX	**C**	(800) 341-7400	**C- / 3.6**	1.88	1.00	0.89 /57	0.35 /31	1.37 /24	1.24	0.86
USS	Federated USG Sec:2-5yrs R	FIGKX	**C-**	(800) 341-7400	**D / 2.2**	1.71	0.68	0.23 /45	-0.22 /14	0.74 /19	0.58	1.14
MMT	Federated VA Muni Cash Svc	VACXX	**C**	(800) 341-7400	**D / 2.0**	0.00	0.03	0.03 /38	0.02 /22	0.02 /10	0.03	0.87
MMT	Federated VA Muni Cash Tr Cash	VCSXX	**C**	(800) 341-7400	**D / 2.0**	0.00	0.03	0.03 /38	0.02 /22	0.02 /10	0.03	1.47
MMT	Federated VA Muni Cash Tr Wealth	VAIXX	**C**	(800) 341-7400	**D / 2.0**	0.00	0.03	0.03 /38	0.02 /22	0.02 /10	0.03	0.61
GES	Fidelity Adv 529 High Income A	FHCAX	**E+**	(800) 522-7297	**D- / 1.2**	2.67	0.21	-3.85 / 8	1.00 /43	3.82 /58	0.00	1.27
GES	Fidelity Adv 529 High Income B	FBBAX	**D-**	(800) 522-7297	**D / 1.6**	2.47	-0.19	-4.60 / 6	0.24 /29	3.04 /46	0.00	2.02
GES	Fidelity Adv 529 High Income C	FHPCX	**E+**	(800) 522-7297	**D- / 1.5**	2.45	-0.24	-4.65 / 6	0.14 /28	2.94 /44	0.00	2.12
GES	Fidelity Adv 529 High Income D	FHIDX	**D-**	(800) 522-7297	**D+ / 2.8**	2.57	0.04	-4.20 / 7	0.65 /36	3.46 /52	0.00	1.62
GES	Fidelity Adv 529 High Income P	FHIPX	**D-**	(800) 522-7297	**D / 1.8**	2.51	-0.09	-4.42 / 6	0.40 /31	3.19 /48	0.00	1.87
GEI	Fidelity Adv 529 Inflatn-Prot Bd A	FIPEX	**E+**	(800) 522-7297	**E / 0.5**	4.36	3.32	0.55 /50	-1.58 / 6	2.13 /33	0.00	0.85
GEI	Fidelity Adv 529 Inflatn-Prot Bd B	FIPGX	**E+**	(800) 522-7297	**E+ / 0.7**	4.18	2.89	-0.20 /29	-2.32 / 3	1.37 /24	0.00	1.60
GEI	Fidelity Adv 529 Inflatn-Prot Bd C	FICPX	**E+**	(800) 522-7297	**E+ / 0.6**	4.17	2.86	-0.27 /28	-2.41 / 3	1.27 /23	0.00	1.70

● Denotes fund is closed to new investors
* Denotes fund is included in Section II

RISK			NET ASSETS		ASSET							FUND MANAGER		MINIMUM		LOADS	
Risk Rating/Pts	3 Yr Avg Standard Deviation	Avg Duration	NAV As of 3/31/16	Total $(Mil)	Cash %	Gov. Bond %	Muni. Bond %	Corp. Bond %	Other %	Portfolio Turnover Ratio	Avg Coupon Rate	Manager Quality Pct	Manager Tenure (Years)	Initial Purch. $	Additional Purch. $	Front End Load	Back End Load
A+ / 9.7	0.7	1.0	8.49	405	7	3	0	37	53	10	1.9	72	21	1,000,000	0	0.0	0.0
A+ / 9.7	0.6	1.0	8.49	83	7	3	0	37	53	10	1.9	62	21	1,000,000	0	0.0	0.0
A+ / 9.6	0.7	1.0	8.50	504	7	3	0	37	53	10	1.9	78	21	100,000	0	0.0	0.0
U /	N/A	2.4	10.32	19	5	17	0	65	13	23	3.3	N/A	3	1,500	100	1.0	0.0
B / 7.9	2.5	2.4	10.32	199	5	17	0	65	13	23	3.3	64	3	1,000,000	0	0.0	0.0
U /	N/A	2.4	10.32	N/A	5	17	0	65	13	23	3.3	N/A	3	250	100	0.0	0.0
B / 7.9	2.5	2.4	10.31	28	5	17	0	65	13	23	3.3	52	3	1,000,000	0	0.0	0.0
D+ / 2.5	5.2	4.3	8.53	407	25	0	0	48	27	17	5.5	24	3	1,500	100	4.5	0.0
D+ / 2.5	5.2	4.3	8.52	64	25	0	0	48	27	17	5.5	13	3	1,500	100	0.0	0.0
D+ / 2.7	5.1	4.3	8.52	164	25	0	0	48	27	17	5.5	13	3	1,500	100	0.0	0.0
D+ / 2.6	5.2	4.3	8.48	73	25	0	0	48	27	17	5.5	26	3	1,500	100	1.0	0.0
D+ / 2.6	5.1	4.3	8.49	99	25	0	0	48	27	17	5.5	31	3	1,000,000	0	0.0	0.0
A+ / 9.9	N/A	N/A	1.00	5,484	100	0	0	0	0	0	0.0	N/A	N/A	500,000	0	0.0	0.0
A+ / 9.9	N/A	N/A	1.00	3,846	100	0	0	0	0	0	0.1	N/A	N/A	1,500	100	0.0	0.0
A+ / 9.9	N/A	N/A	1.00	52	100	0	0	0	0	0	0.1	N/A	N/A	25,000	0	0.0	0.0
A+ / 9.9	N/A	N/A	1.00	1,087	100	0	0	0	0	0	0.0	N/A	N/A	500,000	0	0.0	0.0
C+ / 6.8	2.9	4.7	10.84	378	10	14	0	48	28	30	4.2	54	3	1,500	100	4.5	0.0
C+ / 6.8	2.9	4.7	10.84	22	10	14	0	48	28	30	4.2	35	3	1,500	100	0.0	0.0
C+ / 6.8	2.9	4.7	10.84	95	10	14	0	48	28	30	4.2	36	3	1,500	100	0.0	0.0
C+ / 6.8	2.9	4.7	10.84	5,043	10	14	0	48	28	30	4.2	78	3	1,000,000	0	0.0	0.0
C+ / 6.8	2.9	4.7	10.84	65	10	14	0	48	28	30	4.2	49	3	0	0	0.0	0.0
U /	N/A	4.7	10.84	111	10	14	0	48	28	30	4.2	N/A	3	0	0	0.0	0.0
C+ / 6.8	2.9	4.7	10.84	600	10	14	0	48	28	30	4.2	66	3	1,000,000	0	0.0	0.0
B- / 7.4	2.8	5.1	11.11	520	7	47	0	0	46	58	2.4	50	13	1,000,000	0	0.0	0.0
B- / 7.3	2.8	5.1	11.11	118	7	47	0	0	46	58	2.4	38	13	1,000,000	0	0.0	0.0
U /	N/A	N/A	1.00	2,092	0	0	0	0	100	0	0.0	N/A	23	25,000	0	0.0	0.0
U /	N/A	N/A	1.00	750	100	0	0	0	0	0	0.0	N/A	23	500,000	0	0.0	0.0
A+ / 9.9	N/A	N/A	1.00	20,120	100	0	0	0	0	0	0.1	65	23	500,000	0	0.0	0.0
U /	N/A	N/A	1.00	3,620	100	0	0	0	0	0	0.0	N/A	23	500,000	0	0.0	0.0
U /	N/A	N/A	1.00	677	100	0	0	0	0	0	0.0	N/A	23	500,000	0	0.0	0.0
A+ / 9.9	N/A	N/A	1.00	152	100	0	0	0	0	0	0.0	63	N/A	25,000	0	0.0	0.0
A+ / 9.8	0.5	0.4	9.07	314	12	0	1	34	53	21	1.6	53	18	1,500	100	2.0	0.0
A+ / 9.8	0.6	0.4	9.07	2,298	12	0	1	34	53	21	1.6	78	18	1,000,000	0	0.0	0.0
A+ / 9.8	0.6	0.4	9.07	144	12	0	1	34	53	21	1.6	56	18	1,000,000	0	0.0	0.0
A+ / 9.6	0.7	1.6	10.43	7	0	99	0	0	1	222	1.1	36	11	1,000,000	0	0.0	0.0
B+ / 8.6	1.9	3.4	11.10	54	0	99	0	0	1	252	1.5	N/A	3	1,000,000	0	0.0	0.0
A+ / 9.9	N/A	N/A	1.00	14,020	100	0	0	0	0	0	0.0	63	22	25,000	0	0.0	0.0
U /	0.7	1.6	10.44	77	0	99	0	0	1	222	1.1	N/A	11	1,000,000	0	0.0	0.0
A+ / 9.6	0.7	1.6	10.44	72	0	99	0	0	1	222	1.1	53	11	100,000	0	0.0	0.0
B+ / 8.6	1.9	3.4	11.10	416	0	99	0	0	1	252	1.5	30	3	1,000,000	0	0.0	0.0
B+ / 8.6	1.9	3.4	11.10	14	0	99	0	0	1	252	1.5	18	3	250	100	0.0	0.0
A+ / 9.9	N/A	N/A	1.00	163	100	0	0	0	0	0	0.0	N/A	N/A	10,000	0	0.0	0.0
A+ / 9.9	N/A	N/A	1.00	128	100	0	0	0	0	0	0.0	N/A	N/A	1,000	0	0.0	0.0
A+ / 9.9	N/A	N/A	1.00	43	100	0	0	0	0	0	0.0	N/A	N/A	25,000	0	0.0	0.0
D / 1.8	5.9	N/A	23.48	13	3	0	0	91	6	10	0.0	42	11	1,000	50	4.8	0.0
D / 1.8	5.9	N/A	21.15	N/A	3	0	0	91	6	10	0.0	21	11	1,000	50	0.0	0.0
D / 1.7	5.9	N/A	20.90	5	3	0	0	91	6	10	0.0	19	11	1,000	50	0.0	0.0
D / 1.7	5.9	N/A	22.38	N/A	3	0	0	91	6	10	0.0	31	11	1,000	50	0.0	0.0
D / 1.8	5.9	N/A	21.65	N/A	3	0	0	91	6	10	0.0	25	11	1,000	50	0.0	0.0
D / 2.2	5.5	N/A	16.51	13	0	100	0	0	0	12	0.0	2	11	1,000	50	4.8	0.0
D / 2.2	5.5	N/A	14.94	N/A	0	100	0	0	0	12	0.0	1	11	1,000	50	0.0	0.0
D / 2.2	5.5	N/A	14.73	6	0	100	0	0	0	12	0.0	1	11	1,000	50	0.0	0.0

Fund Type	Fund Name (99 Pct = Best, 0 Pct = Worst)	Ticker Symbol	Overall Investment Rating	Phone	PERFORMANCE: Performance Rating/Pts	Total Return % through 3/31/16: 3 Mo	6 Mo	1Yr / Pct	Annualized: 3Yr / Pct	Annualized: 5Yr / Pct	Incl. in Returns: Dividend Yield	Incl. in Returns: Expense Ratio
GEI	Fidelity Adv 529 Inflatn-Prot Bd D	FIDDX	**E+**	(800) 522-7297	**E+ / 0.9**	4.24	3.15	0.19 /44	-1.94 / 5	1.77 /28	0.00	1.20
GEI	Fidelity Adv 529 Inflatn-Prot Bd P	FIPPX	**E+**	(800) 522-7297	**E+ / 0.7**	4.23	3.04	--	-2.17 / 4	1.52 /26	0.00	1.45
GEI	Fidelity Adv 529 Ltd Term Bond A	FLTAX	**C-**	(800) 522-7297	**D+ / 2.6**	1.48	0.98	0.86 /56	0.90 /41	2.45 /37	0.00	0.88
GEI	Fidelity Adv 529 Ltd Term Bond B	FLTBX	**C-**	(800) 522-7297	**D+ / 2.9**	1.29	0.54	0.07 /40	0.13 /28	1.68 /27	0.00	1.63
GEI	Fidelity Adv 529 Ltd Term Bond C	FLBCX	**C-**	(800) 522-7297	**D+ / 2.8**	1.31	0.55	--	0.05 /24	1.58 /26	0.00	1.73
GEI	Fidelity Adv 529 Ltd Term Bond D	FLDDX	**C**	(800) 522-7297	**C- / 3.7**	1.42	0.83	0.51 /50	0.56 /34	2.11 /32	0.00	1.23
GEI	Fidelity Adv 529 Ltd Term Bond P	FLTPX	**C**	(800) 522-7297	**C- / 3.2**	1.33	0.66	0.26 /45	0.29 /30	1.85 /29	0.00	1.48
GES	Fidelity Adv 529 Strat Inc A	FBBGX	**D**	(800) 522-7297	**D+ / 2.8**	2.98	2.25	-0.86 /23	1.35 /49	3.24 /49	0.00	1.13
GES	Fidelity Adv 529 Strat Inc B	FSMBX	**D**	(800) 522-7297	**C- / 3.7**	2.76	1.85	-1.60 /18	0.59 /35	2.46 /37	0.00	1.88
GES	Fidelity Adv 529 Strat Inc C	FSXMX	**D**	(800) 522-7297	**C- / 3.5**	2.79	1.86	-1.68 /17	0.49 /33	2.37 /36	0.00	1.98
GES	Fidelity Adv 529 Strat Inc P	FSXPX	**D**	(800) 522-7297	**C- / 3.9**	2.78	1.94	-1.45 /19	0.73 /37	2.62 /39	0.00	1.73
MUS	Fidelity Adv CA Muni Inc A	FCMAX	**B+**	(800) 522-7297	**B+ / 8.9**	1.68	3.18	3.64 /91	4.05 /96	6.27 /94	2.80	0.79
MUS ●	Fidelity Adv CA Muni Inc B	FCMBX	**A-**	(800) 522-7297	**A- / 9.2**	1.61	2.87	3.03 /85	3.44 /92	5.65 /90	2.34	1.37
MUS	Fidelity Adv CA Muni Inc C	FCMKX	**B+**	(800) 522-7297	**A- / 9.1**	1.58	2.80	2.87 /84	3.27 /91	5.48 /89	2.18	1.54
MUS	Fidelity Adv CA Muni Inc I	FCMQX	**A**	(800) 522-7297	**A+ / 9.7**	1.82	3.30	3.89 /93	4.29 /97	6.53 /95	3.16	0.55
MUS	Fidelity Adv CA Muni Inc T	FCMTX	**B+**	(800) 522-7297	**B+ / 8.9**	1.70	3.20	3.69 /92	4.10 /96	6.32 /94	2.86	0.72
EM	Fidelity Adv Emerging Mkts Inc A	FMKAX	**D-**	(800) 522-7297	**C- / 3.9**	4.52	5.61	3.52 /79	0.97 /42	5.14 /73	4.76	1.18
EM ●	Fidelity Adv Emerging Mkts Inc B	FBEMX	**D**	(800) 522-7297	**C / 4.4**	4.30	5.20	2.80 /76	0.24 /29	4.40 /66	4.25	1.89
EM	Fidelity Adv Emerging Mkts Inc C	FMKCX	**D**	(800) 522-7297	**C / 4.4**	4.31	5.19	2.76 /76	0.23 /29	4.37 /66	4.22	1.93
EM	Fidelity Adv Emerging Mkts Inc I	FMKIX	**D**	(800) 522-7297	**C+ / 6.3**	4.58	5.65	3.79 /80	1.23 /47	5.43 /74	5.25	0.89
EM	Fidelity Adv Emerging Mkts Inc T	FAEMX	**D-**	(800) 522-7297	**C- / 3.8**	4.52	5.51	3.47 /79	0.93 /41	5.11 /73	4.72	1.22
* LP	Fidelity Adv Float-Rate Hi-Inc A	FFRAX	**D+**	(800) 522-7297	**D- / 1.2**	1.39	-0.70	-2.06 /15	0.71 /37	1.99 /31	3.83	0.98
LP ●	Fidelity Adv Float-Rate Hi-Inc B	FFRBX	**D+**	(800) 522-7297	**D- / 1.4**	1.27	-0.84	-2.43 /14	0.23 /29	1.49 /26	3.45	1.50
LP	Fidelity Adv Float-Rate Hi-Inc C	FFRCX	**D+**	(800) 522-7297	**D- / 1.2**	1.20	-1.07	-2.69 /12	-0.01 /15	1.25 /23	3.17	1.73
LP	Fidelity Adv Float-Rate Hi-Inc I	FFRIX	**C-**	(800) 522-7297	**C- / 3.2**	1.45	-0.59	-1.74 /17	0.97 /42	2.23 /34	4.18	0.74
LP	Fidelity Adv Float-Rate Hi-Inc T	FFRTX	**D+**	(800) 522-7297	**D- / 1.2**	1.37	-0.65	-2.05 /15	0.65 /36	1.92 /30	3.74	1.07
GL	Fidelity Adv Global Bond A	FGBZX	**D-**	(800) 544-8544	**D- / 1.3**	5.50	4.20	1.51 /66	-0.45 /12	--	2.33	1.46
GL	Fidelity Adv Global Bond C	FGBYX	**D-**	(800) 544-8544	**D- / 1.5**	5.27	3.85	0.67 /53	-1.24 / 7	--	1.73	2.25
GL	Fidelity Adv Global Bond I	FGBIX	**D**	(800) 544-8544	**C- / 4.0**	5.55	4.33	1.77 /69	-0.24 /14	--	2.68	1.14
GL	Fidelity Adv Global Bond T	FGBWX	**D-**	(800) 544-8544	**D- / 1.3**	5.40	4.09	1.41 /65	-0.48 /12	--	2.34	1.48
USS	Fidelity Adv Govt Inc A	FVIAX	**C**	(800) 522-7297	**C- / 4.2**	2.65	1.72	1.59 /67	1.71 /56	2.97 /44	1.26	0.77
USS ●	Fidelity Adv Govt Inc B	FVIBX	**C**	(800) 522-7297	**C / 4.6**	2.47	1.26	0.77 /55	0.94 /41	2.21 /34	0.60	1.50
USS	Fidelity Adv Govt Inc C	FVICX	**C**	(800) 522-7297	**C / 4.6**	2.46	1.23	0.71 /53	0.90 /41	2.17 /33	0.55	1.55
USS	Fidelity Adv Govt Inc I	FVIIX	**B**	(800) 522-7297	**C+ / 6.4**	2.62	1.76	1.76 /69	1.95 /60	3.22 /48	1.57	0.50
USS	Fidelity Adv Govt Inc T	FVITX	**C-**	(800) 522-7297	**C- / 4.2**	2.65	1.63	1.50 /66	1.69 /56	2.97 /45	1.27	0.76
* COH	Fidelity Adv Hi Income Advantage A	FAHDX	**D-**	(800) 522-7297	**C- / 3.2**	1.35	0.19	-4.84 / 5	2.63 /72	4.75 /70	4.83	1.02
COH ●	Fidelity Adv Hi Income Advantage B	FAHBX	**D-**	(800) 522-7297	**C- / 3.8**	1.17	-0.08	-5.47 / 4	1.91 /60	4.02 /62	4.30	1.74
COH	Fidelity Adv Hi Income Advantage C	FAHEX	**D-**	(800) 522-7297	**C- / 3.8**	1.27	-0.09	-5.47 / 4	1.90 /59	3.98 /61	4.24	1.77
COH	Fidelity Adv Hi Income Advantage I	FAHCX	**D**	(800) 522-7297	**C+ / 5.7**	1.42	0.35	-4.56 / 6	2.90 /75	5.01 /72	5.26	0.78
COH	Fidelity Adv Hi Income Advantage T	FAHYX	**D-**	(800) 522-7297	**C- / 3.4**	1.45	0.31	-4.78 / 5	2.67 /73	4.77 /70	4.83	1.01
COH	Fidelity Adv High Income A	FHIAX	**E+**	(800) 522-7297	**D- / 1.3**	2.67	0.24	-3.63 / 9	1.19 /46	3.99 /61	5.49	1.03
COH ●	Fidelity Adv High Income B	FHCBX	**E+**	(800) 522-7297	**D / 1.6**	2.51	0.03	-4.31 / 7	0.48 /33	3.27 /49	5.00	1.73
COH	Fidelity Adv High Income C	FHNCX	**E+**	(800) 522-7297	**D- / 1.5**	2.49	-0.01	-4.38 / 7	0.42 /32	3.21 /48	4.92	1.80
COH	Fidelity Adv High Income I	FHNIX	**D-**	(800) 522-7297	**C- / 3.7**	2.72	0.34	-3.56 / 9	1.33 /49	4.17 /64	5.91	0.87
COH	Fidelity Adv High Income T	FHITX	**E+**	(800) 522-7297	**D- / 1.3**	2.67	0.36	-3.66 / 9	1.17 /46	3.97 /61	5.46	1.05
GES	Fidelity Adv Inflation-Protect Bd A	FIPAX	**E+**	(800) 522-7297	**E+ / 0.6**	4.43	3.33	0.65 /52	-1.48 / 6	2.24 /34	0.00	0.78
GES ●	Fidelity Adv Inflation-Protect Bd B	FBIPX	**E+**	(800) 522-7297	**E+ / 0.8**	4.22	2.99	-0.01 /31	-2.15 / 4	1.54 /26	0.00	1.46
GES	Fidelity Adv Inflation-Protect Bd C	FIPCX	**E+**	(800) 522-7297	**E+ / 0.7**	4.14	2.92	-0.10 /30	-2.21 / 4	1.47 /25	0.00	1.54
GES	Fidelity Adv Inflation-Protect Bd I	FIPIX	**D-**	(800) 522-7297	**D- / 1.5**	4.43	3.47	0.90 /57	-1.23 / 7	2.48 /38	0.16	0.52
GES	Fidelity Adv Inflation-Protect Bd T	FIPTX	**E+**	(800) 522-7297	**E+ / 0.6**	4.34	3.33	0.65 /52	-1.50 / 6	2.20 /34	0.00	0.81
MUN	Fidelity Adv Interm Municipal Inc A	FZIAX	**B+**	(800) 522-7297	**C+ / 6.4**	1.21	2.27	2.34 /79	2.40 /82	3.84 /76	2.11	0.69
MUN ●	Fidelity Adv Interm Municipal Inc B	FZIBX	**A**	(800) 522-7297	**B- / 7.4**	1.06	1.98	1.78 /75	1.80 /74	3.24 /72	1.66	1.24

● Denotes fund is closed to new investors
* Denotes fund is included in Section II

RISK			NET ASSETS		ASSET							FUND MANAGER		MINIMUM		LOADS	
Risk Rating/Pts	3 Yr Avg Standard Deviation	Avg Duration	NAV As of 3/31/16	Total $(Mil)	Cash %	Gov. Bond %	Muni. Bond %	Corp. Bond %	Other %	Portfolio Turnover Ratio	Avg Coupon Rate	Manager Quality Pct	Manager Tenure (Years)	Initial Purch. $	Additional Purch. $	Front End Load	Back End Load
D / 2.2	5.5	N/A	15.73	N/A	0	100	0	0	0	12	0.0	2	11	1,000	50	0.0	0.0
D / 2.2	5.5	N/A	15.26	N/A	0	100	0	0	0	12	0.0	2	11	1,000	50	0.0	0.0
B+ / 8.5	1.9	N/A	16.51	21	1	4	0	73	22	15	0.0	43	11	1,000	50	3.8	0.0
B+ / 8.5	2.0	N/A	14.90	N/A	1	4	0	73	22	15	0.0	21	11	1,000	50	0.0	0.0
B+ / 8.5	1.9	N/A	14.71	10	1	4	0	73	22	15	0.0	20	11	1,000	50	0.0	0.0
B+ / 8.5	1.9	N/A	15.75	2	1	4	0	73	22	15	0.0	32	11	1,000	50	0.0	0.0
B+ / 8.5	2.0	N/A	15.22	N/A	1	4	0	73	22	15	0.0	25	11	1,000	50	0.0	0.0
C- / 3.3	4.5	N/A	17.30	41	4	29	0	19	48	9	0.0	36	11	1,000	50	4.8	0.0
C- / 3.3	4.5	N/A	16.00	1	4	29	0	19	48	9	0.0	18	11	1,000	50	0.0	0.0
C- / 3.2	4.5	N/A	15.84	27	4	29	0	19	48	9	0.0	16	11	1,000	50	0.0	0.0
C- / 3.3	4.5	N/A	16.26	N/A	4	29	0	19	48	9	0.0	20	11	1,000	50	0.0	0.0
C / 4.7	3.6	6.0	13.26	48	0	0	100	0	0	10	0.0	75	10	2,500	0	4.0	0.5
C / 4.7	3.6	6.0	13.25	N/A	0	0	100	0	0	10	0.0	49	10	2,500	0	0.0	0.5
C / 4.7	3.6	6.0	13.24	26	0	0	100	0	0	10	0.0	43	10	2,500	0	0.0	0.5
C / 4.8	3.6	6.0	13.27	47	0	0	100	0	0	10	0.0	82	10	2,500	0	0.0	0.5
C / 4.7	3.6	6.0	13.29	8	0	0	100	0	0	10	0.0	77	10	2,500	0	4.0	0.5
E / 0.4	8.0	7.3	13.16	230	2	74	0	22	2	143	0.0	90	21	2,500	0	4.0	1.0
E / 0.4	8.0	7.3	13.32	4	2	74	0	22	2	143	0.0	79	21	2,500	0	0.0	1.0
E / 0.4	8.0	7.3	13.26	96	2	74	0	22	2	143	0.0	78	21	2,500	0	0.0	1.0
E / 0.4	7.9	7.3	12.90	2,731	2	74	0	22	2	143	0.0	92	21	2,500	0	0.0	1.0
E / 0.4	8.0	7.3	13.10	75	2	74	0	22	2	143	0.0	90	21	2,500	0	4.0	1.0
B- / 7.4	2.7	0.3	9.18	718	5	0	0	82	13	26	0.0	71	3	2,500	0	2.8	1.0
B- / 7.4	2.8	0.3	9.17	9	5	0	0	82	13	26	0.0	47	3	2,500	0	0.0	1.0
B- / 7.3	2.8	0.3	9.18	587	5	0	0	82	13	26	0.0	38	3	2,500	0	0.0	1.0
B- / 7.4	2.8	0.3	9.16	1,980	5	0	0	82	13	26	0.0	79	3	2,500	0	0.0	1.0
B- / 7.2	2.8	0.3	9.17	171	5	0	0	82	13	26	0.0	64	3	2,500	0	2.8	1.0
D+ / 2.6	5.1	N/A	9.12	5	0	32	0	24	44	227	0.0	49	4	2,500	0	4.0	0.0
D+ / 2.6	5.2	N/A	9.10	4	0	32	0	24	44	227	0.0	25	4	2,500	0	0.0	0.0
D+ / 2.6	5.1	N/A	9.12	3	0	32	0	24	44	227	0.0	57	4	2,500	0	0.0	0.0
D+ / 2.7	5.1	N/A	9.11	3	0	32	0	24	44	227	0.0	48	4	2,500	0	4.0	0.0
B- / 7.1	2.8	5.1	10.56	255	1	47	0	0	52	83	0.0	53	9	2,500	0	4.0	0.0
B- / 7.0	2.9	5.1	10.55	4	1	47	0	0	52	83	0.0	27	9	2,500	0	0.0	0.0
B- / 7.0	2.9	5.1	10.55	87	1	47	0	0	52	83	0.0	26	9	2,500	0	0.0	0.0
B- / 7.0	2.9	5.1	10.55	452	1	47	0	0	52	83	0.0	61	9	2,500	0	0.0	0.0
B- / 7.0	2.9	5.1	10.55	196	1	47	0	0	52	83	0.0	51	9	2,500	0	4.0	0.0
E+ / 0.6	6.7	3.8	9.91	558	4	0	0	76	20	42	0.0	86	7	2,500	0	4.0	1.0
E+ / 0.6	6.8	3.8	9.84	4	4	0	0	76	20	42	0.0	62	7	2,500	0	0.0	1.0
E+ / 0.6	6.8	3.8	9.90	148	4	0	0	76	20	42	0.0	61	7	2,500	0	0.0	1.0
E+ / 0.6	6.8	3.8	9.30	661	4	0	0	76	20	42	0.0	89	7	2,500	0	0.0	1.0
E+ / 0.6	6.8	3.8	9.97	380	4	0	0	76	20	42	0.0	87	7	2,500	0	4.0	1.0
D- / 1.1	6.0	4.1	7.27	200	2	0	0	95	3	60	0.0	42	15	2,500	0	4.0	1.0
D- / 1.1	6.0	4.1	7.25	4	2	0	0	95	3	60	0.0	22	15	2,500	0	0.0	1.0
D- / 1.1	6.0	4.1	7.25	84	2	0	0	95	3	60	0.0	21	15	2,500	0	0.0	1.0
D- / 1.2	5.9	4.1	7.28	368	2	0	0	95	3	60	0.0	48	15	2,500	0	0.0	1.0
D- / 1.1	5.9	4.1	7.26	64	2	0	0	95	3	60	0.0	41	15	2,500	0	4.0	1.0
D / 2.2	5.5	5.6	12.03	91	0	100	0	0	0	20	0.0	2	12	2,500	0	4.0	0.0
D / 2.2	5.5	5.6	11.62	5	0	100	0	0	0	20	0.0	2	12	2,500	0	0.0	0.0
D+ / 2.3	5.5	5.6	11.56	56	0	100	0	0	0	20	0.0	2	12	2,500	0	0.0	0.0
D / 2.2	5.5	5.6	12.11	152	0	100	0	0	0	20	0.0	3	12	2,500	0	0.0	0.0
D / 2.2	5.5	5.6	12.03	28	0	100	0	0	0	20	0.0	2	12	2,500	0	4.0	0.0
B / 7.6	2.7	4.8	10.58	152	0	0	100	0	0	17	0.0	47	10	2,500	0	4.0	0.5
B / 7.6	2.7	4.8	10.58	1	0	0	100	0	0	17	0.0	29	10	2,500	0	0.0	0.5

Fund Type	Fund Name (99 Pct = Best, 0 Pct = Worst)	Ticker Symbol	Overall Investment Rating	Phone	PERFORMANCE: Performance Rating/Pts	Total Return % through 3/31/16: 3 Mo	6 Mo	1Yr / Pct	Annualized: 3Yr / Pct	5Yr / Pct	Incl. in Returns: Dividend Yield	Expense Ratio
MUN	Fidelity Adv Interm Municipal Inc C	FZICX	**A-**	(800) 522-7297	**C+ / 6.9**	0.93	1.90	1.49 /74	1.59 /70	3.05 /70	1.47	1.44
MUN	Fidelity Adv Interm Municipal Inc I	FZIIX	**A+**	(800) 522-7297	**B+ / 8.5**	1.27	2.40	2.60 /81	2.65 /84	4.11 /78	2.45	0.44
MUN	Fidelity Adv Interm Municipal Inc T	FZITX	**B+**	(800) 522-7297	**C+ / 6.4**	1.12	2.29	2.29 /79	2.40 /82	3.86 /77	2.16	0.65
GL	Fidelity Adv International Bond A	FINWX	**E**	(800) 544-8544	**D- / 1.0**	7.37	6.09	3.21 /78	-1.58 / 6	--	2.07	1.42
GL	Fidelity Adv International Bond C	FINRX	**E**	(800) 544-8544	**D- / 1.1**	7.11	5.61	2.34 /74	-2.36 / 3	--	1.45	2.25
GL	Fidelity Adv International Bond I	FINOX	**D-**	(800) 544-8544	**C- / 3.1**	7.40	6.24	3.36 /78	-1.36 / 7	--	2.40	1.15
GL	Fidelity Adv International Bond T	FINTX	**E**	(800) 544-8544	**D- / 1.0**	7.24	6.00	3.10 /77	-1.61 / 6	--	2.08	1.49
GEI	Fidelity Adv Invt Grade Bond A	FGBAX	**D+**	(800) 522-7297	**C- / 3.4**	3.12	1.76	-0.43 /27	1.48 /52	3.33 /50	2.39	0.77
GEI •	Fidelity Adv Invt Grade Bond B	FGBBX	**C-**	(800) 522-7297	**C- / 4.0**	2.93	1.40	-1.14 /21	0.75 /38	2.61 /39	1.76	1.50
GEI	Fidelity Adv Invt Grade Bond C	FGBCX	**C-**	(800) 522-7297	**C- / 3.9**	2.92	1.38	-1.18 /20	0.72 /37	2.59 /39	1.73	1.52
GEI	Fidelity Adv Invt Grade Bond I	FGBPX	**C**	(800) 522-7297	**C+ / 5.9**	3.05	1.89	-0.16 /30	1.75 /57	3.61 /55	2.75	0.50
GEI	Fidelity Adv Invt Grade Bond T	FGBTX	**D+**	(800) 522-7297	**C- / 3.4**	2.97	1.74	-0.47 /26	1.45 /51	3.31 /50	2.35	0.80
COI	Fidelity Adv Limited Term Bond	FJRLX	**B**	(800) 522-7297	**C / 5.2**	1.67	1.17	1.24 /62	1.29 /48	2.84 /43	1.83	0.45
GEI	Fidelity Adv Limited Term Bond A	FDIAX	**C**	(800) 522-7297	**C- / 3.2**	1.51	1.02	0.93 /57	0.99 /42	2.55 /38	1.48	0.76
GEI •	Fidelity Adv Limited Term Bond B	FIBBX	**C**	(800) 522-7297	**C- / 3.2**	1.42	0.74	0.28 /45	0.27 /30	1.83 /29	0.80	1.46
GEI	Fidelity Adv Limited Term Bond C	FNBCX	**C**	(800) 522-7297	**C- / 3.1**	1.41	0.72	0.24 /45	0.22 /29	1.80 /29	0.76	1.54
GEI	Fidelity Adv Limited Term Bond I	EFIPX	**B**	(800) 522-7297	**C / 5.1**	1.57	1.15	1.19 /61	1.25 /47	2.81 /42	1.78	0.50
GEI	Fidelity Adv Limited Term Bond T	FTBRX	**C**	(800) 522-7297	**C- / 3.3**	1.59	1.10	0.92 /57	1.00 /43	2.59 /39	1.48	0.76
MUN	Fidelity Adv Ltd Term Muni Inc A	FASHX	**C**	(800) 522-7297	**C- / 3.0**	0.65	0.92	1.06 /68	0.93 /51	1.73 /40	1.14	0.81
MUN •	Fidelity Adv Ltd Term Muni Inc B	FBSHX	**C**	(800) 522-7297	**C- / 3.1**	0.41	0.62	0.47 /54	0.28 /32	1.07 /27	0.59	1.40
MUN	Fidelity Adv Ltd Term Muni Inc C	FCSHX	**C**	(800) 522-7297	**D+ / 2.8**	0.47	0.55	0.32 /49	0.18 /30	0.97 /26	0.44	1.55
MUN	Fidelity Adv Ltd Term Muni Inc I	FISHX	**A-**	(800) 522-7297	**C+ / 5.8**	0.71	1.14	1.41 /73	1.18 /58	1.98 /46	1.43	0.55
MUN	Fidelity Adv Ltd Term Muni Inc T	FTSHX	**C**	(800) 522-7297	**C- / 3.1**	0.66	0.94	1.11 /69	0.97 /52	1.76 /40	1.18	0.77
MTG	Fidelity Adv Mortgage Secs A	FMGAX	**C+**	(800) 522-7297	**C / 4.8**	1.79	1.39	1.77 /69	2.17 /65	3.22 /48	1.88	0.81
MTG •	Fidelity Adv Mortgage Secs B	FMSBX	**B-**	(800) 522-7297	**C / 5.4**	1.62	1.04	1.15 /61	1.47 /51	2.51 /38	1.26	1.50
MTG	Fidelity Adv Mortgage Secs C	FOMCX	**C+**	(800) 522-7297	**C / 5.3**	1.52	1.02	1.03 /59	1.44 /51	2.47 /37	1.23	1.53
MTG	Fidelity Adv Mortgage Secs I	FMSCX	**A**	(800) 522-7297	**B- / 7.1**	1.87	1.53	2.16 /73	2.48 /70	3.53 /53	2.25	0.50
MTG	Fidelity Adv Mortgage Secs T	FMSAX	**C+**	(800) 522-7297	**C / 4.9**	1.79	1.47	1.86 /70	2.21 /66	3.26 /49	1.88	0.79
MUH	Fidelity Adv Muni Income A	FAMUX	**C+**	(800) 522-7297	**B+ / 8.6**	1.47	3.09	3.24 /87	3.69 /94	5.82 /91	2.96	0.79
MUH •	Fidelity Adv Muni Income B	FAIBX	**B-**	(800) 522-7297	**A- / 9.0**	1.40	2.80	2.65 /82	3.05 /88	5.14 /86	2.51	1.45
MUH	Fidelity Adv Muni Income C	FAMCX	**B-**	(800) 522-7297	**B+ / 8.9**	1.36	2.78	2.55 /81	2.93 /87	5.03 /86	2.35	1.55
MUH	Fidelity Adv Muni Income I	FMPIX	**B+**	(800) 522-7297	**A / 9.5**	1.61	3.23	3.50 /90	3.96 /96	6.09 /92	3.33	0.54
MUH	Fidelity Adv Muni Income T	FAHIX	**C+**	(800) 522-7297	**B+ / 8.7**	1.54	3.17	3.33 /88	3.72 /94	5.85 /91	2.97	0.78
MUS	Fidelity Adv NY Muni Income A	FNMAX	**B**	(800) 522-7297	**B+ / 8.4**	1.71	3.11	4.02 /94	3.50 /93	5.18 /87	2.60	0.78
MUS •	Fidelity Adv NY Muni Income B	FNYBX	**B+**	(800) 522-7297	**B+ / 8.9**	1.56	2.81	3.42 /89	2.90 /87	4.55 /82	2.13	1.38
MUS	Fidelity Adv NY Muni Income C	FNYCX	**B+**	(800) 522-7297	**B+ / 8.7**	1.52	2.74	3.26 /87	2.74 /85	4.39 /81	1.98	1.52
MUS	Fidelity Adv NY Muni Income I	FEMIX	**A**	(800) 522-7297	**A / 9.5**	1.77	3.24	4.29 /96	3.77 /94	5.44 /88	2.95	0.53
MUS	Fidelity Adv NY Muni Income T	FNYPX	**B**	(800) 522-7297	**B+ / 8.5**	1.65	3.14	4.08 /94	3.56 /93	5.23 /87	2.65	0.73
GEI	Fidelity Adv Short-Fixed Income A	FSFAX	**C+**	(800) 522-7297	**C- / 3.3**	0.83	0.60	0.77 /55	0.76 /38	1.17 /22	0.96	0.70
GEI •	Fidelity Adv Short-Fixed Income B	FBSFX	**C-**	(800) 522-7297	**D / 1.8**	0.65	0.18	-0.03 /31	-0.07 /15	0.37 /16	0.29	1.45
GEI	Fidelity Adv Short-Fixed Income C	FSFCX	**C-**	(800) 522-7297	**D / 1.8**	0.65	0.18	-0.14 /30	-0.11 /15	0.32 /16	0.29	1.55
GEI	Fidelity Adv Short-Fixed Income I	FSXIX	**B**	(800) 522-7297	**C / 4.4**	0.97	0.68	0.92 /57	0.93 /41	1.37 /24	1.13	0.53
GEI	Fidelity Adv Short-Fixed Income T	FASFX	**C+**	(800) 522-7297	**C- / 3.2**	0.93	0.60	0.76 /54	0.75 /38	1.19 /22	0.96	0.70
* GES	Fidelity Adv Strategic Income A	FSTAX	**D**	(800) 522-7297	**C- / 3.4**	2.94	2.24	-0.76 /24	1.44 /51	3.35 /51	3.12	1.00
GES •	Fidelity Adv Strategic Income B	FSINX	**D**	(800) 522-7297	**C- / 4.0**	2.76	1.98	-1.42 /19	0.75 /38	2.65 /40	2.57	1.69
GES	Fidelity Adv Strategic Income C	FSRCX	**D**	(800) 522-7297	**C- / 3.8**	2.76	1.87	-1.50 /18	0.69 /37	2.59 /39	2.50	1.75
GES	Fidelity Adv Strategic Income I	FSRIX	**C-**	(800) 522-7297	**C+ / 5.8**	3.06	2.43	-0.48 /26	1.70 /56	3.61 /55	3.47	0.78
GES	Fidelity Adv Strategic Income T	FSIAX	**D**	(800) 522-7297	**C- / 3.4**	2.94	2.24	-0.76 /24	1.44 /51	3.36 /51	3.12	1.00
COI	Fidelity Advisor Corporate Bond A	FCBAX	**D+**	(800) 522-7297	**C / 4.7**	3.04	2.35	-0.89 /23	2.27 /67	5.01 /72	2.84	0.79
COI	Fidelity Advisor Corporate Bond C	FCCCX	**D+**	(800) 522-7297	**C / 5.1**	2.85	1.97	-1.63 /18	1.49 /52	4.22 /64	2.21	1.55
COI	Fidelity Advisor Corporate Bond I	FCBIX	**C-**	(800) 522-7297	**B- / 7.0**	3.11	2.49	-0.60 /25	2.55 /71	5.30 /74	3.24	0.50
COI	Fidelity Advisor Corporate Bond T	FCBTX	**D+**	(800) 522-7297	**C / 4.6**	3.02	2.31	-0.96 /22	2.20 /66	4.96 /71	2.77	0.86

• Denotes fund is closed to new investors
* Denotes fund is included in Section II

RISK			NET ASSETS		ASSET							FUND MANAGER		MINIMUM		LOADS	
Risk Rating/Pts	3 Yr Avg Standard Deviation	Avg Duration	NAV As of 3/31/16	Total $(Mil)	Cash %	Gov. Bond %	Muni. Bond %	Corp. Bond %	Other %	Portfolio Turnover Ratio	Avg Coupon Rate	Manager Quality Pct	Manager Tenure (Years)	Initial Purch. $	Additional Purch. $	Front End Load	Back End Load
B / 7.6	2.7	4.8	10.58	63	0	0	100	0	0	17	0.0	24	10	2,500	0	0.0	0.5
B / 7.6	2.7	4.8	10.59	689	0	0	100	0	0	17	0.0	57	10	2,500	0	0.0	0.5
B / 7.6	2.6	4.8	10.57	20	0	0	100	0	0	17	0.0	48	10	2,500	0	4.0	0.5
E+ / 0.7	7.0	N/A	8.78	3	10	50	0	15	25	145	0.0	19	4	2,500	0	4.0	0.0
E+ / 0.7	7.0	N/A	8.76	3	10	50	0	15	25	145	0.0	10	4	2,500	0	0.0	0.0
E+ / 0.7	7.0	N/A	8.78	2	10	50	0	15	25	145	0.0	23	4	2,500	0	0.0	0.0
E+ / 0.7	7.0	N/A	8.77	3	10	50	0	15	25	145	0.0	18	4	2,500	0	4.0	0.0
C+ / 5.6	3.2	5.3	7.76	75	6	24	1	39	30	182	0.0	28	12	2,500	0	4.0	0.0
C+ / 5.6	3.2	5.3	7.77	1	6	24	1	39	30	182	0.0	14	12	2,500	0	0.0	0.0
C+ / 5.6	3.2	5.3	7.77	28	6	24	1	39	30	182	0.0	14	12	2,500	0	0.0	0.0
C / 5.5	3.3	5.3	7.77	504	6	24	1	39	30	182	0.0	34	12	2,500	0	0.0	0.0
C / 5.4	3.3	5.3	7.76	20	6	24	1	39	30	182	0.0	26	12	2,500	0	4.0	0.0
B+ / 8.5	2.0	2.6	11.49	829	0	4	0	74	22	44	0.0	71	7	2,500	0	0.0	0.0
B+ / 8.5	1.9	2.6	11.46	315	0	4	0	74	22	44	0.0	46	7	2,500	0	2.8	0.0
B+ / 8.6	1.9	2.6	11.45	1	0	4	0	74	22	44	0.0	26	7	2,500	0	0.0	0.0
B+ / 8.5	2.0	2.6	11.44	111	0	4	0	74	22	44	0.0	24	7	2,500	0	0.0	0.0
B+ / 8.5	2.0	2.6	11.49	446	0	4	0	74	22	44	0.0	55	7	2,500	0	0.0	0.0
B+ / 8.6	1.9	2.6	11.47	193	0	4	0	74	22	44	0.0	47	7	2,500	0	2.8	0.0
B+ / 8.9	1.4	2.7	10.68	381	0	0	100	0	0	21	0.0	47	13	2,500	0	2.8	0.5
A- / 9.0	1.3	2.7	10.67	N/A	0	0	100	0	0	21	0.0	30	13	2,500	0	0.0	0.5
A- / 9.0	1.4	2.7	10.66	64	0	0	100	0	0	21	0.0	25	13	2,500	0	0.0	0.5
A- / 9.0	1.3	2.7	10.67	278	0	0	100	0	0	21	0.0	60	13	2,500	0	0.0	0.5
A- / 9.0	1.4	2.7	10.66	22	0	0	100	0	0	21	0.0	50	13	2,500	0	2.8	0.5
B / 7.8	2.6	3.8	11.36	44	1	0	0	0	99	439	0.0	40	8	2,500	0	4.0	0.0
B / 7.8	2.6	3.8	11.36	1	1	0	0	0	99	439	0.0	22	8	2,500	0	0.0	0.0
B / 7.8	2.6	3.8	11.34	19	1	0	0	0	99	439	0.0	21	8	2,500	0	0.0	0.0
B / 7.8	2.5	3.8	11.35	79	1	0	0	0	99	439	0.0	52	8	2,500	0	0.0	0.0
B / 7.8	2.6	3.8	11.39	24	1	0	0	0	99	439	0.0	41	8	2,500	0	4.0	0.0
C- / 3.5	3.8	6.8	13.55	401	0	0	100	0	0	14	0.0	51	10	2,500	0	4.0	0.0
C- / 3.5	3.8	6.8	13.51	3	0	0	100	0	0	14	0.0	31	10	2,500	0	0.0	0.0
C- / 3.5	3.8	6.8	13.59	131	0	0	100	0	0	14	0.0	28	10	2,500	0	0.0	0.0
C- / 3.5	3.8	6.8	13.48	390	0	0	100	0	0	14	0.0	61	10	2,500	0	0.0	0.0
C- / 3.5	3.8	6.8	13.60	175	0	0	100	0	0	14	0.0	53	10	2,500	0	4.0	0.0
C / 4.7	3.6	6.6	13.63	49	0	0	100	0	0	11	0.0	52	14	2,500	0	4.0	0.5
C / 4.6	3.6	6.6	13.63	1	0	0	100	0	0	11	0.0	31	14	2,500	0	0.0	0.5
C / 4.7	3.6	6.6	13.63	32	0	0	100	0	0	11	0.0	28	14	2,500	0	0.0	0.5
C / 4.7	3.6	6.6	13.62	41	0	0	100	0	0	11	0.0	61	14	2,500	0	0.0	0.5
C / 4.7	3.6	6.6	13.64	9	0	0	100	0	0	11	0.0	54	14	2,500	0	4.0	0.5
A+ / 9.6	0.8	1.7	9.35	197	2	21	0	47	30	75	0.0	74	9	2,500	0	1.5	0.0
A+ / 9.6	0.8	1.7	9.32	1	2	21	0	47	30	75	0.0	39	9	2,500	0	0.0	0.0
A+ / 9.6	0.7	1.7	9.30	88	2	21	0	47	30	75	0.0	38	9	2,500	0	0.0	0.0
A+ / 9.6	0.8	1.7	9.36	497	2	21	0	47	30	75	0.0	79	9	2,500	0	0.0	0.0
A+ / 9.6	0.8	1.7	9.36	94	2	21	0	47	30	75	0.0	74	9	2,500	0	1.5	0.0
C- / 3.2	4.5	4.8	11.56	3,159	3	30	0	19	48	121	0.0	38	17	2,500	0	4.0	0.0
C- / 3.2	4.5	4.8	11.60	58	3	30	0	19	48	121	0.0	20	17	2,500	0	0.0	0.0
C- / 3.2	4.5	4.8	11.53	1,391	3	30	0	19	48	121	0.0	19	17	2,500	0	0.0	0.0
C- / 3.2	4.5	4.8	11.72	2,564	3	30	0	19	48	121	0.0	46	17	2,500	0	0.0	0.0
C- / 3.3	4.4	4.8	11.55	970	3	30	0	19	48	121	0.0	39	17	2,500	0	4.0	0.0
C- / 3.1	4.7	6.7	11.19	32	7	1	2	88	2	50	0.0	35	6	2,500	0	4.0	0.0
C- / 3.1	4.6	6.7	11.19	17	7	1	2	88	2	50	0.0	18	6	2,500	0	0.0	0.0
C- / 3.1	4.7	6.7	11.19	115	7	1	2	88	2	50	0.0	44	6	2,500	0	0.0	0.0
C- / 3.1	4.7	6.7	11.19	8	7	1	2	88	2	50	0.0	34	6	2,500	0	4.0	0.0

99 Pct = Best 0 Pct = Worst					PERFORMANCE							
						Total Return % through 3/31/16					Incl. in Returns	
									Annualized			
Fund Type	Fund Name	Ticker Symbol	Overall Investment Rating	Phone	Performance Rating/Pts	3 Mo	6 Mo	1Yr / Pct	3Yr / Pct	5Yr / Pct	Dividend Yield	Expense Ratio
GL	Fidelity Advisor Glbl Hi Income A	FGHAX	**D-**	(800) 522-7297	**C- / 3.3**	2.93	1.83	-1.36 /19	1.83 /58	--	5.01	1.28
GL	Fidelity Advisor Glbl Hi Income C	FGHCX	**D**	(800) 522-7297	**C- / 3.7**	2.74	1.46	-2.09 /15	1.07 /44	--	4.46	2.12
GL	Fidelity Advisor Glbl Hi Income I	FGHIX	**D+**	(800) 522-7297	**C+ / 5.7**	2.99	1.96	-1.12 /21	2.09 /63	--	5.47	1.02
GL	Fidelity Advisor Glbl Hi Income T	FGHTX	**D-**	(800) 522-7297	**C- / 3.3**	2.93	1.83	-1.36 /19	1.83 /58	--	5.02	1.40
MUN	Fidelity Advisor Muni Inc 2017 A	FAMMX	**C-**	(800) 544-8544	**D- / 1.4**	0.14	0.02	0.24 /47	0.56 /40	--	0.59	0.65
MUN	Fidelity Advisor Muni Inc 2017 I	FAVIX	**C+**	(800) 544-8544	**C / 4.3**	0.21	0.15	0.48 /54	0.81 /47	--	0.86	0.40
MUN	Fidelity Advisor Muni Inc 2019 A	FAPAX	**C**	(800) 544-8544	**C / 4.4**	0.88	1.14	1.59 /74	1.38 /64	--	1.33	0.65
MUN	Fidelity Advisor Muni Inc 2019 I	FACIX	**A-**	(800) 544-8544	**B- / 7.0**	0.94	1.26	1.85 /76	1.63 /71	--	1.62	0.40
MUN	Fidelity Advisor Muni Inc 2021 A	FOMAX	**C**	(800) 544-8544	**B- / 7.5**	1.26	2.40	2.99 /85	2.46 /82	--	1.83	0.65
MUN	Fidelity Advisor Muni Inc 2021 I	FOMIX	**B-**	(800) 544-8544	**B+ / 8.6**	1.32	2.53	3.25 /87	2.71 /85	--	2.13	0.40
MUN	Fidelity Advisor Muni Inc 2023 A	FSODX	**U**	(800) 544-8544	**U /**	1.88	3.67	3.57 /91	--	--	1.76	0.65
MUN	Fidelity Advisor Muni Inc 2023 I	FSWTX	**U**	(800) 544-8544	**U /**	1.94	3.80	3.83 /93	--	--	2.05	0.40
COI	Fidelity Advisor Series ShTm Fd	FYATX	**U**	(800) 522-7297	**U /**	0.99	0.91	1.06 /60	--	--	1.12	0.45
* GEI	Fidelity Advisor Total Bond A	FEPAX	**C-**	(800) 522-7297	**C / 4.6**	3.13	2.28	0.53 /50	1.99 /61	3.66 /56	2.65	0.75
GEI	• Fidelity Advisor Total Bond B	FBEPX	**C-**	(800) 522-7297	**C / 5.2**	2.96	1.92	-0.17 /30	1.31 /48	2.94 /44	2.07	1.45
GEI	Fidelity Advisor Total Bond C	FCEPX	**C-**	(800) 522-7297	**C / 5.0**	2.84	1.79	-0.24 /29	1.24 /47	2.89 /43	2.00	1.53
GEI	Fidelity Advisor Total Bond I	FEPIX	**C+**	(800) 522-7297	**C+ / 6.8**	3.10	2.31	0.77 /55	2.25 /66	3.91 /60	3.01	0.50
GEI	Fidelity Advisor Total Bond T	FEPTX	**C-**	(800) 522-7297	**C / 4.5**	3.03	2.17	0.51 /50	1.98 /61	3.65 /56	2.64	0.77
COI	Fidelity Advisor Total Bond Z	FBKWX	**U**	(800) 544-8544	**U /**	3.14	2.38	0.82 /56	--	--	3.15	0.36
US	Fidelity AZ Inter Treas Index		**C-**	(800) 544-8544	**B- / 7.2**	3.98	2.56	3.26 /78	2.07 /63	4.48 /67	0.00	0.35
MUS	Fidelity AZ Muni Income Fd	FSAZX	**A-**	(800) 544-8544	**A+ / 9.6**	1.75	3.30	4.04 /94	4.05 /96	5.83 /91	2.85	0.55
MMT	Fidelity CA AMT T/F MM Fd	FSPXX	**U**	(800) 544-8544	**U /**	--	--	--	--	--	0.01	0.30
MMT	Fidelity CA AMT T/F MM I	FSBXX	**C**	(800) 544-8544	**D / 2.0**	0.00	0.01	0.02 /36	0.02 /22	0.02 /10	0.02	0.25
MMT	Fidelity CA AMT T/F MM Svc	FSSXX	**U**	(800) 544-8544	**U /**	--	--	--	--	--	0.01	0.50
* MUS	Fidelity CA Ltd Term Tax-Free Bd	FCSTX	**A+**	(800) 544-8544	**B- / 7.4**	0.77	1.20	1.88 /76	1.85 /75	2.51 /59	1.69	0.49
MMT	Fidelity CA Muni Money Market	FCFXX	**U**	(800) 544-8544	**U /**	--	--	--	--	--	0.01	0.50
MUS	Fidelity CA Municipal Inc	FCTFX	**A**	(800) 544-8544	**A+ / 9.7**	1.77	3.35	3.99 /94	4.39 /97	6.62 /95	3.25	0.46
MM	Fidelity Cash-MM III	FCOXX	**C-**	(800) 544-8544	**D / 1.9**	0.02	0.02	0.03 /36	0.02 /19	0.01 / 4	0.03	0.46
MMT	Fidelity Cash-Tax Exempt I	FTCXX	**U**	(800) 522-7297	**U /**	--	--	--	--	--	0.08	0.22
* GEN	Fidelity Conservative Inc Bond	FCONX	**C+**	(800) 544-8544	**C- / 3.1**	0.19	0.36	0.46 /49	0.37 /31	0.55 /17	0.55	0.40
GEN	Fidelity Conservative Inc Bond Inst	FCNVX	**C+**	(800) 544-8544	**C- / 3.4**	0.21	0.40	0.56 /51	0.47 /32	0.65 /18	0.65	0.35
MUN	Fidelity Consrv Inc Muni Bd	FCRDX	**U**	(800) 522-7297	**U /**	0.21	0.31	0.47 /54	--	--	0.36	0.40
MUN	Fidelity Consrv Inc Muni Bd Inst	FMNDX	**U**	(800) 522-7297	**U /**	0.23	0.36	0.57 /57	--	--	0.46	0.35
COI	Fidelity Corporate Bond Fund	FCBFX	**C**	(800) 522-7297	**B / 7.9**	3.13	4.01	0.90 /57	3.11 /77	5.66 /75	4.72	0.45
MUS	Fidelity CT Muni Income Fd	FICNX	**A**	(800) 544-8544	**A / 9.4**	1.81	3.42	4.18 /95	3.54 /93	4.91 /85	2.71	0.48
US	Fidelity DE Inter Treasury Index		**C-**	(800) 544-8544	**B- / 7.2**	3.99	2.54	3.26 /78	2.08 /63	4.48 /67	0.00	0.35
LP	Fidelity Floating Rate High Income	FFRHX	**C-**	(800) 544-8544	**C- / 3.3**	1.46	-0.47	-1.69 /17	1.02 /43	2.30 /35	4.22	0.69
* COH	Fidelity Focused High Income	FHIFX	**D**	(800) 544-8544	**C / 4.9**	2.32	1.92	-2.34 /14	1.80 /57	4.28 /65	4.78	0.85
GL	Fidelity Global Bond Fund	FGBFX	**D**	(800) 544-8544	**C- / 4.0**	5.55	4.33	1.77 /70	-0.24 /14	--	2.68	1.09
GL	Fidelity Global High Income	FGHNX	**D+**	(800) 522-7297	**C+ / 5.7**	2.99	1.96	-1.11 /21	2.10 /63	--	5.48	1.05
* USA	Fidelity GNMA Fund	FGMNX	**B+**	(800) 544-8544	**C+ / 6.6**	1.61	1.50	1.97 /72	2.19 /65	3.40 /51	1.94	0.45
MM	Fidelity Government Cash Reserves	FDRXX	**U**	(800) 544-8544	**U /**	0.01	0.01	0.01 /32	0.01 /17	0.01 / 4	0.01	0.37
USS	Fidelity Government Income Fund	FGOVX	**B**	(800) 544-8544	**C+ / 6.6**	2.73	1.88	1.82 /70	2.00 /61	3.28 /49	1.62	0.45
MM	Fidelity Government Port I	FIGXX	**C**	(800) 544-8544	**D / 2.2**	0.05	0.05	0.06 /39	0.03 /22	0.02 / 7	0.06	0.21
MM	Fidelity Government Port II	FCVXX	**U**	(800) 544-8544	**U /**	0.01	0.01	0.02 /34	0.01 /17	0.01 / 4	0.02	0.36
MM	Fidelity Government Port Select	FGEXX	**C**	(800) 544-8544	**D / 2.1**	0.04	0.04	0.04 /37	0.02 /19	0.02 / 7	0.05	0.26
* COI	Fidelity High Income	SPHIX	**D-**	(800) 544-8544	**D / 2.2**	2.78	0.20	-4.92 / 5	0.78 /39	3.77 /58	6.14	0.72
GEI	Fidelity Inflation-Protected Bd	FINPX	**D-**	(800) 544-8544	**D / 1.6**	4.52	3.50	1.05 /59	-1.14 / 8	2.57 /39	0.23	0.45
MM	Fidelity Inst MM-Treasury Only II	FOXXX	**U**	(800) 544-8544	**U /**	--	--	--	--	--	0.01	0.36
USA	Fidelity Inst MM-Treasury Only Inst	FRSXX	**U**	(800) 544-8544	**U /**	0.04	0.05	0.05 /38	--	--	0.05	0.19
MUN	Fidelity Intermd Muni Inc	FLTMX	**A+**	(800) 544-8544	**B+ / 8.5**	1.19	2.44	2.59 /81	2.68 /85	4.15 /79	2.54	0.36
* GEI	Fidelity Intermediate Bond	FTHRX	**B+**	(800) 544-8544	**C+ / 6.2**	2.43	1.76	1.62 /68	1.80 /57	3.19 /48	2.50	0.45

• Denotes fund is closed to new investors
* Denotes fund is included in Section II

RISK			NET ASSETS		ASSET							FUND MANAGER		MINIMUM		LOADS	
Risk Rating/Pts	3 Yr Avg Standard Deviation	Avg Duration	NAV As of 3/31/16	Total $(Mil)	Cash %	Gov. Bond %	Muni. Bond %	Corp. Bond %	Other %	Portfolio Turnover Ratio	Avg Coupon Rate	Manager Quality Pct	Manager Tenure (Years)	Initial Purch. $	Additional Purch. $	Front End Load	Back End Load
D- / 1.5	6.1	N/A	8.85	6	6	1	0	89	4	44	0.0	95	5	2,500	0	4.0	1.0
D / 1.6	6.1	N/A	8.85	3	6	1	0	89	4	44	0.0	91	5	2,500	0	0.0	1.0
D- / 1.5	6.1	N/A	8.85	3	6	1	0	89	4	44	0.0	96	5	2,500	0	0.0	1.0
D / 1.6	6.1	N/A	8.85	2	6	1	0	89	4	44	0.0	95	5	2,500	0	4.0	1.0
A- / 9.0	1.3	N/A	10.48	12	0	0	100	0	0	3	0.0	44	5	10,000	100	2.8	0.5
A- / 9.0	1.3	N/A	10.48	32	0	0	100	0	0	3	0.0	53	5	10,000	100	0.0	0.5
B- / 7.5	2.7	N/A	10.76	7	0	0	100	0	0	8	0.0	26	5	10,000	100	2.8	0.5
B- / 7.5	2.7	N/A	10.76	25	0	0	100	0	0	8	0.0	32	5	10,000	100	0.0	0.5
C- / 3.9	4.0	N/A	11.09	14	0	0	100	0	0	5	0.0	17	5	10,000	100	2.8	0.5
C- / 3.9	4.0	N/A	11.09	19	0	0	100	0	0	5	0.0	21	5	10,000	100	0.0	0.5
U /	N/A	N/A	10.35	4	0	0	100	0	0	16	0.0	N/A	3	10,000	100	2.8	0.5
U /	N/A	N/A	10.35	20	0	0	100	0	0	16	0.0	N/A	3	10,000	100	0.0	0.5
U /	N/A	N/A	10.00	164	0	2	0	70	28	0	0.0	N/A	1	0	0	0.0	0.0
C / 5.5	3.3	5.2	10.51	1,231	3	22	1	36	38	140	0.0	44	12	2,500	0	4.0	0.0
C / 5.3	3.3	5.2	10.52	3	3	22	1	36	38	140	0.0	23	12	2,500	0	0.0	0.0
C+ / 5.6	3.2	5.2	10.51	154	3	22	1	36	38	140	0.0	24	12	2,500	0	0.0	0.0
C / 5.4	3.3	5.2	10.49	2,408	3	22	1	36	38	140	0.0	52	12	2,500	0	0.0	0.0
C / 5.4	3.3	5.2	10.49	121	3	22	1	36	38	140	0.0	42	12	2,500	0	4.0	0.0
U /	N/A	5.2	10.49	668	3	22	1	36	38	140	0.0	N/A	12	5,000,000	0	0.0	0.0
C- / 3.0	4.7	N/A	16.45	3	0	99	0	0	1	3	0.0	29	10	50	25	0.0	0.0
C / 4.3	3.8	6.5	12.29	168	0	0	100	0	0	17	0.0	68	6	10,000	0	0.0	0.5
U /	N/A	N/A	1.00	286	100	0	0	0	0	0	0.0	N/A	5	25,000	0	0.0	0.0
A+ / 9.9	N/A	N/A	1.00	408	100	0	0	0	0	0	0.0	N/A	5	1,000,000	0	0.0	0.0
U /	N/A	N/A	1.00	N/A	100	0	0	0	0	0	0.0	N/A	5	1,000,000	0	0.0	0.0
B+ / 8.9	1.6	3.0	10.76	816	0	0	100	0	0	25	0.0	78	10	10,000	0	0.0	0.5
U /	N/A	N/A	1.00	6,092	100	0	0	0	0	0	0.0	N/A	5	5,000	0	0.0	0.0
C / 4.6	3.6	6.0	13.24	1,863	0	0	100	0	0	10	0.0	83	10	10,000	0	0.0	0.5
A+ / 9.9	N/A	N/A	1.00	1,129	100	0	0	0	0	0	0.0	65	5	1,000,000	0	0.0	0.0
U /	N/A	N/A	1.00	1,431	100	0	0	0	0	0	0.1	69	8	1,000,000	0	0.0	0.0
A+ / 9.9	0.2	N/A	10.02	1,123	10	0	10	79	1	44	0.0	78	5	2,500	0	0.0	0.0
A+ / 9.9	0.2	N/A	10.02	2,845	10	0	10	79	1	44	0.0	81	5	1,000,000	0	0.0	0.0
U /	N/A	N/A	10.05	79	0	0	100	0	0	51	0.0	N/A	3	10,000	0	0.0	0.0
U /	N/A	N/A	10.05	337	0	0	100	0	0	51	0.0	N/A	3	1,000,000	0	0.0	0.0
C- / 3.2	4.6	6.7	11.19	837	7	1	2	88	2	50	0.0	72	6	2,500	0	0.0	0.0
C / 5.0	3.5	6.5	11.87	443	0	0	100	0	0	13	0.0	58	14	10,000	0	0.0	0.5
C- / 3.0	4.7	N/A	16.16	3	0	100	0	0	0	57	0.0	29	10	50	25	0.0	0.0
B- / 7.2	2.8	0.3	9.17	5,366	5	0	0	82	13	26	0.0	80	3	2,500	0	0.0	1.0
D / 1.6	5.5	4.3	8.10	731	4	0	0	92	4	62	0.0	75	12	2,500	0	0.0	1.0
D+ / 2.6	5.1	N/A	9.12	45	0	32	0	24	44	227	0.0	57	4	2,500	0	0.0	0.0
D- / 1.5	6.1	N/A	8.85	83	6	1	0	89	4	44	0.0	96	5	2,500	0	0.0	1.0
B- / 7.3	2.8	3.4	11.64	6,129	5	0	0	0	95	450	0.0	84	12	2,500	0	0.0	0.0
U /	N/A	N/A	1.00	124,702	100	0	0	0	0	0	0.0	N/A	4	2,500	0	0.0	0.0
C+ / 6.9	2.9	5.1	10.54	3,673	1	47	0	0	52	83	0.0	62	9	2,500	0	0.0	0.0
A+ / 9.9	N/A	N/A	1.00	22,043	100	0	0	0	0	0	0.1	65	12	1,000,000	0	0.0	0.0
U /	N/A	N/A	1.00	485	100	0	0	0	0	0	0.0	N/A	12	1,000,000	0	0.0	0.0
A+ / 9.9	N/A	N/A	1.00	286	100	0	0	0	0	0	0.1	65	12	1,000,000	0	0.0	0.0
D / 1.6	6.1	3.8	8.05	3,916	3	0	0	94	3	37	0.0	18	16	2,500	0	0.0	1.0
D / 2.2	5.5	5.6	12.15	1,499	0	100	0	0	0	20	0.0	3	12	2,500	0	0.0	0.0
U /	N/A	N/A	1.00	307	100	0	0	0	0	0	0.0	N/A	5	1,000,000	0	0.0	0.0
U /	N/A	N/A	1.00	1,023	0	0	0	0	100	0	0.0	N/A	5	10,000,000	0	0.0	0.0
B / 7.6	2.6	4.8	10.57	4,870	0	0	100	0	0	17	0.0	59	10	10,000	0	0.0	0.5
B / 8.1	2.3	3.9	10.93	3,133	0	30	0	53	17	53	0.0	60	7	2,500	0	0.0	0.0

					PERFORMANCE							
99 Pct = Best 0 Pct = Worst						Total Return % through 3/31/16					Incl. in Returns	
									Annualized			
Fund Type	Fund Name	Ticker Symbol	Overall Investment Rating	Phone	Perfor-mance Rating/Pts	3 Mo	6 Mo	1Yr / Pct	3Yr / Pct	5Yr / Pct	Dividend Yield	Expense Ratio
* USS	Fidelity Intermediate Government	FSTGX	**B**	(800) 544-8544	**C / 5.5**	2.18	1.16	1.75 /69	1.38 /50	2.41 /36	1.23	0.45
GL	Fidelity International Bond Rtl	FINUX	**D-**	(800) 544-8544	**C- / 3.1**	7.27	6.12	3.36 /78	-1.36 / 7	--	2.40	1.11
GEI	Fidelity Investment Grade Bond Fd	FBNDX	**C**	(800) 544-8544	**C+ / 6.1**	3.20	1.92	0.01 /31	1.85 /59	3.69 /56	2.80	0.45
USS	Fidelity Limited Term Government	FFXSX	**B-**	(800) 544-8544	**C / 4.4**	1.41	0.54	1.09 /60	0.90 /41	1.36 /24	0.79	0.45
MUN	Fidelity Limited Term Municipal Inc	FSTFX	**A**	(800) 544-8544	**C+ / 5.9**	0.64	1.08	1.39 /73	1.25 /60	2.05 /47	1.50	0.48
MMT	Fidelity MA AMT T/F MM Fd	FMSXX	**U**	(800) 544-8544	**U /**	--	--	--	--	--	0.11	0.30
MMT	Fidelity MA AMT T/F MM Inst	FMAXX	**U**	(800) 544-8544	**U /**	--	--	--	--	--	0.11	0.25
MMT	Fidelity MA AMT T/F MM Svc	FMHXX	**U**	(800) 544-8544	**U /**	--	--	--	--	--	0.11	0.50
US	Fidelity MA Intr Treas Index		**C-**	(800) 544-8544	**B- / 7.3**	4.02	2.58	3.36 /78	2.09 /63	4.50 /67	0.00	0.35
* MUS	Fidelity MA Muni Inc Fd	FDMMX	**A-**	(800) 544-8544	**A / 9.4**	1.66	3.13	3.93 /93	3.75 /94	5.59 /89	3.04	0.46
MUS	Fidelity MD Muni Income Fd	SMDMX	**A-**	(800) 544-8544	**A- / 9.2**	1.76	3.22	3.94 /94	3.31 /91	4.85 /84	2.50	0.55
* MUS	Fidelity MI Muni Inc	FMHTX	**A+**	(800) 544-8544	**A / 9.4**	1.54	3.17	4.11 /95	3.62 /93	5.20 /87	3.03	0.49
MM	Fidelity MM Port F	FMMXX	**C+**	(800) 522-7297	**D+ / 2.7**	0.09	0.14	0.22 /45	0.14 /28	0.16 /15	0.22	0.15
MM	Fidelity MM Port I	FMPXX	**C**	(800) 522-7297	**D+ / 2.6**	0.08	0.12	0.18 /44	0.10 /27	0.12 /15	0.18	0.21
MM	Fidelity MM Port II	FCIXX	**C**	(800) 522-7297	**D / 2.2**	0.05	0.05	0.06 /39	0.03 /22	0.03 /10	0.06	0.36
MM	Fidelity MM Port Inst	FNSXX	**C+**	(800) 544-8544	**D+ / 2.7**	0.09	0.14	0.22 /45	0.14 /28	0.16 /15	0.22	0.18
MM	Fidelity MM Port Select	FMYXX	**C**	(800) 544-8544	**D+ / 2.5**	0.07	0.10	0.13 /42	0.05 /25	0.08 /14	0.13	0.26
MM	Fidelity MM Prime MM Select	FDIXX	**C**	(800) 544-8544	**D+ / 2.4**	0.07	0.10	0.11 /42	0.04 /24	0.05 /12	0.11	0.26
MMT	Fidelity MM Tax Exempt Select	FSXXX	**U**	(800) 544-8544	**U /**	--	--	--	--	--	0.08	0.27
MM	Fidelity MM Treas Only Select	FTYXX	**C-**	(800) 544-8544	**D / 1.9**	0.02	0.02	0.03 /36	0.02 /19	0.01 / 4	0.03	0.26
MM	Fidelity MM Treasury I	FISXX	**C**	(800) 544-8544	**D / 2.1**	0.04	0.05	0.05 /38	0.02 /19	0.02 / 7	0.05	0.21
MM	Fidelity MM Treasury II	FCEXX	**U**	(800) 544-8544	**U /**	0.01	0.01	0.01 /32	0.01 /17	0.01 / 4	0.01	0.36
MM	Fidelity MM Treasury Instl	FRBXX	**U**	(800) 544-8544	**U /**	0.05	0.06	0.06 /39	--	--	0.06	N/A
MM	Fidelity MM Treasury Select	FTUXX	**C**	(800) 544-8544	**D / 2.1**	0.03	0.03	0.04 /37	0.02 /19	0.02 / 7	0.04	0.26
MUS	Fidelity MN Muni Inc	FIMIX	**A+**	(800) 544-8544	**B+ / 8.9**	1.43	2.60	3.57 /91	3.00 /88	4.42 /81	2.65	0.50
MTG	Fidelity Mortgage Securities	FMSFX	**A**	(800) 544-8544	**B- / 7.3**	1.88	1.56	2.21 /73	2.56 /71	3.58 /54	2.30	0.45
MUN	Fidelity Muni Inc 2017	FMIFX	**C+**	(800) 544-8544	**C / 4.3**	0.21	0.15	0.48 /54	0.81 /47	--	0.86	0.40
MUN	Fidelity Muni Inc 2019	FMCFX	**A-**	(800) 544-8544	**B- / 7.0**	0.94	1.26	1.85 /76	1.63 /71	--	1.62	0.40
MUN	Fidelity Muni Inc 2021	FOCFX	**B-**	(800) 544-8544	**B+ / 8.6**	1.32	2.53	3.25 /87	2.71 /85	--	2.13	0.40
MUN	Fidelity Muni Inc 2023	FCHPX	**U**	(800) 544-8544	**U /**	1.94	3.80	3.83 /93	--	--	2.05	0.40
* MUH	Fidelity Municipal Inc	FHIGX	**B**	(800) 544-8544	**A / 9.5**	1.64	3.41	3.75 /92	3.98 /96	6.05 /92	3.36	0.48
MMT	Fidelity Municipal MM Fund	FTEXX	**U**	(800) 544-8544	**U /**	--	--	--	--	--	0.01	0.40
MM	Fidelity NC Cap Mgmt Tr Cash Port		**C**	(800) 544-8544	**D+ / 2.5**	0.08	0.11	0.14 /42	0.05 /25	0.06 /13	0.14	0.24
USS	Fidelity NC Cap Mgmt Tr Term Port		**C**	(800) 544-8544	**D+ / 2.7**	0.10	0.15	0.21 /44	0.13 /28	0.16 /15	0.21	0.26
* EM	Fidelity New Markets Income	FNMIX	**D**	(800) 544-8544	**C+ / 6.5**	4.52	5.88	3.99 /81	1.36 /49	5.56 /75	5.37	0.86
US	Fidelity NH Inter Treas Index		**C-**	(800) 544-8544	**B- / 7.3**	4.02	2.58	3.30 /78	2.09 /63	4.49 /67	0.00	0.35
MMT	Fidelity NJ AMT T/F MM Inst	FSKXX	**C**	(800) 544-8544	**D / 2.2**	0.01	0.01	0.01 /34	0.03 /25	0.03 /12	0.01	0.25
* MUS	Fidelity NJ Muni Income Fd	FNJHX	**B+**	(800) 544-8544	**A- / 9.0**	1.76	4.31	3.24 /87	2.99 /88	5.19 /87	3.08	0.48
MMT	Fidelity NY AMT T/F MM Inst	FNKXX	**U**	(800) 544-8544	**U /**	--	--	--	--	--	0.04	0.25
MMT	Fidelity NY AMT T/F MM Svc	FNOXX	**U**	(800) 544-8544	**U /**	--	--	--	--	--	0.04	0.50
MUS	Fidelity NY Muni Inc Fd	FTFMX	**A-**	(800) 544-8544	**A / 9.5**	1.79	3.35	4.36 /96	3.86 /95	5.52 /89	3.02	0.46
* MUS	Fidelity OH Muni Inc	FOHFX	**B+**	(800) 544-8544	**A+ / 9.7**	1.89	3.64	4.59 /97	4.30 /97	5.80 /91	2.84	0.48
MUS	Fidelity PA Muni Inc	FPXTX	**A**	(800) 544-8544	**A / 9.4**	1.49	2.90	3.54 /90	3.79 /95	5.47 /89	3.06	0.49
MM	Fidelity Prime MM I	FIDXX	**C**	(800) 522-7297	**D+ / 2.5**	0.09	0.12	0.16 /43	0.06 /26	0.08 /14	0.16	0.21
MM	Fidelity Prime MM II	FDOXX	**C**	(800) 522-7297	**D / 2.2**	0.05	0.06	0.06 /39	0.03 /22	0.02 / 8	0.06	0.36
MM	Fidelity Prime MM III	FCDXX	**C-**	(800) 522-7297	**D / 1.9**	0.03	0.03	0.03 /36	0.02 /19	0.01 / 5	0.03	0.46
MM	Fidelity Prime MM Inst	FIPXX	**C**	(800) 544-8544	**D+ / 2.7**	0.10	0.14	0.20 /44	0.11 /27	0.13 /15	0.20	0.18
MM	Fidelity Retirement Government MM	FRTXX	**U**	(800) 544-8544	**U /**	--	--	--	--	--	0.02	0.42
EM	Fidelity Series Emerg Mrkts Dbt	FEDCX	**D+**	(800) 522-7297	**B- / 7.5**	5.08	6.86	4.02 /81	1.67 /55	4.91 /71	6.22	0.82
EM	Fidelity Series Emerg Mrkts Dbt F	FEDFX	**D+**	(800) 522-7297	**B / 7.6**	5.11	6.92	4.13 /82	1.78 /57	5.03 /72	6.32	0.72
COI	Fidelity Series Float Rate Hi Inc	FFHCX	**D+**	(800) 544-8544	**D+ / 2.8**	0.82	-2.46	-3.86 / 8	0.97 /42	--	5.11	0.72
COI	Fidelity Series Float Rate Hi Inc F	FFHFX	**D+**	(800) 544-8544	**C- / 3.0**	0.85	-2.41	-3.76 / 8	1.07 /44	--	5.22	0.62

● Denotes fund is closed to new investors
* Denotes fund is included in Section II

RISK			NET ASSETS		ASSET							FUND MANAGER		MINIMUM		LOADS	
Risk Rating/Pts	3 Yr Avg Standard Deviation	Avg Duration	NAV As of 3/31/16	Total $(Mil)	Cash %	Gov. Bond %	Muni. Bond %	Corp. Bond %	Other %	Portfolio Turnover Ratio	Avg Coupon Rate	Manager Quality Pct	Manager Tenure (Years)	Initial Purch. $	Additional Purch. $	Front End Load	Back End Load
B+ / 8.3	2.2	3.7	10.77	758	0	64	0	0	36	71	0.0	57	8	2,500	0	0.0	0.0
E+ / 0.7	7.0	N/A	8.78	41	10	50	0	15	25	145	0.0	23	4	2,500	0	0.0	0.0
C+ / 5.6	3.2	5.3	7.77	6,752	6	24	1	39	30	182	0.0	38	12	2,500	0	0.0	0.0
A- / 9.0	1.3	2.6	10.11	413	0	70	0	0	30	102	0.0	61	8	2,500	0	0.0	0.0
A- / 9.0	1.4	2.7	10.66	3,073	0	0	100	0	0	21	0.0	60	13	10,000	0	0.0	0.5
U /	N/A	N/A	1.00	200	100	0	0	0	0	0	0.1	67	10	25,000	0	0.0	0.0
U /	N/A	N/A	1.00	418	100	0	0	0	0	0	0.1	67	10	1,000,000	0	0.0	0.0
U /	N/A	N/A	1.00	N/A	100	0	0	0	0	0	0.1	67	10	1,000,000	0	0.0	0.0
C- / 3.0	4.7	N/A	16.31	24	0	99	0	0	1	0	0.0	29	10	50	25	0.0	0.0
C / 4.4	3.7	6.8	12.60	2,289	0	0	100	0	0	8	0.0	55	6	10,000	0	0.0	0.5
C / 4.8	3.6	6.6	11.52	217	0	0	100	0	0	27	0.0	46	14	10,000	0	0.0	0.5
C+ / 5.7	3.2	5.7	12.48	666	0	0	100	0	0	12	0.0	76	10	10,000	0	0.0	0.5
A+ / 9.9	N/A	N/A	1.00	2,056	100	0	0	0	0	0	0.2	72	5	0	0	0.0	0.0
A+ / 9.9	N/A	N/A	1.00	20,157	100	0	0	0	0	0	0.2	70	5	1,000,000	0	0.0	0.0
A+ / 9.9	N/A	N/A	1.00	76	100	0	0	0	0	0	0.1	65	5	1,000,000	0	0.0	0.0
A+ / 9.9	N/A	N/A	1.00	21,413	100	0	0	0	0	0	0.2	72	5	10,000,000	0	0.0	0.0
A+ / 9.9	N/A	N/A	1.00	224	100	0	0	0	0	0	0.1	N/A	5	1,000,000	0	0.0	0.0
A+ / 9.9	N/A	N/A	1.00	1,282	100	0	0	0	0	0	0.1	65	5	1,000,000	0	0.0	0.0
U /	N/A	N/A	1.00	4	100	0	0	0	0	0	0.1	69	8	1,000,000	0	0.0	0.0
A+ / 9.9	N/A	N/A	1.00	180	100	0	0	0	0	0	0.0	65	5	1,000,000	0	0.0	0.0
A+ / 9.9	N/A	N/A	1.00	9,640	100	0	0	0	0	0	0.1	65	14	1,000,000	0	0.0	0.0
U /	N/A	N/A	1.00	557	100	0	0	0	0	0	0.0	N/A	14	1,000,000	0	0.0	0.0
U /	N/A	N/A	1.00	645	100	0	0	0	0	0	0.1	N/A	N/A	10,000,000	0	0.0	0.0
A+ / 9.9	N/A	N/A	1.00	191	100	0	0	0	0	0	0.0	65	14	1,000,000	0	0.0	0.0
B- / 7.1	2.8	5.5	11.84	516	0	0	100	0	0	15	0.0	N/A	6	10,000	0	0.0	0.5
B / 7.8	2.6	3.8	11.39	930	1	0	0	0	99	439	0.0	55	8	2,500	0	0.0	0.0
A- / 9.1	1.3	N/A	10.48	89	0	0	100	0	0	3	0.0	54	5	10,000	0	0.0	0.5
B- / 7.5	2.7	N/A	10.76	55	0	0	100	0	0	8	0.0	32	5	10,000	0	0.0	0.5
C- / 3.9	4.0	N/A	11.09	32	0	0	100	0	0	5	0.0	21	5	10,000	0	0.0	0.5
U /	N/A	N/A	10.35	18	0	0	100	0	0	16	0.0	N/A	3	10,000	0	0.0	0.5
C- / 3.5	3.8	6.6	13.55	5,723	0	0	100	0	0	9	0.0	61	7	10,000	0	0.0	0.5
U /	N/A	N/A	1.00	22,620	100	0	0	0	0	0	0.0	N/A	13	5,000	0	0.0	0.0
A+ / 9.9	N/A	N/A	1.00	4,043	100	0	0	0	0	0	0.1	N/A	3	0	0	0.0	0.0
A+ / 9.9	N/A	0.1	9.68	1,478	20	3	0	74	3	902	0.0	71	1	0	0	0.0	0.0
E / 0.4	8.0	7.3	14.96	3,898	3	73	0	22	2	146	0.0	93	21	2,500	0	0.0	1.0
C- / 3.0	4.7	N/A	16.29	52	0	99	0	0	1	0	0.0	29	10	50	25	0.0	0.0
A+ / 9.9	N/A	N/A	1.00	165	100	0	0	0	0	0	0.0	68	6	1,000,000	0	0.0	0.0
C / 4.3	3.8	6.7	12.00	548	0	0	100	0	0	7	0.0	31	7	10,000	0	0.0	0.5
U /	N/A	N/A	1.00	462	100	0	0	0	0	0	0.0	69	5	1,000,000	0	0.0	0.0
U /	N/A	N/A	1.00	N/A	100	0	0	0	0	0	0.0	69	5	1,000,000	0	0.0	0.0
C / 4.6	3.6	6.6	13.64	1,726	0	0	100	0	0	11	0.0	66	14	10,000	0	0.0	0.5
C- / 3.8	3.9	7.1	12.43	659	0	0	100	0	0	7	0.0	74	10	10,000	0	0.0	0.5
C / 5.1	3.4	6.3	11.39	475	0	0	100	0	0	12	0.0	74	14	10,000	0	0.0	0.5
A+ / 9.9	N/A	N/A	1.00	9,639	100	0	0	0	0	0	0.2	N/A	5	1,000,000	0	0.0	0.0
A+ / 9.9	N/A	N/A	1.00	245	100	0	0	0	0	0	0.1	65	5	1,000,000	0	0.0	0.0
A+ / 9.9	N/A	N/A	1.00	894	100	0	0	0	0	0	0.0	65	5	1,000,000	0	0.0	0.0
A+ / 9.9	N/A	N/A	1.00	46,325	100	0	0	0	0	0	0.2	70	5	10,000,000	0	0.0	0.0
U /	N/A	N/A	1.00	10,997	100	0	0	0	0	0	0.0	N/A	N/A	100,000	0	0.0	0.0
E / 0.5	7.8	N/A	9.49	481	6	70	2	20	2	40	0.0	95	5	0	0	0.0	0.0
E / 0.5	7.8	N/A	9.49	538	6	70	2	20	2	40	0.0	95	5	0	0	0.0	0.0
C / 5.5	3.3	N/A	8.98	191	6	0	0	74	20	42	0.0	75	5	0	0	0.0	0.0
C / 5.5	3.3	N/A	8.98	213	6	0	0	74	20	42	0.0	78	5	0	0	0.0	0.0

I. Index of Bond and Money Market Mutual Funds

Fund Type	Fund Name (99 Pct = Best, 0 Pct = Worst)	Ticker Symbol	Overall Investment Rating	Phone	PERFORMANCE: Performance Rating/Pts	Total Return % through 3/31/16: 3 Mo	6 Mo	1Yr / Pct	Annualized: 3Yr / Pct	5Yr / Pct	Incl. in Returns: Dividend Yield	Expense Ratio
GEI	Fidelity Series Inf-Pro Bd Idx	FSIPX	D	(800) 544-8544	D / 1.7	3.69	2.69	1.55 /67	-0.94 / 9	1.67 /27	0.05	0.20
* GEI	Fidelity Series Inf-Pro Bd Idx F	FFIPX	D	(800) 544-8544	D+ / 2.4	3.72	2.76	1.70 /69	-0.79 / 9	1.80 /29	0.20	0.05
COI	Fidelity Series Short-Term Credit	FYBTX	U	(800) 544-8544	U /	1.07	0.95	1.06 /60	--	--	1.18	0.45
COI	Fidelity Series Short-Term Credit F	FYCTX	U	(800) 544-8544	U /	1.10	1.00	1.16 /61	--	--	1.28	0.35
GL	Fidelity Short Dur High Inc	FSAHX	U	(800) 544-8544	U /	1.20	-1.59	-4.40 / 6	--	--	4.86	1.00
GL	Fidelity Short Dur High Inc A	FSBHX	U	(800) 544-8544	U /	1.13	-1.71	-4.64 / 6	--	--	4.42	1.29
GL	Fidelity Short Dur High Inc C	FSDHX	U	(800) 544-8544	U /	0.95	-2.08	-5.35 / 4	--	--	3.82	2.08
GL	Fidelity Short Dur High Inc I	FSFHX	U	(800) 544-8544	U /	1.20	-1.59	-4.40 / 6	--	--	4.87	1.04
GL	Fidelity Short Dur High Inc T	FSEHX	U	(800) 544-8544	U /	1.13	-1.71	-4.64 / 6	--	--	4.42	1.31
* GEI	● Fidelity Short-Term Bond	FSHBX	B	(800) 544-8544	C / 4.5	0.92	0.75	1.01 /59	0.97 /42	1.38 /24	1.00	0.45
GEI	Fidelity Spartan Infl PB Idx FA	FSIYX	D-	(800) 544-8544	D+ / 2.7	4.60	3.74	1.28 /63	-0.82 / 9	--	0.00	0.10
GEI	Fidelity Spartan Infl PB Idx FAI	FIPDX	D-	(800) 544-8544	D+ / 2.8	4.60	3.68	1.33 /64	-0.77 / 9	--	0.00	0.05
GEI	Fidelity Spartan Infl PB Idx Inst	FIPBX	D-	(800) 544-8544	D+ / 2.7	4.60	3.66	1.31 /63	-0.79 / 9	--	0.00	0.07
GEI	Fidelity Spartan Infl PB Idx Inv	FSIQX	D-	(800) 544-8544	D+ / 2.3	4.60	3.63	1.28 /63	-0.92 / 9	--	0.00	0.20
US	Fidelity Spartan Intrm Treasury Adv	FIBAX	C-	(800) 544-8544	B / 7.6	4.15	2.75	3.58 /79	2.31 /68	4.72 /70	1.91	0.10
US	Fidelity Spartan Intrm Treasury Inv	FIBIX	C-	(800) 544-8544	B- / 7.4	4.03	2.60	3.39 /78	2.18 /65	4.60 /69	1.81	0.20
US	Fidelity Spartan Lg-T Tre Bd In Adv	FLBAX	C-	(800) 544-8544	A+ / 9.6	8.30	6.57	2.67 /75	5.94 /95	9.58 /93	2.58	0.10
US	Fidelity Spartan Lg-T Tre Bd In Inv	FLBIX	C-	(800) 544-8544	A / 9.5	8.28	6.44	2.50 /75	5.81 /94	9.46 /93	2.49	0.20
MM	Fidelity Spartan Money Market	SPRXX	C	(800) 544-8544	D / 2.2	0.05	0.06	0.07 /40	0.03 /22	0.02 / 8	0.07	0.42
MM	Fidelity Spartan Money Market Prem	FZDXX	C	(800) 544-8544	D+ / 2.5	0.08	0.11	0.12 /42	0.05 /25	0.03 /10	0.12	N/A
US	Fidelity Spartan S/T TyBd In Adv	FSBAX	B	(800) 544-8544	C / 4.8	1.58	0.87	1.49 /66	1.04 /43	1.47 /25	0.92	0.10
US	Fidelity Spartan S/T TyBd In Inv	FSBIX	B-	(800) 544-8544	C / 4.6	1.56	0.82	1.39 /65	0.94 /41	1.37 /24	0.82	0.20
GEI	Fidelity Spartan US Bond Idx F	FUBFX	B	(800) 544-8544	B- / 7.3	3.07	2.49	2.02 /72	2.46 /70	3.80 /58	2.48	0.05
COI	Fidelity Spartan US Bond Idx FA	FSITX	B	(800) 544-8544	B- / 7.3	3.07	2.48	1.99 /72	2.42 /69	--	2.45	0.17
COI	Fidelity Spartan US Bond Idx FAI	FXNAX	B	(800) 544-8544	B- / 7.3	3.07	2.49	2.02 /72	2.46 /70	--	2.48	0.05
COI	Fidelity Spartan US Bond Idx Inst	FXSTX	B	(800) 544-8544	B- / 7.3	3.07	2.48	2.00 /72	2.44 /70	--	2.47	0.05
* GEI	Fidelity Spartan US Bond Idx Inv	FBIDX	B-	(800) 544-8544	B- / 7.1	3.04	2.41	1.86 /70	2.29 /67	3.62 /55	2.33	0.22
MM	Fidelity Spartan US Govt MM	FZCXX	U	(800) 544-8544	U /	--	--	--	--	--	0.02	N/A
* GEI	Fidelity Srs Inv Grade Bond	FSIGX	C+	(800) 544-8544	C+ / 6.9	3.13	2.63	1.20 /62	2.23 /66	3.85 /59	2.81	0.45
GEI	Fidelity Srs Inv Grade Bond F	FIBFX	C+	(800) 544-8544	B- / 7.1	3.16	2.68	1.39 /65	2.33 /68	3.95 /61	2.90	0.35
GEI	Fidelity Strat Adv Core Inc MM	FWHBX	C+	(800) 544-8544	C+ / 6.6	2.65	2.31	1.00 /59	2.08 /63	--	2.59	1.01
GEI	Fidelity Strat Adv Core Inc MM L	FQANX	C+	(800) 544-8544	C+ / 6.5	2.65	2.20	1.00 /59	2.08 /63	--	2.59	1.01
GEI	Fidelity Strat Adv Core Inc MM N	FQAOX	C+	(800) 544-8544	C+ / 6.1	2.59	2.18	0.75 /54	1.80 /57	--	2.34	1.26
* COI	Fidelity Strat Adv Short Duration	FAUDX	C+	(800) 544-8544	C- / 3.7	0.48	0.56	0.49 /49	0.63 /36	--	1.23	0.74
GEN	Fidelity Strat Advs Inc Opp FOF	FSADX	D	(800) 544-8544	C- / 3.8	1.88	0.07	-4.16 / 7	1.62 /54	--	5.81	2.26
GEL	Fidelity Strat Advs Inc Opp FOF F	FLTSX	D	(800) 544-8544	C- / 3.8	1.88	0.07	-4.16 / 7	1.62 /54	--	5.81	2.26
GEN	Fidelity Strat Advs Inc Opp FOF L	FQAFX	D	(800) 544-8544	C- / 3.8	1.88	0.07	-4.16 / 7	1.63 /54	--	5.81	2.27
GEN	Fidelity Strat Advs Inc Opp FOF N		D-	(800) 544-8544	D+ / 2.6	1.82	-0.19	-4.53 / 6	0.96 /42	--	5.55	2.51
* GEI	Fidelity Strategic Advisers Cor Inc	FPCIX	C+	(800) 544-8544	C+ / 6.4	2.66	2.27	0.85 /56	2.00 /61	3.77 /58	3.11	0.85
* COH	Fidelity Strategic Advisers Inc Opp	FPIOX	D	(800) 544-8544	C- / 3.9	1.82	-0.32	-4.64 / 6	1.46 /51	3.99 /61	5.69	1.15
* GL	Fidelity Strategic Income Fund	FSICX	D+	(800) 544-8544	C+ / 5.8	2.97	2.38	-0.54 /26	1.70 /56	3.62 /55	3.56	0.71
MMT	Fidelity Tax Exempt MM Premium	FZEXX	U	(800) 522-7297	U /	--	--	--	--	--	0.01	N/A
* MUN	Fidelity Tax Free Bond Fd	FTABX	A-	(800) 544-8544	A+ / 9.6	1.77	3.51	3.81 /93	4.04 /96	6.19 /93	3.39	0.46
GEI	Fidelity Total Bond Fund	FTBFX	C+	(800) 544-8544	B- / 7.0	3.21	2.43	0.83 /56	2.34 /68	3.99 /61	3.06	0.45
MM	● Fidelity Treasury Mny Mkt Advisor B	FDBXX	U	(800) 544-8544	U /	--	--	--	--	--	0.01	1.48
MM	Fidelity Treasury Mny Mkt Dly Mny	FDUXX	U	(800) 522-7297	U /	--	--	--	--	--	0.01	0.73
MM	Fidelity Treasury Money Market Fund	FZFXX	U	(800) 522-7297	U /	--	--	--	--	--	0.01	N/A
MM	Fidelity Treasury Only Money Market	FDLXX	U	(800) 544-8544	U /	--	--	--	--	--	0.01	0.42
MM	Fidelity US Treasury Income Port I	FSIXX	C	(800) 544-8544	D / 2.1	0.03	0.03	0.04 /37	0.02 /20	0.02 / 8	0.04	0.21
GL	Fiera Cap STRONG Nations Curr Inst	SCAFX	E+	(855) 722-3637	E / 0.3	5.95	3.91	0.41 /48	-4.58 / 2	--	0.00	1.08
MM	Financial Sq Treas Instr Fd FST Ca	GCIXX	U	(800) 526-7384	U /	0.01	0.01	0.01 /32	--	--	0.01	0.38
MM	First American Gov Oblig Inst Inv	FVIXX	U	(800) 677-3863	U /	0.01	0.01	0.02 /34	0.01 /17	0.01 / 5	0.02	0.35

● Denotes fund is closed to new investors
* Denotes fund is included in Section II

RISK			NET ASSETS		ASSET							FUND MANAGER		MINIMUM		LOADS	
Risk Rating/Pts	3 Yr Avg Standard Deviation	Avg Duration	NAV As of 3/31/16	Total $(Mil)	Cash %	Gov. Bond %	Muni. Bond %	Corp. Bond %	Other %	Portfolio Turnover Ratio	Avg Coupon Rate	Manager Quality Pct	Manager Tenure (Years)	Initial Purch. $	Additional Purch. $	Front End Load	Back End Load
C- / 3.8	4.1	3.7	9.88	779	0	100	0	0	0	26	0.0	6	2	0	0	0.0	0.0
C- / 3.7	4.2	3.7	9.89	903	0	100	0	0	0	26	0.0	6	2	0	0	0.0	0.0
U /	N/A	N/A	9.99	753	0	2	0	70	28	0	0.0	N/A	1	0	0	0.0	0.0
U /	N/A	N/A	9.99	768	0	2	0	70	28	0	0.0	N/A	1	0	0	0.0	0.0
U /	N/A	N/A	8.94	40	4	0	0	92	4	84	0.0	N/A	3	2,500	0	0.0	1.0
U /	N/A	N/A	8.94	6	4	0	0	92	4	84	0.0	N/A	3	2,500	0	4.0	1.0
U /	N/A	N/A	8.94	5	4	0	0	92	4	84	0.0	N/A	3	2,500	0	0.0	1.0
U /	N/A	N/A	8.94	3	4	0	0	92	4	84	0.0	N/A	3	2,500	0	0.0	1.0
U /	N/A	N/A	8.94	2	4	0	0	92	4	84	0.0	N/A	3	2,500	0	4.0	1.0
A+ / 9.6	0.8	1.7	8.61	5,416	1	26	1	42	30	83	0.0	81	9	2,500	0	0.0	0.0
D / 2.1	5.5	N/A	9.79	282	0	100	0	0	0	42	0.0	4	2	10,000	0	0.0	0.0
D / 2.2	5.5	N/A	9.79	N/A	0	100	0	0	0	42	0.0	4	2	0	0	0.0	0.0
D+ / 2.3	5.4	N/A	9.79	11	0	100	0	0	0	42	0.0	4	2	0	0	0.0	0.0
D / 2.1	5.5	N/A	9.79	301	0	100	0	0	0	42	0.0	3	2	2,500	0	0.0	0.0
C- / 3.0	4.7	6.5	11.26	1,351	0	99	0	0	1	53	0.0	35	2	10,000	0	0.0	0.0
C- / 3.0	4.7	6.5	11.25	145	0	99	0	0	1	53	0.0	32	2	2,500	0	0.0	0.0
E- / 0.1	11.3	17.3	13.74	867	0	99	0	0	1	35	0.0	25	2	10,000	0	0.0	0.0
E- / 0.1	11.3	17.3	13.73	458	0	99	0	0	1	35	0.0	22	2	2,500	0	0.0	0.0
A+ / 9.9	N/A	N/A	1.00	2,129	100	0	0	0	0	0	0.1	65	N/A	2,500	0	0.0	0.0
A+ / 9.9	N/A	N/A	1.00	N/A	100	0	0	0	0	0	0.1	65	N/A	100,000	0	0.0	0.0
A- / 9.0	1.4	2.6	10.54	1,143	0	99	0	0	1	40	0.0	74	2	10,000	0	0.0	0.0
A- / 9.0	1.4	2.6	10.54	52	0	99	0	0	1	40	0.0	70	2	2,500	0	0.0	0.0
C+ / 6.0	3.1	5.4	11.77	2,742	0	42	1	24	33	75	0.0	57	2	0	0	0.0	0.0
C+ / 6.0	3.1	5.4	11.77	6,860	0	42	1	24	33	75	0.0	82	2	10,000	0	0.0	0.0
C+ / 6.0	3.1	5.4	11.77	1,480	0	42	1	24	33	75	0.0	83	2	0	0	0.0	0.0
C+ / 6.1	3.1	5.4	11.77	3,314	0	42	1	24	33	75	0.0	83	2	0	0	0.0	0.0
C+ / 6.0	3.1	5.4	11.77	6,907	0	42	1	24	33	75	0.0	51	2	2,500	0	0.0	0.0
U /	N/A	N/A	1.00	N/A	100	0	0	0	0	0	0.0	N/A	4	100,000	0	0.0	0.0
C / 5.5	3.3	5.4	11.30	11,726	2	19	2	46	31	157	0.0	48	8	0	0	0.0	0.0
C+ / 5.6	3.3	5.4	11.31	11,164	2	19	2	46	31	157	0.0	51	8	0	0	0.0	0.0
C+ / 6.0	3.1	N/A	9.87	41	0	0	0	0	100	115	0.0	45	4	0	0	0.0	0.0
C+ / 6.1	3.1	N/A	9.87	N/A	0	0	0	0	100	115	0.0	46	4	0	0	0.0	0.0
C+ / 6.0	3.1	N/A	9.87	N/A	0	0	0	0	100	115	0.0	37	4	0	0	0.0	0.0
A+ / 9.8	0.6	N/A	9.98	6,398	11	8	2	51	28	16	0.0	78	5	0	0	0.0	0.0
D / 2.0	5.7	N/A	9.26	6	5	0	0	83	12	39	0.0	73	4	0	0	0.0	1.0
D / 2.0	5.7	N/A	9.26	1	5	0	0	83	12	39	0.0	73	4	0	0	0.0	1.0
D / 2.0	5.6	N/A	9.26	N/A	5	0	0	83	12	39	0.0	73	4	0	0	0.0	1.0
D / 2.0	5.7	N/A	9.26	N/A	5	0	0	83	12	39	0.0	42	4	0	0	0.0	1.0
C+ / 6.2	3.1	N/A	10.54	26,747	0	28	2	29	41	120	0.0	46	9	0	0	0.0	0.0
D- / 1.4	5.7	N/A	8.75	3,795	6	0	0	82	12	16	0.0	55	9	0	0	0.0	0.0
C- / 3.2	4.5	4.9	10.36	7,103	2	30	0	20	48	118	0.0	95	17	2,500	0	0.0	0.0
U /	N/A	N/A	1.00	N/A	100	0	0	0	0	0	0.0	N/A	8	100,000	0	0.0	0.0
C- / 4.2	3.8	6.8	11.77	3,110	0	0	100	0	0	5	0.0	62	7	25,000	0	0.0	0.5
C / 5.5	3.3	5.2	10.51	17,503	3	22	1	36	38	140	0.0	57	12	2,500	0	0.0	0.0
U /	N/A	N/A	1.00	5	100	0	0	0	0	0	0.0	N/A	5	1,000	0	0.0	0.0
U /	N/A	N/A	1.00	4,692	100	0	0	0	0	0	0.0	N/A	5	1,000	0	0.0	0.0
U /	N/A	N/A	1.00	N/A	100	0	0	0	0	0	0.0	N/A	5	2,500	0	0.0	0.0
U /	N/A	N/A	1.00	4,505	100	0	0	0	0	0	0.0	N/A	5	25,000	0	0.0	0.0
A+ / 9.9	N/A	N/A	1.00	10,041	100	0	0	0	0	0	0.0	65	5	1,000,000	0	0.0	0.0
C- / 3.1	4.6	N/A	17.27	79	14	69	16	0	1	312	0.0	4	4	100,000	10,000	0.0	0.0
U /	N/A	N/A	1.00	398	100	0	0	0	0	0	0.0	N/A	N/A	10,000,000	0	0.0	0.0
U /	N/A	N/A	1.00	1,383	100	0	0	0	0	0	0.0	N/A	N/A	0	0	0.0	0.0

Fund Type	Fund Name (99 Pct = Best, 0 Pct = Worst)	Ticker Symbol	Overall Investment Rating	Phone	PERFORMANCE: Performance Rating/Pts	Total Return % through 3/31/16: 3 Mo	6 Mo	1Yr / Pct	Annualized: 3Yr / Pct	Annualized: 5Yr / Pct	Incl. in Returns: Dividend Yield	Expense Ratio
MM	First American Gov Oblig Z	FGZXX	**C**	(800) 677-3863	**D / 2.1**	0.04	0.04	0.05 /38	0.02 /20	0.02 / 8	0.05	0.25
MM	First American Prime Oblig A		**U**	(800) 677-3863	**U /**	--	--	--	--	--	0.02	0.80
MM	First American Prime Oblig D	FPDXX	**U**	(800) 677-3863	**U /**	--	--	--	--	--	0.02	0.65
MM	First American Prime Oblig I	FIUXX	**U**	(800) 677-3863	**U /**	0.01	0.02	0.03 /36	0.02 /20	0.01 / 5	0.03	0.45
MM	First American Prime Oblig Inst Inv	FPIXX	**C**	(800) 677-3863	**D / 2.2**	0.04	0.05	0.05 /38	0.03 /22	0.02 / 8	0.05	0.35
MM	First American Prime Oblig Y	FAIXX	**U**	(800) 677-3863	**U /**	0.01	0.01	0.02 /34	0.02 /20	0.01 / 5	0.02	0.50
MM	First American Prime Oblig Z	FPZXX	**C**	(800) 677-3863	**D+ / 2.4**	0.06	0.08	0.10 /41	0.04 /24	0.05 /12	0.10	0.25
MM	First American Treas Oblig Inst Inv	FLIXX	**U**	(800) 677-3863	**U /**	--	--	--	--	--	0.01	0.35
MM	First American Treas Oblig Z	FUZXX	**C-**	(800) 677-3863	**D / 1.9**	0.03	0.04	0.04 /37	0.01 /17	0.01 / 5	0.04	0.25
MM	First American US Treas Money Mkt	FOZXX	**C-**	(800) 677-3863	**D / 1.9**	0.02	0.02	0.02 /34	0.01 /17	--	0.02	0.29
GL	First Eagle High Yield A	FEHAX	**E**	(800) 334-2143	**E- / 0.2**	1.33	-3.62	-8.09 / 1	-1.06 / 8	--	7.09	1.16
GL	First Eagle High Yield C	FEHCX	**E**	(800) 334-2143	**E / 0.3**	1.28	-3.88	-8.67 / 1	-1.76 / 5	--	6.62	1.91
COH	First Eagle High Yield I	FEHIX	**E**	(800) 334-2143	**E / 0.5**	1.53	-3.42	-7.73 / 2	-0.74 /10	2.97 /45	7.72	0.87
MUI	First Inv CA Tax Exempt A	FICAX	**C+**	(800) 423-4026	**B+ / 8.5**	1.42	3.16	3.89 /93	4.00 /96	6.14 /93	3.13	1.06
MUN	First Inv CA Tax Exempt Adv	FICJX	**U**	(800) 423-4026	**U /**	1.58	3.33	4.25 /95	--	--	3.67	0.76
MUI	First Inv CA Tax Exempt B	FICFX	**B**	(800) 423-4026	**A- / 9.0**	1.20	2.69	3.02 /85	3.13 /89	5.31 /88	2.72	1.90
MUN	First Inv CA Tax Exempt Inst	FICLX	**U**	(800) 423-4026	**U /**	1.50	3.33	4.09 /94	--	--	3.67	0.74
MUI	First Inv CT Tax Exempt A	FICTX	**C**	(800) 423-4026	**C+ / 6.2**	1.05	2.30	2.73 /82	2.61 /84	4.89 /84	2.94	1.06
MUN	First Inv CT Tax Exempt Adv	FICYX	**U**	(800) 423-4026	**U /**	1.14	2.42	2.34 /79	--	--	3.19	0.92
MUI	First Inv CT Tax Exempt B	FICUX	**B-**	(800) 423-4026	**B / 7.7**	0.86	1.91	1.93 /77	1.87 /75	4.15 /79	2.34	1.79
MUN	First Inv CT Tax Exempt Inst	FICZX	**U**	(800) 423-4026	**U /**	1.12	2.39	2.91 /84	--	--	3.15	0.75
*COH	First Inv Fund for Income A	FIFIX	**D-**	(800) 423-4026	**D- / 1.5**	2.52	1.64	-2.25 /14	1.41 /50	4.27 /65	4.90	1.23
COH ●	First Inv Fund for Income Adv	FIFKX	**U**	(800) 423-4026	**U /**	2.58	1.76	-1.91 /16	--	--	5.55	0.95
COH	First Inv Fund for Income B	FIFJX	**D**	(800) 423-4026	**C- / 3.3**	2.27	1.14	-2.75 /12	0.63 /36	3.52 /53	4.25	2.03
COH	First Inv Fund for Income Inst	FIFLX	**U**	(800) 423-4026	**U /**	2.63	1.88	-1.69 /17	--	--	5.75	0.80
USS	First Inv Government A	FIGVX	**D+**	(800) 423-4026	**D- / 1.4**	1.88	0.98	0.71 /53	0.95 /42	1.88 /30	1.96	1.19
USL ●	First Inv Government Adv	FIHUX	**U**	(800) 423-4026	**U /**	2.03	1.18	1.08 /60	--	--	2.26	0.89
USS	First Inv Government B	FIGYX	**C-**	(800) 423-4026	**C- / 3.0**	1.77	0.64	-0.07 /31	0.16 /28	1.10 /21	1.22	2.02
USL	First Inv Government Inst	FIHVX	**U**	(800) 423-4026	**U /**	1.98	1.19	1.09 /60	--	--	2.45	0.76
COI	First Inv Investment Grade A	FIIGX	**D+**	(800) 423-4026	**C- / 4.0**	3.24	2.43	0.55 /50	2.15 /64	4.45 /67	3.67	1.15
COI ●	First Inv Investment Grade Advisor	FIIJX	**U**	(800) 423-4026	**U /**	3.35	2.57	0.84 /56	--	--	3.97	0.84
COI	First Inv Investment Grade B	FIIHX	**C-**	(800) 423-4026	**C / 5.1**	3.01	2.01	-0.31 /28	1.27 /48	3.62 /55	3.16	2.03
COI	First Inv Investment Grade Inst	FIIKX	**U**	(800) 423-4026	**U /**	3.43	2.72	1.02 /59	--	--	4.25	0.74
COH	First Inv Life Srs Fd For Income		**D+**	(800) 423-4026	**C+ / 5.8**	2.74	2.06	-1.48 /18	1.90 /59	4.74 /70	5.90	0.85
COI	First Inv Ltd Dur Hi Qual Bd A	FLDKX	**U**	(800) 423-4026	**U /**	1.14	0.61	0.44 /48	--	--	2.06	1.32
COI	First Inv Ltd Dur Hi Qual Bd Adv	FLDLX	**U**	(800) 423-4026	**U /**	1.21	0.71	0.69 /53	--	--	2.53	1.09
COI	First Inv Ltd Dur Hi Qual Bd Inst	FLDMX	**U**	(800) 423-4026	**U /**	1.13	0.71	0.85 /56	--	--	2.69	0.92
MUI	First Inv MA Tax Exempt A	FIMAX	**C-**	(800) 423-4026	**C+ / 6.6**	1.09	2.33	2.62 /81	2.83 /86	5.14 /86	2.97	1.15
MUN	First Inv MA Tax Exempt Adv	FIMHX	**U**	(800) 423-4026	**U /**	1.22	2.52	3.18 /87	--	--	3.36	0.85
MUI	First Inv MA Tax Exempt B	FIMGX	**C+**	(800) 423-4026	**B / 8.0**	0.93	2.00	1.95 /77	2.10 /78	4.39 /81	2.49	1.86
MUN	First Inv MA Tax Exempt Inst	FIMJX	**U**	(800) 423-4026	**U /**	1.22	2.52	2.92 /84	--	--	3.36	0.82
MUI	First Inv MI Tax Exempt A	FTMIX	**C**	(800) 423-4026	**B- / 7.0**	1.27	2.03	2.81 /83	3.01 /88	5.17 /87	3.37	1.13
MUN	First Inv MI Tax Exempt Adv	FTMLX	**U**	(800) 423-4026	**U /**	1.32	2.14	3.05 /85	--	--	3.80	0.79
MUI	First Inv MI Tax Exempt B	FTMJX	**C+**	(800) 423-4026	**B / 8.1**	1.03	1.61	2.06 /78	2.24 /80	4.40 /81	2.92	1.85
MUN	First Inv MI Tax Exempt Inst	FTMMX	**U**	(800) 423-4026	**U /**	1.33	2.07	2.90 /84	--	--	3.82	0.81
MUI	First Inv MN Tax Exempt A	FIMNX	**C-**	(800) 423-4026	**C / 5.0**	1.03	1.86	2.12 /78	2.25 /80	4.59 /82	3.11	1.11
MUN	First Inv MN Tax Exempt Adv	FIMQX	**U**	(800) 423-4026	**U /**	1.10	1.93	2.44 /80	--	--	3.54	0.86
MUI	First Inv MN Tax Exempt B	FIMOX	**C+**	(800) 423-4026	**C+ / 6.8**	0.85	1.49	1.42 /73	1.46 /66	3.82 /76	2.63	1.90
MUN	First Inv MN Tax Exempt Inst	FIMRX	**U**	(800) 423-4026	**U /**	1.09	1.92	2.28 /79	--	--	3.54	0.80
MUI	First Inv NC Tax Exempt A	FMTNX	**C-**	(800) 423-4026	**C / 5.4**	1.08	1.64	2.31 /79	2.39 /81	4.75 /83	3.39	1.10
MUN	First Inv NC Tax Exempt Adv	FMTTX	**U**	(800) 423-4026	**U /**	1.20	1.81	2.65 /82	--	--	3.79	0.79
MUI	First Inv NC Tax Exempt B	FMTQX	**C+**	(800) 423-4026	**B- / 7.2**	0.92	1.30	1.54 /74	1.61 /70	3.97 /77	2.91	1.84

● Denotes fund is closed to new investors
* Denotes fund is included in Section II

RISK			NET ASSETS		ASSET							FUND MANAGER		MINIMUM		LOADS	
Risk Rating/Pts	3 Yr Avg Standard Deviation	Avg Duration	NAV As of 3/31/16	Total $(Mil)	Cash %	Gov. Bond %	Muni. Bond %	Corp. Bond %	Other %	Portfolio Turnover Ratio	Avg Coupon Rate	Manager Quality Pct	Manager Tenure (Years)	Initial Purch. $	Additional Purch. $	Front End Load	Back End Load
A+ / 9.9	N/A	N/A	1.00	7,553	100	0	0	0	0	0	0.1	65	N/A	10,000,000	0	0.0	0.0
U /	N/A	N/A	1.00	1,490	100	0	0	0	0	0	0.0	N/A	N/A	2,500	100	0.0	0.0
U /	N/A	N/A	1.00	513	100	0	0	0	0	0	0.0	N/A	N/A	0	0	0.0	0.0
U /	N/A	N/A	1.00	712	100	0	0	0	0	0	0.0	N/A	N/A	0	0	0.0	0.0
A+ / 9.9	N/A	N/A	1.00	242	100	0	0	0	0	0	0.1	65	N/A	0	0	0.0	0.0
U /	N/A	N/A	1.00	3,246	100	0	0	0	0	0	0.0	N/A	N/A	0	0	0.0	0.0
A+ / 9.9	N/A	N/A	1.00	4,674	100	0	0	0	0	0	0.1	65	N/A	10,000,000	0	0.0	0.0
U /	N/A	N/A	1.00	665	100	0	0	0	0	0	0.0	N/A	N/A	0	0	0.0	0.0
A+ / 9.9	N/A	N/A	1.00	3,038	100	0	0	0	0	0	0.0	63	N/A	10,000,000	0	0.0	0.0
A+ / 9.9	N/A	N/A	1.00	298	100	0	0	0	0	0	0.0	63	N/A	10,000,000	0	0.0	0.0
D- / 1.0	6.6	4.5	8.17	147	8	0	0	77	15	32	0.0	27	N/A	2,500	100	4.5	0.0
D- / 1.0	6.6	4.5	8.17	104	8	0	0	77	15	32	0.0	14	N/A	2,500	100	0.0	0.0
E+ / 0.7	6.5	4.5	8.18	317	8	0	0	77	15	32	0.0	9	N/A	1,000,000	100	0.0	0.0
C- / 3.8	4.1	4.5	13.10	49	2	0	97	0	1	47	5.3	51	25	1,000	0	5.8	0.0
U /	N/A	4.5	13.08	3	2	0	97	0	1	47	5.3	N/A	25	1,000	0	0.0	0.0
C- / 3.8	4.1	4.5	13.02	N/A	2	0	97	0	1	47	5.3	25	25	1,000	0	0.0	0.0
U /	N/A	4.5	13.08	N/A	2	0	97	0	1	47	5.3	N/A	25	2,000,000	0	0.0	0.0
C / 4.8	3.5	3.7	13.65	34	0	0	99	0	1	19	5.1	27	25	1,000	0	5.8	0.0
U /	N/A	3.7	13.54	N/A	0	0	99	0	1	19	5.1	N/A	25	1,000	0	0.0	0.0
C / 4.9	3.5	3.7	13.64	1	0	0	99	0	1	19	5.1	14	25	1,000	0	0.0	0.0
U /	N/A	3.7	13.72	N/A	0	0	99	0	1	19	5.1	N/A	25	2,000,000	0	0.0	0.0
D / 2.0	5.1	4.0	2.37	554	3	0	0	91	6	47	9.4	61	7	1,000	0	5.8	0.0
U /	N/A	4.0	2.37	45	3	0	0	91	6	47	9.4	N/A	7	1,000	0	0.0	0.0
D+ / 2.3	5.0	4.0	2.37	3	3	0	0	91	6	47	9.4	34	7	1,000	0	0.0	0.0
U /	N/A	4.0	2.38	48	3	0	0	91	6	47	9.4	N/A	7	2,000,000	0	0.0	0.0
B / 8.2	2.3	4.6	10.83	261	1	28	0	0	71	82	3.3	41	4	1,000	0	5.8	0.0
U /	N/A	4.6	10.85	57	1	28	0	0	71	82	3.3	N/A	4	1,000	0	0.0	0.0
B / 8.2	2.3	4.6	10.81	2	1	28	0	0	71	82	3.3	20	4	1,000	0	0.0	0.0
U /	N/A	4.6	10.88	14	1	28	0	0	71	82	3.3	N/A	4	2,000,000	0	0.0	0.0
C / 4.3	3.8	5.4	9.69	462	1	2	0	96	1	36	7.7	50	7	1,000	0	5.8	0.0
U /	N/A	5.4	9.73	74	1	2	0	96	1	36	7.7	N/A	7	1,000	0	0.0	0.0
C / 4.3	3.8	5.4	9.62	3	1	2	0	96	1	36	7.7	23	7	1,000	0	0.0	0.0
U /	N/A	5.4	9.72	23	1	2	0	96	1	36	7.7	N/A	7	2,000,000	0	0.0	0.0
D / 2.1	5.1	N/A	5.88	96	3	0	0	90	7	41	0.0	81	7	0	0	0.0	0.0
U /	N/A	2.3	9.71	38	3	8	0	58	31	57	3.5	N/A	N/A	1,000	0	5.8	0.0
U /	N/A	2.3	9.74	46	3	8	0	58	31	57	3.5	N/A	N/A	1,000	0	0.0	0.0
U /	N/A	2.3	9.74	21	3	8	0	58	31	57	3.5	N/A	N/A	2,000,000	0	0.0	0.0
C- / 3.7	4.2	4.0	12.13	22	2	0	97	0	1	11	5.1	17	25	1,000	0	5.8	0.0
U /	N/A	4.0	12.16	N/A	2	0	97	0	1	11	5.1	N/A	25	1,000	0	0.0	0.0
C- / 3.7	4.2	4.0	12.10	N/A	2	0	97	0	1	11	5.1	10	25	1,000	0	0.0	0.0
U /	N/A	4.0	12.16	N/A	2	0	97	0	1	11	5.1	N/A	25	2,000,000	0	0.0	0.0
C- / 4.2	3.9	3.7	12.41	20	0	0	99	0	1	54	5.4	32	25	1,000	0	5.8	0.0
U /	N/A	3.7	12.46	N/A	0	0	99	0	1	54	5.4	N/A	25	1,000	0	0.0	0.0
C- / 4.2	3.9	3.7	12.36	N/A	0	0	99	0	1	54	5.4	16	25	1,000	0	0.0	0.0
U /	N/A	3.7	12.39	N/A	0	0	99	0	1	54	5.4	N/A	25	2,000,000	0	0.0	0.0
C / 5.4	3.3	3.3	12.36	21	0	0	99	0	1	8	5.1	24	25	1,000	0	5.8	0.0
U /	N/A	3.3	12.36	N/A	0	0	99	0	1	8	5.1	N/A	25	1,000	0	0.0	0.0
C / 5.4	3.3	3.3	12.29	N/A	0	0	99	0	1	8	5.1	12	25	1,000	0	0.0	0.0
U /	N/A	3.3	12.37	N/A	0	0	99	0	1	8	5.1	N/A	25	2,000,000	0	0.0	0.0
C / 5.1	3.4	3.2	13.73	20	1	0	98	0	1	11	5.2	26	24	1,000	0	5.8	0.0
U /	N/A	3.2	13.75	N/A	1	0	98	0	1	11	5.2	N/A	24	1,000	0	0.0	0.0
C / 5.1	3.4	3.2	13.70	N/A	1	0	98	0	1	11	5.2	13	24	1,000	0	0.0	0.0

Fund Type	Fund Name (99 Pct = Best; 0 Pct = Worst)	Ticker Symbol	Overall Investment Rating	Phone	PERFORMANCE: Performance Rating/Pts	Total Return % through 3/31/16: 3 Mo	6 Mo	1Yr / Pct	Annualized: 3Yr / Pct	Annualized: 5Yr / Pct	Incl. in Returns: Dividend Yield	Expense Ratio
MUN	First Inv NC Tax Exempt Inst	FMTUX	U	(800) 423-4026	U /	1.13	1.81	2.44 /80	--	--	3.80	0.79
MUI	First Inv NJ Tax Exempt A	FINJX	C	(800) 423-4026	C+ / 6.6	1.66	3.26	2.96 /85	2.63 /84	4.97 /85	3.22	1.04
MUN	First Inv NJ Tax Exempt Adv	FINLX	U	(800) 423-4026	U /	1.65	3.32	3.25 /87	--	--	3.70	0.74
MUI	First Inv NJ Tax Exempt B	FINKX	C+	(800) 423-4026	B / 7.9	1.52	2.87	2.19 /78	1.85 /75	4.19 /79	2.76	1.83
MUN	First Inv NJ Tax Exempt Inst	FINNX	U	(800) 423-4026	U /	1.75	3.37	3.14 /86	--	--	3.74	0.73
MUI	First Inv NY Tax Exempt A	FNYFX	C	(800) 423-4026	B- / 7.0	1.26	2.53	3.21 /87	2.86 /87	5.00 /85	3.35	1.01
MUN	First Inv NY Tax Exempt Adv	FNYHX	U	(800) 423-4026	U /	1.32	2.71	3.51 /90	--	--	3.77	0.71
MUI	First Inv NY Tax Exempt B	FNYGX	B-	(800) 423-4026	B / 8.1	1.10	2.19	2.50 /80	2.12 /78	4.26 /79	2.87	1.74
MUN	First Inv NY Tax Exempt Inst	FNYJX	U	(800) 423-4026	U /	1.31	2.64	3.43 /89	--	--	3.76	0.69
MUI	First Inv OH Tax Exempt A	FIOHX	C+	(800) 423-4026	B- / 7.1	1.31	2.20	2.70 /82	3.02 /88	4.95 /85	2.94	1.10
MUN	First Inv OH Tax Exempt Adv	FIOKX	U	(800) 423-4026	U /	1.38	2.33	1.57 /74	--	--	3.05	0.96
MUI	First Inv OH Tax Exempt B	FIOJX	B-	(800) 423-4026	B / 8.0	1.07	1.78	1.75 /75	2.11 /78	4.10 /78	2.12	1.97
MUN	First Inv OH Tax Exempt Inst	FIOLX	U	(800) 423-4026	U /	1.37	2.41	3.04 /85	--	--	3.05	0.79
MUI	First Inv OR Tax Exempt A	FTORX	C-	(800) 423-4026	C+ / 5.9	1.42	2.62	2.80 /83	2.42 /82	4.87 /84	2.85	1.06
MUN	First Inv OR Tax Exempt Adv	FTOTX	U	(800) 423-4026	U /	1.52	2.75	3.13 /86	--	--	3.35	0.73
MUI	First Inv OR Tax Exempt B	FTOBX	C	(800) 423-4026	B- / 7.5	1.33	2.19	2.08 /78	1.63 /71	4.09 /78	2.33	1.84
MUN	First Inv OR Tax Exempt Inst	FTOUX	U	(800) 423-4026	U /	1.54	2.79	3.02 /85	--	--	3.39	0.73
MUI	First Inv PA Tax Exempt A	FTPAX	C	(800) 423-4026	C+ / 6.7	0.95	1.88	2.61 /81	2.91 /87	5.27 /87	3.41	1.06
MUN	First Inv PA Tax Exempt Adv	FTPEX	U	(800) 423-4026	U /	1.01	2.07	2.90 /84	--	--	3.82	0.78
MUI	First Inv PA Tax Exempt B	FTPDX	C+	(800) 423-4026	B / 7.9	0.79	1.55	1.79 /76	2.09 /78	4.47 /81	2.98	1.89
MUN	First Inv PA Tax Exempt Inst	FTPFX	U	(800) 423-4026	U /	1.01	1.99	2.83 /83	--	--	3.83	0.75
* MUI	First Inv Tax Exempt Income A	FITAX	C	(800) 423-4026	C+ / 6.5	1.03	2.03	2.50 /80	2.82 /86	5.17 /87	3.66	1.00
MUN	First Inv Tax Exempt Income Adv	FITDX	U	(800) 423-4026	U /	1.10	2.16	2.76 /83	--	--	4.14	0.68
MUI	First Inv Tax Exempt Income B	FITCX	B-	(800) 423-4026	B / 7.9	0.97	1.69	1.80 /76	2.08 /78	4.41 /81	3.20	1.75
MUN	First Inv Tax Exempt Income Inst	FITEX	U	(800) 423-4026	U /	1.19	2.26	2.75 /83	--	--	4.12	0.67
MUI	First Inv Tax Exempt Opps A	EIITX	C	(800) 423-4026	B / 7.9	1.41	2.77	3.34 /88	3.44 /92	6.12 /93	2.97	1.04
MUN	First Inv Tax Exempt Opps Adv	EIIAX	U	(800) 423-4026	U /	1.38	2.82	3.45 /90	--	--	3.25	0.83
MUI	First Inv Tax Exempt Opps B	EIIUX	C+	(800) 423-4026	B+ / 8.6	1.20	2.39	2.50 /80	2.69 /85	5.35 /88	2.51	1.77
MUN	First Inv Tax Exempt Opps Inst	EIINX	U	(800) 423-4026	U /	1.43	2.94	3.50 /90	--	--	3.24	0.71
MUI	First Inv VA Tax Exempt A	FIVAX	C-	(800) 423-4026	C+ / 6.1	1.23	2.22	2.68 /82	2.56 /83	4.53 /82	2.83	1.06
MUN	First Inv VA Tax Exempt Adv	FIVCX	U	(800) 423-4026	U /	1.18	2.18	2.75 /83	--	--	3.07	0.87
MUI	First Inv VA Tax Exempt B	FIVBX	C+	(800) 423-4026	B- / 7.2	0.85	1.59	1.54 /74	1.61 /70	3.65 /75	2.12	1.90
MUN	First Inv VA Tax Exempt Inst	FIVDX	U	(800) 423-4026	U /	1.32	2.32	2.96 /85	--	--	3.05	0.74
LP	First Investors Floating Rate A	FRFDX	U	(800) 423-4026	U /	1.65	0.56	0.52 /50	--	--	2.77	1.33
LP	First Investors Floating Rate Adv	FRFEX	U	(800) 423-4026	U /	1.59	0.58	0.66 /53	--	--	3.19	1.03
LP	First Investors Floating Rate Inst	FRFNX	U	(800) 423-4026	U /	1.64	0.69	0.97 /58	--	--	3.40	0.90
GL	First Investors Intl Opptys Bd A	FIOBX	E	(800) 423-4026	E+ / 0.7	8.00	6.62	-1.01 /22	-1.13 / 8	--	2.74	1.38
GL	● First Investors Intl Opptys Bd Adv	FIODX	U	(800) 423-4026	U /	8.01	6.79	-0.88 /23	--	--	3.02	1.04
GL	First Investors Intl Opptys Bd Inst	FIOEX	U	(800) 423-4026	U /	8.01	6.82	-0.76 /24	--	--	3.13	0.90
GEN	● First Investors Strategic Inc Adv	FSIHX	U	(800) 423-4026	U /	2.29	2.07	-1.04 /21	--	--	4.07	0.91
MUN	First Security Municipal Bond A	FSARX	U		U /	2.07	3.54	--	--	--	0.00	N/A
MUN	First Security Municipal Bond Inst	FIFSX	U		U /	2.07	3.54	--	--	--	0.00	N/A
LP	First Trust Short Duration HI A	FDHAX	C-	(800) 621-1675	C- / 4.2	2.37	0.41	-1.34 /19	2.10 /63	--	4.10	1.26
LP	First Trust Short Duration HI C	FDHCX	C-	(800) 621-1675	C / 4.4	2.23	0.08	-2.07 /15	1.32 /49	--	3.44	2.01
LP	First Trust Short Duration HI I	FDHIX	C+	(800) 621-1675	C+ / 6.3	2.43	0.54	-1.09 /21	2.36 /68	--	4.50	1.01
GEI	First Western Fixed Income Inst	FWFIX	A+	(800) 292-6775	B- / 7.5	1.84	1.83	2.15 /73	2.79 /74	--	2.68	0.95
COI	First Western Sht Duration Bd Inst	FWSBX	U	(800) 292-6775	U /	0.85	0.81	1.51 /66	--	--	2.20	0.89
GL	Forward Credit Analysis Long/Sh A	FLSLX	E+	(800) 999-6809	E+ / 0.9	1.97	4.52	5.35 /90	-0.77 / 9	3.62 /55	2.38	2.02
GEL	Forward Credit Analysis Long/Sh Adv	FLSMX	D	(800) 999-6809	C- / 4.2	2.10	4.76	5.79 /92	-0.36 /13	4.15 /64	2.92	1.57
EM	Forward EM Corporate Debt Adv	FFXMX	U	(800) 999-6809	U /	0.33	-1.60	-5.92 / 3	--	--	9.68	1.95
GL	Forward EM Corporate Debt C	FFXCX	E+	(800) 999-6809	E- / 0.2	0.11	-2.03	-6.72 / 2	-3.04 / 2	-0.70 / 2	8.39	2.85
GL	Forward EM Corporate Debt I	FFXIX	E+	(800) 999-6809	E / 0.3	0.34	-1.71	-5.98 / 3	-2.14 / 4	0.22 /16	9.76	1.90

● Denotes fund is closed to new investors
* Denotes fund is included in Section II

RISK			NET ASSETS		ASSET							FUND MANAGER		MINIMUM		LOADS	
Risk Rating/Pts	3 Yr Avg Standard Deviation	Avg Duration	NAV As of 3/31/16	Total $(Mil)	Cash %	Gov. Bond %	Muni. Bond %	Corp. Bond %	Other %	Portfolio Turnover Ratio	Avg Coupon Rate	Manager Quality Pct	Manager Tenure (Years)	Initial Purch. $	Additional Purch. $	Front End Load	Back End Load
U /	N/A	3.2	13.72	N/A	1	0	98	0	1	11	5.2	N/A	24	2,000,000	0	0.0	0.0
C / 4.3	3.8	4.5	13.15	47	1	0	98	0	1	30	5.3	21	25	1,000	0	5.8	0.0
U /	N/A	4.5	13.13	1	1	0	98	0	1	30	5.3	N/A	25	1,000	0	0.0	0.0
C- / 4.2	3.8	4.5	13.09	N/A	1	0	98	0	1	30	5.3	11	25	1,000	0	0.0	0.0
U /	N/A	4.5	13.12	N/A	1	0	98	0	1	30	5.3	N/A	25	2,000,000	0	0.0	0.0
C / 4.6	3.6	4.2	14.77	145	1	0	98	0	1	28	5.2	30	25	1,000	0	5.8	0.0
U /	N/A	4.2	14.76	6	1	0	98	0	1	28	5.2	N/A	25	1,000	0	0.0	0.0
C / 4.6	3.6	4.2	14.75	1	1	0	98	0	1	28	5.2	16	25	1,000	0	0.0	0.0
U /	N/A	4.2	14.78	N/A	1	0	98	0	1	28	5.2	N/A	25	2,000,000	0	0.0	0.0
C / 4.9	3.5	3.9	12.79	22	1	0	98	0	1	81	5.2	39	25	1,000	0	5.8	0.0
U /	N/A	3.9	12.60	N/A	1	0	98	0	1	81	5.2	N/A	25	1,000	0	0.0	0.0
C / 4.9	3.5	3.9	12.75	N/A	1	0	98	0	1	81	5.2	18	25	1,000	0	0.0	0.0
U /	N/A	3.9	12.87	N/A	1	0	98	0	1	81	5.2	N/A	25	2,000,000	0	0.0	0.0
C- / 3.8	4.1	4.4	13.82	50	1	0	98	0	1	25	4.7	14	24	1,000	0	5.8	0.0
U /	N/A	4.4	13.79	3	1	0	98	0	1	25	4.7	N/A	24	1,000	0	0.0	0.0
C- / 3.8	4.1	4.4	13.76	N/A	1	0	98	0	1	25	4.7	8	24	1,000	0	0.0	0.0
U /	N/A	4.4	13.81	N/A	1	0	98	0	1	25	4.7	N/A	24	2,000,000	0	0.0	0.0
C / 4.4	3.7	3.5	13.40	34	0	0	99	0	1	40	5.3	30	25	1,000	0	5.8	0.0
U /	N/A	3.5	13.41	1	0	0	99	0	1	40	5.3	N/A	25	1,000	0	0.0	0.0
C / 4.5	3.7	3.5	13.32	N/A	0	0	99	0	1	40	5.3	15	25	1,000	0	0.0	0.0
U /	N/A	3.5	13.38	N/A	0	0	99	0	1	40	5.3	N/A	25	2,000,000	0	0.0	0.0
C / 4.8	3.6	3.9	9.88	628	0	0	98	0	2	11	5.3	32	25	1,000	0	5.8	0.0
U /	N/A	3.9	9.87	30	0	0	98	0	2	11	5.3	N/A	25	1,000	0	0.0	0.0
C / 4.8	3.6	3.9	9.85	1	0	0	98	0	2	11	5.3	17	25	1,000	0	0.0	0.0
U /	N/A	3.9	9.90	7	0	0	98	0	2	11	5.3	N/A	25	2,000,000	0	0.0	0.0
C- / 3.3	4.5	4.3	17.15	267	1	0	98	0	1	70	5.2	24	25	1,000	0	5.8	0.0
U /	N/A	4.3	17.14	4	1	0	98	0	1	70	5.2	N/A	25	1,000	0	0.0	0.0
C- / 3.2	4.5	4.3	17.06	3	1	0	98	0	1	70	5.2	13	25	1,000	0	0.0	0.0
U /	N/A	4.3	17.20	N/A	1	0	98	0	1	70	5.2	N/A	25	2,000,000	0	0.0	0.0
C / 4.4	3.7	3.9	13.34	44	0	0	100	0	0	38	4.9	22	25	1,000	0	5.8	0.0
U /	N/A	3.9	13.30	N/A	0	0	100	0	0	38	4.9	N/A	25	1,000	0	0.0	0.0
C / 4.4	3.7	3.9	13.23	N/A	0	0	100	0	0	38	4.9	10	25	1,000	0	0.0	0.0
U /	N/A	3.9	13.39	N/A	0	0	100	0	0	38	4.9	N/A	25	2,000,000	0	0.0	0.0
U /	N/A	N/A	9.50	60	7	0	0	46	47	49	0.0	N/A	3	1,000	0	5.8	0.0
U /	N/A	N/A	9.49	56	7	0	0	46	47	49	0.0	N/A	3	1,000	0	0.0	0.0
U /	N/A	N/A	9.48	14	7	0	0	46	47	49	0.0	N/A	3	2,000,000	0	0.0	0.0
E+ / 0.7	7.2	N/A	9.07	69	5	81	0	13	1	61	0.0	28	4	1,000	0	5.8	0.0
U /	N/A	N/A	9.09	63	5	81	0	13	1	61	0.0	N/A	4	1,000	0	0.0	0.0
U /	N/A	N/A	9.12	8	5	81	0	13	1	61	0.0	N/A	4	2,000,000	0	0.0	0.0
U /	N/A	N/A	9.27	N/A	9	14	5	54	18	40	0.0	N/A	3	1,000	0	0.0	0.0
U /	N/A	N/A	10.32	3	0	0	0	0	100	0	0.0	N/A	1	5,000	1,000	2.0	0.0
U /	N/A	N/A	10.32	2	0	0	0	0	100	0	0.0	N/A	1	25,000	1,000	0.0	0.0
C+ / 6.1	3.1	2.2	19.43	44	3	0	0	31	66	58	0.0	94	4	2,500	50	3.5	0.0
C+ / 6.0	3.1	2.2	19.42	24	3	0	0	31	66	58	0.0	88	4	2,500	50	0.0	0.0
C+ / 6.1	3.1	2.2	19.43	92	3	0	0	31	66	58	0.0	96	4	0	0	0.0	0.0
B / 8.1	2.3	N/A	9.81	68	2	12	3	36	47	129	0.0	89	N/A	1,000	100	0.0	0.0
U /	N/A	N/A	9.95	107	3	0	3	48	46	63	0.0	N/A	3	1,000	100	0.0	0.0
D- / 1.3	6.3	N/A	7.70	3	4	5	90	0	1	168	0.0	35	3	4,000	100	5.8	0.0
D- / 1.2	6.3	N/A	7.67	21	4	5	90	0	1	168	0.0	7	3	0	0	0.0	0.0
U /	N/A	N/A	7.32	1	4	9	0	85	2	70	0.0	N/A	5	0	0	0.0	0.0
D / 1.9	5.7	N/A	7.43	1	4	9	0	85	2	70	0.0	7	5	4,000	100	0.0	0.0
D / 2.0	5.7	N/A	7.32	25	4	9	0	85	2	70	0.0	11	5	100,000	0	0.0	0.0

Fund Type	Fund Name (99 Pct = Best, 0 Pct = Worst)	Ticker Symbol	Overall Investment Rating	Phone	PERFORMANCE: Performance Rating/Pts	Total Return % through 3/31/16: 3 Mo	6 Mo	1Yr / Pct	Annualized: 3Yr / Pct	Annualized: 5Yr / Pct	Incl. in Returns: Dividend Yield	Expense Ratio
GL	Forward EM Corporate Debt Inv	FFXRX	E+	(800) 999-6809	E / 0.3	0.16	-1.73	-6.26 / 3	-2.46 / 3	-0.13 / 3	9.15	2.25
COH	Forward High Yield Bond C	AHYIX	E+	(800) 999-6809	E+ / 0.8	0.64	-2.37	-6.29 / 3	-0.36 / 13	2.82 / 42	5.55	2.62
COH	Forward High Yield Bond Inst	AHBAX	E+	(800) 999-6809	D- / 1.4	0.74	-2.04	-5.44 / 4	0.55 / 34	3.76 / 58	6.51	1.72
COH	Forward High Yield Bond Inv	AHBIX	E+	(800) 999-6809	D- / 1.1	0.76	-2.11	-5.79 / 3	0.15 / 28	3.34 / 51	6.07	2.12
COH	Forward High Yield Bond Z		E+	(800) 999-6809	D- / 1.5	0.77	-1.99	-5.35 / 4	0.62 / 35	3.84 / 59	6.64	1.62
GEI	Forward Investment Grd Fxd-Inc Inst	AIFIX	D+	(800) 999-6809	C / 4.6	2.88	1.85	2.12 / 72	0.63 / 36	3.44 / 52	1.27	1.39
GEI	Forward Investment Grd Fxd-Inc Inv	AITIX	U	(800) 999-6809	U /	2.71	1.42	1.30 / 63	--	2.88 / 43	0.56	1.79
GEI	Forward Investment Grd Fxd-Inc Z		D+	(800) 999-6809	C / 4.8	2.92	1.92	2.25 / 73	0.73 / 37	3.52 / 53	1.39	1.29
LP	Forward Select Opportunity Inst	FSOTX	U	(800) 999-6809	U /	-8.00	-13.63	-20.54 / 0	--	--	4.29	1.96
*GEI	FPA New Income Inc	FPNIX	C	(800) 982-4372	D+ / 2.7	0.60	-0.04	0.16 / 43	0.72 / 37	1.24 / 23	1.86	0.58
*USS	Franklin Adjustable US Govt Sec A	FISAX	C-	(800) 342-5236	E+ / 0.9	-0.38	-0.76	-1.11 / 21	-0.24 / 14	0.40 / 17	1.21	0.91
GEI	Franklin Adjustable US Govt Sec A1	FAUGX	U	(800) 342-5236	U /	-0.34	-0.57	-0.85 / 23	--	--	1.36	0.75
USS	Franklin Adjustable US Govt Sec Adv	FAUZX	C-	(800) 342-5236	D / 1.6	-0.31	-0.52	-0.86 / 23	0.01 / 16	0.65 / 18	1.49	0.66
USS	Franklin Adjustable US Govt Sec C	FCSCX	C-	(800) 342-5236	D- / 1.0	-0.47	-0.84	-1.39 / 19	-0.64 / 11	0.02 / 7	0.84	1.31
GEI	Franklin Adjustable US Govt Sec R6		U	(800) 342-5236	U /	-0.29	-0.46	-0.74 / 24	--	--	1.61	0.53
MUS	Franklin Alabama Tax-Free Inc A	FRALX	C	(800) 342-5236	C+ / 6.9	1.47	2.34	2.21 / 78	2.50 / 83	5.48 / 89	3.51	0.72
MUS	Franklin Alabama Tax-Free Inc C	FALEX	C+	(800) 342-5236	B / 7.8	1.32	2.04	1.63 / 75	1.95 / 76	4.90 / 84	3.08	1.27
*MUS	Franklin Arizona Tax-Free Inc A	FTAZX	C	(800) 342-5236	B / 7.8	1.66	2.98	2.53 / 81	2.91 / 87	5.72 / 90	3.49	0.62
MUS	Franklin Arizona Tax-Free Inc Adv	FAZZX	B-	(800) 321-8563	A- / 9.0	1.59	3.03	2.54 / 81	3.00 / 88	5.81 / 91	3.74	0.52
MUS	Franklin Arizona Tax-Free Inc C	FAZIX	C+	(800) 342-5236	B+ / 8.3	1.50	2.75	1.94 / 77	2.37 / 81	5.14 / 86	3.05	1.17
*MUS	Franklin CA Interm Tax-Free A	FKCIX	A-	(800) 342-5236	B+ / 8.8	1.65	2.96	3.14 / 86	3.43 / 92	5.48 / 89	2.67	0.63
MUS	Franklin CA Interm Tax-Free Adv	FRCZX	A	(800) 321-8563	A / 9.3	1.67	3.00	3.23 / 87	3.52 / 93	5.59 / 89	2.83	0.53
MUS	Franklin CA Interm Tax-Free C	FCCIX	A-	(800) 342-5236	B+ / 8.9	1.59	2.67	2.57 / 81	2.89 / 87	4.92 / 85	2.19	1.18
*MUH	Franklin California H/Y Muni A	FCAMX	C+	(800) 342-5236	A+ / 9.8	2.06	4.52	4.98 / 98	5.51 / 99	9.42 / 99	3.70	0.63
MUH	Franklin California H/Y Muni Adv	FVCAX	C+	(800) 321-8563	A+ / 9.9	2.08	4.56	5.07 / 98	5.61 / 99	9.53 / 99	3.96	0.53
MUH	Franklin California H/Y Muni C	FCAHX	C+	(800) 342-5236	A+ / 9.9	2.00	4.31	4.48 / 97	4.97 / 99	8.83 / 99	3.31	1.18
*MUI	● Franklin California Ins Tx-Fr A	FRCIX	B	(800) 342-5236	A / 9.5	1.89	3.53	3.98 / 94	5.10 / 99	7.46 / 97	3.70	0.59
MUI	● Franklin California Ins Tx-Fr Adv	FZCAX	B+	(800) 321-8563	A+ / 9.9	1.91	3.57	4.06 / 94	5.19 / 99	7.55 / 97	3.94	0.50
MUI	● Franklin California Ins Tx-Fr C	FRCAX	B+	(800) 342-5236	A+ / 9.7	1.80	3.28	3.43 / 89	4.53 / 98	6.87 / 96	3.26	1.15
*MUS	Franklin California Tx-Fr Inc A	FKTFX	B-	(800) 342-5236	A / 9.4	1.87	3.98	3.82 / 93	4.67 / 98	7.51 / 97	3.66	0.58
MUS	Franklin California Tx-Fr Inc Adv	FCAVX	B	(800) 321-8563	A+ / 9.8	1.90	4.03	3.92 / 93	4.77 / 98	7.62 / 98	3.92	0.49
MUS	Franklin California Tx-Fr Inc C	FRCTX	B	(800) 342-5236	A+ / 9.6	1.73	3.84	3.39 / 89	4.10 / 96	6.93 / 96	3.28	1.14
*MUS	Franklin Colorado Tax-Free Inc A	FRCOX	C	(800) 342-5236	B / 7.6	1.44	2.50	2.49 / 80	2.87 / 87	5.73 / 90	3.63	0.65
MUS	Franklin Colorado Tax-Free Inc Adv	FCOZX	B-	(800) 321-8563	B+ / 8.9	1.46	2.54	2.59 / 81	2.97 / 88	5.84 / 91	3.88	0.55
MUS	Franklin Colorado Tax-Free Inc C	FCOIX	C+	(800) 342-5236	B / 8.2	1.37	2.28	1.99 / 77	2.33 / 81	5.17 / 87	3.19	1.20
MUS	Franklin CT Tax-Free Inc A	FXCTX	C-	(800) 342-5236	C+ / 5.7	1.64	3.04	2.62 / 81	1.80 / 74	4.54 / 82	3.44	0.68
MUS	Franklin CT Tax-Free Inc Adv	FCNZX	C+	(800) 321-8563	B / 8.1	1.66	3.09	2.63 / 82	1.90 / 76	4.65 / 83	3.69	0.58
MUS	Franklin CT Tax-Free Inc C	FCTIX	C	(800) 342-5236	B- / 7.0	1.49	2.84	2.05 / 77	1.24 / 60	3.98 / 77	3.03	1.23
MUS	● Franklin Double Tax-Free Inc A	FPRTX	E-	(800) 342-5236	E- / 0.2	1.17	1.67	-0.50 / 26	-3.26 / 2	1.47 / 34	4.06	0.76
MUS	● Franklin Double Tax-Free Inc Adv	FDBZX	E-	(800) 321-8563	E / 0.3	1.19	1.62	-0.51 / 26	-3.20 / 2	1.56 / 36	4.34	0.67
MUS	● Franklin Double Tax-Free Inc C	FPRIX	E-	(800) 342-5236	E / 0.3	0.92	1.29	-1.15 / 20	-3.81 / 2	0.89 / 24	3.66	1.32
EM	Franklin Emg Mkt Debt Opportunity	FEMDX	D-	(800) 342-5236	C- / 3.1	3.17	4.56	2.26 / 73	-0.63 / 11	3.07 / 46	5.85	1.09
*MUN	Franklin Fdrl Lmtd Trm T/F Inc A	FFTFX	C-	(800) 342-5236	D / 1.8	0.31	0.24	0.50 / 55	0.57 / 40	1.58 / 37	0.87	0.70
MUN	Franklin Fdrl Lmtd Trm T/F Inc Adv	FTFZX	B+	(800) 342-5236	C / 4.7	0.34	0.42	0.75 / 61	0.75 / 45	1.73 / 40	1.04	0.55
*MUN	Franklin Fed Interm-Trm T/F Inc A	FKITX	B	(800) 342-5236	B / 7.9	1.26	2.32	2.77 / 83	2.54 / 83	4.81 / 84	2.42	0.68
MUN	Franklin Fed Interm-Trm T/F Inc Adv	FITZX	A-	(800) 321-8563	B+ / 8.7	1.36	2.45	2.95 / 84	2.67 / 84	4.92 / 85	2.56	0.58
MUN	Franklin Fed Interm-Trm T/F Inc C	FCITX	B	(800) 342-5236	B / 7.9	1.12	2.04	2.21 / 78	1.98 / 77	4.23 / 79	1.93	1.23
*MUN	Franklin Federal Tax-Free Inc A	FKTIX	C+	(800) 342-5236	B / 8.2	1.46	2.69	2.82 / 83	3.36 / 91	6.09 / 92	3.64	0.62
MUN	Franklin Federal Tax-Free Inc Adv	FAFTX	B	(800) 321-8563	A / 9.3	1.48	2.74	2.92 / 84	3.47 / 92	6.21 / 93	3.90	0.52
MUN	Franklin Federal Tax-Free Inc C	FRFTX	B-	(800) 342-5236	B+ / 8.7	1.32	2.41	2.26 / 79	2.80 / 86	5.51 / 89	3.25	1.17
COI	Franklin Flexible Alpha Bond A	FABFX	U	(800) 342-5236	U /	-0.32	-0.04	--	--	--	0.00	1.82
COI	Franklin Flexible Alpha Bond Adv	FZBAX	U	(800) 342-5236	U /	-0.32	-0.01	--	--	--	0.00	1.57

● Denotes fund is closed to new investors
* Denotes fund is included in Section II

RISK			NET ASSETS		ASSET							FUND MANAGER		MINIMUM		LOADS	
Risk Rating/Pts	3 Yr Avg Standard Deviation	Avg Duration	NAV As of 3/31/16	Total $(Mil)	Cash %	Gov. Bond %	Muni. Bond %	Corp. Bond %	Other %	Portfolio Turnover Ratio	Avg Coupon Rate	Manager Quality Pct	Manager Tenure (Years)	Initial Purch. $	Additional Purch. $	Front End Load	Back End Load
D / 1.9	5.8	N/A	7.39	153	4	9	0	85	2	70	0.0	9	5	4,000	100	0.0	0.0
D / 1.6	5.5	N/A	8.62	1	10	0	0	89	1	206	0.0	12	N/A	4,000	100	0.0	0.0
D / 1.6	5.5	N/A	8.62	19	10	0	0	89	1	206	0.0	28	N/A	100,000	0	0.0	0.0
D / 1.6	5.5	N/A	8.65	67	10	0	0	89	1	206	0.0	19	N/A	4,000	100	0.0	0.0
D / 1.6	5.5	N/A	8.60	5	10	0	0	89	1	206	0.0	30	N/A	0	0	0.0	0.0
C- / 3.9	4.0	6.5	11.20	2	6	48	0	30	16	314	0.9	9	N/A	100,000	0	0.0	0.0
U /	4.1	6.5	11.20	16	6	48	0	30	16	314	0.9	N/A	N/A	4,000	100	0.0	0.0
C- / 3.9	4.0	6.5	11.18	5	6	48	0	30	16	314	0.9	10	N/A	0	0	0.0	0.0
U /	N/A	N/A	19.44	3	0	5	0	15	80	181	0.0	N/A	5	100,000	0	0.0	0.0
A+ / 9.6	0.8	1.3	10.01	5,352	0	7	1	25	67	29	2.1	76	12	1,500	100	0.0	2.0
A+ / 9.8	0.5	0.9	8.44	790	4	2	0	0	94	10	2.4	46	25	1,000	0	2.3	0.0
U /	N/A	0.9	8.44	186	4	2	0	0	94	10	2.4	N/A	25	0	0	2.3	0.0
A+ / 9.8	0.5	0.9	8.45	254	4	2	0	0	94	10	2.4	58	25	1,000,000	0	0.0	0.0
A+ / 9.8	0.5	0.9	8.44	318	4	2	0	0	94	10	2.4	36	25	1,000	0	0.0	0.0
U /	N/A	0.9	8.45	2	4	2	0	0	94	10	2.4	N/A	25	0	0	0.0	0.0
C- / 4.2	3.9	3.8	11.35	228	1	0	98	0	1	6	5.2	21	27	1,000	0	4.3	0.0
C- / 4.2	3.8	3.8	11.49	54	1	0	98	0	1	6	5.2	13	27	1,000	0	0.0	0.0
C- / 3.6	4.2	4.6	11.09	798	1	0	98	0	1	12	5.2	19	24	1,000	0	4.3	0.0
C- / 3.6	4.2	4.6	11.11	58	1	0	98	0	1	12	5.2	21	24	1,000	0	0.0	0.0
C- / 3.6	4.2	4.6	11.26	113	1	0	98	0	1	12	5.2	12	24	1,000	0	0.0	0.0
C / 5.3	3.3	5.3	12.29	951	1	0	98	0	1	5	5.1	61	24	1,000	0	2.3	0.0
C / 5.3	3.3	5.3	12.32	491	1	0	98	0	1	5	5.1	68	24	1,000	0	0.0	0.0
C / 5.4	3.3	5.3	12.34	267	1	0	98	0	1	5	5.1	41	24	1,000	0	0.0	0.0
D / 2.1	4.8	7.0	10.94	1,389	7	0	92	0	1	12	5.7	82	23	1,000	0	4.3	0.0
D / 2.0	4.9	7.0	10.96	569	7	0	92	0	1	12	5.7	83	23	1,000	0	0.0	0.0
D / 2.1	4.8	7.0	11.02	354	7	0	92	0	1	12	5.7	61	23	1,000	0	0.0	0.0
C- / 3.3	4.4	5.4	13.27	1,454	1	0	98	0	1	12	5.3	82	25	1,000	0	4.3	0.0
C- / 3.4	4.4	5.4	13.29	53	1	0	98	0	1	12	5.3	84	25	1,000	0	0.0	0.0
C- / 3.4	4.4	5.4	13.47	186	1	0	98	0	1	12	5.3	60	25	1,000	0	0.0	0.0
C- / 3.2	4.6	6.6	7.59	11,754	6	0	93	0	1	10	5.3	60	25	1,000	0	4.3	0.0
C- / 3.1	4.6	6.6	7.58	1,081	6	0	93	0	1	10	5.3	64	25	1,000	0	0.0	0.0
C- / 3.2	4.5	6.6	7.58	1,413	6	0	93	0	1	10	5.3	41	25	1,000	0	0.0	0.0
C- / 3.5	4.3	4.2	11.93	552	3	0	96	0	1	2	5.2	18	29	1,000	0	4.3	0.0
C- / 3.5	4.3	4.2	11.93	51	3	0	96	0	1	2	5.2	20	29	1,000	0	0.0	0.0
C- / 3.5	4.3	4.2	12.07	111	3	0	96	0	1	2	5.2	12	29	1,000	0	0.0	0.0
C- / 3.8	4.1	3.9	10.71	253	1	0	98	0	1	5	5.1	10	28	1,000	0	4.3	0.0
C- / 3.7	4.2	3.9	10.70	21	1	0	98	0	1	5	5.1	10	28	1,000	0	0.0	0.0
C- / 3.8	4.1	3.9	10.79	68	1	0	98	0	1	5	5.1	8	28	1,000	0	0.0	0.0
E / 0.5	7.9	5.3	9.34	121	13	0	86	0	1	10	5.8	1	30	1,000	0	4.3	0.0
E / 0.5	7.9	5.3	9.35	2	13	0	86	0	1	10	5.8	1	30	1,000	0	0.0	0.0
E / 0.5	7.9	5.3	9.38	24	13	0	86	0	1	10	5.8	0	30	1,000	0	0.0	0.0
E+ / 0.7	7.1	4.7	10.08	497	8	50	3	30	9	18	6.7	41	10	1,000,000	0	0.0	0.0
A / 9.5	0.8	1.6	10.42	887	2	0	97	0	1	20	4.0	58	13	1,000	0	2.3	0.0
A / 9.5	0.8	1.6	10.42	240	2	0	97	0	1	20	4.0	68	13	1,000	0	0.0	0.0
C / 5.4	3.3	4.7	12.48	2,015	3	0	96	0	1	4	5.1	32	24	1,000	0	2.3	0.0
C / 5.4	3.3	4.7	12.51	2,017	3	0	96	0	1	4	5.1	36	24	1,000	0	0.0	0.0
C / 5.4	3.3	4.7	12.51	469	3	0	96	0	1	4	5.1	19	24	1,000	0	0.0	0.0
C- / 3.8	4.1	4.3	12.44	8,296	1	0	98	0	1	5	5.3	32	29	1,000	0	4.3	0.0
C- / 3.8	4.1	4.3	12.45	1,432	1	0	98	0	1	5	5.3	35	29	1,000	0	0.0	0.0
C- / 3.8	4.1	4.3	12.43	1,199	1	0	98	0	1	5	5.3	19	29	1,000	0	0.0	0.0
U /	N/A	N/A	9.84	10	0	0	0	0	100	0	0.0	N/A	1	1,000	0	4.3	0.0
U /	N/A	N/A	9.84	N/A	0	0	0	0	100	0	0.0	N/A	1	0	0	0.0	0.0

Fund Type	Fund Name (99 Pct = Best, 0 Pct = Worst)	Ticker Symbol	Overall Investment Rating	Phone	PERFORMANCE: Performance Rating/Pts	Total Return % through 3/31/16: 3 Mo	6 Mo	1Yr / Pct	Annualized: 3Yr / Pct	Annualized: 5Yr / Pct	Incl. in Returns: Dividend Yield	Expense Ratio
COI	Franklin Flexible Alpha Bond C	FABDX	U	(800) 342-5236	U /	-0.39	-0.17	--	--	--	0.00	2.22
COI	Franklin Flexible Alpha Bond R	FABMX	U	(800) 342-5236	U /	-0.48	-0.23	--	--	--	0.00	2.07
COI	Franklin Flexible Alpha Bond R6	FABNX	U	(800) 342-5236	U /	-0.20	0.13	--	--	--	0.00	1.43
* LP	Franklin Floating Rate Dly-Acc A	FAFRX	D+	(800) 342-5236	D / 1.7	1.46	-1.20	-2.60 /13	0.89 /41	2.28 /35	4.68	0.86
LP	Franklin Floating Rate Dly-Acc Adv	FDAAX	C-	(800) 321-8563	C- / 3.6	1.40	-1.08	-2.36 /14	1.10 /44	2.53 /38	5.05	0.61
LP	Franklin Floating Rate Dly-Acc C	FCFRX	D+	(800) 342-5236	D / 1.8	1.24	-1.40	-2.99 /11	0.45 /32	1.87 /30	4.38	1.26
LP	Franklin Floating Rate Dly-Acc R6		C-	(800) 342-5236	C- / 3.8	1.54	-1.05	-2.28 /14	1.17 /46	2.58 /39	5.12	0.73
* MUS	Franklin Florida Tax-Free Inc A	FRFLX	C-	(800) 342-5236	C+ / 6.6	1.59	2.58	2.55 /81	2.32 /81	4.76 /83	3.76	0.64
MUS	Franklin Florida Tax-Free Inc C	FRFIX	C	(800) 342-5236	B / 7.8	1.42	2.34	1.95 /77	1.78 /74	4.18 /79	3.31	1.19
MUS	Franklin Georgia Tax-Free Inc A	FTGAX	C	(800) 342-5236	B- / 7.4	1.47	2.33	2.63 /82	2.75 /85	5.50 /89	3.48	0.67
MUS	Franklin Georgia Tax-Free Inc C	FGAIX	C+	(800) 342-5236	B / 8.1	1.40	2.02	2.04 /77	2.19 /79	4.93 /85	3.04	1.22
GL	Franklin Global Government Bond A	FGGAX	U	(800) 321-8563	U /	2.77	2.25	-0.70 /24	--	--	1.88	2.55
GL	Franklin Global Government Bond		U	(800) 321-8563	U /	2.89	2.38	-0.54 /26	--	--	2.01	2.30
GL	Franklin Global Government Bond C		U	(800) 321-8563	U /	2.74	2.06	-1.29 /20	--	--	1.37	2.95
GL	Franklin Global Government Bond R		U	(800) 321-8563	U /	2.71	2.12	-1.06 /21	--	--	1.60	2.80
GL	Franklin Global Government Bond R6		U	(800) 321-8563	U /	2.79	2.28	-0.64 /25	--	--	2.01	3.04
* COH	Franklin High Income A	FHAIX	E-	(800) 342-5236	E- / 0.2	1.74	-1.87	-11.00 / 0	-1.74 / 5	2.56 /38	6.76	0.76
COH	Franklin High Income Adv	FVHIX	E-	(800) 321-8563	E / 0.3	1.17	-1.79	-10.86 / 0	-1.76 / 5	2.60 /39	7.24	0.61
COH	Franklin High Income C	FCHIX	E-	(800) 342-5236	E- / 0.2	0.98	-2.69	-11.87 / 0	-2.41 / 3	1.90 /30	6.46	1.26
COH	Franklin High Income R	FHIRX	E-	(800) 342-5236	E- / 0.2	1.01	-2.61	-11.66 / 0	-2.25 / 4	2.05 /32	6.59	1.11
COH	Franklin High Income R6	FHRRX	E-	(800) 342-5236	E / 0.3	1.83	-1.71	-10.71 / 1	-1.45 / 6	2.74 /41	7.40	0.47
* MUH	Franklin High Yld Tax-Free Inc A	FRHIX	C	(800) 342-5236	B+ / 8.7	2.02	4.11	3.68 /92	3.69 /94	6.94 /96	4.05	0.65
MUH	Franklin High Yld Tax-Free Inc Adv	FHYVX	C+	(800) 321-8563	A+ / 9.6	2.03	4.24	3.86 /93	3.81 /95	7.06 /96	4.30	0.55
MUH	Franklin High Yld Tax-Free Inc C	FHYIX	C+	(800) 342-5236	A- / 9.2	1.84	3.85	3.15 /86	3.13 /89	6.37 /94	3.61	1.20
* MUI	● Franklin Insured Tax-Free Inc A	FTFIX	B	(800) 342-5236	B+ / 8.5	1.28	2.28	2.85 /83	3.81 /95	6.06 /92	3.69	0.61
MUI	● Franklin Insured Tax-Free Inc Adv	FINZX	A-	(800) 321-8563	A / 9.4	1.30	2.41	2.95 /84	3.91 /95	6.17 /93	3.95	0.52
MUI	● Franklin Insured Tax-Free Inc C	FRITX	B+	(800) 342-5236	A- / 9.0	1.12	2.05	2.25 /79	3.24 /90	5.47 /89	3.25	1.17
MUS	Franklin Kentucky Tax-Free Inc A	FRKYX	C-	(800) 342-5236	C+ / 6.4	1.24	1.97	2.05 /78	2.37 /81	5.01 /85	3.46	0.78
MUS	Franklin Louisiana Tax-Free Inc A	FKLAX	C	(800) 342-5236	B- / 7.4	1.45	2.59	2.84 /83	2.64 /84	5.21 /87	3.58	0.69
MUS	Franklin Louisiana Tax-Free Inc C	FLAIX	C+	(800) 342-5236	B / 8.1	1.29	2.36	2.24 /79	2.08 /78	4.64 /82	3.15	1.24
* GEI	Franklin Low Dur Totl Return A	FLDAX	C-	(800) 342-5236	D / 1.6	0.44	0.15	-0.73 /24	0.52 /33	1.13 /22	2.17	0.97
GEI	Franklin Low Dur Totl Return Adv	FLDZX	C+	(800) 321-8563	C- / 3.7	0.48	0.26	-0.42 /27	0.80 /39	1.40 /24	2.42	0.72
COI	Franklin Low Dur Totl Return C	FLDCX	C-	(800) 342-5236	D / 1.8	0.32	-0.07	-1.11 /21	0.14 /28	--	1.94	1.37
COI	Franklin Low Dur Totl Return R6	FLRRX	C+	(800) 342-5236	C- / 3.9	0.50	0.31	-0.33 /28	0.90 /41	1.35 /24	2.52	0.55
MUS	Franklin MA Tax-Free Inc A	FMISX	C+	(800) 342-5236	B+ / 8.3	1.55	3.10	3.55 /90	3.35 /91	5.44 /88	3.15	0.67
MUS	Franklin MA Tax-Free Inc Adv	FMAHX	B-	(800) 321-8563	A / 9.3	1.58	3.15	3.65 /91	3.45 /92	5.56 /89	3.39	0.57
MUS	Franklin MA Tax-Free Inc C	FMAIX	C+	(800) 342-5236	B+ / 8.9	1.49	2.88	3.04 /85	2.81 /86	4.88 /84	2.72	1.22
MUS	Franklin Maryland Tax-Free Inc A	FMDTX	C-	(800) 342-5236	C+ / 6.3	1.61	2.90	2.32 /79	2.14 /79	4.89 /84	3.44	0.67
MUS	Franklin Maryland Tax-Free Inc Adv	FMDZX	C+	(800) 321-8563	B / 8.2	1.54	2.86	2.33 /79	2.21 /79	4.99 /85	3.69	0.57
MUS	Franklin Maryland Tax-Free Inc C	FMDIX	C	(800) 342-5236	B- / 7.5	1.44	2.57	1.81 /76	1.58 /69	4.31 /80	2.98	1.22
* MUI	Franklin MI Tax-Free Inc A	FTTMX	C-	(800) 342-5236	C+ / 6.6	1.37	2.36	1.97 /77	2.41 /82	4.47 /81	3.31	0.65
MUI	Franklin MI Tax-Free Inc C	FRMTX	C+	(800) 342-5236	B / 7.7	1.22	2.13	1.48 /74	1.85 /75	3.91 /77	2.87	1.20
MUI	Franklin Michigan Tax-Free Inc Adv	FMTFX	B-	(800) 321-8563	B+ / 8.4	1.39	2.49	2.15 /78	2.53 /83	4.60 /82	3.55	0.55
* MUS	Franklin Missouri Tax-Free Inc A	FRMOX	C-	(800) 342-5236	C+ / 6.1	1.38	2.21	2.41 /80	2.12 /78	4.88 /84	3.38	0.63
MUS	Franklin Missouri Tax-Free Inc Adv	FRMZX	C+	(800) 321-8563	B / 8.2	1.40	2.26	2.59 /81	2.25 /80	4.98 /85	3.62	0.53
MUS	Franklin Missouri Tax-Free Inc C	FMOIX	C	(800) 342-5236	B- / 7.4	1.23	1.91	1.83 /76	1.58 /69	4.30 /80	2.95	1.18
* MUI	Franklin MN Tax-Free Inc A	FMINX	C+	(800) 342-5236	C+ / 6.9	1.23	1.95	2.52 /81	2.53 /83	4.67 /83	2.98	0.65
MUI	Franklin MN Tax-Free Inc Adv	FMNZX	B+	(800) 321-8563	B+ / 8.5	1.26	2.00	2.62 /81	2.63 /84	4.79 /84	3.21	0.55
MUI	Franklin MN Tax-Free Inc C	FMNIX	B-	(800) 342-5236	B / 7.8	1.08	1.73	1.94 /77	1.94 /76	4.11 /78	2.54	1.20
* MUS	Franklin NC Tax-Free Inc A	FXNCX	D+	(800) 342-5236	C- / 4.2	1.25	2.12	2.23 /79	1.39 /64	4.36 /80	3.30	0.63
MUS	Franklin NC Tax-Free Inc Adv	FNCZX	C	(800) 321-8563	B- / 7.4	1.28	2.16	2.33 /79	1.50 /68	4.47 /81	3.55	0.53
MUS	Franklin NC Tax-Free Inc C	FNCIX	C-	(800) 342-5236	C+ / 5.7	1.10	1.81	1.65 /75	0.83 /48	3.79 /76	2.86	1.18

● Denotes fund is closed to new investors
* Denotes fund is included in Section II

RISK			NET ASSETS		ASSET							FUND MANAGER		MINIMUM		LOADS	
Risk Rating/Pts	3 Yr Avg Standard Deviation	Avg Duration	NAV As of 3/31/16	Total $(Mil)	Cash %	Gov. Bond %	Muni. Bond %	Corp. Bond %	Other %	Portfolio Turnover Ratio	Avg Coupon Rate	Manager Quality Pct	Manager Tenure (Years)	Initial Purch. $	Additional Purch. $	Front End Load	Back End Load
U /	N/A	N/A	9.83	N/A	0	0	0	0	100	0	0.0	N/A	1	1,000	0	4.3	0.0
U /	N/A	N/A	9.82	N/A	0	0	0	0	100	0	0.0	N/A	1	1,000	0	0.0	0.0
U /	N/A	N/A	9.85	N/A	0	0	0	0	100	0	0.0	N/A	1	1,000,000	0	0.0	0.0
B- / 7.2	2.8	0.2	8.35	1,321	3	0	0	12	85	47	4.8	69	15	1,000	0	2.3	0.0
B- / 7.2	2.8	0.2	8.35	1,022	3	0	0	12	85	47	4.8	75	15	1,000,000	0	0.0	0.0
B- / 7.3	2.8	0.2	8.35	532	3	0	0	12	85	47	4.8	46	15	1,000	0	0.0	0.0
B- / 7.2	2.8	0.2	8.35	N/A	3	0	0	12	85	47	4.8	78	15	1,000,000	0	0.0	0.0
C- / 3.3	4.5	4.0	11.18	689	2	0	97	0	1	5	5.3	11	29	1,000	0	4.3	0.0
C- / 3.3	4.5	4.0	11.40	89	2	0	97	0	1	5	5.3	8	29	1,000	0	0.0	0.0
C- / 3.6	4.2	4.5	12.32	428	0	0	99	0	1	12	5.2	17	27	1,000	0	4.3	0.0
C- / 3.5	4.2	4.5	12.49	126	0	0	99	0	1	12	5.2	11	27	1,000	0	0.0	0.0
U /	N/A	N/A	9.60	13	6	93	0	0	1	60	0.0	N/A	3	1,000	0	4.3	0.0
U /	N/A	N/A	9.63	N/A	6	93	0	0	1	60	0.0	N/A	3	0	0	0.0	0.0
U /	N/A	N/A	9.59	N/A	6	93	0	0	1	60	0.0	N/A	3	1,000	0	0.0	0.0
U /	N/A	N/A	9.59	N/A	6	93	0	0	1	60	0.0	N/A	3	1,000	0	0.0	0.0
U /	N/A	N/A	9.60	N/A	6	93	0	0	1	60	0.0	N/A	3	1,000,000	0	0.0	0.0
E / 0.4	7.6	4.3	1.66	2,545	5	0	0	93	2	35	6.8	5	25	1,000	0	4.3	0.0
E / 0.5	7.4	4.3	1.66	773	5	0	0	93	2	35	6.8	6	25	1,000	0	0.0	0.0
E / 0.5	7.4	4.3	1.67	520	5	0	0	93	2	35	6.8	4	25	1,000	0	0.0	0.0
E / 0.5	7.3	4.3	1.68	221	5	0	0	93	2	35	6.8	5	25	1,000	0	0.0	0.0
E / 0.5	7.6	4.3	1.66	81	5	0	0	93	2	35	6.8	6	25	1,000	0	0.0	0.0
D / 2.0	5.1	5.9	10.61	5,109	0	0	99	0	1	8	5.6	17	23	1,000	0	4.3	0.0
D / 2.0	5.2	5.9	10.66	2,164	0	0	99	0	1	8	5.6	19	23	1,000	0	0.0	0.0
D / 2.0	5.2	5.9	10.80	1,061	0	0	99	0	1	8	5.6	11	23	1,000	0	0.0	0.0
C / 4.5	3.7	3.0	12.45	1,663	1	0	98	0	1	2	5.2	62	27	1,000	0	4.3	0.0
C / 4.4	3.7	3.0	12.45	58	1	0	98	0	1	2	5.2	68	27	1,000	0	0.0	0.0
C / 4.5	3.7	3.0	12.63	275	1	0	98	0	1	2	5.2	41	27	1,000	0	0.0	0.0
C- / 4.1	3.9	3.9	11.30	173	3	0	96	0	1	6	5.2	17	24	1,000	0	4.3	0.0
C- / 4.0	3.9	4.2	11.49	335	1	0	98	0	1	13	5.3	20	25	1,000	0	4.3	0.0
C- / 4.1	3.9	4.2	11.66	68	1	0	98	0	1	13	5.3	13	25	1,000	0	0.0	0.0
A- / 9.2	1.1	1.3	9.75	1,598	7	11	1	41	40	41	2.5	71	12	1,000	0	2.3	0.0
A- / 9.2	1.1	1.3	9.79	154	7	11	1	41	40	41	2.5	80	12	1,000,000	0	0.0	0.0
A- / 9.2	1.0	1.3	9.73	232	7	11	1	41	40	41	2.5	50	12	1,000	0	0.0	0.0
A- / 9.2	1.1	1.3	9.79	546	7	11	1	41	40	41	2.5	81	12	1,000,000	0	0.0	0.0
C- / 3.3	4.4	5.1	11.96	400	0	0	100	0	0	7	4.9	23	27	1,000	0	4.3	0.0
C- / 3.3	4.5	5.1	11.96	13	0	0	100	0	0	7	4.9	25	27	1,000	0	0.0	0.0
C- / 3.2	4.5	5.1	12.10	62	0	0	100	0	0	7	4.9	14	27	1,000	0	0.0	0.0
C- / 3.5	4.3	4.0	11.36	369	1	0	98	0	1	16	5.1	11	27	1,000	0	4.3	0.0
C- / 3.5	4.3	4.0	11.36	28	1	0	98	0	1	16	5.1	11	27	1,000	0	0.0	0.0
C- / 3.5	4.3	4.0	11.57	117	1	0	98	0	1	16	5.1	8	27	1,000	0	0.0	0.0
C- / 4.1	3.9	4.4	11.80	896	4	0	95	0	1	13	5.2	20	27	1,000	0	4.3	0.0
C- / 4.1	3.9	4.4	11.98	145	4	0	95	0	1	13	5.2	13	27	1,000	0	0.0	0.0
C- / 4.1	3.9	4.4	11.84	40	4	0	95	0	1	13	5.2	23	27	1,000	0	0.0	0.0
C- / 4.0	4.0	4.0	12.04	879	2	0	97	0	1	5	5.2	14	29	1,000	0	4.3	0.0
C- / 3.9	4.0	4.0	12.05	46	2	0	97	0	1	5	5.2	15	29	1,000	0	0.0	0.0
C- / 3.9	4.0	4.0	12.15	167	2	0	97	0	1	5	5.2	9	29	1,000	0	0.0	0.0
C / 5.0	3.5	3.8	12.62	730	1	0	98	0	1	7	4.8	26	27	1,000	0	4.3	0.0
C / 4.9	3.5	3.8	12.63	122	1	0	98	0	1	7	4.8	28	27	1,000	0	0.0	0.0
C / 4.9	3.5	3.8	12.75	218	1	0	98	0	1	7	4.8	15	27	1,000	0	0.0	0.0
C- / 4.0	4.0	3.8	11.97	794	3	0	96	0	1	7	5.1	9	29	1,000	0	4.3	0.0
C- / 4.0	3.9	3.8	11.97	89	3	0	96	0	1	7	5.1	9	29	1,000	0	0.0	0.0
C- / 4.0	3.9	3.8	12.15	206	3	0	96	0	1	7	5.1	7	29	1,000	0	0.0	0.0

Fund Type	Fund Name (99 Pct = Best; 0 Pct = Worst)	Ticker Symbol	Overall Investment Rating	Phone	PERFORMANCE: Performance Rating/Pts	Total Return % through 3/31/16: 3 Mo	6 Mo	1Yr / Pct	Annualized: 3Yr / Pct	5Yr / Pct	Incl. in Returns: Dividend Yield	Expense Ratio
*MUN	Franklin New Jersey TaxFree Inc A	FRNJX	C-	(800) 342-5236	C+ / 5.6	1.36	2.93	2.39 /80	1.84 /75	4.74 /83	3.63	0.64
MUN	Franklin New Jersey TaxFree Inc Adv	FNJZX	C+	(800) 321-8563	B / 8.1	1.47	2.98	2.49 /80	1.95 /76	4.86 /84	3.89	0.54
MUN	Franklin New Jersey TaxFree Inc C	FNIIX	C	(800) 342-5236	B- / 7.0	1.29	2.70	1.90 /76	1.30 /61	4.17 /79	3.21	1.19
*MUS	Franklin New York Tax-Free Inc A	FNYTX	C-	(800) 342-5236	C+ / 6.3	1.34	2.08	2.32 /79	2.25 /80	4.68 /83	3.43	0.61
MUS	Franklin New York Tax-Free Inc Adv	FNYAX	B-	(800) 321-8563	B+ / 8.3	1.36	2.12	2.42 /80	2.38 /81	4.80 /84	3.68	0.51
MUS	Franklin New York Tax-Free Inc C	FNYIX	C+	(800) 342-5236	B- / 7.5	1.12	1.71	1.76 /75	1.69 /72	4.09 /78	3.03	1.16
*MUS	Franklin NY Interm Tax-Free Inc A	FKNIX	B+	(800) 342-5236	B+ / 8.3	1.57	2.51	3.36 /89	2.82 /86	4.77 /83	2.55	0.65
MUS	Franklin NY Interm Tax-Free Inc Adv	FNYZX	A	(800) 321-8563	A- / 9.0	1.59	2.54	3.45 /90	2.91 /87	4.88 /84	2.69	0.55
MUS	Franklin NY Interm Tax-Free Inc C	FKNCX	B+	(800) 342-5236	B+ / 8.3	1.43	2.23	2.79 /83	2.28 /80	4.21 /79	2.06	1.20
MUI	Franklin Ohio Ins Tax-Free Inc Adv	FROZX	B	(800) 321-8563	A / 9.4	1.60	2.98	3.56 /91	3.57 /93	5.68 /90	3.47	0.53
*MUI	Franklin Ohio Tax-Free Inc A	FTOIX	C+	(800) 342-5236	B+ / 8.3	1.58	2.94	3.47 /90	3.45 /92	5.57 /89	3.24	0.63
MUI	Franklin Ohio Tax-Free Inc C	FOITX	B-	(800) 342-5236	B+ / 8.9	1.42	2.62	2.86 /84	2.87 /87	4.98 /85	2.79	1.18
*MUS	Franklin Oregon Tax-Free Inc A	FRORX	C-	(800) 342-5236	C+ / 6.7	1.53	2.70	2.85 /84	2.31 /80	4.78 /83	3.39	0.63
MUS	Franklin Oregon Tax-Free Inc Adv	FOFZX	C+	(800) 321-8563	B+ / 8.5	1.64	2.83	3.03 /85	2.44 /82	4.92 /85	3.63	0.53
MUS	Franklin Oregon Tax-Free Inc C	FORIX	C	(800) 342-5236	B / 7.8	1.46	2.47	2.33 /79	1.78 /74	4.24 /79	2.95	1.18
*MUS	Franklin PA Tax-Free Inc A	FRPAX	C-	(800) 342-5236	B- / 7.0	1.70	2.75	2.39 /80	2.49 /83	5.31 /88	3.63	0.64
MUS	Franklin PA Tax-Free Inc Adv	FPFZX	C+	(800) 321-8563	B+ / 8.6	1.72	2.80	2.49 /80	2.59 /84	5.43 /88	3.89	0.54
MUS	Franklin PA Tax-Free Inc C	FRPTX	C+	(800) 342-5236	B / 7.9	1.54	2.45	1.81 /76	1.94 /76	4.75 /83	3.21	1.19
COI	Franklin Payout 2017 Advisor	FPOBX	U	(800) 342-5236	U /	0.91	0.70	--	--	--	0.00	N/A
COI	Franklin Payout 2017 R6	FPOKX	U	(800) 342-5236	U /	0.91	0.70	--	--	--	0.00	N/A
COI	Franklin Payout 2018 Advisor	FPODX	U	(800) 342-5236	U /	1.41	0.97	--	--	--	0.00	N/A
COI	Franklin Payout 2018 R6	FPOLX	U	(800) 342-5236	U /	1.41	0.97	--	--	--	0.00	N/A
COI	Franklin Payout 2019 Advisor	FPOFX	U	(800) 342-5236	U /	2.22	1.53	--	--	--	0.00	N/A
COI	Franklin Payout 2019 R6	FPOEX	U	(800) 342-5236	U /	2.22	1.53	--	--	--	0.00	N/A
COI	Franklin Payout 2020 Advisor	FPOHX	U	(800) 342-5236	U /	2.74	1.88	--	--	--	0.00	N/A
COI	Franklin Payout 2020 R6	FPOGX	U	(800) 342-5236	U /	2.74	1.78	--	--	--	0.00	N/A
COI	Franklin Payout 2021 Advisor	FPOJX	U	(800) 342-5236	U /	3.64	2.80	--	--	--	0.00	N/A
COI	Franklin Payout 2021 R6	FPOMX	U	(800) 342-5236	U /	3.64	2.80	--	--	--	0.00	N/A
GEI	Franklin Real Return A	FRRAX	D-	(800) 342-5236	E / 0.3	2.29	2.08	-3.38 /10	-1.85 / 5	-0.65 / 2	0.98	1.12
GEI	Franklin Real Return Adv	FARRX	D-	(800) 342-5236	E+ / 0.7	2.39	2.24	-3.11 /11	-1.59 / 6	-0.39 / 2	1.28	0.87
GEI	Franklin Real Return C	FRRCX	D-	(800) 342-5236	E / 0.5	2.19	1.95	-3.64 / 9	-2.24 / 4	-1.04 / 2	0.58	1.52
GEI	Franklin Real Return R6	FRRRX	D-	(800) 342-5236	E+ / 0.8	2.39	2.24	-2.91 /12	-1.45 / 6	-0.31 / 2	1.48	0.73
*GEN	Franklin Strategic Income A	FRSTX	D-	(800) 342-5236	E+ / 0.7	1.44	0.70	-3.68 / 9	0.09 /27	2.80 /42	4.35	0.87
GEN	Franklin Strategic Income Adv	FKSAX	D	(800) 321-8563	D+ / 2.3	1.51	0.82	-3.43 /10	0.34 /31	3.05 /46	4.80	0.62
GEN	Franklin Strategic Income C	FSGCX	D-	(800) 342-5236	D- / 1.2	1.34	0.49	-4.07 / 7	-0.31 /13	2.39 /36	4.12	1.27
GEN	Franklin Strategic Income R	FKSRX	D-	(800) 342-5236	D- / 1.3	1.39	0.57	-3.93 / 8	-0.13 /14	2.55 /38	4.30	1.12
GL	Franklin Strategic Income R6	FGKNX	D	(800) 342-5236	D+ / 2.7	1.54	0.89	-3.40 /10	0.46 /32	3.03 /46	4.94	0.49
MTG	Franklin Strategic Mortgage Port A	FSMFX	B	(800) 342-5236	C / 5.4	1.43	1.00	1.41 /65	2.76 /74	3.74 /57	2.04	1.01
MTG ●	Franklin Strategic Mortgage Port A1	FSMIX	B+	(800) 342-5236	C+ / 5.8	1.36	1.10	1.53 /67	3.01 /76	4.00 /61	2.26	0.76
MTG	Franklin Strategic Mortgage Port Ad	FSMZX	A+	(800) 342-5236	B- / 7.5	1.49	1.12	1.55 /67	2.98 /76	3.98 /61	2.38	0.76
MTG	Franklin Strategic Mortgage Port C		A	(800) 342-5236	C+ / 6.6	1.34	0.80	1.01 /59	2.36 /68	3.34 /51	1.74	1.41
MUS	Franklin Tennessee Muni Bond A	FRTIX	C-	(800) 342-5236	C+ / 6.4	1.58	2.66	2.74 /82	2.18 /79	4.70 /83	3.33	0.72
*GEI	Franklin Total Return A	FKBAX	D+	(800) 342-5236	D+ / 2.8	1.60	1.31	-1.45 /19	1.48 /52	3.42 /52	3.35	0.94
GEI	Franklin Total Return Adv	FBDAX	C-	(800) 321-8563	C / 5.4	1.73	1.52	-1.15 /20	1.76 /57	3.69 /56	3.69	0.69
GEI	Franklin Total Return C	FCTLX	C-	(800) 342-5236	C- / 4.1	1.55	1.16	-1.87 /16	1.08 /44	3.00 /45	3.19	1.34
GEI	Franklin Total Return R	FTRRX	C-	(800) 342-5236	C / 4.4	1.57	1.21	-1.65 /18	1.24 /47	3.16 /48	3.31	1.19
COI	Franklin Total Return R6	FRERX	C-	(800) 342-5236	C+ / 5.7	1.74	1.57	-1.04 /21	1.89 /59	3.77 /58	3.81	0.53
*USS	Franklin US Government Sec A	FKUSX	C	(800) 342-5236	C- / 3.4	1.10	1.13	1.05 /59	1.59 /54	2.48 /38	3.10	0.76
USS	Franklin US Government Sec Adv	FUSAX	B+	(800) 321-8563	C+ / 5.8	1.13	1.20	1.20 /62	1.74 /56	2.63 /39	3.38	0.61
USS	Franklin US Government Sec C	FRUGX	C+	(800) 342-5236	C / 4.6	1.14	0.88	0.70 /53	1.09 /44	1.97 /31	2.75	1.26
USS	Franklin US Government Sec R	FUSRX	B-	(800) 342-5236	C / 4.9	1.17	0.95	0.85 /56	1.23 /47	2.12 /33	2.88	1.11
USA	Franklin US Government Sec R6	FGORX	A-	(800) 342-5236	C+ / 6.0	1.17	1.27	1.49 /66	1.87 /59	2.65 /40	3.52	0.47

● Denotes fund is closed to new investors
* Denotes fund is included in Section II

RISK			NET ASSETS		ASSET							FUND MANAGER		MINIMUM		LOADS	
Risk Rating/Pts	3 Yr Avg Standard Deviation	Avg Duration	NAV As of 3/31/16	Total $(Mil)	Cash %	Gov. Bond %	Muni. Bond %	Corp. Bond %	Other %	Portfolio Turnover Ratio	Avg Coupon Rate	Manager Quality Pct	Manager Tenure (Years)	Initial Purch. $	Additional Purch. $	Front End Load	Back End Load
C- / 4.0	4.0	3.8	11.74	792	1	0	98	0	1	5	5.2	11	28	1,000	0	4.3	0.0
C- / 4.0	4.0	3.8	11.75	91	1	0	98	0	1	5	5.2	12	28	1,000	0	0.0	0.0
C- / 4.0	3.9	3.8	11.89	217	1	0	98	0	1	5	5.2	8	28	1,000	0	0.0	0.0
C / 4.5	3.7	3.8	11.53	4,145	6	0	93	0	1	7	5.2	18	27	1,000	0	4.3	0.0
C / 4.4	3.7	3.8	11.54	257	6	0	93	0	1	7	5.2	20	27	1,000	0	0.0	0.0
C / 4.4	3.7	3.8	11.51	656	6	0	93	0	1	7	5.2	12	27	1,000	0	0.0	0.0
C / 5.2	3.4	5.0	11.89	556	1	0	97	0	2	6	5.0	37	24	1,000	50	2.3	0.0
C / 5.3	3.3	5.0	11.92	388	1	0	97	0	2	6	5.0	42	24	1,000	0	0.0	0.0
C / 5.2	3.4	5.0	11.93	178	1	0	97	0	2	6	5.0	24	24	1,000	50	0.0	0.0
C- / 3.7	4.2	4.4	12.93	80	0	0	99	0	1	14	5.0	36	27	1,000	0	0.0	0.0
C- / 3.6	4.2	4.4	12.92	1,184	0	0	99	0	1	14	5.0	31	27	1,000	0	4.3	0.0
C- / 3.6	4.2	4.4	13.08	322	0	0	99	0	1	14	5.0	18	27	1,000	0	0.0	0.0
C- / 3.5	4.2	4.8	11.91	959	2	0	97	0	1	8	5.1	12	25	1,000	0	4.3	0.0
C- / 3.5	4.3	4.8	11.93	52	2	0	97	0	1	8	5.1	13	25	1,000	0	0.0	0.0
C- / 3.5	4.3	4.8	12.09	190	2	0	97	0	1	8	5.1	8	25	1,000	0	0.0	0.0
C- / 3.5	4.3	3.9	10.34	964	4	0	95	0	1	6	5.2	14	30	1,000	0	4.3	0.0
C- / 3.5	4.3	3.9	10.35	53	4	0	95	0	1	6	5.2	15	30	1,000	0	0.0	0.0
C- / 3.5	4.3	3.9	10.46	282	4	0	95	0	1	6	5.2	10	30	1,000	0	0.0	0.0
U /	N/A	1.8	10.01	2	0	0	0	0	100	0	3.3	N/A	1	1,000,000	0	0.0	0.0
U /	N/A	1.8	10.01	2	0	0	0	0	100	0	3.3	N/A	1	1,000,000	0	0.0	0.0
U /	N/A	2.7	10.05	2	0	0	0	0	100	0	3.4	N/A	1	1,000,000	0	0.0	0.0
U /	N/A	2.7	10.05	2	0	0	0	0	100	0	3.4	N/A	1	1,000,000	0	0.0	0.0
U /	N/A	3.6	10.12	2	0	0	0	0	100	0	3.2	N/A	1	1,000,000	0	0.0	0.0
U /	N/A	3.6	10.12	2	0	0	0	0	100	0	3.2	N/A	1	1,000,000	0	0.0	0.0
U /	N/A	4.4	10.12	2	0	0	0	0	100	0	3.6	N/A	1	1,000,000	0	0.0	0.0
U /	N/A	4.4	10.12	2	0	0	0	0	100	0	3.6	N/A	1	1,000,000	0	0.0	0.0
U /	N/A	5.3	10.25	2	0	0	0	0	100	0	3.4	N/A	1	1,000	0	0.0	0.0
U /	N/A	5.3	10.25	2	0	0	0	0	100	0	3.4	N/A	1	1,000,000	0	0.0	0.0
C- / 3.7	4.2	1.4	9.84	165	6	70	0	7	17	27	2.7	7	12	1,000	0	4.3	0.0
C- / 3.7	4.2	1.4	9.87	34	6	70	0	7	17	27	2.7	7	12	1,000,000	0	0.0	0.0
C- / 3.7	4.2	1.4	9.78	44	6	70	0	7	17	27	2.7	6	12	1,000	0	0.0	0.0
C- / 3.6	4.2	1.4	9.87	2	6	70	0	7	17	27	2.7	8	12	1,000,000	0	0.0	0.0
C- / 3.6	4.2	3.1	9.19	4,403	5	20	3	44	28	73	5.5	21	22	1,000	0	4.3	0.0
C- / 3.6	4.2	3.1	9.20	883	5	20	3	44	28	73	5.5	27	22	1,000	0	0.0	0.0
C- / 3.5	4.3	3.1	9.19	1,623	5	20	3	44	28	73	5.5	14	22	1,000	0	0.0	0.0
C- / 3.5	4.3	3.1	9.16	183	5	20	3	44	28	73	5.5	17	22	1,000	0	0.0	0.0
C- / 3.6	4.2	3.1	9.20	262	5	20	3	44	28	73	5.5	82	22	1,000,000	0	0.0	0.0
B / 8.2	2.2	4.3	9.49	32	0	0	0	0	100	173	3.6	81	23	1,000	0	4.3	0.0
B / 8.2	2.2	4.3	9.49	57	0	0	0	0	100	173	3.6	87	23	1,000	0	4.3	0.0
B / 8.2	2.2	4.3	9.48	13	0	0	0	0	100	173	3.6	86	23	1,000	0	0.0	0.0
B / 8.2	2.2	4.3	9.49	7	0	0	0	0	100	173	3.6	69	23	1,000	0	0.0	0.0
C- / 4.2	3.9	4.4	11.41	297	1	0	98	0	1	12	5.1	15	20	1,000	0	4.3	0.0
C+ / 5.7	3.2	5.1	9.68	3,566	0	17	3	38	42	295	3.8	35	18	1,000	0	4.3	0.0
C / 5.4	3.3	5.1	9.72	452	0	17	3	38	42	295	3.8	41	18	1,000,000	0	0.0	0.0
C / 5.4	3.3	5.1	9.64	443	0	17	3	38	42	295	3.8	23	18	1,000	0	0.0	0.0
C+ / 5.6	3.2	5.1	9.66	67	0	17	3	38	42	295	3.8	27	18	1,000	0	0.0	0.0
C / 4.8	3.6	5.1	9.72	69	0	17	3	38	42	295	3.8	53	18	1,000,000	0	0.0	0.0
B+ / 8.4	2.0	3.7	6.37	4,260	1	0	0	0	99	69	4.4	83	23	1,000	0	4.3	0.0
B+ / 8.5	2.0	3.7	6.39	646	1	0	0	0	99	69	4.4	86	23	1,000	0	0.0	0.0
B+ / 8.4	2.0	3.7	6.33	1,054	1	0	0	0	99	69	4.4	62	23	1,000	0	0.0	0.0
B+ / 8.4	2.1	3.7	6.37	64	1	0	0	0	99	69	4.4	72	23	1,000	0	0.0	0.0
B+ / 8.5	2.0	3.7	6.39	458	1	0	0	0	99	69	4.4	87	23	1,000,000	0	0.0	0.0

99 Pct = Best
0 Pct = Worst

Fund Type	Fund Name	Ticker Symbol	Overall Investment Rating	Phone	PERFORMANCE: Performance Rating/Pts	Total Return % through 3/31/16: 3 Mo	6 Mo	1Yr / Pct	Annualized: 3Yr / Pct	Annualized: 5Yr / Pct	Incl. in Returns: Dividend Yield	Incl. in Returns: Expense Ratio
*MUS	Franklin Virginia Tax-Free Inc A	FRVAX	C-	(800) 342-5236	C+ / 6.4	1.67	2.86	2.87 /84	2.13 /78	4.69 /83	3.43	0.65
MUS	Franklin Virginia Tax-Free Inc Adv	FRVZX	C+	(800) 321-8563	B+ / 8.3	1.69	2.90	2.88 /84	2.22 /79	4.78 /83	3.68	0.55
MUS	Franklin Virginia Tax-Free Inc C	FVAIX	C+	(800) 342-5236	B / 7.6	1.59	2.62	2.27 /79	1.57 /69	4.11 /78	2.98	1.20
GL	Frost Conservative Allocation Inv	FDSFX	D+	(866) 777-7818	C / 5.4	0.30	0.79	-3.35 /10	2.89 /75	1.85 /29	0.57	2.71
GEI	Frost Credit Inst	FCFIX	D	(866) 777-7818	C- / 3.0	-0.87	-3.11	-4.69 / 6	1.45 /51	--	5.29	0.84
GEI	Frost Credit Inv	FCFAX	D	(866) 777-7818	D+ / 2.3	-0.93	-3.24	-4.94 / 5	1.20 /46	--	5.02	1.08
US	Frost Kempner Treasury and Inc Inst	FIKTX	D	(866) 777-7818	D / 1.6	3.29	2.45	0.34 /47	-0.85 / 9	1.84 /29	0.43	0.84
COI	Frost Low Duration Bond Inst	FILDX	C+	(866) 777-7818	C- / 4.0	0.71	0.50	0.55 /50	0.80 /39	1.88 /30	1.42	0.52
COI	Frost Low Duration Bond Inv	FADLX	C+	(866) 777-7818	C- / 3.5	0.65	0.37	0.30 /46	0.54 /34	1.63 /27	1.17	0.77
MUN	Frost Municipal Bond Inst	FIMUX	A+	(866) 777-7818	B+ / 8.3	0.97	1.80	2.52 /81	2.40 /82	3.70 /75	2.47	0.52
MUN	Frost Municipal Bond Inv	FAUMX	A+	(866) 777-7818	B / 8.0	0.91	1.68	2.27 /79	2.11 /78	3.43 /73	2.23	0.77
GEI	Frost Total Return Bond Inst	FIJEX	A-	(866) 777-7818	C+ / 6.4	1.72	0.52	0.01 /31	2.41 /69	4.55 /68	3.74	0.51
GEI	Frost Total Return Bond Inv	FATRX	B+	(866) 777-7818	C+ / 6.0	1.66	0.49	-0.24 /29	2.16 /65	4.29 /65	3.49	0.75
GEI	FX Strategy A	FXFAX	E-	(855) 397-8728	E- / 0.0	-12.07	-26.90	-33.00 / 0	-2.83 / 3	--	0.00	3.75
MM	Gabelli US Treasury Money Mkt A	GBAXX	C	(800) 422-3554	D / 2.1	0.04	0.05	0.05 /38	0.02 /20	0.02 / 8	0.05	0.11
MM	Gabelli US Treasury Money Mkt AAA	GABXX	C	(800) 422-3554	D / 2.1	0.04	0.05	0.05 /38	0.02 /20	0.02 / 8	0.05	0.11
MM	Gabelli US Treasury Money Mkt C	GBCXX	C	(800) 422-3554	D / 2.1	0.04	0.05	0.05 /38	0.02 /20	0.02 / 8	0.05	0.11
GEI	GE Institutional Income Inv	GFIIX	B+	(800) 242-0134	B- / 7.3	2.81	2.54	1.20 /62	2.60 /72	4.06 /62	2.89	0.23
GEI	GE Institutional Income Svc	GEISX	B	(800) 242-0134	C+ / 6.9	2.70	2.39	0.88 /57	2.32 /68	3.80 /58	2.64	0.48
GEI	GE Investments Income 1	GEIMX	B	(800) 242-0134	C+ / 6.3	2.58	2.14	0.49 /49	2.00 /61	3.50 /53	2.26	1.05
*GES	GE RSP Income	GESLX	A-	(800) 242-0134	B- / 7.4	2.77	2.52	1.23 /62	2.66 /73	4.14 /63	2.87	0.17
MMT	General AMT-Free Municipal MM A	DLTXX	U	(800) 645-6561	U /	--	--	--	--	--	0.01	0.71
MMT	General AMT-Free Municipal MM B	DMBXX	U	(800) 645-6561	U /	--	--	--	--	--	0.01	1.01
MMT	General AMT-Free Municipal MM Dr	DLRXX	U	(800) 645-6561	U /	--	--	--	--	--	0.01	0.51
MMT	General AMT-Free Municipal MM R	DTMXX	U	(800) 645-6561	U /	--	--	--	--	--	0.01	0.51
MMT	General New Jersey Municipal MM A	DNJXX	C	(800) 645-6561	D+ / 2.5	0.00	0.09	0.09 /42	0.03 /25	0.02 /10	0.09	0.64
USS	Glenmede Core Fixed Income Port	GTCGX	B	(800) 442-8299	C+ / 6.4	2.52	2.26	1.97 /72	1.84 /58	3.19 /48	2.15	0.53
MUN	Glenmede Intermediate Muni Port	GTCMX	A+	(800) 442-8299	B / 7.9	1.26	1.97	2.42 /80	1.87 /75	2.81 /66	1.47	0.23
GEI	GMO Core Plus Bond III	GUGAX	D+		C+ / 5.6	1.12	0.98	-0.96 /22	1.95 /60	5.24 /73	5.21	0.60
GEI	GMO Core Plus Bond IV	GPBFX	D+		C+ / 5.7	1.12	1.12	-0.94 /22	1.98 /61	5.30 /74	5.21	0.55
GL	GMO Currency Hedged Intl Bond III	GMHBX	C+		A- / 9.1	2.76	3.36	0.09 /41	5.62 /94	7.78 /86	9.59	0.71
GEI	GMO Debt Opportunities VI	GMODX	U		U /	-0.04	0.45	0.97 /58	--	--	1.70	0.34
*EM	● GMO Emerging Country Debt III	GMCDX	D+		B / 8.0	4.26	6.65	2.53 /75	3.02 /77	7.73 /85	7.16	0.56
EM	● GMO Emerging Country Debt IV	GMDFX	D+		B / 8.1	4.39	6.69	2.58 /75	3.07 /77	7.80 /86	7.22	0.51
GL	GMO Global Bond III	GMGBX	C-		C+ / 6.6	5.28	4.65	4.16 /82	1.13 /45	3.61 /55	0.00	0.69
*US	GMO US Treasury	GUSTX	C+		D+ / 2.8	0.16	0.17	0.26 /45	0.15 /28	0.13 /15	0.18	0.10
GEI	Goldman Sachs Bond A	GSFAX	C+	(800) 526-7384	C / 5.5	2.30	1.92	1.83 /70	2.39 /69	4.29 /65	3.21	1.12
GEI	Goldman Sachs Bond C	GSFCX	C+	(800) 526-7384	C+ / 5.7	2.12	1.54	0.97 /58	1.60 /54	3.51 /53	2.59	1.87
GEI	Goldman Sachs Bond Institutional	GSNIX	A	(800) 526-7384	B / 7.6	2.49	2.09	2.17 /73	2.74 /74	4.64 /69	3.67	0.78
GEI	Goldman Sachs Bond IR	GSNTX	A	(800) 526-7384	B- / 7.5	2.47	2.15	2.18 /73	2.65 /73	4.47 /67	3.59	0.87
GEI	Goldman Sachs Bond R	GSNRX	B+	(800) 526-7384	C+ / 6.6	2.34	1.79	1.58 /67	2.10 /64	4.01 /62	3.09	1.38
COI	Goldman Sachs Bond R6	GSFUX	U	(800) 526-7384	U /	2.48	2.06	--	--	--	0.00	N/A
GEI	Goldman Sachs Bond Service	GSNSX	B+	(800) 526-7384	C+ / 6.8	2.37	1.85	1.68 /69	2.24 /66	4.13 /63	3.19	1.29
GEI	Goldman Sachs Core Fixed Inc A	GCFIX	C+	(800) 526-7384	C / 5.0	2.49	2.19	1.56 /67	2.13 /64	3.75 /57	2.47	0.81
GEI	Goldman Sachs Core Fixed Inc C	GCFCX	C+	(800) 526-7384	C / 5.4	2.39	1.90	0.90 /57	1.37 /50	2.99 /45	1.82	1.56
GEI	Goldman Sachs Core Fixed Inc Inst	GSFIX	A	(800) 526-7384	B- / 7.3	2.57	2.35	1.91 /71	2.48 /70	4.10 /63	2.90	0.47
GEI	Goldman Sachs Core Fixed Inc IR	GDFTX	A	(800) 526-7384	B- / 7.2	2.55	2.31	1.82 /70	2.39 /69	4.03 /62	2.82	0.58
GEI	Goldman Sachs Core Fixed Inc R	GDFRX	B	(800) 526-7384	C+ / 6.3	2.42	2.06	1.31 /63	1.88 /59	3.50 /53	2.32	1.07
COI	Goldman Sachs Core Fixed Inc R6	GCFUX	U	(800) 526-7384	U /	2.57	2.26	--	--	--	0.00	N/A
GEI	Goldman Sachs Core Fixed Inc Svc	GSCSX	B+	(800) 526-7384	C+ / 6.4	2.44	2.10	1.40 /65	1.97 /61	3.58 /54	2.41	0.97
EM	Goldman Sachs Dyn Em Mkts Debt A	GDDAX	U	(800) 526-7384	U /	7.43	7.32	0.14 /42	--	--	4.05	3.45
EM	Goldman Sachs Dyn Em Mkts Debt C	GDDCX	U	(800) 526-7384	U /	7.22	6.91	-0.71 /24	--	--	3.51	3.66

● Denotes fund is closed to new investors
* Denotes fund is included in Section II

RISK			NET ASSETS		ASSET							FUND MANAGER		MINIMUM		LOADS	
Risk Rating/Pts	3 Yr Avg Standard Deviation	Avg Duration	NAV As of 3/31/16	Total $(Mil)	Cash %	Gov. Bond %	Muni. Bond %	Corp. Bond %	Other %	Portfolio Turnover Ratio	Avg Coupon Rate	Manager Quality Pct	Manager Tenure (Years)	Initial Purch. $	Additional Purch. $	Front End Load	Back End Load
C- / 4.0	3.9	4.0	11.56	540	1	0	98	0	1	8	5.1	14	29	1,000	0	4.3	0.0
C- / 4.0	3.9	4.0	11.56	53	1	0	98	0	1	8	5.1	14	29	1,000	0	0.0	0.0
C- / 4.0	4.0	4.0	11.74	111	1	0	98	0	1	8	5.1	9	29	1,000	0	0.0	0.0
D+ / 2.5	5.3	N/A	10.37	3	4	25	1	16	54	51	0.0	98	5	2,500	500	0.0	2.0
C- / 3.1	4.6	1.7	9.10	107	5	0	0	42	53	47	0.0	79	4	1,000,000	0	0.0	0.0
C- / 3.1	4.6	1.7	9.09	9	5	0	0	42	53	47	0.0	71	4	2,500	500	0.0	0.0
C- / 4.0	3.9	6.2	10.04	15	18	81	0	0	1	8	0.0	7	10	1,000,000	0	0.0	0.0
A / 9.4	0.9	2.5	10.24	216	2	28	2	20	48	52	0.0	77	14	1,000,000	0	0.0	0.0
A / 9.3	1.0	2.5	10.24	19	2	28	2	20	48	52	0.0	62	14	2,500	500	0.0	0.0
B / 8.2	2.3	4.0	10.62	256	0	0	99	0	1	9	0.0	70	14	1,000,000	0	0.0	0.0
B / 8.1	2.3	4.0	10.61	5	0	0	99	0	1	9	0.0	53	14	2,500	500	0.0	0.0
B / 8.0	2.4	4.1	10.27	1,509	1	25	3	25	46	49	0.0	89	14	1,000,000	0	0.0	0.0
B / 8.0	2.4	4.1	10.27	253	1	25	3	25	46	49	0.0	86	14	2,500	500	0.0	0.0
E- / 0.0	25.3	N/A	8.67	3	33	14	2	25	26	40	0.0	7	5	5,000	2,000	5.8	0.0
A+ / 9.9	N/A	N/A	1.00	8	100	0	0	0	0	0	0.1	63	24	3,000	0	0.0	0.0
A+ / 9.9	N/A	N/A	1.00	1,462	100	0	0	0	0	0	0.1	63	24	10,000	0	0.0	0.0
A+ / 9.9	N/A	N/A	1.00	5	100	0	0	0	0	0	0.1	63	24	3,000	0	0.0	0.0
C+ / 6.9	2.9	5.4	9.45	293	3	20	0	41	36	297	6.3	78	19	5,000,000	0	0.0	0.0
C+ / 6.5	3.0	5.4	9.66	N/A	3	20	0	41	36	297	6.3	61	19	5,000,000	0	0.0	0.0
B- / 7.0	2.9	4.9	11.54	28	3	16	1	43	37	282	5.8	53	19	0	0	0.0	0.0
C+ / 6.9	2.9	5.5	11.59	2,508	0	25	0	40	35	319	5.9	79	20	0	0	0.0	0.0
U /	N/A	N/A	1.00	26	100	0	0	0	0	0	0.0	N/A	N/A	100,000	0	0.0	0.0
U /	N/A	N/A	1.00	178	100	0	0	0	0	0	0.0	N/A	N/A	2,500	100	0.0	0.0
U /	N/A	N/A	1.00	9	100	0	0	0	0	0	0.0	N/A	N/A	10,000	100	0.0	0.0
U /	N/A	N/A	1.00	25	100	0	0	0	0	0	0.0	N/A	N/A	100,000	0	0.0	0.0
A+ / 9.9	0.1	N/A	1.00	195	100	0	0	0	0	0	0.1	63	N/A	2,500	100	0.0	0.0
B- / 7.2	2.8	4.5	11.29	441	0	29	1	49	21	27	0.0	62	17	1,000	0	0.0	0.0
B / 8.2	2.2	4.2	11.10	337	4	0	95	0	1	71	5.1	49	5	0	0	0.0	0.0
C- / 3.1	4.6	4.7	7.20	7	23	66	0	3	8	128	5.4	24	2	0	0	0.0	0.0
C- / 3.1	4.6	4.7	7.22	217	23	66	0	3	8	128	5.4	25	2	125,000,000	0	0.0	0.0
D+ / 2.3	5.5	5.3	8.93	62	12	83	0	0	5	117	6.3	99	2	0	0	0.0	0.0
U /	N/A	N/A	24.67	1,673	0	0	0	0	100	37	0.0	N/A	2	300,000,000	0	0.4	0.4
E / 0.4	8.6	4.7	9.05	861	0	81	0	11	8	18	8.3	99	22	0	0	0.5	0.5
E / 0.4	8.5	4.7	9.04	3,201	0	81	0	11	8	18	8.3	99	22	125,000,000	0	0.5	0.5
D+ / 2.4	5.3	5.4	8.77	38	8	87	0	0	5	84	6.4	92	N/A	0	0	0.0	0.0
A+ / 9.9	0.1	N/A	25.01	3,623	0	99	0	0	1	0	0.0	72	2	0	0	0.0	0.0
B- / 7.3	2.8	6.2	10.28	129	4	29	1	30	36	454	0.0	76	10	1,000	50	3.8	0.0
B- / 7.2	2.8	6.2	10.27	17	4	29	1	30	36	454	0.0	42	10	1,000	50	0.0	0.0
B- / 7.3	2.8	6.2	10.28	278	4	29	1	30	36	454	0.0	84	10	1,000,000	0	0.0	0.0
B- / 7.3	2.8	6.2	10.25	40	4	29	1	30	36	454	0.0	82	10	0	0	0.0	0.0
B- / 7.2	2.8	6.2	10.27	9	4	29	1	30	36	454	0.0	60	10	0	0	0.0	0.0
U /	N/A	6.2	10.28	N/A	4	29	1	30	36	454	0.0	N/A	10	0	0	0.0	0.0
B- / 7.3	2.8	6.2	10.28	N/A	4	29	1	30	36	454	0.0	70	10	0	0	0.0	0.0
B- / 7.3	2.8	4.9	10.53	142	4	20	0	32	44	388	0.0	57	16	1,000	50	3.8	0.0
B- / 7.3	2.8	4.9	10.59	18	4	20	0	32	44	388	0.0	32	16	1,000	50	0.0	0.0
B- / 7.4	2.8	4.9	10.57	696	4	20	0	32	44	388	0.0	75	16	1,000,000	0	0.0	0.0
B- / 7.5	2.7	4.9	10.54	5	4	20	0	32	44	388	0.0	73	16	0	0	0.0	0.0
B- / 7.3	2.8	4.9	10.54	10	4	20	0	32	44	388	0.0	48	16	0	0	0.0	0.0
U /	N/A	4.9	10.57	57	4	20	0	32	44	388	0.0	N/A	16	0	0	0.0	0.0
B- / 7.4	2.8	4.9	10.58	2	4	20	0	32	44	388	0.0	51	16	0	0	0.0	0.0
U /	N/A	N/A	8.24	1	18	55	1	23	3	179	0.0	N/A	3	1,000	50	4.5	2.0
U /	N/A	N/A	8.26	N/A	18	55	1	23	3	179	0.0	N/A	3	1,000	50	0.0	2.0

Fund Type	Fund Name	Ticker Symbol	Overall Investment Rating	Phone	PERFORMANCE: Performance Rating/Pts	Total Return % through 3/31/16: 3 Mo	6 Mo	1Yr / Pct	Annualized: 3Yr / Pct	5Yr / Pct	Incl. in Returns: Dividend Yield	Expense Ratio
	99 Pct = Best; 0 Pct = Worst											
EM	Goldman Sachs Dyn Em Mkts Debt	GDDIX	**U**	(800) 526-7384	**U** /	7.50	7.49	0.37 /47	--	--	4.58	2.57
EM	Goldman Sachs Dyn Em Mkts Debt	GIRDX	**U**	(800) 526-7384	**U** /	7.49	7.46	0.27 /45	--	--	4.50	2.77
EM	Goldman Sachs Dyn Em Mkts Debt R	GDDRX	**U**	(800) 526-7384	**U** /	7.35	7.17	-0.22 /29	--	--	4.00	3.27
MUN	Goldman Sachs Dynamic Muni Inc A	GSMIX	**C**	(800) 526-7384	**B- / 7.5**	1.18	2.97	2.69 /82	2.58 /83	5.77 /91	3.27	1.01
MUN	Goldman Sachs Dynamic Muni Inc C	GSMUX	**C+**	(800) 526-7384	**B / 7.8**	0.99	2.59	1.86 /76	1.82 /74	4.99 /85	2.66	1.76
MUN	Goldman Sachs Dynamic Muni Inc	GSMTX	**B**	(800) 526-7384	**B+ / 8.9**	1.26	3.15	2.98 /85	2.91 /87	6.12 /93	3.74	0.67
MUN	Goldman Sachs Dynamic Muni Inc IR	GUIRX	**B**	(800) 526-7384	**B+ / 8.9**	1.24	3.10	2.95 /84	2.84 /86	5.99 /92	3.65	0.76
MUN	Goldman Sachs Dynamic Muni Inc Sv	GSMEX	**C+**	(800) 526-7384	**B+ / 8.4**	1.13	2.88	2.53 /81	2.42 /82	5.61 /90	3.24	1.16
EM	Goldman Sachs Emg Mkts Debt A	GSDAX	**D**	(800) 526-7384	**C+ / 5.7**	5.00	6.12	4.42 /84	2.35 /68	5.83 /76	4.70	1.25
EM	Goldman Sachs Emg Mkts Debt C	GSCDX	**D**	(800) 526-7384	**C+ / 6.3**	4.72	5.65	3.57 /79	1.59 /54	5.05 /72	4.18	2.00
EM	Goldman Sachs Emg Mkts Debt Inst	GSDIX	**D+**	(800) 526-7384	**B / 7.8**	4.99	6.21	4.69 /85	2.70 /73	6.19 /78	5.25	0.91
EM	Goldman Sachs Emg Mkts Debt IR	GSIRX	**D+**	(800) 526-7384	**B / 7.8**	4.97	6.16	4.60 /85	2.61 /72	6.09 /77	5.17	1.00
EM	Goldman Sachs Emg Mkts Debt R6	GSIUX	**U**	(800) 526-7384	**U** /	4.99	6.21	--	--	--	0.00	N/A
GEI	Goldman Sachs Enhanced Inc A	GEIAX	**C-**	(800) 526-7384	**D- / 1.5**	0.41	0.49	0.29 /46	-0.02 /15	0.09 /14	0.39	0.72
GEI	Goldman Sachs Enhanced Inc Admin	GEADX	**C+**	(800) 526-7384	**D+ / 2.7**	0.43	0.43	0.38 /47	0.06 /25	0.18 /16	0.48	0.63
GEI	Goldman Sachs Enhanced Inc Inst	GEIIX	**C+**	(800) 526-7384	**C- / 3.2**	0.49	0.55	0.63 /52	0.31 /30	0.42 /17	0.73	0.38
GEI	Goldman Sachs Enhanced Inc IR	GHIRX	**C+**	(800) 526-7384	**D+ / 2.9**	0.36	0.51	0.43 /48	0.19 /29	0.33 /16	0.64	0.47
GEI	Goldman Sachs Enhanced Inc R6	GEIUX	**U**	(800) 526-7384	**U** /	0.39	0.55	--	--	--	0.00	N/A
MM	Goldman Sachs Fin Sq Govt Cap	GCGXX	**C-**	(800) 526-7384	**D / 1.9**	0.02	0.02	0.03 /36	0.01 /17	0.01 / 5	0.03	0.38
MM	Goldman Sachs Fin Sq Govt FST	FGTXX	**C**	(800) 526-7384	**D / 2.2**	0.06	0.07	0.08 /40	0.03 /22	0.03 /10	0.08	0.23
MM	Goldman Sachs Fin Sq Govt Pfd	GPGXX	**C**	(800) 526-7384	**D / 2.1**	0.03	0.04	0.04 /37	0.02 /20	0.01 / 5	0.04	0.33
MM	Goldman Sachs Fin Sq Govt Sel	GSGXX	**C**	(800) 526-7384	**D / 2.2**	0.05	0.06	0.06 /39	0.03 /22	0.02 / 8	0.06	0.26
MM	Goldman Sachs Fin Sq MM Adm	FADXX	**C**	(800) 526-7384	**D / 2.1**	0.04	0.04	0.04 /37	0.02 /20	0.01 / 5	0.04	0.48
MM	Goldman Sachs Fin Sq MM FST	FSMXX	**C**	(800) 526-7384	**D+ / 2.7**	0.10	0.14	0.20 /44	0.11 /27	0.13 /15	0.20	0.23
MM	Goldman Sachs Fin Sq MM FST	GCKXX	**C**	(800) 526-7384	**D / 2.2**	0.06	0.07	0.07 /40	0.03 /22	0.02 / 8	0.07	0.38
MM	Goldman Sachs Fin Sq MM Pfd	GPMXX	**C**	(800) 526-7384	**D+ / 2.4**	0.07	0.09	0.10 /41	0.04 /24	0.04 /11	0.10	0.33
MM	Goldman Sachs Fin Sq MM Prm	GPRXX	**C**	(800) 526-7384	**D / 2.1**	0.04	0.04	0.04 /37	0.02 /20	0.01 / 5	0.04	0.58
MM	Goldman Sachs Fin Sq MM Res	GREXX	**C**	(800) 526-7384	**D / 2.1**	0.04	0.04	0.04 /37	0.02 /20	0.01 / 5	0.04	0.88
MM	Goldman Sachs Fin Sq MM Sel	GSMXX	**C**	(800) 526-7384	**D+ / 2.6**	0.09	0.13	0.17 /43	0.08 /26	0.10 /15	0.17	0.26
MM	Goldman Sachs Fin Sq Pr Oblg Adm	FBAXX	**C**	(800) 526-7384	**D / 2.1**	0.03	0.03	0.04 /37	0.02 /20	0.01 / 5	0.04	0.48
MM	Goldman Sachs Fin Sq Pr Oblg C	GPCXX	**U**	(800) 526-7384	**U** /	--	--	--	--	--	0.01	1.23
MM	Goldman Sachs Fin Sq Pr Oblg CM	GFOXX	**C**	(800) 526-7384	**D / 2.1**	0.03	0.03	0.04 /37	0.02 /20	0.01 / 5	0.04	1.03
MM	Goldman Sachs Fin Sq Pr Oblg Cptl	GCPXX	**C**	(800) 526-7384	**D / 2.2**	0.05	0.06	0.07 /40	0.03 /22	0.02 / 8	0.07	0.38
MM	Goldman Sachs Fin Sq Pr Oblg Pfd	GPPXX	**C**	(800) 526-7384	**D+ / 2.3**	0.07	0.08	0.08 /40	0.03 /22	0.03 /10	0.08	0.33
MM	Goldman Sachs Fin Sq Pr Oblg Prm	GOPXX	**C**	(800) 526-7384	**D / 2.1**	0.03	0.03	0.04 /37	0.02 /20	0.01 / 5	0.04	0.58
MM	Goldman Sachs Fin Sq Pr Oblg Res	GBRXX	**U**	(800) 526-7384	**U** /	--	--	--	--	--	0.01	0.88
MM	Goldman Sachs Fin Sq Pr Oblg Sel	GSPXX	**C**	(800) 526-7384	**D+ / 2.5**	0.08	0.11	0.12 /42	0.05 /25	0.06 /13	0.12	0.26
MM	Goldman Sachs Fin Sq Pr Oblg Shs	FPOXX	**C**	(800) 526-7384	**D+ / 2.5**	0.09	0.12	0.15 /43	0.07 /26	0.08 /14	0.15	0.23
MM	Goldman Sachs Fin Sq Pr Oblg Svc	FBSXX	**U**	(800) 526-7384	**U** /	--	--	--	--	--	0.01	0.73
MMT	Goldman Sachs Fin Sq T-E CA FST	ITCXX	**U**		**U** /	0.00	0.01	0.01 /34	0.01 /20	0.01 / 8	0.01	0.41
MMT	Goldman Sachs Fin Sq T-E CA FST	IAMXX	**U**		**U** /	0.00	0.01	0.01 /34	0.01 /20	0.01 / 8	0.01	0.56
MMT	Goldman Sachs Fin Sq T-E CA FST	IECXX	**U**	(800) 526-7384	**U** /	0.00	0.01	0.01 /34	0.01 /20	0.01 / 8	0.01	1.41
MMT	Goldman Sachs Fin Sq T-E CA FST	ICSXX	**U**		**U** /	0.00	0.01	0.01 /34	0.01 /20	0.01 / 8	0.01	0.81
MMT	Goldman Sachs Fin Sq T-E NY FST	IYAXX	**C-**		**D / 1.9**	0.00	0.02	0.02 /36	0.01 /20	0.01 / 8	0.02	0.57
MMT	Goldman Sachs Fin Sq T-E NY FST	IYSXX	**C-**		**D / 1.9**	0.00	0.02	0.02 /36	0.01 /20	0.01 / 8	0.02	0.82
MM	Goldman Sachs Fin Sq Tre Instr Pfd	GPIXX	**C-**	(800) 526-7384	**D / 1.9**	0.02	0.02	0.02 /34	0.01 /17	0.01 / 5	0.02	0.33
MM	Goldman Sachs Fin Sq Tre Instr Sel	GSIXX	**C-**	(800) 526-7384	**D / 1.9**	0.03	0.04	0.04 /37	0.01 /17	0.01 / 5	0.04	0.26
MM	Goldman Sachs Fin Sq Tre Instr Shs	FTIXX	**C**	(800) 526-7384	**D / 2.1**	0.04	0.05	0.05 /38	0.02 /20	0.01 / 5	0.05	0.23
MM	Goldman Sachs Fin Sq Treas Sol	GCFXX	**U**	(800) 526-7384	**U** /	--	--	--	--	--	0.01	0.38
MM	Goldman Sachs Fin Sq Treas Sol	FEDXX	**C**	(800) 526-7384	**D / 2.1**	0.04	0.05	0.06 /39	0.02 /20	0.02 / 8	0.06	0.23
MM	Goldman Sachs Fin Sq Treas Sol Pfd	GPFXX	**C-**	(800) 526-7384	**D / 1.9**	0.02	0.02	0.03 /36	0.01 /17	0.01 / 5	0.03	0.33
MM	Goldman Sachs Fin Sq Treas Sol Sel	GSFXX	**C**	(800) 526-7384	**D / 2.1**	0.04	0.04	0.05 /38	0.02 /20	0.01 / 5	0.05	0.26

• Denotes fund is closed to new investors
* Denotes fund is included in Section II

RISK			NET ASSETS		ASSET							FUND MANAGER		MINIMUM		LOADS	
Risk Rating/Pts	3 Yr Avg Standard Deviation	Avg Duration	NAV As of 3/31/16	Total $(Mil)	Cash %	Gov. Bond %	Muni. Bond %	Corp. Bond %	Other %	Portfolio Turnover Ratio	Avg Coupon Rate	Manager Quality Pct	Manager Tenure (Years)	Initial Purch. $	Additional Purch. $	Front End Load	Back End Load
U /	N/A	N/A	8.26	39	18	55	1	23	3	179	0.0	N/A	3	1,000,000	0	0.0	2.0
U /	N/A	N/A	8.24	N/A	18	55	1	23	3	179	0.0	N/A	3	0	0	0.0	2.0
U /	N/A	N/A	8.26	N/A	18	55	1	23	3	179	0.0	N/A	3	0	0	0.0	2.0
C- / 4.0	3.7	8.1	15.69	178	0	0	99	0	1	14	0.0	27	17	1,000	50	3.8	0.0
C- / 3.9	3.7	8.1	15.69	30	0	0	99	0	1	14	0.0	14	17	1,000	50	0.0	0.0
C- / 4.0	3.7	8.1	15.68	484	0	0	99	0	1	14	0.0	36	17	1,000,000	0	0.0	0.0
C- / 3.9	3.7	8.1	15.67	10	0	0	99	0	1	14	0.0	34	17	0	0	0.0	0.0
C- / 4.0	3.7	8.1	15.77	N/A	0	0	99	0	1	14	0.0	23	17	0	0	0.0	0.0
E+ / 0.7	7.0	7.2	12.25	110	4	64	2	27	3	113	0.0	97	13	1,000	50	4.5	2.0
E+ / 0.7	7.0	7.2	12.24	28	4	64	2	27	3	113	0.0	94	13	1,000	50	0.0	2.0
E+ / 0.7	7.0	7.2	12.26	870	4	64	2	27	3	113	0.0	98	13	1,000,000	0	0.0	2.0
E+ / 0.7	7.0	7.2	12.26	17	4	64	2	27	3	113	0.0	98	13	0	0	0.0	2.0
U /	N/A	7.2	12.26	1	4	64	2	27	3	113	0.0	N/A	13	0	0	0.0	0.0
A+ / 9.8	0.4	0.6	9.41	35	11	5	0	63	21	39	0.0	58	8	1,000	50	1.5	0.0
A+ / 9.8	0.4	0.6	9.43	N/A	11	5	0	63	21	39	0.0	61	8	0	0	0.0	0.0
A+ / 9.9	0.4	0.6	9.40	425	11	5	0	63	21	39	0.0	76	8	1,000,000	0	0.0	0.0
A+ / 9.9	0.4	0.6	9.39	1	11	5	0	63	21	39	0.0	71	8	0	0	0.0	0.0
U /	N/A	0.6	9.40	N/A	11	5	0	63	21	39	0.0	N/A	8	0	0	0.0	0.0
A+ / 9.9	N/A	N/A	1.00	1,318	100	0	0	0	0	0	0.0	65	N/A	10,000,000	0	0.0	0.0
A+ / 9.9	N/A	N/A	1.00	41,405	100	0	0	0	0	0	0.1	63	N/A	10,000,000	0	0.0	0.0
A+ / 9.9	N/A	N/A	1.00	98	100	0	0	0	0	0	0.0	65	N/A	10,000,000	0	0.0	0.0
A+ / 9.9	N/A	N/A	1.00	183	100	0	0	0	0	0	0.1	63	N/A	10,000,000	0	0.0	0.0
A+ / 9.9	N/A	N/A	1.00	360	100	0	0	0	0	0	0.0	63	N/A	10,000,000	0	0.0	0.0
A+ / 9.9	N/A	N/A	1.00	41,455	100	0	0	0	0	0	0.2	70	N/A	10,000,000	0	0.0	0.0
A+ / 9.9	N/A	N/A	1.00	340	100	0	0	0	0	0	0.1	63	N/A	10,000,000	0	0.0	0.0
A+ / 9.9	N/A	N/A	1.00	63	100	0	0	0	0	0	0.1	63	N/A	10,000,000	0	0.0	0.0
A+ / 9.9	N/A	N/A	1.00	N/A	100	0	0	0	0	0	0.0	63	N/A	10,000,000	0	0.0	0.0
A+ / 9.9	N/A	N/A	1.00	N/A	100	0	0	0	0	0	0.0	63	N/A	10,000,000	0	0.0	0.0
A+ / 9.9	N/A	N/A	1.00	2,766	100	0	0	0	0	0	0.2	69	N/A	10,000,000	0	0.0	0.0
A+ / 9.9	N/A	N/A	1.00	1,614	100	0	0	0	0	0	0.0	65	N/A	10,000,000	0	0.0	0.0
U /	N/A	N/A	1.00	22	100	0	0	0	0	0	0.0	N/A	N/A	1,000	0	0.0	0.0
A+ / 9.9	N/A	N/A	1.00	N/A	100	0	0	0	0	0	0.0	65	N/A	10,000,000	0	0.0	0.0
A+ / 9.9	N/A	N/A	1.00	160	100	0	0	0	0	0	0.1	63	N/A	10,000,000	0	0.0	0.0
A+ / 9.9	N/A	N/A	1.00	283	100	0	0	0	0	0	0.1	63	N/A	10,000,000	0	0.0	0.0
A+ / 9.9	N/A	N/A	1.00	N/A	100	0	0	0	0	0	0.0	65	N/A	10,000,000	0	0.0	0.0
U /	N/A	N/A	1.00	63	100	0	0	0	0	0	0.0	N/A	N/A	10,000,000	0	0.0	0.0
A+ / 9.9	N/A	N/A	1.00	109	100	0	0	0	0	0	0.1	65	N/A	10,000,000	0	0.0	0.0
A+ / 9.9	N/A	N/A	1.00	13,683	100	0	0	0	0	0	0.2	N/A	N/A	10,000,000	0	0.0	0.0
U /	N/A	N/A	1.00	758	100	0	0	0	0	0	0.0	N/A	N/A	10,000,000	0	0.0	0.0
U /	N/A	N/A	1.00	182	100	0	0	0	0	0	0.0	N/A	N/A	10,000,000	0	0.0	0.0
U /	N/A	N/A	1.00	N/A	100	0	0	0	0	0	0.0	N/A	N/A	10,000,000	0	0.0	0.0
U /	N/A	N/A	1.00	N/A	100	0	0	0	0	0	0.0	N/A	N/A	10,000,000	0	0.0	0.0
U /	N/A	N/A	1.00	N/A	100	0	0	0	0	0	0.0	N/A	N/A	10,000,000	0	0.0	0.0
A+ / 9.9	N/A	N/A	1.00	N/A	100	0	0	0	0	0	0.0	65	N/A	10,000,000	0	0.0	0.0
A+ / 9.9	N/A	N/A	1.00	N/A	100	0	0	0	0	0	0.0	65	N/A	10,000,000	0	0.0	0.0
A+ / 9.9	N/A	N/A	1.00	51	100	0	0	0	0	0	0.0	63	N/A	10,000,000	0	0.0	0.0
A+ / 9.9	N/A	N/A	1.00	18	100	0	0	0	0	0	0.0	63	N/A	10,000,000	0	0.0	0.0
A+ / 9.9	N/A	N/A	1.00	52,364	100	0	0	0	0	0	0.1	64	N/A	10,000,000	0	0.0	0.0
U /	N/A	N/A	1.00	76	100	0	0	0	0	0	0.0	N/A	N/A	10,000,000	0	0.0	0.0
A+ / 9.9	N/A	N/A	1.00	9,369	100	0	0	0	0	0	0.1	64	N/A	10,000,000	0	0.0	0.0
A+ / 9.9	N/A	N/A	1.00	48	100	0	0	0	0	0	0.0	65	N/A	10,000,000	0	0.0	0.0
A+ / 9.9	N/A	N/A	1.00	9	100	0	0	0	0	0	0.1	64	N/A	10,000,000	0	0.0	0.0

99 Pct = Best 0 Pct = Worst					PERFORMANCE							
						Total Return % through 3/31/16					Incl. in Returns	
									Annualized			
Fund Type	Fund Name	Ticker Symbol	Overall Investment Rating	Phone	Perfor-mance Rating/Pts	3 Mo	6 Mo	1Yr / Pct	3Yr / Pct	5Yr / Pct	Dividend Yield	Expense Ratio
MMT	Goldman Sachs Fin Sq Tx-Ex NY	IENXX	**C-**		**D / 1.9**	0.00	0.02	0.02 /36	0.01 /20	0.01 / 8	0.02	1.42
MM	Goldman Sachs Finan Sq Trs Oblg	GCTXX	**U**	(800) 526-7384	**U /**	0.01	0.01	0.02 /34	0.01 /17	0.01 / 5	0.02	0.38
MM	Goldman Sachs Finan Sq Trs Oblg	GPOXX	**C-**	(800) 526-7384	**D / 1.9**	0.02	0.03	0.03 /36	0.01 /17	0.01 / 5	0.03	0.33
GL	Goldman Sachs Glbl Income A	GSGIX	**B+**	(800) 526-7384	**C+ / 6.4**	2.41	2.58	1.67 /68	3.02 /77	4.30 /65	5.52	1.18
GL	Goldman Sachs Glbl Income C	GSLCX	**B+**	(800) 526-7384	**C+ / 6.7**	2.24	2.21	0.83 /56	2.24 /66	3.51 /53	5.01	1.93
GL	Goldman Sachs Glbl Income Inst	GSGLX	**A+**	(800) 526-7384	**B / 8.0**	2.50	2.75	2.01 /72	3.37 /79	4.66 /69	6.08	0.84
GL	Goldman Sachs Glbl Income IR	GBIRX	**A+**	(800) 526-7384	**B / 8.0**	2.48	2.75	1.96 /72	3.26 /78	4.54 /68	6.04	0.90
GL	Goldman Sachs Glbl Income R6	GBIUX	**U**	(800) 526-7384	**U /**	2.59	2.74	--	--	--	0.00	N/A
GL	Goldman Sachs Glbl Income Svc	GGISX	**A**	(800) 526-7384	**B- / 7.4**	2.28	2.23	1.23 /62	2.74 /74	4.07 /62	5.58	1.34
USS	Goldman Sachs Govt Income A	GSGOX	**C**	(800) 526-7384	**C- / 4.0**	2.49	1.65	1.66 /68	1.53 /53	2.62 /39	1.51	1.05
USS	Goldman Sachs Govt Income C	GSOCX	**C+**	(800) 526-7384	**C / 4.4**	2.30	1.28	0.91 /57	0.79 /39	1.87 /30	0.83	1.80
USS	Goldman Sachs Govt Income Inst	GSOIX	**B+**	(800) 526-7384	**C+ / 6.4**	2.58	1.83	2.01 /72	1.90 /59	2.99 /45	1.91	0.71
USS	Goldman Sachs Govt Income IR	GSOTX	**B+**	(800) 526-7384	**C+ / 6.3**	2.56	1.78	1.92 /71	1.78 /57	2.88 /43	1.82	0.80
USS	Goldman Sachs Govt Income R	GSORX	**B-**	(800) 526-7384	**C / 5.4**	2.43	1.53	1.41 /65	1.28 /48	2.37 /36	1.32	1.30
USS	Goldman Sachs Govt Income R6	GSOUX	**U**	(800) 526-7384	**U /**	2.66	1.83	--	--	--	0.00	N/A
USS	Goldman Sachs Govt Income Svc	GSOSX	**B**	(800) 526-7384	**C+ / 5.6**	2.46	1.57	1.50 /66	1.37 /50	2.46 /37	1.41	1.21
MTG	Goldman Sachs Hi Qual Fltg R A	GSAMX	**C-**	(800) 526-7384	**D- / 1.0**	-0.14	-0.35	-0.81 /23	-0.39 /12	-0.19 / 3	0.23	0.90
MTG	Goldman Sachs Hi Qual Fltg R Inst	GSARX	**C-**	(800) 526-7384	**D / 1.7**	-0.06	-0.18	-0.47 /26	-0.07 /15	0.12 /15	0.57	0.56
MTG	Goldman Sachs Hi Qual Fltg R IR	GTATX	**C-**	(800) 526-7384	**D- / 1.5**	-0.08	-0.23	-0.56 /25	-0.20 /14	--	0.48	0.65
GEI	Goldman Sachs Hi Qual Fltg R R6	GTAUX	**U**	(800) 526-7384	**U /**	-0.06	-0.18	--	--	--	0.00	N/A
MTG	Goldman Sachs Hi Qual Fltg R Svc	GSASX	**C-**	(800) 526-7384	**D- / 1.2**	-0.29	-0.40	-0.93 /22	-0.54 /11	-0.33 / 2	0.10	1.07
COH	Goldman Sachs High Yield A	GSHAX	**E**	(800) 526-7384	**E / 0.5**	1.26	-1.03	-6.37 / 3	0.59 /35	3.70 /56	5.65	1.06
COH	Goldman Sachs High Yield C	GSHCX	**E**	(800) 526-7384	**E+ / 0.6**	1.07	-1.39	-7.04 / 2	-0.15 /14	2.93 /44	5.12	1.81
COH	Goldman Sachs High Yield Inst	GSHIX	**E+**	(800) 526-7384	**D- / 1.4**	1.34	-0.85	-6.01 / 3	0.95 /42	4.06 /62	6.27	0.72
COH	Goldman Sachs High Yield IR	GSHTX	**E+**	(800) 526-7384	**D- / 1.2**	1.32	-0.90	-6.11 / 3	0.80 /39	3.96 /61	6.18	0.81
MUH	Goldman Sachs High Yield Muni A	GHYAX	**C-**	(800) 526-7384	**B+ / 8.8**	2.32	4.72	4.89 /98	4.18 /97	8.14 /98	4.30	0.93
MUH	Goldman Sachs High Yield Muni C	GHYCX	**C-**	(800) 526-7384	**A- / 9.1**	2.14	4.33	4.11 /95	3.41 /92	7.34 /97	3.76	1.68
MUH	Goldman Sachs High Yield Muni Inst	GHYIX	**C**	(800) 526-7384	**A+ / 9.7**	2.40	4.86	5.19 /98	4.45 /97	8.45 /99	4.78	0.59
MUH	Goldman Sachs High Yield Muni IR	GYIRX	**C**	(800) 526-7384	**A+ / 9.7**	2.50	4.84	5.15 /98	4.48 /98	8.43 /99	4.74	0.68
COH	Goldman Sachs High Yield R	GSHRX	**E+**	(800) 526-7384	**E+ / 0.9**	1.19	-1.15	-6.60 / 2	0.34 /31	3.44 /52	5.65	1.31
COH	Goldman Sachs High Yield R6	GSHUX	**U**	(800) 526-7384	**U /**	1.35	-0.84	--	--	--	0.00	0.70
COH	Goldman Sachs High Yield Svc	GSHSX	**E+**	(800) 526-7384	**D- / 1.0**	1.22	-1.11	-6.38 / 3	0.43 /32	3.53 /54	5.74	1.22
LP	Goldman Sachs HY Floating Rate A	GFRAX	**C**	(800) 526-7384	**C- / 3.6**	1.87	0.07	-0.91 /22	1.39 /50	2.45 /37	3.82	0.95
LP	Goldman Sachs HY Floating Rate C	GFRCX	**C-**	(800) 526-7384	**C- / 3.1**	1.58	-0.30	-1.64 /18	0.60 /35	1.69 /27	3.15	1.70
LP	Goldman Sachs HY Floating Rate	GSFRX	**B-**	(800) 526-7384	**C / 5.3**	1.96	0.24	-0.57 /25	1.70 /56	2.82 /42	4.25	0.61
LP	Goldman Sachs HY Floating Rate IR	GFRIX	**C+**	(800) 526-7384	**C / 5.2**	1.93	0.20	-0.65 /25	1.65 /55	2.74 /41	4.16	0.71
LP	Goldman Sachs HY Floating Rate R	GFRRX	**C**	(800) 526-7384	**C- / 4.1**	1.70	-0.15	-1.15 /20	1.10 /44	2.20 /34	3.66	1.17
GEI	Goldman Sachs Infl Prot Secs A	GSAPX	**E+**	(800) 526-7384	**E+ / 0.8**	4.40	3.61	1.09 /60	-1.21 / 7	2.62 /39	0.57	0.96
GEI	Goldman Sachs Infl Prot Secs C	GSCFX	**D-**	(800) 526-7384	**E+ / 0.9**	4.14	3.17	0.39 /48	-1.96 / 4	1.86 /29	0.29	1.71
GEI	Goldman Sachs Infl Prot Secs Inst	GSIPX	**D-**	(800) 526-7384	**D+ / 2.6**	4.46	3.71	1.42 /65	-0.88 / 9	2.96 /44	0.73	0.62
GEI	Goldman Sachs Infl Prot Secs IR	GSTPX	**D-**	(800) 526-7384	**D / 1.8**	4.38	3.62	1.29 /63	-1.01 / 8	2.83 /42	0.69	0.71
GEI	Goldman Sachs Infl Prot Secs R	GSRPX	**D-**	(800) 526-7384	**D- / 1.2**	4.31	3.40	0.79 /55	-1.48 / 6	2.34 /36	0.49	1.22
GEI	Goldman Sachs Infl Prot Secs R6	GSRUX	**U**	(800) 526-7384	**U /**	4.46	3.82	--	--	--	0.00	N/A
GL	Goldman Sachs Inv Gr Cdt A	GSGAX	**D+**	(800) 526-7384	**C / 4.9**	3.27	2.61	-0.54 /26	2.24 /66	4.91 /71	3.13	0.86
GL	Goldman Sachs Inv Gr Cdt Inst	GSGDX	**C-**	(800) 526-7384	**B- / 7.2**	3.36	2.78	-0.30 /28	2.58 /72	5.26 /73	3.59	0.52
GL	Goldman Sachs Inv Gr Cdt IR	GTIRX	**C-**	(800) 526-7384	**B- / 7.1**	3.45	2.73	-0.28 /28	2.53 /71	--	3.50	0.61
COI	Goldman Sachs Inv Gr Cdt R6	GTIUX	**U**	(800) 526-7384	**U /**	3.36	2.78	--	--	--	0.00	N/A
GL	Goldman Sachs Inv Gr Cdt SA-Inst	GSCPX	**C**	(800) 526-7384	**B- / 7.2**	3.47	2.78	-0.19 /29	2.62 /72	5.29 /73	3.59	0.52
MMT	Goldman Sachs Investor T/F MM	FEAXX	**U**	(800) 526-7384	**U /**	0.00	0.01	0.01 /34	0.01 /20	0.01 / 8	0.01	0.48
MMT	Goldman Sachs Investor T/F MM CM	GXCXX	**U**	(800) 526-7384	**U /**	0.00	0.01	0.01 /34	0.01 /20	0.01 / 8	0.01	1.03
MM	Goldman Sachs Investor T/F MM Cptl	GCXXX	**U**	(800) 526-7384	**U /**	0.00	0.01	0.01 /32	0.01 /17	0.01 / 5	0.01	0.38
MMT	Goldman Sachs Investor T/F MM Inst	FTXXX	**U**	(800) 526-7384	**U /**	0.00	0.01	0.01 /34	0.01 /20	0.01 / 8	0.01	0.23

● Denotes fund is closed to new investors
* Denotes fund is included in Section II

RISK			NET ASSETS		ASSET							FUND MANAGER		MINIMUM		LOADS	
Risk Rating/Pts	3 Yr Avg Standard Deviation	Avg Duration	NAV As of 3/31/16	Total $(Mil)	Cash %	Gov. Bond %	Muni. Bond %	Corp. Bond %	Other %	Portfolio Turnover Ratio	Avg Coupon Rate	Manager Quality Pct	Manager Tenure (Years)	Initial Purch. $	Additional Purch. $	Front End Load	Back End Load
A+ / 9.9	N/A	N/A	1.00	N/A	100	0	0	0	0	0	0.0	65	N/A	10,000,000	0	0.0	0.0
U /	N/A	N/A	1.00	515	100	0	0	0	0	0	0.0	N/A	N/A	10,000,000	0	0.0	0.0
A+ / 9.9	N/A	N/A	1.00	119	100	0	0	0	0	0	0.0	65	N/A	10,000,000	0	0.0	0.0
B / 7.6	2.7	5.1	12.24	112	8	44	1	27	20	226	0.0	98	21	1,000	50	3.8	0.0
B- / 7.5	2.7	5.1	12.14	13	8	44	1	27	20	226	0.0	97	21	1,000	50	0.0	0.0
B / 7.6	2.7	5.1	12.22	680	8	44	1	27	20	226	0.0	99	21	1,000,000	0	0.0	0.0
B / 7.6	2.7	5.1	12.20	32	8	44	1	27	20	226	0.0	99	21	0	0	0.0	0.0
U /	N/A	5.1	12.22	1	8	44	1	27	20	226	0.0	N/A	21	0	0	0.0	0.0
B / 7.6	2.7	5.1	12.16	2	8	44	1	27	20	226	0.0	98	21	0	0	0.0	0.0
B / 8.0	2.4	5.1	15.03	160	0	43	1	0	56	471	0.0	57	3	1,000	50	3.8	0.0
B / 8.0	2.4	5.1	15.03	12	0	43	1	0	56	471	0.0	32	3	1,000	50	0.0	0.0
B / 7.9	2.5	5.1	15.01	147	0	43	1	0	56	471	0.0	74	3	1,000,000	0	0.0	0.0
B / 8.0	2.4	5.1	15.02	5	0	43	1	0	56	471	0.0	71	3	0	0	0.0	0.0
B / 7.9	2.5	5.1	15.01	23	0	43	1	0	56	471	0.0	46	3	0	0	0.0	0.0
U /	N/A	5.1	15.01	N/A	0	43	1	0	56	471	0.0	N/A	3	0	0	0.0	0.0
B / 7.9	2.4	5.1	14.99	55	0	43	1	0	56	471	0.0	50	3	0	0	0.0	0.0
A+ / 9.8	0.4	0.2	8.63	11	12	16	6	2	64	64	0.0	53	8	1,000	50	1.5	0.0
A+ / 9.9	0.4	0.2	8.63	361	12	16	6	2	64	64	0.0	73	8	1,000,000	0	0.0	0.0
A+ / 9.9	0.4	0.2	8.61	1	12	16	6	2	64	64	0.0	62	8	0	0	0.0	0.0
U /	N/A	0.2	8.63	N/A	12	16	6	2	64	64	0.0	N/A	8	0	0	0.0	0.0
A+ / 9.8	0.4	0.2	8.67	1	12	16	6	2	64	64	0.0	51	8	0	0	0.0	0.0
D- / 1.3	5.7	4.2	6.02	340	2	0	0	92	6	55	0.0	27	7	1,000	50	4.5	2.0
D- / 1.3	5.7	4.2	6.03	52	2	0	0	92	6	55	0.0	14	7	1,000	50	0.0	2.0
D- / 1.4	5.7	4.2	6.04	3,198	2	0	0	92	6	55	0.0	37	7	1,000,000	0	0.0	2.0
D- / 1.4	5.7	4.2	6.03	9	2	0	0	92	6	55	0.0	33	7	0	0	0.0	2.0
D- / 1.0	5.7	8.8	9.36	261	0	0	99	0	1	14	0.0	27	16	1,000	50	4.5	2.0
D- / 1.0	5.7	8.8	9.36	73	0	0	99	0	1	14	0.0	14	16	1,000	50	0.0	2.0
D- / 1.1	5.7	8.8	9.36	3,750	0	0	99	0	1	14	0.0	36	16	1,000,000	0	0.0	2.0
D- / 1.0	5.7	8.8	9.37	21	0	0	99	0	1	14	0.0	35	16	0	0	0.0	2.0
D- / 1.3	5.7	4.2	6.02	15	2	0	0	92	6	55	0.0	21	7	0	0	0.0	2.0
U /	N/A	4.2	6.05	162	2	0	0	92	6	55	0.0	N/A	7	0	0	0.0	2.0
D- / 1.3	5.7	4.2	6.02	15	2	0	0	92	6	55	0.0	23	7	0	0	0.0	2.0
B / 7.9	2.5	0.7	9.46	6	0	3	0	88	9	55	0.0	89	5	1,000	50	2.3	0.0
B / 8.0	2.4	0.7	9.46	2	0	3	0	88	9	55	0.0	72	5	1,000	50	0.0	0.0
B / 8.0	2.4	0.7	9.47	3,208	0	3	0	88	9	55	0.0	92	5	1,000,000	0	0.0	0.0
B / 7.9	2.5	0.7	9.48	1	0	3	0	88	9	55	0.0	91	5	0	0	0.0	0.0
B / 7.9	2.5	0.7	9.46	N/A	0	3	0	88	9	55	0.0	85	5	0	0	0.0	0.0
D+ / 2.6	5.1	6.6	10.44	40	1	98	0	0	1	161	0.0	4	9	1,000	50	3.8	0.0
D+ / 2.7	5.1	6.6	10.32	6	1	98	0	0	1	161	0.0	2	9	1,000	50	0.0	0.0
D+ / 2.7	5.1	6.6	10.55	120	1	98	0	0	1	161	0.0	4	9	1,000,000	0	0.0	0.0
D+ / 2.7	5.1	6.6	10.49	3	1	98	0	0	1	161	0.0	4	9	0	0	0.0	0.0
D+ / 2.7	5.1	6.6	10.41	10	1	98	0	0	1	161	0.0	3	9	0	0	0.0	0.0
U /	N/A	6.6	10.55	N/A	1	98	0	0	1	161	0.0	N/A	9	0	0	0.0	0.0
C- / 3.5	4.3	6.7	9.08	28	6	10	3	77	4	84	0.0	97	1	1,000	50	3.8	0.0
C- / 3.4	4.3	6.7	9.08	156	6	10	3	77	4	84	0.0	98	1	1,000,000	0	0.0	0.0
C- / 3.5	4.3	6.7	9.09	1	6	10	3	77	4	84	0.0	97	1	0	0	0.0	0.0
U /	N/A	6.7	9.08	N/A	6	10	3	77	4	84	0.0	N/A	1	0	0	0.0	0.0
C- / 3.5	4.3	6.7	9.09	240	6	10	3	77	4	84	0.0	98	1	100,000,000	0	0.0	0.0
U /	N/A	N/A	1.00	89	100	0	0	0	0	0	0.0	N/A	N/A	10,000,000	0	0.0	0.0
U /	N/A	N/A	1.00	N/A	100	0	0	0	0	0	0.0	N/A	N/A	10,000,000	0	0.0	0.0
U /	N/A	N/A	1.00	53	100	0	0	0	0	0	0.0	N/A	N/A	10,000,000	0	0.0	0.0
U /	N/A	N/A	1.00	3,676	100	0	0	0	0	0	0.0	N/A	N/A	10,000,000	0	0.0	0.0

Fund Type	Fund Name (99 Pct = Best, 0 Pct = Worst)	Ticker Symbol	Overall Investment Rating	Phone	PERFORMANCE: Performance Rating/Pts	Total Return % through 3/31/16: 3 Mo	6 Mo	1Yr / Pct	Annualized: 3Yr / Pct	Annualized: 5Yr / Pct	Incl. in Returns: Dividend Yield	Expense Ratio
MMT	Goldman Sachs Investor T/F MM Pfd	GPTXX	**U**	(800) 526-7384	**U /**	0.00	0.01	0.01 /34	0.01 /20	0.01 / 8	0.01	0.33
MMT	Goldman Sachs Investor T/F MM Prm	GXPXX	**U**	(800) 526-7384	**U /**	0.00	0.01	0.01 /34	0.01 /20	0.01 / 8	0.01	0.58
MMT	Goldman Sachs Investor T/F MM Res	GXRXX	**U**	(800) 526-7384	**U /**	0.00	0.01	0.01 /34	0.01 /20	0.01 / 8	0.01	0.88
MMT	Goldman Sachs Investor T/F MM Sel	GSTXX	**U**	(800) 526-7384	**U /**	0.00	0.01	0.01 /34	0.01 /20	0.01 / 8	0.01	0.26
MMT	Goldman Sachs Investor T/F MM Svc	FESXX	**U**	(800) 526-7384	**U /**	0.00	0.01	0.01 /34	0.01 /20	0.01 / 8	0.01	0.73
USA	Goldman Sachs Lmtd Matur Obl	GPPAX	**U**	(800) 526-7384	**U /**	0.24	0.26	0.36 /47	--	--	0.35	3.18
USA	Goldman Sachs Lmtd Matur Obl Inst	GPPIX	**U**	(800) 526-7384	**U /**	0.30	0.38	0.61 /51	--	--	0.60	2.93
EM	Goldman Sachs Local Emg Mkt Debt	GAMDX	**E-**	(800) 526-7384	**E- / 0.0**	10.14	9.49	-3.57 / 9	-8.58 / 0	-3.06 / 1	5.11	1.36
EM	Goldman Sachs Local Emg Mkt Debt	GCMDX	**E-**	(800) 526-7384	**E- / 0.0**	9.92	9.08	-4.41 / 6	-9.25 / 0	-3.79 / 0	4.61	2.14
EM	Goldman Sachs Local Emg Mkt Debt	GIMDX	**E-**	(800) 526-7384	**E- / 0.1**	10.23	9.68	-3.38 /10	-8.27 / 0	-2.73 / 1	5.69	1.05
EM	Goldman Sachs Local Emg Mkt Debt	GLIRX	**E-**	(800) 526-7384	**E- / 0.1**	10.22	9.46	-3.48 /10	-8.40 / 0	-2.85 / 1	5.60	1.14
USS	Goldman Sachs Short Dur Gov A	GSSDX	**C-**	(800) 526-7384	**D / 1.8**	0.97	0.26	0.44 /48	0.29 /30	0.46 /17	0.62	0.93
USS	Goldman Sachs Short Dur Gov C	GSDCX	**C-**	(800) 526-7384	**D / 1.8**	0.80	0.01	-0.02 /31	-0.10 /15	0.06 /13	0.28	1.69
USS	Goldman Sachs Short Dur Gov Inst	GSTGX	**B-**	(800) 526-7384	**C- / 3.8**	1.05	0.43	0.78 /55	0.63 /36	0.80 /19	0.97	0.59
USS	Goldman Sachs Short Dur Gov IR	GTDTX	**C+**	(800) 526-7384	**C- / 3.5**	0.93	0.29	0.59 /51	0.51 /33	0.69 /18	0.88	0.68
USS	Goldman Sachs Short Dur Gov R6	GSTUX	**U**	(800) 526-7384	**U /**	1.06	0.34	--	--	--	0.00	N/A
USS	Goldman Sachs Short Dur Gov Svc	GSDSX	**C**	(800) 526-7384	**D+ / 2.8**	0.84	0.09	0.18 /43	0.10 /27	0.28 /16	0.48	1.10
GEI	Goldman Sachs Short Dur Income A	GDIAX	**C+**	(800) 526-7384	**C- / 3.6**	1.03	0.71	0.91 /57	0.93 /41	--	2.27	0.99
GEI	Goldman Sachs Short Dur Income C	GDICX	**C+**	(800) 526-7384	**C- / 3.6**	0.93	0.51	0.51 /50	0.53 /34	--	1.91	1.74
GEI	Goldman Sachs Short Dur Income	GDFIX	**B+**	(800) 526-7384	**C / 5.1**	1.21	0.99	1.36 /64	1.31 /48	--	2.65	0.64
GEI	Goldman Sachs Short Dur Income IR	GSSRX	**B**	(800) 526-7384	**C / 4.8**	1.09	0.84	1.16 /61	1.18 /46	--	2.56	0.74
GEI	Goldman Sachs Short Dur Income R	GIFRX	**C+**	(800) 526-7384	**C- / 4.0**	1.07	0.69	0.75 /54	0.71 /37	--	2.05	1.22
COI	Goldman Sachs Short Dur Income R6	GDIUX	**U**	(800) 526-7384	**U /**	1.10	0.88	--	--	--	0.00	N/A
MUN	Goldman Sachs Short Dur T/F A	GSDTX	**C**	(800) 526-7384	**D+ / 2.9**	0.33	0.75	0.62 /58	0.46 /37	1.34 /32	0.87	0.76
MUN	Goldman Sachs Short Dur T/F C	GSTCX	**C**	(800) 526-7384	**D+ / 2.8**	0.23	0.55	0.22 /47	0.06 /27	0.91 /24	0.49	1.51
MUN	Goldman Sachs Short Dur T/F Inst	GSDUX	**B+**	(800) 526-7384	**C / 4.9**	0.32	0.83	0.86 /64	0.77 /46	1.64 /38	1.23	0.41
MUN	Goldman Sachs Short Dur T/F IR	GDIRX	**B**	(800) 526-7384	**C / 4.7**	0.39	0.88	0.87 /64	0.71 /44	1.57 /37	1.14	0.51
MUN	Goldman Sachs Short Dur T/F Svc	GSFSX	**C+**	(800) 526-7384	**C- / 3.4**	0.20	0.58	0.36 /50	0.30 /32	1.16 /28	0.73	0.92
* GL	Goldman Sachs Strategic Income A	GSZAX	**D**	(800) 526-7384	**E / 0.5**	-1.67	-2.14	-2.49 /13	-0.42 /12	2.14 /33	4.17	0.91
GL	Goldman Sachs Strategic Income C	GSZCX	**D**	(800) 526-7384	**E / 0.5**	-1.84	-2.49	-3.21 /11	-1.17 / 7	1.38 /24	3.56	1.66
GL	Goldman Sachs Strategic Income Inst	GSZIX	**D**	(800) 526-7384	**D- / 1.2**	-1.58	-1.97	-2.15 /15	-0.08 /15	2.51 /38	4.69	0.57
GL	Goldman Sachs Strategic Income IR	GZIRX	**D**	(800) 526-7384	**D- / 1.1**	-1.61	-2.01	-2.24 /15	-0.17 /14	2.42 /37	4.60	0.66
GL	Goldman Sachs Strategic Income R	GSZRX	**D**	(800) 526-7384	**E+ / 0.7**	-1.73	-2.25	-2.73 /12	-0.67 /10	1.89 /30	4.09	1.16
MTG	Goldman Sachs US Mtge A	GSUAX	**B**	(800) 526-7384	**C / 5.5**	1.82	1.39	1.89 /71	2.50 /71	3.47 /52	2.33	0.95
MTG	Goldman Sachs US Mtge Inst	GSUIX	**A+**	(800) 526-7384	**B / 7.6**	1.91	1.66	2.23 /73	2.87 /75	3.86 /59	2.76	0.62
MTG	Goldman Sachs US Mtge IR	GGIRX	**A+**	(800) 526-7384	**B- / 7.4**	1.88	1.52	2.14 /73	2.75 /74	--	2.67	0.71
MTG	Goldman Sachs US Mtge R6	GGIUX	**U**	(800) 526-7384	**U /**	1.91	1.66	--	--	--	0.00	N/A
MTG	Goldman Sachs US Mtge SA-Inst	GSUPX	**A+**	(800) 526-7384	**B / 7.6**	2.00	1.66	2.23 /73	2.87 /75	3.84 /59	2.76	0.63
GEI	Great Lakes Bond Institutional	GLBNX	**B-**	(855) 278-2020	**C+ / 6.6**	3.25	3.23	1.29 /63	1.95 /60	--	2.47	0.85
COI	Great-West Bond Index Init	MXBIX	**C+**	(866) 831-7129	**C+ / 6.3**	2.46	1.70	1.11 /60	1.94 /60	3.28 /49	1.21	0.50
COI	Great-West Bond Index Inst	MXCOX	**U**	(866) 831-7129	**U /**	2.37	1.68	--	--	--	0.00	N/A
COI	Great-West Bond Index L	MXBJX	**C+**	(866) 831-7129	**C+ / 5.8**	2.36	1.46	0.80 /55	1.67 /55	--	1.77	0.75
COI	Great-West Federated Bond Init	MXFDX	**C-**	(866) 831-7129	**C / 4.6**	1.85	1.18	-0.96 /22	1.21 /46	2.91 /44	2.23	0.70
COI	Great-West Federated Bond Inst	MXIUX	**U**	(866) 831-7129	**U /**	1.68	1.08	--	--	--	0.00	N/A
COI	Great-West Loomis Sayles Bond Init	MXLMX	**D**	(866) 831-7129	**C / 5.1**	3.54	1.59	-2.95 /12	1.61 /54	4.65 /69	2.47	0.90
GEL	Great-West Loomis Sayles Bond Inst	MXUGX	**U**	(866) 831-7129	**U /**	3.73	1.76	--	--	--	0.00	N/A
COH	Great-West Putnam High Yld Bd Init	MXHYX	**D**	(866) 831-7129	**C / 5.0**	3.49	1.46	-3.68 / 9	1.68 /55	4.25 /65	6.44	1.10
COH	Great-West Putnam High Yld Bd Inst	MXFRX	**U**	(866) 831-7129	**U /**	3.56	1.70	--	--	--	0.00	N/A
COI	Great-West Short Duration Bd Init	MXSDX	**B-**	(866) 831-7129	**C- / 4.0**	0.49	0.23	0.38 /47	0.91 /41	2.02 /31	0.94	0.60
COI	Great-West Short Duration Bd Inst	MXXJX	**U**	(866) 831-7129	**U /**	0.51	0.34	--	--	--	0.00	N/A
COI	Great-West Short Duration Bd L	MXTDX	**C+**	(866) 831-7129	**C- / 4.0**	0.53	0.15	0.35 /47	0.88 /40	--	1.06	0.85
GL	Great-West TempletonGlobal Bd Init	MXGBX	**E+**	(866) 831-7129	**E / 0.5**	-0.24	0.98	-4.64 / 6	-1.74 / 5	1.28 /23	4.18	1.30

● Denotes fund is closed to new investors
* Denotes fund is included in Section II

RISK			NET ASSETS		ASSET							FUND MANAGER		MINIMUM		LOADS	
Risk Rating/Pts	3 Yr Avg Standard Deviation	Avg Duration	NAV As of 3/31/16	Total $(Mil)	Cash %	Gov. Bond %	Muni. Bond %	Corp. Bond %	Other %	Portfolio Turnover Ratio	Avg Coupon Rate	Manager Quality Pct	Manager Tenure (Years)	Initial Purch. $	Additional Purch. $	Front End Load	Back End Load
U /	N/A	N/A	1.00	3	100	0	0	0	0	0	0.0	N/A	N/A	10,000,000	0	0.0	0.0
U /	N/A	N/A	1.00	N/A	100	0	0	0	0	0	0.0	N/A	N/A	10,000,000	0	0.0	0.0
U /	N/A	N/A	1.00	7	100	0	0	0	0	0	0.0	N/A	N/A	10,000,000	0	0.0	0.0
U /	N/A	N/A	1.00	204	100	0	0	0	0	0	0.0	N/A	N/A	10,000,000	0	0.0	0.0
U /	N/A	N/A	1.00	64	100	0	0	0	0	0	0.0	N/A	N/A	10,000,000	0	0.0	0.0
U /	N/A	0.2	10.00	N/A	0	0	0	0	100	40	0.0	N/A	2	0	0	0.0	0.0
U /	N/A	0.2	10.00	15	0	0	0	0	100	40	0.0	N/A	2	1,000,000	0	0.0	0.0
E- / 0.1	12.6	N/A	6.36	140	9	74	1	12	4	145	0.0	0	8	1,000	50	4.5	2.0
E- / 0.1	12.5	N/A	6.37	7	9	74	1	12	4	145	0.0	0	8	1,000	50	0.0	2.0
E- / 0.1	12.5	N/A	6.36	391	9	74	1	12	4	145	0.0	1	8	1,000,000	0	0.0	2.0
E- / 0.1	12.5	N/A	6.35	10	9	74	1	12	4	145	0.0	0	8	0	0	0.0	2.0
A+ / 9.7	0.6	2.0	10.10	174	7	54	0	0	39	185	0.0	62	8	1,000	50	1.5	0.0
A+ / 9.7	0.6	2.0	10.03	34	7	54	0	0	39	185	0.0	46	8	1,000	50	0.0	0.0
A+ / 9.7	0.6	2.0	10.07	1,088	7	54	0	0	39	185	0.0	78	8	1,000,000	0	0.0	0.0
A+ / 9.8	0.6	2.0	10.10	19	7	54	0	0	39	185	0.0	N/A	8	0	0	0.0	0.0
U /	N/A	2.0	10.07	74	7	54	0	0	39	185	0.0	N/A	8	0	0	0.0	0.0
A+ / 9.7	0.6	2.0	10.05	31	7	54	0	0	39	185	0.0	54	8	0	0	0.0	0.0
A- / 9.0	1.4	3.1	9.96	7	12	13	3	43	29	139	0.0	73	4	1,000	50	1.5	0.0
A- / 9.0	1.4	3.1	9.96	1	12	13	3	43	29	139	0.0	53	4	1,000	50	0.0	0.0
A- / 9.0	1.3	3.1	9.98	389	12	13	3	43	29	139	0.0	84	4	1,000,000	0	0.0	0.0
A- / 9.0	1.3	3.1	9.97	N/A	12	13	3	43	29	139	0.0	80	4	0	0	0.0	0.0
B+ / 8.9	1.4	3.1	9.98	N/A	12	13	3	43	29	139	0.0	59	4	0	0	0.0	0.0
U /	N/A	3.1	9.97	N/A	12	13	3	43	29	139	0.0	N/A	4	0	0	0.0	0.0
A / 9.3	1.0	2.1	10.56	148	0	0	100	0	0	24	0.0	44	17	1,000	50	1.5	0.0
A / 9.3	1.0	2.1	10.55	34	0	0	100	0	0	24	0.0	33	17	1,000	50	0.0	0.0
A / 9.3	1.0	2.1	10.54	4,307	0	0	100	0	0	24	0.0	59	17	1,000,000	0	0.0	0.0
A / 9.3	1.0	2.1	10.55	4	0	0	100	0	0	24	0.0	57	17	0	0	0.0	0.0
A- / 9.2	1.0	2.1	10.54	N/A	0	0	100	0	0	24	0.0	40	17	0	0	0.0	0.0
C / 5.3	3.4	2.7	9.41	1,386	3	33	2	27	35	188	0.0	44	6	1,000	50	3.8	0.0
C / 5.2	3.4	2.7	9.41	712	3	33	2	27	35	188	0.0	23	6	1,000	50	0.0	0.0
C / 5.3	3.4	2.7	9.41	11,267	3	33	2	27	35	188	0.0	58	6	1,000,000	0	0.0	0.0
C / 5.2	3.4	2.7	9.41	334	3	33	2	27	35	188	0.0	55	6	0	0	0.0	0.0
C / 5.2	3.4	2.7	9.40	9	3	33	2	27	35	188	0.0	37	6	0	0	0.0	0.0
B+ / 8.3	2.2	4.0	10.68	37	0	16	0	0	84	1,367	0.0	73	13	1,000	50	3.8	0.0
B+ / 8.3	2.2	4.0	10.71	60	0	16	0	0	84	1,367	0.0	83	13	1,000,000	0	0.0	0.0
B+ / 8.3	2.2	4.0	10.71	7	0	16	0	0	84	1,367	0.0	80	13	0	0	0.0	0.0
U /	N/A	4.0	10.71	N/A	0	16	0	0	84	1,367	0.0	N/A	13	0	0	0.0	0.0
B+ / 8.3	2.2	4.0	10.69	211	0	16	0	0	84	1,367	0.0	83	13	100,000,000	0	0.0	0.0
C+ / 6.2	3.1	N/A	9.80	92	4	8	15	53	20	33	0.0	44	4	100,000	100	0.0	0.0
C+ / 6.5	3.0	5.6	13.77	351	0	41	1	24	34	57	3.2	73	12	0	0	0.0	0.0
U /	N/A	5.6	9.94	745	0	41	1	24	34	57	3.2	N/A	12	0	0	0.0	0.0
C+ / 6.7	3.0	5.6	9.12	36	0	41	1	24	34	57	3.2	59	12	0	0	0.0	0.0
C / 5.5	3.3	4.7	10.48	31	0	18	0	51	31	57	4.1	33	13	0	0	0.0	0.0
U /	N/A	4.7	9.69	367	0	18	0	51	31	57	4.1	N/A	13	0	0	0.0	0.0
D / 2.2	5.5	4.6	12.30	323	1	34	2	46	17	21	4.3	39	22	0	0	0.0	0.0
U /	N/A	4.6	9.17	382	1	34	2	46	17	21	4.3	N/A	22	0	0	0.0	0.0
D- / 1.1	5.9	3.9	7.72	10	1	1	0	86	12	53	6.0	60	7	0	0	0.0	0.0
U /	N/A	3.9	9.03	269	1	1	0	86	12	53	6.0	N/A	7	0	0	0.0	0.0
A / 9.4	0.9	1.8	10.27	48	0	0	0	80	20	55	2.6	80	13	0	0	0.0	0.0
U /	N/A	1.8	9.91	124	0	0	0	80	20	55	2.6	N/A	13	0	0	0.0	0.0
A / 9.3	1.0	1.8	9.48	N/A	0	0	0	80	20	55	2.6	79	13	0	0	0.0	0.0
D / 1.9	5.7	0.4	8.19	66	13	86	0	0	1	28	3.6	14	11	0	0	0.0	0.0

99 Pct = Best
0 Pct = Worst

Fund Type	Fund Name	Ticker Symbol	Overall Investment Rating	Phone	PERFORMANCE Performance Rating/Pts	Total Return % through 3/31/16 3 Mo	6 Mo	1Yr / Pct	Annualized 3Yr / Pct	Annualized 5Yr / Pct	Incl. in Returns Dividend Yield	Incl. in Returns Expense Ratio
GL	Great-West TempletonGlobal Bd Inst	MXZMX	**U**	(866) 831-7129	**U** /	-0.11	1.24	--	--	--	0.00	N/A
MTG	Great-West US Govt Mtg Secs Init	MXGMX	**B+**	(866) 831-7129	**C+ / 6.0**	1.51	0.94	1.06 /60	1.93 /60	2.78 /41	1.55	0.60
MTG	Great-West US Govt Mtg Secs Inst	MXDQX	**U**	(866) 831-7129	**U** /	1.33	0.88	--	--	--	0.00	N/A
LP	Guggenheim Floating Rate Strat A	GIFAX	**B+**	(800) 820-0888	**C+ / 5.6**	1.12	-0.19	0.29 /46	2.82 /75	--	4.13	1.19
LP	Guggenheim Floating Rate Strat C	GIFCX	**B+**	(800) 820-0888	**C+ / 5.6**	0.91	-0.60	-0.49 /26	2.04 /62	--	3.50	1.91
LP	Guggenheim Floating Rate Strat Inst	GIFIX	**A+**	(800) 820-0888	**B- / 7.3**	1.18	-0.07	0.53 /50	3.06 /77	--	4.49	0.85
LP	Guggenheim Floating Rate Strat P	GIFPX	**U**	(800) 820-0888	**U** /	1.12	-0.19	--	--	--	0.00	1.04
COH	Guggenheim High Yield A	SIHAX	**D-**	(800) 820-0888	**D+ / 2.6**	1.57	-0.52	-3.17 /11	2.35 /68	4.03 /62	6.75	1.27
COH	Guggenheim High Yield C	SIHSX	**D**	(800) 820-0888	**C- / 3.0**	1.37	-0.97	-3.92 / 8	1.56 /53	3.23 /49	6.23	2.01
COH	Guggenheim High Yield Inst	SHYIX	**D+**	(800) 820-0888	**C / 5.0**	1.59	-0.48	-2.96 /11	2.58 /72	4.26 /65	7.37	0.94
COH	Guggenheim High Yield P	SIHPX	**U**	(800) 820-0888	**U** /	1.57	-0.58	--	--	--	0.00	3.36
USS	Guggenheim Investment Grade Bd A	SIUSX	**A**	(800) 820-0888	**B- / 7.1**	1.33	1.17	0.89 /57	3.94 /83	5.04 /72	4.10	1.17
USS	Guggenheim Investment Grade Bd C	SDICX	**A+**	(800) 820-0888	**B- / 7.4**	1.16	0.81	0.15 /43	3.18 /78	4.29 /65	3.55	1.99
COI	Guggenheim Investment Grade Bd	GIUSX	**A+**	(800) 820-0888	**B+ / 8.3**	1.45	1.34	1.13 /61	4.18 /85	--	4.53	0.94
COI	Guggenheim Investment Grade Bd P	SIUPX	**U**	(800) 820-0888	**U** /	1.32	1.14	--	--	--	0.00	3.29
COI	Guggenheim Limited Duration P	GILPX	**U**	(800) 820-0888	**U** /	-0.07	-0.24	--	--	--	0.00	0.94
* GEL	Guggenheim Macro Opportunities A	GIOAX	**D**	(800) 820-0888	**D- / 1.4**	0.18	-1.75	-3.07 /11	1.47 /51	--	5.16	1.57
GEL	Guggenheim Macro Opportunities C	GIOCX	**D**	(800) 820-0888	**D / 1.8**	0.00	-2.12	-3.80 / 8	0.73 /37	--	4.59	2.29
GEL	Guggenheim Macro Opportunities	GIOIX	**C-**	(800) 820-0888	**C / 4.5**	0.27	-1.58	-2.74 /12	1.81 /58	--	5.71	1.25
MUN	Guggenheim Municipal Income A	GIJAX	**C**	(800) 820-0888	**B / 8.1**	1.10	2.90	2.43 /80	3.20 /90	--	2.12	1.17
MUN	Guggenheim Municipal Income P	GIJPX	**U**	(800) 820-0888	**U** /	1.01	2.82	--	--	--	0.00	3.17
GEI	Guggenheim Total Return Bond A	GIBAX	**C+**	(800) 820-0888	**C+ / 6.0**	1.42	0.91	0.52 /50	3.22 /78	--	4.16	1.10
GEI	Guggenheim Total Return Bond C	GIBCX	**B-**	(800) 820-0888	**C+ / 6.4**	1.25	0.56	-0.19 /29	2.48 /70	--	3.60	1.80
GEI	Guggenheim Total Return Bond Inst	GIBIX	**A**	(800) 820-0888	**B / 7.9**	1.50	1.08	0.86 /56	3.58 /81	--	4.67	0.76
COI	Guggenheim Total Return Bond P	GIBLX	**U**	(800) 820-0888	**U** /	1.44	0.95	--	--	--	0.00	1.02
GEI	GuideMark Core Fixed Inc Inst	GICFX	**C+**	(888) 278-5809	**C+ / 6.1**	2.48	1.89	0.97 /58	1.80 /57	--	1.97	0.72
GEI	GuideMark Core Fixed Inc Svc	GMCOX	**C+**	(888) 278-5809	**C+ / 5.7**	2.91	2.26	1.05 /59	1.42 /51	2.82 /42	1.41	1.32
GL	GuideMark Opptnstc Fxd Inc Inst	GIOFX	**D-**	(888) 278-5809	**E / 0.5**	-1.74	-0.77	-4.22 / 7	-1.21 / 7	--	0.90	1.09
GL	GuideMark Opptnstc Fxd Inc Svc	GMIFX	**D-**	(888) 278-5809	**E / 0.4**	-1.52	-0.66	-4.34 / 7	-1.59 / 6	--	0.88	1.67
MUI	GuideMark Tax-Exempt Fixed Inc Svc	GMTEX	**B+**	(888) 278-5809	**B+ / 8.8**	1.66	2.91	3.18 /87	2.67 /84	4.76 /83	2.75	1.38
GL	GuidePath Flexible Income Alloc Ins	GIXFX	**C-**	(888) 278-5809	**C / 4.4**	2.34	1.63	-0.21 /29	0.89 /41	--	1.23	0.69
GL	GuidePath Flexible Income Alloc Svc	GPIFX	**D+**	(888) 278-5809	**D+ / 2.4**	1.60	0.61	-1.51 /18	0.09 /27	--	0.76	1.29
COI	GuideStone Ex-Duration Bond Inst	GEDYX	**C-**	(888) 984-8433	**B+ / 8.6**	6.23	5.01	-1.77 /17	4.38 /86	7.86 /86	6.38	0.59
COI	GuideStone Ex-Duration Bond Inv	GEDZX	**C-**	(888) 984-8433	**B+ / 8.4**	6.06	4.93	-2.12 /15	4.12 /85	7.62 /85	1.20	0.86
COH	GuideStone Flexible Income Inv	GFLZX	**U**	(888) 984-8433	**U** /	1.14	-1.17	-2.31 /14	--	--	3.38	1.23
GL	GuideStone Global Bond Inst	GGBEX	**U**	(888) 984-8433	**U** /	3.86	2.17	--	--	--	0.00	N/A
GL	GuideStone Global Bond Inv	GGBFX	**D-**	(888) 984-8433	**D+ / 2.4**	3.80	1.90	-3.41 /10	0.03 /21	2.81 /42	3.35	0.91
GEI	GuideStone Infl Protected Bd Inst	GIPYX	**U**	(888) 984-8433	**U** /	3.81	2.98	--	--	--	0.00	N/A
GL	GuideStone Infl Protected Bd Inv	GIPZX	**D-**	(888) 984-8433	**D- / 1.1**	3.71	2.89	-0.19 /29	-1.42 / 6	2.12 /33	0.00	0.66
COI	GuideStone Low-Duration Bond Inst	GLDYX	**C+**	(888) 984-8433	**C- / 3.7**	0.53	0.31	0.34 /47	0.73 /37	1.59 /26	1.05	0.42
COI	GuideStone Low-Duration Bond Inv	GLDZX	**C+**	(888) 984-8433	**C- / 3.2**	0.46	0.16	0.07 /40	0.47 /32	1.36 /24	0.44	0.67
COI	GuideStone Med-Duration Bond Inst	GMDYX	**C+**	(888) 984-8433	**C+ / 6.5**	2.32	2.35	0.77 /55	2.08 /63	3.95 /61	3.06	0.48
COI	GuideStone Med-Duration Bond Inv	GMDZX	**C+**	(888) 984-8433	**C+ / 6.1**	2.35	2.28	0.44 /49	1.88 /59	3.76 /58	1.17	0.74
MM	GuideStone Money Market Inst	GMYXX	**C**	(888) 984-8433	**D+ / 2.5**	0.08	0.11	0.15 /43	0.07 /26	0.08 /14	0.15	0.20
MM	GuideStone Money Market Inv	GMZXX	**U**	(888) 984-8433	**U** /	--	--	--	--	--	0.03	0.44
MUN	Gurtin California Muni Val Inst	GCMFX	**A+**	(844) 342-5763	**A+ / 9.8**	0.88	2.16	3.36 /89	4.92 /98	6.71 /95	2.00	0.79
MUN	Gurtin National Muni Val Inst	GNMFX	**A+**	(844) 342-5763	**A / 9.5**	0.64	1.78	2.44 /80	4.24 /97	5.87 /91	2.00	0.93
COI	Hancock Horizon Core Bond A	HHBAX	**D+**	(888) 346-6300	**D / 1.6**	2.01	1.34	0.44 /49	0.59 /35	2.41 /36	2.08	1.06
COI	Hancock Horizon Core Bond C	HHBCX	**C-**	(888) 346-6300	**D / 2.0**	1.81	0.88	-0.33 /28	-0.18 /14	1.63 /27	1.40	1.81
COI	Hancock Horizon Core Bond Inst	HHBTX	**C+**	(888) 346-6300	**C / 4.4**	2.07	1.40	0.69 /53	0.82 /39	2.66 /40	2.42	0.81
MUS	Hancock Horizon LA Tax-Fr Inc Inst	HHLTX	**C-**	(888) 346-6300	**A / 9.5**	1.21	3.34	4.19 /95	3.70 /94	6.19 /93	2.96	1.34
MUS	Hancock Horizon LA Tax-Free Inc A	HHLAX	**C-**	(888) 346-6300	**B+ / 8.4**	1.21	3.21	3.93 /93	3.44 /92	5.93 /92	2.60	1.59

● Denotes fund is closed to new investors
* Denotes fund is included in Section II

RISK			NET ASSETS		ASSET							FUND MANAGER		MINIMUM		LOADS	
Risk Rating/Pts	3 Yr Avg Standard Deviation	Avg Dura-tion	NAV As of 3/31/16	Total $(Mil)	Cash %	Gov. Bond %	Muni. Bond %	Corp. Bond %	Other %	Portfolio Turnover Ratio	Avg Coupon Rate	Manager Quality Pct	Manager Tenure (Years)	Initial Purch. $	Additional Purch. $	Front End Load	Back End Load
U /	N/A	0.4	8.97	298	13	86	0	0	1	28	3.6	N/A	11	0	0	0.0	0.0
B / 7.9	2.5	4.6	12.13	147	0	3	0	2	95	38	3.6	38	23	0	0	0.0	0.0
U /	N/A	4.6	9.88	162	0	3	0	2	95	38	3.6	N/A	23	0	0	0.0	0.0
B+ / 8.4	2.1	4.2	25.27	408	1	0	0	22	77	44	0.4	97	5	2,500	100	3.0	0.0
B+ / 8.4	2.1	4.2	25.25	175	1	0	0	22	77	44	0.4	94	5	2,500	100	0.0	0.0
B+ / 8.4	2.1	4.2	25.29	1,324	1	0	0	22	77	44	0.4	98	5	2,000,000	0	0.0	0.0
U /	N/A	4.2	25.28	80	1	0	0	22	77	44	0.4	N/A	5	0	0	0.0	0.0
D+ / 2.3	4.9	6.9	10.34	70	0	0	0	73	27	72	2.4	89	4	2,500	100	4.0	2.0
D+ / 2.3	4.9	6.9	10.42	17	0	0	0	73	27	72	2.4	75	4	2,500	100	0.0	2.0
D+ / 2.3	4.9	6.9	8.43	128	0	0	0	73	27	72	2.4	91	4	2,000,000	0	0.0	2.0
U /	N/A	6.9	10.34	1	0	0	0	73	27	72	2.4	N/A	4	0	0	0.0	2.0
B / 8.1	2.3	4.0	17.94	130	0	7	8	31	54	57	3.0	98	4	2,500	100	4.0	0.0
B / 8.1	2.3	4.0	17.86	28	0	7	8	31	54	57	3.0	96	4	2,500	100	0.0	0.0
B / 8.1	2.3	4.0	17.92	20	0	7	8	31	54	57	3.0	98	4	2,000,000	0	0.0	0.0
U /	N/A	4.0	17.95	2	0	7	8	31	54	57	3.0	N/A	4	0	0	0.0	0.0
U /	N/A	0.7	24.26	2	6	0	0	29	65	26	2.7	N/A	N/A	0	0	0.0	0.0
C / 5.5	3.3	1.5	24.87	737	2	1	0	32	65	40	5.0	72	5	2,500	100	4.0	0.0
C / 5.4	3.3	1.5	24.85	340	2	1	0	32	65	40	5.0	40	5	2,500	100	0.0	0.0
C / 5.5	3.3	1.5	24.90	1,990	2	1	0	32	65	40	5.0	82	5	2,000,000	0	0.0	0.0
D+ / 2.8	5.0	6.3	12.75	50	6	0	93	0	1	80	3.9	14	4	2,500	100	4.0	0.0
U /	N/A	6.3	12.74	N/A	6	0	93	0	1	80	3.9	N/A	4	0	0	0.0	0.0
C+ / 6.8	2.9	3.9	26.16	494	0	10	4	31	55	74	2.8	91	5	2,500	100	4.0	0.0
C+ / 6.8	2.9	3.9	26.16	144	0	10	4	31	55	74	2.8	81	5	2,500	100	0.0	0.0
C+ / 6.8	2.9	3.9	26.19	2,014	0	10	4	31	55	74	2.8	93	5	2,000,000	0	0.0	0.0
U /	N/A	3.9	26.16	60	0	10	4	31	55	74	2.8	N/A	5	0	0	0.0	0.0
C+ / 6.4	3.0	N/A	9.46	2	0	10	0	37	53	185	0.0	38	6	0	0	0.0	0.0
C+ / 6.2	3.1	N/A	9.54	210	0	10	0	37	53	185	0.0	26	6	0	0	0.0	0.0
C- / 3.5	4.3	N/A	9.05	9	16	37	0	13	34	40	0.0	23	5	0	0	0.0	0.0
C- / 3.5	4.3	N/A	9.06	79	16	37	0	13	34	40	0.0	16	5	0	0	0.0	0.0
C / 4.6	3.6	N/A	11.62	50	0	0	0	0	100	33	0.0	26	10	0	0	0.0	0.0
C+ / 6.1	3.1	N/A	9.62	N/A	5	34	0	27	34	23	0.0	89	4	0	0	0.0	0.0
C+ / 6.4	3.0	N/A	9.55	115	5	34	0	27	34	23	0.0	71	4	0	0	0.0	0.0
E / 0.5	8.1	N/A	3.96	148	4	21	3	66	6	48	0.0	32	15	1,000,000	0	0.0	0.0
E / 0.5	8.1	N/A	17.71	127	4	21	3	66	6	48	0.0	25	15	1,000	100	0.0	0.0
U /	N/A	N/A	9.34	144	8	0	0	26	66	77	0.0	N/A	3	1,000	100	0.0	0.0
U /	N/A	8.7	9.40	320	10	25	1	54	10	57	0.0	N/A	10	1,000,000	0	0.0	0.0
D / 1.8	5.6	8.7	9.39	82	10	25	1	54	10	57	0.0	71	10	1,000	100	0.0	0.0
U /	N/A	N/A	10.36	235	1	98	0	0	1	88	0.0	N/A	6	1,000,000	0	0.0	0.0
D+ / 2.8	5.0	N/A	10.33	72	1	98	0	0	1	88	0.0	20	6	1,000	100	0.0	0.0
A / 9.4	0.9	N/A	8.41	609	0	33	1	36	30	529	0.0	76	13	1,000,000	0	0.0	0.0
A / 9.3	0.9	N/A	13.33	246	0	33	1	36	30	529	0.0	61	13	1,000	100	0.0	0.0
C+ / 6.3	3.1	N/A	6.79	706	0	27	1	30	42	346	0.0	71	11	1,000,000	0	0.0	0.0
C+ / 6.1	3.1	N/A	14.64	197	0	27	1	30	42	346	0.0	58	11	1,000	100	0.0	0.0
A+ / 9.9	N/A	N/A	1.00	226	100	0	0	0	0	0	0.2	67	N/A	1,000,000	0	0.0	0.0
U /	N/A	N/A	1.00	1,142	100	0	0	0	0	0	0.0	N/A	N/A	1,000	100	0.0	0.0
B / 8.0	2.4	N/A	10.17	185	0	0	0	0	100	83	0.0	97	N/A	250,000	0	0.0	0.0
B / 8.0	2.4	N/A	10.09	109	0	0	0	0	100	32	0.0	95	N/A	250,000	0	0.0	0.0
B / 8.1	2.3	3.6	16.02	35	2	3	20	58	17	38	0.0	33	16	1,000	100	4.0	0.0
B / 8.2	2.3	3.6	16.11	2	2	3	20	58	17	38	0.0	16	16	1,000	100	0.0	0.0
B / 8.2	2.3	3.6	16.05	205	2	3	20	58	17	38	0.0	40	16	1,000	100	0.0	0.0
E+ / 0.7	6.8	8.3	17.27	5	5	0	94	0	1	19	0.0	7	5	1,000	100	0.0	0.0
E+ / 0.7	6.8	8.3	17.27	5	5	0	94	0	1	19	0.0	6	5	1,000	100	4.0	0.0

Fund Type	Fund Name	Ticker Symbol	Overall Investment Rating	Phone	Performance Rating/Pts	3 Mo	6 Mo	1Yr / Pct	3Yr / Pct (Annualized)	5Yr / Pct (Annualized)	Dividend Yield	Expense Ratio
99 Pct = Best, 0 Pct = Worst					PERFORMANCE: Total Return % through 3/31/16						Incl. in Returns	
MUN	Hancock Horizon LA Tax-Free Inc C	HHLCX	U	(888) 346-6300	U /	1.21	3.28	4.13 /95	--	--	2.96	2.36
MUS	Hancock Horizon MS Tax-Fr Inc Inst	HHMTX	C	(888) 346-6300	A / 9.3	1.80	3.87	4.43 /96	3.23 /90	5.77 /91	2.91	1.04
MUS	Hancock Horizon MS Tax-Free Inc A	HIMAX	C-	(888) 346-6300	B / 8.2	1.68	3.74	4.17 /95	2.96 /88	5.51 /89	2.55	1.29
MUN	Hancock Horizon MS Tax-Free Inc C	HAMCX	U	(888) 346-6300	U /	1.54	3.37	3.27 /88	--	--	1.63	2.04
GEI	Harbor Bond Admin	HRBDX	C-	(800) 422-1050	C / 5.1	1.99	1.98	-0.08 /30	1.34 /49	3.13 /47	4.64	0.82
* GEI	Harbor Bond Inst	HABDX	C-	(800) 422-1050	C+ / 5.6	2.05	2.12	0.18 /43	1.61 /54	3.38 /51	4.91	0.57
COH	Harbor High Yield Bond Admin	HYFRX	D-	(800) 422-1050	C- / 3.4	2.40	0.42	-4.36 / 7	1.30 /48	3.59 /55	5.31	0.94
COH	Harbor High Yield Bond Inst	HYFAX	D	(800) 422-1050	C- / 3.9	2.36	0.55	-4.13 / 7	1.56 /53	3.84 /59	5.58	0.69
COH	Harbor High Yield Bond Inv	HYFIX	D-	(800) 422-1050	C- / 3.1	2.38	0.35	-4.48 / 6	1.18 /46	3.46 /52	5.18	1.06
MM	Harbor Money Market Admin	HRMXX	C	(800) 422-1050	D+ / 2.6	0.07	0.11	0.14 /42	0.09 /27	0.09 /14	0.14	0.56
MM	Harbor Money Market Inst	HARXX	C	(800) 422-1050	D+ / 2.6	0.07	0.11	0.14 /42	0.09 /27	0.09 /14	0.14	0.31
US	Harbor Real Return Admin	HRRRX	E	(800) 422-1050	E+ / 0.7	3.83	3.15	-0.35 /27	-2.10 / 4	1.97 /31	2.07	0.89
US	Harbor Real Return Inst	HARRX	E+	(800) 422-1050	E+ / 0.9	3.83	3.22	-0.26 /28	-1.88 / 5	2.21 /34	2.26	0.64
GEI	Harbor Unconstrained Bond Adm	HRUBX	D	(800) 422-1050	E+ / 0.7	-0.82	0.04	-3.53 / 9	-0.97 / 9	1.35 /24	2.54	1.60
GEI	Harbor Unconstrained Bond Inst	HAUBX	D	(800) 422-1050	E+ / 0.8	-0.84	0.06	-3.33 /10	-0.73 /10	1.60 /27	2.82	1.35
GL	Hartford Duration Hedged Str Inc A	HABEX	U	(888) 843-7824	U /	0.10	0.94	-2.71 /12	--	--	3.84	1.84
GL	Hartford Duration Hedged Str Inc C	HABGX	U	(888) 843-7824	U /	-0.09	0.56	-3.57 / 9	--	--	3.22	2.60
GL	Hartford Duration Hedged Str Inc I	HABHX	U	(888) 843-7824	U /	0.28	1.07	-2.44 /13	--	--	4.30	1.53
GL	Hartford Duration Hedged Str Inc R3	HABJX	U	(888) 843-7824	U /	0.03	0.67	-3.18 /11	--	--	3.64	2.22
GL	Hartford Duration Hedged Str Inc R4	HABKX	U	(888) 843-7824	U /	0.10	0.82	-2.89 /12	--	--	3.95	1.92
GL	Hartford Duration Hedged Str Inc R5	HABLX	U	(888) 843-7824	U /	0.18	0.97	-2.59 /13	--	--	4.26	1.62
GL	Hartford Duration Hedged Str Inc Y	HABIX	U	(888) 843-7824	U /	0.20	1.02	-2.50 /13	--	--	4.37	1.51
GL	Hartford Emg Markets Local Debt A	HLDAX	E-	(888) 843-7824	E- / 0.1	9.36	9.23	-3.70 / 9	-6.41 / 1	--	5.05	1.47
GL	Hartford Emg Markets Local Debt C	HLDCX	E-	(888) 843-7824	E- / 0.1	9.32	8.95	-4.35 / 7	-7.10 / 1	--	4.48	2.23
GL	Hartford Emg Markets Local Debt I	HLDIX	E-	(888) 843-7824	E- / 0.2	9.61	9.38	-3.45 /10	-6.16 / 1	--	5.55	1.19
GL	Hartford Emg Markets Local Debt R3	HLDRX	E-	(888) 843-7824	E- / 0.1	9.46	8.74	-4.29 / 7	-6.79 / 1	--	4.56	1.81
GL	Hartford Emg Markets Local Debt R4	HLDSX	E-	(888) 843-7824	E- / 0.2	9.36	9.12	-3.82 / 8	-6.44 / 1	--	5.05	1.51
GL	Hartford Emg Markets Local Debt R5	HLDTX	E-	(888) 843-7824	E- / 0.2	9.43	8.97	-3.80 / 8	-6.29 / 1	--	6.58	1.20
GL	Hartford Emg Markets Local Debt Y	HLDYX	E-	(888) 843-7824	E- / 0.2	9.52	9.33	-3.36 /10	-6.10 / 1	--	5.68	1.11
* LP	Hartford Floating Rate A	HFLAX	D	(888) 843-7824	D- / 1.2	1.46	-1.21	-2.65 /13	0.60 /35	2.48 /38	4.18	0.96
LP	• Hartford Floating Rate B	HFLBX	D	(888) 843-7824	D- / 1.1	1.15	-1.59	-3.51 /10	-0.21 /14	1.66 /27	3.53	1.81
LP	Hartford Floating Rate C	HFLCX	D	(888) 843-7824	D- / 1.2	1.16	-1.71	-3.49 /10	-0.18 /14	1.70 /28	3.55	1.71
GL	Hartford Floating Rate High Inc A	HFHAX	D-	(888) 843-7824	E+ / 0.9	1.53	-1.80	-4.02 / 8	0.34 /31	--	5.19	1.12
GL	Hartford Floating Rate High Inc C	HFHCX	D-	(888) 843-7824	E+ / 0.9	1.35	-2.17	-4.74 / 5	-0.41 /12	--	4.56	1.89
GL	Hartford Floating Rate High Inc I	HFHIX	D	(888) 843-7824	D / 2.0	1.60	-1.68	-3.77 / 8	0.60 /35	--	5.61	0.86
GL	Hartford Floating Rate High Inc R3	HFHRX	D-	(888) 843-7824	D- / 1.3	1.57	-1.84	-4.11 / 7	0.11 /27	--	5.03	1.50
GL	Hartford Floating Rate High Inc R4	HFHSX	D-	(888) 843-7824	D / 1.7	1.64	-1.63	-3.86 / 8	0.40 /31	--	5.42	1.20
GL	Hartford Floating Rate High Inc R5	HFHTX	D	(888) 843-7824	C- / 3.6	1.72	-0.51	-2.61 /13	1.03 /43	--	6.72	0.90
GL	Hartford Floating Rate High Inc Y	HFHYX	D	(888) 843-7824	D+ / 2.4	1.61	-1.66	-3.74 / 9	0.64 /36	--	5.66	0.80
LP	Hartford Floating Rate I	HFLIX	D+	(888) 843-7824	C- / 3.3	1.53	-1.06	-2.37 /14	0.87 /40	2.74 /41	4.60	0.70
LP	Hartford Floating Rate R3	HFLRX	D	(888) 843-7824	D / 1.8	1.40	-1.33	-2.88 /12	0.36 /31	2.22 /34	4.04	1.35
LP	Hartford Floating Rate R4	HFLSX	D+	(888) 843-7824	D+ / 2.7	1.34	-1.22	-2.66 /13	0.58 /35	2.45 /37	4.30	1.05
LP	Hartford Floating Rate R5	HFLTX	D+	(888) 843-7824	C- / 3.2	1.41	-1.19	-2.48 /13	0.84 /40	2.73 /41	4.62	0.77
LP	Hartford Floating Rate Y	HFLYX	D+	(888) 843-7824	C- / 3.5	1.55	-1.05	-2.32 /14	0.97 /42	2.82 /42	4.66	0.64
GL	Hartford Global Alpha A	HAPAX	D+	(888) 843-7824	E / 0.3	0.21	-0.21	-1.04 /21	-1.23 / 7	--	0.00	1.44
GL	Hartford Global Alpha C	HAPCX	D+	(888) 843-7824	E / 0.5	0.00	-0.64	-1.80 /16	-1.97 / 4	--	0.00	2.14
GL	Hartford Global Alpha I	HAPIX	D+	(888) 843-7824	E+ / 0.9	0.21	-0.14	-0.87 /23	-1.00 / 8	--	0.07	1.13
GL	Hartford Global Alpha R3	HAPRX	D+	(888) 843-7824	E+ / 0.6	0.00	-0.43	-1.47 /19	-1.65 / 5	--	0.00	1.83
GL	Hartford Global Alpha R4	HAPSX	D+	(888) 843-7824	E+ / 0.7	0.11	-0.32	-1.25 /20	-1.37 / 6	--	0.00	1.53
GL	Hartford Global Alpha R5	HAPTX	D+	(888) 843-7824	E+ / 0.9	0.21	-0.10	-0.93 /22	-1.06 / 8	--	0.00	1.23
GL	Hartford Global Alpha Y	HAPYX	D+	(888) 843-7824	D- / 1.0	0.21	-0.12	-0.74 /24	-0.96 / 9	--	0.09	1.15
COH	Hartford High Yield A	HAHAX	D-	(888) 843-7824	D / 1.7	2.88	1.16	-3.53 /10	1.39 /50	3.78 /58	4.80	1.14

• Denotes fund is closed to new investors
* Denotes fund is included in Section II

RISK			NET ASSETS		ASSET							FUND MANAGER		MINIMUM		LOADS	
Risk Rating/Pts	3 Yr Avg Standard Deviation	Avg Duration	NAV As of 3/31/16	Total $(Mil)	Cash %	Gov. Bond %	Muni. Bond %	Corp. Bond %	Other %	Portfolio Turnover Ratio	Avg Coupon Rate	Manager Quality Pct	Manager Tenure (Years)	Initial Purch. $	Additional Purch. $	Front End Load	Back End Load
U /	N/A	8.3	17.26	N/A	5	0	94	0	1	19	0.0	N/A	5	1,000	100	0.0	0.0
D- / 1.4	6.2	5.8	16.88	8	4	0	95	0	1	3	0.0	7	5	1,000	100	0.0	0.0
D- / 1.4	6.2	5.8	16.88	8	4	0	95	0	1	3	0.0	7	5	1,000	100	4.0	0.0
U /	N/A	5.8	16.91	N/A	4	0	95	0	1	3	0.0	N/A	5	1,000	100	0.0	0.0
C / 4.6	3.6	4.5	11.65	45	0	30	4	17	49	586	3.3	20	N/A	50,000	0	0.0	0.0
C / 4.7	3.6	4.5	11.64	2,718	0	30	4	17	49	586	3.3	27	N/A	1,000	0	0.0	0.0
D- / 1.5	5.6	4.0	9.52	4	9	0	0	90	1	49	6.3	50	14	50,000	0	0.0	1.0
D / 1.6	5.6	4.0	9.50	1,686	9	0	0	90	1	49	6.3	60	14	1,000	0	0.0	1.0
D- / 1.5	5.6	4.0	9.52	92	9	0	0	90	1	49	6.3	45	14	2,500	0	0.0	1.0
A+ / 9.9	N/A	N/A	1.00	2	100	0	0	0	0	0	0.1	69	13	50,000	0	0.0	0.0
A+ / 9.9	N/A	N/A	1.00	121	100	0	0	0	0	0	0.1	70	13	1,000	0	0.0	0.0
D- / 1.3	6.1	7.3	9.21	3	0	84	0	7	9	531	1.9	3	11	50,000	0	0.0	0.0
D- / 1.3	6.1	7.3	9.21	116	0	84	0	7	9	531	1.9	4	11	1,000	0	0.0	0.0
B- / 7.0	2.9	-1.0	9.72	N/A	7	33	2	48	10	784	2.4	21	2	50,000	0	0.0	0.0
B- / 7.1	2.8	-1.0	9.76	19	7	33	2	48	10	784	2.4	27	2	1,000	0	0.0	0.0
U /	N/A	N/A	8.72	8	4	24	1	38	33	50	0.0	N/A	3	2,000	50	4.5	0.0
U /	N/A	N/A	8.71	2	4	24	1	38	33	50	0.0	N/A	3	2,000	50	0.0	0.0
U /	N/A	N/A	8.72	N/A	4	24	1	38	33	50	0.0	N/A	3	2,000	50	0.0	0.0
U /	N/A	N/A	8.71	N/A	4	24	1	38	33	50	0.0	N/A	3	0	0	0.0	0.0
U /	N/A	N/A	8.71	N/A	4	24	1	38	33	50	0.0	N/A	3	0	0	0.0	0.0
U /	N/A	N/A	8.71	N/A	4	24	1	38	33	50	0.0	N/A	3	0	0	0.0	0.0
U /	N/A	N/A	8.71	2	4	24	1	38	33	50	0.0	N/A	3	250,000	0	0.0	0.0
E- / 0.2	11.1	4.7	7.25	5	9	65	0	23	3	122	8.2	1	5	5,000	50	4.5	0.0
E- / 0.2	11.1	4.7	7.25	1	9	65	0	23	3	122	8.2	1	5	5,000	50	0.0	0.0
E- / 0.2	11.1	4.7	7.24	2	9	65	0	23	3	122	8.2	2	5	5,000	50	0.0	0.0
E- / 0.2	11.2	4.7	7.25	N/A	9	65	0	23	3	122	8.2	1	5	0	0	0.0	0.0
E- / 0.2	11.1	4.7	7.25	N/A	9	65	0	23	3	122	8.2	1	5	0	0	0.0	0.0
E- / 0.2	11.2	4.7	7.14	N/A	9	65	0	23	3	122	8.2	2	5	0	0	0.0	0.0
E- / 0.2	11.1	4.7	7.21	84	9	65	0	23	3	122	8.2	2	5	250,000	0	0.0	0.0
C / 5.2	3.4	0.3	8.16	928	3	0	0	76	21	30	8.0	55	N/A	2,000	50	3.0	0.0
C / 5.3	3.3	0.3	8.14	6	3	0	0	76	21	30	8.0	30	N/A	0	0	0.0	0.0
C / 5.4	3.3	0.3	8.14	1,258	3	0	0	76	21	30	8.0	30	N/A	2,000	50	0.0	0.0
C- / 3.7	4.2	0.4	9.20	109	0	0	0	73	27	55	9.4	79	N/A	2,000	50	3.0	0.0
C- / 3.7	4.2	0.4	9.20	84	0	0	0	73	27	55	9.4	47	N/A	2,000	50	0.0	0.0
C- / 3.7	4.2	0.4	9.21	94	0	0	0	73	27	55	9.4	85	N/A	2,000	50	0.0	0.0
C- / 3.7	4.2	0.4	9.20	N/A	0	0	0	73	27	55	9.4	72	N/A	0	0	0.0	0.0
C- / 3.7	4.2	0.4	9.19	1	0	0	0	73	27	55	9.4	81	N/A	0	0	0.0	0.0
C- / 3.9	4.1	0.4	9.19	N/A	0	0	0	73	27	55	9.4	90	N/A	0	0	0.0	0.0
C- / 3.8	4.1	0.4	9.18	3	0	0	0	73	27	55	9.4	86	N/A	250,000	0	0.0	0.0
C / 5.3	3.4	0.3	8.17	1,341	3	0	0	76	21	30	8.0	70	N/A	2,000	50	0.0	0.0
C / 5.2	3.4	0.3	8.18	12	3	0	0	76	21	30	8.0	47	N/A	0	0	0.0	0.0
C / 5.3	3.3	0.3	8.15	9	3	0	0	76	21	30	8.0	54	N/A	0	0	0.0	0.0
C / 5.3	3.3	0.3	8.15	3	3	0	0	76	21	30	8.0	70	N/A	0	0	0.0	0.0
C / 5.2	3.4	0.3	8.15	289	3	0	0	76	21	30	8.0	74	N/A	250,000	0	0.0	0.0
B+ / 8.7	1.8	0.3	9.49	5	17	57	6	14	6	296	0.0	22	4	5,000	50	5.5	0.0
B+ / 8.7	1.8	0.3	9.26	2	17	57	6	14	6	296	0.0	11	4	5,000	50	0.0	0.0
B+ / 8.7	1.8	0.3	9.56	3	17	57	6	14	6	296	0.0	27	4	5,000	50	0.0	0.0
B+ / 8.7	1.8	0.3	9.36	2	17	57	6	14	6	296	0.0	15	4	0	0	0.0	0.0
B+ / 8.7	1.8	0.3	9.45	2	17	57	6	14	6	296	0.0	19	4	0	0	0.0	0.0
B+ / 8.6	1.9	0.3	9.55	2	17	57	6	14	6	296	0.0	26	4	0	0	0.0	0.0
B+ / 8.7	1.8	0.3	9.57	11	17	57	6	14	6	296	0.0	28	4	250,000	0	0.0	0.0
D / 1.8	5.4	4.4	6.91	219	10	0	0	88	2	40	7.4	56	4	2,000	50	4.5	0.0

Fund Type	Fund Name (99 Pct = Best, 0 Pct = Worst)	Ticker Symbol	Overall Investment Rating	Phone	PERFORMANCE: Performance Rating/Pts	Total Return % through 3/31/16: 3 Mo	6 Mo	1Yr / Pct	Annualized: 3Yr / Pct	Annualized: 5Yr / Pct	Incl. in Returns: Dividend Yield	Expense Ratio
COH ●	Hartford High Yield B	HAHBX	D-	(888) 843-7824	C- / 3.0	2.70	0.78	-4.17 / 7	0.64 /36	3.00 /45	4.25	2.02
COH	Hartford High Yield C	HAHCX	D-	(888) 843-7824	C- / 3.0	2.70	0.78	-4.14 / 7	0.69 /37	3.03 /46	4.25	1.83
COH	Hartford High Yield HLS IA		D	(888) 843-7824	C / 5.0	3.05	1.30	-3.33 /10	1.73 /56	4.33 /66	7.23	0.75
COH	Hartford High Yield HLS IB		D	(888) 843-7824	C / 4.5	2.96	1.06	-3.59 / 9	1.46 /51	4.06 /62	7.00	1.00
COH	Hartford High Yield I	HAHIX	D	(888) 843-7824	C / 4.9	2.78	1.14	-3.26 /11	1.65 /55	4.00 /61	5.28	0.81
COH	Hartford High Yield R3	HAHRX	D	(888) 843-7824	C- / 3.9	2.81	1.01	-3.82 / 8	1.14 /45	3.48 /53	4.71	1.47
COH	Hartford High Yield R4	HAHSX	D	(888) 843-7824	C / 4.4	2.73	1.01	-3.53 /10	1.39 /50	3.75 /57	5.03	1.16
COH	Hartford High Yield R5	HAHTX	D	(888) 843-7824	C / 5.1	2.96	1.31	-3.24 /11	1.74 /56	4.07 /63	5.33	0.85
COH	Hartford High Yield Y	HAHYX	D	(888) 843-7824	C / 5.1	2.97	1.33	-3.08 /11	1.75 /57	4.12 /63	5.38	0.73
US	Hartford Inflation Plus A	HIPAX	E+	(888) 843-7824	E / 0.4	3.34	2.75	0.84 /56	-2.20 / 4	1.90 /30	0.00	0.92
US ●	Hartford Inflation Plus B	HIPBX	D-	(888) 843-7824	E / 0.4	3.07	2.36	0.10 /41	-2.95 / 2	1.12 /21	0.00	1.74
US	Hartford Inflation Plus C	HIPCX	E+	(888) 843-7824	E / 0.4	3.08	2.36	0.10 /41	-2.95 / 2	1.12 /21	0.00	1.63
US	Hartford Inflation Plus I	HIPIX	D-	(888) 843-7824	E+ / 0.9	3.38	2.90	1.10 /60	-1.97 / 4	2.14 /33	0.00	0.67
US	Hartford Inflation Plus R3	HIPRX	D-	(888) 843-7824	E+ / 0.6	3.20	2.50	0.47 /49	-2.56 / 3	1.52 /26	0.00	1.23
US	Hartford Inflation Plus R4	HIPSX	D-	(888) 843-7824	E+ / 0.7	3.24	2.75	0.84 /56	-2.26 / 4	1.84 /29	0.00	0.92
US	Hartford Inflation Plus R5	HIPTX	D-	(888) 843-7824	E+ / 0.9	3.39	2.81	1.10 /60	-1.97 / 4	2.14 /33	0.00	0.64
US	Hartford Inflation Plus Y	HIPYX	D-	(888) 843-7824	E+ / 0.9	3.37	2.89	1.10 /60	-1.90 / 5	2.22 /34	0.00	0.52
MUN	Hartford Municipal Income A	HMKAX	U	(888) 843-7824	U /	1.51	3.56	--	--	--	0.00	N/A
MUN	Hartford Municipal Income C	HMKCX	U	(888) 843-7824	U /	1.32	3.16	--	--	--	0.00	N/A
MUN	Hartford Municipal Income I	HMKIX	U	(888) 843-7824	U /	1.57	3.69	--	--	--	0.00	N/A
MUH	Hartford Municipal Opportunities A	HHMAX	C+	(888) 843-7824	B / 8.1	1.56	3.32	4.03 /94	3.07 /89	6.11 /93	2.63	0.90
MUH ●	Hartford Municipal Opportunities B	HHMBX	C+	(888) 843-7824	B+ / 8.4	1.37	2.94	3.26 /87	2.26 /80	5.29 /88	2.01	1.72
MUH	Hartford Municipal Opportunities C	HHMCX	C+	(888) 843-7824	B+ / 8.4	1.37	2.81	3.25 /87	2.26 /80	5.29 /88	2.01	1.66
MUH	Hartford Municipal Opportunities I	HHMIX	B+	(888) 843-7824	A / 9.3	1.73	3.44	4.29 /96	3.32 /91	6.36 /94	3.00	0.65
MUN	Hartford Municipal Real Return A	HTNAX	C-	(888) 843-7824	C / 4.6	1.47	3.53	2.62 /81	1.42 /65	3.98 /77	2.76	0.90
MUN ●	Hartford Municipal Real Return B	HTNBX	C+	(888) 843-7824	C+ / 5.7	1.29	3.17	1.85 /76	0.63 /42	3.19 /71	2.15	1.73
MUN	Hartford Municipal Real Return C	HTNCX	C	(888) 843-7824	C+ / 5.6	1.29	3.16	1.85 /76	0.63 /42	3.18 /71	2.15	1.64
MUN	Hartford Municipal Real Return I	HTNIX	A-	(888) 843-7824	B / 7.9	1.53	3.66	2.88 /84	1.63 /71	4.23 /79	3.14	0.66
MUN	Hartford Municipal Real Return Y	HTNYX	B+	(888) 843-7824	B / 7.9	1.54	3.67	2.87 /84	1.64 /71	4.23 /79	3.14	0.60
MUN	Hartford Municipal Short Duration A	HMJAX	U	(888) 843-7824	U /	0.61	0.93	--	--	--	0.00	N/A
MUN	Hartford Municipal Short Duration C	HMJCX	U	(888) 843-7824	U /	0.42	0.65	--	--	--	0.00	N/A
MUN	Hartford Municipal Short Duration I	HMJIX	U	(888) 843-7824	U /	0.67	1.05	--	--	--	0.00	N/A
MTG	Hartford Quality Bond A	HQBAX	C-	(888) 843-7824	C / 4.7	2.23	1.64	1.69 /69	2.21 /66	--	0.76	1.26
MTG	Hartford Quality Bond C	HQBCX	C	(888) 843-7824	C / 5.5	2.06	1.38	0.94 /57	1.47 /51	--	0.26	2.01
MTG	Hartford Quality Bond I	HQBIX	B	(888) 843-7824	B- / 7.3	2.29	1.90	2.00 /72	2.54 /71	--	1.10	0.98
MTG	Hartford Quality Bond R3	HQBRX	C+	(888) 843-7824	C+ / 6.5	2.16	2.03	1.80 /70	2.02 /62	--	0.91	1.68
MTG	Hartford Quality Bond R4	HQBSX	B	(888) 843-7824	B- / 7.2	2.23	2.35	2.28 /74	2.37 /69	--	1.36	1.38
MTG	Hartford Quality Bond R5	HQBTX	B+	(888) 843-7824	B / 7.7	2.31	2.69	2.76 /76	2.77 /74	--	1.83	1.08
MTG	Hartford Quality Bond Y	HQBYX	B	(888) 843-7824	B- / 7.3	2.32	1.90	2.00 /72	2.51 /71	--	1.10	0.98
COI	Hartford Short Duration A	HSDAX	C+	(888) 843-7824	C- / 3.5	1.21	0.82	0.64 /52	1.03 /43	1.79 /29	1.62	0.91
COI ●	Hartford Short Duration B	HSDBX	B-	(888) 843-7824	C / 4.6	1.21	0.82	0.65 /52	1.06 /44	1.91 /30	1.66	1.76
COI	Hartford Short Duration C	HSDCX	C	(888) 843-7824	C- / 3.0	1.03	0.44	-0.10 /30	0.28 /30	1.04 /21	0.91	1.60
COI	Hartford Short Duration I	HSDIX	B+	(888) 843-7824	C / 5.1	1.29	0.96	0.95 /58	1.33 /49	2.08 /32	1.96	0.55
COI	Hartford Short Duration R3	HSDRX	C+	(888) 843-7824	C- / 4.0	1.24	0.77	0.44 /49	0.77 /38	1.49 /26	1.36	1.23
COI	Hartford Short Duration R4	HSDSX	B-	(888) 843-7824	C / 4.6	1.31	0.92	0.74 /54	1.07 /44	1.81 /29	1.65	0.92
COI	Hartford Short Duration R5	HSDTX	B+	(888) 843-7824	C / 5.1	1.29	0.96	0.94 /57	1.33 /49	2.07 /32	1.96	0.61
COI	Hartford Short Duration Y	HSDYX	B+	(888) 843-7824	C / 5.3	1.40	1.08	1.09 /60	1.42 /51	2.15 /33	2.00	0.50
COH	Hartford SMART529 High Yld 529 A		D-	(888) 843-7824	D / 1.6	2.92	1.14	-3.51 /10	1.25 /47	3.61 /55	0.00	1.85
COH	Hartford SMART529 High Yld 529 B		D-	(888) 843-7824	C- / 3.1	2.75	0.86	-4.04 / 7	0.69 /37	3.04 /46	0.00	2.40
COH	Hartford SMART529 High Yld 529 C		D-	(888) 843-7824	D+ / 2.8	2.69	0.76	-4.24 / 7	0.50 /33	2.85 /43	0.00	2.59
COH	Hartford SMART529 High Yld 529 E		D	(888) 843-7824	C / 4.6	2.93	1.21	-3.31 /10	1.50 /52	3.86 /59	0.00	1.19
US	Hartford SMART529 Infl Plus 529 A		E+	(888) 843-7824	E / 0.3	3.27	2.61	0.62 /52	-2.39 / 3	1.71 /28	0.00	1.85

● Denotes fund is closed to new investors
* Denotes fund is included in Section II

RISK			NET ASSETS		ASSET							FUND MANAGER		MINIMUM		LOADS	
Risk Rating/Pts	3 Yr Avg Standard Deviation	Avg Duration	NAV As of 3/31/16	Total $(Mil)	Cash %	Gov. Bond %	Muni. Bond %	Corp. Bond %	Other %	Portfolio Turnover Ratio	Avg Coupon Rate	Manager Quality Pct	Manager Tenure (Years)	Initial Purch. $	Additional Purch. $	Front End Load	Back End Load
D / 1.7	5.4	4.4	6.87	2	10	0	0	88	2	40	7.4	31	4	0	0	0.0	0.0
D / 1.7	5.4	4.4	6.89	59	10	0	0	88	2	40	7.4	32	4	2,000	50	0.0	0.0
D / 1.6	5.5	4.3	7.78	252	4	0	0	92	4	39	7.5	72	4	0	0	0.0	0.0
D / 1.7	5.5	4.3	7.65	77	4	0	0	92	4	39	7.5	57	4	0	0	0.0	0.0
D / 1.7	5.4	4.4	6.94	29	10	0	0	88	2	40	7.4	69	4	2,000	50	0.0	0.0
D / 1.7	5.4	4.4	6.91	3	10	0	0	88	2	40	7.4	45	4	0	0	0.0	0.0
D / 1.8	5.3	4.4	6.91	1	10	0	0	88	2	40	7.4	56	4	0	0	0.0	0.0
D / 1.7	5.4	4.4	6.91	1	10	0	0	88	2	40	7.4	73	4	0	0	0.0	0.0
D / 1.8	5.4	4.4	6.90	7	10	0	0	88	2	40	7.4	74	4	250,000	0	0.0	0.0
C- / 3.0	4.7	5.1	10.83	243	0	90	0	3	7	155	2.5	4	1	2,000	50	4.5	0.0
C- / 3.1	4.7	5.1	10.40	8	0	90	0	3	7	155	2.5	3	1	0	0	0.0	0.0
C- / 3.0	4.7	5.1	10.39	163	0	90	0	3	7	155	2.5	3	1	2,000	50	0.0	0.0
C- / 3.1	4.7	5.1	11.01	61	0	90	0	3	7	155	2.5	5	1	2,000	50	0.0	0.0
C- / 3.1	4.7	5.1	10.64	59	0	90	0	3	7	155	2.5	4	1	0	0	0.0	0.0
C- / 3.0	4.7	5.1	10.82	17	0	90	0	3	7	155	2.5	4	1	0	0	0.0	0.0
C- / 3.0	4.7	5.1	10.98	3	0	90	0	3	7	155	2.5	5	1	0	0	0.0	0.0
C- / 3.0	4.7	5.1	11.03	95	0	90	0	3	7	155	2.5	5	1	250,000	0	0.0	0.0
U /	N/A	5.6	10.28	5	7	0	92	0	1	0	2.5	N/A	1	2,000	50	4.5	0.0
U /	N/A	5.6	10.28	3	7	0	92	0	1	0	2.5	N/A	1	2,000	50	0.0	0.0
U /	N/A	5.6	10.28	5	7	0	92	0	1	0	2.5	N/A	1	2,000	50	0.0	0.0
C- / 3.9	3.5	5.0	8.68	253	6	0	93	0	1	21	2.4	41	4	2,000	50	4.5	0.0
C- / 4.0	3.4	5.0	8.67	2	6	0	93	0	1	21	2.4	22	4	0	0	0.0	0.0
C- / 4.0	3.5	5.0	8.68	114	6	0	93	0	1	21	2.4	21	4	2,000	50	0.0	0.0
C- / 4.0	3.4	5.0	8.70	261	6	0	93	0	1	21	2.4	52	4	2,000	50	0.0	0.0
C+ / 6.2	3.1	4.4	9.29	105	3	0	96	0	1	26	2.2	24	9	2,000	50	4.5	0.0
C+ / 6.3	3.1	4.4	9.20	1	3	0	96	0	1	26	2.2	13	9	0	0	0.0	0.0
C+ / 6.2	3.1	4.4	9.23	27	3	0	96	0	1	26	2.2	13	9	2,000	50	0.0	0.0
C+ / 6.2	3.1	4.4	9.31	18	3	0	96	0	1	26	2.2	30	9	0	0	0.0	0.0
C+ / 6.1	3.1	4.4	9.26	18	3	0	96	0	1	26	2.2	29	9	250,000	0	0.0	0.0
U /	N/A	2.3	10.08	7	12	0	87	0	1	0	1.4	N/A	1	2,000	50	4.5	0.0
U /	N/A	2.3	10.08	4	12	0	87	0	1	0	1.4	N/A	1	2,000	50	0.0	0.0
U /	N/A	2.3	10.08	5	12	0	87	0	1	0	1.4	N/A	1	2,000	50	0.0	0.0
C+ / 6.0	3.1	4.7	10.26	14	8	1	0	0	91	20	3.1	29	4	2,000	50	4.5	0.0
C+ / 6.0	3.1	4.7	10.19	3	8	1	0	0	91	20	3.1	14	4	2,000	50	0.0	0.0
C+ / 6.1	3.1	4.7	10.28	7	8	1	0	0	91	20	3.1	38	4	2,000	50	0.0	0.0
C+ / 6.1	3.1	4.7	10.24	N/A	8	1	0	0	91	20	3.1	24	4	0	0	0.0	0.0
C+ / 6.0	3.1	4.7	10.26	N/A	8	1	0	0	91	20	3.1	34	4	0	0	0.0	0.0
C+ / 6.1	3.1	4.7	10.28	N/A	8	1	0	0	91	20	3.1	46	4	0	0	0.0	0.0
C+ / 6.2	3.1	4.7	10.28	98	8	1	0	0	91	20	3.1	37	4	250,000	0	0.0	0.0
A- / 9.0	1.3	1.7	9.80	509	0	4	0	71	25	31	2.9	79	4	2,000	50	2.0	0.0
A- / 9.1	1.2	1.7	9.85	4	0	4	0	71	25	31	2.9	80	4	0	0	0.0	0.0
A- / 9.1	1.2	1.7	9.80	129	0	4	0	71	25	31	2.9	48	4	2,000	50	0.0	0.0
A- / 9.1	1.2	1.7	9.82	171	0	4	0	71	25	31	2.9	86	4	2,000	50	0.0	0.0
A- / 9.0	1.3	1.7	9.78	1	0	4	0	71	25	31	2.9	70	4	0	0	0.0	0.0
A- / 9.0	1.3	1.7	9.79	1	0	4	0	71	25	31	2.9	80	4	0	0	0.0	0.0
A- / 9.1	1.2	1.7	9.78	N/A	0	4	0	71	25	31	2.9	86	4	0	0	0.0	0.0
A- / 9.0	1.3	1.7	9.78	50	0	4	0	71	25	31	2.9	87	4	250,000	0	0.0	0.0
D / 1.7	5.4	N/A	18.70	5	4	0	0	87	9	15	0.0	50	12	250	25	4.5	0.0
D / 1.7	5.4	N/A	17.56	N/A	4	0	0	87	9	15	0.0	32	12	250	25	0.0	0.0
D / 1.7	5.4	N/A	17.15	1	4	0	0	87	9	15	0.0	27	12	250	25	0.0	0.0
D / 1.7	5.4	N/A	19.29	1	4	0	0	87	9	15	0.0	59	12	250	25	0.0	0.0
C- / 3.0	4.7	N/A	14.52	4	0	92	0	0	8	15	0.0	4	12	250	25	4.5	0.0

Fund Type	Fund Name (99 Pct = Best, 0 Pct = Worst)	Ticker Symbol	Overall Investment Rating	Phone	PERFORMANCE: Performance Rating/Pts	Total Return % through 3/31/16: 3 Mo	6 Mo	1Yr / Pct	Annualized: 3Yr / Pct	Annualized: 5Yr / Pct	Incl. in Returns: Dividend Yield	Expense Ratio
US	Hartford SMART529 Infl Plus 529 B		**E+**	(888) 843-7824	**E / 0.4**	3.10	2.33	--	-2.93 / 3	1.14 /22	0.00	2.40
US	Hartford SMART529 Infl Plus 529 C		**E+**	(888) 843-7824	**E / 0.4**	3.02	2.23	-0.15 /30	-3.12 / 2	0.96 /20	0.00	2.59
US	Hartford SMART529 Infl Plus 529 E		**D-**	(888) 843-7824	**E+ / 0.8**	3.30	2.74	0.87 /56	-2.14 / 4	1.96 /31	0.00	1.19
GEI	Hartford SMART529 Tot Ret Bd 529		**D+**	(888) 843-7824	**C- / 3.4**	2.61	1.90	0.28 /45	1.54 /53	3.37 /51	0.00	1.85
GEI	Hartford SMART529 Tot Ret Bd 529		**C-**	(888) 843-7824	**C / 4.5**	2.50	1.55	-0.24 /29	0.97 /42	2.80 /42	0.00	2.40
GEI	Hartford SMART529 Tot Ret Bd 529		**D+**	(888) 843-7824	**C- / 4.1**	2.44	1.46	-0.50 /26	0.77 /38	2.60 /39	0.00	2.59
GEI	Hartford SMART529 Tot Ret Bd 529		**C**	(888) 843-7824	**C+ / 6.0**	2.69	2.00	0.55 /51	1.79 /57	3.62 /55	0.00	1.19
GL	Hartford Strategic Income A	HSNAX	**D-**	(888) 843-7824	**D+ / 2.9**	2.97	2.75	-0.95 /22	1.30 /48	3.47 /53	4.10	1.01
GL	● Hartford Strategic Income B	HSNBX	**D**	(888) 843-7824	**C- / 3.9**	3.08	2.53	-1.43 /19	0.62 /35	2.76 /41	3.55	1.82
GL	Hartford Strategic Income C	HSNCX	**D**	(888) 843-7824	**C- / 3.7**	2.89	2.46	-1.60 /18	0.57 /34	2.74 /41	3.49	1.72
GL	Hartford Strategic Income I	HSNIX	**D+**	(888) 843-7824	**C+ / 5.6**	3.02	2.87	-0.70 /24	1.57 /53	3.75 /57	4.53	0.71
GL	Hartford Strategic Income R3	HSNRX	**D**	(888) 843-7824	**C / 4.5**	3.02	2.60	-1.24 /20	0.98 /42	3.15 /47	3.99	1.40
GL	Hartford Strategic Income R4	HSNSX	**D+**	(888) 843-7824	**C / 5.2**	3.09	2.75	-0.94 /22	1.31 /49	3.47 /53	4.30	1.05
GL	Hartford Strategic Income R5	HSNTX	**D+**	(888) 843-7824	**C+ / 5.7**	3.05	2.91	-0.64 /25	1.62 /54	3.74 /57	4.60	0.73
GEL	Hartford Strategic Income R6	HSNVX	**U**	(888) 843-7824	**U /**	3.17	2.92	-0.47 /26	--	--	4.67	0.63
GL	Hartford Strategic Income Y	HSNYX	**D+**	(888) 843-7824	**C+ / 5.9**	3.18	2.94	-0.48 /26	1.71 /56	3.86 /59	4.65	0.63
* GEI	Hartford Total Return Bond A	ITBAX	**D+**	(888) 843-7824	**C- / 3.5**	2.55	1.89	0.32 /46	1.61 /54	3.45 /52	2.42	0.88
GEI	● Hartford Total Return Bond B	ITBBX	**C-**	(888) 843-7824	**C / 4.3**	2.37	1.52	-0.45 /26	0.86 /40	2.69 /40	1.78	1.81
GEI	Hartford Total Return Bond C	HABCX	**C-**	(888) 843-7824	**C / 4.3**	2.46	1.52	-0.40 /27	0.86 /40	2.71 /40	1.80	1.60
COI	Hartford Total Return Bond HLS IA		**C+**	(888) 843-7824	**C+ / 6.6**	2.74	2.09	0.76 /54	2.12 /64	3.96 /61	3.10	0.50
COI	Hartford Total Return Bond HLS IB		**C**	(888) 843-7824	**C+ / 6.1**	2.67	2.01	0.53 /50	1.87 /59	3.71 /57	2.82	0.75
GEI	Hartford Total Return Bond I	ITBIX	**C**	(888) 843-7824	**C+ / 6.2**	2.63	2.05	0.55 /51	1.91 /60	3.77 /58	2.85	0.55
GEI	Hartford Total Return Bond R3	ITBRX	**C-**	(888) 843-7824	**C / 5.1**	2.44	1.63	-0.03 /31	1.29 /48	3.15 /47	2.23	1.16
GEI	Hartford Total Return Bond R4	ITBUX	**C-**	(888) 843-7824	**C+ / 5.7**	2.52	1.80	0.28 /45	1.60 /54	3.45 /52	2.55	0.84
GEI	Hartford Total Return Bond R5	ITBTX	**C**	(888) 843-7824	**C+ / 6.2**	2.60	1.95	0.58 /51	1.90 /59	3.78 /58	2.85	0.55
COI	Hartford Total Return Bond R6	ITBVX	**U**	(888) 843-7824	**U /**	2.60	1.99	0.56 /51	--	--	2.83	0.44
GEI	Hartford Total Return Bond Y	HABYX	**C**	(888) 843-7824	**C+ / 6.4**	2.72	2.10	0.78 /55	2.04 /62	3.88 /60	2.95	0.44
COI	Hartford Ultrashort Bd HLS IA		**U**	(888) 843-7824	**U /**	0.30	0.30	0.23 /45	--	--	0.32	0.45
GES	Hartford Unconstrained Bond A	HTIAX	**D-**	(888) 843-7824	**E / 0.4**	-0.60	-0.24	-2.62 /13	-0.70 /10	2.20 /34	3.40	1.17
GES	● Hartford Unconstrained Bond B	HTIBX	**D-**	(888) 843-7824	**E / 0.5**	-0.89	-0.72	-3.45 /10	-1.47 / 6	1.42 /25	2.79	2.08
GES	Hartford Unconstrained Bond C	HTICX	**D-**	(888) 843-7824	**E / 0.5**	-0.78	-0.71	-3.43 /10	-1.47 / 6	1.44 /25	2.79	1.86
COI	Hartford Unconstrained Bond I	HTIIX	**D**	(888) 843-7824	**D- / 1.1**	-0.64	-0.22	-2.46 /13	-0.48 /12	2.40 /36	3.83	0.77
COI	Hartford Unconstrained Bond R3	HTIRX	**D**	(888) 843-7824	**E+ / 0.7**	-0.67	-0.39	-2.91 /12	-0.99 / 8	1.90 /30	3.25	1.46
COI	Hartford Unconstrained Bond R4	HTISX	**D**	(888) 843-7824	**E+ / 0.9**	-0.60	-0.25	-2.62 /13	-0.70 /10	2.20 /34	3.56	1.15
COI	Hartford Unconstrained Bond R5	HTITX	**D**	(888) 843-7824	**D- / 1.1**	-0.53	-0.10	-2.33 /14	-0.40 /12	2.48 /38	3.87	0.85
GES	Hartford Unconstrained Bond Y	HTIYX	**D**	(888) 843-7824	**D- / 1.1**	-0.53	-0.21	-2.34 /14	-0.40 /12	2.50 /38	3.87	0.73
USS	Hartford US Govt Sec HLS Fd IA	HAUSX	**B**	(888) 843-7824	**C+ / 5.8**	2.03	1.34	1.86 /70	1.55 /53	2.66 /40	1.82	0.48
USS	Hartford US Govt Sec HLS Fd IB	HBUSX	**B-**	(888) 843-7824	**C / 5.3**	1.94	1.25	1.64 /68	1.29 /48	2.41 /37	1.52	0.73
GL	Hartford US Govt Securities HLS IA		**B**	(888) 843-7824	**C+ / 5.8**	2.03	1.34	1.86 /70	1.55 /53	2.66 /40	1.82	0.48
GL	Hartford World Bond A	HWDAX	**C-**	(888) 843-7824	**C- / 3.0**	2.10	1.27	0.55 /51	1.35 /49	--	0.77	1.02
GL	Hartford World Bond C	HWDCX	**C**	(888) 843-7824	**C- / 3.8**	1.93	0.94	-0.13 /30	0.60 /35	--	0.13	1.76
GL	Hartford World Bond I	HWDIX	**B+**	(888) 843-7824	**C+ / 5.8**	2.27	1.51	0.93 /57	1.65 /55	--	1.07	0.76
GL	Hartford World Bond R3	HWDRX	**C+**	(888) 843-7824	**C / 4.6**	2.03	1.13	0.25 /45	1.04 /43	--	0.50	1.39
GL	Hartford World Bond R4	HWDSX	**B**	(888) 843-7824	**C / 5.1**	2.10	1.27	0.57 /51	1.30 /48	--	0.82	1.07
GL	Hartford World Bond R5	HWDTX	**B+**	(888) 843-7824	**C+ / 5.8**	2.18	1.53	0.96 /58	1.64 /55	--	1.10	0.79
GL	Hartford World Bond R6	HWDVX	**U**	(888) 843-7824	**U /**	2.19	1.55	1.03 /59	--	--	1.17	0.67
GL	Hartford World Bond Y	HWDYX	**B+**	(888) 843-7824	**C+ / 5.9**	2.20	1.55	1.03 /59	1.75 /57	--	1.17	0.67
EM	Harvest Fds Intermediate Bond A	HXIAX	**C**	(866) 777-7818	**B+ / 8.5**	1.85	4.57	5.01 /87	5.48 /93	--	4.10	2.07
EM	Harvest Fds Intermediate Bond Inst	HXIIX	**C+**	(866) 777-7818	**A- / 9.2**	1.66	4.44	5.01 /87	5.59 /93	--	4.50	1.90
COI	HC Capital US Corp FI Sec HC Strat	HCXSX	**C**	(800) 242-9596	**B- / 7.5**	4.28	3.49	1.07 /60	2.49 /71	4.32 /66	2.65	0.36
USL	HC Capital US Govt FI Sec HC Strat	HCUSX	**B**	(800) 242-9596	**C+ / 6.3**	2.74	1.81	1.98 /72	1.76 /57	2.58 /39	1.36	0.18
MTG	HC Capital US Mtg/Asst Bckd FI Str	HCASX	**A**	(800) 242-9596	**C+ / 6.8**	1.87	1.58	1.94 /71	2.23 /66	2.95 /44	2.83	0.21

● Denotes fund is closed to new investors
* Denotes fund is included in Section II

RISK			NET ASSETS		ASSET							FUND MANAGER		MINIMUM		LOADS	
Risk Rating/Pts	3 Yr Avg Standard Deviation	Avg Duration	NAV As of 3/31/16	Total $(Mil)	Cash %	Gov. Bond %	Muni. Bond %	Corp. Bond %	Other %	Portfolio Turnover Ratio	Avg Coupon Rate	Manager Quality Pct	Manager Tenure (Years)	Initial Purch. $	Additional Purch. $	Front End Load	Back End Load
C- / 3.0	4.7	N/A	13.62	N/A	0	92	0	0	8	15	0.0	3	12	250	25	0.0	0.0
C- / 3.0	4.7	N/A	13.32	1	0	92	0	0	8	15	0.0	3	12	250	25	0.0	0.0
C- / 3.0	4.7	N/A	15.02	1	0	92	0	0	8	15	0.0	5	12	250	25	0.0	0.0
C / 5.1	3.4	N/A	17.66	15	0	20	1	29	50	9	0.0	26	14	250	25	4.5	0.0
C / 5.1	3.4	N/A	16.39	1	0	20	1	29	50	9	0.0	15	14	250	25	0.0	0.0
C / 5.1	3.4	N/A	15.97	4	0	20	1	29	50	9	0.0	13	14	250	25	0.0	0.0
C / 5.1	3.4	N/A	18.34	1	0	20	1	29	50	9	0.0	33	14	250	25	0.0	0.0
D / 2.1	5.6	6.0	8.42	119	0	26	1	40	33	66	6.8	92	4	2,000	50	4.5	0.0
D / 2.1	5.6	6.0	8.44	3	0	26	1	40	33	66	6.8	86	4	0	0	0.0	0.0
D / 2.1	5.6	6.0	8.45	77	0	26	1	40	33	66	6.8	85	4	2,000	50	0.0	0.0
D / 2.1	5.6	6.0	8.45	25	0	26	1	40	33	66	6.8	94	4	2,000	50	0.0	0.0
D / 2.1	5.5	6.0	8.41	N/A	0	26	1	40	33	66	6.8	90	4	0	0	0.0	0.0
D / 2.1	5.5	6.0	8.42	N/A	0	26	1	40	33	66	6.8	92	4	0	0	0.0	0.0
D / 2.1	5.5	6.0	8.42	1	0	26	1	40	33	66	6.8	94	4	0	0	0.0	0.0
U /	N/A	6.0	8.42	N/A	0	26	1	40	33	66	6.8	N/A	4	0	0	0.0	0.0
D / 2.0	5.6	6.0	8.42	181	0	26	1	40	33	66	6.8	95	4	250,000	0	0.0	0.0
C / 5.2	3.4	5.7	10.32	725	0	11	0	31	58	57	4.1	29	4	2,000	50	4.5	0.0
C / 5.1	3.4	5.7	10.24	8	0	11	0	31	58	57	4.1	14	4	0	0	0.0	0.0
C / 5.2	3.4	5.7	10.34	69	0	11	0	31	58	57	4.1	14	4	2,000	50	0.0	0.0
C / 5.2	3.4	5.7	11.23	2,382	0	0	0	0	100	84	4.2	60	4	0	0	0.0	0.0
C / 5.2	3.4	5.7	11.16	290	0	0	0	0	100	84	4.2	50	4	0	0	0.0	0.0
C / 5.2	3.4	5.7	10.33	24	0	11	0	31	58	57	4.1	37	4	2,000	50	0.0	0.0
C / 5.2	3.4	5.7	10.51	6	0	11	0	31	58	57	4.1	21	4	0	0	0.0	0.0
C / 5.2	3.4	5.7	10.49	15	0	11	0	31	58	57	4.1	29	4	0	0	0.0	0.0
C / 5.2	3.4	5.7	10.49	2	0	11	0	31	58	57	4.1	37	4	0	0	0.0	0.0
U /	N/A	5.7	10.48	N/A	0	11	0	31	58	57	4.1	N/A	4	0	0	0.0	0.0
C / 5.1	3.4	5.7	10.49	1,057	0	11	0	31	58	57	4.1	40	4	250,000	0	0.0	0.0
U /	N/A	0.6	10.02	586	0	0	0	0	100	40	1.4	N/A	3	0	0	0.0	0.0
C / 5.0	3.5	3.3	9.36	51	0	9	0	29	62	67	5.0	10	4	2,000	50	4.5	0.0
C / 5.1	3.4	3.3	9.35	1	0	9	0	29	62	67	5.0	7	4	0	0	0.0	0.0
C / 5.1	3.4	3.3	9.38	12	0	9	0	29	62	67	5.0	7	4	2,000	50	0.0	0.0
C / 5.2	3.4	3.3	9.36	3	0	9	0	29	62	67	5.0	11	4	2,000	50	0.0	0.0
C / 5.0	3.5	3.3	9.35	N/A	0	9	0	29	62	67	5.0	8	4	0	0	0.0	0.0
C / 5.1	3.4	3.3	9.35	N/A	0	9	0	29	62	67	5.0	9	4	0	0	0.0	0.0
C / 5.1	3.4	3.3	9.35	N/A	0	9	0	29	62	67	5.0	11	4	0	0	0.0	0.0
C / 5.1	3.4	3.3	9.33	20	0	9	0	29	62	67	5.0	12	4	250,000	0	0.0	0.0
B / 8.1	2.3	3.8	10.55	421	0	39	0	2	59	37	2.5	60	4	0	0	0.0	0.0
B / 8.1	2.3	3.8	10.52	94	0	39	0	2	59	37	2.5	50	4	0	0	0.0	0.0
B / 8.1	2.3	3.8	10.55	421	0	39	0	2	59	37	2.5	93	4	0	0	0.0	0.0
B+ / 8.5	2.0	3.8	10.27	516	4	66	1	12	17	99	2.2	92	5	2,000	50	4.5	0.0
B+ / 8.5	2.0	3.8	10.25	173	4	66	1	12	17	99	2.2	85	5	2,000	50	0.0	0.0
B+ / 8.5	2.0	3.8	10.29	2,318	4	66	1	12	17	99	2.2	94	5	2,000	50	0.0	0.0
B+ / 8.5	2.0	3.8	10.28	1	4	66	1	12	17	99	2.2	90	5	0	0	0.0	0.0
B+ / 8.5	1.9	3.8	10.28	5	4	66	1	12	17	99	2.2	92	5	0	0	0.0	0.0
B+ / 8.5	2.0	3.8	10.28	N/A	4	66	1	12	17	99	2.2	94	5	0	0	0.0	0.0
U /	N/A	3.8	10.29	1	4	66	1	12	17	99	2.2	N/A	5	0	0	0.0	0.0
B+ / 8.5	2.0	3.8	10.29	480	4	66	1	12	17	99	2.2	95	5	250,000	0	0.0	0.0
D / 2.0	5.7	2.3	10.00	24	5	0	0	91	4	336	0.0	99	3	2,500	100	4.3	1.5
D / 2.0	5.6	2.3	9.99	35	5	0	0	91	4	336	0.0	99	3	1,000,000	0	0.0	1.5
C- / 3.3	4.5	N/A	9.87	268	0	0	0	0	100	158	0.0	45	6	0	0	0.0	0.0
B- / 7.2	2.8	N/A	10.15	229	0	0	0	0	100	100	0.0	76	6	0	0	0.0	0.0
B / 8.1	2.3	N/A	9.85	202	0	0	0	0	100	30	0.0	51	4	0	0	0.0	0.0

Fund Type	Fund Name (99 Pct = Best, 0 Pct = Worst)	Ticker Symbol	Overall Investment Rating	Phone	PERFORMANCE: Performance Rating/Pts	Total Return % through 3/31/16: 3 Mo	6 Mo	1Yr / Pct	Annualized: 3Yr / Pct	5Yr / Pct	Incl. in Returns: Dividend Yield	Expense Ratio
GL	HC Inflation Protected Secs HC Adv	HCPAX	**U**	(800) 242-9596	**U** /	4.39	3.54	1.28 /63	--	--	0.19	0.41
GL	HC Inflation Protected Secs HC Str	HCPBX	**U**	(800) 242-9596	**U** /	4.39	3.43	1.38 /64	--	--	0.19	0.16
GL	Henderson High Yield Opp A	HYOAX	**U**	(866) 443-6337	**U** /	3.51	2.51	-1.34 /19	--	--	5.11	1.39
GL	Henderson High Yield Opp C	HYOCX	**U**	(866) 443-6337	**U** /	3.23	2.08	-2.16 /15	--	--	4.85	2.01
GL	Henderson High Yield Opp I	HYOIX	**U**	(866) 443-6337	**U** /	3.59	2.58	-1.22 /20	--	--	5.73	1.16
GEI	Henderson Strategic Income A	HFAAX	**C**	(866) 443-6337	**C+ / 6.6**	1.37	2.19	0.04 /37	3.82 /82	4.60 /69	2.75	1.17
GEI	Henderson Strategic Income C	HFACX	**C+**	(866) 443-6337	**B- / 7.3**	1.19	1.80	-0.61 /25	3.05 /77	3.80 /58	2.14	1.94
GEI	Henderson Strategic Income I	HFAIX	**B**	(866) 443-6337	**B / 8.2**	1.43	2.41	0.36 /47	4.09 /84	4.84 /71	3.10	0.94
GL	Henderson Unconstrained Bond A	HUNAX	**U**	(866) 443-6337	**U** /	-0.37	0.76	-1.05 /21	--	--	0.96	2.05
GL	Henderson Unconstrained Bond C	HUNCX	**U**	(866) 443-6337	**U** /	-0.65	0.30	-1.87 /16	--	--	0.29	2.80
GL	Henderson Unconstrained Bond I	HUNIX	**U**	(866) 443-6337	**U** /	-0.31	0.89	-0.84 /23	--	--	1.21	1.79
COH	Hennessy Core Bond Institutional	HCBIX	**D+**	(800) 966-4354	**D+ / 2.8**	0.78	-0.23	-1.62 /18	0.47 /32	2.65 /40	0.39	2.60
COH	Hennessy Core Bond Investor	HCBFX	**D+**	(800) 966-4354	**D / 1.7**	0.69	-0.41	-2.07 /15	0.15 /28	2.36 /36	0.10	2.94
GEI	Highland Fixed Income A	HFBAX	**C-**	(877) 665-1287	**C- / 3.5**	2.18	2.18	0.30 /46	1.53 /53	3.04 /46	2.45	0.94
GEI	Highland Fixed Income C	HFBCX	**C-**	(877) 665-1287	**C- / 4.1**	2.00	1.81	-0.44 /27	0.78 /39	2.27 /35	1.82	1.69
GEI	Highland Fixed Income Y	HFBYX	**B-**	(877) 665-1287	**C+ / 6.0**	2.24	2.30	0.55 /51	1.79 /57	3.32 /50	2.81	0.69
LP	Highland Floating Rate Opps A	HFRAX	**E+**	(877) 665-1287	**E / 0.4**	-2.52	-7.02	-10.42 / 1	0.76 /38	3.69 /56	5.79	1.39
LP	Highland Floating Rate Opps C	HFRCX	**E+**	(877) 665-1287	**E / 0.5**	-2.50	-7.25	-10.87 / 0	0.26 /29	3.18 /48	5.45	1.89
LP	Highland Floating Rate Opps Z	HFRZX	**E+**	(877) 665-1287	**E+ / 0.8**	-2.29	-6.74	-10.11 / 1	1.11 /45	4.08 /63	6.39	1.05
MUN	Highland Tax-Exempt A	HTXAX	**C**	(877) 665-1287	**C+ / 6.6**	1.15	2.26	2.47 /80	2.36 /81	4.01 /78	1.96	1.06
MUN	Highland Tax-Exempt C	HTXCX	**C+**	(877) 665-1287	**B- / 7.3**	0.97	1.81	1.63 /75	1.61 /70	3.25 /72	1.32	1.81
MUN	Highland Tax-Exempt Y	HTXYX	**B**	(877) 665-1287	**B+ / 8.6**	1.31	2.37	2.70 /82	2.62 /84	4.29 /80	2.29	0.81
*GES	Homestead Short Term Bond	HOSBX	**B**	(800) 258-3030	**C / 4.6**	0.76	0.72	0.64 /52	1.11 /45	2.06 /32	1.41	0.73
USS	Homestead Short Term Govt Sec	HOSGX	**C+**	(800) 258-3030	**C- / 3.9**	1.16	0.57	0.97 /58	0.66 /36	1.14 /22	0.76	0.71
*COH	Hotchkis and Wiley High Yield A	HWHAX	**E+**	(866) 493-8637	**E+ / 0.7**	1.65	-1.59	-5.48 / 4	1.09 /44	4.32 /66	6.31	0.98
COH	Hotchkis and Wiley High Yield C	HWHCX	**E+**	(866) 493-8637	**E+ / 0.9**	1.55	-1.91	-6.19 / 3	0.39 /31	--	5.86	1.73
COH	Hotchkis and Wiley High Yield I	HWHIX	**D-**	(866) 493-8637	**D / 1.9**	1.71	-1.53	-5.26 / 5	1.39 /50	4.66 /69	6.80	0.73
GL	HSBC Emerging Markets Local Debt	HBMAX	**E-**	(800) 728-8183	**E- / 0.1**	10.21	10.44	-3.24 /11	-7.32 / 1	--	4.08	2.06
GL	HSBC Emerging Markets Local Debt I	HBMIX	**E-**	(800) 728-8183	**E- / 0.1**	10.24	10.54	-2.80 /12	-6.99 / 1	--	4.62	1.71
GL	HSBC Global High Income Bond A	HBIAX	**U**	(800) 782-8183	**U** /	3.15	3.77	--	--	--	0.00	1.56
GL	HSBC Global High Income Bond I	HBIIX	**U**	(800) 782-8183	**U** /	3.31	4.00	--	--	--	0.00	1.21
GL	HSBC Global High Yield Bond A	HBYAX	**U**	(800) 782-8183	**U** /	2.40	2.13	--	--	--	0.00	1.65
GL	HSBC Global High Yield Bond I	HBYIX	**U**	(800) 782-8183	**U** /	2.45	2.36	--	--	--	0.000	1.30
MM	HSBC Prime Money Market A	REAXX	**U**	(800) 728-8183	**U** /	--	--	--	--	--	0.04	0.68
MM	HSBC Prime Money Market D	HIMXX	**C**	(800) 728-8183	**D / 2.1**	0.02	0.03	0.05 /38	0.03 /22	0.02 / 8	0.05	0.53
MM	HSBC Prime Money Market I	HSIXX	**C**	(800) 728-8183	**D+ / 2.7**	0.10	0.15	0.20 /44	0.10 /27	0.11 /15	0.20	0.18
MM	HSBC Prime Money Market Y	RMYXX	**C**	(800) 728-8183	**D+ / 2.5**	0.07	0.09	0.12 /42	0.05 /25	0.04 /11	0.12	0.28
MM	HSBC US Government Money Market	FTRXX	**U**	(800) 728-8183	**U** /	0.00	0.01	0.03 /36	0.02 /20	0.02 / 8	0.03	0.68
MM	● HSBC US Government Money Market	HUBXX	**U**	(800) 728-8183	**U** /	0.00	0.01	0.03 /36	0.02 /20	0.02 / 8	0.03	1.28
MM	HSBC US Government Money Market	HGDXX	**U**	(800) 728-8183	**U** /	0.00	0.01	0.03 /36	0.02 /20	0.02 / 8	0.03	0.53
MM	HSBC US Government Money Market	HGIXX	**C**	(800) 728-8183	**D+ / 2.3**	0.05	0.06	0.07 /40	0.04 /24	0.03 /10	0.07	0.18
MM	HSBC US Government Money Market	RGYXX	**C**	(800) 728-8183	**D / 2.1**	0.02	0.03	0.04 /37	0.03 /22	0.02 / 8	0.04	0.28
MM	HSBC US Treasury Money Market I	HBIXX	**C-**	(800) 728-8183	**D / 1.9**	0.03	0.03	0.03 /36	0.01 /17	0.01 / 5	0.03	0.18
MM	HSBC US Treasury Money Market Y	HTYXX	**U**	(800) 728-8183	**U** /	0.01	0.01	0.01 /32	--	--	0.01	0.28
COH	Hundredfold Select Alternative Svc	SFHYX	**C-**	(855) 582-8006	**C+ / 6.4**	1.99	1.32	-0.54 /26	2.31 /68	4.30 /65	0.24	3.10
USS	Hussman Strategic Total Return	HSTRX	**D+**	(800) 487-7626	**C+ / 5.8**	6.68	6.97	4.43 /84	0.66 /36	1.05 /21	0.42	0.76
GEI	IA 529 CSI Bond Index Port		**B**	(800) 662-7447	**C+ / 6.9**	3.02	2.39	1.64 /68	2.18 /65	3.49 /53	0.00	0.34
GEL	IA 529 CSI Conservative Income Port		**C+**	(800) 662-7447	**C / 4.9**	2.14	1.80	0.99 /58	1.03 /43	2.51 /38	0.00	0.34
COI	ICON Bond A	IOBAX	**D+**	(800) 764-0442	**D / 1.6**	0.26	0.38	-0.72 /24	1.32 /49	2.70 /40	3.61	1.51
GES	ICON Bond C	IOBCX	**C-**	(800) 764-0442	**C- / 3.3**	0.20	0.17	-1.31 /19	0.75 /38	2.08 /32	3.14	2.34
GES	ICON Bond S	IOBZX	**C+**	(800) 764-0442	**C / 4.9**	0.28	0.57	-0.50 /26	1.60 /54	2.95 /44	3.99	1.06
GEL	ID 529 IDeal CSP Income Port		**C-**	(800) 662-7447	**C- / 3.7**	2.04	1.71	0.48 /49	0.38 /31	1.95 /31	0.00	0.84

● Denotes fund is closed to new investors
* Denotes fund is included in Section II

RISK			NET ASSETS		ASSET							FUND MANAGER		MINIMUM		LOADS	
Risk Rating/Pts	3 Yr Avg Standard Deviation	Avg Duration	NAV As of 3/31/16	Total $(Mil)	Cash %	Gov. Bond %	Muni. Bond %	Corp. Bond %	Other %	Portfolio Turnover Ratio	Avg Coupon Rate	Manager Quality Pct	Manager Tenure (Years)	Initial Purch. $	Additional Purch. $	Front End Load	Back End Load
U /	N/A	N/A	10.22	N/A	5	94	0	0	1	27	0.0	N/A	N/A	0	0	0.0	0.0
U /	N/A	N/A	10.23	485	5	94	0	0	1	27	0.0	N/A	N/A	0	0	0.0	0.0
U /	N/A	N/A	9.22	1	6	0	0	92	2	201	0.0	N/A	3	500	0	4.8	0.0
U /	N/A	N/A	9.19	1	6	0	0	92	2	201	0.0	N/A	3	500	0	0.0	0.0
U /	N/A	N/A	9.18	6	6	0	0	92	2	201	0.0	N/A	3	0	0	0.0	0.0
C / 4.8	3.6	N/A	9.02	60	11	9	0	71	9	54	0.0	94	8	500	0	4.8	0.0
C / 4.7	3.6	N/A	8.98	45	11	9	0	71	9	54	0.0	88	8	500	0	0.0	0.0
C / 4.7	3.6	N/A	9.00	281	11	9	0	71	9	54	0.0	96	8	0	0	0.0	0.0
U /	N/A	1.7	9.00	1	17	19	0	38	26	129	0.0	N/A	3	500	0	4.8	0.0
U /	N/A	1.7	8.99	1	17	19	0	38	26	129	0.0	N/A	3	500	0	0.0	0.0
U /	N/A	1.7	9.00	1	17	19	0	38	26	129	0.0	N/A	3	0	0	0.0	0.0
C+ / 6.4	2.5	N/A	6.43	2	2	22	0	63	13	50	0.0	64	9	250,000	0	0.0	0.0
C+ / 6.6	2.5	N/A	7.30	2	2	22	0	63	13	50	0.0	51	9	2,500	0	0.0	0.0
B- / 7.1	2.8	5.1	12.68	121	8	19	4	36	33	57	5.2	42	2	500	100	4.3	0.0
B- / 7.1	2.8	5.1	12.70	7	8	19	4	36	33	57	5.2	22	2	500	100	0.0	0.0
B- / 7.1	2.8	5.1	12.67	5	8	19	4	36	33	57	5.2	51	2	1,000,000	0	0.0	0.0
D / 2.1	5.5	N/A	6.63	157	0	0	0	61	39	55	8.4	73	4	2,500	50	3.5	0.0
D / 2.1	5.5	N/A	6.63	226	0	0	0	61	39	55	8.4	52	4	2,500	50	0.0	0.0
D / 2.1	5.5	N/A	6.63	187	0	0	0	61	39	55	8.4	85	4	2,500	50	0.0	0.0
C / 4.3	3.6	7.0	11.74	25	16	0	83	0	1	26	5.5	20	2	500	100	4.3	0.0
C / 4.3	3.6	7.0	11.73	3	16	0	83	0	1	26	5.5	11	2	500	100	0.0	0.0
C / 4.4	3.5	7.0	12.74	N/A	16	0	83	0	1	26	5.5	27	2	1,000,000	0	0.0	0.0
A / 9.5	0.8	2.6	5.20	545	2	7	22	42	27	26	0.0	84	25	500	0	0.0	0.0
A- / 9.1	1.1	2.2	5.23	72	6	56	2	29	7	20	0.0	58	21	500	0	0.0	0.0
D- / 1.4	5.7	4.5	10.99	572	2	0	0	91	7	44	6.9	42	7	2,500	100	3.8	2.0
D- / 1.4	5.7	4.5	11.04	3	2	0	0	91	7	44	6.9	23	7	2,500	100	0.0	2.0
D- / 1.5	5.6	4.5	11.06	1,722	2	0	0	91	7	44	6.9	54	7	1,000,000	100	0.0	2.0
E- / 0.1	12.2	4.8	7.00	N/A	22	76	0	1	1	186	0.0	1	N/A	1,000	100	4.8	0.0
E- / 0.1	12.2	4.8	7.00	15	22	76	0	1	1	186	0.0	1	N/A	1,000,000	0	0.0	0.0
U /	N/A	N/A	9.83	N/A	0	0	0	0	100	0	0.0	N/A	1	1,000	100	4.8	0.0
U /	N/A	N/A	9.84	25	0	0	0	0	100	0	0.0	N/A	1	1,000,000	0	0.0	0.0
U /	N/A	N/A	9.44	N/A	0	0	0	0	100	0	0.0	N/A	1	1,000	100	4.8	0.0
U /	N/A	N/A	9.45	24	0	0	0	0	100	0	0.0	N/A	1	1,000,000	0	0.0	0.0
U /	N/A	N/A	1.00	27	100	0	0	0	0	0	0.0	N/A	N/A	1,000	100	0.0	0.0
A+ / 9.9	N/A	N/A	1.00	1,317	100	0	0	0	0	0	0.1	67	N/A	1,000	100	0.0	0.0
A+ / 9.9	N/A	N/A	1.00	6,381	100	0	0	0	0	0	0.2	69	N/A	25,000,000	5,000,000	0.0	0.0
A+ / 9.9	N/A	N/A	1.00	432	100	0	0	0	0	0	0.1	N/A	N/A	5,000,000	0	0.0	0.0
U /	N/A	N/A	1.00	1	100	0	0	0	0	0	0.0	N/A	N/A	1,000	100	0.0	0.0
U /	N/A	N/A	1.00	N/A	100	0	0	0	0	0	0.0	N/A	N/A	0	0	0.0	0.0
U /	N/A	N/A	1.00	820	100	0	0	0	0	0	0.0	N/A	N/A	1,000	100	0.0	0.0
A+ / 9.9	N/A	N/A	1.00	585	100	0	0	0	0	0	0.1	N/A	N/A	25,000,000	5,000,000	0.0	0.0
A+ / 9.9	N/A	N/A	1.00	2,902	100	0	0	0	0	0	0.0	67	N/A	5,000,000	0	0.0	0.0
A+ / 9.9	N/A	N/A	1.00	468	100	0	0	0	0	0	0.0	64	N/A	25,000,000	5,000,000	0.0	0.0
U /	N/A	N/A	1.00	1,002	100	0	0	0	0	0	0.0	N/A	N/A	5,000,000	0	0.0	0.0
C- / 3.6	3.7	N/A	21.55	39	26	0	0	50	24	418	0.0	92	12	5,000	1,000	0.0	0.0
D- / 1.4	6.2	N/A	11.80	426	27	59	0	0	14	196	0.0	16	14	1,000	100	0.0	1.5
C+ / 6.3	3.1	N/A	16.73	37	0	46	1	25	28	0	0.0	49	13	25	25	0.0	0.0
B- / 7.5	2.7	N/A	15.26	140	25	49	1	13	12	0	0.0	25	13	25	25	0.0	0.0
B- / 7.4	2.7	5.1	9.04	4	3	3	0	75	19	153	5.7	56	5	1,000	100	4.8	0.0
B- / 7.5	2.7	5.1	9.12	5	3	3	0	75	19	153	5.7	28	5	1,000	100	0.0	0.0
B- / 7.4	2.7	5.1	9.08	73	3	3	0	75	19	153	5.7	55	5	1,000	100	0.0	0.0
B- / 7.3	2.8	N/A	12.48	56	25	48	0	12	15	0	0.0	13	9	25	25	0.0	0.0

99 Pct = Best 0 Pct = Worst Fund Type	Fund Name	Ticker Symbol	Overall Investment Rating	Phone	PERFORMANCE Performance Rating/Pts	Total Return % through 3/31/16 3 Mo	6 Mo	1Yr / Pct	Annualized 3Yr / Pct	5Yr / Pct	Incl. in Returns Dividend Yield	Expense Ratio
COH	Integrity High Income A	IHFAX	**E+**	(800) 601-5593	**D / 1.6**	2.79	0.64	-3.77 / 8	1.30 /48	4.24 /65	5.36	1.64
COH	Integrity High Income C	IHFCX	**D-**	(800) 601-5593	**D+ / 2.7**	2.58	0.40	-4.47 / 6	0.55 /34	3.47 /53	4.81	2.39
COH	Intrepid Income Institutional	ICMUX	**D+**	(866) 996-3863	**D / 1.7**	1.42	0.07	-1.29 /20	0.52 /33	2.29 /35	3.63	0.96
MUS	Invesco California Tax-Free Inc A	CLFAX	**B-**	(800) 959-4246	**A / 9.3**	1.92	4.02	4.84 /97	4.45 /97	7.27 /97	3.62	0.91
MUS ●	Invesco California Tax-Free Inc B	CLFBX	**B**	(800) 959-4246	**A+ / 9.8**	1.93	4.02	4.86 /98	4.54 /98	7.32 /97	3.81	0.88
MUS	Invesco California Tax-Free Inc C	CLFCX	**B**	(800) 959-4246	**A+ / 9.6**	1.80	3.76	4.32 /96	3.96 /96	6.75 /95	3.29	1.41
MUS	Invesco California Tax-Free Inc Y	CLFDX	**B**	(800) 959-4246	**A+ / 9.8**	2.06	4.15	5.10 /98	4.74 /98	7.54 /97	4.02	0.66
COI	Invesco Conservative Income Instl	ICIFX	**U**	(800) 959-4246	**U /**	0.42	0.55	0.69 /53	--	--	0.56	1.02
* GEI	Invesco Core Plus Bond A	ACPSX	**C**	(800) 959-4246	**C+ / 5.9**	2.51	2.39	0.29 /46	3.00 /76	4.38 /66	3.19	0.98
GEI ●	Invesco Core Plus Bond B	CPBBX	**C**	(800) 959-4246	**C+ / 6.4**	2.33	1.93	-0.45 /26	2.21 /66	3.59 /55	2.59	1.73
GEI	Invesco Core Plus Bond C	CPCFX	**C**	(800) 959-4246	**C+ / 6.4**	2.33	1.92	-0.46 /26	2.24 /66	3.57 /54	2.58	1.73
GEI	Invesco Core Plus Bond R	CPBRX	**C+**	(800) 959-4246	**B- / 7.2**	2.45	2.17	0.04 /37	2.75 /74	4.10 /63	3.08	1.23
GEI	Invesco Core Plus Bond R5	CPIIX	**B-**	(800) 959-4246	**B / 7.8**	2.58	2.43	0.51 /50	3.25 /78	4.62 /69	3.55	0.61
COI	Invesco Core Plus Bond R6	CPBFX	**B**	(800) 959-4246	**B / 7.9**	2.60	2.57	0.63 /52	3.31 /79	4.59 /68	3.67	0.54
GEI	Invesco Core Plus Bond Y	CPBYX	**B-**	(800) 959-4246	**B / 7.8**	2.57	2.42	0.53 /50	3.26 /78	4.64 /69	3.57	0.73
* GEI	Invesco Corporate Bond A	ACCBX	**C-**	(800) 959-4246	**C+ / 6.2**	3.67	3.15	-0.49 /26	3.12 /77	5.08 /72	3.49	0.91
GEI ●	Invesco Corporate Bond B	ACCDX	**C**	(800) 959-4246	**B / 7.7**	3.67	3.15	-0.49 /26	3.07 /77	5.07 /72	3.64	0.91
GEI	Invesco Corporate Bond C	ACCEX	**C-**	(800) 959-4246	**C+ / 6.5**	3.42	2.66	-1.32 /19	2.30 /67	4.28 /65	2.66	1.66
COI	Invesco Corporate Bond R	ACCZX	**C-**	(800) 959-4246	**B- / 7.4**	3.61	2.88	-0.88 /23	2.82 /75	--	3.39	1.16
COI	Invesco Corporate Bond R5	ACCWX	**C**	(800) 959-4246	**B / 8.0**	3.63	3.22	-0.22 /29	3.51 /80	5.52 /75	4.05	0.47
COI	Invesco Corporate Bond R6	ICBFX	**C**	(800) 959-4246	**B / 8.0**	3.78	3.22	-0.19 /29	3.52 /80	5.40 /74	4.08	0.46
GEI	Invesco Corporate Bond Y	ACCHX	**C**	(800) 959-4246	**B / 7.9**	3.73	3.13	-0.38 /27	3.33 /79	5.34 /74	3.89	0.66
EM	Invesco Emerg Mkts Flexible Bond A	IAEMX	**E-**	(800) 959-4246	**E- / 0.0**	0.77	0.31	-10.75 / 0	-9.82 / 0	-4.41 / 0	5.35	1.89
EM ●	Invesco Emerg Mkts Flexible Bond B	IBEMX	**E-**	(800) 959-4246	**E- / 0.0**	0.67	0.03	-11.36 / 0	-10.52 / 0	-5.12 / 0	4.72	2.64
EM	Invesco Emerg Mkts Flexible Bond C	ICEMX	**E-**	(800) 959-4246	**E- / 0.0**	0.67	0.03	-11.34 / 0	-10.50 / 0	-5.11 / 0	4.71	2.64
EM	Invesco Emerg Mkts Flexible Bond R	IREMX	**E-**	(800) 959-4246	**E- / 0.0**	0.68	0.16	-11.01 / 0	-10.10 / 0	-4.68 / 0	5.30	2.14
EM	Invesco Emerg Mkts Flexible Bond	IIEMX	**E-**	(800) 959-4246	**E- / 0.0**	0.85	0.46	-10.39 / 1	-9.56 / 0	-4.17 / 0	5.88	1.34
EM	Invesco Emerg Mkts Flexible Bond	IFEMX	**E-**	(800) 959-4246	**E- / 0.0**	0.70	0.46	-10.53 / 1	-9.64 / 0	-4.27 / 0	5.88	1.33
EM	Invesco Emerg Mkts Flexible Bond Y	IYEMX	**E-**	(800) 959-4246	**E- / 0.0**	0.85	0.46	-10.51 / 1	-9.62 / 0	-4.19 / 0	5.88	1.64
* LP	Invesco Floating Rate A	AFRAX	**D**	(800) 959-4246	**D- / 1.4**	1.33	-1.11	-3.45 /10	0.81 /39	2.82 /42	4.98	1.07
LP	Invesco Floating Rate C	AFRCX	**D**	(800) 959-4246	**D / 1.6**	1.21	-1.36	-3.83 / 8	0.34 /31	2.30 /35	4.60	1.57
LP	Invesco Floating Rate R	AFRRX	**D+**	(800) 959-4246	**D+ / 2.5**	1.41	-1.22	-3.54 / 9	0.61 /35	2.57 /39	4.85	1.32
LP	Invesco Floating Rate R5	AFRIX	**D+**	(800) 959-4246	**C- / 3.5**	1.39	-0.98	-3.08 /11	1.12 /45	3.14 /47	5.37	0.81
LP	Invesco Floating Rate R6	AFRFX	**D+**	(800) 959-4246	**C- / 3.6**	1.41	-0.94	-3.12 /11	1.16 /46	3.07 /46	5.47	0.71
LP	Invesco Floating Rate Y	AFRYX	**D+**	(800) 959-4246	**C- / 3.5**	1.39	-1.00	-3.10 /11	1.10 /44	3.07 /46	5.36	0.82
MM	Invesco Gov and Agency Corp	AGCXX	**C**	(800) 959-4246	**D+ / 2.3**	0.05	0.06	0.09 /41	0.04 /24	0.03 /10	0.09	0.17
MM	Invesco Gov and Agency CshMgt		**C**	(800) 959-4246	**D+ / 2.3**	0.03	0.04	0.08 /40	0.04 /24	0.03 /10	0.07	0.24
MM	Invesco Gov and Agency Inst	AGPXX	**C**	(800) 959-4246	**D+ / 2.3**	0.05	0.07	0.10 /41	0.04 /24	0.04 /12	0.10	0.14
MM	Invesco Gov and Agency Psnl		**C**	(800) 959-4246	**D / 2.2**	0.03	0.04	0.07 /40	0.03 /22	0.03 /10	0.07	0.89
MM	Invesco Gov and Agency Pvt	GPVXX	**C**	(800) 959-4246	**D / 2.2**	0.03	0.04	0.07 /40	0.03 /22	0.03 /10	0.07	0.64
MM	Invesco Gov and Agency Res		**C**	(800) 959-4246	**D / 2.2**	0.03	0.04	0.07 /40	0.03 /22	0.03 /10	0.07	0.34
MM	Invesco Gov and Agency Rsv		**C**	(800) 959-4246	**D / 2.2**	0.03	0.04	0.07 /40	0.03 /22	0.03 /10	0.07	1.14
MM	Invesco Gov TaxAdvantage Corp	TACXX	**C**	(800) 959-4246	**D+ / 2.5**	0.03	0.05	0.14 /42	0.06 /26	0.05 /12	0.14	0.23
MM	Invesco Gov TaxAdvantage CshMgt		**C**	(800) 959-4246	**D+ / 2.5**	0.03	0.04	0.13 /42	0.06 /26	0.05 /12	0.13	0.30
MM	Invesco Gov TaxAdvantage Inst	TSPXX	**C**	(800) 959-4246	**D+ / 2.5**	0.04	0.05	0.15 /43	0.06 /26	0.05 /12	0.15	0.20
MM	Invesco Gov TaxAdvantage Psnl		**C**	(800) 959-4246	**D+ / 2.5**	0.02	0.03	0.13 /42	0.06 /26	0.05 /12	0.13	0.95
MM	Invesco Gov TaxAdvantage Pvt	TXPXX	**C**	(800) 959-4246	**D+ / 2.5**	0.02	0.03	0.13 /42	0.06 /26	0.05 /12	0.13	0.70
MM	Invesco Gov TaxAdvantage Rs		**C**	(800) 959-4246	**D+ / 2.5**	0.02	0.03	0.13 /42	0.06 /26	0.05 /12	0.13	0.40
MM	Invesco Gov TaxAdvantage Rsv		**C**	(800) 959-4246	**D+ / 2.5**	0.02	0.03	0.13 /42	0.06 /26	0.05 /12	0.13	1.20
* COH	Invesco High Yield A	AMHYX	**E+**	(800) 959-4246	**D- / 1.4**	1.67	0.85	-3.95 / 8	1.24 /47	4.25 /65	5.63	1.02
COH ●	Invesco High Yield B	AHYBX	**E+**	(800) 959-4246	**D / 1.8**	1.48	0.48	-4.65 / 6	0.49 /33	3.48 /53	5.08	1.77
COH	Invesco High Yield C	AHYCX	**E+**	(800) 959-4246	**D / 1.8**	1.48	0.47	-4.74 / 5	0.45 /32	3.46 /52	5.04	1.77

● Denotes fund is closed to new investors
* Denotes fund is included in Section II

RISK			NET ASSETS		ASSET							FUND MANAGER		MINIMUM		LOADS	
Risk Rating/Pts	3 Yr Avg Standard Deviation	Avg Duration	NAV As of 3/31/16	Total $(Mil)	Cash %	Gov. Bond %	Muni. Bond %	Corp. Bond %	Other %	Portfolio Turnover Ratio	Avg Coupon Rate	Manager Quality Pct	Manager Tenure (Years)	Initial Purch. $	Additional Purch. $	Front End Load	Back End Load
D- / 1.4	5.6	N/A	7.12	23	0	0	0	99	1	35	0.0	49	8	1,000	50	4.3	0.0
D- / 1.4	5.6	N/A	7.14	5	0	0	0	99	1	35	0.0	26	8	1,000	50	0.0	0.0
C+ / 6.4	2.5	1.9	8.84	75	34	0	0	58	8	51	0.0	57	6	250,000	100	0.0	2.0
C- / 3.2	4.3	7.7	12.40	331	1	0	97	0	2	12	5.2	59	7	1,000	50	4.3	0.0
C- / 3.2	4.3	7.7	12.51	14	1	0	97	0	2	12	5.2	61	7	1,000	50	0.0	0.0
C- / 3.2	4.4	7.7	12.48	42	1	0	97	0	2	12	5.2	40	7	1,000	50	0.0	0.0
C- / 3.1	4.4	7.7	12.45	30	1	0	97	0	2	12	5.2	72	7	1,000	50	0.0	0.0
U /	N/A	N/A	10.01	83	26	0	0	43	31	64	0.0	N/A	2	1,000,000	0	0.0	0.0
C / 5.2	3.4	5.3	10.70	570	1	12	0	47	40	537	3.9	81	7	1,000	50	4.3	0.0
C / 5.3	3.4	5.3	10.69	7	1	12	0	47	40	537	3.9	49	7	1,000	50	0.0	0.0
C / 5.1	3.4	5.3	10.69	84	1	12	0	47	40	537	3.9	50	7	1,000	50	0.0	0.0
C / 5.1	3.4	5.3	10.69	7	1	12	0	47	40	537	3.9	73	7	0	0	0.0	0.0
C / 5.1	3.4	5.3	10.69	N/A	1	12	0	47	40	537	3.9	85	7	10,000,000	0	0.0	0.0
C / 5.1	3.4	5.3	10.69	243	1	12	0	47	40	537	3.9	90	7	10,000,000	0	0.0	0.0
C / 5.1	3.4	5.3	10.70	126	1	12	0	47	40	537	3.9	86	7	1,000	50	0.0	0.0
C- / 3.0	4.7	6.9	7.09	903	2	8	0	85	5	228	4.6	53	6	1,000	50	4.3	0.0
C- / 3.0	4.7	6.9	7.10	16	2	8	0	85	5	228	4.6	53	6	1,000	50	0.0	0.0
C- / 3.0	4.7	6.9	7.12	72	2	8	0	85	5	228	4.6	28	6	1,000	50	0.0	0.0
D+ / 2.9	4.8	6.9	7.09	7	2	8	0	85	5	228	4.6	51	6	0	0	0.0	0.0
D+ / 2.9	4.8	6.9	7.09	4	2	8	0	85	5	228	4.6	81	6	10,000,000	0	0.0	0.0
C- / 3.0	4.7	6.9	7.09	23	2	8	0	85	5	228	4.6	82	6	10,000,000	0	0.0	0.0
D+ / 2.9	4.8	6.9	7.10	29	2	8	0	85	5	228	4.6	58	6	1,000	50	0.0	0.0
E- / 0.2	10.0	5.5	6.38	6	6	66	0	27	1	50	6.9	0	3	1,000	50	4.3	0.0
E- / 0.2	10.0	5.5	6.38	N/A	6	66	0	27	1	50	6.9	0	3	1,000	50	0.0	0.0
E- / 0.2	9.9	5.5	6.39	1	6	66	0	27	1	50	6.9	0	3	1,000	50	0.0	0.0
E- / 0.2	9.9	5.5	6.37	N/A	6	66	0	27	1	50	6.9	0	3	0	0	0.0	0.0
E- / 0.2	9.9	5.5	6.38	N/A	6	66	0	27	1	50	6.9	0	3	10,000,000	0	0.0	0.0
E- / 0.2	10.0	5.5	6.37	60	6	66	0	27	1	50	6.9	0	3	10,000,000	0	0.0	0.0
E- / 0.2	9.9	5.5	6.38	N/A	6	66	0	27	1	50	6.9	0	3	1,000	50	0.0	0.0
C / 5.5	3.3	N/A	7.15	649	0	0	0	25	75	59	0.0	61	10	1,000	50	2.5	0.0
C / 5.4	3.3	N/A	7.12	452	0	0	0	25	75	59	0.0	43	10	1,000	50	0.0	0.0
C / 5.5	3.3	N/A	7.17	11	0	0	0	25	75	59	0.0	53	10	0	0	0.0	0.0
C / 5.3	3.3	N/A	7.16	3	0	0	0	25	75	59	0.0	76	10	10,000,000	0	0.0	0.0
C / 5.4	3.3	N/A	7.15	119	0	0	0	25	75	59	0.0	79	10	10,000,000	0	0.0	0.0
C / 5.5	3.3	N/A	7.14	568	0	0	0	25	75	59	0.0	76	10	1,000	50	0.0	0.0
A+ / 9.9	N/A	N/A	1.00	793	100	0	0	0	0	0	0.1	67	N/A	1,000,000	0	0.0	0.0
A+ / 9.9	N/A	N/A	1.00	160	100	0	0	0	0	0	0.1	67	N/A	1,000,000	0	0.0	0.0
A+ / 9.9	N/A	N/A	1.00	3,472	100	0	0	0	0	0	0.1	N/A	N/A	1,000,000	0	0.0	0.0
A+ / 9.9	N/A	N/A	1.00	10	100	0	0	0	0	0	0.1	67	N/A	1,000	0	0.0	0.0
A+ / 9.9	N/A	N/A	1.00	399	100	0	0	0	0	0	0.1	67	N/A	100,000	0	0.0	0.0
A+ / 9.9	N/A	N/A	1.00	59	100	0	0	0	0	0	0.1	67	N/A	1,000,000	0	0.0	0.0
A+ / 9.9	N/A	N/A	1.00	292	100	0	0	0	0	0	0.1	67	N/A	1,000	0	0.0	0.0
A+ / 9.9	N/A	N/A	1.00	N/A	100	0	0	0	0	0	0.1	69	N/A	1,000,000	0	0.0	0.0
A+ / 9.9	N/A	N/A	1.00	39	100	0	0	0	0	0	0.1	69	N/A	1,000,000	0	0.0	0.0
A+ / 9.9	N/A	N/A	1.00	17	100	0	0	0	0	0	0.2	69	N/A	1,000,000	0	0.0	0.0
A+ / 9.9	N/A	N/A	1.00	2	100	0	0	0	0	0	0.1	69	N/A	1,000	0	0.0	0.0
A+ / 9.9	N/A	N/A	1.00	6	100	0	0	0	0	0	0.1	69	N/A	100,000	0	0.0	0.0
A+ / 9.9	N/A	N/A	1.00	2	100	0	0	0	0	0	0.1	69	N/A	1,000,000	0	0.0	0.0
A+ / 9.9	N/A	N/A	1.00	46	100	0	0	0	0	0	0.1	69	N/A	1,000	0	0.0	0.0
D- / 1.0	6.0	4.2	3.94	757	3	0	0	93	4	110	6.4	44	11	1,000	50	4.3	0.0
D- / 1.1	6.0	4.2	3.95	10	3	0	0	93	4	110	6.4	23	11	1,000	50	0.0	0.0
D- / 1.0	6.0	4.2	3.93	97	3	0	0	93	4	110	6.4	22	11	1,000	50	0.0	0.0

Fund Type	Fund Name	Ticker Symbol	Overall Investment Rating	Phone	Performance Rating/Pts	3 Mo	6 Mo	1Yr / Pct	3Yr / Pct (Annualized)	5Yr / Pct (Annualized)	Dividend Yield	Expense Ratio
99 Pct = Best, 0 Pct = Worst					PERFORMANCE	Total Return % through 3/31/16					Incl. in Returns	
COH ●	Invesco High Yield Investor	HYINX	D-	(800) 959-4246	C- / 3.8	1.67	0.62	-4.14 / 7	1.25 /47	4.27 /65	5.91	0.97
* MUH●	Invesco High Yield Municipal A	ACTHX	C+	(800) 959-4246	A+ / 9.8	1.97	4.79	5.96 /99	5.60 /99	8.79 /99	4.62	0.93
MUH●	Invesco High Yield Municipal B	ACTGX	C+	(800) 959-4246	A+ / 9.9	1.96	4.78	5.95 /99	5.63 /99	8.86 /99	4.82	0.93
MUH●	Invesco High Yield Municipal C	ACTFX	C+	(800) 959-4246	A+ / 9.9	1.80	4.34	5.24 /98	4.84 /98	7.98 /98	4.15	1.67
MUH●	Invesco High Yield Municipal R5	ACTNX	C+	(800) 959-4246	A+ / 9.9	2.05	4.84	6.14 /99	5.84 /99	8.97 /99	5.09	0.68
MUH●	Invesco High Yield Municipal Y	ACTDX	C+	(800) 959-4246	A+ / 9.9	2.02	4.91	6.22 /99	5.86 /99	9.05 /99	5.07	0.68
COH	Invesco High Yield R5	AHIYX	D	(800) 959-4246	C / 4.4	1.75	0.77	-3.65 / 9	1.55 /53	4.56 /68	6.23	0.69
COH	Invesco High Yield R6	HYIFX	D	(800) 959-4246	C / 4.7	1.77	1.07	-3.54 / 9	1.72 /56	4.58 /68	6.31	0.61
COH	Invesco High Yield Y	AHHYX	D	(800) 959-4246	C / 4.3	1.47	0.73	-3.92 / 8	1.57 /53	4.51 /68	6.13	0.77
GEI	Invesco Income Allocation A	ALAAX	C-	(800) 959-4246	B- / 7.3	2.93	3.68	-0.05 /31	4.30 /86	5.83 /76	3.43	1.14
GEI ●	Invesco Income Allocation B	BLIAX	C-	(800) 959-4246	B / 7.9	2.70	3.26	-0.74 /24	3.54 /80	5.05 /72	2.85	1.89
GEI	Invesco Income Allocation C	CLIAX	C-	(800) 959-4246	B / 7.9	2.71	3.26	-0.83 /23	3.50 /80	5.03 /72	2.85	1.89
GEI	Invesco Income Allocation R	RLIAX	C	(800) 959-4246	B+ / 8.3	2.89	3.57	-0.28 /28	4.04 /84	5.57 /75	3.40	1.39
GEI	Invesco Income Allocation R5	ILAAX	C	(800) 959-4246	B+ / 8.6	2.98	3.79	0.09 /41	4.55 /88	6.09 /77	3.87	0.85
GEI	Invesco Income Allocation Y	ALAYX	C	(800) 959-4246	B+ / 8.6	2.98	3.79	0.18 /44	4.55 /88	6.07 /77	3.87	0.89
GL	Invesco Intl Tot Rtn Bd A	AUBAX	D	(800) 959-4246	C- / 4.1	7.51	5.84	3.49 /79	0.53 /34	1.13 /22	1.08	1.72
GL ●	Invesco Intl Tot Rtn Bd B	AUBBX	D	(800) 959-4246	C / 4.7	7.32	5.46	2.74 /76	-0.22 /14	0.39 /17	0.42	2.47
GL	Invesco Intl Tot Rtn Bd C	AUBCX	D	(800) 959-4246	C / 4.6	7.33	5.36	2.74 /76	-0.25 /13	0.35 /16	0.42	2.47
GL	Invesco Intl Tot Rtn Bd R5	AUBIX	D+	(800) 959-4246	C+ / 6.5	7.68	5.97	3.75 /80	0.78 /39	1.39 /24	1.37	1.16
GL	Invesco Intl Tot Rtn Bd R6	AUBFX	D+	(800) 959-4246	C+ / 6.5	7.68	5.97	3.85 /80	0.78 /39	1.31 /23	1.37	1.16
GL	Invesco Intl Tot Rtn Bd Y	AUBYX	D+	(800) 959-4246	C+ / 6.5	7.58	5.98	3.75 /80	0.78 /39	1.39 /24	1.37	1.47
* MUN	Invesco Intm Term Municipal Inc A	VKLMX	A+	(800) 959-4246	B+ / 8.6	1.58	3.05	3.45 /90	3.21 /90	4.89 /84	2.49	0.90
MUN●	Invesco Intm Term Municipal Inc B	VKLBX	A+	(800) 959-4246	A- / 9.2	1.56	3.01	3.52 /90	3.20 /90	4.87 /84	2.56	0.90
MUN	Invesco Intm Term Municipal Inc C	VKLCX	A	(800) 959-4246	B+ / 8.5	1.40	2.60	2.74 /82	2.46 /82	4.12 /78	1.88	1.62
MUN	Invesco Intm Term Municipal Inc Y	VKLIX	A+	(800) 959-4246	A / 9.3	1.55	3.08	3.70 /92	3.47 /92	5.14 /86	2.80	0.65
* MUN	Invesco Limited Term Muni Inc A	ATFAX	B+	(800) 959-4246	C+ / 5.9	0.91	1.44	1.69 /75	1.72 /73	3.81 /76	2.05	0.63
MUN●	Invesco Limited Term Muni Inc A2	AITFX	A+	(800) 959-4246	B- / 7.4	0.88	1.48	1.94 /77	1.95 /76	4.07 /78	2.33	0.38
MUN	Invesco Limited Term Muni Inc C	ATFCX	U	(800) 959-4246	U /	0.64	0.99	0.94 /65	--	--	1.37	1.38
MUN	Invesco Limited Term Muni Inc R5	ATFIX	A+	(800) 959-4246	B / 7.8	0.89	1.50	1.99 /77	2.00 /77	4.07 /78	2.40	0.36
MUN	Invesco Limited Term Muni Inc Y	ATFYX	A+	(800) 959-4246	B / 7.8	0.88	1.48	1.94 /77	1.98 /77	4.05 /78	2.35	0.38
MM	Invesco Liquid Assets Corp	LPCXX	C	(800) 959-4246	D+ / 2.6	0.09	0.13	0.17 /43	0.08 /26	0.09 /14	0.17	0.20
MM	Invesco Liquid Assets CshMgt		C	(800) 959-4246	D+ / 2.5	0.07	0.10	0.12 /42	0.05 /25	0.05 /12	0.12	0.27
MM	Invesco Liquid Assets Inst	LAPXX	C	(800) 959-4246	D+ / 2.7	0.09	0.14	0.20 /44	0.11 /27	0.12 /15	0.20	0.17
MM	Invesco Liquid Assets Psnl		C-	(800) 959-4246	D / 1.9	0.02	0.02	0.02 /34	0.02 /20	0.02 / 8	0.02	0.92
MM	Invesco Liquid Assets Pvt	LPVXX	C-	(800) 959-4246	D / 1.9	0.02	0.03	0.03 /36	0.02 /20	0.02 / 8	0.03	0.67
MM	Invesco Liquid Assets Rs		C	(800) 959-4246	D / 2.2	0.05	0.05	0.06 /39	0.03 /22	0.03 /10	0.06	0.37
MM	Invesco Liquid Assets Rsv		C-	(800) 959-4246	D / 1.9	0.02	0.02	0.02 /34	0.02 /20	0.02 / 8	0.02	1.17
MM ●	Invesco Money Market AX	ACZXX	U	(800) 959-4246	U /	--	--	--	--	--	0.06	0.82
MM ●	Invesco Money Market B		U	(800) 959-4246	U /	--	--	--	--	--	0.06	1.57
MM ●	Invesco Money Market BX	ACYXX	U	(800) 959-4246	U /	--	--	--	--	--	0.06	1.57
MM	Invesco Money Market C		U	(800) 959-4246	U /	--	--	--	--	--	0.06	1.57
MM	Invesco Money Market CashResrv	AIMXX	U	(800) 959-4246	U /	--	--	--	--	--	0.06	0.82
MM ●	Invesco Money Market CX	ACXXX	U	(800) 959-4246	U /	--	--	--	--	--	0.06	1.57
MM ●	Invesco Money Market Inv	INAXX	U	(800) 959-4246	U /	--	--	--	--	--	0.06	0.67
MM	Invesco Money Market R		U	(800) 959-4246	U /	--	--	--	--	--	0.06	1.07
MM	Invesco Money Market Y		U	(800) 959-4246	U /	--	--	--	--	--	0.06	0.67
* MUN	Invesco Municipal Income A	VKMMX	B	(800) 959-4246	A- / 9.0	1.81	3.58	4.26 /95	3.99 /96	6.51 /94	3.96	0.93
MUN●	Invesco Municipal Income B	VMIBX	B	(800) 959-4246	A- / 9.2	1.56	3.13	3.42 /89	3.17 /90	5.69 /90	3.40	1.68
MUN	Invesco Municipal Income C	VMICX	B	(800) 959-4246	A- / 9.2	1.64	3.21	3.49 /90	3.17 /90	5.68 /90	3.40	1.68
MUN	Invesco Municipal Income Inv	VMINX	U	(800) 959-4246	U /	1.86	3.66	4.40 /96	--	--	4.27	0.81
MUN	Invesco Municipal Income Y	VMIIX	A-	(800) 959-4246	A+ / 9.7	1.80	3.70	4.44 /96	4.23 /97	6.78 /96	4.38	0.68
MUS	Invesco NY Tax Free Income A	VNYAX	C+	(800) 959-4246	B+ / 8.3	1.45	3.16	3.78 /92	3.35 /91	6.17 /93	3.46	1.03

● Denotes fund is closed to new investors
* Denotes fund is included in Section II

RISK			NET ASSETS		ASSET							FUND MANAGER		MINIMUM		LOADS	
Risk Rating/Pts	3 Yr Avg Standard Deviation	Avg Duration	NAV As of 3/31/16	Total $(Mil)	Cash %	Gov. Bond %	Muni. Bond %	Corp. Bond %	Other %	Portfolio Turnover Ratio	Avg Coupon Rate	Manager Quality Pct	Manager Tenure (Years)	Initial Purch. $	Additional Purch. $	Front End Load	Back End Load
D- / 1.2	5.9	4.2	3.94	103	3	0	0	93	4	110	6.4	45	11	1,000	50	0.0	0.0
D- / 1.4	5.4	8.5	10.18	4,880	2	0	97	0	1	17	5.9	73	14	1,000	50	4.3	0.0
D- / 1.3	5.4	8.5	10.23	59	2	0	97	0	1	17	5.9	73	14	1,000	50	0.0	0.0
D- / 1.4	5.4	8.5	10.15	1,188	2	0	97	0	1	17	5.9	41	14	1,000	50	0.0	0.0
D- / 1.4	5.4	8.5	10.18	2	2	0	97	0	1	17	5.9	79	14	10,000,000	0	0.0	0.0
D- / 1.3	5.5	8.5	10.20	1,606	2	0	97	0	1	17	5.9	78	14	1,000	50	0.0	0.0
D- / 1.2	5.9	4.2	3.93	89	3	0	0	93	4	110	6.4	56	11	10,000,000	0	0.0	0.0
D- / 1.1	6.0	4.2	3.94	131	3	0	0	93	4	110	6.4	62	11	10,000,000	0	0.0	0.0
D- / 1.3	5.7	4.2	3.95	110	3	0	0	93	4	110	6.4	59	11	1,000	50	0.0	0.0
D+ / 2.4	5.4	4.5	10.88	306	6	8	0	34	52	1	7.8	95	N/A	1,000	50	5.5	0.0
D+ / 2.4	5.3	4.5	10.90	3	6	8	0	34	52	1	7.8	89	N/A	1,000	50	0.0	0.0
D+ / 2.4	5.3	4.5	10.89	105	6	8	0	34	52	1	7.8	89	N/A	1,000	50	0.0	0.0
D+ / 2.4	5.3	4.5	10.89	3	6	8	0	34	52	1	7.8	93	N/A	0	0	0.0	0.0
D+ / 2.4	5.4	4.5	10.88	1	6	8	0	34	52	1	7.8	96	N/A	10,000,000	0	0.0	0.0
D+ / 2.4	5.4	4.5	10.88	20	6	8	0	34	52	1	7.8	96	N/A	1,000	50	0.0	0.0
D- / 1.1	6.3	7.3	10.27	26	3	53	4	33	7	135	4.6	86	9	1,000	50	4.3	0.0
D- / 1.1	6.2	7.3	10.26	1	3	53	4	33	7	135	4.6	60	9	1,000	50	0.0	0.0
D- / 1.1	6.2	7.3	10.25	5	3	53	4	33	7	135	4.6	59	9	1,000	50	0.0	0.0
D- / 1.1	6.3	7.3	10.27	N/A	3	53	4	33	7	135	4.6	89	9	10,000,000	0	0.0	0.0
D- / 1.1	6.3	7.3	10.27	N/A	3	53	4	33	7	135	4.6	89	9	10,000,000	0	0.0	0.0
D- / 1.1	6.2	7.3	10.26	6	3	53	4	33	7	135	4.6	89	9	1,000	50	0.0	0.0
C+ / 6.5	3.0	5.0	11.32	655	1	0	97	0	2	12	4.6	69	11	1,000	50	2.5	0.0
C+ / 6.5	3.0	5.0	11.55	5	1	0	97	0	2	12	4.6	66	11	1,000	50	0.0	0.0
C+ / 6.4	3.0	5.0	11.29	210	1	0	97	0	2	12	4.6	37	11	1,000	50	0.0	0.0
C+ / 6.5	3.0	5.0	11.31	216	1	0	97	0	2	12	4.6	78	11	1,000	50	0.0	0.0
B+ / 8.3	2.2	3.0	11.55	1,206	0	0	97	0	3	15	4.0	44	5	1,000	50	2.5	0.0
B+ / 8.3	2.2	3.0	11.55	93	0	0	97	0	3	15	4.0	53	5	1,000	50	1.0	0.0
U /	N/A	3.0	11.54	282	0	0	97	0	3	15	4.0	N/A	5	1,000	50	0.0	0.0
B+ / 8.3	2.2	3.0	11.54	16	0	0	97	0	3	15	4.0	55	5	10,000,000	0	0.0	0.0
B+ / 8.3	2.2	3.0	11.54	706	0	0	97	0	3	15	4.0	53	5	1,000	50	0.0	0.0
A+ / 9.9	N/A	N/A	1.00	2,997	100	0	0	0	0	0	0.2	69	N/A	1,000,000	0	0.0	0.0
A+ / 9.9	N/A	N/A	1.00	186	100	0	0	0	0	0	0.1	N/A	N/A	1,000,000	0	0.0	0.0
A+ / 9.9	N/A	N/A	1.00	18,315	100	0	0	0	0	0	0.2	70	N/A	10,000,000	0	0.0	0.0
A+ / 9.9	N/A	N/A	1.00	64	100	0	0	0	0	0	0.0	N/A	N/A	1,000	0	0.0	0.0
A+ / 9.9	N/A	N/A	1.00	220	100	0	0	0	0	0	0.0	N/A	N/A	100,000	0	0.0	0.0
A+ / 9.9	N/A	N/A	1.00	13	100	0	0	0	0	0	0.1	65	N/A	1,000,000	0	0.0	0.0
A+ / 9.9	N/A	N/A	1.00	133	100	0	0	0	0	0	0.0	N/A	N/A	1,000	0	0.0	0.0
U /	N/A	N/A	1.00	117	100	0	0	0	0	0	0.1	70	N/A	1,000	50	0.0	0.0
U /	N/A	N/A	1.00	15	100	0	0	0	0	0	0.1	70	N/A	1,000	50	0.0	0.0
U /	N/A	N/A	1.00	2	100	0	0	0	0	0	0.1	70	N/A	1,000	50	0.0	0.0
U /	N/A	N/A	1.00	87	100	0	0	0	0	0	0.1	70	N/A	1,000	50	0.0	0.0
U /	N/A	N/A	1.00	782	100	0	0	0	0	0	0.1	70	N/A	1,000	50	0.0	0.0
U /	N/A	N/A	1.00	6	100	0	0	0	0	0	0.1	70	N/A	1,000	50	0.0	0.0
U /	N/A	N/A	1.00	150	100	0	0	0	0	0	0.1	70	N/A	1,000	50	0.0	0.0
U /	N/A	N/A	1.00	37	100	0	0	0	0	0	0.1	70	N/A	0	0	0.0	0.0
U /	N/A	N/A	1.00	24	100	0	0	0	0	0	0.1	70	N/A	1,000	50	0.0	0.0
C- / 4.0	4.0	6.7	13.75	1,792	2	0	97	0	1	10	5.3	57	11	1,000	50	4.3	0.0
C- / 4.0	4.0	6.7	13.71	9	2	0	97	0	1	10	5.3	29	11	1,000	50	0.0	0.0
C- / 4.0	4.0	6.7	13.68	167	2	0	97	0	1	10	5.3	29	11	1,000	50	0.0	0.0
U /	N/A	6.7	13.76	115	2	0	97	0	1	10	5.3	N/A	11	1,000	50	0.0	0.0
C- / 4.0	4.0	6.7	13.74	460	2	0	97	0	1	10	5.3	69	11	1,000	50	0.0	0.0
C- / 3.4	4.3	6.6	16.04	133	1	0	98	0	1	13	4.9	26	9	1,000	50	4.3	0.0

99 Pct = Best 0 Pct = Worst Fund Type	Fund Name	Ticker Symbol	Overall Investment Rating	Phone	PERFORMANCE Performance Rating/Pts	Total Return % through 3/31/16 3 Mo	6 Mo	1Yr / Pct	Annualized 3Yr / Pct	5Yr / Pct	Incl. in Returns Dividend Yield	Expense Ratio
MUS	● Invesco NY Tax Free Income B	VBNYX	**B**	(800) 959-4246	**A / 9.3**	1.44	3.16	3.78 /92	3.33 /91	6.29 /94	3.62	1.03
MUS	Invesco NY Tax Free Income C	VNYCX	**C+**	(800) 959-4246	**B+ / 8.6**	1.27	2.79	3.02 /85	2.56 /83	5.38 /88	2.88	1.78
MUS	Invesco NY Tax Free Income Y	VNYYX	**B**	(800) 959-4246	**A / 9.4**	1.57	3.36	4.10 /94	3.61 /93	6.43 /94	3.86	0.78
MUS	Invesco PA Tax Free Income A	VKMPX	**C+**	(800) 959-4246	**B / 8.1**	1.47	3.19	3.72 /92	3.06 /89	5.86 /91	3.29	1.04
MUS	● Invesco PA Tax Free Income B	VKPAX	**B-**	(800) 959-4246	**A- / 9.1**	1.48	3.13	3.66 /92	3.06 /89	5.97 /92	3.45	1.04
MUS	Invesco PA Tax Free Income C	VKPCX	**C+**	(800) 959-4246	**B+ / 8.4**	1.30	2.83	2.93 /84	2.32 /81	5.09 /86	2.75	1.79
MUS	Invesco PA Tax Free Income Y	VKPYX	**B-**	(800) 959-4246	**A / 9.3**	1.60	3.32	3.98 /94	3.34 /91	6.15 /93	3.69	0.79
MM	Invesco Premier Portfoilo Inst	IPPXX	**C**	(800) 959-4246	**D+ / 2.5**	0.08	0.12	0.15 /43	0.07 /26	0.08 /14	0.15	0.25
MMT	Invesco Premier Tax-Ex Port Inst	PEIXX	**C**	(800) 959-4246	**D / 2.1**	0.00	0.01	0.03 /38	0.02 /22	0.02 /10	0.03	0.25
MM	Invesco Premier US Gv Mny Port Inst	IUGXX	**C**	(800) 959-4246	**D / 2.2**	0.04	0.06	0.07 /40	0.03 /22	0.03 /10	0.07	0.25
GL	Invesco Premium Income A	PIAFX	**D**	(800) 959-4246	**C / 4.8**	2.82	3.33	-0.50 /26	2.68 /73	--	4.75	1.28
GL	Invesco Premium Income C	PICFX	**D+**	(800) 959-4246	**C+ / 6.0**	2.59	2.90	-1.20 /20	1.93 /60	--	4.22	2.03
GL	Invesco Premium Income R	PIRFX	**D+**	(800) 959-4246	**C+ / 6.9**	2.78	3.22	-0.73 /24	2.46 /70	--	4.80	1.53
GL	Invesco Premium Income R5	IPNFX	**C-**	(800) 959-4246	**B / 7.6**	2.87	3.44	-0.26 /28	2.97 /76	--	5.26	0.90
GL	Invesco Premium Income R6	PIFFX	**C-**	(800) 959-4246	**B / 7.6**	2.87	3.44	-0.26 /28	2.97 /76	--	5.26	0.90
GL	Invesco Premium Income Y	PIYFX	**C-**	(800) 959-4246	**B / 7.6**	2.87	3.44	-0.17 /30	2.97 /76	--	5.26	1.03
LP	Invesco Senior Loan A	VSLAX	**D-**	(800) 959-4246	**E+ / 0.9**	0.71	-2.68	-5.42 / 4	0.83 /39	3.49 /53	5.99	1.92
LP	Invesco Senior Loan B	VSLBX	**D-**	(800) 959-4246	**D / 1.6**	0.71	-2.68	-5.42 / 4	0.74 /38	3.25 /49	6.19	2.67
LP	Invesco Senior Loan C	VSLCX	**D-**	(800) 959-4246	**D- / 1.1**	0.70	-2.87	-5.95 / 3	0.19 /29	2.78 /41	5.39	2.67
LP	Invesco Senior Loan IB	XPRTX	**D**	(800) 959-4246	**D+ / 2.6**	0.78	-2.55	-5.16 / 5	1.09 /44	3.66 /56	6.46	1.67
LP	Invesco Senior Loan IC	XSLCX	**D**	(800) 959-4246	**D / 2.2**	0.91	-2.62	-5.30 / 4	0.99 /42	3.59 /55	6.30	1.82
MUH	Invesco Sh Dur High Yield Muni A	ISHAX	**U**	(800) 959-4246	**U /**	1.67	3.69	--	--	--	0.00	1.77
MUH	Invesco Sh Dur High Yield Muni C	ISHCX	**U**	(800) 959-4246	**U /**	1.40	3.24	--	--	--	0.00	2.52
MUH	Invesco Sh Dur High Yield Muni R5	ISHFX	**U**	(800) 959-4246	**U /**	1.63	3.77	--	--	--	0.00	1.52
MUH	Invesco Sh Dur High Yield Muni Y	ISHYX	**U**	(800) 959-4246	**U /**	1.63	3.77	--	--	--	0.00	1.52
US	Invesco Sh Dur Infl Pro A	LMTAX	**C**	(800) 959-4246	**C- / 3.0**	2.22	1.83	1.83 /70	0.53 /34	0.47 /17	0.20	0.92
US	● Invesco Sh Dur Infl Pro A2	SHTIX	**C+**	(800) 959-4246	**C- / 3.8**	2.24	1.81	1.91 /71	0.55 /34	0.49 /17	0.22	0.82
US	Invesco Sh Dur Infl Pro R5	ALMIX	**B**	(800) 959-4246	**C / 4.5**	2.38	1.94	1.97 /72	0.61 /35	0.54 /17	0.29	0.59
US	Invesco Sh Dur Infl Pro Y	LMTYX	**B-**	(800) 959-4246	**C / 4.4**	2.28	1.80	1.90 /71	0.55 /34	0.50 /17	0.26	0.67
GEI	Invesco Short Term Bond A	STBAX	**C+**	(800) 959-4246	**C- / 3.3**	1.01	0.73	0.56 /51	1.09 /44	1.63 /27	1.91	0.69
GEI	Invesco Short Term Bond C	STBCX	**C+**	(800) 959-4246	**C- / 3.9**	0.93	0.68	0.33 /46	0.74 /38	1.29 /23	1.62	1.19
GEI	Invesco Short Term Bond R	STBRX	**C+**	(800) 959-4246	**C- / 3.8**	0.92	0.56	0.22 /44	0.74 /38	1.29 /23	1.62	1.04
GEI	Invesco Short Term Bond R5	ISTBX	**B+**	(800) 959-4246	**C / 4.9**	0.95	0.86	0.82 /56	1.26 /47	1.80 /29	2.22	0.44
COI	Invesco Short Term Bond R6	ISTFX	**B+**	(800) 959-4246	**C / 5.1**	1.07	0.98	0.94 /57	1.35 /49	1.70 /28	2.22	0.43
GEI	Invesco Short Term Bond Y	STBYX	**B+**	(800) 959-4246	**C / 4.8**	1.04	0.81	0.71 /53	1.25 /47	1.79 /29	2.11	0.54
MM	Invesco STIC Prime Corp	SSCXX	**C**	(800) 959-4246	**D+ / 2.6**	0.07	0.10	0.18 /44	0.10 /27	0.09 /14	0.18	0.22
MM	Invesco STIC Prime CshMgt		**C**	(800) 959-4246	**D+ / 2.6**	0.06	0.08	0.16 /43	0.09 /27	0.08 /14	0.16	0.29
MM	Invesco STIC Prime Inst	SRIXX	**C**	(800) 959-4246	**D+ / 2.6**	0.08	0.11	0.19 /44	0.10 /27	0.09 /14	0.19	0.19
MM	Invesco STIC Prime Psnl		**C**	(800) 959-4246	**D+ / 2.5**	0.04	0.06	0.14 /42	0.08 /26	0.07 /14	0.14	0.94
MM	Invesco STIC Prime Pvt	SPVXX	**C**	(800) 959-4246	**D+ / 2.5**	0.04	0.06	0.14 /42	0.08 /26	0.07 /14	0.14	0.69
MM	Invesco STIC Prime Rs		**C**	(800) 959-4246	**D+ / 2.5**	0.05	0.07	0.15 /43	0.07 /26	0.07 /14	0.15	0.39
MM	Invesco STIC Prime Rsv		**C**	(800) 959-4246	**D+ / 2.5**	0.04	0.06	0.14 /42	0.08 /27	0.07 /14	0.14	1.19
GL	Invesco Strategic Income A	SIZAX	**U**	(800) 959-4246	**U /**	-3.83	-3.57	-4.27 / 7	--	--	3.30	2.04
GL	Invesco Strategic Income C	SIZCX	**U**	(800) 959-4246	**U /**	-4.16	-4.08	-5.03 / 5	--	--	2.61	2.79
GL	Invesco Strategic Income R	SIZRX	**U**	(800) 959-4246	**U /**	-4.08	-3.88	-4.69 / 6	--	--	3.10	2.29
GL	Invesco Strategic Income R5	SIZFX	**U**	(800) 959-4246	**U /**	-3.89	-3.57	-4.04 / 8	--	--	3.70	1.83
GL	Invesco Strategic Income R6	SIZSX	**U**	(800) 959-4246	**U /**	-3.79	-3.57	-4.04 / 8	--	--	3.70	1.83
GL	Invesco Strategic Income Y	SIZYX	**U**	(800) 959-4246	**U /**	-3.79	-3.57	-4.04 / 8	--	--	3.69	1.79
GEI	Invesco Strategic Real Return A	SRRAX	**U**	(800) 959-4246	**U /**	2.98	1.77	-1.16 /20	--	--	2.91	2.47
GEI	Invesco Strategic Real Return C	SRRCX	**U**	(800) 959-4246	**U /**	2.74	1.34	-1.95 /16	--	--	2.18	3.22
GEI	Invesco Strategic Real Return R	SRRQX	**U**	(800) 959-4246	**U /**	2.83	1.56	-1.49 /18	--	--	2.64	2.72
GEI	Invesco Strategic Real Return R5	SRRFX	**U**	(800) 959-4246	**U /**	3.02	1.88	-0.93 /22	--	--	3.22	2.39

● Denotes fund is closed to new investors
* Denotes fund is included in Section II

RISK			NET ASSETS		ASSET							FUND MANAGER		MINIMUM		LOADS	
Risk Rating/Pts	3 Yr Avg Standard Deviation	Avg Duration	NAV As of 3/31/16	Total $(Mil)	Cash %	Gov. Bond %	Muni. Bond %	Corp. Bond %	Other %	Portfolio Turnover Ratio	Avg Coupon Rate	Manager Quality Pct	Manager Tenure (Years)	Initial Purch. $	Additional Purch. $	Front End Load	Back End Load
C- / 3.4	4.3	6.6	16.07	2	1	0	98	0	1	13	4.9	25	9	1,000	50	0.0	0.0
C- / 3.4	4.3	6.6	16.02	26	1	0	98	0	1	13	4.9	13	9	1,000	50	0.0	0.0
C- / 3.4	4.3	6.6	16.03	15	1	0	98	0	1	13	4.9	33	9	1,000	50	0.0	0.0
C- / 3.3	4.2	7.1	16.70	115	2	0	97	0	1	13	5.1	23	7	1,000	50	4.3	0.0
C- / 3.3	4.2	7.1	16.73	1	2	0	97	0	1	13	5.1	23	7	1,000	50	0.0	0.0
C- / 3.3	4.3	7.1	16.72	10	2	0	97	0	1	13	5.1	12	7	1,000	50	0.0	0.0
C- / 3.3	4.3	7.1	16.72	4	2	0	97	0	1	13	5.1	29	7	1,000	50	0.0	0.0
A+ / 9.9	N/A	N/A	1.00	8,324	100	0	0	0	0	0	0.2	67	N/A	1,000,000	0	0.0	0.0
A+ / 9.9	N/A	N/A	1.00	130	100	0	0	0	0	0	0.0	67	N/A	1,000,000	0	0.0	0.0
A+ / 9.9	N/A	N/A	1.00	2,048	100	0	0	0	0	0	0.1	N/A	N/A	1,000,000	0	0.0	0.0
D- / 1.1	6.4	4.7	9.90	49	6	16	0	34	44	120	6.1	98	3	1,000	50	5.5	0.0
D- / 1.2	6.4	4.7	9.90	16	6	16	0	34	44	120	6.1	96	3	1,000	50	0.0	0.0
D- / 1.2	6.4	4.7	9.90	N/A	6	16	0	34	44	120	6.1	97	3	0	0	0.0	0.0
D- / 1.1	6.4	4.7	9.91	N/A	6	16	0	34	44	120	6.1	98	3	10,000,000	0	0.0	0.0
D- / 1.2	6.4	4.7	9.91	41	6	16	0	34	44	120	6.1	98	3	10,000,000	0	0.0	0.0
D- / 1.2	6.4	4.7	9.91	11	6	16	0	34	44	120	6.1	98	3	1,000	50	0.0	0.0
C- / 3.7	4.2	N/A	6.02	117	0	0	0	74	26	59	0.0	54	9	1,000	100	3.3	0.0
C- / 3.6	4.2	N/A	6.02	2	0	0	0	74	26	59	0.0	49	9	1,000	100	0.0	0.0
C- / 3.6	4.2	N/A	6.04	117	0	0	0	74	26	59	0.0	32	9	1,000	100	0.0	0.0
C- / 3.6	4.2	N/A	6.03	538	0	0	0	74	26	59	0.0	61	9	1,000	100	0.0	0.0
C- / 3.6	4.2	N/A	6.03	45	0	0	0	74	26	59	0.0	57	9	1,000	100	0.0	0.0
U /	N/A	N/A	10.26	21	0	0	0	0	100	0	0.0	N/A	1	1,000	50	2.5	0.0
U /	N/A	N/A	10.24	8	0	0	0	0	100	0	0.0	N/A	1	1,000	50	0.0	0.0
U /	N/A	N/A	10.26	1	0	0	0	0	100	0	0.0	N/A	1	10,000,000	0	0.0	0.0
U /	N/A	N/A	10.26	10	0	0	0	0	100	0	0.0	N/A	1	1,000	50	0.0	0.0
A / 9.4	0.9	1.5	10.60	34	0	100	0	0	0	106	0.6	74	7	1,000	50	2.5	0.0
A / 9.4	0.9	1.5	10.60	25	0	100	0	0	0	106	0.6	78	7	1,000	50	1.0	0.0
A / 9.3	1.0	1.5	10.61	1	0	100	0	0	0	106	0.6	75	7	10,000,000	0	0.0	0.0
A / 9.4	0.9	1.5	10.60	14	0	100	0	0	0	106	0.6	74	7	1,000	50	0.0	0.0
A- / 9.2	1.1	2.0	8.54	387	4	11	0	56	29	250	2.7	82	7	1,000	50	2.5	0.0
A- / 9.2	1.1	2.0	8.54	445	4	11	0	56	29	250	2.7	75	7	1,000	50	0.0	0.0
A / 9.3	1.0	2.0	8.55	4	4	11	0	56	29	250	2.7	73	7	0	0	0.0	0.0
A / 9.3	1.0	2.0	8.53	1	4	11	0	56	29	250	2.7	86	7	10,000,000	0	0.0	0.0
A / 9.3	1.0	2.0	8.55	64	4	11	0	56	29	250	2.7	88	7	10,000,000	0	0.0	0.0
A / 9.3	1.0	2.0	8.54	58	4	11	0	56	29	250	2.7	85	7	1,000	50	0.0	0.0
A+ / 9.9	N/A	N/A	1.00	96	100	0	0	0	0	0	0.2	70	N/A	1,000,000	0	0.0	0.0
A+ / 9.9	N/A	N/A	1.00	449	100	0	0	0	0	0	0.2	70	N/A	1,000,000	0	0.0	0.0
A+ / 9.9	N/A	N/A	1.00	1,863	100	0	0	0	0	0	0.2	70	N/A	1,000,000	0	0.0	0.0
A+ / 9.9	N/A	N/A	1.00	111	100	0	0	0	0	0	0.1	70	N/A	1,000	0	0.0	0.0
A+ / 9.9	N/A	N/A	1.00	165	100	0	0	0	0	0	0.1	70	N/A	100,000	0	0.0	0.0
A+ / 9.9	N/A	N/A	1.00	17	100	0	0	0	0	0	0.2	69	N/A	1,000,000	0	0.0	0.0
A+ / 9.9	N/A	N/A	1.00	28	100	0	0	0	0	0	0.1	70	N/A	1,000	0	0.0	0.0
U /	N/A	N/A	9.20	19	4	8	1	27	60	145	0.0	N/A	2	1,000	50	4.3	0.0
U /	N/A	N/A	9.19	4	4	8	1	27	60	145	0.0	N/A	2	1,000	50	0.0	0.0
U /	N/A	N/A	9.19	N/A	4	8	1	27	60	145	0.0	N/A	2	0	0	0.0	0.0
U /	N/A	N/A	9.20	N/A	4	8	1	27	60	145	0.0	N/A	2	10,000,000	0	0.0	0.0
U /	N/A	N/A	9.20	N/A	4	8	1	27	60	145	0.0	N/A	2	10,000,000	0	0.0	0.0
U /	N/A	N/A	9.20	12	4	8	1	27	60	145	0.0	N/A	2	1,000	50	0.0	0.0
U /	N/A	N/A	9.45	10	2	44	0	27	27	25	0.0	N/A	2	1,000	50	2.5	0.0
U /	N/A	N/A	9.44	N/A	2	44	0	27	27	25	0.0	N/A	2	1,000	50	0.0	0.0
U /	N/A	N/A	9.45	N/A	2	44	0	27	27	25	0.0	N/A	2	0	0	0.0	0.0
U /	N/A	N/A	9.45	N/A	2	44	0	27	27	25	0.0	N/A	2	10,000,000	0	0.0	0.0

Fund Type	Fund Name (99 Pct = Best, 0 Pct = Worst)	Ticker Symbol	Overall Investment Rating	Phone	PERFORMANCE: Performance Rating/Pts	Total Return % through 3/31/16: 3 Mo	6 Mo	1Yr / Pct	Annualized: 3Yr / Pct	Annualized: 5Yr / Pct	Incl. in Returns: Dividend Yield	Incl. in Returns: Expense Ratio
GEI	Invesco Strategic Real Return R6	SRRSX	**U**	(800) 959-4246	**U** /	3.02	1.88	-0.93 /22	--	--	3.22	2.39
GEI	Invesco Strategic Real Return Y	SRRYX	**U**	(800) 959-4246	**U** /	3.02	1.88	-0.93 /22	--	--	3.21	2.22
MMT	Invesco Tax-Exempt Cash A	ACSXX	**U**	(800) 959-4246	**U** /	--	--	--	--	--	0.11	0.74
MMT ●	Invesco Tax-Exempt Cash Inv	TEIXX	**U**	(800) 959-4246	**U** /	--	--	--	--	--	0.11	0.64
MMT	Invesco Tax-Exempt Cash Y		**U**	(800) 959-4246	**U** /	--	--	--	--	--	0.11	0.64
MMT	Invesco Tax-Free Cash Rsv Corp	TFOXX	**U**	(800) 959-4246	**U** /	--	--	--	--	--	0.01	0.33
MMT	Invesco Tax-Free Cash Rsv CshMgt		**U**	(800) 959-4246	**U** /	--	--	--	--	--	0.01	0.40
MMT	Invesco Tax-Free Cash Rsv Inst	TFPXX	**U**	(800) 959-4246	**U** /	--	--	--	--	--	0.01	0.30
MMT	Invesco Tax-Free Cash Rsv Psnl		**U**	(800) 959-4246	**U** /	--	--	--	--	--	0.01	1.05
MM	Invesco Treasury Corp	TYCXX	**C**	(800) 959-4246	**D** / **2.2**	0.04	0.05	0.06 /39	0.03 /22	0.03 /10	0.06	0.21
MM	Invesco Treasury CshMgt		**C**	(800) 959-4246	**D** / **2.2**	0.03	0.03	0.05 /38	0.03 /22	0.03 /10	0.05	0.28
MM	Invesco Treasury Inst	TRPXX	**C**	(800) 959-4246	**D** / **2.2**	0.05	0.06	0.07 /40	0.03 /22	0.03 /10	0.07	0.18
MM	Invesco Treasury Psnl		**C**	(800) 959-4246	**D** / **2.1**	0.02	0.03	0.04 /37	0.02 /20	0.03 /10	0.04	0.93
MM	Invesco Treasury Pvt	TPFXX	**C**	(800) 959-4246	**D** / **2.1**	0.02	0.03	0.04 /37	0.02 /20	0.02 / 8	0.04	0.68
MM	Invesco Treasury Rs		**C**	(800) 959-4246	**D** / **2.1**	0.02	0.03	0.04 /37	0.02 /20	0.03 /10	0.04	0.38
MM	Invesco Treasury Rsv		**C**	(800) 959-4246	**D** / **2.1**	0.02	0.03	0.04 /37	0.02 /20	0.03 /10	0.04	1.18
* USS	Invesco US Government A	AGOVX	**C-**	(800) 959-4246	**C-** / **3.2**	2.45	1.54	1.27 /63	1.26 /47	2.55 /38	1.51	0.96
USS ●	Invesco US Government B	AGVBX	**C-**	(800) 959-4246	**C-** / **3.8**	2.27	1.17	0.41 /48	0.51 /33	1.78 /28	0.84	1.71
USS	Invesco US Government C	AGVCX	**C-**	(800) 959-4246	**C-** / **3.8**	2.28	1.06	0.41 /48	0.51 /33	1.78 /28	0.84	1.71
USS ●	Invesco US Government Investor	AGIVX	**C+**	(800) 959-4246	**C** / **5.3**	2.46	1.55	1.29 /63	1.27 /48	2.57 /39	1.60	0.92
USS	Invesco US Government R	AGVRX	**C+**	(800) 959-4246	**C** / **4.8**	2.39	1.41	1.02 /59	1.01 /43	2.31 /35	1.33	1.21
USS	Invesco US Government R5	AGOIX	**B**	(800) 959-4246	**C+** / **5.9**	2.54	1.60	1.63 /68	1.61 /54	2.93 /44	1.93	0.60
USS	Invesco US Government Y	AGVYX	**B-**	(800) 959-4246	**C+** / **5.7**	2.51	1.55	1.41 /65	1.51 /52	2.80 /42	1.82	0.71
USS	Invesco US Mortgage A	VKMGX	**B**	(800) 959-4246	**C+** / **5.6**	1.94	1.73	2.37 /74	2.61 /72	3.34 /51	3.72	0.96
USS ●	Invesco US Mortgage B	VUSBX	**B+**	(800) 959-4246	**C+** / **6.1**	1.76	1.36	1.60 /68	1.83 /58	2.58 /39	3.13	1.72
USS	Invesco US Mortgage C	VUSCX	**B+**	(800) 959-4246	**C+** / **6.1**	1.68	1.27	1.60 /68	1.83 /58	2.56 /39	3.13	1.72
MTG	Invesco US Mortgage R5	VUSJX	**A+**	(800) 959-4246	**B** / **7.7**	2.03	1.82	2.69 /75	2.91 /75	3.62 /55	4.19	0.67
USS	Invesco US Mortgage Y	VUSIX	**A+**	(800) 959-4246	**B** / **7.7**	1.99	1.85	2.62 /75	2.87 /75	3.61 /55	4.12	0.72
GEN	Iron Strategic Income Fd Inst	IFUNX	**D+**	(800) 408-4682	**C-** / **3.0**	1.57	0.52	-2.46 /13	0.89 /41	2.15 /33	2.91	1.57
GEN	Iron Strategic Income Fd Inv	IRNIX	**D**	(800) 408-4682	**D** / **2.2**	1.56	0.43	-2.72 /12	0.56 /34	1.80 /29	2.59	1.92
* GEI	Ivy Bond A	IBOAX	**D+**	(800) 777-6472	**C-** / **3.5**	2.38	1.41	0.18 /44	2.05 /62	3.83 /59	2.29	1.02
GEI ●	Ivy Bond B	IBOBX	**C-**	(800) 777-6472	**C** / **4.5**	2.15	0.93	-0.75 /24	1.09 /44	2.82 /42	1.50	2.00
GEI	Ivy Bond C	IBOCX	**C-**	(800) 777-6472	**C** / **4.8**	2.21	1.04	-0.57 /25	1.27 /48	3.05 /46	1.68	1.80
GEI	Ivy Bond Fund Y	IBOYX	**C+**	(800) 777-6472	**C+** / **6.3**	2.39	1.43	0.22 /44	2.09 /63	3.88 /60	2.47	0.99
GEI	Ivy Bond I	IVBIX	**C+**	(800) 777-6472	**C+** / **6.7**	2.45	1.54	0.45 /49	2.34 /68	4.15 /64	2.70	0.74
COI	Ivy Bond R	IYBDX	**C**	(800) 777-6472	**C+** / **5.7**	2.31	1.25	-0.14 /30	1.74 /56	--	2.11	1.32
COI	Ivy Bond R6	IBNDX	**C+**	(800) 777-6472	**C+** / **6.8**	2.49	1.61	0.60 /51	2.43 /69	4.20 /64	2.85	0.58
EM	Ivy Emerging Mkts Loc Curr Debt A	IECAX	**U**	(800) 777-6472	**U** /	8.67	8.14	-0.79 /23	--	--	0.00	2.00
EM	Ivy Emerging Mkts Loc Curr Debt C	IECCX	**U**	(800) 777-6472	**U** /	8.49	7.82	-1.47 /19	--	--	0.00	2.50
EM	Ivy Emerging Mkts Loc Curr Debt E	IECEX	**U**	(800) 777-6472	**U** /	8.67	8.14	-0.79 /23	--	--	0.00	1.72
EM	Ivy Emerging Mkts Loc Curr Debt I	IECIX	**U**	(800) 777-6472	**U** /	8.78	8.37	-0.45 /26	--	--	0.00	1.62
EM	Ivy Emerging Mkts Loc Curr Debt R	IECRX	**U**	(800) 777-6472	**U** /	8.70	8.16	-0.91 /22	--	--	0.00	2.33
EM	Ivy Emerging Mkts Loc Curr Debt R6	IMMCX	**U**	(800) 777-6472	**U** /	8.78	8.37	-0.45 /26	--	--	0.00	1.47
EM	Ivy Emerging Mkts Loc Curr Debt Y	IECYX	**U**	(800) 777-6472	**U** /	8.67	8.14	-0.79 /23	--	--	0.00	1.86
GEI	Ivy Fond E	IVBEX	**D+**	(800) 777-6472	**C-** / **3.3**	2.37	1.40	0.12 /42	1.96 /61	3.75 /57	2.23	1.35
GL	Ivy Global Bond A	IVSAX	**D-**	(800) 777-6472	**E+** / **0.6**	2.40	2.58	-1.54 /18	-0.48 /12	1.26 /23	2.80	1.22
GL ●	Ivy Global Bond B	IVSBX	**D-**	(800) 777-6472	**E+** / **0.9**	2.22	2.19	-2.29 /14	-1.26 / 7	0.48 /17	2.19	2.10
GL	Ivy Global Bond C	IVSCX	**D-**	(800) 777-6472	**E+** / **0.9**	2.11	2.08	-2.39 /14	-1.26 / 7	0.48 /17	2.19	1.87
GL	Ivy Global Bond I	IVSIX	**D-**	(800) 777-6472	**D** / **1.9**	2.48	2.61	-1.39 /19	-0.27 /13	1.49 /26	3.23	0.87
GL	Ivy Global Bond R	IYGOX	**D-**	(800) 777-6472	**D-** / **1.1**	2.29	2.33	-2.03 /15	-1.01 / 8	--	2.47	1.46
GL	Ivy Global Bond R6	IVBDX	**D**	(800) 777-6472	**D+** / **2.4**	2.47	2.71	-1.30 /20	-0.23 /14	1.51 /26	3.22	0.70
GL	Ivy Global Bond Y	IVSYX	**D-**	(800) 777-6472	**D-** / **1.5**	2.40	2.58	-1.54 /18	-0.52 /11	1.24 /23	2.97	1.12

● Denotes fund is closed to new investors
* Denotes fund is included in Section II

RISK			NET ASSETS		ASSET							FUND MANAGER		MINIMUM		LOADS	
Risk Rating/Pts	3 Yr Avg Standard Deviation	Avg Duration	NAV As of 3/31/16	Total $(Mil)	Cash %	Gov. Bond %	Muni. Bond %	Corp. Bond %	Other %	Portfolio Turnover Ratio	Avg Coupon Rate	Manager Quality Pct	Manager Tenure (Years)	Initial Purch. $	Additional Purch. $	Front End Load	Back End Load
U /	N/A	N/A	9.45	N/A	2	44	0	27	27	25	0.0	N/A	2	10,000,000	0	0.0	0.0
U /	N/A	N/A	9.45	7	2	44	0	27	27	25	0.0	N/A	2	1,000	50	0.0	0.0
U /	N/A	N/A	1.00	38	100	0	0	0	0	0	0.1	72	N/A	1,000	50	0.0	0.0
U /	N/A	N/A	1.00	7	100	0	0	0	0	0	0.1	72	N/A	1,000	50	0.0	0.0
U /	N/A	N/A	1.00	13	100	0	0	0	0	0	0.1	72	N/A	1,000	50	0.0	0.0
U /	N/A	N/A	1.00	1	100	0	0	0	0	0	0.0	67	N/A	1,000,000	0	0.0	0.0
U /	N/A	N/A	1.00	44	100	0	0	0	0	0	0.0	67	N/A	1,000,000	0	0.0	0.0
U /	N/A	N/A	1.00	565	100	0	0	0	0	0	0.0	67	N/A	1,000,000	0	0.0	0.0
U /	N/A	N/A	1.00	3	100	0	0	0	0	0	0.0	67	N/A	10,000	0	0.0	0.0
A+ / 9.9	N/A	N/A	1.00	1,727	100	0	0	0	0	0	0.1	N/A	N/A	1,000,000	0	0.0	0.0
A+ / 9.9	N/A	N/A	1.00	4,398	100	0	0	0	0	0	0.1	N/A	N/A	1,000,000	0	0.0	0.0
A+ / 9.9	N/A	N/A	1.00	6,989	100	0	0	0	0	0	0.1	N/A	N/A	1,000,000	0	0.0	0.0
A+ / 9.9	N/A	N/A	1.00	123	100	0	0	0	0	0	0.0	N/A	N/A	1,000	0	0.0	0.0
A+ / 9.9	N/A	N/A	1.00	449	100	0	0	0	0	0	0.0	N/A	N/A	100,000	0	0.0	0.0
A+ / 9.9	N/A	N/A	1.00	332	100	0	0	0	0	0	0.0	N/A	N/A	1,000,000	0	0.0	0.0
A+ / 9.9	N/A	N/A	1.00	33	100	0	0	0	0	0	0.0	N/A	N/A	1,000	0	0.0	0.0
B- / 7.5	2.7	5.0	9.05	626	8	44	0	5	43	76	2.6	40	7	1,000	50	4.3	0.0
B- / 7.4	2.7	5.0	9.08	10	8	44	0	5	43	76	2.6	20	7	1,000	50	0.0	0.0
B- / 7.4	2.7	5.0	9.04	48	8	44	0	5	43	76	2.6	20	7	1,000	50	0.0	0.0
B- / 7.4	2.7	5.0	9.06	41	8	44	0	5	43	76	2.6	40	7	1,000	50	0.0	0.0
B- / 7.4	2.7	5.0	9.06	6	8	44	0	5	43	76	2.6	32	7	0	0	0.0	0.0
B- / 7.5	2.7	5.0	9.05	2	8	44	0	5	43	76	2.6	51	7	10,000,000	0	0.0	0.0
B- / 7.4	2.7	5.0	9.06	19	8	44	0	5	43	76	2.6	49	7	1,000	50	0.0	0.0
B / 8.2	2.2	4.5	12.35	402	0	0	0	2	98	500	3.8	92	N/A	1,000	50	4.3	0.0
B / 8.2	2.2	4.5	12.29	1	0	0	0	2	98	500	3.8	83	N/A	1,000	50	0.0	0.0
B / 8.2	2.3	4.5	12.26	13	0	0	0	2	98	500	3.8	83	N/A	1,000	50	0.0	0.0
B / 8.2	2.3	4.5	12.39	131	0	0	0	2	98	500	3.8	83	N/A	10,000,000	0	0.0	0.0
B / 8.2	2.2	4.5	12.40	26	0	0	0	2	98	500	3.8	93	N/A	1,000	50	0.0	0.0
C / 5.1	3.4	N/A	10.34	154	30	3	0	51	16	191	0.0	79	10	10,000	1,000	0.0	1.0
C / 5.0	3.5	N/A	10.42	9	30	3	0	51	16	191	0.0	62	10	10,000	1,000	0.0	1.0
C+ / 5.8	3.2	5.5	10.54	702	0	12	1	46	41	182	4.2	43	13	750	0	5.8	0.0
C+ / 5.8	3.2	5.5	10.54	7	0	12	1	46	41	182	4.2	19	13	750	0	0.0	0.0
C+ / 5.9	3.2	5.5	10.54	34	0	12	1	46	41	182	4.2	22	13	750	0	0.0	0.0
C+ / 5.9	3.2	5.5	10.54	3	0	12	1	46	41	182	4.2	45	13	10,000,000	0	0.0	0.0
C+ / 5.8	3.2	5.5	10.54	14	0	12	1	46	41	182	4.2	54	9	0	0	0.0	0.0
C+ / 5.8	3.2	5.5	10.54	3	0	12	1	46	41	182	4.2	51	13	0	0	0.0	0.0
C+ / 5.9	3.2	5.5	10.54	2	0	12	1	46	41	182	4.2	80	13	1,000,000	0	0.0	0.0
U /	N/A	4.5	8.77	20	4	79	0	11	6	40	5.0	N/A	N/A	750	0	5.8	0.0
U /	N/A	4.5	8.69	2	4	79	0	11	6	40	5.0	N/A	N/A	750	0	0.0	0.0
U /	N/A	4.5	8.77	2	4	79	0	11	6	40	5.0	N/A	N/A	750	0	5.8	0.0
U /	N/A	4.5	8.80	8	4	79	0	11	6	40	5.0	N/A	N/A	0	0	0.0	0.0
U /	N/A	4.5	8.75	2	4	79	0	11	6	40	5.0	N/A	N/A	0	0	0.0	0.0
U /	N/A	4.5	8.80	1	4	79	0	11	6	40	5.0	N/A	N/A	0	0	0.0	0.0
U /	N/A	4.5	8.77	3	4	79	0	11	6	40	5.0	N/A	N/A	0	0	0.0	0.0
C+ / 5.8	3.2	5.5	10.54	4	0	12	1	46	41	182	4.2	40	9	750	0	5.8	0.0
C- / 3.2	4.6	2.8	9.17	132	2	26	1	62	9	26	5.2	45	8	750	0	5.8	0.0
C- / 3.2	4.6	2.8	9.16	3	2	26	1	62	9	26	5.2	22	8	750	0	0.0	0.0
C- / 3.2	4.5	2.8	9.16	21	2	26	1	62	9	26	5.2	23	8	750	0	0.0	0.0
C- / 3.2	4.5	2.8	9.16	23	2	26	1	62	9	26	5.2	53	8	0	0	0.0	0.0
C- / 3.2	4.6	2.8	9.15	1	2	26	1	62	9	26	5.2	29	8	0	0	0.0	0.0
C- / 3.2	4.6	2.8	9.17	N/A	2	26	1	62	9	26	5.2	54	8	1,000,000	0	0.0	0.0
C- / 3.2	4.6	2.8	9.17	2	2	26	1	62	9	26	5.2	44	8	0	0	0.0	0.0

Fund Type	Fund Name (99 Pct = Best, 0 Pct = Worst)	Ticker Symbol	Overall Investment Rating	Phone	PERFORMANCE: Performance Rating/Pts	Total Return % through 3/31/16: 3 Mo	6 Mo	1Yr / Pct	Annualized: 3Yr / Pct	Annualized: 5Yr / Pct	Incl. in Returns: Dividend Yield	Expense Ratio
*COH	Ivy High Income A	WHIAX	E	(800) 777-6472	E / 0.4	1.49	-3.68	-7.85 / 1	0.38 /31	4.66 /69	7.70	0.94
COH ●	Ivy High Income B	WHIBX	E	(800) 777-6472	E+ / 0.6	1.32	-4.03	-8.52 / 1	-0.36 /13	3.88 /60	7.39	1.67
COH	Ivy High Income C	WRHIX	E	(800) 777-6472	E+ / 0.6	1.33	-4.01	-8.49 / 1	-0.31 /13	3.94 /60	7.42	1.64
COH	Ivy High Income E	IVHEX	E	(800) 777-6472	E / 0.3	1.45	-3.79	-8.10 / 1	0.06 /25	4.29 /65	7.42	1.26
COH	Ivy High Income I	IVHIX	E+	(800) 777-6472	D- / 1.2	1.56	-3.56	-7.62 / 2	0.64 /36	4.93 /71	8.45	0.69
COH	Ivy High Income R	IYHIX	E	(800) 777-6472	E+ / 0.8	1.42	-3.84	-8.17 / 1	0.05 /24	--	7.81	1.29
COH	Ivy High Income R6	IHIFX	E+	(800) 777-6472	D- / 1.3	1.60	-3.47	-7.46 / 2	0.73 /37	4.99 /72	8.63	0.54
COH	Ivy High Income Y	WHIYX	E+	(800) 777-6472	D- / 1.0	1.51	-3.69	-7.86 / 1	0.39 /31	4.67 /69	8.17	0.95
*GES	Ivy Limited-Term Bond A	WLTAX	C-	(800) 777-6472	D+ / 2.8	1.58	1.17	0.93 /57	0.59 /35	1.53 /26	1.34	0.88
GES ●	Ivy Limited-Term Bond B	WLTBX	C-	(800) 777-6472	D / 1.8	1.39	0.77	0.11 /41	-0.25 /14	0.69 /18	0.57	1.72
GES	Ivy Limited-Term Bond C	WLBCX	C-	(800) 777-6472	D+ / 2.5	1.41	0.82	0.21 /44	-0.15 /14	0.79 /19	0.66	1.64
GES	Ivy Limited-Term Bond E	IVLEX	C-	(800) 777-6472	D+ / 2.4	1.55	1.11	0.81 /55	0.47 /32	1.43 /25	1.23	1.03
GES	Ivy Limited-Term Bond I	ILTIX	C+	(800) 777-6472	C / 4.5	1.64	1.29	1.17 /61	0.84 /40	1.79 /29	1.62	0.63
COI	Ivy Limited-Term Bond R	IYLTX	C	(800) 777-6472	C- / 3.3	1.50	1.00	0.57 /51	0.24 /29	--	1.02	1.23
COI	Ivy Limited-Term Bond R6	ILMDX	B-	(800) 777-6472	C / 4.6	1.68	1.36	1.32 /64	0.92 /41	1.83 /29	1.76	0.48
GES	Ivy Limited-Term Bond Y	WLTYX	C+	(800) 777-6472	C- / 4.0	1.58	1.17	0.93 /57	0.59 /35	1.53 /26	1.38	0.89
MM	Ivy Money Market A	WRAXX	U	(800) 777-6472	U /	--	--	--	--	--	0.02	0.69
MM ●	Ivy Money Market B	WRBXX	U	(800) 777-6472	U /	0.00	0.01	0.02 /34	0.02 /20	0.02 / 8	0.02	1.74
MM ●	Ivy Money Market C	WRCXX	U	(800) 777-6472	U /	--	--	--	--	--	0.02	1.63
MM	Ivy Money Market E	IVEXX	U	(800) 777-6472	U /	--	--	--	--	--	0.02	0.73
MUN	Ivy Municipal Bond A	WMBAX	B	(800) 777-6472	B- / 7.0	1.17	2.62	2.83 /83	2.46 /82	5.00 /85	2.18	1.01
*MUN ●	Ivy Municipal Bond B	WMBBX	B+	(800) 777-6472	B / 7.6	0.99	2.25	2.09 /78	1.69 /72	4.22 /79	1.55	1.77
MUN	Ivy Municipal Bond C	WMBCX	B+	(800) 777-6472	B / 7.6	0.99	2.25	2.09 /78	1.70 /72	4.22 /79	1.55	1.76
MUN	Ivy Municipal Bond I	IMBIX	A+	(800) 777-6472	B+ / 8.7	1.21	2.72	3.05 /85	2.68 /85	5.23 /87	2.48	0.80
MUN	Ivy Municipal Bond Y	WMBYX	A	(800) 777-6472	B+ / 8.5	1.17	2.61	2.83 /83	2.46 /82	5.00 /85	2.27	1.05
MUH	Ivy Municipal High Income A	IYIAX	C	(800) 777-6472	B / 8.2	0.95	2.80	3.53 /90	3.35 /91	6.77 /96	3.85	0.87
MUH ●	Ivy Municipal High Income B	IYIBX	C	(800) 777-6472	B+ / 8.5	0.77	2.42	2.77 /83	2.56 /83	5.94 /92	3.28	1.64
MUH	Ivy Municipal High Income C	IYICX	C	(800) 777-6472	B+ / 8.5	0.78	2.44	2.80 /83	2.60 /84	5.99 /92	3.31	1.60
MUH	Ivy Municipal High Income I	WYMHX	C+	(800) 777-6472	A / 9.3	0.99	2.89	3.71 /92	3.54 /93	6.95 /96	4.20	0.70
MUH	Ivy Municipal High Income Y	IYIYX	C+	(800) 777-6472	A- / 9.2	0.95	2.78	3.52 /90	3.36 /91	6.78 /96	4.01	0.95
GEI	J Hancock Absolute Ret Curr A	JCUAX	D	(800) 257-3336	C+ / 6.1	4.36	3.39	5.86 /93	1.64 /55	1.00 /20	0.00	1.35
GEI	J Hancock Absolute Ret Curr I	JCUIX	D+	(800) 257-3336	B / 7.7	4.49	3.54	6.21 /94	2.02 /62	1.40 /24	0.00	1.03
GEI	J Hancock Absolute Ret Curr NAV		D+	(800) 257-3336	B / 7.9	4.56	3.73	6.38 /95	2.15 /64	1.58 /26	0.00	0.92
GEI	J Hancock Active Bond 1	JIADX	B-	(800) 257-3336	C+ / 6.9	2.30	1.56	0.41 /48	2.55 /71	4.26 /65	3.33	0.68
GEI	J Hancock Active Bond NAV		B-	(800) 257-3336	B- / 7.0	2.32	1.59	0.46 /49	2.60 /72	4.31 /66	3.38	0.63
*GEI	J Hancock Bond A	JHNBX	C-	(800) 257-3336	C / 5.0	2.28	1.56	0.20 /44	2.48 /70	4.58 /68	3.16	0.94
GEI ●	J Hancock Bond B	JHBBX	C-	(800) 257-3336	C / 5.5	2.05	1.15	-0.56 /25	1.75 /57	3.84 /59	2.59	1.64
GEI	J Hancock Bond C	JHCBX	C-	(800) 257-3336	C+ / 5.6	2.11	1.21	-0.50 /26	1.77 /57	3.85 /59	2.59	1.64
GEI	J Hancock Bond I	JHBIX	B-	(800) 257-3336	B- / 7.3	2.29	1.71	0.51 /50	2.80 /74	4.94 /71	3.60	0.63
COI	J Hancock Bond R2	JHRBX	C+	(800) 257-3336	C+ / 6.6	2.20	1.45	0.10 /41	2.41 /69	4.58 /68	3.19	1.04
COI	J Hancock Bond R4	JBFRX	U	(800) 257-3336	U /	2.30	1.64	0.58 /51	--	--	3.61	0.89
COI	J Hancock Bond R6	JHBSX	B-	(800) 257-3336	B- / 7.5	2.39	1.77	0.63 /52	2.94 /76	5.03 /72	3.71	0.54
MUS	J Hancock CA Tax Free Income A	TACAX	B	(800) 257-3336	A- / 9.1	1.69	3.93	3.88 /93	4.15 /96	7.02 /96	3.43	0.83
MUS ●	J Hancock CA Tax Free Income B	TSCAX	B	(800) 257-3336	A / 9.3	1.60	3.55	3.20 /87	3.41 /92	6.24 /93	2.84	1.68
MUS	J Hancock CA Tax Free Income C	TCCAX	B	(800) 257-3336	A / 9.3	1.51	3.55	3.11 /86	3.37 /92	6.22 /93	2.84	1.68
GEI	J Hancock Core Bond 1	JICDX	C+	(800) 257-3336	C+ / 6.8	2.85	2.18	1.33 /64	2.23 /66	4.11 /63	1.67	0.69
GEI	J Hancock Core Bond NAV		C+	(800) 257-3336	C+ / 6.9	2.79	2.14	1.38 /64	2.26 /67	4.16 /64	1.73	0.64
COH	J Hancock Core High Yld A	JYIAX	E	(800) 257-3336	E / 0.4	1.71	-1.93	-7.58 / 2	-0.19 /14	3.90 /60	7.44	1.08
COH	J Hancock Core High Yld C	JYICX	E	(800) 257-3336	E / 0.5	1.53	-2.19	-8.18 / 1	-0.96 / 9	--	6.94	1.83
COH	J Hancock Core High Yld I	JYIIX	E	(800) 257-3336	D- / 1.1	1.89	-1.69	-7.24 / 2	0.18 /28	4.24 /65	8.02	0.81
GL	J Hancock Core High Yld NAV		U	(800) 257-3336	U /	1.81	-1.64	-7.12 / 2	--	--	8.16	0.69
GL	J Hancock Core High Yld R2	JCHYX	U	(800) 257-3336	U /	1.70	-1.95	-7.65 / 2	--	--	7.66	1.21

● Denotes fund is closed to new investors
* Denotes fund is included in Section II

RISK			NET ASSETS		ASSET							FUND MANAGER		MINIMUM		LOADS	
Risk Rating/Pts	3 Yr Avg Standard Deviation	Avg Duration	NAV As of 3/31/16	Total $(Mil)	Cash %	Gov. Bond %	Muni. Bond %	Corp. Bond %	Other %	Portfolio Turnover Ratio	Avg Coupon Rate	Manager Quality Pct	Manager Tenure (Years)	Initial Purch. $	Additional Purch. $	Front End Load	Back End Load
D- / 1.2	5.9	3.2	6.91	1,798	2	0	0	72	26	44	7.5	22	3	750	0	5.8	0.0
D- / 1.1	5.9	3.2	6.91	82	2	0	0	72	26	44	7.5	12	3	750	0	0.0	0.0
D- / 1.1	5.9	3.2	6.91	998	2	0	0	72	26	44	7.5	12	3	750	0	0.0	0.0
D- / 1.2	5.9	3.2	6.91	8	2	0	0	72	26	44	7.5	17	3	750	0	5.8	0.0
D- / 1.2	5.9	3.2	6.91	1,182	2	0	0	72	26	44	7.5	28	3	0	0	0.0	0.0
D- / 1.1	5.9	3.2	6.91	59	2	0	0	72	26	44	7.5	16	3	0	0	0.0	0.0
D- / 1.2	5.9	3.2	6.91	49	2	0	0	72	26	44	7.5	31	3	1,000,000	0	0.0	0.0
D- / 1.1	5.9	3.2	6.91	390	2	0	0	72	26	44	7.5	22	3	10,000,000	0	0.0	0.0
B+ / 8.7	1.8	2.8	10.87	1,577	3	12	1	72	12	39	3.4	35	2	750	0	2.5	0.0
B+ / 8.7	1.8	2.8	10.87	14	3	12	1	72	12	39	3.4	16	2	750	0	0.0	0.0
B+ / 8.7	1.8	2.8	10.87	130	3	12	1	72	12	39	3.4	18	2	750	0	0.0	0.0
B+ / 8.7	1.8	2.8	10.87	4	3	12	1	72	12	39	3.4	32	2	750	0	2.5	0.0
B+ / 8.7	1.8	2.8	10.87	54	3	12	1	72	12	39	3.4	43	2	0	0	0.0	0.0
B+ / 8.7	1.8	2.8	10.87	1	3	12	1	72	12	39	3.4	33	2	0	0	0.0	0.0
B+ / 8.7	1.8	2.8	10.87	3	3	12	1	72	12	39	3.4	55	2	1,000,000	0	0.0	0.0
B+ / 8.7	1.8	2.8	10.87	17	3	12	1	72	12	39	3.4	35	2	10,000,000	0	0.0	0.0
U /	N/A	N/A	1.00	166	100	0	0	0	0	0	0.0	N/A	16	750	0	0.0	0.0
U /	N/A	N/A	1.00	6	100	0	0	0	0	0	0.0	N/A	16	750	0	0.0	0.0
U /	N/A	N/A	1.00	45	100	0	0	0	0	0	0.0	N/A	16	750	0	0.0	0.0
U /	N/A	N/A	1.00	7	100	0	0	0	0	0	0.0	N/A	16	750	0	0.0	0.0
C+ / 6.2	3.1	5.6	12.13	178	2	0	95	0	3	8	3.8	36	16	750	0	4.3	0.0
C+ / 6.2	3.1	5.6	12.13	2	2	0	95	0	3	8	3.8	18	16	750	0	0.0	0.0
C+ / 6.2	3.1	5.6	12.13	31	2	0	95	0	3	8	3.8	18	16	750	0	0.0	0.0
C+ / 6.2	3.1	5.6	12.13	9	2	0	95	0	3	8	3.8	43	16	0	0	0.0	0.0
C+ / 6.2	3.1	5.6	12.13	1	2	0	95	0	3	8	3.8	36	16	10,000,000	0	0.0	0.0
D+ / 2.4	4.6	7.4	5.28	390	1	0	94	3	2	9	5.5	26	7	750	0	4.3	0.0
D+ / 2.4	4.7	7.4	5.28	14	1	0	94	3	2	9	5.5	13	7	750	0	0.0	0.0
D+ / 2.4	4.6	7.4	5.28	237	1	0	94	3	2	9	5.5	14	7	750	0	0.0	0.0
D+ / 2.4	4.6	7.4	5.28	701	1	0	94	3	2	9	5.5	31	7	0	0	0.0	0.0
D+ / 2.4	4.6	7.4	5.28	21	1	0	94	3	2	9	5.5	27	7	10,000,000	0	0.0	0.0
E / 0.4	8.2	N/A	8.85	20	0	99	0	0	1	0	0.0	99	5	1,000	0	3.0	0.0
E / 0.4	8.2	N/A	9.07	205	0	99	0	0	1	0	0.0	99	5	250,000	0	0.0	0.0
E / 0.4	8.2	N/A	9.17	775	0	99	0	0	1	0	0.0	99	5	0	0	0.0	0.0
C+ / 5.9	3.2	5.4	10.03	294	3	11	0	40	46	63	3.1	71	11	0	0	0.0	0.0
C+ / 6.0	3.1	5.4	10.02	1,779	3	11	0	40	46	63	3.1	73	11	0	0	0.0	0.0
C / 5.3	3.3	5.0	15.69	1,836	1	8	0	44	47	66	0.0	N/A	14	1,000	0	4.0	0.0
C / 5.3	3.3	5.0	15.68	23	1	8	0	44	47	66	0.0	37	14	1,000	0	0.0	0.0
C / 5.3	3.3	5.0	15.69	295	1	8	0	44	47	66	0.0	38	14	1,000	0	0.0	0.0
C / 5.4	3.3	5.0	15.69	1,016	1	8	0	44	47	66	0.0	79	14	250,000	0	0.0	0.0
C / 5.5	3.3	5.0	15.70	53	1	8	0	44	47	66	0.0	78	14	0	0	0.0	0.0
U /	N/A	5.0	15.70	N/A	1	8	0	44	47	66	0.0	N/A	14	0	0	0.0	0.0
C / 5.4	3.3	5.0	15.71	114	1	8	0	44	47	66	0.0	87	14	1,000,000	0	0.0	0.0
C- / 3.7	3.7	10.9	11.13	248	3	0	96	0	1	19	0.0	79	N/A	1,000	0	4.0	0.0
C- / 3.7	3.7	10.9	11.14	2	3	0	96	0	1	19	0.0	49	N/A	1,000	0	0.0	0.0
C- / 3.7	3.7	10.9	11.13	36	3	0	96	0	1	19	0.0	47	N/A	1,000	0	0.0	0.0
C+ / 5.8	3.2	5.6	13.19	197	0	33	0	21	46	408	2.9	46	9	0	0	0.0	0.0
C+ / 5.8	3.2	5.6	13.17	1,134	0	33	0	21	46	408	2.9	48	9	0	0	0.0	0.0
E+ / 0.6	6.8	N/A	8.91	266	5	0	0	92	3	28	0.0	12	7	1,000	0	4.0	0.0
E+ / 0.6	6.7	N/A	8.91	51	5	0	0	92	3	28	0.0	8	7	1,000	0	0.0	0.0
E+ / 0.6	6.7	N/A	8.92	175	5	0	0	92	3	28	0.0	15	7	250,000	0	0.0	0.0
U /	N/A	N/A	8.92	67	5	0	0	92	3	28	0.0	N/A	7	0	0	0.0	0.0
U /	N/A	N/A	8.91	N/A	5	0	0	92	3	28	0.0	N/A	7	0	0	0.0	0.0

Fund Type	Fund Name (99 Pct = Best; 0 Pct = Worst)	Ticker Symbol	Overall Investment Rating	Phone	PERFORMANCE: Performance Rating/Pts	Total Return % through 3/31/16: 3 Mo	6 Mo	1Yr / Pct	Annualized: 3Yr / Pct	5Yr / Pct	Incl. in Returns: Dividend Yield	Expense Ratio
GL	J Hancock Core High Yld R4	JCHRX	**U**	(800) 257-3336	**U /**	1.74	-1.87	-7.47 / 2	--	--	7.87	1.06
GL	J Hancock Core High Yld R6	JHCHX	**U**	(800) 257-3336	**U /**	1.82	-1.71	-7.14 / 2	--	--	8.26	0.71
EM	J Hancock Emerg Markets Debt A	JMKAX	**E**	(800) 257-3336	**D- / 1.2**	6.29	7.85	0.02 /33	-0.86 / 9	2.67 /40	4.83	1.20
EM	J Hancock Emerg Markets Debt C	JMKCX	**U**	(800) 257-3336	**U /**	6.24	7.61	-0.78 /23	--	--	4.22	1.90
EM	J Hancock Emerg Markets Debt I	JMKIX	**D-**	(800) 257-3336	**C- / 3.9**	6.37	8.01	0.40 /48	-0.50 /12	3.06 /46	5.40	0.89
EM	J Hancock Emerg Markets Debt NAV		**U**	(800) 257-3336	**U /**	6.40	8.08	0.51 /50	--	--	5.52	0.78
EM	J Hancock Emerg Markets Debt R2	JHEMX	**U**	(800) 257-3336	**U /**	6.34	7.95	0.21 /44	--	--	5.32	1.30
EM	J Hancock Emerg Markets Debt R4	JHMDX	**U**	(800) 257-3336	**U /**	6.36	8.01	0.31 /46	--	--	5.42	1.15
EM	J Hancock Emerg Markets Debt R6	JEMIX	**U**	(800) 257-3336	**U /**	6.41	8.10	0.48 /49	--	--	5.59	0.80
GEI	J Hancock Fltng Rate Inc 1	JFIHX	**D**	(800) 257-3336	**E+ / 0.8**	0.38	-3.01	-5.36 / 4	-0.22 /14	2.08 /32	5.43	0.76
GEI	J Hancock Fltng Rate Inc A	JFIAX	**D-**	(800) 257-3336	**E / 0.4**	0.27	-3.20	-5.73 / 4	-0.63 /11	1.65 /27	4.88	1.13
GEI ●	J Hancock Fltng Rate Inc B	JFIBX	**D**	(800) 257-3336	**E / 0.4**	0.11	-3.53	-6.38 / 3	-1.26 / 7	0.94 /20	4.28	1.83
GEI	J Hancock Fltng Rate Inc C	JFIGX	**D**	(800) 257-3336	**E / 0.4**	-0.01	-3.51	-6.45 / 3	-1.23 / 7	0.99 /20	4.28	1.83
GEI	J Hancock Fltng Rate Inc I	JFIIX	**D**	(800) 257-3336	**E+ / 0.8**	0.37	-2.92	-5.41 / 4	-0.29 /13	2.01 /31	5.36	0.82
GEI	J Hancock Fltng Rate Inc NAV		**D**	(800) 257-3336	**E+ / 0.9**	0.40	-2.98	-5.30 / 4	-0.17 /14	2.13 /33	5.48	0.71
LP	J Hancock Fltng Rate Inc R6	JFIRX	**D**	(800) 257-3336	**E+ / 0.9**	0.38	-3.00	-5.32 / 4	-0.13 /15	2.15 /33	5.46	0.72
COH	J Hancock Focused High Yield A	JHHBX	**E**	(800) 257-3336	**D- / 1.0**	1.65	-0.39	-5.02 / 5	0.76 /38	2.61 /39	6.62	0.95
COH ●	J Hancock Focused High Yield B	TSHYX	**E+**	(800) 257-3336	**D- / 1.1**	1.47	-0.77	-5.77 / 3	-0.10 /15	1.78 /28	6.07	1.70
COH	J Hancock Focused High Yield C	JHYCX	**E+**	(800) 257-3336	**D- / 1.2**	1.79	-0.76	-5.74 / 4	0.01 /16	1.85 /29	6.10	1.70
COH	J Hancock Focused High Yield I	JYHIX	**D-**	(800) 257-3336	**C- / 3.3**	2.03	0.04	-4.53 / 6	1.03 /43	2.92 /44	7.14	0.70
GL	J Hancock Global Bond 1	JIGDX	**D+**	(800) 257-3336	**C+ / 5.8**	6.20	5.07	3.59 /79	0.55 /34	2.76 /41	0.02	0.83
GL	J Hancock Global Bond NAV		**D+**	(800) 257-3336	**C+ / 5.8**	6.12	5.03	3.55 /79	0.56 /34	2.79 /42	0.06	0.78
GEI	J Hancock Global Income A	JYGAX	**E**	(800) 257-3336	**D- / 1.2**	4.20	4.10	-1.54 /18	-0.09 /15	2.97 /45	5.58	1.25
GEI	J Hancock Global Income I	JYGIX	**D-**	(800) 257-3336	**C- / 3.8**	4.39	4.26	-1.14 /21	0.21 /29	3.28 /49	6.11	0.94
GEI	J Hancock Global Income NAV		**D**	(800) 257-3336	**C- / 4.1**	4.32	4.22	-1.04 /21	0.40 /31	3.42 /52	6.32	0.83
USS	J Hancock Government Inc A	JHGIX	**C**	(800) 257-3336	**C- / 3.7**	2.11	1.31	1.23 /62	1.54 /53	2.94 /44	2.16	1.09
USS ●	J Hancock Government Inc B	TSGIX	**C**	(800) 257-3336	**C- / 4.2**	2.03	1.03	0.47 /49	0.76 /38	2.14 /33	1.50	1.84
USS	J Hancock Government Inc C	TCGIX	**C+**	(800) 257-3336	**C- / 4.2**	1.92	0.93	0.47 /49	0.76 /38	2.14 /33	1.50	1.84
COH	J Hancock High Yield 1	JIHDX	**E**	(800) 257-3336	**E / 0.4**	1.21	-3.25	-8.82 / 1	-1.22 / 7	2.84 /43	8.29	0.77
MUH	J Hancock High Yield Muni Bond A	JHTFX	**C-**	(800) 257-3336	**B+ / 8.4**	2.11	4.06	3.96 /94	3.19 /90	6.44 /94	4.38	0.98
MUH ●	J Hancock High Yield Muni Bond B	TSHTX	**C**	(800) 257-3336	**B+ / 8.7**	1.93	3.67	3.19 /87	2.42 /82	5.65 /90	3.83	1.73
MUH	J Hancock High Yield Muni Bond C	JCTFX	**C**	(800) 257-3336	**B+ / 8.7**	1.93	3.67	3.19 /87	2.42 /82	5.65 /90	3.83	1.73
COH	J Hancock High Yield NAV		**E**	(800) 257-3336	**E / 0.4**	1.24	-3.26	-8.75 / 1	-1.18 / 7	2.89 /43	8.44	0.72
* GL	J Hancock Income A	JHFIX	**C-**	(800) 257-3336	**C / 4.7**	2.25	2.35	0.95 /58	2.09 /63	3.71 /57	2.80	0.82
GL ●	J Hancock Income B	STIBX	**C**	(800) 257-3336	**C / 5.3**	2.08	2.00	0.26 /45	1.38 /50	2.99 /45	2.22	1.52
GL	J Hancock Income C	JSTCX	**C**	(800) 257-3336	**C / 5.3**	2.08	2.00	0.26 /45	1.38 /50	2.99 /45	2.22	1.52
GL	J Hancock Income I	JSTIX	**B**	(800) 257-3336	**B- / 7.1**	2.33	2.51	1.26 /63	2.47 /70	4.09 /63	3.22	0.50
GL	J Hancock Income R1	JSTRX	**C+**	(800) 257-3336	**C+ / 6.0**	2.17	2.18	0.62 /52	1.75 /57	3.42 /52	2.58	1.16
GEL	J Hancock Income R2	JSNSX	**C+**	(800) 257-3336	**C+ / 6.4**	2.24	2.31	0.87 /56	2.03 /62	3.70 /57	2.83	0.91
GL	J Hancock Income R3	JSNHX	**C+**	(800) 257-3336	**C+ / 6.1**	2.21	2.24	0.73 /54	1.86 /59	3.50 /53	2.70	1.06
GL	J Hancock Income R4	JSNFX	**B-**	(800) 257-3336	**C+ / 6.8**	2.31	2.29	1.12 /61	2.26 /67	3.86 /59	3.08	0.76
GL	J Hancock Income R5	JSNVX	**B**	(800) 257-3336	**B- / 7.2**	2.36	2.55	1.32 /64	2.47 /70	4.10 /63	3.28	0.46
GEL	J Hancock Income R6	JSNWX	**B+**	(800) 257-3336	**B- / 7.3**	2.52	2.57	1.38 /64	2.58 /72	4.16 /64	3.33	0.41
GEI	J Hancock Inv Quality Bond 1	JIQBX	**C**	(800) 257-3336	**C+ / 6.3**	2.98	2.31	1.13 /61	1.81 /58	3.93 /60	1.87	0.68
GEI	J Hancock Inv Quality Bond NAV		**C**	(800) 257-3336	**C+ / 6.3**	3.00	2.34	1.10 /60	1.86 /59	3.97 /61	1.93	0.63
GEI	J Hancock Invest Gr Bond A	TAUSX	**C-**	(800) 257-3336	**C / 4.7**	2.27	1.55	0.71 /53	2.21 /66	3.97 /61	2.51	0.88
GEI ●	J Hancock Invest Gr Bond B	TSUSX	**C**	(800) 257-3336	**C / 5.3**	2.18	1.28	0.06 /39	1.48 /52	3.22 /48	1.87	1.63
GEI	J Hancock Invest Gr Bond C	TCUSX	**C**	(800) 257-3336	**C / 5.3**	2.18	1.28	0.06 /39	1.48 /52	3.22 /49	1.87	1.63
GEI	J Hancock Invest Gr Bond I	TIUSX	**B-**	(800) 257-3336	**B- / 7.1**	2.43	1.78	1.07 /60	2.51 /71	4.30 /65	2.87	0.62
COI	J Hancock Invest Gr Bond R2	JIGBX	**U**	(800) 257-3336	**U /**	2.28	1.58	0.83 /56	--	--	2.73	1.02
COI	J Hancock Invest Gr Bond R4	JIGMX	**U**	(800) 257-3336	**U /**	2.33	1.67	0.97 /58	--	--	2.87	0.87
COI	J Hancock Invest Gr Bond R6	JIGEX	**U**	(800) 257-3336	**U /**	2.47	1.85	1.24 /62	--	--	3.03	0.52

● Denotes fund is closed to new investors
* Denotes fund is included in Section II

RISK			NET ASSETS		ASSET							FUND MANAGER		MINIMUM		LOADS	
Risk Rating/Pts	3 Yr Avg Standard Deviation	Avg Duration	NAV As of 3/31/16	Total $(Mil)	Cash %	Gov. Bond %	Muni. Bond %	Corp. Bond %	Other %	Portfolio Turnover Ratio	Avg Coupon Rate	Manager Quality Pct	Manager Tenure (Years)	Initial Purch. $	Additional Purch. $	Front End Load	Back End Load
U /	N/A	N/A	8.91	N/A	5	0	0	92	3	28	0.0	N/A	7	0	0	0.0	0.0
U /	N/A	N/A	8.91	N/A	5	0	0	92	3	28	0.0	N/A	7	1,000,000	0	0.0	0.0
E / 0.4	8.7	N/A	8.91	1	9	43	0	46	2	27	0.0	36	3	1,000	0	4.0	0.0
U /	N/A	N/A	8.91	N/A	9	43	0	46	2	27	0.0	N/A	3	1,000	0	0.0	0.0
E / 0.3	8.7	N/A	8.92	6	9	43	0	46	2	27	0.0	48	3	250,000	0	0.0	0.0
U /	N/A	N/A	8.91	537	9	43	0	46	2	27	0.0	N/A	3	0	0	0.0	0.0
U /	N/A	N/A	8.91	N/A	9	43	0	46	2	27	0.0	N/A	3	0	0	0.0	0.0
U /	N/A	N/A	8.91	N/A	9	43	0	46	2	27	0.0	N/A	3	0	0	0.0	0.0
U /	N/A	N/A	8.91	N/A	9	43	0	46	2	27	0.0	N/A	3	1,000,000	0	0.0	0.0
C / 5.3	3.4	0.5	8.08	22	2	0	0	80	18	40	4.1	40	9	0	0	0.0	0.0
C / 5.3	3.4	0.5	8.09	184	2	0	0	80	18	40	4.1	28	9	1,000	0	2.5	0.0
C / 5.5	3.3	0.5	8.09	20	2	0	0	80	18	40	4.1	16	9	1,000	0	0.0	0.0
C+ / 5.6	3.2	0.5	8.12	144	2	0	0	80	18	40	4.1	16	9	1,000	0	0.0	0.0
C / 5.3	3.4	0.5	8.09	131	2	0	0	80	18	40	4.1	37	9	250,000	0	0.0	0.0
C / 5.3	3.4	0.5	8.09	1,745	2	0	0	80	18	40	4.1	41	9	0	0	0.0	0.0
C / 5.4	3.3	0.5	8.09	24	2	0	0	80	18	40	4.1	31	9	1,000,000	0	0.0	0.0
D- / 1.0	6.1	3.5	3.22	254	6	0	0	88	6	80	0.0	30	8	1,000	0	4.0	0.0
D- / 1.0	6.1	3.5	3.22	19	6	0	0	88	6	80	0.0	14	8	1,000	0	0.0	0.0
D- / 1.2	5.9	3.5	3.22	78	6	0	0	88	6	80	0.0	16	8	1,000	0	0.0	0.0
E+ / 0.9	6.2	3.5	3.22	33	6	0	0	88	6	80	0.0	37	8	250,000	0	0.0	0.0
D+ / 2.9	4.8	6.3	12.50	61	11	52	3	23	11	61	3.9	86	1	0	0	0.0	0.0
D+ / 2.9	4.8	6.3	12.48	432	11	52	3	23	11	61	3.9	86	1	0	0	0.0	0.0
E+ / 0.7	7.0	5.3	8.90	3	2	47	0	47	4	63	7.6	9	7	1,000	0	4.0	0.0
E+ / 0.7	7.0	5.3	8.90	N/A	2	47	0	47	4	63	7.6	10	7	250,000	0	0.0	0.0
E+ / 0.8	6.9	5.3	8.90	389	2	47	0	47	4	63	7.6	11	7	0	0	0.0	0.0
B / 8.1	2.3	4.2	9.64	280	2	26	0	0	72	77	0.0	62	18	1,000	0	4.0	0.0
B / 7.9	2.4	4.2	9.64	4	2	26	0	0	72	77	0.0	33	18	1,000	0	0.0	0.0
B / 8.1	2.3	4.2	9.64	19	2	26	0	0	72	77	0.0	35	18	1,000	0	0.0	0.0
E+ / 0.7	6.6	3.9	7.37	317	2	0	0	90	8	59	8.2	7	10	0	0	0.0	0.0
D / 2.0	4.8	9.5	8.25	150	5	0	94	0	1	30	0.0	17	N/A	1,000	0	4.0	0.0
D / 2.0	4.8	9.5	8.25	6	5	0	94	0	1	30	0.0	10	N/A	1,000	0	0.0	0.0
D / 2.0	4.8	9.5	8.25	44	5	0	94	0	1	30	0.0	10	N/A	1,000	0	0.0	0.0
E+ / 0.7	6.5	3.9	7.29	186	2	0	0	90	8	59	8.2	7	10	0	0	0.0	0.0
C+ / 6.5	3.0	3.6	6.47	907	6	26	3	47	18	51	0.0	96	17	1,000	0	4.0	0.0
C+ / 6.4	3.0	3.6	6.47	102	6	26	3	47	18	51	0.0	93	17	1,000	0	0.0	0.0
C+ / 6.5	3.0	3.6	6.47	419	6	26	3	47	18	51	0.0	93	17	1,000	0	0.0	0.0
C+ / 6.3	3.1	3.6	6.46	2,504	6	26	3	47	18	51	0.0	97	17	250,000	0	0.0	0.0
C+ / 6.3	3.1	3.6	6.49	15	6	26	3	47	18	51	0.0	95	17	0	0	0.0	0.0
C+ / 6.3	3.1	3.6	6.46	10	6	26	3	47	18	51	0.0	74	17	0	0	0.0	0.0
C+ / 6.4	3.0	3.6	6.47	3	6	26	3	47	18	51	0.0	95	17	0	0	0.0	0.0
C+ / 6.4	3.0	3.6	6.47	130	6	26	3	47	18	51	0.0	97	17	0	0	0.0	0.0
C+ / 6.4	3.0	3.6	6.46	12	6	26	3	47	18	51	0.0	97	17	0	0	0.0	0.0
C+ / 6.3	3.1	3.6	6.47	190	6	26	3	47	18	51	0.0	85	17	1,000,000	0	0.0	0.0
C / 4.9	3.5	5.4	12.26	74	0	13	1	30	56	133	6.6	31	6	0	0	0.0	0.0
C / 4.8	3.5	5.4	12.24	512	0	13	1	30	56	133	6.6	31	6	0	0	0.0	0.0
C+ / 6.0	3.1	4.5	10.49	361	2	14	0	36	48	69	0.0	50	18	1,000	0	4.0	0.0
C+ / 5.9	3.2	4.5	10.50	7	2	14	0	36	48	69	0.0	27	18	1,000	0	0.0	0.0
C+ / 5.8	3.2	4.5	10.50	35	2	14	0	36	48	69	0.0	27	18	1,000	0	0.0	0.0
C+ / 6.0	3.1	4.5	10.50	46	2	14	0	36	48	69	0.0	61	18	250,000	0	0.0	0.0
U /	N/A	4.5	10.49	N/A	2	14	0	36	48	69	0.0	N/A	18	0	0	0.0	0.0
U /	N/A	4.5	10.49	N/A	2	14	0	36	48	69	0.0	N/A	18	0	0	0.0	0.0
U /	N/A	4.5	10.50	N/A	2	14	0	36	48	69	0.0	N/A	18	1,000,000	0	0.0	0.0

Fund Type	Fund Name (99 Pct = Best; 0 Pct = Worst)	Ticker Symbol	Overall Investment Rating	Phone	PERFORMANCE: Performance Rating/Pts	Total Return % through 3/31/16: 3 Mo	6 Mo	1Yr / Pct	Annualized: 3Yr / Pct	Annualized: 5Yr / Pct	Incl. in Returns: Dividend Yield	Expense Ratio
MM	J Hancock Money Market A	JHMXX	U	(800) 257-3336	U /	--	--	--	--	--	0.01	0.98
MM	● J Hancock Money Market C	JMCXX	U	(800) 257-3336	U /	--	--	--	--	--	0.01	1.73
GEI	J Hancock Real Return Bond 1	JIRRX	E+	(800) 257-3336	E+ / 0.9	4.26	3.49	-0.17 /30	-1.93 / 5	2.22 /34	1.12	0.83
GEI	J Hancock Real Return Bond NAV		E+	(800) 257-3336	E+ / 0.9	4.31	3.53	-0.07 /31	-1.87 / 5	2.29 /35	1.14	0.78
USS	J Hancock Sh Tm Govt Inc NAV		C+	(800) 257-3336	C- / 3.6	0.94	0.39	0.81 /55	0.49 /33	1.05 /21	1.64	0.62
GEL	J Hancock Short Duration Opp A	JMBAX	D	(800) 257-3336	D- / 1.2	1.33	1.05	-2.09 /15	0.09 /27	1.68 /27	3.55	1.16
GEL	J Hancock Short Duration Opp I	JMBIX	D+	(800) 257-3336	D+ / 2.9	1.41	1.11	-1.88 /16	0.33 /30	1.96 /31	3.98	0.85
GEL	J Hancock Short Duration Opp NAV		D+	(800) 257-3336	C- / 3.3	1.45	1.28	-1.64 /18	0.56 /34	2.16 /33	4.11	0.74
* GL	J Hancock Strat Income Opp A	JIPAX	C-	(800) 257-3336	C / 4.7	1.77	2.01	0.01 /32	2.27 /67	3.92 /60	2.70	1.12
GL	J Hancock Strat Income Opp C	JIPCX	C	(800) 257-3336	C / 5.2	1.59	1.65	-0.70 /24	1.56 /53	3.20 /48	2.11	1.82
GL	J Hancock Strat Income Opp I	JIPIX	B	(800) 257-3336	B- / 7.1	1.94	2.26	0.32 /46	2.65 /73	4.29 /65	3.12	0.81
GL	J Hancock Strat Income Opp NAV		B+	(800) 257-3336	B- / 7.4	1.87	2.22	0.43 /48	2.90 /75	4.49 /67	3.24	0.69
GL	J Hancock Strat Income Opp R2	JIPPX	C+	(800) 257-3336	C+ / 6.4	1.74	2.04	-0.05 /31	2.22 /66	3.94 /61	2.76	1.21
GEI	J Hancock Strat Income Opp R6	JIPRX	B	(800) 257-3336	B- / 7.2	1.86	2.21	0.42 /48	2.69 /73	4.31 /66	3.22	0.71
* MUN	J Hancock Tax Free Bond A	TAMBX	C	(800) 257-3336	B / 8.1	1.41	3.11	3.09 /86	3.17 /90	5.66 /90	3.65	0.93
MUN ●	J Hancock Tax Free Bond B	TSMBX	C+	(800) 257-3336	B+ / 8.4	1.23	2.74	2.33 /79	2.40 /82	4.87 /84	3.07	1.68
MUN	J Hancock Tax Free Bond C	TBMBX	C	(800) 257-3336	B+ / 8.3	1.13	2.63	2.22 /79	2.37 /81	4.86 /84	3.07	1.68
COH	J Hancock US High Yield Bd 1	JIHLX	D	(800) 257-3336	C- / 3.5	1.57	-1.08	-4.84 / 5	1.38 /50	3.90 /60	6.99	0.83
COH	J Hancock US High Yield Bd NAV		D	(800) 257-3336	C- / 3.6	1.58	-1.06	-4.80 / 5	1.44 /51	3.95 /61	7.05	0.78
GL	J Hancock VIT Active Bond NAV		B+	(800) 257-3336	B- / 7.5	2.45	1.61	0.83 /56	2.90 /75	4.50 /68	5.24	0.64
GL	J Hancock VIT Core Bond NAV		B-	(800) 257-3336	B- / 7.1	2.93	2.27	1.61 /68	2.37 /69	4.23 /64	1.71	0.62
GL	J Hancock VIT Global Bond I		D+	(800) 257-3336	C / 5.5	5.85	4.61	3.13 /77	0.48 /33	2.62 /39	2.53	0.81
GL	J Hancock VIT Global Bond NAV		D+	(800) 257-3336	C / 5.5	5.87	4.63	3.15 /78	0.49 /33	2.64 /39	2.54	0.76
COH	J Hancock VIT High Yield I		E	(800) 257-3336	E / 0.4	1.04	-3.13	-8.97 / 1	-1.19 / 7	2.94 /44	8.70	0.78
COH	J Hancock VIT High Yield NAV		E	(800) 257-3336	E / 0.4	1.05	-3.13	-9.03 / 1	-1.21 / 7	2.95 /44	8.89	0.73
GEL	J Hancock VIT Inv Qual Bd I		C	(800) 257-3336	C+ / 6.2	3.04	2.32	0.99 /58	1.79 /57	4.03 /62	1.83	0.69
GEL	J Hancock VIT Inv Qual Bd II		C-	(800) 257-3336	C+ / 5.8	2.95	2.14	0.78 /55	1.58 /54	3.82 /58	1.63	0.89
GEL	J Hancock VIT Inv Qual Bd NAV		C	(800) 257-3336	C+ / 6.3	2.96	2.28	1.04 /59	1.84 /58	4.07 /63	1.89	0.64
GL	J Hancock VIT Real Return Bd I		E+	(800) 257-3336	D- / 1.3	4.49	3.54	-0.25 /29	-1.29 / 7	2.84 /43	6.56	1.00
GL	J Hancock VIT Real Return Bd II		E+	(800) 257-3336	D- / 1.2	4.47	3.50	-0.38 /27	-1.46 / 6	2.66 /40	6.44	1.20
GL	J Hancock VIT Real Return Bd NAV		E+	(800) 257-3336	D- / 1.4	4.56	3.59	-0.12 /30	-1.22 / 7	2.91 /44	6.70	0.95
GES	J Hancock VIT Strat Inc Opps I	JESNX	B+	(800) 257-3336	B- / 7.5	1.84	2.26	0.35 /47	2.99 /76	4.59 /68	2.50	0.74
GES	J Hancock VIT Strat Inc Opps II		B	(800) 257-3336	B- / 7.2	1.83	2.24	0.15 /43	2.78 /74	4.39 /66	2.29	0.94
GES	J Hancock VIT Strat Inc Opps NAV		B+	(800) 257-3336	B- / 7.5	1.84	2.31	0.40 /48	3.03 /77	4.64 /69	2.56	0.69
GEI	J Hancock VIT Total Bd Mkt B NAV		B-	(800) 257-3336	B- / 7.0	3.07	2.34	1.71 /69	2.27 /67	3.60 /55	2.81	0.51
GEN	J Hancock VIT Value I	JEVLX	D+	(800) 257-3336	B / 7.7	-0.84	-1.55	-12.81 / 0	5.82 /94	8.02 /87	0.54	0.82
GEN	J Hancock VIT Value II		D+	(800) 257-3336	B- / 7.5	-0.85	-1.61	-12.98 / 0	5.62 /94	7.81 /86	0.32	1.02
GEN	J Hancock VIT Value NAV		D+	(800) 257-3336	B / 7.8	-0.84	-1.51	-12.78 / 0	5.88 /95	8.07 /87	0.59	0.77
MUS	Jamestown VA Tax Exempt	JTEVX	A+	(866) 738-1126	B- / 7.4	1.26	1.86	2.37 /80	1.53 /68	2.48 /59	2.03	0.88
GEI	Janus Aspen Flexible Bond Inst	JAFLX	B+	(800) 295-2687	C+ / 6.5	2.14	1.32	0.52 /50	2.23 /66	4.15 /64	2.35	0.59
GEI	Janus Aspen Flexible Bond Svc		B	(800) 295-2687	C+ / 6.0	2.05	1.13	0.29 /46	1.97 /61	3.88 /60	1.98	0.85
EM	Janus Emerging Markets A	JMFAX	E-	(800) 295-2687	E- / 0.2	1.61	6.01	-10.08 / 1	-2.48 / 3	-4.67 / 0	0.00	1.97
EM	Janus Emerging Markets C	JMFCX	E-	(800) 295-2687	E- / 0.2	1.35	5.78	-10.71 / 1	-3.15 / 2	-5.35 / 0	0.00	2.68
EM	● Janus Emerging Markets D	JMFDX	E-	(800) 295-2687	E / 0.4	1.62	6.25	-9.81 / 1	-2.15 / 4	-4.46 / 0	0.34	1.67
EM	Janus Emerging Markets I	JMFIX	E-	(800) 295-2687	E / 0.4	1.74	6.28	-9.63 / 1	-2.01 / 4	-4.32 / 0	0.38	1.52
EM	Janus Emerging Markets S	JMFSX	E-	(800) 295-2687	E / 0.3	1.62	6.01	-9.67 / 1	-2.37 / 3	-4.62 / 0	0.25	2.05
EM	Janus Emerging Markets T	JMFTX	E-	(800) 295-2687	E / 0.3	1.61	6.16	-9.88 / 1	-2.29 / 4	-4.51 / 0	0.25	1.77
* GEI	Janus Flexible Bond A	JDFAX	C-	(800) 295-2687	C- / 3.9	2.17	1.24	0.32 /46	2.00 /61	3.84 /59	2.28	0.79
GEI	Janus Flexible Bond C	JFICX	C+	(800) 295-2687	C / 4.7	1.90	0.88	-0.37 /27	1.26 /47	3.07 /46	1.72	1.53
COI	● Janus Flexible Bond D	JANFX	B+	(800) 295-2687	C+ / 6.4	2.22	1.34	0.51 /50	2.19 /65	4.03 /62	2.60	0.60
GEI	Janus Flexible Bond I	JFLEX	B+	(800) 295-2687	C+ / 6.5	2.23	1.36	0.55 /51	2.22 /66	4.07 /63	2.64	0.57
COI	Janus Flexible Bond N	JDFNX	B+	(800) 295-2687	C+ / 6.6	2.16	1.34	0.58 /51	2.32 /68	4.11 /63	2.76	0.44

● Denotes fund is closed to new investors
* Denotes fund is included in Section II

RISK			NET ASSETS		ASSET							FUND MANAGER		MINIMUM		LOADS	
Risk Rating/Pts	3 Yr Avg Standard Deviation	Avg Duration	NAV As of 3/31/16	Total $(Mil)	Cash %	Gov. Bond %	Muni. Bond %	Corp. Bond %	Other %	Portfolio Turnover Ratio	Avg Coupon Rate	Manager Quality Pct	Manager Tenure (Years)	Initial Purch. $	Additional Purch. $	Front End Load	Back End Load
U /	N/A	N/A	1.00	417	100	0	0	0	0	0	0.0	N/A	N/A	1,000	0	0.0	0.0
U /	N/A	N/A	1.00	25	100	0	0	0	0	0	0.0	N/A	N/A	1,000	0	0.0	0.0
D- / 1.4	6.2	6.9	11.26	82	0	87	0	7	6	52	2.6	2	8	0	0	0.0	0.0
D- / 1.4	6.2	6.9	11.13	805	0	87	0	7	6	52	2.6	2	8	0	0	0.0	0.0
A- / 9.1	1.1	N/A	9.65	275	2	82	0	0	16	31	0.0	52	N/A	0	0	0.0	0.0
C / 5.4	3.3	1.7	9.39	28	1	8	0	63	28	61	5.2	37	7	1,000	0	2.5	0.0
C / 5.5	3.3	1.7	9.37	24	1	8	0	63	28	61	5.2	43	7	250,000	0	0.0	0.0
C / 5.4	3.3	1.7	9.39	1,319	1	8	0	63	28	61	5.2	52	7	0	0	0.0	0.0
C+ / 6.4	3.1	3.6	10.48	1,170	5	25	3	45	22	37	0.0	97	10	1,000	0	4.0	0.0
C+ / 6.4	3.1	3.6	10.48	447	5	25	3	45	22	37	0.0	94	10	1,000	0	0.0	0.0
C+ / 6.2	3.1	3.6	10.49	2,057	5	25	3	45	22	37	0.0	98	10	250,000	0	0.0	0.0
C+ / 6.3	3.1	3.6	10.48	1,779	5	25	3	45	22	37	0.0	98	10	0	0	0.0	0.0
C+ / 6.3	3.1	3.6	10.49	21	5	25	3	45	22	37	0.0	97	10	0	0	0.0	0.0
C+ / 6.4	3.0	3.6	10.49	21	5	25	3	45	22	37	0.0	90	10	1,000,000	0	0.0	0.0
D+ / 2.9	4.3	10.9	10.12	536	2	0	97	0	1	10	0.0	23	N/A	1,000	0	4.0	0.0
C- / 3.0	4.2	10.9	10.12	7	2	0	97	0	1	10	0.0	12	N/A	1,000	0	0.0	0.0
D+ / 2.9	4.3	10.9	10.11	59	2	0	97	0	1	10	0.0	12	N/A	1,000	0	0.0	0.0
D / 1.7	5.4	4.6	10.30	74	2	0	0	95	3	40	6.5	55	11	0	0	0.0	0.0
D / 1.7	5.4	4.6	10.29	259	2	0	0	95	3	40	6.5	57	11	0	0	0.0	0.0
C+ / 6.1	3.1	5.5	9.63	552	1	11	0	41	47	60	0.0	98	11	0	0	0.0	0.0
C+ / 5.9	3.2	5.6	13.34	1,023	0	31	0	21	48	425	3.0	97	9	0	0	0.0	0.0
D+ / 2.9	4.8	6.4	12.49	44	9	55	3	19	14	81	4.1	84	8	0	0	0.0	0.0
D+ / 2.8	4.9	6.4	12.44	488	9	55	3	19	14	81	4.1	85	8	0	0	0.0	0.0
E+ / 0.7	6.5	3.9	4.87	86	2	1	0	87	10	74	8.5	7	19	0	0	0.0	0.0
E+ / 0.7	6.5	3.9	4.80	85	2	1	0	87	10	74	8.5	7	19	0	0	0.0	0.0
C / 4.8	3.6	5.4	11.17	167	0	10	1	33	56	97	6.7	30	10	0	0	0.0	0.0
C / 4.9	3.5	5.4	11.17	91	0	10	1	33	56	97	6.7	25	10	0	0	0.0	0.0
C / 4.8	3.5	5.4	11.13	25	0	10	1	33	56	97	6.7	31	10	0	0	0.0	0.0
E+ / 0.9	6.4	7.2	11.40	5	0	85	0	6	9	60	2.1	23	8	0	0	0.0	0.0
E+ / 0.9	6.4	7.2	11.23	30	0	85	0	6	9	60	2.1	20	8	0	0	0.0	0.0
D- / 1.0	6.4	7.2	11.24	38	0	85	0	6	9	60	2.1	25	8	0	0	0.0	0.0
C+ / 6.3	3.1	3.5	13.31	464	5	25	3	44	23	49	0.0	92	12	0	0	0.0	0.0
C+ / 6.3	3.1	3.5	13.34	50	5	25	3	44	23	49	0.0	91	12	0	0	0.0	0.0
C+ / 6.3	3.1	3.5	13.27	85	5	25	3	44	23	49	0.0	92	12	0	0	0.0	0.0
C+ / 5.8	3.2	5.7	10.41	157	0	43	1	24	32	67	5.6	49	11	0	0	0.0	0.0
E- / 0.0	13.8	N/A	19.99	473	3	0	0	0	97	26	0.0	99	19	0	0	0.0	0.0
E- / 0.0	13.8	N/A	19.90	26	3	0	0	0	97	26	0.0	99	19	0	0	0.0	0.0
E- / 0.0	13.8	N/A	19.96	35	3	0	0	0	97	26	0.0	99	19	0	0	0.0	0.0
B+ / 8.4	2.1	3.6	10.21	26	8	0	91	0	1	16	0.0	41	11	5,000	0	0.0	0.0
B- / 7.4	2.7	5.7	11.92	356	0	36	0	36	28	111	3.7	68	9	0	0	0.0	0.0
B- / 7.4	2.7	5.7	12.92	340	0	36	0	36	28	111	3.7	54	9	0	0	0.0	0.0
E- / 0.0	16.8	N/A	7.58	N/A	5	0	0	0	95	131	0.0	9	4	2,500	0	5.8	0.0
E- / 0.0	16.8	N/A	7.50	N/A	5	0	0	0	95	131	0.0	7	4	2,500	0	0.0	0.0
E- / 0.0	16.8	N/A	7.55	7	5	0	0	0	95	131	0.0	12	4	2,500	0	0.0	0.0
E- / 0.0	16.8	N/A	7.58	37	5	0	0	0	95	131	0.0	13	4	1,000,000	0	0.0	0.0
E- / 0.0	16.8	N/A	7.55	1	5	0	0	0	95	131	0.0	10	4	2,500	0	0.0	0.0
E- / 0.0	16.8	N/A	7.56	4	5	0	0	0	95	131	0.0	11	4	2,500	0	0.0	0.0
B- / 7.5	2.7	5.7	10.46	717	0	36	0	36	28	124	3.7	56	9	2,500	0	4.8	0.0
B / 7.6	2.7	5.7	10.46	361	0	36	0	36	28	124	3.7	31	9	2,500	0	0.0	0.0
B- / 7.5	2.7	5.7	10.46	650	0	36	0	36	28	124	3.7	83	9	2,500	100	0.0	0.0
B / 7.6	2.7	5.7	10.46	5,280	0	36	0	36	28	124	3.7	68	9	1,000,000	0	0.0	0.0
B- / 7.4	2.7	5.7	10.45	603	0	36	0	36	28	124	3.7	85	9	0	0	0.0	0.0

99 Pct = Best 0 Pct = Worst Fund Type	Fund Name	Ticker Symbol	Overall Investment Rating	Phone	PERFORMANCE Performance Rating/Pts	Total Return % through 3/31/16 3 Mo	6 Mo	1Yr / Pct	Annualized 3Yr / Pct	5Yr / Pct	Incl. in Returns Dividend Yield	Expense Ratio
GEI	Janus Flexible Bond R	JDFRX	**C+**	(800) 295-2687	**C / 5.4**	2.07	1.05	-0.07 /31	1.59 /54	3.43 /52	2.01	1.19
GEI	Janus Flexible Bond S	JADFX	**B-**	(800) 295-2687	**C+ / 5.8**	2.04	1.08	0.18 /44	1.85 /59	3.68 /56	2.26	0.94
GEI	Janus Flexible Bond T	JAFIX	**B**	(800) 295-2687	**C+ / 6.3**	2.21	1.31	0.44 /49	2.11 /64	3.94 /61	2.52	0.69
GL	Janus Global Bond A	JGBAX	**D**	(800) 295-2687	**D+ / 2.9**	3.78	2.53	-1.27 /20	1.32 /49	2.87 /43	1.77	1.04
GL	Janus Global Bond C	JGBCX	**D**	(800) 295-2687	**C- / 3.7**	3.60	2.27	-1.99 /16	0.52 /33	2.09 /32	1.12	1.81
GL	● Janus Global Bond D	JGBDX	**C-**	(800) 295-2687	**C / 5.5**	3.94	2.74	-1.08 /21	1.47 /51	3.00 /45	2.04	0.89
GL	Janus Global Bond I	JGBIX	**C-**	(800) 295-2687	**C+ / 5.7**	3.85	2.67	-1.03 /21	1.57 /53	3.10 /47	2.09	0.80
GL	Janus Global Bond N	JGLNX	**U**	(800) 295-2687	**U /**	3.88	2.83	-0.92 /22	--	--	2.20	0.70
GL	Janus Global Bond S	JGBSX	**D+**	(800) 295-2687	**C / 5.2**	3.77	2.59	-1.07 /21	1.31 /49	2.81 /42	2.05	1.19
GL	Janus Global Bond T	JHBTX	**D+**	(800) 295-2687	**C / 5.3**	3.81	2.59	-1.16 /20	1.36 /49	2.92 /44	1.97	0.96
GL	Janus Global Unconstrained Bond A	JUCAX	**U**	(800) 295-2687	**U /**	2.03	3.29	0.34 /47	--	--	1.96	1.07
GL	Janus Global Unconstrained Bond C	JUCCX	**U**	(800) 295-2687	**U /**	1.85	2.90	-0.44 /27	--	--	1.29	1.80
GL	Janus Global Unconstrained Bond D	JUCDX	**U**	(800) 295-2687	**U /**	1.92	3.27	0.23 /45	--	--	2.06	1.14
GL	Janus Global Unconstrained Bond I	JUCIX	**U**	(800) 295-2687	**U /**	2.10	3.42	0.62 /52	--	--	2.34	0.76
GL	Janus Global Unconstrained Bond N	JUCNX	**U**	(800) 295-2687	**U /**	2.10	3.44	0.61 /51	--	--	2.34	0.77
GL	Janus Global Unconstrained Bond S	JUCSX	**U**	(800) 295-2687	**U /**	2.00	3.20	0.16 /43	--	--	1.89	1.36
GL	Janus Global Unconstrained Bond T	JUCTX	**U**	(800) 295-2687	**U /**	1.94	3.31	0.28 /45	--	--	2.11	1.01
COH	Janus High Yield N	JHYNX	**D+**	(800) 295-2687	**C+ / 6.0**	2.33	0.67	-1.67 /17	2.26 /67	4.64 /69	5.97	0.61
GL	Janus High-Yield A	JHYAX	**D**	(800) 295-2687	**C- / 3.1**	2.23	0.58	-1.91 /16	1.92 /60	4.32 /66	5.33	0.98
GL	Janus High-Yield C	JDHCX	**D**	(800) 295-2687	**C- / 4.0**	2.07	0.13	-2.65 /13	1.18 /46	3.58 /54	4.93	1.70
GL	● Janus High-Yield D	JNHYX	**D+**	(800) 295-2687	**C+ / 5.8**	2.29	0.57	-1.83 /16	2.13 /64	4.54 /68	5.80	0.77
GL	Janus High-Yield I	JHYFX	**D+**	(800) 295-2687	**C+ / 5.8**	2.31	0.61	-1.75 /17	2.17 /65	4.60 /69	5.89	0.70
GL	Janus High-Yield R	JHYRX	**D**	(800) 295-2687	**C / 4.6**	2.15	0.28	-2.41 /14	1.48 /52	3.93 /60	5.19	1.37
GL	Janus High-Yield S	JDHYX	**D+**	(800) 295-2687	**C / 5.1**	2.21	0.41	-2.13 /15	1.76 /57	4.16 /64	5.47	1.12
GL	Janus High-Yield T	JAHYX	**D+**	(800) 295-2687	**C+ / 5.6**	2.29	0.55	-1.89 /16	2.01 /61	4.44 /67	5.74	0.87
GL	Janus Multi Sector Income A	JMUAX	**U**	(800) 295-2687	**U /**	1.24	0.77	-0.31 /28	--	--	4.17	2.29
GL	Janus Multi Sector Income C	JMUCX	**U**	(800) 295-2687	**U /**	1.27	0.54	-0.85 /23	--	--	3.72	3.04
GL	Janus Multi Sector Income D	JMUDX	**U**	(800) 295-2687	**U /**	1.50	1.00	--	--	--	4.58	2.22
GL	Janus Multi Sector Income I	JMUIX	**U**	(800) 295-2687	**U /**	1.32	0.96	0.03 /35	--	--	4.73	2.02
GL	Janus Multi Sector Income N	JMTNX	**U**	(800) 295-2687	**U /**	1.43	1.08	0.14 /42	--	--	4.72	2.02
GL	Janus Multi Sector Income S	JMUSX	**U**	(800) 295-2687	**U /**	1.34	0.85	-0.14 /30	--	--	4.44	2.52
GL	Janus Multi Sector Income T	JMUTX	**U**	(800) 295-2687	**U /**	1.38	0.95	-0.04 /31	--	--	4.54	2.26
COI	Janus Short Term Bond N	JSHNX	**B**	(800) 295-2687	**C / 4.6**	0.99	0.68	0.74 /54	1.12 /45	1.69 /27	1.40	0.59
GL	Janus Short-Term Bond A	JSHAX	**C**	(800) 295-2687	**D+ / 2.9**	0.92	0.51	0.77 /55	0.83 /40	1.41 /25	1.07	0.90
GL	Janus Short-Term Bond C	JSHCX	**C-**	(800) 295-2687	**D / 1.8**	0.40	0.14	-0.26 /28	-0.03 /15	0.66 /18	0.40	1.67
GL	● Janus Short-Term Bond D	JNSTX	**C+**	(800) 295-2687	**C- / 4.2**	0.95	0.59	0.60 /51	0.86 /40	1.54 /26	1.26	0.76
GL	Janus Short-Term Bond I	JSHIX	**B**	(800) 295-2687	**C / 4.6**	0.98	0.64	1.02 /59	1.07 /44	1.66 /27	1.35	0.65
GL	Janus Short-Term Bond S	JSHSX	**C+**	(800) 295-2687	**C- / 3.5**	0.55	0.43	0.36 /47	0.57 /34	1.24 /23	1.02	1.09
GL	Janus Short-Term Bond T	JASBX	**C+**	(800) 295-2687	**C- / 3.9**	0.93	0.54	0.50 /49	0.76 /38	1.44 /25	1.16	0.84
GEI	JNL/PPM America Strategic Income		**D**	(800) 392-2909	**C- / 4.1**	2.43	1.25	-3.21 /11	1.17 /46	--	0.00	0.76
GEI	JNL/PPM America Total Return A		**D**	(800) 392-2909	**C- / 3.7**	2.71	2.09	-0.36 /27	0.41 /31	3.48 /53	2.42	0.85
GL	John Hancock Glbl Sht Dur Crdt NAV		**U**	(800) 257-3336	**U /**	2.37	2.35	-1.74 /17	--	--	6.36	0.97
GL	John Hancock II Asia Pac TR Bd NA		**D+**	(800) 257-3336	**C+ / 6.3**	5.33	7.66	3.58 /79	0.72 /37	--	2.77	0.77
GES	Johnson Fixed Income	JFINX	**B**	(800) 541-0170	**B- / 7.3**	3.19	2.59	1.73 /69	2.42 /69	3.67 /56	2.12	0.85
MUN	Johnson Municipal Income	JMUNX	**A+**	(800) 541-0170	**B+ / 8.7**	1.27	2.08	2.76 /83	2.75 /85	3.79 /76	1.90	0.66
MM	JPMorgan 100% US Tr Sc MM	VPIXX	**U**	(800) 480-4111	**U /**	0.01	0.01	0.01 /32	--	--	0.01	0.31
MM	JPMorgan 100% US Tr Sc MM Cptl	CJTXX	**C-**	(800) 480-4111	**D / 1.9**	0.03	0.03	0.03 /36	0.01 /17	0.01 / 5	0.03	0.21
MMT	JPMorgan CA Mun MM E-trade	JCEXX	**C**	(800) 480-4111	**D / 2.1**	0.00	0.02	0.02 /36	0.02 /22	0.02 /10	0.02	1.07
MMT	JPMorgan CA Mun MM Morgan	VCAXX	**C-**	(800) 480-4111	**D / 1.9**	0.00	0.02	0.02 /36	0.01 /20	0.01 / 8	0.02	0.62
MMT	JPMorgan CA Mun MM Svc	JCVXX	**C-**	(800) 480-4111	**D / 1.9**	0.00	0.02	0.02 /36	0.01 /20	0.01 / 8	0.02	1.07
MUH	JPMorgan CA Tax Free Bond A	JCBAX	**B**	(800) 480-4111	**B / 7.9**	1.44	2.57	3.17 /87	2.86 /87	4.60 /82	2.70	0.96
MUH	JPMorgan CA Tax Free Bond C	JCBCX	**B+**	(800) 480-4111	**B+ / 8.3**	1.32	2.32	2.66 /82	2.33 /81	4.08 /78	2.31	1.47

● Denotes fund is closed to new investors
* Denotes fund is included in Section II

RISK			NET ASSETS		ASSET							FUND MANAGER		MINIMUM		LOADS	
Risk Rating/Pts	3 Yr Avg Standard Deviation	Avg Duration	NAV As of 3/31/16	Total $(Mil)	Cash %	Gov. Bond %	Muni. Bond %	Corp. Bond %	Other %	Portfolio Turnover Ratio	Avg Coupon Rate	Manager Quality Pct	Manager Tenure (Years)	Initial Purch. $	Additional Purch. $	Front End Load	Back End Load
B- / 7.5	2.7	5.7	10.46	47	0	36	0	36	28	124	3.7	41	9	2,500	0	0.0	0.0
B- / 7.5	2.7	5.7	10.46	71	0	36	0	36	28	124	3.7	49	9	2,500	0	0.0	0.0
B- / 7.4	2.7	5.7	10.46	1,531	0	36	0	36	28	124	3.7	58	9	2,500	0	0.0	0.0
C- / 3.7	4.2	6.1	9.69	15	0	52	0	37	11	191	3.5	92	6	2,500	0	4.8	0.0
C- / 3.7	4.2	6.1	9.70	5	0	52	0	37	11	191	3.5	84	6	2,500	0	0.0	0.0
C- / 3.7	4.2	6.1	9.69	9	0	52	0	37	11	191	3.5	93	6	2,500	100	0.0	0.0
C- / 3.7	4.2	6.1	9.68	28	0	52	0	37	11	191	3.5	94	6	1,000,000	0	0.0	0.0
U /	N/A	6.1	9.68	205	0	52	0	37	11	191	3.5	N/A	6	0	0	0.0	0.0
C- / 3.6	4.2	6.1	9.70	N/A	0	52	0	37	11	191	3.5	92	6	2,500	0	0.0	0.0
C- / 3.6	4.2	6.1	9.69	7	0	52	0	37	11	191	3.5	93	6	2,500	0	0.0	0.0
U /	N/A	3.6	9.70	78	0	0	0	0	100	107	3.0	N/A	2	2,500	0	4.8	0.0
U /	N/A	3.6	9.69	41	0	0	0	0	100	107	3.0	N/A	2	2,500	0	0.0	0.0
U /	N/A	3.6	9.70	13	0	0	0	0	100	107	3.0	N/A	2	2,500	100	0.0	0.0
U /	N/A	3.6	9.70	976	0	0	0	0	100	107	3.0	N/A	2	1,000,000	0	0.0	0.0
U /	N/A	3.6	9.70	3	0	0	0	0	100	107	3.0	N/A	2	0	0	0.0	0.0
U /	N/A	3.6	9.70	1	0	0	0	0	100	107	3.0	N/A	2	2,500	0	0.0	0.0
U /	N/A	3.6	9.69	153	0	0	0	0	100	107	3.0	N/A	2	2,500	0	0.0	0.0
D / 2.1	5.0	3.7	8.01	18	10	0	0	85	5	71	7.2	87	13	0	0	0.0	0.0
D+ / 2.6	5.1	3.7	8.01	127	10	0	0	85	5	71	7.2	96	13	2,500	0	4.8	0.0
D+ / 2.7	5.0	3.7	8.01	49	10	0	0	85	5	71	7.2	91	13	2,500	0	0.0	0.0
D+ / 2.7	5.1	3.7	8.01	308	10	0	0	85	5	71	7.2	96	13	2,500	100	0.0	0.0
D+ / 2.8	5.0	3.7	8.01	201	10	0	0	85	5	71	7.2	97	13	1,000,000	0	0.0	0.0
D+ / 2.8	5.0	3.7	8.00	2	10	0	0	85	5	71	7.2	93	13	2,500	0	0.0	0.0
D+ / 2.7	5.1	3.7	8.02	2	10	0	0	85	5	71	7.2	95	13	2,500	0	0.0	0.0
D+ / 2.7	5.0	3.7	8.01	1,122	10	0	0	85	5	71	7.2	96	13	2,500	0	0.0	0.0
U /	N/A	N/A	9.54	10	3	11	0	54	32	132	0.0	N/A	2	2,500	0	4.8	0.0
U /	N/A	N/A	9.55	3	3	11	0	54	32	132	0.0	N/A	2	2,500	0	0.0	0.0
U /	N/A	N/A	9.55	9	3	11	0	54	32	132	0.0	N/A	2	2,500	100	0.0	0.0
U /	N/A	N/A	9.54	7	3	11	0	54	32	132	0.0	N/A	2	1,000,000	0	0.0	0.0
U /	N/A	N/A	9.55	2	3	11	0	54	32	132	0.0	N/A	2	0	0	0.0	0.0
U /	N/A	N/A	9.55	2	3	11	0	54	32	132	0.0	N/A	2	2,500	0	0.0	0.0
U /	N/A	N/A	9.55	23	3	11	0	54	32	132	0.0	N/A	2	2,500	0	0.0	0.0
A / 9.3	1.0	1.6	3.03	36	4	25	0	64	7	84	2.3	84	9	0	0	0.0	0.0
A- / 9.1	1.1	1.6	3.03	142	4	25	0	64	7	84	2.3	88	9	2,500	0	2.5	0.0
A / 9.4	0.9	1.6	3.02	57	4	25	0	64	7	84	2.3	60	9	2,500	0	0.0	0.0
A- / 9.2	1.1	1.6	3.03	191	4	25	0	64	7	84	2.3	88	9	2,500	100	0.0	0.0
A- / 9.1	1.1	1.6	3.03	501	4	25	0	64	7	84	2.3	90	9	1,000,000	0	0.0	0.0
A / 9.4	0.9	1.6	3.02	3	4	25	0	64	7	84	2.3	84	9	2,500	0	0.0	0.0
A- / 9.1	1.1	1.6	3.03	1,526	4	25	0	64	7	84	2.3	87	9	2,500	0	0.0	0.0
D+ / 2.5	5.2	5.0	10.54	105	4	0	0	84	12	81	5.7	38	4	0	0	0.0	0.0
C- / 3.3	4.4	5.4	11.74	979	3	12	0	58	27	88	4.5	11	7	0	0	0.0	0.0
U /	N/A	N/A	8.59	310	0	0	0	0	100	62	0.0	N/A	3	0	0	0.0	0.0
D+ / 2.5	5.3	N/A	9.29	406	3	44	0	51	2	35	0.0	87	3	0	0	0.0	0.0
C+ / 6.1	3.1	5.5	17.06	258	3	22	9	51	15	28	4.2	57	21	2,000	100	0.0	0.0
B / 7.8	2.6	4.4	17.50	71	1	0	98	0	1	18	4.5	73	21	2,000	100	0.0	0.0
U /	N/A	N/A	1.00	1,790	100	0	0	0	0	0	0.0	N/A	N/A	5,000,000	0	0.0	0.0
A+ / 9.9	N/A	N/A	1.00	9,151	100	0	0	0	0	0	0.0	64	N/A	50,000,000	0	0.0	0.0
A+ / 9.9	N/A	N/A	1.00	1,085	100	0	0	0	0	0	0.0	N/A	N/A	0	0	0.0	0.0
A+ / 9.9	N/A	N/A	1.00	283	100	0	0	0	0	0	0.0	N/A	N/A	1,000	25	0.0	0.0
A+ / 9.9	N/A	N/A	1.00	216	100	0	0	0	0	0	0.0	N/A	N/A	10,000,000	0	0.0	0.0
C / 5.2	2.9	4.9	11.15	83	3	0	96	0	1	4	4.3	58	12	1,000	50	3.8	0.0
C / 5.2	2.9	4.9	11.06	58	3	0	96	0	1	4	4.3	39	12	1,000	50	0.0	0.0

Fund Type	Fund Name (99 Pct = Best, 0 Pct = Worst)	Ticker Symbol	Overall Investment Rating	Phone	PERFORMANCE: Performance Rating/Pts	Total Return % through 3/31/16: 3 Mo	6 Mo	1Yr / Pct	Annualized: 3Yr / Pct	Annualized: 5Yr / Pct	Incl. in Returns: Dividend Yield	Expense Ratio
MUH	JPMorgan CA Tax Free Bond I	JPICX	**A-**	(800) 480-4111	**A- / 9.0**	1.50	2.58	3.26 /88	2.93 /87	4.70 /83	2.97	0.54
MUH	JPMorgan CA Tax Free Bond Sel	JPCBX	**A-**	(800) 480-4111	**A- / 9.0**	1.54	2.68	3.31 /88	2.92 /87	4.66 /83	2.85	0.72
* GEI	JPMorgan Core Bond A	PGBOX	**C+**	(800) 480-4111	**C / 5.0**	2.78	1.90	1.79 /70	2.07 /63	3.52 /53	2.07	0.98
GEI	JPMorgan Core Bond C	OBOCX	**B-**	(800) 480-4111	**C+ / 5.6**	2.60	1.55	1.18 /61	1.42 /51	2.84 /43	1.47	1.47
GEI	JPMorgan Core Bond R2	JCBZX	**B**	(800) 480-4111	**C+ / 6.2**	2.64	1.70	1.45 /66	1.81 /58	3.25 /49	1.91	1.35
GEI	JPMorgan Core Bond R5	JCBRX	**A**	(800) 480-4111	**B- / 7.1**	2.78	1.99	2.04 /72	2.36 /68	3.82 /59	2.47	0.55
GEI	JPMorgan Core Bond R6	JCBUX	**A**	(800) 480-4111	**B- / 7.3**	2.80	2.03	2.14 /73	2.45 /70	3.89 /60	2.57	0.41
GEI	JPMorgan Core Bond Sel	WOBDX	**A-**	(800) 480-4111	**C+ / 6.9**	2.83	1.92	1.98 /72	2.24 /66	3.70 /57	2.33	0.73
* GL	JPMorgan Core Plus Bond A	ONIAX	**C+**	(800) 480-4111	**C+ / 5.8**	2.66	1.91	0.86 /56	2.69 /73	4.10 /63	2.80	1.00
GL	JPMorgan Core Plus Bond C	OBDCX	**B-**	(800) 480-4111	**C+ / 6.2**	2.50	1.44	0.16 /43	2.02 /62	3.42 /52	2.21	1.49
GL	JPMorgan Core Plus Bond Inst	JCBIX	**A**	(800) 480-4111	**B / 7.7**	2.86	2.06	1.26 /63	3.01 /76	4.40 /66	3.19	0.54
GL	JPMorgan Core Plus Bond R2	JCPZX	**B+**	(800) 480-4111	**C+ / 6.7**	2.68	1.69	0.55 /51	2.32 /68	3.70 /57	2.49	1.36
GL	JPMorgan Core Plus Bond R6	JCPUX	**A**	(800) 480-4111	**B / 7.7**	2.74	1.96	1.19 /61	3.04 /77	4.45 /67	3.24	0.43
GL	JPMorgan Core Plus Bond Sel	HLIPX	**A-**	(800) 480-4111	**B- / 7.5**	2.85	1.99	1.11 /60	2.85 /75	4.24 /65	3.05	0.69
GEI	JPMorgan Corporate Bond A	CBRAX	**C-**	(800) 480-4111	**C+ / 6.4**	3.90	3.83	0.74 /54	2.92 /76	--	2.93	1.08
GEI	JPMorgan Corporate Bond C	CBRCX	**C-**	(800) 480-4111	**B- / 7.2**	3.88	3.61	0.25 /45	2.41 /69	--	2.56	1.90
GEI	JPMorgan Corporate Bond R6	CBFVX	**C**	(800) 480-4111	**B / 8.1**	4.09	4.13	1.12 /61	3.32 /79	--	3.41	0.44
GEI	JPMorgan Corporate Bond Sel	CBFSX	**C**	(800) 480-4111	**B / 8.0**	4.06	4.07	1.01 /59	3.22 /78	--	3.31	0.74
EM	JPMorgan Emerg Mkt Corp Debt A	JEMAX	**U**	(800) 480-4111	**U /**	4.28	4.06	0.92 /57	--	--	3.65	3.75
EM	JPMorgan Emerg Mkt Corp Debt C	JEFMX	**U**	(800) 480-4111	**U /**	4.15	3.70	0.46 /49	--	--	3.23	4.22
EM	JPMorgan Emerg Mkt Corp Debt R6	JCDRX	**U**	(800) 480-4111	**U /**	4.40	4.21	1.43 /65	--	--	4.29	2.01
EM	JPMorgan Emerg Mkt Corp Debt Sel	JEDSX	**U**	(800) 480-4111	**U /**	4.34	4.18	1.16 /61	--	--	3.82	2.39
EM	JPMorgan Emerg Mkt Debt A	JEDAX	**D-**	(800) 480-4111	**C- / 3.0**	4.33	5.57	1.53 /67	0.35 /31	4.65 /69	5.04	1.62
EM	JPMorgan Emerg Mkt Debt C	JEDCX	**D-**	(800) 480-4111	**C- / 3.8**	4.07	5.16	0.99 /58	-0.18 /14	4.10 /63	4.72	1.98
EM	JPMorgan Emerg Mkt Debt R5	JEMRX	**D**	(800) 480-4111	**C+ / 5.6**	4.26	5.62	1.90 /71	0.77 /38	5.09 /72	5.69	0.96
EM	JPMorgan Emerg Mkt Debt R6	JEMVX	**D**	(800) 480-4111	**C+ / 5.7**	4.30	5.67	1.96 /72	0.83 /39	5.08 /72	5.78	0.84
EM	JPMorgan Emerg Mkt Debt Sel	JEMDX	**D**	(800) 480-4111	**C / 5.3**	4.37	5.68	1.81 /70	0.59 /35	4.89 /71	5.51	1.13
EM	JPMorgan Emg Mkts Loc Curr Db A	JECAX	**E-**	(800) 480-4111	**E- / 0.0**	9.50	9.35	-3.99 / 8	-8.17 / 1	--	0.00	1.97
EM	JPMorgan Emg Mkts Loc Curr Db C	JECCX	**E-**	(800) 480-4111	**E- / 0.1**	9.34	9.04	-4.51 / 6	-8.63 / 0	--	0.00	2.49
EM	JPMorgan Emg Mkts Loc Curr Db R2	JECZX	**E-**	(800) 480-4111	**E- / 0.1**	9.42	9.12	-4.24 / 7	-8.39 / 0	--	0.00	2.26
EM	JPMorgan Emg Mkts Loc Curr Db R5	JECRX	**E-**	(800) 480-4111	**E- / 0.1**	9.67	9.52	-3.59 / 9	-7.76 / 1	--	0.00	1.55
EM	JPMorgan Emg Mkts Loc Curr Db R6	JECUX	**E-**	(800) 480-4111	**E- / 0.1**	9.66	9.51	-3.59 / 9	-7.72 / 1	--	0.00	1.03
EM	JPMorgan Emg Mkts Loc Curr Db Sel	JECSX	**E-**	(800) 480-4111	**E- / 0.1**	9.58	9.58	-3.73 / 9	-7.91 / 1	--	0.00	1.27
MM	JPMorgan Federal MM Agency	VFIXX	**C-**	(800) 480-4111	**D / 1.9**	0.02	0.03	0.03 /36	0.02 /20	0.01 / 5	0.03	0.34
MM	JPMorgan Federal MM Inst	JFMXX	**C**	(800) 480-4111	**D / 2.1**	0.03	0.04	0.04 /37	0.02 /20	0.02 / 8	0.04	0.34
MM	JPMorgan Federal MM Morgan	VFVXX	**U**	(800) 480-4111	**U /**	--	--	--	--	--	0.01	0.64
MM	JPMorgan Federal MM Prem	VFPXX	**U**	(800) 480-4111	**U /**	--	--	--	--	--	0.01	0.49
MM	JPMorgan Federal MM Res	JFRXX	**U**	(800) 480-4111	**U /**	--	--	--	--	--	0.01	0.74
LP	JPMorgan Floating Rate Income A	JPHAX	**D**	(800) 480-4111	**D- / 1.2**	1.10	-1.38	-3.26 /11	0.57 /34	--	4.23	1.27
LP	JPMorgan Floating Rate Income C	JPHCX	**D**	(800) 480-4111	**D- / 1.3**	1.08	-1.53	-3.64 / 9	0.08 /26	--	3.83	1.75
LP	JPMorgan Floating Rate Income R6	JPHRX	**U**	(800) 480-4111	**U /**	1.29	-1.20	-2.80 /12	--	--	4.71	0.68
LP	JPMorgan Floating Rate Income Sel	JPHSX	**D+**	(800) 480-4111	**C- / 3.0**	1.27	-1.15	-2.90 /12	0.83 /40	--	4.60	0.93
GL	JPMorgan Global Bond Opptys A	GBOAX	**C-**	(800) 480-4111	**C / 5.3**	2.40	2.70	-0.63 /25	2.55 /71	--	5.66	1.28
GL	JPMorgan Global Bond Opptys C	GBOCX	**C-**	(800) 480-4111	**C+ / 6.2**	2.31	2.43	-1.08 /21	2.15 /64	--	5.54	1.80
GL	JPMorgan Global Bond Opptys R6	GBONX	**C+**	(800) 480-4111	**B- / 7.5**	2.49	2.90	-0.26 /28	2.97 /76	--	6.25	0.72
GL	JPMorgan Global Bond Opptys Select	GBOSX	**C+**	(800) 480-4111	**B- / 7.4**	2.46	2.83	-0.39 /27	2.83 /75	--	6.12	0.98
* USS	JPMorgan Government Bond A	OGGAX	**C-**	(800) 480-4111	**C / 4.3**	2.87	2.05	1.87 /71	1.57 /53	3.58 /54	2.10	1.12
USS	JPMorgan Government Bond C	OGVCX	**C-**	(800) 480-4111	**C / 4.7**	2.70	1.66	1.11 /60	0.86 /40	2.83 /42	1.44	1.53
USS	JPMorgan Government Bond R2	JGBZX	**C**	(800) 480-4111	**C+ / 5.6**	2.81	1.91	1.62 /68	1.31 /49	3.31 /50	1.94	1.41
USS	JPMorgan Government Bond Sel	HLGAX	**C+**	(800) 480-4111	**C+ / 6.5**	2.94	2.18	2.17 /73	1.85 /59	3.85 /59	2.47	0.79
* COH	JPMorgan High Yield A	OHYAX	**E+**	(800) 480-4111	**D- / 1.5**	2.46	0.29	-4.73 / 6	1.25 /47	3.82 /59	5.73	1.37
COH	JPMorgan High Yield C	OGHCX	**D-**	(800) 480-4111	**D+ / 2.6**	2.32	0.02	-5.15 / 5	0.68 /36	3.22 /49	5.33	1.85

● Denotes fund is closed to new investors
* Denotes fund is included in Section II

RISK			NET ASSETS		ASSET							FUND MANAGER		MINIMUM		LOADS	
Risk Rating/Pts	3 Yr Avg Standard Deviation	Avg Duration	NAV As of 3/31/16	Total $(Mil)	Cash %	Gov. Bond %	Muni. Bond %	Corp. Bond %	Other %	Portfolio Turnover Ratio	Avg Coupon Rate	Manager Quality Pct	Manager Tenure (Years)	Initial Purch. $	Additional Purch. $	Front End Load	Back End Load
C / 5.1	2.9	4.9	10.92	134	3	0	96	0	1	4	4.3	60	12	3,000,000	0	0.0	0.0
C / 5.2	2.9	4.9	11.15	38	3	0	96	0	1	4	4.3	60	12	1,000,000	0	0.0	0.0
B / 7.6	2.7	5.0	11.81	3,135	3	29	0	24	44	15	2.7	57	25	1,000	50	3.8	0.0
B / 7.6	2.7	5.0	11.88	994	3	29	0	24	44	15	2.7	36	25	1,000	50	0.0	0.0
B / 7.6	2.7	5.0	11.79	114	3	29	0	24	44	15	2.7	48	25	0	0	0.0	0.0
B / 7.6	2.7	5.0	11.78	451	3	29	0	24	44	15	2.7	73	25	0	0	0.0	0.0
B / 7.6	2.7	5.0	11.81	13,187	3	29	0	24	44	15	2.7	76	25	15,000,000	0	0.0	0.0
B / 7.6	2.7	5.0	11.80	12,054	3	29	0	24	44	15	2.7	N/A	25	1,000,000	0	0.0	0.0
B- / 7.1	2.8	5.7	8.22	870	5	19	0	36	40	52	4.1	98	20	1,000	50	3.8	0.0
B- / 7.2	2.8	5.7	8.26	268	5	19	0	36	40	52	4.1	96	20	1,000	50	0.0	0.0
B- / 7.0	2.9	5.7	8.23	835	5	19	0	36	40	52	4.1	98	20	3,000,000	0	0.0	0.0
B- / 7.2	2.8	5.7	8.22	36	5	19	0	36	40	52	4.1	97	20	0	0	0.0	0.0
B- / 7.1	2.9	5.7	8.22	2,387	5	19	0	36	40	52	4.1	98	20	15,000,000	0	0.0	0.0
C+ / 6.9	2.9	5.7	8.22	454	5	19	0	36	40	52	4.1	98	20	1,000,000	0	0.0	0.0
C- / 3.2	4.5	N/A	9.94	119	0	0	0	0	100	74	0.0	45	3	1,000	50	3.8	0.0
C- / 3.2	4.5	N/A	9.94	N/A	0	0	0	0	100	74	0.0	30	3	1,000	50	0.0	0.0
C- / 3.2	4.6	N/A	9.96	1,739	0	0	0	0	100	74	0.0	60	3	15,000,000	0	0.0	0.0
C- / 3.1	4.6	N/A	9.96	31	0	0	0	0	100	74	0.0	55	3	1,000,000	0	0.0	0.0
U /	N/A	N/A	9.90	N/A	7	3	0	87	3	81	0.0	N/A	3	1,000	50	3.8	0.0
U /	N/A	N/A	9.90	N/A	7	3	0	87	3	81	0.0	N/A	3	1,000	50	0.0	0.0
U /	N/A	N/A	9.90	175	7	3	0	87	3	81	0.0	N/A	3	15,000,000	0	0.0	0.0
U /	N/A	N/A	9.92	2	7	3	0	87	3	81	0.0	N/A	3	1,000,000	0	0.0	0.0
E+ / 0.7	7.1	6.5	7.91	53	6	83	0	8	3	164	6.3	81	7	1,000	50	3.8	0.0
E+ / 0.7	7.1	6.5	7.88	9	6	83	0	8	3	164	6.3	59	7	1,000	50	0.0	0.0
E+ / 0.7	7.2	6.5	7.98	1	6	83	0	8	3	164	6.3	88	7	0	0	0.0	0.0
E+ / 0.7	7.2	6.5	7.93	767	6	83	0	8	3	164	6.3	89	7	15,000,000	0	0.0	0.0
E+ / 0.7	7.1	6.5	7.92	76	6	83	0	8	3	164	6.3	86	7	1,000,000	0	0.0	0.0
E- / 0.1	11.7	N/A	7.95	1	35	64	0	0	1	134	0.0	1	4	1,000	50	3.8	0.0
E- / 0.2	11.7	N/A	7.84	N/A	35	64	0	0	1	134	0.0	0	4	1,000	50	0.0	0.0
E- / 0.1	11.7	N/A	7.90	N/A	35	64	0	0	1	134	0.0	0	4	0	0	0.0	0.0
E- / 0.2	11.6	N/A	8.05	N/A	35	64	0	0	1	134	0.0	1	4	0	0	0.0	0.0
E- / 0.2	11.6	N/A	8.06	76	35	64	0	0	1	134	0.0	1	4	15,000,000	0	0.0	0.0
E- / 0.1	11.7	N/A	8.01	2	35	64	0	0	1	134	0.0	1	4	1,000,000	0	0.0	0.0
A+ / 9.9	N/A	N/A	1.00	234	100	0	0	0	0	0	0.0	65	N/A	5,000,000	0	0.0	0.0
A+ / 9.9	N/A	N/A	1.00	3,601	100	0	0	0	0	0	0.0	65	N/A	10,000,000	0	0.0	0.0
U /	N/A	N/A	1.00	130	100	0	0	0	0	0	0.0	N/A	N/A	1,000	25	0.0	0.0
U /	N/A	N/A	1.00	158	100	0	0	0	0	0	0.0	N/A	N/A	1,000,000	0	0.0	0.0
U /	N/A	N/A	1.00	5	100	0	0	0	0	0	0.0	N/A	N/A	10,000,000	25	0.0	0.0
C+ / 6.1	3.1	N/A	9.10	79	5	0	0	39	56	16	0.0	60	5	1,000	50	2.3	0.0
C+ / 5.9	3.2	N/A	9.08	22	5	0	0	39	56	16	0.0	41	5	1,000	50	0.0	0.0
U /	N/A	N/A	9.11	816	5	0	0	39	56	16	0.0	N/A	5	15,000,000	0	0.0	0.0
C+ / 6.1	3.1	N/A	9.11	913	5	0	0	39	56	16	0.0	74	5	1,000,000	0	0.0	0.0
C / 4.4	3.7	N/A	9.82	84	2	15	0	58	25	90	0.0	97	4	1,000	50	3.8	0.0
C / 4.5	3.7	N/A	9.79	29	2	15	0	58	25	90	0.0	96	4	1,000	50	0.0	0.0
C / 4.4	3.7	N/A	9.84	149	2	15	0	58	25	90	0.0	98	4	15,000,000	0	0.0	0.0
C / 4.5	3.7	N/A	9.84	901	2	15	0	58	25	90	0.0	98	4	1,000,000	0	0.0	0.0
C+ / 5.7	3.2	4.9	10.87	562	6	47	0	0	47	18	2.6	39	20	1,000	50	3.8	0.0
C+ / 5.8	3.2	4.9	10.84	74	6	47	0	0	47	18	2.6	21	20	1,000	50	0.0	0.0
C+ / 5.8	3.2	4.9	10.86	63	6	47	0	0	47	18	2.6	32	20	0	0	0.0	0.0
C+ / 5.7	3.2	4.9	10.87	604	6	47	0	0	47	18	2.6	49	20	1,000,000	0	0.0	0.0
D- / 1.5	5.6	5.1	6.87	929	3	0	0	91	6	52	0.0	47	18	1,000	50	3.8	0.0
D- / 1.5	5.6	5.1	6.88	206	3	0	0	91	6	52	0.0	29	18	1,000	50	0.0	0.0

99 Pct = Best
0 Pct = Worst

Fund Type	Fund Name	Ticker Symbol	Overall Investment Rating	Phone	PERFORMANCE: Performance Rating/Pts	Total Return % through 3/31/16: 3 Mo	6 Mo	1Yr / Pct	Annualized: 3Yr / Pct	Annualized: 5Yr / Pct	Incl. in Returns: Dividend Yield	Incl. in Returns: Expense Ratio
COH	JPMorgan High Yield R2	JHYZX	**D-**	(800) 480-4111	**C- / 3.0**	2.37	0.13	-5.05 / 5	0.91 /41	3.51 /53	5.61	1.80
COH	JPMorgan High Yield R5	JYHRX	**D**	(800) 480-4111	**C- / 4.1**	2.50	0.42	-4.48 / 6	1.45 /51	4.08 /63	6.16	0.91
COH	JPMorgan High Yield R6	JHYUX	**D**	(800) 480-4111	**C / 4.3**	2.51	0.43	-4.44 / 6	1.53 /53	4.14 /63	6.21	0.77
COH	JPMorgan High Yield Sel	OHYFX	**D**	(800) 480-4111	**C- / 4.0**	2.34	0.26	-4.53 / 6	1.40 /50	4.02 /62	6.13	1.10
COI	JPMorgan Inflation Managed Bond A	JIMAX	**D+**	(800) 480-4111	**D- / 1.0**	2.30	2.18	1.16 /61	-0.45 /12	1.41 /25	1.48	1.22
COI	JPMorgan Inflation Managed Bond C	JIMCX	**D+**	(800) 480-4111	**D- / 1.2**	2.05	1.80	0.43 /48	-1.13 / 8	0.75 /19	0.91	1.58
COI	JPMorgan Inflation Managed Bond	JIMZX	**D+**	(800) 480-4111	**D / 1.6**	2.13	2.05	0.81 /55	-0.70 /10	1.16 /22	1.28	1.80
COI	JPMorgan Inflation Managed Bond	JIMRX	**C-**	(800) 480-4111	**C- / 3.0**	2.37	2.29	1.29 /63	-0.26 /13	1.61 /27	1.75	0.65
GEI	JPMorgan Inflation Managed Bond	JIMMX	**C-**	(800) 480-4111	**C- / 3.1**	2.27	2.33	1.37 /64	-0.17 /14	1.68 /27	1.84	0.49
COI	JPMorgan Inflation Managed Bond	JRBSX	**C-**	(800) 480-4111	**D+ / 2.9**	2.35	2.27	1.23 /62	-0.31 /13	1.56 /26	1.69	0.75
GEI	JPMorgan Intermediate T/F Bd A	JITAX	**C+**	(800) 480-4111	**C / 5.5**	1.22	2.30	2.84 /76	2.35 /68	3.52 /53	2.34	0.93
GEI	JPMorgan Intermediate T/F Bd C	JITCX	**C+**	(800) 480-4111	**C+ / 6.0**	1.08	2.00	2.18 /73	1.67 /55	2.83 /42	1.78	1.43
GEI	JPMorgan Intermediate T/F Bd Inst	JITIX	**A-**	(800) 480-4111	**B- / 7.5**	1.41	2.49	3.17 /78	2.62 /72	3.80 /58	2.74	0.67
GEI	JPMorgan Intermediate T/F Bd Sel	VSITX	**A-**	(800) 480-4111	**B- / 7.4**	1.29	2.43	3.05 /77	2.52 /71	3.70 /57	2.63	0.52
GEI	JPMorgan Limited Duration Bd A	ONUAX	**C+**	(800) 480-4111	**C- / 3.1**	0.27	0.05	0.19 /44	1.12 /45	2.09 /32	0.68	0.97
GEI	JPMorgan Limited Duration Bd C	OGUCX	**C+**	(800) 480-4111	**C- / 3.3**	0.26	-0.09	-0.30 /28	0.62 /35	1.59 /26	0.20	1.47
GEI	JPMorgan Limited Duration Bd R6	JUSUX	**A-**	(800) 480-4111	**C / 5.1**	0.49	0.29	0.67 /53	1.56 /53	2.56 /39	1.17	0.40
GEI	JPMorgan Limited Duration Bd Sel	HLGFX	**B+**	(800) 480-4111	**C / 4.8**	0.34	0.18	0.45 /49	1.37 /50	2.34 /36	0.95	0.65
MM	JPMorgan Liquid Assets MM Agency	AJLXX	**C**	(800) 480-4111	**D+ / 2.4**	0.07	0.08	0.10 /41	0.04 /24	0.05 /13	0.10	0.33
MM	JPMorgan Liquid Assets MM C	OPCXX	**U**	(800) 480-4111	**U /**	--	--	--	--	--	0.01	1.18
MM	JPMorgan Liquid Assets MM Cptl	CJLXX	**C**	(800) 480-4111	**D+ / 2.6**	0.09	0.12	0.18 /44	0.10 /27	0.12 /15	0.18	0.23
MM	JPMorgan Liquid Assets MM E	JLEXX	**U**	(800) 480-4111	**U /**	--	--	--	--	--	0.01	1.08
MM	JPMorgan Liquid Assets MM Inst	IJLXX	**C**	(800) 480-4111	**D+ / 2.5**	0.08	0.11	0.15 /43	0.07 /26	0.09 /14	0.15	0.28
MM	JPMorgan Liquid Assets MM Inv	HLPXX	**U**	(800) 480-4111	**U /**	--	--	--	--	--	0.02	0.53
MM	JPMorgan Liquid Assets MM Morg	MJLXX	**U**	(800) 480-4111	**U /**	--	--	--	--	--	0.01	0.63
MM	JPMorgan Liquid Assets MM Prem	PJLXX	**C-**	(800) 480-4111	**D / 1.9**	0.02	0.03	0.03 /36	0.02 /20	0.01 / 5	0.03	0.48
MM	JPMorgan Liquid Assets MM Rsv	HPIXX	**U**	(800) 480-4111	**U /**	--	--	--	--	--	0.01	0.73
MM	JPMorgan Liquid Assets MM Svc	OPSXX	**U**	(800) 480-4111	**U /**	--	--	--	--	--	0.01	1.08
GEI	JPMorgan Managed Income Instl	JMGIX	**C+**	(800) 480-4111	**C- / 3.2**	0.27	0.31	0.52 /50	0.42 /32	0.50 /17	0.51	0.35
GEI	JPMorgan Managed Income Select	JMGSX	**C+**	(800) 480-4111	**C- / 3.0**	0.24	0.26	0.32 /46	0.32 /30	0.40 /17	0.41	0.55
MTG	JPMorgan Mortgage Backed Sec A	OMBAX	**B**	(800) 480-4111	**C / 5.4**	2.07	1.30	2.45 /74	2.32 /68	3.40 /51	2.48	1.05
MTG	JPMorgan Mortgage Backed Sec C	OBBCX	**A-**	(800) 480-4111	**C+ / 6.1**	1.92	1.10	1.93 /71	1.82 /58	2.90 /44	2.16	1.55
MTG	JPMorgan Mortgage Backed Sec R6	JMBUX	**A+**	(800) 480-4111	**B- / 7.5**	2.12	1.46	2.76 /76	2.72 /73	3.82 /59	3.06	0.47
MTG	JPMorgan Mortgage Backed Sec Sel	OMBIX	**A+**	(800) 480-4111	**B- / 7.3**	2.00	1.37	2.58 /75	2.57 /72	3.66 /56	2.89	0.76
MUN	JPMorgan Muni Income A	OTBAX	**A+**	(800) 480-4111	**B / 7.8**	1.48	2.71	3.27 /88	2.77 /86	3.90 /77	2.44	1.01
MUN	JPMorgan Muni Income C	OMICX	**A+**	(800) 480-4111	**B / 8.2**	1.36	2.44	2.70 /82	2.17 /79	3.31 /72	1.99	1.52
MUN	JPMorgan Muni Income Sel	HLTAX	**A+**	(800) 480-4111	**A- / 9.1**	1.55	2.85	3.55 /90	3.06 /89	4.18 /79	2.80	0.74
MMT	JPMorgan Muni MM Agency	JMAXX	**U**	(800) 480-4111	**U /**	0.00	0.01	0.02 /36	0.01 /20	0.03 /13	0.02	0.32
MMT	JPMorgan Muni MM E-trade	JMEXX	**U**	(800) 480-4111	**U /**	0.00	0.01	0.01 /35	0.01 /20	0.01 / 8	0.01	1.07
MMT	JPMorgan Muni MM Inst	IJMXX	**U**	(800) 480-4111	**U /**	0.01	0.01	0.02 /36	0.02 /22	0.05 /14	0.02	0.27
MMT	JPMorgan Muni MM Morgan	MJMXX	**U**	(800) 480-4111	**U /**	0.00	0.01	0.01 /35	0.01 /20	0.01 / 8	0.01	0.62
MMT	JPMorgan Muni MM Prem	HTOXX	**U**	(800) 480-4111	**U /**	0.00	0.01	0.01 /35	0.01 /20	0.01 / 8	0.01	0.47
MMT	JPMorgan Muni MM Rsv	OGIXX	**U**	(800) 480-4111	**U /**	0.00	0.01	0.01 /35	0.01 /20	0.01 / 8	0.01	0.72
MMT	JPMorgan Muni MM Svc	SJMXX	**U**	(800) 480-4111	**U /**	0.00	0.01	0.01 /35	0.01 /20	0.01 / 8	0.01	1.07
MMT	JPMorgan NY Mun MM E-trade	JNEXX	**U**	(800) 480-4111	**U /**	--	--	--	--	--	0.01	1.08
MMT	JPMorgan NY Mun MM Morgan	VNYXX	**U**	(800) 480-4111	**U /**	--	--	--	--	--	0.01	0.63
MMT	JPMorgan NY Muni MM Svc	JNVXX	**U**	(800) 480-4111	**U /**	--	--	--	--	--	0.01	1.08
MUS	JPMorgan NY T/F Bond A	VANTX	**B+**	(800) 480-4111	**C+ / 6.4**	1.28	2.23	2.67 /82	2.10 /78	3.65 /75	2.90	0.94
MUS	JPMorgan NY T/F Bond C	JCNTX	**A**	(800) 480-4111	**C+ / 6.9**	1.11	1.73	1.95 /77	1.37 /64	2.90 /67	2.32	1.44
MUS	JPMorgan NY T/F Bond Inst	JNYIX	**A+**	(800) 480-4111	**B+ / 8.4**	1.36	2.36	2.93 /84	2.35 /81	3.89 /77	3.27	0.53
MUS	JPMorgan NY T/F Bond Sel	VINTX	**A+**	(800) 480-4111	**B / 8.2**	1.32	2.29	2.79 /83	2.19 /79	3.72 /75	3.13	0.69
MUI	JPMorgan OH Municipal A	ONOHX	**A-**	(800) 480-4111	**C+ / 6.7**	1.39	2.10	2.71 /82	2.21 /79	3.57 /75	2.78	1.06

● Denotes fund is closed to new investors
* Denotes fund is included in Section II

RISK			NET ASSETS		ASSET							FUND MANAGER		MINIMUM		LOADS	
Risk Rating/Pts	3 Yr Avg Standard Deviation	Avg Duration	NAV As of 3/31/16	Total $(Mil)	Cash %	Gov. Bond %	Muni. Bond %	Corp. Bond %	Other %	Portfolio Turnover Ratio	Avg Coupon Rate	Manager Quality Pct	Manager Tenure (Years)	Initial Purch. $	Additional Purch. $	Front End Load	Back End Load
D- / 1.5	5.6	5.1	6.86	9	3	0	0	91	6	52	0.0	36	18	0	0	0.0	0.0
D- / 1.5	5.6	5.1	6.91	60	3	0	0	91	6	52	0.0	55	18	0	0	0.0	0.0
D / 1.6	5.6	5.1	6.90	4,011	3	0	0	91	6	52	0.0	58	18	15,000,000	0	0.0	0.0
D- / 1.5	5.6	5.1	6.90	4,895	3	0	0	91	6	52	0.0	53	18	1,000,000	0	0.0	0.0
B- / 7.5	2.7	2.3	10.28	45	1	36	0	29	34	28	2.6	13	6	1,000	50	3.8	0.0
B- / 7.5	2.7	2.3	10.23	4	1	36	0	29	34	28	2.6	8	6	1,000	50	0.0	0.0
B- / 7.5	2.7	2.3	10.28	1	1	36	0	29	34	28	2.6	11	6	0	0	0.0	0.0
B- / 7.5	2.7	2.3	10.32	12	1	36	0	29	34	28	2.6	15	6	0	0	0.0	0.0
B- / 7.5	2.7	2.3	10.29	817	1	36	0	29	34	28	2.6	14	6	15,000,000	0	0.0	0.0
B- / 7.5	2.7	2.3	10.28	691	1	36	0	29	34	28	2.6	14	6	1,000,000	0	0.0	0.0
B- / 7.0	2.7	7.6	11.30	238	3	0	96	0	1	21	4.3	81	11	1,000	50	3.8	0.0
C+ / 6.9	2.7	7.6	11.04	69	3	0	96	0	1	21	4.3	53	11	1,000	50	0.0	0.0
B- / 7.0	2.7	7.6	11.12	4,097	3	0	96	0	1	21	4.3	86	11	3,000,000	0	0.0	0.0
B- / 7.0	2.7	7.6	11.14	332	3	0	96	0	1	21	4.3	85	11	1,000,000	0	0.0	0.0
A+ / 9.6	0.7	1.0	9.97	197	10	0	0	14	76	24	1.5	87	21	1,000	50	2.3	0.0
A+ / 9.7	0.7	1.0	9.87	51	10	0	0	14	76	24	1.5	78	21	1,000	50	0.0	0.0
A+ / 9.7	0.7	1.0	9.99	737	10	0	0	14	76	24	1.5	91	21	15,000,000	0	0.0	0.0
A+ / 9.6	0.7	1.0	9.97	318	10	0	0	14	76	24	1.5	90	21	1,000,000	0	0.0	0.0
A+ / 9.9	N/A	N/A	1.00	75	100	0	0	0	0	0	0.1	65	N/A	5,000,000	0	0.0	0.0
U /	N/A	N/A	1.00	496	100	0	0	0	0	0	0.0	N/A	N/A	1,000	25	0.0	0.0
A+ / 9.9	N/A	N/A	1.00	1,961	100	0	0	0	0	0	0.2	70	N/A	50,000,000	0	0.0	0.0
U /	N/A	N/A	1.00	1,759	100	0	0	0	0	0	0.0	68	N/A	0	0	0.0	0.0
A+ / 9.9	N/A	N/A	1.00	6,357	100	0	0	0	0	0	0.2	68	N/A	10,000,000	0	0.0	0.0
U /	N/A	N/A	1.00	143	100	0	0	0	0	0	0.0	N/A	N/A	1,000,000	0	0.0	0.0
U /	N/A	N/A	1.00	1,622	100	0	0	0	0	0	0.0	N/A	N/A	1,000	25	0.0	0.0
A+ / 9.9	N/A	N/A	1.00	187	100	0	0	0	0	0	0.0	65	N/A	1,000,000	0	0.0	0.0
U /	N/A	N/A	1.00	151	100	0	0	0	0	0	0.0	N/A	N/A	10,000,000	0	0.0	0.0
U /	N/A	N/A	1.00	53	100	0	0	0	0	0	0.0	N/A	N/A	10,000,000	0	0.0	0.0
A+ / 9.9	0.2	3.4	10.01	5,905	7	4	0	66	23	112	4.4	78	6	3,000,000	0	0.0	0.0
A+ / 9.9	0.2	3.4	10.01	1	7	4	0	66	23	112	4.4	75	6	1,000,000	0	0.0	0.0
B+ / 8.5	2.0	3.7	11.66	203	8	0	0	3	89	7	3.6	81	16	1,000	50	3.8	0.0
B+ / 8.6	1.9	3.7	11.36	19	8	0	0	3	89	7	3.6	61	16	1,000	50	0.0	0.0
B+ / 8.5	1.9	3.7	11.38	1,373	8	0	0	3	89	7	3.6	88	16	15,000,000	0	0.0	0.0
B+ / 8.6	1.9	3.7	11.38	1,131	8	0	0	3	89	7	3.6	86	16	1,000,000	0	0.0	0.0
B- / 7.3	2.8	4.8	10.09	75	7	0	92	0	1	9	4.6	59	10	1,000	50	3.8	0.0
B- / 7.3	2.8	4.8	10.00	16	7	0	92	0	1	9	4.6	38	10	1,000	50	0.0	0.0
B- / 7.3	2.8	4.8	10.03	243	7	0	92	0	1	9	4.6	74	10	1,000,000	0	0.0	0.0
U /	N/A	N/A	1.00	162	100	0	0	0	0	0	0.0	N/A	N/A	5,000,000	0	0.0	0.0
U /	N/A	N/A	1.00	1,977	100	0	0	0	0	0	0.0	N/A	N/A	0	0	0.0	0.0
U /	N/A	N/A	1.00	148	100	0	0	0	0	0	0.0	N/A	N/A	10,000,000	0	0.0	0.0
U /	N/A	N/A	1.00	397	100	0	0	0	0	0	0.0	N/A	N/A	1,000	25	0.0	0.0
U /	N/A	N/A	1.00	29	100	0	0	0	0	0	0.0	N/A	N/A	1,000,000	0	0.0	0.0
U /	N/A	N/A	1.00	10	100	0	0	0	0	0	0.0	N/A	N/A	10,000,000	0	0.0	0.0
U /	N/A	N/A	1.00	452	100	0	0	0	0	0	0.0	N/A	N/A	10,000,000	0	0.0	0.0
U /	N/A	N/A	1.00	411	100	0	0	0	0	0	0.0	N/A	N/A	0	0	0.0	0.0
U /	N/A	N/A	1.00	478	100	0	0	0	0	0	0.0	N/A	N/A	1,000	25	0.0	0.0
U /	N/A	N/A	1.00	75	100	0	0	0	0	0	0.0	N/A	N/A	10,000,000	0	0.0	0.0
B / 7.9	2.5	4.6	7.09	170	0	0	99	0	1	12	4.9	46	11	1,000	50	3.8	0.0
B / 7.9	2.5	4.6	7.08	105	0	0	99	0	1	12	4.9	25	11	1,000	50	0.0	0.0
B / 7.9	2.5	4.6	7.12	135	0	0	99	0	1	12	4.9	55	11	3,000,000	0	0.0	0.0
B / 7.9	2.5	4.6	7.12	46	0	0	99	0	1	12	4.9	49	11	1,000,000	0	0.0	0.0
B / 7.8	2.6	4.6	11.00	51	0	0	99	0	1	3	4.6	46	22	1,000	50	3.8	0.0

					PERFORMANCE							
99 Pct = Best 0 Pct = Worst						Total Return % through 3/31/16					Incl. in Returns	
									Annualized			
Fund Type	Fund Name	Ticker Symbol	Overall Investment Rating	Phone	Perfor-mance Rating/Pts	3 Mo	6 Mo	1Yr / Pct	3Yr / Pct	5Yr / Pct	Dividend Yield	Expense Ratio
MUI	JPMorgan OH Municipal C	JOMCX	**A+**	(800) 480-4111	**B- / 7.5**	1.23	1.85	2.13 /78	1.61 /70	2.96 /68	2.23	1.57
MUI	JPMorgan OH Municipal Sel	HLOMX	**A+**	(800) 480-4111	**B+ / 8.5**	1.47	2.33	2.98 /85	2.48 /82	3.83 /76	3.15	0.82
MM	JPMorgan Prime MM Agency	VMIXX	**C**	(800) 480-4111	**D+ / 2.4**	0.07	0.08	0.09 /41	0.04 /24	0.05 /13	0.09	0.31
MM	JPMorgan Prime MM C	JXCXX	**U**	(800) 480-4111	**U /**	--	--	--	--	--	0.01	1.16
MM	JPMorgan Prime MM Capital	CJPXX	**C**	(800) 480-4111	**D+ / 2.6**	0.08	0.12	0.17 /43	0.09 /27	0.11 /15	0.17	0.21
MM	JPMorgan Prime MM CshMgt	JCMXX	**U**	(800) 480-4111	**U /**	--	--	--	--	--	0.01	0.96
MM	JPMorgan Prime MM Direct	JMDXX	**C**	(800) 480-4111	**D+ / 2.4**	0.06	0.07	0.09 /41	0.05 /25	0.04 /12	0.09	0.31
MM	JPMorgan Prime MM Eagle	JPEXX	**U**	(800) 480-4111	**U /**	--	--	--	--	--	0.01	0.71
MM	JPMorgan Prime MM IM	JIMXX	**C**	(800) 480-4111	**D+ / 2.7**	0.09	0.13	0.19 /44	0.11 /27	--	0.19	0.16
MM	JPMorgan Prime MM Inst	JINXX	**C**	(800) 480-4111	**D+ / 2.5**	0.08	0.10	0.14 /42	0.06 /26	0.08 /14	0.14	0.26
MM	JPMorgan Prime MM Morgan	VMVXX	**U**	(800) 480-4111	**U /**	0.01	0.01	0.02 /35	0.01 /17	0.01 / 5	0.02	0.51
MM	JPMorgan Prime MM Prem	VPMXX	**C-**	(800) 480-4111	**D / 2.0**	0.02	0.02	0.03 /36	0.02 /21	0.01 / 5	0.03	0.46
MM	JPMorgan Prime MM Rsv	JRVXX	**U**	(800) 480-4111	**U /**	--	--	--	--	--	0.01	0.71
* GEI	JPMorgan Short Duration Bond A	OGLVX	**C-**	(800) 480-4111	**D / 1.7**	0.79	0.27	0.46 /49	0.40 /31	0.78 /19	0.64	0.95
GEI	JPMorgan Short Duration Bond C	OSTCX	**C-**	(800) 480-4111	**D / 1.8**	0.66	0.02	-0.06 /31	-0.11 /15	0.27 /16	0.14	1.41
GEI	JPMorgan Short Duration Bond R6	JSDUX	**B**	(800) 480-4111	**C- / 4.2**	0.90	0.52	0.88 /57	0.88 /40	1.28 /23	1.16	0.36
GEI	JPMorgan Short Duration Bond Sel	HLLVX	**C+**	(800) 480-4111	**C- / 3.8**	0.84	0.40	0.71 /53	0.65 /36	1.04 /21	0.90	0.65
COH	JPMorgan Short Duration Hi Yld A	JSDHX	**D**	(800) 480-4111	**D / 1.7**	1.66	-0.06	-2.54 /13	0.79 /39	--	4.60	1.27
COH	JPMorgan Short Duration Hi Yld C	JSDCX	**D**	(800) 480-4111	**D / 1.8**	1.66	-0.30	-3.02 /11	0.27 /30	--	4.20	1.88
COH	JPMorgan Short Duration Hi Yld R6	JSDRX	**D+**	(800) 480-4111	**C- / 4.1**	1.87	0.15	-2.21 /15	1.19 /46	--	5.16	0.71
COH	JPMorgan Short Duration Hi Yld Sel	JSDSX	**D+**	(800) 480-4111	**C- / 3.7**	1.73	-0.02	-2.35 /14	1.00 /43	--	5.02	0.96
MUN	JPMorgan Short Term Muni Bond A	OSTAX	**C+**	(800) 480-4111	**C- / 3.9**	0.78	1.18	1.54 /74	0.87 /49	1.20 /29	0.76	0.89
MUN	JPMorgan Short Term Muni Bond C	STMCX	**C+**	(800) 480-4111	**C- / 4.0**	0.64	0.91	0.99 /67	0.36 /34	0.69 /21	0.24	1.40
MUN	JPMorgan Short Term Muni Bond Inst	JIMIX	**A+**	(800) 480-4111	**C+ / 6.8**	0.89	1.42	2.04 /77	1.35 /63	1.70 /39	1.27	0.48
MUN	JPMorgan Short Term Muni Bond Sel	PGUIX	**A**	(800) 480-4111	**C+ / 6.2**	0.84	1.29	1.80 /76	1.12 /56	1.44 /34	1.03	0.54
GL	JPMorgan SmartAllocation Income A	SAIAX	**C-**	(800) 480-4111	**C- / 3.9**	2.89	2.08	0.37 /47	1.58 /54	--	2.22	5.26
GL	JPMorgan SmartAllocation Income C	SAICX	**C-**	(800) 480-4111	**C / 4.8**	2.73	1.79	-0.13 /30	1.07 /44	--	1.67	5.92
GL	JPMorgan SmartAllocation Income	SAIRX	**C**	(800) 480-4111	**C / 5.3**	2.81	1.94	0.16 /43	1.34 /49	--	1.89	5.64
GL	JPMorgan SmartAllocation Income	SIARX	**C+**	(800) 480-4111	**C+ / 6.5**	3.00	2.30	0.87 /56	2.05 /62	--	2.73	4.95
GL	JPMorgan SmartAllocation Income	SINRX	**C+**	(800) 480-4111	**C+ / 6.6**	2.94	2.33	0.86 /56	2.10 /64	--	2.79	4.88
GL	JPMorgan SmartAllocation Income	SIASX	**C+**	(800) 480-4111	**C+ / 6.2**	2.93	2.18	0.65 /52	1.83 /58	--	2.17	4.69
* GL	JPMorgan Strategic Income Opp A	JSOAX	**D+**	(800) 480-4111	**E+ / 0.8**	1.05	-0.09	-2.00 /16	-0.09 /15	1.35 /24	3.71	1.27
GL	JPMorgan Strategic Income Opp C	JSOCX	**D+**	(800) 480-4111	**D- / 1.1**	0.93	-0.34	-2.45 /13	-0.59 /11	0.85 /19	3.31	1.74
GL	JPMorgan Strategic Income Opp R5	JSORX	**C-**	(800) 480-4111	**D+ / 2.9**	1.16	0.16	-1.50 /18	0.39 /31	1.81 /29	4.35	0.74
GL	JPMorgan Strategic Income Opp Sel	JSOSX	**C-**	(800) 480-4111	**D+ / 2.3**	1.20	0.05	-1.73 /17	0.19 /29	1.61 /27	4.12	0.97
GEN	JPMorgan Tax Aware High Inc A	JTIAX	**C+**	(800) 480-4111	**C+ / 6.0**	1.43	2.22	2.60 /75	2.71 /73	4.73 /70	2.54	1.21
GEN	JPMorgan Tax Aware High Inc C	JTICX	**B**	(800) 480-4111	**C+ / 6.7**	1.31	1.96	2.07 /72	2.18 /65	4.21 /64	2.13	1.72
GEN	JPMorgan Tax Aware High Inc Sel	JTISX	**A-**	(800) 480-4111	**B / 7.6**	1.46	2.28	2.70 /75	2.81 /74	4.84 /71	2.74	0.96
MUN	JPMorgan Tax Aware Inc Opps A	JTAAX	**C-**	(800) 480-4111	**D- / 1.3**	0.25	0.44	0.48 /54	0.43 /36	1.36 /32	1.70	1.13
MUN	JPMorgan Tax Aware Inc Opps C	JTACX	**C-**	(800) 480-4111	**D / 1.6**	0.18	0.11	-0.13 /30	-0.21 /14	0.70 /21	1.07	1.64
MUN	JPMorgan Tax Aware Inc Opps Sel	JTASX	**B**	(800) 480-4111	**C- / 4.1**	0.27	0.49	0.60 /57	0.52 /39	1.45 /34	1.89	0.88
MUI	JPMorgan Tax Aware Real Return A	TXRAX	**D**	(800) 480-4111	**D- / 1.2**	0.97	3.09	2.02 /77	-0.23 /14	1.63 /38	2.61	0.97
MUI	JPMorgan Tax Aware Real Return C	TXRCX	**D**	(800) 480-4111	**D- / 1.5**	0.81	2.86	1.44 /73	-0.86 / 9	0.98 /26	2.05	1.49
MUI	JPMorgan Tax Aware Real Return	TXRIX	**C-**	(800) 480-4111	**C / 4.3**	1.03	3.33	2.28 /79	0.03 /24	1.88 /43	2.97	0.56
MUN	JPMorgan Tax Aware Real Return R6	TXRRX	**U**	(800) 480-4111	**U /**	1.05	3.27	2.37 /80	--	--	3.06	0.45
MUI	JPMorgan Tax Aware Real Return	TXRSX	**C-**	(800) 480-4111	**C- / 3.8**	0.99	3.14	2.12 /78	-0.12 /15	1.74 /40	2.81	0.73
MUN	JPMorgan Tax Aware Real Return	JTARX	**D+**	(800) 480-4111	**C- / 4.0**	1.27	3.17	2.48 /80	-0.12 /15	1.95 /45	3.23	1.01
MUN	JPMorgan Tax Free Bond A	PMBAX	**B+**	(800) 480-4111	**A- / 9.0**	1.82	3.58	3.91 /93	3.92 /95	5.18 /87	3.58	1.00
MUN	JPMorgan Tax Free Bond C	JTFCX	**B+**	(800) 480-4111	**A- / 9.1**	1.58	3.17	3.13 /86	3.16 /90	4.44 /81	3.06	1.49
MUN	JPMorgan Tax Free Bond Sel	PRBIX	**A**	(800) 480-4111	**A+ / 9.6**	1.80	3.61	4.04 /94	4.06 /96	5.36 /88	3.93	0.72
MMT	JPMorgan Tax Free MM Agency	VTIXX	**C**	(800) 480-4111	**D / 2.1**	0.00	0.02	0.03 /38	0.02 /22	0.01 / 9	0.03	0.31
MMT	JPMorgan Tax Free MM Direct	JTDXX	**C**	(800) 480-4111	**D / 2.1**	0.00	0.02	0.03 /38	0.02 /22	0.02 /10	0.03	0.31

● Denotes fund is closed to new investors
* Denotes fund is included in Section II

RISK			NET ASSETS		ASSET							FUND MANAGER		MINIMUM		LOADS	
Risk Rating/Pts	3 Yr Avg Standard Deviation	Avg Duration	NAV As of 3/31/16	Total $(Mil)	Cash %	Gov. Bond %	Muni. Bond %	Corp. Bond %	Other %	Portfolio Turnover Ratio	Avg Coupon Rate	Manager Quality Pct	Manager Tenure (Years)	Initial Purch. $	Additional Purch. $	Front End Load	Back End Load
B / 7.8	2.6	4.6	11.06	27	0	0	99	0	1	3	4.6	28	22	1,000	50	0.0	0.0
B / 7.8	2.6	4.6	10.93	55	0	0	99	0	1	3	4.6	56	22	1,000,000	0	0.0	0.0
A+ / 9.9	N/A	N/A	1.00	7,155	100	0	0	0	0	0	0.1	65	N/A	5,000,000	0	0.0	0.0
U /	N/A	N/A	1.00	36	100	0	0	0	0	0	0.0	N/A	N/A	1,000	25	0.0	0.0
A+ / 9.9	N/A	N/A	1.00	67,255	100	0	0	0	0	0	0.2	69	N/A	50,000,000	0	0.0	0.0
U /	N/A	N/A	1.00	337	100	0	0	0	0	0	0.0	N/A	N/A	10,000,000	0	0.0	0.0
A+ / 9.9	N/A	N/A	1.00	1,389	100	0	0	0	0	0	0.1	67	N/A	0	0	0.0	0.0
U /	N/A	N/A	1.00	383	100	0	0	0	0	0	0.0	N/A	N/A	1,000	0	0.0	0.0
A+ / 9.9	N/A	N/A	1.00	2,062	100	0	0	0	0	0	0.2	70	N/A	50,000,000	0	0.0	0.0
A+ / 9.9	N/A	N/A	1.00	20,678	100	0	0	0	0	0	0.1	67	N/A	10,000,000	0	0.0	0.0
U /	N/A	N/A	1.00	1,829	100	0	0	0	0	0	0.0	N/A	N/A	1,000	25	0.0	0.0
A+ / 9.9	N/A	N/A	1.00	2,172	100	0	0	0	0	0	0.0	65	N/A	1,000,000	0	0.0	0.0
U /	N/A	N/A	1.00	907	100	0	0	0	0	0	0.0	N/A	N/A	10,000,000	0	0.0	0.0
A+ / 9.6	0.7	1.8	10.86	545	0	58	0	23	19	41	2.1	56	10	1,000	50	2.3	0.0
A+ / 9.6	0.7	1.8	10.93	109	0	58	0	23	19	41	2.1	39	10	1,000	50	0.0	0.0
A+ / 9.7	0.7	1.8	10.87	3,176	0	58	0	23	19	41	2.1	80	10	15,000,000	0	0.0	0.0
A+ / 9.6	0.7	1.8	10.88	7,039	0	58	0	23	19	41	2.1	73	10	1,000,000	0	0.0	0.0
C- / 4.1	3.4	N/A	9.05	3	2	0	0	82	16	73	0.0	55	3	1,000	50	2.3	0.0
C- / 4.1	3.4	N/A	9.04	N/A	2	0	0	82	16	73	0.0	37	3	1,000	50	0.0	0.0
C- / 4.1	3.4	N/A	9.05	26	2	0	0	82	16	73	0.0	74	3	15,000,000	0	0.0	0.0
C- / 4.1	3.4	N/A	9.04	108	2	0	0	82	16	73	0.0	64	3	1,000,000	0	0.0	0.0
A- / 9.0	1.4	3.3	10.69	38	3	0	96	0	1	53	4.2	47	10	1,000	50	2.3	0.0
B+ / 8.9	1.4	3.3	10.77	17	3	0	96	0	1	53	4.2	31	10	1,000	50	0.0	0.0
B+ / 8.9	1.4	3.3	10.74	2,325	3	0	96	0	1	53	4.2	71	10	3,000,000	0	0.0	0.0
B+ / 8.9	1.4	3.3	10.72	151	3	0	96	0	1	53	4.2	56	10	1,000,000	0	0.0	0.0
C+ / 5.8	3.2	N/A	14.68	1	1	19	0	46	34	28	0.0	94	4	500	50	3.8	0.0
C+ / 5.9	3.2	N/A	14.66	N/A	1	19	0	46	34	28	0.0	90	4	500	50	0.0	0.0
C+ / 5.9	3.2	N/A	14.68	N/A	1	19	0	46	34	28	0.0	92	4	0	0	0.0	0.0
C+ / 5.8	3.2	N/A	14.70	N/A	1	19	0	46	34	28	0.0	96	4	0	0	0.0	0.0
C+ / 5.9	3.2	N/A	14.70	150	1	19	0	46	34	28	0.0	96	4	15,000,000	0	0.0	0.0
C+ / 5.9	3.2	N/A	14.74	N/A	1	19	0	46	34	28	0.0	95	4	1,000,000	0	0.0	0.0
B+ / 8.4	2.1	N/A	11.08	1,596	34	1	0	45	20	255	4.6	58	8	1,000	50	3.8	0.0
B+ / 8.4	2.1	N/A	11.05	1,220	34	1	0	45	20	255	4.6	40	8	1,000	50	0.0	0.0
B+ / 8.4	2.1	N/A	11.12	632	34	1	0	45	20	255	4.6	80	8	0	0	0.0	0.0
B+ / 8.4	2.1	N/A	11.11	9,862	34	1	0	45	20	255	4.6	74	8	1,000,000	0	0.0	0.0
C+ / 6.6	3.0	4.8	11.03	50	4	0	79	5	12	10	4.4	84	9	1,000	50	3.8	0.0
C+ / 6.7	3.0	4.8	11.01	24	4	0	79	5	12	10	4.4	68	9	1,000	50	0.0	0.0
C+ / 6.7	3.0	4.8	11.03	47	4	0	79	5	12	10	4.4	86	9	1,000,000	0	0.0	0.0
A+ / 9.7	0.6	2.1	10.13	94	0	1	82	9	8	246	3.3	61	5	1,000	50	3.8	0.0
A+ / 9.7	0.6	2.1	10.02	15	0	1	82	9	8	246	3.3	39	5	1,000	50	0.0	0.0
A+ / 9.8	0.6	2.1	10.13	193	0	1	82	9	8	246	3.3	71	5	1,000,000	0	0.0	0.0
C+ / 6.0	3.1	3.1	9.59	49	1	0	98	0	1	18	4.3	8	11	1,000	50	3.8	0.0
C+ / 6.0	3.1	3.1	9.57	38	1	0	98	0	1	18	4.3	7	11	1,000	50	0.0	0.0
C+ / 6.0	3.1	3.1	9.61	1,222	1	0	98	0	1	18	4.3	10	11	3,000,000	0	0.0	0.0
U /	N/A	3.1	9.61	188	1	0	98	0	1	18	4.3	N/A	11	15,000,000	0	0.0	0.0
C+ / 6.1	3.1	3.1	9.60	119	1	0	98	0	1	18	4.3	9	11	1,000,000	0	0.0	0.0
C / 4.9	3.5	N/A	10.04	11	0	0	100	0	0	6	0.0	8	9	0	0	0.0	0.0
C / 4.5	3.7	6.7	12.61	156	7	0	92	0	1	90	4.7	N/A	11	1,000	50	3.8	0.0
C / 4.5	3.7	6.7	12.51	28	7	0	92	0	1	90	4.7	37	11	1,000	50	0.0	0.0
C / 4.5	3.7	6.7	12.56	124	7	0	92	0	1	90	4.7	74	11	1,000,000	0	0.0	0.0
A+ / 9.9	N/A	N/A	1.00	340	100	0	0	0	0	0	0.0	N/A	27	5,000,000	0	0.0	0.0
A+ / 9.9	N/A	N/A	1.00	N/A	100	0	0	0	0	0	0.0	N/A	27	0	0	0.0	0.0

99 Pct = Best
0 Pct = Worst

Fund Type	Fund Name	Ticker Symbol	Overall Investment Rating	Phone	PERFORMANCE: Performance Rating/Pts	Total Return % through 3/31/16: 3 Mo	6 Mo	1Yr / Pct	Annualized: 3Yr / Pct	Annualized: 5Yr / Pct	Incl. in Returns: Dividend Yield	Expense Ratio
MMT	JPMorgan Tax Free MM Eagle	JTEXX	C	(800) 480-4111	D / 2.1	0.00	0.02	0.03 /38	0.02 /22	0.02 /10	0.03	0.71
MMT	JPMorgan Tax Free MM Inst	JTFXX	C	(800) 480-4111	D / 2.1	0.00	0.02	0.03 /38	0.02 /22	0.02 /10	0.03	0.26
MMT	JPMorgan Tax Free MM Morgan	VTMXX	C	(800) 480-4111	D / 2.1	0.00	0.02	0.03 /38	0.02 /22	0.01 / 9	0.03	0.61
MMT	JPMorgan Tax Free MM Prem	VXPXX	C	(800) 480-4111	D / 2.1	0.00	0.02	0.03 /38	0.02 /22	0.01 / 9	0.03	0.46
MMT	JPMorgan Tax Free MM Rsv	RTJXX	C-	(800) 480-4111	D / 2.0	0.00	0.02	0.02 /36	0.01 /21	0.01 / 9	0.03	0.71
GEI	JPMorgan Total Return A	JMTAX	C+	(800) 480-4111	C / 4.9	2.68	2.29	0.51 /50	2.14 /64	4.05 /62	2.95	1.13
GEI	JPMorgan Total Return C	JMTCX	C+	(800) 480-4111	C / 5.4	2.52	2.05	-0.09 /30	1.48 /52	3.38 /51	2.37	1.64
COI	JPMorgan Total Return R2	JMTTX	U	(800) 480-4111	U /	2.65	2.11	0.15 /43	--	--	2.50	1.32
GEI	JPMorgan Total Return R5	JMTRX	A-	(800) 480-4111	B- / 7.0	2.83	2.49	0.79 /55	2.36 /68	4.27 /65	3.24	0.69
COI	JPMorgan Total Return R6	JMTIX	U	(800) 480-4111	U /	2.74	2.41	0.76 /54	--	--	3.31	0.57
GEI	JPMorgan Total Return Sel	JMTSX	B+	(800) 480-4111	C+ / 6.8	2.80	2.44	0.72 /54	2.26 /67	4.17 /64	3.17	0.85
US	JPMorgan Treasury and Agency A	OTABX	C-	(800) 480-4111	D / 1.6	0.84	0.19	0.73 /54	0.24 /29	0.56 /17	0.50	1.03
US	JPMorgan Treasury and Agency Sel	OGTFX	C+	(800) 480-4111	C- / 3.6	0.99	0.40	1.05 /59	0.50 /33	0.82 /19	0.71	0.78
GL	JPMorgan Unconstrained Debt A	JSIAX	C-	(800) 480-4111	C- / 3.4	1.16	1.48	-0.32 /28	1.57 /53	2.58 /39	3.94	1.14
GL	JPMorgan Unconstrained Debt C	JINCX	C	(800) 480-4111	C / 4.3	1.08	1.29	-0.81 /23	1.08 /44	2.08 /32	3.62	1.65
GL	JPMorgan Unconstrained Debt R2	JISZX	C	(800) 480-4111	C / 4.8	1.12	1.39	-0.59 /25	1.34 /49	2.35 /36	3.82	1.80
GL	JPMorgan Unconstrained Debt R5	JSIRX	B-	(800) 480-4111	C+ / 6.1	1.33	1.78	0.14 /42	2.06 /63	3.06 /46	4.53	0.65
GL	JPMorgan Unconstrained Debt R6	JSIMX	B	(800) 480-4111	C+ / 6.2	1.35	1.82	0.21 /44	2.10 /64	--	4.61	0.59
GL	JPMorgan Unconstrained Debt Select	JSISX	C+	(800) 480-4111	C+ / 5.8	1.30	1.60	-0.05 /31	1.85 /59	2.86 /43	4.36	0.84
MM	JPMorgan US Govt MM Agency	OGAXX	C-	(800) 480-4111	D / 2.0	0.03	0.03	0.03 /36	0.02 /21	0.01 / 5	0.03	0.31
MM	JPMorgan US Govt MM Cptl	OGVXX	C	(800) 480-4111	D / 2.2	0.04	0.05	0.06 /39	0.03 /23	0.02 / 9	0.06	0.21
MM	JPMorgan US Govt MM Direct	JGDXX	U	(800) 480-4111	U /	0.02	0.02	0.02 /35	0.01 /17	0.01 / 5	0.02	0.31
MM	JPMorgan US Govt MM Eagle	JJGXX	U	(800) 480-4111	U /	--	--	--	--	--	0.01	0.71
MM	JPMorgan US Govt MM IM	MGMXX	C	(800) 480-4111	D / 2.2	0.05	0.06	0.07 /40	0.03 /23	--	0.07	0.16
MM	JPMorgan US Govt MM Inst	IJGXX	C	(800) 480-4111	D / 2.1	0.04	0.04	0.05 /38	0.02 /21	0.02 / 9	0.05	0.26
MM	JPMorgan US Govt MM Investor	JGMXX	U	(800) 480-4111	U /	--	--	--	--	--	0.01	0.51
MM	JPMorgan US Govt MM Morgan	MJGXX	U	(800) 480-4111	U /	--	--	--	--	--	0.01	0.61
MM	JPMorgan US Govt MM Prem	OGSXX	U	(800) 480-4111	U /	--	--	--	--	--	0.01	0.46
MM	JPMorgan US Govt MM Rsv	RJGXX	U	(800) 480-4111	U /	--	--	--	--	--	0.01	0.71
MM	JPMorgan US Govt MM Svc	SJGXX	U	(800) 480-4111	U /	--	--	--	--	--	0.01	1.06
MM	JPMorgan US Treas Plus MM Agency	AJTXX	C-	(800) 480-4111	D / 1.9	0.02	0.02	0.02 /35	0.01 /17	0.01 / 6	0.02	0.31
MM	JPMorgan US Treas Plus MM Direct	JUDXX	U	(800) 480-4111	U /	--	--	--	--	--	0.01	0.31
MM	JPMorgan US Treas Plus MM IM	MJPXX	C	(800) 480-4111	D / 2.1	0.04	0.05	0.05 /38	0.02 /21	--	0.05	0.16
MM	JPMorgan US Treas Plus MM Inst	IJTXX	C-	(800) 480-4111	D / 2.0	0.03	0.04	0.04 /37	0.01 /17	0.01 / 6	0.04	0.26
MUS	Kansas Municipal	KSMUX	A+	(800) 601-5593	B+ / 8.3	1.32	2.52	3.22 /87	3.00 /88	4.38 /80	2.71	1.17
COI	Knights of Columbus Core Bond Inst	KCCIX	U	(844) 523-8637	U /	2.70	2.15	1.64 /68	--	--	2.20	1.19
COI	Knights of Columbus Core Bond S	KCCSX	U	(844) 523-8637	U /	2.69	2.13	--	--	--	0.00	1.31
COI	Knights of Columbus Ltd Dur Bd Inst	KCLIX	U	(844) 523-8637	U /	0.77	0.32	0.54 /50	--	--	0.94	1.22
COI	Knights of Columbus Ltd Dur Bd S	KCLSX	U	(844) 523-8637	U /	0.76	0.43	--	--	--	0.00	1.48
GEI	KP Fixed Income Instl	KPFIX	U	(855) 457-3637	U /	2.97	2.39	1.72 /69	--	--	2.10	0.35
COI	KS 529 LearningQuest ESP Dvsd Bd		C-	(800) 345-6488	C- / 4.0	2.77	2.21	1.09 /60	1.72 /56	3.23 /49	0.00	1.03
COI	KS 529 LearningQuest ESP Dvsd Bd		C-	(800) 345-6488	C / 4.6	2.51	1.76	0.29 /46	0.93 /41	2.45 /37	0.00	1.78
GL	KS 529 LearningQuest ESP If Pr Bd		D+	(800) 345-6488	E / 0.4	1.99	1.37	0.45 /49	-1.46 / 6	1.02 /20	0.00	0.96
GL	KS 529 LearningQuest ESP If Pr Bd		D+	(800) 345-6488	E / 0.5	1.63	0.81	-0.48 /26	-2.25 / 4	0.26 /16	0.00	1.71
GL	KS 529 LearningQuest ESP ShTm A		C-	(800) 345-6488	D- / 1.0	1.18	0.88	0.29 /46	0.15 /28	0.74 /19	0.00	0.97
GL	KS 529 LearningQuest ESP ShTm C		C-	(800) 345-6488	D- / 1.3	0.96	0.48	-0.48 /26	-0.63 /11	--	0.00	1.72
GL	KS 529 LearningQuest ESP ShTm		C+	(800) 345-6488	C- / 3.5	1.37	0.95	0.54 /50	0.41 /31	1.06 /21	0.00	0.55
COI	KS 529 LearningQuest ESP Tot Bd		B-	(800) 345-6488	B- / 7.0	3.09	2.43	1.65 /68	2.22 /66	3.55 /54	0.00	0.25
GL	KS 529 Schwab CSP Short-Term		C+	(800) 345-6488	C- / 3.4	1.25	1.03	0.66 /53	0.32 /30	1.05 /21	0.00	0.68
GL	Laudus Mondrian Global Govt Fxd Inc	LMGDX	D-	(800) 407-0256	C- / 3.1	9.18	8.02	5.17 /89	-1.37 / 7	--	0.00	1.76
GL	Laudus Mondrian Intl Govt Fxd Inc	LIFNX	D	(800) 407-0256	C- / 3.9	9.00	7.61	7.27 /97	-1.10 / 8	-0.86 / 2	0.00	0.76
GL	Lazard Emerg Mkts Multi Asset Inst	EMMIX	E-	(800) 821-6474	E- / 0.1	2.93	4.81	-7.92 / 1	-5.83 / 1	-3.81 / 0	0.99	1.28

● Denotes fund is closed to new investors
* Denotes fund is included in Section II

RISK			NET ASSETS		ASSET							FUND MANAGER		MINIMUM		LOADS	
Risk Rating/Pts	3 Yr Avg Standard Deviation	Avg Duration	NAV As of 3/31/16	Total $(Mil)	Cash %	Gov. Bond %	Muni. Bond %	Corp. Bond %	Other %	Portfolio Turnover Ratio	Avg Coupon Rate	Manager Quality Pct	Manager Tenure (Years)	Initial Purch. $	Additional Purch. $	Front End Load	Back End Load
A+ / 9.9	N/A	N/A	1.00	1,278	100	0	0	0	0	0	0.0	N/A	27	1,000	0	0.0	0.0
A+ / 9.9	N/A	N/A	1.00	9,315	100	0	0	0	0	0	0.0	N/A	27	10,000,000	0	0.0	0.0
A+ / 9.9	N/A	N/A	1.00	109	100	0	0	0	0	0	0.0	N/A	27	1,000	25	0.0	0.0
A+ / 9.9	N/A	N/A	1.00	2,859	100	0	0	0	0	0	0.0	N/A	27	1,000,000	0	0.0	0.0
A+ / 9.9	N/A	N/A	1.00	4,238	100	0	0	0	0	0	0.0	N/A	27	10,000,000	0	0.0	0.0
B- / 7.5	2.7	5.0	9.82	163	12	6	0	50	32	394	4.7	71	8	1,000	50	3.8	0.0
B- / 7.4	2.7	5.0	9.80	43	12	6	0	50	32	394	4.7	41	8	1,000	50	0.0	0.0
U /	N/A	5.0	9.84	2	12	6	0	50	32	394	4.7	N/A	8	0	0	0.0	0.0
B- / 7.5	2.7	5.0	9.85	10	12	6	0	50	32	394	4.7	78	8	0	0	0.0	0.0
U /	N/A	5.0	9.84	28	12	6	0	50	32	394	4.7	N/A	8	15,000,000	0	0.0	0.0
B- / 7.4	2.7	5.0	9.85	240	12	6	0	50	32	394	4.7	74	8	1,000,000	0	0.0	0.0
A / 9.3	1.0	2.1	9.43	33	0	88	0	11	1	23	1.9	49	11	1,000	50	2.3	0.0
A / 9.3	1.0	2.1	9.43	71	0	88	0	11	1	23	1.9	59	11	1,000,000	0	0.0	0.0
B- / 7.3	2.8	3.4	9.69	90	16	6	0	37	41	179	4.4	94	6	1,000	50	3.8	0.0
B- / 7.3	2.8	3.4	9.64	6	16	6	0	37	41	179	4.4	90	6	1,000	50	0.0	0.0
B- / 7.2	2.8	3.4	9.68	N/A	16	6	0	37	41	179	4.4	92	6	0	0	0.0	0.0
B- / 7.1	2.8	3.4	9.73	3	16	6	0	37	41	179	4.4	96	6	0	0	0.0	0.0
B- / 7.2	2.8	3.4	9.72	380	16	6	0	37	41	179	4.4	96	6	15,000,000	0	0.0	0.0
B- / 7.2	2.8	3.4	9.71	2,299	16	6	0	37	41	179	4.4	95	6	1,000,000	0	0.0	0.0
A+ / 9.9	N/A	N/A	1.00	8,037	100	0	0	0	0	0	0.0	65	N/A	5,000,000	0	0.0	0.0
A+ / 9.9	N/A	N/A	1.00	24,812	100	0	0	0	0	0	0.1	65	N/A	50,000,000	0	0.0	0.0
U /	N/A	N/A	1.00	866	100	0	0	0	0	0	0.0	N/A	N/A	0	0	0.0	0.0
U /	N/A	N/A	1.00	406	100	0	0	0	0	0	0.0	N/A	N/A	1,000	0	0.0	0.0
A+ / 9.9	N/A	N/A	1.00	278	100	0	0	0	0	0	0.1	65	N/A	50,000,000	0	0.0	0.0
A+ / 9.9	N/A	N/A	1.00	8,704	100	0	0	0	0	0	0.1	65	N/A	10,000,000	0	0.0	0.0
U /	N/A	N/A	1.00	3,797	100	0	0	0	0	0	0.0	N/A	N/A	1,000,000	0	0.0	0.0
U /	N/A	N/A	1.00	1,890	100	0	0	0	0	0	0.0	N/A	N/A	1,000	25	0.0	0.0
U /	N/A	N/A	1.00	7,156	100	0	0	0	0	0	0.0	N/A	N/A	1,000,000	0	0.0	0.0
U /	N/A	N/A	1.00	15	100	0	0	0	0	0	0.0	N/A	N/A	10,000,000	0	0.0	0.0
U /	N/A	N/A	1.00	316	100	0	0	0	0	0	0.0	N/A	N/A	10,000,000	0	0.0	0.0
A+ / 9.9	N/A	N/A	1.00	1,082	100	0	0	0	0	0	0.0	64	N/A	5,000,000	0	0.0	0.0
U /	N/A	N/A	1.00	639	100	0	0	0	0	0	0.0	N/A	N/A	0	0	0.0	0.0
A+ / 9.9	N/A	N/A	1.00	5,415	100	0	0	0	0	0	0.1	64	N/A	50,000,000	0	0.0	0.0
A+ / 9.9	N/A	N/A	1.00	8,736	100	0	0	0	0	0	0.0	64	N/A	10,000,000	0	0.0	0.0
B- / 7.0	2.9	4.1	11.02	57	0	0	100	0	0	11	4.9	N/A	20	1,000	50	2.5	0.0
U /	N/A	6.3	9.96	44	0	0	0	0	100	68	0.0	N/A	1	25,000	250	0.0	2.0
U /	N/A	6.3	9.96	N/A	0	0	0	0	100	68	0.0	N/A	1	100,000	0	0.0	2.0
U /	N/A	2.3	9.97	43	0	0	0	0	100	77	0.0	N/A	1	25,000	250	0.0	2.0
U /	N/A	2.3	9.98	N/A	0	0	0	0	100	77	0.0	N/A	1	100,000	0	0.0	2.0
U /	N/A	N/A	10.07	977	10	42	0	22	26	496	0.0	N/A	2	0	0	0.0	0.0
C+ / 6.4	3.0	N/A	7.41	1	0	31	1	32	36	0	0.0	54	N/A	100	50	4.5	0.0
C+ / 6.6	3.0	N/A	6.93	2	0	31	1	32	36	0	0.0	30	N/A	100	50	0.0	0.0
B+ / 8.3	2.2	N/A	6.66	N/A	0	86	0	5	9	0	0.0	18	N/A	100	50	4.5	0.0
B / 8.2	2.3	N/A	6.23	N/A	0	86	0	5	9	0	0.0	10	N/A	100	50	0.0	0.0
A- / 9.1	1.1	N/A	6.87	24	56	19	0	11	14	0	0.0	73	N/A	500	50	4.5	0.0
A- / 9.1	1.2	N/A	6.28	12	56	19	0	11	14	0	0.0	39	N/A	500	50	0.0	0.0
A- / 9.1	1.1	N/A	7.42	305	60	16	0	12	12	0	0.0	80	N/A	500	50	0.0	0.0
C+ / 5.9	3.2	N/A	8.00	13	0	47	1	26	26	0	0.0	76	N/A	500	50	0.0	0.0
A- / 9.1	1.2	N/A	13.77	156	0	0	0	0	100	0	0.0	78	N/A	1,000	50	0.0	0.0
D- / 1.4	6.2	N/A	9.16	9	2	97	0	0	1	62	0.0	23	N/A	100	0	0.0	2.0
D- / 1.3	6.3	6.4	9.93	120	2	93	0	0	5	50	0.0	30	N/A	100	0	0.0	2.0
E- / 0.1	12.4	N/A	7.73	156	4	24	0	0	72	109	0.0	2	5	100,000	50	0.0	1.0

99 Pct = Best 0 Pct = Worst Fund Type	Fund Name	Ticker Symbol	Overall Investment Rating	Phone	PERFORMANCE Performance Rating/Pts	Total Return % through 3/31/16 3 Mo	6 Mo	1Yr / Pct	Annualized 3Yr / Pct	5Yr / Pct	Incl. in Returns Dividend Yield	Expense Ratio
GL	Lazard Emerg Mkts Multi Asset Open	EMMOX	E-	(800) 821-6474	E- / 0.1	2.93	4.74	-8.11 / 1	-6.11 / 1	-4.10 / 0	0.66	2.23
EM	Lazard Emerging Markets Income	LEIIX	U	(800) 821-6474	U /	5.25	4.39	-1.60 /18	--	--	0.18	5.15
EM	Lazard Emerging Markets Income	LEIOX	U	(800) 821-6474	U /	5.24	4.25	-1.78 /17	--	--	0.00	13.96
EM	Lazard Explorer Total Ret Ptf Instl	LETIX	U	(800) 821-6474	U /	2.17	2.69	-2.95 /12	--	--	3.41	1.30
EM	Lazard Explorer Total Ret Ptf Open	LETOX	U	(800) 821-6474	U /	2.09	2.52	-3.15 /11	--	--	3.05	1.78
GL	Lazard Global Fixed Inc Pfolio Inst	LZGIX	D	(800) 821-6474	C- / 3.5	5.09	3.64	2.65 /75	-0.21 /14	--	2.02	4.12
GL	Lazard Global Fixed Inc Pfolio Open	LZGOX	D	(800) 821-6474	C- / 3.0	5.02	3.50	2.35 /74	-0.46 /12	--	1.74	20.84
COH	Lazard US Corporate Income Inst	LZHYX	C-	(800) 821-6474	B- / 7.3	2.88	2.84	-0.34 /28	3.06 /77	5.08 /72	4.91	0.71
COH	Lazard US Corporate Income Open	LZHOX	C-	(800) 821-6474	C+ / 6.7	2.80	2.47	-0.61 /25	2.70 /73	4.73 /70	4.61	1.55
COI	Lazard US Short Dur Fixed Inc Inst	UMNIX	C-	(800) 821-6474	D / 1.7	0.40	0.20	0.21 /44	-0.25 /14	1.33 /23	1.12	0.52
COI	Lazard US Short Dur Fixed Inc Open	UMNOX	C-	(800) 821-6474	D+ / 2.6	0.33	1.07	1.04 /59	-0.15 /14	1.27 /23	1.95	17.62
COI	Leader Short-Term Bond A	LCAMX	D+	(800) 711-9164	E+ / 0.6	-1.83	-4.26	-5.49 / 4	-0.06 /15	--	2.34	1.43
COI	Leader Short-Term Bond C	LCMCX	D+	(800) 711-9164	E / 0.5	-1.94	-4.47	-5.93 / 3	-0.56 /11	--	1.86	1.93
GEI	Leader Short-Term Bond Inst	LCCIX	D+	(800) 711-9164	D- / 1.1	-1.80	-4.08	-5.05 / 5	0.42 /32	1.58 /26	2.90	0.93
GEI	Leader Short-Term Bond Inv	LCCMX	D+	(800) 711-9164	E+ / 0.7	-1.84	-4.26	-5.48 / 4	-0.09 /15	1.09 /21	2.37	1.43
GEI	Leader Total Return A	LCATX	E+	(800) 711-9164	E / 0.3	-2.09	-7.49	-11.14 / 0	-0.77 /10	--	4.75	1.58
GEI	Leader Total Return C	LCCTX	E+	(800) 711-9164	E / 0.3	-2.20	-7.66	-11.57 / 0	-1.11 / 8	--	4.26	2.08
GL	Leader Total Return Inst	LCTIX	E+	(800) 711-9164	E / 0.4	-1.87	-7.19	-10.63 / 1	-0.10 /15	2.38 /36	5.37	1.08
GL	Leader Total Return Inv	LCTRX	E+	(800) 711-9164	E / 0.3	-2.19	-7.48	-11.20 / 0	-0.65 /10	1.82 /29	4.83	1.58
MUN	Lee Financial Tactical Inv	LOVIX	C		A+ / 9.9	1.54	6.47	-4.76 / 5	6.55 /99	--	0.75	1.36
MUS	Lee Fnl Hawaii-Muni Bond Inv	SURFX	A+		A- / 9.0	1.26	2.22	2.83 /83	3.17 /90	4.65 /83	2.69	1.05
GL	Legg Mason BW Global High Yield A	LBHAX	U	(877) 534-4627	U /	4.16	3.17	-2.89 /12	--	--	4.08	1.80
GL	Legg Mason BW Global High Yield C	LBHCX	U	(877) 534-4627	U /	3.86	2.68	-3.71 / 9	--	--	3.52	2.69
GL	Legg Mason BW Global High Yield FI	LBHFX	U	(877) 534-4627	U /	4.16	3.16	-2.89 /12	--	--	4.26	1.87
GL	Legg Mason BW Global High Yield I	LMYIX	U	(877) 534-4627	U /	4.25	3.33	-2.57 /13	--	--	4.60	1.38
GL	Legg Mason BW Global High Yield IS	LMZIX	D	(877) 534-4627	C+ / 5.6	4.13	3.24	-2.63 /13	1.65 /55	4.82 /70	4.67	1.28
GL	Legg Mason BW Global Opportunities	LOBAX	U	(877) 534-4627	U /	8.25	7.54	-0.80 /23	--	--	0.94	1.18
GEI	Legg Mason CO Sc Ch All Fixed Inc		D+	(877) 534-4627	C / 4.4	2.44	2.20	0.33 /46	1.81 /58	3.84 /59	0.00	0.82
GEI	Legg Mason CO Sc Ch All Fixed Inc		C-	(877) 534-4627	C / 4.7	2.28	1.85	-0.36 /27	1.11 /45	3.11 /47	0.00	1.52
GEI	Legg Mason CO Sc Ch All Fixed Inc		C-	(877) 534-4627	C / 5.1	2.31	1.89	-0.20 /29	1.31 /49	3.31 /50	0.00	1.32
GEI	Legg Mason CO Sc Ch All Fixed Inc		C-	(877) 534-4627	C / 5.5	2.41	2.05	--	1.51 /52	3.54 /54	0.00	1.09
GEI	Legg Mason WY Sch Ch Fix Inc 80%		C	(877) 534-4627	C / 4.7	0.95	1.79	-0.58 /25	2.31 /68	3.30 /50	0.00	0.86
GEI	Legg Mason WY Sch Ch Fix Inc 80%		C+	(877) 534-4627	C / 5.0	0.78	1.45	-1.22 /20	1.61 /54	2.59 /39	0.00	1.56
GEI	Legg Mason WY Sch Ch Fix Inc 80%		C+	(877) 534-4627	C / 5.4	0.82	1.53	-1.06 /21	1.80 /57	2.80 /42	0.00	1.36
GEI	Legg Mason WY Sch Ch Fix Inc 80%		C+	(877) 534-4627	C+ / 5.7	0.91	1.65	-0.90 /22	1.96 /61	2.98 /45	0.00	1.09
GEI	LeggMason CO SC Yr to Enr Le Th 1		D+	(877) 534-4627	E+ / 0.8	0.80	0.51	-0.22 /29	-0.29 /13	0.32 /16	0.00	0.71
GEI	LeggMason CO SC Yr to Enr Le Th 1		C-	(877) 534-4627	D- / 1.0	0.64	0.16	-0.87 /23	-0.99 / 8	-0.39 / 2	0.00	1.41
GEI	LeggMason CO SC Yr to Enr Le Th 1		C-	(877) 534-4627	D- / 1.1	0.62	0.23	-0.77 /23	-0.79 / 9	-0.18 / 3	0.00	1.21
GEI	LeggMason CO SC Yr to Enr Le Th 1		C-	(877) 534-4627	D- / 1.2	0.68	0.23	-0.67 /24	-0.74 /10	-0.14 / 3	0.00	1.09
GEI	LeggMason CO Sch Ch Fix Inc 80%		C	(877) 534-4627	C / 4.7	0.95	1.79	-0.58 /25	2.31 /68	3.30 /50	0.00	0.81
GEI	LeggMason CO Sch Ch Fix Inc 80%		C+	(877) 534-4627	C / 5.0	0.78	1.45	-1.22 /20	1.61 /54	2.59 /39	0.00	1.51
GEI	LeggMason CO Sch Ch Fix Inc 80%		C+	(877) 534-4627	C / 5.4	0.82	1.53	-1.06 /21	1.80 /58	2.80 /42	0.00	1.31
GEI	LeggMason CO Sch Ch Fix Inc 80%		C+	(877) 534-4627	C+ / 5.7	0.91	1.65	-0.90 /23	1.96 /61	2.98 /45	0.00	1.09
GEI	LeggMason WY SC Yr To Enr Le Th		D+	(877) 534-4627	E+ / 0.8	0.80	0.51	-0.22 /29	-0.29 /13	0.32 /16	0.00	0.86
GEI	LeggMason WY SC Yr To Enr Le Th		C-	(877) 534-4627	D- / 1.0	0.64	0.16	-0.87 /23	-0.99 / 8	-0.39 / 2	0.00	1.56
GEI	LeggMason WY SC Yr To Enr Le Th		C-	(877) 534-4627	D- / 1.1	0.62	0.23	-0.77 /24	-0.79 / 9	-0.18 / 3	0.00	1.36
GEI	LeggMason WY SC Yr To Enr Le Th		C-	(877) 534-4627	D- / 1.2	0.68	0.23	-0.67 /25	-0.74 /10	-0.14 / 3	0.00	1.09
GEI	LeggMason WY Sch Ch All Fixed Inc		D+	(877) 534-4627	C / 4.4	2.44	2.20	0.33 /46	1.81 /58	3.84 /59	0.00	0.82
GEI	LeggMason WY Sch Ch All Fixed Inc		C-	(877) 534-4627	C / 4.7	2.28	1.85	-0.36 /27	1.11 /45	3.11 /47	0.00	1.52
GEI	LeggMason WY Sch Ch All Fixed Inc		C-	(877) 534-4627	C / 5.1	2.31	1.89	-0.20 /29	1.31 /49	3.31 /50	0.00	1.32
GEI	LeggMason WY Sch Ch All Fixed Inc		C-	(877) 534-4627	C / 5.5	2.41	2.05	--	1.51 /52	3.54 /54	0.00	1.09
GEI	Leland Currency Strategy A	GHCAX	U	(877) 270-2848	U /	-0.90	0.75	6.85 /96	--	--	0.31	16.35

• Denotes fund is closed to new investors
* Denotes fund is included in Section II

RISK			NET ASSETS		ASSET							FUND MANAGER		MINIMUM		LOADS	
Risk Rating/Pts	3 Yr Avg Standard Deviation	Avg Duration	NAV As of 3/31/16	Total $(Mil)	Cash %	Gov. Bond %	Muni. Bond %	Corp. Bond %	Other %	Portfolio Turnover Ratio	Avg Coupon Rate	Manager Quality Pct	Manager Tenure (Years)	Initial Purch. $	Additional Purch. $	Front End Load	Back End Load
E- / 0.1	12.5	N/A	7.74	1	4	24	0	0	72	109	0.0	2	5	2,500	50	0.0	1.0
U /	N/A	0.4	8.85	13	0	0	0	0	100	125	2.2	N/A	2	100,000	50	0.0	1.0
U /	N/A	0.4	8.83	N/A	0	0	0	0	100	125	2.2	N/A	2	2,500	50	0.0	1.0
U /	N/A	6.4	8.67	239	34	37	0	27	2	182	6.1	N/A	3	100,000	50	0.0	1.0
U /	N/A	6.4	8.72	1	34	37	0	27	2	182	6.1	N/A	3	2,500	50	0.0	1.0
C- / 3.1	4.6	4.8	9.14	6	4	51	11	32	2	78	3.9	58	4	100,000	50	0.0	1.0
C- / 3.1	4.6	4.8	9.14	N/A	4	51	11	32	2	78	3.9	48	4	2,500	50	0.0	1.0
D+ / 2.5	4.7	0.9	4.72	237	4	0	0	95	1	28	3.1	95	13	100,000	50	0.0	1.0
D+ / 2.7	4.6	0.9	4.74	2	4	0	0	95	1	28	3.1	93	13	2,500	50	0.0	1.0
A- / 9.1	1.3	1.0	9.90	100	1	7	5	37	50	46	3.0	33	5	100,000	50	0.0	0.0
A- / 9.0	1.3	1.0	9.91	N/A	1	7	5	37	50	46	3.0	36	5	2,500	50	0.0	0.0
B / 7.8	2.5	1.7	8.99	27	27	1	0	49	23	71	3.8	37	11	2,500	100	1.5	0.0
B / 7.8	2.5	1.7	9.03	14	27	1	0	49	23	71	3.8	23	11	2,500	100	0.0	0.0
B / 7.9	2.5	1.7	9.07	283	27	1	0	49	23	71	3.8	71	11	2,000,000	0	0.0	0.0
B / 7.8	2.5	1.7	9.01	224	27	1	0	49	23	71	3.8	45	11	2,500	100	0.0	0.0
D+ / 2.4	5.4	2.4	9.07	12	4	0	0	74	22	174	5.0	14	6	2,500	100	1.5	0.0
D+ / 2.4	5.4	2.4	9.14	6	4	0	0	74	22	174	5.0	12	6	2,500	100	0.0	0.0
D+ / 2.4	5.3	2.4	9.05	44	4	0	0	74	22	174	5.0	59	6	2,000,000	0	0.0	0.0
D+ / 2.4	5.3	2.4	9.08	21	4	0	0	74	22	174	5.0	39	6	2,500	100	0.0	0.0
E / 0.3	9.4	N/A	11.20	46	7	0	0	11	82	104	5.2	99	5	2,500	100	0.0	0.0
C+ / 6.6	3.0	5.6	11.31	166	2	0	97	0	1	6	5.2	70	1	10,000	100	0.0	0.0
U /	N/A	4.4	8.40	N/A	10	0	0	79	11	54	5.8	N/A	7	1,000	50	4.3	0.0
U /	N/A	4.4	8.39	N/A	10	0	0	79	11	54	5.8	N/A	7	1,000	50	0.0	0.0
U /	N/A	4.4	8.40	N/A	10	0	0	79	11	54	5.8	N/A	7	0	0	0.0	0.0
U /	N/A	4.4	8.40	1	10	0	0	79	11	54	5.8	N/A	7	1,000,000	0	0.0	0.0
D / 1.6	6.1	4.4	8.39	27	10	0	0	79	11	54	5.8	95	7	0	0	0.0	0.0
U /	7.2	7.9	10.63	14	2	78	0	15	5	52	4.6	N/A	10	1,000	50	4.3	0.0
C / 4.9	3.5	N/A	21.38	18	0	37	0	35	28	0	0.0	35	15	250	50	3.5	0.0
C / 4.8	3.5	N/A	19.31	1	0	37	0	35	28	0	0.0	18	15	250	50	0.0	0.0
C / 4.9	3.5	N/A	19.90	15	0	37	0	35	28	0	0.0	22	15	250	50	0.0	0.0
C / 4.9	3.5	N/A	20.86	2	0	37	0	35	28	0	0.0	28	15	250	50	0.0	0.0
B- / 7.2	2.8	N/A	17.07	261	0	0	0	0	100	0	0.0	92	17	250	50	3.5	0.0
B- / 7.2	2.8	N/A	15.41	18	0	0	0	0	100	0	0.0	85	17	250	50	0.0	0.0
B- / 7.3	2.8	N/A	15.91	238	0	0	0	0	100	0	0.0	88	17	250	50	0.0	0.0
B- / 7.2	2.8	N/A	16.60	35	0	0	0	0	100	0	0.0	89	17	250	50	0.0	0.0
A- / 9.1	1.2	N/A	13.88	123	0	0	0	0	100	0	0.0	24	17	250	50	3.5	0.0
A- / 9.1	1.2	N/A	12.55	9	0	0	0	0	100	0	0.0	13	17	250	50	0.0	0.0
A- / 9.1	1.2	N/A	12.92	129	0	0	0	0	100	0	0.0	15	17	250	50	0.0	0.0
A- / 9.1	1.2	N/A	13.26	17	0	0	0	0	100	0	0.0	16	17	250	50	0.0	0.0
B- / 7.2	2.8	N/A	17.07	261	0	0	0	0	100	0	0.0	92	17	250	50	3.5	0.0
B- / 7.2	2.8	N/A	15.41	18	0	0	0	0	100	0	0.0	85	17	250	50	0.0	0.0
B- / 7.3	2.8	N/A	15.91	238	0	0	0	0	100	0	0.0	88	17	250	50	0.0	0.0
B- / 7.2	2.8	N/A	16.60	35	0	0	0	0	100	0	0.0	89	17	250	50	0.0	0.0
A- / 9.1	1.2	N/A	13.88	123	0	0	0	0	100	0	0.0	24	N/A	250	50	3.5	0.0
A- / 9.1	1.2	N/A	12.55	9	0	0	0	0	100	0	0.0	13	N/A	250	50	0.0	0.0
A- / 9.1	1.2	N/A	12.92	129	0	0	0	0	100	0	0.0	15	N/A	250	50	0.0	0.0
A- / 9.1	1.2	N/A	13.26	17	0	0	0	0	100	0	0.0	16	N/A	250	50	0.0	0.0
C / 4.8	3.5	N/A	21.38	18	0	0	0	0	100	0	0.0	35	16	250	50	3.5	0.0
C / 4.8	3.5	N/A	19.31	1	0	0	0	0	100	0	0.0	19	16	250	50	0.0	0.0
C / 4.9	3.5	N/A	19.90	15	0	0	0	0	100	0	0.0	22	16	250	50	0.0	0.0
C / 4.9	3.5	N/A	20.86	2	0	0	0	0	100	0	0.0	28	16	250	50	0.0	0.0
U /	N/A	N/A	12.12	7	100	0	0	0	0	0	0.0	N/A	2	2,500	250	5.8	1.0

Fund Type	Fund Name	Ticker Symbol	Overall Investment Rating	Phone	PERFORMANCE: Performance Rating/Pts	Total Return % through 3/31/16: 3 Mo	6 Mo	1Yr / Pct	Annualized: 3Yr / Pct	5Yr / Pct	Incl. in Returns: Dividend Yield	Expense Ratio
GEI	Leland Currency Strategy C	GHCCX	U	(877) 270-2848	U /	-1.07	0.42	5.88 /93	--	--	0.33	17.10
GEI	Leland Currency Strategy I	GHCIX	U	(877) 270-2848	U /	-0.82	0.92	6.94 /97	--	--	0.32	16.10
GEI	LKCM Fixed Income Institutional	LKFIX	B-	(800) 688-5526	C / 4.7	2.49	2.04	0.98 /58	1.17 /46	2.58 /39	2.42	0.70
GL	LM BW Absolute Return Opptys FI	LBAFX	D	(877) 534-4627	D+ / 2.6	2.95	2.66	-3.70 / 9	0.11 /27	--	2.62	1.12
GL	LM BW Global Opportunities Bond A	GOBAX	D-	(877) 534-4627	D+ / 2.9	8.24	7.62	-0.68 /24	0.19 /29	3.55 /54	1.05	0.94
GL	LM BW Global Opportunities Bond C	LGOCX	D-	(877) 534-4627	C- / 3.6	8.21	7.24	-1.39 /19	-0.54 /11	2.78 /41	0.51	1.70
GL	LM BW Global Opportunities Bond C1	GOBCX	D-	(877) 534-4627	C- / 4.2	8.18	7.39	-1.06 /21	-0.23 /14	3.09 /47	0.74	1.40
GL	LM BW Global Opportunities Bond FI	GOBFX	D	(877) 534-4627	C / 5.0	8.34	7.55	-0.65 /25	0.17 /28	3.40 /51	1.05	0.99
GL	LM BW Global Opportunities Bond I	GOBIX	D	(877) 534-4627	C / 5.5	8.41	7.79	-0.42 /27	0.43 /32	3.81 /58	1.26	0.69
GL	LM BW Global Opportunities Bond IS	GOBSX	D	(877) 534-4627	C+ / 5.7	8.41	7.78	-0.30 /28	0.55 /34	3.91 /60	1.37	0.58
GL	LM BW Global Opportunities Bond R	LBORX	D	(877) 534-4627	C / 4.5	8.27	7.50	-0.98 /22	-0.11 /15	--	0.89	1.36
GL	LM BW International Opptys Bd A	LWOAX	E+	(877) 534-4627	D / 1.8	8.84	7.49	-0.98 /22	-0.18 /14	--	0.00	1.18
GL	LM BW International Opptys Bd C	LIOCX	D-	(877) 534-4627	D+ / 2.9	8.61	7.14	-1.69 /17	-0.93 / 9	--	0.00	1.92
GL	LM BW International Opptys Bd FI	LWOFX	D	(877) 534-4627	C / 4.6	8.83	7.47	-0.89 /23	-0.11 /15	--	0.00	1.12
GL	LM BW International Opptys Bd I	LWOIX	D	(877) 534-4627	C / 4.9	8.91	7.56	-0.72 /24	0.07 /26	--	0.00	0.83
GL	LM BW International Opptys Bd IS	LMOTX	D	(877) 534-4627	C / 5.1	9.01	7.76	-0.54 /26	0.15 /28	3.17 /48	0.00	0.69
GL	LM BW International Opptys Bd R	LWORX	D-	(877) 534-4627	C- / 3.9	8.76	7.40	-1.16 /20	-0.43 /12	--	0.00	1.44
GEI	LM Capital Opportunistic Bond Inst	LMCOX	U	(866) 777-7818	U /	2.95	2.31	0.92 /57	--	--	2.94	3.37
GEN	Logan Circle Part Core Plus I		U	(866) 777-7818	U /	3.05	2.45	0.95 /58	--	--	2.32	4.72
GEN	Logan Circle Part Core Plus R		U	(866) 777-7818	U /	3.04	2.45	1.16 /61	--	--	2.43	4.97
GES	Loomis Sayles Bond Admin	LBFAX	D-	(800) 633-3330	C- / 3.3	2.71	1.70	-3.77 / 8	0.72 /37	3.60 /55	2.32	1.14
GES	Loomis Sayles Bond Inst	LSBDX	D	(800) 633-3330	C / 4.4	2.81	1.95	-3.25 /11	1.27 /48	4.16 /64	2.81	0.64
COI	Loomis Sayles Bond N	LSBNX	D	(800) 633-3330	C / 4.4	2.83	1.92	-3.25 /11	1.28 /48	--	2.90	0.57
* GES	Loomis Sayles Bond Ret	LSBRX	D	(800) 633-3330	C- / 3.7	2.68	1.75	-3.58 / 9	0.93 /41	3.83 /59	2.57	0.89
EM	Loomis Sayles Emerg Mkts Opptys A	LEOAX	U	(800) 225-5478	U /	2.43	3.36	-0.45 /26	--	--	2.10	1.72
EM	Loomis Sayles Emerg Mkts Opptys C	LEOCX	U	(800) 225-5478	U /	2.28	2.35	-1.53 /18	--	--	2.07	2.46
EM	● Loomis Sayles Emerg Mkts Opptys N	LEONX	U	(800) 225-5478	U /	2.52	2.88	-0.47 /26	--	--	3.14	8.29
EM	Loomis Sayles Emerg Mkts Opptys Y	LEOYX	U	(800) 225-5478	U /	2.52	2.98	-0.48 /26	--	--	3.13	1.47
* GEI	Loomis Sayles Fixed Inc Fd	LSFIX	D+	(800) 633-3330	C+ / 5.6	3.03	2.26	-2.49 /13	1.86 /59	4.68 /69	4.72	0.57
GL	Loomis Sayles Glbl Bd Inst	LSGBX	D	(800) 633-3330	C- / 3.6	5.32	4.20	1.69 /69	-0.41 /12	1.40 /24	0.00	0.78
GL	Loomis Sayles Glbl Bd Ret	LSGLX	D	(800) 633-3330	C- / 3.1	5.26	4.05	1.45 /66	-0.64 /11	1.15 /22	0.00	1.03
USL	Loomis Sayles Infl Prot Sec Inst	LSGSX	D-	(800) 633-3330	D- / 1.5	4.37	3.52	1.23 /62	-1.20 / 7	2.60 /39	0.72	0.80
GEI	Loomis Sayles Infl Prot Sec Rtl	LIPRX	D-	(800) 633-3330	D- / 1.2	4.39	3.27	0.88 /57	-1.48 / 6	2.32 /35	0.58	1.03
* COH	Loomis Sayles Inst High Income Inst	LSHIX	D-	(800) 633-3330	C- / 3.7	2.56	-0.85	-8.73 / 1	1.91 /60	4.39 /66	6.80	0.68
GEI	Loomis Sayles Intm Dur Bd Inst	LSDIX	A-	(800) 633-3330	C+ / 6.5	2.23	1.44	1.39 /65	2.10 /64	3.35 /51	2.39	0.47
COI	Loomis Sayles Intm Dur Bd Rtl	LSDRX	B+	(800) 633-3330	C+ / 6.0	2.17	1.31	1.14 /61	1.81 /58	3.05 /46	2.14	0.71
GEI	Loomis Sayles Invst Gr Fix Inc I	LSIGX	D+	(800) 633-3330	C+ / 5.8	3.99	3.77	-0.04 /31	1.37 /50	4.02 /62	2.22	0.48
MUN	Lord Abbett AMT Free Municipal Bd A	LATAX	C+	(888) 522-2388	B+ / 8.8	1.99	3.99	3.96 /94	3.07 /89	6.82 /96	3.14	0.89
MUN	Lord Abbett AMT Free Municipal Bd	LATCX	C	(888) 522-2388	B+ / 8.6	1.83	3.61	3.24 /87	2.38 /81	6.05 /92	2.60	1.53
MUN	Lord Abbett AMT Free Municipal Bd F	LATFX	C+	(888) 522-2388	A / 9.3	2.01	4.04	4.06 /94	3.17 /90	6.92 /96	3.31	0.79
MUN	Lord Abbett AMT Free Municipal Bd I	LMCIX	C+	(888) 522-2388	A / 9.3	2.04	4.09	4.16 /95	3.27 /91	7.04 /96	3.40	0.69
* COH	Lord Abbett Bond Debenture A	LBNDX	D+	(888) 522-2388	C / 5.5	1.61	0.61	-3.45 /10	2.94 /76	4.89 /71	4.51	0.82
COH	● Lord Abbett Bond Debenture B	LBNBX	D	(888) 522-2388	C / 5.0	1.28	0.22	-4.31 / 7	2.14 /64	4.13 /63	3.81	1.62
COH	Lord Abbett Bond Debenture C	BDLAX	D	(888) 522-2388	C / 5.4	1.46	0.30	-4.03 / 8	2.29 /67	4.22 /64	3.97	1.50
COH	Lord Abbett Bond Debenture F	LBDFX	D+	(888) 522-2388	C+ / 6.7	1.63	0.65	-3.37 /10	3.09 /77	5.08 /72	4.71	0.72
COH	Lord Abbett Bond Debenture I	LBNYX	D+	(888) 522-2388	C+ / 6.9	1.66	0.70	-3.29 /10	3.18 /78	5.18 /73	4.82	0.62
COH	Lord Abbett Bond Debenture P	LBNPX	D+	(888) 522-2388	C+ / 6.4	1.46	0.49	-3.57 / 9	2.89 /75	4.86 /71	4.57	1.07
COH	Lord Abbett Bond Debenture R2	LBNQX	D+	(888) 522-2388	C+ / 5.9	1.51	0.41	-3.83 / 8	2.59 /72	4.57 /68	4.21	1.22
COH	Lord Abbett Bond Debenture R3	LBNRX	D+	(888) 522-2388	C+ / 6.0	1.40	0.46	-3.87 / 8	2.65 /73	4.65 /69	4.32	1.12
GEL	Lord Abbett Bond Debenture R4	LBNSX	U	(888) 522-2388	U /	1.60	0.59	--	--	--	0.00	N/A
GEL	Lord Abbett Bond Debenture R5	LBNTX	U	(888) 522-2388	U /	1.66	0.70	--	--	--	0.00	N/A
GEL	Lord Abbett Bond Debenture R6	LBNVX	U	(888) 522-2388	U /	1.55	0.74	--	--	--	0.00	N/A

99 Pct = Best
0 Pct = Worst

● Denotes fund is closed to new investors
* Denotes fund is included in Section II

RISK			NET ASSETS		ASSET							FUND MANAGER		MINIMUM		LOADS	
Risk Rating/Pts	3 Yr Avg Standard Deviation	Avg Duration	NAV As of 3/31/16	Total $(Mil)	Cash %	Gov. Bond %	Muni. Bond %	Corp. Bond %	Other %	Portfolio Turnover Ratio	Avg Coupon Rate	Manager Quality Pct	Manager Tenure (Years)	Initial Purch. $	Additional Purch. $	Front End Load	Back End Load
U /	N/A	N/A	12.01	1	100	0	0	0	0	0	0.0	N/A	2	2,500	250	0.0	1.0
U /	N/A	N/A	12.13	19	100	0	0	0	0	0	0.0	N/A	2	5,000,000	10,000	0.0	1.0
B+ / 8.6	1.9	3.3	10.70	209	2	13	0	83	2	46	3.3	57	19	2,000	1,000	0.0	1.0
C- / 3.0	4.7	N/A	11.52	3	3	67	0	27	3	43	0.0	71	5	0	0	0.0	0.0
E+ / 0.6	7.1	7.9	10.64	291	2	78	0	15	5	52	4.6	78	10	1,000	50	4.3	0.0
E+ / 0.6	7.2	7.9	10.55	31	2	78	0	15	5	52	4.6	46	10	1,000	50	0.0	0.0
E+ / 0.6	7.1	7.9	10.58	15	2	78	0	15	5	52	4.6	58	10	1,000	50	0.0	0.0
E+ / 0.6	7.1	7.9	10.52	69	2	78	0	15	5	52	4.6	77	10	0	0	0.0	0.0
E+ / 0.6	7.2	7.9	10.57	1,540	2	78	0	15	5	52	4.6	84	10	1,000,000	0	0.0	0.0
E+ / 0.6	7.1	7.9	10.57	1,299	2	78	0	15	5	52	4.6	86	10	0	0	0.0	0.0
E+ / 0.6	7.2	7.9	10.61	16	2	78	0	15	5	52	4.6	64	10	0	0	0.0	0.0
E / 0.5	7.7	8.0	11.20	14	4	81	0	12	3	43	4.7	61	7	1,000	50	4.3	0.0
E / 0.5	7.8	8.0	11.10	N/A	4	81	0	12	3	43	4.7	34	7	1,000	50	0.0	0.0
E / 0.5	7.8	8.0	11.22	6	4	81	0	12	3	43	4.7	66	7	0	0	0.0	0.0
E / 0.5	7.7	8.0	11.24	85	4	81	0	12	3	43	4.7	75	7	1,000,000	0	0.0	0.0
E / 0.5	7.8	8.0	11.25	25	4	81	0	12	3	43	4.7	77	7	0	0	0.0	0.0
E / 0.5	7.8	8.0	11.17	N/A	4	81	0	12	3	43	4.7	51	7	0	0	0.0	0.0
U /	N/A	5.7	10.11	10	0	22	0	53	25	26	0.0	N/A	3	1,000,000	0	0.0	0.0
U /	N/A	N/A	9.92	10	8	14	0	36	42	798	0.0	N/A	2	5,000,000	0	0.0	0.0
U /	N/A	N/A	9.93	N/A	8	14	0	36	42	798	0.0	N/A	2	500,000	0	0.0	0.0
D- / 1.4	6.2	4.5	13.08	221	3	30	1	47	19	22	4.7	28	25	0	0	0.0	0.0
D- / 1.4	6.2	4.5	13.19	10,642	3	30	1	47	19	22	4.7	44	25	100,000	50	0.0	0.0
D- / 1.4	6.2	4.5	13.17	101	3	30	1	47	19	22	4.7	26	25	1,000,000	0	0.0	0.0
D- / 1.4	6.2	4.5	13.12	4,961	3	30	1	47	19	22	4.7	33	25	2,500	50	0.0	0.0
U /	N/A	N/A	9.73	N/A	13	16	0	69	2	37	0.0	N/A	2	2,500	100	4.3	0.0
U /	N/A	N/A	9.62	N/A	13	16	0	69	2	37	0.0	N/A	2	2,500	100	0.0	0.0
U /	N/A	N/A	9.64	N/A	13	16	0	69	2	37	0.0	N/A	2	1,000,000	0	0.0	0.0
U /	N/A	N/A	9.64	24	13	16	0	69	2	37	0.0	N/A	2	100,000	100	0.0	0.0
D / 1.7	5.9	4.2	12.60	1,209	2	24	2	54	18	15	4.6	61	21	3,000,000	50,000	0.0	0.0
D+ / 2.9	4.8	6.8	15.63	1,114	0	48	1	35	16	117	3.8	50	16	100,000	0	0.0	0.0
D+ / 2.9	4.8	6.8	15.42	386	0	48	1	35	16	117	3.8	42	16	2,500	50	0.0	0.0
D+ / 2.3	5.1	8.1	10.51	23	3	96	0	0	1	135	0.6	6	4	100,000	0	0.0	0.0
D+ / 2.4	5.1	8.1	10.46	4	3	96	0	0	1	135	0.6	3	4	2,500	50	0.0	0.0
E / 0.4	8.0	4.3	6.00	643	4	9	0	60	27	19	5.1	51	20	3,000,000	50,000	0.0	0.0
B / 8.1	2.3	3.8	10.38	128	0	18	1	46	35	151	2.9	77	11	100,000	0	0.0	0.0
B / 8.1	2.3	3.8	10.38	20	0	18	1	46	35	151	2.9	79	11	2,500	50	0.0	0.0
C- / 3.0	4.7	4.6	12.00	476	1	37	0	49	13	26	4.2	34	22	3,000,000	50,000	0.0	0.0
D+ / 2.5	5.0	7.4	16.21	133	0	0	98	0	2	21	5.2	12	6	1,000	0	2.3	0.0
D+ / 2.6	5.0	7.4	16.20	27	0	0	98	0	2	21	5.2	8	6	1,000	0	0.0	0.0
D+ / 2.6	5.0	7.4	16.21	44	0	0	98	0	2	21	5.2	13	6	0	0	0.0	0.0
D+ / 2.6	5.0	7.4	16.22	1	0	0	98	0	2	21	5.2	14	6	1,000,000	0	0.0	0.0
D / 1.8	5.4	4.6	7.43	4,180	2	2	0	72	24	88	0.0	92	29	1,000	0	2.3	0.0
D / 1.8	5.4	4.6	7.45	72	2	2	0	72	24	88	0.0	85	29	1,000	0	0.0	0.0
D / 1.7	5.4	4.6	7.45	1,858	2	2	0	72	24	88	0.0	87	29	1,000	0	0.0	0.0
D / 1.8	5.4	4.6	7.42	1,874	2	2	0	72	24	88	0.0	93	29	0	0	0.0	0.0
D / 1.8	5.4	4.6	7.39	464	2	2	0	72	24	88	0.0	94	29	1,000,000	0	0.0	0.0
D / 1.8	5.4	4.6	7.59	35	2	2	0	72	24	88	0.0	92	29	0	0	0.0	0.0
D / 1.7	5.4	4.6	7.43	4	2	2	0	72	24	88	0.0	90	29	0	0	0.0	0.0
D / 1.8	5.3	4.6	7.41	109	2	2	0	72	24	88	0.0	91	29	0	0	0.0	0.0
U /	N/A	4.6	7.43	N/A	2	2	0	72	24	88	0.0	N/A	29	0	0	0.0	0.0
U /	N/A	4.6	7.39	N/A	2	2	0	72	24	88	0.0	N/A	29	0	0	0.0	0.0
U /	N/A	4.6	7.39	11	2	2	0	72	24	88	0.0	N/A	29	0	0	0.0	0.0

Fund Type	Fund Name (99 Pct = Best, 0 Pct = Worst)	Ticker Symbol	Overall Investment Rating	Phone	PERFORMANCE: Performance Rating/Pts	Total Return % through 3/31/16: 3 Mo	6 Mo	1Yr / Pct	Annualized: 3Yr / Pct	Annualized: 5Yr / Pct	Incl. in Returns: Dividend Yield	Expense Ratio
GEI	Lord Abbett Core Fixed Income A	LCRAX	**C**	(888) 522-2388	**C / 5.2**	2.65	1.79	0.72 /54	1.93 /60	3.70 /57	2.34	0.85
GEI	● Lord Abbett Core Fixed Income B	LCRBX	**C**	(888) 522-2388	**C / 4.7**	2.45	1.47	-0.09 /30	1.11 /45	2.88 /43	1.59	1.65
GEI	Lord Abbett Core Fixed Income C	LCRCX	**C**	(888) 522-2388	**C / 5.1**	2.50	1.46	0.08 /40	1.29 /48	3.02 /45	1.76	1.47
GEI	Lord Abbett Core Fixed Income F	LCRFX	**B**	(888) 522-2388	**C+ / 6.4**	2.66	1.91	0.81 /55	2.02 /62	3.79 /58	2.47	0.75
GEI	Lord Abbett Core Fixed Income I	LCRYX	**B**	(888) 522-2388	**C+ / 6.5**	2.69	1.87	0.91 /57	2.12 /64	3.90 /60	2.58	0.65
GEI	● Lord Abbett Core Fixed Income P	LCRPX	**C+**	(888) 522-2388	**C+ / 5.8**	2.58	1.77	0.52 /50	1.70 /56	3.45 /52	2.18	1.10
GEI	Lord Abbett Core Fixed Income R2	LCRQX	**C+**	(888) 522-2388	**C / 5.5**	2.54	1.57	0.22 /44	1.52 /53	3.28 /49	1.98	1.25
GEI	Lord Abbett Core Fixed Income R3	LCRRX	**C+**	(888) 522-2388	**C+ / 5.7**	2.57	1.62	0.32 /46	1.62 /54	3.37 /51	2.08	1.15
COI	Lord Abbett Core Fixed Income R4	LCRSX	**U**	(888) 522-2388	**U /**	2.64	1.77	--	--	--	0.00	N/A
COI	Lord Abbett Core Fixed Income R5	LCRTX	**U**	(888) 522-2388	**U /**	2.71	1.90	--	--	--	0.00	N/A
COI	Lord Abbett Core Fixed Income R6	LCRVX	**U**	(888) 522-2388	**U /**	2.72	1.94	--	--	--	0.00	N/A
EM	Lord Abbett Em Mkts Corp Debt A	LCDAX	**U**	(888) 522-2388	**U /**	4.35	4.63	3.96 /81	--	--	4.35	2.62
EM	Lord Abbett Em Mkts Corp Debt C	LEDCX	**U**	(888) 522-2388	**U /**	4.18	4.28	3.25 /78	--	--	3.77	3.41
EM	Lord Abbett Em Mkts Corp Debt F	LCDFX	**U**	(888) 522-2388	**U /**	4.43	4.72	4.08 /82	--	--	4.49	2.52
EM	Lord Abbett Em Mkts Corp Debt R2	LCDQX	**U**	(888) 522-2388	**U /**	4.40	4.74	4.19 /82	--	--	4.66	3.02
EM	Lord Abbett Em Mkts Corp Debt R3	LCDRX	**U**	(888) 522-2388	**U /**	4.40	4.73	4.19 /82	--	--	4.66	2.92
EM	Lord Abbett Em Mkts Corp Debt R4	LCDSX	**U**	(888) 522-2388	**U /**	4.34	4.60	--	--	--	0.00	2.67
EM	Lord Abbett Em Mkts Corp Debt R5	LCDTX	**U**	(888) 522-2388	**U /**	4.47	4.81	--	--	--	0.00	2.42
EM	Lord Abbett Em Mkts Corp Debt R6	LCDVX	**U**	(888) 522-2388	**U /**	4.42	4.77	--	--	--	0.00	2.36
EM	Lord Abbett Em Mkts Local Bond A	LEMAX	**U**	(888) 522-2388	**U /**	8.95	8.75	-4.68 / 6	--	--	6.04	3.01
EM	Lord Abbett Em Mkts Local Bond C	LEMCX	**U**	(888) 522-2388	**U /**	8.66	8.27	-5.36 / 4	--	--	5.47	3.79
EM	Lord Abbett Em Mkts Local Bond F	LEMFX	**U**	(888) 522-2388	**U /**	8.87	8.70	-4.59 / 6	--	--	6.28	2.91
EM	Lord Abbett Em Mkts Local Bond I	LEMLX	**U**	(888) 522-2388	**U /**	8.90	8.76	-4.49 / 6	--	--	6.38	2.81
EM	Lord Abbett Em Mkts Local Bond R2	LEMQX	**U**	(888) 522-2388	**U /**	8.90	8.75	-4.49 / 6	--	--	6.38	3.41
EM	Lord Abbett Em Mkts Local Bond R3	LEMRX	**U**	(888) 522-2388	**U /**	8.90	8.76	-4.49 / 6	--	--	6.38	3.31
EM	Lord Abbett Em Mkts Local Bond R4	LEMKX	**U**	(888) 522-2388	**U /**	8.84	8.65	--	--	--	0.00	3.06
EM	Lord Abbett Em Mkts Local Bond R5	LEMTX	**U**	(888) 522-2388	**U /**	8.91	8.78	--	--	--	0.00	2.81
EM	Lord Abbett Em Mkts Local Bond R6	LEMVX	**U**	(888) 522-2388	**U /**	8.92	8.81	--	--	--	0.00	2.76
GL	Lord Abbett Emerg Mkts Currency A	LDMAX	**E-**	(888) 522-2388	**E- / 0.2**	4.10	5.03	-2.47 /13	-4.61 / 2	-2.68 / 1	2.78	0.98
GL	● Lord Abbett Emerg Mkts Currency B	LDMBX	**E-**	(888) 522-2388	**E- / 0.2**	3.89	4.40	-3.23 /11	-5.39 / 1	-3.48 / 1	2.05	1.78
GL	Lord Abbett Emerg Mkts Currency C	LDMCX	**E-**	(888) 522-2388	**E- / 0.2**	3.93	4.69	-3.03 /11	-5.21 / 1	-3.29 / 1	2.24	1.61
GL	Lord Abbett Emerg Mkts Currency F	LDMFX	**E-**	(888) 522-2388	**E- / 0.2**	4.12	5.08	-2.20 /15	-4.47 / 2	-2.58 / 1	2.94	0.88
GL	Lord Abbett Emerg Mkts Currency I	LDMYX	**E-**	(888) 522-2388	**E / 0.3**	4.16	5.14	-2.29 /14	-4.38 / 2	-2.49 / 1	3.04	0.78
GL	Lord Abbett Emerg Mkts Currency R2	LDMQX	**E-**	(888) 522-2388	**E- / 0.2**	4.00	4.81	-2.85 /12	-4.98 / 1	-3.08 / 1	2.44	1.38
GL	Lord Abbett Emerg Mkts Currency R3	LDMRX	**E-**	(888) 522-2388	**E- / 0.2**	4.04	4.89	-2.59 /13	-4.84 / 1	-2.96 / 1	2.55	1.28
GL	Lord Abbett Emerg Mkts Currency R4	LDMSX	**U**	(888) 522-2388	**U /**	4.09	5.02	--	--	--	0.00	1.03
GL	Lord Abbett Emerg Mkts Currency R5	LDMTX	**U**	(888) 522-2388	**U /**	4.16	5.15	--	--	--	0.00	0.78
GL	Lord Abbett Emerg Mkts Currency R6	LDMVX	**U**	(888) 522-2388	**U /**	4.19	5.21	--	--	--	0.00	0.75
* LP	Lord Abbett Floating Rate A	LFRAX	**C+**	(888) 522-2388	**C / 4.9**	1.69	0.43	-0.01 /31	2.08 /63	3.65 /56	4.39	0.80
LP	Lord Abbett Floating Rate C	LARCX	**C+**	(888) 522-2388	**C / 4.8**	1.54	0.23	-0.63 /25	1.42 /51	2.99 /45	3.85	1.48
LP	Lord Abbett Floating Rate F	LFRFX	**B+**	(888) 522-2388	**C+ / 6.1**	1.71	0.47	0.08 /40	2.17 /65	3.75 /57	4.59	0.70
LP	Lord Abbett Floating Rate I	LFRIX	**A-**	(888) 522-2388	**C+ / 6.3**	1.74	0.64	0.19 /44	2.28 /67	3.87 /60	4.69	0.60
LP	Lord Abbett Floating Rate R2	LFRRX	**B-**	(888) 522-2388	**C / 5.2**	1.59	0.23	-0.51 /26	1.68 /55	3.24 /49	4.09	1.20
LP	Lord Abbett Floating Rate R3	LRRRX	**B**	(888) 522-2388	**C / 5.5**	1.62	0.39	-0.30 /28	1.82 /58	3.37 /51	4.19	1.10
LP	Lord Abbett Floating Rate R4	LRRKX	**U**	(888) 522-2388	**U /**	1.68	0.52	--	--	--	0.00	N/A
LP	Lord Abbett Floating Rate R5	LRRTX	**U**	(888) 522-2388	**U /**	1.74	0.66	--	--	--	0.00	N/A
LP	Lord Abbett Floating Rate R6	LRRVX	**U**	(888) 522-2388	**U /**	1.76	0.67	--	--	--	0.00	N/A
* COH	Lord Abbett High Yield A	LHYAX	**D**	(888) 522-2388	**C / 5.4**	1.97	0.12	-3.28 /10	2.85 /75	5.54 /75	5.87	0.94
COH	● Lord Abbett High Yield B	LHYBX	**D**	(888) 522-2388	**C / 4.9**	1.78	-0.27	-4.07 / 7	2.04 /62	4.72 /70	5.20	1.74
COH	Lord Abbett High Yield C	LHYCX	**D**	(888) 522-2388	**C / 5.3**	1.96	-0.06	-3.80 / 8	2.23 /66	4.88 /71	5.34	1.59
COH	Lord Abbett High Yield F	LHYFX	**D+**	(888) 522-2388	**C+ / 6.7**	2.14	0.31	-3.06 /11	3.00 /76	5.67 /75	6.10	0.84
COH	Lord Abbett High Yield I	LAHYX	**D+**	(888) 522-2388	**C+ / 6.7**	2.02	0.24	-3.17 /11	3.08 /77	5.76 /76	6.23	0.74

● Denotes fund is closed to new investors
* Denotes fund is included in Section II

RISK			NET ASSETS		ASSET							FUND MANAGER		MINIMUM		LOADS	
Risk Rating/Pts	3 Yr Avg Standard Deviation	Avg Duration	NAV As of 3/31/16	Total $(Mil)	Cash %	Gov. Bond %	Muni. Bond %	Corp. Bond %	Other %	Portfolio Turnover Ratio	Avg Coupon Rate	Manager Quality Pct	Manager Tenure (Years)	Initial Purch. $	Additional Purch. $	Front End Load	Back End Load
C+ / 6.7	3.0	5.6	10.97	476	0	37	0	22	41	494	0.0	44	18	1,500	0	2.3	0.0
C+ / 6.8	2.9	5.6	10.94	5	0	37	0	22	41	494	0.0	22	18	1,000	0	0.0	0.0
C+ / 6.7	3.0	5.6	10.92	89	0	37	0	22	41	494	0.0	26	18	1,500	0	0.0	0.0
C+ / 6.9	2.9	5.6	10.97	413	0	37	0	22	41	494	0.0	49	18	0	0	0.0	0.0
C+ / 6.9	2.9	5.6	10.97	343	0	37	0	22	41	494	0.0	52	18	1,000,000	0	0.0	0.0
C+ / 6.8	2.9	5.6	11.01	N/A	0	37	0	22	41	494	0.0	38	18	0	0	0.0	0.0
C+ / 6.8	2.9	5.6	10.97	N/A	0	37	0	22	41	494	0.0	32	18	0	0	0.0	0.0
C+ / 6.7	2.9	5.6	10.97	22	0	37	0	22	41	494	0.0	35	18	0	0	0.0	0.0
U /	N/A	5.6	10.97	N/A	0	37	0	22	41	494	0.0	N/A	18	0	0	0.0	0.0
U /	N/A	5.6	10.97	N/A	0	37	0	22	41	494	0.0	N/A	18	0	0	0.0	0.0
U /	N/A	5.6	10.97	33	0	37	0	22	41	494	0.0	N/A	18	0	0	0.0	0.0
U /	N/A	N/A	14.91	12	3	5	0	91	1	293	0.0	N/A	N/A	1,000	0	2.3	0.0
U /	N/A	N/A	14.91	1	3	5	0	91	1	293	0.0	N/A	N/A	1,000	0	0.0	0.0
U /	N/A	N/A	14.92	11	3	5	0	91	1	293	0.0	N/A	N/A	0	0	0.0	0.0
U /	N/A	N/A	14.91	N/A	3	5	0	91	1	293	0.0	N/A	N/A	0	0	0.0	0.0
U /	N/A	N/A	14.91	N/A	3	5	0	91	1	293	0.0	N/A	N/A	0	0	0.0	0.0
U /	N/A	N/A	14.91	N/A	3	5	0	91	1	293	0.0	N/A	N/A	0	0	0.0	0.0
U /	N/A	N/A	14.92	N/A	3	5	0	91	1	293	0.0	N/A	N/A	0	0	0.0	0.0
U /	N/A	N/A	14.91	N/A	3	5	0	91	1	293	0.0	N/A	N/A	0	0	0.0	0.0
U /	N/A	N/A	10.65	6	5	85	0	8	2	39	0.0	N/A	3	1,000	0	2.3	0.0
U /	N/A	N/A	10.64	1	5	85	0	8	2	39	0.0	N/A	3	1,000	0	0.0	0.0
U /	N/A	N/A	10.64	N/A	5	85	0	8	2	39	0.0	N/A	3	0	0	0.0	0.0
U /	N/A	N/A	10.64	2	5	85	0	8	2	39	0.0	N/A	3	1,000,000	0	0.0	0.0
U /	N/A	N/A	10.64	N/A	5	85	0	8	2	39	0.0	N/A	3	0	0	0.0	0.0
U /	N/A	N/A	10.64	N/A	5	85	0	8	2	39	0.0	N/A	3	0	0	0.0	0.0
U /	N/A	N/A	10.64	N/A	5	85	0	8	2	39	0.0	N/A	3	0	0	0.0	0.0
U /	N/A	N/A	10.64	N/A	5	85	0	8	2	39	0.0	N/A	3	0	0	0.0	0.0
U /	N/A	N/A	10.64	N/A	5	85	0	8	2	39	0.0	N/A	3	0	0	0.0	0.0
E / 0.5	7.9	0.1	5.27	21	3	1	0	40	56	113	2.4	4	9	1,000	0	2.3	0.0
E / 0.5	8.0	0.1	5.29	N/A	3	1	0	40	56	113	2.4	3	9	1,000	0	0.0	0.0
E / 0.5	8.0	0.1	5.30	5	3	1	0	40	56	113	2.4	3	9	1,000	0	0.0	0.0
E / 0.5	8.1	0.1	5.27	9	3	1	0	40	56	113	2.4	4	9	0	0	0.0	0.0
E / 0.5	8.1	0.1	5.26	375	3	1	0	40	56	113	2.4	5	9	1,000,000	0	0.0	0.0
E / 0.5	8.0	0.1	5.28	N/A	3	1	0	40	56	113	2.4	3	9	0	0	0.0	0.0
E / 0.5	8.1	0.1	5.26	N/A	3	1	0	40	56	113	2.4	4	9	0	0	0.0	0.0
U /	N/A	0.1	5.27	N/A	3	1	0	40	56	113	2.4	N/A	9	0	0	0.0	0.0
U /	N/A	0.1	5.26	N/A	3	1	0	40	56	113	2.4	N/A	9	0	0	0.0	0.0
U /	N/A	0.1	5.26	N/A	3	1	0	40	56	113	2.4	N/A	9	0	0	0.0	0.0
B / 8.1	2.4	0.3	8.85	2,199	4	0	0	19	77	77	0.0	94	4	1,500	0	2.3	0.0
B / 8.1	2.3	0.3	8.86	1,401	4	0	0	19	77	77	0.0	87	4	1,500	0	0.0	0.0
B / 8.1	2.3	0.3	8.84	2,036	4	0	0	19	77	77	0.0	95	4	0	0	0.0	0.0
B / 8.1	2.3	0.3	8.86	353	4	0	0	19	77	77	0.0	94	4	1,000,000	0	0.0	0.0
B / 8.1	2.3	0.3	8.86	1	4	0	0	19	77	77	0.0	91	4	0	0	0.0	0.0
B / 8.1	2.3	0.3	8.86	28	4	0	0	19	77	77	0.0	91	4	0	0	0.0	0.0
U /	N/A	0.3	8.85	N/A	4	0	0	19	77	77	0.0	N/A	4	0	0	0.0	0.0
U /	N/A	0.3	8.86	N/A	4	0	0	19	77	77	0.0	N/A	4	0	0	0.0	0.0
U /	N/A	0.3	8.86	9	4	0	0	19	77	77	0.0	N/A	4	0	0	0.0	0.0
D- / 1.5	5.6	4.6	6.92	1,240	2	0	0	83	15	93	0.0	91	18	1,500	0	2.3	0.0
D- / 1.5	5.6	4.6	6.89	6	2	0	0	83	15	93	0.0	80	18	1,000	0	0.0	0.0
D- / 1.5	5.6	4.6	6.89	362	2	0	0	83	15	93	0.0	84	18	1,500	0	0.0	0.0
D- / 1.4	5.6	4.6	6.92	928	2	0	0	83	15	93	0.0	92	18	0	0	0.0	0.0
D / 1.6	5.6	4.6	6.95	1,898	2	0	0	83	15	93	0.0	93	18	1,000,000	0	0.0	0.0

Fund Type	Fund Name (99 Pct = Best, 0 Pct = Worst)	Ticker Symbol	Overall Investment Rating	Phone	PERFORMANCE: Performance Rating/Pts	Total Return % through 3/31/16: 3 Mo	6 Mo	1Yr / Pct	Annualized: 3Yr / Pct	Annualized: 5Yr / Pct	Incl. in Returns: Dividend Yield	Expense Ratio
MUH	Lord Abbett High Yield Muni Bd F	HYMFX	**C**	(888) 522-2388	**A+ / 9.6**	2.38	4.49	4.57 /97	3.72 /94	7.34 /97	4.68	0.77
COH ●	Lord Abbett High Yield P	LHYPX	**D+**	(888) 522-2388	**C+ / 6.0**	1.91	0.05	-3.51 /10	2.61 /72	5.31 /74	5.76	1.19
COH	Lord Abbett High Yield R2	LHYQX	**D+**	(888) 522-2388	**C+ / 5.7**	1.88	-0.04	-3.72 / 9	2.43 /69	5.15 /73	5.62	1.34
COH	Lord Abbett High Yield R3	LHYRX	**D+**	(888) 522-2388	**C+ / 5.9**	1.90	0.00	-3.63 / 9	2.58 /72	5.25 /73	5.72	1.24
COH	Lord Abbett High Yield R4	LHYSX	**U**	(888) 522-2388	**U /**	1.97	0.12	--	--	--	0.00	N/A
COH	Lord Abbett High Yield R5	LHYTX	**U**	(888) 522-2388	**U /**	2.03	0.26	--	--	--	0.00	N/A
COH	Lord Abbett High Yield R6	LHYVX	**U**	(888) 522-2388	**U /**	2.20	0.44	--	--	--	0.00	N/A
* COI	Lord Abbett Income A	LAGVX	**D+**	(888) 522-2388	**C / 4.8**	3.04	1.92	-1.93 /16	1.99 /61	4.76 /70	4.43	0.88
COI ●	Lord Abbett Income B	LAVBX	**D+**	(888) 522-2388	**C / 4.7**	3.22	1.52	-2.35 /14	1.31 /49	4.01 /62	3.72	1.68
COI	Lord Abbett Income C	LAUSX	**D+**	(888) 522-2388	**C / 5.0**	3.26	1.61	-2.17 /15	1.47 /52	4.15 /64	3.88	1.53
COI	Lord Abbett Income F	LAUFX	**D+**	(888) 522-2388	**C+ / 6.0**	3.07	1.97	-1.84 /16	2.09 /63	4.85 /71	4.63	0.78
COI	Lord Abbett Income I	LAUYX	**C-**	(888) 522-2388	**C+ / 6.2**	3.09	2.02	-1.74 /17	2.19 /65	4.96 /71	4.73	0.68
COI	Lord Abbett Income R2	LAUQX	**D+**	(888) 522-2388	**C / 5.5**	3.30	1.72	-1.93 /16	1.73 /56	4.42 /67	4.11	1.28
COI	Lord Abbett Income R3	LAURX	**D+**	(888) 522-2388	**C / 5.3**	2.96	1.77	-2.20 /15	1.70 /56	4.46 /67	4.23	1.18
COI	Lord Abbett Income R4	LAUKX	**U**	(888) 522-2388	**U /**	3.41	2.27	--	--	--	0.00	N/A
COI	Lord Abbett Income R5	LAUTX	**U**	(888) 522-2388	**U /**	3.09	2.02	--	--	--	0.00	N/A
COI	Lord Abbett Income R6	LAUVX	**U**	(888) 522-2388	**U /**	3.12	2.07	--	--	--	0.00	N/A
GEN	Lord Abbett Inflation Focused A	LIFAX	**D-**	(888) 522-2388	**E- / 0.2**	-0.93	0.09	-2.96 /11	-3.53 / 2	--	4.18	0.84
GEN	Lord Abbett Inflation Focused C	LIFCX	**D-**	(888) 522-2388	**E- / 0.2**	-1.07	-0.29	-3.62 / 9	-4.22 / 2	--	3.64	1.54
GEN	Lord Abbett Inflation Focused F	LIFFX	**D-**	(888) 522-2388	**E- / 0.2**	-0.91	0.05	-2.94 /12	-3.48 / 2	--	4.38	0.74
GEN	Lord Abbett Inflation Focused I	LIFIX	**D-**	(888) 522-2388	**E- / 0.2**	-0.88	0.19	-2.77 /12	-3.34 / 2	--	4.49	0.64
GEN	Lord Abbett Inflation Focused R2	LIFQX	**D-**	(888) 522-2388	**E- / 0.2**	-1.03	-0.11	-3.35 /10	-3.93 / 2	--	3.87	1.24
GEN	Lord Abbett Inflation Focused R3	LIFRX	**D-**	(888) 522-2388	**E- / 0.2**	-1.00	-0.14	-3.25 /11	-3.84 / 2	--	3.98	1.14
GEI	Lord Abbett Inflation Focused R4	LIFKX	**U**	(888) 522-2388	**U /**	-0.94	0.06	--	--	--	0.00	N/A
GEI	Lord Abbett Inflation Focused R5	LIFTX	**U**	(888) 522-2388	**U /**	-0.88	0.18	--	--	--	0.00	N/A
GEI	Lord Abbett Inflation Focused R6	LIFVX	**U**	(888) 522-2388	**U /**	-0.86	0.24	--	--	--	0.00	N/A
* MUN	Lord Abbett Interm Tax Free A	LISAX	**B+**	(888) 522-2388	**B+ / 8.5**	1.58	3.10	3.30 /88	3.01 /88	5.08 /86	2.63	0.71
MUN ●	Lord Abbett Interm Tax Free B	LISBX	**B**	(888) 522-2388	**B / 8.2**	1.39	2.71	2.49 /80	2.20 /79	4.25 /79	1.91	1.51
MUN	Lord Abbett Interm Tax Free C	LISCX	**B+**	(888) 522-2388	**B+ / 8.4**	1.33	2.70	2.57 /81	2.36 /81	4.38 /81	2.08	1.34
MUN	Lord Abbett Interm Tax Free F	LISFX	**A-**	(888) 522-2388	**A- / 9.1**	1.51	3.06	3.31 /88	3.11 /89	5.17 /87	2.79	0.61
MUN	Lord Abbett Interm Tax Free I	LAIIX	**A**	(888) 522-2388	**A- / 9.2**	1.63	3.21	3.51 /90	3.22 /90	5.28 /88	2.89	0.51
MUN ●	Lord Abbett Interm Tax Free P	LISPX	**A-**	(888) 522-2388	**B+ / 8.8**	1.52	2.99	3.06 /86	2.77 /86	4.83 /84	2.46	0.96
* GEI	Lord Abbett Shrt Duration Inc A	LALDX	**C+**	(888) 522-2388	**C- / 4.0**	1.22	0.57	0.68 /53	1.44 /51	2.72 /41	3.84	0.59
GEI ●	Lord Abbett Shrt Duration Inc B	LLTBX	**C+**	(888) 522-2388	**C- / 3.6**	1.03	0.40	-0.10 /30	0.64 /36	1.96 /31	3.12	1.39
GEI	Lord Abbett Shrt Duration Inc C	LDLAX	**C+**	(888) 522-2388	**C- / 3.9**	1.06	0.49	0.07 /40	0.79 /39	2.04 /32	3.27	1.26
GEI	Lord Abbett Shrt Duration Inc F	LDLFX	**B+**	(888) 522-2388	**C / 5.3**	1.24	0.84	0.78 /55	1.54 /53	2.87 /43	4.02	0.49
GEI	Lord Abbett Shrt Duration Inc I	LLDYX	**B+**	(888) 522-2388	**C / 5.5**	1.27	0.89	0.88 /57	1.63 /55	2.96 /44	4.12	0.39
GEI	Lord Abbett Shrt Duration Inc R2	LDLQX	**C+**	(888) 522-2388	**C- / 4.2**	1.13	0.37	0.29 /46	0.97 /42	2.32 /35	3.53	0.99
GEI	Lord Abbett Shrt Duration Inc R3	LDLRX	**C+**	(888) 522-2388	**C / 4.4**	0.92	0.42	0.17 /43	1.07 /44	2.39 /36	3.63	0.89
COI	Lord Abbett Shrt Duration Inc R4	LDLKX	**U**	(888) 522-2388	**U /**	1.20	0.77	--	--	--	0.00	N/A
COI	Lord Abbett Shrt Duration Inc R5	LDLTX	**U**	(888) 522-2388	**U /**	1.03	0.65	--	--	--	0.00	N/A
COI	Lord Abbett Shrt Duration Inc R6	LDLVX	**U**	(888) 522-2388	**U /**	1.29	0.93	--	--	--	0.00	N/A
* MUN	Lord Abbett Shrt Duration Tax-Fr A	LSDAX	**C**	(888) 522-2388	**C- / 3.2**	0.52	0.65	0.92 /65	0.76 /46	1.58 /37	1.02	0.70
MUN	Lord Abbett Shrt Duration Tax-Fr C	LSDCX	**C**	(888) 522-2388	**C- / 3.0**	0.37	0.35	0.30 /49	0.13 /29	0.91 /25	0.42	1.32
MUN	Lord Abbett Shrt Duration Tax-Fr F	LSDFX	**B+**	(888) 522-2388	**C / 5.2**	0.54	0.70	1.02 /67	0.86 /49	1.66 /38	1.14	0.60
MUN	Lord Abbett Shrt Duration Tax-Fr I	LISDX	**A-**	(888) 522-2388	**C / 5.4**	0.56	0.75	1.12 /69	0.95 /51	1.77 /41	1.24	0.50
MUS	Lord Abbett Tax Free CA A	LCFIX	**B-**	(888) 522-2388	**A+ / 9.6**	1.93	4.04	4.48 /97	4.57 /98	7.56 /98	3.26	0.82
MUS	Lord Abbett Tax Free CA C	CALAX	**B-**	(888) 522-2388	**A+ / 9.6**	1.87	3.81	3.83 /93	3.91 /95	6.90 /96	2.71	1.45
MUS	Lord Abbett Tax Free CA F	LCFFX	**B**	(888) 522-2388	**A+ / 9.8**	1.96	4.09	4.58 /97	4.67 /98	7.67 /98	3.43	0.72
MUN	Lord Abbett Tax Free CA I	CAILX	**B**	(888) 522-2388	**A+ / 9.8**	2.07	4.24	4.68 /97	4.78 /98	7.81 /98	3.52	0.62
* MUN	Lord Abbett Tax Free Natl A	LANSX	**C+**	(888) 522-2388	**A- / 9.1**	2.12	4.06	4.18 /95	3.57 /93	7.16 /97	3.45	0.77
MUN ●	Lord Abbett Tax Free Natl B	LANBX	**C+**	(888) 522-2388	**B+ / 8.9**	1.92	3.64	3.36 /89	2.75 /85	6.32 /94	2.74	1.57

● Denotes fund is closed to new investors
* Denotes fund is included in Section II

RISK			NET ASSETS		ASSET							FUND MANAGER		MINIMUM		LOADS	
Risk Rating/Pts	3 Yr Avg Standard Deviation	Avg Duration	NAV As of 3/31/16	Total $(Mil)	Cash %	Gov. Bond %	Muni. Bond %	Corp. Bond %	Other %	Portfolio Turnover Ratio	Avg Coupon Rate	Manager Quality Pct	Manager Tenure (Years)	Initial Purch. $	Additional Purch. $	Front End Load	Back End Load
E+ / 0.9	5.8	8.7	11.79	429	1	0	98	0	1	31	5.6	14	12	0	0	0.0	0.0
D- / 1.5	5.6	4.6	7.02	N/A	2	0	0	83	15	93	0.0	89	18	0	0	0.0	0.0
D- / 1.5	5.6	4.6	6.96	7	2	0	0	83	15	93	0.0	87	18	0	0	0.0	0.0
D- / 1.5	5.6	4.6	6.96	50	2	0	0	83	15	93	0.0	89	18	0	0	0.0	0.0
U /	N/A	4.6	6.92	3	2	0	0	83	15	93	0.0	N/A	18	0	0	0.0	0.0
U /	N/A	4.6	6.95	N/A	2	0	0	83	15	93	0.0	N/A	18	0	0	0.0	0.0
U /	N/A	4.6	6.96	46	2	0	0	83	15	93	0.0	N/A	18	0	0	0.0	0.0
C- / 3.0	4.7	5.3	2.71	958	1	4	1	72	22	163	0.0	36	18	1,500	0	2.3	0.0
D+ / 2.9	4.8	5.3	2.72	5	1	4	1	72	22	163	0.0	19	18	500	0	0.0	0.0
C- / 3.0	4.7	5.3	2.73	267	1	4	1	72	22	163	0.0	22	18	1,500	0	0.0	0.0
D+ / 2.9	4.8	5.3	2.71	394	1	4	1	72	22	163	0.0	37	18	0	0	0.0	0.0
C- / 3.1	4.7	5.3	2.71	104	1	4	1	72	22	163	0.0	42	18	1,000,000	0	0.0	0.0
D+ / 2.9	4.8	5.3	2.74	3	1	4	1	72	22	163	0.0	28	18	0	0	0.0	0.0
C- / 3.0	4.7	5.3	2.72	52	1	4	1	72	22	163	0.0	28	18	0	0	0.0	0.0
U /	N/A	5.3	2.72	1	1	4	1	72	22	163	0.0	N/A	18	0	0	0.0	0.0
U /	N/A	5.3	2.71	N/A	1	4	1	72	22	163	0.0	N/A	18	0	0	0.0	0.0
U /	N/A	5.3	2.71	3	1	4	1	72	22	163	0.0	N/A	18	0	0	0.0	0.0
C- / 3.6	4.2	1.9	11.90	291	2	3	0	46	49	62	0.0	6	5	1,500	0	2.3	0.0
C- / 3.7	4.2	1.9	11.91	50	2	3	0	46	49	62	0.0	5	5	1,500	0	0.0	0.0
C- / 3.7	4.2	1.9	11.90	117	2	3	0	46	49	62	0.0	6	5	0	0	0.0	0.0
C- / 3.6	4.2	1.9	11.90	135	2	3	0	46	49	62	0.0	6	5	1,000,000	0	0.0	0.0
C- / 3.6	4.2	1.9	11.89	N/A	2	3	0	46	49	62	0.0	5	5	0	0	0.0	0.0
C- / 3.6	4.2	1.9	11.89	N/A	2	3	0	46	49	62	0.0	5	5	0	0	0.0	0.0
U /	N/A	1.9	11.90	N/A	2	3	0	46	49	62	0.0	N/A	5	0	0	0.0	0.0
U /	N/A	1.9	11.90	N/A	2	3	0	46	49	62	0.0	N/A	5	0	0	0.0	0.0
U /	N/A	1.9	11.90	N/A	2	3	0	46	49	62	0.0	N/A	5	0	0	0.0	0.0
C / 5.1	3.4	5.4	10.98	1,790	0	0	99	0	1	12	4.9	42	10	1,000	0	2.3	0.0
C / 5.1	3.4	5.4	10.97	2	0	0	99	0	1	12	4.9	21	10	1,000	0	0.0	0.0
C / 5.0	3.5	5.4	10.96	616	0	0	99	0	1	12	4.9	24	10	1,000	0	0.0	0.0
C / 5.0	3.5	5.4	10.97	1,719	0	0	99	0	1	12	4.9	43	10	0	0	0.0	0.0
C / 5.1	3.4	5.4	10.98	228	0	0	99	0	1	12	4.9	50	10	1,000,000	0	0.0	0.0
C / 5.1	3.4	5.4	10.98	N/A	0	0	99	0	1	12	4.9	35	10	0	0	0.0	0.0
B+ / 8.9	1.4	1.9	4.32	10,883	2	3	0	47	48	59	0.0	87	18	1,500	0	2.3	0.0
B+ / 8.9	1.5	1.9	4.33	17	2	3	0	47	48	59	0.0	59	18	1,000	0	0.0	0.0
B+ / 8.9	1.5	1.9	4.35	6,846	2	3	0	47	48	59	0.0	71	18	1,500	0	0.0	0.0
B+ / 8.9	1.5	1.9	4.32	11,149	2	3	0	47	48	59	0.0	87	18	0	0	0.0	0.0
B+ / 8.9	1.5	1.9	4.32	4,779	2	3	0	47	48	59	0.0	88	18	1,000,000	0	0.0	0.0
B+ / 8.9	1.5	1.9	4.32	24	2	3	0	47	48	59	0.0	78	18	0	0	0.0	0.0
B+ / 8.9	1.4	1.9	4.32	227	2	3	0	47	48	59	0.0	79	18	0	0	0.0	0.0
U /	N/A	1.9	4.33	5	2	3	0	47	48	59	0.0	N/A	18	0	0	0.0	0.0
U /	N/A	1.9	4.31	2	2	3	0	47	48	59	0.0	N/A	18	0	0	0.0	0.0
U /	N/A	1.9	4.32	184	2	3	0	47	48	59	0.0	N/A	18	0	0	0.0	0.0
A- / 9.2	1.1	2.2	15.76	1,069	1	0	98	0	1	26	3.7	55	8	1,000	0	2.3	0.0
A / 9.3	1.0	2.2	15.76	194	1	0	98	0	1	26	3.7	34	8	1,000	0	0.0	0.0
A / 9.3	1.0	2.2	15.76	713	1	0	98	0	1	26	3.7	59	8	0	0	0.0	0.0
A / 9.3	1.0	2.2	15.76	51	1	0	98	0	1	26	3.7	N/A	8	1,000,000	0	0.0	0.0
D+ / 2.9	4.6	7.5	11.10	206	0	0	99	0	1	15	5.3	52	10	1,000	0	2.3	0.0
D+ / 2.9	4.6	7.5	11.11	46	0	0	99	0	1	15	5.3	31	10	1,000	0	0.0	0.0
D+ / 2.9	4.6	7.5	11.10	40	0	0	99	0	1	15	5.3	56	10	0	0	0.0	0.0
D+ / 2.9	4.6	7.5	11.10	4	0	0	99	0	1	15	5.3	61	10	1,000,000	0	0.0	0.0
D+ / 2.5	5.0	7.3	11.49	1,492	0	0	98	0	2	29	5.4	16	10	1,000	0	2.3	0.0
D+ / 2.5	5.0	7.3	11.55	3	0	0	98	0	2	29	5.4	9	10	1,000	0	0.0	0.0

Fund Type	Fund Name (99 Pct = Best, 0 Pct = Worst)	Ticker Symbol	Overall Investment Rating	Phone	PERFORMANCE: Performance Rating/Pts	Total Return % through 3/31/16: 3 Mo	6 Mo	1Yr / Pct	Annualized: 3Yr / Pct	5Yr / Pct	Incl. in Returns: Dividend Yield	Expense Ratio
MUN	Lord Abbett Tax Free Natl C	LTNSX	**C+**	(888) 522-2388	**A- / 9.1**	1.88	3.65	3.54 /90	2.92 /87	6.48 /94	2.91	1.40
MUN	Lord Abbett Tax Free Natl F	LANFX	**C+**	(888) 522-2388	**A / 9.5**	2.05	4.11	4.28 /96	3.66 /94	7.27 /97	3.62	0.67
MUN	Lord Abbett Tax Free Natl I	LTNIX	**C+**	(888) 522-2388	**A+ / 9.6**	2.07	4.06	4.28 /96	3.72 /94	7.37 /97	3.71	0.57
MUS	Lord Abbett Tax Free NJ A	LANJX	**C+**	(888) 522-2388	**B+ / 8.7**	2.04	4.37	3.41 /89	3.10 /89	6.25 /93	3.22	0.86
MUS	Lord Abbett Tax Free NJ F	LNJFX	**C+**	(888) 522-2388	**A / 9.3**	2.06	4.63	3.71 /92	3.27 /91	6.39 /94	3.39	0.76
MUN	Lord Abbett Tax Free NJ I	LINJX	**C+**	(888) 522-2388	**A / 9.4**	2.09	4.70	3.87 /93	3.42 /92	6.55 /95	3.53	0.66
MUS	Lord Abbett Tax Free NY A	LANYX	**B-**	(888) 522-2388	**A- / 9.0**	1.77	3.64	3.97 /94	3.53 /93	6.02 /92	2.90	0.80
MUS	Lord Abbett Tax Free NY C	NYLAX	**B-**	(888) 522-2388	**A- / 9.0**	1.70	3.31	3.39 /89	2.89 /87	5.34 /88	2.33	1.44
MUS	Lord Abbett Tax Free NY F	LNYFX	**B**	(888) 522-2388	**A / 9.5**	1.88	3.78	4.16 /95	3.65 /94	6.14 /93	3.06	0.70
MUN	Lord Abbett Tax Free NY I	NYLIX	**B**	(888) 522-2388	**A / 9.5**	1.90	3.74	4.26 /95	3.76 /94	6.26 /93	3.16	0.60
* GEI	Lord Abbett Total Return A	LTRAX	**C**	(888) 522-2388	**C / 5.5**	2.80	2.04	0.55 /51	2.08 /63	4.09 /63	2.78	0.84
GEI ●	Lord Abbett Total Return B	LTRBX	**C**	(888) 522-2388	**C / 5.0**	2.71	1.73	-0.24 /29	1.27 /48	3.26 /49	2.05	1.64
GEI	Lord Abbett Total Return C	LTRCX	**C**	(888) 522-2388	**C / 5.3**	2.64	1.71	-0.10 /30	1.43 /51	3.43 /52	2.19	1.47
GEI	Lord Abbett Total Return F	LTRFX	**B-**	(888) 522-2388	**C+ / 6.6**	2.82	2.18	0.65 /52	2.18 /65	4.21 /64	2.94	0.74
GEI	Lord Abbett Total Return I	LTRYX	**B**	(888) 522-2388	**C+ / 6.8**	2.85	2.23	0.76 /54	2.28 /67	4.30 /65	3.04	0.64
GEI ●	Lord Abbett Total Return P	LTRPX	**C+**	(888) 522-2388	**C+ / 6.1**	2.73	2.01	0.32 /46	1.83 /58	3.83 /59	2.59	1.09
GEI	Lord Abbett Total Return R2	LTRQX	**C+**	(888) 522-2388	**C+ / 5.8**	2.70	1.93	0.16 /43	1.67 /55	3.70 /57	2.44	1.24
GEI	Lord Abbett Total Return R3	LTRRX	**C+**	(888) 522-2388	**C+ / 6.0**	2.73	1.98	0.26 /45	1.78 /57	3.79 /58	2.55	1.14
COI	Lord Abbett Total Return R4	LTRKX	**U**	(888) 522-2388	**U /**	2.79	2.12	--	--	--	0.00	N/A
COI	Lord Abbett Total Return R5	LTRTX	**U**	(888) 522-2388	**U /**	2.88	2.20	--	--	--	0.00	N/A
COI	Lord Abbett Total Return R6	LTRHX	**U**	(888) 522-2388	**U /**	2.82	2.10	--	--	--	0.00	N/A
* MUH	Lord Abbett Tx Fr High Yld Muni A	HYMAX	**C-**	(888) 522-2388	**A- / 9.2**	2.35	4.44	4.47 /97	3.59 /93	7.23 /97	4.48	0.87
MUH	Lord Abbett Tx Fr High Yld Muni C	HYMCX	**C-**	(888) 522-2388	**A- / 9.1**	2.20	4.03	3.83 /93	2.94 /88	6.54 /95	3.97	1.50
MUH	Lord Abbett Tx Fr High Yld Muni I	HYMIX	**C**	(888) 522-2388	**A+ / 9.6**	2.40	4.45	4.67 /97	3.72 /94	7.37 /97	4.77	0.67
MUH ●	Lord Abbett Tx Fr High Yld Muni P	HYMPX	**C**	(888) 522-2388	**A / 9.4**	2.30	4.33	4.24 /95	3.41 /92	7.02 /96	4.36	1.12
MM	Lord Abbett US G and G Spns MM A	LACXX	**U**	(888) 522-2388	**U /**	--	--	--	--	--	0.02	0.66
MM	Lord Abbett US G and G Spns MM C	LCCXX	**U**	(888) 522-2388	**U /**	--	--	--	--	--	0.02	0.66
GEI	LWAS DFA Two Year Fixed Income	DFCFX	**C+**	(800) 984-9472	**C- / 3.4**	0.68	0.40	0.65 /52	0.47 /33	0.63 /18	0.61	0.29
USS	LWAS DFA Two Year Government	DFYGX	**C+**	(800) 984-9472	**C- / 3.4**	0.75	0.23	0.51 /50	0.44 /32	0.56 /18	0.43	0.28
COI	Madison Core Bond A	MBOAX	**C-**	(800) 877-6089	**C- / 3.8**	2.78	2.05	1.33 /64	1.59 /54	2.64 /39	2.03	0.90
COI	Madison Core Bond B	MBOBX	**C**	(800) 877-6089	**C / 4.5**	2.49	1.67	0.57 /51	0.83 /40	1.86 /30	1.39	1.65
COI	Madison Core Bond R6	MCBRX	**U**	(800) 877-6089	**U /**	2.85	2.31	1.70 /69	--	--	2.39	0.52
COI	Madison Core Bond Y	MBOYX	**B+**	(800) 877-6089	**C+ / 6.3**	2.75	2.11	1.51 /66	1.84 /58	2.88 /43	2.40	0.65
GEI	Madison Corporate Bond Y	COINX	**C**	(800) 877-6089	**C+ / 6.9**	3.62	2.82	1.07 /60	2.19 /65	3.88 /60	2.77	0.65
COH	Madison High Income A	MHNAX	**D-**	(800) 877-6089	**D+ / 2.9**	3.60	2.10	-3.24 /11	1.59 /54	3.80 /58	5.10	1.00
COH	Madison High Income B	MHNBX	**D-**	(800) 877-6089	**C- / 3.5**	3.33	1.62	-4.06 / 7	0.80 /39	3.01 /45	4.41	1.75
COH	Madison High Income Y	MHNYX	**D**	(800) 877-6089	**C / 5.5**	3.54	2.11	-3.16 /11	1.86 /59	4.08 /63	5.90	0.75
GEI	Madison High Quality Bond Y	MIIBX	**B**	(800) 877-6089	**C / 4.9**	1.73	1.24	1.48 /66	1.07 /44	1.61 /27	1.04	0.49
MUN	Madison Tax Free National Y	GTFHX	**B+**	(800) 877-6089	**A- / 9.1**	1.78	3.04	3.73 /92	2.94 /88	4.49 /81	2.32	0.85
MUS	Madison Tax Free Virginia Y	GTVAX	**A**	(800) 877-6089	**B+ / 8.7**	1.44	2.57	3.11 /86	2.68 /85	3.95 /77	2.30	0.85
MUS	Maine Municipal	MEMUX	**A**	(800) 601-5593	**B / 7.9**	1.10	2.61	3.22 /87	2.51 /83	4.27 /80	2.32	1.29
MUN	MainStay California Tx Fr Opp A	MSCAX	**B-**	(800) 624-6782	**A+ / 9.8**	2.12	5.30	6.31 /99	5.25 /99	--	3.35	0.88
MUN	MainStay California Tx Fr Opp C	MSCCX	**B-**	(800) 624-6782	**A+ / 9.9**	2.05	5.15	5.98 /99	4.85 /98	--	3.20	1.30
MUN	MainStay California Tx Fr Opp I	MCOIX	**B-**	(800) 624-6782	**A+ / 9.9**	2.19	5.43	6.69 /99	5.53 /99	--	3.76	0.63
MUN	MainStay California Tx Fr Opp Inv	MSCVX	**B-**	(800) 624-6782	**A+ / 9.7**	2.12	5.28	6.36 /99	5.13 /99	--	3.29	1.04
LP	MainStay Floating Rate A	MXFAX	**C-**	(800) 624-6782	**C- / 3.4**	2.02	0.13	-0.37 /27	1.42 /51	2.70 /40	3.48	1.08
LP	MainStay Floating Rate B	MXFBX	**C-**	(800) 624-6782	**C- / 3.5**	1.84	-0.23	-1.11 /21	0.71 /37	1.92 /30	2.83	1.80
LP	MainStay Floating Rate C	MXFCX	**C-**	(800) 624-6782	**C- / 3.4**	1.72	-0.34	-1.21 /20	0.67 /36	1.91 /30	2.84	1.80
LP	MainStay Floating Rate I	MXFIX	**B-**	(800) 624-6782	**C / 5.4**	1.97	0.15	-0.12 /30	1.67 /55	2.96 /44	3.84	0.83
LP	MainStay Floating Rate Inv	MXFNX	**C-**	(800) 624-6782	**C- / 3.4**	2.02	0.13	-0.37 /27	1.43 /51	2.68 /40	3.49	1.05
GL	MainStay Global High Income A	MGHAX	**E**	(800) 624-6782	**D- / 1.3**	5.80	8.12	4.33 /83	-1.23 / 7	3.37 /51	5.66	1.17
GL	MainStay Global High Income B	MGHBX	**E**	(800) 624-6782	**D- / 1.5**	5.65	7.75	3.42 /79	-2.13 / 4	2.45 /37	5.08	2.09

● Denotes fund is closed to new investors
* Denotes fund is included in Section II

RISK			NET ASSETS		ASSET							FUND MANAGER		MINIMUM		LOADS	
Risk Rating/Pts	3 Yr Avg Standard Deviation	Avg Duration	NAV As of 3/31/16	Total $(Mil)	Cash %	Gov. Bond %	Muni. Bond %	Corp. Bond %	Other %	Portfolio Turnover Ratio	Avg Coupon Rate	Manager Quality Pct	Manager Tenure (Years)	Initial Purch. $	Additional Purch. $	Front End Load	Back End Load
D+ / 2.5	5.0	7.3	11.50	186	0	0	98	0	2	29	5.4	10	10	1,000	0	0.0	0.0
D+ / 2.5	5.0	7.3	11.48	249	0	0	98	0	2	29	5.4	18	10	0	0	0.0	0.0
D+ / 2.5	5.0	7.3	11.48	9	0	0	98	0	2	29	5.4	19	10	1,000,000	0	0.0	0.0
D+ / 2.6	5.0	7.4	4.99	91	1	0	98	0	1	17	5.2	12	10	1,000	0	2.3	0.0
D+ / 2.5	5.0	7.4	5.00	8	1	0	98	0	1	17	5.2	13	10	0	0	0.0	0.0
D+ / 2.6	5.0	7.4	5.00	N/A	1	0	98	0	1	17	5.2	15	10	1,000,000	0	0.0	0.0
C- / 3.4	4.4	6.8	11.43	296	1	0	98	0	1	10	5.1	28	10	1,000	0	2.3	0.0
C- / 3.4	4.4	6.8	11.42	62	1	0	98	0	1	10	5.1	16	10	1,000	0	0.0	0.0
C- / 3.4	4.4	6.8	11.45	37	1	0	98	0	1	10	5.1	31	10	0	0	0.0	0.0
C- / 3.4	4.4	6.8	11.44	2	1	0	98	0	1	10	5.1	34	10	1,000,000	0	0.0	0.0
C+ / 6.4	3.0	5.2	10.38	1,295	0	31	0	30	39	434	0.0	52	18	1,500	0	2.3	0.0
C+ / 6.3	3.1	5.2	10.37	10	0	31	0	30	39	434	0.0	27	18	1,000	0	0.0	0.0
C+ / 6.4	3.0	5.2	10.37	206	0	31	0	30	39	434	0.0	31	18	1,500	0	0.0	0.0
C+ / 6.5	3.0	5.2	10.38	588	0	31	0	30	39	434	0.0	57	18	0	0	0.0	0.0
C+ / 6.5	3.0	5.2	10.40	290	0	31	0	30	39	434	0.0	61	18	1,000,000	0	0.0	0.0
C+ / 6.6	3.0	5.2	10.43	3	0	31	0	30	39	434	0.0	44	18	0	0	0.0	0.0
C+ / 6.5	3.0	5.2	10.38	7	0	31	0	30	39	434	0.0	39	18	0	0	0.0	0.0
C+ / 6.4	3.0	5.2	10.38	136	0	31	0	30	39	434	0.0	42	18	0	0	0.0	0.0
U /	N/A	5.2	10.38	5	0	31	0	30	39	434	0.0	N/A	18	0	0	0.0	0.0
U /	N/A	5.2	10.39	39	0	31	0	30	39	434	0.0	N/A	18	0	0	0.0	0.0
U /	N/A	5.2	10.39	N/A	0	31	0	30	39	434	0.0	N/A	18	0	0	0.0	0.0
E+ / 0.9	5.8	8.7	11.78	1,177	1	0	98	0	1	31	5.6	13	12	1,000	0	2.3	0.0
E+ / 0.9	5.8	8.7	11.78	415	1	0	98	0	1	31	5.6	9	12	1,000	0	0.0	0.0
E+ / 0.9	5.8	8.7	11.76	47	1	0	98	0	1	31	5.6	14	12	1,000,000	0	0.0	0.0
E+ / 0.9	5.8	8.7	11.79	N/A	1	0	98	0	1	31	5.6	11	12	0	0	0.0	0.0
U /	N/A	N/A	1.00	588	100	0	0	0	0	0	0.0	N/A	N/A	1,000	0	0.0	0.0
U /	N/A	N/A	1.00	75	100	0	0	0	0	0	0.0	N/A	N/A	1,000	0	0.0	0.0
A+ / 9.8	0.5	1.6	10.00	85	0	66	1	31	2	238	1.5	74	N/A	0	0	0.0	0.0
A+ / 9.8	0.5	1.8	9.88	122	0	99	0	0	1	262	0.9	71	N/A	0	0	0.0	0.0
B- / 7.5	2.7	5.0	10.11	33	2	26	9	34	29	57	25.9	58	7	1,000	50	4.5	0.0
B / 7.6	2.7	5.0	10.11	3	2	26	9	34	29	57	25.9	33	7	1,000	50	0.0	0.0
U /	N/A	5.0	10.11	2	2	26	9	34	29	57	25.9	N/A	7	500,000	50,000	0.0	0.0
B- / 7.4	2.7	5.0	10.07	183	2	26	9	34	29	57	25.9	71	7	25,000	50	0.0	0.0
C / 4.6	3.7	6.4	11.42	23	2	0	7	90	1	37	23.8	41	9	25,000	50	0.0	0.0
D- / 1.4	5.6	3.9	5.76	21	3	0	0	96	1	28	16.5	61	11	1,000	50	4.5	0.0
D- / 1.5	5.6	3.9	5.91	2	3	0	0	96	1	28	16.5	34	11	1,000	50	0.0	0.0
D- / 1.5	5.6	3.9	5.67	1	3	0	0	96	1	28	16.5	76	11	25,000	50	0.0	0.0
B+ / 8.9	1.5	2.8	11.09	107	2	60	0	36	2	35	42.6	56	16	25,000	50	0.0	0.0
C / 4.6	3.6	5.9	11.15	28	1	0	98	0	1	15	23.5	34	19	25,000	50	0.0	0.0
C+ / 5.7	3.2	5.7	11.73	22	2	0	97	0	1	12	24.0	38	19	25,000	50	0.0	0.0
B- / 7.1	2.8	4.5	11.18	18	0	0	100	0	0	16	4.7	47	13	1,000	50	2.5	0.0
D+ / 2.5	5.2	N/A	10.41	85	0	0	99	0	1	50	0.0	62	3	25,000	0	4.5	0.0
D+ / 2.5	5.2	N/A	10.41	15	0	0	99	0	1	50	0.0	47	3	2,500	50	0.0	0.0
D+ / 2.5	5.2	N/A	10.41	71	0	0	99	0	1	50	0.0	76	3	5,000,000	0	0.0	0.0
D+ / 2.5	5.2	N/A	10.41	N/A	0	0	99	0	1	50	0.0	58	3	2,500	50	4.5	0.0
B / 7.9	2.5	N/A	9.03	301	0	3	0	79	18	31	0.0	88	12	25,000	0	3.0	0.0
B / 7.8	2.6	N/A	9.04	8	0	3	0	79	18	31	0.0	73	12	1,000	50	0.0	0.0
B / 7.8	2.6	N/A	9.03	164	0	3	0	79	18	31	0.0	73	12	1,000	50	0.0	0.0
B / 7.8	2.6	N/A	9.03	763	0	3	0	79	18	31	0.0	91	12	5,000,000	0	0.0	0.0
B / 7.9	2.5	N/A	9.03	29	0	3	0	79	18	31	0.0	88	12	1,000	50	3.0	0.0
E / 0.3	8.7	3.6	9.72	101	4	58	0	36	2	19	0.0	25	5	25,000	0	4.5	0.0
E / 0.3	8.7	3.6	9.56	7	4	58	0	36	2	19	0.0	11	5	1,000	50	0.0	0.0

Fund Type	Fund Name (99 Pct = Best, 0 Pct = Worst)	Ticker Symbol	Overall Investment Rating	Phone	PERFORMANCE: Performance Rating/Pts	Total Return % through 3/31/16: 3 Mo	6 Mo	1Yr / Pct	Annualized 3Yr / Pct	Annualized 5Yr / Pct	Incl. in Returns: Dividend Yield	Expense Ratio
GL	MainStay Global High Income C	MHYCX	E	(800) 624-6782	D- / 1.5	5.64	7.62	3.41 /79	-2.13 / 4	2.45 /37	5.07	2.09
GL	MainStay Global High Income I	MGHIX	D-	(800) 624-6782	C- / 4.1	5.86	8.24	4.59 /85	-0.98 / 8	3.62 /55	6.17	0.92
GL	MainStay Global High Income Inv	MGHHX	E	(800) 624-6782	D- / 1.1	5.80	8.16	4.20 /82	-1.39 / 6	3.23 /49	5.43	1.34
USS	MainStay Government Fund A	MGVAX	C-	(800) 624-6782	D+ / 2.9	1.70	1.21	1.14 /61	1.23 /47	2.45 /37	2.19	0.98
USS	MainStay Government Fund B	MCSGX	C-	(800) 624-6782	C- / 3.1	1.56	0.82	0.12 /42	0.21 /29	1.47 /25	1.28	2.01
USS	MainStay Government Fund C	MGVCX	C	(800) 624-6782	C- / 3.2	1.56	0.83	0.24 /45	0.25 /29	1.47 /25	1.28	2.01
USS	MainStay Government Fund I	MGOIX	B+	(800) 624-6782	C+ / 5.6	1.86	1.44	1.50 /66	1.51 /52	2.71 /41	2.52	0.73
USS	MainStay Government Fund Inv	MGVNX	C-	(800) 624-6782	D+ / 2.3	1.75	1.20	0.98 /58	1.00 /43	2.25 /34	1.93	1.26
COH	MainStay High Yield Corp Bond A	MHCAX	D	(800) 624-6782	C- / 3.2	2.48	0.56	-1.63 /18	1.83 /58	4.64 /69	6.37	0.99
COH	MainStay High Yield Corp Bond B	MKHCX	D	(800) 624-6782	C- / 3.8	2.26	0.11	-2.49 /13	1.01 /43	3.82 /59	5.81	1.76
COH	MainStay High Yield Corp Bond C	MYHCX	D	(800) 624-6782	C- / 3.8	2.26	0.11	-2.50 /13	1.00 /43	3.82 /59	5.81	1.76
COH	MainStay High Yield Corp Bond I	MHYIX	D+	(800) 624-6782	C+ / 5.9	2.55	0.70	-1.38 /19	2.08 /63	4.90 /71	6.94	0.74
COH	MainStay High Yield Corp Bond Inv	MHHIX	D	(800) 624-6782	C- / 3.0	2.28	0.40	-1.75 /17	1.77 /57	4.57 /68	6.37	1.01
COH	MainStay High Yield Corp Bond R1	MHHRX	D+	(800) 624-6782	C+ / 5.6	2.33	0.45	-1.49 /18	1.93 /60	--	6.84	0.84
COH	MainStay High Yield Corp Bond R2	MHYRX	D+	(800) 624-6782	C / 5.2	2.45	0.51	-1.74 /17	1.73 /56	4.55 /68	6.56	1.09
COH	MainStay High Yield Corp Bond R6	MHYSX	U	(800) 624-6782	U /	2.60	0.79	-1.21 /20	--	--	7.12	0.58
MUH	MainStay High Yield Muni Bond A	MMHAX	C+	(800) 624-6782	A+ / 9.8	2.65	5.98	6.37 /99	5.59 /99	9.50 /99	3.83	0.90
MUH	MainStay High Yield Muni Bond C	MMHDX	C+	(800) 624-6782	A+ / 9.9	2.46	5.58	5.56 /99	4.78 /98	8.65 /99	3.26	1.67
MUH	MainStay High Yield Muni Bond I	MMHIX	C+	(800) 624-6782	A+ / 9.9	2.71	6.02	6.64 /99	5.82 /99	9.76 /99	4.26	0.65
MUH	MainStay High Yield Muni Bond Inv	MMHVX	C+	(800) 624-6782	A+ / 9.8	2.65	5.88	6.35 /99	5.53 /99	9.46 /99	3.81	0.92
COH	MainStay High Yield Opps A	MYHAX	E	(800) 624-6782	E / 0.4	1.63	-0.48	-7.27 / 2	-0.55 /11	2.87 /43	5.51	1.50
COH	MainStay High Yield Opps C	MYHYX	E	(800) 624-6782	E / 0.5	1.38	-0.81	-7.94 / 1	-1.27 / 7	2.13 /33	5.07	2.21
COH	MainStay High Yield Opps I	MYHIX	E	(800) 624-6782	E+ / 0.9	1.69	-0.36	-7.02 / 2	-0.33 /13	3.12 /47	6.02	1.25
COH	MainStay High Yield Opps Investor	MYHNX	E	(800) 624-6782	E / 0.4	1.67	-0.44	-7.15 / 2	-0.50 /12	2.91 /44	5.61	1.46
GEI	MainStay Indexed Bond A	MIXAX	C	(800) 624-6782	C / 4.7	2.70	1.98	1.06 /60	1.78 /57	3.00 /45	2.08	0.74
GEI	MainStay Indexed Bond I	MIXIX	B	(800) 624-6782	C+ / 6.7	2.79	2.16	1.41 /65	2.13 /64	3.36 /51	2.49	0.49
GEI	MainStay Indexed Bond Inv	MIXNX	C-	(800) 624-6782	C / 4.4	2.65	1.89	0.79 /55	1.60 /54	2.83 /42	1.90	0.97
MM	MainStay Money Market Fund Inv	MKTXX	U	(800) 624-6782	U /	--	--	--	--	--	0.01	0.90
MUN	MainStay NY Tax Free Opp A	MNOAX	C+	(800) 624-6782	A / 9.3	1.44	4.56	4.66 /97	4.44 /97	--	3.39	0.85
MUN	MainStay NY Tax Free Opp C	MNOCX	B-	(800) 624-6782	A+ / 9.7	1.37	4.41	4.35 /96	4.05 /96	--	3.25	1.22
MUN	MainStay NY Tax Free Opp I	MNOIX	B-	(800) 624-6782	A+ / 9.8	1.50	4.69	4.92 /98	4.67 /98	--	3.79	0.60
MUN	MainStay NY Tax Free Opp Inv	MNOVX	C+	(800) 624-6782	A- / 9.2	1.53	4.55	4.72 /97	4.28 /97	--	3.35	0.97
COH	MainStay Sht Duration Hi Yield A	MDHAX	C-	(800) 624-6782	C / 5.1	1.14	-0.02	-0.62 /25	2.61 /72	--	5.05	1.01
COH	MainStay Sht Duration Hi Yield C	MDHCX	C-	(800) 624-6782	C / 4.8	0.82	-0.56	-1.59 /18	1.71 /56	--	4.32	1.87
COH	MainStay Sht Duration Hi Yield I	MDHIX	C	(800) 624-6782	C+ / 6.8	1.10	0.00	-0.38 /27	2.86 /75	--	5.47	0.76
COH	MainStay Sht Duration Hi Yield Inv	MDHVX	C-	(800) 624-6782	C / 4.8	1.01	-0.19	-0.85 /23	2.45 /70	--	4.94	1.12
COH	MainStay Sht Duration Hi Yield R2	MDHRX	C-	(800) 624-6782	C+ / 6.2	1.01	-0.18	-0.83 /23	2.50 /71	--	5.11	1.11
GES	MainStay Tax Adv Sht-Tm Bd A	MSTAX	C+	(800) 624-6782	C- / 3.2	0.67	0.76	1.28 /63	0.52 /33	0.77 /19	0.64	1.12
GES	MainStay Tax Adv Sht-Tm Bd I	MSTIX	B	(800) 624-6782	C / 4.3	0.84	0.88	1.54 /67	0.81 /39	1.03 /21	0.90	0.87
GES	MainStay Tax Adv Sht-Tm Bd	MYTBX	C	(800) 624-6782	D+ / 2.6	0.64	0.61	0.95 /58	0.18 /28	0.41 /17	0.21	1.48
MUN	MainStay Tax Free Bond Fund A	MTBAX	C+	(800) 624-6782	A- / 9.1	1.61	4.34	4.27 /96	4.18 /97	6.98 /96	3.19	0.78
MUN	MainStay Tax Free Bond Fund B	MKTBX	B	(800) 624-6782	A+ / 9.6	1.45	4.21	4.03 /94	3.88 /95	6.64 /95	3.10	1.09
MUN	MainStay Tax Free Bond Fund C	MTFCX	B	(800) 624-6782	A+ / 9.6	1.45	4.21	4.03 /94	3.88 /95	6.63 /95	3.10	1.09
MUN	MainStay Tax Free Bond Fund I	MTBIX	B	(800) 624-6782	A+ / 9.8	1.57	4.46	4.53 /97	4.44 /97	7.22 /97	3.58	0.53
MUN	MainStay Tax Free Bond Fund Inv	MKINX	C+	(800) 624-6782	A- / 9.1	1.51	4.33	4.28 /96	4.14 /96	6.91 /96	3.20	0.84
GEI	MainStay Total Return Bond A	MTMAX	D+	(800) 624-6782	C- / 3.0	2.89	1.96	-0.52 /26	1.36 /49	3.51 /53	2.37	0.86
GEI	MainStay Total Return Bond B	MTMBX	C-	(800) 624-6782	C- / 3.7	2.74	1.65	-1.11 /21	0.57 /34	2.67 /40	1.88	1.76
GEI	MainStay Total Return Bond C	MTMCX	C-	(800) 624-6782	C- / 3.7	2.74	1.65	-1.11 /21	0.54 /34	2.65 /40	1.88	1.76
GEI	MainStay Total Return Bond I	MTMIX	C+	(800) 624-6782	C+ / 5.9	3.01	2.21	0.02 /33	1.70 /56	3.84 /59	3.03	0.62
GEI	MainStay Total Return Bond Inv	MTMNX	D+	(800) 624-6782	C- / 3.0	3.02	2.12	-0.36 /27	1.32 /49	3.45 /52	2.50	1.01
COI	MainStay Total Return Bond R1	MTMRX	C+	(800) 624-6782	C+ / 5.7	2.98	2.16	-0.07 /31	1.61 /54	--	2.93	0.72
COI	MainStay Total Return Bond R2	MTRTX	C	(800) 624-6782	C / 5.3	2.92	2.03	-0.28 /28	1.37 /50	--	2.63	0.97

• Denotes fund is closed to new investors
* Denotes fund is included in Section II

RISK			NET ASSETS		ASSET							FUND MANAGER		MINIMUM		LOADS	
Risk Rating/Pts	3 Yr Avg Standard Deviation	Avg Duration	NAV As of 3/31/16	Total $(Mil)	Cash %	Gov. Bond %	Muni. Bond %	Corp. Bond %	Other %	Portfolio Turnover Ratio	Avg Coupon Rate	Manager Quality Pct	Manager Tenure (Years)	Initial Purch. $	Additional Purch. $	Front End Load	Back End Load
E / 0.3	8.7	3.6	9.57	35	4	58	0	36	2	19	0.0	11	5	1,000	50	0.0	0.0
E / 0.4	8.7	3.6	9.73	14	4	58	0	36	2	19	0.0	32	5	5,000,000	0	0.0	0.0
E / 0.3	8.7	3.6	9.81	25	4	58	0	36	2	19	0.0	22	5	1,000	50	4.5	0.0
B+ / 8.3	2.1	4.6	8.54	93	1	9	0	0	90	13	0.0	60	5	25,000	0	4.5	0.0
B+ / 8.3	2.2	4.6	8.54	8	1	9	0	0	90	13	0.0	26	5	1,000	50	0.0	0.0
B+ / 8.4	2.1	4.6	8.54	22	1	9	0	0	90	13	0.0	29	5	1,000	50	0.0	0.0
B+ / 8.3	2.2	4.6	8.63	5	1	9	0	0	90	13	0.0	75	5	5,000,000	0	0.0	0.0
B+ / 8.4	2.1	4.6	8.58	42	1	9	0	0	90	13	0.0	53	5	1,000	50	4.5	0.0
D+ / 2.4	4.9	3.5	5.34	3,169	5	0	0	92	3	38	0.0	81	16	25,000	0	4.5	0.0
D+ / 2.4	4.9	3.5	5.31	126	5	0	0	92	3	38	0.0	46	16	1,000	50	0.0	0.0
D+ / 2.3	4.9	3.5	5.31	611	5	0	0	92	3	38	0.0	46	16	1,000	50	0.0	0.0
D+ / 2.4	4.9	3.5	5.34	4,680	5	0	0	92	3	38	0.0	85	16	5,000,000	0	0.0	0.0
D+ / 2.4	4.8	3.5	5.38	274	5	0	0	92	3	38	0.0	79	16	1,000	50	4.5	0.0
D+ / 2.4	4.8	3.5	5.33	N/A	5	0	0	92	3	38	0.0	83	16	0	0	0.0	0.0
D+ / 2.3	4.9	3.5	5.34	9	5	0	0	92	3	38	0.0	77	16	0	0	0.0	0.0
U /	N/A	3.5	5.34	17	5	0	0	92	3	38	0.0	N/A	16	250,000	0	0.0	0.0
D- / 1.2	5.8	N/A	12.38	730	2	0	97	0	1	31	0.0	55	6	25,000	0	4.5	0.0
D- / 1.3	5.8	N/A	12.35	353	2	0	97	0	1	31	0.0	30	6	2,500	50	0.0	0.0
D- / 1.3	5.8	N/A	12.38	1,137	2	0	97	0	1	31	0.0	66	6	5,000,000	0	0.0	0.0
D- / 1.3	5.8	N/A	12.36	4	2	0	97	0	1	31	0.0	55	6	2,500	50	4.5	0.0
D- / 1.1	5.9	N/A	9.94	147	4	0	0	89	7	15	0.0	10	9	25,000	0	4.5	0.0
D- / 1.1	6.0	N/A	9.89	91	4	0	0	89	7	15	0.0	7	9	1,000	50	0.0	0.0
D- / 1.1	5.9	N/A	9.96	176	4	0	0	89	7	15	0.0	12	9	5,000,000	0	0.0	0.0
D- / 1.1	6.0	N/A	9.89	5	4	0	0	89	7	15	0.0	10	9	1,000	50	4.5	0.0
C+ / 6.7	3.0	4.5	10.98	37	0	39	1	25	35	155	0.0	38	12	25,000	0	3.0	0.0
C+ / 6.8	2.9	4.5	10.99	219	0	39	1	25	35	155	0.0	51	12	5,000,000	0	0.0	0.0
C+ / 6.6	3.0	4.5	11.03	5	0	39	1	25	35	155	0.0	32	12	1,000	50	3.0	0.0
U /	N/A	N/A	1.00	57	100	0	0	0	0	0	0.0	N/A	7	1,000	50	0.0	0.0
D+ / 2.7	5.0	N/A	10.57	78	0	0	99	0	1	19	0.0	40	4	25,000	0	4.5	0.0
D+ / 2.7	5.1	N/A	10.57	29	0	0	99	0	1	19	0.0	27	4	2,500	50	0.0	0.0
D+ / 2.7	5.1	N/A	10.57	38	0	0	99	0	1	19	0.0	44	4	5,000,000	0	0.0	0.0
D+ / 2.7	5.1	N/A	10.57	N/A	0	0	99	0	1	19	0.0	34	4	2,500	50	4.5	0.0
C / 4.5	3.2	N/A	9.40	133	5	0	0	89	6	54	0.0	95	4	25,000	0	3.0	0.0
C / 4.6	3.2	N/A	9.39	42	5	0	0	89	6	54	0.0	87	4	2,500	50	0.0	0.0
C / 4.6	3.2	N/A	9.40	339	5	0	0	89	6	54	0.0	96	4	5,000,000	0	0.0	0.0
C / 4.5	3.2	N/A	9.39	5	5	0	0	89	6	54	0.0	93	4	2,500	50	3.0	0.0
C / 4.5	3.2	N/A	9.39	N/A	5	0	0	89	6	54	0.0	94	4	0	0	0.0	0.0
A+ / 9.7	0.7	2.0	9.60	101	6	40	0	52	2	7	0.0	66	1	25,000	0	1.0	0.0
A+ / 9.6	0.7	2.0	9.60	191	6	40	0	52	2	7	0.0	78	1	5,000,000	0	0.0	0.0
A+ / 9.6	0.7	2.0	9.63	4	6	40	0	52	2	7	0.0	50	1	1,000	50	1.0	0.0
C- / 3.0	4.5	7.2	10.16	893	5	0	94	0	1	46	0.0	49	7	25,000	0	4.5	0.0
C- / 3.0	4.5	7.2	10.15	18	5	0	94	0	1	46	0.0	39	7	1,000	50	0.0	0.0
C- / 3.0	4.5	7.2	10.16	220	5	0	94	0	1	46	0.0	39	7	1,000	50	0.0	0.0
C- / 3.0	4.5	7.2	10.16	659	5	0	94	0	1	46	0.0	57	7	5,000,000	0	0.0	0.0
C- / 3.0	4.5	7.2	10.20	17	5	0	94	0	1	46	0.0	47	7	1,000	50	4.5	0.0
C+ / 6.3	3.1	3.7	10.48	483	3	15	0	58	24	28	0.0	34	5	25,000	0	4.5	0.0
C+ / 6.3	3.1	3.7	10.49	8	3	15	0	58	24	28	0.0	16	5	1,000	50	0.0	0.0
C+ / 6.4	3.0	3.7	10.50	27	3	15	0	58	24	28	0.0	16	5	1,000	50	0.0	0.0
C+ / 6.3	3.1	3.7	10.48	938	3	15	0	58	24	28	0.0	44	5	5,000,000	0	0.0	0.0
C+ / 6.1	3.1	3.7	10.54	9	3	15	0	58	24	28	0.0	32	5	1,000	50	4.5	0.0
C+ / 6.3	3.1	3.7	10.48	4	3	15	0	58	24	28	0.0	49	5	0	0	0.0	0.0
C+ / 6.3	3.1	3.7	10.48	1	3	15	0	58	24	28	0.0	41	5	0	0	0.0	0.0

Fund Type	Fund Name (99 Pct = Best, 0 Pct = Worst)	Ticker Symbol	Overall Investment Rating	Phone	PERFORMANCE: Performance Rating/Pts	Total Return % through 3/31/16: 3 Mo	6 Mo	1Yr / Pct	Annualized: 3Yr / Pct	5Yr / Pct	Incl. in Returns: Dividend Yield	Expense Ratio
COI	MainStay Total Return Bond R6	MTRDX	U	(800) 624-6782	U /	3.02	2.24	0.09 /41	--	--	3.09	0.53
GL	MainStay Unconstrained Bond A	MASAX	D-	(800) 624-6782	E+ / 0.6	1.07	0.22	-4.02 / 8	0.07 /26	2.92 /44	3.58	1.04
GL	MainStay Unconstrained Bond B	MASBX	D-	(800) 624-6782	E+ / 0.8	0.88	-0.16	-4.77 / 5	-0.75 /10	2.04 /32	2.97	1.81
GL	MainStay Unconstrained Bond C	MSICX	D-	(800) 624-6782	E+ / 0.8	0.88	-0.04	-4.66 / 6	-0.72 /10	2.07 /32	2.97	1.81
GL	MainStay Unconstrained Bond I	MSDIX	D-	(800) 624-6782	D / 1.7	1.13	0.35	-3.77 / 8	0.31 /30	3.17 /48	4.00	0.79
GL	MainStay Unconstrained Bond Inv	MSYDX	D-	(800) 624-6782	E+ / 0.6	1.06	0.34	-3.89 / 8	0.02 /18	2.82 /42	3.53	1.06
COI	Manning & Napier Core Bond I	EXCIX	U	(800) 466-3863	U /	2.10	1.68	--	--	--	0.00	N/A
COI	Manning & Napier Core Bond S	EXCRX	C+	(800) 466-3863	C+ / 5.7	2.10	1.62	0.94 /57	1.57 /54	3.89 /60	1.77	0.71
MUN	Manning & Napier Diversified TE Srs	EXDVX	B+	(800) 466-3863	C+ / 5.6	0.86	1.22	2.01 /77	0.80 /47	2.60 /61	0.90	0.57
GL	Manning & Napier Glb Fxd Inc Srs I	MNGIX	D	(800) 466-3863	D+ / 2.8	3.83	2.71	-0.21 /29	-0.33 /13	--	0.00	0.72
GL	Manning & Napier Glb Fxd Inc Srs S	MNGSX	U	(800) 466-3863	U /	3.84	2.71	-0.32 /28	--	--	0.00	0.87
GL	Manning & Napier High Yield Bond I	MNHAX	D+	(800) 466-3863	C+ / 6.3	3.21	1.95	-1.81 /16	2.24 /66	--	6.49	0.91
COI	Manning & Napier Unconstrained Bd I	MNCPX	U	(800) 466-3863	U /	1.54	1.12	-0.46 /26	--	--	2.94	0.51
* COI	Manning & Napier Unconstrained Bd	EXCPX	C-	(800) 466-3863	C- / 3.9	1.44	0.98	-0.76 /24	0.81 /39	3.51 /53	2.41	0.76
USS	Manor Bond Fund	MNRBX	C-	(800) 787-3334	D / 2.0	0.96	0.34	0.44 /49	-0.15 /14	0.17 /16	0.05	1.00
GEI	MassMutual Premier Core Bond A	MMCBX	D+	(800) 542-6767	D+ / 2.7	2.00	0.90	-0.98 /22	1.47 /52	3.23 /49	2.44	0.97
GEI	MassMutual Premier Core Bond Adm	MCBLX	C	(800) 542-6767	C / 5.4	2.08	0.92	-0.77 /24	1.71 /56	3.48 /53	2.83	0.72
COI	MassMutual Premier Core Bond I	MCZZX	C+	(800) 542-6767	C+ / 5.9	2.16	1.10	-0.49 /26	2.01 /61	3.80 /58	3.09	0.42
GEI	MassMutual Premier Core Bond R3	MCBNX	C-	(800) 542-6767	C / 4.5	1.96	0.75	-1.19 /20	1.23 /47	2.97 /45	2.38	1.12
COI	MassMutual Premier Core Bond R4	MCZRX	U	(800) 542-6767	U /	2.01	0.87	-0.92 /22	--	--	2.82	0.87
GEI	MassMutual Premier Core Bond R5	MCBDX	C	(800) 542-6767	C+ / 5.7	2.06	0.98	-0.60 /25	1.86 /59	3.65 /56	2.97	0.52
GEI	MassMutual Premier Core Bond Svc	MCBYX	C	(800) 542-6767	C+ / 5.6	2.07	0.99	-0.69 /24	1.80 /58	3.59 /55	2.90	0.62
GEI	MassMutual Premier Diversified Bd A	MDVAX	C-	(800) 542-6767	C- / 3.1	2.37	1.58	-0.79 /23	1.61 /54	3.63 /55	1.92	1.17
COI	MassMutual Premier Diversified Bd I	MDBZX	B	(800) 542-6767	C+ / 6.6	2.51	1.87	-0.09 /30	2.31 /68	4.62 /69	2.45	0.62
GEI	MassMutual Premier Dvsfd Bd Adm	MDBLX	C+	(800) 542-6767	C+ / 5.9	2.47	1.70	-0.48 /26	1.91 /60	3.89 /60	2.33	0.92
GEI	MassMutual Premier Dvsfd Bd Svc	MDBYX	C+	(800) 542-6767	C+ / 6.0	2.47	1.75	-0.42 /27	1.98 /61	3.96 /61	2.38	0.82
COI	MassMutual Premier Dvsfd Bond R4	MDBFX	U	(800) 542-6767	U /	2.39	1.57	-0.61 /25	--	--	2.42	1.07
GEI	MassMutual Premier Dvsfd Bond R5	MDBSX	B-	(800) 542-6767	C+ / 6.2	2.50	1.80	-0.29 /28	2.09 /63	4.03 /62	2.54	0.72
COH	MassMutual Premier High Yield A	MPHAX	D	(800) 542-6767	C- / 3.6	1.59	0.09	-2.55 /13	2.74 /74	5.82 /76	6.09	1.14
COH	MassMutual Premier High Yield Adm	MPHLX	D+	(800) 542-6767	C+ / 6.7	1.59	0.17	-2.35 /14	2.99 /76	6.05 /77	6.78	0.89
COH	MassMutual Premier High Yield I	MPHZX	C-	(800) 542-6767	B- / 7.2	1.69	0.24	-2.05 /15	3.32 /79	6.46 /79	7.03	0.59
COH	MassMutual Premier High Yield R3	MPHNX	D+	(800) 542-6767	C+ / 6.0	1.57	-0.07	-2.66 /13	2.51 /71	5.55 /75	6.69	1.29
COH	MassMutual Premier High Yield R4	MPHRX	U	(800) 542-6767	U /	1.48	0.01	-2.52 /13	--	--	7.04	1.04
COH	MassMutual Premier High Yield R5	MPHSX	C-	(800) 542-6767	B- / 7.0	1.56	0.12	-2.16 /15	3.15 /77	6.25 /78	6.88	0.69
COH	MassMutual Premier High Yield Svc	DLHYX	D+	(800) 542-6767	C+ / 6.8	1.56	0.14	-2.25 /15	3.06 /77	6.20 /78	6.78	0.79
GEI	MassMutual Premier Infl-PI A	MPSAX	E+	(800) 542-6767	E+ / 0.6	4.46	3.63	0.90 /57	-1.25 / 7	2.51 /38	0.56	1.16
GEI	MassMutual Premier Infl-PI Adm	MIPLX	D-	(800) 542-6767	D / 1.8	4.56	3.75	1.28 /63	-0.98 / 8	2.72 /41	0.86	0.91
GEI	MassMutual Premier Infl-PI I	MIPZX	D	(800) 542-6767	C- / 3.0	4.60	3.99	1.59 /67	-0.68 /10	3.06 /46	1.15	0.61
GEI	MassMutual Premier Infl-PI R3	MIPNX	D-	(800) 542-6767	D- / 1.3	4.37	3.45	0.74 /54	-1.46 / 6	2.24 /34	0.70	1.31
GEI	MassMutual Premier Infl-PI R4	MIPRX	U	(800) 542-6767	U /	4.37	3.64	1.11 /60	--	--	0.97	1.06
GEI	MassMutual Premier Infl-PI R5	MIPSX	D-	(800) 542-6767	D+ / 2.8	4.49	3.87	1.38 /64	-0.80 / 9	2.95 /44	1.04	0.71
GEI	MassMutual Premier Infl-PI Svc	MIPYX	D-	(800) 542-6767	D+ / 2.5	4.50	3.78	1.29 /63	-0.90 / 9	2.85 /43	0.96	0.81
GEI	MassMutual Premier Short Dur Bd A	MSHAX	C-	(800) 542-6767	D / 2.2	1.10	0.20	0.30 /46	0.94 /41	1.65 /27	2.08	0.95
GEI	MassMutual Premier Short Dur Bd	MSTLX	B	(800) 542-6767	C / 4.6	1.20	0.30	0.50 /49	1.19 /46	1.88 /30	2.35	0.70
COI	MassMutual Premier Short Dur Bd I	MSTZX	B+	(800) 542-6767	C / 5.2	1.29	0.41	0.80 /55	1.48 /52	2.19 /33	2.64	0.40
GEI	MassMutual Premier Short Dur Bd R3	MSDNX	C+	(800) 542-6767	C- / 3.8	1.09	0.09	0.19 /44	0.72 /37	1.39 /24	2.33	1.10
COI	MassMutual Premier Short Dur Bd R4	MPSDX	U	(800) 542-6767	U /	1.19	0.22	0.41 /48	--	--	2.45	0.85
GEI	MassMutual Premier Short Dur Bd R5	MSTDX	B+	(800) 542-6767	C / 5.0	1.28	0.32	0.70 /53	1.37 /50	2.04 /32	2.54	0.50
GEI	MassMutual Premier Short Dur Bd	MSBYX	B	(800) 542-6767	C / 4.9	1.29	0.30	0.69 /53	1.30 /48	1.99 /31	2.44	0.60
COI	MassMutual Select Total Ret Bd A	MPTRX	U	(800) 542-6767	U /	2.43	1.90	1.00 /59	--	--	1.70	0.94
GL	MassMutual Select Total Ret Bd Adm	MSPLX	C	(800) 542-6767	C+ / 5.6	2.44	1.87	1.17 /61	1.39 /50	2.90 /44	1.85	0.69
GL	MassMutual Select Total Ret Bd I	MSPZX	C+	(800) 542-6767	C+ / 6.2	2.53	2.08	1.48 /66	1.76 /57	3.25 /49	2.15	0.39

● Denotes fund is closed to new investors
* Denotes fund is included in Section II

RISK			NET ASSETS		ASSET							FUND MANAGER		MINIMUM		LOADS	
Risk Rating/Pts	3 Yr Avg Standard Deviation	Avg Duration	NAV As of 3/31/16	Total $(Mil)	Cash %	Gov. Bond %	Muni. Bond %	Corp. Bond %	Other %	Portfolio Turnover Ratio	Avg Coupon Rate	Manager Quality Pct	Manager Tenure (Years)	Initial Purch. $	Additional Purch. $	Front End Load	Back End Load
U /	N/A	3.7	10.48	N/A	3	15	0	58	24	28	0.0	N/A	5	250,000	0	0.0	0.0
C- / **3.5**	4.3	4.3	8.44	450	7	0	0	88	5	22	0.0	71	7	25,000	0	4.5	0.0
C- / **3.4**	4.3	4.3	8.40	18	7	0	0	88	5	22	0.0	36	7	1,000	50	0.0	0.0
C- / **3.4**	4.4	4.3	8.40	254	7	0	0	88	5	22	0.0	37	7	1,000	50	0.0	0.0
C- / **3.4**	4.3	4.3	8.45	809	7	0	0	88	5	22	0.0	79	7	5,000,000	0	0.0	0.0
C- / **3.4**	4.4	4.3	8.51	31	7	0	0	88	5	22	0.0	69	7	1,000	50	4.5	0.0
U /	N/A	N/A	9.92	84	0	0	0	0	100	88	0.0	N/A	11	10,000,000	0	0.0	0.0
C+ / **6.4**	3.0	N/A	10.67	149	0	0	0	0	100	88	0.0	50	11	2,000	0	0.0	0.0
B+ / **8.7**	1.8	N/A	11.14	347	3	0	96	0	1	33	0.0	30	12	2,000	0	0.0	0.0
D+ / **2.9**	4.8	N/A	9.48	74	3	50	0	39	8	54	0.0	53	4	1,000,000	0	0.0	0.0
U /	N/A	N/A	9.46	144	3	50	0	39	8	54	0.0	N/A	4	2,000	0	0.0	0.0
D+ / **2.3**	5.4	N/A	8.36	64	4	0	0	95	1	109	0.0	97	13	1,000,000	0	0.0	0.0
U /	N/A	N/A	9.23	42	5	4	0	76	15	53	0.0	N/A	11	10,000,000	0	0.0	0.0
C+ / **6.4**	3.0	N/A	10.24	827	5	4	0	76	15	53	0.0	29	11	2,000	0	0.0	0.0
B+ / **8.9**	1.5	2.1	10.52	1	1	98	0	0	1	29	2.1	25	18	1,000	25	0.0	0.0
C+ / **6.0**	3.1	5.6	10.70	159	0	1	1	58	40	361	3.4	29	21	0	0	4.8	0.0
C+ / **6.3**	3.1	5.6	10.79	91	0	1	1	58	40	361	3.4	37	21	0	0	0.0	0.0
C+ / **6.1**	3.1	5.6	10.89	582	0	1	1	58	40	361	3.4	64	21	0	0	0.0	0.0
C+ / **6.0**	3.1	5.6	10.91	1	0	1	1	58	40	361	3.4	23	21	0	0	0.0	0.0
U /	N/A	5.6	10.66	14	0	1	1	58	40	361	3.4	N/A	21	0	0	0.0	0.0
C+ / **6.2**	3.1	5.6	10.92	426	0	1	1	58	40	361	3.4	41	21	0	0	0.0	0.0
C+ / **6.2**	3.1	5.6	10.86	120	0	1	1	58	40	361	3.4	39	21	0	0	0.0	0.0
C+ / **6.9**	2.9	5.6	9.93	36	0	11	0	50	39	362	3.2	39	17	0	0	4.8	0.0
B- / **7.1**	2.9	5.6	10.61	19	0	11	0	50	39	362	3.2	82	17	0	0	0.0	0.0
C+ / **6.8**	2.9	5.6	9.95	35	0	11	0	50	39	362	3.2	47	17	0	0	0.0	0.0
C+ / **6.8**	2.9	5.6	9.97	17	0	11	0	50	39	362	3.2	50	17	0	0	0.0	0.0
U /	N/A	5.6	9.87	3	0	11	0	50	39	362	3.2	N/A	17	0	0	0.0	0.0
C+ / **6.9**	2.9	5.6	9.85	72	0	11	0	50	39	362	3.2	56	17	0	0	0.0	0.0
D / **1.9**	5.3	3.6	8.32	26	2	0	0	94	4	76	7.7	91	6	0	0	5.8	0.0
D / **1.9**	5.3	3.6	8.33	25	2	0	0	94	4	76	7.7	93	6	0	0	0.0	0.0
D / **1.9**	5.3	3.6	8.40	130	2	0	0	94	4	76	7.7	95	6	0	0	0.0	0.0
D / **1.9**	5.3	3.6	8.43	8	2	0	0	94	4	76	7.7	90	6	0	0	0.0	0.0
U /	N/A	3.6	8.25	10	2	0	0	94	4	76	7.7	N/A	6	0	0	0.0	0.0
D / **1.9**	5.3	3.6	8.44	34	2	0	0	94	4	76	7.7	94	6	0	0	0.0	0.0
D / **1.9**	5.2	3.6	8.44	59	2	0	0	94	4	76	7.7	94	6	0	0	0.0	0.0
D+ / **2.3**	5.4	5.8	10.30	22	0	53	0	26	21	59	2.4	3	13	0	0	4.8	0.0
D+ / **2.3**	5.4	5.8	10.55	13	0	53	0	26	21	59	2.4	3	13	0	0	0.0	0.0
D+ / **2.3**	5.4	5.8	10.47	176	0	53	0	26	21	59	2.4	4	13	0	0	0.0	0.0
D+ / **2.3**	5.4	5.8	10.28	1	0	53	0	26	21	59	2.4	3	13	0	0	0.0	0.0
U /	N/A	5.8	10.26	4	0	53	0	26	21	59	2.4	N/A	13	0	0	0.0	0.0
D+ / **2.3**	5.4	5.8	10.47	58	0	53	0	26	21	59	2.4	4	13	0	0	0.0	0.0
D+ / **2.3**	5.4	5.8	10.44	75	0	53	0	26	21	59	2.4	4	13	0	0	0.0	0.0
A- / **9.2**	1.1	2.9	10.10	91	2	23	0	43	32	59	2.0	77	18	0	0	3.5	0.0
A- / **9.2**	1.1	2.9	10.16	34	2	23	0	43	32	59	2.0	83	18	0	0	0.0	0.0
A- / **9.2**	1.1	2.9	10.23	180	2	23	0	43	32	59	2.0	89	18	0	0	0.0	0.0
A / **9.3**	1.0	2.9	10.19	3	2	23	0	43	32	59	2.0	70	18	0	0	0.0	0.0
U /	N/A	2.9	10.22	7	2	23	0	43	32	59	2.0	N/A	18	0	0	0.0	0.0
A- / **9.2**	1.1	2.9	10.26	192	2	23	0	43	32	59	2.0	86	18	0	0	0.0	0.0
A- / **9.2**	1.1	2.9	10.20	64	2	23	0	43	32	59	2.0	85	18	0	0	0.0	0.0
U /	N/A	N/A	10.11	2	0	27	2	18	53	264	0.0	N/A	N/A	0	0	4.8	0.0
C+ / **5.9**	3.2	N/A	10.08	88	0	27	2	18	53	264	0.0	93	N/A	0	0	0.0	0.0
C+ / **5.9**	3.2	N/A	10.13	529	0	27	2	18	53	264	0.0	95	N/A	0	0	0.0	0.0

99 Pct = Best
0 Pct = Worst

Fund Type	Fund Name	Ticker Symbol	Overall Investment Rating	Phone	PERFORMANCE: Performance Rating/Pts	Total Return % through 3/31/16: 3 Mo	6 Mo	1Yr / Pct	Annualized: 3Yr / Pct	Annualized: 5Yr / Pct	Incl. in Returns: Dividend Yield	Expense Ratio
GL	MassMutual Select Total Ret Bd R3	MSPNX	**C-**	(800) 542-6767	**C / 4.9**	2.34	1.77	0.77 /55	1.04 /43	2.51 /38	1.46	1.09
GL	MassMutual Select Total Ret Bd R4	MSPGX	**C**	(800) 542-6767	**C / 5.4**	2.42	1.89	1.09 /60	1.28 /48	2.77 /41	1.67	0.84
GL	MassMutual Select Total Ret Bd R5	MSPSX	**C**	(800) 542-6767	**C+ / 5.9**	2.54	1.99	1.38 /64	1.60 /54	3.10 /47	2.06	0.49
GL	MassMutual Select Total Ret Bd Svc	MSPHX	**C**	(800) 542-6767	**C+ / 5.8**	2.53	2.03	1.23 /62	1.50 /52	2.99 /45	1.90	0.59
GEI	MassMutual Strategic Bond A	MSBAX	**C-**	(800) 542-6767	**C / 5.0**	2.94	2.67	1.01 /59	2.36 /68	3.94 /61	2.41	1.14
GEI	MassMutual Strategic Bond Adm	MSBLX	**C+**	(800) 542-6767	**B- / 7.4**	2.93	2.85	1.28 /63	2.64 /72	4.20 /64	2.69	0.89
COI	MassMutual Strategic Bond I	MSBZX	**B-**	(800) 542-6767	**B / 7.7**	3.03	2.88	1.62 /68	2.90 /75	4.44 /67	3.02	0.59
GEI	MassMutual Strategic Bond R3	MSBNX	**C+**	(800) 542-6767	**C+ / 6.7**	2.86	2.57	0.79 /55	2.14 /64	3.67 /56	2.43	1.29
COI	MassMutual Strategic Bond R4	MSBRX	**U**	(800) 542-6767	**U /**	2.84	2.64	1.08 /60	--	--	2.79	1.04
GEI	MassMutual Strategic Bond R5	MBSSX	**B-**	(800) 542-6767	**B / 7.7**	3.03	2.88	1.51 /66	2.85 /75	4.40 /66	2.92	0.69
GEI	MassMutual Strategic Bond Service	MBSYX	**B-**	(800) 542-6767	**B / 7.6**	3.03	2.79	1.43 /65	2.76 /74	4.32 /66	2.83	0.79
GL	Matson Money Fxd Inc VI Inst	FMVFX	**U**	(866) 780-0357	**U /**	1.41	0.65	0.53 /50	--	--	0.00	1.56
EM	Matthews Asia Strategic Income Inst	MINCX	**D+**	(800) 789-2742	**C+ / 6.0**	3.24	6.11	2.22 /73	1.05 /44	--	3.61	1.07
EM	Matthews Asia Strategic Income Inv	MAINX	**D+**	(800) 789-2742	**C+ / 5.7**	3.28	5.98	1.99 /72	0.88 /40	--	3.38	1.27
MUN	McDonnell Intermediate Muni Bond A	MIMAX	**B+**	(800) 225-5478	**B / 7.6**	1.45	2.45	3.01 /85	2.42 /82	--	1.23	1.23
MUN	McDonnell Intermediate Muni Bond C	MIMCX	**B**	(800) 225-5478	**B / 7.6**	1.27	2.09	2.26 /79	1.66 /71	--	0.55	2.01
MUN	McDonnell Intermediate Muni Bond Y	MIMYX	**A+**	(800) 225-5478	**B+ / 8.8**	1.51	2.57	3.26 /88	2.71 /85	--	1.50	0.99
USA	MD Sass Sht Trm US Gv Agcy Inc	MDSIX	**C+**	(855) 637-3863	**C- / 3.7**	0.95	0.57	0.47 /49	0.63 /36	--	2.51	0.65
GL	Meeder Total Return Bond	FLBDX	**D+**	(800) 325-3539	**D+ / 2.8**	1.94	0.90	-1.89 /16	0.24 /29	--	2.44	1.73
GES	Metropolitan West Alpha Trak 500 M	MWATX	**C**	(800) 496-8298	**A+ / 9.9**	0.97	7.85	0.53 /50	11.58 /99	11.75 /98	0.53	2.38
LP	Metropolitan West Floating Rt Inc I	MWFLX	**U**	(800) 496-8298	**U /**	0.58	0.20	0.48 /49	--	--	3.62	0.70
LP	Metropolitan West Floating Rt Inc M	MWFRX	**U**	(800) 496-8298	**U /**	0.54	0.10	0.19 /44	--	--	3.42	1.07
COH	Metropolitan West High Yield Bond I	MWHIX	**D**	(800) 496-8298	**C- / 3.8**	0.82	0.63	-2.34 /14	1.08 /44	3.27 /49	4.47	0.61
COH	Metropolitan West High Yield Bond M	MWHYX	**D**	(800) 496-8298	**C- / 3.3**	0.76	0.51	-2.58 /13	0.83 /40	3.01 /45	4.22	0.89
GEI	Metropolitan West Interm Bond I	MWIIX	**A-**	(800) 496-8298	**C+ / 6.0**	1.87	1.29	1.26 /63	1.78 /57	3.72 /57	1.40	0.49
GEI	Metropolitan West Interm Bond M	MWIMX	**B+**	(800) 496-8298	**C+ / 5.6**	1.81	1.08	1.02 /59	1.56 /53	3.48 /53	1.16	0.73
GEI	Metropolitan West Low Dur Bd Adm	MWLNX	**C+**	(800) 496-8298	**C- / 3.8**	0.33	0.16	0.14 /42	0.80 /39	2.01 /31	1.03	0.68
GEI	Metropolitan West Low Dur Bd I	MWLIX	**B+**	(800) 496-8298	**C / 4.5**	0.42	0.32	0.43 /48	1.18 /46	2.38 /36	1.35	0.39
* GEI	Metropolitan West Low Dur Bd M	MWLDX	**B-**	(800) 496-8298	**C- / 4.1**	0.38	0.22	0.32 /46	0.96 /42	2.20 /34	1.12	0.63
GEI	Metropolitan West Strategic Inc I	MWSIX	**B**	(800) 496-8298	**C / 4.8**	-0.15	-0.30	-0.33 /28	1.61 /54	3.57 /54	3.80	2.13
GEI	Metropolitan West Strategic Inc M	MWSTX	**B-**	(800) 496-8298	**C / 4.4**	-0.08	-0.30	-0.65 /25	1.37 /50	3.32 /50	3.46	2.41
GEI	Metropolitan West Tot Ret Bond Adm	MWTNX	**B+**	(800) 496-8298	**C+ / 6.8**	2.35	1.85	0.96 /58	2.31 /68	4.46 /67	1.48	0.80
GEI	Metropolitan West Tot Ret Bond I	MWTIX	**A-**	(800) 496-8298	**B- / 7.4**	2.41	2.00	1.28 /63	2.69 /73	4.87 /71	1.80	0.44
* GEI	Metropolitan West Tot Ret Bond M	MWTRX	**B+**	(800) 496-8298	**B- / 7.0**	2.36	1.79	0.96 /58	2.45 /70	4.63 /69	1.58	0.69
COI	Metropolitan West Tot Ret Bond Plan	MWTSX	**A**	(800) 496-8298	**B- / 7.4**	2.45	2.01	1.31 /63	2.72 /73	--	1.86	0.40
GEI	Metropolitan West Ultra Short Bnd I	MWUIX	**C+**	(800) 496-8298	**C- / 3.5**	0.21	0.17	0.33 /46	0.60 /35	1.47 /25	0.80	0.48
GEI	Metropolitan West Ultra Short Bnd M	MWUSX	**C+**	(800) 496-8298	**C- / 3.1**	-0.06	-0.14	0.17 /43	0.44 /32	1.31 /23	0.64	0.66
GEL	Metropolitan West Uncons Bond I	MWCIX	**A-**	(800) 496-8298	**C+ / 5.9**	0.53	0.61	0.25 /45	2.10 /64	--	2.22	0.80
* GEL	Metropolitan West Uncons Bond M	MWCRX	**B+**	(800) 496-8298	**C / 5.5**	0.55	0.55	-0.05 /31	1.83 /58	--	1.91	1.04
GL	MFS Absolute Return Fund A	MRNAX	**D+**	(800) 225-2606	**E / 0.4**	1.93	0.33	-2.03 /15	-1.07 / 8	-0.62 / 2	0.59	1.47
GL	MFS Absolute Return Fund B	MRNBX	**D+**	(800) 225-2606	**E / 0.5**	1.66	-0.22	-2.86 /12	-1.84 / 5	-1.39 / 1	0.00	2.22
GL	MFS Absolute Return Fund C	MRNCX	**D+**	(800) 225-2606	**E / 0.5**	1.66	-0.11	-2.86 /12	-1.83 / 5	-1.38 / 1	0.00	2.22
GL	MFS Absolute Return Fund I	MRNIX	**D+**	(800) 225-2606	**D- / 1.1**	1.87	0.34	-1.90 /16	-0.82 / 9	-0.37 / 2	0.86	1.22
GL	MFS Absolute Return Fund R1	MRNRX	**D+**	(800) 225-2606	**E / 0.5**	1.55	-0.22	-2.85 /12	-1.84 / 5	-1.39 / 1	0.00	2.22
GL	MFS Absolute Return Fund R2	MRNSX	**D+**	(800) 225-2606	**E+ / 0.7**	1.75	0.09	-2.40 /14	-1.36 / 7	-0.90 / 2	0.34	1.72
GL	MFS Absolute Return Fund R3	MRNTX	**D+**	(800) 225-2606	**E+ / 0.9**	1.93	0.22	-2.04 /15	-1.07 / 8	-0.63 / 2	0.60	1.47
GL	MFS Absolute Return Fund R4	MRNUX	**D+**	(800) 225-2606	**D- / 1.1**	1.99	0.34	-1.79 /17	-0.82 / 9	-0.38 / 2	0.86	1.22
MUS	MFS AL Municipal Bond Fund A	MFALX	**B-**	(800) 225-2606	**B / 8.0**	1.52	2.95	3.74 /92	3.02 /88	5.34 /88	3.40	1.09
MUS	MFS AL Municipal Bond Fund B	MBABX	**B-**	(800) 225-2606	**B+ / 8.3**	1.34	2.57	2.96 /85	2.25 /80	4.56 /82	2.80	1.84
MUS	MFS AR Municipal Bond Fund A	MFARX	**C+**	(800) 225-2606	**B- / 7.5**	1.34	2.73	3.35 /89	2.67 /84	4.64 /82	2.85	0.90
MUS	MFS AR Municipal Bond Fund B	MBARX	**C+**	(800) 225-2606	**B / 8.0**	1.15	2.34	2.57 /81	1.90 /76	3.84 /76	2.22	1.65
MUS	MFS CA Municipal Bond Fund A	MCFTX	**B-**	(800) 225-2606	**A / 9.3**	2.19	4.32	5.22 /98	4.37 /97	7.34 /97	3.39	0.87

• Denotes fund is closed to new investors
* Denotes fund is included in Section II

RISK			NET ASSETS		ASSET							FUND MANAGER		MINIMUM		LOADS	
Risk Rating/Pts	3 Yr Avg Standard Deviation	Avg Duration	NAV As of 3/31/16	Total $(Mil)	Cash %	Gov. Bond %	Muni. Bond %	Corp. Bond %	Other %	Portfolio Turnover Ratio	Avg Coupon Rate	Manager Quality Pct	Manager Tenure (Years)	Initial Purch. $	Additional Purch. $	Front End Load	Back End Load
C+ / 5.7	3.2	N/A	10.08	46	0	27	2	18	53	264	0.0	90	N/A	0	0	0.0	0.0
C+ / 5.8	3.2	N/A	10.15	318	0	27	2	18	53	264	0.0	92	N/A	0	0	0.0	0.0
C+ / 5.9	3.2	N/A	10.11	125	0	27	2	18	53	264	0.0	94	N/A	0	0	0.0	0.0
C+ / 5.8	3.2	N/A	10.15	203	0	27	2	18	53	264	0.0	93	N/A	0	0	0.0	0.0
C / 5.1	3.4	5.8	10.16	44	0	31	0	32	37	191	4.1	51	12	0	0	4.8	0.0
C / 5.0	3.5	5.8	10.19	39	0	31	0	32	37	191	4.1	61	12	0	0	0.0	0.0
C / 5.0	3.5	5.8	10.20	84	0	31	0	32	37	191	4.1	85	12	0	0	0.0	0.0
C / 5.2	3.4	5.8	10.07	5	0	31	0	32	37	191	4.1	44	12	0	0	0.0	0.0
U /	N/A	5.8	10.13	22	0	31	0	32	37	191	4.1	N/A	12	0	0	0.0	0.0
C / 5.0	3.5	5.8	10.21	58	0	31	0	32	37	191	4.1	73	12	0	0	0.0	0.0
C / 5.1	3.4	5.8	10.21	51	0	31	0	32	37	191	4.1	71	12	0	0	0.0	0.0
U /	N/A	N/A	25.16	20	19	54	1	21	5	11	0.0	N/A	2	0	0	0.0	0.0
D / 1.9	5.7	3.6	10.22	11	3	28	0	59	10	34	0.0	91	5	3,000,000	100	0.0	0.0
D / 1.9	5.7	3.6	10.23	52	3	28	0	59	10	34	0.0	89	5	2,500	100	0.0	0.0
C+ / 6.1	3.1	N/A	10.21	14	7	0	92	0	1	10	0.0	34	4	2,500	100	3.0	0.0
C+ / 5.8	3.2	N/A	10.21	6	7	0	92	0	1	10	0.0	16	4	2,500	100	0.0	0.0
C+ / 6.2	3.1	N/A	10.22	69	7	0	92	0	1	10	0.0	43	4	100,000	100	0.0	0.0
A / 9.5	0.8	N/A	9.79	99	2	16	0	0	82	100	0.0	72	5	10,000	1,000	0.0	0.0
C / 5.0	3.5	N/A	9.27	214	5	42	0	29	24	82	0.0	77	5	2,500	100	0.0	0.0
E- / 0.2	11.5	0.6	7.22	2	10	47	0	6	37	30	5.3	99	18	5,000	0	0.0	0.0
U /	N/A	0.2	9.80	138	7	4	0	68	21	49	4.0	N/A	3	3,000,000	50,000	0.0	0.0
U /	N/A	0.2	9.80	8	7	4	0	68	21	49	4.0	N/A	3	5,000	0	0.0	0.0
D+ / 2.7	4.6	3.3	9.09	570	5	2	0	86	7	61	5.2	55	14	3,000,000	50,000	0.0	0.0
D+ / 2.7	4.6	3.3	9.09	497	5	2	0	86	7	61	5.2	45	14	5,000	0	0.0	0.0
B+ / 8.8	1.7	3.3	10.58	1,093	0	38	0	22	40	253	2.2	80	14	3,000,000	50,000	0.0	0.0
B+ / 8.7	1.8	3.3	10.58	199	0	38	0	22	40	253	2.2	74	14	5,000	0	0.0	0.0
A+ / 9.7	0.7	1.1	11.27	7	2	20	0	22	56	30	2.0	81	19	2,500	0	0.0	0.0
A+ / 9.7	0.7	1.1	8.73	1,914	2	20	0	22	56	30	2.0	87	19	3,000,000	50,000	0.0	0.0
A+ / 9.6	0.7	1.1	8.73	1,492	2	20	0	22	56	30	2.0	83	19	5,000	0	0.0	0.0
B+ / 8.9	1.4	1.7	7.98	61	2	6	0	12	80	32	4.3	90	13	3,000,000	50,000	0.0	0.0
A- / 9.0	1.4	1.7	7.99	59	2	6	0	12	80	32	4.3	88	13	5,000	0	0.0	0.0
B- / 7.1	2.8	5.0	10.84	291	0	37	1	17	45	246	2.6	N/A	19	2,500	0	0.0	0.0
B- / 7.0	2.9	5.0	10.83	46,187	0	37	1	17	45	246	2.6	79	19	3,000,000	50,000	0.0	0.0
B- / 7.1	2.8	5.0	10.83	16,460	0	37	1	17	45	246	2.6	73	19	5,000	0	0.0	0.0
B- / 7.2	2.8	5.0	10.20	10,660	0	37	1	17	45	246	2.6	89	19	25,000,000	50,000	0.0	0.0
A+ / 9.9	0.4	0.4	4.28	75	5	17	0	18	60	16	1.4	81	13	3,000,000	50,000	0.0	0.0
A+ / 9.8	0.5	0.4	4.27	78	5	17	0	18	60	16	1.4	78	13	5,000	0	0.0	0.0
B+ / 8.8	1.6	1.4	11.71	1,396	1	11	2	20	66	18	3.0	92	5	3,000,000	50,000	0.0	0.0
B+ / 8.8	1.7	1.4	11.72	826	1	11	2	20	66	18	3.0	90	5	5,000	0	0.0	0.0
B+ / 8.4	2.1	1.4	9.25	3	4	7	0	72	17	30	1.9	26	5	1,000	50	4.3	0.0
B+ / 8.4	2.1	1.4	9.18	N/A	4	7	0	72	17	30	1.9	13	5	1,000	50	0.0	0.0
B+ / 8.4	2.1	1.4	9.18	2	4	7	0	72	17	30	1.9	13	5	1,000	50	0.0	0.0
B+ / 8.4	2.1	1.4	9.26	1	4	7	0	72	17	30	1.9	33	5	0	0	0.0	0.0
B+ / 8.4	2.0	1.4	9.19	N/A	4	7	0	72	17	30	1.9	13	5	0	0	0.0	0.0
B+ / 8.4	2.1	1.4	9.24	N/A	4	7	0	72	17	30	1.9	20	5	0	0	0.0	0.0
B+ / 8.4	2.1	1.4	9.25	N/A	4	7	0	72	17	30	1.9	26	5	0	0	0.0	0.0
B+ / 8.4	2.1	1.4	9.25	N/A	4	7	0	72	17	30	1.9	33	5	0	0	0.0	0.0
C / 4.5	3.7	5.2	10.49	53	0	0	99	0	1	22	5.2	36	17	1,000	50	4.3	0.0
C / 4.5	3.7	5.2	10.49	1	0	0	99	0	1	22	5.2	18	17	1,000	50	0.0	0.0
C- / 4.2	3.9	5.6	10.07	160	0	0	99	0	1	20	4.7	21	17	1,000	50	4.3	0.0
C- / 4.2	3.9	5.6	10.08	7	0	0	99	0	1	20	4.7	11	17	1,000	50	0.0	0.0
C- / 3.2	4.6	6.6	6.14	281	0	0	99	0	1	24	4.9	47	17	1,000	50	4.3	0.0

99 Pct = Best
0 Pct = Worst

Fund Type	Fund Name	Ticker Symbol	Overall Investment Rating	Phone	PERFORMANCE: Performance Rating/Pts	Total Return % through 3/31/16: 3 Mo	6 Mo	1Yr / Pct	Annualized: 3Yr / Pct	Annualized: 5Yr / Pct	Incl. in Returns: Dividend Yield	Expense Ratio
MUS	MFS CA Municipal Bond Fund B	MBCAX	B-	(800) 225-2606	A / 9.5	2.00	3.93	4.42 /96	3.58 /93	6.52 /94	2.80	1.62
MUS	MFS CA Municipal Bond Fund C	MCCAX	B-	(800) 225-2606	A / 9.4	1.96	3.84	4.26 /95	3.43 /92	6.35 /94	2.65	1.62
* GEI	MFS Corporate Bond A	MFBFX	C-	(800) 225-2606	C+ / 6.1	3.90	3.60	1.03 /59	2.79 /74	4.63 /69	3.22	0.82
GEI	MFS Corporate Bond B	MFBBX	C-	(800) 225-2606	C+ / 6.6	3.72	3.22	0.27 /45	2.05 /62	3.86 /59	2.62	1.57
GEI	MFS Corporate Bond C	MFBCX	C-	(800) 225-2606	C+ / 6.7	3.72	3.22	0.34 /47	2.05 /62	3.87 /60	2.62	1.57
GEI	MFS Corporate Bond I	MBDIX	C+	(800) 225-2606	B / 7.9	3.97	3.80	1.28 /63	3.07 /77	4.89 /71	3.61	0.57
GEI	MFS Corporate Bond R1	MFBGX	C-	(800) 225-2606	C+ / 6.7	3.72	3.29	0.34 /47	2.05 /62	3.87 /60	2.62	1.57
GEI	MFS Corporate Bond R2	MBRRX	C	(800) 225-2606	B- / 7.4	3.84	3.47	0.78 /55	2.53 /71	4.37 /66	3.12	1.07
GEI	MFS Corporate Bond R3	MFBHX	C+	(800) 225-2606	B / 7.7	3.90	3.60	1.03 /59	2.79 /74	4.63 /69	3.36	0.82
GEI	MFS Corporate Bond R4	MFBJX	C+	(800) 225-2606	B / 8.0	3.96	3.80	1.35 /64	3.07 /77	4.89 /71	3.61	0.57
COI	MFS Corporate Bond R5	MFBKX	C+	(800) 225-2606	B / 8.0	4.00	3.79	1.39 /65	3.13 /77	--	3.72	0.46
* EM	MFS Emerging Markets Debt A	MEDAX	D	(800) 225-2606	C / 5.5	4.24	4.70	1.10 /60	0.90 /41	4.66 /69	4.22	1.12
EM	MFS Emerging Markets Debt B	MEDBX	D-	(800) 225-2606	C- / 4.0	4.11	4.30	0.36 /47	0.14 /28	3.90 /60	3.67	1.87
EM	MFS Emerging Markets Debt C	MEDCX	D-	(800) 225-2606	C- / 4.0	4.11	4.38	0.36 /47	0.16 /28	3.89 /60	3.66	1.87
EM	MFS Emerging Markets Debt I	MEDIX	D	(800) 225-2606	C+ / 5.9	4.38	4.83	1.35 /64	1.15 /45	4.92 /71	4.66	0.87
EM	MFS Emerging Markets Debt R1	MEDDX	D-	(800) 225-2606	C- / 4.0	3.99	4.26	0.32 /46	0.13 /28	3.87 /60	3.62	1.87
EM	MFS Emerging Markets Debt R2	MEDEX	D	(800) 225-2606	C / 5.0	4.19	4.58	0.82 /56	0.65 /36	4.40 /66	4.12	1.37
EM	MFS Emerging Markets Debt R3	MEDFX	D	(800) 225-2606	C / 5.4	4.26	4.64	1.05 /59	0.89 /41	4.66 /69	4.36	1.12
EM	MFS Emerging Markets Debt R4	MEDGX	D	(800) 225-2606	C+ / 5.9	4.32	4.77	1.30 /63	1.14 /45	4.92 /71	4.61	0.87
EM	MFS Emerging Markets Debt R5	MEDHX	D	(800) 225-2606	C+ / 6.2	4.41	4.96	1.48 /66	1.28 /48	5.00 /72	4.79	0.76
EM	MFS Emerging Mkts Debt Loc Curr A	EMLAX	E-	(800) 225-2606	E- / 0.0	9.62	9.03	-5.62 / 4	-7.54 / 1	--	4.66	1.48
EM	MFS Emerging Mkts Debt Loc Curr B	EMLBX	E-	(800) 225-2606	E- / 0.1	9.59	8.79	-6.19 / 3	-8.20 / 1	--	4.11	2.23
EM	MFS Emerging Mkts Debt Loc Curr C	EMLCX	E-	(800) 225-2606	E- / 0.1	9.59	8.79	-6.19 / 3	-8.20 / 1	--	4.11	2.23
EM	MFS Emerging Mkts Debt Loc Curr I	EMLIX	E-	(800) 225-2606	E- / 0.1	9.86	9.34	-5.25 / 5	-7.31 / 1	--	5.12	1.23
EM	MFS Emerging Mkts Debt Loc Curr	EMLJX	E-	(800) 225-2606	E- / 0.1	9.41	8.62	-6.31 / 3	-8.23 / 0	--	4.11	2.23
EM	MFS Emerging Mkts Debt Loc Curr	EMLKX	E-	(800) 225-2606	E- / 0.1	9.72	9.06	-5.72 / 4	-7.76 / 1	--	4.61	1.73
EM	MFS Emerging Mkts Debt Loc Curr	EMLLX	E-	(800) 225-2606	E- / 0.1	9.61	9.02	-5.60 / 4	-7.50 / 1	--	4.87	1.48
EM	MFS Emerging Mkts Debt Loc Curr	EMLMX	E-	(800) 225-2606	E- / 0.1	9.85	9.33	-5.24 / 5	-7.26 / 1	--	5.12	1.23
EM	MFS Emerging Mkts Debt Loc Curr	EMLNX	E-	(800) 225-2606	E- / 0.1	9.88	9.40	-5.14 / 5	-7.21 / 1	--	5.22	1.18
MUS	MFS GA Municipal Bond Fund A	MMGAX	C+	(800) 225-2606	B / 7.7	1.50	2.77	3.27 /88	2.83 /86	5.30 /88	3.06	1.04
MUS	MFS GA Municipal Bond Fund B	MBGAX	C+	(800) 225-2606	B / 8.1	1.31	2.38	2.49 /80	2.05 /77	4.49 /81	2.44	1.79
GL	MFS Global Bond Fund A	MGBAX	E+	(800) 225-2606	D- / 1.1	5.84	4.97	3.04 /77	-2.27 / 4	0.44 /17	1.29	1.19
GL	MFS Global Bond Fund B	MGBBX	E	(800) 225-2606	E+ / 0.7	5.68	4.48	2.28 /74	-2.96 / 2	-0.38 / 2	0.63	1.94
GL	MFS Global Bond Fund C	MGBDX	E	(800) 225-2606	E+ / 0.7	5.68	4.48	2.28 /74	-2.99 / 2	-0.38 / 2	0.63	1.94
GL	MFS Global Bond Fund I	MGBJX	E+	(800) 225-2606	D- / 1.4	5.81	5.00	3.18 /78	-2.01 / 4	0.59 /18	1.59	0.94
GL	MFS Global Bond Fund R1	MGBKX	E	(800) 225-2606	E+ / 0.7	5.55	4.48	2.28 /74	-2.96 / 2	-0.40 / 2	0.63	1.94
GL	MFS Global Bond Fund R2	MGBLX	E	(800) 225-2606	D- / 1.0	5.81	4.74	2.79 /76	-2.50 / 3	0.10 /14	1.11	1.44
GL	MFS Global Bond Fund R3	MGBMX	E+	(800) 225-2606	D- / 1.2	5.87	4.99	3.16 /78	-2.22 / 4	0.38 /17	1.35	1.19
GL	MFS Global Bond Fund R4	MGBNX	E+	(800) 225-2606	D- / 1.4	5.93	5.12	3.30 /78	-1.98 / 4	0.63 /18	1.59	0.94
GL	MFS Global Bond Fund R5	MGBOX	E+	(800) 225-2606	D / 1.6	5.98	5.20	3.47 /79	-1.84 / 5	--	1.74	0.82
COH	MFS Global High Yield A	MHOAX	E+	(800) 225-2606	D / 1.7	2.52	1.35	-3.79 / 8	1.40 /50	3.96 /61	6.09	1.14
COH	MFS Global High Yield B	MHOBX	D-	(800) 225-2606	D+ / 2.8	2.33	0.98	-4.49 / 6	0.60 /35	3.16 /48	5.58	1.89
COH	MFS Global High Yield C	MHOCX	D-	(800) 225-2606	C- / 3.0	2.52	1.15	-4.36 / 7	0.70 /37	3.21 /48	5.57	1.89
COH	MFS Global High Yield I	MHOIX	D	(800) 225-2606	C / 4.7	2.59	1.48	-3.55 / 9	1.60 /54	4.18 /64	6.62	0.89
COH	MFS Global High Yield R1	MHORX	D-	(800) 225-2606	D+ / 2.9	2.33	0.98	-4.50 / 6	0.65 /36	3.15 /47	5.57	1.89
COH	MFS Global High Yield R2	MHOSX	D	(800) 225-2606	C- / 3.8	2.46	1.23	-4.02 / 8	1.11 /45	3.67 /56	6.10	1.39
COH	MFS Global High Yield R3	MHOTX	D	(800) 225-2606	C / 4.3	2.52	1.35	-3.79 / 8	1.40 /50	3.96 /61	6.36	1.14
COH	MFS Global High Yield R4	MHOUX	D	(800) 225-2606	C / 4.7	2.58	1.49	-3.65 / 9	1.57 /53	4.32 /66	6.62	0.89
COH	MFS Global High Yield R5	MHOVX	D	(800) 225-2606	C / 4.9	2.61	1.53	-3.62 / 9	1.70 /56	4.23 /65	6.73	0.79
GL	MFS Global Multi-Asset A	GLMAX	E	(800) 225-2606	E / 0.3	2.14	0.58	-7.27 / 2	-0.66 /10	-0.49 / 2	0.00	2.51
GL	MFS Global Multi-Asset B	GLMBX	E	(800) 225-2606	E / 0.5	1.94	0.24	-8.02 / 1	-1.40 / 6	-1.23 / 1	0.00	3.26
GL	MFS Global Multi-Asset C	GLMCX	E	(800) 225-2606	E / 0.5	2.07	0.25	-7.91 / 1	-1.40 / 6	-1.22 / 1	0.00	3.26

- ● Denotes fund is closed to new investors
- * Denotes fund is included in Section II

RISK			NET ASSETS		ASSET							FUND MANAGER		MINIMUM		LOADS	
Risk Rating/Pts	3 Yr Avg Standard Deviation	Avg Duration	NAV As of 3/31/16	Total $(Mil)	Cash %	Gov. Bond %	Muni. Bond %	Corp. Bond %	Other %	Portfolio Turnover Ratio	Avg Coupon Rate	Manager Quality Pct	Manager Tenure (Years)	Initial Purch. $	Additional Purch. $	Front End Load	Back End Load
C- / 3.1	4.6	6.6	6.14	3	0	0	99	0	1	24	4.9	23	17	1,000	50	0.0	0.0
C- / 3.1	4.6	6.6	6.16	34	0	0	99	0	1	24	4.9	21	17	1,000	50	0.0	0.0
C- / 4.0	4.0	6.4	13.83	1,654	5	0	0	93	2	29	4.6	58	11	1,000	50	4.3	0.0
C- / 4.0	4.0	6.4	13.80	72	5	0	0	93	2	29	4.6	33	11	1,000	50	0.0	0.0
C- / 4.0	4.0	6.4	13.79	261	5	0	0	93	2	29	4.6	33	11	1,000	50	0.0	0.0
C- / 4.0	4.0	6.4	13.83	675	5	0	0	93	2	29	4.6	73	11	0	0	0.0	0.0
C- / 4.0	4.0	6.4	13.80	7	5	0	0	93	2	29	4.6	33	11	0	0	0.0	0.0
C- / 4.0	4.0	6.4	13.83	59	5	0	0	93	2	29	4.6	49	11	0	0	0.0	0.0
C- / 4.0	4.0	6.4	13.83	65	5	0	0	93	2	29	4.6	58	11	0	0	0.0	0.0
C- / 4.0	4.0	6.4	13.84	146	5	0	0	93	2	29	4.6	74	11	0	0	0.0	0.0
C- / 4.1	3.9	6.4	13.82	44	5	0	0	93	2	29	4.6	84	11	0	0	0.0	0.0
E+ / 0.8	6.9	6.0	14.24	569	9	58	0	30	3	55	5.7	89	18	1,000	50	0.0	0.0
E+ / 0.8	6.8	6.0	14.30	32	9	58	0	30	3	55	5.7	75	18	1,000	50	0.0	0.0
E+ / 0.8	6.9	6.0	14.29	220	9	58	0	30	3	55	5.7	76	18	1,000	50	0.0	0.0
E+ / 0.8	6.9	6.0	14.21	2,262	9	58	0	30	3	55	5.7	91	18	0	0	0.0	0.0
E+ / 0.8	6.9	6.0	14.30	1	9	58	0	30	3	55	5.7	75	18	0	0	0.0	0.0
E+ / 0.8	6.9	6.0	14.30	25	9	58	0	30	3	55	5.7	87	18	0	0	0.0	0.0
E+ / 0.8	6.9	6.0	14.25	44	9	58	0	30	3	55	5.7	89	18	0	0	0.0	0.0
E+ / 0.8	6.9	6.0	14.25	70	9	58	0	30	3	55	5.7	91	18	0	0	0.0	0.0
E+ / 0.8	6.9	6.0	14.24	739	9	58	0	30	3	55	5.7	92	18	0	0	0.0	0.0
E- / 0.1	12.5	4.4	6.79	3	26	66	0	6	2	102	7.3	1	5	1,000	0	4.3	0.0
E- / 0.1	12.5	4.4	6.80	N/A	26	66	0	6	2	102	7.3	1	5	1,000	0	0.0	0.0
E- / 0.1	12.5	4.4	6.80	1	26	66	0	6	2	102	7.3	1	5	1,000	0	0.0	0.0
E- / 0.1	12.5	4.4	6.79	1	26	66	0	6	2	102	7.3	1	5	0	0	0.0	0.0
E- / 0.1	12.5	4.4	6.80	N/A	26	66	0	6	2	102	7.3	1	5	0	0	0.0	0.0
E- / 0.1	12.5	4.4	6.80	N/A	26	66	0	6	2	102	7.3	1	5	0	0	0.0	0.0
E- / 0.1	12.4	4.4	6.80	N/A	26	66	0	6	2	102	7.3	1	5	0	0	0.0	0.0
E- / 0.1	12.5	4.4	6.80	N/A	26	66	0	6	2	102	7.3	1	5	0	0	0.0	0.0
E- / 0.1	12.5	4.4	6.80	323	26	66	0	6	2	102	7.3	1	5	0	0	0.0	0.0
C- / 4.0	4.0	5.6	11.02	61	1	0	98	0	1	16	5.2	22	17	1,000	50	4.3	0.0
C- / 4.0	4.0	5.6	11.06	1	1	0	98	0	1	16	5.2	11	17	1,000	50	0.0	0.0
D- / 1.0	6.6	6.6	8.86	14	9	43	0	39	9	143	3.8	11	6	1,000	50	0.0	0.0
E+ / 0.9	6.6	6.6	8.81	1	9	43	0	39	9	143	3.8	8	6	1,000	50	0.0	0.0
D- / 1.0	6.6	6.6	8.81	2	9	43	0	39	9	143	3.8	7	6	1,000	50	0.0	0.0
D- / 1.0	6.5	6.6	8.81	2	9	43	0	39	9	143	3.8	13	6	0	0	0.0	0.0
E+ / 0.9	6.6	6.6	8.81	N/A	9	43	0	39	9	143	3.8	8	6	0	0	0.0	0.0
D- / 1.0	6.6	6.6	8.81	N/A	9	43	0	39	9	143	3.8	9	6	0	0	0.0	0.0
D- / 1.0	6.6	6.6	8.82	N/A	9	43	0	39	9	143	3.8	11	6	0	0	0.0	0.0
D- / 1.0	6.6	6.6	8.82	N/A	9	43	0	39	9	143	3.8	13	6	0	0	0.0	0.0
E+ / 0.9	6.6	6.6	8.81	634	9	43	0	39	9	143	3.8	15	6	0	0	0.0	0.0
D- / 1.4	5.7	4.4	5.80	237	70	1	0	27	2	18	6.4	53	11	1,000	50	4.3	0.0
D- / 1.4	5.6	4.4	5.81	16	70	1	0	27	2	18	6.4	28	11	1,000	50	0.0	0.0
D- / 1.4	5.7	4.4	5.80	66	70	1	0	27	2	18	6.4	30	11	1,000	50	0.0	0.0
D- / 1.5	5.6	4.4	5.80	85	70	1	0	27	2	18	6.4	61	11	0	0	0.0	0.0
D- / 1.5	5.6	4.4	5.81	N/A	70	1	0	27	2	18	6.4	30	11	0	0	0.0	0.0
D- / 1.4	5.6	4.4	5.81	N/A	70	1	0	27	2	18	6.4	42	11	0	0	0.0	0.0
D- / 1.5	5.6	4.4	5.80	8	70	1	0	27	2	18	6.4	53	11	0	0	0.0	0.0
D- / 1.4	5.7	4.4	5.83	7	70	1	0	27	2	18	6.4	59	11	0	0	0.0	0.0
D- / 1.4	5.7	4.4	5.79	4	70	1	0	27	2	18	6.4	68	11	0	0	0.0	0.0
E+ / 0.9	6.6	N/A	8.61	6	9	30	0	20	41	39	0.0	40	5	1,000	50	5.8	0.0
E+ / 0.9	6.6	N/A	8.40	1	9	30	0	20	41	39	0.0	20	5	1,000	50	0.0	0.0
E+ / 0.9	6.7	N/A	8.40	1	9	30	0	20	41	39	0.0	20	5	1,000	50	0.0	0.0

99 Pct = Best 0 Pct = Worst					PERFORMANCE							
						Total Return % through 3/31/16					Incl. in Returns	
									Annualized			
Fund Type	Fund Name	Ticker Symbol	Overall Investment Rating	Phone	Performance Rating/Pts	3 Mo	6 Mo	1Yr / Pct	3Yr / Pct	5Yr / Pct	Dividend Yield	Expense Ratio
GL	MFS Global Multi-Asset I	GLMIX	**E**	(800) 225-2606	**E+ / 0.9**	2.24	0.69	-7.03 / 2	-0.40 /12	-0.24 / 2	0.00	2.26
GL	MFS Global Multi-Asset R1	GLMRX	**E**	(800) 225-2606	**E / 0.5**	2.06	0.25	-7.89 / 1	-1.40 / 6	-1.22 / 1	0.00	3.26
GL	MFS Global Multi-Asset R2	GLMSX	**E**	(800) 225-2606	**E+ / 0.6**	2.15	0.47	-7.60 / 2	-0.92 / 9	-0.75 / 2	0.00	2.76
GL	MFS Global Multi-Asset R3	GLMTX	**E**	(800) 225-2606	**E+ / 0.7**	2.14	0.58	-7.28 / 2	-0.68 /10	-0.49 / 2	0.00	2.51
GL	MFS Global Multi-Asset R4	GLMUX	**E**	(800) 225-2606	**E+ / 0.9**	2.24	0.80	-7.03 / 2	-0.40 /12	-0.24 / 2	0.00	2.26
* USS	MFS Government Securities Fund A	MFGSX	**C-**	(800) 225-2606	**C- / 3.7**	2.40	1.69	1.51 /66	1.50 /52	2.64 /39	1.89	0.88
USS	MFS Government Securities Fund B	MFGBX	**C**	(800) 225-2606	**C / 4.3**	2.32	1.31	0.75 /54	0.74 /38	1.88 /30	1.23	1.63
USS	MFS Government Securities Fund C	MFGDX	**C**	(800) 225-2606	**C / 4.3**	2.31	1.31	0.75 /54	0.74 /38	1.87 /30	1.23	1.63
USS	MFS Government Securities Fund I	MGSIX	**B**	(800) 225-2606	**C+ / 6.1**	2.47	1.82	1.66 /68	1.72 /56	2.88 /43	2.22	0.63
USS	MFS Government Securities Fund R1	MFGGX	**C**	(800) 225-2606	**C / 4.3**	2.32	1.31	0.75 /54	0.74 /38	1.88 /30	1.23	1.63
USS	MFS Government Securities Fund R2	MGVSX	**C+**	(800) 225-2606	**C / 5.3**	2.34	1.56	1.26 /63	1.25 /47	2.38 /36	1.73	1.13
USS	MFS Government Securities Fund R3	MFGHX	**B-**	(800) 225-2606	**C+ / 5.8**	2.51	1.69	1.51 /66	1.50 /52	2.64 /39	1.97	0.88
USS	MFS Government Securities Fund R4	MFGJX	**B+**	(800) 225-2606	**C+ / 6.2**	2.47	1.81	1.76 /69	1.75 /57	2.88 /43	2.22	0.63
USL	MFS Government Securities Fund R5	MFGKX	**B+**	(800) 225-2606	**C+ / 6.4**	2.50	1.87	1.88 /71	1.87 /59	--	2.33	0.52
COH	MFS High Income Fund 529A	EAHIX	**D**	(800) 225-2606	**C / 4.4**	2.38	0.62	-3.95 / 8	1.55 /53	4.11 /63	5.47	1.05
COH	MFS High Income Fund 529B	EMHBX	**D-**	(800) 225-2606	**D+ / 2.9**	2.19	0.23	-4.68 / 6	0.77 /38	3.32 /50	4.92	1.80
COH	MFS High Income Fund 529C	EMHCX	**D-**	(800) 225-2606	**C- / 3.0**	2.51	0.55	-4.65 / 6	0.78 /39	3.33 /50	4.91	1.80
COH	MFS High Income Fund A	MHITX	**D**	(800) 225-2606	**C / 4.5**	2.38	0.63	-3.92 / 8	1.57 /53	4.15 /64	5.51	0.95
COH	MFS High Income Fund B	MHIBX	**D-**	(800) 225-2606	**C- / 3.1**	2.52	0.57	-4.60 / 6	0.83 /40	3.38 /51	4.97	1.70
COH	MFS High Income Fund C	MHICX	**D-**	(800) 225-2606	**D+ / 2.8**	2.20	0.26	-4.88 / 5	0.74 /38	3.32 /50	4.97	1.70
COH	MFS High Income Fund I	MHIIX	**D**	(800) 225-2606	**C / 5.0**	2.77	1.06	-3.67 / 9	1.83 /58	4.41 /67	6.00	0.70
COH	MFS High Income Fund R1	MHIGX	**D-**	(800) 225-2606	**D+ / 2.8**	2.20	0.26	-4.90 / 5	0.73 /37	3.32 /50	4.98	1.70
COH	MFS High Income Fund R2	MIHRX	**D**	(800) 225-2606	**C- / 3.9**	2.32	0.51	-4.43 / 6	1.32 /49	3.84 /59	5.49	1.20
COH	MFS High Income Fund R3	MHIHX	**D**	(800) 225-2606	**C / 4.5**	2.38	0.63	-3.92 / 8	1.57 /54	4.15 /64	5.75	0.95
COH	MFS High Income Fund R4	MHIJX	**D**	(800) 225-2606	**C / 4.9**	2.45	0.75	-3.95 / 8	1.83 /58	4.35 /66	6.01	0.70
COH	MFS High Income Fund R5	MHIKX	**D**	(800) 225-2606	**C / 5.1**	2.47	0.81	-3.59 / 9	1.91 /60	--	6.11	0.62
USS	MFS Inflation Adjusted Bond A	MIAAX	**E+**	(800) 225-2606	**E+ / 0.6**	4.52	3.54	0.82 /56	-1.48 / 6	2.21 /34	0.58	1.02
USS	MFS Inflation Adjusted Bond B	MIABX	**E+**	(800) 225-2606	**E+ / 0.7**	4.24	3.07	0.03 /35	-2.22 / 4	1.45 /25	0.13	1.77
USS	MFS Inflation Adjusted Bond C	MIACX	**E+**	(800) 225-2606	**E+ / 0.7**	4.32	3.01	-0.03 /31	-2.33 / 3	1.35 /24	0.06	1.77
USS	MFS Inflation Adjusted Bond I	MIAIX	**D-**	(800) 225-2606	**D- / 1.4**	4.55	3.51	0.92 /57	-1.35 / 7	2.37 /36	0.71	0.77
USS	MFS Inflation Adjusted Bond R1	MIALX	**E+**	(800) 225-2606	**E+ / 0.7**	4.22	3.02	-0.13 /30	-2.33 / 3	1.35 /24	0.06	1.77
USS	MFS Inflation Adjusted Bond R2	MIATX	**D-**	(800) 225-2606	**D- / 1.0**	4.44	3.26	0.39 /48	-1.83 / 5	1.86 /29	0.38	1.27
USS	MFS Inflation Adjusted Bond R3	MIAHX	**D-**	(800) 225-2606	**D- / 1.2**	4.39	3.39	0.66 /53	-1.59 / 6	2.10 /32	0.55	1.02
USS	MFS Inflation Adjusted Bond R4	MIAJX	**D-**	(800) 225-2606	**D- / 1.4**	4.45	3.51	0.92 /57	-1.36 / 7	2.35 /36	0.71	0.77
GEI	MFS Inflation Adjusted Bond R5	MIAKX	**D-**	(800) 225-2606	**D- / 1.5**	4.56	3.65	1.08 /60	-1.25 / 7	--	0.77	0.67
GEI	MFS Limited Maturity 529A	EALMX	**C-**	(800) 225-2606	**D / 1.8**	0.96	0.60	0.44 /49	0.54 /34	1.18 /22	1.08	0.96
GEI	MFS Limited Maturity 529B	EBLMX	**C-**	(800) 225-2606	**D / 1.6**	0.77	0.22	-0.32 /28	-0.22 /14	0.44 /17	0.35	1.71
GEI	MFS Limited Maturity 529C	ELDCX	**C-**	(800) 225-2606	**D- / 1.5**	0.75	0.18	-0.40 /27	-0.31 /13	0.32 /16	0.26	1.71
GEI	MFS Limited Maturity A	MQLFX	**C-**	(800) 225-2606	**D / 2.0**	0.80	0.63	0.49 /49	0.59 /35	1.23 /23	1.13	0.86
GEI	• MFS Limited Maturity B	MQLBX	**C-**	(800) 225-2606	**D / 1.7**	0.62	0.09	-0.26 /28	-0.16 /14	0.47 /17	0.41	1.61
GEI	MFS Limited Maturity C	MQLCX	**C-**	(800) 225-2606	**D- / 1.5**	0.59	0.04	-0.35 /27	-0.31 /13	0.38 /17	0.31	1.61
GEI	MFS Limited Maturity I	MQLIX	**B-**	(800) 225-2606	**C- / 3.9**	0.84	0.54	0.64 /52	0.74 /38	1.35 /24	1.31	0.61
GEI	MFS Limited Maturity Initial		**B**	(800) 225-2606	**C- / 4.2**	0.89	0.79	0.88 /57	0.86 /40	1.07 /21	1.36	0.44
GEI	MFS Limited Maturity R1	MQLGX	**C-**	(800) 225-2606	**D / 1.6**	0.59	0.20	-0.36 /27	-0.26 /13	0.37 /16	0.31	1.61
GEI	MFS Limited Maturity R2	MLMRX	**C+**	(800) 225-2606	**C- / 3.0**	0.74	0.34	0.08 /40	0.29 /30	0.95 /20	0.91	1.11
GEI	MFS Limited Maturity R3	MQLHX	**C+**	(800) 225-2606	**C- / 3.6**	0.78	0.58	0.56 /51	0.55 /34	1.16 /22	1.06	0.86
GEI	MFS Limited Maturity R4	MQLJX	**B-**	(800) 225-2606	**C- / 4.0**	1.01	0.70	0.65 /52	0.74 /38	1.38 /24	1.31	0.61
COI	MFS Limited Maturity R5	MQLKX	**B-**	(800) 225-2606	**C- / 4.0**	0.86	0.57	0.56 /51	0.77 /38	--	1.39	0.52
MUS	MFS MA Municipal Bond A	MFSSX	**C**	(800) 225-2606	**B / 7.9**	1.65	3.08	3.77 /92	2.88 /87	5.58 /89	3.27	0.86
MUS	MFS MA Municipal Bond B	MBMAX	**C+**	(800) 225-2606	**B / 8.2**	1.46	2.68	2.97 /85	2.09 /78	4.77 /83	2.64	1.61
MUS	MFS MD Municipal Bond A	MFSMX	**C**	(800) 225-2606	**B- / 7.0**	1.46	2.80	3.08 /86	2.39 /82	4.93 /85	3.23	0.97
MUS	MFS MD Municipal Bond B	MBMDX	**C+**	(800) 225-2606	**B / 7.6**	1.28	2.32	2.31 /79	1.60 /70	4.13 /79	2.63	1.72

• Denotes fund is closed to new investors
* Denotes fund is included in Section II

RISK			NET ASSETS		ASSET							FUND MANAGER		MINIMUM		LOADS	
Risk Rating/Pts	3 Yr Avg Standard Deviation	Avg Duration	NAV As of 3/31/16	Total $(Mil)	Cash %	Gov. Bond %	Muni. Bond %	Corp. Bond %	Other %	Portfolio Turnover Ratio	Avg Coupon Rate	Manager Quality Pct	Manager Tenure (Years)	Initial Purch. $	Additional Purch. $	Front End Load	Back End Load
E+ / 0.9	6.6	N/A	8.67	13	9	30	0	20	41	39	0.0	49	5	0	0	0.0	0.0
E+ / 0.9	6.6	N/A	8.43	N/A	9	30	0	20	41	39	0.0	20	5	0	0	0.0	0.0
E+ / 0.9	6.6	N/A	8.56	N/A	9	30	0	20	41	39	0.0	32	5	0	0	0.0	0.0
E+ / 0.9	6.6	N/A	8.60	1	9	30	0	20	41	39	0.0	40	5	0	0	0.0	0.0
E+ / 0.9	6.6	N/A	8.67	N/A	9	30	0	20	41	39	0.0	49	5	0	0	0.0	0.0
B / 7.7	2.6	4.8	10.18	728	0	45	0	1	54	67	3.3	51	10	1,000	0	4.3	0.0
B / 7.7	2.6	4.8	10.17	23	0	45	0	1	54	67	3.3	27	10	1,000	0	0.0	0.0
B / 7.7	2.6	4.8	10.20	49	0	45	0	1	54	67	3.3	27	10	1,000	0	0.0	0.0
B / 7.7	2.6	4.8	10.17	46	0	45	0	1	54	67	3.3	60	10	0	0	0.0	0.0
B / 7.7	2.6	4.8	10.17	5	0	45	0	1	54	67	3.3	27	10	0	0	0.0	0.0
B / 7.7	2.6	4.8	10.17	123	0	45	0	1	54	67	3.3	42	10	0	0	0.0	0.0
B / 7.7	2.6	4.8	10.18	112	0	45	0	1	54	67	3.3	51	10	0	0	0.0	0.0
B / 7.7	2.6	4.8	10.18	85	0	45	0	1	54	67	3.3	60	10	0	0	0.0	0.0
B / 7.7	2.6	4.8	10.17	1,031	0	45	0	1	54	67	3.3	83	10	0	0	0.0	0.0
D / 1.7	5.4	4.3	3.20	3	3	0	0	93	4	43	6.4	61	10	250	0	0.0	0.0
D / 1.6	5.5	4.3	3.20	N/A	3	0	0	93	4	43	6.4	33	10	250	0	0.0	0.0
D / 1.6	5.5	4.3	3.21	1	3	0	0	93	4	43	6.4	33	10	250	0	0.0	0.0
D / 1.7	5.4	4.3	3.20	424	3	0	0	93	4	43	6.4	62	10	1,000	50	0.0	0.0
D / 1.6	5.5	4.3	3.21	21	3	0	0	93	4	43	6.4	35	10	1,000	50	0.0	0.0
D / 1.7	5.4	4.3	3.21	61	3	0	0	93	4	43	6.4	33	10	1,000	50	0.0	0.0
D / 1.7	5.5	4.3	3.20	53	3	0	0	93	4	43	6.4	75	10	0	0	0.0	0.0
D / 1.6	5.5	4.3	3.20	1	3	0	0	93	4	43	6.4	32	10	0	0	0.0	0.0
D / 1.7	5.4	4.3	3.20	14	3	0	0	93	4	43	6.4	52	10	0	0	0.0	0.0
D / 1.8	5.4	4.3	3.20	7	3	0	0	93	4	43	6.4	62	10	0	0	0.0	0.0
D / 1.8	5.4	4.3	3.20	N/A	3	0	0	93	4	43	6.4	76	10	0	0	0.0	0.0
D / 1.8	5.4	4.3	3.20	797	3	0	0	93	4	43	6.4	78	10	0	0	0.0	0.0
D+ / 2.4	5.3	5.2	10.48	51	1	98	0	0	1	26	1.1	4	13	1,000	0	4.3	0.0
D+ / 2.4	5.3	5.2	10.43	12	1	98	0	0	1	26	1.1	3	13	1,000	0	0.0	0.0
D+ / 2.5	5.3	5.2	10.44	13	1	98	0	0	1	26	1.1	3	13	1,000	0	0.0	0.0
D+ / 2.4	5.3	5.2	10.49	8	1	98	0	0	1	26	1.1	5	13	0	0	0.0	0.0
D+ / 2.4	5.3	5.2	10.42	N/A	1	98	0	0	1	26	1.1	3	13	0	0	0.0	0.0
D+ / 2.4	5.3	5.2	10.46	2	1	98	0	0	1	26	1.1	4	13	0	0	0.0	0.0
D+ / 2.4	5.3	5.2	10.47	2	1	98	0	0	1	26	1.1	4	13	0	0	0.0	0.0
D+ / 2.5	5.3	5.2	10.48	N/A	1	98	0	0	1	26	1.1	5	13	0	0	0.0	0.0
D+ / 2.4	5.3	5.2	10.51	1,139	1	98	0	0	1	26	1.1	3	13	0	0	0.0	0.0
A / 9.5	0.8	1.4	5.99	52	3	8	0	73	16	37	2.0	64	18	250	0	2.5	0.0
A+ / 9.6	0.8	1.4	5.97	2	3	8	0	73	16	37	2.0	36	18	250	0	0.0	0.0
A / 9.5	0.8	1.4	5.99	27	3	8	0	73	16	37	2.0	33	18	250	0	0.0	0.0
A+ / 9.6	0.8	1.4	5.99	469	3	8	0	73	16	37	2.0	70	18	1,000	50	2.5	0.0
A / 9.5	0.8	1.4	5.97	6	3	8	0	73	16	37	2.0	36	18	1,000	50	0.0	0.0
A+ / 9.6	0.7	1.4	5.98	120	3	8	0	73	16	37	2.0	34	18	1,000	50	0.0	0.0
A+ / 9.6	0.8	1.4	5.96	220	3	8	0	73	16	37	2.0	75	18	0	0	0.0	0.0
A+ / 9.7	0.7	1.4	10.23	504	0	5	0	76	19	24	2.2	80	4	0	0	0.0	0.0
A / 9.5	0.8	1.4	5.97	1	3	8	0	73	16	37	2.0	34	18	0	0	0.0	0.0
A+ / 9.6	0.7	1.4	5.98	4	3	8	0	73	16	37	2.0	54	18	0	0	0.0	0.0
A / 9.5	0.8	1.4	5.99	3	3	8	0	73	16	37	2.0	62	18	0	0	0.0	0.0
A / 9.5	0.8	1.4	5.99	7	3	8	0	73	16	37	2.0	75	18	0	0	0.0	0.0
A+ / 9.6	0.8	1.4	5.97	510	3	8	0	73	16	37	2.0	79	18	0	0	0.0	0.0
C- / 3.4	4.3	5.7	11.43	225	0	0	99	0	1	13	5.0	17	17	1,000	50	4.3	0.0
C- / 3.4	4.3	5.7	11.45	3	0	0	99	0	1	13	5.0	9	17	1,000	50	0.0	0.0
C / 4.3	3.8	5.5	11.09	82	0	0	99	0	1	18	5.6	19	17	1,000	50	4.3	0.0
C / 4.3	3.8	5.5	11.08	2	0	0	99	0	1	18	5.6	10	17	1,000	50	0.0	0.0

99 Pct = Best
0 Pct = Worst

Fund Type	Fund Name	Ticker Symbol	Overall Investment Rating	Phone	PERFORMANCE Performance Rating/Pts	Total Return % through 3/31/16 3 Mo	6 Mo	1Yr / Pct	Annualized 3Yr / Pct	5Yr / Pct	Incl. in Returns Dividend Yield	Expense Ratio
MUS	MFS MS Municipal Bond A	MISSX	C+	(800) 225-2606	B / 7.9	1.53	3.13	3.59 /91	2.92 /87	5.22 /87	3.25	0.96
MUS	MFS MS Municipal Bond B	MBMSX	B-	(800) 225-2606	B+ / 8.3	1.36	2.78	2.90 /84	2.22 /79	4.50 /81	2.73	1.71
* MUH	MFS Municipal High Income A	MMHYX	C+	(800) 225-2606	A+ / 9.6	2.50	4.75	5.72 /99	4.79 /98	8.16 /98	3.98	0.72
MUH	MFS Municipal High Income B	MMHBX	C+	(800) 225-2606	A+ / 9.7	2.30	4.34	5.03 /98	3.98 /96	7.31 /97	3.39	1.72
MUH	MFS Municipal High Income C	MMHCX	C+	(800) 225-2606	A+ / 9.6	2.25	4.23	4.67 /97	3.75 /94	7.08 /97	3.18	1.72
MUH	MFS Municipal High Income I	MMIIX	C+	(800) 225-2606	A+ / 9.9	2.50	4.75	5.72 /99	4.78 /98	8.15 /98	4.16	0.72
* MUN	MFS Municipal Income A	MFIAX	C+	(800) 225-2606	B+ / 8.5	1.82	3.45	4.09 /94	3.46 /92	6.33 /94	3.37	0.80
MUN	MFS Municipal Income A1	MMIDX	B-	(800) 225-2606	B+ / 8.8	1.88	3.69	4.46 /96	3.71 /94	6.59 /95	3.60	0.55
MUN	MFS Municipal Income B	MMIBX	B-	(800) 225-2606	B+ / 8.8	1.52	3.06	3.31 /88	2.68 /85	5.53 /89	2.78	1.55
MUN	MFS Municipal Income B1	MMIGX	B	(800) 225-2606	A- / 9.0	1.57	3.18	3.55 /90	2.92 /87	5.78 /91	3.00	1.55
MUN	MFS Municipal Income C	MMICX	B-	(800) 225-2606	B+ / 8.8	1.63	3.05	3.30 /88	2.67 /85	5.51 /89	2.77	1.55
MUN	MFS Municipal Income I	MIMIX	B+	(800) 225-2606	A / 9.5	1.89	3.58	4.35 /96	3.71 /94	6.56 /95	3.77	0.55
* MUN	MFS Municipal Lmtd Maturity A	MTLFX	B+	(800) 225-2606	C+ / 5.6	0.96	1.54	2.09 /78	1.51 /68	2.70 /64	1.65	0.80
MUN ●	MFS Municipal Lmtd Maturity B	MTLBX	B+	(800) 225-2606	C / 5.4	0.90	1.29	1.46 /73	0.80 /47	1.96 /45	0.95	1.55
MUN	MFS Municipal Lmtd Maturity C	MTLCX	B	(800) 225-2606	C / 5.0	0.87	1.23	1.35 /72	0.65 /43	1.85 /43	0.85	1.55
MUN	MFS Municipal Lmtd Maturity I	MTLIX	A+	(800) 225-2606	B / 7.6	1.12	1.74	2.37 /80	1.70 /72	2.85 /66	1.84	0.55
MUS	MFS NC Municipal Bond A	MSNCX	C+	(800) 225-2606	B- / 7.5	1.49	2.94	3.47 /90	2.57 /83	5.17 /87	3.16	0.86
MUS	MFS NC Municipal Bond B	MBNCX	C+	(800) 225-2606	B / 7.9	1.31	2.48	2.71 /82	1.78 /74	4.37 /80	2.57	1.61
MUS	MFS NC Municipal Bond C	MCNCX	C+	(800) 225-2606	B / 7.9	1.30	2.56	2.70 /82	1.80 /74	4.39 /81	2.56	1.61
MUS	MFS NY Municipal Bond A	MSNYX	C+	(800) 225-2606	B / 8.1	1.73	3.43	4.04 /94	3.05 /88	5.56 /89	3.24	0.88
MUS	MFS NY Municipal Bond B	MBNYX	C+	(800) 225-2606	B+ / 8.4	1.55	3.05	3.28 /88	2.29 /80	4.79 /84	2.66	1.63
MUS	MFS NY Municipal Bond C	MCNYX	C+	(800) 225-2606	B+ / 8.5	1.64	3.05	3.36 /89	2.31 /80	4.78 /83	2.65	1.63
MUS	MFS PA Municipal Bond A	MFPAX	C+	(800) 225-2606	B / 8.2	1.73	3.42	4.15 /95	3.15 /90	5.74 /91	3.31	0.95
MUS	MFS PA Municipal Bond B	MBPAX	C+	(800) 225-2606	B+ / 8.5	1.44	3.02	3.26 /88	2.36 /81	4.93 /85	2.70	1.70
MUS	MFS SC Municipal Bond A	MFSCX	C	(800) 225-2606	B- / 7.3	1.56	3.00	3.51 /90	2.46 /82	4.87 /84	2.81	0.90
MUS	MFS SC Municipal Bond B	MBSCX	C+	(800) 225-2606	B / 7.8	1.38	2.63	2.74 /82	1.68 /72	4.09 /78	2.20	1.65
GES	MFS Strategic Income A	MFIOX	C-	(800) 225-2606	C / 5.5	3.01	2.20	-0.68 /24	1.54 /53	3.56 /54	3.65	1.11
GES	MFS Strategic Income B	MIOBX	D+	(800) 225-2606	C- / 4.2	2.83	1.82	-1.30 /20	0.86 /40	2.84 /43	3.05	1.86
GES	MFS Strategic Income C	MIOCX	D+	(800) 225-2606	C- / 4.2	2.84	1.82	-1.31 /19	0.86 /40	2.87 /43	3.05	1.86
GES	MFS Strategic Income I	MFIIX	C-	(800) 225-2606	C+ / 6.1	3.24	2.33	-0.28 /28	1.84 /58	3.85 /59	4.06	0.86
MUS	MFS TN Municipal Bond A	MSTNX	C-	(800) 225-2606	C+ / 6.9	1.59	3.05	3.31 /88	2.30 /80	4.84 /84	2.82	0.94
MUS	MFS TN Municipal Bond B	MBTNX	C	(800) 225-2606	B / 7.6	1.41	2.68	2.55 /81	1.54 /69	4.04 /78	2.21	1.69
GEI	MFS Total Return Bond 529A	EARBX	B	(800) 225-2606	C+ / 6.7	2.91	2.21	0.66 /53	2.24 /66	3.85 /59	2.73	0.98
GEI	MFS Total Return Bond 529B	EBRBX	C	(800) 225-2606	C / 5.2	2.68	1.78	-0.19 /29	1.38 /50	2.97 /45	1.99	1.73
GEI	MFS Total Return Bond 529C	ECRBX	C	(800) 225-2606	C / 5.2	2.78	1.78	-0.19 /29	1.38 /50	2.97 /45	1.99	1.73
* GEI	MFS Total Return Bond A	MRBFX	B	(800) 225-2606	C+ / 6.9	3.01	2.33	0.80 /55	2.29 /67	3.90 /60	2.76	0.88
GEI	MFS Total Return Bond B	MRBBX	C+	(800) 225-2606	C / 5.5	2.72	1.85	-0.04 /31	1.53 /53	3.13 /47	2.14	1.63
GEI	MFS Total Return Bond C	MRBCX	C+	(800) 225-2606	C / 5.3	2.70	1.80	-0.14 /30	1.43 /51	3.03 /46	2.04	1.63
GEI	MFS Total Return Bond I	MRBIX	B+	(800) 225-2606	B- / 7.1	3.05	2.31	0.86 /56	2.45 /70	4.06 /62	3.04	0.63
GEI	MFS Total Return Bond R1	MRBGX	C	(800) 225-2606	C / 5.3	2.70	1.80	-0.14 /30	1.40 /50	3.01 /45	2.04	1.63
GEI	MFS Total Return Bond R2	MRRRX	C+	(800) 225-2606	C+ / 6.2	2.83	2.05	0.35 /47	1.94 /60	3.54 /54	2.54	1.13
GEI	MFS Total Return Bond R3	MRBHX	B	(800) 225-2606	C+ / 6.6	2.89	2.18	0.60 /51	2.16 /65	3.78 /58	2.79	0.88
GEI	MFS Total Return Bond R4	MRBJX	B+	(800) 225-2606	B- / 7.1	3.05	2.31	0.95 /58	2.45 /70	4.06 /62	3.04	0.63
GEI	MFS Total Return Bond R5	MRBKX	B+	(800) 225-2606	B- / 7.3	3.08	2.37	0.97 /58	2.55 /71	4.11 /63	3.14	0.53
MUS	MFS VA Municipal Bond A	MSVAX	C+	(800) 225-2606	B / 8.0	1.74	3.22	3.94 /94	2.89 /87	5.12 /86	3.09	0.88
MUS	MFS VA Municipal Bond B	MBVAX	C+	(800) 225-2606	B+ / 8.3	1.56	2.84	3.09 /86	2.13 /78	4.34 /80	2.49	1.63
MUS	MFS VA Municipal Bond C	MVACX	C+	(800) 225-2606	B+ / 8.3	1.55	2.83	3.17 /87	2.16 /79	4.33 /80	2.49	1.63
MUS	MFS WV Municipal Bond A	MFWVX	C+	(800) 225-2606	B- / 7.4	1.48	2.91	3.23 /87	2.54 /83	4.79 /84	2.93	0.93
MUS	MFS WV Municipal Bond B	MBWVX	C+	(800) 225-2606	B / 7.9	1.38	2.62	2.55 /81	1.81 /74	4.01 /78	2.32	1.68
MTG	Mgd Acct Srs BlackRock US Mtg Inst	MSUMX	A+	(800) 441-7762	B / 7.9	1.75	1.67	2.09 /72	3.28 /78	4.59 /68	2.56	0.59
MTG	Mgd Acct Srs BlackRock US Mtg Inv	BMPAX	B-	(800) 441-7762	C+ / 6.0	1.68	1.52	1.69 /69	2.97 /76	4.25 /65	2.18	0.89
MTG	Mgd Acct Srs BlackRock US Mtg Inv	BMPCX	B	(800) 441-7762	C+ / 6.4	1.50	1.15	0.94 /57	2.21 /66	3.48 /53	1.53	1.63

● Denotes fund is closed to new investors
* Denotes fund is included in Section II

RISK			NET ASSETS		ASSET							FUND MANAGER		MINIMUM		LOADS	
Risk Rating/Pts	3 Yr Avg Standard Deviation	Avg Duration	NAV As of 3/31/16	Total $(Mil)	Cash %	Gov. Bond %	Muni. Bond %	Corp. Bond %	Other %	Portfolio Turnover Ratio	Avg Coupon Rate	Manager Quality Pct	Manager Tenure (Years)	Initial Purch. $	Additional Purch. $	Front End Load	Back End Load
C / 4.3	3.8	5.6	10.02	88	0	0	99	0	1	16	5.2	28	17	1,000	50	4.3	0.0
C- / 4.2	3.8	5.6	10.03	2	0	0	99	0	1	16	5.2	15	17	1,000	50	0.0	0.0
D / 1.8	5.1	7.6	8.31	2,014	3	0	96	0	1	12	5.4	48	14	1,000	50	4.3	0.0
D / 1.9	5.1	7.6	8.32	31	3	0	96	0	1	12	5.4	26	14	1,000	50	0.0	0.0
D / 1.9	5.1	7.6	8.32	280	3	0	96	0	1	12	5.4	20	14	1,000	50	0.0	0.0
D / 1.8	5.1	7.6	8.30	1,388	3	0	96	0	1	12	5.4	48	14	0	0	0.0	0.0
C- / 3.8	4.1	6.4	8.89	865	0	0	99	0	1	17	5.2	34	18	1,000	50	4.3	0.0
C- / 3.8	4.1	6.4	8.90	551	0	0	99	0	1	17	5.2	40	18	1,000	50	4.3	0.0
C- / 3.8	4.1	6.4	8.90	28	0	0	99	0	1	17	5.2	16	18	1,000	50	0.0	0.0
C- / 3.7	4.1	6.4	8.90	N/A	0	0	99	0	1	17	5.2	20	18	1,000	50	0.0	0.0
C- / 3.7	4.1	6.4	8.92	180	0	0	99	0	1	17	5.2	16	18	1,000	50	0.0	0.0
C- / 3.8	4.1	6.4	8.88	472	0	0	99	0	1	17	5.2	41	18	0	0	0.0	0.0
B+ / 8.6	1.8	3.2	8.21	697	1	0	98	0	1	15	4.5	51	18	1,000	50	2.5	0.0
B+ / 8.7	1.8	3.2	8.21	2	1	0	98	0	1	15	4.5	28	18	1,000	50	0.0	0.0
B+ / 8.7	1.8	3.2	8.22	138	1	0	98	0	1	15	4.5	24	18	1,000	50	0.0	0.0
B+ / 8.7	1.8	3.2	8.21	646	1	0	98	0	1	15	4.5	59	18	0	0	0.0	0.0
C- / 4.0	3.9	5.5	12.01	289	0	0	99	0	1	16	5.2	18	17	1,000	50	4.3	0.0
C- / 4.0	4.0	5.5	11.99	4	0	0	99	0	1	16	5.2	10	17	1,000	50	0.0	0.0
C- / 4.0	4.0	5.5	12.00	57	0	0	99	0	1	16	5.2	10	17	1,000	50	0.0	0.0
C- / 3.3	4.4	6.0	11.31	169	1	0	98	0	1	25	5.3	18	17	1,000	50	4.3	0.0
C- / 3.4	4.4	6.0	11.28	5	1	0	98	0	1	25	5.3	11	17	1,000	50	0.0	0.0
C- / 3.3	4.4	6.0	11.30	27	1	0	98	0	1	25	5.3	10	17	1,000	50	0.0	0.0
C- / 3.6	4.2	6.5	10.50	116	1	0	98	0	1	23	5.2	24	17	1,000	50	4.3	0.0
C- / 3.5	4.3	6.5	10.52	6	1	0	98	0	1	23	5.2	12	17	1,000	50	0.0	0.0
C- / 3.6	4.2	5.6	12.35	176	0	0	99	0	1	22	5.2	13	17	1,000	50	4.3	0.0
C- / 3.7	4.2	5.6	12.34	4	0	0	99	0	1	22	5.2	8	17	1,000	50	0.0	0.0
C / 4.6	3.7	5.2	6.36	210	42	5	0	48	5	29	5.0	46	11	1,000	0	0.0	0.0
C / 4.6	3.7	5.2	6.32	25	42	5	0	48	5	29	5.0	25	11	1,000	0	0.0	0.0
C / 4.6	3.6	5.2	6.30	41	42	5	0	48	5	29	5.0	25	11	1,000	0	0.0	0.0
C / 4.7	3.6	5.2	6.36	16	42	5	0	48	5	29	5.0	58	11	0	0	0.0	0.0
C- / 3.6	4.2	5.7	10.70	106	0	0	99	0	1	18	5.1	11	17	1,000	50	4.3	0.0
C- / 3.7	4.2	5.7	10.69	2	0	0	99	0	1	18	5.1	8	17	1,000	50	0.0	0.0
C+ / 6.7	3.0	5.3	10.72	6	3	19	0	42	36	72	3.9	57	10	250	0	0.0	0.0
C+ / 6.6	3.0	5.3	10.75	N/A	3	19	0	42	36	72	3.9	29	10	250	0	0.0	0.0
C+ / 6.4	3.0	5.3	10.75	3	3	19	0	42	36	72	3.9	28	10	250	0	0.0	0.0
C+ / 6.7	3.0	5.3	10.74	1,767	3	19	0	42	36	72	3.9	59	10	1,000	50	0.0	0.0
C+ / 6.5	3.0	5.3	10.75	29	3	19	0	42	36	72	3.9	32	10	1,000	50	0.0	0.0
C+ / 6.6	3.0	5.3	10.75	148	3	19	0	42	36	72	3.9	30	10	1,000	50	0.0	0.0
C+ / 6.6	3.0	5.3	10.74	1,065	3	19	0	42	36	72	3.9	69	10	0	0	0.0	0.0
C+ / 6.6	3.0	5.3	10.75	4	3	19	0	42	36	72	3.9	29	10	0	0	0.0	0.0
C+ / 6.6	3.0	5.3	10.73	48	3	19	0	42	36	72	3.9	45	10	0	0	0.0	0.0
C+ / 6.7	3.0	5.3	10.73	87	3	19	0	42	36	72	3.9	54	10	0	0	0.0	0.0
C+ / 6.6	3.0	5.3	10.74	114	3	19	0	42	36	72	3.9	68	10	0	0	0.0	0.0
C+ / 6.5	3.0	5.3	10.74	1,398	3	19	0	42	36	72	3.9	73	10	0	0	0.0	0.0
C- / 3.8	4.1	5.9	11.51	251	0	0	99	0	1	20	5.2	21	17	1,000	50	4.3	0.0
C- / 3.9	4.0	5.9	11.50	2	0	0	99	0	1	20	5.2	12	17	1,000	50	0.0	0.0
C- / 3.8	4.1	5.9	11.51	25	0	0	99	0	1	20	5.2	11	17	1,000	50	0.0	0.0
C- / 4.2	3.9	5.5	11.37	121	0	0	99	0	1	22	5.1	19	17	1,000	50	4.3	0.0
C- / 4.1	3.9	5.5	11.37	1	0	0	99	0	1	22	5.1	11	17	1,000	50	0.0	0.0
B- / 7.4	2.7	0.9	10.43	201	0	1	0	0	99	1,710	4.9	80	7	2,000,000	0	0.0	0.0
B- / 7.4	2.8	0.9	10.41	81	0	1	0	0	99	1,710	4.9	70	7	1,000	50	4.0	0.0
B- / 7.3	2.8	0.9	10.41	21	0	1	0	0	99	1,710	4.9	37	7	1,000	50	0.0	0.0

99 Pct = Best 0 Pct = Worst Fund Type	Fund Name	Ticker Symbol	Overall Investment Rating	Phone	PERFORMANCE Performance Rating/Pts	Total Return % through 3/31/16 3 Mo	6 Mo	1Yr / Pct	Annualized 3Yr / Pct	5Yr / Pct	Incl. in Returns Dividend Yield	Expense Ratio
COI	Miller Intermediate Bond A	MIFAX	**U**	(877) 441-4434	**U /**	0.87	1.67	-0.45 /26	--	--	1.22	2.05
COI	Miller Intermediate Bond C	MIFCX	**U**	(877) 441-4434	**U /**	0.69	1.34	-0.79 /23	--	--	0.36	2.80
COI	Miller Intermediate Bond I	MIFIX	**U**	(877) 441-4434	**U /**	1.00	1.87	-0.23 /29	--	--	1.46	1.80
GL	Mirae Global Dynamic Bond A	MAGDX	**D+**	(888) 335-3417	**C- / 3.6**	2.92	2.63	0.48 /49	1.52 /53	--	1.75	5.20
GL	Mirae Global Dynamic Bond C	MCGDX	**D+**	(888) 335-3417	**C / 4.4**	2.79	2.39	-0.18 /29	0.79 /39	--	1.18	5.68
GL	Mirae Global Dynamic Bond I	MDBIX	**C-**	(888) 335-3417	**C+ / 6.2**	2.96	2.75	0.71 /53	1.76 /57	--	2.06	2.03
GEL	MO 529 MOST CSP Direct Vngd Csv		**C+**	(800) 662-7447	**C / 4.9**	2.22	1.85	1.35 /64	1.02 /43	2.55 /38	0.00	0.55
COI	MO 529 MOST CSP Direct Vngd		**B**	(800) 662-7447	**B / 8.1**	2.70	3.29	0.95 /58	3.55 /80	4.58 /68	0.00	0.55
GES	Morgan Stanley Gl Fxd Inc Opps A	DINAX	**D-**	(800) 869-6397	**D / 1.7**	0.55	-0.45	-3.54 / 9	1.72 /56	4.50 /68	3.22	1.04
GES ●	Morgan Stanley Gl Fxd Inc Opps B	DINBX	**D**	(800) 869-6397	**D+ / 2.8**	0.38	-0.78	-4.34 / 7	0.92 /41	3.73 /57	2.65	1.88
GEI	Morgan Stanley Gl Fxd Inc Opps C	MSIPX	**U**	(800) 869-6397	**U /**	0.21	-0.92	--	--	--	0.00	1.74
GES	Morgan Stanley Gl Fxd Inc Opps I	DINDX	**D+**	(800) 869-6397	**C / 4.8**	0.45	-0.44	-3.34 /10	2.03 /62	4.80 /70	3.69	0.70
GEI	Morgan Stanley Gl Fxd Inc Opps IS	MGFOX	**U**	(800) 869-6397	**U /**	0.46	-0.42	-3.29 /10	--	--	3.73	0.64
GES ●	Morgan Stanley Gl Fxd Inc Opps L	DINCX	**D**	(800) 869-6397	**C- / 3.6**	0.31	-0.74	-3.93 / 8	1.41 /50	4.07 /63	3.13	1.26
MM	Morgan Stanley Liquid Asset	DWLXX	**U**	(800) 869-6397	**U /**	0.01	0.01	0.02 /35	0.01 /18	0.01 / 6	0.02	0.45
USS	Morgan Stanley Mortgage Sec Tr A	MTGAX	**B**	(800) 869-6397	**C+ / 5.9**	0.72	0.63	0.94 /58	3.23 /78	4.96 /71	5.04	1.58
USS ●	Morgan Stanley Mortgage Sec Tr B	MTGBX	**A-**	(800) 869-6397	**C+ / 6.6**	0.57	0.30	0.27 /45	2.62 /72	4.35 /66	4.68	2.61
MTG	Morgan Stanley Mortgage Sec Tr C	MSMTX	**U**	(800) 869-6397	**U /**	0.65	0.38	--	--	--	0.00	15.92
USS	Morgan Stanley Mortgage Sec Tr I	MTGDX	**A+**	(800) 869-6397	**B / 7.9**	0.94	0.80	1.38 /64	3.63 /81	5.34 /74	5.66	1.35
USS ●	Morgan Stanley Mortgage Sec Tr L	MTGCX	**A**	(800) 869-6397	**B- / 7.2**	0.66	0.49	0.65 /52	2.96 /76	4.59 /68	5.01	1.81
MMT	Morgan Stanley T/F Daily Inc MM	DSTXX	**U**	(800) 869-6397	**U /**	--	--	--	--	--	0.01	0.54
USS	Morgan Stanley US Govt Sec Tr A	USGAX	**C+**	(800) 869-6397	**C / 4.3**	2.29	1.89	1.52 /67	1.89 /59	3.33 /50	2.30	0.99
USS ●	Morgan Stanley US Govt Sec Tr B	USGBX	**A-**	(800) 869-6397	**C+ / 6.4**	2.41	2.02	1.66 /68	1.91 /60	3.34 /51	2.42	0.96
USL	Morgan Stanley US Govt Sec Tr C	MSGVX	**U**	(800) 869-6397	**U /**	2.09	1.51	--	--	--	0.00	N/A
USS	Morgan Stanley US Govt Sec Tr I	USGDX	**A**	(800) 869-6397	**C+ / 6.8**	2.38	2.08	1.90 /71	2.17 /65	3.58 /54	2.77	0.77
USS ●	Morgan Stanley US Govt Sec Tr L	USGCX	**B+**	(800) 869-6397	**C+ / 5.8**	2.33	1.87	1.27 /63	1.58 /54	2.92 /44	2.15	1.22
GEI	MSIF Corporate Bond A	MIGAX	**C-**	(800) 354-8185	**B+ / 8.7**	8.87	8.27	4.16 /82	4.45 /87	6.05 /77	2.43	1.88
COI	MSIF Corporate Bond C	MSBOX	**U**	(800) 354-8185	**U /**	8.60	7.79	--	--	--	0.00	38.20
GEI	MSIF Corporate Bond I	MPFDX	**C**	(800) 354-8185	**A / 9.4**	8.88	8.38	4.43 /84	4.75 /89	6.29 /78	2.87	1.15
GEI ●	MSIF Corporate Bond L	MGILX	**C**	(800) 354-8185	**A- / 9.2**	8.78	8.12	3.87 /81	4.16 /85	5.71 /75	2.27	1.73
EM	MSIF EM Fixed Income Oppty A	MEAPX	**E+**	(800) 354-8185	**D+ / 2.6**	7.04	8.26	2.53 /75	0.16 /28	--	5.25	2.85
EM	MSIF EM Fixed Income Oppty C	MSEDX	**U**	(800) 354-8185	**U /**	6.93	7.91	--	--	--	0.00	4.60
EM	MSIF EM Fixed Income Oppty I	MEAIX	**D**	(800) 354-8185	**C / 5.4**	7.15	8.50	2.95 /76	0.52 /33	--	5.78	1.91
EM	MSIF EM Fixed Income Oppty IS	MRDPX	**U**	(800) 354-8185	**U /**	7.15	8.38	2.96 /76	--	--	5.79	21.21
EM ●	MSIF EM Fixed Income Oppty L	MEALX	**D-**	(800) 354-8185	**C- / 4.2**	7.05	8.21	2.35 /74	-0.09 /15	--	5.31	4.10
COH	MSIF High Yield A	MSYPX	**D-**	(800) 354-8185	**C- / 3.5**	1.77	-1.67	-3.43 /10	2.49 /71	--	6.60	1.53
COH	MSIF High Yield C	MSHDX	**U**	(800) 354-8185	**U /**	1.54	-2.03	--	--	--	0.00	2.15
COH	MSIF High Yield I	MSYIX	**D+**	(800) 354-8185	**C+ / 6.2**	1.83	-1.49	-3.06 /11	2.84 /75	--	7.29	1.17
COH	MSIF High Yield IS	MSHYX	**U**	(800) 354-8185	**U /**	1.83	-1.47	-3.13 /11	--	--	7.32	1.57
COH ●	MSIF High Yield L	MSYLX	**D**	(800) 354-8185	**C / 5.0**	1.62	-1.79	-3.65 / 9	2.22 /66	--	6.65	1.84
COI	MSIF Short Duration Income A	MLDAX	**C+**	(800) 354-8185	**C- / 4.2**	3.18	2.98	2.44 /74	1.49 /52	1.76 /28	1.30	1.12
COI ●	MSIF Short Duration Income C	MSLDX	**U**	(800) 354-8185	**U /**	2.92	2.49	--	--	--	0.00	6.63
GES	MSIF Short Duration Income I	MPLDX	**A**	(800) 354-8185	**C+ / 6.7**	3.22	3.00	2.77 /76	1.79 /57	2.00 /31	1.67	0.53
COI ●	MSIF Short Duration Income L	MSJLX	**B+**	(800) 354-8185	**C+ / 5.6**	3.11	2.78	2.07 /72	1.16 /46	--	1.00	1.70
USS	MSIF Trust Core Plus Fix Inc A	MFXAX	**C+**	(800) 354-8185	**B+ / 8.3**	6.63	6.39	4.43 /84	4.14 /85	5.45 /74	3.20	1.07
COI	MSIF Trust Core Plus Fix Inc C	MSCKX	**U**	(800) 354-8185	**U /**	6.34	5.96	--	--	--	0.00	14.06
USS	MSIF Trust Core Plus Fix Inc I	MPFIX	**B-**	(800) 354-8185	**A- / 9.2**	6.65	6.60	4.81 /86	4.46 /87	5.76 /76	3.69	0.73
COI ●	MSIF Trust Core Plus Fix Inc L	MSIOX	**C+**	(800) 354-8185	**B+ / 8.9**	6.43	6.27	4.18 /82	3.89 /83	--	3.11	1.76
MM	MSILF Govt Portfolio Adm	MGOXX	**U**	(800) 354-8185	**U /**	0.02	0.03	0.05 /38	0.04 /24	0.04 /12	0.05	0.36
MM	MSILF Govt Portfolio Adv	MAYXX	**U**	(800) 354-8185	**U /**	--	--	--	--	--	0.03	0.46
MM	MSILF Govt Portfolio Cash Mgmt	MSGXX	**U**	(800) 354-8185	**U /**	0.02	0.03	0.05 /38	0.04 /24	0.04 /12	0.05	0.36
MM	MSILF Govt Portfolio Inst	MVRXX	**C**	(800) 354-8185	**D+ / 2.5**	0.06	0.07	0.09 /41	0.06 /26	0.05 /13	0.09	0.21

● Denotes fund is closed to new investors
* Denotes fund is included in Section II

RISK			NET ASSETS		ASSET							FUND MANAGER		MINIMUM		LOADS	
Risk Rating/Pts	3 Yr Avg Standard Deviation	Avg Duration	NAV As of 3/31/16	Total $(Mil)	Cash %	Gov. Bond %	Muni. Bond %	Corp. Bond %	Other %	Portfolio Turnover Ratio	Avg Coupon Rate	Manager Quality Pct	Manager Tenure (Years)	Initial Purch. $	Additional Purch. $	Front End Load	Back End Load
U /	N/A	N/A	15.29	1	0	0	0	0	100	85	0.0	N/A	2	2,500	100	5.8	0.0
U /	N/A	N/A	15.38	N/A	0	0	0	0	100	85	0.0	N/A	2	2,500	100	0.0	0.0
U /	N/A	N/A	15.30	45	0	0	0	0	100	85	0.0	N/A	2	1,000,000	100	0.0	0.0
C / 4.6	3.6	3.7	10.17	1	15	14	0	69	2	106	0.0	93	4	2,000	100	4.5	0.0
C / 4.5	3.7	3.7	10.14	1	15	14	0	69	2	106	0.0	88	4	2,000	100	0.0	0.0
C / 4.7	3.6	3.7	10.18	11	15	14	0	69	2	106	0.0	95	4	250,000	25,000	0.0	0.0
B / 7.8	2.5	N/A	14.29	185	25	48	1	13	13	0	0.0	28	10	25	25	0.0	0.0
C / 5.1	3.4	N/A	16.00	256	0	42	1	19	38	0	0.0	94	10	25	25	0.0	0.0
D+ / 2.8	4.9	2.2	5.35	97	4	25	0	38	33	102	4.5	41	6	1,000	100	4.3	0.0
D+ / 2.8	5.0	2.2	5.37	1	4	25	0	38	33	102	4.5	18	6	1,000	100	0.0	0.0
U /	N/A	2.2	5.34	18	4	25	0	38	33	102	4.5	N/A	6	1,000	100	0.0	0.0
D+ / 2.9	4.9	2.2	5.40	157	4	25	0	38	33	102	4.5	53	6	5,000,000	0	0.0	0.0
U /	N/A	2.2	5.40	60	4	25	0	38	33	102	4.5	N/A	6	10,000,000	0	0.0	0.0
D+ / 2.8	4.9	2.2	5.34	12	4	25	0	38	33	102	4.5	32	6	1,000	100	0.0	0.0
U /	N/A	N/A	1.00	4,659	100	0	0	0	0	0	0.0	N/A	N/A	5,000	100	0.0	0.0
B / 8.0	2.4	3.6	8.33	56	0	0	0	3	97	299	3.2	96	8	1,000	100	4.3	0.0
B / 8.0	2.4	3.6	8.15	N/A	0	0	0	3	97	299	3.2	94	8	1,000	100	0.0	0.0
U /	N/A	3.6	8.27	1	0	0	0	3	97	299	3.2	N/A	8	1,000	100	0.0	0.0
B / 8.0	2.4	3.6	8.19	39	0	0	0	3	97	299	3.2	97	8	5,000,000	0	0.0	0.0
B / 8.0	2.4	3.6	8.26	2	0	0	0	3	97	299	3.2	96	8	1,000	100	0.0	0.0
U /	N/A	N/A	1.00	1,373	100	0	0	0	0	0	0.0	N/A	N/A	5,000	100	0.0	0.0
B / 8.1	2.3	4.6	8.85	51	0	32	9	3	56	317	3.4	81	5	1,000	100	4.3	0.0
B / 8.1	2.3	4.6	8.85	420	0	32	9	3	56	317	3.4	81	5	1,000	100	0.0	0.0
U /	N/A	4.6	8.92	N/A	0	32	9	3	56	317	3.4	N/A	5	1,000	100	0.0	0.0
B / 8.0	2.4	4.6	8.85	87	0	32	9	3	56	317	3.4	85	5	5,000,000	0	0.0	0.0
B / 8.1	2.3	4.6	8.92	13	0	32	9	3	56	317	3.4	71	5	1,000	100	0.0	0.0
D- / 1.2	6.4	6.6	11.54	1	3	1	0	95	1	45	0.0	90	5	1,000	0	4.3	0.0
U /	N/A	6.6	11.49	N/A	3	1	0	95	1	45	0.0	N/A	5	1,000	0	0.0	0.0
D- / 1.2	6.3	6.6	11.52	31	3	1	0	95	1	45	0.0	92	5	5,000,000	0	0.0	0.0
D- / 1.1	6.4	6.6	11.52	2	3	1	0	95	1	45	0.0	87	5	1,000	0	0.0	0.0
E / 0.4	8.6	5.3	9.12	1	5	56	0	37	2	95	5.5	77	4	1,000	0	4.3	2.0
U /	N/A	5.3	9.10	N/A	5	56	0	37	2	95	5.5	N/A	4	1,000	0	0.0	2.0
E / 0.4	8.6	5.3	9.14	21	5	56	0	37	2	95	5.5	85	4	5,000,000	0	0.0	2.0
U /	N/A	5.3	9.14	1	5	56	0	37	2	95	5.5	N/A	4	10,000,000	0	0.0	2.0
E / 0.4	8.6	5.3	9.11	1	5	56	0	37	2	95	5.5	66	4	1,000	0	0.0	2.0
D- / 1.4	5.6	3.7	9.28	55	0	0	0	98	2	62	0.0	89	4	1,000	0	4.3	0.0
U /	N/A	3.7	9.27	2	0	0	0	98	2	62	0.0	N/A	4	1,000	0	0.0	0.0
D- / 1.4	5.7	3.7	9.29	38	0	0	0	98	2	62	0.0	91	4	5,000,000	0	0.0	0.0
U /	N/A	3.7	9.29	15	0	0	0	98	2	62	0.0	N/A	4	10,000,000	0	0.0	0.0
D- / 1.4	5.6	3.7	9.28	1	0	0	0	98	2	62	0.0	85	4	1,000	0	0.0	0.0
B+ / 8.5	2.0	1.8	7.88	50	1	8	0	75	16	41	0.0	87	5	1,000	0	4.3	0.0
U /	N/A	1.8	7.84	N/A	1	8	0	75	16	41	0.0	N/A	5	1,000	0	0.0	0.0
B+ / 8.5	2.0	1.8	7.86	99	1	8	0	75	16	41	0.0	92	5	5,000,000	0	0.0	0.0
B+ / 8.5	2.0	1.8	7.86	N/A	1	8	0	75	16	41	0.0	82	5	1,000	0	0.0	0.0
C- / 3.3	4.5	5.2	10.61	4	1	17	1	36	45	348	7.7	97	5	1,000	0	4.3	0.0
U /	N/A	5.2	10.56	1	1	17	1	36	45	348	7.7	N/A	5	1,000	0	0.0	0.0
C- / 3.3	4.5	5.2	10.59	168	1	17	1	36	45	348	7.7	98	5	5,000,000	0	0.0	0.0
C- / 3.3	4.5	5.2	10.60	N/A	1	17	1	36	45	348	7.7	93	5	1,000	0	0.0	0.0
U /	N/A	N/A	1.00	5	100	0	0	0	0	0	0.1	N/A	N/A	10,000,000	0	0.0	0.0
U /	N/A	N/A	1.00	830	100	0	0	0	0	0	0.0	N/A	N/A	10,000,000	0	0.0	0.0
U /	N/A	N/A	1.00	105	100	0	0	0	0	0	0.1	N/A	N/A	1,000,000	0	0.0	0.0
A+ / 9.9	N/A	N/A	1.00	34,972	100	0	0	0	0	0	0.1	68	N/A	10,000,000	0	0.0	0.0

99 Pct = Best
0 Pct = Worst

Fund Type	Fund Name	Ticker Symbol	Overall Investment Rating	Phone	PERFORMANCE: Performance Rating/Pts	Total Return % through 3/31/16: 3 Mo	6 Mo	1Yr / Pct	Annualized: 3Yr / Pct	Annualized: 5Yr / Pct	Incl. in Returns: Dividend Yield	Expense Ratio
MM	MSILF Govt Portfolio Inv	MVVXX	**C**	(800) 354-8185	**D+ / 2.3**	0.03	0.04	0.06 /39	0.05 /25	0.04 /12	0.06	0.31
MM	MSILF Govt Portfolio IS	MGSXX	**C**	(800) 354-8185	**D+ / 2.4**	0.04	0.06	0.08 /40	0.05 /25	0.05 /13	0.08	0.26
MM	MSILF Govt Portfolio Part	MPCXX	**U**	(800) 354-8185	**U /**	--	--	--	--	--	0.03	0.71
MM	MSILF Govt Sec Portfolio Adm	MGAXX	**U**	(800) 354-8185	**U /**	--	--	--	--	--	0.01	0.49
MM	MSILF Govt Sec Portfolio Cash Mgmt	MCHXX	**U**	(800) 354-8185	**U /**	--	--	--	--	--	0.01	0.49
MM	MSILF Govt Sec Portfolio Inst	MUIXX	**C**	(800) 354-8185	**D / 2.1**	0.04	0.04	0.05 /39	0.02 /21	0.02 / 9	0.05	0.34
MM	MSILF Govt Sec Portfolio Inv	MVIXX	**U**	(800) 354-8185	**U /**	0.01	0.01	0.02 /35	0.01 /17	0.01 / 6	0.02	0.44
MM	MSILF Govt Sec Portfolio IS	MSVXX	**C-**	(800) 354-8185	**D / 2.0**	0.02	0.03	0.03 /36	0.02 /21	0.01 / 6	0.03	0.39
MM	MSILF Money Mkt Adm	MANXX	**C**	(800) 354-8185	**D+ / 2.4**	0.07	0.09	0.09 /41	0.04 /24	0.03 /10	0.09	0.37
MM	MSILF Money Mkt Adv	MVSXX	**C**	(800) 354-8185	**D / 2.2**	0.04	0.05	0.06 /39	0.03 /23	0.02 / 9	0.06	0.47
MM	MSILF Money Mkt Cshmgt	MSHXX	**C**	(800) 354-8185	**D+ / 2.4**	0.07	0.09	0.09 /41	0.04 /24	0.03 /10	0.09	0.37
MM	MSILF Money Mkt Inst	MPUXX	**C+**	(800) 354-8185	**D+ / 2.7**	0.11	0.16	0.24 /45	0.13 /28	0.14 /15	0.24	0.22
MM	MSILF Money Mkt Inv	MIOXX	**C**	(800) 354-8185	**D+ / 2.5**	0.08	0.11	0.14 /42	0.06 /26	0.05 /13	0.14	0.32
MM	MSILF Money Mkt IS	MMRXX	**C**	(800) 354-8185	**D+ / 2.6**	0.09	0.14	0.19 /44	0.08 /27	0.09 /14	0.19	0.27
MM	MSILF Money Mkt Part	MMNXX	**U**	(800) 354-8185	**U /**	--	--	--	--	--	0.01	0.72
MM	MSILF Prime Portfolio Adm	MPMXX	**C**	(800) 354-8185	**D+ / 2.3**	0.05	0.07	0.09 /41	0.04 /24	0.03 /10	0.09	0.36
MM	MSILF Prime Portfolio Adv	MAVXX	**C**	(800) 354-8185	**D / 2.2**	0.03	0.04	0.06 /39	0.03 /23	0.02 / 9	0.06	0.46
MM	MSILF Prime Portfolio Inst	MPFXX	**C**	(800) 354-8185	**D+ / 2.6**	0.09	0.13	0.17 /43	0.09 /27	0.11 /15	0.17	0.21
MM	MSILF Prime Portfolio Inv	MPVXX	**C**	(800) 354-8185	**D+ / 2.5**	0.07	0.08	0.10 /41	0.05 /25	0.04 /12	0.10	0.31
MM	MSILF Prime Portfolio IS	MPEXX	**C**	(800) 354-8185	**D+ / 2.5**	0.08	0.10	0.12 /42	0.06 /26	0.07 /14	0.12	0.26
MM	MSILF Prime Portfolio Part	MPNXX	**U**	(800) 354-8185	**U /**	--	--	--	--	--	0.03	0.71
MMT	MSILF T/E Portfolio Cshmgt	MTMXX	**U**	(800) 354-8185	**U /**	--	--	--	--	--	0.01	0.40
MMT	MSILF T/E Portfolio Inst	MTXXX	**U**	(800) 354-8185	**U /**	0.01	0.01	0.01 /35	0.01 /21	0.02 /10	0.01	0.25
MMT	MSILF T/E Portfolio Inst Select	MXSXX	**U**	(800) 354-8185	**U /**	--	--	--	--	--	0.01	0.30
MM	MSILF Treasury Portfolio Adm	MTTXX	**U**	(800) 354-8185	**U /**	0.02	0.02	0.04 /37	0.03 /23	0.03 /10	0.04	0.36
MM	MSILF Treasury Portfolio Adv	MAOXX	**U**	(800) 354-8185	**U /**	0.00	0.01	0.02 /35	0.03 /23	0.02 / 9	0.02	0.46
MM	MSILF Treasury Portfolio Cshmgt	MREXX	**U**	(800) 354-8185	**U /**	0.01	0.02	0.04 /37	0.03 /23	0.03 /10	0.04	0.36
MM	MSILF Treasury Portfolio Inst	MISXX	**C**	(800) 354-8185	**D+ / 2.4**	0.05	0.07	0.08 /40	0.05 /25	0.04 /12	0.08	0.21
MM	MSILF Treasury Portfolio Inv	MTNXX	**C**	(800) 354-8185	**D / 2.2**	0.03	0.04	0.05 /39	0.04 /24	0.03 /10	0.05	0.31
MM	MSILF Treasury Portfolio IS	MTSXX	**C**	(800) 354-8185	**D+ / 2.3**	0.04	0.05	0.07 /40	0.04 /24	0.03 /10	0.07	0.26
MM	MSILF Treasury Portfolio Part	MTCXX	**U**	(800) 354-8185	**U /**	0.00	0.01	0.02 /35	0.03 /23	0.03 /10	0.02	0.71
MM	MSILF Treasury Securities Admin	MAMXX	**U**	(800) 354-8185	**U /**	--	--	--	--	--	0.01	0.37
MM	MSILF Treasury Securities Adv	MVYXX	**U**	(800) 354-8185	**U /**	--	--	--	--	--	0.01	0.47
MM	MSILF Treasury Securities Cshmgt	MHSXX	**U**	(800) 354-8185	**U /**	--	--	--	--	--	0.01	0.37
MM	MSILF Treasury Securities Inst	MSUXX	**C**	(800) 354-8185	**D / 2.1**	0.03	0.04	0.04 /37	0.02 /21	0.02 / 9	0.04	0.22
MM	MSILF Treasury Securities Inv	MNVXX	**U**	(800) 354-8185	**U /**	0.01	0.01	0.02 /35	0.01 /18	0.01 / 6	0.02	0.32
MM	MSILF Treasury Securities IS	MSSXX	**C-**	(800) 354-8185	**D / 2.0**	0.02	0.02	0.03 /36	0.02 /21	0.01 / 6	0.03	0.27
COI	Mutual of America Inst Bond	MABOX	**C+**	(800) 914-8716	**C+ / 6.8**	3.11	2.12	1.70 /69	2.15 /64	3.47 /53	3.22	0.88
COH	Muzinich Credit Opportunities Inst	MZCIX	**U**	(855) 689-4642	**U /**	2.72	3.11	2.35 /74	--	--	2.29	1.45
COH	Muzinich Credit Opportunities SIns	MZCSX	**A+**	(855) 689-4642	**B+ / 8.8**	2.74	3.23	2.50 /75	4.85 /90	--	2.35	1.35
COI	Nationwide Bond A	NBDAX	**C+**	(800) 848-0920	**C / 5.4**	2.95	2.21	1.25 /62	1.91 /60	3.78 /58	1.99	0.89
COI	Nationwide Bond C	GBDCX	**C**	(800) 848-0920	**C / 5.0**	2.76	1.73	0.38 /47	1.16 /46	3.02 /45	1.29	1.65
GEI	Nationwide Bond Index A	GBIAX	**C**	(800) 848-0920	**C / 5.4**	2.89	2.15	1.21 /62	1.87 /59	3.13 /47	1.81	0.68
GEI	Nationwide Bond Index C	GBICX	**C**	(800) 848-0920	**C / 5.1**	2.73	1.81	0.54 /50	1.18 /46	2.46 /37	1.20	1.36
GEI	Nationwide Bond Index Inst	GBXIX	**B**	(800) 848-0920	**B- / 7.0**	2.99	2.35	1.63 /68	2.25 /67	3.55 /54	2.26	0.27
COI	Nationwide Bond Inst	NWIBX	**B+**	(800) 848-0920	**C+ / 6.9**	3.01	2.36	1.44 /65	2.25 /67	--	2.33	0.58
COI	Nationwide Bond Inst Svc	MUIBX	**B+**	(800) 848-0920	**C+ / 6.8**	3.00	2.23	1.40 /65	2.18 /65	4.03 /62	2.29	0.63
COI	Nationwide Bond R	GBDRX	**C+**	(800) 848-0920	**C+ / 5.9**	2.97	2.05	0.89 /57	1.63 /55	3.49 /53	1.69	1.33
COI	Nationwide Core Plus Bond A	NWCPX	**U**	(800) 848-0920	**U /**	2.39	1.91	1.43 /65	--	--	2.64	0.83
GEI	Nationwide Core Plus Bond Inst	NWCIX	**A**	(800) 848-0920	**B- / 7.1**	2.47	2.07	1.76 /69	2.41 /69	4.25 /65	3.08	0.49
COI	Nationwide Core Plus Bond Inst Svc	NWCSX	**U**	(800) 848-0920	**U /**	2.45	2.04	1.79 /70	--	--	3.01	0.59
USS	Nationwide Govt Bond A	NUSAX	**D+**	(800) 848-0920	**C- / 3.4**	2.54	1.67	0.41 /48	0.84 /40	2.42 /37	1.48	1.16

● Denotes fund is closed to new investors
* Denotes fund is included in Section II

RISK			NET ASSETS		ASSET							FUND MANAGER		MINIMUM		LOADS	
Risk Rating/Pts	3 Yr Avg Standard Deviation	Avg Duration	NAV As of 3/31/16	Total $(Mil)	Cash %	Gov. Bond %	Muni. Bond %	Corp. Bond %	Other %	Portfolio Turnover Ratio	Avg Coupon Rate	Manager Quality Pct	Manager Tenure (Years)	Initial Purch. $	Additional Purch. $	Front End Load	Back End Load
A+ / 9.9	N/A	N/A	1.00	36	100	0	0	0	0	0	0.1	68	N/A	10,000,000	0	0.0	0.0
A+ / 9.9	N/A	N/A	1.00	1,537	100	0	0	0	0	0	0.1	68	N/A	10,000,000	0	0.0	0.0
U /	N/A	N/A	1.00	N/A	100	0	0	0	0	0	0.0	N/A	N/A	10,000,000	0	0.0	0.0
U /	N/A	N/A	1.00	N/A	100	0	0	0	0	0	0.0	N/A	N/A	10,000,000	0	0.0	0.0
U /	N/A	N/A	1.00	1	100	0	0	0	0	0	0.0	N/A	N/A	1,000,000	0	0.0	0.0
A+ / 9.9	N/A	N/A	1.00	16	100	0	0	0	0	0	0.1	65	N/A	10,000,000	0	0.0	0.0
U /	N/A	N/A	1.00	N/A	100	0	0	0	0	0	0.0	N/A	N/A	10,000,000	0	0.0	0.0
A+ / 9.9	N/A	N/A	1.00	N/A	100	0	0	0	0	0	0.0	65	N/A	10,000,000	0	0.0	0.0
A+ / 9.9	N/A	N/A	1.00	2	100	0	0	0	0	0	0.1	64	N/A	10,000,000	0	0.0	0.0
A+ / 9.9	N/A	N/A	1.00	4	100	0	0	0	0	0	0.1	65	N/A	10,000,000	0	0.0	0.0
A+ / 9.9	N/A	N/A	1.00	30	100	0	0	0	0	0	0.1	64	N/A	1,000,000	0	0.0	0.0
A+ / 9.9	N/A	N/A	1.00	4,542	100	0	0	0	0	0	0.2	71	N/A	200,000,000	0	0.0	0.0
A+ / 9.9	N/A	N/A	1.00	N/A	100	0	0	0	0	0	0.1	N/A	N/A	10,000,000	0	0.0	0.0
A+ / 9.9	N/A	N/A	1.00	405	100	0	0	0	0	0	0.2	68	N/A	10,000,000	0	0.0	0.0
U /	N/A	N/A	1.00	3	100	0	0	0	0	0	0.0	N/A	N/A	10,000,000	0	0.0	0.0
A+ / 9.9	N/A	N/A	1.00	N/A	100	0	0	0	0	0	0.1	N/A	N/A	10,000,000	0	0.0	0.0
A+ / 9.9	N/A	N/A	1.00	201	100	0	0	0	0	0	0.1	67	N/A	10,000,000	0	0.0	0.0
A+ / 9.9	N/A	N/A	1.00	18,414	100	0	0	0	0	0	0.2	69	N/A	10,000,000	0	0.0	0.0
A+ / 9.9	N/A	N/A	1.00	122	100	0	0	0	0	0	0.1	N/A	N/A	10,000,000	0	0.0	0.0
A+ / 9.9	N/A	N/A	1.00	75	100	0	0	0	0	0	0.1	N/A	N/A	10,000,000	0	0.0	0.0
U /	N/A	N/A	1.00	3	100	0	0	0	0	0	0.0	N/A	N/A	10,000,000	0	0.0	0.0
U /	N/A	N/A	1.00	26	100	0	0	0	0	0	0.0	N/A	N/A	1,000,000	0	0.0	0.0
U /	N/A	N/A	1.00	37	100	0	0	0	0	0	0.0	N/A	N/A	10,000,000	0	0.0	0.0
U /	N/A	N/A	1.00	N/A	100	0	0	0	0	0	0.0	N/A	N/A	10,000,000	0	0.0	0.0
U /	N/A	N/A	1.00	2	100	0	0	0	0	0	0.0	N/A	N/A	10,000,000	0	0.0	0.0
U /	N/A	N/A	1.00	691	100	0	0	0	0	0	0.0	N/A	N/A	10,000,000	0	0.0	0.0
U /	N/A	N/A	1.00	54	100	0	0	0	0	0	0.0	N/A	N/A	1,000,000	0	0.0	0.0
A+ / 9.9	N/A	N/A	1.00	19,284	100	0	0	0	0	0	0.1	67	N/A	10,000,000	0	0.0	0.0
A+ / 9.9	N/A	N/A	1.00	42	100	0	0	0	0	0	0.1	67	N/A	10,000,000	0	0.0	0.0
A+ / 9.9	N/A	N/A	1.00	288	100	0	0	0	0	0	0.1	67	N/A	10,000,000	0	0.0	0.0
U /	N/A	N/A	1.00	N/A	100	0	0	0	0	0	0.0	N/A	N/A	10,000,000	0	0.0	0.0
U /	N/A	N/A	1.00	N/A	100	0	0	0	0	0	0.0	N/A	N/A	10,000,000	0	0.0	0.0
U /	N/A	N/A	1.00	10	100	0	0	0	0	0	0.0	N/A	N/A	10,000,000	0	0.0	0.0
U /	N/A	N/A	1.00	108	100	0	0	0	0	0	0.0	N/A	N/A	1,000,000	0	0.0	0.0
A+ / 9.9	N/A	N/A	1.00	19,877	100	0	0	0	0	0	0.0	66	N/A	10,000,000	0	0.0	0.0
U /	N/A	N/A	1.00	61	100	0	0	0	0	0	0.0	N/A	N/A	10,000,000	0	0.0	0.0
A+ / 9.9	N/A	N/A	1.00	239	100	0	0	0	0	0	0.0	66	N/A	10,000,000	0	0.0	0.0
C+ / 5.6	3.2	4.9	9.98	17	1	7	0	57	35	18	3.5	75	20	25,000	5,000	0.0	0.0
U /	N/A	N/A	10.50	20	0	0	0	0	100	598	0.0	N/A	3	1,000,000	100	0.0	1.0
C+ / 6.5	2.5	N/A	10.50	158	0	0	0	0	100	598	0.0	99	3	100,000,000	100	0.0	1.0
B- / 7.1	2.8	5.3	9.74	14	0	34	0	51	15	76	0.0	71	12	2,000	100	2.3	0.0
B- / 7.0	2.9	5.3	9.75	3	0	34	0	51	15	76	0.0	38	12	2,000	100	0.0	0.0
C+ / 6.5	3.0	5.7	11.21	176	2	40	1	24	33	297	0.0	40	7	2,000	100	2.3	0.0
C+ / 6.5	3.0	5.7	11.21	2	2	40	1	24	33	297	0.0	21	7	2,000	100	0.0	0.0
C+ / 6.5	3.0	5.7	11.19	675	2	40	1	24	33	297	0.0	52	7	1,000,000	0	0.0	0.0
B- / 7.0	2.9	5.3	9.76	332	0	34	0	51	15	76	0.0	81	12	1,000,000	0	0.0	0.0
B- / 7.0	2.9	5.3	9.75	51	0	34	0	51	15	76	0.0	79	12	50,000	0	0.0	0.0
C+ / 6.9	2.9	5.3	9.75	1	0	34	0	51	15	76	0.0	54	12	0	0	0.0	0.0
U /	N/A	5.1	10.23	4	1	7	0	49	43	78	0.0	N/A	14	2,000	100	4.3	0.0
B / 7.7	2.6	5.1	10.23	949	1	7	0	49	43	78	0.0	78	14	1,000,000	0	0.0	0.0
U /	N/A	5.1	10.24	4	1	7	0	49	43	78	0.0	N/A	14	50,000	0	0.0	0.0
C+ / 5.6	3.2	6.0	10.27	18	2	65	0	0	33	28	0.0	21	19	2,000	100	2.3	0.0

Fund Type	Fund Name (99 Pct = Best, 0 Pct = Worst)	Ticker Symbol	Overall Investment Rating	Phone	PERFORMANCE: Performance Rating/Pts	Total Return % through 3/31/16: 3 Mo	6 Mo	1Yr / Pct	Annualized: 3Yr / Pct	5Yr / Pct	Incl. in Returns: Dividend Yield	Expense Ratio
USS	Nationwide Govt Bond C	GGBCX	**D+**	(800) 848-0920	**C- / 3.2**	2.48	1.44	-0.17 /30	0.18 /28	1.76 /28	0.85	1.83
USS	Nationwide Govt Bond Inst Svc	NAUGX	**C-**	(800) 848-0920	**C / 5.0**	2.61	1.81	0.69 /53	1.12 /45	2.69 /40	1.80	0.87
USS	Nationwide Govt Bond R	GGBRX	**D+**	(800) 848-0920	**C- / 3.8**	2.44	1.58	0.03 /35	0.47 /33	2.10 /32	1.14	1.53
COH	Nationwide High Yield Bond A	GGHAX	**E**	(800) 848-0920	**E+ / 0.6**	1.03	-1.24	-6.10 / 3	0.49 /33	3.29 /50	5.13	1.78
COH	Nationwide High Yield Bond C	GHHCX	**E+**	(800) 848-0920	**E+ / 0.9**	0.91	-1.48	-6.71 / 2	-0.07 /15	2.77 /41	4.78	2.29
COH	Nationwide High Yield Bond Inst	GGYIX	**E+**	(800) 848-0920	**D / 1.7**	0.93	-1.06	-5.89 / 3	0.75 /38	3.54 /54	5.71	1.41
COH	Nationwide High Yield Bond Inst Svc	GGYSX	**E+**	(800) 848-0920	**D- / 1.4**	0.89	-1.30	-6.20 / 3	0.53 /34	--	5.54	1.61
GEI	Nationwide HighMark Bond A	NWJGX	**C+**	(800) 848-0920	**C+ / 5.6**	3.19	2.26	1.20 /62	1.99 /61	3.58 /54	1.96	0.90
GEI	Nationwide HighMark Bond C	NWJHX	**C+**	(800) 848-0920	**C+ / 5.8**	3.12	2.08	0.77 /55	1.56 /53	3.16 /48	1.60	1.35
COI	Nationwide HighMark Bond I	NWJIX	**U**	(800) 848-0920	**U /**	3.33	2.43	1.59 /67	--	--	2.37	0.50
GEI	Nationwide HighMark Bond IS	NWJJX	**B+**	(800) 848-0920	**C+ / 6.9**	3.27	2.42	1.49 /66	2.19 /65	3.82 /59	2.19	0.74
MUS	Nationwide HighMark CA Int TF Bd A	NWJKX	**A+**	(800) 848-0920	**B / 8.0**	1.45	2.00	2.45 /80	2.62 /84	3.65 /75	2.08	0.89
MUS	Nationwide HighMark CA Int TF Bd C	NWJLX	**A+**	(800) 848-0920	**B / 8.1**	1.35	1.78	2.01 /77	2.17 /79	3.18 /71	1.69	1.38
MUN	Nationwide HighMark CA Int TF Bd I	NWJMX	**U**	(800) 848-0920	**U /**	1.61	2.13	2.84 /83	--	--	2.40	0.57
MUS	Nationwide HighMark CA Int TF Bd IS	NWJNX	**A+**	(800) 848-0920	**B+ / 8.8**	1.50	2.01	2.68 /82	2.86 /87	3.88 /77	2.35	0.66
MUN	Nationwide HighMark Natl Int TFB A	NWJOX	**A-**	(800) 848-0920	**B- / 7.0**	1.22	1.80	2.25 /79	2.04 /77	3.15 /71	1.78	1.08
MUN	Nationwide HighMark Natl Int TFB C	NWJPX	**A**	(800) 848-0920	**B- / 7.3**	1.20	1.67	1.88 /76	1.58 /70	2.70 /64	1.37	1.57
MUN	Nationwide HighMark Natl Int TFB I	NWJQX	**U**	(800) 848-0920	**U /**	1.29	2.04	2.65 /82	--	--	2.11	0.77
MUN	Nationwide HighMark Natl Int TFB IS	NWJRX	**A+**	(800) 848-0920	**B+ / 8.3**	1.28	2.02	2.60 /81	2.29 /80	3.41 /73	2.06	0.85
GEI	Nationwide HighMark Sht Term Bd A	NWJSX	**C**	(800) 848-0920	**D+ / 2.6**	1.07	0.62	0.63 /52	0.56 /34	1.13 /22	1.00	0.78
GEI	Nationwide HighMark Sht Term Bd C	NWJTX	**C**	(800) 848-0920	**D+ / 2.7**	0.95	0.29	0.08 /40	0.07 /26	0.67 /18	0.58	1.29
COI	Nationwide HighMark Sht Term Bd I	NWJUX	**U**	(800) 848-0920	**U /**	1.14	0.77	0.94 /58	--	--	1.33	0.45
GEI	Nationwide HighMark Sht Term Bd IS	NWJVX	**B-**	(800) 848-0920	**C / 4.3**	1.13	0.74	0.88 /57	0.86 /40	1.41 /25	1.28	0.53
GEI	Nationwide Infl-Prot Secs A	NIFAX	**D-**	(800) 848-0920	**D- / 1.1**	4.32	3.54	0.83 /56	-0.98 / 8	--	0.00	0.84
GEI	Nationwide Infl-Prot Secs Inst	NIFIX	**D**	(800) 848-0920	**D+ / 2.8**	4.41	3.74	1.15 /61	-0.69 /10	--	0.00	0.34
MM	Nationwide Money Market Isnt	GMIXX	**U**	(800) 848-0920	**U /**	--	--	--	--	--	0.01	0.49
MUN	Nationwide Ziegler Wisconsin TE A	NWJWX	**D+**	(800) 848-0920	**C- / 3.6**	1.38	2.53	1.69 /75	0.57 /40	2.85 /66	2.79	1.03
MUN	Nationwide Ziegler Wisconsin TE C	NWKGX	**D+**	(800) 848-0920	**C- / 3.9**	1.17	2.21	1.14 /69	0.12 /28	2.38 /56	2.42	1.53
MUN	Nationwide Ziegler Wisconsin TE I	NWJYX	**U**	(800) 848-0920	**U /**	1.45	2.68	1.99 /77	--	--	3.15	0.74
MUN	Nationwide Ziegler Wisconsin TE IS	NWJZX	**C**	(800) 848-0920	**C+ / 6.0**	1.44	2.66	1.94 /77	0.81 /47	3.11 /70	3.10	0.78
USS	Natixis Loomis Say Ltd Trm Gv&Agy	NEFLX	**C-**	(800) 225-5478	**D+ / 2.6**	0.93	0.27	0.48 /49	0.62 /35	1.45 /25	1.40	0.77
USS	Natixis Loomis Say Ltd Trm Gv&Agy	NECLX	**C-**	(800) 225-5478	**D / 1.7**	0.76	-0.08	-0.25 /29	-0.12 /15	0.70 /18	0.70	1.53
USS	Natixis Loomis Say Ltd Trm Gv&Agy	NELYX	**C+**	(800) 225-5478	**C / 4.3**	1.08	0.40	0.82 /56	0.91 /41	1.70 /28	1.69	0.52
* GEI	Natixis Loomis Sayles Cor Pl Bd A	NEFRX	**D**	(800) 225-5478	**C- / 3.5**	3.96	3.15	-1.10 /21	1.46 /51	4.33 /66	2.53	0.74
GEI	Natixis Loomis Sayles Cor Pl Bd C	NECRX	**D**	(800) 225-5478	**C- / 4.1**	3.77	2.83	-1.80 /17	0.71 /37	3.57 /54	1.93	1.49
COI	• Natixis Loomis Sayles Cor Pl Bd N	NERNX	**C-**	(800) 225-5478	**C+ / 6.2**	4.10	3.35	-0.74 /24	1.80 /58	--	2.98	0.40
GEI	Natixis Loomis Sayles Cor Pl Bd Y	NERYX	**D+**	(800) 225-5478	**C+ / 6.0**	3.99	3.28	-0.84 /23	1.70 /56	4.59 /68	2.88	0.49
COH	Natixis Loomis Sayles High Income A	NEFHX	**E**	(800) 225-5478	**E+ / 0.6**	2.14	-0.60	-6.30 / 3	0.29 /30	3.33 /50	5.25	1.13
COH	Natixis Loomis Sayles High Income C	NEHCX	**E**	(800) 225-5478	**E+ / 0.8**	1.95	-0.98	-7.00 / 2	-0.46 /12	2.59 /39	4.66	1.88
COH	Natixis Loomis Sayles High Income Y	NEHYX	**E+**	(800) 225-5478	**D / 1.6**	2.21	-0.46	-6.07 / 3	0.49 /33	3.59 /55	5.78	0.88
COI	Natixis Loomis Sayles Inv Gr Bd Adm	LIGAX	**D**	(800) 225-5478	**C- / 4.1**	3.48	3.11	-1.64 /18	0.68 /36	3.33 /50	1.78	1.08
* GEI	Natixis Loomis Sayles Invst Gr Bd A	LIGRX	**D-**	(800) 225-5478	**D+ / 2.6**	3.59	3.31	-1.32 /19	0.95 /42	3.61 /55	1.92	0.83
GEI	Natixis Loomis Sayles Invst Gr Bd C	LGBCX	**D**	(800) 225-5478	**C- / 3.1**	3.35	2.80	-2.14 /15	0.18 /28	2.81 /42	1.21	1.58
COI	• Natixis Loomis Sayles Invst Gr Bd N	LGBNX	**D+**	(800) 225-5478	**C / 5.2**	3.60	3.36	-1.00 /22	1.25 /47	--	2.42	0.47
GEI	Natixis Loomis Sayles Invst Gr Bd Y	LSIIX	**D+**	(800) 225-5478	**C / 5.1**	3.56	3.36	-1.14 /21	1.19 /46	3.85 /59	2.27	0.58
LP	Natixis Loomis Sayles Sen FR & FI A	LSFAX	**D**	(800) 225-5478	**D / 1.8**	0.50	-2.53	-2.80 /12	1.67 /55	--	5.78	1.10
LP	Natixis Loomis Sayles Sen FR & FI C	LSFCX	**D+**	(800) 225-5478	**D+ / 2.6**	0.32	-2.91	-3.53 /10	0.90 /41	--	5.22	1.86
LP	Natixis Loomis Sayles Sen FR & FI Y	LSFYX	**C-**	(800) 225-5478	**C / 4.5**	0.56	-2.40	-2.65 /13	1.90 /59	--	6.26	0.86
GES	Natixis Loomis Sayles Strat Alpha A	LABAX	**D**	(800) 225-5478	**E / 0.5**	0.03	-1.02	-3.24 /11	-0.21 /14	1.56 /26	2.95	1.10
GES	Natixis Loomis Sayles Strat Alpha C	LABCX	**D**	(800) 225-5478	**E+ / 0.7**	-0.15	-1.29	-3.98 / 8	-0.94 / 9	0.81 /19	2.31	1.85
GES	Natixis Loomis Sayles Strat Alpha Y	LASYX	**D**	(800) 225-5478	**D- / 1.4**	0.11	-0.88	-2.98 /11	0.05 /24	1.81 /29	3.36	0.86
* GEL	Natixis Loomis Sayles Strat Inc A	NEFZX	**D-**	(800) 225-5478	**D+ / 2.8**	1.59	1.56	-5.57 / 4	2.10 /64	4.47 /67	3.30	0.94

• Denotes fund is closed to new investors
* Denotes fund is included in Section II

RISK			NET ASSETS		ASSET							FUND MANAGER		MINIMUM		LOADS	
Risk Rating/Pts	3 Yr Avg Standard Deviation	Avg Duration	NAV As of 3/31/16	Total $(Mil)	Cash %	Gov. Bond %	Muni. Bond %	Corp. Bond %	Other %	Portfolio Turnover Ratio	Avg Coupon Rate	Manager Quality Pct	Manager Tenure (Years)	Initial Purch. $	Additional Purch. $	Front End Load	Back End Load
C+ / 5.8	3.2	6.0	10.27	1	2	65	0	0	33	28	0.0	13	19	2,000	100	0.0	0.0
C+ / 5.6	3.2	6.0	10.27	38	2	65	0	0	33	28	0.0	28	19	50,000	0	0.0	0.0
C+ / 5.7	3.2	6.0	10.28	1	2	65	0	0	33	28	0.0	15	19	0	0	0.0	0.0
D- / 1.4	5.7	4.3	5.48	17	7	0	0	92	1	43	8.0	25	6	2,000	100	4.3	0.0
D- / 1.4	5.7	4.3	5.51	5	7	0	0	92	1	43	8.0	15	6	2,000	100	0.0	0.0
D- / 1.4	5.7	4.3	5.51	4	7	0	0	92	1	43	8.0	32	6	1,000,000	0	0.0	0.0
D- / 1.4	5.7	4.3	5.51	1	7	0	0	92	1	43	8.0	26	6	50,000	0	0.0	0.0
C+ / 6.7	3.0	5.0	10.79	22	1	14	3	54	28	43	7.0	49	3	2,000	100	2.3	0.0
C+ / 6.7	3.0	5.0	10.73	7	1	14	3	54	28	43	7.0	35	3	2,000	100	0.0	0.0
U /	N/A	5.0	10.99	194	1	14	3	54	28	43	7.0	N/A	3	1,000,000	0	0.0	0.0
C+ / 6.8	2.9	5.0	11.00	320	1	14	3	54	28	43	7.0	57	3	50,000	0	0.0	0.0
B- / 7.2	2.8	4.8	10.47	52	2	0	97	0	1	8	0.0	54	3	2,000	100	2.3	0.0
B- / 7.1	2.8	4.8	10.43	32	2	0	97	0	1	8	0.0	38	3	2,000	100	0.0	0.0
U /	N/A	4.8	10.53	56	2	0	97	0	1	8	0.0	N/A	3	1,000,000	0	0.0	0.0
B- / 7.2	2.8	4.8	10.52	53	2	0	97	0	1	8	0.0	68	3	50,000	0	0.0	0.0
B / 7.6	2.7	4.7	11.13	10	1	0	98	0	1	14	0.0	40	20	2,000	100	2.3	0.0
B / 7.7	2.6	4.7	11.15	4	1	0	98	0	1	14	0.0	28	20	2,000	100	0.0	0.0
U /	N/A	4.7	11.14	28	1	0	98	0	1	14	0.0	N/A	20	1,000,000	0	0.0	0.0
B / 7.7	2.6	4.7	11.14	20	1	0	98	0	1	14	0.0	50	20	50,000	0	0.0	0.0
A / 9.4	0.9	1.9	9.96	72	2	2	0	56	40	35	0.0	60	12	2,000	100	2.3	0.0
A / 9.4	0.9	1.9	10.08	17	2	2	0	56	40	35	0.0	43	12	2,000	100	0.0	0.0
U /	N/A	1.9	9.98	219	2	2	0	56	40	35	0.0	N/A	12	1,000,000	0	0.0	0.0
A / 9.4	0.9	1.9	9.98	66	2	2	0	56	40	35	0.0	76	12	50,000	0	0.0	0.0
D+ / 2.4	5.1	7.7	9.66	N/A	0	99	0	0	1	30	0.0	4	4	2,000	100	2.3	0.0
D+ / 2.4	5.1	7.7	9.71	155	0	99	0	0	1	30	0.0	5	4	1,000,000	0	0.0	0.0
U /	N/A	N/A	1.00	495	100	0	0	0	0	0	0.0	N/A	N/A	1,000,000	0	0.0	0.0
C / 5.3	3.3	5.9	9.99	87	0	0	99	0	1	3	4.7	9	3	2,000	100	2.3	0.0
C / 5.3	3.3	5.9	9.97	10	0	0	99	0	1	3	4.7	7	3	2,000	100	0.0	0.0
U /	N/A	5.9	9.99	N/A	0	0	99	0	1	3	4.7	N/A	3	1,000,000	0	0.0	0.0
C / 5.5	3.3	5.9	9.99	1	0	0	99	0	1	3	4.7	10	3	50,000	0	0.0	0.0
A- / 9.1	1.2	2.0	11.52	460	1	30	0	0	69	48	2.2	56	15	2,500	100	2.3	0.0
A- / 9.1	1.2	2.0	11.53	85	1	30	0	0	69	48	2.2	31	15	2,500	100	0.0	0.0
A- / 9.1	1.2	2.0	11.56	435	1	30	0	0	69	48	2.2	72	15	100,000	100	0.0	0.0
D+ / 2.9	4.8	6.8	12.57	787	1	19	0	55	25	175	4.3	18	20	2,500	100	4.3	0.0
D+ / 2.9	4.8	6.8	12.57	323	1	19	0	55	25	175	4.3	10	20	2,500	100	0.0	0.0
D+ / 2.9	4.8	6.8	12.67	2,001	1	19	0	55	25	175	4.3	29	20	1,000,000	0	0.0	0.0
D+ / 2.9	4.8	6.8	12.66	2,926	1	19	0	55	25	175	4.3	23	20	100,000	100	0.0	0.0
E / 0.5	7.2	4.7	3.84	32	4	8	0	73	15	69	5.4	14	14	2,500	100	4.3	0.0
E / 0.5	7.2	4.7	3.85	11	4	8	0	73	15	69	5.4	9	14	2,500	100	0.0	0.0
E / 0.5	7.3	4.7	3.83	111	4	8	0	73	15	69	5.4	17	14	100,000	100	0.0	0.0
D+ / 2.6	5.1	4.6	11.15	39	3	28	1	52	16	23	4.5	14	20	0	0	0.0	0.0
D+ / 2.6	5.2	4.6	11.18	1,337	3	28	1	52	16	23	4.5	19	20	2,500	100	4.3	0.0
D+ / 2.6	5.1	4.6	11.07	1,083	3	28	1	52	16	23	4.5	11	20	2,500	100	0.0	0.0
D+ / 2.6	5.1	4.6	11.17	37	3	28	1	52	16	23	4.5	23	20	1,000,000	0	0.0	0.0
D+ / 2.6	5.1	4.6	11.18	5,084	3	28	1	52	16	23	4.5	25	20	100,000	100	0.0	0.0
C / 5.4	3.3	N/A	9.39	270	3	0	0	67	30	67	0.0	88	5	2,500	100	3.5	0.0
C / 5.3	3.3	N/A	9.36	268	3	0	0	67	30	67	0.0	73	5	2,500	100	0.0	0.0
C / 5.4	3.3	N/A	9.39	1,081	3	0	0	67	30	67	0.0	91	5	100,000	100	0.0	0.0
C+ / 6.4	3.0	N/A	9.38	74	13	6	0	51	30	87	0.0	21	6	2,500	100	4.3	0.0
C+ / 6.3	3.1	N/A	9.35	56	13	6	0	51	30	87	0.0	11	6	2,500	100	0.0	0.0
C+ / 6.5	3.0	N/A	9.37	1,109	13	6	0	51	30	87	0.0	27	6	100,000	100	0.0	0.0
E+ / 0.6	7.3	3.8	13.83	2,666	3	20	1	41	35	23	4.2	79	21	2,500	100	4.3	0.0

99 Pct = Best
0 Pct = Worst

Fund Type	Fund Name	Ticker Symbol	Overall Investment Rating	Phone	PERFORMANCE Performance Rating/Pts	Total Return % through 3/31/16 3 Mo	6 Mo	1Yr / Pct	Annualized 3Yr / Pct	5Yr / Pct	Incl. in Returns Dividend Yield	Expense Ratio
GEL	Natixis Loomis Sayles Strat Inc Adm	NEZAX	D	(800) 225-5478	C / 4.5	1.62	1.45	-5.81 / 3	1.87 /59	4.23 /65	3.20	1.19
GEL	Natixis Loomis Sayles Strat Inc C	NECZX	D-	(800) 225-5478	C- / 3.5	1.46	1.23	-6.26 / 3	1.37 /50	3.71 /57	2.63	1.69
GEL ●	Natixis Loomis Sayles Strat Inc N	NEZNX	D	(800) 225-5478	C+ / 5.6	1.75	1.74	-5.26 / 5	2.44 /70	--	3.78	0.62
GEL	Natixis Loomis Sayles Strat Inc Y	NEZYX	D	(800) 225-5478	C / 5.5	1.72	1.70	-5.33 / 4	2.37 /69	4.74 /70	3.70	0.69
MUN	Navigator Duration Neutral Bond A	NDNAX	U	(877) 766-2264	U /	-2.08	1.65	1.43 /73	--	--	1.18	1.71
MUN	Navigator Duration Neutral Bond C	NDNCX	U	(877) 766-2264	U /	-2.30	1.23	0.64 /58	--	--	0.54	2.46
MUN	Navigator Duration Neutral Bond I	NDNIX	U	(877) 766-2264	U /	-2.02	1.79	1.68 /75	--	--	1.47	1.46
MUS	Nebraska Municipal	NEMUX	B+	(800) 601-5593	B+ / 8.6	1.26	2.73	3.63 /91	3.23 /90	4.55 /82	2.53	1.20
GEN	Neiman Tactical Income A	NTAFX	E+		E- / 0.2	-0.33	-3.07	-4.97 / 5	-2.31 / 3	--	1.68	2.25
COH	Neiman Tactical Income C	NTCFX	U		U /	-1.85	-4.84	-7.15 / 2	--	--	0.48	3.00
EM	Neuberger Berman Emg Mkts Debt A	NERAX	U	(800) 877-9700	U /	7.75	8.46	-0.68 /24	--	--	4.80	1.53
EM	Neuberger Berman Emg Mkts Debt C	NERCX	U	(800) 877-9700	U /	7.70	8.07	-1.42 /19	--	--	4.27	2.21
EM	Neuberger Berman Emg Mkts Debt	NERIX	U	(800) 877-9700	U /	7.98	8.67	-0.31 /28	--	--	5.38	1.07
LP	Neuberger Berman Floating Rt Inc A	NFIAX	D+	(800) 877-9700	D / 1.6	1.35	-0.72	-1.24 /20	1.22 /47	2.87 /43	3.53	1.22
LP	Neuberger Berman Floating Rt Inc C	NFICX	C-	(800) 877-9700	D+ / 2.7	1.17	-1.08	-1.97 /16	0.47 /33	2.10 /32	2.93	1.96
LP	Neuberger Berman Floating Rt Inc I	NFIIX	C+	(800) 877-9700	C / 4.9	1.43	-0.54	-0.88 /23	1.59 /54	3.25 /49	4.06	0.84
COH	Neuberger Berman High Inc Bd A	NHIAX	E+	(800) 877-9700	D- / 1.2	2.75	0.87	-4.66 / 6	0.95 /42	3.56 /54	5.11	1.09
COH	Neuberger Berman High Inc Bd C	NHICX	E+	(800) 877-9700	D / 1.6	2.57	0.52	-5.31 / 4	0.26 /29	2.83 /42	4.60	1.82
COH	Neuberger Berman High Inc Bd Inst	NHILX	D	(800) 877-9700	C- / 4.2	2.84	1.07	-4.25 / 7	1.39 /50	4.00 /61	5.75	0.69
COH ●	Neuberger Berman High Inc Bd Inv	NHINX	D	(800) 877-9700	C- / 4.0	2.93	1.11	-4.40 / 6	1.24 /47	3.87 /60	5.60	0.84
COH	Neuberger Berman High Inc Bd R3	NHIRX	D-	(800) 877-9700	C- / 3.0	2.69	0.75	-4.86 / 5	0.76 /38	3.34 /51	5.10	1.32
COH	Neuberger Berman High Inc Bd R6	NRHIX	D	(800) 877-9700	C / 4.4	2.85	1.10	-4.19 / 7	1.47 /52	--	5.83	0.62
MUN	Neuberger Berman Muni Int Bd A	NMNAX	C+	(800) 877-9700	B- / 7.1	1.35	2.36	2.59 /81	2.48 /82	4.16 /79	1.79	1.04
MUN	Neuberger Berman Muni Int Bd C	NMNCX	B-	(800) 877-9700	B / 7.7	1.26	2.07	1.92 /76	1.75 /73	3.41 /73	1.13	1.80
MUN	Neuberger Berman Muni Int Bd Inst	NMNLX	A-	(800) 877-9700	B+ / 8.9	1.53	2.62	3.05 /85	2.89 /87	4.57 /82	2.23	0.66
MUN	Neuberger Berman Muni Int Bd Inv	NMUIX	A-	(800) 877-9700	B+ / 8.8	1.49	2.55	2.90 /84	2.74 /85	4.43 /81	2.08	0.84
MUN	Neuberger Berman NY Muni Inc Inst	NMIIX	A+	(800) 877-9700	B+ / 8.8	1.44	2.45	3.11 /86	2.82 /86	--	2.30	0.89
GEI	Neuberger Berman Short Dur Bd A	NSHAX	C-	(800) 877-9700	D / 1.7	0.75	0.51	0.45 /49	0.43 /32	1.11 /21	0.83	1.41
GEI	Neuberger Berman Short Dur Bd C	NSHCX	C-	(800) 877-9700	D- / 1.5	0.56	0.02	-0.27 /28	-0.31 /13	0.34 /16	0.13	2.17
GEI	Neuberger Berman Short Dur Bd Inst	NSHLX	B	(800) 877-9700	C- / 4.2	0.81	0.69	0.84 /56	0.83 /40	1.50 /26	1.22	1.05
GEI	Neuberger Berman Short Dur Bd Inv	NSBIX	C+	(800) 877-9700	C- / 3.8	0.89	0.59	0.64 /52	0.63 /36	1.30 /23	1.02	1.28
GEI	Neuberger Berman Short Dur Bd Tr	NSBTX	C+	(800) 877-9700	C- / 3.6	0.77	0.54	0.66 /53	0.54 /34	1.21 /22	0.92	1.44
COH	Neuberger Berman Short Dur HI A	NHSAX	D-	(800) 877-9700	D / 1.8	2.18	1.31	-1.80 /17	1.17 /46	--	3.58	1.22
COH	Neuberger Berman Short Dur HI C	NHSCX	D	(800) 877-9700	D+ / 2.8	1.89	0.84	-2.62 /13	0.38 /31	--	2.99	1.99
COH	Neuberger Berman Short Dur HI Inst	NHSIX	D+	(800) 877-9700	C / 5.0	2.16	1.38	-1.55 /18	1.50 /52	--	4.12	0.81
GES	Neuberger Berman Strat Inc A	NSTAX	D	(800) 877-9700	D- / 1.5	1.69	1.12	-2.14 /15	1.00 /43	3.73 /57	3.15	1.26
GES	Neuberger Berman Strat Inc C	NSTCX	D	(800) 877-9700	D+ / 2.5	1.52	0.78	-2.81 /12	0.29 /30	3.01 /45	2.59	2.00
GES	Neuberger Berman Strat Inc Inst	NSTLX	D+	(800) 877-9700	C / 4.7	1.78	1.32	-1.75 /17	1.40 /50	4.14 /64	3.69	0.87
GL	Neuberger Berman Strat Inc R6	NRSIX	D+	(800) 877-9700	C / 4.8	1.80	1.26	-1.69 /17	1.44 /51	--	3.76	0.80
GES	Neuberger Berman Strat Inc Tr	NSTTX	D+	(800) 877-9700	C- / 4.0	1.70	1.14	-2.10 /15	1.04 /43	3.78 /58	3.33	1.23
GEI	Neuberger Core Bond A	NCRAX	C-	(800) 877-9700	C- / 3.9	2.60	1.91	1.04 /59	1.67 /55	3.20 /48	2.25	1.01
GEI	Neuberger Core Bond C	NCRCX	C-	(800) 877-9700	C / 4.6	2.42	1.54	0.30 /46	0.92 /41	2.45 /37	1.62	1.76
GEI	Neuberger Core Bond Inst	NCRLX	B	(800) 877-9700	C+ / 6.6	2.59	2.11	1.44 /65	2.05 /62	3.60 /55	2.74	0.62
GEI ●	Neuberger Core Bond Inv	NCRIX	C+	(800) 877-9700	C+ / 5.9	2.50	1.91	1.04 /59	1.64 /55	3.20 /48	2.35	1.15
MUH	Neuberger Municipal High Inc A	NMHAX	U	(800) 877-9700	U /	2.28	4.64	--	--	--	0.00	1.38
MUH	Neuberger Municipal High Inc C	NMHCX	U	(800) 877-9700	U /	2.20	4.36	--	--	--	0.00	2.13
MUH	Neuberger Municipal High Inc Inst	NMHIX	U	(800) 877-9700	U /	2.47	4.93	--	--	--	0.00	1.01
GEI	New Covenant Income	NCICX	B+	(877) 835-4531	C+ / 6.0	2.15	1.67	1.61 /68	1.67 /55	2.73 /41	1.76	0.95
MUS	New Hampshire Municipal	NHMUX	A+	(800) 601-5593	B / 7.8	1.18	2.24	2.99 /85	2.47 /82	3.70 /75	2.13	1.73
GL	NJ 529 NJBest CSP Income Port		C-	(800) 342-5236	C- / 3.0	0.70	1.21	-1.74 /17	0.47 /33	1.92 /30	0.00	0.96
COH	Nomura High Yield I	NPHIX	D	(800) 535-2726	C / 4.7	2.97	0.93	-4.63 / 6	2.35 /68	--	7.26	1.45
GEI	North Country Intermediate Bond	NCBDX	B	(888) 350-2990	C+ / 5.9	2.82	2.22	1.85 /70	1.45 /51	2.64 /40	1.71	0.89

● Denotes fund is closed to new investors
* Denotes fund is included in Section II

RISK			NET ASSETS		ASSET							FUND MANAGER		MINIMUM		LOADS	
Risk Rating/Pts	3 Yr Avg Standard Deviation	Avg Duration	NAV As of 3/31/16	Total $(Mil)	Cash %	Gov. Bond %	Muni. Bond %	Corp. Bond %	Other %	Portfolio Turnover Ratio	Avg Coupon Rate	Manager Quality Pct	Manager Tenure (Years)	Initial Purch. $	Additional Purch. $	Front End Load	Back End Load
E+ / 0.6	7.3	3.8	13.79	138	3	20	1	41	35	23	4.2	72	21	0	0	0.0	0.0
E+ / 0.6	7.3	3.8	13.94	3,634	3	20	1	41	35	23	4.2	48	21	2,500	100	0.0	0.0
E+ / 0.6	7.3	3.8	13.82	119	3	20	1	41	35	23	4.2	86	21	1,000,000	0	0.0	0.0
E+ / 0.6	7.3	3.8	13.82	5,389	3	20	1	41	35	23	4.2	85	21	100,000	100	0.0	0.0
U /	N/A	N/A	10.14	1	11	0	88	0	1	81	0.0	N/A	N/A	5,000	500	3.8	0.0
U /	N/A	N/A	10.05	1	11	0	88	0	1	81	0.0	N/A	N/A	5,000	500	0.0	0.0
U /	N/A	N/A	10.11	78	11	0	88	0	1	81	0.0	N/A	N/A	25,000	0	0.0	0.0
C / 4.7	3.6	4.4	10.67	43	0	0	100	0	0	12	4.9	45	20	1,000	50	2.5	0.0
D+ / 2.5	5.3	N/A	9.04	25	84	1	0	11	4	184	0.0	4	N/A	2,500	100	5.8	0.0
U /	N/A	N/A	9.04	N/A	84	1	0	11	4	184	0.0	N/A	N/A	2,500	100	0.0	0.0
U /	N/A	5.5	8.63	N/A	5	68	0	24	3	100	7.6	N/A	N/A	1,000	100	4.3	0.0
U /	N/A	5.5	8.63	N/A	5	68	0	24	3	100	7.6	N/A	N/A	1,000	100	0.0	0.0
U /	N/A	5.5	8.63	112	5	68	0	24	3	100	7.6	N/A	N/A	1,000,000	0	0.0	0.0
B / 7.7	2.6	0.5	9.64	19	4	0	1	71	24	44	4.8	86	7	1,000	100	4.3	0.0
B / 7.7	2.6	0.5	9.64	25	4	0	1	71	24	44	4.8	59	7	1,000	100	0.0	0.0
B / 7.6	2.6	0.5	9.64	196	4	0	1	71	24	44	4.8	90	7	1,000,000	0	0.0	0.0
D- / 1.2	5.9	4.1	8.16	94	3	0	0	92	5	24	6.4	36	11	1,000	100	4.3	0.0
D- / 1.2	5.8	4.1	8.18	33	3	0	0	92	5	24	6.4	19	11	1,000	100	0.0	0.0
D- / 1.3	5.8	4.1	8.18	2,817	3	0	0	92	5	24	6.4	52	11	1,000,000	0	0.0	0.0
D- / 1.1	6.0	4.1	8.17	157	3	0	0	92	5	24	6.4	45	11	2,000	100	0.0	0.0
D- / 1.2	5.8	4.1	8.17	6	3	0	0	92	5	24	6.4	31	11	0	0	0.0	0.0
D- / 1.3	5.8	4.1	8.18	709	3	0	0	92	5	24	6.4	55	11	0	0	0.0	0.0
C / 5.2	3.4	4.7	11.98	7	1	0	98	0	1	22	4.1	28	N/A	1,000	100	4.0	0.0
C / 5.3	3.4	4.7	11.99	3	1	0	98	0	1	22	4.1	15	N/A	1,000	100	0.0	0.0
C / 5.2	3.4	4.7	11.99	143	1	0	98	0	1	22	4.1	40	N/A	1,000,000	0	0.0	0.0
C / 5.3	3.4	4.7	12.00	16	1	0	98	0	1	22	4.1	36	N/A	2,000	100	0.0	0.0
C+ / 6.1	3.1	4.8	17.79	63	0	0	99	0	1	17	4.6	46	N/A	1,000,000	0	0.0	0.0
A+ / 9.7	0.7	1.6	7.51	5	0	31	0	28	41	75	1.8	62	10	1,000	100	2.5	0.0
A+ / 9.7	0.7	1.6	7.51	3	0	31	0	28	41	75	1.8	34	10	1,000	100	0.0	0.0
A+ / 9.7	0.6	1.6	7.88	33	0	31	0	28	41	75	1.8	80	10	1,000,000	0	0.0	0.0
A+ / 9.7	0.7	1.6	7.89	30	0	31	0	28	41	75	1.8	73	10	2,000	100	0.0	0.0
A+ / 9.7	0.6	1.6	7.52	3	0	31	0	28	41	75	1.8	71	10	1,000	100	0.0	0.0
C- / 3.4	3.9	2.4	9.41	3	1	0	0	89	10	45	5.8	69	N/A	1,000	100	4.3	0.0
C- / 3.4	3.9	2.4	9.40	1	1	0	0	89	10	45	5.8	37	N/A	1,000	100	0.0	0.0
C- / 3.4	3.9	2.4	9.40	183	1	0	0	89	10	45	5.8	81	N/A	1,000,000	0	0.0	0.0
C / 4.5	3.7	4.2	10.64	316	0	16	0	38	46	357	4.2	34	8	1,000	100	4.3	0.0
C / 4.4	3.7	4.2	10.63	187	0	16	0	38	46	357	4.2	17	8	1,000	100	0.0	0.0
C / 4.5	3.7	4.2	10.63	1,232	0	16	0	38	46	357	4.2	46	8	1,000,000	0	0.0	0.0
C / 4.5	3.7	4.2	10.62	249	0	16	0	38	46	357	4.2	93	8	0	0	0.0	0.0
C / 4.4	3.8	4.2	10.63	25	0	16	0	38	46	357	4.2	34	8	1,000	100	0.0	0.0
C+ / 6.4	3.0	5.2	10.43	32	0	32	0	26	42	240	3.2	35	8	1,000	100	4.3	0.0
C+ / 6.4	3.0	5.2	10.44	5	0	32	0	26	42	240	3.2	18	8	1,000	100	0.0	0.0
C+ / 6.8	2.9	5.2	10.46	276	0	32	0	26	42	240	3.2	50	8	1,000,000	0	0.0	0.0
C+ / 6.7	2.9	5.2	10.44	12	0	32	0	26	42	240	3.2	37	8	2,000	100	0.0	0.0
U /	N/A	5.9	10.35	N/A	0	0	99	0	1	0	4.3	N/A	1	1,000	100	4.3	0.0
U /	N/A	5.9	10.35	N/A	0	0	99	0	1	0	4.3	N/A	1	1,000	100	0.0	0.0
U /	N/A	5.9	10.35	104	0	0	99	0	1	0	4.3	N/A	1	1,000,000	0	0.0	0.0
B+ / 8.4	2.1	3.8	23.31	297	28	16	0	21	35	115	0.0	62	4	500	100	0.0	0.0
B / 8.0	2.4	4.7	10.94	5	0	0	100	0	0	13	4.7	60	13	1,000	50	2.5	0.0
B- / 7.5	2.7	N/A	15.85	19	0	0	0	0	100	0	0.0	82	13	25	25	0.0	0.0
D- / 1.0	6.0	4.8	8.71	24	4	0	0	89	7	106	0.0	84	4	250,000	1,000	0.0	2.0
B / 8.0	2.4	N/A	10.37	80	2	38	0	59	1	51	0.0	44	13	1,000	100	0.0	0.0

Fund Type	Fund Name (99 Pct = Best, 0 Pct = Worst)	Ticker Symbol	Overall Investment Rating	Phone	PERFORMANCE: Performance Rating/Pts	Total Return % through 3/31/16: 3 Mo	6 Mo	1Yr / Pct	Annualized: 3Yr / Pct	Annualized: 5Yr / Pct	Incl. in Returns: Dividend Yield	Expense Ratio
GES	Northeast Investors Trust	NTHEX	**E-**	(800) 225-6704	**E- / 0.0**	-10.32	-17.94	-25.81 / 0	-9.21 / 0	-2.75 / 1	9.27	1.27
MUS	Northern AZ Tax Exempt	NOAZX	**A-**	(800) 595-9111	**A / 9.4**	1.75	3.12	4.06 /94	3.54 /93	5.66 /90	3.12	0.61
* MTG	Northern Bond Index	NOBOX	**B+**	(800) 595-9111	**B- / 7.2**	2.95	2.33	1.89 /71	2.37 /69	3.66 /56	2.54	0.18
MUS	Northern CA Intermediate T/E	NCITX	**A-**	(800) 595-9111	**A / 9.4**	1.72	3.03	4.02 /94	3.44 /92	5.17 /87	2.54	0.50
MUS	Northern CA T/E Bond	NCATX	**B+**	(800) 595-9111	**A+ / 9.8**	1.81	3.59	4.96 /98	4.87 /98	7.66 /98	3.12	0.62
GEI	Northern Core Bond	NOCBX	**C+**	(800) 637-1380	**C+ / 6.9**	2.59	2.06	1.00 /59	2.32 /68	4.06 /62	2.10	0.51
* GL	Northern Fixed Income	NOFIX	**C+**	(800) 595-9111	**C+ / 6.8**	2.57	2.17	0.52 /50	2.35 /68	4.09 /63	2.71	0.49
* MUH	Northern High Yield Muni	NHYMX	**B**	(800) 595-9111	**A+ / 9.8**	1.85	4.17	4.80 /97	4.25 /97	7.58 /98	3.62	0.86
* COH	Northern HY Fixed Income	NHFIX	**D-**	(800) 595-9111	**D / 2.0**	0.56	-0.76	-4.43 / 6	1.32 /49	4.25 /65	6.11	0.82
MM	Northern Inst Fds Prime Oblg Pf Shs	NPAXX	**C**	(800) 637-1380	**D+ / 2.5**	0.08	0.12	0.14 /42	0.07 /26	0.07 /14	0.14	0.17
MM	Northern Inst Fds Prime Oblg Ptf S	NPCXX	**C**	(800) 637-1380	**D+ / 2.5**	0.08	0.12	0.14 /42	0.07 /26	0.06 /14	0.14	0.42
MM	Northern Inst Treasury Port Shares	NITXX	**C**	(800) 637-1380	**D / 2.2**	0.05	0.06	0.06 /39	0.03 /23	0.02 / 9	0.06	0.22
MMT	Northern Instl Muni Port Shares	NMUXX	**U**	(800) 637-1380	**U /**	0.00	0.01	0.02 /36	0.01 /21	0.02 /11	0.02	0.22
USA	Northern Instl US Gvt Select WC	WCGXX	**U**	(800) 637-1380	**U /**	0.04	0.05	0.05 /38	--	--	0.05	0.21
* MUN	Northern Intermed Tax Exempt	NOITX	**A**	(800) 595-9111	**A- / 9.0**	1.42	2.95	3.53 /90	2.88 /87	4.61 /82	1.99	0.50
EM	Northern Multi Mgr EM Debt Oppty	NMEDX	**U**	(800) 595-9111	**U /**	5.71	6.21	-2.25 /15	--	--	0.62	1.09
GEI	Northern Multi-Mgr HY Oppty	NMHYX	**E+**	(800) 595-9111	**D- / 1.4**	2.78	-0.03	-5.19 / 5	0.65 /36	3.67 /56	6.01	1.00
* GEI	Northern Short Bond	BSBAX	**C+**	(800) 637-1380	**C- / 3.8**	0.89	0.55	0.41 /48	0.66 /36	1.41 /25	1.31	0.44
USS	Northern Short-Int US Govt	NSIUX	**C+**	(800) 595-9111	**C- / 3.9**	1.45	0.79	1.37 /64	0.51 /33	1.22 /22	0.56	0.48
* MUH	Northern Short-Interm Tax-Ex	NSITX	**B+**	(800) 595-9111	**C+ / 5.8**	0.67	0.90	1.41 /73	1.02 /54	1.50 /35	1.17	0.48
* MUN	Northern Tax Exempt	NOTEX	**B+**	(800) 595-9111	**A+ / 9.6**	1.54	3.55	4.28 /96	3.87 /95	6.14 /93	3.32	0.49
* MTG	Northern Tax-Advtged Ult-Sh Fxd Inc	NTAUX	**C+**	(800) 595-9111	**C- / 3.4**	0.29	0.32	0.41 /48	0.52 /33	0.76 /19	0.66	0.26
* GEI	Northern Ultra-Short Fixed Income	NUSFX	**B-**	(800) 595-9111	**C- / 3.9**	0.66	0.57	0.69 /53	0.74 /38	1.06 /21	0.91	0.27
USS	Northern US Government	NOUGX	**C+**	(800) 595-9111	**C / 4.8**	2.26	1.23	1.98 /72	0.90 /41	2.16 /33	0.83	0.82
US	Northern US Treasury Index	BTIAX	**C+**	(800) 637-1380	**C+ / 6.7**	3.16	2.16	2.25 /73	1.97 /61	3.40 /52	1.43	0.29
* MUN	Nuveen All Amer Muni A	FLAAX	**C+**	(800) 257-8787	**A- / 9.2**	1.86	3.72	4.37 /96	4.32 /97	7.51 /97	3.56	0.70
MUN	Nuveen All Amer Muni C	FACCX	**U**	(800) 257-8787	**U /**	1.75	3.32	3.56 /91	--	--	2.95	1.50
MUN ●	Nuveen All Amer Muni C2	FAACX	**B-**	(800) 257-8787	**A / 9.5**	1.73	3.45	3.83 /93	3.76 /94	6.93 /96	3.21	1.25
MUN	Nuveen All Amer Muni I	FAARX	**B**	(800) 257-8787	**A+ / 9.8**	1.90	3.81	4.56 /97	4.54 /98	7.69 /98	3.90	0.50
MUS	Nuveen AZ Muni Bond A	FAZTX	**B-**	(800) 257-8787	**B+ / 8.5**	1.81	3.54	4.05 /94	3.49 /93	5.72 /90	3.15	0.88
MUN	Nuveen AZ Muni Bond C	FZCCX	**U**	(800) 257-8787	**U /**	1.61	3.12	3.29 /88	--	--	2.47	1.68
MUS ●	Nuveen AZ Muni Bond C2	FAZCX	**B+**	(800) 257-8787	**A- / 9.0**	1.67	3.26	3.48 /90	2.94 /88	5.14 /86	2.74	1.43
MUS	Nuveen AZ Muni Bond I	NMARX	**A-**	(800) 257-8787	**A / 9.5**	1.85	3.62	4.31 /96	3.72 /94	5.93 /92	3.44	0.68
MUH	Nuveen CA High Yield Muni Bd A	NCHAX	**C**	(800) 257-8787	**A+ / 9.9**	2.38	5.76	6.23 /99	6.89 /99	11.74 /99	3.92	0.85
MUN	Nuveen CA High Yield Muni Bd C	NAWSX	**U**	(800) 257-8787	**U /**	2.18	5.34	5.39 /98	--	--	3.31	1.64
MUH ●	Nuveen CA High Yield Muni Bd C2	NCHCX	**C**	(800) 257-8787	**A+ / 9.9**	2.14	5.47	5.54 /98	6.28 /99	11.11 /99	3.55	1.40
MUH	Nuveen CA High Yield Muni Bd I	NCHRX	**C**	(800) 257-8787	**A+ / 9.9**	2.33	5.96	6.43 /99	7.14 /99	12.00 /99	4.37	0.65
MUS	Nuveen CA Muni Bond A	NCAAX	**B+**	(800) 257-8787	**A+ / 9.8**	2.13	4.75	5.72 /99	5.51 /99	8.39 /99	3.47	0.77
MUN	Nuveen CA Muni Bond C	NAKFX	**U**	(800) 257-8787	**U /**	1.94	4.44	4.89 /98	--	--	2.85	1.56
MUS ●	Nuveen CA Muni Bond C2	NCACX	**B+**	(800) 257-8787	**A+ / 9.9**	1.99	4.55	5.11 /98	4.92 /98	7.81 /98	3.06	1.32
MUS	Nuveen CA Muni Bond I	NCSPX	**B+**	(800) 257-8787	**A+ / 9.9**	2.17	4.92	5.89 /99	5.72 /99	8.60 /99	3.78	0.57
MUS	Nuveen CO Muni Bond A	FCOTX	**B**	(800) 257-8787	**A / 9.3**	1.71	3.76	4.71 /97	4.38 /97	6.60 /95	3.40	0.86
MUN	Nuveen CO Muni Bond C	FAFKX	**U**	(800) 257-8787	**U /**	1.41	3.25	3.86 /93	--	--	2.74	1.65
MUS ●	Nuveen CO Muni Bond C2	FCOCX	**B+**	(800) 257-8787	**A / 9.5**	1.57	3.48	4.15 /95	3.81 /95	6.03 /92	3.01	1.41
MUS	Nuveen CO Muni Bond I	FCORX	**B+**	(800) 257-8787	**A+ / 9.8**	1.75	3.75	4.90 /98	4.57 /98	6.82 /96	3.72	0.66
GES	Nuveen Core Bond A	FAIIX	**C-**	(800) 257-8787	**C- / 4.2**	2.35	1.72	-0.20 /29	1.68 /55	2.86 /43	2.54	0.85
COI	Nuveen Core Bond C	NTIBX	**C-**	(800) 257-8787	**C- / 4.2**	2.18	1.35	-0.86 /23	0.94 /41	2.08 /32	1.86	1.61
GES	Nuveen Core Bond I	FINIX	**C+**	(800) 257-8787	**C+ / 6.1**	2.42	1.74	0.04 /37	1.93 /60	3.08 /46	2.86	0.59
COI	Nuveen Core Bond R6	NTIFX	**U**	(800) 257-8787	**U /**	2.48	1.87	0.16 /43	--	--	2.88	0.56
MUS	Nuveen CT Muni Bond A	FCTTX	**B-**	(800) 257-8787	**B / 8.2**	1.47	3.18	3.67 /92	3.24 /90	5.20 /87	3.16	0.79
MUN	Nuveen CT Muni Bond C	FDCDX	**U**	(800) 257-8787	**U /**	1.28	2.69	2.87 /84	--	--	2.53	1.59
MUS ●	Nuveen CT Muni Bond C2	FCTCX	**B**	(800) 257-8787	**B+ / 8.7**	1.34	2.90	3.10 /86	2.67 /85	4.63 /82	2.75	1.34

● Denotes fund is closed to new investors
* Denotes fund is included in Section II

RISK			NET ASSETS		ASSET							FUND MANAGER		MINIMUM		LOADS	
Risk Rating/Pts	3 Yr Avg Standard Deviation	Avg Duration	NAV As of 3/31/16	Total $(Mil)	Cash %	Gov. Bond %	Muni. Bond %	Corp. Bond %	Other %	Portfolio Turnover Ratio	Avg Coupon Rate	Manager Quality Pct	Manager Tenure (Years)	Initial Purch. $	Additional Purch. $	Front End Load	Back End Load
E- / 0.2	10.9	6.5	3.83	237	0	0	0	73	27	8	7.8	0	N/A	1,000	0	0.0	0.0
C / 4.7	3.6	5.2	10.96	109	4	0	95	0	1	85	4.9	53	17	2,500	50	0.0	0.0
C+ / 6.7	3.0	5.2	10.74	2,631	0	42	1	25	32	81	3.6	42	9	2,500	50	0.0	0.0
C / 4.6	3.6	5.3	11.03	509	2	0	97	0	1	106	4.5	49	17	2,500	50	0.0	0.0
C- / 3.2	4.5	6.4	12.06	189	2	0	96	0	2	194	4.4	72	19	2,500	50	0.0	0.0
C+ / 5.7	3.2	5.2	10.40	246	3	20	0	35	42	814	3.7	50	5	2,500	50	0.0	0.0
C / 5.2	3.4	5.2	10.23	1,353	3	14	0	41	42	664	4.7	97	5	2,500	50	0.0	0.0
C- / 3.1	4.1	6.0	9.02	570	7	0	91	0	2	8	5.9	72	18	2,500	50	0.0	0.0
D- / 1.5	5.6	4.4	6.42	5,124	4	0	0	93	3	91	7.6	51	9	2,500	50	0.0	2.0
A+ / 9.9	N/A	N/A	1.00	3,067	100	0	0	0	0	0	0.1	67	N/A	20,000,000	0	0.0	0.0
A+ / 9.9	N/A	N/A	1.00	42	100	0	0	0	0	0	0.1	67	N/A	20,000,000	0	0.0	0.0
A+ / 9.9	N/A	N/A	1.00	24,611	100	0	0	0	0	0	0.1	66	N/A	5,000,000	0	0.0	0.0
U /	N/A	N/A	1.00	4,462	100	0	0	0	0	0	0.0	N/A	N/A	5,000,000	0	0.0	0.0
U /	N/A	N/A	1.00	214	0	0	0	0	100	0	0.0	N/A	N/A	5,000,000	0	0.0	0.0
C / 5.3	3.3	5.1	10.82	3,157	14	0	85	0	1	128	4.2	41	18	2,500	50	0.0	0.0
U /	N/A	N/A	8.89	66	6	82	0	10	2	273	0.0	N/A	N/A	100,000	50	0.0	2.0
D / 1.9	5.8	4.2	9.01	403	5	2	0	81	12	54	7.2	25	5	2,500	50	0.0	2.0
A- / 9.2	1.1	2.7	18.86	560	1	29	0	39	31	277	2.8	63	6	2,500	50	0.0	0.0
B+ / 8.9	1.6	2.6	9.97	166	0	85	0	0	15	671	1.2	42	10	2,500	50	0.0	0.0
B+ / 8.7	1.3	2.6	10.48	1,161	2	0	97	0	1	23	4.3	59	9	2,500	50	0.0	0.0
C- / 3.8	4.1	6.0	10.89	1,062	6	0	93	0	1	165	4.9	45	18	2,500	50	0.0	0.0
A+ / 9.9	0.3	1.1	10.12	3,363	1	3	69	23	4	132	2.7	76	7	2,500	50	0.0	0.0
A+ / 9.8	0.5	1.2	10.18	1,542	4	14	1	72	9	63	1.4	81	7	2,500	50	0.0	0.0
B / 8.0	2.4	3.5	9.87	26	2	80	0	0	18	546	1.5	35	10	2,500	50	0.0	0.0
C+ / 6.0	3.1	4.9	22.13	123	3	96	0	0	1	51	1.8	57	7	2,500	50	0.0	0.0
D+ / 2.9	4.6	7.2	11.72	1,132	1	0	98	0	1	18	5.0	45	6	3,000	100	4.2	0.0
U /	N/A	7.2	11.73	105	1	0	98	0	1	18	5.0	N/A	6	3,000	100	0.0	0.0
D+ / 2.9	4.6	7.2	11.72	308	1	0	98	0	1	18	5.0	30	6	3,000	100	0.0	0.0
D+ / 2.9	4.6	7.2	11.77	1,372	1	0	98	0	1	18	5.0	53	6	100,000	0	0.0	0.0
C- / 4.2	3.7	7.1	10.95	49	3	0	96	0	1	14	5.3	52	5	3,000	100	4.2	0.0
U /	N/A	7.1	10.95	3	3	0	96	0	1	14	5.3	N/A	5	3,000	100	0.0	0.0
C- / 4.2	3.7	7.1	10.95	7	3	0	96	0	1	14	5.3	34	5	3,000	100	0.0	0.0
C / 4.3	3.6	7.1	10.98	43	3	0	96	0	1	14	5.3	62	5	100,000	0	0.0	0.0
E+ / 0.6	6.8	9.8	9.80	405	2	0	96	0	2	10	4.6	N/A	10	3,000	100	4.2	0.0
U /	N/A	9.8	9.79	51	2	0	96	0	2	10	4.6	N/A	10	3,000	100	0.0	0.0
E / 0.5	6.8	9.8	9.78	50	2	0	96	0	2	10	4.6	41	10	3,000	100	0.0	0.0
E+ / 0.6	6.8	9.8	9.78	325	2	0	96	0	2	10	4.6	76	10	100,000	0	0.0	0.0
C- / 3.3	4.1	8.4	11.39	400	1	0	98	0	1	14	4.5	91	13	3,000	100	4.2	0.0
U /	N/A	8.4	11.35	55	1	0	98	0	1	14	4.5	N/A	13	3,000	100	0.0	0.0
C- / 3.3	4.1	8.4	11.36	57	1	0	98	0	1	14	4.5	85	13	3,000	100	0.0	0.0
C- / 3.3	4.1	8.4	11.39	650	1	0	98	0	1	14	4.5	93	13	100,000	0	0.0	0.0
C- / 3.7	4.0	7.9	10.96	82	2	0	97	0	1	8	5.0	74	5	3,000	100	4.2	0.0
U /	N/A	7.9	10.92	7	2	0	97	0	1	8	5.0	N/A	5	3,000	100	0.0	0.0
C- / 3.6	4.0	7.9	10.93	11	2	0	97	0	1	8	5.0	47	5	3,000	100	0.0	0.0
C- / 3.6	4.0	7.9	10.94	87	2	0	97	0	1	8	5.0	79	5	100,000	0	0.0	0.0
C+ / 6.4	3.0	4.8	9.89	15	2	10	0	44	44	44	4.2	37	16	3,000	100	3.0	0.0
C+ / 6.3	3.1	4.8	9.86	1	2	10	0	44	44	44	4.2	27	16	3,000	100	0.0	0.0
C+ / 6.4	3.0	4.8	9.85	120	2	10	0	44	44	44	4.2	45	16	100,000	0	0.0	0.0
U /	N/A	4.8	9.86	54	2	10	0	44	44	44	4.2	N/A	16	5,000,000	0	0.0	0.0
C / 4.4	3.8	6.9	10.89	168	1	0	98	0	1	16	5.1	39	5	3,000	100	4.2	0.0
U /	N/A	6.9	10.87	5	1	0	98	0	1	16	5.1	N/A	5	3,000	100	0.0	0.0
C / 4.4	3.7	6.9	10.88	39	1	0	98	0	1	16	5.1	24	5	3,000	100	0.0	0.0

99 Pct = Best 0 Pct = Worst					PERFORMANCE							
						Total Return % through 3/31/16					Incl. in Returns	
									Annualized			
Fund Type	Fund Name	Ticker Symbol	Overall Investment Rating	Phone	Performance Rating/Pts	3 Mo	6 Mo	1Yr / Pct	3Yr / Pct	5Yr / Pct	Dividend Yield	Expense Ratio
MUS	Nuveen CT Muni Bond I	FCTRX	B+	(800) 257-8787	A / 9.3	1.52	3.19	3.89 /93	3.43 /92	5.40 /88	3.51	0.59
MUS	Nuveen GA Muni Bond A	FGATX	B-	(800) 257-8787	B+ / 8.3	1.40	2.70	3.61 /91	3.36 /91	5.73 /90	3.38	0.83
MUN	Nuveen GA Muni Bond C	FGCCX	U	(800) 257-8787	U /	1.20	2.29	2.79 /83	--	--	2.74	1.62
MUS ●	Nuveen GA Muni Bond C2	FGACX	B+	(800) 257-8787	B+ / 8.8	1.27	2.34	3.07 /86	2.78 /86	5.14 /86	3.01	1.38
MUS	Nuveen GA Muni Bond I	FGARX	A-	(800) 257-8787	A / 9.4	1.44	2.79	3.79 /92	3.55 /93	5.95 /92	3.70	0.63
GL	Nuveen Global Total Return Bond A	NGTAX	E	(800) 257-8787	E / 0.3	3.63	2.55	-1.88 /16	-2.03 / 4	--	3.84	1.89
GL	Nuveen Global Total Return Bond C	NGTCX	E	(800) 257-8787	E / 0.4	3.49	2.16	-2.57 /13	-2.72 / 3	--	3.23	2.64
GL	Nuveen Global Total Return Bond I	NGTIX	E	(800) 257-8787	E+ / 0.8	3.69	2.62	-1.67 /17	-1.78 / 5	--	4.28	1.64
GL	Nuveen Global Total Return Bond R3	NGTRX	E	(800) 257-8787	E+ / 0.6	3.62	2.42	-2.12 /15	-2.25 / 4	--	3.76	2.14
GL	Nuveen High Income Bond A	FJSIX	E-	(800) 257-8787	E- / 0.1	0.39	-5.44	-12.80 / 0	-2.70 / 3	1.74 /28	7.49	1.01
GL	Nuveen High Income Bond C	FCSIX	E-	(800) 257-8787	E- / 0.1	0.25	-5.78	-13.48 / 0	-3.40 / 2	1.04 /21	6.87	1.76
GL	Nuveen High Income Bond I	FJSYX	E-	(800) 257-8787	E- / 0.2	0.37	-5.38	-12.70 / 0	-2.47 / 3	2.03 /32	8.07	0.76
GL	Nuveen High Income Bond R3	FANSX	E-	(800) 257-8787	E- / 0.2	0.40	-5.48	-13.08 / 0	-2.95 / 2	1.49 /26	7.44	1.25
* MUH	Nuveen High Yield Muni Bond A	NHMAX	C	(800) 257-8787	A+ / 9.9	2.87	5.46	6.17 /99	6.24 /99	10.93 /99	5.15	0.83
MUH	Nuveen High Yield Muni Bond C	NHCCX	U	(800) 257-8787	U /	2.67	5.04	5.33 /98	--	--	4.59	1.63
MUH ●	Nuveen High Yield Muni Bond C2	NHMCX	C	(800) 257-8787	A+ / 9.9	2.73	5.17	5.58 /99	5.67 /99	10.31 /99	4.83	1.38
MUH	Nuveen High Yield Muni Bond I	NHMRX	C	(800) 257-8787	A+ / 9.9	2.92	5.57	6.39 /99	6.45 /99	11.14 /99	5.58	0.63
MUN	Nuveen Infl Protected Muni Bd A	NITAX	D	(800) 257-8787	C- / 3.1	1.48	3.90	2.83 /83	0.29 /32	3.54 /74	2.41	1.00
MUN	Nuveen Infl Protected Muni Bd C	NAADX	U	(800) 257-8787	U /	1.27	3.46	1.96 /77	--	--	1.64	1.81
MUN ●	Nuveen Infl Protected Muni Bd C2	NIPCX	D	(800) 257-8787	C- / 3.8	1.34	3.61	2.25 /79	-0.25 /14	2.99 /69	1.92	1.55
MUN	Nuveen Infl Protected Muni Bd I	NIPIX	C-	(800) 257-8787	C+ / 5.9	1.52	3.98	3.00 /85	0.49 /38	3.75 /76	2.65	0.79
GL	Nuveen Inflation Protected Sec A	FAIPX	E+	(800) 257-8787	E+ / 0.7	4.22	3.16	0.36 /47	-1.06 / 8	2.56 /39	0.00	0.92
GL	Nuveen Inflation Protected Sec C	FCIPX	D-	(800) 257-8787	D- / 1.0	4.08	2.81	-0.27 /28	-1.63 / 5	1.93 /30	0.00	1.66
GL	Nuveen Inflation Protected Sec I	FYIPX	D	(800) 257-8787	D+ / 2.7	4.27	3.31	0.63 /52	-0.66 /10	2.92 /44	0.00	0.66
GL	Nuveen Inflation Protected Sec R3	FRIPX	D-	(800) 257-8787	D- / 1.3	4.16	3.09	0.09 /41	-1.29 / 7	2.30 /35	0.00	1.15
GL	Nuveen Inflation Protected Sec R6	FISFX	U	(800) 257-8787	U /	4.36	3.40	0.81 /55	--	--	0.00	0.52
USS	Nuveen Intermediate Government Bd	FIGAX	C	(800) 257-8787	C- / 3.1	1.77	0.97	1.04 /59	0.96 /42	1.93 /30	1.05	1.02
USS	Nuveen Intermediate Government Bd	FYGYX	B	(800) 257-8787	C / 5.2	1.95	1.22	1.43 /65	1.22 /47	2.18 /33	1.34	0.77
USS	Nuveen Intermediate Govt Bd C	FYGCX	C	(800) 257-8787	C- / 3.2	1.71	0.72	0.42 /48	0.20 /29	1.18 /22	0.35	1.77
USS	Nuveen Intermediate Govt Bd R3	FYGRX	C+	(800) 257-8787	C / 4.3	1.83	1.08	1.01 /59	0.77 /38	1.69 /27	0.82	1.27
* MUN	Nuveen Intmdt Duration Muni Bond A	NMBAX	A-	(800) 257-8787	B+ / 8.4	1.66	3.04	3.60 /91	3.09 /89	4.60 /82	2.67	0.69
MUN	Nuveen Intmdt Duration Muni Bond C	NNCCX	U	(800) 257-8787	U /	1.47	2.65	2.80 /83	--	--	1.99	1.49
MUN ●	Nuveen Intmdt Duration Muni Bond	NNSCX	A	(800) 257-8787	B+ / 8.6	1.53	2.78	3.06 /86	2.54 /83	4.02 /78	2.24	1.24
MUN	Nuveen Intmdt Duration Muni Bond I	NUVBX	A+	(800) 257-8787	A / 9.3	1.71	3.25	3.90 /93	3.32 /91	4.81 /84	2.94	0.49
MUS	Nuveen KS Muni Bond A	FKSTX	C+	(800) 257-8787	B+ / 8.6	1.63	3.03	3.90 /93	3.59 /93	5.96 /92	3.46	0.84
MUN	Nuveen KS Muni Bond C	FAFOX	U	(800) 257-8787	U /	1.35	2.56	3.02 /85	--	--	2.86	1.64
MUS ●	Nuveen KS Muni Bond C2	FCKSX	B-	(800) 257-8787	A- / 9.0	1.41	2.66	3.24 /87	3.02 /88	5.38 /88	3.08	1.39
MUS	Nuveen KS Muni Bond I	FRKSX	B+	(800) 257-8787	A / 9.5	1.59	3.13	4.01 /94	3.80 /95	6.17 /93	3.81	0.64
MUS	Nuveen KY Muni Bond A	FKYTX	B-	(800) 257-8787	B / 8.2	1.52	2.62	3.47 /90	3.24 /90	5.36 /88	3.42	0.80
MUN	Nuveen KY Muni Bond C	FKCCX	U	(800) 257-8787	U /	1.32	2.31	2.74 /82	--	--	2.77	1.59
MUS ●	Nuveen KY Muni Bond C2	FKYCX	B+	(800) 257-8787	B+ / 8.7	1.39	2.35	3.01 /85	2.69 /85	4.79 /84	3.04	1.35
MUS	Nuveen KY Muni Bond I	FKYRX	A-	(800) 257-8787	A / 9.3	1.57	2.73	3.79 /92	3.47 /92	5.59 /89	3.79	0.60
MUS	Nuveen LA Muni Bond A	FTLAX	B-	(800) 257-8787	A- / 9.1	1.35	3.03	3.60 /91	4.32 /97	6.69 /95	3.62	0.85
MUN	Nuveen LA Muni Bond C	FAFLX	U	(800) 257-8787	U /	1.08	2.65	2.72 /82	--	--	3.01	1.64
MUS ●	Nuveen LA Muni Bond C2	FTLCX	B	(800) 257-8787	A / 9.4	1.14	2.78	2.99 /85	3.75 /94	6.11 /93	3.27	1.40
MUS	Nuveen LA Muni Bond I	FTLRX	B	(800) 257-8787	A+ / 9.7	1.32	3.13	3.72 /92	4.50 /98	6.88 /96	3.97	0.65
* MUN	Nuveen Ltd Term Muni A	FLTDX	B+	(800) 257-8787	C+ / 5.8	0.90	1.47	2.04 /77	1.65 /71	2.82 /66	1.79	0.64
MUN	Nuveen Ltd Term Muni C	FAFJX	U	(800) 257-8787	U /	0.71	1.07	1.27 /71	--	--	1.17	1.43
MUN ●	Nuveen Ltd Term Muni C2	FLTCX	A	(800) 257-8787	C+ / 6.4	0.81	1.28	1.57 /74	1.27 /60	2.45 /58	1.46	0.99
MUN	Nuveen Ltd Term Muni I	FLTRX	A+	(800) 257-8787	B / 7.7	0.95	1.56	2.22 /79	1.82 /74	3.02 /69	2.00	0.44
MUS	Nuveen MA Muni Bond A	NMAAX	C+	(800) 257-8787	B+ / 8.4	1.49	3.25	3.84 /93	3.46 /92	5.84 /91	3.20	0.81
MUN	Nuveen MA Muni Bond C	NAAGX	U	(800) 257-8787	U /	1.29	2.86	3.02 /85	--	--	2.55	1.61

● Denotes fund is closed to new investors
* Denotes fund is included in Section II

RISK			NET ASSETS		ASSET							FUND MANAGER		MINIMUM		LOADS	
Risk Rating/Pts	3 Yr Avg Standard Deviation	Avg Duration	NAV As of 3/31/16	Total $(Mil)	Cash %	Gov. Bond %	Muni. Bond %	Corp. Bond %	Other %	Portfolio Turnover Ratio	Avg Coupon Rate	Manager Quality Pct	Manager Tenure (Years)	Initial Purch. $	Additional Purch. $	Front End Load	Back End Load
C / 4.5	3.7	6.9	10.92	74	1	0	98	0	1	16	5.1	46	5	100,000	0	0.0	0.0
C / 4.6	3.6	6.7	11.16	95	2	0	97	0	1	11	5.5	47	9	3,000	100	4.2	0.0
U /	N/A	6.7	11.11	7	2	0	97	0	1	11	5.5	N/A	9	3,000	100	0.0	0.0
C / 4.6	3.7	6.7	11.11	29	2	0	97	0	1	11	5.5	29	9	3,000	100	0.0	0.0
C / 4.6	3.6	6.7	11.12	47	2	0	97	0	1	11	5.5	54	9	100,000	0	0.0	0.0
D- / 1.0	6.5	N/A	17.79	1	3	32	0	57	8	89	0.0	12	5	3,000	100	4.8	0.0
D- / 1.0	6.5	N/A	17.88	N/A	3	32	0	57	8	89	0.0	8	5	3,000	100	0.0	0.0
D- / 1.0	6.5	N/A	17.85	12	3	32	0	57	8	89	0.0	15	5	100,000	0	0.0	0.0
D- / 1.0	6.6	N/A	17.85	N/A	3	32	0	57	8	89	0.0	10	5	0	0	0.0	0.0
E+ / 0.6	7.6	4.4	6.77	140	3	0	0	85	12	80	7.9	8	11	3,000	100	4.8	0.0
E+ / 0.6	7.6	4.4	6.77	38	3	0	0	85	12	80	7.9	6	11	3,000	100	0.0	0.0
E+ / 0.6	7.5	4.4	6.79	194	3	0	0	85	12	80	7.9	9	11	100,000	0	0.0	0.0
E+ / 0.6	7.6	4.4	6.92	1	3	0	0	85	12	80	7.9	7	11	0	0	0.0	0.0
E+ / 0.7	6.2	10.5	17.40	4,146	2	0	96	0	2	15	6.4	70	16	3,000	100	4.2	0.0
U /	N/A	10.5	17.38	643	2	0	96	0	2	15	6.4	N/A	16	3,000	100	0.0	0.0
E+ / 0.7	6.2	10.5	17.39	1,236	2	0	96	0	2	15	6.4	44	16	3,000	100	0.0	0.0
E+ / 0.7	6.1	10.5	17.40	6,482	2	0	96	0	2	15	6.4	77	16	100,000	0	0.0	0.0
C- / 3.1	4.6	4.5	10.61	21	0	0	100	0	0	20	4.3	6	5	3,000	100	3.0	0.0
U /	N/A	4.5	10.60	1	0	0	100	0	0	20	4.3	N/A	5	3,000	100	0.0	0.0
C- / 3.2	4.6	4.5	10.61	6	0	0	100	0	0	20	4.3	5	5	3,000	100	0.0	0.0
C- / 3.2	4.5	4.5	10.63	15	0	0	100	0	0	20	4.3	6	5	100,000	0	0.0	0.0
D+ / 2.6	5.1	4.3	11.11	73	4	85	0	5	6	34	0.0	28	12	3,000	100	4.3	0.0
D+ / 2.7	5.1	4.3	10.97	13	4	85	0	5	6	34	0.0	16	12	3,000	100	0.0	0.0
D+ / 2.7	5.0	4.3	11.23	347	4	85	0	5	6	34	0.0	40	12	100,000	0	0.0	0.0
D+ / 2.6	5.1	4.3	11.02	12	4	85	0	5	6	34	0.0	23	12	0	0	0.0	0.0
U /	N/A	4.3	11.25	3	4	85	0	5	6	34	0.0	N/A	12	5,000,000	0	0.0	0.0
B+ / 8.5	1.9	3.7	8.89	13	3	59	3	1	34	59	4.6	47	14	3,000	100	3.0	0.0
B+ / 8.6	1.9	3.7	8.90	62	3	59	3	1	34	59	4.6	57	14	100,000	0	0.0	0.0
B+ / 8.5	1.9	3.7	8.91	1	3	59	3	1	34	59	4.6	25	14	3,000	100	0.0	0.0
B+ / 8.6	1.9	3.7	8.90	N/A	3	59	3	1	34	59	4.6	41	14	0	0	0.0	0.0
C+ / 5.9	3.2	5.6	9.35	1,064	0	0	98	0	2	19	4.8	53	9	3,000	100	3.0	0.0
U /	N/A	5.6	9.36	33	0	0	98	0	2	19	4.8	N/A	9	3,000	100	0.0	0.0
C+ / 6.0	3.1	5.6	9.37	102	0	0	98	0	2	19	4.8	36	9	3,000	100	0.0	0.0
C+ / 6.0	3.1	5.6	9.38	3,895	0	0	98	0	2	19	4.8	64	9	100,000	0	0.0	0.0
C- / 3.6	4.2	6.9	11.10	143	3	0	96	0	1	8	5.5	35	5	3,000	100	4.2	0.0
U /	N/A	6.9	11.07	10	3	0	96	0	1	8	5.5	N/A	5	3,000	100	0.0	0.0
C- / 3.6	4.2	6.9	11.08	41	3	0	96	0	1	8	5.5	21	5	3,000	100	0.0	0.0
C- / 3.6	4.2	6.9	11.14	34	3	0	96	0	1	8	5.5	41	5	100,000	0	0.0	0.0
C / 4.7	3.6	6.1	11.22	297	2	0	97	0	1	7	5.3	43	9	3,000	100	4.2	0.0
U /	N/A	6.1	11.22	6	2	0	97	0	1	7	5.3	N/A	9	3,000	100	0.0	0.0
C / 4.8	3.6	6.1	11.22	45	2	0	97	0	1	7	5.3	28	9	3,000	100	0.0	0.0
C / 4.8	3.6	6.1	11.22	30	2	0	97	0	1	7	5.3	51	9	100,000	0	0.0	0.0
C- / 3.3	4.2	7.7	11.54	85	4	0	95	0	1	12	5.4	59	5	3,000	100	4.2	0.0
U /	N/A	7.7	11.48	7	4	0	95	0	1	12	5.4	N/A	5	3,000	100	0.0	0.0
C- / 3.3	4.3	7.7	11.48	22	4	0	95	0	1	12	5.4	38	5	3,000	100	0.0	0.0
C- / 3.3	4.3	7.7	11.56	13	4	0	95	0	1	12	5.4	69	5	100,000	0	0.0	0.0
B+ / 8.7	1.8	3.3	11.15	1,197	0	0	99	0	1	20	4.3	57	10	3,000	100	2.5	0.0
U /	N/A	3.3	11.10	85	0	0	99	0	1	20	4.3	N/A	10	3,000	100	0.0	0.0
B+ / 8.7	1.8	3.3	11.11	466	0	0	99	0	1	20	4.3	43	10	3,000	100	0.0	0.0
B+ / 8.7	1.8	3.3	11.10	2,676	0	0	99	0	1	20	4.3	70	10	100,000	0	0.0	0.0
C- / 3.7	4.0	7.3	10.29	87	2	0	97	0	1	11	5.1	39	5	3,000	100	4.2	0.0
U /	N/A	7.3	10.20	6	2	0	97	0	1	11	5.1	N/A	5	3,000	100	0.0	0.0

Fund Type	Fund Name	Ticker Symbol	Overall Investment Rating	Phone	PERFORMANCE Performance Rating/Pts	Total Return % through 3/31/16 3 Mo	6 Mo	1Yr / Pct	Annualized 3Yr / Pct	Annualized 5Yr / Pct	Incl. in Returns Dividend Yield	Expense Ratio
MUS ●	Nuveen MA Muni Bond C2	NMACX	**B**	(800) 257-8787	**A- / 9.0**	1.35	2.97	3.36 /89	2.90 /87	5.27 /87	2.78	1.36
MUS	Nuveen MA Muni Bond I	NBMAX	**B+**	(800) 257-8787	**A / 9.5**	1.53	3.34	4.13 /95	3.68 /94	6.06 /92	3.52	0.62
MUS	Nuveen MD Muni Bond A	NMDAX	**C+**	(800) 257-8787	**B / 8.0**	1.51	2.89	3.94 /94	2.93 /87	5.19 /87	3.33	0.83
MUN	Nuveen MD Muni Bond C	NACCX	**U**	(800) 257-8787	**U /**	1.33	2.50	3.06 /86	--	--	2.71	1.63
MUS ●	Nuveen MD Muni Bond C2	NMDCX	**B-**	(800) 257-8787	**B+ / 8.5**	1.48	2.71	3.38 /89	2.37 /81	4.63 /82	2.93	1.38
MUS	Nuveen MD Muni Bond I	NMMDX	**B+**	(800) 257-8787	**A- / 9.2**	1.66	3.00	4.17 /95	3.13 /89	5.41 /88	3.69	0.63
MUS	Nuveen MI Muni Bond A	FMITX	**B-**	(800) 257-8787	**B+ / 8.9**	1.51	3.47	4.25 /95	3.96 /96	5.98 /92	3.26	0.84
MUN	Nuveen MI Muni Bond C	FAFNX	**U**	(800) 257-8787	**U /**	1.32	3.09	3.37 /89	--	--	2.65	1.63
MUS ●	Nuveen MI Muni Bond C2	FLMCX	**B**	(800) 257-8787	**A / 9.3**	1.39	3.13	3.64 /91	3.36 /92	5.40 /88	2.90	1.39
MUS	Nuveen MI Muni Bond I	NMMIX	**B+**	(800) 257-8787	**A+ / 9.7**	1.56	3.58	4.47 /97	4.18 /97	6.20 /93	3.61	0.64
MUS	Nuveen Minnesota Intmdt Muni Bd A	FAMAX	**A+**	(800) 257-8787	**B+ / 8.4**	1.46	2.77	3.67 /92	3.11 /89	4.67 /83	2.74	0.82
MUN	Nuveen Minnesota Intmdt Muni Bd C	NIBCX	**U**	(800) 257-8787	**U /**	1.27	2.38	2.86 /84	--	--	2.04	1.62
MUS	Nuveen Minnesota Intmdt Muni Bd	FACMX	**A+**	(800) 257-8787	**B+ / 8.7**	1.34	2.53	3.19 /87	2.62 /84	4.19 /79	2.36	1.27
MUN ●	Nuveen Minnesota Intmdt Muni Bd	NIBMX	**A+**	(800) 257-8787	**B+ / 8.6**	1.33	2.49	3.10 /86	2.55 /83	4.08 /78	2.27	1.38
MUS	Nuveen Minnesota Intmdt Muni Bd I	FAMTX	**A+**	(800) 257-8787	**A / 9.3**	1.61	2.97	3.97 /94	3.34 /91	4.88 /84	3.01	0.63
MUS	Nuveen Minnesota Municipal Bond A	FJMNX	**C+**	(800) 257-8787	**B+ / 8.9**	1.72	3.42	4.54 /97	3.87 /95	6.70 /95	3.41	0.84
MUN	Nuveen Minnesota Municipal Bond C	NTCCX	**U**	(800) 257-8787	**U /**	1.53	3.12	3.76 /92	--	--	2.81	1.64
MUS	Nuveen Minnesota Municipal Bond	FCMNX	**B-**	(800) 257-8787	**A / 9.3**	1.58	3.17	4.06 /94	3.39 /92	6.20 /93	3.10	1.29
MUN ●	Nuveen Minnesota Municipal Bond	NMBCX	**B-**	(800) 257-8787	**A / 9.3**	1.59	3.23	4.06 /94	3.33 /91	6.13 /93	3.01	1.39
MUS	Nuveen Minnesota Municipal Bond I	FYMNX	**B**	(800) 257-8787	**A+ / 9.7**	1.77	3.52	4.76 /97	4.08 /96	6.90 /96	3.76	0.64
MUS	Nuveen MO Muni Bond A	FMOTX	**B-**	(800) 257-8787	**B+ / 8.8**	1.69	3.36	4.44 /96	3.76 /94	6.10 /92	3.45	0.79
MUN	Nuveen MO Muni Bond C	FAFPX	**U**	(800) 257-8787	**U /**	1.50	2.97	3.63 /91	--	--	2.83	1.59
MUS ●	Nuveen MO Muni Bond C2	FMOCX	**B**	(800) 257-8787	**A- / 9.2**	1.56	3.10	3.90 /93	3.19 /90	5.53 /89	3.09	1.34
MUS	Nuveen MO Muni Bond I	FMMRX	**B+**	(800) 257-8787	**A+ / 9.6**	1.74	3.47	4.66 /97	3.95 /95	6.30 /94	3.81	0.59
MUS	Nuveen NC Muni Bond A	FLNCX	**C+**	(800) 257-8787	**B+ / 8.3**	1.58	3.21	3.51 /90	3.36 /92	5.62 /90	2.93	0.78
MUN	Nuveen NC Muni Bond C	FDCCX	**U**	(800) 257-8787	**U /**	1.47	2.89	2.68 /82	--	--	2.26	1.58
MUS ●	Nuveen NC Muni Bond C2	FCNCX	**B-**	(800) 257-8787	**B+ / 8.9**	1.53	3.02	3.02 /85	2.84 /86	5.06 /86	2.50	1.33
MUS	Nuveen NC Muni Bond I	FCNRX	**B+**	(800) 257-8787	**A / 9.4**	1.71	3.38	3.76 /92	3.59 /93	5.84 /91	3.21	0.58
MUS	Nuveen Nebraska Municipal Bond A	FNTAX	**C**	(800) 257-8787	**B+ / 8.3**	1.36	3.05	3.72 /92	3.34 /91	5.42 /88	2.77	0.92
MUN	Nuveen Nebraska Municipal Bond C	NAAFX	**U**	(800) 257-8787	**U /**	1.19	2.76	2.90 /84	--	--	2.11	1.72
MUS	Nuveen Nebraska Municipal Bond C1	FNTCX	**C+**	(800) 257-8787	**B+ / 8.9**	1.25	2.92	3.24 /87	2.87 /87	4.94 /85	2.42	1.38
MUN ●	Nuveen Nebraska Municipal Bond C2	NCNBX	**C+**	(800) 257-8787	**B+ / 8.8**	1.25	2.80	3.08 /86	2.73 /85	4.83 /84	2.37	1.47
MUS	Nuveen Nebraska Municipal Bond I	FNTYX	**C+**	(800) 257-8787	**A / 9.4**	1.51	3.25	3.90 /93	3.51 /93	5.63 /90	3.06	0.72
MUS	Nuveen NJ Muni Bond A	NNJAX	**C+**	(800) 257-8787	**B+ / 8.9**	2.07	4.34	4.22 /95	3.74 /94	6.52 /94	3.21	0.81
MUN	Nuveen NJ Muni Bond C	NJCCX	**U**	(800) 257-8787	**U /**	1.88	3.95	3.42 /89	--	--	2.59	1.61
MUS ●	Nuveen NJ Muni Bond C2	NNJCX	**B-**	(800) 257-8787	**A- / 9.2**	1.86	4.09	3.69 /92	3.16 /90	5.93 /92	2.85	1.36
MUS	Nuveen NJ Muni Bond I	NMNJX	**B**	(800) 257-8787	**A+ / 9.7**	2.11	4.55	4.54 /97	3.99 /96	6.74 /95	3.65	0.61
MUS	Nuveen NM Muni Bond A	FNMTX	**C+**	(800) 257-8787	**B / 7.8**	1.44	3.02	3.77 /92	2.74 /85	4.77 /83	2.97	0.85
MUN	Nuveen NM Muni Bond C	FNCCX	**U**	(800) 257-8787	**U /**	1.34	2.61	2.94 /84	--	--	2.31	1.65
MUS ●	Nuveen NM Muni Bond C2	FNMCX	**B-**	(800) 257-8787	**B+ / 8.3**	1.31	2.76	3.24 /87	2.21 /79	4.20 /79	2.59	1.40
MUS	Nuveen NM Muni Bond I	FNMRX	**B+**	(800) 257-8787	**A- / 9.0**	1.49	3.12	3.88 /93	2.93 /87	4.97 /85	3.31	0.65
GEN	Nuveen NWQ Flexible Income A	NWQAX	**D+**	(800) 257-8787	**C+ / 5.8**	2.67	3.90	0.37 /47	2.94 /76	6.08 /77	5.14	1.49
GEN	Nuveen NWQ Flexible Income C	NWQCX	**D+**	(800) 257-8787	**C+ / 6.6**	2.53	3.57	-0.35 /28	2.17 /65	5.30 /74	4.61	2.24
GEN	Nuveen NWQ Flexible Income I	NWQIX	**C-**	(800) 257-8787	**B / 7.9**	2.73	4.09	0.63 /52	3.21 /78	6.37 /79	5.65	1.25
MUS	Nuveen NY Muni Bond A	NNYAX	**B-**	(800) 257-8787	**B+ / 8.8**	1.54	3.59	4.20 /95	3.78 /94	5.64 /90	3.48	0.77
MUN	Nuveen NY Muni Bond C	NAJPX	**U**	(800) 257-8787	**U /**	1.34	3.09	3.37 /89	--	--	2.83	1.57
MUS ●	Nuveen NY Muni Bond C2	NNYCX	**B**	(800) 257-8787	**A- / 9.2**	1.40	3.22	3.65 /91	3.19 /90	5.05 /86	3.10	1.32
MUS	Nuveen NY Muni Bond I	NTNYX	**B+**	(800) 257-8787	**A+ / 9.6**	1.59	3.60	4.33 /96	3.96 /96	5.83 /91	3.84	0.57
MUS	Nuveen OH Muni Bond A	FOHTX	**C+**	(800) 257-8787	**B+ / 8.9**	1.90	3.70	4.30 /96	3.79 /95	6.01 /92	3.33	0.80
MUN	Nuveen OH Muni Bond C	FAFMX	**U**	(800) 257-8787	**U /**	1.71	3.32	3.51 /90	--	--	2.73	1.59
MUS ●	Nuveen OH Muni Bond C2	FOHCX	**B-**	(800) 257-8787	**A- / 9.2**	1.76	3.42	3.72 /92	3.24 /90	5.44 /88	2.93	1.35
MUS	Nuveen OH Muni Bond I	NXOHX	**B**	(800) 257-8787	**A+ / 9.7**	1.96	3.81	4.52 /97	4.01 /96	6.22 /93	3.69	0.60

99 Pct = Best; 0 Pct = Worst

● Denotes fund is closed to new investors
* Denotes fund is included in Section II

RISK			NET ASSETS		ASSET							FUND MANAGER		MINIMUM		LOADS	
Risk Rating/Pts	3 Yr Avg Standard Deviation	Avg Duration	NAV As of 3/31/16	Total $(Mil)	Cash %	Gov. Bond %	Muni. Bond %	Corp. Bond %	Other %	Portfolio Turnover Ratio	Avg Coupon Rate	Manager Quality Pct	Manager Tenure (Years)	Initial Purch. $	Additional Purch. $	Front End Load	Back End Load
C- / 3.8	3.9	7.3	10.21	23	2	0	97	0	1	11	5.1	26	5	3,000	100	0.0	0.0
C- / 3.8	3.9	7.3	10.28	154	2	0	97	0	1	11	5.1	48	5	100,000	0	0.0	0.0
C- / 4.1	3.9	6.5	10.88	63	3	0	95	0	2	20	3.8	31	5	3,000	100	4.2	0.0
U /	N/A	6.5	10.84	10	3	0	95	0	2	20	3.8	N/A	5	3,000	100	0.0	0.0
C- / 4.1	3.9	6.5	10.85	30	3	0	95	0	2	20	3.8	18	5	3,000	100	0.0	0.0
C- / 4.2	3.9	6.5	10.89	71	3	0	95	0	2	20	3.8	37	5	100,000	0	0.0	0.0
C- / 3.7	4.0	7.7	11.79	114	1	0	98	0	1	19	4.7	55	9	3,000	100	4.2	0.0
U /	N/A	7.7	11.76	8	1	0	98	0	1	19	4.7	N/A	9	3,000	100	0.0	0.0
C- / 3.6	4.0	7.7	11.76	21	1	0	98	0	1	19	4.7	34	9	3,000	100	0.0	0.0
C- / 3.6	4.0	7.7	11.78	43	1	0	98	0	1	19	4.7	62	9	100,000	0	0.0	0.0
C+ / 6.7	3.0	6.2	10.63	89	2	0	97	0	1	11	4.6	63	22	3,000	100	3.0	0.0
U /	N/A	6.2	10.57	12	2	0	97	0	1	11	4.6	N/A	22	3,000	100	0.0	0.0
C+ / 6.7	3.0	6.2	10.66	2	2	0	97	0	1	11	4.6	45	22	3,000	100	0.0	0.0
C+ / 6.8	2.9	6.2	10.59	7	2	0	97	0	1	11	4.6	43	22	3,000	100	0.0	0.0
C+ / 6.7	3.0	6.2	10.58	223	2	0	97	0	1	11	4.6	75	22	100,000	0	0.0	0.0
D+ / 2.9	4.4	9.6	11.94	143	2	0	97	0	1	10	4.5	39	28	3,000	100	4.2	0.0
U /	N/A	9.6	11.93	18	2	0	97	0	1	10	4.5	N/A	28	3,000	100	0.0	0.0
C- / 3.0	4.3	9.6	11.89	13	2	0	97	0	1	10	4.5	26	28	3,000	100	0.0	0.0
C- / 3.0	4.3	9.6	11.95	9	2	0	97	0	1	10	4.5	26	28	3,000	100	0.0	0.0
C- / 3.0	4.3	9.6	11.93	124	2	0	97	0	1	10	4.5	47	28	100,000	0	0.0	0.0
C- / 3.8	3.9	7.3	11.52	213	0	0	99	0	1	8	4.5	50	5	3,000	100	4.2	0.0
U /	N/A	7.3	11.48	14	0	0	99	0	1	8	4.5	N/A	5	3,000	100	0.0	0.0
C- / 3.8	3.9	7.3	11.49	28	0	0	99	0	1	8	4.5	33	5	3,000	100	0.0	0.0
C- / 3.8	3.9	7.3	11.51	221	0	0	99	0	1	8	4.5	58	5	100,000	0	0.0	0.0
C- / 3.8	3.9	7.5	11.14	176	0	0	99	0	1	11	4.4	38	9	3,000	100	4.2	0.0
U /	N/A	7.5	11.14	12	0	0	99	0	1	11	4.4	N/A	9	3,000	100	0.0	0.0
C- / 3.7	3.9	7.5	11.15	37	0	0	99	0	1	11	4.4	23	9	3,000	100	0.0	0.0
C- / 3.8	3.9	7.5	11.19	249	0	0	99	0	1	11	4.4	43	9	100,000	0	0.0	0.0
D+ / 2.6	4.6	10.4	11.01	25	3	0	96	0	1	27	4.9	19	6	3,000	100	4.2	0.0
U /	N/A	10.4	10.98	2	3	0	96	0	1	27	4.9	N/A	6	3,000	100	0.0	0.0
D+ / 2.6	4.6	10.4	10.93	3	3	0	96	0	1	27	4.9	13	6	3,000	100	0.0	0.0
D+ / 2.6	4.6	10.4	11.01	4	3	0	96	0	1	27	4.9	12	6	3,000	100	0.0	0.0
D+ / 2.6	4.6	10.4	11.02	26	3	0	96	0	1	27	4.9	22	6	100,000	0	0.0	0.0
C- / 3.1	4.3	8.1	11.60	145	1	0	98	0	1	11	4.3	36	5	3,000	100	4.2	0.0
U /	N/A	8.1	11.55	11	1	0	98	0	1	11	4.3	N/A	5	3,000	100	0.0	0.0
C- / 3.1	4.3	8.1	11.55	41	1	0	98	0	1	11	4.3	22	5	3,000	100	0.0	0.0
C- / 3.1	4.3	8.1	11.64	111	1	0	98	0	1	11	4.3	43	5	100,000	0	0.0	0.0
C / 4.4	3.8	6.7	10.61	52	3	0	96	0	1	19	5.2	25	5	3,000	100	4.2	0.0
U /	N/A	6.7	10.63	3	3	0	96	0	1	19	5.2	N/A	5	3,000	100	0.0	0.0
C / 4.3	3.8	6.7	10.62	11	3	0	96	0	1	19	5.2	15	5	3,000	100	0.0	0.0
C / 4.3	3.8	6.7	10.67	19	3	0	96	0	1	19	5.2	29	5	100,000	0	0.0	0.0
D / 1.9	5.8	N/A	20.70	61	6	0	0	43	51	125	0.0	91	7	3,000	100	4.8	0.0
D / 1.8	5.8	N/A	20.67	35	6	0	0	43	51	125	0.0	82	7	3,000	100	0.0	0.0
D / 1.8	5.8	N/A	20.73	101	6	0	0	43	51	125	0.0	93	7	100,000	0	0.0	0.0
C- / 3.7	4.0	7.6	11.21	290	2	0	97	0	1	23	5.2	50	5	3,000	100	4.2	0.0
U /	N/A	7.6	11.19	20	2	0	97	0	1	23	5.2	N/A	5	3,000	100	0.0	0.0
C- / 3.7	4.0	7.6	11.20	69	2	0	97	0	1	23	5.2	30	5	3,000	100	0.0	0.0
C- / 3.7	4.0	7.6	11.22	362	2	0	97	0	1	23	5.2	55	5	100,000	0	0.0	0.0
C- / 3.1	4.3	8.3	11.78	296	3	0	96	0	1	16	5.1	36	9	3,000	100	4.2	0.0
U /	N/A	8.3	11.72	14	3	0	96	0	1	16	5.1	N/A	9	3,000	100	0.0	0.0
C- / 3.1	4.4	8.3	11.74	57	3	0	96	0	1	16	5.1	22	9	3,000	100	0.0	0.0
C- / 3.1	4.3	8.3	11.74	199	3	0	96	0	1	16	5.1	43	9	100,000	0	0.0	0.0

Fund Type	Fund Name (99 Pct = Best, 0 Pct = Worst)	Ticker Symbol	Overall Investment Rating	Phone	Performance Rating/Pts	3 Mo	6 Mo	1Yr / Pct	3Yr / Pct (Annualized)	5Yr / Pct (Annualized)	Dividend Yield	Expense Ratio
MUS	Nuveen Oregon Intmdt Muni Bd A	FOTAX	**A**	(800) 257-8787	**B / 7.8**	1.52	2.59	3.27 /88	2.54 /83	4.07 /78	2.54	0.84
MUN	Nuveen Oregon Intmdt Muni Bd C	NAFOX	**U**	(800) 257-8787	**U /**	1.32	2.19	2.45 /80	--	--	1.83	1.64
MUN ●	Nuveen Oregon Intmdt Muni Bd C2	NIMOX	**A**	(800) 257-8787	**B / 8.0**	1.38	2.30	2.69 /82	1.95 /76	3.50 /74	2.05	1.39
MUS	Nuveen Oregon Intmdt Muni Bd I	FORCX	**A+**	(800) 257-8787	**B+ / 8.8**	1.55	2.67	3.54 /90	2.71 /85	4.29 /80	2.78	0.64
MUS	Nuveen PA Muni Bond A	FPNTX	**B**	(800) 257-8787	**A- / 9.1**	1.60	3.46	4.17 /95	4.15 /96	6.36 /94	3.44	0.81
MUN	Nuveen PA Muni Bond C	FPCCX	**U**	(800) 257-8787	**U /**	1.40	3.06	3.34 /89	--	--	2.81	1.61
MUS ●	Nuveen PA Muni Bond C2	FPMBX	**B+**	(800) 257-8787	**A / 9.4**	1.46	3.26	3.66 /92	3.60 /93	5.80 /91	3.02	1.36
MUS	Nuveen PA Muni Bond I	NBPAX	**B+**	(800) 257-8787	**A+ / 9.7**	1.55	3.55	4.35 /96	4.36 /97	6.57 /95	3.76	0.61
USS	Nuveen Preferred Securities A	NPSAX	**C+**	(800) 257-8787	**B- / 7.5**	-0.45	1.77	1.39 /65	4.53 /88	7.18 /83	5.33	1.07
USS	Nuveen Preferred Securities C	NPSCX	**C+**	(800) 257-8787	**B / 7.9**	-0.58	1.38	0.68 /53	3.75 /82	6.39 /79	4.82	1.82
USS	Nuveen Preferred Securities I	NPSRX	**B**	(800) 257-8787	**B+ / 8.6**	-0.33	1.89	1.64 /68	4.78 /89	7.45 /84	5.84	0.82
COI	Nuveen Preferred Securities R3	NPSTX	**B-**	(800) 257-8787	**B / 8.2**	-0.50	1.65	1.17 /61	4.26 /86	6.91 /81	5.34	1.32
* MUH	Nuveen Short Dur Hi Yld Muni A	NVHAX	**A**	(800) 257-8787	**A- / 9.2**	1.82	2.98	3.38 /89	4.00 /96	--	3.21	0.79
MUH	Nuveen Short Dur Hi Yld Muni C	NVCCX	**U**	(800) 257-8787	**U /**	1.51	2.45	2.53 /81	--	--	2.48	1.59
MUH ●	Nuveen Short Dur Hi Yld Muni C2	NVHCX	**A**	(800) 257-8787	**A- / 9.2**	1.68	2.60	2.73 /82	3.44 /92	--	2.77	1.34
MUH	Nuveen Short Dur Hi Yld Muni I	NVHIX	**A**	(800) 257-8787	**A+ / 9.7**	1.86	3.06	3.56 /91	4.22 /97	--	3.47	0.59
GEI	Nuveen Short Term Bond A	FALTX	**C**	(800) 257-8787	**D+ / 2.9**	0.59	0.37	0.29 /46	0.90 /41	1.50 /26	1.47	0.73
GEI	Nuveen Short Term Bond C	FBSCX	**C**	(800) 257-8787	**D+ / 2.5**	0.40	-0.02	-0.50 /26	0.15 /28	0.70 /18	0.72	1.48
GEI	Nuveen Short Term Bond I	FLTIX	**B**	(800) 257-8787	**C / 4.6**	0.64	0.58	0.62 /52	1.17 /46	1.73 /28	1.73	0.48
COI	Nuveen Short Term Bond R3	NSSRX	**C+**	(800) 257-8787	**C- / 3.4**	0.52	0.22	-0.12 /30	0.59 /35	--	1.20	0.98
COI	Nuveen Short Term Bond R6	NSSFX	**U**	(800) 257-8787	**U /**	0.65	0.59	0.63 /52	--	--	1.75	0.46
MUN	Nuveen Short Term Municipal Bond A	FSHAX	**C+**	(800) 257-8787	**C- / 3.0**	0.52	0.44	0.89 /64	0.79 /47	1.78 /41	0.86	0.71
MUN	Nuveen Short Term Municipal Bond C	NAAEX	**U**	(800) 257-8787	**U /**	0.33	0.07	0.24 /47	--	--	0.33	1.50
MUN ●	Nuveen Short Term Municipal Bond	NSVCX	**B-**	(800) 257-8787	**C- / 3.9**	0.44	0.37	0.54 /56	0.46 /37	--	0.54	1.06
MUN	Nuveen Short Term Municipal Bond I	FSHYX	**A-**	(800) 257-8787	**C / 5.4**	0.56	0.53	0.97 /66	0.96 /52	1.96 /45	1.06	0.50
COI	Nuveen Strategic Income A	FCDDX	**D-**	(800) 257-8787	**D- / 1.2**	1.86	0.31	-4.41 / 6	1.01 /43	3.80 /58	4.92	0.92
COI	Nuveen Strategic Income C	FCBCX	**D-**	(800) 257-8787	**D- / 1.5**	1.67	-0.09	-5.04 / 5	0.26 /29	3.03 /46	4.32	1.67
COI	Nuveen Strategic Income I	FCBYX	**D**	(800) 257-8787	**C- / 3.9**	2.01	0.52	-4.09 / 7	1.28 /48	4.08 /63	5.50	0.67
COI	Nuveen Strategic Income R3	FABSX	**D**	(800) 257-8787	**D+ / 2.9**	1.80	0.20	-4.61 / 6	0.79 /39	3.53 /54	4.89	1.17
GEL	Nuveen Strategic Income R6	FSFRX	**U**	(800) 257-8787	**U /**	2.06	0.57	-4.04 / 8	--	--	5.45	0.61
MUN	Nuveen Strategic Municipal Opptys A	NSAOX	**U**	(800) 257-8787	**U /**	2.26	4.80	5.39 /98	--	--	2.48	1.38
MUN	Nuveen Strategic Municipal Opptys C	NSCOX	**U**	(800) 257-8787	**U /**	2.16	4.38	4.63 /97	--	--	1.75	2.18
MUN	Nuveen Strategic Municipal Opptys I	NSIOX	**U**	(800) 257-8787	**U /**	2.40	4.89	5.68 /99	--	--	2.73	1.18
GEI	Nuveen Symphony Credit Oppty A	NCOAX	**E**	(800) 257-8787	**E / 0.3**	2.90	-2.79	-8.51 / 1	-0.26 /13	3.73 /57	6.85	1.02
GEI	Nuveen Symphony Credit Oppty C	NCFCX	**E**	(800) 257-8787	**E / 0.5**	2.70	-3.13	-9.19 / 1	-0.99 / 8	2.95 /44	6.36	1.77
GEI	Nuveen Symphony Credit Oppty I	NCOIX	**U**	(800) 257-8787	**U /**	2.97	-2.66	-8.26 / 1	--	3.99 /61	7.48	0.77
COH	Nuveen Symphony Credit Oppty R6	NCSRX	**U**	(800) 257-8787	**U /**	2.96	-2.60	-8.21 / 1	--	--	7.47	0.69
LP	Nuveen Symphony Floating Rt Inc A	NFRAX	**C-**	(800) 257-8787	**C- / 3.4**	1.54	-0.83	-2.59 /13	1.90 /59	--	4.79	0.96
LP	Nuveen Symphony Floating Rt Inc C	NFFCX	**C-**	(800) 257-8787	**C- / 3.4**	1.34	-1.17	-3.34 /10	1.13 /45	--	4.13	1.71
LP	Nuveen Symphony Floating Rt Inc I	NFRIX	**C**	(800) 257-8787	**C / 5.4**	1.61	-0.70	-2.35 /14	2.16 /65	--	5.18	0.70
LP	Nuveen Symphony Floating Rt Inc R6	NFRFX	**U**	(800) 257-8787	**U /**	1.66	-0.65	-2.30 /14	--	--	5.18	0.68
COH	Nuveen Symphony High Yield Bond A	NSYAX	**E**	(800) 257-8787	**E+ / 0.8**	1.57	-2.19	-7.59 / 2	1.18 /46	--	6.05	1.61
COH	Nuveen Symphony High Yield Bond	NSYCX	**E**	(800) 257-8787	**D- / 1.0**	1.31	-2.65	-8.35 / 1	0.37 /31	--	5.52	2.34
COH	Nuveen Symphony High Yield Bond I	NSYIX	**D-**	(800) 257-8787	**D+ / 2.8**	1.64	-2.12	-7.40 / 2	1.39 /50	--	6.63	1.36
MUS	Nuveen TN Muni Bond A	FTNTX	**C+**	(800) 257-8787	**B+ / 8.3**	1.46	3.06	3.78 /92	3.34 /91	5.80 /91	3.04	0.79
MUN	Nuveen TN Muni Bond C	FTNDX	**U**	(800) 257-8787	**U /**	1.18	2.56	2.95 /85	--	--	2.39	1.58
MUS ●	Nuveen TN Muni Bond C2	FTNCX	**C+**	(800) 257-8787	**B+ / 8.8**	1.24	2.69	3.21 /87	2.77 /86	5.20 /87	2.64	1.34
MUS	Nuveen TN Muni Bond I	FTNRX	**B**	(800) 257-8787	**A / 9.4**	1.43	3.08	3.99 /94	3.55 /93	6.01 /92	3.38	0.59
MUN	Nuveen US Infrastructure Bd A	NUSNX	**U**	(800) 257-8787	**U /**	3.35	3.02	-0.92 /22	--	--	4.13	1.89
MUN	Nuveen US Infrastructure Bd C	NUSCX	**U**	(800) 257-8787	**U /**	3.21	2.62	-1.63 /18	--	--	3.53	2.61
MUN	Nuveen US Infrastructure Bd I	NUSIX	**U**	(800) 257-8787	**U /**	3.41	3.09	-0.67 /25	--	--	4.56	1.60
MUS	Nuveen VA Muni Bond A	FVATX	**C+**	(800) 257-8787	**B / 8.2**	1.83	3.49	4.15 /95	3.13 /89	5.52 /89	3.09	0.80

Performance: Total Return % through 3/31/16; Incl. in Returns: Dividend Yield, Expense Ratio.

● Denotes fund is closed to new investors
* Denotes fund is included in Section II

RISK			NET ASSETS		ASSET							FUND MANAGER		MINIMUM		LOADS	
Risk Rating/Pts	3 Yr Avg Standard Deviation	Avg Duration	NAV As of 3/31/16	Total $(Mil)	Cash %	Gov. Bond %	Muni. Bond %	Corp. Bond %	Other %	Portfolio Turnover Ratio	Avg Coupon Rate	Manager Quality Pct	Manager Tenure (Years)	Initial Purch. $	Additional Purch. $	Front End Load	Back End Load
C+ / 6.7	3.0	6.0	10.47	53	4	0	95	0	1	7	4.7	42	19	3,000	100	3.0	0.0
U /	N/A	6.0	10.41	3	4	0	95	0	1	7	4.7	N/A	19	3,000	100	0.0	0.0
C+ / 6.6	3.0	6.0	10.44	8	4	0	95	0	1	7	4.7	25	19	3,000	100	0.0	0.0
C+ / 6.5	3.0	6.0	10.48	157	4	0	95	0	1	7	4.7	46	19	100,000	0	0.0	0.0
C- / 3.8	3.9	7.7	11.23	119	4	0	95	0	1	10	4.8	70	5	3,000	100	4.2	0.0
U /	N/A	7.7	11.18	15	4	0	95	0	1	10	4.8	N/A	5	3,000	100	0.0	0.0
C- / 3.9	3.9	7.7	11.19	40	4	0	95	0	1	10	4.8	47	5	3,000	100	0.0	0.0
C- / 3.8	3.9	7.7	11.20	152	4	0	95	0	1	10	4.8	77	5	100,000	0	0.0	0.0
C / 4.6	3.6	4.6	16.61	434	4	0	0	66	30	18	0.0	99	10	3,000	100	4.8	0.0
C / 4.6	3.7	4.6	16.63	227	4	0	0	66	30	18	0.0	99	10	3,000	100	0.0	0.0
C / 4.6	3.7	4.6	16.62	1,421	4	0	0	66	30	18	0.0	99	10	100,000	0	0.0	0.0
C / 4.6	3.7	4.6	16.73	2	4	0	0	66	30	18	0.0	98	10	0	0	0.0	0.0
C / 5.1	2.9	N/A	10.20	778	2	0	96	0	2	17	0.0	90	3	3,000	100	2.5	0.0
U /	N/A	N/A	10.19	107	2	0	96	0	2	17	0.0	N/A	3	3,000	100	0.0	0.0
C / 5.0	3.0	N/A	10.20	41	2	0	96	0	2	17	0.0	82	3	3,000	100	0.0	0.0
C / 5.0	3.0	N/A	10.21	2,434	2	0	96	0	2	17	0.0	91	3	100,000	0	0.0	0.0
A / 9.4	0.9	1.2	9.83	99	2	5	1	47	45	43	4.9	83	6	3,000	100	2.3	0.0
A / 9.5	0.8	1.2	9.86	31	2	5	1	47	45	43	4.9	55	6	3,000	100	0.0	0.0
A / 9.4	0.9	1.2	9.84	432	2	5	1	47	45	43	4.9	88	6	100,000	0	0.0	0.0
A / 9.4	0.9	1.2	9.84	N/A	2	5	1	47	45	43	4.9	75	6	0	0	0.0	0.0
U /	N/A	1.2	9.85	66	2	5	1	47	45	43	4.9	N/A	6	5,000,000	0	0.0	0.0
A+ / 9.6	0.7	1.9	10.12	172	1	0	98	0	1	36	3.8	75	14	3,000	100	2.5	0.0
U /	N/A	1.9	10.10	7	1	0	98	0	1	36	3.8	N/A	14	3,000	100	0.0	0.0
A+ / 9.6	0.7	1.9	10.11	13	1	0	98	0	1	36	3.8	58	14	3,000	100	0.0	0.0
A+ / 9.6	0.8	1.9	10.12	467	1	0	98	0	1	36	3.8	79	14	100,000	0	0.0	0.0
D+ / 2.5	5.2	4.3	10.25	201	2	8	0	79	11	47	5.5	16	16	3,000	100	4.3	0.0
D+ / 2.5	5.2	4.3	10.19	92	2	8	0	79	11	47	5.5	9	16	3,000	100	0.0	0.0
D+ / 2.5	5.3	4.3	10.24	482	2	8	0	79	11	47	5.5	21	16	100,000	0	0.0	0.0
D+ / 2.5	5.2	4.3	10.29	8	2	8	0	79	11	47	5.5	14	16	0	0	0.0	0.0
U /	N/A	4.3	10.25	33	2	8	0	79	11	47	5.5	N/A	16	5,000,000	0	0.0	0.0
U /	N/A	N/A	10.40	1	0	0	100	0	0	0	0.0	N/A	2	3,000	100	3.0	0.0
U /	N/A	N/A	10.40	N/A	0	0	100	0	0	0	0.0	N/A	2	3,000	100	0.0	0.0
U /	N/A	N/A	10.41	55	0	0	100	0	0	0	0.0	N/A	2	100,000	0	0.0	0.0
D- / 1.3	6.3	3.2	18.41	102	8	0	0	86	6	40	0.0	14	6	3,000	100	4.8	0.0
D- / 1.3	6.3	3.2	18.39	87	8	0	0	86	6	40	0.0	9	6	3,000	100	0.0	0.0
U /	6.3	3.2	18.42	416	8	0	0	86	6	40	0.0	N/A	6	100,000	0	0.0	0.0
U /	N/A	3.2	18.44	8	8	0	0	86	6	40	0.0	N/A	6	5,000,000	0	0.0	0.0
C+ / 6.3	3.1	0.9	19.09	109	4	0	0	78	18	42	0.0	91	5	3,000	100	3.0	0.0
C+ / 6.3	3.1	0.9	19.09	42	4	0	0	78	18	42	0.0	81	5	3,000	100	0.0	0.0
C+ / 6.3	3.1	0.9	19.10	648	4	0	0	78	18	42	0.0	93	5	100,000	0	0.0	0.0
U /	N/A	0.9	19.11	N/A	4	0	0	78	18	42	0.0	N/A	5	5,000,000	0	0.0	0.0
E+ / 0.6	6.9	N/A	15.44	3	0	0	0	92	8	154	0.0	37	4	3,000	100	4.8	0.0
E+ / 0.6	6.9	N/A	15.39	1	0	0	0	92	8	154	0.0	18	4	3,000	100	0.0	0.0
E+ / 0.6	6.9	N/A	15.44	9	0	0	0	92	8	154	0.0	44	4	100,000	0	0.0	0.0
C- / 3.4	4.2	7.5	12.08	294	1	0	98	0	1	3	4.6	29	9	3,000	100	4.2	0.0
U /	N/A	7.5	12.04	15	1	0	98	0	1	3	4.6	N/A	9	3,000	100	0.0	0.0
C- / 3.4	4.2	7.5	12.06	82	1	0	98	0	1	3	4.6	17	9	3,000	100	0.0	0.0
C- / 3.4	4.2	7.5	12.06	73	1	0	98	0	1	3	4.6	35	9	100,000	0	0.0	0.0
U /	N/A	N/A	19.56	1	2	0	62	34	2	15	0.0	N/A	2	3,000	100	4.3	0.0
U /	N/A	N/A	19.57	N/A	2	0	62	34	2	15	0.0	N/A	2	3,000	100	0.0	0.0
U /	N/A	N/A	19.56	8	2	0	62	34	2	15	0.0	N/A	2	100,000	0	0.0	0.0
C- / 3.7	4.2	6.9	11.29	189	2	0	97	0	1	22	4.0	27	5	3,000	100	4.2	0.0

Fund Type	Fund Name (99 Pct = Best, 0 Pct = Worst)	Ticker Symbol	Overall Investment Rating	Phone	PERFORMANCE: Performance Rating/Pts	Total Return % through 3/31/16: 3 Mo	6 Mo	1Yr / Pct	Annualized: 3Yr / Pct	5Yr / Pct	Incl. in Returns: Dividend Yield	Expense Ratio
MUN	Nuveen VA Muni Bond C	FVCCX	**U**	(800) 257-8787	**U /**	1.64	3.08	3.32 /88	--	--	2.43	1.59
MUS ●	Nuveen VA Muni Bond C2	FVACX	**B-**	(800) 257-8787	**B+ / 8.7**	1.61	3.22	3.60 /91	2.53 /83	4.93 /85	2.70	1.35
MUS	Nuveen VA Muni Bond I	NMVAX	**B**	(800) 257-8787	**A / 9.3**	1.79	3.58	4.34 /96	3.31 /91	5.72 /90	3.40	0.60
MUS	Nuveen WI Muni Bond A	FWIAX	**C+**	(800) 257-8787	**B+ / 8.3**	1.42	3.10	3.54 /90	3.40 /92	5.76 /91	3.39	0.87
MUN	Nuveen WI Muni Bond C	FWCCX	**U**	(800) 257-8787	**U /**	1.32	2.80	2.74 /82	--	--	2.77	1.67
MUS ●	Nuveen WI Muni Bond C2	FWICX	**C+**	(800) 257-8787	**B+ / 8.9**	1.28	2.91	2.97 /85	2.84 /86	5.20 /87	2.99	1.42
MUS	Nuveen WI Muni Bond I	FWIRX	**B-**	(800) 257-8787	**A / 9.4**	1.47	3.30	3.76 /92	3.62 /93	5.98 /92	3.75	0.67
COI	NY 529 CSP Direct Bd Mkt Idx Port		**B**	(800) 662-7447	**B- / 7.0**	3.01	2.37	1.67 /68	2.27 /67	3.60 /55	0.00	0.25
GEI	NY 529 CSP Direct Inf-Prot Secs		**D-**	(800) 662-7447	**D+ / 2.7**	4.59	3.73	1.48 /66	-0.82 / 9	2.89 /43	0.00	0.25
COI	NY 529 CSP Direct Int Accum Port		**C+**	(800) 662-7447	**C- / 3.1**	0.16	0.33	0.50 /49	0.30 /30	0.33 /16	0.00	0.25
COH	Oaktree High Yield Bond Adv	OHYDX	**U**		**U /**	3.08	2.03	-2.62 /13	--	--	6.31	4.14
COH	Oaktree High Yield Bond Inst	OHYIX	**U**		**U /**	3.14	2.15	-2.37 /14	--	--	6.57	3.89
USA	OH CollegeAdv 529 BR GNMA Opt A		**C-**	(800) 441-7762	**C- / 3.9**	1.48	1.64	1.73 /69	1.61 /54	2.89 /43	0.00	1.08
USA	OH CollegeAdv 529 BR GNMA Opt C		**C**	(800) 441-7762	**C / 4.4**	1.38	1.29	1.03 /59	0.86 /40	2.12 /33	0.00	1.83
MUH	OH CollegeAdv 529 BR Hi Yd Bd Opt		**D-**	(800) 441-7762	**D / 1.7**	1.56	-0.55	-4.79 / 5	1.73 /73	4.59 /82	0.00	1.21
MUH	OH CollegeAdv 529 BR Hi Yd Bd Opt		**D-**	(800) 441-7762	**D+ / 2.9**	1.37	-0.96	-5.48 / 4	0.96 /52	3.82 /76	0.00	1.96
USS	OH CollegeAdv 529 BR Inf Pr Bd Op		**E+**	(800) 441-7762	**E / 0.5**	3.54	2.83	-0.42 /27	-1.74 / 5	1.83 /29	0.00	0.93
USS	OH CollegeAdv 529 BR Inf Pr Bd Op		**E+**	(800) 441-7762	**E / 0.5**	3.35	2.42	-1.13 /21	-2.47 / 3	1.05 /21	0.00	1.68
MM	OH CollegeAdv 529 BR Mny Mkt Opt		**C-**	(800) 441-7762	**D / 2.0**	0.03	0.03	0.03 /36	0.01 /18	0.01 / 6	0.03	0.96
MM	OH CollegeAdv 529 BR Mny Mkt Opt		**C-**	(800) 441-7762	**D / 2.0**	0.03	0.03	0.03 /36	0.01 /18	0.01 / 6	0.03	1.71
GEI	OH CollegeAdv 529 BR WF TR Bd		**C-**	(800) 441-7762	**C- / 4.1**	2.59	1.85	0.80 /55	1.72 /56	3.52 /53	0.00	1.24
GEI	OH CollegeAdv 529 BR WF TR Bd		**C-**	(800) 441-7762	**C / 4.5**	2.38	1.43	0.08 /40	0.96 /42	2.73 /41	0.00	1.99
MUS	Oklahoma Municipal	OKMUX	**B+**	(800) 601-5593	**B+ / 8.5**	1.34	3.01	3.98 /94	3.03 /88	4.75 /83	2.28	1.20
* GEI	Old Westbury Fixed Income	OWFIX	**C+**	(800) 607-2200	**C / 4.7**	1.93	1.31	1.42 /65	0.94 /41	2.09 /32	1.31	0.74
* MUN	Old Westbury Muni Bond	OWMBX	**A+**	(800) 607-2200	**B- / 7.1**	1.15	1.85	2.35 /80	1.37 /64	2.60 /61	1.29	0.70
* MUS	Oppeneheimer Rochester CA Muni A	OPCAX	**C**	(888) 470-0862	**A- / 9.0**	1.78	3.94	4.19 /95	4.09 /96	9.04 /99	5.11	1.07
MUS ●	Oppeneheimer Rochester CA Muni B	OCABX	**C**	(888) 470-0862	**A- / 9.2**	1.60	3.56	3.41 /89	3.26 /90	8.14 /98	4.62	1.84
MUS	Oppeneheimer Rochester CA Muni C	OCACX	**C**	(888) 470-0862	**A / 9.3**	1.73	3.71	3.43 /89	3.32 /91	8.22 /98	4.65	1.82
MUS	Oppeneheimer Rochester CA Muni Y	OCAYX	**C+**	(888) 470-0862	**A+ / 9.8**	1.84	4.07	4.44 /96	4.33 /97	9.30 /99	5.61	0.83
* MUH	Oppeneheimer Rochester Hi Yld Mun	ORNAX	**C-**	(888) 470-0862	**A / 9.5**	2.89	5.69	6.68 /99	4.44 /97	9.32 /99	6.20	0.99
MUH ●	Oppeneheimer Rochester Hi Yld Mun	ORNBX	**C**	(888) 470-0862	**A+ / 9.7**	2.69	5.13	5.86 /99	3.63 /93	8.45 /99	5.75	1.75
MUH	Oppeneheimer Rochester Hi Yld Mun	ORNCX	**C**	(888) 470-0862	**A+ / 9.7**	2.72	5.18	5.92 /99	3.63 /93	8.46 /99	5.81	1.75
MUH	Oppeneheimer Rochester Hi Yld Mun	ORNYX	**C**	(888) 470-0862	**A+ / 9.9**	2.93	5.62	6.84 /99	4.60 /98	9.49 /99	6.67	0.84
MUS	Oppeneheimer Rochester LT CA	OLCAX	**C+**	(888) 470-0862	**C+ / 6.2**	1.23	2.37	1.16 /70	1.77 /73	4.01 /78	3.51	0.89
MUS ●	Oppeneheimer Rochester LT CA	OLCBX	**C**	(888) 470-0862	**C+ / 5.6**	1.00	1.90	0.33 /50	0.97 /52	3.11 /70	2.70	1.69
MUS	Oppeneheimer Rochester LT CA	OLCCX	**C+**	(888) 470-0862	**C+ / 5.8**	1.05	2.01	0.72 /60	1.01 /53	3.23 /71	2.86	1.65
MUS	Oppeneheimer Rochester LT CA	OLCYX	**A**	(888) 470-0862	**B / 8.0**	1.28	2.49	1.71 /75	2.01 /77	4.24 /79	3.83	0.65
MUS	Oppeneheimer Rochester NJ Muni A	ONJAX	**D**	(888) 470-0862	**C / 4.6**	1.40	2.91	1.29 /72	1.74 /73	6.03 /92	4.81	1.17
MUS ●	Oppeneheimer Rochester NJ Muni B	ONJBX	**D**	(888) 470-0862	**C+ / 5.9**	1.21	2.63	0.53 /56	0.98 /52	5.21 /87	4.27	1.93
MUS	Oppeneheimer Rochester NJ Muni C	ONJCX	**D**	(888) 470-0862	**C+ / 5.8**	1.22	2.53	0.44 /53	0.98 /52	5.25 /87	4.30	1.92
MUS	Oppeneheimer Rochester NJ Muni Y	ONJYX	**C-**	(888) 470-0862	**B / 7.9**	1.43	2.98	1.43 /73	1.89 /75	6.20 /93	5.19	1.02
* MUS	Oppeneheimer Rochester PA Muni A	OPATX	**D+**	(888) 470-0862	**C+ / 6.1**	0.46	1.15	2.17 /78	2.50 /83	6.41 /94	5.54	0.95
MUS ●	Oppeneheimer Rochester PA Muni B	OPABX	**D+**	(888) 470-0862	**B- / 7.1**	0.28	0.68	1.41 /73	1.71 /72	5.57 /89	5.07	1.71
MUS	Oppeneheimer Rochester PA Muni C	OPACX	**D+**	(888) 470-0862	**B- / 7.2**	0.29	0.69	1.43 /73	1.74 /73	5.61 /90	5.09	1.70
MUS	Oppeneheimer Rochester PA Muni Y	OPAYX	**C-**	(888) 470-0862	**B+ / 8.4**	0.50	1.12	2.32 /79	2.65 /84	6.56 /95	5.97	0.80
GEI	Oppeneheimer Rochester Ul Sht Dur	OSDIX	**U**	(888) 470-0862	**U /**	0.25	0.28	0.55 /51	--	--	0.75	0.35
GL	Oppeneheimer Rochester Ul Sht Dur	OSDYX	**C+**	(888) 470-0862	**C- / 3.3**	0.25	0.28	0.55 /51	0.42 /32	--	0.75	0.38
USL	Oppenheimer 529 BS FI Port 4		**C+**	(888) 470-0862	**C- / 4.2**	1.59	0.89	0.59 /51	0.83 /40	2.23 /34	0.00	0.68
USL	Oppenheimer 529 BS FI Port A		**C-**	(888) 470-0862	**D- / 1.3**	1.49	0.74	--	0.30 /30	1.06 /21	0.00	0.78
USL	Oppenheimer 529 BS FI Port C		**C**	(888) 470-0862	**D+ / 2.8**	1.53	0.76	-0.15 /30	0.05 /24	0.80 /19	0.00	1.03
USL	Oppenheimer 529 BS FI Port G		**C**	(888) 470-0862	**C- / 3.2**	1.52	0.76	--	0.29 /30	1.04 /21	0.00	0.78
USL	Oppenheimer 529 BS FI Port H		**C+**	(888) 470-0862	**C- / 3.7**	1.60	0.95	0.32 /46	0.56 /34	1.31 /23	0.00	0.53

● Denotes fund is closed to new investors
* Denotes fund is included in Section II

RISK			NET ASSETS		ASSET							FUND MANAGER		MINIMUM		LOADS	
Risk Rating/Pts	3 Yr Avg Standard Deviation	Avg Duration	NAV As of 3/31/16	Total $(Mil)	Cash %	Gov. Bond %	Muni. Bond %	Corp. Bond %	Other %	Portfolio Turnover Ratio	Avg Coupon Rate	Manager Quality Pct	Manager Tenure (Years)	Initial Purch. $	Additional Purch. $	Front End Load	Back End Load
U /	N/A	6.9	11.28	14	2	0	97	0	1	22	4.0	N/A	5	3,000	100	0.0	0.0
C- / 3.6	4.2	6.9	11.27	43	2	0	97	0	1	22	4.0	15	5	3,000	100	0.0	0.0
C- / 3.7	4.1	6.9	11.25	159	2	0	97	0	1	22	4.0	32	5	100,000	0	0.0	0.0
C- / 3.1	4.7	7.0	10.93	56	1	0	98	0	1	5	5.0	20	5	3,000	100	4.2	0.0
U /	N/A	7.0	10.94	4	1	0	98	0	1	5	5.0	N/A	5	3,000	100	0.0	0.0
C- / 3.0	4.7	7.0	10.94	13	1	0	98	0	1	5	5.0	12	5	3,000	100	0.0	0.0
C- / 3.1	4.7	7.0	10.96	38	1	0	98	0	1	5	5.0	24	5	100,000	0	0.0	0.0
C+ / 6.3	3.1	N/A	16.43	260	0	46	1	25	28	0	0.0	79	7	25	25	0.0	0.0
D / 2.1	5.5	N/A	16.41	234	1	98	0	0	1	0	0.0	4	N/A	25	25	0.0	0.0
A+ / 9.9	0.1	N/A	12.15	799	0	0	0	0	100	0	0.0	77	7	25	25	0.0	0.0
U /	N/A	N/A	9.45	1	0	0	0	0	100	46	0.0	N/A	2	25,000	2,500	0.0	0.0
U /	N/A	N/A	9.45	23	0	0	0	0	100	46	0.0	N/A	2	1,000,000	100,000	0.0	0.0
B- / 7.1	2.8	N/A	12.36	5	0	4	0	0	96	0	0.0	71	N/A	25	25	4.0	0.0
B- / 7.1	2.9	N/A	11.77	3	0	4	0	0	96	0	0.0	39	N/A	25	25	0.0	0.0
D- / 1.5	5.6	N/A	16.31	20	4	0	0	79	17	0	0.0	83	N/A	25	25	4.0	0.0
D- / 1.5	5.6	N/A	15.52	8	4	0	0	79	17	0	0.0	53	N/A	25	25	0.0	0.0
D+ / 2.7	5.1	N/A	11.99	8	0	99	0	0	1	0	0.0	5	N/A	25	25	4.0	0.0
D+ / 2.7	5.1	N/A	11.41	5	0	99	0	0	1	0	0.0	3	N/A	25	25	0.0	0.0
A+ / 9.9	N/A	N/A	1.00	84	100	0	0	0	0	0	0.0	64	7	25	25	0.0	0.0
A+ / 9.9	N/A	N/A	1.00	30	100	0	0	0	0	0	0.0	64	7	25	25	0.0	0.0
C+ / 5.9	3.2	N/A	12.66	36	0	33	0	20	47	0	0.0	32	N/A	25	25	4.0	0.0
C+ / 5.7	3.2	N/A	12.06	14	0	33	0	20	47	0	0.0	16	N/A	25	25	0.0	0.0
C / 5.0	3.5	5.2	11.92	42	0	0	100	0	0	15	4.7	43	20	1,000	50	2.5	0.0
B+ / 8.4	1.7	8.5	11.29	583	0	44	4	45	7	67	0.0	45	4	1,000	100	0.0	0.0
B+ / 8.3	2.2	6.3	12.09	1,507	1	2	96	0	1	31	0.0	36	18	1,000	100	0.0	0.0
D / 1.7	5.9	5.8	8.39	889	0	0	99	0	1	21	0.0	19	14	1,000	50	4.8	0.0
D / 1.7	5.9	5.8	8.40	2	0	0	99	0	1	21	0.0	10	14	1,000	50	0.0	0.0
D / 1.7	5.9	5.8	8.36	259	0	0	99	0	1	21	0.0	10	14	1,000	50	0.0	0.0
D / 1.7	5.9	5.8	8.39	158	0	0	99	0	1	21	0.0	24	14	1,000	50	0.0	0.0
E / 0.5	7.0	8.2	7.10	3,093	0	0	99	0	1	16	0.0	11	15	1,000	50	4.8	0.0
E / 0.5	7.1	8.2	7.13	35	0	0	99	0	1	16	0.0	7	15	1,000	50	0.0	0.0
E / 0.5	7.1	8.2	7.07	1,311	0	0	99	0	1	16	0.0	8	15	1,000	50	0.0	0.0
E / 0.5	7.0	8.2	7.09	805	0	0	99	0	1	16	0.0	12	15	1,000	50	0.0	0.0
C+ / 6.2	3.1	3.0	3.24	277	0	0	100	0	0	39	0.0	31	12	1,000	50	2.3	0.0
C+ / 6.2	3.1	3.0	3.34	N/A	0	0	100	0	0	39	0.0	15	12	1,000	50	0.0	0.0
C+ / 6.1	3.1	3.0	3.23	148	0	0	100	0	0	39	0.0	16	12	1,000	50	0.0	0.0
C+ / 6.5	3.0	3.0	3.25	148	0	0	100	0	0	39	0.0	41	12	1,000	50	0.0	0.0
E+ / 0.9	6.7	4.7	9.43	261	0	0	100	0	0	7	0.0	6	14	1,000	50	4.8	0.0
E+ / 0.9	6.7	4.7	9.46	3	0	0	100	0	0	7	0.0	4	14	1,000	50	0.0	0.0
E+ / 0.9	6.7	4.7	9.44	123	0	0	100	0	0	7	0.0	4	14	1,000	50	0.0	0.0
E+ / 0.9	6.6	4.7	9.44	24	0	0	100	0	0	7	0.0	6	14	1,000	50	0.0	0.0
D- / 1.0	6.5	6.3	10.39	533	0	0	100	0	0	12	0.0	7	17	1,000	50	4.8	0.0
D- / 1.1	6.5	6.3	10.38	7	0	0	100	0	0	12	0.0	5	17	1,000	50	0.0	0.0
D- / 1.0	6.5	6.3	10.36	220	0	0	100	0	0	12	0.0	6	17	1,000	50	0.0	0.0
D- / 1.1	6.5	6.3	10.39	28	0	0	100	0	0	12	0.0	7	17	1,000	50	0.0	0.0
U /	N/A	0.5	5.00	14	0	0	0	0	100	106	0.0	N/A	5	5,000,000	0	0.0	0.0
A+ / 9.9	0.2	0.5	5.00	285	0	0	0	0	100	106	0.0	80	5	250,000	0	0.0	0.0
B+ / 8.4	2.1	N/A	10.25	27	0	0	0	0	100	0	0.0	57	9	25	15	0.0	0.0
B+ / 8.8	1.6	N/A	6.80	4	0	0	0	0	100	0	0.0	50	9	25	15	3.5	0.0
B+ / 8.8	1.6	N/A	6.65	7	0	0	0	0	100	0	0.0	42	9	25	15	0.0	0.0
B+ / 8.9	1.6	N/A	9.34	8	0	0	0	0	100	0	0.0	50	9	25	15	0.0	0.0
B+ / 8.9	1.5	N/A	9.55	5	0	0	0	0	100	0	0.0	61	9	25	15	0.0	0.0

Fund Type	Fund Name (99 Pct = Best; 0 Pct = Worst)	Ticker Symbol	Overall Investment Rating	Phone	PERFORMANCE: Performance Rating/Pts	Total Return % through 3/31/16: 3 Mo	6 Mo	1Yr / Pct	Annualized: 3Yr / Pct	Annualized: 5Yr / Pct	Incl. in Returns: Dividend Yield	Expense Ratio
USL	Oppenheimer 529 BS Idx FI Port 4		B-	(888) 470-0862	C / 5.2	1.87	1.34	1.34 /64	1.25 /47	2.52 /38	0.00	0.22
GEI	Oppenheimer 529 SE AC Div Bond A		C-	(888) 470-0862	C- / 3.5	2.66	2.02	0.89 /57	1.57 /54	3.09 /47	0.00	1.00
GEI	Oppenheimer 529 SE AC Div Bond B		C-	(888) 470-0862	C / 4.5	2.50	1.67	0.18 /44	0.83 /40	2.32 /35	0.00	2.06
GEI	Oppenheimer 529 SE AC Div Bond C		C-	(888) 470-0862	C / 4.4	2.49	1.67	0.18 /44	0.82 /39	2.32 /35	0.00	2.06
GES	Oppenheimer 529 SE Global Str Inc		D-	(888) 470-0862	E+ / 0.7	1.78	0.44	-2.91 /12	0.10 /27	2.43 /37	0.00	1.02
GES	Oppenheimer 529 SE Global Str Inc		D-	(888) 470-0862	D- / 1.0	1.59	0.05	-3.63 / 9	-0.65 /10	1.66 /27	0.00	1.94
GES	Oppenheimer 529 SE Global Str Inc		D-	(888) 470-0862	D- / 1.0	1.59	0.05	-3.63 / 9	-0.65 /10	1.66 /27	0.00	1.94
GES	Oppenheimer 529 SE Inst Mny Mkt A		C-	(888) 470-0862	E+ / 0.8	0.04	0.04	0.04 /37	0.01 /16	0.01 / 3	0.00	0.35
GES	Oppenheimer 529 SE Inst Mny Mkt C		C	(888) 470-0862	D / 2.0	0.05	0.05	0.05 /38	0.02 /18	0.01 / 3	0.00	1.65
GEI	Oppenheimer 529 SE School Yrs 3		C-	(888) 470-0862	C- / 3.1	0.97	0.59	-1.24 /20	0.52 /33	1.48 /25	0.00	1.95
GEI	Oppenheimer 529 SE School Yrs A		C-	(888) 470-0862	D / 1.8	1.14	0.99	-0.49 /26	1.27 /48	2.24 /34	0.00	0.94
GEI	Oppenheimer 529 SE Ultra Cons 3		C-	(888) 470-0862	C / 4.5	1.01	1.09	-1.55 /18	1.31 /49	2.33 /35	0.00	1.91
GEI	Oppenheimer 529 SE Ultra Cons A		D+	(888) 470-0862	C- / 3.7	1.24	1.47	-0.76 /24	2.10 /64	3.13 /47	0.00	1.01
GES	Oppenheimer 529 TEP School Yrs		B	(888) 470-0862	C / 5.1	1.02	1.02	--	1.52 /53	2.35 /36	0.00	0.54
GES	Oppenheimer 529 TEP Sh Term Yld		C	(888) 470-0862	D+ / 2.3	0.08	0.08	0.08 /40	0.03 /21	0.02 / 7	0.00	0.35
MM	Oppenheimer Cash Reserves A	CRSXX	U	(888) 470-0862	U /	--	--	--	--	--	0.01	0.91
MM	● Oppenheimer Cash Reserves B	CRBXX	U	(888) 470-0862	U /	--	--	--	--	--	0.01	1.46
MM	Oppenheimer Cash Reserves C	CSCXX	U	(888) 470-0862	U /	--	--	--	--	--	0.01	1.46
* GEI	Oppenheimer Core Bond A	OPIGX	C	(888) 470-0862	C / 5.5	2.40	2.06	0.85 /56	2.85 /75	4.87 /71	2.86	0.98
GEI	● Oppenheimer Core Bond B	OIGBX	C+	(888) 470-0862	C+ / 6.2	2.21	1.66	0.04 /37	2.06 /63	4.11 /63	2.20	1.73
GEI	Oppenheimer Core Bond C	OPBCX	C+	(888) 470-0862	C+ / 6.3	2.21	1.66	0.05 /38	2.11 /64	4.10 /63	2.20	1.73
COI	Oppenheimer Core Bond I	OPBIX	B+	(888) 470-0862	B / 7.8	2.34	2.24	1.19 /62	3.22 /78	--	3.34	0.54
GEI	Oppenheimer Core Bond R	OPBNX	B-	(888) 470-0862	B- / 7.1	2.33	1.91	0.54 /50	2.62 /72	4.62 /69	2.70	1.23
GEI	Oppenheimer Core Bond Y	OPBYX	B-	(888) 470-0862	B / 7.6	2.48	2.19	1.09 /60	2.94 /76	5.09 /72	3.25	0.73
COI	Oppenheimer Corporate Bond A	OFIAX	D+	(888) 470-0862	C / 5.2	2.88	2.81	-0.94 /22	2.80 /74	5.28 /73	2.87	1.02
COI	Oppenheimer Corporate Bond C	OFICX	C-	(888) 470-0862	C+ / 5.9	2.60	2.44	-1.77 /17	2.01 /62	4.47 /67	2.27	1.78
COI	Oppenheimer Corporate Bond I	OFIIX	C	(888) 470-0862	B / 7.8	2.99	3.04	-0.51 /26	3.26 /78	--	3.45	0.57
COI	Oppenheimer Corporate Bond R	OFINX	C-	(888) 470-0862	C+ / 6.8	2.72	2.69	-1.28 /20	2.52 /71	4.99 /72	2.77	1.28
COI	Oppenheimer Corporate Bond Y	OFIYX	C	(888) 470-0862	B- / 7.5	2.84	2.94	-0.79 /23	3.02 /77	5.50 /75	3.26	0.78
EM	Oppenheimer Em Mkts Local Debt A	OEMAX	E-	(888) 470-0862	E- / 0.2	10.19	9.74	-0.01 /31	-5.76 / 1	-1.19 / 1	5.85	1.54
EM	Oppenheimer Em Mkts Local Debt C	OEMCX	E-	(888) 470-0862	E- / 0.2	9.84	9.34	-0.74 /24	-6.47 / 1	-1.93 / 1	5.42	2.32
EM	Oppenheimer Em Mkts Local Debt I	OEMIX	E-	(888) 470-0862	E / 0.3	10.29	10.11	0.39 /48	-5.36 / 1	-0.93 / 2	6.53	1.09
EM	Oppenheimer Em Mkts Local Debt R	OEMNX	E-	(888) 470-0862	E- / 0.2	10.13	9.61	-0.25 /29	-6.00 / 1	-1.43 / 1	5.90	1.82
EM	Oppenheimer Em Mkts Local Debt Y	OEMYX	E-	(888) 470-0862	E / 0.3	10.27	10.06	0.29 /46	-5.45 / 1	-0.87 / 2	6.44	1.28
GL	Oppenheimer Global High Yield A	OGYAX	U	(888) 470-0862	U /	2.94	0.86	-3.37 /10	--	--	4.91	1.79
GL	Oppenheimer Global High Yield C	OGYCX	U	(888) 470-0862	U /	2.67	0.41	-4.13 / 7	--	--	4.45	2.76
GL	Oppenheimer Global High Yield I	OGYIX	U	(888) 470-0862	U /	3.03	1.03	-3.02 /11	--	--	5.52	1.26
GL	Oppenheimer Global High Yield R	OGYNX	U	(888) 470-0862	U /	2.89	0.74	-3.59 / 9	--	--	4.91	2.65
GL	Oppenheimer Global High Yield Y	OGYYX	U	(888) 470-0862	U /	3.02	1.01	-3.08 /11	--	--	5.46	1.69
* GES	Oppenheimer Global Strategic Inc A	OPSIX	D-	(888) 470-0862	E+ / 0.7	1.48	0.40	-3.16 /11	0.06 /25	2.51 /38	4.05	1.04
GES	● Oppenheimer Global Strategic Inc B	OPSGX	D-	(888) 470-0862	D- / 1.0	1.55	0.03	-3.62 / 9	-0.72 /10	1.66 /27	3.46	1.79
GES	Oppenheimer Global Strategic Inc C	OSICX	D-	(888) 470-0862	D- / 1.0	1.57	0.03	-3.64 / 9	-0.69 /10	1.79 /29	3.47	1.79
GEI	Oppenheimer Global Strategic Inc I	OSIIX	D	(888) 470-0862	D+ / 2.9	1.85	0.60	-2.52 /13	0.47 /33	2.83 /42	4.68	0.60
GES	Oppenheimer Global Strategic Inc R	OSINX	D-	(888) 470-0862	D- / 1.4	1.68	0.28	-3.15 /11	-0.21 /14	2.18 /33	3.98	1.29
GES	Oppenheimer Global Strategic Inc Y	OSIYX	D	(888) 470-0862	D+ / 2.4	1.54	0.52	-2.93 /12	0.31 /30	2.74 /41	4.49	0.79
MM	Oppenheimer Insti MM E	IOEXX	C+	(888) 470-0862	D+ / 2.7	0.10	0.15	0.22 /45	0.14 /28	0.16 /16	0.22	0.10
MM	Oppenheimer Insti MM L	IOLXX	C	(888) 470-0862	D+ / 2.6	0.08	0.12	0.17 /43	0.09 /27	0.10 /15	0.17	0.15
* GL	Oppenheimer Intl Bond A	OIBAX	E+	(888) 470-0862	E+ / 0.6	4.04	3.05	-0.50 /26	-1.20 / 7	1.08 /21	3.12	1.02
GL	● Oppenheimer Intl Bond B	OIBBX	E+	(888) 470-0862	E+ / 0.8	3.87	2.68	-1.09 /21	-1.93 / 5	0.29 /16	2.53	1.77
GL	Oppenheimer Intl Bond C	OIBCX	E+	(888) 470-0862	E+ / 0.8	3.87	2.68	-1.08 /21	-1.88 / 5	0.39 /17	2.53	1.77
GL	Oppenheimer Intl Bond I	OIBIX	D-	(888) 470-0862	D / 1.8	4.16	3.27	-0.07 /31	-0.76 /10	1.43 /25	3.71	0.57
GL	Oppenheimer Intl Bond R	OIBNX	E+	(888) 470-0862	D- / 1.1	3.99	2.93	-0.76 /24	-1.49 / 6	0.74 /19	3.03	1.27

● Denotes fund is closed to new investors
* Denotes fund is included in Section II

RISK			NET ASSETS		ASSET							FUND MANAGER		MINIMUM		LOADS	
Risk Rating/Pts	3 Yr Avg Standard Deviation	Avg Duration	NAV As of 3/31/16	Total $(Mil)	Cash %	Gov. Bond %	Muni. Bond %	Corp. Bond %	Other %	Portfolio Turnover Ratio	Avg Coupon Rate	Manager Quality Pct	Manager Tenure (Years)	Initial Purch. $	Additional Purch. $	Front End Load	Back End Load
B+ / 8.3	2.1	N/A	13.65	86	0	0	0	0	100	0	0.0	74	9	25	15	0.0	0.0
C+ / 6.6	3.0	N/A	18.15	3	0	0	0	0	100	0	0.0	32	11	250	25	4.8	0.0
C+ / 6.7	3.0	N/A	16.40	N/A	0	0	0	0	100	0	0.0	17	11	250	25	0.0	0.0
C+ / 6.6	3.0	N/A	16.45	1	0	0	0	0	100	0	0.0	16	11	250	25	0.0	0.0
C- / 3.6	4.2	N/A	41.08	12	0	0	0	0	100	0	0.0	12	11	250	25	4.8	0.0
C- / 3.6	4.2	N/A	37.69	N/A	0	0	0	0	100	0	0.0	8	11	250	25	0.0	0.0
C- / 3.6	4.2	N/A	37.73	3	0	0	0	0	100	0	0.0	8	11	250	25	0.0	0.0
A+ / 9.9	N/A	N/A	23.35	18	0	0	0	0	100	0	0.0	62	11	250	25	4.8	0.0
A+ / 9.9	0.1	N/A	22.13	6	0	0	0	0	100	0	0.0	62	11	250	25	0.0	0.0
B / 8.2	2.2	N/A	23.88	3	0	0	0	0	100	0	0.0	45	11	250	25	0.0	0.0
B / 8.2	2.2	N/A	26.60	8	0	0	0	0	100	0	0.0	78	11	250	25	4.8	0.0
C / 5.5	3.3	N/A	12.03	3	0	0	0	0	100	0	0.0	78	11	250	25	0.0	0.0
C / 5.4	3.3	N/A	13.09	8	0	0	0	0	100	0	0.0	90	11	250	25	4.8	0.0
B+ / 8.8	1.7	N/A	12.85	6	0	0	0	0	100	0	0.0	85	11	250	25	0.0	0.0
A+ / 9.9	0.1	N/A	12.54	15	0	0	0	0	100	0	0.0	62	11	250	25	0.0	0.0
U /	N/A	N/A	1.00	440	100	0	0	0	0	0	0.0	N/A	6	1,000	0	0.0	0.0
U /	N/A	N/A	1.00	13	100	0	0	0	0	0	0.0	N/A	6	1,000	0	0.0	0.0
U /	N/A	N/A	1.00	253	100	0	0	0	0	0	0.0	N/A	6	1,000	0	0.0	0.0
C+ / 5.9	3.2	5.6	6.86	563	11	1	0	44	44	85	0.0	79	7	1,000	0	4.8	0.0
C+ / 6.0	3.1	5.6	6.86	10	11	1	0	44	44	85	0.0	46	7	1,000	0	0.0	0.0
C+ / 6.0	3.1	5.6	6.87	136	11	1	0	44	44	85	0.0	48	7	1,000	0	0.0	0.0
C+ / 5.9	3.2	5.6	6.85	616	11	1	0	44	44	85	0.0	91	7	5,000,000	0	0.0	0.0
C+ / 5.9	3.2	5.6	6.86	55	11	1	0	44	44	85	0.0	71	7	1,000	0	0.0	0.0
C / 5.4	3.3	5.6	6.82	135	11	1	0	44	44	85	0.0	77	7	1,000	0	0.0	0.0
C- / 3.4	4.4	6.6	10.62	124	6	0	0	91	3	100	0.0	66	6	1,000	50	4.8	0.0
C- / 3.4	4.3	6.6	10.61	32	6	0	0	91	3	100	0.0	37	6	1,000	50	0.0	0.0
C- / 3.4	4.3	6.6	10.62	N/A	6	0	0	91	3	100	0.0	83	6	5,000,000	0	0.0	0.0
C- / 3.4	4.3	6.6	10.62	9	6	0	0	91	3	100	0.0	54	6	1,000	50	0.0	0.0
C- / 3.4	4.4	6.6	10.61	7	6	0	0	91	3	100	0.0	76	6	1,000	50	0.0	0.0
E- / 0.2	11.0	4.9	7.40	31	0	72	0	27	1	107	0.0	2	1	1,000	0	4.8	0.0
E- / 0.2	11.0	4.9	7.40	8	0	72	0	27	1	107	0.0	1	1	1,000	0	0.0	0.0
E- / 0.2	11.0	4.9	7.40	2	0	72	0	27	1	107	0.0	3	1	5,000,000	0	0.0	0.0
E- / 0.2	11.0	4.9	7.40	1	0	72	0	27	1	107	0.0	2	1	1,000	0	0.0	0.0
E- / 0.2	11.0	4.9	7.40	3	0	72	0	27	1	107	0.0	3	1	0	0	0.0	0.0
U /	N/A	4.3	8.89	27	3	0	0	95	2	67	0.0	N/A	3	1,000	0	4.8	0.0
U /	N/A	4.3	8.88	4	3	0	0	95	2	67	0.0	N/A	3	1,000	0	0.0	0.0
U /	N/A	4.3	8.89	22	3	0	0	95	2	67	0.0	N/A	3	5,000,000	0	0.0	0.0
U /	N/A	4.3	8.89	1	3	0	0	95	2	67	0.0	N/A	3	1,000	0	0.0	0.0
U /	N/A	4.3	8.89	1	3	0	0	95	2	67	0.0	N/A	3	0	0	0.0	0.0
C- / 3.4	4.3	4.2	3.81	3,710	6	10	0	63	21	79	0.0	11	7	1,000	0	4.8	0.0
C- / 3.6	4.2	4.2	3.83	58	6	10	0	63	21	79	0.0	8	7	1,000	0	0.0	0.0
C- / 3.5	4.3	4.2	3.81	889	6	10	0	63	21	79	0.0	7	7	1,000	0	0.0	0.0
C- / 3.5	4.3	4.2	3.80	46	6	10	0	63	21	79	0.0	16	7	5,000,000	0	0.0	0.0
C- / 3.5	4.3	4.2	3.82	152	6	10	0	63	21	79	0.0	9	7	1,000	0	0.0	0.0
C- / 3.5	4.3	4.2	3.81	362	6	10	0	63	21	79	0.0	14	7	1,000	0	0.0	0.0
A+ / 9.9	N/A	N/A	1.00	6,447	100	0	0	0	0	0	0.2	72	10	0	0	0.0	0.0
A+ / 9.9	N/A	N/A	1.00	759	100	0	0	0	0	0	0.2	69	10	1,000,000	0	0.0	0.0
D+ / 2.3	5.4	5.3	5.70	1,725	4	62	0	30	4	111	0.0	25	3	1,000	0	4.8	0.0
D / 2.0	5.6	5.3	5.68	25	4	62	0	30	4	111	0.0	13	3	1,000	0	0.0	0.0
D / 2.0	5.6	5.3	5.68	518	4	62	0	30	4	111	0.0	14	3	1,000	0	0.0	0.0
D+ / 2.3	5.5	5.3	5.69	1,398	4	62	0	30	4	111	0.0	37	3	5,000,000	0	0.0	0.0
D+ / 2.3	5.4	5.3	5.68	147	4	62	0	30	4	111	0.0	19	3	1,000	0	0.0	0.0

Fund Type	Fund Name (99 Pct = Best, 0 Pct = Worst)	Ticker Symbol	Overall Investment Rating	Phone	PERFORMANCE: Perfor-mance Rating/Pts	Total Return % through 3/31/16: 3 Mo	6 Mo	1Yr / Pct	Annualized: 3Yr / Pct	Annualized: 5Yr / Pct	Incl. in Returns: Dividend Yield	Expense Ratio
GL	Oppenheimer Intl Bond Y	OIBYX	**D-**	(888) 470-0862	**D / 1.6**	4.10	3.36	-0.26 /28	-0.89 / 9	1.35 /24	3.52	0.77
* USS	Oppenheimer Limited Term Govt A	OPGVX	**C**	(888) 470-0862	**D+ / 2.5**	0.77	0.12	0.42 /48	0.64 /36	1.12 /21	1.71	0.92
USS ●	Oppenheimer Limited Term Govt B	OGSBX	**C-**	(888) 470-0862	**D / 1.6**	0.57	-0.27	-0.39 /27	-0.15 /14	0.32 /16	0.94	1.68
USS	Oppenheimer Limited Term Govt C	OLTCX	**C-**	(888) 470-0862	**D / 1.6**	0.57	-0.27	-0.39 /27	-0.19 /14	0.30 /16	0.95	1.66
USA	Oppenheimer Limited Term Govt I	OLTIX	**B-**	(888) 470-0862	**C / 4.3**	0.83	0.27	0.73 /54	1.00 /43	--	2.07	0.47
USS	Oppenheimer Limited Term Govt R	OLTNX	**C+**	(888) 470-0862	**C- / 3.1**	0.69	0.20	0.22 /44	0.37 /31	0.84 /19	1.45	1.17
USS	Oppenheimer Limited Term Govt Y	OLTYX	**B-**	(888) 470-0862	**C / 4.3**	0.84	0.27	0.72 /54	1.01 /43	1.46 /25	2.06	0.66
* USS	Oppenheimer Limited-Term Bond A	OUSGX	**C**	(888) 470-0862	**C- / 3.2**	0.69	0.22	0.10 /41	1.12 /45	2.72 /41	2.25	0.91
USS ●	Oppenheimer Limited-Term Bond B	UGTBX	**C**	(888) 470-0862	**D+ / 2.7**	0.50	-0.18	-0.82 /23	0.28 /30	1.92 /30	1.48	1.66
USS	Oppenheimer Limited-Term Bond C	OUSCX	**C**	(888) 470-0862	**D+ / 2.7**	0.50	-0.18	-0.81 /23	0.28 /30	1.92 /30	1.49	1.65
USL	Oppenheimer Limited-Term Bond I	OUSIX	**U**	(888) 470-0862	**U /**	0.78	0.41	0.37 /47	--	--	2.68	0.46
USS	Oppenheimer Limited-Term Bond R	OUSNX	**C+**	(888) 470-0862	**C- / 3.8**	0.62	0.08	-0.20 /29	0.83 /40	2.46 /37	2.00	1.16
USS	Oppenheimer Limited-Term Bond Y	OUSYX	**B**	(888) 470-0862	**C / 4.8**	0.74	0.32	0.40 /48	1.32 /49	2.96 /44	2.48	0.65
* MUS	Oppenheimer Ltd Term NY Muni A	LTNYX	**D-**	(888) 470-0862	**D- / 1.0**	0.65	1.19	-1.39 /19	-0.29 /13	2.68 /63	3.76	0.84
MUS ●	Oppenheimer Ltd Term NY Muni B	LTBBX	**D-**	(888) 470-0862	**E+ / 0.9**	0.47	1.16	-2.12 /15	-0.97 / 9	1.92 /44	3.09	1.59
MUS	Oppenheimer Ltd Term NY Muni C	LTNCX	**D-**	(888) 470-0862	**D- / 1.0**	0.48	1.17	-2.11 /15	-0.94 / 9	1.98 /46	3.11	1.59
MUN	Oppenheimer Ltd Term NY Muni Y	LTBYX	**D-**	(888) 470-0862	**D / 1.8**	0.71	1.31	-1.15 /20	-0.06 /15	2.92 /67	4.10	0.59
MM	Oppenheimer Money Market A	OMBXX	**U**	(888) 470-0862	**U /**	--	--	--	--	--	0.01	0.64
MUN ●	Oppenheimer Rochester AMT-Fr	OTFBX	**C+**	(888) 470-0862	**A+ / 9.7**	1.94	4.71	5.25 /98	3.93 /95	9.29 /99	5.20	1.73
MUN	Oppenheimer Rochester AMT-Fr	OMFCX	**C+**	(888) 470-0862	**A+ / 9.7**	1.95	4.56	5.11 /98	3.90 /95	9.30 /99	5.21	1.73
MUN	Oppenheimer Rochester AMT-Fr	OMFYX	**C+**	(888) 470-0862	**A+ / 9.9**	2.18	5.05	6.12 /99	4.92 /98	10.39 /99	6.16	0.73
* MUS	Oppenheimer Rochester AMT-Fr NY	OPNYX	**D**	(888) 470-0862	**C+ / 6.3**	1.43	2.86	3.60 /91	2.12 /78	7.33 /97	4.98	0.96
MUS ●	Oppenheimer Rochester AMT-Fr NY	ONYBX	**D+**	(888) 470-0862	**B- / 7.2**	1.25	2.48	2.81 /83	1.29 /61	6.44 /94	4.46	1.73
MUS	Oppenheimer Rochester AMT-Fr NY	ONYCX	**D+**	(888) 470-0862	**B- / 7.2**	1.16	2.39	2.73 /82	1.31 /62	6.51 /94	4.47	1.71
MUN	Oppenheimer Rochester AMT-Fr NY	ONYYX	**C-**	(888) 470-0862	**B+ / 8.6**	1.39	2.98	3.74 /92	2.36 /81	7.57 /98	5.46	0.71
* MUN	Oppenheimer Rochester AMT-Free	OPTAX	**C**	(888) 470-0862	**A / 9.5**	2.11	4.91	5.85 /99	4.70 /98	10.14 /99	5.62	0.98
MUS ●	Oppenheimer Rochester AZ Muni A	ORAZX	**E**	(888) 470-0862	**D- / 1.1**	1.13	2.83	0.03 /38	0.20 /30	5.72 /90	4.75	1.73
MUS ●	Oppenheimer Rochester AZ Muni B	ORBZX	**E+**	(888) 470-0862	**D / 1.6**	1.05	2.56	-0.71 /24	-0.49 /12	4.96 /85	4.24	2.51
MUS ●	Oppenheimer Rochester AZ Muni C	ORCZX	**E+**	(888) 470-0862	**D- / 1.5**	0.95	2.46	-0.71 /24	-0.52 /11	4.93 /85	4.24	2.51
MUN ●	Oppenheimer Rochester AZ Muni Y	ORYZX	**D-**	(888) 470-0862	**C- / 4.1**	1.23	2.92	0.04 /39	0.26 /31	5.79 /91	4.99	1.51
MUN	Oppenheimer Rochester Int Term Mu	ORRWX	**A-**	(888) 470-0862	**A- / 9.1**	1.95	4.14	4.74 /97	3.46 /92	4.86 /84	2.24	1.18
MUN	Oppenheimer Rochester Int Term Mu	ORRCX	**B+**	(888) 470-0862	**B+ / 8.9**	1.53	3.52	3.87 /93	2.62 /84	4.03 /78	1.55	1.94
MUN	Oppenheimer Rochester Int Term Mu	ORRYX	**A**	(888) 470-0862	**A+ / 9.6**	1.77	4.01	4.96 /98	3.66 /94	5.09 /86	2.50	0.95
* MUN	Oppenheimer Rochester Ltd Term M	OPITX	**D**	(888) 470-0862	**D- / 1.5**	0.81	1.74	-1.22 /20	0.27 /32	3.40 /73	3.99	0.92
MUN ●	Oppenheimer Rochester Ltd Term M	OIMBX	**D**	(888) 470-0862	**D- / 1.3**	0.64	1.37	-1.82 /16	-0.48 /12	2.61 /62	3.33	1.68
MUN	Oppenheimer Rochester Ltd Term M	OITCX	**D**	(888) 470-0862	**D- / 1.3**	0.64	1.38	-1.89 /16	-0.48 /12	2.64 /62	3.35	1.67
MUN	Oppenheimer Rochester Ltd Term M	OPIYX	**D+**	(888) 470-0862	**C- / 4.0**	0.87	1.87	-0.98 /22	0.52 /39	3.67 /75	4.33	0.67
MUS ●	Oppenheimer Rochester MA Muni A	ORMAX	**D**	(888) 470-0862	**C / 5.0**	1.30	2.94	2.29 /79	1.77 /73	6.14 /93	4.51	1.63
MUS ●	Oppenheimer Rochester MA Muni B	ORBAX	**D+**	(888) 470-0862	**C+ / 6.3**	1.22	2.57	1.63 /75	1.02 /54	5.38 /88	3.99	2.42
MUS ●	Oppenheimer Rochester MA Muni C	ORCAX	**D+**	(888) 470-0862	**C+ / 6.3**	1.22	2.58	1.64 /75	1.02 /54	5.37 /88	4.01	2.38
MUS ●	Oppenheimer Rochester MA Muni Y	ORYAX	**C-**	(888) 470-0862	**B / 7.9**	1.40	2.93	2.39 /80	1.82 /74	6.18 /93	4.74	1.36
MUS ●	Oppenheimer Rochester MD Muni A	ORMDX	**E**	(888) 470-0862	**E+ / 0.6**	0.99	0.87	0.68 /59	-0.60 /11	4.76 /83	5.14	1.30
MUS ●	Oppenheimer Rochester MD Muni B	ORYBX	**E**	(888) 470-0862	**E+ / 0.9**	0.81	0.51	-0.07 /31	-1.33 / 7	3.98 /77	4.66	2.10
MUS ●	Oppenheimer Rochester MD Muni C	ORYCX	**E**	(888) 470-0862	**E+ / 0.9**	0.81	0.61	-0.06 /31	-1.34 / 7	3.98 /77	4.67	2.05
MUN ●	Oppenheimer Rochester MD Muni Y	ORYYX	**E+**	(888) 470-0862	**D- / 1.5**	1.10	0.96	0.67 /59	-0.59 /11	4.82 /84	5.39	1.05
MUS ●	Oppenheimer Rochester MI Muni A	ORMIX	**E+**	(888) 470-0862	**D- / 1.1**	1.02	2.30	0.56 /56	0.23 /31	5.16 /86	5.30	1.44
MUS ●	Oppenheimer Rochester MI Muni B	ORMBX	**D-**	(888) 470-0862	**D / 1.6**	0.85	1.92	-0.19 /29	-0.48 /12	4.40 /81	4.81	2.18
MUS ●	Oppenheimer Rochester MI Muni C	ORMCX	**D-**	(888) 470-0862	**D- / 1.5**	0.85	1.81	-0.18 /29	-0.51 /11	4.39 /81	4.83	2.18
MUS ●	Oppenheimer Rochester MI Muni Y	ORMYX	**D**	(888) 470-0862	**C- / 3.9**	1.03	2.18	0.45 /53	0.24 /31	5.14 /86	5.59	1.18
MUS ●	Oppenheimer Rochester MN Muni A	OPAMX	**C+**	(888) 470-0862	**B+ / 8.7**	1.24	2.67	3.47 /90	4.07 /96	7.46 /97	3.52	1.25
MUS ●	Oppenheimer Rochester MN Muni B	OPBMX	**B-**	(888) 470-0862	**A- / 9.1**	1.14	2.30	2.71 /82	3.33 /91	6.67 /95	2.97	2.01
MUS ●	Oppenheimer Rochester MN Muni C	OPCMX	**B-**	(888) 470-0862	**A- / 9.1**	1.14	2.30	2.79 /83	3.33 /91	6.67 /95	2.97	2.01

● Denotes fund is closed to new investors
* Denotes fund is included in Section II

RISK			NET ASSETS		ASSET							FUND MANAGER		MINIMUM		LOADS	
Risk Rating/Pts	3 Yr Avg Standard Deviation	Avg Duration	NAV As of 3/31/16	Total $(Mil)	Cash %	Gov. Bond %	Muni. Bond %	Corp. Bond %	Other %	Portfolio Turnover Ratio	Avg Coupon Rate	Manager Quality Pct	Manager Tenure (Years)	Initial Purch. $	Additional Purch. $	Front End Load	Back End Load
D / 2.1	5.6	5.3	5.70	2,403	4	62	0	30	4	111	0.0	33	3	1,000	0	0.0	0.0
A / 9.4	0.9	2.2	4.48	562	0	40	0	1	59	155	0.0	63	7	1,000	0	2.3	0.0
A / 9.3	1.0	2.2	4.48	8	0	40	0	1	59	155	0.0	34	7	1,000	0	0.0	0.0
A / 9.3	1.0	2.2	4.47	180	0	40	0	1	59	155	0.0	32	7	1,000	0	0.0	0.0
A / 9.3	1.0	2.2	4.48	362	0	40	0	1	59	155	0.0	79	7	1,000,000	0	0.0	0.0
A / 9.3	0.9	2.2	4.48	31	0	40	0	1	59	155	0.0	53	7	1,000	0	0.0	0.0
A / 9.3	1.0	2.2	4.49	66	0	40	0	1	59	155	0.0	80	7	1,000	0	0.0	0.0
A- / 9.0	1.3	2.1	4.54	716	11	1	0	59	29	83	0.0	84	7	1,000	0	2.3	0.0
A- / 9.0	1.3	2.1	4.53	12	11	1	0	59	29	83	0.0	51	7	1,000	0	0.0	0.0
A- / 9.0	1.3	2.1	4.53	181	11	1	0	59	29	83	0.0	51	7	1,000	0	0.0	0.0
U /	N/A	2.1	4.55	140	11	1	0	59	29	83	0.0	N/A	7	1,000,000	0	0.0	0.0
A- / 9.0	1.3	2.1	4.54	35	11	1	0	59	29	83	0.0	76	7	1,000	0	0.0	0.0
A- / 9.0	1.3	2.1	4.56	263	11	1	0	59	29	83	0.0	87	7	1,000	0	0.0	0.0
C- / 3.3	4.4	3.0	3.00	1,818	0	0	99	0	1	9	0.0	6	17	1,000	50	2.3	0.0
C- / 3.4	4.4	3.0	3.00	8	0	0	99	0	1	9	0.0	5	17	1,000	50	0.0	0.0
C- / 3.3	4.4	3.0	2.99	766	0	0	99	0	1	9	0.0	5	17	1,000	50	0.0	0.0
C- / 3.3	4.4	3.0	3.00	157	0	0	99	0	1	9	0.0	7	17	0	0	0.0	0.0
U /	N/A	N/A	1.00	1,803	100	0	0	0	0	0	0.0	N/A	6	1,000	0	0.0	0.0
D- / 1.3	6.3	6.9	6.94	8	0	0	99	0	1	9	0.0	12	14	1,000	0	0.0	0.0
D- / 1.3	6.2	6.9	6.93	413	0	0	99	0	1	9	0.0	12	14	1,000	0	0.0	0.0
D- / 1.3	6.2	6.9	6.96	437	0	0	99	0	1	9	0.0	28	14	1,000	0	0.0	0.0
E+ / 0.7	6.8	9.3	11.11	951	0	0	98	0	2	7	0.0	5	14	1,000	0	4.8	0.0
E+ / 0.6	6.8	9.3	11.12	2	0	0	98	0	2	7	0.0	3	14	1,000	0	0.0	0.0
E+ / 0.6	6.8	9.3	11.11	120	0	0	98	0	2	7	0.0	3	14	1,000	0	0.0	0.0
E+ / 0.7	6.8	9.3	11.12	50	0	0	98	0	2	7	0.0	6	14	1,000	0	0.0	0.0
D- / 1.3	6.2	6.9	6.98	1,309	0	0	99	0	1	9	0.0	23	14	1,000	0	4.8	0.0
E+ / 0.8	6.9	4.9	10.31	25	0	0	100	0	0	17	0.0	3	10	1,000	0	4.8	0.0
E+ / 0.8	6.9	4.9	10.31	1	0	0	100	0	0	17	0.0	2	10	1,000	0	0.0	0.0
E+ / 0.8	6.9	4.9	10.31	12	0	0	100	0	0	17	0.0	2	10	1,000	0	0.0	0.0
E+ / 0.8	6.8	4.9	10.32	4	0	0	100	0	0	17	0.0	3	10	1,000	0	0.0	0.0
C / 5.0	3.5	5.1	4.42	130	0	0	100	0	0	56	0.0	59	6	1,000	0	2.3	0.0
C / 4.9	3.5	5.1	4.41	37	0	0	100	0	0	56	0.0	31	6	1,000	0	0.0	0.0
C / 5.0	3.5	5.1	4.42	32	0	0	100	0	0	56	0.0	72	6	1,000	0	0.0	0.0
C- / 4.2	3.9	2.6	4.50	1,163	0	0	100	0	0	16	0.0	8	14	1,000	0	2.3	0.0
C / 4.3	3.8	2.6	4.50	12	0	0	100	0	0	16	0.0	7	14	1,000	0	0.0	0.0
C / 4.3	3.8	2.6	4.48	641	0	0	100	0	0	16	0.0	6	14	1,000	0	0.0	0.0
C / 4.3	3.8	2.6	4.50	255	0	0	100	0	0	16	0.0	9	14	1,000	0	0.0	0.0
D / 1.8	5.8	5.4	10.38	31	0	0	100	0	0	16	0.0	7	10	1,000	0	4.8	0.0
D / 1.8	5.8	5.4	10.38	1	0	0	100	0	0	16	0.0	6	10	1,000	0	0.0	0.0
D / 1.8	5.8	5.4	10.36	15	0	0	100	0	0	16	0.0	6	10	1,000	0	0.0	0.0
D / 1.9	5.8	5.4	10.38	5	0	0	100	0	0	16	0.0	7	10	1,000	0	0.0	0.0
E / 0.4	8.2	6.8	9.44	22	0	0	100	0	0	7	0.0	1	10	1,000	0	4.8	0.0
E / 0.5	8.1	6.8	9.42	1	0	0	100	0	0	7	0.0	1	10	1,000	0	0.0	0.0
E / 0.4	8.2	6.8	9.41	22	0	0	100	0	0	7	0.0	1	10	1,000	0	0.0	0.0
E / 0.4	8.1	6.8	9.45	3	0	0	100	0	0	7	0.0	1	10	1,000	0	0.0	0.0
D / 1.9	5.8	3.6	8.31	27	0	0	100	0	0	8	0.0	5	10	1,000	0	4.8	0.0
D / 1.9	5.8	3.6	8.31	1	0	0	100	0	0	8	0.0	3	10	1,000	0	0.0	0.0
D / 1.9	5.8	3.6	8.29	17	0	0	100	0	0	8	0.0	3	10	1,000	0	0.0	0.0
D / 1.9	5.8	3.6	8.29	2	0	0	100	0	0	8	0.0	5	10	1,000	0	0.0	0.0
C- / 3.5	4.3	4.3	13.12	85	0	0	100	0	0	13	0.0	52	10	1,000	0	4.8	0.0
C- / 3.4	4.3	4.3	13.11	2	0	0	100	0	0	13	0.0	28	10	1,000	0	0.0	0.0
C- / 3.5	4.3	4.3	13.11	38	0	0	100	0	0	13	0.0	29	10	1,000	0	0.0	0.0

Fund Type	Fund Name	Ticker Symbol	Overall Investment Rating	Phone	PERFORMANCE: Performance Rating/Pts	Total Return % through 3/31/16: 3 Mo	6 Mo	1Yr / Pct	Annualized 3Yr / Pct	Annualized 5Yr / Pct	Incl. in Returns: Dividend Yield	Expense Ratio
	99 Pct = Best, 0 Pct = Worst											
MUN ●	Oppenheimer Rochester MN Muni Y	OPYMX	**B**	(888) 470-0862	**A+ / 9.6**	1.25	2.71	3.56 /91	4.15 /96	7.54 /97	3.78	1.00
* MUS	Oppenheimer Rochester Muni A	RMUNX	**D**	(888) 470-0862	**C / 4.3**	1.93	2.68	2.03 /77	1.46 /67	6.55 /95	6.08	0.97
MUS ●	Oppenheimer Rochester Muni B	RMUBX	**D**	(888) 470-0862	**C / 5.2**	1.72	2.25	1.18 /70	0.59 /41	5.60 /90	5.54	1.82
MUS	Oppenheimer Rochester Muni C	RMUCX	**D**	(888) 470-0862	**C / 5.2**	1.73	2.26	1.12 /69	0.60 /41	5.63 /90	5.55	1.82
MUS	Oppenheimer Rochester Muni Y	RMUYX	**D+**	(888) 470-0862	**B / 7.7**	1.96	2.75	2.18 /78	1.61 /70	6.70 /95	6.53	0.82
MUS ●	Oppenheimer Rochester NC Muni A	OPNCX	**D-**	(888) 470-0862	**C- / 3.8**	1.56	3.03	1.90 /76	1.30 /61	6.03 /92	4.72	1.50
MUS ●	Oppenheimer Rochester NC Muni B	OPCBX	**D**	(888) 470-0862	**C / 5.1**	1.38	2.66	1.15 /70	0.53 /39	5.21 /87	4.21	2.27
MUS ●	Oppenheimer Rochester NC Muni C	OPCCX	**D**	(888) 470-0862	**C / 5.2**	1.38	2.66	1.15 /70	0.58 /41	5.25 /87	4.21	2.26
MUN ●	Oppenheimer Rochester NC Muni Y	OPCYX	**D+**	(888) 470-0862	**B- / 7.2**	1.57	3.04	1.94 /77	1.35 /63	6.10 /92	4.99	1.27
MUS ●	Oppenheimer Rochester Ohio Muni A	OROHX	**C-**	(888) 470-0862	**B+ / 8.5**	2.35	4.42	4.02 /94	3.46 /92	6.85 /96	4.92	1.32
MUS ●	Oppenheimer Rochester Ohio Muni B	OROBX	**C**	(888) 470-0862	**B+ / 8.9**	2.17	3.94	3.26 /88	2.70 /85	6.06 /92	4.43	2.07
MUS ●	Oppenheimer Rochester Ohio Muni C	OROCX	**C**	(888) 470-0862	**B+ / 8.9**	2.18	3.95	3.27 /88	2.70 /85	6.04 /92	4.44	2.07
MUS ●	Oppenheimer Rochester Ohio Muni Y	OROYX	**C**	(888) 470-0862	**A / 9.5**	2.36	4.42	4.05 /94	3.50 /93	6.88 /96	5.19	1.04
MUN	Oppenheimer Rochester Sht Term	ORSTX	**A**	(888) 470-0862	**C+ / 6.1**	0.50	1.21	1.64 /75	1.82 /74	2.56 /61	1.85	0.86
MUN	Oppenheimer Rochester Sht Term	ORSCX	**A-**	(888) 470-0862	**C+ / 5.6**	0.33	0.85	0.90 /64	1.05 /54	1.77 /41	1.16	1.62
MUN	Oppenheimer Rochester Sht Term	ORSYX	**A+**	(888) 470-0862	**B / 7.9**	0.55	1.33	1.89 /76	2.07 /78	2.81 /66	2.14	0.61
MUS ●	Oppenheimer Rochester VA Muni A	ORVAX	**E-**	(888) 470-0862	**E+ / 0.6**	1.01	2.57	-0.52 /26	-0.69 /10	5.33 /88	6.35	1.29
MUS ●	Oppenheimer Rochester VA Muni B	ORVBX	**E**	(888) 470-0862	**E+ / 0.8**	0.83	2.21	-1.26 /20	-1.43 / 6	4.54 /82	5.92	2.04
MUS ●	Oppenheimer Rochester VA Muni C	ORVCX	**E**	(888) 470-0862	**E+ / 0.9**	0.96	2.21	-1.14 /21	-1.39 / 6	4.57 /82	5.93	2.05
MUS ●	Oppenheimer Rochester VA Muni Y	ORVYX	**E**	(888) 470-0862	**D- / 1.5**	1.13	2.68	-0.39 /27	-0.64 /11	5.41 /88	6.67	1.05
LP	Oppenheimer Sen Floating Rate Pl A	OSFAX	**U**	(888) 470-0862	**U /**	0.37	-3.60	-5.05 / 5	--	--	5.45	2.39
LP	Oppenheimer Sen Floating Rate Pl C	OSFCX	**U**	(888) 470-0862	**U /**	0.18	-3.98	-5.70 / 4	--	--	4.81	3.17
LP	Oppenheimer Sen Floating Rate Pl I	OSFIX	**U**	(888) 470-0862	**U /**	0.45	-3.43	-4.58 / 6	--	--	6.05	1.71
LP	Oppenheimer Sen Floating Rate Pl Y	OSFYX	**U**	(888) 470-0862	**U /**	0.43	-3.47	-4.69 / 6	--	--	5.92	2.02
* LP	Oppenheimer Sen-Floating Rate A	OOSAX	**D+**	(888) 470-0862	**D- / 1.4**	0.97	-1.77	-2.61 /13	1.11 /45	2.77 /41	4.59	1.08
LP ●	Oppenheimer Sen-Floating Rate B	OOSBX	**D+**	(888) 470-0862	**D / 1.8**	0.85	-2.01	-3.21 /11	0.58 /35	2.17 /33	4.24	1.59
LP	Oppenheimer Sen-Floating Rate C	OOSCX	**D+**	(888) 470-0862	**D- / 1.5**	0.66	-2.25	-3.45 /10	0.36 /31	2.12 /33	3.99	1.83
LP	Oppenheimer Sen-Floating Rate I	OOSIX	**C-**	(888) 470-0862	**C- / 4.1**	1.05	-1.63	-2.33 /14	1.43 /51	2.99 /45	5.08	0.76
LP	Oppenheimer Sen-Floating Rate R	OOSNX	**C-**	(888) 470-0862	**D+ / 2.9**	0.91	-2.02	-2.98 /11	0.84 /40	2.48 /38	4.50	1.34
LP	Oppenheimer Sen-Floating Rate Y	OOSYX	**C-**	(888) 470-0862	**C- / 3.9**	1.03	-1.66	-2.39 /14	1.35 /49	3.03 /46	5.01	0.83
* GL	Opportunistic Income A	ENIAX	**B+**	(800) 342-5734	**C / 5.3**	0.50	0.29	0.30 /46	1.68 /55	2.58 /39	2.53	0.52
GEI	Optimum Fixed Income A	OAFIX	**D**	(800) 523-1918	**D- / 1.4**	1.96	1.45	-0.63 /25	0.69 /37	2.82 /42	2.58	1.17
GEI	Optimum Fixed Income C	OCFIX	**D**	(800) 523-1918	**D+ / 2.3**	1.85	1.11	-1.39 /19	-0.03 /15	2.11 /33	1.94	1.92
GEI	Optimum Fixed Income I	OIFIX	**C-**	(800) 523-1918	**C / 4.4**	1.96	1.61	-0.48 /26	0.95 /42	3.12 /47	2.96	0.92
* GES	Osterweis Strategic Income	OSTIX	**D+**	(800) 700-3316	**C- / 4.0**	0.47	-1.29	-2.39 /14	1.45 /51	3.45 /52	5.89	0.82
COH	PACE High Yield Invst A	PHIAX	**E+**	(888) 793-8637	**D- / 1.5**	3.20	2.22	-2.96 /11	0.93 /41	3.87 /60	5.60	1.26
COH	PACE High Yield Invst C	PHYCX	**D-**	(888) 793-8637	**C- / 3.1**	3.11	2.02	-3.41 /10	0.47 /33	3.40 /52	5.28	1.73
COH	PACE High Yield Invst P	PHYPX	**D-**	(888) 793-8637	**C- / 3.4**	3.33	2.29	-2.80 /12	1.14 /45	4.09 /63	5.89	1.09
COH	PACE High Yield Invst Y	PHDYX	**D**	(888) 793-8637	**C / 4.6**	3.34	2.43	-2.65 /13	1.21 /46	4.15 /64	6.04	1.03
GL	PACE International Fx Inc Inve A	PWFAX	**D**	(888) 793-8637	**C / 4.4**	7.11	6.14	4.51 /84	0.95 /42	1.02 /21	2.70	1.27
GL	PACE International Fx Inc Inve C	PWFCX	**D+**	(888) 793-8637	**C+ / 5.6**	7.02	6.02	4.03 /81	0.47 /33	0.54 /17	2.39	1.76
GL	PACE International Fx Inc Inve P	PCGLX	**D+**	(888) 793-8637	**C+ / 5.9**	7.25	6.33	4.79 /86	1.15 /45	1.23 /23	3.03	1.08
GL	PACE International Fx Inc Inve Y	PWFYX	**C-**	(888) 793-8637	**C+ / 6.8**	7.27	6.45	4.79 /86	1.15 /45	1.23 /23	3.08	1.09
GEI	PACE Intrm Fixed Inc Inve A	PIFAX	**C-**	(888) 793-8637	**D+ / 2.7**	1.72	0.97	1.03 /59	1.14 /45	2.23 /34	1.31	1.03
GEI	PACE Intrm Fixed Inc Inve C	PIICX	**C+**	(888) 793-8637	**C- / 4.0**	1.71	0.76	0.57 /51	0.67 /36	1.72 /28	0.91	1.53
GEI	PACE Intrm Fixed Inc Inve P	PCIFX	**C+**	(888) 793-8637	**C / 4.5**	1.93	1.24	1.35 /64	1.44 /51	2.50 /38	1.65	0.83
GEI	PACE Intrm Fixed Inc Inve Y	PIFYX	**B**	(888) 793-8637	**C / 5.4**	1.93	1.16	1.35 /64	1.42 /51	2.48 /38	1.69	0.86
USS	PACE Mtg Backed Sec Fixed Inc Inv	PFXAX	**C+**	(888) 793-8637	**C / 4.4**	1.83	1.37	1.77 /70	2.02 /62	2.67 /40	2.03	1.07
USS	PACE Mtg Backed Sec Fixed Inc Inv	PFXCX	**B-**	(888) 793-8637	**C / 5.4**	1.58	1.00	1.14 /61	1.49 /52	2.13 /33	1.59	1.59
USS	PACE Mtg Backed Sec Fixed Inc Inv	PCGTX	**B+**	(888) 793-8637	**C+ / 5.9**	1.79	1.40	1.92 /71	2.24 /66	2.91 /44	2.31	0.91
USS	PACE Mtg Backed Sec Fixed Inc Inv	PFXYX	**A**	(888) 793-8637	**C+ / 6.8**	1.87	1.48	2.00 /72	2.27 /67	2.91 /44	2.36	0.86
MUN	PACE Muni Fxd Inc Inve A	PMUAX	**B+**	(888) 793-8637	**B / 7.7**	1.62	3.10	3.69 /92	2.77 /86	4.32 /80	2.37	0.92

● Denotes fund is closed to new investors
* Denotes fund is included in Section II

RISK			NET ASSETS		ASSET							FUND MANAGER		MINIMUM		LOADS	
Risk Rating/Pts	3 Yr Avg Standard Deviation	Avg Duration	NAV As of 3/31/16	Total $(Mil)	Cash %	Gov. Bond %	Muni. Bond %	Corp. Bond %	Other %	Portfolio Turnover Ratio	Avg Coupon Rate	Manager Quality Pct	Manager Tenure (Years)	Initial Purch. $	Additional Purch. $	Front End Load	Back End Load
C- / 3.4	4.3	4.3	13.12	18	0	0	100	0	0	13	0.0	55	10	1,000	0	0.0	0.0
E+ / 0.6	7.2	7.4	14.72	4,506	0	0	99	0	1	13	0.0	4	17	1,000	50	4.8	0.0
E+ / 0.6	7.2	7.4	14.70	16	0	0	99	0	1	13	0.0	2	17	1,000	50	0.0	0.0
E+ / 0.6	7.2	7.4	14.68	858	0	0	99	0	1	13	0.0	2	17	1,000	50	0.0	0.0
E+ / 0.6	7.2	7.4	14.72	222	0	0	99	0	1	13	0.0	4	17	1,000	50	0.0	0.0
E+ / 0.9	6.6	5.5	10.93	40	0	0	100	0	0	15	0.0	5	10	1,000	0	4.8	0.0
E+ / 0.9	6.6	5.5	10.93	1	0	0	100	0	0	15	0.0	3	10	1,000	0	0.0	0.0
D- / 1.0	6.6	5.5	10.93	26	0	0	100	0	0	15	0.0	4	10	1,000	0	0.0	0.0
E+ / 0.9	6.7	5.5	10.93	6	0	0	100	0	0	15	0.0	5	10	1,000	0	0.0	0.0
D- / 1.5	6.1	5.4	10.22	46	0	0	99	0	1	9	0.0	10	10	1,000	0	4.8	0.0
D- / 1.5	6.1	5.4	10.21	1	0	0	99	0	1	9	0.0	7	10	1,000	0	0.0	0.0
D- / 1.5	6.1	5.4	10.20	20	0	0	99	0	1	9	0.0	7	10	1,000	0	0.0	0.0
D- / 1.5	6.1	5.4	10.21	8	0	0	99	0	1	9	0.0	10	10	1,000	0	0.0	0.0
A / 9.3	1.0	1.7	3.75	387	0	0	99	0	1	58	0.0	90	6	1,000	0	2.3	0.0
A / 9.4	0.9	1.7	3.75	94	0	0	99	0	1	58	0.0	77	6	1,000	0	0.0	0.0
A / 9.3	1.0	1.7	3.75	368	0	0	99	0	1	58	0.0	92	6	1,000	0	0.0	0.0
E / 0.3	8.9	9.1	8.01	56	0	0	100	0	0	11	0.0	1	10	1,000	0	4.8	0.0
E / 0.3	8.8	9.1	7.99	2	0	0	100	0	0	11	0.0	0	10	1,000	0	0.0	0.0
E / 0.3	8.8	9.1	7.99	24	0	0	100	0	0	11	0.0	1	10	1,000	0	0.0	0.0
E / 0.3	8.8	9.1	8.01	8	0	0	100	0	0	11	0.0	1	10	1,000	0	0.0	0.0
U /	N/A	0.2	8.73	17	0	0	0	25	75	68	0.0	N/A	3	1,000	50	3.5	0.0
U /	N/A	0.2	8.73	11	0	0	0	25	75	68	0.0	N/A	3	1,000	50	0.0	0.0
U /	N/A	0.2	8.74	N/A	0	0	0	25	75	68	0.0	N/A	3	5,000,000	0	0.0	0.0
U /	N/A	0.2	8.74	8	0	0	0	25	75	68	0.0	N/A	3	0	0	0.0	0.0
C+ / 6.9	2.9	0.2	7.58	3,882	0	0	0	22	78	39	0.0	77	17	1,000	50	3.5	0.0
C+ / 6.9	2.9	0.2	7.58	46	0	0	0	22	78	39	0.0	53	17	1,000	50	0.0	0.0
C+ / 6.9	2.9	0.2	7.58	2,842	0	0	0	22	78	39	0.0	44	17	1,000	50	0.0	0.0
C+ / 6.9	2.9	0.2	7.56	914	0	0	0	22	78	39	0.0	84	17	5,000,000	0	0.0	0.0
C+ / 6.9	2.9	0.2	7.57	37	0	0	0	22	78	39	0.0	68	17	1,000	50	0.0	0.0
C+ / 6.8	2.9	0.2	7.56	3,921	0	0	0	22	78	39	0.0	84	17	0	0	0.0	0.0
A- / 9.2	1.1	2.9	8.09	2,143	6	0	0	16	78	42	0.0	94	9	100,000	1,000	0.0	0.0
C+ / 5.6	3.2	4.7	9.38	40	0	23	1	33	43	482	3.6	14	9	1,000	100	4.5	0.0
C+ / 5.6	3.2	4.7	9.37	153	0	23	1	33	43	482	3.6	9	9	1,000	100	0.0	0.0
C+ / 5.7	3.2	4.7	9.37	1,893	0	23	1	33	43	482	3.6	17	9	0	0	0.0	0.0
C / 5.2	3.4	1.2	10.57	4,772	17	0	0	80	3	58	0.0	89	14	5,000	100	0.0	0.0
D- / 1.5	5.6	4.4	9.11	4	5	0	0	92	3	57	6.8	38	1	1,000	100	4.5	0.0
D- / 1.4	5.6	4.4	9.11	3	5	0	0	92	3	57	6.8	25	1	1,000	100	0.0	0.0
D- / 1.5	5.6	4.4	9.13	392	5	0	0	92	3	57	6.8	44	1	10,000	500	2.0	0.0
D- / 1.4	5.6	4.4	9.15	1	5	0	0	92	3	57	6.8	46	1	5,000,000	0	0.0	0.0
D+ / 2.7	5.1	6.2	10.39	45	2	48	0	42	8	40	3.6	90	21	1,000	100	4.5	1.0
D+ / 2.6	5.1	6.2	10.40	3	2	48	0	42	8	40	3.6	84	21	1,000	100	0.0	1.0
D+ / 2.7	5.1	6.2	10.39	505	2	48	0	42	8	40	3.6	92	21	10,000	500	2.0	1.0
D+ / 2.6	5.1	6.2	10.36	4	2	48	0	42	8	40	3.6	92	21	5,000,000	0	0.0	1.0
B+ / 8.5	2.0	3.5	12.29	19	2	45	0	33	20	476	2.5	46	4	1,000	100	4.5	0.0
B+ / 8.5	2.0	3.5	12.31	2	2	45	0	33	20	476	2.5	31	4	1,000	100	0.0	0.0
B+ / 8.5	2.0	3.5	12.30	406	2	45	0	33	20	476	2.5	57	4	10,000	500	2.0	0.0
B+ / 8.5	2.0	3.5	12.29	N/A	2	45	0	33	20	476	2.5	58	4	5,000,000	0	0.0	0.0
B / 8.0	2.4	3.3	13.02	46	0	7	0	0	93	1,360	2.5	83	3	1,000	100	4.5	0.0
B / 8.1	2.4	3.3	13.03	12	0	7	0	0	93	1,360	2.5	66	3	1,000	100	0.0	0.0
B / 8.0	2.4	3.3	13.02	414	0	7	0	0	93	1,360	2.5	87	3	10,000	500	2.0	0.0
B / 8.0	2.4	3.3	13.02	48	0	7	0	0	93	1,360	2.5	87	3	5,000,000	0	0.0	0.0
C+ / 6.0	3.1	5.0	13.38	52	1	0	98	0	1	21	5.0	44	16	1,000	100	4.5	0.0

99 Pct = Best 0 Pct = Worst Fund Type	Fund Name	Ticker Symbol	Overall Investment Rating	Phone	PERFORMANCE Performance Rating/Pts	Total Return % through 3/31/16 3 Mo	6 Mo	1Yr / Pct	Annualized 3Yr / Pct	5Yr / Pct	Incl. in Returns Dividend Yield	Expense Ratio
MUN	PACE Muni Fxd Inc Inve C	PMUCX	**A-**	(888) 793-8637	**B+ / 8.4**	1.54	2.89	3.21 /87	2.27 /80	3.81 /76	1.95	1.42
MUN	PACE Muni Fxd Inc Inve P	PCMNX	**A**	(888) 793-8637	**B+ / 8.7**	1.74	3.29	4.00 /94	3.05 /89	4.59 /82	2.65	0.67
MUN	PACE Muni Fxd Inc Inve Y	PMUYX	**A+**	(888) 793-8637	**A- / 9.1**	1.65	3.19	3.91 /93	3.02 /88	4.57 /82	2.69	0.70
COI	PACE Strat Fxd Inc Inve A	PBNAX	**D**	(888) 793-8637	**D / 2.0**	2.69	2.56	-0.15 /30	0.92 /41	3.98 /61	2.50	1.07
COI	PACE Strat Fxd Inc Inve C	PBNCX	**D+**	(888) 793-8637	**C- / 3.8**	2.68	2.43	-0.61 /25	0.47 /33	3.51 /53	2.15	1.54
COI	PACE Strat Fxd Inc Inve P	PCSIX	**D+**	(888) 793-8637	**C / 4.3**	2.88	2.82	0.14 /42	1.21 /46	4.25 /65	2.84	0.82
COI	PACE Strat Fxd Inc Inve Y	PSFYX	**D+**	(888) 793-8637	**C / 5.1**	2.87	2.79	0.08 /40	1.17 /46	4.22 /64	2.84	0.93
USS	Pacific Advisors Govt Secs A	PADGX	**D+**	(800) 282-6693	**E / 0.3**	0.17	0.54	-0.68 /24	-1.08 / 8	-0.45 / 2	0.00	6.37
USS	Pacific Advisors Govt Secs C	PGGCX	**D+**	(800) 282-6693	**E / 0.4**	-0.01	0.16	-1.42 /19	-1.82 / 5	-1.19 / 1	0.00	7.09
GES	Pacific Advisors Inc & Eq A	PADIX	**C-**	(800) 282-6693	**B- / 7.3**	2.90	5.56	1.17 /61	4.31 /86	5.28 /73	0.95	2.66
GES	Pacific Advisors Inc & Eq C	PIECX	**C-**	(800) 282-6693	**B / 7.8**	2.70	5.17	0.42 /48	3.54 /80	4.49 /67	0.43	3.41
MUN	Pacific Capital T/F Sh-Interm Y	PTFSX	**A**	(888) 739-1390	**C+ / 5.9**	0.69	0.98	1.50 /74	1.06 /55	1.35 /32	1.09	0.34
MUI	Pacific Capital Tax-Free Secs Y	PTXFX	**A+**	(888) 739-1390	**A- / 9.1**	1.47	2.61	3.68 /92	3.06 /89	4.48 /81	2.91	0.32
MTG	Pacific Financial Tactical Inst	PFGTX	**C-**	(888) 451-8734	**D- / 1.5**	0.00	-0.41	-2.02 /16	0.01 /16	1.05 /21	1.16	2.47
MTG	Pacific Financial Tactical Inv	PFTLX	**D+**	(888) 451-8734	**E+ / 0.8**	-0.21	-0.83	-2.78 /12	-0.77 /10	0.30 /16	0.99	3.22
GEI	Pacific Funds Core Income Class A	PLIAX	**D+**	(800) 722-2333	**C / 4.3**	2.87	2.24	-0.27 /28	2.04 /62	4.37 /66	2.81	1.13
GL	Pacific Funds Core Income Class Adv	PLIDX	**C**	(800) 722-2333	**C+ / 6.7**	2.92	2.36	-0.02 /31	2.29 /67	4.56 /68	3.18	0.88
LP	Pacific Funds Core Income Class C	PLNCX	**C-**	(800) 722-2333	**C / 4.8**	2.67	1.85	-1.03 /21	1.25 /47	--	2.17	1.88
GEI	Pacific Funds Core Income Class I	PLIIX	**C**	(800) 722-2333	**C+ / 6.8**	2.94	2.39	0.03 /36	2.32 /68	4.62 /69	3.23	0.73
COI	Pacific Funds Core Income Class P		**U**	(800) 722-2333	**U /**	2.92	2.36	--	--	--	0.00	0.73
LP	Pacific Funds Floating Rate Inc A	PLFLX	**C+**	(800) 722-2333	**C / 4.3**	1.56	0.93	0.71 /53	1.78 /57	--	3.87	1.29
LP	Pacific Funds Floating Rate Inc Adv	PLFDX	**B+**	(800) 722-2333	**C+ / 6.2**	1.61	1.05	0.96 /58	2.03 /62	--	4.24	1.04
LP	Pacific Funds Floating Rate Inc C	PLBCX	**C+**	(800) 722-2333	**C / 4.3**	1.37	0.55	-0.04 /31	1.01 /43	--	3.24	2.04
LP	Pacific Funds Floating Rate Inc I	PLFRX	**B+**	(800) 722-2333	**C+ / 6.2**	1.63	1.08	1.02 /59	2.05 /62	--	4.30	0.89
LP	Pacific Funds Floating Rate Inc P		**B+**	(800) 722-2333	**C+ / 6.2**	1.62	1.06	0.96 /58	2.03 /62	--	4.24	0.89
COH	Pacific Funds High Income A	PLAHX	**E**	(800) 722-2333	**E+ / 0.6**	2.41	-0.53	-5.79 / 3	0.26 /29	--	4.48	1.52
COH	Pacific Funds High Income Adv	PLHYX	**E+**	(800) 722-2333	**D / 1.6**	2.35	-0.52	-5.66 / 4	0.44 /32	--	4.93	1.27
COH	Pacific Funds High Income C	PLCHX	**E**	(800) 722-2333	**E+ / 0.8**	2.10	-0.92	-6.52 / 3	-0.51 /11	--	3.87	2.27
COH	Pacific Funds High Income I	PLHIX	**E+**	(800) 722-2333	**D / 1.6**	2.36	-0.51	-5.57 / 4	0.47 /33	--	5.01	1.12
COH	Pacific Funds High Income P		**U**	(800) 722-2333	**U /**	2.37	-0.42	-5.60 / 4	--	--	4.98	1.12
COH	Pacific Funds Ltd Dur Hi Inc A	PLLDX	**U**	(800) 722-2333	**U /**	2.50	0.15	-2.94 /12	--	--	4.48	1.35
COH	Pacific Funds Ltd Dur Hi Inc Adv	PLLYX	**U**	(800) 722-2333	**U /**	2.56	0.38	-2.70 /12	--	--	4.88	1.10
COH	Pacific Funds Ltd Dur Hi Inc C	PLLCX	**U**	(800) 722-2333	**U /**	2.43	-0.11	-3.56 / 9	--	--	3.85	2.10
COH	Pacific Funds Ltd Dur Hi Inc I	PLLIX	**U**	(800) 722-2333	**U /**	2.68	0.41	-2.53 /13	--	--	4.93	0.95
COI	Pacific Funds Shrt Duration Inc A	PLADX	**C**	(800) 722-2333	**C- / 3.2**	1.02	0.73	0.15 /43	1.22 /47	--	1.56	1.09
COI	Pacific Funds Shrt Duration Inc Adv	PLDSX	**B**	(800) 722-2333	**C / 5.1**	1.08	0.85	0.40 /48	1.47 /52	--	1.86	0.84
COI	Pacific Funds Shrt Duration Inc C	PLCSX	**C**	(800) 722-2333	**C- / 3.1**	0.84	0.36	-0.58 /25	0.46 /32	--	0.88	1.84
COI	Pacific Funds Shrt Duration Inc I	PLSDX	**B**	(800) 722-2333	**C / 5.2**	1.19	0.97	0.54 /50	1.48 /52	--	1.91	0.69
GEL	Pacific Funds Strategic Income A	PLSTX	**D**	(800) 722-2333	**C- / 3.5**	3.03	1.34	-2.16 /15	1.90 /59	--	4.05	1.30
GEL	Pacific Funds Strategic Income Adv	PLSFX	**D+**	(800) 722-2333	**C+ / 6.0**	2.99	1.47	-2.01 /16	2.13 /64	--	4.49	1.05
GEL	Pacific Funds Strategic Income C	PLCNX	**D**	(800) 722-2333	**C- / 4.1**	2.74	0.97	-2.90 /12	1.14 /45	--	3.47	2.05
GEN	Pacific Funds Strategic Income I	PLSRX	**D+**	(800) 722-2333	**C+ / 6.0**	3.02	1.50	-1.98 /16	2.14 /64	--	4.56	0.90
GL	Palmer Square Income Plus	PSYPX	**U**	(866) 933-9033	**U /**	-4.70	-6.47	-5.93 / 3	--	--	3.75	0.76
GEI	Parnassus Income Fd-Fixed Inc	PRFIX	**B+**	(800) 999-3505	**C+ / 6.1**	2.35	1.94	1.59 /67	1.71 /56	2.74 /41	1.96	0.78
COI	Parnassus Income Fd-Fixed Inc Inst	PFPLX	**U**	(800) 999-3505	**U /**	2.40	2.10	--	--	--	0.00	N/A
COH	Pax High Yield A	PXHAX	**E**	(800) 767-1729	**E / 0.3**	0.04	-3.21	-7.39 / 2	-0.92 / 9	2.15 /33	6.06	0.99
COH	Pax High Yield I	PXHIX	**E+**	(800) 767-1729	**E+ / 0.6**	0.10	-2.97	-7.21 / 2	-0.69 /10	2.40 /36	6.62	0.74
COH	Pax High Yield Inv	PAXHX	**E**	(800) 767-1729	**E / 0.5**	0.04	-3.22	-7.53 / 2	-0.96 / 9	2.13 /33	6.35	0.99
COH	Pax High Yield R	PXHRX	**E**	(800) 767-1729	**E / 0.4**	-0.02	-3.33	-7.76 / 2	-1.17 / 7	1.95 /31	6.09	1.24
MUS	Payden CA Muni Inc Investor	PYCRX	**A+**	(888) 409-8007	**B+ / 8.9**	1.41	2.45	2.86 /84	2.94 /88	4.42 /81	1.99	0.70
MM	Payden Cash Rsv MM Investor	PBHXX	**U**	(888) 409-8007	**U /**	--	--	--	--	--	0.02	0.37
COI	Payden Core Bond Adviser	PYCWX	**C+**	(888) 409-8007	**C+ / 6.5**	2.14	1.90	0.94 /58	2.16 /65	3.83 /59	2.56	0.85

• Denotes fund is closed to new investors
* Denotes fund is included in Section II

RISK			NET ASSETS		ASSET							FUND MANAGER		MINIMUM		LOADS	
Risk Rating/Pts	3 Yr Avg Standard Deviation	Avg Duration	NAV As of 3/31/16	Total $(Mil)	Cash %	Gov. Bond %	Muni. Bond %	Corp. Bond %	Other %	Portfolio Turnover Ratio	Avg Coupon Rate	Manager Quality Pct	Manager Tenure (Years)	Initial Purch. $	Additional Purch. $	Front End Load	Back End Load
C+ / 5.9	3.2	5.0	13.39	11	1	0	98	0	1	21	5.0	29	16	1,000	100	0.0	0.0
C+ / 5.9	3.2	5.0	13.39	352	1	0	98	0	1	21	5.0	53	16	10,000	500	2.0	0.0
C+ / 5.9	3.2	5.0	13.39	N/A	1	0	98	0	1	21	5.0	52	16	5,000,000	0	0.0	0.0
C- / 3.9	4.0	4.9	13.80	13	0	35	1	35	29	154	3.4	16	1	1,000	100	4.5	0.0
C- / 3.9	4.1	4.9	13.81	11	0	35	1	35	29	154	3.4	11	1	1,000	100	0.0	0.0
C- / 3.9	4.0	4.9	13.80	852	0	35	1	35	29	154	3.4	21	1	10,000	500	2.0	0.0
C- / 3.9	4.0	4.9	13.78	3	0	35	1	35	29	154	3.4	20	1	5,000,000	0	0.0	0.0
B+ / 8.8	1.6	3.2	8.96	1	0	38	0	26	36	183	0.7	20	6	1,000	25	4.8	2.0
B+ / 8.8	1.6	3.2	8.52	N/A	0	38	0	26	36	183	0.7	11	6	10,000	500	0.0	2.0
D / 2.1	5.6	5.0	11.94	12	7	0	0	46	47	13	5.3	99	15	1,000	25	4.8	2.0
D / 2.1	5.6	5.0	11.46	3	7	0	0	46	47	13	5.3	98	15	10,000	500	0.0	2.0
A- / 9.0	1.3	N/A	10.25	106	1	0	98	0	1	24	0.0	56	12	0	0	0.0	0.0
C+ / 5.8	3.2	N/A	10.37	273	1	0	98	0	1	17	0.0	52	12	0	0	0.0	0.0
B+ / 8.7	1.8	N/A	9.57	13	32	13	0	10	45	123	0.0	38	9	5,000	250	0.0	0.0
B+ / 8.7	1.8	N/A	9.31	107	32	13	0	10	45	123	0.0	18	9	5,000	250	0.0	0.0
C / 4.8	3.5	N/A	10.45	196	3	13	0	68	16	53	0.0	50	N/A	1,000	50	4.3	0.0
C / 4.8	3.5	N/A	10.47	249	3	13	0	68	16	53	0.0	97	N/A	0	0	0.0	0.0
C / 4.9	3.5	N/A	10.45	141	3	13	0	68	16	53	0.0	93	N/A	1,000	50	0.0	0.0
C / 4.9	3.5	N/A	10.46	4	3	13	0	68	16	53	0.0	62	N/A	500,000	0	0.0	0.0
U /	N/A	N/A	10.49	16	3	13	0	68	16	53	0.0	N/A	N/A	0	0	0.0	0.0
B / 7.9	2.5	N/A	9.76	191	0	0	0	11	89	80	0.0	92	5	1,000	50	3.0	0.0
B / 7.9	2.4	N/A	9.79	230	0	0	0	11	89	80	0.0	94	5	0	0	0.0	0.0
B / 7.9	2.5	N/A	9.74	161	0	0	0	11	89	80	0.0	85	5	1,000	50	0.0	0.0
B / 8.0	2.4	N/A	9.77	92	0	0	0	11	89	80	0.0	94	5	500,000	0	0.0	0.0
B / 7.9	2.5	N/A	9.77	1	0	0	0	11	89	80	0.0	94	5	0	0	0.0	0.0
E+ / 0.7	6.6	N/A	9.44	10	7	0	0	87	6	60	0.0	16	5	1,000	50	4.3	0.0
E+ / 0.7	6.5	N/A	9.44	2	7	0	0	87	6	60	0.0	19	5	0	0	0.0	0.0
E+ / 0.7	6.6	N/A	9.43	4	7	0	0	87	6	60	0.0	9	5	1,000	50	0.0	0.0
E+ / 0.7	6.6	N/A	9.37	N/A	7	0	0	87	6	60	0.0	19	5	500,000	0	0.0	0.0
U /	N/A	N/A	9.36	114	7	0	0	87	6	60	0.0	N/A	5	0	0	0.0	0.0
U /	N/A	N/A	8.91	8	6	0	0	59	35	49	0.0	N/A	3	1,000	50	3.0	0.0
U /	N/A	N/A	8.91	2	6	0	0	59	35	49	0.0	N/A	3	0	0	0.0	0.0
U /	N/A	N/A	8.90	3	6	0	0	59	35	49	0.0	N/A	3	1,000	50	0.0	0.0
U /	N/A	N/A	8.92	21	6	0	0	59	35	49	0.0	N/A	3	500,000	0	0.0	0.0
B+ / 8.6	1.9	N/A	10.26	70	5	6	0	77	12	78	0.0	76	5	1,000	50	3.0	0.0
B+ / 8.6	1.9	N/A	10.26	129	5	6	0	77	12	78	0.0	83	5	0	0	0.0	0.0
B+ / 8.7	1.8	N/A	10.24	44	5	6	0	77	12	78	0.0	46	5	1,000	50	0.0	0.0
B+ / 8.7	1.8	N/A	10.25	2	5	6	0	77	12	78	0.0	84	5	500,000	0	0.0	0.0
D+ / 2.3	5.5	N/A	10.09	52	1	0	0	83	16	157	0.0	72	5	1,000	50	4.3	0.0
D / 2.2	5.5	N/A	10.09	115	1	0	0	83	16	157	0.0	79	5	0	0	0.0	0.0
D / 2.2	5.5	N/A	10.07	44	1	0	0	83	16	157	0.0	39	5	1,000	50	0.0	0.0
D / 2.2	5.5	N/A	10.03	1	1	0	0	83	16	157	0.0	78	5	500,000	0	0.0	0.0
U /	N/A	N/A	9.08	353	16	0	0	45	39	14	0.0	N/A	N/A	1,000,000	0	0.0	2.0
B / 7.8	2.6	4.6	16.74	196	5	25	0	41	29	53	3.1	47	3	2,000	50	0.0	0.0
U /	N/A	4.6	16.74	10	5	25	0	41	29	53	3.1	N/A	3	100,000	50	0.0	0.0
D / 1.6	5.5	4.5	6.17	6	2	0	0	92	6	74	6.9	9	1	1,000	50	4.5	0.0
D / 1.6	5.5	4.5	6.14	164	2	0	0	92	6	74	6.9	10	1	250,000	0	0.0	0.0
D / 1.6	5.5	4.5	6.16	229	2	0	0	92	6	74	6.9	9	1	1,000	50	0.0	0.0
D / 1.6	5.5	4.5	6.16	1	2	0	0	92	6	74	6.9	8	1	0	0	0.0	0.0
B- / 7.0	2.9	4.1	10.41	48	4	0	95	0	1	45	4.3	63	N/A	5,000	250	0.0	0.0
U /	N/A	N/A	1.00	324	100	0	0	0	0	0	0.0	N/A	N/A	5,000	250	0.0	0.0
C+ / 5.8	3.2	5.1	10.65	23	0	16	0	48	36	31	4.0	72	19	5,000	250	0.0	0.0

Fund Type	Fund Name	Ticker Symbol	Overall Investment Rating	Phone	PERFORMANCE Performance Rating/Pts	Total Return % through 3/31/16 3 Mo	6 Mo	1Yr / Pct	Annualized 3Yr / Pct	5Yr / Pct	Incl. in Returns Dividend Yield	Expense Ratio
99 Pct = Best *0 Pct = Worst*												
GEI	Payden Core Bond Investor	PYCBX	**B-**	(888) 409-8007	**B- / 7.1**	2.20	2.02	1.19 /62	2.49 /71	4.13 /63	2.81	0.60
COI	Payden Corporate Bond Investor	PYACX	**C+**	(888) 409-8007	**B+ / 8.4**	3.12	3.18	1.66 /68	4.10 /84	5.84 /76	3.07	0.81
EM	Payden Em Mkts Corp Bd Adv	PYCAX	**U**	(888) 409-8007	**U /**	3.51	3.11	0.50 /49	--	--	4.09	1.63
EM	Payden Em Mkts Corp Bd Inv	PYCEX	**U**	(888) 409-8007	**U /**	3.46	3.25	0.83 /56	--	--	4.34	1.42
EM	Payden Em Mkts Corp Bd SI	PYCIX	**U**	(888) 409-8007	**U /**	3.59	3.40	1.03 /59	--	--	4.42	1.39
EM	Payden Emerg Mkts Bond Investor	PYEMX	**D**	(888) 409-8007	**C / 5.5**	4.54	5.56	1.78 /70	0.72 /37	4.83 /70	5.20	0.78
EM	Payden Emerging Market Bond Adv	PYEWX	**D**	(888) 409-8007	**C / 5.0**	4.43	5.39	1.42 /65	0.44 /32	4.56 /68	4.99	1.03
EM	Payden Emerging Market Bond SI	PYEIX	**D**	(888) 409-8007	**C+ / 5.6**	4.50	5.55	1.79 /70	0.77 /38	--	5.29	0.77
EM	Payden Emerging Markets Lcl Bd Adv	PYEAX	**E-**	(888) 409-8007	**E- / 0.0**	9.26	8.42	-4.01 / 8	-8.77 / 0	--	4.92	1.21
EM	Payden Emerging Markets Lcl Bd Inv	PYELX	**E-**	(888) 409-8007	**E- / 0.1**	9.35	8.57	-3.76 / 9	-8.57 / 0	--	5.17	0.96
LP	Payden Floating Rate Adv	PYFAX	**U**	(888) 409-8007	**U /**	1.43	0.65	1.10 /60	--	--	3.04	1.14
LP	Payden Floating Rate Inv	PYFRX	**U**	(888) 409-8007	**U /**	1.40	0.77	1.24 /62	--	--	3.28	0.90
LP	Payden Floating Rate SI	PYFIX	**U**	(888) 409-8007	**U /**	1.52	0.82	1.34 /64	--	--	3.38	0.89
GL	Payden Global Fixed Inc Investor	PYGFX	**B**	(888) 409-8007	**B / 7.6**	2.02	2.62	1.03 /59	2.96 /76	4.15 /64	1.83	1.05
GL	Payden Global Low Duration Investor	PYGSX	**C+**	(888) 409-8007	**C- / 3.6**	0.60	0.40	0.10 /41	0.68 /36	1.68 /27	1.20	0.69
USA	Payden GNMA Adv	PYGWX	**B-**	(888) 409-8007	**C+ / 5.9**	1.77	1.54	1.77 /70	1.67 /55	3.02 /45	3.18	0.85
USA	Payden GNMA Investor	PYGNX	**B**	(888) 409-8007	**C+ / 6.3**	1.72	1.67	1.92 /71	1.89 /59	3.27 /49	3.43	0.61
COH	Payden High Income Adviser	PYHWX	**D+**	(888) 409-8007	**C+ / 5.7**	2.42	2.22	-1.38 /19	1.85 /59	4.34 /66	5.07	0.93
COH	Payden High Income Investor	PYHRX	**D+**	(888) 409-8007	**C+ / 6.0**	2.49	2.34	-1.41 /19	2.02 /62	4.55 /68	5.38	0.68
USS	Payden Kravitz Cash Bal Plan Adv	PKCBX	**D+**	(888) 409-8007	**D- / 1.4**	-0.30	-0.59	-0.87 /23	-0.21 /14	0.89 /20	1.98	1.73
USS	Payden Kravitz Cash Bal Plan Ret	PKCRX	**D+**	(888) 409-8007	**D- / 1.1**	-0.41	-0.73	-1.13 /21	-0.49 /12	0.63 /18	2.03	1.97
USS	Payden Kravitz Cash Bal Plan SI	PKBIX	**U**	(888) 409-8007	**U /**	-0.29	-0.53	-0.62 /25	--	1.11 /21	2.01	1.47
GEI	Payden Limited Maturity Investor	PYLMX	**C+**	(888) 409-8007	**C- / 3.5**	0.41	0.38	0.33 /46	0.55 /34	0.72 /19	0.75	0.57
* GEI	Payden Low Duration Investor	PYSBX	**C+**	(888) 409-8007	**C- / 3.8**	0.78	0.57	0.54 /50	0.69 /37	1.44 /25	1.13	0.55
USS	Payden US Government Adv	PYUWX	**C+**	(888) 409-8007	**C- / 3.6**	1.15	0.42	0.49 /49	0.55 /34	1.19 /22	1.24	0.84
US	Payden US Government Investor	PYUSX	**C+**	(888) 409-8007	**C- / 4.0**	1.12	0.45	0.73 /54	0.77 /38	1.43 /25	1.48	0.59
MUN	Performance Trust Muni Bond Inst	PTIMX	**B**	(800) 737-3676	**A+ / 9.7**	2.51	4.46	5.39 /98	4.60 /98	--	2.33	0.86
MUN	Performance Trust Muni Bond Rtl	PTRMX	**B**	(800) 737-3676	**A+ / 9.7**	2.49	4.37	5.21 /98	4.42 /97	--	2.09	1.11
GEI	Performance Trust Strategic Bond	PTIAX	**A**	(800) 737-3676	**B / 8.2**	1.49	2.84	3.45 /79	4.10 /84	6.37 /79	5.02	0.89
US	Permanent Portfolio Short-Tm Treas	PRTBX	**C-**	(800) 531-5142	**D- / 1.2**	-0.02	-0.18	-0.49 /26	-0.59 /11	-0.59 / 2	0.00	1.20
COH	Permanent Portfolio Versatile Bd	PRVBX	**D-**	(800) 531-5142	**C- / 3.0**	3.53	-0.16	-4.44 / 6	0.70 /37	1.75 /28	4.65	1.19
GL	PF Currency Strategies P		**D-**	(800) 722-2333	**C- / 3.5**	-0.61	1.48	0.35 /47	0.53 /34	--	2.09	0.90
EM	PF Emerging Mkts Debt P		**E+**	(800) 722-2333	**D / 1.8**	7.78	8.03	2.92 /76	-1.97 / 4	--	0.10	1.08
LP	PF Floating Rate Loan P		**C-**	(800) 722-2333	**C- / 3.4**	1.78	-0.79	-2.40 /14	0.90 /41	2.55 /38	5.30	1.03
GEI	PF Inflation Managed P		**E+**	(800) 722-2333	**E+ / 0.7**	3.93	2.46	-0.80 /23	-2.02 / 4	2.22 /34	0.00	0.68
COI	PF Managed Bond P		**C**	(800) 722-2333	**C+ / 6.7**	2.72	2.98	1.31 /63	2.09 /63	3.41 /52	2.33	0.64
GEI	PF Short Duration Bond P		**C+**	(800) 722-2333	**C- / 3.6**	0.82	0.35	0.35 /47	0.62 /35	1.07 /21	2.06	0.64
MM	PFM Government Series		**C**	(800) 338-3383	**D+ / 2.3**	0.06	0.07	0.08 /40	0.04 /24	0.04 /12	0.08	0.22
MM	PFM Prime Series Colorado Investors		**C+**	(800) 338-3383	**D+ / 2.7**	0.11	0.16	0.22 /45	0.14 /28	--	0.22	0.17
COI	PIA BBB Bond MACS	PBBBX	**C-**	(800) 251-1970	**B- / 7.1**	4.65	3.43	-0.89 /23	2.43 /70	5.12 /73	4.00	0.15
COH	PIA High Yield Institutional	PHYSX	**C-**	(800) 251-1970	**C+ / 6.9**	2.90	1.08	-1.14 /21	2.72 /74	5.21 /73	6.49	0.90
MTG	PIA Short-Term Securities Adv	PIASX	**C+**	(800) 251-1970	**C- / 3.3**	0.55	0.48	0.34 /47	0.45 /32	0.45 /17	0.94	0.40
MUS	PIMCO CA Interm Muni Bond A	PCMBX	**A+**	(800) 426-0107	**B / 7.9**	1.42	2.72	3.33 /88	2.36 /81	3.76 /76	2.09	0.78
MUS	PIMCO CA Interm Muni Bond C	PCFCX	**A**	(800) 426-0107	**B / 7.6**	1.24	2.35	2.57 /81	1.60 /70	2.99 /69	1.41	1.53
MUS	PIMCO CA Interm Muni Bond D	PCIDX	**A+**	(800) 426-0107	**B+ / 8.5**	1.42	2.72	3.33 /88	2.36 /81	3.76 /76	2.14	0.78
MUS	PIMCO CA Interm Muni Bond Inst	PCIMX	**A+**	(800) 426-0107	**B+ / 8.8**	1.50	2.89	3.66 /92	2.70 /85	4.10 /78	2.46	0.45
MUS	PIMCO CA Interm Muni Bond P	PCIPX	**A+**	(800) 426-0107	**B+ / 8.7**	1.48	2.84	3.56 /91	2.59 /84	3.99 /77	2.36	0.55
MUS	PIMCO CA Sh Duration Muni Inc A	PCDAX	**C-**	(800) 426-0107	**D / 1.6**	0.36	0.41	0.54 /56	0.34 /33	0.33 /17	0.53	0.73
MUS	PIMCO CA Sh Duration Muni Inc C	PCSCX	**C**	(800) 426-0107	**D+ / 2.8**	0.29	0.27	0.25 /47	0.04 /25	0.03 /12	0.25	1.03
MUS	PIMCO CA Sh Duration Muni Inc D	PCDDX	**C+**	(800) 426-0107	**C- / 3.6**	0.36	0.41	0.54 /56	0.34 /34	0.33 /17	0.54	0.73
MUS	PIMCO CA Sh Duration Muni Inc Inst	PCDIX	**B+**	(800) 426-0107	**C / 4.8**	0.45	0.61	0.94 /66	0.74 /45	0.73 /22	0.94	0.33
MUS	PIMCO CA Sh Duration Muni Inc P	PCDPX	**B**	(800) 426-0107	**C / 4.5**	0.43	0.56	0.84 /63	0.64 /42	0.63 /20	0.84	0.43

• Denotes fund is closed to new investors
* Denotes fund is included in Section II

RISK			NET ASSETS		ASSET							FUND MANAGER		MINIMUM		LOADS	
Risk Rating/Pts	3 Yr Avg Standard Deviation	Avg Duration	NAV As of 3/31/16	Total $(Mil)	Cash %	Gov. Bond %	Muni. Bond %	Corp. Bond %	Other %	Portfolio Turnover Ratio	Avg Coupon Rate	Manager Quality Pct	Manager Tenure (Years)	Initial Purch. $	Additional Purch. $	Front End Load	Back End Load
C+ / 5.8	3.2	5.1	10.67	692	0	16	0	48	36	31	4.0	66	19	100,000	250	0.0	0.0
C- / 3.0	4.5	7.1	10.97	75	2	1	0	94	3	112	4.5	91	N/A	5,000	250	0.0	0.0
U /	N/A	4.9	9.65	N/A	1	13	0	85	1	93	5.2	N/A	3	5,000	250	0.0	0.0
U /	N/A	4.9	9.62	2	1	13	0	85	1	93	5.2	N/A	3	100,000	250	0.0	0.0
U /	N/A	4.9	9.64	36	1	13	0	85	1	93	5.2	N/A	3	50,000,000	250	0.0	0.0
E+ / 0.6	7.5	6.7	13.14	416	2	78	0	18	2	54	6.2	87	16	100,000	250	0.0	0.0
E+ / 0.6	7.5	6.7	13.15	28	2	78	0	18	2	54	6.2	83	16	5,000	250	0.0	0.0
E+ / 0.6	7.5	6.7	13.12	554	2	78	0	18	2	54	6.2	88	16	50,000,000	250	0.0	0.0
E- / 0.1	11.8	5.2	6.82	N/A	1	78	0	18	3	106	6.6	0	N/A	5,000	250	0.0	0.0
E- / 0.1	11.8	5.2	6.82	139	1	78	0	18	3	106	6.6	0	N/A	100,000	250	0.0	0.0
U /	N/A	0.3	9.81	N/A	8	0	0	21	71	39	4.0	N/A	3	5,000	250	0.0	0.0
U /	N/A	0.3	9.79	48	8	0	0	21	71	39	4.0	N/A	3	100,000	250	0.0	0.0
U /	N/A	0.3	9.80	118	8	0	0	21	71	39	4.0	N/A	3	50,000,000	250	0.0	0.0
C+ / 5.6	3.3	6.1	8.88	91	1	51	0	44	4	44	2.7	98	N/A	5,000	250	0.0	0.0
A / 9.3	1.0	1.5	9.99	133	1	27	0	52	20	35	1.9	86	N/A	5,000	250	0.0	0.0
B- / 7.3	2.8	4.4	9.81	23	0	0	0	0	100	15	4.6	71	N/A	5,000	250	0.0	0.0
B- / 7.4	2.8	4.4	9.81	256	0	0	0	0	100	15	4.6	78	N/A	100,000	250	0.0	0.0
D / 2.0	5.2	3.9	6.25	13	4	0	0	90	6	32	5.7	81	12	5,000	250	0.0	0.0
D / 2.0	5.2	3.9	6.23	578	4	0	0	90	6	32	5.7	84	12	100,000	250	0.0	0.0
B+ / 8.3	2.2	1.5	10.08	54	4	8	0	40	48	85	2.9	40	N/A	25,000	0	0.0	0.0
B+ / 8.3	2.1	1.5	9.71	28	4	8	0	40	48	85	2.9	31	N/A	25,000	0	0.0	0.0
U /	2.1	1.5	10.22	110	4	8	0	40	48	85	2.9	N/A	N/A	25,000	0	0.0	0.0
A+ / 9.8	0.4	0.5	9.43	429	3	23	0	46	28	39	1.1	79	N/A	5,000	250	0.0	0.0
A / 9.5	0.8	1.4	10.05	835	2	26	0	50	22	31	1.8	76	N/A	5,000	250	0.0	0.0
A- / 9.0	1.4	2.5	10.65	1	0	6	0	1	93	32	2.5	48	N/A	5,000	250	0.0	0.0
A- / 9.0	1.3	2.5	10.64	143	0	6	0	1	93	32	2.5	61	N/A	100,000	250	0.0	0.0
D+ / 2.9	4.8	N/A	24.23	99	1	0	98	0	1	32	0.0	50	5	1,000,000	500	0.0	2.0
C- / 3.0	4.7	N/A	24.29	26	1	0	98	0	1	32	0.0	45	5	2,500	500	0.0	2.0
C+ / 6.6	3.0	N/A	22.60	392	0	0	39	2	59	80	0.0	96	6	5,000	500	0.0	2.0
A+ / 9.9	0.1	0.2	64.81	20	0	99	0	0	1	1	0.2	40	13	1,000	100	0.0	0.0
E+ / 0.9	6.0	7.1	54.77	11	0	0	0	99	1	38	4.9	36	13	1,000	100	0.0	0.0
E / 0.3	9.0	N/A	9.75	127	0	0	0	0	100	141	0.0	80	4	0	0	0.0	0.0
E / 0.3	9.2	N/A	9.14	108	4	66	0	28	2	105	0.0	13	4	0	0	0.0	0.0
B- / 7.2	2.8	N/A	9.14	80	4	0	0	10	86	69	0.0	76	6	0	0	0.0	0.0
D / 1.7	5.9	N/A	8.73	52	0	90	0	3	7	139	0.0	2	8	0	0	0.0	0.0
C / 4.5	3.7	N/A	10.57	422	0	26	3	24	47	578	0.0	56	2	0	0	0.0	0.0
A / 9.4	0.9	N/A	9.84	76	2	7	0	46	45	60	0.0	71	5	0	0	0.0	0.0
A+ / 9.9	N/A	N/A	1.00	164	100	0	0	0	0	0	0.1	N/A	N/A	1,000,000	0	0.0	0.0
A+ / 9.9	N/A	N/A	1.00	314	100	0	0	0	0	0	0.2	71	N/A	50,000	0	0.0	0.0
D+ / 2.4	5.1	7.2	9.13	218	1	14	0	84	1	18	0.0	32	13	1,000	50	0.0	0.0
D+ / 2.5	4.7	4.0	9.56	126	4	0	0	95	1	26	0.0	92	6	1,000,000	100	0.0	0.0
A+ / 9.8	0.5	1.0	10.01	165	1	18	0	55	26	60	0.0	75	N/A	1,000	50	0.0	0.0
B- / 7.5	2.7	4.9	9.97	43	8	0	91	0	1	10	4.9	46	5	1,000	50	2.3	0.0
B- / 7.5	2.7	4.9	9.97	12	8	0	91	0	1	10	4.9	24	5	1,000	50	0.0	0.0
B- / 7.5	2.7	4.9	9.97	3	8	0	91	0	1	10	4.9	46	5	1,000	50	0.0	0.0
B- / 7.5	2.7	4.9	9.97	51	8	0	91	0	1	10	4.9	59	5	1,000,000	0	0.0	0.0
B- / 7.5	2.7	4.9	9.97	16	8	0	91	0	1	10	4.9	55	5	1,000,000	0	0.0	0.0
A+ / 9.6	0.7	2.2	9.94	40	0	0	100	0	0	36	3.7	55	5	1,000	50	2.3	0.0
A+ / 9.6	0.7	2.2	9.94	2	0	0	100	0	0	36	3.7	44	5	1,000	50	0.0	0.0
A+ / 9.6	0.7	2.2	9.94	3	0	0	100	0	0	36	3.7	55	5	1,000	50	0.0	0.0
A+ / 9.6	0.7	2.2	9.94	72	0	0	100	0	0	36	3.7	75	5	1,000,000	0	0.0	0.0
A+ / 9.6	0.7	2.2	9.94	23	0	0	100	0	0	36	3.7	71	5	1,000,000	0	0.0	0.0

99 Pct = Best
0 Pct = Worst

Fund Type	Fund Name	Ticker Symbol	Overall Investment Rating	Phone	PERFORMANCE: Performance Rating/Pts	Total Return % through 3/31/16: 3 Mo	6 Mo	1Yr / Pct	Annualized: 3Yr / Pct	Annualized: 5Yr / Pct	Incl. in Returns: Dividend Yield	Expense Ratio
MUN	PIMCO California Municipal Bd A	PCTTX	**A-**	(800) 426-0107	**A+ / 9.7**	2.46	5.38	5.86 /99	4.39 /97	--	2.38	0.79
MUN	PIMCO California Municipal Bd C	PCTGX	**A-**	(800) 426-0107	**A+ / 9.6**	2.28	4.99	5.09 /98	3.61 /93	--	1.71	1.54
MUN	PIMCO California Municipal Bd D	PCTDX	**A-**	(800) 426-0107	**A+ / 9.8**	2.45	5.37	5.86 /99	4.39 /97	--	2.43	0.79
MUN	PIMCO California Municipal Bd Inst	PCTIX	**A**	(800) 426-0107	**A+ / 9.9**	2.54	5.55	6.23 /99	4.75 /98	--	2.76	0.44
MUN	PIMCO California Municipal Bd P	PCTPX	**A-**	(800) 426-0107	**A+ / 9.9**	2.51	5.50	6.12 /99	4.65 /98	--	2.67	0.54
GEI	PIMCO Credit Absolute Return A	PZCRX	**D-**	(800) 426-0107	**E / 0.4**	-0.43	-1.29	-4.21 / 7	-0.82 / 9	--	2.39	1.30
GEI	PIMCO Credit Absolute Return C	PCCRX	**D**	(800) 426-0107	**E / 0.4**	-0.54	-1.58	-4.83 / 5	-1.51 / 6	--	1.87	2.05
GEI	PIMCO Credit Absolute Return D	PDCRX	**D**	(800) 426-0107	**E+ / 0.7**	-0.43	-1.26	-4.18 / 7	-0.81 / 9	--	2.43	1.30
GEI	PIMCO Credit Absolute Return Inst	PCARX	**D**	(800) 426-0107	**D- / 1.0**	-0.32	-1.00	-3.77 / 8	-0.38 /13	--	2.77	0.90
GEI	PIMCO Credit Absolute Return P	PPCRX	**D**	(800) 426-0107	**E+ / 0.9**	-0.43	-1.06	-3.97 / 8	-0.49 /12	--	2.68	1.00
GES	PIMCO Diversified Income A	PDVAX	**D**	(800) 426-0107	**C- / 3.4**	2.23	2.98	-0.19 /29	1.28 /48	4.05 /62	6.17	1.16
GES	PIMCO Diversified Income Admin	PDAAX	**D+**	(800) 426-0107	**C / 5.5**	2.26	3.06	-0.04 /31	1.43 /51	4.21 /64	6.56	1.01
GES	PIMCO Diversified Income C	PDICX	**D**	(800) 426-0107	**C- / 3.7**	2.05	2.61	-0.92 /22	0.53 /34	3.28 /49	5.65	1.91
GES	PIMCO Diversified Income D	PDVDX	**D**	(800) 426-0107	**C / 5.2**	2.23	2.98	-0.19 /29	1.28 /48	4.05 /62	6.41	1.16
GES	PIMCO Diversified Income Inst	PDIIX	**D+**	(800) 426-0107	**C+ / 5.9**	2.32	3.18	0.21 /44	1.68 /55	4.47 /67	6.81	0.76
GES	PIMCO Diversified Income P	PDVPX	**D+**	(800) 426-0107	**C+ / 5.8**	2.30	3.13	0.11 /41	1.58 /54	4.37 /66	6.71	0.86
EM	PIMCO EM Corporate Bond A	PECZX	**E-**	(800) 426-0107	**E / 0.3**	4.10	4.32	-2.34 /14	-2.42 / 3	1.50 /26	4.33	1.35
EM	PIMCO EM Corporate Bond C	PECCX	**E-**	(800) 426-0107	**E / 0.4**	3.92	3.94	-3.06 /11	-3.14 / 2	0.74 /19	3.74	2.10
EM	PIMCO EM Corporate Bond D	PECDX	**E**	(800) 426-0107	**E+ / 0.6**	4.10	4.32	-2.35 /14	-2.42 / 3	1.49 /26	4.49	1.35
EM	PIMCO EM Corporate Bond Inst	PEMIX	**E**	(800) 426-0107	**E+ / 0.7**	4.20	4.52	-1.95 /16	-2.03 / 4	1.88 /30	4.90	0.95
EM	PIMCO EM Corporate Bond P	PMIPX	**E**	(800) 426-0107	**E+ / 0.7**	4.17	4.47	-2.05 /15	-2.13 / 4	1.78 /28	4.80	1.05
EM	PIMCO Em Mkts Full Spectrum Bd A	PFSSX	**E-**	(800) 426-0107	**E- / 0.1**	7.22	6.86	-3.67 / 9	-5.57 / 1	--	4.38	2.34
EM	PIMCO Em Mkts Full Spectrum Bd C	PFSCX	**E-**	(800) 426-0107	**E- / 0.1**	7.04	6.47	-4.39 / 7	-6.28 / 1	--	3.79	3.09
EM	PIMCO Em Mkts Full Spectrum Bd D	PFSYX	**E-**	(800) 426-0107	**E- / 0.2**	7.22	6.86	-3.67 / 9	-5.57 / 1	--	4.55	2.34
EM	PIMCO Em Mkts Full Spectrum Bd	PFSIX	**E-**	(800) 426-0107	**E- / 0.2**	7.32	7.07	-3.29 /10	-5.19 / 1	--	4.95	1.94
EM	PIMCO Em Mkts Full Spectrum Bd P	PFSPX	**E-**	(800) 426-0107	**E- / 0.2**	7.30	7.02	-3.39 /10	-5.29 / 1	--	4.85	2.04
EM	PIMCO Emerging Local Bond A	PELAX	**E-**	(800) 426-0107	**E- / 0.0**	9.77	8.85	-4.80 / 5	-8.77 / 0	-3.27 / 1	4.30	1.35
EM	PIMCO Emerging Local Bond Admin	PEBLX	**E-**	(800) 426-0107	**E- / 0.1**	9.82	8.95	-4.61 / 6	-8.59 / 0	-3.08 / 1	4.66	1.15
EM	PIMCO Emerging Local Bond C	PELCX	**E-**	(800) 426-0107	**E- / 0.0**	9.58	8.45	-5.50 / 4	-9.45 / 0	-3.99 / 0	3.73	2.10
EM	PIMCO Emerging Local Bond D	PLBDX	**E-**	(800) 426-0107	**E- / 0.0**	9.77	8.85	-4.80 / 5	-8.78 / 0	-3.27 / 1	4.47	1.35
EM	PIMCO Emerging Local Bond Inst	PELBX	**E-**	(800) 426-0107	**E- / 0.1**	9.88	9.09	-4.37 / 7	-8.36 / 0	-2.83 / 1	4.92	0.90
EM	PIMCO Emerging Local Bond P	PELPX	**E-**	(800) 426-0107	**E- / 0.1**	9.86	9.04	-4.47 / 6	-8.45 / 0	-2.93 / 1	4.82	1.00
EM	PIMCO Emerging Markets Bond A	PAEMX	**E**	(800) 426-0107	**D- / 1.0**	5.45	6.73	0.02 /33	-1.06 / 8	3.16 /48	4.58	1.20
EM	PIMCO Emerging Markets Bond	PEBAX	**D-**	(800) 426-0107	**D+ / 2.9**	5.48	6.79	0.14 /42	-0.92 / 9	3.32 /50	4.88	1.08
EM	PIMCO Emerging Markets Bond C	PEBCX	**E**	(800) 426-0107	**D- / 1.1**	5.27	6.35	-0.72 /24	-1.79 / 5	2.39 /36	4.02	1.95
EM	PIMCO Emerging Markets Bond D	PEMDX	**E+**	(800) 426-0107	**D+ / 2.6**	5.45	6.73	0.02 /33	-1.06 / 8	3.16 /48	4.76	1.20
EM	PIMCO Emerging Markets Bond Inst	PEBIX	**D-**	(800) 426-0107	**C- / 3.3**	5.54	6.92	0.39 /48	-0.67 /10	3.58 /54	5.13	0.83
EM	PIMCO Emerging Markets Bond P	PEMPX	**D-**	(800) 426-0107	**C- / 3.1**	5.52	6.87	0.29 /46	-0.77 /10	3.47 /53	5.03	0.93
GL	PIMCO Emerging Markets Currency	PLMAX	**E-**	(800) 426-0107	**E- / 0.2**	5.19	5.00	-1.69 /17	-4.48 / 2	-2.75 / 1	2.02	1.25
GL	PIMCO Emerging Markets Currency	PDEVX	**E-**	(800) 426-0107	**E / 0.3**	5.22	5.08	-1.55 /18	-4.34 / 2	-2.60 / 1	2.25	1.10
GL	PIMCO Emerging Markets Currency	PLMCX	**E-**	(800) 426-0107	**E- / 0.2**	5.00	4.62	-2.41 /14	-5.19 / 1	-3.47 / 1	1.37	2.00
GL	PIMCO Emerging Markets Currency	PLMDX	**E-**	(800) 426-0107	**E / 0.3**	5.18	5.00	-1.69 /17	-4.48 / 2	-2.75 / 1	2.10	1.25
GL	PIMCO Emerging Markets Currency	PLMIX	**E-**	(800) 426-0107	**E / 0.3**	5.28	5.21	-1.30 /20	-4.10 / 2	-2.36 / 1	2.50	0.85
GL	PIMCO Emerging Markets Currency	PLMPX	**E-**	(800) 426-0107	**E / 0.3**	5.26	5.15	-1.40 /19	-4.20 / 2	-2.45 / 1	2.40	0.95
GEI	PIMCO Extended Duration Inst	PEDIX	**C-**	(800) 426-0107	**A+ / 9.9**	11.81	9.92	0.73 /54	8.72 /99	15.27 /99	2.87	0.51
GEI	PIMCO Extended Duration P	PEDPX	**C-**	(800) 426-0107	**A+ / 9.9**	11.78	9.87	0.63 /52	8.61 /99	15.16 /99	2.78	0.61
* GEI	PIMCO Fixed Income SHares C	FXICX	**D**	(800) 988-8380	**C- / 3.9**	-0.95	0.21	-1.98 /16	1.31 /49	4.44 /67	11.47	0.01
GL	PIMCO Fixed Income SHares LD	FXIDX	**U**	(800) 988-8380	**U /**	-0.85	-1.23	-0.25 /29	--	--	3.40	0.10
* GEI	PIMCO Fixed Income SHares M	FXIMX	**C-**	(800) 988-8380	**B- / 7.1**	3.78	4.15	0.05 /38	2.31 /68	5.01 /72	4.57	0.04
US	PIMCO Fixed Income SHares R	FXIRX	**E**	(800) 988-8380	**E+ / 0.7**	3.03	2.27	-2.26 /14	-1.69 / 5	4.48 /67	5.15	0.07
MUN	PIMCO Fixed Income SHares TE	FXIEX	**B+**	(800) 988-8380	**A / 9.3**	1.25	4.39	6.45 /99	2.84 /86	--	2.96	0.05
GES	PIMCO Floating Income A	PFIAX	**E+**	(800) 426-0107	**E+ / 0.6**	-0.57	0.82	-2.82 /12	-0.73 /10	0.77 /19	4.63	0.97

• Denotes fund is closed to new investors
* Denotes fund is included in Section II

RISK			NET ASSETS		ASSET							FUND MANAGER		MINIMUM		LOADS	
Risk Rating/Pts	3 Yr Avg Standard Deviation	Avg Duration	NAV As of 3/31/16	Total $(Mil)	Cash %	Gov. Bond %	Muni. Bond %	Corp. Bond %	Other %	Portfolio Turnover Ratio	Avg Coupon Rate	Manager Quality Pct	Manager Tenure (Years)	Initial Purch. $	Additional Purch. $	Front End Load	Back End Load
C- / 4.1	3.9	6.5	10.81	6	1	0	98	0	1	8	4.9	79	4	1,000	50	2.3	0.0
C- / 4.1	3.9	6.5	10.81	2	1	0	98	0	1	8	4.9	48	4	1,000	50	0.0	0.0
C- / 4.1	3.9	6.5	10.81	1	1	0	98	0	1	8	4.9	79	4	1,000	50	0.0	0.0
C- / 4.2	3.9	6.5	10.81	5	1	0	98	0	1	8	4.9	86	4	1,000,000	0	0.0	0.0
C- / 4.2	3.9	6.5	10.81	N/A	1	0	98	0	1	8	4.9	85	4	1,000,000	0	0.0	0.0
C / 5.2	3.4	1.4	9.34	16	23	11	0	30	36	148	0.0	15	5	1,000	50	3.8	0.0
C / 5.3	3.3	1.4	9.26	7	23	11	0	30	36	148	0.0	9	5	1,000	50	0.0	0.0
C / 5.3	3.4	1.4	9.32	6	23	11	0	30	36	148	0.0	15	5	1,000	50	0.0	0.0
C / 5.2	3.4	1.4	9.32	351	23	11	0	30	36	148	0.0	24	5	1,000,000	0	0.0	0.0
C / 5.1	3.4	1.4	9.30	17	23	11	0	30	36	148	0.0	20	5	1,000,000	0	0.0	0.0
D / 2.0	5.7	5.3	10.15	147	3	16	2	54	25	59	5.5	18	11	1,000	50	3.8	0.0
D / 2.0	5.7	5.3	10.15	9	3	16	2	54	25	59	5.5	21	11	1,000,000	0	0.0	0.0
D / 2.0	5.7	5.3	10.15	104	3	16	2	54	25	59	5.5	10	11	1,000	50	0.0	0.0
D / 2.0	5.7	5.3	10.15	46	3	16	2	54	25	59	5.5	18	11	1,000	50	0.0	0.0
D / 2.0	5.7	5.3	10.15	1,872	3	16	2	54	25	59	5.5	26	11	1,000,000	0	0.0	0.0
D / 2.0	5.7	5.3	10.15	54	3	16	2	54	25	59	5.5	24	11	1,000,000	0	0.0	0.0
E / 0.5	7.8	4.9	9.83	1	6	3	0	89	2	98	6.2	9	N/A	1,000	50	3.8	0.0
E / 0.5	7.8	4.9	9.83	N/A	6	3	0	89	2	98	6.2	7	N/A	1,000	50	0.0	0.0
E / 0.5	7.8	4.9	9.83	N/A	6	3	0	89	2	98	6.2	9	N/A	1,000	50	0.0	0.0
E / 0.5	7.8	4.9	9.83	139	6	3	0	89	2	98	6.2	12	N/A	1,000,000	0	0.0	0.0
E / 0.5	7.8	4.9	9.83	1	6	3	0	89	2	98	6.2	11	N/A	1,000,000	0	0.0	0.0
E- / 0.2	9.9	N/A	7.31	1	16	42	0	40	2	28	0.0	2	3	1,000	50	3.8	0.0
E- / 0.2	9.9	N/A	7.31	N/A	16	42	0	40	2	28	0.0	1	3	1,000	50	0.0	0.0
E- / 0.2	9.9	N/A	7.31	2	16	42	0	40	2	28	0.0	2	3	1,000	50	0.0	0.0
E- / 0.2	9.9	N/A	7.31	339	16	42	0	40	2	28	0.0	3	3	1,000,000	0	0.0	0.0
E- / 0.2	9.9	N/A	7.31	4	16	42	0	40	2	28	0.0	3	3	1,000,000	0	0.0	0.0
E- / 0.1	12.5	4.6	7.21	49	17	64	0	16	3	60	5.2	0	10	1,000	50	3.8	0.0
E- / 0.1	12.5	4.6	7.21	9	17	64	0	16	3	60	5.2	0	10	1,000,000	0	0.0	0.0
E- / 0.1	12.5	4.6	7.21	24	17	64	0	16	3	60	5.2	0	10	1,000	50	0.0	0.0
E- / 0.1	12.5	4.6	7.21	30	17	64	0	16	3	60	5.2	0	10	1,000	50	0.0	0.0
E- / 0.1	12.5	4.6	7.21	4,857	17	64	0	16	3	60	5.2	0	10	1,000,000	0	0.0	0.0
E- / 0.1	12.5	4.6	7.21	109	17	64	0	16	3	60	5.2	0	10	1,000,000	0	0.0	0.0
E / 0.3	9.1	5.6	9.70	162	10	42	0	46	2	22	5.7	30	5	1,000	50	3.8	0.0
E / 0.3	9.1	5.6	9.70	5	10	42	0	46	2	22	5.7	34	5	1,000,000	0	0.0	0.0
E / 0.3	9.1	5.6	9.70	71	10	42	0	46	2	22	5.7	15	5	1,000	50	0.0	0.0
E / 0.3	9.1	5.6	9.70	135	10	42	0	46	2	22	5.7	30	5	1,000	50	0.0	0.0
E / 0.3	9.1	5.6	9.70	1,017	10	42	0	46	2	22	5.7	41	5	1,000,000	0	0.0	0.0
E / 0.3	9.1	5.6	9.70	113	10	42	0	46	2	22	5.7	38	5	1,000,000	0	0.0	0.0
E+ / 0.6	7.4	0.7	8.75	18	16	48	0	34	2	76	4.5	4	11	1,000	50	3.8	0.0
E+ / 0.6	7.4	0.7	8.75	5	16	48	0	34	2	76	4.5	5	11	1,000,000	0	0.0	0.0
E+ / 0.6	7.5	0.7	8.75	8	16	48	0	34	2	76	4.5	3	11	1,000	50	0.0	0.0
E+ / 0.6	7.4	0.7	8.75	16	16	48	0	34	2	76	4.5	4	11	1,000	50	0.0	0.0
E+ / 0.6	7.4	0.7	8.75	3,945	16	48	0	34	2	76	4.5	5	11	1,000,000	0	0.0	0.0
E+ / 0.6	7.4	0.7	8.75	7	16	48	0	34	2	76	4.5	5	11	1,000,000	0	0.0	0.0
E- / 0.0	18.0	26.5	8.66	400	0	0	0	0	100	68	0.4	4	9	1,000,000	0	0.0	0.0
E- / 0.0	18.0	26.5	8.66	60	0	0	0	0	100	68	0.4	4	9	1,000,000	0	0.0	0.0
D+ / 2.9	4.8	N/A	10.22	1,522	0	60	4	28	8	95	0.0	43	7	0	0	0.0	0.0
U /	N/A	N/A	9.65	30	0	0	0	0	100	1,135	0.0	N/A	3	0	0	0.0	0.0
D+ / 2.7	5.0	N/A	10.13	1,533	0	16	14	23	47	473	0.0	20	7	0	0	0.0	0.0
E+ / 0.9	6.7	N/A	9.21	157	0	80	0	8	12	126	0.0	5	9	0	0	0.0	0.0
C / 4.4	3.7	N/A	10.07	96	2	9	87	0	2	72	0.0	44	4	0	0	0.0	0.0
D / 2.2	5.5	0.1	7.67	115	2	15	2	53	28	65	5.4	29	11	1,000	50	2.3	0.0

99 Pct = Best
0 Pct = Worst

Fund Type	Fund Name	Ticker Symbol	Overall Investment Rating	Phone	PERFORMANCE: Performance Rating/Pts	Total Return % through 3/31/16: 3 Mo	6 Mo	1Yr / Pct	Annualized: 3Yr / Pct	Annualized: 5Yr / Pct	Incl. in Returns: Dividend Yield	Expense Ratio
GES	PIMCO Floating Income Admin	PFTAX	**E+**	(800) 426-0107	**D- / 1.0**	-0.54	0.89	-2.68 /13	-0.59 /11	0.92 /20	4.89	0.82
GES	PIMCO Floating Income C	PFNCX	**E+**	(800) 426-0107	**E+ / 0.7**	-0.64	0.67	-3.11 /11	-1.03 / 8	0.47 /17	4.42	1.27
GES	PIMCO Floating Income D	PFIDX	**E+**	(800) 426-0107	**E+ / 0.9**	-0.57	0.82	-2.82 /12	-0.73 /10	0.77 /19	4.73	0.97
GES	PIMCO Floating Income Inst	PFIIX	**D-**	(800) 426-0107	**D- / 1.2**	-0.48	1.01	-2.44 /14	-0.34 /13	1.17 /22	5.14	0.57
GES	PIMCO Floating Income P	PFTPX	**D-**	(800) 426-0107	**D- / 1.1**	-0.51	0.96	-2.54 /13	-0.44 /12	1.07 /21	5.04	0.67
GL	PIMCO Foreign Bd Fd (Unhgd) A	PFUAX	**E+**	(800) 426-0107	**D / 1.6**	7.08	6.65	1.90 /71	-0.70 /10	1.20 /22	1.36	0.94
GL	PIMCO Foreign Bd Fd (Unhgd)	PFUUX	**D**	(800) 426-0107	**C- / 4.2**	7.12	6.73	2.06 /72	-0.55 /11	1.36 /24	1.56	0.79
GL	PIMCO Foreign Bd Fd (Unhgd) C	PFRCX	**E+**	(800) 426-0107	**D / 1.8**	6.89	6.26	1.14 /61	-1.44 / 6	0.45 /17	0.69	1.69
GL	PIMCO Foreign Bd Fd (Unhgd) D	PFBDX	**D-**	(800) 426-0107	**C- / 3.8**	7.08	6.65	1.90 /71	-0.70 /10	1.20 /22	1.41	0.94
GL	PIMCO Foreign Bd Fd (Unhgd) Inst	PFUIX	**D**	(800) 426-0107	**C / 4.6**	7.19	6.86	2.31 /74	-0.31 /13	1.61 /27	1.79	0.54
GL	PIMCO Foreign Bd Fd (Unhgd) P	PFUPX	**D**	(800) 426-0107	**C / 4.5**	7.16	6.81	2.21 /73	-0.41 /12	1.50 /26	1.70	0.64
GL	PIMCO Foreign Bond (US Hedged) A	PFOAX	**C+**	(800) 426-0107	**B / 7.6**	2.68	3.24	0.19 /44	4.04 /84	6.09 /77	6.32	0.92
GL	PIMCO Foreign Bond (US Hedged)	PFRAX	**B**	(800) 426-0107	**B+ / 8.4**	2.72	3.32	0.34 /47	4.20 /85	6.25 /78	6.71	0.77
GL	PIMCO Foreign Bond (US Hedged) C	PFOCX	**C+**	(800) 426-0107	**B / 7.8**	2.52	2.89	-0.53 /26	3.28 /79	5.31 /74	5.82	1.67
GL	PIMCO Foreign Bond (US Hedged) D	PFODX	**B**	(800) 426-0107	**B+ / 8.3**	2.68	3.24	0.19 /44	4.04 /84	6.09 /77	6.56	0.92
GL	PIMCO Foreign Bond (US Hedged)	PFORX	**B**	(800) 426-0107	**B+ / 8.6**	2.78	3.45	0.59 /51	4.46 /87	6.52 /79	6.96	0.52
GL	PIMCO Foreign Bond (US Hedged) P	PFBPX	**B**	(800) 426-0107	**B+ / 8.5**	2.75	3.40	0.49 /49	4.35 /86	6.41 /79	6.86	0.62
GL	PIMCO Foreign Bond (US Hedged) R	PFRRX	**B-**	(800) 426-0107	**B / 8.1**	2.62	3.11	-0.06 /31	3.78 /82	5.83 /76	6.30	1.17
GL	PIMCO Glb Advantage Strategy Bd A	PGSAX	**E+**	(800) 426-0107	**E / 0.3**	2.81	3.19	-1.33 /19	-2.32 / 3	0.28 /16	1.72	1.11
GL	PIMCO Glb Advantage Strategy Bd C	PAFCX	**E+**	(800) 426-0107	**E / 0.4**	2.63	2.82	-2.06 /15	-3.05 / 2	-0.46 / 2	1.06	1.86
GL	PIMCO Glb Advantage Strategy Bd D	PGSDX	**E+**	(800) 426-0107	**E+ / 0.6**	2.81	3.19	-1.33 /19	-2.32 / 3	0.28 /16	1.79	1.11
GL	PIMCO Glb Advantage Strategy Bd I	PSAIX	**E+**	(800) 426-0107	**E+ / 0.8**	2.90	3.39	-0.94 /22	-1.93 / 5	0.68 /18	2.18	0.71
GL	PIMCO Glb Advantage Strategy Bd P	PGBPX	**E+**	(800) 426-0107	**E+ / 0.7**	2.88	3.34	-1.04 /21	-2.03 / 4	0.58 /18	2.08	0.81
GL	PIMCO Glb Advantage Strategy Bd R	PSBRX	**E+**	(800) 426-0107	**E / 0.5**	2.75	3.06	-1.57 /18	-2.57 / 3	0.03 / 9	1.54	1.36
GL	PIMCO Global Bond (Unhedged)	PADMX	**D**	(800) 426-0107	**C / 4.4**	5.08	3.70	2.29 /74	0.03 /21	2.37 /36	1.56	0.82
GL	PIMCO Global Bond (Unhedged) D	PGBDX	**D**	(800) 426-0107	**C- / 4.1**	5.04	3.63	2.13 /73	-0.12 /15	2.22 /34	1.41	0.97
GL	PIMCO Global Bond (Unhedged) Inst	PIGLX	**D+**	(800) 426-0107	**C / 4.8**	5.14	3.83	2.54 /75	0.28 /30	2.63 /39	1.80	0.57
GL	PIMCO Global Bond (Unhedged) P	PGOPX	**D+**	(800) 426-0107	**C / 4.6**	5.11	3.78	2.44 /74	0.18 /28	2.52 /38	1.70	0.67
GL	PIMCO Global Bond (US Hedged) A	PAIIX	**C-**	(800) 426-0107	**C+ / 5.8**	2.26	2.24	-0.44 /27	2.91 /75	5.22 /73	3.89	0.91
GL	PIMCO Global Bond (US Hedged)	PGDAX	**C+**	(800) 426-0107	**B- / 7.5**	2.29	2.29	-0.34 /28	3.01 /76	5.33 /74	4.14	0.81
GL	PIMCO Global Bond (US Hedged) C	PCIIX	**C**	(800) 426-0107	**C+ / 6.1**	2.07	1.86	-1.19 /20	2.14 /64	4.43 /67	3.27	1.66
GL	PIMCO Global Bond (US Hedged)	PGBIX	**B-**	(800) 426-0107	**B / 7.7**	2.34	2.41	-0.10 /30	3.26 /78	5.59 /75	4.38	0.56
GL	PIMCO Global Bond (US Hedged) P	PGNPX	**B-**	(800) 426-0107	**B / 7.6**	2.33	2.37	-0.19 /29	3.16 /78	5.48 /74	4.29	0.66
USA	PIMCO GNMA A	PAGNX	**C**	(800) 426-0107	**C- / 4.1**	1.49	1.47	1.58 /67	1.70 /56	2.99 /45	1.92	0.90
USA	PIMCO GNMA C	PCGNX	**C+**	(800) 426-0107	**C / 4.5**	1.32	1.11	0.84 /56	0.95 /42	2.23 /34	1.27	1.65
USA	PIMCO GNMA D	PGNDX	**B**	(800) 426-0107	**C+ / 5.9**	1.49	1.47	1.58 /67	1.70 /56	2.99 /45	2.00	0.90
USA	PIMCO GNMA Inst	PDMIX	**B+**	(800) 426-0107	**C+ / 6.6**	1.58	1.66	1.97 /72	2.10 /64	3.40 /52	2.39	0.50
USA	PIMCO GNMA P	PPGNX	**B+**	(800) 426-0107	**C+ / 6.4**	1.56	1.61	1.88 /71	2.00 /61	3.30 /50	2.29	0.60
MM	PIMCO Government Money Market A	AMAXX	**C**	(800) 426-0107	**D / 2.2**	0.03	0.06	0.06 /39	0.03 /23	0.03 /11	0.06	0.33
MM	PIMCO Government Money Market C	AMGXX	**C**	(800) 426-0107	**D / 2.2**	0.03	0.06	0.06 /40	0.03 /23	0.03 /11	0.06	0.33
MM	PIMCO Government Money Market M	PGFXX	**C**	(800) 426-0107	**D+ / 2.5**	0.07	0.10	0.11 /42	0.05 /25	0.04 /12	0.11	0.18
MM	PIMCO Government Money Market P	PGPXX	**C**	(800) 426-0107	**D+ / 2.3**	0.05	0.07	0.08 /40	0.03 /23	0.03 /11	0.08	0.28
*COH	PIMCO High Yield A	PHDAX	**D**	(800) 426-0107	**C- / 4.2**	2.60	1.97	-2.02 /15	2.14 /64	4.51 /68	5.15	0.91
COH	PIMCO High Yield Admin	PHYAX	**D+**	(800) 426-0107	**C+ / 6.2**	2.63	2.02	-1.92 /16	2.24 /66	4.61 /69	5.44	0.81
COH	PIMCO High Yield C	PHDCX	**D**	(800) 426-0107	**C / 4.6**	2.42	1.60	-2.74 /12	1.39 /50	3.73 /57	4.59	1.66
COH	PIMCO High Yield D	PHYDX	**D+**	(800) 426-0107	**C+ / 6.0**	2.60	1.97	-2.02 /15	2.14 /64	4.51 /68	5.34	0.91
COH	PIMCO High Yield Inst	PHIYX	**D+**	(800) 426-0107	**C+ / 6.6**	2.69	2.15	-1.68 /17	2.50 /71	4.87 /71	5.69	0.56
MUH	PIMCO High Yield Muni Bond A	PYMAX	**C+**	(800) 426-0107	**A+ / 9.8**	2.83	5.90	7.10 /99	4.55 /98	7.59 /98	3.83	0.85
MUH	PIMCO High Yield Muni Bond C	PYMCX	**C+**	(800) 426-0107	**A+ / 9.7**	2.65	5.52	6.31 /99	3.78 /94	6.79 /96	3.20	1.60
MUH	PIMCO High Yield Muni Bond D	PYMDX	**C+**	(800) 426-0107	**A+ / 9.9**	2.83	5.90	7.10 /99	4.55 /98	7.59 /98	3.91	0.85
MUH	PIMCO High Yield Muni Bond Inst	PHMIX	**C+**	(800) 426-0107	**A+ / 9.9**	2.90	6.05	7.42 /99	4.87 /98	7.89 /98	4.20	0.55
MUH	PIMCO High Yield Muni Bond P	PYMPX	**C+**	(800) 426-0107	**A+ / 9.9**	2.88	6.00	7.31 /99	4.76 /98	7.79 /98	4.11	0.65

- ● Denotes fund is closed to new investors
- * Denotes fund is included in Section II

RISK			NET ASSETS		ASSET							FUND MANAGER		MINIMUM		LOADS	
Risk Rating/Pts	3 Yr Avg Standard Deviation	Avg Duration	NAV As of 3/31/16	Total $(Mil)	Cash %	Gov. Bond %	Muni. Bond %	Corp. Bond %	Other %	Portfolio Turnover Ratio	Avg Coupon Rate	Manager Quality Pct	Manager Tenure (Years)	Initial Purch. $	Additional Purch. $	Front End Load	Back End Load
D / 2.2	5.5	0.1	7.67	N/A	2	15	2	53	28	65	5.4	34	11	1,000,000	0	0.0	0.0
D / 2.2	5.5	0.1	7.67	85	2	15	2	53	28	65	5.4	22	11	1,000	50	0.0	0.0
D / 2.2	5.5	0.1	7.67	14	2	15	2	53	28	65	5.4	29	11	1,000	50	0.0	0.0
D / 2.2	5.5	0.1	7.67	77	2	15	2	53	28	65	5.4	41	11	1,000,000	0	0.0	0.0
D / 2.2	5.5	0.1	7.67	19	2	15	2	53	28	65	5.4	38	11	1,000,000	0	0.0	0.0
E+ / 0.8	6.6	7.4	9.66	90	0	67	4	17	12	312	2.2	42	2	1,000	50	3.8	0.0
E+ / 0.8	6.6	7.4	9.66	19	0	67	4	17	12	312	2.2	47	2	1,000,000	0	0.0	0.0
E+ / 0.8	6.6	7.4	9.66	25	0	67	4	17	12	312	2.2	22	2	1,000	50	0.0	0.0
E+ / 0.8	6.6	7.4	9.66	338	0	67	4	17	12	312	2.2	42	2	1,000	50	0.0	0.0
E+ / 0.8	6.6	7.4	9.66	716	0	67	4	17	12	312	2.2	57	2	1,000,000	0	0.0	0.0
E+ / 0.8	6.6	7.4	9.66	73	0	67	4	17	12	312	2.2	53	2	1,000,000	0	0.0	0.0
C / 4.7	3.4	7.3	10.16	496	0	72	2	17	9	317	2.1	99	2	1,000	50	3.8	0.0
C / 4.7	3.4	7.3	10.16	72	0	72	2	17	9	317	2.1	99	2	1,000,000	0	0.0	0.0
C / 4.7	3.4	7.3	10.16	92	0	72	2	17	9	317	2.1	99	2	1,000	50	0.0	0.0
C / 4.7	3.4	7.3	10.16	1,104	0	72	2	17	9	317	2.1	99	2	1,000	50	0.0	0.0
C / 4.7	3.4	7.3	10.16	4,971	0	72	2	17	9	317	2.1	99	2	1,000,000	0	0.0	0.0
C / 4.7	3.4	7.3	10.16	943	0	72	2	17	9	317	2.1	99	2	1,000,000	0	0.0	0.0
C / 4.7	3.4	7.3	10.16	41	0	72	2	17	9	317	2.1	99	2	0	0	0.0	0.0
D / 2.1	5.6	4.6	10.06	14	0	50	3	28	19	141	3.0	10	5	1,000	50	3.8	0.0
D / 2.1	5.6	4.6	10.06	8	0	50	3	28	19	141	3.0	7	5	1,000	50	0.0	0.0
D / 2.1	5.6	4.6	10.06	7	0	50	3	28	19	141	3.0	10	5	1,000	50	0.0	0.0
D / 2.1	5.6	4.6	10.06	903	0	50	3	28	19	141	3.0	13	5	1,000,000	0	0.0	0.0
D / 2.1	5.6	4.6	10.06	4	0	50	3	28	19	141	3.0	12	5	1,000,000	0	0.0	0.0
D / 2.1	5.6	4.6	10.06	4	0	50	3	28	19	141	3.0	9	5	0	0	0.0	0.0
D+ / 2.9	4.8	6.4	9.18	122	15	62	1	16	6	358	2.4	73	2	1,000,000	0	0.0	0.0
D+ / 2.9	4.8	6.4	9.18	19	15	62	1	16	6	358	2.4	62	2	1,000	50	0.0	0.0
D+ / 2.9	4.8	6.4	9.18	409	15	62	1	16	6	358	2.4	80	2	1,000,000	0	0.0	0.0
D+ / 2.9	4.8	6.4	9.18	1	15	62	1	16	6	358	2.4	77	2	1,000,000	0	0.0	0.0
C / 5.0	3.5	6.0	10.00	72	18	54	2	18	8	338	2.2	98	2	1,000	50	3.8	0.0
C / 5.0	3.5	6.0	10.00	7	18	54	2	18	8	338	2.2	98	2	1,000,000	0	0.0	0.0
C / 5.0	3.5	6.0	10.00	26	18	54	2	18	8	338	2.2	96	2	1,000	50	0.0	0.0
C / 5.0	3.5	6.0	10.00	493	18	54	2	18	8	338	2.2	99	2	1,000,000	0	0.0	0.0
C / 5.0	3.5	6.0	10.00	50	18	54	2	18	8	338	2.2	99	2	1,000,000	0	0.0	0.0
B / 7.7	2.6	3.4	11.36	232	0	4	0	0	96	1,880	2.8	76	4	1,000	50	3.8	0.0
B / 7.7	2.6	3.4	11.36	92	0	4	0	0	96	1,880	2.8	44	4	1,000	50	0.0	0.0
B / 7.7	2.6	3.4	11.36	102	0	4	0	0	96	1,880	2.8	76	4	1,000	50	0.0	0.0
B / 7.7	2.6	3.4	11.36	347	0	4	0	0	96	1,880	2.8	86	4	1,000,000	0	0.0	0.0
B / 7.7	2.6	3.4	11.36	90	0	4	0	0	96	1,880	2.8	84	4	1,000,000	0	0.0	0.0
A+ / 9.9	N/A	N/A	1.00	7	100	0	0	0	0	0	0.1	66	5	1,000	50	0.0	0.0
A+ / 9.9	N/A	N/A	1.00	4	100	0	0	0	0	0	0.1	66	5	1,000	50	0.0	0.0
A+ / 9.9	N/A	N/A	1.00	182	100	0	0	0	0	0	0.1	66	5	1,000,000	0	0.0	0.0
A+ / 9.9	N/A	N/A	1.00	1	100	0	0	0	0	0	0.1	66	5	1,000,000	0	0.0	0.0
D / 1.9	5.3	3.9	8.37	618	6	0	0	92	2	39	6.4	85	6	1,000	50	3.8	0.0
D / 1.9	5.3	3.9	8.37	355	6	0	0	92	2	39	6.4	86	6	1,000,000	0	0.0	0.0
D / 1.8	5.3	3.9	8.37	348	6	0	0	92	2	39	6.4	57	6	1,000	50	0.0	0.0
D / 1.8	5.3	3.9	8.37	297	6	0	0	92	2	39	6.4	85	6	1,000	50	0.0	0.0
D / 1.9	5.3	3.9	8.37	6,793	6	0	0	92	2	39	6.4	89	6	1,000,000	0	0.0	0.0
D / 1.9	5.1	7.0	8.96	204	11	0	88	0	1	32	5.5	43	5	1,000	50	2.3	0.0
D / 1.9	5.1	7.0	8.96	89	11	0	88	0	1	32	5.5	22	5	1,000	50	0.0	0.0
D / 1.9	5.1	7.0	8.96	48	11	0	88	0	1	32	5.5	43	5	1,000	50	0.0	0.0
D / 1.9	5.1	7.0	8.96	313	11	0	88	0	1	32	5.5	54	5	1,000,000	0	0.0	0.0
D / 1.9	5.1	7.0	8.96	111	11	0	88	0	1	32	5.5	50	5	1,000,000	0	0.0	0.0

99 Pct = Best 0 Pct = Worst					PERFORMANCE							
						Total Return % through 3/31/16					Incl. in Returns	
									Annualized			
Fund Type	Fund Name	Ticker Symbol	Overall Investment Rating	Phone	Performance Rating/Pts	3 Mo	6 Mo	1Yr / Pct	3Yr / Pct	5Yr / Pct	Dividend Yield	Expense Ratio
COH	PIMCO High Yield P	PHLPX	**D+**	(800) 426-0107	**C+ / 6.4**	2.66	2.10	-1.78 /17	2.40 /69	4.77 /70	5.59	0.66
COH	PIMCO High Yield R	PHYRX	**D+**	(800) 426-0107	**C+ / 5.6**	2.54	1.85	-2.26 /14	1.89 /59	4.25 /65	5.09	1.16
GL	PIMCO High Yield Spectrum A	PHSAX	**D**	(800) 426-0107	**C- / 4.0**	2.85	1.57	-2.62 /13	2.11 /64	5.03 /72	6.44	0.96
GL	PIMCO High Yield Spectrum C	PHSCX	**D**	(800) 426-0107	**C / 4.4**	2.67	1.21	-3.34 /10	1.35 /49	4.25 /65	5.92	1.71
GL	PIMCO High Yield Spectrum D	PHSDX	**D+**	(800) 426-0107	**C+ / 5.8**	2.85	1.57	-2.62 /13	2.10 /64	5.03 /72	6.68	0.96
GL	PIMCO High Yield Spectrum Inst	PHSIX	**D+**	(800) 426-0107	**C+ / 6.4**	2.93	1.74	-2.29 /14	2.46 /70	5.40 /74	7.04	0.61
GL	PIMCO High Yield Spectrum P	PHSPX	**D+**	(800) 426-0107	**C+ / 6.2**	2.91	1.70	-2.38 /14	2.36 /68	5.29 /73	6.94	0.71
* GEI	PIMCO Income Fund A	PONAX	**C+**	(800) 426-0107	**B / 7.6**	1.64	2.04	2.00 /72	4.09 /84	7.53 /84	6.99	0.85
GEI	PIMCO Income Fund Adm	PIINX	**B**	(800) 426-0107	**B+ / 8.4**	1.68	2.12	2.15 /73	4.24 /85	7.70 /85	7.42	0.84
GEI	PIMCO Income Fund C	PONCX	**C+**	(800) 426-0107	**B / 7.8**	1.46	1.66	1.22 /62	3.38 /79	6.82 /81	6.48	1.60
GEI	PIMCO Income Fund D	PONDX	**B**	(800) 426-0107	**B+ / 8.4**	1.66	2.07	2.06 /72	4.17 /85	7.64 /85	7.32	0.79
GEI	PIMCO Income Fund Inst	PIMIX	**B+**	(800) 426-0107	**B+ / 8.6**	1.74	2.24	2.41 /74	4.48 /87	7.94 /87	7.68	0.45
GEI	PIMCO Income Fund P	PONPX	**B**	(800) 426-0107	**B+ / 8.5**	1.72	2.19	2.30 /74	4.39 /86	7.85 /86	7.57	0.55
GEI	PIMCO Income Fund R	PONRX	**B-**	(800) 426-0107	**B / 8.2**	1.58	1.91	1.73 /69	3.85 /83	7.29 /83	7.00	1.10
* COI	PIMCO Investment Grade Corp A	PBDAX	**D+**	(800) 426-0107	**C+ / 5.8**	3.21	3.08	0.08 /40	2.64 /72	5.48 /74	4.24	0.91
COI	PIMCO Investment Grade Corp	PGCAX	**C-**	(800) 426-0107	**B- / 7.5**	3.25	3.15	0.23 /45	2.80 /74	5.64 /75	4.55	0.76
COI	PIMCO Investment Grade Corp C	PBDCX	**D+**	(800) 426-0107	**C+ / 6.1**	3.03	2.70	-0.66 /25	1.88 /59	4.70 /70	3.66	1.66
COI	PIMCO Investment Grade Corp D	PBDDX	**C-**	(800) 426-0107	**B- / 7.3**	3.21	3.08	0.08 /40	2.64 /72	5.48 /74	4.40	0.91
COI	PIMCO Investment Grade Corp Inst	PIGIX	**C**	(800) 426-0107	**B / 7.8**	3.31	3.28	0.47 /49	3.05 /77	5.90 /76	4.80	0.51
COI	PIMCO Investment Grade Corp P	PBDPX	**C-**	(800) 426-0107	**B / 7.7**	3.28	3.23	0.38 /47	2.95 /76	5.80 /76	4.70	0.61
COI	PIMCO Long Dur Total Return D	PLRDX	**U**	(800) 426-0107	**U /**	6.58	5.19	-0.84 /23	--	--	4.77	0.92
GEI	PIMCO Long Dur Total Return Inst	PLRIX	**C-**	(800) 426-0107	**B+ / 8.7**	6.69	5.40	-0.44 /27	4.26 /86	7.90 /86	5.16	0.52
GEI	PIMCO Long Dur Total Return P	PLRPX	**C-**	(800) 426-0107	**B+ / 8.6**	6.66	5.35	-0.54 /26	4.16 /85	7.79 /86	5.07	0.62
GEI	PIMCO Long Term Credit D	PTCDX	**U**	(800) 426-0107	**U /**	6.73	6.33	-1.67 /17	--	--	6.08	0.98
GEI	PIMCO Long Term Credit Inst	PTCIX	**C-**	(800) 426-0107	**A- / 9.0**	6.83	6.53	-1.29 /20	4.81 /89	9.24 /92	6.47	0.58
USL	PIMCO Long Term US Govt A	PFGAX	**C-**	(800) 426-0107	**B+ / 8.7**	7.72	5.78	1.53 /67	4.97 /90	8.81 /90	2.09	0.85
USL	PIMCO Long Term US Govt Admin	PLGBX	**C-**	(800) 426-0107	**A / 9.3**	7.74	5.83	1.63 /68	5.08 /91	8.93 /91	2.22	0.75
USL	PIMCO Long Term US Govt C	PFGCX	**C-**	(800) 426-0107	**B+ / 8.8**	7.53	5.37	0.76 /54	4.19 /85	8.00 /87	1.50	1.60
USL	PIMCO Long Term US Govt D	PLGDX	**U**	(800) 426-0107	**U /**	7.70	5.74	1.47 /66	--	--	2.08	0.90
USL	PIMCO Long Term US Govt Inst	PGOVX	**C-**	(800) 426-0107	**A / 9.4**	7.81	5.97	1.89 /71	5.34 /92	9.19 /92	2.43	0.50
USL	PIMCO Long Term US Govt P	PLTPX	**C-**	(800) 426-0107	**A / 9.3**	7.78	5.92	1.79 /70	5.24 /92	9.08 /91	2.35	0.60
* GEI	PIMCO Low Duration A	PTLAX	**C-**	(800) 426-0107	**D- / 1.4**	0.39	0.82	-0.06 /31	0.19 /29	1.38 /24	2.12	0.80
GEI	PIMCO Low Duration Admin	PLDAX	**C**	(800) 426-0107	**C- / 3.0**	0.41	0.86	0.03 /35	0.28 /30	1.48 /25	2.26	0.71
GEI	PIMCO Low Duration C	PTLCX	**C-**	(800) 426-0107	**D / 1.8**	0.32	0.67	-0.35 /28	-0.11 /15	1.08 /21	1.87	1.10
GEI	PIMCO Low Duration D	PLDDX	**C**	(800) 426-0107	**D+ / 2.9**	0.40	0.84	-0.01 /31	0.24 /29	1.44 /25	2.22	0.75
GEI	PIMCO Low Duration Fund II P	PDRPX	**C**	(800) 426-0107	**C- / 3.3**	0.64	0.92	0.54 /50	0.35 /31	1.39 /24	1.66	0.60
GEI	PIMCO Low Duration II Admin	PDFAX	**C**	(800) 426-0107	**C- / 3.0**	0.61	0.86	0.39 /48	0.20 /29	1.24 /23	1.52	0.75
GEI	PIMCO Low Duration II Inst	PLDTX	**C+**	(800) 426-0107	**C- / 3.5**	0.67	0.98	0.64 /52	0.45 /32	1.49 /26	1.77	0.50
GEI	PIMCO Low Duration III Admin	PDRAX	**C-**	(800) 426-0107	**D+ / 2.8**	0.12	0.38	-0.37 /27	0.23 /29	1.57 /26	1.84	0.75
GEI	PIMCO Low Duration III Inst	PLDIX	**C**	(800) 426-0107	**C- / 3.2**	0.18	0.50	-0.12 /30	0.48 /33	1.82 /29	2.09	0.50
COI	PIMCO Low Duration III P	PLUPX	**C**	(800) 426-0107	**C- / 3.0**	0.16	0.45	-0.22 /29	0.38 /31	1.72 /28	1.99	0.60
GEI	PIMCO Low Duration Inst	PTLDX	**C**	(800) 426-0107	**C- / 3.5**	0.47	0.99	0.28 /45	0.53 /34	1.73 /28	2.50	0.46
GEI	PIMCO Low Duration P	PLDPX	**C**	(800) 426-0107	**C- / 3.3**	0.44	0.94	0.18 /44	0.43 /32	1.63 /27	2.40	0.56
GEI	PIMCO Low Duration R	PLDRX	**C-**	(800) 426-0107	**D / 1.8**	0.33	0.70	-0.30 /28	-0.06 /15	1.13 /22	1.92	1.05
COI	PIMCO Moderate Duration Admin	PMAOX	**U**	(800) 426-0107	**U /**	1.49	1.48	--	--	--	0.00	0.71
GEI	PIMCO Moderate Duration Fund P	PMOPX	**C+**	(800) 426-0107	**C / 5.2**	1.53	1.55	0.41 /48	1.41 /50	3.06 /46	2.54	0.56
GEI	PIMCO Moderate Duration Inst	PMDRX	**C+**	(800) 426-0107	**C / 5.4**	1.55	1.60	0.51 /50	1.51 /52	3.16 /48	2.64	0.46
MM	PIMCO Money Market A	PYAXX	**C-**	(800) 426-0107	**D / 2.0**	0.00	0.01	0.02 /35	0.02 /21	0.03 /11	0.02	0.47
MM	PIMCO Money Market Admin	PMAXX	**C**	(800) 426-0107	**D+ / 2.3**	0.03	0.04	0.05 /39	0.03 /23	0.04 /12	0.05	0.32
MM	PIMCO Money Market C	PKCXX	**C-**	(800) 426-0107	**D / 2.0**	0.00	0.01	0.02 /35	0.02 /21	0.03 /11	0.02	0.47
MM	PIMCO Money Market Inst	PMIXX	**C**	(800) 426-0107	**D+ / 2.3**	0.03	0.04	0.05 /39	0.03 /23	0.04 /12	0.05	0.32
MTG	PIMCO Mortgage Opportunities A	PMZAX	**A-**	(800) 426-0107	**C+ / 6.0**	0.77	0.81	1.80 /70	3.01 /76	--	3.58	1.01

• Denotes fund is closed to new investors
* Denotes fund is included in Section II

RISK			NET ASSETS		ASSET							FUND MANAGER		MINIMUM		LOADS	
Risk Rating/Pts	3 Yr Avg Standard Deviation	Avg Duration	NAV As of 3/31/16	Total $(Mil)	Cash %	Gov. Bond %	Muni. Bond %	Corp. Bond %	Other %	Portfolio Turnover Ratio	Avg Coupon Rate	Manager Quality Pct	Manager Tenure (Years)	Initial Purch. $	Additional Purch. $	Front End Load	Back End Load
D / 1.9	5.3	3.9	8.37	955	6	0	0	92	2	39	6.4	88	6	1,000,000	0	0.0	0.0
D / 1.8	5.3	3.9	8.37	33	6	0	0	92	2	39	6.4	79	6	0	0	0.0	0.0
D / 1.9	5.8	3.6	9.22	11	5	0	0	93	2	34	7.1	96	6	1,000	50	3.8	0.0
D / 1.9	5.8	3.6	9.22	6	5	0	0	93	2	34	7.1	93	6	1,000	50	0.0	0.0
D / 1.9	5.7	3.6	9.22	25	5	0	0	93	2	34	7.1	96	6	1,000	50	0.0	0.0
D / 1.9	5.7	3.6	9.22	1,672	5	0	0	93	2	34	7.1	97	6	1,000,000	0	0.0	0.0
D / 1.9	5.7	3.6	9.22	127	5	0	0	93	2	34	7.1	97	6	1,000,000	0	0.0	0.0
C / 4.7	3.6	3.4	11.77	7,072	22	12	0	21	45	164	2.7	97	9	1,000	50	3.8	0.0
C / 4.7	3.6	3.4	11.77	272	22	12	0	21	45	164	2.7	97	9	1,000,000	0	0.0	0.0
C / 4.7	3.6	3.4	11.77	6,457	22	12	0	21	45	164	2.7	95	9	1,000	50	0.0	0.0
C / 4.7	3.6	3.4	11.77	9,186	22	12	0	21	45	164	2.7	97	9	1,000	50	0.0	0.0
C / 4.7	3.6	3.4	11.77	22,253	22	12	0	21	45	164	2.7	98	9	1,000,000	0	0.0	0.0
C / 4.7	3.6	3.4	11.77	10,551	22	12	0	21	45	164	2.7	98	9	1,000,000	0	0.0	0.0
C / 4.7	3.6	3.4	11.77	202	22	12	0	21	45	164	2.7	96	9	0	0	0.0	0.0
D+ / 2.8	5.0	6.2	10.15	948	0	29	0	58	13	86	4.2	43	14	1,000	50	3.8	0.0
D+ / 2.8	5.0	6.2	10.15	192	0	29	0	58	13	86	4.2	49	14	1,000,000	0	0.0	0.0
D+ / 2.8	5.0	6.2	10.15	534	0	29	0	58	13	86	4.2	23	14	1,000	50	0.0	0.0
D+ / 2.8	5.0	6.2	10.15	509	0	29	0	58	13	86	4.2	43	14	1,000	50	0.0	0.0
D+ / 2.8	5.0	6.2	10.15	4,143	0	29	0	58	13	86	4.2	59	14	1,000,000	0	0.0	0.0
D+ / 2.8	5.0	6.2	10.15	943	0	29	0	58	13	86	4.2	55	14	1,000,000	0	0.0	0.0
U /	N/A	13.6	11.29	1	0	0	0	0	100	76	4.3	N/A	9	1,000	50	0.0	0.0
E / 0.3	8.7	13.6	11.29	2,968	0	0	0	0	100	76	4.3	8	9	1,000,000	0	0.0	0.0
E / 0.3	8.7	13.6	11.29	11	0	0	0	0	100	76	4.3	8	9	1,000,000	0	0.0	0.0
U /	N/A	11.5	11.40	2	0	0	0	0	100	71	5.7	N/A	7	1,000	50	0.0	0.0
E / 0.3	8.9	11.5	11.40	3,014	0	0	0	0	100	71	5.7	13	7	1,000,000	0	0.0	0.0
E- / 0.2	10.9	17.0	6.44	159	0	81	0	1	18	244	2.6	24	9	1,000	50	3.8	0.0
E- / 0.2	10.9	17.0	6.44	28	0	81	0	1	18	244	2.6	27	9	1,000,000	0	0.0	0.0
E- / 0.2	10.9	17.0	6.44	32	0	81	0	1	18	244	2.6	13	9	1,000	50	0.0	0.0
U /	N/A	17.0	6.44	24	0	81	0	1	18	244	2.6	N/A	9	1,000	50	0.0	0.0
E- / 0.2	10.9	17.0	6.44	305	0	81	0	1	18	244	2.6	34	9	1,000,000	0	0.0	0.0
E- / 0.2	10.9	17.0	6.44	82	0	81	0	1	18	244	2.6	31	9	1,000,000	0	0.0	0.0
B+ / 8.7	1.7	1.2	9.87	1,088	0	23	0	43	34	110	2.4	37	2	1,000	50	2.3	0.0
B+ / 8.7	1.7	1.2	9.87	179	0	23	0	43	34	110	2.4	40	2	1,000,000	0	0.0	0.0
B+ / 8.7	1.7	1.2	9.87	575	0	23	0	43	34	110	2.4	29	2	1,000	50	0.0	0.0
B+ / 8.7	1.7	1.2	9.87	837	0	23	0	43	34	110	2.4	39	2	1,000	50	0.0	0.0
B+ / 8.9	1.5	1.2	9.73	1	0	12	1	46	41	170	2.2	48	2	1,000,000	0	0.0	0.0
B+ / 8.9	1.5	1.2	9.73	10	0	12	1	46	41	170	2.2	43	2	1,000,000	0	0.0	0.0
B+ / 8.9	1.5	1.2	9.73	364	0	12	1	46	41	170	2.2	51	2	1,000,000	0	0.0	0.0
B+ / 8.8	1.6	1.2	9.48	6	0	23	2	40	35	159	2.1	40	2	1,000,000	0	0.0	0.0
B+ / 8.8	1.6	1.2	9.48	165	0	23	2	40	35	159	2.1	48	2	1,000,000	0	0.0	0.0
B+ / 8.8	1.6	1.2	9.48	33	0	23	2	40	35	159	2.1	47	2	1,000,000	0	0.0	0.0
B+ / 8.7	1.7	1.2	9.87	6,544	0	23	0	43	34	110	2.4	49	2	1,000,000	0	0.0	0.0
B+ / 8.7	1.7	1.2	9.87	849	0	23	0	43	34	110	2.4	45	2	1,000,000	0	0.0	0.0
B+ / 8.7	1.7	1.2	9.87	92	0	23	0	43	34	110	2.4	30	2	0	0	0.0	0.0
U /	N/A	3.3	10.13	9	0	0	0	0	100	254	3.2	N/A	2	1,000,000	0	0.0	0.0
B / 7.6	2.6	3.3	10.13	7	0	0	0	0	100	254	3.2	45	2	1,000,000	0	0.0	0.0
B / 7.7	2.6	3.3	10.13	1,460	0	0	0	0	100	254	3.2	49	2	1,000,000	0	0.0	0.0
A+ / 9.9	N/A	N/A	1.00	164	100	0	0	0	0	0	0.0	N/A	5	1,000	50	0.0	0.0
A+ / 9.9	N/A	N/A	1.00	79	100	0	0	0	0	0	0.1	66	5	1,000,000	0	0.0	0.0
A+ / 9.9	N/A	N/A	1.00	77	100	0	0	0	0	0	0.0	N/A	5	1,000	50	0.0	0.0
A+ / 9.9	N/A	N/A	1.00	241	100	0	0	0	0	0	0.1	66	5	1,000,000	0	0.0	0.0
B+ / 8.6	1.9	N/A	10.94	52	0	22	0	2	76	1,133	0.0	93	4	1,000	50	3.8	0.0

99 Pct = Best 0 Pct = Worst Fund Type	Fund Name	Ticker Symbol	Overall Investment Rating	Phone	PERFORMANCE Performance Rating/Pts	Total Return % through 3/31/16 3 Mo	6 Mo	1Yr / Pct	Annualized 3Yr / Pct	5Yr / Pct	Incl. in Returns Dividend Yield	Expense Ratio
MTG	PIMCO Mortgage Opportunities C	PMZCX	**A-**	(800) 426-0107	**C+ / 6.3**	0.59	0.43	1.04 /59	2.24 /66	--	2.96	1.76
MTG	PIMCO Mortgage Opportunities D	PMZDX	**A+**	(800) 426-0107	**B- / 7.5**	0.77	0.81	1.80 /70	3.00 /76	--	3.72	1.01
MTG	PIMCO Mortgage Opportunities Inst	PMZIX	**A+**	(800) 426-0107	**B / 7.9**	0.86	1.00	2.20 /73	3.42 /79	--	4.12	0.61
MTG	PIMCO Mortgage Opportunities P	PMZPX	**A+**	(800) 426-0107	**B / 7.8**	0.82	0.93	2.08 /72	3.31 /79	--	4.00	0.71
MTG	PIMCO Mortgage-Backd Sec A	PMRAX	**C+**	(800) 426-0107	**C / 5.1**	1.57	1.40	2.03 /72	2.28 /67	3.23 /49	2.02	0.90
MTG	PIMCO Mortgage-Backd Sec Admin	PMTAX	**A**	(800) 426-0107	**B- / 7.0**	1.60	1.47	2.17 /73	2.44 /70	3.39 /51	2.24	0.75
MTG	PIMCO Mortgage-Backd Sec C	PMRCX	**B**	(800) 426-0107	**C / 5.5**	1.39	1.03	1.28 /63	1.53 /53	2.47 /37	1.36	1.65
MTG	PIMCO Mortgage-Backd Sec D	PTMDX	**A**	(800) 426-0107	**C+ / 6.8**	1.57	1.40	2.03 /72	2.28 /67	3.23 /49	2.10	0.90
MTG	PIMCO Mortgage-Backd Sec Inst	PTRIX	**A+**	(800) 426-0107	**B- / 7.4**	1.66	1.60	2.43 /74	2.69 /73	3.65 /56	2.49	0.50
MTG	PIMCO Mortgage-Backd Sec P	PMRPX	**A+**	(800) 426-0107	**B- / 7.3**	1.64	1.55	2.33 /74	2.59 /72	3.54 /54	2.39	0.60
MUN	PIMCO Municipal Bond A	PMLAX	**B**	(800) 426-0107	**A / 9.3**	1.57	4.37	4.53 /97	3.78 /94	6.01 /92	3.09	0.75
MUN	PIMCO Municipal Bond Admin	PMNAX	**B+**	(800) 426-0107	**A+ / 9.6**	1.58	4.40	4.59 /97	3.84 /95	6.10 /93	3.21	0.69
MUN	PIMCO Municipal Bond C	PMLCX	**B**	(800) 426-0107	**A / 9.3**	1.45	4.12	4.02 /94	3.26 /90	5.49 /89	2.67	1.25
MUN	PIMCO Municipal Bond D	PMBDX	**B**	(800) 426-0107	**A+ / 9.6**	1.57	4.38	4.53 /97	3.78 /95	6.01 /92	3.16	0.75
MUN	PIMCO Municipal Bond Inst	PFMIX	**B+**	(800) 426-0107	**A+ / 9.7**	1.64	4.53	4.85 /98	4.10 /96	6.34 /94	3.46	0.44
MUN	PIMCO Municipal Bond P	PMUPX	**B+**	(800) 426-0107	**A+ / 9.7**	1.62	4.48	4.75 /97	3.99 /96	6.23 /93	3.36	0.54
MUN	PIMCO Natl Intmdt Mncpl Bd A	PMNTX	**B**	(800) 426-0107	**B+ / 8.4**	1.36	3.48	3.74 /92	2.80 /86	--	1.79	0.80
MUN	PIMCO Natl Intmdt Mncpl Bd C	PMNNX	**B**	(800) 426-0107	**B+ / 8.4**	1.25	3.23	3.23 /87	2.30 /80	--	1.35	1.30
MUN	PIMCO Natl Intmdt Mncpl Bd D	PMNDX	**B+**	(800) 426-0107	**A- / 9.0**	1.36	3.48	3.74 /92	2.80 /86	--	1.84	0.80
MUN	PIMCO Natl Intmdt Mncpl Bd Inst	PMNIX	**A-**	(800) 426-0107	**A- / 9.2**	1.45	3.66	4.10 /95	3.16 /90	--	2.18	0.45
MUN	PIMCO Natl Intmdt Mncpl Bd P	PMNPX	**A-**	(800) 426-0107	**A- / 9.2**	1.42	3.61	4.00 /94	3.06 /89	--	2.08	0.55
MUS	PIMCO NY Muni Bond A	PNYAX	**A-**	(800) 426-0107	**B+ / 8.9**	1.62	3.22	3.56 /91	3.48 /93	4.88 /84	3.13	0.78
MUS	PIMCO NY Muni Bond C	PBFCX	**B+**	(800) 426-0107	**B+ / 8.7**	1.44	2.85	2.80 /83	2.71 /85	4.10 /78	2.47	1.53
MUS	PIMCO NY Muni Bond D	PNYDX	**A**	(800) 426-0107	**A / 9.3**	1.62	3.22	3.56 /91	3.48 /93	4.88 /84	3.20	0.78
MUS	PIMCO NY Muni Bond Inst	PNYIX	**A**	(800) 426-0107	**A / 9.5**	1.70	3.39	3.89 /93	3.82 /95	5.23 /87	3.52	0.45
MUS	PIMCO NY Muni Bond P	PNYPX	**A**	(800) 426-0107	**A / 9.5**	1.68	3.34	3.79 /92	3.72 /94	5.12 /86	3.42	0.55
* GEI	PIMCO Real Return A	PRTNX	**E**	(800) 426-0107	**E / 0.4**	4.02	3.06	-0.70 /24	-2.04 / 4	2.24 /34	0.54	0.90
GEI	PIMCO Real Return Administrative	PARRX	**E**	(800) 426-0107	**E+ / 0.8**	4.06	3.13	-0.56 /25	-1.90 / 5	2.39 /36	0.71	0.75
GL	PIMCO Real Return Asset D	PRTDX	**U**	(800) 426-0107	**U /**	7.32	6.36	-1.97 /16	--	--	1.53	1.01
GEI	PIMCO Real Return Asset Inst	PRAIX	**E**	(800) 426-0107	**D- / 1.1**	7.41	6.55	-1.60 /18	-1.96 / 4	4.84 /71	1.89	0.61
GEI	PIMCO Real Return Asset P	PRTPX	**E**	(800) 426-0107	**D- / 1.0**	7.38	6.50	-1.70 /17	-2.06 / 4	4.74 /70	1.80	0.71
GEI	PIMCO Real Return C	PRTCX	**E**	(800) 426-0107	**E / 0.5**	3.90	2.81	-1.19 /20	-2.53 / 3	1.73 /28	0.08	1.40
GEI	PIMCO Real Return D	PRRDX	**E**	(800) 426-0107	**E+ / 0.8**	4.02	3.06	-0.70 /24	-2.04 / 4	2.24 /34	0.56	0.90
GEI	PIMCO Real Return Institutional	PRRIX	**E+**	(800) 426-0107	**D- / 1.0**	4.12	3.18	-0.39 /27	-1.68 / 5	2.63 /39	0.87	0.50
COI	PIMCO Real Return Ltd Duration D	PPDRX	**U**	(800) 426-0107	**U /**	2.17	2.13	--	--	--	0.00	0.85
COI	PIMCO Real Return Ltd Duration Inst	PPIRX	**U**	(800) 426-0107	**U /**	2.17	2.13	--	--	--	0.00	0.45
COI	PIMCO Real Return Ltd Duration P	PPPRX	**U**	(800) 426-0107	**U /**	2.17	2.13	--	--	--	0.00	0.55
GEI	PIMCO Real Return P	PRLPX	**E+**	(800) 426-0107	**D- / 1.0**	4.09	3.21	-0.41 /27	-1.75 / 5	2.54 /38	0.85	0.60
GEI	PIMCO Real Return R	PRRRX	**E**	(800) 426-0107	**E+ / 0.6**	3.96	2.93	-0.94 /22	-2.29 / 4	1.98 /31	0.32	1.15
COI	PIMCO Senior Floating Rate Fd A	PSRZX	**C-**	(800) 426-0107	**C- / 3.1**	1.66	-0.09	-0.64 /25	1.42 /51	--	3.59	1.01
COI	PIMCO Senior Floating Rate Fd C	PSRWX	**C-**	(800) 426-0107	**D+ / 2.8**	1.47	-0.46	-1.39 /19	0.66 /36	--	2.91	1.76
COI	PIMCO Senior Floating Rate Fd D	PSRDX	**C+**	(800) 426-0107	**C / 4.3**	1.66	-0.09	-0.64 /25	1.42 /51	--	3.67	1.01
COI	PIMCO Senior Floating Rate Fd Inst	PSRIX	**C+**	(800) 426-0107	**C / 4.8**	1.74	0.06	-0.35 /28	1.72 /56	--	3.98	0.71
COI	PIMCO Senior Floating Rate Fd P	PSRPX	**C+**	(800) 426-0107	**C / 4.6**	1.71	0.01	-0.45 /27	1.62 /54	--	3.88	0.81
COI	PIMCO Short Asset Investment A	PAIAX	**C-**	(800) 426-0107	**D / 1.6**	0.19	0.37	0.42 /48	0.33 /30	--	0.61	0.71
COI	PIMCO Short Asset Investment	PAIQX	**C+**	(800) 426-0107	**C- / 3.3**	0.21	0.42	0.52 /50	0.43 /32	--	0.72	0.61
COI	PIMCO Short Asset Investment D	PAIUX	**C+**	(800) 426-0107	**C- / 3.1**	0.19	0.37	0.42 /48	0.34 /31	--	0.62	0.71
COI	PIMCO Short Asset Investment Inst	PAIDX	**B-**	(800) 426-0107	**C- / 3.8**	0.27	0.54	0.77 /55	0.69 /37	--	0.97	0.36
COI	PIMCO Short Asset Investment P	PAIPX	**C+**	(800) 426-0107	**C- / 3.6**	0.25	0.49	0.67 /53	0.59 /35	--	0.87	0.46
MUN	PIMCO Short Duration Muni Inc A	PSDAX	**C-**	(800) 426-0107	**D / 1.9**	0.43	0.56	0.63 /58	0.51 /39	0.56 /19	0.85	0.73
MUN	PIMCO Short Duration Muni Inc Adm	PSDMX	**B+**	(800) 426-0107	**C / 4.6**	0.48	0.64	0.81 /62	0.67 /43	0.78 /22	1.04	0.58
MUN	PIMCO Short Duration Muni Inc C	PSDCX	**C+**	(800) 426-0107	**C- / 3.2**	0.36	0.41	0.33 /50	0.22 /31	0.27 /17	0.57	1.03

- Denotes fund is closed to new investors

* Denotes fund is included in Section II

RISK			NET ASSETS		ASSET							FUND MANAGER		MINIMUM		LOADS	
Risk Rating/Pts	3 Yr Avg Standard Deviation	Avg Duration	NAV As of 3/31/16	Total $(Mil)	Cash %	Gov. Bond %	Muni. Bond %	Corp. Bond %	Other %	Portfolio Turnover Ratio	Avg Coupon Rate	Manager Quality Pct	Manager Tenure (Years)	Initial Purch. $	Additional Purch. $	Front End Load	Back End Load
B+ / 8.5	1.9	N/A	10.94	23	0	22	0	2	76	1,133	0.0	87	4	1,000	50	0.0	0.0
B+ / 8.6	1.9	N/A	10.94	70	0	22	0	2	76	1,133	0.0	93	4	1,000	50	0.0	0.0
B+ / 8.6	1.9	N/A	10.94	1,402	0	22	0	2	76	1,133	0.0	96	4	1,000,000	0	0.0	0.0
B+ / 8.6	1.9	N/A	10.94	543	0	22	0	2	76	1,133	0.0	95	4	1,000,000	0	0.0	0.0
B / 8.0	2.4	3.0	10.56	30	0	0	0	0	100	1,501	2.7	53	4	1,000	50	3.8	0.0
B / 8.0	2.4	3.0	10.56	5	0	0	0	0	100	1,501	2.7	59	4	1,000,000	0	0.0	0.0
B / 8.0	2.4	3.0	10.56	11	0	0	0	0	100	1,501	2.7	29	4	1,000	50	0.0	0.0
B / 8.0	2.4	3.0	10.56	42	0	0	0	0	100	1,501	2.7	53	4	1,000	50	0.0	0.0
B / 8.0	2.4	3.0	10.56	118	0	0	0	0	100	1,501	2.7	73	4	1,000,000	0	0.0	0.0
B / 8.0	2.4	3.0	10.56	10	0	0	0	0	100	1,501	2.7	69	4	1,000,000	0	0.0	0.0
C- / 3.4	4.3	5.7	9.90	267	6	0	93	0	1	17	5.1	38	5	1,000	50	2.3	0.0
C- / 3.4	4.3	5.7	9.90	N/A	6	0	93	0	1	17	5.1	40	5	1,000,000	0	0.0	0.0
C- / 3.4	4.3	5.7	9.90	121	6	0	93	0	1	17	5.1	24	5	1,000	50	0.0	0.0
C- / 3.4	4.3	5.7	9.90	12	6	0	93	0	1	17	5.1	38	5	1,000	50	0.0	0.0
C- / 3.4	4.3	5.7	9.90	168	6	0	93	0	1	17	5.1	48	5	1,000,000	0	0.0	0.0
C- / 3.4	4.3	5.7	9.90	124	6	0	93	0	1	17	5.1	44	5	1,000,000	0	0.0	0.0
C / 4.8	3.6	5.2	10.63	17	6	0	93	0	1	25	4.8	32	4	1,000	50	2.3	0.0
C / 4.8	3.6	5.2	10.63	5	6	0	93	0	1	25	4.8	20	4	1,000	50	0.0	0.0
C / 4.8	3.6	5.2	10.63	3	6	0	93	0	1	25	4.8	32	4	1,000	50	0.0	0.0
C / 4.8	3.6	5.2	10.63	26	6	0	93	0	1	25	4.8	43	4	1,000,000	0	0.0	0.0
C / 4.8	3.6	5.2	10.63	14	6	0	93	0	1	25	4.8	40	4	1,000,000	0	0.0	0.0
C / 5.0	3.5	5.3	11.43	70	2	0	97	0	1	10	5.1	56	5	1,000	50	2.3	0.0
C / 5.0	3.5	5.3	11.43	14	2	0	97	0	1	10	5.1	31	5	1,000	50	0.0	0.0
C / 5.0	3.5	5.3	11.43	13	2	0	97	0	1	10	5.1	56	5	1,000	50	0.0	0.0
C / 5.0	3.5	5.3	11.43	56	2	0	97	0	1	10	5.1	73	5	1,000,000	0	0.0	0.0
C / 5.0	3.5	5.3	11.43	10	2	0	97	0	1	10	5.1	69	5	1,000,000	0	0.0	0.0
D- / 1.1	6.3	7.4	10.92	1,920	0	92	0	3	5	117	2.0	1	9	1,000	50	3.8	0.0
D- / 1.1	6.3	7.4	10.92	648	0	92	0	3	5	117	2.0	2	9	1,000,000	0	0.0	0.0
U /	N/A	15.2	8.22	2	0	0	0	0	100	99	2.7	N/A	9	1,000	50	0.0	0.0
E- / 0.2	10.4	15.2	8.22	1,618	0	0	0	0	100	99	2.7	0	9	1,000,000	0	0.0	0.0
E- / 0.2	10.4	15.2	8.22	5	0	0	0	0	100	99	2.7	0	9	1,000,000	0	0.0	0.0
D- / 1.1	6.3	7.4	10.92	828	0	92	0	3	5	117	2.0	1	9	1,000	50	0.0	0.0
D- / 1.1	6.3	7.4	10.92	900	0	92	0	3	5	117	2.0	1	9	1,000	50	0.0	0.0
D- / 1.1	6.3	7.4	10.92	5,573	0	92	0	3	5	117	2.0	2	9	1,000,000	0	0.0	0.0
U /	N/A	N/A	9.89	N/A	0	0	0	0	100	0	0.0	N/A	1	1,000	50	0.0	0.0
U /	N/A	N/A	9.89	3	0	0	0	0	100	0	0.0	N/A	1	1,000,000	0	0.0	0.0
U /	N/A	N/A	9.89	N/A	0	0	0	0	100	0	0.0	N/A	1	1,000,000	0	0.0	0.0
D- / 1.1	6.3	7.4	10.92	738	0	92	0	3	5	117	2.0	2	9	1,000,000	0	0.0	0.0
D- / 1.1	6.3	7.4	10.92	338	0	92	0	3	5	117	2.0	1	9	0	0	0.0	0.0
B / 8.2	2.3	0.9	9.65	64	8	0	0	76	16	33	4.5	85	5	1,000	50	2.3	1.0
B / 8.2	2.3	0.9	9.65	53	8	0	0	76	16	33	4.5	58	5	1,000	50	0.0	1.0
B / 8.2	2.3	0.9	9.65	14	8	0	0	76	16	33	4.5	85	5	1,000	50	0.0	1.0
B / 8.2	2.3	0.9	9.65	836	8	0	0	76	16	33	4.5	89	5	1,000,000	0	0.0	1.0
B / 8.2	2.3	0.9	9.65	13	8	0	0	76	16	33	4.5	88	5	1,000,000	0	0.0	1.0
A+ / 9.9	0.3	0.2	10.00	59	12	8	2	60	18	2,324	2.4	75	4	1,000	50	2.3	0.0
A+ / 9.9	0.3	0.2	10.00	N/A	12	8	2	60	18	2,324	2.4	78	4	1,000,000	0	0.0	0.0
A+ / 9.9	0.3	0.2	10.00	5	12	8	2	60	18	2,324	2.4	75	4	1,000	50	0.0	0.0
A+ / 9.9	0.3	0.2	10.00	599	12	8	2	60	18	2,324	2.4	84	4	1,000,000	0	0.0	0.0
A+ / 9.9	0.3	0.2	10.00	55	12	8	2	60	18	2,324	2.4	82	4	1,000,000	0	0.0	0.0
A+ / 9.7	0.7	1.7	8.47	102	7	0	92	0	1	28	3.2	60	2	1,000	50	2.3	0.0
A+ / 9.7	0.7	1.7	8.47	N/A	7	0	92	0	1	28	3.2	72	2	1,000,000	0	0.0	0.0
A+ / 9.7	0.7	1.7	8.47	15	7	0	92	0	1	28	3.2	49	2	1,000	50	0.0	0.0

99 Pct = Best
0 Pct = Worst

Fund Type	Fund Name	Ticker Symbol	Overall Investment Rating	Phone	PERFORMANCE: Performance Rating/Pts	Total Return % through 3/31/16: 3 Mo	6 Mo	1Yr / Pct	Annualized 3Yr / Pct	Annualized 5Yr / Pct	Incl. in Returns: Dividend Yield	Expense Ratio
MUN	PIMCO Short Duration Muni Inc D	PSDDX	**B**	(800) 426-0107	**C- / 4.1**	0.43	0.56	0.63 /58	0.51 /39	0.56 /19	0.86	0.73
MUN	PIMCO Short Duration Muni Inc Inst	PSDIX	**A-**	(800) 426-0107	**C / 5.3**	0.52	0.75	1.03 /67	0.91 /50	0.97 /26	1.26	0.33
MUN	PIMCO Short Duration Muni Inc P	PSDPX	**B+**	(800) 426-0107	**C / 5.0**	0.50	0.70	0.93 /65	0.81 /47	0.87 /23	1.16	0.43
* GEI	PIMCO Short Term A	PSHAX	**C-**	(800) 426-0107	**D / 1.7**	-0.38	0.41	0.20 /44	0.57 /34	0.95 /20	1.52	0.71
GEI	PIMCO Short Term Admin	PSFAX	**C+**	(800) 426-0107	**C- / 3.3**	-0.38	0.41	0.20 /44	0.57 /34	0.95 /20	1.55	0.71
GEI	PIMCO Short Term C	PFTCX	**C**	(800) 426-0107	**D+ / 2.8**	-0.45	0.26	-0.09 /30	0.27 /30	0.65 /18	1.25	1.01
GEI	PIMCO Short Term D	PSHDX	**C+**	(800) 426-0107	**C- / 3.3**	-0.38	0.41	0.20 /44	0.57 /34	0.95 /20	1.55	0.71
GEI	PIMCO Short Term Inst	PTSHX	**C+**	(800) 426-0107	**C- / 3.8**	-0.32	0.53	0.45 /49	0.82 /39	1.20 /22	1.80	0.46
GEI	PIMCO Short Term P	PTSPX	**C+**	(800) 426-0107	**C- / 3.6**	-0.34	0.48	0.35 /47	0.72 /37	1.10 /21	1.70	0.56
GEI	PIMCO Short Term R	PTSRX	**C**	(800) 426-0107	**D+ / 2.9**	-0.44	0.29	-0.04 /31	0.32 /30	0.70 /18	1.30	0.96
MTG	PIMCO StkPlus Intl (DH) A	PIPAX	**E**	(800) 426-0107	**D- / 1.3**	-7.05	-0.60	-15.26 / 0	3.56 /81	6.13 /77	6.37	1.16
MTG	PIMCO StkPlus Intl (DH) C	PIPCX	**E**	(800) 426-0107	**D / 1.6**	-7.23	-0.83	-15.85 / 0	2.86 /75	5.34 /74	6.58	1.91
MTG	PIMCO StkPlus Intl (DH) D	PIPDX	**D-**	(800) 426-0107	**C- / 3.3**	-7.04	-0.45	-15.27 / 0	3.56 /81	6.13 /77	6.57	1.16
MTG	PIMCO StkPlus Intl (DH) I	PISIX	**D-**	(800) 426-0107	**C- / 4.2**	-6.89	-0.32	-14.79 / 0	4.01 /84	6.55 /80	6.63	0.76
USS	PIMCO StocksPLUS Short A	PSSAX	**E-**	(800) 426-0107	**E- / 0.0**	-1.91	-7.63	-6.53 / 3	-12.27 / 0	-10.75 / 0	4.18	1.04
USS	PIMCO StocksPLUS Short C	PSSCX	**E-**	(800) 426-0107	**E- / 0.0**	-2.07	-8.02	-6.85 / 2	-12.93 / 0	-11.38 / 0	3.89	1.79
USS	PIMCO StocksPLUS Short D	PSSDX	**E-**	(800) 426-0107	**E- / 0.0**	-1.92	-7.61	-6.43 / 3	-12.32 / 0	-10.76 / 0	4.30	1.04
USS	PIMCO StocksPLUS Short I	PSTIX	**E-**	(800) 426-0107	**E- / 0.0**	-1.86	-7.52	-5.91 / 3	-11.98 / 0	-10.41 / 0	4.48	0.64
USS	PIMCO StocksPLUS Short P	PSPLX	**E-**	(800) 426-0107	**E- / 0.0**	-1.86	-7.56	-5.96 / 3	-12.06 / 0	-10.51 / 0	4.42	0.74
* GEI	PIMCO Total Return A	PTTAX	**D**	(800) 426-0107	**D+ / 2.9**	1.68	2.05	-0.11 /30	1.12 /45	3.25 /49	2.72	0.85
GEI	PIMCO Total Return Admin	PTRAX	**C-**	(800) 426-0107	**C / 5.0**	1.72	2.12	0.03 /35	1.26 /47	3.40 /52	2.95	0.71
GEI	PIMCO Total Return C	PTTCX	**D**	(800) 426-0107	**C- / 3.3**	1.50	1.68	-0.84 /23	0.37 /31	2.49 /38	2.09	1.60
GEI	PIMCO Total Return D	PTTDX	**C-**	(800) 426-0107	**C / 4.9**	1.71	2.10	-0.01 /31	1.22 /47	3.36 /51	2.92	0.75
GEI	PIMCO Total Return Fund II P	PMTPX	**C-**	(800) 426-0107	**C / 5.1**	2.61	2.25	0.53 /50	1.17 /46	3.07 /46	2.60	0.60
GEI	PIMCO Total Return II Admin	PRADX	**C-**	(800) 426-0107	**C / 4.8**	2.57	2.18	0.38 /47	1.02 /43	2.91 /44	2.45	0.75
GEI	PIMCO Total Return II Inst	PMBIX	**C-**	(800) 426-0107	**C / 5.3**	2.63	2.30	0.63 /52	1.27 /48	3.17 /48	2.70	0.50
GEI	PIMCO Total Return III Admin	PRFAX	**D+**	(800) 426-0107	**C / 4.7**	1.81	1.91	-0.32 /28	1.14 /45	2.95 /44	2.89	0.76
GEI	PIMCO Total Return III Inst	PTSAX	**C-**	(800) 426-0107	**C / 5.2**	1.87	2.04	-0.08 /30	1.39 /50	3.21 /48	3.14	0.51
GEI	PIMCO Total Return III P	PRAPX	**C-**	(800) 426-0107	**C / 5.0**	1.85	1.99	-0.18 /29	1.29 /48	3.10 /47	3.04	0.61
GEI	PIMCO Total Return Inst	PTTRX	**C-**	(800) 426-0107	**C / 5.5**	1.78	2.24	0.28 /45	1.52 /53	3.66 /56	3.20	0.46
COI	PIMCO Total Return IV A	PTUZX	**D**	(800) 426-0107	**D / 1.9**	2.05	2.35	-0.14 /30	0.76 /38	--	1.65	0.85
COI	PIMCO Total Return IV C	PTUCX	**D**	(800) 426-0107	**D+ / 2.9**	1.89	1.99	-0.87 /23	0.07 /26	--	0.98	1.60
COI	PIMCO Total Return IV Inst	PTUIX	**C-**	(800) 426-0107	**C / 4.9**	2.14	2.52	0.21 /44	1.11 /45	--	2.06	0.50
COI	PIMCO Total Return IV P	PTUPX	**C-**	(800) 426-0107	**C / 4.7**	2.11	2.46	0.09 /41	1.01 /43	--	1.94	0.60
GEI	PIMCO Total Return P	PTTPX	**C-**	(800) 426-0107	**C / 5.3**	1.75	2.19	0.18 /44	1.42 /51	3.55 /54	3.10	0.56
GEI	PIMCO Total Return R	PTRRX	**D+**	(800) 426-0107	**C / 4.3**	1.62	1.93	-0.35 /28	0.87 /40	3.00 /45	2.57	1.10
GEI	PIMCO Unconstrained Bond A	PUBAX	**D**	(800) 426-0107	**E / 0.3**	-0.70	0.05	-3.50 /10	-1.45 / 6	0.77 /19	5.72	1.30
GEI	PIMCO Unconstrained Bond Admin	PUBFX	**U**	(800) 426-0107	**U /**	-0.68	0.12	-3.36 /10	--	--	6.09	1.15
GEI	PIMCO Unconstrained Bond C	PUBCX	**D**	(800) 426-0107	**E / 0.4**	-0.88	-0.31	-4.16 / 7	-2.15 / 4	0.07 /14	5.12	2.05
GEI	PIMCO Unconstrained Bond D	PUBDX	**D**	(800) 426-0107	**E+ / 0.6**	-0.70	0.05	-3.50 /10	-1.45 / 6	0.77 /19	5.94	1.30
GEI	PIMCO Unconstrained Bond Inst	PFIUX	**D**	(800) 426-0107	**E+ / 0.7**	-0.61	0.25	-3.12 /11	-1.06 / 8	1.17 /22	6.36	0.90
GEI	PIMCO Unconstrained Bond P	PUCPX	**D**	(800) 426-0107	**E+ / 0.7**	-0.63	0.20	-3.21 /11	-1.15 / 8	1.07 /21	6.26	1.00
GEI	PIMCO Unconstrained Bond R	PUBRX	**D**	(800) 426-0107	**E / 0.5**	-0.76	-0.07	-3.65 / 9	-1.68 / 5	0.52 /17	5.68	1.55
MUN	PIMCO Unconstrained Tax Mnged Bd	ATMAX	**D**	(800) 426-0107	**E+ / 0.6**	-0.65	1.84	-1.36 /19	-0.51 /11	0.93 /25	4.45	1.10
MUN	PIMCO Unconstrained Tax Mnged Bd	ATMCX	**D**	(800) 426-0107	**E+ / 0.8**	-0.83	1.47	-2.04 /15	-1.21 / 7	0.26 /17	3.82	1.85
MUN	PIMCO Unconstrained Tax Mnged Bd	ATMDX	**D**	(800) 426-0107	**D- / 1.3**	-0.65	1.84	-1.36 /19	-0.51 /11	0.93 /25	4.63	1.10
MUN	PIMCO Unconstrained Tax Mnged Bd	PUTIX	**D**	(800) 426-0107	**D / 1.7**	-0.56	2.03	-0.97 /22	-0.12 /15	1.32 /32	5.03	0.70
MUN	PIMCO Unconstrained Tax Mnged Bd	PUTPX	**D**	(800) 426-0107	**D / 1.6**	-0.58	1.98	-1.07 /21	-0.22 /14	1.22 /30	4.93	0.80
EM	PIMCO VIT Emerging Mkt Bond Adm		**D-**	(800) 426-0107	**C- / 3.2**	4.82	6.31	0.61 /51	-0.65 /10	3.68 /56	5.25	1.00
* MUN	Pioneer AMT-Free Muni A	PBMFX	**C+**	(800) 225-6292	**A / 9.3**	1.97	4.26	5.10 /98	4.38 /97	7.80 /98	3.32	0.85
MUN	Pioneer AMT-Free Muni C	MNBCX	**C+**	(800) 225-6292	**A / 9.5**	1.80	3.90	4.34 /96	3.61 /93	6.97 /96	2.75	1.60
MUN	Pioneer AMT-Free Muni Y	PBYMX	**B-**	(800) 225-6292	**A+ / 9.8**	1.97	4.40	5.31 /98	4.64 /98	8.05 /98	3.74	0.65

● Denotes fund is closed to new investors
* Denotes fund is included in Section II

RISK			NET ASSETS		ASSET							FUND MANAGER		MINIMUM		LOADS	
Risk Rating/Pts	3 Yr Avg Standard Deviation	Avg Duration	NAV As of 3/31/16	Total $(Mil)	Cash %	Gov. Bond %	Muni. Bond %	Corp. Bond %	Other %	Portfolio Turnover Ratio	Avg Coupon Rate	Manager Quality Pct	Manager Tenure (Years)	Initial Purch. $	Additional Purch. $	Front End Load	Back End Load
A+ / 9.7	0.7	1.7	8.47	3	7	0	92	0	1	28	3.2	60	2	1,000	50	0.0	0.0
A+ / 9.7	0.7	1.7	8.47	62	7	0	92	0	1	28	3.2	79	2	1,000,000	0	0.0	0.0
A+ / 9.7	0.7	1.7	8.47	68	7	0	92	0	1	28	3.2	76	2	1,000,000	0	0.0	0.0
A / 9.3	1.0	0.3	9.66	619	9	0	0	71	20	283	2.6	83	5	1,000	50	2.3	0.0
A / 9.3	1.0	0.3	9.66	1,407	9	0	0	71	20	283	2.6	84	5	1,000,000	0	0.0	0.0
A / 9.3	1.0	0.3	9.66	178	9	0	0	71	20	283	2.6	76	5	1,000	50	0.0	0.0
A / 9.3	1.0	0.3	9.66	431	9	0	0	71	20	283	2.6	84	5	1,000	50	0.0	0.0
A / 9.3	1.0	0.3	9.66	8,464	9	0	0	71	20	283	2.6	87	5	1,000,000	0	0.0	0.0
A / 9.3	1.0	0.3	9.66	1,155	9	0	0	71	20	283	2.6	86	5	1,000,000	0	0.0	0.0
A / 9.3	1.0	0.3	9.66	104	9	0	0	71	20	283	2.6	77	5	0	0	0.0	0.0
E- / 0.0	14.6	5.6	6.33	380	18	60	0	20	2	814	4.7	94	1	1,000	50	3.8	0.0
E- / 0.0	14.5	5.6	5.90	198	18	60	0	20	2	814	4.7	90	1	1,000	50	0.0	0.0
E- / 0.0	14.6	5.6	6.34	293	18	60	0	20	2	814	4.7	94	1	1,000	50	0.0	0.0
E- / 0.0	14.6	5.6	6.62	1,402	18	60	0	20	2	814	4.7	96	1	1,000,000	0	0.0	0.0
E / 0.3	9.3	5.9	10.27	54	14	42	1	35	8	403	0.0	0	2	1,000	50	3.8	0.0
E / 0.3	9.2	5.9	9.92	20	14	42	1	35	8	403	0.0	0	2	1,000	50	0.0	0.0
E / 0.3	9.1	5.9	10.24	44	14	42	1	35	8	403	0.0	0	2	1,000	50	0.0	0.0
E / 0.3	9.3	5.9	10.55	1,689	14	42	1	35	8	403	0.0	0	2	1,000,000	0	0.0	0.0
E / 0.3	9.3	5.9	10.55	58	14	42	1	35	8	403	0.0	0	2	1,000,000	0	0.0	0.0
C / 4.3	3.8	4.6	10.18	7,657	0	43	5	16	36	265	3.3	15	2	1,000	50	3.8	0.0
C / 4.3	3.8	4.6	10.18	6,252	0	43	5	16	36	265	3.3	17	2	1,000,000	0	0.0	0.0
C / 4.3	3.8	4.6	10.18	4,054	0	43	5	16	36	265	3.3	9	2	1,000	50	0.0	0.0
C / 4.3	3.8	4.6	10.18	5,386	0	43	5	16	36	265	3.3	17	2	1,000	50	0.0	0.0
C / 5.2	3.4	4.8	9.68	11	0	23	2	16	59	363	4.1	18	2	1,000,000	0	0.0	0.0
C / 5.2	3.4	4.8	9.68	14	0	23	2	16	59	363	4.1	16	2	1,000,000	0	0.0	0.0
C / 5.2	3.4	4.8	9.68	781	0	23	2	16	59	363	4.1	20	2	1,000,000	0	0.0	0.0
C / 4.5	3.7	4.5	9.04	58	0	33	5	18	44	291	3.8	16	2	1,000,000	0	0.0	0.0
C / 4.5	3.7	4.5	9.04	949	0	33	5	18	44	291	3.8	21	2	1,000,000	0	0.0	0.0
C / 4.5	3.7	4.5	9.04	51	0	33	5	18	44	291	3.8	19	2	1,000,000	0	0.0	0.0
C / 4.3	3.8	4.6	10.18	58,520	0	43	5	16	36	265	3.3	21	2	1,000,000	0	0.0	0.0
C / 4.8	3.6	4.6	10.37	14	11	45	6	16	22	245	2.9	19	2	1,000	50	3.8	0.0
C / 4.8	3.6	4.6	10.37	3	11	45	6	16	22	245	2.9	11	2	1,000	50	0.0	0.0
C / 4.8	3.6	4.6	10.37	1,340	11	45	6	16	22	245	2.9	27	2	1,000,000	0	0.0	0.0
C / 4.8	3.6	4.6	10.37	N/A	11	45	6	16	22	245	2.9	25	2	1,000,000	0	0.0	0.0
C / 4.3	3.8	4.6	10.18	4,618	0	43	5	16	36	265	3.3	19	2	1,000,000	0	0.0	0.0
C / 4.3	3.8	4.6	10.18	1,429	0	43	5	16	36	265	3.3	12	2	0	0	0.0	0.0
C+ / 6.2	3.1	2.9	10.19	314	0	36	2	32	30	270	4.5	10	2	1,000	50	3.8	0.0
U /	N/A	2.9	10.19	2	0	36	2	32	30	270	4.5	N/A	2	1,000,000	0	0.0	0.0
C+ / 6.2	3.1	2.9	10.20	347	0	36	2	32	30	270	4.5	8	2	1,000	50	0.0	0.0
C+ / 6.2	3.1	2.9	10.19	127	0	36	2	32	30	270	4.5	10	2	1,000	50	0.0	0.0
C+ / 6.2	3.1	2.9	10.19	2,852	0	36	2	32	30	270	4.5	14	2	1,000,000	0	0.0	0.0
C+ / 6.1	3.1	2.9	10.19	1,150	0	36	2	32	30	270	4.5	13	2	1,000,000	0	0.0	0.0
C+ / 6.1	3.1	2.9	10.19	8	0	36	2	32	30	270	4.5	9	2	0	0	0.0	0.0
C+ / 6.2	3.1	-0.9	9.91	20	14	8	75	0	3	297	4.1	20	1	1,000	50	3.8	0.0
C+ / 6.2	3.1	-0.9	9.91	7	14	8	75	0	3	297	4.1	11	1	1,000	50	0.0	0.0
C+ / 6.2	3.1	-0.9	9.91	16	14	8	75	0	3	297	4.1	20	1	1,000	50	0.0	0.0
C+ / 6.3	3.1	-0.9	9.91	78	14	8	75	0	3	297	4.1	29	1	1,000,000	0	0.0	0.0
C+ / 6.2	3.1	-0.9	9.91	41	14	8	75	0	3	297	4.1	27	1	1,000,000	0	0.0	0.0
E / 0.4	8.5	5.3	12.11	220	1	53	0	44	2	28	5.8	42	7	0	0	0.0	0.0
D+ / 2.6	5.1	6.9	14.77	727	1	0	98	0	1	29	4.8	30	10	1,000	100	4.5	0.0
D+ / 2.6	5.1	6.9	14.65	60	1	0	98	0	1	29	4.8	15	10	1,000	500	0.0	0.0
D+ / 2.6	5.1	6.9	14.72	327	1	0	98	0	1	29	4.8	37	10	5,000,000	0	0.0	0.0

99 Pct = Best 0 Pct = Worst Fund Type	Fund Name	Ticker Symbol	Overall Investment Rating	Phone	PERFORMANCE Performance Rating/Pts	Total Return % through 3/31/16 3 Mo	6 Mo	1Yr / Pct	Annualized 3Yr / Pct	5Yr / Pct	Incl. in Returns Dividend Yield	Expense Ratio
* GEI	Pioneer Bond Fund A	PIOBX	**C+**	(800) 225-6292	**C / 4.7**	1.83	1.65	0.51 / 50	2.39 / 69	4.03 / 62	2.63	0.93
GEI	Pioneer Bond Fund C	PCYBX	**B-**	(800) 225-6292	**C / 5.3**	1.66	1.29	-0.26 / 28	1.56 / 53	3.16 / 48	2.01	1.63
COI	Pioneer Bond Fund K	PBFKX	**A**	(800) 225-6292	**B- / 7.2**	1.82	1.74	0.79 / 55	2.70 / 73	4.24 / 65	3.13	0.47
GEI	Pioneer Bond Fund R	PBFRX	**B+**	(800) 225-6292	**C+ / 6.1**	1.66	1.42	0.17 / 43	2.04 / 62	3.65 / 56	2.50	1.21
GEI	Pioneer Bond Fund Y	PICYX	**A**	(800) 225-6292	**B- / 7.1**	1.91	1.79	0.76 / 54	2.63 / 72	4.26 / 65	3.03	0.58
GL	Pioneer Dynamic Credit A	RCRAX	**D**	(800) 225-6292	**E+ / 0.9**	2.18	-0.34	-1.60 / 18	0.19 / 29	--	4.19	1.14
GL	Pioneer Dynamic Credit C	RCRCX	**D**	(800) 225-6292	**D- / 1.2**	2.10	-0.61	-2.24 / 15	-0.56 / 11	--	3.63	1.90
GL	Pioneer Dynamic Credit Y	RCRYX	**D+**	(800) 225-6292	**C- / 3.2**	2.23	-0.10	-1.29 / 20	0.48 / 33	--	4.69	0.93
COH	Pioneer Floating Rate Fund Class A	FLARX	**C-**	(800) 225-6292	**C- / 3.3**	1.27	0.06	0.36 / 47	1.77 / 57	3.05 / 46	3.23	1.10
COH	Pioneer Floating Rate Fund Class C	FLRCX	**C**	(800) 225-6292	**C- / 4.1**	1.09	-0.28	-0.34 / 28	1.04 / 43	2.30 / 35	2.67	1.84
LP	Pioneer Floating Rate Fund Class K	FLRKX	**A-**	(800) 225-6292	**C+ / 6.1**	1.36	0.11	0.75 / 54	2.12 / 64	3.26 / 49	3.78	0.73
COH	Pioneer Floating Rate Fund Class Y	FLYRX	**B+**	(800) 225-6292	**C+ / 6.1**	1.36	0.11	0.77 / 55	2.14 / 64	3.41 / 52	3.78	0.82
GL	Pioneer Global High Yield A	PGHYX	**E**	(800) 225-6292	**E / 0.3**	2.44	-0.05	-5.29 / 4	-1.55 / 6	1.37 / 24	5.94	1.17
GL	Pioneer Global High Yield C	PGYCX	**E**	(800) 225-6292	**E / 0.3**	2.27	-0.40	-5.97 / 3	-2.22 / 4	0.70 / 18	5.49	1.87
GL	Pioneer Global High Yield Y	GHYYX	**E+**	(800) 225-6292	**E+ / 0.6**	2.40	-0.06	-5.18 / 5	-1.28 / 7	1.67 / 27	6.56	0.87
GL	Pioneer Global Multisector Income A	PGABX	**D**	(800) 225-6292	**D / 1.6**	2.63	2.09	-0.36 / 27	0.77 / 38	2.42 / 37	3.39	2.67
GL	Pioneer Global Multisector Income C	PGCBX	**D**	(800) 225-6292	**D+ / 2.4**	2.40	1.63	-1.24 / 20	-0.13 / 15	1.54 / 26	2.64	2.56
GL	Pioneer Global Multisector Income Y	PGYBX	**D+**	(800) 225-6292	**C / 4.7**	2.67	2.21	-0.17 / 30	1.01 / 43	2.73 / 41	3.79	1.39
MUH	Pioneer High Income Municipal A	PIMAX	**C-**	(800) 225-6292	**B+ / 8.5**	2.55	5.83	6.18 / 99	2.90 / 87	6.59 / 95	5.13	0.89
MUH	Pioneer High Income Municipal C	HICMX	**C**	(800) 225-6292	**B+ / 8.9**	2.36	5.44	5.38 / 98	2.12 / 78	5.80 / 91	4.63	1.65
MUH	Pioneer High Income Municipal Y	HIMYX	**C+**	(800) 225-6292	**A / 9.5**	2.62	5.82	6.24 / 99	3.03 / 88	6.75 / 95	5.55	0.71
* COH	Pioneer High Yield A	TAHYX	**E**	(800) 225-6292	**E+ / 0.9**	1.70	-0.11	-6.62 / 2	0.97 / 42	2.96 / 44	4.99	1.17
COH	Pioneer High Yield C	PYICX	**E+**	(800) 225-6292	**D- / 1.2**	1.52	-0.41	-7.18 / 2	0.28 / 30	2.27 / 35	4.44	1.89
COH	Pioneer High Yield R	TYHRX	**E+**	(800) 225-6292	**D / 1.6**	1.65	-0.21	-6.87 / 2	0.65 / 36	2.62 / 39	4.79	1.51
COH	Pioneer High Yield Y	TYHYX	**D-**	(800) 225-6292	**C- / 3.3**	1.78	0.05	-6.23 / 3	1.31 / 49	3.30 / 50	5.53	0.88
* GL	Pioneer Multi-Asset Ultrasht Inc A	MAFRX	**C-**	(800) 225-6292	**D / 1.8**	0.09	0.11	0.40 / 48	0.62 / 35	--	1.18	0.63
GL	Pioneer Multi-Asset Ultrasht Inc C	MCFRX	**C+**	(800) 225-6292	**D+ / 2.9**	0.12	-0.04	0.11 / 41	0.33 / 30	--	0.92	0.94
GL	Pioneer Multi-Asset Ultrasht Inc C2	MAUCX	**C+**	(800) 225-6292	**C- / 3.0**	0.11	0.05	0.10 / 41	0.33 / 30	--	0.91	0.95
GL	Pioneer Multi-Asset Ultrasht Inc K	MAUKX	**B**	(800) 225-6292	**C- / 4.0**	0.24	0.21	0.63 / 52	0.87 / 40	--	1.44	0.41
GL	Pioneer Multi-Asset Ultrasht Inc Y	MYFRX	**B-**	(800) 225-6292	**C- / 3.8**	0.22	0.27	0.54 / 50	0.77 / 38	--	1.34	0.51
GEI	Pioneer Short Term Income A	STABX	**C+**	(800) 225-6292	**D+ / 2.9**	0.36	0.32	0.65 / 52	0.96 / 42	1.77 / 28	1.55	0.82
GEI	Pioneer Short Term Income C	PSHCX	**C+**	(800) 225-6292	**C- / 3.6**	0.30	0.20	0.31 / 46	0.65 / 36	1.27 / 23	1.36	1.06
COI	Pioneer Short Term Income C2	STIIX	**C+**	(800) 225-6292	**C- / 3.6**	0.20	0.11	0.32 / 46	0.71 / 37	1.31 / 23	1.37	1.04
COI	Pioneer Short Term Income K	STIKX	**B+**	(800) 225-6292	**C / 4.5**	0.33	0.37	0.97 / 58	1.10 / 45	1.86 / 30	1.92	0.50
GEI	Pioneer Short Term Income Y	PSHYX	**B+**	(800) 225-6292	**C / 4.5**	0.30	0.32	0.75 / 54	1.17 / 46	2.02 / 31	1.81	0.60
* GES	Pioneer Strategic Income A	PSRAX	**D+**	(800) 225-6292	**C- / 3.1**	2.05	1.45	-0.70 / 24	1.60 / 54	3.65 / 56	3.35	1.05
GES	Pioneer Strategic Income C	PSRCX	**C-**	(800) 225-6292	**C- / 3.9**	1.81	1.12	-1.45 / 19	0.88 / 40	2.93 / 44	2.83	1.72
GEN	Pioneer Strategic Income K	STRKX	**C**	(800) 225-6292	**C+ / 6.1**	2.16	1.68	-0.26 / 28	2.04 / 62	3.97 / 61	3.95	0.61
GES	Pioneer Strategic Income R	STIRX	**C-**	(800) 225-6292	**C / 4.6**	1.95	1.28	-1.05 / 21	1.23 / 47	3.29 / 50	3.18	1.38
GES	Pioneer Strategic Income Y	STRYX	**C**	(800) 225-6292	**C+ / 5.8**	2.04	1.52	-0.48 / 26	1.88 / 59	3.94 / 61	3.83	0.73
MM	Plan Investment Government/REPO	PIFXX	**C**	(800) 441-7762	**D+ / 2.3**	0.05	0.06	0.06 / 40	0.03 / 23	0.04 / 12	0.06	0.30
MM	Plan Investment Money Market Port	PIMXX	**C**	(800) 441-7762	**D+ / 2.5**	0.06	0.10	0.12 / 42	0.06 / 26	0.07 / 14	0.12	0.25
GEI	Plan Investment Ultrashort Dur Bd	PIFDX	**C+**	(800) 621-9215	**C- / 3.4**	0.37	0.37	0.61 / 51	0.45 / 32	--	0.61	0.43
GEI	Plan Investment Ultrashort Dur Gvt	PIFUX	**C+**	(800) 621-9215	**D+ / 2.8**	0.34	0.13	0.31 / 46	0.18 / 28	--	0.16	0.58
GEI	PMC Core Fixed Income Fund	PMFIX	**C-**	(866) 762-7338	**C / 5.1**	2.50	1.54	-0.01 / 31	1.33 / 49	3.08 / 46	1.37	1.43
MM	PNC Advtg Inst Money Market Inst	PABXX	**C**	(800) 551-2145	**D+ / 2.5**	0.04	0.05	0.08 / 40	0.06 / 26	0.06 / 14	0.08	0.22
MM	PNC Advtg Inst Treasury MM Adv	PAYXX	**U**	(800) 551-2145	**U /**	--	--	--	--	--	0.02	0.36
MM	PNC Advtg Inst Treasury MM Inst	PAIXX	**U**	(800) 551-2145	**U /**	--	--	--	--	--	0.02	0.26
MM	PNC Advtg Inst Treasury MM Svc	PAEXX	**U**	(800) 551-2145	**U /**	--	--	--	--	--	0.02	0.51
GES	PNC Bond A	PAAAX	**C-**	(800) 551-2145	**C- / 3.8**	2.71	2.12	0.72 / 54	1.69 / 56	2.96 / 44	1.74	0.86
GES	PNC Bond C	PFDCX	**C**	(800) 551-2145	**C / 4.5**	2.53	1.84	0.03 / 35	0.85 / 40	2.14 / 33	1.05	1.58
GES	PNC Bond I	PFDIX	**B-**	(800) 551-2145	**C+ / 6.3**	2.87	2.31	0.99 / 58	1.84 / 58	3.17 / 48	1.99	0.58

● Denotes fund is closed to new investors
* Denotes fund is included in Section II

RISK			NET ASSETS		ASSET							FUND MANAGER		MINIMUM		LOADS	
Risk Rating/Pts	3 Yr Avg Standard Deviation	Avg Duration	NAV As of 3/31/16	Total $(Mil)	Cash %	Gov. Bond %	Muni. Bond %	Corp. Bond %	Other %	Portfolio Turnover Ratio	Avg Coupon Rate	Manager Quality Pct	Manager Tenure (Years)	Initial Purch. $	Additional Purch. $	Front End Load	Back End Load
B / 7.9	2.5	4.6	9.62	1,145	3	8	2	46	41	81	3.8	85	18	1,000	100	4.5	0.0
B / 7.9	2.5	4.6	9.51	134	3	8	2	46	41	81	3.8	53	18	1,000	500	0.0	0.0
B / 8.0	2.4	4.6	9.61	314	3	8	2	46	41	81	3.8	91	18	5,000,000	0	0.0	0.0
B / 7.9	2.4	4.6	9.70	148	3	8	2	46	41	81	3.8	76	18	0	0	0.0	0.0
B / 7.9	2.5	4.6	9.53	1,945	3	8	2	46	41	81	3.8	88	18	5,000,000	0	0.0	0.0
C / 5.1	3.4	3.7	8.99	47	4	0	0	64	32	81	5.2	75	5	1,000	100	4.5	0.0
C / 5.0	3.5	3.7	8.97	44	4	0	0	64	32	81	5.2	42	5	1,000	500	0.0	0.0
C / 5.1	3.4	3.7	9.03	203	4	0	0	64	32	81	5.2	83	5	5,000,000	0	0.0	0.0
B / 8.0	1.9	1.2	6.63	179	4	1	0	62	33	24	4.4	92	9	1,000	100	4.5	0.0
B / 7.9	2.0	1.2	6.64	88	4	1	0	62	33	24	4.4	84	9	1,000	500	0.0	0.0
B+ / 8.5	2.0	1.2	6.63	1	4	1	0	62	33	24	4.4	94	9	5,000,000	0	0.0	0.0
B / 8.0	1.9	1.2	6.65	362	4	1	0	62	33	24	4.4	94	9	5,000,000	0	0.0	0.0
D- / 1.4	6.2	3.6	8.23	214	0	5	0	76	19	32	6.5	17	15	1,000	100	4.5	0.0
D- / 1.4	6.1	3.6	8.21	199	0	5	0	76	19	32	6.5	10	15	1,000	500	0.0	0.0
D- / 1.5	6.1	3.6	8.08	310	0	5	0	76	19	32	6.5	23	15	5,000,000	0	0.0	0.0
C- / 4.2	3.9	5.1	10.34	13	5	42	3	29	21	34	4.3	87	9	1,000	100	4.5	0.0
C- / 4.2	3.9	5.1	10.37	4	5	42	3	29	21	34	4.3	59	9	1,000	500	0.0	0.0
C- / 4.2	3.9	5.1	10.43	12	5	42	3	29	21	34	4.3	90	9	5,000,000	0	0.0	0.0
D / 1.8	5.1	7.0	7.45	266	0	0	100	0	0	29	6.5	16	10	1,000	100	4.5	0.0
D / 1.7	5.2	7.0	7.45	156	0	0	100	0	0	29	6.5	9	10	1,000	500	0.0	0.0
D / 1.8	5.1	7.0	7.35	153	0	0	100	0	0	29	6.5	17	10	5,000,000	0	0.0	0.0
E+ / 0.8	6.4	3.4	8.80	579	2	1	0	64	33	32	5.4	35	9	1,000	100	4.5	0.0
E+ / 0.8	6.4	3.4	8.99	265	2	1	0	64	33	32	5.4	18	9	1,000	500	0.0	0.0
E+ / 0.8	6.3	3.4	9.96	30	2	1	0	64	33	32	5.4	26	9	0	0	0.0	0.0
E+ / 0.8	6.4	3.4	8.81	232	2	1	0	64	33	32	5.4	46	9	5,000,000	0	0.0	0.0
A+ / 9.9	0.4	0.3	9.92	673	5	3	0	32	60	45	2.0	84	N/A	1,000	100	2.5	0.0
A+ / 9.9	0.3	0.3	9.91	523	5	3	0	32	60	45	2.0	78	N/A	1,000	500	0.0	0.0
A+ / 9.9	0.4	0.3	9.91	10	5	3	0	32	60	45	2.0	78	N/A	1,000	500	0.0	0.0
A+ / 9.9	0.4	0.3	9.93	5	5	3	0	32	60	45	2.0	88	N/A	5,000,000	0	0.0	0.0
A+ / 9.9	0.3	0.3	9.93	1,439	5	3	0	32	60	45	2.0	87	N/A	5,000,000	0	0.0	0.0
A+ / 9.8	0.5	0.7	9.52	220	2	9	0	38	51	48	2.2	86	10	1,000	100	2.5	0.0
A+ / 9.8	0.6	0.7	9.50	103	2	9	0	38	51	48	2.2	79	10	1,000	500	0.0	0.0
A+ / 9.8	0.6	0.7	9.50	4	2	9	0	38	51	48	2.2	81	10	1,000	500	0.0	0.0
A+ / 9.8	0.5	0.7	9.52	17	2	9	0	38	51	48	2.2	88	10	5,000,000	0	0.0	0.0
A+ / 9.8	0.6	0.7	9.49	277	2	9	0	38	51	48	2.2	88	10	5,000,000	0	0.0	0.0
C+ / 5.6	3.3	4.5	10.33	1,274	0	11	3	50	36	62	4.6	61	17	1,000	100	4.5	0.0
C / 5.5	3.3	4.5	10.10	946	0	11	3	50	36	62	4.6	36	17	1,000	500	0.0	0.0
C / 5.5	3.3	4.5	10.35	214	0	11	3	50	36	62	4.6	80	17	5,000,000	0	0.0	0.0
C / 5.4	3.3	4.5	10.49	224	0	11	3	50	36	62	4.6	46	17	0	0	0.0	0.0
C+ / 5.7	3.2	4.5	10.32	3,855	0	11	3	50	36	62	4.6	76	17	5,000,000	0	0.0	0.0
A+ / 9.9	N/A	N/A	1.00	171	100	0	0	0	0	0	0.1	66	N/A	0	0	0.0	0.0
A+ / 9.9	N/A	N/A	1.00	291	100	0	0	0	0	0	0.1	67	N/A	0	0	0.0	0.0
A+ / 9.9	0.3	0.7	9.97	353	1	15	2	27	55	160	0.0	77	4	1,000,000	0	0.0	0.0
A+ / 9.9	0.3	0.8	10.00	54	3	45	0	0	52	88	0.0	62	4	1,000,000	0	0.0	0.0
C+ / 5.8	3.2	N/A	16.78	250	5	24	0	36	35	132	0.0	24	7	1,000	50	0.0	0.0
A+ / 9.9	N/A	N/A	1.00	905	100	0	0	0	0	0	0.1	69	N/A	3,000,000	0	0.0	0.0
U /	N/A	N/A	1.00	70	100	0	0	0	0	0	0.0	N/A	N/A	3,000,000	0	0.0	0.0
U /	N/A	N/A	1.00	305	100	0	0	0	0	0	0.0	N/A	N/A	3,000,000	0	0.0	0.0
U /	N/A	N/A	1.00	1	100	0	0	0	0	0	0.0	N/A	N/A	3,000,000	0	0.0	0.0
B- / 7.0	2.9	5.2	10.46	3	3	47	0	23	27	66	0.0	39	14	1,000	50	4.5	0.0
B- / 7.1	2.8	5.2	10.43	N/A	3	47	0	23	27	66	0.0	19	14	1,000	50	0.0	0.0
B- / 7.0	2.9	5.2	10.44	84	3	47	0	23	27	66	0.0	44	14	0	0	0.0	0.0

Fund Type	Fund Name (99 Pct = Best, 0 Pct = Worst)	Ticker Symbol	Overall Investment Rating	Phone	PERFORMANCE: Performance Rating/Pts	Total Return % through 3/31/16: 3 Mo	6 Mo	1Yr / Pct	Annualized: 3Yr / Pct	Annualized: 5Yr / Pct	Incl. in Returns: Dividend Yield	Expense Ratio
MM	PNC Government Money Market A	PGAXX	**C**	(800) 551-2145	**D / 2.1**	0.02	0.03	0.04 /38	0.03 /23	0.02 / 9	0.04	0.61
MM	PNC Government Money Market Adv	PAGXX	**U**	(800) 551-2145	**U /**	0.02	0.03	--	--	--	0.00	N/A
MM	PNC Government Money Market I	PKIXX	**C**	(800) 551-2145	**D / 2.1**	0.02	0.03	0.04 /38	0.03 /23	0.02 / 9	0.04	0.36
USS	PNC Government Mortgage A	POMAX	**C-**	(800) 551-2145	**C- / 3.3**	1.55	1.15	1.10 /60	1.51 /52	2.20 /34	2.17	1.01
USS	PNC Government Mortgage C	PGTCX	**C**	(800) 551-2145	**C- / 4.1**	1.37	0.66	0.34 /47	0.79 /39	1.44 /25	1.53	1.73
USS	PNC Government Mortgage I	PTGIX	**B+**	(800) 551-2145	**C+ / 6.0**	1.72	1.27	1.46 /66	1.80 /58	2.47 /37	2.52	0.73
COH	PNC High Yield Bond Fund A	PAHBX	**E**	(800) 551-2145	**E+ / 0.8**	4.01	0.05	-5.68 / 4	0.38 /31	3.69 /56	5.40	1.19
COH	PNC High Yield Bond Fund I	PIHBX	**D-**	(800) 551-2145	**D+ / 2.9**	4.22	0.16	-5.33 / 4	0.68 /36	3.98 /61	5.91	0.93
GES	PNC Intermediate Bond A	PBFAX	**C-**	(800) 551-2145	**D / 1.7**	2.07	1.15	0.63 /52	0.86 /40	2.19 /33	1.15	0.81
GES	PNC Intermediate Bond C	PIBCX	**C-**	(800) 551-2145	**C- / 3.0**	1.89	0.81	-0.08 /30	0.13 /28	1.42 /25	0.50	1.53
GES	PNC Intermediate Bond I	PIKIX	**B-**	(800) 551-2145	**C / 5.0**	2.23	1.36	0.95 /58	1.13 /45	2.43 /37	1.43	0.53
MUN	PNC Intermediate Tax Exempt Bond	PTBIX	**B+**	(800) 551-2145	**B+ / 8.3**	1.62	2.79	3.18 /87	3.01 /88	4.55 /82	2.30	0.89
MUN	PNC Intermediate Tax Exempt Bond	PITCX	**A-**	(800) 551-2145	**B / 8.2**	1.34	2.34	2.40 /80	2.17 /79	3.72 /76	1.62	1.61
MUN	PNC Intermediate Tax Exempt Bond I	PTIIX	**A+**	(800) 551-2145	**A- / 9.1**	1.67	2.86	3.44 /89	3.15 /90	4.72 /83	2.52	0.61
GEI	PNC Ltd Maturity Bond A	PLFAX	**C**	(800) 551-2145	**D / 2.2**	0.83	0.47	0.50 /49	0.46 /32	0.66 /18	0.49	0.76
GEI	PNC Ltd Maturity Bond C	PFLCX	**C**	(800) 551-2145	**D+ / 2.3**	0.69	0.20	0.01 /32	-0.02 /15	0.10 /14	0.01	1.48
GEI	PNC Ltd Maturity Bond I	PMYIX	**C+**	(800) 551-2145	**C- / 3.7**	0.89	0.57	0.69 /53	0.56 /34	0.82 /19	0.69	0.48
MUS	PNC MD Tax Exempt Bond A	PDATX	**B+**	(800) 551-2145	**C+ / 6.9**	1.51	2.12	2.78 /83	2.08 /78	3.43 /73	2.14	0.89
MUS	PNC MD Tax Exempt Bond C	PDACX	**B+**	(800) 551-2145	**C+ / 6.9**	1.35	1.82	2.06 /78	1.32 /62	2.64 /62	1.51	1.61
MUS	PNC MD Tax Exempt Bond I	PDITX	**A+**	(800) 551-2145	**B+ / 8.3**	1.49	2.17	3.02 /85	2.28 /80	3.65 /75	2.44	0.61
MM	PNC Money Market A	PEAXX	**U**	(800) 551-2145	**U /**	--	--	--	--	--	0.05	0.61
MM	PNC Money Market C	PECXX	**U**	(800) 551-2145	**U /**	--	--	--	--	--	0.05	1.36
MM	PNC Money Market I	PCIXX	**U**	(800) 551-2145	**U /**	--	--	--	--	--	0.05	0.36
MUS	PNC Ohio Intermediate Tax-Ex Bond	POXAX	**B+**	(800) 551-2145	**B- / 7.0**	1.39	2.36	2.76 /83	2.11 /78	3.82 /76	1.83	0.89
MUS	PNC Ohio Intermediate Tax-Ex Bond	POXCX	**B+**	(800) 551-2145	**B- / 7.1**	1.23	2.00	2.13 /78	1.39 /64	3.07 /70	1.19	1.61
MUS	PNC Ohio Intermediate Tax-Ex Bond	POXIX	**A+**	(800) 551-2145	**B+ / 8.5**	1.57	2.50	3.14 /86	2.38 /81	4.08 /78	2.16	0.61
MUN	PNC Tax Exempt Limited Mat Bond A	PDLAX	**C**	(800) 551-2145	**C- / 3.4**	0.78	1.01	1.34 /72	0.94 /51	1.73 /40	1.19	0.83
MUN	PNC Tax Exempt Limited Mat Bond I	PDLIX	**A**	(800) 551-2145	**C+ / 6.3**	0.75	1.13	1.61 /74	1.21 /59	1.97 /46	1.50	0.55
MMT	PNC Tax Exempt Money Market A	PXAXX	**U**	(800) 551-2145	**U /**	0.01	0.01	0.02 /36	0.02 /23	0.02 /11	0.02	0.56
MMT	PNC Tax Exempt Money Market	PXTXX	**U**	(800) 551-2145	**U /**	0.01	0.01	0.03 /39	0.02 /23	0.02 /11	0.03	0.41
MMT	PNC Tax Exempt Money Market I	PXIXX	**U**	(800) 551-2145	**U /**	0.01	0.01	0.02 /36	0.02 /23	0.02 /11	0.02	0.31
GEI	PNC Total Return Advantage A	PTVAX	**C-**	(800) 551-2145	**C- / 3.0**	2.75	1.72	-0.45 /27	1.37 /50	3.03 /46	2.11	0.84
GEI	PNC Total Return Advantage C	PTVCX	**C-**	(800) 551-2145	**C- / 3.8**	2.57	1.36	-1.15 /20	0.65 /36	2.28 /35	1.50	1.56
GEI	PNC Total Return Advantage I	PTVIX	**C+**	(800) 551-2145	**C+ / 5.6**	2.82	1.84	-0.19 /29	1.62 /54	3.30 /50	2.48	0.56
MM	PNC Treasury Money Market A	PRAXX	**U**	(800) 551-2145	**U /**	0.01	0.01	0.02 /35	0.01 /18	0.01 / 6	0.02	0.61
MM	PNC Treasury Money Market I	PDIXX	**U**	(800) 551-2145	**U /**	0.01	0.01	0.02 /35	0.01 /18	0.01 / 6	0.02	0.36
GEI	PNC Ultra Short Bond A	PSBAX	**C-**	(800) 551-2145	**D- / 1.5**	0.27	0.11	0.13 /42	-0.03 /15	0.06 /13	0.13	0.61
GEI	PNC Ultra Short Bond I	PNCIX	**C+**	(800) 551-2145	**D+ / 2.9**	0.34	0.25	0.40 /48	0.24 /29	0.33 /16	0.40	0.33
GEI	Power Income A	PWRAX	**D+**	(877) 779-7462	**D- / 1.0**	0.31	-1.05	-1.58 /18	0.76 /38	1.13 /22	1.54	1.95
GEI	Power Income C	PWRCX	**U**	(877) 779-7462	**U /**	0.11	-1.34	-2.30 /14	--	--	1.30	2.64
GEI	Power Income I	PWRIX	**C-**	(877) 779-7462	**C- / 3.6**	0.31	-0.88	-1.35 /19	1.03 /43	1.39 /24	1.75	1.71
GES	Praxis Interm Income A	MIIAX	**C**	(800) 977-2947	**C- / 3.8**	2.51	1.84	1.38 /65	2.03 /62	3.34 /51	2.26	0.95
GES	Praxis Interm Income I	MIIIX	**B+**	(800) 977-2947	**C+ / 6.3**	2.52	1.94	1.78 /70	2.41 /69	3.73 /57	2.74	0.54
GEI	Principal Bond Market Index Inst	PNIIX	**B+**	(800) 222-5852	**B- / 7.3**	2.97	2.27	1.63 /68	2.49 /71	3.65 /56	1.90	0.28
GEI	Principal Bond Market Index J	PBIJX	**C+**	(800) 222-5852	**C+ / 5.9**	2.82	1.97	1.13 /61	1.61 /54	2.86 /43	1.51	0.70
GEI	Principal Bond Market Index R1	PBIMX	**C**	(800) 222-5852	**C / 5.2**	2.73	1.78	0.67 /53	1.21 /46	2.51 /38	1.06	1.17
GEI	Principal Bond Market Index R2	PBINX	**C+**	(800) 222-5852	**C / 5.4**	2.73	1.85	0.83 /56	1.34 /49	2.64 /40	1.04	1.04
GEI	Principal Bond Market Index R3	PBOIX	**C+**	(800) 222-5852	**C+ / 5.8**	2.83	1.98	1.05 /59	1.55 /53	2.84 /43	1.34	0.86
GEI	Principal Bond Market Index R4	PBIPX	**C+**	(800) 222-5852	**C+ / 6.2**	2.82	2.09	1.25 /62	1.75 /57	3.02 /45	1.72	0.67
GEI	Principal Bond Market Index R5	PBIQX	**B-**	(800) 222-5852	**C+ / 6.4**	2.91	2.15	1.31 /63	1.86 /59	3.14 /47	1.60	0.55
MUS	Principal CA Municipal A	SRCMX	**B**	(800) 222-5852	**A+ / 9.7**	2.04	4.30	4.96 /98	5.05 /99	7.85 /98	4.23	0.81
MUS	Principal CA Municipal C	SRCCX	**B**	(800) 222-5852	**A+ / 9.7**	1.83	3.84	4.10 /95	4.06 /96	6.83 /96	3.49	1.74

• Denotes fund is closed to new investors
* Denotes fund is included in Section II

RISK			NET ASSETS		ASSET							FUND MANAGER		MINIMUM		LOADS	
Risk Rating/Pts	3 Yr Avg Standard Deviation	Avg Duration	NAV As of 3/31/16	Total $(Mil)	Cash %	Gov. Bond %	Muni. Bond %	Corp. Bond %	Other %	Portfolio Turnover Ratio	Avg Coupon Rate	Manager Quality Pct	Manager Tenure (Years)	Initial Purch. $	Additional Purch. $	Front End Load	Back End Load
A+ / 9.9	N/A	N/A	1.00	361	100	0	0	0	0	0	0.0	67	N/A	1,000	50	0.0	0.0
U /	N/A	N/A	1.00	11	100	0	0	0	0	0	0.0	N/A	N/A	0	0	0.0	0.0
A+ / 9.9	N/A	N/A	1.00	1,701	100	0	0	0	0	0	0.0	67	N/A	0	0	0.0	0.0
B / 8.0	2.4	3.7	9.24	9	2	6	0	0	92	30	0.0	69	14	1,000	50	4.5	0.0
B / 8.0	2.4	3.7	9.23	1	2	6	0	0	92	30	0.0	37	14	1,000	50	0.0	0.0
B / 7.9	2.4	3.7	9.25	42	2	6	0	0	92	30	0.0	76	14	0	0	0.0	0.0
D- / 1.1	5.9	4.1	7.10	1	7	0	0	90	3	40	0.0	22	8	1,000	50	4.5	0.0
D- / 1.1	6.0	4.1	7.10	12	7	0	0	90	3	40	0.0	29	8	0	0	0.0	0.0
B+ / 8.4	2.1	3.8	11.00	4	1	42	0	40	17	47	0.0	35	14	1,000	50	4.5	0.0
B+ / 8.4	2.1	3.8	11.04	N/A	1	42	0	40	17	47	0.0	17	14	1,000	50	0.0	0.0
B+ / 8.3	2.1	3.8	11.00	295	1	42	0	40	17	47	0.0	42	14	0	0	0.0	0.0
C+ / 5.8	3.2	5.3	9.72	3	0	0	100	0	0	23	0.0	52	9	1,000	50	3.0	0.0
C+ / 6.1	3.1	5.3	9.62	N/A	0	0	100	0	0	23	0.0	28	9	1,000	50	0.0	0.0
C+ / 6.0	3.1	5.3	9.76	79	0	0	100	0	0	23	0.0	58	9	0	0	0.0	0.0
A+ / 9.7	0.7	1.7	10.22	5	1	37	0	32	30	58	0.0	62	14	1,000	50	2.0	0.0
A+ / 9.7	0.6	1.7	10.22	1	1	37	0	32	30	58	0.0	44	14	1,000	50	0.0	0.0
A+ / 9.7	0.6	1.7	10.19	298	1	37	0	32	30	58	0.0	72	14	0	0	0.0	0.0
C+ / 6.9	2.9	4.7	11.21	N/A	7	0	92	0	1	9	0.0	31	9	1,000	50	3.0	0.0
B- / 7.1	2.8	4.7	11.21	N/A	7	0	92	0	1	9	0.0	17	9	1,000	50	0.0	0.0
C+ / 6.9	2.9	4.7	11.21	48	7	0	92	0	1	9	0.0	37	9	0	0	0.0	0.0
U /	N/A	N/A	1.00	149	100	0	0	0	0	0	0.1	68	N/A	1,000	50	0.0	0.0
U /	N/A	N/A	1.00	N/A	100	0	0	0	0	0	0.1	68	N/A	1,000	50	0.0	0.0
U /	N/A	N/A	1.00	1,230	100	0	0	0	0	0	0.1	68	N/A	0	0	0.0	0.0
B- / 7.0	2.9	5.2	10.94	4	5	0	94	0	1	15	0.0	35	7	1,000	50	3.0	0.0
C+ / 6.8	2.9	5.2	10.92	1	5	0	94	0	1	15	0.0	17	7	1,000	50	0.0	0.0
C+ / 6.9	2.9	5.2	10.98	40	5	0	94	0	1	15	0.0	42	7	0	0	0.0	0.0
B+ / 8.8	1.6	2.9	10.48	N/A	2	0	97	0	1	36	0.0	40	9	1,000	50	3.0	0.0
B+ / 8.8	1.6	2.9	10.47	132	2	0	97	0	1	36	0.0	51	9	0	0	0.0	0.0
U /	N/A	N/A	1.00	41	100	0	0	0	0	0	0.0	N/A	N/A	1,000	50	0.0	0.0
U /	N/A	N/A	1.00	198	100	0	0	0	0	0	0.0	N/A	N/A	0	0	0.0	0.0
U /	N/A	N/A	1.00	349	100	0	0	0	0	0	0.0	N/A	N/A	0	0	0.0	0.0
C+ / 6.9	2.9	5.2	10.74	11	1	26	0	38	35	51	0.0	32	14	1,000	50	4.5	0.0
C+ / 6.9	2.9	5.2	10.76	1	1	26	0	38	35	51	0.0	17	14	1,000	50	0.0	0.0
C+ / 6.9	2.9	5.2	10.73	174	1	26	0	38	35	51	0.0	39	14	0	0	0.0	0.0
U /	N/A	N/A	1.00	177	100	0	0	0	0	0	0.0	N/A	N/A	1,000	50	0.0	0.0
U /	N/A	N/A	1.00	423	100	0	0	0	0	0	0.0	N/A	N/A	0	0	0.0	0.0
A+ / 9.9	0.2	0.9	9.95	1	2	41	0	29	28	90	0.0	57	14	1,000	50	1.0	0.0
A+ / 9.9	0.2	0.9	9.94	393	2	41	0	29	28	90	0.0	72	14	0	0	0.0	0.0
B / 7.7	2.6	N/A	9.57	27	100	0	0	0	0	554	0.0	66	6	1,000	100	5.0	0.0
U /	N/A	N/A	9.52	3	100	0	0	0	0	554	0.0	N/A	6	2,500	500	0.0	0.0
B / 7.7	2.6	N/A	9.57	182	100	0	0	0	0	554	0.0	78	6	100,000	0	0.0	0.0
B / 7.6	2.6	4.8	10.52	85	0	25	3	41	31	16	0.0	56	22	2,500	100	3.8	2.0
B / 7.7	2.6	4.8	10.47	365	0	25	3	41	31	16	0.0	75	22	100,000	0	0.0	2.0
C+ / 6.8	2.9	5.7	11.11	1,164	0	42	1	24	33	320	3.1	71	7	0	0	0.0	0.0
C+ / 6.6	3.0	5.7	10.92	31	0	42	1	24	33	320	3.1	33	7	1,000	100	0.0	0.0
C+ / 6.5	3.0	5.7	10.92	2	0	42	1	24	33	320	3.1	22	7	0	0	0.0	0.0
C+ / 6.6	3.0	5.7	10.93	3	0	42	1	24	33	320	3.1	25	7	0	0	0.0	0.0
C+ / 6.5	3.0	5.7	10.91	15	0	42	1	24	33	320	3.1	30	7	0	0	0.0	0.0
C+ / 6.7	3.0	5.7	10.92	36	0	42	1	24	33	320	3.1	37	7	0	0	0.0	0.0
C+ / 6.6	3.0	5.7	10.96	28	0	42	1	24	33	320	3.1	40	7	0	0	0.0	0.0
C- / 3.1	4.6	5.2	10.68	240	2	0	97	0	1	27	5.2	76	3	1,000	100	3.8	0.0
C- / 3.1	4.6	5.2	10.70	29	2	0	97	0	1	27	5.2	37	3	1,000	100	0.0	0.0

Fund Type	Fund Name (99 Pct = Best, 0 Pct = Worst)	Ticker Symbol	Overall Investment Rating	Phone	PERFORMANCE: Performance Rating/Pts	Total Return % through 3/31/16: 3 Mo	6 Mo	1Yr / Pct	Annualized: 3Yr / Pct	5Yr / Pct	Incl. in Returns: Dividend Yield	Expense Ratio
MUN	Principal CA Municipal Inst	PCMFX	**B+**	(800) 222-5852	**A+ / 9.9**	2.08	4.49	5.24 /98	5.11 /99	7.89 /98	4.57	95.60
MUN	Principal CA Municipal P	PLBTX	**U**	(800) 222-5852	**U /**	2.10	4.52	--	--	--	0.00	0.60
GL	Principal Capital Securities S	PCSFX	**U**	(800) 222-5852	**U /**	-0.81	0.34	0.23 /45	--	--	5.80	0.11
GEI	Principal Core Plus Bond A	PRBDX	**C-**	(800) 222-5852	**C- / 3.8**	2.51	1.61	0.05 /38	1.64 /55	3.28 /49	1.80	1.01
GEI	Principal Core Plus Bond C	PBMCX	**C-**	(800) 222-5852	**C- / 4.0**	2.31	1.18	-0.81 /23	0.78 /39	2.40 /36	1.01	2.02
GEI	Principal Core Plus Bond Inst	PMSIX	**B-**	(800) 222-5852	**C+ / 6.3**	2.61	1.80	0.42 /48	2.03 /62	3.67 /56	2.24	0.50
GEI	Principal Core Plus Bond J	PBMJX	**C+**	(800) 222-5852	**C+ / 5.7**	2.51	1.72	0.07 /40	1.66 /55	3.26 /49	1.88	0.82
GEI	Principal Core Plus Bond R1	PBOMX	**C**	(800) 222-5852	**C / 4.7**	2.40	1.37	-0.44 /27	1.14 /45	2.77 /41	1.38	1.38
GEI	Principal Core Plus Bond R2	PBMNX	**C**	(800) 222-5852	**C / 4.9**	2.45	1.45	-0.31 /28	1.26 /47	2.92 /44	1.53	1.25
GEI	Principal Core Plus Bond R3	PBMMX	**C**	(800) 222-5852	**C / 5.3**	2.49	1.53	-0.14 /30	1.44 /51	3.09 /47	1.70	1.07
GEI	Principal Core Plus Bond R4	PBMSX	**C+**	(800) 222-5852	**C+ / 5.6**	2.48	1.59	0.04 /37	1.65 /55	3.28 /49	1.84	0.88
GEI	Principal Core Plus Bond R5	PBMPX	**C+**	(800) 222-5852	**C+ / 5.8**	2.56	1.68	0.17 /43	1.75 /57	3.40 /52	2.00	0.76
COH	Principal Dynamic HY Exp A	PDYAX	**U**	(800) 222-5852	**U /**	0.70	-3.06	-5.81 / 3	--	--	5.07	1.72
COH	Principal Dynamic HY Exp Instl	PDYIX	**U**	(800) 222-5852	**U /**	0.86	-2.87	-5.44 / 4	--	--	5.42	1.37
* GL	Principal Glb Divers Income A	PGBAX	**D**	(800) 222-5852	**C / 4.9**	2.21	2.10	-2.01 /16	2.56 /71	5.04 /72	4.83	1.09
GL	Principal Glb Divers Income C	PGDCX	**D+**	(800) 222-5852	**C / 5.2**	2.02	1.73	-2.69 /12	1.78 /57	4.27 /65	4.27	1.85
GL	Principal Glb Divers Income Inst	PGDIX	**C-**	(800) 222-5852	**B- / 7.1**	2.31	2.28	-1.70 /17	2.87 /75	5.38 /74	5.37	0.78
GL	Principal Glb Divers Income P	PGDPX	**C-**	(800) 222-5852	**B- / 7.0**	2.29	2.25	-1.69 /17	2.84 /75	5.33 /74	5.32	0.83
MTG	Principal Govt & High Qual Bd A	CMPGX	**B-**	(800) 222-5852	**C / 5.1**	2.11	1.40	1.64 /68	1.84 /58	2.97 /45	3.01	0.90
MTG	Principal Govt & High Qual Bd C	CCUGX	**C+**	(800) 222-5852	**C / 4.6**	1.91	1.00	0.91 /57	1.00 /43	2.12 /33	2.27	1.66
MTG	Principal Govt & High Qual Bd Inst	PMRIX	**A**	(800) 222-5852	**C+ / 6.6**	2.08	1.45	1.91 /71	2.09 /63	3.24 /49	3.36	0.52
MTG	Principal Govt & High Qual Bd J	PMRJX	**B+**	(800) 222-5852	**C+ / 6.0**	2.01	1.31	1.63 /68	1.73 /56	2.83 /42	3.08	0.80
MTG	Principal Govt & High Qual Bd P	PGSPX	**A-**	(800) 222-5852	**C+ / 6.3**	2.03	1.36	1.74 /69	1.90 /59	3.08 /46	3.18	0.75
MTG	Principal Govt & High Qual Bd R1	PMGRX	**B-**	(800) 222-5852	**C / 5.2**	1.90	1.17	1.15 /61	1.31 /49	2.47 /37	2.60	1.38
MTG	Principal Govt & High Qual Bd R2	PFMRX	**B**	(800) 222-5852	**C / 5.5**	2.02	1.23	1.28 /63	1.47 /52	2.60 /39	2.73	1.25
MTG	Principal Govt & High Qual Bd R3	PRCMX	**B+**	(800) 222-5852	**C+ / 5.9**	2.06	1.32	1.46 /66	1.65 /55	2.78 /41	2.91	1.07
MTG	Principal Govt & High Qual Bd R4	PMRDX	**B+**	(800) 222-5852	**C+ / 6.1**	2.01	1.32	1.65 /68	1.81 /58	2.98 /45	3.10	0.88
MTG	Principal Govt & High Qual Bd R5	PMREX	**A-**	(800) 222-5852	**C+ / 6.4**	2.14	1.47	1.86 /71	1.97 /61	3.10 /47	3.21	0.76
*COH	Principal High Yield A	CPHYX	**D-**	(800) 222-5852	**D+ / 2.7**	1.99	0.20	-3.85 / 8	1.67 /55	4.51 /68	5.88	0.88
COH	Principal High Yield C	CCHIX	**D-**	(800) 222-5852	**C- / 3.2**	1.95	-0.01	-4.39 / 7	0.98 /42	3.76 /58	5.28	1.63
COH	Principal High Yield Fund I A	PYHAX	**E+**	(800) 222-5852	**D- / 1.3**	2.69	0.51	-4.93 / 5	1.04 /43	3.80 /58	5.22	1.23
COH	Principal High Yield Fund I Inst	PYHIX	**D**	(800) 222-5852	**C- / 4.2**	2.79	0.72	-4.35 / 7	1.41 /50	4.12 /63	5.85	0.65
COH	Principal High Yield Inst	PHYTX	**D**	(800) 222-5852	**C / 5.2**	2.24	0.35	-3.48 /10	2.00 /61	4.85 /71	6.44	0.60
COH	Principal High Yield P	PYHPX	**D**	(800) 222-5852	**C / 5.1**	2.20	0.46	-3.53 /10	1.96 /61	4.79 /70	6.29	0.71
COI	Principal Income Fd A	CMPIX	**C-**	(800) 222-5852	**C / 4.6**	2.61	1.29	-0.36 /27	1.76 /57	3.79 /58	3.13	0.88
COI	Principal Income Fd C	CNMCX	**C-**	(800) 222-5852	**C- / 4.1**	2.40	0.78	-1.24 /20	0.94 /41	2.98 /45	2.39	1.67
COI	Principal Income Fd Inst	PIOIX	**C+**	(800) 222-5852	**C+ / 6.3**	2.70	1.37	-0.08 /31	2.10 /64	4.17 /64	3.58	0.50
COI	Principal Income Fd J	PIOJX	**C**	(800) 222-5852	**C+ / 5.7**	2.64	1.24	-0.28 /28	1.76 /57	3.72 /57	3.27	0.79
COI	Principal Income Fd P	PIMPX	**C**	(800) 222-5852	**C+ / 6.0**	2.67	1.29	-0.26 /28	1.92 /60	4.01 /62	3.39	0.67
COI	Principal Income Fd R1	PIOMX	**C-**	(800) 222-5852	**C / 4.8**	2.49	1.05	-0.83 /23	1.26 /47	3.30 /50	2.71	1.37
COI	Principal Income Fd R2	PIONX	**C-**	(800) 222-5852	**C / 5.0**	2.63	1.12	-0.70 /24	1.39 /50	3.45 /52	2.84	1.24
COI	Principal Income Fd R3	PIOOX	**C-**	(800) 222-5852	**C / 5.4**	2.56	1.10	-0.52 /26	1.57 /54	3.61 /55	3.02	1.06
COI	Principal Income Fd R4	PIOPX	**C**	(800) 222-5852	**C+ / 5.7**	2.72	1.30	-0.33 /28	1.76 /57	3.81 /58	3.20	0.87
COI	Principal Income Fd R5	PIOQX	**C**	(800) 222-5852	**C+ / 5.9**	2.64	1.25	-0.22 /29	1.85 /59	3.94 /61	3.33	0.75
COI	Principal Income Fd R6	PICNX	**U**	(800) 222-5852	**U /**	2.69	1.35	-0.03 /31	--	--	3.52	1.22
GEI	Principal Infl Prot A	PITAX	**E+**	(800) 222-5852	**E / 0.5**	3.56	2.91	-0.47 /26	-1.69 / 5	2.00 /31	0.66	0.95
GEI	Principal Infl Prot C	PPOCX	**E+**	(800) 222-5852	**E+ / 0.6**	3.44	2.45	-1.26 /20	-2.43 / 3	1.22 /22	0.54	2.08
GEI	Principal Infl Prot Inst	PIPIX	**D-**	(800) 222-5852	**D- / 1.3**	3.65	3.13	-0.11 /30	-1.20 / 7	2.47 /37	0.80	0.39
GEI	Principal Infl Prot J	PIPJX	**E+**	(800) 222-5852	**E+ / 0.8**	3.51	2.78	-0.78 /23	-1.80 / 5	1.81 /29	0.64	1.03
GEI	Principal Infl Prot R1	PISPX	**E+**	(800) 222-5852	**E+ / 0.7**	3.43	2.68	-0.93 /22	-2.05 / 4	1.59 /26	0.64	1.27
GEI	Principal Infl Prot R2	PBSAX	**E+**	(800) 222-5852	**E+ / 0.8**	3.54	2.82	-0.77 /24	-1.92 / 5	1.74 /28	0.66	1.14
GEI	Principal Infl Prot R3	PIFPX	**E+**	(800) 222-5852	**E+ / 0.9**	3.51	2.71	-0.60 /25	-1.77 / 5	1.90 /30	0.70	0.96

● Denotes fund is closed to new investors
* Denotes fund is included in Section II

RISK			NET ASSETS		ASSET							FUND MANAGER		MINIMUM		LOADS	
Risk Rating/Pts	3 Yr Avg Standard Deviation	Avg Duration	NAV As of 3/31/16	Total $(Mil)	Cash %	Gov. Bond %	Muni. Bond %	Corp. Bond %	Other %	Portfolio Turnover Ratio	Avg Coupon Rate	Manager Quality Pct	Manager Tenure (Years)	Initial Purch. $	Additional Purch. $	Front End Load	Back End Load
C- / 3.1	4.6	5.2	10.68	2	2	0	97	0	1	27	5.2	78	3	0	0	0.0	0.0
U /	N/A	5.2	10.68	44	2	0	97	0	1	27	5.2	N/A	3	0	0	0.0	0.0
U /	N/A	N/A	9.55	203	6	0	0	81	13	10	0.0	N/A	2	0	0	0.0	0.0
C+ / 6.5	3.0	5.5	10.85	95	0	14	0	44	42	208	3.5	37	16	1,000	100	3.8	0.0
C+ / 6.6	3.0	5.5	10.85	8	0	14	0	44	42	208	3.5	17	16	1,000	100	0.0	0.0
C+ / 6.8	2.9	5.5	10.84	3,865	0	14	0	44	42	208	3.5	51	16	1,000,000	0	0.0	0.0
C+ / 6.6	3.0	5.5	10.92	156	0	14	0	44	42	208	3.5	38	16	1,000	100	0.0	0.0
C+ / 6.8	2.9	5.5	10.84	6	0	14	0	44	42	208	3.5	25	16	0	0	0.0	0.0
C+ / 6.7	3.0	5.5	10.74	11	0	14	0	44	42	208	3.5	27	16	0	0	0.0	0.0
C+ / 6.6	3.0	5.5	10.78	29	0	14	0	44	42	208	3.5	31	16	0	0	0.0	0.0
C+ / 6.6	3.0	5.5	10.98	21	0	14	0	44	42	208	3.5	38	16	0	0	0.0	0.0
C+ / 6.6	3.0	5.5	10.79	56	0	14	0	44	42	208	3.5	40	16	0	0	0.0	0.0
U /	N/A	1.2	8.70	7	1	0	0	48	51	94	5.7	N/A	N/A	1,000	100	3.8	0.0
U /	N/A	1.2	8.73	7	1	0	0	48	51	94	5.7	N/A	N/A	0	0	0.0	0.0
D+ / 2.3	5.4	3.9	13.18	2,041	8	13	0	35	44	77	6.3	98	6	1,000	100	3.8	0.0
D+ / 2.3	5.5	3.9	13.11	2,440	8	13	0	35	44	77	6.3	95	6	1,000	100	0.0	0.0
D+ / 2.3	5.4	3.9	13.13	3,309	8	13	0	35	44	77	6.3	98	6	1,000,000	0	0.0	0.0
D+ / 2.3	5.4	3.9	13.12	2,541	8	13	0	35	44	77	6.3	98	6	0	0	0.0	0.0
B / 8.2	2.3	5.3	10.94	310	1	4	0	0	95	31	3.5	42	6	1,000	100	2.3	0.0
B / 8.1	2.3	5.3	10.93	60	1	4	0	0	95	31	3.5	20	6	1,000	100	0.0	0.0
B / 8.2	2.2	5.3	10.94	989	1	4	0	0	95	31	3.5	52	6	1,000,000	0	0.0	0.0
B / 8.2	2.2	5.3	10.95	141	1	4	0	0	95	31	3.5	40	6	1,000	100	0.0	0.0
B / 8.2	2.2	5.3	10.96	12	1	4	0	0	95	31	3.5	46	6	0	0	0.0	0.0
B+ / 8.3	2.2	5.3	10.95	3	1	4	0	0	95	31	3.5	29	6	0	0	0.0	0.0
B / 8.2	2.3	5.3	10.95	11	1	4	0	0	95	31	3.5	31	6	0	0	0.0	0.0
B / 8.2	2.3	5.3	10.95	17	1	4	0	0	95	31	3.5	36	6	0	0	0.0	0.0
B / 8.2	2.2	5.3	10.95	10	1	4	0	0	95	31	3.5	43	6	0	0	0.0	0.0
B / 8.1	2.3	5.3	10.96	23	1	4	0	0	95	31	3.5	45	6	0	0	0.0	0.0
D / 1.8	5.4	3.8	6.80	848	2	2	0	87	9	45	6.7	71	7	1,000	100	3.8	0.0
D / 1.7	5.4	3.8	6.87	366	2	2	0	87	9	45	6.7	40	7	1,000	100	0.0	0.0
D- / 1.3	5.8	4.2	9.24	4	3	0	0	88	9	50	6.4	39	9	1,000	100	3.8	0.0
D- / 1.3	5.8	4.2	9.24	840	3	0	0	88	9	50	6.4	52	9	1,000,000	0	0.0	0.0
D / 1.7	5.4	3.8	6.76	1,527	2	2	0	87	9	45	6.7	81	7	1,000,000	0	0.0	0.0
D / 1.8	5.4	3.8	6.81	493	2	2	0	87	9	45	6.7	80	7	0	0	0.0	0.0
C / 5.5	3.3	5.0	9.44	260	4	13	0	55	28	12	4.0	50	11	1,000	100	2.3	0.0
C / 5.5	3.3	5.0	9.49	65	4	13	0	55	28	12	4.0	25	11	1,000	100	0.0	0.0
C+ / 5.6	3.3	5.0	9.46	2,588	4	13	0	55	28	12	4.0	N/A	11	1,000,000	0	0.0	0.0
C / 5.5	3.3	5.0	9.46	91	4	13	0	55	28	12	4.0	50	11	1,000	100	0.0	0.0
C+ / 5.6	3.3	5.0	9.46	28	4	13	0	55	28	12	4.0	56	11	0	0	0.0	0.0
C / 5.4	3.3	5.0	9.47	17	4	13	0	55	28	12	4.0	33	11	0	0	0.0	0.0
C / 5.5	3.3	5.0	9.48	3	4	13	0	55	28	12	4.0	38	11	0	0	0.0	0.0
C / 5.5	3.3	5.0	9.48	33	4	13	0	55	28	12	4.0	43	11	0	0	0.0	0.0
C / 5.4	3.3	5.0	9.48	26	4	13	0	55	28	12	4.0	49	11	0	0	0.0	0.0
C+ / 5.6	3.2	5.0	9.46	46	4	13	0	55	28	12	4.0	54	11	0	0	0.0	0.0
U /	N/A	5.0	9.46	6	4	13	0	55	28	12	4.0	N/A	11	0	0	0.0	0.0
D+ / 2.4	5.1	7.2	8.44	13	0	99	0	0	1	55	3.7	3	6	1,000	100	3.8	0.0
D+ / 2.4	5.2	7.2	8.12	4	0	99	0	0	1	55	3.7	2	6	1,000	100	0.0	0.0
D+ / 2.4	5.1	7.2	8.51	1,664	0	99	0	0	1	55	3.7	4	6	1,000,000	0	0.0	0.0
D+ / 2.4	5.1	7.2	8.26	8	0	99	0	0	1	55	3.7	2	6	1,000	100	0.0	0.0
D+ / 2.4	5.1	7.2	8.14	1	0	99	0	0	1	55	3.7	2	6	0	0	0.0	0.0
D+ / 2.4	5.1	7.2	8.19	1	0	99	0	0	1	55	3.7	2	6	0	0	0.0	0.0
D+ / 2.4	5.1	7.2	8.26	5	0	99	0	0	1	55	3.7	2	6	0	0	0.0	0.0

Fund Type	Fund Name (99 Pct = Best, 0 Pct = Worst)	Ticker Symbol	Overall Investment Rating	Phone	PERFORMANCE: Performance Rating/Pts	Total Return % through 3/31/16: 3 Mo	6 Mo	1Yr / Pct	Annualized: 3Yr / Pct	5Yr / Pct	Incl. in Returns: Dividend Yield	Expense Ratio
GEI	Principal Infl Prot R4	PIFSX	**D-**	(800) 222-5852	**D- / 1.0**	3.60	2.86	-0.43 /27	-1.58 / 6	2.10 /32	0.74	0.77
GEI	Principal Infl Prot R5	PBPPX	**D-**	(800) 222-5852	**D- / 1.1**	3.58	2.99	-0.29 /28	-1.48 / 6	2.22 /34	0.75	0.65
MUN	Principal Opportunistic Muni C	PMODX	**C**	(800) 222-5852	**A / 9.5**	1.61	4.46	5.20 /98	3.54 /93	--	2.81	1.97
MUH	Principal Opportunistic Muni Inst	POMFX	**C**	(800) 222-5852	**A+ / 9.8**	1.95	5.06	6.24 /99	4.44 /97	--	3.78	0.83
MUH	Principal Opportunistic Muni P	PMOQX	**U**	(800) 222-5852	**U /**	1.86	5.08	6.33 /99	--	--	3.77	1.06
MUN	Principal Opportunistic Munil A	PMOAX	**C**	(800) 222-5852	**A / 9.5**	1.79	4.94	5.98 /99	4.35 /97	--	3.40	1.11
* USS	Principal Preferred Sec A	PPSAX	**C+**	(800) 222-5852	**B / 7.9**	-0.10	1.84	1.39 /65	4.72 /89	6.45 /79	4.67	1.07
USS	Principal Preferred Sec C	PRFCX	**C+**	(800) 222-5852	**B / 8.1**	-0.20	1.47	0.64 /52	3.95 /83	5.67 /75	4.11	1.82
USS	Principal Preferred Sec Inst	PPSIX	**B**	(800) 222-5852	**B+ / 8.8**	-0.02	2.00	1.71 /69	5.04 /91	6.78 /81	5.20	0.76
USS	Principal Preferred Sec J	PPSJX	**B-**	(800) 222-5852	**B+ / 8.5**	-0.10	1.89	1.42 /65	4.59 /88	6.29 /78	4.97	1.06
COI	Principal Preferred Sec P	PPSPX	**B**	(800) 222-5852	**B+ / 8.7**	-0.04	1.97	1.63 /68	4.97 /90	6.70 /80	5.12	0.83
USS	Principal Preferred Sec R1	PUSAX	**B-**	(800) 222-5852	**B / 8.2**	-0.24	1.60	0.89 /57	4.16 /85	5.88 /76	4.40	1.58
USS	Principal Preferred Sec R2	PPRSX	**B-**	(800) 222-5852	**B / 8.2**	-0.20	1.67	1.03 /59	4.29 /86	6.03 /77	4.55	1.45
USS	Principal Preferred Sec R3	PNARX	**B-**	(800) 222-5852	**B+ / 8.4**	-0.06	1.76	1.20 /62	4.53 /88	6.24 /78	4.71	1.27
USS	Principal Preferred Sec R4	PQARX	**B**	(800) 222-5852	**B+ / 8.5**	-0.01	1.85	1.39 /65	4.70 /89	6.40 /79	4.91	1.08
USS	Principal Preferred Sec R5	PPARX	**B**	(800) 222-5852	**B+ / 8.6**	-0.08	1.91	1.51 /66	4.84 /90	6.55 /80	5.01	0.96
MTG	Principal Real Estate Dbt Inc A	PRDYX	**U**	(800) 222-5852	**U /**	0.22	-1.08	-1.58 /18	--	--	3.47	1.14
MTG	Principal Real Estate Dbt Inc Inst	PRDIX	**U**	(800) 222-5852	**U /**	0.40	-0.83	-1.18 /20	--	--	3.91	0.84
MTG	Principal Real Estate Dbt Inc P	PDIFX	**U**	(800) 222-5852	**U /**	0.37	-0.86	--	--	--	0.00	0.89
GEI	Principal Short-Term Income Fd A	SRHQX	**C+**	(800) 222-5852	**C- / 3.5**	1.12	0.74	0.86 /56	1.06 /44	1.84 /29	1.48	0.68
GEI	Principal Short-Term Income Fd C	STCCX	**C**	(800) 222-5852	**D+ / 2.9**	0.91	0.30	-0.03 /31	0.19 /29	0.98 /20	0.62	1.57
GEI	Principal Short-Term Income Fd Inst	PSHIX	**B+**	(800) 222-5852	**C / 5.0**	1.10	0.86	1.02 /59	1.32 /49	2.10 /32	1.75	0.43
GEI	Principal Short-Term Income Fd J	PSJIX	**B**	(800) 222-5852	**C / 4.4**	1.03	0.65	0.75 /54	0.98 /42	1.69 /28	1.48	0.70
COI	Principal Short-Term Income Fd P	PSTPX	**B+**	(800) 222-5852	**C / 5.0**	1.16	0.82	1.03 /59	1.26 /47	2.01 /31	1.67	0.52
GEI	Principal Short-Term Income Fd R1	PSIMX	**C+**	(800) 222-5852	**C- / 3.4**	0.89	0.36	0.16 /43	0.46 /32	1.24 /23	0.90	1.30
GEI	Principal Short-Term Income Fd R2	PSINX	**C+**	(800) 222-5852	**C- / 3.7**	1.00	0.51	0.37 /47	0.62 /35	1.39 /24	1.03	1.17
GEI	Principal Short-Term Income Fd R3	PSIOX	**C+**	(800) 222-5852	**C- / 4.0**	1.05	0.59	0.55 /51	0.77 /38	1.57 /26	1.20	0.99
GEI	Principal Short-Term Income Fd R4	PSIPX	**B**	(800) 222-5852	**C / 4.4**	1.09	0.69	0.75 /54	0.97 /42	1.77 /28	1.40	0.80
GEI	Principal Short-Term Income Fd R5	PSIQX	**B**	(800) 222-5852	**C / 4.6**	1.04	0.66	0.78 /55	1.11 /45	1.89 /30	1.51	0.68
MUN	Principal Tax-Exempt Bond Fd A	PTEAX	**C+**	(800) 222-5852	**B+ / 8.8**	1.48	3.37	3.97 /94	3.75 /94	6.35 /94	3.32	0.81
MUN	Principal Tax-Exempt Bond Fd C	PTBCX	**C+**	(800) 222-5852	**B+ / 8.9**	1.27	2.95	3.26 /88	2.90 /87	5.51 /89	2.64	1.78
MUN	Principal Tax-Exempt Bond Fd Inst	PITEX	**B**	(800) 222-5852	**A+ / 9.6**	1.65	3.60	4.27 /96	3.85 /95	6.42 /94	3.59	0.60
MUN	Principal Tax-Exempt Bond Fd P	PTETX	**U**	(800) 222-5852	**U /**	1.67	3.63	--	--	--	0.00	0.61
MM	ProFunds Money Market Inv	MPIXX	**U**	(888) 776-3637	**U /**	--	--	--	--	--	0.02	1.03
MM	ProFunds Money Market Svc	MPSXX	**U**	(888) 776-3637	**U /**	--	--	--	--	--	0.02	N/A
MTG	ProFunds-Falling US Dollar Inv	FDPIX	**E-**	(888) 776-3637	**E- / 0.2**	3.73	0.72	1.92 /71	-6.03 / 1	-5.87 / 0	0.00	2.46
MTG	ProFunds-Falling US Dollar Svc	FDPSX	**E-**	(888) 776-3637	**E- / 0.1**	3.41	0.17	0.82 /56	-7.00 / 1	-6.83 / 0	0.00	3.46
USA	ProFunds-US Government Plus Inv	GVPIX	**C-**	(888) 776-3637	**A+ / 9.7**	11.00	7.60	-1.01 /22	6.34 /96	11.68 /98	0.00	1.40
USA	ProFunds-US Government Plus Svc	GVPSX	**C-**	(888) 776-3637	**A / 9.3**	10.69	6.98	-2.08 /15	5.21 /92	10.55 /96	0.00	2.40
GEI	Prudential Absolute Return Bond A	PADAX	**D+**	(800) 225-1852	**E+ / 0.9**	0.00	0.00	-1.89 /16	0.45 /32	1.39 /24	2.04	1.22
GEI	Prudential Absolute Return Bond C	PADCX	**D+**	(800) 225-1852	**D- / 1.2**	-0.18	-0.38	-2.60 /13	-0.27 /13	0.66 /18	1.37	1.97
GEI	Prudential Absolute Return Bond Q	PADQX	**C-**	(800) 225-1852	**C- / 3.3**	0.08	0.14	-1.48 /18	0.77 /38	1.74 /28	2.44	0.85
GEI	Prudential Absolute Return Bond Z	PADZX	**C-**	(800) 225-1852	**C- / 3.1**	0.06	0.11	-1.63 /18	0.70 /37	1.67 /27	2.38	0.97
MUS	Prudential CA Muni Income A	PBCAX	**B-**	(800) 225-1852	**B+ / 8.6**	1.71	3.53	3.83 /93	3.54 /93	6.34 /94	3.48	0.94
MUS ●	Prudential CA Muni Income B	PCAIX	**B**	(800) 225-1852	**A- / 9.2**	1.56	3.40	3.57 /91	3.29 /91	6.08 /92	3.39	1.19
MUS	Prudential CA Muni Income C	PCICX	**B-**	(800) 225-1852	**B+ / 8.9**	1.43	3.06	3.07 /86	2.78 /86	5.56 /89	2.90	1.69
MUS	Prudential CA Muni Income Z	PCIZX	**B+**	(800) 225-1852	**A / 9.5**	1.68	3.57	4.00 /94	3.81 /95	6.62 /95	3.89	0.69
COI	Prudential Core Bond A	TPCAX	**D+**	(800) 225-1852	**D- / 1.5**	2.96	2.29	1.28 /63	0.35 /31	2.51 /38	2.24	0.95
COI	Prudential Core Bond C	TPCCX	**D+**	(800) 225-1852	**D+ / 2.8**	2.77	1.93	0.53 /50	-0.33 /13	1.81 /29	1.61	N/A
COI	Prudential Core Bond Q	TPCQX	**C**	(800) 225-1852	**C / 4.6**	3.02	2.44	1.56 /67	0.65 /36	2.82 /42	2.62	N/A
COI	Prudential Core Bond R	TPCRX	**C-**	(800) 225-1852	**C- / 3.4**	2.91	2.20	1.08 /60	-0.01 /16	2.11 /33	2.15	N/A
GEI	Prudential Core Bond Z	TAIBX	**C**	(800) 225-1852	**C / 4.6**	2.92	2.44	1.46 /66	0.64 /36	2.81 /42	2.62	0.70

● Denotes fund is closed to new investors
* Denotes fund is included in Section II

RISK			NET ASSETS		ASSET							FUND MANAGER		MINIMUM		LOADS	
Risk Rating/Pts	3 Yr Avg Standard Deviation	Avg Duration	NAV As of 3/31/16	Total $(Mil)	Cash %	Gov. Bond %	Muni. Bond %	Corp. Bond %	Other %	Portfolio Turnover Ratio	Avg Coupon Rate	Manager Quality Pct	Manager Tenure (Years)	Initial Purch. $	Additional Purch. $	Front End Load	Back End Load
D+ / 2.4	5.1	7.2	8.34	2	0	99	0	0	1	55	3.7	3	6	0	0	0.0	0.0
D+ / 2.4	5.1	7.2	8.40	5	0	99	0	0	1	55	3.7	3	6	0	0	0.0	0.0
D- / 1.4	6.2	5.8	10.59	14	2	0	97	0	1	55	5.5	9	4	1,000	100	0.0	0.0
E+ / 0.9	6.2	5.8	10.60	N/A	2	0	97	0	1	55	5.5	16	4	0	0	0.0	0.0
U /	N/A	5.8	10.61	51	2	0	97	0	1	55	5.5	N/A	4	0	0	0.0	0.0
D- / 1.4	6.2	5.8	10.60	40	2	0	97	0	1	55	5.5	15	4	1,000	100	3.8	0.0
C / 4.4	3.8	5.1	10.03	847	6	0	0	57	37	17	6.5	99	14	1,000	100	3.8	0.0
C / 4.4	3.7	5.1	10.02	811	6	0	0	57	37	17	6.5	98	14	1,000	100	0.0	0.0
C / 4.4	3.8	5.1	9.97	2,083	6	0	0	57	37	17	6.5	99	14	0	0	0.0	0.0
C / 4.4	3.8	5.1	9.79	48	6	0	0	57	37	17	6.5	99	14	1,000	100	0.0	0.0
C / 4.4	3.8	5.1	9.96	1,334	6	0	0	57	37	17	6.5	98	14	0	0	0.0	0.0
C / 4.4	3.8	5.1	9.92	2	6	0	0	57	37	17	6.5	98	14	0	0	0.0	0.0
C / 4.4	3.7	5.1	9.87	2	6	0	0	57	37	17	6.5	99	14	0	0	0.0	0.0
C / 4.4	3.8	5.1	9.91	4	6	0	0	57	37	17	6.5	99	14	0	0	0.0	0.0
C / 4.4	3.8	5.1	9.89	1	6	0	0	57	37	17	6.5	99	14	0	0	0.0	0.0
C / 4.4	3.7	5.1	9.93	4	6	0	0	57	37	17	6.5	99	14	0	0	0.0	0.0
U /	N/A	4.4	9.51	22	1	0	0	6	93	42	3.8	N/A	2	1,000	100	3.8	0.0
U /	N/A	4.4	9.52	22	1	0	0	6	93	42	3.8	N/A	2	0	0	0.0	0.0
U /	N/A	4.4	9.52	N/A	1	0	0	6	93	42	3.8	N/A	2	0	0	0.0	0.0
A / 9.4	0.9	1.9	12.17	314	0	8	0	62	30	56	2.7	81	6	1,000	100	2.3	0.0
A / 9.4	0.9	1.9	12.18	87	0	8	0	62	30	56	2.7	45	6	1,000	100	0.0	0.0
A / 9.4	0.9	1.9	12.16	2,207	0	8	0	62	30	56	2.7	86	6	1,000,000	0	0.0	0.0
A / 9.4	0.9	1.9	12.16	134	0	8	0	62	30	56	2.7	78	6	1,000	100	0.0	0.0
A / 9.4	0.9	1.9	12.17	95	0	8	0	62	30	56	2.7	86	6	0	0	0.0	0.0
A / 9.4	0.9	1.9	12.16	1	0	8	0	62	30	56	2.7	55	6	0	0	0.0	0.0
A / 9.4	0.9	1.9	12.17	2	0	8	0	62	30	56	2.7	61	6	0	0	0.0	0.0
A / 9.4	0.9	1.9	12.17	12	0	8	0	62	30	56	2.7	71	6	0	0	0.0	0.0
A / 9.4	0.9	1.9	12.17	12	0	8	0	62	30	56	2.7	78	6	0	0	0.0	0.0
A / 9.4	0.9	1.9	12.17	10	0	8	0	62	30	56	2.7	82	6	0	0	0.0	0.0
C- / 3.3	4.5	5.1	7.46	255	2	0	97	0	1	21	5.5	33	3	1,000	100	3.8	0.0
C- / 3.3	4.5	5.1	7.48	23	2	0	97	0	1	21	5.5	15	3	1,000	100	0.0	0.0
C- / 3.3	4.5	5.1	7.47	1	2	0	97	0	1	21	5.5	36	3	0	0	0.0	0.0
U /	N/A	5.1	7.46	29	2	0	97	0	1	21	5.5	N/A	3	0	0	0.0	0.0
U /	N/A	N/A	1.00	312	100	0	0	0	0	0	0.0	N/A	N/A	15,000	100	0.0	0.0
U /	N/A	N/A	1.00	24	100	0	0	0	0	0	0.0	N/A	N/A	5,000	100	0.0	0.0
E+ / 0.8	6.9	N/A	18.08	6	100	0	0	0	0	0	0.0	2	7	15,000	100	0.0	0.0
E+ / 0.8	6.9	N/A	17.27	2	100	0	0	0	0	0	0.0	1	7	5,000	100	0.0	0.0
E- / 0.0	16.4	N/A	56.92	104	61	38	0	0	1	2,626	0.0	7	7	15,000	100	0.0	0.0
E- / 0.0	16.5	N/A	53.63	9	61	38	0	0	1	2,626	0.0	5	7	5,000	100	0.0	0.0
B / 7.9	2.4	1.4	9.31	254	2	4	0	53	41	64	-15.8	52	5	2,500	100	4.5	0.0
B / 7.9	2.5	1.4	9.34	135	2	4	0	53	41	64	-15.8	27	5	2,500	100	0.0	0.0
B / 7.9	2.5	1.4	9.33	157	2	4	0	53	41	64	-15.8	61	5	0	0	0.0	0.0
B / 8.0	2.4	1.4	9.35	1,420	2	4	0	53	41	64	-15.8	59	5	0	0	0.0	0.0
C- / 3.9	4.1	6.6	10.95	132	0	0	99	0	1	10	4.7	38	12	2,500	100	4.0	0.0
C- / 3.9	4.1	6.6	10.95	5	0	0	99	0	1	10	4.7	31	12	2,500	100	0.0	0.0
C- / 3.9	4.1	6.6	10.95	36	0	0	99	0	1	10	4.7	20	12	2,500	100	0.0	0.0
C- / 3.8	4.1	6.6	10.95	59	0	0	99	0	1	10	4.7	44	12	0	0	0.0	0.0
C+ / 6.7	3.0	N/A	9.98	4	0	0	0	0	100	535	0.0	18	1	2,500	100	4.5	0.0
C+ / 6.7	3.0	N/A	9.99	1	0	0	0	0	100	535	0.0	11	1	2,500	100	0.0	0.0
C+ / 6.7	3.0	N/A	9.98	N/A	0	0	0	0	100	535	0.0	24	1	0	0	0.0	0.0
C+ / 6.7	3.0	N/A	9.98	N/A	0	0	0	0	100	535	0.0	14	1	0	0	0.0	0.0
C+ / 6.7	3.0	N/A	9.98	89	0	0	0	0	100	535	0.0	15	1	0	0	0.0	0.0

Fund Type	Fund Name (99 Pct = Best, 0 Pct = Worst)	Ticker Symbol	Overall Investment Rating	Phone	PERFORMANCE: Performance Rating/Pts	Total Return % through 3/31/16: 3 Mo	6 Mo	1Yr / Pct	Annualized: 3Yr / Pct	5Yr / Pct	Incl. in Returns: Dividend Yield	Expense Ratio
GEI	Prudential Core Short-Term Bond Fd		**B+**	(800) 225-1852	**C / 4.8**	0.46	0.58	1.08 /60	1.28 /48	1.94 /30	1.62	0.07
MTG	Prudential Corporate Bond A	PCWAX	**C-**	(800) 225-1852	**C+ / 5.8**	4.90	4.18	2.67 /75	2.27 /67	3.18 /48	2.20	N/A
MTG	Prudential Corporate Bond C	PCWCX	**C**	(800) 225-1852	**C+ / 6.2**	4.53	3.62	1.66 /68	1.42 /51	2.36 /36	1.61	N/A
MTG	Prudential Corporate Bond Q	PCWQX	**B-**	(800) 225-1852	**B / 7.7**	4.77	4.11	2.63 /75	2.42 /69	3.38 /51	2.53	N/A
MTG	Prudential Corporate Bond R	PCWRX	**C+**	(800) 225-1852	**C+ / 6.8**	4.66	3.88	2.13 /73	1.75 /57	2.66 /40	2.02	N/A
MTG	Prudential Corporate Bond Z	TGMBX	**B-**	(800) 225-1852	**B / 7.8**	4.87	4.12	2.73 /75	2.46 /70	3.40 /52	2.54	1.02
GL	Prudential Emg Mkts Debt Loc Curr A	EMDAX	**E-**	(800) 225-1852	**E- / 0.1**	9.07	8.67	-3.33 /10	-7.47 / 1	-2.89 / 1	5.53	2.36
GL	Prudential Emg Mkts Debt Loc Curr C	EMDCX	**E-**	(800) 225-1852	**E- / 0.1**	9.71	9.09	-3.33 /10	-7.94 / 1	-3.30 / 1	5.06	3.11
GL	Prudential Emg Mkts Debt Loc Curr Q	EMDQX	**E-**	(800) 225-1852	**E- / 0.2**	9.91	9.77	-2.22 /15	-6.87 / 1	-2.34 / 1	6.04	2.01
GL	Prudential Emg Mkts Debt Loc Curr Z	EMDZX	**E-**	(800) 225-1852	**E- / 0.2**	10.09	9.75	-2.23 /15	-6.89 / 1	-2.36 / 1	6.00	2.11
LP	Prudential Floating Rate Inc A	FRFAX	**C**	(800) 225-1852	**C- / 4.1**	1.58	-0.21	-0.25 /29	1.94 /60	3.29 /50	3.47	1.56
LP	Prudential Floating Rate Inc C	FRFCX	**C**	(800) 225-1852	**C- / 4.1**	1.40	-0.58	-0.99 /22	1.12 /45	2.52 /38	2.83	2.31
LP	Prudential Floating Rate Inc Q	PFRIX	**B+**	(800) 225-1852	**C+ / 6.2**	1.65	-0.07	0.30 /46	2.27 /67	3.63 /55	3.83	N/A
LP	Prudential Floating Rate Inc Z	FRFZX	**B+**	(800) 225-1852	**C+ / 6.0**	1.54	-0.07	0.02 /33	2.17 /65	3.57 /54	3.86	1.31
GL	Prudential Global Total Return A	GTRAX	**D**	(800) 225-1852	**C / 5.3**	5.56	4.37	3.41 /79	1.74 /56	3.56 /54	3.28	1.21
GL	● Prudential Global Total Return B	PBTRX	**D**	(800) 225-1852	**C+ / 6.0**	5.38	4.15	2.66 /75	0.99 /42	2.79 /42	2.71	1.96
GL	Prudential Global Total Return C	PCTRX	**D**	(800) 225-1852	**C+ / 6.0**	5.38	4.16	2.66 /75	0.99 /42	2.83 /42	2.72	1.96
GL	Prudential Global Total Return Q	PGTQX	**C-**	(800) 225-1852	**B / 7.8**	5.59	4.52	3.59 /79	2.34 /68	4.04 /62	3.74	0.82
GL	Prudential Global Total Return Z	PZTRX	**D+**	(800) 225-1852	**B / 7.6**	5.60	4.64	3.66 /80	2.04 /62	3.81 /58	3.66	0.96
USS	Prudential Government Income A	PGVAX	**C-**	(800) 225-1852	**C- / 4.0**	2.79	1.72	1.43 /65	1.74 /56	3.06 /46	0.95	1.01
USS	● Prudential Government Income B	PBGPX	**C**	(800) 225-1852	**C / 4.7**	2.59	1.35	0.58 /51	0.98 /42	2.27 /35	0.28	1.76
USS	Prudential Government Income C	PRICX	**C**	(800) 225-1852	**C / 4.7**	2.58	1.35	0.68 /53	0.98 /42	2.29 /35	0.28	1.76
USS	Prudential Government Income R	JDRVX	**C+**	(800) 225-1852	**C+ / 5.7**	2.72	1.60	1.07 /60	1.49 /52	2.78 /41	0.76	1.51
USS	Prudential Government Income Z	PGVZX	**B**	(800) 225-1852	**C+ / 6.5**	2.86	1.85	1.68 /69	1.99 /61	3.32 /50	1.24	0.76
MM	Prudential Government Money Mkt A	PBMXX	**U**	(800) 225-1852	**U /**	--	--	--	--	--	0.01	0.59
MM	● Prudential Government Money Mkt B	MJBXX	**U**	(800) 225-1852	**U /**	--	--	--	--	--	0.01	0.47
MM	Prudential Government Money Mkt C	MJCXX	**U**	(800) 225-1852	**U /**	--	--	--	--	--	0.01	0.47
MM	Prudential Government Money Mkt Z	PMZXX	**U**	(800) 225-1852	**U /**	--	--	--	--	--	0.01	0.47
*COH	Prudential High Yield A	PBHAX	**D**	(800) 225-1852	**C- / 4.1**	3.24	1.29	-2.11 /15	2.32 /68	4.90 /71	6.18	0.83
COH	● Prudential High Yield B	PBHYX	**D**	(800) 225-1852	**C / 5.3**	3.12	1.04	-2.61 /13	1.81 /58	4.38 /66	5.96	1.33
COH	Prudential High Yield C	PRHCX	**D**	(800) 225-1852	**C / 4.8**	3.06	0.91	-2.86 /12	1.56 /53	4.12 /63	5.70	1.58
COH	Prudential High Yield Q	PHYQX	**D+**	(800) 225-1852	**C+ / 6.6**	3.33	1.29	-1.92 /16	2.58 /72	6.11 /77	6.87	0.46
COH	Prudential High Yield R	JDYRX	**D+**	(800) 225-1852	**C+ / 5.8**	3.18	1.17	-2.35 /14	2.07 /63	4.64 /69	6.22	1.33
COH	Prudential High Yield Z	PHYZX	**D+**	(800) 225-1852	**C+ / 6.7**	3.31	1.44	-1.83 /16	2.60 /72	5.18 /73	6.76	0.58
MUH	Prudential Muni High Income A	PRHAX	**C+**	(800) 225-1852	**A / 9.4**	1.97	4.06	4.86 /98	4.52 /98	7.51 /97	3.95	0.87
MUH	● Prudential Muni High Income B	PMHYX	**C+**	(800) 225-1852	**A+ / 9.8**	1.91	4.03	4.61 /97	4.30 /97	7.27 /97	3.88	1.12
MUH	Prudential Muni High Income C	PHICX	**C+**	(800) 225-1852	**A / 9.5**	1.79	3.68	4.10 /95	3.75 /94	6.72 /95	3.40	1.62
MUH	Prudential Muni High Income Z	PHIZX	**C+**	(800) 225-1852	**A+ / 9.8**	2.05	4.20	5.14 /98	4.79 /98	7.79 /98	4.38	0.62
*MUN	Prudential National Muni A	PRNMX	**C+**	(800) 225-1852	**B / 8.1**	1.46	3.21	3.38 /89	2.99 /88	5.60 /90	3.41	0.84
MUN	● Prudential National Muni B	PBHMX	**B-**	(800) 225-1852	**B+ / 8.8**	1.46	3.15	3.12 /86	2.73 /85	5.35 /88	3.31	1.09
MUN	Prudential National Muni C	PNMCX	**C+**	(800) 225-1852	**B+ / 8.3**	1.28	2.83	2.63 /82	2.23 /79	4.82 /84	2.83	1.59
MUN	Prudential National Muni Z	DNMZX	**B**	(800) 225-1852	**A- / 9.2**	1.59	3.34	3.63 /91	3.24 /90	5.87 /91	3.80	0.59
COI	Prudential Short Dur Mtl Sec Bd A	SDMAX	**U**	(800) 225-1852	**U /**	1.22	0.53	--	--	--	2.52	1.54
COI	Prudential Short Dur Mtl Sec Bd C	SDMCX	**U**	(800) 225-1852	**U /**	1.14	0.23	-0.67 /25	--	--	1.92	2.29
COI	Prudential Short Dur Mtl Sec Bd Q	SDMQX	**U**	(800) 225-1852	**U /**	1.38	0.63	0.24 /45	--	--	2.84	1.05
COI	Prudential Short Dur Mtl Sec Bd Z	SDMZX	**U**	(800) 225-1852	**U /**	1.38	0.73	0.24 /45	--	--	2.84	1.29
COH	Prudential Short Duration HY Inc A	HYSAX	**C-**	(800) 225-1852	**C+ / 5.6**	1.84	1.88	1.21 /62	2.45 /70	--	6.14	1.11
COH	Prudential Short Duration HY Inc C	HYSCX	**C-**	(800) 225-1852	**C+ / 5.7**	1.65	1.62	0.46 /49	1.69 /56	--	5.59	1.86
COH	Prudential Short Duration HY Inc Q	HYSQX	**B-**	(800) 225-1852	**B- / 7.5**	1.92	2.17	1.56 /67	2.79 /74	--	6.69	0.77
COH	Prudential Short Duration HY Inc Z	HYSZX	**C+**	(800) 225-1852	**B- / 7.4**	1.90	2.01	1.36 /64	2.71 /73	--	6.61	0.86
*COI	Prudential Short-Term Corp Bond A	PBSMX	**C+**	(800) 225-1852	**C- / 3.8**	1.61	1.23	1.25 /62	1.42 /51	2.37 /36	2.42	0.78
COI	● Prudential Short-Term Corp Bond B	PSMBX	**C+**	(800) 225-1852	**C- / 3.9**	1.43	0.85	0.49 /49	0.67 /36	1.61 /27	1.74	1.53

● Denotes fund is closed to new investors
* Denotes fund is included in Section II

RISK			NET ASSETS		ASSET							FUND MANAGER		MINIMUM		LOADS	
Risk Rating/Pts	3 Yr Avg Standard Deviation	Avg Duration	NAV As of 3/31/16	Total $(Mil)	Cash %	Gov. Bond %	Muni. Bond %	Corp. Bond %	Other %	Portfolio Turnover Ratio	Avg Coupon Rate	Manager Quality Pct	Manager Tenure (Years)	Initial Purch. $	Additional Purch. $	Front End Load	Back End Load
A+ / 9.8	0.5	0.2	9.28	2,998	0	0	0	47	53	34	1.7	91	N/A	2,500	100	0.0	0.0
C / 5.0	3.5	N/A	11.01	N/A	2	0	4	82	12	1,221	0.0	39	1	2,500	100	4.5	0.0
C / 5.1	3.4	N/A	10.98	1	2	0	4	82	12	1,221	0.0	18	1	2,500	100	0.0	0.0
C / 5.1	3.4	N/A	10.98	N/A	2	0	4	82	12	1,221	0.0	44	1	0	0	0.0	0.0
C / 5.1	3.4	N/A	10.98	N/A	2	0	4	82	12	1,221	0.0	25	1	0	0	0.0	0.0
C / 5.1	3.4	N/A	10.99	20	2	0	4	82	12	1,221	0.0	45	1	0	0	0.0	0.0
E- / 0.1	12.6	5.3	6.35	3	3	86	0	9	2	101	6.6	1	5	2,500	100	4.5	0.0
E- / 0.0	12.7	5.3	6.44	1	3	86	0	9	2	101	6.6	1	5	2,500	100	0.0	0.0
E- / 0.0	12.7	5.3	6.46	N/A	3	86	0	9	2	101	6.6	1	5	0	0	0.0	0.0
E- / 0.0	12.7	5.3	6.47	26	3	86	0	9	2	101	6.6	1	5	0	0	0.0	0.0
B / 8.0	2.4	1.8	9.59	50	4	0	0	14	82	64	4.6	93	5	2,500	100	3.3	0.0
B / 7.9	2.4	1.8	9.59	36	4	0	0	14	82	64	4.6	85	5	2,500	100	0.0	0.0
B / 8.0	2.4	1.8	9.60	N/A	4	0	0	14	82	64	4.6	95	5	0	0	0.0	0.0
B / 8.1	2.4	1.8	9.60	149	4	0	0	14	82	64	4.6	94	5	0	0	0.0	0.0
E+ / 0.9	6.4	8.2	6.60	156	3	44	1	23	29	95	2.1	95	14	2,500	100	4.5	0.0
E+ / 0.8	6.4	8.2	6.60	4	3	44	1	23	29	95	2.1	91	14	2,500	100	0.0	0.0
E+ / 0.8	6.4	8.2	6.59	29	3	44	1	23	29	95	2.1	91	14	2,500	100	0.0	0.0
E+ / 0.9	6.4	8.2	6.68	28	3	44	1	23	29	95	2.1	97	14	0	0	0.0	0.0
E+ / 0.8	6.5	8.2	6.63	127	3	44	1	23	29	95	2.1	96	14	0	0	0.0	0.0
B- / 7.1	2.8	5.3	9.75	370	0	28	0	1	71	817	2.5	55	13	2,500	100	4.5	0.0
C+ / 6.9	2.9	5.3	9.76	3	0	28	0	1	71	817	2.5	29	13	2,500	100	0.0	0.0
C+ / 6.9	2.9	5.3	9.77	13	0	28	0	1	71	817	2.5	29	13	2,500	100	0.0	0.0
C+ / 6.9	2.9	5.3	9.76	15	0	28	0	1	71	817	2.5	44	13	0	0	0.0	0.0
B- / 7.0	2.9	5.3	9.73	111	0	28	0	1	71	817	2.5	68	13	0	0	0.0	0.0
U /	N/A	N/A	1.00	485	100	0	0	0	0	0	0.0	N/A	N/A	2,500	100	0.0	0.0
U /	N/A	N/A	1.00	21	100	0	0	0	0	0	0.0	N/A	N/A	2,500	100	0.0	0.0
U /	N/A	N/A	1.00	18	100	0	0	0	0	0	0.0	N/A	N/A	2,500	100	0.0	0.0
U /	N/A	N/A	1.00	107	100	0	0	0	0	0	0.0	N/A	N/A	0	0	0.0	0.0
D- / 1.5	5.6	4.3	5.13	1,149	4	0	0	93	3	48	6.6	86	17	2,500	100	4.5	0.0
D- / 1.5	5.6	4.3	5.12	185	4	0	0	93	3	48	6.6	74	17	2,500	100	0.0	0.0
D- / 1.4	5.7	4.3	5.12	215	4	0	0	93	3	48	6.6	59	17	2,500	100	0.0	0.0
D / 1.6	5.5	4.3	5.13	203	4	0	0	93	3	48	6.6	89	17	0	0	0.0	0.0
D- / 1.5	5.6	4.3	5.13	50	4	0	0	93	3	48	6.6	81	17	0	0	0.0	0.0
D- / 1.5	5.6	4.3	5.14	1,796	4	0	0	93	3	48	6.6	89	17	0	0	0.0	0.0
D / 1.8	5.1	7.2	10.39	398	3	0	96	0	1	10	5.3	39	12	2,500	100	4.0	0.0
D / 1.9	5.1	7.2	10.40	58	3	0	96	0	1	10	5.3	34	12	2,500	100	0.0	0.0
D / 1.9	5.1	7.2	10.39	122	3	0	96	0	1	10	5.3	21	12	2,500	100	0.0	0.0
D / 1.9	5.1	7.2	10.38	257	3	0	96	0	1	10	5.3	49	12	0	0	0.0	0.0
C- / 3.7	4.2	6.7	15.27	599	1	0	98	0	1	15	5.0	21	12	2,500	100	4.0	0.0
C- / 3.7	4.2	6.7	15.32	26	1	0	98	0	1	15	5.0	16	12	2,500	100	0.0	0.0
C- / 3.6	4.2	6.7	15.31	31	1	0	98	0	1	15	5.0	11	12	2,500	100	0.0	0.0
C- / 3.6	4.2	6.7	15.26	32	1	0	98	0	1	15	5.0	26	12	0	0	0.0	0.0
U /	N/A	2.7	9.58	9	7	4	0	52	37	51	1.2	N/A	3	2,500	100	3.3	0.0
U /	N/A	2.7	9.59	8	7	4	0	52	37	51	1.2	N/A	3	2,500	100	0.0	0.0
U /	N/A	2.7	9.59	85	7	4	0	52	37	51	1.2	N/A	3	0	0	0.0	0.0
U /	N/A	2.7	9.59	10	7	4	0	52	37	51	1.2	N/A	3	0	0	0.0	0.0
C / 5.3	2.8	2.2	8.96	434	3	0	0	93	4	56	7.1	94	2	2,500	100	3.3	0.0
C / 5.1	2.9	2.2	8.96	298	3	0	0	93	4	56	7.1	88	2	2,500	100	0.0	0.0
C / 5.2	2.9	2.2	8.97	20	3	0	0	93	4	56	7.1	96	2	0	0	0.0	0.0
C / 5.3	2.9	2.2	8.96	842	3	0	0	93	4	56	7.1	95	2	0	0	0.0	0.0
B+ / 8.9	1.5	2.6	11.11	1,631	1	0	0	88	11	49	3.3	83	17	2,500	100	3.3	0.0
B+ / 8.8	1.6	2.6	11.11	26	1	0	0	88	11	49	3.3	52	17	2,500	100	0.0	0.0

Fund Type	Fund Name (99 Pct = Best, 0 Pct = Worst)	Ticker Symbol	Overall Investment Rating	Phone	PERFORMANCE: Performance Rating/Pts	Total Return % through 3/31/16: 3 Mo	6 Mo	1Yr / Pct	Annualized: 3Yr / Pct	Annualized: 5Yr / Pct	Incl. in Returns: Dividend Yield	Expense Ratio
COI	Prudential Short-Term Corp Bond C	PIFCX	**C+**	(800) 225-1852	**C- / 3.9**	1.43	0.86	0.50 /49	0.67 /36	1.61 /27	1.75	1.53
COI	Prudential Short-Term Corp Bond Q	PSTQX	**A**	(800) 225-1852	**C+ / 6.1**	1.70	1.41	1.70 /69	1.84 /58	2.69 /40	2.85	0.43
COI	Prudential Short-Term Corp Bond R	JDTRX	**B**	(800) 225-1852	**C / 4.9**	1.55	1.11	1.00 /59	1.18 /46	2.11 /33	2.25	1.28
COI	Prudential Short-Term Corp Bond Z	PIFZX	**A-**	(800) 225-1852	**C+ / 5.9**	1.67	1.36	1.60 /68	1.68 /55	2.63 /39	2.75	0.53
MUH	Prudential Sht Dur Muni High Inc A	PDSAX	**U**	(800) 225-1852	**U /**	1.50	2.57	3.07 /86	--	--	2.00	1.48
MUH	Prudential Sht Dur Muni High Inc C	PDSCX	**U**	(800) 225-1852	**U /**	1.31	2.19	2.30 /79	--	--	1.33	2.23
MUH	Prudential Sht Dur Muni High Inc Z	PDSZX	**U**	(800) 225-1852	**U /**	1.56	2.70	3.33 /88	--	--	2.31	1.23
* GES	Prudential Total Return Bond A	PDBAX	**C-**	(800) 225-1852	**C / 5.2**	3.11	2.04	0.49 /49	2.55 /71	4.66 /69	2.42	0.87
GES ●	Prudential Total Return Bond B	PRDBX	**C-**	(800) 225-1852	**C+ / 6.3**	2.98	1.84	-0.05 /31	2.04 /62	4.13 /63	2.07	1.62
GES	Prudential Total Return Bond C	PDBCX	**C-**	(800) 225-1852	**C+ / 5.8**	2.85	1.66	-0.27 /28	1.78 /57	3.87 /60	1.85	1.62
GES	Prudential Total Return Bond Q	PTRQX	**C+**	(800) 225-1852	**B / 7.6**	3.21	2.20	0.85 /56	2.91 /75	5.01 /72	2.89	0.49
GES	Prudential Total Return Bond R	DTBRX	**C**	(800) 225-1852	**C+ / 6.8**	3.04	1.94	0.27 /45	2.31 /68	4.40 /67	2.31	1.37
GES	Prudential Total Return Bond Z	PDBZX	**C+**	(800) 225-1852	**B- / 7.5**	3.18	2.16	0.66 /53	2.82 /75	4.92 /71	2.78	0.62
GL	Putnam Absolute Return 100 A	PARTX	**C-**	(800) 225-1581	**D- / 1.2**	-1.01	-1.03	-1.72 /17	0.07 /26	0.15 /15	1.60	0.67
GL	Putnam Absolute Return 100 B	PARPX	**C-**	(800) 225-1581	**D- / 1.3**	-1.01	-1.11	-1.90 /16	-0.13 /15	-0.04 / 3	1.33	0.87
GL	Putnam Absolute Return 100 C	PARQX	**D+**	(800) 225-1581	**E+ / 0.8**	-1.22	-1.49	-2.47 /13	-0.67 /10	-0.60 / 2	0.84	1.42
GL	Putnam Absolute Return 100 M	PARZX	**C-**	(800) 225-1581	**D- / 1.2**	-1.01	-1.09	-1.78 /17	0.02 /18	0.10 /14	1.54	0.72
GL	Putnam Absolute Return 100 R	PRARX	**C-**	(800) 225-1581	**D- / 1.2**	-1.00	-1.10	-1.89 /16	-0.16 /14	-0.08 / 3	0.00	0.92
GL	Putnam Absolute Return 100 Y	PARYX	**C-**	(800) 225-1581	**D / 1.8**	-0.91	-0.87	-1.45 /19	0.33 /30	0.42 /17	1.87	0.42
GL	Putnam Absolute Return 300 A	PTRNX	**D**	(800) 225-1581	**E / 0.5**	-3.10	-3.26	-4.76 / 5	-0.51 /11	-0.03 / 3	4.77	0.84
GL	Putnam Absolute Return 300 B	PTRBX	**D**	(800) 225-1581	**E / 0.5**	-3.11	-3.31	-4.91 / 5	-0.70 /10	-0.24 / 2	4.59	1.04
GL	Putnam Absolute Return 300 C	PTRGX	**D**	(800) 225-1581	**E / 0.4**	-3.22	-3.53	-5.41 / 4	-1.25 / 7	-0.78 / 2	3.93	1.59
GL	Putnam Absolute Return 300 M	PZARX	**D**	(800) 225-1581	**E / 0.5**	-3.11	-3.30	-4.80 / 5	-0.55 /11	-0.09 / 3	4.76	0.89
GL	Putnam Absolute Return 300 R	PTRKX	**D**	(800) 225-1581	**E / 0.5**	-3.19	-3.37	-5.06 / 5	-0.78 / 9	-0.29 / 2	4.04	1.09
GL	Putnam Absolute Return 300 Y	PYTRX	**D**	(800) 225-1581	**E+ / 0.7**	-2.99	-3.07	-4.48 / 6	-0.28 /13	0.21 /16	5.11	0.59
GL	Putnam Absolute Return 500 A	PJMDX	**D**	(800) 225-1581	**E+ / 0.8**	-1.03	-1.51	-3.29 /10	1.20 /46	2.16 /33	4.60	1.15
GL	Putnam Absolute Return 500 B	PJMBX	**D**	(800) 225-1581	**D- / 1.4**	-1.13	-1.81	-3.96 / 8	0.46 /32	1.39 /24	4.05	1.90
GL	Putnam Absolute Return 500 C	PJMCX	**D**	(800) 225-1581	**D- / 1.4**	-1.23	-1.86	-4.01 / 8	0.45 /32	1.38 /24	4.21	1.90
GL	Putnam Absolute Return 500 M	PJMMX	**D**	(800) 225-1581	**E+ / 0.9**	-1.04	-1.65	-3.70 / 9	0.73 /38	1.66 /27	4.34	1.65
GL	Putnam Absolute Return 500 R	PJMRX	**D**	(800) 225-1581	**D+ / 2.8**	-1.01	-1.51	-3.40 /10	0.98 /42	1.91 /30	1.26	1.40
GL	Putnam Absolute Return 500 Y	PJMYX	**D+**	(800) 225-1581	**C- / 3.7**	-0.84	-1.33	-2.95 /12	1.47 /52	2.42 /37	5.13	0.90
GL	Putnam Absolute Return 700 A	PDMAX	**D-**	(800) 225-1581	**E+ / 0.8**	-1.26	-2.17	-5.06 / 5	1.48 /52	2.53 /38	6.87	1.27
GL	Putnam Absolute Return 700 B	PDMBX	**D-**	(800) 225-1581	**D- / 1.3**	-1.47	-2.58	-5.83 / 3	0.72 /37	1.75 /28	6.59	2.02
GL	Putnam Absolute Return 700 C	PDMCX	**D-**	(800) 225-1581	**D- / 1.3**	-1.47	-2.54	-5.80 / 3	0.72 /37	1.75 /28	6.73	2.02
GL	Putnam Absolute Return 700 M	PDMMX	**D-**	(800) 225-1581	**E+ / 0.8**	-1.37	-2.47	-5.63 / 4	0.98 /42	2.01 /31	6.69	1.77
GL	Putnam Absolute Return 700 R	PDMRX	**D**	(800) 225-1581	**D+ / 2.6**	-1.27	-2.31	-5.31 / 4	1.25 /47	2.28 /35	7.03	1.52
GL	Putnam Absolute Return 700 Y	PDMYX	**D**	(800) 225-1581	**C- / 3.5**	-1.17	-2.01	-4.83 / 5	1.75 /57	2.79 /42	7.53	1.02
USS	Putnam American Government A	PAGVX	**C-**	(800) 225-1581	**D- / 1.4**	0.53	0.25	-1.17 /20	0.87 /40	2.22 /34	2.56	0.89
USS	Putnam American Government B	PAMBX	**C-**	(800) 225-1581	**D / 1.7**	0.30	-0.16	-1.95 /16	0.11 /27	1.45 /25	1.90	1.64
USS	Putnam American Government C	PAMIX	**C-**	(800) 225-1581	**D / 1.6**	0.30	-0.16	-2.05 /15	0.10 /27	1.44 /25	1.89	1.64
USS	Putnam American Government M	PAMMX	**C-**	(800) 225-1581	**D- / 1.3**	0.36	0.14	-1.51 /18	0.63 /36	1.94 /31	2.32	1.14
USS	Putnam American Government R	PAMRX	**C**	(800) 225-1581	**C- / 3.1**	0.37	0.14	-1.52 /18	0.60 /35	1.95 /31	2.42	1.14
USL	Putnam American Government R5	PAMDX	**C+**	(800) 225-1581	**C- / 4.1**	0.46	0.37	-1.04 /21	1.13 /45	--	2.93	0.61
USL	Putnam American Government R6	PAMEX	**C+**	(800) 225-1581	**C- / 4.2**	0.47	0.30	-0.94 /22	1.20 /46	--	3.04	0.54
USS	Putnam American Government Y	PATYX	**C+**	(800) 225-1581	**C- / 4.0**	0.46	0.25	-1.04 /21	1.09 /44	2.44 /37	2.93	0.64
MUI	Putnam AMT Free Ins Mun A	PPNAX	**B**	(800) 225-1581	**B / 8.2**	1.48	2.87	3.08 /86	3.31 /91	5.73 /90	3.39	0.78
MUI	Putnam AMT Free Ins Mun B	PTFIX	**B+**	(800) 225-1581	**B+ / 8.6**	1.39	2.56	2.45 /80	2.68 /85	5.09 /86	2.92	1.40
MUI	Putnam AMT Free Ins Mun C	PAMTX	**B**	(800) 225-1581	**B+ / 8.4**	1.29	2.47	2.29 /79	2.52 /83	4.93 /85	2.76	1.55
MUI	Putnam AMT Free Ins Mun M	PPMTX	**B**	(800) 225-1581	**B / 8.2**	1.48	2.79	2.80 /83	3.05 /89	5.46 /89	3.15	1.05
MUI	Putnam AMT Free Ins Mun Y	PAMYX	**A**	(800) 225-1581	**A / 9.4**	1.54	2.99	3.32 /88	3.55 /93	5.99 /92	3.76	0.55
MUS	Putnam AZ Tax Exempt Inc A	PTAZX	**B-**	(800) 225-1581	**B / 7.7**	1.57	2.68	2.91 /84	2.80 /86	5.16 /87	2.84	0.92
MUS	Putnam AZ Tax Exempt Inc B	PAZBX	**B**	(800) 225-1581	**B / 8.2**	1.41	2.36	2.27 /79	2.20 /79	4.51 /81	2.33	1.55

● Denotes fund is closed to new investors
* Denotes fund is included in Section II

RISK			NET ASSETS		ASSET							FUND MANAGER		MINIMUM		LOADS	
Risk Rating/Pts	3 Yr Avg Standard Deviation	Avg Duration	NAV As of 3/31/16	Total $(Mil)	Cash %	Gov. Bond %	Muni. Bond %	Corp. Bond %	Other %	Portfolio Turnover Ratio	Avg Coupon Rate	Manager Quality Pct	Manager Tenure (Years)	Initial Purch. $	Additional Purch. $	Front End Load	Back End Load
B+ / 8.9	1.5	2.6	11.11	1,551	1	0	0	88	11	49	3.3	52	17	2,500	100	0.0	0.0
B+ / 8.9	1.5	2.6	11.15	141	1	0	0	88	11	49	3.3	89	17	0	0	0.0	0.0
B+ / 8.9	1.5	2.6	11.11	162	1	0	0	88	11	49	3.3	76	17	0	0	0.0	0.0
B+ / 8.9	1.6	2.6	11.14	5,752	1	0	0	88	11	49	3.3	87	17	0	0	0.0	0.0
U /	N/A	3.8	10.26	61	14	0	85	0	1	31	4.2	N/A	2	2,500	100	3.3	0.0
U /	N/A	3.8	10.25	21	14	0	85	0	1	31	4.2	N/A	2	2,500	100	0.0	0.0
U /	N/A	3.8	10.26	64	14	0	85	0	1	31	4.2	N/A	2	0	0	0.0	0.0
C- / 4.1	3.9	6.3	14.36	3,122	2	10	1	52	35	114	2.9	44	14	2,500	100	4.5	0.0
C- / 4.1	3.9	6.3	14.36	45	2	10	1	52	35	114	2.9	29	14	2,500	100	0.0	0.0
C- / 4.1	3.9	6.3	14.34	472	2	10	1	52	35	114	2.9	23	14	2,500	100	0.0	0.0
C- / 4.1	3.9	6.3	14.34	2,717	2	10	1	52	35	114	2.9	56	14	0	0	0.0	0.0
C- / 4.1	3.9	6.3	14.39	570	2	10	1	52	35	114	2.9	36	14	0	0	0.0	0.0
C- / 4.1	3.9	6.3	14.31	6,567	2	10	1	52	35	114	2.9	53	14	0	0	0.0	0.0
A- / 9.2	1.1	-0.2	9.79	110	4	3	0	58	35	105	2.4	68	8	500	0	1.0	0.0
A- / 9.2	1.1	-0.2	9.77	2	4	3	0	58	35	105	2.4	56	8	500	0	0.0	0.0
A- / 9.2	1.1	-0.2	9.74	24	4	3	0	58	35	105	2.4	37	8	500	0	0.0	0.0
A- / 9.2	1.1	-0.2	9.77	2	4	3	0	58	35	105	2.4	62	8	500	0	0.8	0.0
A- / 9.1	1.1	-0.2	9.87	N/A	4	3	0	58	35	105	2.4	55	8	500	0	0.0	0.0
A- / 9.1	1.1	-0.2	9.82	104	4	3	0	58	35	105	2.4	78	8	500	0	0.0	0.0
C+ / 6.7	3.0	-1.0	9.39	317	0	4	0	37	59	486	4.3	42	8	500	0	1.0	0.0
C+ / 6.7	3.0	-1.0	9.35	8	0	4	0	37	59	486	4.3	36	8	500	0	0.0	0.0
C+ / 6.7	2.9	-1.0	9.33	115	0	4	0	37	59	486	4.3	21	8	500	0	0.0	0.0
C+ / 6.8	2.9	-1.0	9.36	9	0	4	0	37	59	486	4.3	40	8	500	0	0.8	0.0
C+ / 6.8	2.9	-1.0	9.41	N/A	0	4	0	37	59	486	4.3	34	8	500	0	0.0	0.0
C+ / 6.7	3.0	-1.0	9.41	257	0	4	0	37	59	486	4.3	50	8	500	0	0.0	0.0
C / 4.9	3.5	4.1	10.56	380	22	1	0	17	60	510	3.0	91	8	500	0	5.8	0.0
C / 5.0	3.5	4.1	10.46	32	22	1	0	17	60	510	3.0	81	8	500	0	0.0	0.0
C / 5.0	3.5	4.1	10.42	206	22	1	0	17	60	510	3.0	81	8	500	0	0.0	0.0
C / 4.9	3.5	4.1	10.48	10	22	1	0	17	60	510	3.0	86	8	500	0	3.5	0.0
C / 5.0	3.5	4.1	10.81	1	22	1	0	17	60	510	3.0	89	8	500	0	0.0	0.0
C / 5.0	3.5	4.1	10.60	537	22	1	0	17	60	510	3.0	93	8	500	0	0.0	0.0
D+ / 2.7	5.1	5.9	10.95	388	0	1	0	22	77	563	5.6	93	8	500	0	5.8	0.0
D+ / 2.7	5.0	5.9	10.73	30	0	1	0	22	77	563	5.6	86	8	500	0	0.0	0.0
D+ / 2.7	5.0	5.9	10.71	206	0	1	0	22	77	563	5.6	86	8	500	0	0.0	0.0
D+ / 2.7	5.1	5.9	10.78	7	0	1	0	22	77	563	5.6	89	8	500	0	3.5	0.0
D+ / 2.7	5.0	5.9	10.84	2	0	1	0	22	77	563	5.6	91	8	500	0	0.0	0.0
D+ / 2.7	5.0	5.9	10.96	695	0	1	0	22	77	563	5.6	95	8	500	0	0.0	0.0
B+ / 8.8	1.7	2.8	8.76	425	0	26	0	0	74	970	4.0	71	9	500	0	4.0	0.0
B+ / 8.7	1.8	2.8	8.68	5	0	26	0	0	74	970	4.0	39	9	500	0	0.0	0.0
B+ / 8.7	1.8	2.8	8.72	21	0	26	0	0	74	970	4.0	39	9	500	0	0.0	0.0
B+ / 8.7	1.8	2.8	8.83	1	0	26	0	0	74	970	4.0	58	9	500	0	3.3	0.0
B+ / 8.7	1.8	2.8	8.77	5	0	26	0	0	74	970	4.0	56	9	500	0	0.0	0.0
B+ / 8.7	1.8	2.8	8.74	1	0	26	0	0	74	970	4.0	82	9	0	0	0.0	0.0
B+ / 8.7	1.8	2.8	8.73	1	0	26	0	0	74	970	4.0	83	9	0	0	0.0	0.0
B+ / 8.8	1.7	2.8	8.73	41	0	26	0	0	74	970	4.0	78	9	500	0	0.0	0.0
C / 4.8	3.6	6.1	15.46	328	0	0	100	0	0	10	4.9	46	14	500	0	4.0	0.0
C / 4.7	3.6	6.1	15.48	3	0	0	100	0	0	10	4.9	27	14	500	0	0.0	0.0
C / 4.8	3.6	6.1	15.50	29	0	0	100	0	0	10	4.9	24	14	500	0	0.0	0.0
C / 4.8	3.6	6.1	15.51	1	0	0	100	0	0	10	4.9	38	14	500	0	3.3	0.0
C / 4.8	3.6	6.1	15.47	42	0	0	100	0	0	10	4.9	55	14	500	0	0.0	0.0
C / 5.2	3.4	5.7	9.30	44	0	0	99	0	1	23	4.9	36	17	500	0	4.0	0.0
C / 5.1	3.4	5.7	9.29	1	0	0	99	0	1	23	4.9	21	17	500	0	0.0	0.0

99 Pct = Best
0 Pct = Worst

Fund Type	Fund Name	Ticker Symbol	Overall Investment Rating	Phone	PERFORMANCE Perfor-mance Rating/Pts	Total Return % through 3/31/16 3 Mo	6 Mo	1Yr / Pct	Annualized 3Yr / Pct	5Yr / Pct	Incl. in Returns Dividend Yield	Expense Ratio
MUS	Putnam AZ Tax Exempt Inc C	PAZCX	**B**	(800) 225-1581	**B / 8.0**	1.37	2.28	2.11 /78	2.04 /77	4.36 /80	2.18	1.70
MUS	Putnam AZ Tax Exempt Inc M	PAZMX	**B-**	(800) 225-1581	**B / 7.6**	1.49	2.53	2.62 /81	2.55 /83	4.88 /84	2.58	1.20
MUS	Putnam AZ Tax Exempt Inc Y	PAZYX	**A-**	(800) 225-1581	**A- / 9.0**	1.62	2.79	3.13 /86	3.06 /89	5.41 /88	3.17	0.70
*MUS	Putnam CA Tax Exempt Income A	PCTEX	**B-**	(800) 225-1581	**B+ / 8.7**	1.71	3.19	3.57 /91	3.71 /94	6.81 /96	3.45	0.74
MUS	Putnam CA Tax Exempt Income B	PCTBX	**B**	(800) 225-1581	**A- / 9.0**	1.55	3.00	3.05 /85	3.05 /89	6.17 /93	2.97	1.37
MUS	Putnam CA Tax Exempt Income C	PCTCX	**B**	(800) 225-1581	**B+ / 8.9**	1.50	2.90	2.87 /84	2.87 /87	5.99 /92	2.80	1.52
MUS	Putnam CA Tax Exempt Income M	PCLMX	**B-**	(800) 225-1581	**B+ / 8.6**	1.64	3.18	3.41 /89	3.42 /92	6.52 /95	3.22	1.02
MUS	Putnam CA Tax Exempt Income Y	PCIYX	**B+**	(800) 225-1581	**A+ / 9.6**	1.75	3.42	3.90 /93	3.96 /96	7.07 /97	3.79	0.52
*GES	Putnam Diversified Income A	PDINX	**E+**	(800) 225-1581	**E- / 0.2**	-4.67	-3.87	-7.23 / 2	-0.93 / 9	1.10 /21	5.13	0.98
GES	Putnam Diversified Income B	PSIBX	**E+**	(800) 225-1581	**E / 0.3**	-4.75	-4.11	-7.86 / 1	-1.64 / 5	0.37 /17	4.57	1.73
GES	Putnam Diversified Income C	PDVCX	**E+**	(800) 225-1581	**E / 0.3**	-4.79	-4.14	-7.91 / 1	-1.69 / 5	0.35 /16	4.60	1.73
GES	Putnam Diversified Income M	PDVMX	**E+**	(800) 225-1581	**E- / 0.2**	-4.65	-4.01	-7.54 / 2	-1.20 / 7	0.85 /19	5.02	1.23
GES	Putnam Diversified Income R	PDVRX	**E+**	(800) 225-1581	**E / 0.3**	-4.63	-3.85	-7.40 / 2	-1.16 / 8	0.87 /19	5.12	1.23
GEL	Putnam Diversified Income R6	PDVGX	**U**	(800) 225-1581	**U /**	-4.63	-3.73	-6.97 / 2	--	--	5.75	0.64
GES	Putnam Diversified Income Y	PDVYX	**E+**	(800) 225-1581	**E / 0.4**	-4.53	-3.65	-6.91 / 2	-0.65 /11	1.38 /24	5.68	0.73
EM	Putnam Emerging Markets Income A	PEMWX	**E**	(800) 225-1581	**D- / 1.4**	6.11	7.71	2.39 /74	-0.94 / 9	--	3.11	2.48
EM	Putnam Emerging Markets Income B	PEMHX	**E+**	(800) 225-1581	**D / 1.7**	5.92	7.32	1.64 /68	-1.67 / 5	--	2.64	3.23
EM	Putnam Emerging Markets Income C	PEMJX	**E+**	(800) 225-1581	**D / 1.7**	5.92	7.32	1.55 /67	-1.68 / 5	--	2.66	3.23
EM	Putnam Emerging Markets Income M	PEMKX	**E**	(800) 225-1581	**D- / 1.3**	5.95	7.60	2.03 /72	-1.18 / 7	--	2.91	2.73
EM	Putnam Emerging Markets Income Y	PEMOX	**D-**	(800) 225-1581	**C- / 4.1**	6.13	7.81	2.64 /75	-0.69 /10	--	3.47	2.23
COH	Putnam Floating Rate Income A	PFLRX	**C-**	(800) 225-1581	**C- / 4.2**	1.99	-0.30	-1.05 /21	1.42 /51	3.09 /47	4.26	0.99
COH	Putnam Floating Rate Income B	PFRBX	**C-**	(800) 225-1581	**C- / 4.2**	1.81	-0.40	-1.36 /19	1.17 /46	2.86 /43	4.10	1.19
COH	Putnam Floating Rate Income C	PFICX	**D+**	(800) 225-1581	**C- / 3.2**	1.68	-0.67	-1.79 /17	0.66 /36	2.32 /35	3.54	1.74
COH	Putnam Floating Rate Income M	PFLMX	**C-**	(800) 225-1581	**C- / 4.1**	1.85	-0.44	-1.22 /20	1.33 /49	3.02 /45	4.23	1.04
COH	Putnam Floating Rate Income R	PFLLX	**C-**	(800) 225-1581	**C- / 4.1**	1.80	-0.42	-1.41 /19	1.12 /45	2.81 /42	4.05	1.24
COH	Putnam Floating Rate Income Y	PFRYX	**C-**	(800) 225-1581	**C / 5.1**	2.05	-0.17	-0.80 /23	1.67 /55	3.35 /51	4.56	0.74
GL	Putnam Global Income A	PGGIX	**D**	(800) 225-1581	**D- / 1.1**	1.51	1.30	-1.47 /19	0.39 /31	1.79 /29	3.11	1.11
GL	Putnam Global Income B	PGLBX	**D**	(800) 225-1581	**D- / 1.4**	1.24	0.85	-2.22 /15	-0.36 /13	1.02 /21	2.49	1.86
GL	Putnam Global Income C	PGGLX	**D**	(800) 225-1581	**D- / 1.3**	1.24	0.85	-2.29 /14	-0.39 /12	1.03 /21	2.50	1.86
GL	Putnam Global Income M	PGGMX	**D**	(800) 225-1581	**D- / 1.1**	1.39	1.12	-1.72 /17	0.15 /28	1.53 /26	2.93	1.36
GL	Putnam Global Income R	PGBRX	**D**	(800) 225-1581	**D+ / 2.4**	1.37	1.12	-1.79 /17	0.11 /27	1.53 /26	3.01	1.36
GL	Putnam Global Income R5	PGGDX	**D+**	(800) 225-1581	**C- / 3.6**	1.51	1.29	-1.33 /19	0.66 /36	--	3.55	0.83
GL	Putnam Global Income R6	PGGEX	**D+**	(800) 225-1581	**C- / 3.7**	1.53	1.41	-1.19 /20	0.72 /37	--	3.61	0.76
GL	Putnam Global Income Y	PGGYX	**D+**	(800) 225-1581	**C- / 3.5**	1.48	1.33	-1.32 /19	0.63 /36	2.03 /32	3.49	0.86
COH	Putnam High Yield Advantage A	PHYIX	**E+**	(800) 225-1581	**D- / 1.2**	3.25	0.47	-4.61 / 6	1.12 /45	4.03 /62	5.70	1.03
COH	Putnam High Yield Advantage B	PHYBX	**E+**	(800) 225-1581	**D- / 1.4**	3.13	0.11	-5.41 / 4	0.38 /31	3.26 /49	5.31	1.78
COH	Putnam High Yield Advantage C	PHYLX	**E+**	(800) 225-1581	**D- / 1.4**	2.96	0.14	-5.41 / 4	0.38 /31	3.24 /49	5.35	1.78
COH	Putnam High Yield Advantage M	PHYMX	**E+**	(800) 225-1581	**D- / 1.1**	3.01	0.17	-4.99 / 5	0.86 /40	3.75 /57	5.55	1.28
COH	Putnam High Yield Advantage R	PFJAX	**D-**	(800) 225-1581	**D+ / 2.6**	3.01	0.17	-4.99 / 5	0.86 /40	3.75 /57	5.74	1.28
COH	Putnam High Yield Advantage Y	PHAYX	**D**	(800) 225-1581	**C- / 3.7**	3.34	0.55	-4.38 / 7	1.39 /50	4.29 /65	5.88	0.78
*COH	Putnam High Yield Trust A	PHIGX	**E+**	(800) 225-1581	**D- / 1.5**	2.85	0.48	-4.74 / 6	1.28 /48	3.95 /61	5.68	1.00
COH	Putnam High Yield Trust B	PHBBX	**E+**	(800) 225-1581	**D / 1.8**	2.65	0.10	-5.48 / 4	0.52 /34	3.17 /48	5.12	1.75
COH	Putnam High Yield Trust C	PCHYX	**E+**	(800) 225-1581	**D / 1.8**	2.68	0.10	-5.42 / 4	0.52 /34	3.18 /48	5.14	1.75
COH	Putnam High Yield Trust M	PHIMX	**E+**	(800) 225-1581	**D- / 1.5**	2.92	0.49	-4.84 / 5	1.03 /43	3.72 /57	5.42	1.25
COH	Putnam High Yield Trust R	PHDRX	**D-**	(800) 225-1581	**C- / 3.4**	2.87	0.41	-4.92 / 5	1.04 /43	3.69 /56	5.82	1.25
COH	Putnam High Yield Trust Y	PHYYX	**D**	(800) 225-1581	**C / 4.4**	2.97	0.62	-4.44 / 6	1.52 /53	4.22 /64	6.35	0.75
*GES	Putnam Income Fund A	PINCX	**D+**	(800) 225-1581	**D- / 1.0**	-0.62	-1.12	-3.88 / 8	0.94 /41	3.54 /54	2.72	0.86
GES	Putnam Income Fund B	PNCBX	**D+**	(800) 225-1581	**D- / 1.3**	-0.67	-1.35	-4.49 / 6	0.24 /29	2.78 /41	2.08	1.61
GES	Putnam Income Fund C	PUICX	**D+**	(800) 225-1581	**D- / 1.2**	-0.67	-1.49	-4.49 / 6	0.21 /29	2.78 /41	2.08	1.61
GES	Putnam Income Fund M	PNCMX	**D+**	(800) 225-1581	**D- / 1.0**	-0.53	-1.24	-4.01 / 8	0.71 /37	3.28 /49	2.62	1.11
GES	Putnam Income Fund R	PIFRX	**D+**	(800) 225-1581	**D / 1.7**	-0.54	-1.23	-4.11 / 7	0.70 /37	3.29 /50	2.63	1.11
COI	Putnam Income Fund R5	PINFX	**C-**	(800) 225-1581	**C- / 3.3**	-0.53	-0.94	-3.64 / 9	1.22 /47	--	3.15	0.57

• Denotes fund is closed to new investors
* Denotes fund is included in Section II

RISK			NET ASSETS		ASSET							FUND MANAGER		MINIMUM		LOADS	
Risk Rating/Pts	3 Yr Avg Standard Deviation	Avg Duration	NAV As of 3/31/16	Total $(Mil)	Cash %	Gov. Bond %	Muni. Bond %	Corp. Bond %	Other %	Portfolio Turnover Ratio	Avg Coupon Rate	Manager Quality Pct	Manager Tenure (Years)	Initial Purch. $	Additional Purch. $	Front End Load	Back End Load
C / 5.2	3.4	5.7	9.31	2	0	0	99	0	1	23	4.9	18	17	500	0	0.0	0.0
C / 5.2	3.4	5.7	9.32	1	0	0	99	0	1	23	4.9	29	17	500	0	3.3	0.0
C / 5.1	3.4	5.7	9.31	2	0	0	99	0	1	23	4.9	44	17	0	0	0.0	0.0
C- / 3.9	4.0	6.9	8.30	1,228	0	0	100	0	0	14	4.7	45	14	500	0	4.0	0.0
C- / 4.1	3.9	6.9	8.30	5	0	0	100	0	0	14	4.7	29	14	500	0	0.0	0.0
C- / 4.0	4.0	6.9	8.35	52	0	0	100	0	0	14	4.7	23	14	500	0	0.0	0.0
C- / 4.0	3.9	6.9	8.28	3	0	0	100	0	0	14	4.7	38	14	500	0	3.3	0.0
C- / 4.1	3.9	6.9	8.33	63	0	0	100	0	0	14	4.7	57	14	500	0	0.0	0.0
D / 2.1	5.5	-1.4	6.63	1,440	0	7	0	27	66	725	6.2	88	22	500	0	4.0	0.0
D / 2.1	5.5	-1.4	6.57	58	0	7	0	27	66	725	6.2	72	22	500	0	0.0	0.0
D / 2.1	5.6	-1.4	6.52	760	0	7	0	27	66	725	6.2	72	22	500	0	0.0	0.0
D / 2.2	5.5	-1.4	6.52	136	0	7	0	27	66	725	6.2	84	22	500	0	3.3	0.0
D / 2.1	5.6	-1.4	6.56	4	0	7	0	27	66	725	6.2	85	22	500	0	0.0	0.0
U /	N/A	-1.4	6.57	10	0	7	0	27	66	725	6.2	N/A	22	0	0	0.0	0.0
D / 2.1	5.6	-1.4	6.57	1,271	0	7	0	27	66	725	6.2	91	22	500	0	0.0	0.0
E / 0.3	8.9	5.1	8.58	9	2	53	1	42	2	18	5.9	34	3	500	0	4.0	0.0
E / 0.3	8.9	5.1	8.56	N/A	2	53	1	42	2	18	5.9	17	3	500	0	0.0	0.0
E / 0.3	8.9	5.1	8.57	N/A	2	53	1	42	2	18	5.9	17	3	500	0	0.0	0.0
E / 0.3	8.9	5.1	8.58	N/A	2	53	1	42	2	18	5.9	27	3	500	0	3.3	0.0
E / 0.3	8.9	5.1	8.58	3	2	53	1	42	2	18	5.9	41	3	500	0	0.0	0.0
C / 5.5	2.8	0.4	8.33	272	4	0	0	77	19	79	4.4	86	11	500	0	1.0	0.0
C+ / 5.7	2.7	0.4	8.32	15	4	0	0	77	19	79	4.4	82	11	500	0	0.0	0.0
C+ / 5.6	2.7	0.4	8.32	89	4	0	0	77	19	79	4.4	60	11	500	0	0.0	0.0
C+ / 5.7	2.7	0.4	8.32	4	4	0	0	77	19	79	4.4	85	11	500	0	0.8	0.0
C+ / 5.7	2.7	0.4	8.32	N/A	4	0	0	77	19	79	4.4	81	11	500	0	0.0	0.0
C / 5.5	2.8	0.4	8.34	258	4	0	0	77	19	79	4.4	89	11	500	0	0.0	0.0
C / 4.9	3.5	4.3	11.86	154	0	36	0	26	38	296	4.4	81	22	500	0	4.0	0.0
C / 4.9	3.5	4.3	11.80	5	0	36	0	26	38	296	4.4	50	22	500	0	0.0	0.0
C / 4.8	3.5	4.3	11.80	21	0	36	0	26	38	296	4.4	49	22	500	0	0.0	0.0
C / 4.9	3.5	4.3	11.74	9	0	36	0	26	38	296	4.4	74	22	500	0	3.3	0.0
C / 4.8	3.6	4.3	11.83	8	0	36	0	26	38	296	4.4	73	22	0	0	0.0	0.0
C / 4.8	3.6	4.3	11.85	N/A	0	36	0	26	38	296	4.4	86	22	0	0	0.0	0.0
C / 5.0	3.5	4.3	11.85	N/A	0	36	0	26	38	296	4.4	87	22	0	0	0.0	0.0
C / 4.8	3.5	4.3	11.85	60	0	36	0	26	38	296	4.4	86	22	0	0	0.0	0.0
D- / 1.2	5.8	4.1	5.46	292	4	0	0	93	3	29	6.3	40	14	500	0	4.0	1.0
D- / 1.2	5.9	4.1	5.33	13	4	0	0	93	3	29	6.3	21	14	500	0	0.0	1.0
D- / 1.3	5.8	4.1	5.31	16	4	0	0	93	3	29	6.3	21	14	500	0	0.0	1.0
D- / 1.3	5.8	4.1	5.44	74	4	0	0	93	3	29	6.3	33	14	500	0	3.3	1.0
D- / 1.3	5.8	4.1	5.44	23	4	0	0	93	3	29	6.3	33	14	500	0	0.0	1.0
D- / 1.3	5.8	4.1	5.71	92	4	0	0	93	3	29	6.3	50	14	0	0	0.0	1.0
D- / 1.1	5.9	4.0	7.10	752	4	0	0	90	6	47	6.2	45	14	500	0	4.0	0.0
D- / 1.2	5.9	4.0	7.09	12	4	0	0	90	6	47	6.2	23	14	500	0	0.0	0.0
D- / 1.2	5.9	4.0	7.03	45	4	0	0	90	6	47	6.2	23	14	500	0	0.0	0.0
D- / 1.2	5.9	4.0	7.14	12	4	0	0	90	6	47	6.2	37	14	500	0	3.3	0.0
D- / 1.2	5.9	4.0	6.94	8	4	0	0	90	6	47	6.2	37	14	500	0	0.0	0.0
D- / 1.2	5.9	4.0	6.94	154	4	0	0	90	6	47	6.2	54	14	500	0	0.0	0.0
B- / 7.3	2.8	2.4	6.78	974	0	0	0	26	74	793	4.9	51	9	500	0	4.0	0.0
B- / 7.1	2.8	2.4	6.72	28	0	0	0	26	74	793	4.9	28	9	500	0	0.0	0.0
B- / 7.2	2.8	2.4	6.73	205	0	0	0	26	74	793	4.9	27	9	500	0	0.0	0.0
B- / 7.2	2.8	2.4	6.62	93	0	0	0	26	74	793	4.9	44	9	500	0	3.3	0.0
B- / 7.2	2.8	2.4	6.73	29	0	0	0	26	74	793	4.9	42	9	0	0	0.0	0.0
B- / 7.2	2.8	2.4	6.86	5	0	0	0	26	74	793	4.9	61	9	0	0	0.0	0.0

Fund Type	Fund Name (99 Pct = Best, 0 Pct = Worst)	Ticker Symbol	Overall Investment Rating	Phone	PERFORMANCE: Performance Rating/Pts	Total Return % through 3/31/16: 3 Mo	6 Mo	1Yr / Pct	Annualized: 3Yr / Pct	Annualized: 5Yr / Pct	Incl. in Returns: Dividend Yield	Expense Ratio
COI	Putnam Income Fund R6	PINHX	C-	(800) 225-1581	C- / 3.4	-0.52	-0.94	-3.50 /10	1.31 /49	--	3.14	0.50
GES	Putnam Income Fund Y	PNCYX	C-	(800) 225-1581	C- / 3.2	-0.55	-1.01	-3.61 / 9	1.21 /46	3.79 /58	3.02	0.61
MUN	Putnam Intermediate-Term Muni Inc	PIMEX	B-	(800) 225-1581	C+ / 5.9	1.14	2.03	2.24 /79	2.03 /77	--	1.08	1.76
MUN	Putnam Intermediate-Term Muni Inc	PIMBX	A-	(800) 225-1581	B- / 7.0	1.09	1.83	1.63 /75	1.45 /66	--	0.54	2.36
MUN	Putnam Intermediate-Term Muni Inc	PIMFX	B	(800) 225-1581	C+ / 6.5	0.96	1.65	1.38 /73	1.27 /60	--	0.39	2.51
MUN	Putnam Intermediate-Term Muni Inc	PIMMX	A	(800) 225-1581	B / 7.7	1.18	2.00	1.99 /77	1.81 /74	--	0.88	2.01
MUN	Putnam Intermediate-Term Muni Inc	PIMYX	A-	(800) 225-1581	B- / 7.0	1.20	2.16	2.50 /80	2.28 /80	--	1.33	1.51
MUS	Putnam MA Tax Exempt Inc II A	PXMAX	C+	(800) 225-1581	B- / 7.5	1.43	2.60	2.74 /82	2.67 /85	5.27 /87	2.86	0.77
MUS	Putnam MA Tax Exempt Inc II B	PMABX	C+	(800) 225-1581	B / 8.0	1.28	2.29	2.11 /78	2.04 /77	4.62 /82	2.37	1.39
MUS	Putnam MA Tax Exempt Inc II C	PMMCX	C+	(800) 225-1581	B / 7.8	1.24	2.20	1.95 /77	1.88 /75	4.45 /81	2.21	1.54
MUS	Putnam MA Tax Exempt Inc II M	PMAMX	C	(800) 225-1581	B- / 7.3	1.36	2.46	2.46 /80	2.39 /82	4.98 /85	2.62	1.04
MUS	Putnam MA Tax Exempt Inc II Y	PMAYX	B	(800) 225-1581	B+ / 8.9	1.48	2.71	2.96 /85	2.93 /87	5.51 /89	3.20	0.54
MUS	Putnam MI Tax Exempt Inc II A	PXMIX	C+	(800) 225-1581	B- / 7.0	1.05	2.05	2.55 /81	2.49 /83	4.90 /84	2.92	0.86
MUS	Putnam MI Tax Exempt Inc II B	PMEBX	B	(800) 225-1581	B / 7.8	1.01	1.84	2.02 /77	1.89 /75	4.25 /79	2.42	1.49
MUS	Putnam MI Tax Exempt Inc II C	PMGCX	B-	(800) 225-1581	B- / 7.5	0.97	1.76	1.87 /76	1.73 /73	4.11 /78	2.27	1.64
MUS	Putnam MI Tax Exempt Inc II M	PMIMX	C+	(800) 225-1581	C+ / 6.9	1.09	2.02	2.37 /80	2.24 /80	4.61 /82	2.68	1.14
MUS	Putnam MI Tax Exempt Inc II Y	PMIYX	B+	(800) 225-1581	B+ / 8.7	1.21	2.26	2.77 /83	2.75 /85	5.15 /86	3.26	0.64
MUS	Putnam MN Tax Exempt Inc II A	PXMNX	B+	(800) 225-1581	B / 7.7	1.13	2.10	2.75 /83	2.84 /86	4.89 /84	2.80	0.83
MUS	Putnam MN Tax Exempt Inc II B	PMTBX	B+	(800) 225-1581	B / 8.1	0.98	1.69	2.13 /78	2.21 /79	4.26 /80	2.32	1.45
MUS	Putnam MN Tax Exempt Inc II C	PMOCX	B+	(800) 225-1581	B / 8.0	1.05	1.72	1.98 /77	2.06 /78	4.12 /78	2.16	1.60
MUS	Putnam MN Tax Exempt Inc II M	PMNMX	B	(800) 225-1581	B- / 7.4	1.07	1.86	2.38 /80	2.56 /83	4.61 /82	2.57	1.10
MUS	Putnam MN Tax Exempt Inc II Y	PMNYX	A	(800) 225-1581	A- / 9.0	1.29	2.21	2.99 /85	3.10 /89	5.15 /86	3.14	0.60
MM	Putnam Money Market T	PMMXX	U	(800) 225-1581	U /	--	--	--	--	--	0.01	0.75
MUS	Putnam NJ Tax Exempt Income A	PTNJX	C	(800) 225-1581	C+ / 6.8	1.56	3.07	2.82 /83	2.23 /79	4.86 /84	3.15	0.78
MUS	Putnam NJ Tax Exempt Income B	PNJBX	C+	(800) 225-1581	B / 7.6	1.30	2.64	2.19 /78	1.57 /69	4.20 /79	2.67	1.40
MUS	Putnam NJ Tax Exempt Income C	PNJCX	C+	(800) 225-1581	B- / 7.4	1.37	2.67	2.03 /77	1.45 /66	4.08 /78	2.51	1.55
MUS	Putnam NJ Tax Exempt Income M	PNJMX	C	(800) 225-1581	C+ / 6.5	1.38	2.93	2.54 /81	1.95 /76	4.58 /82	2.91	1.05
MUS	Putnam NJ Tax Exempt Income Y	PNJYX	B	(800) 225-1581	B+ / 8.5	1.50	3.06	3.04 /85	2.42 /82	5.09 /86	3.50	0.55
*MUS	Putnam NY Tax Exempt Income A	PTEIX	B-	(800) 225-1581	B / 8.0	1.62	2.86	3.56 /91	2.91 /87	5.18 /87	3.23	0.74
MUS	Putnam NY Tax Exempt Income B	PEIBX	B	(800) 225-1581	B+ / 8.4	1.59	2.67	2.92 /84	2.31 /80	4.56 /82	2.74	1.37
MUS	Putnam NY Tax Exempt Income C	PNNCX	B-	(800) 225-1581	B / 8.2	1.43	2.59	2.76 /83	2.11 /78	4.39 /81	2.59	1.52
MUS	Putnam NY Tax Exempt Income M	PNYMX	C+	(800) 225-1581	B / 7.9	1.55	2.84	3.27 /88	2.62 /84	4.91 /85	2.98	1.02
MUS	Putnam NY Tax Exempt Income Y	PNYYX	A-	(800) 225-1581	A- / 9.2	1.67	3.09	3.79 /93	3.17 /90	5.43 /88	3.57	0.52
MUS	Putnam OH Tax Exempt Inc II A	PXOHX	B	(800) 225-1581	B / 7.7	1.62	2.87	3.18 /87	2.71 /85	4.84 /84	2.97	0.80
MUS	Putnam OH Tax Exempt Inc II B	POXBX	B+	(800) 225-1581	B / 8.1	1.47	2.56	2.54 /81	2.07 /78	4.19 /79	2.49	1.42
MUS	Putnam OH Tax Exempt Inc II C	POOCX	B+	(800) 225-1581	B / 8.0	1.43	2.37	2.38 /80	1.92 /76	4.03 /78	2.34	1.57
MUS	Putnam OH Tax Exempt Inc II M	POHMX	B	(800) 225-1581	B- / 7.5	1.56	2.62	2.89 /84	2.43 /82	4.52 /82	2.74	1.07
MUS	Putnam OH Tax Exempt Inc II Y	POTYX	A	(800) 225-1581	A- / 9.0	1.68	2.98	3.51 /90	2.93 /87	5.07 /86	3.32	0.57
MUS	Putnam PA Tax Exempt Income A	PTEPX	B-	(800) 225-1581	B / 7.8	1.65	2.80	3.25 /87	2.79 /86	5.09 /86	3.05	0.78
MUS	Putnam PA Tax Exempt Income B	PPNBX	B	(800) 225-1581	B / 8.2	1.50	2.38	2.63 /82	2.13 /79	4.42 /81	2.57	1.40
MUS	Putnam PA Tax Exempt Income C	PPNCX	B	(800) 225-1581	B / 8.1	1.46	2.30	2.47 /80	2.01 /77	4.28 /80	2.42	1.55
MUS	Putnam PA Tax Exempt Income M	PPAMX	C+	(800) 225-1581	B / 7.6	1.58	2.55	2.86 /84	2.48 /82	4.78 /83	2.82	1.05
MUS	Putnam PA Tax Exempt Income Y	PPTYX	A-	(800) 225-1581	A- / 9.1	1.70	2.92	3.49 /90	3.02 /88	5.32 /88	3.40	0.55
GES	Putnam Ret Income Fd Lifestyle 3 A	PISFX	D+	(800) 225-1581	C+ / 6.5	1.47	3.12	-2.66 /13	3.82 /82	4.54 /68	2.43	1.87
GES	Putnam Ret Income Fd Lifestyle 3 B	PBIOX	D+	(800) 225-1581	C+ / 6.9	1.20	2.67	-3.40 /10	3.04 /77	3.73 /57	1.79	2.62
GES	Putnam Ret Income Fd Lifestyle 3 C	PCIOX	D+	(800) 225-1581	C+ / 6.9	1.29	2.76	-3.32 /10	3.03 /77	3.75 /57	1.78	2.62
GES	Putnam Ret Income Fd Lifestyle 3 M	PMIOX	D+	(800) 225-1581	C+ / 6.4	1.32	2.92	-2.89 /12	3.56 /81	4.24 /65	2.23	2.12
GES	Putnam Ret Income Fd Lifestyle 3 R	PRIOX	C-	(800) 225-1581	B / 7.6	1.32	2.91	-2.91 /12	3.57 /81	4.22 /64	2.29	2.12
GES	Putnam Ret Income Fd Lifestyle 3 Y	PIIYX	C-	(800) 225-1581	B / 8.1	1.43	3.23	-2.44 /14	4.08 /84	4.78 /70	2.76	1.62
GEI	Putnam Ret Income Fund Lifestyle2 A	PRYAX	D+	(800) 225-1581	C- / 4.0	0.27	0.99	-2.42 /14	2.46 /70	--	2.44	2.18
GEI	Putnam Ret Income Fund Lifestyle2 B	PRLBX	D+	(800) 225-1581	C / 4.5	0.21	0.68	-3.13 /11	1.71 /56	--	1.95	2.93
GEI	Putnam Ret Income Fund Lifestyle2	PRYCX	D+	(800) 225-1581	C / 4.5	0.21	0.68	-3.13 /11	1.71 /56	--	1.95	2.93

● Denotes fund is closed to new investors
* Denotes fund is included in Section II

RISK			NET ASSETS		ASSET							FUND MANAGER		MINIMUM		LOADS	
Risk Rating/Pts	3 Yr Avg Standard Deviation	Avg Duration	NAV As of 3/31/16	Total $(Mil)	Cash %	Gov. Bond %	Muni. Bond %	Corp. Bond %	Other %	Portfolio Turnover Ratio	Avg Coupon Rate	Manager Quality Pct	Manager Tenure (Years)	Initial Purch. $	Additional Purch. $	Front End Load	Back End Load
B- / 7.2	2.8	2.4	6.88	5	0	0	0	26	74	793	4.9	66	9	0	0	0.0	0.0
B- / 7.2	2.8	2.4	6.88	735	0	0	0	26	74	793	4.9	62	9	0	0	0.0	0.0
B- / 7.4	2.7	4.3	10.31	18	8	0	91	0	1	1	4.3	36	3	500	0	4.0	0.0
B- / 7.3	2.8	4.3	10.32	N/A	8	0	91	0	1	1	4.3	20	3	500	0	0.0	0.0
B- / 7.3	2.8	4.3	10.31	1	8	0	91	0	1	1	4.3	17	3	500	0	0.0	0.0
B- / 7.3	2.8	4.3	10.32	N/A	8	0	91	0	1	1	4.3	28	3	500	0	0.0	0.0
B- / 7.4	2.8	4.3	10.31	N/A	8	0	91	0	1	1	4.3	43	3	500	0	3.3	0.0
C- / 4.1	3.9	6.1	9.80	244	1	0	98	0	1	8	4.7	20	14	500	0	4.0	0.0
C- / 4.1	3.9	6.1	9.79	3	1	0	98	0	1	8	4.7	12	14	500	0	0.0	0.0
C- / 4.1	3.9	6.1	9.82	30	1	0	98	0	1	8	4.7	11	14	500	0	0.0	0.0
C- / 4.1	3.9	6.1	9.80	3	1	0	98	0	1	8	4.7	16	14	500	0	3.3	0.0
C- / 4.1	3.9	6.1	9.83	39	1	0	98	0	1	8	4.7	24	14	0	0	0.0	0.0
C / 5.3	3.3	5.5	9.27	60	2	0	97	0	1	12	4.8	31	17	500	0	4.0	0.0
C / 5.2	3.4	5.5	9.27	1	2	0	97	0	1	12	4.8	17	17	500	0	0.0	0.0
C / 5.2	3.4	5.5	9.28	3	2	0	97	0	1	12	4.8	15	17	500	0	0.0	0.0
C / 5.3	3.3	5.5	9.28	N/A	2	0	97	0	1	12	4.8	24	17	500	0	3.3	0.0
C / 5.2	3.4	5.5	9.29	9	2	0	97	0	1	12	4.8	36	17	0	0	0.0	0.0
C+ / 6.0	3.1	5.5	9.45	87	1	0	98	0	1	6	4.6	45	17	500	0	4.0	0.0
C+ / 5.9	3.2	5.5	9.42	1	1	0	98	0	1	6	4.6	27	17	500	0	0.0	0.0
C+ / 5.9	3.2	5.5	9.44	18	1	0	98	0	1	6	4.6	23	17	500	0	0.0	0.0
C+ / 6.0	3.1	5.5	9.44	N/A	1	0	98	0	1	6	4.6	37	17	500	0	3.3	0.0
C+ / 5.8	3.2	5.5	9.47	5	1	0	98	0	1	6	4.6	54	17	0	0	0.0	0.0
U /	N/A	N/A	1.00	29	100	0	0	0	0	0	0.0	N/A	N/A	500	0	0.0	0.0
C / 4.5	3.7	5.7	9.43	146	0	0	100	0	0	10	4.5	17	17	500	0	4.0	0.0
C / 4.5	3.7	5.7	9.41	4	0	0	100	0	0	10	4.5	10	17	500	0	0.0	0.0
C / 4.5	3.7	5.7	9.44	22	0	0	100	0	0	10	4.5	10	17	500	0	0.0	0.0
C / 4.5	3.7	5.7	9.43	2	0	0	100	0	0	10	4.5	13	17	500	0	3.3	0.0
C / 4.5	3.7	5.7	9.44	19	0	0	100	0	0	10	4.5	20	17	0	0	0.0	0.0
C / 4.6	3.6	6.4	8.70	931	0	0	99	0	1	15	4.9	33	14	500	0	4.0	0.0
C / 4.6	3.6	6.4	8.69	11	0	0	99	0	1	15	4.9	19	14	500	0	0.0	0.0
C / 4.6	3.6	6.4	8.70	61	0	0	99	0	1	15	4.9	16	14	500	0	0.0	0.0
C / 4.6	3.6	6.4	8.71	1	0	0	99	0	1	15	4.9	25	14	500	0	3.3	0.0
C / 4.6	3.6	6.4	8.71	50	0	0	99	0	1	15	4.9	41	14	0	0	0.0	0.0
C / 5.5	3.3	5.8	9.19	117	0	0	99	0	1	16	4.7	37	17	500	0	4.0	0.0
C / 5.4	3.3	5.8	9.18	2	0	0	99	0	1	16	4.7	21	17	500	0	0.0	0.0
C / 5.5	3.3	5.8	9.19	11	0	0	99	0	1	16	4.7	18	17	500	0	0.0	0.0
C+ / 5.7	3.2	5.8	9.19	1	0	0	99	0	1	16	4.7	31	17	500	0	3.3	0.0
C / 5.5	3.3	5.8	9.20	12	0	0	99	0	1	16	4.7	45	17	0	0	0.0	0.0
C / 5.0	3.5	6.2	9.30	160	0	0	100	0	0	22	4.7	35	17	500	0	4.0	0.0
C / 4.9	3.5	6.2	9.28	4	0	0	100	0	0	22	4.7	18	17	500	0	0.0	0.0
C / 5.0	3.5	6.2	9.30	25	0	0	100	0	0	22	4.7	17	17	500	0	0.0	0.0
C / 5.0	3.5	6.2	9.30	4	0	0	100	0	0	22	4.7	26	17	500	0	3.3	0.0
C / 4.9	3.5	6.2	9.31	8	0	0	100	0	0	22	4.7	41	17	0	0	0.0	0.0
D- / 1.2	6.4	5.7	10.82	24	30	4	0	12	54	53	4.5	95	12	500	0	4.0	0.0
D- / 1.2	6.4	5.7	10.77	1	30	4	0	12	54	53	4.5	89	12	500	0	0.0	0.0
D- / 1.2	6.4	5.7	10.78	3	30	4	0	12	54	53	4.5	89	12	500	0	0.0	0.0
D- / 1.2	6.4	5.7	10.79	N/A	30	4	0	12	54	53	4.5	93	12	500	0	3.3	0.0
D- / 1.2	6.4	5.7	10.81	N/A	30	4	0	12	54	53	4.5	93	12	500	0	0.0	0.0
D- / 1.1	6.4	5.7	10.84	1	30	4	0	12	54	53	4.5	96	12	500	0	0.0	0.0
C- / 3.8	4.1	N/A	9.89	12	20	8	0	20	52	40	0.0	91	5	500	0	4.0	0.0
C- / 3.8	4.1	N/A	9.77	N/A	20	8	0	20	52	40	0.0	81	5	500	0	0.0	0.0
C- / 3.8	4.1	N/A	9.77	N/A	20	8	0	20	52	40	0.0	81	5	500	0	0.0	0.0

99 Pct = Best
0 Pct = Worst

Fund Type	Fund Name	Ticker Symbol	Overall Investment Rating	Phone	PERFORMANCE: Performance Rating/Pts	Total Return % through 3/31/16: 3 Mo	6 Mo	1Yr / Pct	Annualized: 3Yr / Pct	Annualized: 5Yr / Pct	Incl. in Returns: Dividend Yield	Incl. in Returns: Expense Ratio
GEI	Putnam Ret Income Fund Lifestyle2	PRLMX	**D+**	(800) 225-1581	**C- / 3.9**	0.27	0.83	-2.69 /12	2.22 /66	--	2.19	2.43
GEI	Putnam Ret Income Fund Lifestyle2	PRLRX	**C-**	(800) 225-1581	**C / 5.5**	0.16	0.83	-2.69 /12	2.22 /66	--	2.26	2.43
GEI	Putnam Ret Income Fund Lifestyle2 Y	PRLYX	**C-**	(800) 225-1581	**C+ / 6.4**	0.33	1.10	-2.19 /15	2.73 /74	--	2.77	1.93
* COI	Putnam Short Duration Income A	PSDTX	**C+**	(800) 225-1581	**C- / 3.3**	0.17	0.33	0.34 /47	0.47 /33	--	0.52	0.54
COI	Putnam Short Duration Income B	PSDBX	**C**	(800) 225-1581	**D / 2.0**	0.08	0.13	-0.15 /30	0.04 /23	--	0.13	0.94
COI	Putnam Short Duration Income C	PSDLX	**C-**	(800) 225-1581	**D / 1.9**	0.08	0.03	-0.15 /30	0.04 /23	--	0.13	0.94
COI	Putnam Short Duration Income M	PSDGX	**C+**	(800) 225-1581	**C- / 3.2**	0.16	0.31	0.29 /46	0.42 /32	--	0.47	0.59
COI	Putnam Short Duration Income R	PSDRX	**C**	(800) 225-1581	**D+ / 2.5**	0.08	0.23	-0.05 /31	0.08 /26	--	0.13	0.94
GEI	Putnam Short Duration Income R6	PSDQX	**C+**	(800) 225-1581	**C- / 3.5**	0.20	0.38	0.44 /49	0.57 /34	--	0.63	0.43
COI	Putnam Short Duration Income Y	PSDYX	**C+**	(800) 225-1581	**C- / 3.5**	0.20	0.38	0.44 /49	0.57 /34	--	0.62	0.44
MUN	Putnam Short-Term Municipal Inc A	PSMEX	**C+**	(800) 225-1581	**C- / 3.2**	0.45	0.41	0.55 /56	0.48 /38	--	0.54	1.42
MUN	Putnam Short-Term Municipal Inc B	PSMFX	**C+**	(800) 225-1581	**C- / 3.2**	0.30	0.21	0.25 /47	0.26 /31	--	0.35	1.62
MUN	Putnam Short-Term Municipal Inc C	PSMTX	**C-**	(800) 225-1581	**D / 1.9**	0.20	0.00	-0.09 /30	0.01 /18	--	0.01	2.17
MUN	Putnam Short-Term Municipal Inc M	PSMMX	**C+**	(800) 225-1581	**C- / 3.1**	0.34	0.29	0.40 /52	0.40 /35	--	0.50	1.47
MUN	Putnam Short-Term Municipal Inc Y	PSMYX	**B+**	(800) 225-1581	**C / 4.6**	0.41	0.43	0.70 /60	0.70 /44	--	0.80	1.17
* MUN	Putnam Tax Exempt Income A	PTAEX	**B-**	(800) 225-1581	**B / 8.1**	1.46	2.88	2.93 /84	3.10 /89	5.72 /90	3.52	0.75
MUN	Putnam Tax Exempt Income B	PTBEX	**B**	(800) 225-1581	**B+ / 8.4**	1.30	2.56	2.28 /79	2.45 /82	5.05 /86	3.04	1.38
MUN	Putnam Tax Exempt Income C	PTECX	**B**	(800) 225-1581	**B / 8.2**	1.26	2.48	2.13 /78	2.29 /80	4.91 /85	2.88	1.53
MUN	Putnam Tax Exempt Income M	PTXMX	**B-**	(800) 225-1581	**B / 8.0**	1.38	2.72	2.63 /82	2.84 /86	5.42 /88	3.26	1.03
MUN	Putnam Tax Exempt Income Y	PTEYX	**A-**	(800) 225-1581	**A- / 9.2**	1.51	2.98	3.15 /86	3.36 /92	5.96 /92	3.87	0.53
* COH	Putnam Tax-Free Hi-Yield A	PTHAX	**C-**	(800) 225-1581	**B / 8.0**	2.25	4.26	4.69 /85	4.33 /86	7.63 /85	3.97	0.80
COH	Putnam Tax-Free Hi-Yield B	PTHYX	**C**	(800) 225-1581	**B+ / 8.3**	2.17	3.94	4.12 /82	3.71 /82	7.00 /82	3.52	1.42
COH	Putnam Tax-Free Hi-Yield C	PTCCX	**C-**	(800) 225-1581	**B / 8.2**	2.14	3.86	3.97 /81	3.55 /80	6.84 /81	3.37	1.57
COH	Putnam Tax-Free Hi-Yield M	PTYMX	**C-**	(800) 225-1581	**B / 7.9**	2.19	4.04	4.41 /84	4.05 /84	7.35 /84	3.75	1.07
COH	Putnam Tax-Free Hi-Yield Y	PTFYX	**C**	(800) 225-1581	**B+ / 8.9**	2.38	4.36	5.00 /87	4.58 /88	7.91 /86	4.35	0.57
* USS	Putnam US Govt Income Tr A	PGSIX	**D+**	(800) 225-1581	**D- / 1.3**	-0.90	-0.15	-1.41 /19	0.98 /42	2.09 /32	2.56	0.85
USS	Putnam US Govt Income Tr B	PGSBX	**D+**	(800) 225-1581	**D / 1.6**	-1.08	-0.52	-2.15 /15	0.26 /30	1.34 /23	1.91	1.58
USS	Putnam US Govt Income Tr C	PGVCX	**D+**	(800) 225-1581	**D- / 1.5**	-1.09	-0.59	-2.23 /15	0.22 /29	1.31 /23	1.92	1.60
USS	Putnam US Govt Income Tr M	PGSMX	**D+**	(800) 225-1581	**D- / 1.2**	-0.96	-0.29	-1.67 /17	0.73 /38	1.83 /29	2.30	1.09
USS	Putnam US Govt Income Tr R	PGVRX	**C-**	(800) 225-1581	**D+ / 2.9**	-0.98	-0.29	-1.69 /17	0.72 /37	1.83 /29	2.41	1.10
USS	Putnam US Govt Income Tr Y	PUSYX	**C**	(800) 225-1581	**C- / 3.9**	-0.84	-0.02	-1.23 /20	1.23 /47	2.33 /35	2.97	0.60
COI	Quality Income	SQIFX	**C+**	(800) 332-5580	**D+ / 2.8**	0.13	0.08	-0.08 /31	0.24 /29	--	1.03	0.90
GL	Quantified Managed Income Investor	QBDSX	**U**	(855) 747-9555	**U /**	2.02	1.53	-1.75 /17	--	--	3.81	1.79
COI	Rainier High Yield Institutional	RAIHX	**D**	(800) 248-6314	**C / 5.3**	1.94	0.71	-2.82 /12	1.96 /61	4.82 /70	5.69	0.73
COH	Rainier High Yield Original	RIMYX	**D**	(800) 248-6314	**C / 5.2**	1.86	0.78	-2.57 /13	1.91 /60	--	5.85	1.11
COI	Rainier Interm Fixed Income Inst	RAIFX	**U**	(800) 248-6314	**U /**	2.21	1.68	1.95 /71	--	--	2.06	2.92
GEI	Rainier Interm Fixed Income Orig	RIMFX	**B+**	(800) 248-6314	**C+ / 5.9**	2.17	1.61	1.85 /70	1.58 /54	2.85 /43	1.97	0.75
EM	RBC BlueBay Em Mkt Corporate Bd	RECAX	**U**	(800) 422-2766	**U /**	2.99	2.76	-1.26 /20	--	--	3.60	35.45
EM	RBC BlueBay Em Mkt Corporate Bd I	RBECX	**D-**	(800) 422-2766	**D+ / 2.6**	3.13	2.89	-0.97 /22	0.31 /30	--	4.04	1.74
EM	RBC BlueBay EM Unconstrained FI I	RUFIX	**U**	(800) 422-2766	**U /**	-1.15	1.43	-4.31 / 7	--	--	0.47	2.50
EM	RBC BlueBay Emerg Mkt Select Bd A	RESAX	**U**	(800) 422-2766	**U /**	4.61	5.09	-2.26 /14	--	--	0.00	3.84
EM	RBC BlueBay Emerg Mkt Select Bd I	RBESX	**E-**	(800) 422-2766	**E / 0.3**	4.72	5.32	-2.05 /15	-3.30 / 2	--	0.00	1.14
GL	RBC BlueBay Global High Yield Bd A	RHYAX	**U**	(800) 422-2766	**U /**	1.20	0.90	-1.12 /21	--	--	3.47	2.38
GL	RBC BlueBay Global High Yield Bd I	RGHYX	**C-**	(800) 422-2766	**C+ / 6.1**	1.26	1.05	-0.91 /22	2.90 /75	--	3.94	1.33
MM	RBC Prime Money Market Fund	TKSXX	**U**	(800) 422-2766	**U /**	--	--	--	--	--	0.01	0.92
MM	● RBC Prime Money Market Inst 1	TPNXX	**C**	(800) 422-2766	**D+ / 2.5**	0.06	0.08	0.11 /42	0.05 /25	0.07 /14	0.11	0.18
MM	RBC Prime Money Market Inst 2	TKIXX	**C**	(800) 422-2766	**D / 2.1**	0.03	0.04	0.04 /38	0.02 /21	0.02 / 9	0.04	0.27
COI	RBC Short Duration Fixed Income F	RSHFX	**U**	(800) 422-2766	**U /**	1.03	0.75	1.16 /61	--	--	1.66	2.07
COI	RBC Short Duration Fixed Income I	RSDIX	**U**	(800) 422-2766	**U /**	1.05	0.90	1.26 /63	--	--	1.76	1.68
COI	RBC Ultra-Short Fixed Income F	RULFX	**U**	(800) 422-2766	**U /**	0.64	0.66	1.14 /61	--	--	1.33	3.04
COI	RBC Ultra-Short Fixed Income I	RUSIX	**U**	(800) 422-2766	**U /**	0.66	0.71	1.22 /62	--	--	1.41	1.65
MM	RBC US Govt Money Market Fd Inst	TUGXX	**C**	(800) 422-2766	**D+ / 2.3**	0.05	0.06	0.06 /40	0.03 /23	0.02 / 9	0.06	0.17

● Denotes fund is closed to new investors
* Denotes fund is included in Section II

RISK			NET ASSETS		ASSET							FUND MANAGER		MINIMUM		LOADS	
Risk Rating/Pts	3 Yr Avg Standard Deviation	Avg Duration	NAV As of 3/31/16	Total $(Mil)	Cash %	Gov. Bond %	Muni. Bond %	Corp. Bond %	Other %	Portfolio Turnover Ratio	Avg Coupon Rate	Manager Quality Pct	Manager Tenure (Years)	Initial Purch. $	Additional Purch. $	Front End Load	Back End Load
C- / 3.8	4.1	N/A	9.88	N/A	20	8	0	20	52	40	0.0	89	5	500	0	3.3	0.0
C- / 3.8	4.1	N/A	9.88	N/A	20	8	0	20	52	40	0.0	89	5	500	0	0.0	0.0
C- / 3.9	4.1	N/A	9.90	N/A	20	8	0	20	52	40	0.0	93	5	500	0	0.0	0.0
A+ / 9.9	0.2	0.2	10.02	1,408	1	0	0	92	7	46	1.4	80	5	500	0	0.0	0.0
A+ / 9.9	0.2	0.2	10.00	2	1	0	0	92	7	46	1.4	61	5	500	0	0.0	0.0
A+ / 9.9	0.2	0.2	10.00	20	1	0	0	92	7	46	1.4	61	5	500	0	0.0	0.0
A+ / 9.9	0.2	0.2	10.01	9	1	0	0	92	7	46	1.4	79	5	500	0	0.0	0.0
A+ / 9.9	0.3	0.2	10.01	1	1	0	0	92	7	46	1.4	62	5	500	0	0.0	0.0
A+ / 9.9	0.2	0.2	10.03	2	1	0	0	92	7	46	1.4	82	5	0	0	0.0	0.0
A+ / 9.9	0.2	0.2	10.03	962	1	0	0	92	7	46	1.4	83	5	0	0	0.0	0.0
A+ / 9.8	0.5	1.7	10.03	10	3	0	96	0	1	45	3.9	69	3	500	0	1.0	0.0
A+ / 9.8	0.5	1.7	10.02	N/A	3	0	96	0	1	45	3.9	55	3	500	0	0.0	0.0
A+ / 9.8	0.5	1.7	10.02	N/A	3	0	96	0	1	45	3.9	46	3	500	0	0.0	0.0
A+ / 9.8	0.5	1.7	10.02	N/A	3	0	96	0	1	45	3.9	61	3	500	0	0.8	0.0
A+ / 9.8	0.5	1.7	10.02	4	3	0	96	0	1	45	3.9	77	3	500	0	0.0	0.0
C / 4.7	3.6	6.0	8.79	879	0	0	99	0	1	16	5.0	40	14	500	0	4.0	0.0
C / 4.6	3.6	6.0	8.79	7	0	0	99	0	1	16	5.0	21	14	500	0	0.0	0.0
C / 4.7	3.6	6.0	8.81	38	0	0	99	0	1	16	5.0	19	14	500	0	0.0	0.0
C / 4.6	3.6	6.0	8.82	6	0	0	99	0	1	16	5.0	30	14	500	0	3.3	0.0
C / 4.6	3.6	6.0	8.81	42	0	0	99	0	1	16	5.0	46	14	500	0	0.0	0.0
D / 2.2	4.8	7.4	12.69	781	0	0	98	1	1	17	5.1	99	14	500	0	4.0	1.0
D / 2.2	4.8	7.4	12.72	13	0	0	98	1	1	17	5.1	99	14	500	0	0.0	1.0
D / 2.2	4.8	7.4	12.72	73	0	0	98	1	1	17	5.1	99	14	500	0	0.0	1.0
D / 2.2	4.8	7.4	12.69	9	0	0	98	1	1	17	5.1	99	14	500	0	3.3	1.0
D / 2.2	4.8	7.4	12.74	150	0	0	98	1	1	17	5.1	99	14	500	0	0.0	1.0
B / 7.6	2.7	1.3	13.15	786	0	0	0	0	100	1,388	5.8	85	9	500	0	4.0	0.0
B / 7.6	2.7	1.3	13.08	16	0	0	0	0	100	1,388	5.8	58	9	500	0	0.0	0.0
B / 7.6	2.7	1.3	13.02	65	0	0	0	0	100	1,388	5.8	56	9	500	0	0.0	0.0
B / 7.7	2.6	1.3	13.20	14	0	0	0	0	100	1,388	5.8	80	9	500	0	3.3	0.0
B / 7.6	2.6	1.3	13.01	24	0	0	0	0	100	1,388	5.8	80	9	500	0	0.0	0.0
B / 7.6	2.7	1.3	13.02	101	0	0	0	0	100	1,388	5.8	88	9	500	0	0.0	0.0
A+ / 9.9	0.4	0.4	9.83	67	4	15	7	14	60	242	3.1	70	4	5,000	100	0.0	0.0
U /	N/A	N/A	9.07	22	13	24	20	8	35	872	0.0	N/A	3	10,000	1,000	0.0	0.0
D / 2.0	5.7	4.0	10.77	47	1	0	0	98	1	34	6.9	53	7	100,000	1,000	0.0	0.0
D- / 1.3	5.8	4.0	10.80	1	1	0	0	98	1	34	6.9	76	7	2,500	250	0.0	0.0
U /	N/A	N/A	12.72	39	0	37	0	62	1	205	6.9	N/A	8	100,000	1,000	0.0	0.0
B+ / 8.4	2.1	N/A	12.72	22	0	37	0	62	1	205	6.9	58	8	2,500	250	0.0	0.0
U /	N/A	N/A	9.39	N/A	19	3	0	77	1	172	0.0	N/A	5	2,500	100	4.3	2.0
D / 1.6	6.0	N/A	9.40	18	19	3	0	77	1	172	0.0	79	5	1,000,000	10,000	0.0	2.0
U /	N/A	N/A	9.42	14	0	0	0	0	100	693	0.0	N/A	2	1,000,000	10,000	0.0	2.0
U /	N/A	N/A	9.08	N/A	21	74	0	3	2	282	0.0	N/A	5	2,500	100	4.3	2.0
E / 0.3	8.8	N/A	9.10	18	21	74	0	3	2	282	0.0	7	5	1,000,000	10,000	0.0	2.0
U /	N/A	N/A	9.62	1	12	0	0	77	11	128	0.0	N/A	5	2,500	100	4.3	2.0
C- / 3.6	4.2	N/A	9.62	33	12	0	0	77	11	128	0.0	98	5	1,000,000	10,000	0.0	2.0
U /	N/A	N/A	1.00	1,225	100	0	0	0	0	0	0.0	N/A	N/A	0	0	0.0	0.0
A+ / 9.9	N/A	N/A	1.00	431	100	0	0	0	0	0	0.1	N/A	N/A	10,000,000	0	0.0	0.0
A+ / 9.9	N/A	N/A	1.00	275	100	0	0	0	0	0	0.0	66	N/A	1,000,000	0	0.0	0.0
U /	N/A	N/A	9.92	1	0	0	0	67	33	57	0.0	N/A	3	10,000	1,000	0.0	0.0
U /	N/A	N/A	9.92	13	0	0	0	67	33	57	0.0	N/A	3	10,000	1,000	0.0	0.0
U /	N/A	N/A	9.87	4	4	0	0	61	35	63	0.0	N/A	3	10,000	1,000	0.0	0.0
U /	N/A	N/A	9.87	14	4	0	0	61	35	63	0.0	N/A	3	10,000	1,000	0.0	0.0
A+ / 9.9	N/A	N/A	1.00	1,224	100	0	0	0	0	0	0.1	66	N/A	10,000,000	0	0.0	0.0

Fund Type	Fund Name (99 Pct = Best, 0 Pct = Worst)	Ticker Symbol	Overall Investment Rating	Phone	PERFORMANCE: Performance Rating/Pts	Total Return % through 3/31/16: 3 Mo	6 Mo	1Yr / Pct	Annualized: 3Yr / Pct	Annualized: 5Yr / Pct	Incl. in Returns: Dividend Yield	Expense Ratio
MM	RBC US Govt Money Market Fd Inst	TIMXX	**C-**	(800) 422-2766	**D / 2.0**	0.03	0.03	0.03 /36	0.02 /21	0.02 / 9	0.03	0.27
COH	Redwood Managed Volatility I	RWDIX	**U**		**U /**	3.32	-0.60	-1.94 /16	--	--	1.25	2.17
COH	Redwood Managed Volatility N	RWDNX	**U**		**U /**	3.19	-0.79	-2.21 /15	--	--	1.04	2.43
COH	Redwood Managed Volatility Y	RWDYX	**U**		**U /**	3.30	-0.60	-1.80 /17	--	--	1.24	2.16
GEI	RidgeWorth Seix Core Bond A	STGIX	**C-**	(888) 784-3863	**C- / 4.2**	2.82	2.00	0.99 /58	1.94 /60	3.62 /55	1.68	0.62
GEI	RidgeWorth Seix Core Bond I	STIGX	**B-**	(888) 784-3863	**C+ / 6.7**	2.75	2.07	1.16 /61	2.16 /65	3.89 /60	1.93	0.45
COI	RidgeWorth Seix Core Bond IS	STGZX	**C+**	(888) 784-3863	**C+ / 6.6**	2.88	2.14	0.96 /58	2.09 /63	3.85 /59	2.01	N/A
GEI	RidgeWorth Seix Core Bond R	SCIGX	**C+**	(888) 784-3863	**C+ / 6.0**	2.75	1.87	0.76 /54	1.75 /57	3.41 /52	1.55	0.85
COH	RidgeWorth Seix Corporate Bond A	SAINX	**D**	(888) 784-3863	**C- / 4.2**	3.75	2.52	-0.55 /25	2.08 /63	4.25 /65	2.50	0.99
COH	RidgeWorth Seix Corporate Bond C	STIFX	**D+**	(888) 784-3863	**C / 5.2**	3.47	2.18	-1.25 /20	1.41 /50	3.56 /54	1.94	1.67
COH	RidgeWorth Seix Corporate Bond I	STICX	**C-**	(888) 784-3863	**C+ / 6.9**	3.70	2.65	-0.33 /28	2.40 /69	4.56 /68	2.86	0.69
LP	RidgeWorth Seix Fltng Rt Hg Inc A	SFRAX	**D+**	(888) 784-3863	**D+ / 2.9**	1.93	-0.72	-1.85 /16	1.27 /48	2.82 /42	4.31	0.91
LP	RidgeWorth Seix Fltng Rt Hg Inc C	SFRCX	**D+**	(888) 784-3863	**C- / 3.0**	1.79	-1.01	-2.42 /14	0.66 /36	2.16 /33	3.82	1.50
LP	RidgeWorth Seix Fltng Rt Hg Inc I	SAMBX	**C-**	(888) 784-3863	**C / 4.7**	2.00	-0.58	-1.57 /18	1.56 /53	3.11 /47	4.72	0.61
LP	RidgeWorth Seix Fltng Rt Hg Inc IS	SFRZX	**C-**	(888) 784-3863	**C / 4.8**	1.90	-0.53	-1.46 /19	1.61 /54	3.13 /47	4.83	0.47
MUS	RidgeWorth Seix GA Tax Ex Bond A	SGTEX	**C+**	(888) 784-3863	**B / 8.0**	1.43	2.91	3.36 /89	3.20 /90	5.35 /88	2.25	0.73
MUS	RidgeWorth Seix GA Tax Ex Bond I	SGATX	**B+**	(888) 784-3863	**A- / 9.2**	1.46	2.97	3.46 /90	3.32 /91	5.49 /89	2.46	0.64
MUS	RidgeWorth Seix Hi Grade Muni Bd A	SFLTX	**B+**	(888) 784-3863	**B+ / 8.8**	1.45	3.24	3.67 /92	4.07 /96	6.45 /94	1.90	0.81
MUS	RidgeWorth Seix Hi Grade Muni Bd I	SCFTX	**A**	(888) 784-3863	**A+ / 9.7**	1.57	3.40	3.82 /93	4.25 /97	6.61 /95	2.13	0.70
COH	RidgeWorth Seix High Income A	SAHIX	**E**	(888) 784-3863	**E+ / 0.7**	2.95	0.08	-5.77 / 3	0.51 /33	3.32 /50	6.11	0.99
COH	RidgeWorth Seix High Income I	STHTX	**D-**	(888) 784-3863	**D+ / 2.9**	3.18	0.36	-5.41 / 4	0.78 /39	3.60 /55	6.66	0.77
COH	RidgeWorth Seix High Income IS	STHZX	**D-**	(888) 784-3863	**C- / 3.1**	3.22	0.44	-5.40 / 4	0.86 /40	3.66 /56	6.82	0.63
COH	RidgeWorth Seix High Income R	STHIX	**E+**	(888) 784-3863	**D / 1.6**	2.90	-0.02	-5.96 / 3	0.34 /31	3.07 /46	6.21	1.21
COH	RidgeWorth Seix High Yield A	HYPSX	**E**	(888) 784-3863	**E+ / 0.7**	1.95	-0.90	-5.43 / 4	0.61 /35	3.42 /52	5.59	0.87
COH	RidgeWorth Seix High Yield I	SAMHX	**D-**	(888) 784-3863	**D+ / 2.7**	2.00	-0.82	-5.31 / 4	0.83 /40	3.65 /56	6.10	0.58
COH	RidgeWorth Seix High Yield R	HYLSX	**E+**	(888) 784-3863	**D- / 1.4**	1.91	-1.02	-5.59 / 4	0.38 /31	3.14 /47	5.65	1.04
MUN	RidgeWorth Seix Inv Grade T/E Bd A	SISIX	**B+**	(888) 784-3863	**B- / 7.2**	1.31	2.72	2.86 /84	2.71 /85	4.60 /82	2.00	0.91
MUN	RidgeWorth Seix Inv Grade T/E Bd I	STTBX	**A+**	(888) 784-3863	**B+ / 8.9**	1.35	2.71	2.93 /84	2.87 /87	4.78 /84	2.25	0.68
US	RidgeWorth Seix Ltd Dur I	SAMLX	**C+**	(888) 784-3863	**D+ / 2.8**	0.21	0.16	0.25 /45	0.21 /29	0.46 /17	0.25	0.46
MUS	RidgeWorth Seix NC Tax Exempt A	SNCIX	**C+**	(888) 784-3863	**B / 7.8**	1.31	2.71	3.20 /87	3.07 /89	5.01 /85	2.00	0.79
MUS	RidgeWorth Seix NC Tax Exempt I	CNCFX	**B+**	(888) 784-3863	**A- / 9.2**	1.35	2.89	3.36 /89	3.22 /90	5.16 /87	2.25	0.69
MUS	RidgeWorth Seix Short-Trm Muni Bd	CMDTX	**B-**	(888) 784-3863	**C / 4.3**	0.41	0.29	0.40 /52	0.66 /43	2.97 /68	0.41	0.63
MUS	RidgeWorth Seix Short-Trm Muni Bd	SMMAX	**C-**	(888) 784-3863	**D / 1.7**	0.38	0.20	0.23 /47	0.51 /39	2.82 /66	0.23	0.76
GEI	RidgeWorth Seix Sh-Term Bond A	STSBX	**C-**	(888) 784-3863	**D / 2.0**	0.94	0.45	0.57 /51	0.58 /35	1.09 /21	0.46	0.81
GEI	RidgeWorth Seix Sh-Term Bond C	SCBSX	**C**	(888) 784-3863	**D+ / 2.5**	0.70	0.10	--	0.02 /18	0.44 /17	0.00	1.58
GEI	RidgeWorth Seix Sh-Term Bond I	SSBTX	**B-**	(888) 784-3863	**C- / 4.0**	0.89	0.45	0.67 /53	0.78 /39	1.32 /23	0.67	0.67
COI	RidgeWorth Seix Total Return Bd A	CBPSX	**C-**	(888) 784-3863	**C- / 3.9**	2.58	1.90	1.00 /59	1.82 /58	3.67 /56	1.61	0.71
COI	RidgeWorth Seix Total Return Bd I	SAMFX	**C+**	(888) 784-3863	**C+ / 6.6**	2.61	1.96	1.23 /62	2.09 /63	3.94 /61	1.94	0.44
COI	RidgeWorth Seix Total Return Bd IS	SAMZX	**B-**	(888) 784-3863	**C+ / 6.8**	2.65	2.03	1.46 /66	2.20 /66	4.01 /62	2.07	0.31
COI	RidgeWorth Seix Total Return Bd R	SCBLX	**C**	(888) 784-3863	**C+ / 5.6**	2.47	1.76	0.72 /54	1.50 /52	3.36 /51	1.34	1.06
GEI	RidgeWorth Seix Ultra Short Bond I	SISSX	**C+**	(888) 784-3863	**C- / 3.5**	0.33	0.42	0.41 /48	0.58 /35	0.89 /20	0.81	0.37
* USS	RidgeWorth Seix US Gvt Sec U/S Bd	SIGVX	**C+**	(888) 784-3863	**D+ / 2.8**	0.02	-0.19	-0.13 /30	0.26 /30	0.73 /19	0.77	0.39
MTG	RidgeWorth Seix US Mtg A	SLTMX	**B**	(888) 784-3863	**C+ / 5.7**	1.83	1.39	1.70 /69	2.29 /67	3.13 /47	1.46	1.33
MTG	RidgeWorth Seix US Mtg C	SCLFX	**C+**	(888) 784-3863	**C / 5.4**	1.65	1.02	0.86 /56	1.51 /52	2.33 /35	0.77	2.05
MTG	RidgeWorth Seix US Mtg I	SLMTX	**A**	(888) 784-3863	**B- / 7.1**	1.88	1.49	1.81 /70	2.50 /71	3.33 /50	1.70	1.16
MUS	RidgeWorth Seix VA Interm Muni A	CVIAX	**B**	(888) 784-3863	**C+ / 6.8**	1.48	2.72	3.26 /88	2.43 /82	3.80 /76	2.11	0.74
MUS	RidgeWorth Seix VA Interm Muni I	CRVTX	**A+**	(888) 784-3863	**B+ / 8.6**	1.51	2.78	3.27 /88	2.52 /83	3.94 /77	2.32	0.65
COI	River Canyon Total Return Bond Inst	RCTIX	**U**	(800) 245-0371	**U /**	-0.15	-0.05	3.22 /78	--	--	5.46	N/A
GEI	● RiverNorth/DoubleLine Strat Inc I	RNSIX	**C**	(888) 848-7549	**B- / 7.0**	2.35	3.04	0.65 /52	3.03 /77	6.25 /78	6.30	1.40
GEI	● RiverNorth/DoubleLine Strat Inc R	RNDLX	**C-**	(888) 848-7549	**C+ / 6.5**	2.18	2.80	0.30 /46	2.76 /74	6.00 /77	6.04	1.65
GEI	RiverNorth/Oaktree High Income I	RNHIX	**D**	(888) 848-7549	**C- / 4.2**	2.46	1.89	-2.88 /12	1.75 /57	--	6.47	1.82
GEI	RiverNorth/Oaktree High Income R	RNOTX	**D**	(888) 848-7549	**C- / 3.6**	2.40	1.76	-3.14 /11	1.45 /51	--	6.20	2.07

● Denotes fund is closed to new investors
* Denotes fund is included in Section II

RISK			NET ASSETS		ASSET							FUND MANAGER		MINIMUM		LOADS	
Risk Rating/Pts	3 Yr Avg Standard Deviation	Avg Duration	NAV As of 3/31/16	Total $(Mil)	Cash %	Gov. Bond %	Muni. Bond %	Corp. Bond %	Other %	Portfolio Turnover Ratio	Avg Coupon Rate	Manager Quality Pct	Manager Tenure (Years)	Initial Purch. $	Additional Purch. $	Front End Load	Back End Load
A+ / 9.9	N/A	N/A	1.00	558	100	0	0	0	0	0	0.0	66	N/A	1,000,000	0	0.0	0.0
U /	N/A	N/A	14.40	31	2	0	3	86	9	519	0.0	N/A	3	250,000	1,000	0.0	0.0
U /	N/A	N/A	14.38	19	2	0	3	86	9	519	0.0	N/A	3	10,000	500	0.0	0.0
U /	N/A	N/A	14.46	171	2	0	3	86	9	519	0.0	N/A	3	20,000,000	1,000	0.0	1.0
C+ / 6.2	3.1	5.7	10.86	10	2	38	0	25	35	168	2.9	40	12	2,000	1,000	4.8	0.0
C+ / 6.2	3.1	5.7	10.86	255	2	38	0	25	35	168	2.9	48	12	0	0	0.0	0.0
C+ / 6.1	3.1	5.7	10.86	N/A	2	38	0	25	35	168	2.9	72	12	2,500,000	0	0.0	0.0
C+ / 6.0	3.1	5.7	10.87	3	2	38	0	25	35	168	2.9	34	12	0	0	0.0	0.0
D / 2.1	4.8	7.1	8.50	1	3	0	0	96	1	90	3.8	91	12	2,000	1,000	4.8	0.0
D / 2.2	4.8	7.1	8.46	8	3	0	0	96	1	90	3.8	82	12	5,000	1,000	0.0	0.0
D+ / 2.3	4.8	7.1	8.46	9	3	0	0	96	1	90	3.8	93	12	0	0	0.0	0.0
C+ / 6.1	3.1	0.3	8.33	143	3	0	0	81	16	29	4.6	85	10	2,000	1,000	2.5	0.0
C+ / 6.0	3.1	0.3	8.33	55	3	0	0	81	16	29	4.6	71	10	5,000	1,000	0.0	0.0
C+ / 6.0	3.1	0.3	8.33	3,046	3	0	0	81	16	29	4.6	89	10	0	0	0.0	0.0
C+ / 6.1	3.1	0.3	8.33	1,128	3	0	0	81	16	29	4.6	90	10	2,500,000	0	0.0	0.0
C / 4.3	3.8	5.9	10.98	4	4	0	95	0	1	55	5.0	36	13	2,000	1,000	4.8	0.0
C / 4.4	3.7	5.9	10.96	108	4	0	95	0	1	55	5.0	40	13	0	0	0.0	0.0
C / 4.5	3.7	6.2	12.36	14	10	0	89	0	1	228	4.3	76	22	2,000	1,000	4.8	0.0
C / 4.6	3.6	6.2	12.36	99	10	0	89	0	1	228	4.3	82	22	0	0	0.0	0.0
E+ / 0.7	6.6	3.6	5.92	43	10	0	0	87	3	86	6.6	19	5	2,000	1,000	4.8	0.0
E+ / 0.7	6.5	3.6	5.92	545	10	0	0	87	3	86	6.6	26	5	0	0	0.0	0.0
E+ / 0.7	6.5	3.6	5.92	1	10	0	0	87	3	86	6.6	28	5	2,500,000	0	0.0	0.0
E+ / 0.7	6.5	3.6	5.92	15	10	0	0	87	3	86	6.6	17	5	0	0	0.0	0.0
D- / 1.2	5.9	3.5	7.61	7	12	0	0	87	1	72	6.3	26	9	2,000	1,000	4.8	0.0
D- / 1.2	5.9	3.5	7.80	522	12	0	0	87	1	72	6.3	32	9	0	0	0.0	0.0
D- / 1.2	5.8	3.5	7.80	1	12	0	0	87	1	72	6.3	21	9	0	0	0.0	0.0
B- / 7.0	2.9	5.4	12.24	25	8	0	91	0	1	144	4.6	52	24	2,000	1,000	4.8	0.0
B- / 7.0	2.9	5.4	12.22	629	8	0	91	0	1	144	4.6	59	24	0	0	0.0	0.0
A+ / 9.9	0.3	0.1	9.83	7	1	0	0	0	99	45	0.6	74	14	0	0	0.0	0.0
C- / 4.2	3.8	5.6	10.50	1	6	0	93	0	1	51	4.9	31	11	2,000	1,000	4.8	0.0
C / 4.3	3.8	5.6	10.53	29	6	0	93	0	1	51	4.9	35	11	0	0	0.0	0.0
A / 9.3	1.0	1.6	9.98	32	6	0	93	0	1	148	3.9	56	5	0	0	0.0	0.0
A / 9.4	0.9	1.6	9.98	7	6	0	93	0	1	148	3.9	52	5	2,000	1,000	2.5	0.0
A / 9.5	0.8	1.9	10.01	2	0	28	3	39	30	199	2.0	63	8	2,000	1,000	2.5	0.0
A / 9.5	0.8	1.9	10.00	2	0	28	3	39	30	199	2.0	42	8	5,000	1,000	0.0	0.0
A+ / 9.6	0.8	1.9	9.98	50	0	28	3	39	30	199	2.0	76	8	0	0	0.0	0.0
C+ / 6.0	3.1	5.7	11.02	32	2	42	0	23	33	173	2.8	58	14	2,000	1,000	4.8	0.0
C+ / 6.1	3.1	5.7	10.66	970	2	42	0	23	33	173	2.8	74	14	0	0	0.0	0.0
C+ / 6.3	3.1	5.7	10.67	56	2	42	0	23	33	173	2.8	78	14	2,500,000	0	0.0	0.0
C+ / 6.2	3.1	5.7	10.67	50	2	42	0	23	33	173	2.8	47	14	0	0	0.0	0.0
A+ / 9.9	0.4	0.3	9.93	105	5	0	4	46	45	54	2.3	79	10	0	0	0.0	0.0
A+ / 9.9	0.3	0.3	10.03	1,556	3	0	0	0	97	34	1.7	73	10	0	0	0.0	0.0
B / 7.8	2.6	4.6	11.31	7	0	8	0	0	92	165	3.8	45	9	2,000	1,000	2.5	0.0
B / 7.6	2.6	4.6	11.33	6	0	8	0	0	92	165	3.8	22	9	5,000	1,000	0.0	0.0
B / 7.7	2.6	4.6	11.33	25	0	8	0	0	92	165	3.8	51	9	0	0	0.0	0.0
C+ / 6.6	3.0	5.5	10.06	4	5	0	94	0	1	59	5.0	38	5	2,000	1,000	4.8	0.0
C+ / 6.4	3.0	5.5	10.06	65	5	0	94	0	1	59	5.0	40	5	0	0	0.0	0.0
U /	N/A	N/A	9.88	26	15	0	0	0	85	45	0.0	N/A	2	100,000	10,000	0.0	0.0
C- / 3.9	4.0	N/A	10.29	1,672	14	9	6	24	47	29	0.0	85	6	100,000	100	0.0	2.0
C- / 4.0	4.0	N/A	10.30	220	14	9	6	24	47	29	0.0	82	6	5,000	100	0.0	2.0
D+ / 2.6	5.1	N/A	8.98	77	0	1	0	70	29	70	0.0	73	4	100,000	100	0.0	2.0
D+ / 2.7	5.1	N/A	8.97	8	0	1	0	70	29	70	0.0	59	4	5,000	100	0.0	2.0

99 Pct = Best
0 Pct = Worst

Fund Type	Fund Name	Ticker Symbol	Overall Investment Rating	Phone	PERFORMANCE Performance Rating/Pts	Total Return % through 3/31/16 3 Mo	6 Mo	1Yr / Pct	Annualized 3Yr / Pct	5Yr / Pct	Incl. in Returns Dividend Yield	Expense Ratio
COH	● RiverPark Sht-Tm Hi Yield Instl	RPHIX	A+	(888) 564-4517	B- / 7.1	0.97	1.24	1.49 /66	2.66 /73	3.22 /49	3.13	0.87
COH	● RiverPark Sht-Tm High Yield Rtl	RPHYX	A+	(888) 564-4517	C+ / 6.5	0.92	1.02	1.14 /61	2.33 /68	2.92 /44	2.89	1.18
MUN	Robinson Tax Advantaged Income A	ROBAX	U	(800) 207-7108	U /	2.80	9.55	6.88 /99	--	--	4.24	7.41
MUN	Robinson Tax Advantaged Income C	ROBCX	U	(800) 207-7108	U /	2.63	9.21	6.16 /99	--	--	3.85	8.16
MUN	Robinson Tax Advantaged Income	ROBNX	U	(800) 207-7108	U /	2.86	9.67	7.13 /99	--	--	4.72	7.16
COI	Rockefeller Core Taxable Bond Instl	RCFIX	U	(855) 369-6209	U /	2.62	2.28	2.10 /72	--	--	1.46	0.86
MUN	Rockefeller Int TxEx Natl Bd Instl	RCTEX	U	(855) 369-6209	U /	0.89	1.47	1.79 /76	--	--	0.58	0.86
MUN	Rockefeller Int TxEx NY Bd Instl	RCNYX	U	(855) 369-6209	U /	0.79	1.27	1.55 /74	--	--	0.42	0.95
LP	RS Floating Rate A	RSFLX	D	(800) 766-3863	D- / 1.5	2.68	-0.02	-2.81 /12	0.51 /33	2.46 /37	5.12	1.08
LP	RS Floating Rate C	RSFCX	D-	(800) 766-3863	D- / 1.2	2.47	-0.52	-3.68 / 9	-0.32 /13	1.65 /27	4.41	1.85
LP	RS Floating Rate K	RSFKX	U	(800) 766-3863	U /	2.54	-0.26	-3.30 /10	--	1.95 /31	4.71	1.58
LP	RS Floating Rate Y	RSFYX	D	(800) 766-3863	C- / 3.3	2.73	0.09	-2.69 /12	0.70 /37	2.71 /41	5.47	0.82
MUH	RS High Income Municipal Bond A	RSHMX	C+	(800) 766-3863	B+ / 8.9	1.59	3.44	4.17 /95	3.76 /94	6.82 /96	3.72	1.02
MUH	RS High Income Municipal Bond C	RSHCX	C+	(800) 766-3863	A- / 9.0	1.40	3.05	3.37 /89	2.97 /88	5.98 /92	3.11	1.77
MUH	RS High Income Municipal Bond Y	RHMYX	B-	(800) 766-3863	A+ / 9.7	1.74	3.66	4.50 /97	4.03 /96	7.08 /97	4.09	0.73
COH	RS High Yield Fund A	GUHYX	E	(800) 766-3863	E+ / 0.7	2.17	-0.75	-4.77 / 5	0.22 /29	3.54 /54	6.44	1.16
COH	RS High Yield Fund C	RHYCX	E	(800) 766-3863	E+ / 0.9	2.00	-1.08	-5.41 / 4	-0.53 /11	2.79 /42	5.96	1.90
COH	RS High Yield Fund K	RHYKX	E+	(800) 766-3863	D- / 1.1	2.08	-0.91	-5.06 / 5	-0.17 /14	3.15 /47	6.32	1.52
COH	RS High Yield Fund Y	RSYYX	E+	(800) 766-3863	D / 1.7	2.23	-0.65	-4.59 / 6	0.40 /31	3.75 /57	6.95	0.90
COI	RS Investment Quality Bond A	GUIQX	C-	(800) 766-3863	C / 4.7	2.97	1.70	0.52 /50	2.09 /63	3.58 /54	2.76	1.05
COI	RS Investment Quality Bond C	RIQCX	C-	(800) 766-3863	C / 4.9	2.75	1.26	-0.45 /27	1.25 /47	2.74 /41	2.01	1.88
COI	RS Investment Quality Bond K	RIQKX	C	(800) 766-3863	C+ / 5.7	2.87	1.50	0.02 /33	1.68 /55	3.17 /48	2.47	1.46
COI	RS Investment Quality Bond Y	RSQYX	C+	(800) 766-3863	C+ / 6.8	3.03	1.83	0.76 /54	2.27 /67	3.77 /58	3.10	0.78
GEI	RS Low Duration Bond Fund A	RLDAX	C-	(800) 766-3863	D / 1.8	0.69	0.08	0.39 /48	0.54 /34	1.19 /22	1.17	0.90
GEI	RS Low Duration Bond Fund C	RLDCX	C-	(800) 766-3863	D / 1.6	0.50	-0.25	-0.33 /28	-0.21 /14	0.44 /17	0.47	1.64
GEI	RS Low Duration Bond Fund K	RLDKX	C	(800) 766-3863	D+ / 2.7	0.58	-0.09	--	0.12 /27	0.78 /19	0.80	1.33
GEI	RS Low Duration Bond Fund Y	RSDYX	C+	(800) 766-3863	C- / 3.9	0.75	0.19	0.61 /52	0.79 /39	1.42 /25	1.41	0.61
GEI	RS Strategic Income A	RSIAX	D+	(800) 766-3863	D+ / 2.7	1.87	1.22	-0.01 /31	1.00 /43	3.25 /49	3.05	1.14
GEI	RS Strategic Income C	RSICX	D+	(800) 766-3863	C- / 3.0	1.77	0.82	-0.78 /23	0.23 /29	2.41 /37	2.37	1.96
GEI	RS Strategic Income K	RINKX	D+	(800) 766-3863	C- / 3.7	1.76	1.02	-0.38 /27	0.59 /35	2.82 /42	2.78	1.57
GEI	RS Strategic Income Y	RSRYX	C-	(800) 766-3863	C / 5.0	1.92	1.32	0.29 /46	1.25 /47	3.46 /52	3.38	0.87
MUN	RS Tax-Exempt Fund A	GUTEX	C+	(800) 766-3863	B / 7.7	1.55	2.81	3.34 /89	2.65 /84	5.00 /85	3.05	0.96
MUN	RS Tax-Exempt Fund C	RETCX	C+	(800) 766-3863	B / 7.9	1.26	2.40	2.52 /81	1.80 /74	4.15 /79	2.38	1.72
MUN	RS Tax-Exempt Fund Y	RSTYX	B+	(800) 766-3863	B+ / 8.9	1.58	2.87	3.45 /90	2.73 /85	5.13 /86	3.27	0.69
GL	Russell Glbl Opportunistic Credit A	RGCAX	D-	(800) 832-6688	D+ / 2.4	4.48	4.25	--	0.38 /31	3.69 /56	3.45	1.58
GL	Russell Glbl Opportunistic Credit C	RGCCX	D-	(800) 832-6688	C- / 3.0	4.37	3.94	-0.70 /24	-0.34 /13	2.95 /44	2.89	2.33
GL	Russell Glbl Opportunistic Credit E	RCCEX	D	(800) 832-6688	C / 4.5	4.59	4.36	0.11 /41	0.42 /32	3.72 /57	3.58	1.58
GL	Russell Glbl Opportunistic Credit S	RGCSX	D	(800) 832-6688	C / 4.9	4.62	4.46	0.24 /45	0.66 /36	3.96 /61	3.80	1.33
GL	Russell Glbl Opportunistic Credit Y	RGCYX	D	(800) 832-6688	C / 5.0	4.52	4.38	0.31 /46	0.71 /37	4.05 /62	3.87	1.13
COI	Russell Investment Grade Bond A	RFAAX	C	(800) 832-6688	C / 4.8	2.77	2.22	1.38 /65	1.99 /61	3.34 /51	1.56	0.82
COI	Russell Investment Grade Bond C	RFACX	C	(800) 832-6688	C / 5.1	2.58	1.81	0.58 /51	1.22 /47	2.57 /39	0.89	1.57
COI	Russell Investment Grade Bond E	RFAEX	B-	(800) 832-6688	C+ / 6.5	2.77	2.22	1.33 /64	1.99 /61	3.36 /51	1.61	0.82
COI	Russell Investment Grade Bond I	RFASX	B	(800) 832-6688	B- / 7.1	2.88	2.39	1.67 /68	2.33 /68	3.68 /56	1.94	0.49
COI	Russell Investment Grade Bond S	RFATX	B	(800) 832-6688	C+ / 6.9	2.82	2.35	1.59 /67	2.25 /67	3.60 /55	1.87	0.57
COI	Russell Investment Grade Bond Y	RFAYX	B+	(800) 832-6688	B- / 7.3	2.89	2.45	1.84 /70	2.45 /70	3.80 /58	2.06	0.37
GEI	Russell Short Duration Bond A	RSBTX	C-	(800) 832-6688	D- / 1.5	1.09	0.66	0.49 /49	0.59 /35	1.40 /25	1.01	1.01
GEI	Russell Short Duration Bond C	RSBCX	C-	(800) 832-6688	D / 1.8	0.92	0.31	-0.21 /29	-0.14 /14	0.65 /18	0.36	1.76
GEI	Russell Short Duration Bond E	RSBEX	C+	(800) 832-6688	C- / 3.7	1.09	0.66	0.53 /50	0.61 /35	1.41 /25	1.05	1.01
GEI	Russell Short Duration Bond S	RFBSX	B-	(800) 832-6688	C- / 4.2	1.18	0.78	0.79 /55	0.85 /40	1.66 /27	1.30	0.76
GEI	Russell Short Duration Bond Y	RSBYX	B-	(800) 832-6688	C / 4.4	1.14	0.82	0.82 /56	0.94 /42	1.75 /28	1.38	0.56
GEI	Russell Strategic Bond A	RFDAX	C-	(800) 832-6688	C / 4.9	3.04	2.10	1.13 /61	2.03 /62	3.61 /55	1.93	1.04
GEI	Russell Strategic Bond C	RFCCX	C	(800) 832-6688	C / 5.2	2.82	1.72	0.46 /49	1.28 /48	2.83 /42	1.25	1.79

● Denotes fund is closed to new investors
* Denotes fund is included in Section II

RISK			NET ASSETS		ASSET							FUND MANAGER		MINIMUM		LOADS	
Risk Rating/Pts	3 Yr Avg Standard Deviation	Avg Duration	NAV As of 3/31/16	Total $(Mil)	Cash %	Gov. Bond %	Muni. Bond %	Corp. Bond %	Other %	Portfolio Turnover Ratio	Avg Coupon Rate	Manager Quality Pct	Manager Tenure (Years)	Initial Purch. $	Additional Purch. $	Front End Load	Back End Load
A- / 9.0	0.8	N/A	9.75	616	1	0	0	83	16	90	0.0	97	6	100,000	100	0.0	0.0
A- / 9.0	0.8	N/A	9.71	250	1	0	0	83	16	90	0.0	96	6	1,000	100	0.0	0.0
U /	N/A	N/A	10.25	18	0	0	97	0	3	0	0.0	N/A	2	2,500	100	5.8	0.0
U /	N/A	N/A	10.25	4	0	0	97	0	3	0	0.0	N/A	2	2,500	100	0.0	0.0
U /	N/A	N/A	10.25	73	0	0	97	0	3	0	0.0	N/A	2	1,000,000	100,000	0.0	0.0
U /	N/A	N/A	10.19	79	0	0	0	0	100	88	0.0	N/A	N/A	1,000,000	10,000	0.0	0.0
U /	N/A	N/A	10.19	79	0	0	0	0	100	43	0.0	N/A	3	1,000,000	10,000	0.0	0.0
U /	N/A	N/A	10.19	39	0	0	0	0	100	51	0.0	N/A	3	1,000,000	10,000	0.0	0.0
C- / 4.1	3.9	1.6	9.19	215	2	0	0	85	13	39	5.3	48	7	2,500	100	2.3	0.0
C- / 4.1	3.9	1.6	9.19	376	2	0	0	85	13	39	5.3	26	7	2,500	100	0.0	0.0
U /	3.9	1.6	9.19	2	2	0	0	85	13	39	5.3	N/A	7	1,000	0	0.0	0.0
C- / 4.2	3.9	1.6	9.19	419	2	0	0	85	13	39	5.3	59	7	0	100	0.0	0.0
C- / 3.0	4.2	4.5	10.96	54	3	0	96	0	1	25	5.6	48	2	2,500	100	3.8	0.0
D+ / 2.9	4.3	4.5	10.96	37	3	0	96	0	1	25	5.6	24	2	2,500	100	0.0	0.0
D+ / 2.9	4.3	4.5	10.97	48	3	0	96	0	1	25	5.6	56	2	0	100	0.0	0.0
E+ / 0.9	6.1	3.7	5.88	27	4	0	0	91	5	221	6.7	18	7	2,500	100	3.8	0.0
E+ / 0.9	6.2	3.7	5.89	22	4	0	0	91	5	221	6.7	10	7	2,500	100	0.0	0.0
E+ / 0.9	6.2	3.7	5.90	18	4	0	0	91	5	221	6.7	13	7	1,000	0	0.0	0.0
D- / 1.0	6.1	3.7	5.85	6	4	0	0	91	5	221	6.7	21	7	0	100	0.0	0.0
C+ / 5.7	3.2	5.7	9.79	50	0	10	1	59	30	51	4.6	62	12	2,500	100	3.8	0.0
C+ / 5.7	3.2	5.7	9.78	10	0	10	1	59	30	51	4.6	34	12	2,500	100	0.0	0.0
C+ / 5.7	3.2	5.7	9.80	5	0	10	1	59	30	51	4.6	48	12	1,000	0	0.0	0.0
C+ / 5.9	3.2	5.7	9.78	6	0	10	1	59	30	51	4.6	75	12	0	100	0.0	0.0
A / 9.3	1.0	1.8	9.99	308	4	0	0	47	49	38	2.9	59	12	2,500	100	2.3	0.0
A / 9.3	0.9	1.8	9.99	149	4	0	0	47	49	38	2.9	34	12	2,500	100	0.0	0.0
A / 9.3	0.9	1.8	9.99	4	4	0	0	47	49	38	2.9	44	12	1,000	0	0.0	0.0
A / 9.4	0.9	1.8	9.99	390	4	0	0	47	49	38	2.9	74	12	0	100	0.0	0.0
C / 5.4	3.3	2.7	9.79	38	5	13	0	64	18	87	4.1	33	7	2,500	100	3.8	0.0
C / 5.2	3.4	2.7	9.84	13	5	13	0	64	18	87	4.1	15	7	2,500	100	0.0	0.0
C / 5.4	3.3	2.7	9.84	3	5	13	0	64	18	87	4.1	23	7	1,000	0	0.0	0.0
C / 5.2	3.4	2.7	9.74	13	5	13	0	64	18	87	4.1	39	7	0	100	0.0	0.0
C / 4.6	3.6	4.4	10.61	92	3	0	96	0	1	14	5.0	25	23	2,500	100	3.8	0.0
C / 4.7	3.6	4.4	10.60	43	3	0	96	0	1	14	5.0	13	23	2,500	100	0.0	0.0
C / 4.7	3.6	4.4	10.60	52	3	0	96	0	1	14	5.0	28	23	0	100	0.0	0.0
D / 1.6	6.1	4.4	9.13	5	3	32	0	42	23	125	0.0	82	N/A	0	0	3.8	0.0
D / 1.6	6.1	4.4	9.09	8	3	32	0	42	23	125	0.0	52	N/A	0	0	0.0	0.0
D- / 1.5	6.1	4.4	9.15	29	3	32	0	42	23	125	0.0	83	N/A	0	0	0.0	0.0
D- / 1.5	6.1	4.4	9.16	999	3	32	0	42	23	125	0.0	87	N/A	0	0	0.0	0.0
D / 1.6	6.1	4.4	9.16	600	3	32	0	42	23	125	0.0	87	N/A	10,000,000	0	0.0	0.0
C+ / 6.5	3.0	5.4	22.02	9	0	20	0	26	54	187	0.0	71	27	0	0	3.8	0.0
C+ / 6.5	3.0	5.4	21.83	18	0	20	0	26	54	187	0.0	39	27	0	0	0.0	0.0
C+ / 6.5	3.0	5.4	22.00	23	0	20	0	26	54	187	0.0	72	27	0	0	0.0	0.0
C+ / 6.5	3.0	5.4	22.01	278	0	20	0	26	54	187	0.0	81	27	100,000	0	0.0	0.0
C+ / 6.5	3.0	5.4	21.99	676	0	20	0	26	54	187	0.0	79	27	0	0	0.0	0.0
C+ / 6.5	3.0	5.4	22.03	164	0	20	0	26	54	187	0.0	84	27	10,000,000	0	0.0	0.0
A- / 9.2	1.1	1.5	19.09	27	0	25	0	28	47	183	0.0	60	5	0	0	3.8	0.0
A- / 9.2	1.1	1.5	18.94	52	0	25	0	28	47	183	0.0	35	5	0	0	0.0	0.0
A- / 9.2	1.1	1.5	19.13	25	0	25	0	28	47	183	0.0	60	5	0	0	0.0	0.0
A- / 9.2	1.1	1.5	19.11	546	0	25	0	28	47	183	0.0	74	5	0	0	0.0	0.0
A- / 9.2	1.1	1.5	19.11	151	0	25	0	28	47	183	0.0	77	5	10,000,000	0	0.0	0.0
C+ / 6.0	3.1	5.4	10.94	59	0	21	0	28	51	159	0.0	43	N/A	0	0	3.8	0.0
C+ / 5.9	3.2	5.4	10.93	60	0	21	0	28	51	159	0.0	22	N/A	0	0	0.0	0.0

Fund Type	Fund Name (99 Pct = Best, 0 Pct = Worst)	Ticker Symbol	Overall Investment Rating	Phone	PERFORMANCE: Performance Rating/Pts	Total Return % through 3/31/16: 3 Mo	6 Mo	1Yr / Pct	Annualized: 3Yr / Pct	Annualized: 5Yr / Pct	Incl. in Returns: Dividend Yield	Incl. in Returns: Expense Ratio
GEI	Russell Strategic Bond E	RFCEX	C+	(800) 832-6688	C+ / 6.6	3.06	2.12	1.23 /62	2.05 /62	3.64 /55	2.02	1.04
GEI	Russell Strategic Bond I	RFCSX	B-	(800) 832-6688	B- / 7.0	3.12	2.18	1.45 /66	2.33 /68	3.93 /60	2.32	0.71
GEI	Russell Strategic Bond S	RFCTX	B-	(800) 832-6688	B- / 7.0	3.07	2.13	1.38 /65	2.28 /67	3.87 /60	2.24	0.79
GEI	Russell Strategic Bond Y	RFCYX	B	(800) 832-6688	B- / 7.2	3.14	2.24	1.56 /67	2.45 /70	4.04 /62	2.43	0.59
MUN	Russell Tax Exempt Bond A	RTEAX	A+	(800) 832-6688	B / 7.9	1.56	2.83	3.30 /88	2.81 /86	3.81 /76	2.31	0.84
MUN	Russell Tax Exempt Bond C	RTECX	A+	(800) 832-6688	B / 8.1	1.41	2.44	2.58 /81	2.08 /78	3.08 /70	1.71	1.59
MUN	Russell Tax Exempt Bond E	RTBEX	A+	(800) 832-6688	B+ / 8.9	1.57	2.81	3.30 /88	2.84 /86	3.85 /77	2.44	0.84
MUN	Russell Tax Exempt Bond S	RLVSX	A+	(800) 832-6688	A- / 9.1	1.61	2.95	3.57 /91	3.09 /89	4.10 /78	2.70	0.59
MUH	Russell Tax Exempt High Yield Bd A	RTHAX	U	(800) 832-6688	U /	2.81	5.91	--	--	--	0.00	N/A
MUH	Russell Tax Exempt High Yield Bd C	RTHCX	U	(800) 832-6688	U /	2.63	5.51	--	--	--	0.00	N/A
MUH	Russell Tax Exempt High Yield Bd E	RTHEX	U	(800) 832-6688	U /	2.81	5.82	--	--	--	0.00	N/A
MUH	Russell Tax Exempt High Yield Bd S	RTHSX	U	(800) 832-6688	U /	2.85	6.04	--	--	--	0.00	N/A
COI	Ryan Labs Core Bond	RLCBX	U		U /	2.80	1.72	0.68 /53	--	--	2.27	N/A
EM	Rydex Emerging Markets Bond Strat	RYIEX	U	(800) 820-0888	U /	7.70	8.76	5.13 /88	--	--	15.87	1.73
EM	Rydex Emerging Markets Bond Strat	RYFTX	U	(800) 820-0888	U /	6.91	7.70	3.73 /80	--	--	17.19	2.26
EM	Rydex Emerging Markets Bond Strat	RYGTX	U	(800) 820-0888	U /	7.12	8.40	4.82 /86	--	--	16.79	1.76
USL	Rydex Govt Lg Bd 1.2x Strgy A	RYABX	C-	(800) 820-0888	A+ / 9.7	10.88	7.88	0.11 /41	7.66 /99	12.92 /99	1.56	1.20
USL	Rydex Govt Lg Bd 1.2x Strgy C	RYCGX	C-	(800) 820-0888	A+ / 9.7	10.69	7.49	-0.64 /25	6.77 /97	12.00 /98	0.93	1.95
GL	Rydex Govt Lg Bd 1.2x Strgy H	RYHBX	U	(800) 820-0888	U /	10.89	7.91	0.25 /45	--	--	1.64	1.18
USL	Rydex Govt Lg Bd 1.2x Strgy Inv	RYGBX	C-	(800) 820-0888	A+ / 9.9	10.94	7.99	0.32 /46	7.82 /99	13.09 /99	1.88	0.95
COH	Rydex High Yld Stratgy A	RYHDX	C-	(800) 820-0888	B / 8.0	4.15	5.00	1.66 /68	4.39 /86	6.54 /79	3.65	1.55
COH	Rydex High Yld Stratgy C	RYHHX	C-	(800) 820-0888	B / 8.2	3.96	4.64	0.70 /53	3.56 /81	5.71 /75	4.21	2.30
COH	Rydex High Yld Stratgy H	RYHGX	C-	(800) 820-0888	B+ / 8.8	4.02	4.87	1.36 /64	4.42 /87	6.56 /80	3.84	1.51
USS	Rydex Inv Govt Lg Bd Stgy A	RYAQX	E-	(800) 820-0888	E- / 0.0	-8.91	-7.82	-4.47 / 6	-8.17 / 1	-12.35 / 0	0.00	3.41
USS	Rydex Inv Govt Lg Bd Stgy C	RYJCX	E-	(800) 820-0888	E- / 0.0	-9.07	-8.17	-5.18 / 5	-8.85 / 0	-13.00 / 0	0.00	4.15
GL	Rydex Inv Govt Lg Bd Stgy H	RYHJX	U	(800) 820-0888	U /	-8.91	-7.77	-4.47 / 6	--	--	0.00	3.08
USS	Rydex Inv Govt Lg Bd Stgy Inv	RYJUX	E-	(800) 820-0888	E- / 0.0	-8.86	-7.70	-4.22 / 7	-7.96 / 1	-12.12 / 0	0.00	3.16
COH	Rydex Inv High Yld Strtgy A	RYILX	E-	(800) 820-0888	E- / 0.0	-5.53	-7.29	-6.81 / 2	-9.25 / 0	-10.94 / 0	0.00	1.56
COH	Rydex Inv High Yld Strtgy C	RYIYX	E-	(800) 820-0888	E- / 0.0	-5.74	-7.69	-7.59 / 2	-9.70 / 0	-11.47 / 0	0.00	2.29
COH	Rydex Inv High Yld Strtgy H	RYIHX	E-	(800) 820-0888	E- / 0.0	-5.36	-7.20	-6.67 / 2	-8.89 / 0	-10.71 / 0	0.00	1.55
GEI	Rydex Strengthening Dlr 2x Strtgy A	RYSDX	D-	(800) 820-0888	C- / 3.5	-8.62	-4.91	-11.01 / 0	5.09 /91	4.20 /64	0.00	1.71
GEI	Rydex Strengthening Dlr 2x Strtgy C	RYSJX	D-	(800) 820-0888	C / 4.3	-8.81	-5.27	-11.69 / 0	4.29 /86	3.41 /52	0.00	2.47
GEI	Rydex Strengthening Dlr 2x Strtgy H	RYSBX	D	(800) 820-0888	C+ / 5.8	-8.62	-4.89	-11.00 / 0	5.08 /91	4.22 /64	0.00	1.71
GEI	Rydex Wekng Dlr 2x Stgry A	RYWDX	E-	(800) 820-0888	E- / 0.0	8.28	2.53	6.54 /95	-9.53 / 0	-9.21 / 0	0.00	1.73
GEI	Rydex Wekng Dlr 2x Stgry C	RYWJX	E-	(800) 820-0888	E- / 0.0	8.03	2.14	5.74 /92	-10.21 / 0	-9.88 / 0	0.00	2.49
GEI	Rydex Wekng Dlr 2x Stgry H	RYWBX	E-	(800) 820-0888	E- / 0.1	8.29	2.62	6.54 /95	-9.52 / 0	-9.20 / 0	0.00	1.73
* GES	SA Global Fixed Income Fund	SAXIX	B-	(800) 366-7266	C / 4.5	1.52	1.01	1.07 /60	0.86 /40	1.48 /25	0.68	0.74
* GEI	SA US Fixed Income Fund	SAUFX	C+	(800) 366-7266	D+ / 2.8	0.68	0.21	0.35 /47	0.10 /27	0.20 /16	0.21	0.65
MUS	Sanford C Bernstein CA Muni	SNCAX	A+	(212) 486-5800	B / 7.8	1.29	2.12	2.61 /81	1.81 /74	3.14 /70	2.14	0.63
MUN	Sanford C Bernstein Diversified Mun	SNDPX	A+	(800) 221-5672	B / 8.0	1.25	2.13	2.56 /81	1.93 /76	3.12 /70	2.03	0.55
* GES	Sanford C Bernstein II Int Dur Inst	SIIDX	B	(800) 221-5672	B- / 7.5	3.07	2.46	1.64 /68	2.64 /72	3.83 /59	3.25	0.58
* GES	Sanford C Bernstein Interm Duration	SNIDX	B-	(212) 486-5800	B- / 7.3	3.07	2.44	1.58 /67	2.49 /71	3.72 /57	3.13	0.59
MUS	Sanford C Bernstein New York Muni	SNNYX	A+	(212) 486-5800	B / 8.0	1.25	2.27	2.86 /84	1.85 /75	3.04 /69	2.31	0.61
MUS	Sanford C Bernstein Sh Dur CA Mun	SDCMX	U	(212) 486-5800	U /	0.08	-0.09	-0.17 /30	--	0.39 /18	0.01	0.83
MUS	Sanford C Bernstein Sh Dur NY Mun	SDNYX	C+	(212) 486-5800	C- / 3.0	0.20	0.21	0.27 /48	0.16 /29	0.72 /21	0.35	0.70
MUN	Sanford C Bernstein Sh-Dur Dvrs	SDDMX	C+	(212) 486-5800	C- / 3.4	0.28	0.31	0.45 /53	0.28 /32	0.75 /22	0.37	0.63
GES	Sanford C Bernstein Short Dur Plus	SNSDX	C+	(212) 486-5800	C- / 3.4	0.70	0.29	0.41 /48	0.47 /33	0.58 /18	0.75	0.64
USS	Sanford C Bernstein US Govt Sh Dur	SNGSX	C-	(212) 486-5800	D / 1.7	0.35	-0.17	-0.24 /29	-0.05 /15	0.20 /16	0.32	0.84
GEI	Saratoga Adv Tr Inv Qlty Bond C	SQBCX	C-	(800) 807-3863	D- / 1.5	2.14	1.32	0.37 /47	-0.10 /15	0.65 /18	0.14	2.31
GEI	Saratoga Adv Tr Inv Qlty Bond I	SIBPX	C	(800) 807-3863	C- / 3.2	2.21	1.46	0.94 /58	0.63 /36	1.48 /25	0.70	1.31
MUN	Saratoga Adv Tr-Municipal Bond C	SMBCX	D+	(800) 807-3863	D- / 1.4	0.75	1.44	0.87 /64	-0.11 /15	1.12 /28	0.10	4.02
MUN	Saratoga Adv Tr-Municipal Bond I	SMBPX	C-	(800) 807-3863	D+ / 2.7	0.76	1.35	0.94 /66	0.39 /35	1.68 /39	0.27	3.00

● Denotes fund is closed to new investors
* Denotes fund is included in Section II

RISK			NET ASSETS		ASSET							FUND MANAGER		MINIMUM		LOADS	
Risk Rating/Pts	3 Yr Avg Standard Deviation	Avg Duration	NAV As of 3/31/16	Total $(Mil)	Cash %	Gov. Bond %	Muni. Bond %	Corp. Bond %	Other %	Portfolio Turnover Ratio	Avg Coupon Rate	Manager Quality Pct	Manager Tenure (Years)	Initial Purch. $	Additional Purch. $	Front End Load	Back End Load
C+ / 6.0	3.1	5.4	10.86	116	0	21	0	28	51	159	0.0	43	N/A	0	0	0.0	0.0
C+ / 6.0	3.1	5.4	10.82	1,084	0	21	0	28	51	159	0.0	54	N/A	100,000	0	0.0	0.0
C+ / 6.0	3.1	5.4	10.97	3,064	0	21	0	28	51	159	0.0	52	N/A	0	0	0.0	0.0
C+ / 6.0	3.1	5.4	10.83	1,298	0	21	0	28	51	159	0.0	58	N/A	10,000,000	0	0.0	0.0
B / 8.0	2.4	5.2	23.53	21	0	0	91	0	9	28	0.0	78	3	0	0	3.8	0.0
B / 8.0	2.4	5.2	23.40	29	0	0	91	0	9	28	0.0	46	3	0	0	0.0	0.0
B / 8.0	2.4	5.2	23.48	52	0	0	91	0	9	28	0.0	79	3	0	0	0.0	0.0
B / 8.0	2.4	5.2	23.44	1,286	0	0	91	0	9	28	0.0	84	3	0	0	0.0	0.0
U /	N/A	8.6	10.40	2	0	0	0	0	100	0	0.0	N/A	1	0	0	3.8	0.0
U /	N/A	8.6	10.38	1	0	0	0	0	100	0	0.0	N/A	1	0	0	0.0	0.0
U /	N/A	8.6	10.40	17	0	0	0	0	100	0	0.0	N/A	1	0	0	0.0	0.0
U /	N/A	8.6	10.40	259	0	0	0	0	100	0	0.0	N/A	1	0	0	0.0	0.0
U /	N/A	N/A	10.00	71	1	16	0	28	55	161	0.0	N/A	N/A	1,000,000	0	0.0	0.0
U /	N/A	N/A	18.19	N/A	88	10	0	0	2	655	0.0	N/A	3	2,500	0	4.8	0.0
U /	N/A	N/A	17.63	N/A	88	10	0	0	2	655	0.0	N/A	3	2,500	0	0.0	0.0
U /	N/A	N/A	18.05	N/A	88	10	0	0	2	655	0.0	N/A	3	2,500	0	0.0	0.0
E- / 0.0	15.6	13.8	58.50	10	3	96	0	0	1	1,932	3.6	25	22	2,500	0	4.8	0.0
E- / 0.0	15.6	13.8	58.13	3	3	96	0	0	1	1,932	3.6	12	22	2,500	0	0.0	0.0
U /	N/A	13.8	58.55	71	3	96	0	0	1	1,932	3.6	N/A	22	2,500	0	0.0	0.0
E- / 0.0	15.6	13.8	58.12	59	3	96	0	0	1	1,932	3.6	29	22	2,500	0	0.0	0.0
E+ / 0.9	6.2	0.1	23.32	12	89	2	0	8	1	393	0.0	98	9	2,500	0	4.8	0.0
E+ / 0.8	6.2	0.1	21.25	2	89	2	0	8	1	393	0.0	96	9	2,500	0	0.0	0.0
E+ / 0.9	6.1	0.1	23.31	741	89	2	0	8	1	393	0.0	98	9	2,500	0	0.0	0.0
E- / 0.0	13.3	N/A	33.11	18	79	20	0	0	1	2,190	0.0	33	8	2,500	0	4.8	0.0
E- / 0.0	13.3	N/A	29.46	28	79	20	0	0	1	2,190	0.0	16	8	2,500	0	0.0	0.0
U /	N/A	N/A	33.12	21	79	20	0	0	1	2,190	0.0	N/A	8	2,500	0	0.0	0.0
E- / 0.0	13.3	N/A	34.27	89	79	20	0	0	1	2,190	0.0	40	8	2,500	0	0.0	0.0
E+ / 0.8	6.3	N/A	17.92	3	100	0	0	0	0	784	0.0	1	9	2,500	0	4.8	0.0
E+ / 0.8	6.2	N/A	16.92	2	100	0	0	0	0	784	0.0	0	9	2,500	0	0.0	0.0
E+ / 0.8	6.2	N/A	18.18	7	100	0	0	0	0	784	0.0	1	9	2,500	0	0.0	0.0
E- / 0.0	14.2	0.1	47.68	2	98	1	0	0	1	299	0.0	99	11	2,500	0	4.8	0.0
E- / 0.0	14.2	0.1	43.60	2	98	1	0	0	1	299	0.0	99	11	2,500	0	0.0	0.0
E- / 0.0	14.1	0.1	47.49	10	98	1	0	0	1	299	0.0	99	11	2,500	0	0.0	0.0
E- / 0.0	14.1	N/A	12.55	1	86	13	0	0	1	219	0.0	0	11	2,500	0	4.8	0.0
E- / 0.0	14.1	N/A	11.43	1	86	13	0	0	1	219	0.0	0	11	2,500	0	0.0	0.0
E- / 0.0	14.0	N/A	12.54	3	86	13	0	0	1	219	0.0	0	11	2,500	0	0.0	0.0
A- / 9.0	1.3	2.7	9.73	733	1	28	4	62	5	72	3.0	58	17	100,000	0	0.0	0.0
A+ / 9.8	0.5	1.5	10.21	607	1	52	0	44	3	202	1.8	58	17	100,000	0	0.0	0.0
B / 7.9	2.4	4.1	14.55	1,085	1	0	97	1	1	16	5.0	39	26	25,000	0	0.0	0.0
B / 8.1	2.3	4.1	14.63	5,047	0	0	97	1	2	15	5.0	47	27	25,000	0	0.0	0.0
C+ / 5.6	3.2	5.2	15.21	629	0	18	0	30	52	266	3.4	62	11	3,000,000	0	0.0	0.0
C+ / 5.6	3.3	5.4	13.32	3,375	0	21	0	29	50	249	3.5	56	11	25,000	0	0.0	0.0
B / 8.0	2.4	4.2	14.26	1,503	2	0	96	0	2	17	5.0	43	27	25,000	0	0.0	0.0
U /	0.5	1.6	12.42	19	3	0	90	6	1	32	4.9	N/A	22	25,000	0	0.0	0.0
A+ / 9.8	0.6	1.6	12.46	54	3	0	95	1	1	26	4.4	51	22	25,000	0	0.0	0.0
A+ / 9.7	0.6	1.4	12.60	160	1	0	96	2	1	25	4.6	55	22	25,000	0	0.0	0.0
A+ / 9.7	0.7	1.8	11.73	328	9	19	0	26	46	86	1.6	62	11	25,000	0	0.0	0.0
A+ / 9.8	0.5	1.8	12.47	22	2	57	0	0	41	58	1.5	49	11	25,000	0	0.0	0.0
B+ / 8.8	1.7	N/A	9.70	N/A	0	0	0	0	100	68	0.0	20	6	250	0	0.0	2.0
B+ / 8.7	1.7	N/A	9.69	9	0	0	0	0	100	68	0.0	38	6	250	0	0.0	2.0
B+ / 8.3	2.1	N/A	9.69	N/A	0	0	0	0	100	21	0.0	10	6	250	0	0.0	2.0
B+ / 8.4	2.1	N/A	9.66	1	0	0	0	0	100	21	0.0	15	6	250	0	0.0	2.0

Fund Type	Fund Name (99 Pct = Best, 0 Pct = Worst)	Ticker Symbol	Overall Investment Rating	Phone	PERFORMANCE: Performance Rating/Pts	Total Return % through 3/31/16: 3 Mo	6 Mo	1Yr / Pct	Annualized: 3Yr / Pct	5Yr / Pct	Incl. in Returns: Dividend Yield	Expense Ratio
MUS	Saturna Idaho Tax-Exempt	NITEX	A+	(800) 728-8762	A- / 9.2	1.91	3.04	3.68 /92	3.23 /90	4.09 /78	3.52	0.66
GL	Saturna Sustainable Bond	SEBFX	U	(800) 728-8762	U /	1.32	0.83	-0.62 /25	--	--	2.02	N/A
GES	SC 529 CO FS Conservative A	CNATX	C	(800) 345-6611	C- / 3.5	1.35	2.03	0.27 /45	2.10 /64	2.32 /35	0.00	0.99
GES	SC 529 CO FS Conservative B		C+	(800) 345-6611	C / 4.6	1.12	1.57	-0.66 /25	1.20 /46	1.47 /25	0.00	1.74
GES	● SC 529 CO FS Conservative BX		B	(800) 345-6611	C / 5.2	1.21	1.72	-0.35 /28	1.55 /53	1.78 /28	0.00	1.44
GES	SC 529 CO FS Conservative C	CNBTX	B-	(800) 345-6611	C / 5.1	1.25	1.70	-0.36 /27	1.49 /52	1.66 /27	0.00	1.74
GES	SC 529 CO FS Conservative CX		B	(800) 345-6611	C+ / 5.6	1.26	1.76	-0.14 /30	1.74 /56	2.00 /31	0.00	1.24
GES	SC 529 CO FS Conservative Dir		A+	(800) 345-6611	B- / 7.1	1.55	2.27	0.96 /58	2.58 /72	2.74 /41	0.00	0.54
GES	SC 529 CO FS Conservative E	CNETX	B	(800) 345-6611	C+ / 5.6	1.30	1.86	-0.14 /30	1.75 /57	1.99 /31	0.00	1.24
GES	SC 529 CO FS Conservative Z		A	(800) 345-6611	C+ / 6.5	1.39	2.07	0.39 /48	2.26 /67	2.51 /38	0.00	0.74
COH	SC 529 CO FS Income Opps A	CINAX	D	(800) 345-6611	C / 4.7	2.62	2.74	-1.37 /19	2.59 /72	5.06 /72	0.00	1.43
COH	SC 529 CO FS Income Opps B		D	(800) 345-6611	C / 5.4	2.42	2.28	-2.18 /15	1.72 /56	4.21 /64	0.00	2.18
COH	SC 529 CO FS Income Opps C	CICNX	D+	(800) 345-6611	C+ / 5.8	2.50	2.46	-1.92 /16	1.98 /61	4.39 /66	0.00	2.18
COH	SC 529 CO FS Income Opps E	CINEX	D+	(800) 345-6611	C+ / 6.3	2.56	2.56	-1.71 /17	2.24 /66	4.73 /70	0.00	1.68
GEI	SC 529 CO FS Total Return Bond A	CBADX	C-	(800) 345-6611	C / 4.4	2.71	1.71	0.91 /57	1.68 /55	3.36 /51	0.00	1.09
GEI	SC 529 CO FS Total Return Bond B		C-	(800) 345-6611	C / 4.4	2.52	1.34	0.06 /39	0.83 /40	2.52 /38	0.00	1.84
GEI	SC 529 CO FS Total Return Bond C	CBCDX	C	(800) 345-6611	C / 4.8	2.54	1.44	0.31 /46	1.08 /44	2.69 /40	0.00	1.84
GEI	SC 529 CO FS Total Return Bond E	CEDBX	C	(800) 345-6611	C / 5.3	2.62	1.52	0.56 /51	1.32 /49	3.02 /45	0.00	1.34
USS	SC 529 CO FS US Govt Mortgage A	CAGMX	C+	(800) 345-6611	C- / 3.9	1.27	0.93	1.14 /61	1.99 /61	3.69 /56	0.00	1.25
USS	SC 529 CO FS US Govt Mortgage B		C+	(800) 345-6611	C / 4.5	1.08	0.43	0.21 /44	1.12 /45	2.85 /43	0.00	2.00
USS	SC 529 CO FS US Govt Mortgage C	CGCBX	B-	(800) 345-6611	C / 5.0	1.16	0.65	0.50 /50	1.38 /50	3.02 /45	0.00	2.00
USS	SC 529 CO FS US Govt Mortgage E	CEGDX	B-	(800) 345-6611	C / 5.4	1.16	0.68	0.75 /54	1.63 /55	3.36 /51	0.00	1.50
GL	Schroder Abs Rtn EMD & Currency	SARVX	D+	(800) 464-3108	C / 5.1	7.48	5.76	2.06 /72	0.09 /27	--	0.00	1.59
GL	Schroder Abs Rtn EMD & Currency	SARNX	D+	(800) 464-3108	C / 5.5	7.51	5.89	2.28 /74	0.30 /30	--	0.00	1.34
MUN	Schroder Broad Tax-Aware Val Bd	STWVX	U	(800) 464-3108	U /	1.86	3.71	3.19 /87	--	--	2.64	0.95
COI	Schroder Broad Tax-Aware Val Bd	STWTX	C	(800) 464-3108	B+ / 8.8	2.01	3.83	3.41 /79	4.56 /88	--	2.85	0.70
EM	Schroder Emerg Mkts Mlt Sctr Bd Adv	SMSVX	U	(800) 464-3108	U /	6.63	7.38	1.14 /61	--	--	1.53	2.05
EM	Schroder Emerg Mkts Mlt Sctr Bd Inv	SMSNX	U	(800) 464-3108	U /	6.78	7.52	1.37 /64	--	--	1.75	1.80
EM	Schroder Emerg Mkts Mlt Sctr Bd R6	SMSRX	U	(800) 464-3108	U /	6.79	7.60	1.60 /68	--	--	1.87	1.65
GL	Schroder Global Strategic Bond Adv	SGBVX	U	(800) 464-3108	U /	-1.06	-1.14	-4.31 / 7	--	--	0.18	1.50
GL	Schroder Global Strategic Bond Inv	SGBNX	U	(800) 464-3108	U /	-1.04	-1.15	-4.20 / 7	--	--	0.06	1.25
COI	Schroder Long Dur Inv-Gr Bd Inv	STWLX	C-	(800) 464-3108	A- / 9.1	6.40	5.59	-2.12 /15	5.31 /92	--	4.12	1.16
COI	Schroder Short Duration Bond Inv	SDBNX	U	(800) 464-3108	U /	1.09	0.88	--	--	--	0.00	2.66
COI	Schroder Short Duration Bond R6	SDBRX	U	(800) 464-3108	U /	1.13	0.96	--	--	--	0.00	2.51
GES	Schroder Total Return Fix Inc Adv	SBBVX	C-	(800) 464-3108	C / 4.5	2.19	1.10	-0.74 /24	1.11 /45	3.22 /49	2.57	0.89
GES	Schroder Total Return Fix Inc Inv	SBBIX	C-	(800) 464-3108	C / 5.0	2.26	1.24	-0.49 /26	1.36 /50	3.48 /53	2.82	0.64
MM	Schwab Adv Cash Reserves Prem	SWZXX	U	(800) 407-0256	U /	--	--	--	--	--	0.01	0.72
MM	Schwab Adv Cash Reserves Sweep	SWQXX	U	(800) 407-0256	U /	--	--	--	--	--	0.01	0.72
MMT	Schwab AMT Tax-Free Money	SWFXX	C	(800) 407-0256	D / 2.1	0.00	0.02	0.02 /36	0.02 /23	0.02 /11	0.02	0.70
MMT	Schwab AMT Tax-Free Money Val	SWWXX	C	(800) 407-0256	D / 2.1	0.00	0.02	0.02 /36	0.02 /23	0.02 /11	0.02	0.57
MMT	Schwab CA Muni Money Sweep	SWCXX	C	(800) 407-0256	D / 2.1	0.00	0.02	0.03 /39	0.02 /23	0.02 /11	0.03	0.69
MMT	Schwab CA Muni Money Val Adv	SWKXX	C	(800) 407-0256	D / 2.1	0.00	0.02	0.03 /39	0.02 /23	0.02 /11	0.03	0.56
MUS	Schwab California Tax-Free Bond Fd	SWCAX	A+	(800) 407-0256	A / 9.3	1.53	2.58	3.46 /90	3.45 /92	5.00 /85	2.16	0.60
MM	Schwab Cash Reserves	SWSXX	U	(800) 407-0256	U /	--	--	--	--	--	0.06	0.70
USA	Schwab GNMA	SWGSX	B+	(800) 407-0256	C+ / 6.6	1.86	1.79	2.21 /73	2.04 /62	3.00 /45	2.28	0.64
GL	Schwab Intermediate-Term Bond	SWIIX	B+	(800) 407-0256	C+ / 6.1	2.24	1.63	1.62 /68	1.76 /57	2.76 /41	1.85	0.62
MMT	Schwab MA Muni Money Sweep	SWDXX	C	(800) 407-0256	D+ / 2.3	0.00	0.04	0.04 /40	0.02 /23	0.03 /13	0.04	0.75
MMT	Schwab Muni Money Premier	SWOXX	C	(800) 407-0256	D / 2.1	0.00	0.02	0.03 /39	0.02 /23	0.02 /11	0.03	0.55
MMT	Schwab Muni Money Sel	SWLXX	C	(800) 407-0256	D / 2.1	0.00	0.02	0.03 /39	0.02 /23	0.02 /11	0.03	0.55
MMT	Schwab Muni Money Sweep	SWXXX	C	(800) 407-0256	D / 2.1	0.00	0.02	0.03 /39	0.02 /23	0.02 /11	0.03	0.68
MMT	Schwab Muni Money Val Adv	SWTXX	C	(800) 407-0256	D / 2.1	0.00	0.02	0.03 /39	0.02 /23	0.02 /11	0.03	0.55
MMT	Schwab NY Muni Money Swep	SWNXX	C	(800) 407-0256	D / 2.1	0.00	0.02	0.02 /37	0.02 /23	0.02 /11	0.02	0.71

● Denotes fund is closed to new investors
* Denotes fund is included in Section II

RISK			NET ASSETS		ASSET							FUND MANAGER		MINIMUM		LOADS	
Risk Rating/Pts	3 Yr Avg Standard Deviation	Avg Duration	NAV As of 3/31/16	Total $(Mil)	Cash %	Gov. Bond %	Muni. Bond %	Corp. Bond %	Other %	Portfolio Turnover Ratio	Avg Coupon Rate	Manager Quality Pct	Manager Tenure (Years)	Initial Purch. $	Additional Purch. $	Front End Load	Back End Load
B- / 7.3	2.8	6.4	5.53	18	2	0	97	0	1	7	4.8	80	21	1,000	25	0.0	0.0
U /	N/A	N/A	9.74	7	3	8	0	85	4	4	0.0	N/A	1	10,000	25	0.0	0.0
B+ / 8.3	2.2	N/A	15.05	84	15	18	0	24	43	0	0.0	93	N/A	250	50	5.8	0.0
B+ / 8.3	2.2	N/A	13.60	3	15	18	0	24	43	0	0.0	83	N/A	250	50	0.0	0.0
B+ / 8.3	2.2	N/A	14.21	1	15	18	0	24	43	0	0.0	88	N/A	250	50	0.0	0.0
B+ / 8.3	2.2	N/A	13.79	45	15	18	0	24	43	0	0.0	87	N/A	250	50	0.0	0.0
B+ / 8.3	2.2	N/A	14.46	5	15	18	0	24	43	0	0.0	90	N/A	250	50	0.0	0.0
B+ / 8.5	2.0	N/A	15.76	69	15	18	0	24	43	0	0.0	94	N/A	250	50	0.0	0.0
B+ / 8.3	2.2	N/A	14.79	4	15	18	0	24	43	0	0.0	90	N/A	250	50	0.0	0.0
B+ / 8.3	2.1	N/A	15.29	3	15	18	0	24	43	0	0.0	94	N/A	250	50	0.0	0.0
D / 1.7	5.4	3.6	25.87	5	3	0	0	92	5	7	7.7	90	N/A	250	50	4.8	0.0
D / 1.7	5.5	3.6	22.85	N/A	3	0	0	92	5	7	7.7	74	N/A	250	50	0.0	0.0
D / 1.7	5.4	3.6	22.95	2	3	0	0	92	5	7	7.7	81	N/A	250	50	0.0	0.0
D / 1.7	5.4	3.6	24.08	N/A	3	0	0	92	5	7	7.7	86	N/A	250	50	0.0	0.0
C+ / 6.6	3.0	4.9	17.81	4	0	12	1	44	43	320	5.7	37	N/A	250	50	3.3	0.0
C+ / 6.6	3.0	4.9	15.84	N/A	0	12	1	44	43	320	5.7	17	N/A	250	50	0.0	0.0
C+ / 6.7	3.0	4.9	16.15	3	0	12	1	44	43	320	5.7	22	N/A	250	50	0.0	0.0
C+ / 6.6	3.0	4.9	16.08	N/A	0	12	1	44	43	320	5.7	27	N/A	250	50	0.0	0.0
B+ / 8.6	1.9	5.2	15.13	1	0	0	0	9	91	121	6.0	90	N/A	250	50	4.8	0.0
B+ / 8.6	1.9	5.2	14.04	N/A	0	0	0	9	91	121	6.0	74	N/A	250	50	0.0	0.0
B+ / 8.6	1.9	5.2	13.95	1	0	0	0	9	91	121	6.0	82	N/A	250	50	0.0	0.0
B / 7.7	2.6	5.2	14.78	N/A	0	0	0	9	91	121	6.0	90	N/A	250	50	0.0	0.0
C- / 3.1	4.7	N/A	9.91	4	2	97	0	0	1	207	0.0	73	5	2,500	1,000	0.0	0.0
D+ / 2.9	4.8	N/A	9.88	71	2	97	0	0	1	207	0.0	80	5	250,000	1,000	0.0	0.0
U /	N/A	7.3	11.05	2	0	0	90	9	1	36	0.0	N/A	5	2,500	1,000	0.0	0.0
D / 1.6	5.8	7.3	11.06	124	0	0	90	9	1	36	0.0	92	5	250,000	1,000	0.0	0.0
U /	N/A	5.9	9.19	2	1	51	3	40	5	209	0.0	N/A	3	2,500	1,000	0.0	0.0
U /	N/A	5.9	9.18	8	1	51	3	40	5	209	0.0	N/A	3	250,000	1,000	0.0	0.0
U /	N/A	5.9	9.19	20	1	51	3	40	5	209	0.0	N/A	3	5,000,000	0	0.0	0.0
U /	N/A	N/A	8.95	N/A	0	31	2	54	13	73	0.0	N/A	2	2,500	1,000	0.0	0.0
U /	N/A	N/A	8.98	N/A	0	31	2	54	13	73	0.0	N/A	2	250,000	1,000	0.0	0.0
E / 0.3	9.1	14.6	8.98	46	3	26	1	65	5	126	0.0	42	5	250,000	1,000	0.0	0.0
U /	N/A	1.8	10.03	1	0	0	0	0	100	0	0.0	N/A	1	250,000	1,000	0.0	0.0
U /	N/A	1.8	10.03	24	0	0	0	0	100	0	0.0	N/A	1	5,000,000	0	0.0	0.0
C / 5.2	3.4	5.5	9.89	1	0	13	1	58	28	93	0.0	20	12	2,500	1,000	0.0	0.0
C / 5.2	3.4	5.5	9.88	154	0	13	1	58	28	93	0.0	25	12	250,000	1,000	0.0	0.0
U /	N/A	N/A	1.00	18,239	100	0	0	0	0	0	0.0	N/A	12	0	0	0.0	0.0
U /	N/A	N/A	1.00	5,241	100	0	0	0	0	0	0.0	N/A	12	0	0	0.0	0.0
A+ / 9.9	N/A	N/A	1.00	3,531	100	0	0	0	0	0	0.0	N/A	N/A	0	0	0.0	0.0
A+ / 9.9	N/A	N/A	1.00	371	100	0	0	0	0	0	0.0	N/A	N/A	25,000	500	0.0	0.0
A+ / 9.9	N/A	N/A	1.00	6,496	100	0	0	0	0	0	0.0	N/A	N/A	0	0	0.0	0.0
A+ / 9.9	N/A	N/A	1.00	667	100	0	0	0	0	0	0.0	N/A	N/A	25,000	500	0.0	0.0
C+ / 6.8	2.9	5.0	12.15	443	0	0	100	0	0	77	0.0	80	8	100	0	0.0	0.0
U /	N/A	N/A	1.00	40,312	100	0	0	0	0	0	0.1	N/A	N/A	0	0	0.0	0.0
B- / 7.3	2.8	4.0	10.21	321	0	0	0	0	100	325	0.0	80	13	100	0	0.0	0.0
B+ / 8.3	2.2	3.7	10.28	345	0	41	0	21	38	127	0.0	95	9	100	0	0.0	0.0
A+ / 9.9	N/A	N/A	1.00	495	100	0	0	0	0	0	0.0	N/A	N/A	0	0	0.0	0.0
A+ / 9.9	N/A	N/A	1.00	729	100	0	0	0	0	0	0.0	N/A	N/A	3,000,000	1	0.0	0.0
A+ / 9.9	N/A	N/A	1.00	305	100	0	0	0	0	0	0.0	N/A	N/A	1,000,000	1	0.0	0.0
A+ / 9.9	N/A	N/A	1.00	11,316	100	0	0	0	0	0	0.0	N/A	N/A	0	0	0.0	0.0
A+ / 9.9	N/A	N/A	1.00	530	100	0	0	0	0	0	0.0	N/A	N/A	25,000	500	0.0	0.0
A+ / 9.9	N/A	N/A	1.00	1,749	100	0	0	0	0	0	0.0	N/A	N/A	0	0	0.0	0.0

Fund Type	Fund Name (99 Pct = Best, 0 Pct = Worst)	Ticker Symbol	Overall Investment Rating	Phone	PERFORMANCE: Performance Rating/Pts	Total Return % through 3/31/16: 3 Mo	6 Mo	1Yr / Pct	Annualized: 3Yr / Pct	5Yr / Pct	Incl. in Returns: Dividend Yield	Expense Ratio
MMT	Schwab NY Muni Money Val Adv	SWYXX	**C**	(800) 407-0256	**D / 2.1**	0.00	0.02	0.02 /37	0.02 /23	0.02 /11	0.02	0.58
MMT	Schwab PA Muni Money Fund Sweep	SWEXX	**C-**	(800) 407-0256	**D / 2.0**	0.00	0.01	0.01 /35	0.01 /21	0.01 / 9	0.01	0.74
MM	Schwab Retirement Advantage	SWIXX	**C-**	(800) 407-0256	**D / 2.0**	0.02	0.02	0.03 /37	0.02 /21	0.01 / 6	0.03	0.61
USS	Schwab Short-Term Bond Market	SWBDX	**B**	(800) 407-0256	**C / 4.8**	1.58	0.87	1.40 /65	1.05 /44	1.54 /26	1.06	0.61
* MUN	Schwab Tax-Free Bond Fund	SWNTX	**A+**	(800) 407-0256	**A- / 9.0**	1.45	2.50	3.21 /87	2.99 /88	4.65 /83	2.14	0.57
* USL	Schwab Total Bond Market Fd	SWLBX	**B**	(800) 407-0256	**C+ / 6.9**	2.89	2.16	1.58 /67	2.20 /66	3.46 /52	2.17	0.54
GEI	Schwab Trs Inflation Prot Sec Index	SWRSX	**D-**	(800) 407-0256	**D+ / 2.3**	4.40	3.66	1.24 /62	-0.90 / 9	2.73 /41	0.74	0.61
MM	Schwab Value Adv Money Investor	SWVXX	**C**	(800) 407-0256	**D / 2.1**	0.03	0.03	0.04 /38	0.02 /21	0.02 / 9	0.04	0.58
MM	Schwab Value Adv Money Prem	SWAXX	**C**	(800) 407-0256	**D+ / 2.4**	0.07	0.10	0.11 /42	0.04 /24	0.04 /12	0.11	0.37
MM	Schwab Value Adv Money Select	SWBXX	**C**	(800) 407-0256	**D+ / 2.3**	0.05	0.06	0.07 /40	0.03 /23	0.02 / 9	0.07	0.48
MM	Schwab Value Adv Money Ultra	SNAXX	**C**	(800) 407-0256	**D+ / 2.5**	0.08	0.11	0.14 /42	0.06 /26	0.06 /14	0.14	0.35
GEI	Scout Core Bond Fund Institutional	SCCIX	**A**	(800) 996-2862	**C+ / 6.8**	3.21	2.50	2.95 /76	1.87 /59	3.76 /58	1.68	0.61
COI	Scout Core Bond Fund Y	SCCYX	**A-**	(800) 996-2862	**C+ / 6.1**	3.12	2.31	2.57 /75	1.48 /52	--	1.32	0.97
GEI	Scout Core Plus Bond Fund Inst	SCPZX	**A**	(800) 996-2862	**C+ / 6.8**	3.61	2.45	2.95 /76	1.84 /58	4.49 /67	1.49	0.56
COI	Scout Core Plus Bond Fund Y	SCPYX	**B+**	(800) 996-2862	**C+ / 6.1**	3.54	2.28	2.59 /75	1.44 /51	4.14 /64	1.08	0.96
COI	Scout Low Duration Bond	SCLDX	**B**	(800) 996-2862	**C / 4.5**	0.88	0.58	0.73 /54	1.08 /44	--	1.12	1.03
GEL	Scout Unconstrained Bond Inst	SUBFX	**C-**	(800) 996-2862	**C / 4.7**	3.32	2.93	4.23 /83	0.23 /29	--	0.52	0.81
GEN	Scout Unconstrained Bond Y	SUBYX	**D+**	(800) 996-2862	**C- / 4.1**	3.22	2.76	3.87 /81	-0.07 /15	--	0.00	1.11
MMT	Scudder CAT Tax Exempt Cash Inst	SCIXX	**C**	(800) 728-3337	**D+ / 2.3**	0.01	0.02	0.03 /39	0.03 /25	0.03 /13	0.02	0.22
MMT	Scudder T/E Cash Mngd	TXMXX	**C**	(800) 728-3337	**D+ / 2.3**	0.00	0.02	0.02 /37	0.03 /25	0.02 /11	0.02	0.41
MUH	SEI Asset Alloc-Def Strat All A	STDAX	**C**	(800) 342-5734	**A+ / 9.9**	3.55	4.93	-0.19 /29	7.15 /99	8.98 /99	3.71	1.35
COI	SEI Catholic Values Fixed Income A	CFVAX	**U**	(800) 342-5734	**U /**	3.05	2.67	--	--	--	0.00	N/A
COI	SEI Catholic Values Fixed Income Y	CFVYX	**U**	(800) 342-5734	**U /**	3.07	2.78	--	--	--	0.00	N/A
USA	SEI Daily Inc Tr-GNMA Bond A	SEGMX	**B+**	(800) 342-5734	**B- / 7.2**	1.94	1.79	1.86 /71	2.52 /71	3.42 /52	1.88	0.69
MM	SEI Daily Inc Tr-Government A	SEOXX	**C**	(800) 342-5734	**D / 2.1**	0.03	0.03	0.04 /38	0.03 /23	0.03 /11	0.04	0.58
MM	SEI Daily Inc Tr-Money Market A	TCMXX	**C**	(800) 342-5734	**D+ / 2.4**	0.07	0.09	0.11 /42	0.04 /24	0.05 /13	0.11	0.67
MM	SEI Daily Inc Tr-Prime Obligation A	TCPXX	**C**	(800) 342-5734	**D+ / 2.4**	0.07	0.08	0.09 /41	0.04 /24	0.04 /12	0.09	0.53
* USS	SEI Daily Inc Tr-Sh Dur Gov Bd A	TCSGX	**C+**	(800) 342-5734	**C- / 3.6**	0.99	0.60	0.61 /52	0.54 /34	0.98 /20	0.80	0.73
USS	SEI Daily Inc Tr-Sh Dur Gov Bd Y	SDGFX	**U**	(800) 342-5734	**U /**	0.86	0.19	-0.19 /29	--	--	0.00	0.43
GES	SEI Daily Inc Tr-Ultra Sh Dur Bd A	SECPX	**C+**	(800) 342-5734	**C- / 3.6**	0.46	0.47	0.58 /51	0.61 /35	0.91 /20	0.90	0.72
GEI	SEI Daily Inc Tr-Ultra Sh Dur Bd Y	SECYX	**U**	(800) 342-5734	**U /**	0.48	0.51	--	--	--	0.00	N/A
* EM	SEI Inst Intl Emerging Mkts Debt A	SITEX	**E-**	(800) 342-5734	**E / 0.3**	7.81	7.56	-1.31 /19	-3.98 / 2	1.13 /22	0.48	1.61
EM	SEI Inst Intl Emerging Mkts Debt Y	SIEDX	**U**	(800) 342-5734	**U /**	7.91	7.67	-1.14 /21	--	--	0.54	1.36
GL	SEI Inst Intl International Fx In A	SEFIX	**A**	(800) 342-5734	**B / 8.0**	3.15	3.75	1.69 /69	3.47 /80	4.25 /65	5.63	1.07
* COI	SEI Inst Inv Core Fixed Income A	SCOAX	**A**	(800) 342-5734	**B / 7.8**	2.80	2.50	1.80 /70	2.95 /76	4.60 /69	2.67	0.38
* COH	SEI Inst Inv High Yield Bond A	SGYAX	**D**	(800) 342-5734	**C- / 3.9**	2.02	-1.08	-4.87 / 5	1.57 /54	5.03 /72	6.87	0.56
COI	SEI Inst Inv Intermediate Dur Cr A	SIDCX	**U**	(800) 342-5734	**U /**	3.02	2.17	-1.00 /22	--	--	0.00	0.35
COI	SEI Inst Inv Limited Duration Bd A	SLDBX	**U**	(800) 342-5734	**U /**	1.12	0.78	1.21 /62	--	--	1.25	0.34
* GEI	SEI Inst Inv Long Dur Credit A	SLDAX	**C-**	(800) 342-5734	**A / 9.3**	6.58	6.44	0.61 /52	5.26 /92	--	3.93	0.37
* COI	SEI Inst Inv Long Duration A	LDRAX	**C-**	(800) 342-5734	**A- / 9.0**	7.12	5.95	-0.15 /30	4.74 /89	8.55 /89	3.99	0.37
GEI	SEI Inst Inv Tr Real Return Plus Fd	RRPAX	**C-**	(800) 342-5734	**D / 1.8**	2.11	1.58	1.47 /66	-0.56 /11	0.73 /19	0.00	0.29
* GEI	SEI Inst Inv Ultra Short Dur Bd A	SUSAX	**B**	(800) 342-5734	**C- / 4.2**	0.52	0.65	0.86 /56	0.89 /41	1.15 /22	1.26	0.22
* EM	SEI Insti Inv Tr Emer Mrk Dbt Fd A	SEDAX	**E**	(800) 342-5734	**E+ / 0.7**	8.13	8.16	-0.21 /29	-3.03 / 2	2.08 /32	0.93	0.93
GEI	SEI Institutional Mgd Real Return A	SRAAX	**D+**	(800) 342-5734	**D- / 1.3**	2.03	1.41	1.11 /60	-0.93 / 9	0.38 /17	0.00	0.80
GEI	SEI Institutional Mgd Real Return Y	SRYRX	**U**	(800) 342-5734	**U /**	2.03	1.51	1.21 /62	--	--	0.00	0.55
* COI	SEI Instl Managed Tr-Core Fix Inc A	TRLVX	**B**	(800) 342-5734	**C+ / 6.9**	2.70	2.16	1.14 /61	2.52 /71	4.31 /66	2.34	0.86
COI	SEI Instl Managed Tr-Core Fix Inc I	SCXIX	**B-**	(800) 342-5734	**C+ / 6.5**	2.56	2.05	0.92 /57	2.28 /67	4.08 /63	2.13	1.11
COI	SEI Instl Managed Tr-Core Fix Inc Y	SCFYX	**U**	(800) 342-5734	**U /**	2.67	2.29	--	--	--	0.00	0.63
* GEI	SEI Instl Managed Tr-High Yld Bd A	SHYAX	**D-**	(800) 342-5734	**D- / 1.3**	1.65	-1.91	-5.90 / 3	0.64 /36	4.02 /62	6.19	1.08
GEI	SEI Instl Managed Tr-High Yld Bd I	SEIYX	**D-**	(800) 342-5734	**E+ / 0.9**	1.61	-2.04	-6.53 / 3	0.13 /28	3.12 /47	5.89	1.32
COH	SEI Instl Managed Tr-High Yld Bd Y	SIYYX	**U**	(800) 342-5734	**U /**	1.56	-1.79	-5.66 / 4	--	--	6.46	0.83
GEI	SEI Instl Mgd Tr-Enhanced Inc A	SEEAX	**C+**	(800) 342-5734	**C- / 3.5**	0.68	0.30	-0.40 /27	0.90 /41	1.59 /26	2.16	1.05

● Denotes fund is closed to new investors
* Denotes fund is included in Section II

RISK			NET ASSETS		ASSET							FUND MANAGER		MINIMUM		LOADS	
Risk Rating/Pts	3 Yr Avg Standard Deviation	Avg Duration	NAV As of 3/31/16	Total $(Mil)	Cash %	Gov. Bond %	Muni. Bond %	Corp. Bond %	Other %	Portfolio Turnover Ratio	Avg Coupon Rate	Manager Quality Pct	Manager Tenure (Years)	Initial Purch. $	Additional Purch. $	Front End Load	Back End Load
A+ / 9.9	N/A	N/A	1.00	204	100	0	0	0	0	0	0.0	N/A	N/A	25,000	500	0.0	0.0
A+ / 9.9	N/A	N/A	1.00	501	100	0	0	0	0	0	0.0	N/A	N/A	0	0	0.0	0.0
A+ / 9.9	N/A	N/A	1.00	674	100	0	0	0	0	0	0.0	66	18	25,000	1	0.0	0.0
A- / 9.0	1.3	2.7	9.35	419	0	68	0	25	7	63	0.0	73	12	100	0	0.0	0.0
B- / 7.2	2.8	4.8	11.99	681	0	0	99	0	1	92	0.0	70	8	100	0	0.0	0.0
C+ / 6.5	3.0	5.3	9.61	1,324	0	43	1	22	34	82	0.0	85	18	100	0	0.0	0.0
D / 2.1	5.3	7.8	11.16	275	0	100	0	0	0	33	0.0	4	10	100	0	0.0	0.0
A+ / 9.9	N/A	N/A	1.00	6,397	100	0	0	0	0	0	0.0	66	24	25,000	500	0.0	0.0
A+ / 9.9	N/A	N/A	1.00	1,067	100	0	0	0	0	0	0.1	66	24	3,000,000	1	0.0	0.0
A+ / 9.9	N/A	N/A	1.00	1,168	100	0	0	0	0	0	0.1	66	24	1,000,000	1	0.0	0.0
A+ / 9.9	N/A	N/A	1.00	2,686	100	0	0	0	0	0	0.1	67	24	10,000,000	1	0.0	0.0
B+ / 8.4	2.1	4.1	11.72	200	15	32	0	29	24	158	3.7	80	15	100,000	100	0.0	0.0
B+ / 8.4	2.1	4.1	11.72	3	15	32	0	29	24	158	3.7	80	15	1,000	100	0.0	0.0
B / 8.1	2.3	3.5	32.36	791	15	39	0	30	16	187	2.3	80	20	100,000	100	0.0	0.0
B / 8.1	2.3	3.5	32.35	52	15	39	0	30	16	187	2.3	75	20	1,000	100	0.0	0.0
A / 9.4	0.9	1.8	10.04	56	1	16	0	39	44	69	3.1	85	4	1,000	100	0.0	0.0
C / 4.9	3.5	3.0	11.52	1,237	30	5	0	54	11	116	2.8	89	5	100,000	100	0.0	0.0
C / 4.9	3.5	3.0	11.53	94	30	5	0	54	11	116	2.8	84	5	1,000	100	0.0	0.0
A+ / 9.9	N/A	N/A	1.00	380	100	0	0	0	0	0	0.0	67	N/A	1,000,000	0	0.0	0.0
A+ / 9.9	N/A	N/A	1.00	69	100	0	0	0	0	0	0.0	67	N/A	100,000	1,000	0.0	0.0
E / 0.5	7.5	N/A	14.31	8	3	0	0	32	65	33	0.0	99	13	100,000	1,000	0.0	0.0
U /	N/A	N/A	9.99	88	0	0	0	0	100	0	0.0	N/A	1	500	100	0.0	0.0
U /	N/A	N/A	10.00	1	0	0	0	0	100	0	0.0	N/A	1	500	100	0.0	0.0
B- / 7.0	2.9	3.6	10.84	127	22	0	0	0	78	758	0.0	87	1	0	0	0.0	0.0
A+ / 9.9	N/A	N/A	1.00	1,892	100	0	0	0	0	0	0.0	N/A	1	0	0	0.0	0.0
A+ / 9.9	N/A	N/A	1.00	255	100	0	0	0	0	0	0.1	66	N/A	0	0	0.0	0.0
A+ / 9.9	N/A	N/A	1.00	5,868	100	0	0	0	0	0	0.1	66	N/A	0	0	0.0	0.0
A / 9.3	0.9	1.6	10.51	814	21	43	0	0	36	151	0.0	59	13	0	0	0.0	0.0
U /	N/A	1.6	10.51	52	21	43	0	0	36	151	0.0	N/A	13	0	0	0.0	0.0
A+ / 9.8	0.4	0.7	9.30	202	0	14	5	47	34	106	0.0	80	17	0	0	0.0	0.0
U /	N/A	0.7	9.30	37	0	14	5	47	34	106	0.0	N/A	17	100,000	1,000	0.0	0.5
E / 0.3	9.6	6.3	9.39	1,364	3	85	0	10	2	71	0.0	6	10	100,000	1,000	0.0	1.0
U /	N/A	6.3	9.41	100	3	85	0	10	2	71	0.0	N/A	10	100,000	1,000	0.0	1.0
C+ / 6.6	2.8	7.6	10.16	494	0	63	2	30	5	78	0.0	99	8	100,000	1,000	0.0	1.0
C+ / 6.8	2.9	6.8	10.42	5,306	0	30	0	28	42	316	0.0	90	7	100,000	1,000	0.0	0.0
D / 2.0	5.2	4.8	8.25	2,434	5	0	0	79	16	55	0.0	70	7	100,000	1,000	0.0	0.0
U /	N/A	2.1	9.90	1,358	0	6	3	89	2	0	0.0	N/A	1	100,000	1,000	0.0	0.0
U /	N/A	7.1	10.00	1,004	0	35	3	38	24	62	0.0	N/A	2	100,000	1,000	0.0	0.0
E / 0.3	8.2	14.0	10.10	3,226	0	3	8	87	2	151	0.0	28	4	100,000	1,000	0.0	0.0
E / 0.3	8.6	13.7	8.56	2,842	0	20	6	70	4	73	0.0	37	12	100,000	1,000	0.0	0.0
B+ / 8.3	2.2	2.8	9.66	168	0	100	0	0	0	41	0.0	15	7	100,000	1,000	0.0	0.0
A+ / 9.9	0.4	1.5	9.97	631	48	0	1	28	23	112	0.0	86	5	100,000	1,000	0.0	0.0
E / 0.3	9.6	6.4	9.44	1,832	4	84	0	9	3	78	0.0	7	10	100,000	1,000	0.0	0.0
B+ / 8.3	2.2	3.0	10.05	277	1	98	0	0	1	37	0.0	11	3	100,000	1,000	0.0	0.3
U /	N/A	3.0	10.07	27	1	98	0	0	1	37	0.0	N/A	3	100,000	1,000	0.0	0.3
C+ / 6.5	3.0	5.2	11.46	2,020	0	29	0	29	42	350	0.0	84	6	100,000	1,000	0.0	0.6
C+ / 6.5	3.0	5.2	11.45	9	0	29	0	29	42	350	0.0	79	6	100,000	1,000	0.0	0.6
U /	N/A	5.2	11.46	59	0	29	0	29	42	350	0.0	N/A	6	100,000	1,000	0.0	0.6
D+ / 2.5	5.3	2.6	6.59	1,513	5	0	0	78	17	56	0.0	31	12	100,000	1,000	0.0	1.0
D+ / 2.5	5.2	2.6	6.37	6	5	0	0	78	17	56	0.0	21	12	100,000	1,000	0.0	1.0
U /	N/A	2.6	6.59	185	5	0	0	78	17	56	0.0	N/A	12	100,000	1,000	0.0	1.0
A- / 9.1	1.2	1.0	7.40	189	5	4	1	39	51	89	0.0	83	10	100,000	1,000	0.0	0.8

Fund Type	99 Pct = Best 0 Pct = Worst Fund Name	Ticker Symbol	Overall Investment Rating	Phone	PERFORMANCE Perfor-mance Rating/Pts	Total Return % through 3/31/16 3 Mo	6 Mo	1Yr / Pct	Annualized 3Yr / Pct	5Yr / Pct	Incl. in Returns Dividend Yield	Expense Ratio
GEI	SEI Instl Mgd Tr-Enhanced Inc I	SEIIX	**C**	(800) 342-5734	**D+ / 2.9**	0.54	0.02	-0.67 /25	0.61 /35	1.30 /23	1.89	1.26
GL	SEI Instl Mgd Tr-Enhanced Inc Y	SNHYX	**U**	(800) 342-5734	**U /**	0.54	0.23	-0.39 /27	--	--	2.30	0.77
MM	SEI Liquid Asset Tr Prime Oblig A	TPRXX	**U**	(800) 342-5734	**U /**	--	--	--	--	--	0.02	0.75
MUS	SEI Tax-Exempt Tr-CA Muni Bond A	SBDAX	**A+**	(800) 342-5734	**B+ / 8.9**	1.55	2.56	3.36 /89	2.80 /86	4.26 /80	1.95	0.85
* MUN	SEI Tax-Exempt Tr-Intrm Term Muni	SEIMX	**A+**	(800) 342-5734	**B+ / 8.8**	1.52	2.86	3.57 /91	2.79 /86	4.51 /82	2.46	0.85
MUN	SEI Tax-Exempt Tr-Intrm Term Muni	SINYX	**U**	(800) 342-5734	**U /**	1.57	3.07	--	--	--	0.00	0.60
MUS	SEI Tax-Exempt Tr-MA Muni Bond A	SMAAX	**B+**	(800) 342-5734	**B+ / 8.6**	1.55	2.65	3.46 /90	2.51 /83	4.03 /78	1.83	0.85
MUI	SEI Tax-Exempt Tr-NJ Muni Bond A	SENJX	**A+**	(800) 342-5734	**B / 7.9**	1.36	2.58	2.51 /80	1.86 /75	3.30 /72	2.09	0.85
MUI	SEI Tax-Exempt Tr-NY Muni Bond A	SENYX	**A+**	(800) 342-5734	**B+ / 8.3**	1.33	2.27	3.14 /86	2.27 /80	3.54 /74	1.76	0.85
MUS	SEI Tax-Exempt Tr-PA Muni Bond A	SEPAX	**A+**	(800) 342-5734	**B / 8.1**	1.39	2.19	3.15 /86	2.05 /77	3.82 /76	1.97	0.83
* MUN	SEI Tax-Exempt Tr-Shrt Dur Muni A	SUMAX	**C+**	(800) 342-5734	**C- / 3.4**	0.09	0.17	0.21 /46	0.34 /34	0.63 /20	0.31	0.85
MUN	SEI Tax-Exempt Tr-Shrt Dur Muni Y	SHYMX	**U**	(800) 342-5734	**U /**	0.25	0.29	--	--	--	0.00	0.60
* MUN	SEI Tax-Exempt Tr-Tax Advtg Inc A	SEATX	**B**	(800) 342-5734	**A+ / 9.8**	1.75	4.80	5.66 /99	4.38 /97	6.99 /96	3.68	1.08
MUN	SEI Tax-Exempt Tr-Tax Advtg Inc Y	STAYX	**U**	(800) 342-5734	**U /**	1.81	4.93	--	--	--	0.00	0.83
MMT	SEI Tax-Exempt Tr-Tax Free A	TXEXX	**U**	(800) 342-5734	**U /**	0.00	0.01	0.02 /36	0.01 /21	0.01 / 9	0.02	0.68
* GEI	SEI US Fixed Income A	SUFAX	**C+**	(800) 342-5734	**C+ / 6.5**	2.72	2.09	1.39 /65	2.20 /66	3.85 /59	1.95	0.86
GEI	SEI US Fixed Income Y	SUSWX	**U**	(800) 342-5734	**U /**	2.78	2.22	1.64 /68	--	--	2.19	0.61
GEN	Semper MBS Total Return Fund Inst	SEMMX	**U**	(888) 263-6443	**U /**	-1.10	-0.71	1.43 /65	--	--	5.74	0.90
GEN	Semper MBS Total Return Fund Inv	SEMPX	**U**	(888) 263-6443	**U /**	-1.17	-0.83	1.18 /61	--	--	5.49	1.13
GES	Semper Short Duration Inst	SEMIX	**B**	(888) 263-6443	**C / 4.7**	0.04	0.13	1.11 /60	1.28 /48	2.13 /33	3.25	1.06
GES	Semper Short Duration Inv	SEMRX	**C**	(888) 263-6443	**D+ / 2.8**	0.00	0.03	1.02 /59	0.09 /27	0.82 /19	3.06	1.84
USS	Sentinel Government Securities A	SEGSX	**C-**	(800) 282-3863	**D+ / 2.6**	1.81	1.38	1.23 /62	0.32 /30	1.83 /29	2.36	0.92
USS	Sentinel Government Securities C	SCGGX	**D+**	(800) 282-3863	**D / 1.7**	1.60	1.05	0.50 /50	-0.48 /12	1.03 /21	1.58	1.73
USS	Sentinel Government Securities I	SIBWX	**C**	(800) 282-3863	**C- / 4.1**	1.86	1.47	1.45 /66	0.55 /34	2.07 /32	2.62	0.68
USS	Sentinel Low Duration Bond A	SSIGX	**C-**	(800) 282-3863	**D- / 1.2**	0.33	0.24	-0.66 /25	-0.28 /13	0.18 /16	2.27	0.93
USS	Sentinel Low Duration Bond I	SSBDX	**U**	(800) 282-3863	**U /**	0.39	0.48	-0.30 /28	--	--	2.54	0.66
USS	Sentinel Low Duration Bond S	SSSGX	**C-**	(800) 282-3863	**D- / 1.4**	0.29	0.16	-0.71 /24	-0.43 /12	-0.05 / 3	2.12	1.02
GL	Sentinel Total Return Bond A	SATRX	**C-**	(800) 282-3863	**C / 4.3**	1.71	0.90	-0.84 /23	1.75 /57	4.03 /62	2.07	0.96
GL	Sentinel Total Return Bond C	SCTRX	**C-**	(800) 282-3863	**C- / 4.0**	1.49	0.47	-1.60 /18	1.07 /44	3.47 /53	1.26	1.75
GL	Sentinel Total Return Bond I	SITRX	**C**	(800) 282-3863	**C+ / 5.7**	1.75	1.00	-0.67 /25	1.90 /59	4.19 /64	2.29	0.80
GL	Sentinel Total Return Bond R3	SBRRX	**U**	(800) 282-3863	**U /**	1.71	0.90	-0.84 /23	--	--	2.12	1.34
GL	Sentinel Total Return Bond R6	STRRX	**U**	(800) 282-3863	**U /**	1.76	1.10	-0.55 /26	--	--	2.31	0.84
GEI	Sextant Bond Income Fund	SBIFX	**C-**	(800) 728-8762	**C+ / 6.7**	3.76	2.19	0.71 /53	2.10 /64	4.23 /65	3.17	1.17
GEI	Sextant Short-Term Bond Fund	STBFX	**B-**	(800) 728-8762	**C / 4.5**	0.88	0.97	1.30 /63	0.94 /42	1.13 /22	1.09	1.19
LP	● Shenkman Floating Rate Hi Inc Inst	SFHIX	**U**	(855) 743-6562	**U /**	1.52	-0.39	-1.55 /18	--	--	4.53	0.83
COH	Shenkman Short Duration Hi Inc A	SCFAX	**C-**	(855) 743-6562	**C- / 3.9**	1.02	0.57	-0.07 /31	2.05 /62	--	2.90	1.74
COH	Shenkman Short Duration Hi Inc C	SCFCX	**U**	(855) 743-6562	**U /**	0.84	0.21	-0.88 /23	--	--	2.27	2.50
COH	Shenkman Short Duration Hi Inc F	SCFFX	**U**	(855) 743-6562	**U /**	1.19	0.79	0.17 /43	--	--	3.23	1.56
COH	Shenkman Short Duration Hi Inc Inst	SCFIX	**B**	(855) 743-6562	**C+ / 6.1**	1.21	0.84	0.26 /45	2.46 /70	--	3.32	1.61
USS	Sht-Tm US Government Bond Direct	STUSX	**U**	(800) 955-9988	**U /**	0.61	0.16	0.27 /45	--	0.02 / 7	0.08	0.97
USS	Sht-Tm US Government Bond K	STUKX	**C-**	(800) 955-9988	**D- / 1.3**	0.50	-0.09	-0.18 /29	-0.51 /11	-0.51 / 2	0.01	1.47
GL	Sierra Strategic Income A	SSIZX	**C-**	(866) 738-4363	**C- / 3.4**	2.12	2.02	-0.42 /27	2.05 /62	--	2.58	2.02
GL	Sierra Strategic Income C	SSICX	**C**	(866) 738-4363	**C / 5.0**	1.93	1.69	-1.05 /21	1.44 /51	--	2.16	2.63
GL	Sierra Strategic Income I	SSIIX	**C+**	(866) 738-4363	**C+ / 6.1**	2.12	2.03	-0.42 /27	2.05 /62	--	2.73	2.00
GL	Sierra Strategic Income R	SSIRX	**B**	(866) 738-4363	**C+ / 6.7**	2.18	2.18	-0.12 /30	2.40 /69	--	3.15	1.62
GL	● Sierra Strategic Income Y	SSIYX	**B**	(866) 738-4363	**C+ / 6.7**	2.18	2.18	-0.12 /30	2.40 /69	--	3.15	1.61
MUS	Sit MN Tax Free Income	SMTFX	**A**	(800) 332-5580	**A / 9.4**	1.54	3.06	3.89 /93	3.61 /93	5.74 /91	3.21	0.82
MUN	Sit Tax Free Income Fund	SNTIX	**B**	(800) 332-5580	**A+ / 9.8**	1.76	4.16	4.78 /97	4.69 /98	7.09 /97	3.37	0.86
* USS	Sit US Government Securities Fund	SNGVX	**B**	(800) 332-5580	**C / 4.5**	0.90	1.11	1.60 /68	0.85 /40	1.38 /24	1.77	0.80
GEI	SMI Bond	SMIUX	**U**	(877) 764-3863	**U /**	2.59	0.14	--	--	--	0.00	N/A
GES	Spirit of America Income Fd A	SOAIX	**C-**	(800) 452-4892	**C+ / 6.9**	3.07	3.11	0.99 /58	3.66 /81	7.21 /83	4.31	1.15
MUH	Spirit of America Municipal TF Bd A	SOAMX	**D+**	(800) 452-4892	**B- / 7.5**	1.82	3.79	3.88 /93	2.60 /84	5.85 /91	3.18	1.10

● Denotes fund is closed to new investors
* Denotes fund is included in Section II

RISK			NET ASSETS		ASSET							FUND MANAGER		MINIMUM		LOADS	
Risk Rating/Pts	3 Yr Avg Standard Deviation	Avg Duration	NAV As of 3/31/16	Total $(Mil)	Cash %	Gov. Bond %	Muni. Bond %	Corp. Bond %	Other %	Portfolio Turnover Ratio	Avg Coupon Rate	Manager Quality Pct	Manager Tenure (Years)	Initial Purch. $	Additional Purch. $	Front End Load	Back End Load
A- / 9.1	1.2	1.0	7.38	N/A	5	4	1	39	51	89	0.0	77	10	100,000	1,000	0.0	0.8
U /	N/A	1.0	7.39	18	5	4	1	39	51	89	0.0	N/A	10	100,000	1,000	0.0	0.8
U /	N/A	N/A	1.00	1,555	100	0	0	0	0	0	0.0	N/A	N/A	0	0	0.0	0.0
C+ / 6.4	3.0	4.9	11.03	280	1	0	98	0	1	13	0.0	53	17	100,000	1,000	0.0	0.0
C+ / 6.3	3.1	5.3	11.86	1,572	0	0	99	0	1	10	0.0	48	17	100,000	1,000	0.0	0.5
U /	N/A	5.3	11.87	19	0	0	99	0	1	10	0.0	N/A	17	100,000	1,000	0.0	0.5
C / 5.2	3.4	5.6	10.87	60	0	0	99	0	1	16	0.0	32	6	100,000	1,000	0.0	0.0
B / 7.9	2.5	4.5	10.55	108	0	0	99	0	1	15	0.0	42	3	100,000	1,000	0.0	0.0
B / 7.6	2.7	4.6	10.94	175	2	0	97	0	1	17	0.0	48	17	100,000	1,000	0.0	0.0
B / 7.7	2.6	4.8	10.89	126	2	0	97	0	1	19	0.0	42	17	100,000	1,000	0.0	0.0
A+ / 9.9	0.3	1.2	10.04	1,507	0	0	98	1	1	37	0.0	72	5	100,000	1,000	0.0	0.0
U /	N/A	1.2	10.04	18	0	0	98	1	1	37	0.0	N/A	5	100,000	1,000	0.0	0.0
C- / 3.1	4.5	7.1	10.35	1,108	0	8	70	7	15	22	0.0	59	9	100,000	1,000	0.0	0.0
U /	N/A	7.1	10.34	33	0	8	70	7	15	22	0.0	N/A	9	100,000	1,000	0.0	0.0
U /	N/A	N/A	1.00	1,129	100	0	0	0	0	0	0.0	N/A	N/A	100,000	0	0.0	0.0
C+ / 6.2	2.9	7.1	10.39	1,137	17	30	0	20	33	313	0.0	54	2	100,000	1,000	0.0	0.6
U /	N/A	7.1	10.39	94	17	30	0	20	33	313	0.0	N/A	2	100,000	1,000	0.0	0.6
U /	N/A	N/A	10.59	364	0	0	0	0	100	166	0.0	N/A	3	1,000,000	1,000	0.0	0.0
U /	N/A	N/A	10.58	54	0	0	0	0	100	166	0.0	N/A	3	2,500	1,000	0.0	0.0
A / 9.3	1.0	N/A	9.89	42	23	0	9	1	67	56	0.0	88	1	1,000,000	1,000	0.0	0.0
A / 9.3	1.0	N/A	9.88	1	23	0	9	1	67	56	0.0	51	1	2,500	1,000	0.0	0.0
B- / 7.5	2.7	5.1	10.04	179	6	1	0	0	93	150	4.0	22	4	1,000	50	2.3	0.0
B / 7.6	2.7	5.1	10.06	25	6	1	0	0	93	150	4.0	11	4	1,000	50	0.0	0.0
B- / 7.5	2.7	5.1	10.04	38	6	1	0	0	93	150	4.0	27	4	1,000,000	0	0.0	0.0
B+ / 8.8	1.6	2.1	8.42	108	2	0	0	51	47	27	3.5	47	4	1,000	50	1.0	0.0
U /	N/A	2.1	8.43	38	2	0	0	51	47	27	3.5	N/A	4	1,000,000	0	0.0	0.0
B+ / 8.8	1.7	2.1	8.43	273	2	0	0	51	47	27	3.5	41	4	1,000	50	0.0	0.0
C+ / 5.9	3.2	4.7	10.35	292	23	8	0	40	29	441	4.3	95	6	1,000	50	2.3	0.0
C+ / 5.9	3.2	4.7	10.32	38	23	8	0	40	29	441	4.3	90	6	1,000	50	0.0	0.0
C+ / 6.0	3.1	4.7	10.36	419	23	8	0	40	29	441	4.3	96	6	1,000,000	0	0.0	0.0
U /	N/A	4.7	10.35	1	23	8	0	40	29	441	4.3	N/A	6	0	0	0.0	0.0
U /	N/A	4.7	10.36	1	23	8	0	40	29	441	4.3	N/A	6	1,000,000	0	0.0	0.0
C- / 3.3	4.2	7.0	5.17	8	5	13	33	48	1	4	6.6	22	21	1,000	25	0.0	0.0
A- / 9.1	1.2	2.6	5.04	8	3	12	0	84	1	13	5.4	75	21	1,000	25	0.0	0.0
U /	N/A	N/A	9.42	262	0	0	0	0	100	70	0.0	N/A	2	1,000,000	100,000	0.0	1.0
B- / 7.4	2.2	N/A	9.82	7	5	0	0	82	13	57	0.0	93	4	1,000	100	3.0	1.0
U /	N/A	N/A	9.79	8	5	0	0	82	13	57	0.0	N/A	4	1,000	100	0.0	1.0
U /	N/A	N/A	9.80	48	5	0	0	82	13	57	0.0	N/A	4	1,000	100	0.0	1.0
B- / 7.3	2.3	N/A	9.81	77	5	0	0	82	13	57	0.0	95	4	1,000,000	100,000	0.0	1.0
U /	0.4	1.5	10.19	6	2	94	0	0	4	33	1.4	N/A	13	1,000	100	0.0	0.0
A+ / 9.8	0.5	1.5	10.04	1	2	94	0	0	4	33	1.4	34	13	1,000	100	0.0	0.0
C+ / 6.7	3.0	N/A	20.57	44	12	3	24	21	40	149	0.0	96	5	10,000	1,000	5.8	0.0
C+ / 6.8	2.9	N/A	20.53	51	12	3	24	21	40	149	0.0	93	5	10,000	1,000	0.0	0.0
C+ / 6.7	3.0	N/A	20.60	48	12	3	24	21	40	149	0.0	96	5	10,000	1,000	0.0	0.0
C+ / 6.8	2.9	N/A	20.51	230	12	3	24	21	40	149	0.0	97	5	100,000	1,000	0.0	0.0
C+ / 6.7	3.0	N/A	20.47	3	12	3	24	21	40	149	0.0	97	5	20,000,000	0	0.0	0.0
C / 5.0	3.5	4.8	10.63	507	4	0	94	0	2	10	4.5	69	23	5,000	100	0.0	0.0
C- / 3.0	4.7	5.7	9.80	156	0	0	96	0	4	31	4.5	55	28	5,000	100	0.0	0.0
A / 9.3	1.0	1.0	11.07	664	4	1	0	0	95	14	6.2	79	29	5,000	100	0.0	0.0
U /	N/A	N/A	9.78	8	0	0	0	0	100	400	0.0	N/A	1	500	50	0.0	2.0
C- / 3.1	4.7	N/A	11.91	211	5	0	72	8	15	9	0.0	73	7	500	50	4.8	0.0
E+ / 0.9	5.7	10.3	9.67	106	0	0	100	0	0	7	5.5	7	7	500	50	4.8	0.0

Fund Type	Fund Name (99 Pct = Best, 0 Pct = Worst)	Ticker Symbol	Overall Investment Rating	Phone	PERFORMANCE: Performance Rating/Pts	Total Return % through 3/31/16: 3 Mo	6 Mo	1Yr / Pct	Annualized 3Yr / Pct	Annualized 5Yr / Pct	Incl. in Returns: Dividend Yield	Expense Ratio
COH	SSgA High Yield Bond A	SSHGX	**U**	(800) 843-2639	**U /**	2.18	0.69	-3.33 /10	--	--	5.58	1.13
COH	SSgA High Yield Bond C	SSHHX	**U**	(800) 843-2639	**U /**	1.92	0.32	-4.18 / 7	--	--	5.02	1.88
COH	SSgA High Yield Bond I	SSHJX	**U**	(800) 843-2639	**U /**	2.22	0.94	-3.09 /11	--	--	6.03	0.88
COH	SSgA High Yield Bond K	SSHKX	**U**	(800) 843-2639	**U /**	2.26	1.03	-2.91 /12	--	--	6.23	0.68
COH ●	SSgA High Yield Bond N	SSHYX	**D**	(800) 843-2639	**C / 4.7**	2.22	0.78	-3.14 /11	1.64 /55	4.34 /66	5.99	0.93
GL	STAAR AltCat	SITAX	**E-**	(800) 332-7738	**E / 0.5**	-2.09	1.31	-10.70 / 1	-0.69 /10	0.05 /12	0.00	2.45
GEI	STAAR Inv Trust General Bond Fund	SITGX	**C-**	(800) 332-7738	**D / 1.6**	1.24	-0.01	-1.26 /20	-0.14 /14	0.56 /18	0.47	1.55
COI	STAAR Inv Trust Shrt Term Bond	SITBX	**C-**	(800) 332-7738	**D / 1.6**	0.22	0.11	-0.11 /30	-0.23 /14	0.23 /16	0.00	1.49
GEN	Stadion Alternative Income A	TACFX	**D+**	(866) 383-7636	**C / 4.9**	3.02	4.22	4.74 /86	1.92 /60	--	1.63	4.16
GEL	Stadion Alternative Income C	TACCX	**U**	(866) 383-7636	**U /**	2.88	3.88	--	--	--	0.00	N/A
GEL	Stadion Alternative Income I	TACSX	**C+**	(866) 383-7636	**B / 7.7**	3.12	4.41	5.10 /88	2.21 /66	--	1.06	4.14
COI	State Farm Bond A	BNSAX	**C-**	(800) 447-4930	**C+ / 5.8**	3.44	2.94	2.29 /74	2.08 /63	3.50 /53	2.27	0.66
COI	State Farm Bond B	BNSBX	**C**	(800) 447-4930	**C+ / 6.3**	3.35	2.74	1.89 /71	1.67 /55	3.09 /47	1.95	1.06
COI	State Farm Bond Inst	SFBIX	**C+**	(800) 447-4930	**B- / 7.4**	3.41	2.97	2.54 /75	2.30 /67	3.74 /57	2.58	0.41
COI	State Farm Bond LegA	SFBAX	**C-**	(800) 447-4930	**C+ / 5.7**	3.35	2.85	2.20 /73	2.05 /62	3.48 /53	2.27	0.66
COI	State Farm Bond LegB	SFBBX	**C**	(800) 447-4930	**C+ / 6.3**	3.25	2.65	1.80 /70	1.64 /55	3.09 /47	1.95	1.06
COI	State Farm Bond R1	SRBOX	**C**	(800) 447-4930	**C+ / 6.5**	3.36	2.78	1.97 /72	1.75 /57	3.17 /48	2.03	0.98
COI	State Farm Bond R2	SRBTX	**C+**	(800) 447-4930	**C+ / 6.7**	3.32	2.79	2.08 /72	1.92 /60	3.36 /51	2.22	0.78
COI	State Farm Bond R3	SRBHX	**C+**	(800) 447-4930	**B- / 7.3**	3.39	3.03	2.47 /74	2.23 /66	3.67 /56	2.51	0.48
GEI	State Farm Interim	SFITX	**C+**	(800) 447-4930	**C / 4.4**	1.38	0.76	1.35 /64	0.84 /40	1.39 /24	1.13	0.16
* MUN	State Farm Muni Bond	SFBDX	**A+**	(800) 447-4930	**A- / 9.1**	1.38	2.28	3.31 /88	3.12 /89	4.49 /81	3.01	0.15
MUH	State Farm Tax Advant Bond A	TANAX	**C+**	(800) 447-4930	**B+ / 8.6**	1.65	2.76	3.63 /91	3.30 /91	4.70 /83	2.22	0.66
MUH	State Farm Tax Advant Bond B	TANBX	**C+**	(800) 447-4930	**B+ / 8.9**	1.54	2.55	3.13 /86	2.86 /87	4.28 /80	1.89	1.06
MUH	State Farm Tax Advant Bond LegA	SFTAX	**C+**	(800) 447-4930	**B+ / 8.6**	1.65	2.76	3.63 /91	3.30 /91	4.70 /83	2.22	0.66
MUH	State Farm Tax Advant Bond LegB	SFTBX	**C+**	(800) 447-4930	**A- / 9.0**	1.62	2.63	3.30 /88	2.92 /87	4.30 /80	1.88	1.06
COI	State Street Aggregate Bond Index	SSAFX	**U**	(800) 882-0052	**U /**	3.06	2.53	1.94 /71	--	--	2.02	0.28
COI	State Street Aggregate Bond Index A	SSFCX	**U**	(800) 882-0052	**U /**	2.92	3.87	3.12 /77	--	--	4.07	1.25
COI	State Street Aggregate Bond Index I	SSFDX	**U**	(800) 882-0052	**U /**	3.07	4.00	3.38 /78	--	--	4.48	1.00
COI	State Street Aggregate Bond Index K	SSFEX	**U**	(800) 882-0052	**U /**	3.07	2.53	1.92 /71	--	--	3.07	0.80
MM	State Street Inst Liq Reserves Inv	SSVXX	**U**	(800) 882-0052	**U /**	0.01	0.01	0.01 /33	--	--	0.01	0.47
MM	State Street Inst Liq Reserves Prem	SSIXX	**C**	(800) 882-0052	**D+ / 2.7**	0.09	0.13	0.19 /44	0.11 /27	0.14 /15	0.19	0.12
MM	State Street TreasPls MM Prem		**C-**	(800) 882-0052	**D / 2.0**	0.04	0.04	0.04 /38	0.01 /18	0.01 / 6	0.04	0.13
MM	State Street US Govt MM Premier	GVMXX	**C**	(800) 882-0052	**D / 2.1**	0.05	0.05	0.05 /39	0.02 /21	0.02 / 9	0.05	0.12
COI	Sterling Capital Corporate A	SCCMX	**C-**	(800) 228-1872	**C / 5.3**	1.98	1.70	0.77 /55	1.97 /61	--	2.76	0.86
COI	Sterling Capital Corporate C	SCCNX	**C-**	(800) 228-1872	**C / 4.7**	1.81	1.25	-0.06 /31	1.15 /45	--	2.09	1.61
GEL	Sterling Capital Corporate Inst	SCCPX	**C**	(800) 228-1872	**C+ / 6.7**	2.15	1.83	1.02 /59	2.24 /66	--	3.07	0.61
USS	Sterling Capital Interm US Govt A	BGVAX	**C**	(800) 228-1872	**C- / 3.9**	2.17	1.36	1.13 /61	1.05 /44	2.17 /33	1.66	0.96
USS ●	Sterling Capital Interm US Govt B	BUSGX	**C**	(800) 228-1872	**C- / 3.4**	1.99	0.89	0.38 /47	0.27 /30	1.40 /25	0.96	1.71
USS	Sterling Capital Interm US Govt C	BIUCX	**C**	(800) 228-1872	**C- / 3.4**	1.99	0.89	0.38 /47	0.27 /30	1.39 /24	0.96	1.71
USS	Sterling Capital Interm US Govt I	BBGVX	**B**	(800) 228-1872	**C / 5.3**	2.23	1.49	1.39 /65	1.28 /48	2.42 /37	1.95	0.71
MUS	Sterling Capital KY Interm TxFr A	BKTAX	**B**	(800) 228-1872	**C+ / 6.8**	1.23	1.99	2.60 /81	1.79 /74	3.58 /75	2.24	1.02
MUS	Sterling Capital KY Interm TxFr C	BKCAX	**C+**	(800) 228-1872	**C+ / 6.3**	1.14	1.61	1.94 /77	1.07 /55	--	1.55	1.77
MUS	Sterling Capital KY Interm TxFr I	BKITX	**A**	(800) 228-1872	**B / 8.1**	1.39	2.12	2.86 /84	2.08 /78	3.84 /76	2.53	0.77
MUS	Sterling Capital MD Interm TxFr A	BMAAX	**B+**	(800) 228-1872	**B- / 7.2**	1.41	2.36	2.74 /82	1.90 /76	3.42 /73	1.72	0.95
MUS	Sterling Capital MD Interm TxFr C	BMDCX	**B**	(800) 228-1872	**C+ / 6.5**	1.23	1.89	1.97 /77	1.12 /56	--	1.02	1.70
MUS	Sterling Capital MD Interm TxFr I	BMAIX	**A**	(800) 228-1872	**B+ / 8.3**	1.47	2.48	3.08 /86	2.16 /79	3.68 /75	2.00	0.70
MUS	Sterling Capital NC Interm TxFr A	BNCAX	**B+**	(800) 228-1872	**B / 7.7**	1.45	2.37	3.03 /85	2.14 /79	3.63 /75	2.10	0.89
MUS	Sterling Capital NC Interm TxFr C	BBNCX	**B**	(800) 228-1872	**B- / 7.2**	1.35	2.07	2.35 /80	1.38 /64	--	1.40	1.64
MUS	Sterling Capital NC Interm TxFr I	BBNTX	**A**	(800) 228-1872	**B+ / 8.5**	1.51	2.49	3.28 /88	2.39 /82	3.89 /77	2.39	0.64
MUS	Sterling Capital SC Interm TxFr A	BASCX	**A-**	(800) 228-1872	**B / 7.8**	1.53	2.43	3.03 /85	2.24 /80	3.84 /76	1.80	0.91
MUS	Sterling Capital SC Interm TxFr C	BSCCX	**B+**	(800) 228-1872	**B- / 7.2**	1.25	1.95	2.17 /78	1.44 /66	--	1.10	1.66
MUS	Sterling Capital SC Interm TxFr I	BSCIX	**A+**	(800) 228-1872	**B+ / 8.5**	1.50	2.56	3.20 /87	2.46 /82	4.10 /78	2.09	0.66

● Denotes fund is closed to new investors
* Denotes fund is included in Section II

RISK			NET ASSETS		ASSET							FUND MANAGER		MINIMUM		LOADS	
Risk Rating/Pts	3 Yr Avg Standard Deviation	Avg Duration	NAV As of 3/31/16	Total $(Mil)	Cash %	Gov. Bond %	Muni. Bond %	Corp. Bond %	Other %	Portfolio Turnover Ratio	Avg Coupon Rate	Manager Quality Pct	Manager Tenure (Years)	Initial Purch. $	Additional Purch. $	Front End Load	Back End Load
U /	N/A	4.3	7.16	N/A	6	0	0	93	1	100	0.0	N/A	5	2,000	0	3.8	0.0
U /	N/A	4.3	7.15	N/A	6	0	0	93	1	100	0.0	N/A	5	2,000	0	0.0	0.0
U /	N/A	4.3	7.17	N/A	6	0	0	93	1	100	0.0	N/A	5	1,000,000	0	0.0	0.0
U /	N/A	4.3	7.17	N/A	6	0	0	93	1	100	0.0	N/A	5	10,000,000	0	0.0	0.0
D- / 1.5	5.6	4.3	7.16	72	6	0	0	93	1	100	0.0	N/A	5	1,000	100	0.0	0.0
E- / 0.2	11.6	N/A	13.10	3	4	0	0	0	96	25	0.0	39	19	1,000	50	0.0	0.0
B+ / 8.7	1.8	N/A	9.71	2	0	7	4	87	2	13	3.9	30	19	1,000	50	0.0	0.0
A+ / 9.8	0.5	1.4	8.93	1	1	0	5	92	2	3	3.5	45	19	1,000	50	0.0	0.0
C- / 3.9	4.0	N/A	10.06	3	2	0	0	0	98	485	0.0	36	4	1,000	250	5.8	0.0
U /	N/A	N/A	10.03	N/A	2	0	0	0	98	485	0.0	N/A	4	1,000	250	0.0	0.0
C- / 3.9	4.0	N/A	10.04	80	2	0	0	0	98	485	0.0	47	4	500,000	0	0.0	0.0
C / 4.9	3.5	3.4	11.45	431	1	13	0	68	18	10	0.0	57	16	250	50	3.0	0.0
C / 4.9	3.5	3.4	11.44	11	1	13	0	68	18	10	0.0	42	16	250	50	0.0	0.0
C / 4.9	3.5	3.4	11.44	252	1	13	0	68	18	10	0.0	70	16	250	50	0.0	0.0
C / 4.9	3.5	3.4	11.45	128	1	13	0	68	18	10	0.0	57	16	250	50	3.0	0.0
C / 4.9	3.5	3.4	11.46	3	1	13	0	68	18	10	0.0	42	16	250	50	0.0	0.0
C / 4.9	3.5	3.4	11.45	4	1	13	0	68	18	10	0.0	45	16	0	0	0.0	0.0
C / 5.0	3.5	3.4	11.43	10	1	13	0	68	18	10	0.0	52	16	0	0	0.0	0.0
C / 4.9	3.5	3.4	11.45	2	1	13	0	68	18	10	0.0	63	16	0	0	0.0	0.0
B+ / 8.8	1.7	2.4	10.07	378	10	89	0	0	1	12	0.0	47	18	250	50	0.0	0.0
B- / 7.0	2.9	3.9	8.88	699	5	0	94	0	1	10	0.0	72	18	250	50	0.0	0.0
C- / 3.2	4.0	4.6	12.05	460	3	0	96	0	1	6	0.0	32	16	250	50	3.0	0.0
C- / 3.1	4.1	4.6	12.04	3	3	0	96	0	1	6	0.0	20	16	250	50	0.0	0.0
C- / 3.2	4.0	4.6	12.03	76	3	0	96	0	1	6	0.0	32	16	250	50	3.0	0.0
C- / 3.2	4.1	4.6	12.04	N/A	3	0	96	0	1	6	0.0	22	16	250	50	0.0	0.0
U /	N/A	N/A	10.14	95	2	41	0	23	34	62	0.0	N/A	2	0	0	0.0	0.0
U /	N/A	5.7	10.01	N/A	0	0	0	0	100	62	0.0	N/A	2	2,000	0	3.8	0.0
U /	N/A	5.7	10.01	5	0	0	0	0	100	62	0.0	N/A	2	1,000,000	0	0.0	0.0
U /	N/A	5.7	10.01	54	0	0	0	0	100	62	0.0	N/A	2	10,000,000	0	0.0	0.0
U /	N/A	N/A	1.00	314	100	0	0	0	0	0	0.0	N/A	N/A	25,000,000	0	0.0	0.0
A+ / 9.9	N/A	N/A	1.00	43,990	100	0	0	0	0	0	0.2	70	N/A	500,000,000	0	0.0	0.0
A+ / 9.9	N/A	N/A	1.00	1,788	100	0	0	0	0	0	0.0	64	N/A	500,000,000	0	0.0	0.0
A+ / 9.9	N/A	N/A	1.00	10,613	100	0	0	0	0	0	0.1	64	N/A	500,000,000	0	0.0	0.0
C / 5.0	3.5	N/A	10.13	N/A	3	0	0	94	3	34	0.0	54	5	1,000	0	2.0	0.0
C / 5.2	3.4	N/A	10.11	N/A	3	0	0	94	3	34	0.0	29	5	1,000	0	0.0	0.0
C / 5.0	3.5	N/A	10.13	65	3	0	0	94	3	34	0.0	51	5	1,000,000	0	0.0	0.0
B / 8.2	2.2	3.4	10.24	8	3	76	0	3	18	62	0.0	44	13	1,000	0	2.0	0.0
B / 8.2	2.2	3.4	10.20	N/A	3	76	0	3	18	62	0.0	23	13	1,000	0	0.0	0.0
B / 8.2	2.3	3.4	10.22	1	3	76	0	3	18	62	0.0	22	13	1,000	0	0.0	0.0
B / 8.2	2.2	3.4	10.25	21	3	76	0	3	18	62	0.0	53	13	1,000,000	0	0.0	0.0
C+ / 6.7	3.0	5.3	10.58	4	3	0	96	0	1	17	0.0	24	13	1,000	0	2.0	0.0
C+ / 6.6	3.0	5.3	10.59	N/A	3	0	96	0	1	17	0.0	13	13	1,000	0	0.0	0.0
C+ / 6.6	3.0	5.3	10.57	8	3	0	96	0	1	17	0.0	31	13	1,000,000	0	0.0	0.0
C+ / 6.8	2.9	5.4	11.26	6	3	0	96	0	1	18	0.0	27	13	1,000	0	2.0	0.0
B- / 7.0	2.9	5.4	11.26	1	3	0	96	0	1	18	0.0	14	13	1,000	0	0.0	0.0
C+ / 6.8	2.9	5.4	11.28	28	3	0	96	0	1	18	0.0	34	13	1,000,000	0	0.0	0.0
C+ / 6.1	3.1	5.3	11.05	49	3	0	96	0	1	17	0.0	27	16	1,000	0	2.0	0.0
C+ / 6.3	3.1	5.3	11.05	5	3	0	96	0	1	17	0.0	14	16	1,000	0	0.0	0.0
C+ / 6.1	3.1	5.3	11.05	146	3	0	96	0	1	17	0.0	35	16	1,000,000	0	0.0	0.0
C+ / 6.5	3.0	5.3	11.27	18	3	0	96	0	1	13	0.0	33	16	1,000	0	2.0	0.0
C+ / 6.4	3.0	5.3	11.26	2	3	0	96	0	1	13	0.0	16	16	1,000	0	0.0	0.0
C+ / 6.6	3.0	5.3	11.19	65	3	0	96	0	1	13	0.0	41	16	1,000,000	0	0.0	0.0

Fund Type	Fund Name (99 Pct = Best, 0 Pct = Worst)	Ticker Symbol	Overall Investment Rating	Phone	PERFORMANCE: Performance Rating/Pts	Total Return % through 3/31/16: 3 Mo	6 Mo	1Yr / Pct	Annualized: 3Yr / Pct	Annualized: 5Yr / Pct	Incl. in Returns: Dividend Yield	Expense Ratio
COI	Sterling Capital Sec Opp Inst	SCSPX	**A**	(800) 228-1872	**B- / 7.1**	1.97	1.49	2.03 /72	2.47 /70	--	2.61	0.61
COI	Sterling Capital Securitized Opp A	SCSSX	**B**	(800) 228-1872	**C+ / 5.7**	1.80	1.26	1.68 /69	2.18 /65	--	2.31	0.86
COI	Sterling Capital Securitized Opp C	SCSTX	**B-**	(800) 228-1872	**C / 5.3**	1.62	0.89	0.92 /57	1.45 /51	--	1.61	1.61
USS	Sterling Capital Short Dur Bd A	BSGAX	**C**	(800) 228-1872	**C- / 3.0**	0.88	0.64	0.59 /51	0.77 /38	1.58 /26	2.69	0.80
USS	Sterling Capital Short Dur Bd C	BBSCX	**C**	(800) 228-1872	**D+ / 2.6**	0.69	0.38	-0.05 /31	0.02 /18	--	1.99	1.55
USS	Sterling Capital Short Dur Bd Inst	BBSGX	**B**	(800) 228-1872	**C / 4.5**	0.94	0.76	0.84 /56	1.02 /43	1.81 /29	3.00	0.55
GEI	Sterling Capital Tot Rtn Bd A	BICAX	**C-**	(800) 228-1872	**C / 4.5**	2.73	2.29	1.47 /66	2.39 /69	3.74 /57	3.04	0.81
GEI	● Sterling Capital Tot Rtn Bd B	BICBX	**C+**	(800) 228-1872	**C+ / 5.8**	2.53	1.90	0.70 /53	1.62 /54	2.96 /44	2.46	1.56
GEI	Sterling Capital Tot Rtn Bd C	BICCX	**C+**	(800) 228-1872	**C+ / 5.7**	2.44	1.81	0.61 /52	1.60 /54	2.96 /44	2.47	1.56
GEI	Sterling Capital Tot Rtn Bd I	BIBTX	**B+**	(800) 228-1872	**B- / 7.4**	2.69	2.31	1.62 /68	2.61 /72	4.00 /61	3.47	0.56
GEI	Sterling Capital Tot Rtn Bd R	BICRX	**B-**	(800) 228-1872	**C+ / 6.6**	2.55	2.07	1.11 /60	2.11 /64	3.45 /52	2.97	1.06
COI	Sterling Capital Ultra Short Bd A	BUSRX	**C+**	(800) 228-1872	**D+ / 2.8**	0.39	0.32	0.44 /49	0.26 /30	--	1.25	0.78
COI	Sterling Capital Ultra Short Bd Ins	BUSIX	**C+**	(800) 228-1872	**C- / 3.4**	0.35	0.44	0.59 /51	0.48 /33	--	1.51	0.53
MUS	Sterling Capital VA Interm TxFr A	BVAAX	**B-**	(800) 228-1872	**B- / 7.3**	1.42	2.32	2.89 /84	1.95 /76	3.34 /73	2.01	0.90
MUS	Sterling Capital VA Interm TxFr C	BVACX	**C+**	(800) 228-1872	**C+ / 6.7**	1.32	1.94	2.13 /78	1.19 /58	--	1.32	1.65
MUS	Sterling Capital VA Interm TxFr I	BVATX	**A-**	(800) 228-1872	**B+ / 8.3**	1.57	2.44	3.15 /86	2.20 /79	3.62 /75	2.30	0.65
MUS	Sterling Capital WVA Interm TxFr A	BWVAX	**A-**	(800) 228-1872	**B / 7.6**	1.40	2.38	3.06 /86	2.10 /78	3.68 /75	2.03	0.90
MUS	Sterling Capital WVA Interm TxFr C	BWVCX	**B+**	(800) 228-1872	**B- / 7.0**	1.21	2.00	2.30 /79	1.34 /63	--	1.33	1.65
MUS	Sterling Capital WVA Interm TxFr I	OWVAX	**A+**	(800) 228-1872	**B+ / 8.4**	1.46	2.50	3.32 /88	2.35 /81	3.94 /77	2.31	0.65
GES	Steward Select Bond Fd Indv	SEAKX	**C+**	(877) 420-4440	**C / 5.2**	2.30	1.48	1.26 /63	1.21 /46	2.07 /32	1.76	0.96
GES	Steward Select Bond Fd Inst	SEACX	**B-**	(877) 420-4440	**C+ / 5.9**	2.42	1.66	1.65 /68	1.58 /54	2.44 /37	2.10	0.62
* EM	Stone Harbor Emerging Debt Inst	SHMDX	**D**	(866) 699-8125	**C+ / 6.3**	6.82	8.10	3.61 /79	0.52 /34	3.84 /59	6.79	0.68
EM	Stone Harbor Emg Mks Crp Dbt Fd	SHCDX	**C-**	(866) 699-8125	**B- / 7.5**	4.80	4.71	2.65 /75	2.17 /65	--	5.21	1.40
EM	Stone Harbor Emg Mkts Dbt All Inst	SHADX	**U**	(866) 699-8125	**U /**	8.75	9.20	0.08 /40	--	--	2.85	1.72
GEI	Stone Harbor High Yield Bond Inst	SHHYX	**D**	(866) 699-8125	**C- / 3.6**	2.53	1.85	-4.38 / 7	0.97 /42	4.05 /62	6.40	0.62
COI	Stone Harbor Investment Grade Inst	SHIGX	**U**	(866) 699-8125	**U /**	3.18	2.52	1.05 /59	--	--	1.19	2.09
GEN	Stone Harbor Strategic Income Inst	SHSIX	**U**	(866) 699-8125	**U /**	3.60	3.59	-0.78 /23	--	--	3.95	1.65
USS	Stratus Govt Securities Inst	STGSX	**C**	(888) 769-2362	**C- / 3.1**	1.41	0.64	0.62 /52	0.17 /28	1.44 /25	1.95	0.94
USL	● SunAmerica 2020 High Watermark A	HWKAX	**D-**	(800) 858-8850	**E+ / 0.9**	2.26	0.82	1.15 /61	0.14 /28	4.03 /62	2.30	2.10
USL	● SunAmerica 2020 High Watermark C		**D-**	(800) 858-8850	**D / 1.6**	2.13	0.55	0.44 /49	-0.52 /11	3.36 /51	1.63	2.98
USL	● SunAmerica 2020 High Watermark I		**D+**	(800) 858-8850	**C / 4.3**	2.48	1.11	1.66 /68	0.61 /35	4.55 /68	2.93	1.92
COH	SunAmerica Flexible Credit A	SHNAX	**D**	(800) 858-8850	**C- / 3.1**	1.86	0.87	-1.26 /20	1.86 /59	4.18 /64	3.94	1.60
COH	SunAmerica Flexible Credit C	SHNCX	**D**	(800) 858-8850	**C / 4.3**	1.70	0.56	-1.86 /16	1.22 /47	3.52 /53	3.49	2.26
COH	SunAmerica Flexible Credit W	SHNWX	**U**	(800) 858-8850	**U /**	1.60	0.66	-1.07 /21	--	--	4.35	1.47
LP	SunAmerica Sr Floating Rate A	SASFX	**D+**	(800) 858-8850	**D- / 1.5**	1.40	-0.86	-2.03 /15	1.04 /43	2.29 /35	4.12	1.77
LP	SunAmerica Sr Floating Rate C	NFRCX	**C-**	(800) 858-8850	**C- / 3.2**	1.46	-1.00	-2.32 /14	0.78 /39	2.01 /31	3.97	2.16
GES	SunAmerica Strategic Bond A	SDIAX	**D-**	(800) 858-8850	**D- / 1.5**	2.79	1.59	-2.07 /15	0.97 /42	3.26 /49	3.97	1.30
GES	SunAmerica Strategic Bond B	SDIBX	**D**	(800) 858-8850	**D+ / 2.7**	2.32	1.26	-3.01 /11	0.29 /30	2.51 /38	3.51	1.97
GES	SunAmerica Strategic Bond C	NAICX	**D**	(800) 858-8850	**D+ / 2.9**	2.64	1.28	-2.67 /13	0.33 /30	2.61 /39	3.53	1.94
GEL	SunAmerica Strategic Bond W	SDIWX	**U**	(800) 858-8850	**U /**	2.52	1.69	-2.19 /15	--	--	4.37	1.17
USS	SunAmerica US Gov Sec A	SGTAX	**D+**	(800) 858-8850	**D- / 1.4**	1.59	1.10	0.31 /46	0.66 /36	2.39 /36	1.67	1.37
USS	SunAmerica US Gov Sec C	NASBX	**D+**	(800) 858-8850	**D+ / 2.8**	1.54	0.78	-0.23 /29	0.01 /16	1.75 /28	1.11	2.14
GEI	SunAmerica VAL Co I Cap Conse Fd	VCCCX	**B**	(800) 858-8850	**C+ / 6.8**	2.79	2.17	1.45 /66	2.18 /65	3.65 /56	1.93	0.63
USS	SunAmerica VAL Co I Gov Sec Fd	VCGSX	**C+**	(800) 858-8850	**C+ / 6.3**	2.93	2.08	2.17 /73	1.72 /56	3.67 /56	2.44	0.64
GEI	SunAmerica VAL Co I Infln Prot Fd	VCTPX	**D-**	(800) 858-8850	**D- / 1.1**	3.22	2.35	-0.18 /29	-1.30 / 7	2.30 /35	1.18	0.58
GL	SunAmerica VAL Co I Intl Govt Bd Fd	VCIFX	**D+**	(800) 858-8850	**C+ / 5.9**	6.51	5.93	3.96 /81	0.41 /32	2.11 /33	2.57	0.65
* GEI	SunAmerica VAL Co II Core Bond Fd	VCCBX	**C+**	(800) 858-8850	**C+ / 6.4**	2.67	2.01	0.66 /53	1.99 /61	3.63 /55	2.06	0.80
GEI	SunAmerica VAL Co II High Yld Bd	VCHYX	**D+**	(800) 858-8850	**C / 4.9**	2.81	1.39	-2.95 /12	1.57 /54	4.12 /63	5.21	0.99
* GEI	SunAmerica VAL Co II Strat Bond	VCSBX	**D+**	(800) 858-8850	**C / 5.2**	2.78	1.93	-1.35 /19	1.51 /52	3.79 /58	3.63	0.88
* MUS	T Rowe Price CA Tax Free Bond	PRXCX	**A-**	(800) 638-5660	**A+ / 9.8**	1.81	3.93	4.56 /97	4.39 /97	6.82 /96	3.30	0.49
* COI	T Rowe Price Corporate Income	PRPIX	**C**	(800) 638-5660	**B / 7.7**	3.51	3.14	0.29 /46	2.99 /76	5.36 /74	3.39	0.62
COH	T Rowe Price Credit Opptys	PRCPX	**U**	(800) 638-5660	**U /**	2.28	-1.50	-5.98 / 3	--	--	6.42	1.89

● Denotes fund is closed to new investors
* Denotes fund is included in Section II

RISK			NET ASSETS		ASSET							FUND MANAGER		MINIMUM		LOADS	
Risk Rating/Pts	3 Yr Avg Standard Deviation	Avg Duration	NAV As of 3/31/16	Total $(Mil)	Cash %	Gov. Bond %	Muni. Bond %	Corp. Bond %	Other %	Portfolio Turnover Ratio	Avg Coupon Rate	Manager Quality Pct	Manager Tenure (Years)	Initial Purch. $	Additional Purch. $	Front End Load	Back End Load
B / 8.1	2.4	N/A	10.00	47	0	1	0	1	98	20	0.0	91	5	1,000,000	0	0.0	0.0
B / 8.1	2.3	N/A	9.99	N/A	0	1	0	1	98	20	0.0	88	5	1,000	0	2.0	0.0
B / 8.1	2.3	N/A	9.98	N/A	0	1	0	1	98	20	0.0	72	5	1,000	0	0.0	0.0
A / 9.4	0.9	1.6	8.80	8	0	2	2	63	33	56	0.0	78	5	1,000	0	2.0	0.0
A / 9.4	0.9	1.6	8.80	2	0	2	2	63	33	56	0.0	45	5	1,000	0	0.0	0.0
A / 9.4	0.9	1.6	8.80	74	0	2	2	63	33	56	0.0	84	5	1,000,000	0	0.0	0.0
C+ / 6.4	3.0	4.5	10.60	61	2	5	3	42	48	41	0.0	61	8	1,000	0	5.8	0.0
C+ / 6.4	3.0	4.5	10.61	1	2	5	3	42	48	41	0.0	35	8	1,000	0	0.0	0.0
C+ / 6.6	3.0	4.5	10.61	6	2	5	3	42	48	41	0.0	35	8	1,000	0	0.0	0.0
C+ / 6.7	3.0	4.5	10.60	611	2	5	3	42	48	41	0.0	76	8	1,000,000	0	0.0	0.0
C+ / 6.5	3.0	4.5	10.55	N/A	2	5	3	42	48	41	0.0	51	8	1,000	0	0.0	0.0
A+ / 9.9	0.3	N/A	9.83	8	2	0	2	53	43	66	0.0	71	4	1,000	0	0.5	0.0
A+ / 9.9	0.3	N/A	9.82	39	2	0	2	53	43	66	0.0	79	4	1,000,000	0	0.0	0.0
C+ / 5.7	3.2	5.2	12.09	36	2	0	97	0	1	16	0.0	22	16	1,000	0	2.0	0.0
C+ / 5.8	3.2	5.2	12.09	1	2	0	97	0	1	16	0.0	11	16	1,000	0	0.0	0.0
C+ / 5.7	3.2	5.2	12.09	82	2	0	97	0	1	16	0.0	27	16	1,000,000	0	0.0	0.0
C+ / 6.8	2.9	5.2	10.22	36	3	0	96	0	1	10	0.0	31	16	1,000	0	2.0	0.0
C+ / 6.6	3.0	5.2	10.22	1	3	0	96	0	1	10	0.0	15	16	1,000	0	0.0	0.0
C+ / 6.6	3.0	5.2	10.23	63	3	0	96	0	1	10	0.0	37	16	1,000,000	0	0.0	0.0
B- / 7.2	2.8	3.8	24.88	14	2	24	0	60	14	13	0.0	28	6	200	0	0.0	0.0
B- / 7.2	2.8	3.8	24.76	138	2	24	0	60	14	13	0.0	38	6	25,000	1,000	0.0	0.0
E / 0.4	8.7	6.4	10.02	1,541	0	0	0	0	100	75	7.1	85	9	1,000,000	250,000	0.0	0.0
D / 1.6	6.0	N/A	8.74	17	1	3	0	94	2	62	0.0	97	9	1,000,000	250,000	0.0	0.0
U /	N/A	N/A	8.95	66	3	82	1	12	2	11	0.0	N/A	2	1,000,000	250,000	0.0	0.0
D / 1.6	6.0	4.7	7.81	245	0	0	0	0	100	52	8.3	37	9	1,000,000	250,000	0.0	0.0
U /	N/A	N/A	10.38	16	11	20	0	36	33	51	0.0	N/A	3	1,000,000	250,000	0.0	0.0
U /	N/A	N/A	9.50	36	8	23	0	53	16	8	0.0	N/A	3	1,000,000	250,000	0.0	0.0
B+ / 8.5	2.0	N/A	10.15	36	2	66	0	7	25	21	0.0	25	15	250,000	0	0.0	0.0
C- / 3.8	4.1	N/A	9.06	21	2	97	0	0	1	0	0.0	13	12	500	100	5.8	0.0
C- / 3.8	4.1	N/A	9.09	3	2	97	0	0	1	0	0.0	9	12	500	100	0.0	0.0
C- / 3.8	4.1	N/A	9.08	8	2	97	0	0	1	0	0.0	19	12	0	0	0.0	0.0
D+ / 2.8	4.4	2.1	3.29	125	2	0	0	83	15	74	5.2	85	15	500	100	4.8	0.0
D+ / 2.8	4.5	2.1	3.31	62	2	0	0	83	15	74	5.2	62	15	500	100	0.0	0.0
U /	N/A	2.1	3.29	90	2	0	0	83	15	74	5.2	N/A	7	50,000	0	0.0	0.0
B- / 7.3	2.8	N/A	7.64	107	2	0	0	79	19	41	0.0	81	7	500	100	3.8	0.0
B- / 7.2	2.8	N/A	7.64	163	2	0	0	79	19	41	0.0	73	7	500	100	0.0	0.0
C- / 3.0	4.7	5.6	3.28	175	2	17	0	73	8	137	5.1	18	14	500	100	4.8	0.0
D+ / 2.9	4.8	5.6	3.27	31	2	17	0	73	8	137	5.1	11	14	500	100	0.0	0.0
D+ / 2.9	4.8	5.6	3.29	151	2	17	0	73	8	137	5.1	11	14	500	100	0.0	0.0
U /	N/A	5.6	3.27	30	2	17	0	73	8	137	5.1	N/A	14	50,000	0	0.0	0.0
C+ / 6.9	2.9	4.8	9.59	156	3	42	0	0	55	57	3.4	27	2	500	100	4.8	0.0
C+ / 6.8	2.9	4.8	9.59	32	3	42	0	0	55	57	3.4	14	2	500	100	0.0	0.0
C+ / 6.4	3.0	5.8	9.91	235	7	26	0	29	38	193	3.4	50	14	0	0	0.0	0.0
C / 5.5	3.3	5.6	10.85	154	7	37	0	5	51	7	2.9	44	5	0	0	0.0	0.0
C- / 3.4	4.3	7.0	10.75	460	3	64	0	26	7	33	2.0	5	12	0	0	0.0	0.0
D / 1.9	5.5	7.0	11.41	182	2	87	0	9	2	43	3.9	83	7	0	0	0.0	0.0
C+ / 5.6	3.2	5.7	11.17	1,180	9	24	0	34	33	153	3.6	40	14	0	0	0.0	0.0
D+ / 2.6	5.2	4.3	7.32	493	7	0	0	89	4	36	6.3	55	7	0	0	0.0	0.0
C- / 3.1	4.6	5.4	11.09	763	4	21	0	67	8	132	4.8	29	14	0	0	0.0	0.0
C- / 3.9	4.0	5.1	11.77	532	0	0	100	0	0	6	5.0	74	13	2,500	100	0.0	0.0
D+ / 2.9	4.6	7.2	9.51	790	0	0	0	0	100	49	4.3	62	13	2,500	100	0.0	0.0
U /	N/A	N/A	7.85	32	7	0	0	86	7	133	0.0	N/A	1	2,500	100	0.0	2.0

Fund Type	Fund Name (99 Pct = Best, 0 Pct = Worst)	Ticker Symbol	Overall Investment Rating	Phone	PERFORMANCE: Performance Rating/Pts	Total Return % through 3/31/16: 3 Mo	6 Mo	1Yr / Pct	Annualized: 3Yr / Pct	Annualized: 5Yr / Pct	Incl. in Returns: Dividend Yield	Expense Ratio
COH	T Rowe Price Credit Opptys Adv	PAOPX	**U**	(800) 638-5660	**U /**	2.13	-1.67	-6.31 / 3	--	--	6.33	2.65
EM	T Rowe Price Em Mkts Loc Cur	PRELX	**E-**	(800) 638-5660	**E- / 0.1**	9.63	10.05	-2.98 /11	-7.68 / 1	--	5.25	1.35
EM	T Rowe Price Emerg Mkts Corp Bd	PACEX	**D**	(800) 638-5660	**C+ / 5.7**	4.66	5.54	2.70 /75	1.31 /49	--	4.66	1.54
EM	T Rowe Price Emerg Mkts Corp Bd	TRECX	**D+**	(800) 638-5660	**C+ / 5.9**	4.68	5.59	2.80 /76	1.41 /50	--	4.75	1.21
EM	T Rowe Price Emerging Markets Bd	PREMX	**D**	(800) 638-5660	**C+ / 5.7**	5.08	6.81	4.29 /83	0.89 /41	4.31 /66	6.17	0.93
EM	T Rowe Price Emerging Markets Bd A	PAIKX	**U**	(800) 638-5660	**U /**	5.01	6.67	--	--	--	0.00	1.36
EM	T Rowe Price Emerging Markets Bd I	PRXIX	**U**	(800) 638-5660	**U /**	5.11	6.79	--	--	--	0.00	0.77
EM	T Rowe Price Emg Mkts Loc Cur Adv	PAELX	**E-**	(800) 638-5660	**E- / 0.1**	9.79	10.18	-2.93 /12	-7.77 / 1	--	5.15	1.77
LP	T Rowe Price Floating Rate	PRFRX	**B**	(800) 638-5660	**C / 5.4**	1.66	0.66	0.62 /52	2.19 /65	--	3.92	0.81
LP	T Rowe Price Floating Rate Advisor	PAFRX	**B**	(800) 638-5660	**C / 5.3**	1.62	0.69	0.59 /51	2.12 /64	--	3.80	1.12
MUS	T Rowe Price GA Tax-Free Bd	GTFBX	**A-**	(800) 638-5660	**A / 9.4**	1.57	3.04	3.77 /92	3.64 /93	5.85 /91	3.07	0.53
GL	T Rowe Price Global High Inc Bd	RPIHX	**U**	(800) 638-5660	**U /**	4.03	4.10	0.56 /51	--	--	6.38	1.03
GL	T Rowe Price Global High Inc Bd Adv	PAIHX	**U**	(800) 638-5660	**U /**	4.00	4.03	0.41 /48	--	--	6.22	1.46
GL	T Rowe Price Global High Inc Bd I	RPOIX	**U**	(800) 638-5660	**U /**	4.08	4.21	--	--	--	0.00	0.99
GES	T Rowe Price Global MS Bd	PRSNX	**C**	(800) 638-5660	**B- / 7.4**	3.26	4.35	2.14 /73	2.24 /66	3.84 /59	3.44	0.82
GES	T Rowe Price Global MS Bd Adv	PRSAX	**C**	(800) 638-5660	**B- / 7.1**	3.21	4.25	1.94 /71	2.06 /63	3.67 /56	3.25	1.20
* USA	T Rowe Price GNMA	PRGMX	**B**	(800) 638-5660	**C+ / 5.9**	1.42	1.32	1.53 /67	1.71 /56	2.79 /42	2.99	0.59
* COH ●	T Rowe Price High Yield	PRHYX	**D**	(800) 638-5660	**C / 4.7**	2.67	1.29	-3.12 /11	2.12 /64	4.81 /70	6.22	0.74
COH ●	T Rowe Price High Yield Adv	PAHIX	**D**	(800) 638-5660	**C / 4.3**	2.79	1.22	-3.46 /10	1.90 /60	4.54 /68	5.87	1.00
COH	T Rowe Price High Yield I	PRHIX	**U**	(800) 638-5660	**U /**	2.87	1.51	--	--	--	0.00	0.60
US	T Rowe Price Infla-Protect Bond	PRIPX	**D-**	(800) 638-5660	**D / 1.7**	4.05	3.17	1.20 /62	-1.01 / 8	2.54 /38	0.10	0.58
EM	T Rowe Price Ins Emerging Mkts Bd	TREBX	**D+**	(800) 638-5660	**B- / 7.4**	4.80	6.50	4.90 /87	2.12 /64	4.84 /71	5.89	0.70
GEI	T Rowe Price Inst Core Plus	TICPX	**B-**	(800) 638-5660	**B- / 7.0**	2.98	2.44	1.26 /63	2.33 /68	4.01 /62	2.93	0.45
COH	T Rowe Price Inst Credit Opptys	TRXPX	**U**	(800) 638-5660	**U /**	2.46	-1.15	-5.87 / 3	--	--	6.75	0.66
GL	T Rowe Price Inst Glbl Mlti-Sec Bd	RPGMX	**U**	(800) 638-5660	**U /**	3.39	4.44	2.40 /74	--	--	3.58	0.57
EM	T Rowe Price Inst Intl Bd	RPIIX	**D**	(800) 638-5660	**C / 4.6**	8.27	7.78	5.79 /92	-0.44 /12	0.51 /17	1.93	0.55
COI	T Rowe Price Inst Long Dur Cr	RPLCX	**U**	(800) 638-5660	**U /**	6.31	6.32	-0.07 /31	--	--	3.82	0.45
COI	T Rowe Price Instl Core Plus F	PFCPX	**C+**	(800) 638-5660	**C+ / 6.9**	2.95	2.48	1.23 /62	2.23 /66	3.89 /60	2.80	0.56
LP	T Rowe Price Instl Fltng Rate	RPIFX	**A-**	(800) 638-5660	**C+ / 6.2**	1.75	0.76	0.94 /58	2.69 /73	3.55 /54	4.30	0.56
* LP	T Rowe Price Instl Fltng Rate F	PFFRX	**B+**	(800) 638-5660	**C+ / 6.1**	1.83	0.79	0.91 /57	2.56 /71	3.46 /52	4.17	0.69
* COH ●	T Rowe Price Instl High Yield	TRHYX	**D**	(800) 638-5660	**C / 4.4**	2.97	1.27	-3.65 / 9	1.99 /61	4.67 /69	6.66	0.50
MUH	T Rowe Price Int Tax-Fr Hi Yld	PRIHX	**U**	(800) 638-5660	**U /**	1.90	3.40	4.09 /94	--	--	2.49	2.72
MUH	T Rowe Price Int Tax-Fr Hi Yld Adv	PRAHX	**U**	(800) 638-5660	**U /**	1.88	3.35	3.89 /93	--	--	2.40	3.50
* GL	T Rowe Price Intl Bond	RPIBX	**D-**	(800) 638-5660	**C- / 3.9**	8.22	7.43	5.61 /91	-0.77 /10	0.20 /16	1.71	0.83
GL	T Rowe Price Intl Bond Adv	PAIBX	**D-**	(800) 638-5660	**C- / 3.3**	8.14	7.28	5.28 /89	-1.09 / 8	-0.09 / 3	1.42	1.06
GL	T Rowe Price Intl Bond I	RPISX	**U**	(800) 638-5660	**U /**	8.24	7.49	--	--	--	0.00	0.67
COI	T Rowe Price Ltd Dur Inf Foc Bd I	TRLDX	**U**	(800) 638-5660	**U /**	1.62	1.00	--	--	--	0.00	0.36
MUS	T Rowe Price MD ShTm Tax-Free Bd	PRMDX	**B**	(800) 638-5660	**C / 4.4**	0.54	0.52	0.85 /63	0.59 /41	0.82 /23	0.66	0.53
* MUS	T Rowe Price MD Tax Free Bd	MDXBX	**A**	(800) 638-5660	**A / 9.3**	1.56	2.88	3.68 /92	3.49 /93	5.78 /91	3.45	0.45
MMT	T Rowe Price MD Tax-Free Money	TMDXX	**U**	(800) 638-5660	**U /**	--	--	--	--	--	0.01	0.58
* GEI	T Rowe Price New Income	PRCIX	**C+**	(800) 638-5660	**C+ / 6.5**	2.66	2.11	1.10 /60	2.03 /62	3.54 /54	2.53	0.60
GEI	T Rowe Price New Income Adv	PANIX	**C+**	(800) 638-5660	**C+ / 6.1**	2.61	2.01	0.87 /56	1.81 /58	3.32 /50	2.31	0.84
COI	T Rowe Price New Income I	PRXEX	**U**	(800) 638-5660	**U /**	2.59	2.19	--	--	--	0.00	0.46
GEI	T Rowe Price New Income R	RRNIX	**C**	(800) 638-5660	**C / 5.5**	2.42	1.85	0.56 /51	1.45 /51	2.96 /44	2.00	1.22
MUS	T Rowe Price NJ Tax-Free Bond	NJTFX	**B+**	(800) 638-5660	**A / 9.5**	1.59	3.53	3.66 /92	3.67 /94	5.90 /91	3.22	0.51
MUS	T Rowe Price NY Tax Free Bd	PRNYX	**B+**	(800) 638-5660	**A / 9.5**	1.54	3.27	4.10 /95	3.70 /94	5.84 /91	3.30	0.49
MM	T Rowe Price Prime Reserve	PRRXX	**U**	(800) 638-5660	**U /**	--	--	--	--	--	0.01	0.53
* GES	T Rowe Price Short Term Bond	PRWBX	**C+**	(800) 638-5660	**C- / 3.9**	0.79	0.53	0.64 /52	0.70 /37	1.24 /23	1.49	0.52
GES	T Rowe Price Short Term Bond Adv	PASHX	**C+**	(800) 638-5660	**C- / 3.2**	0.72	0.18	0.36 /47	0.35 /31	0.90 /20	1.20	0.81
* GES	T Rowe Price Spectrum Income	RPSIX	**C-**	(800) 638-5660	**B- / 7.1**	3.67	3.97	0.62 /52	2.24 /66	4.06 /62	3.27	0.67
MM	T Rowe Price Summit Cash Reserves	TSCXX	**U**	(800) 638-5660	**U /**	0.01	0.01	0.01 /33	0.01 /18	0.01 / 6	0.01	0.45
MUN	T Rowe Price Summit Muni Inc Adv	PAIMX	**B+**	(800) 638-5660	**A / 9.5**	1.72	3.49	3.83 /93	3.74 /94	--	3.04	0.75

● Denotes fund is closed to new investors
* Denotes fund is included in Section II

RISK			NET ASSETS		ASSET							FUND MANAGER		MINIMUM		LOADS	
Risk Rating/Pts	3 Yr Avg Standard Deviation	Avg Duration	NAV As of 3/31/16	Total $(Mil)	Cash %	Gov. Bond %	Muni. Bond %	Corp. Bond %	Other %	Portfolio Turnover Ratio	Avg Coupon Rate	Manager Quality Pct	Manager Tenure (Years)	Initial Purch. $	Additional Purch. $	Front End Load	Back End Load
U /	N/A	N/A	7.83	N/A	7	0	0	86	7	133	0.0	N/A	1	2,500	100	0.0	2.0
E- / 0.1	12.2	N/A	6.57	168	4	92	0	3	1	82	0.0	1	4	2,500	100	0.0	2.0
D- / 1.4	6.2	5.5	9.89	1	8	2	0	83	7	106	6.7	92	4	2,500	100	0.0	2.0
D- / 1.4	6.2	5.5	9.89	85	8	2	0	83	7	106	6.7	93	4	2,500	100	0.0	2.0
E / 0.5	7.9	6.1	11.82	4,379	5	66	0	22	7	45	6.2	90	22	2,500	100	0.0	2.0
U /	N/A	6.1	11.82	N/A	5	66	0	22	7	45	6.2	N/A	22	2,500	100	0.0	2.0
U /	N/A	6.1	11.81	10	5	66	0	22	7	45	6.2	N/A	22	1,000,000	0	0.0	2.0
E- / 0.1	12.2	N/A	6.57	N/A	4	92	0	3	1	82	0.0	1	4	2,500	100	0.0	2.0
B+ / 8.4	2.1	0.4	9.68	577	7	0	0	73	20	55	5.3	95	5	2,500	100	0.0	2.0
B+ / 8.4	2.1	0.4	9.68	32	7	0	0	73	20	55	5.3	95	5	2,500	100	0.0	2.0
C / 4.4	3.7	4.7	11.79	303	0	0	100	0	0	3	5.1	53	19	2,500	100	0.0	0.0
U /	N/A	N/A	9.58	26	0	0	0	0	100	0	0.0	N/A	1	2,500	100	0.0	2.0
U /	N/A	N/A	9.58	N/A	0	0	0	0	100	0	0.0	N/A	1	2,500	100	0.0	2.0
U /	N/A	N/A	9.58	1	0	0	0	0	100	0	0.0	N/A	1	1,000,000	0	0.0	2.0
C- / 4.0	4.0	3.9	11.04	282	6	32	0	35	27	114	4.3	64	8	2,500	100	0.0	0.0
C- / 4.0	4.0	3.9	11.05	9	6	32	0	35	27	114	4.3	57	8	2,500	100	0.0	0.0
B / 7.8	2.6	3.8	9.50	1,549	0	0	0	0	100	430	4.6	77	8	2,500	100	0.0	0.0
D- / 1.4	5.7	3.5	6.25	7,796	4	0	0	90	6	59	6.8	82	20	2,500	100	0.0	2.0
D- / 1.3	5.7	3.5	6.24	92	4	0	0	90	6	59	6.8	75	20	2,500	100	0.0	2.0
U /	N/A	3.5	6.26	994	4	0	0	90	6	59	6.8	N/A	20	1,000,000	0	0.0	2.0
D+ / 2.4	5.3	4.9	11.95	357	0	0	0	0	100	178	1.2	6	14	2,500	100	0.0	0.0
E+ / 0.8	6.9	5.8	8.54	305	4	61	0	24	11	54	6.1	97	10	1,000,000	0	0.0	2.0
C+ / 5.7	3.2	5.4	10.37	604	2	22	1	30	45	150	3.4	54	N/A	1,000,000	0	0.0	0.0
U /	N/A	N/A	7.68	21	4	0	0	88	8	240	0.0	N/A	1	1,000,000	0	0.0	2.0
U /	N/A	6.3	9.69	232	6	32	0	34	28	148	4.1	N/A	3	1,000,000	0	0.0	0.0
E+ / 0.9	6.4	7.3	8.78	347	3	69	1	23	4	90	3.5	52	9	1,000,000	0	0.0	2.0
U /	N/A	N/A	10.30	34	3	7	0	88	2	65	0.0	N/A	3	1,000,000	0	0.0	0.0
C+ / 5.7	3.2	5.4	10.37	N/A	2	22	1	30	45	150	3.4	73	N/A	2,500	100	0.0	0.0
B+ / 8.3	2.2	0.5	9.82	2,607	7	0	0	70	23	48	5.0	97	7	1,000,000	0	0.0	2.0
B / 8.2	2.3	0.5	9.82	756	7	0	0	70	23	48	5.0	96	7	2,500	100	0.0	2.0
D- / 1.1	6.0	3.5	8.26	1,815	1	0	0	92	7	66	6.8	76	1	1,000,000	0	0.0	2.0
U /	N/A	N/A	10.40	36	0	0	99	0	1	5	0.0	N/A	2	2,500	100	0.0	2.0
U /	N/A	N/A	10.39	1	0	0	99	0	1	5	0.0	N/A	2	2,500	100	0.0	2.0
E+ / 0.8	6.5	7.4	8.92	5,206	3	68	1	24	4	73	3.5	40	4	2,500	100	0.0	2.0
E+ / 0.8	6.6	7.4	8.93	27	3	68	1	24	4	73	3.5	30	4	2,500	100	0.0	2.0
U /	N/A	7.4	8.93	13	3	68	1	24	4	73	3.5	N/A	4	1,000,000	0	0.0	2.0
U /	N/A	1.6	5.03	N/A	0	72	0	18	10	92	1.0	N/A	6	1,000,000	0	0.0	0.0
A / 9.5	0.8	1.8	5.23	211	0	0	100	0	0	19	4.7	66	20	2,500	100	0.0	0.0
C / 4.9	3.5	4.0	10.98	2,142	0	0	99	0	1	7	5.0	54	16	2,500	100	0.0	0.0
U /	N/A	N/A	1.00	136	100	0	0	0	0	0	0.0	N/A	15	2,500	100	0.0	0.0
C+ / 6.0	3.1	5.4	9.55	26,684	1	17	1	30	51	145	3.4	44	16	2,500	100	0.0	0.0
C+ / 6.0	3.1	5.4	9.53	52	1	17	1	30	51	145	3.4	36	16	2,500	100	0.0	0.0
U /	N/A	5.4	9.54	178	1	17	1	30	51	145	3.4	N/A	16	1,000,000	0	0.0	0.0
C+ / 6.1	3.1	5.4	9.54	8	1	17	1	30	51	145	3.4	27	16	2,500	100	0.0	0.0
C / 4.3	3.8	4.5	12.24	369	1	0	98	0	1	7	5.0	49	16	2,500	100	0.0	0.0
C- / 4.1	3.9	4.4	11.90	457	1	0	98	0	1	3	5.1	47	16	2,500	100	0.0	0.0
U /	N/A	N/A	1.00	6,562	100	0	0	0	0	0	0.0	N/A	7	2,500	100	0.0	0.0
A / 9.4	0.9	1.9	4.73	5,432	2	6	0	48	44	53	22.4	72	21	2,500	100	0.0	0.0
A / 9.3	1.0	1.9	4.72	106	2	6	0	48	44	53	22.4	54	21	2,500	100	0.0	0.0
C- / 3.6	4.2	5.2	12.23	5,844	2	23	0	37	38	14	4.7	77	18	2,500	100	0.0	0.0
U /	N/A	N/A	1.00	5,297	100	0	0	0	0	0	0.0	N/A	7	25,000	1,000	0.0	0.0
C- / 3.6	4.2	4.7	12.10	2	1	0	98	0	1	17	5.2	38	17	25,000	1,000	0.0	0.0

Fund Type	Fund Name (99 Pct = Best, 0 Pct = Worst)	Ticker Symbol	Overall Investment Rating	Phone	PERFORMANCE: Performance Rating/Pts	Total Return % through 3/31/16: 3 Mo	6 Mo	1Yr / Pct	Annualized: 3Yr / Pct	5Yr / Pct	Incl. in Returns: Dividend Yield	Expense Ratio
* MUN	T Rowe Price Summit Muni Income	PRINX	B+	(800) 638-5660	A+ / 9.6	1.70	3.62	4.08 /94	3.99 /96	6.59 /95	3.29	0.50
* MUN	T Rowe Price Summit Muni Intmdt	PRSMX	A+	(800) 638-5660	A- / 9.1	1.53	2.82	3.55 /91	3.13 /89	4.67 /83	2.55	0.50
MUN	T Rowe Price Summit Muni Intmdt	PAIFX	A+	(800) 638-5660	B+ / 8.9	1.39	2.69	3.30 /88	2.84 /86	--	2.30	0.75
* MUH	T Rowe Price Tax-Free High Yield	PRFHX	C+	(800) 638-5660	A+ / 9.7	1.94	4.03	4.23 /95	4.69 /98	8.04 /98	3.91	0.69
MUH	T Rowe Price Tax-Free High Yield Ad	PATFX	C+	(800) 638-5660	A / 9.5	1.94	3.86	3.95 /94	4.35 /97	--	3.57	1.03
* MUN	T Rowe Price Tax-Free Income	PRTAX	B+	(800) 638-5660	A / 9.4	1.56	3.11	3.48 /90	3.63 /93	6.03 /92	3.68	0.51
MUN	T Rowe Price Tax-Free Income Adv	PATAX	B+	(800) 638-5660	A- / 9.2	1.48	2.94	3.22 /87	3.28 /91	5.68 /90	3.34	0.86
* MUN	T Rowe Price Tax-Free Sh-Intmdt	PRFSX	A-	(800) 638-5660	C+ / 6.0	0.67	0.84	1.36 /72	1.13 /56	2.09 /49	1.34	0.49
MUN	T Rowe Price Tax-Free Sh-Intmdt	PATIX	B	(800) 638-5660	C / 4.9	0.58	0.66	1.00 /67	0.77 /46	--	0.99	0.83
COI	T Rowe Price Ultra Short Term Bond	TRBUX	C+	(800) 638-5660	C- / 3.5	0.65	0.47	0.68 /53	0.51 /33	--	0.88	0.45
* GEI	T Rowe Price US Bond Enhanced	PBDIX	B	(800) 638-5660	C+ / 6.8	2.90	2.24	1.60 /68	2.31 /68	3.68 /56	2.82	0.30
US	T Rowe Price US Treas Intmdt	PRTIX	C-	(800) 638-5660	C+ / 6.2	3.45	2.09	2.87 /76	1.48 /52	3.52 /53	1.61	0.51
US	T Rowe Price US Treas Long-Term	PRULX	C-	(800) 638-5660	A / 9.3	7.88	6.29	2.21 /73	5.08 /91	8.75 /90	2.35	0.51
MM	T Rowe Price US Treasury Money	PRTXX	U	(800) 638-5660	U /	--	--	--	--	--	0.01	0.44
* MUS	T Rowe Price VA Tax-Free Bond	PRVAX	B+	(800) 638-5660	A / 9.4	1.51	3.12	3.79 /93	3.48 /93	5.61 /90	3.26	0.47
MMT	Tax Free Money Fd Inv Prem	BTXXX	U	(800) 728-3337	U /	--	--	--	--	--	0.02	0.84
MMT	Tax-Exempt CA MM Institutional	TXIXX	C	(800) 728-3337	D+ / 2.3	0.03	0.04	0.04 /40	0.02 /23	0.03 /13	0.04	0.39
USA	TCG Advantage Money Market Inst	GAIXX	U	(866) 707-8588	U /	0.08	0.14	0.32 /46	--	--	0.32	3.23
USA	TCG Cash Reserve Mny Mkt Inst	CRIXX	U	(866) 707-8588	U /	0.09	0.14	0.24 /45	--	--	0.24	3.23
USA	TCG Daily Liquidity Mny Mkt Inst	DLIXX	U	(866) 707-8588	U /	0.08	0.14	0.26 /45	--	--	0.26	3.23
USA	TCG Liquid Assets Money Market Inst	LSIXX	U	(866) 707-8588	U /	0.09	0.14	0.27 /45	--	--	0.27	3.23
USA	TCG Liquidity Plus Mny Mkt Inst	LPIXX	U	(866) 707-8588	U /	0.09	0.14	0.28 /45	--	--	0.28	3.23
USA	TCG Max Money Market Inst	GXIXX	U	(866) 707-8588	U /	0.09	0.14	0.29 /46	--	--	0.28	3.23
USA	TCG Premier Money Market Inst	GRIXX	U	(866) 707-8588	U /	0.08	0.14	0.27 /45	--	--	0.27	3.23
USA	TCG Primary Liquidity Mny Mkt Inst	GQIXX	U	(866) 707-8588	U /	0.09	0.14	0.28 /45	--	--	0.28	3.23
USA	TCG Select Money Market Inst	GLIXX	U	(866) 707-8588	U /	0.08	0.14	0.28 /46	--	--	0.28	3.23
USA	TCG Ultra Money Market Inst	GUIXX	U	(866) 707-8588	U /	0.09	0.15	0.29 /46	--	--	0.29	3.23
USS	TCW Core Fixed Income I	TGCFX	B+	(800) 386-3829	C+ / 6.6	2.51	1.97	1.27 /63	2.09 /63	3.83 /59	1.64	0.50
* USS	TCW Core Fixed Income N	TGFNX	B	(800) 386-3829	C+ / 6.1	2.46	1.86	0.95 /58	1.78 /57	3.72 /57	1.41	0.79
EM	TCW Emerging Markets Income I	TGEIX	D-	(800) 386-3829	C- / 3.2	4.59	5.38	2.32 /74	-0.77 /10	3.61 /55	4.96	0.88
EM	TCW Emerging Markets Income N	TGINX	D-	(800) 386-3829	D+ / 2.8	4.60	5.28	2.05 /72	-1.02 / 8	3.31 /50	4.79	1.16
GL	TCW Emg Mkts Local Currency Inc I	TGWIX	E-	(800) 386-3829	E- / 0.1	10.06	8.25	-3.40 /10	-6.71 / 1	-1.55 / 1	0.00	1.00
GL	TCW Emg Mkts Local Currency Inc N	TGWNX	E-	(800) 386-3829	E- / 0.2	10.21	8.39	-3.29 /10	-6.71 / 1	-1.57 / 1	0.00	1.25
GL	TCW Global Bond I	TGGBX	D+	(800) 386-3829	C / 4.4	4.31	3.20	2.78 /76	0.11 /27	--	0.99	1.37
GL	TCW Global Bond N	TGGFX	D+	(800) 386-3829	C / 4.4	4.31	3.20	2.78 /76	0.11 /27	--	0.99	1.64
COH	TCW High Yield Bond I	TGHYX	C-	(800) 386-3829	B- / 7.4	1.60	2.17	0.20 /44	2.97 /76	4.11 /63	4.32	1.03
COH	TCW High Yield Bond N	TGHNX	C-	(800) 386-3829	C+ / 6.9	1.36	1.85	-0.24 /29	2.66 /73	3.88 /60	4.00	1.38
MTG	TCW Short Term Bond I	TGSMX	C+	(800) 386-3829	C- / 3.3	0.24	0.24	0.26 /45	0.47 /33	0.98 /20	0.72	1.57
MTG	TCW Total Return Bond I	TGLMX	A+	(800) 386-3829	B / 7.8	2.06	1.56	1.85 /70	3.14 /77	5.25 /73	2.19	0.60
* MTG	TCW Total Return Bond N	TGMNX	A	(800) 386-3829	B- / 7.5	2.05	1.42	1.59 /67	2.84 /75	4.93 /71	1.92	0.88
COI	TD Asset Mgmt Short-Term Bond Adv	TDSHX	U		U /	0.96	0.64	0.75 /54	--	--	1.04	0.93
COI	TD Asset Mgmt Short-Term Bond Inst	TDSBX	B-		C- / 4.0	0.96	0.64	0.75 /54	0.71 /37	1.02 /21	1.04	0.68
COI	TDAM 1 to 5 Year Corporate Bond Ptf	TDFPX	U		U /	1.72	1.32	1.60 /68	--	--	1.47	1.76
COI	TDAM 5 to 10 Year Corporate Bd Ptf	TDFSX	U		U /	4.20	3.72	2.52 /75	--	--	2.68	2.37
GEI	TDAM Core Bond Adv	TDCBX	B+		C+ / 6.9	3.00	2.43	1.69 /69	2.18 /65	--	1.75	2.37
GEI	TDAM Core Bond Inst	TDBFX	B		C+ / 6.9	3.00	2.43	1.69 /69	2.18 /65	--	1.75	2.12
COH	TDAM High Yield Bond Adv	TDHYX	D+		C+ / 6.0	2.39	2.55	-2.30 /14	2.15 /64	--	4.89	2.65
COH	TDAM High Yield Bond Inst	TDHBX	D+		C+ / 6.0	2.40	2.44	-2.29 /14	2.15 /64	--	4.89	2.40
MM	TDAM Inst Treasury Obligs MM Com	TTCXX	U		U /	0.00	0.01	0.02 /35	0.01 /18	0.01 / 6	0.02	0.93
MM	TDAM Inst Treasury Obligs MM IS	TDVXX	U		U /	0.00	0.01	0.02 /35	0.01 /18	0.01 / 6	0.02	0.43
MMT	TDAM Instl Muni Mny Mkt Inst	TICXX	U		U /	--	--	--	--	--	0.01	0.36
MMT	TDAM Municipal Investor	WTMXX	U		U /	--	--	--	--	--	0.01	0.95

● Denotes fund is closed to new investors
* Denotes fund is included in Section II

RISK			NET ASSETS		ASSET							FUND MANAGER		MINIMUM		LOADS	
Risk Rating/Pts	3 Yr Avg Standard Deviation	Avg Duration	NAV As of 3/31/16	Total $(Mil)	Cash %	Gov. Bond %	Muni. Bond %	Corp. Bond %	Other %	Portfolio Turnover Ratio	Avg Coupon Rate	Manager Quality Pct	Manager Tenure (Years)	Initial Purch. $	Additional Purch. $	Front End Load	Back End Load
C- / 3.6	4.2	4.7	12.10	1,078	1	0	98	0	1	17	5.2	46	17	25,000	1,000	0.0	0.0
C+ / 6.8	2.9	4.3	12.11	4,037	1	0	98	0	1	12	5.0	68	23	25,000	1,000	0.0	0.0
C+ / 6.9	2.9	4.3	12.10	7	1	0	98	0	1	12	5.0	55	23	25,000	1,000	0.0	0.0
D+ / 2.3	4.9	5.2	12.09	3,558	0	0	99	0	1	4	5.4	49	14	2,500	100	0.0	2.0
D+ / 2.3	5.0	5.2	12.10	18	0	0	99	0	1	4	5.4	37	14	2,500	100	0.0	2.0
C- / 4.2	3.9	4.4	10.44	1,914	0	0	99	0	1	8	5.2	47	9	2,500	100	0.0	0.0
C- / 4.2	3.9	4.4	10.45	637	0	0	99	0	1	8	5.2	35	9	2,500	100	0.0	0.0
B+ / 8.9	1.5	2.7	5.65	2,092	1	0	98	0	1	19	4.9	54	22	2,500	100	0.0	0.0
B+ / 8.9	1.4	2.7	5.64	7	1	0	98	0	1	19	4.9	43	22	2,500	100	0.0	0.0
A+ / 9.8	0.4	N/A	4.99	239	1	14	0	63	22	128	0.0	78	3	2,500	100	0.0	0.0
C+ / 6.5	3.0	5.8	11.14	610	0	25	2	32	41	54	3.6	55	16	2,500	100	0.0	0.5
C- / 4.2	3.9	5.3	5.98	443	0	94	0	0	6	61	2.4	28	9	2,500	100	0.0	0.0
E- / 0.2	10.8	16.7	13.52	398	1	94	0	0	5	46	3.5	15	13	2,500	100	0.0	0.0
U /	N/A	N/A	1.00	2,068	100	0	0	0	0	0	0.0	N/A	7	2,500	100	0.0	0.0
C- / 4.1	3.9	4.3	12.24	1,131	1	0	98	0	1	6	5.0	41	19	2,500	100	0.0	0.0
U /	N/A	N/A	1.00	141	100	0	0	0	0	0	0.0	N/A	N/A	2,000	0	0.0	0.0
A+ / 9.9	N/A	N/A	1.00	86	100	0	0	0	0	0	0.0	66	N/A	100,000	0	0.0	0.0
U /	N/A	N/A	1.00	25	0	0	0	0	100	0	0.0	N/A	2	500	50	0.0	0.0
U /	N/A	N/A	1.00	25	0	0	0	0	100	0	0.0	N/A	2	500	50	0.0	0.0
U /	N/A	N/A	1.00	25	0	0	0	0	100	0	0.0	N/A	2	500	50	0.0	0.0
U /	N/A	N/A	1.00	25	0	0	0	0	100	0	0.0	N/A	2	500	50	0.0	0.0
U /	N/A	N/A	1.00	25	0	0	0	0	100	0	0.0	N/A	2	500	50	0.0	0.0
U /	N/A	N/A	1.00	25	0	0	0	0	100	0	0.0	N/A	2	500	50	0.0	0.0
U /	N/A	N/A	1.00	25	0	0	0	0	100	0	0.0	N/A	2	500	50	0.0	0.0
U /	N/A	N/A	1.00	25	0	0	0	0	100	0	0.0	N/A	2	500	50	0.0	0.0
U /	N/A	N/A	1.00	25	0	0	0	0	100	0	0.0	N/A	2	500	50	0.0	0.0
U /	N/A	N/A	1.00	25	0	0	0	0	100	0	0.0	N/A	2	500	50	0.0	0.0
B / 7.6	2.7	5.0	11.18	1,157	1	35	0	19	45	333	2.8	79	6	2,000	250	0.0	0.0
B / 7.6	2.7	5.0	11.16	536	1	35	0	19	45	333	2.8	68	6	2,000	250	0.0	0.0
E+ / 0.7	7.0	5.8	7.72	2,153	5	56	0	37	2	173	6.1	37	6	2,000	250	0.0	0.0
E+ / 0.7	7.0	5.8	9.95	462	5	56	0	37	2	173	6.1	30	6	2,000	250	0.0	0.0
E- / 0.2	11.2	4.4	8.53	110	3	95	0	1	1	250	7.3	1	6	2,000	250	0.0	0.0
E- / 0.2	11.2	4.4	8.53	144	3	95	0	1	1	250	7.3	1	6	2,000	250	0.0	0.0
C- / 3.8	4.1	5.3	9.95	8	5	46	0	19	30	147	3.5	75	5	2,000	250	0.0	0.0
C- / 3.8	4.1	5.3	9.95	7	5	46	0	19	30	147	3.5	75	5	2,000	250	0.0	0.0
D+ / 2.7	4.6	3.1	6.06	19	2	6	0	88	4	196	4.4	95	5	2,000	250	0.0	0.0
D+ / 2.7	4.5	3.1	6.10	7	2	6	0	88	4	196	4.4	93	5	2,000	250	0.0	0.0
A+ / 9.9	0.3	0.4	8.69	9	5	13	0	31	51	9	1.4	76	6	2,000	250	0.0	0.0
B / 7.6	2.7	5.0	10.28	6,930	5	20	0	2	73	288	2.9	85	6	2,000	250	0.0	0.0
B / 7.7	2.6	5.0	10.61	2,586	5	20	0	2	73	288	2.9	79	6	2,000	250	0.0	0.0
U /	N/A	1.7	10.20	N/A	3	11	3	61	22	120	0.0	N/A	7	0	0	0.0	0.0
A+ / 9.6	0.8	1.7	10.20	54	3	11	3	61	22	120	0.0	77	7	0	0	0.0	0.0
U /	N/A	2.6	10.13	56	0	0	0	0	100	70	0.0	N/A	N/A	0	0	0.0	0.0
U /	N/A	6.2	10.45	41	0	0	0	0	100	72	0.0	N/A	N/A	0	0	0.0	0.0
C+ / 6.8	2.9	5.4	10.14	N/A	0	0	0	0	100	62	0.0	52	N/A	0	0	0.0	0.0
C+ / 6.7	3.0	5.4	10.14	38	0	0	0	0	100	62	0.0	52	N/A	0	0	0.0	0.0
D+ / 2.6	4.6	4.3	9.22	N/A	0	0	0	0	100	23	0.0	88	3	0	0	0.0	0.0
D+ / 2.6	4.6	4.3	9.22	8	0	0	0	0	100	23	0.0	88	3	0	0	0.0	0.0
U /	N/A	N/A	1.00	524	100	0	0	0	0	0	0.0	N/A	N/A	0	0	0.0	0.0
U /	N/A	N/A	1.00	195	100	0	0	0	0	0	0.0	N/A	N/A	0	0	0.0	0.0
U /	N/A	N/A	1.00	37	100	0	0	0	0	0	0.0	N/A	N/A	0	0	0.0	0.0
U /	N/A	N/A	1.00	424	100	0	0	0	0	0	0.0	N/A	21	0	0	0.0	0.0

Fund Type	Fund Name (99 Pct = Best, 0 Pct = Worst)	Ticker Symbol	Overall Investment Rating	Phone	PERFORMANCE: Performance Rating/Pts	Total Return % through 3/31/16: 3 Mo	6 Mo	1Yr / Pct	Annualized: 3Yr / Pct	Annualized: 5Yr / Pct	Incl. in Returns: Dividend Yield	Expense Ratio
EM	Templeton Emerging Markets Bond A	FEMGX	**U**	(800) 342-5236	**U /**	2.65	5.54	2.26 /73	--	--	2.79	2.37
EM	Templeton Emerging Markets Bond		**U**	(800) 342-5236	**U /**	2.64	5.69	2.39 /74	--	--	3.05	2.12
EM	Templeton Emerging Markets Bond C		**U**	(800) 342-5236	**U /**	2.64	5.33	1.90 /71	--	--	2.45	2.77
EM	Templeton Emerging Markets Bond R		**U**	(800) 342-5236	**U /**	2.77	5.55	2.17 /73	--	--	2.71	2.62
EM	Templeton Emerging Markets Bond		**U**	(800) 342-5236	**U /**	2.76	5.73	2.58 /75	--	--	3.12	2.02
* GL	Templeton Global Bond A	TPINX	**E**	(800) 342-5236	**E / 0.5**	0.03	2.30	-4.31 / 7	-0.63 /11	1.93 /30	3.00	0.91
GL	Templeton Global Bond Adv	TGBAX	**E+**	(800) 321-8563	**D- / 1.1**	0.09	2.35	-4.16 / 7	-0.41 /12	2.18 /33	3.41	0.66
GL	Templeton Global Bond C	TEGBX	**E**	(800) 342-5236	**E+ / 0.7**	-0.07	2.00	-4.76 / 5	-1.05 / 8	1.52 /26	2.71	1.31
GL	Templeton Global Bond R	FGBRX	**E**	(800) 342-5236	**E+ / 0.8**	0.05	2.17	-4.55 / 6	-0.88 / 9	1.68 /27	2.88	1.16
GL	Templeton Global Bond R6	FBNRX	**E+**	(800) 342-5236	**D- / 1.2**	0.13	2.43	-4.02 / 8	-0.37 /13	2.09 /32	3.55	0.53
* GL	Templeton Global Total Return A	TGTRX	**E**	(800) 342-5236	**E / 0.4**	0.06	2.21	-5.04 / 5	-1.03 / 8	2.43 /37	3.45	1.04
GL	Templeton Global Total Return Adv	TTRZX	**E**	(800) 321-8563	**E+ / 0.9**	0.20	2.43	-4.79 / 5	-0.75 /10	2.70 /40	3.85	0.79
GL	Templeton Global Total Return C	TTRCX	**E**	(800) 342-5236	**E+ / 0.6**	0.04	2.10	-5.42 / 4	-1.40 / 6	2.04 /32	3.19	1.44
GL	Templeton Global Total Return R		**E**	(800) 342-5236	**E+ / 0.6**	0.08	2.18	-5.27 / 4	-1.26 / 7	2.19 /33	3.34	1.29
GL	Templeton Global Total Return R6	FTTRX	**E**	(800) 342-5236	**D- / 1.0**	0.24	2.50	-4.59 / 6	-0.65 /11	2.76 /41	3.98	0.68
GL	Templeton Hard Currency A	ICPHX	**E**	(800) 342-5236	**E- / 0.0**	-0.51	0.00	-6.16 / 3	-6.45 / 1	-4.14 / 0	0.00	1.24
GL	Templeton Hard Currency Advisor	ICHHX	**E**	(800) 321-8563	**E- / 0.1**	-0.51	0.13	-5.98 / 3	-6.19 / 1	-3.90 / 0	0.00	0.99
GL	Templeton International Bond A	TBOAX	**E**	(800) 342-5236	**E- / 0.2**	1.39	3.79	-3.65 / 9	-2.73 / 3	0.28 /16	2.09	1.15
GL	Templeton International Bond Adv	FIBZX	**E**	(800) 321-8563	**E / 0.5**	1.55	3.91	-3.39 /10	-2.42 / 3	0.57 /18	2.45	0.90
GL	Templeton International Bond C	FCNBX	**E**	(800) 342-5236	**E / 0.3**	1.29	3.58	-4.02 / 8	-3.07 / 2	-0.09 / 3	1.79	1.54
GL	Templeton International Bond R		**E**	(800) 342-5236	**E / 0.3**	1.42	3.65	-3.79 / 8	-2.90 / 3	0.07 /14	1.94	1.40
GEI	TETON Westwood Interm Bond A	WEAIX	**C-**	(800) 422-3554	**D+ / 2.3**	2.43	1.98	1.56 /67	0.64 /36	1.76 /28	1.43	1.47
GEI	TETON Westwood Interm Bond AAA	WEIBX	**C+**	(800) 422-3554	**C / 4.6**	2.45	2.02	1.65 /68	0.71 /37	1.88 /30	1.58	1.37
GEI	TETON Westwood Interm Bond C	WECIX	**C-**	(800) 422-3554	**C- / 3.1**	2.20	1.54	0.81 /55	-0.06 /15	1.09 /21	0.85	2.12
GEI	TETON Westwood Interm Bond I	WEIIX	**B-**	(800) 422-3554	**C / 5.1**	2.51	2.06	1.82 /70	0.97 /42	2.11 /33	1.83	1.12
COH	Third Avenue Focused Credit Inst	TFCIX	**E-**	(800) 443-1021	**E- / 0.0**	-7.31	-26.37	-33.59 / 0	-12.93 / 0	-5.22 / 0	22.27	0.88
COH	Third Avenue Focused Credit Inv	TFCVX	**E-**	(800) 443-1021	**E- / 0.0**	-7.30	-26.48	-33.70 / 0	-13.13 / 0	-5.44 / 0	21.87	1.13
* GEI	Thompson Bond	THOPX	**D**	(800) 999-0887	**D- / 1.2**	0.38	-1.50	-3.43 /10	-0.13 /15	2.30 /35	4.80	0.72
MUS	Thornburg CA Ltd Term Muni A	LTCAX	**A+**	(800) 847-0200	**B- / 7.0**	0.82	1.37	1.84 /76	1.96 /77	3.36 /73	1.29	0.94
MUS	Thornburg CA Ltd Term Muni C	LTCCX	**A+**	(800) 847-0200	**B- / 7.3**	0.76	1.25	1.61 /74	1.68 /72	3.09 /70	1.09	1.18
MUS	Thornburg CA Ltd Term Muni Inst	LTCIX	**A+**	(800) 847-0200	**B / 8.2**	0.96	1.60	2.23 /79	2.29 /80	3.71 /75	1.62	0.63
MUN	Thornburg Intermediate Muni A	THIMX	**A+**	(800) 847-0200	**B / 8.1**	1.16	2.49	2.75 /83	2.62 /84	4.64 /82	1.96	0.92
MUN	Thornburg Intermediate Muni C	THMCX	**A+**	(800) 847-0200	**B+ / 8.3**	1.08	2.33	2.43 /80	2.30 /80	4.31 /80	1.69	1.28
MUN	Thornburg Intermediate Muni Inst	THMIX	**A+**	(800) 847-0200	**A- / 9.0**	1.30	2.71	3.12 /86	2.96 /88	4.98 /85	2.28	0.62
* GES	Thornburg Limited Term Income A	THIFX	**B-**	(800) 847-0200	**C / 4.9**	1.75	1.15	1.02 /59	1.57 /54	3.32 /50	1.88	0.87
GES	Thornburg Limited Term Income C	THICX	**B**	(800) 847-0200	**C / 5.1**	1.78	1.03	0.79 /55	1.34 /49	3.08 /47	1.68	1.10
GES	Thornburg Limited Term Income Inst	THIIX	**A-**	(800) 847-0200	**C+ / 6.2**	1.84	1.24	1.37 /64	1.93 /60	3.69 /56	2.25	0.52
GES	Thornburg Limited Term Income R3	THIRX	**B**	(800) 847-0200	**C / 5.4**	1.72	1.08	0.90 /57	1.46 /51	3.23 /49	1.79	1.11
COI	Thornburg Limited Term Income R4	THRIX	**U**	(800) 847-0200	**U /**	1.72	1.01	0.90 /57	--	--	1.79	1.66
COI	Thornburg Limited Term Income R5	THRRX	**B+**	(800) 847-0200	**C+ / 6.0**	1.81	1.28	1.26 /63	1.82 /58	--	2.15	0.67
* MUN	Thornburg Limited Term Muni A	LTMFX	**A-**	(800) 847-0200	**C+ / 6.1**	0.84	1.38	1.89 /76	1.51 /68	2.88 /67	1.50	0.73
MUN	Thornburg Limited Term Muni C	LTMCX	**A**	(800) 847-0200	**C+ / 6.5**	0.79	1.26	1.66 /75	1.29 /61	2.62 /62	1.30	0.96
MUN	Thornburg Limited Term Muni Inst	LTMIX	**A+**	(800) 847-0200	**B / 7.7**	0.85	1.46	2.21 /79	1.84 /75	3.22 /71	1.83	0.41
USS	Thornburg Limited Term US Govt A	LTUSX	**C+**	(800) 847-0200	**C- / 3.6**	1.55	0.80	1.17 /61	0.80 /39	1.53 /26	1.52	0.92
USS	● Thornburg Limited Term US Govt B	LTUBX	**C-**	(800) 847-0200	**D- / 1.4**	1.23	0.13	-0.18 /29	-0.56 /11	0.15 /15	0.20	7.08
USS	Thornburg Limited Term US Govt C	LTUCX	**C+**	(800) 847-0200	**C- / 3.7**	1.55	0.66	0.90 /57	0.51 /33	1.24 /23	1.27	1.21
USS	Thornburg Limited Term US Govt Inst	LTUIX	**B**	(800) 847-0200	**C / 4.9**	1.71	0.96	1.50 /66	1.12 /45	1.86 /30	1.86	0.62
USS	Thornburg Limited Term US Govt R3	LTURX	**C+**	(800) 847-0200	**C- / 4.2**	1.61	0.76	1.10 /60	0.73 /38	1.45 /25	1.47	1.35
USS	Thornburg Limited Term US Govt R4	LTUGX	**U**	(800) 847-0200	**U /**	1.61	0.76	1.11 /61	--	--	1.47	1.13
USS	Thornburg Limited Term US Govt R5	LTGRX	**B**	(800) 847-0200	**C / 4.8**	1.69	0.92	1.42 /65	1.08 /44	--	1.79	2.02
COI	Thornburg Low Duration Income A	TLDAX	**U**	(800) 847-0200	**U /**	0.94	0.56	0.73 /54	--	--	0.71	2.10
COI	Thornburg Low Duration Income I	TLDIX	**U**	(800) 847-0200	**U /**	0.99	0.74	0.93 /57	--	--	0.92	1.89

● Denotes fund is closed to new investors
* Denotes fund is included in Section II

RISK			NET ASSETS		ASSET							FUND MANAGER		MINIMUM		LOADS	
Risk Rating/Pts	3 Yr Avg Standard Deviation	Avg Duration	NAV As of 3/31/16	Total $(Mil)	Cash %	Gov. Bond %	Muni. Bond %	Corp. Bond %	Other %	Portfolio Turnover Ratio	Avg Coupon Rate	Manager Quality Pct	Manager Tenure (Years)	Initial Purch. $	Additional Purch. $	Front End Load	Back End Load
U /	N/A	N/A	8.37	13	0	0	0	0	100	43	0.0	N/A	3	1,000	0	4.3	0.0
U /	N/A	N/A	8.39	1	0	0	0	0	100	43	0.0	N/A	3	1,000	0	0.0	0.0
U /	N/A	N/A	8.37	1	0	0	0	0	100	43	0.0	N/A	3	1,000	0	0.0	0.0
U /	N/A	N/A	8.36	N/A	0	0	0	0	100	43	0.0	N/A	3	1,000	0	0.0	0.0
U /	N/A	N/A	8.39	N/A	0	0	0	0	100	43	0.0	N/A	3	1,000,000	0	0.0	0.0
D- / 1.1	6.4	0.4	11.49	16,012	20	78	0	0	2	43	4.6	39	15	1,000	0	4.3	0.0
D- / 1.1	6.4	0.4	11.44	25,546	20	78	0	0	2	43	4.6	47	15	1,000	0	0.0	0.0
D- / 1.1	6.4	0.4	11.51	5,083	20	78	0	0	2	43	4.6	27	15	1,000	0	0.0	0.0
D- / 1.1	6.5	0.4	11.49	337	20	78	0	0	2	43	4.6	32	15	1,000	0	0.0	0.0
D- / 1.1	6.5	0.4	11.44	3,095	20	78	0	0	2	43	4.6	48	15	1,000,000	0	0.0	0.0
E+ / 0.8	6.9	0.8	11.40	1,420	10	76	0	11	3	32	5.1	28	8	1,000	0	4.3	0.0
E+ / 0.7	6.9	0.8	11.42	2,813	10	76	0	11	3	32	5.1	36	8	1,000	0	0.0	0.0
E+ / 0.7	6.9	0.8	11.39	581	10	76	0	11	3	32	5.1	19	8	1,000	0	0.0	0.0
E+ / 0.8	6.9	0.8	11.41	9	10	76	0	11	3	32	5.1	22	8	1,000	0	0.0	0.0
E+ / 0.7	7.0	0.8	11.42	1,198	10	76	0	11	3	32	5.1	39	8	1,000,000	0	0.0	0.0
D / 1.6	6.0	0.3	7.77	70	63	36	0	0	1	0	0.0	1	15	1,000	0	2.3	0.0
D / 1.6	6.0	0.3	7.86	23	63	36	0	0	1	0	0.0	2	15	1,000,000	0	0.0	0.0
D / 1.6	6.0	0.5	10.10	111	18	80	0	0	2	43	4.0	8	9	1,000	0	4.3	0.0
D / 1.6	6.1	0.5	10.11	294	18	80	0	0	2	43	4.0	9	9	1,000	0	0.0	0.0
D / 1.6	6.0	0.5	10.11	14	18	80	0	0	2	43	4.0	7	9	1,000	0	0.0	0.0
D / 1.6	6.0	0.5	10.11	1	18	80	0	0	2	43	4.0	7	9	1,000	0	0.0	0.0
B+ / 8.3	2.1	4.4	11.48	1	8	28	0	63	1	65	0.0	28	17	1,000	0	4.0	0.0
B+ / 8.3	2.1	4.4	11.49	4	8	28	0	63	1	65	0.0	30	17	1,000	0	0.0	0.0
B+ / 8.3	2.1	4.4	10.90	1	8	28	0	63	1	65	0.0	15	17	1,000	0	0.0	0.0
B+ / 8.4	2.1	4.4	11.49	14	8	28	0	63	1	65	0.0	37	17	500,000	0	0.0	0.0
E- / 0.1	11.5	3.3	5.20	413	5	8	0	59	28	48	10.3	0	7	100,000	0	0.0	2.0
E- / 0.1	11.5	3.3	5.21	200	5	8	0	59	28	48	10.3	0	7	2,500	1,000	0.0	2.0
C / 4.6	3.6	2.2	10.53	2,055	0	5	3	89	3	29	6.6	28	24	1,000	100	0.0	0.0
B+ / 8.6	1.9	3.4	13.94	186	5	0	94	0	1	14	3.7	72	5	5,000	100	1.5	0.0
B+ / 8.6	1.9	3.4	13.95	67	5	0	94	0	1	14	3.7	55	5	5,000	100	0.0	0.0
B+ / 8.6	1.9	3.4	13.96	441	5	0	94	0	1	14	3.7	81	5	2,500,000	100	0.0	0.0
B / 7.7	2.6	4.6	14.38	455	2	0	97	0	1	13	4.0	58	5	5,000	100	2.0	0.0
B / 7.7	2.6	4.6	14.40	168	2	0	97	0	1	13	4.0	47	5	5,000	100	0.0	0.0
B / 7.7	2.6	4.6	14.37	861	2	0	97	0	1	13	4.0	75	5	2,500,000	100	0.0	0.0
B+ / 8.5	2.0	2.9	13.35	1,104	1	4	3	63	29	19	3.0	70	9	5,000	100	1.5	0.0
B+ / 8.4	2.0	2.9	13.33	638	1	4	3	63	29	19	3.0	56	9	5,000	100	0.0	0.0
B+ / 8.5	2.0	2.9	13.35	2,319	1	4	3	63	29	19	3.0	81	9	2,500,000	100	0.0	0.0
B+ / 8.5	2.0	2.9	13.36	164	1	4	3	63	29	19	3.0	61	9	0	0	0.0	0.0
U /	N/A	2.9	13.34	6	1	4	3	63	29	19	3.0	N/A	9	0	0	0.0	0.0
B+ / 8.4	2.0	2.9	13.35	103	1	4	3	63	29	19	3.0	84	9	0	0	0.0	0.0
B+ / 8.7	1.8	3.3	14.61	1,696	2	0	97	0	1	19	3.9	52	5	5,000	100	1.5	0.0
B+ / 8.7	1.8	3.3	14.64	739	2	0	97	0	1	19	3.9	45	5	5,000	100	0.0	0.0
B+ / 8.7	1.8	3.3	14.61	5,098	2	0	97	0	1	19	3.9	69	5	2,500,000	100	0.0	0.0
B+ / 8.8	1.6	2.7	13.28	114	8	30	0	5	57	14	2.7	51	9	5,000	100	1.5	0.0
B+ / 8.8	1.6	2.7	13.25	N/A	8	30	0	5	57	14	2.7	15	9	5,000	100	0.0	0.0
B+ / 8.8	1.7	2.7	13.36	52	8	30	0	5	57	14	2.7	40	9	5,000	100	0.0	0.0
B+ / 8.8	1.6	2.7	13.28	130	8	30	0	5	57	14	2.7	64	9	2,500,000	100	0.0	0.0
B+ / 8.8	1.6	2.7	13.29	21	8	30	0	5	57	14	2.7	48	9	0	0	0.0	0.0
U /	N/A	2.7	13.28	1	8	30	0	5	57	14	2.7	N/A	9	0	0	0.0	0.0
B+ / 8.8	1.7	2.7	13.29	2	8	30	0	5	57	14	2.7	60	9	0	0	0.0	0.0
U /	N/A	1.6	12.40	11	9	29	1	37	24	29	1.9	N/A	3	5,000	100	1.5	0.0
U /	N/A	1.6	12.40	12	9	29	1	37	24	29	1.9	N/A	3	2,500,000	100	0.0	0.0

99 Pct = Best 0 Pct = Worst Fund Type	Fund Name	Ticker Symbol	Overall Investment Rating	Phone	PERFORMANCE Performance Rating/Pts	Total Return % through 3/31/16 3 Mo	6 Mo	1Yr / Pct	Annualized 3Yr / Pct	5Yr / Pct	Incl. in Returns Dividend Yield	Expense Ratio
MUN	Thornburg Low Duration Municipal A	TLMAX	**U**	(800) 847-0200	**U /**	0.28	0.15	0.40 /52	--	--	0.16	2.85
MUN	Thornburg Low Duration Municipal I	TLMIX	**U**	(800) 847-0200	**U /**	0.32	0.15	0.51 /55	--	--	0.35	0.82
MUS	Thornburg NM Intermediate Muni A	THNMX	**A+**	(800) 847-0200	**B / 7.6**	1.03	1.97	2.40 /80	2.25 /80	3.48 /74	2.17	0.98
MUS	Thornburg NM Intermediate Muni D	THNDX	**A+**	(800) 847-0200	**B / 8.0**	1.05	1.92	2.25 /79	2.00 /77	3.24 /72	1.99	1.20
MUS	Thornburg NM Intermediate Muni I	THNIX	**A+**	(800) 847-0200	**B+ / 8.5**	1.19	2.21	2.81 /83	2.59 /84	3.84 /76	2.54	0.65
MUN	Thornburg NY Interm Muni I	TNYIX	**A+**	(800) 847-0200	**B+ / 8.7**	1.26	2.58	3.14 /86	2.62 /84	4.55 /82	2.39	0.76
MUN	Thornburg NY Intermediate Muni A	THNYX	**A+**	(800) 847-0200	**B / 7.8**	1.18	2.42	2.82 /83	2.29 /80	4.22 /79	2.04	1.05
GES	Thornburg Strategic Income Fd A	TSIAX	**D+**	(800) 847-0200	**C- / 3.1**	1.81	0.91	-1.23 /20	1.74 /56	4.29 /65	3.69	1.23
GES	Thornburg Strategic Income Fd C	TSICX	**D+**	(800) 847-0200	**C- / 4.2**	1.77	0.73	-1.76 /17	1.17 /46	3.71 /57	3.31	1.97
GES	Thornburg Strategic Income Fd I	TSIIX	**C-**	(800) 847-0200	**C+ / 5.9**	1.98	1.16	-0.91 /22	2.07 /63	4.64 /69	4.20	0.89
GL	Thornburg Strategic Income Fd R3	TSIRX	**C-**	(800) 847-0200	**C / 5.2**	1.81	0.91	-1.23 /20	1.69 /56	--	3.86	2.70
GL	Thornburg Strategic Income Fd R4	TSRIX	**U**	(800) 847-0200	**U /**	1.90	1.00	-1.22 /20	--	--	3.86	2.64
GL	Thornburg Strategic Income Fd R5	TSRRX	**C-**	(800) 847-0200	**C+ / 5.8**	1.96	1.12	-0.89 /23	2.01 /62	--	4.12	1.55
MUN	Thornburg Strategic Municipal Inc A	TSSAX	**A-**	(800) 847-0200	**B+ / 8.6**	1.29	2.59	2.85 /84	3.21 /90	6.43 /94	2.22	1.31
MUN	Thornburg Strategic Municipal Inc C	TSSCX	**A-**	(800) 847-0200	**B+ / 8.8**	1.22	2.51	2.55 /81	2.90 /87	6.13 /93	1.97	1.70
MUN	Thornburg Strategic Municipal Inc I	TSSIX	**A**	(800) 847-0200	**A / 9.3**	1.37	2.81	3.16 /86	3.53 /93	6.76 /95	2.57	0.93
*COH	● Thrivent Diversified Inc Plus A	AAHYX	**D**	(800) 847-4836	**C / 4.8**	0.95	1.64	-1.85 /16	2.92 /76	5.09 /72	3.53	1.10
COH	Thrivent Diversified Inc Plus S	THYFX	**C-**	(800) 847-4836	**B- / 7.3**	0.88	1.80	-1.58 /18	3.21 /78	5.38 /74	4.02	0.81
USS	● Thrivent Government Bond A	TBFAX	**C-**	(800) 847-4836	**C / 4.9**	3.09	1.92	1.74 /69	1.42 /51	2.99 /45	1.03	1.08
USS	Thrivent Government Bond S	TBFIX	**C**	(800) 847-4836	**C+ / 6.3**	3.11	1.98	1.87 /71	1.72 /56	3.32 /50	1.28	0.57
COH	● Thrivent High Yield A	LBHYX	**D-**	(800) 847-4836	**D+ / 2.6**	2.48	0.76	-3.21 /11	1.66 /55	4.59 /68	5.33	0.80
COH	Thrivent High Yield S	LBHIX	**D**	(800) 847-4836	**C / 5.4**	2.55	0.68	-2.92 /12	1.97 /61	4.89 /71	5.89	0.49
GES	● Thrivent Income A	LUBIX	**C-**	(800) 847-4836	**C / 5.2**	3.12	2.73	-0.02 /31	2.56 /71	4.46 /67	3.15	0.77
GES	Thrivent Income S	LBIIX	**C+**	(800) 847-4836	**B / 7.6**	3.20	2.90	0.33 /47	2.89 /75	4.85 /71	3.65	0.40
GEI	● Thrivent Limited Maturity Bond A	LBLAX	**C+**	(800) 847-4836	**C- / 4.1**	0.87	0.57	0.44 /49	0.84 /40	1.34 /23	1.49	0.62
GEI	Thrivent Limited Maturity Bond S	THLIX	**B**	(800) 847-4836	**C / 4.5**	0.92	0.68	0.75 /54	1.08 /44	1.61 /27	1.72	0.37
*MUN	● Thrivent Municipal Bond A	AAMBX	**B-**	(800) 847-4836	**B / 8.1**	1.33	2.90	3.34 /89	3.33 /91	5.48 /89	3.19	0.75
MUN	Thrivent Municipal Bond S	TMBIX	**A-**	(800) 847-4836	**A / 9.4**	1.39	3.03	3.60 /91	3.60 /93	5.76 /91	3.59	0.49
GEI	● Thrivent Oppty Income Plus A	AAINX	**U**	(800) 847-4836	**U /**	2.06	1.41	-0.68 /24	--	--	3.63	0.98
GEI	Thrivent Oppty Income Plus S	IIINX	**U**	(800) 847-4836	**U /**	2.12	1.52	-0.47 /26	--	--	4.02	0.67
GEI	TIAA-CREF Bond Index Inst	TBIIX	**B**	(800) 842-2252	**B- / 7.3**	3.11	2.44	1.98 /72	2.41 /69	3.67 /56	2.23	0.12
GEI	TIAA-CREF Bond Index Prem	TBIPX	**B**	(800) 842-2252	**B- / 7.1**	3.07	2.36	1.83 /70	2.26 /67	3.51 /53	2.08	0.27
GEI	TIAA-CREF Bond Index Retail	TBILX	**B-**	(800) 842-2252	**C+ / 6.7**	2.93	2.27	1.54 /67	2.06 /63	3.29 /50	1.90	0.45
GEI	TIAA-CREF Bond Index Retire	TBIRX	**B-**	(800) 842-2252	**C+ / 6.8**	2.95	2.31	1.63 /68	2.15 /65	3.39 /51	1.98	0.37
GEI	TIAA-CREF Bond Inst	TIBDX	**B+**	(800) 842-2252	**B / 7.7**	3.18	2.66	2.04 /72	2.84 /75	4.40 /67	2.66	0.31
GEI	TIAA-CREF Bond Plus Inst	TIBFX	**B**	(800) 842-2252	**B / 7.6**	3.03	2.38	1.55 /67	2.78 /74	4.57 /68	2.97	0.32
GEI	TIAA-CREF Bond Plus Prem	TBPPX	**B**	(800) 842-2252	**B- / 7.4**	2.99	2.41	1.39 /65	2.63 /72	4.41 /67	2.82	0.47
GEI	TIAA-CREF Bond Plus Retail	TCBPX	**B-**	(800) 842-2252	**B- / 7.2**	2.95	2.22	1.23 /62	2.45 /70	4.23 /65	2.66	0.64
GEI	TIAA-CREF Bond Plus Retire	TCBRX	**B**	(800) 842-2252	**B- / 7.3**	3.06	2.35	1.39 /65	2.53 /71	4.32 /66	2.72	0.57
GEI	TIAA-CREF Bond Prem	TIDPX	**B**	(800) 842-2252	**B / 7.6**	3.14	2.58	1.89 /71	2.72 /74	4.25 /65	2.51	0.47
GEI	TIAA-CREF Bond Retail	TIORX	**B**	(800) 842-2252	**B- / 7.4**	3.06	2.49	1.74 /69	2.55 /71	4.08 /63	2.36	0.62
GEI	TIAA-CREF Bond Retire	TIDRX	**B**	(800) 842-2252	**B- / 7.4**	3.07	2.51	1.80 /70	2.58 /72	4.13 /63	2.41	0.56
EM	TIAA-CREF Emerging Mkts Debt Inst	TEDNX	**U**	(800) 842-2252	**U /**	5.58	6.09	1.15 /61	--	--	4.86	0.66
EM	TIAA-CREF Emerging Mkts Debt	TEDPX	**U**	(800) 842-2252	**U /**	5.54	6.01	1.00 /59	--	--	4.72	0.86
EM	TIAA-CREF Emerging Mkts Debt Ret	TEDTX	**U**	(800) 842-2252	**U /**	5.52	5.97	0.91 /57	--	--	4.63	0.94
EM	TIAA-CREF Emerging Mkts Debt Rtl	TEDLX	**U**	(800) 842-2252	**U /**	5.48	5.92	0.84 /56	--	--	4.56	0.97
COH	TIAA-CREF High Yield Fund Inst	TIHYX	**D-**	(800) 842-2252	**C- / 3.7**	2.71	0.85	-3.87 / 8	1.65 /55	4.74 /70	6.10	0.36
COH	TIAA-CREF High Yield Fund Premier	TIHPX	**D-**	(800) 842-2252	**C- / 3.5**	2.79	0.78	-3.90 / 8	1.54 /53	4.60 /69	5.94	0.51
COH	TIAA-CREF High Yield Fund Retail	TIYRX	**D-**	(800) 842-2252	**C- / 3.1**	2.64	0.72	-4.09 / 7	1.36 /50	4.45 /67	5.82	0.64
COH	TIAA-CREF High Yield Fund Retire	TIHRX	**D-**	(800) 842-2252	**C- / 3.3**	2.76	0.72	-4.00 / 8	1.44 /51	4.50 /68	5.83	0.61
GEI	TIAA-CREF Infltn Linkd Bd Inst	TIILX	**D-**	(800) 842-2252	**D- / 1.3**	3.50	2.64	0.41 /48	-1.16 / 8	2.62 /39	0.32	0.26
GEI	TIAA-CREF Infltn Linkd Bd Prmr	TIKPX	**D-**	(800) 842-2252	**D- / 1.2**	3.51	2.63	0.31 /46	-1.30 / 7	2.47 /37	0.22	0.42

● Denotes fund is closed to new investors
* Denotes fund is included in Section II

RISK			NET ASSETS		ASSET							FUND MANAGER		MINIMUM		LOADS	
Risk Rating/Pts	3 Yr Avg Standard Deviation	Avg Duration	NAV As of 3/31/16	Total $(Mil)	Cash %	Gov. Bond %	Muni. Bond %	Corp. Bond %	Other %	Portfolio Turnover Ratio	Avg Coupon Rate	Manager Quality Pct	Manager Tenure (Years)	Initial Purch. $	Additional Purch. $	Front End Load	Back End Load
U /	N/A	1.4	12.36	4	1	0	98	0	1	16	3.3	N/A	3	5,000	100	1.5	0.0
U /	N/A	1.4	12.35	42	1	0	98	0	1	16	3.3	N/A	3	2,500,000	100	0.0	0.0
B / 7.8	2.5	4.8	13.67	139	2	0	97	0	1	19	4.7	48	5	5,000	100	2.0	0.0
B / 7.8	2.5	4.8	13.68	28	2	0	97	0	1	19	4.7	39	5	5,000	100	0.0	0.0
B / 7.8	2.5	4.8	13.67	62	2	0	97	0	1	19	4.7	61	5	2,500,000	100	0.0	0.0
B / 7.7	2.6	4.9	13.36	31	3	0	96	0	1	8	4.4	60	5	2,500,000	100	0.0	0.0
B / 7.8	2.6	4.9	13.36	47	3	0	96	0	1	8	4.4	48	5	5,000	100	2.0	0.0
C / 4.8	3.6	3.3	11.10	295	8	2	0	71	19	38	5.1	83	9	5,000	100	4.5	0.0
C / 4.7	3.6	3.3	11.09	280	8	2	0	71	19	38	5.1	60	9	5,000	100	0.0	0.0
C / 4.6	3.6	3.3	11.08	449	8	2	0	71	19	38	5.1	88	9	2,500,000	100	0.0	0.0
C / 4.8	3.6	3.3	11.09	2	8	2	0	71	19	38	5.1	95	9	0	0	0.0	0.0
U /	N/A	3.3	11.10	3	8	2	0	71	19	38	5.1	N/A	9	0	0	0.0	0.0
C / 4.8	3.6	3.3	11.08	5	8	2	0	71	19	38	5.1	96	9	0	0	0.0	0.0
C / 5.3	3.3	5.8	15.38	74	1	0	98	0	1	12	4.2	53	7	5,000	100	2.0	0.0
C / 5.4	3.3	5.8	15.40	35	1	0	98	0	1	12	4.2	43	7	5,000	100	0.0	0.0
C / 5.3	3.3	5.8	15.40	169	1	0	98	0	1	12	4.2	69	7	2,500,000	100	0.0	0.0
D+ / 2.4	4.8	4.2	6.79	581	3	3	0	25	69	137	5.9	94	12	2,000	50	4.5	0.0
D+ / 2.4	4.8	4.2	6.73	110	3	3	0	25	69	137	5.9	96	12	50,000	0	0.0	0.0
C / 4.7	3.6	5.5	10.11	10	1	82	0	7	10	145	2.3	27	6	2,000	50	2.0	0.0
C / 4.7	3.6	5.5	10.11	46	1	82	0	7	10	145	2.3	35	6	50,000	0	0.0	0.0
D / 1.6	5.5	4.2	4.54	455	3	0	0	90	7	38	6.0	69	19	2,000	50	4.5	0.0
D / 1.7	5.4	4.2	4.54	197	3	0	0	90	7	38	6.0	80	19	50,000	0	0.0	0.0
C- / 4.1	3.9	5.9	9.00	352	3	4	0	78	15	92	4.3	54	7	2,000	50	4.5	0.0
C- / 4.2	3.8	5.9	8.99	429	3	4	0	78	15	92	4.3	74	7	50,000	0	0.0	0.0
A- / 9.2	1.1	1.8	12.36	362	4	25	0	36	35	89	2.2	72	17	2,500	100	0.0	0.0
A- / 9.2	1.1	1.8	12.36	382	4	25	0	36	35	89	2.2	78	17	50,000	0	0.0	0.0
C / 4.4	3.7	6.0	11.73	1,480	0	0	98	0	2	8	4.7	41	14	2,000	50	4.5	0.0
C / 4.4	3.7	6.0	11.73	122	0	0	98	0	2	8	4.7	50	14	50,000	0	0.0	0.0
U /	N/A	3.1	9.92	249	1	13	0	29	57	165	4.4	N/A	14	2,000	50	4.5	0.0
U /	N/A	3.1	9.92	152	1	13	0	29	57	165	4.4	N/A	14	50,000	0	0.0	0.0
C+ / 6.2	3.1	5.6	10.98	6,063	0	0	0	0	100	20	3.1	56	N/A	10,000,000	1,000	0.0	0.0
C+ / 6.1	3.1	5.6	10.98	53	0	0	0	0	100	20	3.1	50	N/A	5,000,000	0	0.0	0.0
C+ / 6.2	3.1	5.6	10.98	21	0	0	0	0	100	20	3.1	43	N/A	2,500	100	0.0	0.0
C+ / 6.3	3.1	5.6	10.98	121	0	0	0	0	100	20	3.1	48	N/A	0	0	0.0	0.0
C+ / 5.7	3.2	5.8	10.45	2,659	0	24	1	35	40	328	3.8	76	13	2,000,000	1,000	0.0	0.0
C+ / 5.7	3.2	5.5	10.47	2,382	0	18	4	39	39	285	3.9	77	10	2,000,000	1,000	0.0	0.0
C+ / 5.6	3.2	5.5	10.47	27	0	18	4	39	39	285	3.9	71	10	1,000,000	0	0.0	0.0
C+ / 5.7	3.2	5.5	10.49	264	0	18	4	39	39	285	3.9	60	10	2,500	100	0.0	0.0
C+ / 5.9	3.2	5.5	10.49	198	0	18	4	39	39	285	3.9	69	10	0	0	0.0	0.0
C+ / 5.8	3.2	5.8	10.46	30	0	24	1	35	40	328	3.8	73	13	1,000,000	0	0.0	0.0
C+ / 5.7	3.2	5.8	10.63	79	0	24	1	35	40	328	3.8	61	13	2,500	100	0.0	0.0
C+ / 5.8	3.2	5.8	10.64	234	0	24	1	35	40	328	3.8	63	13	0	0	0.0	0.0
U /	N/A	6.5	9.35	218	0	0	0	0	100	115	5.9	N/A	N/A	2,000,000	1,000	0.0	0.0
U /	N/A	6.5	9.35	1	0	0	0	0	100	115	5.9	N/A	N/A	1,000,000	0	0.0	0.0
U /	N/A	6.5	9.35	3	0	0	0	0	100	115	5.9	N/A	N/A	0	0	0.0	0.0
U /	N/A	6.5	9.35	1	0	0	0	0	100	115	5.9	N/A	N/A	2,500	100	0.0	0.0
E+ / 0.9	6.2	4.3	9.01	2,235	0	8	0	78	14	71	6.4	56	10	2,000,000	1,000	0.0	2.0
E+ / 0.9	6.2	4.3	9.02	73	0	8	0	78	14	71	6.4	52	10	0	0	0.0	2.0
E+ / 0.9	6.1	4.3	9.05	440	0	8	0	78	14	71	6.4	46	10	2,500	100	0.0	2.0
E+ / 0.9	6.1	4.3	9.02	247	0	8	0	78	14	71	6.4	49	10	0	0	0.0	2.0
D+ / 2.5	5.2	5.9	11.53	1,891	0	98	0	0	2	17	1.1	3	8	2,000,000	1,000	0.0	0.0
D+ / 2.5	5.2	5.9	11.50	11	0	98	0	0	2	17	1.1	3	8	0	0	0.0	0.0

Fund Type	Fund Name (99 Pct = Best, 0 Pct = Worst)	Ticker Symbol	Overall Investment Rating	Phone	Performance Rating/Pts	3 Mo	6 Mo	1Yr / Pct	3Yr / Pct (Annualized)	5Yr / Pct (Annualized)	Dividend Yield	Expense Ratio
GEI	TIAA-CREF Infltn Linkd Bd Retail	TCILX	D-	(800) 842-2252	D- / 1.1	3.50	2.55	0.18 /44	-1.46 / 6	2.31 /35	0.09	0.57
GEI	TIAA-CREF Infltn Linkd Bd Retire	TIKRX	D-	(800) 842-2252	D- / 1.1	3.57	2.61	0.22 /44	-1.39 / 6	2.38 /36	0.13	0.51
MM	TIAA-CREF Money Market Inst	TCIXX	C	(800) 842-2252	D+ / 2.3	0.06	0.08	0.08 /40	0.03 /23	0.03 /11	0.08	0.13
GEI	TIAA-CREF Sh Trm Bond Inst	TISIX	B-	(800) 842-2252	C / 4.5	0.91	0.75	1.17 /61	0.97 /42	1.85 /29	1.64	0.27
GEI	TIAA-CREF Sh Trm Bond Prmr	TSTPX	C+	(800) 842-2252	C- / 4.2	0.88	0.67	1.02 /59	0.82 /39	1.69 /28	1.49	0.42
GEI	TIAA-CREF Sh Trm Bond Retail	TCTRX	C+	(800) 842-2252	C- / 3.8	0.74	0.60	0.77 /55	0.63 /36	1.52 /26	1.34	0.58
GEI	TIAA-CREF Sh Trm Bond Retire	TISRX	C+	(800) 842-2252	C- / 4.0	0.85	0.62	0.92 /57	0.72 /37	1.59 /26	1.39	0.52
COI	TIAA-CREF Short-Term Bond Indx	TNSHX	U	(800) 842-2252	U /	0.93	0.52	--	--	--	0.00	N/A
COI	TIAA-CREF Short-Term Bond Indx	TPSHX	U	(800) 842-2252	U /	0.89	0.45	--	--	--	0.00	N/A
COI	TIAA-CREF Short-Term Bond Indx	TESHX	U	(800) 842-2252	U /	0.87	0.40	--	--	--	0.00	N/A
COI	TIAA-CREF Short-Term Bond Indx	TRSHX	U	(800) 842-2252	U /	0.84	0.35	--	--	--	0.00	N/A
COI	TIAACREF Social Choice Bond Inst	TSBIX	B+	(800) 842-2252	B / 8.1	2.64	2.01	1.63 /68	3.67 /81	--	2.45	0.45
COI	TIAACREF Social Choice Bond Prmr	TSBPX	B+	(800) 842-2252	B / 8.0	2.51	1.84	1.38 /65	3.48 /80	--	2.31	0.61
COI	TIAACREF Social Choice Bond Ret	TSBBX	B+	(800) 842-2252	B / 8.0	2.48	1.89	1.38 /65	3.41 /79	--	2.21	0.70
COI	TIAACREF Social Choice Bond Rtl	TSBRX	B+	(800) 842-2252	B / 7.9	2.47	1.87	1.25 /62	3.33 /79	--	2.18	0.73
MUN	TIAA-CREF T/E Bond Inst	TITIX	B+	(800) 842-2252	B / 8.2	1.37	2.83	2.61 /81	2.12 /78	4.65 /83	2.00	0.35
MUN	TIAA-CREF T/E Bond Retail	TIXRX	B	(800) 842-2252	B / 7.8	1.30	2.67	2.21 /78	1.80 /74	4.36 /80	1.71	0.63
GES	Timothy Plan Fixed Income A	TFIAX	D+	(800) 662-0201	D / 1.7	2.61	1.26	0.31 /46	0.88 /40	2.30 /35	2.50	1.29
GES	Timothy Plan Fixed Income C	TFICX	C-	(800) 662-0201	D+ / 2.9	2.25	0.75	-0.49 /26	0.09 /27	1.54 /26	1.80	2.04
COI	Timothy Plan Fixed Income I	TPFIX	U	(800) 662-0201	U /	2.65	1.45	0.62 /52	--	--	2.94	1.04
COH	Timothy Plan High Yield A	TPHAX	E+	(800) 662-0201	D- / 1.1	3.50	1.39	-3.04 /11	0.44 /32	3.20 /48	4.31	1.31
COH	Timothy Plan High Yield C	TPHCX	E+	(800) 662-0201	D- / 1.4	3.33	1.04	-3.71 / 9	-0.30 /13	2.45 /37	3.50	2.06
COH	Timothy Plan High Yield I	TPHIX	U	(800) 662-0201	U /	3.61	1.56	-2.74 /12	--	--	4.82	1.07
COH	Toews Hedged High Yield Bond	THHYX	C+	(877) 558-6397	B- / 7.4	1.90	1.20	1.27 /63	2.89 /75	4.53 /68	1.07	1.66
GL	Toews Unconstrained Income	TUIFX	U	(877) 558-6397	U /	2.53	1.62	0.92 /57	--	--	1.11	1.62
GEI	Touchstone Active Bond A	TOBAX	C-	(800) 543-0407	C / 4.4	3.18	2.80	0.63 /52	2.03 /62	3.66 /56	2.87	1.16
GEI	Touchstone Active Bond C	TODCX	C+	(800) 543-0407	C / 5.1	2.92	2.33	-0.15 /30	1.23 /47	2.87 /43	2.52	2.03
COI	Touchstone Active Bond Instl	TOBIX	B+	(800) 543-0407	B- / 7.1	3.27	2.98	0.97 /58	2.35 /68	3.94 /61	3.35	0.92
COI	Touchstone Active Bond Y	TOBYX	B+	(800) 543-0407	C+ / 6.9	3.15	2.84	0.79 /55	2.26 /67	3.87 /60	3.27	0.88
GES	Touchstone Flexible Income A	FFSAX	C	(800) 543-0407	C / 5.3	1.69	2.08	2.13 /73	2.92 /76	4.44 /67	2.77	1.36
GES	Touchstone Flexible Income C	FRACX	C+	(800) 543-0407	C+ / 6.5	1.43	1.64	1.33 /64	2.14 /64	3.67 /56	2.26	2.11
GEL	Touchstone Flexible Income Inst	TFSLX	A-	(800) 543-0407	B / 8.0	1.77	2.25	2.57 /75	3.31 /79	--	3.27	0.96
GES	Touchstone Flexible Income Y	MXIIX	A-	(800) 543-0407	B / 7.9	1.75	2.20	2.38 /74	3.18 /78	4.69 /70	3.18	1.02
COH	Touchstone High Yield A	THYAX	E	(800) 543-0407	E+ / 0.7	1.99	0.13	-5.78 / 3	0.40 /31	3.57 /54	5.37	1.15
COH	Touchstone High Yield C	THYCX	E	(800) 543-0407	E+ / 0.9	1.68	-0.25	-6.51 / 3	-0.35 /13	2.77 /41	4.85	1.87
COH	Touchstone High Yield Inst	THIYX	D-	(800) 543-0407	D+ / 2.8	2.03	0.30	-5.44 / 4	0.78 /39	--	5.83	0.75
COH	Touchstone High Yield Y	THYYX	E+	(800) 543-0407	D / 2.2	2.00	0.25	-5.62 / 4	0.65 /36	3.83 /59	5.75	0.87
MUI	Touchstone Ohio Tax-Free Bond A	TOHAX	B	(800) 543-0407	B / 7.8	1.39	2.35	3.02 /85	3.13 /89	4.92 /85	2.90	1.08
MUI	Touchstone Ohio Tax-Free Bond C	TOHCX	B+	(800) 543-0407	B / 8.2	1.13	1.98	2.18 /78	2.34 /81	4.14 /79	2.31	1.92
GEI	Touchstone Tot Rtn Bond A	TCPAX	C-	(800) 543-0407	C- / 4.0	2.77	1.63	0.90 /57	1.89 /59	3.64 /55	2.50	1.27
GEI	Touchstone Tot Rtn Bond C	TCPCX	C	(800) 543-0407	C / 4.9	2.69	1.25	0.16 /43	1.16 /46	--	1.90	2.28
GEI	Touchstone Tot Rtn Bond Inst	TCPNX	B	(800) 543-0407	C+ / 6.9	2.86	1.82	1.29 /63	2.30 /67	--	3.02	0.62
GEI	Touchstone Tot Rtn Bond Y	TCPYX	B-	(800) 543-0407	C+ / 6.7	2.93	1.86	1.23 /62	2.16 /65	3.95 /61	2.85	0.71
GEI	Touchstone Ut Sh Dr Fxd Inc A	TSDAX	C	(800) 543-0407	D+ / 2.6	0.42	0.47	0.63 /52	0.55 /34	0.93 /20	1.25	0.99
GEI	Touchstone Ut Sh Dr Fxd Inc C	TSDCX	C+	(800) 543-0407	D+ / 2.7	0.31	0.23	0.14 /42	0.09 /27	0.37 /17	0.79	1.48
GEI	Touchstone Ut Sh Dr Fxd Inc Inst	TSDIX	B	(800) 543-0407	C- / 4.2	0.49	0.62	0.93 /57	0.88 /41	1.22 /22	1.57	0.48
GEI	Touchstone Ut Sh Dr Fxd Inc Y	TSYYX	B	(800) 543-0407	C- / 4.1	0.48	0.59	0.88 /57	0.83 /40	1.18 /22	1.53	0.52
USS	Touchstone Ut Sh Dr Fxd Inc Z	TSDOX	B-	(800) 543-0407	C- / 3.6	0.42	0.47	0.63 /52	0.59 /35	1.00 /20	1.28	0.76
COH	Transamerica Bond I2		D+	(888) 233-4339	C+ / 5.6	2.82	1.33	-2.90 /12	2.01 /62	4.91 /71	4.75	0.70
COI	Transamerica Bond R6	TABSX	U	(888) 233-4339	U /	2.82	1.33	--	--	--	0.00	0.70
GEI	Transamerica Core Bond I2		B+	(888) 233-4339	C+ / 6.9	2.50	1.80	1.51 /67	2.32 /68	3.69 /56	2.37	0.52
EM	Transamerica Emerging Mkts Debt A	EMTAX	E	(888) 233-4339	E+ / 0.9	5.56	6.63	0.49 /49	-0.98 / 9	--	4.56	1.11

Performance: Total Return % through 3/31/16; Incl. in Returns: Dividend Yield, Expense Ratio.

• Denotes fund is closed to new investors
* Denotes fund is included in Section II

RISK			NET ASSETS		ASSET							FUND MANAGER		MINIMUM		LOADS	
Risk Rating/Pts	3 Yr Avg Standard Deviation	Avg Duration	NAV As of 3/31/16	Total $(Mil)	Cash %	Gov. Bond %	Muni. Bond %	Corp. Bond %	Other %	Portfolio Turnover Ratio	Avg Coupon Rate	Manager Quality Pct	Manager Tenure (Years)	Initial Purch. $	Additional Purch. $	Front End Load	Back End Load
D+ / 2.6	5.2	5.9	11.25	125	0	98	0	0	2	17	1.1	3	8	2,500	100	0.0	0.0
D+ / 2.5	5.2	5.9	11.61	217	0	98	0	0	2	17	1.1	3	8	0	0	0.0	0.0
A+ / 9.9	N/A	N/A	1.00	339	100	0	0	0	0	0	0.1	64	17	2,000,000	1,000	0.0	0.0
A- / 9.1	1.1	1.6	10.34	1,268	0	0	0	0	100	114	2.4	74	10	2,000,000	1,000	0.0	0.0
A- / 9.1	1.1	1.6	10.35	12	0	0	0	0	100	114	2.4	68	10	0	0	0.0	0.0
A- / 9.2	1.1	1.6	10.34	139	0	0	0	0	100	114	2.4	56	10	2,500	100	0.0	0.0
A- / 9.2	1.1	1.6	10.35	97	0	0	0	0	100	114	2.4	60	10	0	0	0.0	0.0
U /	N/A	1.9	10.03	103	0	0	0	0	100	0	1.3	N/A	1	10,000,000	1,000	0.0	0.0
U /	N/A	1.9	10.03	1	0	0	0	0	100	0	1.3	N/A	1	0	0	0.0	0.0
U /	N/A	1.9	10.03	5	0	0	0	0	100	0	1.3	N/A	1	0	0	0.0	0.0
U /	N/A	1.9	10.03	2	0	0	0	0	100	0	1.3	N/A	1	2,500	100	0.0	0.0
C / 5.4	3.3	5.9	10.32	376	0	0	0	0	100	459	3.3	94	4	2,000,000	1,000	0.0	0.0
C / 5.4	3.3	5.9	10.31	29	0	0	0	0	100	459	3.3	93	4	0	0	0.0	0.0
C / 5.5	3.3	5.9	10.32	223	0	0	0	0	100	459	3.3	92	4	0	0	0.0	0.0
C+ / 5.6	3.2	5.9	10.31	65	0	0	0	0	100	459	3.3	92	4	2,500	100	0.0	0.0
C / 5.3	3.3	5.4	10.72	50	0	0	0	0	100	155	4.6	22	6	2,000,000	1,000	0.0	0.0
C / 5.3	3.3	5.4	10.73	296	0	0	0	0	100	155	4.6	17	6	2,500	100	0.0	0.0
B- / 7.0	2.9	4.2	10.31	78	2	32	0	31	35	28	0.0	19	12	1,000	0	4.5	0.0
B- / 7.1	2.8	4.2	9.93	9	2	32	0	31	35	28	0.0	10	12	1,000	0	0.0	0.0
U /	N/A	4.2	10.24	N/A	2	32	0	31	35	28	0.0	N/A	12	25,000	5,000	0.0	0.0
D- / 1.0	6.0	N/A	8.57	42	6	0	0	93	1	39	0.0	22	9	1,000	0	4.5	0.0
D- / 1.0	6.0	N/A	8.67	3	6	0	0	93	1	39	0.0	12	9	1,000	0	0.0	0.0
U /	N/A	N/A	8.58	1	6	0	0	93	1	39	0.0	N/A	9	25,000	5,000	0.0	0.0
C / 4.5	3.2	N/A	10.71	317	0	0	0	0	100	797	0.0	96	6	10,000	100	0.0	0.0
U /	N/A	N/A	9.96	91	50	31	0	11	8	632	0.0	N/A	3	10,000	100	0.0	0.0
C+ / 6.8	2.9	5.9	10.31	26	2	23	0	43	32	349	0.0	68	15	2,500	50	4.8	0.0
C+ / 6.9	2.9	5.9	9.56	7	2	23	0	43	32	349	0.0	36	15	2,500	50	0.0	0.0
C+ / 6.7	3.0	5.9	10.30	7	2	23	0	43	32	349	0.0	82	15	500,000	50	0.0	0.0
C+ / 6.9	2.9	5.9	10.30	64	2	23	0	43	32	349	0.0	81	15	2,500	50	0.0	0.0
C+ / 6.2	3.1	4.6	10.58	58	5	14	3	37	41	102	6.5	88	14	2,500	50	5.8	0.0
C+ / 5.9	3.2	4.6	10.44	45	5	14	3	37	41	102	6.5	66	14	2,500	50	0.0	0.0
C+ / 6.1	3.1	4.6	10.61	82	5	14	3	37	41	102	6.5	91	14	500,000	50	0.0	0.0
C+ / 6.3	3.1	4.6	10.61	358	5	14	3	37	41	102	6.5	90	14	2,500	50	0.0	0.0
E+ / 0.9	6.2	4.5	7.74	23	2	0	0	97	1	35	0.0	20	17	2,500	50	4.8	0.0
E+ / 0.9	6.2	4.5	7.72	18	2	0	0	97	1	35	0.0	11	17	2,500	50	0.0	0.0
E+ / 0.9	6.2	4.5	7.95	73	2	0	0	97	1	35	0.0	28	17	500,000	50	0.0	0.0
E+ / 0.9	6.1	4.5	7.95	84	2	0	0	97	1	35	0.0	25	17	2,500	50	0.0	0.0
C / 5.5	3.3	4.4	11.87	52	1	0	98	0	1	23	0.0	51	30	2,500	50	4.8	0.0
C / 5.5	3.3	4.4	11.88	7	1	0	98	0	1	23	0.0	27	30	2,500	50	0.0	0.0
C+ / 6.6	3.0	5.5	10.22	6	6	6	3	33	52	19	0.0	42	5	2,500	50	4.8	0.0
C+ / 6.6	3.0	5.5	10.21	3	6	6	3	33	52	19	0.0	22	5	2,500	50	0.0	0.0
C+ / 6.5	3.0	5.5	10.23	149	6	6	3	33	52	19	0.0	56	5	500,000	50	0.0	0.0
C+ / 6.4	3.0	5.5	10.24	42	6	6	3	33	52	19	0.0	50	5	2,500	50	0.0	0.0
A+ / 9.9	0.3	0.7	9.30	10	7	0	4	38	51	132	0.0	80	8	2,500	50	2.0	0.0
A+ / 9.9	0.3	0.7	9.30	9	7	0	4	38	51	132	0.0	59	8	2,500	50	0.0	0.0
A+ / 9.9	0.3	0.7	9.30	105	7	0	4	38	51	132	0.0	87	8	500,000	50	0.0	0.0
A+ / 9.9	0.3	0.7	9.30	241	7	0	4	38	51	132	0.0	86	8	2,500	50	0.0	0.0
A+ / 9.9	0.3	0.7	9.30	224	7	0	4	38	51	132	0.0	81	8	2,500	50	0.0	0.0
D / 1.7	5.5	5.1	9.06	470	3	12	0	65	20	46	11.8	83	9	0	0	0.0	0.0
U /	N/A	5.1	9.06	N/A	3	12	0	65	20	46	11.8	N/A	9	0	0	0.0	0.0
B- / 7.1	2.8	4.9	10.12	1,322	6	27	0	24	43	17	14.1	62	1	0	0	0.0	0.0
E / 0.4	8.6	5.0	9.74	43	6	61	2	29	2	237	12.8	32	5	1,000	50	4.8	0.0

Fund Type	Fund Name (99 Pct = Best, 0 Pct = Worst)	Ticker Symbol	Overall Investment Rating	Phone	PERFORMANCE Perfor-mance Rating/Pts	Total Return % through 3/31/16 3 Mo	6 Mo	1Yr / Pct	Annualized 3Yr / Pct	Annualized 5Yr / Pct	Incl. in Returns Dividend Yield	Expense Ratio
EM	Transamerica Emerging Mkts Debt C	EMTCX	**E**	(888) 233-4339	**D- / 1.3**	5.29	6.19	-0.27 /28	-1.67 / 5	--	4.05	1.85
EM	Transamerica Emerging Mkts Debt I	EMTIX	**D-**	(888) 233-4339	**C- / 3.5**	5.66	6.75	0.78 /55	-0.63 /11	--	5.18	0.81
EM	Transamerica Emerging Mkts Debt I2		**D-**	(888) 233-4339	**C- / 3.7**	5.69	6.91	0.98 /58	-0.53 /11	--	5.27	0.71
EM	Transamerica Emerging Mkts Debt	TAEDX	**U**	(888) 233-4339	**U /**	5.58	6.81	--	--	--	0.00	0.71
COI	Transamerica Flexible Income A	IDITX	**C-**	(888) 233-4339	**C- / 3.0**	1.30	0.42	-0.81 /23	1.81 /58	4.15 /64	3.40	0.89
COI ●	Transamerica Flexible Income B	IFLBX	**C-**	(888) 233-4339	**C- / 3.7**	1.06	-0.05	-1.67 /17	0.95 /42	3.28 /50	2.67	1.72
COI	Transamerica Flexible Income C	IFLLX	**C-**	(888) 233-4339	**C- / 4.0**	1.13	0.06	-1.52 /18	1.09 /44	3.41 /52	2.86	1.60
COI	Transamerica Flexible Income I	TFXIX	**C+**	(888) 233-4339	**C+ / 5.9**	1.37	0.55	-0.53 /26	2.09 /63	4.44 /67	3.85	0.61
COI	Transamerica Flexible Income I2		**C+**	(888) 233-4339	**C+ / 5.9**	1.39	0.49	-0.55 /26	2.15 /65	4.54 /68	3.94	0.51
GEL	Transamerica Flexible Income R6	TAFLX	**U**	(888) 233-4339	**U /**	1.40	0.61	--	--	--	0.00	0.52
LP	Transamerica Floating Rate A	TFLAX	**U**	(888) 233-4339	**U /**	1.91	0.98	1.45 /66	--	--	3.53	1.12
LP	Transamerica Floating Rate C	TFLCX	**U**	(888) 233-4339	**U /**	1.72	0.60	0.70 /53	--	--	2.95	1.88
LP	Transamerica Floating Rate I	TFLIX	**U**	(888) 233-4339	**U /**	1.76	1.09	1.36 /64	--	--	3.94	0.89
LP	Transamerica Floating Rate I2		**U**	(888) 233-4339	**U /**	1.98	1.12	1.73 /69	--	--	3.98	0.81
GL	Transamerica Global Bond A	ATGBX	**U**	(888) 233-4339	**U /**	7.61	7.48	3.79 /80	--	--	0.68	1.15
GL	Transamerica Global Bond C	CTGBX	**U**	(888) 233-4339	**U /**	7.40	6.97	2.95 /76	--	--	0.04	1.90
GL	Transamerica Global Bond I	ITGBX	**U**	(888) 233-4339	**U /**	7.61	7.52	3.95 /81	--	--	0.96	0.93
GL	Transamerica Global Bond I2		**U**	(888) 233-4339	**U /**	7.73	7.63	4.06 /82	--	--	0.95	0.80
GES	Transamerica High Yield Bond A	IHIYX	**D-**	(888) 233-4339	**D- / 1.3**	2.39	-0.05	-4.45 / 6	1.26 /47	4.62 /69	5.56	1.01
GES ●	Transamerica High Yield Bond B	INCBX	**D-**	(888) 233-4339	**D / 1.7**	2.16	-0.37	-5.25 / 5	0.43 /32	3.81 /58	4.94	1.81
GES	Transamerica High Yield Bond C	INCLX	**D-**	(888) 233-4339	**D / 1.7**	2.21	-0.31	-5.16 / 5	0.48 /33	3.88 /60	5.09	1.74
COH	Transamerica High Yield Bond I	TDHIX	**D**	(888) 233-4339	**C- / 4.2**	2.44	0.09	-4.25 / 7	1.47 /52	4.91 /71	6.09	0.74
GES	Transamerica High Yield Bond I2		**D**	(888) 233-4339	**C / 4.4**	2.46	0.14	-4.13 / 7	1.58 /54	5.02 /72	6.19	0.64
COH	Transamerica High Yield Bond R6	TAHBX	**U**	(888) 233-4339	**U /**	2.47	0.15	--	--	--	0.00	0.64
MUH	Transamerica High Yield Muni A	THAYX	**U**	(888) 233-4339	**U /**	2.31	4.98	6.31 /99	--	--	2.44	1.30
MUH	Transamerica High Yield Muni C	THCYX	**U**	(888) 233-4339	**U /**	2.17	4.68	5.69 /99	--	--	1.97	2.05
MUH	Transamerica High Yield Muni I	THYIX	**U**	(888) 233-4339	**U /**	2.26	5.05	6.36 /99	--	--	2.66	1.08
GEI	Transamerica Inflation Opptys A	TIOAX	**U**	(888) 233-4339	**U /**	2.98	1.79	-1.22 /20	--	--	0.00	0.99
GEI	Transamerica Inflation Opptys C	TIOCX	**U**	(888) 233-4339	**U /**	2.79	1.38	-2.05 /15	--	--	0.00	1.78
GEI	Transamerica Inflation Opptys I	ITIOX	**U**	(888) 233-4339	**U /**	3.08	1.89	-1.02 /21	--	--	0.00	0.79
GEI	Transamerica Inflation Opptys I2		**U**	(888) 233-4339	**U /**	3.08	1.89	-0.92 /22	--	--	0.00	0.66
COI	Transamerica Intermediate Bond I2		**U**	(888) 233-4339	**U /**	2.48	2.11	1.14 /61	--	--	1.66	0.42
MUN	Transamerica Intermediate Muni A	TAMUX	**A+**	(888) 233-4339	**A+ / 9.8**	1.87	3.58	4.84 /97	5.79 /99	--	1.53	0.96
MUN	Transamerica Intermediate Muni C	TCMUX	**A+**	(888) 233-4339	**A+ / 9.9**	1.74	3.30	4.26 /95	5.17 /99	--	1.05	1.71
MUN	Transamerica Intermediate Muni I	TIMUX	**A+**	(888) 233-4339	**A+ / 9.9**	1.86	3.59	5.00 /98	5.89 /99	--	1.68	0.71
GEI	Transamerica Prt Core Bond	DVGCX	**C+**	(888) 233-4339	**C+ / 6.5**	2.52	1.93	0.71 /53	2.09 /63	3.76 /58	1.88	0.97
COI	Transamerica Prt High Quality Bond	DVHQX	**C+**	(888) 233-4339	**C- / 3.2**	0.89	0.44	0.54 /50	0.31 /30	0.90 /20	1.52	1.00
COH	Transamerica Prt High Yield Bond	DVHYX	**D**	(888) 233-4339	**C / 4.8**	2.92	0.79	-3.75 / 9	1.69 /56	4.48 /67	5.76	1.19
USS	Transamerica Prt Inflation-Prot Sec	DVIGX	**E+**	(888) 233-4339	**E+ / 0.9**	3.63	2.77	-0.41 /27	-1.73 / 5	2.08 /32	0.12	1.03
GEI	Transamerica Prt Inst Core Bond	DICBX	**B-**	(888) 233-4339	**B- / 7.0**	2.54	2.03	1.06 /60	2.39 /69	4.07 /63	2.22	0.72
GEI	Transamerica Prt Inst High Qual Bd	DIHQX	**B-**	(888) 233-4339	**C- / 3.9**	1.04	0.58	0.87 /56	0.65 /36	1.26 /23	1.75	0.77
COH	Transamerica Prt Inst High Yld Bd	DIHYX	**D**	(888) 233-4339	**C / 5.2**	2.95	0.83	-3.57 / 9	1.93 /60	4.72 /70	5.98	0.92
USS	Transamerica Prt Inst Infl Prot Sec	DIIGX	**D-**	(888) 233-4339	**D- / 1.2**	3.72	2.95	-0.10 /30	-1.37 / 7	2.47 /37	0.20	0.78
* COI	Transamerica Short-Term Bond A	ITAAX	**C+**	(888) 233-4339	**C- / 3.5**	0.81	0.43	0.40 /48	1.27 /48	2.35 /36	2.02	0.84
COI	Transamerica Short-Term Bond C	ITACX	**C**	(888) 233-4339	**C- / 3.2**	0.63	0.06	-0.36 /27	0.47 /33	1.58 /26	1.31	1.60
COI	Transamerica Short-Term Bond I	TSTIX	**B+**	(888) 233-4339	**C / 5.2**	0.97	0.52	0.68 /53	1.50 /52	2.56 /39	2.28	0.63
COI	Transamerica Short-Term Bond I2		**B+**	(888) 233-4339	**C / 5.3**	0.89	0.57	0.68 /53	1.57 /54	2.66 /40	2.38	0.53
COI	Transamerica Short-Term Bond R6	TASTX	**U**	(888) 233-4339	**U /**	0.89	0.57	--	--	--	0.00	0.53
GEI	Transamerica Total Return I2		**C-**	(888) 233-4339	**C / 5.4**	1.91	2.46	0.43 /48	1.36 /50	3.34 /51	2.97	0.78
USA	TransWestern Inst Sht Dur Govt Bond	TWSGX	**C+**	(855) 881-2380	**C- / 4.2**	0.94	0.34	0.48 /49	1.04 /44	1.59 /26	1.69	0.70
GES	Tributary Income Inst	FOINX	**A**	(800) 662-4203	**B- / 7.3**	2.86	2.01	1.75 /69	2.53 /71	3.98 /61	2.60	1.12
COI	Tributary Income Inst Plus	FOIPX	**A**	(800) 662-4203	**B- / 7.4**	2.87	2.05	1.79 /70	2.64 /73	--	2.74	0.90

● Denotes fund is closed to new investors
* Denotes fund is included in Section II

RISK			NET ASSETS		ASSET							FUND MANAGER		MINIMUM		LOADS	
Risk Rating/Pts	3 Yr Avg Standard Deviation	Avg Duration	NAV As of 3/31/16	Total $(Mil)	Cash %	Gov. Bond %	Muni. Bond %	Corp. Bond %	Other %	Portfolio Turnover Ratio	Avg Coupon Rate	Manager Quality Pct	Manager Tenure (Years)	Initial Purch. $	Additional Purch. $	Front End Load	Back End Load
E / 0.4	8.5	5.0	9.70	14	6	61	2	29	2	237	12.8	17	5	1,000	50	0.0	0.0
E / 0.4	8.5	5.0	9.75	566	6	61	2	29	2	237	12.8	43	5	1,000,000	0	0.0	0.0
E / 0.4	8.5	5.0	9.75	74	6	61	2	29	2	237	12.8	46	5	0	0	0.0	0.0
U /	N/A	5.0	9.74	N/A	6	61	2	29	2	237	12.8	N/A	5	0	0	0.0	0.0
C+ / 6.8	2.9	3.4	9.05	74	0	12	0	59	29	27	14.4	73	11	1,000	50	4.8	0.0
C+ / 6.7	3.0	3.4	9.06	2	0	12	0	59	29	27	14.4	37	11	1,000	50	0.0	0.0
C+ / 6.9	2.9	3.4	8.99	61	0	12	0	59	29	27	14.4	42	11	1,000	50	0.0	0.0
C+ / 6.6	3.0	3.4	9.06	148	0	12	0	59	29	27	14.4	81	11	1,000,000	0	0.0	0.0
C+ / 6.9	2.9	3.4	9.06	131	0	12	0	59	29	27	14.4	83	11	0	0	0.0	0.0
U /	N/A	3.4	9.06	1	0	12	0	59	29	27	14.4	N/A	11	0	0	0.0	0.0
U /	N/A	N/A	9.73	4	5	0	0	79	16	41	4.8	N/A	3	1,000	50	4.8	0.0
U /	N/A	N/A	9.73	5	5	0	0	79	16	41	4.8	N/A	3	1,000	50	0.0	0.0
U /	N/A	N/A	9.70	4	5	0	0	79	16	41	4.8	N/A	3	1,000,000	0	0.0	0.0
U /	N/A	N/A	9.73	340	5	0	0	79	16	41	4.8	N/A	3	0	0	0.0	0.0
U /	N/A	5.6	9.61	N/A	8	70	5	14	3	195	7.1	N/A	N/A	1,000	50	4.8	0.0
U /	N/A	5.6	9.58	N/A	8	70	5	14	3	195	7.1	N/A	N/A	1,000	50	0.0	0.0
U /	N/A	5.6	9.61	N/A	8	70	5	14	3	195	7.1	N/A	N/A	1,000,000	0	0.0	0.0
U /	N/A	5.6	9.62	44	8	70	5	14	3	195	7.1	N/A	N/A	0	0	0.0	0.0
D / 2.1	5.6	4.0	8.51	123	2	0	0	95	3	61	8.6	45	10	1,000	50	4.8	0.0
D / 2.1	5.6	4.0	8.52	3	2	0	0	95	3	61	8.6	22	10	1,000	50	0.0	0.0
D / 2.0	5.6	4.0	8.47	52	2	0	0	95	3	61	8.6	24	10	1,000	50	0.0	0.0
D / 1.6	5.5	4.0	8.57	117	2	0	0	95	3	61	8.6	57	10	1,000,000	0	0.0	0.0
D / 2.1	5.6	4.0	8.59	747	2	0	0	95	3	61	8.6	58	10	0	0	0.0	0.0
U /	N/A	4.0	8.59	1	2	0	0	95	3	61	8.6	N/A	10	0	0	0.0	0.0
U /	N/A	6.0	11.76	47	3	0	96	0	1	78	13.2	N/A	3	1,000	50	3.3	0.0
U /	N/A	6.0	11.77	8	3	0	96	0	1	78	13.2	N/A	3	1,000	50	0.0	0.0
U /	N/A	6.0	11.77	36	3	0	96	0	1	78	13.2	N/A	3	1,000,000	0	0.0	0.0
U /	N/A	6.3	9.68	1	1	75	0	17	7	35	8.6	N/A	2	1,000	50	4.8	0.0
U /	N/A	6.3	9.58	N/A	1	75	0	17	7	35	8.6	N/A	2	1,000	50	0.0	0.0
U /	N/A	6.3	9.71	N/A	1	75	0	17	7	35	8.6	N/A	2	1,000,000	0	0.0	0.0
U /	N/A	6.3	9.72	180	1	75	0	17	7	35	8.6	N/A	2	0	0	0.0	0.0
U /	N/A	5.2	10.20	1,129	0	34	0	34	32	50	11.6	N/A	2	0	0	0.0	0.0
C+ / 5.6	3.2	5.3	11.52	258	8	0	91	0	1	55	7.9	97	4	1,000	50	4.8	0.0
C+ / 5.7	3.2	5.3	11.50	110	8	0	91	0	1	55	7.9	95	4	1,000	50	0.0	0.0
C+ / 5.7	3.2	5.3	11.57	496	8	0	91	0	1	55	7.9	97	4	1,000,000	0	0.0	0.0
C+ / 6.0	3.1	5.1	13.06	385	0	33	0	34	33	46	11.8	45	5	5,000	0	0.0	0.0
A+ / 9.6	0.7	1.7	11.20	107	0	12	0	27	61	70	9.6	58	26	5,000	0	0.0	0.0
D- / 1.4	5.7	3.9	8.03	118	4	0	0	95	1	44	8.6	66	16	5,000	0	0.0	0.0
D+ / 2.5	5.1	7.2	11.14	120	0	99	0	0	1	54	9.9	4	6	5,000	0	0.0	0.0
C+ / 6.0	3.1	5.1	10.80	365	0	33	0	34	33	46	11.8	57	5	5,000	0	0.0	0.0
A+ / 9.6	0.7	1.7	10.17	55	0	12	0	27	61	70	9.6	73	26	5,000	0	0.0	0.0
D- / 1.4	5.6	3.9	8.02	315	4	0	0	95	1	44	8.6	77	16	5,000	0	0.0	0.0
D+ / 2.5	5.1	7.2	9.77	81	0	99	0	0	1	54	9.9	5	6	5,000	0	0.0	0.0
A- / 9.2	1.1	1.5	10.13	896	1	0	0	70	29	66	9.2	87	5	1,000	50	2.5	0.0
A- / 9.2	1.1	1.5	10.11	674	1	0	0	70	29	66	9.2	60	5	1,000	50	0.0	0.0
A- / 9.2	1.1	1.5	9.96	883	1	0	0	70	29	66	9.2	89	5	1,000,000	0	0.0	0.0
A- / 9.2	1.1	1.5	9.95	925	1	0	0	70	29	66	9.2	90	5	0	0	0.0	0.0
U /	N/A	1.5	9.95	N/A	1	0	0	70	29	66	9.2	N/A	5	0	0	0.0	0.0
C / 4.8	3.6	4.6	10.12	584	0	30	2	24	44	62	14.5	22	8	0	0	0.0	0.0
A- / 9.0	1.3	N/A	9.90	357	0	15	0	0	85	25	0.0	73	5	2,000,000	500,000	0.0	0.3
B- / 7.3	2.8	5.1	10.41	7	1	17	2	24	56	52	3.7	77	13	1,000	50	0.0	0.0
B- / 7.3	2.8	5.1	10.41	187	1	17	2	24	56	52	3.7	89	13	5,000,000	50	0.0	0.0

Fund Type	Fund Name (99 Pct = Best, 0 Pct = Worst)	Ticker Symbol	Overall Investment Rating	Phone	Performance Rating/Pts	3 Mo	6 Mo	1Yr / Pct	Annualized 3Yr / Pct	Annualized 5Yr / Pct	Dividend Yield	Expense Ratio
MUN	Tributary Nebraska Tax Free InstlP	FONPX	**C-**	(800) 662-4203	**D+ / 2.8**	1.15	1.28	0.37 /51	-0.16 /14	0.19 /16	0.80	0.78
COI	Tributary Short/Int Bond Inst Plus	FOSPX	**B+**	(800) 662-4203	**C / 4.9**	1.16	0.88	1.31 /63	1.21 /46	--	1.95	0.80
GEI	Tributary Short/Intmdt Bond Inst	FOSIX	**B-**	(800) 662-4203	**C / 4.5**	1.12	0.68	1.09 /60	0.95 /42	1.87 /30	1.74	1.04
GEI	Trust for Credit UltSh Dur Gov Inv	TCUYX	**C-**	(800) 342-5828	**D / 1.8**	0.07	-0.04	-0.02 /31	0.01 /16	--	0.40	0.40
MTG	Trust for Credit UltSh Dur Gov TCU	TCUUX	**C**	(800) 342-5828	**D / 2.2**	0.07	-0.03	0.01 /32	0.04 /23	0.24 /16	0.43	0.37
USS	Trust for Credit Uns Sh Dur Ptf Inv	TCUEX	**C+**	(800) 342-5828	**C- / 3.2**	0.75	0.20	0.49 /49	0.33 /30	--	0.69	0.39
GEI	Trust for Credit Uns Sh Dur TCU	TCUDX	**C+**	(800) 342-5828	**C- / 3.2**	0.75	0.21	0.52 /50	0.36 /31	0.71 /18	0.72	0.36
USS	UBS Core Plus Bond A	BNBDX	**C-**	(888) 793-8637	**C / 4.4**	2.18	1.65	0.16 /43	2.20 /66	3.74 /57	2.01	1.75
USS	UBS Core Plus Bond C	BNOCX	**C**	(888) 793-8637	**C / 5.5**	1.99	1.32	-0.42 /27	1.67 /55	3.22 /49	1.64	2.38
USS	UBS Core Plus Bond P	BPBDX	**B-**	(888) 793-8637	**C+ / 6.8**	2.23	1.74	0.38 /48	2.41 /69	3.98 /61	2.33	1.45
GL	UBS Fixed Income Opportunities A	FNOAX	**D-**	(888) 793-8637	**E- / 0.1**	-4.72	-4.60	-7.52 / 2	-3.61 / 2	-1.25 / 1	0.46	1.90
GL	UBS Fixed Income Opportunities C	FNOCX	**D-**	(888) 793-8637	**E- / 0.1**	-4.84	-4.74	-8.00 / 1	-4.08 / 2	-1.74 / 1	0.06	2.48
GL	UBS Fixed Income Opportunities P	FNOYX	**D-**	(888) 793-8637	**E- / 0.2**	-4.61	-4.43	-7.33 / 2	-3.35 / 2	-0.99 / 2	0.69	1.70
MUN	UBS Municipal Bond A	UMBAX	**U**	(888) 793-8637	**U /**	1.55	3.46	4.36 /96	--	--	1.54	1.46
MUN	UBS Municipal Bond C	UMBCX	**U**	(888) 793-8637	**U /**	1.56	3.35	3.89 /93	--	--	1.14	1.98
MUN	UBS Municipal Bond P	UMBPX	**U**	(888) 793-8637	**U /**	1.69	3.67	4.60 /97	--	--	1.81	1.23
MMT	UBS PaineWebber RMA CA Muni	RCAXX	**U**	(800) 647-1568	**U /**	--	--	--	--	--	0.01	0.63
MM	UBS PaineWebber RMA Money Fund	RMAXX	**U**	(800) 647-1568	**U /**	--	--	--	--	--	0.01	0.56
MM	UBS PaineWebber RMA Retirement	PWRXX	**U**	(800) 647-1568	**U /**	--	--	--	--	--	0.01	0.68
MM	UBS Select Prime Inst	SELXX	**C**	(888) 793-8637	**D+ / 2.6**	0.07	0.11	0.14 /42	0.07 /26	0.09 /14	0.14	0.18
MM	UBS Select Prime Investor	SPIXX	**U**	(888) 793-8637	**U /**	--	--	--	--	--	0.02	0.60
MM	UBS Select Prime Pfd	SPPXX	**C**	(888) 793-8637	**D+ / 2.7**	0.08	0.13	0.18 /44	0.11 /27	0.13 /15	0.18	0.18
MMT	UBS Select Tax-Free Investor	SFRXX	**C-**	(888) 793-8637	**D / 2.0**	0.00	0.01	0.02 /37	0.01 /21	0.01 / 9	0.02	0.92
MM	UBS Select Treas Inst	SETXX	**C**	(888) 793-8637	**D / 2.1**	0.03	0.04	0.05 /39	0.02 /21	0.02 / 9	0.05	0.18
MM	UBS Select Treas Pfd	STPXX	**C**	(888) 793-8637	**D+ / 2.3**	0.04	0.05	0.06 /40	0.03 /23	0.02 / 9	0.06	0.18
MM	UBS Select Treasury Investor	STRXX	**U**	(888) 793-8637	**U /**	0.00	0.01	0.02 /35	0.01 /18	0.01 / 6	0.02	0.60
GEI	Universal Inst Core Plus Fxd Inc I	UFIPX	**B**	(800) 869-6397	**B / 7.9**	3.22	2.92	1.13 /61	3.15 /78	4.75 /70	3.41	0.80
GEI	Universal Inst Core Plus Fxd Inc II	UCFIX	**B**	(800) 869-6397	**B / 7.6**	3.03	2.73	0.85 /56	2.87 /75	4.46 /67	3.25	1.05
EM	Universal Inst Emer Mrkt Debt I	UEMDX	**D-**	(800) 869-6397	**C- / 4.2**	4.70	6.27	1.36 /64	-0.15 /14	3.98 /61	5.45	1.08
EM	Universal Inst Emer Mrkt Debt II	UEDBX	**D-**	(800) 869-6397	**C- / 4.1**	4.73	6.16	1.32 /64	-0.17 /14	3.92 /60	5.43	1.33
US	US Global Inv Govt Ultra-Short Bond	UGSDX	**C+**	(800) 873-8637	**C- / 3.3**	0.61	0.22	0.38 /48	0.44 /32	0.27 /16	0.37	1.07
GL	US Global Inv Near-Term Tax Free	NEARX	**B+**	(800) 873-8637	**C / 5.4**	0.37	0.65	1.43 /65	1.57 /54	2.38 /36	1.42	1.08
USS	US Govt Securities Direct	CAUSX	**B+**	(800) 955-9988	**C+ / 6.2**	3.55	2.61	2.82 /76	1.45 /51	2.38 /36	2.50	0.83
USS	US Govt Securities K	CAUKX	**C**	(800) 955-9988	**C- / 4.2**	2.36	1.23	1.24 /62	0.57 /34	1.64 /27	0.94	1.33
MUS	USAA California Bond Adviser	UXABX	**B-**	(800) 382-8722	**A / 9.4**	1.33	2.67	3.68 /92	4.07 /96	7.95 /98	3.41	0.83
*MUS	USAA California Bond Fund	USCBX	**B**	(800) 382-8722	**A+ / 9.7**	1.38	2.78	3.93 /94	4.33 /97	8.23 /98	3.65	0.57
GEN	USAA Flexible Income Adviser	UAFIX	**U**	(800) 382-8722	**U /**	6.33	2.40	-3.12 /11	--	--	4.13	1.56
GEN	USAA Flexible Income Fund	USFIX	**U**	(800) 382-8722	**U /**	6.32	2.41	-3.00 /11	--	--	4.26	0.93
GEN	USAA Flexible Income Institutional	UIFIX	**U**	(800) 382-8722	**U /**	6.42	2.57	-2.61 /13	--	--	4.43	0.86
USA	USAA Government Securities Adviser	UAGNX	**B+**	(800) 382-8722	**C / 5.5**	1.97	1.12	1.29 /63	1.47 /52	2.12 /33	1.97	1.05
USA	USAA Government Securities Fund	USGNX	**B+**	(800) 382-8722	**C+ / 6.0**	1.92	1.24	1.52 /67	1.75 /57	2.51 /38	2.20	0.51
USS	USAA Government Securities Inst	UIGSX	**U**	(800) 382-8722	**U /**	2.03	1.36	--	--	--	0.00	0.69
GL	USAA High Income Adviser	UHYOX	**E+**	(800) 382-8722	**E+ / 0.9**	2.44	-1.91	-7.59 / 2	0.18 /28	3.56 /54	6.21	1.21
*COH	USAA High Income Fund	USHYX	**E+**	(800) 382-8722	**D- / 1.1**	2.67	-1.62	-7.31 / 2	0.43 /32	3.80 /58	6.54	0.89
COH	USAA High Income Institutional	UIHIX	**E+**	(800) 382-8722	**D- / 1.2**	2.57	-1.57	-7.22 / 2	0.54 /34	3.94 /61	6.67	0.80
*USS	USAA Income Fund	USAIX	**C+**	(800) 382-8722	**C+ / 6.5**	3.04	2.04	0.26 /45	2.16 /65	4.02 /62	3.62	0.53
COI	USAA Income Fund Adv	UINCX	**C+**	(800) 382-8722	**C+ / 6.1**	2.97	1.90	--	1.88 /59	3.73 /57	3.37	0.79
USS	USAA Income Fund Inst	UIINX	**B-**	(800) 382-8722	**C+ / 6.7**	3.04	2.13	0.36 /47	2.23 /66	4.14 /64	3.72	0.46
COI	USAA Intmdt-Trm Bd Fd Adv	UITBX	**C**	(800) 382-8722	**C / 5.1**	2.51	1.04	-1.27 /20	1.55 /53	4.09 /63	3.85	0.89
GEI	USAA Intmdt-Trm Bd Fd Inst	UIITX	**C+**	(800) 382-8722	**C+ / 5.8**	2.69	1.21	-0.95 /22	1.94 /60	4.48 /67	4.18	0.58
*GEI	USAA Intmdt-Trm Bd Fund	USIBX	**C+**	(800) 382-8722	**C+ / 5.6**	2.67	1.17	-1.04 /21	1.83 /58	4.37 /66	4.09	0.68
MM	USAA Money Market Fund	USAXX	**U**	(800) 382-8722	**U /**	--	--	--	--	--	0.01	0.63

PERFORMANCE: Total Return % through 3/31/16; Incl. in Returns: Dividend Yield, Expense Ratio.

● Denotes fund is closed to new investors
* Denotes fund is included in Section II

RISK			NET ASSETS		ASSET							FUND MANAGER		MINIMUM		LOADS	
Risk Rating/Pts	3 Yr Avg Standard Deviation	Avg Duration	NAV As of 3/31/16	Total $(Mil)	Cash %	Gov. Bond %	Muni. Bond %	Corp. Bond %	Other %	Portfolio Turnover Ratio	Avg Coupon Rate	Manager Quality Pct	Manager Tenure (Years)	Initial Purch. $	Additional Purch. $	Front End Load	Back End Load
B / 7.7	2.6	N/A	10.05	57	0	0	0	0	100	0	0.0	8	N/A	5,000,000	50	0.0	0.0
A- / 9.2	1.1	2.0	9.41	112	0	20	2	27	51	51	2.4	84	13	5,000,000	50	0.0	0.0
A- / 9.2	1.1	2.0	9.38	12	0	20	2	27	51	51	2.4	73	13	1,000	50	0.0	0.0
A+ / 9.9	0.2	0.6	9.50	15	1	64	0	0	35	196	0.0	58	21	0	0	0.0	0.0
A+ / 9.9	0.2	0.6	9.50	399	1	64	0	0	35	196	0.0	58	N/A	0	0	0.0	0.0
A+ / 9.8	0.6	N/A	9.72	23	2	70	0	0	28	206	0.0	60	21	0	0	0.0	0.0
A+ / 9.8	0.6	N/A	9.72	431	2	70	0	0	28	206	0.0	61	21	0	0	0.0	0.0
C+ / 6.5	3.0	4.2	9.10	5	21	21	1	20	37	744	2.8	82	4	1,000	100	4.5	0.0
C+ / 6.5	3.0	4.2	9.06	1	21	21	1	20	37	744	2.8	59	4	1,000	100	0.0	0.0
C+ / 6.3	3.1	4.2	9.08	30	21	21	1	20	37	744	2.8	86	4	1,000	100	0.0	0.0
C / 4.3	3.8	N/A	8.47	4	6	25	2	58	9	19	0.0	6	6	1,000	100	4.5	0.0
C / 4.3	3.8	N/A	8.45	2	6	25	2	58	9	19	0.0	5	6	1,000	100	0.0	0.0
C- / 4.2	3.9	N/A	8.48	7	6	25	2	58	9	19	0.0	6	6	1,000	100	0.0	0.0
U /	N/A	N/A	10.32	14	0	0	99	0	1	72	4.7	N/A	2	1,000	100	2.3	0.0
U /	N/A	N/A	10.32	5	0	0	99	0	1	72	4.7	N/A	2	1,000	100	0.0	0.0
U /	N/A	N/A	10.32	61	0	0	99	0	1	72	4.7	N/A	2	5,000,000	0	0.0	0.0
U /	N/A	N/A	1.00	912	100	0	0	0	0	0	0.0	N/A	28	0	0	0.0	0.0
U /	N/A	N/A	1.00	4,710	100	0	0	0	0	0	0.0	N/A	N/A	0	0	0.0	0.0
U /	N/A	N/A	1.00	498	100	0	0	0	0	0	0.0	N/A	N/A	0	0	0.0	0.0
A+ / 9.9	N/A	N/A	1.00	4,300	100	0	0	0	0	0	0.1	68	15	1,000,000	0	0.0	0.0
U /	N/A	N/A	1.00	390	100	0	0	0	0	0	0.0	N/A	15	100,000	0	0.0	0.0
A+ / 9.9	N/A	N/A	1.00	7,300	100	0	0	0	0	0	0.2	70	15	99,000,000	0	0.0	0.0
A+ / 9.9	N/A	N/A	1.00	21	100	0	0	0	0	0	0.0	N/A	8	100,000	0	0.0	0.0
A+ / 9.9	N/A	N/A	1.00	3,611	100	0	0	0	0	0	0.1	66	12	1,000,000	0	0.0	0.0
A+ / 9.9	N/A	N/A	1.00	4,081	100	0	0	0	0	0	0.1	66	8	50,000,000	0	0.0	0.0
U /	N/A	N/A	1.00	264	100	0	0	0	0	0	0.0	N/A	8	100,000	0	0.0	0.0
C / 5.4	3.3	5.5	10.58	84	1	18	0	36	45	320	0.0	87	5	0	0	0.0	0.0
C+ / 5.6	3.3	5.5	10.53	107	1	18	0	36	45	320	0.0	84	5	0	0	0.0	0.0
E / 0.5	8.1	6.5	7.80	215	2	73	0	22	3	81	0.0	60	14	0	0	0.0	0.0
E / 0.5	8.1	6.5	7.75	19	2	73	0	22	3	81	0.0	59	14	0	0	0.0	0.0
A- / 9.2	1.1	N/A	2.01	62	16	83	0	0	1	33	0.0	64	27	5,000	100	0.0	0.0
B+ / 8.9	1.5	5.9	2.25	112	12	0	87	0	1	12	6.0	94	26	5,000	100	0.0	0.0
B / 7.8	2.6	4.5	10.57	18	1	90	0	0	9	18	3.0	50	13	1,000	100	0.0	0.0
B / 7.8	2.6	4.5	10.58	5	1	90	0	0	9	18	3.0	23	13	1,000	100	0.0	0.0
D+ / 2.9	4.4	9.2	11.28	8	0	0	99	0	1	4	4.9	50	10	3,000	50	0.0	1.0
D+ / 2.9	4.4	9.2	11.29	697	0	0	99	0	1	4	4.9	59	10	3,000	50	0.0	0.0
U /	N/A	N/A	8.74	5	7	19	5	28	41	90	0.0	N/A	8	3,000	50	0.0	1.0
U /	N/A	N/A	8.74	58	7	19	5	28	41	90	0.0	N/A	8	3,000	50	0.0	0.0
U /	N/A	N/A	8.76	25	7	19	5	28	41	90	0.0	N/A	8	1,000,000	0	0.0	0.0
B+ / 8.4	2.1	2.1	10.01	5	1	14	4	0	81	15	5.4	72	4	3,000	50	0.0	0.0
B+ / 8.5	2.0	2.1	10.01	432	1	14	4	0	81	15	5.4	81	4	3,000	50	0.0	0.0
U /	N/A	2.1	10.02	99	1	14	4	0	81	15	5.4	N/A	4	1,000,000	0	0.0	1.0
D / 2.0	5.6	2.9	7.37	9	1	0	0	85	14	16	7.6	75	17	3,000	50	0.0	1.0
D- / 1.4	5.6	2.9	7.36	1,015	1	0	0	85	14	16	7.6	24	17	3,000	50	0.0	1.0
D- / 1.4	5.7	2.9	7.35	910	1	0	0	85	14	16	7.6	27	17	1,000,000	0	0.0	1.0
C+ / 6.1	3.1	3.7	12.88	3,163	0	11	8	64	17	10	5.8	82	4	3,000	50	0.0	0.0
C+ / 6.1	3.1	3.7	12.85	181	0	11	8	64	17	10	5.8	56	4	3,000	50	0.0	0.0
C+ / 6.2	3.1	3.7	12.87	2,866	0	11	8	64	17	10	5.8	84	4	1,000,000	0	0.0	0.0
C+ / 6.3	3.1	3.2	10.31	90	1	6	4	74	15	13	8.9	49	14	3,000	50	0.0	0.0
C+ / 6.4	3.0	3.2	10.32	1,587	1	6	4	74	15	13	8.9	56	14	1,000,000	0	0.0	0.0
C+ / 6.3	3.1	3.2	10.32	1,704	1	6	4	74	15	13	8.9	52	14	3,000	50	0.0	0.0
U /	N/A	N/A	1.00	5,632	100	0	0	0	0	0	0.0	N/A	10	1,000	50	0.0	0.0

Fund Type	Fund Name (99 Pct = Best, 0 Pct = Worst)	Ticker Symbol	Overall Investment Rating	Phone	PERFORMANCE: Performance Rating/Pts	Total Return % through 3/31/16: 3 Mo	6 Mo	1Yr / Pct	Annualized: 3Yr / Pct	Annualized: 5Yr / Pct	Incl. in Returns: Dividend Yield	Expense Ratio
MUS	USAA New York Bond Adv	UNYBX	**C+**	(800) 382-8722	**B+ / 8.6**	1.28	2.72	3.26 /88	2.84 /86	5.73 /90	3.26	0.90
GEI	USAA New York Bond Fund	USNYX	**C+**	(800) 382-8722	**B / 8.0**	1.32	2.89	3.45 /79	3.15 /77	6.00 /77	3.45	0.66
GES	USAA Real Return Fund	USRRX	**E**	(800) 382-8722	**E+ / 0.6**	3.75	3.60	-3.81 / 8	-1.85 / 5	1.16 /22	0.95	1.15
GES	USAA Real Return Institutional	UIRRX	**E**	(800) 382-8722	**E+ / 0.7**	3.64	3.48	-3.72 / 9	-1.71 / 5	1.36 /24	1.15	0.96
COI	USAA Short Term Bond Adv	UASBX	**C+**	(800) 382-8722	**C- / 4.1**	1.14	0.50	0.33 /47	0.84 /40	1.71 /28	1.43	0.85
GEI	USAA Short Term Bond Inst	UISBX	**B**	(800) 382-8722	**C / 4.6**	1.11	0.56	0.57 /51	1.16 /46	2.10 /32	1.77	0.50
* GEI	USAA Short Term Bond Retail Fund	USSBX	**B-**	(800) 382-8722	**C / 4.5**	1.20	0.62	0.57 /51	1.04 /44	1.98 /31	1.67	0.62
MUN	USAA T/E Short Term Adviser	UTESX	**C+**	(800) 382-8722	**C- / 3.4**	0.25	0.36	0.44 /53	0.58 /41	1.60 /37	1.20	0.98
* MUN	USAA T/E Short Term Bond Fund	USSTX	**B+**	(800) 382-8722	**C / 4.9**	0.31	0.58	0.60 /57	0.83 /48	1.85 /43	1.45	0.55
MMT	USAA Tax Exempt-CA MM	UCAXX	**C**	(800) 382-8722	**D+ / 2.5**	0.00	0.09	0.10 /43	0.04 /26	0.03 /13	0.10	0.58
MMT	USAA Tax Exempt-Money Market	USEXX	**C**	(800) 382-8722	**D / 2.1**	0.00	0.02	0.02 /37	0.02 /23	0.02 /11	0.02	0.56
MMT	USAA Tax Exempt-NY MM	UNYXX	**C**	(800) 382-8722	**D / 2.1**	0.00	0.01	0.02 /37	0.02 /23	0.02 /11	0.02	0.77
MMT	USAA Tax VA Exempt MM	UVAXX	**C**	(800) 382-8722	**D+ / 2.3**	0.00	0.02	0.02 /37	0.03 /25	0.03 /13	0.02	0.65
MUN	USAA Tax-Ex Intm-Trm Adviser	UTEIX	**A+**	(800) 382-8722	**B+ / 8.7**	1.46	2.75	3.24 /87	2.88 /87	5.11 /86	2.95	0.88
MUN	USAA Tax-Ex L Term Adviser	UTELX	**B**	(800) 382-8722	**A- / 9.1**	1.42	2.90	3.60 /91	3.46 /92	6.51 /94	3.88	0.99
* MUN	USAA Tax-Exempt Interm-Term Fund	USATX	**A+**	(800) 382-8722	**A- / 9.1**	1.45	2.88	3.43 /89	3.12 /89	5.34 /88	3.20	0.55
* MUN	USAA Tax-Exempt Long Term Fund	USTEX	**B+**	(800) 382-8722	**A / 9.5**	1.49	3.04	3.88 /93	3.81 /95	6.86 /96	4.15	0.55
MUN	USAA Ultra Short-Term Bond Fund	UUSTX	**B-**	(800) 382-8722	**C- / 4.0**	0.29	0.01	-0.23 /29	0.65 /43	1.34 /32	1.24	0.58
GEI	USAA Ultra Short-Term Bond Inst	UUSIX	**U**	(800) 382-8722	**U /**	0.28	0.02	-0.22 /29	--	--	1.25	0.53
MUS	USAA Virginia Bond Adv	UVABX	**B**	(800) 382-8722	**A- / 9.0**	1.21	2.60	3.20 /87	3.32 /91	5.66 /90	3.30	0.84
* GEI	USAA Virginia Bond Fund	USVAX	**C+**	(800) 382-8722	**B / 8.2**	1.35	2.81	3.53 /79	3.58 /81	5.88 /76	3.53	0.59
COH	Value Line Core Bond Fund	VAGIX	**C-**	(800) 243-2729	**C / 5.5**	2.73	2.20	1.43 /65	1.24 /47	3.38 /51	1.73	1.26
MUH	Value Line Tax Exempt Fund	VLHYX	**C+**	(800) 243-2729	**B+ / 8.4**	1.25	2.46	2.92 /84	2.44 /82	4.40 /81	2.66	1.19
EM	Van Eck Unconstrained EM Bd A	EMBAX	**E-**	(800) 826-1115	**E- / 0.1**	4.16	5.23	-8.88 / 1	-5.32 / 1	--	6.09	1.32
EM	Van Eck Unconstrained EM Bd C	EMBCX	**E-**	(800) 826-1115	**E- / 0.1**	4.13	4.74	-9.59 / 1	-5.95 / 1	--	6.66	2.60
EM	Van Eck Unconstrained EM Bd I	EMBUX	**E-**	(800) 826-1115	**E- / 0.2**	4.27	5.32	-8.67 / 1	-5.02 / 1	--	6.39	0.95
EM	Van Eck Unconstrained EM Bd Y	EMBYX	**E-**	(800) 826-1115	**E- / 0.1**	4.28	5.34	-8.69 / 1	-5.07 / 1	--	6.41	1.08
COH	Vanguard 529 High Yield Bond Port		**C-**	(800) 662-7447	**C+ / 6.7**	2.25	1.76	-1.24 /20	2.59 /72	5.31 /74	0.00	0.38
COI	Vanguard 529 Income		**C**	(800) 662-7447	**C / 4.4**	2.00	1.61	0.77 /55	0.75 /38	2.41 /37	0.00	0.25
GEI	Vanguard 529 Inflation Pro Sec Port		**D-**	(800) 662-7447	**D+ / 2.3**	4.55	3.69	1.37 /64	-0.94 / 9	2.78 /42	0.00	0.32
GEI	Vanguard 529 Interest Acc Port		**C+**	(800) 662-7447	**D+ / 2.9**	0.17	0.34	0.42 /48	0.20 /29	0.22 /16	0.00	0.25
GEI	Vanguard 529 ND Income Fd		**C**	(800) 662-7447	**C- / 4.0**	2.00	1.45	0.61 /52	0.56 /34	2.02 /31	0.00	0.85
GEI	Vanguard 529 PA Income Port		**B+**	(800) 662-7447	**B+ / 8.3**	2.70	3.25	1.24 /62	3.85 /83	4.88 /71	0.00	0.52
GEI	Vanguard 529 PA Infl Pro Sec Port		**D-**	(800) 662-7447	**D / 1.7**	4.46	3.63	1.20 /62	-1.10 / 8	2.60 /39	0.00	0.54
GEI	Vanguard 529 Ttl Bond Mkt Index Por		**B-**	(800) 662-7447	**C+ / 6.9**	3.03	2.35	1.61 /68	2.19 /65	3.50 /53	0.00	0.28
MUS	Vanguard CA Interm-Term T-E Adm	VCADX	**A+**	(800) 662-7447	**A / 9.5**	1.65	3.07	4.13 /95	3.81 /95	5.62 /90	2.75	0.12
* MUS	Vanguard CA Interm-Term T-E Inv	VCAIX	**A+**	(800) 662-7447	**A / 9.5**	1.63	3.02	4.04 /94	3.73 /94	5.54 /89	2.66	0.20
MUS	Vanguard CA Long-Term Tax-Exmpt	VCLAX	**B+**	(800) 662-7447	**A+ / 9.8**	1.89	4.08	5.05 /98	4.87 /98	7.15 /97	3.47	0.12
MUS	Vanguard CA Long-Term Tax-Exmpt	VCITX	**B+**	(800) 662-7447	**A+ / 9.8**	1.87	4.04	4.96 /98	4.79 /98	7.06 /97	3.40	0.20
MMT	Vanguard CA T/F MM Inv	VCTXX	**U**	(800) 662-7447	**U /**	--	--	--	--	--	0.01	0.16
EM	Vanguard Em Mkt Govt Bd Idx	VGAVX	**U**	(800) 662-7447	**U /**	4.66	6.24	3.86 /81	--	--	4.72	0.33
EM	Vanguard Em Mkt Govt Bd Idx Inv	VGOVX	**U**	(800) 662-7447	**U /**	4.61	6.17	3.64 /80	--	--	4.57	0.49
US	Vanguard Extnd Durtn Trea Idx Inst	VEDTX	**C-**	(800) 662-7447	**A+ / 9.9**	11.70	9.30	1.34 /64	8.82 /99	15.40 /99	2.77	0.08
US	Vanguard Extnd Durtn Trea Idx	VEDIX	**C-**	(800) 662-7447	**A+ / 9.9**	11.71	9.32	1.37 /64	8.84 /99	15.46 /99	2.79	0.06
MM	Vanguard Federal M/M Inv	VMFXX	**C**	(800) 662-7447	**D+ / 2.4**	0.07	0.09	0.10 /41	0.04 /24	0.03 /11	0.10	0.11
USA	Vanguard GNMA Adm	VFIJX	**A-**	(800) 662-7447	**B- / 7.3**	1.87	1.85	2.28 /74	2.55 /71	3.45 /52	2.40	0.11
* USA	Vanguard GNMA Inv	VFIIX	**B+**	(800) 662-7447	**B- / 7.1**	1.85	1.81	2.18 /73	2.45 /70	3.35 /51	2.30	0.21
COH	Vanguard High-Yield Corporate Adm	VWEAX	**C-**	(800) 662-7447	**B- / 7.0**	2.24	1.77	-1.09 /21	2.78 /74	5.55 /75	5.74	0.13
* COH	Vanguard High-Yield Corporate Inv	VWEHX	**C-**	(800) 662-7447	**C+ / 6.8**	2.22	1.72	-1.19 /20	2.68 /73	5.44 /74	5.64	0.23
MUH	Vanguard High-Yield Tax-Exempt	VWALX	**B**	(800) 662-7447	**A+ / 9.8**	1.85	4.11	4.81 /97	4.49 /98	6.90 /96	3.68	0.12
* MUH	Vanguard High-Yield Tax-Exempt Inv	VWAHX	**B**	(800) 662-7447	**A+ / 9.8**	1.83	4.07	4.73 /97	4.40 /97	6.82 /96	3.60	0.20
USS	Vanguard Infltn Pro Sec Adm	VAIPX	**D-**	(800) 662-7447	**D+ / 2.8**	4.56	3.72	1.51 /67	-0.77 /10	2.99 /45	0.82	0.10

• Denotes fund is closed to new investors
* Denotes fund is included in Section II

RISK			NET ASSETS		ASSET							FUND MANAGER		MINIMUM		LOADS	
Risk Rating/Pts	3 Yr Avg Standard Deviation	Avg Duration	NAV As of 3/31/16	Total $(Mil)	Cash %	Gov. Bond %	Muni. Bond %	Corp. Bond %	Other %	Portfolio Turnover Ratio	Avg Coupon Rate	Manager Quality Pct	Manager Tenure (Years)	Initial Purch. $	Additional Purch. $	Front End Load	Back End Load
C- / 3.3	4.1	8.7	12.25	6	2	0	97	0	1	5	4.7	19	6	3,000	50	0.0	1.0
C- / 3.4	4.0	8.7	12.28	211	2	0	97	0	1	5	4.7	84	6	3,000	50	0.0	0.0
E+ / 0.8	6.9	N/A	9.47	27	6	40	0	14	40	24	0.0	5	6	3,000	50	0.0	0.0
E+ / 0.8	6.8	N/A	9.47	79	6	40	0	14	40	24	0.0	5	6	3,000	50	0.0	0.0
A- / 9.1	1.1	1.6	9.10	15	0	7	8	64	21	31	5.5	73	14	3,000	50	0.0	0.0
A- / 9.2	1.1	1.6	9.09	2,030	0	7	8	64	21	31	5.5	82	14	1,000,000	0	0.0	0.0
A- / 9.1	1.1	1.6	9.10	1,386	0	7	8	64	21	31	5.5	77	14	3,000	50	0.0	0.0
A+ / 9.7	0.6	2.3	10.59	31	0	0	100	0	0	30	5.0	62	13	3,000	50	0.0	1.0
A+ / 9.8	0.6	2.3	10.59	1,759	0	0	100	0	0	30	5.0	76	13	3,000	50	0.0	0.0
A+ / 9.9	0.1	N/A	1.00	306	100	0	0	0	0	0	0.1	N/A	5	3,000	50	0.0	0.0
A+ / 9.9	N/A	N/A	1.00	2,637	100	0	0	0	0	0	0.0	N/A	10	3,000	50	0.0	0.0
A+ / 9.9	N/A	N/A	1.00	86	100	0	0	0	0	0	0.0	67	10	3,000	50	0.0	0.0
A+ / 9.9	N/A	N/A	1.00	172	100	0	0	0	0	0	0.0	68	6	3,000	50	0.0	0.0
B- / 7.2	2.8	6.3	13.61	42	0	0	100	0	0	4	4.9	60	13	3,000	50	0.0	1.0
C- / 3.7	4.0	8.0	13.71	11	0	0	99	0	1	7	5.3	38	N/A	3,000	50	0.0	1.0
B- / 7.3	2.8	6.3	13.61	4,321	0	0	100	0	0	4	4.9	75	13	3,000	50	0.0	0.0
C- / 3.7	4.0	8.0	13.73	2,415	0	0	99	0	1	7	5.3	50	N/A	3,000	50	0.0	0.0
A+ / 9.7	0.6	N/A	9.94	404	1	0	9	67	23	31	0.0	80	6	3,000	50	0.0	0.0
U /	N/A	N/A	9.94	20	1	0	9	67	23	31	0.0	N/A	6	1,000,000	0	0.0	0.0
C- / 4.0	3.8	7.6	11.51	23	0	0	99	0	1	12	5.3	41	10	3,000	50	0.0	1.0
C- / 3.9	3.8	7.6	11.52	647	0	0	99	0	1	12	5.3	91	10	3,000	50	0.0	0.0
C / 4.7	3.1	5.2	15.05	72	1	20	2	41	36	111	0.0	88	6	1,000	250	0.0	0.0
C- / 3.7	3.7	6.1	10.12	69	1	0	98	0	1	4	0.0	20	6	1,000	250	0.0	0.0
E- / 0.2	10.0	N/A	6.87	10	5	68	4	4	19	410	0.0	3	4	1,000	100	5.8	0.0
E- / 0.2	10.0	N/A	6.67	4	5	68	4	4	19	410	0.0	2	4	1,000	100	0.0	0.0
E- / 0.2	10.1	N/A	6.95	118	5	68	4	4	19	410	0.0	3	4	1,000,000	0	0.0	0.0
E- / 0.2	10.0	N/A	6.93	24	5	68	4	4	19	410	0.0	3	4	1,000	100	0.0	0.0
D / 2.1	5.0	N/A	23.13	135	5	2	0	88	5	0	0.0	91	14	3,000	50	0.0	0.0
B- / 7.3	2.8	N/A	15.78	761	25	48	0	12	15	0	0.0	30	14	3,000	50	0.0	0.0
D / 2.1	5.5	N/A	17.70	120	1	98	0	0	1	0	0.0	3	N/A	3,000	50	0.0	0.0
A+ / 9.9	0.1	N/A	11.96	444	0	0	0	0	100	0	0.0	74	N/A	3,000	50	0.0	0.0
B / 7.6	2.7	N/A	13.27	61	25	48	1	13	13	0	0.0	17	10	25	25	0.0	0.0
C / 5.3	3.4	N/A	15.57	145	0	38	1	20	41	0	0.0	95	10	25	25	0.0	0.0
D / 2.1	5.5	N/A	14.29	23	1	98	0	0	1	0	0.0	3	10	25	25	0.0	0.0
C+ / 6.2	3.1	N/A	17.01	191	0	46	1	25	28	0	0.0	49	14	3,000	50	0.0	0.0
C+ / 5.9	3.2	5.5	11.97	9,426	0	0	99	0	1	17	4.3	82	5	50,000	100	0.0	0.0
C+ / 5.9	3.2	5.5	11.97	1,552	0	0	99	0	1	17	4.3	80	5	3,000	100	0.0	0.0
C- / 3.6	4.2	5.2	12.34	3,003	0	0	99	0	1	14	4.7	80	5	50,000	100	0.0	0.0
C- / 3.6	4.2	5.2	12.34	460	0	0	99	0	1	14	4.7	78	5	3,000	100	0.0	0.0
U /	N/A	N/A	1.00	3,386	100	0	0	0	0	0	0.0	N/A	N/A	3,000	100	0.0	0.0
U /	N/A	6.0	19.19	140	0	0	0	0	100	20	5.7	N/A	3	10,000	100	0.0	0.0
U /	N/A	6.0	9.59	9	0	0	0	0	100	20	5.7	N/A	3	3,000	100	0.0	0.0
E- / 0.0	17.8	24.7	37.90	526	0	99	0	0	1	16	3.7	12	3	5,000,000	0	0.0	0.0
E- / 0.0	17.8	24.7	95.14	243	0	99	0	0	1	16	3.7	12	3	100,000,000	0	0.0	0.0
A+ / 9.9	N/A	N/A	1.00	3,495	100	0	0	0	0	0	0.1	66	9	3,000	100	0.0	0.0
B- / 7.1	2.8	4.0	10.79	17,487	0	2	0	0	98	685	3.6	88	10	50,000	0	0.0	0.0
B- / 7.1	2.8	4.0	10.79	8,509	0	2	0	0	98	685	3.6	87	10	3,000	100	0.0	0.0
D / 2.2	5.0	4.5	5.59	13,309	2	3	0	92	3	35	5.8	92	8	50,000	0	0.0	0.0
D / 2.2	5.0	4.5	5.59	3,608	2	3	0	92	3	35	5.8	91	8	3,000	100	0.0	0.0
C- / 3.1	4.1	4.7	11.43	7,965	3	0	94	0	3	21	4.5	74	6	50,000	100	0.0	0.0
C- / 3.1	4.1	4.7	11.43	1,748	3	0	94	0	3	21	4.5	71	6	3,000	100	0.0	0.0
D / 2.0	5.5	7.6	26.36	10,770	2	97	0	0	1	39	0.9	6	5	10,000	100	0.0	0.0

99 Pct = Best
0 Pct = Worst

Fund Type	Fund Name	Ticker Symbol	Overall Investment Rating	Phone	PERFORMANCE: Performance Rating/Pts	Total Return % through 3/31/16: 3 Mo	6 Mo	1Yr / Pct	Annualized 3Yr / Pct	Annualized 5Yr / Pct	Incl. in Returns: Dividend Yield	Expense Ratio
USS	Vanguard Infltn Pro Sec Inst	VIPIX	D-	(800) 662-7447	D+ / 2.9	4.58	3.79	1.55 /67	-0.74 /10	3.02 /46	0.85	0.07
* USS	Vanguard Infltn Pro Sec Inv	VIPSX	D-	(800) 662-7447	D+ / 2.7	4.60	3.68	1.43 /65	-0.86 / 9	2.89 /43	0.72	0.20
GEI	Vanguard Interm-Term Bd Index Adm	VBILX	C	(800) 662-7447	B / 7.8	4.02	3.03	2.82 /76	2.73 /74	5.16 /73	2.60	0.10
* GEI	Vanguard Interm-Term Bd Index Inv	VBIIX	C	(800) 662-7447	B / 7.8	4.00	3.00	2.76 /76	2.64 /73	5.06 /72	2.54	0.20
GEI	Vanguard Interm-Term Invst-Grd Adm	VFIDX	B-	(800) 662-7447	B / 8.1	3.52	3.33	2.86 /76	3.11 /77	5.08 /72	3.03	0.10
* GEI	Vanguard Interm-Term Invst-Grd Inv	VFICX	B-	(800) 662-7447	B / 8.0	3.50	3.28	2.76 /76	3.01 /76	4.97 /71	2.93	0.20
MUN	Vanguard Interm-Term Tax-Exempt	VWIUX	A+	(800) 662-7447	A- / 9.2	1.59	2.98	3.73 /92	3.28 /91	4.99 /85	2.87	0.12
* MUN	Vanguard Interm-Term Tax-Exempt	VWITX	A+	(800) 662-7447	A- / 9.2	1.57	2.94	3.65 /91	3.19 /90	4.91 /85	2.78	0.20
US	Vanguard Interm-Term Treasury Adm	VFIUX	C+	(800) 662-7447	B- / 7.0	3.42	2.17	3.16 /78	2.01 /62	3.80 /58	1.68	0.10
* US	Vanguard Interm-Term Treasury Inv	VFITX	C	(800) 662-7447	C+ / 6.8	3.40	2.12	3.06 /77	1.91 /60	3.70 /57	1.58	0.20
GEI	Vanguard Interm-Tm Bd Idx Inst	VBIMX	C	(800) 662-7447	B / 7.8	4.02	3.05	2.85 /76	2.76 /74	5.19 /73	2.63	0.07
COI	Vanguard Interm-Tm Bd Idx Inst Plus	VBIUX	C	(800) 662-7447	B / 7.9	4.03	3.06	2.87 /76	2.78 /74	--	2.65	0.05
COI	Vanguard Intm-Term Corp Bd Idx	VICSX	C	(800) 662-7447	B / 8.1	4.09	3.63	2.31 /74	3.31 /79	5.73 /76	3.25	0.10
COI	Vanguard Intm-Term Corp Bd Idx Inst	VICBX	C+	(800) 662-7447	B / 8.2	4.13	3.63	2.32 /74	3.34 /79	5.76 /76	3.28	0.07
* USS	Vanguard Intm-Term Govt Bd Idx	VSIGX	C+	(800) 662-7447	B- / 7.0	3.27	2.08	3.01 /77	2.02 /62	3.72 /57	1.59	0.10
USS	Vanguard Intm-Term Govt Bd Idx Inst	VIIGX	C+	(800) 662-7447	B- / 7.0	3.31	2.10	3.06 /77	2.05 /62	3.77 /58	1.60	0.07
MUN	Vanguard Lmtd-Term Tax-Exempt	VMLUX	A+	(800) 662-7447	C+ / 6.5	0.64	1.03	1.65 /75	1.35 /63	1.94 /45	1.55	0.12
* MUN	Vanguard Lmtd-Term Tax-Exempt Inv	VMLTX	A	(800) 662-7447	C+ / 6.4	0.62	0.99	1.57 /74	1.27 /60	1.86 /43	1.46	0.20
GEL	Vanguard Long Term Bd Idx Inst	VBLLX	C-	(800) 662-7447	A- / 9.1	7.37	6.32	0.35 /47	4.76 /89	8.56 /89	3.91	0.07
COI	Vanguard Long Term Bd Idx Inst Plus	VBLIX	C-	(800) 662-7447	A- / 9.1	7.38	6.34	0.38 /48	4.78 /89	--	3.93	0.05
* GEL	Vanguard Long Term Bd Idx Investor	VBLTX	C-	(800) 662-7447	A- / 9.0	7.35	6.28	0.26 /45	4.64 /88	8.42 /89	3.82	0.20
COI	Vanguard Long-Term Corp Bd Idx	VLTCX	C-	(800) 662-7447	B+ / 8.7	6.96	5.79	-1.14 /21	4.33 /86	7.89 /86	4.47	0.10
COI	Vanguard Long-Term Corp Bd Idx	VLCIX	C-	(800) 662-7447	B+ / 8.7	6.96	5.82	-1.13 /21	4.36 /86	7.91 /86	4.49	0.07
USL	Vanguard Long-Term Govt Bd Idx	VLGSX	C-	(800) 662-7447	A+ / 9.6	8.21	6.52	2.76 /76	5.88 /95	9.43 /93	2.56	0.10
USL	Vanguard Long-Term Govt Bd Idx	VLGIX	C-	(800) 662-7447	A+ / 9.6	8.24	6.56	2.77 /76	5.92 /95	9.47 /93	2.58	0.07
GEI	• Vanguard Long-Term Inv Gr Adm	VWETX	C-	(800) 662-7447	A / 9.4	6.73	6.86	1.35 /64	5.42 /93	8.80 /90	4.25	0.12
* GEI	• Vanguard Long-Term Inv Gr Inv	VWESX	C-	(800) 662-7447	A / 9.3	6.71	6.81	1.25 /62	5.31 /92	8.70 /90	4.16	0.22
MUN	Vanguard Long-Term Tax-Exempt	VWLUX	A-	(800) 662-7447	A+ / 9.8	1.88	4.03	4.86 /98	4.45 /97	6.48 /94	3.62	0.12
* MUN	Vanguard Long-Term Tax-Exempt Inv	VWLTX	A-	(800) 662-7447	A+ / 9.8	1.86	3.99	4.77 /97	4.37 /97	6.39 /94	3.54	0.20
US	Vanguard Long-Term Treasury Adm	VUSUX	C-	(800) 662-7447	A+ / 9.6	8.29	6.56	2.64 /75	5.94 /95	9.57 /93	2.67	0.10
* US	Vanguard Long-Term Treasury Inv	VUSTX	C-	(800) 662-7447	A+ / 9.6	8.26	6.51	2.54 /75	5.83 /95	9.46 /93	2.58	0.20
* MUS	Vanguard MA Tax-Exempt Inv	VMATX	B+	(800) 662-7447	A+ / 9.7	1.72	3.61	4.47 /97	4.10 /96	5.62 /90	2.98	0.16
MTG	Vanguard Mort-Backed Secs Idx Adm	VMBSX	A+	(800) 662-7447	B- / 7.2	1.76	1.64	2.17 /73	2.52 /71	3.09 /47	1.63	0.10
MTG	Vanguard Mort-Backed Secs Idx Inst	VMBIX	U	(800) 662-7447	U /	1.79	1.67	2.18 /73	--	--	1.66	0.07
MUS	Vanguard NJ Long-Term Tax-Exmpt	VNJUX	B+	(800) 662-7447	A+ / 9.6	1.85	4.50	4.00 /94	3.85 /95	5.86 /91	3.52	0.12
MUS	Vanguard NJ Long-Term Tax-Exmpt	VNJTX	B+	(800) 662-7447	A+ / 9.6	1.83	4.46	3.92 /93	3.76 /94	5.77 /91	3.45	0.20
MMT	Vanguard NJ T/E Money Market	VNJXX	U	(800) 662-7447	U /	0.01	0.01	0.01 /35	0.01 /21	0.02 /11	0.01	0.16
MUS	Vanguard NY Long-Term Tax-Exmpt	VNYUX	A-	(800) 662-7447	A+ / 9.8	1.78	3.85	4.94 /98	4.45 /97	6.03 /92	3.25	0.12
MUS	Vanguard NY Long-Term Tax-Exmpt	VNYTX	A-	(800) 662-7447	A+ / 9.8	1.76	3.81	4.85 /98	4.36 /97	5.94 /92	3.17	0.20
MMT	Vanguard NY Tx-Ex MM Inv	VYFXX	U	(800) 662-7447	U /	0.01	0.01	0.01 /35	0.01 /21	0.02 /11	0.01	0.16
COI	Vanguard OH College Adv Income		C	(800) 662-7447	C / 4.7	2.15	1.81	1.26 /63	0.87 /40	2.46 /37	0.00	0.27
* MUS	Vanguard OH Long-Term Tax-Exmpt	VOHIX	B+	(800) 662-7447	A+ / 9.8	1.80	3.80	4.85 /98	4.47 /97	6.26 /93	3.26	0.16
MMT	Vanguard OH Tax Exempt MM	VOHXX	U	(800) 662-7447	U /	0.01	0.01	0.01 /35	0.01 /21	0.03 /13	0.01	0.16
MUS	Vanguard PA Long-Term Tax-Exmpt	VPALX	A-	(800) 662-7447	A+ / 9.7	1.54	3.43	4.39 /96	4.35 /97	6.04 /92	3.59	0.12
MUS	Vanguard PA Long-Term Tax-Exmpt	VPAIX	A-	(800) 662-7447	A+ / 9.7	1.52	3.39	4.31 /96	4.27 /97	5.95 /92	3.51	0.20
MMT	Vanguard PA T/F MM Inv	VPTXX	U	(800) 662-7447	U /	--	--	--	--	--	0.01	0.16
MM	Vanguard Prime M/M Inv	VMMXX	C	(800) 662-7447	D+ / 2.5	0.09	0.12	0.13 /42	0.05 /25	0.05 /13	0.13	0.16
MM	Vanguard Prime MM Adm	VMRXX	C	(800) 662-7447	D+ / 2.6	0.10	0.15	0.19 /44	0.10 /27	0.10 /15	0.19	0.10
GES	Vanguard Short-Term Bd Idx Admiral	VBIRX	B+	(800) 662-7447	C / 5.1	1.58	0.93	1.49 /66	1.24 /47	1.78 /29	1.32	0.10
COI	Vanguard Short-Term Bd Idx Ins Plus	VBIPX	B+	(800) 662-7447	C / 5.2	1.59	0.96	1.54 /67	1.29 /48	--	1.37	0.05
COI	Vanguard Short-Term Bd Idx Inst	VBITX	B+	(800) 662-7447	C / 5.2	1.59	0.94	1.52 /67	1.27 /48	--	1.35	0.07
* GES	Vanguard Short-Term Bd Idx Investor	VBISX	B	(800) 662-7447	C / 4.9	1.57	0.89	1.43 /65	1.15 /45	1.69 /28	1.25	0.20

• Denotes fund is closed to new investors
* Denotes fund is included in Section II

RISK			NET ASSETS		ASSET							FUND MANAGER		MINIMUM		LOADS	
Risk Rating/Pts	3 Yr Avg Standard Deviation	Avg Duration	NAV As of 3/31/16	Total $(Mil)	Cash %	Gov. Bond %	Muni. Bond %	Corp. Bond %	Other %	Portfolio Turnover Ratio	Avg Coupon Rate	Manager Quality Pct	Manager Tenure (Years)	Initial Purch. $	Additional Purch. $	Front End Load	Back End Load
D / 2.0	5.5	7.6	10.74	7,659	2	97	0	0	1	39	0.9	6	5	5,000,000	100	0.0	0.0
D / 2.0	5.5	7.6	13.43	4,731	2	97	0	0	1	39	0.9	5	5	3,000	100	0.0	0.0
C- / 3.2	4.5	6.4	11.64	10,653	0	58	0	40	2	60	3.0	31	8	10,000	100	0.0	0.0
C- / 3.2	4.5	6.4	11.64	1,422	0	58	0	40	2	60	3.0	28	8	3,000	100	0.0	0.0
C / 4.7	3.6	5.5	9.91	19,947	1	7	0	77	15	88	3.4	75	8	50,000	0	0.0	0.0
C / 4.7	3.6	5.5	9.91	2,745	1	7	0	77	15	88	3.4	72	8	3,000	100	0.0	0.0
C+ / 6.5	3.0	5.1	14.39	43,453	3	0	96	0	1	12	4.7	71	3	50,000	0	0.0	0.0
C+ / 6.5	3.0	5.1	14.39	4,558	3	0	96	0	1	12	4.7	N/A	3	3,000	100	0.0	0.0
C / 4.6	3.6	5.4	11.59	5,006	0	97	0	0	3	63	2.0	50	15	50,000	0	0.0	0.0
C / 4.6	3.6	5.4	11.59	1,370	0	97	0	0	3	63	2.0	46	15	3,000	100	0.0	0.0
C- / 3.2	4.5	6.4	11.64	2,473	0	58	0	40	2	60	3.0	32	8	5,000,000	100	0.0	0.0
C- / 3.2	4.5	6.4	11.64	1,181	0	58	0	40	2	60	3.0	69	8	100,000,000	100	0.0	0.0
C- / 3.2	4.6	6.3	23.34	494	1	0	0	98	1	56	3.8	79	7	10,000	0	0.0	0.0
C- / 3.2	4.6	6.3	28.84	353	1	0	0	98	1	56	3.8	79	7	5,000,000	0	0.0	0.0
C / 5.0	3.5	5.2	22.35	560	0	99	0	0	1	35	2.2	45	3	10,000	0	0.0	0.0
C / 5.0	3.5	5.2	27.74	235	0	99	0	0	1	35	2.2	47	3	5,000,000	0	0.0	0.0
A- / 9.1	1.2	1.8	11.05	19,724	2	0	97	0	1	16	3.7	76	8	50,000	0	0.0	0.0
A- / 9.1	1.2	1.8	11.05	2,074	2	0	97	0	1	16	3.7	73	8	3,000	100	0.0	0.0
E / 0.3	9.1	13.9	14.04	2,232	0	43	5	50	2	39	4.9	9	3	5,000,000	100	0.0	0.0
E / 0.3	9.1	13.9	14.04	2,474	0	43	5	50	2	39	4.9	32	3	100,000,000	100	0.0	0.0
E / 0.3	9.1	13.9	14.04	2,516	0	43	5	50	2	39	4.9	9	3	3,000	100	0.0	0.0
E / 0.3	8.6	12.8	23.76	75	0	0	0	99	1	64	5.5	23	7	10,000	0	0.0	0.0
E / 0.3	8.6	12.8	29.49	306	0	0	0	99	1	64	5.5	23	7	5,000,000	0	0.0	0.0
E- / 0.2	11.0	16.2	26.97	213	0	99	0	0	1	24	3.7	48	3	10,000	0	0.0	0.0
E- / 0.2	11.0	16.2	34.23	115	0	99	0	0	1	24	3.7	49	3	5,000,000	0	0.0	0.0
E / 0.3	8.5	13.1	10.43	10,110	5	3	15	75	2	21	4.7	26	8	50,000	0	0.0	0.0
E / 0.3	8.5	13.1	10.43	3,910	5	3	15	75	2	21	4.7	23	8	3,000	100	0.0	0.0
C- / 3.9	4.0	4.9	11.87	8,537	2	0	97	0	1	18	4.8	75	6	50,000	100	0.0	0.0
C- / 3.9	4.0	4.9	11.87	977	2	0	97	0	1	18	4.8	73	6	3,000	100	0.0	0.0
E- / 0.2	11.2	16.6	13.11	2,625	0	97	0	0	3	59	3.6	26	15	50,000	0	0.0	0.0
E- / 0.1	11.2	16.6	13.11	1,213	0	97	0	0	3	59	3.6	24	15	3,000	100	0.0	0.0
C- / 3.9	4.1	5.1	11.03	1,379	0	0	99	0	1	15	4.6	55	8	3,000	100	0.0	0.0
B / 8.2	2.3	3.7	21.35	500	0	0	0	0	100	713	4.5	69	7	10,000	0	0.0	0.0
U /	N/A	3.7	28.93	43	0	0	0	0	100	713	4.5	N/A	7	5,000,000	0	0.0	0.0
C- / 3.9	4.1	5.3	12.22	1,787	1	0	98	0	1	25	4.5	48	3	50,000	100	0.0	0.0
C- / 3.9	4.1	5.3	12.22	252	1	0	98	0	1	25	4.5	44	3	3,000	100	0.0	0.0
U /	N/A	N/A	1.00	1,352	100	0	0	0	0	0	0.0	N/A	5	3,000	100	0.0	0.0
C / 4.3	3.8	5.0	12.03	3,740	0	0	99	0	1	17	4.7	80	3	50,000	100	0.0	0.0
C / 4.3	3.8	5.0	12.03	461	0	0	99	0	1	17	4.7	78	3	3,000	100	0.0	0.0
U /	N/A	N/A	1.00	2,175	100	0	0	0	0	0	0.0	N/A	5	3,000	100	0.0	0.0
B- / 7.3	2.8	N/A	15.21	244	25	48	0	12	15	0	0.0	34	7	25	0	0.0	0.0
C- / 3.6	4.2	5.2	12.78	1,088	0	0	99	0	1	21	4.5	64	8	3,000	100	0.0	0.0
U /	N/A	N/A	1.00	530	100	0	0	0	0	0	0.0	N/A	1	3,000	100	0.0	0.0
C / 4.3	3.8	4.8	11.79	3,012	0	0	99	0	1	16	4.8	77	5	50,000	100	0.0	0.0
C / 4.3	3.8	4.8	11.79	377	0	0	99	0	1	16	4.8	75	5	3,000	100	0.0	0.0
U /	N/A	N/A	1.00	2,084	100	0	0	0	0	0	0.0	N/A	1	3,000	100	0.0	0.0
A+ / 9.9	N/A	N/A	1.00	106,544	100	0	0	0	0	0	0.1	66	13	3,000	100	0.0	0.0
A+ / 9.9	N/A	N/A	1.00	29,470	100	0	0	0	0	0	0.2	69	13	5,000,000	100	0.0	0.0
A- / 9.0	1.3	2.7	10.56	14,861	0	72	0	26	2	45	1.9	76	3	10,000	100	0.0	0.0
A- / 9.0	1.3	2.7	10.56	3,595	0	72	0	26	2	45	1.9	84	3	100,000,000	100	0.0	0.0
A- / 9.0	1.3	2.7	10.56	4,756	0	72	0	26	2	45	1.9	84	3	5,000,000	100	0.0	0.0
A- / 9.0	1.3	2.7	10.56	2,311	0	72	0	26	2	45	1.9	73	3	3,000	100	0.0	0.0

Fund Type	Fund Name (99 Pct = Best, 0 Pct = Worst)	Ticker Symbol	Overall Investment Rating	Phone	PERFORMANCE: Performance Rating/Pts	Total Return % through 3/31/16: 3 Mo	6 Mo	1Yr / Pct	Annualized: 3Yr / Pct	5Yr / Pct	Incl. in Returns: Dividend Yield	Expense Ratio
* COI	Vanguard Short-Term Crp Bd Idx	VSCSX	A	(800) 662-7447	C+ / 6.2	1.75	1.40	1.78 /70	1.89 /59	2.84 /43	2.00	0.10
COI	Vanguard Short-Term Crp Bd Idx Inst	VSTBX	A	(800) 662-7447	C+ / 6.3	1.76	1.44	1.83 /70	1.93 /60	2.87 /43	2.03	0.07
USS	Vanguard Short-Term Federal Adm	VSGDX	B	(800) 662-7447	C / 4.7	1.28	0.88	1.46 /66	1.01 /43	1.48 /25	0.99	0.10
* USS	Vanguard Short-Term Federal Inv	VSGBX	B-	(800) 662-7447	C / 4.5	1.26	0.74	1.36 /64	0.91 /41	1.38 /24	0.89	0.20
USS	Vanguard Short-Term Gvt Bd Idx	VSBSX	B-	(800) 662-7447	C- / 3.9	0.86	0.41	0.89 /57	0.68 /37	0.80 /19	0.70	0.10
USS	Vanguard Short-Term Gvt Bd Idx Inst	VSBIX	B-	(800) 662-7447	C- / 4.0	0.89	0.43	0.89 /57	0.72 /37	0.83 /19	0.73	0.07
MUN	Vanguard Short-Term Tax-Exempt	VWSUX	B	(800) 662-7447	C / 4.3	0.32	0.38	0.73 /61	0.61 /42	0.91 /25	0.79	0.12
* MUN	Vanguard Short-Term Tax-Exempt	VWSTX	B	(800) 662-7447	C- / 4.1	0.30	0.34	0.64 /58	0.53 /39	0.83 /23	0.70	0.20
US	Vanguard Short-Term Treasury Adm	VFIRX	B-	(800) 662-7447	C / 4.3	1.24	0.66	1.25 /63	0.83 /40	1.17 /22	0.81	0.10
* US	Vanguard Short-Term Treasury Inv	VFISX	B-	(800) 662-7447	C- / 4.1	1.22	0.61	1.15 /61	0.73 /38	1.07 /21	0.71	0.20
GEI	Vanguard Sh-Term Invest-Grade	VFSUX	A	(800) 662-7447	C+ / 6.1	1.73	1.45	1.83 /70	1.78 /57	2.35 /36	2.07	0.10
GEI	Vanguard Sh-Term Invest-Grade Inst	VFSIX	A	(800) 662-7447	C+ / 6.1	1.74	1.47	1.86 /71	1.81 /58	2.39 /36	2.10	0.07
* GEI	Vanguard Sh-Term Invest-Grade Inv	VFSTX	A-	(800) 662-7447	C+ / 5.9	1.71	1.41	1.73 /69	1.67 /55	2.25 /34	1.97	0.20
GEI	Vanguard ST Inf Prot Sec Idx Adm	VTAPX	C-	(800) 662-7447	D / 1.8	1.82	1.40	1.32 /64	-0.54 /11	--	0.00	0.08
GEI	Vanguard ST Inf Prot Sec Idx Inst	VTSPX	C-	(800) 662-7447	D / 1.8	1.82	1.40	1.36 /64	-0.51 /11	--	0.00	0.05
* GEI	Vanguard ST Inf Prot Sec Idx Inv	VTIPX	C-	(800) 662-7447	D / 1.7	1.78	1.40	1.24 /62	-0.63 /11	--	0.00	0.17
MUN	Vanguard Tax Exempt Bond Index	VTEAX	U	(800) 662-7447	U /	1.48	3.26	--	--	--	0.00	N/A
MUN	Vanguard Tax Exempt Bond Index	VTEBX	U	(800) 662-7447	U /	1.46	3.23	--	--	--	0.00	N/A
MMT	Vanguard Tax Exempt Money Mkt	VMSXX	U	(800) 662-7447	U /	0.01	0.01	0.01 /35	0.01 /21	0.02 /11	0.01	0.16
COI	Vanguard Total Bond Mkt II Idx Inst	VTBNX	B	(800) 662-7447	B- / 7.1	3.06	2.31	1.73 /69	2.34 /68	3.66 /56	2.36	0.05
* COI	Vanguard Total Bond Mkt II Idx Inv	VTBIX	B	(800) 662-7447	B- / 7.0	3.04	2.28	1.66 /68	2.27 /67	3.59 /55	2.29	0.10
GES	Vanguard Total Bond Mrkt Idx IPLUS	VBMPX	B	(800) 662-7447	B- / 7.2	3.06	2.44	1.81 /70	2.39 /69	3.73 /57	2.43	0.05
GES	Vanguard Total Bond Mrkt Index Adm	VBTLX	B	(800) 662-7447	B- / 7.2	3.05	2.43	1.79 /70	2.37 /69	3.70 /57	2.41	0.07
GES	Vanguard Total Bond Mrkt Index Inst	VBTIX	B	(800) 662-7447	B- / 7.2	3.06	2.43	1.80 /70	2.38 /69	3.72 /57	2.42	0.06
* GES	Vanguard Total Bond Mrkt Index Inv	VBMFX	B	(800) 662-7447	B- / 7.0	3.03	2.38	1.69 /69	2.25 /67	3.58 /54	2.32	0.20
GL	Vanguard Total Internatl Bd Idx Adm	VTABX	U	(800) 662-7447	U /	3.45	3.95	2.35 /74	--	--	1.54	0.14
GL	Vanguard Total Internatl Bd Idx Ins	VTIFX	U	(800) 662-7447	U /	3.46	4.02	2.42 /74	--	--	1.59	0.09
GL	Vanguard Total Internatl Bd Idx Inv	VTIBX	U	(800) 662-7447	U /	3.44	3.88	2.33 /74	--	--	1.53	0.17
MM	Vanguard Treas MM Inv	VUSXX	C	(800) 662-7447	D+ / 2.3	0.05	0.06	0.07 /40	0.03 /23	0.02 / 9	0.07	0.09
GEI	Vanguard Ultra-Short-Term Bond	VUSFX	U	(800) 662-7447	U /	0.51	0.43	0.72 /54	--	--	0.72	N/A
GEI	Vanguard Ultra-Short-Term Bond Inv	VUBFX	U	(800) 662-7447	U /	0.49	0.39	0.64 /52	--	--	0.64	N/A
GEI	Vanguard WY College Inv Bon In Port		B-	(800) 662-7447	C+ / 6.7	3.00	2.32	1.51 /67	2.04 /62	3.34 /51	0.00	0.52
GEI	Vanguard WY College Inv Income		C	(800) 662-7447	C / 4.5	2.07	1.71	0.78 /55	0.83 /40	2.34 /36	0.00	0.52
GEI	Vantagepoint Core Bond Index I	VPCIX	B	(800) 669-7400	C+ / 6.6	2.93	2.17	1.46 /66	2.05 /62	3.32 /50	2.49	0.41
GEI	Vantagepoint Core Bond Index II	VPCDX	B	(800) 669-7400	B- / 7.0	2.96	2.25	1.64 /68	2.24 /66	3.53 /54	2.67	0.21
COI	Vantagepoint Core Bond Index T	VQCIX	B+	(800) 669-7400	B- / 7.1	3.00	2.39	1.81 /70	2.31 /68	--	2.74	0.21
COH	Vantagepoint High Yield T	VQHYX	U	(800) 669-7400	U /	2.59	0.14	-4.84 / 5	--	--	6.20	0.88
USL	Vantagepoint Inflation Focused Inv	VPTSX	E+	(800) 669-7400	D- / 1.3	4.19	3.56	0.87 /57	-1.45 / 6	2.22 /34	0.31	0.65
GEI	Vantagepoint Inflation Focused T	VQTSX	D-	(800) 669-7400	D- / 1.5	4.18	3.65	1.07 /60	-1.22 / 7	--	0.49	0.40
GEI	Vantagepoint Low Duration Bond Inv	VPIPX	C+	(800) 669-7400	C- / 3.9	0.98	0.62	0.41 /48	0.75 /38	1.42 /25	1.01	0.62
COI	Vantagepoint Low Duration Bond T	VQIPX	B	(800) 669-7400	C / 4.4	1.04	0.65	0.66 /53	1.00 /43	--	1.26	0.37
US	Victory CEMP Market Neutral Inc A	CBHAX	D+	(888) 944-4367	D / 1.6	3.27	2.16	4.95 /87	0.32 /30	--	1.92	1.17
US	Victory CEMP Market Neutral Inc C	CBHCX	C-	(888) 944-4367	C- / 3.4	3.06	1.75	4.15 /82	-0.44 /12	--	0.86	1.91
US	Victory CEMP Market Neutral Inc I	CBHIX	C+	(888) 944-4367	C / 5.4	3.31	2.25	5.23 /89	0.61 /35	--	2.42	0.96
USS	Victory INCORE Fund For Income A	IPFIX	C+	(800) 539-3863	C- / 4.2	2.07	1.13	1.34 /64	1.21 /46	2.02 /31	4.86	0.94
USS	Victory INCORE Fund For Income C	VFFCX	C	(800) 539-3863	C- / 3.6	1.92	0.67	0.48 /49	0.42 /32	1.24 /23	4.22	1.72
USA	Victory INCORE Fund For Income I	VFFIX	B+	(800) 539-3863	C+ / 5.6	2.13	1.26	1.51 /67	1.49 /52	2.30 /35	5.23	0.65
USS	Victory INCORE Fund For Income R	GGIFX	B-	(800) 539-3863	C / 5.0	2.07	1.02	1.22 /62	1.17 /46	2.00 /31	4.94	0.95
USA	Victory INCORE Fund For Income R6	VFFRX	U	(800) 539-3863	U /	2.13	1.27	1.63 /68	--	--	5.25	0.99
USA	Victory INCORE Fund For Income Y	VFFYX	B+	(800) 539-3863	C / 5.5	2.11	1.23	1.45 /66	1.43 /51	--	5.16	0.90
USS	Victory INCORE Total Return Bond A	MUCAX	D+	(800) 539-3863	C- / 4.1	2.32	0.88	-1.36 /19	1.55 /53	3.60 /55	3.07	1.10
USS	Victory INCORE Total Return Bond C	MUCCX	D+	(800) 539-3863	C- / 3.6	2.14	0.52	-2.07 /15	0.80 /39	2.84 /43	2.36	2.08

• Denotes fund is closed to new investors
* Denotes fund is included in Section II

RISK			NET ASSETS		ASSET							FUND MANAGER		MINIMUM		LOADS	
Risk Rating/Pts	3 Yr Avg Standard Deviation	Avg Duration	NAV As of 3/31/16	Total $(Mil)	Cash %	Gov. Bond %	Muni. Bond %	Corp. Bond %	Other %	Portfolio Turnover Ratio	Avg Coupon Rate	Manager Quality Pct	Manager Tenure (Years)	Initial Purch. $	Additional Purch. $	Front End Load	Back End Load
B+ / 8.8	1.6	2.8	21.72	1,542	0	0	0	99	1	62	3.7	89	7	10,000	0	0.0	0.0
B+ / 8.8	1.7	2.8	26.59	836	0	0	0	99	1	62	3.7	89	7	5,000,000	0	0.0	0.0
A- / 9.2	1.1	2.4	10.82	4,392	2	84	0	0	14	361	1.6	77	11	50,000	0	0.0	0.0
A- / 9.2	1.1	2.4	10.82	821	2	84	0	0	14	361	1.6	73	11	3,000	100	0.0	0.0
A+ / 9.7	0.7	1.9	20.40	313	1	98	0	0	1	64	1.5	76	3	10,000	0	0.0	0.0
A+ / 9.7	0.7	1.9	25.63	63	1	98	0	0	1	64	1.5	77	3	5,000,000	0	0.0	0.0
A+ / 9.8	0.4	1.5	15.82	11,235	0	0	99	0	1	32	2.7	77	20	50,000	0	0.0	0.0
A+ / 9.8	0.4	1.5	15.82	1,303	0	0	99	0	1	32	2.7	75	20	3,000	100	0.0	0.0
A / 9.3	1.0	2.4	10.76	6,362	0	97	0	0	3	87	1.4	77	16	50,000	0	0.0	0.0
A / 9.3	1.0	2.4	10.76	1,014	0	97	0	0	3	87	1.4	74	16	3,000	100	0.0	0.0
A- / 9.0	1.3	2.6	10.69	34,148	0	14	0	64	22	79	3.2	88	8	50,000	0	0.0	0.0
A- / 9.0	1.3	2.6	10.69	9,343	0	14	0	64	22	79	3.2	88	8	5,000,000	100	0.0	0.0
A- / 9.0	1.3	2.6	10.69	9,770	0	14	0	64	22	79	3.2	86	8	3,000	100	0.0	0.0
B+ / 8.6	1.8	2.4	24.61	2,658	0	99	0	0	1	26	0.9	18	4	10,000	100	0.0	0.0
B+ / 8.7	1.8	2.4	24.62	4,449	0	99	0	0	1	26	0.9	18	4	5,000,000	100	0.0	0.0
B+ / 8.6	1.8	2.4	24.57	4,436	0	99	0	0	1	26	0.9	17	4	3,000	100	0.0	0.0
U /	N/A	N/A	20.54	32	0	0	0	0	100	0	0.0	N/A	1	10,000	1	0.0	0.0
U /	N/A	N/A	10.27	1	0	0	0	0	100	0	0.0	N/A	1	3,000	1	0.0	0.0
U /	N/A	N/A	1.00	17,184	100	0	0	0	0	0	0.0	N/A	28	3,000	100	0.0	0.0
C+ / 6.2	3.1	N/A	10.86	36,290	4	45	1	25	25	108	0.0	81	6	5,000,000	100	0.0	0.0
C+ / 6.2	3.1	N/A	10.86	54,644	4	45	1	25	25	108	0.0	79	6	3,000	100	0.0	0.0
C+ / 6.3	3.1	5.5	10.90	25,266	0	47	1	26	26	72	3.3	57	24	100,000,000	100	0.0	0.0
C+ / 6.3	3.1	5.5	10.90	63,296	0	47	1	26	26	72	3.3	55	24	10,000	100	0.0	0.0
C+ / 6.3	3.1	5.5	10.90	30,243	0	47	1	26	26	72	3.3	56	24	5,000,000	100	0.0	0.0
C+ / 6.3	3.1	5.5	10.90	6,621	0	47	1	26	26	72	3.3	51	24	3,000	100	0.0	0.0
U /	N/A	7.1	21.76	15,360	1	75	3	18	3	13	2.7	N/A	3	10,000	100	0.0	0.0
U /	N/A	7.1	32.66	13,620	1	75	3	18	3	13	2.7	N/A	3	5,000,000	100	0.0	0.0
U /	N/A	7.1	10.88	19,559	1	75	3	18	3	13	2.7	N/A	3	3,000	100	0.0	0.0
A+ / 9.9	N/A	N/A	1.00	9,329	100	0	0	0	0	0	0.1	66	19	50,000	100	0.0	0.0
U /	N/A	0.9	20.00	509	24	23	0	26	27	0	1.9	N/A	1	50,000	100	0.0	0.0
U /	N/A	0.9	10.00	49	24	23	0	26	27	0	1.9	N/A	1	3,000	100	0.0	0.0
C+ / 6.3	3.1	N/A	15.46	37	0	47	1	21	31	0	0.0	43	7	25	15	0.0	0.0
B- / 7.5	2.7	N/A	14.27	247	25	48	0	10	17	0	0.0	20	7	25	15	0.0	0.0
C+ / 6.7	3.0	5.6	10.29	27	1	42	1	24	32	160	3.2	46	1	0	0	0.0	0.0
C+ / 6.7	3.0	5.6	10.36	13	1	42	1	24	32	160	3.2	53	1	0	0	0.0	0.0
C+ / 6.7	3.0	5.6	10.29	1,641	1	42	1	24	32	160	3.2	82	1	0	0	0.0	0.0
U /	N/A	4.2	8.59	361	6	0	0	90	4	76	5.7	N/A	2	0	0	0.0	0.0
D / 2.0	5.3	8.1	10.70	23	1	84	0	8	7	75	1.3	6	8	0	0	0.0	0.0
D / 2.0	5.3	8.1	10.72	497	1	84	0	8	7	75	1.3	3	8	0	0	0.0	0.0
A / 9.3	1.0	1.7	10.04	59	3	16	1	60	20	75	2.0	72	12	0	0	0.0	0.0
A / 9.4	0.9	1.7	10.04	724	3	16	1	60	20	75	2.0	82	12	0	0	0.0	0.0
B- / 7.1	2.9	N/A	9.42	29	20	0	0	0	80	135	0.0	48	N/A	2,500	50	5.8	0.0
B- / 7.0	2.9	N/A	9.36	1	20	0	0	0	80	135	0.0	26	N/A	2,500	50	0.0	0.0
B- / 7.0	2.9	N/A	9.45	48	20	0	0	0	80	135	0.0	60	N/A	100,000	50	0.0	0.0
B+ / 8.6	1.9	2.8	9.91	390	0	24	0	0	76	44	7.3	60	10	2,500	250	2.0	0.0
B+ / 8.5	1.9	2.8	9.83	72	0	24	0	0	76	44	7.3	32	10	2,500	250	0.0	0.0
B+ / 8.5	1.9	2.8	9.90	449	0	24	0	0	76	44	7.3	74	10	2,000,000	0	0.0	0.0
B+ / 8.6	1.9	2.8	9.91	85	0	24	0	0	76	44	7.3	59	10	0	0	0.0	0.0
U /	N/A	2.8	9.90	5	0	24	0	0	76	44	7.3	N/A	10	0	0	0.0	0.0
B+ / 8.6	1.9	2.8	9.91	6	0	24	0	0	76	44	7.3	73	10	0	0	0.0	0.0
C / 5.2	3.4	6.3	9.61	16	0	4	1	57	38	259	3.4	53	4	2,500	250	2.0	0.0
C / 5.2	3.4	6.3	9.68	3	0	4	1	57	38	259	3.4	29	4	2,500	250	0.0	0.0

99 Pct = Best
0 Pct = Worst

Fund Type	Fund Name	Ticker Symbol	Overall Investment Rating	Phone	PERFORMANCE: Performance Rating/Pts	Total Return % through 3/31/16: 3 Mo	6 Mo	1Yr / Pct	Annualized: 3Yr / Pct	5Yr / Pct	Incl. in Returns: Dividend Yield	Expense Ratio
COI	Victory INCORE Total Return Bond	MUCRX	**U**	(800) 539-3863	**U /**	2.38	0.91	-1.10 /21	--	--	3.39	1.53
USS	Victory INCORE Total Return Bond Y	MUCYX	**C-**	(800) 539-3863	**C / 5.5**	2.37	1.00	-1.12 /21	1.80 /58	3.87 /60	3.37	0.73
MUN	Victory National Muni A	VNMAX	**A+**	(800) 539-3863	**B- / 7.5**	1.16	2.23	3.00 /85	2.05 /78	3.68 /75	2.08	1.09
MUN	Victory National Muni Y	VNMYX	**A+**	(800) 539-3863	**B+ / 8.4**	1.13	2.27	3.18 /87	2.32 /81	--	2.39	1.10
MUS	Victory OH Muni Bond A	SOHTX	**A+**	(800) 539-3863	**B / 8.1**	1.53	2.46	2.78 /83	2.62 /84	3.89 /77	2.77	1.06
MUS	Viking Tax-Free Fund For MT Fd	VMTTX	**B+**	(800) 601-5593	**B / 8.0**	1.15	2.27	3.35 /89	2.58 /83	4.50 /81	2.72	1.15
MUS	Viking Tax-Free Fund For ND Fd	VNDFX	**B+**	(800) 601-5593	**B / 8.2**	1.37	2.52	3.98 /94	2.76 /86	4.40 /81	2.47	1.24
COH	Virtus Bond Fund A	SAVAX	**D+**	(800) 243-1574	**C- / 3.8**	1.93	1.39	0.18 /44	1.69 /56	3.62 /55	2.87	1.13
COH ●	Virtus Bond Fund B	SAVBX	**D+**	(800) 243-1574	**C / 4.3**	1.90	1.07	-0.46 /26	0.96 /42	2.85 /43	2.31	1.88
COH	Virtus Bond Fund C	SAVCX	**D+**	(800) 243-1574	**C / 4.3**	1.79	1.06	-0.46 /26	0.95 /42	2.85 /43	2.31	1.88
COH	Virtus Bond Fund I	SAVYX	**C-**	(800) 243-1574	**C+ / 6.1**	2.05	1.49	0.42 /48	1.95 /60	3.89 /60	3.18	0.88
MUS	Virtus California T/E Bond A	CTESX	**B+**	(800) 243-1574	**A- / 9.2**	1.65	3.08	4.03 /94	4.04 /96	6.28 /94	2.89	1.18
MUS	Virtus California T/E Bond I	CTXEX	**A-**	(800) 243-1574	**A+ / 9.7**	1.64	3.13	4.30 /96	4.25 /97	6.52 /95	3.23	0.93
EM	Virtus Emerging Markets Debt A	VEDAX	**E**	(800) 243-1574	**D- / 1.1**	4.14	4.79	0.96 /58	-0.74 /10	--	4.18	1.49
EM	Virtus Emerging Markets Debt C	VEDCX	**E**	(800) 243-1574	**D- / 1.2**	3.96	4.29	0.11 /41	-1.45 / 6	--	3.60	2.24
EM	Virtus Emerging Markets Debt I	VIEDX	**D-**	(800) 243-1574	**C- / 3.2**	4.21	4.80	1.10 /60	-0.50 /12	--	4.60	1.24
COH	Virtus High Yield A	PHCHX	**D-**	(800) 243-1574	**D+ / 2.9**	2.05	1.04	-2.65 /13	1.55 /53	4.59 /68	5.13	1.33
COH ●	Virtus High Yield B	PHCCX	**D-**	(800) 243-1574	**C- / 3.2**	1.93	0.45	-3.45 /10	0.76 /38	3.81 /58	4.72	2.08
COH	Virtus High Yield C	PGHCX	**D-**	(800) 243-1574	**C- / 3.1**	1.91	0.44	-3.65 / 9	0.74 /38	3.82 /59	4.67	2.08
COH	Virtus High Yield I	PHCIX	**D**	(800) 243-1574	**C / 5.2**	2.11	1.16	-2.42 /14	1.80 /58	--	5.59	1.08
GEI	Virtus Low Duration Income A	HIMZX	**C+**	(800) 243-1574	**C- / 3.9**	0.99	0.52	0.89 /57	1.34 /49	2.55 /38	1.87	1.11
GEI	Virtus Low Duration Income C	PCMZX	**C+**	(800) 243-1574	**C- / 3.6**	0.91	0.25	0.24 /45	0.62 /35	1.80 /29	1.17	1.86
GEI	Virtus Low Duration Income I	HIBIX	**B+**	(800) 243-1574	**C / 5.5**	1.05	0.74	1.14 /61	1.63 /55	2.80 /42	2.16	0.86
GES	Virtus Multi-Sec Intermediate Bd A	NAMFX	**D-**	(800) 243-1574	**D / 1.6**	2.14	1.43	-1.19 /20	0.79 /39	3.51 /53	4.25	1.11
GES ●	Virtus Multi-Sec Intermediate Bd B	NBMFX	**D-**	(800) 243-1574	**D / 2.2**	1.96	1.06	-1.93 /16	0.04 /24	2.71 /41	3.66	1.86
GES	Virtus Multi-Sec Intermediate Bd C	NCMFX	**D-**	(800) 243-1574	**D / 2.2**	2.04	1.04	-1.92 /16	0.03 /21	2.73 /41	3.61	1.86
GES	Virtus Multi-Sec Intermediate Bd I	VMFIX	**D**	(800) 243-1574	**C / 4.5**	2.26	1.51	-0.90 /23	1.06 /44	3.78 /58	4.62	0.86
GL	Virtus Multi-Sec Intermediate Bd R6	VMFRX	**U**	(800) 243-1574	**U /**	2.17	1.44	-0.92 /22	--	--	4.70	0.79
* GES	Virtus Multi-Sector Short Term Bd A	NARAX	**C-**	(800) 243-1574	**C- / 3.1**	1.15	0.57	0.06 /39	0.94 /42	2.79 /42	2.78	0.97
GES ●	Virtus Multi-Sector Short Term Bd B	PBARX	**C-**	(800) 243-1574	**C- / 3.2**	1.03	0.32	-0.45 /27	0.45 /32	2.30 /35	2.35	1.47
GES	Virtus Multi-Sector Short Term Bd C	PSTCX	**C**	(800) 243-1574	**C- / 3.8**	1.07	0.44	-0.20 /29	0.75 /38	2.55 /38	2.55	1.22
GES	Virtus Multi-Sector Short Term Bd I	PIMSX	**C+**	(800) 243-1574	**C / 4.6**	0.99	0.48	0.30 /46	1.20 /46	3.05 /46	3.10	0.72
GES	Virtus Multi-Sector Short Term Bd T	PMSTX	**C-**	(800) 243-1574	**D+ / 2.7**	0.95	0.19	-0.70 /24	0.18 /28	2.00 /31	2.06	1.72
LP	Virtus Senior Floating Rate Fund A	PSFRX	**C-**	(800) 243-1574	**C- / 3.4**	1.77	-0.11	-0.96 /22	1.47 /52	2.98 /45	3.79	1.20
LP	Virtus Senior Floating Rate Fund C	PFSRX	**C-**	(800) 243-1574	**C- / 3.3**	1.59	-0.47	-1.79 /17	0.71 /37	2.19 /34	3.14	1.95
LP	Virtus Senior Floating Rate Fund I	PSFIX	**C+**	(800) 243-1574	**C / 5.3**	1.83	0.02	-0.72 /24	1.72 /56	3.22 /49	4.16	0.95
GEN	Virtus Strat Income A	VASBX	**U**	(800) 243-1574	**U /**	1.00	0.87	-0.15 /30	--	--	3.49	2.42
GEN	Virtus Strat Income C	VSBCX	**U**	(800) 243-1574	**U /**	0.72	0.51	-1.08 /21	--	--	2.88	3.17
GEL	Virtus Strat Income I	VISBX	**U**	(800) 243-1574	**U /**	0.96	0.89	-0.10 /30	--	--	3.89	2.17
MUN	Virtus Tax Exempt Bond A	HXBZX	**B**	(800) 243-1574	**B / 8.0**	1.41	2.51	2.98 /85	2.69 /85	5.24 /87	2.42	1.00
MUN	Virtus Tax Exempt Bond C	PXCZX	**B-**	(800) 243-1574	**B / 7.9**	1.23	2.14	2.22 /79	1.90 /76	4.44 /81	1.76	1.75
MUN	Virtus Tax Exempt Bond I	HXBIX	**A-**	(800) 243-1574	**A- / 9.0**	1.47	2.63	3.24 /87	2.94 /88	5.50 /89	2.74	0.75
EM	Voya Diversified Emerg Mkts Dbt A	IADEX	**D-**	(800) 992-0180	**C- / 3.7**	4.67	4.75	0.92 /57	0.51 /33	--	4.53	8.56
EM	Voya Diversified Emerg Mkts Dbt C	ICDEX	**D-**	(800) 992-0180	**C- / 3.4**	4.48	4.29	0.11 /41	-0.23 /14	--	4.22	9.31
EM	Voya Diversified Emerg Mkts Dbt I	IIDEX	**D**	(800) 992-0180	**C / 5.5**	4.80	4.92	1.21 /62	0.79 /39	--	5.25	8.17
EM	Voya Diversified Emerg Mkts Dbt W	IWDEX	**D**	(800) 992-0180	**C / 5.4**	4.80	4.77	1.18 /61	0.77 /38	--	5.22	8.31
EM	Voya Emerg Markets Corporate Debt	IMCDX	**C-**	(800) 992-0180	**B / 7.9**	4.32	4.64	2.45 /74	2.77 /74	--	4.89	1.03
EM	Voya Emerg Mkts Hard Curr Debt P	IHCSX	**C-**	(800) 992-0180	**B+ / 8.6**	4.84	6.77	4.40 /84	3.38 /79	--	5.42	0.82
EM	Voya Emg Mkts Local Currency Debt	ILCDX	**E-**	(800) 992-0180	**E- / 0.1**	8.15	8.47	-2.62 /13	-7.58 / 1	--	0.00	0.98
LP	Voya Floating Rate A	IFRAX	**C+**	(800) 992-0180	**C / 4.4**	1.45	-0.11	-0.27 /28	1.92 /60	3.33 /50	3.84	1.09
LP	Voya Floating Rate C	IFRCX	**C+**	(800) 992-0180	**C- / 4.1**	1.26	-0.48	-1.01 /22	1.16 /46	2.56 /39	3.18	1.84
LP	Voya Floating Rate I	IFRIX	**B+**	(800) 992-0180	**C+ / 6.0**	1.51	0.02	-0.01 /31	2.18 /65	3.57 /54	4.20	0.78

● Denotes fund is closed to new investors
* Denotes fund is included in Section II

RISK			NET ASSETS		ASSET							FUND MANAGER		MINIMUM		LOADS	
Risk Rating/Pts	3 Yr Avg Standard Deviation	Avg Duration	NAV As of 3/31/16	Total $(Mil)	Cash %	Gov. Bond %	Muni. Bond %	Corp. Bond %	Other %	Portfolio Turnover Ratio	Avg Coupon Rate	Manager Quality Pct	Manager Tenure (Years)	Initial Purch. $	Additional Purch. $	Front End Load	Back End Load
U /	N/A	6.3	9.63	2	0	4	1	57	38	259	3.4	N/A	4	0	0	0.0	0.0
C / 5.2	3.4	6.3	9.63	81	0	4	1	57	38	259	3.4	64	4	1,000,000	0	0.0	0.0
B / 7.9	2.5	4.3	11.09	60	4	0	95	0	1	97	4.4	45	22	2,500	250	2.0	0.0
B / 7.9	2.5	4.3	11.08	3	4	0	95	0	1	97	4.4	56	22	0	0	0.0	0.0
B / 7.6	2.7	4.3	11.39	41	4	0	96	0	0	29	4.3	58	22	2,500	250	2.0	0.0
C+ / 5.6	3.2	4.5	10.31	72	0	0	100	0	0	13	4.6	36	17	1,000	50	2.5	0.0
C / 5.5	3.3	4.8	10.55	26	0	0	100	0	0	18	4.2	41	17	1,000	50	2.5	0.0
C- / 3.9	3.5	4.3	11.01	46	2	8	1	55	34	64	4.7	88	4	2,500	100	3.8	0.0
C- / 3.9	3.5	4.3	10.73	N/A	2	8	1	55	34	64	4.7	70	4	2,500	100	0.0	0.0
C- / 3.9	3.5	4.3	10.77	12	2	8	1	55	34	64	4.7	70	4	2,500	100	0.0	0.0
C- / 3.9	3.5	4.3	11.18	22	2	8	1	55	34	64	4.7	90	4	100,000	0	0.0	0.0
C / 4.3	3.8	6.3	12.06	20	1	0	98	0	1	24	5.0	N/A	20	2,500	100	2.8	0.0
C / 4.3	3.8	6.3	12.03	11	1	0	98	0	1	24	5.0	75	20	100,000	0	0.0	0.0
E / 0.5	8.0	N/A	8.75	1	2	35	0	60	3	47	0.0	39	4	2,500	100	3.8	0.0
E / 0.5	8.0	N/A	8.74	N/A	2	35	0	60	3	47	0.0	20	4	2,500	100	0.0	0.0
E / 0.5	8.0	N/A	8.74	26	2	35	0	60	3	47	0.0	47	4	100,000	0	0.0	0.0
D / 1.8	5.4	3.9	3.92	58	5	0	0	83	12	94	6.5	63	5	2,500	100	3.8	0.0
D / 1.8	5.3	3.9	3.81	N/A	5	0	0	83	12	94	6.5	35	5	2,500	100	0.0	0.0
D / 1.8	5.4	3.9	3.85	3	5	0	0	83	12	94	6.5	34	5	2,500	100	0.0	0.0
D / 1.8	5.3	3.9	3.92	7	5	0	0	83	12	94	6.5	77	5	100,000	0	0.0	0.0
B+ / 8.9	1.6	2.3	10.76	96	3	6	0	31	60	58	3.6	78	4	2,500	100	2.3	0.0
B+ / 8.9	1.6	2.3	10.77	49	3	6	0	31	60	58	3.6	48	4	2,500	100	0.0	0.0
B+ / 8.9	1.5	2.3	10.76	180	3	6	0	31	60	58	3.6	85	4	100,000	0	0.0	0.0
D+ / 2.8	4.9	4.1	9.69	98	0	7	0	61	32	66	5.6	28	22	2,500	100	3.8	0.0
D+ / 2.8	4.9	4.1	9.66	2	0	7	0	61	32	66	5.6	14	22	2,500	100	0.0	0.0
D+ / 2.8	4.9	4.1	9.78	75	0	7	0	61	32	66	5.6	14	22	2,500	100	0.0	0.0
D+ / 2.8	4.9	4.1	9.70	110	0	7	0	61	32	66	5.6	37	22	100,000	0	0.0	0.0
U /	N/A	4.1	9.69	2	0	7	0	61	32	66	5.6	N/A	22	0	0	0.0	0.0
B / 8.2	2.3	2.2	4.65	1,412	0	3	0	47	50	37	4.5	59	23	2,500	100	2.3	0.0
B / 8.1	2.4	2.2	4.62	N/A	0	3	0	47	50	37	4.5	40	23	2,500	100	0.0	0.0
B / 8.1	2.4	2.2	4.71	1,322	0	3	0	47	50	37	4.5	48	23	2,500	100	0.0	0.0
B / 8.1	2.3	2.2	4.65	3,843	0	3	0	47	50	37	4.5	71	23	100,000	0	0.0	0.0
B / 8.0	2.4	2.2	4.69	522	0	3	0	47	50	37	4.5	30	23	2,500	100	0.0	0.0
B / 7.7	2.6	0.4	9.18	232	0	0	0	28	72	34	4.4	91	8	2,500	100	2.8	0.0
B / 7.8	2.5	0.4	9.19	119	0	0	0	28	72	34	4.4	79	8	2,500	100	0.0	0.0
B / 7.8	2.6	0.4	9.17	230	0	0	0	28	72	34	4.4	92	8	100,000	0	0.0	0.0
U /	N/A	N/A	9.53	1	0	0	0	0	100	97	0.0	N/A	2	2,500	100	3.8	0.0
U /	N/A	N/A	9.52	1	0	0	0	0	100	97	0.0	N/A	2	2,500	100	0.0	0.0
U /	N/A	N/A	9.52	26	0	0	0	0	100	97	0.0	N/A	2	100,000	0	0.0	0.0
C / 4.9	3.5	5.4	11.52	73	2	0	97	0	1	22	4.7	30	4	2,500	100	2.8	0.0
C / 5.0	3.5	5.4	11.52	29	2	0	97	0	1	22	4.7	15	4	2,500	100	0.0	0.0
C / 5.0	3.5	5.4	11.52	101	2	0	97	0	1	22	4.7	37	4	100,000	0	0.0	0.0
E+ / 0.8	6.9	N/A	8.96	N/A	6	47	0	44	3	74	0.0	85	3	1,000	0	2.5	0.0
E+ / 0.8	6.8	N/A	8.86	N/A	6	47	0	44	3	74	0.0	57	3	1,000	0	0.0	0.0
E+ / 0.8	6.9	N/A	8.96	1	6	47	0	44	3	74	0.0	88	3	250,000	0	0.0	0.0
E+ / 0.8	6.8	N/A	8.96	N/A	6	47	0	44	3	74	0.0	88	3	1,000	0	0.0	0.0
D / 2.0	5.6	4.7	9.60	90	0	0	0	0	100	52	4.8	98	3	0	0	0.0	0.0
E+ / 0.7	7.1	5.5	9.36	136	0	0	0	0	100	32	5.3	99	3	0	0	0.0	0.0
E- / 0.2	11.7	3.4	7.43	83	0	0	0	0	100	22	6.4	1	3	0	0	0.0	0.0
B+ / 8.3	2.1	N/A	9.70	40	12	0	0	9	79	60	0.0	92	N/A	1,000	0	2.5	0.0
B+ / 8.4	2.1	N/A	9.70	51	12	0	0	9	79	60	0.0	85	N/A	1,000	0	0.0	0.0
B+ / 8.4	2.1	N/A	9.70	891	12	0	0	9	79	60	0.0	94	N/A	250,000	0	0.0	0.0

Fund Type	Fund Name (99 Pct = Best, 0 Pct = Worst)	Ticker Symbol	Overall Investment Rating	Phone	PERFORMANCE: Performance Rating/Pts	Total Return % through 3/31/16: 3 Mo	6 Mo	1Yr / Pct	Annualized: 3Yr / Pct	Annualized: 5Yr / Pct	Incl. in Returns: Dividend Yield	Expense Ratio
LP	Voya Floating Rate P	IFRPX	**U**	(800) 992-0180	**U** /	1.67	0.35	0.55 /51	--	--	4.88	0.77
LP	Voya Floating Rate R	IFRRX	**B-**	(800) 992-0180	**C / 5.1**	1.49	-0.23	-0.52 /26	1.67 /55	3.06 /46	3.69	1.34
LP	Voya Floating Rate W	IFRWX	**B+**	(800) 992-0180	**C+ / 6.0**	1.50	0.02	-0.01 /31	2.17 /65	3.60 /55	4.19	0.84
GL	Voya Global Bond A	INGBX	**U**	(800) 992-0180	**U** /	5.96	4.49	2.12 /73	--	1.34 /23	4.09	0.98
GL	● Voya Global Bond B	IGBBX	**D-**	(800) 992-0180	**C- / 3.1**	5.81	4.13	1.44 /65	-0.74 /10	0.60 /18	3.46	1.73
GL	Voya Global Bond C	IGBCX	**D-**	(800) 992-0180	**C- / 3.0**	5.80	4.12	1.45 /66	-0.77 /10	0.58 /18	3.47	1.73
GL	Voya Global Bond I	IGBIX	**D**	(800) 992-0180	**C / 5.0**	6.07	4.67	2.43 /74	0.25 /29	1.64 /27	4.50	0.61
GL	Voya Global Bond O	IGBOX	**D**	(800) 992-0180	**C / 4.5**	5.99	4.49	2.17 /73	-0.03 /15	1.35 /24	4.29	0.98
GEI	Voya Global Bond Portfolio Adv	IOSAX	**D**	(800) 992-0180	**C- / 3.7**	6.32	4.72	1.86 /71	-0.49 /12	0.91 /20	0.00	1.20
GEI	Voya Global Bond Portfolio Inl	IOSIX	**D**	(800) 992-0180	**C / 4.8**	6.42	4.95	2.41 /74	0.03 /21	1.42 /25	0.00	0.70
GEI	Voya Global Bond Portfolio Svc	IOSSX	**D**	(800) 992-0180	**C / 4.3**	6.32	4.85	2.12 /73	-0.22 /14	1.16 /22	0.00	0.95
GL	Voya Global Bond R	IGBRX	**D**	(800) 992-0180	**C- / 4.1**	6.03	4.49	1.99 /72	-0.26 /13	--	3.97	1.23
GL	Voya Global Bond R6	IGBZX	**U**	(800) 992-0180	**U** /	6.05	4.77	2.45 /74	--	--	4.51	0.59
GL	Voya Global Bond W	IGBWX	**D**	(800) 992-0180	**C / 5.0**	6.06	4.62	2.34 /74	0.23 /29	1.59 /26	4.55	0.73
* USA	Voya GNMA Income A	LEXNX	**B**	(800) 992-0180	**C / 5.5**	1.66	1.49	2.21 /73	2.07 /63	3.10 /47	2.92	0.92
USA	● Voya GNMA Income B	LEXBX	**B-**	(800) 992-0180	**C / 5.1**	1.36	0.99	1.32 /64	1.26 /47	2.30 /35	2.25	1.67
USA	Voya GNMA Income C	LEGNX	**B-**	(800) 992-0180	**C / 5.2**	1.36	1.01	1.46 /66	1.30 /48	2.34 /36	2.26	1.67
USA	Voya GNMA Income I	LEINX	**A**	(800) 992-0180	**B- / 7.0**	1.62	1.52	2.50 /75	2.35 /68	3.38 /51	3.27	0.65
USA	Voya GNMA Income W	IGMWX	**A**	(800) 992-0180	**B- / 7.0**	1.61	1.50	2.46 /74	2.33 /68	3.36 /51	3.24	0.67
COH	Voya High Yield Bond A	IHYAX	**D**	(800) 992-0180	**C / 5.1**	2.73	1.55	-1.54 /18	2.28 /67	5.36 /74	5.18	1.09
COH	● Voya High Yield Bond B	INYBX	**D**	(800) 992-0180	**C / 4.8**	2.55	1.18	-2.28 /14	1.50 /52	4.56 /68	4.54	1.84
COH	Voya High Yield Bond C	IMYCX	**D**	(800) 992-0180	**C / 4.7**	2.43	1.06	-2.38 /14	1.48 /52	4.58 /68	4.57	1.84
COH	Voya High Yield Bond I	IHYIX	**C-**	(800) 992-0180	**C+ / 6.9**	2.83	1.73	-1.19 /20	2.66 /73	5.76 /76	5.69	0.68
COH	Voya High Yield Bond P	IHYPX	**U**	(800) 992-0180	**U** /	2.97	2.03	-0.60 /25	--	--	6.30	0.68
COH	Voya High Yield Bond R	IRSTX	**U**	(800) 992-0180	**U** /	2.67	1.43	-1.77 /17	--	--	5.06	1.34
COH	Voya High Yield Bond W	IHYWX	**D+**	(800) 992-0180	**C+ / 6.7**	2.79	1.69	-1.27 /20	2.56 /71	--	5.59	0.84
COH	Voya High Yield Institutional	IPIMX	**D+**	(800) 992-0180	**C+ / 6.1**	3.27	1.66	-1.34 /19	2.08 /63	4.75 /70	6.34	0.50
COH	Voya High Yield Service	IPHYX	**D+**	(800) 992-0180	**C+ / 5.6**	3.10	1.53	-1.69 /17	1.82 /58	4.49 /67	6.09	0.75
COH	Voya High Yield Service 2	IPYSX	**D+**	(800) 992-0180	**C / 5.4**	3.17	1.46	-1.72 /17	1.68 /55	4.34 /66	5.93	1.00
COI	Voya Intermediate Bond A	IIBAX	**C+**	(800) 992-0180	**C+ / 6.4**	2.70	2.41	1.09 /60	2.73 /74	4.71 /70	2.38	0.67
COI	● Voya Intermediate Bond B	IIBBX	**C**	(800) 992-0180	**C+ / 6.2**	2.41	1.92	0.31 /46	1.95 /60	3.90 /60	1.68	1.42
COI	Voya Intermediate Bond C	IICCX	**C+**	(800) 992-0180	**C+ / 6.2**	2.42	1.94	0.35 /47	1.98 /61	3.90 /60	1.72	1.42
COI	Voya Intermediate Bond I	IICIX	**B**	(800) 992-0180	**B / 7.8**	2.69	2.48	1.32 /64	3.09 /77	5.02 /72	2.77	0.33
COI	Voya Intermediate Bond O	IDBOX	**B**	(800) 992-0180	**B- / 7.5**	2.70	2.41	1.09 /60	2.74 /74	4.69 /70	2.45	0.67
GEI	Voya Intermediate Bond Port Adv	IIBPX	**B-**	(800) 992-0180	**B- / 7.1**	2.66	2.38	0.76 /54	2.50 /71	4.48 /67	3.21	1.04
GEI	Voya Intermediate Bond Port I	IPIIX	**B**	(800) 992-0180	**B / 7.6**	2.72	2.31	0.94 /58	2.93 /76	4.94 /71	3.29	0.54
* GEI	Voya Intermediate Bond Port S	IPISX	**B-**	(800) 992-0180	**B- / 7.2**	2.65	2.13	0.67 /53	2.64 /73	4.67 /69	3.04	0.79
COI	Voya Intermediate Bond R	IIBOX	**B-**	(800) 992-0180	**B- / 7.1**	2.54	2.29	0.85 /56	2.48 /70	4.45 /67	2.21	0.92
COI	Voya Intermediate Bond R6	IIBZX	**U**	(800) 992-0180	**U** /	2.69	2.59	1.43 /65	--	--	2.78	0.32
COI	Voya Intermediate Bond W	IIBWX	**B**	(800) 992-0180	**B / 7.7**	2.67	2.44	1.25 /63	3.00 /76	5.19 /73	2.70	0.42
COI	Voya Investment Grade Credit P	IIGPX	**C+**	(800) 992-0180	**B+ / 8.8**	3.70	4.46	0.90 /57	4.55 /88	--	3.87	0.61
GEI	Voya Investment Grade Credit SMA	ISCFX	**C+**	(800) 992-0180	**B+ / 8.8**	3.74	4.42	1.00 /59	4.65 /88	5.32 /74	3.97	0.65
GEI	Voya Limited Maturity Bond Adv	IMBAX	**C+**	(800) 992-0180	**C- / 3.4**	0.71	0.30	0.35 /47	0.47 /33	0.64 /18	0.55	1.03
GEI	Voya Limited Maturity Bond Inst	ILBPX	**B+**	(800) 992-0180	**C / 4.6**	0.89	0.69	1.03 /59	1.10 /45	1.25 /23	1.21	0.28
GEI	Voya Limited Maturity Bond Svc	ILMBX	**B**	(800) 992-0180	**C- / 4.2**	0.79	0.59	0.75 /54	0.85 /40	1.00 /20	0.94	0.53
MM	Voya Liquid Assets Inst	IPLXX	**C**	(800) 992-0180	**D / 2.1**	0.04	0.04	0.05 /39	0.02 /21	0.04 /12	0.05	0.28
* LP	Voya Money Market Port I	IVMXX	**C-**	(800) 992-0180	**D / 1.9**	0.03	0.03	0.03 /36	0.02 /18	0.02 / 7	0.03	0.39
MTG	Voya Securitized Credit P	VSCFX	**U**	(800) 992-0180	**U** /	1.05	0.91	3.42 /79	--	--	4.97	0.72
LP	Voya Senior Income A	XSIAX	**C-**	(800) 992-0180	**C / 4.8**	1.85	-0.90	-1.91 /16	2.47 /70	4.26 /65	5.58	2.46
LP	● Voya Senior Income B	XSIBX	**C-**	(800) 992-0180	**C / 4.9**	1.56	-1.25	-2.58 /13	1.90 /60	3.72 /57	5.22	3.21
LP	Voya Senior Income C	XSICX	**C-**	(800) 992-0180	**C / 5.0**	1.64	-1.17	-2.42 /14	1.93 /60	3.74 /57	5.20	2.96
LP	Voya Senior Income I	XSIIX	**C**	(800) 992-0180	**C+ / 6.4**	1.84	-0.78	-1.67 /17	2.75 /74	4.53 /68	6.01	2.21

● Denotes fund is closed to new investors
* Denotes fund is included in Section II

RISK			NET ASSETS		ASSET							FUND MANAGER		MINIMUM		LOADS	
Risk Rating/Pts	3 Yr Avg Standard Deviation	Avg Duration	NAV As of 3/31/16	Total $(Mil)	Cash %	Gov. Bond %	Muni. Bond %	Corp. Bond %	Other %	Portfolio Turnover Ratio	Avg Coupon Rate	Manager Quality Pct	Manager Tenure (Years)	Initial Purch. $	Additional Purch. $	Front End Load	Back End Load
U /	N/A	N/A	9.69	22	12	0	0	9	79	60	0.0	N/A	N/A	0	0	0.0	0.0
B+ / 8.4	2.1	N/A	9.69	108	12	0	0	9	79	60	0.0	91	N/A	0	0	0.0	0.0
B+ / 8.4	2.1	N/A	9.72	98	12	0	0	9	79	60	0.0	94	N/A	1,000	0	0.0	0.0
U /	5.7	6.5	10.02	58	2	34	0	33	31	396	3.6	N/A	5	1,000	0	2.5	0.0
D / 1.9	5.8	6.5	9.92	N/A	2	34	0	33	31	396	3.6	40	5	1,000	0	0.0	0.0
D / 1.9	5.7	6.5	9.96	25	2	34	0	33	31	396	3.6	39	5	1,000	0	0.0	0.0
D / 1.9	5.8	6.5	9.98	91	2	34	0	33	31	396	3.6	80	5	250,000	0	0.0	0.0
D / 1.9	5.7	6.5	9.81	2	2	34	0	33	31	396	3.6	71	5	1,000	0	0.0	0.0
D / 1.7	5.9	6.8	10.43	27	3	34	0	34	29	296	3.7	6	5	0	0	0.0	0.0
D / 1.8	5.9	6.8	10.61	174	3	34	0	34	29	296	3.7	7	5	0	0	0.0	0.0
D / 1.8	5.9	6.8	10.60	43	3	34	0	34	29	296	3.7	6	5	0	0	0.0	0.0
D / 1.9	5.7	6.5	10.00	5	2	34	0	33	31	396	3.6	57	5	0	0	0.0	0.0
U /	N/A	6.5	10.02	185	2	34	0	33	31	396	3.6	N/A	5	1,000,000	0	0.0	0.0
D / 2.0	5.7	6.5	9.80	83	2	34	0	33	31	396	3.6	79	5	1,000	0	0.0	0.0
B+ / 8.3	2.2	2.4	8.63	630	0	0	0	0	100	511	4.4	87	7	1,000	0	2.5	0.0
B+ / 8.3	2.2	2.4	8.57	N/A	0	0	0	0	100	511	4.4	60	7	1,000	0	0.0	0.0
B+ / 8.3	2.2	2.4	8.58	108	0	0	0	0	100	511	4.4	61	7	1,000	0	0.0	0.0
B+ / 8.3	2.2	2.4	8.64	503	0	0	0	0	100	511	4.4	90	7	250,000	0	0.0	0.0
B+ / 8.3	2.2	2.4	8.65	119	0	0	0	0	100	511	4.4	90	7	1,000	0	0.0	0.0
D / 2.0	5.2	4.2	7.62	78	0	0	0	99	1	37	6.3	87	9	1,000	0	2.5	0.0
D / 2.0	5.2	4.2	7.61	N/A	0	0	0	99	1	37	6.3	63	9	1,000	0	0.0	0.0
D / 2.0	5.2	4.2	7.61	13	0	0	0	99	1	37	6.3	62	9	1,000	0	0.0	0.0
D / 2.0	5.2	4.2	7.61	347	0	0	0	99	1	37	6.3	91	9	250,000	0	0.0	0.0
U /	N/A	4.2	7.61	103	0	0	0	99	1	37	6.3	N/A	9	0	0	0.0	0.0
U /	N/A	4.2	7.62	N/A	0	0	0	99	1	37	6.3	N/A	9	0	0	0.0	0.0
D / 2.0	5.2	4.2	7.63	83	0	0	0	99	1	37	6.3	90	9	1,000	0	0.0	0.0
D / 1.9	5.3	4.3	9.49	64	1	0	0	98	1	78	6.5	83	2	0	0	0.0	0.0
D / 1.9	5.3	4.3	9.48	467	1	0	0	98	1	78	6.5	77	2	0	0	0.0	0.0
D / 1.9	5.3	4.3	9.50	5	1	0	0	98	1	78	6.5	72	2	0	0	0.0	0.0
C+ / 5.7	3.2	5.2	10.09	489	2	23	0	30	45	587	3.5	85	7	1,000	0	2.5	0.0
C+ / 5.6	3.3	5.2	10.06	N/A	2	23	0	30	45	587	3.5	57	7	1,000	0	0.0	0.0
C+ / 5.6	3.2	5.2	10.07	32	2	23	0	30	45	587	3.5	58	7	1,000	0	0.0	0.0
C+ / 5.6	3.3	5.2	10.08	1,127	2	23	0	30	45	587	3.5	89	7	250,000	0	0.0	0.0
C+ / 5.6	3.2	5.2	10.09	34	2	23	0	30	45	587	3.5	85	7	1,000	0	0.0	0.0
C+ / 5.8	3.2	5.2	12.73	322	0	14	0	38	48	428	4.0	62	7	0	0	0.0	0.0
C+ / 5.7	3.2	5.2	12.86	1,250	0	14	0	38	48	428	4.0	80	7	0	0	0.0	0.0
C+ / 5.8	3.2	5.2	12.77	3,240	0	14	0	38	48	428	4.0	72	7	0	0	0.0	0.0
C+ / 5.8	3.2	5.2	10.10	146	2	23	0	30	45	587	3.5	81	7	0	0	0.0	0.0
U /	N/A	5.2	10.08	596	2	23	0	30	45	587	3.5	N/A	7	1,000,000	0	0.0	0.0
C+ / 5.6	3.3	5.2	10.07	586	2	23	0	30	45	587	3.5	88	7	1,000	0	0.0	0.0
C- / 3.2	4.6	6.8	10.71	126	1	3	0	94	2	436	4.1	94	4	0	0	0.0	0.0
C- / 3.1	4.6	6.8	10.70	4	1	3	0	94	2	436	4.1	93	4	0	0	0.0	0.0
A+ / 9.7	0.6	1.8	9.90	26	2	30	0	45	23	433	2.2	69	7	0	0	0.0	0.0
A+ / 9.7	0.7	1.8	10.18	148	2	30	0	45	23	433	2.2	86	7	0	0	0.0	0.0
A+ / 9.7	0.6	1.8	10.23	98	2	30	0	45	23	433	2.2	81	7	0	0	0.0	0.0
A+ / 9.9	N/A	N/A	1.00	82	100	0	0	0	0	0	0.1	66	12	0	0	0.0	0.0
A+ / 9.9	N/A	N/A	1.00	541	0	0	0	0	100	0	0.0	62	12	0	0	0.0	0.0
U /	N/A	4.2	9.99	144	0	0	0	0	100	33	3.8	N/A	N/A	0	0	0.0	0.0
C / 5.3	3.4	0.1	12.24	199	0	0	0	20	80	63	7.6	93	N/A	1,000	0	2.5	0.0
C / 5.3	3.3	0.1	12.18	N/A	0	0	0	20	80	63	7.6	89	N/A	1,000	0	0.0	0.0
C / 5.3	3.3	0.1	12.21	225	0	0	0	20	80	63	7.6	90	N/A	1,000	0	0.0	0.0
C / 5.3	3.4	0.1	12.20	34	0	0	0	20	80	63	7.6	95	N/A	250,000	0	0.0	0.0

Fund Type	Fund Name (99 Pct = Best, 0 Pct = Worst)	Ticker Symbol	Overall Investment Rating	Phone	PERFORMANCE: Performance Rating/Pts	Total Return % through 3/31/16: 3 Mo	6 Mo	1Yr / Pct	Annualized: 3Yr / Pct	Annualized: 5Yr / Pct	Incl. in Returns: Dividend Yield	Expense Ratio
LP	Voya Senior Income W	XSIWX	C	(800) 992-0180	C+ / 6.4	1.84	-0.77	-1.66 /17	2.69 /73	4.53 /68	5.99	2.21
COI	Voya Short Term Bond A	IASBX	C+	(800) 992-0180	C- / 3.2	0.70	0.47	0.65 /52	1.09 /44	--	1.52	0.89
COI	Voya Short Term Bond C	ICSBX	C	(800) 992-0180	D+ / 2.9	0.51	0.10	-0.21 /29	0.32 /30	--	0.80	1.64
COI	Voya Short Term Bond I	IISBX	B+	(800) 992-0180	C / 4.9	0.66	0.61	0.82 /56	1.35 /49	--	1.83	0.59
COI	Voya Short Term Bond R	VSTRX	U	(800) 992-0180	U /	0.64	0.34	0.39 /48	--	--	1.30	1.14
COI	Voya Short Term Bond W	IWSBX	B+	(800) 992-0180	C / 4.9	0.75	0.58	0.87 /57	1.32 /49	--	1.78	0.64
GEI	Voya Strategic Income Opptys A	ISIAX	C-	(800) 992-0180	C / 4.7	0.20	0.36	0.25 /45	2.13 /64	--	0.54	2.82
GEI	Voya Strategic Income Opptys C	ISICX	C-	(800) 992-0180	C / 4.3	-0.10	-0.06	-0.57 /25	1.27 /48	--	0.14	3.57
GEI	Voya Strategic Income Opptys I	IISIX	C+	(800) 992-0180	C+ / 6.6	0.20	0.81	0.91 /57	2.48 /70	--	0.81	2.43
GEI	Voya Strategic Income Opptys R	ISIRX	C-	(800) 992-0180	C / 5.4	0.00	0.37	0.17 /43	1.80 /58	--	0.57	3.07
GEI	Voya Strategic Income Opptys W	ISIWX	C	(800) 992-0180	C+ / 5.7	0.20	0.17	0.17 /43	2.03 /62	--	0.78	2.57
GEI	Voya US Bond Index Adv	ILUAX	C+	(800) 992-0180	C+ / 5.9	2.86	2.12	1.10 /60	1.61 /54	2.89 /43	1.78	0.91
GEI	Voya US Bond Index I	ILBAX	B-	(800) 992-0180	C+ / 6.9	3.04	2.36	1.68 /69	2.16 /65	3.41 /52	2.24	0.41
GEI	Voya US Bond Index S	ILABX	C+	(800) 992-0180	C+ / 6.4	2.96	2.25	1.34 /64	1.87 /59	3.14 /47	2.01	0.66
GEI	VY BlackRock Infl Pro Bond Adv	IBRAX	E+	(800) 992-0180	E+ / 0.7	3.60	2.57	-0.75 /24	-2.02 / 4	1.61 /27	0.01	1.32
GEI	VY BlackRock Infl Pro Bond Inst	IBRIX	D-	(800) 992-0180	D- / 1.1	3.70	2.85	-0.26 /28	-1.45 / 6	2.21 /34	0.46	0.57
GEI	VY BlackRock Infl Pro Bond Svc	IBRSX	E+	(800) 992-0180	E+ / 0.9	3.62	2.67	-0.46 /26	-1.70 / 5	1.96 /31	0.27	0.82
GEI	VY Pioneer High Yield I	IPHIX	D-	(800) 992-0180	C- / 3.1	1.76	-0.30	-6.32 / 3	1.21 /46	3.56 /54	5.40	0.77
GEI	VY Pioneer High Yield S	IPHSX	D-	(800) 992-0180	D+ / 2.6	1.70	-0.42	-6.48 / 3	0.96 /42	3.31 /50	5.14	1.02
MTG	WA Adjustable Rate Income A	ARMZX	C-	(877) 534-4627	D / 1.7	0.29	0.18	-0.05 /31	0.54 /34	1.20 /22	1.39	0.82
COI	WA Adjustable Rate Income C	LWAIX	C-	(877) 534-4627	D- / 1.3	0.09	-0.33	-0.98 /22	-0.35 /13	0.37 /17	0.59	1.73
MTG	● WA Adjustable Rate Income C1	ARMGX	C-	(877) 534-4627	D / 1.6	0.16	-0.20	-0.73 /24	-0.06 /15	0.59 /18	0.86	1.41
MTG	WA Adjustable Rate Income I	SBAYX	C+	(877) 534-4627	C- / 3.6	0.33	0.27	0.11 /41	0.71 /37	1.40 /25	1.59	0.67
COI	WA Adjustable Rate Income IS	ARMLX	U	(877) 534-4627	U /	0.35	0.31	0.09 /41	--	--	1.68	0.56
MUS	WA CA Municipals A	SHRCX	C+	(877) 534-4627	B / 8.0	1.56	3.10	3.08 /86	3.04 /88	6.40 /94	3.94	0.72
MUS	WA CA Municipals C	SCACX	B-	(877) 534-4627	B+ / 8.5	1.43	2.88	2.57 /81	2.46 /82	5.81 /91	3.56	1.29
MUS	WA CA Municipals I	LMCUX	B+	(877) 534-4627	A- / 9.1	1.53	3.16	3.20 /87	3.14 /89	6.54 /95	4.23	0.70
COI	WA Core Bond A	WABAX	C+	(888) 425-6432	C+ / 6.0	2.85	2.51	1.59 /67	2.81 /74	4.02 /62	2.11	0.82
COI	WA Core Bond C	WABCX	C+	(888) 425-6432	C+ / 6.6	2.70	2.28	0.95 /58	2.09 /63	3.28 /50	1.57	1.64
COI	● WA Core Bond C1	LWACX	B	(888) 425-6432	B- / 7.2	2.76	2.38	1.28 /63	2.45 /70	3.63 /55	1.89	1.28
COI	WA Core Bond FI	WAPIX	B+	(888) 425-6432	B / 7.7	2.87	2.59	1.68 /69	2.92 /76	4.12 /63	2.29	0.80
COI	WA Core Bond I	WATFX	A-	(888) 425-6432	B / 8.0	2.96	2.74	2.04 /72	3.21 /78	4.39 /66	2.63	0.52
COI	WA Core Bond IS	WACSX	A-	(888) 425-6432	B / 8.0	2.96	2.84	2.05 /72	3.27 /78	4.46 /67	2.64	0.45
COI	WA Core Bond R	WABRX	B	(888) 425-6432	B- / 7.3	2.79	2.38	1.34 /64	2.55 /71	3.75 /57	1.95	1.29
COI	WA Core Plus Bond C	WAPCX	C+	(888) 425-6432	C+ / 6.5	2.23	2.16	0.60 /51	2.16 /65	3.68 /56	2.12	1.52
COI	● WA Core Plus Bond C1	LWCPX	C+	(888) 425-6432	B- / 7.1	2.30	2.34	0.93 /57	2.50 /71	4.00 /62	2.45	1.24
* GEI	WA Core Plus Bond FI	WACIX	B	(888) 425-6432	B / 7.6	2.39	2.52	1.29 /63	2.92 /76	4.46 /67	2.80	0.81
GEI	WA Core Plus Bond I	WACPX	B	(888) 425-6432	B / 7.9	2.57	2.79	1.66 /68	3.25 /78	4.77 /70	3.17	0.49
GEI	WA Core Plus Bond IS	WAPSX	B	(888) 425-6432	B / 8.0	2.49	2.71	1.69 /69	3.28 /79	4.79 /70	3.20	0.43
COI	WA Core Plus Bond R	WAPRX	C+	(888) 425-6432	B- / 7.3	2.43	2.45	1.02 /59	2.59 /72	4.09 /63	2.54	1.25
COI	WA Core Plus BondA	WAPAX	C	(888) 425-6432	C+ / 6.0	2.50	2.58	1.33 /64	2.87 /75	4.41 /67	2.64	0.78
COI	WA Corporate Bond A	SIGAX	C-	(877) 534-4627	C+ / 6.3	2.66	3.15	-0.70 /24	3.36 /79	5.36 /74	4.11	1.03
COI	● WA Corporate Bond B	HBDIX	C-	(877) 534-4627	C+ / 6.6	2.40	2.80	-1.48 /18	2.46 /70	4.49 /67	3.51	1.96
COI	WA Corporate Bond C	LWBOX	C-	(877) 534-4627	C+ / 6.9	2.52	2.82	-1.31 /19	2.62 /72	4.63 /69	3.67	1.87
COI	● WA Corporate Bond C1	SBILX	C-	(877) 534-4627	B- / 7.3	2.56	2.97	-1.15 /20	2.89 /75	4.82 /70	3.87	1.54
COI	WA Corporate Bond I	SIGYX	C	(877) 534-4627	B / 8.1	2.83	3.39	-0.30 /28	3.69 /82	5.72 /76	4.61	0.70
COI	WA Corporate Bond P	LCBPX	C-	(877) 534-4627	B / 7.7	2.63	3.08	-0.84 /23	3.21 /78	5.20 /73	4.15	1.16
EM	WA Emerging Markets Debt A	LWEAX	E-	(888) 425-6432	E+ / 0.6	4.18	5.20	-0.16 /30	-1.65 / 5	2.35 /36	4.53	1.40
EM	WA Emerging Markets Debt A2	WEMDX	U	(888) 425-6432	U /	4.19	5.22	0.02 /33	--	--	4.52	1.29
EM	WA Emerging Markets Debt C	WAEOX	E	(888) 425-6432	E+ / 0.7	3.96	5.01	-0.68 /24	-2.36 / 3	1.74 /28	4.01	2.14
EM	● WA Emerging Markets Debt C1	LWECX	E	(888) 425-6432	E+ / 0.9	4.16	5.33	-0.33 /28	-2.04 / 4	1.95 /31	4.32	1.90
EM	WA Emerging Markets Debt FI	LMWDX	D-	(888) 425-6432	C- / 3.3	4.42	7.82	2.15 /73	-0.94 / 9	--	7.18	1.90

● Denotes fund is closed to new investors
* Denotes fund is included in Section II

RISK			NET ASSETS		ASSET							FUND MANAGER		MINIMUM		LOADS	
Risk Rating/Pts	3 Yr Avg Standard Deviation	Avg Duration	NAV As of 3/31/16	Total $(Mil)	Cash %	Gov. Bond %	Muni. Bond %	Corp. Bond %	Other %	Portfolio Turnover Ratio	Avg Coupon Rate	Manager Quality Pct	Manager Tenure (Years)	Initial Purch. $	Additional Purch. $	Front End Load	Back End Load
C / 5.3	3.3	0.1	12.24	27	0	0	0	20	80	63	7.6	95	N/A	1,000	0	0.0	0.0
A / 9.5	0.8	1.8	9.88	10	0	5	0	63	32	95	2.9	87	4	1,000	0	2.5	0.0
A / 9.4	0.9	1.8	9.88	1	0	5	0	63	32	95	2.9	66	4	1,000	0	0.0	0.0
A / 9.5	0.8	1.8	9.88	10	0	5	0	63	32	95	2.9	89	4	250,000	0	0.0	0.0
U /	N/A	1.8	9.88	N/A	0	5	0	63	32	95	2.9	N/A	4	0	0	0.0	0.0
A / 9.4	0.9	1.8	9.89	1	0	5	0	63	32	95	2.9	90	4	1,000	0	0.0	0.0
C / 5.4	3.3	N/A	9.94	2	5	8	0	33	54	158	0.0	83	4	1,000	0	2.5	0.0
C / 5.4	3.3	N/A	9.78	N/A	5	8	0	33	54	158	0.0	50	4	1,000	0	0.0	0.0
C / 5.5	3.3	N/A	9.99	6	5	8	0	33	54	158	0.0	89	4	250,000	0	0.0	0.0
C / 5.3	3.4	N/A	9.86	3	5	8	0	33	54	158	0.0	75	4	0	0	0.0	0.0
C+ / 5.7	3.2	N/A	9.90	N/A	5	8	0	33	54	158	0.0	81	4	1,000	0	0.0	0.0
C+ / 6.3	3.1	5.4	10.78	28	0	42	1	27	30	209	3.3	31	4	0	0	0.0	0.0
C+ / 6.0	3.1	5.4	10.84	3,190	0	42	1	27	30	209	3.3	45	4	0	0	0.0	0.0
C+ / 6.3	3.1	5.4	10.80	269	0	42	1	27	30	209	3.3	38	4	0	0	0.0	0.0
D+ / 2.4	5.2	7.0	9.20	55	15	72	0	0	13	527	1.2	2	6	0	0	0.0	0.0
D+ / 2.4	5.2	7.0	9.53	323	15	72	0	0	13	527	1.2	3	6	0	0	0.0	0.0
D+ / 2.3	5.2	7.0	9.45	199	15	72	0	0	13	527	1.2	3	6	0	0	0.0	0.0
D- / 1.2	6.4	3.6	10.82	92	5	0	0	66	29	35	6.0	73	10	0	0	0.0	0.0
D- / 1.1	6.5	3.6	10.81	4	5	0	0	66	29	35	6.0	58	10	0	0	0.0	0.0
A+ / 9.6	0.7	0.6	8.84	133	2	1	1	37	59	34	1.8	77	4	1,000	50	2.3	0.0
A+ / 9.7	0.7	0.6	8.80	2	2	1	1	37	59	34	1.8	39	4	1,000	50	0.0	0.0
A+ / 9.6	0.7	0.6	8.78	31	2	1	1	37	59	34	1.8	48	4	1,000	50	0.0	0.0
A+ / 9.6	0.7	0.6	8.82	9	2	1	1	37	59	34	1.8	83	4	1,000,000	0	0.0	0.0
U /	N/A	0.6	8.82	13	2	1	1	37	59	34	1.8	N/A	4	1,000,000	0	0.0	0.0
C- / 4.0	4.0	6.0	16.62	433	0	0	99	0	1	7	4.8	28	12	1,000	50	4.3	0.0
C- / 4.0	3.9	6.0	16.58	77	0	0	99	0	1	7	4.8	17	12	1,000	50	0.0	0.0
C- / 4.0	3.9	6.0	16.62	85	0	0	99	0	1	7	4.8	31	12	1,000,000	0	0.0	0.0
C+ / 6.2	3.1	6.2	12.41	350	0	30	0	31	39	85	3.0	87	22	1,000	50	4.3	0.0
C+ / 6.2	3.1	6.2	12.42	35	0	30	0	31	39	85	3.0	71	22	1,000	50	0.0	0.0
C+ / 6.1	3.1	6.2	12.42	20	0	30	0	31	39	85	3.0	81	22	1,000	50	0.0	0.0
C+ / 6.2	3.1	6.2	12.42	247	0	30	0	31	39	85	3.0	89	22	0	0	0.0	0.0
C+ / 6.2	3.1	6.2	12.41	2,747	0	30	0	31	39	85	3.0	91	22	1,000,000	0	0.0	0.0
C+ / 6.1	3.1	6.2	12.43	1,841	0	30	0	31	39	85	3.0	92	22	0	0	0.0	0.0
C+ / 6.2	3.1	6.2	12.42	9	0	30	0	31	39	85	3.0	84	22	0	0	0.0	0.0
C / 5.5	3.3	6.7	11.63	141	0	30	0	34	36	93	3.9	69	3	1,000	50	0.0	0.0
C / 5.4	3.3	6.7	11.62	28	0	30	0	34	36	93	3.9	80	3	1,000	50	0.0	0.0
C / 5.4	3.3	6.7	11.63	1,541	0	30	0	34	36	93	3.9	80	3	0	0	0.0	0.0
C / 5.3	3.4	6.7	11.63	10,233	0	30	0	34	36	93	3.9	86	3	1,000,000	0	0.0	0.0
C / 5.4	3.3	6.7	11.62	3,483	0	30	0	34	36	93	3.9	87	3	0	0	0.0	0.0
C / 5.4	3.3	6.7	11.61	69	0	30	0	34	36	93	3.9	82	3	0	0	0.0	0.0
C / 5.4	3.3	6.7	11.62	609	0	30	0	34	36	93	3.9	87	3	1,000	50	4.3	0.0
D+ / 2.8	4.9	6.7	11.93	239	0	2	1	88	9	95	5.2	80	6	1,000	50	4.3	0.0
D+ / 2.9	4.8	6.7	11.89	4	0	2	1	88	9	95	5.2	46	6	1,000	50	0.0	0.0
D+ / 2.9	4.9	6.7	11.93	3	0	2	1	88	9	95	5.2	50	6	1,000	50	0.0	0.0
D+ / 2.8	4.9	6.7	11.86	14	0	2	1	88	9	95	5.2	60	6	1,000	50	0.0	0.0
D+ / 2.8	4.9	6.7	11.94	25	0	2	1	88	9	95	5.2	87	6	1,000,000	0	0.0	0.0
D+ / 2.8	4.9	6.7	11.92	65	0	2	1	88	9	95	5.2	76	6	0	50	0.0	0.0
E / 0.4	8.3	6.7	4.73	8	5	65	0	29	1	31	5.8	17	3	1,000	50	4.3	0.0
U /	N/A	6.7	4.72	3	5	65	0	29	1	31	5.8	N/A	3	1,000	50	4.3	0.0
E / 0.4	8.3	6.7	4.72	1	5	65	0	29	1	31	5.8	10	3	1,000	50	0.0	0.0
E / 0.4	8.4	6.7	4.76	N/A	5	65	0	29	1	31	5.8	12	3	1,000	50	0.0	0.0
E / 0.4	8.3	6.7	4.72	N/A	5	65	0	29	1	31	5.8	33	3	0	0	0.0	0.0

Fund Type	Fund Name (99 Pct = Best, 0 Pct = Worst)	Ticker Symbol	Overall Investment Rating	Phone	PERFORMANCE: Performance Rating/Pts	Total Return % through 3/31/16: 3 Mo	6 Mo	1Yr / Pct	Annualized: 3Yr / Pct	Annualized: 5Yr / Pct	Incl. in Returns: Dividend Yield	Incl. in Returns: Expense Ratio
EM	WA Emerging Markets Debt Inst	SEMDX	E+	(888) 425-6432	D- / 1.5	4.19	5.53	0.42 /48	-1.29 / 7	2.74 /41	4.91	0.95
EM	WA Emerging Markets Debt IS	LWISX	E+	(888) 425-6432	D / 1.7	4.43	5.57	0.51 /50	-1.17 / 8	--	5.00	1.10
GL	● WA Global Government Bond A	WAOAX	E	(888) 425-6432	E+ / 0.7	1.12	0.64	-1.59 /18	-0.22 /14	1.95 /31	8.01	1.60
GL	● WA Global Government Bond C	WAOCX	E+	(888) 425-6432	E+ / 0.8	0.88	0.21	-2.47 /13	-1.04 / 8	1.12 /22	7.81	2.46
EM	● WA Global Government Bond I	WAFIX	D-	(888) 425-6432	D+ / 2.5	1.24	0.87	-1.32 /19	0.10 /27	2.25 /34	8.38	1.27
GL	● WA Global Government Bond R	WAORX	E+	(888) 425-6432	D- / 1.3	0.99	0.55	-1.85 /16	-0.46 /12	1.69 /28	8.10	2.09
COH	WA Global High Yield Bond A	SAHYX	E-	(877) 534-4627	E / 0.3	1.34	-1.00	-6.59 / 3	-1.54 / 6	2.51 /38	6.77	1.14
COH	● WA Global High Yield Bond B	SBHYX	E	(877) 534-4627	E / 0.3	0.99	-1.43	-7.09 / 2	-2.21 / 4	1.85 /29	6.44	1.89
GL	WA Global High Yield Bond C	LWGOX	E	(877) 534-4627	E / 0.3	1.18	-1.34	-7.07 / 2	-2.24 / 4	1.97 /31	6.33	1.90
COH	● WA Global High Yield Bond C1	SHYCX	E	(877) 534-4627	E / 0.3	1.23	-1.19	-6.89 / 2	-1.96 / 4	2.07 /32	6.56	1.61
COH	WA Global High Yield Bond I	SHYOX	E	(877) 534-4627	E / 0.5	1.40	-0.91	-6.38 / 3	-1.28 / 7	2.83 /42	7.31	0.85
GL	WA Global High Yield Bond IS	LWGSX	E	(877) 534-4627	E+ / 0.6	1.43	-0.84	-6.13 / 3	-1.19 / 7	--	7.44	0.78
GL	WA Global Strategic Income A	SDSAX	D-	(877) 534-4627	E+ / 0.8	0.74	-1.27	-3.57 / 9	0.42 /32	3.96 /61	8.54	1.12
GL	● WA Global Strategic Income B	SLDSX	D-	(877) 534-4627	E+ / 0.9	0.54	-1.76	-4.30 / 7	-0.39 /12	3.12 /47	8.10	1.94
GL	WA Global Strategic Income C	LWSIX	D-	(877) 534-4627	D- / 1.0	0.73	-1.45	-4.10 / 7	-0.33 /13	3.19 /48	8.17	1.85
GL	● WA Global Strategic Income C1	SDSIX	D-	(877) 534-4627	D- / 1.2	0.64	-1.45	-3.93 / 8	0.02 /18	3.52 /53	8.51	1.53
GL	WA Global Strategic Income I	SDSYX	D	(877) 534-4627	D+ / 2.8	0.97	-1.09	-3.11 /11	0.75 /38	4.24 /65	9.18	0.85
GL	WA Global Strategic Income IS	WAGIX	U	(877) 534-4627	U /	0.78	-1.10	-3.19 /11	--	--	9.29	0.73
COH	WA High Yield A	WAYAX	E-	(888) 425-6432	E- / 0.2	0.72	-3.50	-8.96 / 1	-1.13 / 8	2.78 /42	6.64	0.93
COH	WA High Yield A2	WHAYX	U	(888) 425-6432	U /	0.72	-3.47	-8.90 / 1	--	--	6.66	0.92
COH	WA High Yield C	WAYCX	E	(888) 425-6432	E- / 0.2	0.53	-3.77	-9.63 / 1	-2.13 / 4	1.86 /30	6.13	1.77
COH	WA High Yield I	WAHYX	E	(888) 425-6432	E / 0.4	0.77	-3.29	-8.71 / 1	-1.07 / 8	2.92 /44	7.22	0.68
COH	WA High Yield IS	WAHSX	E	(888) 425-6432	E / 0.4	0.81	-3.27	-8.64 / 1	-1.00 / 8	2.97 /45	7.29	0.63
COH	WA High Yield R	WAYRX	E	(888) 425-6432	E / 0.3	0.64	-3.56	-9.24 / 1	-1.65 / 5	2.33 /35	6.58	1.54
GEI	WA Inflation Indexed Plus Bond A	WAFAX	E+	(888) 425-6432	E / 0.4	3.14	2.10	-0.99 /22	-1.95 / 4	2.00 /31	0.32	0.73
GEI	WA Inflation Indexed Plus Bond C	WAFCX	E+	(888) 425-6432	E / 0.4	3.02	1.77	-1.61 /18	-2.70 / 3	1.22 /22	0.28	1.47
GEI	● WA Inflation Indexed Plus Bond C1	LWICX	E+	(888) 425-6432	E / 0.5	2.99	1.94	-1.40 /19	-2.46 / 3	1.46 /25	0.29	1.30
USS	WA Inflation Indexed Plus Bond FI	WATPX	E+	(888) 425-6432	E+ / 0.7	3.07	2.03	-1.09 /21	-2.01 / 4	1.87 /30	0.33	0.75
USS	WA Inflation Indexed Plus Bond I	WAIIX	D-	(888) 425-6432	E+ / 0.9	3.21	2.18	-0.78 /23	-1.67 / 5	2.28 /35	0.36	0.41
USS	WA Inflation Indexed Plus Bond IS	WAFSX	D-	(888) 425-6432	E+ / 0.9	3.20	2.26	-0.68 /24	-1.55 / 6	2.36 /36	0.37	0.26
GEI	WA Inflation Indexed Plus Bond R	WAFRX	E+	(888) 425-6432	E+ / 0.6	3.08	1.84	-1.38 /19	-2.31 / 3	1.64 /27	0.31	1.09
MM	WA Inst Cash Reserves Inst	CARXX	C	(800) 331-1792	D+ / 2.7	0.09	0.14	0.20 /44	0.12 /28	0.14 /15	0.20	0.22
MM	WA Inst Cash Reserves Inv	LCRXX	U	(800) 331-1792	U /	0.08	0.12	0.15 /43	--	--	0.15	0.33
MMT	WA Inst Cash Reserves L	CFRXX	C	(800) 331-1792	D+ / 2.7	0.08	0.12	0.16 /45	0.07 /27	0.09 /15	0.16	0.33
MM	WA Inst Cash Reserves S	CFSXX	C	(800) 331-1792	D+ / 2.4	0.07	0.09	0.10 /41	0.04 /24	0.03 /11	0.10	0.48
MM	WA Inst Cash Reserves SVB	SVLXX	C-	(800) 331-1792	D / 1.9	0.02	0.02	0.02 /35	0.01 /18	0.01 / 6	0.02	0.49
MM	WA Inst Govt Reserves Inst	INGXX	C	(888) 425-6432	D+ / 2.5	0.05	0.07	0.09 /41	0.06 /26	0.05 /13	0.09	0.21
MM	WA Inst Govt Reserves Inv		U	(888) 425-6432	U /	0.03	0.04	0.04 /38	--	--	0.04	0.31
MM	WA Inst Liquid Reserves Inst	CILXX	C	(800) 331-1792	D+ / 2.7	0.09	0.15	0.21 /44	0.12 /28	0.14 /15	0.21	0.23
MM	WA Inst Liquid Reserves Inv	LLRXX	U	(800) 331-1792	U /	0.08	0.12	0.16 /43	--	--	0.16	0.33
MM	WA Inst Liquid Reserves SVB Inst	SVIXX	C	(800) 331-1792	D+ / 2.5	0.07	0.10	0.13 /42	0.05 /25	0.07 /14	0.13	0.33
MMT	WA Inst Tax Free Reserves Inv	LTFXX	U	(800) 331-1792	U /	0.01	0.01	0.01 /35	--	--	0.01	0.45
MM	WA Inst US Treas Reserves Inst	CIIXX	C	(800) 331-1792	D+ / 2.3	0.03	0.04	0.04 /38	0.03 /23	0.02 / 9	0.04	0.21
MUS	WA Int Maturity California Muni A	ITCAX	A-	(877) 534-4627	B+ / 8.3	1.19	2.60	2.98 /85	2.98 /88	4.98 /85	2.74	0.80
MUS	WA Int Maturity California Muni C	SIMLX	A-	(877) 534-4627	B+ / 8.4	1.16	2.42	2.49 /80	2.41 /82	4.36 /80	2.22	1.38
MUS	WA Int Maturity California Muni I	SICYX	A	(877) 534-4627	A- / 9.1	1.23	2.68	3.13 /86	3.14 /89	5.13 /86	2.95	0.74
MUS	WA Int Maturity New York Muni A	IMNYX	B+	(877) 534-4627	B / 7.6	1.14	1.87	2.71 /82	2.33 /81	4.52 /82	2.82	0.76
MUS	WA Int Maturity New York Muni C	SINLX	B+	(877) 534-4627	B / 7.7	1.11	1.69	2.10 /78	1.76 /73	3.89 /77	2.29	1.38
MUS	WA Int Maturity New York Muni I	LMIIX	A	(877) 534-4627	B+ / 8.5	1.29	2.06	2.86 /84	2.51 /83	4.67 /83	3.03	0.72
COI	WA Intermediate Bond A	WATAX	C+	(888) 425-6432	C / 4.3	2.30	2.10	1.80 /70	1.80 /58	3.20 /48	1.95	0.83
COI	WA Intermediate Bond C	WATCX	C+	(888) 425-6432	C / 4.8	2.00	1.69	0.90 /57	1.03 /43	2.44 /37	1.25	1.62
GEI	WA Intermediate Bond I	WATIX	A	(888) 425-6432	C+ / 6.9	2.36	2.24	2.12 /73	2.19 /65	3.57 /54	2.35	0.50

● Denotes fund is closed to new investors
* Denotes fund is included in Section II

RISK			NET ASSETS		ASSET							FUND MANAGER		MINIMUM		LOADS	
Risk Rating/Pts	3 Yr Avg Standard Deviation	Avg Duration	NAV As of 3/31/16	Total $(Mil)	Cash %	Gov. Bond %	Muni. Bond %	Corp. Bond %	Other %	Portfolio Turnover Ratio	Avg Coupon Rate	Manager Quality Pct	Manager Tenure (Years)	Initial Purch. $	Additional Purch. $	Front End Load	Back End Load
E / 0.4	8.3	6.7	4.72	105	5	65	0	29	1	31	5.8	24	3	1,000,000	0	0.0	0.0
E / 0.4	8.4	6.7	4.71	N/A	5	65	0	29	1	31	5.8	27	3	1,000,000	0	0.0	0.0
D- / 1.3	6.3	5.2	8.15	N/A	15	82	0	2	1	127	4.1	56	18	1,000	50	4.3	0.0
D- / 1.2	6.3	5.2	8.05	N/A	15	82	0	2	1	127	4.1	28	18	1,000	50	0.0	0.0
D- / 1.3	6.3	5.2	8.18	8	15	82	0	2	1	127	4.1	73	18	1,000,000	0	0.0	0.0
D- / 1.3	6.3	5.2	8.15	N/A	15	82	0	2	1	127	4.1	46	18	0	0	0.0	0.0
E+ / 0.7	6.5	4.4	5.83	151	1	1	0	90	8	71	6.6	6	10	1,000	50	4.3	0.0
E+ / 0.7	6.4	4.4	5.86	3	1	1	0	90	8	71	6.6	5	10	1,000	50	0.0	0.0
D- / 1.1	6.4	4.4	5.84	6	1	1	0	90	8	71	6.6	10	10	1,000	50	0.0	0.0
E+ / 0.7	6.5	4.4	5.90	42	1	1	0	90	8	71	6.6	6	10	1,000	50	0.0	0.0
E+ / 0.8	6.4	4.4	5.83	33	1	1	0	90	8	71	6.6	7	10	1,000,000	0	0.0	0.0
D- / 1.2	6.4	4.4	5.83	89	1	1	0	90	8	71	6.6	25	10	0	0	0.0	0.0
C- / 3.2	4.5	2.8	6.04	264	3	17	0	58	22	37	5.6	82	4	1,000	50	4.3	0.0
C- / 3.3	4.4	2.8	5.97	3	3	17	0	58	22	37	5.6	48	4	1,000	50	0.0	0.0
C- / 3.2	4.5	2.8	6.04	6	3	17	0	58	22	37	5.6	51	4	1,000	50	0.0	0.0
C- / 3.3	4.5	2.8	6.05	32	3	17	0	58	22	37	5.6	69	4	1,000	50	0.0	0.0
C- / 3.2	4.5	2.8	6.08	57	3	17	0	58	22	37	5.6	87	4	1,000,000	0	0.0	0.0
U /	N/A	2.8	6.07	N/A	3	17	0	58	22	37	5.6	N/A	4	1,000,000	0	0.0	0.0
E+ / 0.8	6.3	4.3	7.29	11	0	0	0	90	10	82	6.7	7	11	1,000	50	4.3	0.0
U /	N/A	4.3	7.31	13	0	0	0	90	10	82	6.7	N/A	11	1,000	50	4.3	0.0
E+ / 0.8	6.2	4.3	7.23	2	0	0	0	90	10	82	6.7	6	11	1,000	50	0.0	0.0
E+ / 0.8	6.3	4.3	7.24	169	0	0	0	90	10	82	6.7	8	11	1,000,000	0	0.0	0.0
E+ / 0.8	6.3	4.3	7.36	132	0	0	0	90	10	82	6.7	8	11	0	0	0.0	0.0
E+ / 0.8	6.3	4.3	7.24	N/A	0	0	0	90	10	82	6.7	6	11	0	0	0.0	0.0
D+ / 2.8	5.0	6.1	11.17	22	11	88	0	0	1	69	0.9	2	15	1,000	50	4.3	0.0
D+ / 2.8	5.0	6.1	10.93	1	11	88	0	0	1	69	0.9	2	15	1,000	50	0.0	0.0
D+ / 2.8	4.9	6.1	11.03	2	11	88	0	0	1	69	0.9	2	15	1,000	50	0.0	0.0
D+ / 2.8	5.0	6.1	11.08	1	11	88	0	0	1	69	0.9	4	15	0	0	0.0	0.0
D+ / 2.8	5.0	6.1	11.25	103	11	88	0	0	1	69	0.9	5	15	1,000,000	0	0.0	0.0
D+ / 2.8	5.0	6.1	11.29	385	11	88	0	0	1	69	0.9	5	15	0	0	0.0	0.0
D+ / 2.8	5.0	6.1	11.05	1	11	88	0	0	1	69	0.9	2	15	0	0	0.0	0.0
A+ / 9.9	N/A	N/A	1.00	9,729	100	0	0	0	0	0	0.2	70	N/A	1,000,000	50	0.0	0.0
U /	N/A	N/A	1.00	194	100	0	0	0	0	0	0.2	N/A	N/A	1,000,000	50	0.0	0.0
A+ / 9.9	N/A	N/A	1.00	636	100	0	0	0	0	0	0.2	67	N/A	1,000,000	50	0.0	0.0
A+ / 9.9	N/A	N/A	1.00	104	100	0	0	0	0	0	0.1	66	N/A	1,000,000	50	0.0	0.0
A+ / 9.9	N/A	N/A	1.00	166	100	0	0	0	0	0	0.0	66	N/A	0	0	0.0	0.0
A+ / 9.9	N/A	N/A	1.00	8,196	100	0	0	0	0	0	0.1	68	N/A	1,000,000	50	0.0	0.0
U /	N/A	N/A	1.00	74	100	0	0	0	0	0	0.0	N/A	N/A	1,000,000	50	0.0	0.0
A+ / 9.9	N/A	N/A	1.00	5,507	100	0	0	0	0	0	0.2	70	N/A	1,000,000	50	0.0	0.0
U /	N/A	N/A	1.00	156	100	0	0	0	0	0	0.2	N/A	N/A	1,000,000	50	0.0	0.0
A+ / 9.9	N/A	N/A	1.00	350	100	0	0	0	0	0	0.1	N/A	N/A	0	0	0.0	0.0
U /	N/A	N/A	1.00	127	100	0	0	0	0	0	0.0	N/A	N/A	1,000,000	50	0.0	0.0
A+ / 9.9	N/A	N/A	1.00	11,715	100	0	0	0	0	0	0.0	N/A	24	1,000,000	50	0.0	0.0
C+ / 5.8	3.2	4.9	9.10	78	0	0	100	0	0	4	4.8	51	4	1,000	50	2.3	0.0
C+ / 5.7	3.2	4.9	9.09	114	0	0	100	0	0	4	4.8	31	4	1,000	50	0.0	0.0
C+ / 5.8	3.2	4.9	9.13	32	0	0	100	0	0	4	4.8	55	4	1,000,000	0	0.0	0.0
C+ / 6.4	3.0	4.6	9.04	147	0	0	99	0	1	5	5.1	34	4	1,000	50	2.3	0.0
C+ / 6.1	3.1	4.6	9.05	71	0	0	99	0	1	5	5.1	19	4	1,000	50	0.0	0.0
C+ / 6.1	3.1	4.6	9.03	49	0	0	99	0	1	5	5.1	37	4	1,000,000	0	0.0	0.0
B / 8.0	2.4	4.3	11.09	2	0	28	1	42	29	59	2.7	78	7	1,000	50	4.3	0.0
B / 8.1	2.3	4.3	11.10	1	0	28	1	42	29	59	2.7	45	7	1,000	50	0.0	0.0
B / 8.1	2.4	4.3	11.09	271	0	28	1	42	29	59	2.7	78	7	1,000,000	0	0.0	0.0

99 Pct = Best
0 Pct = Worst

Fund Type	Fund Name	Ticker Symbol	Overall Investment Rating	Phone	PERFORMANCE: Performance Rating/Pts	Total Return % through 3/31/16: 3 Mo	6 Mo	1Yr / Pct	Annualized: 3Yr / Pct	Annualized: 5Yr / Pct	Incl. in Returns: Dividend Yield	Expense Ratio
GEI	WA Intermediate Bond IS	WABSX	**A**	(888) 425-6432	**B- / 7.1**	2.37	2.27	2.27 /73	2.27 /67	3.63 /55	2.41	0.45
COI	WA Intermediate Bond R	WATRX	**B**	(888) 425-6432	**C+ / 5.8**	2.21	1.93	1.48 /66	1.53 /53	2.93 /44	1.73	1.15
* MUN	WA Intermediate-Term Muni A	SBLTX	**B+**	(877) 534-4627	**B / 7.7**	1.37	2.49	2.83 /83	2.26 /80	4.86 /84	3.01	0.75
MUN	WA Intermediate-Term Muni C	SMLLX	**B+**	(877) 534-4627	**B / 7.7**	1.23	2.21	2.25 /79	1.68 /72	4.25 /79	2.52	1.32
MUN	WA Intermediate-Term Muni I	SBTYX	**A**	(877) 534-4627	**B+ / 8.5**	1.40	2.56	3.13 /86	2.41 /82	5.02 /85	3.22	0.62
MM	WA Liquid Reserves Service	LQSXX	**U**	(800) 331-1792	**U /**	0.01	0.01	--	--	--	0.00	N/A
GL	WA Macro Opportunities A	LAAAX	**U**	(800) 228-2121	**U /**	1.79	2.87	-0.22 /29	--	--	2.49	1.60
GL	WA Macro Opportunities C	LAACX	**U**	(800) 228-2121	**U /**	1.60	2.50	-0.89 /23	--	--	2.06	2.39
GL	WA Macro Opportunities FI	LAFIX	**U**	(800) 228-2121	**U /**	1.69	2.95	-0.24 /29	--	--	2.39	1.73
GL	WA Macro Opportunities I	LAOIX	**U**	(800) 228-2121	**U /**	1.79	3.02	0.02 /33	--	--	2.93	1.42
GL	WA Macro Opportunities IS	LAOSX	**U**	(800) 228-2121	**U /**	1.79	3.10	0.19 /44	--	--	3.00	1.29
MUN ●	WA Managed Municipals 1	SMMOX	**B**	(877) 534-4627	**A- / 9.2**	1.62	3.08	3.16 /87	3.35 /91	6.81 /96	3.74	0.58
* MUN	WA Managed Municipals A	SHMMX	**C+**	(877) 534-4627	**B / 8.1**	1.53	2.96	3.01 /85	3.26 /91	6.70 /95	3.50	0.66
MUN ●	WA Managed Municipals B	SMMBX	**C+**	(877) 534-4627	**B+ / 8.7**	1.41	2.69	2.43 /80	2.67 /85	6.09 /92	3.10	1.24
MUN	WA Managed Municipals C	SMMCX	**C+**	(877) 534-4627	**B+ / 8.7**	1.40	2.68	2.44 /80	2.68 /85	6.12 /93	3.10	1.24
MUN	WA Managed Municipals I	SMMYX	**B**	(877) 534-4627	**A- / 9.2**	1.61	3.06	3.16 /87	3.38 /92	6.83 /96	3.74	0.57
MUS	WA Massachusetts Municipals A	SLMMX	**C+**	(877) 534-4627	**B / 8.2**	1.64	3.48	4.10 /95	3.13 /89	5.80 /91	3.00	0.87
MUS	WA Massachusetts Municipals C	SMALX	**B-**	(877) 534-4627	**B+ / 8.8**	1.51	3.21	3.54 /90	2.57 /83	5.23 /87	2.60	1.47
MUS	WA Massachusetts Municipals I	LHMIX	**B+**	(877) 534-4627	**A / 9.3**	1.67	3.56	4.18 /95	3.26 /91	5.94 /92	3.28	0.86
USS ●	WA Mortgage Backed Securities 1	SGVSX	**A+**	(877) 534-4627	**B / 7.7**	0.71	0.02	0.72 /54	3.52 /80	4.85 /71	3.59	0.71
* USS	WA Mortgage Backed Securities A	SGVAX	**B+**	(877) 534-4627	**C+ / 5.6**	0.56	-0.21	0.37 /47	3.23 /78	4.58 /68	3.19	0.95
USS ●	WA Mortgage Backed Securities B	HGVSX	**B+**	(877) 534-4627	**C+ / 6.1**	0.34	-0.54	-0.39 /27	2.43 /70	3.80 /58	2.55	1.78
MTG	WA Mortgage Backed Securities C	LWMSX	**B+**	(877) 534-4627	**C+ / 6.2**	0.40	-0.45	-0.30 /28	2.48 /70	3.82 /59	2.64	1.73
USS ●	WA Mortgage Backed Securities C1	SGSLX	**A**	(877) 534-4627	**C+ / 6.7**	0.54	-0.31	0.03 /36	2.78 /74	4.06 /62	2.89	1.49
USS	WA Mortgage Backed Securities I	SGSYX	**A+**	(877) 534-4627	**B / 7.8**	0.63	0.03	0.68 /53	3.59 /81	4.91 /71	3.63	0.63
MUH	WA Municipal High Income A	STXAX	**C**	(877) 534-4627	**B+ / 8.4**	2.64	4.40	3.81 /93	3.15 /90	7.02 /96	3.99	0.81
MUH	WA Municipal High Income C	SMHLX	**C+**	(877) 534-4627	**B+ / 8.9**	2.51	4.05	3.15 /86	2.58 /83	6.41 /94	3.61	1.38
MUH	WA Municipal High Income I	LMHIX	**C+**	(877) 534-4627	**A / 9.4**	2.68	4.41	3.89 /93	3.33 /91	7.17 /97	4.32	0.72
MUS	WA New Jersey Municipals A	SHNJX	**C+**	(877) 534-4627	**C+ / 6.8**	1.44	3.22	3.15 /86	2.24 /80	4.98 /85	3.55	0.76
MUS	WA New Jersey Municipals C	SNJLX	**B**	(877) 534-4627	**B / 7.8**	1.31	2.94	2.66 /82	1.67 /72	4.38 /81	3.15	1.34
MUS	WA New Jersey Municipals I	LNJIX	**A-**	(877) 534-4627	**B+ / 8.5**	1.48	3.22	3.32 /88	2.38 /81	5.12 /86	3.88	0.68
* MUS	WA New York Municipals A	SBNYX	**C**	(877) 534-4627	**B- / 7.3**	1.34	2.50	3.25 /87	2.57 /83	5.27 /87	3.38	0.73
MUS ●	WA New York Municipals B	SMNBX	**C+**	(877) 534-4627	**B / 8.0**	1.14	2.15	2.67 /82	1.92 /76	4.62 /82	2.97	1.36
MUS	WA New York Municipals C	SBYLX	**C+**	(877) 534-4627	**B / 8.0**	1.13	2.14	2.67 /82	1.96 /77	4.66 /83	2.97	1.30
MUS	WA New York Municipals I	SNPYX	**B**	(877) 534-4627	**B+ / 8.8**	1.37	2.48	3.38 /89	2.70 /85	5.41 /88	3.66	0.62
MUS	WA Oregon Municipals A	SHORX	**B-**	(877) 534-4627	**B- / 7.4**	1.55	2.70	3.38 /89	2.59 /84	4.99 /85	3.17	0.85
MUS	WA Oregon Municipals C	SORLX	**B+**	(877) 534-4627	**B / 8.1**	1.42	2.43	2.83 /83	2.06 /78	4.42 /81	2.77	1.42
MUS	WA Oregon Municipals I	LMOOX	**A**	(877) 534-4627	**B+ / 8.8**	1.58	2.67	3.44 /89	2.74 /85	5.12 /86	3.46	0.80
MUS	WA Pennsylvania Municipals A	SBPAX	**C+**	(877) 534-4627	**B / 8.0**	2.16	3.01	3.59 /91	2.93 /87	5.03 /86	3.35	0.71
MUS	WA Pennsylvania Municipals C	SPALX	**B-**	(877) 534-4627	**B+ / 8.5**	2.04	2.74	3.02 /85	2.35 /81	4.43 /81	2.95	1.28
MUS	WA Pennsylvania Municipals I	LPPIX	**B+**	(877) 534-4627	**A- / 9.1**	2.19	3.07	3.70 /92	3.04 /88	5.15 /86	3.60	0.64
MM	WA Premium Liquid Reserves	CIPXX	**C-**	(800) 331-1792	**D / 2.0**	0.02	0.02	0.03 /37	0.02 /21	0.01 / 6	0.03	0.50
MM	WA Premium US Treasury Reserves	CIMXX	**U**	(800) 331-1792	**U /**	0.01	0.01	0.02 /35	0.01 /18	0.01 / 6	0.02	0.50
MUN	WA Short Duration Muni Income A	SHDAX	**C+**	(877) 534-4627	**C- / 3.1**	0.44	0.50	0.48 /54	0.80 /47	1.44 /34	1.04	0.65
MUN	WA Short Duration Muni Income A2	SHDQX	**U**	(877) 534-4627	**U /**	0.41	0.45	0.43 /53	--	--	0.99	0.68
MUN	WA Short Duration Muni Income C	SHDLX	**C+**	(877) 534-4627	**C- / 3.7**	0.36	0.33	0.13 /44	0.45 /37	1.08 /27	0.71	1.01
MUN	WA Short Duration Muni Income I	SMDYX	**B+**	(877) 534-4627	**C / 5.0**	0.46	0.54	0.56 /56	0.88 /49	1.54 /36	1.14	0.57
COI	WA Short Term Yield IS	LGSTX	**U**	(877) 534-4627	**U /**	0.22	0.18	0.20 /44	--	--	0.30	0.44
US	WA Short-Term Bond A	SBSTX	**C-**	(877) 534-4627	**D / 1.8**	0.58	0.27	0.10 /41	0.55 /34	1.11 /21	1.37	0.79
COI	WA Short-Term Bond C	LWSOX	**C-**	(877) 534-4627	**D- / 1.5**	0.38	-0.14	-0.68 /24	-0.24 /14	0.34 /16	0.61	1.61
US ●	WA Short-Term Bond C1	SSTLX	**C+**	(877) 534-4627	**C- / 3.1**	0.77	0.15	0.09 /41	0.37 /31	0.91 /20	1.13	1.05
US	WA Short-Term Bond I	SBSYX	**B-**	(877) 534-4627	**C- / 4.0**	0.64	0.39	0.36 /47	0.83 /40	1.44 /25	1.66	0.49

● Denotes fund is closed to new investors
* Denotes fund is included in Section II

RISK			NET ASSETS		ASSET							FUND MANAGER		MINIMUM		LOADS	
Risk Rating/Pts	3 Yr Avg Standard Deviation	Avg Duration	NAV As of 3/31/16	Total $(Mil)	Cash %	Gov. Bond %	Muni. Bond %	Corp. Bond %	Other %	Portfolio Turnover Ratio	Avg Coupon Rate	Manager Quality Pct	Manager Tenure (Years)	Initial Purch. $	Additional Purch. $	Front End Load	Back End Load
B / 8.1	2.4	4.3	11.10	209	0	28	1	42	29	59	2.7	80	7	0	0	0.0	0.0
B / 8.0	2.4	4.3	11.09	N/A	0	28	1	42	29	59	2.7	66	7	0	0	0.0	0.0
C+ / 6.2	3.1	4.5	6.61	1,329	0	0	100	0	0	7	4.8	31	12	1,000	50	2.3	0.0
C+ / 6.1	3.1	4.5	6.62	712	0	0	100	0	0	7	4.8	18	12	1,000	50	0.0	0.0
C+ / 6.2	3.1	4.5	6.61	630	0	0	100	0	0	7	4.8	35	12	1,000,000	0	0.0	0.0
U /	N/A	N/A	1.00	N/A	100	0	0	0	0	0	0.0	N/A	N/A	0	0	0.0	0.0
U /	N/A	5.3	10.25	51	5	48	0	39	8	105	4.2	N/A	3	1,000	50	4.3	0.0
U /	N/A	5.3	10.15	28	5	48	0	39	8	105	4.2	N/A	3	1,000	50	0.0	0.0
U /	N/A	5.3	10.25	29	5	48	0	39	8	105	4.2	N/A	3	0	0	0.0	0.0
U /	N/A	5.3	10.24	463	5	48	0	39	8	105	4.2	N/A	3	1,000,000	0	0.0	0.0
U /	N/A	5.3	10.26	141	5	48	0	39	8	105	4.2	N/A	3	0	0	0.0	0.0
C- / 3.6	4.2	5.7	16.76	23	0	0	99	0	1	7	5.1	29	12	0	0	0.0	0.0
C- / 3.6	4.2	5.7	16.81	3,047	0	0	99	0	1	7	5.1	27	12	1,000	50	4.3	0.0
C- / 3.6	4.2	5.7	16.81	25	0	0	99	0	1	7	5.1	16	12	1,000	50	0.0	0.0
C- / 3.6	4.2	5.7	16.82	743	0	0	99	0	1	7	5.1	16	12	1,000	50	0.0	0.0
C- / 3.6	4.2	5.7	16.84	1,094	0	0	99	0	1	7	5.1	30	12	1,000,000	0	0.0	0.0
C- / 4.0	4.0	6.8	13.14	64	0	0	100	0	0	15	4.9	34	4	1,000	50	4.3	0.0
C- / 4.0	4.0	6.8	13.12	15	0	0	100	0	0	15	4.9	20	4	1,000	50	0.0	0.0
C- / 4.0	4.0	6.8	13.13	24	0	0	100	0	0	15	4.9	36	4	1,000,000	0	0.0	0.0
B+ / 8.3	2.2	4.9	10.73	35	9	1	0	4	86	137	3.8	97	N/A	0	0	0.0	0.0
B+ / 8.4	2.1	4.9	10.71	595	9	1	0	4	86	137	3.8	97	N/A	1,000	50	4.3	0.0
B+ / 8.3	2.1	4.9	10.72	7	9	1	0	4	86	137	3.8	93	N/A	1,000	50	0.0	0.0
B+ / 8.3	2.2	4.9	10.71	32	9	1	0	4	86	137	3.8	90	N/A	1,000	50	0.0	0.0
B+ / 8.4	2.1	4.9	10.73	18	9	1	0	4	86	137	3.8	95	N/A	1,000	50	0.0	0.0
B+ / 8.3	2.2	4.9	10.76	244	9	1	0	4	86	137	3.8	98	N/A	1,000,000	0	0.0	0.0
D+ / 2.4	4.8	6.6	14.58	338	0	0	99	0	1	8	5.8	20	10	1,000	50	4.3	0.0
D+ / 2.4	4.8	6.6	14.50	118	0	0	99	0	1	8	5.8	13	10	1,000	50	0.0	0.0
D+ / 2.4	4.8	6.6	14.50	323	0	0	99	0	1	8	5.8	23	10	1,000,000	0	0.0	0.0
C+ / 5.6	3.2	5.4	12.72	187	0	0	99	0	1	5	5.4	29	12	1,000	50	4.3	0.0
C / 5.5	3.3	5.4	12.73	52	0	0	99	0	1	5	5.4	17	12	1,000	50	0.0	0.0
C / 5.5	3.3	5.4	12.73	37	0	0	99	0	1	5	5.4	32	12	1,000,000	0	0.0	0.0
C- / 4.2	3.9	5.2	13.72	554	0	0	100	0	0	3	5.2	21	18	1,000	50	4.3	0.0
C- / 4.2	3.9	5.2	13.70	5	0	0	100	0	0	3	5.2	12	18	1,000	50	0.0	0.0
C- / 4.2	3.9	5.2	13.70	97	0	0	100	0	0	3	5.2	13	18	1,000	50	0.0	0.0
C- / 4.2	3.9	5.2	13.71	115	0	0	100	0	0	3	5.2	23	18	1,000,000	0	0.0	0.0
C / 5.5	3.3	5.3	10.67	51	0	0	100	0	0	11	4.5	41	10	1,000	50	4.3	0.0
C / 5.5	3.3	5.3	10.62	17	0	0	100	0	0	11	4.5	26	10	1,000	50	0.0	0.0
C / 5.5	3.3	5.3	10.67	16	0	0	100	0	0	11	4.5	45	10	1,000,000	0	0.0	0.0
C- / 4.0	4.0	5.9	13.19	126	0	0	100	0	0	3	5.1	28	9	1,000	50	4.3	0.0
C- / 4.0	4.0	5.9	13.13	72	0	0	100	0	0	3	5.1	17	9	1,000	50	0.0	0.0
C- / 4.1	3.9	5.9	13.18	27	0	0	100	0	0	3	5.1	32	9	1,000,000	0	0.0	0.0
A+ / 9.9	N/A	N/A	1.00	126	100	0	0	0	0	0	0.0	66	N/A	100,000	50	0.0	0.0
U /	N/A	N/A	1.00	72	100	0	0	0	0	0	0.0	N/A	25	100,000	50	0.0	0.0
A / 9.5	0.8	1.6	5.12	381	0	0	100	0	0	30	3.2	70	13	1,000	50	2.3	0.0
U /	N/A	1.6	5.12	1	0	0	100	0	0	30	3.2	N/A	13	1,000	50	2.3	0.0
A / 9.4	0.8	1.6	5.12	1,019	0	0	100	0	0	30	3.2	51	13	1,000	50	0.0	0.0
A / 9.5	0.8	1.6	5.12	384	0	0	100	0	0	30	3.2	74	13	1,000,000	0	0.0	0.0
U /	N/A	0.2	9.99	N/A	0	0	0	0	100	15	0.0	N/A	2	1,000,000	0	0.0	0.0
A+ / 9.6	0.8	1.7	3.85	39	0	2	0	56	42	34	1.9	76	4	1,000	50	2.3	0.0
A / 9.4	0.9	1.7	3.85	7	0	2	0	56	42	34	1.9	38	4	1,000	50	0.0	0.0
A / 9.4	0.9	1.7	3.86	60	0	2	0	56	42	34	1.9	62	4	1,000	50	0.0	0.0
A+ / 9.6	0.8	1.7	3.85	124	0	2	0	56	42	34	1.9	83	4	1,000,000	0	0.0	0.0

99 Pct = Best
0 Pct = Worst

Fund Type	Fund Name	Ticker Symbol	Overall Investment Rating	Phone	PERFORMANCE: Performance Rating/Pts	Total Return % through 3/31/16: 3 Mo	6 Mo	1Yr / Pct	Annualized: 3Yr / Pct	Annualized: 5Yr / Pct	Incl. in Returns: Dividend Yield	Expense Ratio
COI	WA Short-Term Bond IS	LWSTX	B-	(877) 534-4627	C- / 4.1	0.65	0.42	0.41 /48	0.87 /40	1.34 /24	1.70	0.45
COI	WA Short-Term Bond R	LWARX	U	(877) 534-4627	U /	0.50	0.08	-0.22 /29	--	--	1.08	1.19
MMT	WA Tax Free Reserves A	LWAXX	U	(800) 331-1792	U /	--	--	--	--	--	0.02	0.72
MMT	WA Tax Free Reserves B	LTBXX	U	(800) 331-1792	U /	0.00	0.01	0.02 /37	0.02 /23	0.02 /11	0.02	1.63
MMT	WA Tax Free Reserves C	LTCXX	U	(800) 331-1792	U /	--	--	--	--	--	0.02	1.12
MMT	WA Tax Free Reserves N	CIXXX	U	(800) 331-1792	U /	--	--	--	--	--	0.02	0.87
GL	WA Total Return Unconstrained A	WAUAX	D+	(888) 425-6432	D- / 1.1	-0.37	-0.15	-1.13 /21	0.62 /35	1.97 /31	2.90	1.18
GL	WA Total Return Unconstrained C	WAUCX	D+	(888) 425-6432	D- / 1.3	-0.44	-0.51	-1.74 /17	-0.16 /14	1.19 /22	2.29	1.90
GL	WA Total Return Unconstrained FI	WARIX	C-	(888) 425-6432	C- / 3.0	-0.37	-0.17	-1.14 /21	0.58 /35	1.99 /31	3.01	1.18
GL	WA Total Return Unconstrained I	WAARX	C-	(888) 425-6432	C- / 3.5	-0.31	-0.04	-0.89 /23	0.86 /40	2.26 /34	3.27	0.91
GL	WA Total Return Unconstrained IS	WAASX	C-	(888) 425-6432	C- / 3.7	-0.19	0.01	-0.69 /24	0.96 /42	2.31 /35	3.38	0.81
GL	WA Total Return Unconstrained R	WAURX	D+	(888) 425-6432	D / 1.9	-0.43	-0.29	-1.43 /19	0.30 /30	1.67 /27	2.71	1.46
* COI	Waddell & Reed Adv Bond Fund A	UNBDX	D+	(888) 923-3355	C- / 3.1	3.17	2.62	1.43 /65	1.41 /50	3.40 /52	1.93	0.96
COI ●	Waddell & Reed Adv Bond Fund B	WBABX	D+	(888) 923-3355	C- / 3.3	2.86	1.97	0.13 /42	0.06 /25	2.11 /33	0.78	2.26
COI	Waddell & Reed Adv Bond Fund C	WCABX	C-	(888) 923-3355	C- / 4.2	3.11	2.33	0.67 /53	0.48 /33	2.46 /37	1.15	1.87
COI	Waddell & Reed Adv Bond Fund Y	WYABX	C+	(888) 923-3355	C+ / 6.4	3.42	2.90	1.87 /71	1.70 /56	3.70 /57	2.30	0.67
MM	Waddell & Reed Adv Cash Mgmt A	UNCXX	U	(888) 923-3355	U /	0.00	0.01	0.02 /35	0.02 /21	0.02 / 9	0.02	0.82
MM ●	Waddell & Reed Adv Cash Mgmt B	WCBXX	U	(888) 923-3355	U /	--	--	--	--	--	0.02	1.83
* GL	Waddell & Reed Adv Global Bond A	UNHHX	D-	(888) 923-3355	E / 0.5	2.07	2.05	-1.59 /18	-0.64 /11	1.14 /22	2.43	1.19
GL ●	Waddell & Reed Adv Global Bond B	WGBBX	D-	(888) 923-3355	E / 0.5	1.75	1.36	-3.19 /11	-1.94 / 5	-0.12 / 3	1.20	2.54
GL	Waddell & Reed Adv Global Bond C	WGBCX	D-	(888) 923-3355	E+ / 0.7	1.58	1.65	-2.71 /12	-1.46 / 6	0.30 /16	1.71	2.02
GL	Waddell & Reed Adv Global Bond Y	WGBYX	D-	(888) 923-3355	D / 1.8	2.19	2.23	-1.24 /20	-0.28 /13	1.53 /26	2.95	0.83
USS	Waddell & Reed Adv Gov Secs A	UNGVX	D	(888) 923-3355	D- / 1.5	2.54	1.59	1.44 /65	0.33 /30	2.03 /32	1.36	1.07
USS ●	Waddell & Reed Adv Gov Secs B	WGVBX	D	(888) 923-3355	D- / 1.4	2.26	1.02	0.27 /45	-0.83 / 9	0.85 /19	0.26	2.24
USS	Waddell & Reed Adv Gov Secs C	WGVCX	D+	(888) 923-3355	D / 1.7	2.32	1.16	0.60 /51	-0.50 /12	1.19 /22	0.60	1.88
USS	Waddell & Reed Adv Gov Secs Y	WGVYX	C-	(888) 923-3355	C / 4.5	2.61	1.75	1.75 /69	0.64 /36	2.35 /36	1.72	0.74
* COH	Waddell & Reed Adv High Income A	UNHIX	E	(888) 923-3355	E+ / 0.7	2.46	-1.93	-6.30 / 3	1.06 /44	5.21 /73	7.15	1.01
COH ●	Waddell & Reed Adv High Income B	WBHIX	E+	(888) 923-3355	E+ / 0.9	2.14	-2.53	-7.42 / 2	-0.09 /15	4.03 /62	6.30	2.18
COH	Waddell & Reed Adv High Income C	WCHIX	E+	(888) 923-3355	D- / 1.2	2.26	-2.31	-7.03 / 2	0.29 /30	4.39 /66	6.75	1.79
COH	Waddell & Reed Adv High Income Y	WYHIX	D-	(888) 923-3355	C- / 3.2	2.53	-1.80	-6.05 / 3	1.33 /49	5.50 /75	7.88	0.74
* MUN	Waddell & Reed Adv Muni Bond A	UNMBX	B+	(888) 923-3355	B / 7.6	1.21	2.78	2.95 /85	2.76 /86	5.23 /87	2.63	0.90
MUN ●	Waddell & Reed Adv Muni Bond B	WBMBX	B+	(888) 923-3355	B / 7.8	0.99	2.30	2.13 /78	1.81 /74	4.20 /79	1.82	1.82
MUN	Waddell & Reed Adv Muni Bond C	WCMBX	B+	(888) 923-3355	B / 7.9	1.00	2.34	2.20 /78	1.93 /76	4.32 /80	1.89	1.76
* MUH	Waddell & Reed Adv Muni High Inc A	UMUHX	C+	(888) 923-3355	B+ / 8.3	0.42	2.17	2.92 /84	3.71 /94	6.59 /95	4.12	0.90
MUH ●	Waddell & Reed Adv Muni High Inc B	WBMHX	C+	(888) 923-3355	B+ / 8.4	0.20	1.69	1.94 /77	2.71 /85	5.57 /89	3.35	1.87
MUH	Waddell & Reed Adv Muni High Inc C	WCMHX	C+	(888) 923-3355	B+ / 8.6	0.23	1.76	2.08 /78	2.86 /87	5.71 /90	3.48	1.73
US	Wasatch Hoisington US Treasury	WHOSX	C-	(800) 551-1700	A+ / 9.6	9.18	7.16	0.87 /57	6.80 /97	11.69 /98	1.97	0.67
GEI	Wasatch-1st Source Income Investor	FMEQX	C+	(800) 766-8938	C- / 4.1	1.77	1.27	1.48 /66	1.13 /45	2.03 /32	1.75	0.73
MUH	Wasmer Schroeder Hi Yld Muni Inst	WSHYX	U	(888) 263-6443	U /	2.03	4.03	5.00 /98	--	--	4.74	1.08
GL	Wavelength Interest Rate Neutral	WAVLX	U		U /	3.16	3.11	-4.00 / 8	--	--	2.16	2.58
GEN	Weitz Core Plus Income Ins	WCPBX	U	(800) 232-4161	U /	3.65	2.02	2.06 /72	--	--	2.34	2.55
GEN	Weitz Core Plus Income Inv	WCPNX	U	(800) 232-4161	U /	3.60	1.91	1.78 /70	--	--	2.16	3.18
MUS	Weitz Nebraska Tax Free Income Fd	WNTFX	A	(800) 232-4161	C+ / 6.1	0.60	0.78	1.20 /70	1.22 /59	2.35 /55	1.89	0.75
GEI	Weitz Short Intm Income Inst	WEFIX	B	(800) 232-4161	C / 4.7	1.34	0.92	0.83 /56	1.09 /44	1.97 /31	2.10	0.61
COI	Weitz Short Intm Income Inv	WSHNX	C+	(800) 232-4161	C- / 4.2	1.36	0.80	0.58 /51	0.85 /40	--	1.85	0.89
USA	Wells Fargo 100% Trsry MM Inst	WOTXX	U	(800) 222-8222	U /	0.02	0.03	0.03 /36	--	--	0.03	0.39
MTG	Wells Fargo Adj Rate Govt A	ESAAX	C-	(800) 222-8222	D- / 1.3	-0.15	-0.38	-0.42 /27	0.13 /28	0.71 /18	0.78	0.79
MTG	Wells Fargo Adj Rate Govt Adm	ESADX	C+	(800) 222-8222	D+ / 2.7	-0.11	-0.32	-0.28 /28	0.27 /30	0.85 /19	0.94	0.73
MTG ●	Wells Fargo Adj Rate Govt B	ESABX	C-	(800) 222-8222	D- / 1.1	-0.32	-0.75	-1.16 /20	-0.65 /11	-0.04 / 3	0.05	1.54
MTG	Wells Fargo Adj Rate Govt C	ESACX	C-	(800) 222-8222	D- / 1.1	-0.32	-0.75	-1.15 /21	-0.62 /11	-0.04 / 3	0.05	1.54
MTG	Wells Fargo Adj Rate Govt I	EKIZX	C+	(800) 222-8222	D+ / 2.9	-0.08	-0.24	-0.14 /30	0.41 /32	0.98 /20	1.08	0.46
MUS	Wells Fargo CA Ltd Tax Fr A	SFCIX	A+	(800) 222-8222	B- / 7.2	0.91	1.38	1.91 /76	2.16 /79	3.01 /69	1.48	0.83

● Denotes fund is closed to new investors
* Denotes fund is included in Section II

RISK			NET ASSETS		ASSET							FUND MANAGER		MINIMUM		LOADS	
Risk Rating/Pts	3 Yr Avg Standard Deviation	Avg Duration	NAV As of 3/31/16	Total $(Mil)	Cash %	Gov. Bond %	Muni. Bond %	Corp. Bond %	Other %	Portfolio Turnover Ratio	Avg Coupon Rate	Manager Quality Pct	Manager Tenure (Years)	Initial Purch. $	Additional Purch. $	Front End Load	Back End Load
A / 9.5	0.8	1.7	3.85	440	0	2	0	56	42	34	1.9	82	4	0	0	0.0	0.0
U /	N/A	1.7	3.85	N/A	0	2	0	56	42	34	1.9	N/A	4	0	0	0.0	0.0
U /	N/A	N/A	1.00	124	100	0	0	0	0	0	0.0	N/A	N/A	1,000	50	0.0	0.0
U /	N/A	N/A	1.00	N/A	100	0	0	0	0	0	0.0	N/A	N/A	1,000	50	0.0	0.0
U /	N/A	N/A	1.00	1	100	0	0	0	0	0	0.0	N/A	N/A	1,000	50	0.0	0.0
U /	N/A	N/A	1.00	62	100	0	0	0	0	0	0.0	N/A	N/A	0	0	0.0	0.0
B / 7.7	2.6	1.6	10.04	233	1	29	0	46	24	62	3.4	85	10	1,000	50	4.3	0.0
B / 7.7	2.6	1.6	10.04	18	1	29	0	46	24	62	3.4	56	10	1,000	50	0.0	0.0
B / 7.7	2.6	1.6	10.03	199	1	29	0	46	24	62	3.4	84	10	0	0	0.0	0.0
B / 7.7	2.6	1.6	10.04	571	1	29	0	46	24	62	3.4	88	10	1,000,000	0	0.0	0.0
B / 7.6	2.7	1.6	10.03	120	1	29	0	46	24	62	3.4	89	10	0	0	0.0	0.0
B / 7.6	2.7	1.6	10.04	1	1	29	0	46	24	62	3.4	77	10	0	0	0.0	0.0
C / 5.2	3.4	5.4	6.33	1,179	0	13	1	72	14	58	4.1	36	1	750	0	5.8	0.0
C+ / 5.6	3.2	5.4	6.32	3	0	13	1	72	14	58	4.1	12	1	750	0	0.0	0.0
C / 5.4	3.3	5.4	6.33	10	0	13	1	72	14	58	4.1	16	1	750	0	0.0	0.0
C / 5.5	3.3	5.4	6.34	2	0	13	1	72	14	58	4.1	47	1	0	0	0.0	0.0
U /	N/A	N/A	1.00	1,465	100	0	0	0	0	0	0.0	N/A	18	750	0	0.0	0.0
U /	N/A	N/A	1.00	1	100	0	0	0	0	0	0.0	N/A	18	750	0	0.0	0.0
C- / 3.3	4.4	2.7	3.55	562	3	22	1	65	9	16	4.9	40	14	750	0	5.8	0.0
C- / 3.2	4.5	2.7	3.54	2	3	22	1	65	9	16	4.9	13	14	750	0	0.0	0.0
C- / 3.3	4.5	2.7	3.54	6	3	22	1	65	9	16	4.9	19	14	750	0	0.0	0.0
C- / 3.3	4.5	2.7	3.55	47	3	22	1	65	9	16	4.9	52	14	0	0	0.0	0.0
C+ / 6.5	3.0	4.4	5.56	257	0	52	0	3	45	63	3.2	15	1	750	0	4.3	0.0
C+ / 6.5	3.0	4.4	5.56	1	0	52	0	3	45	63	3.2	8	1	750	0	0.0	0.0
C+ / 6.5	3.0	4.4	5.56	4	0	52	0	3	45	63	3.2	9	1	750	0	0.0	0.0
C+ / 6.5	3.0	4.4	5.56	3	0	52	0	3	45	63	3.2	20	1	0	0	0.0	0.0
D- / 1.2	5.9	3.4	6.22	1,549	2	0	0	76	22	43	7.4	40	8	750	0	5.8	0.0
D- / 1.2	5.9	3.4	6.22	5	2	0	0	76	22	43	7.4	14	8	750	0	0.0	0.0
D- / 1.2	5.9	3.4	6.22	30	2	0	0	76	22	43	7.4	20	8	750	0	0.0	0.0
D- / 1.2	5.9	3.4	6.22	265	2	0	0	76	22	43	7.4	49	8	0	0	0.0	0.0
C+ / 6.2	3.1	5.8	7.65	876	1	0	98	0	1	20	3.9	46	16	750	0	4.3	0.0
C+ / 6.1	3.1	5.8	7.64	1	1	0	98	0	1	20	3.9	20	16	750	0	0.0	0.0
C+ / 6.0	3.1	5.8	7.64	15	1	0	98	0	1	20	3.9	22	16	750	0	0.0	0.0
C- / 3.3	4.0	6.8	4.90	836	1	0	97	0	2	7	5.7	57	8	750	0	4.3	0.0
C- / 3.2	4.0	6.8	4.90	1	1	0	97	0	2	7	5.7	26	8	750	0	0.0	0.0
C- / 3.3	4.0	6.8	4.90	24	1	0	97	0	2	7	5.7	29	8	750	0	0.0	0.0
E- / 0.0	13.2	20.3	18.59	382	1	98	0	0	1	131	2.6	21	20	2,000	100	0.0	2.0
B+ / 8.6	1.9	3.2	10.21	107	2	21	3	46	28	44	3.8	48	8	2,000	100	0.0	2.0
U /	N/A	6.0	10.79	105	4	0	95	0	1	16	5.3	N/A	2	100,000	500	0.0	1.0
U /	N/A	N/A	9.45	17	6	31	0	54	9	107	0.0	N/A	3	100,000	100	0.0	0.0
U /	N/A	N/A	10.15	15	3	30	2	35	30	8	0.0	N/A	N/A	1,000,000	25	0.0	0.0
U /	N/A	N/A	10.15	5	3	30	2	35	30	8	0.0	N/A	N/A	2,500	25	0.0	0.0
B+ / 8.9	1.5	2.2	10.12	64	5	0	89	0	6	12	4.1	54	31	2,500	25	0.0	0.0
A- / 9.0	1.3	2.2	12.30	1,156	1	22	0	44	33	30	3.2	75	20	1,000,000	25	0.0	0.0
A- / 9.0	1.3	2.2	12.28	101	1	22	0	44	33	30	3.2	72	20	2,500	25	0.0	0.0
U /	N/A	N/A	1.00	2,168	0	0	0	0	100	0	0.0	N/A	N/A	10,000,000	0	0.0	0.0
A+ / 9.9	0.4	0.7	9.01	182	6	0	0	0	94	10	2.3	69	8	1,000	100	2.0	0.0
A+ / 9.8	0.4	0.7	9.01	76	6	0	0	0	94	10	2.3	76	8	1,000,000	0	0.0	0.0
A+ / 9.8	0.4	0.7	9.01	N/A	6	0	0	0	94	10	2.3	36	8	1,000	100	0.0	0.0
A+ / 9.9	0.4	0.7	9.01	108	6	0	0	0	94	10	2.3	38	8	1,000	100	0.0	0.0
A+ / 9.8	0.4	0.7	9.01	823	6	0	0	0	94	10	2.3	79	8	1,000,000	0	0.0	0.0
B+ / 8.9	1.4	2.9	10.96	203	2	0	96	0	2	31	3.4	88	7	1,000	100	2.0	0.0

Fund Type	Fund Name	Ticker Symbol	Overall Investment Rating	Phone	PERFORMANCE Performance Rating/Pts	Total Return % through 3/31/16 3 Mo	6 Mo	1Yr / Pct	Annualized 3Yr / Pct	5Yr / Pct	Incl. in Returns Dividend Yield	Expense Ratio
MUS	Wells Fargo CA Ltd Tax Fr Adm	SCTIX	A+	(800) 222-8222	B+ / 8.3	1.05	1.59	2.21 /79	2.41 /82	3.24 /72	1.71	0.77
MUS	Wells Fargo CA Ltd Tax Fr C	SFCCX	A+	(800) 222-8222	C+ / 6.5	0.73	1.01	1.25 /71	1.40 /65	2.25 /52	0.78	1.58
MMT	Wells Fargo CA Muni MM A	SGCXX	C	(800) 222-8222	D / 2.1	0.00	0.03	0.03 /39	0.02 /23	0.02 /11	0.03	0.63
MMT	Wells Fargo CA Muni MM Adm	WCMXX	C	(800) 222-8222	D / 2.1	0.00	0.03	0.03 /39	0.02 /23	0.02 /11	0.03	0.36
MMT	Wells Fargo CA Muni MM Prmr	WCTXX	C	(800) 222-8222	D+ / 2.3	0.01	0.03	0.04 /40	0.02 /23	0.02 /11	0.04	0.24
MMT	Wells Fargo CA Muni MM S	WFCXX	C	(800) 222-8222	D / 2.1	0.00	0.03	0.03 /39	0.02 /23	0.02 /11	0.03	0.53
MMT	Wells Fargo CA Muni MM Sweep		C	(800) 222-8222	D / 2.1	0.00	0.03	0.03 /39	0.02 /23	0.02 /11	0.03	0.98
MUS	Wells Fargo CA Tax Fr A	SCTAX	A-	(800) 222-8222	A / 9.4	1.78	3.49	4.19 /95	4.78 /98	7.32 /97	2.77	0.83
MUS	Wells Fargo CA Tax Fr Adm	SGCAX	A	(800) 222-8222	A+ / 9.8	1.82	3.67	4.48 /97	5.01 /99	7.54 /97	3.09	0.77
MUS	● Wells Fargo CA Tax Fr B	SGCBX	A	(800) 222-8222	A+ / 9.6	1.57	3.16	3.48 /90	4.03 /96	6.54 /95	2.17	1.58
MUS	Wells Fargo CA Tax Fr C	SCTCX	A-	(800) 222-8222	A+ / 9.6	1.58	3.16	3.40 /89	4.00 /96	6.52 /95	2.17	1.58
MM	Wells Fargo Cash Inv MM Sel	WFQXX	C+	(800) 222-8222	D+ / 2.7	0.10	0.15	0.21 /44	0.13 /28	0.13 /15	0.21	0.19
MUS	Wells Fargo CO Tax Fr A	NWCOX	A-	(800) 222-8222	A- / 9.0	1.63	3.46	4.04 /94	4.21 /97	5.93 /92	2.81	0.93
MUS	Wells Fargo CO Tax Fr Adm	NCOTX	A+	(800) 222-8222	A+ / 9.8	1.69	3.58	4.30 /96	4.47 /98	6.19 /93	3.18	0.87
MUS	Wells Fargo CO Tax Fr C	WCOTX	A	(800) 222-8222	A / 9.3	1.45	3.08	3.28 /88	3.44 /92	5.14 /86	2.21	1.68
GEI	Wells Fargo Conv Income Inst	WCIIX	U	(800) 222-8222	U /	0.26	0.29	0.42 /48	--	--	0.52	0.38
* GEI	Wells Fargo Core Bond A	MBFAX	C-	(800) 222-8222	C / 4.7	2.82	2.10	1.32 /64	2.14 /64	3.95 /61	1.31	0.85
GEI	Wells Fargo Core Bond Adm	MNTRX	C+	(800) 222-8222	C+ / 6.8	2.74	2.09	1.32 /64	2.21 /66	4.04 /62	1.45	0.79
GEI	● Wells Fargo Core Bond B	MBFBX	C	(800) 222-8222	C / 5.4	2.57	1.73	0.50 /50	1.36 /50	3.15 /47	0.64	1.60
GEI	Wells Fargo Core Bond C	MBFCX	C	(800) 222-8222	C / 5.4	2.58	1.74	0.50 /50	1.39 /50	3.17 /48	0.64	1.60
GEI	Wells Fargo Core Bond I	MBFIX	B-	(800) 222-8222	B- / 7.3	2.81	2.23	1.60 /68	2.50 /71	4.31 /66	1.72	0.52
COI	Wells Fargo Core Bond R	WTRRX	C+	(800) 222-8222	C+ / 6.3	2.66	1.93	0.99 /58	1.88 /59	3.68 /56	1.13	1.10
COI	Wells Fargo Core Bond R4	MBFRX	B-	(800) 222-8222	B- / 7.2	2.87	2.26	1.58 /67	2.42 /69	--	1.62	0.62
COI	Wells Fargo Core Bond R6	WTRIX	B	(800) 222-8222	B- / 7.4	2.90	2.34	1.73 /69	2.55 /71	--	1.77	0.47
USS	Wells Fargo Core Plus Bond A	STYAX	C-	(800) 222-8222	C+ / 5.7	3.36	2.88	1.40 /65	2.66 /73	4.07 /63	1.98	0.94
COI	Wells Fargo Core Plus Bond Adm	WIPDX	C+	(800) 222-8222	B / 7.7	3.31	2.94	1.51 /67	2.78 /74	4.21 /64	2.18	0.88
USS	● Wells Fargo Core Plus Bond B	STYBX	C	(800) 222-8222	C+ / 6.3	3.17	2.51	0.63 /52	1.88 /59	3.28 /50	1.24	1.69
USS	Wells Fargo Core Plus Bond C	WFIPX	C	(800) 222-8222	C+ / 6.3	3.05	2.40	0.63 /52	1.87 /59	3.27 /49	1.32	1.69
USS	Wells Fargo Core Plus Bond Inst	WIPIX	B-	(800) 222-8222	B / 7.8	3.33	3.00	1.64 /68	2.92 /76	4.38 /66	2.31	0.61
MUN	Wells Fargo CoreBuilder A	WFCMX	A	(800) 222-8222	A+ / 9.9	1.12	3.74	4.74 /97	5.14 /99	8.06 /98	3.33	N/A
MM	Wells Fargo Csh Inv MM Adm	WFAXX	C	(800) 222-8222	D+ / 2.3	0.05	0.06	0.06 /40	0.03 /23	0.02 / 9	0.06	0.35
MM	Wells Fargo Csh Inv MM I	WFIXX	C	(800) 222-8222	D+ / 2.5	0.08	0.11	0.14 /42	0.06 /26	0.06 /14	0.14	0.23
MM	Wells Fargo Csh Inv MM S	NWIXX	U	(800) 222-8222	U /	0.01	0.01	0.02 /35	0.01 /18	0.01 / 6	0.02	0.52
GES	Wells Fargo Dvsfd Inc Bldr A	EKSAX	C-	(800) 222-8222	B / 7.7	4.46	6.11	0.17 /43	4.34 /86	5.81 /76	3.13	1.07
GES	Wells Fargo Dvsfd Inc Bldr Adm	EKSDX	C-	(800) 222-8222	B+ / 8.8	4.39	6.11	0.28 /46	4.54 /88	5.96 /77	3.50	0.99
GES	● Wells Fargo Dvsfd Inc Bldr B	EKSBX	C-	(800) 222-8222	B / 8.2	4.08	5.71	-0.56 /25	3.56 /81	5.02 /72	2.59	1.82
GES	Wells Fargo Dvsfd Inc Bldr C	EKSCX	C-	(800) 222-8222	B / 8.2	4.09	5.72	-0.57 /25	3.56 /81	5.02 /72	2.59	1.82
GES	Wells Fargo Dvsfd Inc Bldr Inst	EKSYX	C-	(800) 222-8222	B+ / 8.9	4.25	6.21	0.47 /49	4.69 /89	6.17 /78	3.69	0.74
USS	Wells Fargo Govt Secs A	SGVDX	C	(800) 222-8222	C- / 4.1	2.52	1.67	1.55 /67	1.82 /58	2.89 /43	0.74	0.87
USS	Wells Fargo Govt Secs Adm	WGSDX	B+	(800) 222-8222	C+ / 6.6	2.48	1.78	1.76 /69	2.03 /62	3.11 /47	0.98	0.81
USS	● Wells Fargo Govt Secs B	WGSBX	C+	(800) 222-8222	C / 4.9	2.34	1.30	0.80 /55	1.07 /44	2.15 /33	0.04	1.62
USS	Wells Fargo Govt Secs C	WGSCX	C+	(800) 222-8222	C / 4.9	2.34	1.30	0.80 /55	1.06 /44	2.13 /33	0.04	1.62
USS	Wells Fargo Govt Secs I	SGVIX	B+	(800) 222-8222	C+ / 6.9	2.61	1.86	1.92 /71	2.20 /66	3.28 /50	1.13	0.54
MM	Wells Fargo Gv MM Adm	WGAXX	U	(800) 222-8222	U /	--	--	--	--	--	0.01	0.34
MM	Wells Fargo Gv MM I	GVIXX	C	(800) 222-8222	D / 2.2	0.03	0.04	0.04 /38	0.02 /21	0.02 / 9	0.04	0.22
MM	Wells Fargo Gv MM Select	WFFXX	U	(800) 222-8222	U /	0.05	0.06	--	--	--	0.00	N/A
MM	Wells Fargo Heritage MM Adm	SHMXX	C	(800) 222-8222	D+ / 2.3	0.05	0.05	0.06 /40	0.03 /23	0.02 / 9	0.06	0.34
MM	Wells Fargo Heritage MM Inst	SHIXX	C	(800) 222-8222	D+ / 2.5	0.08	0.11	0.13 /42	0.05 /25	0.05 /13	0.13	0.22
MM	Wells Fargo Heritage MM Sel	WFJXX	C	(800) 222-8222	D+ / 2.7	0.10	0.14	0.20 /44	0.12 /28	0.12 /15	0.20	0.18
MM	Wells Fargo Heritage MM Svc	WHTXX	C	(800) 222-8222	D / 2.0	0.02	0.03	0.03 /37	0.02 /21	0.01 / 6	0.03	0.51
MUH	Wells Fargo Hi Yld Muni Bd A	WHYMX	B-	(800) 222-8222	A+ / 9.9	1.76	4.59	5.32 /98	6.33 /99	--	3.22	1.08
MUH	Wells Fargo Hi Yld Muni Bd Adm	WHYDX	B	(800) 222-8222	A+ / 9.9	1.78	4.54	5.32 /98	6.44 /99	--	3.47	1.02

99 Pct = Best; 0 Pct = Worst

● Denotes fund is closed to new investors
* Denotes fund is included in Section II

RISK			NET ASSETS		ASSET							FUND MANAGER		MINIMUM		LOADS	
Risk Rating/Pts	3 Yr Avg Standard Deviation	Avg Duration	NAV As of 3/31/16	Total $(Mil)	Cash %	Gov. Bond %	Muni. Bond %	Corp. Bond %	Other %	Portfolio Turnover Ratio	Avg Coupon Rate	Manager Quality Pct	Manager Tenure (Years)	Initial Purch. $	Additional Purch. $	Front End Load	Back End Load
B+ / 8.9	1.4	2.9	10.80	254	2	0	96	0	2	31	3.4	91	7	1,000,000	0	0.0	0.0
B+ / 8.9	1.4	2.9	10.96	37	2	0	96	0	2	31	3.4	71	7	1,000	100	0.0	0.0
A+ / 9.9	N/A	N/A	1.00	439	100	0	0	0	0	0	0.0	N/A	N/A	1,000	100	0.0	0.0
A+ / 9.9	N/A	N/A	1.00	N/A	100	0	0	0	0	0	0.0	N/A	N/A	1,000,000	0	0.0	0.0
A+ / 9.9	N/A	N/A	1.00	692	100	0	0	0	0	0	0.0	N/A	N/A	10,000,000	0	0.0	0.0
A+ / 9.9	N/A	N/A	1.00	55	100	0	0	0	0	0	0.0	N/A	N/A	100,000	0	0.0	0.0
A+ / 9.9	N/A	N/A	1.00	N/A	100	0	0	0	0	0	0.0	N/A	N/A	0	0	0.0	0.0
C / 4.5	3.7	5.9	12.15	521	1	0	97	0	2	30	3.9	89	7	1,000	100	4.5	0.0
C / 4.5	3.7	5.9	12.18	300	1	0	97	0	2	30	3.9	91	7	1,000,000	0	0.0	0.0
C / 4.6	3.7	5.9	12.40	N/A	1	0	97	0	2	30	3.9	75	7	1,000	100	0.0	0.0
C / 4.4	3.7	5.9	12.39	59	1	0	97	0	2	30	3.9	72	7	1,000	100	0.0	0.0
A+ / 9.9	N/A	N/A	1.00	5,887	100	0	0	0	0	0	0.2	71	13	50,000,000	0	0.0	0.0
C / 5.0	3.5	6.2	11.21	38	0	0	100	0	0	23	4.7	84	11	1,000	100	4.5	0.0
C / 5.0	3.5	6.2	11.21	59	0	0	100	0	0	23	4.7	88	11	1,000,000	0	0.0	0.0
C / 5.0	3.5	6.2	11.22	6	0	0	100	0	0	23	4.7	56	11	1,000	100	0.0	0.0
U /	N/A	0.4	9.99	588	1	1	9	65	24	80	1.0	N/A	3	1,000,000	0	0.0	0.0
C+ / 5.8	3.2	5.6	13.27	721	0	33	0	21	46	586	2.9	44	13	1,000	100	4.5	0.0
C+ / 5.8	3.2	5.6	12.95	523	0	33	0	21	46	586	2.9	47	13	1,000,000	0	0.0	0.0
C+ / 5.8	3.2	5.6	13.22	1	0	33	0	21	46	586	2.9	23	13	1,000	100	0.0	0.0
C+ / 5.8	3.2	5.6	13.14	67	0	33	0	21	46	586	2.9	23	13	1,000	100	0.0	0.0
C+ / 5.8	3.2	5.6	12.93	1,941	0	33	0	21	46	586	2.9	57	13	1,000,000	0	0.0	0.0
C+ / 5.7	3.2	5.6	12.95	17	0	33	0	21	46	586	2.9	58	13	0	0	0.0	0.0
C+ / 5.9	3.2	5.6	12.94	41	0	33	0	21	46	586	2.9	81	13	0	0	0.0	0.0
C+ / 5.8	3.2	5.6	12.94	380	0	33	0	21	46	586	2.9	84	13	0	0	0.0	0.0
C / 4.9	3.5	5.7	12.30	263	0	14	3	40	43	322	4.3	85	11	1,000	100	4.5	0.0
C / 4.9	3.5	5.7	12.28	70	0	14	3	40	43	322	4.3	82	11	1,000,000	0	0.0	0.0
C / 5.0	3.5	5.7	12.34	N/A	0	14	3	40	43	322	4.3	58	11	1,000	100	0.0	0.0
C / 5.1	3.4	5.7	12.29	20	0	14	3	40	43	322	4.3	59	11	1,000	100	0.0	0.0
C / 5.0	3.5	5.7	12.31	64	0	14	3	40	43	322	4.3	89	11	1,000,000	0	0.0	0.0
C / 4.3	3.8	N/A	12.00	423	3	0	96	0	1	37	0.0	91	8	0	0	0.0	0.0
A+ / 9.9	N/A	N/A	1.00	302	100	0	0	0	0	0	0.1	66	13	1,000,000	0	0.0	0.0
A+ / 9.9	N/A	N/A	1.00	5,211	100	0	0	0	0	0	0.1	N/A	13	10,000,000	0	0.0	0.0
U /	N/A	N/A	1.00	1,190	100	0	0	0	0	0	0.0	N/A	13	100,000	0	0.0	0.0
D- / 1.1	6.4	5.5	5.74	132	2	0	0	73	25	63	5.5	96	9	1,000	100	5.8	0.0
D- / 1.1	6.4	5.5	5.62	52	2	0	0	73	25	63	5.5	97	9	1,000,000	0	0.0	0.0
D- / 1.2	6.4	5.5	5.76	1	2	0	0	73	25	63	5.5	93	9	1,000	100	0.0	0.0
D- / 1.2	6.4	5.5	5.75	109	2	0	0	73	25	63	5.5	93	9	1,000	100	0.0	0.0
D- / 1.3	6.3	5.5	5.61	83	2	0	0	73	25	63	5.5	98	9	1,000,000	0	0.0	0.0
B- / 7.4	2.7	5.0	11.38	507	0	39	0	1	60	349	3.3	60	6	1,000	100	4.5	0.0
B- / 7.4	2.8	5.0	11.37	219	0	39	0	1	60	349	3.3	73	6	1,000,000	0	0.0	0.0
B- / 7.4	2.7	5.0	11.38	N/A	0	39	0	1	60	349	3.3	35	6	1,000	100	0.0	0.0
B- / 7.5	2.7	5.0	11.38	27	0	39	0	1	60	349	3.3	35	6	1,000	100	0.0	0.0
B- / 7.4	2.7	5.0	11.37	470	0	39	0	1	60	349	3.3	78	6	1,000,000	0	0.0	0.0
U /	N/A	N/A	1.00	346	100	0	0	0	0	0	0.0	N/A	17	1,000,000	0	0.0	0.0
A+ / 9.9	N/A	N/A	1.00	14,718	100	0	0	0	0	0	0.0	66	17	10,000,000	0	0.0	0.0
U /	N/A	N/A	1.00	6,885	100	0	0	0	0	0	0.0	N/A	17	50,000,000	0	0.0	0.0
A+ / 9.9	N/A	N/A	1.00	313	100	0	0	0	0	0	0.1	66	N/A	1,000,000	0	0.0	0.0
A+ / 9.9	N/A	N/A	1.00	8,269	100	0	0	0	0	0	0.1	N/A	N/A	10,000,000	0	0.0	0.0
A+ / 9.9	N/A	N/A	1.00	33,831	100	0	0	0	0	0	0.2	70	N/A	50,000,000	0	0.0	0.0
A+ / 9.9	N/A	N/A	1.00	850	100	0	0	0	0	0	0.0	66	N/A	100,000	0	0.0	0.0
D+ / 2.6	4.5	7.1	10.66	32	0	0	98	0	2	62	4.3	95	3	1,000	100	4.5	0.0
D+ / 2.6	4.5	7.1	10.66	23	0	0	98	0	2	62	4.3	95	3	1,000,000	0	0.0	0.0

Fund Type	Fund Name	Ticker Symbol	Overall Investment Rating	Phone	Performance Rating/Pts	3 Mo	6 Mo	1Yr / Pct	3Yr / Pct	5Yr / Pct	Dividend Yield	Expense Ratio
99 Pct = Best 0 Pct = Worst					PERFORMANCE	Total Return % through 3/31/16			Annualized		Incl. in Returns	
MUH	Wells Fargo Hi Yld Muni Bd C	WHYCX	B-	(800) 222-8222	A+ / 9.9	1.57	4.10	4.54 /97	5.58 /99	--	2.64	1.83
MUH	Wells Fargo Hi Yld Muni Bd Inst	WHYIX	B-	(800) 222-8222	A+ / 9.9	1.82	4.72	5.58 /99	6.60 /99	--	3.61	0.75
COH	Wells Fargo High Inc A	SHBAX	E+	(800) 222-8222	E+ / 0.8	3.07	1.90	-3.49 /10	0.13 /28	3.43 /52	5.13	1.02
COH	Wells Fargo High Inc Adm	WFNDX	D-	(800) 222-8222	D+ / 2.8	3.08	1.95	-3.31 /10	0.28 /30	3.55 /54	5.47	0.96
COH ●	Wells Fargo High Inc B	WFNBX	E+	(800) 222-8222	D- / 1.1	2.89	1.53	-4.21 / 7	-0.61 /11	2.66 /40	4.60	1.77
COH	Wells Fargo High Inc C	WFNCX	E+	(800) 222-8222	D- / 1.1	2.90	1.53	-4.20 / 7	-0.61 /11	2.66 /40	4.60	1.77
COH	Wells Fargo High Inc I	SHYYX	D-	(800) 222-8222	C- / 3.3	3.15	2.10	-3.18 /11	0.53 /34	3.83 /59	5.77	0.69
COH	Wells Fargo High Yld Bd Fd A	EKHAX	D	(800) 222-8222	C+ / 5.7	3.63	5.08	-0.59 /25	2.69 /73	4.85 /71	3.91	1.04
COH	Wells Fargo High Yld Bd Fd Adm	EKHYX	C-	(800) 222-8222	B / 7.9	3.68	5.18	-0.05 /31	3.03 /77	5.15 /73	4.31	0.98
COH ●	Wells Fargo High Yld Bd Fd B	EKHBX	D+	(800) 222-8222	C+ / 6.6	3.78	5.03	-1.01 /22	2.03 /62	4.13 /63	3.34	1.79
COH	Wells Fargo High Yld Bd Fd C	EKHCX	D+	(800) 222-8222	C+ / 6.3	3.45	4.70	-1.32 /19	1.93 /60	4.07 /63	3.35	1.79
GL	Wells Fargo Intl Bd A	ESIYX	E	(800) 222-8222	E+ / 0.8	8.49	5.13	1.10 /60	-1.54 / 6	0.14 /15	0.00	1.06
GL	Wells Fargo Intl Bd Adm	ESIDX	D-	(800) 222-8222	D+ / 2.7	8.59	5.23	1.30 /63	-1.38 / 6	0.32 /16	0.00	1.00
GL ●	Wells Fargo Intl Bd B	ESIUX	E	(800) 222-8222	D- / 1.0	8.24	4.75	0.31 /46	-2.28 / 4	-0.61 / 2	0.00	1.81
GL	Wells Fargo Intl Bd C	ESIVX	E	(800) 222-8222	D- / 1.0	8.21	4.69	0.32 /46	-2.30 / 3	-0.62 / 2	0.00	1.81
GL	Wells Fargo Intl Bd I	ESICX	D-	(800) 222-8222	D+ / 2.8	8.55	5.21	1.39 /65	-1.26 / 7	0.46 /17	0.00	0.73
GL	Wells Fargo Intl Bd R6	ESIRX	D-	(800) 222-8222	C- / 3.0	8.54	5.30	1.49 /66	-1.17 / 8	--	0.00	0.68
* MUN	Wells Fargo Intm Tax/AMT Fr A	WFTAX	A	(800) 222-8222	B / 8.0	1.22	2.68	2.74 /82	2.75 /85	4.73 /83	2.10	0.80
MUN	Wells Fargo Intm Tax/AMT Fr Adm	WFITX	A+	(800) 222-8222	B+ / 8.8	1.24	2.73	2.84 /83	2.85 /86	4.85 /84	2.27	0.74
MUN	Wells Fargo Intm Tax/AMT Fr C	WFTFX	A	(800) 222-8222	B / 7.9	1.04	2.31	1.99 /77	1.99 /77	3.95 /77	1.44	1.55
MUN	Wells Fargo Intm Tax/AMT Fr I	WITIX	A+	(800) 222-8222	A- / 9.0	1.19	2.72	2.93 /84	3.00 /88	5.02 /85	2.43	0.47
MM	Wells Fargo MM Svc	WMOXX	U	(800) 222-8222	U /	0.01	0.01	0.01 /33	0.01 /18	0.01 / 6	0.01	0.72
MUS	Wells Fargo MN Tax Free A	NMTFX	A+	(800) 222-8222	B / 7.6	1.24	2.43	2.96 /85	2.89 /87	4.79 /84	2.82	0.89
MUS	Wells Fargo MN Tax Free Adm	NWMIX	A+	(800) 222-8222	A- / 9.0	1.20	2.46	3.12 /86	3.12 /89	5.05 /86	3.20	0.83
MUS	Wells Fargo MN Tax Free C	WMTCX	A+	(800) 222-8222	B / 8.0	0.97	1.96	2.11 /78	2.10 /78	3.99 /77	2.22	1.64
MMT	Wells Fargo Mu Cash Mgmt MM Adm	WUCXX	C	(800) 222-8222	D+ / 2.3	0.00	0.02	0.02 /37	0.03 /25	0.03 /13	0.02	0.36
MMT	Wells Fargo Mu Cash Mgmt MM I	EMMXX	C	(800) 222-8222	D+ / 2.3	0.01	0.02	0.03 /39	0.03 /25	0.04 /14	0.03	0.24
MMT	Wells Fargo Mu Cash Mgmt MM S	EISXX	C	(800) 222-8222	D+ / 2.3	0.01	0.02	0.03 /39	0.03 /25	0.03 /13	0.03	0.53
* MUN	Wells Fargo Muni Bd A	WMFAX	B+	(800) 222-8222	B+ / 8.9	1.18	3.51	3.77 /92	4.12 /96	6.52 /95	2.79	0.80
MUN	Wells Fargo Muni Bd Adm	WMFDX	A	(800) 222-8222	A+ / 9.7	1.22	3.58	3.82 /93	4.24 /97	6.65 /95	3.06	0.74
MUN ●	Wells Fargo Muni Bd B	WMFBX	B+	(800) 222-8222	A- / 9.2	0.91	3.13	3.01 /85	3.32 /91	5.70 /90	2.20	1.55
MUN	Wells Fargo Muni Bd C	WMFCX	B+	(800) 222-8222	A- / 9.2	0.91	3.13	2.91 /84	3.32 /91	5.71 /90	2.19	1.55
MUN	Wells Fargo Muni Bd Inst	WMBIX	A	(800) 222-8222	A+ / 9.7	1.25	3.65	4.07 /94	4.39 /97	6.82 /96	3.20	0.47
MMT	Wells Fargo Municipal MM A	WMUXX	C	(800) 222-8222	D+ / 2.3	0.00	0.01	0.02 /37	0.03 /25	0.03 /13	0.02	0.83
MMT	Wells Fargo Municipal MM Prmr	WMTXX	U	(800) 222-8222	U /	--	--	--	--	--	0.02	0.44
MMT	Wells Fargo Municipal MM Svc	WMSXX	C	(800) 222-8222	D+ / 2.3	0.00	0.01	0.02 /37	0.03 /25	0.03 /13	0.02	0.73
MMT	Wells Fargo Natl TF MM A	NWMXX	C	(800) 222-8222	D / 2.2	0.00	0.01	0.02 /37	0.02 /23	0.02 /11	0.02	0.63
MMT	Wells Fargo Natl TF MM Adm	WNTXX	C	(800) 222-8222	D / 2.2	0.00	0.01	0.02 /37	0.02 /23	0.02 /11	0.02	0.36
MMT	Wells Fargo Natl TF MM Prmr	WFNXX	U	(800) 222-8222	U /	--	--	--	--	--	0.02	0.24
MMT	Wells Fargo Natl TF MM S	MMIXX	C	(800) 222-8222	D / 2.2	0.00	0.01	0.02 /37	0.02 /23	0.02 /11	0.02	0.53
MMT	Wells Fargo Natl TF MM Sw		C	(800) 222-8222	D / 2.2	0.00	0.01	0.02 /37	0.02 /23	0.02 /11	0.02	0.98
MUS	Wells Fargo NC TF A	ENCMX	B+	(800) 222-8222	B / 8.0	1.09	2.34	2.74 /83	3.30 /91	5.33 /88	2.84	0.94
MUS	Wells Fargo NC TF C	ENCCX	A-	(800) 222-8222	B+ / 8.3	0.91	1.87	1.98 /77	2.50 /83	4.54 /82	2.24	1.69
MUS	Wells Fargo NC TF Inst	ENCYX	A+	(800) 222-8222	A / 9.3	1.16	2.49	3.05 /85	3.62 /93	5.65 /90	3.28	0.61
MUS	Wells Fargo PA Tax Fr A	EKVAX	A	(800) 222-8222	B+ / 8.8	1.16	2.52	3.69 /92	4.05 /96	6.12 /93	3.12	0.90
MUS ●	Wells Fargo PA Tax Fr B	EKVBX	A	(800) 222-8222	A- / 9.1	0.99	2.07	2.84 /83	3.25 /90	5.32 /88	2.53	1.65
MUS	Wells Fargo PA Tax Fr C	EKVCX	A	(800) 222-8222	A- / 9.1	0.90	2.06	2.84 /83	3.25 /90	5.32 /88	2.53	1.65
MUS	Wells Fargo PA Tax Fr Inst	EKVYX	A+	(800) 222-8222	A+ / 9.7	1.22	2.65	3.94 /94	4.30 /97	6.38 /94	3.51	0.57
GEI	Wells Fargo Real Return A	IPBAX	E+	(800) 222-8222	D- / 1.0	4.97	4.81	1.10 /60	-0.83 / 9	2.61 /39	0.57	1.45
GEI	Wells Fargo Real Return Adm	IPBIX	D	(800) 222-8222	C- / 3.5	5.14	5.06	1.46 /66	-0.54 /11	2.87 /43	0.76	1.39
GEI ●	Wells Fargo Real Return B	IPBBX	E+	(800) 222-8222	D- / 1.3	4.83	4.62	0.41 /48	-1.56 / 6	1.85 /29	0.23	2.20
GEI	Wells Fargo Real Return C	IPBCX	E+	(800) 222-8222	D- / 1.3	4.83	4.50	0.41 /48	-1.57 / 6	1.85 /29	0.23	2.20

● Denotes fund is closed to new investors
* Denotes fund is included in Section II

RISK			NET ASSETS		ASSET							FUND MANAGER		MINIMUM		LOADS	
Risk Rating/Pts	3 Yr Avg Standard Deviation	Avg Duration	NAV As of 3/31/16	Total $(Mil)	Cash %	Gov. Bond %	Muni. Bond %	Corp. Bond %	Other %	Portfolio Turnover Ratio	Avg Coupon Rate	Manager Quality Pct	Manager Tenure (Years)	Initial Purch. $	Additional Purch. $	Front End Load	Back End Load
D+ / 2.6	4.5	7.1	10.66	8	0	0	98	0	2	62	4.3	90	3	1,000	100	0.0	0.0
D+ / 2.6	4.5	7.1	10.66	65	0	0	98	0	2	62	4.3	96	3	1,000,000	0	0.0	0.0
D- / 1.5	5.6	4.3	6.33	218	7	0	0	90	3	51	5.9	18	18	1,000	100	4.5	0.0
D / 1.6	5.6	4.3	6.40	24	7	0	0	90	3	51	5.9	21	18	1,000,000	0	0.0	0.0
D- / 1.5	5.6	4.3	6.33	N/A	7	0	0	90	3	51	5.9	10	18	1,000	100	0.0	0.0
D- / 1.5	5.6	4.3	6.33	15	7	0	0	90	3	51	5.9	10	18	1,000	100	0.0	0.0
D- / 1.5	5.6	4.3	6.39	74	7	0	0	90	3	51	5.9	27	18	1,000,000	0	0.0	0.0
D- / 1.2	5.9	5.5	3.14	173	1	0	0	89	10	55	5.4	90	3	1,000	100	4.5	0.0
D- / 1.1	6.0	5.5	3.15	30	1	0	0	89	10	55	5.4	92	3	1,000,000	0	0.0	0.0
D- / 1.0	6.0	5.5	3.15	1	1	0	0	89	10	55	5.4	80	3	1,000	100	0.0	0.0
D- / 1.2	5.9	5.5	3.14	55	1	0	0	89	10	55	5.4	78	3	1,000	100	0.0	0.0
E+ / 0.6	7.3	5.7	10.22	51	0	71	2	25	2	136	3.6	20	23	1,000	100	4.5	0.0
E+ / 0.6	7.3	5.7	10.24	229	0	71	2	25	2	136	3.6	24	23	1,000,000	0	0.0	0.0
E+ / 0.6	7.3	5.7	10.12	N/A	0	71	2	25	2	136	3.6	11	23	1,000	100	0.0	0.0
E+ / 0.6	7.3	5.7	10.02	6	0	71	2	25	2	136	3.6	11	23	1,000	100	0.0	0.0
E+ / 0.6	7.3	5.7	10.28	519	0	71	2	25	2	136	3.6	26	23	1,000,000	0	0.0	0.0
E+ / 0.6	7.4	5.7	10.30	16	0	71	2	25	2	136	3.6	28	23	0	0	0.0	0.0
B- / 7.0	2.9	4.4	11.73	574	1	0	98	0	1	38	3.8	53	15	1,000	100	3.0	0.0
B- / 7.1	2.9	4.4	11.74	777	1	0	98	0	1	38	3.8	58	15	1,000,000	0	0.0	0.0
C+ / 6.9	2.9	4.4	11.73	57	1	0	98	0	1	38	3.8	28	15	1,000	100	0.0	0.0
B- / 7.0	2.9	4.4	11.74	1,126	1	0	98	0	1	38	3.8	63	15	1,000,000	0	0.0	0.0
U /	N/A	N/A	1.00	257	100	0	0	0	0	0	0.0	N/A	N/A	100,000	0	0.0	0.0
B / 7.7	2.6	4.3	10.93	44	3	0	96	0	1	20	4.6	74	8	1,000	100	4.5	0.0
B / 7.7	2.6	4.3	10.92	118	3	0	96	0	1	20	4.6	81	8	1,000,000	0	0.0	0.0
B / 7.7	2.6	4.3	10.92	10	3	0	96	0	1	20	4.6	41	8	1,000	100	0.0	0.0
A+ / 9.9	N/A	N/A	1.00	1	100	0	0	0	0	0	0.0	67	N/A	1,000,000	0	0.0	0.0
A+ / 9.9	N/A	N/A	1.00	1,206	100	0	0	0	0	0	0.0	67	N/A	10,000,000	0	0.0	0.0
A+ / 9.9	N/A	N/A	1.00	83	100	0	0	0	0	0	0.0	67	N/A	100,000	0	0.0	0.0
C / 4.5	3.7	4.9	10.48	1,511	3	0	96	0	1	27	3.1	80	16	1,000	100	4.5	0.0
C / 4.6	3.6	4.9	10.48	257	3	0	96	0	1	27	3.1	83	16	1,000,000	0	0.0	0.0
C / 4.6	3.7	4.9	10.48	1	3	0	96	0	1	27	3.1	47	16	1,000	100	0.0	0.0
C / 4.6	3.6	4.9	10.47	178	3	0	96	0	1	27	3.1	47	16	1,000	100	0.0	0.0
C / 4.6	3.7	4.9	10.48	874	3	0	96	0	1	27	3.1	85	16	1,000,000	0	0.0	0.0
A+ / 9.9	N/A	N/A	1.00	138	100	0	0	0	0	0	0.0	68	N/A	1,000	100	0.0	0.0
U /	N/A	N/A	1.00	14	100	0	0	0	0	0	0.0	68	6	10,000,000	0	0.0	0.0
A+ / 9.9	N/A	N/A	1.00	158	100	0	0	0	0	0	0.0	68	N/A	100,000	0	0.0	0.0
A+ / 9.9	N/A	N/A	1.00	172	100	0	0	0	0	0	0.0	N/A	N/A	1,000	100	0.0	0.0
A+ / 9.9	N/A	N/A	1.00	177	100	0	0	0	0	0	0.0	N/A	N/A	1,000,000	0	0.0	0.0
U /	N/A	N/A	1.00	1,684	100	0	0	0	0	0	0.0	N/A	N/A	10,000,000	0	0.0	0.0
A+ / 9.9	N/A	N/A	1.00	137	100	0	0	0	0	0	0.0	N/A	N/A	100,000	0	0.0	0.0
A+ / 9.9	N/A	N/A	1.00	628	100	0	0	0	0	0	0.0	N/A	N/A	0	0	0.0	0.0
C+ / 5.7	3.2	4.2	10.49	36	4	0	95	0	1	12	4.9	59	7	1,000	100	4.5	0.0
C+ / 5.8	3.2	4.2	10.49	5	4	0	95	0	1	12	4.9	33	7	1,000	100	0.0	0.0
C+ / 5.7	3.2	4.2	10.49	59	4	0	95	0	1	12	4.9	76	7	1,000,000	0	0.0	0.0
C+ / 5.7	3.2	4.2	11.94	52	1	0	98	0	1	15	4.5	85	7	1,000	100	4.5	0.0
C+ / 5.6	3.2	4.2	11.89	1	1	0	98	0	1	15	4.5	58	7	1,000	100	0.0	0.0
C+ / 5.7	3.2	4.2	11.91	17	1	0	98	0	1	15	4.5	58	7	1,000	100	0.0	0.0
C+ / 5.7	3.2	4.2	11.94	127	1	0	98	0	1	15	4.5	88	7	1,000,000	0	0.0	0.0
D / 1.9	5.8	3.8	9.93	19	6	65	0	14	15	57	1.6	4	11	1,000	100	4.5	0.0
D / 1.8	5.8	3.8	10.02	16	6	65	0	14	15	57	1.6	4	11	1,000,000	0	0.0	0.0
D / 1.8	5.8	3.8	9.76	N/A	6	65	0	14	15	57	1.6	2	11	1,000	100	0.0	0.0
D / 1.9	5.8	3.8	9.76	6	6	65	0	14	15	57	1.6	2	11	1,000	100	0.0	0.0

Fund Type	Fund Name	Ticker Symbol	Overall Investment Rating	Phone	PERFORMANCE: Performance Rating/Pts	Total Return % through 3/31/16: 3 Mo	6 Mo	1Yr / Pct	Annualized: 3Yr / Pct	5Yr / Pct	Incl. in Returns: Dividend Yield	Expense Ratio
USS	Wells Fargo Sh Dur Gov A	MSDAX	**C-**	(800) 222-8222	**D / 1.8**	0.84	0.39	0.45 /49	0.44 /32	1.00 /20	1.33	0.78
USS	Wells Fargo Sh Dur Gov Adm	MNSGX	**C+**	(800) 222-8222	**C- / 3.7**	0.88	0.38	0.53 /50	0.59 /35	1.18 /22	1.53	0.72
USS ●	Wells Fargo Sh Dur Gov B	MSDBX	**C-**	(800) 222-8222	**D- / 1.5**	0.66	-0.07	-0.39 /27	-0.33 /13	0.24 /16	0.61	1.53
USS	Wells Fargo Sh Dur Gov C	MSDCX	**C-**	(800) 222-8222	**D- / 1.5**	0.66	-0.07	-0.38 /27	-0.33 /13	0.23 /16	0.61	1.53
USS	Wells Fargo Sh Dur Gov I	WSGIX	**B-**	(800) 222-8222	**C- / 4.0**	0.92	0.47	0.81 /55	0.77 /38	1.36 /24	1.71	0.45
USS	Wells Fargo Sh Dur Gov R6	MSDRX	**B-**	(800) 222-8222	**C- / 4.2**	0.93	0.60	0.86 /56	0.82 /39	--	1.76	0.40
GEI	Wells Fargo Sh-Tm Bd A	SSTVX	**C+**	(800) 222-8222	**C- / 3.4**	0.87	0.62	0.80 /55	1.01 /43	1.41 /25	1.08	0.81
GEI	Wells Fargo Sh-Tm Bd C	WFSHX	**C+**	(800) 222-8222	**C- / 3.0**	0.70	0.26	0.06 /39	0.26 /30	0.64 /18	0.38	1.56
GEI	Wells Fargo Sh-Tm Bd I	SSHIX	**B+**	(800) 222-8222	**C / 5.0**	1.04	0.85	1.05 /59	1.30 /48	1.72 /28	1.35	0.48
COH	Wells Fargo Sh-Tm Hi Yld A	SSTHX	**C+**	(800) 222-8222	**C / 5.2**	1.31	1.69	1.52 /67	2.16 /65	3.12 /47	2.79	0.93
COH	Wells Fargo Sh-Tm Hi Yld Adm	WDHYX	**A**	(800) 222-8222	**C+ / 6.8**	1.35	1.77	1.80 /70	2.32 /68	3.28 /50	3.04	0.87
COH	Wells Fargo Sh-Tm Hi Yld C	WFHYX	**C+**	(800) 222-8222	**C / 5.2**	1.13	1.32	0.77 /55	1.40 /50	2.35 /36	2.14	1.68
COH	Wells Fargo Sh-Tm Hi Yld Inst	STYIX	**A**	(800) 222-8222	**B- / 7.1**	1.51	1.85	1.95 /71	2.47 /70	--	3.18	0.60
* MUN	Wells Fargo ST Muni Bd A	WSMAX	**C+**	(800) 222-8222	**C- / 3.5**	0.26	0.60	0.79 /62	0.87 /49	1.59 /37	1.00	0.75
MUN	Wells Fargo ST Muni Bd Adm	WSTMX	**B+**	(800) 222-8222	**C / 4.7**	0.17	0.52	0.52 /55	0.81 /47	1.55 /36	1.05	0.69
MUN	Wells Fargo ST Muni Bd C	WSSCX	**C+**	(800) 222-8222	**D+ / 2.8**	0.09	0.23	-0.05 /31	0.12 /29	0.83 /23	0.28	1.50
MUN	Wells Fargo ST Muni Bd I	WSBIX	**A**	(800) 222-8222	**C+ / 5.6**	0.32	0.71	1.00 /67	1.07 /55	1.81 /42	1.23	0.42
* MUN	Wells Fargo Str Muni Bd A	VMPAX	**A-**	(800) 222-8222	**C+ / 5.9**	0.58	1.57	1.96 /77	2.18 /79	3.08 /70	1.50	0.81
MUN	Wells Fargo Str Muni Bd Adm	VMPYX	**A+**	(800) 222-8222	**B / 8.2**	0.72	1.75	2.09 /78	2.32 /81	3.23 /71	1.68	0.75
MUN ●	Wells Fargo Str Muni Bd B	VMPIX	**A+**	(800) 222-8222	**C+ / 6.6**	0.51	1.31	1.20 /70	1.42 /65	2.32 /54	0.82	1.56
MUN	Wells Fargo Str Muni Bd C	DHICX	**A**	(800) 222-8222	**C+ / 6.5**	0.40	1.19	1.20 /70	1.42 /65	2.31 /54	0.82	1.56
MUN	Wells Fargo Str Muni Bd I	STRIX	**A+**	(800) 222-8222	**B+ / 8.3**	0.66	1.74	2.30 /79	2.52 /83	--	1.89	0.48
GL	Wells Fargo Strategic Income A	WSIAX	**D-**	(800) 222-8222	**E / 0.5**	0.61	-0.18	-4.32 / 7	-0.58 /11	--	1.30	1.54
GL	Wells Fargo Strategic Income Ad	WSIDX	**D-**	(800) 222-8222	**D- / 1.0**	0.63	-0.15	-4.17 / 7	-0.43 /12	--	1.39	1.48
GL	Wells Fargo Strategic Income C	WSICX	**D-**	(800) 222-8222	**E+ / 0.6**	0.45	-0.58	-4.99 / 5	-1.31 / 7	--	0.89	2.29
GL	Wells Fargo Strategic Income I	WSINX	**D-**	(800) 222-8222	**D- / 1.1**	0.60	-0.13	-4.04 / 8	-0.30 /13	--	1.66	1.21
MM	Wells Fargo Treas Pls MM I	PISXX	**C**	(800) 222-8222	**D / 2.2**	0.03	0.04	0.04 /38	0.02 /21	0.02 / 9	0.04	0.23
GES	Wells Fargo Ult ST Inc A	SADAX	**C-**	(800) 222-8222	**D / 1.7**	0.33	0.40	0.32 /46	0.35 /31	0.57 /18	0.77	0.78
GES	Wells Fargo Ult ST Inc Adm	WUSDX	**C+**	(800) 222-8222	**C- / 3.5**	0.36	0.59	0.58 /51	0.50 /33	0.74 /19	0.94	0.72
GES	Wells Fargo Ult ST Inc C	WUSTX	**C-**	(800) 222-8222	**D- / 1.4**	0.16	0.04	-0.42 /27	-0.39 /12	-0.18 / 3	0.06	1.53
GES	Wells Fargo Ult ST Inc Instl	SADIX	**B-**	(800) 222-8222	**C- / 3.9**	0.41	0.69	0.79 /55	0.71 /37	0.94 /20	1.14	0.45
* MUN	Wells Fargo Ult-Sh Mun Inc A	SMAVX	**C-**	(800) 222-8222	**D- / 1.4**	-0.02	0.08	0.03 /38	0.14 /29	0.47 /19	0.32	0.74
MUN	Wells Fargo Ult-Sh Mun Inc Adm	WUSMX	**C+**	(800) 222-8222	**C- / 3.1**	-0.01	0.11	0.10 /43	0.28 /32	0.58 /20	0.40	0.68
MUN	Wells Fargo Ult-Sh Mun Inc C	WFUSX	**C-**	(800) 222-8222	**D- / 1.3**	-0.11	-0.19	-0.51 /26	-0.51 /11	-0.22 / 3	0.00	1.49
MUN	Wells Fargo Ult-Sh Mun Inc I	SMAIX	**B-**	(800) 222-8222	**C- / 3.7**	0.05	0.23	0.33 /50	0.44 /37	0.77 /22	0.62	0.41
COI	Wells Fargo VT Total Rtn Bd 2		**C+**	(800) 222-8222	**C+ / 6.5**	2.84	2.11	1.22 /62	2.01 /62	3.86 /59	1.29	0.92
MUS	Wells Fargo WI Tax Fr A	WWTFX	**A+**	(800) 222-8222	**B / 7.7**	0.99	2.37	2.76 /83	3.00 /88	4.21 /79	2.12	0.90
MUS	Wells Fargo WI Tax Fr C	WWTCX	**A+**	(800) 222-8222	**B / 8.1**	0.81	2.00	2.00 /77	2.24 /80	3.44 /73	1.48	1.65
USL	WesMark Govt Bond Fund	WMBDX	**C+**	(800) 341-7400	**C / 5.3**	2.22	1.34	1.81 /70	1.21 /46	2.16 /33	1.68	1.00
MUI	WesMark West Virginia Muni Bond	WMKMX	**A+**	(800) 341-7400	**B+ / 8.7**	1.46	2.45	2.88 /84	2.62 /84	3.77 /76	2.11	1.06
MUI	Westcore CO Tax Exempt	WTCOX	**A+**	(800) 392-2673	**A- / 9.1**	1.52	3.01	3.53 /90	3.07 /89	4.49 /81	2.67	0.77
COH	Westcore Flexible Income Inst	WILTX	**C-**	(800) 392-2673	**B- / 7.5**	3.81	3.21	-0.27 /28	3.44 /80	5.44 /74	5.16	1.04
COH	Westcore Flexible Income Rtl	WTLTX	**C-**	(800) 392-2673	**B- / 7.3**	3.75	3.01	-0.41 /27	3.27 /78	5.30 /74	5.06	0.88
GEI	Westcore Plus Bond Inst	WIIBX	**B+**	(800) 392-2673	**B- / 7.4**	3.01	2.24	1.33 /64	2.62 /72	4.07 /63	3.34	0.55
* GEI	Westcore Plus Bond Rtl	WTIBX	**B**	(800) 392-2673	**B- / 7.2**	3.05	2.24	1.20 /62	2.46 /70	3.92 /60	3.19	0.70
MM	Western Asset Inst US Tr Ob MM Inst	LUIXX	**U**	(888) 425-6432	**U /**	0.05	0.06	0.08 /40	--	--	0.08	N/A
COH	Western Asset Short Dur High Inc A	SHIAX	**E**	(877) 534-4627	**E- / 0.1**	-1.95	-6.29	-11.38 / 0	-2.38 / 3	2.08 /32	7.45	0.95
COH	Western Asset Short Dur High Inc C	LWHIX	**E**	(877) 534-4627	**E- / 0.1**	-2.31	-6.81	-12.20 / 0	-3.10 / 2	1.32 /23	6.82	1.66
COH ●	Western Asset Short Dur High Inc C1	SHICX	**E**	(877) 534-4627	**E- / 0.1**	-2.22	-6.62	-11.82 / 0	-2.81 / 3	1.63 /27	7.17	1.37
COH	Western Asset Short Dur High Inc I	SHIYX	**E**	(877) 534-4627	**E- / 0.2**	-1.88	-6.14	-11.11 / 0	-2.10 / 4	2.33 /35	7.88	0.66
COH	Western Asset Short Dur High Inc R	LWSRX	**U**	(877) 534-4627	**U /**	-2.09	-6.48	-11.65 / 0	--	--	7.33	1.30
GEI	Western Asset Ultra Sh Oblig IS	LWAUX	**U**	(877) 534-4627	**U /**	0.08	0.12	0.19 /44	--	--	0.19	N/A

99 Pct = Best; 0 Pct = Worst

● Denotes fund is closed to new investors
* Denotes fund is included in Section II

RISK			NET ASSETS		ASSET							FUND MANAGER		MINIMUM		LOADS	
Risk Rating/Pts	3 Yr Avg Standard Deviation	Avg Duration	NAV As of 3/31/16	Total $(Mil)	Cash %	Gov. Bond %	Muni. Bond %	Corp. Bond %	Other %	Portfolio Turnover Ratio	Avg Coupon Rate	Manager Quality Pct	Manager Tenure (Years)	Initial Purch. $	Additional Purch. $	Front End Load	Back End Load
A / 9.5	0.8	1.8	10.00	64	1	30	0	0	69	500	2.3	59	13	1,000	100	2.0	0.0
A / 9.5	0.8	1.8	10.01	131	1	30	0	0	69	500	2.3	69	13	1,000,000	0	0.0	0.0
A / 9.5	0.8	1.8	10.00	N/A	1	30	0	0	69	500	2.3	32	13	1,000	100	0.0	0.0
A / 9.5	0.8	1.8	10.01	30	1	30	0	0	69	500	2.3	32	13	1,000	100	0.0	0.0
A / 9.5	0.8	1.8	10.01	644	1	30	0	0	69	500	2.3	76	13	1,000,000	0	0.0	0.0
A / 9.5	0.8	1.8	10.03	215	1	30	0	0	69	500	2.3	77	13	0	0	0.0	0.0
A+ / 9.6	0.7	2.0	8.74	285	4	3	5	52	36	57	2.3	84	12	1,000	100	2.0	0.0
A+ / 9.6	0.7	2.0	8.73	14	4	3	5	52	36	57	2.3	54	12	1,000	100	0.0	0.0
A / 9.5	0.8	2.0	8.75	288	4	3	5	52	36	57	2.3	87	12	1,000,000	0	0.0	0.0
B / 7.9	2.0	1.3	8.03	305	6	0	1	89	4	40	4.9	94	18	1,000	100	3.0	0.0
B / 7.9	2.0	1.3	8.03	332	6	0	1	89	4	40	4.9	95	18	1,000,000	0	0.0	0.0
B / 7.9	2.0	1.3	8.03	121	6	0	1	89	4	40	4.9	88	18	1,000	100	0.0	0.0
B / 7.9	2.0	1.3	8.02	643	6	0	1	89	4	40	4.9	96	18	1,000,000	0	0.0	0.0
A+ / 9.8	0.6	1.4	9.94	3,394	0	0	98	0	2	24	2.5	81	16	1,000	100	2.0	0.0
A+ / 9.8	0.6	1.4	9.94	93	0	0	98	0	2	24	2.5	78	16	1,000,000	0	0.0	0.0
A+ / 9.8	0.6	1.4	9.94	88	0	0	98	0	2	24	2.5	48	16	1,000	100	0.0	0.0
A+ / 9.8	0.5	1.4	9.96	2,171	0	0	98	0	2	24	2.5	85	16	1,000,000	0	0.0	0.0
B+ / 8.9	1.5	2.2	8.99	662	4	0	95	0	1	39	2.5	86	6	1,000	100	4.0	0.0
B+ / 8.9	1.5	2.2	8.99	504	4	0	95	0	1	39	2.5	88	6	1,000,000	0	0.0	0.0
B+ / 8.9	1.5	2.2	8.97	1	4	0	95	0	1	39	2.5	61	6	1,000	100	0.0	0.0
B+ / 8.9	1.5	2.2	9.02	153	4	0	95	0	1	39	2.5	61	6	1,000	100	0.0	0.0
B+ / 8.9	1.6	2.2	8.99	432	4	0	95	0	1	39	2.5	90	6	1,000,000	0	0.0	0.0
C- / 4.0	3.9	0.2	8.95	1	7	15	2	60	16	53	5.2	41	3	1,000	100	4.0	0.0
C- / 4.0	3.9	0.2	8.98	1	7	15	2	60	16	53	5.2	47	3	1,000,000	0	0.0	0.0
C- / 4.0	3.9	0.2	8.92	1	7	15	2	60	16	53	5.2	22	3	1,000	100	0.0	0.0
C- / 4.1	3.9	0.2	8.94	22	7	15	2	60	16	53	5.2	51	3	1,000,000	0	0.0	0.0
A+ / 9.9	N/A	N/A	1.00	10,108	100	0	0	0	0	0	0.0	66	N/A	10,000,000	0	0.0	0.0
A+ / 9.9	0.3	0.5	8.45	319	4	0	4	52	40	70	3.5	76	14	1,000	100	2.0	0.0
A+ / 9.9	0.4	0.5	8.42	33	4	0	4	52	40	70	3.5	81	14	1,000,000	0	0.0	0.0
A+ / 9.9	0.4	0.5	8.44	8	4	0	4	52	40	70	3.5	43	14	1,000	100	0.0	0.0
A+ / 9.9	0.3	0.5	8.45	1,056	4	0	4	52	40	70	3.5	85	14	1,000,000	0	0.0	0.0
A+ / 9.9	0.3	0.6	9.61	1,244	0	0	97	0	3	44	1.7	60	16	1,000	100	2.0	0.0
A+ / 9.9	0.2	0.6	9.61	301	0	0	97	0	3	44	1.7	75	16	1,000,000	0	0.0	0.0
A+ / 9.9	0.3	0.6	9.47	34	0	0	97	0	3	44	1.7	41	16	1,000	100	0.0	0.0
A+ / 9.9	0.2	0.6	9.61	4,016	0	0	97	0	3	44	1.7	80	16	5,000,000	0	0.0	0.0
C+ / 5.7	3.2	5.6	10.65	77	0	31	1	21	47	565	2.9	63	13	0	0	0.0	0.0
B / 8.0	2.4	4.1	11.03	156	3	0	96	0	1	28	3.9	83	15	1,000	100	4.5	0.0
B / 8.0	2.4	4.1	11.03	11	3	0	96	0	1	28	3.9	54	15	1,000	100	0.0	0.0
B- / 7.2	2.8	3.9	10.12	259	2	9	19	0	70	13	0.0	56	18	1,000	100	0.0	0.0
C+ / 6.9	2.9	5.1	10.67	122	1	0	98	0	1	15	0.0	47	10	1,000	100	0.0	0.0
C+ / 6.0	3.1	5.0	11.76	206	8	0	91	0	1	30	0.0	55	11	2,500	25	0.0	0.0
D / 2.2	5.0	4.4	8.32	13	4	0	0	89	7	37	0.0	96	13	500,000	0	0.0	2.0
D+ / 2.3	4.9	4.4	8.43	48	4	0	0	89	7	37	0.0	95	13	2,500	25	0.0	2.0
C+ / 6.5	3.0	4.8	10.65	114	1	14	6	45	34	51	0.0	74	13	500,000	0	0.0	0.0
C+ / 6.3	3.1	4.8	10.78	1,248	1	14	6	45	34	51	0.0	61	13	2,500	25	0.0	0.0
U /	N/A	N/A	1.00	70	100	0	0	0	0	0	0.1	N/A	N/A	1,000,000	50	0.0	0.0
D- / 1.0	6.1	2.2	4.93	308	0	0	0	85	15	47	7.0	5	10	1,000	50	2.3	0.0
D- / 1.0	6.0	2.2	4.92	76	0	0	0	85	15	47	7.0	4	10	1,000	50	0.0	0.0
E+ / 0.9	6.1	2.2	4.95	77	0	0	0	85	15	47	7.0	5	10	1,000	50	0.0	0.0
E+ / 0.9	6.1	2.2	4.95	168	0	0	0	85	15	47	7.0	6	10	1,000,000	0	0.0	0.0
U /	N/A	2.2	4.92	N/A	0	0	0	85	15	47	7.0	N/A	10	0	0	0.0	0.0
U /	N/A	0.2	10.00	8	0	0	0	0	100	0	0.0	N/A	1	1,000,000	0	0.0	0.0

Fund Type	Fund Name (99 Pct = Best, 0 Pct = Worst)	Ticker Symbol	Overall Investment Rating	Phone	PERFORMANCE: Performance Rating/Pts	Total Return % through 3/31/16: 3 Mo	6 Mo	1Yr / Pct	Annualized: 3Yr / Pct	5Yr / Pct	Incl. in Returns: Dividend Yield	Expense Ratio
COH	Westwood Opportunistic Hi Yld Inst	WWHYX	**U**	(866) 777-7818	**U /**	2.23	0.04	-3.72 / 9	--	--	5.58	4.00
COH	Westwood Opportunistic Hi Yld Ultra	WHYUX	**U**	(866) 777-7818	**U /**	2.25	0.07	-3.67 / 9	--	--	5.64	6.23
COH	Westwood Short Dur High Yield Inst	WHGHX	**D+**	(866) 777-7818	**C- / 3.3**	0.82	0.60	-1.59 /18	0.64 /36	--	4.52	0.94
COH	Westwood Short Dur High Yld A	WSDAX	**U**	(866) 777-7818	**U /**	0.75	0.48	-1.82 /16	--	--	4.18	1.19
GL	Westwood Worldwide Inc Oppty Inst	WWIOX	**U**	(866) 777-7818	**U /**	-1.04	1.92	--	--	--	0.00	2.49
GEI	William Blair Bond I	WBFIX	**C+**	(800) 742-7272	**B- / 7.0**	2.95	3.07	1.25 /63	2.26 /67	4.37 /66	3.79	0.60
COI	William Blair Bond Institutional	BBFIX	**B-**	(800) 742-7272	**B- / 7.2**	2.97	3.10	1.31 /63	2.38 /69	4.50 /68	3.85	0.41
GEI	William Blair Bond N	WBBNX	**C+**	(800) 742-7272	**C+ / 6.7**	2.98	2.96	1.06 /60	2.10 /64	4.21 /64	3.58	0.85
GEI	William Blair Income I	BIFIX	**B**	(800) 742-7272	**C / 5.4**	1.86	1.71	1.23 /62	1.38 /50	3.00 /45	3.11	0.59
GEI	William Blair Income N	WBRRX	**B-**	(800) 742-7272	**C / 4.9**	1.68	1.46	0.86 /56	1.14 /45	2.75 /41	2.85	0.84
GEI	William Blair Low Duration I	WBLIX	**C+**	(800) 742-7272	**C- / 3.6**	0.70	0.74	0.45 /49	0.55 /34	1.23 /23	2.52	0.60
GEI	William Blair Low Duration Inst	WBLJX	**C+**	(800) 742-7272	**C- / 3.8**	0.70	0.75	0.47 /49	0.66 /36	1.35 /24	2.54	0.43
GEI	William Blair Low Duration N	WBLNX	**C+**	(800) 742-7272	**C- / 3.3**	0.65	0.54	0.26 /45	0.39 /31	1.07 /21	2.32	0.75
GES	Wilmington Broad Market Bond A	AKIRX	**C-**	(800) 336-9970	**C / 4.5**	2.89	2.07	1.10 /60	2.03 /62	3.42 /52	1.87	1.10
GES	Wilmington Broad Market Bond Inst	ARKIX	**B-**	(800) 336-9970	**B- / 7.1**	3.02	2.26	1.43 /65	2.37 /69	3.78 /58	2.29	0.85
GEI	Wilmington Intermediate Trm Bd A	GVITX	**C-**	(800) 336-9970	**C- / 3.0**	2.17	1.34	1.31 /63	1.25 /47	2.47 /37	1.27	1.15
GEI	Wilmington Intermediate Trm Bd Inst	ARIFX	**B+**	(800) 336-9970	**C+ / 5.8**	2.26	1.50	1.53 /67	1.54 /53	2.78 /42	1.65	0.90
MUN	Wilmington Muni Bond A	WTABX	**B+**	(800) 336-9970	**B- / 7.4**	1.46	2.65	3.40 /89	2.68 /85	4.27 /80	1.59	1.10
MUN	Wilmington Muni Bond Inst	WTAIX	**A+**	(800) 336-9970	**A- / 9.0**	1.60	2.85	3.66 /92	2.96 /88	4.54 /82	1.90	0.85
MUS	Wilmington NY Municipal Bond A	VNYFX	**B**	(800) 336-9970	**B- / 7.2**	1.53	2.61	3.48 /90	2.54 /83	3.87 /77	1.68	1.19
MUS	Wilmington NY Municipal Bond Inst	VNYIX	**A+**	(800) 336-9970	**B+ / 8.9**	1.50	2.64	3.65 /91	2.80 /86	4.11 /78	2.00	0.94
MM	Wilmington Prime MM Admn	AKIXX	**C**	(800) 336-9970	**D / 2.2**	0.03	0.04	0.05 /39	0.02 /21	0.03 /11	0.05	0.98
MM	Wilmington Prime MM Institutional	WPSXX	**C**	(800) 336-9970	**D / 2.2**	0.03	0.04	0.05 /39	0.02 /21	--	0.05	0.48
MM	Wilmington Prime MM Select	VSMXX	**C**	(800) 336-9970	**D / 2.2**	0.03	0.04	0.05 /39	0.02 /21	0.02 / 9	0.05	0.73
MM	Wilmington Prime MM Service	VSIXX	**U**	(800) 336-9970	**U /**	0.01	0.01	0.01 /33	0.01 /18	0.01 / 6	0.01	0.98
COI	Wilmington Short-Term Bd A	MVSAX	**C+**	(800) 336-9970	**C- / 3.1**	1.17	0.69	0.67 /53	0.71 /37	1.10 /21	0.96	1.15
COI	Wilmington Short-Term Bd Inst	MVSTX	**B**	(800) 336-9970	**C / 4.4**	1.23	0.81	0.92 /57	0.92 /41	1.35 /24	1.23	0.90
MMT	Wilmington Tax-Exempt MM Admn	AFIXX	**U**	(800) 336-9970	**U /**	--	--	--	--	--	0.01	1.00
MMT	Wilmington Tax-Exempt MM Select	AKXXX	**U**	(800) 336-9970	**U /**	--	--	--	--	--	0.01	0.75
MMT	Wilmington Tax-Exempt MM Service	ATFXX	**U**	(800) 336-9970	**U /**	--	--	--	--	--	0.01	1.00
MM	Wilmington U.S. Treasury MM Admn	ARMXX	**U**	(800) 336-9970	**U /**	0.01	0.01	0.01 /33	0.01 /18	0.01 / 6	0.01	0.97
MM	Wilmington U.S. Treasury MM Select	VSTXX	**U**	(800) 336-9970	**U /**	0.01	0.01	0.01 /33	0.01 /18	0.01 / 7	0.01	0.72
MM	Wilmington US Government MM	AIIXX	**U**	(800) 336-9970	**U /**	0.01	0.01	0.02 /35	0.01 /18	0.01 / 7	0.02	0.97
MM	Wilmington US Government MM Inst	WGOXX	**U**	(800) 336-9970	**U /**	0.01	0.01	0.02 /35	0.01 /18	--	0.02	0.47
MM	Wilmington US Government MM	AKGXX	**U**	(800) 336-9970	**U /**	0.01	0.01	0.02 /35	0.01 /18	0.01 / 7	0.02	0.72
MM	Wilmington US Government MM	AGAXX	**U**	(800) 336-9970	**U /**	--	--	--	--	--	0.01	0.97
MTG	Wright Current Income	WCIFX	**A-**	(800) 232-0013	**C+ / 6.2**	2.01	1.49	1.57 /67	1.89 /59	2.78 /42	3.46	1.24
GEN	Zeo Strategic Income I	ZEOIX	**A+**	(855) 936-3863	**C+ / 6.7**	0.99	0.41	1.41 /65	2.78 /74	--	3.35	1.30
GL	Ziegler Strategic Income Inst	ZLSIX	**D-**	(877) 568-7633	**E / 0.4**	0.39	-0.63	-2.48 /13	-2.31 / 3	--	3.76	2.40

• Denotes fund is closed to new investors
* Denotes fund is included in Section II

RISK			NET ASSETS		ASSET							FUND MANAGER		MINIMUM		LOADS	
Risk Rating/Pts	3 Yr Avg Standard Deviation	Avg Duration	NAV As of 3/31/16	Total $(Mil)	Cash %	Gov. Bond %	Muni. Bond %	Corp. Bond %	Other %	Portfolio Turnover Ratio	Avg Coupon Rate	Manager Quality Pct	Manager Tenure (Years)	Initial Purch. $	Additional Purch. $	Front End Load	Back End Load
U /	N/A	N/A	9.12	N/A	9	0	0	89	2	37	0.0	N/A	2	5,000	0	0.0	0.0
U /	N/A	N/A	9.11	4	9	0	0	89	2	37	0.0	N/A	2	250,000	0	0.0	0.0
C / 4.5	3.2	3.0	9.05	77	1	0	0	98	1	44	0.0	53	5	100,000	0	0.0	0.0
U /	N/A	3.0	9.05	1	1	0	0	98	1	44	0.0	N/A	5	5,000	0	2.3	0.0
U /	N/A	N/A	9.22	7	0	0	0	0	100	0	0.0	N/A	N/A	5,000	0	0.0	0.0
C+ / 5.6	3.2	5.1	10.45	285	1	6	0	41	52	32	5.1	60	9	500,000	0	0.0	0.0
C+ / 5.7	3.2	5.1	10.44	107	1	6	0	41	52	32	5.1	79	9	5,000,000	0	0.0	0.0
C+ / 5.6	3.2	5.1	10.56	150	1	6	0	41	52	32	5.1	55	9	2,500	1,000	0.0	0.0
B+ / 8.4	2.1	3.2	8.93	62	4	6	0	26	64	21	4.1	56	14	500,000	0	0.0	0.0
B+ / 8.4	2.1	3.2	8.99	34	4	6	0	26	64	21	4.1	48	14	2,500	1,000	0.0	0.0
A / 9.3	1.0	1.0	9.17	109	5	0	0	17	78	106	2.8	60	7	500,000	0	0.0	0.0
A / 9.4	0.9	1.0	9.17	26	5	0	0	17	78	106	2.8	72	7	5,000,000	0	0.0	0.0
A / 9.3	1.0	1.0	9.17	7	5	0	0	17	78	106	2.8	54	7	2,500	1,000	0.0	0.0
C+ / 5.9	3.2	5.4	9.91	5	0	33	0	42	25	45	5.7	42	20	1,000	25	4.5	0.0
C+ / 5.9	3.2	5.4	9.75	406	0	33	0	42	25	45	5.7	54	20	1,000,000	25	0.0	0.0
B / 8.2	2.3	3.8	10.00	4	1	45	0	50	4	45	0.0	41	20	1,000	25	4.5	0.0
B+ / 8.3	2.2	3.8	10.00	120	1	45	0	50	4	45	0.0	54	20	1,000,000	25	0.0	0.0
C+ / 6.2	3.1	5.4	13.47	38	1	0	93	0	6	50	0.0	43	5	1,000	25	4.5	0.0
C+ / 6.1	3.1	5.4	13.48	263	1	0	93	0	6	50	0.0	53	5	1,000,000	25	0.0	0.0
C+ / 6.2	3.1	5.5	10.86	21	3	0	96	0	1	31	0.0	40	4	1,000	25	4.5	0.0
C+ / 6.3	3.1	5.5	10.86	62	3	0	96	0	1	31	0.0	50	4	1,000,000	25	0.0	0.0
A+ / 9.9	N/A	N/A	1.00	293	100	0	0	0	0	0	0.1	N/A	N/A	1,000	25	0.0	0.0
A+ / 9.9	N/A	N/A	1.00	276	100	0	0	0	0	0	0.1	N/A	N/A	5,000,000	25	0.0	0.0
A+ / 9.9	N/A	N/A	1.00	2,466	100	0	0	0	0	0	0.1	N/A	N/A	100,000	25	0.0	0.0
U /	N/A	N/A	1.00	737	100	0	0	0	0	0	0.0	N/A	N/A	0	0	0.0	0.0
A / 9.5	0.8	1.5	10.06	8	1	32	0	49	18	138	0.0	76	20	1,000	25	1.8	0.0
A / 9.5	0.8	1.5	10.06	137	1	32	0	49	18	138	0.0	82	20	1,000,000	25	0.0	0.0
U /	N/A	N/A	1.00	55	100	0	0	0	0	0	0.0	N/A	N/A	1,000	25	0.0	0.0
U /	N/A	N/A	1.00	418	100	0	0	0	0	0	0.0	N/A	N/A	100,000	25	0.0	0.0
U /	N/A	N/A	1.00	66	100	0	0	0	0	0	0.0	N/A	N/A	0	0	0.0	0.0
U /	N/A	N/A	1.00	567	100	0	0	0	0	0	0.0	N/A	28	1,000	25	0.0	0.0
U /	N/A	N/A	1.00	245	100	0	0	0	0	0	0.0	N/A	28	100,000	25	0.0	0.0
U /	N/A	N/A	1.00	1,669	100	0	0	0	0	0	0.0	N/A	N/A	1,000	25	0.0	0.0
U /	N/A	N/A	1.00	14	100	0	0	0	0	0	0.0	N/A	N/A	5,000,000	25	0.0	0.0
U /	N/A	N/A	1.00	958	100	0	0	0	0	0	0.0	N/A	N/A	100,000	25	0.0	0.0
U /	N/A	N/A	1.00	729	100	0	0	0	0	0	0.0	N/A	N/A	0	0	0.0	0.0
B+ / 8.3	2.1	3.9	9.41	68	4	0	0	2	94	27	5.1	55	7	1,000	0	0.0	0.0
A- / 9.0	1.4	N/A	9.83	210	0	0	0	0	100	143	0.0	97	5	5,000	1,000	0.0	1.0
C- / 4.2	3.9	N/A	8.63	49	12	0	0	45	43	107	0.0	10	4	100,000	1,000	0.0	0.0

Section II

Analysis of Largest Bond and Money Market Mutual Funds

A summary analysis of the 381 largest retail

Fixed Income Mutual Funds

receiving a TheStreet Investment Rating.

Funds are listed in alphabetical order.

Section II Contents

1. Fund Name The name of the mutual fund as stated in its prospectus, which can sometimes differ slightly from the name that the company uses for advertising. If you cannot find the paritcular mutual fund you are interested in, or if you have any doubts regarding the precise name, verify the information with your broker or on your account statement. Also, use the fund's ticker symbol for confirmation.

2. Ticker Symbol The unique alphabetic symbol used for identifying and trading a specific mutual fund. No two funds can have the same ticker symbol, and the ticker symbol for mutual funds always ends with an "X".

A handful of funds currently show no associated ticker symbol. This means that the fund is either small or new since the NASD only assigns a ticker symbols to funds with at least $25 million in assets or 1,000 shareholders.

3. Investment Rating Our overall rating is measured on a scale from A to E based on each fund's risk-adjusted performance. Please see page 11 for specific descriptions of each letter grade. Also refer to page 7 for information on how our ratings are derived. Most important, when using this rating, please be sure to consider the warnings beginning on page 13 regarding the ratings' limitations and the underlying assumptions.

4. Major Rating Factors A synopsis of the key ratios and sub-factors that have most influenced the rating of a particular mutual fund, including an examination of the fund's performance, risk, and managerial performance. There may be additional factors which have influenced the rating but do not appear due to space limitations.

5. Services Offered Services and/or benefits offered by the fund.

6. Address The address of the company managing the fund.

7. Phone The telephone number of the company managing the fund. Call this number to receive a prospectus or other information about the fund.

8. Fund Family The umbrella group of mutual funds to which the fund belongs. In many cases, investors may move their assets from one fund to another within the same family at little or no cost.

9. Fund Type The mutual fund's peer category based on its investment objective as stated in its prospectus.

COH	Corporate - High Yield	MMT	Money Market - Tax Free
COI	Corporate - Inv. Grade	MTG	Mortgage
EM	Emerging Market	MUH	Municipal - High Yield
GEN	General	MUI	Municipal - Insured
GEI	General - Inv. Grade	MUN	Municipal - National
GEL	General - Long Term	MUS	Municipal - Single State
GES	General - Short & Interm.	USL	U.S. Gov.- Long Term
GL	Global	USS	U.S. Gov. - Short & Interm
LP	Loan Participation	USA	U.S. Gov. - Agency
MM	Money Market	US	U.S. Gov. - Treasury

A blank fund type means that the mutual fund has not yet been categorized.

How to Read the Annualized Total Return Graph

The annualized total return graph provides a clearer picture of a fund's yearly financial performance. In addition to the solid line denoting the fund's calendar year returns for the last six years, the graph also shows the yearly return for a benchmark bond index for easy comparison using a dotted line. In the case of most bond funds, the index used is the Lehman Brothers Aggregate Bond Index; and for municipal bond funds, the index used is Lehman Brothers Municipals Index.

The top of the shaded area of the graph denotes the average returns for all funds within the same fund type. If the solid line falls into the shaded area, that means that the fund has performed below the average for its type.

How to Read the Historical Data Table

NAV:
The fund's share price as of the date indicated. A fund's NAV is computed by dividing the value of the fund's asset holdings, less accrued fees and expenses, by the number of its shares outstanding.

Risk Rating/Pts:
A letter grade rating based solely on the mutual fund's risk as determined by its monthly performance volatility over the trailing three years. Pts are rating points where 0=worst and 10=best.

Data Date:
The quarter-end or year-end as of date used for evaluating the mutual fund.

Data Date	Investment Rating	Net Assets ($Mil)	NAV	Performance Rating/Pts	Total Return Y-T-D	Risk Rating/Pts
3-16	C+	105	38.99	C+ / 6.3	20.69%	D+ / 2.9
2015	C	179	9.51	C+ / 6.4	-2.28%	D+ / 2.9
2014	C	470	10.45	C / 4.3	2.77%	C+ / 5.7
2013	B-	424	1.00	D- / 1.2	1.04%	B+ / 8.9
2012	B	159	42.37	C+ / 6.2	-1.66%	C / 5.3
2011	B-	155	41.31	C+ / 6.4	-1.41%	C+ / 5.2

Investment Rating:
Our overall opinion of the fund's risk-adjusted performance at the specified time period.

Net Assets $(Mil):
The total value of all of the fund's asset holdings (in millions) including stocks, bonds, cash, and other financial instruments, less accrued expenses and fees.

Performance Rating/Pts:
A letter grade rating based solely on the mutual fund's return to shareholders over the trailing three years, without any consideration for the amount of risk the fund poses.
Pts are rating points where 0=worst and 10=best

Total Return Y-T-D:
The fund's total return to shareholders since the beginning of the calendar year specified.

AB Global Bond A (ANAGX) C Fair

Fund Family: Alliance Bernstein Funds **Phone:** (800) 221-5672
Address: P.O. Box 786003, San Antonio, TX 78278
Fund Type: GL - Global

Major Rating Factors: Middle of the road best describes AB Global Bond A whose TheStreet.com Investment Rating is currently a C (Fair). The fund has a performance rating of C (Fair) based on an average return of 2.37% over the last three years and 2.97% over the last three months. Factored into the performance evaluation is an expense ratio of 0.85% (average) and a 4.3% front-end load that is levied at the time of purchase.

The fund's risk rating is currently C+ (Fair). Volatility, as measured by standard deviation, is considered average for fixed income funds at 3.13. Another risk factor is the fund's fairly average duration of 5.5 years (i.e. average interest rate risk).

Douglas J. Peebles has been running the fund for 24 years and currently receives a manager quality ranking of 97 (0=worst, 99=best). If you desire an average level of risk, then this fund may be an option.

Services Offered: Automated phone transactions, check writing, payroll deductions, bank draft capabilities, an IRA investment plan, a 401K investment plan and a systematic withdrawal plan.

Data Date	Investment Rating	Net Assets ($Mil)	NAV	Perfor-mance Rating/Pts	Total Return Y-T-D	Risk Rating/Pts
3-16	C	1,077	8.36	C / 5.4	2.97%	C+/ 6.0
2015	C-	1,071	8.16	C / 4.6	0.48%	C+/ 5.7
2014	D	1,082	8.42	C- / 3.0	4.76%	C+/ 5.7
2013	D	1,238	8.24	D / 2.0	-2.15%	C+/ 6.7
2012	C+	1,579	8.62	C- / 3.6	7.02%	B- / 7.2
2011	C-	1,501	8.35	C / 5.3	4.44%	C / 4.5

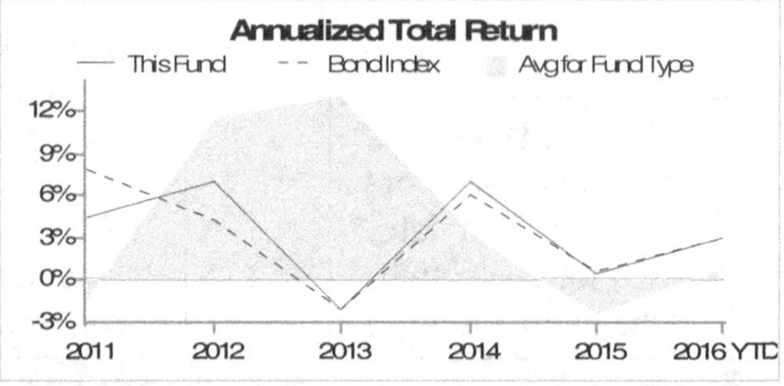

AB High Income A (AGDAX) D Weak

Fund Family: Alliance Bernstein Funds **Phone:** (800) 221-5672
Address: P.O. Box 786003, San Antonio, TX 78278
Fund Type: GL - Global

Major Rating Factors: AB High Income A has adopted a very risky asset allocation strategy and currently receives an overall TheStreet.com Investment Rating of D (Weak). Volatility, as measured by standard deviation, is considered above average for fixed income funds at 5.50. Another risk factor is the fund's below average duration of 4.8 years (i.e. lower interest rate risk). Unfortunately, the high level of risk (D, Weak) has only provided investors with average performance.

The fund's performance rating is currently C- (Fair). It has registered an average return of 1.92% over the last three years and is up 3.44% over the last three months. Factored into the performance evaluation is an expense ratio of 0.85% (average) and a 4.3% front-end load that is levied at the time of purchase.

Douglas J. Peebles has been running the fund for 14 years and currently receives a manager quality ranking of 96 (0=worst, 99=best). If you are comfortable owning a very high risk investment, then this fund may be an option.

Services Offered: Automated phone transactions, check writing, payroll deductions, bank draft capabilities, an IRA investment plan, a 401K investment plan and a systematic withdrawal plan.

Data Date	Investment Rating	Net Assets ($Mil)	NAV	Perfor-mance Rating/Pts	Total Return Y-T-D	Risk Rating/Pts
3-16	D	1,882	8.15	C- / 3.7	3.44%	D / 2.2
2015	D	1,795	8.02	D / 2.2	-3.98%	D+/ 2.7
2014	C-	2,201	8.95	B- / 7.4	1.68%	D / 1.9
2013	C	2,589	9.38	A- / 9.2	6.62%	E+/ 0.9
2012	C+	2,563	9.50	A- / 9.1	18.54%	E / 0.5
2011	C+	1,755	8.60	A+/ 9.6	2.05%	E / 0.3

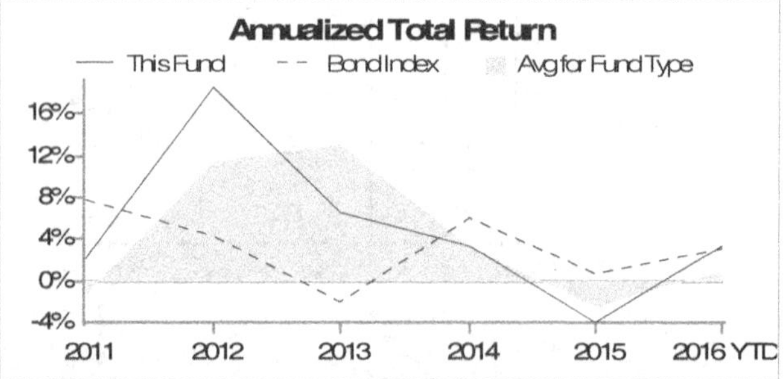

AB High Income Municipal A (ABTHX) C Fair

Fund Family: Alliance Bernstein Funds **Phone:** (800) 221-5672
Address: P.O. Box 786003, San Antonio, TX 78278
Fund Type: MUH - Municipal - High Yield

Major Rating Factors: AB High Income Municipal A has adopted a very risky asset allocation strategy and currently receives an overall TheStreet.com Investment Rating of C (Fair). Volatility, as measured by standard deviation, is considered high for fixed income funds at 6.33. Another risk factor is the fund's fairly average duration of 6.3 years (i.e. average interest rate risk). The high level of risk (E+, Very Weak) did however, reward investors with excellent performance.

The fund's performance rating is currently A+ (Excellent). It has registered an average return of 4.78% over the last three years (7.92% taxable equivalent) and is up 2.26% over the last three months (3.74% taxable equivalent). Factored into the performance evaluation is an expense ratio of 0.87% (average) and a 3.0% front-end load that is levied at the time of purchase.

Michael G. Brooks has been running the fund for 6 years and currently receives a manager quality ranking of 18 (0=worst, 99=best). If you are comfortable owning a very high risk investment, this fund may be an option.

Services Offered: Automated phone transactions, payroll deductions, bank draft capabilities, an IRA investment plan, a 401K investment plan, wire transfers and a systematic withdrawal plan.

Data Date	Investment Rating	Net Assets ($Mil)	NAV	Perfor-mance Rating/Pts	Total Return Y-T-D	Risk Rating/Pts
3-16	C	805	11.51	A+/ 9.7	2.26%	E+/ 0.8
2015	C	738	11.37	A+/ 9.7	5.31%	E+/ 0.6
2014	C+	677	11.29	A+/ 9.9	17.19%	E+/ 0.6
2013	D+	522	10.11	B / 8.0	-7.95%	E+/ 0.6
2012	U	639	11.55	U / --	16.59%	U / --
2011	U	304	10.40	U / --	12.91%	U / --

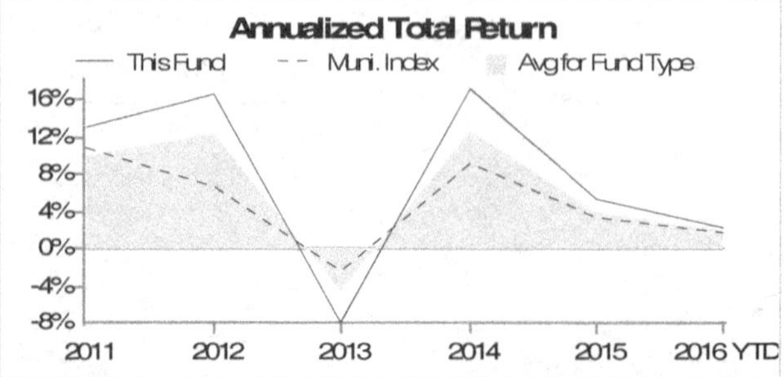

AB Municipal Income (MISHX) C Fair

Fund Family: Alliance Bernstein Funds **Phone:** (800) 221-5672
Address: P.O. Box 786003, San Antonio, TX 78278
Fund Type: MUH - Municipal - High Yield
Major Rating Factors: AB Municipal Income has adopted a very risky asset allocation strategy and currently receives an overall TheStreet.com Investment Rating of C (Fair). Volatility, as measured by standard deviation, is considered high for fixed income funds at 6.51. The high level of risk (E+, Very Weak) did however, reward investors with excellent performance.

The fund's performance rating is currently A+ (Excellent). It has registered an average return of 5.93% over the last three years (9.82% taxable equivalent) and is up 2.75% over the last three months (4.55% taxable equivalent). Factored into the performance evaluation is an expense ratio of 0.01% (very low).

Terrance T. Hults has been running the fund for 6 years and currently receives a manager quality ranking of 38 (0=worst, 99=best). If you are comfortable owning a very high risk investment, this fund may be an option.
Services Offered: Automated phone transactions, bank draft capabilities and wire transfers.

Data Date	Investment Rating	Net Assets ($Mil)	NAV	Performance Rating/Pts	Total Return Y-T-D	Risk Rating/Pts
3-16	C	1,031	11.48	A+ / 9.9	2.75%	E+ / 0.7
2015	C	851	11.29	A+ / 9.9	5.82%	E+ / 0.6
2014	C+	528	11.16	A+ / 9.9	18.14%	E+ / 0.6
2013	C+	287	9.92	A+ / 9.6	-6.71%	E+ / 0.9

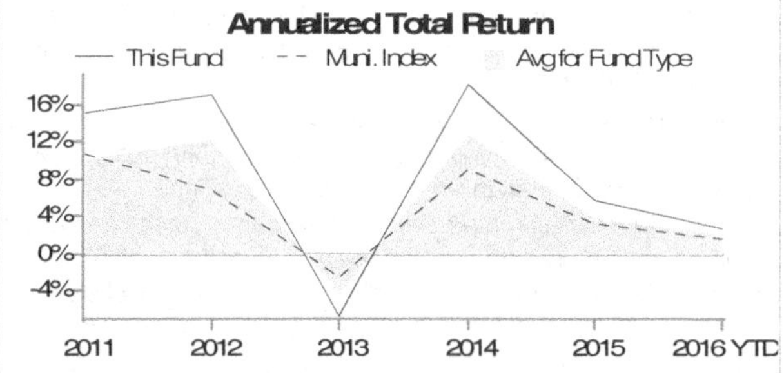

AB Municipal Income Natl A (ALTHX) B Good

Fund Family: Alliance Bernstein Funds **Phone:** (800) 221-5672
Address: P.O. Box 786003, San Antonio, TX 78278
Fund Type: MUN - Municipal - National
Major Rating Factors: Strong performance is the major factor driving the B (Good) TheStreet.com Investment Rating for AB Municipal Income Natl A. The fund currently has a performance rating of B+ (Good) based on an average return of 3.23% over the last three years (5.35% taxable equivalent) and 1.75% over the last three months (2.90% taxable equivalent). Factored into the performance evaluation is an expense ratio of 0.80% (low) and a 3.0% front-end load that is levied at the time of purchase.

The fund's risk rating is currently C (Fair). Volatility, as measured by standard deviation, is considered average for fixed income funds at 3.82. Another risk factor is the fund's below average duration of 4.8 years (i.e. lower interest rate risk).

Terrance T. Hults has been running the fund for 21 years and currently receives a manager quality ranking of 35 (0=worst, 99=best). If you desire an average level of risk and strong performance, then this fund is a good option.
Services Offered: Automated phone transactions, check writing, payroll deductions, bank draft capabilities and a systematic withdrawal plan.

Data Date	Investment Rating	Net Assets ($Mil)	NAV	Performance Rating/Pts	Total Return Y-T-D	Risk Rating/Pts
3-16	B	635	10.43	B+ / 8.7	1.75%	C / 4.3
2015	B-	613	10.33	B+ / 8.5	2.94%	C- / 4.1
2014	B+	588	10.38	B+ / 8.4	10.02%	C- / 3.8
2013	C	620	9.78	C+ / 6.2	-4.39%	C- / 4.2
2012	A+	775	10.60	B / 8.0	8.47%	C / 4.6
2011	A+	652	10.14	B / 8.2	10.71%	C / 5.2

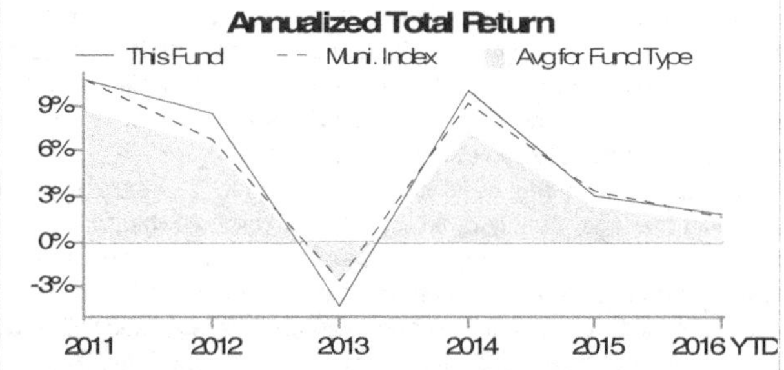

American Funds Bd Fd of Amer A (ABNDX) C- Fair

Fund Family: American Funds **Phone:** (800) 421-0180
Address: 333 South Hope Street, Los Angeles, CA 90071
Fund Type: GEI - General - Investment Grade
Major Rating Factors: Middle of the road best describes American Funds Bd Fd of Amer A whose TheStreet.com Investment Rating is currently a C- (Fair). The fund has a performance rating of C (Fair) based on an average return of 2.19% over the last three years and 2.92% over the last three months. Factored into the performance evaluation is an expense ratio of 0.60% (low) and a 3.8% front-end load that is levied at the time of purchase.

The fund's risk rating is currently C+ (Fair). Volatility, as measured by standard deviation, is considered average for fixed income funds at 3.17. Another risk factor is the fund's fairly average duration of 5.4 years (i.e. average interest rate risk).

John H. Smet has been running the fund for 27 years and currently receives a manager quality ranking of 47 (0=worst, 99=best). If you desire an average level of risk, then this fund may be an option.
Services Offered: Automated phone transactions, payroll deductions, bank draft capabilities, an IRA investment plan, a 401K investment plan, a Keogh investment plan, wire transfers and a systematic withdrawal plan.

Data Date	Investment Rating	Net Assets ($Mil)	NAV	Performance Rating/Pts	Total Return Y-T-D	Risk Rating/Pts
3-16	C-	19,401	12.90	C / 5.2	2.92%	C+ / 5.8
2015	C-	18,548	12.59	C- / 3.6	0.23%	C+ / 5.9
2014	C-	18,663	12.81	C- / 3.5	5.53%	C+ / 6.7
2013	C-	19,325	12.40	D+ / 2.8	-1.99%	B- / 7.3
2012	C	24,142	12.95	C- / 3.1	5.89%	B / 7.6
2011	C	23,472	12.55	C- / 4.2	6.51%	C+ / 6.8

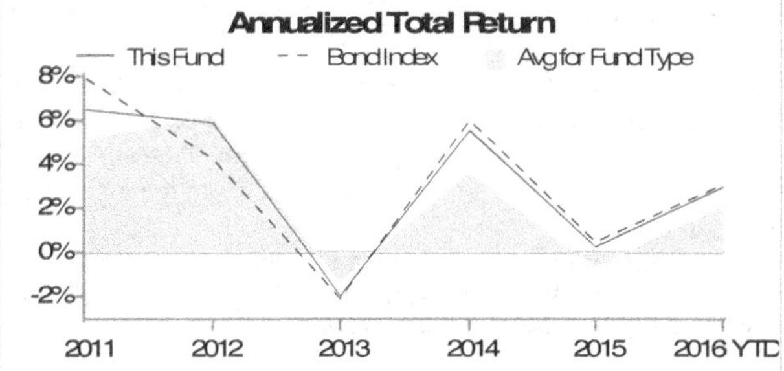

American Funds Cap World Bond A (CWBFX) D Weak

Fund Family: American Funds **Phone:** (800) 421-0180
Address: 333 South Hope Street, Los Angeles, CA 90071
Fund Type: GL - Global
Major Rating Factors: American Funds Cap World Bond A receives a TheStreet.com Investment Rating of D (Weak). The fund has a performance rating of C- (Fair) based on an average return of 0.44% over the last three years and 5.40% over the last three months. Factored into the performance evaluation is an expense ratio of 0.93% (average) and a 3.8% front-end load that is levied at the time of purchase.

The fund's risk rating is currently C- (Fair). Volatility, as measured by standard deviation, is considered average for fixed income funds at 4.74. Another risk factor is the fund's fairly average duration of 6.4 years (i.e. average interest rate risk).

Robert H. Neithart has been running the fund for 17 years and currently receives a manager quality ranking of 83 (0=worst, 99=best). If you desire an average level of risk, then this fund may be an option.
Services Offered: Automated phone transactions, payroll deductions, bank draft capabilities, an IRA investment plan, a 401K investment plan, a Keogh investment plan, wire transfers and a systematic withdrawal plan.

Data Date	Investment Rating	Net Assets ($Mil)	NAV	Performance Rating/Pts	Total Return Y-T-D	Risk Rating/Pts
3-16	D	6,381	19.85	C- / 3.1	5.40%	C- / 3.0
2015	D-	6,138	18.91	E+ / 0.7	-4.19%	C- / 3.3
2014	E+	7,028	19.85	D- / 1.4	1.59%	C- / 3.3
2013	E+	7,237	20.11	D / 1.9	-2.92%	C- / 3.0
2012	E-	8,376	21.20	D+ / 2.7	7.43%	D / 2.1
2011	E	7,868	20.47	D+ / 2.7	3.80%	D+ / 2.4

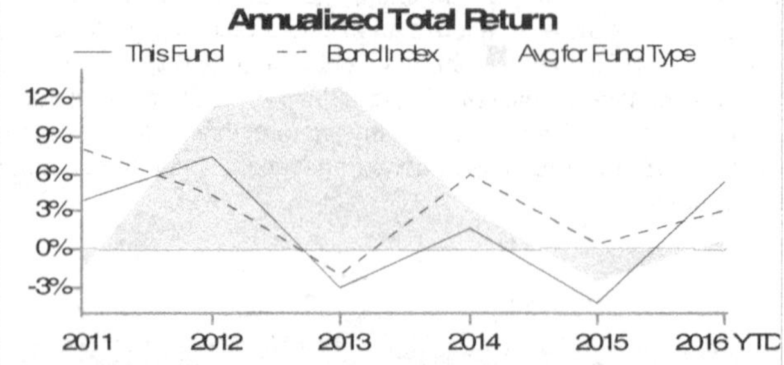

American Funds High Inc Muni Bnd A (AMHIX) C+ Fair

Fund Family: American Funds **Phone:** (800) 421-0180
Address: 333 South Hope Street, Los Angeles, CA 90071
Fund Type: MUH - Municipal - High Yield
Major Rating Factors: American Funds High Inc Muni Bnd A has adopted a risky asset allocation strategy and currently receives an overall TheStreet.com Investment Rating of C+ (Fair). Volatility, as measured by standard deviation, is considered above average for fixed income funds at 4.53. Another risk factor is the fund's fairly average duration of 7.0 years (i.e. average interest rate risk). The high level of risk (D+, Weak) did however, reward investors with excellent performance.

The fund's performance rating is currently A+ (Excellent). It has registered an average return of 4.95% over the last three years (8.20% taxable equivalent) and is up 2.20% over the last three months (3.64% taxable equivalent). Factored into the performance evaluation is an expense ratio of 0.68% (low) and a 3.8% front-end load that is levied at the time of purchase.

Neil L. Langberg has been running the fund for 22 years and currently receives a manager quality ranking of 78 (0=worst, 99=best). If you are comfortable owning a high risk investment, this fund may be an option.
Services Offered: Automated phone transactions, payroll deductions, an IRA investment plan, a Keogh investment plan and a systematic withdrawal plan.

Data Date	Investment Rating	Net Assets ($Mil)	NAV	Performance Rating/Pts	Total Return Y-T-D	Risk Rating/Pts
3-16	C+	3,159	15.81	A+ / 9.7	2.20%	D+ / 2.5
2015	C+	2,931	15.62	A+ / 9.7	4.39%	D / 2.2
2014	B	2,563	15.58	A+ / 9.8	14.04%	D- / 1.4
2013	C+	2,121	14.26	B+ / 8.6	-3.41%	D+ / 2.3
2012	A+	2,441	15.42	A+ / 9.7	14.18%	C- / 3.0
2011	B+	1,887	14.10	A- / 9.0	9.90%	D+ / 2.6

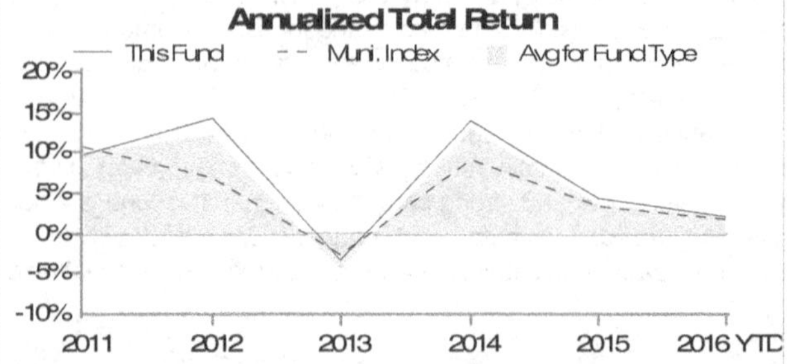

American Funds High Income Tr A (AHITX) E Very Weak

Fund Family: American Funds **Phone:** (800) 421-0180
Address: 333 South Hope Street, Los Angeles, CA 90071
Fund Type: COH - Corporate - High Yield
Major Rating Factors: American Funds High Income Tr A has adopted a very risky asset allocation strategy and currently receives an overall TheStreet.com Investment Rating of E (Very Weak). Volatility, as measured by standard deviation, is considered above average for fixed income funds at 6.04. Unfortunately, the high level of risk (D-, Weak) failed to pay off as investors endured poor performance.

The fund's performance rating is currently E (Very Weak). It has registered an average return of -0.21% over the last three years and is up 2.77% over the last three months. Factored into the performance evaluation is an expense ratio of 0.67% (low) and a 3.8% front-end load that is levied at the time of purchase.

David C. Barclay has been running the fund for 27 years and currently receives a manager quality ranking of 12 (0=worst, 99=best). If you can tolerate very high levels of risk in the hope of improved future returns, holding this fund may be an option.
Services Offered: Automated phone transactions, payroll deductions, an IRA investment plan, a 401K investment plan, a Keogh investment plan, wire transfers and a systematic withdrawal plan.

Data Date	Investment Rating	Net Assets ($Mil)	NAV	Performance Rating/Pts	Total Return Y-T-D	Risk Rating/Pts
3-16	E	11,033	9.46	E / 0.5	2.77%	D- / 1.0
2015	E	10,974	9.35	E+ / 0.7	-7.42%	D- / 1.2
2014	D	13,458	10.75	C+ / 6.0	0.53%	D / 2.2
2013	C	14,340	11.36	B+ / 8.8	6.44%	D- / 1.2
2012	C-	14,368	11.36	B / 7.8	14.52%	D- / 1.0
2011	C	11,619	10.66	B+ / 8.7	1.98%	E+ / 0.9

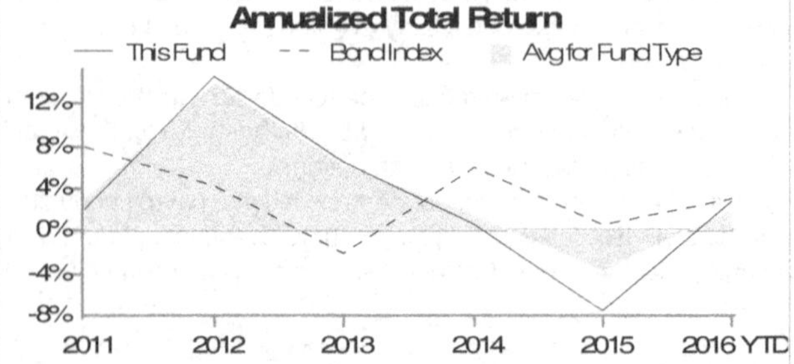

American Funds Intm Bd Fd Amr A (AIBAX) C+ Fair

Fund Family: American Funds **Phone:** (800) 421-0180
Address: 333 South Hope Street, Los Angeles, CA 90071
Fund Type: GEI - General - Investment Grade
Major Rating Factors: A moderate risk profile coupled with stable earnings characterizes American Funds Intm Bd Fd Amr A which receives a TheStreet.com Investment Rating of C+ (Fair). Volatility, as measured by standard deviation, is considered low for fixed income funds at 1.84. Another risk factor is the fund's very low average duration of 2.9 years (i.e. low interest rate risk). The fund's risk rating is currently B+ (Good).

The fund's performance rating is currently C- (Fair). It has registered an average return of 1.13% over the last three years and is up 1.74% over the last three months. Factored into the performance evaluation is an expense ratio of 0.61% (low) and a 2.5% front-end load that is levied at the time of purchase.

John H. Smet has been running the fund for 25 years and currently receives a manager quality ranking of 50 (0=worst, 99=best). If you desire stability with a moderate level of risk then this fund is an excellent option.
Services Offered: Automated phone transactions, payroll deductions, an IRA investment plan, a 401K investment plan, a Keogh investment plan, wire transfers and a systematic withdrawal plan.

Data Date	Investment Rating	Net Assets ($Mil)	NAV	Performance Rating/Pts	Total Return Y-T-D	Risk Rating/Pts
3-16	C+	7,095	13.63	C- / 3.7	1.74%	B+ / 8.6
2015	C	6,795	13.43	C- / 3.0	0.92%	B+ / 8.6
2014	D+	6,346	13.51	D- / 1.5	1.92%	B+ / 8.8
2013	D+	6,303	13.42	D- / 1.4	-1.17%	B+ / 8.9
2012	C-	7,162	13.76	D- / 1.3	2.70%	B+ / 8.8
2011	C	6,601	13.63	D / 2.2	3.71%	A- / 9.0

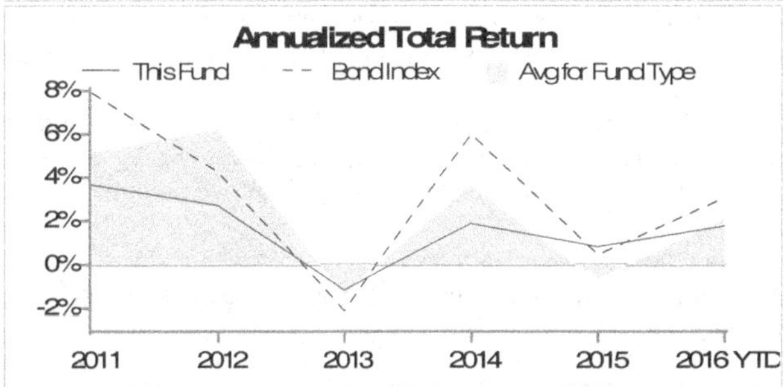

American Funds Ltd Term T/E Bond A (LTEBX) B+ Good

Fund Family: American Funds **Phone:** (800) 421-0180
Address: 333 South Hope Street, Los Angeles, CA 90071
Fund Type: MUN - Municipal - National
Major Rating Factors: A moderate risk profile coupled with stable earnings characterizes American Funds Ltd Term T/E Bond A which receives a TheStreet.com Investment Rating of B+ (Good). Volatility, as measured by standard deviation, is considered low for fixed income funds at 1.94. Another risk factor is the fund's very low average duration of 3.0 years (i.e. low interest rate risk). The fund's risk rating is currently B+ (Good).

The fund's performance rating is currently C (Fair). It has registered an average return of 1.57% over the last three years (2.60% taxable equivalent) and is up 0.91% over the last three months (1.51% taxable equivalent). Factored into the performance evaluation is an expense ratio of 0.57% (very low) and a 2.5% front-end load that is levied at the time of purchase.

Neil L. Langberg has been running the fund for 23 years and currently receives a manager quality ranking of 49 (0=worst, 99=best). If you desire stability with a moderate level of risk then this fund is an excellent option.
Services Offered: Automated phone transactions, payroll deductions, an IRA investment plan, a 401K investment plan, a Keogh investment plan and a systematic withdrawal plan.

Data Date	Investment Rating	Net Assets ($Mil)	NAV	Performance Rating/Pts	Total Return Y-T-D	Risk Rating/Pts
3-16	B+	2,850	15.97	C / 5.5	0.91%	B+ / 8.5
2015	A	2,762	15.91	C+ / 6.7	1.40%	B+ / 8.4
2014	C+	2,661	16.06	C- / 3.8	3.36%	B / 8.1
2013	A+	2,580	15.92	C+ / 6.2	-0.15%	B / 7.9
2012	C	2,703	16.34	C- / 3.9	3.81%	C+ / 6.6
2011	C+	2,309	16.16	C / 5.3	7.48%	C+ / 6.2

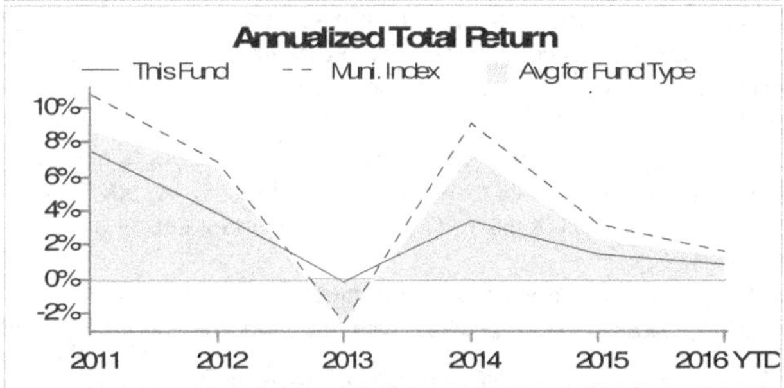

American Funds Preservation A (PPVAX) C Fair

Fund Family: American Funds **Phone:** (800) 421-0180
Address: 333 South Hope Street, Los Angeles, CA 90071
Fund Type: GEI - General - Investment Grade
Major Rating Factors: A moderate risk profile coupled with stable earnings characterizes American Funds Preservation A which receives a TheStreet.com Investment Rating of C (Fair). Volatility, as measured by standard deviation, is considered low for fixed income funds at 1.71. Another risk factor is the fund's below average duration of 3.3 years (i.e. lower interest rate risk). The fund's risk rating is currently B+ (Good).

The fund's performance rating is currently C- (Fair). It has registered an average return of 0.98% over the last three years and is up 1.53% over the last three months. Factored into the performance evaluation is an expense ratio of 0.71% (low) and a 2.5% front-end load that is levied at the time of purchase.

John H. Smet has been running the fund for 4 years and currently receives a manager quality ranking of 47 (0=worst, 99=best). If you desire stability with a moderate level of risk then this fund is an excellent option.
Services Offered: Automated phone transactions, bank draft capabilities, wire transfers and a systematic withdrawal plan.

Data Date	Investment Rating	Net Assets ($Mil)	NAV	Performance Rating/Pts	Total Return Y-T-D	Risk Rating/Pts
3-16	C	678	10.00	C- / 3.4	1.53%	B+ / 8.8
2015	C	604	9.87	D+ / 2.8	0.56%	B+ / 8.8
2014	U	443	9.93	U / --	1.90%	U / --
2013	U	333	9.84	U / --	-1.10%	U / --
2012	U	256	10.06	U / --	0.00%	U / --

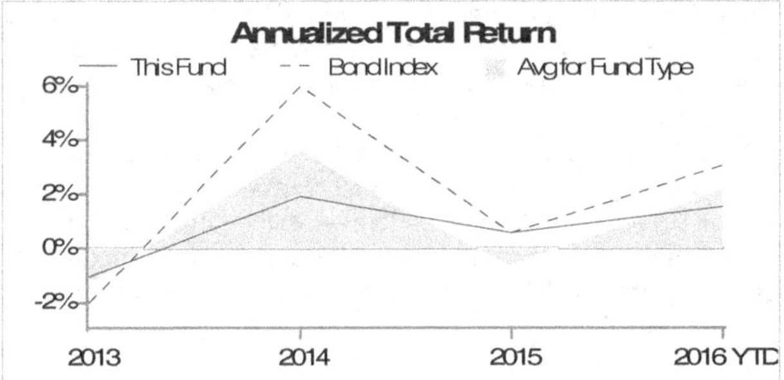

American Funds Sh-T Bd of Amr A (ASBAX) C- Fair

Fund Family: American Funds **Phone:** (800) 421-0180
Address: 333 South Hope Street, Los Angeles, CA 90071
Fund Type: GES - General - Short & Inter. Term
Major Rating Factors: Disappointing performance is the major factor driving the C- (Fair) TheStreet.com Investment Rating for American Funds Sh-T Bd of Amr A. The fund currently has a performance rating of D (Weak) based on an average return of 0.44% over the last three years and 0.87% over the last three months. Factored into the performance evaluation is an expense ratio of 0.60% (low) and a 2.5% front-end load that is levied at the time of purchase.

The fund's risk rating is currently A (Excellent). Volatility, as measured by standard deviation, is considered very low for fixed income funds at 0.82. Another risk factor is the fund's very low average duration of 1.5 years (i.e. low interest rate risk).

John R. Queen has been running the fund for 5 years and currently receives a manager quality ranking of 57 (0=worst, 99=best). This fund offers only a moderate level of risk but investors looking for strong performance are still waiting.

Services Offered: Automated phone transactions, bank draft capabilities, an IRA investment plan, a 401K investment plan, wire transfers and a systematic withdrawal plan.

Data Date	Investment Rating	Net Assets ($Mil)	NAV	Performance Rating/Pts	Total Return Y-T-D	Risk Rating/Pts
3-16	C-	3,082	9.99	D / 1.7	0.87%	A / 9.5
2015	C	2,998	9.92	D+ / 2.3	0.36%	A / 9.5
2014	D+	2,972	9.98	E+ / 0.6	0.46%	A+ / 9.7
2013	D+	3,112	9.98	E / 0.4	-0.32%	A+ / 9.7
2012	D+	3,188	10.07	E / 0.5	0.81%	A+ / 9.7
2011	C-	3,246	10.08	D- / 1.3	1.08%	A+ / 9.7

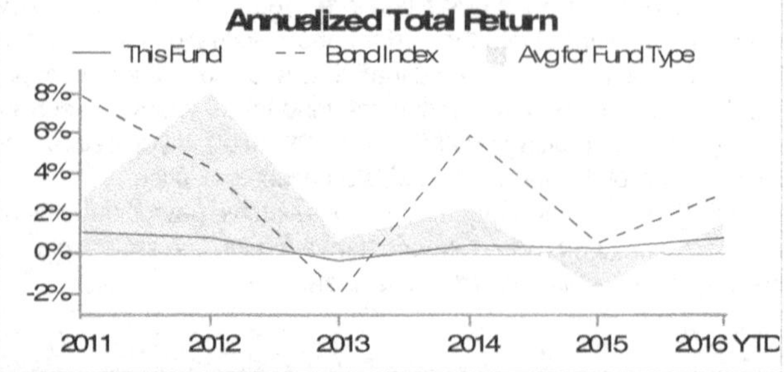

American Funds ST T/E Bnd Fd A (ASTEX) C- Fair

Fund Family: American Funds **Phone:** (800) 421-0180
Address: 333 South Hope Street, Los Angeles, CA 90071
Fund Type: MUN - Municipal - National
Major Rating Factors: Disappointing performance is the major factor driving the C- (Fair) TheStreet.com Investment Rating for American Funds ST T/E Bnd Fd A. The fund currently has a performance rating of D (Weak) based on an average return of 0.58% over the last three years (0.96% taxable equivalent) and 0.44% over the last three months (0.73% taxable equivalent). Factored into the performance evaluation is an expense ratio of 0.58% (low) and a 2.5% front-end load that is levied at the time of purchase.

The fund's risk rating is currently A (Excellent). Volatility, as measured by standard deviation, is considered very low for fixed income funds at 0.92. Another risk factor is the fund's very low average duration of 1.9 years (i.e. low interest rate risk).

Brenda S. Ellerin has been running the fund for 7 years and currently receives a manager quality ranking of 54 (0=worst, 99=best). This fund offers only a moderate level of risk but investors looking for strong performance are still waiting.

Services Offered: Automated phone transactions, check writing, payroll deductions, bank draft capabilities, wire transfers and a systematic withdrawal plan.

Data Date	Investment Rating	Net Assets ($Mil)	NAV	Performance Rating/Pts	Total Return Y-T-D	Risk Rating/Pts
3-16	C-	673	10.17	D / 1.8	0.44%	A / 9.4
2015	C	671	10.15	C- / 3.1	0.44%	A / 9.3
2014	C-	737	10.21	D- / 1.4	0.95%	A / 9.4
2013	C	735	10.22	D / 2.0	0.41%	A / 9.4
2012	C-	663	10.29	E+ / 0.9	1.63%	A / 9.4
2011	U	560	10.26	U / --	2.62%	U / --

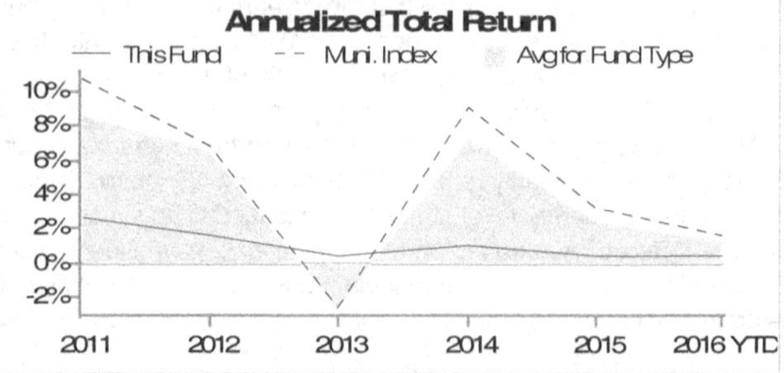

American Funds T/E Bd of America A (AFTEX) B+ Good

Fund Family: American Funds **Phone:** (800) 421-0180
Address: 333 South Hope Street, Los Angeles, CA 90071
Fund Type: MUN - Municipal - National
Major Rating Factors: Strong performance is the major factor driving the B+ (Good) TheStreet.com Investment Rating for American Funds T/E Bd of America A. The fund currently has a performance rating of B+ (Good) based on an average return of 3.52% over the last three years (5.83% taxable equivalent) and 1.54% over the last three months (2.55% taxable equivalent). Factored into the performance evaluation is an expense ratio of 0.54% (very low) and a 3.8% front-end load that is levied at the time of purchase.

The fund's risk rating is currently C (Fair). Volatility, as measured by standard deviation, is considered average for fixed income funds at 3.50. Another risk factor is the fund's fairly average duration of 5.5 years (i.e. average interest rate risk).

Neil L. Langberg has been running the fund for 37 years and currently receives a manager quality ranking of 56 (0=worst, 99=best). If you desire an average level of risk and strong performance, then this fund is a good option.

Services Offered: Automated phone transactions, payroll deductions, an IRA investment plan, a 401K investment plan, wire transfers and a systematic withdrawal plan.

Data Date	Investment Rating	Net Assets ($Mil)	NAV	Performance Rating/Pts	Total Return Y-T-D	Risk Rating/Pts
3-16	B+	8,142	13.19	B+ / 8.6	1.54%	C / 4.9
2015	B	7,769	13.09	B+ / 8.7	3.12%	C / 4.7
2014	A-	7,071	13.11	B+ / 8.6	9.67%	C / 4.3
2013	B	6,590	12.37	B- / 7.4	-2.73%	C / 4.3
2012	B+	7,663	13.16	B- / 7.4	8.91%	C / 4.3
2011	B	6,626	12.52	B- / 7.1	10.22%	C / 4.4

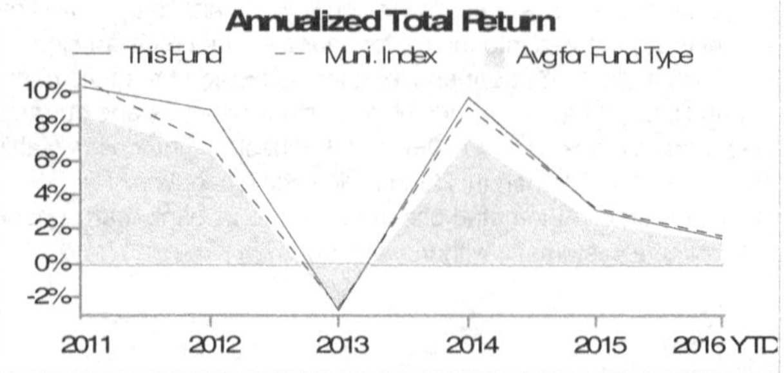

American Funds Tax-Exempt of CA A (TAFTX) B+ Good

Fund Family: American Funds **Phone:** (800) 421-0180
Address: 333 South Hope Street, Los Angeles, CA 90071
Fund Type: MUS - Municipal - Single State

Major Rating Factors: Exceptional performance is the major factor driving the B+ (Good) TheStreet.com Investment Rating for American Funds Tax-Exempt of CA A. The fund currently has a performance rating of A- (Excellent) based on an average return of 4.06% over the last three years (6.72% taxable equivalent) and 1.67% over the last three months (2.77% taxable equivalent). Factored into the performance evaluation is an expense ratio of 0.62% (low) and a 3.8% front-end load that is levied at the time of purchase.

The fund's risk rating is currently C (Fair). Volatility, as measured by standard deviation, is considered average for fixed income funds at 3.70. Another risk factor is the fund's fairly average duration of 5.4 years (i.e. average interest rate risk).

Neil L. Langberg has been running the fund for 30 years and currently receives a manager quality ranking of 74 (0=worst, 99=best). If you desire an average level of risk and strong performance, then this fund is a good option.

Services Offered: Automated phone transactions, payroll deductions, an IRA investment plan, a 401K investment plan and a systematic withdrawal plan.

Data Date	Investment Rating	Net Assets ($Mil)	NAV	Performance Rating/Pts	Total Return Y-T-D	Risk Rating/Pts
3-16	B+	1,535	17.97	A- / 9.1	1.67%	C / 4.5
2015	B+	1,458	17.81	A- / 9.1	3.38%	C / 4.3
2014	A	1,337	17.81	A- / 9.1	10.77%	C- / 4.1
2013	B+	1,208	16.65	B+ / 8.5	-2.31%	C- / 3.8
2012	A-	1,353	17.69	B+ / 8.7	9.96%	C- / 3.1
2011	B+	1,231	16.70	B+ / 8.8	11.61%	D+ / 2.8

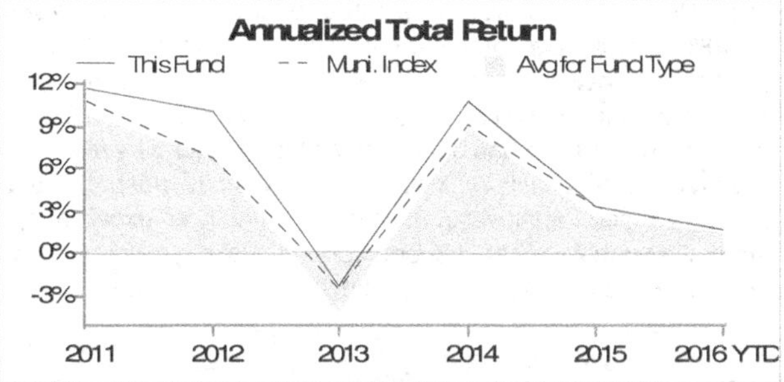

American Funds US Govt Sec A (AMUSX) C+ Fair

Fund Family: American Funds **Phone:** (800) 421-0180
Address: 333 South Hope Street, Los Angeles, CA 90071
Fund Type: USS - US Government - Short & Inter. Term

Major Rating Factors: A moderate risk profile coupled with stable earnings characterizes American Funds US Govt Sec A which receives a TheStreet.com Investment Rating of C+ (Fair). Volatility, as measured by standard deviation, is considered low for fixed income funds at 2.86. Another risk factor is the fund's below average duration of 5.0 years (i.e. lower interest rate risk). The fund's risk rating is currently B- (Good).

The fund's performance rating is currently C (Fair). It has registered an average return of 1.98% over the last three years and is up 2.57% over the last three months. Factored into the performance evaluation is an expense ratio of 0.65% (low) and a 3.8% front-end load that is levied at the time of purchase.

Fergus MacDonald has been running the fund for 6 years and currently receives a manager quality ranking of 66 (0=worst, 99=best). If you desire stability with a moderate level of risk then this fund is an excellent option.

Services Offered: Payroll deductions, an IRA investment plan, a 401K investment plan, a Keogh investment plan, wire transfers and a systematic withdrawal plan.

Data Date	Investment Rating	Net Assets ($Mil)	NAV	Performance Rating/Pts	Total Return Y-T-D	Risk Rating/Pts
3-16	C+	2,929	14.18	C / 5.0	2.57%	B- / 7.0
2015	C-	2,629	13.85	C- / 3.8	1.52%	B- / 7.0
2014	D	2,626	14.03	D / 1.8	4.84%	B / 7.6
2013	D	2,914	13.52	D- / 1.0	-3.16%	B / 7.8
2012	D-	4,165	14.21	D / 1.8	2.10%	C+ / 6.9
2011	D	4,136	14.41	D+ / 2.5	7.77%	B- / 7.4

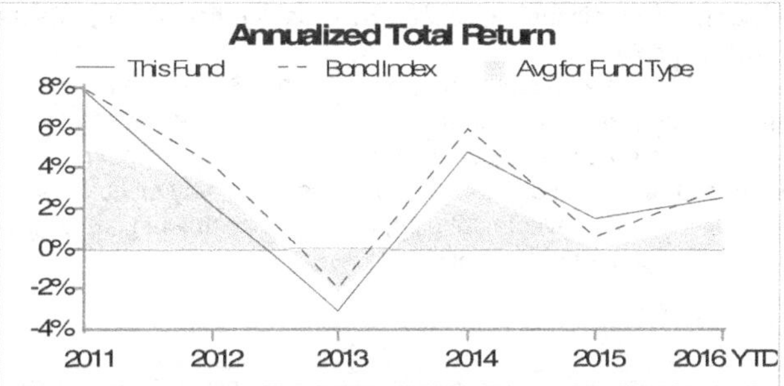

AMG Mgrs Bond Svc (MGFIX) C- Fair

Fund Family: Managers Funds LLC **Phone:** (800) 835-3879
Address: 800 Connecticut Ave., Norwalk, CT 06854
Fund Type: GEL - General - Long Term

Major Rating Factors: Middle of the road best describes AMG Mgrs Bond Svc whose TheStreet.com Investment Rating is currently a C- (Fair). The fund has a performance rating of C+ (Fair) based on an average return of 1.98% over the last three years and 2.89% over the last three months. Factored into the performance evaluation is an expense ratio of 1.03% (average).

The fund's risk rating is currently C (Fair). Volatility, as measured by standard deviation, is considered average for fixed income funds at 3.68. Another risk factor is the fund's below average duration of 4.4 years (i.e. lower interest rate risk).

Daniel J. Fuss has been running the fund for 22 years and currently receives a manager quality ranking of 52 (0=worst, 99=best). If you desire an average level of risk, then this fund may be an option.

Services Offered: Automated phone transactions, payroll deductions, bank draft capabilities, an IRA investment plan and a systematic withdrawal plan.

Data Date	Investment Rating	Net Assets ($Mil)	NAV	Performance Rating/Pts	Total Return Y-T-D	Risk Rating/Pts
3-16	C-	1,542	26.76	C+ / 6.3	2.89%	C / 4.5
2015	C-	1,576	26.20	C+ / 5.6	-2.15%	C / 5.1
2014	B+	1,946	27.88	B- / 7.5	5.81%	C / 4.9
2013	B+	1,545	27.33	B / 8.2	1.08%	C / 4.5
2012	B+	2,373	27.93	B / 7.6	12.04%	C / 4.4
2011	C	2,121	25.97	B- / 7.5	6.06%	D+ / 2.8

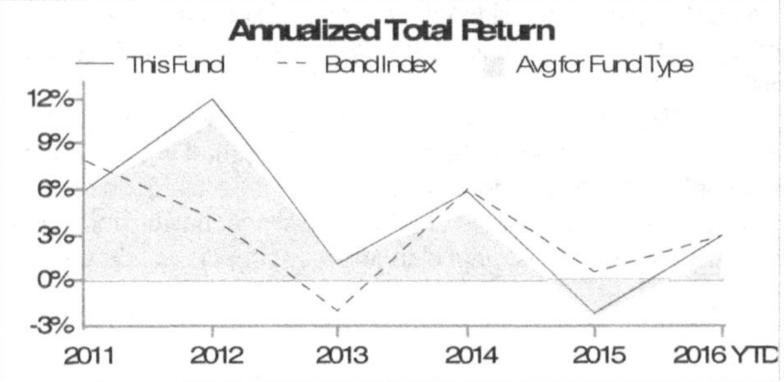

Aquila Hawaiian Tax Free Trust A (HULAX) B+ Good

Fund Family: Aquila Funds **Phone:** (800) 437-1020
Address: 380 Madison Aveneue, New York, NY 10017
Fund Type: MUN - Municipal - National
Major Rating Factors: A moderate risk profile coupled with stable earnings characterizes Aquila Hawaiian Tax Free Trust A which receives a TheStreet.com Investment Rating of B+ (Good). Volatility, as measured by standard deviation, is considered low for fixed income funds at 2.71. Another risk factor is the fund's below average duration of 4.5 years (i.e. lower interest rate risk). The fund's risk rating is currently B- (Good).

The fund's performance rating is currently C+ (Fair). It has registered an average return of 2.12% over the last three years (3.51% taxable equivalent) and is up 1.48% over the last three months (2.45% taxable equivalent). Factored into the performance evaluation is an expense ratio of 0.81% (low) and a 4.0% front-end load that is levied at the time of purchase.

Stephen K. Rodgers has been running the fund for 31 years and currently receives a manager quality ranking of 38 (0=worst, 99=best). If you desire stability with a moderate level of risk then this fund is an excellent option.
Services Offered: Automated phone transactions, payroll deductions, bank draft capabilities, wire transfers and a systematic withdrawal plan.

Data Date	Investment Rating	Net Assets ($Mil)	NAV	Performance Rating/Pts	Total Return Y-T-D	Risk Rating/Pts
3-16	B+	672	11.61	C+ / 6.4	1.48%	B- / 7.5
2015	B	662	11.50	C+ / 6.4	2.07%	B- / 7.3
2014	D+	675	11.53	C- / 3.7	5.40%	C+ / 6.3
2013	D+	687	11.23	D+ / 2.9	-2.55%	C+ / 6.4
2012	D	773	11.83	D+ / 2.8	4.25%	C+ / 6.6
2011	B-	748	11.65	C- / 3.9	7.39%	B / 7.9

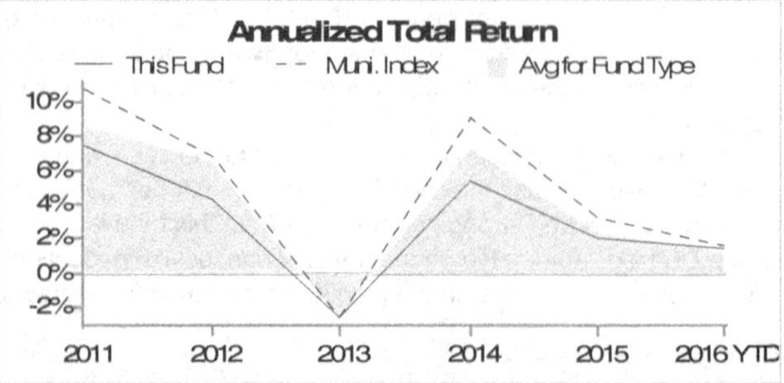

Baird Core Plus Bond Inv (BCOSX) C+ Fair

Fund Family: Baird Funds **Phone:** (866) 442-2473
Address: 777 East Wisconsin Avenue, Milwaukee, WI 53202
Fund Type: GEI - General - Investment Grade
Major Rating Factors: Strong performance is the major factor driving the C+ (Fair) TheStreet.com Investment Rating for Baird Core Plus Bond Inv. The fund currently has a performance rating of B- (Good) based on an average return of 2.43% over the last three years and 3.07% over the last three months. Factored into the performance evaluation is an expense ratio of 0.55% (very low).

The fund's risk rating is currently C+ (Fair). Volatility, as measured by standard deviation, is considered average for fixed income funds at 3.25. Another risk factor is the fund's fairly average duration of 5.5 years (i.e. average interest rate risk).

Gary A. Elfe has been running the fund for 16 years and currently receives a manager quality ranking of 54 (0=worst, 99=best). If you desire an average level of risk and strong performance, then this fund is a good option.
Services Offered: Automated phone transactions, payroll deductions, bank draft capabilities, an IRA investment plan, a Keogh investment plan, wire transfers and a systematic withdrawal plan.

Data Date	Investment Rating	Net Assets ($Mil)	NAV	Performance Rating/Pts	Total Return Y-T-D	Risk Rating/Pts
3-16	C+	2,291	11.54	B- / 7.1	3.07%	C+ / 5.6
2015	C	2,173	11.26	C+ / 6.1	-0.11%	C / 5.5
2014	B	2,192	11.55	C+ / 5.8	6.27%	C+ / 6.1
2013	B+	1,046	11.16	C+ / 5.9	-1.61%	C+ / 6.7
2012	A	1,035	11.67	C+ / 5.9	7.80%	B- / 7.0
2011	A-	329	11.18	C / 5.5	7.57%	B- / 7.1

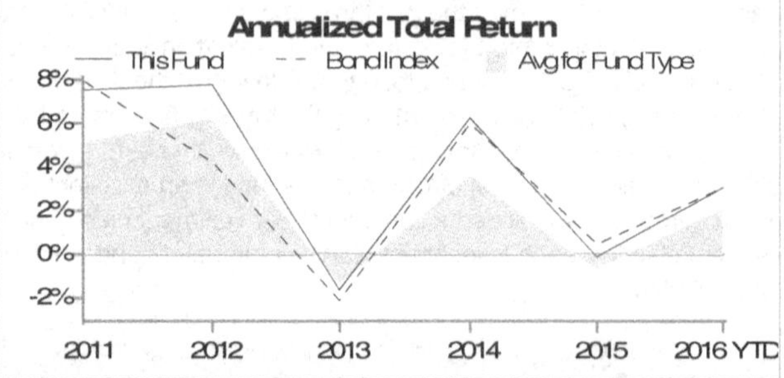

Berwyn Income Fund (BERIX) C+ Fair

Fund Family: Berwyn Funds **Phone:** (800) 992-6757
Address: C/O Ultimus Fund Solutions LLC, Cincinnati, OH 45246
Fund Type: GES - General - Short & Inter. Term
Major Rating Factors: Strong performance is the major factor driving the C+ (Fair) TheStreet.com Investment Rating for Berwyn Income Fund. The fund currently has a performance rating of B+ (Good) based on an average return of 5.11% over the last three years and 3.08% over the last three months. Factored into the performance evaluation is an expense ratio of 0.64% (low) and a 1.0% back-end load levied at the time of sale.

The fund's risk rating is currently C- (Fair). Volatility, as measured by standard deviation, is considered average for fixed income funds at 4.70. Another risk factor is the fund's below average duration of 3.3 years (i.e. lower interest rate risk).

Lee S. Grout has been running the fund for 11 years and currently receives a manager quality ranking of 99 (0=worst, 99=best). If you desire an average level of risk and strong performance, then this fund is a good option.
Services Offered: Automated phone transactions, payroll deductions, bank draft capabilities, an IRA investment plan and a systematic withdrawal plan.

Data Date	Investment Rating	Net Assets ($Mil)	NAV	Performance Rating/Pts	Total Return Y-T-D	Risk Rating/Pts
3-16	C+	1,694	13.19	B+ / 8.7	3.08%	C- / 3.1
2015	C	1,747	12.85	B+ / 8.3	-3.30%	C- / 3.0
2014	C+	2,575	13.61	B+ / 8.6	3.32%	D / 2.1
2013	B+	2,107	14.01	A+ / 9.9	15.83%	D+ / 2.3
2012	E	1,448	13.15	C / 4.7	7.96%	D / 2.1
2011	D	1,312	12.87	C+ / 6.5	3.09%	D+ / 2.4

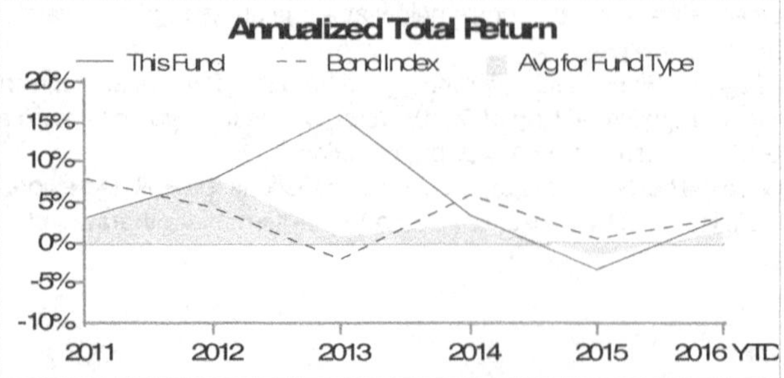

BlackRock Alloc Target Srs M (BRAMX) B+ Good

Fund Family: BlackRock Funds **Phone:** (800) 441-7762
Address: c/o PFPC, Inc., Providence, RI 02940
Fund Type: GEI - General - Investment Grade
Major Rating Factors: Strong performance is the major factor driving the B+ (Good) TheStreet.com Investment Rating for BlackRock Alloc Target Srs M. The fund currently has a performance rating of B (Good) based on an average return of 2.93% over the last three years and 2.15% over the last three months. Factored into the performance evaluation is an expense ratio of 0.14% (very low).

The fund's risk rating is currently C+ (Fair). Volatility, as measured by standard deviation, is considered average for fixed income funds at 3.09.

Matthew Marra has been running the fund for 5 years and currently receives a manager quality ranking of 86 (0=worst, 99=best). If you desire an average level of risk and strong performance, then this fund is a good option.
Services Offered: Automated phone transactions, bank draft capabilities, wire transfers and a systematic withdrawal plan.

Data Date	Investment Rating	Net Assets ($Mil)	NAV	Performance Rating/Pts	Total Return Y-T-D	Risk Rating/Pts
3-16	B+	553	9.93	B / 7.7	2.15%	C+ / 6.2
2015	B	533	9.80	B- / 7.4	1.52%	C+ / 5.9
2014	C+	464	9.98	C+ / 5.6	7.11%	C+ / 5.8

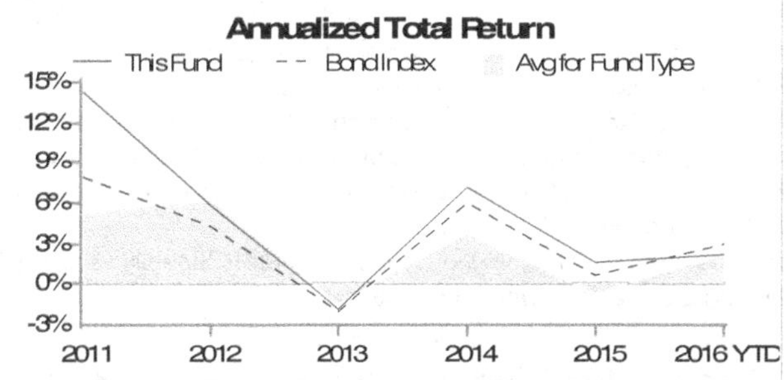

BlackRock Floating Rate Inc Inv A (BFRAX) C+ Fair

Fund Family: BlackRock Funds **Phone:** (800) 441-7762
Address: c/o PFPC, Inc., Providence, RI 02940
Fund Type: LP - Loan Participation
Major Rating Factors: A moderate risk profile coupled with stable earnings characterizes BlackRock Floating Rate Inc Inv A which receives a TheStreet.com Investment Rating of C+ (Fair). Volatility, as measured by standard deviation, is considered low for fixed income funds at 2.23. Another risk factor is the fund's very low average duration of 0.2 years (i.e. low interest rate risk). The fund's risk rating is currently B (Good).

The fund's performance rating is currently C (Fair). It has registered an average return of 2.03% over the last three years and is up 1.16% over the last three months. Factored into the performance evaluation is an expense ratio of 0.99% (average) and a 2.5% front-end load that is levied at the time of purchase.

Leland T. Hart has been running the fund for 7 years and currently receives a manager quality ranking of 95 (0=worst, 99=best). If you desire stability with a moderate level of risk then this fund is an excellent option.
Services Offered: Automated phone transactions, payroll deductions, bank draft capabilities, an IRA investment plan, a 401K investment plan, wire transfers and a systematic withdrawal plan.

Data Date	Investment Rating	Net Assets ($Mil)	NAV	Performance Rating/Pts	Total Return Y-T-D	Risk Rating/Pts
3-16	C+	541	9.91	C / 4.5	1.16%	B / 8.2
2015	B+	540	9.89	C+ / 6.1	0.71%	B+ / 8.4
2014	B+	567	10.21	C / 4.6	1.20%	B / 8.2
2013	B+	750	10.51	B- / 7.3	5.09%	C / 5.2
2012	E+	501	10.39	C- / 3.2	8.29%	C- / 4.1
2011	C-	338	10.03	C+ / 6.8	2.41%	D+ / 2.8

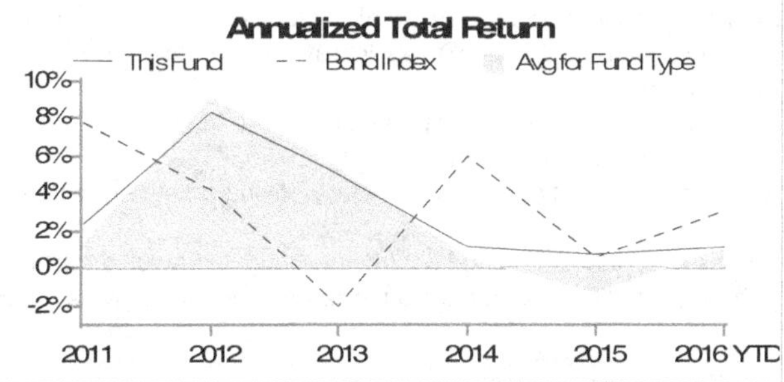

BlackRock Glbl Long/Short Crd Iv A (BGCAX) D+ Weak

Fund Family: BlackRock Funds **Phone:** (800) 441-7762
Address: c/o PFPC, Inc., Providence, RI 02940
Fund Type: GL - Global
Major Rating Factors: Very poor performance is the major factor driving the D+ (Weak) TheStreet.com Investment Rating for BlackRock Glbl Long/Short Crd Iv A. The fund currently has a performance rating of E+ (Very Weak) based on an average return of 0.38% over the last three years and -0.82% over the last three months. Factored into the performance evaluation is an expense ratio of 1.99% (high) and a 4.0% front-end load that is levied at the time of purchase.

The fund's risk rating is currently B+ (Good). Volatility, as measured by standard deviation, is considered low for fixed income funds at 2.17.

Michael E. J. Phelps has been running the fund for 5 years and currently receives a manager quality ranking of 79 (0=worst, 99=best). This fund offers only a moderate level of risk but investors looking for strong performance are still waiting.
Services Offered: Automated phone transactions, payroll deductions, bank draft capabilities, wire transfers and a systematic withdrawal plan.

Data Date	Investment Rating	Net Assets ($Mil)	NAV	Performance Rating/Pts	Total Return Y-T-D	Risk Rating/Pts
3-16	D+	552	9.68	E+ / 0.7	-0.82%	B+ / 8.3
2015	C-	683	9.76	D / 2.2	-1.22%	B / 8.2
2014	C	1,180	10.36	D+ / 2.8	0.67%	B+ / 8.6
2013	U	1,713	10.79	U / --	3.49%	U / --
2012	U	162	10.54	U / --	6.76%	U / --

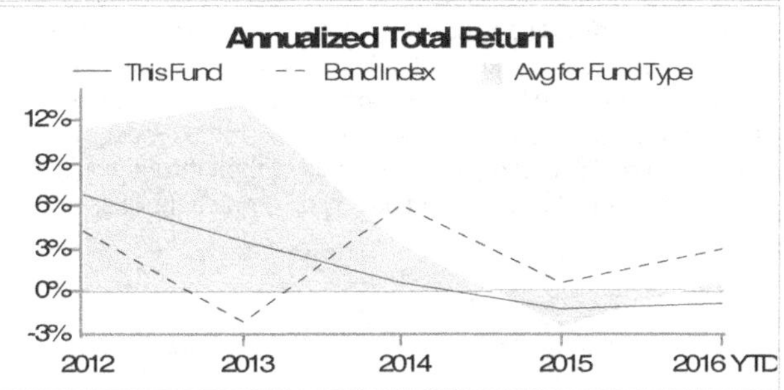

BlackRock High Yield Bond Inv A (BHYAX) D- Weak

Fund Family: BlackRock Funds **Phone:** (800) 441-7762
Address: c/o PFPC, Inc., Providence, RI 02940
Fund Type: COH - Corporate - High Yield
Major Rating Factors: BlackRock High Yield Bond Inv A has adopted a very risky asset allocation strategy and currently receives an overall TheStreet.com Investment Rating of D- (Weak). Volatility, as measured by standard deviation, is considered above average for fixed income funds at 5.62. Unfortunately, the high level of risk (D-, Weak) failed to pay off as investors endured very poor performance.

The fund's performance rating is currently D+ (Weak). It has registered an average return of 1.88% over the last three years and is up 1.56% over the last three months. Factored into the performance evaluation is an expense ratio of 0.94% (average) and a 4.0% front-end load that is levied at the time of purchase.

James E. Keenan has been running the fund for 9 years and currently receives a manager quality ranking of 77 (0=worst, 99=best). If you can tolerate very high levels of risk in the hope of improved future returns, holding this fund may be an option.
Services Offered: Payroll deductions, bank draft capabilities, an IRA investment plan and a systematic withdrawal plan.

Data Date	Investment Rating	Net Assets ($Mil)	NAV	Performance Rating/Pts	Total Return Y-T-D	Risk Rating/Pts
3-16	D-	2,893	7.15	D+ / 2.4	1.56%	D- / 1.5
2015	D	2,622	7.13	D+ / 2.8	-4.33%	D- / 1.2
2014	C	2,927	7.88	B+ / 8.3	3.04%	D / 1.8
2013	B-	4,283	8.21	A+ / 9.6	8.95%	D- / 1.3
2012	C+	3,550	8.09	A- / 9.1	16.77%	D- / 1.0
2011	C+	2,243	7.39	A / 9.4	2.88%	D- / 1.1

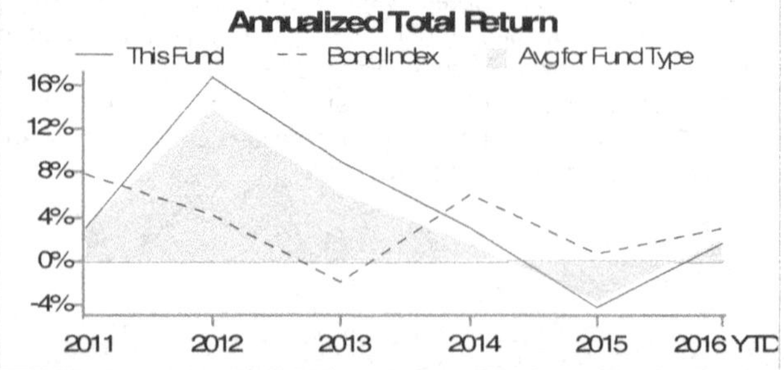

BlackRock Low Duration Bond Inv A (BLDAX) C Fair

Fund Family: BlackRock Funds **Phone:** (800) 441-7762
Address: c/o PFPC, Inc., Providence, RI 02940
Fund Type: GEI - General - Investment Grade
Major Rating Factors: Disappointing performance is the major factor driving the C (Fair) TheStreet.com Investment Rating for BlackRock Low Duration Bond Inv A. The fund currently has a performance rating of D+ (Weak) based on an average return of 0.90% over the last three years and 0.65% over the last three months. Factored into the performance evaluation is an expense ratio of 0.84% (low) and a 2.3% front-end load that is levied at the time of purchase.

The fund's risk rating is currently A- (Excellent). Volatility, as measured by standard deviation, is considered very low for fixed income funds at 1.05. Another risk factor is the fund's very low average duration of 1.8 years (i.e. low interest rate risk).

Thomas F. Musmanno has been running the fund for 8 years and currently receives a manager quality ranking of 75 (0=worst, 99=best). This fund offers only a moderate level of risk but investors looking for strong performance are still waiting.
Services Offered: Automated phone transactions, payroll deductions, bank draft capabilities, an IRA investment plan, wire transfers and a systematic withdrawal plan.

Data Date	Investment Rating	Net Assets ($Mil)	NAV	Performance Rating/Pts	Total Return Y-T-D	Risk Rating/Pts
3-16	C	830	9.61	D+ / 2.9	0.65%	A- / 9.2
2015	C+	843	9.58	C- / 4.0	0.48%	A- / 9.2
2014	C	777	9.68	D+ / 2.4	1.18%	A- / 9.1
2013	C+	1,605	9.75	C- / 3.1	0.99%	A- / 9.1
2012	C	578	9.83	D / 1.7	4.84%	A- / 9.1
2011	C	516	9.59	D+ / 2.7	1.86%	B+ / 8.7

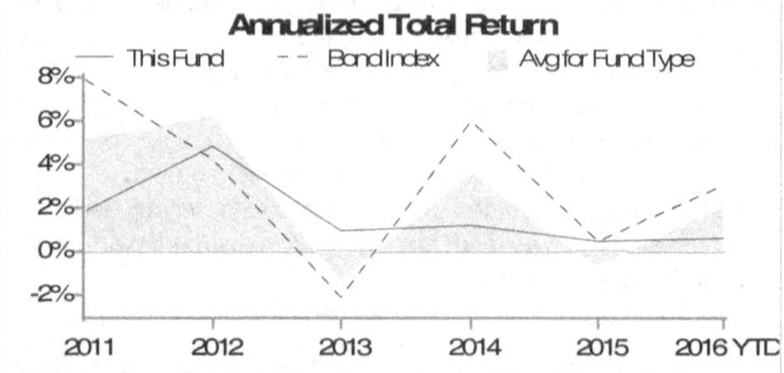

BlackRock Natl Muni Inv A (MDNLX) B- Good

Fund Family: BlackRock Funds **Phone:** (800) 441-7762
Address: c/o PFPC, Inc., Providence, RI 02940
Fund Type: MUN - Municipal - National
Major Rating Factors: Strong performance is the major factor driving the B- (Good) TheStreet.com Investment Rating for BlackRock Natl Muni Inv A. The fund currently has a performance rating of B (Good) based on an average return of 3.44% over the last three years (5.70% taxable equivalent) and 1.07% over the last three months (1.77% taxable equivalent). Factored into the performance evaluation is an expense ratio of 0.85% (average) and a 4.3% front-end load that is levied at the time of purchase.

The fund's risk rating is currently C (Fair). Volatility, as measured by standard deviation, is considered average for fixed income funds at 3.74.

Walter O'Connor has been running the fund for 20 years and currently receives a manager quality ranking of 46 (0=worst, 99=best). If you desire an average level of risk and strong performance, then this fund is a good option.
Services Offered: Payroll deductions, bank draft capabilities and a systematic withdrawal plan.

Data Date	Investment Rating	Net Assets ($Mil)	NAV	Performance Rating/Pts	Total Return Y-T-D	Risk Rating/Pts
3-16	B-	2,615	11.05	B / 8.2	1.07%	C / 4.4
2015	B-	2,592	11.01	B+ / 8.6	3.35%	C- / 4.2
2014	B+	2,177	11.00	B+ / 8.6	10.06%	C- / 3.3
2013	C+	1,716	10.35	B / 7.6	-3.20%	C- / 3.5
2012	B+	2,055	11.09	B / 8.2	9.63%	C- / 3.4
2011	A+	1,339	10.50	B / 8.1	11.36%	C / 4.4

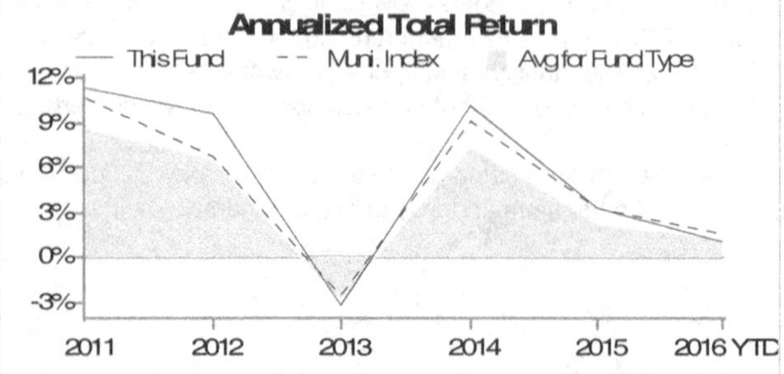

BlackRock Strat Muni Opps Inv A (MEMTX) B- Good

Fund Family: BlackRock Funds **Phone:** (800) 441-7762
Address: c/o PFPC, Inc., Providence, RI 02940
Fund Type: MUN - Municipal - National
Major Rating Factors: Strong performance is the major factor driving the B- (Good) TheStreet.com Investment Rating for BlackRock Strat Muni Opps Inv A. The fund currently has a performance rating of B+ (Good) based on an average return of 3.31% over the last three years (5.48% taxable equivalent) and 1.29% over the last three months (2.14% taxable equivalent). Factored into the performance evaluation is an expense ratio of 0.93% (average) and a 4.3% front-end load that is levied at the time of purchase.

The fund's risk rating is currently C- (Fair). Volatility, as measured by standard deviation, is considered average for fixed income funds at 3.86.

Theodore R. Jaeckel, Jr. has been running the fund for 10 years and currently receives a manager quality ranking of 43 (0=worst, 99=best). If you desire an average level of risk and strong performance, then this fund is a good option.

Services Offered: Automated phone transactions, payroll deductions, wire transfers and a systematic withdrawal plan.

Data Date	Investment Rating	Net Assets ($Mil)	NAV	Performance Rating/Pts	Total Return Y-T-D	Risk Rating/Pts
3-16	B-	1,025	11.61	B+ / 8.4	1.29%	C- / 4.2
2015	B-	934	11.53	B+ / 8.7	3.41%	C- / 4.0
2014	C+	618	11.45	B / 7.9	9.36%	C- / 3.2
2013	C	190	10.77	C+ / 6.9	-3.09%	C- / 3.7
2012	B+	216	11.51	B / 7.6	8.17%	C- / 3.9
2011	B+	105	11.02	B- / 7.2	11.06%	C / 4.8

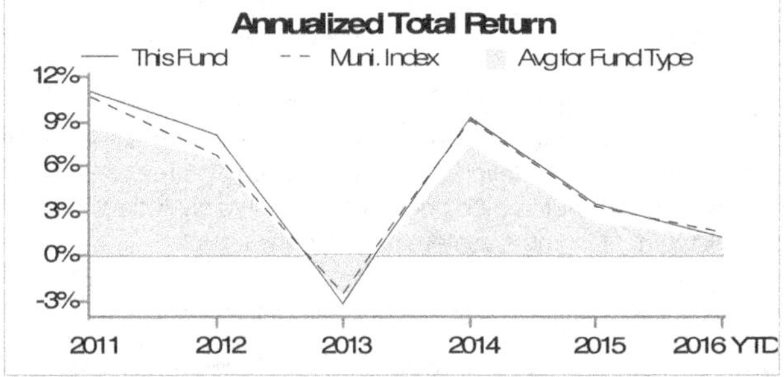

BlackRock Total Return Inv A (MDHQX) C Fair

Fund Family: BlackRock Funds **Phone:** (800) 441-7762
Address: c/o PFPC, Inc., Providence, RI 02940
Fund Type: GEI - General - Investment Grade
Major Rating Factors: Middle of the road best describes BlackRock Total Return Inv A whose TheStreet.com Investment Rating is currently a C (Fair). The fund has a performance rating of C+ (Fair) based on an average return of 3.01% over the last three years and 2.52% over the last three months. Factored into the performance evaluation is an expense ratio of 0.86% (average) and a 4.0% front-end load that is levied at the time of purchase.

The fund's risk rating is currently C (Fair). Volatility, as measured by standard deviation, is considered average for fixed income funds at 3.32. Another risk factor is the fund's fairly average duration of 5.2 years (i.e. average interest rate risk).

Richard M. Rieder has been running the fund for 6 years and currently receives a manager quality ranking of 79 (0=worst, 99=best). If you desire an average level of risk, then this fund may be an option.

Services Offered: Automated phone transactions, bank draft capabilities, an IRA investment plan, wire transfers and a systematic withdrawal plan.

Data Date	Investment Rating	Net Assets ($Mil)	NAV	Performance Rating/Pts	Total Return Y-T-D	Risk Rating/Pts
3-16	C	2,538	11.73	C+ / 6.0	2.52%	C / 5.4
2015	C-	2,291	11.51	C+ / 5.6	0.03%	C / 5.2
2014	B	1,236	11.86	C+ / 6.4	7.74%	C+ / 6.0
2013	C	965	11.40	C / 4.5	-0.50%	C+ / 6.5
2012	B-	1,102	11.83	C / 4.9	9.70%	C+ / 6.5
2011	D+	973	11.18	C- / 4.1	4.30%	C+ / 5.7

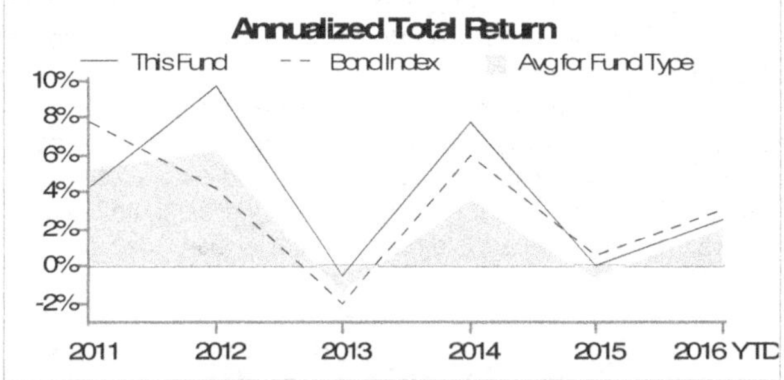

BNY Mellon Bond M (MPBFX) B Good

Fund Family: Mellon Funds **Phone:** (800) 645-6561
Address: One Mellon Center, Pittsburgh, PA 15258
Fund Type: GEI - General - Investment Grade
Major Rating Factors: BNY Mellon Bond M receives a TheStreet.com Investment Rating of B (Good). The fund has a performance rating of C+ (Fair) based on an average return of 1.92% over the last three years and 2.91% over the last three months. Factored into the performance evaluation is an expense ratio of 0.55% (very low).

The fund's risk rating is currently C+ (Fair). Volatility, as measured by standard deviation, is considered average for fixed income funds at 2.95. Another risk factor is the fund's fairly average duration of 5.2 years (i.e. average interest rate risk).

John F. Flahive has been running the fund for 11 years and currently receives a manager quality ranking of 44 (0=worst, 99=best). If you desire an average level of risk, then this fund may be an option.

Services Offered: Automated phone transactions, bank draft capabilities, an IRA investment plan and a systematic withdrawal plan.

Data Date	Investment Rating	Net Assets ($Mil)	NAV	Performance Rating/Pts	Total Return Y-T-D	Risk Rating/Pts
3-16	B	1,007	12.94	C+ / 6.6	2.91%	C+ / 6.7
2015	C+	994	12.66	C+ / 5.7	0.70%	C+ / 6.7
2014	C	1,032	12.92	C- / 4.1	4.63%	C+ / 6.6
2013	C	1,100	12.72	C- / 3.8	-2.29%	B- / 7.5
2012	B-	1,300	13.58	C- / 3.4	6.04%	B+ / 8.4
2011	C+	1,332	13.32	C- / 3.1	5.48%	B+ / 8.7

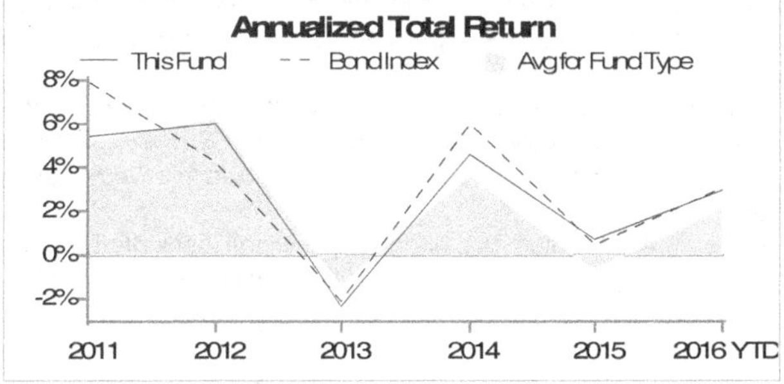

BNY Mellon Inter Bond M (MPIBX) B- Good

Fund Family: Mellon Funds **Phone:** (800) 645-6561
Address: One Mellon Center, Pittsburgh, PA 15258
Fund Type: GEI - General - Investment Grade

Major Rating Factors: A moderate risk profile coupled with stable earnings characterizes BNY Mellon Inter Bond M which receives a TheStreet.com Investment Rating of B- (Good). Volatility, as measured by standard deviation, is considered low for fixed income funds at 1.99. Another risk factor is the fund's below average duration of 3.1 years (i.e. lower interest rate risk). The fund's risk rating is currently B+ (Good).

The fund's performance rating is currently C (Fair). It has registered an average return of 0.99% over the last three years and is up 1.97% over the last three months. Factored into the performance evaluation is an expense ratio of 0.55% (very low).

John F. Flahive has been running the fund for 10 years and currently receives a manager quality ranking of 41 (0=worst, 99=best). If you desire stability with a moderate level of risk then this fund is an excellent option.

Services Offered: Automated phone transactions, bank draft capabilities, an IRA investment plan and a systematic withdrawal plan.

Data Date	Investment Rating	Net Assets ($Mil)	NAV	Performance Rating/Pts	Total Return Y-T-D	Risk Rating/Pts
3-16	B-	861	12.67	C / 4.8	1.97%	B+ / 8.5
2015	C+	857	12.49	C / 4.5	0.58%	B+ / 8.4
2014	C	904	12.66	D+ / 2.5	1.95%	B+ / 8.5
2013	C+	927	12.67	C- / 3.0	-1.30%	B+ / 8.6
2012	C	930	13.20	D / 2.2	4.15%	B+ / 8.8
2011	C	976	13.03	D+ / 2.5	4.11%	B+ / 8.9

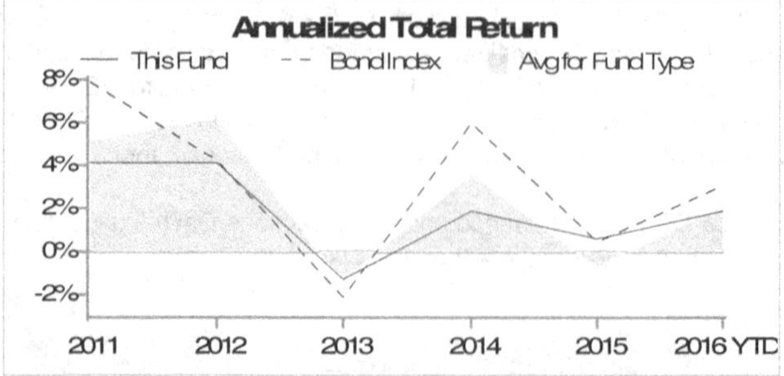

BNY Mellon National ST Muni Bd M (MPSTX) C+ Fair

Fund Family: Mellon Funds **Phone:** (800) 645-6561
Address: One Mellon Center, Pittsburgh, PA 15258
Fund Type: MUI - Municipal - Insured

Major Rating Factors: A moderate risk profile coupled with stable earnings characterizes BNY Mellon National ST Muni Bd M which receives a TheStreet.com Investment Rating of C+ (Fair). Volatility, as measured by standard deviation, is considered very low for fixed income funds at 0.78. Another risk factor is the fund's very low average duration of 1.5 years (i.e. low interest rate risk). The fund's risk rating is currently A (Excellent).

The fund's performance rating is currently C- (Fair). It has registered an average return of 0.42% over the last three years and is up 0.20% over the last three months. Factored into the performance evaluation is an expense ratio of 0.50% (very low).

J. Christopher Nicholl has been running the fund for 1 year and currently receives a manager quality ranking of 53 (0=worst, 99=best). If you desire stability with a moderate level of risk then this fund is an excellent option.

Services Offered: Automated phone transactions, bank draft capabilities, an IRA investment plan and a systematic withdrawal plan.

Data Date	Investment Rating	Net Assets ($Mil)	NAV	Performance Rating/Pts	Total Return Y-T-D	Risk Rating/Pts
3-16	C+	1,009	12.81	C- / 3.6	0.20%	A / 9.5
2015	B+	1,016	12.81	C / 5.3	0.37%	A / 9.5
2014	C	1,197	12.88	D / 2.0	0.71%	A / 9.5
2013	B-	1,272	12.90	D+ / 2.9	0.34%	A+ / 9.6
2012	C-	1,281	12.97	D- / 1.0	1.09%	A+ / 9.6
2011	C+	1,177	12.97	D+ / 2.3	2.21%	A / 9.5

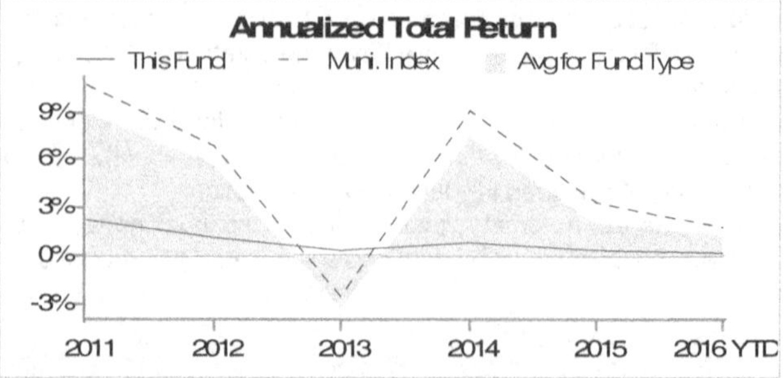

BNY Mellon Natl Int Muni M (MPNIX) A+ Excellent

Fund Family: Mellon Funds **Phone:** (800) 645-6561
Address: One Mellon Center, Pittsburgh, PA 15258
Fund Type: MUN - Municipal - National

Major Rating Factors: Strong performance is the major factor driving the A+ (Excellent) TheStreet.com Investment Rating for BNY Mellon Natl Int Muni M. The fund currently has a performance rating of B+ (Good) based on an average return of 2.64% over the last three years (4.37% taxable equivalent) and 1.28% over the last three months (2.12% taxable equivalent). Factored into the performance evaluation is an expense ratio of 0.50% (very low).

The fund's risk rating is currently B- (Good). Volatility, as measured by standard deviation, is considered low for fixed income funds at 2.75. Another risk factor is the fund's below average duration of 4.3 years (i.e. lower interest rate risk).

John F. Flahive has been running the fund for 16 years and currently receives a manager quality ranking of 54 (0=worst, 99=best). If you desire only a moderate level of risk and strong performance, then this fund is an excellent option.

Services Offered: Automated phone transactions, bank draft capabilities, an IRA investment plan and a systematic withdrawal plan.

Data Date	Investment Rating	Net Assets ($Mil)	NAV	Performance Rating/Pts	Total Return Y-T-D	Risk Rating/Pts
3-16	A+	2,108	13.83	B+ / 8.7	1.28%	B- / 7.4
2015	A+	2,063	13.74	B+ / 8.8	2.64%	B- / 7.0
2014	A-	1,918	13.75	B- / 7.1	5.99%	C+ / 5.9
2013	A+	1,665	13.34	B / 7.9	-1.46%	C+ / 6.1
2012	B	1,770	13.93	C+ / 6.0	5.25%	C / 5.5
2011	A	1,613	13.69	B- / 7.1	9.34%	C / 5.5

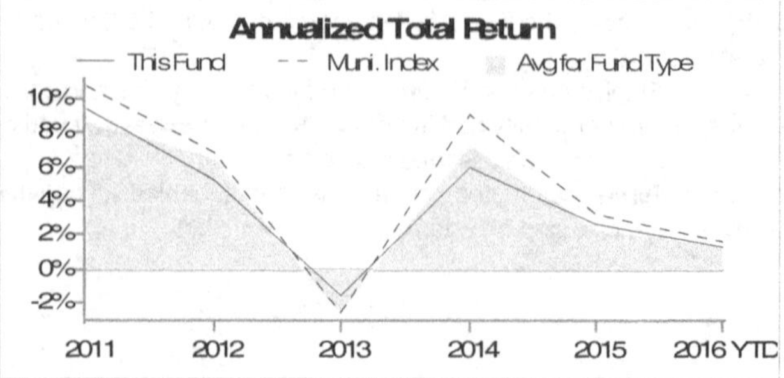

Calvert Short Duration Income A (CSDAX) C- Fair

Fund Family: Calvert Group **Phone:** (800) 368-2745
Address: 4550 Montgomery Avenue, Bethesda, MD 20814
Fund Type: COI - Corporate - Investment Grade
Major Rating Factors: Disappointing performance is the major factor driving the C- (Fair) TheStreet.com Investment Rating for Calvert Short Duration Income A. The fund currently has a performance rating of D- (Weak) based on an average return of 0.73% over the last three years and 1.25% over the last three months. Factored into the performance evaluation is an expense ratio of 1.14% (above average), a 2.8% front-end load that is levied at the time of purchase and a 2.0% back-end load levied at the time of sale.

The fund's risk rating is currently B+ (Good). Volatility, as measured by standard deviation, is considered low for fixed income funds at 1.46. Another risk factor is the fund's very low average duration of 2.5 years (i.e. low interest rate risk).

Matthew Duch has been running the fund for 7 years and currently receives a manager quality ranking of 56 (0=worst, 99=best). This fund offers only a moderate level of risk but investors looking for strong performance are still waiting.
Services Offered: Automated phone transactions, payroll deductions, bank draft capabilities, an IRA investment plan, a 401K investment plan, a Keogh investment plan and a systematic withdrawal plan.

Data Date	Investment Rating	Net Assets ($Mil)	NAV	Perfor-mance Rating/Pts	Total Return Y-T-D	Risk Rating/Pts
3-16	C-	669	15.92	D- / 1.4	1.25%	B+ / 8.9
2015	C-	695	15.81	D / 1.9	0.24%	B+ / 8.9
2014	C-	853	16.06	D / 1.9	0.67%	B+ / 8.8
2013	C-	1,104	16.26	D / 1.8	0.67%	B+ / 8.7
2012	D+	1,252	16.46	D- / 1.3	6.47%	B+ / 8.7
2011	D+	1,518	15.82	D / 1.7	0.38%	B+ / 8.7

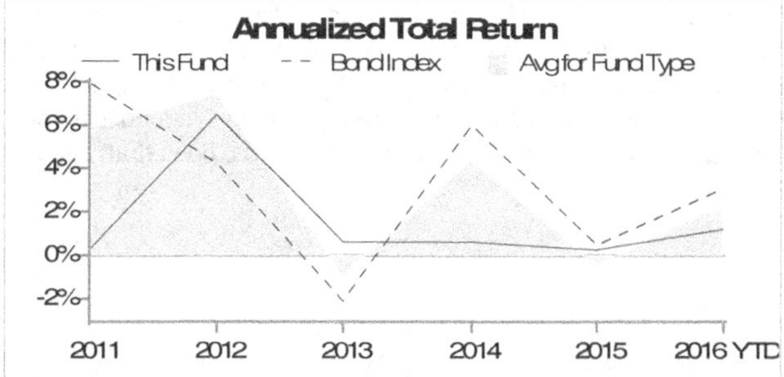

CGCM Core Fixed Inc Invest (TIIUX) B- Good

Fund Family: Consulting Group Capital Markets **Phone:** (800) 444-4273
Address: 2000 Westchester Avenue, Purchase, NY 10577
Fund Type: GEI - General - Investment Grade
Major Rating Factors: CGCM Core Fixed Inc Invest receives a TheStreet.com Investment Rating of B- (Good). The fund has a performance rating of C+ (Fair) based on an average return of 2.22% over the last three years and 2.61% over the last three months. Factored into the performance evaluation is an expense ratio of 0.54% (very low).

The fund's risk rating is currently C+ (Fair). Volatility, as measured by standard deviation, is considered average for fixed income funds at 3.11. Another risk factor is the fund's below average duration of 4.0 years (i.e. lower interest rate risk).

S. Kenneth Leech has been running the fund for 2 years and currently receives a manager quality ranking of 51 (0=worst, 99=best). If you desire an average level of risk, then this fund may be an option.
Services Offered: Payroll deductions and a systematic withdrawal plan.

Data Date	Investment Rating	Net Assets ($Mil)	NAV	Perfor-mance Rating/Pts	Total Return Y-T-D	Risk Rating/Pts
3-16	B-	661	8.24	C+ / 6.8	2.61%	C+ / 6.1
2015	C+	798	8.09	C+ / 6.4	0.59%	C+ / 5.9
2014	B-	776	8.31	C / 5.5	5.70%	C+ / 6.3
2013	B	870	8.19	C / 5.1	-1.95%	B- / 7.2
2012	A-	933	8.57	C / 5.4	7.91%	B- / 7.4
2011	B	1,254	8.54	C / 4.7	6.42%	B- / 7.2

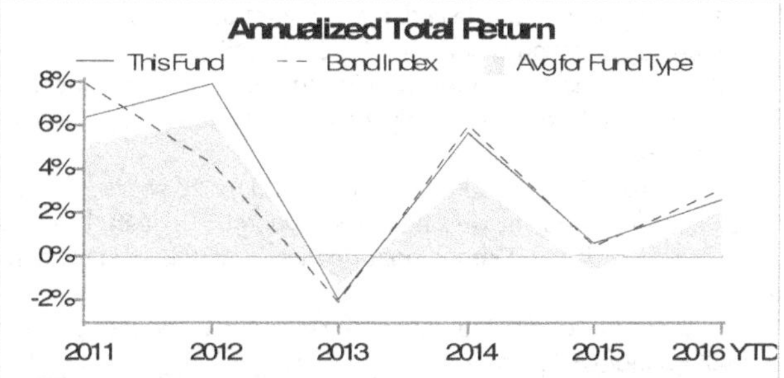

CNR Fixed Income Opportunities N (RIMOX) D+ Weak

Fund Family: CNR Funds **Phone:** (888) 889-0799
Address: c/o SEI Inv Distribution Co., Oaks, PA 19456
Fund Type: GEI - General - Investment Grade
Major Rating Factors: CNR Fixed Income Opportunities N receives a TheStreet.com Investment Rating of D+ (Weak). The fund has a performance rating of C (Fair) based on an average return of 1.49% over the last three years and -0.74% over the last three months. Factored into the performance evaluation is an expense ratio of 1.12% (average).

The fund's risk rating is currently C- (Fair). Volatility, as measured by standard deviation, is considered average for fixed income funds at 3.98.

Stefan P. Pinter has been running the fund for 5 years and currently receives a manager quality ranking of 90 (0=worst, 99=best). If you desire an average level of risk, then this fund may be an option.
Services Offered: Automated phone transactions, payroll deductions, bank draft capabilities, an IRA investment plan, wire transfers and a systematic withdrawal plan.

Data Date	Investment Rating	Net Assets ($Mil)	NAV	Perfor-mance Rating/Pts	Total Return Y-T-D	Risk Rating/Pts
3-16	D+	1,678	24.29	C / 4.3	-0.74%	C- / 4.0
2015	C	1,613	24.47	B / 7.6	1.81%	C- / 4.1
2014	C	1,338	25.73	C / 5.5	-0.04%	C / 5.4
2013	A+	1,125	27.26	B+ / 8.7	6.46%	C / 4.8
2012	D	653	27.20	C+ / 5.7	10.70%	C- / 3.2
2011	U	498	26.16	U / --	2.04%	U / --

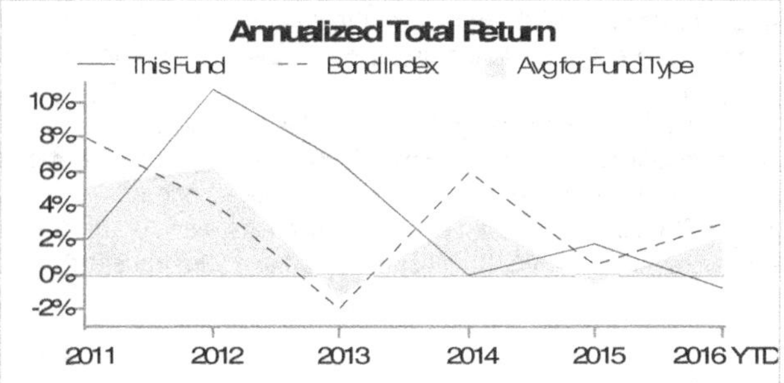

Cohen and Steers Pref Sec&Inc A (CPXAX) B- Good

Fund Family: Cohen & Steers Funds **Phone:** (800) 330-7348
Address: 280 Park Avenue, New York, NY 10017
Fund Type: GEI - General - Investment Grade
Major Rating Factors: Exceptional performance is the major factor driving the B- (Good) TheStreet.com Investment Rating for Cohen and Steers Pref Sec&Inc A. The fund currently has a performance rating of A- (Excellent) based on an average return of 5.55% over the last three years and 0.08% over the last three months. Factored into the performance evaluation is an expense ratio of 1.19% (above average).

The fund's risk rating is currently C- (Fair). Volatility, as measured by standard deviation, is considered average for fixed income funds at 4.35.

Joseph M. Harvey has been running the fund for 6 years and currently receives a manager quality ranking of 99 (0=worst, 99=best). If you desire an average level of risk and strong performance, then this fund is a good option.
Services Offered: Automated phone transactions, bank draft capabilities and wire transfers.

Data Date	Investment Rating	Net Assets ($Mil)	NAV	Performance Rating/Pts	Total Return Y-T-D	Risk Rating/Pts
3-16	B-	821	13.39	A- / 9.1	0.08%	C- / 3.4
2015	B+	738	13.57	A+ / 9.8	5.78%	C- / 3.9
2014	A	568	13.56	A+ / 9.7	11.61%	D+ / 2.9
2013	B	431	12.87	A / 9.4	2.55%	D / 2.2
2012	U	414	13.34	U / --	22.04%	U / --
2011	U	109	11.69	U / --	3.32%	U / --

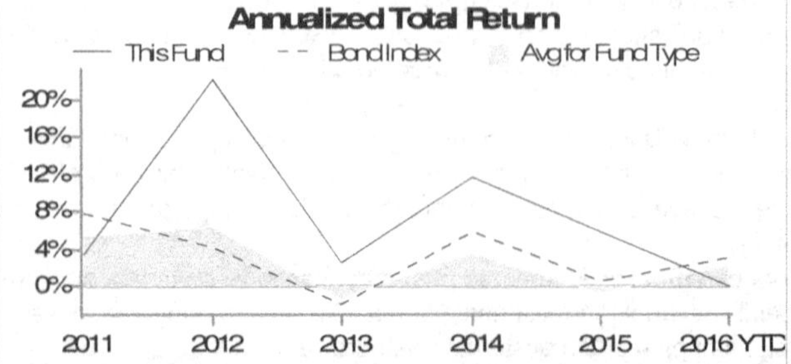

Colorado Bond Shares Tax-Exempt (HICOX) A+ Excellent

Fund Family: Freedom Funds Management Company **Phone:** (800) 572-0069
Address: 1200 17th Street, Denver, CO 80202
Fund Type: MUS - Municipal - Single State
Major Rating Factors: Strong performance is the major factor driving the A+ (Excellent) TheStreet.com Investment Rating for Colorado Bond Shares Tax-Exempt. The fund currently has a performance rating of B+ (Good) based on an average return of 4.05% over the last three years (6.71% taxable equivalent) and 1.27% over the last three months (2.10% taxable equivalent). Factored into the performance evaluation is an expense ratio of 0.58% (low) and a 4.8% front-end load that is levied at the time of purchase.

The fund's risk rating is currently A- (Excellent). Volatility, as measured by standard deviation, is considered very low for fixed income funds at 1.15. Another risk factor is the fund's fairly average duration of 6.1 years (i.e. average interest rate risk).

Fred R. Kelly, Jr. has been running the fund for 26 years and currently receives a manager quality ranking of 98 (0=worst, 99=best). If you desire only a moderate level of risk and strong performance, then this fund is an excellent option.
Services Offered: Automated phone transactions, bank draft capabilities and a systematic withdrawal plan.

Data Date	Investment Rating	Net Assets ($Mil)	NAV	Performance Rating/Pts	Total Return Y-T-D	Risk Rating/Pts
3-16	A+	984	9.14	B+ / 8.8	1.27%	A- / 9.1
2015	A+	944	9.13	A- / 9.0	4.50%	A- / 9.1
2014	A+	905	9.10	C+ / 6.4	5.76%	A- / 9.1
2013	A+	860	8.99	C+ / 6.7	1.60%	A- / 9.1
2012	B+	894	9.23	C- / 3.6	5.14%	A / 9.3
2011	B+	800	9.17	C- / 3.4	6.36%	A / 9.5

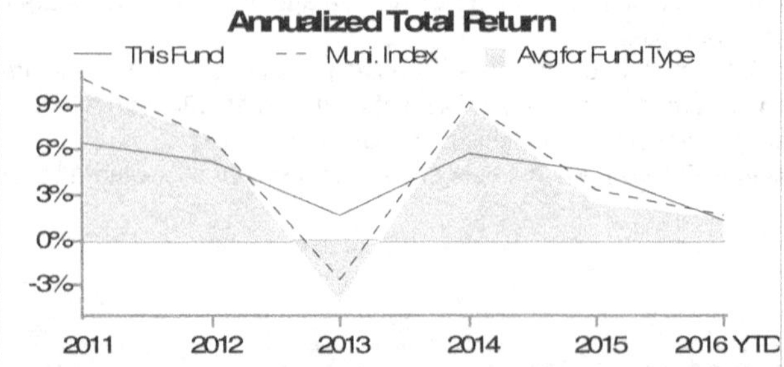

Columbia Act Ptf MMrg Core Pl Bd A (CMCPX) B- Good

Fund Family: Columbia Threadneedle Investments **Phone:** (800) 345-6611
Address: One Financial Center, Boston, MA 02111
Fund Type: COI - Corporate - Investment Grade
Major Rating Factors: A moderate risk profile coupled with stable earnings characterizes Columbia Act Ptf MMrg Core Pl Bd A which receives a TheStreet.com Investment Rating of B- (Good). Volatility, as measured by standard deviation, is considered low for fixed income funds at 2.85. Another risk factor is the fund's below average duration of 4.9 years (i.e. lower interest rate risk). The fund's risk rating is currently B- (Good).

The fund's performance rating is currently C+ (Fair). It has registered an average return of 1.76% over the last three years and is up 2.59% over the last three months. Factored into the performance evaluation is an expense ratio of 0.81% (low).

Brian Lavin has been running the fund for 4 years and currently receives a manager quality ranking of 59 (0=worst, 99=best). If you desire stability with a moderate level of risk then this fund is an excellent option.
Services Offered: Automated phone transactions, bank draft capabilities, an IRA investment plan, a 401K investment plan and wire transfers.

Data Date	Investment Rating	Net Assets ($Mil)	NAV	Performance Rating/Pts	Total Return Y-T-D	Risk Rating/Pts
3-16	B-	5,507	10.13	C+ / 6.0	2.59%	B- / 7.1
2015	C	5,217	9.92	C / 5.2	-0.36%	B- / 7.0
2014	U	4,546	10.17	U / --	5.17%	U / --
2013	U	4,115	9.88	U / --	-1.72%	U / --
2012	U	4,966	10.27	U / --	0.00%	U / --

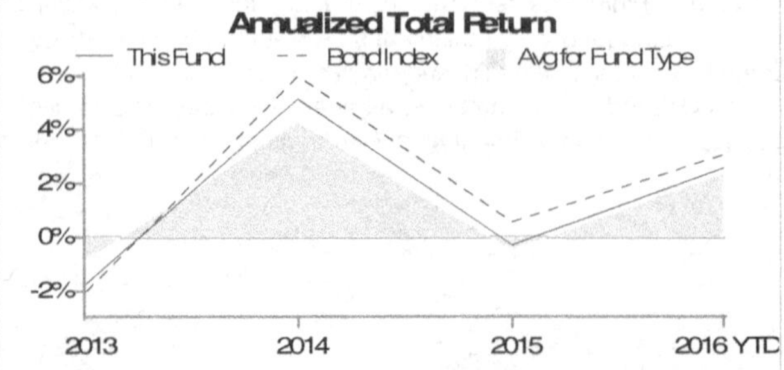

Columbia AMT-Free Tax-Exempt Bond A (INTAX) B Good

Fund Family: Columbia Threadneedle Investments **Phone:** (800) 345-6611
Address: One Financial Center, Boston, MA 02111
Fund Type: MUN - Municipal - National
Major Rating Factors: Exceptional performance is the major factor driving the B (Good) TheStreet.com Investment Rating for Columbia AMT-Free Tax-Exempt Bond A. The fund currently has a performance rating of A (Excellent) based on an average return of 4.32% over the last three years (7.15% taxable equivalent) and 1.45% over the last three months (2.40% taxable equivalent). Factored into the performance evaluation is an expense ratio of 0.83% (low) and a 3.0% front-end load that is levied at the time of purchase.

The fund's risk rating is currently C- (Fair). Volatility, as measured by standard deviation, is considered average for fixed income funds at 4.06. Another risk factor is the fund's above average duration of 7.4 years (i.e. higher interest rate risk).

Catherine M. Stienstra has been running the fund for 9 years and currently receives a manager quality ranking of 70 (0=worst, 99=best). If you desire an average level of risk and strong performance, then this fund is a good option.
Services Offered: Automated phone transactions, payroll deductions, bank draft capabilities, an IRA investment plan, a 401K investment plan, a Keogh investment plan, wire transfers and a systematic withdrawal plan.

Data Date	Investment Rating	Net Assets ($Mil)	NAV	Performance Rating/Pts	Total Return Y-T-D	Risk Rating/Pts
3-16	B	611	4.09	A / 9.4	1.45%	C- / 3.5
2015	B	592	4.07	A / 9.4	3.95%	C- / 3.2
2014	B+	559	4.09	A / 9.3	12.26%	D+ / 2.9
2013	C+	520	3.80	B- / 7.5	-3.64%	C- / 3.1
2012	B	632	4.11	B+ / 8.3	10.73%	D+ / 2.9
2011	C+	593	3.87	B- / 7.2	11.19%	C- / 3.5

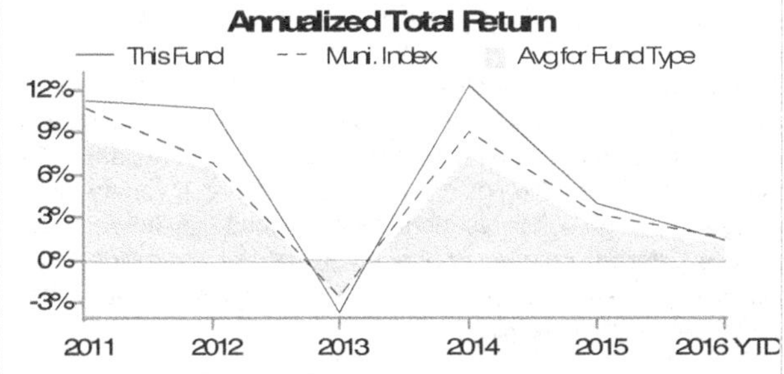

Columbia CMG Ultra Short Term Bond (CMGUX) C+ Fair

Fund Family: Columbia Threadneedle Investments **Phone:** (800) 345-6611
Address: One Financial Center, Boston, MA 02111
Fund Type: GEI - General - Investment Grade
Major Rating Factors: A moderate risk profile coupled with stable earnings characterizes Columbia CMG Ultra Short Term Bond which receives a TheStreet.com Investment Rating of C+ (Fair). Volatility, as measured by standard deviation, is considered very low for fixed income funds at 0.26. Another risk factor is the fund's very low average duration of 0.5 years (i.e. low interest rate risk). The fund's risk rating is currently A+ (Excellent).

The fund's performance rating is currently C- (Fair). It has registered an average return of 0.46% over the last three years and is up 0.41% over the last three months. Factored into the performance evaluation is an expense ratio of 0.26% (very low).

Leonard A. Aplet has been running the fund for 4 years and currently receives a manager quality ranking of 77 (0=worst, 99=best). If you desire stability with a moderate level of risk then this fund is an excellent option.
Services Offered: Automated phone transactions and bank draft capabilities.

Data Date	Investment Rating	Net Assets ($Mil)	NAV	Performance Rating/Pts	Total Return Y-T-D	Risk Rating/Pts
3-16	C+	1,463	9.00	C- / 3.3	0.41%	A+ / 9.9
2015	B	1,446	8.98	C / 4.3	0.30%	A+ / 9.9
2014	C	1,687	8.99	D / 1.6	0.36%	A+ / 9.9
2013	C	1,952	8.99	D- / 1.5	0.35%	A+ / 9.9
2012	C-	1,491	9.01	E+ / 0.6	1.38%	A+ / 9.9
2011	C-	931	8.97	D- / 1.4	0.78%	A+ / 9.9

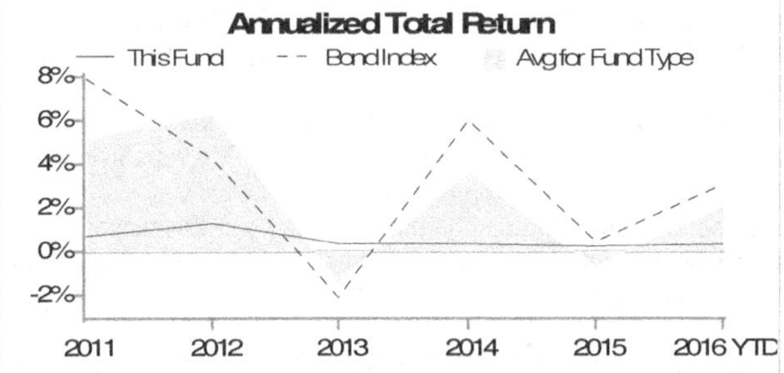

Columbia High Yield Bond A (INEAX) D Weak

Fund Family: Columbia Threadneedle Investments **Phone:** (800) 345-6611
Address: One Financial Center, Boston, MA 02111
Fund Type: COH - Corporate - High Yield
Major Rating Factors: Columbia High Yield Bond A has adopted a very risky asset allocation strategy and currently receives an overall TheStreet.com Investment Rating of D (Weak). Volatility, as measured by standard deviation, is considered above average for fixed income funds at 5.35. Another risk factor is the fund's below average duration of 4.2 years (i.e. lower interest rate risk). Unfortunately, the high level of risk (D, Weak) has only provided investors with average performance.

The fund's performance rating is currently C (Fair). It has registered an average return of 2.77% over the last three years and is up 2.75% over the last three months. Factored into the performance evaluation is an expense ratio of 1.07% (average) and a 4.8% front-end load that is levied at the time of purchase.

Brian J. Lavin has been running the fund for 6 years and currently receives a manager quality ranking of 92 (0=worst, 99=best). If you are comfortable owning a very high risk investment, then this fund may be an option.
Services Offered: Automated phone transactions, payroll deductions, bank draft capabilities, an IRA investment plan, a 401K investment plan and a systematic withdrawal plan.

Data Date	Investment Rating	Net Assets ($Mil)	NAV	Performance Rating/Pts	Total Return Y-T-D	Risk Rating/Pts
3-16	D	1,151	2.80	C / 5.0	2.75%	D / 1.8
2015	D	1,084	2.76	C / 4.7	-1.53%	D / 1.7
2014	C-	1,195	2.94	B / 7.6	3.68%	D / 1.9
2013	C	1,341	2.98	A- / 9.1	5.90%	E+ / 0.9
2012	C-	1,285	2.97	B+ / 8.3	15.61%	E+ / 0.8
2011	C	1,163	2.73	A- / 9.2	5.10%	E+ / 0.6

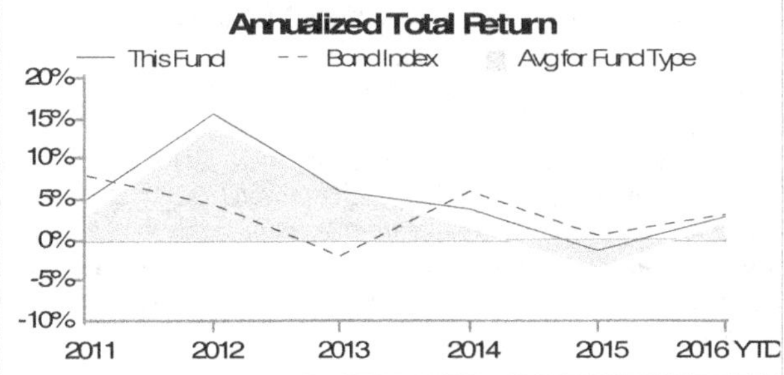

Columbia Income Opportunities A (AIOAX) D Weak

Fund Family: Columbia Threadneedle Investments **Phone:** (800) 345-6611
Address: One Financial Center, Boston, MA 02111
Fund Type: COH - Corporate - High Yield
Major Rating Factors: Columbia Income Opportunities A has adopted a very risky asset allocation strategy and currently receives an overall TheStreet.com Investment Rating of D (Weak). Volatility, as measured by standard deviation, is considered above average for fixed income funds at 5.50. Another risk factor is the fund's below average duration of 4.6 years (i.e. lower interest rate risk). Unfortunately, the high level of risk (D, Weak) has only provided investors with average performance.

The fund's performance rating is currently C (Fair). It has registered an average return of 2.64% over the last three years and is up 2.53% over the last three months. Factored into the performance evaluation is an expense ratio of 1.11% (average) and a 4.8% front-end load that is levied at the time of purchase.

Brian J. Lavin has been running the fund for 13 years and currently receives a manager quality ranking of 90 (0=worst, 99=best). If you are comfortable owning a very high risk investment, then this fund may be an option.

Services Offered: Automated phone transactions, payroll deductions, bank draft capabilities, an IRA investment plan, a 401K investment plan, wire transfers and a systematic withdrawal plan.

Data Date	Investment Rating	Net Assets ($Mil)	NAV	Performance Rating/Pts	Total Return Y-T-D	Risk Rating/Pts
3-16	D	1,482	9.41	C / 4.8	2.53%	D / 1.6
2015	D	1,376	9.29	C / 4.4	-1.15%	D- / 1.4
2014	D	1,636	9.90	C+ / 6.9	3.69%	D / 1.9
2013	C	1,508	10.02	B+ / 8.8	4.65%	D- / 1.4
2012	C	983	10.06	B / 8.0	14.11%	D- / 1.3
2011	C+	765	9.31	B+ / 8.6	6.15%	D / 1.6

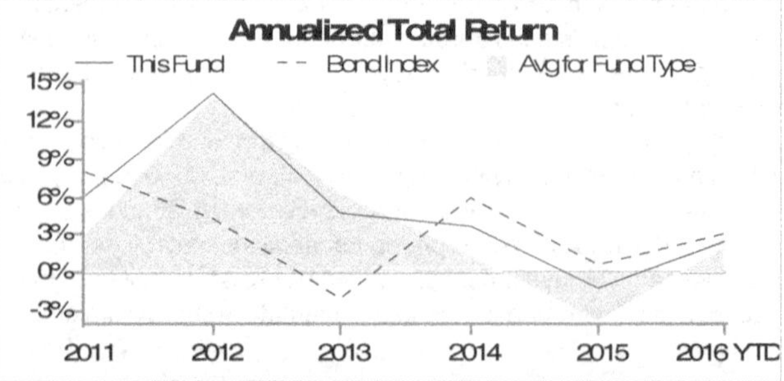

Columbia Strategic Income A (COSIX) D Weak

Fund Family: Columbia Threadneedle Investments **Phone:** (800) 345-6611
Address: One Financial Center, Boston, MA 02111
Fund Type: GES - General - Short & Inter. Term
Major Rating Factors: Columbia Strategic Income A receives a TheStreet.com Investment Rating of D (Weak). The fund has a performance rating of C- (Fair) based on an average return of 1.82% over the last three years and 2.22% over the last three months. Factored into the performance evaluation is an expense ratio of 1.05% (average) and a 4.8% front-end load that is levied at the time of purchase.

The fund's risk rating is currently C- (Fair). Volatility, as measured by standard deviation, is considered average for fixed income funds at 4.46. Another risk factor is the fund's very low average duration of 2.6 years (i.e. low interest rate risk).

Brian J. Lavin has been running the fund for 6 years and currently receives a manager quality ranking of 77 (0=worst, 99=best). If you desire an average level of risk, then this fund may be an option.

Services Offered: Automated phone transactions, check writing, payroll deductions, bank draft capabilities, an IRA investment plan and a systematic withdrawal plan.

Data Date	Investment Rating	Net Assets ($Mil)	NAV	Performance Rating/Pts	Total Return Y-T-D	Risk Rating/Pts
3-16	D	1,546	5.73	C- / 3.7	2.22%	C- / 3.3
2015	D	1,488	5.66	D+ / 2.7	0.24%	C- / 3.7
2014	D-	1,257	5.88	C / 4.4	3.67%	C- / 3.2
2013	C-	1,271	6.00	C+ / 6.3	0.07%	C- / 3.1
2012	D	1,508	6.42	C+ / 6.3	11.60%	D+ / 2.5
2011	D-	1,285	6.03	C / 5.0	6.11%	C- / 3.8

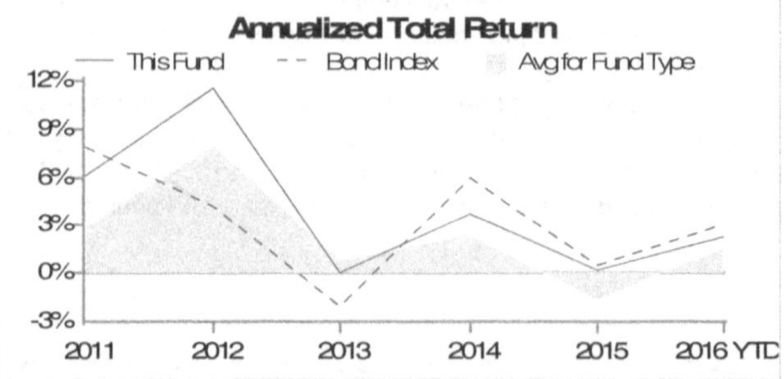

Columbia Tax-Exempt A (COLTX) B+ Good

Fund Family: Columbia Threadneedle Investments **Phone:** (800) 345-6611
Address: One Financial Center, Boston, MA 02111
Fund Type: MUN - Municipal - National
Major Rating Factors: Strong performance is the major factor driving the B+ (Good) TheStreet.com Investment Rating for Columbia Tax-Exempt A. The fund currently has a performance rating of B+ (Good) based on an average return of 3.75% over the last three years (6.21% taxable equivalent) and 1.05% over the last three months (1.74% taxable equivalent). Factored into the performance evaluation is an expense ratio of 0.76% (low) and a 3.0% front-end load that is levied at the time of purchase.

The fund's risk rating is currently C (Fair). Volatility, as measured by standard deviation, is considered average for fixed income funds at 3.76. Another risk factor is the fund's fairly average duration of 6.9 years (i.e. average interest rate risk).

Kimberly A. Campbell has been running the fund for 14 years and currently receives a manager quality ranking of 56 (0=worst, 99=best). If you desire an average level of risk and strong performance, then this fund is a good option.

Services Offered: Automated phone transactions, check writing, payroll deductions, bank draft capabilities, an IRA investment plan and a systematic withdrawal plan.

Data Date	Investment Rating	Net Assets ($Mil)	NAV	Performance Rating/Pts	Total Return Y-T-D	Risk Rating/Pts
3-16	B+	3,274	14.00	B+ / 8.9	1.05%	C / 4.3
2015	B	3,263	13.99	A- / 9.1	3.56%	C- / 4.1
2014	A-	3,334	14.08	B+ / 8.7	11.00%	C- / 3.8
2013	C+	3,280	13.24	B- / 7.2	-3.41%	C- / 3.5
2012	C+	3,794	14.29	B / 7.6	8.99%	D+ / 2.8
2011	C	3,736	13.65	B- / 7.4	11.95%	C- / 3.0

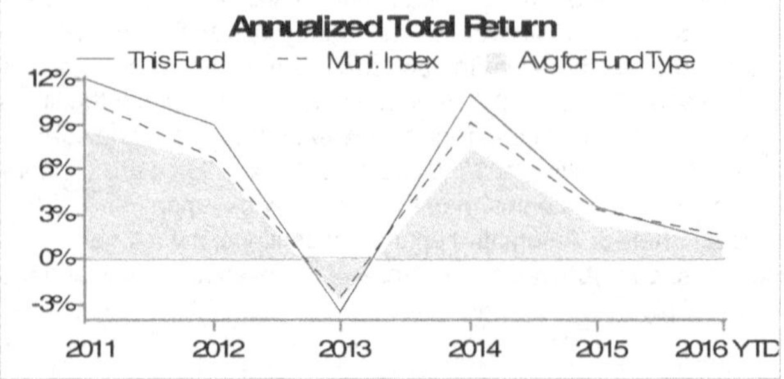

Columbia Total Return Bond A (LIBAX) C- Fair

Fund Family: Columbia Threadneedle Investments **Phone:** (800) 345-6611
Address: One Financial Center, Boston, MA 02111
Fund Type: COI - Corporate - Investment Grade
Major Rating Factors: Middle of the road best describes Columbia Total Return Bond A whose TheStreet.com Investment Rating is currently a C- (Fair). The fund has a performance rating of C (Fair) based on an average return of 1.74% over the last three years and 2.70% over the last three months. Factored into the performance evaluation is an expense ratio of 0.91% (average) and a 3.0% front-end load that is levied at the time of purchase.

The fund's risk rating is currently C+ (Fair). Volatility, as measured by standard deviation, is considered average for fixed income funds at 2.98. Another risk factor is the fund's fairly average duration of 5.4 years (i.e. average interest rate risk).

Carl W. Pappo has been running the fund for 11 years and currently receives a manager quality ranking of 55 (0=worst, 99=best). If you desire an average level of risk, then this fund may be an option.
Services Offered: Automated phone transactions, payroll deductions, bank draft capabilities, an IRA investment plan, a 401K investment plan, wire transfers and a systematic withdrawal plan.

Data Date	Investment Rating	Net Assets ($Mil)	NAV	Perfor-mance Rating/Pts	Total Return Y-T-D	Risk Rating/Pts
3-16	C-	1,107	9.11	C / 4.6	2.70%	C+/ 6.6
2015	C-	1,105	8.92	C- / 3.0	0.11%	C+/ 6.6
2014	C-	1,274	9.19	C- / 3.6	5.20%	C+/ 6.8
2013	C-	1,604	8.95	C- / 3.0	-2.55%	B- / 7.0
2012	C+	428	9.47	C- / 3.8	7.09%	B- / 7.0
2011	C+	249	9.28	C / 4.9	6.42%	C+/ 6.5

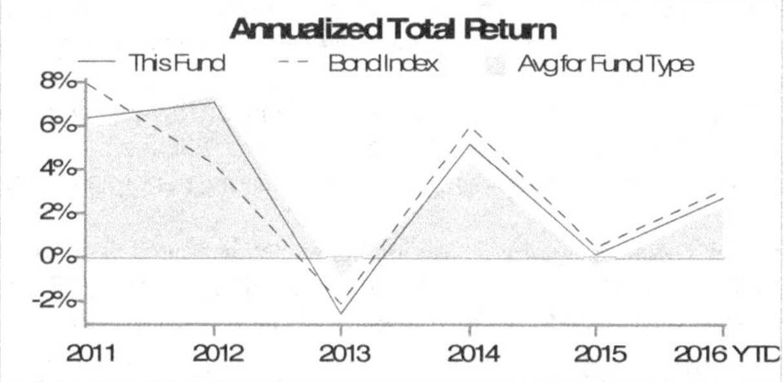

Columbia US Government Mortgage A (AUGAX) B- Good

Fund Family: Columbia Threadneedle Investments **Phone:** (800) 345-6611
Address: One Financial Center, Boston, MA 02111
Fund Type: USS - US Government - Short & Inter. Term
Major Rating Factors: A moderate risk profile coupled with stable earnings characterizes Columbia US Government Mortgage A which receives a TheStreet.com Investment Rating of B- (Good). Volatility, as measured by standard deviation, is considered low for fixed income funds at 1.87. Another risk factor is the fund's below average duration of 4.6 years (i.e. lower interest rate risk). The fund's risk rating is currently B+ (Good).

The fund's performance rating is currently C (Fair). It has registered an average return of 1.99% over the last three years and is up 1.28% over the last three months. Factored into the performance evaluation is an expense ratio of 0.97% (average) and a 3.0% front-end load that is levied at the time of purchase.

Jason J. Callan has been running the fund for 7 years and currently receives a manager quality ranking of 90 (0=worst, 99=best). If you desire stability with a moderate level of risk then this fund is an excellent option.
Services Offered: Automated phone transactions, payroll deductions, bank draft capabilities, an IRA investment plan, a 401K investment plan, a Keogh investment plan, wire transfers and a systematic withdrawal plan.

Data Date	Investment Rating	Net Assets ($Mil)	NAV	Perfor-mance Rating/Pts	Total Return Y-T-D	Risk Rating/Pts
3-16	B-	667	5.46	C / 4.7	1.28%	B+/ 8.6
2015	B	640	5.42	C / 5.2	1.07%	B+/ 8.6
2014	B-	568	5.52	C- / 3.8	5.51%	B+/ 8.4
2013	B	581	5.37	C- / 4.1	-1.54%	B+/ 8.4
2012	A	737	5.62	C / 4.7	6.95%	B+/ 8.6
2011	A+	568	5.52	C / 4.6	8.80%	B+/ 8.7

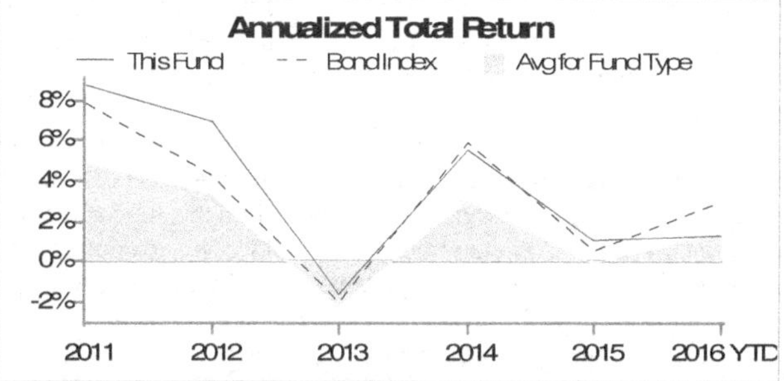

Commerce Bond (CFBNX) B+ Good

Fund Family: Commerce Funds **Phone:** (800) 995-6365
Address: PO Box 219525, Kansas, MO 64121
Fund Type: GEI - General - Investment Grade
Major Rating Factors: A moderate risk profile coupled with stable earnings characterizes Commerce Bond which receives a TheStreet.com Investment Rating of B+ (Good). Volatility, as measured by standard deviation, is considered low for fixed income funds at 2.72. Another risk factor is the fund's fairly average duration of 5.0 years (i.e. average interest rate risk). The fund's risk rating is currently B- (Good).

The fund's performance rating is currently C+ (Fair). It has registered an average return of 2.33% over the last three years and is up 2.38% over the last three months. Factored into the performance evaluation is an expense ratio of 0.68% (low).

Scott M. Colbert has been running the fund for 22 years and currently receives a manager quality ranking of 73 (0=worst, 99=best). If you desire stability with a moderate level of risk then this fund is an excellent option.
Services Offered: Automated phone transactions, payroll deductions, bank draft capabilities, an IRA investment plan, a 401K investment plan, a Keogh investment plan, wire transfers and a systematic withdrawal plan.

Data Date	Investment Rating	Net Assets ($Mil)	NAV	Perfor-mance Rating/Pts	Total Return Y-T-D	Risk Rating/Pts
3-16	B+	1,062	19.98	C+/ 6.7	2.38%	B- / 7.4
2015	B+	981	19.67	C+/ 6.6	0.11%	B- / 7.3
2014	A-	879	20.35	C+/ 5.8	5.86%	B- / 7.5
2013	A	779	20.01	C+/ 6.0	-0.56%	B / 8.1
2012	A+	784	20.95	C / 5.4	7.26%	B / 8.2
2011	A-	734	20.35	C / 4.5	6.80%	B+/ 8.3

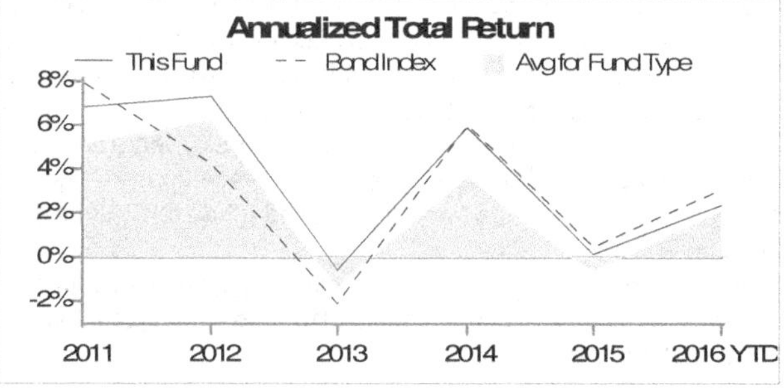

Delaware Diversified Income A (DPDFX) D Weak

Fund Family: Delaware Investments **Phone:** (800) 523-1918
Address: P.O. Box 219656, Kansas City, MO 64121
Fund Type: GES - General - Short & Inter. Term
Major Rating Factors: Disappointing performance is the major factor driving the D (Weak) TheStreet.com Investment Rating for Delaware Diversified Income A. The fund currently has a performance rating of D+ (Weak) based on an average return of 1.47% over the last three years and 2.30% over the last three months. Factored into the performance evaluation is an expense ratio of 0.90% (average) and a 4.5% front-end load that is levied at the time of purchase.

The fund's risk rating is currently C (Fair). Volatility, as measured by standard deviation, is considered average for fixed income funds at 3.60. Another risk factor is the fund's fairly average duration of 5.3 years (i.e. average interest rate risk).

Paul C. Grillo, Jr. has been running the fund for 15 years and currently receives a manager quality ranking of 23 (0=worst, 99=best). This fund offers an average level of risk, but investors looking for strong performance will be frustrated.
Services Offered: Automated phone transactions, payroll deductions, bank draft capabilities, an IRA investment plan, a 401K investment plan, a Keogh investment plan, wire transfers and a systematic withdrawal plan.

Data Date	Investment Rating	Net Assets ($Mil)	NAV	Performance Rating/Pts	Total Return Y-T-D	Risk Rating/Pts
3-16	D	1,500	8.71	D+ / 2.9	2.30%	C / 4.7
2015	D	1,568	8.57	D / 1.9	-1.15%	C / 4.7
2014	D	2,035	8.97	C- / 3.4	5.11%	C / 5.1
2013	D+	2,956	8.89	C- / 3.6	-1.37%	C+ / 5.6
2012	D+	4,750	9.35	C- / 3.4	6.86%	C+ / 6.0
2011	C	4,482	9.16	C+ / 5.8	6.39%	C / 4.9

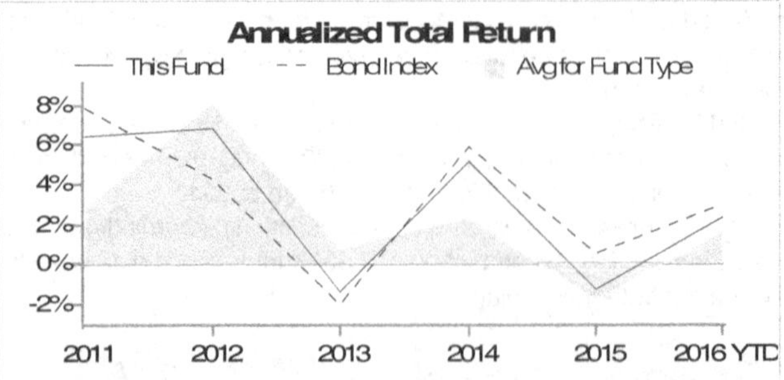

Deutsche CA Tax Free Inc A (KCTAX) B- Good

Fund Family: Deutsche Funds **Phone:** (800) 728-3337
Address: P.O. Box 219151, Kansas City, MO 64121
Fund Type: MUS - Municipal - Single State
Major Rating Factors: Strong performance is the major factor driving the B- (Good) TheStreet.com Investment Rating for Deutsche CA Tax Free Inc A. The fund currently has a performance rating of B+ (Good) based on an average return of 3.67% over the last three years (6.08% taxable equivalent) and 1.50% over the last three months (2.48% taxable equivalent). Factored into the performance evaluation is an expense ratio of 0.93% (average) and a 2.8% front-end load that is levied at the time of purchase.

The fund's risk rating is currently C- (Fair). Volatility, as measured by standard deviation, is considered average for fixed income funds at 4.21. Another risk factor is the fund's below average duration of 4.8 years (i.e. lower interest rate risk).

Matthew J. Caggiano has been running the fund for 17 years and currently receives a manager quality ranking of 36 (0=worst, 99=best). If you desire an average level of risk and strong performance, then this fund is a good option.
Services Offered: Automated phone transactions, payroll deductions, bank draft capabilities, wire transfers and a systematic withdrawal plan.

Data Date	Investment Rating	Net Assets ($Mil)	NAV	Performance Rating/Pts	Total Return Y-T-D	Risk Rating/Pts
3-16	B-	546	7.77	B+ / 8.9	1.50%	C- / 3.6
2015	C+	533	7.72	A- / 9.0	2.68%	C- / 3.3
2014	B	522	7.80	A / 9.4	11.60%	D / 2.2
2013	C+	497	7.26	B / 8.1	-3.68%	D+ / 2.7
2012	B	560	7.84	B+ / 8.5	10.81%	D+ / 2.5
2011	C-	453	7.36	B- / 7.1	10.69%	D+ / 2.9

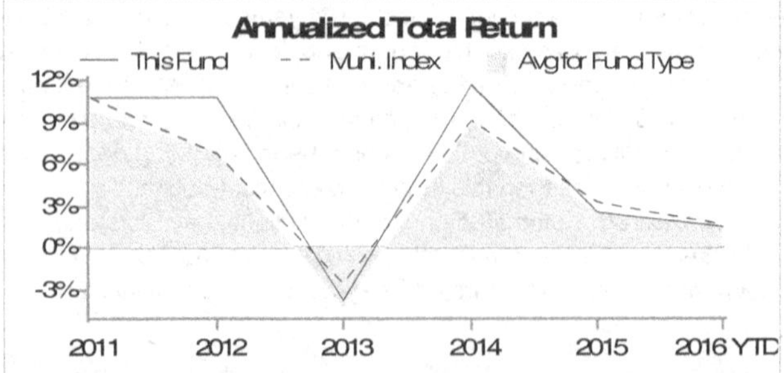

Deutsche High Income A (KHYAX) E+ Very Weak

Fund Family: Deutsche Funds **Phone:** (800) 728-3337
Address: P.O. Box 219151, Kansas City, MO 64121
Fund Type: COH - Corporate - High Yield
Major Rating Factors: Deutsche High Income A has adopted a very risky asset allocation strategy and currently receives an overall TheStreet.com Investment Rating of E+ (Very Weak). Volatility, as measured by standard deviation, is considered above average for fixed income funds at 5.35. Unfortunately, the high level of risk (D, Weak) failed to pay off as investors endured very poor performance.

The fund's performance rating is currently D- (Weak). It has registered an average return of 1.42% over the last three years and is up 1.74% over the last three months. Factored into the performance evaluation is an expense ratio of 0.94% (average), a 4.5% front-end load that is levied at the time of purchase and a 2.0% back-end load levied at the time of sale.

Gary A. Russell has been running the fund for 10 years and currently receives a manager quality ranking of 57 (0=worst, 99=best). If you can tolerate very high levels of risk in the hope of improved future returns, holding this fund may be an option.
Services Offered: Automated phone transactions, payroll deductions, bank draft capabilities, an IRA investment plan, a 401K investment plan and a systematic withdrawal plan.

Data Date	Investment Rating	Net Assets ($Mil)	NAV	Performance Rating/Pts	Total Return Y-T-D	Risk Rating/Pts
3-16	E+	802	4.39	D- / 1.1	1.74%	D / 1.8
2015	D-	820	4.37	D / 1.6	-3.47%	D / 1.6
2014	D	1,007	4.78	C+ / 6.2	1.90%	D / 2.0
2013	C	1,203	4.97	B+ / 8.9	7.04%	E+ / 0.9
2012	D	1,311	4.95	B / 7.7	14.73%	E+ / 0.7
2011	C-	1,236	4.63	B+ / 8.3	4.02%	D- / 1.2

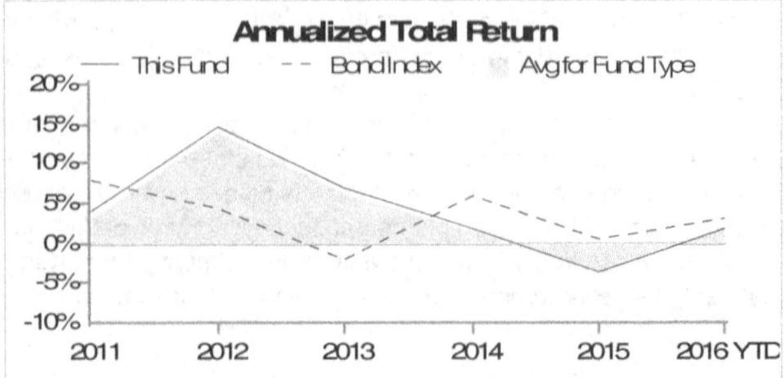

Deutsche Managed Municipal Bd A (SMLAX) B- Good

Fund Family: Deutsche Funds **Phone:** (800) 728-3337
Address: P.O. Box 219151, Kansas City, MO 64121
Fund Type: MUN - Municipal - National

Major Rating Factors: Strong performance is the major factor driving the B- (Good) TheStreet.com Investment Rating for Deutsche Managed Municipal Bd A. The fund currently has a performance rating of B+ (Good) based on an average return of 3.51% over the last three years (5.81% taxable equivalent) and 1.41% over the last three months (2.33% taxable equivalent). Factored into the performance evaluation is an expense ratio of 0.81% (low) and a 2.8% front-end load that is levied at the time of purchase.

The fund's risk rating is currently C- (Fair). Volatility, as measured by standard deviation, is considered average for fixed income funds at 4.17. Another risk factor is the fund's below average duration of 4.6 years (i.e. lower interest rate risk).

Ashton P. Goodfield has been running the fund for 28 years and currently receives a manager quality ranking of 33 (0=worst, 99=best). If you desire an average level of risk and strong performance, then this fund is a good option.

Services Offered: Automated phone transactions, check writing, payroll deductions, bank draft capabilities, an IRA investment plan, a 401K investment plan, wire transfers and a systematic withdrawal plan.

Data Date	Investment Rating	Net Assets ($Mil)	NAV	Perfor-mance Rating/Pts	Total Return Y-T-D	Risk Rating/Pts
3-16	B-	1,968	9.37	B+ / 8.8	1.41%	C- / 3.7
2015	C+	1,941	9.32	B+ / 8.9	2.94%	C- / 3.5
2014	B+	1,980	9.40	A- / 9.1	11.18%	D+ / 2.8
2013	C	1,901	8.80	C+ / 6.9	-3.94%	C- / 3.6
2012	B	2,363	9.53	B- / 7.5	9.52%	C- / 3.6
2011	C+	1,970	9.07	B- / 7.4	9.70%	C- / 3.3

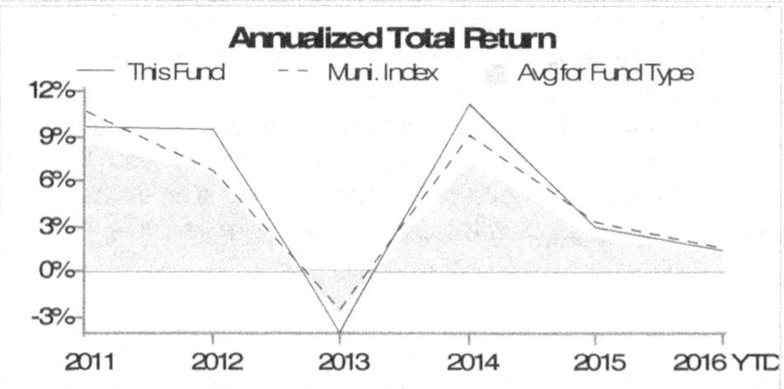

Deutsche Strategic Govt Sec A (KUSAX) C- Fair

Fund Family: Deutsche Funds **Phone:** (800) 728-3337
Address: P.O. Box 219151, Kansas City, MO 64121
Fund Type: USS - US Government - Short & Inter. Term

Major Rating Factors: A moderate risk profile coupled with stable earnings characterizes Deutsche Strategic Govt Sec A which receives a TheStreet.com Investment Rating of C- (Fair). Volatility, as measured by standard deviation, is considered low for fixed income funds at 2.86. Another risk factor is the fund's below average duration of 3.4 years (i.e. lower interest rate risk). The fund's risk rating is currently B- (Good).

The fund's performance rating is currently C- (Fair). It has registered an average return of 0.88% over the last three years and is up 1.38% over the last three months. Factored into the performance evaluation is an expense ratio of 0.81% (low) and a 2.8% front-end load that is levied at the time of purchase.

William J. Chepolis has been running the fund for 14 years and currently receives a manager quality ranking of 43 (0=worst, 99=best). If you desire stability with a moderate level of risk then this fund is an excellent option.

Services Offered: Automated phone transactions, payroll deductions, bank draft capabilities, an IRA investment plan, a 401K investment plan and a systematic withdrawal plan.

Data Date	Investment Rating	Net Assets ($Mil)	NAV	Perfor-mance Rating/Pts	Total Return Y-T-D	Risk Rating/Pts
3-16	C-	949	8.10	C- / 3.0	1.38%	B- / 7.0
2015	D+	956	8.04	D+ / 2.5	-0.04%	C+ / 6.6
2014	D-	1,089	8.30	D / 2.2	6.02%	C+ / 6.2
2013	D-	1,197	8.09	E+ / 0.8	-4.37%	B- / 7.2
2012	C-	1,571	8.79	D / 2.0	2.36%	B+ / 8.5
2011	C+	1,676	9.00	C- / 3.3	7.13%	B+ / 8.6

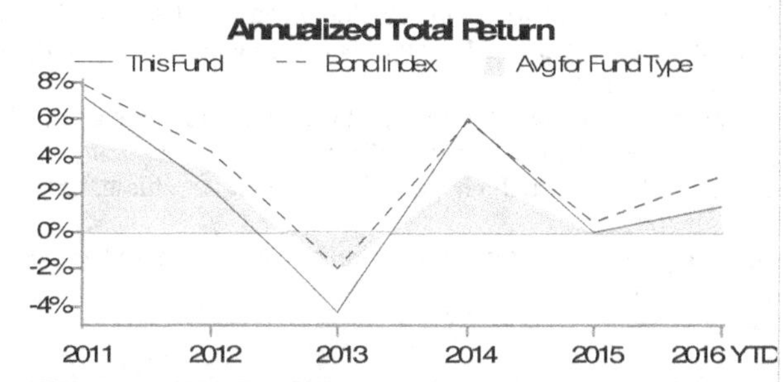

DFA CA Sht Trm Muni Bd Inst (DFCMX) A- Excellent

Fund Family: Dimensional Fund Advisors **Phone:** (800) 984-9472
Address: 6300 Bee Cave Road, Austin, TX 78746
Fund Type: MUS - Municipal - Single State

Major Rating Factors: A moderate risk profile coupled with stable earnings characterizes DFA CA Sht Trm Muni Bd Inst which receives a TheStreet.com Investment Rating of A- (Excellent). Volatility, as measured by standard deviation, is considered very low for fixed income funds at 0.93. Another risk factor is the fund's very low average duration of 2.6 years (i.e. low interest rate risk). The fund's risk rating is currently A (Excellent).

The fund's performance rating is currently C (Fair). It has registered an average return of 0.95% over the last three years (1.57% taxable equivalent) and is up 0.64% over the last three months (1.06% taxable equivalent). Factored into the performance evaluation is an expense ratio of 0.22% (very low).

David A. Plecha has been running the fund for 9 years and currently receives a manager quality ranking of 77 (0=worst, 99=best). If you desire stability with a moderate level of risk then this fund is an excellent option.

Services Offered: Automated phone transactions, bank draft capabilities and wire transfers.

Data Date	Investment Rating	Net Assets ($Mil)	NAV	Perfor-mance Rating/Pts	Total Return Y-T-D	Risk Rating/Pts
3-16	A-	816	10.35	C / 5.5	0.64%	A / 9.4
2015	A+	833	10.31	C+ / 6.5	1.02%	A / 9.4
2014	C+	724	10.29	D / 2.1	0.80%	A+ / 9.7
2013	B	547	10.29	C- / 3.4	0.65%	A+ / 9.6
2012	C-	403	10.31	D- / 1.0	0.94%	A / 9.4
2011	C	328	10.35	D / 2.1	2.68%	A / 9.4

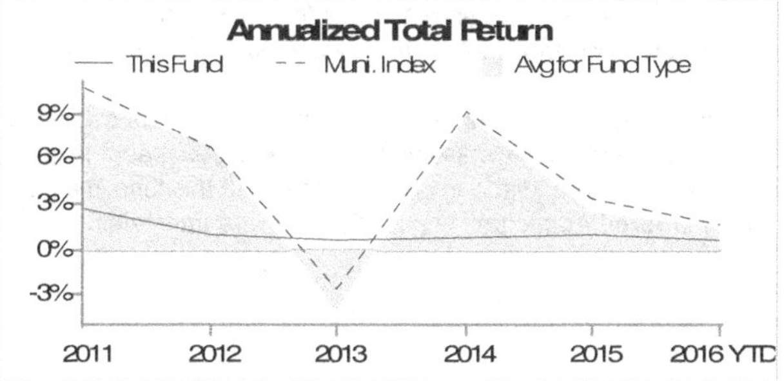

DFA Five Year Glbl Fixed Inc Inst (DFGBX) A- Excellent

Fund Family: Dimensional Fund Advisors **Phone:** (800) 984-9472
Address: 6300 Bee Cave Road, Austin, TX 78746
Fund Type: GL - Global
Major Rating Factors: A moderate risk profile coupled with stable earnings characterizes DFA Five Year Glbl Fixed Inc Inst which receives a TheStreet.com Investment Rating of A- (Excellent). Volatility, as measured by standard deviation, is considered low for fixed income funds at 2.25. Another risk factor is the fund's below average duration of 3.7 years (i.e. lower interest rate risk). The fund's risk rating is currently B (Good).

The fund's performance rating is currently C+ (Fair). It has registered an average return of 1.95% over the last three years and is up 2.32% over the last three months. Factored into the performance evaluation is an expense ratio of 0.27% (very low).

David A. Plecha has been running the fund for 17 years and currently receives a manager quality ranking of 96 (0=worst, 99=best). If you desire stability with a moderate level of risk then this fund is an excellent option.
Services Offered: Bank draft capabilities and wire transfers.

Data Date	Investment Rating	Net Assets ($Mil)	NAV	Perfor-mance Rating/Pts	Total Return Y-T-D	Risk Rating/Pts
3-16	A-	11,737	11.11	C+/ 6.5	2.32%	B / 8.2
2015	B+	11,298	10.90	C+/ 6.4	1.45%	B / 8.1
2014	C+	10,019	10.93	C- / 3.5	2.87%	B+/ 8.3
2013	B-	7,954	10.84	C- / 4.0	-0.41%	B / 8.1
2012	C-	6,477	11.15	D+/ 2.6	4.80%	B- / 7.4
2011	C-	5,180	10.91	D+/ 2.3	4.51%	B+/ 8.3

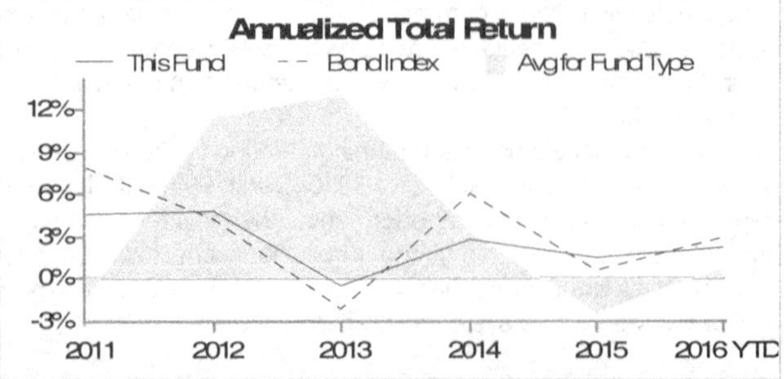

DFA Infltn Protected Sec Port Inst (DIPSX) D- Weak

Fund Family: Dimensional Fund Advisors **Phone:** (800) 984-9472
Address: 6300 Bee Cave Road, Austin, TX 78746
Fund Type: US - US Treasury
Major Rating Factors: DFA Infltn Protected Sec Port Inst has adopted a very risky asset allocation strategy and currently receives an overall TheStreet.com Investment Rating of D- (Weak). Volatility, as measured by standard deviation, is considered above average for fixed income funds at 6.03. Unfortunately, the high level of risk (D-, Weak) failed to pay off as investors endured very poor performance.

The fund's performance rating is currently D+ (Weak). It has registered an average return of -0.84% over the last three years and is up 5.01% over the last three months. Factored into the performance evaluation is an expense ratio of 0.12% (very low).

David A. Plecha has been running the fund for 10 years and currently receives a manager quality ranking of 5 (0=worst, 99=best). If you can tolerate very high levels of risk in the hope of improved future returns, holding this fund may be an option.
Services Offered: Automated phone transactions and wire transfers.

Data Date	Investment Rating	Net Assets ($Mil)	NAV	Perfor-mance Rating/Pts	Total Return Y-T-D	Risk Rating/Pts
3-16	D-	3,272	11.95	D+/ 2.8	5.01%	D- / 1.3
2015	E+	3,065	11.38	D- / 1.0	-1.22%	D- / 1.2
2014	E	2,737	11.60	D- / 1.4	3.36%	D- / 1.2
2013	E+	2,401	11.46	D+/ 2.8	-9.27%	D / 2.0
2012	C	2,591	12.80	C+/ 6.9	7.45%	D+/ 2.9
2011	D+	1,934	12.23	C+/ 6.2	14.54%	C- / 3.1

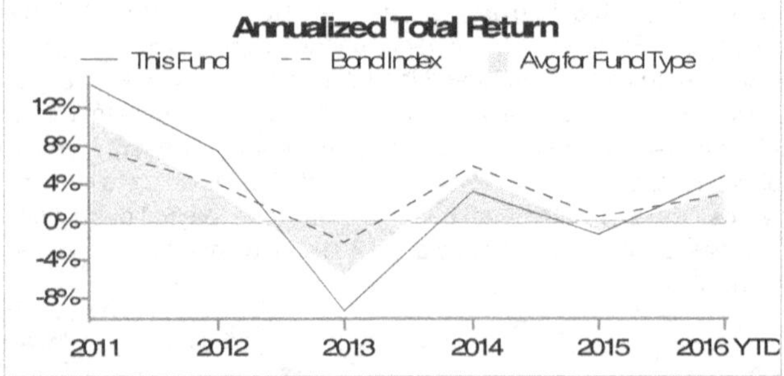

DFA Intmdt Govt Fx Inc Inst (DFIGX) C+ Fair

Fund Family: Dimensional Fund Advisors **Phone:** (800) 984-9472
Address: 6300 Bee Cave Road, Austin, TX 78746
Fund Type: USS - US Government - Short & Inter. Term
Major Rating Factors: Strong performance is the major factor driving the C+ (Fair) TheStreet.com Investment Rating for DFA Intmdt Govt Fx Inc Inst. The fund currently has a performance rating of B- (Good) based on an average return of 2.31% over the last three years and 3.71% over the last three months. Factored into the performance evaluation is an expense ratio of 0.12% (very low).

The fund's risk rating is currently C (Fair). Volatility, as measured by standard deviation, is considered average for fixed income funds at 3.73. Another risk factor is the fund's fairly average duration of 5.7 years (i.e. average interest rate risk).

David A. Plecha has been running the fund for 6 years and currently receives a manager quality ranking of 51 (0=worst, 99=best). If you desire an average level of risk and strong performance, then this fund is a good option.
Services Offered: Bank draft capabilities and wire transfers.

Data Date	Investment Rating	Net Assets ($Mil)	NAV	Perfor-mance Rating/Pts	Total Return Y-T-D	Risk Rating/Pts
3-16	C+	3,412	12.86	B- / 7.5	3.71%	C / 4.4
2015	C	3,359	12.46	C+/ 6.1	1.77%	C / 4.7
2014	D	4,099	12.55	C- / 3.3	5.18%	C+/ 5.7
2013	D	3,294	12.26	C- / 3.3	-3.52%	C+/ 5.7
2012	D	3,158	13.02	C- / 3.7	3.71%	C+/ 5.6
2011	D-	2,484	12.92	C- / 3.1	9.43%	C+/ 6.1

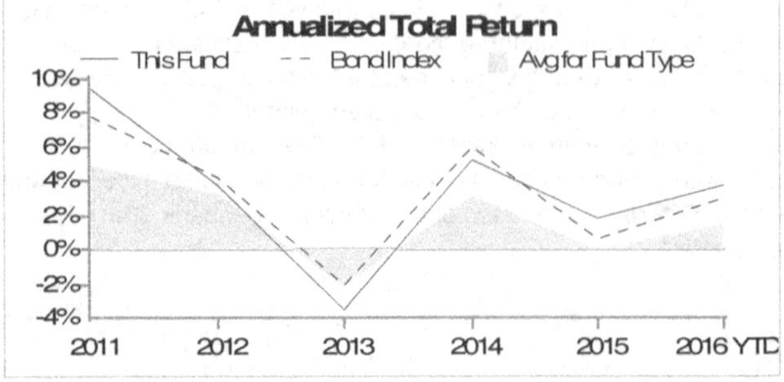

DFA Intmdt Term Municipal Bd Inst (DFTIX) B+ Good

Fund Family: Dimensional Fund Advisors **Phone:** (800) 984-9472
Address: 6300 Bee Cave Road, Austin, TX 78746
Fund Type: MUN - Municipal - National
Major Rating Factors: Strong performance is the major factor driving the B+ (Good) TheStreet.com Investment Rating for DFA Intmdt Term Municipal Bd Inst. The fund currently has a performance rating of B+ (Good) based on an average return of 2.32% over the last three years (3.84% taxable equivalent) and 1.19% over the last three months (1.97% taxable equivalent). Factored into the performance evaluation is an expense ratio of 0.23% (very low).

The fund's risk rating is currently C (Fair). Volatility, as measured by standard deviation, is considered average for fixed income funds at 3.35. Another risk factor is the fund's below average duration of 4.8 years (i.e. lower interest rate risk).

David A. Plecha currently receives a manager quality ranking of 29 (0=worst, 99=best). If you desire an average level of risk and strong performance, then this fund is a good option.
Services Offered: Automated phone transactions, bank draft capabilities and wire transfers.

Data Date	Investment Rating	Net Assets ($Mil)	NAV	Performance Rating/Pts	Total Return Y-T-D	Risk Rating/Pts
3-16	B+	1,086	10.26	B+ / 8.3	1.19%	C / 5.3
2015	B+	963	10.18	B+ / 8.4	2.60%	C / 5.1
2014	U	561	10.07	U / --	5.49%	U / --
2013	U	310	9.70	U / --	-2.05%	U / --
2012	U	101	10.01	U / --	0.00%	U / --

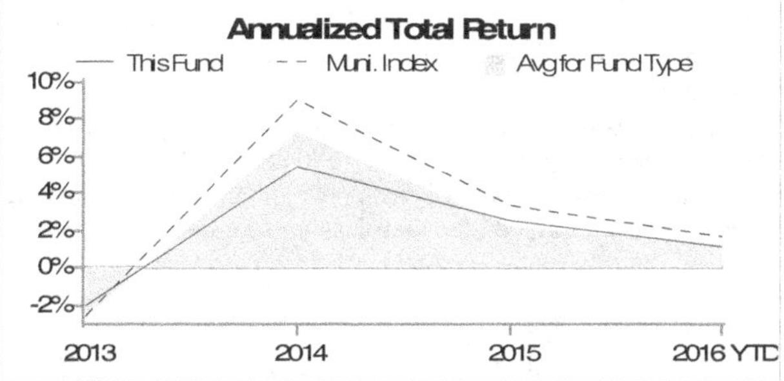

DFA Int-Term Extended Quality Inst (DFTEX) C Fair

Fund Family: Dimensional Fund Advisors **Phone:** (800) 984-9472
Address: 6300 Bee Cave Road, Austin, TX 78746
Fund Type: GL - Global
Major Rating Factors: DFA Int-Term Extended Quality Inst has adopted a risky asset allocation strategy and currently receives an overall TheStreet.com Investment Rating of C (Fair). Volatility, as measured by standard deviation, is considered above average for fixed income funds at 4.92. Another risk factor is the fund's fairly average duration of 6.9 years (i.e. average interest rate risk). The high level of risk (D+, Weak) did however, reward investors with excellent performance.

The fund's performance rating is currently B (Good). It has registered an average return of 3.05% over the last three years and is up 4.00% over the last three months. Factored into the performance evaluation is an expense ratio of 0.22% (very low).

David A. Plecha has been running the fund for 6 years and currently receives a manager quality ranking of 98 (0=worst, 99=best). If you are comfortable owning a high risk investment, this fund may be an option.
Services Offered: Automated phone transactions, bank draft capabilities and wire transfers.

Data Date	Investment Rating	Net Assets ($Mil)	NAV	Performance Rating/Pts	Total Return Y-T-D	Risk Rating/Pts
3-16	C	1,165	10.80	B / 8.0	4.00%	D+ / 2.8
2015	C-	1,094	10.46	C+ / 6.9	1.28%	D+ / 2.6
2014	C-	2,313	10.73	C+ / 6.1	8.07%	C- / 3.5
2013	D+	1,523	10.28	C / 5.3	-3.81%	C- / 4.0
2012	U	919	10.99	U / --	8.27%	U / --
2011	U	378	10.45	U / --	9.37%	U / --

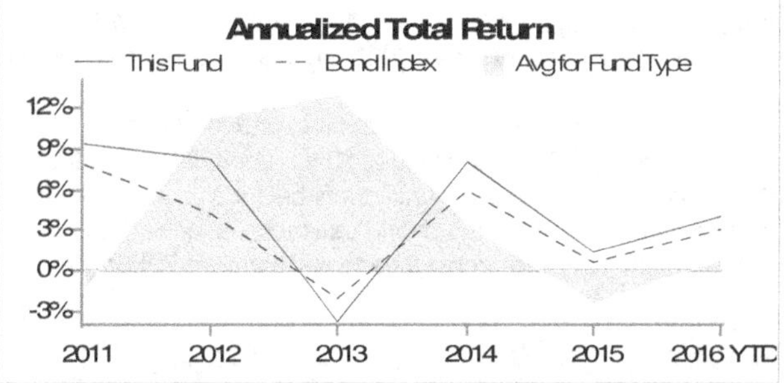

DFA Investment Grade Portfolio (DFAPX) C+ Fair

Fund Family: Dimensional Fund Advisors **Phone:** (800) 984-9472
Address: 6300 Bee Cave Road, Austin, TX 78746
Fund Type: GL - Global
Major Rating Factors: Strong performance is the major factor driving the C+ (Fair) TheStreet.com Investment Rating for DFA Investment Grade Portfolio. The fund currently has a performance rating of B (Good) based on an average return of 2.67% over the last three years and 3.36% over the last three months. Factored into the performance evaluation is an expense ratio of 0.22% (very low).

The fund's risk rating is currently C (Fair). Volatility, as measured by standard deviation, is considered average for fixed income funds at 3.79.

David A. Plecha has been running the fund for 5 years and currently receives a manager quality ranking of 98 (0=worst, 99=best). If you desire an average level of risk and strong performance, then this fund is a good option.
Services Offered: Automated phone transactions, bank draft capabilities, an IRA investment plan, a 401K investment plan and wire transfers.

Data Date	Investment Rating	Net Assets ($Mil)	NAV	Performance Rating/Pts	Total Return Y-T-D	Risk Rating/Pts
3-16	C+	4,807	10.94	B / 7.7	3.36%	C / 4.3
2015	C	4,368	10.64	C+ / 6.8	1.61%	C / 4.3
2014	D+	2,612	10.73	C / 4.5	6.23%	C / 5.4
2013	U	1,717	10.35	U / --	-2.87%	U / --
2012	U	991	10.90	U / --	5.31%	U / --
2011	U	278	10.60	U / --	0.00%	U / --

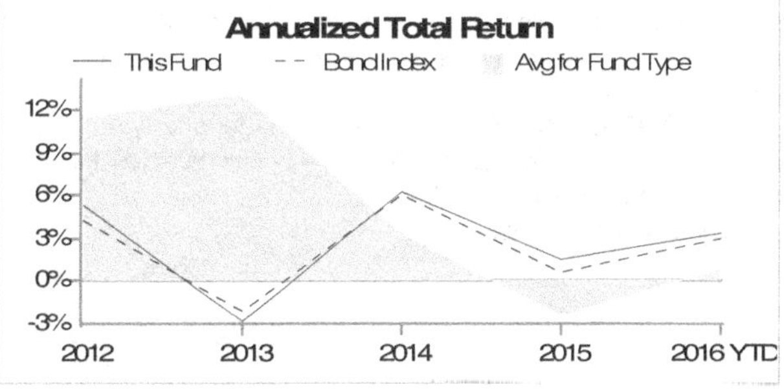

DFA One-Yr Fixed Inc Inst (DFIHX) C+ Fair

Fund Family: Dimensional Fund Advisors **Phone:** (800) 984-9472
Address: 6300 Bee Cave Road, Austin, TX 78746
Fund Type: GES - General - Short & Inter. Term
Major Rating Factors: A moderate risk profile coupled with stable earnings characterizes DFA One-Yr Fixed Inc Inst which receives a TheStreet.com Investment Rating of C+ (Fair). Volatility, as measured by standard deviation, is considered very low for fixed income funds at 0.29. Another risk factor is the fund's very low average duration of 1.0 years (i.e. low interest rate risk). The fund's risk rating is currently A+ (Excellent).

The fund's performance rating is currently C- (Fair). It has registered an average return of 0.40% over the last three years and is up 0.45% over the last three months. Factored into the performance evaluation is an expense ratio of 0.17% (very low).

David A. Plecha has been running the fund for 33 years and currently receives a manager quality ranking of 76 (0=worst, 99=best). If you desire stability with a moderate level of risk then this fund is an excellent option.
Services Offered: Bank draft capabilities and wire transfers.

Data Date	Investment Rating	Net Assets ($Mil)	NAV	Performance Rating/Pts	Total Return Y-T-D	Risk Rating/Pts
3-16	C+	7,350	10.31	C- / 3.2	0.45%	A+ / 9.9
2015	B	7,610	10.28	C- / 4.2	0.31%	A+ / 9.9
2014	C	8,750	10.30	D- / 1.4	0.26%	A+ / 9.9
2013	C	8,540	10.31	D- / 1.2	0.34%	A+ / 9.9
2012	C-	7,636	10.32	E+ / 0.6	0.93%	A+ / 9.9
2011	C-	7,086	10.30	D- / 1.2	0.59%	A+ / 9.9

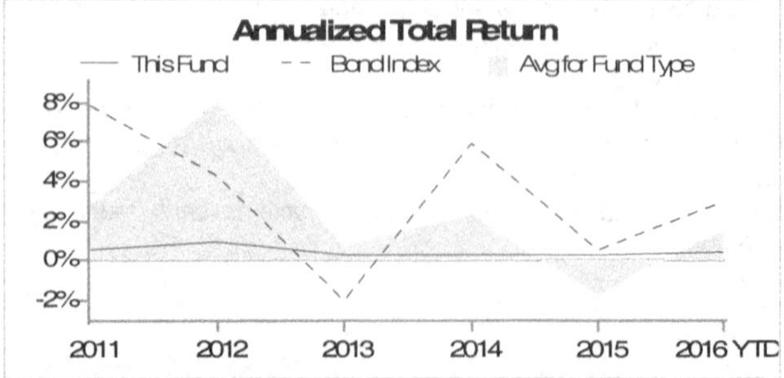

DFA S/T Extended Quality Port Inst (DFEQX) A- Excellent

Fund Family: Dimensional Fund Advisors **Phone:** (800) 984-9472
Address: 6300 Bee Cave Road, Austin, TX 78746
Fund Type: GL - Global
Major Rating Factors: A moderate risk profile coupled with stable earnings characterizes DFA S/T Extended Quality Port Inst which receives a TheStreet.com Investment Rating of A- (Excellent). Volatility, as measured by standard deviation, is considered low for fixed income funds at 1.52. Another risk factor is the fund's very low average duration of 2.8 years (i.e. low interest rate risk). The fund's risk rating is currently B+ (Good).

The fund's performance rating is currently C+ (Fair). It has registered an average return of 1.54% over the last three years and is up 1.74% over the last three months. Factored into the performance evaluation is an expense ratio of 0.22% (very low).

David J. Williams has been running the fund for 8 years and currently receives a manager quality ranking of 93 (0=worst, 99=best). If you desire stability with a moderate level of risk then this fund is an excellent option.
Services Offered: Automated phone transactions, bank draft capabilities, an IRA investment plan, wire transfers and a systematic withdrawal plan.

Data Date	Investment Rating	Net Assets ($Mil)	NAV	Performance Rating/Pts	Total Return Y-T-D	Risk Rating/Pts
3-16	A-	4,106	10.87	C+ / 5.7	1.74%	B+ / 8.9
2015	A-	3,943	10.73	C+ / 5.9	1.15%	B+ / 8.9
2014	C+	3,961	10.79	D+ / 2.8	1.68%	B+ / 8.9
2013	B-	2,628	10.78	C- / 3.4	0.41%	A- / 9.0
2012	C	2,049	10.91	D / 1.9	3.63%	B+ / 8.9
2011	U	1,367	10.75	U / --	2.93%	U / --

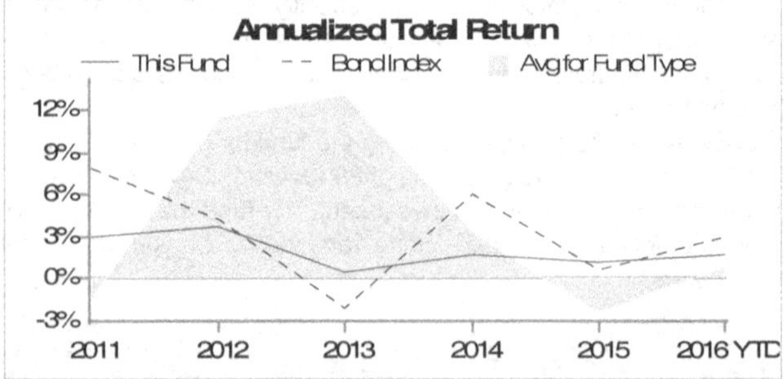

DFA Selectively Hedged Glb FI Ptf (DFSHX) D Weak

Fund Family: Dimensional Fund Advisors **Phone:** (800) 984-9472
Address: 6300 Bee Cave Road, Austin, TX 78746
Fund Type: GL - Global
Major Rating Factors: Disappointing performance is the major factor driving the D (Weak) TheStreet.com Investment Rating for DFA Selectively Hedged Glb FI Ptf. The fund currently has a performance rating of D (Weak) based on an average return of -0.97% over the last three years and 3.13% over the last three months. Factored into the performance evaluation is an expense ratio of 0.17% (very low).

The fund's risk rating is currently C- (Fair). Volatility, as measured by standard deviation, is considered average for fixed income funds at 4.11. Another risk factor is the fund's very low average duration of 2.8 years (i.e. low interest rate risk).

David A. Plecha currently receives a manager quality ranking of 31 (0=worst, 99=best). This fund offers an average level of risk, but investors looking for strong performance will be frustrated.

Services Offered: N/A

Data Date	Investment Rating	Net Assets ($Mil)	NAV	Performance Rating/Pts	Total Return Y-T-D	Risk Rating/Pts
3-16	D	942	9.56	D / 1.7	3.13%	C- / 3.8
2015	D	952	9.27	D- / 1.1	-3.17%	C- / 4.1
2014	E+	1,094	9.68	E+ / 0.7	-1.57%	C- / 3.6
2013	E+	956	9.99	D / 1.9	-1.11%	C- / 3.1
2012	E-	873	10.24	D / 1.7	4.22%	D+ / 2.4
2011	E	751	10.07	D / 2.2	0.85%	C- / 3.1

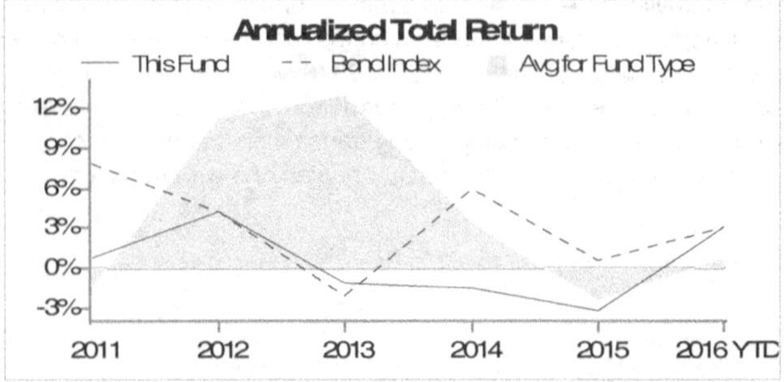

DFA Short Term Municipal Bd Inst (DFSMX) B+ Good

Fund Family: Dimensional Fund Advisors **Phone:** (800) 984-9472
Address: 6300 Bee Cave Road, Austin, TX 78746
Fund Type: MUN - Municipal - National
Major Rating Factors: A moderate risk profile coupled with stable earnings characterizes DFA Short Term Municipal Bd Inst which receives a TheStreet.com Investment Rating of B+ (Good). Volatility, as measured by standard deviation, is considered very low for fixed income funds at 0.96. Another risk factor is the fund's very low average duration of 2.6 years (i.e. low interest rate risk). The fund's risk rating is currently A (Excellent).

The fund's performance rating is currently C (Fair). It has registered an average return of 0.86% over the last three years (1.42% taxable equivalent) and is up 0.57% over the last three months (0.94% taxable equivalent). Factored into the performance evaluation is an expense ratio of 0.22% (very low).

David A. Plecha has been running the fund for 14 years and currently receives a manager quality ranking of 77 (0=worst, 99=best). If you desire stability with a moderate level of risk then this fund is an excellent option.
Services Offered: Automated phone transactions, bank draft capabilities and wire transfers.

Data Date	Investment Rating	Net Assets ($Mil)	NAV	Performance Rating/Pts	Total Return Y-T-D	Risk Rating/Pts
3-16	B+	2,192	10.23	C / 5.2	0.57%	A / 9.3
2015	A+	2,213	10.20	C+/ 6.4	1.15%	A / 9.4
2014	C	2,150	10.18	D / 1.8	0.57%	A+/ 9.7
2013	B-	1,842	10.21	D+/ 2.8	0.46%	A+/ 9.7
2012	C-	1,572	10.25	E+/ 0.9	0.73%	A / 9.5
2011	C	1,527	10.31	D / 1.9	2.38%	A / 9.5

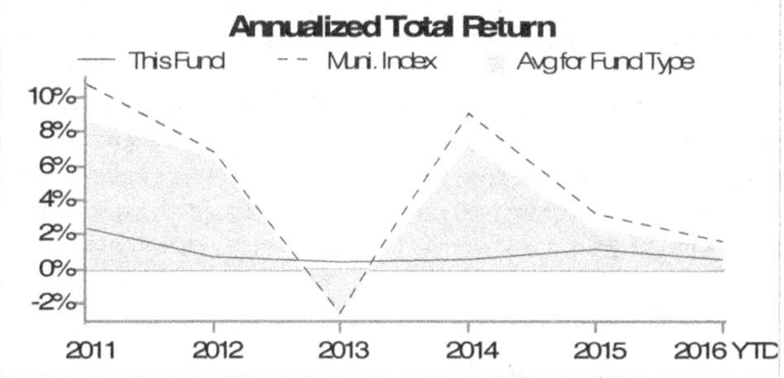

DFA Short-Term Government Inst (DFFGX) B Good

Fund Family: Dimensional Fund Advisors **Phone:** (800) 984-9472
Address: 6300 Bee Cave Road, Austin, TX 78746
Fund Type: USS - US Government - Short & Inter. Term
Major Rating Factors: A moderate risk profile coupled with stable earnings characterizes DFA Short-Term Government Inst which receives a TheStreet.com Investment Rating of B (Good). Volatility, as measured by standard deviation, is considered low for fixed income funds at 1.43. Another risk factor is the fund's very low average duration of 2.8 years (i.e. low interest rate risk). The fund's risk rating is currently B+ (Good).

The fund's performance rating is currently C (Fair). It has registered an average return of 1.11% over the last three years and is up 1.67% over the last three months. Factored into the performance evaluation is an expense ratio of 0.19% (very low).

David A. Plecha has been running the fund for 28 years and currently receives a manager quality ranking of 71 (0=worst, 99=best). If you desire stability with a moderate level of risk then this fund is an excellent option.
Services Offered: Bank draft capabilities and wire transfers.

Data Date	Investment Rating	Net Assets ($Mil)	NAV	Performance Rating/Pts	Total Return Y-T-D	Risk Rating/Pts
3-16	B	2,089	10.77	C / 4.9	1.67%	B+/ 8.9
2015	B	2,144	10.62	C / 4.9	0.99%	A- / 9.0
2014	C-	2,144	10.65	D / 1.8	1.25%	A- / 9.2
2013	C	1,807	10.62	D / 2.1	-0.45%	A- / 9.1
2012	C-	1,603	10.77	D- / 1.3	1.59%	A- / 9.1
2011	C-	1,358	10.79	D / 1.7	3.39%	A- / 9.0

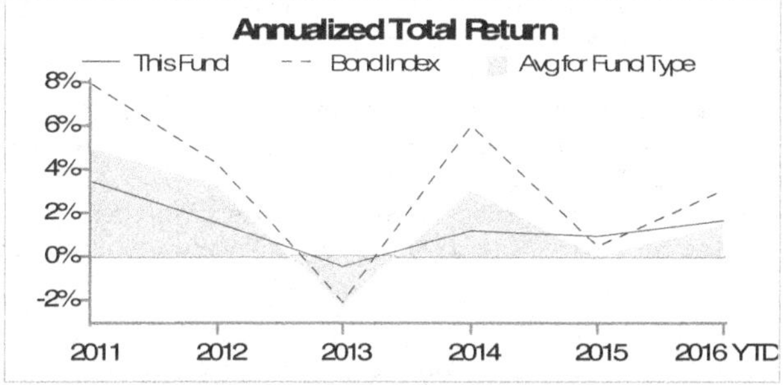

DFA Two Year Glbl Fixed Inc Inst (DFGFX) C+ Fair

Fund Family: Dimensional Fund Advisors **Phone:** (800) 984-9472
Address: 6300 Bee Cave Road, Austin, TX 78746
Fund Type: GL - Global
Major Rating Factors: A moderate risk profile coupled with stable earnings characterizes DFA Two Year Glbl Fixed Inc Inst which receives a TheStreet.com Investment Rating of C+ (Fair). Volatility, as measured by standard deviation, is considered very low for fixed income funds at 0.43. Another risk factor is the fund's very low average duration of 1.5 years (i.e. low interest rate risk). The fund's risk rating is currently A+ (Excellent).

The fund's performance rating is currently C- (Fair). It has registered an average return of 0.52% over the last three years and is up 0.61% over the last three months. Factored into the performance evaluation is an expense ratio of 0.18% (very low).

David A. Plecha has been running the fund for 17 years and currently receives a manager quality ranking of 83 (0=worst, 99=best). If you desire stability with a moderate level of risk then this fund is an excellent option.
Services Offered: Bank draft capabilities and wire transfers.

Data Date	Investment Rating	Net Assets ($Mil)	NAV	Performance Rating/Pts	Total Return Y-T-D	Risk Rating/Pts
3-16	C+	4,961	9.96	C- / 3.5	0.61%	A+/ 9.8
2015	B	5,310	9.93	C / 4.4	0.33%	A+/ 9.9
2014	C	6,153	9.90	D- / 1.5	0.38%	A+/ 9.9
2013	C	5,659	10.01	D- / 1.4	0.46%	A+/ 9.9
2012	C-	4,653	10.04	E+/ 0.6	1.03%	A+/ 9.9
2011	C-	4,723	10.08	D- / 1.3	0.78%	A+/ 9.9

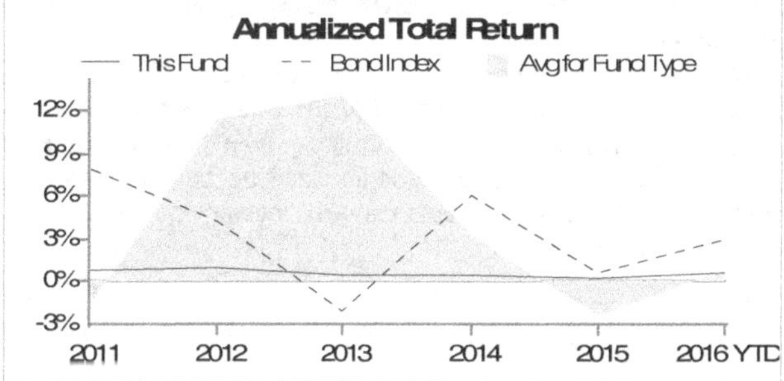

DFA World ex US Govt Fxd Inc Inst (DWFIX) C+ Fair

Fund Family: Dimensional Fund Advisors **Phone:** (800) 984-9472
Address: 6300 Bee Cave Road, Austin, TX 78746
Fund Type: GL - Global
Major Rating Factors: Exceptional performance is the major factor driving the C+ (Fair) TheStreet.com Investment Rating for DFA World ex US Govt Fxd Inc Inst. The fund currently has a performance rating of A- (Excellent) based on an average return of 4.77% over the last three years and 4.43% over the last three months. Factored into the performance evaluation is an expense ratio of 0.22% (very low).

The fund's risk rating is currently C- (Fair). Volatility, as measured by standard deviation, is considered average for fixed income funds at 4.37. Another risk factor is the fund's above average duration of 8.2 years (i.e. higher interest rate risk).

David A. Plecha has been running the fund for 5 years and currently receives a manager quality ranking of 99 (0=worst, 99=best). If you desire an average level of risk and strong performance, then this fund is a good option.
Services Offered: Automated phone transactions, bank draft capabilities, an IRA investment plan, a 401K investment plan and wire transfers.

Data Date	Investment Rating	Net Assets ($Mil)	NAV	Performance Rating/Pts	Total Return Y-T-D	Risk Rating/Pts
3-16	C+	636	10.14	A- / 9.0	4.43%	C- / 3.1
2015	C	565	9.71	B / 8.2	0.85%	D+ / 2.8
2014	A-	385	10.34	B / 8.1	12.28%	C / 4.5
2013	U	262	10.03	U / --	-2.16%	U / --
2012	U	164	10.44	U / --	6.69%	U / --

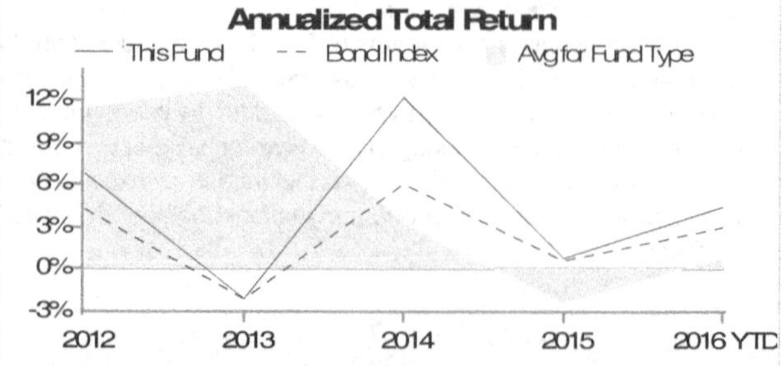

Dodge & Cox Income Fund (DODIX) B+ Good

Fund Family: Dodge & Cox **Phone:** (800) 621-3979
Address: 555 California Street, San Francisco, CA 94104
Fund Type: GEI - General - Investment Grade
Major Rating Factors: A moderate risk profile coupled with stable earnings characterizes Dodge & Cox Income Fund which receives a TheStreet.com Investment Rating of B+ (Good). Volatility, as measured by standard deviation, is considered low for fixed income funds at 2.75. Another risk factor is the fund's below average duration of 4.0 years (i.e. lower interest rate risk). The fund's risk rating is currently B- (Good).

The fund's performance rating is currently C+ (Fair). It has registered an average return of 2.42% over the last three years and is up 2.37% over the last three months. Factored into the performance evaluation is an expense ratio of 0.44% (very low).

Charles F. Pohl currently receives a manager quality ranking of 85 (0=worst, 99=best). If you desire stability with a moderate level of risk then this fund is an excellent option.
Services Offered: Automated phone transactions, payroll deductions, bank draft capabilities, an IRA investment plan and a systematic withdrawal plan.

Data Date	Investment Rating	Net Assets ($Mil)	NAV	Performance Rating/Pts	Total Return Y-T-D	Risk Rating/Pts
3-16	B+	43,341	13.47	C+ / 6.9	2.37%	B- / 7.4
2015	B+	43,898	13.29	C+ / 6.6	-0.59%	B / 7.7
2014	A	39,128	13.78	C+ / 6.2	5.48%	B- / 7.5
2013	A	24,599	13.53	C+ / 6.4	0.64%	B- / 7.5
2012	B	26,539	13.86	C / 4.4	7.94%	B / 7.6
2011	C+	23,698	13.30	C / 4.4	4.76%	C+ / 6.9

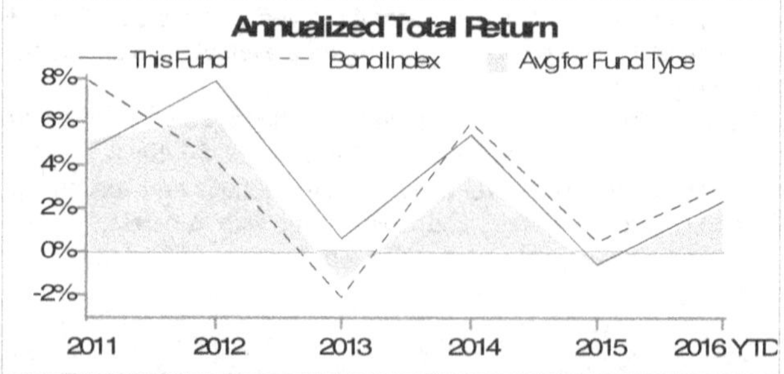

DoubleLine Core Fixed Income N (DLFNX) B Good

Fund Family: DoubleLine Funds **Phone:** (877) 354-6311
Address: C/O US Bancorp Fund Services L, Milwaukee, WI 53201
Fund Type: GL - Global
Major Rating Factors: Strong performance is the major factor driving the B (Good) TheStreet.com Investment Rating for DoubleLine Core Fixed Income N. The fund currently has a performance rating of B- (Good) based on an average return of 2.52% over the last three years and 2.49% over the last three months. Factored into the performance evaluation is an expense ratio of 0.75% (low).

The fund's risk rating is currently C+ (Fair). Volatility, as measured by standard deviation, is considered average for fixed income funds at 3.11. Another risk factor is the fund's below average duration of 4.7 years (i.e. lower interest rate risk).

Jeffrey E. Gundlach has been running the fund for 6 years and currently receives a manager quality ranking of 97 (0=worst, 99=best). If you desire an average level of risk and strong performance, then this fund is a good option.
Services Offered: Automated phone transactions, payroll deductions, bank draft capabilities, an IRA investment plan, a 401K investment plan, wire transfers and a systematic withdrawal plan.

Data Date	Investment Rating	Net Assets ($Mil)	NAV	Performance Rating/Pts	Total Return Y-T-D	Risk Rating/Pts
3-16	B	950	10.86	B- / 7.0	2.49%	C+ / 6.1
2015	C+	845	10.67	C+ / 6.7	0.39%	C+ / 5.9
2014	B	511	10.98	C+ / 6.1	6.60%	C+ / 6.2
2013	A	388	10.70	B- / 7.2	-1.36%	C+ / 6.4
2012	U	795	11.33	U / --	7.89%	U / --
2011	U	413	10.95	U / --	11.12%	U / --

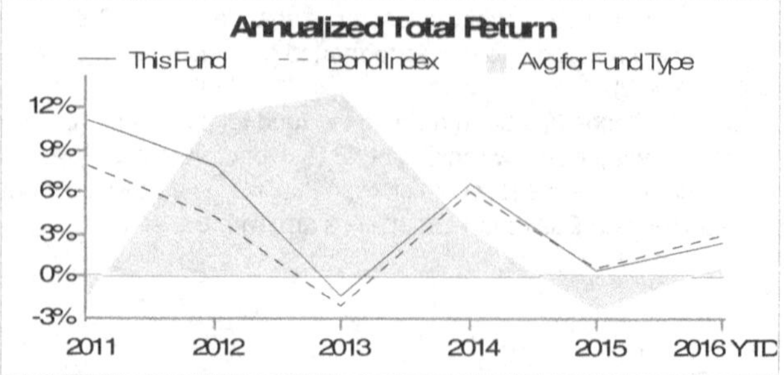

DoubleLine Low Duration Bond N (DLSNX) B+ Good

Fund Family: DoubleLine Funds **Phone:** (877) 354-6311
Address: C/O US Bancorp Fund Services L, Milwaukee, WI 53201
Fund Type: COI - Corporate - Investment Grade
Major Rating Factors: A moderate risk profile coupled with stable earnings characterizes DoubleLine Low Duration Bond N which receives a TheStreet.com Investment Rating of B+ (Good). Volatility, as measured by standard deviation, is considered very low for fixed income funds at 0.80. Another risk factor is the fund's very low average duration of 1.1 years (i.e. low interest rate risk). The fund's risk rating is currently A (Excellent).

The fund's performance rating is currently C (Fair). It has registered an average return of 1.21% over the last three years and is up 0.66% over the last three months. Factored into the performance evaluation is an expense ratio of 0.71% (low).

Bonnie N. Baha has been running the fund for 5 years and currently receives a manager quality ranking of 88 (0=worst, 99=best). If you desire stability with a moderate level of risk then this fund is an excellent option.
Services Offered: Automated phone transactions, payroll deductions, bank draft capabilities, an IRA investment plan, a 401K investment plan, wire transfers and a systematic withdrawal plan.

Data Date	Investment Rating	Net Assets ($Mil)	NAV	Performance Rating/Pts	Total Return Y-T-D	Risk Rating/Pts
3-16	B+	1,160	9.99	C / 4.7	0.66%	A / 9.5
2015	A	1,140	9.98	C+ / 5.9	0.81%	A+ / 9.6
2014	B-	1,081	10.12	D+ / 2.8	1.35%	A+ / 9.6
2013	U	996	10.17	U / --	1.29%	U / --
2012	U	214	10.19	U / --	3.32%	U / --

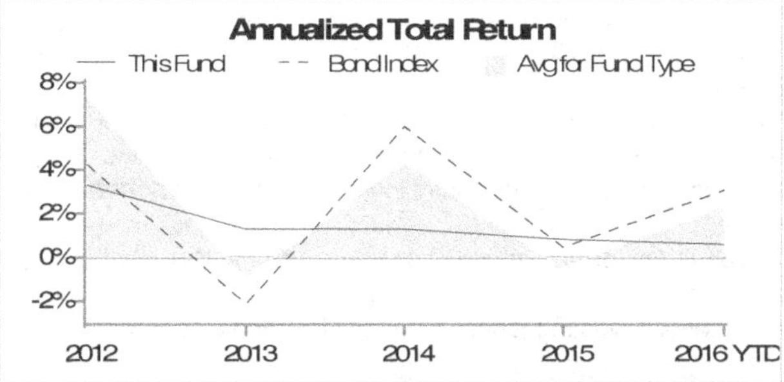

DoubleLine Total Return Bond N (DLTNX) A+ Excellent

Fund Family: DoubleLine Funds **Phone:** (877) 354-6311
Address: C/O US Bancorp Fund Services L, Milwaukee, WI 53201
Fund Type: GES - General - Short & Inter. Term
Major Rating Factors: Strong performance is the major factor driving the A+ (Excellent) TheStreet.com Investment Rating for DoubleLine Total Return Bond N. The fund currently has a performance rating of B (Good) based on an average return of 2.93% over the last three years and 1.69% over the last three months. Factored into the performance evaluation is an expense ratio of 0.72% (low).

The fund's risk rating is currently B (Good). Volatility, as measured by standard deviation, is considered low for fixed income funds at 2.62. Another risk factor is the fund's below average duration of 3.6 years (i.e. lower interest rate risk).

Jeffrey E. Gundlach has been running the fund for 6 years and currently receives a manager quality ranking of 88 (0=worst, 99=best). If you desire only a moderate level of risk and strong performance, then this fund is an excellent option.
Services Offered: Automated phone transactions, payroll deductions, bank draft capabilities, an IRA investment plan, a 401K investment plan, wire transfers and a systematic withdrawal plan.

Data Date	Investment Rating	Net Assets ($Mil)	NAV	Performance Rating/Pts	Total Return Y-T-D	Risk Rating/Pts
3-16	A+	11,714	10.87	B / 7.6	1.69%	B / 7.7
2015	A	10,359	10.78	B / 7.8	2.07%	B- / 7.5
2014	A+	7,798	10.97	C+ / 6.7	6.47%	B- / 7.4
2013	A+	6,995	10.78	B- / 7.4	-0.23%	B / 7.9
2012	U	8,995	11.33	U / --	9.00%	U / --
2011	U	4,463	11.02	U / --	9.16%	U / --

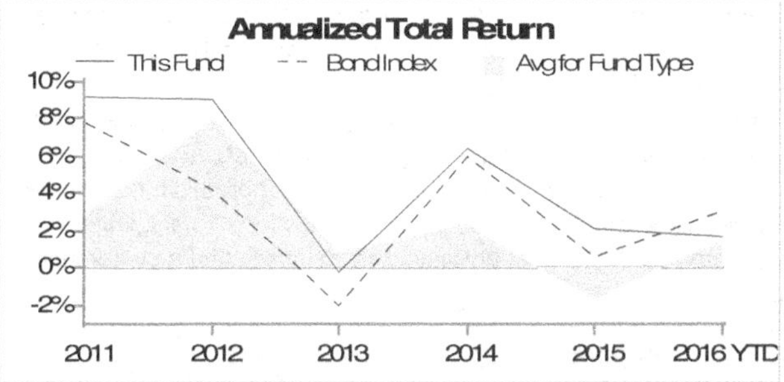

Dreyfus Bond Market Index Inv (DBMIX) B- Good

Fund Family: Dreyfus Funds **Phone:** (800) 645-6561
Address: 144 Glenn Curtiss Boulevard, Uniondale, NY 11556
Fund Type: COI - Corporate - Investment Grade
Major Rating Factors: Dreyfus Bond Market Index Inv receives a TheStreet.com Investment Rating of B- (Good). The fund has a performance rating of C+ (Fair) based on an average return of 2.00% over the last three years and 2.88% over the last three months. Factored into the performance evaluation is an expense ratio of 0.41% (very low).

The fund's risk rating is currently C+ (Fair). Volatility, as measured by standard deviation, is considered average for fixed income funds at 2.99. Another risk factor is the fund's fairly average duration of 5.7 years (i.e. average interest rate risk).

Nancy G. Rogers has been running the fund for 6 years and currently receives a manager quality ranking of 72 (0=worst, 99=best). If you desire an average level of risk, then this fund may be an option.
Services Offered: Automated phone transactions, payroll deductions, bank draft capabilities, an IRA investment plan, a 401K investment plan, a Keogh investment plan, wire transfers and a systematic withdrawal plan.

Data Date	Investment Rating	Net Assets ($Mil)	NAV	Performance Rating/Pts	Total Return Y-T-D	Risk Rating/Pts
3-16	B-	1,086	10.53	C+ / 6.5	2.88%	C+ / 6.6
2015	C	1,022	10.29	C / 5.3	0.05%	C+ / 6.4
2014	C	1,178	10.56	C- / 3.8	5.56%	B- / 7.0
2013	C-	878	10.32	C- / 3.2	-2.59%	B- / 7.4
2012	C	1,046	11.02	D+ / 2.9	3.69%	B- / 7.4
2011	C	946	10.97	C- / 3.3	7.42%	B / 8.0

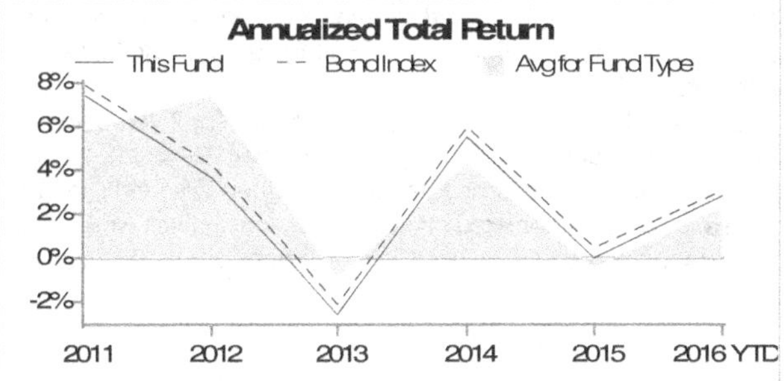

Dreyfus Interm Term Inc A (DRITX) | D+ | Weak

Fund Family: Dreyfus Funds **Phone:** (800) 645-6561
Address: 144 Glenn Curtiss Boulevard, Uniondale, NY 11556
Fund Type: GEI - General - Investment Grade
Major Rating Factors: Disappointing performance is the major factor driving the D+ (Weak) TheStreet.com Investment Rating for Dreyfus Interm Term Inc A. The fund currently has a performance rating of D+ (Weak) based on an average return of 1.37% over the last three years and 2.10% over the last three months. Factored into the performance evaluation is an expense ratio of 0.91% (average) and a 4.5% front-end load that is levied at the time of purchase.

The fund's risk rating is currently C+ (Fair). Volatility, as measured by standard deviation, is considered average for fixed income funds at 3.12. Another risk factor is the fund's fairly average duration of 5.6 years (i.e. average interest rate risk).

David R. Bowser has been running the fund for 8 years and currently receives a manager quality ranking of 28 (0=worst, 99=best). This fund offers an average level of risk, but investors looking for strong performance will be frustrated.
Services Offered: Automated phone transactions, check writing, payroll deductions, bank draft capabilities, an IRA investment plan, a 401K investment plan, a Keogh investment plan, wire transfers and a systematic withdrawal plan.

Data Date	Investment Rating	Net Assets ($Mil)	NAV	Performance Rating/Pts	Total Return Y-T-D	Risk Rating/Pts
3-16	D+	561	13.49	D+ / 2.7	2.10%	C+ / 6.0
2015	D+	571	13.29	D / 1.8	-1.44%	C+ / 5.9
2014	D+	708	13.91	C- / 3.5	4.77%	C+ / 6.4
2013	C	758	13.61	C- / 4.1	-1.31%	C+ / 6.7
2012	B-	960	14.14	C- / 4.2	7.18%	B- / 7.3
2011	C+	983	13.63	C / 4.9	7.31%	C+ / 6.7

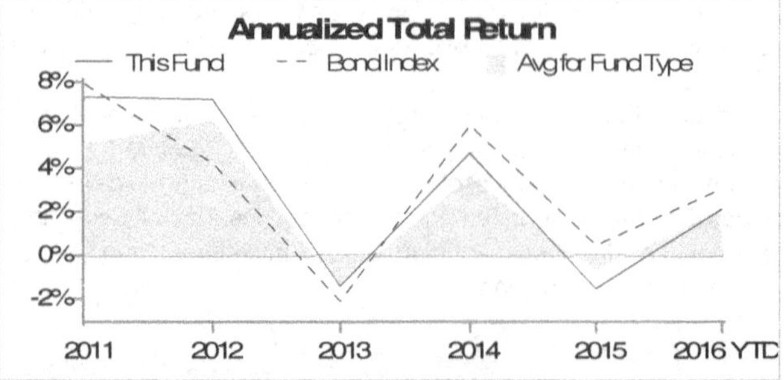

Dreyfus Intermediate Muni Bd (DITEX) | A | Excellent

Fund Family: Dreyfus Funds **Phone:** (800) 645-6561
Address: 144 Glenn Curtiss Boulevard, Uniondale, NY 11556
Fund Type: MUN - Municipal - National
Major Rating Factors: Exceptional performance is the major factor driving the A (Excellent) TheStreet.com Investment Rating for Dreyfus Intermediate Muni Bd. The fund currently has a performance rating of A- (Excellent) based on an average return of 3.04% over the last three years (5.03% taxable equivalent) and 1.48% over the last three months (2.45% taxable equivalent). Factored into the performance evaluation is an expense ratio of 0.73% (low).

The fund's risk rating is currently C+ (Fair). Volatility, as measured by standard deviation, is considered average for fixed income funds at 3.19. Another risk factor is the fund's below average duration of 4.8 years (i.e. lower interest rate risk).

Thomas C. Casey has been running the fund for 5 years and currently receives a manager quality ranking of 51 (0=worst, 99=best). If you desire an average level of risk and strong performance, then this fund is a good option.
Services Offered: Automated phone transactions, check writing, payroll deductions, bank draft capabilities, wire transfers and a systematic withdrawal plan.

Data Date	Investment Rating	Net Assets ($Mil)	NAV	Performance Rating/Pts	Total Return Y-T-D	Risk Rating/Pts
3-16	A	782	14.09	A- / 9.1	1.48%	C+ / 5.8
2015	A	766	13.97	A- / 9.1	3.00%	C / 5.5
2014	B+	789	14.02	B- / 7.5	7.21%	C / 5.2
2013	A-	790	13.44	B / 7.7	-1.86%	C / 5.4
2012	B	960	14.23	C+ / 6.4	4.88%	C / 5.3
2011	A	897	14.03	C+ / 6.9	10.00%	C+ / 5.6

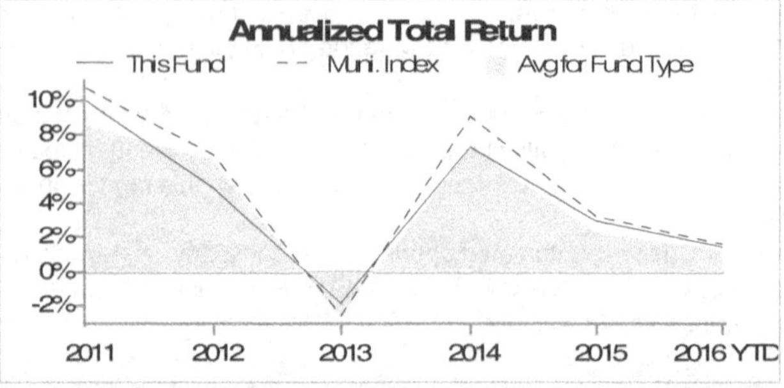

Dreyfus Municipal Bond (DRTAX) | B+ | Good

Fund Family: Dreyfus Funds **Phone:** (800) 645-6561
Address: 144 Glenn Curtiss Boulevard, Uniondale, NY 11556
Fund Type: MUN - Municipal - National
Major Rating Factors: Exceptional performance is the major factor driving the B+ (Good) TheStreet.com Investment Rating for Dreyfus Municipal Bond. The fund currently has a performance rating of A (Excellent) based on an average return of 3.69% over the last three years (6.11% taxable equivalent) and 1.62% over the last three months (2.68% taxable equivalent). Factored into the performance evaluation is an expense ratio of 0.72% (low).

The fund's risk rating is currently C- (Fair). Volatility, as measured by standard deviation, is considered average for fixed income funds at 3.89. Another risk factor is the fund's below average duration of 5.0 years (i.e. lower interest rate risk).

Daniel A. Marques has been running the fund for 7 years and currently receives a manager quality ranking of 47 (0=worst, 99=best). If you desire an average level of risk and strong performance, then this fund is a good option.
Services Offered: Automated phone transactions, check writing, payroll deductions, bank draft capabilities, wire transfers and a systematic withdrawal plan.

Data Date	Investment Rating	Net Assets ($Mil)	NAV	Performance Rating/Pts	Total Return Y-T-D	Risk Rating/Pts
3-16	B+	1,453	11.98	A / 9.5	1.62%	C- / 4.1
2015	B+	1,436	11.88	A / 9.5	3.60%	C- / 4.0
2014	A	1,474	11.85	A- / 9.0	10.51%	C- / 3.9
2013	B	1,448	11.10	B / 7.6	-3.56%	C / 4.4
2012	B+	1,683	11.91	B- / 7.3	7.30%	C / 4.3
2011	A	1,674	11.48	B / 8.0	10.37%	C / 4.3

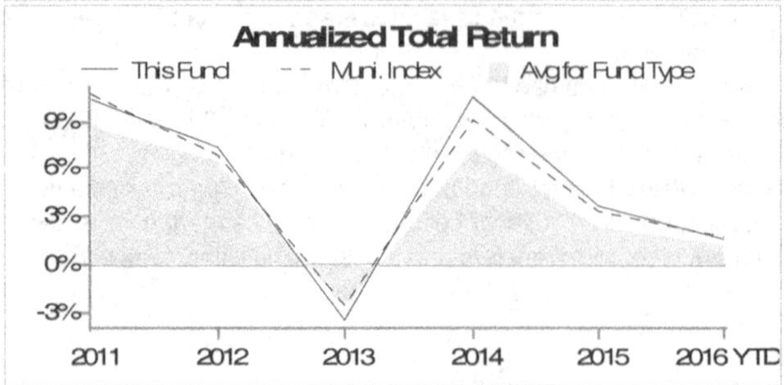

Dreyfus NY Tax Exempt Bond (DRNYX) B+ Good

Fund Family: Dreyfus Funds **Phone:** (800) 645-6561
Address: 144 Glenn Curtiss Boulevard, Uniondale, NY 11556
Fund Type: MUS - Municipal - Single State
Major Rating Factors: Exceptional performance is the major factor driving the B+ (Good) TheStreet.com Investment Rating for Dreyfus NY Tax Exempt Bond. The fund currently has a performance rating of A- (Excellent) based on an average return of 2.92% over the last three years (4.84% taxable equivalent) and 1.58% over the last three months (2.62% taxable equivalent). Factored into the performance evaluation is an expense ratio of 0.72% (low).

The fund's risk rating is currently C (Fair). Volatility, as measured by standard deviation, is considered average for fixed income funds at 3.68. Another risk factor is the fund's fairly average duration of 5.2 years (i.e. average interest rate risk).

David Belton has been running the fund for 7 years and currently receives a manager quality ranking of 31 (0=worst, 99=best). If you desire an average level of risk and strong performance, then this fund is a good option.
Services Offered: Automated phone transactions, check writing, payroll deductions, bank draft capabilities, wire transfers and a systematic withdrawal plan.

Data Date	Investment Rating	Net Assets ($Mil)	NAV	Performance Rating/Pts	Total Return Y-T-D	Risk Rating/Pts
3-16	B+	1,178	15.14	A- / 9.1	1.58%	C / 4.5
2015	B+	1,172	15.02	A- / 9.1	3.61%	C / 4.3
2014	B	1,194	14.98	B / 7.9	8.96%	C- / 4.0
2013	C-	1,171	14.24	C+ / 5.7	-4.68%	C / 4.4
2012	B	1,408	15.50	C+ / 6.9	6.36%	C / 4.3
2011	A-	1,378	15.11	B- / 7.3	9.88%	C / 4.9

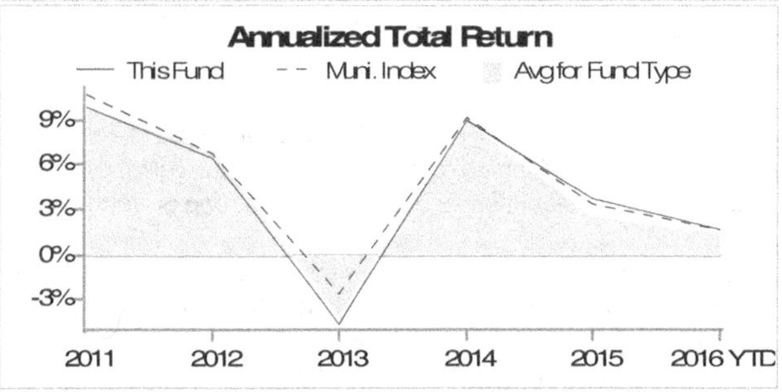

Dupree KY Tax Free Income (KYTFX) A+ Excellent

Fund Family: Dupree Funds **Phone:** (800) 866-0614
Address: P.O. Box 1149, Lexington, KY 40507
Fund Type: MUS - Municipal - Single State
Major Rating Factors: Exceptional performance is the major factor driving the A+ (Excellent) TheStreet.com Investment Rating for Dupree KY Tax Free Income. The fund currently has a performance rating of A- (Excellent) based on an average return of 3.17% over the last three years (5.25% taxable equivalent) and 1.53% over the last three months (2.53% taxable equivalent). Factored into the performance evaluation is an expense ratio of 0.55% (very low).

The fund's risk rating is currently C+ (Fair). Volatility, as measured by standard deviation, is considered average for fixed income funds at 3.08. Another risk factor is the fund's fairly average duration of 5.2 years (i.e. average interest rate risk).

Vincent Harrison has been running the fund for 17 years and currently receives a manager quality ranking of 61 (0=worst, 99=best). If you desire an average level of risk and strong performance, then this fund is a good option.
Services Offered: Automated phone transactions, payroll deductions, bank draft capabilities, an IRA investment plan, wire transfers and a systematic withdrawal plan.

Data Date	Investment Rating	Net Assets ($Mil)	NAV	Performance Rating/Pts	Total Return Y-T-D	Risk Rating/Pts
3-16	A+	1,001	7.96	A- / 9.1	1.53%	C+ / 6.3
2015	A	989	7.90	A- / 9.0	2.51%	C+ / 5.9
2014	A	988	7.96	B / 8.2	7.66%	C / 5.1
2013	A	930	7.65	B / 8.1	-2.02%	C / 5.3
2012	B+	996	8.09	C+ / 6.8	6.09%	C / 5.1
2011	B+	951	7.89	C+ / 6.2	10.09%	C+ / 5.9

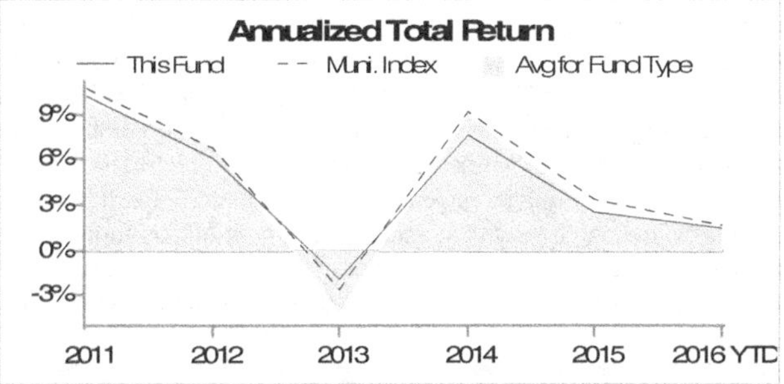

Eaton Vance Float Rate Advtage A (EAFAX) D+ Weak

Fund Family: Eaton Vance Funds **Phone:** (800) 262-1122
Address: The Eaton Vance Building, Boston, MA 02109
Fund Type: LP - Loan Participation
Major Rating Factors: Eaton Vance Float Rate Advtage A receives a TheStreet.com Investment Rating of D+ (Weak). The fund has a performance rating of C- (Fair) based on an average return of 1.42% over the last three years and 2.31% over the last three months. Factored into the performance evaluation is an expense ratio of 1.36% (above average) and a 2.3% front-end load that is levied at the time of purchase.

The fund's risk rating is currently C (Fair). Volatility, as measured by standard deviation, is considered average for fixed income funds at 3.30. Another risk factor is the fund's very low average duration of 0.3 years (i.e. low interest rate risk).

Scott H. Page has been running the fund for 20 years and currently receives a manager quality ranking of 84 (0=worst, 99=best). If you desire an average level of risk, then this fund may be an option.
Services Offered: Automated phone transactions, payroll deductions, bank draft capabilities, an IRA investment plan, a 401K investment plan, wire transfers and a systematic withdrawal plan.

Data Date	Investment Rating	Net Assets ($Mil)	NAV	Performance Rating/Pts	Total Return Y-T-D	Risk Rating/Pts
3-16	D+	1,487	10.20	C- / 3.4	2.31%	C / 5.4
2015	D+	1,549	10.10	D+ / 2.9	-1.84%	C+ / 6.1
2014	A-	1,984	10.79	C / 5.4	0.69%	B / 7.9
2013	A-	2,280	11.20	B+ / 8.3	5.62%	C / 4.5
2012	D-	1,048	11.10	C+ / 6.2	10.53%	D / 2.1
2011	B	682	10.58	A+ / 9.7	3.06%	D- / 1.1

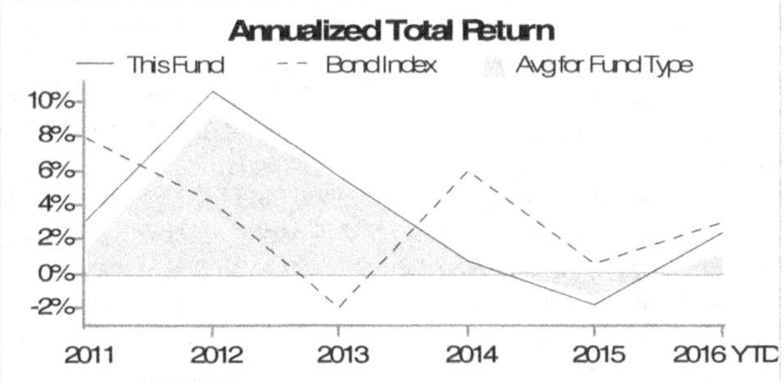

Eaton Vance Floating Rate A (EVBLX) C- Fair

Fund Family: Eaton Vance Funds **Phone:** (800) 262-1122
Address: The Eaton Vance Building, Boston, MA 02109
Fund Type: LP - Loan Participation
Major Rating Factors: Disappointing performance is the major factor driving the C- (Fair) TheStreet.com Investment Rating for Eaton Vance Floating Rate A. The fund currently has a performance rating of D+ (Weak) based on an average return of 0.94% over the last three years and 1.85% over the last three months. Factored into the performance evaluation is an expense ratio of 1.03% (average) and a 2.3% front-end load that is levied at the time of purchase.

The fund's risk rating is currently B- (Good). Volatility, as measured by standard deviation, is considered low for fixed income funds at 2.72. Another risk factor is the fund's very low average duration of 0.3 years (i.e. low interest rate risk).

Scott H. Page has been running the fund for 15 years and currently receives a manager quality ranking of 76 (0=worst, 99=best). This fund offers only a moderate level of risk but investors looking for strong performance are still waiting.
Services Offered: Automated phone transactions, payroll deductions, bank draft capabilities, an IRA investment plan, a 401K investment plan and a systematic withdrawal plan.

Data Date	Investment Rating	Net Assets ($Mil)	NAV	Performance Rating/Pts	Total Return Y-T-D	Risk Rating/Pts
3-16	C-	1,069	8.76	D+ / 2.5	1.85%	B- / 7.4
2015	C-	1,204	8.69	D+ / 2.3	-1.91%	B- / 7.5
2014	B	1,688	9.21	C- / 4.0	0.37%	B+ / 8.6
2013	B+	2,739	9.50	C+ / 6.9	4.54%	C+ / 6.1
2012	E+	1,695	9.43	C- / 3.8	8.12%	C- / 3.5
2011	C	1,421	9.10	B / 8.0	2.13%	D / 2.0

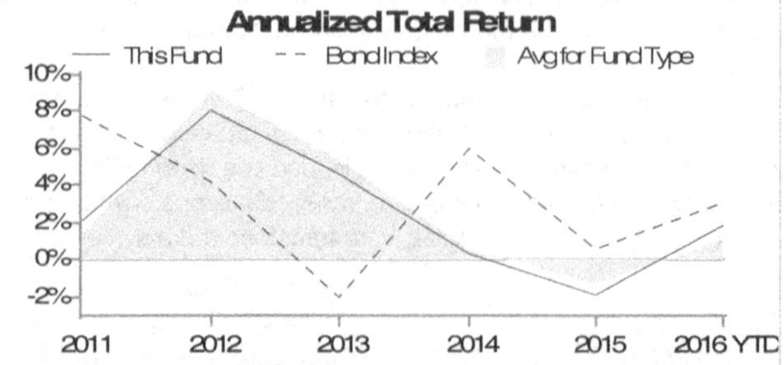

Eaton Vance Income Fd of Boston A (EVIBX) D Weak

Fund Family: Eaton Vance Funds **Phone:** (800) 262-1122
Address: The Eaton Vance Building, Boston, MA 02109
Fund Type: COH - Corporate - High Yield
Major Rating Factors: Eaton Vance Income Fd of Boston A has adopted a very risky asset allocation strategy and currently receives an overall TheStreet.com Investment Rating of D (Weak). Volatility, as measured by standard deviation, is considered above average for fixed income funds at 5.04. Another risk factor is the fund's below average duration of 3.8 years (i.e. lower interest rate risk). Unfortunately, the high level of risk (D, Weak) has only provided investors with average performance.

The fund's performance rating is currently C (Fair). It has registered an average return of 2.72% over the last three years and is up 3.26% over the last three months. Factored into the performance evaluation is an expense ratio of 1.00% (average) and a 4.8% front-end load that is levied at the time of purchase.

Michael W. Weilheimer has been running the fund for 15 years and currently receives a manager quality ranking of 91 (0=worst, 99=best). If you are comfortable owning a very high risk investment, then this fund may be an option.
Services Offered: Automated phone transactions, payroll deductions, bank draft capabilities, an IRA investment plan, a 401K investment plan and a systematic withdrawal plan.

Data Date	Investment Rating	Net Assets ($Mil)	NAV	Performance Rating/Pts	Total Return Y-T-D	Risk Rating/Pts
3-16	D	1,351	5.49	C / 4.9	3.26%	D / 2.1
2015	D	1,258	5.40	C- / 3.9	-2.05%	D / 2.2
2014	C	1,490	5.86	C+ / 6.8	2.54%	C- / 3.3
2013	C+	1,906	6.06	A- / 9.1	7.29%	D / 1.8
2012	C	1,966	6.00	B / 7.8	13.40%	D / 1.6
2011	B-	1,445	5.66	A+ / 9.6	4.58%	E+ / 0.9

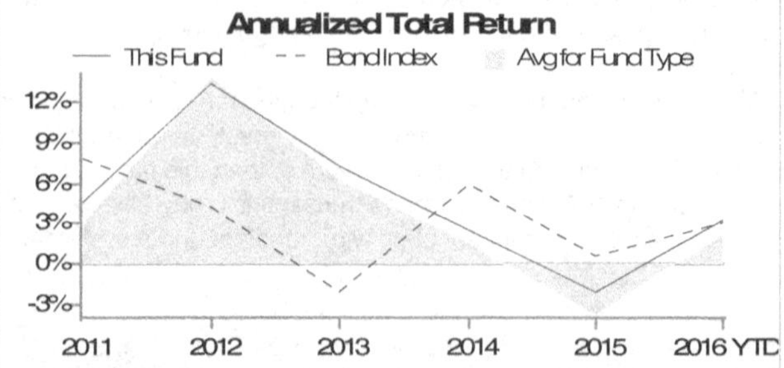

Eaton Vance National Muni Inc A (EANAX) C- Fair

Fund Family: Eaton Vance Funds **Phone:** (800) 262-1122
Address: The Eaton Vance Building, Boston, MA 02109
Fund Type: MUN - Municipal - National
Major Rating Factors: Eaton Vance National Muni Inc A has adopted a very risky asset allocation strategy and currently receives an overall TheStreet.com Investment Rating of C- (Fair). Volatility, as measured by standard deviation, is considered high for fixed income funds at 6.58. Another risk factor is the fund's fairly average duration of 5.8 years (i.e. average interest rate risk). The high level of risk (E+, Very Weak) did however, reward investors with excellent performance.

The fund's performance rating is currently B+ (Good). It has registered an average return of 3.64% over the last three years (6.03% taxable equivalent) and is up 1.37% over the last three months (2.27% taxable equivalent). Factored into the performance evaluation is an expense ratio of 0.76% (low) and a 4.8% front-end load that is levied at the time of purchase.

Craig R. Brandon has been running the fund for 3 years and currently receives a manager quality ranking of 7 (0=worst, 99=best). If you are comfortable owning a very high risk investment, this fund may be an option.
Services Offered: Automated phone transactions, payroll deductions, bank draft capabilities, an IRA investment plan and a systematic withdrawal plan.

Data Date	Investment Rating	Net Assets ($Mil)	NAV	Performance Rating/Pts	Total Return Y-T-D	Risk Rating/Pts
3-16	C-	1,879	10.00	B+ / 8.6	1.37%	E+ / 0.9
2015	C-	1,890	9.96	A- / 9.0	4.30%	E+ / 0.7
2014	C+	2,061	9.93	A+ / 9.6	14.83%	E / 0.5
2013	D-	1,957	9.04	C+ / 6.1	-7.46%	E / 0.5
2012	B-	2,854	10.26	A- / 9.0	14.21%	D- / 1.4
2011	C+	2,805	9.41	A+ / 9.8	11.72%	E / 0.3

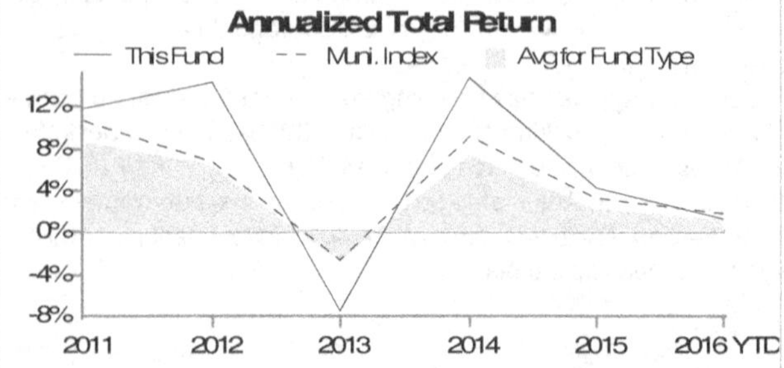

Eaton Vance Short Dur Strat Inc A (ETSIX) D Weak

Fund Family: Eaton Vance Funds **Phone:** (800) 262-1122
Address: The Eaton Vance Building, Boston, MA 02109
Fund Type: GL - Global
Major Rating Factors: Very poor performance is the major factor driving the D (Weak) TheStreet.com Investment Rating for Eaton Vance Short Dur Strat Inc A. The fund currently has a performance rating of E+ (Very Weak) based on an average return of 0.08% over the last three years and -0.90% over the last three months. Factored into the performance evaluation is an expense ratio of 1.06% (average) and a 2.3% front-end load that is levied at the time of purchase.

The fund's risk rating is currently C (Fair). Volatility, as measured by standard deviation, is considered average for fixed income funds at 3.53. Another risk factor is the fund's very low average duration of 0.5 years (i.e. low interest rate risk).

Mark S. Venezia has been running the fund for 26 years and currently receives a manager quality ranking of 69 (0=worst, 99=best). This fund offers an average level of risk, but investors looking for strong performance will be frustrated.
Services Offered: Automated phone transactions, payroll deductions, bank draft capabilities, an IRA investment plan, a Keogh investment plan and a systematic withdrawal plan.

Data Date	Investment Rating	Net Assets ($Mil)	NAV	Performance Rating/Pts	Total Return Y-T-D	Risk Rating/Pts
3-16	D	1,039	7.13	E+ / 0.9	-0.90%	C / 4.9
2015	D+	1,176	7.27	C- / 3.1	-0.81%	C+ / 5.7
2014	C-	857	7.64	C / 4.5	4.34%	C / 5.5
2013	D	1,039	7.83	C- / 3.9	0.36%	C / 5.0
2012	E+	1,476	8.18	D+ / 2.8	8.51%	C / 5.2
2011	D	1,615	7.90	C / 4.3	0.99%	C / 5.3

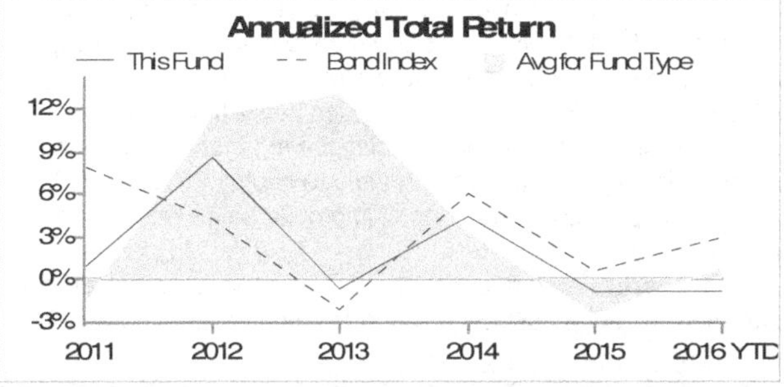

Elfun Tax Exempt Income (ELFTX) B+ Good

Fund Family: GE Investment Funds **Phone:** (800) 242-0134
Address: PO Box 9838, Providence, RI 02940
Fund Type: MUN - Municipal - National
Major Rating Factors: Exceptional performance is the major factor driving the B+ (Good) TheStreet.com Investment Rating for Elfun Tax Exempt Income. The fund currently has a performance rating of A (Excellent) based on an average return of 3.40% over the last three years (5.63% taxable equivalent) and 1.56% over the last three months (2.58% taxable equivalent). Factored into the performance evaluation is an expense ratio of 0.21% (very low).

The fund's risk rating is currently C (Fair). Volatility, as measured by standard deviation, is considered average for fixed income funds at 3.77. Another risk factor is the fund's fairly average duration of 6.7 years (i.e. average interest rate risk).

Michael J. Caufield has been running the fund for 16 years and currently receives a manager quality ranking of 42 (0=worst, 99=best). If you desire an average level of risk and strong performance, then this fund is a good option.
Services Offered: Automated phone transactions, payroll deductions, bank draft capabilities, an IRA investment plan, wire transfers and a systematic withdrawal plan.

Data Date	Investment Rating	Net Assets ($Mil)	NAV	Performance Rating/Pts	Total Return Y-T-D	Risk Rating/Pts
3-16	B+	1,583	11.95	A / 9.3	1.56%	C / 4.3
2015	B	1,585	11.88	A- / 9.2	3.22%	C- / 3.8
2014	B+	1,621	11.97	B+ / 8.8	9.85%	C- / 3.5
2013	B-	1,569	11.34	B- / 7.4	-4.05%	C- / 3.9
2012	B+	1,785	12.32	B / 7.8	7.45%	C- / 3.8
2011	A+	1,731	11.97	B / 7.6	10.57%	C / 4.9

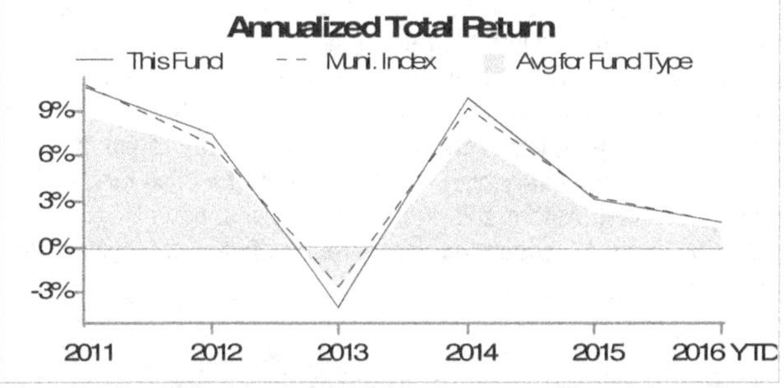

Federated Bond Fund A (FDBAX) D+ Weak

Fund Family: Federated Investors Funds **Phone:** (800) 341-7400
Address: 4000 Ericcson Drive, Warrendale, PA 15086
Fund Type: COI - Corporate - Investment Grade
Major Rating Factors: Federated Bond Fund A receives a TheStreet.com Investment Rating of D+ (Weak). The fund has a performance rating of C (Fair) based on an average return of 2.31% over the last three years and 3.35% over the last three months. Factored into the performance evaluation is an expense ratio of 1.21% (above average) and a 4.5% front-end load that is levied at the time of purchase.

The fund's risk rating is currently C- (Fair). Volatility, as measured by standard deviation, is considered average for fixed income funds at 4.25. Another risk factor is the fund's fairly average duration of 5.5 years (i.e. average interest rate risk).

Brian S. Ruffner has been running the fund for 3 years and currently receives a manager quality ranking of 50 (0=worst, 99=best). If you desire an average level of risk, then this fund may be an option.
Services Offered: Automated phone transactions, payroll deductions, bank draft capabilities, an IRA investment plan, a 401K investment plan, wire transfers and a systematic withdrawal plan.

Data Date	Investment Rating	Net Assets ($Mil)	NAV	Performance Rating/Pts	Total Return Y-T-D	Risk Rating/Pts
3-16	D+	663	8.93	C / 4.6	3.35%	C- / 3.5
2015	D	681	8.73	D+ / 2.5	-1.95%	C- / 4.0
2014	C	892	9.40	C+ / 5.7	5.85%	C / 4.8
2013	C+	889	9.27	C+ / 6.3	0.83%	C / 4.6
2012	C+	943	9.62	C+ / 5.8	10.22%	C / 4.7
2011	C	733	9.17	C+ / 6.3	5.98%	C- / 4.1

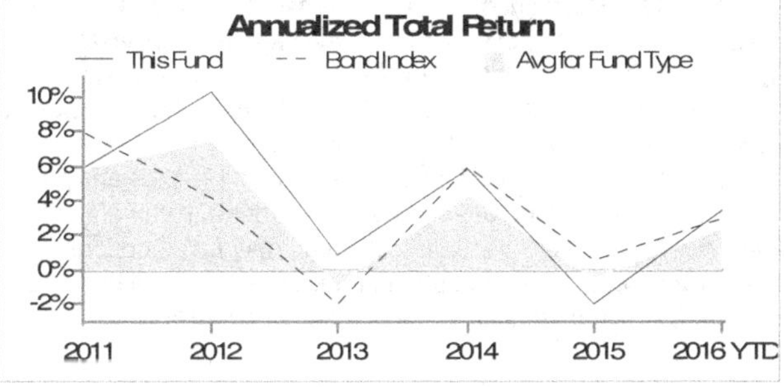

Federated High Income Bond A (FHIIX) D- Weak

Fund Family: Federated Investors Funds **Phone:** (800) 341-7400
Address: 4000 Ericcson Drive, Warrendale, PA 15086
Fund Type: COH - Corporate - High Yield
Major Rating Factors: Federated High Income Bond A has adopted a very risky asset allocation strategy and currently receives an overall TheStreet.com Investment Rating of D- (Weak). Volatility, as measured by standard deviation, is considered above average for fixed income funds at 5.42. Unfortunately, the high level of risk (D, Weak) failed to pay off as investors endured very poor performance.

The fund's performance rating is currently D+ (Weak). It has registered an average return of 1.97% over the last three years and is up 3.40% over the last three months. Factored into the performance evaluation is an expense ratio of 1.25% (above average), a 4.5% front-end load that is levied at the time of purchase and a 2.0% back-end load levied at the time of sale.

Mark E. Durbiano has been running the fund for 29 years and currently receives a manager quality ranking of 80 (0=worst, 99=best). If you can tolerate very high levels of risk in the hope of improved future returns, holding this fund may be an option.
Services Offered: Automated phone transactions, payroll deductions, bank draft capabilities, an IRA investment plan, wire transfers and a systematic withdrawal plan.

Data Date	Investment Rating	Net Assets ($Mil)	NAV	Performance Rating/Pts	Total Return Y-T-D	Risk Rating/Pts
3-16	D-	610	7.06	D+ / 2.4	3.40%	D / 1.7
2015	D-	634	6.92	D / 1.6	-3.28%	D / 1.8
2014	D	776	7.56	C+ / 6.2	2.14%	D+ / 2.7
2013	C+	887	7.84	B+ / 8.8	6.69%	D / 1.7
2012	C-	940	7.82	B- / 7.4	14.28%	D- / 1.5
2011	C+	806	7.36	A- / 9.1	4.66%	D- / 1.1

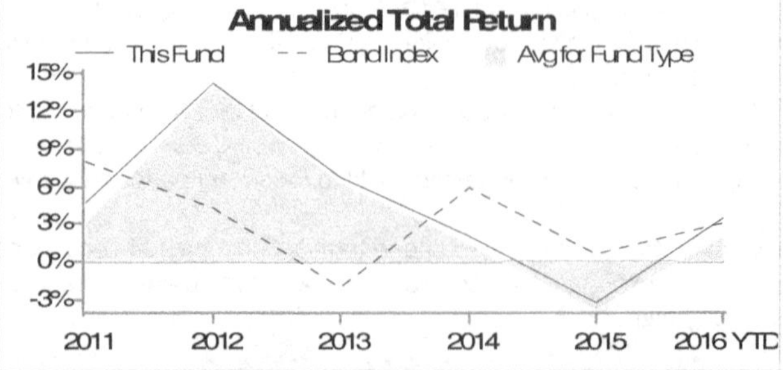

Federated Instl High Yld Bond (FIHBX) D+ Weak

Fund Family: Federated Investors Funds **Phone:** (800) 341-7400
Address: 4000 Ericcson Drive, Warrendale, PA 15086
Fund Type: COH - Corporate - High Yield
Major Rating Factors: Federated Instl High Yld Bond has adopted a very risky asset allocation strategy and currently receives an overall TheStreet.com Investment Rating of D+ (Weak). Volatility, as measured by standard deviation, is considered above average for fixed income funds at 5.56. Unfortunately, the high level of risk (D, Weak) has only provided investors with average performance.

The fund's performance rating is currently C+ (Fair). It has registered an average return of 2.83% over the last three years and is up 3.52% over the last three months. Factored into the performance evaluation is an expense ratio of 0.57% (very low) and a 2.0% back-end load levied at the time of sale.

Mark E. Durbiano has been running the fund for 14 years and currently receives a manager quality ranking of 91 (0=worst, 99=best). If you are comfortable owning a very high risk investment, then this fund may be an option.
Services Offered: Automated phone transactions, payroll deductions, bank draft capabilities, an IRA investment plan, wire transfers and a systematic withdrawal plan.

Data Date	Investment Rating	Net Assets ($Mil)	NAV	Performance Rating/Pts	Total Return Y-T-D	Risk Rating/Pts
3-16	D+	4,361	9.27	C+ / 6.3	3.52%	D / 1.6
2015	D+	4,282	9.09	C+ / 5.6	-2.29%	D / 1.6
2014	C+	3,612	9.88	B / 8.1	3.08%	D+ / 2.4
2013	B	3,095	10.21	A+ / 9.7	7.31%	D / 1.6
2012	B-	2,090	10.19	B+ / 8.9	15.16%	D- / 1.5
2011	B	755	9.56	A / 9.5	5.68%	D- / 1.3

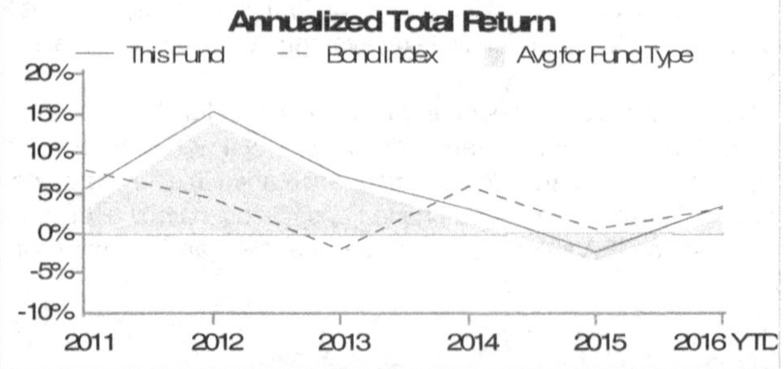

Federated Muni & Stock Advantage A (FMUAX) C- Fair

Fund Family: Federated Investors Funds **Phone:** (800) 341-7400
Address: 4000 Ericcson Drive, Warrendale, PA 15086
Fund Type: MUH - Municipal - High Yield
Major Rating Factors: Federated Muni & Stock Advantage A has adopted a very risky asset allocation strategy and currently receives an overall TheStreet.com Investment Rating of C- (Fair). Volatility, as measured by standard deviation, is considered above average for fixed income funds at 5.45. Another risk factor is the fund's above average duration of 7.2 years (i.e. higher interest rate risk). The high level of risk (D-, Weak) did however, reward investors with excellent performance.

The fund's performance rating is currently B+ (Good). It has registered an average return of 4.15% over the last three years (6.87% taxable equivalent) and is up 2.32% over the last three months (3.84% taxable equivalent). Factored into the performance evaluation is an expense ratio of 1.09% (average) and a 5.5% front-end load that is levied at the time of purchase.

John L. Nichol has been running the fund for 13 years and currently receives a manager quality ranking of 94 (0=worst, 99=best). If you are comfortable owning a very high risk investment, this fund may be an option.
Services Offered: Automated phone transactions, payroll deductions, bank draft capabilities, wire transfers and a systematic withdrawal plan.

Data Date	Investment Rating	Net Assets ($Mil)	NAV	Performance Rating/Pts	Total Return Y-T-D	Risk Rating/Pts
3-16	C-	609	12.31	B+ / 8.6	2.32%	D- / 1.4
2015	C-	590	12.11	A- / 9.0	-0.97%	D- / 1.1
2014	C+	556	12.57	A / 9.4	7.00%	D- / 1.3
2013	A-	390	12.20	A+ / 9.9	8.79%	D+ / 2.6
2012	C+	307	11.59	B / 8.1	9.07%	D / 1.9
2011	C	275	11.05	B / 8.0	11.67%	D / 2.1

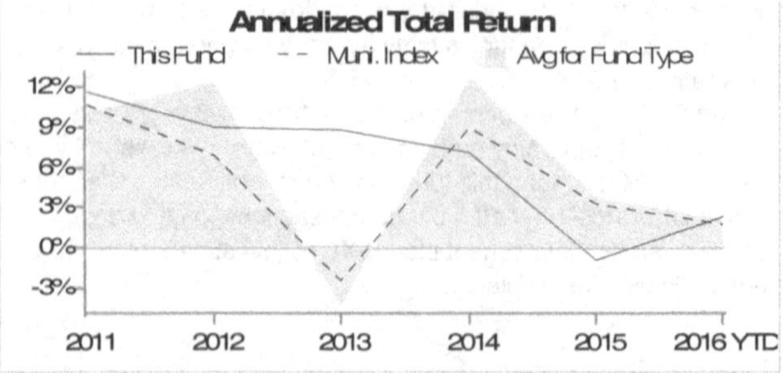

Federated Muni Ultrashrt A (FMUUX) C- Fair

Fund Family: Federated Investors Funds **Phone:** (800) 341-7400
Address: 4000 Ericcson Drive, Warrendale, PA 15086
Fund Type: MUI - Municipal - Insured
Major Rating Factors: Disappointing performance is the major factor driving the C- (Fair) TheStreet.com Investment Rating for Federated Muni Ultrashrt A. The fund currently has a performance rating of D- (Weak) based on an average return of -0.08% over the last three years and -0.14% over the last three months. Factored into the performance evaluation is an expense ratio of 1.03% (average) and a 2.0% front-end load that is levied at the time of purchase.

The fund's risk rating is currently A+ (Excellent). Volatility, as measured by standard deviation, is considered very low for fixed income funds at 0.33. Another risk factor is the fund's very low average duration of 0.4 years (i.e. low interest rate risk).

Jeffrey A. Kozemchak has been running the fund for 16 years and currently receives a manager quality ranking of 49 (0=worst, 99=best). This fund offers only a moderate level of risk but investors looking for strong performance are still waiting.
Services Offered: Automated phone transactions, payroll deductions, bank draft capabilities, wire transfers and a systematic withdrawal plan.

Data Date	Investment Rating	Net Assets ($Mil)	NAV	Performance Rating/Pts	Total Return Y-T-D	Risk Rating/Pts
3-16	C-	846	9.97	D- / 1.1	-0.14%	A+ / 9.9
2015	C	911	9.99	D+ / 2.3	-0.35%	A+ / 9.9
2014	D+	1,289	10.04	E+ / 0.7	0.33%	A+ / 9.9
2013	C-	1,597	10.03	E+ / 0.7	0.09%	A+ / 9.9
2012	C-	2,069	10.05	E / 0.4	0.59%	A+ / 9.9
2011	C-	1,991	10.04	D- / 1.3	1.24%	A+ / 9.9

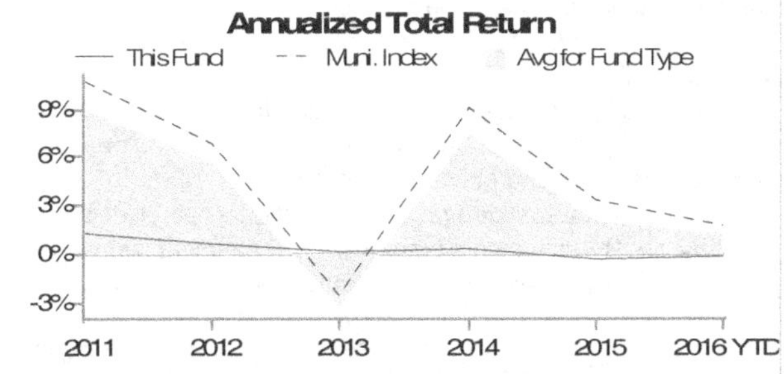

Fidelity Adv Float-Rate Hi-Inc A (FFRAX) D+ Weak

Fund Family: Fidelity Advisor **Phone:** (800) 522-7297
Address: 245 Summer Street, Boston, MA 02210
Fund Type: LP - Loan Participation
Major Rating Factors: Disappointing performance is the major factor driving the D+ (Weak) TheStreet.com Investment Rating for Fidelity Adv Float-Rate Hi-Inc A. The fund currently has a performance rating of D- (Weak) based on an average return of 0.71% over the last three years and 1.39% over the last three months. Factored into the performance evaluation is an expense ratio of 0.98% (average), a 2.8% front-end load that is levied at the time of purchase and a 1.0% back-end load levied at the time of sale.

The fund's risk rating is currently B- (Good). Volatility, as measured by standard deviation, is considered low for fixed income funds at 2.73. Another risk factor is the fund's very low average duration of 0.3 years (i.e. low interest rate risk).

Eric Mollenhauer has been running the fund for 3 years and currently receives a manager quality ranking of 71 (0=worst, 99=best). This fund offers only a moderate level of risk but investors looking for strong performance are still waiting.
Services Offered: Automated phone transactions, payroll deductions, bank draft capabilities, an IRA investment plan, a 401K investment plan, a Keogh investment plan, wire transfers and a systematic withdrawal plan.

Data Date	Investment Rating	Net Assets ($Mil)	NAV	Performance Rating/Pts	Total Return Y-T-D	Risk Rating/Pts
3-16	D+	718	9.18	D- / 1.2	1.39%	B- / 7.4
2015	C-	772	9.14	D / 1.7	-1.44%	B / 8.0
2014	C	1,038	9.63	D+ / 2.6	0.02%	B+ / 8.4
2013	C	1,693	9.98	C / 4.9	3.62%	C / 5.4
2012	E	1,333	9.94	D+ / 2.4	6.61%	C- / 3.9
2011	E+	1,536	9.65	C / 4.9	1.43%	C- / 3.3

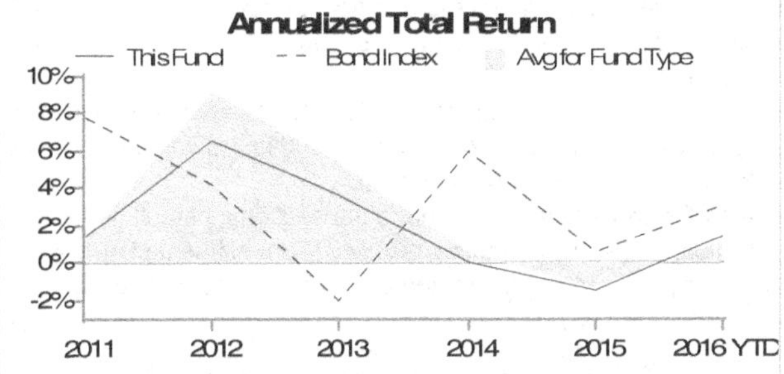

Fidelity Adv Hi Income Advantage A (FAHDX) D- Weak

Fund Family: Fidelity Advisor **Phone:** (800) 522-7297
Address: 245 Summer Street, Boston, MA 02210
Fund Type: COH - Corporate - High Yield
Major Rating Factors: Fidelity Adv Hi Income Advantage A has adopted a very risky asset allocation strategy and currently receives an overall TheStreet.com Investment Rating of D- (Weak). Volatility, as measured by standard deviation, is considered high for fixed income funds at 6.74. Another risk factor is the fund's below average duration of 3.8 years (i.e. lower interest rate risk). Unfortunately, the high level of risk (E+, Very Weak) has only provided investors with average performance.

The fund's performance rating is currently C- (Fair). It has registered an average return of 2.63% over the last three years and is up 1.35% over the last three months. Factored into the performance evaluation is an expense ratio of 1.02% (average), a 4.0% front-end load that is levied at the time of purchase and a 1.0% back-end load levied at the time of sale.

Harley J. Lank has been running the fund for 7 years and currently receives a manager quality ranking of 86 (0=worst, 99=best). If you are comfortable owning a very high risk investment, then this fund may be an option.
Services Offered: Automated phone transactions, payroll deductions, bank draft capabilities, an IRA investment plan, a 401K investment plan, a Keogh investment plan, wire transfers and a systematic withdrawal plan.

Data Date	Investment Rating	Net Assets ($Mil)	NAV	Performance Rating/Pts	Total Return Y-T-D	Risk Rating/Pts
3-16	D-	558	9.91	C- / 3.2	1.35%	E+ / 0.6
2015	D	591	9.89	C / 5.1	-3.01%	E+ / 0.8
2014	C	666	10.69	B+ / 8.8	3.86%	D- / 1.2
2013	C	701	10.73	A / 9.5	9.99%	E / 0.3
2012	C-	714	10.32	B+ / 8.6	18.03%	E- / 0.2
2011	C	617	9.30	A+ / 9.7	-0.21%	E- / 0.1

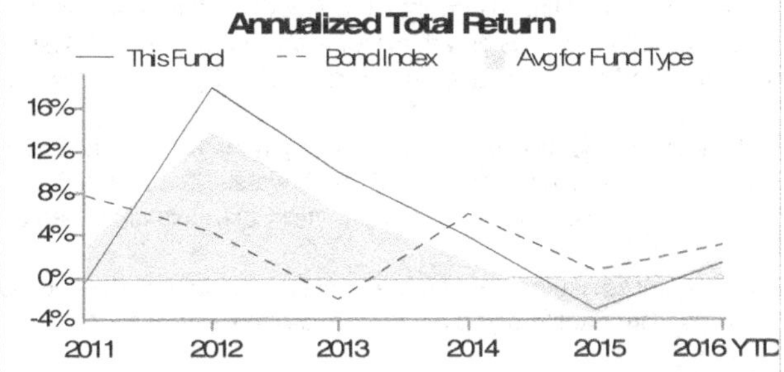

Fidelity Adv Strategic Income A (FSTAX) D Weak

Fund Family: Fidelity Advisor **Phone:** (800) 522-7297
Address: 245 Summer Street, Boston, MA 02210
Fund Type: GES - General - Short & Inter. Term
Major Rating Factors: Fidelity Adv Strategic Income A receives a TheStreet.com Investment Rating of D (Weak). The fund has a performance rating of C- (Fair) based on an average return of 1.44% over the last three years and 2.94% over the last three months. Factored into the performance evaluation is an expense ratio of 1.00% (average) and a 4.0% front-end load that is levied at the time of purchase.

The fund's risk rating is currently C- (Fair). Volatility, as measured by standard deviation, is considered average for fixed income funds at 4.47. Another risk factor is the fund's below average duration of 4.8 years (i.e. lower interest rate risk).

Mark J. Notkin has been running the fund for 17 years and currently receives a manager quality ranking of 38 (0=worst, 99=best). If you desire an average level of risk, then this fund may be an option.

Services Offered: Automated phone transactions, payroll deductions, bank draft capabilities, an IRA investment plan, a 401K investment plan, a Keogh investment plan, wire transfers and a systematic withdrawal plan.

Data Date	Investment Rating	Net Assets ($Mil)	NAV	Performance Rating/Pts	Total Return Y-T-D	Risk Rating/Pts
3-16	D	3,159	11.56	C- / 3.4	2.94%	C- / 3.2
2015	D	3,268	11.32	D / 1.7	-1.84%	C- / 3.7
2014	D	3,792	11.92	C- / 4.1	3.52%	C / 4.3
2013	C-	4,206	12.10	C+ / 5.6	0.08%	C- / 4.1
2012	D-	5,573	12.69	C / 5.4	10.57%	C- / 3.0
2011	D+	4,668	12.07	C+ / 6.4	4.47%	D+ / 2.9

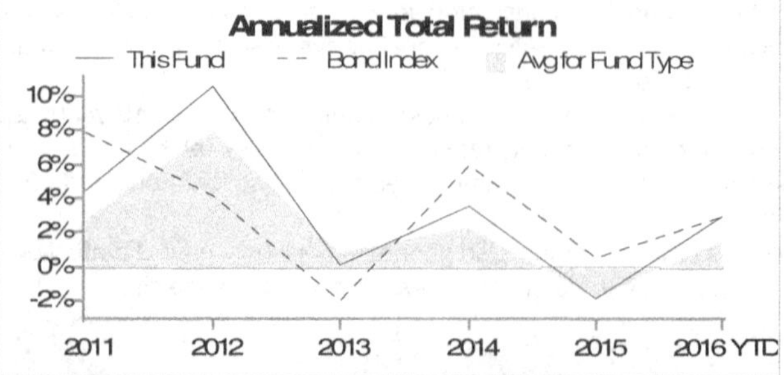

Fidelity Advisor Total Bond A (FEPAX) C- Fair

Fund Family: Fidelity Advisor **Phone:** (800) 522-7297
Address: 245 Summer Street, Boston, MA 02210
Fund Type: GEI - General - Investment Grade
Major Rating Factors: Middle of the road best describes Fidelity Advisor Total Bond A whose TheStreet.com Investment Rating is currently a C- (Fair). The fund has a performance rating of C (Fair) based on an average return of 1.99% over the last three years and 3.13% over the last three months. Factored into the performance evaluation is an expense ratio of 0.75% (low) and a 4.0% front-end load that is levied at the time of purchase.

The fund's risk rating is currently C (Fair). Volatility, as measured by standard deviation, is considered average for fixed income funds at 3.27. Another risk factor is the fund's fairly average duration of 5.2 years (i.e. average interest rate risk).

Ford O'Neil has been running the fund for 12 years and currently receives a manager quality ranking of 44 (0=worst, 99=best). If you desire an average level of risk, then this fund may be an option.

Services Offered: Automated phone transactions, payroll deductions, bank draft capabilities, an IRA investment plan, a 401K investment plan, a Keogh investment plan, wire transfers and a systematic withdrawal plan.

Data Date	Investment Rating	Net Assets ($Mil)	NAV	Performance Rating/Pts	Total Return Y-T-D	Risk Rating/Pts
3-16	C-	1,231	10.51	C / 4.6	3.13%	C / 5.5
2015	D+	1,141	10.26	D+ / 2.4	-0.73%	C+ / 5.7
2014	D+	738	10.68	C- / 3.6	5.22%	C+ / 6.3
2013	C-	515	10.44	C- / 3.6	-1.33%	B- / 7.0
2012	C+	663	10.96	C- / 3.5	6.27%	B / 7.8
2011	B+	1,320	10.92	C / 5.1	6.98%	B- / 7.1

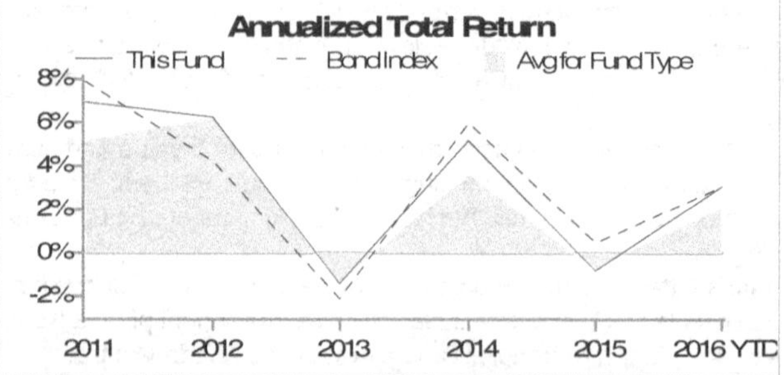

Fidelity CA Ltd Term Tax-Free Bd (FCSTX) A+ Excellent

Fund Family: Fidelity Investments **Phone:** (800) 544-8544
Address: 245 Summer Street, Boston, MA 02210
Fund Type: MUS - Municipal - Single State
Major Rating Factors: Strong performance is the major factor driving the A+ (Excellent) TheStreet.com Investment Rating for Fidelity CA Ltd Term Tax-Free Bd. The fund currently has a performance rating of B- (Good) based on an average return of 1.85% over the last three years (3.06% taxable equivalent) and 0.77% over the last three months (1.28% taxable equivalent). Factored into the performance evaluation is an expense ratio of 0.49% (very low) and a 0.5% back-end load levied at the time of sale.

The fund's risk rating is currently B+ (Good). Volatility, as measured by standard deviation, is considered low for fixed income funds at 1.56. Another risk factor is the fund's very low average duration of 3.0 years (i.e. low interest rate risk).

Jamie Pagliocco has been running the fund for 10 years and currently receives a manager quality ranking of 78 (0=worst, 99=best). If you desire only a moderate level of risk and strong performance, then this fund is an excellent option.

Services Offered: Automated phone transactions, payroll deductions, bank draft capabilities, wire transfers and a systematic withdrawal plan.

Data Date	Investment Rating	Net Assets ($Mil)	NAV	Performance Rating/Pts	Total Return Y-T-D	Risk Rating/Pts
3-16	A+	816	10.76	B- / 7.4	0.77%	B+ / 8.9
2015	A+	788	10.72	B / 7.8	1.70%	B+ / 8.9
2014	B+	782	10.73	C- / 4.2	3.25%	B+ / 8.8
2013	A	689	10.59	C / 5.2	0.30%	B+ / 8.8
2012	C+	790	10.80	D+ / 2.3	2.44%	B+ / 8.9
2011	B-	721	10.77	C- / 3.4	4.74%	B+ / 8.7

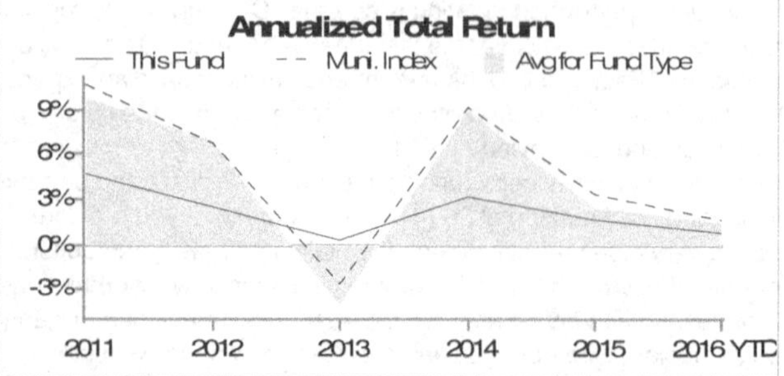

Fidelity Conservative Inc Bond (FCONX) C+ Fair

Fund Family: Fidelity Investments **Phone:** (800) 544-8544
Address: 245 Summer Street, Boston, MA 02210
Fund Type: GEN - General

Major Rating Factors: A moderate risk profile coupled with stable earnings characterizes Fidelity Conservative Inc Bond which receives a TheStreet.com Investment Rating of C+ (Fair). Volatility, as measured by standard deviation, is considered very low for fixed income funds at 0.17. The fund's risk rating is currently A+ (Excellent).

The fund's performance rating is currently C- (Fair). It has registered an average return of 0.37% over the last three years and is up 0.19% over the last three months. Factored into the performance evaluation is an expense ratio of 0.40% (very low).

James K. Miller has been running the fund for 5 years and currently receives a manager quality ranking of 78 (0=worst, 99=best). If you desire stability with a moderate level of risk then this fund is an excellent option.

Services Offered: Automated phone transactions, bank draft capabilities and wire transfers.

Data Date	Investment Rating	Net Assets ($Mil)	NAV	Performance Rating/Pts	Total Return Y-T-D	Risk Rating/Pts
3-16	C+	1,123	10.02	C- / 3.1	0.19%	A+ / 9.9
2015	B	1,089	10.02	C / 4.5	0.35%	A+ / 9.9
2014	C	1,433	10.03	D / 1.6	0.21%	A+ / 9.9
2013	U	1,563	10.04	U / --	0.62%	U / --
2012	U	1,033	10.03	U / --	1.38%	U / --
2011	U	363	9.97	U / --	0.00%	U / --

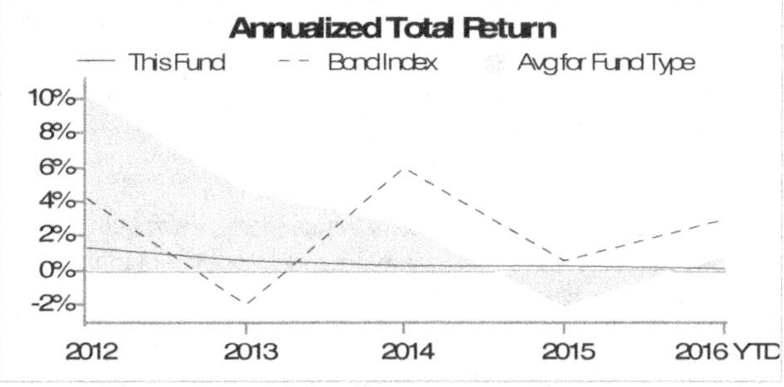

Fidelity Focused High Income (FHIFX) D Weak

Fund Family: Fidelity Investments **Phone:** (800) 544-8544
Address: 245 Summer Street, Boston, MA 02210
Fund Type: COH - Corporate - High Yield

Major Rating Factors: Fidelity Focused High Income has adopted a very risky asset allocation strategy and currently receives an overall TheStreet.com Investment Rating of D (Weak). Volatility, as measured by standard deviation, is considered above average for fixed income funds at 5.48. Another risk factor is the fund's below average duration of 4.3 years (i.e. lower interest rate risk). Unfortunately, the high level of risk (D, Weak) has only provided investors with average performance.

The fund's performance rating is currently C (Fair). It has registered an average return of 1.80% over the last three years and is up 2.32% over the last three months. Factored into the performance evaluation is an expense ratio of 0.85% (average) and a 1.0% back-end load levied at the time of sale.

Matthew J. Conti has been running the fund for 12 years and currently receives a manager quality ranking of 75 (0=worst, 99=best). If you are comfortable owning a very high risk investment, then this fund may be an option.

Services Offered: Automated phone transactions, payroll deductions, bank draft capabilities, an IRA investment plan, a Keogh investment plan, wire transfers and a systematic withdrawal plan.

Data Date	Investment Rating	Net Assets ($Mil)	NAV	Performance Rating/Pts	Total Return Y-T-D	Risk Rating/Pts
3-16	D	731	8.10	C / 4.9	2.32%	D / 1.6
2015	D	727	8.01	C / 4.7	-1.93%	D / 1.7
2014	C-	592	8.55	C+ / 6.5	2.45%	C- / 3.1
2013	B-	744	9.00	B+ / 8.9	4.44%	D+ / 2.4
2012	C	929	9.39	B- / 7.5	11.69%	D / 1.8
2011	C+	781	8.95	B+ / 8.3	5.87%	D / 2.0

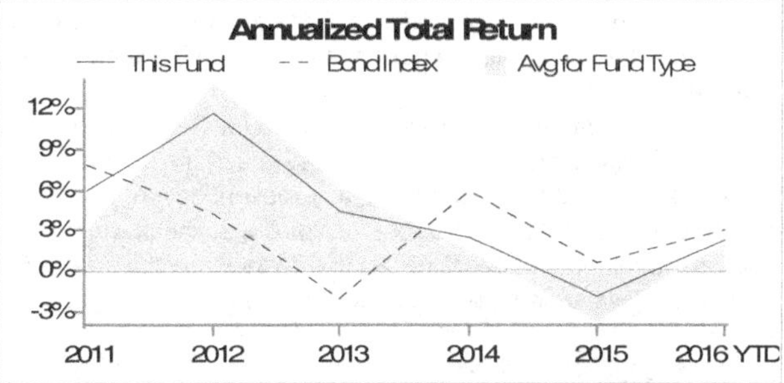

Fidelity GNMA Fund (FGMNX) B+ Good

Fund Family: Fidelity Investments **Phone:** (800) 544-8544
Address: 245 Summer Street, Boston, MA 02210
Fund Type: USA - US Government/Agency

Major Rating Factors: A moderate risk profile coupled with stable earnings characterizes Fidelity GNMA Fund which receives a TheStreet.com Investment Rating of B+ (Good). Volatility, as measured by standard deviation, is considered low for fixed income funds at 2.78. Another risk factor is the fund's below average duration of 3.4 years (i.e. lower interest rate risk). The fund's risk rating is currently B- (Good).

The fund's performance rating is currently C+ (Fair). It has registered an average return of 2.19% over the last three years and is up 1.61% over the last three months. Factored into the performance evaluation is an expense ratio of 0.45% (very low).

William W. Irving has been running the fund for 12 years and currently receives a manager quality ranking of 84 (0=worst, 99=best). If you desire stability with a moderate level of risk then this fund is an excellent option.

Services Offered: Automated phone transactions, check writing, payroll deductions, bank draft capabilities, an IRA investment plan, a 401K investment plan, a Keogh investment plan, wire transfers and a systematic withdrawal plan.

Data Date	Investment Rating	Net Assets ($Mil)	NAV	Performance Rating/Pts	Total Return Y-T-D	Risk Rating/Pts
3-16	B+	6,129	11.64	C+ / 6.6	1.61%	B- / 7.3
2015	B+	5,911	11.52	C+ / 6.9	1.20%	B- / 7.0
2014	C	6,442	11.66	C- / 4.0	6.26%	C+ / 6.9
2013	C	6,901	11.21	C- / 3.4	-2.17%	B / 7.7
2012	C+	10,916	11.74	C- / 3.0	2.98%	B+ / 8.4
2011	B+	8,976	11.84	C- / 3.8	7.91%	B+ / 8.6

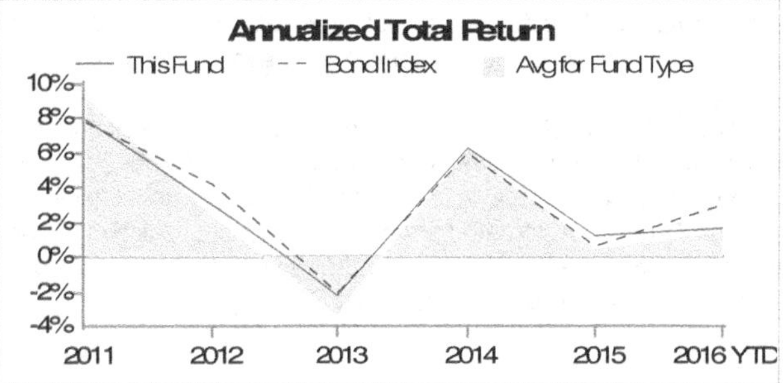

Fidelity High Income (SPHIX) D- Weak

Fund Family: Fidelity Investments **Phone:** (800) 544-8544
Address: 245 Summer Street, Boston, MA 02210
Fund Type: COI - Corporate - Investment Grade

Major Rating Factors: Fidelity High Income has adopted a very risky asset allocation strategy and currently receives an overall TheStreet.com Investment Rating of D- (Weak). Volatility, as measured by standard deviation, is considered above average for fixed income funds at 6.06. Unfortunately, the high level of risk (D, Weak) failed to pay off as investors endured very poor performance.

The fund's performance rating is currently D (Weak). It has registered an average return of 0.78% over the last three years and is up 2.78% over the last three months. Factored into the performance evaluation is an expense ratio of 0.72% (low) and a 1.0% back-end load levied at the time of sale.

Frederick D. Hoff, Jr. has been running the fund for 16 years and currently receives a manager quality ranking of 18 (0=worst, 99=best). If you can tolerate very high levels of risk in the hope of improved future returns, holding this fund may be an option.

Services Offered: Automated phone transactions, payroll deductions, bank draft capabilities, an IRA investment plan, a Keogh investment plan, wire transfers and a systematic withdrawal plan.

Data Date	Investment Rating	Net Assets ($Mil)	NAV	Performance Rating/Pts	Total Return Y-T-D	Risk Rating/Pts
3-16	D-	3,916	8.05	D / 2.2	2.78%	D / 1.6
2015	D-	4,163	7.95	D / 1.7	-5.40%	D / 1.9
2014	C	5,365	8.90	B- / 7.5	1.53%	D+ / 2.9
2013	C+	6,001	9.37	A / 9.4	6.68%	E+ / 0.9
2012	C-	6,494	9.34	B+ / 8.4	14.89%	E+ / 0.6
2011	C+	4,580	8.64	A / 9.3	3.41%	E+ / 0.9

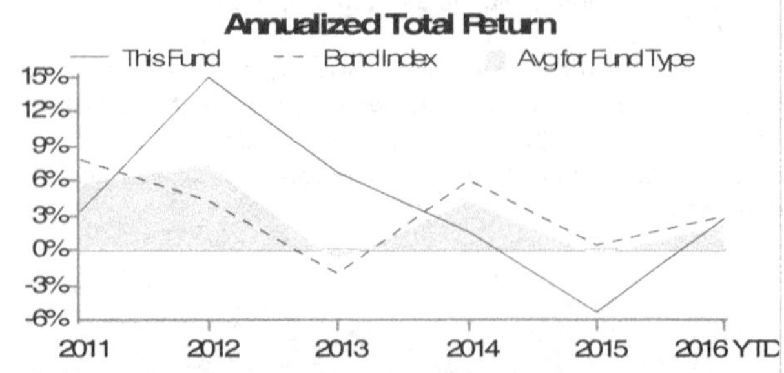

Fidelity Intermediate Bond (FTHRX) B+ Good

Fund Family: Fidelity Investments **Phone:** (800) 544-8544
Address: 245 Summer Street, Boston, MA 02210
Fund Type: GEI - General - Investment Grade

Major Rating Factors: A moderate risk profile coupled with stable earnings characterizes Fidelity Intermediate Bond which receives a TheStreet.com Investment Rating of B+ (Good). Volatility, as measured by standard deviation, is considered low for fixed income funds at 2.30. Another risk factor is the fund's below average duration of 3.9 years (i.e. lower interest rate risk). The fund's risk rating is currently B (Good).

The fund's performance rating is currently C+ (Fair). It has registered an average return of 1.80% over the last three years and is up 2.43% over the last three months. Factored into the performance evaluation is an expense ratio of 0.45% (very low).

Robert Galusza has been running the fund for 7 years and currently receives a manager quality ranking of 60 (0=worst, 99=best). If you desire stability with a moderate level of risk then this fund is an excellent option.

Services Offered: Automated phone transactions, check writing, payroll deductions, bank draft capabilities, an IRA investment plan, a 401K investment plan, a Keogh investment plan and a systematic withdrawal plan.

Data Date	Investment Rating	Net Assets ($Mil)	NAV	Performance Rating/Pts	Total Return Y-T-D	Risk Rating/Pts
3-16	B+	3,133	10.93	C+ / 6.2	2.43%	B / 8.1
2015	B	3,080	10.73	C+ / 5.7	0.68%	B / 8.0
2014	C+	3,342	10.93	C- / 3.6	3.31%	B / 8.2
2013	B+	3,325	10.83	C / 4.7	-0.64%	B / 8.2
2012	B-	4,067	11.14	C- / 3.6	4.93%	B / 8.0
2011	B	4,277	10.88	C / 5.0	6.15%	B- / 7.1

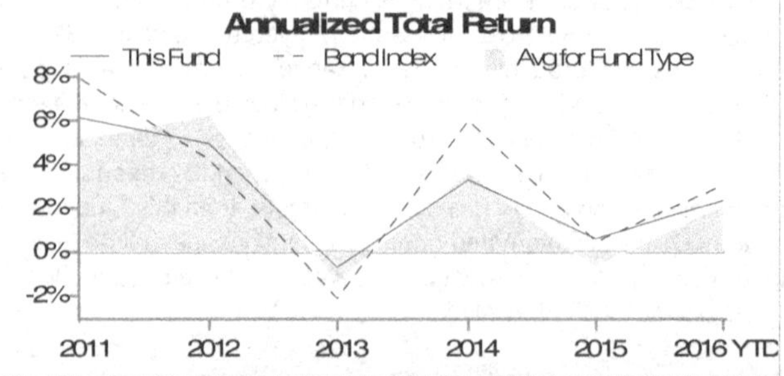

Fidelity Intermediate Government (FSTGX) B Good

Fund Family: Fidelity Investments **Phone:** (800) 544-8544
Address: 245 Summer Street, Boston, MA 02210
Fund Type: USS - US Government - Short & Inter. Term

Major Rating Factors: A moderate risk profile coupled with stable earnings characterizes Fidelity Intermediate Government which receives a TheStreet.com Investment Rating of B (Good). Volatility, as measured by standard deviation, is considered low for fixed income funds at 2.15. Another risk factor is the fund's below average duration of 3.7 years (i.e. lower interest rate risk). The fund's risk rating is currently B+ (Good).

The fund's performance rating is currently C (Fair). It has registered an average return of 1.38% over the last three years and is up 2.18% over the last three months. Factored into the performance evaluation is an expense ratio of 0.45% (very low).

William W. Irving has been running the fund for 8 years and currently receives a manager quality ranking of 57 (0=worst, 99=best). If you desire stability with a moderate level of risk then this fund is an excellent option.

Services Offered: Automated phone transactions, check writing, payroll deductions, bank draft capabilities, an IRA investment plan, a Keogh investment plan and a systematic withdrawal plan.

Data Date	Investment Rating	Net Assets ($Mil)	NAV	Performance Rating/Pts	Total Return Y-T-D	Risk Rating/Pts
3-16	B	758	10.77	C / 5.5	2.18%	B+ / 8.3
2015	C+	714	10.57	C / 5.0	0.81%	B+ / 8.3
2014	C-	770	10.68	D+ / 2.3	2.60%	B+ / 8.6
2013	C	869	10.54	D+ / 2.6	-1.26%	B+ / 8.5
2012	D+	1,097	10.85	D / 1.8	1.97%	B / 8.0
2011	D+	1,184	10.97	D / 2.2	5.71%	B / 8.1

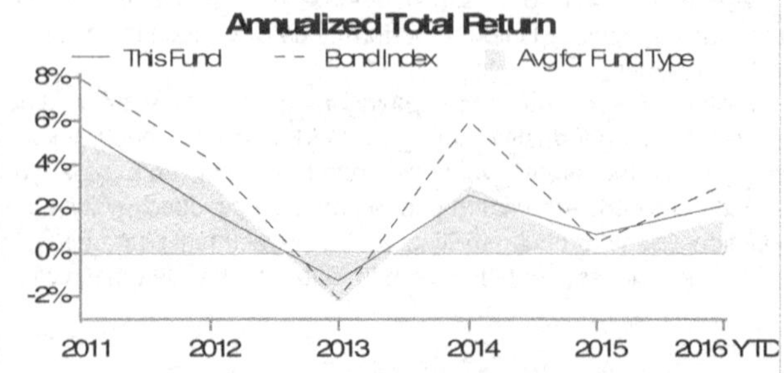

Fidelity MA Muni Inc Fd (FDMMX) A- Excellent

Fund Family: Fidelity Investments **Phone:** (800) 544-8544
Address: 245 Summer Street, Boston, MA 02210
Fund Type: MUS - Municipal - Single State
Major Rating Factors: Exceptional performance is the major factor driving the A- (Excellent) TheStreet.com Investment Rating for Fidelity MA Muni Inc Fd. The fund currently has a performance rating of A (Excellent) based on an average return of 3.75% over the last three years (6.21% taxable equivalent) and 1.66% over the last three months (2.75% taxable equivalent). Factored into the performance evaluation is an expense ratio of 0.46% (very low) and a 0.5% back-end load levied at the time of sale.

The fund's risk rating is currently C (Fair). Volatility, as measured by standard deviation, is considered average for fixed income funds at 3.74. Another risk factor is the fund's fairly average duration of 6.8 years (i.e. average interest rate risk).

Kevin J. Ramundo has been running the fund for 6 years and currently receives a manager quality ranking of 55 (0=worst, 99=best). If you desire an average level of risk and strong performance, then this fund is a good option.
Services Offered: Automated phone transactions, check writing, payroll deductions, bank draft capabilities and a systematic withdrawal plan.

Data Date	Investment Rating	Net Assets ($Mil)	NAV	Performance Rating/Pts	Total Return Y-T-D	Risk Rating/Pts
3-16	A-	2,289	12.60	A / 9.4	1.66%	C / 4.4
2015	B	2,232	12.50	A / 9.3	3.36%	C- / 3.8
2014	B+	2,170	12.52	B+ / 8.8	9.96%	C- / 3.6
2013	B-	1,981	11.79	B- / 7.5	-3.46%	C- / 3.9
2012	B+	2,547	12.69	B / 7.6	7.18%	C / 4.3
2011	A+	2,220	12.32	B- / 7.4	10.37%	C / 5.3

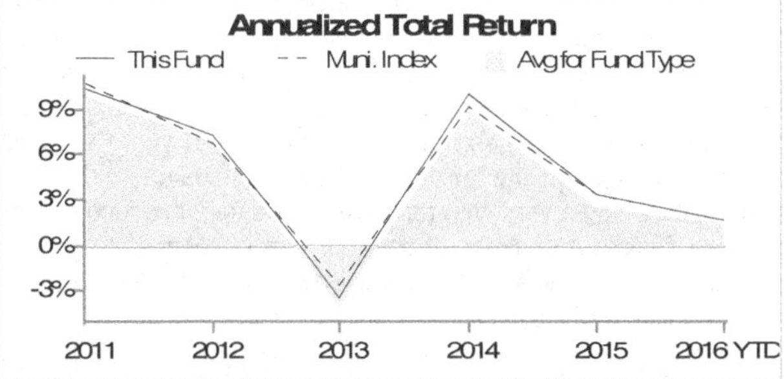

Fidelity MI Muni Inc (FMHTX) A+ Excellent

Fund Family: Fidelity Investments **Phone:** (800) 544-8544
Address: 245 Summer Street, Boston, MA 02210
Fund Type: MUS - Municipal - Single State
Major Rating Factors: Exceptional performance is the major factor driving the A+ (Excellent) TheStreet.com Investment Rating for Fidelity MI Muni Inc. The fund currently has a performance rating of A (Excellent) based on an average return of 3.62% over the last three years (5.99% taxable equivalent) and 1.54% over the last three months (2.55% taxable equivalent). Factored into the performance evaluation is an expense ratio of 0.49% (very low) and a 0.5% back-end load levied at the time of sale.

The fund's risk rating is currently C+ (Fair). Volatility, as measured by standard deviation, is considered average for fixed income funds at 3.22. Another risk factor is the fund's fairly average duration of 5.7 years (i.e. average interest rate risk).

Jamie Pagliocco has been running the fund for 10 years and currently receives a manager quality ranking of 76 (0=worst, 99=best). If you desire an average level of risk and strong performance, then this fund is a good option.
Services Offered: Automated phone transactions, check writing, payroll deductions, bank draft capabilities and a systematic withdrawal plan.

Data Date	Investment Rating	Net Assets ($Mil)	NAV	Performance Rating/Pts	Total Return Y-T-D	Risk Rating/Pts
3-16	A+	666	12.48	A / 9.4	1.54%	C+ / 5.7
2015	A	633	12.38	A / 9.4	3.61%	C / 5.4
2014	A+	569	12.33	B+ / 8.5	9.23%	C / 5.2
2013	B+	529	11.70	B- / 7.0	-2.75%	C+ / 5.7
2012	A	693	12.54	C+ / 6.7	6.19%	C+ / 6.0
2011	A	610	12.24	C+ / 6.1	9.20%	C+ / 6.5

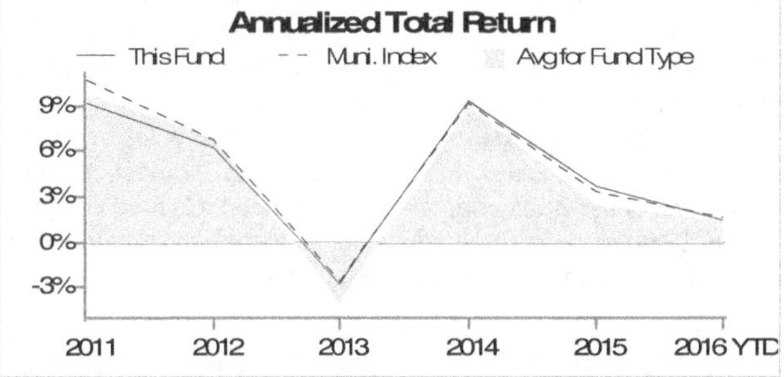

Fidelity Municipal Inc (FHIGX) B Good

Fund Family: Fidelity Investments **Phone:** (800) 544-8544
Address: 245 Summer Street, Boston, MA 02210
Fund Type: MUH - Municipal - High Yield
Major Rating Factors: Exceptional performance is the major factor driving the B (Good) TheStreet.com Investment Rating for Fidelity Municipal Inc. The fund currently has a performance rating of A (Excellent) based on an average return of 3.98% over the last three years (6.59% taxable equivalent) and 1.64% over the last three months (2.72% taxable equivalent). Factored into the performance evaluation is an expense ratio of 0.48% (very low) and a 0.5% back-end load levied at the time of sale.

The fund's risk rating is currently C- (Fair). Volatility, as measured by standard deviation, is considered average for fixed income funds at 3.79. Another risk factor is the fund's fairly average duration of 6.6 years (i.e. average interest rate risk).

Jamie Pagliocco has been running the fund for 7 years and currently receives a manager quality ranking of 61 (0=worst, 99=best). If you desire an average level of risk and strong performance, then this fund is a good option.
Services Offered: Automated phone transactions, check writing, payroll deductions, bank draft capabilities and a systematic withdrawal plan.

Data Date	Investment Rating	Net Assets ($Mil)	NAV	Performance Rating/Pts	Total Return Y-T-D	Risk Rating/Pts
3-16	B	5,723	13.55	A / 9.5	1.64%	C- / 3.5
2015	B-	5,756	13.44	A / 9.5	3.31%	C- / 3.0
2014	B+	5,733	13.53	A- / 9.2	10.59%	C- / 3.0
2013	B	5,331	12.68	B / 8.2	-2.94%	C- / 3.4
2012	B+	6,783	13.57	B / 8.2	7.92%	C- / 3.5
2011	B+	5,761	13.03	B / 7.6	10.64%	C- / 4.1

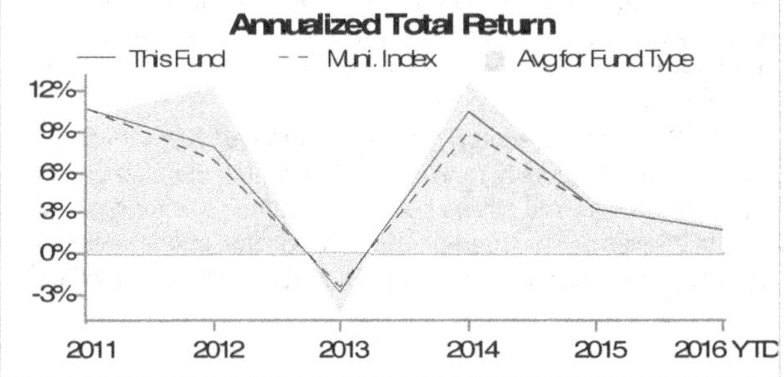

Fidelity New Markets Income (FNMIX) D Weak

Fund Family: Fidelity Investments **Phone:** (800) 544-8544
Address: 245 Summer Street, Boston, MA 02210
Fund Type: EM - Emerging Market

Major Rating Factors: Fidelity New Markets Income has adopted a very risky asset allocation strategy and currently receives an overall TheStreet.com Investment Rating of D (Weak). Volatility, as measured by standard deviation, is considered high for fixed income funds at 8.02. Another risk factor is the fund's above average duration of 7.3 years (i.e. higher interest rate risk). Unfortunately, the high level of risk (E, Very Weak) has only provided investors with average performance.

The fund's performance rating is currently C+ (Fair). It has registered an average return of 1.36% over the last three years and is up 4.52% over the last three months. Factored into the performance evaluation is an expense ratio of 0.86% (average) and a 1.0% back-end load levied at the time of sale.

John H. Carlson has been running the fund for 21 years and currently receives a manager quality ranking of 93 (0=worst, 99=best). If you are comfortable owning a very high risk investment, then this fund may be an option.

Services Offered: Automated phone transactions, payroll deductions, bank draft capabilities, an IRA investment plan, a 401K investment plan, a Keogh investment plan and a systematic withdrawal plan.

Data Date	Investment Rating	Net Assets ($Mil)	NAV	Performance Rating/Pts	Total Return Y-T-D	Risk Rating/Pts
3-16	D	3,898	14.96	C+ / 6.5	4.52%	E / 0.4
2015	E+	3,978	14.52	D / 1.9	0.24%	E / 0.3
2014	D-	4,513	15.26	C / 5.5	4.32%	E / 0.3
2013	D	4,514	15.59	B- / 7.2	-6.41%	E+ / 0.6
2012	B	7,243	17.80	A+ / 9.7	20.02%	D- / 1.3
2011	B-	4,134	15.83	A / 9.3	7.94%	D- / 1.5

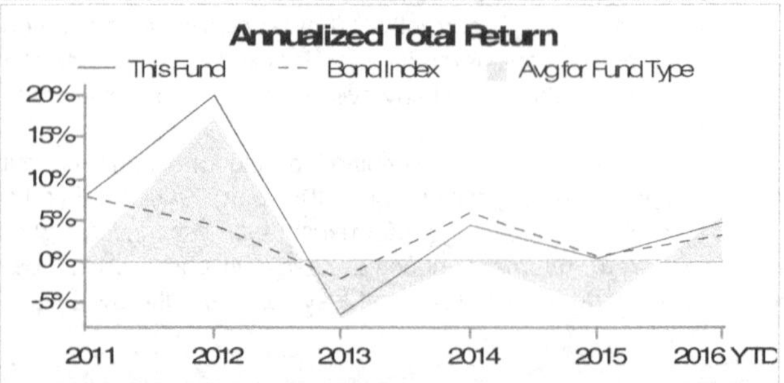

Fidelity NJ Muni Income Fd (FNJHX) B+ Good

Fund Family: Fidelity Investments **Phone:** (800) 544-8544
Address: 245 Summer Street, Boston, MA 02210
Fund Type: MUS - Municipal - Single State

Major Rating Factors: Exceptional performance is the major factor driving the B+ (Good) TheStreet.com Investment Rating for Fidelity NJ Muni Income Fd. The fund currently has a performance rating of A- (Excellent) based on an average return of 2.99% over the last three years (4.95% taxable equivalent) and 1.76% over the last three months (2.91% taxable equivalent). Factored into the performance evaluation is an expense ratio of 0.48% (very low) and a 0.5% back-end load levied at the time of sale.

The fund's risk rating is currently C (Fair). Volatility, as measured by standard deviation, is considered average for fixed income funds at 3.81. Another risk factor is the fund's fairly average duration of 6.7 years (i.e. average interest rate risk).

Jamie Pagliocco has been running the fund for 7 years and currently receives a manager quality ranking of 31 (0=worst, 99=best). If you desire an average level of risk and strong performance, then this fund is a good option.

Services Offered: Automated phone transactions, payroll deductions, bank draft capabilities, wire transfers and a systematic withdrawal plan.

Data Date	Investment Rating	Net Assets ($Mil)	NAV	Performance Rating/Pts	Total Return Y-T-D	Risk Rating/Pts
3-16	B+	548	12.00	A- / 9.0	1.76%	C / 4.3
2015	B-	548	11.88	B+ / 8.9	1.98%	C- / 3.8
2014	B+	601	12.06	B+ / 8.4	8.94%	C- / 4.2
2013	B	580	11.44	B- / 7.2	-2.91%	C / 4.5
2012	B+	683	12.25	C+ / 6.8	6.38%	C / 4.9
2011	B+	607	11.93	C+ / 6.8	9.71%	C / 5.0

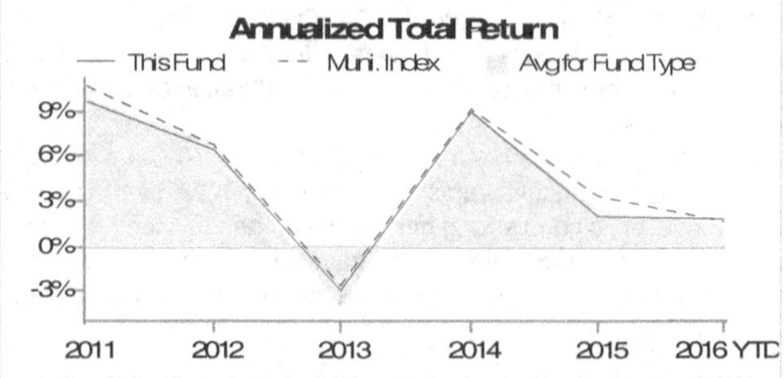

Fidelity OH Muni Inc (FOHFX) B+ Good

Fund Family: Fidelity Investments **Phone:** (800) 544-8544
Address: 245 Summer Street, Boston, MA 02210
Fund Type: MUS - Municipal - Single State

Major Rating Factors: Exceptional performance is the major factor driving the B+ (Good) TheStreet.com Investment Rating for Fidelity OH Muni Inc. The fund currently has a performance rating of A+ (Excellent) based on an average return of 4.30% over the last three years (7.12% taxable equivalent) and 1.89% over the last three months (3.13% taxable equivalent). Factored into the performance evaluation is an expense ratio of 0.48% (very low) and a 0.5% back-end load levied at the time of sale.

The fund's risk rating is currently C- (Fair). Volatility, as measured by standard deviation, is considered average for fixed income funds at 3.90. Another risk factor is the fund's above average duration of 7.1 years (i.e. higher interest rate risk).

Jamie Pagliocco has been running the fund for 10 years and currently receives a manager quality ranking of 74 (0=worst, 99=best). If you desire an average level of risk and strong performance, then this fund is a good option.

Services Offered: Automated phone transactions, check writing, payroll deductions, bank draft capabilities and a systematic withdrawal plan.

Data Date	Investment Rating	Net Assets ($Mil)	NAV	Performance Rating/Pts	Total Return Y-T-D	Risk Rating/Pts
3-16	B+	659	12.43	A+ / 9.7	1.89%	C- / 3.8
2015	B	634	12.29	A+ / 9.6	4.24%	C- / 3.6
2014	A	597	12.26	A- / 9.0	10.26%	C- / 3.9
2013	B	535	11.48	B- / 7.4	-3.16%	C / 4.4
2012	A-	646	12.39	B- / 7.3	7.14%	C / 5.1
2011	A-	537	12.01	C+ / 6.5	9.62%	C+ / 5.8

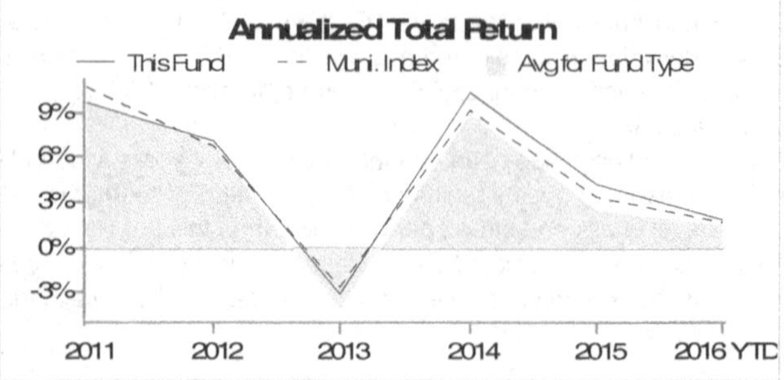

Fidelity Series Inf-Pro Bd Idx F (FFIPX) D Weak

Fund Family: Fidelity Investments **Phone:** (800) 544-8544
Address: 245 Summer Street, Boston, MA 02210
Fund Type: GEI - General - Investment Grade
Major Rating Factors: Disappointing performance is the major factor driving the D (Weak) TheStreet.com Investment Rating for Fidelity Series Inf-Pro Bd Idx F. The fund currently has a performance rating of D+ (Weak) based on an average return of -0.79% over the last three years and 3.72% over the last three months. Factored into the performance evaluation is an expense ratio of 0.05% (very low).

The fund's risk rating is currently C- (Fair). Volatility, as measured by standard deviation, is considered average for fixed income funds at 4.15. Another risk factor is the fund's below average duration of 3.7 years (i.e. lower interest rate risk).

Brandon Bettencourt has been running the fund for 2 years and currently receives a manager quality ranking of 6 (0=worst, 99=best). This fund offers an average level of risk, but investors looking for strong performance will be frustrated.
Services Offered: Automated phone transactions, payroll deductions, bank draft capabilities, an IRA investment plan, a 401K investment plan, wire transfers and a systematic withdrawal plan.

Data Date	Investment Rating	Net Assets ($Mil)	NAV	Performance Rating/Pts	Total Return Y-T-D	Risk Rating/Pts
3-16	D	903	9.89	D+ / 2.4	3.72%	C- / 3.7
2015	D	903	9.54	D- / 1.3	-0.77%	C- / 3.8
2014	E+	591	9.65	E+ / 0.7	0.95%	C / 4.5
2013	D-	717	10.05	D / 2.1	-5.65%	C / 5.1
2012	C-	3,692	11.36	C- / 3.6	4.92%	C+ / 6.4
2011	U	2,310	11.11	U / --	8.73%	U / --

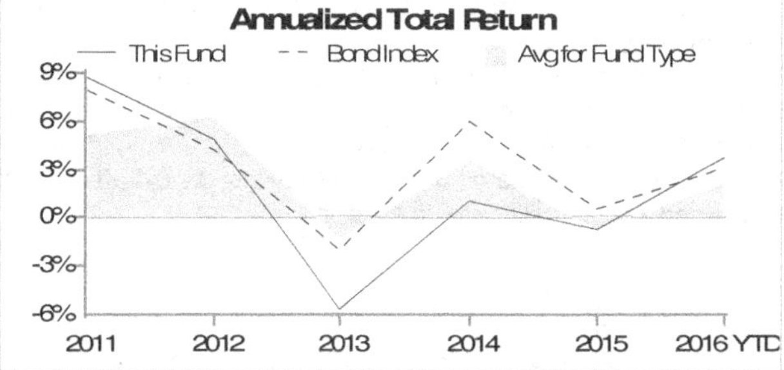

Fidelity Short-Term Bond (FSHBX) B Good

Fund Family: Fidelity Investments **Phone:** (800) 544-8544
Address: 245 Summer Street, Boston, MA 02210
Fund Type: GEI - General - Investment Grade
Major Rating Factors: A moderate risk profile coupled with stable earnings characterizes Fidelity Short-Term Bond which receives a TheStreet.com Investment Rating of B (Good). Volatility, as measured by standard deviation, is considered very low for fixed income funds at 0.75. Another risk factor is the fund's very low average duration of 1.6 years (i.e. low interest rate risk). The fund's risk rating is currently A+ (Excellent).

The fund's performance rating is currently C (Fair). It has registered an average return of 0.97% over the last three years and is up 0.92% over the last three months. Factored into the performance evaluation is an expense ratio of 0.45% (very low).

Robert Galusza has been running the fund for 9 years and currently receives a manager quality ranking of 81 (0=worst, 99=best). If you desire stability with a moderate level of risk then this fund is an excellent option.
Services Offered: Automated phone transactions, check writing, payroll deductions, bank draft capabilities, an IRA investment plan, a 401K investment plan, a Keogh investment plan and a systematic withdrawal plan. However, the fund is currently closed to new investors.

Data Date	Investment Rating	Net Assets ($Mil)	NAV	Performance Rating/Pts	Total Return Y-T-D	Risk Rating/Pts
3-16	B	5,416	8.61	C / 4.5	0.92%	A+ / 9.6
2015	B+	5,234	8.55	C / 5.2	0.67%	A+ / 9.6
2014	C	6,150	8.58	D / 2.1	0.93%	A+ / 9.6
2013	C+	6,894	8.58	D+ / 2.4	0.57%	A / 9.5
2012	C-	7,199	8.60	D- / 1.2	2.37%	A / 9.5
2011	C	7,844	8.49	D / 2.0	1.78%	A / 9.5

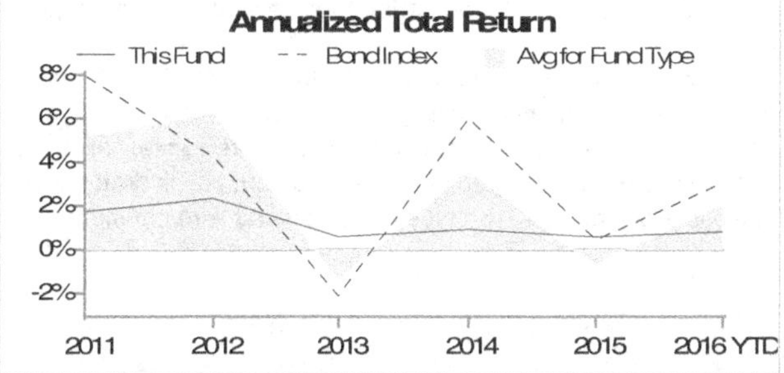

Fidelity Spartan US Bond Idx Inv (FBIDX) B- Good

Fund Family: Fidelity Investments **Phone:** (800) 544-8544
Address: 245 Summer Street, Boston, MA 02210
Fund Type: GEI - General - Investment Grade
Major Rating Factors: Strong performance is the major factor driving the B- (Good) TheStreet.com Investment Rating for Fidelity Spartan US Bond Idx Inv. The fund currently has a performance rating of B- (Good) based on an average return of 2.29% over the last three years and 3.04% over the last three months. Factored into the performance evaluation is an expense ratio of 0.22% (very low).

The fund's risk rating is currently C+ (Fair). Volatility, as measured by standard deviation, is considered average for fixed income funds at 3.13. Another risk factor is the fund's fairly average duration of 5.4 years (i.e. average interest rate risk).

Brandon Bettencourt has been running the fund for 2 years and currently receives a manager quality ranking of 51 (0=worst, 99=best). If you desire an average level of risk and strong performance, then this fund is a good option.
Services Offered: Automated phone transactions, payroll deductions, bank draft capabilities, an IRA investment plan, a 401K investment plan, a Keogh investment plan and wire transfers.

Data Date	Investment Rating	Net Assets ($Mil)	NAV	Performance Rating/Pts	Total Return Y-T-D	Risk Rating/Pts
3-16	B-	6,907	11.77	B- / 7.1	3.04%	C+ / 6.0
2015	C	6,797	11.49	C+ / 6.1	0.38%	C+ / 5.9
2014	C	6,574	11.74	C- / 4.2	5.90%	C+ / 6.8
2013	C	5,365	11.36	C- / 3.7	-2.36%	B- / 7.2
2012	C	6,228	11.89	C- / 3.2	4.07%	B- / 7.3
2011	C+	6,976	11.78	C- / 3.6	7.67%	B / 8.1

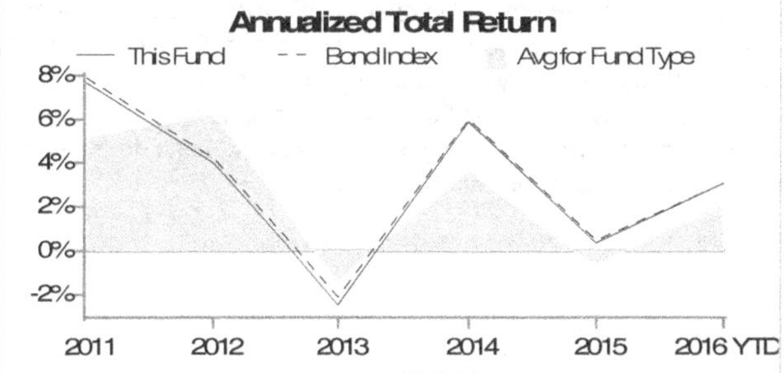

Fidelity Srs Inv Grade Bond (FSIGX) C+ Fair

Fund Family: Fidelity Investments **Phone:** (800) 544-8544
Address: 245 Summer Street, Boston, MA 02210
Fund Type: GEI - General - Investment Grade
Major Rating Factors: Middle of the road best describes Fidelity Srs Inv Grade Bond whose TheStreet.com Investment Rating is currently a C+ (Fair). The fund has a performance rating of C+ (Fair) based on an average return of 2.23% over the last three years and 3.13% over the last three months. Factored into the performance evaluation is an expense ratio of 0.45% (very low).

The fund's risk rating is currently C (Fair). Volatility, as measured by standard deviation, is considered average for fixed income funds at 3.26. Another risk factor is the fund's fairly average duration of 5.4 years (i.e. average interest rate risk).

Ford O'Neil has been running the fund for 8 years and currently receives a manager quality ranking of 48 (0=worst, 99=best). If you desire an average level of risk, then this fund may be an option.
Services Offered: Automated phone transactions, bank draft capabilities, wire transfers and a systematic withdrawal plan.

Data Date	Investment Rating	Net Assets ($Mil)	NAV	Performance Rating/Pts	Total Return Y-T-D	Risk Rating/Pts
3-16	C+	11,726	11.30	C+ / 6.9	3.13%	C / 5.5
2015	C	12,304	11.03	C+ / 5.6	-0.24%	C / 5.5
2014	C	12,889	11.45	C / 4.8	5.88%	C+ / 6.2
2013	C+	11,959	11.11	C / 4.7	-1.96%	C+ / 6.8
2012	B-	13,653	11.59	C- / 4.2	5.50%	B- / 7.5
2011	B-	14,261	11.68	C / 4.5	7.75%	B- / 7.3

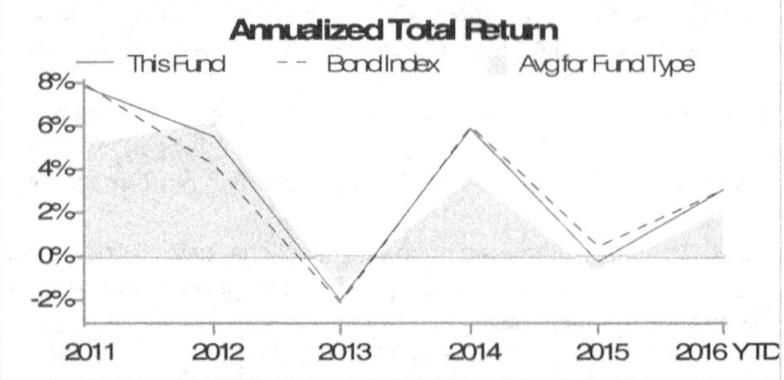

Fidelity Strat Adv Short Duration (FAUDX) C+ Fair

Fund Family: Fidelity Investments **Phone:** (800) 544-8544
Address: 245 Summer Street, Boston, MA 02210
Fund Type: COI - Corporate - Investment Grade
Major Rating Factors: A moderate risk profile coupled with stable earnings characterizes Fidelity Strat Adv Short Duration which receives a TheStreet.com Investment Rating of C+ (Fair). Volatility, as measured by standard deviation, is considered very low for fixed income funds at 0.59. The fund's risk rating is currently A+ (Excellent).

The fund's performance rating is currently C- (Fair). It has registered an average return of 0.63% over the last three years and is up 0.48% over the last three months. Factored into the performance evaluation is an expense ratio of 0.74% (low).

Gregory H. Pappas has been running the fund for 5 years and currently receives a manager quality ranking of 78 (0=worst, 99=best). If you desire stability with a moderate level of risk then this fund is an excellent option.
Services Offered: Automated phone transactions, bank draft capabilities, an IRA investment plan, a 401K investment plan and wire transfers.

Data Date	Investment Rating	Net Assets ($Mil)	NAV	Performance Rating/Pts	Total Return Y-T-D	Risk Rating/Pts
3-16	C+	6,398	9.98	C- / 3.7	0.48%	A+ / 9.8
2015	B+	7,192	9.97	C / 4.8	0.48%	A+ / 9.8
2014	C	7,100	10.03	D / 1.9	0.69%	A+ / 9.8
2013	U	6,511	10.06	U / --	0.54%	U / --
2012	U	4,985	10.09	U / --	1.81%	U / --

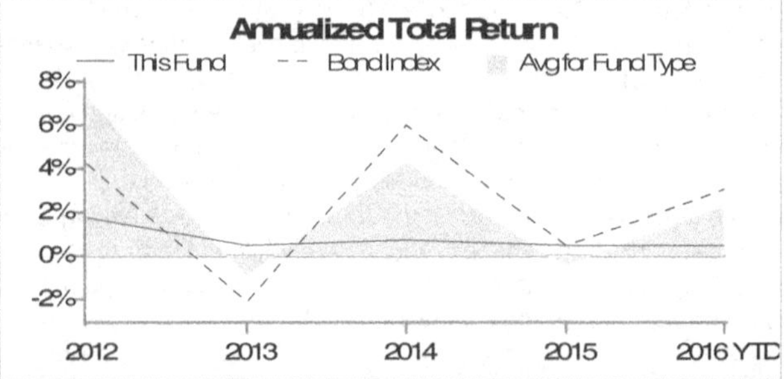

Fidelity Strategic Advisers Cor Inc (FPCIX) C+ Fair

Fund Family: Fidelity Investments **Phone:** (800) 544-8544
Address: 245 Summer Street, Boston, MA 02210
Fund Type: GEI - General - Investment Grade
Major Rating Factors: Middle of the road best describes Fidelity Strategic Advisers Cor Inc whose TheStreet.com Investment Rating is currently a C+ (Fair). The fund has a performance rating of C+ (Fair) based on an average return of 2.00% over the last three years and 2.66% over the last three months. Factored into the performance evaluation is an expense ratio of 0.85% (average).

The fund's risk rating is currently C+ (Fair). Volatility, as measured by standard deviation, is considered average for fixed income funds at 3.08.

Gregory Pappas has been running the fund for 9 years and currently receives a manager quality ranking of 46 (0=worst, 99=best). If you desire an average level of risk, then this fund may be an option.
Services Offered: Automated phone transactions, bank draft capabilities, wire transfers and a systematic withdrawal plan.

Data Date	Investment Rating	Net Assets ($Mil)	NAV	Performance Rating/Pts	Total Return Y-T-D	Risk Rating/Pts
3-16	C+	26,747	10.54	C+ / 6.4	2.66%	C+ / 6.2
2015	C	28,195	10.34	C+ / 5.8	-0.02%	C+ / 6.2
2014	C+	19,161	10.66	C / 5.4	5.37%	C+ / 6.3
2013	B	16,225	10.43	C / 5.2	-1.57%	B- / 7.0
2012	A-	11,891	10.90	C / 5.2	7.82%	B / 7.6
2011	B+	7,515	10.57	C / 5.3	5.99%	B- / 7.1

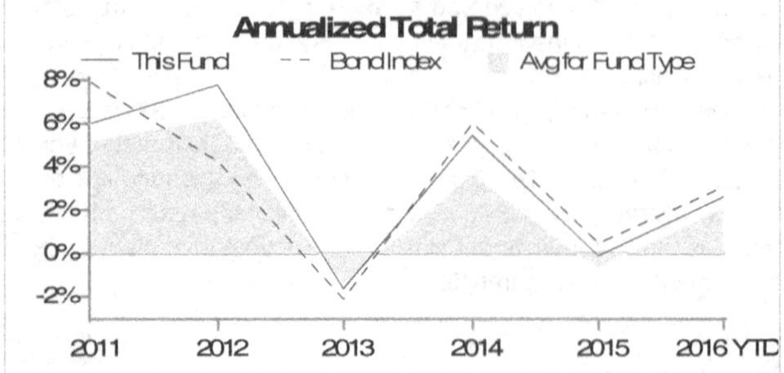

Fidelity Strategic Advisers Inc Opp (FPIOX) D Weak

Fund Family: Fidelity Investments **Phone:** (800) 544-8544
Address: 245 Summer Street, Boston, MA 02210
Fund Type: COH - Corporate - High Yield
Major Rating Factors: Fidelity Strategic Advisers Inc Opp has adopted a very risky asset allocation strategy and currently receives an overall TheStreet.com Investment Rating of D (Weak). Volatility, as measured by standard deviation, is considered above average for fixed income funds at 5.67. Unfortunately, the high level of risk (D-, Weak) has only provided investors with average performance.

The fund's performance rating is currently C- (Fair). It has registered an average return of 1.46% over the last three years and is up 1.82% over the last three months. Factored into the performance evaluation is an expense ratio of 1.15% (above average).

Greg Pappas has been running the fund for 9 years and currently receives a manager quality ranking of 55 (0=worst, 99=best). If you are comfortable owning a very high risk investment, then this fund may be an option.
Services Offered: Automated phone transactions, bank draft capabilities, wire transfers and a systematic withdrawal plan.

Data Date	Investment Rating	Net Assets ($Mil)	NAV	Performance Rating/Pts	Total Return Y-T-D	Risk Rating/Pts
3-16	D	3,795	8.75	C- / 3.9	1.82%	D- / 1.4
2015	D	3,973	8.71	C / 4.4	-3.86%	D- / 1.5
2014	C	4,144	9.75	B / 8.0	1.80%	D / 1.9
2013	C+	4,307	10.26	A+ / 9.6	8.06%	E+ / 0.8
2012	C	3,952	10.11	B+ / 8.7	15.25%	E / 0.5
2011	C+	2,660	9.35	A / 9.4	2.00%	E+ / 0.6

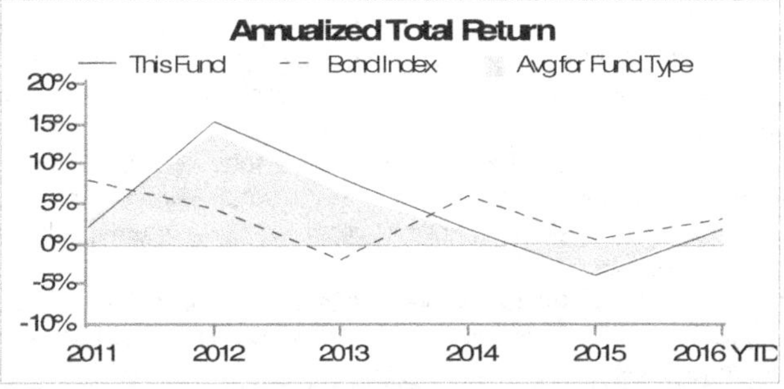

Fidelity Strategic Income Fund (FSICX) D+ Weak

Fund Family: Fidelity Investments **Phone:** (800) 544-8544
Address: 245 Summer Street, Boston, MA 02210
Fund Type: GL - Global
Major Rating Factors: Fidelity Strategic Income Fund receives a TheStreet.com Investment Rating of D+ (Weak). The fund has a performance rating of C+ (Fair) based on an average return of 1.70% over the last three years and 2.97% over the last three months. Factored into the performance evaluation is an expense ratio of 0.71% (low).

The fund's risk rating is currently C- (Fair). Volatility, as measured by standard deviation, is considered average for fixed income funds at 4.49. Another risk factor is the fund's below average duration of 4.9 years (i.e. lower interest rate risk).

Mark J. Notkin has been running the fund for 17 years and currently receives a manager quality ranking of 95 (0=worst, 99=best). If you desire an average level of risk, then this fund may be an option.
Services Offered: Automated phone transactions, payroll deductions, bank draft capabilities, an IRA investment plan, a 401K investment plan, a Keogh investment plan, wire transfers and a systematic withdrawal plan.

Data Date	Investment Rating	Net Assets ($Mil)	NAV	Performance Rating/Pts	Total Return Y-T-D	Risk Rating/Pts
3-16	D+	7,103	10.36	C+ / 5.8	2.97%	C- / 3.2
2015	D+	7,334	10.15	C- / 4.0	-1.62%	C- / 3.6
2014	C-	8,370	10.69	C+ / 5.8	3.78%	C- / 4.2
2013	C+	8,407	10.85	B- / 7.2	0.38%	C- / 4.0
2012	C	10,493	11.37	C+ / 6.8	10.90%	D+ / 2.9
2011	C	8,547	10.81	B- / 7.2	4.64%	D+ / 2.8

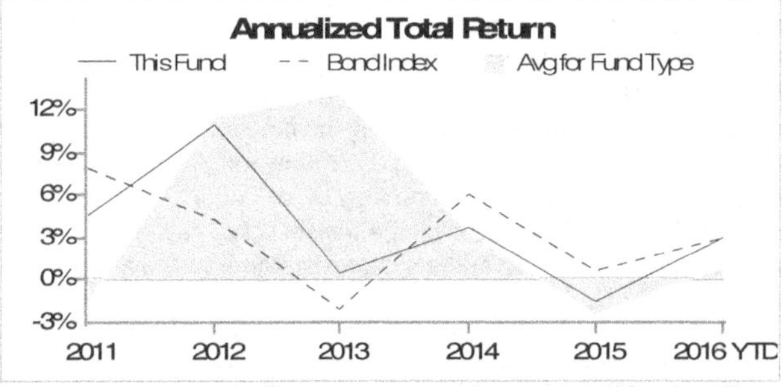

Fidelity Tax Free Bond Fd (FTABX) A- Excellent

Fund Family: Fidelity Investments **Phone:** (800) 544-8544
Address: 245 Summer Street, Boston, MA 02210
Fund Type: MUN - Municipal - National
Major Rating Factors: Exceptional performance is the major factor driving the A- (Excellent) TheStreet.com Investment Rating for Fidelity Tax Free Bond Fd. The fund currently has a performance rating of A+ (Excellent) based on an average return of 4.04% over the last three years (6.69% taxable equivalent) and 1.77% over the last three months (2.93% taxable equivalent). Factored into the performance evaluation is an expense ratio of 0.46% (very low) and a 0.5% back-end load levied at the time of sale.

The fund's risk rating is currently C- (Fair). Volatility, as measured by standard deviation, is considered average for fixed income funds at 3.83. Another risk factor is the fund's fairly average duration of 6.8 years (i.e. average interest rate risk).

Jamie Pagliocco has been running the fund for 7 years and currently receives a manager quality ranking of 62 (0=worst, 99=best). If you desire an average level of risk and strong performance, then this fund is a good option.
Services Offered: Automated phone transactions, payroll deductions, bank draft capabilities, wire transfers and a systematic withdrawal plan.

Data Date	Investment Rating	Net Assets ($Mil)	NAV	Performance Rating/Pts	Total Return Y-T-D	Risk Rating/Pts
3-16	A-	3,110	11.77	A+ / 9.6	1.77%	C- / 4.2
2015	B	2,983	11.66	A / 9.5	3.21%	C- / 3.7
2014	A+	2,819	11.71	A / 9.3	10.73%	C- / 4.2
2013	B+	2,208	10.97	B+ / 8.4	-2.83%	C- / 4.0
2012	A+	2,481	11.72	B / 8.2	8.18%	C / 4.4
2011	A	2,005	11.22	B / 7.6	10.90%	C / 4.8

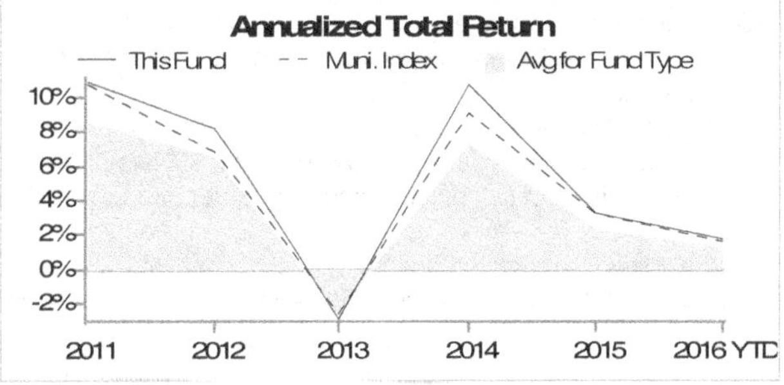

First Inv Fund for Income A (FIFIX) D- Weak

Fund Family: First Investors Funds **Phone:** (800) 423-4026
Address: 110 Wall Street, New York, NY 10005
Fund Type: COH - Corporate - High Yield
Major Rating Factors: First Inv Fund for Income A has adopted a very risky asset allocation strategy and currently receives an overall TheStreet.com Investment Rating of D- (Weak). Volatility, as measured by standard deviation, is considered above average for fixed income funds at 5.10. Unfortunately, the high level of risk (D, Weak) failed to pay off as investors endured very poor performance.

The fund's performance rating is currently D- (Weak). It has registered an average return of 1.41% over the last three years and is up 2.52% over the last three months. Factored into the performance evaluation is an expense ratio of 1.23% (above average) and a 5.8% front-end load that is levied at the time of purchase.

Clinton J. Comeaux has been running the fund for 7 years and currently receives a manager quality ranking of 61 (0=worst, 99=best). If you can tolerate very high levels of risk in the hope of improved future returns, holding this fund may be an option.
Services Offered: Automated phone transactions, payroll deductions, bank draft capabilities, an IRA investment plan, a 401K investment plan and a systematic withdrawal plan.

Data Date	Investment Rating	Net Assets ($Mil)	NAV	Performance Rating/Pts	Total Return Y-T-D	Risk Rating/Pts
3-16	D-	554	2.37	D- / 1.5	2.52%	D / 2.0
2015	D-	552	2.34	D / 1.8	-2.28%	D / 1.9
2014	D-	603	2.52	C / 4.9	0.56%	D+/ 2.7
2013	C+	658	2.64	B+/ 8.8	6.22%	D- / 1.5
2012	D+	614	2.63	B- / 7.3	13.11%	D- / 1.4
2011	C-	537	2.47	B / 7.8	5.25%	D / 1.6

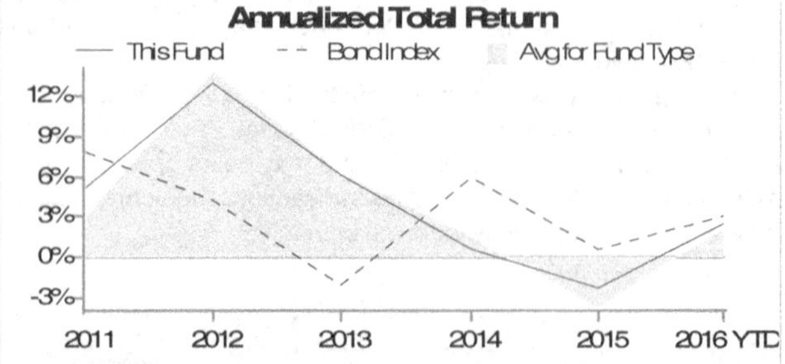

First Inv Tax Exempt Income A (FITAX) C Fair

Fund Family: First Investors Funds **Phone:** (800) 423-4026
Address: 110 Wall Street, New York, NY 10005
Fund Type: MUI - Municipal - Insured
Major Rating Factors: Middle of the road best describes First Inv Tax Exempt Income A whose TheStreet.com Investment Rating is currently a C (Fair). The fund has a performance rating of C+ (Fair) based on an average return of 2.82% over the last three years and 1.03% over the last three months. Factored into the performance evaluation is an expense ratio of 1.00% (average) and a 5.8% front-end load that is levied at the time of purchase.

The fund's risk rating is currently C (Fair). Volatility, as measured by standard deviation, is considered average for fixed income funds at 3.57. Another risk factor is the fund's below average duration of 3.9 years (i.e. lower interest rate risk).

Clark D. Wagner has been running the fund for 25 years and currently receives a manager quality ranking of 32 (0=worst, 99=best). If you desire an average level of risk, then this fund may be an option.
Services Offered: Automated phone transactions, payroll deductions, bank draft capabilities, wire transfers and a systematic withdrawal plan.

Data Date	Investment Rating	Net Assets ($Mil)	NAV	Performance Rating/Pts	Total Return Y-T-D	Risk Rating/Pts
3-16	C	628	9.88	C+/ 6.5	1.03%	C / 4.8
2015	C+	626	9.87	B- / 7.3	2.54%	C / 4.5
2014	C	644	10.01	C+/ 6.7	8.88%	C- / 3.7
2013	D+	639	9.56	C / 5.0	-3.18%	C- / 4.1
2012	D	722	10.27	C / 4.9	7.23%	C- / 4.0
2011	C	705	9.97	C / 5.1	10.32%	C / 5.4

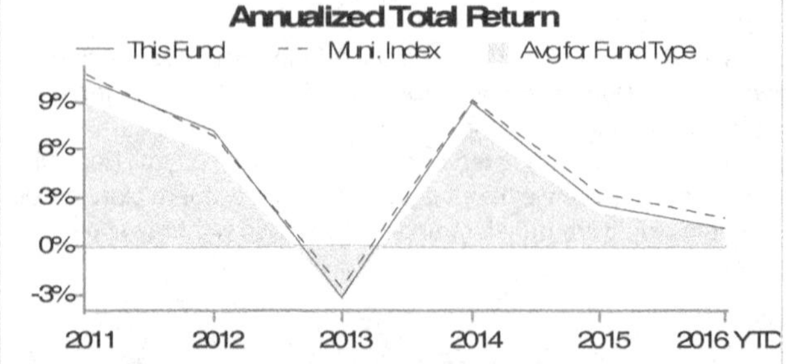

FPA New Income Inc (FPNIX) C Fair

Fund Family: FPA Funds **Phone:** (800) 982-4372
Address: 11400 West Olympic Blvd, Los Angeles, CA 90064
Fund Type: GEI - General - Investment Grade
Major Rating Factors: Disappointing performance is the major factor driving the C (Fair) TheStreet.com Investment Rating for FPA New Income Inc. The fund currently has a performance rating of D+ (Weak) based on an average return of 0.72% over the last three years and 0.60% over the last three months. Factored into the performance evaluation is an expense ratio of 0.58% (low) and a 2.0% back-end load levied at the time of sale.

The fund's risk rating is currently A+ (Excellent). Volatility, as measured by standard deviation, is considered very low for fixed income funds at 0.77. Another risk factor is the fund's very low average duration of 1.3 years (i.e. low interest rate risk).

Thomas H. Atteberry has been running the fund for 12 years and currently receives a manager quality ranking of 76 (0=worst, 99=best). This fund offers only a moderate level of risk but investors looking for strong performance are still waiting.
Services Offered: Automated phone transactions, payroll deductions, bank draft capabilities, an IRA investment plan and a systematic withdrawal plan.

Data Date	Investment Rating	Net Assets ($Mil)	NAV	Performance Rating/Pts	Total Return Y-T-D	Risk Rating/Pts
3-16	C	5,352	10.01	D+/ 2.7	0.60%	A+/ 9.6
2015	C	5,357	9.95	C- / 3.2	0.15%	A / 9.5
2014	C+	5,622	10.12	D / 2.2	2.07%	A+/ 9.6
2013	C	5,176	10.27	D / 1.8	0.67%	A+/ 9.7
2012	C-	5,043	10.64	E+/ 0.6	2.18%	A+/ 9.9
2011	C-	4,432	10.65	D- / 1.3	2.23%	A+/ 9.9

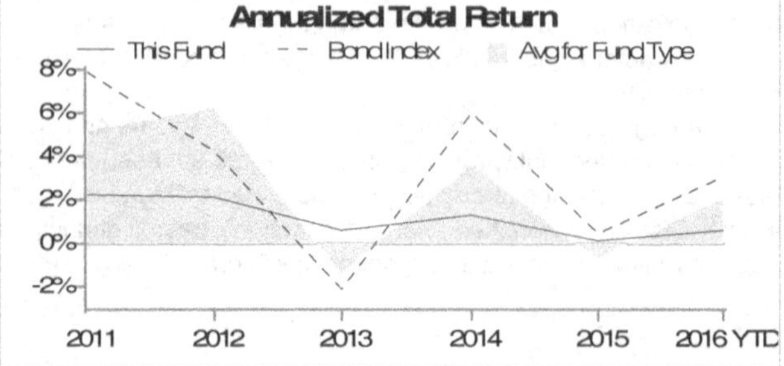

Franklin Adjustable US Govt Sec A (FISAX) C- Fair

Fund Family: Franklin Templeton Investments **Phone:** (800) 342-5236
Address: One Franklin Parkway, San Mateo, CA 94403
Fund Type: USS - US Government - Short & Inter. Term
Major Rating Factors: Very poor performance is the major factor driving the C- (Fair) TheStreet.com Investment Rating for Franklin Adjustable US Govt Sec A. The fund currently has a performance rating of E+ (Very Weak) based on an average return of -0.24% over the last three years and -0.38% over the last three months. Factored into the performance evaluation is an expense ratio of 0.91% (average) and a 2.3% front-end load that is levied at the time of purchase.

The fund's risk rating is currently A+ (Excellent). Volatility, as measured by standard deviation, is considered very low for fixed income funds at 0.47. Another risk factor is the fund's very low average duration of 0.9 years (i.e. low interest rate risk).

Roger A. Bayston has been running the fund for 25 years and currently receives a manager quality ranking of 46 (0=worst, 99=best). This fund offers only a moderate level of risk but investors looking for strong performance are still waiting.
Services Offered: Automated phone transactions, payroll deductions, bank draft capabilities, an IRA investment plan, a 401K investment plan, a Keogh investment plan, wire transfers and a systematic withdrawal plan.

Data Date	Investment Rating	Net Assets ($Mil)	NAV	Performance Rating/Pts	Total Return Y-T-D	Risk Rating/Pts
3-16	C-	790	8.44	E+ / 0.9	-0.38%	A+ / 9.8
2015	C	842	8.50	D / 2.0	-0.68%	A+ / 9.8
2014	C-	1,030	8.66	D- / 1.1	0.65%	A+ / 9.8
2013	C-	1,086	8.70	E+ / 0.9	-0.16%	A+ / 9.8
2012	C-	1,278	8.84	E / 0.5	1.42%	A+ / 9.8
2011	C-	1,471	8.85	D- / 1.3	1.72%	A+ / 9.9

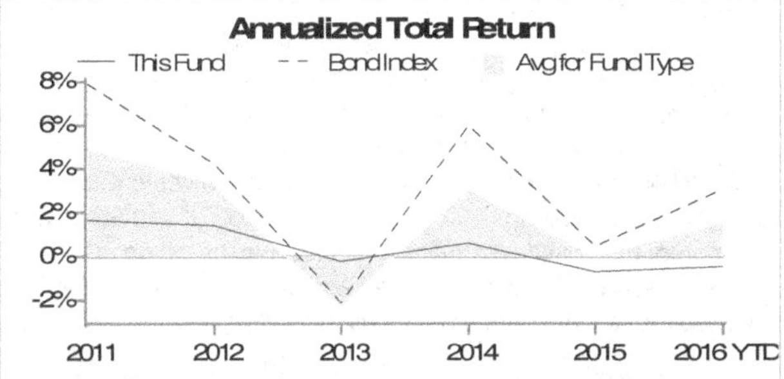

Franklin Arizona Tax-Free Inc A (FTAZX) C Fair

Fund Family: Franklin Templeton Investments **Phone:** (800) 342-5236
Address: One Franklin Parkway, San Mateo, CA 94403
Fund Type: MUS - Municipal - Single State
Major Rating Factors: Strong performance is the major factor driving the C (Fair) TheStreet.com Investment Rating for Franklin Arizona Tax-Free Inc A. The fund currently has a performance rating of B (Good) based on an average return of 2.91% over the last three years (4.82% taxable equivalent) and 1.66% over the last three months (2.75% taxable equivalent). Factored into the performance evaluation is an expense ratio of 0.62% (low) and a 4.3% front-end load that is levied at the time of purchase.

The fund's risk rating is currently C- (Fair). Volatility, as measured by standard deviation, is considered average for fixed income funds at 4.23. Another risk factor is the fund's below average duration of 4.6 years (i.e. lower interest rate risk).

Carrie Higgins has been running the fund for 24 years and currently receives a manager quality ranking of 19 (0=worst, 99=best). If you desire an average level of risk and strong performance, then this fund is a good option.
Services Offered: Automated phone transactions, payroll deductions, bank draft capabilities, wire transfers and a systematic withdrawal plan.

Data Date	Investment Rating	Net Assets ($Mil)	NAV	Performance Rating/Pts	Total Return Y-T-D	Risk Rating/Pts
3-16	C	798	11.09	B / 7.8	1.66%	C- / 3.6
2015	C	786	11.00	B / 7.6	1.86%	C- / 3.4
2014	B	810	11.21	B+ / 8.4	11.08%	C- / 3.1
2013	D	807	10.50	C / 5.1	-4.98%	C- / 3.5
2012	C+	975	11.50	C+ / 6.9	8.81%	C- / 3.3
2011	B-	872	10.99	C+ / 6.9	10.82%	C / 4.3

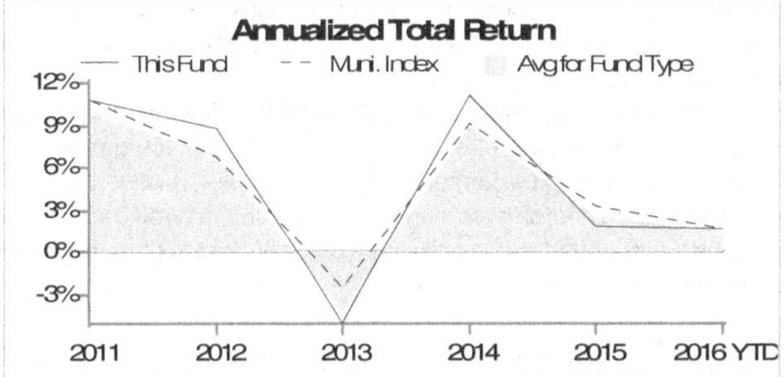

Franklin CA Interm Tax-Free A (FKCIX) A- Excellent

Fund Family: Franklin Templeton Investments **Phone:** (800) 342-5236
Address: One Franklin Parkway, San Mateo, CA 94403
Fund Type: MUS - Municipal - Single State
Major Rating Factors: Strong performance is the major factor driving the A- (Excellent) TheStreet.com Investment Rating for Franklin CA Interm Tax-Free A. The fund currently has a performance rating of B+ (Good) based on an average return of 3.43% over the last three years (5.68% taxable equivalent) and 1.65% over the last three months (2.73% taxable equivalent). Factored into the performance evaluation is an expense ratio of 0.63% (low) and a 2.3% front-end load that is levied at the time of purchase.

The fund's risk rating is currently C (Fair). Volatility, as measured by standard deviation, is considered average for fixed income funds at 3.32. Another risk factor is the fund's fairly average duration of 5.3 years (i.e. average interest rate risk).

John W. Wiley has been running the fund for 24 years and currently receives a manager quality ranking of 61 (0=worst, 99=best). If you desire an average level of risk and strong performance, then this fund is a good option.
Services Offered: Automated phone transactions, payroll deductions, bank draft capabilities, wire transfers and a systematic withdrawal plan.

Data Date	Investment Rating	Net Assets ($Mil)	NAV	Performance Rating/Pts	Total Return Y-T-D	Risk Rating/Pts
3-16	A-	951	12.29	B+ / 8.8	1.65%	C / 5.3
2015	B+	924	12.17	B+ / 8.8	2.68%	C / 5.1
2014	A-	875	12.19	B / 8.1	8.34%	C / 4.8
2013	B+	781	11.60	B / 7.8	-1.69%	C / 4.8
2012	B	791	12.18	C+ / 6.9	6.38%	C / 4.4
2011	B+	643	11.84	B- / 7.2	10.41%	C / 4.8

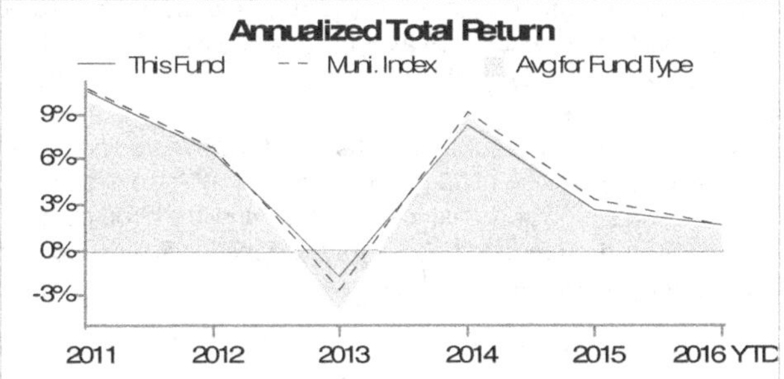

Franklin California H/Y Muni A (FCAMX) C+ Fair

Fund Family: Franklin Templeton Investments **Phone:** (800) 342-5236
Address: One Franklin Parkway, San Mateo, CA 94403
Fund Type: MUH - Municipal - High Yield
Major Rating Factors: Franklin California H/Y Muni A has adopted a very risky asset allocation strategy and currently receives an overall TheStreet.com Investment Rating of C+ (Fair). Volatility, as measured by standard deviation, is considered above average for fixed income funds at 4.84. Another risk factor is the fund's above average duration of 7.0 years (i.e. higher interest rate risk). The high level of risk (D, Weak) did however, reward investors with excellent performance.

The fund's performance rating is currently A+ (Excellent). It has registered an average return of 5.51% over the last three years (9.12% taxable equivalent) and is up 2.06% over the last three months (3.41% taxable equivalent). Factored into the performance evaluation is an expense ratio of 0.63% (low) and a 4.3% front-end load that is levied at the time of purchase.

John W. Wiley has been running the fund for 23 years and currently receives a manager quality ranking of 82 (0=worst, 99=best). If you are comfortable owning a very high risk investment, this fund may be an option.
Services Offered: Automated phone transactions, payroll deductions, bank draft capabilities and a systematic withdrawal plan.

Data Date	Investment Rating	Net Assets ($Mil)	NAV	Performance Rating/Pts	Total Return Y-T-D	Risk Rating/Pts
3-16	C+	1,389	10.94	A+ / 9.8	2.06%	D / 2.1
2015	C+	1,332	10.82	A+ / 9.8	5.24%	D / 1.7
2014	B-	1,262	10.70	A+ / 9.8	14.68%	D- / 1.1
2013	C+	1,094	9.77	A- / 9.1	-3.71%	D- / 1.5
2012	A-	1,303	10.61	A+ / 9.8	13.39%	D / 1.9
2011	A-	1,073	9.77	A+ / 9.8	14.58%	D / 1.7

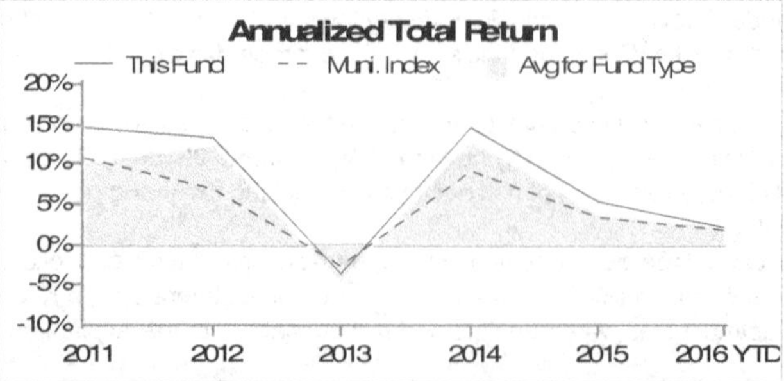

Franklin California Ins Tx-Fr A (FRCIX) B Good

Fund Family: Franklin Templeton Investments **Phone:** (800) 342-5236
Address: One Franklin Parkway, San Mateo, CA 94403
Fund Type: MUI - Municipal - Insured
Major Rating Factors: Exceptional performance is the major factor driving the B (Good) TheStreet.com Investment Rating for Franklin California Ins Tx-Fr A. The fund currently has a performance rating of A (Excellent) based on an average return of 5.10% over the last three years and 1.89% over the last three months. Factored into the performance evaluation is an expense ratio of 0.59% (low) and a 4.3% front-end load that is levied at the time of purchase.

The fund's risk rating is currently C- (Fair). Volatility, as measured by standard deviation, is considered average for fixed income funds at 4.40. Another risk factor is the fund's fairly average duration of 5.4 years (i.e. average interest rate risk).

John W. Wiley has been running the fund for 25 years and currently receives a manager quality ranking of 82 (0=worst, 99=best). If you desire an average level of risk and strong performance, then this fund is a good option.
Services Offered: Automated phone transactions, payroll deductions, bank draft capabilities, wire transfers and a systematic withdrawal plan. However, the fund is currently closed to new investors.

Data Date	Investment Rating	Net Assets ($Mil)	NAV	Performance Rating/Pts	Total Return Y-T-D	Risk Rating/Pts
3-16	B	1,454	13.27	A / 9.5	1.89%	C- / 3.3
2015	B-	1,447	13.15	A / 9.5	4.39%	C- / 3.1
2014	A-	1,533	13.10	A / 9.4	13.00%	C- / 3.2
2013	B-	1,575	12.09	B / 8.0	-3.35%	C- / 3.3
2012	B	1,958	13.02	B / 8.1	9.60%	D+ / 2.9
2011	C	1,775	12.36	C+ / 6.8	12.40%	C- / 3.4

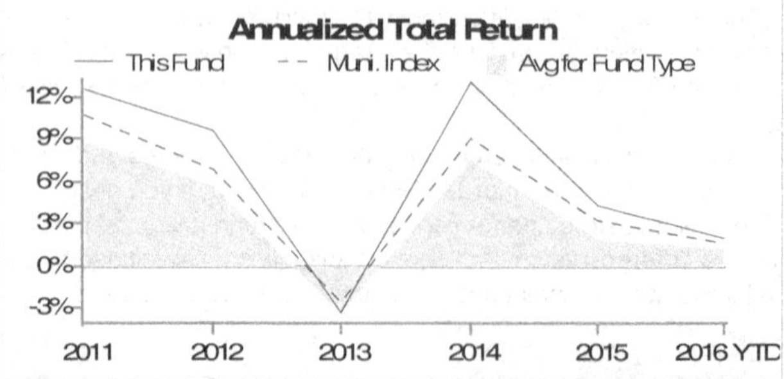

Franklin California Tx-Fr Inc A (FKTFX) B- Good

Fund Family: Franklin Templeton Investments **Phone:** (800) 342-5236
Address: One Franklin Parkway, San Mateo, CA 94403
Fund Type: MUS - Municipal - Single State
Major Rating Factors: Exceptional performance is the major factor driving the B- (Good) TheStreet.com Investment Rating for Franklin California Tx-Fr Inc A. The fund currently has a performance rating of A (Excellent) based on an average return of 4.67% over the last three years (7.73% taxable equivalent) and 1.87% over the last three months (3.10% taxable equivalent). Factored into the performance evaluation is an expense ratio of 0.58% (low) and a 4.3% front-end load that is levied at the time of purchase.

The fund's risk rating is currently C- (Fair). Volatility, as measured by standard deviation, is considered average for fixed income funds at 4.55. Another risk factor is the fund's fairly average duration of 6.6 years (i.e. average interest rate risk).

John W. Wiley has been running the fund for 25 years and currently receives a manager quality ranking of 60 (0=worst, 99=best). If you desire an average level of risk and strong performance, then this fund is a good option.
Services Offered: Automated phone transactions, payroll deductions, bank draft capabilities and a systematic withdrawal plan.

Data Date	Investment Rating	Net Assets ($Mil)	NAV	Performance Rating/Pts	Total Return Y-T-D	Risk Rating/Pts
3-16	B-	11,754	7.59	A / 9.4	1.87%	C- / 3.2
2015	C+	11,552	7.52	A / 9.3	3.61%	D+ / 2.9
2014	B+	11,560	7.55	A / 9.5	13.54%	D+ / 2.8
2013	C	10,843	6.94	B- / 7.3	-3.85%	D+ / 2.5
2012	B-	12,695	7.54	B / 8.2	10.16%	D+ / 2.6
2011	C	11,738	7.14	B / 7.7	11.34%	D+ / 2.6

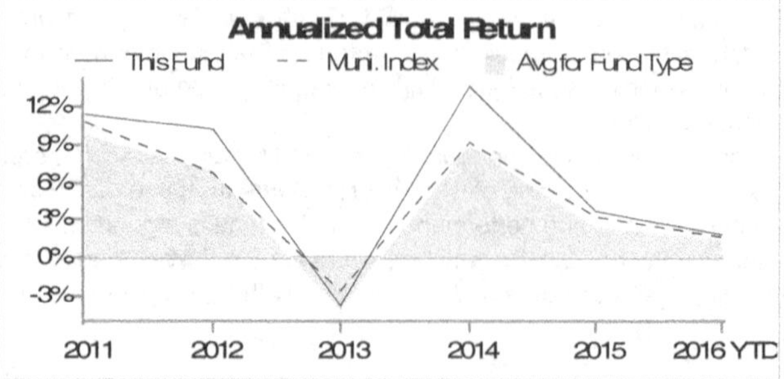

Franklin Colorado Tax-Free Inc A (FRCOX) C Fair

Fund Family: Franklin Templeton Investments **Phone:** (800) 342-5236
Address: One Franklin Parkway, San Mateo, CA 94403
Fund Type: MUS - Municipal - Single State
Major Rating Factors: Strong performance is the major factor driving the C (Fair) TheStreet.com Investment Rating for Franklin Colorado Tax-Free Inc A. The fund currently has a performance rating of B (Good) based on an average return of 2.87% over the last three years (4.75% taxable equivalent) and 1.44% over the last three months (2.38% taxable equivalent). Factored into the performance evaluation is an expense ratio of 0.65% (low) and a 4.3% front-end load that is levied at the time of purchase.

The fund's risk rating is currently C- (Fair). Volatility, as measured by standard deviation, is considered average for fixed income funds at 4.28. Another risk factor is the fund's below average duration of 4.2 years (i.e. lower interest rate risk).

Stella S. Wong has been running the fund for 29 years and currently receives a manager quality ranking of 18 (0=worst, 99=best). If you desire an average level of risk and strong performance, then this fund is a good option.
Services Offered: Automated phone transactions, payroll deductions, bank draft capabilities, wire transfers and a systematic withdrawal plan.

Data Date	Investment Rating	Net Assets ($Mil)	NAV	Performance Rating/Pts	Total Return Y-T-D	Risk Rating/Pts
3-16	C	552	11.93	B / 7.6	1.44%	C- / 3.5
2015	C	539	11.87	B- / 7.4	2.00%	C- / 3.2
2014	C+	539	12.09	B / 8.1	10.97%	D+ / 2.8
2013	D	530	11.34	C / 5.2	-5.32%	C- / 3.2
2012	C	653	12.44	C+ / 6.7	8.42%	C- / 3.0
2011	B+	543	11.92	B- / 7.5	12.08%	C / 4.3

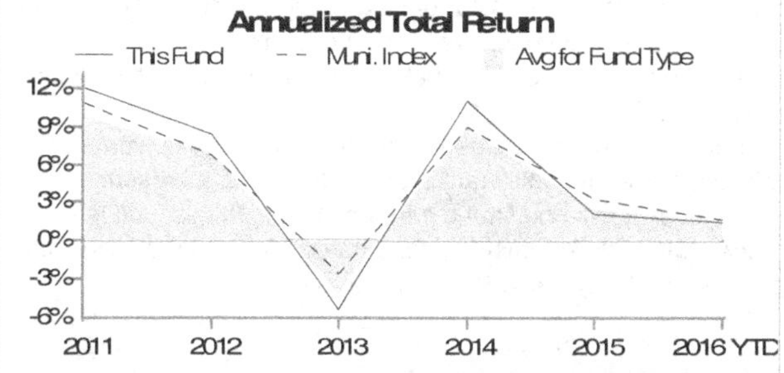

Franklin Fdrl Lmtd Trm T/F Inc A (FFTFX) C- Fair

Fund Family: Franklin Templeton Investments **Phone:** (800) 342-5236
Address: One Franklin Parkway, San Mateo, CA 94403
Fund Type: MUN - Municipal - National
Major Rating Factors: Disappointing performance is the major factor driving the C- (Fair) TheStreet.com Investment Rating for Franklin Fdrl Lmtd Trm T/F Inc A. The fund currently has a performance rating of D (Weak) based on an average return of 0.57% over the last three years (0.94% taxable equivalent) and 0.31% over the last three months (0.51% taxable equivalent). Factored into the performance evaluation is an expense ratio of 0.70% (low) and a 2.3% front-end load that is levied at the time of purchase.

The fund's risk rating is currently A (Excellent). Volatility, as measured by standard deviation, is considered very low for fixed income funds at 0.79. Another risk factor is the fund's very low average duration of 1.6 years (i.e. low interest rate risk).

James P. Conn has been running the fund for 13 years and currently receives a manager quality ranking of 58 (0=worst, 99=best). This fund offers only a moderate level of risk but investors looking for strong performance are still waiting.
Services Offered: Automated phone transactions, payroll deductions, bank draft capabilities, an IRA investment plan, a 401K investment plan, wire transfers and a systematic withdrawal plan.

Data Date	Investment Rating	Net Assets ($Mil)	NAV	Performance Rating/Pts	Total Return Y-T-D	Risk Rating/Pts
3-16	C-	887	10.42	D / 1.8	0.31%	A / 9.5
2015	C+	868	10.41	C- / 3.4	0.42%	A / 9.5
2014	C	906	10.46	D / 1.8	1.09%	A / 9.5
2013	B-	968	10.45	C- / 3.3	0.37%	A / 9.3
2012	C-	762	10.55	D- / 1.5	1.96%	A- / 9.0
2011	C+	673	10.53	D+ / 2.7	4.03%	A- / 9.0

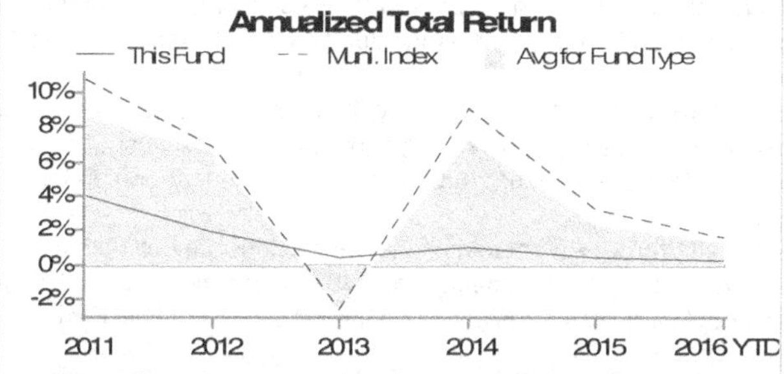

Franklin Fed Interm-Trm T/F Inc A (FKITX) B Good

Fund Family: Franklin Templeton Investments **Phone:** (800) 342-5236
Address: One Franklin Parkway, San Mateo, CA 94403
Fund Type: MUN - Municipal - National
Major Rating Factors: Strong performance is the major factor driving the B (Good) TheStreet.com Investment Rating for Franklin Fed Interm-Trm T/F Inc A. The fund currently has a performance rating of B (Good) based on an average return of 2.54% over the last three years (4.21% taxable equivalent) and 1.26% over the last three months (2.09% taxable equivalent). Factored into the performance evaluation is an expense ratio of 0.68% (low) and a 2.3% front-end load that is levied at the time of purchase.

The fund's risk rating is currently C (Fair). Volatility, as measured by standard deviation, is considered average for fixed income funds at 3.29. Another risk factor is the fund's below average duration of 4.7 years (i.e. lower interest rate risk).

John B. Pomeroy has been running the fund for 24 years and currently receives a manager quality ranking of 32 (0=worst, 99=best). If you desire an average level of risk and strong performance, then this fund is a good option.
Services Offered: Automated phone transactions, payroll deductions, bank draft capabilities and a systematic withdrawal plan.

Data Date	Investment Rating	Net Assets ($Mil)	NAV	Performance Rating/Pts	Total Return Y-T-D	Risk Rating/Pts
3-16	B	2,015	12.48	B / 7.9	1.26%	C / 5.4
2015	B	1,895	12.40	B / 8.0	2.45%	C / 5.1
2014	C+	1,806	12.41	C+ / 6.4	6.86%	C / 4.9
2013	B	1,880	11.93	B- / 7.1	-2.49%	C / 4.7
2012	B-	2,175	12.57	C+ / 6.7	5.55%	C / 4.3
2011	B+	1,649	12.24	B- / 7.2	11.20%	C / 4.7

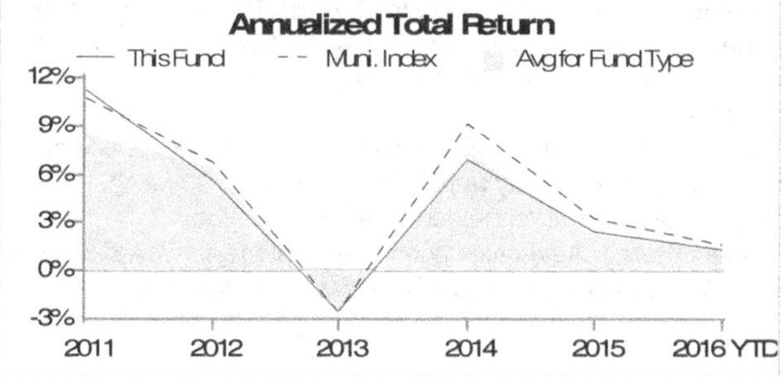

Franklin Federal Tax-Free Inc A (FKTIX) C+ Fair

Fund Family: Franklin Templeton Investments **Phone:** (800) 342-5236
Address: One Franklin Parkway, San Mateo, CA 94403
Fund Type: MUN - Municipal - National
Major Rating Factors: Strong performance is the major factor driving the C+ (Fair) TheStreet.com Investment Rating for Franklin Federal Tax-Free Inc A. The fund currently has a performance rating of B (Good) based on an average return of 3.36% over the last three years (5.56% taxable equivalent) and 1.46% over the last three months (2.42% taxable equivalent). Factored into the performance evaluation is an expense ratio of 0.62% (low) and a 4.3% front-end load that is levied at the time of purchase.

The fund's risk rating is currently C- (Fair). Volatility, as measured by standard deviation, is considered average for fixed income funds at 4.08. Another risk factor is the fund's below average duration of 4.3 years (i.e. lower interest rate risk).

Sheila A. Amoroso has been running the fund for 29 years and currently receives a manager quality ranking of 32 (0=worst, 99=best). If you desire an average level of risk and strong performance, then this fund is a good option.
Services Offered: Automated phone transactions, payroll deductions, bank draft capabilities and a systematic withdrawal plan.

Data Date	Investment Rating	Net Assets ($Mil)	NAV	Performance Rating/Pts	Total Return Y-T-D	Risk Rating/Pts
3-16	C+	8,296	12.44	B / 8.2	1.46%	C- / 3.8
2015	C+	8,244	12.38	B / 8.1	2.44%	C- / 3.6
2014	B+	8,622	12.55	B+ / 8.6	11.21%	C- / 3.3
2013	C	8,059	11.74	C+ / 6.7	-4.46%	C- / 3.6
2012	B	9,320	12.78	B- / 7.5	9.03%	C- / 3.6
2011	A-	8,265	12.19	B / 7.6	12.12%	C / 4.6

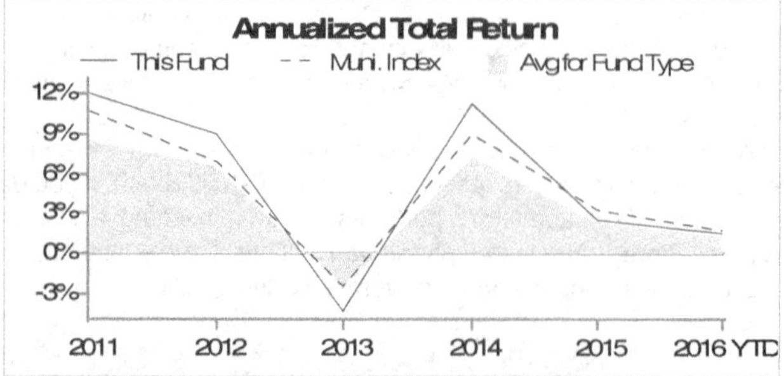

Franklin Floating Rate Dly-Acc A (FAFRX) D+ Weak

Fund Family: Franklin Templeton Investments **Phone:** (800) 342-5236
Address: One Franklin Parkway, San Mateo, CA 94403
Fund Type: LP - Loan Participation
Major Rating Factors: Disappointing performance is the major factor driving the D+ (Weak) TheStreet.com Investment Rating for Franklin Floating Rate Dly-Acc A. The fund currently has a performance rating of D (Weak) based on an average return of 0.89% over the last three years and 1.46% over the last three months. Factored into the performance evaluation is an expense ratio of 0.86% (average) and a 2.3% front-end load that is levied at the time of purchase.

The fund's risk rating is currently B- (Good). Volatility, as measured by standard deviation, is considered low for fixed income funds at 2.81. Another risk factor is the fund's very low average duration of 0.2 years (i.e. low interest rate risk).

Richard S. Hsu has been running the fund for 15 years and currently receives a manager quality ranking of 69 (0=worst, 99=best). This fund offers only a moderate level of risk but investors looking for strong performance are still waiting.
Services Offered: Automated phone transactions, payroll deductions, bank draft capabilities, an IRA investment plan, a 401K investment plan, a Keogh investment plan, wire transfers and a systematic withdrawal plan.

Data Date	Investment Rating	Net Assets ($Mil)	NAV	Performance Rating/Pts	Total Return Y-T-D	Risk Rating/Pts
3-16	D+	1,321	8.35	D / 1.7	1.46%	B- / 7.2
2015	C-	1,493	8.33	D / 2.2	-2.12%	B- / 7.2
2014	B	1,743	8.91	C- / 4.0	0.49%	B+ / 8.5
2013	B	2,022	9.21	C+ / 6.4	4.53%	C+ / 5.7
2012	E+	1,327	9.13	C- / 3.2	8.06%	C / 4.8
2011	E+	1,213	8.83	C / 5.2	0.89%	D+ / 2.8

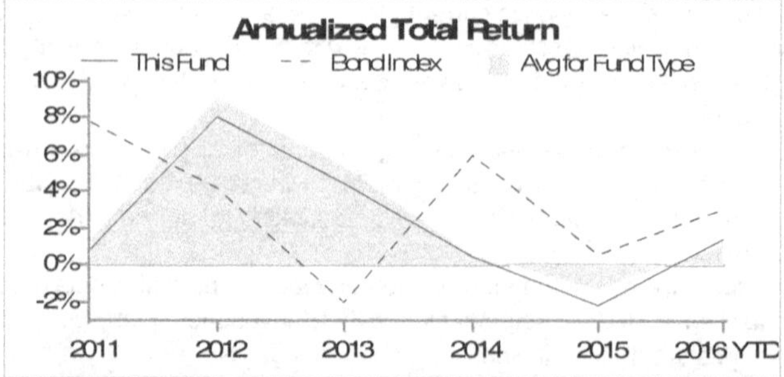

Franklin Florida Tax-Free Inc A (FRFLX) C- Fair

Fund Family: Franklin Templeton Investments **Phone:** (800) 342-5236
Address: One Franklin Parkway, San Mateo, CA 94403
Fund Type: MUS - Municipal - Single State
Major Rating Factors: Middle of the road best describes Franklin Florida Tax-Free Inc A whose TheStreet.com Investment Rating is currently a C- (Fair). The fund has a performance rating of C+ (Fair) based on an average return of 2.32% over the last three years (3.84% taxable equivalent) and 1.59% over the last three months (2.63% taxable equivalent). Factored into the performance evaluation is an expense ratio of 0.64% (low) and a 4.3% front-end load that is levied at the time of purchase.

The fund's risk rating is currently C- (Fair). Volatility, as measured by standard deviation, is considered average for fixed income funds at 4.46. Another risk factor is the fund's below average duration of 4.0 years (i.e. lower interest rate risk).

Stella S. Wong has been running the fund for 29 years and currently receives a manager quality ranking of 11 (0=worst, 99=best). If you desire an average level of risk, then this fund may be an option.
Services Offered: Automated phone transactions, payroll deductions, bank draft capabilities, wire transfers and a systematic withdrawal plan.

Data Date	Investment Rating	Net Assets ($Mil)	NAV	Performance Rating/Pts	Total Return Y-T-D	Risk Rating/Pts
3-16	C-	689	11.18	C+ / 6.6	1.59%	C- / 3.3
2015	C-	688	11.11	C+ / 6.8	2.53%	C- / 3.0
2014	D+	717	11.28	C+ / 6.3	9.86%	C- / 3.0
2013	E+	771	10.73	D / 1.6	-6.22%	C- / 3.7
2012	C+	1,024	11.91	C / 5.5	6.57%	C / 5.4
2011	A	994	11.69	C+ / 6.4	10.11%	C+ / 6.1

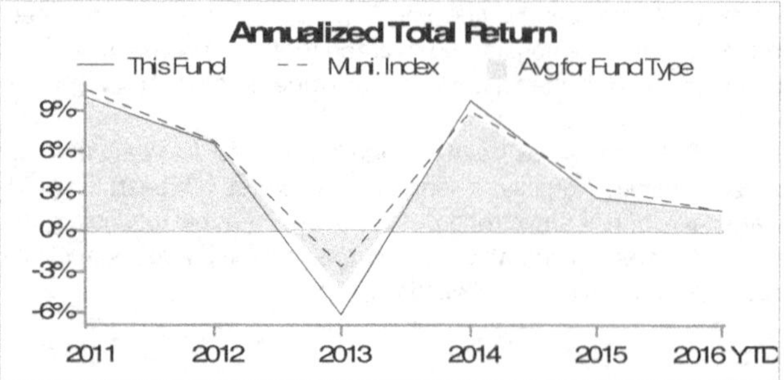

Franklin High Income A (FHAIX) E- Very Weak

Fund Family: Franklin Templeton Investments **Phone:** (800) 342-5236
Address: One Franklin Parkway, San Mateo, CA 94403
Fund Type: COH - Corporate - High Yield
Major Rating Factors: Franklin High Income A has adopted a very risky asset allocation strategy and currently receives an overall TheStreet.com Investment Rating of E- (Very Weak). Volatility, as measured by standard deviation, is considered high for fixed income funds at 7.63. Unfortunately, the high level of risk (E, Very Weak) failed to pay off as investors endured poor performance.

The fund's performance rating is currently E- (Very Weak). It has registered an average return of -1.74% over the last three years and is up 1.74% over the last three months. Factored into the performance evaluation is an expense ratio of 0.76% (low) and a 4.3% front-end load that is levied at the time of purchase.

Christopher J. Molumphy has been running the fund for 25 years and currently receives a manager quality ranking of 5 (0=worst, 99=best). If you can tolerate very high levels of risk in the hope of improved future returns, holding this fund may be an option.
Services Offered: Automated phone transactions, payroll deductions, bank draft capabilities, an IRA investment plan, a 401K investment plan, a Keogh investment plan and a systematic withdrawal plan.

Data Date	Investment Rating	Net Assets ($Mil)	NAV	Performance Rating/Pts	Total Return Y-T-D	Risk Rating/Pts
3-16	E-	2,545	1.66	E- / 0.2	1.74%	E / 0.4
2015	E-	2,961	1.66	E / 0.3	-10.74%	E / 0.5
2014	D-	3,624	1.98	C+ / 5.7	-0.39%	D- / 1.3
2013	C+	3,804	2.11	A / 9.5	7.64%	E+ / 0.8
2012	C-	3,704	2.09	B+ / 8.3	15.71%	E+ / 0.6
2011	C-	2,547	1.94	B+ / 8.7	4.55%	E+ / 0.8

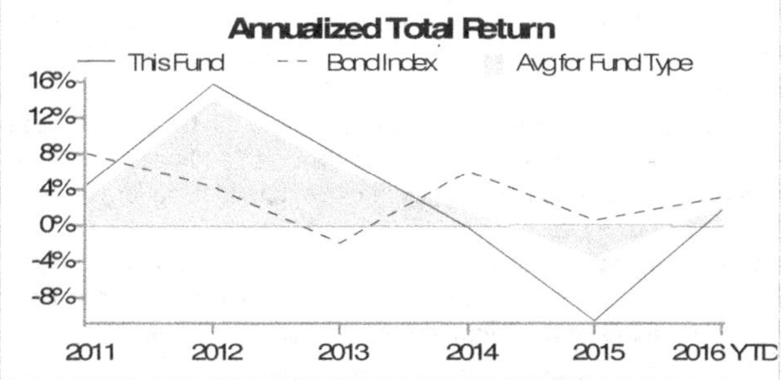

Franklin High Yld Tax-Free Inc A (FRHIX) C Fair

Fund Family: Franklin Templeton Investments **Phone:** (800) 342-5236
Address: One Franklin Parkway, San Mateo, CA 94403
Fund Type: MUH - Municipal - High Yield
Major Rating Factors: Franklin High Yld Tax-Free Inc A has adopted a very risky asset allocation strategy and currently receives an overall TheStreet.com Investment Rating of C (Fair). Volatility, as measured by standard deviation, is considered above average for fixed income funds at 5.13. Another risk factor is the fund's fairly average duration of 5.9 years (i.e. average interest rate risk). The high level of risk (D, Weak) did however, reward investors with excellent performance.

The fund's performance rating is currently B+ (Good). It has registered an average return of 3.69% over the last three years (6.11% taxable equivalent) and is up 2.02% over the last three months (3.35% taxable equivalent). Factored into the performance evaluation is an expense ratio of 0.65% (low) and a 4.3% front-end load that is levied at the time of purchase.

John W. Wiley has been running the fund for 23 years and currently receives a manager quality ranking of 17 (0=worst, 99=best). If you are comfortable owning a very high risk investment, this fund may be an option.
Services Offered: Automated phone transactions, payroll deductions, bank draft capabilities, wire transfers and a systematic withdrawal plan.

Data Date	Investment Rating	Net Assets ($Mil)	NAV	Performance Rating/Pts	Total Return Y-T-D	Risk Rating/Pts
3-16	C	5,109	10.61	B+ / 8.7	2.02%	D / 2.0
2015	C-	5,003	10.51	B+ / 8.5	3.18%	D / 1.6
2014	C+	5,175	10.63	A- / 9.2	13.87%	D- / 1.0
2013	D-	5,076	9.77	C+ / 5.6	-6.73%	D / 1.7
2012	B+	6,489	10.94	A- / 9.0	11.06%	D+ / 2.3
2011	A	5,427	10.28	A+ / 9.6	12.39%	D / 2.2

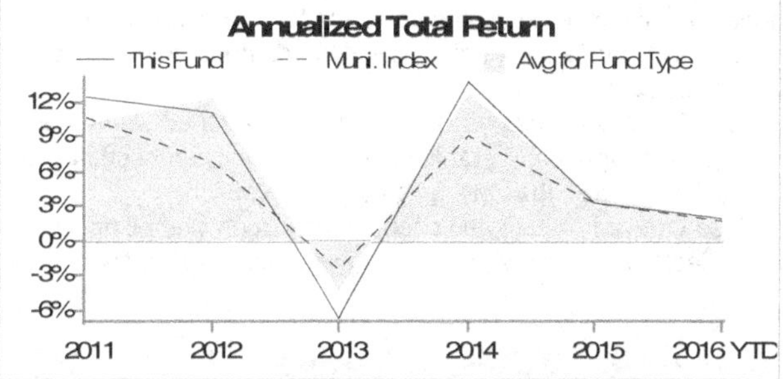

Franklin Insured Tax-Free Inc A (FTFIX) B Good

Fund Family: Franklin Templeton Investments **Phone:** (800) 342-5236
Address: One Franklin Parkway, San Mateo, CA 94403
Fund Type: MUI - Municipal - Insured
Major Rating Factors: Strong performance is the major factor driving the B (Good) TheStreet.com Investment Rating for Franklin Insured Tax-Free Inc A. The fund currently has a performance rating of B+ (Good) based on an average return of 3.81% over the last three years and 1.28% over the last three months. Factored into the performance evaluation is an expense ratio of 0.61% (low) and a 4.3% front-end load that is levied at the time of purchase.

The fund's risk rating is currently C (Fair). Volatility, as measured by standard deviation, is considered average for fixed income funds at 3.66. Another risk factor is the fund's below average duration of 3.0 years (i.e. lower interest rate risk).

John B. Pomeroy has been running the fund for 27 years and currently receives a manager quality ranking of 62 (0=worst, 99=best). If you desire an average level of risk and strong performance, then this fund is a good option.
Services Offered: Automated phone transactions, payroll deductions, bank draft capabilities, wire transfers and a systematic withdrawal plan. However, the fund is currently closed to new investors.

Data Date	Investment Rating	Net Assets ($Mil)	NAV	Performance Rating/Pts	Total Return Y-T-D	Risk Rating/Pts
3-16	B	1,663	12.45	B+ / 8.5	1.28%	C / 4.5
2015	B	1,679	12.41	B+ / 8.5	3.17%	C / 4.4
2014	A-	1,810	12.50	B+ / 8.5	11.15%	C- / 4.1
2013	C	1,930	11.71	C+ / 6.3	-3.80%	C- / 4.1
2012	C+	2,547	12.63	C+ / 6.4	7.92%	C- / 3.8
2011	B-	2,180	12.13	C+ / 6.5	11.37%	C / 4.9

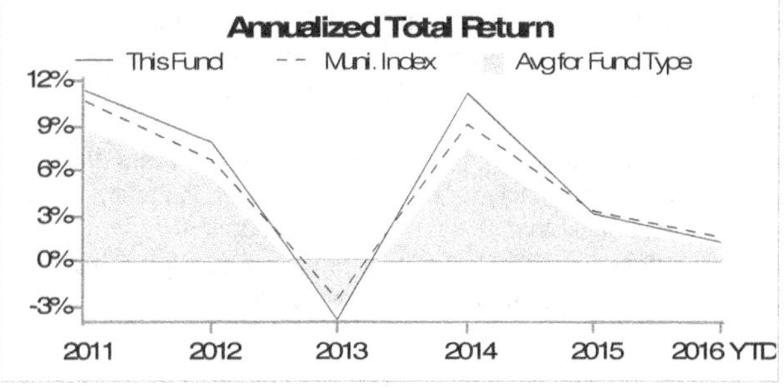

Franklin Low Dur Totl Return A (FLDAX) C- Fair

Fund Family: Franklin Templeton Investments **Phone:** (800) 342-5236
Address: One Franklin Parkway, San Mateo, CA 94403
Fund Type: GEI - General - Investment Grade
Major Rating Factors: Disappointing performance is the major factor driving the C- (Fair) TheStreet.com Investment Rating for Franklin Low Dur Totl Return A. The fund currently has a performance rating of D (Weak) based on an average return of 0.52% over the last three years and 0.44% over the last three months. Factored into the performance evaluation is an expense ratio of 0.97% (average) and a 2.3% front-end load that is levied at the time of purchase.

The fund's risk rating is currently A- (Excellent). Volatility, as measured by standard deviation, is considered very low for fixed income funds at 1.05. Another risk factor is the fund's very low average duration of 1.3 years (i.e. low interest rate risk).

Christopher J. Molumphy has been running the fund for 12 years and currently receives a manager quality ranking of 71 (0=worst, 99=best). This fund offers only a moderate level of risk but investors looking for strong performance are still waiting.

Services Offered: Automated phone transactions, payroll deductions, bank draft capabilities, an IRA investment plan, a 401K investment plan, a Keogh investment plan and a systematic withdrawal plan.

Data Date	Investment Rating	Net Assets ($Mil)	NAV	Perfor-mance Rating/Pts	Total Return Y-T-D	Risk Rating/Pts
3-16	C-	1,598	9.75	D / 1.6	0.44%	A- / 9.2
2015	C	1,637	9.74	D+ / 2.7	-0.59%	A / 9.3
2014	C-	1,585	10.00	D / 1.8	0.19%	B+ / 8.9
2013	C	1,315	10.13	D+ / 2.3	1.22%	B+ / 8.7
2012	D	967	10.24	D- / 1.2	4.08%	B+ / 8.3
2011	C-	721	10.09	D / 1.7	0.60%	B+ / 8.9

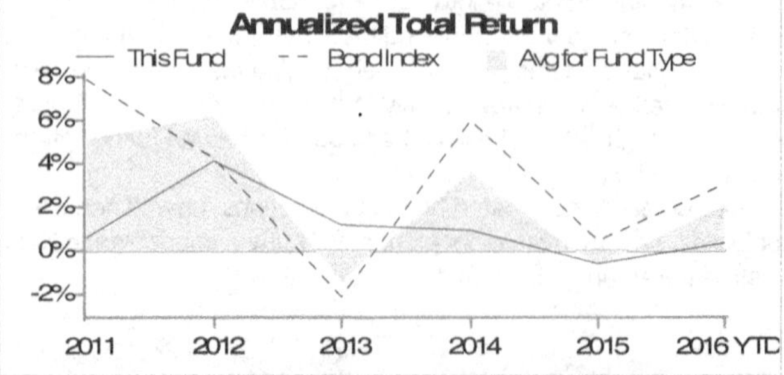

Franklin MI Tax-Free Inc A (FTTMX) C- Fair

Fund Family: Franklin Templeton Investments **Phone:** (800) 342-5236
Address: One Franklin Parkway, San Mateo, CA 94403
Fund Type: MUI - Municipal - Insured
Major Rating Factors: Middle of the road best describes Franklin MI Tax-Free Inc A whose TheStreet.com Investment Rating is currently a C- (Fair). The fund has a performance rating of C+ (Fair) based on an average return of 2.41% over the last three years and 1.37% over the last three months. Factored into the performance evaluation is an expense ratio of 0.65% (low) and a 4.3% front-end load that is levied at the time of purchase.

The fund's risk rating is currently C- (Fair). Volatility, as measured by standard deviation, is considered average for fixed income funds at 3.93. Another risk factor is the fund's below average duration of 4.4 years (i.e. lower interest rate risk).

John B. Pomeroy has been running the fund for 27 years and currently receives a manager quality ranking of 20 (0=worst, 99=best). If you desire an average level of risk, then this fund may be an option.

Services Offered: Automated phone transactions, payroll deductions, bank draft capabilities, wire transfers and a systematic withdrawal plan.

Data Date	Investment Rating	Net Assets ($Mil)	NAV	Perfor-mance Rating/Pts	Total Return Y-T-D	Risk Rating/Pts
3-16	C-	896	11.80	C+ / 6.6	1.37%	C- / 4.1
2015	C-	894	11.74	C+ / 6.6	0.80%	C- / 3.9
2014	B	954	12.06	B- / 7.4	10.95%	C / 4.3
2013	D-	967	11.30	D+ / 2.4	-5.15%	C / 5.1
2012	C-	1,256	12.36	C / 4.3	6.09%	C / 5.3
2011	C+	1,207	12.07	C / 5.2	9.88%	C+ / 6.2

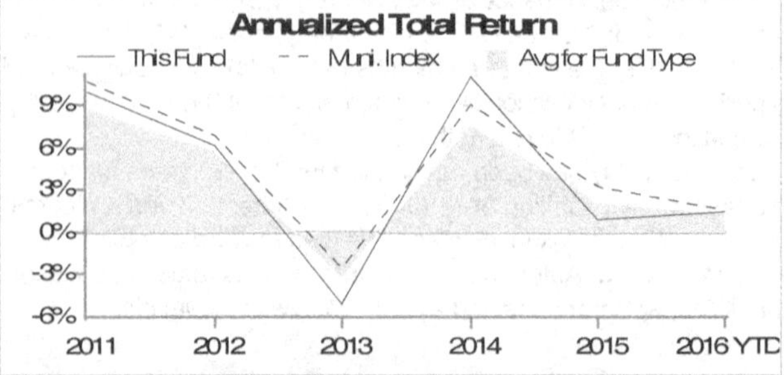

Franklin Missouri Tax-Free Inc A (FRMOX) C- Fair

Fund Family: Franklin Templeton Investments **Phone:** (800) 342-5236
Address: One Franklin Parkway, San Mateo, CA 94403
Fund Type: MUS - Municipal - Single State
Major Rating Factors: Middle of the road best describes Franklin Missouri Tax-Free Inc A whose TheStreet.com Investment Rating is currently a C- (Fair). The fund has a performance rating of C+ (Fair) based on an average return of 2.12% over the last three years (3.51% taxable equivalent) and 1.38% over the last three months (2.29% taxable equivalent). Factored into the performance evaluation is an expense ratio of 0.63% (low) and a 4.3% front-end load that is levied at the time of purchase.

The fund's risk rating is currently C- (Fair). Volatility, as measured by standard deviation, is considered average for fixed income funds at 3.97. Another risk factor is the fund's below average duration of 4.0 years (i.e. lower interest rate risk).

Stella S. Wong has been running the fund for 29 years and currently receives a manager quality ranking of 14 (0=worst, 99=best). If you desire an average level of risk, then this fund may be an option.

Services Offered: Automated phone transactions, payroll deductions, bank draft capabilities, wire transfers and a systematic withdrawal plan.

Data Date	Investment Rating	Net Assets ($Mil)	NAV	Perfor-mance Rating/Pts	Total Return Y-T-D	Risk Rating/Pts
3-16	C-	879	12.04	C+ / 6.1	1.38%	C- / 4.0
2015	C-	865	11.98	C+ / 6.5	2.37%	C- / 3.7
2014	C-	877	12.13	C+ / 6.1	9.08%	C- / 3.5
2013	D-	915	11.56	C- / 3.1	-5.83%	C- / 3.9
2012	C	1,135	12.73	C+ / 6.0	6.82%	C- / 3.9
2011	B+	957	12.36	C+ / 6.8	11.66%	C / 5.3

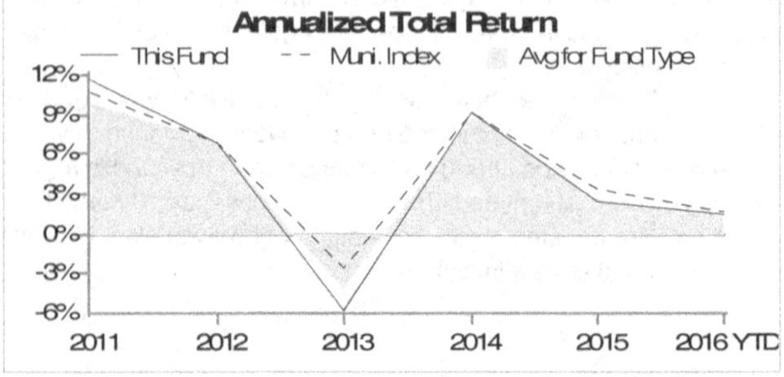

Franklin MN Tax-Free Inc A (FMINX) C+ Fair

Fund Family: Franklin Templeton Investments **Phone:** (800) 342-5236
Address: One Franklin Parkway, San Mateo, CA 94403
Fund Type: MUI - Municipal - Insured
Major Rating Factors: Middle of the road best describes Franklin MN Tax-Free Inc A whose TheStreet.com Investment Rating is currently a C+ (Fair). The fund has a performance rating of C+ (Fair) based on an average return of 2.53% over the last three years and 1.23% over the last three months. Factored into the performance evaluation is an expense ratio of 0.65% (low) and a 4.3% front-end load that is levied at the time of purchase.

The fund's risk rating is currently C (Fair). Volatility, as measured by standard deviation, is considered average for fixed income funds at 3.48. Another risk factor is the fund's below average duration of 3.8 years (i.e. lower interest rate risk).

John B. Pomeroy has been running the fund for 27 years and currently receives a manager quality ranking of 26 (0=worst, 99=best). If you desire an average level of risk, then this fund may be an option.
Services Offered: Automated phone transactions, payroll deductions, bank draft capabilities, wire transfers and a systematic withdrawal plan.

Data Date	Investment Rating	Net Assets ($Mil)	NAV	Performance Rating/Pts	Total Return Y-T-D	Risk Rating/Pts
3-16	C+	730	12.62	C+ / 6.9	1.23%	C / 5.0
2015	C	720	12.56	B- / 7.0	2.15%	C / 4.8
2014	C+	712	12.69	C+ / 6.4	8.17%	C / 4.4
2013	C-	739	12.12	C / 5.3	-3.77%	C / 4.5
2012	C	891	13.00	C+ / 5.6	6.60%	C / 4.7
2011	B	769	12.61	C+ / 5.9	10.94%	C+ / 5.8

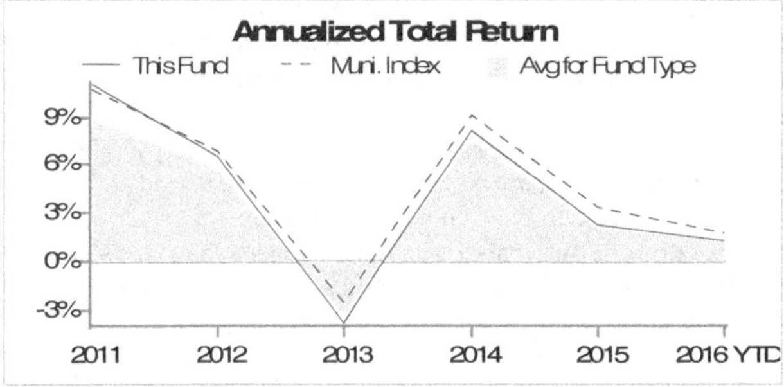

Franklin NC Tax-Free Inc A (FXNCX) D+ Weak

Fund Family: Franklin Templeton Investments **Phone:** (800) 342-5236
Address: One Franklin Parkway, San Mateo, CA 94403
Fund Type: MUS - Municipal - Single State
Major Rating Factors: Franklin NC Tax-Free Inc A receives a TheStreet.com Investment Rating of D+ (Weak). The fund has a performance rating of C- (Fair) based on an average return of 1.39% over the last three years (2.30% taxable equivalent) and 1.25% over the last three months (2.07% taxable equivalent). Factored into the performance evaluation is an expense ratio of 0.63% (low) and a 4.3% front-end load that is levied at the time of purchase.

The fund's risk rating is currently C- (Fair). Volatility, as measured by standard deviation, is considered average for fixed income funds at 3.95. Another risk factor is the fund's below average duration of 3.8 years (i.e. lower interest rate risk).

Stella S. Wong has been running the fund for 29 years and currently receives a manager quality ranking of 9 (0=worst, 99=best). If you desire an average level of risk, then this fund may be an option.
Services Offered: Automated phone transactions, payroll deductions, bank draft capabilities, wire transfers and a systematic withdrawal plan.

Data Date	Investment Rating	Net Assets ($Mil)	NAV	Performance Rating/Pts	Total Return Y-T-D	Risk Rating/Pts
3-16	D+	794	11.97	C- / 4.2	1.25%	C- / 4.0
2015	D+	799	11.92	C- / 4.0	1.55%	C- / 3.8
2014	D	834	12.16	C / 5.3	8.67%	C- / 3.4
2013	E+	889	11.64	D / 1.9	-6.75%	C- / 3.8
2012	C	1,146	12.93	C+ / 5.8	6.96%	C- / 4.2
2011	A	984	12.53	B- / 7.5	11.30%	C / 4.8

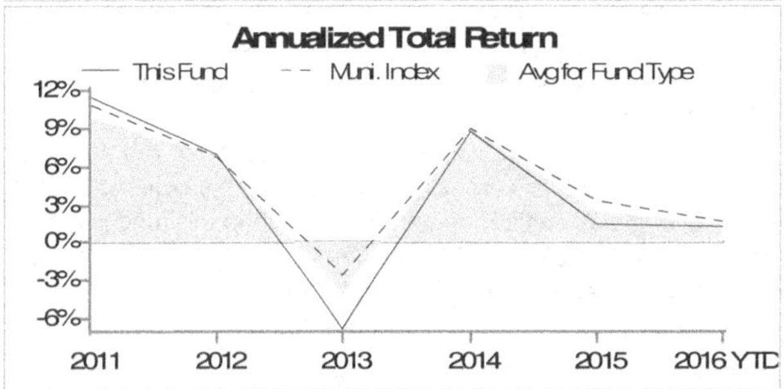

Franklin New Jersey TaxFree Inc A (FRNJX) C- Fair

Fund Family: Franklin Templeton Investments **Phone:** (800) 342-5236
Address: One Franklin Parkway, San Mateo, CA 94403
Fund Type: MUN - Municipal - National
Major Rating Factors: Middle of the road best describes Franklin New Jersey TaxFree Inc A whose TheStreet.com Investment Rating is currently a C- (Fair). The fund has a performance rating of C+ (Fair) based on an average return of 1.84% over the last three years (3.05% taxable equivalent) and 1.36% over the last three months (2.25% taxable equivalent). Factored into the performance evaluation is an expense ratio of 0.64% (low) and a 4.3% front-end load that is levied at the time of purchase.

The fund's risk rating is currently C- (Fair). Volatility, as measured by standard deviation, is considered average for fixed income funds at 3.97. Another risk factor is the fund's below average duration of 3.8 years (i.e. lower interest rate risk).

Stella S. Wong has been running the fund for 28 years and currently receives a manager quality ranking of 11 (0=worst, 99=best). If you desire an average level of risk, then this fund may be an option.
Services Offered: Automated phone transactions, payroll deductions, bank draft capabilities, wire transfers and a systematic withdrawal plan.

Data Date	Investment Rating	Net Assets ($Mil)	NAV	Performance Rating/Pts	Total Return Y-T-D	Risk Rating/Pts
3-16	C-	792	11.74	C+ / 5.6	1.36%	C- / 4.0
2015	C-	815	11.69	C+ / 5.6	1.33%	C- / 3.7
2014	D+	903	11.99	C+ / 5.8	8.92%	C- / 3.6
2013	D-	1,011	11.46	D+ / 2.5	-5.50%	C- / 3.7
2012	D+	1,271	12.58	C / 5.2	6.13%	C- / 4.0
2011	B+	1,130	12.31	B- / 7.0	10.89%	C / 4.7

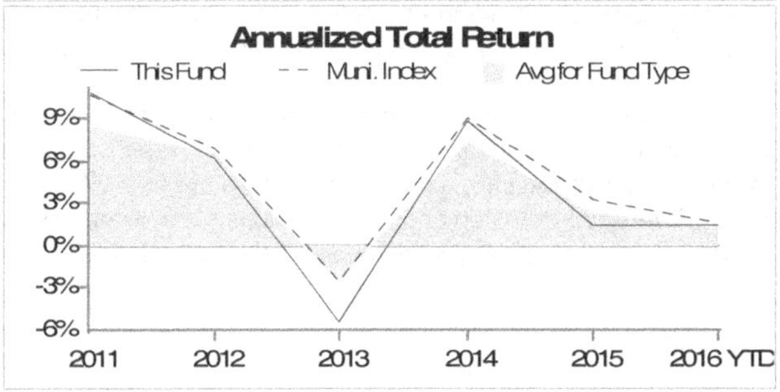

Franklin New York Tax-Free Inc A (FNYTX) C- Fair

Fund Family: Franklin Templeton Investments **Phone:** (800) 342-5236
Address: One Franklin Parkway, San Mateo, CA 94403
Fund Type: MUS - Municipal - Single State
Major Rating Factors: Middle of the road best describes Franklin New York Tax-Free Inc A whose TheStreet.com Investment Rating is currently a C- (Fair). The fund has a performance rating of C+ (Fair) based on an average return of 2.25% over the last three years (3.73% taxable equivalent) and 1.34% over the last three months (2.22% taxable equivalent). Factored into the performance evaluation is an expense ratio of 0.61% (low) and a 4.3% front-end load that is levied at the time of purchase.

The fund's risk rating is currently C (Fair). Volatility, as measured by standard deviation, is considered average for fixed income funds at 3.69. Another risk factor is the fund's below average duration of 3.8 years (i.e. lower interest rate risk).

John B. Pomeroy has been running the fund for 27 years and currently receives a manager quality ranking of 18 (0=worst, 99=best). If you desire an average level of risk, then this fund may be an option.
Services Offered: Automated phone transactions, payroll deductions, bank draft capabilities, an IRA investment plan and a systematic withdrawal plan.

Data Date	Investment Rating	Net Assets ($Mil)	NAV	Performance Rating/Pts	Total Return Y-T-D	Risk Rating/Pts
3-16	C-	4,145	11.53	C+ / 6.3	1.34%	C / 4.5
2015	C	4,178	11.48	C+ / 6.5	1.51%	C / 4.3
2014	C	4,451	11.72	C+ / 6.5	9.28%	C- / 4.0
2013	D-	4,637	11.15	C- / 3.4	-4.65%	C- / 4.2
2012	D+	5,692	12.13	C / 4.8	6.40%	C / 4.3
2011	B-	5,401	11.84	C+ / 6.1	10.01%	C / 5.2

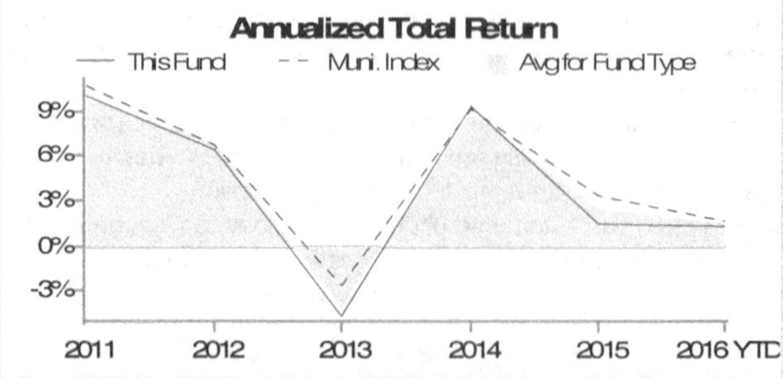

Franklin NY Interm Tax-Free Inc A (FKNIX) B+ Good

Fund Family: Franklin Templeton Investments **Phone:** (800) 342-5236
Address: One Franklin Parkway, San Mateo, CA 94403
Fund Type: MUS - Municipal - Single State
Major Rating Factors: Strong performance is the major factor driving the B+ (Good) TheStreet.com Investment Rating for Franklin NY Interm Tax-Free Inc A. The fund currently has a performance rating of B+ (Good) based on an average return of 2.82% over the last three years (4.67% taxable equivalent) and 1.57% over the last three months (2.60% taxable equivalent). Factored into the performance evaluation is an expense ratio of 0.65% (low) and a 2.3% front-end load that is levied at the time of purchase.

The fund's risk rating is currently C (Fair). Volatility, as measured by standard deviation, is considered average for fixed income funds at 3.40. Another risk factor is the fund's below average duration of 5.0 years (i.e. lower interest rate risk).

John B. Pomeroy has been running the fund for 24 years and currently receives a manager quality ranking of 37 (0=worst, 99=best). If you desire an average level of risk and strong performance, then this fund is a good option.
Services Offered: Automated phone transactions, payroll deductions, bank draft capabilities and a systematic withdrawal plan.

Data Date	Investment Rating	Net Assets ($Mil)	NAV	Performance Rating/Pts	Total Return Y-T-D	Risk Rating/Pts
3-16	B+	556	11.89	B+ / 8.3	1.57%	C / 5.2
2015	B	534	11.78	B / 8.1	2.79%	C / 5.0
2014	C+	531	11.77	C+ / 6.2	7.03%	C / 4.7
2013	C+	599	11.31	C+ / 6.5	-2.63%	C / 4.5
2012	C	642	11.94	C+ / 6.0	4.90%	C- / 4.1
2011	C+	554	11.71	C+ / 6.6	10.92%	C / 4.6

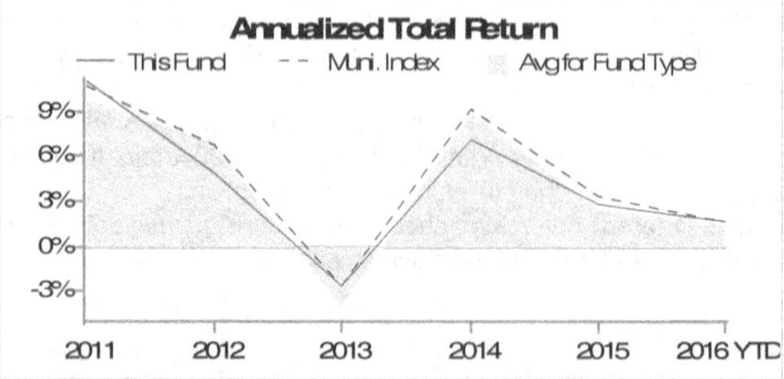

Franklin Ohio Tax-Free Inc A (FTOIX) C+ Fair

Fund Family: Franklin Templeton Investments **Phone:** (800) 342-5236
Address: One Franklin Parkway, San Mateo, CA 94403
Fund Type: MUI - Municipal - Insured
Major Rating Factors: Strong performance is the major factor driving the C+ (Fair) TheStreet.com Investment Rating for Franklin Ohio Tax-Free Inc A. The fund currently has a performance rating of B+ (Good) based on an average return of 3.45% over the last three years and 1.58% over the last three months. Factored into the performance evaluation is an expense ratio of 0.63% (low) and a 4.3% front-end load that is levied at the time of purchase.

The fund's risk rating is currently C- (Fair). Volatility, as measured by standard deviation, is considered average for fixed income funds at 4.20. Another risk factor is the fund's below average duration of 4.4 years (i.e. lower interest rate risk).

John B. Pomeroy has been running the fund for 27 years and currently receives a manager quality ranking of 31 (0=worst, 99=best). If you desire an average level of risk and strong performance, then this fund is a good option.
Services Offered: Automated phone transactions, payroll deductions, bank draft capabilities, wire transfers and a systematic withdrawal plan.

Data Date	Investment Rating	Net Assets ($Mil)	NAV	Performance Rating/Pts	Total Return Y-T-D	Risk Rating/Pts
3-16	C+	1,184	12.92	B+ / 8.3	1.58%	C- / 3.6
2015	C+	1,155	12.82	B / 8.2	3.31%	C- / 3.4
2014	C+	1,149	12.85	B / 7.8	10.24%	C- / 3.1
2013	D	1,170	12.11	C / 5.0	-4.42%	C- / 3.4
2012	D+	1,423	13.13	C / 5.4	7.43%	C- / 3.6
2011	C+	1,234	12.68	C / 5.3	10.79%	C+ / 5.7

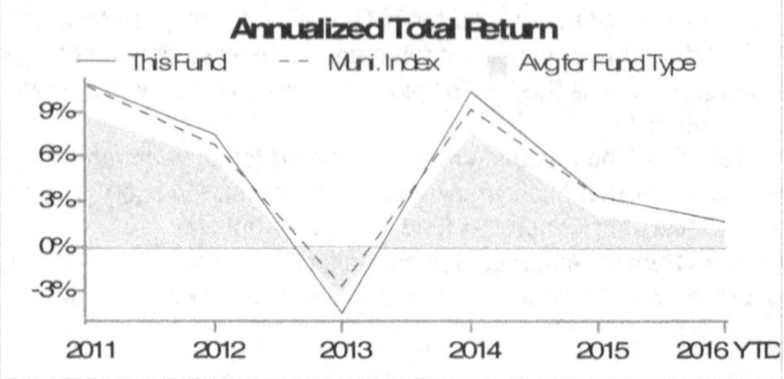

Franklin Oregon Tax-Free Inc A (FRORX) C- Fair

Fund Family: Franklin Templeton Investments **Phone:** (800) 342-5236
Address: One Franklin Parkway, San Mateo, CA 94403
Fund Type: MUS - Municipal - Single State
Major Rating Factors: Middle of the road best describes Franklin Oregon Tax-Free Inc A whose TheStreet.com Investment Rating is currently a C- (Fair). The fund has a performance rating of C+ (Fair) based on an average return of 2.31% over the last three years (3.83% taxable equivalent) and 1.53% over the last three months (2.53% taxable equivalent). Factored into the performance evaluation is an expense ratio of 0.63% (low) and a 4.3% front-end load that is levied at the time of purchase.

The fund's risk rating is currently C- (Fair). Volatility, as measured by standard deviation, is considered average for fixed income funds at 4.24. Another risk factor is the fund's below average duration of 4.8 years (i.e. lower interest rate risk).

John W. Wiley has been running the fund for 25 years and currently receives a manager quality ranking of 12 (0=worst, 99=best). If you desire an average level of risk, then this fund may be an option.
Services Offered: Automated phone transactions, payroll deductions, bank draft capabilities, wire transfers and a systematic withdrawal plan.

Data Date	Investment Rating	Net Assets ($Mil)	NAV	Performance Rating/Pts	Total Return Y-T-D	Risk Rating/Pts
3-16	C-	959	11.91	C+ / 6.7	1.53%	C- / 3.5
2015	C-	937	11.83	C+ / 6.7	2.32%	C- / 3.3
2014	D+	944	11.99	C+ / 6.4	9.78%	C- / 3.0
2013	E+	933	11.36	D+ / 2.4	-6.27%	C- / 3.5
2012	C	1,178	12.57	C+ / 5.7	6.86%	C- / 4.2
2011	B+	1,005	12.19	C+ / 6.8	11.03%	C / 5.3

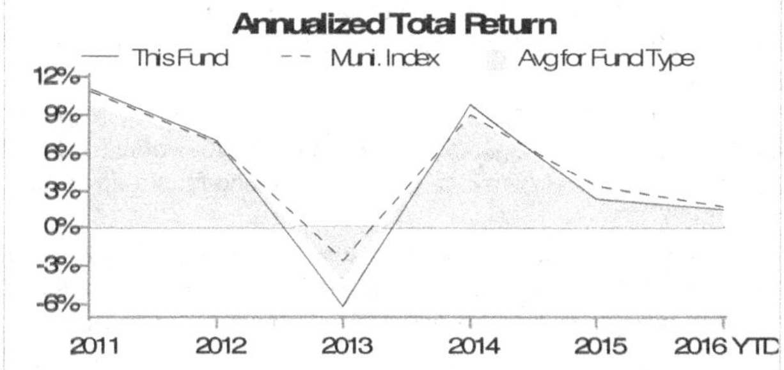

Franklin PA Tax-Free Inc A (FRPAX) C- Fair

Fund Family: Franklin Templeton Investments **Phone:** (800) 342-5236
Address: One Franklin Parkway, San Mateo, CA 94403
Fund Type: MUS - Municipal - Single State
Major Rating Factors: Strong performance is the major factor driving the C- (Fair) TheStreet.com Investment Rating for Franklin PA Tax-Free Inc A. The fund currently has a performance rating of B- (Good) based on an average return of 2.49% over the last three years (4.12% taxable equivalent) and 1.70% over the last three months (2.82% taxable equivalent). Factored into the performance evaluation is an expense ratio of 0.64% (low) and a 4.3% front-end load that is levied at the time of purchase.

The fund's risk rating is currently C- (Fair). Volatility, as measured by standard deviation, is considered average for fixed income funds at 4.30. Another risk factor is the fund's below average duration of 3.9 years (i.e. lower interest rate risk).

Stella S. Wong has been running the fund for 30 years and currently receives a manager quality ranking of 14 (0=worst, 99=best). If you desire an average level of risk and strong performance, then this fund is a good option.
Services Offered: Automated phone transactions, payroll deductions, bank draft capabilities, wire transfers and a systematic withdrawal plan.

Data Date	Investment Rating	Net Assets ($Mil)	NAV	Performance Rating/Pts	Total Return Y-T-D	Risk Rating/Pts
3-16	C-	964	10.34	B- / 7.0	1.70%	C- / 3.5
2015	C-	958	10.26	C+ / 6.7	1.89%	C- / 3.2
2014	C	991	10.47	B- / 7.2	10.62%	D+ / 2.9
2013	D-	1,036	9.87	C- / 3.2	-6.15%	C- / 3.2
2012	C	1,285	10.93	C+ / 6.4	7.41%	C- / 3.3
2011	A-	1,071	10.57	B- / 7.4	11.67%	C / 4.7

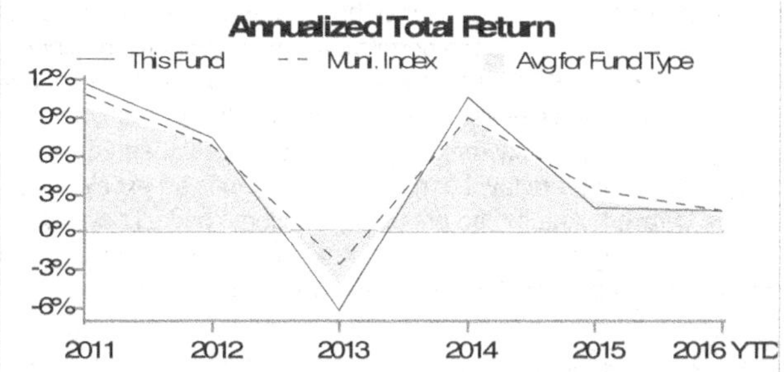

Franklin Strategic Income A (FRSTX) D- Weak

Fund Family: Franklin Templeton Investments **Phone:** (800) 342-5236
Address: One Franklin Parkway, San Mateo, CA 94403
Fund Type: GEN - General
Major Rating Factors: Very poor performance is the major factor driving the D- (Weak) TheStreet.com Investment Rating for Franklin Strategic Income A. The fund currently has a performance rating of E+ (Very Weak) based on an average return of 0.09% over the last three years and 1.44% over the last three months. Factored into the performance evaluation is an expense ratio of 0.87% (average) and a 4.3% front-end load that is levied at the time of purchase.

The fund's risk rating is currently C- (Fair). Volatility, as measured by standard deviation, is considered average for fixed income funds at 4.21. Another risk factor is the fund's below average duration of 3.1 years (i.e. lower interest rate risk).

Christopher J. Molumphy has been running the fund for 22 years and currently receives a manager quality ranking of 21 (0=worst, 99=best). This fund offers an average level of risk, but investors looking for strong performance will be frustrated.
Services Offered: Automated phone transactions, payroll deductions, an IRA investment plan, a 401K investment plan, a Keogh investment plan, wire transfers and a systematic withdrawal plan.

Data Date	Investment Rating	Net Assets ($Mil)	NAV	Performance Rating/Pts	Total Return Y-T-D	Risk Rating/Pts
3-16	D-	4,403	9.19	E+ / 0.7	1.44%	C- / 3.6
2015	D	4,774	9.15	D- / 1.2	-4.26%	C- / 3.9
2014	D	5,230	10.00	C / 4.7	1.67%	C- / 4.0
2013	C	4,939	10.46	B- / 7.3	3.20%	D+ / 2.7
2012	D-	4,490	10.68	C+ / 6.0	12.35%	D / 2.1
2011	E+	3,319	10.09	C / 5.2	2.65%	D+ / 2.9

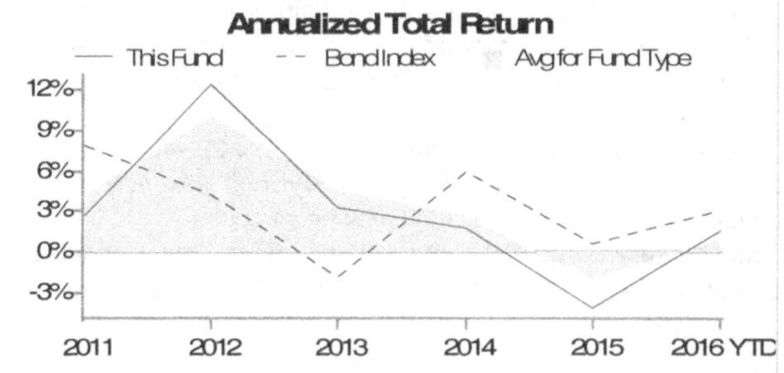

Franklin Total Return A (FKBAX) D+ Weak

Fund Family: Franklin Templeton Investments **Phone:** (800) 342-5236
Address: One Franklin Parkway, San Mateo, CA 94403
Fund Type: GEI - General - Investment Grade
Major Rating Factors: Disappointing performance is the major factor driving the D+ (Weak) TheStreet.com Investment Rating for Franklin Total Return A. The fund currently has a performance rating of D+ (Weak) based on an average return of 1.48% over the last three years and 1.60% over the last three months. Factored into the performance evaluation is an expense ratio of 0.94% (average) and a 4.3% front-end load that is levied at the time of purchase.

The fund's risk rating is currently C+ (Fair). Volatility, as measured by standard deviation, is considered average for fixed income funds at 3.20. Another risk factor is the fund's fairly average duration of 5.1 years (i.e. average interest rate risk).

Christopher J. Molumphy has been running the fund for 18 years and currently receives a manager quality ranking of 35 (0=worst, 99=best). This fund offers an average level of risk, but investors looking for strong performance will be frustrated.
Services Offered: Automated phone transactions, payroll deductions, bank draft capabilities, an IRA investment plan, a 401K investment plan, a Keogh investment plan, wire transfers and a systematic withdrawal plan.

Data Date	Investment Rating	Net Assets ($Mil)	NAV	Performance Rating/Pts	Total Return Y-T-D	Risk Rating/Pts
3-16	D+	3,566	9.68	D+ / 2.8	1.60%	C+ / 5.7
2015	D+	3,536	9.56	D+ / 2.4	-1.59%	C+ / 5.6
2014	D	3,282	10.04	C- / 3.7	4.47%	C / 5.3
2013	C-	2,969	9.85	C- / 4.1	-0.98%	C+ / 5.7
2012	C+	3,225	10.33	C / 4.5	8.33%	C+ / 6.0
2011	C	2,266	10.04	C / 4.3	5.53%	C+ / 6.5

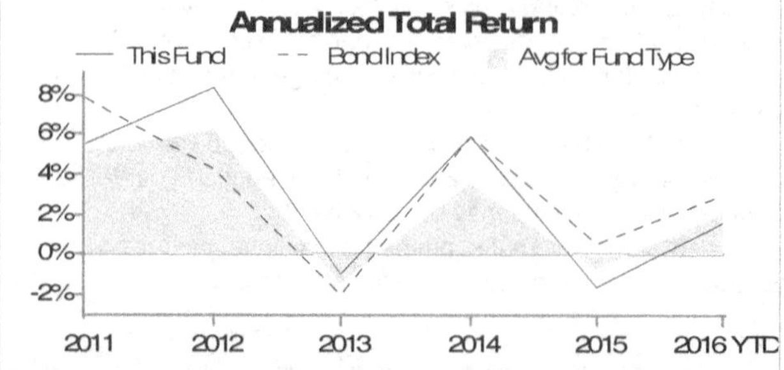

Franklin US Government Sec A (FKUSX) C Fair

Fund Family: Franklin Templeton Investments **Phone:** (800) 342-5236
Address: One Franklin Parkway, San Mateo, CA 94403
Fund Type: USS - US Government - Short & Inter. Term
Major Rating Factors: A moderate risk profile coupled with stable earnings characterizes Franklin US Government Sec A which receives a TheStreet.com Investment Rating of C (Fair). Volatility, as measured by standard deviation, is considered low for fixed income funds at 2.03. Another risk factor is the fund's below average duration of 3.7 years (i.e. lower interest rate risk). The fund's risk rating is currently B+ (Good).

The fund's performance rating is currently C- (Fair). It has registered an average return of 1.59% over the last three years and is up 1.10% over the last three months. Factored into the performance evaluation is an expense ratio of 0.76% (low) and a 4.3% front-end load that is levied at the time of purchase.

Roger A. Bayston has been running the fund for 23 years and currently receives a manager quality ranking of 83 (0=worst, 99=best). If you desire stability with a moderate level of risk then this fund is an excellent option.
Services Offered: Automated phone transactions, payroll deductions, bank draft capabilities, an IRA investment plan, a 401K investment plan, a Keogh investment plan and a systematic withdrawal plan.

Data Date	Investment Rating	Net Assets ($Mil)	NAV	Performance Rating/Pts	Total Return Y-T-D	Risk Rating/Pts
3-16	C	4,260	6.37	C- / 3.4	1.10%	B+ / 8.4
2015	C	4,137	6.35	C- / 3.6	0.94%	B+ / 8.3
2014	D	4,279	6.50	D / 1.7	4.31%	B / 8.2
2013	D+	4,782	6.45	D- / 1.2	-1.68%	B+ / 8.5
2012	D+	6,614	6.80	D- / 1.4	1.53%	B+ / 8.6
2011	C	6,603	6.94	D+ / 2.6	6.81%	B+ / 8.8

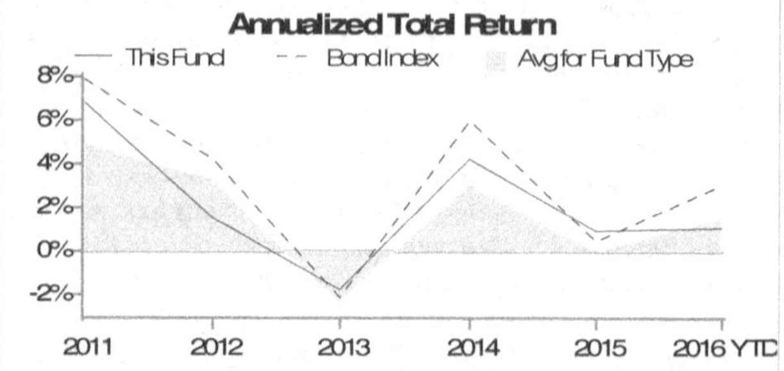

Franklin Virginia Tax-Free Inc A (FRVAX) C- Fair

Fund Family: Franklin Templeton Investments **Phone:** (800) 342-5236
Address: One Franklin Parkway, San Mateo, CA 94403
Fund Type: MUS - Municipal - Single State
Major Rating Factors: Middle of the road best describes Franklin Virginia Tax-Free Inc A whose TheStreet.com Investment Rating is currently a C- (Fair). The fund has a performance rating of C+ (Fair) based on an average return of 2.13% over the last three years (3.53% taxable equivalent) and 1.67% over the last three months (2.77% taxable equivalent). Factored into the performance evaluation is an expense ratio of 0.65% (low) and a 4.3% front-end load that is levied at the time of purchase.

The fund's risk rating is currently C- (Fair). Volatility, as measured by standard deviation, is considered average for fixed income funds at 3.93. Another risk factor is the fund's below average duration of 4.0 years (i.e. lower interest rate risk).

Stella S. Wong has been running the fund for 29 years and currently receives a manager quality ranking of 14 (0=worst, 99=best). If you desire an average level of risk, then this fund may be an option.
Services Offered: Automated phone transactions, payroll deductions, bank draft capabilities, wire transfers and a systematic withdrawal plan.

Data Date	Investment Rating	Net Assets ($Mil)	NAV	Performance Rating/Pts	Total Return Y-T-D	Risk Rating/Pts
3-16	C-	540	11.56	C+ / 6.4	1.67%	C- / 4.0
2015	C-	536	11.47	C+ / 6.0	1.77%	C- / 3.8
2014	C-	554	11.69	C+ / 6.1	9.13%	C- / 3.5
2013	D-	592	11.13	D+ / 2.7	-5.80%	C- / 3.8
2012	C-	772	12.24	C / 5.4	6.80%	C- / 4.2
2011	B+	676	11.89	C+ / 6.6	10.72%	C / 5.4

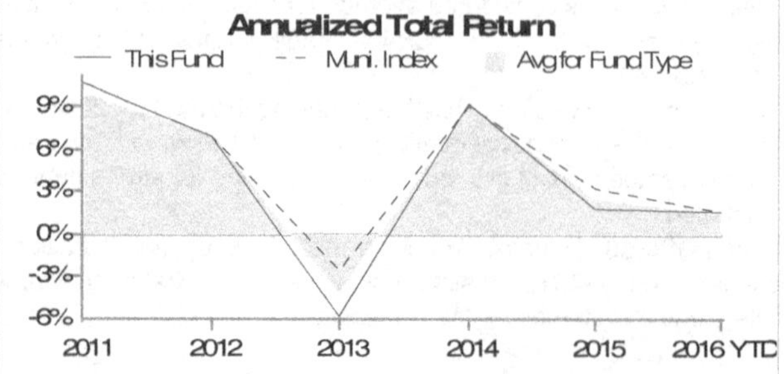

GE RSP Income (GESLX) A- Excellent

Fund Family: GE Investment Funds **Phone:** (800) 242-0134
Address: PO Box 9838, Providence, RI 02940
Fund Type: GES - General - Short & Inter. Term
Major Rating Factors: Strong performance is the major factor driving the A- (Excellent) TheStreet.com Investment Rating for GE RSP Income. The fund currently has a performance rating of B- (Good) based on an average return of 2.66% over the last three years and 2.77% over the last three months. Factored into the performance evaluation is an expense ratio of 0.17% (very low).

The fund's risk rating is currently C+ (Fair). Volatility, as measured by standard deviation, is considered average for fixed income funds at 2.91. Another risk factor is the fund's fairly average duration of 5.5 years (i.e. average interest rate risk).

William M. Healey has been running the fund for 20 years and currently receives a manager quality ranking of 79 (0=worst, 99=best). If you desire an average level of risk and strong performance, then this fund is a good option.
Services Offered: N/A

Data Date	Investment Rating	Net Assets ($Mil)	NAV	Performance Rating/Pts	Total Return Y-T-D	Risk Rating/Pts
3-16	A-	2,508	11.59	B- / 7.4	2.77%	C+/ 6.9
2015	B	2,465	11.36	C+/ 6.8	0.35%	C+/ 6.8
2014	B	2,608	11.67	C / 5.3	5.83%	B- / 7.2
2013	B+	2,601	11.33	C+/ 5.9	-0.84%	B- / 7.3
2012	B+	2,932	11.75	C / 4.6	5.87%	B / 7.8
2011	B+	2,755	11.67	C- / 4.1	8.01%	B+/ 8.4

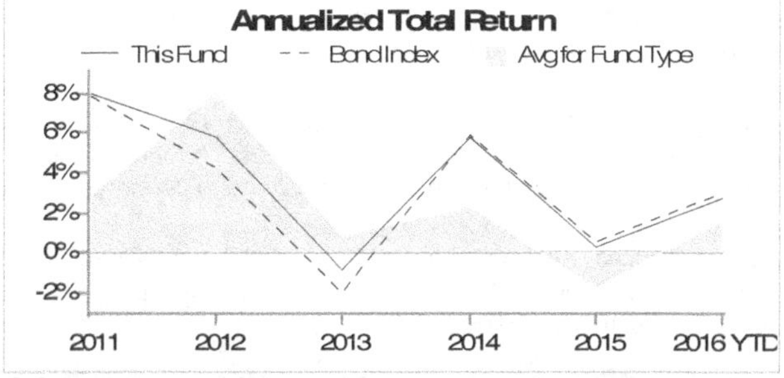

GMO Emerging Country Debt III (GMCDX) D+ Weak

Fund Family: GMO Funds **Phone:** N/A
Address: 40 Rowes Wharf, Boston, MA 02110
Fund Type: EM - Emerging Market
Major Rating Factors: GMO Emerging Country Debt III has adopted a very risky asset allocation strategy and currently receives an overall TheStreet.com Investment Rating of D+ (Weak). Volatility, as measured by standard deviation, is considered high for fixed income funds at 8.55. Another risk factor is the fund's below average duration of 4.7 years (i.e. lower interest rate risk). The high level of risk (E, Very Weak) did however, reward investors with excellent performance.

The fund's performance rating is currently B (Good). It has registered an average return of 3.02% over the last three years and is up 4.26% over the last three months. Factored into the performance evaluation is an expense ratio of 0.56% (very low), a 0.5% front-end load that is levied at the time of purchase and a 0.5% back-end load levied at the time of sale.

Thomas F. Cooper has been running the fund for 22 years and currently receives a manager quality ranking of 99 (0=worst, 99=best). If you are comfortable owning a very high risk investment, this fund may be an option.
Services Offered: However, the fund is currently closed to new investors.

Data Date	Investment Rating	Net Assets ($Mil)	NAV	Performance Rating/Pts	Total Return Y-T-D	Risk Rating/Pts
3-16	D+	861	9.05	B / 8.0	4.26%	E / 0.4
2015	D+	828	8.68	C+/ 6.1	0.02%	E / 0.4
2014	C-	855	9.33	B+/ 8.8	5.98%	E- / 0.2
2013	C	492	9.61	A+/ 9.6	-1.18%	E- / 0.2
2012	B-	573	10.32	A+/ 9.9	26.73%	E- / 0.2
2011	B-	597	8.84	A+/ 9.8	7.50%	E+/ 0.7

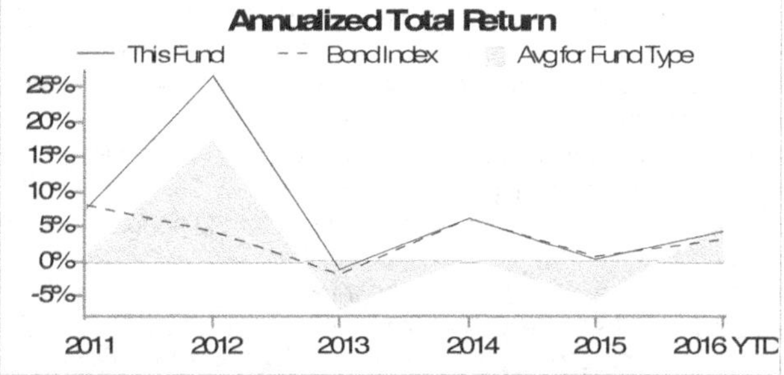

GMO US Treasury (GUSTX) C+ Fair

Fund Family: GMO Funds **Phone:** N/A
Address: 40 Rowes Wharf, Boston, MA 02110
Fund Type: US - US Treasury
Major Rating Factors: Disappointing performance is the major factor driving the C+ (Fair) TheStreet.com Investment Rating for GMO US Treasury. The fund currently has a performance rating of D+ (Weak) based on an average return of 0.15% over the last three years and 0.16% over the last three months. Factored into the performance evaluation is an expense ratio of 0.10% (very low).

The fund's risk rating is currently A+ (Excellent). Volatility, as measured by standard deviation, is considered very low for fixed income funds at 0.07.

Benjamin L. Inker has been running the fund for 2 years and currently receives a manager quality ranking of 72 (0=worst, 99=best). This fund offers only a moderate level of risk but investors looking for strong performance are still waiting.
Services Offered: Automated phone transactions, bank draft capabilities, wire transfers and a systematic withdrawal plan.

Data Date	Investment Rating	Net Assets ($Mil)	NAV	Performance Rating/Pts	Total Return Y-T-D	Risk Rating/Pts
3-16	C+	3,623	25.01	D+/ 2.8	0.16%	A+/ 9.9
2015	B-	3,972	24.99	C- / 3.8	0.11%	A+/ 9.9
2014	C-	2,187	25.00	D- / 1.1	0.08%	A+/ 9.9
2013	C-	1,802	25.00	E+/ 0.8	0.14%	A+/ 9.9
2012	D+	2,959	25.00	E / 0.3	0.10%	A+/ 9.9
2011	U	1,980	25.00	U / --	0.09%	U / --

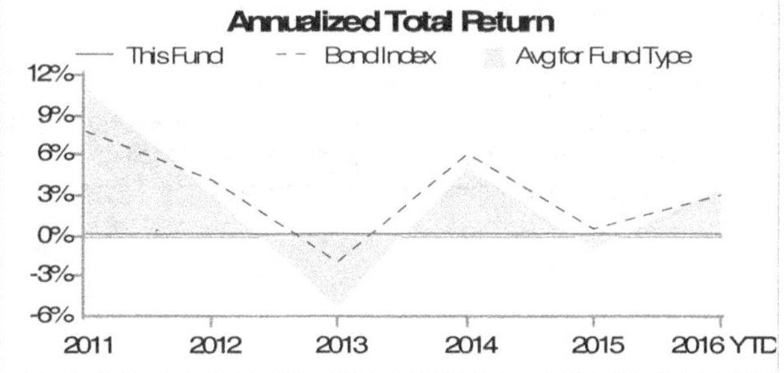

Goldman Sachs Strategic Income A (GSZAX) D Weak

Fund Family: Goldman Sachs Funds **Phone:** (800) 526-7384
Address: P.O. Box 06050, Chicago, IL 60050
Fund Type: GL - Global

Major Rating Factors: Very poor performance is the major factor driving the D (Weak) TheStreet.com Investment Rating for Goldman Sachs Strategic Income A. The fund currently has a performance rating of E (Very Weak) based on an average return of -0.42% over the last three years and -1.67% over the last three months. Factored into the performance evaluation is an expense ratio of 0.91% (average) and a 3.8% front-end load that is levied at the time of purchase.

The fund's risk rating is currently C (Fair). Volatility, as measured by standard deviation, is considered average for fixed income funds at 3.36. Another risk factor is the fund's very low average duration of 2.7 years (i.e. low interest rate risk).

Jonathan A. Beinner has been running the fund for 6 years and currently receives a manager quality ranking of 44 (0=worst, 99=best). This fund offers an average level of risk, but investors looking for strong performance will be frustrated.

Services Offered: Automated phone transactions, payroll deductions, bank draft capabilities, an IRA investment plan, a 401K investment plan, wire transfers and a systematic withdrawal plan.

Data Date	Investment Rating	Net Assets ($Mil)	NAV	Performance Rating/Pts	Total Return Y-T-D	Risk Rating/Pts
3-16	D	1,386	9.41	E / 0.5	-1.67%	C / 5.3
2015	D+	1,703	9.62	D / 2.1	-2.40%	C+/ 5.9
2014	C	2,987	10.28	C / 5.0	-0.84%	C+/ 5.7
2013	B+	2,945	10.66	B- / 7.3	6.07%	C / 5.1
2012	U	522	10.34	U / --	13.34%	U / --
2011	U	732	9.49	U / --	-2.49%	U / --

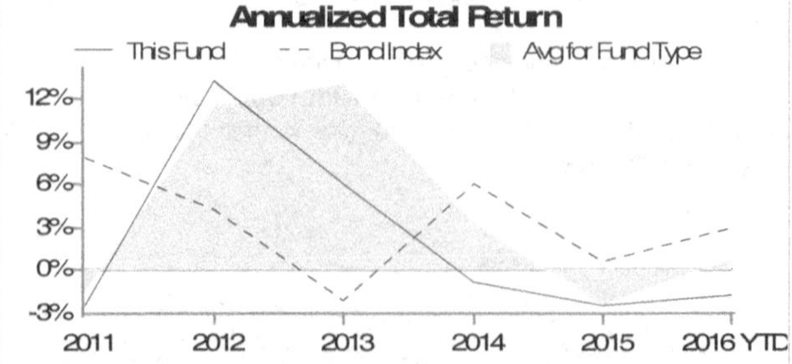

Guggenheim Macro Opportunities A (GIOAX) D Weak

Fund Family: Guggenheim Investments Funds **Phone:** (800) 820-0888
Address: 9601 Blackwell Road, Rockville, MD 20850
Fund Type: GEL - General - Long Term

Major Rating Factors: Disappointing performance is the major factor driving the D (Weak) TheStreet.com Investment Rating for Guggenheim Macro Opportunities A. The fund currently has a performance rating of D- (Weak) based on an average return of 1.47% over the last three years and 0.18% over the last three months. Factored into the performance evaluation is an expense ratio of 1.57% (above average) and a 4.0% front-end load that is levied at the time of purchase.

The fund's risk rating is currently C (Fair). Volatility, as measured by standard deviation, is considered average for fixed income funds at 3.29. Another risk factor is the fund's very low average duration of 1.5 years (i.e. low interest rate risk).

Byron S. Minerd has been running the fund for 5 years and currently receives a manager quality ranking of 72 (0=worst, 99=best). This fund offers an average level of risk, but investors looking for strong performance will be frustrated.

Services Offered: Automated phone transactions, payroll deductions, bank draft capabilities, an IRA investment plan, wire transfers and a systematic withdrawal plan.

Data Date	Investment Rating	Net Assets ($Mil)	NAV	Performance Rating/Pts	Total Return Y-T-D	Risk Rating/Pts
3-16	D	737	24.87	D- / 1.4	0.18%	C / 5.5
2015	C-	779	25.16	C / 4.6	-1.51%	C+/ 5.7
2014	A-	644	26.83	B- / 7.5	5.14%	C / 5.3
2013	U	325	26.70	U / --	3.82%	U / --
2012	U	128	27.05	U / --	14.38%	U / --

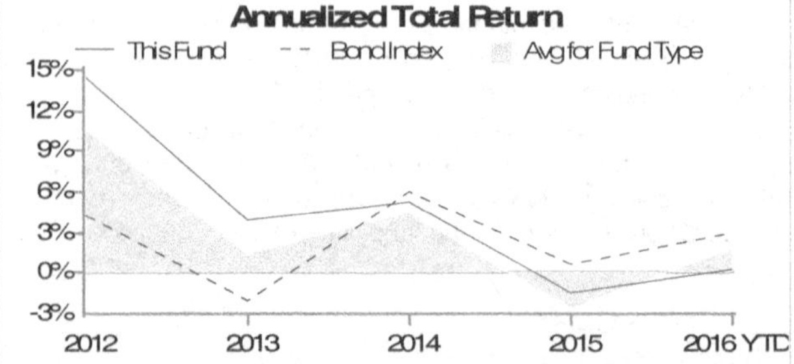

Harbor Bond Inst (HABDX) C- Fair

Fund Family: Harbor Funds **Phone:** (800) 422-1050
Address: 111 South Wacker Drive, Chicago, IL 60606
Fund Type: GEI - General - Investment Grade

Major Rating Factors: Middle of the road best describes Harbor Bond Inst whose TheStreet.com Investment Rating is currently a C- (Fair). The fund has a performance rating of C+ (Fair) based on an average return of 1.61% over the last three years and 2.05% over the last three months. Factored into the performance evaluation is an expense ratio of 0.57% (very low).

The fund's risk rating is currently C (Fair). Volatility, as measured by standard deviation, is considered average for fixed income funds at 3.61. Another risk factor is the fund's below average duration of 4.5 years (i.e. lower interest rate risk).

Mark R. Kiesel currently receives a manager quality ranking of 27 (0=worst, 99=best). If you desire an average level of risk, then this fund may be an option.

Services Offered: Automated phone transactions, payroll deductions, bank draft capabilities, an IRA investment plan, wire transfers and a systematic withdrawal plan.

Data Date	Investment Rating	Net Assets ($Mil)	NAV	Performance Rating/Pts	Total Return Y-T-D	Risk Rating/Pts
3-16	C-	2,718	11.64	C+/ 5.6	2.05%	C / 4.7
2015	C-	2,776	11.47	C+/ 5.8	0.23%	C / 4.8
2014	C	3,886	12.06	C+/ 5.7	4.78%	C / 5.2
2013	C	6,345	11.95	C / 4.9	-1.46%	C / 5.5
2012	C+	7,688	12.48	C / 4.9	9.32%	C+/ 6.1
2011	D+	7,300	12.19	C- / 3.9	3.48%	C+/ 6.3

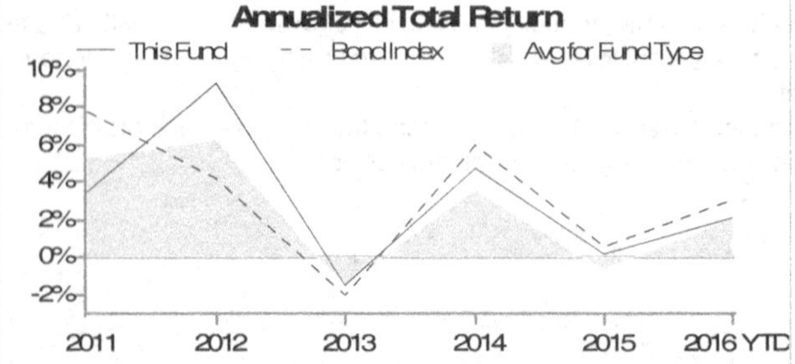

Hartford Floating Rate A (HFLAX) D Weak

Fund Family: Hartford Mutual Funds **Phone:** (888) 843-7824
Address: P.O. Box 64387, St. Paul, MN 55164
Fund Type: LP - Loan Participation
Major Rating Factors: Disappointing performance is the major factor driving the D (Weak) TheStreet.com Investment Rating for Hartford Floating Rate A. The fund currently has a performance rating of D- (Weak) based on an average return of 0.60% over the last three years and 1.46% over the last three months. Factored into the performance evaluation is an expense ratio of 0.96% (average) and a 3.0% front-end load that is levied at the time of purchase.

The fund's risk rating is currently C (Fair). Volatility, as measured by standard deviation, is considered average for fixed income funds at 3.38. Another risk factor is the fund's very low average duration of 0.3 years (i.e. low interest rate risk).

Brion S. Johnson currently receives a manager quality ranking of 55 (0=worst, 99=best). This fund offers an average level of risk, but investors looking for strong performance will be frustrated.
Services Offered: Automated phone transactions, payroll deductions, bank draft capabilities, an IRA investment plan, a 401K investment plan, a Keogh investment plan, wire transfers and a systematic withdrawal plan.

Data Date	Investment Rating	Net Assets ($Mil)	NAV	Performance Rating/Pts	Total Return Y-T-D	Risk Rating/Pts
3-16	D	928	8.16	D- / 1.2	1.46%	C / 5.2
2015	D	997	8.13	D / 1.8	-2.14%	C / 5.2
2014	C	1,443	8.66	C- / 3.8	-0.25%	B- / 7.3
2013	B	2,064	9.03	B- / 7.1	5.08%	C / 4.7
2012	E	1,777	8.94	C- / 4.2	9.18%	D+ / 2.3
2011	C-	1,754	8.59	B / 7.7	1.59%	D / 2.1

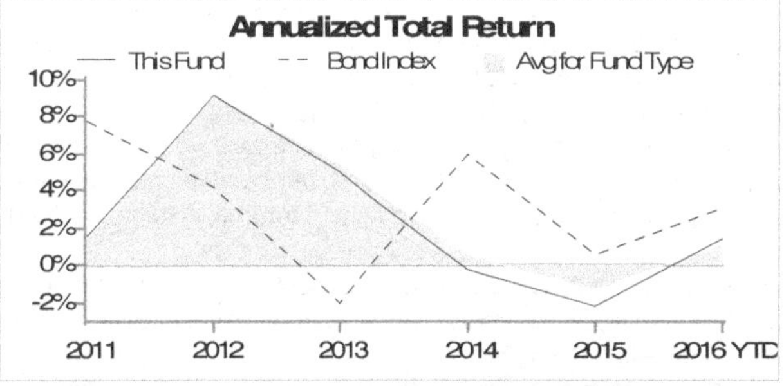

Hartford Total Return Bond A (ITBAX) D+ Weak

Fund Family: Hartford Mutual Funds **Phone:** (888) 843-7824
Address: P.O. Box 64387, St. Paul, MN 55164
Fund Type: GEI - General - Investment Grade
Major Rating Factors: Hartford Total Return Bond A receives a TheStreet.com Investment Rating of D+ (Weak). The fund has a performance rating of C- (Fair) based on an average return of 1.61% over the last three years and 2.55% over the last three months. Factored into the performance evaluation is an expense ratio of 0.88% (average) and a 4.5% front-end load that is levied at the time of purchase.

The fund's risk rating is currently C (Fair). Volatility, as measured by standard deviation, is considered average for fixed income funds at 3.39. Another risk factor is the fund's fairly average duration of 5.7 years (i.e. average interest rate risk).

Campe E. Goodman has been running the fund for 4 years and currently receives a manager quality ranking of 29 (0=worst, 99=best). If you desire an average level of risk, then this fund may be an option.
Services Offered: Automated phone transactions, payroll deductions, bank draft capabilities, an IRA investment plan, a 401K investment plan, wire transfers and a systematic withdrawal plan.

Data Date	Investment Rating	Net Assets ($Mil)	NAV	Performance Rating/Pts	Total Return Y-T-D	Risk Rating/Pts
3-16	D+	725	10.32	C- / 3.5	2.55%	C / 5.2
2015	D+	677	10.13	D / 2.1	-0.93%	C / 5.3
2014	D	613	10.48	C- / 3.5	5.24%	C+ / 5.8
2013	C-	570	10.40	C- / 3.2	-1.78%	C+ / 6.7
2012	C+	710	10.84	C- / 3.3	7.10%	B / 8.1
2011	C+	669	10.74	C- / 3.7	6.26%	B / 7.8

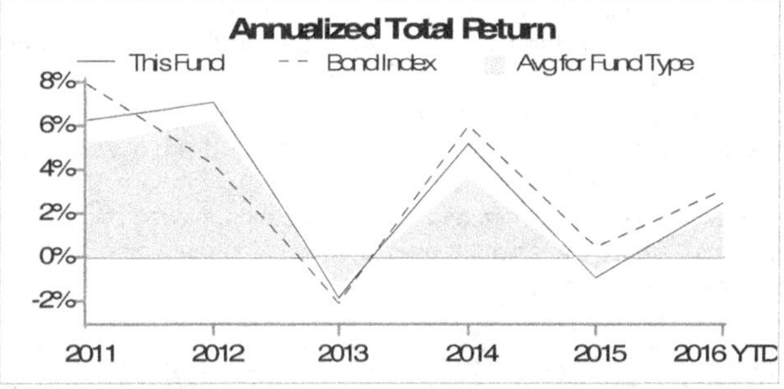

Homestead Short Term Bond (HOSBX) B Good

Fund Family: Homestead Funds **Phone:** (800) 258-3030
Address: c/o BFDS, Kansas, MO 64121
Fund Type: GES - General - Short & Inter. Term
Major Rating Factors: A moderate risk profile coupled with stable earnings characterizes Homestead Short Term Bond which receives a TheStreet.com Investment Rating of B (Good). Volatility, as measured by standard deviation, is considered very low for fixed income funds at 0.82. Another risk factor is the fund's very low average duration of 2.6 years (i.e. low interest rate risk). The fund's risk rating is currently A (Excellent).

The fund's performance rating is currently C (Fair). It has registered an average return of 1.11% over the last three years and is up 0.76% over the last three months. Factored into the performance evaluation is an expense ratio of 0.73% (low).

Douglas G. Kern has been running the fund for 25 years and currently receives a manager quality ranking of 84 (0=worst, 99=best). If you desire stability with a moderate level of risk then this fund is an excellent option.
Services Offered: Automated phone transactions, payroll deductions, bank draft capabilities, an IRA investment plan and a systematic withdrawal plan.

Data Date	Investment Rating	Net Assets ($Mil)	NAV	Performance Rating/Pts	Total Return Y-T-D	Risk Rating/Pts
3-16	B	545	5.20	C / 4.6	0.76%	A / 9.5
2015	A	542	5.18	C+ / 6.0	0.43%	A / 9.4
2014	B	571	5.23	C- / 3.4	1.56%	A / 9.4
2013	A-	535	5.22	C- / 4.2	1.64%	A / 9.5
2012	C+	426	5.22	D / 2.1	4.58%	A / 9.4
2011	B	374	5.12	C- / 3.5	1.90%	B+ / 8.7

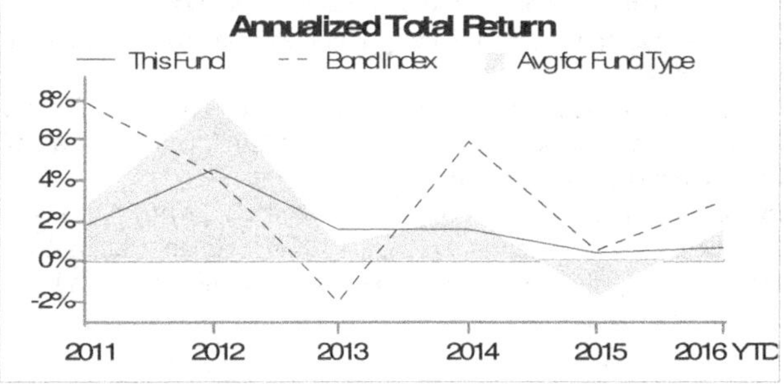

Hotchkis and Wiley High Yield A (HWHAX) E+ Very Weak

Fund Family: Hotchkis & Wiley Funds **Phone:** (866) 493-8637
Address: 725 S. Figueroa Street, Los Angeles, CA 90017
Fund Type: COH - Corporate - High Yield

Major Rating Factors: Hotchkis and Wiley High Yield A has adopted a very risky asset allocation strategy and currently receives an overall TheStreet.com Investment Rating of E+ (Very Weak). Volatility, as measured by standard deviation, is considered above average for fixed income funds at 5.66. Unfortunately, the high level of risk (D-, Weak) failed to pay off as investors endured poor performance.

The fund's performance rating is currently E+ (Very Weak). It has registered an average return of 1.09% over the last three years and is up 1.65% over the last three months. Factored into the performance evaluation is an expense ratio of 0.98% (average), a 3.8% front-end load that is levied at the time of purchase and a 2.0% back-end load levied at the time of sale.

Mark T. Hudoff has been running the fund for 7 years and currently receives a manager quality ranking of 42 (0=worst, 99=best). If you can tolerate very high levels of risk in the hope of improved future returns, holding this fund may be an option.

Services Offered: Automated phone transactions, payroll deductions, bank draft capabilities, an IRA investment plan, a 401K investment plan, wire transfers and a systematic withdrawal plan.

Data Date	Investment Rating	Net Assets ($Mil)	NAV	Perfor-mance Rating/Pts	Total Return Y-T-D	Risk Rating/Pts
3-16	E+	572	10.99	E+ / 0.7	1.65%	D- / 1.4
2015	D-	565	10.98	D- / 1.4	-4.56%	D / 1.8
2014	C-	604	12.32	B- / 7.1	0.90%	D+ / 2.7
2013	C+	490	12.99	A+ / 9.6	8.85%	E+ / 0.8
2012	C+	177	12.80	A- / 9.2	17.61%	E / 0.4
2011	U	96	11.71	U / --	1.91%	U / --

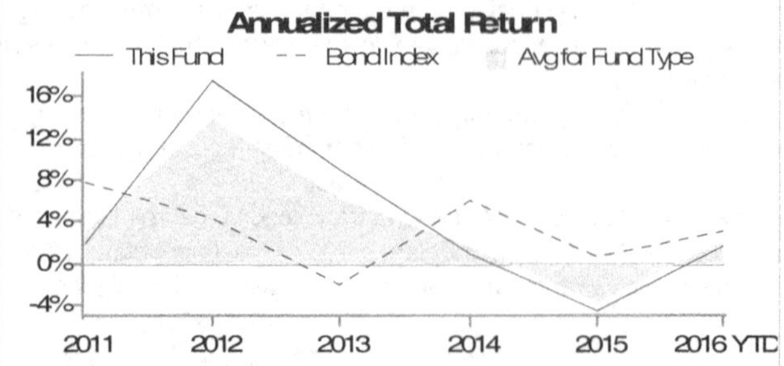

Invesco Core Plus Bond A (ACPSX) C Fair

Fund Family: Invesco Investments Funds **Phone:** (800) 959-4246
Address: P.O. Box 4739, Houston, TX 77210
Fund Type: GEI - General - Investment Grade

Major Rating Factors: Middle of the road best describes Invesco Core Plus Bond A whose TheStreet.com Investment Rating is currently a C (Fair). The fund has a performance rating of C+ (Fair) based on an average return of 3.00% over the last three years and 2.51% over the last three months. Factored into the performance evaluation is an expense ratio of 0.98% (average) and a 4.3% front-end load that is levied at the time of purchase.

The fund's risk rating is currently C (Fair). Volatility, as measured by standard deviation, is considered average for fixed income funds at 3.39. Another risk factor is the fund's fairly average duration of 5.3 years (i.e. average interest rate risk).

Chuck Burge has been running the fund for 7 years and currently receives a manager quality ranking of 81 (0=worst, 99=best). If you desire an average level of risk, then this fund may be an option.

Services Offered: Automated phone transactions, payroll deductions, bank draft capabilities, an IRA investment plan, a 401K investment plan, wire transfers and a systematic withdrawal plan.

Data Date	Investment Rating	Net Assets ($Mil)	NAV	Perfor-mance Rating/Pts	Total Return Y-T-D	Risk Rating/Pts
3-16	C	570	10.70	C+ / 5.9	2.51%	C / 5.2
2015	C-	534	10.52	C / 5.4	0.28%	C / 5.1
2014	C+	383	10.86	C / 5.3	7.01%	C+ / 5.9
2013	C	313	10.57	C / 4.4	-0.44%	C+ / 6.4
2012	C	330	10.99	C- / 3.4	7.95%	B- / 7.1
2011	U	240	10.57	U / --	5.41%	U / --

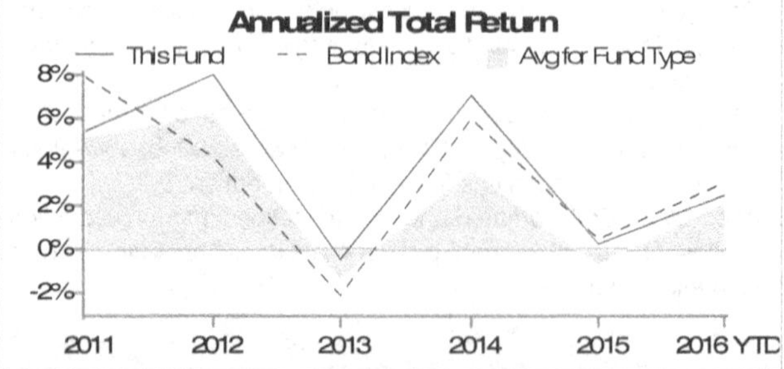

Invesco Corporate Bond A (ACCBX) C- Fair

Fund Family: Invesco Investments Funds **Phone:** (800) 959-4246
Address: P.O. Box 4739, Houston, TX 77210
Fund Type: GEI - General - Investment Grade

Major Rating Factors: Middle of the road best describes Invesco Corporate Bond A whose TheStreet.com Investment Rating is currently a C- (Fair). The fund has a performance rating of C+ (Fair) based on an average return of 3.12% over the last three years and 3.67% over the last three months. Factored into the performance evaluation is an expense ratio of 0.91% (average) and a 4.3% front-end load that is levied at the time of purchase.

The fund's risk rating is currently C- (Fair). Volatility, as measured by standard deviation, is considered average for fixed income funds at 4.74. Another risk factor is the fund's fairly average duration of 6.9 years (i.e. average interest rate risk).

Chuck Burge has been running the fund for 6 years and currently receives a manager quality ranking of 53 (0=worst, 99=best). If you desire an average level of risk, then this fund may be an option.

Services Offered: Automated phone transactions, payroll deductions, bank draft capabilities, an IRA investment plan, a 401K investment plan, a Keogh investment plan, wire transfers and a systematic withdrawal plan.

Data Date	Investment Rating	Net Assets ($Mil)	NAV	Perfor-mance Rating/Pts	Total Return Y-T-D	Risk Rating/Pts
3-16	C-	903	7.09	C+ / 6.2	3.67%	C- / 3.0
2015	D+	854	6.90	C- / 4.2	-1.62%	D+ / 2.8
2014	C+	838	7.28	C+ / 6.9	8.00%	C- / 3.8
2013	C	766	7.01	C+ / 6.4	-0.05%	C- / 3.8
2012	C	889	7.29	C+ / 5.8	11.44%	C- / 3.9
2011	D-	789	6.82	C / 5.0	5.89%	C- / 3.8

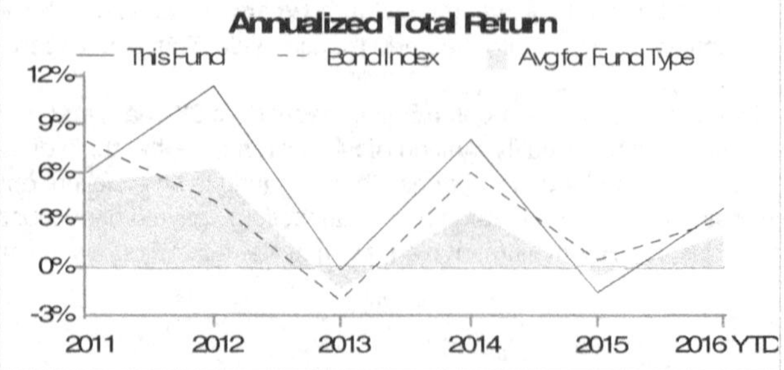

Invesco Floating Rate A (AFRAX) D Weak

Fund Family: Invesco Investments Funds **Phone:** (800) 959-4246
Address: P.O. Box 4739, Houston, TX 77210
Fund Type: LP - Loan Participation
Major Rating Factors: Disappointing performance is the major factor driving the D (Weak) TheStreet.com Investment Rating for Invesco Floating Rate A. The fund currently has a performance rating of D- (Weak) based on an average return of 0.81% over the last three years and 1.33% over the last three months. Factored into the performance evaluation is an expense ratio of 1.07% (average) and a 2.5% front-end load that is levied at the time of purchase.

The fund's risk rating is currently C (Fair). Volatility, as measured by standard deviation, is considered average for fixed income funds at 3.29.

Thomas Ewald has been running the fund for 10 years and currently receives a manager quality ranking of 61 (0=worst, 99=best). This fund offers an average level of risk, but investors looking for strong performance will be frustrated.

Services Offered: Automated phone transactions, payroll deductions, an IRA investment plan and a systematic withdrawal plan.

Data Date	Investment Rating	Net Assets ($Mil)	NAV	Perfor-mance Rating/Pts	Total Return Y-T-D	Risk Rating/Pts
3-16	D	649	7.15	D- / 1.4	1.33%	C / 5.5
2015	C-	690	7.14	D+ / 2.3	-2.87%	B- / 7.4
2014	B+	868	7.72	C / 5.3	0.86%	B / 7.9
2013	A-	1,093	7.99	B / 7.9	5.88%	C / 5.1
2012	D-	513	7.87	C / 5.0	10.12%	C- / 3.0
2011	C	415	7.51	B / 8.2	1.55%	D / 1.8

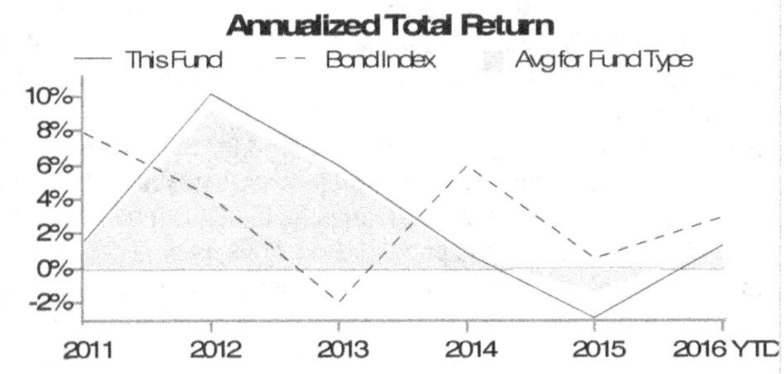

Invesco High Yield A (AMHYX) E+ Very Weak

Fund Family: Invesco Investments Funds **Phone:** (800) 959-4246
Address: P.O. Box 4739, Houston, TX 77210
Fund Type: COH - Corporate - High Yield
Major Rating Factors: Invesco High Yield A has adopted a very risky asset allocation strategy and currently receives an overall TheStreet.com Investment Rating of E+ (Very Weak). Volatility, as measured by standard deviation, is considered above average for fixed income funds at 6.01. Unfortunately, the high level of risk (D-, Weak) failed to pay off as investors endured very poor performance.

The fund's performance rating is currently D- (Weak). It has registered an average return of 1.24% over the last three years and is up 1.67% over the last three months. Factored into the performance evaluation is an expense ratio of 1.02% (average) and a 4.3% front-end load that is levied at the time of purchase.

Darren S. Hughes has been running the fund for 11 years and currently receives a manager quality ranking of 44 (0=worst, 99=best). If you can tolerate very high levels of risk in the hope of improved future returns, holding this fund may be an option.

Services Offered: Automated phone transactions, payroll deductions, bank draft capabilities, an IRA investment plan, a 401K investment plan, a Keogh investment plan, wire transfers and a systematic withdrawal plan.

Data Date	Investment Rating	Net Assets ($Mil)	NAV	Perfor-mance Rating/Pts	Total Return Y-T-D	Risk Rating/Pts
3-16	E+	757	3.94	D- / 1.4	1.67%	D- / 1.0
2015	D-	752	3.93	D / 2.2	-3.09%	E+ / 0.9
2014	D	863	4.29	B- / 7.1	1.12%	D- / 1.4
2013	C	1,068	4.49	A- / 9.2	7.04%	E+ / 0.8
2012	C-	1,097	4.44	B+ / 8.4	17.51%	E+ / 0.6
2011	C-	865	4.01	B+ / 8.8	1.43%	E / 0.4

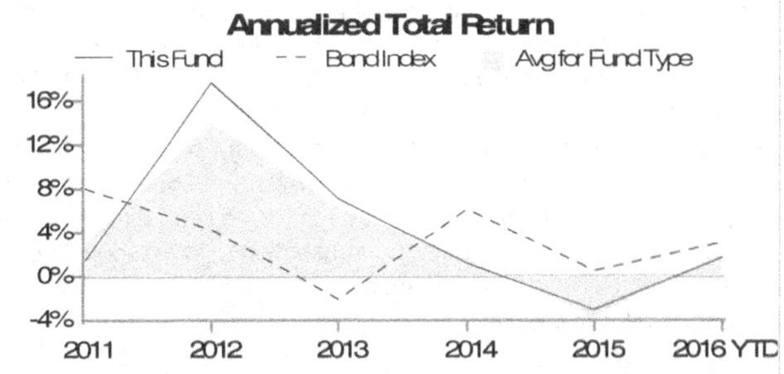

Invesco High Yield Municipal A (ACTHX) C+ Fair

Fund Family: Invesco Investments Funds **Phone:** (800) 959-4246
Address: P.O. Box 4739, Houston, TX 77210
Fund Type: MUH - Municipal - High Yield
Major Rating Factors: Invesco High Yield Municipal A has adopted a very risky asset allocation strategy and currently receives an overall TheStreet.com Investment Rating of C+ (Fair). Volatility, as measured by standard deviation, is considered above average for fixed income funds at 5.39. Another risk factor is the fund's above average duration of 8.5 years (i.e. higher interest rate risk). The high level of risk (D-, Weak) did however, reward investors with excellent performance.

The fund's performance rating is currently A+ (Excellent). It has registered an average return of 5.60% over the last three years (9.27% taxable equivalent) and is up 1.97% over the last three months (3.26% taxable equivalent). Factored into the performance evaluation is an expense ratio of 0.93% (average) and a 4.3% front-end load that is levied at the time of purchase.

James D. Phillips has been running the fund for 14 years and currently receives a manager quality ranking of 73 (0=worst, 99=best). If you are comfortable owning a very high risk investment, this fund may be an option.

Services Offered: Automated phone transactions, payroll deductions, bank draft capabilities, an IRA investment plan, a 401K investment plan, wire transfers and a systematic withdrawal plan. However, the fund is currently closed to new investors.

Data Date	Investment Rating	Net Assets ($Mil)	NAV	Perfor-mance Rating/Pts	Total Return Y-T-D	Risk Rating/Pts
3-16	C+	4,880	10.18	A+ / 9.8	1.97%	D- / 1.4
2015	C	4,797	10.10	A+ / 9.8	6.25%	D- / 1.0
2014	C+	4,779	9.99	A+ / 9.8	16.55%	E+ / 0.9
2013	C-	4,019	9.04	B- / 7.5	-5.56%	D- / 1.5
2012	A	4,872	10.12	A+ / 9.7	13.92%	D+ / 2.4
2011	B+	3,545	9.40	A+ / 9.6	11.30%	D / 1.9

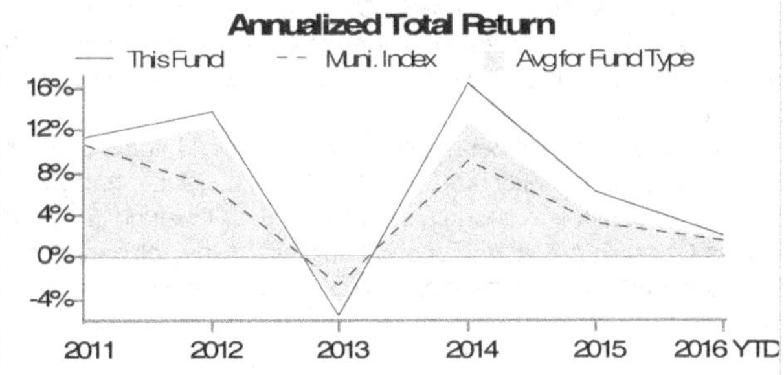

Invesco Intm Term Municipal Inc A (VKLMX) A+ Excellent

Fund Family: Invesco Investments Funds **Phone:** (800) 959-4246
Address: P.O. Box 4739, Houston, TX 77210
Fund Type: MUN - Municipal - National
Major Rating Factors: Strong performance is the major factor driving the A+ (Excellent) TheStreet.com Investment Rating for Invesco Intm Term Municipal Inc A. The fund currently has a performance rating of B+ (Good) based on an average return of 3.21% over the last three years (5.32% taxable equivalent) and 1.58% over the last three months (2.62% taxable equivalent). Factored into the performance evaluation is an expense ratio of 0.90% (average) and a 2.5% front-end load that is levied at the time of purchase.

The fund's risk rating is currently C+ (Fair). Volatility, as measured by standard deviation, is considered average for fixed income funds at 3.00. Another risk factor is the fund's fairly average duration of 5.0 years (i.e. average interest rate risk).

Robert J. Stryker has been running the fund for 11 years and currently receives a manager quality ranking of 69 (0=worst, 99=best). If you desire an average level of risk and strong performance, then this fund is a good option.
Services Offered: Automated phone transactions, payroll deductions, bank draft capabilities, an IRA investment plan, a 401K investment plan, wire transfers and a systematic withdrawal plan.

Data Date	Investment Rating	Net Assets ($Mil)	NAV	Performance Rating/Pts	Total Return Y-T-D	Risk Rating/Pts
3-16	A+	655	11.32	B+ / 8.6	1.58%	C+ / 6.5
2015	A	605	11.21	B+ / 8.7	2.87%	C+ / 6.2
2014	A-	475	11.20	B- / 7.5	7.77%	C+ / 5.6
2013	B+	397	10.73	C+ / 6.6	-1.80%	C+ / 5.9
2012	B+	390	11.28	C+ / 6.1	5.95%	C+ / 5.8
2011	B+	315	11.05	C+ / 6.4	8.75%	C / 5.5

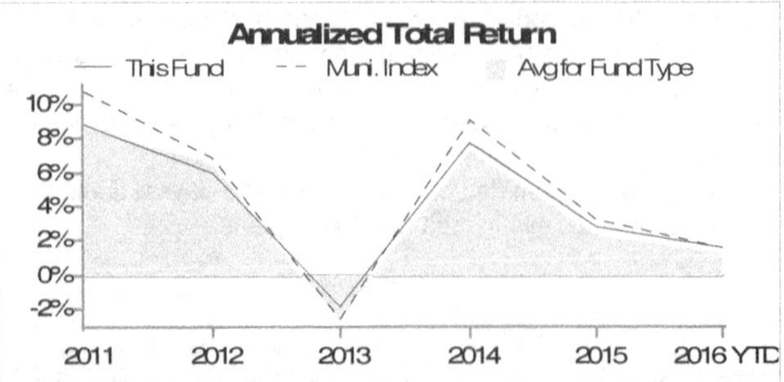

Invesco Limited Term Muni Inc A (ATFAX) B+ Good

Fund Family: Invesco Investments Funds **Phone:** (800) 959-4246
Address: P.O. Box 4739, Houston, TX 77210
Fund Type: MUN - Municipal - National
Major Rating Factors: A moderate risk profile coupled with stable earnings characterizes Invesco Limited Term Muni Inc A which receives a TheStreet.com Investment Rating of B+ (Good). Volatility, as measured by standard deviation, is considered low for fixed income funds at 2.16. Another risk factor is the fund's below average duration of 3.0 years (i.e. lower interest rate risk). The fund's risk rating is currently B+ (Good).

The fund's performance rating is currently C+ (Fair). It has registered an average return of 1.72% over the last three years (2.85% taxable equivalent) and is up 0.91% over the last three months (1.51% taxable equivalent). Factored into the performance evaluation is an expense ratio of 0.63% (low) and a 2.5% front-end load that is levied at the time of purchase.

Robert J. Stryker has been running the fund for 5 years and currently receives a manager quality ranking of 44 (0=worst, 99=best). If you desire stability with a moderate level of risk then this fund is an excellent option.
Services Offered: Automated phone transactions, payroll deductions, bank draft capabilities, an IRA investment plan, a 401K investment plan, wire transfers and a systematic withdrawal plan.

Data Date	Investment Rating	Net Assets ($Mil)	NAV	Performance Rating/Pts	Total Return Y-T-D	Risk Rating/Pts
3-16	B+	1,206	11.55	C+ / 5.9	0.91%	B+ / 8.3
2015	A	1,135	11.50	C+ / 6.9	1.40%	B / 8.1
2014	B-	930	11.60	C / 4.9	4.39%	B- / 7.2
2013	A	975	11.43	C+ / 6.9	-0.78%	C+ / 6.5
2012	C+	1,158	11.86	C / 5.0	4.91%	C+ / 5.9
2011	A-	1,036	11.68	C+ / 5.7	8.85%	C+ / 6.9

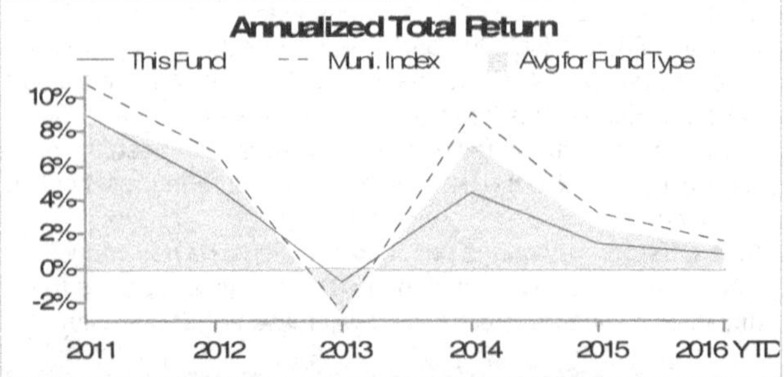

Invesco Municipal Income A (VKMMX) B Good

Fund Family: Invesco Investments Funds **Phone:** (800) 959-4246
Address: P.O. Box 4739, Houston, TX 77210
Fund Type: MUN - Municipal - National
Major Rating Factors: Exceptional performance is the major factor driving the B (Good) TheStreet.com Investment Rating for Invesco Municipal Income A. The fund currently has a performance rating of A- (Excellent) based on an average return of 3.99% over the last three years (6.61% taxable equivalent) and 1.81% over the last three months (3.00% taxable equivalent). Factored into the performance evaluation is an expense ratio of 0.93% (average) and a 4.3% front-end load that is levied at the time of purchase.

The fund's risk rating is currently C- (Fair). Volatility, as measured by standard deviation, is considered average for fixed income funds at 3.95. Another risk factor is the fund's fairly average duration of 6.7 years (i.e. average interest rate risk).

Robert J. Stryker has been running the fund for 11 years and currently receives a manager quality ranking of 57 (0=worst, 99=best). If you desire an average level of risk and strong performance, then this fund is a good option.
Services Offered: Automated phone transactions, payroll deductions, bank draft capabilities, a 401K investment plan, wire transfers and a systematic withdrawal plan.

Data Date	Investment Rating	Net Assets ($Mil)	NAV	Performance Rating/Pts	Total Return Y-T-D	Risk Rating/Pts
3-16	B	1,792	13.75	A- / 9.0	1.81%	C- / 4.0
2015	C+	1,703	13.64	B+ / 8.9	3.70%	C- / 3.2
2014	B+	1,635	13.72	B+ / 8.8	11.00%	C- / 3.4
2013	C+	1,540	12.89	C+ / 6.9	-3.47%	C- / 3.8
2012	B-	1,535	13.93	B- / 7.5	8.93%	C- / 3.4
2011	B+	1,453	13.34	B+ / 8.9	10.92%	D+ / 2.8

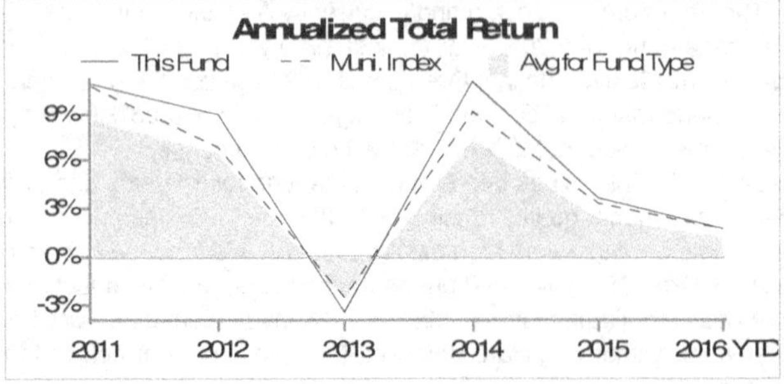

Invesco US Government A (AGOVX) C- Fair

Fund Family: Invesco Investments Funds **Phone:** (800) 959-4246
Address: P.O. Box 4739, Houston, TX 77210
Fund Type: USS - US Government - Short & Inter. Term
Major Rating Factors: A moderate risk profile coupled with stable earnings characterizes Invesco US Government A which receives a TheStreet.com Investment Rating of C- (Fair). Volatility, as measured by standard deviation, is considered low for fixed income funds at 2.70. Another risk factor is the fund's below average duration of 5.0 years (i.e. lower interest rate risk). The fund's risk rating is currently B- (Good).

The fund's performance rating is currently C- (Fair). It has registered an average return of 1.26% over the last three years and is up 2.45% over the last three months. Factored into the performance evaluation is an expense ratio of 0.96% (average) and a 4.3% front-end load that is levied at the time of purchase.

Brian Schneider has been running the fund for 7 years and currently receives a manager quality ranking of 40 (0=worst, 99=best). If you desire stability with a moderate level of risk then this fund is an excellent option.
Services Offered: Automated phone transactions, payroll deductions, bank draft capabilities, an IRA investment plan, a 401K investment plan, a Keogh investment plan, wire transfers and a systematic withdrawal plan.

Data Date	Investment Rating	Net Assets ($Mil)	NAV	Performance Rating/Pts	Total Return Y-T-D	Risk Rating/Pts
3-16	C-	626	9.05	C- / 3.2	2.45%	B- / 7.5
2015	D+	602	8.87	D / 1.9	0.18%	B- / 7.4
2014	D	627	8.99	D- / 1.4	3.85%	B / 7.8
2013	D	678	8.83	E+ / 0.9	-2.88%	B- / 7.5
2012	E+	849	9.30	D- / 1.5	2.21%	C+ / 6.3
2011	E+	928	9.34	D / 1.9	7.23%	C+ / 6.4

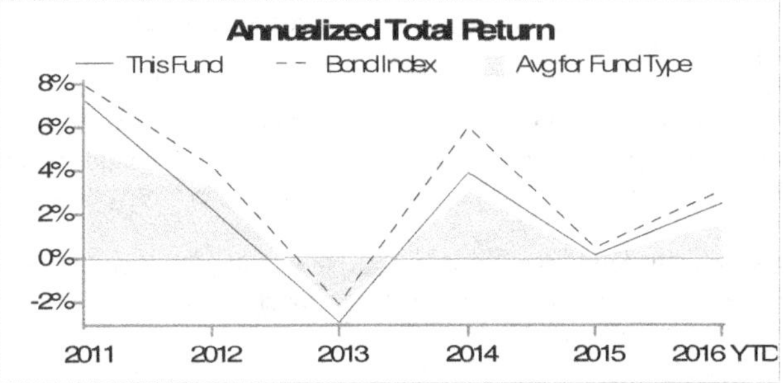

Ivy Bond A (IBOAX) D+ Weak

Fund Family: Ivy Funds **Phone:** (800) 777-6472
Address: PO Box 29217, Shawnee Mission, KS 66201
Fund Type: GEI - General - Investment Grade
Major Rating Factors: Ivy Bond A receives a TheStreet.com Investment Rating of D+ (Weak). The fund has a performance rating of C- (Fair) based on an average return of 2.05% over the last three years and 2.38% over the last three months. Factored into the performance evaluation is an expense ratio of 1.02% (average) and a 5.8% front-end load that is levied at the time of purchase.

The fund's risk rating is currently C+ (Fair). Volatility, as measured by standard deviation, is considered average for fixed income funds at 3.17. Another risk factor is the fund's fairly average duration of 5.5 years (i.e. average interest rate risk).

David W. Land, CFA has been running the fund for 13 years and currently receives a manager quality ranking of 43 (0=worst, 99=best). If you desire an average level of risk, then this fund may be an option.
Services Offered: Automated phone transactions, payroll deductions, bank draft capabilities, an IRA investment plan, a 401K investment plan, a Keogh investment plan, wire transfers and a systematic withdrawal plan.

Data Date	Investment Rating	Net Assets ($Mil)	NAV	Performance Rating/Pts	Total Return Y-T-D	Risk Rating/Pts
3-16	D+	702	10.54	C- / 3.5	2.38%	C+ / 5.8
2015	D+	702	10.35	D+ / 2.6	-0.31%	C+ / 5.7
2014	C-	673	10.64	C- / 3.8	5.91%	C+ / 6.5
2013	C	539	10.30	C- / 3.4	-0.94%	B / 7.6
2012	B-	537	10.71	C- / 3.4	6.99%	B / 8.2
2011	C+	410	10.38	C- / 4.0	6.90%	B / 7.7

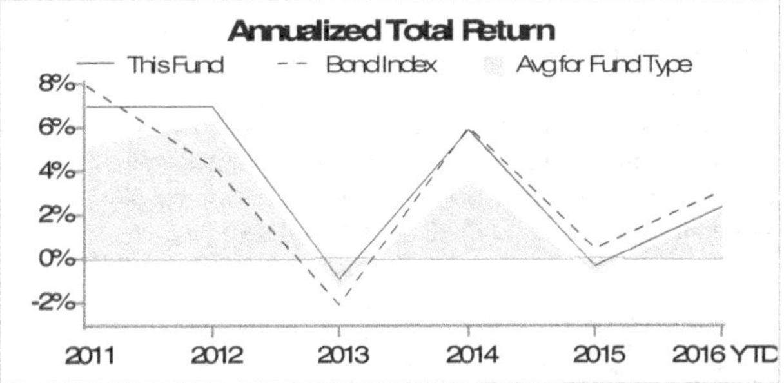

Ivy High Income A (WHIAX) E Very Weak

Fund Family: Ivy Funds **Phone:** (800) 777-6472
Address: PO Box 29217, Shawnee Mission, KS 66201
Fund Type: COH - Corporate - High Yield
Major Rating Factors: Ivy High Income A has adopted a very risky asset allocation strategy and currently receives an overall TheStreet.com Investment Rating of E (Very Weak). Volatility, as measured by standard deviation, is considered above average for fixed income funds at 5.90. Unfortunately, the high level of risk (D-, Weak) failed to pay off as investors endured poor performance.

The fund's performance rating is currently E (Very Weak). It has registered an average return of 0.38% over the last three years and is up 1.49% over the last three months. Factored into the performance evaluation is an expense ratio of 0.94% (average) and a 5.8% front-end load that is levied at the time of purchase.

William M. Nelson has been running the fund for 3 years and currently receives a manager quality ranking of 22 (0=worst, 99=best). If you can tolerate very high levels of risk in the hope of improved future returns, holding this fund may be an option.
Services Offered: Payroll deductions, bank draft capabilities, an IRA investment plan, a 401K investment plan, a Keogh investment plan and a systematic withdrawal plan.

Data Date	Investment Rating	Net Assets ($Mil)	NAV	Performance Rating/Pts	Total Return Y-T-D	Risk Rating/Pts
3-16	E	1,798	6.91	E / 0.4	1.49%	D- / 1.2
2015	E+	2,358	6.94	E+ / 0.9	-7.41%	D- / 1.5
2014	B-	3,285	8.07	B / 7.6	1.48%	C- / 3.7
2013	A-	3,743	8.64	A+ / 9.8	10.20%	D+ / 2.6
2012	B	2,777	8.54	A- / 9.0	16.89%	D / 2.0
2011	B	1,395	7.97	A- / 9.2	6.12%	D / 1.9

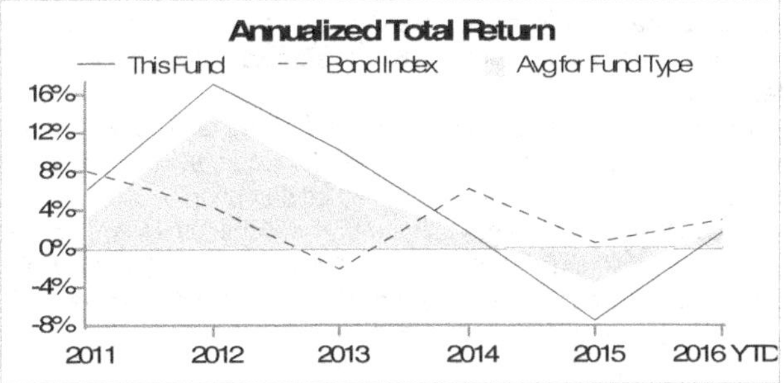

Ivy Limited-Term Bond A (WLTAX) C- Fair

Fund Family: Ivy Funds **Phone:** (800) 777-6472
Address: PO Box 29217, Shawnee Mission, KS 66201
Fund Type: GES - General - Short & Inter. Term

Major Rating Factors: Disappointing performance is the major factor driving the C- (Fair) TheStreet.com Investment Rating for Ivy Limited-Term Bond A. The fund currently has a performance rating of D+ (Weak) based on an average return of 0.59% over the last three years and 1.58% over the last three months. Factored into the performance evaluation is an expense ratio of 0.88% (average) and a 2.5% front-end load that is levied at the time of purchase.

The fund's risk rating is currently B+ (Good). Volatility, as measured by standard deviation, is considered low for fixed income funds at 1.79. Another risk factor is the fund's very low average duration of 2.8 years (i.e. low interest rate risk).

Susan K. Regan has been running the fund for 2 years and currently receives a manager quality ranking of 35 (0=worst, 99=best). This fund offers only a moderate level of risk but investors looking for strong performance are still waiting.

Services Offered: Payroll deductions, bank draft capabilities, an IRA investment plan, a 401K investment plan, a Keogh investment plan and a systematic withdrawal plan.

Data Date	Investment Rating	Net Assets ($Mil)	NAV	Performance Rating/Pts	Total Return Y-T-D	Risk Rating/Pts
3-16	C-	1,577	10.87	D+ / 2.8	1.58%	B+ / 8.7
2015	C-	1,515	10.74	D+ / 2.4	0.45%	B+ / 8.7
2014	D	1,520	10.84	D- / 1.2	0.85%	B+ / 8.7
2013	C-	1,368	10.90	D- / 1.5	-0.73%	B+ / 8.8
2012	D+	1,179	11.20	D- / 1.1	2.67%	B+ / 8.9
2011	C-	1,014	11.13	D / 1.8	2.99%	A- / 9.1

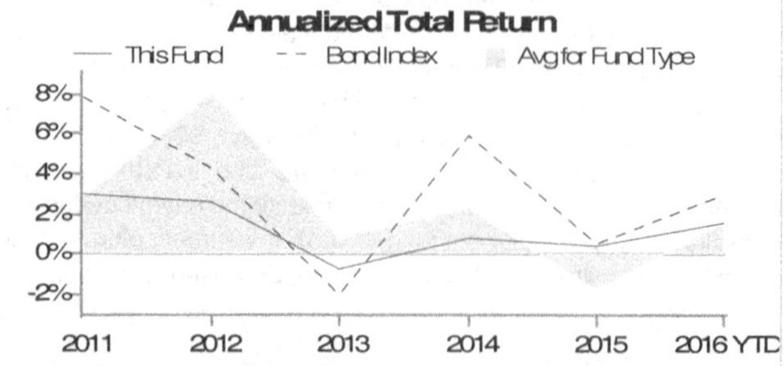

J Hancock Bond A (JHNBX) C- Fair

Fund Family: John Hancock Funds **Phone:** (800) 257-3336
Address: 601 Congress Street, Boston, MA 02210
Fund Type: GEI - General - Investment Grade

Major Rating Factors: Middle of the road best describes J Hancock Bond A whose TheStreet.com Investment Rating is currently a C- (Fair). The fund has a performance rating of C (Fair) based on an average return of 2.48% over the last three years and 2.28% over the last three months. Factored into the performance evaluation is an expense ratio of 0.94% (average) and a 4.0% front-end load that is levied at the time of purchase.

The fund's risk rating is currently C (Fair). Volatility, as measured by standard deviation, is considered average for fixed income funds at 3.33. Another risk factor is the fund's fairly average duration of 5.0 years (i.e. average interest rate risk).

If you desire an average level of risk, then this fund may be an option.

Services Offered: Automated phone transactions, payroll deductions, bank draft capabilities, an IRA investment plan, a 401K investment plan, a Keogh investment plan and a systematic withdrawal plan.

Data Date	Investment Rating	Net Assets ($Mil)	NAV	Performance Rating/Pts	Total Return Y-T-D	Risk Rating/Pts
3-16	C-	1,836	15.69	C / 5.0	2.28%	C / 5.3
2015	C-	1,768	15.46	C / 5.1	-0.18%	C / 5.2
2014	B	1,522	16.02	C+ / 6.5	6.63%	C / 5.4
2013	C+	1,316	15.75	C+ / 6.0	0.46%	C / 5.4
2012	A-	1,295	16.42	C+ / 6.7	11.49%	C+ / 5.9
2011	B	962	15.44	C+ / 6.6	4.95%	C / 4.9

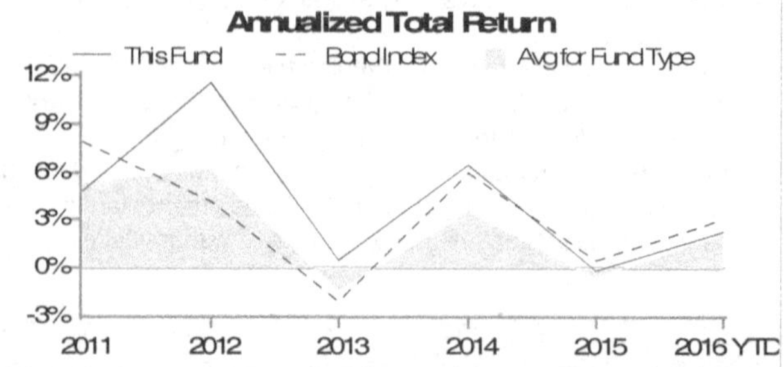

J Hancock Income A (JHFIX) C- Fair

Fund Family: John Hancock Funds **Phone:** (800) 257-3336
Address: 601 Congress Street, Boston, MA 02210
Fund Type: GL - Global

Major Rating Factors: Middle of the road best describes J Hancock Income A whose TheStreet.com Investment Rating is currently a C- (Fair). The fund has a performance rating of C (Fair) based on an average return of 2.09% over the last three years and 2.25% over the last three months. Factored into the performance evaluation is an expense ratio of 0.82% (low) and a 4.0% front-end load that is levied at the time of purchase.

The fund's risk rating is currently C+ (Fair). Volatility, as measured by standard deviation, is considered average for fixed income funds at 3.02. Another risk factor is the fund's below average duration of 3.6 years (i.e. lower interest rate risk).

Daniel S. Janis, III has been running the fund for 17 years and currently receives a manager quality ranking of 96 (0=worst, 99=best). If you desire an average level of risk, then this fund may be an option.

Services Offered: Automated phone transactions, check writing, payroll deductions, bank draft capabilities, an IRA investment plan, a 401K investment plan, a Keogh investment plan and a systematic withdrawal plan.

Data Date	Investment Rating	Net Assets ($Mil)	NAV	Performance Rating/Pts	Total Return Y-T-D	Risk Rating/Pts
3-16	C-	907	6.47	C / 4.7	2.25%	C+ / 6.5
2015	C	908	6.37	C / 5.2	0.44%	C+ / 6.1
2014	C	1,050	6.56	C+ / 5.6	3.70%	C / 4.8
2013	D	1,336	6.58	C+ / 5.8	2.00%	D+ / 2.4
2012	D-	1,754	6.75	C+ / 6.4	11.57%	D / 1.8
2011	D-	1,774	6.40	C+ / 6.2	1.68%	D+ / 2.6

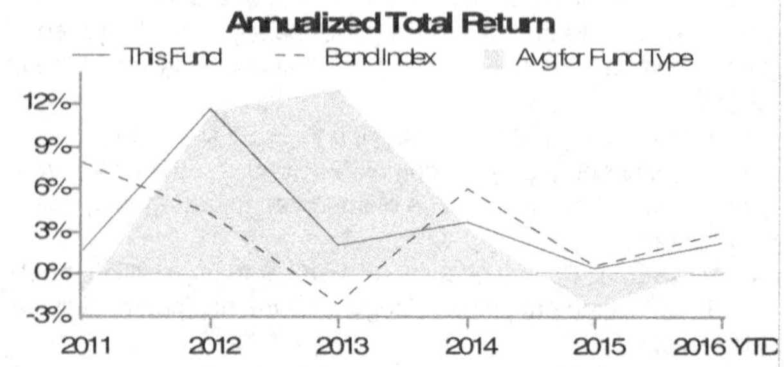

J Hancock Strat Income Opp A (JIPAX) C- Fair

Fund Family: John Hancock Funds **Phone:** (800) 257-3336
Address: 601 Congress Street, Boston, MA 02210
Fund Type: GL - Global
Major Rating Factors: Middle of the road best describes J Hancock Strat Income Opp A whose TheStreet.com Investment Rating is currently a C- (Fair). The fund has a performance rating of C (Fair) based on an average return of 2.27% over the last three years and 1.77% over the last three months. Factored into the performance evaluation is an expense ratio of 1.12% (average) and a 4.0% front-end load that is levied at the time of purchase.

The fund's risk rating is currently C+ (Fair). Volatility, as measured by standard deviation, is considered average for fixed income funds at 3.05. Another risk factor is the fund's below average duration of 3.6 years (i.e. lower interest rate risk).

Daniel S. Janis, III has been running the fund for 10 years and currently receives a manager quality ranking of 97 (0=worst, 99=best). If you desire an average level of risk, then this fund may be an option.
Services Offered: Automated phone transactions, payroll deductions, bank draft capabilities, wire transfers and a systematic withdrawal plan.

Data Date	Investment Rating	Net Assets ($Mil)	NAV	Performance Rating/Pts	Total Return Y-T-D	Risk Rating/Pts
3-16	C-	1,170	10.48	C / 4.7	1.77%	C+ / 6.4
2015	C+	1,141	10.36	C+ / 6.1	0.79%	C+ / 6.1
2014	C+	1,089	10.86	C+ / 6.3	4.45%	C / 4.7
2013	D	1,186	10.79	C+ / 6.1	2.41%	D / 2.1
2012	D-	1,022	11.13	C+ / 6.6	11.84%	D / 1.6
2011	U	675	10.46	U / --	1.53%	U / --

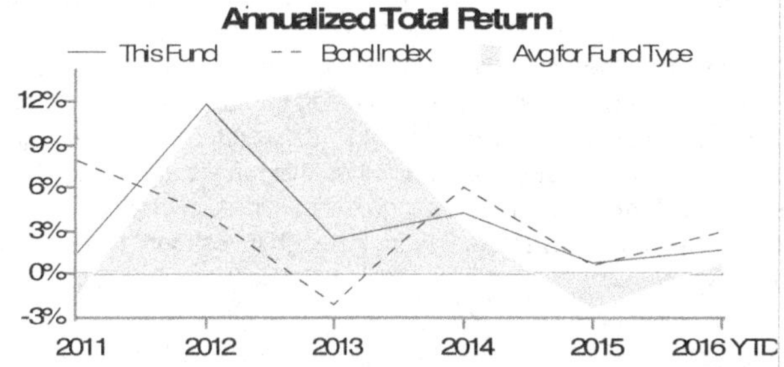

J Hancock Tax Free Bond A (TAMBX) C Fair

Fund Family: John Hancock Funds **Phone:** (800) 257-3336
Address: 601 Congress Street, Boston, MA 02210
Fund Type: MUN - Municipal - National
Major Rating Factors: J Hancock Tax Free Bond A has adopted a risky asset allocation strategy and currently receives an overall TheStreet.com Investment Rating of C (Fair). Volatility, as measured by standard deviation, is considered above average for fixed income funds at 4.25. Another risk factor is the fund's very high average duration of 10.9 years (i.e. very high interest rate risk). The high level of risk (D+, Weak) did however, reward investors with excellent performance.

The fund's performance rating is currently B (Good). It has registered an average return of 3.17% over the last three years (5.25% taxable equivalent) and is up 1.41% over the last three months (2.33% taxable equivalent). Factored into the performance evaluation is an expense ratio of 0.93% (average) and a 4.0% front-end load that is levied at the time of purchase.

Christopher P. Conkey currently receives a manager quality ranking of 23 (0=worst, 99=best). If you are comfortable owning a high risk investment, this fund may be an option.
Services Offered: Automated phone transactions, payroll deductions, bank draft capabilities, wire transfers and a systematic withdrawal plan.

Data Date	Investment Rating	Net Assets ($Mil)	NAV	Performance Rating/Pts	Total Return Y-T-D	Risk Rating/Pts
3-16	C	536	10.12	B / 8.1	1.41%	D+ / 2.9
2015	C	520	10.07	B / 8.2	2.63%	D+ / 2.7
2014	C	408	10.20	B+ / 8.4	11.27%	D / 1.9
2013	D-	378	9.55	C / 4.4	-5.07%	D+ / 2.8
2012	C-	465	10.48	C+ / 6.5	8.47%	D+ / 2.9
2011	C-	424	10.06	C+ / 6.4	10.22%	C- / 3.6

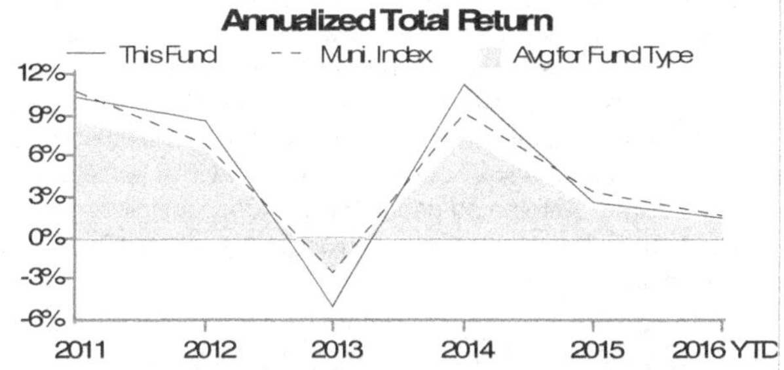

Janus Flexible Bond A (JDFAX) C- Fair

Fund Family: Janus Funds **Phone:** (800) 295-2687
Address: 151 Detroit Street, Denver, CO 80206
Fund Type: GEI - General - Investment Grade
Major Rating Factors: A moderate risk profile coupled with stable earnings characterizes Janus Flexible Bond A which receives a TheStreet.com Investment Rating of C- (Fair). Volatility, as measured by standard deviation, is considered low for fixed income funds at 2.68. Another risk factor is the fund's fairly average duration of 5.7 years (i.e. average interest rate risk). The fund's risk rating is currently B- (Good).

The fund's performance rating is currently C- (Fair). It has registered an average return of 2.00% over the last three years and is up 2.17% over the last three months. Factored into the performance evaluation is an expense ratio of 0.79% (low) and a 4.8% front-end load that is levied at the time of purchase.

Darrell W. Watters has been running the fund for 9 years and currently receives a manager quality ranking of 56 (0=worst, 99=best). If you desire stability with a moderate level of risk then this fund is an excellent option.
Services Offered: Automated phone transactions, payroll deductions, bank draft capabilities, an IRA investment plan, a 401K investment plan, wire transfers and a systematic withdrawal plan.

Data Date	Investment Rating	Net Assets ($Mil)	NAV	Performance Rating/Pts	Total Return Y-T-D	Risk Rating/Pts
3-16	C-	717	10.46	C- / 3.9	2.17%	B- / 7.5
2015	C-	698	10.30	D+ / 2.9	-0.14%	B- / 7.3
2014	C	661	10.56	C- / 3.9	4.72%	B- / 7.3
2013	B-	637	10.37	C / 4.5	-0.28%	B / 7.7
2012	C+	829	10.82	C- / 3.7	7.83%	B- / 7.2
2011	C+	512	10.54	C- / 3.7	6.45%	B / 8.0

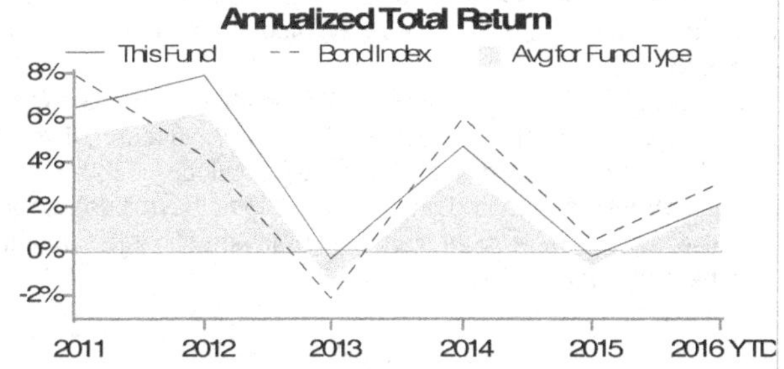

JPMorgan Core Bond A (PGBOX) C+ Fair

Fund Family: JPMorgan Funds **Phone:** (800) 480-4111
Address: 522 Fifth Avenue, New York, NY 10036
Fund Type: GEI - General - Investment Grade
Major Rating Factors: A moderate risk profile coupled with stable earnings characterizes JPMorgan Core Bond A which receives a TheStreet.com Investment Rating of C+ (Fair). Volatility, as measured by standard deviation, is considered low for fixed income funds at 2.67. Another risk factor is the fund's below average duration of 5.0 years (i.e. lower interest rate risk). The fund's risk rating is currently B (Good).

The fund's performance rating is currently C (Fair). It has registered an average return of 2.07% over the last three years and is up 2.78% over the last three months. Factored into the performance evaluation is an expense ratio of 0.98% (average) and a 3.8% front-end load that is levied at the time of purchase.

Douglas S. Swanson has been running the fund for 25 years and currently receives a manager quality ranking of 57 (0=worst, 99=best). If you desire stability with a moderate level of risk then this fund is an excellent option.
Services Offered: Automated phone transactions, payroll deductions, bank draft capabilities, an IRA investment plan, a Keogh investment plan and a systematic withdrawal plan.

Data Date	Investment Rating	Net Assets ($Mil)	NAV	Performance Rating/Pts	Total Return Y-T-D	Risk Rating/Pts
3-16	C+	3,135	11.81	C / 5.0	2.78%	B / 7.6
2015	C-	2,956	11.55	C- / 3.4	0.51%	B- / 7.5
2014	C-	4,754	11.76	C- / 3.1	5.04%	B / 7.7
2013	C-	5,210	11.48	D+ / 2.6	-1.92%	B / 8.1
2012	C+	6,565	12.07	D+ / 2.8	4.82%	B+ / 8.3
2011	B	5,635	11.85	C- / 3.6	7.18%	B+ / 8.6

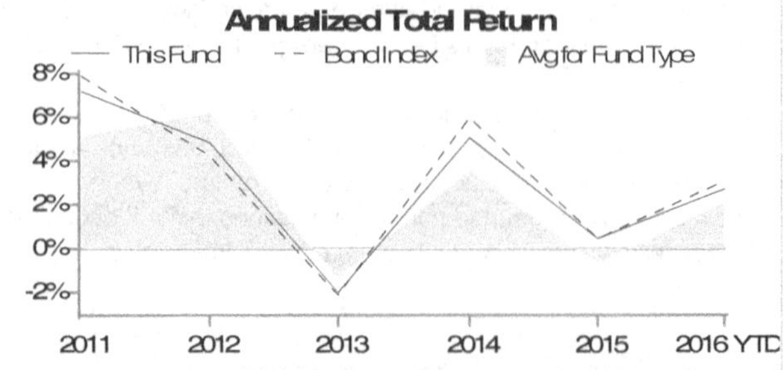

JPMorgan Core Plus Bond A (ONIAX) C+ Fair

Fund Family: JPMorgan Funds **Phone:** (800) 480-4111
Address: 522 Fifth Avenue, New York, NY 10036
Fund Type: GL - Global
Major Rating Factors: A moderate risk profile coupled with stable earnings characterizes JPMorgan Core Plus Bond A which receives a TheStreet.com Investment Rating of C+ (Fair). Volatility, as measured by standard deviation, is considered low for fixed income funds at 2.83. Another risk factor is the fund's fairly average duration of 5.7 years (i.e. average interest rate risk). The fund's risk rating is currently B- (Good).

The fund's performance rating is currently C+ (Fair). It has registered an average return of 2.69% over the last three years and is up 2.66% over the last three months. Factored into the performance evaluation is an expense ratio of 1.00% (average) and a 3.8% front-end load that is levied at the time of purchase.

Mark M. Jackson has been running the fund for 20 years and currently receives a manager quality ranking of 98 (0=worst, 99=best). If you desire stability with a moderate level of risk then this fund is an excellent option.
Services Offered: Automated phone transactions, payroll deductions, bank draft capabilities, an IRA investment plan, a Keogh investment plan and a systematic withdrawal plan.

Data Date	Investment Rating	Net Assets ($Mil)	NAV	Performance Rating/Pts	Total Return Y-T-D	Risk Rating/Pts
3-16	C+	870	8.22	C+ / 5.8	2.66%	B- / 7.1
2015	C	795	8.06	C / 5.1	0.02%	B- / 7.0
2014	B	517	8.31	C / 4.9	6.04%	B- / 7.4
2013	B	335	8.16	C / 4.9	0.07%	B / 7.7
2012	B	569	8.51	C / 4.3	6.97%	B / 7.7
2011	B+	379	8.26	C / 4.8	6.64%	B / 7.8

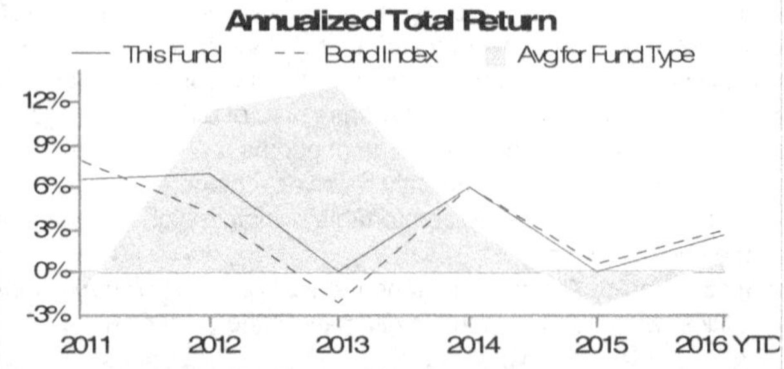

JPMorgan Government Bond A (OGGAX) C- Fair

Fund Family: JPMorgan Funds **Phone:** (800) 480-4111
Address: 522 Fifth Avenue, New York, NY 10036
Fund Type: USS - US Government - Short & Inter. Term
Major Rating Factors: Middle of the road best describes JPMorgan Government Bond A whose TheStreet.com Investment Rating is currently a C- (Fair). The fund has a performance rating of C (Fair) based on an average return of 1.57% over the last three years and 2.87% over the last three months. Factored into the performance evaluation is an expense ratio of 1.12% (average) and a 3.8% front-end load that is levied at the time of purchase.

The fund's risk rating is currently C+ (Fair). Volatility, as measured by standard deviation, is considered average for fixed income funds at 3.22. Another risk factor is the fund's below average duration of 4.9 years (i.e. lower interest rate risk).

Michael J. Sais has been running the fund for 20 years and currently receives a manager quality ranking of 39 (0=worst, 99=best). If you desire an average level of risk, then this fund may be an option.
Services Offered: Automated phone transactions, payroll deductions, bank draft capabilities, an IRA investment plan, a 401K investment plan, wire transfers and a systematic withdrawal plan.

Data Date	Investment Rating	Net Assets ($Mil)	NAV	Performance Rating/Pts	Total Return Y-T-D	Risk Rating/Pts
3-16	C-	562	10.87	C / 4.3	2.87%	C+ / 5.7
2015	D+	605	10.62	D+ / 2.5	0.71%	C+ / 5.6
2014	D-	655	10.93	D / 2.1	5.25%	C+ / 6.0
2013	D-	708	10.85	D / 1.8	-3.85%	C / 5.5
2012	E+	799	11.63	D+ / 2.8	3.28%	C / 5.2
2011	D-	597	11.55	C- / 3.2	10.33%	C+ / 5.8

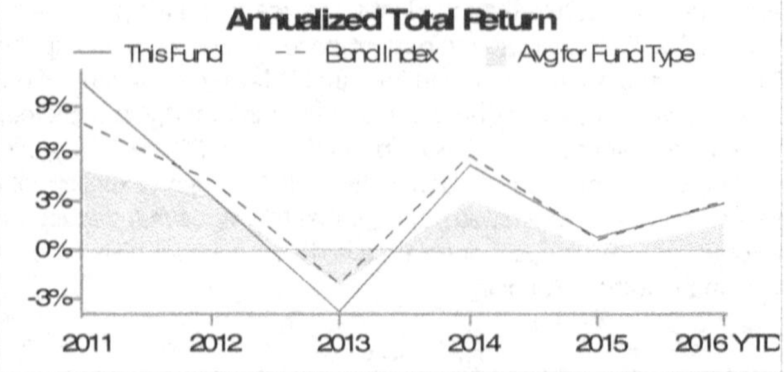

JPMorgan High Yield A (OHYAX) E+ Very Weak

Fund Family: JPMorgan Funds **Phone:** (800) 480-4111
Address: 522 Fifth Avenue, New York, NY 10036
Fund Type: COH - Corporate - High Yield

Major Rating Factors: JPMorgan High Yield A has adopted a very risky asset allocation strategy and currently receives an overall TheStreet.com Investment Rating of E+ (Very Weak). Volatility, as measured by standard deviation, is considered above average for fixed income funds at 5.62. Unfortunately, the high level of risk (D-, Weak) failed to pay off as investors endured very poor performance.

The fund's performance rating is currently D- (Weak). It has registered an average return of 1.25% over the last three years and is up 2.46% over the last three months. Factored into the performance evaluation is an expense ratio of 1.37% (above average) and a 3.8% front-end load that is levied at the time of purchase.

James P. Shanahan, Jr. has been running the fund for 18 years and currently receives a manager quality ranking of 47 (0=worst, 99=best). If you can tolerate very high levels of risk in the hope of improved future returns, holding this fund may be an option.

Services Offered: Automated phone transactions, payroll deductions, bank draft capabilities, an IRA investment plan, a 401K investment plan, wire transfers and a systematic withdrawal plan.

Data Date	Investment Rating	Net Assets ($Mil)	NAV	Performance Rating/Pts	Total Return Y-T-D	Risk Rating/Pts
3-16	E+	929	6.87	D- / 1.5	2.46%	D- / 1.5
2015	D-	811	6.80	D / 1.7	-4.75%	D / 1.6
2014	C-	809	7.55	B- / 7.1	2.37%	D+ / 2.6
2013	C+	1,020	7.95	B+ / 8.9	6.85%	D- / 1.3
2012	C-	1,021	8.10	B / 7.7	14.48%	D- / 1.0
2011	C	1,012	7.59	B+ / 8.7	2.26%	D- / 1.2

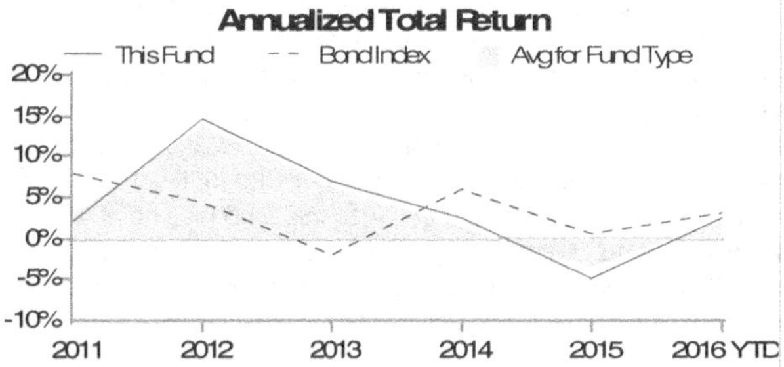

JPMorgan Short Duration Bond A (OGLVX) C- Fair

Fund Family: JPMorgan Funds **Phone:** (800) 480-4111
Address: 522 Fifth Avenue, New York, NY 10036
Fund Type: GEI - General - Investment Grade

Major Rating Factors: Disappointing performance is the major factor driving the C- (Fair) TheStreet.com Investment Rating for JPMorgan Short Duration Bond A. The fund currently has a performance rating of D (Weak) based on an average return of 0.40% over the last three years and 0.79% over the last three months. Factored into the performance evaluation is an expense ratio of 0.95% (average) and a 2.3% front-end load that is levied at the time of purchase.

The fund's risk rating is currently A+ (Excellent). Volatility, as measured by standard deviation, is considered very low for fixed income funds at 0.74. Another risk factor is the fund's very low average duration of 1.8 years (i.e. low interest rate risk).

Gregg F. Hrivnak has been running the fund for 10 years and currently receives a manager quality ranking of 56 (0=worst, 99=best). This fund offers only a moderate level of risk but investors looking for strong performance are still waiting.

Services Offered: Automated phone transactions, payroll deductions, bank draft capabilities, an IRA investment plan, a 401K investment plan, wire transfers and a systematic withdrawal plan.

Data Date	Investment Rating	Net Assets ($Mil)	NAV	Performance Rating/Pts	Total Return Y-T-D	Risk Rating/Pts
3-16	C-	545	10.86	D / 1.7	0.79%	A+ / 9.6
2015	C	533	10.79	D+ / 2.4	0.17%	A+ / 9.6
2014	D+	230	10.85	E+ / 0.8	0.47%	A+ / 9.7
2013	C-	242	10.87	E+ / 0.9	-0.22%	A+ / 9.6
2012	D+	292	10.98	E+ / 0.6	1.41%	A+ / 9.6
2011	C-	263	10.94	D- / 1.4	1.43%	A+ / 9.7

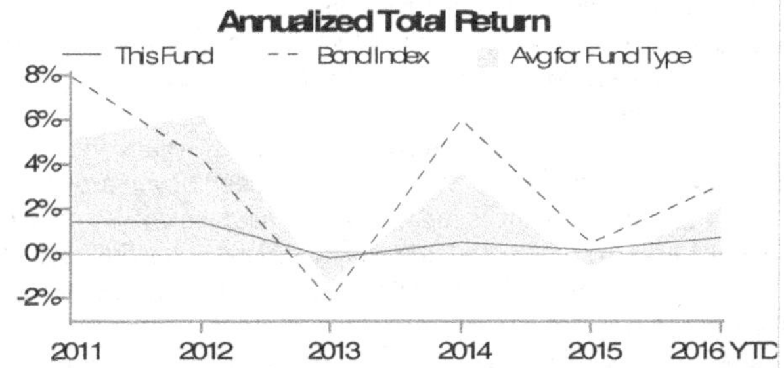

JPMorgan Strategic Income Opp A (JSOAX) D+ Weak

Fund Family: JPMorgan Funds **Phone:** (800) 480-4111
Address: 522 Fifth Avenue, New York, NY 10036
Fund Type: GL - Global

Major Rating Factors: Very poor performance is the major factor driving the D+ (Weak) TheStreet.com Investment Rating for JPMorgan Strategic Income Opp A. The fund currently has a performance rating of E+ (Very Weak) based on an average return of -0.09% over the last three years and 1.05% over the last three months. Factored into the performance evaluation is an expense ratio of 1.27% (above average) and a 3.8% front-end load that is levied at the time of purchase.

The fund's risk rating is currently B+ (Good). Volatility, as measured by standard deviation, is considered low for fixed income funds at 2.09.

William H. Eigen, III has been running the fund for 8 years and currently receives a manager quality ranking of 58 (0=worst, 99=best). This fund offers only a moderate level of risk but investors looking for strong performance are still waiting.

Services Offered: Automated phone transactions, payroll deductions, bank draft capabilities, a 401K investment plan, a Keogh investment plan, wire transfers and a systematic withdrawal plan.

Data Date	Investment Rating	Net Assets ($Mil)	NAV	Performance Rating/Pts	Total Return Y-T-D	Risk Rating/Pts
3-16	D+	1,596	11.08	E+ / 0.8	1.05%	B+ / 8.4
2015	D+	1,967	11.07	D- / 1.4	-2.37%	B / 7.9
2014	C	3,774	11.69	D+ / 2.7	-0.14%	B+ / 8.8
2013	C-	4,694	11.86	C- / 3.9	2.78%	C+ / 6.6
2012	E	2,293	11.80	D / 2.0	7.82%	C / 4.9
2011	E+	2,366	11.31	D+ / 2.7	-0.28%	C / 5.2

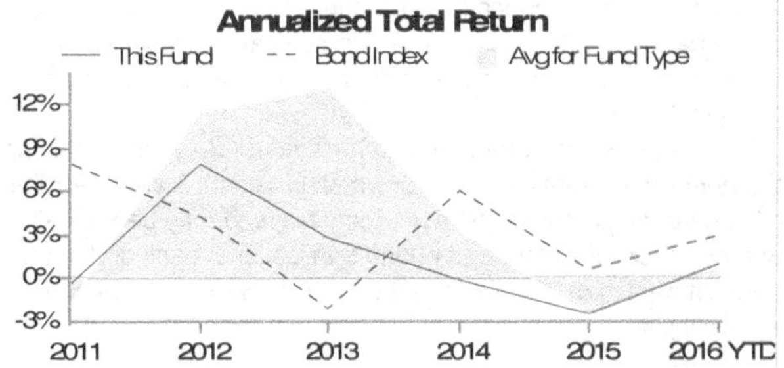

Loomis Sayles Bond Ret (LSBRX) D Weak

Fund Family: Loomis Sayles Funds **Phone:** (800) 633-3330
Address: PO Box 219594, Kansas, MO 61421
Fund Type: GES - General - Short & Inter. Term
Major Rating Factors: Loomis Sayles Bond Ret has adopted a very risky asset allocation strategy and currently receives an overall TheStreet.com Investment Rating of D (Weak). Volatility, as measured by standard deviation, is considered above average for fixed income funds at 6.21. Another risk factor is the fund's below average duration of 4.5 years (i.e. lower interest rate risk). Unfortunately, the high level of risk (D-, Weak) has only provided investors with average performance.

The fund's performance rating is currently C- (Fair). It has registered an average return of 0.93% over the last three years and is up 2.68% over the last three months. Factored into the performance evaluation is an expense ratio of 0.89% (average).

Daniel J. Fuss has been running the fund for 25 years and currently receives a manager quality ranking of 33 (0=worst, 99=best). If you are comfortable owning a very high risk investment, then this fund may be an option.
Services Offered: Automated phone transactions, payroll deductions, bank draft capabilities, an IRA investment plan, wire transfers and a systematic withdrawal plan.

Data Date	Investment Rating	Net Assets ($Mil)	NAV	Performance Rating/Pts	Total Return Y-T-D	Risk Rating/Pts
3-16	D	4,961	13.12	C- / 3.7	2.68%	D- / 1.4
2015	D	5,355	12.82	D / 2.1	-7.06%	D / 2.0
2014	C	8,498	14.76	B+ / 8.4	4.49%	D / 1.7
2013	C+	8,370	15.09	A- / 9.2	5.52%	D- / 1.5
2012	C+	8,771	15.06	B+ / 8.5	14.77%	D- / 1.4
2011	C-	8,051	13.88	B / 8.0	3.48%	D / 1.8

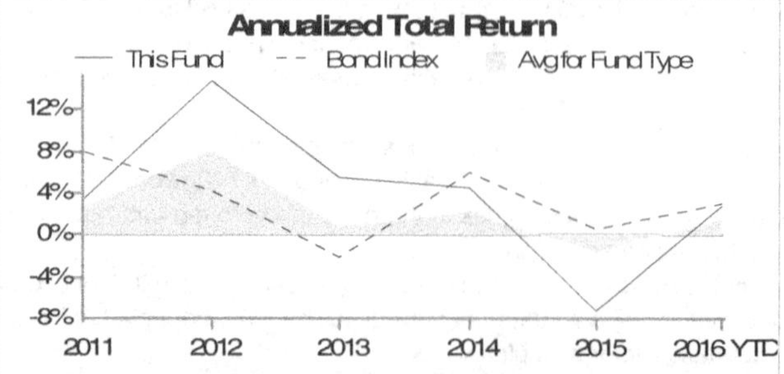

Loomis Sayles Fixed Inc Fd (LSFIX) D+ Weak

Fund Family: Loomis Sayles Funds **Phone:** (800) 633-3330
Address: PO Box 219594, Kansas, MO 61421
Fund Type: GEI - General - Investment Grade
Major Rating Factors: Loomis Sayles Fixed Inc Fd has adopted a very risky asset allocation strategy and currently receives an overall TheStreet.com Investment Rating of D+ (Weak). Volatility, as measured by standard deviation, is considered above average for fixed income funds at 5.91. Another risk factor is the fund's below average duration of 4.2 years (i.e. lower interest rate risk). Unfortunately, the high level of risk (D, Weak) has only provided investors with average performance.

The fund's performance rating is currently C+ (Fair). It has registered an average return of 1.86% over the last three years and is up 3.03% over the last three months. Factored into the performance evaluation is an expense ratio of 0.57% (very low).

Daniel J. Fuss has been running the fund for 21 years and currently receives a manager quality ranking of 61 (0=worst, 99=best). If you are comfortable owning a very high risk investment, then this fund may be an option.
Services Offered: Automated phone transactions, bank draft capabilities, an IRA investment plan, a 401K investment plan, wire transfers and a systematic withdrawal plan.

Data Date	Investment Rating	Net Assets ($Mil)	NAV	Performance Rating/Pts	Total Return Y-T-D	Risk Rating/Pts
3-16	D+	1,209	12.60	C+ / 5.6	3.03%	D / 1.7
2015	D	1,190	12.23	C- / 4.1	-6.03%	D / 2.0
2014	C+	1,442	13.90	B+ / 8.7	4.62%	D / 1.7
2013	B-	1,213	14.45	A+ / 9.6	6.88%	D- / 1.5
2012	C+	1,172	14.43	B+ / 8.8	15.65%	D- / 1.5
2011	C-	904	13.19	B / 7.9	3.90%	D / 1.8

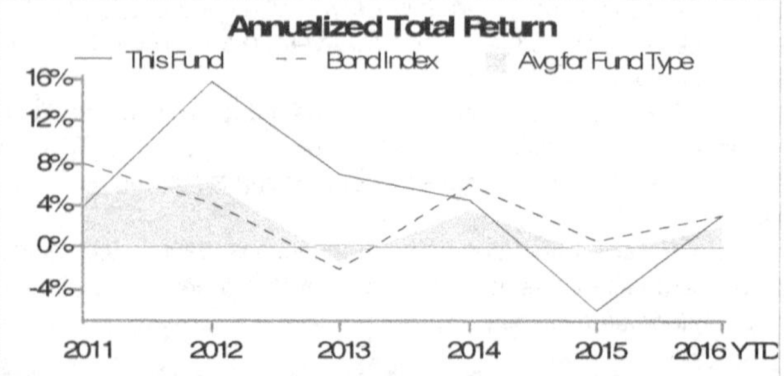

Loomis Sayles Inst High Income Inst (LSHIX) D- Weak

Fund Family: Loomis Sayles Funds **Phone:** (800) 633-3330
Address: PO Box 219594, Kansas, MO 61421
Fund Type: COH - Corporate - High Yield
Major Rating Factors: Loomis Sayles Inst High Income Inst has adopted a very risky asset allocation strategy and currently receives an overall TheStreet.com Investment Rating of D- (Weak). Volatility, as measured by standard deviation, is considered high for fixed income funds at 7.95. Another risk factor is the fund's below average duration of 4.3 years (i.e. lower interest rate risk). Unfortunately, the high level of risk (E, Very Weak) has only provided investors with average performance.

The fund's performance rating is currently C- (Fair). It has registered an average return of 1.91% over the last three years and is up 2.56% over the last three months. Factored into the performance evaluation is an expense ratio of 0.68% (low).

Daniel J. Fuss has been running the fund for 20 years and currently receives a manager quality ranking of 51 (0=worst, 99=best). If you are comfortable owning a very high risk investment, then this fund may be an option.
Services Offered: Automated phone transactions, bank draft capabilities, an IRA investment plan, a 401K investment plan, wire transfers and a systematic withdrawal plan.

Data Date	Investment Rating	Net Assets ($Mil)	NAV	Performance Rating/Pts	Total Return Y-T-D	Risk Rating/Pts
3-16	D-	643	6.00	C- / 3.7	2.56%	E / 0.4
2015	D-	593	5.85	C- / 3.2	-10.27%	E / 0.5
2014	C+	657	7.24	A+ / 9.6	5.17%	E+ / 0.9
2013	C+	667	7.65	A+ / 9.9	15.07%	E / 0.4
2012	C	626	7.47	B+ / 8.8	17.98%	E / 0.3
2011	C-	518	6.79	B+ / 8.9	-0.08%	E / 0.4

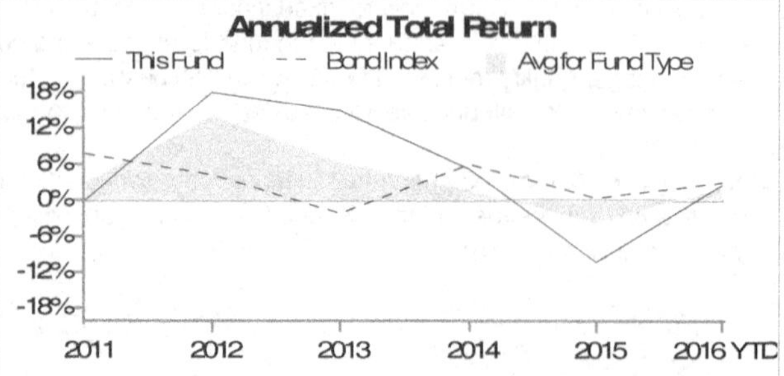

Lord Abbett Bond Debenture A (LBNDX) D+ Weak

Fund Family: Lord Abbett Funds **Phone:** (888) 522-2388
Address: 90 Hudson Street, Jersey City, NJ 07302
Fund Type: COH - Corporate - High Yield

Major Rating Factors: Lord Abbett Bond Debenture A has adopted a very risky asset allocation strategy and currently receives an overall TheStreet.com Investment Rating of D+ (Weak). Volatility, as measured by standard deviation, is considered above average for fixed income funds at 5.38. Another risk factor is the fund's below average duration of 4.6 years (i.e. lower interest rate risk). Unfortunately, the high level of risk (D, Weak) has only provided investors with average performance.

The fund's performance rating is currently C (Fair). It has registered an average return of 2.94% over the last three years and is up 1.61% over the last three months. Factored into the performance evaluation is an expense ratio of 0.82% (low) and a 2.3% front-end load that is levied at the time of purchase.

Christopher J. Towle has been running the fund for 29 years and currently receives a manager quality ranking of 92 (0=worst, 99=best). If you are comfortable owning a very high risk investment, then this fund may be an option.

Services Offered: Automated phone transactions, payroll deductions, an IRA investment plan, a 401K investment plan and a systematic withdrawal plan.

Data Date	Investment Rating	Net Assets ($Mil)	NAV	Performance Rating/Pts	Total Return Y-T-D	Risk Rating/Pts
3-16	D+	4,180	7.43	C / 5.5	1.61%	D / 1.8
2015	C-	4,175	7.40	C+/ 6.9	-1.74%	D / 2.0
2014	C+	4,513	7.93	B+/ 8.3	4.52%	D+/ 2.4
2013	C+	4,771	8.15	A- / 9.1	7.79%	D- / 1.4
2012	D	4,840	8.14	B- / 7.1	13.22%	D- / 1.3
2011	D+	4,329	7.63	B- / 7.4	3.88%	D / 1.7

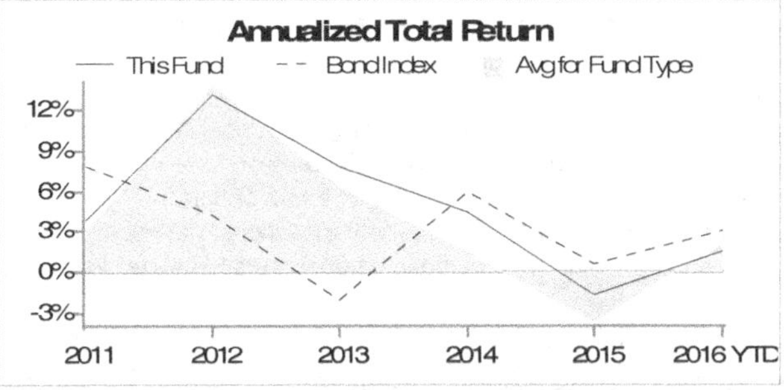

Lord Abbett Floating Rate A (LFRAX) C+ Fair

Fund Family: Lord Abbett Funds **Phone:** (888) 522-2388
Address: 90 Hudson Street, Jersey City, NJ 07302
Fund Type: LP - Loan Participation

Major Rating Factors: A moderate risk profile coupled with stable earnings characterizes Lord Abbett Floating Rate A which receives a TheStreet.com Investment Rating of C+ (Fair). Volatility, as measured by standard deviation, is considered low for fixed income funds at 2.36. Another risk factor is the fund's very low average duration of 0.3 years (i.e. low interest rate risk). The fund's risk rating is currently B (Good).

The fund's performance rating is currently C (Fair). It has registered an average return of 2.08% over the last three years and is up 1.69% over the last three months. Factored into the performance evaluation is an expense ratio of 0.80% (low) and a 2.3% front-end load that is levied at the time of purchase.

Jeffrey D. Lapin has been running the fund for 4 years and currently receives a manager quality ranking of 94 (0=worst, 99=best). If you desire stability with a moderate level of risk then this fund is an excellent option.

Services Offered: Automated phone transactions, payroll deductions, bank draft capabilities, a 401K investment plan, wire transfers and a systematic withdrawal plan.

Data Date	Investment Rating	Net Assets ($Mil)	NAV	Performance Rating/Pts	Total Return Y-T-D	Risk Rating/Pts
3-16	C+	2,199	8.85	C / 4.9	1.69%	B / 8.1
2015	B	2,270	8.80	C+/ 6.2	0.35%	B- / 7.5
2014	A-	2,600	9.16	C / 5.4	0.93%	B / 8.0
2013	A-	3,595	9.50	B / 7.9	5.89%	C / 4.9
2012	E+	1,449	9.41	C- / 4.2	10.12%	D+/ 2.9
2011	D-	1,100	9.01	C+/ 5.8	1.44%	D+/ 2.7

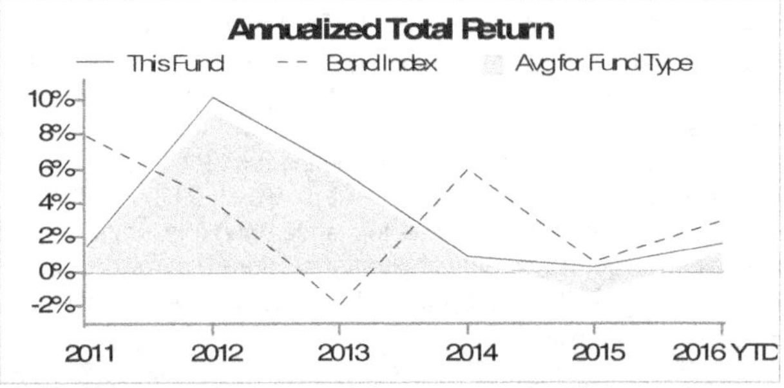

Lord Abbett High Yield A (LHYAX) D Weak

Fund Family: Lord Abbett Funds **Phone:** (888) 522-2388
Address: 90 Hudson Street, Jersey City, NJ 07302
Fund Type: COH - Corporate - High Yield

Major Rating Factors: Lord Abbett High Yield A has adopted a very risky asset allocation strategy and currently receives an overall TheStreet.com Investment Rating of D (Weak). Volatility, as measured by standard deviation, is considered above average for fixed income funds at 5.60. Another risk factor is the fund's below average duration of 4.6 years (i.e. lower interest rate risk). Unfortunately, the high level of risk (D-, Weak) has only provided investors with average performance.

The fund's performance rating is currently C (Fair). It has registered an average return of 2.85% over the last three years and is up 1.97% over the last three months. Factored into the performance evaluation is an expense ratio of 0.94% (average) and a 2.3% front-end load that is levied at the time of purchase.

Christopher J. Towle has been running the fund for 18 years and currently receives a manager quality ranking of 91 (0=worst, 99=best). If you are comfortable owning a very high risk investment, then this fund may be an option.

Services Offered: Automated phone transactions, payroll deductions, an IRA investment plan, a 401K investment plan and a systematic withdrawal plan.

Data Date	Investment Rating	Net Assets ($Mil)	NAV	Performance Rating/Pts	Total Return Y-T-D	Risk Rating/Pts
3-16	D	1,240	6.92	C / 5.4	1.97%	D- / 1.5
2015	D+	965	6.89	C+/ 6.7	-2.26%	D / 1.6
2014	C+	842	7.46	B+/ 8.7	3.47%	D / 2.0
2013	B-	870	7.81	A+/ 9.8	9.70%	D- / 1.1
2012	C+	752	7.85	B+/ 8.8	16.51%	E+/ 0.8
2011	C+	609	7.40	A- / 9.2	3.15%	E+/ 0.9

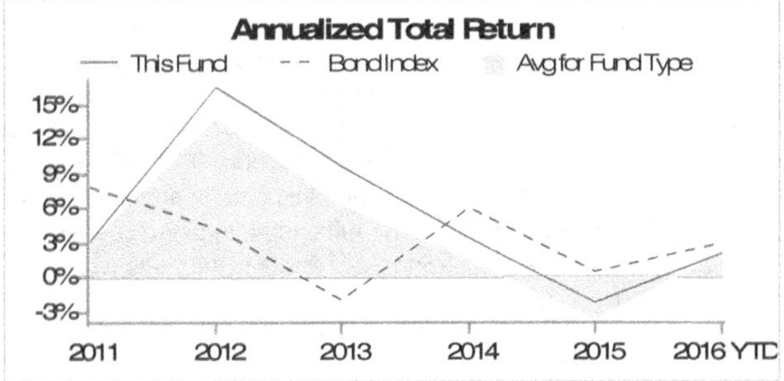

Lord Abbett Income A (LAGVX) D+ Weak

Fund Family: Lord Abbett Funds **Phone:** (888) 522-2388
Address: 90 Hudson Street, Jersey City, NJ 07302
Fund Type: COI - Corporate - Investment Grade
Major Rating Factors: Lord Abbett Income A receives a TheStreet.com Investment Rating of D+ (Weak). The fund has a performance rating of C (Fair) based on an average return of 1.99% over the last three years and 3.04% over the last three months. Factored into the performance evaluation is an expense ratio of 0.88% (average) and a 2.3% front-end load that is levied at the time of purchase.

The fund's risk rating is currently C- (Fair). Volatility, as measured by standard deviation, is considered average for fixed income funds at 4.73. Another risk factor is the fund's fairly average duration of 5.3 years (i.e. average interest rate risk).

Andrew H. O'Brien has been running the fund for 18 years and currently receives a manager quality ranking of 36 (0=worst, 99=best). If you desire an average level of risk, then this fund may be an option.
Services Offered: Automated phone transactions, payroll deductions, an IRA investment plan, a 401K investment plan and a systematic withdrawal plan.

Data Date	Investment Rating	Net Assets ($Mil)	NAV	Performance Rating/Pts	Total Return Y-T-D	Risk Rating/Pts
3-16	D+	958	2.71	C / 4.8	3.04%	C- / 3.0
2015	D	978	2.66	C- / 3.0	-3.09%	C- / 3.6
2014	B-	1,129	2.87	B- / 7.3	7.23%	C- / 4.1
2013	B	1,024	2.82	B / 7.7	0.28%	C- / 4.2
2012	A-	1,191	3.00	B- / 7.5	12.51%	C / 4.6
2011	C+	788	2.85	B- / 7.3	6.55%	C- / 3.4

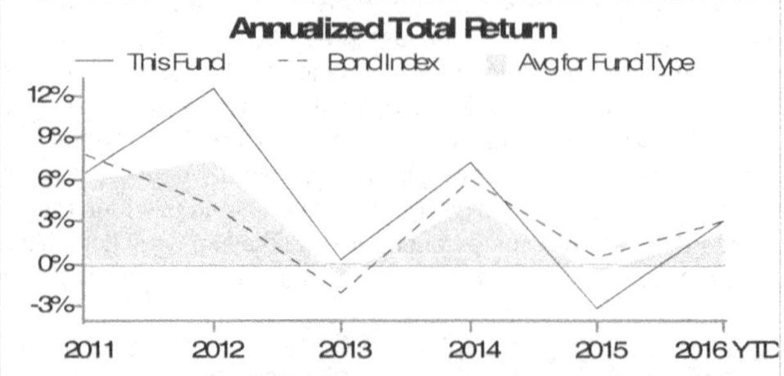

Lord Abbett Interm Tax Free A (LISAX) B+ Good

Fund Family: Lord Abbett Funds **Phone:** (888) 522-2388
Address: 90 Hudson Street, Jersey City, NJ 07302
Fund Type: MUN - Municipal - National
Major Rating Factors: Strong performance is the major factor driving the B+ (Good) TheStreet.com Investment Rating for Lord Abbett Interm Tax Free A. The fund currently has a performance rating of B+ (Good) based on an average return of 3.01% over the last three years (4.98% taxable equivalent) and 1.58% over the last three months (2.62% taxable equivalent). Factored into the performance evaluation is an expense ratio of 0.71% (low) and a 2.3% front-end load that is levied at the time of purchase.

The fund's risk rating is currently C (Fair). Volatility, as measured by standard deviation, is considered average for fixed income funds at 3.41. Another risk factor is the fund's fairly average duration of 5.4 years (i.e. average interest rate risk).

Daniel S. Solender has been running the fund for 10 years and currently receives a manager quality ranking of 42 (0=worst, 99=best). If you desire an average level of risk and strong performance, then this fund is a good option.
Services Offered: Automated phone transactions, payroll deductions, an IRA investment plan, a 401K investment plan, a Keogh investment plan and a systematic withdrawal plan.

Data Date	Investment Rating	Net Assets ($Mil)	NAV	Performance Rating/Pts	Total Return Y-T-D	Risk Rating/Pts
3-16	B+	1,790	10.98	B+ / 8.5	1.58%	C / 5.1
2015	B+	1,709	10.88	B+ / 8.6	2.86%	C / 4.9
2014	B+	1,541	10.88	B / 7.6	8.35%	C / 4.9
2013	B-	1,596	10.34	C+ / 6.5	-2.82%	C / 5.2
2012	A-	2,181	11.01	C+ / 6.9	6.40%	C / 5.5
2011	B+	1,484	10.65	C+ / 6.9	9.87%	C / 4.9

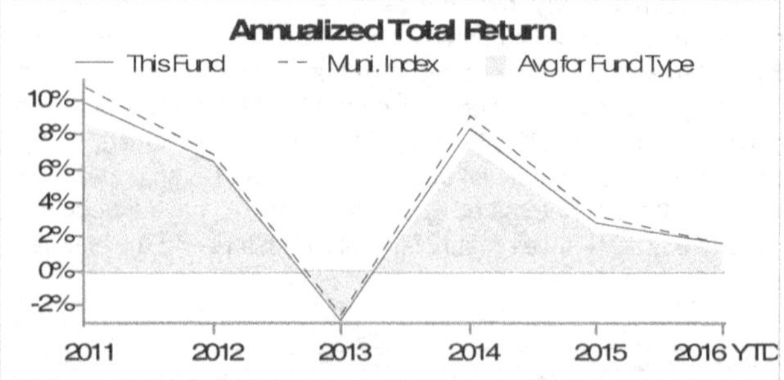

Lord Abbett Shrt Duration Inc A (LALDX) C+ Fair

Fund Family: Lord Abbett Funds **Phone:** (888) 522-2388
Address: 90 Hudson Street, Jersey City, NJ 07302
Fund Type: GEI - General - Investment Grade
Major Rating Factors: A moderate risk profile coupled with stable earnings characterizes Lord Abbett Shrt Duration Inc A which receives a TheStreet.com Investment Rating of C+ (Fair). Volatility, as measured by standard deviation, is considered low for fixed income funds at 1.41. Another risk factor is the fund's very low average duration of 1.9 years (i.e. low interest rate risk). The fund's risk rating is currently B+ (Good).

The fund's performance rating is currently C- (Fair). It has registered an average return of 1.44% over the last three years and is up 1.22% over the last three months. Factored into the performance evaluation is an expense ratio of 0.59% (low) and a 2.3% front-end load that is levied at the time of purchase.

Andrew H. O'Brien has been running the fund for 18 years and currently receives a manager quality ranking of 87 (0=worst, 99=best). If you desire stability with a moderate level of risk then this fund is an excellent option.
Services Offered: Automated phone transactions, payroll deductions, an IRA investment plan, a 401K investment plan and a systematic withdrawal plan.

Data Date	Investment Rating	Net Assets ($Mil)	NAV	Performance Rating/Pts	Total Return Y-T-D	Risk Rating/Pts
3-16	C+	10,883	4.32	C- / 4.0	1.22%	B+ / 8.9
2015	B-	11,056	4.31	C / 4.5	0.43%	A- / 9.0
2014	B-	12,594	4.46	C- / 3.3	1.73%	B+ / 8.9
2013	A-	13,132	4.55	C / 4.8	1.62%	B+ / 8.8
2012	C+	11,684	4.65	D+ / 2.7	6.64%	B+ / 8.8
2011	C+	7,070	4.54	C- / 3.7	3.16%	B / 7.6

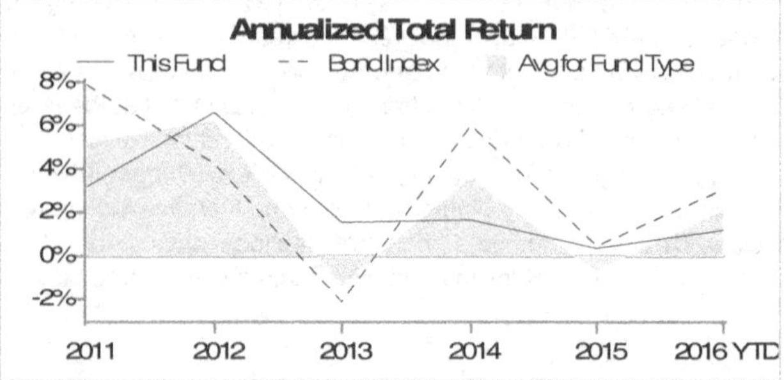

Lord Abbett Shrt Duration Tax-Fr A (LSDAX) C Fair

Fund Family: Lord Abbett Funds **Phone:** (888) 522-2388
Address: 90 Hudson Street, Jersey City, NJ 07302
Fund Type: MUN - Municipal - National
Major Rating Factors: A moderate risk profile coupled with stable earnings characterizes Lord Abbett Shrt Duration Tax-Fr A which receives a TheStreet.com Investment Rating of C (Fair). Volatility, as measured by standard deviation, is considered very low for fixed income funds at 1.05. Another risk factor is the fund's very low average duration of 2.2 years (i.e. low interest rate risk). The fund's risk rating is currently A- (Excellent).

The fund's performance rating is currently C- (Fair). It has registered an average return of 0.76% over the last three years (1.26% taxable equivalent) and is up 0.52% over the last three months (0.86% taxable equivalent). Factored into the performance evaluation is an expense ratio of 0.70% (low) and a 2.3% front-end load that is levied at the time of purchase.

Daniel S. Solender has been running the fund for 8 years and currently receives a manager quality ranking of 55 (0=worst, 99=best). If you desire stability with a moderate level of risk then this fund is an excellent option.
Services Offered: Automated phone transactions, payroll deductions, bank draft capabilities, an IRA investment plan, a 401K investment plan, wire transfers and a systematic withdrawal plan.

Data Date	Investment Rating	Net Assets ($Mil)	NAV	Performance Rating/Pts	Total Return Y-T-D	Risk Rating/Pts
3-16	C	1,069	15.76	C- / 3.2	0.52%	A- / 9.2
2015	B-	1,078	15.72	C / 4.4	0.71%	A- / 9.2
2014	C	1,255	15.77	D / 2.0	1.58%	A- / 9.2
2013	C+	1,363	15.70	D+ / 2.7	0.02%	A / 9.3
2012	C	1,564	15.91	D- / 1.4	2.16%	A / 9.4
2011	C+	1,273	15.82	D+ / 2.6	3.46%	A / 9.4

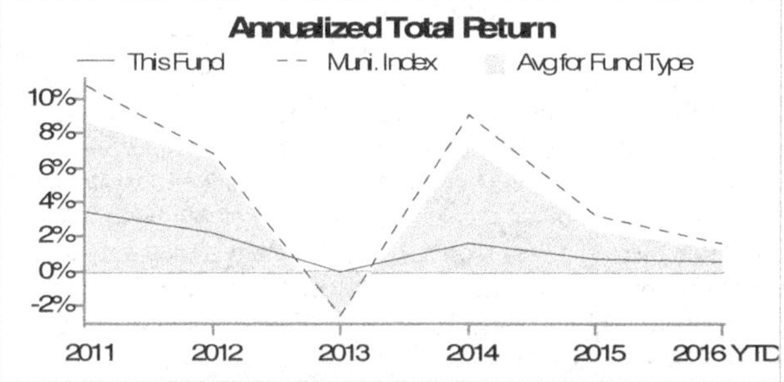

Lord Abbett Tax Free Natl A (LANSX) C+ Fair

Fund Family: Lord Abbett Funds **Phone:** (888) 522-2388
Address: 90 Hudson Street, Jersey City, NJ 07302
Fund Type: MUN - Municipal - National
Major Rating Factors: Lord Abbett Tax Free Natl A has adopted a risky asset allocation strategy and currently receives an overall TheStreet.com Investment Rating of C+ (Fair). Volatility, as measured by standard deviation, is considered above average for fixed income funds at 5.04. Another risk factor is the fund's above average duration of 7.3 years (i.e. higher interest rate risk). The high level of risk (D+, Weak) did however, reward investors with excellent performance.

The fund's performance rating is currently A- (Excellent). It has registered an average return of 3.57% over the last three years (5.91% taxable equivalent) and is up 2.12% over the last three months (3.51% taxable equivalent). Factored into the performance evaluation is an expense ratio of 0.77% (low) and a 2.3% front-end load that is levied at the time of purchase.

Daniel S. Solender has been running the fund for 10 years and currently receives a manager quality ranking of 16 (0=worst, 99=best). If you are comfortable owning a high risk investment, this fund may be an option.
Services Offered: Automated phone transactions, payroll deductions, an IRA investment plan, a 401K investment plan and a systematic withdrawal plan.

Data Date	Investment Rating	Net Assets ($Mil)	NAV	Performance Rating/Pts	Total Return Y-T-D	Risk Rating/Pts
3-16	C+	1,492	11.49	A- / 9.1	2.12%	D+ / 2.5
2015	C	1,445	11.35	B+ / 8.9	3.28%	D / 2.2
2014	C+	1,440	11.39	A+ / 9.6	12.83%	D- / 1.1
2013	C	1,379	10.49	B / 7.8	-6.11%	D / 2.0
2012	A	1,769	11.62	A+ / 9.7	13.75%	D+ / 2.5
2011	A-	1,431	10.65	A- / 9.2	11.08%	D+ / 2.6

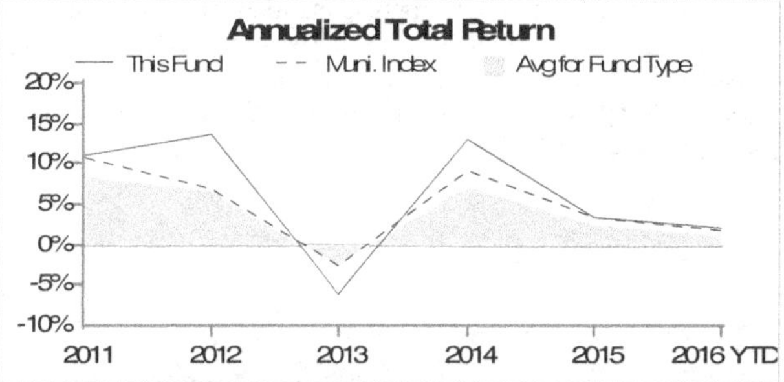

Lord Abbett Total Return A (LTRAX) C Fair

Fund Family: Lord Abbett Funds **Phone:** (888) 522-2388
Address: 90 Hudson Street, Jersey City, NJ 07302
Fund Type: GEI - General - Investment Grade
Major Rating Factors: Middle of the road best describes Lord Abbett Total Return A whose TheStreet.com Investment Rating is currently a C (Fair). The fund has a performance rating of C (Fair) based on an average return of 2.08% over the last three years and 2.80% over the last three months. Factored into the performance evaluation is an expense ratio of 0.84% (low) and a 2.3% front-end load that is levied at the time of purchase.

The fund's risk rating is currently C+ (Fair). Volatility, as measured by standard deviation, is considered average for fixed income funds at 3.03. Another risk factor is the fund's fairly average duration of 5.2 years (i.e. average interest rate risk).

Andrew H. O'Brien has been running the fund for 18 years and currently receives a manager quality ranking of 52 (0=worst, 99=best). If you desire an average level of risk, then this fund may be an option.
Services Offered: Automated phone transactions, payroll deductions, an IRA investment plan, a 401K investment plan and a systematic withdrawal plan.

Data Date	Investment Rating	Net Assets ($Mil)	NAV	Performance Rating/Pts	Total Return Y-T-D	Risk Rating/Pts
3-16	C	1,295	10.38	C / 5.5	2.80%	C+ / 6.4
2015	C-	1,223	10.17	C / 4.3	-0.64%	C+ / 6.5
2014	C+	959	10.55	C / 5.0	6.12%	C+ / 6.6
2013	B-	829	10.30	C / 5.0	-1.40%	B- / 7.2
2012	B+	959	10.77	C / 4.6	7.73%	B / 8.0
2011	B-	777	10.57	C / 4.7	7.20%	C+ / 6.9

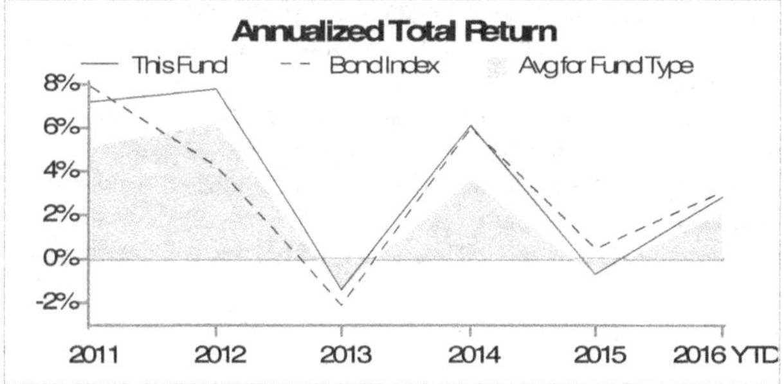

Lord Abbett Tx Fr High Yld Muni A (HYMAX) C- Fair

Fund Family: Lord Abbett Funds **Phone:** (888) 522-2388
Address: 90 Hudson Street, Jersey City, NJ 07302
Fund Type: MUH - Municipal - High Yield
Major Rating Factors: Lord Abbett Tx Fr High Yld Muni A has adopted a very risky asset allocation strategy and currently receives an overall TheStreet.com Investment Rating of C- (Fair). Volatility, as measured by standard deviation, is considered high for fixed income funds at 5.84. Another risk factor is the fund's above average duration of 8.7 years (i.e. higher interest rate risk). The high level of risk (E+, Very Weak) did however, reward investors with excellent performance.

The fund's performance rating is currently A- (Excellent). It has registered an average return of 3.59% over the last three years (5.95% taxable equivalent) and is up 2.35% over the last three months (3.89% taxable equivalent). Factored into the performance evaluation is an expense ratio of 0.87% (average) and a 2.3% front-end load that is levied at the time of purchase.

Daniel S. Solender has been running the fund for 12 years and currently receives a manager quality ranking of 13 (0=worst, 99=best). If you are comfortable owning a very high risk investment, this fund may be an option.
Services Offered: Automated phone transactions, payroll deductions, bank draft capabilities, an IRA investment plan, a 401K investment plan, wire transfers and a systematic withdrawal plan.

Data Date	Investment Rating	Net Assets ($Mil)	NAV	Performance Rating/Pts	Total Return Y-T-D	Risk Rating/Pts
3-16	C-	1,177	11.78	A- / 9.2	2.35%	E+ / 0.9
2015	C-	1,139	11.64	A- / 9.2	3.66%	E+ / 0.6
2014	C+	1,165	11.76	A+ / 9.8	14.50%	E+ / 0.6
2013	D-	982	10.77	C / 5.5	-6.99%	D- / 1.0
2012	A-	1,250	12.16	A+ / 9.7	17.99%	D / 2.1
2011	C+	866	10.84	A- / 9.2	4.55%	D- / 1.3

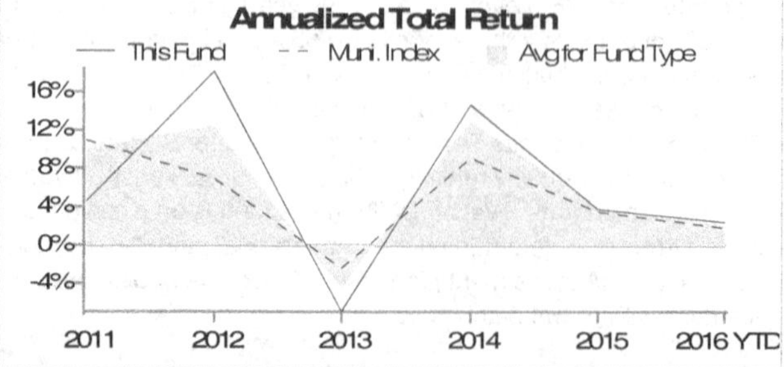

Manning & Napier Unconstrained Bd S (EXCPX) C- Fair

Fund Family: Manning & Napier Funds **Phone:** (800) 466-3863
Address: 290 Woodcliff Drive, Fairport, NY 14450
Fund Type: COI - Corporate - Investment Grade
Major Rating Factors: Middle of the road best describes Manning & Napier Unconstrained Bd S whose TheStreet.com Investment Rating is currently a C- (Fair). The fund has a performance rating of C- (Fair) based on an average return of 0.81% over the last three years and 1.44% over the last three months. Factored into the performance evaluation is an expense ratio of 0.76% (low).

The fund's risk rating is currently C+ (Fair). Volatility, as measured by standard deviation, is considered average for fixed income funds at 3.04.

R. Keith Harwood has been running the fund for 11 years and currently receives a manager quality ranking of 29 (0=worst, 99=best). If you desire an average level of risk, then this fund may be an option.
Services Offered: Automated phone transactions, payroll deductions, bank draft capabilities and wire transfers.

Data Date	Investment Rating	Net Assets ($Mil)	NAV	Performance Rating/Pts	Total Return Y-T-D	Risk Rating/Pts
3-16	C-	827	10.24	C- / 3.9	1.44%	C+ / 6.4
2015	C-	835	10.12	C / 4.4	-0.88%	C+ / 6.3
2014	C	680	10.53	C / 5.5	3.18%	C / 5.2
2013	B-	654	10.65	B- / 7.0	-0.02%	C / 4.6
2012	B	631	11.27	C+ / 6.8	10.94%	C / 4.7

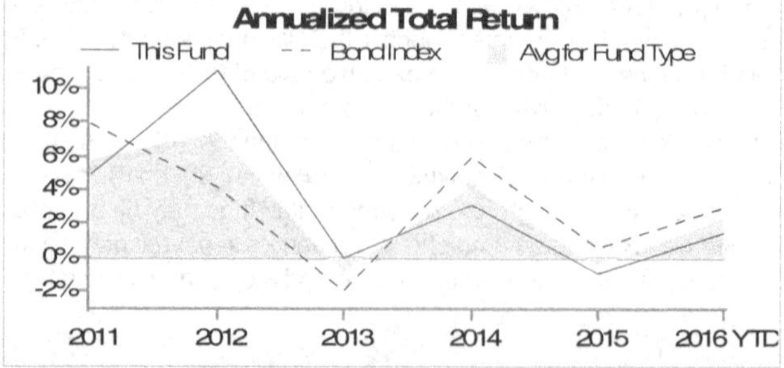

Metropolitan West Low Dur Bd M (MWLDX) B- Good

Fund Family: Metropolitan West Fund **Phone:** (800) 496-8298
Address: 11766 Wilshire Boulevard, Los Angeles, CA 90025
Fund Type: GEI - General - Investment Grade
Major Rating Factors: A moderate risk profile coupled with stable earnings characterizes Metropolitan West Low Dur Bd M which receives a TheStreet.com Investment Rating of B- (Good). Volatility, as measured by standard deviation, is considered very low for fixed income funds at 0.72. Another risk factor is the fund's very low average duration of 1.1 years (i.e. low interest rate risk). The fund's risk rating is currently A+ (Excellent).

The fund's performance rating is currently C- (Fair). It has registered an average return of 0.96% over the last three years and is up 0.38% over the last three months. Factored into the performance evaluation is an expense ratio of 0.63% (low).

Stephen M. Kane has been running the fund for 19 years and currently receives a manager quality ranking of 83 (0=worst, 99=best). If you desire stability with a moderate level of risk then this fund is an excellent option.
Services Offered: Automated phone transactions, check writing, payroll deductions, bank draft capabilities and a systematic withdrawal plan.

Data Date	Investment Rating	Net Assets ($Mil)	NAV	Performance Rating/Pts	Total Return Y-T-D	Risk Rating/Pts
3-16	B-	1,492	8.73	C- / 4.1	0.38%	A+ / 9.6
2015	A	1,515	8.72	C+ / 5.8	0.21%	A / 9.5
2014	B+	1,991	8.80	C / 4.3	1.39%	B+ / 8.9
2013	A	1,858	8.79	C / 5.4	1.92%	B+ / 8.8
2012	B	1,128	8.79	C- / 4.1	7.54%	B / 7.9
2011	D+	1,232	8.43	C- / 3.8	1.12%	C+ / 6.3

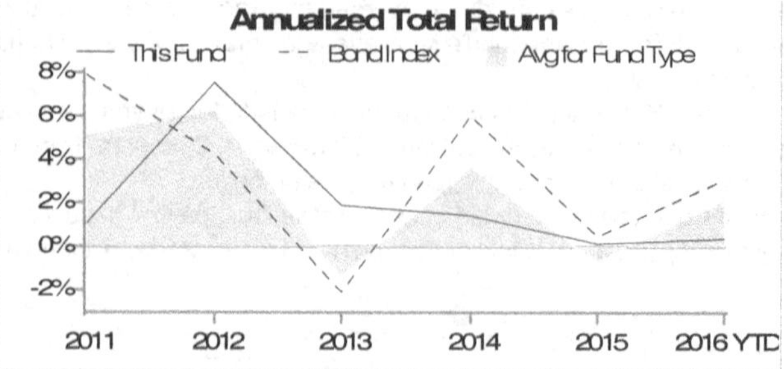

Metropolitan West Tot Ret Bond M (MWTRX) B+ Good

Fund Family: Metropolitan West Fund **Phone:** (800) 496-8298
Address: 11766 Wilshire Boulevard, Los Angeles, CA 90025
Fund Type: GEI - General - Investment Grade

Major Rating Factors: Strong performance is the major factor driving the B+ (Good) TheStreet.com Investment Rating for Metropolitan West Tot Ret Bond M. The fund currently has a performance rating of B- (Good) based on an average return of 2.45% over the last three years and 2.36% over the last three months. Factored into the performance evaluation is an expense ratio of 0.69% (low).

The fund's risk rating is currently B- (Good). Volatility, as measured by standard deviation, is considered low for fixed income funds at 2.84. Another risk factor is the fund's fairly average duration of 5.0 years (i.e. average interest rate risk).

Stephen M. Kane has been running the fund for 19 years and currently receives a manager quality ranking of 73 (0=worst, 99=best). If you desire only a moderate level of risk and strong performance, then this fund is an excellent option.

Services Offered: Automated phone transactions, check writing, payroll deductions, bank draft capabilities and a systematic withdrawal plan.

Data Date	Investment Rating	Net Assets ($Mil)	NAV	Perfor-mance Rating/Pts	Total Return Y-T-D	Risk Rating/Pts
3-16	B+	16,460	10.83	B- / 7.0	2.36%	B- / 7.1
2015	B	16,048	10.62	C+/ 6.9	-0.04%	C+/ 6.9
2014	A+	14,117	10.91	B- / 7.3	5.83%	C+/ 6.5
2013	A+	10,074	10.55	B- / 7.3	0.20%	B- / 7.1
2012	A+	10,124	10.90	B- / 7.4	11.41%	C+/ 6.7
2011	B+	8,354	10.37	C / 5.4	5.20%	C+/ 6.8

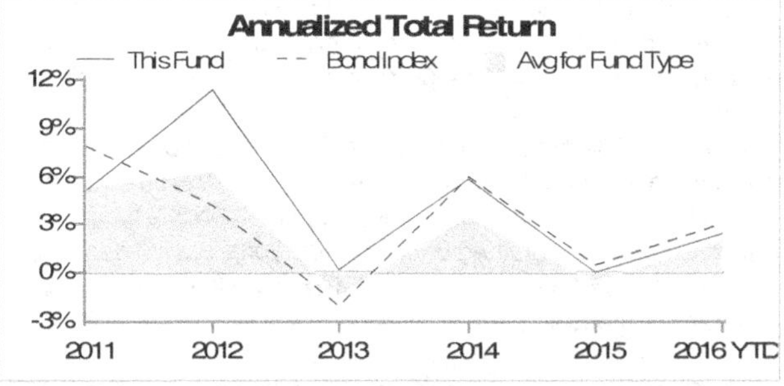

Metropolitan West Uncons Bond M (MWCRX) B+ Good

Fund Family: Metropolitan West Fund **Phone:** (800) 496-8298
Address: 11766 Wilshire Boulevard, Los Angeles, CA 90025
Fund Type: GEL - General - Long Term

Major Rating Factors: A moderate risk profile coupled with stable earnings characterizes Metropolitan West Uncons Bond M which receives a TheStreet.com Investment Rating of B+ (Good). Volatility, as measured by standard deviation, is considered low for fixed income funds at 1.66. Another risk factor is the fund's very low average duration of 1.4 years (i.e. low interest rate risk). The fund's risk rating is currently B+ (Good).

The fund's performance rating is currently C (Fair). It has registered an average return of 1.83% over the last three years and is up 0.55% over the last three months. Factored into the performance evaluation is an expense ratio of 1.04% (average).

Stephen M. Kane has been running the fund for 5 years and currently receives a manager quality ranking of 90 (0=worst, 99=best). If you desire stability with a moderate level of risk then this fund is an excellent option.

Services Offered: Automated phone transactions, payroll deductions, bank draft capabilities, an IRA investment plan, a 401K investment plan, wire transfers and a systematic withdrawal plan.

Data Date	Investment Rating	Net Assets ($Mil)	NAV	Perfor-mance Rating/Pts	Total Return Y-T-D	Risk Rating/Pts
3-16	B+	826	11.72	C / 5.5	0.55%	B+/ 8.8
2015	A+	866	11.71	C+/ 6.9	-0.04%	B+/ 8.7
2014	A+	463	11.93	B / 7.9	3.36%	C+/ 6.8
2013	U	266	11.76	U / --	2.87%	U / --
2012	U	64	11.74	U / --	15.78%	U / --

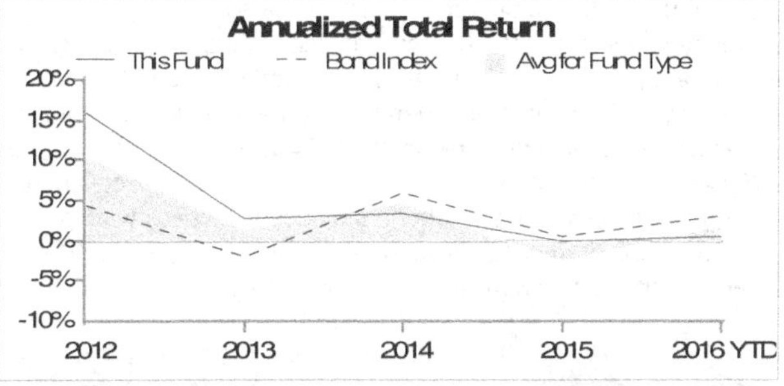

MFS Corporate Bond A (MFBFX) C- Fair

Fund Family: MFS Funds **Phone:** (800) 225-2606
Address: P.O. Box 55824, Boston, MA 02205
Fund Type: GEI - General - Investment Grade

Major Rating Factors: Middle of the road best describes MFS Corporate Bond A whose TheStreet.com Investment Rating is currently a C- (Fair). The fund has a performance rating of C+ (Fair) based on an average return of 2.79% over the last three years and 3.90% over the last three months. Factored into the performance evaluation is an expense ratio of 0.82% (low) and a 4.3% front-end load that is levied at the time of purchase.

The fund's risk rating is currently C- (Fair). Volatility, as measured by standard deviation, is considered average for fixed income funds at 3.95. Another risk factor is the fund's fairly average duration of 6.4 years (i.e. average interest rate risk).

Richard O. Hawkins has been running the fund for 11 years and currently receives a manager quality ranking of 58 (0=worst, 99=best). If you desire an average level of risk, then this fund may be an option.

Services Offered: Automated phone transactions, check writing, payroll deductions, bank draft capabilities, an IRA investment plan, wire transfers and a systematic withdrawal plan.

Data Date	Investment Rating	Net Assets ($Mil)	NAV	Perfor-mance Rating/Pts	Total Return Y-T-D	Risk Rating/Pts
3-16	C-	1,654	13.83	C+/ 6.1	3.90%	C- / 4.0
2015	D+	1,548	13.42	C- / 3.9	-0.36%	C / 4.3
2014	C+	1,500	13.98	C+/ 6.6	5.69%	C / 4.8
2013	C	1,463	13.71	C+/ 5.7	-0.51%	C / 4.6
2012	C+	1,746	14.29	C+/ 6.1	10.44%	C / 4.5
2011	C+	1,137	13.50	C+/ 6.8	6.40%	C- / 4.0

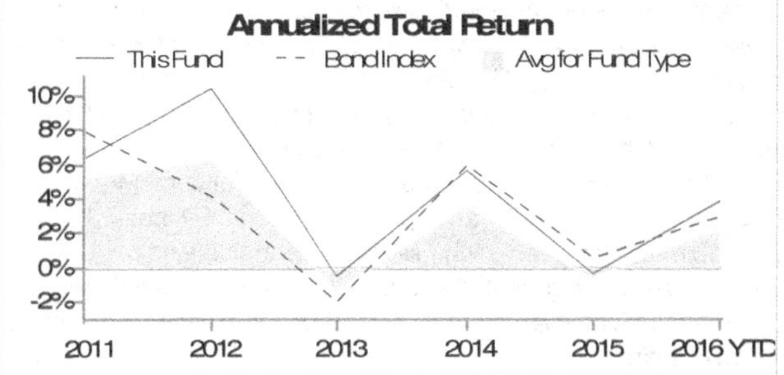

MFS Emerging Markets Debt A (MEDAX) — D — Weak

Fund Family: MFS Funds **Phone:** (800) 225-2606
Address: P.O. Box 55824, Boston, MA 02205
Fund Type: EM - Emerging Market

Major Rating Factors: MFS Emerging Markets Debt A has adopted a very risky asset allocation strategy and currently receives an overall TheStreet.com Investment Rating of D (Weak). Volatility, as measured by standard deviation, is considered high for fixed income funds at 6.87. Another risk factor is the fund's fairly average duration of 6.0 years (i.e. average interest rate risk). Unfortunately, the high level of risk (E+, Very Weak) has only provided investors with average performance.

The fund's performance rating is currently C (Fair). It has registered an average return of 0.90% over the last three years and is up 4.24% over the last three months. Factored into the performance evaluation is an expense ratio of 1.12% (average).

Matthew W. Ryan has been running the fund for 18 years and currently receives a manager quality ranking of 89 (0=worst, 99=best). If you are comfortable owning a very high risk investment, then this fund may be an option.

Services Offered: Automated phone transactions, payroll deductions, bank draft capabilities, an IRA investment plan, a 401K investment plan, wire transfers and a systematic withdrawal plan.

Data Date	Investment Rating	Net Assets ($Mil)	NAV	Performance Rating/Pts	Total Return Y-T-D	Risk Rating/Pts
3-16	D	569	14.24	C / 5.5	4.24%	E+ / 0.8
2015	E	565	13.81	D- / 1.1	-0.77%	E / 0.5
2014	D-	1,289	14.54	C / 4.3	4.37%	E+ / 0.6
2013	E+	1,452	14.56	C / 4.6	-6.40%	E+ / 0.6
2012	C+	1,527	16.36	A- / 9.0	18.83%	E+ / 0.9
2011	D	1,115	14.55	B- / 7.0	5.84%	D / 2.0

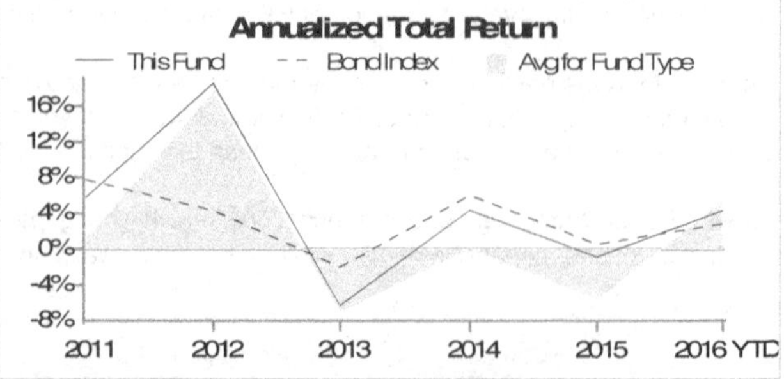

MFS Government Securities Fund A (MFGSX) — C- — Fair

Fund Family: MFS Funds **Phone:** (800) 225-2606
Address: P.O. Box 55824, Boston, MA 02205
Fund Type: USS - US Government - Short & Inter. Term

Major Rating Factors: A moderate risk profile coupled with stable earnings characterizes MFS Government Securities Fund A which receives a TheStreet.com Investment Rating of C- (Fair). Volatility, as measured by standard deviation, is considered low for fixed income funds at 2.62. Another risk factor is the fund's below average duration of 4.8 years (i.e. lower interest rate risk). The fund's risk rating is currently B (Good).

The fund's performance rating is currently C- (Fair). It has registered an average return of 1.50% over the last three years and is up 2.40% over the last three months. Factored into the performance evaluation is an expense ratio of 0.88% (average) and a 4.3% front-end load that is levied at the time of purchase.

Geoffrey L. Schechter has been running the fund for 10 years and currently receives a manager quality ranking of 51 (0=worst, 99=best). If you desire stability with a moderate level of risk then this fund is an excellent option.

Services Offered: Automated phone transactions, check writing, payroll deductions, bank draft capabilities, an IRA investment plan, a 401K investment plan, wire transfers and a systematic withdrawal plan.

Data Date	Investment Rating	Net Assets ($Mil)	NAV	Performance Rating/Pts	Total Return Y-T-D	Risk Rating/Pts
3-16	C-	728	10.18	C- / 3.7	2.40%	B / 7.7
2015	C-	690	9.99	D / 2.2	0.27%	B / 7.6
2014	C-	692	10.16	D+ / 2.7	4.63%	B / 7.7
2013	D-	696	9.92	E / 0.5	-2.96%	B / 7.9
2012	D-	888	10.48	D- / 1.3	2.08%	B / 7.6
2011	C-	990	10.58	D+ / 2.4	7.19%	B+ / 8.3

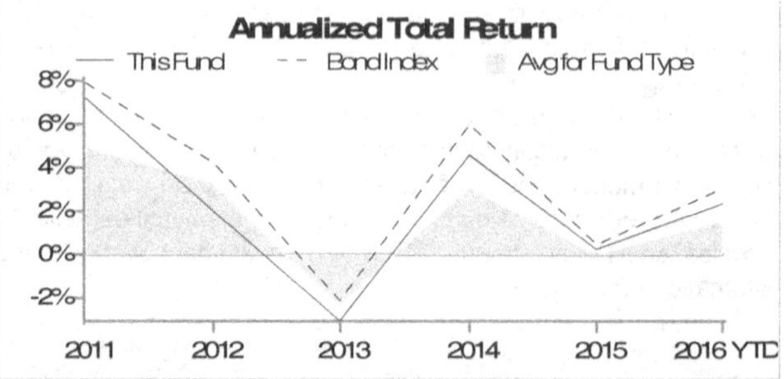

MFS Municipal High Income A (MMHYX) — C+ — Fair

Fund Family: MFS Funds **Phone:** (800) 225-2606
Address: P.O. Box 55824, Boston, MA 02205
Fund Type: MUH - Municipal - High Yield

Major Rating Factors: MFS Municipal High Income A has adopted a very risky asset allocation strategy and currently receives an overall TheStreet.com Investment Rating of C+ (Fair). Volatility, as measured by standard deviation, is considered above average for fixed income funds at 5.12. Another risk factor is the fund's above average duration of 7.6 years (i.e. higher interest rate risk). The high level of risk (D, Weak) did however, reward investors with excellent performance.

The fund's performance rating is currently A+ (Excellent). It has registered an average return of 4.79% over the last three years (7.93% taxable equivalent) and is up 2.50% over the last three months (4.14% taxable equivalent). Factored into the performance evaluation is an expense ratio of 0.72% (low) and a 4.3% front-end load that is levied at the time of purchase.

Geoffrey L. Schechter has been running the fund for 14 years and currently receives a manager quality ranking of 48 (0=worst, 99=best). If you are comfortable owning a very high risk investment, this fund may be an option.

Services Offered: Automated phone transactions, payroll deductions, bank draft capabilities, an IRA investment plan, a 401K investment plan and a systematic withdrawal plan.

Data Date	Investment Rating	Net Assets ($Mil)	NAV	Performance Rating/Pts	Total Return Y-T-D	Risk Rating/Pts
3-16	C+	2,014	8.31	A+ / 9.6	2.50%	D / 1.8
2015	C	1,911	8.19	A / 9.5	5.03%	D- / 1.4
2014	B-	1,527	8.14	A+ / 9.8	14.74%	E+ / 0.9
2013	D+	1,407	7.43	B- / 7.0	-6.02%	D / 1.7
2012	A	2,107	8.31	A+ / 9.7	13.94%	D+ / 2.3
2011	A-	1,761	7.64	A+ / 9.7	11.22%	D / 2.1

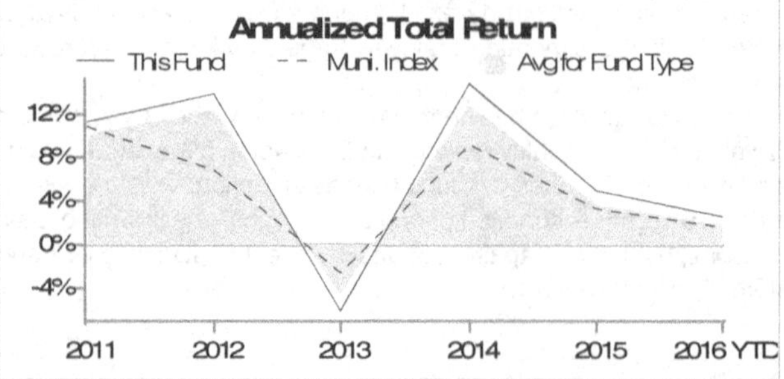

MFS Municipal Income A (MFIAX) C+ Fair

Fund Family: MFS Funds **Phone:** (800) 225-2606
Address: P.O. Box 55824, Boston, MA 02205
Fund Type: MUN - Municipal - National

Major Rating Factors: Strong performance is the major factor driving the C+ (Fair) TheStreet.com Investment Rating for MFS Municipal Income A. The fund currently has a performance rating of B+ (Good) based on an average return of 3.46% over the last three years (5.73% taxable equivalent) and 1.82% over the last three months (3.01% taxable equivalent). Factored into the performance evaluation is an expense ratio of 0.80% (low) and a 4.3% front-end load that is levied at the time of purchase.

The fund's risk rating is currently C- (Fair). Volatility, as measured by standard deviation, is considered average for fixed income funds at 4.09. Another risk factor is the fund's fairly average duration of 6.3 years (i.e. average interest rate risk).

Geoffrey L. Schechter has been running the fund for 18 years and currently receives a manager quality ranking of 34 (0=worst, 99=best). If you desire an average level of risk and strong performance, then this fund is a good option.

Services Offered: Automated phone transactions, check writing, payroll deductions, bank draft capabilities, an IRA investment plan, a 401K investment plan and a systematic withdrawal plan.

Data Date	Investment Rating	Net Assets ($Mil)	NAV	Performance Rating/Pts	Total Return Y-T-D	Risk Rating/Pts
3-16	C+	865	8.89	B+ / 8.5	1.82%	C- / 3.8
2015	C+	808	8.81	B+ / 8.3	3.33%	C- / 3.6
2014	B+	764	8.83	A / 9.3	10.85%	D+ / 2.6
2013	D+	726	8.25	C+ / 5.9	-4.99%	D+ / 2.9
2012	B	1,009	9.01	B / 7.9	10.46%	C- / 3.0
2011	B	894	8.48	B / 7.6	10.62%	C- / 3.8

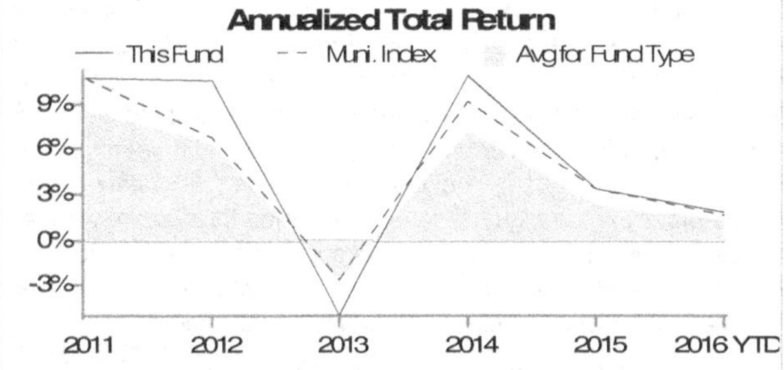

MFS Municipal Lmtd Maturity A (MTLFX) B+ Good

Fund Family: MFS Funds **Phone:** (800) 225-2606
Address: P.O. Box 55824, Boston, MA 02205
Fund Type: MUN - Municipal - National

Major Rating Factors: A moderate risk profile coupled with stable earnings characterizes MFS Municipal Lmtd Maturity A which receives a TheStreet.com Investment Rating of B+ (Good). Volatility, as measured by standard deviation, is considered low for fixed income funds at 1.84. Another risk factor is the fund's below average duration of 3.2 years (i.e. lower interest rate risk). The fund's risk rating is currently B+ (Good).

The fund's performance rating is currently C+ (Fair). It has registered an average return of 1.51% over the last three years (2.50% taxable equivalent) and is up 0.96% over the last three months (1.59% taxable equivalent). Factored into the performance evaluation is an expense ratio of 0.80% (low) and a 2.5% front-end load that is levied at the time of purchase.

Geoffrey L. Schechter has been running the fund for 18 years and currently receives a manager quality ranking of 51 (0=worst, 99=best). If you desire stability with a moderate level of risk then this fund is an excellent option.

Services Offered: Automated phone transactions, check writing, payroll deductions, bank draft capabilities, an IRA investment plan, a 401K investment plan and a systematic withdrawal plan.

Data Date	Investment Rating	Net Assets ($Mil)	NAV	Performance Rating/Pts	Total Return Y-T-D	Risk Rating/Pts
3-16	B+	697	8.21	C+ / 5.6	0.96%	B+ / 8.6
2015	A	680	8.17	C+ / 6.5	1.75%	B+ / 8.6
2014	C	677	8.16	C- / 3.0	3.12%	B+ / 8.5
2013	B	706	8.04	C- / 4.0	-0.84%	B+ / 8.6
2012	C+	653	8.25	D+ / 2.5	3.05%	B+ / 8.6
2011	B+	630	8.17	C- / 4.1	6.03%	B+ / 8.5

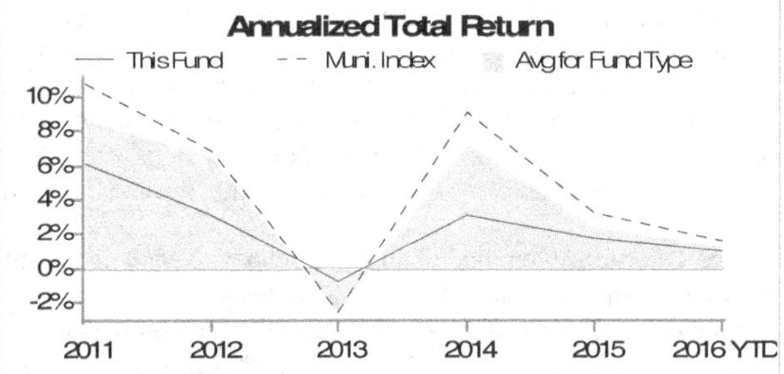

MFS Total Return Bond A (MRBFX) B Good

Fund Family: MFS Funds **Phone:** (800) 225-2606
Address: P.O. Box 55824, Boston, MA 02205
Fund Type: GEI - General - Investment Grade

Major Rating Factors: MFS Total Return Bond A receives a TheStreet.com Investment Rating of B (Good). The fund has a performance rating of C+ (Fair) based on an average return of 2.29% over the last three years and 3.01% over the last three months. Factored into the performance evaluation is an expense ratio of 0.88% (average).

The fund's risk rating is currently C+ (Fair). Volatility, as measured by standard deviation, is considered average for fixed income funds at 2.97. Another risk factor is the fund's fairly average duration of 5.3 years (i.e. average interest rate risk).

Robert D. Persons has been running the fund for 10 years and currently receives a manager quality ranking of 59 (0=worst, 99=best). If you desire an average level of risk, then this fund may be an option.

Services Offered: Automated phone transactions, check writing, payroll deductions, bank draft capabilities, an IRA investment plan, a 401K investment plan, wire transfers and a systematic withdrawal plan.

Data Date	Investment Rating	Net Assets ($Mil)	NAV	Performance Rating/Pts	Total Return Y-T-D	Risk Rating/Pts
3-16	B	1,767	10.74	C+ / 6.9	3.01%	C+ / 6.7
2015	C+	1,617	10.50	C+ / 5.7	-0.53%	C+ / 6.6
2014	B	1,380	10.90	C+ / 5.6	5.68%	C+ / 6.8
2013	C	1,076	10.67	C- / 3.8	-1.04%	B- / 7.0
2012	C+	1,090	11.11	C- / 3.8	7.40%	B- / 7.5
2011	B-	954	10.70	C / 5.1	6.47%	C+ / 6.6

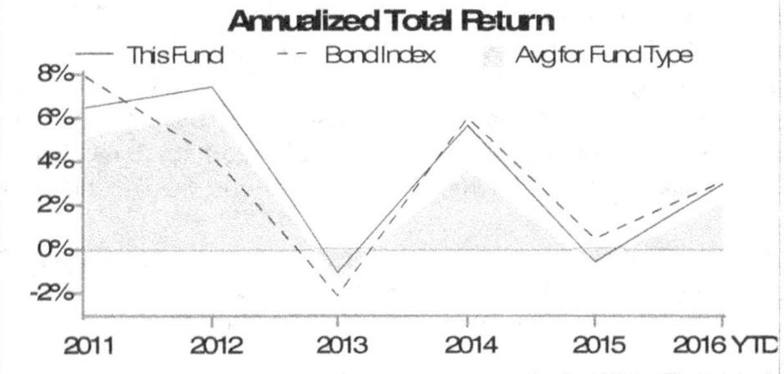

Natixis Loomis Sayles Cor Pl Bd A (NEFRX) D Weak

Fund Family: Natixis Funds **Phone:** (800) 225-5478
Address: P.O. Box 219579, Kansas City, MO 64121
Fund Type: GEI - General - Investment Grade
Major Rating Factors: Natixis Loomis Sayles Cor Pl Bd A has adopted a risky asset allocation strategy and currently receives an overall TheStreet.com Investment Rating of D (Weak). Volatility, as measured by standard deviation, is considered above average for fixed income funds at 4.76. Another risk factor is the fund's fairly average duration of 6.8 years (i.e. average interest rate risk). Unfortunately, the high level of risk (D+, Weak) has only provided investors with average performance.

The fund's performance rating is currently C- (Fair). It has registered an average return of 1.46% over the last three years and is up 3.96% over the last three months. Factored into the performance evaluation is an expense ratio of 0.74% (low) and a 4.3% front-end load that is levied at the time of purchase.

Peter W. Palfrey has been running the fund for 20 years and currently receives a manager quality ranking of 18 (0=worst, 99=best). If you are comfortable owning a high risk investment, then this fund may be an option.

Services Offered: Automated phone transactions, payroll deductions, bank draft capabilities, an IRA investment plan, a 401K investment plan, a Keogh investment plan, wire transfers and a systematic withdrawal plan.

Data Date	Investment Rating	Net Assets ($Mil)	NAV	Performance Rating/Pts	Total Return Y-T-D	Risk Rating/Pts
3-16	D	787	12.57	C- / 3.5	3.96%	D+ / 2.9
2015	D	809	12.19	D- / 1.3	-4.20%	C- / 3.1
2014	D+	851	13.04	C / 5.5	6.18%	C- / 3.9
2013	C+	418	12.76	C+ / 6.4	-0.82%	C / 4.4
2012	A-	559	13.39	C+ / 6.7	11.31%	C+ / 5.7
2011	C	319	12.68	C / 5.2	7.68%	C+ / 5.6

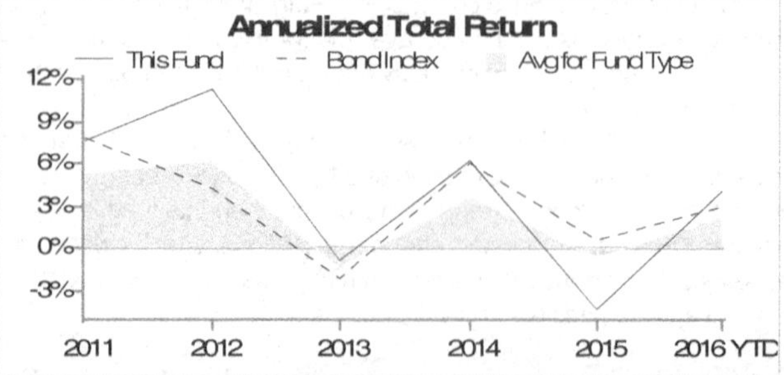

Natixis Loomis Sayles Invst Gr Bd A (LIGRX) D- Weak

Fund Family: Natixis Funds **Phone:** (800) 225-5478
Address: P.O. Box 219579, Kansas City, MO 64121
Fund Type: GEI - General - Investment Grade
Major Rating Factors: Natixis Loomis Sayles Invst Gr Bd A has adopted a risky asset allocation strategy and currently receives an overall TheStreet.com Investment Rating of D- (Weak). Volatility, as measured by standard deviation, is considered above average for fixed income funds at 5.17. Unfortunately, the high level of risk (D+, Weak) failed to pay off as investors endured very poor performance.

The fund's performance rating is currently D+ (Weak). It has registered an average return of 0.95% over the last three years and is up 3.59% over the last three months. Factored into the performance evaluation is an expense ratio of 0.83% (low) and a 4.3% front-end load that is levied at the time of purchase.

Daniel J. Fuss has been running the fund for 20 years and currently receives a manager quality ranking of 19 (0=worst, 99=best). If you can tolerate high levels of risk in the hope of improved future returns, holding this fund may be an option.

Services Offered: Automated phone transactions, payroll deductions, bank draft capabilities, an IRA investment plan, a 401K investment plan, a Keogh investment plan, wire transfers and a systematic withdrawal plan.

Data Date	Investment Rating	Net Assets ($Mil)	NAV	Performance Rating/Pts	Total Return Y-T-D	Risk Rating/Pts
3-16	D-	1,337	11.18	D+ / 2.6	3.59%	D+ / 2.6
2015	D-	1,432	10.84	D- / 1.2	-5.33%	D+ / 2.8
2014	D	1,983	11.86	C+ / 5.6	4.88%	D+ / 2.8
2013	C-	2,358	11.89	C+ / 6.7	1.02%	D+ / 2.7
2012	C-	3,024	12.62	C+ / 6.5	11.98%	D+ / 2.7
2011	D	2,825	11.94	C+ / 6.0	4.82%	D+ / 2.9

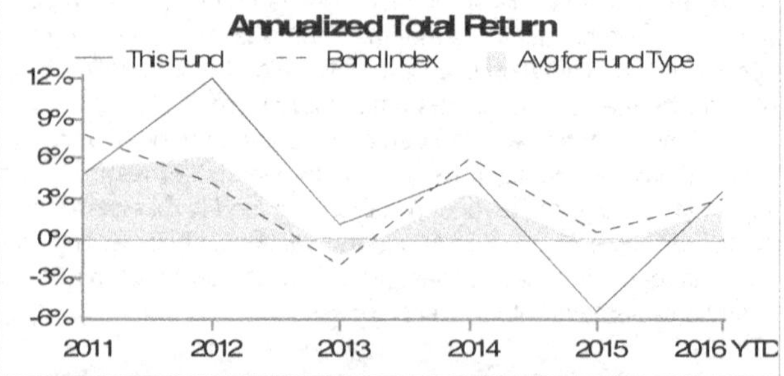

Natixis Loomis Sayles Strat Inc A (NEFZX) D- Weak

Fund Family: Natixis Funds **Phone:** (800) 225-5478
Address: P.O. Box 219579, Kansas City, MO 64121
Fund Type: GEL - General - Long Term
Major Rating Factors: Natixis Loomis Sayles Strat Inc A has adopted a very risky asset allocation strategy and currently receives an overall TheStreet.com Investment Rating of D- (Weak). Volatility, as measured by standard deviation, is considered high for fixed income funds at 7.30. Unfortunately, the high level of risk (E+, Very Weak) failed to pay off as investors endured very poor performance.

The fund's performance rating is currently D+ (Weak). It has registered an average return of 2.10% over the last three years and is up 1.59% over the last three months. Factored into the performance evaluation is an expense ratio of 0.94% (average) and a 4.3% front-end load that is levied at the time of purchase.

Daniel J. Fuss has been running the fund for 21 years and currently receives a manager quality ranking of 79 (0=worst, 99=best). If you can tolerate very high levels of risk in the hope of improved future returns, holding this fund may be an option.

Services Offered: Automated phone transactions, payroll deductions, bank draft capabilities, an IRA investment plan, a 401K investment plan, a Keogh investment plan, wire transfers and a systematic withdrawal plan.

Data Date	Investment Rating	Net Assets ($Mil)	NAV	Performance Rating/Pts	Total Return Y-T-D	Risk Rating/Pts
3-16	D-	2,666	13.83	D+ / 2.8	1.59%	E+ / 0.6
2015	D-	2,875	13.67	D+ / 2.7	-7.64%	E+ / 0.7
2014	C	4,433	16.29	B+ / 8.7	5.65%	D- / 1.0
2013	C+	5,601	16.36	A+ / 9.6	10.87%	E+ / 0.6
2012	D	5,068	15.47	B- / 7.3	13.56%	E+ / 0.8
2011	D+	5,356	14.37	B / 7.7	3.35%	D- / 1.4

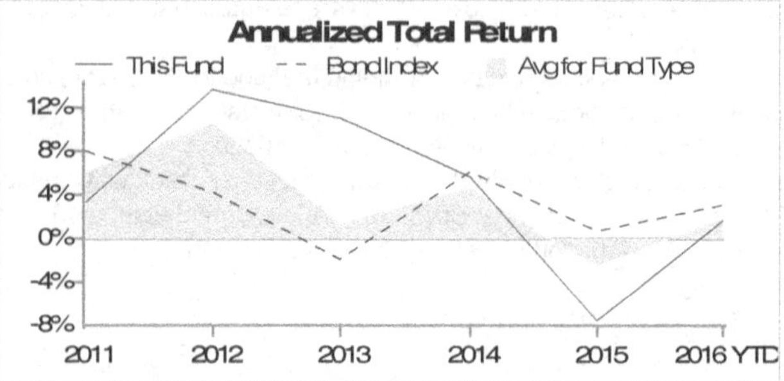

Northern Bond Index (NOBOX) B+ Good

Fund Family: Northern Funds **Phone:** (800) 595-9111
Address: PO Box 75986, Chicago, IL 60675
Fund Type: MTG - Mortgage
Major Rating Factors: Strong performance is the major factor driving the B+ (Good) TheStreet.com Investment Rating for Northern Bond Index. The fund currently has a performance rating of B- (Good) based on an average return of 2.37% over the last three years and 2.95% over the last three months. Factored into the performance evaluation is an expense ratio of 0.18% (very low).

The fund's risk rating is currently C+ (Fair). Volatility, as measured by standard deviation, is considered average for fixed income funds at 2.96. Another risk factor is the fund's fairly average duration of 5.2 years (i.e. average interest rate risk).

Louis R. D'Arienzo has been running the fund for 9 years and currently receives a manager quality ranking of 42 (0=worst, 99=best). If you desire an average level of risk and strong performance, then this fund is a good option.
Services Offered: Automated phone transactions, payroll deductions, bank draft capabilities, an IRA investment plan, a 401K investment plan, wire transfers and a systematic withdrawal plan.

Data Date	Investment Rating	Net Assets ($Mil)	NAV	Performance Rating/Pts	Total Return Y-T-D	Risk Rating/Pts
3-16	B+	2,631	10.74	B- / 7.2	2.95%	C+/ 6.7
2015	C+	2,497	10.50	C+/ 6.2	0.50%	C+/ 6.5
2014	C	2,579	10.74	C- / 4.2	5.93%	B- / 7.0
2013	C	2,232	10.42	C- / 3.8	-2.29%	B- / 7.4
2012	C	2,614	10.96	C- / 3.2	4.05%	B- / 7.2
2011	C	2,328	10.91	C- / 3.3	7.63%	B / 7.9

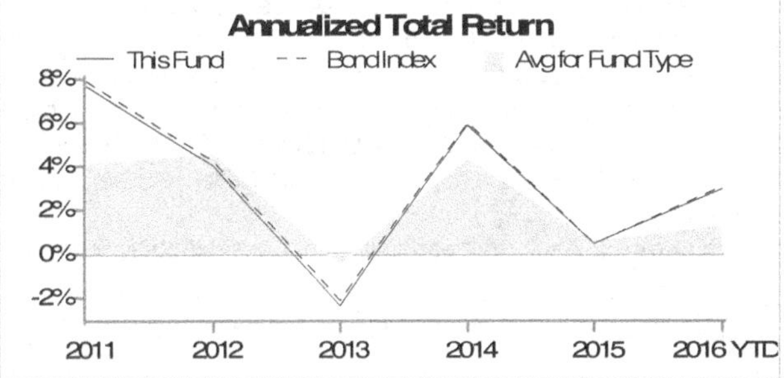

Northern Fixed Income (NOFIX) C+ Fair

Fund Family: Northern Funds **Phone:** (800) 595-9111
Address: PO Box 75986, Chicago, IL 60675
Fund Type: GL - Global
Major Rating Factors: Middle of the road best describes Northern Fixed Income whose TheStreet.com Investment Rating is currently a C+ (Fair). The fund has a performance rating of C+ (Fair) based on an average return of 2.35% over the last three years and 2.57% over the last three months. Factored into the performance evaluation is an expense ratio of 0.49% (very low).

The fund's risk rating is currently C (Fair). Volatility, as measured by standard deviation, is considered average for fixed income funds at 3.41. Another risk factor is the fund's fairly average duration of 5.2 years (i.e. average interest rate risk).

Bradley Camden has been running the fund for 5 years and currently receives a manager quality ranking of 97 (0=worst, 99=best). If you desire an average level of risk, then this fund may be an option.
Services Offered: Automated phone transactions, payroll deductions, bank draft capabilities, an IRA investment plan, a 401K investment plan, wire transfers and a systematic withdrawal plan.

Data Date	Investment Rating	Net Assets ($Mil)	NAV	Performance Rating/Pts	Total Return Y-T-D	Risk Rating/Pts
3-16	C+	1,353	10.23	C+/ 6.8	2.57%	C / 5.2
2015	C	1,380	10.04	C+/ 6.2	-0.16%	C / 5.0
2014	C+	1,945	10.40	C+/ 5.6	6.19%	C+/ 5.6
2013	B	1,534	10.09	C+/ 5.7	-1.49%	C+/ 6.4
2012	B	1,763	10.63	C / 4.5	7.15%	B- / 7.5
2011	C+	1,632	10.43	C- / 3.6	7.22%	B / 8.2

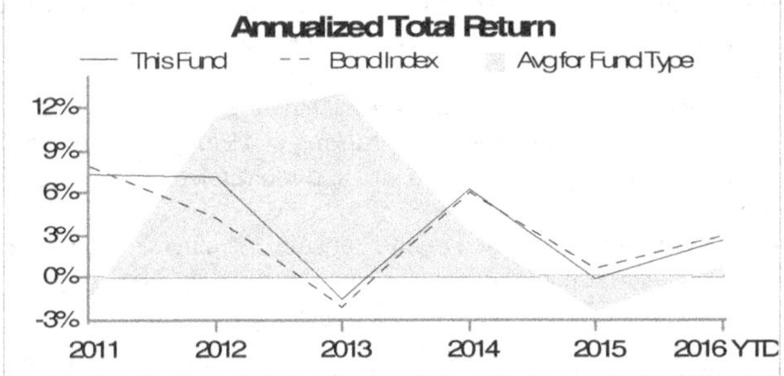

Northern High Yield Muni (NHYMX) B Good

Fund Family: Northern Funds **Phone:** (800) 595-9111
Address: PO Box 75986, Chicago, IL 60675
Fund Type: MUH - Municipal - High Yield
Major Rating Factors: Exceptional performance is the major factor driving the B (Good) TheStreet.com Investment Rating for Northern High Yield Muni. The fund currently has a performance rating of A+ (Excellent) based on an average return of 4.25% over the last three years (7.04% taxable equivalent) and 1.85% over the last three months (3.06% taxable equivalent). Factored into the performance evaluation is an expense ratio of 0.86% (average).

The fund's risk rating is currently C- (Fair). Volatility, as measured by standard deviation, is considered average for fixed income funds at 4.12. Another risk factor is the fund's fairly average duration of 6.0 years (i.e. average interest rate risk).

M. Jane McCart has been running the fund for 18 years and currently receives a manager quality ranking of 72 (0=worst, 99=best). If you desire an average level of risk and strong performance, then this fund is a good option.
Services Offered: Automated phone transactions, payroll deductions, bank draft capabilities, an IRA investment plan, a 401K investment plan, wire transfers and a systematic withdrawal plan.

Data Date	Investment Rating	Net Assets ($Mil)	NAV	Performance Rating/Pts	Total Return Y-T-D	Risk Rating/Pts
3-16	B	570	9.02	A+/ 9.8	1.85%	C- / 3.1
2015	B-	490	8.93	A+/ 9.7	4.50%	D+/ 2.8
2014	B+	298	8.88	A+/ 9.7	12.41%	D / 2.2
2013	B	241	8.26	B+/ 8.9	-4.46%	D+/ 2.9
2012	A	348	9.06	A+/ 9.7	12.47%	D+/ 2.5
2011	A+	543	8.42	A / 9.4	11.47%	D+/ 2.7

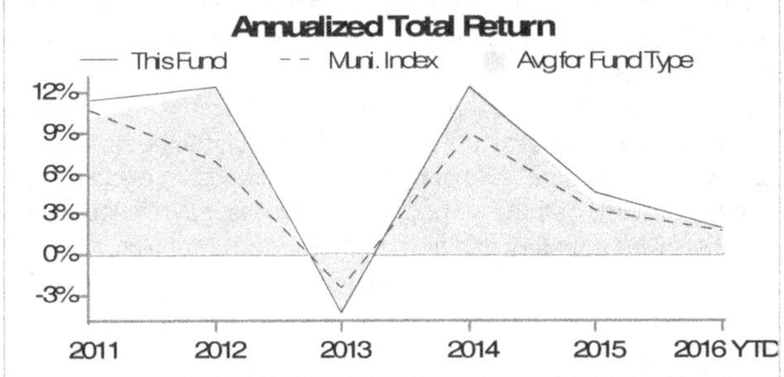

Northern HY Fixed Income (NHFIX) D- Weak

Fund Family: Northern Funds **Phone:** (800) 595-9111
Address: PO Box 75986, Chicago, IL 60675
Fund Type: COH - Corporate - High Yield
Major Rating Factors: Northern HY Fixed Income has adopted a very risky asset allocation strategy and currently receives an overall TheStreet.com Investment Rating of D- (Weak). Volatility, as measured by standard deviation, is considered above average for fixed income funds at 5.61. Unfortunately, the high level of risk (D-, Weak) failed to pay off as investors endured very poor performance.

The fund's performance rating is currently D (Weak). It has registered an average return of 1.32% over the last three years and is up 0.56% over the last three months. Factored into the performance evaluation is an expense ratio of 0.82% (low) and a 2.0% back-end load levied at the time of sale.

Richard J. Inzunza has been running the fund for 9 years and currently receives a manager quality ranking of 51 (0=worst, 99=best). If you can tolerate very high levels of risk in the hope of improved future returns, holding this fund may be an option.
Services Offered: Bank draft capabilities and a systematic withdrawal plan.

Data Date	Investment Rating	Net Assets ($Mil)	NAV	Performance Rating/Pts	Total Return Y-T-D	Risk Rating/Pts
3-16	D-	5,124	6.42	D / 2.0	0.56%	D- / 1.5
2015	D	4,982	6.48	C / 4.5	-3.04%	D / 1.7
2014	C-	4,814	7.08	B / 7.6	2.11%	D / 2.2
2013	C+	5,575	7.49	A / 9.5	7.69%	D- / 1.1
2012	C-	5,926	7.55	B+ / 8.4	15.05%	E+ / 0.6
2011	D+	4,806	7.04	B / 7.6	3.72%	D- / 1.5

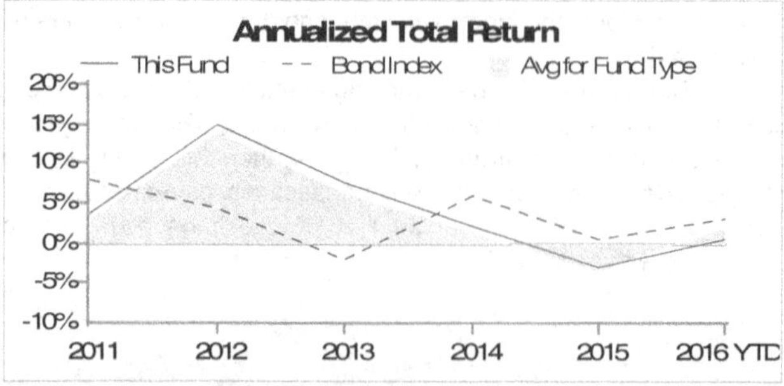

Northern Intermed Tax Exempt (NOITX) A Excellent

Fund Family: Northern Funds **Phone:** (800) 595-9111
Address: PO Box 75986, Chicago, IL 60675
Fund Type: MUN - Municipal - National
Major Rating Factors: Exceptional performance is the major factor driving the A (Excellent) TheStreet.com Investment Rating for Northern Intermed Tax Exempt. The fund currently has a performance rating of A- (Excellent) based on an average return of 2.88% over the last three years (4.77% taxable equivalent) and 1.42% over the last three months (2.35% taxable equivalent). Factored into the performance evaluation is an expense ratio of 0.50% (very low).

The fund's risk rating is currently C (Fair). Volatility, as measured by standard deviation, is considered average for fixed income funds at 3.33. Another risk factor is the fund's fairly average duration of 5.1 years (i.e. average interest rate risk).

Timothy T. A. McGregor has been running the fund for 18 years and currently receives a manager quality ranking of 41 (0=worst, 99=best). If you desire an average level of risk and strong performance, then this fund is a good option.
Services Offered: Automated phone transactions, payroll deductions, bank draft capabilities, wire transfers and a systematic withdrawal plan.

Data Date	Investment Rating	Net Assets ($Mil)	NAV	Performance Rating/Pts	Total Return Y-T-D	Risk Rating/Pts
3-16	A	3,157	10.82	A- / 9.0	1.42%	C / 5.3
2015	B+	3,079	10.72	B+ / 8.9	2.78%	C / 5.1
2014	B	2,969	10.69	B- / 7.3	6.84%	C / 4.7
2013	B+	2,279	10.24	B / 7.6	-2.23%	C / 4.8
2012	C+	2,449	10.75	C+ / 5.8	5.02%	C / 4.7
2011	B	2,179	10.68	C+ / 6.2	10.09%	C / 5.5

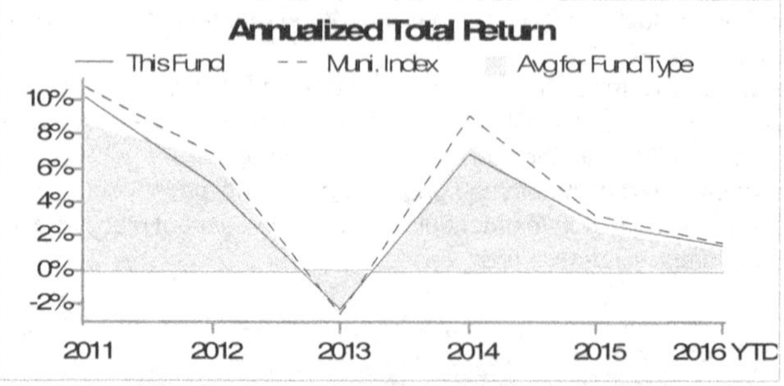

Northern Short Bond (BSBAX) C+ Fair

Fund Family: Northern Institutional Funds **Phone:** (800) 637-1380
Address: 801 S. Canal St., Chicago, IL 60607
Fund Type: GEI - General - Investment Grade
Major Rating Factors: A moderate risk profile coupled with stable earnings characterizes Northern Short Bond which receives a TheStreet.com Investment Rating of C+ (Fair). Volatility, as measured by standard deviation, is considered very low for fixed income funds at 1.08. Another risk factor is the fund's very low average duration of 2.7 years (i.e. low interest rate risk). The fund's risk rating is currently A- (Excellent).

The fund's performance rating is currently C- (Fair). It has registered an average return of 0.66% over the last three years and is up 0.89% over the last three months. Factored into the performance evaluation is an expense ratio of 0.44% (very low).

Bradley Camden has been running the fund for 6 years and currently receives a manager quality ranking of 63 (0=worst, 99=best). If you desire stability with a moderate level of risk then this fund is an excellent option.
Services Offered: Automated phone transactions, payroll deductions, bank draft capabilities, wire transfers and a systematic withdrawal plan.

Data Date	Investment Rating	Net Assets ($Mil)	NAV	Performance Rating/Pts	Total Return Y-T-D	Risk Rating/Pts
3-16	C+	560	18.86	C- / 3.8	0.89%	A- / 9.2
2015	B-	561	18.76	C / 4.4	0.19%	A- / 9.2
2014	C	627	18.96	D / 2.2	0.60%	A- / 9.1
2013	B-	339	19.10	C- / 3.1	0.59%	A- / 9.2
2012	C	223	19.26	D- / 1.4	3.07%	A / 9.3
2011	C	137	18.97	D / 1.8	2.26%	A / 9.5

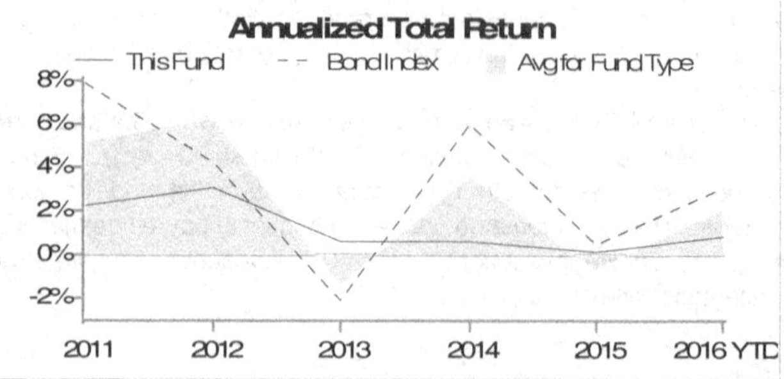

Northern Short-Interm Tax-Ex (NSITX) B+ Good

Fund Family: Northern Funds **Phone:** (800) 595-9111
Address: PO Box 75986, Chicago, IL 60675
Fund Type: MUH - Municipal - High Yield
Major Rating Factors: A moderate risk profile coupled with stable earnings characterizes Northern Short-Interm Tax-Ex which receives a TheStreet.com Investment Rating of B+ (Good). Volatility, as measured by standard deviation, is considered low for fixed income funds at 1.28. Another risk factor is the fund's very low average duration of 2.6 years (i.e. low interest rate risk). The fund's risk rating is currently B+ (Good).

The fund's performance rating is currently C+ (Fair). It has registered an average return of 1.02% over the last three years (1.69% taxable equivalent) and is up 0.67% over the last three months (1.11% taxable equivalent). Factored into the performance evaluation is an expense ratio of 0.48% (very low).

Timothy P. Blair has been running the fund for 9 years and currently receives a manager quality ranking of 59 (0=worst, 99=best). If you desire stability with a moderate level of risk then this fund is an excellent option.
Services Offered: Automated phone transactions, payroll deductions, bank draft capabilities, wire transfers and a systematic withdrawal plan.

Data Date	Investment Rating	Net Assets ($Mil)	NAV	Performance Rating/Pts	Total Return Y-T-D	Risk Rating/Pts
3-16	B+	1,161	10.48	C+ / 5.8	0.67%	B+ / 8.7
2015	A	1,188	10.44	C+ / 6.7	1.15%	B+ / 8.7
2014	C	1,402	10.45	D+ / 2.4	1.38%	B+ / 8.7
2013	B-	1,216	10.45	C- / 3.5	0.08%	B+ / 8.8
2012	D	1,062	10.60	D- / 1.2	1.25%	B+ / 8.6
2011	C-	1,113	10.68	D+ / 2.5	3.30%	B+ / 8.4

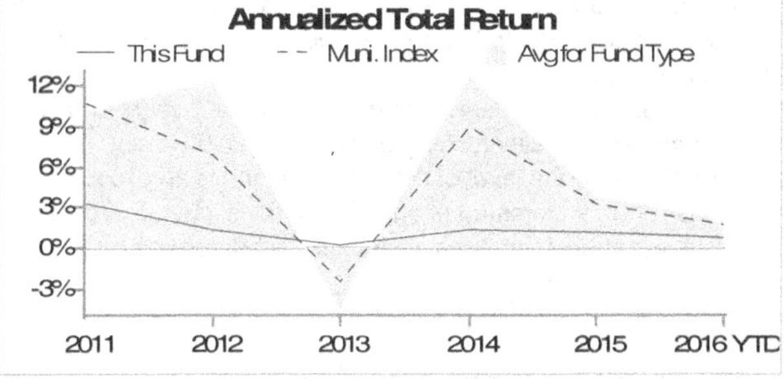

Northern Tax Exempt (NOTEX) B+ Good

Fund Family: Northern Funds **Phone:** (800) 595-9111
Address: PO Box 75986, Chicago, IL 60675
Fund Type: MUN - Municipal - National
Major Rating Factors: Exceptional performance is the major factor driving the B+ (Good) TheStreet.com Investment Rating for Northern Tax Exempt. The fund currently has a performance rating of A+ (Excellent) based on an average return of 3.87% over the last three years (6.41% taxable equivalent) and 1.54% over the last three months (2.55% taxable equivalent). Factored into the performance evaluation is an expense ratio of 0.49% (very low).

The fund's risk rating is currently C- (Fair). Volatility, as measured by standard deviation, is considered average for fixed income funds at 4.14. Another risk factor is the fund's fairly average duration of 6.0 years (i.e. average interest rate risk).

Timothy T. A. McGregor has been running the fund for 18 years and currently receives a manager quality ranking of 45 (0=worst, 99=best). If you desire an average level of risk and strong performance, then this fund is a good option.
Services Offered: Automated phone transactions, payroll deductions, bank draft capabilities, wire transfers and a systematic withdrawal plan.

Data Date	Investment Rating	Net Assets ($Mil)	NAV	Performance Rating/Pts	Total Return Y-T-D	Risk Rating/Pts
3-16	B+	1,062	10.89	A+ / 9.6	1.54%	C- / 3.8
2015	B	994	10.81	A / 9.5	3.69%	C- / 3.5
2014	B+	823	10.79	A- / 9.1	10.46%	C- / 3.3
2013	B	808	10.13	B+ / 8.4	-3.65%	C- / 3.5
2012	B	1,211	11.02	B / 7.9	7.93%	C- / 3.2
2011	B+	1,056	10.79	B- / 7.4	11.86%	C / 4.4

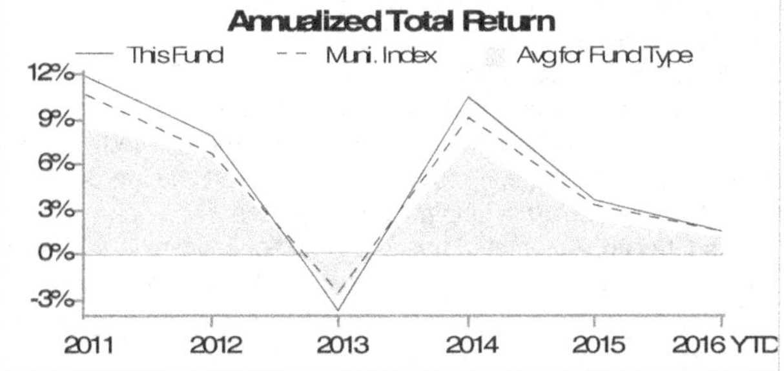

Northern Tax-Advtged Ult-Sh Fxd Inc (NTAUX) C+ Fair

Fund Family: Northern Funds **Phone:** (800) 595-9111
Address: PO Box 75986, Chicago, IL 60675
Fund Type: MTG - Mortgage
Major Rating Factors: A moderate risk profile coupled with stable earnings characterizes Northern Tax-Advtged Ult-Sh Fxd Inc which receives a TheStreet.com Investment Rating of C+ (Fair). Volatility, as measured by standard deviation, is considered very low for fixed income funds at 0.33. Another risk factor is the fund's very low average duration of 1.1 years (i.e. low interest rate risk). The fund's risk rating is currently A+ (Excellent).

The fund's performance rating is currently C- (Fair). It has registered an average return of 0.52% over the last three years and is up 0.29% over the last three months. Factored into the performance evaluation is an expense ratio of 0.26% (very low).

Patrick Quinn has been running the fund for 7 years and currently receives a manager quality ranking of 76 (0=worst, 99=best). If you desire stability with a moderate level of risk then this fund is an excellent option.
Services Offered: Automated phone transactions, payroll deductions, bank draft capabilities, wire transfers and a systematic withdrawal plan.

Data Date	Investment Rating	Net Assets ($Mil)	NAV	Performance Rating/Pts	Total Return Y-T-D	Risk Rating/Pts
3-16	C+	3,363	10.12	C- / 3.4	0.29%	A+ / 9.9
2015	B+	3,311	10.11	C / 4.8	0.35%	A+ / 9.9
2014	C	2,904	10.14	D / 1.8	0.52%	A+ / 9.9
2013	C	2,632	10.15	D / 1.8	0.75%	A+ / 9.9
2012	C-	1,827	10.14	E+ / 0.6	1.35%	A+ / 9.9
2011	U	1,252	10.09	U / --	0.93%	U / --

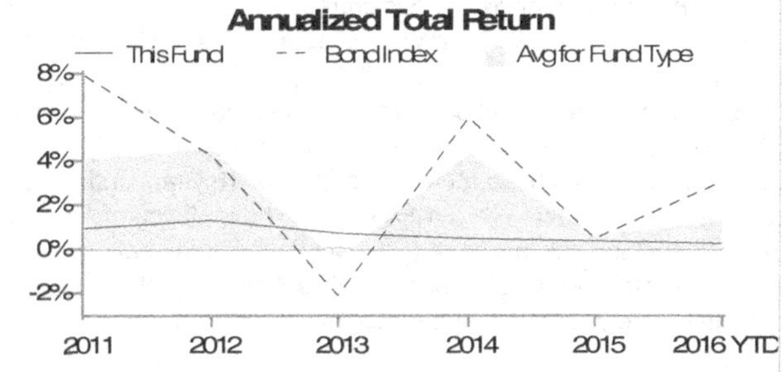

Northern Ultra-Short Fixed Income (NUSFX) B- Good

Fund Family: Northern Funds **Phone:** (800) 595-9111
Address: PO Box 75986, Chicago, IL 60675
Fund Type: GEI - General - Investment Grade
Major Rating Factors: A moderate risk profile coupled with stable earnings characterizes Northern Ultra-Short Fixed Income which receives a TheStreet.com Investment Rating of B- (Good). Volatility, as measured by standard deviation, is considered very low for fixed income funds at 0.52. Another risk factor is the fund's very low average duration of 1.2 years (i.e. low interest rate risk). The fund's risk rating is currently A+ (Excellent).

The fund's performance rating is currently C- (Fair). It has registered an average return of 0.74% over the last three years and is up 0.66% over the last three months. Factored into the performance evaluation is an expense ratio of 0.27% (very low).

Carol H. Sullivan has been running the fund for 7 years and currently receives a manager quality ranking of 81 (0=worst, 99=best). If you desire stability with a moderate level of risk then this fund is an excellent option.
Services Offered: Automated phone transactions, payroll deductions, bank draft capabilities, wire transfers and a systematic withdrawal plan.

Data Date	Investment Rating	Net Assets ($Mil)	NAV	Performance Rating/Pts	Total Return Y-T-D	Risk Rating/Pts
3-16	B-	1,542	10.18	C- / 3.9	0.66%	A+ / 9.8
2015	B+	1,570	10.14	C / 4.9	0.51%	A+ / 9.8
2014	C	1,636	10.18	D / 2.0	0.55%	A+ / 9.7
2013	C+	1,450	10.21	D / 2.2	0.77%	A+ / 9.6
2012	C-	944	10.21	E+ / 0.7	2.43%	A+ / 9.8
2011	U	451	10.09	U / --	0.87%	U / --

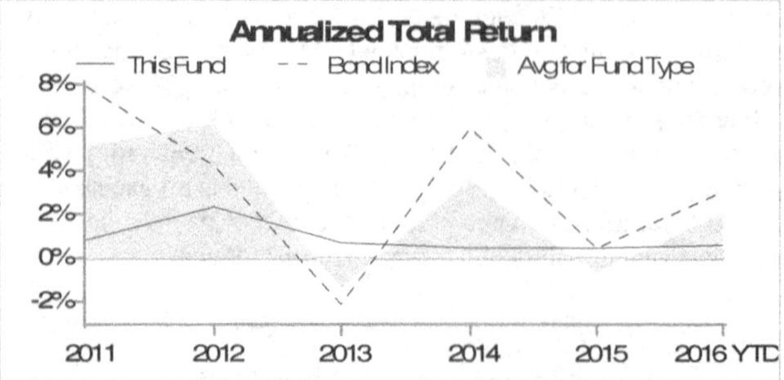

Nuveen All Amer Muni A (FLAAX) C+ Fair

Fund Family: Nuveen Investor Services **Phone:** (800) 257-8787
Address: P.O. Box 8530, Boston, MA 02266
Fund Type: MUN - Municipal - National
Major Rating Factors: Nuveen All Amer Muni A has adopted a risky asset allocation strategy and currently receives an overall TheStreet.com Investment Rating of C+ (Fair). Volatility, as measured by standard deviation, is considered above average for fixed income funds at 4.58. Another risk factor is the fund's above average duration of 7.2 years (i.e. higher interest rate risk). The high level of risk (D+, Weak) did however, reward investors with excellent performance.

The fund's performance rating is currently A- (Excellent). It has registered an average return of 4.32% over the last three years (7.15% taxable equivalent) and is up 1.86% over the last three months (3.08% taxable equivalent). Factored into the performance evaluation is an expense ratio of 0.70% (low) and a 4.2% front-end load that is levied at the time of purchase.

John V. Miller has been running the fund for 6 years and currently receives a manager quality ranking of 45 (0=worst, 99=best). If you are comfortable owning a high risk investment, this fund may be an option.
Services Offered: Automated phone transactions, payroll deductions, bank draft capabilities, wire transfers and a systematic withdrawal plan.

Data Date	Investment Rating	Net Assets ($Mil)	NAV	Performance Rating/Pts	Total Return Y-T-D	Risk Rating/Pts
3-16	C+	1,132	11.72	A- / 9.2	1.86%	D+ / 2.9
2015	C+	1,066	11.61	A- / 9.1	3.77%	D+ / 2.9
2014	B-	937	11.63	A / 9.5	13.38%	D / 1.6
2013	C	898	10.70	B / 7.9	-4.75%	D / 2.1
2012	A-	1,195	11.70	A / 9.3	11.30%	D+ / 2.6
2011	A+	475	10.98	A / 9.5	13.00%	D+ / 2.6

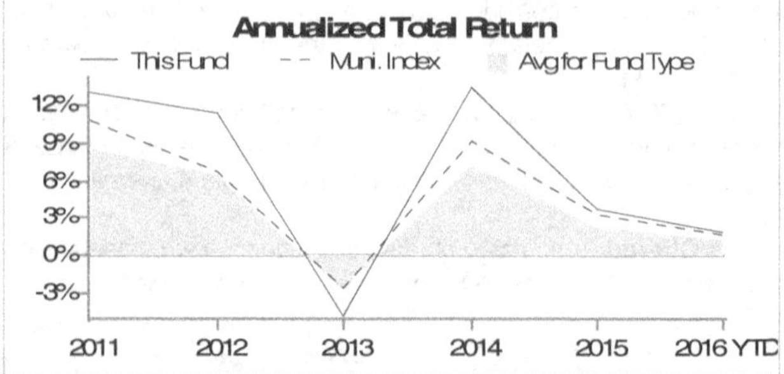

Nuveen High Yield Muni Bond A (NHMAX) C Fair

Fund Family: Nuveen Investor Services **Phone:** (800) 257-8787
Address: P.O. Box 8530, Boston, MA 02266
Fund Type: MUH - Municipal - High Yield
Major Rating Factors: Nuveen High Yield Muni Bond A has adopted a very risky asset allocation strategy and currently receives an overall TheStreet.com Investment Rating of C (Fair). Volatility, as measured by standard deviation, is considered high for fixed income funds at 6.15. Another risk factor is the fund's very high average duration of 10.4 years (i.e. very high interest rate risk). The high level of risk (E+, Very Weak) did however, reward investors with excellent performance.

The fund's performance rating is currently A+ (Excellent). It has registered an average return of 6.24% over the last three years (10.33% taxable equivalent) and is up 2.87% over the last three months (4.75% taxable equivalent). Factored into the performance evaluation is an expense ratio of 0.83% (low) and a 4.2% front-end load that is levied at the time of purchase.

John V. Miller has been running the fund for 16 years and currently receives a manager quality ranking of 70 (0=worst, 99=best). If you are comfortable owning a very high risk investment, this fund may be an option.
Services Offered: Automated phone transactions, payroll deductions, bank draft capabilities, wire transfers and a systematic withdrawal plan.

Data Date	Investment Rating	Net Assets ($Mil)	NAV	Performance Rating/Pts	Total Return Y-T-D	Risk Rating/Pts
3-16	C	4,146	17.40	A+ / 9.9	2.87%	E+ / 0.7
2015	C	3,798	17.14	A+ / 9.9	4.83%	E / 0.5
2014	C+	3,440	17.27	A+ / 9.9	19.13%	E / 0.5
2013	C+	2,416	15.36	A+ / 9.6	-4.69%	E / 0.5
2012	B+	2,896	17.14	A+ / 9.9	20.92%	D- / 1.2
2011	B-	1,922	15.08	A+ / 9.8	11.36%	E+ / 0.7

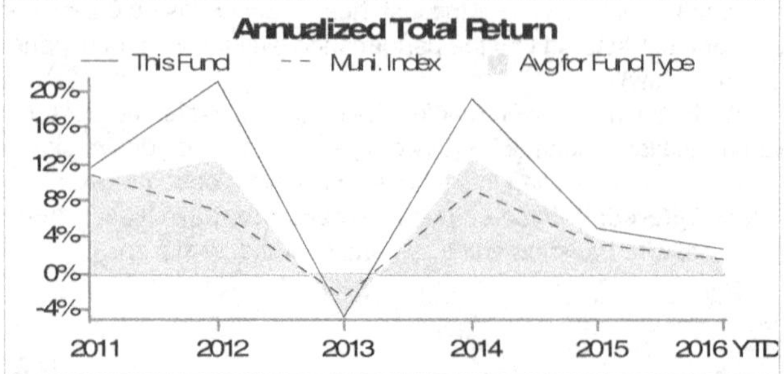

Nuveen Intmdt Duration Muni Bond A (NMBAX) A- Excellent

Fund Family: Nuveen Investor Services **Phone:** (800) 257-8787
Address: P.O. Box 8530, Boston, MA 02266
Fund Type: MUN - Municipal - National
Major Rating Factors: Strong performance is the major factor driving the A- (Excellent) TheStreet.com Investment Rating for Nuveen Intmdt Duration Muni Bond A. The fund currently has a performance rating of B+ (Good) based on an average return of 3.09% over the last three years (5.12% taxable equivalent) and 1.66% over the last three months (2.75% taxable equivalent). Factored into the performance evaluation is an expense ratio of 0.69% (low) and a 3.0% front-end load that is levied at the time of purchase.

The fund's risk rating is currently C+ (Fair). Volatility, as measured by standard deviation, is considered average for fixed income funds at 3.15. Another risk factor is the fund's fairly average duration of 5.6 years (i.e. average interest rate risk).

Paul L. Brennan has been running the fund for 9 years and currently receives a manager quality ranking of 53 (0=worst, 99=best). If you desire an average level of risk and strong performance, then this fund is a good option.
Services Offered: Automated phone transactions, payroll deductions, bank draft capabilities, wire transfers and a systematic withdrawal plan.

Data Date	Investment Rating	Net Assets ($Mil)	NAV	Performance Rating/Pts	Total Return Y-T-D	Risk Rating/Pts
3-16	A-	1,064	9.35	B+ / 8.4	1.66%	C+ / 5.9
2015	B+	589	9.26	B+ / 8.4	2.84%	C+ / 5.6
2014	B+	1,111	9.26	C+ / 6.9	7.31%	C / 5.4
2013	B-	643	8.89	C+ / 5.8	-1.78%	C+ / 6.1
2012	B-	485	9.34	C / 4.9	5.79%	C+ / 6.4
2011	B	389	9.14	C+ / 5.8	7.71%	C+ / 6.0

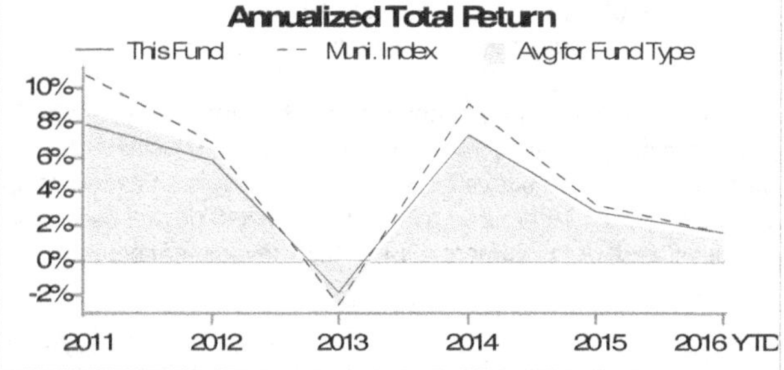

Nuveen Ltd Term Muni A (FLTDX) B+ Good

Fund Family: Nuveen Investor Services **Phone:** (800) 257-8787
Address: P.O. Box 8530, Boston, MA 02266
Fund Type: MUN - Municipal - National
Major Rating Factors: A moderate risk profile coupled with stable earnings characterizes Nuveen Ltd Term Muni A which receives a TheStreet.com Investment Rating of B+ (Good). Volatility, as measured by standard deviation, is considered low for fixed income funds at 1.79. Another risk factor is the fund's below average duration of 3.3 years (i.e. lower interest rate risk). The fund's risk rating is currently B+ (Good).

The fund's performance rating is currently C+ (Fair). It has registered an average return of 1.65% over the last three years (2.73% taxable equivalent) and is up 0.90% over the last three months (1.49% taxable equivalent). Factored into the performance evaluation is an expense ratio of 0.64% (low) and a 2.5% front-end load that is levied at the time of purchase.

Paul L. Brennan has been running the fund for 10 years and currently receives a manager quality ranking of 57 (0=worst, 99=best). If you desire stability with a moderate level of risk then this fund is an excellent option.
Services Offered: Automated phone transactions, payroll deductions, bank draft capabilities, wire transfers and a systematic withdrawal plan.

Data Date	Investment Rating	Net Assets ($Mil)	NAV	Performance Rating/Pts	Total Return Y-T-D	Risk Rating/Pts
3-16	B+	1,197	11.15	C+ / 5.8	0.90%	B+ / 8.7
2015	A	1,168	11.10	C+ / 6.9	1.68%	B+ / 8.7
2014	C+	1,136	11.12	C- / 3.2	3.05%	B+ / 8.6
2013	B+	1,307	11.00	C / 4.9	-0.08%	B+ / 8.6
2012	C	1,362	11.22	D+ / 2.5	2.89%	B+ / 8.3
2011	B-	1,071	11.16	C- / 4.0	6.22%	B / 8.0

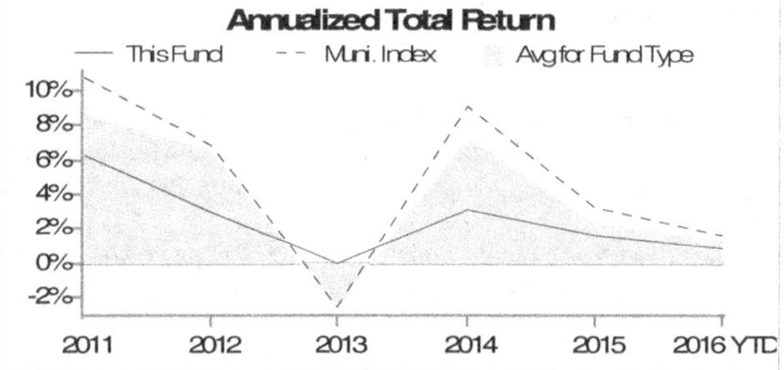

Nuveen Short Dur Hi Yld Muni A (NVHAX) A Excellent

Fund Family: Nuveen Investor Services **Phone:** (800) 257-8787
Address: P.O. Box 8530, Boston, MA 02266
Fund Type: MUH - Municipal - High Yield
Major Rating Factors: Exceptional performance is the major factor driving the A (Excellent) TheStreet.com Investment Rating for Nuveen Short Dur Hi Yld Muni A. The fund currently has a performance rating of A- (Excellent) based on an average return of 4.00% over the last three years (6.62% taxable equivalent) and 1.82% over the last three months (3.01% taxable equivalent). Factored into the performance evaluation is an expense ratio of 0.79% (low) and a 2.5% front-end load that is levied at the time of purchase.

The fund's risk rating is currently C (Fair). Volatility, as measured by standard deviation, is considered average for fixed income funds at 2.94.

John V. Miller has been running the fund for 3 years and currently receives a manager quality ranking of 90 (0=worst, 99=best). If you desire an average level of risk and strong performance, then this fund is a good option.
Services Offered: Automated phone transactions, payroll deductions, bank draft capabilities, wire transfers and a systematic withdrawal plan.

Data Date	Investment Rating	Net Assets ($Mil)	NAV	Performance Rating/Pts	Total Return Y-T-D	Risk Rating/Pts
3-16	A	778	10.20	A- / 9.2	1.82%	C / 5.1
2015	U	780	10.10	U / --	2.81%	U / --
2014	U	575	10.16	U / --	9.76%	U / --
2013	U	269	9.59	U / --	0.00%	U / --

Asset Composition
For: Nuveen Short Dur Hi Yld Muni A

Cash & Cash Equivalent:	2%
Government Bonds:	0%
Municipal Bonds:	96%
Corporate Bonds:	0%
Other:	2%

Old Westbury Fixed Income (OWFIX) C+ Fair

Fund Family: Old Westbury Funds **Phone:** (800) 607-2200
Address: 630 5th Ave., New York, NY 10111
Fund Type: GEI - General - Investment Grade

Major Rating Factors: A moderate risk profile coupled with stable earnings characterizes Old Westbury Fixed Income which receives a TheStreet.com Investment Rating of C+ (Fair). Volatility, as measured by standard deviation, is considered low for fixed income funds at 1.74. Another risk factor is the fund's above average duration of 8.5 years (i.e. higher interest rate risk). The fund's risk rating is currently B+ (Good).

The fund's performance rating is currently C (Fair). It has registered an average return of 0.94% over the last three years and is up 1.93% over the last three months. Factored into the performance evaluation is an expense ratio of 0.74% (low).

David W. Rossmiller has been running the fund for 4 years and currently receives a manager quality ranking of 45 (0=worst, 99=best). If you desire stability with a moderate level of risk then this fund is an excellent option.

Services Offered: Automated phone transactions, payroll deductions, bank draft capabilities, an IRA investment plan, a 401K investment plan and a Keogh investment plan.

Data Date	Investment Rating	Net Assets ($Mil)	NAV	Performance Rating/Pts	Total Return Y-T-D	Risk Rating/Pts
3-16	C+	583	11.29	C / 4.7	1.93%	B+ / 8.4
2015	C+	583	11.11	C / 4.4	0.58%	B+ / 8.4
2014	C-	564	11.19	D / 2.2	1.49%	B+ / 8.6
2013	C	535	11.20	D+ / 2.9	-0.92%	B+ / 8.5
2012	D	484	11.56	D / 2.0	3.19%	B / 7.6
2011	D-	456	11.50	D / 2.1	4.41%	B / 7.7

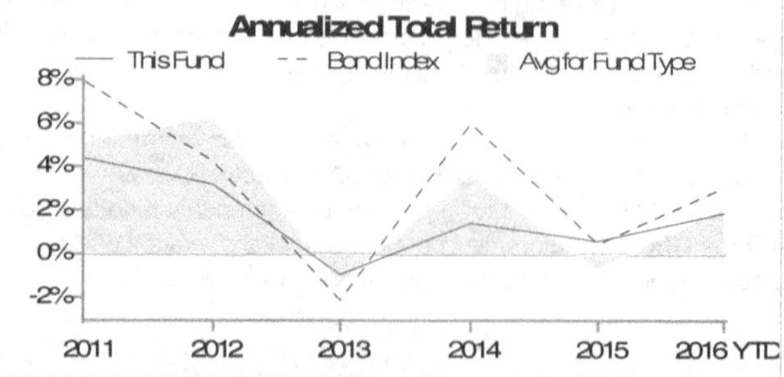

Old Westbury Muni Bond (OWMBX) A+ Excellent

Fund Family: Old Westbury Funds **Phone:** (800) 607-2200
Address: 630 5th Ave., New York, NY 10111
Fund Type: MUN - Municipal - National

Major Rating Factors: Strong performance is the major factor driving the A+ (Excellent) TheStreet.com Investment Rating for Old Westbury Muni Bond. The fund currently has a performance rating of B- (Good) based on an average return of 1.37% over the last three years (2.27% taxable equivalent) and 1.15% over the last three months (1.90% taxable equivalent). Factored into the performance evaluation is an expense ratio of 0.70% (low).

The fund's risk rating is currently B+ (Good). Volatility, as measured by standard deviation, is considered low for fixed income funds at 2.16. Another risk factor is the fund's fairly average duration of 6.3 years (i.e. average interest rate risk).

Bruce A. Whiteford has been running the fund for 18 years and currently receives a manager quality ranking of 36 (0=worst, 99=best). If you desire only a moderate level of risk and strong performance, then this fund is an excellent option.

Services Offered: Automated phone transactions, payroll deductions, bank draft capabilities, a 401K investment plan and a Keogh investment plan.

Data Date	Investment Rating	Net Assets ($Mil)	NAV	Performance Rating/Pts	Total Return Y-T-D	Risk Rating/Pts
3-16	A+	1,507	12.09	B- / 7.1	1.15%	B+ / 8.3
2015	A	1,378	11.99	B- / 7.3	1.84%	B / 8.2
2014	C	1,340	11.94	C- / 3.2	2.61%	B / 8.0
2013	B+	1,199	11.82	C / 5.0	-1.35%	B / 7.8
2012	D-	1,097	12.18	C- / 3.2	2.57%	C+ / 5.7
2011	C-	946	12.17	C / 5.0	6.53%	C / 5.1

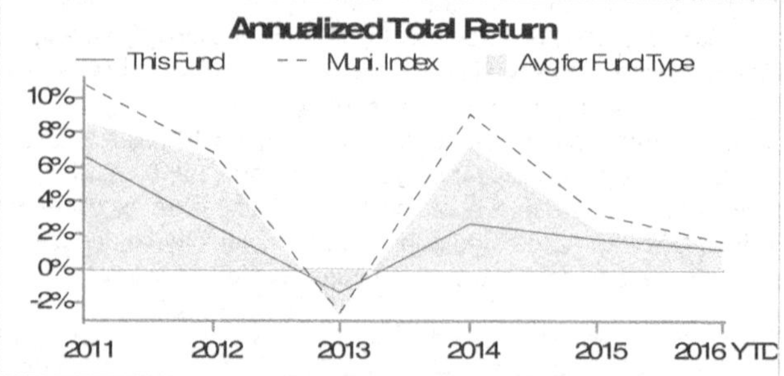

Oppeneheimer Rochester CA Muni A (OPCAX) C Fair

Fund Family: OppenheimerFunds **Phone:** (888) 470-0862
Address: P.O. Box 219534, Denver, CO 80217
Fund Type: MUS - Municipal - Single State

Major Rating Factors: Oppeneheimer Rochester CA Muni A has adopted a very risky asset allocation strategy and currently receives an overall TheStreet.com Investment Rating of C (Fair). Volatility, as measured by standard deviation, is considered above average for fixed income funds at 5.93. Another risk factor is the fund's fairly average duration of 5.8 years (i.e. average interest rate risk). The high level of risk (D, Weak) did however, reward investors with excellent performance.

The fund's performance rating is currently A- (Excellent). It has registered an average return of 4.09% over the last three years (6.77% taxable equivalent) and is up 1.78% over the last three months (2.95% taxable equivalent). Factored into the performance evaluation is an expense ratio of 1.07% (average) and a 4.8% front-end load that is levied at the time of purchase.

Daniel G Loughran has been running the fund for 14 years and currently receives a manager quality ranking of 19 (0=worst, 99=best). If you are comfortable owning a very high risk investment, this fund may be an option.

Services Offered: Automated phone transactions, check writing, payroll deductions, bank draft capabilities, an IRA investment plan, a 401K investment plan, wire transfers and a systematic withdrawal plan.

Data Date	Investment Rating	Net Assets ($Mil)	NAV	Performance Rating/Pts	Total Return Y-T-D	Risk Rating/Pts
3-16	C	889	8.39	A- / 9.0	1.78%	D / 1.7
2015	C	876	8.36	A- / 9.1	3.75%	D- / 1.2
2014	C+	937	8.51	A+ / 9.8	14.78%	E+ / 0.8
2013	C	879	7.85	A- / 9.1	-5.53%	D- / 1.0
2012	B+	1,144	8.84	A+ / 9.9	18.37%	D- / 1.3
2011	C+	970	7.92	A+ / 9.9	13.33%	E- / 0.2

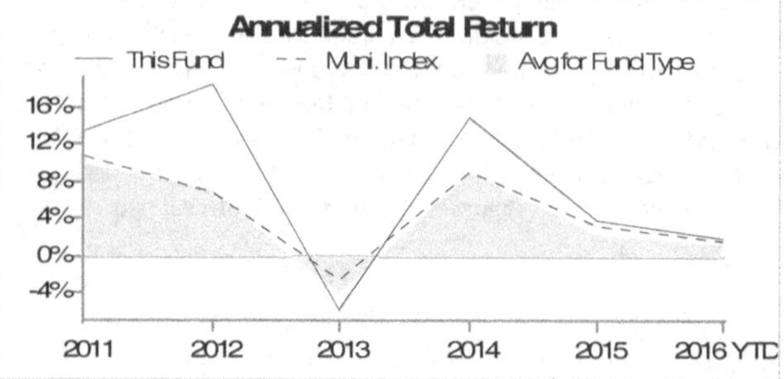

Oppeneheimer Rochester Hi Yld Mun A (ORNAX) C- Fair

Fund Family: OppenheimerFunds **Phone:** (888) 470-0862
Address: P.O. Box 219534, Denver, CO 80217
Fund Type: MUH - Municipal - High Yield

Major Rating Factors: Oppeneheimer Rochester Hi Yld Mun A has adopted a very risky asset allocation strategy and currently receives an overall TheStreet.com Investment Rating of C- (Fair). Volatility, as measured by standard deviation, is considered high for fixed income funds at 7.04. Another risk factor is the fund's above average duration of 8.2 years (i.e. higher interest rate risk). The high level of risk (E, Very Weak) did however, reward investors with excellent performance.

The fund's performance rating is currently A (Excellent). It has registered an average return of 4.44% over the last three years (7.35% taxable equivalent) and is up 2.89% over the last three months (4.79% taxable equivalent). Factored into the performance evaluation is an expense ratio of 0.99% (average) and a 4.8% front-end load that is levied at the time of purchase.

Daniel G Loughran has been running the fund for 15 years and currently receives a manager quality ranking of 11 (0=worst, 99=best). If you are comfortable owning a very high risk investment, this fund may be an option.

Services Offered: Automated phone transactions, check writing, payroll deductions, bank draft capabilities, wire transfers and a systematic withdrawal plan.

Data Date	Investment Rating	Net Assets ($Mil)	NAV	Performance Rating/Pts	Total Return Y-T-D	Risk Rating/Pts
3-16	C-	3,093	7.10	A / 9.5	2.89%	E / 0.5
2015	C-	3,003	7.02	A / 9.4	4.79%	E / 0.4
2014	C+	3,296	7.16	A+ / 9.8	16.13%	E / 0.4
2013	C-	3,296	6.61	B+ / 8.4	-6.63%	E / 0.4
2012	B	4,393	7.63	A+ / 9.9	18.85%	E+ / 0.9
2011	C+	3,739	6.87	A+ / 9.9	11.72%	E- / 0.1

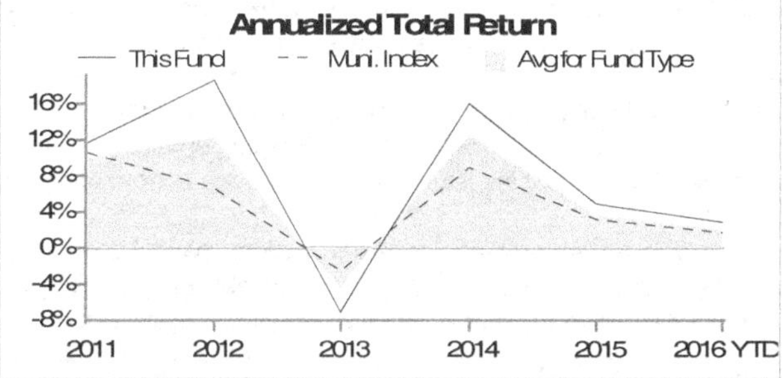

Oppeneheimer Rochester PA Muni A (OPATX) D+ Weak

Fund Family: OppenheimerFunds **Phone:** (888) 470-0862
Address: P.O. Box 219534, Denver, CO 80217
Fund Type: MUS - Municipal - Single State

Major Rating Factors: Oppeneheimer Rochester PA Muni A has adopted a very risky asset allocation strategy and currently receives an overall TheStreet.com Investment Rating of D+ (Weak). Volatility, as measured by standard deviation, is considered above average for fixed income funds at 6.51. Another risk factor is the fund's fairly average duration of 6.3 years (i.e. average interest rate risk). Unfortunately, the high level of risk (D-, Weak) has only provided investors with average performance.

The fund's performance rating is currently C+ (Fair). It has registered an average return of 2.50% over the last three years (4.14% taxable equivalent) and is up 0.46% over the last three months (0.76% taxable equivalent). Factored into the performance evaluation is an expense ratio of 0.95% (average) and a 4.8% front-end load that is levied at the time of purchase.

Daniel G Loughran has been running the fund for 17 years and currently receives a manager quality ranking of 7 (0=worst, 99=best). If you are comfortable owning a very high risk investment, then this fund may be an option.

Services Offered: Automated phone transactions, check writing, payroll deductions, bank draft capabilities, wire transfers and a systematic withdrawal plan.

Data Date	Investment Rating	Net Assets ($Mil)	NAV	Performance Rating/Pts	Total Return Y-T-D	Risk Rating/Pts
3-16	D+	533	10.39	C+ / 6.1	0.46%	D- / 1.0
2015	C-	537	10.50	B / 8.0	3.95%	E+ / 0.7
2014	C	592	10.70	A- / 9.1	15.35%	E / 0.5
2013	E	596	9.83	D / 1.9	-9.35%	E+ / 0.6
2012	B	818	11.52	A / 9.5	12.51%	D- / 1.5
2011	C+	735	10.83	A+ / 9.9	11.31%	E / 0.5

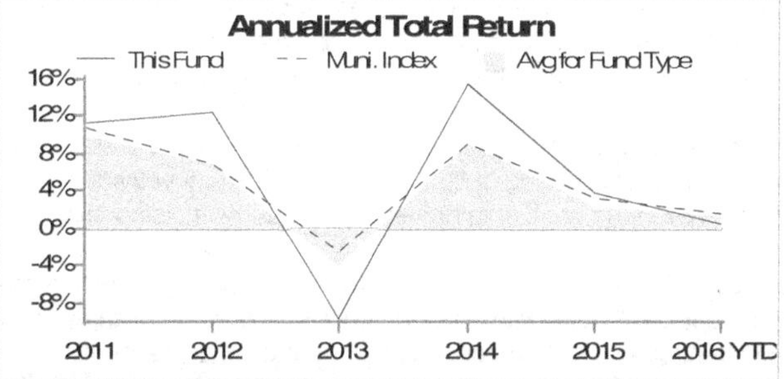

Oppenheimer Core Bond A (OPIGX) C Fair

Fund Family: OppenheimerFunds **Phone:** (888) 470-0862
Address: P.O. Box 219534, Denver, CO 80217
Fund Type: GEI - General - Investment Grade

Major Rating Factors: Middle of the road best describes Oppenheimer Core Bond A whose TheStreet.com Investment Rating is currently a C (Fair). The fund has a performance rating of C (Fair) based on an average return of 2.85% over the last three years and 2.40% over the last three months. Factored into the performance evaluation is an expense ratio of 0.98% (average) and a 4.8% front-end load that is levied at the time of purchase.

The fund's risk rating is currently C+ (Fair). Volatility, as measured by standard deviation, is considered average for fixed income funds at 3.16. Another risk factor is the fund's fairly average duration of 5.6 years (i.e. average interest rate risk).

Krishna K. Memani has been running the fund for 7 years and currently receives a manager quality ranking of 79 (0=worst, 99=best). If you desire an average level of risk, then this fund may be an option.

Services Offered: Automated phone transactions, check writing, payroll deductions, an IRA investment plan, a 401K investment plan, wire transfers and a systematic withdrawal plan.

Data Date	Investment Rating	Net Assets ($Mil)	NAV	Performance Rating/Pts	Total Return Y-T-D	Risk Rating/Pts
3-16	C	563	6.86	C / 5.5	2.40%	C+ / 5.9
2015	C	508	6.74	C / 5.3	0.51%	C+ / 5.7
2014	B-	479	6.92	C+ / 5.7	6.76%	C+ / 6.0
2013	B+	363	6.73	C+ / 6.1	0.10%	C+ / 6.5
2012	A-	453	7.00	C+ / 6.0	9.72%	C+ / 6.6
2011	E	405	6.63	C- / 3.7	7.44%	D+ / 2.6

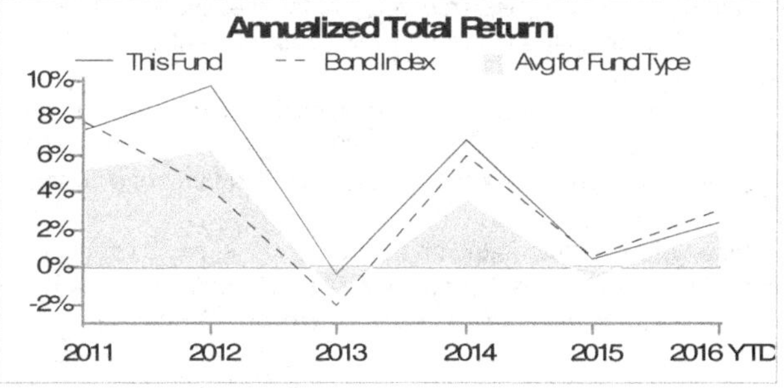

Oppenheimer Global Strategic Inc A (OPSIX) D- Weak

Fund Family: OppenheimerFunds **Phone:** (888) 470-0862
Address: P.O. Box 219534, Denver, CO 80217
Fund Type: GES - General - Short & Inter. Term

Major Rating Factors: Very poor performance is the major factor driving the D- (Weak) TheStreet.com Investment Rating for Oppenheimer Global Strategic Inc A. The fund currently has a performance rating of E+ (Very Weak) based on an average return of 0.06% over the last three years and 1.48% over the last three months. Factored into the performance evaluation is an expense ratio of 1.04% (average) and a 4.8% front-end load that is levied at the time of purchase.

The fund's risk rating is currently C- (Fair). Volatility, as measured by standard deviation, is considered average for fixed income funds at 4.32. Another risk factor is the fund's below average duration of 4.2 years (i.e. lower interest rate risk).

Krishna K. Memani has been running the fund for 7 years and currently receives a manager quality ranking of 11 (0=worst, 99=best). This fund offers an average level of risk, but investors looking for strong performance will be frustrated.

Services Offered: Automated phone transactions, payroll deductions, bank draft capabilities, an IRA investment plan, a 401K investment plan, a Keogh investment plan, wire transfers and a systematic withdrawal plan.

Data Date	Investment Rating	Net Assets ($Mil)	NAV	Performance Rating/Pts	Total Return Y-T-D	Risk Rating/Pts
3-16	D-	3,710	3.81	E+ / 0.7	1.48%	C- / 3.4
2015	D-	3,805	3.79	D- / 1.2	-2.35%	D+ / 2.8
2014	D-	4,528	4.05	C / 4.3	2.63%	C- / 3.3
2013	D-	5,326	4.13	C / 4.5	-0.28%	D+ / 2.3
2012	C-	6,398	4.36	B- / 7.1	13.48%	D / 1.8
2011	E+	5,798	4.07	C / 4.8	0.86%	D / 2.1

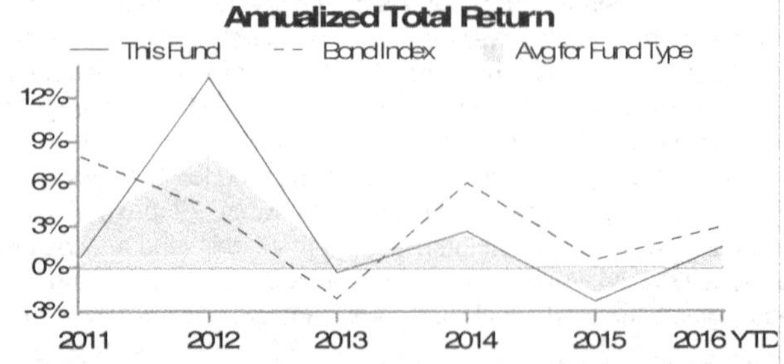

Oppenheimer Intl Bond A (OIBAX) E+ Very Weak

Fund Family: OppenheimerFunds **Phone:** (888) 470-0862
Address: P.O. Box 219534, Denver, CO 80217
Fund Type: GL - Global

Major Rating Factors: Oppenheimer Intl Bond A has adopted a risky asset allocation strategy and currently receives an overall TheStreet.com Investment Rating of E+ (Very Weak). Volatility, as measured by standard deviation, is considered above average for fixed income funds at 5.40. Unfortunately, the high level of risk (D+, Weak) failed to pay off as investors endured poor performance.

The fund's performance rating is currently E+ (Very Weak). It has registered an average return of -1.20% over the last three years and is up 4.04% over the last three months. Factored into the performance evaluation is an expense ratio of 1.02% (average) and a 4.8% front-end load that is levied at the time of purchase.

Hemant Baijal has been running the fund for 3 years and currently receives a manager quality ranking of 25 (0=worst, 99=best). If you can tolerate high levels of risk in the hope of improved future returns, holding this fund may be an option.

Services Offered: Automated phone transactions, payroll deductions, bank draft capabilities, an IRA investment plan, a 401K investment plan, a Keogh investment plan, wire transfers and a systematic withdrawal plan.

Data Date	Investment Rating	Net Assets ($Mil)	NAV	Performance Rating/Pts	Total Return Y-T-D	Risk Rating/Pts
3-16	E+	1,725	5.70	E+ / 0.6	4.04%	D+ / 2.3
2015	D-	1,797	5.52	E / 0.4	-3.72%	D+ / 2.7
2014	E	2,838	5.92	D- / 1.3	0.32%	D- / 1.5
2013	E-	4,379	6.08	E+ / 0.9	-3.90%	E+ / 0.9
2012	E-	5,869	6.58	C- / 3.5	10.77%	E / 0.4
2011	E-	6,130	6.21	D / 2.1	-0.28%	D- / 1.0

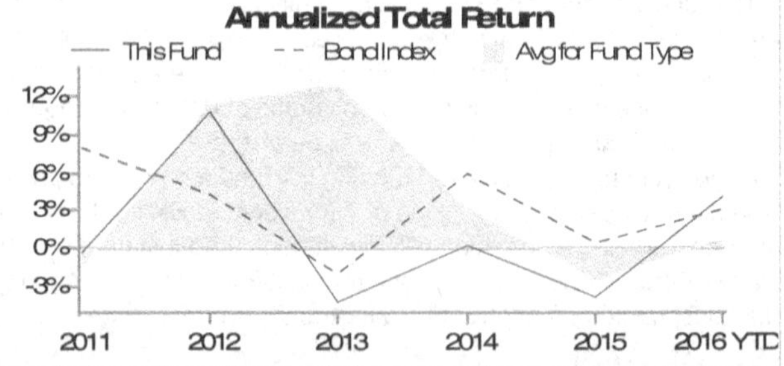

Oppenheimer Limited Term Govt A (OPGVX) C Fair

Fund Family: OppenheimerFunds **Phone:** (888) 470-0862
Address: P.O. Box 219534, Denver, CO 80217
Fund Type: USS - US Government - Short & Inter. Term

Major Rating Factors: Disappointing performance is the major factor driving the C (Fair) TheStreet.com Investment Rating for Oppenheimer Limited Term Govt A. The fund currently has a performance rating of D+ (Weak) based on an average return of 0.64% over the last three years and 0.77% over the last three months. Factored into the performance evaluation is an expense ratio of 0.92% (average) and a 2.3% front-end load that is levied at the time of purchase.

The fund's risk rating is currently A (Excellent). Volatility, as measured by standard deviation, is considered very low for fixed income funds at 0.94. Another risk factor is the fund's very low average duration of 2.2 years (i.e. low interest rate risk).

Peter A. Strzalkowski has been running the fund for 7 years and currently receives a manager quality ranking of 63 (0=worst, 99=best). This fund offers only a moderate level of risk but investors looking for strong performance are still waiting.

Services Offered: Automated phone transactions, payroll deductions, bank draft capabilities, an IRA investment plan, a 401K investment plan, a Keogh investment plan, wire transfers and a systematic withdrawal plan.

Data Date	Investment Rating	Net Assets ($Mil)	NAV	Performance Rating/Pts	Total Return Y-T-D	Risk Rating/Pts
3-16	C	562	4.48	D+ / 2.5	0.77%	A / 9.4
2015	C	546	4.46	D+ / 2.8	0.43%	A / 9.3
2014	C-	585	9.04	D- / 1.5	1.17%	A / 9.4
2013	C-	671	9.15	D- / 1.5	0.20%	A / 9.5
2012	C-	816	9.33	D- / 1.1	2.54%	A / 9.4
2011	C	866	9.31	D / 1.9	1.55%	A- / 9.2

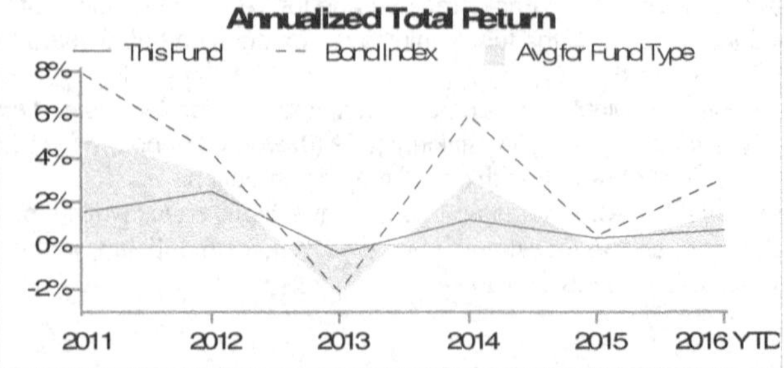

Oppenheimer Limited-Term Bond A (OUSGX) C Fair

Fund Family: OppenheimerFunds **Phone:** (888) 470-0862
Address: P.O. Box 219534, Denver, CO 80217
Fund Type: USS - US Government - Short & Inter. Term
Major Rating Factors: A moderate risk profile coupled with stable earnings characterizes Oppenheimer Limited-Term Bond A which receives a TheStreet.com Investment Rating of C (Fair). Volatility, as measured by standard deviation, is considered very low for fixed income funds at 1.28. Another risk factor is the fund's very low average duration of 2.1 years (i.e. low interest rate risk). The fund's risk rating is currently A- (Excellent).

The fund's performance rating is currently C- (Fair). It has registered an average return of 1.12% over the last three years and is up 0.69% over the last three months. Factored into the performance evaluation is an expense ratio of 0.91% (average) and a 2.3% front-end load that is levied at the time of purchase.

Peter A. Strzalkowski has been running the fund for 7 years and currently receives a manager quality ranking of 84 (0=worst, 99=best). If you desire stability with a moderate level of risk then this fund is an excellent option.
Services Offered: Automated phone transactions, payroll deductions, bank draft capabilities, an IRA investment plan, a 401K investment plan, a Keogh investment plan and a systematic withdrawal plan.

Data Date	Investment Rating	Net Assets ($Mil)	NAV	Performance Rating/Pts	Total Return Y-T-D	Risk Rating/Pts
3-16	C	716	4.54	C- / 3.2	0.69%	A- / 9.0
2015	C+	713	4.53	C- / 3.7	0.45%	A- / 9.0
2014	C-	705	9.24	D / 2.2	1.74%	B+ / 8.7
2013	A-	613	9.37	C / 5.0	0.65%	B+ / 8.5
2012	D	761	9.56	D+ / 2.5	3.89%	B- / 7.0
2011	D+	739	9.63	C- / 3.4	7.47%	C+ / 6.7

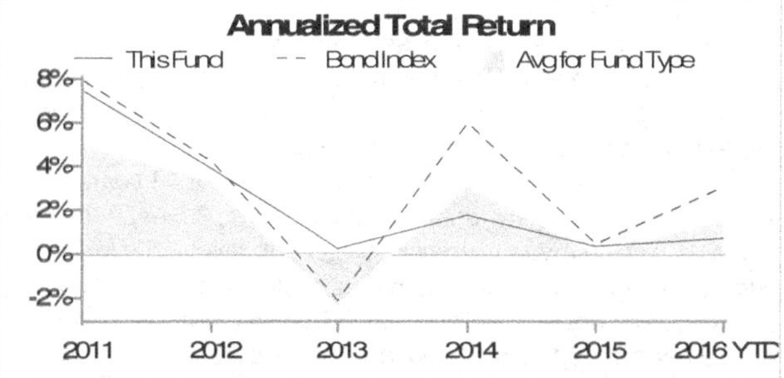

Oppenheimer Ltd Term NY Muni A (LTNYX) D- Weak

Fund Family: OppenheimerFunds **Phone:** (888) 470-0862
Address: P.O. Box 219534, Denver, CO 80217
Fund Type: MUS - Municipal - Single State
Major Rating Factors: Disappointing performance is the major factor driving the D- (Weak) TheStreet.com Investment Rating for Oppenheimer Ltd Term NY Muni A. The fund currently has a performance rating of D- (Weak) based on an average return of -0.29% over the last three years and 0.65% over the last three months (1.08% taxable equivalent). Factored into the performance evaluation is an expense ratio of 0.84% (low) and a 2.3% front-end load that is levied at the time of purchase.

The fund's risk rating is currently C- (Fair). Volatility, as measured by standard deviation, is considered average for fixed income funds at 4.44. Another risk factor is the fund's very low average duration of 3.0 years (i.e. low interest rate risk).

Daniel G Loughran has been running the fund for 17 years and currently receives a manager quality ranking of 6 (0=worst, 99=best). This fund offers an average level of risk, but investors looking for strong performance will be frustrated.
Services Offered: Automated phone transactions, payroll deductions, bank draft capabilities and a systematic withdrawal plan.

Data Date	Investment Rating	Net Assets ($Mil)	NAV	Performance Rating/Pts	Total Return Y-T-D	Risk Rating/Pts
3-16	D-	1,818	3.00	D- / 1.0	0.65%	C- / 3.3
2015	D	1,855	3.01	D / 1.9	-1.01%	C- / 3.1
2014	D	2,344	3.16	C / 4.8	7.16%	C- / 3.8
2013	D-	2,792	3.06	E+ / 0.9	-6.29%	C / 5.3
2012	A-	3,803	3.39	C+ / 5.7	6.13%	C+ / 6.8
2011	A+	3,250	3.32	B- / 7.5	7.76%	C / 5.5

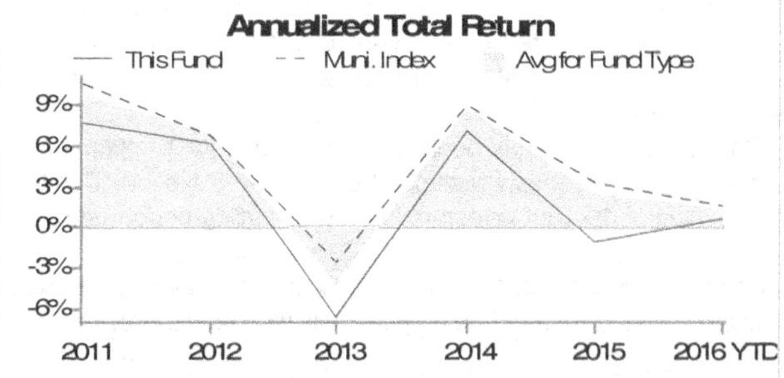

Oppenheimer Rochester AMT-Fr NY M A (OPNYX) D Weak

Fund Family: OppenheimerFunds **Phone:** (888) 470-0862
Address: P.O. Box 219534, Denver, CO 80217
Fund Type: MUS - Municipal - Single State
Major Rating Factors: Oppenheimer Rochester AMT-Fr NY M A has adopted a very risky asset allocation strategy and currently receives an overall TheStreet.com Investment Rating of D (Weak). Volatility, as measured by standard deviation, is considered high for fixed income funds at 6.78. Another risk factor is the fund's above average duration of 9.3 years (i.e. higher interest rate risk). Unfortunately, the high level of risk (E+, Very Weak) has only provided investors with average performance.

The fund's performance rating is currently C+ (Fair). It has registered an average return of 2.12% over the last three years (3.51% taxable equivalent) and is up 1.43% over the last three months (2.37% taxable equivalent). Factored into the performance evaluation is an expense ratio of 0.96% (average) and a 4.8% front-end load that is levied at the time of purchase.

Daniel G Loughran has been running the fund for 14 years and currently receives a manager quality ranking of 5 (0=worst, 99=best). If you are comfortable owning a very high risk investment, then this fund may be an option.
Services Offered: Automated phone transactions, payroll deductions, bank draft capabilities, wire transfers and a systematic withdrawal plan.

Data Date	Investment Rating	Net Assets ($Mil)	NAV	Performance Rating/Pts	Total Return Y-T-D	Risk Rating/Pts
3-16	D	951	11.11	C+ / 6.3	1.43%	E+ / 0.7
2015	C-	936	11.10	B / 7.6	4.18%	E+ / 0.6
2014	C-	983	11.24	B+ / 8.8	14.21%	E / 0.5
2013	E	963	10.42	D / 1.8	-10.67%	E+ / 0.6
2012	B	1,199	12.33	A+ / 9.6	13.66%	D- / 1.3
2011	C+	1,013	11.47	A+ / 9.9	13.09%	E / 0.3

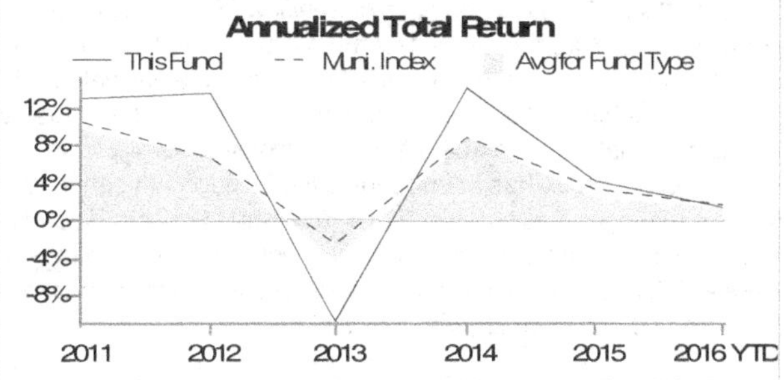

Oppenheimer Rochester AMT-Free Muni (OPTAX) C Fair

Fund Family: OppenheimerFunds **Phone:** (888) 470-0862
Address: P.O. Box 219534, Denver, CO 80217
Fund Type: MUN - Municipal - National
Major Rating Factors: Oppenheimer Rochester AMT-Free Muni has adopted a very risky asset allocation strategy and currently receives an overall TheStreet.com Investment Rating of C (Fair). Volatility, as measured by standard deviation, is considered above average for fixed income funds at 6.23. Another risk factor is the fund's fairly average duration of 6.9 years (i.e. average interest rate risk). The high level of risk (D-, Weak) did however, reward investors with excellent performance.

The fund's performance rating is currently A (Excellent). It has registered an average return of 4.70% over the last three years (7.78% taxable equivalent) and is up 2.11% over the last three months (3.49% taxable equivalent). Factored into the performance evaluation is an expense ratio of 0.98% (average) and a 4.8% front-end load that is levied at the time of purchase.

Daniel G Loughran has been running the fund for 14 years and currently receives a manager quality ranking of 23 (0=worst, 99=best). If you are comfortable owning a very high risk investment, this fund may be an option.
Services Offered: Automated phone transactions, check writing, payroll deductions, bank draft capabilities, an IRA investment plan, a 401K investment plan, wire transfers and a systematic withdrawal plan.

Data Date	Investment Rating	Net Assets ($Mil)	NAV	Performance Rating/Pts	Total Return Y-T-D	Risk Rating/Pts
3-16	C	1,309	6.98	A / 9.5	2.11%	D- / 1.3
2015	C	1,273	6.94	A / 9.5	5.19%	E+ / 0.8
2014	C+	1,319	7.01	A+ / 9.8	15.64%	E+ / 0.6
2013	C	1,332	6.43	A / 9.3	-6.68%	E+ / 0.6
2012	B	1,924	7.29	A+ / 9.9	18.96%	E+ / 0.9
2011	C+	1,591	6.49	A+ / 9.9	16.40%	E- / 0.2

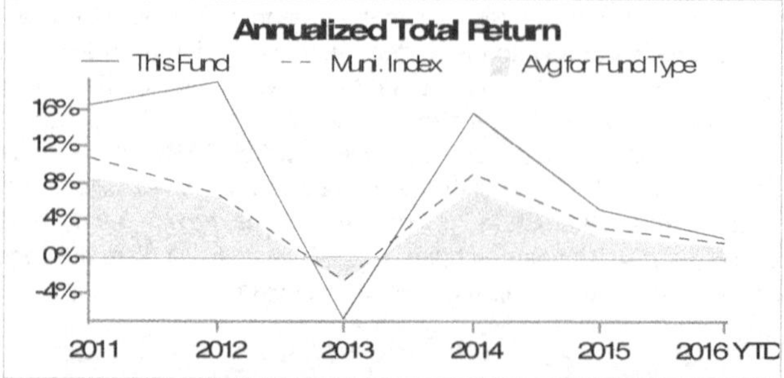

Oppenheimer Rochester Ltd Term M A (OPITX) D Weak

Fund Family: OppenheimerFunds **Phone:** (888) 470-0862
Address: P.O. Box 219534, Denver, CO 80217
Fund Type: MUN - Municipal - National
Major Rating Factors: Disappointing performance is the major factor driving the D (Weak) TheStreet.com Investment Rating for Oppenheimer Rochester Ltd Term M A. The fund currently has a performance rating of D- (Weak) based on an average return of 0.27% over the last three years (0.45% taxable equivalent) and 0.81% over the last three months (1.34% taxable equivalent). Factored into the performance evaluation is an expense ratio of 0.92% (average) and a 2.3% front-end load that is levied at the time of purchase.

The fund's risk rating is currently C- (Fair). Volatility, as measured by standard deviation, is considered average for fixed income funds at 3.86. Another risk factor is the fund's very low average duration of 2.6 years (i.e. low interest rate risk).

Daniel G Loughran has been running the fund for 14 years and currently receives a manager quality ranking of 8 (0=worst, 99=best). This fund offers an average level of risk, but investors looking for strong performance will be frustrated.
Services Offered: Automated phone transactions, payroll deductions, bank draft capabilities, wire transfers and a systematic withdrawal plan.

Data Date	Investment Rating	Net Assets ($Mil)	NAV	Performance Rating/Pts	Total Return Y-T-D	Risk Rating/Pts
3-16	D	1,163	4.50	D- / 1.5	0.81%	C- / 4.2
2015	D	1,212	4.51	D+ / 2.4	-1.71%	C- / 4.0
2014	B-	1,794	14.34	C+ / 6.6	7.20%	C / 4.9
2013	C	2,430	13.92	C / 4.7	-4.08%	C+ / 5.8
2012	A+	3,477	15.11	B- / 7.0	7.47%	C+ / 6.8
2011	A+	2,557	14.67	B / 8.2	8.52%	C / 5.4

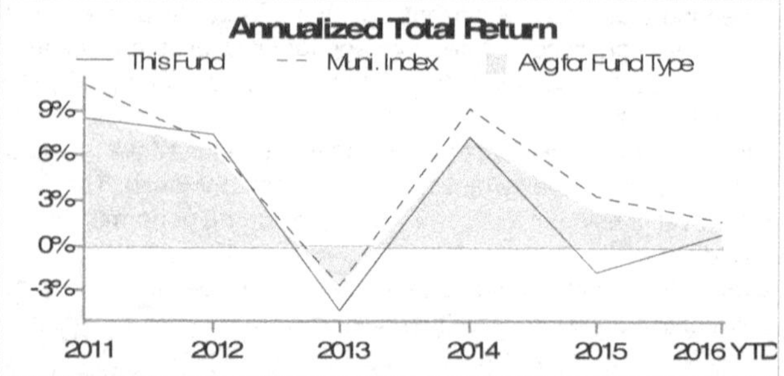

Oppenheimer Rochester Muni A (RMUNX) D Weak

Fund Family: OppenheimerFunds **Phone:** (888) 470-0862
Address: P.O. Box 219534, Denver, CO 80217
Fund Type: MUS - Municipal - Single State
Major Rating Factors: Oppenheimer Rochester Muni A has adopted a very risky asset allocation strategy and currently receives an overall TheStreet.com Investment Rating of D (Weak). Volatility, as measured by standard deviation, is considered high for fixed income funds at 7.16. Another risk factor is the fund's above average duration of 7.4 years (i.e. higher interest rate risk). Unfortunately, the high level of risk (E+, Very Weak) has only provided investors with average performance.

The fund's performance rating is currently C (Fair). It has registered an average return of 1.46% over the last three years (2.42% taxable equivalent) and is up 1.93% over the last three months (3.20% taxable equivalent). Factored into the performance evaluation is an expense ratio of 0.97% (average) and a 4.8% front-end load that is levied at the time of purchase.

Daniel G Loughran has been running the fund for 17 years and currently receives a manager quality ranking of 4 (0=worst, 99=best). If you are comfortable owning a very high risk investment, then this fund may be an option.
Services Offered: Automated phone transactions, payroll deductions, bank draft capabilities and a systematic withdrawal plan.

Data Date	Investment Rating	Net Assets ($Mil)	NAV	Performance Rating/Pts	Total Return Y-T-D	Risk Rating/Pts
3-16	D	4,506	14.72	C / 4.3	1.93%	E+ / 0.6
2015	D	4,461	14.68	C / 5.2	1.95%	E / 0.4
2014	C-	4,988	15.35	B+ / 8.8	14.44%	E / 0.5
2013	E-	4,957	14.29	E / 0.4	-10.87%	E+ / 0.6
2012	B	6,731	17.02	A / 9.5	12.94%	D / 1.6
2011	C+	6,117	15.98	A+ / 9.9	11.52%	E / 0.4

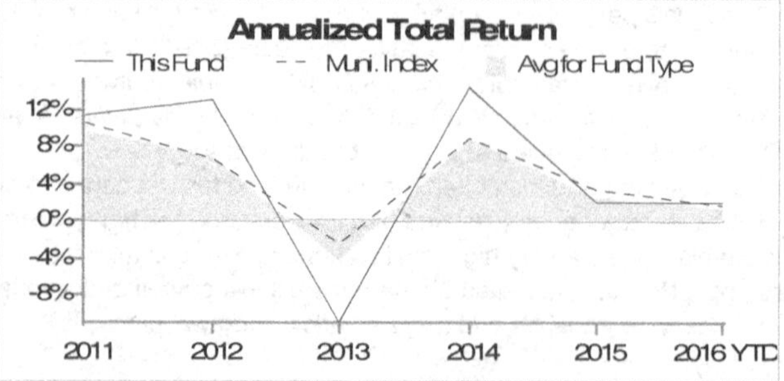

Oppenheimer Sen-Floating Rate A (OOSAX) D+ Weak

Fund Family: OppenheimerFunds **Phone:** (888) 470-0862
Address: P.O. Box 219534, Denver, CO 80217
Fund Type: LP - Loan Participation

Major Rating Factors: Disappointing performance is the major factor driving the D+ (Weak) TheStreet.com Investment Rating for Oppenheimer Sen-Floating Rate A. The fund currently has a performance rating of D- (Weak) based on an average return of 1.11% over the last three years and 0.97% over the last three months. Factored into the performance evaluation is an expense ratio of 1.08% (average) and a 3.5% front-end load that is levied at the time of purchase.

The fund's risk rating is currently C+ (Fair). Volatility, as measured by standard deviation, is considered average for fixed income funds at 2.90. Another risk factor is the fund's very low average duration of 0.2 years (i.e. low interest rate risk).

Joseph J. Welsh has been running the fund for 17 years and currently receives a manager quality ranking of 77 (0=worst, 99=best). This fund offers an average level of risk, but investors looking for strong performance will be frustrated.

Services Offered: Automated phone transactions, payroll deductions, bank draft capabilities, an IRA investment plan, a Keogh investment plan, wire transfers and a systematic withdrawal plan.

Data Date	Investment Rating	Net Assets ($Mil)	NAV	Performance Rating/Pts	Total Return Y-T-D	Risk Rating/Pts
3-16	D+	3,882	7.58	D- / 1.4	0.97%	C+ / 6.9
2015	C-	4,237	7.60	D+ / 2.6	-2.06%	B- / 7.0
2014	B	5,602	8.11	C / 4.4	0.55%	B+ / 8.4
2013	A	7,097	8.43	B / 7.6	6.41%	C+ / 5.7
2012	D-	3,055	8.30	C / 4.8	8.44%	C- / 3.2
2011	C+	2,457	8.06	B / 8.1	2.37%	D / 2.2

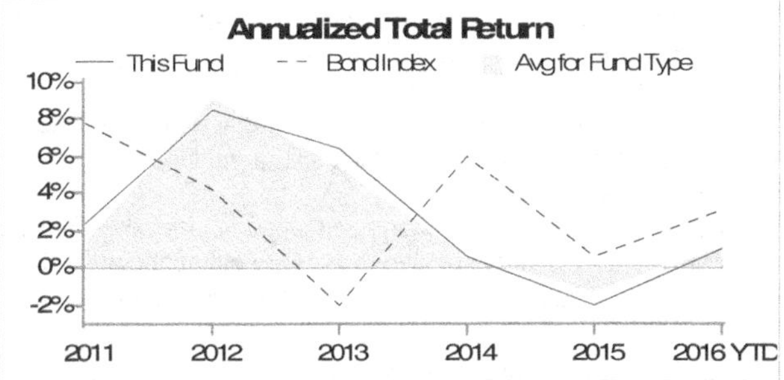

Opportunistic Income A (ENIAX) B+ Good

Fund Family: SEI Financial Management Corp **Phone:** (800) 342-5734
Address: One Freedom Valley Drive, Oaks, PA 19456
Fund Type: GL - Global

Major Rating Factors: A moderate risk profile coupled with stable earnings characterizes Opportunistic Income A which receives a TheStreet.com Investment Rating of B+ (Good). Volatility, as measured by standard deviation, is considered very low for fixed income funds at 1.11. Another risk factor is the fund's very low average duration of 2.9 years (i.e. low interest rate risk). The fund's risk rating is currently A- (Excellent).

The fund's performance rating is currently C (Fair). It has registered an average return of 1.68% over the last three years and is up 0.50% over the last three months. Factored into the performance evaluation is an expense ratio of 0.52% (very low).

Timothy E. Smith has been running the fund for 9 years and currently receives a manager quality ranking of 94 (0=worst, 99=best). If you desire stability with a moderate level of risk then this fund is an excellent option.

Services Offered: Automated phone transactions, bank draft capabilities, an IRA investment plan, a 401K investment plan and wire transfers.

Data Date	Investment Rating	Net Assets ($Mil)	NAV	Performance Rating/Pts	Total Return Y-T-D	Risk Rating/Pts
3-16	B+	2,143	8.09	C / 5.3	0.50%	A- / 9.2
2015	A+	2,169	8.05	C+ / 6.9	0.91%	A- / 9.2
2014	A-	1,967	8.18	C / 4.7	2.07%	A- / 9.0

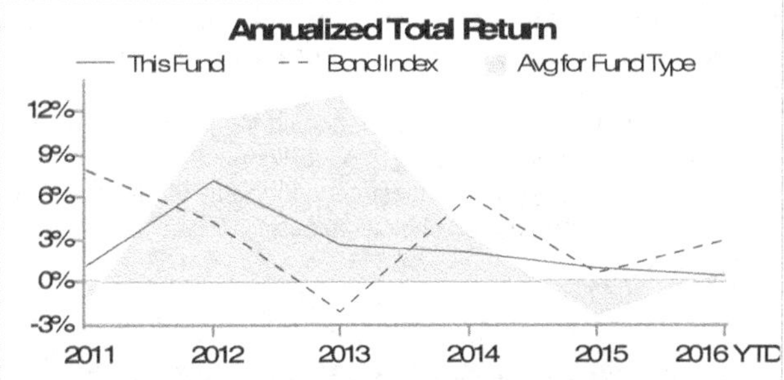

Osterweis Strategic Income (OSTIX) D+ Weak

Fund Family: Osterweis Funds **Phone:** (800) 700-3316
Address: One Maritime Plaza, San Francisco, CA 94111
Fund Type: GES - General - Short & Inter. Term

Major Rating Factors: Osterweis Strategic Income receives a TheStreet.com Investment Rating of D+ (Weak). The fund has a performance rating of C- (Fair) based on an average return of 1.45% over the last three years and 0.47% over the last three months. Factored into the performance evaluation is an expense ratio of 0.82% (low).

The fund's risk rating is currently C (Fair). Volatility, as measured by standard deviation, is considered average for fixed income funds at 3.39. Another risk factor is the fund's very low average duration of 1.2 years (i.e. low interest rate risk).

Carl P. Kaufman has been running the fund for 14 years and currently receives a manager quality ranking of 89 (0=worst, 99=best). If you desire an average level of risk, then this fund may be an option.

Services Offered: Automated phone transactions, payroll deductions, bank draft capabilities, an IRA investment plan, a 401K investment plan, a Keogh investment plan, wire transfers and a systematic withdrawal plan.

Data Date	Investment Rating	Net Assets ($Mil)	NAV	Performance Rating/Pts	Total Return Y-T-D	Risk Rating/Pts
3-16	D+	4,772	10.57	C- / 4.0	0.47%	C / 5.2
2015	C	5,252	10.66	C+ / 6.4	-0.93%	C / 5.0
2014	A	6,269	11.39	C+ / 5.9	1.26%	B / 7.7
2013	A+	5,664	11.84	B+ / 8.4	6.58%	B / 7.6
2012	C	2,749	11.65	C / 5.0	8.55%	C / 5.3
2011	C+	1,952	11.33	C+ / 5.9	4.06%	C / 5.4

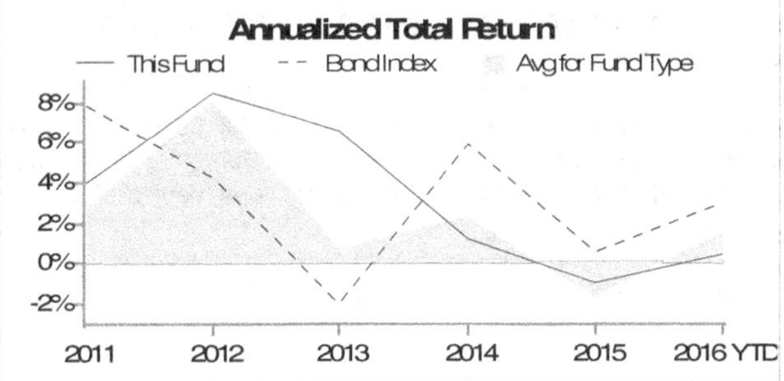

Payden Low Duration Investor (PYSBX) C+ Fair

Fund Family: Payden & Rygel Funds **Phone:** (888) 409-8007
Address: P.O. Box 1611, Milwaukee, WI 53201
Fund Type: GEI - General - Investment Grade

Major Rating Factors: A moderate risk profile coupled with stable earnings characterizes Payden Low Duration Investor which receives a TheStreet.com Investment Rating of C+ (Fair). Volatility, as measured by standard deviation, is considered very low for fixed income funds at 0.83. Another risk factor is the fund's very low average duration of 1.4 years (i.e. low interest rate risk). The fund's risk rating is currently A (Excellent).

The fund's performance rating is currently C- (Fair). It has registered an average return of 0.69% over the last three years and is up 0.78% over the last three months. Factored into the performance evaluation is an expense ratio of 0.55% (very low).

David Ballantine currently receives a manager quality ranking of 76 (0=worst, 99=best). If you desire stability with a moderate level of risk then this fund is an excellent option.

Services Offered: Automated phone transactions, payroll deductions, bank draft capabilities, an IRA investment plan, a 401K investment plan, a Keogh investment plan, wire transfers and a systematic withdrawal plan.

Data Date	Investment Rating	Net Assets ($Mil)	NAV	Performance Rating/Pts	Total Return Y-T-D	Risk Rating/Pts
3-16	C+	835	10.05	C- / 3.8	0.78%	A / 9.5
2015	B	910	10.00	C / 4.7	0.43%	A / 9.5
2014	C+	939	10.07	D+ / 2.5	0.71%	A / 9.3
2013	C+	960	10.15	C- / 3.0	0.56%	A- / 9.1
2012	C	585	10.24	D- / 1.5	4.27%	A- / 9.2
2011	C	519	10.00	D / 1.8	1.10%	A / 9.4

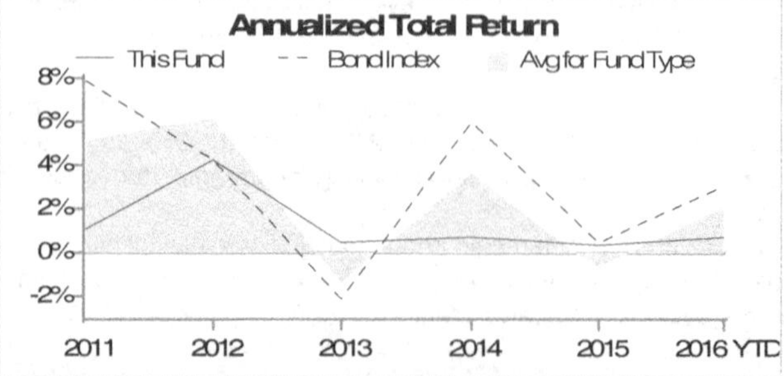

PIMCO Fixed Income SHares C (FXICX) D Weak

Fund Family: Allianz Global Investors **Phone:** (800) 988-8380
Address: 1345 Avenue of the Americas, New York, NY 10105
Fund Type: GEI - General - Investment Grade

Major Rating Factors: PIMCO Fixed Income SHares C has adopted a risky asset allocation strategy and currently receives an overall TheStreet.com Investment Rating of D (Weak). Volatility, as measured by standard deviation, is considered above average for fixed income funds at 4.82. Unfortunately, the high level of risk (D+, Weak) has only provided investors with average performance.

The fund's performance rating is currently C- (Fair). It has registered an average return of 1.31% over the last three years but is down -0.95% over the last three months. Factored into the performance evaluation is an expense ratio of 0.01% (very low).

Curtis A. Mewbourne, II has been running the fund for 7 years and currently receives a manager quality ranking of 43 (0=worst, 99=best). If you are comfortable owning a high risk investment, then this fund may be an option.

Services Offered: Automated phone transactions, bank draft capabilities and wire transfers.

Data Date	Investment Rating	Net Assets ($Mil)	NAV	Performance Rating/Pts	Total Return Y-T-D	Risk Rating/Pts
3-16	D	1,522	10.22	C- / 3.9	-0.95%	D+ / 2.9
2015	C-	1,554	10.42	B- / 7.2	1.73%	C- / 3.2
2014	C	1,971	11.43	B- / 7.4	2.78%	D+ / 2.8
2013	C+	3,134	12.19	B+ / 8.8	1.67%	D / 1.6

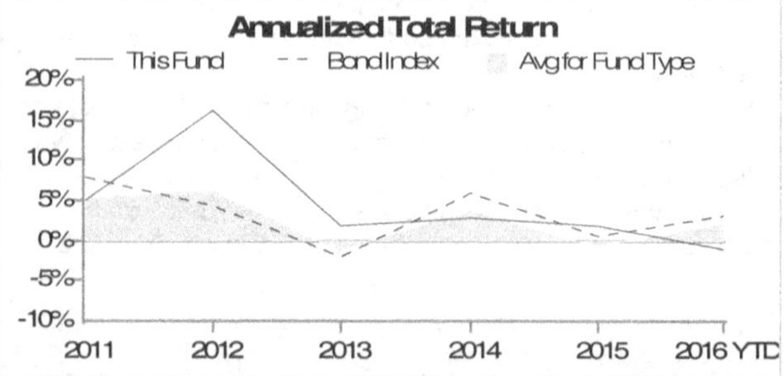

PIMCO Fixed Income SHares M (FXIMX) C- Fair

Fund Family: Allianz Global Investors **Phone:** (800) 988-8380
Address: 1345 Avenue of the Americas, New York, NY 10105
Fund Type: GEI - General - Investment Grade

Major Rating Factors: PIMCO Fixed Income SHares M has adopted a risky asset allocation strategy and currently receives an overall TheStreet.com Investment Rating of C- (Fair). Volatility, as measured by standard deviation, is considered above average for fixed income funds at 5.04. The high level of risk (D+, Weak) did however, reward investors with excellent performance.

The fund's performance rating is currently B- (Good). It has registered an average return of 2.31% over the last three years and is up 3.78% over the last three months. Factored into the performance evaluation is an expense ratio of 0.04% (very low).

Curtis A. Mewbourne, II has been running the fund for 7 years and currently receives a manager quality ranking of 20 (0=worst, 99=best). If you are comfortable owning a high risk investment, this fund may be an option.

Services Offered: Automated phone transactions, bank draft capabilities and wire transfers.

Data Date	Investment Rating	Net Assets ($Mil)	NAV	Performance Rating/Pts	Total Return Y-T-D	Risk Rating/Pts
3-16	C-	1,533	10.13	B- / 7.1	3.78%	D+ / 2.7
2015	C-	1,578	9.87	C+ / 6.0	-0.45%	D+ / 2.6
2014	C+	1,998	10.37	C+ / 6.8	4.87%	C- / 3.9
2013	B+	2,981	10.58	B / 7.9	-0.56%	C / 4.5

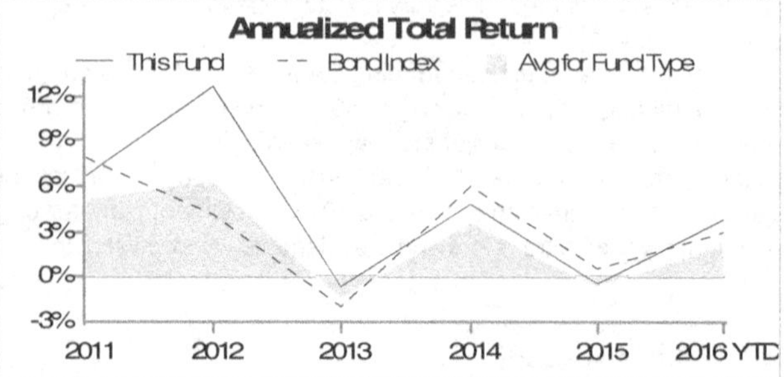

PIMCO High Yield A (PHDAX) D Weak

Fund Family: PIMCO Funds **Phone:** (800) 426-0107
Address: 840 Newport Center Drive, Newport Beach, CA 92660
Fund Type: COH - Corporate - High Yield
Major Rating Factors: PIMCO High Yield A has adopted a very risky asset allocation strategy and currently receives an overall TheStreet.com Investment Rating of D (Weak). Volatility, as measured by standard deviation, is considered above average for fixed income funds at 5.31. Another risk factor is the fund's below average duration of 3.9 years (i.e. lower interest rate risk). Unfortunately, the high level of risk (D, Weak) has only provided investors with average performance.

The fund's performance rating is currently C- (Fair). It has registered an average return of 2.14% over the last three years and is up 2.60% over the last three months. Factored into the performance evaluation is an expense ratio of 0.91% (average) and a 3.8% front-end load that is levied at the time of purchase.

Andrew R. Jessop has been running the fund for 6 years and currently receives a manager quality ranking of 85 (0=worst, 99=best). If you are comfortable owning a very high risk investment, then this fund may be an option.
Services Offered: Automated phone transactions, payroll deductions, bank draft capabilities, an IRA investment plan, a 401K investment plan, wire transfers and a systematic withdrawal plan.

Data Date	Investment Rating	Net Assets ($Mil)	NAV	Perfor-mance Rating/Pts	Total Return Y-T-D	Risk Rating/Pts
3-16	D	618	8.37	C- / 4.2	2.60%	D / 1.9
2015	D	637	8.26	C- / 3.6	-2.22%	D / 1.8
2014	C-	758	9.14	B- / 7.0	2.95%	D+ / 2.6
2013	C	1,064	9.61	B+ / 8.7	5.40%	D- / 1.2
2012	C-	1,256	9.64	B / 7.8	14.17%	D- / 1.0
2011	C-	1,176	8.98	B+ / 8.6	3.64%	E+ / 0.8

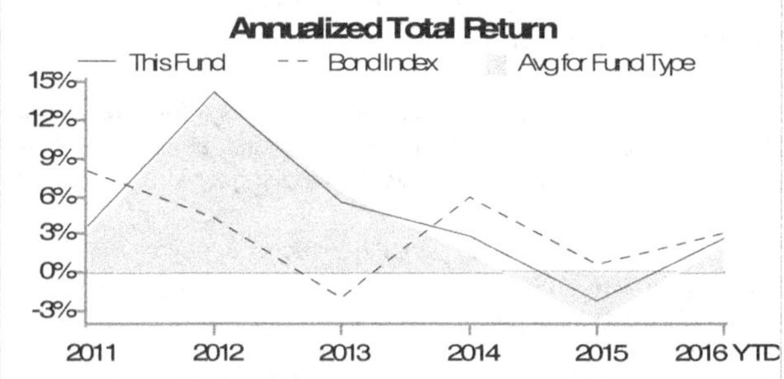

PIMCO Income Fund A (PONAX) C+ Fair

Fund Family: PIMCO Funds **Phone:** (800) 426-0107
Address: 840 Newport Center Drive, Newport Beach, CA 92660
Fund Type: GEI - General - Investment Grade
Major Rating Factors: Strong performance is the major factor driving the C+ (Fair) TheStreet.com Investment Rating for PIMCO Income Fund A. The fund currently has a performance rating of B (Good) based on an average return of 4.09% over the last three years and 1.64% over the last three months. Factored into the performance evaluation is an expense ratio of 0.85% (average) and a 3.8% front-end load that is levied at the time of purchase.

The fund's risk rating is currently C (Fair). Volatility, as measured by standard deviation, is considered average for fixed income funds at 3.62. Another risk factor is the fund's below average duration of 3.4 years (i.e. lower interest rate risk).

Daniel J. Ivascyn has been running the fund for 9 years and currently receives a manager quality ranking of 97 (0=worst, 99=best). If you desire an average level of risk and strong performance, then this fund is a good option.
Services Offered: Automated phone transactions, payroll deductions, bank draft capabilities, an IRA investment plan, a 401K investment plan, a Keogh investment plan, wire transfers and a systematic withdrawal plan.

Data Date	Investment Rating	Net Assets ($Mil)	NAV	Perfor-mance Rating/Pts	Total Return Y-T-D	Risk Rating/Pts
3-16	C+	7,072	11.77	B / 7.6	1.64%	C / 4.7
2015	B-	6,548	11.73	B / 8.1	2.19%	C / 4.5
2014	A+	5,179	12.33	A- / 9.2	6.79%	C- / 4.1
2013	A+	4,856	12.26	A+ / 9.6	4.43%	C / 4.4
2012	A+	3,065	12.36	A+ / 9.8	21.72%	C- / 4.1
2011	C	741	10.85	C+ / 6.5	5.95%	C- / 4.0

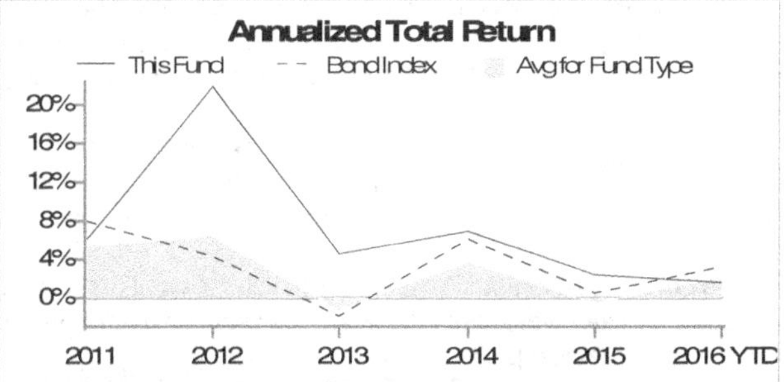

PIMCO Investment Grade Corp A (PBDAX) D+ Weak

Fund Family: PIMCO Funds **Phone:** (800) 426-0107
Address: 840 Newport Center Drive, Newport Beach, CA 92660
Fund Type: COI - Corporate - Investment Grade
Major Rating Factors: PIMCO Investment Grade Corp A has adopted a risky asset allocation strategy and currently receives an overall TheStreet.com Investment Rating of D+ (Weak). Volatility, as measured by standard deviation, is considered above average for fixed income funds at 4.95. Another risk factor is the fund's fairly average duration of 6.2 years (i.e. average interest rate risk). Unfortunately, the high level of risk (D+, Weak) has only provided investors with average performance.

The fund's performance rating is currently C+ (Fair). It has registered an average return of 2.64% over the last three years and is up 3.21% over the last three months. Factored into the performance evaluation is an expense ratio of 0.91% (average) and a 3.8% front-end load that is levied at the time of purchase.

Mark R. Kiesel has been running the fund for 14 years and currently receives a manager quality ranking of 43 (0=worst, 99=best). If you are comfortable owning a high risk investment, then this fund may be an option.
Services Offered: Automated phone transactions, payroll deductions, bank draft capabilities, an IRA investment plan, a 401K investment plan, wire transfers and a systematic withdrawal plan.

Data Date	Investment Rating	Net Assets ($Mil)	NAV	Perfor-mance Rating/Pts	Total Return Y-T-D	Risk Rating/Pts
3-16	D+	948	10.15	C+ / 5.8	3.21%	D+ / 2.8
2015	D+	916	9.92	C / 4.9	-0.14%	D+ / 2.7
2014	C+	956	10.55	B- / 7.5	8.33%	C- / 3.1
2013	C-	1,202	10.24	C+ / 6.4	-2.08%	C- / 3.4
2012	B	1,728	11.12	B / 7.9	14.55%	C- / 3.5
2011	D-	1,055	10.35	C / 5.4	6.45%	C- / 3.3

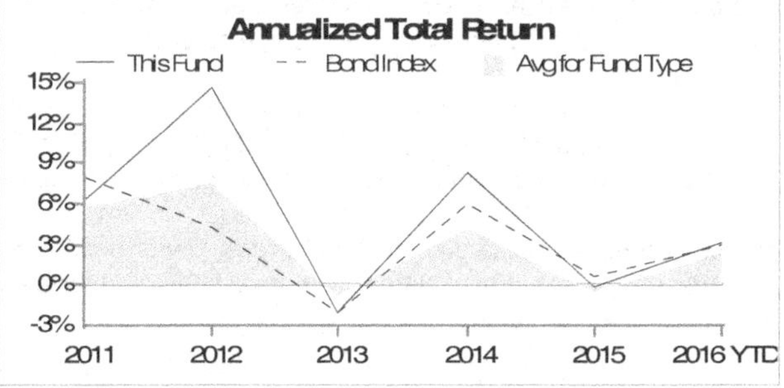

PIMCO Low Duration A (PTLAX) C- Fair

Fund Family: PIMCO Funds **Phone:** (800) 426-0107
Address: 840 Newport Center Drive, Newport Beach, CA 92660
Fund Type: GEI - General - Investment Grade
Major Rating Factors: Disappointing performance is the major factor driving the C- (Fair) TheStreet.com Investment Rating for PIMCO Low Duration A. The fund currently has a performance rating of D- (Weak) based on an average return of 0.19% over the last three years and 0.39% over the last three months. Factored into the performance evaluation is an expense ratio of 0.80% (low) and a 2.3% front-end load that is levied at the time of purchase.

The fund's risk rating is currently B+ (Good). Volatility, as measured by standard deviation, is considered low for fixed income funds at 1.74. Another risk factor is the fund's very low average duration of 1.2 years (i.e. low interest rate risk).

Jerome M. Schneider has been running the fund for 2 years and currently receives a manager quality ranking of 37 (0=worst, 99=best). This fund offers only a moderate level of risk but investors looking for strong performance are still waiting.
Services Offered: Automated phone transactions, payroll deductions, bank draft capabilities, an IRA investment plan, a 401K investment plan, wire transfers and a systematic withdrawal plan.

Data Date	Investment Rating	Net Assets ($Mil)	NAV	Performance Rating/Pts	Total Return Y-T-D	Risk Rating/Pts
3-16	C-	1,088	9.87	D- / 1.4	0.39%	B+ / 8.7
2015	C-	1,212	9.86	D+ / 2.5	0.32%	B+ / 8.7
2014	D+	1,731	10.04	D / 2.0	0.43%	B+ / 8.5
2013	C-	3,306	10.33	D+ / 2.4	-0.23%	B+ / 8.4
2012	C-	3,650	10.51	D / 1.8	5.81%	B+ / 8.4
2011	D-	3,449	10.29	D+ / 2.5	1.35%	B- / 7.1

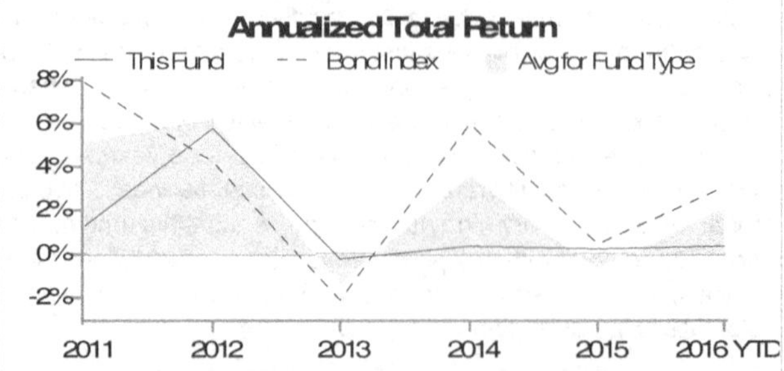

PIMCO Real Return A (PRTNX) E Very Weak

Fund Family: PIMCO Funds **Phone:** (800) 426-0107
Address: 840 Newport Center Drive, Newport Beach, CA 92660
Fund Type: GEI - General - Investment Grade
Major Rating Factors: PIMCO Real Return A has adopted a very risky asset allocation strategy and currently receives an overall TheStreet.com Investment Rating of E (Very Weak). Volatility, as measured by standard deviation, is considered above average for fixed income funds at 6.25. Unfortunately, the high level of risk (D-, Weak) failed to pay off as investors endured poor performance.

The fund's performance rating is currently E (Very Weak). It has registered an average return of -2.04% over the last three years and is up 4.02% over the last three months. Factored into the performance evaluation is an expense ratio of 0.90% (average) and a 3.8% front-end load that is levied at the time of purchase.

Mihir P. Worah has been running the fund for 9 years and currently receives a manager quality ranking of 1 (0=worst, 99=best). If you can tolerate very high levels of risk in the hope of improved future returns, holding this fund may be an option.
Services Offered: Automated phone transactions, payroll deductions, bank draft capabilities, an IRA investment plan, a 401K investment plan, wire transfers and a systematic withdrawal plan.

Data Date	Investment Rating	Net Assets ($Mil)	NAV	Performance Rating/Pts	Total Return Y-T-D	Risk Rating/Pts
3-16	E	1,920	10.92	E / 0.4	4.02%	D- / 1.1
2015	E	1,949	10.51	E / 0.4	-3.14%	D- / 1.0
2014	E	2,319	10.92	E+ / 0.6	3.01%	D- / 1.1
2013	E	2,988	10.97	E+ / 0.9	-9.41%	D / 2.2
2012	D+	5,124	12.27	C+ / 5.7	8.82%	C- / 3.3
2011	D+	4,726	11.79	C+ / 6.1	11.11%	C- / 3.4

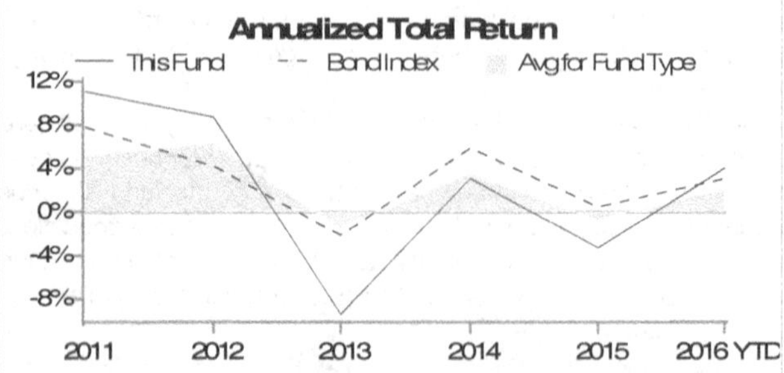

PIMCO Short Term A (PSHAX) C- Fair

Fund Family: PIMCO Funds **Phone:** (800) 426-0107
Address: 840 Newport Center Drive, Newport Beach, CA 92660
Fund Type: GEI - General - Investment Grade
Major Rating Factors: Disappointing performance is the major factor driving the C- (Fair) TheStreet.com Investment Rating for PIMCO Short Term A. The fund currently has a performance rating of D (Weak) based on an average return of 0.57% over the last three years and -0.38% over the last three months. Factored into the performance evaluation is an expense ratio of 0.71% (low) and a 2.3% front-end load that is levied at the time of purchase.

The fund's risk rating is currently A (Excellent). Volatility, as measured by standard deviation, is considered very low for fixed income funds at 0.98. Another risk factor is the fund's very low average duration of 0.3 years (i.e. low interest rate risk).

Jerome M. Schneider has been running the fund for 5 years and currently receives a manager quality ranking of 83 (0=worst, 99=best). This fund offers only a moderate level of risk but investors looking for strong performance are still waiting.
Services Offered: Automated phone transactions, payroll deductions, bank draft capabilities, an IRA investment plan, a 401K investment plan, wire transfers and a systematic withdrawal plan.

Data Date	Investment Rating	Net Assets ($Mil)	NAV	Performance Rating/Pts	Total Return Y-T-D	Risk Rating/Pts
3-16	C-	619	9.66	D / 1.7	-0.38%	A / 9.3
2015	B-	603	9.73	C / 4.3	1.11%	A / 9.3
2014	C	685	9.75	D / 1.7	0.71%	A / 9.5
2013	C-	1,100	9.85	D- / 1.3	0.59%	A / 9.4
2012	D+	1,364	9.88	E+ / 0.7	3.18%	A / 9.5
2011	D+	1,159	9.68	D- / 1.5	0.06%	A- / 9.2

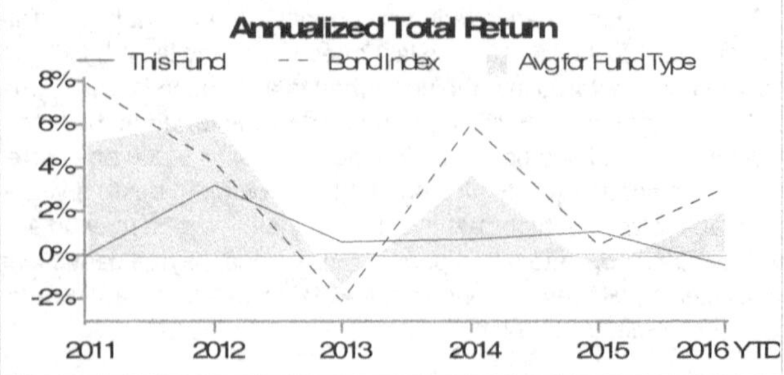

PIMCO Total Return A (PTTAX) D Weak

Fund Family: PIMCO Funds **Phone:** (800) 426-0107
Address: 840 Newport Center Drive, Newport Beach, CA 92660
Fund Type: GEI - General - Investment Grade
Major Rating Factors: Disappointing performance is the major factor driving the D (Weak) TheStreet.com Investment Rating for PIMCO Total Return A. The fund currently has a performance rating of D+ (Weak) based on an average return of 1.12% over the last three years and 1.68% over the last three months. Factored into the performance evaluation is an expense ratio of 0.85% (average) and a 3.8% front-end load that is levied at the time of purchase.

The fund's risk rating is currently C (Fair). Volatility, as measured by standard deviation, is considered average for fixed income funds at 3.80. Another risk factor is the fund's below average duration of 4.6 years (i.e. lower interest rate risk).

Mark R. Kiesel has been running the fund for 2 years and currently receives a manager quality ranking of 15 (0=worst, 99=best). This fund offers an average level of risk, but investors looking for strong performance will be frustrated.
Services Offered: Automated phone transactions, payroll deductions, bank draft capabilities, an IRA investment plan, a 401K investment plan, wire transfers and a systematic withdrawal plan.

Data Date	Investment Rating	Net Assets ($Mil)	NAV	Performance Rating/Pts	Total Return Y-T-D	Risk Rating/Pts
3-16	D	7,657	10.18	D+ / 2.9	1.68%	C / 4.3
2015	D+	8,439	10.07	D+ / 2.7	0.33%	C / 4.4
2014	D	14,122	10.66	C- / 4.0	4.28%	C / 4.9
2013	D	21,616	10.69	C- / 3.1	-2.30%	C / 5.1
2012	C	27,665	11.24	C / 4.4	9.95%	C+ / 5.8
2011	D	26,136	10.87	C- / 3.5	3.75%	C+ / 6.3

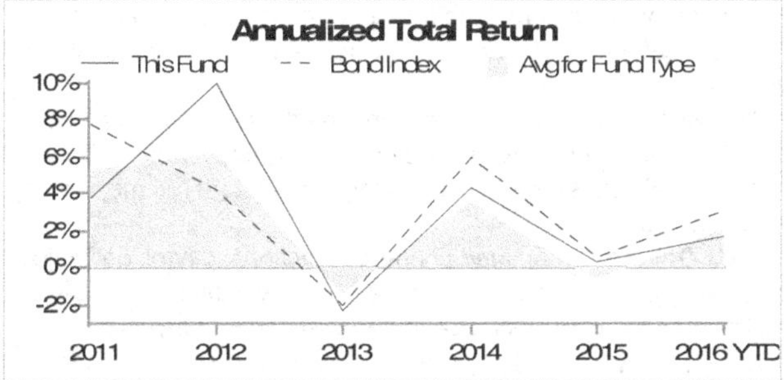

Pioneer AMT-Free Muni A (PBMFX) C+ Fair

Fund Family: Pioneer Investments **Phone:** (800) 225-6292
Address: P.O. Box 55014, Boston, MA 02205
Fund Type: MUN - Municipal - National
Major Rating Factors: Pioneer AMT-Free Muni A has adopted a risky asset allocation strategy and currently receives an overall TheStreet.com Investment Rating of C+ (Fair). Volatility, as measured by standard deviation, is considered above average for fixed income funds at 5.14. Another risk factor is the fund's fairly average duration of 6.9 years (i.e. average interest rate risk). The high level of risk (D+, Weak) did however, reward investors with excellent performance.

The fund's performance rating is currently A (Excellent). It has registered an average return of 4.38% over the last three years (7.25% taxable equivalent) and is up 1.97% over the last three months (3.26% taxable equivalent). Factored into the performance evaluation is an expense ratio of 0.85% (average) and a 4.5% front-end load that is levied at the time of purchase.

David J. Eurkus has been running the fund for 10 years and currently receives a manager quality ranking of 30 (0=worst, 99=best). If you are comfortable owning a high risk investment, this fund may be an option.
Services Offered: Automated phone transactions, payroll deductions, bank draft capabilities, an IRA investment plan, a 401K investment plan, wire transfers and a systematic withdrawal plan.

Data Date	Investment Rating	Net Assets ($Mil)	NAV	Performance Rating/Pts	Total Return Y-T-D	Risk Rating/Pts
3-16	C+	727	14.77	A / 9.3	1.97%	D+ / 2.6
2015	C	708	14.60	A / 9.3	4.50%	D / 2.0
2014	B-	698	14.49	A / 9.5	13.62%	D- / 1.2
2013	C-	648	13.25	B- / 7.5	-5.33%	D / 1.8
2012	B+	823	14.56	A / 9.3	12.86%	D / 2.0
2011	B	765	13.40	A- / 9.0	11.75%	D / 2.0

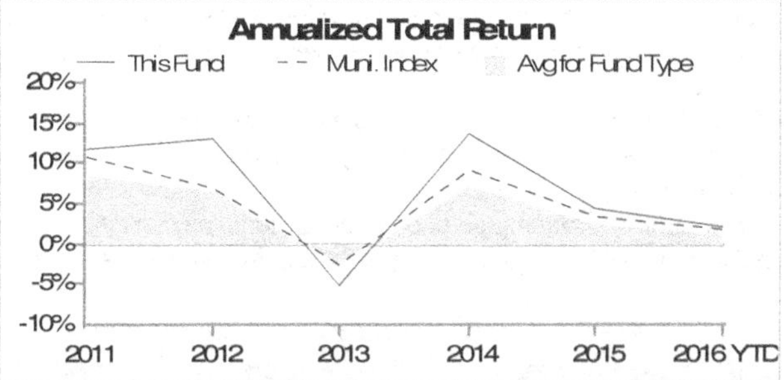

Pioneer Bond Fund A (PIOBX) C+ Fair

Fund Family: Pioneer Investments **Phone:** (800) 225-6292
Address: P.O. Box 55014, Boston, MA 02205
Fund Type: GEI - General - Investment Grade
Major Rating Factors: A moderate risk profile coupled with stable earnings characterizes Pioneer Bond Fund A which receives a TheStreet.com Investment Rating of C+ (Fair). Volatility, as measured by standard deviation, is considered low for fixed income funds at 2.47. Another risk factor is the fund's below average duration of 4.6 years (i.e. lower interest rate risk). The fund's risk rating is currently B (Good).

The fund's performance rating is currently C (Fair). It has registered an average return of 2.39% over the last three years and is up 1.83% over the last three months. Factored into the performance evaluation is an expense ratio of 0.93% (average) and a 4.5% front-end load that is levied at the time of purchase.

Kenneth J. Taubes has been running the fund for 18 years and currently receives a manager quality ranking of 85 (0=worst, 99=best). If you desire stability with a moderate level of risk then this fund is an excellent option.
Services Offered: Automated phone transactions, payroll deductions, bank draft capabilities, an IRA investment plan, a 401K investment plan, a Keogh investment plan and a systematic withdrawal plan.

Data Date	Investment Rating	Net Assets ($Mil)	NAV	Performance Rating/Pts	Total Return Y-T-D	Risk Rating/Pts
3-16	C+	1,145	9.62	C / 4.7	1.83%	B / 7.9
2015	C+	1,034	9.51	C / 4.9	-0.01%	B / 7.9
2014	B+	949	9.80	C / 5.2	5.94%	B / 7.6
2013	B+	531	9.60	C / 4.9	0.49%	B / 8.0
2012	B+	544	9.93	C / 4.3	8.64%	B / 8.2
2011	B-	423	9.53	C / 4.4	5.09%	B- / 7.4

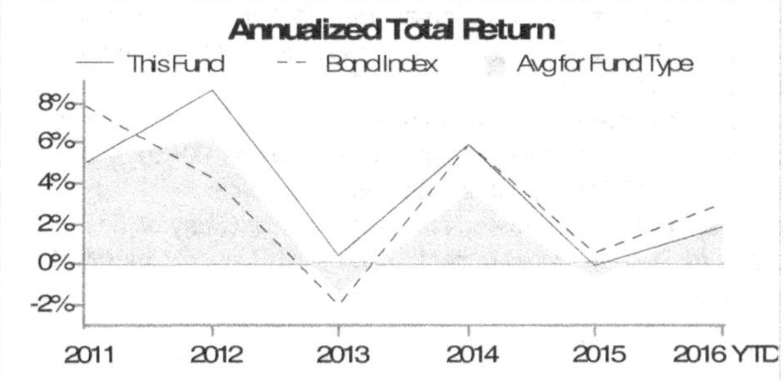

Pioneer High Yield A (TAHYX) E Very Weak

Fund Family: Pioneer Investments **Phone:** (800) 225-6292
Address: P.O. Box 55014, Boston, MA 02205
Fund Type: COH - Corporate - High Yield

Major Rating Factors: Pioneer High Yield A has adopted a very risky asset allocation strategy and currently receives an overall TheStreet.com Investment Rating of E (Very Weak). Volatility, as measured by standard deviation, is considered high for fixed income funds at 6.37. Unfortunately, the high level of risk (E+, Very Weak) failed to pay off as investors endured poor performance.

The fund's performance rating is currently E+ (Very Weak). It has registered an average return of 0.97% over the last three years and is up 1.70% over the last three months. Factored into the performance evaluation is an expense ratio of 1.17% (above average) and a 4.5% front-end load that is levied at the time of purchase.

Andrew D. Feltus has been running the fund for 9 years and currently receives a manager quality ranking of 35 (0=worst, 99=best). If you can tolerate very high levels of risk in the hope of improved future returns, holding this fund may be an option.

Services Offered: Automated phone transactions, payroll deductions, bank draft capabilities, an IRA investment plan, a 401K investment plan, a Keogh investment plan, wire transfers and a systematic withdrawal plan.

Data Date	Investment Rating	Net Assets ($Mil)	NAV	Performance Rating/Pts	Total Return Y-T-D	Risk Rating/Pts
3-16	E	579	8.80	E+ / 0.9	1.70%	E+ / 0.8
2015	E+	579	8.76	D / 2.0	-4.89%	E+ / 0.6
2014	D	826	9.74	B- / 7.1	-0.15%	E+ / 0.9
2013	C	1,182	10.67	A / 9.4	12.31%	E- / 0.2
2012	D-	1,254	10.33	B- / 7.4	14.98%	E- / 0.1
2011	C-	1,370	9.46	A / 9.3	-1.74%	E- / 0.2

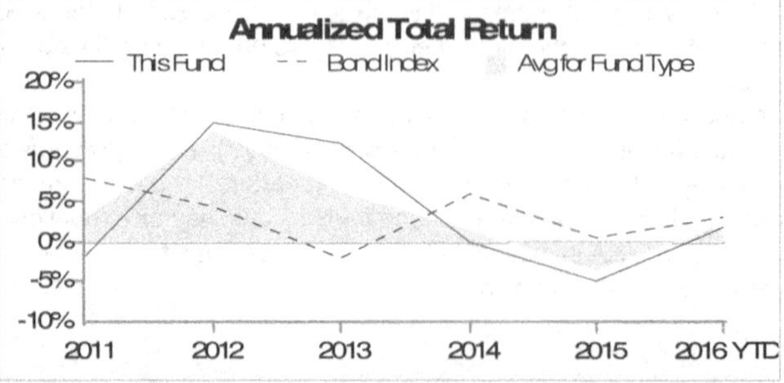

Pioneer Multi-Asset Ultrasht Inc A (MAFRX) C- Fair

Fund Family: Pioneer Investments **Phone:** (800) 225-6292
Address: P.O. Box 55014, Boston, MA 02205
Fund Type: GL - Global

Major Rating Factors: Disappointing performance is the major factor driving the C- (Fair) TheStreet.com Investment Rating for Pioneer Multi-Asset Ultrasht Inc A. The fund currently has a performance rating of D (Weak) based on an average return of 0.62% over the last three years and 0.09% over the last three months. Factored into the performance evaluation is an expense ratio of 0.63% (low) and a 2.5% front-end load that is levied at the time of purchase.

The fund's risk rating is currently A+ (Excellent). Volatility, as measured by standard deviation, is considered very low for fixed income funds at 0.37. Another risk factor is the fund's very low average duration of 0.3 years (i.e. low interest rate risk).

Craig D. Sterling currently receives a manager quality ranking of 84 (0=worst, 99=best). This fund offers only a moderate level of risk but investors looking for strong performance are still waiting.

Services Offered: Automated phone transactions, payroll deductions, bank draft capabilities, an IRA investment plan, wire transfers and a systematic withdrawal plan.

Data Date	Investment Rating	Net Assets ($Mil)	NAV	Performance Rating/Pts	Total Return Y-T-D	Risk Rating/Pts
3-16	C-	673	9.92	D / 1.8	0.09%	A+ / 9.9
2015	C+	696	9.94	C- / 3.3	0.52%	A+ / 9.9
2014	C	708	10.01	D / 1.7	0.70%	A+ / 9.8
2013	U	533	10.06	U / --	0.88%	U / --
2012	U	283	10.08	U / --	2.90%	U / --
2011	U	26	9.96	U / --	0.00%	U / --

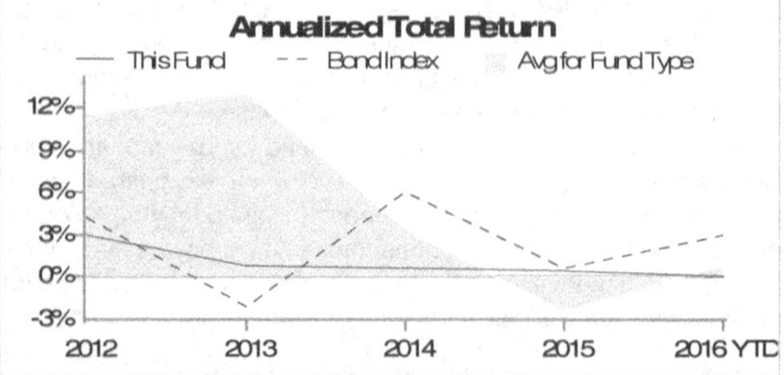

Pioneer Strategic Income A (PSRAX) D+ Weak

Fund Family: Pioneer Investments **Phone:** (800) 225-6292
Address: P.O. Box 55014, Boston, MA 02205
Fund Type: GES - General - Short & Inter. Term

Major Rating Factors: Pioneer Strategic Income A receives a TheStreet.com Investment Rating of D+ (Weak). The fund has a performance rating of C- (Fair) based on an average return of 1.60% over the last three years and 2.05% over the last three months. Factored into the performance evaluation is an expense ratio of 1.05% (average) and a 4.5% front-end load that is levied at the time of purchase.

The fund's risk rating is currently C+ (Fair). Volatility, as measured by standard deviation, is considered average for fixed income funds at 3.25. Another risk factor is the fund's below average duration of 4.5 years (i.e. lower interest rate risk).

Kenneth J. Taubes has been running the fund for 17 years and currently receives a manager quality ranking of 61 (0=worst, 99=best). If you desire an average level of risk, then this fund may be an option.

Services Offered: Automated phone transactions, payroll deductions, bank draft capabilities, a 401K investment plan and a systematic withdrawal plan.

Data Date	Investment Rating	Net Assets ($Mil)	NAV	Performance Rating/Pts	Total Return Y-T-D	Risk Rating/Pts
3-16	D+	1,274	10.33	C- / 3.1	2.05%	C+ / 5.6
2015	D+	1,271	10.21	D+ / 2.7	-1.46%	C+ / 6.1
2014	C+	1,523	10.73	C / 5.5	4.62%	C / 5.5
2013	C	1,872	10.81	C+ / 5.9	1.51%	C / 4.9
2012	C	2,142	11.28	C+ / 5.7	11.22%	C / 4.6
2011	C-	1,687	10.63	C+ / 6.2	3.13%	C- / 3.6

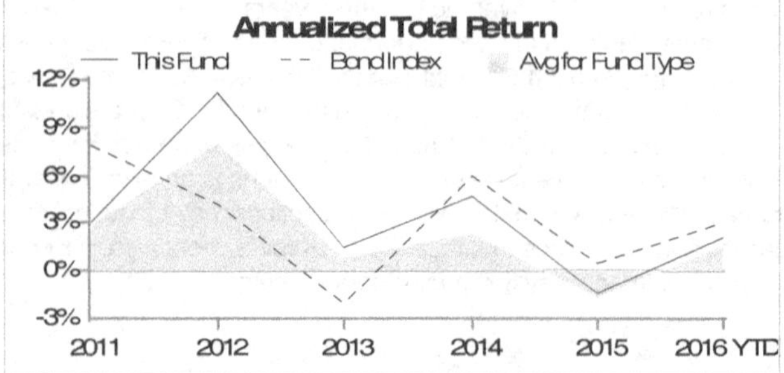

Principal Glb Divers Income A (PGBAX) D Weak

Fund Family: Principal Financial Group **Phone:** (800) 222-5852
Address: P.O. Box 8024, Boston, MA 02266
Fund Type: GL - Global

Major Rating Factors: Principal Glb Divers Income A has adopted a risky asset allocation strategy and currently receives an overall TheStreet.com Investment Rating of D (Weak). Volatility, as measured by standard deviation, is considered above average for fixed income funds at 5.44. Another risk factor is the fund's below average duration of 3.9 years (i.e. lower interest rate risk). Unfortunately, the high level of risk (D+, Weak) has only provided investors with average performance.

The fund's performance rating is currently C (Fair). It has registered an average return of 2.56% over the last three years and is up 2.21% over the last three months. Factored into the performance evaluation is an expense ratio of 1.09% (average) and a 3.8% front-end load that is levied at the time of purchase.

Kelly A. Grossman has been running the fund for 6 years and currently receives a manager quality ranking of 98 (0=worst, 99=best). If you are comfortable owning a high risk investment, then this fund may be an option.

Services Offered: Automated phone transactions, payroll deductions, bank draft capabilities, an IRA investment plan, a 401K investment plan, wire transfers and a systematic withdrawal plan.

Data Date	Investment Rating	Net Assets ($Mil)	NAV	Performance Rating/Pts	Total Return Y-T-D	Risk Rating/Pts
3-16	D	2,041	13.18	C / 4.9	2.21%	D+ / 2.3
2015	D+	2,124	13.05	C+ / 5.9	-2.52%	D / 1.6
2014	C+	2,437	14.03	B+ / 8.4	6.20%	D+ / 2.3
2013	C	2,597	14.12	B+ / 8.7	5.79%	D- / 1.2
2012	C-	2,202	13.96	B+ / 8.4	15.65%	E / 0.4
2011	D	1,033	12.86	B+ / 8.3	2.70%	E- / 0.2

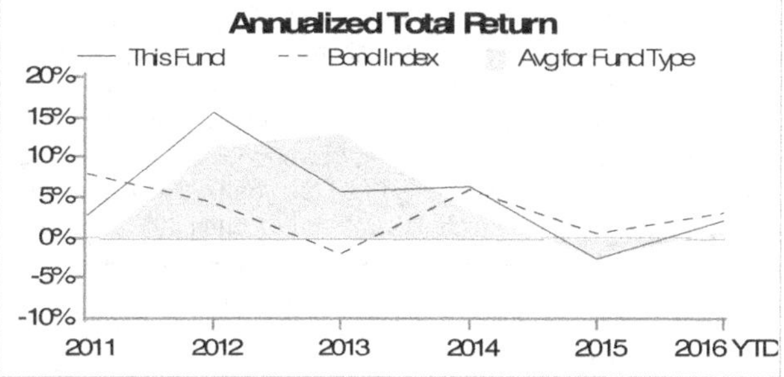

Principal High Yield A (CPHYX) D- Weak

Fund Family: Principal Financial Group **Phone:** (800) 222-5852
Address: P.O. Box 8024, Boston, MA 02266
Fund Type: COH - Corporate - High Yield

Major Rating Factors: Principal High Yield A has adopted a very risky asset allocation strategy and currently receives an overall TheStreet.com Investment Rating of D- (Weak). Volatility, as measured by standard deviation, is considered above average for fixed income funds at 5.36. Unfortunately, the high level of risk (D, Weak) failed to pay off as investors endured very poor performance.

The fund's performance rating is currently D+ (Weak). It has registered an average return of 1.67% over the last three years and is up 1.99% over the last three months. Factored into the performance evaluation is an expense ratio of 0.88% (average) and a 3.8% front-end load that is levied at the time of purchase.

Darrin E. Smith has been running the fund for 7 years and currently receives a manager quality ranking of 71 (0=worst, 99=best). If you can tolerate very high levels of risk in the hope of improved future returns, holding this fund may be an option.

Services Offered: Automated phone transactions, payroll deductions, bank draft capabilities, an IRA investment plan, a 401K investment plan, wire transfers and a systematic withdrawal plan.

Data Date	Investment Rating	Net Assets ($Mil)	NAV	Performance Rating/Pts	Total Return Y-T-D	Risk Rating/Pts
3-16	D-	848	6.80	D+ / 2.7	1.99%	D / 1.8
2015	D	847	6.77	D+ / 2.7	-2.95%	D / 1.8
2014	C-	1,100	7.39	B- / 7.1	2.11%	D+ / 2.6
2013	C+	1,947	7.76	A- / 9.1	7.01%	D- / 1.3
2012	C	1,864	7.87	B / 8.0	15.25%	D- / 1.1
2011	C-	1,692	7.39	B+ / 8.3	3.65%	D- / 1.0

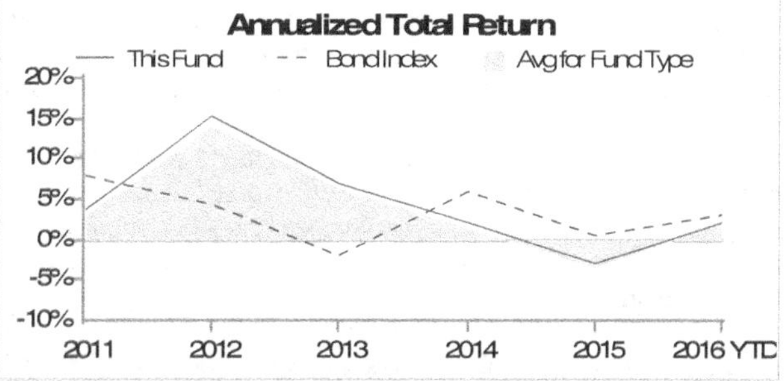

Principal Preferred Sec A (PPSAX) C+ Fair

Fund Family: Principal Financial Group **Phone:** (800) 222-5852
Address: P.O. Box 8024, Boston, MA 02266
Fund Type: USS - US Government - Short & Inter. Term

Major Rating Factors: Strong performance is the major factor driving the C+ (Fair) TheStreet.com Investment Rating for Principal Preferred Sec A. The fund currently has a performance rating of B (Good) based on an average return of 4.72% over the last three years and -0.10% over the last three months. Factored into the performance evaluation is an expense ratio of 1.07% (average) and a 3.8% front-end load that is levied at the time of purchase.

The fund's risk rating is currently C (Fair). Volatility, as measured by standard deviation, is considered average for fixed income funds at 3.75. Another risk factor is the fund's fairly average duration of 5.1 years (i.e. average interest rate risk).

Lewis P. Jacoby, IV has been running the fund for 14 years and currently receives a manager quality ranking of 99 (0=worst, 99=best). If you desire an average level of risk and strong performance, then this fund is a good option.

Services Offered: Automated phone transactions, payroll deductions, bank draft capabilities, an IRA investment plan, a 401K investment plan, a Keogh investment plan, wire transfers and a systematic withdrawal plan.

Data Date	Investment Rating	Net Assets ($Mil)	NAV	Performance Rating/Pts	Total Return Y-T-D	Risk Rating/Pts
3-16	C+	847	10.03	B / 7.9	-0.10%	C / 4.4
2015	B+	770	10.16	A- / 9.2	4.69%	C / 4.7
2014	A	829	10.27	A / 9.3	11.24%	C- / 3.7
2013	C	962	9.87	B / 7.7	1.47%	D / 2.2
2012	B-	1,217	10.53	A- / 9.0	18.87%	D / 1.6
2011	D-	765	9.42	B+ / 8.3	1.17%	E- / 0.0

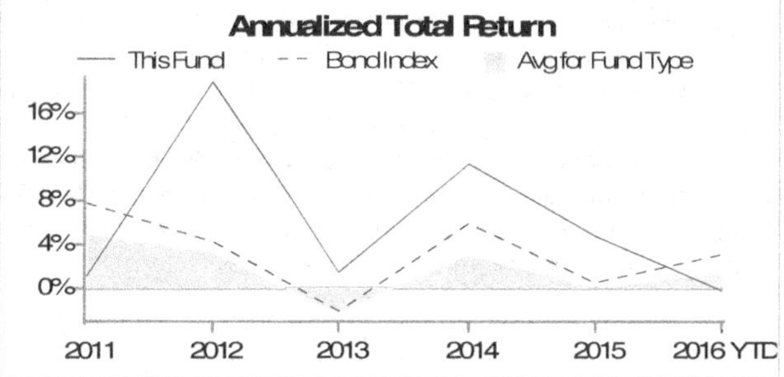

Prudential High Yield A (PBHAX) D Weak

Fund Family: Prudential Investments **Phone:** (800) 225-1852
Address: Gateway Center Three, Newark, NJ 07102
Fund Type: COH - Corporate - High Yield

Major Rating Factors: Prudential High Yield A has adopted a very risky asset allocation strategy and currently receives an overall TheStreet.com Investment Rating of D (Weak). Volatility, as measured by standard deviation, is considered above average for fixed income funds at 5.60. Another risk factor is the fund's below average duration of 4.3 years (i.e. lower interest rate risk). Unfortunately, the high level of risk (D-, Weak) has only provided investors with average performance.

The fund's performance rating is currently C- (Fair). It has registered an average return of 2.32% over the last three years and is up 3.24% over the last three months. Factored into the performance evaluation is an expense ratio of 0.83% (low) and a 4.5% front-end load that is levied at the time of purchase.

Paul E. Appleby has been running the fund for 17 years and currently receives a manager quality ranking of 86 (0=worst, 99=best). If you are comfortable owning a very high risk investment, then this fund may be an option.

Services Offered: Payroll deductions, an IRA investment plan, a 401K investment plan and a systematic withdrawal plan.

Data Date	Investment Rating	Net Assets ($Mil)	NAV	Performance Rating/Pts	Total Return Y-T-D	Risk Rating/Pts
3-16	D	1,149	5.13	C- / 4.1	3.24%	D- / 1.5
2015	D	1,112	5.05	D+ / 2.7	-2.87%	D / 1.9
2014	C-	1,264	5.53	C+ / 6.9	2.53%	D+ / 2.6
2013	C+	1,342	5.73	A- / 9.1	6.95%	D / 1.6
2012	C	1,401	5.71	B / 8.0	14.07%	D- / 1.4
2011	C+	1,118	5.36	A- / 9.1	4.78%	D- / 1.4

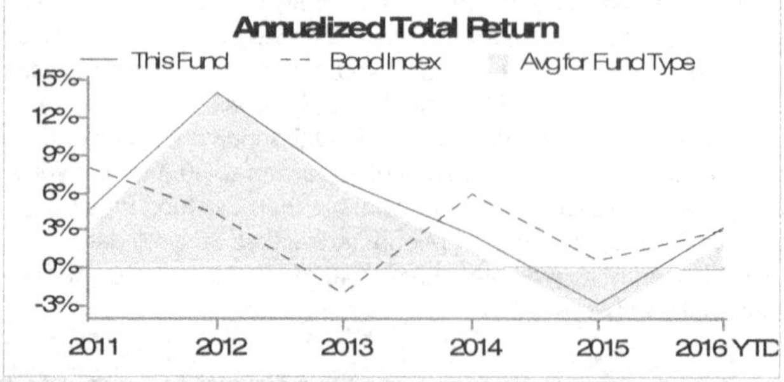

Prudential National Muni A (PRNMX) C+ Fair

Fund Family: Prudential Investments **Phone:** (800) 225-1852
Address: Gateway Center Three, Newark, NJ 07102
Fund Type: MUN - Municipal - National

Major Rating Factors: Strong performance is the major factor driving the C+ (Fair) TheStreet.com Investment Rating for Prudential National Muni A. The fund currently has a performance rating of B (Good) based on an average return of 2.99% over the last three years (4.95% taxable equivalent) and 1.46% over the last three months (2.42% taxable equivalent). Factored into the performance evaluation is an expense ratio of 0.84% (low) and a 4.0% front-end load that is levied at the time of purchase.

The fund's risk rating is currently C- (Fair). Volatility, as measured by standard deviation, is considered average for fixed income funds at 4.19. Another risk factor is the fund's fairly average duration of 6.7 years (i.e. average interest rate risk).

Robert S. Tipp has been running the fund for 12 years and currently receives a manager quality ranking of 21 (0=worst, 99=best). If you desire an average level of risk and strong performance, then this fund is a good option.

Services Offered: Payroll deductions, a 401K investment plan and a systematic withdrawal plan.

Data Date	Investment Rating	Net Assets ($Mil)	NAV	Performance Rating/Pts	Total Return Y-T-D	Risk Rating/Pts
3-16	C+	599	15.27	B / 8.1	1.46%	C- / 3.7
2015	C	597	15.18	B / 8.1	3.00%	C- / 3.4
2014	C+	630	15.28	B / 8.0	9.85%	D+ / 2.6
2013	C-	622	14.43	C+ / 5.7	-4.38%	C- / 3.6
2012	C+	742	15.67	C+ / 6.7	8.69%	C- / 3.8
2011	C+	724	14.96	C+ / 6.6	10.27%	C / 4.3

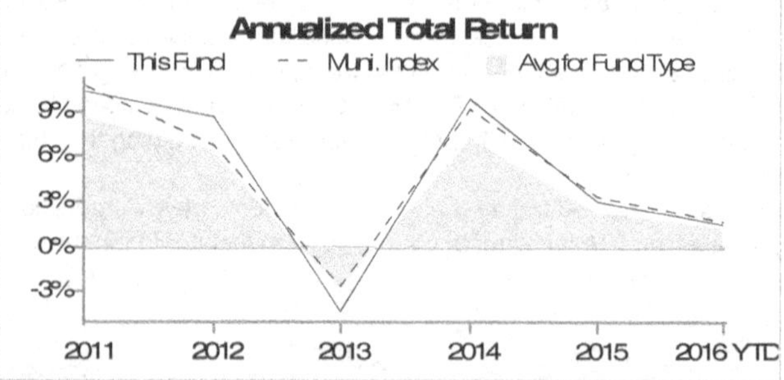

Prudential Short-Term Corp Bond A (PBSMX) C+ Fair

Fund Family: Prudential Investments **Phone:** (800) 225-1852
Address: Gateway Center Three, Newark, NJ 07102
Fund Type: COI - Corporate - Investment Grade

Major Rating Factors: A moderate risk profile coupled with stable earnings characterizes Prudential Short-Term Corp Bond A which receives a TheStreet.com Investment Rating of C+ (Fair). Volatility, as measured by standard deviation, is considered low for fixed income funds at 1.52. Another risk factor is the fund's very low average duration of 2.6 years (i.e. low interest rate risk). The fund's risk rating is currently B+ (Good).

The fund's performance rating is currently C- (Fair). It has registered an average return of 1.42% over the last three years and is up 1.61% over the last three months. Factored into the performance evaluation is an expense ratio of 0.78% (low) and a 3.3% front-end load that is levied at the time of purchase.

Malcolm J. Dalrymple has been running the fund for 17 years and currently receives a manager quality ranking of 83 (0=worst, 99=best). If you desire stability with a moderate level of risk then this fund is an excellent option.

Services Offered: Payroll deductions, an IRA investment plan, a 401K investment plan and a systematic withdrawal plan.

Data Date	Investment Rating	Net Assets ($Mil)	NAV	Performance Rating/Pts	Total Return Y-T-D	Risk Rating/Pts
3-16	C+	1,631	11.11	C- / 3.8	1.61%	B+ / 8.9
2015	C+	1,803	11.00	C- / 3.8	0.81%	B+ / 8.9
2014	C	2,189	11.19	D+ / 2.4	1.41%	B+ / 8.8
2013	C+	2,785	11.33	C- / 3.2	0.89%	B+ / 8.7
2012	C-	2,597	11.56	D / 1.7	5.23%	B+ / 8.5
2011	C	1,761	11.35	D+ / 2.8	2.77%	B / 8.2

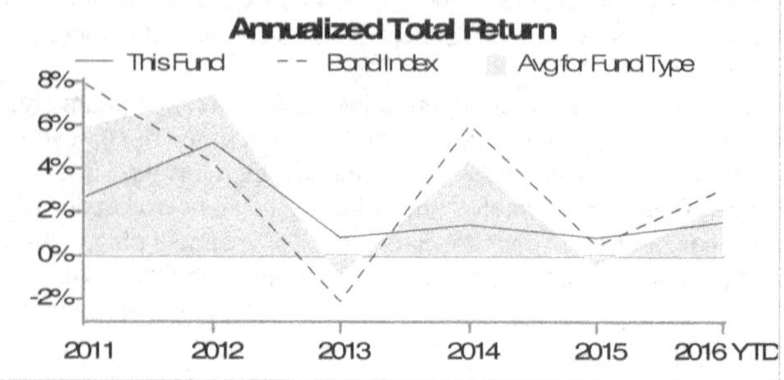

Prudential Total Return Bond A (PDBAX) C- Fair

Fund Family: Prudential Investments **Phone:** (800) 225-1852
Address: Gateway Center Three, Newark, NJ 07102
Fund Type: GES - General - Short & Inter. Term
Major Rating Factors: Middle of the road best describes Prudential Total Return Bond A whose TheStreet.com Investment Rating is currently a C- (Fair). The fund has a performance rating of C (Fair) based on an average return of 2.55% over the last three years and 3.11% over the last three months. Factored into the performance evaluation is an expense ratio of 0.87% (average) and a 4.5% front-end load that is levied at the time of purchase.

The fund's risk rating is currently C- (Fair). Volatility, as measured by standard deviation, is considered average for fixed income funds at 3.89. Another risk factor is the fund's fairly average duration of 6.3 years (i.e. average interest rate risk).

Robert S. Tipp has been running the fund for 14 years and currently receives a manager quality ranking of 44 (0=worst, 99=best). If you desire an average level of risk, then this fund may be an option.
Services Offered: Payroll deductions, an IRA investment plan, a 401K investment plan, wire transfers and a systematic withdrawal plan.

Data Date	Investment Rating	Net Assets ($Mil)	NAV	Performance Rating/Pts	Total Return Y-T-D	Risk Rating/Pts
3-16	C-	3,122	14.36	C / 5.2	3.11%	C- / 4.1
2015	D+	3,051	14.01	C- / 3.9	-0.37%	C- / 4.2
2014	C-	1,862	14.46	C / 5.5	6.78%	C / 4.8
2013	C	1,145	14.02	C / 5.4	-1.17%	C / 5.2
2012	B	1,207	14.68	C+ / 5.7	9.59%	C+ / 6.1
2011	B	647	13.99	C / 5.5	7.57%	C+ / 6.3

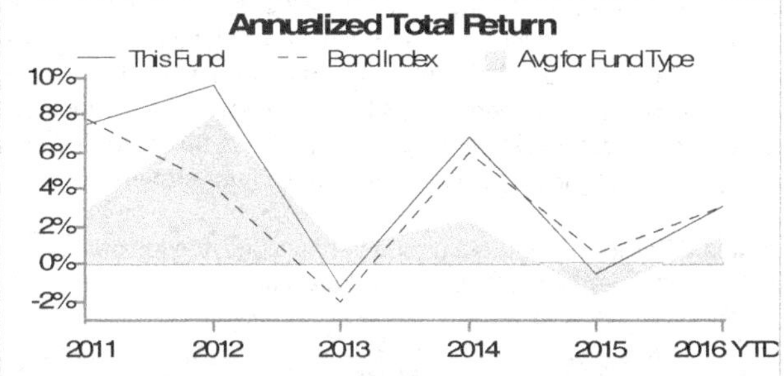

Putnam CA Tax Exempt Income A (PCTEX) B- Good

Fund Family: Putnam Funds **Phone:** (800) 225-1581
Address: One Post Office Square, Boston, MA 02109
Fund Type: MUS - Municipal - Single State
Major Rating Factors: Strong performance is the major factor driving the B- (Good) TheStreet.com Investment Rating for Putnam CA Tax Exempt Income A. The fund currently has a performance rating of B+ (Good) based on an average return of 3.71% over the last three years (6.14% taxable equivalent) and 1.71% over the last three months (2.83% taxable equivalent). Factored into the performance evaluation is an expense ratio of 0.74% (low) and a 4.0% front-end load that is levied at the time of purchase.

The fund's risk rating is currently C- (Fair). Volatility, as measured by standard deviation, is considered average for fixed income funds at 3.99. Another risk factor is the fund's fairly average duration of 6.9 years (i.e. average interest rate risk).

Paul M. Drury has been running the fund for 14 years and currently receives a manager quality ranking of 45 (0=worst, 99=best). If you desire an average level of risk and strong performance, then this fund is a good option.
Services Offered: Automated phone transactions, payroll deductions and a systematic withdrawal plan.

Data Date	Investment Rating	Net Assets ($Mil)	NAV	Performance Rating/Pts	Total Return Y-T-D	Risk Rating/Pts
3-16	B-	1,228	8.30	B+ / 8.7	1.71%	C- / 3.9
2015	C+	1,221	8.23	B+ / 8.8	3.01%	C- / 3.4
2014	B+	1,266	8.29	A- / 9.0	10.92%	C- / 3.1
2013	C+	1,269	7.77	B / 7.8	-3.20%	C- / 3.1
2012	B	1,563	8.36	B+ / 8.5	9.58%	D+ / 2.5
2011	B	1,486	7.95	B+ / 8.4	11.70%	D+ / 2.7

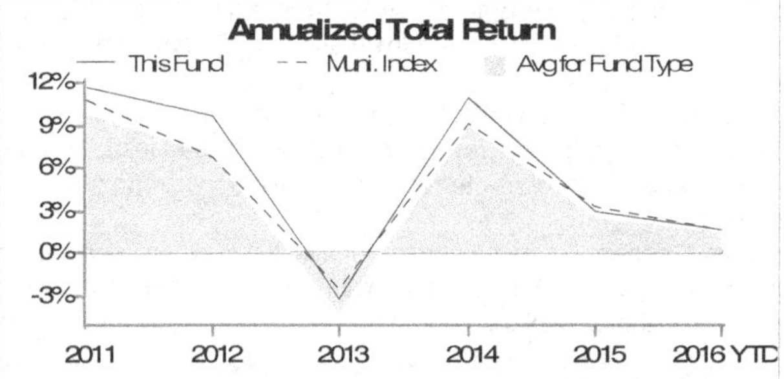

Putnam Diversified Income A (PDINX) E+ Very Weak

Fund Family: Putnam Funds **Phone:** (800) 225-1581
Address: One Post Office Square, Boston, MA 02109
Fund Type: GES - General - Short & Inter. Term
Major Rating Factors: Putnam Diversified Income A has adopted a very risky asset allocation strategy and currently receives an overall TheStreet.com Investment Rating of E+ (Very Weak). Volatility, as measured by standard deviation, is considered above average for fixed income funds at 5.53. Unfortunately, the high level of risk (D, Weak) failed to pay off as investors endured poor performance.

The fund's performance rating is currently E- (Very Weak). It has registered an average return of -0.93% over the last three years and is down -4.67% over the last three months. Factored into the performance evaluation is an expense ratio of 0.98% (average) and a 4.0% front-end load that is levied at the time of purchase.

D. William Kohli has been running the fund for 22 years and currently receives a manager quality ranking of 88 (0=worst, 99=best). If you can tolerate very high levels of risk in the hope of improved future returns, holding this fund may be an option.
Services Offered: Automated phone transactions, payroll deductions, an IRA investment plan, a 401K investment plan and a systematic withdrawal plan.

Data Date	Investment Rating	Net Assets ($Mil)	NAV	Performance Rating/Pts	Total Return Y-T-D	Risk Rating/Pts
3-16	E+	1,440	6.63	E- / 0.2	-4.67%	D / 2.1
2015	D	1,785	7.05	C- / 3.6	-2.92%	C- / 3.2
2014	C	2,276	7.61	C+ / 6.1	0.96%	C / 4.4
2013	C-	2,551	7.92	B / 7.7	7.85%	D / 1.9
2012	E+	1,752	7.77	C / 5.1	12.72%	D / 1.8
2011	C-	1,916	7.31	B / 8.1	-3.61%	D- / 1.3

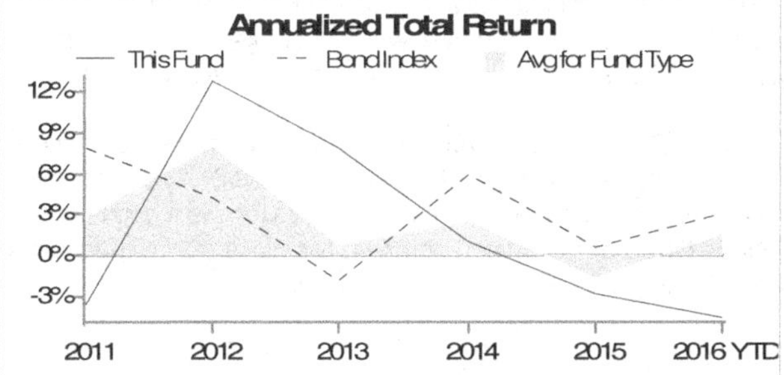

Putnam High Yield Trust A (PHIGX) E+ Very Weak

Fund Family: Putnam Funds **Phone:** (800) 225-1581
Address: One Post Office Square, Boston, MA 02109
Fund Type: COH - Corporate - High Yield
Major Rating Factors: Putnam High Yield Trust A has adopted a very risky asset allocation strategy and currently receives an overall TheStreet.com Investment Rating of E+ (Very Weak). Volatility, as measured by standard deviation, is considered above average for fixed income funds at 5.92. Unfortunately, the high level of risk (D-, Weak) failed to pay off as investors endured very poor performance.

The fund's performance rating is currently D- (Weak). It has registered an average return of 1.28% over the last three years and is up 2.85% over the last three months. Factored into the performance evaluation is an expense ratio of 1.00% (average) and a 4.0% front-end load that is levied at the time of purchase.

Paul D. Scanlon has been running the fund for 14 years and currently receives a manager quality ranking of 45 (0=worst, 99=best). If you can tolerate very high levels of risk in the hope of improved future returns, holding this fund may be an option.
Services Offered: Automated phone transactions, payroll deductions, an IRA investment plan and a systematic withdrawal plan.

Data Date	Investment Rating	Net Assets ($Mil)	NAV	Performance Rating/Pts	Total Return Y-T-D	Risk Rating/Pts
3-16	E+	752	7.10	D- / 1.5	2.85%	D- / 1.1
2015	D-	832	7.01	D- / 1.5	-5.04%	D- / 1.3
2014	C-	920	7.80	B- / 7.2	1.79%	D+/ 2.3
2013	C	1,113	8.07	A- / 9.0	7.69%	E+/ 0.7
2012	D	1,187	7.95	B / 7.7	15.66%	E / 0.5
2011	C-	1,164	7.33	B+/ 8.8	1.67%	E+/ 0.6

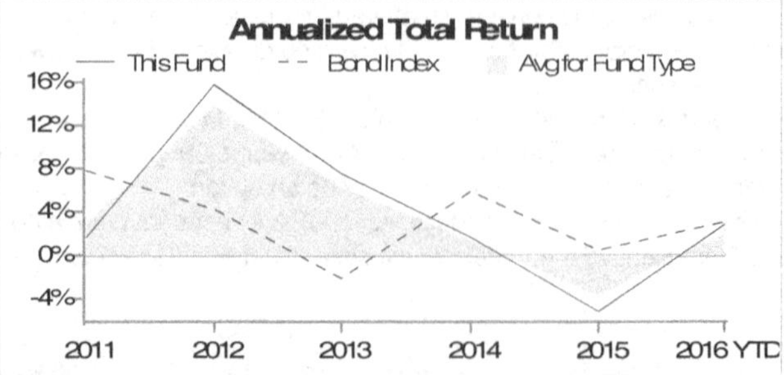

Putnam Income Fund A (PINCX) D+ Weak

Fund Family: Putnam Funds **Phone:** (800) 225-1581
Address: One Post Office Square, Boston, MA 02109
Fund Type: GES - General - Short & Inter. Term
Major Rating Factors: Disappointing performance is the major factor driving the D+ (Weak) TheStreet.com Investment Rating for Putnam Income Fund A. The fund currently has a performance rating of D- (Weak) based on an average return of 0.94% over the last three years and -0.62% over the last three months. Factored into the performance evaluation is an expense ratio of 0.86% (average) and a 4.0% front-end load that is levied at the time of purchase.

The fund's risk rating is currently B- (Good). Volatility, as measured by standard deviation, is considered low for fixed income funds at 2.78. Another risk factor is the fund's very low average duration of 2.3 years (i.e. low interest rate risk).

Michael V. Salm has been running the fund for 9 years and currently receives a manager quality ranking of 51 (0=worst, 99=best). This fund offers only a moderate level of risk but investors looking for strong performance are still waiting.
Services Offered: Automated phone transactions, payroll deductions, an IRA investment plan, a 401K investment plan, a Keogh investment plan and a systematic withdrawal plan.

Data Date	Investment Rating	Net Assets ($Mil)	NAV	Performance Rating/Pts	Total Return Y-T-D	Risk Rating/Pts
3-16	D+	974	6.78	D- / 1.0	-0.62%	B- / 7.3
2015	C-	1,073	6.87	C- / 3.2	-1.75%	B- / 7.5
2014	B+	1,066	7.20	C+/ 6.0	5.13%	C+/ 6.9
2013	A	779	7.14	B- / 7.0	2.06%	C+/ 6.6
2012	B	876	7.27	C / 5.3	10.59%	C+/ 6.3
2011	B	842	6.77	B / 8.1	5.13%	C- / 3.3

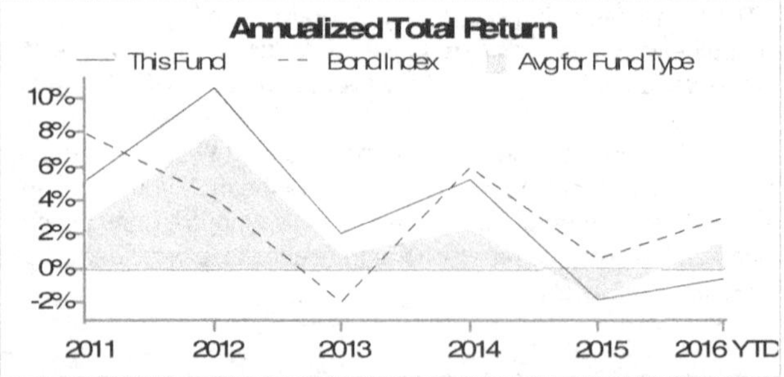

Putnam NY Tax Exempt Income A (PTEIX) B- Good

Fund Family: Putnam Funds **Phone:** (800) 225-1581
Address: One Post Office Square, Boston, MA 02109
Fund Type: MUS - Municipal - Single State
Major Rating Factors: Strong performance is the major factor driving the B- (Good) TheStreet.com Investment Rating for Putnam NY Tax Exempt Income A. The fund currently has a performance rating of B (Good) based on an average return of 2.91% over the last three years (4.82% taxable equivalent) and 1.62% over the last three months (2.68% taxable equivalent). Factored into the performance evaluation is an expense ratio of 0.74% (low) and a 4.0% front-end load that is levied at the time of purchase.

The fund's risk rating is currently C (Fair). Volatility, as measured by standard deviation, is considered average for fixed income funds at 3.63. Another risk factor is the fund's fairly average duration of 6.4 years (i.e. average interest rate risk).

Paul M. Drury has been running the fund for 14 years and currently receives a manager quality ranking of 33 (0=worst, 99=best). If you desire an average level of risk and strong performance, then this fund is a good option.
Services Offered: Automated phone transactions, payroll deductions, bank draft capabilities and a systematic withdrawal plan.

Data Date	Investment Rating	Net Assets ($Mil)	NAV	Performance Rating/Pts	Total Return Y-T-D	Risk Rating/Pts
3-16	B-	931	8.70	B / 8.0	1.62%	C / 4.6
2015	C+	919	8.63	B / 7.8	2.81%	C / 4.5
2014	B-	950	8.69	B- / 7.4	9.51%	C- / 4.1
2013	D	953	8.23	C- / 4.0	-4.54%	C- / 4.0
2012	C+	1,183	8.95	C+/ 6.2	7.26%	C / 4.3
2011	B	1,095	8.66	B- / 7.0	9.73%	C / 4.7

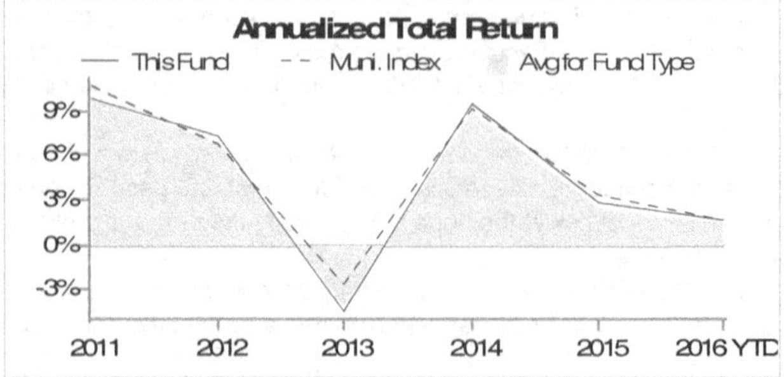

Putnam Short Duration Income A (PSDTX) C+ Fair

Fund Family: Putnam Funds **Phone:** (800) 225-1581
Address: One Post Office Square, Boston, MA 02109
Fund Type: COI - Corporate - Investment Grade

Major Rating Factors: A moderate risk profile coupled with stable earnings characterizes Putnam Short Duration Income A which receives a TheStreet.com Investment Rating of C+ (Fair). Volatility, as measured by standard deviation, is considered very low for fixed income funds at 0.23. Another risk factor is the fund's very low average duration of 0.2 years (i.e. low interest rate risk). The fund's risk rating is currently A+ (Excellent).

The fund's performance rating is currently C- (Fair). It has registered an average return of 0.47% over the last three years and is up 0.17% over the last three months. Factored into the performance evaluation is an expense ratio of 0.54% (very low).

Joanne M. Driscoll has been running the fund for 5 years and currently receives a manager quality ranking of 80 (0=worst, 99=best). If you desire stability with a moderate level of risk then this fund is an excellent option.

Services Offered: Automated phone transactions, payroll deductions, bank draft capabilities, wire transfers and a systematic withdrawal plan.

Data Date	Investment Rating	Net Assets ($Mil)	NAV	Performance Rating/Pts	Total Return Y-T-D	Risk Rating/Pts
3-16	C+	1,408	10.02	C- / 3.3	0.17%	A+ / 9.9
2015	B+	1,339	10.02	C / 4.6	0.27%	A+ / 9.9
2014	C	1,479	10.04	D / 1.6	0.51%	A+ / 9.9
2013	U	1,176	10.04	U / --	0.59%	U / --
2012	U	419	10.04	U / --	0.94%	U / --

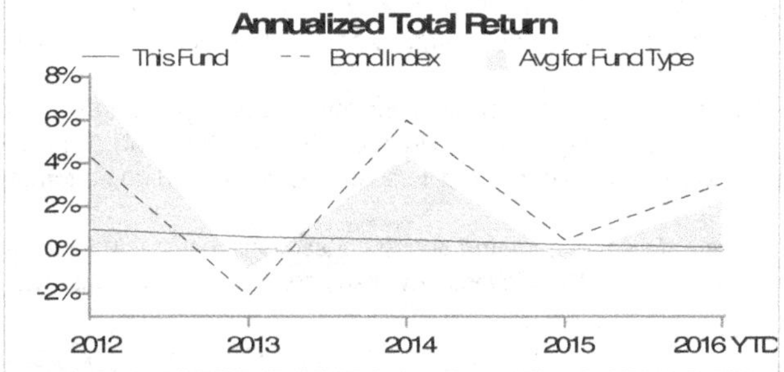

Putnam Tax Exempt Income A (PTAEX) B- Good

Fund Family: Putnam Funds **Phone:** (800) 225-1581
Address: One Post Office Square, Boston, MA 02109
Fund Type: MUN - Municipal - National

Major Rating Factors: Strong performance is the major factor driving the B- (Good) TheStreet.com Investment Rating for Putnam Tax Exempt Income A. The fund currently has a performance rating of B (Good) based on an average return of 3.10% over the last three years (5.13% taxable equivalent) and 1.46% over the last three months (2.42% taxable equivalent). Factored into the performance evaluation is an expense ratio of 0.75% (low) and a 4.0% front-end load that is levied at the time of purchase.

The fund's risk rating is currently C (Fair). Volatility, as measured by standard deviation, is considered average for fixed income funds at 3.59. Another risk factor is the fund's fairly average duration of 6.0 years (i.e. average interest rate risk).

Paul M. Drury has been running the fund for 14 years and currently receives a manager quality ranking of 40 (0=worst, 99=best). If you desire an average level of risk and strong performance, then this fund is a good option.

Services Offered: Automated phone transactions, payroll deductions, bank draft capabilities and a systematic withdrawal plan.

Data Date	Investment Rating	Net Assets ($Mil)	NAV	Performance Rating/Pts	Total Return Y-T-D	Risk Rating/Pts
3-16	B-	879	8.79	B / 8.1	1.46%	C / 4.7
2015	C+	874	8.74	B / 8.0	2.64%	C / 4.5
2014	B+	904	8.84	B / 8.2	9.92%	C- / 4.2
2013	C	910	8.37	C+ / 6.2	-4.10%	C- / 4.0
2012	B+	1,153	9.08	B- / 7.5	8.79%	C- / 4.1
2011	A-	1,090	8.68	B / 8.0	10.77%	C- / 4.1

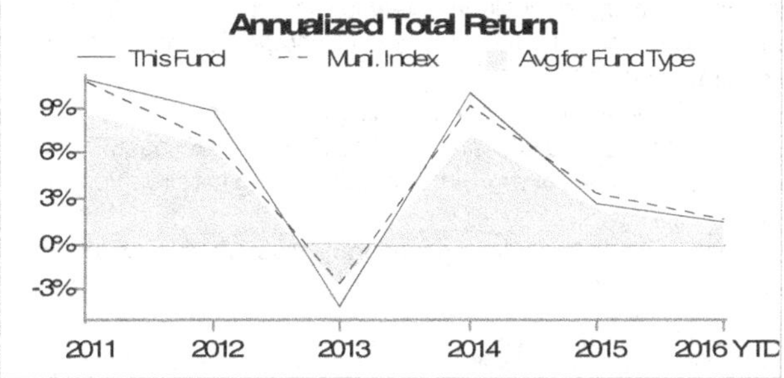

Putnam Tax-Free Hi-Yield A (PTHAX) C- Fair

Fund Family: Putnam Funds **Phone:** (800) 225-1581
Address: One Post Office Square, Boston, MA 02109
Fund Type: COH - Corporate - High Yield

Major Rating Factors: Putnam Tax-Free Hi-Yield A has adopted a very risky asset allocation strategy and currently receives an overall TheStreet.com Investment Rating of C- (Fair). Volatility, as measured by standard deviation, is considered above average for fixed income funds at 4.79. Another risk factor is the fund's above average duration of 7.4 years (i.e. higher interest rate risk). The high level of risk (D, Weak) did however, reward investors with excellent performance.

The fund's performance rating is currently B (Good). It has registered an average return of 4.33% over the last three years and is up 2.25% over the last three months. Factored into the performance evaluation is an expense ratio of 0.80% (low), a 4.0% front-end load that is levied at the time of purchase and a 1.0% back-end load levied at the time of sale.

Paul M. Drury has been running the fund for 14 years and currently receives a manager quality ranking of 99 (0=worst, 99=best). If you are comfortable owning a very high risk investment, this fund may be an option.

Services Offered: Automated phone transactions, payroll deductions, bank draft capabilities, an IRA investment plan, a 401K investment plan, wire transfers and a systematic withdrawal plan.

Data Date	Investment Rating	Net Assets ($Mil)	NAV	Performance Rating/Pts	Total Return Y-T-D	Risk Rating/Pts
3-16	C-	781	12.69	B / 8.0	2.25%	D / 2.2
2015	C-	771	12.53	B / 8.1	4.35%	D / 1.9
2014	D+	815	12.53	B / 7.9	13.70%	D- / 1.1
2013	D-	770	11.53	C / 4.3	-5.41%	D / 2.0
2012	D+	951	12.76	C+ / 6.5	13.01%	D+ / 2.4
2011	C-	877	11.81	B / 7.8	10.62%	D / 1.9

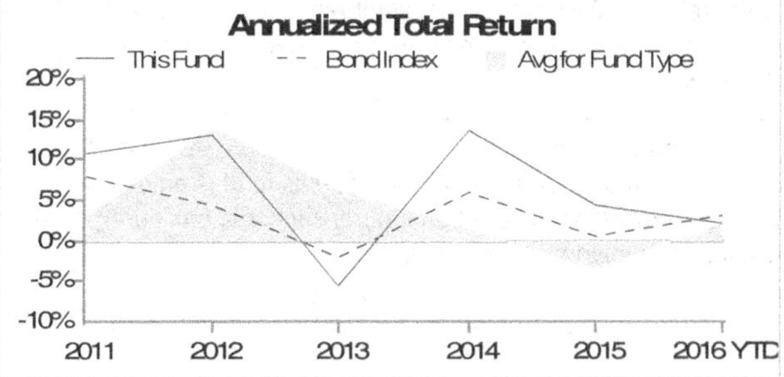

Putnam US Govt Income Tr A (PGSIX) D+ Weak

Fund Family: Putnam Funds **Phone:** (800) 225-1581
Address: One Post Office Square, Boston, MA 02109
Fund Type: USS - US Government - Short & Inter. Term
Major Rating Factors: Disappointing performance is the major factor driving the D+ (Weak) TheStreet.com Investment Rating for Putnam US Govt Income Tr A. The fund currently has a performance rating of D- (Weak) based on an average return of 0.98% over the last three years and -0.90% over the last three months. Factored into the performance evaluation is an expense ratio of 0.85% (average) and a 4.0% front-end load that is levied at the time of purchase.

The fund's risk rating is currently B (Good). Volatility, as measured by standard deviation, is considered low for fixed income funds at 2.66. Another risk factor is the fund's very low average duration of 1.3 years (i.e. low interest rate risk).

Michael V. Salm has been running the fund for 9 years and currently receives a manager quality ranking of 85 (0=worst, 99=best). This fund offers only a moderate level of risk but investors looking for strong performance are still waiting.

Services Offered: Automated phone transactions, payroll deductions, an IRA investment plan, a 401K investment plan and a systematic withdrawal plan.

Data Date	Investment Rating	Net Assets ($Mil)	NAV	Performance Rating/Pts	Total Return Y-T-D	Risk Rating/Pts
3-16	D+	786	13.15	D- / 1.3	-0.90%	B / 7.6
2015	C	811	13.36	C- / 4.2	-0.26%	B- / 7.3
2014	C-	881	13.73	C- / 3.0	5.49%	B- / 7.3
2013	D+	930	13.26	D / 1.9	-0.48%	B / 8.0
2012	D+	1,203	13.53	D- / 1.4	3.31%	B+ / 8.6
2011	B	1,287	13.73	C / 5.2	4.73%	C+ / 6.7

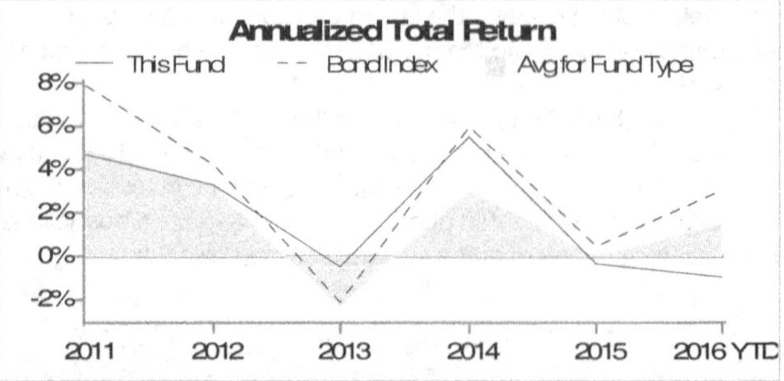

RidgeWorth Seix US Gvt Sec U/S Bd I (SIGVX) C+ Fair

Fund Family: RidgeWorth Funds **Phone:** (888) 784-3863
Address: 50 Hurt Plaza, Atlanta, GA 30303
Fund Type: USS - US Government - Short & Inter. Term
Major Rating Factors: Disappointing performance is the major factor driving the C+ (Fair) TheStreet.com Investment Rating for RidgeWorth Seix US Gvt Sec U/S Bd I. The fund currently has a performance rating of D+ (Weak) based on an average return of 0.26% over the last three years and 0.02% over the last three months. Factored into the performance evaluation is an expense ratio of 0.39% (very low).

The fund's risk rating is currently A+ (Excellent). Volatility, as measured by standard deviation, is considered very low for fixed income funds at 0.30. Another risk factor is the fund's very low average duration of 0.3 years (i.e. low interest rate risk).

Chad K. Stephens has been running the fund for 10 years and currently receives a manager quality ranking of 73 (0=worst, 99=best). This fund offers only a moderate level of risk but investors looking for strong performance are still waiting.

Services Offered: Automated phone transactions and a systematic withdrawal plan.

Data Date	Investment Rating	Net Assets ($Mil)	NAV	Performance Rating/Pts	Total Return Y-T-D	Risk Rating/Pts
3-16	C+	1,556	10.03	D+ / 2.8	0.02%	A+ / 9.9
2015	B	1,520	10.05	C- / 4.1	-0.03%	A+ / 9.9
2014	C	1,728	10.13	D / 1.8	0.91%	A+ / 9.9
2013	C	2,099	10.11	D / 1.6	0.05%	A+ / 9.9
2012	C-	2,388	10.17	E+ / 0.7	1.55%	A+ / 9.9
2011	C	1,818	10.10	D- / 1.5	1.41%	A+ / 9.8

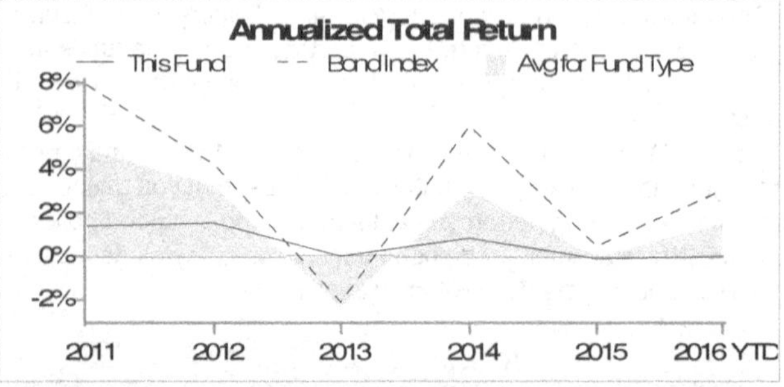

SA Global Fixed Income Fund (SAXIX) B- Good

Fund Family: SA Funds **Phone:** (800) 366-7266
Address: 3055 Olin Avenue, San Jose, CA 95128
Fund Type: GES - General - Short & Inter. Term
Major Rating Factors: A moderate risk profile coupled with stable earnings characterizes SA Global Fixed Income Fund which receives a TheStreet.com Investment Rating of B- (Good). Volatility, as measured by standard deviation, is considered very low for fixed income funds at 1.26. Another risk factor is the fund's very low average duration of 2.7 years (i.e. low interest rate risk). The fund's risk rating is currently A- (Excellent).

The fund's performance rating is currently C (Fair). It has registered an average return of 0.86% over the last three years and is up 1.52% over the last three months. Factored into the performance evaluation is an expense ratio of 0.74% (low).

David A. Plecha has been running the fund for 17 years and currently receives a manager quality ranking of 58 (0=worst, 99=best). If you desire stability with a moderate level of risk then this fund is an excellent option.

Services Offered: Automated phone transactions, bank draft capabilities, an IRA investment plan and wire transfers.

Data Date	Investment Rating	Net Assets ($Mil)	NAV	Performance Rating/Pts	Total Return Y-T-D	Risk Rating/Pts
3-16	B-	733	9.73	C / 4.5	1.52%	A- / 9.0
2015	B-	741	9.60	C / 4.4	0.27%	A- / 9.0
2014	C	751	9.65	D+ / 2.3	1.47%	A- / 9.2
2013	C-	631	9.62	D / 1.9	-0.49%	A- / 9.0
2012	D+	564	9.86	D- / 1.1	2.80%	A- / 9.0
2011	C-	563	9.99	D- / 1.5	1.73%	A / 9.3

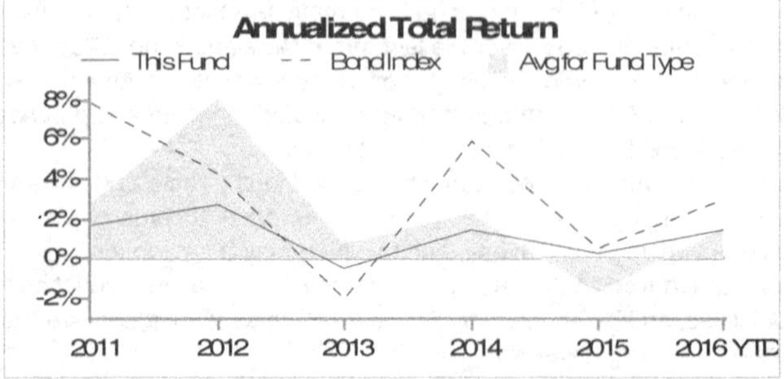

SA US Fixed Income Fund (SAUFX) C+ Fair

Fund Family: SA Funds **Phone:** (800) 366-7266
Address: 3055 Olin Avenue, San Jose, CA 95128
Fund Type: GEI - General - Investment Grade
Major Rating Factors: Disappointing performance is the major factor driving the C+ (Fair) TheStreet.com Investment Rating for SA US Fixed Income Fund. The fund currently has a performance rating of D+ (Weak) based on an average return of 0.10% over the last three years and 0.68% over the last three months. Factored into the performance evaluation is an expense ratio of 0.65% (low).

The fund's risk rating is currently A+ (Excellent). Volatility, as measured by standard deviation, is considered very low for fixed income funds at 0.48. Another risk factor is the fund's very low average duration of 1.5 years (i.e. low interest rate risk).

David A. Plecha has been running the fund for 17 years and currently receives a manager quality ranking of 58 (0=worst, 99=best). This fund offers only a moderate level of risk but investors looking for strong performance are still waiting.
Services Offered: Bank draft capabilities, an IRA investment plan, a 401K investment plan and wire transfers.

Data Date	Investment Rating	Net Assets ($Mil)	NAV	Performance Rating/Pts	Total Return Y-T-D	Risk Rating/Pts
3-16	C+	607	10.21	D+ / 2.8	0.68%	A+ / 9.8
2015	C	610	10.15	D+ / 2.9	0.06%	A+ / 9.8
2014	D+	594	10.17	E+ / 0.8	-0.17%	A+ / 9.9
2013	C-	459	10.19	E+ / 0.7	-0.27%	A+ / 9.9
2012	C-	392	10.22	E / 0.5	0.31%	A+ / 9.9
2011	C-	345	10.22	D- / 1.2	0.44%	A+ / 9.9

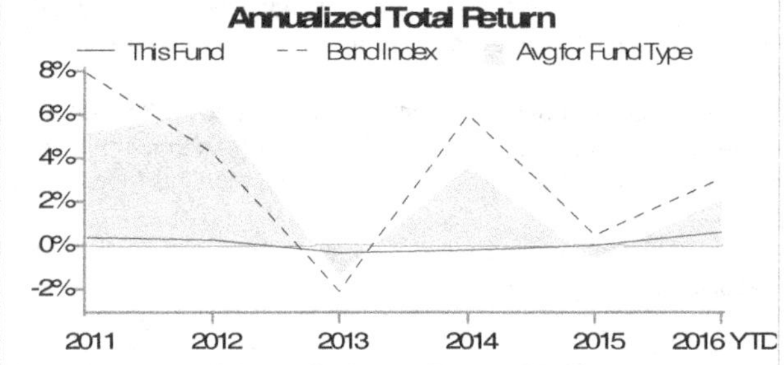

Sanford C Bernstein II Int Dur Inst (SIIDX) B Good

Fund Family: Alliance Bernstein Funds **Phone:** (800) 221-5672
Address: P.O. Box 786003, San Antonio, TX 78278
Fund Type: GES - General - Short & Inter. Term
Major Rating Factors: Strong performance is the major factor driving the B (Good) TheStreet.com Investment Rating for Sanford C Bernstein II Int Dur Inst. The fund currently has a performance rating of B- (Good) based on an average return of 2.64% over the last three years and 3.07% over the last three months. Factored into the performance evaluation is an expense ratio of 0.58% (low).

The fund's risk rating is currently C+ (Fair). Volatility, as measured by standard deviation, is considered average for fixed income funds at 3.23. Another risk factor is the fund's fairly average duration of 5.2 years (i.e. average interest rate risk).

Greg Wilensky has been running the fund for 11 years and currently receives a manager quality ranking of 62 (0=worst, 99=best). If you desire an average level of risk and strong performance, then this fund is a good option.
Services Offered: Payroll deductions, bank draft capabilities, wire transfers and a systematic withdrawal plan.

Data Date	Investment Rating	Net Assets ($Mil)	NAV	Performance Rating/Pts	Total Return Y-T-D	Risk Rating/Pts
3-16	B	629	15.21	B- / 7.5	3.07%	C+ / 5.6
2015	C+	613	14.86	C+ / 6.5	0.42%	C / 5.5
2014	C+	647	15.42	C / 5.1	6.59%	C+ / 6.3
2013	C+	701	15.35	C / 4.3	-2.03%	C+ / 6.9
2012	B	1,039	16.23	C / 4.5	5.53%	B- / 7.3
2011	B+	1,132	15.95	C+ / 5.6	6.88%	C+ / 6.7

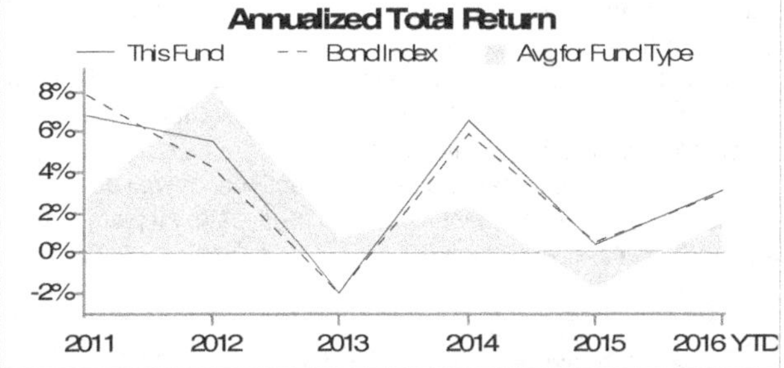

Sanford C Bernstein Interm Duration (SNIDX) B- Good

Fund Family: Bernstein Funds **Phone:** (212) 486-5800
Address: 1345 Avenue of the Americas, New York, NY 10105
Fund Type: GES - General - Short & Inter. Term
Major Rating Factors: Strong performance is the major factor driving the B- (Good) TheStreet.com Investment Rating for Sanford C Bernstein Interm Duration. The fund currently has a performance rating of B- (Good) based on an average return of 2.49% over the last three years and 3.07% over the last three months. Factored into the performance evaluation is an expense ratio of 0.59% (low).

The fund's risk rating is currently C+ (Fair). Volatility, as measured by standard deviation, is considered average for fixed income funds at 3.25. Another risk factor is the fund's fairly average duration of 5.4 years (i.e. average interest rate risk).

Greg Wilensky has been running the fund for 11 years and currently receives a manager quality ranking of 56 (0=worst, 99=best). If you desire an average level of risk and strong performance, then this fund is a good option.
Services Offered: Bank draft capabilities, wire transfers and a systematic withdrawal plan.

Data Date	Investment Rating	Net Assets ($Mil)	NAV	Performance Rating/Pts	Total Return Y-T-D	Risk Rating/Pts
3-16	B-	3,375	13.32	B- / 7.3	3.07%	C+ / 5.6
2015	C	3,338	13.01	C+ / 6.3	0.31%	C / 5.5
2014	C+	3,597	13.53	C / 5.0	6.59%	C+ / 6.3
2013	C	3,840	13.35	C- / 4.0	-2.36%	C+ / 6.9
2012	C+	4,616	14.09	C / 4.3	5.26%	B- / 7.0
2011	B+	4,986	13.86	C / 5.5	6.82%	C+ / 6.5

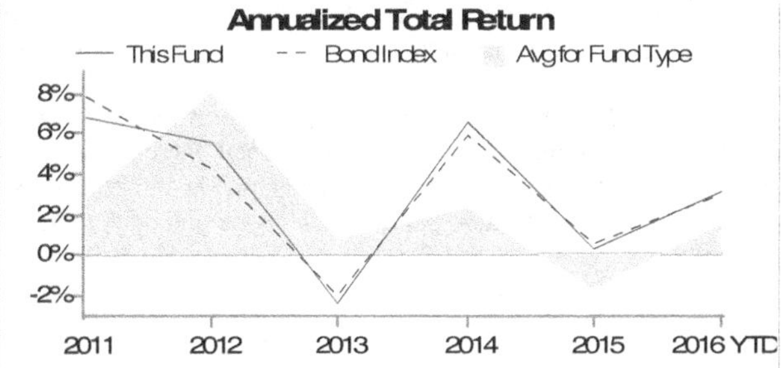

Schwab Tax-Free Bond Fund (SWNTX) A+ Excellent

Fund Family: Schwab Funds **Phone:** (800) 407-0256
Address: P.O. Box 8283, Boston, MA 02266
Fund Type: MUN - Municipal - National
Major Rating Factors: Exceptional performance is the major factor driving the A+ (Excellent) TheStreet.com Investment Rating for Schwab Tax-Free Bond Fund. The fund currently has a performance rating of A- (Excellent) based on an average return of 2.99% over the last three years (4.95% taxable equivalent) and 1.45% over the last three months (2.40% taxable equivalent). Factored into the performance evaluation is an expense ratio of 0.57% (very low).

The fund's risk rating is currently B- (Good). Volatility, as measured by standard deviation, is considered low for fixed income funds at 2.81. Another risk factor is the fund's below average duration of 4.8 years (i.e. lower interest rate risk).

Kenneth M. Salinger has been running the fund for 8 years and currently receives a manager quality ranking of 70 (0=worst, 99=best). If you desire only a moderate level of risk and strong performance, then this fund is an excellent option.
Services Offered: Automated phone transactions, payroll deductions, bank draft capabilities and wire transfers.

Data Date	Investment Rating	Net Assets ($Mil)	NAV	Performance Rating/Pts	Total Return Y-T-D	Risk Rating/Pts
3-16	A+	681	11.99	A- / 9.0	1.45%	B- / 7.2
2015	A+	650	11.88	B+ / 8.9	2.65%	C+ / 6.9
2014	A	642	11.89	B / 7.6	6.54%	C+ / 5.8
2013	A+	591	11.53	B / 8.2	-1.32%	C+ / 6.2
2012	A	713	11.96	C+ / 6.9	5.55%	C+ / 5.9
2011	A+	533	11.76	B- / 7.1	9.57%	C+ / 6.5

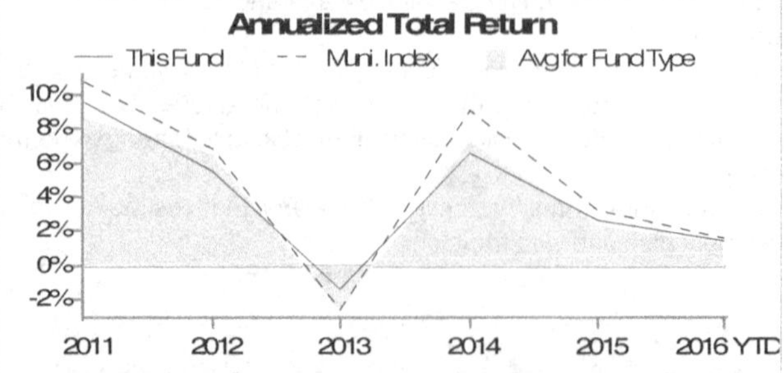

Schwab Total Bond Market Fd (SWLBX) B Good

Fund Family: Schwab Funds **Phone:** (800) 407-0256
Address: P.O. Box 8283, Boston, MA 02266
Fund Type: USL - US Government - Long Term
Major Rating Factors: Schwab Total Bond Market Fd receives a TheStreet.com Investment Rating of B (Good). The fund has a performance rating of C+ (Fair) based on an average return of 2.20% over the last three years and 2.89% over the last three months. Factored into the performance evaluation is an expense ratio of 0.54% (very low).

The fund's risk rating is currently C+ (Fair). Volatility, as measured by standard deviation, is considered average for fixed income funds at 3.00. Another risk factor is the fund's fairly average duration of 5.3 years (i.e. average interest rate risk).

Steven Hung has been running the fund for 18 years and currently receives a manager quality ranking of 85 (0=worst, 99=best). If you desire an average level of risk, then this fund may be an option.
Services Offered: Automated phone transactions, payroll deductions, bank draft capabilities, an IRA investment plan, a 401K investment plan, a Keogh investment plan and wire transfers.

Data Date	Investment Rating	Net Assets ($Mil)	NAV	Performance Rating/Pts	Total Return Y-T-D	Risk Rating/Pts
3-16	B	1,324	9.61	C+ / 6.9	2.89%	C+ / 6.5
2015	C+	1,355	9.39	C+ / 5.9	0.29%	C+ / 6.4
2014	C	1,266	9.57	C- / 4.0	5.83%	B- / 7.1
2013	C	890	9.25	C- / 3.4	-2.38%	B / 7.6
2012	C	927	9.70	C- / 3.0	3.80%	B / 7.6
2011	C-	948	9.59	C- / 3.2	7.40%	B / 7.6

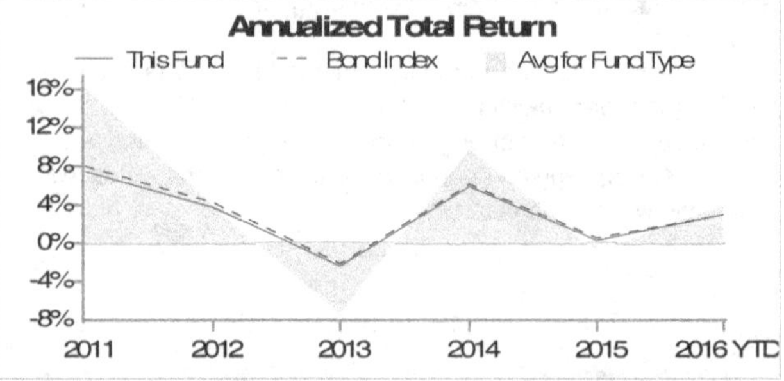

SEI Daily Inc Tr-Sh Dur Gov Bd A (TCSGX) C+ Fair

Fund Family: SEI Financial Management Corp **Phone:** (800) 342-5734
Address: One Freedom Valley Drive, Oaks, PA 19456
Fund Type: USS - US Government - Short & Inter. Term
Major Rating Factors: A moderate risk profile coupled with stable earnings characterizes SEI Daily Inc Tr-Sh Dur Gov Bd A which receives a TheStreet.com Investment Rating of C+ (Fair). Volatility, as measured by standard deviation, is considered very low for fixed income funds at 0.94. Another risk factor is the fund's very low average duration of 1.6 years (i.e. low interest rate risk). The fund's risk rating is currently A (Excellent).

The fund's performance rating is currently C- (Fair). It has registered an average return of 0.54% over the last three years and is up 0.99% over the last three months. Factored into the performance evaluation is an expense ratio of 0.73% (low).

Michael F. Garrett has been running the fund for 13 years and currently receives a manager quality ranking of 59 (0=worst, 99=best). If you desire stability with a moderate level of risk then this fund is an excellent option.
Services Offered: Automated phone transactions and bank draft capabilities.

Data Date	Investment Rating	Net Assets ($Mil)	NAV	Performance Rating/Pts	Total Return Y-T-D	Risk Rating/Pts
3-16	C+	814	10.51	C- / 3.6	0.99%	A / 9.3
2015	C	782	10.43	D+ / 2.9	-0.57%	A / 9.3
2014	C-	715	10.50	D- / 1.5	0.73%	A / 9.5
2013	C	716	10.52	D / 1.7	-0.37%	A / 9.4
2012	C-	708	10.65	D- / 1.0	1.48%	A / 9.5
2011	C	733	10.70	D / 1.8	2.36%	A+ / 9.6

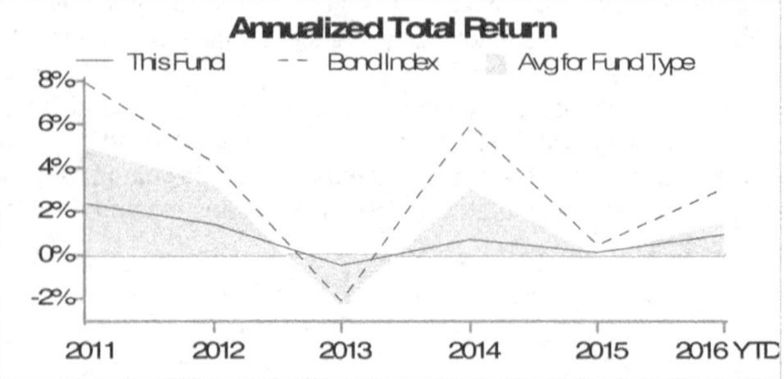

SEI Inst Intl Emerging Mkts Debt A (SITEX) E- Very Weak

Fund Family: SEI Financial Management Corp **Phone:** (800) 342-5734
Address: One Freedom Valley Drive, Oaks, PA 19456
Fund Type: EM - Emerging Market
Major Rating Factors: SEI Inst Intl Emerging Mkts Debt A has adopted a very risky asset allocation strategy and currently receives an overall TheStreet.com Investment Rating of E- (Very Weak). Volatility, as measured by standard deviation, is considered high for fixed income funds at 9.56. Unfortunately, the high level of risk (E, Very Weak) failed to pay off as investors endured poor performance.

The fund's performance rating is currently E (Very Weak). It has registered an average return of -3.98% over the last three years and is up 7.81% over the last three months. Factored into the performance evaluation is an expense ratio of 1.61% (above average) and a 1.0% back-end load levied at the time of sale.

Peter J. Wilby has been running the fund for 10 years and currently receives a manager quality ranking of 6 (0=worst, 99=best). If you can tolerate very high levels of risk in the hope of improved future returns, holding this fund may be an option.
Services Offered: Automated phone transactions, payroll deductions and bank draft capabilities.

Data Date	Investment Rating	Net Assets ($Mil)	NAV	Performance Rating/Pts	Total Return Y-T-D	Risk Rating/Pts
3-16	E-	1,364	9.39	E / 0.3	7.81%	E / 0.3
2015	E-	1,258	8.71	E- / 0.1	-9.12%	E / 0.3
2014	E-	1,322	9.63	E+ / 0.8	-1.20%	E / 0.3
2013	E	1,164	10.02	D+ / 2.3	-9.59%	E / 0.4
2012	B-	1,221	11.57	A / 9.4	17.54%	D- / 1.1
2011	C+	905	10.88	B+ / 8.9	4.74%	D / 1.7

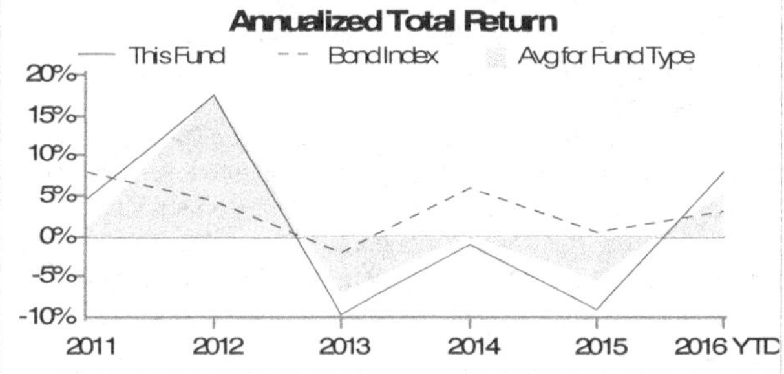

SEI Inst Inv Core Fixed Income A (SCOAX) A Excellent

Fund Family: SEI Financial Management Corp **Phone:** (800) 342-5734
Address: One Freedom Valley Drive, Oaks, PA 19456
Fund Type: COI - Corporate - Investment Grade
Major Rating Factors: Strong performance is the major factor driving the A (Excellent) TheStreet.com Investment Rating for SEI Inst Inv Core Fixed Income A. The fund currently has a performance rating of B (Good) based on an average return of 2.95% over the last three years and 2.80% over the last three months. Factored into the performance evaluation is an expense ratio of 0.38% (very low).

The fund's risk rating is currently C+ (Fair). Volatility, as measured by standard deviation, is considered average for fixed income funds at 2.93. Another risk factor is the fund's fairly average duration of 6.8 years (i.e. average interest rate risk).

Douglas S. Swanson has been running the fund for 7 years and currently receives a manager quality ranking of 90 (0=worst, 99=best). If you desire an average level of risk and strong performance, then this fund is a good option.
Services Offered: Automated phone transactions, bank draft capabilities, an IRA investment plan, a 401K investment plan and wire transfers.

Data Date	Investment Rating	Net Assets ($Mil)	NAV	Performance Rating/Pts	Total Return Y-T-D	Risk Rating/Pts
3-16	A	5,306	10.42	B / 7.8	2.80%	C+ / 6.8
2015	B-	5,180	10.20	B- / 7.2	0.85%	C+ / 5.9
2014	A-	6,295	10.59	C+ / 6.1	6.76%	B- / 7.1

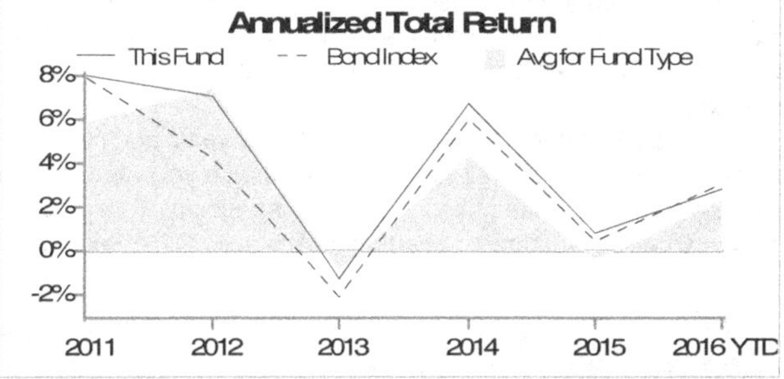

SEI Inst Inv High Yield Bond A (SGYAX) D Weak

Fund Family: SEI Financial Management Corp **Phone:** (800) 342-5734
Address: One Freedom Valley Drive, Oaks, PA 19456
Fund Type: COH - Corporate - High Yield
Major Rating Factors: SEI Inst Inv High Yield Bond A has adopted a very risky asset allocation strategy and currently receives an overall TheStreet.com Investment Rating of D (Weak). Volatility, as measured by standard deviation, is considered above average for fixed income funds at 5.17. Another risk factor is the fund's below average duration of 4.8 years (i.e. lower interest rate risk). Unfortunately, the high level of risk (D, Weak) has only provided investors with average performance.

The fund's performance rating is currently C- (Fair). It has registered an average return of 1.57% over the last three years and is up 2.02% over the last three months. Factored into the performance evaluation is an expense ratio of 0.56% (very low).

Michael E. Schroer has been running the fund for 7 years and currently receives a manager quality ranking of 70 (0=worst, 99=best). If you are comfortable owning a very high risk investment, then this fund may be an option.
Services Offered: Automated phone transactions, bank draft capabilities, an IRA investment plan, a 401K investment plan and wire transfers.

Data Date	Investment Rating	Net Assets ($Mil)	NAV	Performance Rating/Pts	Total Return Y-T-D	Risk Rating/Pts
3-16	D	2,434	8.25	C- / 3.9	2.02%	D / 2.0
2015	D	2,296	8.22	C / 4.4	-4.16%	D / 2.1
2014	B+	2,205	9.22	B+ / 8.6	2.54%	C- / 3.6

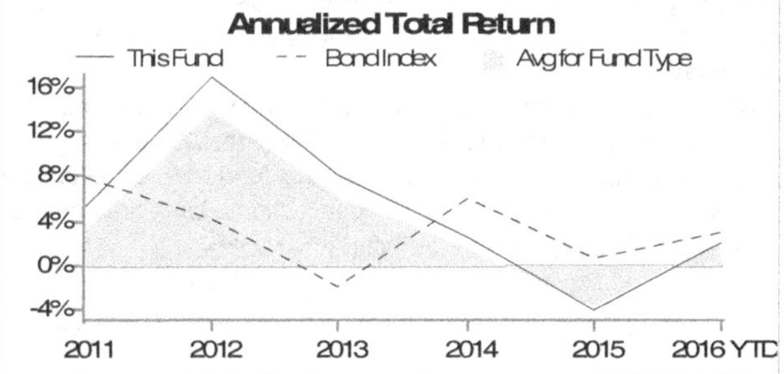

SEI Inst Inv Long Dur Credit A (SLDAX) C- Fair

Fund Family: SEI Financial Management Corp **Phone:** (800) 342-5734
Address: One Freedom Valley Drive, Oaks, PA 19456
Fund Type: GEI - General - Investment Grade
Major Rating Factors: SEI Inst Inv Long Dur Credit A has adopted a very risky asset allocation strategy and currently receives an overall TheStreet.com Investment Rating of C- (Fair). Volatility, as measured by standard deviation, is considered high for fixed income funds at 8.21. Another risk factor is the fund's very high average duration of 13.9 years (i.e. very high interest rate risk). The high level of risk (E, Very Weak) did however, reward investors with excellent performance.

The fund's performance rating is currently A (Excellent). It has registered an average return of 5.26% over the last three years and is up 6.58% over the last three months. Factored into the performance evaluation is an expense ratio of 0.37% (very low).

Jack Sommers has been running the fund for 4 years and currently receives a manager quality ranking of 28 (0=worst, 99=best). If you are comfortable owning a very high risk investment, this fund may be an option.
Services Offered: Automated phone transactions, bank draft capabilities, an IRA investment plan, a 401K investment plan and wire transfers.

Data Date	Investment Rating	Net Assets ($Mil)	NAV	Performance Rating/Pts	Total Return Y-T-D	Risk Rating/Pts
3-16	C-	3,226	10.10	A / 9.3	6.58%	E / 0.3
2015	D+	3,024	9.57	B- / 7.2	-2.71%	E / 0.3
2014	U	3,151	10.47	U / --	17.04%	U / --

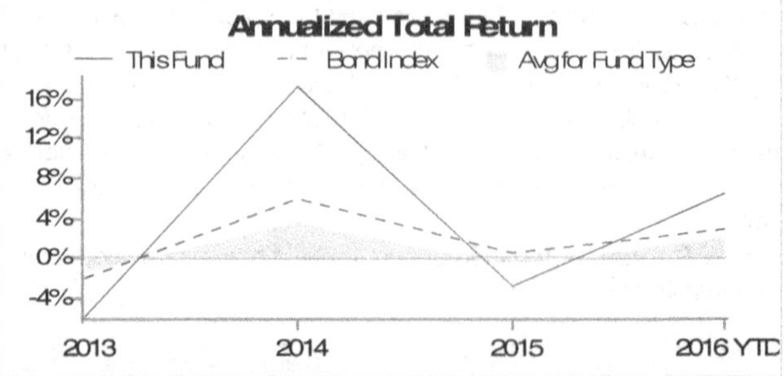

SEI Inst Inv Long Duration A (LDRAX) C- Fair

Fund Family: SEI Financial Management Corp **Phone:** (800) 342-5734
Address: One Freedom Valley Drive, Oaks, PA 19456
Fund Type: COI - Corporate - Investment Grade
Major Rating Factors: SEI Inst Inv Long Duration A has adopted a very risky asset allocation strategy and currently receives an overall TheStreet.com Investment Rating of C- (Fair). Volatility, as measured by standard deviation, is considered high for fixed income funds at 8.58. Another risk factor is the fund's very high average duration of 13.7 years (i.e. very high interest rate risk). The high level of risk (E, Very Weak) did however, reward investors with excellent performance.

The fund's performance rating is currently A- (Excellent). It has registered an average return of 4.74% over the last three years and is up 7.12% over the last three months. Factored into the performance evaluation is an expense ratio of 0.37% (very low).

Tad Rivelle has been running the fund for 12 years and currently receives a manager quality ranking of 37 (0=worst, 99=best). If you are comfortable owning a very high risk investment, this fund may be an option.
Services Offered: Automated phone transactions.

Data Date	Investment Rating	Net Assets ($Mil)	NAV	Performance Rating/Pts	Total Return Y-T-D	Risk Rating/Pts
3-16	C-	2,842	8.56	A- / 9.0	7.12%	E / 0.3
2015	D	2,781	8.07	C+ / 5.8	-3.69%	E / 0.3
2014	C-	3,967	9.13	A- / 9.1	19.00%	E / 0.3

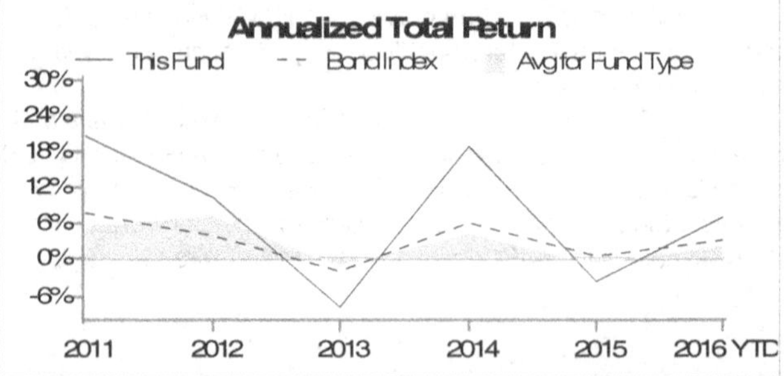

SEI Inst Inv Ultra Short Dur Bd A (SUSAX) B Good

Fund Family: SEI Financial Management Corp **Phone:** (800) 342-5734
Address: One Freedom Valley Drive, Oaks, PA 19456
Fund Type: GEI - General - Investment Grade
Major Rating Factors: A moderate risk profile coupled with stable earnings characterizes SEI Inst Inv Ultra Short Dur Bd A which receives a TheStreet.com Investment Rating of B (Good). Volatility, as measured by standard deviation, is considered very low for fixed income funds at 0.36. Another risk factor is the fund's very low average duration of 1.5 years (i.e. low interest rate risk). The fund's risk rating is currently A+ (Excellent).

The fund's performance rating is currently C- (Fair). It has registered an average return of 0.89% over the last three years and is up 0.52% over the last three months. Factored into the performance evaluation is an expense ratio of 0.22% (very low).

Timothy E. Smith has been running the fund for 5 years and currently receives a manager quality ranking of 86 (0=worst, 99=best). If you desire stability with a moderate level of risk then this fund is an excellent option.
Services Offered: Automated phone transactions, bank draft capabilities, a 401K investment plan and wire transfers.

Data Date	Investment Rating	Net Assets ($Mil)	NAV	Performance Rating/Pts	Total Return Y-T-D	Risk Rating/Pts
3-16	B	631	9.97	C- / 4.2	0.52%	A+ / 9.9
2015	A-	614	9.95	C / 5.4	0.73%	A+ / 9.9
2014	C+	742	10.00	D+ / 2.3	0.74%	A+ / 9.8
2013	U	612	10.03	U / --	0.92%	U / --
2012	U	406	10.04	U / --	2.80%	U / --

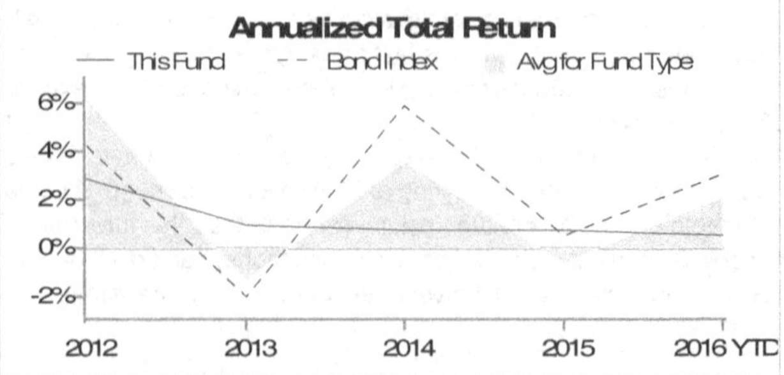

SEI Insti Inv Tr Emer Mrk Dbt Fd A (SEDAX) E Very Weak

Fund Family: SEI Financial Management Corp **Phone:** (800) 342-5734
Address: One Freedom Valley Drive, Oaks, PA 19456
Fund Type: EM - Emerging Market
Major Rating Factors: SEI Insti Inv Tr Emer Mrk Dbt Fd A has adopted a very risky asset allocation strategy and currently receives an overall TheStreet.com Investment Rating of E (Very Weak). Volatility, as measured by standard deviation, is considered high for fixed income funds at 9.59. Unfortunately, the high level of risk (E, Very Weak) failed to pay off as investors endured poor performance.

The fund's performance rating is currently E+ (Very Weak). It has registered an average return of -3.03% over the last three years and is up 8.13% over the last three months. Factored into the performance evaluation is an expense ratio of 0.93% (average).

Peter J. Wilby has been running the fund for 10 years and currently receives a manager quality ranking of 7 (0=worst, 99=best). If you can tolerate very high levels of risk in the hope of improved future returns, holding this fund may be an option.

Services Offered: Automated phone transactions, bank draft capabilities, an IRA investment plan, a 401K investment plan and wire transfers.

Data Date	Investment Rating	Net Assets ($Mil)	NAV	Performance Rating/Pts	Total Return Y-T-D	Risk Rating/Pts
3-16	E	1,832	9.44	E+ / 0.7	8.13%	E / 0.3
2015	E-	1,771	8.73	E- / 0.2	-8.10%	E / 0.3
2014	E	1,658	9.59	D / 2.2	-0.25%	E / 0.3

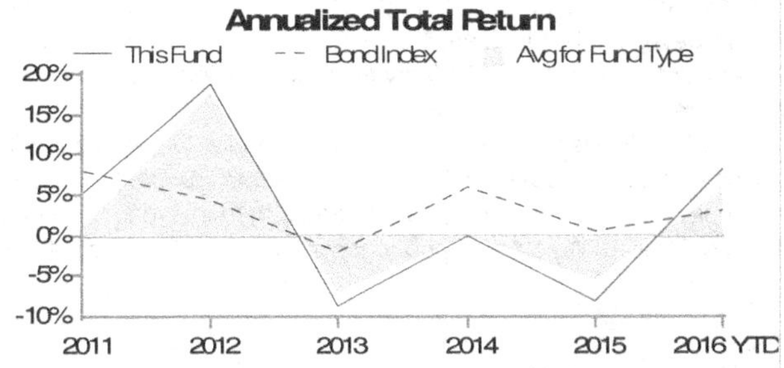

SEI Instl Managed Tr-Core Fix Inc A (TRLVX) B Good

Fund Family: SEI Financial Management Corp **Phone:** (800) 342-5734
Address: One Freedom Valley Drive, Oaks, PA 19456
Fund Type: COI - Corporate - Investment Grade
Major Rating Factors: SEI Instl Managed Tr-Core Fix Inc A receives a TheStreet.com Investment Rating of B (Good). The fund has a performance rating of C+ (Fair) based on an average return of 2.52% over the last three years and 2.70% over the last three months. Factored into the performance evaluation is an expense ratio of 0.86% (average) and a 0.6% back-end load levied at the time of sale.

The fund's risk rating is currently C+ (Fair). Volatility, as measured by standard deviation, is considered average for fixed income funds at 3.02. Another risk factor is the fund's fairly average duration of 5.2 years (i.e. average interest rate risk).

Thomas Wolfe has been running the fund for 6 years and currently receives a manager quality ranking of 84 (0=worst, 99=best). If you desire an average level of risk, then this fund may be an option.

Services Offered: Automated phone transactions, bank draft capabilities, wire transfers and a systematic withdrawal plan.

Data Date	Investment Rating	Net Assets ($Mil)	NAV	Performance Rating/Pts	Total Return Y-T-D	Risk Rating/Pts
3-16	B	2,020	11.46	C+/ 6.9	2.70%	C+/ 6.5
2015	C+	2,025	11.22	C+/ 6.4	0.27%	C+/ 6.3
2014	B+	2,065	11.58	C+/ 6.0	6.56%	C+/ 6.9
2013	B+	1,920	11.14	C+/ 5.6	-1.56%	B / 7.6
2012	A+	2,190	11.64	C+/ 6.2	8.08%	C+/ 6.9
2011	A	2,110	11.09	C+/ 6.2	7.24%	C+/ 6.6

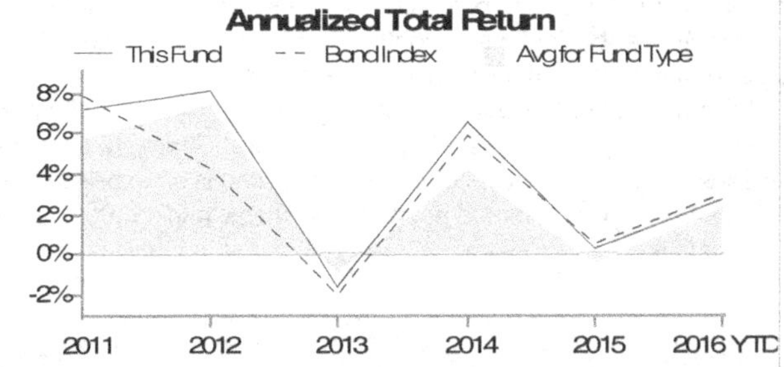

SEI Instl Managed Tr-High Yld Bd A (SHYAX) D- Weak

Fund Family: SEI Financial Management Corp **Phone:** (800) 342-5734
Address: One Freedom Valley Drive, Oaks, PA 19456
Fund Type: GEI - General - Investment Grade
Major Rating Factors: SEI Instl Managed Tr-High Yld Bd A has adopted a risky asset allocation strategy and currently receives an overall TheStreet.com Investment Rating of D- (Weak). Volatility, as measured by standard deviation, is considered above average for fixed income funds at 5.28. Unfortunately, the high level of risk (D+, Weak) failed to pay off as investors endured very poor performance.

The fund's performance rating is currently D- (Weak). It has registered an average return of 0.64% over the last three years and is up 1.65% over the last three months. Factored into the performance evaluation is an expense ratio of 1.08% (average) and a 1.0% back-end load levied at the time of sale.

Robert L. Cook has been running the fund for 12 years and currently receives a manager quality ranking of 31 (0=worst, 99=best). If you can tolerate high levels of risk in the hope of improved future returns, holding this fund may be an option.

Services Offered: Automated phone transactions, payroll deductions, bank draft capabilities, wire transfers and a systematic withdrawal plan.

Data Date	Investment Rating	Net Assets ($Mil)	NAV	Performance Rating/Pts	Total Return Y-T-D	Risk Rating/Pts
3-16	D-	1,513	6.59	D- / 1.3	1.65%	D+/ 2.5
2015	D-	1,492	6.58	D / 1.9	-5.06%	D / 1.9
2014	B+	1,703	7.44	B / 7.8	1.91%	C / 4.3
2013	B+	2,055	7.75	A+/ 9.6	6.95%	D+/ 2.4
2012	B	1,848	7.72	A / 9.3	15.78%	D- / 1.5
2011	B-	1,668	7.13	A+/ 9.7	4.26%	D- / 1.0

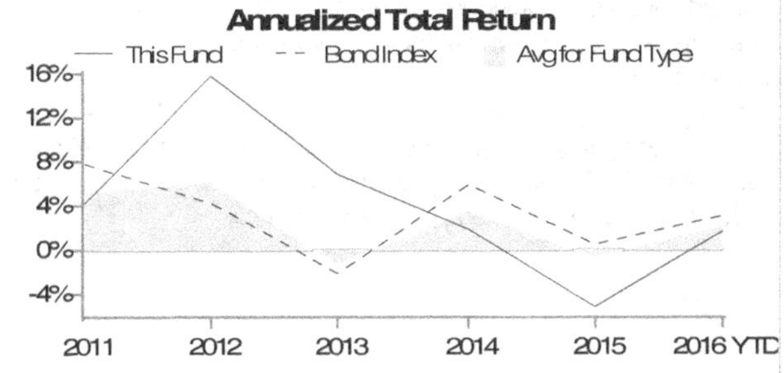

SEI Tax-Exempt Tr-Intrm Term Muni A (SEIMX) A+ Excellent

Fund Family: SEI Financial Management Corp **Phone:** (800) 342-5734
Address: One Freedom Valley Drive, Oaks, PA 19456
Fund Type: MUN - Municipal - National
Major Rating Factors: Strong performance is the major factor driving the A+ (Excellent) TheStreet.com Investment Rating for SEI Tax-Exempt Tr-Intrm Term Muni A. The fund currently has a performance rating of B+ (Good) based on an average return of 2.79% over the last three years (4.62% taxable equivalent) and 1.52% over the last three months (2.52% taxable equivalent). Factored into the performance evaluation is an expense ratio of 0.85% (average) and a 0.5% back-end load levied at the time of sale.

The fund's risk rating is currently C+ (Fair). Volatility, as measured by standard deviation, is considered average for fixed income funds at 3.05. Another risk factor is the fund's fairly average duration of 5.3 years (i.e. average interest rate risk).

Joseph R. Baxter has been running the fund for 17 years and currently receives a manager quality ranking of 48 (0=worst, 99=best). If you desire an average level of risk and strong performance, then this fund is a good option.
Services Offered: Automated phone transactions and bank draft capabilities.

Data Date	Investment Rating	Net Assets ($Mil)	NAV	Perfor-mance Rating/Pts	Total Return Y-T-D	Risk Rating/Pts
3-16	A+	1,572	11.86	B+ / 8.8	1.52%	C+/ 6.3
2015	A	1,567	11.75	B+ / 8.8	2.74%	C+/ 6.1
2014	B+	1,389	11.73	B- / 7.1	6.60%	C / 5.5
2013	A-	1,127	11.29	B- / 7.3	-1.93%	C+/ 5.7
2012	B+	1,013	11.83	C+/ 6.5	5.30%	C+/ 5.7
2011	A	940	11.56	C+/ 6.7	9.09%	C+/ 5.7

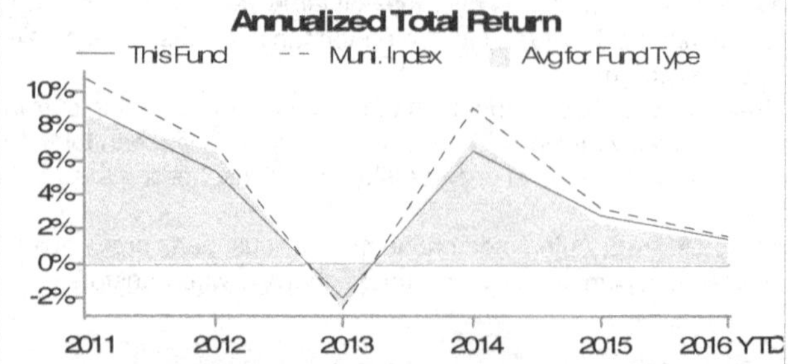

SEI Tax-Exempt Tr-Shrt Dur Muni A (SUMAX) C+ Fair

Fund Family: SEI Financial Management Corp **Phone:** (800) 342-5734
Address: One Freedom Valley Drive, Oaks, PA 19456
Fund Type: MUN - Municipal - National
Major Rating Factors: A moderate risk profile coupled with stable earnings characterizes SEI Tax-Exempt Tr-Shrt Dur Muni A which receives a TheStreet.com Investment Rating of C+ (Fair). Volatility, as measured by standard deviation, is considered very low for fixed income funds at 0.29. Another risk factor is the fund's very low average duration of 1.2 years (i.e. low interest rate risk). The fund's risk rating is currently A+ (Excellent).

The fund's performance rating is currently C- (Fair). It has registered an average return of 0.34% over the last three years (0.56% taxable equivalent) and is up 0.09% over the last three months (0.15% taxable equivalent). Factored into the performance evaluation is an expense ratio of 0.85% (average).

William J. Furrer has been running the fund for 5 years and currently receives a manager quality ranking of 72 (0=worst, 99=best). If you desire stability with a moderate level of risk then this fund is an excellent option.
Services Offered: Automated phone transactions, bank draft capabilities and wire transfers.

Data Date	Investment Rating	Net Assets ($Mil)	NAV	Perfor-mance Rating/Pts	Total Return Y-T-D	Risk Rating/Pts
3-16	C+	1,507	10.04	C- / 3.4	0.09%	A+/ 9.9
2015	B+	1,451	10.04	C / 4.9	0.18%	A+/ 9.9
2014	C	1,211	10.05	D / 1.7	0.54%	A+/ 9.9
2013	C+	1,030	10.04	D / 2.0	0.39%	A+/ 9.9
2012	C-	841	10.06	E+/ 0.7	0.89%	A+/ 9.9
2011	C	672	10.07	D / 1.6	1.52%	A+/ 9.9

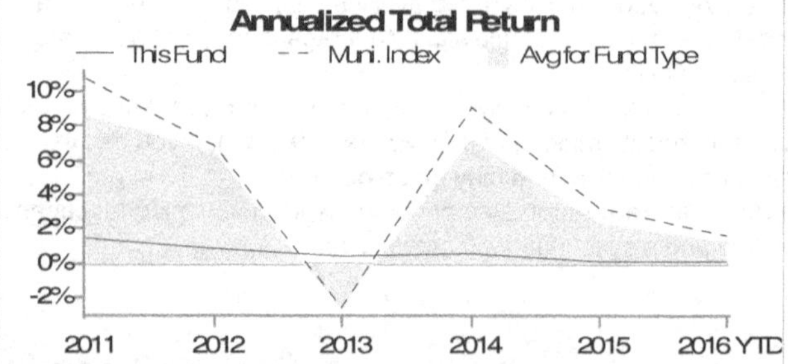

SEI Tax-Exempt Tr-Tax Advtg Inc A (SEATX) B Good

Fund Family: SEI Financial Management Corp **Phone:** (800) 342-5734
Address: One Freedom Valley Drive, Oaks, PA 19456
Fund Type: MUN - Municipal - National
Major Rating Factors: Exceptional performance is the major factor driving the B (Good) TheStreet.com Investment Rating for SEI Tax-Exempt Tr-Tax Advtg Inc A. The fund currently has a performance rating of A+ (Excellent) based on an average return of 4.38% over the last three years (7.25% taxable equivalent) and 1.75% over the last three months (2.90% taxable equivalent). Factored into the performance evaluation is an expense ratio of 1.08% (average).

The fund's risk rating is currently C- (Fair). Volatility, as measured by standard deviation, is considered average for fixed income funds at 4.50. Another risk factor is the fund's above average duration of 7.1 years (i.e. higher interest rate risk).

Lewis P. Jacoby, IV has been running the fund for 9 years and currently receives a manager quality ranking of 59 (0=worst, 99=best). If you desire an average level of risk and strong performance, then this fund is a good option.
Services Offered: Automated phone transactions.

Data Date	Investment Rating	Net Assets ($Mil)	NAV	Perfor-mance Rating/Pts	Total Return Y-T-D	Risk Rating/Pts
3-16	B	1,108	10.35	A+/ 9.8	1.75%	C- / 3.1
2015	B	1,082	10.26	A+/ 9.8	5.50%	D+/ 2.8
2014	B+	852	10.11	A+/ 9.8	11.24%	D / 2.1
2013	B	593	9.43	B+/ 8.7	-3.46%	C- / 3.2
2012	A+	484	10.20	A+/ 9.8	15.97%	C- / 3.5

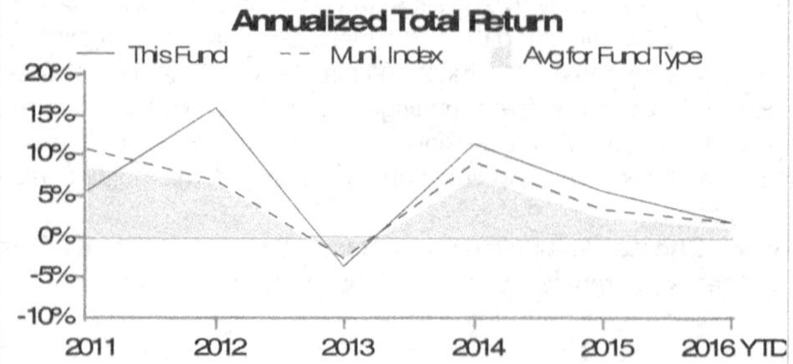

SEI US Fixed Income A (SUFAX) C+ Fair

Fund Family: SEI Financial Management Corp **Phone:** (800) 342-5734
Address: One Freedom Valley Drive, Oaks, PA 19456
Fund Type: GEI - General - Investment Grade
Major Rating Factors: Middle of the road best describes SEI US Fixed Income A whose TheStreet.com Investment Rating is currently a C+ (Fair). The fund has a performance rating of C+ (Fair) based on an average return of 2.20% over the last three years and 2.72% over the last three months. Factored into the performance evaluation is an expense ratio of 0.86% (average) and a 0.6% back-end load levied at the time of sale.

The fund's risk rating is currently C+ (Fair). Volatility, as measured by standard deviation, is considered average for fixed income funds at 2.90. Another risk factor is the fund's above average duration of 7.1 years (i.e. higher interest rate risk).

S. Kenneth Leech has been running the fund for 2 years and currently receives a manager quality ranking of 54 (0=worst, 99=best). If you desire an average level of risk, then this fund may be an option.
Services Offered: Automated phone transactions, bank draft capabilities and wire transfers.

Data Date	Investment Rating	Net Assets ($Mil)	NAV	Performance Rating/Pts	Total Return Y-T-D	Risk Rating/Pts
3-16	C+	1,137	10.39	C+ / 6.5	2.72%	C+ / 6.2
2015	C	1,121	10.16	C+ / 5.7	0.33%	C+ / 6.0
2014	B-	1,134	10.44	C / 4.7	5.91%	B- / 7.2
2013	B-	1,009	10.08	C / 4.4	-2.24%	B / 7.8
2012	B+	941	10.52	C- / 4.2	6.00%	B / 8.2
2011	U	1,026	10.47	U / --	7.62%	U / --

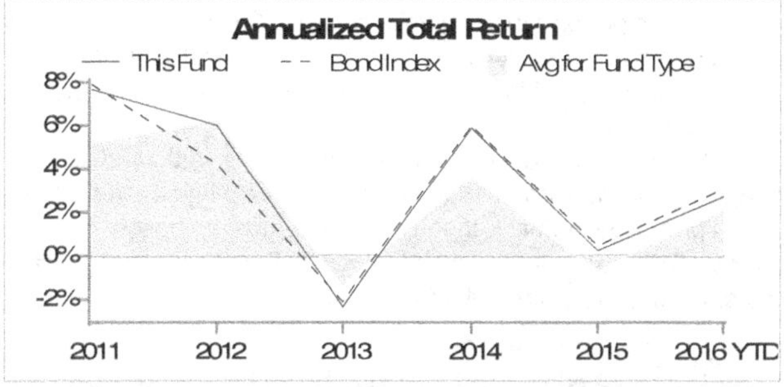

Sit US Government Securities Fund (SNGVX) B Good

Fund Family: Sit Mutual Funds **Phone:** (800) 332-5580
Address: P.O. Box 9763, Providence, RI 02940
Fund Type: USS - US Government - Short & Inter. Term
Major Rating Factors: A moderate risk profile coupled with stable earnings characterizes Sit US Government Securities Fund which receives a TheStreet.com Investment Rating of B (Good). Volatility, as measured by standard deviation, is considered very low for fixed income funds at 1.02. Another risk factor is the fund's very low average duration of 1.0 years (i.e. low interest rate risk). The fund's risk rating is currently A (Excellent).

The fund's performance rating is currently C (Fair). It has registered an average return of 0.85% over the last three years and is up 0.90% over the last three months. Factored into the performance evaluation is an expense ratio of 0.80% (low).

Michael C. Brilley has been running the fund for 29 years and currently receives a manager quality ranking of 79 (0=worst, 99=best). If you desire stability with a moderate level of risk then this fund is an excellent option.
Services Offered: Automated phone transactions, check writing, payroll deductions, bank draft capabilities, an IRA investment plan, a 401K investment plan, a Keogh investment plan, wire transfers and a systematic withdrawal plan.

Data Date	Investment Rating	Net Assets ($Mil)	NAV	Performance Rating/Pts	Total Return Y-T-D	Risk Rating/Pts
3-16	B	664	11.07	C / 4.5	0.90%	A / 9.3
2015	B+	601	11.01	C / 5.1	1.48%	A- / 9.2
2014	C	586	11.06	D / 2.1	2.21%	A- / 9.2
2013	C-	790	11.02	D- / 1.2	-2.24%	A- / 9.2
2012	C	1,739	11.36	D- / 1.3	1.75%	A / 9.4
2011	C+	1,536	11.27	D+ / 2.4	2.72%	A / 9.5

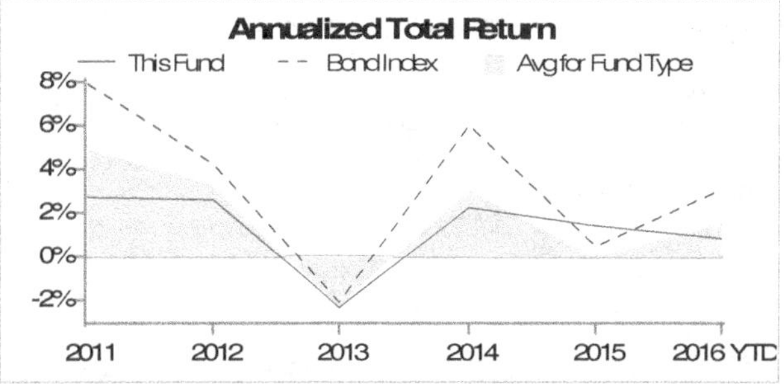

State Farm Muni Bond (SFBDX) A+ Excellent

Fund Family: State Farm Funds **Phone:** (800) 447-4930
Address: P.O. Box 219548, Kansas City, MO 64121
Fund Type: MUN - Municipal - National
Major Rating Factors: Exceptional performance is the major factor driving the A+ (Excellent) TheStreet.com Investment Rating for State Farm Muni Bond. The fund currently has a performance rating of A- (Excellent) based on an average return of 3.12% over the last three years (5.17% taxable equivalent) and 1.38% over the last three months (2.29% taxable equivalent). Factored into the performance evaluation is an expense ratio of 0.15% (very low).

The fund's risk rating is currently B- (Good). Volatility, as measured by standard deviation, is considered low for fixed income funds at 2.89. Another risk factor is the fund's below average duration of 3.9 years (i.e. lower interest rate risk).

Robert Reardon has been running the fund for 18 years and currently receives a manager quality ranking of 72 (0=worst, 99=best). If you desire only a moderate level of risk and strong performance, then this fund is an excellent option.
Services Offered: Automated phone transactions, payroll deductions, bank draft capabilities, wire transfers and a systematic withdrawal plan.

Data Date	Investment Rating	Net Assets ($Mil)	NAV	Performance Rating/Pts	Total Return Y-T-D	Risk Rating/Pts
3-16	A+	699	8.88	A- / 9.1	1.38%	B- / 7.0
2015	A+	681	8.82	A- / 9.0	2.96%	C+ / 6.6
2014	A-	658	8.84	B- / 7.4	6.76%	C+ / 5.7
2013	A	631	8.57	B / 7.8	-1.54%	C+ / 5.8
2012	B	680	9.02	C+ / 6.1	4.86%	C+ / 5.7
2011	A	618	8.91	C+ / 6.1	9.63%	C+ / 6.7

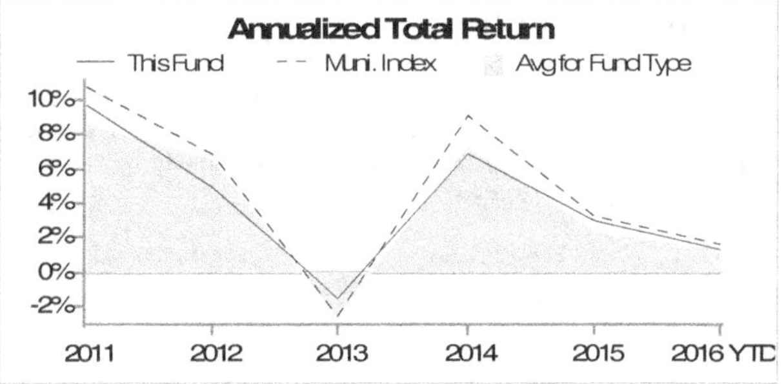

Stone Harbor Emerging Debt Inst (SHMDX) D Weak

Fund Family: Stone Harbor Investment Funds **Phone:** (866) 699-8125
Address: 31 West 52nd Street, New York, NY 10019
Fund Type: EM - Emerging Market

Major Rating Factors: Stone Harbor Emerging Debt Inst has adopted a very risky asset allocation strategy and currently receives an overall TheStreet.com Investment Rating of D (Weak). Volatility, as measured by standard deviation, is considered high for fixed income funds at 8.69. Another risk factor is the fund's fairly average duration of 6.4 years (i.e. average interest rate risk). Unfortunately, the high level of risk (E, Very Weak) has only provided investors with average performance.

The fund's performance rating is currently C+ (Fair). It has registered an average return of 0.52% over the last three years and is up 6.82% over the last three months. Factored into the performance evaluation is an expense ratio of 0.68% (low).

Pablo Cisilino has been running the fund for 9 years and currently receives a manager quality ranking of 85 (0=worst, 99=best). If you are comfortable owning a very high risk investment, then this fund may be an option.

Services Offered: Automated phone transactions, bank draft capabilities, wire transfers and a systematic withdrawal plan.

Data Date	Investment Rating	Net Assets ($Mil)	NAV	Performance Rating/Pts	Total Return Y-T-D	Risk Rating/Pts
3-16	D	1,541	10.02	C+ / 6.3	6.82%	E / 0.4
2015	E	1,646	9.48	D- / 1.1	-0.90%	E / 0.4
2014	E+	2,094	10.19	C- / 3.3	2.87%	E / 0.4
2013	E+	1,887	10.40	C- / 3.8	-8.77%	E / 0.4
2012	B-	1,720	11.97	A / 9.5	17.00%	E+ / 0.7
2011	B	986	10.83	A / 9.3	5.68%	D- / 1.5

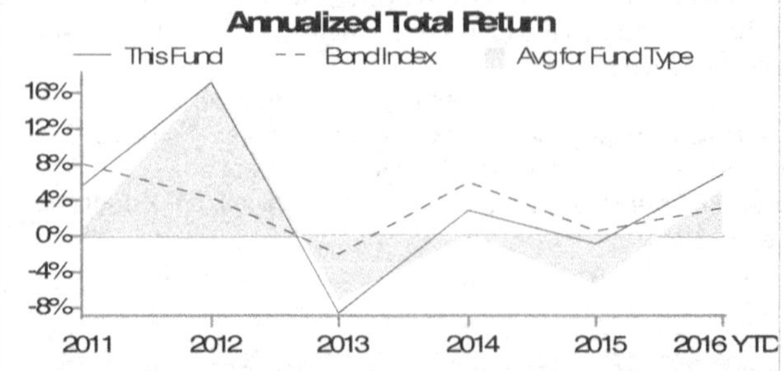

SunAmerica VAL Co II Core Bond Fd (VCCBX) C+ Fair

Fund Family: SunAmerica Funds **Phone:** (800) 858-8850
Address: C/O BFDS, Kansas City, MO 64121
Fund Type: GEI - General - Investment Grade

Major Rating Factors: Middle of the road best describes SunAmerica VAL Co II Core Bond Fd whose TheStreet.com Investment Rating is currently a C+ (Fair). The fund has a performance rating of C+ (Fair) based on an average return of 1.99% over the last three years and 2.67% over the last three months. Factored into the performance evaluation is an expense ratio of 0.80% (low).

The fund's risk rating is currently C+ (Fair). Volatility, as measured by standard deviation, is considered average for fixed income funds at 3.23. Another risk factor is the fund's fairly average duration of 5.7 years (i.e. average interest rate risk).

Robert A. Vanden Assem has been running the fund for 14 years and currently receives a manager quality ranking of 40 (0=worst, 99=best). If you desire an average level of risk, then this fund may be an option.

Services Offered: N/A

Data Date	Investment Rating	Net Assets ($Mil)	NAV	Performance Rating/Pts	Total Return Y-T-D	Risk Rating/Pts
3-16	C+	1,180	11.17	C+ / 6.4	2.67%	C+ / 5.6
2015	C	1,179	10.88	C / 5.5	-0.20%	C / 5.5
2014	C+	956	11.13	C / 5.2	5.44%	C+ / 5.9
2013	C+	866	10.83	C / 5.0	-1.81%	C+ / 6.4
2012	B+	603	11.03	C / 5.3	7.38%	C+ / 6.8
2011	B+	495	10.75	C / 5.3	6.21%	C+ / 6.9

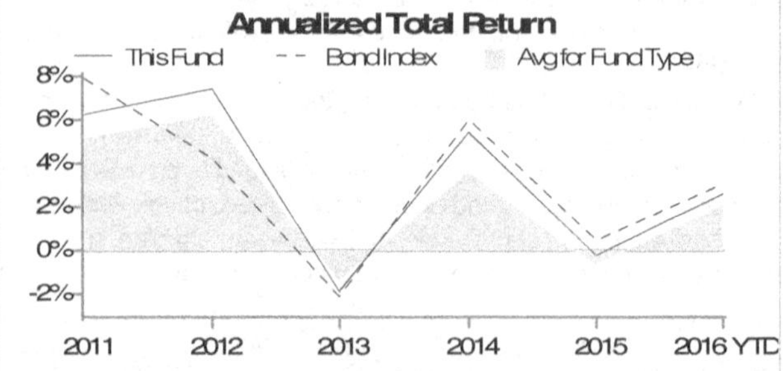

SunAmerica VAL Co II Strat Bond (VCSBX) D+ Weak

Fund Family: SunAmerica Funds **Phone:** (800) 858-8850
Address: C/O BFDS, Kansas City, MO 64121
Fund Type: GEI - General - Investment Grade

Major Rating Factors: SunAmerica VAL Co II Strat Bond receives a TheStreet.com Investment Rating of D+ (Weak). The fund has a performance rating of C (Fair) based on an average return of 1.51% over the last three years and 2.78% over the last three months. Factored into the performance evaluation is an expense ratio of 0.88% (average).

The fund's risk rating is currently C- (Fair). Volatility, as measured by standard deviation, is considered average for fixed income funds at 4.61. Another risk factor is the fund's fairly average duration of 5.4 years (i.e. average interest rate risk).

Robert A. Vanden Assem has been running the fund for 14 years and currently receives a manager quality ranking of 29 (0=worst, 99=best). If you desire an average level of risk, then this fund may be an option.

Services Offered: N/A

Data Date	Investment Rating	Net Assets ($Mil)	NAV	Performance Rating/Pts	Total Return Y-T-D	Risk Rating/Pts
3-16	D+	763	11.09	C / 5.2	2.78%	C- / 3.1
2015	D	768	10.79	C- / 3.6	-1.93%	C- / 3.2
2014	C-	778	11.50	C+ / 6.3	3.95%	C- / 3.7
2013	C+	713	11.60	B / 7.6	0.26%	C- / 3.3
2012	C+	676	11.57	B- / 7.4	12.41%	D+ / 2.7
2011	D+	529	10.80	C+ / 6.5	4.33%	C- / 3.1

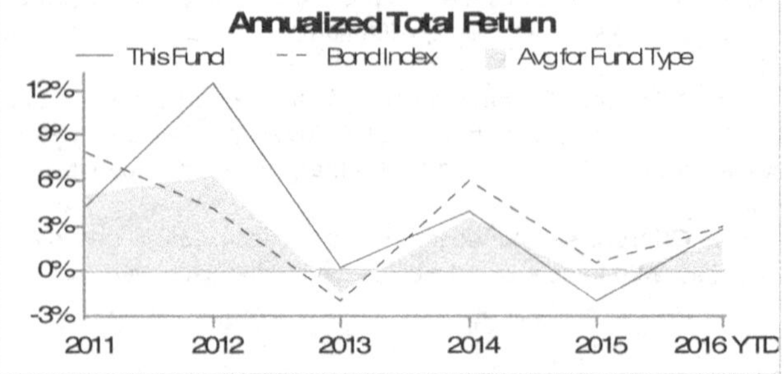

T Rowe Price CA Tax Free Bond (PRXCX) A- Excellent

Fund Family: T Rowe Price Funds **Phone:** (800) 638-5660
Address: 100 East Pratt Street, Baltimore, MD 21202
Fund Type: MUS - Municipal - Single State

Major Rating Factors: Exceptional performance is the major factor driving the A- (Excellent) TheStreet.com Investment Rating for T Rowe Price CA Tax Free Bond. The fund currently has a performance rating of A+ (Excellent) based on an average return of 4.39% over the last three years (7.27% taxable equivalent) and 1.81% over the last three months (3.00% taxable equivalent). Factored into the performance evaluation is an expense ratio of 0.49% (very low).

The fund's risk rating is currently C- (Fair). Volatility, as measured by standard deviation, is considered average for fixed income funds at 4.00. Another risk factor is the fund's fairly average duration of 5.1 years (i.e. average interest rate risk).

Konstantine B. Mallas has been running the fund for 13 years and currently receives a manager quality ranking of 74 (0=worst, 99=best). If you desire an average level of risk and strong performance, then this fund is a good option.

Services Offered: Automated phone transactions, check writing, payroll deductions, bank draft capabilities, wire transfers and a systematic withdrawal plan.

Data Date	Investment Rating	Net Assets ($Mil)	NAV	Performance Rating/Pts	Total Return Y-T-D	Risk Rating/Pts
3-16	A-	532	11.77	A+ / 9.8	1.81%	C- / 3.9
2015	B+	513	11.65	A+ / 9.7	3.84%	C- / 3.7
2014	A	500	11.61	A+ / 9.6	11.41%	C- / 3.5
2013	B+	399	10.81	B+ / 8.7	-2.76%	C- / 3.8
2012	A+	414	11.55	B+ / 8.7	9.28%	C- / 4.0
2011	A	347	11.00	B / 7.9	10.35%	C / 4.3

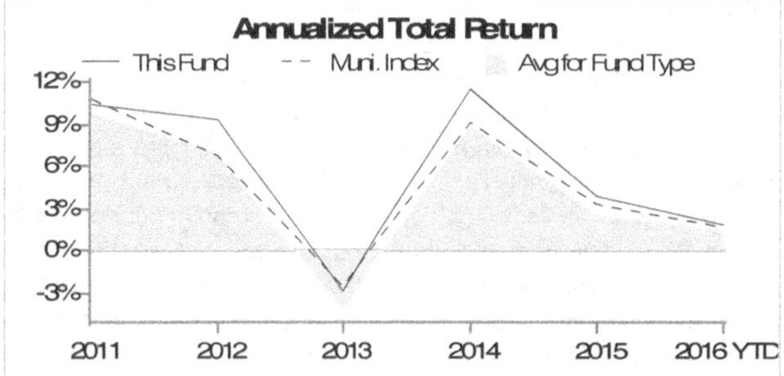

T Rowe Price Corporate Income (PRPIX) C Fair

Fund Family: T Rowe Price Funds **Phone:** (800) 638-5660
Address: 100 East Pratt Street, Baltimore, MD 21202
Fund Type: COI - Corporate - Investment Grade

Major Rating Factors: T Rowe Price Corporate Income has adopted a risky asset allocation strategy and currently receives an overall TheStreet.com Investment Rating of C (Fair). Volatility, as measured by standard deviation, is considered above average for fixed income funds at 4.58. Another risk factor is the fund's above average duration of 7.2 years (i.e. higher interest rate risk). The high level of risk (D+, Weak) did however, reward investors with excellent performance.

The fund's performance rating is currently B (Good). It has registered an average return of 2.99% over the last three years and is up 3.51% over the last three months. Factored into the performance evaluation is an expense ratio of 0.62% (low).

David A. Tiberii has been running the fund for 13 years and currently receives a manager quality ranking of 62 (0=worst, 99=best). If you are comfortable owning a high risk investment, this fund may be an option.

Services Offered: Automated phone transactions, check writing, payroll deductions, bank draft capabilities, an IRA investment plan, a 401K investment plan, a Keogh investment plan, wire transfers and a systematic withdrawal plan.

Data Date	Investment Rating	Net Assets ($Mil)	NAV	Performance Rating/Pts	Total Return Y-T-D	Risk Rating/Pts
3-16	C	790	9.51	B / 7.7	3.51%	D+ / 2.9
2015	C-	708	9.26	C+ / 6.8	-0.67%	D+ / 2.8
2014	C+	623	9.71	B / 7.6	8.26%	C- / 3.4
2013	C+	554	9.45	B- / 7.3	-1.42%	C- / 3.7
2012	B-	683	10.16	B- / 7.4	11.16%	C- / 3.4
2011	C+	577	9.65	C+ / 6.6	7.68%	C- / 4.0

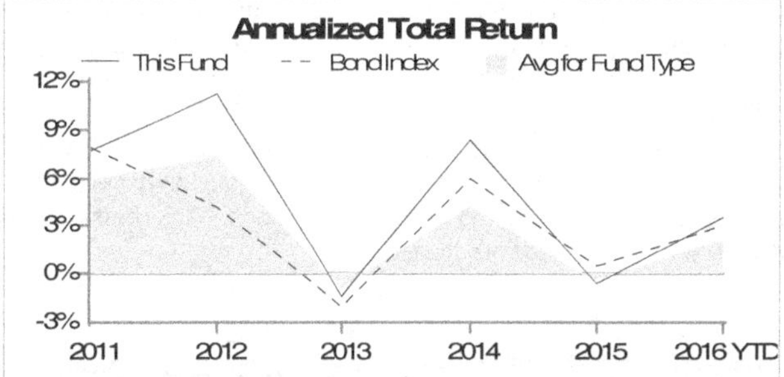

T Rowe Price GNMA (PRGMX) B Good

Fund Family: T Rowe Price Funds **Phone:** (800) 638-5660
Address: 100 East Pratt Street, Baltimore, MD 21202
Fund Type: USA - US Government/Agency

Major Rating Factors: A moderate risk profile coupled with stable earnings characterizes T Rowe Price GNMA which receives a TheStreet.com Investment Rating of B (Good). Volatility, as measured by standard deviation, is considered low for fixed income funds at 2.57. Another risk factor is the fund's below average duration of 3.8 years (i.e. lower interest rate risk). The fund's risk rating is currently B (Good).

The fund's performance rating is currently C+ (Fair). It has registered an average return of 1.71% over the last three years and is up 1.42% over the last three months. Factored into the performance evaluation is an expense ratio of 0.59% (low).

Andrew McCormick has been running the fund for 8 years and currently receives a manager quality ranking of 77 (0=worst, 99=best). If you desire stability with a moderate level of risk then this fund is an excellent option.

Services Offered: Automated phone transactions, check writing, payroll deductions, bank draft capabilities, an IRA investment plan, a 401K investment plan, a Keogh investment plan, wire transfers and a systematic withdrawal plan.

Data Date	Investment Rating	Net Assets ($Mil)	NAV	Performance Rating/Pts	Total Return Y-T-D	Risk Rating/Pts
3-16	B	1,549	9.50	C+ / 5.9	1.42%	B / 7.8
2015	B	1,559	9.43	C+ / 6.3	0.86%	B- / 7.5
2014	C	1,644	9.64	C- / 3.5	5.43%	B- / 7.3
2013	C-	1,534	9.43	D+ / 2.6	-2.41%	B / 8.1
2012	C+	1,810	10.01	D+ / 2.5	2.84%	B+ / 8.8
2011	B	1,671	10.14	C- / 3.3	6.46%	A- / 9.0

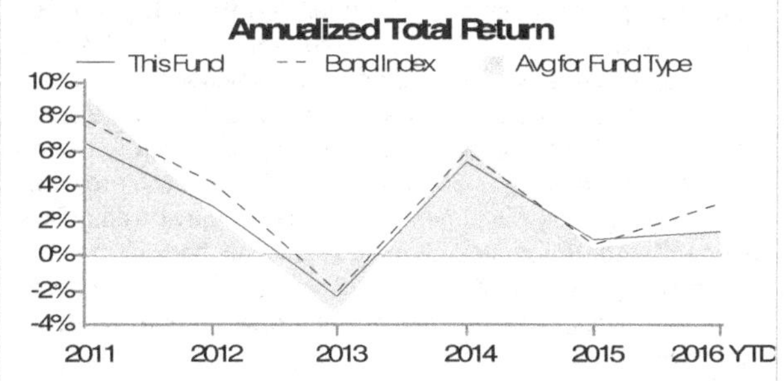

T Rowe Price High Yield (PRHYX) D Weak

Fund Family: T Rowe Price Funds **Phone:** (800) 638-5660
Address: 100 East Pratt Street, Baltimore, MD 21202
Fund Type: COH - Corporate - High Yield
Major Rating Factors: T Rowe Price High Yield has adopted a very risky asset allocation strategy and currently receives an overall TheStreet.com Investment Rating of D (Weak). Volatility, as measured by standard deviation, is considered above average for fixed income funds at 5.65. Another risk factor is the fund's below average duration of 3.5 years (i.e. lower interest rate risk). Unfortunately, the high level of risk (D-, Weak) has only provided investors with average performance.

The fund's performance rating is currently C (Fair). It has registered an average return of 2.12% over the last three years and is up 2.67% over the last three months. Factored into the performance evaluation is an expense ratio of 0.74% (low) and a 2.0% back-end load levied at the time of sale.

Mark J. Vaselkiv has been running the fund for 20 years and currently receives a manager quality ranking of 82 (0=worst, 99=best). If you are comfortable owning a very high risk investment, then this fund may be an option.
Services Offered: Automated phone transactions, check writing, payroll deductions, bank draft capabilities, an IRA investment plan, a 401K investment plan, a Keogh investment plan, wire transfers and a systematic withdrawal plan. However, the fund is currently closed to new investors.

Data Date	Investment Rating	Net Assets ($Mil)	NAV	Performance Rating/Pts	Total Return Y-T-D	Risk Rating/Pts
3-16	D	7,796	6.25	C / 4.7	2.67%	D- / 1.4
2015	D	8,036	6.18	C / 4.8	-3.26%	D- / 1.4
2014	C-	8,379	6.78	B / 7.9	2.00%	D / 1.8
2013	C+	8,739	7.15	A+ / 9.7	9.07%	E+ / 0.7
2012	C-	7,902	6.98	B+ / 8.5	15.24%	E / 0.5
2011	C	6,667	6.49	A- / 9.1	3.19%	E+ / 0.9

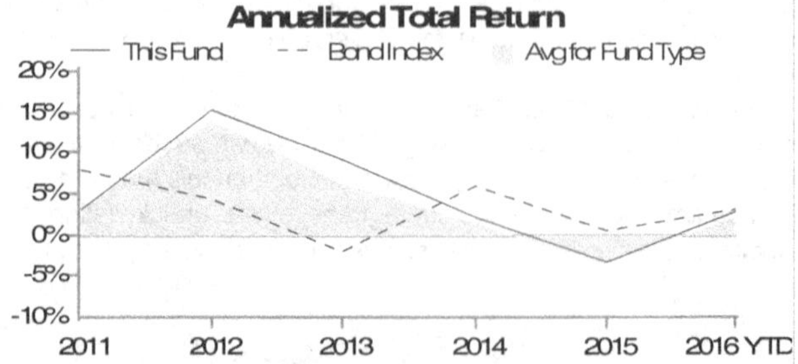

T Rowe Price Instl Fltng Rate F (PFFRX) B+ Good

Fund Family: T Rowe Price Funds **Phone:** (800) 638-5660
Address: 100 East Pratt Street, Baltimore, MD 21202
Fund Type: LP - Loan Participation
Major Rating Factors: A moderate risk profile coupled with stable earnings characterizes T Rowe Price Instl Fltng Rate F which receives a TheStreet.com Investment Rating of B+ (Good). Volatility, as measured by standard deviation, is considered low for fixed income funds at 2.25. Another risk factor is the fund's very low average duration of 0.4 years (i.e. low interest rate risk). The fund's risk rating is currently B (Good).

The fund's performance rating is currently C+ (Fair). It has registered an average return of 2.56% over the last three years and is up 1.83% over the last three months. Factored into the performance evaluation is an expense ratio of 0.69% (low) and a 2.0% back-end load levied at the time of sale.

Paul M. Massaro has been running the fund for 7 years and currently receives a manager quality ranking of 96 (0=worst, 99=best). If you desire stability with a moderate level of risk then this fund is an excellent option.
Services Offered: Automated phone transactions, bank draft capabilities, an IRA investment plan and wire transfers.

Data Date	Investment Rating	Net Assets ($Mil)	NAV	Performance Rating/Pts	Total Return Y-T-D	Risk Rating/Pts
3-16	B+	756	9.82	C+ / 6.1	1.83%	B / 8.2
2015	A-	871	9.74	C+ / 6.9	1.35%	B / 7.8
2014	A-	638	10.02	C / 5.0	1.58%	B+ / 8.5
2013	B+	856	10.28	B- / 7.2	5.12%	C / 5.2
2012	U	658	10.20	U / --	8.17%	U / --
2011	U	382	9.90	U / --	1.80%	U / --

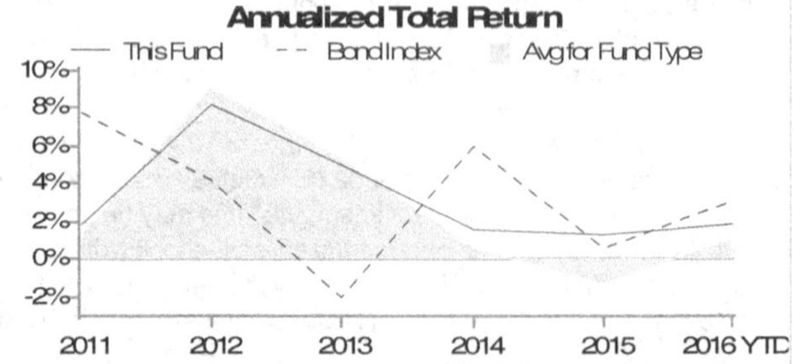

T Rowe Price Instl High Yield (TRHYX) D Weak

Fund Family: T Rowe Price Funds **Phone:** (800) 638-5660
Address: 100 East Pratt Street, Baltimore, MD 21202
Fund Type: COH - Corporate - High Yield
Major Rating Factors: T Rowe Price Instl High Yield has adopted a very risky asset allocation strategy and currently receives an overall TheStreet.com Investment Rating of D (Weak). Volatility, as measured by standard deviation, is considered above average for fixed income funds at 5.97. Another risk factor is the fund's below average duration of 3.5 years (i.e. lower interest rate risk). Unfortunately, the high level of risk (D-, Weak) has only provided investors with average performance.

The fund's performance rating is currently C (Fair). It has registered an average return of 1.99% over the last three years and is up 2.97% over the last three months. Factored into the performance evaluation is an expense ratio of 0.50% (very low) and a 2.0% back-end load levied at the time of sale.

Mark J. Vaselkiv has been running the fund for 1 year and currently receives a manager quality ranking of 76 (0=worst, 99=best). If you are comfortable owning a very high risk investment, then this fund may be an option.
Services Offered: Automated phone transactions, bank draft capabilities, an IRA investment plan, a 401K investment plan, a Keogh investment plan, wire transfers and a systematic withdrawal plan. However, the fund is currently closed to new investors.

Data Date	Investment Rating	Net Assets ($Mil)	NAV	Performance Rating/Pts	Total Return Y-T-D	Risk Rating/Pts
3-16	D	1,815	8.26	C / 4.4	2.97%	D- / 1.1
2015	D	1,925	8.15	C- / 3.8	-3.90%	D- / 1.2
2014	C-	2,249	9.07	B / 7.8	2.28%	D / 1.8
2013	C+	2,872	9.71	A+ / 9.6	8.53%	E+ / 0.9
2012	C	2,611	9.76	B+ / 8.5	14.79%	E+ / 0.6
2011	C	1,801	9.19	B+ / 8.8	3.50%	D- / 1.3

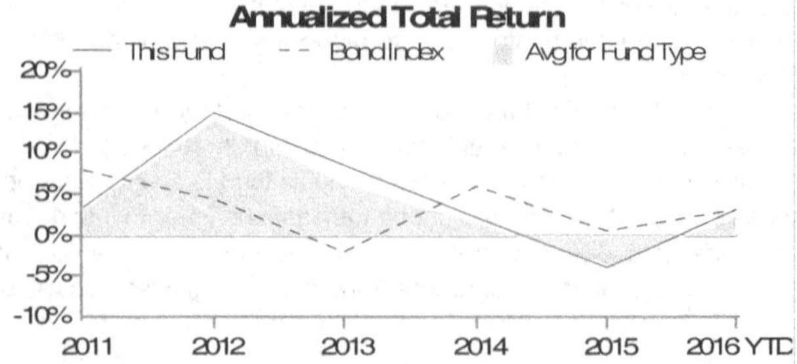

T Rowe Price Intl Bond (RPIBX) D- Weak

Fund Family: T Rowe Price Funds **Phone:** (800) 638-5660
Address: 100 East Pratt Street, Baltimore, MD 21202
Fund Type: GL - Global
Major Rating Factors: T Rowe Price Intl Bond has adopted a very risky asset allocation strategy and currently receives an overall TheStreet.com Investment Rating of D- (Weak). Volatility, as measured by standard deviation, is considered high for fixed income funds at 6.54. Another risk factor is the fund's above average duration of 7.4 years (i.e. higher interest rate risk). Unfortunately, the high level of risk (E+, Very Weak) has only provided investors with average performance.

The fund's performance rating is currently C- (Fair). It has registered an average return of -0.77% over the last three years and is up 8.22% over the last three months. Factored into the performance evaluation is an expense ratio of 0.83% (low) and a 2.0% back-end load levied at the time of sale.

Christopher J. Rothery has been running the fund for 4 years and currently receives a manager quality ranking of 40 (0=worst, 99=best). If you are comfortable owning a very high risk investment, then this fund may be an option.
Services Offered: Automated phone transactions, check writing, payroll deductions, bank draft capabilities, an IRA investment plan, a 401K investment plan, a Keogh investment plan, wire transfers and a systematic withdrawal plan.

Data Date	Investment Rating	Net Assets ($Mil)	NAV	Performance Rating/Pts	Total Return Y-T-D	Risk Rating/Pts
3-16	D-	5,206	8.92	C- / 3.9	8.22%	E+ / 0.8
2015	E	5,231	8.27	E / 0.3	-5.71%	D- / 1.5
2014	E-	4,523	8.94	E- / 0.2	-3.77%	D- / 1.2
2013	E	4,906	9.50	D- / 1.2	-3.81%	D- / 1.4
2012	E-	4,972	10.10	D+ / 2.3	6.11%	E / 0.5
2011	E-	4,719	9.74	D / 2.1	2.63%	D- / 1.0

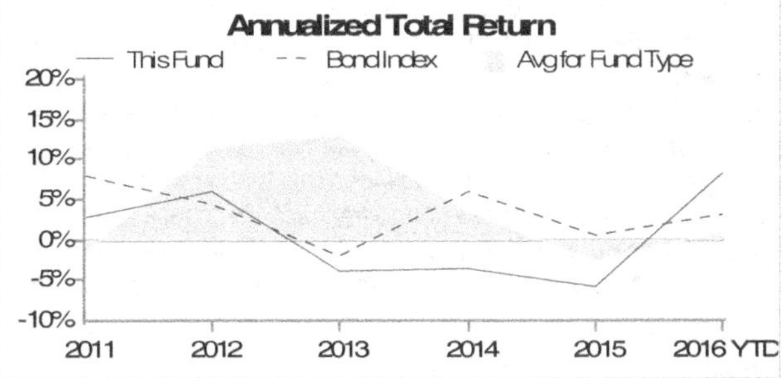

T Rowe Price MD Tax Free Bd (MDXBX) A Excellent

Fund Family: T Rowe Price Funds **Phone:** (800) 638-5660
Address: 100 East Pratt Street, Baltimore, MD 21202
Fund Type: MUS - Municipal - Single State
Major Rating Factors: Exceptional performance is the major factor driving the A (Excellent) TheStreet.com Investment Rating for T Rowe Price MD Tax Free Bd. The fund currently has a performance rating of A (Excellent) based on an average return of 3.49% over the last three years (5.78% taxable equivalent) and 1.56% over the last three months (2.58% taxable equivalent). Factored into the performance evaluation is an expense ratio of 0.45% (very low).

The fund's risk rating is currently C (Fair). Volatility, as measured by standard deviation, is considered average for fixed income funds at 3.53. Another risk factor is the fund's below average duration of 4.0 years (i.e. lower interest rate risk).

Hugh D. McGuirk has been running the fund for 16 years and currently receives a manager quality ranking of 54 (0=worst, 99=best). If you desire an average level of risk and strong performance, then this fund is a good option.
Services Offered: Automated phone transactions, check writing, payroll deductions, bank draft capabilities, an IRA investment plan, a 401K investment plan, a Keogh investment plan, wire transfers and a systematic withdrawal plan.

Data Date	Investment Rating	Net Assets ($Mil)	NAV	Performance Rating/Pts	Total Return Y-T-D	Risk Rating/Pts
3-16	A	2,142	10.98	A / 9.3	1.56%	C / 4.9
2015	A-	2,073	10.90	A / 9.3	3.18%	C / 4.7
2014	A+	2,020	10.95	B+ / 8.9	9.35%	C / 4.4
2013	A-	1,875	10.39	B / 8.2	-2.75%	C / 4.6
2012	A	2,100	11.09	B / 7.7	7.57%	C / 4.9
2011	A+	1,848	10.71	B+ / 8.4	10.09%	C / 5.0

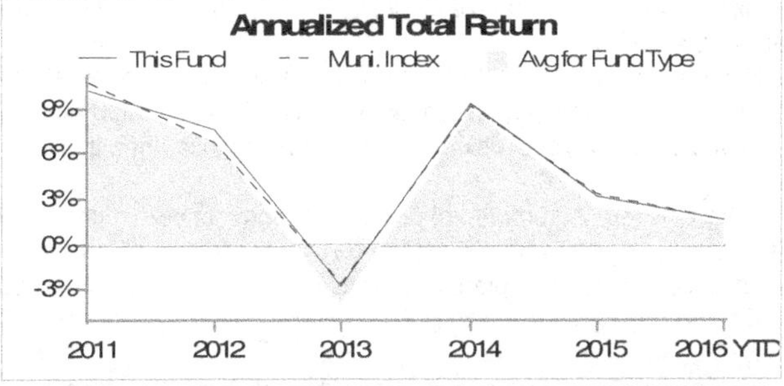

T Rowe Price New Income (PRCIX) C+ Fair

Fund Family: T Rowe Price Funds **Phone:** (800) 638-5660
Address: 100 East Pratt Street, Baltimore, MD 21202
Fund Type: GEI - General - Investment Grade
Major Rating Factors: Middle of the road best describes T Rowe Price New Income whose TheStreet.com Investment Rating is currently a C+ (Fair). The fund has a performance rating of C+ (Fair) based on an average return of 2.03% over the last three years and 2.66% over the last three months. Factored into the performance evaluation is an expense ratio of 0.60% (low).

The fund's risk rating is currently C+ (Fair). Volatility, as measured by standard deviation, is considered average for fixed income funds at 3.12. Another risk factor is the fund's fairly average duration of 5.4 years (i.e. average interest rate risk).

Daniel O. Shackelford has been running the fund for 16 years and currently receives a manager quality ranking of 44 (0=worst, 99=best). If you desire an average level of risk, then this fund may be an option.
Services Offered: Automated phone transactions, check writing, payroll deductions, bank draft capabilities, an IRA investment plan, a 401K investment plan, a Keogh investment plan, wire transfers and a systematic withdrawal plan.

Data Date	Investment Rating	Net Assets ($Mil)	NAV	Performance Rating/Pts	Total Return Y-T-D	Risk Rating/Pts
3-16	C+	26,684	9.55	C+ / 6.5	2.66%	C+ / 6.0
2015	C	27,969	9.36	C+ / 5.8	0.16%	C+ / 5.9
2014	C	28,136	9.58	C / 4.7	5.75%	C+ / 6.4
2013	C	21,532	9.30	C- / 4.1	-2.26%	C+ / 6.9
2012	B	20,368	9.85	C- / 3.9	5.87%	B / 7.9
2011	B	15,142	9.68	C / 4.3	6.25%	B / 8.0

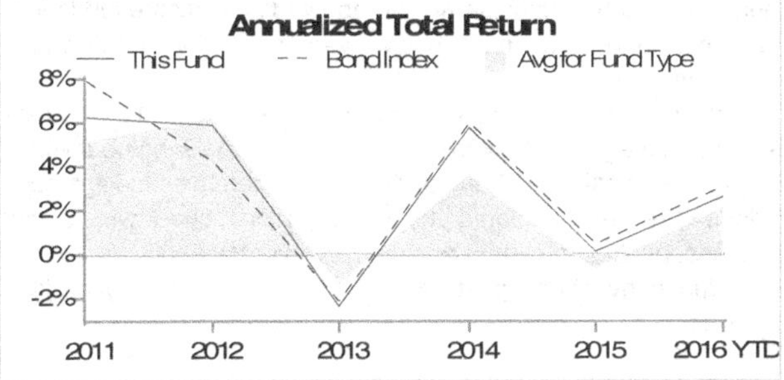

T Rowe Price Short Term Bond (PRWBX) C+ Fair

Fund Family: T Rowe Price Funds **Phone:** (800) 638-5660
Address: 100 East Pratt Street, Baltimore, MD 21202
Fund Type: GES - General - Short & Inter. Term
Major Rating Factors: A moderate risk profile coupled with stable earnings characterizes T Rowe Price Short Term Bond which receives a TheStreet.com Investment Rating of C+ (Fair). Volatility, as measured by standard deviation, is considered very low for fixed income funds at 0.90. Another risk factor is the fund's very low average duration of 1.9 years (i.e. low interest rate risk). The fund's risk rating is currently A (Excellent).

The fund's performance rating is currently C- (Fair). It has registered an average return of 0.70% over the last three years and is up 0.79% over the last three months. Factored into the performance evaluation is an expense ratio of 0.52% (very low).

Edward A. Wiese has been running the fund for 21 years and currently receives a manager quality ranking of 72 (0=worst, 99=best). If you desire stability with a moderate level of risk then this fund is an excellent option.
Services Offered: Automated phone transactions, check writing, payroll deductions, bank draft capabilities, an IRA investment plan, a 401K investment plan, a Keogh investment plan, wire transfers and a systematic withdrawal plan.

Data Date	Investment Rating	Net Assets ($Mil)	NAV	Perfor-mance Rating/Pts	Total Return Y-T-D	Risk Rating/Pts
3-16	C+	5,432	4.73	C- / 3.9	0.79%	A / 9.4
2015	B	5,617	4.71	C / 4.6	0.59%	A / 9.4
2014	C	6,314	4.75	D / 2.0	0.60%	A / 9.4
2013	C+	6,202	4.79	D+ / 2.4	0.30%	A / 9.4
2012	C-	5,848	4.85	D- / 1.1	2.87%	A / 9.4
2011	C	5,294	4.81	D / 2.1	1.46%	A / 9.4

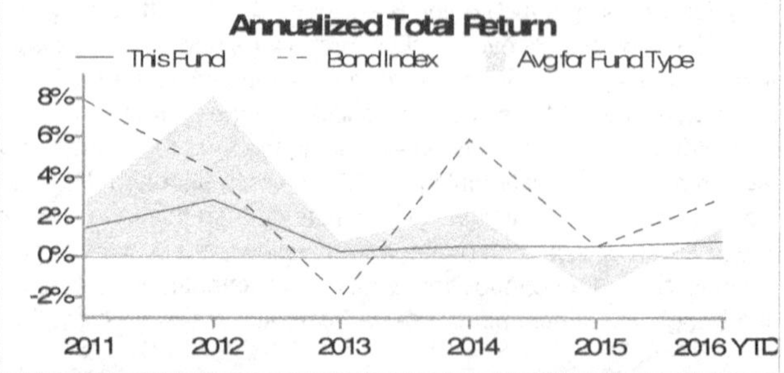

T Rowe Price Spectrum Income (RPSIX) C- Fair

Fund Family: T Rowe Price Funds **Phone:** (800) 638-5660
Address: 100 East Pratt Street, Baltimore, MD 21202
Fund Type: GES - General - Short & Inter. Term
Major Rating Factors: Strong performance is the major factor driving the C- (Fair) TheStreet.com Investment Rating for T Rowe Price Spectrum Income. The fund currently has a performance rating of B- (Good) based on an average return of 2.24% over the last three years and 3.67% over the last three months. Factored into the performance evaluation is an expense ratio of 0.67% (low).

The fund's risk rating is currently C- (Fair). Volatility, as measured by standard deviation, is considered average for fixed income funds at 4.23. Another risk factor is the fund's fairly average duration of 5.2 years (i.e. average interest rate risk).

Edmund M. Notzon III, Ph.D has been running the fund for 18 years and currently receives a manager quality ranking of 77 (0=worst, 99=best). If you desire an average level of risk and strong performance, then this fund is a good option.
Services Offered: Automated phone transactions, check writing, payroll deductions, bank draft capabilities, an IRA investment plan, a 401K investment plan, a Keogh investment plan, wire transfers and a systematic withdrawal plan.

Data Date	Investment Rating	Net Assets ($Mil)	NAV	Perfor-mance Rating/Pts	Total Return Y-T-D	Risk Rating/Pts
3-16	C-	5,844	12.23	B- / 7.1	3.67%	C- / 3.6
2015	C-	6,054	11.89	C+ / 5.6	-2.11%	C- / 4.1
2014	C+	6,722	12.70	C+ / 6.6	3.88%	C / 4.6
2013	B	6,472	12.76	B / 8.1	3.02%	C- / 3.8
2012	D+	6,600	13.00	C+ / 6.1	10.17%	D+ / 2.7
2011	E+	5,981	12.31	C / 5.4	4.16%	D+ / 2.8

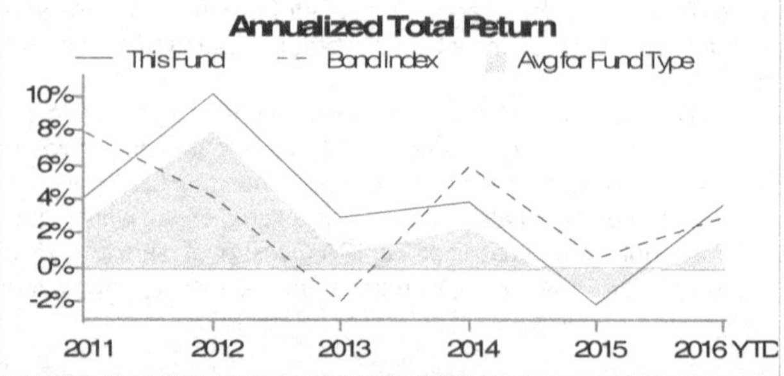

T Rowe Price Summit Muni Income (PRINX) B+ Good

Fund Family: T Rowe Price Funds **Phone:** (800) 638-5660
Address: 100 East Pratt Street, Baltimore, MD 21202
Fund Type: MUN - Municipal - National
Major Rating Factors: Exceptional performance is the major factor driving the B+ (Good) TheStreet.com Investment Rating for T Rowe Price Summit Muni Income. The fund currently has a performance rating of A+ (Excellent) based on an average return of 3.99% over the last three years (6.61% taxable equivalent) and 1.70% over the last three months (2.82% taxable equivalent). Factored into the performance evaluation is an expense ratio of 0.50% (very low).

The fund's risk rating is currently C- (Fair). Volatility, as measured by standard deviation, is considered average for fixed income funds at 4.22. Another risk factor is the fund's below average duration of 4.7 years (i.e. lower interest rate risk).

Konstantine B. Mallas has been running the fund for 17 years and currently receives a manager quality ranking of 46 (0=worst, 99=best). If you desire an average level of risk and strong performance, then this fund is a good option.
Services Offered: Automated phone transactions, check writing, payroll deductions, bank draft capabilities, an IRA investment plan, a 401K investment plan, a Keogh investment plan, wire transfers and a systematic withdrawal plan.

Data Date	Investment Rating	Net Assets ($Mil)	NAV	Perfor-mance Rating/Pts	Total Return Y-T-D	Risk Rating/Pts
3-16	B+	1,078	12.10	A+ / 9.6	1.70%	C- / 3.6
2015	B	1,006	11.99	A+ / 9.6	3.47%	C- / 3.4
2014	A-	965	11.99	A / 9.5	11.56%	D+ / 2.9
2013	B+	733	11.14	B+ / 8.5	-3.74%	C- / 3.5
2012	A+	824	12.01	A- / 9.0	9.87%	C- / 3.8
2011	A+	575	11.35	B+ / 8.7	10.63%	C / 4.3

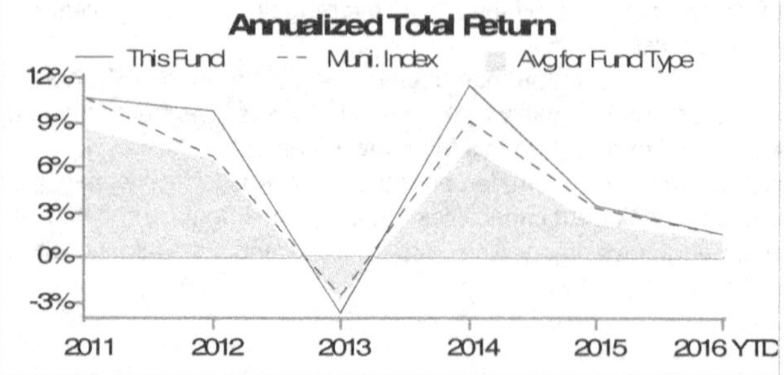

T Rowe Price Summit Muni Intmdt (PRSMX) A+ Excellent

Fund Family: T Rowe Price Funds **Phone:** (800) 638-5660
Address: 100 East Pratt Street, Baltimore, MD 21202
Fund Type: MUN - Municipal - National
Major Rating Factors: Exceptional performance is the major factor driving the A+ (Excellent) TheStreet.com Investment Rating for T Rowe Price Summit Muni Intmdt. The fund currently has a performance rating of A- (Excellent) based on an average return of 3.13% over the last three years (5.18% taxable equivalent) and 1.53% over the last three months (2.53% taxable equivalent). Factored into the performance evaluation is an expense ratio of 0.50% (very low).

The fund's risk rating is currently C+ (Fair). Volatility, as measured by standard deviation, is considered average for fixed income funds at 2.94. Another risk factor is the fund's below average duration of 4.3 years (i.e. lower interest rate risk).

Charles B. Hill has been running the fund for 23 years and currently receives a manager quality ranking of 68 (0=worst, 99=best). If you desire an average level of risk and strong performance, then this fund is a good option.
Services Offered: Automated phone transactions, check writing, payroll deductions, bank draft capabilities, an IRA investment plan, a 401K investment plan, a Keogh investment plan, wire transfers and a systematic withdrawal plan.

Data Date	Investment Rating	Net Assets ($Mil)	NAV	Performance Rating/Pts	Total Return Y-T-D	Risk Rating/Pts
3-16	A+	4,037	12.11	A- / 9.1	1.53%	C+/ 6.8
2015	A+	3,904	12.00	A- / 9.1	2.82%	C+/ 6.4
2014	A	3,932	11.98	B / 7.8	7.05%	C+/ 5.6
2013	A+	2,976	11.49	B / 8.0	-1.16%	C+/ 6.0
2012	B	2,296	11.96	C+/ 6.0	5.29%	C+/ 5.7
2011	A	1,862	11.69	C+/ 6.3	8.94%	C+/ 6.3

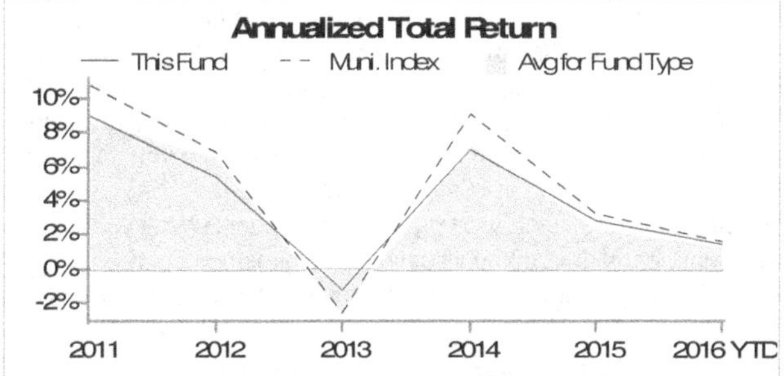

T Rowe Price Tax-Free High Yield (PRFHX) C+ Fair

Fund Family: T Rowe Price Funds **Phone:** (800) 638-5660
Address: 100 East Pratt Street, Baltimore, MD 21202
Fund Type: MUH - Municipal - High Yield
Major Rating Factors: T Rowe Price Tax-Free High Yield has adopted a risky asset allocation strategy and currently receives an overall TheStreet.com Investment Rating of C+ (Fair). Volatility, as measured by standard deviation, is considered above average for fixed income funds at 4.94. Another risk factor is the fund's fairly average duration of 5.2 years (i.e. average interest rate risk). The high level of risk (D+, Weak) did however, reward investors with excellent performance.

The fund's performance rating is currently A+ (Excellent). It has registered an average return of 4.69% over the last three years (7.77% taxable equivalent) and is up 1.94% over the last three months (3.21% taxable equivalent). Factored into the performance evaluation is an expense ratio of 0.69% (low) and a 2.0% back-end load levied at the time of sale.

James M. Murphy has been running the fund for 14 years and currently receives a manager quality ranking of 49 (0=worst, 99=best). If you are comfortable owning a high risk investment, this fund may be an option.
Services Offered: Automated phone transactions, payroll deductions, bank draft capabilities, an IRA investment plan, a 401K investment plan, a Keogh investment plan, wire transfers and a systematic withdrawal plan.

Data Date	Investment Rating	Net Assets ($Mil)	NAV	Performance Rating/Pts	Total Return Y-T-D	Risk Rating/Pts
3-16	C+	3,558	12.09	A+/ 9.7	1.94%	D+/ 2.3
2015	C+	3,362	11.97	A+/ 9.7	3.82%	D / 1.9
2014	B-	3,240	12.00	A+/ 9.8	14.99%	D- / 1.2
2013	C+	2,267	10.89	B+/ 8.6	-4.51%	D / 2.0
2012	A+	2,554	11.92	A+/ 9.7	13.66%	D+/ 2.8
2011	A+	1,779	10.96	A+/ 9.8	10.97%	D+/ 2.4

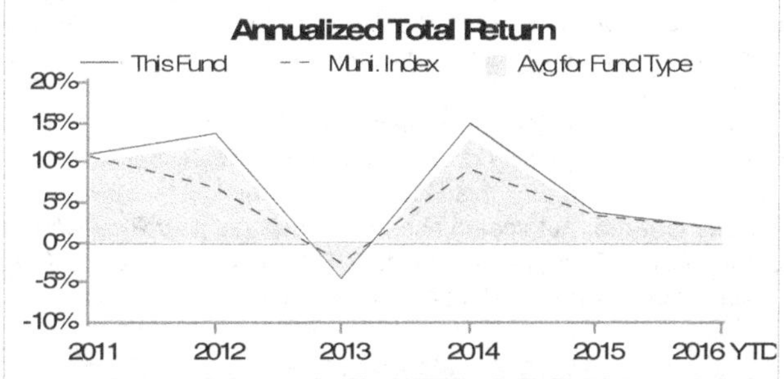

T Rowe Price Tax-Free Income (PRTAX) B+ Good

Fund Family: T Rowe Price Funds **Phone:** (800) 638-5660
Address: 100 East Pratt Street, Baltimore, MD 21202
Fund Type: MUN - Municipal - National
Major Rating Factors: Exceptional performance is the major factor driving the B+ (Good) TheStreet.com Investment Rating for T Rowe Price Tax-Free Income. The fund currently has a performance rating of A (Excellent) based on an average return of 3.63% over the last three years (6.01% taxable equivalent) and 1.56% over the last three months (2.58% taxable equivalent). Factored into the performance evaluation is an expense ratio of 0.51% (very low).

The fund's risk rating is currently C- (Fair). Volatility, as measured by standard deviation, is considered average for fixed income funds at 3.85. Another risk factor is the fund's below average duration of 4.4 years (i.e. lower interest rate risk).

Konstantine B. Mallas has been running the fund for 9 years and currently receives a manager quality ranking of 47 (0=worst, 99=best). If you desire an average level of risk and strong performance, then this fund is a good option.
Services Offered: Automated phone transactions, check writing, payroll deductions, bank draft capabilities, an IRA investment plan, a 401K investment plan, a Keogh investment plan, wire transfers and a systematic withdrawal plan.

Data Date	Investment Rating	Net Assets ($Mil)	NAV	Performance Rating/Pts	Total Return Y-T-D	Risk Rating/Pts
3-16	B+	1,914	10.44	A / 9.4	1.56%	C- / 4.2
2015	B+	1,854	10.37	A / 9.4	3.13%	C- / 4.0
2014	A	1,822	10.44	A / 9.3	10.53%	C- / 3.6
2013	B+	1,681	9.82	B / 8.2	-3.41%	C- / 4.0
2012	A	1,888	10.57	B / 8.2	8.58%	C- / 4.2
2011	A+	1,699	10.12	B / 8.0	10.25%	C / 4.5

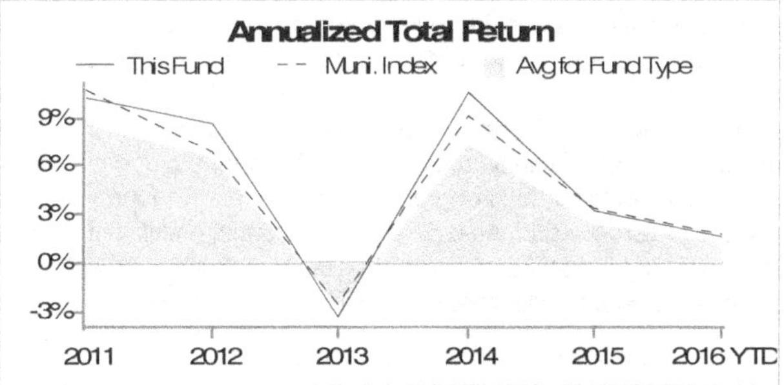

T Rowe Price Tax-Free Sh-Intmdt (PRFSX) A- Excellent

Fund Family: T Rowe Price Funds **Phone:** (800) 638-5660
Address: 100 East Pratt Street, Baltimore, MD 21202
Fund Type: MUN - Municipal - National

Major Rating Factors: A moderate risk profile coupled with stable earnings characterizes T Rowe Price Tax-Free Sh-Intmdt which receives a TheStreet.com Investment Rating of A- (Excellent). Volatility, as measured by standard deviation, is considered low for fixed income funds at 1.50. Another risk factor is the fund's very low average duration of 2.7 years (i.e. low interest rate risk). The fund's risk rating is currently B+ (Good).

The fund's performance rating is currently C+ (Fair). It has registered an average return of 1.13% over the last three years (1.87% taxable equivalent) and is up 0.67% over the last three months (1.11% taxable equivalent). Factored into the performance evaluation is an expense ratio of 0.49% (very low).

Charles B. Hill has been running the fund for 22 years and currently receives a manager quality ranking of 54 (0=worst, 99=best). If you desire stability with a moderate level of risk then this fund is an excellent option.

Services Offered: Automated phone transactions, check writing, payroll deductions, bank draft capabilities, an IRA investment plan, a 401K investment plan, a Keogh investment plan, wire transfers and a systematic withdrawal plan.

Data Date	Investment Rating	Net Assets ($Mil)	NAV	Performance Rating/Pts	Total Return Y-T-D	Risk Rating/Pts
3-16	A-	2,092	5.65	C+ / 6.0	0.67%	B+ / 8.9
2015	A+	2,081	5.63	B- / 7.1	1.05%	B+ / 8.9
2014	B-	2,112	5.65	C- / 3.4	1.90%	B+ / 8.9
2013	A+	1,916	5.63	C / 5.5	0.53%	B+ / 8.9
2012	C+	1,922	5.69	D / 2.2	2.15%	A- / 9.0
2011	B+	1,566	5.67	C- / 3.7	4.60%	B+ / 8.9

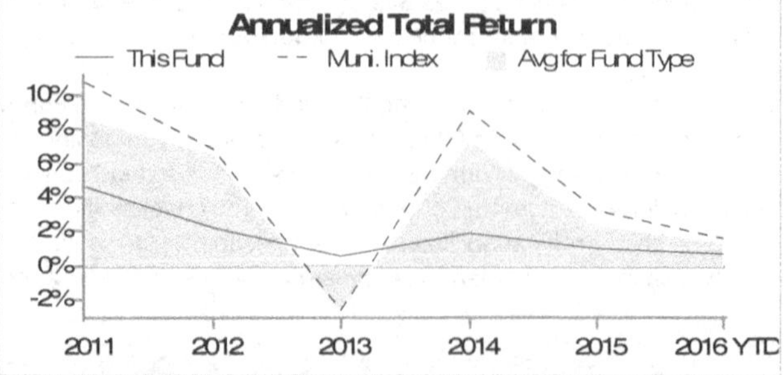

T Rowe Price US Bond Enhanced Index (PBDIX) B Good

Fund Family: T Rowe Price Funds **Phone:** (800) 638-5660
Address: 100 East Pratt Street, Baltimore, MD 21202
Fund Type: GEI - General - Investment Grade

Major Rating Factors: T Rowe Price US Bond Enhanced Index receives a TheStreet.com Investment Rating of B (Good). The fund has a performance rating of C+ (Fair) based on an average return of 2.31% over the last three years and 2.90% over the last three months. Factored into the performance evaluation is an expense ratio of 0.30% (very low) and a 0.5% back-end load levied at the time of sale.

The fund's risk rating is currently C+ (Fair). Volatility, as measured by standard deviation, is considered average for fixed income funds at 3.01. Another risk factor is the fund's fairly average duration of 5.8 years (i.e. average interest rate risk).

Robert M. Larkins has been running the fund for 16 years and currently receives a manager quality ranking of 55 (0=worst, 99=best). If you desire an average level of risk, then this fund may be an option.

Services Offered: Automated phone transactions, payroll deductions, bank draft capabilities, an IRA investment plan, a 401K investment plan, a Keogh investment plan, wire transfers and a systematic withdrawal plan.

Data Date	Investment Rating	Net Assets ($Mil)	NAV	Performance Rating/Pts	Total Return Y-T-D	Risk Rating/Pts
3-16	B	610	11.14	C+ / 6.8	2.90%	C+ / 6.5
2015	C+	595	10.90	C+ / 5.9	0.28%	C+ / 6.3
2014	C+	616	11.19	C / 4.3	6.12%	B- / 7.0
2013	C	556	10.87	C- / 3.7	-2.18%	B- / 7.5
2012	C	833	11.52	C- / 3.2	4.42%	B- / 7.5
2011	C+	1,194	11.53	C- / 3.5	7.42%	B / 8.0

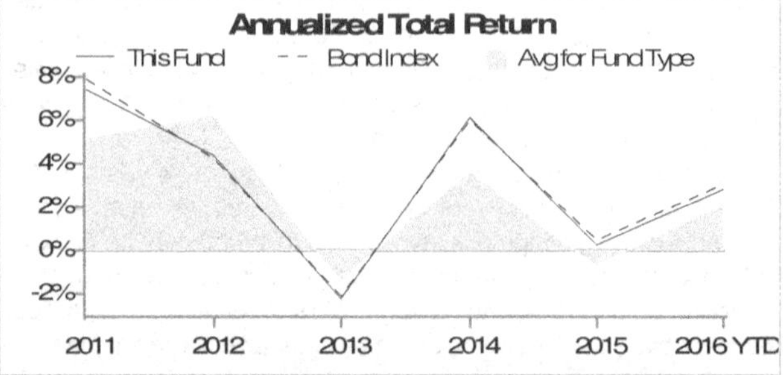

T Rowe Price VA Tax-Free Bond (PRVAX) B+ Good

Fund Family: T Rowe Price Funds **Phone:** (800) 638-5660
Address: 100 East Pratt Street, Baltimore, MD 21202
Fund Type: MUS - Municipal - Single State

Major Rating Factors: Exceptional performance is the major factor driving the B+ (Good) TheStreet.com Investment Rating for T Rowe Price VA Tax-Free Bond. The fund currently has a performance rating of A (Excellent) based on an average return of 3.48% over the last three years (5.76% taxable equivalent) and 1.51% over the last three months (2.50% taxable equivalent). Factored into the performance evaluation is an expense ratio of 0.47% (very low).

The fund's risk rating is currently C- (Fair). Volatility, as measured by standard deviation, is considered average for fixed income funds at 3.91. Another risk factor is the fund's below average duration of 4.3 years (i.e. lower interest rate risk).

Hugh D. McGuirk has been running the fund for 19 years and currently receives a manager quality ranking of 41 (0=worst, 99=best). If you desire an average level of risk and strong performance, then this fund is a good option.

Services Offered: Automated phone transactions, check writing, payroll deductions, bank draft capabilities, an IRA investment plan, a 401K investment plan, wire transfers and a systematic withdrawal plan.

Data Date	Investment Rating	Net Assets ($Mil)	NAV	Performance Rating/Pts	Total Return Y-T-D	Risk Rating/Pts
3-16	B+	1,131	12.24	A / 9.4	1.51%	C- / 4.1
2015	B	1,069	12.15	A / 9.3	3.36%	C- / 3.9
2014	B+	985	12.16	B+ / 8.8	9.84%	C- / 3.6
2013	B	878	11.46	B / 7.9	-3.50%	C- / 4.0
2012	B+	1,004	12.31	B- / 7.4	7.31%	C / 4.3
2011	A+	859	11.88	B / 7.6	10.69%	C / 5.3

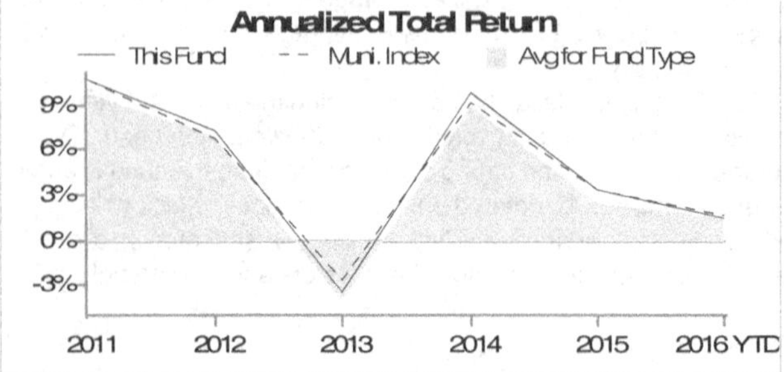

TCW Core Fixed Income N (TGFNX) B Good

Fund Family: TCW Funds **Phone:** (800) 386-3829
Address: 865 S Figueroa St, Los Angeles, CA 90017
Fund Type: USS - US Government - Short & Inter. Term
Major Rating Factors: A moderate risk profile coupled with stable earnings characterizes TCW Core Fixed Income N which receives a TheStreet.com Investment Rating of B (Good). Volatility, as measured by standard deviation, is considered low for fixed income funds at 2.66. Another risk factor is the fund's fairly average duration of 5.0 years (i.e. average interest rate risk). The fund's risk rating is currently B (Good).

The fund's performance rating is currently C+ (Fair). It has registered an average return of 1.78% over the last three years and is up 2.46% over the last three months. Factored into the performance evaluation is an expense ratio of 0.79% (low).

Tad Rivelle has been running the fund for 6 years and currently receives a manager quality ranking of 68 (0=worst, 99=best). If you desire stability with a moderate level of risk then this fund is an excellent option.

Services Offered: Automated phone transactions, payroll deductions, bank draft capabilities, wire transfers and a systematic withdrawal plan.

Data Date	Investment Rating	Net Assets ($Mil)	NAV	Perfor-mance Rating/Pts	Total Return Y-T-D	Risk Rating/Pts
3-16	B	536	11.16	C+ / 6.1	2.46%	B / 7.6
2015	C+	537	10.93	C / 5.3	-0.31%	B- / 7.5
2014	B+	608	11.22	C / 5.4	5.37%	B- / 7.4
2013	B+	695	10.85	C / 5.3	-1.89%	B / 8.0
2012	A+	565	11.23	C / 5.2	6.68%	B / 8.1
2011	B+	277	10.84	C / 5.2	6.62%	B- / 7.0

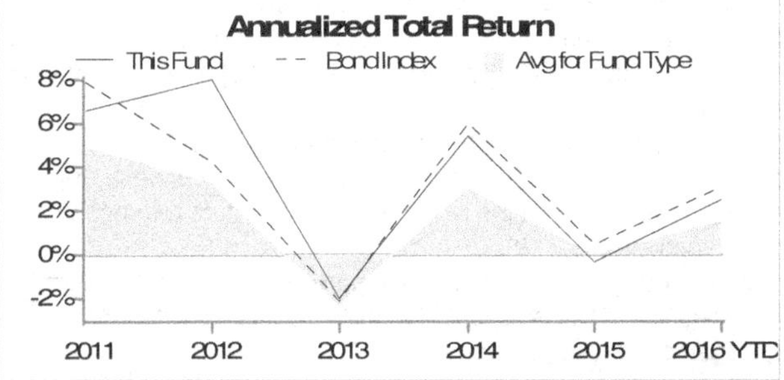

TCW Total Return Bond N (TGMNX) A Excellent

Fund Family: TCW Funds **Phone:** (800) 386-3829
Address: 865 S Figueroa St, Los Angeles, CA 90017
Fund Type: MTG - Mortgage
Major Rating Factors: Strong performance is the major factor driving the A (Excellent) TheStreet.com Investment Rating for TCW Total Return Bond N. The fund currently has a performance rating of B- (Good) based on an average return of 2.84% over the last three years and 2.05% over the last three months. Factored into the performance evaluation is an expense ratio of 0.88% (average).

The fund's risk rating is currently B (Good). Volatility, as measured by standard deviation, is considered low for fixed income funds at 2.61. Another risk factor is the fund's below average duration of 5.0 years (i.e. lower interest rate risk).

Mitchell A. Flack has been running the fund for 6 years and currently receives a manager quality ranking of 79 (0=worst, 99=best). If you desire only a moderate level of risk and strong performance, then this fund is an excellent option.

Services Offered: Automated phone transactions, payroll deductions, bank draft capabilities, wire transfers and a systematic withdrawal plan.

Data Date	Investment Rating	Net Assets ($Mil)	NAV	Perfor-mance Rating/Pts	Total Return Y-T-D	Risk Rating/Pts
3-16	A	2,586	10.61	B- / 7.5	2.05%	B / 7.7
2015	A	2,409	10.45	B- / 7.5	0.72%	B / 7.6
2014	A+	2,212	10.64	B / 7.8	5.48%	C+/ 6.5
2013	A+	2,417	10.34	B / 8.0	1.42%	B- / 7.1
2012	A+	2,475	10.63	B- / 7.4	13.05%	B- / 7.1
2011	B-	1,786	9.97	C / 5.1	3.88%	C+/ 6.4

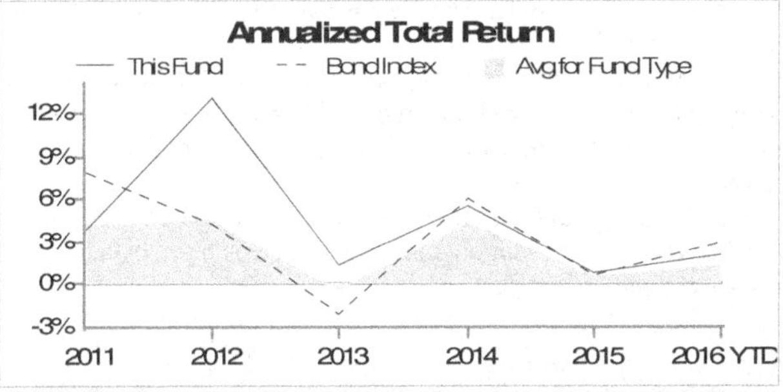

Templeton Global Bond A (TPINX) E Very Weak

Fund Family: Franklin Templeton Investments **Phone:** (800) 342-5236
Address: One Franklin Parkway, San Mateo, CA 94403
Fund Type: GL - Global
Major Rating Factors: Templeton Global Bond A has adopted a very risky asset allocation strategy and currently receives an overall TheStreet.com Investment Rating of E (Very Weak). Volatility, as measured by standard deviation, is considered above average for fixed income funds at 6.43. Unfortunately, the high level of risk (D-, Weak) failed to pay off as investors endured poor performance.

The fund's performance rating is currently E (Very Weak). It has registered an average return of -0.63% over the last three years and is up 0.03% over the last three months. Factored into the performance evaluation is an expense ratio of 0.91% (average) and a 4.3% front-end load that is levied at the time of purchase.

Michael Hasenstab has been running the fund for 15 years and currently receives a manager quality ranking of 39 (0=worst, 99=best). If you can tolerate very high levels of risk in the hope of improved future returns, holding this fund may be an option.

Services Offered: Automated phone transactions, payroll deductions, bank draft capabilities, an IRA investment plan, a 401K investment plan and a systematic withdrawal plan.

Data Date	Investment Rating	Net Assets ($Mil)	NAV	Perfor-mance Rating/Pts	Total Return Y-T-D	Risk Rating/Pts
3-16	E	16,012	11.49	E / 0.5	0.03%	D- / 1.1
2015	E+	18,502	11.58	D- / 1.2	-4.26%	D- / 1.5
2014	D-	22,017	12.46	C / 5.5	1.58%	E+/ 0.7
2013	D-	26,428	13.14	C+/ 6.1	2.22%	E / 0.3
2012	E+	25,903	13.38	C+/ 6.6	15.80%	E- / 0.2
2011	E-	24,080	12.41	C- / 3.1	-2.37%	D- / 1.0

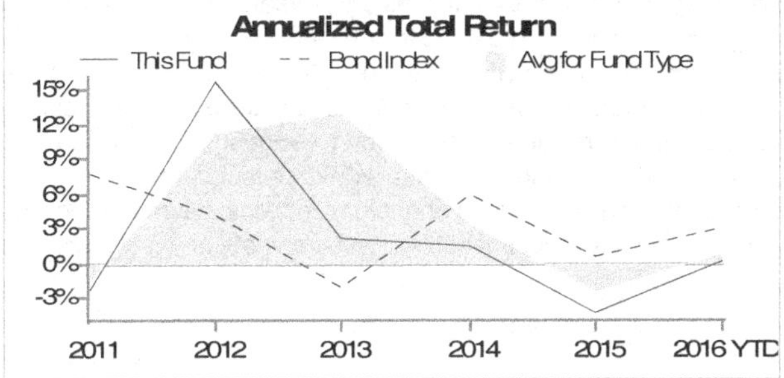

Templeton Global Total Return A (TGTRX) E Very Weak

Fund Family: Franklin Templeton Investments **Phone:** (800) 342-5236
Address: One Franklin Parkway, San Mateo, CA 94403
Fund Type: GL - Global
Major Rating Factors: Templeton Global Total Return A has adopted a very risky asset allocation strategy and currently receives an overall TheStreet.com Investment Rating of E (Very Weak). Volatility, as measured by standard deviation, is considered high for fixed income funds at 6.91. Unfortunately, the high level of risk (E+, Very Weak) failed to pay off as investors endured poor performance.

The fund's performance rating is currently E (Very Weak). It has registered an average return of -1.03% over the last three years and is up 0.06% over the last three months. Factored into the performance evaluation is an expense ratio of 1.04% (average) and a 4.3% front-end load that is levied at the time of purchase.

Michael Hasenstab has been running the fund for 8 years and currently receives a manager quality ranking of 28 (0=worst, 99=best). If you can tolerate very high levels of risk in the hope of improved future returns, holding this fund may be an option.

Services Offered: Automated phone transactions, payroll deductions, bank draft capabilities, an IRA investment plan, a 401K investment plan, wire transfers and a systematic withdrawal plan.

Data Date	Investment Rating	Net Assets ($Mil)	NAV	Performance Rating/Pts	Total Return Y-T-D	Risk Rating/Pts
3-16	E	1,420	11.40	E / 0.4	0.06%	E+ / 0.8
2015	E+	1,696	11.48	D- / 1.1	-4.88%	D- / 1.1
2014	D-	1,986	12.54	C+ / 6.3	0.37%	E / 0.5
2013	D+	2,166	13.48	B / 8.2	3.55%	E- / 0.2
2012	C-	1,402	13.62	B+ / 8.6	19.03%	E- / 0.2
2011	E	898	12.25	C / 4.4	-1.08%	E / 0.5

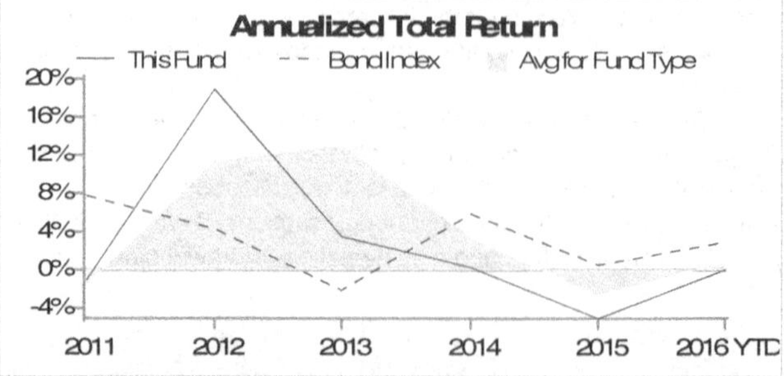

Thompson Bond (THOPX) D Weak

Fund Family: Thompson IM Funds **Phone:** (800) 999-0887
Address: 918 Deming Way, Madison, WI 53717
Fund Type: GEI - General - Investment Grade
Major Rating Factors: Disappointing performance is the major factor driving the D (Weak) TheStreet.com Investment Rating for Thompson Bond. The fund currently has a performance rating of D- (Weak) based on an average return of -0.13% over the last three years and 0.38% over the last three months. Factored into the performance evaluation is an expense ratio of 0.72% (low).

The fund's risk rating is currently C (Fair). Volatility, as measured by standard deviation, is considered average for fixed income funds at 3.62. Another risk factor is the fund's very low average duration of 2.2 years (i.e. low interest rate risk).

John W. Thompson has been running the fund for 24 years and currently receives a manager quality ranking of 28 (0=worst, 99=best). This fund offers an average level of risk, but investors looking for strong performance will be frustrated.

Services Offered: Automated phone transactions, payroll deductions, bank draft capabilities, an IRA investment plan, a 401K investment plan, wire transfers and a systematic withdrawal plan.

Data Date	Investment Rating	Net Assets ($Mil)	NAV	Performance Rating/Pts	Total Return Y-T-D	Risk Rating/Pts
3-16	D	2,055	10.53	D- / 1.2	0.38%	C / 4.6
2015	C-	2,503	10.60	D / 2.2	-2.86%	B- / 7.3
2014	B	3,525	11.40	C / 4.6	0.96%	B / 7.6
2013	A+	2,353	11.74	B- / 7.4	2.82%	B / 7.9
2012	B	1,354	11.86	C / 4.7	9.34%	B- / 7.2
2011	D-	679	11.24	C / 5.2	3.04%	C- / 3.4

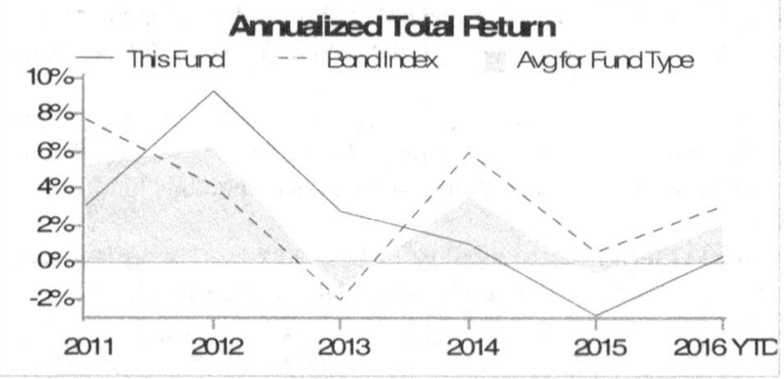

Thornburg Limited Term Income A (THIFX) B- Good

Fund Family: Thornburg Funds **Phone:** (800) 847-0200
Address: 119 East Marcy Street, Santa Fe, NM 87501
Fund Type: GES - General - Short & Inter. Term
Major Rating Factors: A moderate risk profile coupled with stable earnings characterizes Thornburg Limited Term Income A which receives a TheStreet.com Investment Rating of B- (Good). Volatility, as measured by standard deviation, is considered low for fixed income funds at 2.02. Another risk factor is the fund's very low average duration of 2.9 years (i.e. low interest rate risk). The fund's risk rating is currently B+ (Good).

The fund's performance rating is currently C (Fair). It has registered an average return of 1.57% over the last three years and is up 1.75% over the last three months. Factored into the performance evaluation is an expense ratio of 0.87% (average) and a 1.5% front-end load that is levied at the time of purchase.

Jason H. Brady has been running the fund for 9 years and currently receives a manager quality ranking of 70 (0=worst, 99=best). If you desire stability with a moderate level of risk then this fund is an excellent option.

Services Offered: Automated phone transactions, payroll deductions, bank draft capabilities, an IRA investment plan, wire transfers and a systematic withdrawal plan.

Data Date	Investment Rating	Net Assets ($Mil)	NAV	Performance Rating/Pts	Total Return Y-T-D	Risk Rating/Pts
3-16	B-	1,104	13.35	C / 4.9	1.75%	B+ / 8.5
2015	B-	984	13.18	C / 5.0	0.47%	B+ / 8.4
2014	B-	933	13.38	C- / 4.1	3.47%	B / 8.2
2013	A-	936	13.28	C / 5.1	-0.17%	B+ / 8.4
2012	B	1,137	13.73	C- / 3.7	7.50%	B+ / 8.5
2011	C+	702	13.21	C- / 4.1	5.08%	B / 7.6

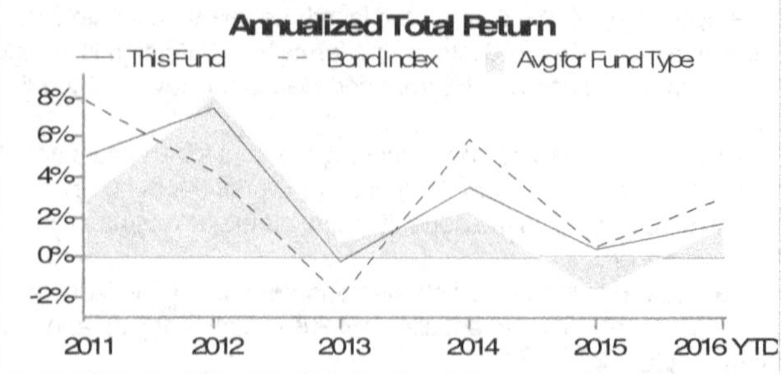

Thornburg Limited Term Muni A (LTMFX) A- Excellent

Fund Family: Thornburg Funds **Phone:** (800) 847-0200
Address: 119 East Marcy Street, Santa Fe, NM 87501
Fund Type: MUN - Municipal - National

Major Rating Factors: A moderate risk profile coupled with stable earnings characterizes Thornburg Limited Term Muni A which receives a TheStreet.com Investment Rating of A- (Excellent). Volatility, as measured by standard deviation, is considered low for fixed income funds at 1.80. Another risk factor is the fund's below average duration of 3.3 years (i.e. lower interest rate risk). The fund's risk rating is currently B+ (Good).

The fund's performance rating is currently C+ (Fair). It has registered an average return of 1.51% over the last three years (2.50% taxable equivalent) and is up 0.84% over the last three months (1.39% taxable equivalent). Factored into the performance evaluation is an expense ratio of 0.73% (low) and a 1.5% front-end load that is levied at the time of purchase.

Christopher M. Ryon has been running the fund for 5 years and currently receives a manager quality ranking of 52 (0=worst, 99=best). If you desire stability with a moderate level of risk then this fund is an excellent option.

Services Offered: Automated phone transactions, payroll deductions, bank draft capabilities, an IRA investment plan, wire transfers and a systematic withdrawal plan.

Data Date	Investment Rating	Net Assets ($Mil)	NAV	Performance Rating/Pts	Total Return Y-T-D	Risk Rating/Pts
3-16	A-	1,696	14.61	C+ / 6.1	0.84%	B+ / 8.7
2015	A+	1,692	14.54	B- / 7.1	1.50%	B+ / 8.7
2014	B-	1,858	14.55	C- / 3.6	2.99%	B+ / 8.5
2013	A+	2,190	14.37	C+ / 5.8	-0.19%	B+ / 8.4
2012	C+	2,232	14.66	C- / 3.2	3.07%	B / 8.1
2011	B	1,798	14.51	C / 4.7	6.70%	B- / 7.2

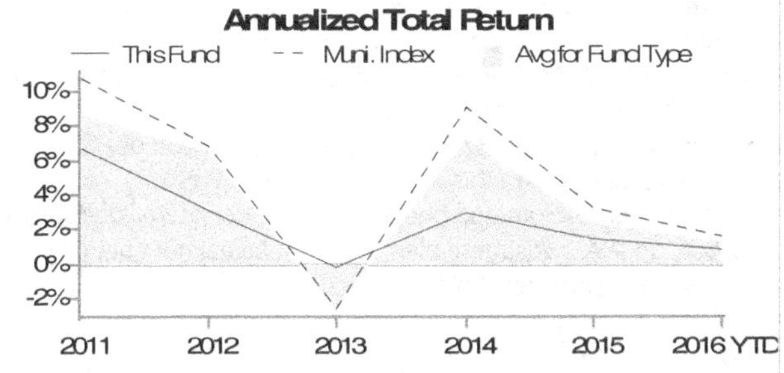

Thrivent Diversified Inc Plus A (AAHYX) D Weak

Fund Family: Thrivent Mutual Funds **Phone:** (800) 847-4836
Address: P.O. Box 219348, Kansas City, MO 64121
Fund Type: COH - Corporate - High Yield

Major Rating Factors: Thrivent Diversified Inc Plus A has adopted a risky asset allocation strategy and currently receives an overall TheStreet.com Investment Rating of D (Weak). Volatility, as measured by standard deviation, is considered above average for fixed income funds at 4.83. Another risk factor is the fund's below average duration of 4.2 years (i.e. lower interest rate risk). Unfortunately, the high level of risk (D+, Weak) has only provided investors with average performance.

The fund's performance rating is currently C (Fair). It has registered an average return of 2.92% over the last three years and is up 0.95% over the last three months. Factored into the performance evaluation is an expense ratio of 1.10% (average) and a 4.5% front-end load that is levied at the time of purchase.

Paul J. Ocenasek has been running the fund for 12 years and currently receives a manager quality ranking of 94 (0=worst, 99=best). If you are comfortable owning a high risk investment, then this fund may be an option.

Services Offered: Automated phone transactions, payroll deductions, bank draft capabilities, an IRA investment plan, a 401K investment plan, a Keogh investment plan, wire transfers and a systematic withdrawal plan. However, the fund is currently closed to new investors.

Data Date	Investment Rating	Net Assets ($Mil)	NAV	Performance Rating/Pts	Total Return Y-T-D	Risk Rating/Pts
3-16	D	581	6.79	C / 4.8	0.95%	D+ / 2.4
2015	C-	586	6.79	B / 7.6	-0.62%	D+ / 2.4
2014	C+	567	7.10	B+ / 8.3	3.54%	D / 2.1
2013	C+	459	7.25	A / 9.4	10.40%	D- / 1.3
2012	D-	290	6.82	B- / 7.2	14.08%	E+ / 0.8
2011	E+	200	6.22	C+ / 6.7	1.74%	D- / 1.2

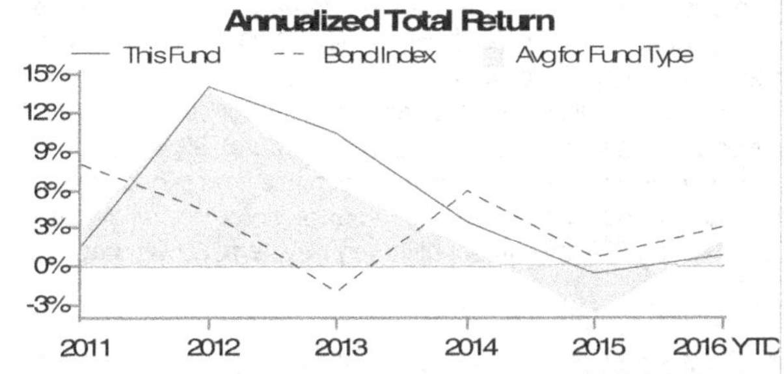

Thrivent Municipal Bond A (AAMBX) B- Good

Fund Family: Thrivent Mutual Funds **Phone:** (800) 847-4836
Address: P.O. Box 219348, Kansas City, MO 64121
Fund Type: MUN - Municipal - National

Major Rating Factors: Strong performance is the major factor driving the B- (Good) TheStreet.com Investment Rating for Thrivent Municipal Bond A. The fund currently has a performance rating of B (Good) based on an average return of 3.33% over the last three years (5.51% taxable equivalent) and 1.33% over the last three months (2.20% taxable equivalent). Factored into the performance evaluation is an expense ratio of 0.75% (low) and a 4.5% front-end load that is levied at the time of purchase.

The fund's risk rating is currently C (Fair). Volatility, as measured by standard deviation, is considered average for fixed income funds at 3.74. Another risk factor is the fund's fairly average duration of 6.0 years (i.e. average interest rate risk).

Janet I. Grangaard has been running the fund for 14 years and currently receives a manager quality ranking of 41 (0=worst, 99=best). If you desire an average level of risk and strong performance, then this fund is a good option.

Services Offered: Automated phone transactions, payroll deductions, bank draft capabilities and a systematic withdrawal plan. However, the fund is currently closed to new investors.

Data Date	Investment Rating	Net Assets ($Mil)	NAV	Performance Rating/Pts	Total Return Y-T-D	Risk Rating/Pts
3-16	B-	1,480	11.73	B / 8.1	1.33%	C / 4.4
2015	C+	1,463	11.67	B / 8.2	3.10%	C- / 4.2
2014	B-	1,454	11.71	B / 7.7	9.61%	C- / 3.7
2013	C-	1,361	11.07	C+ / 5.9	-3.55%	C- / 4.0
2012	B-	1,537	11.91	C+ / 6.2	7.58%	C / 4.8
2011	B	1,367	11.49	C+ / 6.1	10.58%	C+ / 5.7

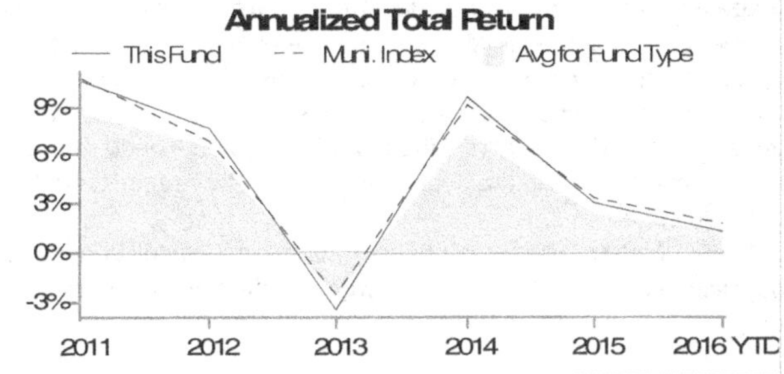

Transamerica Short-Term Bond A (ITAAX) C+ Fair

Fund Family: Transamerica Funds **Phone:** (888) 233-4339
Address: P.O. Box 219945, Kansas City, MO 64121
Fund Type: COI - Corporate - Investment Grade
Major Rating Factors: A moderate risk profile coupled with stable earnings characterizes Transamerica Short-Term Bond A which receives a TheStreet.com Investment Rating of C+ (Fair). Volatility, as measured by standard deviation, is considered very low for fixed income funds at 1.09. Another risk factor is the fund's very low average duration of 1.5 years (i.e. low interest rate risk). The fund's risk rating is currently A- (Excellent).

The fund's performance rating is currently C- (Fair). It has registered an average return of 1.27% over the last three years and is up 0.81% over the last three months. Factored into the performance evaluation is an expense ratio of 0.84% (low) and a 2.5% front-end load that is levied at the time of purchase.

Doug Weih has been running the fund for 5 years and currently receives a manager quality ranking of 87 (0=worst, 99=best). If you desire stability with a moderate level of risk then this fund is an excellent option.
Services Offered: Automated phone transactions, payroll deductions, bank draft capabilities, an IRA investment plan, a Keogh investment plan, wire transfers and a systematic withdrawal plan.

Data Date	Investment Rating	Net Assets ($Mil)	NAV	Performance Rating/Pts	Total Return Y-T-D	Risk Rating/Pts
3-16	C+	896	10.13	C- / 3.5	0.81%	A- / 9.2
2015	B-	944	10.10	C / 4.5	0.30%	A- / 9.2
2014	B-	1,017	10.28	C- / 3.3	1.37%	A- / 9.0
2013	B+	984	10.38	C / 4.5	2.20%	A- / 9.0
2012	C+	800	10.47	D+ / 2.3	6.55%	B+ / 8.9
2011	C+	765	10.19	C- / 3.0	1.85%	B+ / 8.8

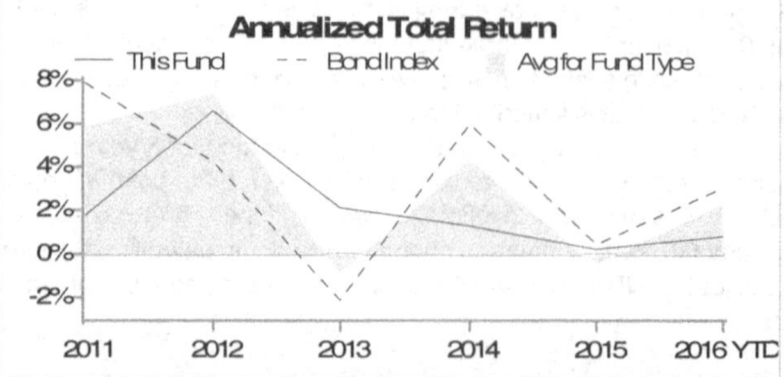

USAA California Bond Fund (USCBX) B Good

Fund Family: USAA Group **Phone:** (800) 382-8722
Address: 9800 Fredricksburg Road, San Antonio, TX 78288
Fund Type: MUS - Municipal - Single State
Major Rating Factors: USAA California Bond Fund has adopted a risky asset allocation strategy and currently receives an overall TheStreet.com Investment Rating of B (Good). Volatility, as measured by standard deviation, is considered above average for fixed income funds at 4.36. Another risk factor is the fund's above average duration of 9.2 years (i.e. higher interest rate risk). The high level of risk (D+, Weak) did however, reward investors with excellent performance.

The fund's performance rating is currently A+ (Excellent). It has registered an average return of 4.33% over the last three years (7.17% taxable equivalent) and is up 1.38% over the last three months (2.29% taxable equivalent). Factored into the performance evaluation is an expense ratio of 0.57% (very low).

John C. Bonnell has been running the fund for 10 years and currently receives a manager quality ranking of 59 (0=worst, 99=best). If you are comfortable owning a high risk investment, this fund may be an option.
Services Offered: Automated phone transactions, payroll deductions, bank draft capabilities, an IRA investment plan and a systematic withdrawal plan.

Data Date	Investment Rating	Net Assets ($Mil)	NAV	Performance Rating/Pts	Total Return Y-T-D	Risk Rating/Pts
3-16	B	697	11.29	A+ / 9.7	1.38%	D+ / 2.9
2015	B-	683	11.23	A+ / 9.8	3.66%	D+ / 2.7
2014	B	666	11.25	A+ / 9.7	12.61%	D / 1.6
2013	B	600	10.39	A+ / 9.7	-2.95%	D / 2.0
2012	B+	679	11.15	A+ / 9.7	11.16%	D / 1.8
2011	B+	625	10.44	A / 9.4	14.74%	D / 1.9

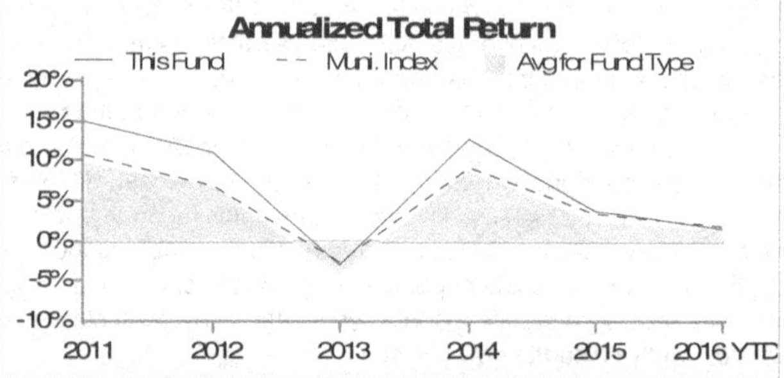

USAA High Income Fund (USHYX) E+ Very Weak

Fund Family: USAA Group **Phone:** (800) 382-8722
Address: 9800 Fredricksburg Road, San Antonio, TX 78288
Fund Type: COH - Corporate - High Yield
Major Rating Factors: USAA High Income Fund has adopted a very risky asset allocation strategy and currently receives an overall TheStreet.com Investment Rating of E+ (Very Weak). Volatility, as measured by standard deviation, is considered above average for fixed income funds at 5.64. Unfortunately, the high level of risk (D-, Weak) failed to pay off as investors endured very poor performance.

The fund's performance rating is currently D- (Weak). It has registered an average return of 0.43% over the last three years and is up 2.67% over the last three months. Factored into the performance evaluation is an expense ratio of 0.89% (average) and a 1.0% back-end load levied at the time of sale.

R. Matthew Freund has been running the fund for 17 years and currently receives a manager quality ranking of 24 (0=worst, 99=best). If you can tolerate very high levels of risk in the hope of improved future returns, holding this fund may be an option.
Services Offered: Automated phone transactions, payroll deductions, bank draft capabilities, an IRA investment plan, wire transfers and a systematic withdrawal plan.

Data Date	Investment Rating	Net Assets ($Mil)	NAV	Performance Rating/Pts	Total Return Y-T-D	Risk Rating/Pts
3-16	E+	1,015	7.36	D- / 1.1	2.67%	D- / 1.4
2015	D-	1,105	7.29	D- / 1.3	-8.56%	D / 1.6
2014	B	1,389	8.45	B+ / 8.6	3.53%	D+ / 2.9
2013	B	1,338	8.69	A+ / 9.7	8.47%	D- / 1.5
2012	B-	1,154	8.66	A / 9.3	16.53%	D- / 1.1
2011	C+	1,323	8.04	A+ / 9.6	2.53%	E+ / 0.7

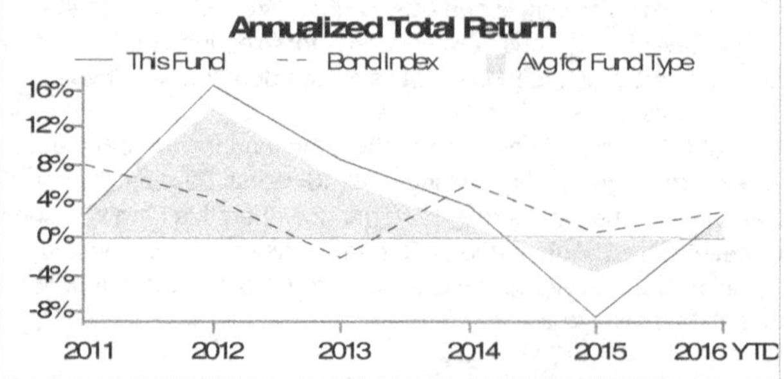

USAA Income Fund (USAIX) C+ Fair

Fund Family: USAA Group **Phone:** (800) 382-8722
Address: 9800 Fredricksburg Road, San Antonio, TX 78288
Fund Type: USS - US Government - Short & Inter. Term
Major Rating Factors: Middle of the road best describes USAA Income Fund whose TheStreet.com Investment Rating is currently a C+ (Fair). The fund has a performance rating of C+ (Fair) based on an average return of 2.16% over the last three years and 3.04% over the last three months. Factored into the performance evaluation is an expense ratio of 0.53% (very low).

The fund's risk rating is currently C+ (Fair). Volatility, as measured by standard deviation, is considered average for fixed income funds at 3.12. Another risk factor is the fund's below average duration of 3.7 years (i.e. lower interest rate risk).

Julianne Bass has been running the fund for 4 years and currently receives a manager quality ranking of 82 (0=worst, 99=best). If you desire an average level of risk, then this fund may be an option.
Services Offered: Automated phone transactions, payroll deductions, bank draft capabilities, an IRA investment plan, wire transfers and a systematic withdrawal plan.

Data Date	Investment Rating	Net Assets ($Mil)	NAV	Performance Rating/Pts	Total Return Y-T-D	Risk Rating/Pts
3-16	C+	3,163	12.88	C+ / 6.5	3.04%	C+ / 6.1
2015	C	3,458	12.60	C+ / 5.8	-1.11%	C+ / 6.2
2014	B+	3,228	13.20	C+ / 5.8	5.89%	B- / 7.1
2013	A	2,628	12.94	C+ / 6.2	-0.18%	B / 7.8
2012	A+	2,790	13.47	C / 5.0	7.00%	B+ / 8.3
2011	A	3,242	13.08	C+ / 5.8	6.87%	B- / 7.0

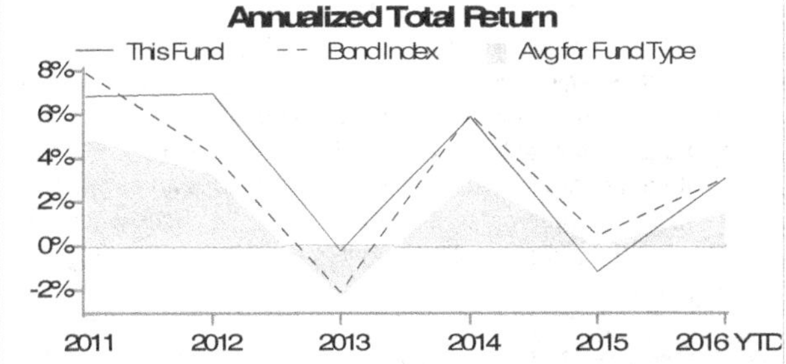

USAA Intmdt-Trm Bd Fund (USIBX) C+ Fair

Fund Family: USAA Group **Phone:** (800) 382-8722
Address: 9800 Fredricksburg Road, San Antonio, TX 78288
Fund Type: GEI - General - Investment Grade
Major Rating Factors: Middle of the road best describes USAA Intmdt-Trm Bd Fund whose TheStreet.com Investment Rating is currently a C+ (Fair). The fund has a performance rating of C+ (Fair) based on an average return of 1.83% over the last three years and 2.67% over the last three months. Factored into the performance evaluation is an expense ratio of 0.68% (low).

The fund's risk rating is currently C+ (Fair). Volatility, as measured by standard deviation, is considered average for fixed income funds at 3.07. Another risk factor is the fund's below average duration of 3.2 years (i.e. lower interest rate risk).

R. Matthew Freund has been running the fund for 14 years and currently receives a manager quality ranking of 52 (0=worst, 99=best). If you desire an average level of risk, then this fund may be an option.
Services Offered: Automated phone transactions, payroll deductions, bank draft capabilities, an IRA investment plan, wire transfers and a systematic withdrawal plan.

Data Date	Investment Rating	Net Assets ($Mil)	NAV	Performance Rating/Pts	Total Return Y-T-D	Risk Rating/Pts
3-16	C+	1,704	10.32	C+ / 5.6	2.67%	C+ / 6.3
2015	C	1,967	10.15	C / 5.2	-2.32%	C+ / 6.4
2014	A+	2,020	10.83	B- / 7.3	5.75%	C+ / 6.3
2013	A+	1,747	10.68	B / 8.1	1.30%	C+ / 6.2
2012	A+	1,795	11.01	B / 8.1	11.23%	C+ / 5.8
2011	A	1,822	10.40	B / 8.1	6.35%	C / 4.3

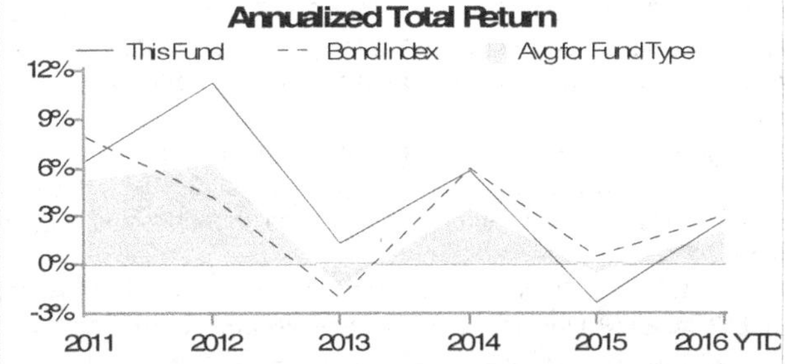

USAA Short Term Bond Retail Fund (USSBX) B- Good

Fund Family: USAA Group **Phone:** (800) 382-8722
Address: 9800 Fredricksburg Road, San Antonio, TX 78288
Fund Type: GEI - General - Investment Grade
Major Rating Factors: A moderate risk profile coupled with stable earnings characterizes USAA Short Term Bond Retail Fund which receives a TheStreet.com Investment Rating of B- (Good). Volatility, as measured by standard deviation, is considered very low for fixed income funds at 1.13. Another risk factor is the fund's very low average duration of 1.6 years (i.e. low interest rate risk). The fund's risk rating is currently A- (Excellent).

The fund's performance rating is currently C (Fair). It has registered an average return of 1.04% over the last three years and is up 1.20% over the last three months. Factored into the performance evaluation is an expense ratio of 0.62% (low).

R. Matthew Freund has been running the fund for 14 years and currently receives a manager quality ranking of 77 (0=worst, 99=best). If you desire stability with a moderate level of risk then this fund is an excellent option.
Services Offered: Automated phone transactions, check writing, payroll deductions, bank draft capabilities, an IRA investment plan, wire transfers and a systematic withdrawal plan.

Data Date	Investment Rating	Net Assets ($Mil)	NAV	Performance Rating/Pts	Total Return Y-T-D	Risk Rating/Pts
3-16	B-	1,386	9.10	C / 4.5	1.20%	A- / 9.1
2015	B+	1,786	9.03	C / 5.1	0.00%	A- / 9.2
2014	B-	1,690	9.18	C- / 3.1	1.66%	A- / 9.2
2013	B+	1,625	9.19	C- / 3.9	1.01%	A / 9.3
2012	C+	1,648	9.28	D / 1.9	4.09%	A / 9.5
2011	B	2,043	9.14	C- / 3.2	2.46%	A- / 9.0

Asset Composition
For: USAA Short Term Bond Retail Fund

Cash & Cash Equivalent:	0%
Government Bonds:	7%
Municipal Bonds:	8%
Corporate Bonds:	64%
Other:	21%

USAA T/E Short Term Bond Fund (USSTX) — B+ Good

Fund Family: USAA Group **Phone:** (800) 382-8722
Address: 9800 Fredricksburg Road, San Antonio, TX 78288
Fund Type: MUN - Municipal - National
Major Rating Factors: A moderate risk profile coupled with stable earnings characterizes USAA T/E Short Term Bond Fund which receives a TheStreet.com Investment Rating of B+ (Good). Volatility, as measured by standard deviation, is considered very low for fixed income funds at 0.60. Another risk factor is the fund's very low average duration of 2.3 years (i.e. low interest rate risk). The fund's risk rating is currently A+ (Excellent).

The fund's performance rating is currently C (Fair). It has registered an average return of 0.83% over the last three years (1.37% taxable equivalent) and is up 0.31% over the last three months (0.51% taxable equivalent). Factored into the performance evaluation is an expense ratio of 0.55% (very low).

Regina G. Shafer has been running the fund for 13 years and currently receives a manager quality ranking of 76 (0=worst, 99=best). If you desire stability with a moderate level of risk then this fund is an excellent option.
Services Offered: Automated phone transactions, check writing, payroll deductions, bank draft capabilities, an IRA investment plan and a systematic withdrawal plan.

Data Date	Investment Rating	Net Assets ($Mil)	NAV	Performance Rating/Pts	Total Return Y-T-D	Risk Rating/Pts
3-16	B+	1,759	10.59	C / 4.9	0.31%	A+ / 9.8
2015	A+	1,806	10.59	C+ / 6.6	0.57%	A+ / 9.7
2014	B	1,994	10.69	C- / 3.4	1.54%	A+ / 9.6
2013	A+	2,087	10.70	C+ / 5.6	0.65%	A / 9.5
2012	B-	2,168	10.83	D+ / 2.6	2.52%	A / 9.4
2011	A	2,029	10.79	C- / 3.7	4.42%	A / 9.4

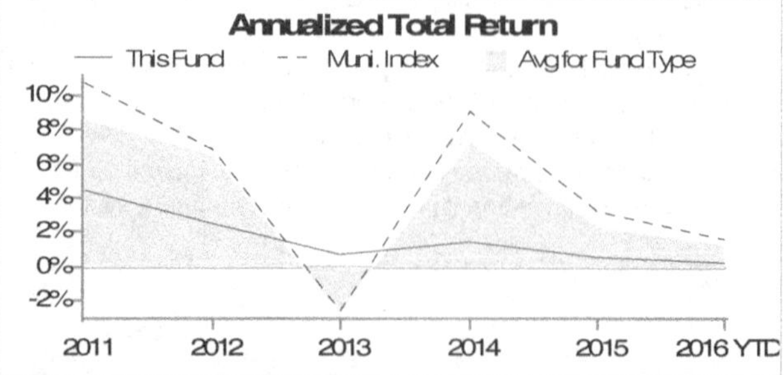

USAA Tax-Exempt Interm-Term Fund (USATX) — A+ Excellent

Fund Family: USAA Group **Phone:** (800) 382-8722
Address: 9800 Fredricksburg Road, San Antonio, TX 78288
Fund Type: MUN - Municipal - National
Major Rating Factors: Exceptional performance is the major factor driving the A+ (Excellent) TheStreet.com Investment Rating for USAA Tax-Exempt Interm-Term Fund. The fund currently has a performance rating of A- (Excellent) based on an average return of 3.12% over the last three years (5.17% taxable equivalent) and 1.45% over the last three months (2.40% taxable equivalent). Factored into the performance evaluation is an expense ratio of 0.55% (very low).

The fund's risk rating is currently B- (Good). Volatility, as measured by standard deviation, is considered low for fixed income funds at 2.76. Another risk factor is the fund's fairly average duration of 6.3 years (i.e. average interest rate risk).

Regina G. Shafer has been running the fund for 13 years and currently receives a manager quality ranking of 75 (0=worst, 99=best). If you desire only a moderate level of risk and strong performance, then this fund is an excellent option.
Services Offered: Automated phone transactions, payroll deductions, bank draft capabilities, an IRA investment plan and a systematic withdrawal plan.

Data Date	Investment Rating	Net Assets ($Mil)	NAV	Performance Rating/Pts	Total Return Y-T-D	Risk Rating/Pts
3-16	A+	4,321	13.61	A- / 9.1	1.45%	B- / 7.3
2015	A+	4,034	13.52	A- / 9.2	2.62%	B- / 7.0
2014	A+	3,757	13.61	B+ / 8.6	7.37%	C+ / 5.7
2013	A+	2,996	13.12	B+ / 8.8	-1.04%	C+ / 5.8
2012	A+	3,321	13.75	B / 7.9	7.21%	C+ / 5.6
2011	A+	3,104	13.31	B+ / 8.6	10.17%	C / 4.8

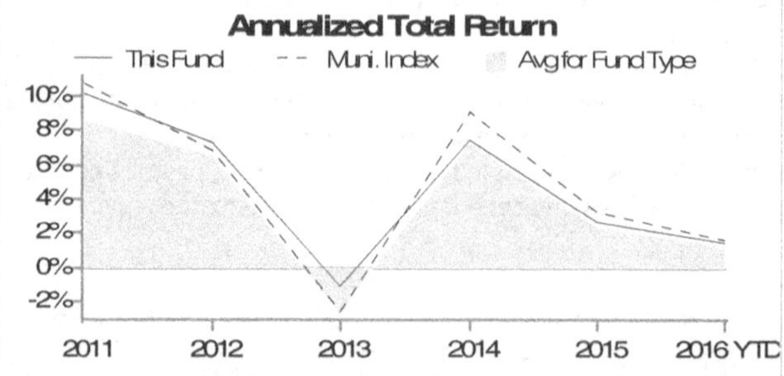

USAA Tax-Exempt Long Term Fund (USTEX) — B+ Good

Fund Family: USAA Group **Phone:** (800) 382-8722
Address: 9800 Fredricksburg Road, San Antonio, TX 78288
Fund Type: MUN - Municipal - National
Major Rating Factors: Exceptional performance is the major factor driving the B+ (Good) TheStreet.com Investment Rating for USAA Tax-Exempt Long Term Fund. The fund currently has a performance rating of A (Excellent) based on an average return of 3.81% over the last three years (6.31% taxable equivalent) and 1.49% over the last three months (2.47% taxable equivalent). Factored into the performance evaluation is an expense ratio of 0.55% (very low).

The fund's risk rating is currently C- (Fair). Volatility, as measured by standard deviation, is considered average for fixed income funds at 3.98. Another risk factor is the fund's above average duration of 7.9 years (i.e. higher interest rate risk).

John C. Bonnell currently receives a manager quality ranking of 50 (0=worst, 99=best). If you desire an average level of risk and strong performance, then this fund is a good option.
Services Offered: Automated phone transactions, payroll deductions, bank draft capabilities, an IRA investment plan and a systematic withdrawal plan.

Data Date	Investment Rating	Net Assets ($Mil)	NAV	Performance Rating/Pts	Total Return Y-T-D	Risk Rating/Pts
3-16	B+	2,415	13.73	A / 9.5	1.49%	C- / 3.7
2015	B	2,357	13.66	A / 9.5	3.32%	C- / 3.4
2014	A-	2,345	13.79	A / 9.5	10.54%	C- / 3.1
2013	A-	2,457	13.01	A- / 9.2	-2.79%	C- / 3.4
2012	A-	2,826	13.94	A- / 9.2	9.81%	D+ / 2.8
2011	A+	2,357	13.21	A / 9.4	12.50%	D+ / 2.8

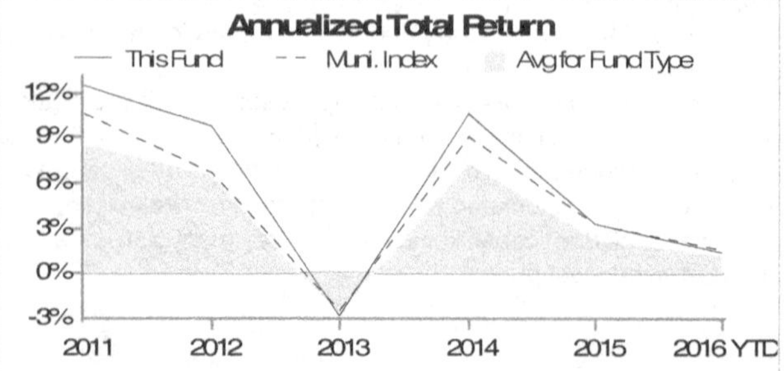

USAA Virginia Bond Fund (USVAX) C+ Fair

Fund Family: USAA Group **Phone:** (800) 382-8722
Address: 9800 Fredricksburg Road, San Antonio, TX 78288
Fund Type: GEI - General - Investment Grade
Major Rating Factors: Strong performance is the major factor driving the C+ (Fair) TheStreet.com Investment Rating for USAA Virginia Bond Fund. The fund currently has a performance rating of B (Good) based on an average return of 3.58% over the last three years and 1.35% over the last three months. Factored into the performance evaluation is an expense ratio of 0.59% (low).

The fund's risk rating is currently C- (Fair). Volatility, as measured by standard deviation, is considered average for fixed income funds at 3.82. Another risk factor is the fund's above average duration of 7.6 years (i.e. higher interest rate risk).

John C. Bonnell has been running the fund for 10 years and currently receives a manager quality ranking of 91 (0=worst, 99=best). If you desire an average level of risk and strong performance, then this fund is a good option.
Services Offered: Automated phone transactions, bank draft capabilities, an IRA investment plan and a systematic withdrawal plan.

Data Date	Investment Rating	Net Assets ($Mil)	NAV	Performance Rating/Pts	Total Return Y-T-D	Risk Rating/Pts
3-16	C+	647	11.52	B / 8.2	1.35%	C- / 3.9
2015	C+	632	11.46	B+ / 8.4	2.78%	C- / 3.7
2014	C+	631	11.56	B- / 7.4	10.78%	C- / 3.7
2013	C	578	10.84	C+ / 6.1	-3.15%	C- / 4.1
2012	D-	660	11.64	C- / 4.2	7.77%	C / 4.5
2011	C-	606	11.22	C / 5.0	10.99%	C / 5.0

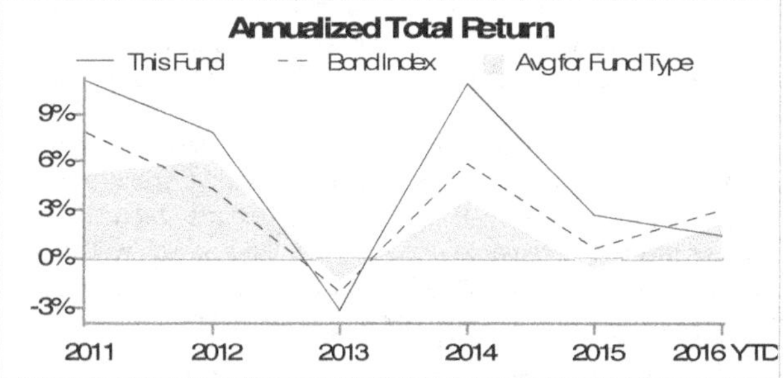

Vanguard CA Interm-Term T-E Inv (VCAIX) A+ Excellent

Fund Family: Vanguard Funds **Phone:** (800) 662-7447
Address: Vanguard Financial Center, Valley Forge, PA 19482
Fund Type: MUS - Municipal - Single State
Major Rating Factors: Exceptional performance is the major factor driving the A+ (Excellent) TheStreet.com Investment Rating for Vanguard CA Interm-Term T-E Inv. The fund currently has a performance rating of A (Excellent) based on an average return of 3.73% over the last three years (6.18% taxable equivalent) and 1.63% over the last three months (2.70% taxable equivalent). Factored into the performance evaluation is an expense ratio of 0.20% (very low).

The fund's risk rating is currently C+ (Fair). Volatility, as measured by standard deviation, is considered average for fixed income funds at 3.17. Another risk factor is the fund's fairly average duration of 5.5 years (i.e. average interest rate risk).

James M. D'Arcy has been running the fund for 5 years and currently receives a manager quality ranking of 80 (0=worst, 99=best). If you desire an average level of risk and strong performance, then this fund is a good option.
Services Offered: Automated phone transactions, check writing, payroll deductions, bank draft capabilities and a systematic withdrawal plan.

Data Date	Investment Rating	Net Assets ($Mil)	NAV	Performance Rating/Pts	Total Return Y-T-D	Risk Rating/Pts
3-16	A+	1,552	11.97	A / 9.5	1.63%	C+ / 5.9
2015	A	1,509	11.85	A / 9.5	3.18%	C / 5.4
2014	A+	1,471	11.81	B+ / 8.7	8.00%	C / 5.0
2013	A+	1,200	11.27	B+ / 8.8	-0.83%	C / 5.2
2012	A	1,344	11.74	B- / 7.5	6.63%	C / 5.0
2011	B+	1,224	11.37	C+ / 6.7	10.16%	C / 5.0

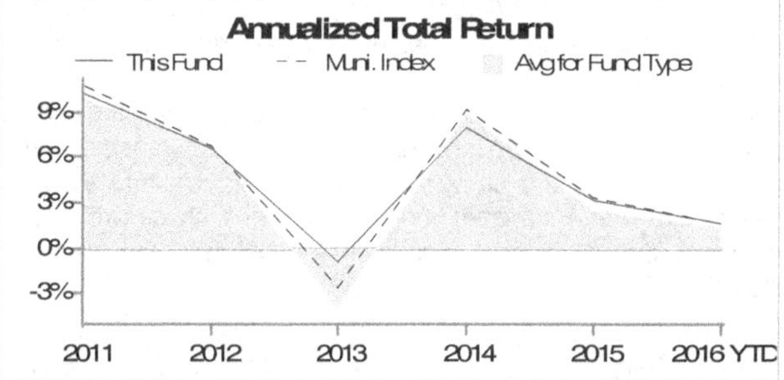

Vanguard GNMA Inv (VFIIX) B+ Good

Fund Family: Vanguard Funds **Phone:** (800) 662-7447
Address: Vanguard Financial Center, Valley Forge, PA 19482
Fund Type: USA - US Government/Agency
Major Rating Factors: Strong performance is the major factor driving the B+ (Good) TheStreet.com Investment Rating for Vanguard GNMA Inv. The fund currently has a performance rating of B- (Good) based on an average return of 2.45% over the last three years and 1.85% over the last three months. Factored into the performance evaluation is an expense ratio of 0.21% (very low).

The fund's risk rating is currently B- (Good). Volatility, as measured by standard deviation, is considered low for fixed income funds at 2.83. Another risk factor is the fund's below average duration of 4.0 years (i.e. lower interest rate risk).

Michael F. Garrett has been running the fund for 10 years and currently receives a manager quality ranking of 87 (0=worst, 99=best). If you desire only a moderate level of risk and strong performance, then this fund is an excellent option.
Services Offered: Automated phone transactions, check writing, payroll deductions, bank draft capabilities, an IRA investment plan, a Keogh investment plan, wire transfers and a systematic withdrawal plan.

Data Date	Investment Rating	Net Assets ($Mil)	NAV	Performance Rating/Pts	Total Return Y-T-D	Risk Rating/Pts
3-16	B+	8,509	10.79	B- / 7.1	1.85%	B- / 7.1
2015	B+	8,577	10.66	B- / 7.1	1.33%	C+ / 6.8
2014	C	9,140	10.82	C- / 4.0	6.65%	C+ / 6.8
2013	C-	9,541	10.42	C- / 3.0	-2.22%	B / 7.7
2012	C+	14,100	10.91	D+ / 2.7	2.35%	B+ / 8.6
2011	B	14,881	11.07	C- / 3.5	7.69%	B+ / 8.7

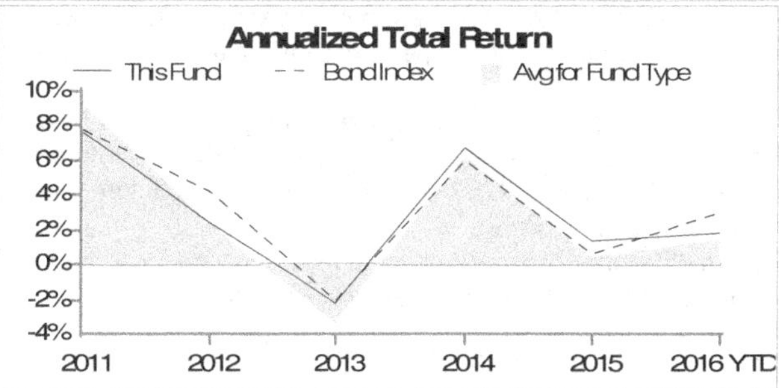

Vanguard High-Yield Corporate Inv (VWEHX) C- Fair

Fund Family: Vanguard Funds **Phone:** (800) 662-7447
Address: Vanguard Financial Center, Valley Forge, PA 19482
Fund Type: COH - Corporate - High Yield
Major Rating Factors: Vanguard High-Yield Corporate Inv has adopted a very risky asset allocation strategy and currently receives an overall TheStreet.com Investment Rating of C- (Fair). Volatility, as measured by standard deviation, is considered above average for fixed income funds at 5.00. Another risk factor is the fund's below average duration of 4.5 years (i.e. lower interest rate risk). Unfortunately, the high level of risk (D, Weak) has only provided investors with average performance.

The fund's performance rating is currently C+ (Fair). It has registered an average return of 2.68% over the last three years and is up 2.22% over the last three months. Factored into the performance evaluation is an expense ratio of 0.23% (very low).

Michael L Hong has been running the fund for 8 years and currently receives a manager quality ranking of 91 (0=worst, 99=best). If you are comfortable owning a very high risk investment, then this fund may be an option.
Services Offered: Automated phone transactions, check writing, payroll deductions, bank draft capabilities, an IRA investment plan, a Keogh investment plan, wire transfers and a systematic withdrawal plan.

Data Date	Investment Rating	Net Assets ($Mil)	NAV	Performance Rating/Pts	Total Return Y-T-D	Risk Rating/Pts
3-16	C-	3,608	5.59	C+ / 6.8	2.22%	D / 2.2
2015	C-	3,804	5.54	C+ / 6.9	-1.39%	D / 2.2
2014	C+	4,151	5.97	B+ / 8.3	4.58%	D+ / 2.7
2013	B	4,371	6.03	A / 9.5	4.54%	D / 1.8
2012	B-	5,638	6.11	B+ / 8.9	14.36%	D- / 1.5
2011	C+	5,170	5.69	B+ / 8.9	7.13%	D / 1.6

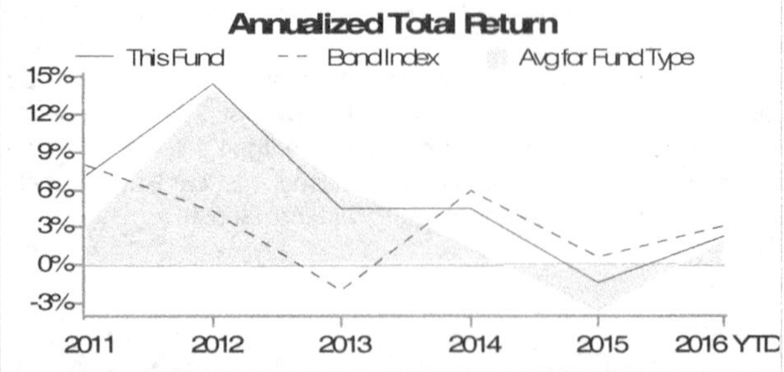

Vanguard High-Yield Tax-Exempt Inv (VWAHX) B Good

Fund Family: Vanguard Funds **Phone:** (800) 662-7447
Address: Vanguard Financial Center, Valley Forge, PA 19482
Fund Type: MUH - Municipal - High Yield
Major Rating Factors: Exceptional performance is the major factor driving the B (Good) TheStreet.com Investment Rating for Vanguard High-Yield Tax-Exempt Inv. The fund currently has a performance rating of A+ (Excellent) based on an average return of 4.40% over the last three years (7.29% taxable equivalent) and 1.83% over the last three months (3.03% taxable equivalent). Factored into the performance evaluation is an expense ratio of 0.20% (very low).

The fund's risk rating is currently C- (Fair). Volatility, as measured by standard deviation, is considered average for fixed income funds at 4.10. Another risk factor is the fund's below average duration of 4.7 years (i.e. lower interest rate risk).

Mathew M. Kiselak has been running the fund for 6 years and currently receives a manager quality ranking of 71 (0=worst, 99=best). If you desire an average level of risk and strong performance, then this fund is a good option.
Services Offered: Automated phone transactions, check writing, payroll deductions, bank draft capabilities, an IRA investment plan, wire transfers and a systematic withdrawal plan.

Data Date	Investment Rating	Net Assets ($Mil)	NAV	Performance Rating/Pts	Total Return Y-T-D	Risk Rating/Pts
3-16	B	1,748	11.43	A+ / 9.8	1.83%	C- / 3.1
2015	B	1,628	11.32	A+ / 9.8	4.13%	D+ / 2.9
2014	B+	1,516	11.28	A+ / 9.6	11.62%	D+ / 2.7
2013	B+	1,264	10.50	B+ / 8.6	-3.22%	C- / 3.4
2012	A	1,606	11.29	A- / 9.0	9.36%	C- / 3.1
2011	A	1,371	10.72	A- / 9.0	10.98%	C- / 3.1

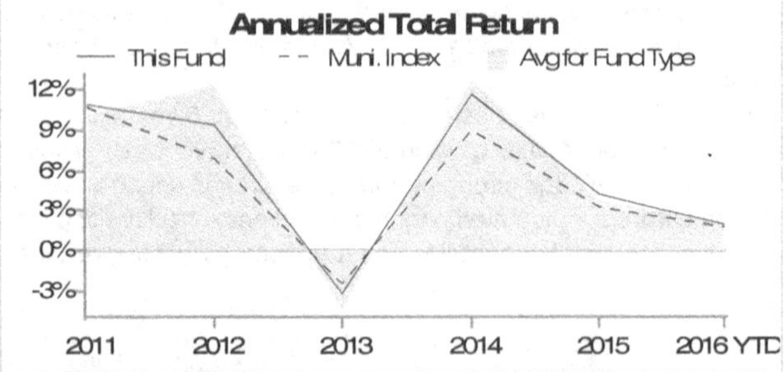

Vanguard Infltn Pro Sec Inv (VIPSX) D- Weak

Fund Family: Vanguard Funds **Phone:** (800) 662-7447
Address: Vanguard Financial Center, Valley Forge, PA 19482
Fund Type: USS - US Government - Short & Inter. Term
Major Rating Factors: Vanguard Infltn Pro Sec Inv has adopted a very risky asset allocation strategy and currently receives an overall TheStreet.com Investment Rating of D- (Weak). Volatility, as measured by standard deviation, is considered above average for fixed income funds at 5.46. Unfortunately, the high level of risk (D, Weak) failed to pay off as investors endured very poor performance.

The fund's performance rating is currently D+ (Weak). It has registered an average return of -0.86% over the last three years and is up 4.60% over the last three months. Factored into the performance evaluation is an expense ratio of 0.20% (very low).

Gemma Wright-Casparius has been running the fund for 5 years and currently receives a manager quality ranking of 5 (0=worst, 99=best). If you can tolerate very high levels of risk in the hope of improved future returns, holding this fund may be an option.
Services Offered: Automated phone transactions, check writing, payroll deductions, bank draft capabilities and wire transfers.

Data Date	Investment Rating	Net Assets ($Mil)	NAV	Performance Rating/Pts	Total Return Y-T-D	Risk Rating/Pts
3-16	D-	4,731	13.43	D+ / 2.7	4.60%	D / 2.0
2015	D-	4,847	12.84	D- / 1.0	-1.83%	D / 2.0
2014	E+	5,604	13.18	D / 1.6	3.83%	D- / 1.5
2013	E+	6,578	12.98	D+ / 2.3	-8.92%	D+ / 2.4
2012	C-	16,075	14.53	C+ / 6.0	6.77%	C- / 3.1
2011	D	15,220	14.11	C+ / 5.8	13.24%	C- / 3.3

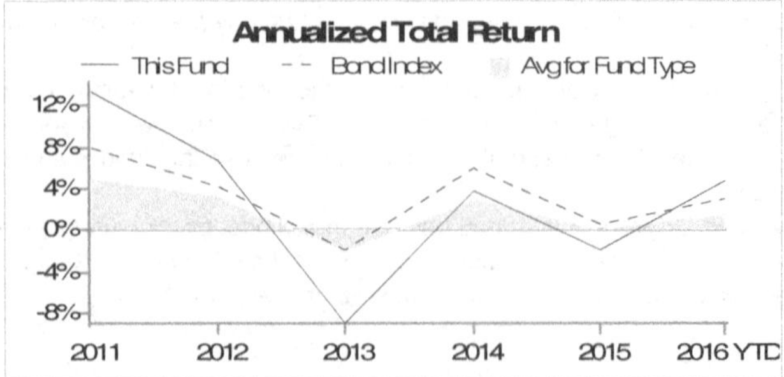

Vanguard Interm-Term Bd Index Inv (VBIIX) C Fair

Fund Family: Vanguard Funds **Phone:** (800) 662-7447
Address: Vanguard Financial Center, Valley Forge, PA 19482
Fund Type: GEI - General - Investment Grade
Major Rating Factors: Strong performance is the major factor driving the C (Fair) TheStreet.com Investment Rating for Vanguard Interm-Term Bd Index Inv. The fund currently has a performance rating of B (Good) based on an average return of 2.64% over the last three years and 4.00% over the last three months. Factored into the performance evaluation is an expense ratio of 0.20% (very low).

The fund's risk rating is currently C- (Fair). Volatility, as measured by standard deviation, is considered average for fixed income funds at 4.47. Another risk factor is the fund's fairly average duration of 6.4 years (i.e. average interest rate risk).

Joshua C. Barrickman has been running the fund for 8 years and currently receives a manager quality ranking of 28 (0=worst, 99=best). If you desire an average level of risk and strong performance, then this fund is a good option.
Services Offered: Automated phone transactions, check writing, payroll deductions, bank draft capabilities, an IRA investment plan, a Keogh investment plan, wire transfers and a systematic withdrawal plan.

Data Date	Investment Rating	Net Assets ($Mil)	NAV	Performance Rating/Pts	Total Return Y-T-D	Risk Rating/Pts
3-16	C	1,422	11.64	B / 7.8	4.00%	C- / 3.2
2015	C-	1,402	11.26	C+ / 6.5	1.21%	C- / 3.1
2014	D+	1,551	11.46	C / 5.2	6.85%	C- / 4.1
2013	C-	1,558	11.09	C / 5.3	-3.54%	C / 4.5
2012	C+	2,120	11.96	C+ / 6.3	6.91%	C / 4.5
2011	C-	2,129	11.77	C / 4.9	10.62%	C / 5.2

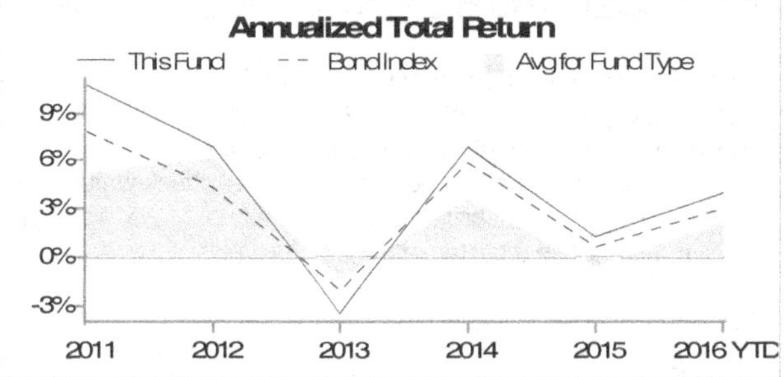

Vanguard Interm-Term Invst-Grd Inv (VFICX) B- Good

Fund Family: Vanguard Funds **Phone:** (800) 662-7447
Address: Vanguard Financial Center, Valley Forge, PA 19482
Fund Type: GEI - General - Investment Grade
Major Rating Factors: Strong performance is the major factor driving the B- (Good) TheStreet.com Investment Rating for Vanguard Interm-Term Invst-Grd Inv. The fund currently has a performance rating of B (Good) based on an average return of 3.01% over the last three years and 3.50% over the last three months. Factored into the performance evaluation is an expense ratio of 0.20% (very low).

The fund's risk rating is currently C (Fair). Volatility, as measured by standard deviation, is considered average for fixed income funds at 3.61. Another risk factor is the fund's fairly average duration of 5.5 years (i.e. average interest rate risk).

Gregory S. Nassour has been running the fund for 8 years and currently receives a manager quality ranking of 72 (0=worst, 99=best). If you desire an average level of risk and strong performance, then this fund is a good option.
Services Offered: Automated phone transactions, check writing, payroll deductions, bank draft capabilities, an IRA investment plan, a Keogh investment plan, wire transfers and a systematic withdrawal plan.

Data Date	Investment Rating	Net Assets ($Mil)	NAV	Performance Rating/Pts	Total Return Y-T-D	Risk Rating/Pts
3-16	B-	2,745	9.91	B / 8.0	3.50%	C / 4.7
2015	C+	2,669	9.64	B- / 7.2	1.53%	C / 4.7
2014	C+	2,874	9.83	C+ / 6.1	5.81%	C / 5.1
2013	B-	3,143	9.67	C+ / 6.6	-1.37%	C / 5.1
2012	B+	4,957	10.32	C+ / 6.8	9.14%	C / 5.1
2011	C+	4,661	9.99	C+ / 6.1	7.52%	C / 5.1

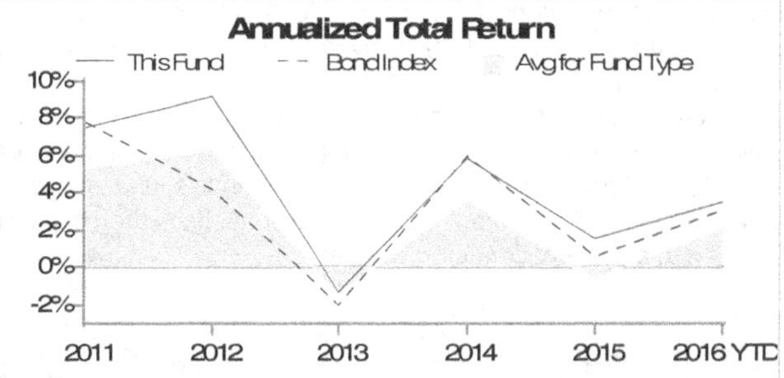

Vanguard Interm-Term Tax-Exempt Inv (VWITX) A+ Excellent

Fund Family: Vanguard Funds **Phone:** (800) 662-7447
Address: Vanguard Financial Center, Valley Forge, PA 19482
Fund Type: MUN - Municipal - National
Major Rating Factors: Exceptional performance is the major factor driving the A+ (Excellent) TheStreet.com Investment Rating for Vanguard Interm-Term Tax-Exempt Inv. The fund currently has a performance rating of A- (Excellent) based on an average return of 3.19% over the last three years (5.28% taxable equivalent) and 1.57% over the last three months (2.60% taxable equivalent). Factored into the performance evaluation is an expense ratio of 0.20% (very low).

The fund's risk rating is currently C+ (Fair). Volatility, as measured by standard deviation, is considered average for fixed income funds at 3.02. Another risk factor is the fund's fairly average duration of 5.1 years (i.e. average interest rate risk).

If you desire an average level of risk and strong performance, then this fund is a good option.
Services Offered: Automated phone transactions, check writing, payroll deductions, bank draft capabilities, an IRA investment plan, wire transfers and a systematic withdrawal plan.

Data Date	Investment Rating	Net Assets ($Mil)	NAV	Performance Rating/Pts	Total Return Y-T-D	Risk Rating/Pts
3-16	A+	4,558	14.39	A- / 9.2	1.57%	C+ / 6.5
2015	A+	4,422	14.26	A- / 9.1	2.86%	C+ / 6.1
2014	A	4,702	14.27	B / 8.0	7.25%	C / 5.2
2013	A	4,624	13.72	B / 8.1	-1.55%	C / 5.5
2012	B+	6,892	14.38	C+ / 6.6	5.70%	C / 5.3
2011	B+	7,060	14.03	C+ / 6.5	9.62%	C+ / 5.6

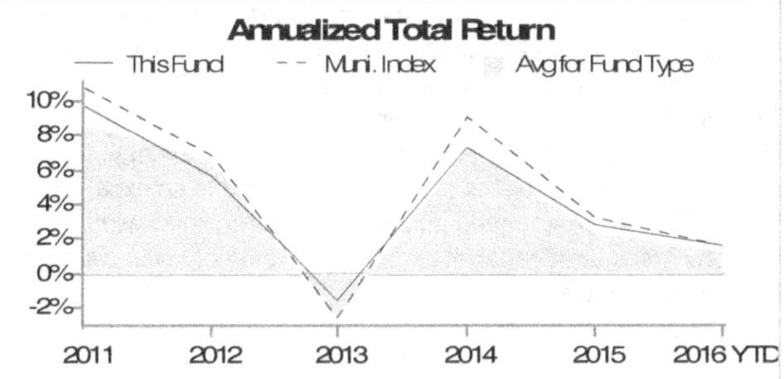

Vanguard Interm-Term Treasury Inv (VFITX) C Fair

Fund Family: Vanguard Funds **Phone:** (800) 662-7447
Address: Vanguard Financial Center, Valley Forge, PA 19482
Fund Type: US - US Treasury
Major Rating Factors: Middle of the road best describes Vanguard Interm-Term Treasury Inv whose TheStreet.com Investment Rating is currently a C (Fair). The fund has a performance rating of C+ (Fair) based on an average return of 1.91% over the last three years and 3.40% over the last three months. Factored into the performance evaluation is an expense ratio of 0.20% (very low).

The fund's risk rating is currently C (Fair). Volatility, as measured by standard deviation, is considered average for fixed income funds at 3.63. Another risk factor is the fund's fairly average duration of 5.4 years (i.e. average interest rate risk).

David R. Glocke has been running the fund for 15 years and currently receives a manager quality ranking of 46 (0=worst, 99=best). If you desire an average level of risk, then this fund may be an option.
Services Offered: Automated phone transactions, check writing, payroll deductions, bank draft capabilities, an IRA investment plan, a Keogh investment plan, wire transfers and a systematic withdrawal plan.

Data Date	Investment Rating	Net Assets ($Mil)	NAV	Performance Rating/Pts	Total Return Y-T-D	Risk Rating/Pts
3-16	C	1,370	11.59	C+ / 6.8	3.40%	C / 4.6
2015	C-	1,307	11.26	C+ / 5.6	1.50%	C / 4.8
2014	D	1,358	11.37	D+ / 2.8	4.32%	C+ / 5.8
2013	D	1,469	11.12	C- / 3.2	-3.09%	C+ / 5.6
2012	D-	2,081	11.70	C- / 3.5	2.67%	C / 5.0
2011	E+	2,349	11.70	C- / 3.1	9.80%	C / 4.6

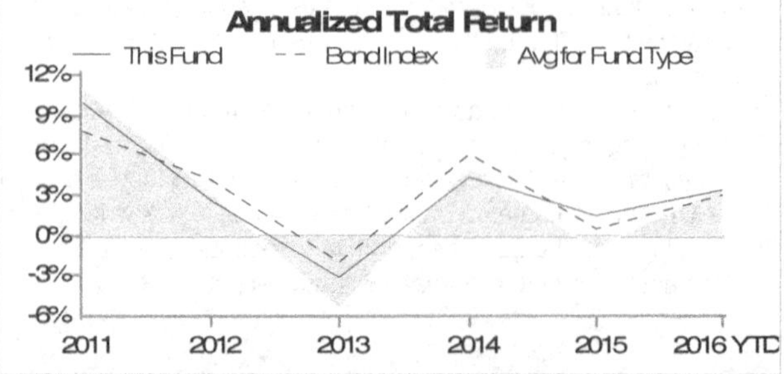

Vanguard Intm-Term Govt Bd Idx Adm (VSIGX) C+ Fair

Fund Family: Vanguard Funds **Phone:** (800) 662-7447
Address: Vanguard Financial Center, Valley Forge, PA 19482
Fund Type: USS - US Government - Short & Inter. Term
Major Rating Factors: Strong performance is the major factor driving the C+ (Fair) TheStreet.com Investment Rating for Vanguard Intm-Term Govt Bd Idx Adm. The fund currently has a performance rating of B- (Good) based on an average return of 2.02% over the last three years and 3.27% over the last three months. Factored into the performance evaluation is an expense ratio of 0.10% (very low).

The fund's risk rating is currently C (Fair). Volatility, as measured by standard deviation, is considered average for fixed income funds at 3.47. Another risk factor is the fund's fairly average duration of 5.2 years (i.e. average interest rate risk).

Joshua C. Barrickman has been running the fund for 3 years and currently receives a manager quality ranking of 45 (0=worst, 99=best). If you desire an average level of risk and strong performance, then this fund is a good option.
Services Offered: Automated phone transactions, bank draft capabilities, wire transfers and a systematic withdrawal plan.

Data Date	Investment Rating	Net Assets ($Mil)	NAV	Performance Rating/Pts	Total Return Y-T-D	Risk Rating/Pts
3-16	C+	560	22.35	B- / 7.0	3.27%	C / 5.0
2015	C	434	21.72	C+ / 5.9	1.65%	C / 5.2
2014	D	262	21.73	D+ / 2.8	4.22%	C+ / 6.1
2013	D+	158	21.18	C- / 3.5	-2.74%	C+ / 5.8
2012	U	52	22.13	U / --	2.63%	U / --
2011	U	12	22.12	U / --	9.66%	U / --

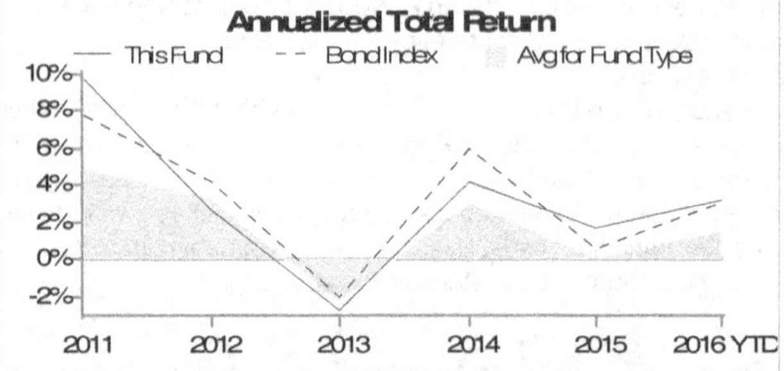

Vanguard Lmtd-Term Tax-Exempt Inv (VMLTX) A Excellent

Fund Family: Vanguard Funds **Phone:** (800) 662-7447
Address: Vanguard Financial Center, Valley Forge, PA 19482
Fund Type: MUN - Municipal - National
Major Rating Factors: A moderate risk profile coupled with stable earnings characterizes Vanguard Lmtd-Term Tax-Exempt Inv which receives a TheStreet.com Investment Rating of A (Excellent). Volatility, as measured by standard deviation, is considered very low for fixed income funds at 1.24. Another risk factor is the fund's very low average duration of 1.8 years (i.e. low interest rate risk). The fund's risk rating is currently A- (Excellent).

The fund's performance rating is currently C+ (Fair). It has registered an average return of 1.27% over the last three years (2.10% taxable equivalent) and is up 0.62% over the last three months (1.03% taxable equivalent). Factored into the performance evaluation is an expense ratio of 0.20% (very low).

Marlin G. Brown has been running the fund for 8 years and currently receives a manager quality ranking of 73 (0=worst, 99=best). If you desire stability with a moderate level of risk then this fund is an excellent option.
Services Offered: Automated phone transactions, check writing, payroll deductions, bank draft capabilities, an IRA investment plan, wire transfers and a systematic withdrawal plan.

Data Date	Investment Rating	Net Assets ($Mil)	NAV	Performance Rating/Pts	Total Return Y-T-D	Risk Rating/Pts
3-16	A	2,074	11.05	C+ / 6.4	0.62%	A- / 9.1
2015	A+	2,037	11.02	B- / 7.3	1.32%	A- / 9.1
2014	C+	2,270	11.04	C- / 3.1	1.79%	A- / 9.1
2013	A-	2,341	11.02	C / 4.6	0.49%	A- / 9.1
2012	C	2,693	11.15	D / 1.7	1.77%	A- / 9.2
2011	B-	3,182	11.16	C- / 3.0	3.71%	A- / 9.2

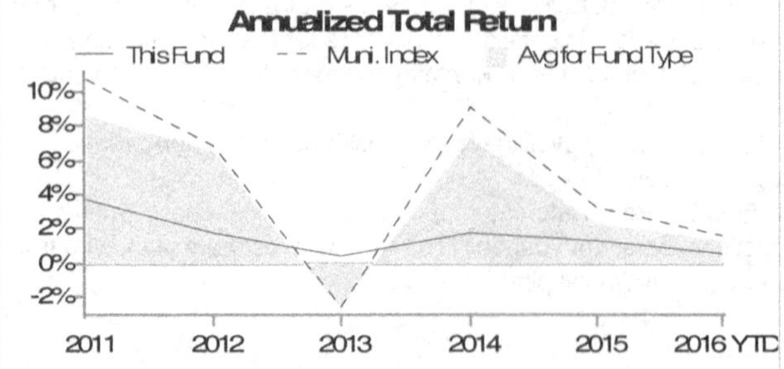

Vanguard Long Term Bd Idx Investor (VBLTX) C- Fair

Fund Family: Vanguard Funds **Phone:** (800) 662-7447
Address: Vanguard Financial Center, Valley Forge, PA 19482
Fund Type: GEL - General - Long Term
Major Rating Factors: Vanguard Long Term Bd Idx Investor has adopted a very risky asset allocation strategy and currently receives an overall TheStreet.com Investment Rating of C- (Fair). Volatility, as measured by standard deviation, is considered high for fixed income funds at 9.06. Another risk factor is the fund's very high average duration of 13.9 years (i.e. very high interest rate risk). The high level of risk (E, Very Weak) did however, reward investors with excellent performance.

The fund's performance rating is currently A- (Excellent). It has registered an average return of 4.64% over the last three years and is up 7.35% over the last three months. Factored into the performance evaluation is an expense ratio of 0.20% (very low).

Joshua C. Barrickman has been running the fund for 3 years and currently receives a manager quality ranking of 9 (0=worst, 99=best). If you are comfortable owning a very high risk investment, this fund may be an option.
Services Offered: Automated phone transactions, check writing, payroll deductions, bank draft capabilities, an IRA investment plan, a Keogh investment plan, wire transfers and a systematic withdrawal plan.

Data Date	Investment Rating	Net Assets ($Mil)	NAV	Performance Rating/Pts	Total Return Y-T-D	Risk Rating/Pts
3-16	C-	2,516	14.04	A- / 9.0	7.35%	E / 0.3
2015	D	2,449	13.20	C+ / 5.8	-3.47%	E- / 0.2
2014	C-	2,594	14.26	B+ / 8.9	19.72%	E / 0.3
2013	D-	2,019	12.41	C+ / 6.4	-9.13%	E- / 0.2
2012	C+	2,904	14.27	A- / 9.2	8.49%	E / 0.3
2011	D	2,727	13.91	B- / 7.4	22.06%	D- / 1.2

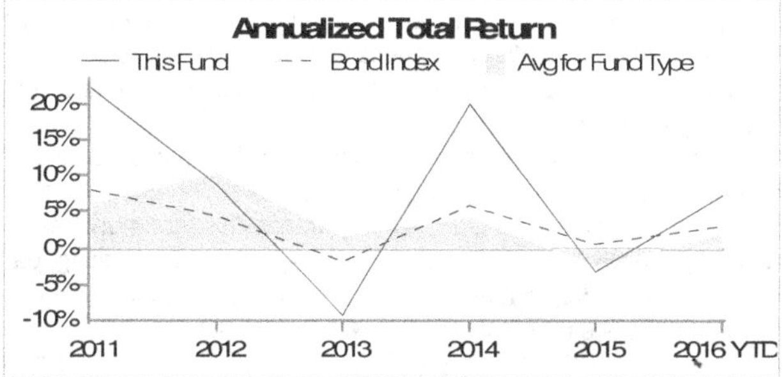

Vanguard Long-Term Inv Gr Inv (VWESX) C- Fair

Fund Family: Vanguard Funds **Phone:** (800) 662-7447
Address: Vanguard Financial Center, Valley Forge, PA 19482
Fund Type: GEI - General - Investment Grade
Major Rating Factors: Vanguard Long-Term Inv Gr Inv has adopted a very risky asset allocation strategy and currently receives an overall TheStreet.com Investment Rating of C- (Fair). Volatility, as measured by standard deviation, is considered high for fixed income funds at 8.46. Another risk factor is the fund's very high average duration of 13.1 years (i.e. very high interest rate risk). The high level of risk (E, Very Weak) did however, reward investors with excellent performance.

The fund's performance rating is currently A (Excellent). It has registered an average return of 5.31% over the last three years and is up 6.71% over the last three months. Factored into the performance evaluation is an expense ratio of 0.22% (very low).

Lucius T. Hill, III has been running the fund for 8 years and currently receives a manager quality ranking of 23 (0=worst, 99=best). If you are comfortable owning a very high risk investment, this fund may be an option.
Services Offered: Automated phone transactions, check writing, payroll deductions, bank draft capabilities, an IRA investment plan, a Keogh investment plan, wire transfers and a systematic withdrawal plan. However, the fund is currently closed to new investors.

Data Date	Investment Rating	Net Assets ($Mil)	NAV	Performance Rating/Pts	Total Return Y-T-D	Risk Rating/Pts
3-16	C-	3,910	10.43	A / 9.3	6.71%	E / 0.3
2015	D+	4,042	9.90	B / 7.7	-2.21%	E / 0.3
2014	C	4,482	10.75	A / 9.4	18.17%	E / 0.4
2013	D+	3,962	9.65	B / 8.0	-5.87%	E / 0.4
2012	C+	4,472	10.85	A / 9.3	11.66%	E / 0.5
2011	D	4,121	10.29	B- / 7.4	17.18%	D- / 1.3

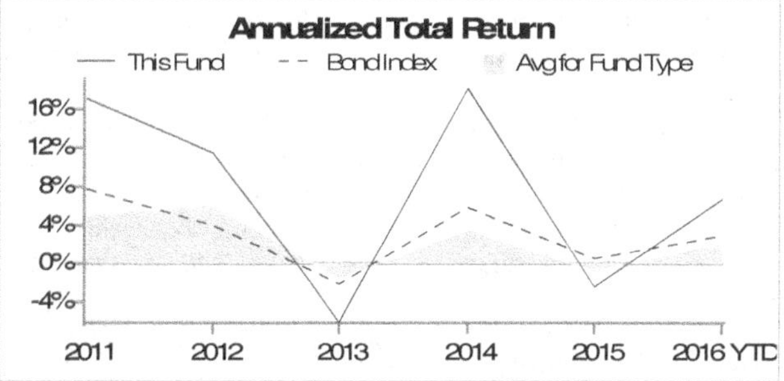

Vanguard Long-Term Tax-Exempt Inv (VWLTX) A- Excellent

Fund Family: Vanguard Funds **Phone:** (800) 662-7447
Address: Vanguard Financial Center, Valley Forge, PA 19482
Fund Type: MUN - Municipal - National
Major Rating Factors: Exceptional performance is the major factor driving the A- (Excellent) TheStreet.com Investment Rating for Vanguard Long-Term Tax-Exempt Inv. The fund currently has a performance rating of A+ (Excellent) based on an average return of 4.37% over the last three years (7.24% taxable equivalent) and 1.86% over the last three months (3.08% taxable equivalent). Factored into the performance evaluation is an expense ratio of 0.20% (very low).

The fund's risk rating is currently C- (Fair). Volatility, as measured by standard deviation, is considered average for fixed income funds at 4.00. Another risk factor is the fund's below average duration of 4.9 years (i.e. lower interest rate risk).

Mathew M. Kiselak has been running the fund for 6 years and currently receives a manager quality ranking of 73 (0=worst, 99=best). If you desire an average level of risk and strong performance, then this fund is a good option.
Services Offered: Automated phone transactions, check writing, payroll deductions, bank draft capabilities, an IRA investment plan, wire transfers and a systematic withdrawal plan.

Data Date	Investment Rating	Net Assets ($Mil)	NAV	Performance Rating/Pts	Total Return Y-T-D	Risk Rating/Pts
3-16	A-	977	11.87	A+ / 9.8	1.86%	C- / 3.9
2015	B+	931	11.75	A+ / 9.7	3.97%	C- / 3.8
2014	A	955	11.74	A / 9.4	11.07%	C- / 3.7
2013	A-	943	11.01	B+ / 8.4	-2.95%	C- / 4.2
2012	A	1,094	11.80	B / 8.1	8.08%	C / 4.4
2011	A	1,093	11.33	B / 7.7	10.69%	C / 4.5

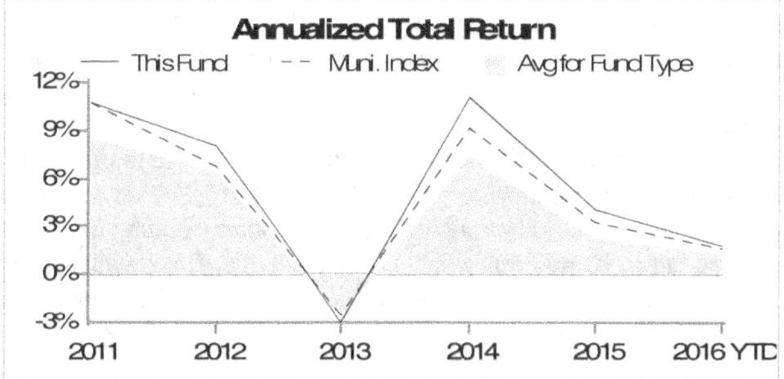

Vanguard Long-Term Treasury Inv (VUSTX) C- Fair

Fund Family: Vanguard Funds **Phone:** (800) 662-7447
Address: Vanguard Financial Center, Valley Forge, PA 19482
Fund Type: US - US Treasury
Major Rating Factors: Vanguard Long-Term Treasury Inv has adopted a very risky asset allocation strategy and currently receives an overall TheStreet.com Investment Rating of C- (Fair). Volatility, as measured by standard deviation, is considered high for fixed income funds at 11.20. Another risk factor is the fund's very high average duration of 16.5 years (i.e. very high interest rate risk). The high level of risk (E-, Very Weak) did however, reward investors with excellent performance.

The fund's performance rating is currently A+ (Excellent). It has registered an average return of 5.83% over the last three years and is up 8.26% over the last three months. Factored into the performance evaluation is an expense ratio of 0.20% (very low).

David R. Glocke has been running the fund for 15 years and currently receives a manager quality ranking of 24 (0=worst, 99=best). If you are comfortable owning a very high risk investment, this fund may be an option.
Services Offered: Automated phone transactions, check writing, payroll deductions, bank draft capabilities, an IRA investment plan, a Keogh investment plan, wire transfers and a systematic withdrawal plan.

Data Date	Investment Rating	Net Assets ($Mil)	NAV	Performance Rating/Pts	Total Return Y-T-D	Risk Rating/Pts
3-16	C-	1,213	13.11	A+ / 9.6	8.26%	E- / 0.1
2015	D+	1,074	12.19	B- / 7.3	-1.54%	E- / 0.1
2014	C-	1,190	13.05	B+ / 8.9	25.28%	E- / 0.2
2013	E	963	10.90	C- / 3.2	-13.03%	E- / 0.1
2012	C-	1,491	13.07	B+ / 8.5	3.47%	E- / 0.1
2011	E+	1,605	13.34	C+ / 6.4	29.28%	E- / 0.1

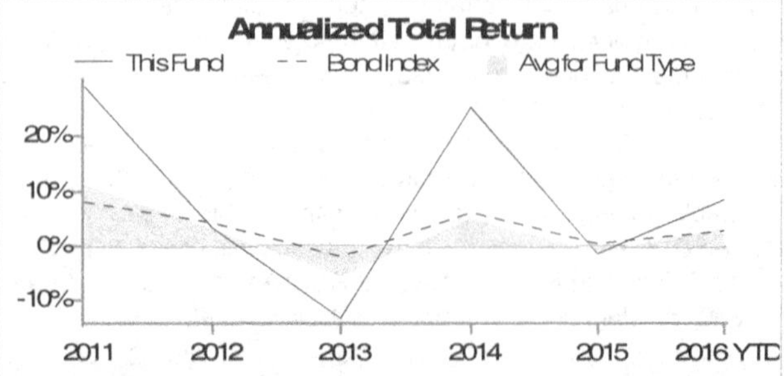

Vanguard MA Tax-Exempt Inv (VMATX) B+ Good

Fund Family: Vanguard Funds **Phone:** (800) 662-7447
Address: Vanguard Financial Center, Valley Forge, PA 19482
Fund Type: MUS - Municipal - Single State
Major Rating Factors: Exceptional performance is the major factor driving the B+ (Good) TheStreet.com Investment Rating for Vanguard MA Tax-Exempt Inv. The fund currently has a performance rating of A+ (Excellent) based on an average return of 4.10% over the last three years (6.79% taxable equivalent) and 1.72% over the last three months (2.85% taxable equivalent). Factored into the performance evaluation is an expense ratio of 0.16% (very low).

The fund's risk rating is currently C- (Fair). Volatility, as measured by standard deviation, is considered average for fixed income funds at 4.07. Another risk factor is the fund's fairly average duration of 5.1 years (i.e. average interest rate risk).

Marlin G. Brown has been running the fund for 8 years and currently receives a manager quality ranking of 55 (0=worst, 99=best). If you desire an average level of risk and strong performance, then this fund is a good option.
Services Offered: Automated phone transactions, check writing, payroll deductions, bank draft capabilities, wire transfers and a systematic withdrawal plan.

Data Date	Investment Rating	Net Assets ($Mil)	NAV	Performance Rating/Pts	Total Return Y-T-D	Risk Rating/Pts
3-16	B+	1,379	11.03	A+ / 9.7	1.72%	C- / 3.9
2015	B+	1,286	10.92	A+ / 9.6	3.95%	C- / 3.6
2014	B+	1,170	10.85	B+ / 8.9	10.29%	C- / 3.6
2013	B	981	10.22	B / 7.6	-3.32%	C- / 4.1
2012	B	1,111	10.92	C+ / 6.9	6.46%	C / 4.5
2011	B+	971	10.59	C+ / 6.7	10.41%	C / 5.1

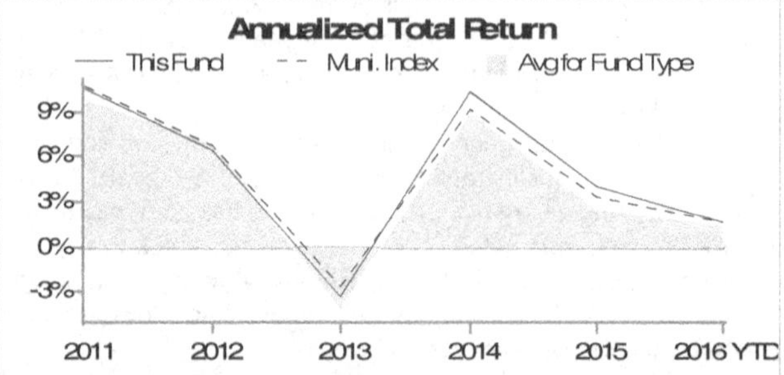

Vanguard OH Long-Term Tax-Exmpt Inv (VOHIX) B+ Good

Fund Family: Vanguard Funds **Phone:** (800) 662-7447
Address: Vanguard Financial Center, Valley Forge, PA 19482
Fund Type: MUS - Municipal - Single State
Major Rating Factors: Exceptional performance is the major factor driving the B+ (Good) TheStreet.com Investment Rating for Vanguard OH Long-Term Tax-Exmpt Inv. The fund currently has a performance rating of A+ (Excellent) based on an average return of 4.47% over the last three years (7.40% taxable equivalent) and 1.80% over the last three months (2.98% taxable equivalent). Factored into the performance evaluation is an expense ratio of 0.16% (very low).

The fund's risk rating is currently C- (Fair). Volatility, as measured by standard deviation, is considered average for fixed income funds at 4.23. Another risk factor is the fund's fairly average duration of 5.2 years (i.e. average interest rate risk).

Marlin G. Brown has been running the fund for 8 years and currently receives a manager quality ranking of 64 (0=worst, 99=best). If you desire an average level of risk and strong performance, then this fund is a good option.
Services Offered: Automated phone transactions, check writing, payroll deductions, bank draft capabilities and a systematic withdrawal plan.

Data Date	Investment Rating	Net Assets ($Mil)	NAV	Performance Rating/Pts	Total Return Y-T-D	Risk Rating/Pts
3-16	B+	1,088	12.78	A+ / 9.8	1.80%	C- / 3.6
2015	B	1,019	12.65	A+ / 9.7	4.25%	C- / 3.4
2014	A	978	12.61	A / 9.3	11.20%	C- / 3.5
2013	B	872	11.81	B / 8.0	-3.16%	C- / 3.9
2012	B+	1,023	12.71	B- / 7.5	7.47%	C / 4.5
2011	A-	899	12.28	B- / 7.2	10.08%	C / 5.2

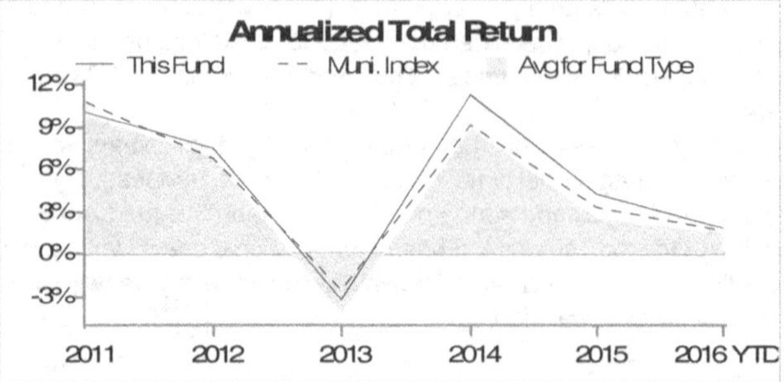

Vanguard Short-Term Bd Idx Investor (VBISX) B Good

Fund Family: Vanguard Funds **Phone:** (800) 662-7447
Address: Vanguard Financial Center, Valley Forge, PA 19482
Fund Type: GES - General - Short & Inter. Term
Major Rating Factors: A moderate risk profile coupled with stable earnings characterizes Vanguard Short-Term Bd Idx Investor which receives a TheStreet.com Investment Rating of B (Good). Volatility, as measured by standard deviation, is considered very low for fixed income funds at 1.31. Another risk factor is the fund's very low average duration of 2.7 years (i.e. low interest rate risk). The fund's risk rating is currently A- (Excellent).

The fund's performance rating is currently C (Fair). It has registered an average return of 1.15% over the last three years and is up 1.57% over the last three months. Factored into the performance evaluation is an expense ratio of 0.20% (very low).

Joshua C. Barrickman has been running the fund for 3 years and currently receives a manager quality ranking of 73 (0=worst, 99=best). If you desire stability with a moderate level of risk then this fund is an excellent option.
Services Offered: Automated phone transactions, check writing, payroll deductions, bank draft capabilities, an IRA investment plan, a Keogh investment plan, wire transfers and a systematic withdrawal plan.

Data Date	Investment Rating	Net Assets ($Mil)	NAV	Performance Rating/Pts	Total Return Y-T-D	Risk Rating/Pts
3-16	B	2,311	10.56	C / 4.9	1.57%	A- / 9.0
2015	B	2,325	10.43	C / 5.0	0.85%	A- / 9.0
2014	C	2,667	10.48	D / 2.0	1.16%	A / 9.3
2013	C	3,003	10.49	D+ / 2.4	0.07%	A- / 9.2
2012	C-	3,185	10.63	D- / 1.3	1.95%	A- / 9.1
2011	C	3,802	10.61	D / 1.9	2.96%	A / 9.3

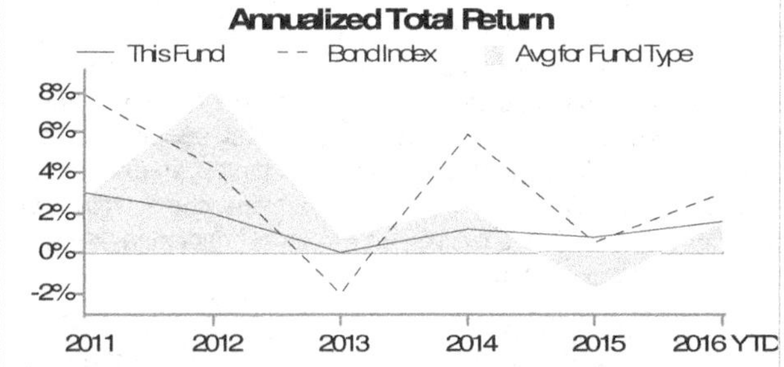

Vanguard Short-Term Crp Bd Idx Adm (VSCSX) A Excellent

Fund Family: Vanguard Funds **Phone:** (800) 662-7447
Address: Vanguard Financial Center, Valley Forge, PA 19482
Fund Type: COI - Corporate - Investment Grade
Major Rating Factors: A moderate risk profile coupled with stable earnings characterizes Vanguard Short-Term Crp Bd Idx Adm which receives a TheStreet.com Investment Rating of A (Excellent). Volatility, as measured by standard deviation, is considered low for fixed income funds at 1.64. Another risk factor is the fund's very low average duration of 2.8 years (i.e. low interest rate risk). The fund's risk rating is currently B+ (Good).

The fund's performance rating is currently C+ (Fair). It has registered an average return of 1.89% over the last three years and is up 1.75% over the last three months. Factored into the performance evaluation is an expense ratio of 0.10% (very low).

Joshua C. Barrickman has been running the fund for 7 years and currently receives a manager quality ranking of 89 (0=worst, 99=best). If you desire stability with a moderate level of risk then this fund is an excellent option.
Services Offered: Automated phone transactions, bank draft capabilities, wire transfers and a systematic withdrawal plan.

Data Date	Investment Rating	Net Assets ($Mil)	NAV	Performance Rating/Pts	Total Return Y-T-D	Risk Rating/Pts
3-16	A	1,542	21.72	C+ / 6.2	1.75%	B+ / 8.8
2015	A	1,341	21.45	C+ / 6.6	1.23%	B+ / 8.8
2014	B	937	21.63	C- / 3.8	1.98%	B+ / 8.7
2013	A-	198	21.64	C / 5.1	1.37%	B+ / 8.5
2012	U	33	21.79	U / --	5.74%	U / --
2011	U	4	21.09	U / --	2.91%	U / --

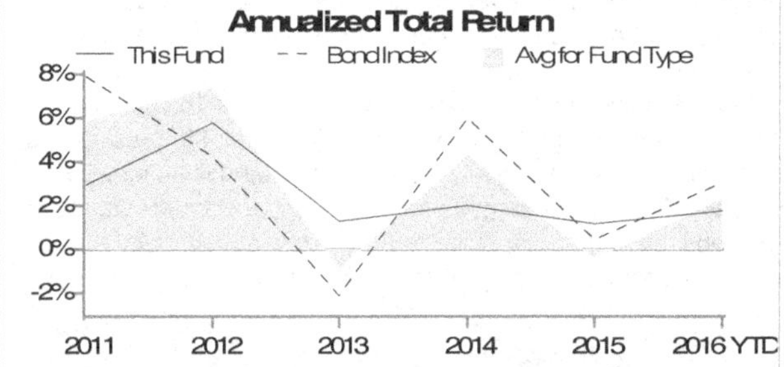

Vanguard Short-Term Federal Inv (VSGBX) B- Good

Fund Family: Vanguard Funds **Phone:** (800) 662-7447
Address: Vanguard Financial Center, Valley Forge, PA 19482
Fund Type: USS - US Government - Short & Inter. Term
Major Rating Factors: A moderate risk profile coupled with stable earnings characterizes Vanguard Short-Term Federal Inv which receives a TheStreet.com Investment Rating of B- (Good). Volatility, as measured by standard deviation, is considered very low for fixed income funds at 1.07. Another risk factor is the fund's very low average duration of 2.4 years (i.e. low interest rate risk). The fund's risk rating is currently A- (Excellent).

The fund's performance rating is currently C (Fair). It has registered an average return of 0.91% over the last three years and is up 1.26% over the last three months. Factored into the performance evaluation is an expense ratio of 0.20% (very low).

Ronald M. Reardon has been running the fund for 11 years and currently receives a manager quality ranking of 73 (0=worst, 99=best). If you desire stability with a moderate level of risk then this fund is an excellent option.
Services Offered: Automated phone transactions, check writing, payroll deductions, bank draft capabilities, an IRA investment plan, a Keogh investment plan, wire transfers and a systematic withdrawal plan.

Data Date	Investment Rating	Net Assets ($Mil)	NAV	Performance Rating/Pts	Total Return Y-T-D	Risk Rating/Pts
3-16	B-	821	10.82	C / 4.5	1.26%	A- / 9.2
2015	B	826	10.71	C / 4.7	0.73%	A- / 9.2
2014	C	928	10.76	D / 1.8	1.17%	A / 9.4
2013	C	1,520	10.70	D / 1.8	-0.35%	A / 9.4
2012	C-	1,999	10.80	D- / 1.0	1.44%	A / 9.3
2011	C-	2,284	10.84	D / 1.6	2.76%	A / 9.4

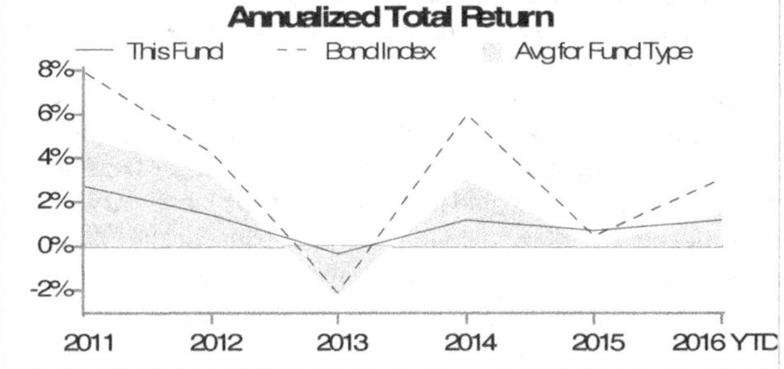

Vanguard Short-Term Tax-Exempt Inv (VWSTX) B Good

Fund Family: Vanguard Funds **Phone:** (800) 662-7447
Address: Vanguard Financial Center, Valley Forge, PA 19482
Fund Type: MUN - Municipal - National
Major Rating Factors: A moderate risk profile coupled with stable earnings characterizes Vanguard Short-Term Tax-Exempt Inv which receives a TheStreet.com Investment Rating of B (Good). Volatility, as measured by standard deviation, is considered very low for fixed income funds at 0.42. Another risk factor is the fund's very low average duration of 1.5 years (i.e. low interest rate risk). The fund's risk rating is currently A+ (Excellent).

The fund's performance rating is currently C- (Fair). It has registered an average return of 0.53% over the last three years (0.88% taxable equivalent) and is up 0.30% over the last three months (0.50% taxable equivalent). Factored into the performance evaluation is an expense ratio of 0.20% (very low).

Pamela W. Tynan has been running the fund for 20 years and currently receives a manager quality ranking of 75 (0=worst, 99=best). If you desire stability with a moderate level of risk then this fund is an excellent option.
Services Offered: Automated phone transactions, check writing, payroll deductions, bank draft capabilities, an IRA investment plan, wire transfers and a systematic withdrawal plan.

Data Date	Investment Rating	Net Assets ($Mil)	NAV	Performance Rating/Pts	Total Return Y-T-D	Risk Rating/Pts
3-16	B	1,303	15.82	C- / 4.1	0.30%	A+ / 9.8
2015	A	1,361	15.80	C / 5.5	0.45%	A+ / 9.8
2014	C+	1,670	15.84	D / 2.0	0.65%	A+ / 9.9
2013	B-	1,817	15.85	D+ / 2.5	0.47%	A+ / 9.9
2012	C-	2,071	15.91	E+ / 0.8	0.99%	A+ / 9.9
2011	C	2,662	15.92	D / 1.6	1.60%	A+ / 9.9

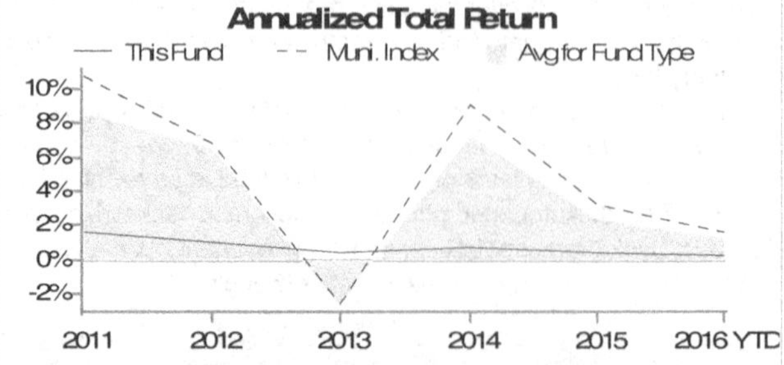

Vanguard Short-Term Treasury Inv (VFISX) B- Good

Fund Family: Vanguard Funds **Phone:** (800) 662-7447
Address: Vanguard Financial Center, Valley Forge, PA 19482
Fund Type: US - US Treasury
Major Rating Factors: A moderate risk profile coupled with stable earnings characterizes Vanguard Short-Term Treasury Inv which receives a TheStreet.com Investment Rating of B- (Good). Volatility, as measured by standard deviation, is considered very low for fixed income funds at 0.95. Another risk factor is the fund's very low average duration of 2.4 years (i.e. low interest rate risk). The fund's risk rating is currently A (Excellent).

The fund's performance rating is currently C- (Fair). It has registered an average return of 0.73% over the last three years and is up 1.22% over the last three months. Factored into the performance evaluation is an expense ratio of 0.20% (very low).

David R. Glocke has been running the fund for 16 years and currently receives a manager quality ranking of 74 (0=worst, 99=best). If you desire stability with a moderate level of risk then this fund is an excellent option.
Services Offered: Automated phone transactions, check writing, payroll deductions, bank draft capabilities, an IRA investment plan, a Keogh investment plan, wire transfers and a systematic withdrawal plan.

Data Date	Investment Rating	Net Assets ($Mil)	NAV	Performance Rating/Pts	Total Return Y-T-D	Risk Rating/Pts
3-16	B-	1,014	10.76	C- / 4.1	1.22%	A / 9.3
2015	B-	986	10.65	C / 4.3	0.45%	A / 9.4
2014	C-	1,049	10.69	D- / 1.5	0.71%	A+ / 9.6
2013	C-	1,167	10.68	D- / 1.5	-0.10%	A / 9.5
2012	D+	1,484	10.74	E+ / 0.8	0.69%	A / 9.4
2011	C-	1,786	10.79	D- / 1.4	2.26%	A / 9.5

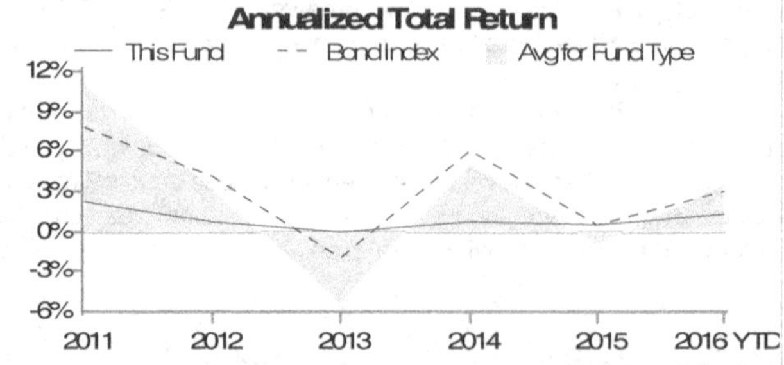

Vanguard Sh-Term Invest-Grade Inv (VFSTX) A- Excellent

Fund Family: Vanguard Funds **Phone:** (800) 662-7447
Address: Vanguard Financial Center, Valley Forge, PA 19482
Fund Type: GEI - General - Investment Grade
Major Rating Factors: A moderate risk profile coupled with stable earnings characterizes Vanguard Sh-Term Invest-Grade Inv which receives a TheStreet.com Investment Rating of A- (Excellent). Volatility, as measured by standard deviation, is considered very low for fixed income funds at 1.34. Another risk factor is the fund's very low average duration of 2.6 years (i.e. low interest rate risk). The fund's risk rating is currently A- (Excellent).

The fund's performance rating is currently C+ (Fair). It has registered an average return of 1.67% over the last three years and is up 1.71% over the last three months. Factored into the performance evaluation is an expense ratio of 0.20% (very low).

Gregory S. Nassour has been running the fund for 8 years and currently receives a manager quality ranking of 86 (0=worst, 99=best). If you desire stability with a moderate level of risk then this fund is an excellent option.
Services Offered: Automated phone transactions, check writing, payroll deductions, bank draft capabilities, an IRA investment plan, a Keogh investment plan, wire transfers and a systematic withdrawal plan.

Data Date	Investment Rating	Net Assets ($Mil)	NAV	Performance Rating/Pts	Total Return Y-T-D	Risk Rating/Pts
3-16	A-	9,770	10.69	C+ / 5.9	1.71%	A- / 9.0
2015	A	9,987	10.56	C+ / 6.2	1.03%	A- / 9.0
2014	B-	10,954	10.66	C- / 3.2	1.76%	A- / 9.0
2013	B	11,732	10.70	C- / 3.9	0.97%	A- / 9.0
2012	C	12,229	10.83	D / 2.0	4.52%	A- / 9.0
2011	C+	13,189	10.64	C- / 3.1	1.93%	B+ / 8.4

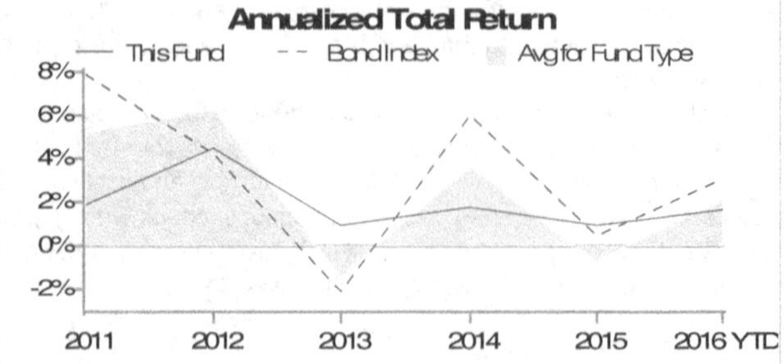

Vanguard ST Inf Prot Sec Idx Inv (VTIPX) C- Fair

Fund Family: Vanguard Funds **Phone:** (800) 662-7447
Address: Vanguard Financial Center, Valley Forge, PA 19482
Fund Type: GEI - General - Investment Grade
Major Rating Factors: Disappointing performance is the major factor driving the C- (Fair) TheStreet.com Investment Rating for Vanguard ST Inf Prot Sec Idx Inv. The fund currently has a performance rating of D (Weak) based on an average return of -0.63% over the last three years and 1.78% over the last three months. Factored into the performance evaluation is an expense ratio of 0.17% (very low).

The fund's risk rating is currently B+ (Good). Volatility, as measured by standard deviation, is considered low for fixed income funds at 1.84. Another risk factor is the fund's very low average duration of 2.3 years (i.e. low interest rate risk).

Gemma Wright-Casparius has been running the fund for 4 years and currently receives a manager quality ranking of 17 (0=worst, 99=best). This fund offers only a moderate level of risk but investors looking for strong performance are still waiting.
Services Offered: Automated phone transactions, payroll deductions, bank draft capabilities and wire transfers.

Data Date	Investment Rating	Net Assets ($Mil)	NAV	Performance Rating/Pts	Total Return Y-T-D	Risk Rating/Pts
3-16	C-	4,436	24.57	D / 1.7	1.78%	B+ / 8.6
2015	C-	4,617	24.14	D / 1.8	-0.21%	B+ / 8.7
2014	U	4,596	24.19	U / --	-1.28%	U / --
2013	U	3,917	24.68	U / --	-1.62%	U / --

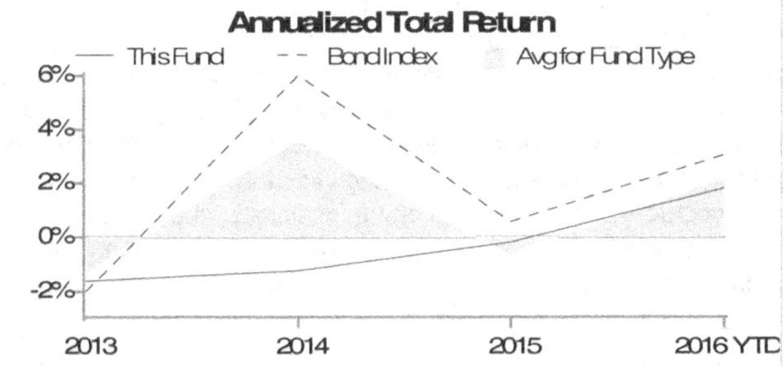

Vanguard Total Bond Mkt II Idx Inv (VTBIX) B Good

Fund Family: Vanguard Funds **Phone:** (800) 662-7447
Address: Vanguard Financial Center, Valley Forge, PA 19482
Fund Type: COI - Corporate - Investment Grade
Major Rating Factors: Strong performance is the major factor driving the B (Good) TheStreet.com Investment Rating for Vanguard Total Bond Mkt II Idx Inv. The fund currently has a performance rating of B- (Good) based on an average return of 2.27% over the last three years and 3.04% over the last three months. Factored into the performance evaluation is an expense ratio of 0.10% (very low).

The fund's risk rating is currently C+ (Fair). Volatility, as measured by standard deviation, is considered average for fixed income funds at 3.10.

Joshua C. Barrickman has been running the fund for 6 years and currently receives a manager quality ranking of 79 (0=worst, 99=best). If you desire an average level of risk and strong performance, then this fund is a good option.
Services Offered: Automated phone transactions, payroll deductions, bank draft capabilities, an IRA investment plan, a 401K investment plan, wire transfers and a systematic withdrawal plan.

Data Date	Investment Rating	Net Assets ($Mil)	NAV	Performance Rating/Pts	Total Return Y-T-D	Risk Rating/Pts
3-16	B	54,644	10.86	B- / 7.0	3.04%	C+ / 6.2
2015	C	55,324	10.60	C+ / 6.0	0.28%	C+ / 6.1
2014	C	54,268	10.84	C- / 4.2	5.93%	B- / 7.0
2013	C	47,497	10.49	C- / 3.7	-2.26%	B- / 7.2
2012	C	45,758	10.97	C- / 3.2	3.91%	B- / 7.2
2011	U	35,626	10.87	U / --	6.61%	U / --

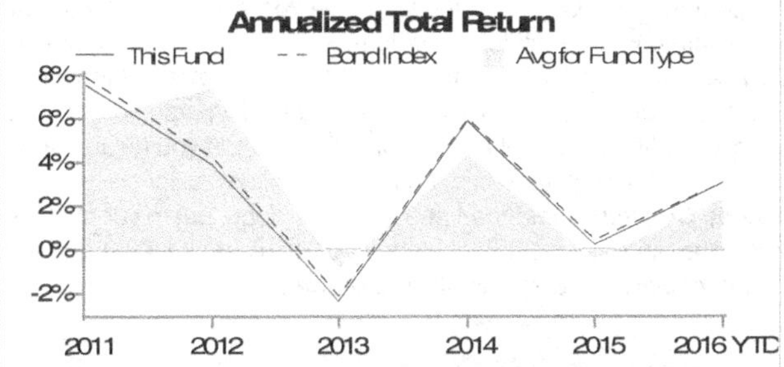

Vanguard Total Bond Mrkt Index Inv (VBMFX) B Good

Fund Family: Vanguard Funds **Phone:** (800) 662-7447
Address: Vanguard Financial Center, Valley Forge, PA 19482
Fund Type: GES - General - Short & Inter. Term
Major Rating Factors: Strong performance is the major factor driving the B (Good) TheStreet.com Investment Rating for Vanguard Total Bond Mrkt Index Inv. The fund currently has a performance rating of B- (Good) based on an average return of 2.25% over the last three years and 3.03% over the last three months. Factored into the performance evaluation is an expense ratio of 0.20% (very low).

The fund's risk rating is currently C+ (Fair). Volatility, as measured by standard deviation, is considered average for fixed income funds at 3.07. Another risk factor is the fund's fairly average duration of 5.5 years (i.e. average interest rate risk).

Kenneth E. Volpert has been running the fund for 24 years and currently receives a manager quality ranking of 51 (0=worst, 99=best). If you desire an average level of risk and strong performance, then this fund is a good option.
Services Offered: Automated phone transactions, check writing, payroll deductions, bank draft capabilities, an IRA investment plan, a Keogh investment plan, wire transfers and a systematic withdrawal plan.

Data Date	Investment Rating	Net Assets ($Mil)	NAV	Performance Rating/Pts	Total Return Y-T-D	Risk Rating/Pts
3-16	B	6,621	10.90	B- / 7.0	3.03%	C+ / 6.3
2015	C	6,565	10.64	C+ / 6.0	0.30%	C+ / 6.1
2014	C	7,076	10.87	C- / 4.1	5.76%	B- / 7.0
2013	C	7,939	10.56	C- / 3.7	-2.26%	B- / 7.2
2012	C	11,794	11.09	C- / 3.2	4.05%	B- / 7.1
2011	C+	12,584	11.00	C- / 3.5	7.56%	B / 7.8

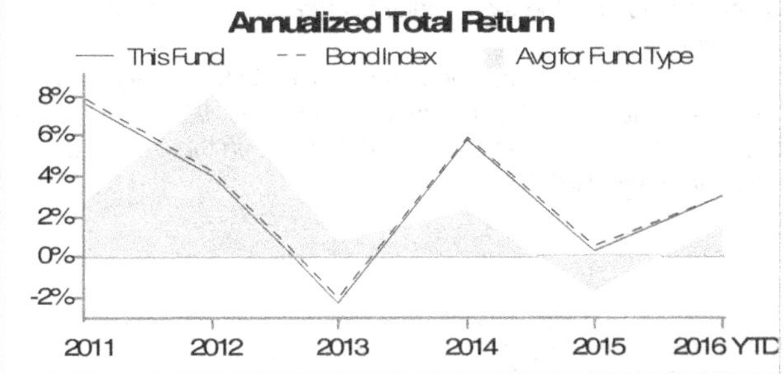

Virtus Multi-Sector Short Term Bd A (NARAX) C- Fair

Fund Family: Virtus Mutual Funds **Phone:** (800) 243-1574
Address: C/O State Street Bank & Trust, Boston, MA 02266
Fund Type: GES - General - Short & Inter. Term

Major Rating Factors: A moderate risk profile coupled with stable earnings characterizes Virtus Multi-Sector Short Term Bd A which receives a TheStreet.com Investment Rating of C- (Fair). Volatility, as measured by standard deviation, is considered low for fixed income funds at 2.25. Another risk factor is the fund's very low average duration of 2.2 years (i.e. low interest rate risk). The fund's risk rating is currently B (Good).

The fund's performance rating is currently C- (Fair). It has registered an average return of 0.94% over the last three years and is up 1.15% over the last three months. Factored into the performance evaluation is an expense ratio of 0.97% (average) and a 2.3% front-end load that is levied at the time of purchase.

David L. Albrycht has been running the fund for 23 years and currently receives a manager quality ranking of 59 (0=worst, 99=best). If you desire stability with a moderate level of risk then this fund is an excellent option.

Services Offered: Automated phone transactions, check writing, payroll deductions, an IRA investment plan, a 401K investment plan, a Keogh investment plan and a systematic withdrawal plan.

Data Date	Investment Rating	Net Assets ($Mil)	NAV	Performance Rating/Pts	Total Return Y-T-D	Risk Rating/Pts
3-16	C-	1,412	4.65	C- / 3.1	1.15%	B / 8.2
2015	C	1,496	4.63	C- / 3.3	0.07%	B / 8.1
2014	C-	1,811	4.76	C- / 3.6	1.03%	B- / 7.0
2013	B-	3,560	4.86	C+ / 6.0	1.52%	C+ / 5.7
2012	C	3,259	4.96	C / 5.0	9.40%	C / 4.8
2011	C	2,364	4.73	C+ / 6.2	3.10%	C- / 4.2

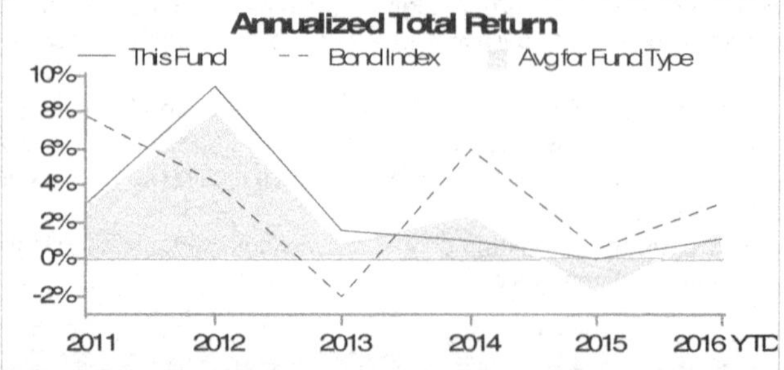

Voya GNMA Income A (LEXNX) B Good

Fund Family: Voya Investments LLC **Phone:** (800) 992-0180
Address: 7337 East Doubletree Ranch Roa, Scottsdale, AZ 85258
Fund Type: USA - US Government/Agency

Major Rating Factors: A moderate risk profile coupled with stable earnings characterizes Voya GNMA Income A which receives a TheStreet.com Investment Rating of B (Good). Volatility, as measured by standard deviation, is considered low for fixed income funds at 2.19. Another risk factor is the fund's very low average duration of 2.4 years (i.e. low interest rate risk). The fund's risk rating is currently B+ (Good).

The fund's performance rating is currently C (Fair). It has registered an average return of 2.07% over the last three years and is up 1.66% over the last three months. Factored into the performance evaluation is an expense ratio of 0.92% (average) and a 2.5% front-end load that is levied at the time of purchase.

Jeffrey Dutra has been running the fund for 7 years and currently receives a manager quality ranking of 87 (0=worst, 99=best). If you desire stability with a moderate level of risk then this fund is an excellent option.

Services Offered: Automated phone transactions, payroll deductions, bank draft capabilities, an IRA investment plan, a 401K investment plan, a Keogh investment plan and a systematic withdrawal plan.

Data Date	Investment Rating	Net Assets ($Mil)	NAV	Performance Rating/Pts	Total Return Y-T-D	Risk Rating/Pts
3-16	B	630	8.63	C / 5.5	1.66%	B+ / 8.3
2015	B	541	8.55	C+ / 5.6	1.60%	B / 8.1
2014	C-	525	8.68	D+ / 2.7	4.93%	B / 8.2
2013	C-	601	8.56	D+ / 2.4	-1.84%	B+ / 8.4
2012	C+	744	9.02	D+ / 2.3	2.87%	B+ / 8.8
2011	C+	653	9.14	C- / 3.0	7.43%	B+ / 8.8

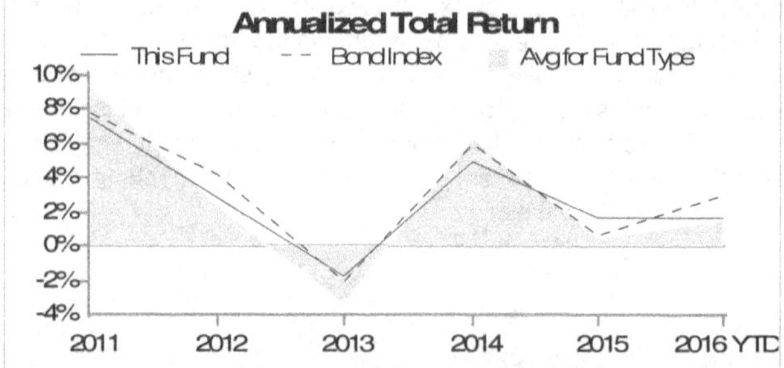

Voya Intermediate Bond Port S (IPISX) B- Good

Fund Family: Voya Investments LLC **Phone:** (800) 992-0180
Address: 7337 East Doubletree Ranch Roa, Scottsdale, AZ 85258
Fund Type: GEI - General - Investment Grade

Major Rating Factors: Strong performance is the major factor driving the B- (Good) TheStreet.com Investment Rating for Voya Intermediate Bond Port S. The fund currently has a performance rating of B- (Good) based on an average return of 2.64% over the last three years and 2.65% over the last three months. Factored into the performance evaluation is an expense ratio of 0.79% (low).

The fund's risk rating is currently C+ (Fair). Volatility, as measured by standard deviation, is considered average for fixed income funds at 3.18. Another risk factor is the fund's fairly average duration of 5.2 years (i.e. average interest rate risk).

Christine Hurtsellers has been running the fund for 7 years and currently receives a manager quality ranking of 72 (0=worst, 99=best). If you desire an average level of risk and strong performance, then this fund is a good option.

Services Offered: N/A

Data Date	Investment Rating	Net Assets ($Mil)	NAV	Performance Rating/Pts	Total Return Y-T-D	Risk Rating/Pts
3-16	B-	3,240	12.77	B- / 7.2	2.65%	C+ / 5.8
2015	C+	3,171	12.44	C+ / 6.9	-0.02%	C+ / 5.7
2014	B+	3,478	12.83	C+ / 6.7	6.48%	C+ / 5.9
2013	A	1,120	12.43	B- / 7.0	-0.38%	C+ / 6.4
2012	A+	1,229	12.89	C+ / 6.6	9.08%	C+ / 6.7
2011	C+	1,247	12.34	C / 4.7	7.30%	C+ / 6.7

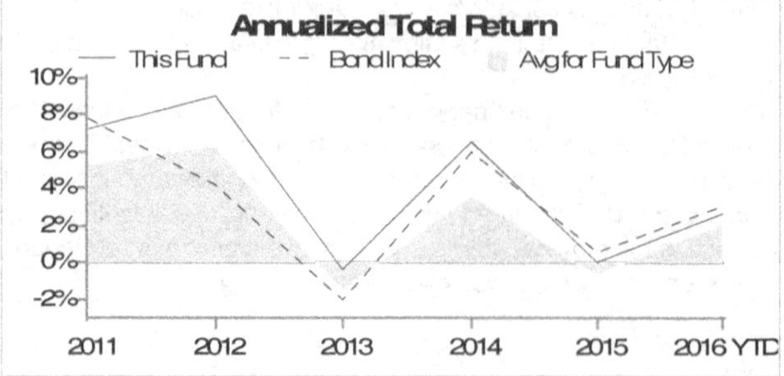

Voya Money Market Port I (IVMXX) C- Fair

Fund Family: Voya Investments LLC **Phone:** (800) 992-0180
Address: 7337 East Doubletree Ranch Roa, Scottsdale, AZ 85258
Fund Type: LP - Loan Participation
Major Rating Factors: Disappointing performance is the major factor driving the C- (Fair) TheStreet.com Investment Rating for Voya Money Market Port I. The fund currently has a performance rating of D (Weak) based on an average return of 0.02% over the last three years and 0.03% over the last three months. Factored into the performance evaluation is an expense ratio of 0.39% (very low).

The fund's risk rating is currently A+ (Excellent). Volatility, as measured by standard deviation, is considered very low for fixed income funds at 0.02.

David S. Yealy has been running the fund for 12 years and currently receives a manager quality ranking of 62 (0=worst, 99=best). This fund offers only a moderate level of risk but investors looking for strong performance are still waiting.

Services Offered: N/A

Data Date	Investment Rating	Net Assets ($Mil)	NAV	Performance Rating/Pts	Total Return Y-T-D	Risk Rating/Pts
3-16	C-	541	1.00	D / 1.9	0.03%	A+ / 9.9
2012	D+	988	1.00	E / 0.3	0.03%	A+ / 9.9

Asset Composition
For: Voya Money Market Port I

Cash & Cash Equivalent:	0%
Government Bonds:	0%
Municipal Bonds:	0%
Corporate Bonds:	0%
Other:	100%

WA Core Plus Bond FI (WACIX) B Good

Fund Family: Western Asset Funds **Phone:** (888) 425-6432
Address: 100 Light Street, Baltimore, MD 21202
Fund Type: GEI - General - Investment Grade
Major Rating Factors: Strong performance is the major factor driving the B (Good) TheStreet.com Investment Rating for WA Core Plus Bond FI. The fund currently has a performance rating of B (Good) based on an average return of 2.92% over the last three years and 2.39% over the last three months. Factored into the performance evaluation is an expense ratio of 0.81% (low).

The fund's risk rating is currently C (Fair). Volatility, as measured by standard deviation, is considered average for fixed income funds at 3.31. Another risk factor is the fund's fairly average duration of 6.7 years (i.e. average interest rate risk).

S. Kenneth Leech has been running the fund for 3 years and currently receives a manager quality ranking of 80 (0=worst, 99=best). If you desire an average level of risk and strong performance, then this fund is a good option.
Services Offered: Automated phone transactions, bank draft capabilities, an IRA investment plan, a 401K investment plan, wire transfers and a systematic withdrawal plan.

Data Date	Investment Rating	Net Assets ($Mil)	NAV	Performance Rating/Pts	Total Return Y-T-D	Risk Rating/Pts
3-16	B	1,541	11.63	B / 7.6	2.39%	C / 5.4
2015	B-	1,541	11.44	B- / 7.5	1.00%	C / 5.4
2014	B+	1,853	11.64	C+ / 6.5	7.35%	C+ / 6.2
2013	B+	3,110	11.19	C+ / 5.8	-1.32%	B- / 7.0
2012	A	2,934	11.67	C+ / 6.4	8.25%	C+ / 6.6
2011	C+	2,121	11.10	B- / 7.1	6.37%	C- / 3.5

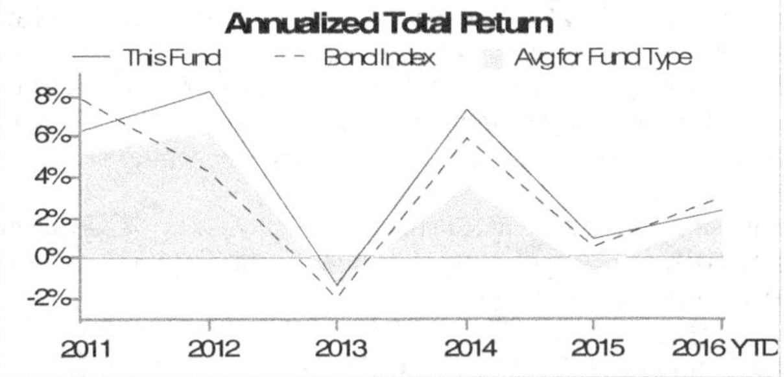

WA Intermediate-Term Muni A (SBLTX) B+ Good

Fund Family: Legg Mason Partners Funds **Phone:** (877) 534-4627
Address: 100 Light Street, Baltimore, MD 21202
Fund Type: MUN - Municipal - National
Major Rating Factors: Strong performance is the major factor driving the B+ (Good) TheStreet.com Investment Rating for WA Intermediate-Term Muni A. The fund currently has a performance rating of B (Good) based on an average return of 2.26% over the last three years (3.74% taxable equivalent) and 1.37% over the last three months (2.27% taxable equivalent). Factored into the performance evaluation is an expense ratio of 0.75% (low) and a 2.3% front-end load that is levied at the time of purchase.

The fund's risk rating is currently C+ (Fair). Volatility, as measured by standard deviation, is considered average for fixed income funds at 3.08. Another risk factor is the fund's below average duration of 4.5 years (i.e. lower interest rate risk).

David Fare has been running the fund for 12 years and currently receives a manager quality ranking of 31 (0=worst, 99=best). If you desire an average level of risk and strong performance, then this fund is a good option.
Services Offered: Automated phone transactions, payroll deductions, bank draft capabilities, an IRA investment plan and a systematic withdrawal plan.

Data Date	Investment Rating	Net Assets ($Mil)	NAV	Performance Rating/Pts	Total Return Y-T-D	Risk Rating/Pts
3-16	B+	1,329	6.61	B / 7.7	1.37%	C+ / 6.2
2015	B	1,348	6.57	B / 7.8	2.21%	C+ / 5.8
2014	B	1,296	6.63	B- / 7.2	7.45%	C / 4.6
2013	B-	1,215	6.37	C+ / 6.9	-3.37%	C / 4.7
2012	B-	1,459	6.81	C+ / 6.6	7.22%	C / 4.6
2011	A	1,321	6.56	B- / 7.1	10.70%	C / 5.4

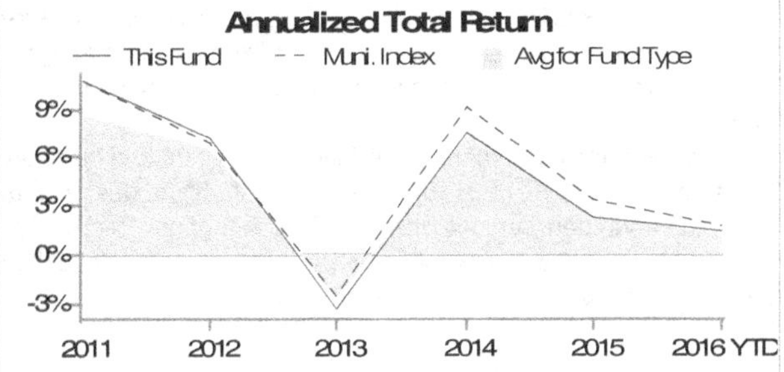

WA Managed Municipals A (SHMMX) C+ Fair

Fund Family: Legg Mason Partners Funds **Phone:** (877) 534-4627
Address: 100 Light Street, Baltimore, MD 21202
Fund Type: MUN - Municipal - National
Major Rating Factors: Strong performance is the major factor driving the C+ (Fair) TheStreet.com Investment Rating for WA Managed Municipals A. The fund currently has a performance rating of B (Good) based on an average return of 3.26% over the last three years (5.40% taxable equivalent) and 1.53% over the last three months (2.53% taxable equivalent). Factored into the performance evaluation is an expense ratio of 0.66% (low) and a 4.3% front-end load that is levied at the time of purchase.

The fund's risk rating is currently C- (Fair). Volatility, as measured by standard deviation, is considered average for fixed income funds at 4.21. Another risk factor is the fund's fairly average duration of 5.7 years (i.e. average interest rate risk).

David Fare has been running the fund for 12 years and currently receives a manager quality ranking of 27 (0=worst, 99=best). If you desire an average level of risk and strong performance, then this fund is a good option.
Services Offered: Automated phone transactions, payroll deductions, bank draft capabilities and a systematic withdrawal plan.

Data Date	Investment Rating	Net Assets ($Mil)	NAV	Performance Rating/Pts	Total Return Y-T-D	Risk Rating/Pts
3-16	C+	3,047	16.81	B / 8.1	1.53%	C- / 3.6
2015	C	2,983	16.70	B / 8.2	2.75%	C- / 3.4
2014	B	2,755	16.88	B+ / 8.7	10.92%	D+ / 2.8
2013	C	2,761	15.83	B / 7.7	-4.35%	D+ / 2.4
2012	B-	3,670	17.23	B / 8.0	10.13%	D+ / 2.6
2011	B+	3,462	16.27	B+ / 8.9	12.90%	D+ / 2.6

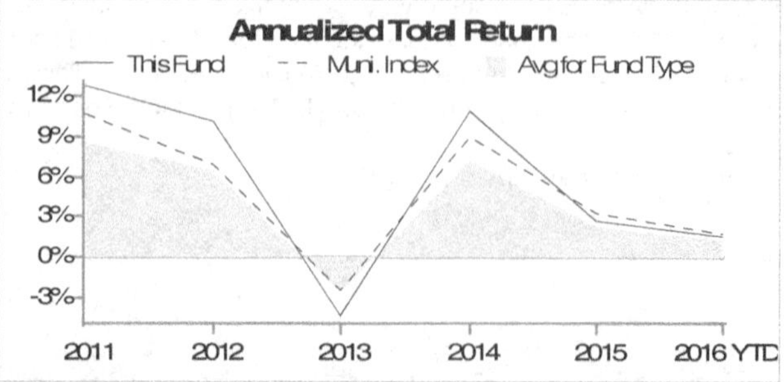

WA Mortgage Backed Securities A (SGVAX) B+ Good

Fund Family: Legg Mason Partners Funds **Phone:** (877) 534-4627
Address: 100 Light Street, Baltimore, MD 21202
Fund Type: USS - US Government - Short & Inter. Term
Major Rating Factors: A moderate risk profile coupled with stable earnings characterizes WA Mortgage Backed Securities A which receives a TheStreet.com Investment Rating of B+ (Good). Volatility, as measured by standard deviation, is considered low for fixed income funds at 2.12. Another risk factor is the fund's below average duration of 4.9 years (i.e. lower interest rate risk). The fund's risk rating is currently B+ (Good).

The fund's performance rating is currently C+ (Fair). It has registered an average return of 3.23% over the last three years and is up 0.56% over the last three months. Factored into the performance evaluation is an expense ratio of 0.95% (average) and a 4.3% front-end load that is levied at the time of purchase.

S. Kenneth Leech currently receives a manager quality ranking of 97 (0=worst, 99=best). If you desire stability with a moderate level of risk then this fund is an excellent option.
Services Offered: Automated phone transactions, payroll deductions, bank draft capabilities, an IRA investment plan, a 401K investment plan, wire transfers and a systematic withdrawal plan.

Data Date	Investment Rating	Net Assets ($Mil)	NAV	Performance Rating/Pts	Total Return Y-T-D	Risk Rating/Pts
3-16	B+	595	10.71	C+ / 5.6	0.56%	B+ / 8.4
2015	A	550	10.73	B- / 7.2	1.98%	B / 8.2
2014	A	464	10.90	C+ / 5.8	6.46%	B / 8.1
2013	A	491	10.66	C / 5.4	1.71%	B+ / 8.4
2012	B+	507	10.88	C / 4.4	7.77%	B / 8.1
2011	B-	480	10.53	C- / 3.4	6.24%	B+ / 8.6

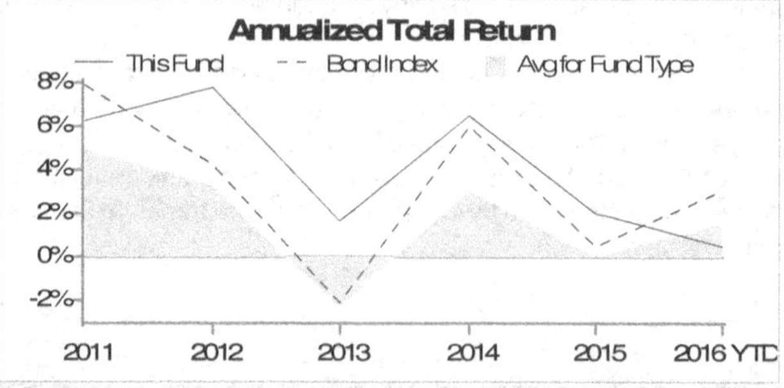

WA New York Municipals A (SBNYX) C Fair

Fund Family: Legg Mason Partners Funds **Phone:** (877) 534-4627
Address: 100 Light Street, Baltimore, MD 21202
Fund Type: MUS - Municipal - Single State
Major Rating Factors: Strong performance is the major factor driving the C (Fair) TheStreet.com Investment Rating for WA New York Municipals A. The fund currently has a performance rating of B- (Good) based on an average return of 2.57% over the last three years (4.26% taxable equivalent) and 1.34% over the last three months (2.22% taxable equivalent). Factored into the performance evaluation is an expense ratio of 0.73% (low) and a 4.3% front-end load that is levied at the time of purchase.

The fund's risk rating is currently C- (Fair). Volatility, as measured by standard deviation, is considered average for fixed income funds at 3.86. Another risk factor is the fund's fairly average duration of 5.2 years (i.e. average interest rate risk).

David Fare has been running the fund for 18 years and currently receives a manager quality ranking of 21 (0=worst, 99=best). If you desire an average level of risk and strong performance, then this fund is a good option.
Services Offered: Automated phone transactions, payroll deductions, bank draft capabilities and a systematic withdrawal plan.

Data Date	Investment Rating	Net Assets ($Mil)	NAV	Performance Rating/Pts	Total Return Y-T-D	Risk Rating/Pts
3-16	C	554	13.72	B- / 7.3	1.34%	C- / 4.2
2015	C	543	13.65	B- / 7.5	3.18%	C- / 4.0
2014	C	539	13.72	C+ / 6.9	9.83%	C- / 3.6
2013	D-	545	12.98	C- / 3.1	-5.86%	D+ / 2.9
2012	C-	796	14.34	C+ / 5.9	7.56%	C- / 3.5
2011	C+	733	13.83	C+ / 6.7	10.73%	C- / 4.2

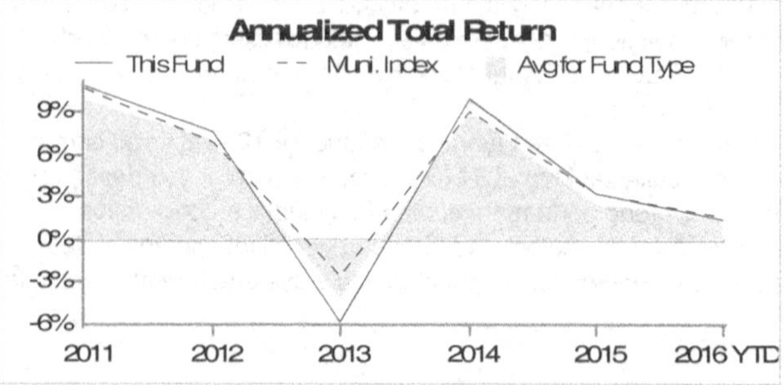

Waddell & Reed Adv Bond Fund A (UNBDX) D+ Weak

Fund Family: Waddell & Reed Funds **Phone:** (888) 923-3355
Address: 6300 Lamar Avenue, Shawnee Mission, KS 66201
Fund Type: COI - Corporate - Investment Grade
Major Rating Factors: Waddell & Reed Adv Bond Fund A receives a TheStreet.com Investment Rating of D+ (Weak). The fund has a performance rating of C- (Fair) based on an average return of 1.41% over the last three years and 3.17% over the last three months. Factored into the performance evaluation is an expense ratio of 0.96% (average) and a 5.8% front-end load that is levied at the time of purchase.

The fund's risk rating is currently C (Fair). Volatility, as measured by standard deviation, is considered average for fixed income funds at 3.40. Another risk factor is the fund's fairly average duration of 5.4 years (i.e. average interest rate risk).

Rick Perry has been running the fund for 1 year and currently receives a manager quality ranking of 36 (0=worst, 99=best). If you desire an average level of risk, then this fund may be an option.
Services Offered: Payroll deductions, bank draft capabilities, an IRA investment plan, a 401K investment plan, a Keogh investment plan and a systematic withdrawal plan.

Data Date	Investment Rating	Net Assets ($Mil)	NAV	Performance Rating/Pts	Total Return Y-T-D	Risk Rating/Pts
3-16	D+	1,179	6.33	C- / 3.1	3.17%	C / 5.2
2015	D	1,187	6.16	D / 1.7	0.13%	C / 5.1
2014	D-	1,242	6.35	D / 1.8	3.54%	C / 5.5
2013	D-	1,305	6.30	D / 2.0	-2.33%	C+ / 5.8
2012	D-	1,631	6.63	D+ / 2.4	5.37%	C+ / 6.3
2011	D+	1,369	6.47	D+ / 2.9	7.29%	B- / 7.5

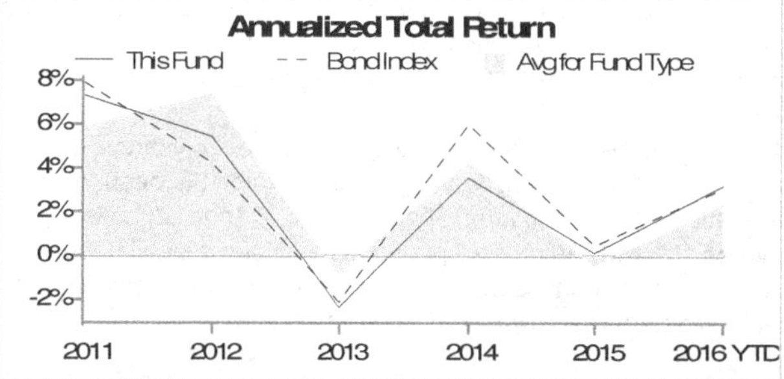

Waddell & Reed Adv Global Bond A (UNHHX) D- Weak

Fund Family: Waddell & Reed Funds **Phone:** (888) 923-3355
Address: 6300 Lamar Avenue, Shawnee Mission, KS 66201
Fund Type: GL - Global
Major Rating Factors: Very poor performance is the major factor driving the D- (Weak) TheStreet.com Investment Rating for Waddell & Reed Adv Global Bond A. The fund currently has a performance rating of E (Very Weak) based on an average return of -0.64% over the last three years and 2.07% over the last three months. Factored into the performance evaluation is an expense ratio of 1.19% (above average) and a 5.8% front-end load that is levied at the time of purchase.

The fund's risk rating is currently C- (Fair). Volatility, as measured by standard deviation, is considered average for fixed income funds at 4.42. Another risk factor is the fund's very low average duration of 2.7 years (i.e. low interest rate risk).

Mark G. Beischel has been running the fund for 14 years and currently receives a manager quality ranking of 40 (0=worst, 99=best). This fund offers an average level of risk, but investors looking for strong performance will be frustrated.
Services Offered: Payroll deductions, bank draft capabilities, an IRA investment plan, a 401K investment plan, a Keogh investment plan and a systematic withdrawal plan.

Data Date	Investment Rating	Net Assets ($Mil)	NAV	Performance Rating/Pts	Total Return Y-T-D	Risk Rating/Pts
3-16	D-	562	3.55	E / 0.5	2.07%	C- / 3.3
2015	D-	624	3.49	E+ / 0.8	-3.56%	C- / 3.4
2014	D-	772	3.72	E+ / 0.8	-0.55%	C / 5.0
2013	D	789	3.88	D+ / 2.7	1.66%	C+ / 5.7
2012	E+	799	3.97	D / 1.8	6.79%	C+ / 5.9
2011	D-	776	3.90	D+ / 2.6	0.79%	C+ / 6.9

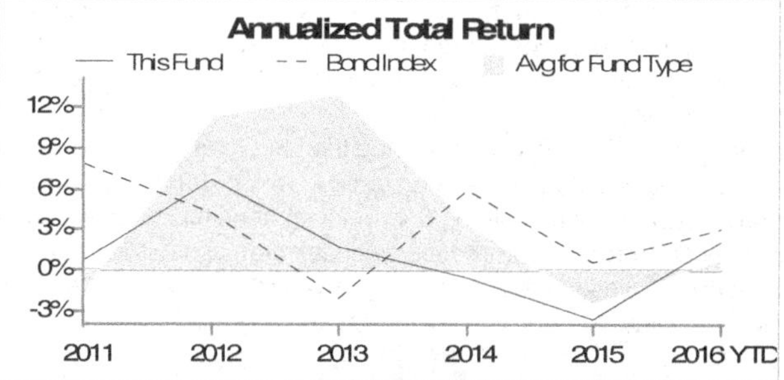

Waddell & Reed Adv High Income A (UNHIX) E Very Weak

Fund Family: Waddell & Reed Funds **Phone:** (888) 923-3355
Address: 6300 Lamar Avenue, Shawnee Mission, KS 66201
Fund Type: COH - Corporate - High Yield
Major Rating Factors: Waddell & Reed Adv High Income A has adopted a very risky asset allocation strategy and currently receives an overall TheStreet.com Investment Rating of E (Very Weak). Volatility, as measured by standard deviation, is considered above average for fixed income funds at 5.88. Unfortunately, the high level of risk (D-, Weak) failed to pay off as investors endured poor performance.

The fund's performance rating is currently E+ (Very Weak). It has registered an average return of 1.06% over the last three years and is up 2.46% over the last three months. Factored into the performance evaluation is an expense ratio of 1.01% (average) and a 5.8% front-end load that is levied at the time of purchase.

William M. Nelson has been running the fund for 8 years and currently receives a manager quality ranking of 40 (0=worst, 99=best). If you can tolerate very high levels of risk in the hope of improved future returns, holding this fund may be an option.
Services Offered: Payroll deductions, bank draft capabilities, an IRA investment plan, a 401K investment plan, a Keogh investment plan and a systematic withdrawal plan.

Data Date	Investment Rating	Net Assets ($Mil)	NAV	Performance Rating/Pts	Total Return Y-T-D	Risk Rating/Pts
3-16	E	1,549	6.22	E+ / 0.7	2.46%	D- / 1.2
2015	E+	1,742	6.18	D- / 1.2	-6.87%	D- / 1.4
2014	B-	1,967	7.12	B+ / 8.3	1.92%	C- / 3.0
2013	B	1,841	7.60	A+ / 9.9	10.81%	D / 1.7
2012	B-	1,641	7.55	A- / 9.1	19.07%	D- / 1.5
2011	C	1,280	6.86	B+ / 8.4	4.89%	D / 1.7

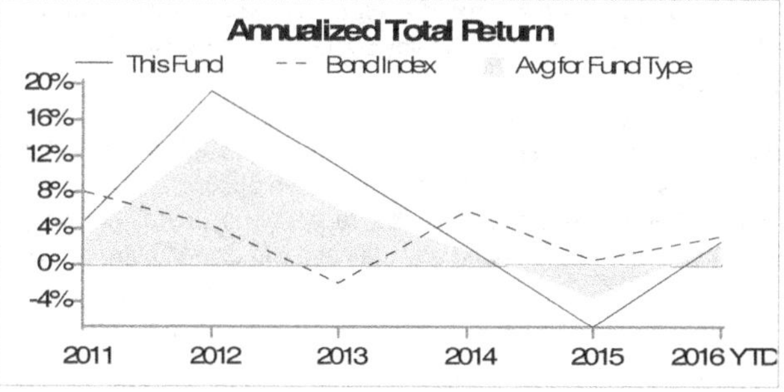

Waddell & Reed Adv Muni Bond A (UNMBX) B+ Good

Fund Family: Waddell & Reed Funds **Phone:** (888) 923-3355
Address: 6300 Lamar Avenue, Shawnee Mission, KS 66201
Fund Type: MUN - Municipal - National
Major Rating Factors: Strong performance is the major factor driving the B+ (Good) TheStreet.com Investment Rating for Waddell & Reed Adv Muni Bond A. The fund currently has a performance rating of B (Good) based on an average return of 2.76% over the last three years (4.57% taxable equivalent) and 1.21% over the last three months (2.00% taxable equivalent). Factored into the performance evaluation is an expense ratio of 0.90% (average) and a 4.3% front-end load that is levied at the time of purchase.

The fund's risk rating is currently C+ (Fair). Volatility, as measured by standard deviation, is considered average for fixed income funds at 3.10. Another risk factor is the fund's fairly average duration of 5.8 years (i.e. average interest rate risk).

Bryan J. Bailey has been running the fund for 16 years and currently receives a manager quality ranking of 46 (0=worst, 99=best). If you desire an average level of risk and strong performance, then this fund is a good option.
Services Offered: Automated phone transactions, payroll deductions, bank draft capabilities, an IRA investment plan, a 401K investment plan, a Keogh investment plan and a systematic withdrawal plan.

Data Date	Investment Rating	Net Assets ($Mil)	NAV	Perfor-mance Rating/Pts	Total Return Y-T-D	Risk Rating/Pts
3-16	B+	876	7.65	B / 7.6	1.21%	C+/ 6.2
2015	B	861	7.60	B / 7.9	2.68%	C+/ 5.7
2014	B+	862	7.61	B- / 7.4	8.59%	C / 5.0
2013	C	836	7.23	C+/ 5.6	-3.29%	C / 5.0
2012	B+	971	7.72	C+/ 6.6	7.65%	C / 5.3
2011	B+	811	7.42	C+/ 6.5	9.84%	C / 5.4

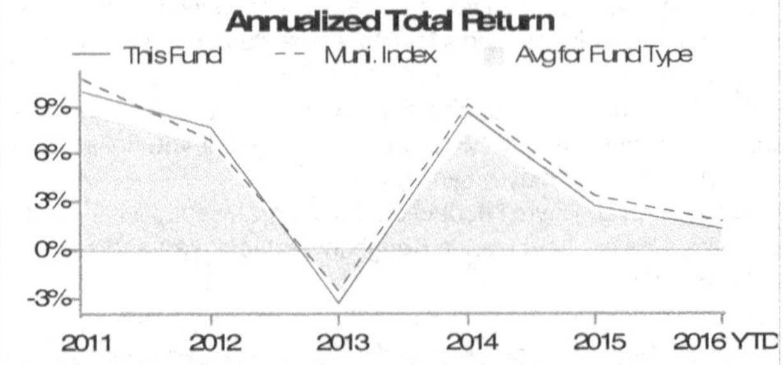

Waddell & Reed Adv Muni High Inc A (UMUHX) C+ Fair

Fund Family: Waddell & Reed Funds **Phone:** (888) 923-3355
Address: 6300 Lamar Avenue, Shawnee Mission, KS 66201
Fund Type: MUH - Municipal - High Yield
Major Rating Factors: Strong performance is the major factor driving the C+ (Fair) TheStreet.com Investment Rating for Waddell & Reed Adv Muni High Inc A. The fund currently has a performance rating of B+ (Good) based on an average return of 3.71% over the last three years (6.14% taxable equivalent) and 0.42% over the last three months (0.70% taxable equivalent). Factored into the performance evaluation is an expense ratio of 0.90% (average) and a 4.3% front-end load that is levied at the time of purchase.

The fund's risk rating is currently C- (Fair). Volatility, as measured by standard deviation, is considered average for fixed income funds at 3.96. Another risk factor is the fund's fairly average duration of 6.8 years (i.e. average interest rate risk).

Michael J. Walls has been running the fund for 8 years and currently receives a manager quality ranking of 57 (0=worst, 99=best). If you desire an average level of risk and strong performance, then this fund is a good option.
Services Offered: Payroll deductions, bank draft capabilities, an IRA investment plan, a 401K investment plan, a Keogh investment plan and a systematic withdrawal plan.

Data Date	Investment Rating	Net Assets ($Mil)	NAV	Perfor-mance Rating/Pts	Total Return Y-T-D	Risk Rating/Pts
3-16	C+	836	4.90	B+ / 8.3	0.42%	C- / 3.3
2015	C+	835	4.93	A- / 9.2	3.78%	D+/ 2.8
2014	B+	802	4.96	A / 9.4	12.72%	D+/ 2.3
2013	C-	724	4.62	C+/ 6.6	-4.02%	C- / 3.0
2012	A	817	5.05	A- / 9.0	11.19%	C- / 3.1
2011	A	665	4.76	A / 9.5	9.34%	D+/ 2.4

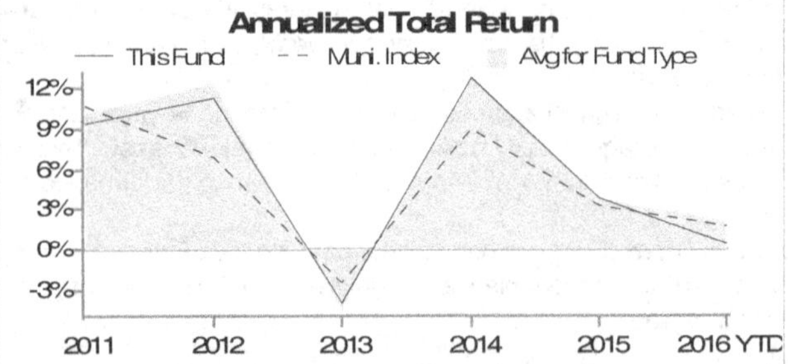

Wells Fargo Core Bond A (MBFAX) C- Fair

Fund Family: Wells Fargo Advantage Funds **Phone:** (800) 222-8222
Address: PO Box 8266, Boston, MA 02266
Fund Type: GEI - General - Investment Grade
Major Rating Factors: Middle of the road best describes Wells Fargo Core Bond A whose TheStreet.com Investment Rating is currently a C- (Fair). The fund has a performance rating of C (Fair) based on an average return of 2.14% over the last three years and 2.82% over the last three months. Factored into the performance evaluation is an expense ratio of 0.85% (average) and a 4.5% front-end load that is levied at the time of purchase.

The fund's risk rating is currently C+ (Fair). Volatility, as measured by standard deviation, is considered average for fixed income funds at 3.18. Another risk factor is the fund's fairly average duration of 5.6 years (i.e. average interest rate risk).

Thomas O'Connor has been running the fund for 13 years and currently receives a manager quality ranking of 44 (0=worst, 99=best). If you desire an average level of risk, then this fund may be an option.
Services Offered: Automated phone transactions, payroll deductions, bank draft capabilities, wire transfers and a systematic withdrawal plan.

Data Date	Investment Rating	Net Assets ($Mil)	NAV	Perfor-mance Rating/Pts	Total Return Y-T-D	Risk Rating/Pts
3-16	C-	721	13.27	C / 4.7	2.82%	C+/ 5.8
2015	D+	571	12.95	D+/ 2.9	0.21%	C+/ 5.6
2014	D+	447	13.10	C- / 3.4	5.76%	C+/ 6.4
2013	C-	352	12.58	C- / 3.1	-2.28%	B- / 7.0
2012	C+	460	13.21	C- / 3.5	6.13%	B / 7.7
2011	B	433	13.17	C- / 4.0	8.20%	B / 8.2

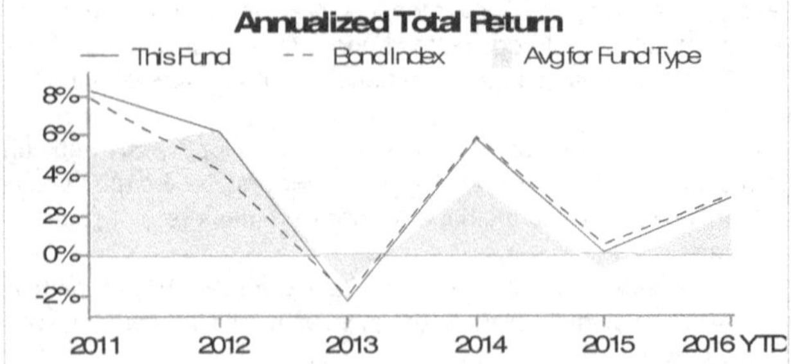

Wells Fargo Intm Tax/AMT Fr A (WFTAX) A Excellent

Fund Family: Wells Fargo Advantage Funds **Phone:** (800) 222-8222
Address: PO Box 8266, Boston, MA 02266
Fund Type: MUN - Municipal - National

Major Rating Factors: Strong performance is the major factor driving the A (Excellent) TheStreet.com Investment Rating for Wells Fargo Intm Tax/AMT Fr A. The fund currently has a performance rating of B (Good) based on an average return of 2.75% over the last three years (4.55% taxable equivalent) and 1.22% over the last three months (2.02% taxable equivalent). Factored into the performance evaluation is an expense ratio of 0.80% (low) and a 3.0% front-end load that is levied at the time of purchase.

The fund's risk rating is currently B- (Good). Volatility, as measured by standard deviation, is considered low for fixed income funds at 2.87. Another risk factor is the fund's below average duration of 4.4 years (i.e. lower interest rate risk).

Lyle J. Fitterer has been running the fund for 15 years and currently receives a manager quality ranking of 53 (0=worst, 99=best). If you desire only a moderate level of risk and strong performance, then this fund is an excellent option.

Services Offered: Automated phone transactions, payroll deductions, bank draft capabilities, an IRA investment plan, a 401K investment plan, a Keogh investment plan, wire transfers and a systematic withdrawal plan.

Data Date	Investment Rating	Net Assets ($Mil)	NAV	Performance Rating/Pts	Total Return Y-T-D	Risk Rating/Pts
3-16	A	574	11.73	B / 8.0	1.22%	B- / 7.0
2015	A	592	11.65	B / 8.1	2.05%	C+ / 6.6
2014	B+	216	11.67	B- / 7.2	7.30%	C+ / 5.6
2013	A-	245	11.14	B- / 7.0	-1.65%	C+ / 6.0
2012	B+	357	11.69	C+ / 6.4	6.44%	C+ / 5.8
2011	A+	242	11.32	B- / 7.2	9.34%	C+ / 5.6

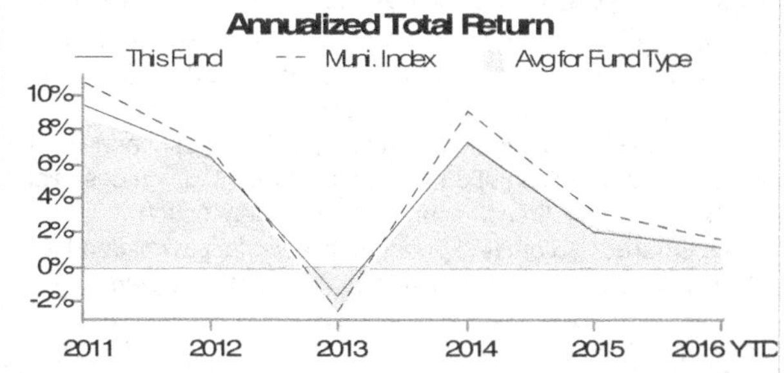

Wells Fargo Muni Bd A (WMFAX) B+ Good

Fund Family: Wells Fargo Advantage Funds **Phone:** (800) 222-8222
Address: PO Box 8266, Boston, MA 02266
Fund Type: MUN - Municipal - National

Major Rating Factors: Strong performance is the major factor driving the B+ (Good) TheStreet.com Investment Rating for Wells Fargo Muni Bd A. The fund currently has a performance rating of B+ (Good) based on an average return of 4.12% over the last three years (6.82% taxable equivalent) and 1.18% over the last three months (1.95% taxable equivalent). Factored into the performance evaluation is an expense ratio of 0.80% (low) and a 4.5% front-end load that is levied at the time of purchase.

The fund's risk rating is currently C (Fair). Volatility, as measured by standard deviation, is considered average for fixed income funds at 3.66. Another risk factor is the fund's below average duration of 4.9 years (i.e. lower interest rate risk).

Lyle J. Fitterer has been running the fund for 16 years and currently receives a manager quality ranking of 80 (0=worst, 99=best). If you desire an average level of risk and strong performance, then this fund is a good option.

Services Offered: Automated phone transactions, payroll deductions, bank draft capabilities, an IRA investment plan, a 401K investment plan, a Keogh investment plan, wire transfers and a systematic withdrawal plan.

Data Date	Investment Rating	Net Assets ($Mil)	NAV	Performance Rating/Pts	Total Return Y-T-D	Risk Rating/Pts
3-16	B+	1,511	10.48	B+ / 8.9	1.18%	C / 4.5
2015	B+	2,017	10.43	A- / 9.1	3.26%	C / 4.4
2014	A+	1,625	10.45	A- / 9.2	11.08%	C- / 4.2
2013	B+	1,620	9.76	B / 8.2	-1.94%	C / 4.5
2012	A+	1,819	10.34	B+ / 8.4	10.28%	C / 5.5
2011	A+	1,547	9.80	B+ / 8.9	10.11%	C / 4.5

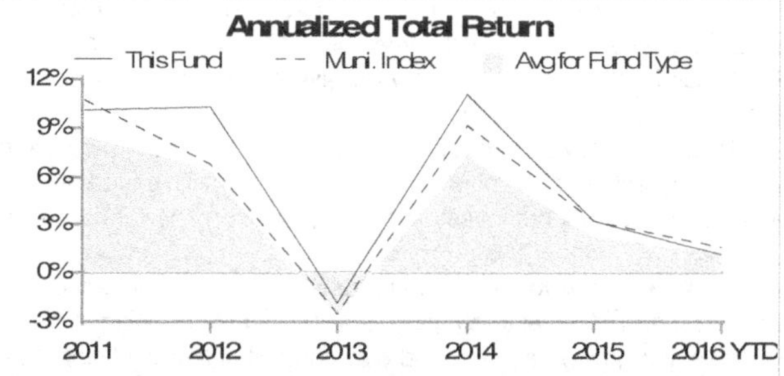

Wells Fargo ST Muni Bd A (WSMAX) C+ Fair

Fund Family: Wells Fargo Advantage Funds **Phone:** (800) 222-8222
Address: PO Box 8266, Boston, MA 02266
Fund Type: MUN - Municipal - National

Major Rating Factors: A moderate risk profile coupled with stable earnings characterizes Wells Fargo ST Muni Bd A which receives a TheStreet.com Investment Rating of C+ (Fair). Volatility, as measured by standard deviation, is considered very low for fixed income funds at 0.57. Another risk factor is the fund's very low average duration of 1.4 years (i.e. low interest rate risk). The fund's risk rating is currently A+ (Excellent).

The fund's performance rating is currently C- (Fair). It has registered an average return of 0.87% over the last three years (1.44% taxable equivalent) and is up 0.26% over the last three months (0.43% taxable equivalent). Factored into the performance evaluation is an expense ratio of 0.75% (low) and a 2.0% front-end load that is levied at the time of purchase.

Lyle J. Fitterer has been running the fund for 16 years and currently receives a manager quality ranking of 81 (0=worst, 99=best). If you desire stability with a moderate level of risk then this fund is an excellent option.

Services Offered: Automated phone transactions, payroll deductions, bank draft capabilities, an IRA investment plan, a Keogh investment plan, wire transfers and a systematic withdrawal plan.

Data Date	Investment Rating	Net Assets ($Mil)	NAV	Performance Rating/Pts	Total Return Y-T-D	Risk Rating/Pts
3-16	C+	3,394	9.94	C- / 3.5	0.26%	A+ / 9.8
2015	B+	3,540	9.94	C / 5.1	0.54%	A+ / 9.8
2014	C+	2,101	9.99	D+ / 2.5	1.56%	A+ / 9.8
2013	B+	1,687	9.94	C- / 3.5	0.71%	A+ / 9.7
2012	C+	1,553	9.99	D- / 1.5	2.32%	A+ / 9.7
2011	B+	1,306	9.94	C- / 3.6	3.24%	A / 9.3

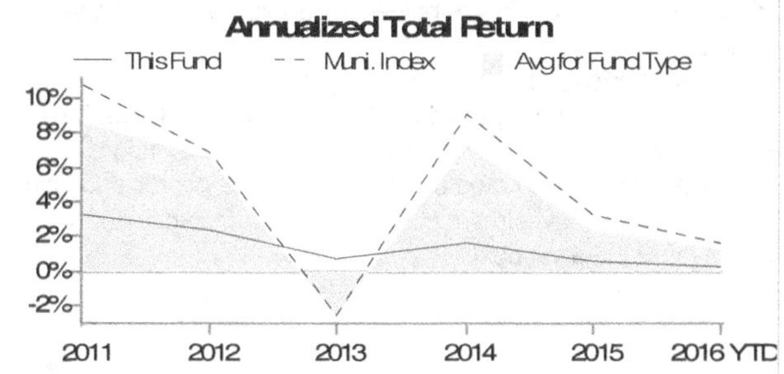

Wells Fargo Str Muni Bd A (VMPAX) A- Excellent

Fund Family: Wells Fargo Advantage Funds **Phone:** (800) 222-8222
Address: PO Box 8266, Boston, MA 02266
Fund Type: MUN - Municipal - National
Major Rating Factors: A moderate risk profile coupled with stable earnings characterizes Wells Fargo Str Muni Bd A which receives a TheStreet.com Investment Rating of A- (Excellent). Volatility, as measured by standard deviation, is considered low for fixed income funds at 1.54. Another risk factor is the fund's very low average duration of 2.2 years (i.e. low interest rate risk). The fund's risk rating is currently B+ (Good).

The fund's performance rating is currently C+ (Fair). It has registered an average return of 2.18% over the last three years (3.61% taxable equivalent) and is up 0.58% over the last three months (0.96% taxable equivalent). Factored into the performance evaluation is an expense ratio of 0.81% (low) and a 4.0% front-end load that is levied at the time of purchase.

Lyle J. Fitterer has been running the fund for 6 years and currently receives a manager quality ranking of 86 (0=worst, 99=best). If you desire stability with a moderate level of risk then this fund is an excellent option.
Services Offered: Automated phone transactions, payroll deductions, bank draft capabilities, wire transfers and a systematic withdrawal plan.

Data Date	Investment Rating	Net Assets ($Mil)	NAV	Performance Rating/Pts	Total Return Y-T-D	Risk Rating/Pts
3-16	A-	662	8.99	C+ / 5.9	0.58%	B+ / 8.9
2015	A+	638	8.98	B- / 7.3	1.53%	B+ / 8.8
2014	B+	603	8.99	C / 4.5	4.55%	B+ / 8.9
2013	A-	569	8.80	C / 4.6	0.60%	A- / 9.0
2012	C+	578	8.95	D+ / 2.3	4.33%	A / 9.5
2011	B	445	8.81	D+ / 2.9	5.10%	A / 9.5

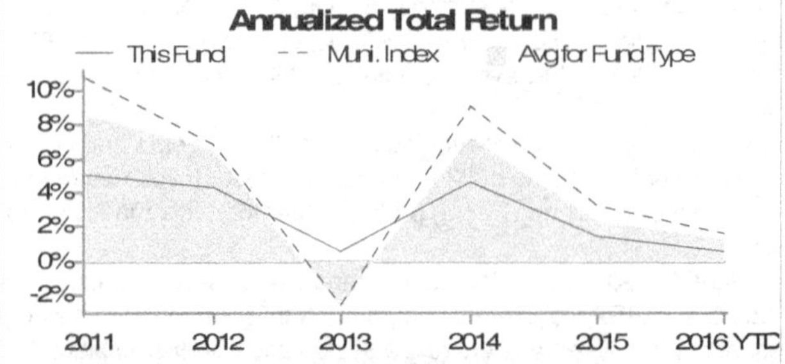

Wells Fargo Ult-Sh Mun Inc A (SMAVX) C- Fair

Fund Family: Wells Fargo Advantage Funds **Phone:** (800) 222-8222
Address: PO Box 8266, Boston, MA 02266
Fund Type: MUN - Municipal - National
Major Rating Factors: Disappointing performance is the major factor driving the C- (Fair) TheStreet.com Investment Rating for Wells Fargo Ult-Sh Mun Inc A. The fund currently has a performance rating of D- (Weak) based on an average return of 0.14% over the last three years (0.23% taxable equivalent) and -0.02% over the last three months. Factored into the performance evaluation is an expense ratio of 0.74% (low) and a 2.0% front-end load that is levied at the time of purchase.

The fund's risk rating is currently A+ (Excellent). Volatility, as measured by standard deviation, is considered very low for fixed income funds at 0.33. Another risk factor is the fund's very low average duration of 0.6 years (i.e. low interest rate risk).

Lyle J. Fitterer has been running the fund for 16 years and currently receives a manager quality ranking of 60 (0=worst, 99=best). This fund offers only a moderate level of risk but investors looking for strong performance are still waiting.
Services Offered: Automated phone transactions, payroll deductions, bank draft capabilities, an IRA investment plan, a 401K investment plan, a Keogh investment plan, wire transfers and a systematic withdrawal plan.

Data Date	Investment Rating	Net Assets ($Mil)	NAV	Performance Rating/Pts	Total Return Y-T-D	Risk Rating/Pts
3-16	C-	1,244	9.61	D- / 1.4	-0.02%	A+ / 9.9
2015	C	1,287	9.62	D+ / 2.8	0.11%	A+ / 9.9
2014	D+	1,114	4.82	E+ / 0.8	0.29%	A+ / 9.9
2013	C-	1,734	4.82	D- / 1.0	0.31%	A+ / 9.9
2012	C-	2,307	4.82	E / 0.5	0.73%	A+ / 9.9
2011	C	2,686	4.81	D / 1.7	1.29%	A+ / 9.8

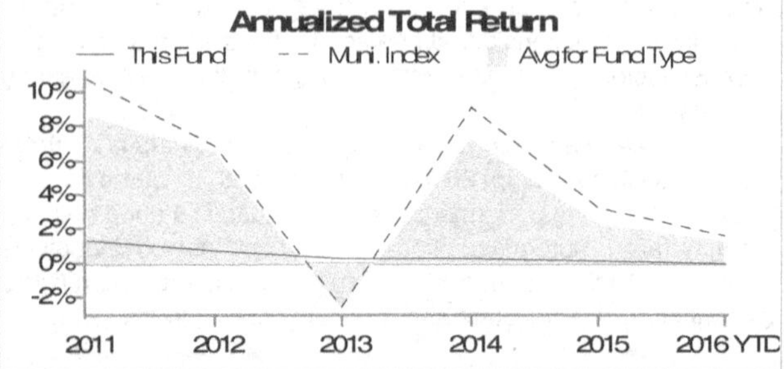

Westcore Plus Bond Rtl (WTIBX) B Good

Fund Family: Westcore Funds **Phone:** (800) 392-2673
Address: 370 17th Street, Denver, CO 80202
Fund Type: GEI - General - Investment Grade
Major Rating Factors: Strong performance is the major factor driving the B (Good) TheStreet.com Investment Rating for Westcore Plus Bond Rtl. The fund currently has a performance rating of B- (Good) based on an average return of 2.46% over the last three years and 3.05% over the last three months. Factored into the performance evaluation is an expense ratio of 0.70% (low).

The fund's risk rating is currently C+ (Fair). Volatility, as measured by standard deviation, is considered average for fixed income funds at 3.06. Another risk factor is the fund's below average duration of 4.8 years (i.e. lower interest rate risk).

Mark R. McKissick has been running the fund for 13 years and currently receives a manager quality ranking of 61 (0=worst, 99=best). If you desire an average level of risk and strong performance, then this fund is a good option.
Services Offered: Automated phone transactions, payroll deductions, bank draft capabilities, an IRA investment plan, a 401K investment plan, wire transfers and a systematic withdrawal plan.

Data Date	Investment Rating	Net Assets ($Mil)	NAV	Performance Rating/Pts	Total Return Y-T-D	Risk Rating/Pts
3-16	B	1,248	10.78	B- / 7.2	3.05%	C+ / 6.3
2015	C+	1,311	10.55	C+ / 6.3	0.01%	C+ / 6.2
2014	C+	1,357	10.92	C / 5.1	5.90%	C+ / 6.7
2013	B+	1,215	10.71	C / 5.3	-1.23%	B- / 7.5
2012	C+	1,457	11.24	C- / 3.6	5.67%	B / 7.8
2011	B+	1,398	11.04	C- / 4.0	7.55%	B+ / 8.5

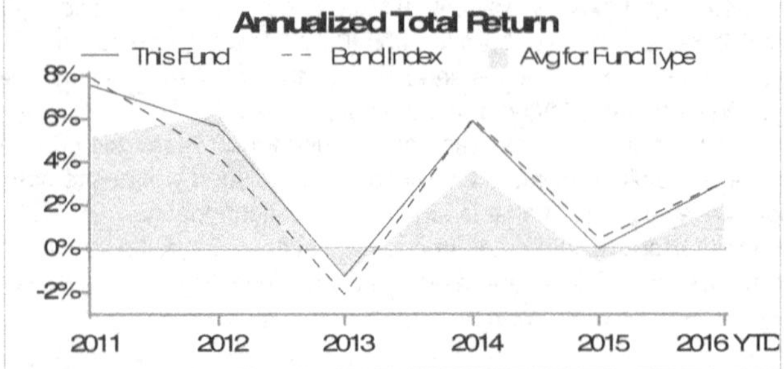

Section III

Top 200 Bond Mutual Funds

A compilation of those

Fixed Income Mutual Funds

receiving the highest TheStreet Investment Ratings.

Funds are listed in order by Overall Investment Rating.

Section III Contents

This section contains a summary analysis of each of the top 200 bond mutual funds as determined by their overall TheStreet Investment Rating. You can use this section to identify those mutual funds that have achieved the best possible combination of total return on investment and reduced risk over the past three years. Consult each fund's individual Performance Rating and Risk Rating to find the fund that best matches your investing style.

In order to optimize the utility of our top and bottom fund lists, rather than listing all funds in a multi-class series, a single fund from each series is selected for display as the primary share class. Whenever possible, the selected fund is one that a retail investor would be most likely to choose. This share class may not be appropriate for every investor, so please consult with your financial advisor, the fund company, and the fund's prospectus before placing your trade.

1. Fund Type

The mutual fund's peer category based on its investment objective as stated in its prospectus.

COH	Corporate - High Yield	MMT	Money Market - Tax Free
COI	Corporate - Inv. Grade	MTG	Mortgage
EM	Emerging Market	MUH	Municipal - High Yield
GEN	General	MUI	Municipal - Insured
GEI	General - Inv. Grade	MUN	Municipal - National
GEL	General - Long Term	MUS	Municipal - Single State
GES	General - Short & Interm.	USL	U.S. Gov.- Long Term
GL	Global	USS	U.S. Gov. - Short & Interm
LP	Loan Participation	USA	U.S. Gov. - Agency
MM	Money Market	US	U.S. Gov. - Treasury

A blank fund type means that the mutual fund has not yet been categorized.

2. Fund Name

The name of the mutual fund as stated in its prospectus, which can sometimes differ slightly from the name that the company uses for advertising. If you cannot find the particular mutual fund you are interested in, or if you have any doubts regarding the precise name, verify the information with your broker or on your account statement. Also, use the fund's ticker symbol for confirmation. (See column 3.)

3. Ticker Symbol

The unique alphabetic symbol used for identifying and trading a specific mutual fund. No two funds can have the same ticker symbol, and the ticker symbol for mutual funds always ends with an "X".

A handful of funds currently show no associated ticker symbol. This means that the fund is either small or new since the NASD only assigns a ticker symbol to funds with at least $25 million in assets or 1,000 shareholders.

4. Overall Investment Rating

Our overall rating is measured on a scale from A to E based on each fund's risk-adjusted performance. Please see page 11 for specific descriptions of each letter grade. Also, refer to page 7 for information on how our ratings are derived. Most important, when using this rating, please be sure to consider the warnings beginning on page 13 regarding the ratings' limitations and the underlying assumptions.

5. Phone

The telephone number of the company managing the fund. Call this number to receive a prospectus or other information about the fund.

6. Net Asset Value (NAV)

The fund's share price as of the date indicated. A fund's NAV is computed by dividing the value of the fund's asset holdings, less accrued fees and expenses, by the number of its shares outstanding.

7. Performance Rating/Points

A letter grade rating based solely on the mutual fund's financial performance over the trailing three years, without any consideration for the amount of risk the fund poses. Like the overall Investment Rating, the Performance Rating is measured on a scale from A to E for ease of interpretation. The points score indicates where the Performance Rating falls on a scale of 0 to 10.

In the case of funds investing in municipal or other tax-free securities, this rating is based on the taxable equivalent return of the fund assuming the maximum marginal U.S. tax rate (35%).

8. 1-Year Total Return

The total return the fund has provided investors over the preceding twelve months. This total return figure is computed based on the fund's dividend distributions and share price appreciation/depreciation during the period, net of the expenses and fees it imposes on its shareholders. Although the total return figure does not reflect an adjustment for any loads the fund may carry, such adjustments have been made in deriving TheStreet Investment Ratings.

9. 1-Year Total Return Percentile

The fund's percentile rank based on its one-year performance compared to that of all other fixed income funds in existence for at least one year. A score of 99 is the best possible, indicating that the fund outperformed 99% of the other mutual funds. Zero is the worst possible percentile score.

In the case of funds investing in municipal or other tax-free securities, this percentile rank is based on the taxable equivalent return of the fund assuming the maximum marginal U.S. tax rate (35%).

10. 3-Year Total Return

The total annual return the fund has provided investors over the preceding three years.

11. 3-Year Total Return Percentile

The fund's percentile rank based on its three-year performance compared to that of all other fixed income funds in existence for at least three years. A score of 99 is the best possible, indicating that the fund outperformed 99% of the other mutual funds. Zero is the worst possible percentile score.

In the case of funds investing in municipal or other tax-free securities, this percentile rank is based on the taxable equivalent return of the fund assuming the maximum marginal U.S. tax rate (35%).

12. 5-Year Total Return

The total annual return the fund has provided investors over the preceding five years.

13. 5-Year Total Return Percentile

The fund's percentile rank based on its five-year performance compared to that of all other fixed income funds in existence for at least five years. A score of 99 is the best possible, indicating that the fund outperformed 99% of the other mutual funds. Zero is the worst possible percentile score.

In the case of funds investing in municipal or other tax-free securities, this percentile rank is based on the taxable equivalent return of the fund assuming the maximum marginal U.S. tax rate (35%).

14. Risk Rating/Points

A letter grade rating based solely on the mutual fund's risk as determined by its monthly performance volatility over the trailing three years and the underlying credit risk and interest rate risk of its investment portfolio. The risk rating does not take into consideration the overall financial performance the fund has achieved or the total return it has provided to its shareholders. Like the overall Investment Rating, the Risk Rating is measured on a scale from A to E for ease of interpretation. The points score indicates where the Risk Rating falls on a scale of 0 to 10.

15. Manager Quality Percentile

The manager quality percentile is based on a ranking of the fund's alpha, a statistical measure representing the difference between a fund's actual returns and its expected performance given its level of risk. Fund managers who have been able to exceed the fund's statistically expected performance receive a high percentile rank with 99 representing the best possible score. At the other end of the spectrum, fund managers who have actually detracted from the fund's expected performance receive a low percentile rank with 0 representing the worst possible score.

16. Manager Tenure

The number of years the current manager has been managing the fund. Since fund managers who deliver substandard returns are usually replaced, a long tenure is usually a good sign that shareholders are satisfied that the fund is achieving its stated objectives.

99 Pct = Best
0 Pct = Worst

Fund Type	Fund Name	Ticker Symbol	Overall Investment Rating	Phone	Net Asset Value As of 3/31/16	PERFORMANCE: Performance Rating/Pts	Annualized Total Return Through 3/31/16: 1Yr / Pct	3Yr / Pct	5Yr / Pct	RISK: Risk Rating/Pts	FUND MGR: Mgr. Quality Pct	Mgr. Tenure (Years)
MUS	Vanguard CA Interm-Term T-E Inv	VCAIX	**A+**	(800) 662-7447	11.97	**A /9.5**	4.04 /94	3.73 /94	5.54 /89	**C+ / 5.9**	80	5
MUS	Fidelity MI Muni Inc	FMHTX	**A+**	(800) 544-8544	12.48	**A /9.4**	4.11 /95	3.62 /93	5.20 /87	**C+ / 5.7**	76	10
MUS	Schwab California Tax-Free Bond	SWCAX	**A+**	(800) 407-0256	12.15	**A /9.3**	3.46 /90	3.45 /92	5.00 /85	**C+ / 6.8**	80	8
MUS	Saturna Idaho Tax-Exempt	NITEX	**A+**	(800) 728-8762	5.53	**A- /9.2**	3.68 /92	3.23 /90	4.09 /78	**B- / 7.3**	80	21
MUN	Vanguard Interm-Term Tax-Exempt	VWITX	**A+**	(800) 662-7447	14.39	**A- /9.2**	3.65 /91	3.19 /90	4.91 /85	**C+ / 6.5**	N/A	3
MUS	Dupree TN Tax-Free Income	TNTIX	**A+**	(800) 866-0614	11.72	**A- /9.2**	3.11 /86	3.27 /91	4.95 /85	**C+ / 5.8**	61	12
MUN	T Rowe Price Summit Muni Intmdt	PRSMX	**A+**	(800) 638-5660	12.11	**A- /9.1**	3.55 /91	3.13 /89	4.67 /83	**C+ / 6.8**	68	23
MUS	Dupree KY Tax Free Income	KYTFX	**A+**	(800) 866-0614	7.96	**A- /9.1**	3.24 /87	3.17 /90	4.87 /84	**C+ / 6.3**	61	17
MUN	USAA Tax-Exempt Interm-Term	USATX	**A+**	(800) 382-8722	13.61	**A- /9.1**	3.43 /89	3.12 /89	5.34 /88	**B- / 7.3**	75	13
MUN	Federated Interm Muni Trust Y	FIMYX	**A+**	(800) 341-7400	10.31	**A- /9.1**	3.82 /93	2.99 /88	4.78 /83	**B- / 7.0**	N/A	21
MUI	Westcore CO Tax Exempt	WTCOX	**A+**	(800) 392-2673	11.76	**A- /9.1**	3.53 /90	3.07 /89	4.49 /81	**C+ / 6.0**	55	11
MUI	Pacific Capital Tax-Free Secs Y	PTXFX	**A+**	(888) 739-1390	10.37	**A- /9.1**	3.68 /92	3.06 /89	4.48 /81	**C+ / 5.8**	52	12
MUN	State Farm Muni Bond	SFBDX	**A+**	(800) 447-4930	8.88	**A- /9.1**	3.31 /88	3.12 /89	4.49 /81	**B- / 7.0**	72	18
MUS	Lee Fnl Hawaii-Muni Bond Inv	SURFX	**A+**		11.31	**A- /9.0**	2.83 /83	3.17 /90	4.65 /83	**C+ / 6.6**	70	1
MUN	BMO Intermediate Tax Free Y	MITFX	**A+**	(800) 236-3863	11.45	**A- /9.0**	3.02 /85	3.04 /88	4.91 /84	**B- / 7.0**	N/A	22
MUN	Schwab Tax-Free Bond Fund	SWNTX	**A+**	(800) 407-0256	11.99	**A- /9.0**	3.21 /87	2.99 /88	4.65 /83	**B- / 7.2**	70	8
MUS	Fidelity MN Muni Inc	FIMIX	**A+**	(800) 544-8544	11.84	**B+ /8.9**	3.57 /91	3.00 /88	4.42 /81	**B- / 7.1**	N/A	6
MUS	Payden CA Muni Inc Investor	PYCRX	**A+**	(888) 409-8007	10.41	**B+ /8.9**	2.86 /84	2.94 /88	4.42 /81	**B- / 7.0**	63	N/A
MUS	SEI Tax-Exempt Tr-CA Muni Bond	SBDAX	**A+**	(800) 342-5734	11.03	**B+ /8.9**	3.36 /89	2.80 /86	4.26 /80	**C+ / 6.4**	53	17
MUS	Colorado Bond Shares	HICOX	**A+**	(800) 572-0069	9.14	**B+ /8.8**	4.61 /97	4.05 /96	4.80 /84	**A- / 9.1**	98	26
MUN	SEI Tax-Exempt Tr-Intrm Term	SEIMX	**A+**	(800) 342-5734	11.86	**B+ /8.8**	3.57 /91	2.79 /86	4.51 /82	**C+ / 6.3**	48	17
MUS	CA Tax-Free Income Direct	CFNTX	**A+**	(800) 955-9988	11.82	**B+ /8.7**	2.67 /82	2.73 /85	4.71 /83	**B / 7.6**	61	13
MUI	WesMark West Virginia Muni Bond	WMKMX	**A+**	(800) 341-7400	10.67	**B+ /8.7**	2.88 /84	2.62 /84	3.77 /76	**C+ / 6.9**	47	10
MUN	Invesco Intm Term Municipal Inc A	VKLMX	**A+**	(800) 959-4246	11.32	**B+ /8.6**	3.45 /90	3.21 /90	4.89 /84	**C+ / 6.5**	69	11
MUS	Nuveen Minnesota Intmdt Muni Bd	FAMAX	**A+**	(800) 257-8787	10.63	**B+ /8.4**	3.67 /92	3.11 /89	4.67 /83	**C+ / 6.7**	63	22
MUN	BNY Mellon NY Int TxEx Inv	MNYIX	**A+**	(800) 645-6561	11.46	**B+ /8.4**	3.13 /86	2.26 /80	4.02 /78	**B- / 7.2**	39	9
MUI	SEI Tax-Exempt Tr-NY Muni Bond	SENYX	**A+**	(800) 342-5734	10.94	**B+ /8.3**	3.14 /86	2.27 /80	3.54 /74	**B / 7.6**	48	17
MUS	Kansas Municipal	KSMUX	**A+**	(800) 601-5593	11.02	**B+ /8.3**	3.22 /87	3.00 /88	4.38 /80	**B- / 7.0**	N/A	20
MUS	SEI Tax-Exempt Tr-PA Muni Bond	SEPAX	**A+**	(800) 342-5734	10.89	**B /8.1**	3.15 /86	2.05 /77	3.82 /76	**B / 7.7**	42	17
MUS	Victory OH Muni Bond A	SOHTX	**A+**	(800) 539-3863	11.39	**B /8.1**	2.78 /83	2.62 /84	3.89 /77	**B / 7.6**	58	22
MUN	Thornburg Intermediate Muni A	THIMX	**A+**	(800) 847-0200	14.38	**B /8.1**	2.75 /83	2.62 /84	4.64 /82	**B / 7.7**	58	5
MUI	BNY Mellon PA Inter Muni Bond M	MPPIX	**A+**	(800) 645-6561	12.51	**B /8.1**	2.55 /81	1.95 /76	3.73 /76	**B- / 7.1**	30	16
MUN	Frost Municipal Bond Inv	FAUMX	**A+**	(866) 777-7818	10.61	**B /8.0**	2.27 /79	2.11 /78	3.43 /73	**B / 8.1**	53	14
GEI	Ave Maria Bond	AVEFX	**A+**	(866) 283-6274	11.27	**B /8.0**	2.51 /75	3.08 /77	3.70 /56	**B / 8.1**	97	13
MUS	Nationwide HighMark CA Int TF Bd	NWJKX	**A+**	(800) 848-0920	10.47	**B /8.0**	2.45 /80	2.62 /84	3.65 /75	**B- / 7.2**	54	3
MUI	SEI Tax-Exempt Tr-NJ Muni Bond	SENJX	**A+**	(800) 342-5734	10.55	**B /7.9**	2.51 /80	1.86 /75	3.30 /72	**B / 7.9**	42	3
MUN	Russell Tax Exempt Bond A	RTEAX	**A+**	(800) 832-6688	23.53	**B /7.9**	3.30 /88	2.81 /86	3.81 /76	**B / 8.0**	78	3
MUS	PIMCO CA Interm Muni Bond A	PCMBX	**A+**	(800) 426-0107	9.97	**B /7.9**	3.33 /88	2.36 /81	3.76 /76	**B- / 7.5**	46	5
MUS	Delaware Tax Free MN Intmdt A	DXCCX	**A+**	(800) 523-1918	11.33	**B /7.9**	2.90 /84	2.65 /84	4.29 /80	**B- / 7.3**	52	13
MUN	Glenmede Intermediate Muni Port	GTCMX	**A+**	(800) 442-8299	11.10	**B /7.9**	2.42 /80	1.87 /75	2.81 /66	**B / 8.2**	49	5
MUN	JPMorgan Muni Income A	OTBAX	**A+**	(800) 480-4111	10.09	**B /7.8**	3.27 /88	2.77 /86	3.90 /77	**B- / 7.3**	59	10
MUS	New Hampshire Municipal	NHMUX	**A+**	(800) 601-5593	10.94	**B /7.8**	2.99 /85	2.47 /82	3.70 /75	**B / 8.0**	60	13
MUS	Brown Advisory Maryland Bond Inv	BIAMX	**A+**	(800) 540-6807	10.80	**B /7.8**	2.66 /82	1.70 /72	2.72 /64	**B+ / 8.4**	46	2
MUN	Thornburg NY Intermediate Muni A	THNYX	**A+**	(800) 847-0200	13.36	**B /7.8**	2.82 /83	2.29 /80	4.22 /79	**B / 7.8**	48	5
MUS	Wells Fargo WI Tax Fr A	WWTFX	**A+**	(800) 222-8222	11.03	**B /7.7**	2.76 /83	3.00 /88	4.21 /79	**B / 8.0**	83	15
MUS	Wells Fargo MN Tax Free A	NMTFX	**A+**	(800) 222-8222	10.93	**B /7.6**	2.96 /85	2.89 /87	4.79 /84	**B / 7.7**	74	8
GES	DoubleLine Total Return Bond N	DLTNX	**A+**	(877) 354-6311	10.87	**B /7.6**	2.20 /73	2.93 /76	5.11 /72	**B / 7.7**	88	6
MUS	Thornburg NM Intermediate Muni A	THNMX	**A+**	(800) 847-0200	13.67	**B /7.6**	2.40 /80	2.25 /80	3.48 /74	**B / 7.8**	48	5
MUN	Victory National Muni A	VNMAX	**A+**	(800) 539-3863	11.09	**B- /7.5**	3.00 /85	2.05 /78	3.68 /75	**B / 7.9**	45	22
MUS	Jamestown VA Tax Exempt	JTEVX	**A+**	(866) 738-1126	10.21	**B- /7.4**	2.37 /80	1.53 /68	2.48 /59	**B+ / 8.4**	41	11
MUN	Cavanal Hill Intmdt TxFr Bd NL Inv	APTFX	**A+**	(800) 762-7085	11.25	**B- /7.4**	1.89 /76	1.63 /71	3.39 /73	**B / 8.1**	35	23
MUS	Fidelity CA Ltd Term Tax-Free Bd	FCSTX	**A+**	(800) 544-8544	10.76	**B- /7.4**	1.88 /76	1.85 /75	2.51 /59	**B+ / 8.9**	78	10

• Denotes fund is closed to new investors

99 Pct = Best
0 Pct = Worst

						PERFORMANCE				RISK	FUND MGR	
							Annualized Total Return Through 3/31/16					
Fund Type	Fund Name	Ticker Symbol	Overall Investment Rating	Phone	Net Asset Value As of 3/31/16	Performance Rating/Pts	1Yr / Pct	3Yr / Pct	5Yr / Pct	Risk Rating/Pts	Mgr. Quality Pct	Mgr. Tenure (Years)
MUI	CNR CA Tax-Exempt Bond N	CCTEX	**A+**	(888) 889-0799	10.78	**B- /7.3**	1.73 /75	1.64 /71	2.70 /64	**B+ / 8.5**	51	7
MTG	Vanguard Mort-Backed Secs Idx	VMBSX	**A+**	(800) 662-7447	21.35	**B- /7.2**	2.17 /73	2.52 /71	3.09 /47	**B / 8.2**	69	7
MUS	Wells Fargo CA Ltd Tax Fr A	SFCIX	**A+**	(800) 222-8222	10.96	**B- /7.2**	1.91 /76	2.16 /79	3.01 /69	**B+ / 8.9**	88	7
MUN	Old Westbury Muni Bond	OWMBX	**A+**	(800) 607-2200	12.09	**B- /7.1**	2.35 /80	1.37 /64	2.60 /61	**B+ / 8.3**	36	18
MUS	Thornburg CA Ltd Term Muni A	LTCAX	**A+**	(800) 847-0200	13.94	**B- /7.0**	1.84 /76	1.96 /77	3.36 /73	**B+ / 8.6**	72	5
MUS	Dupree KY Tax Free Short-to-Med	KYSMX	**A+**	(800) 866-0614	5.41	**C+ /6.8**	2.02 /77	1.32 /62	2.63 /62	**B+ / 8.8**	58	17
MUS	Sit MN Tax Free Income	SMTFX	**A**	(800) 332-5580	10.63	**A /9.4**	3.89 /93	3.61 /93	5.74 /91	**C / 5.0**	69	23
MUS	Fidelity PA Muni Inc	FPXTX	**A**	(800) 544-8544	11.39	**A /9.4**	3.54 /90	3.79 /95	5.47 /89	**C / 5.1**	74	14
MUS	Fidelity CT Muni Income Fd	FICNX	**A**	(800) 544-8544	11.87	**A /9.4**	4.18 /95	3.54 /93	4.91 /85	**C / 5.0**	58	14
MUS	T Rowe Price MD Tax Free Bd	MDXBX	**A**	(800) 638-5660	10.98	**A /9.3**	3.68 /92	3.49 /93	5.78 /91	**C / 4.9**	54	16
MUS	Dupree AL Tax Free Income	DUALX	**A**	(800) 866-0614	12.56	**A- /9.2**	3.13 /86	3.41 /92	5.50 /89	**C+ / 5.6**	68	15
MUS	Dupree NC Tax Free Income	NTFIX	**A**	(800) 866-0614	11.78	**A- /9.2**	3.48 /90	3.21 /90	5.42 /88	**C / 5.1**	49	12
MUN	Dreyfus Intermediate Muni Bd	DITEX	**A**	(800) 645-6561	14.09	**A- /9.1**	3.63 /91	3.04 /88	4.75 /83	**C+ / 5.8**	51	5
MUN	Northern Intermed Tax Exempt	NOITX	**A**	(800) 595-9111	10.82	**A- /9.0**	3.53 /90	2.88 /87	4.61 /82	**C / 5.3**	41	18
MUS	AB Municipal Income II AZ A	AAZAX	**A**	(800) 221-5672	11.30	**B+ /8.9**	4.67 /97	3.45 /92	5.25 /87	**C / 5.3**	62	21
MUS	Wells Fargo PA Tax Fr A	EKVAX	**A**	(800) 222-8222	11.94	**B+ /8.8**	3.69 /92	4.05 /96	6.12 /93	**C+ / 5.7**	85	7
MUS	Aquila Tax-Free Fd for Utah A	UTAHX	**A**	(800) 437-1020	10.56	**B+ /8.8**	3.41 /89	3.87 /95	5.60 /90	**C+ / 6.0**	84	7
MUS	Madison Tax Free Virginia Y	GTVAX	**A**	(800) 877-6089	11.73	**B+ /8.7**	3.11 /86	2.68 /85	3.95 /77	**C+ / 5.7**	38	19
MUI	Commerce Kansas T/F Intm Bond	KTXIX	**A**	(800) 995-6365	19.64	**B+ /8.4**	2.72 /82	2.47 /82	4.23 /79	**C+ / 6.0**	34	16
MUS	Commerce Missouri T/F Intm Bd	CFMOX	**A**	(800) 995-6365	19.74	**B+ /8.3**	2.92 /84	2.22 /79	4.05 /78	**C+ / 6.4**	33	17
GL	SEI Inst Intl International Fx In A	SEFIX	**A**	(800) 342-5734	10.16	**B /8.0**	1.69 /69	3.47 /80	4.25 /65	**C+ / 6.6**	99	8
MUN	Wells Fargo Intm Tax/AMT Fr A	WFTAX	**A**	(800) 222-8222	11.73	**B /8.0**	2.74 /82	2.75 /85	4.73 /83	**B- / 7.0**	53	15
MUS	Maine Municipal	MEMUX	**A**	(800) 601-5593	11.18	**B /7.9**	3.22 /87	2.51 /83	4.27 /80	**B- / 7.1**	47	13
MUS	Nuveen Oregon Intmdt Muni Bd A	FOTAX	**A**	(800) 257-8787	10.47	**B /7.8**	3.27 /88	2.54 /83	4.07 /78	**C+ / 6.7**	42	19
MUS	Columbia AMT Fr NY Intm Muni Bd	LNYAX	**A**	(800) 345-6611	12.23	**B /7.7**	3.17 /87	2.51 /83	4.02 /78	**B- / 7.3**	48	18
MUS	Columbia AMT-Fr SC Intm Muni Bd	NSCIX	**A**	(800) 345-6611	10.52	**B /7.7**	3.30 /88	2.36 /81	4.08 /78	**B- / 7.1**	40	5
MUS	Aquila Churchill Tax-Free of KY A	CHTFX	**A**	(800) 437-1020	10.88	**B /7.6**	2.75 /83	2.83 /86	4.43 /81	**B- / 7.5**	62	7
MUS	Columbia AMT-Fr GA Intm Muni Bd	NGIMX	**A**	(800) 345-6611	10.85	**B- /7.5**	3.02 /85	2.36 /81	3.83 /76	**B- / 7.5**	47	5
MUS	AI KS Tax-Exempt Bond A	IKSTX	**A**	(866) 410-2006	11.18	**B- /7.5**	2.40 /80	2.89 /87	3.95 /77	**B- / 7.2**	60	16
MTG	TCW Total Return Bond N	TGMNX	**A**	(800) 386-3829	10.61	**B- /7.5**	1.59 /67	2.84 /75	4.93 /71	**B / 7.7**	79	6
GES	Tributary Income Inst	FOINX	**A**	(800) 662-4203	10.41	**B- /7.3**	1.75 /69	2.53 /71	3.98 /61	**B- / 7.3**	77	13
MTG	Advisors Series Trust PIA MBS	PMTGX	**A**	(800) 251-1970	9.76	**B- /7.2**	1.85 /70	2.58 /72	3.05 /46	**B / 8.0**	62	10
GEI	Nationwide Core Plus Bond Inst	NWCIX	**A**	(800) 848-0920	10.23	**B- /7.1**	1.76 /69	2.41 /69	4.25 /65	**B / 7.7**	78	14
MUN	Dreyfus Tax Sensitive Tot Ret Bd A	DSDAX	**A**	(800) 645-6561	23.22	**B- /7.1**	2.91 /84	2.59 /84	3.84 /76	**B / 7.7**	60	15
USS	Guggenheim Investment Grade Bd	SIUSX	**A**	(800) 820-0888	17.94	**B- /7.1**	0.89 /57	3.94 /83	5.04 /72	**B / 8.1**	98	4
GEI	WA Intermediate Bond IS	WABSX	**A**	(888) 425-6432	11.10	**B- /7.1**	2.27 /73	2.27 /67	3.63 /55	**B / 8.1**	80	7
MUS	Dupree TN Tax-Free Sh-to-Med	TTSMX	**A**	(800) 866-0614	10.88	**C+ /6.8**	1.97 /77	1.37 /64	2.18 /51	**B+ / 8.6**	45	12
GEI	Scout Core Bond Fund Institutional	SCCIX	**A**	(800) 996-2862	11.72	**C+ /6.8**	2.95 /76	1.87 /59	3.76 /58	**B+ / 8.4**	80	15
MTG	HC Capital US Mtg/Asst Bckd FI	HCASX	**A**	(800) 242-9596	9.85	**C+ /6.8**	1.94 /71	2.23 /66	2.95 /44	**B / 8.1**	51	4
MTG	Federated Mortgage Fund Inst	FGFIX	**A**	(800) 341-7400	9.69	**C+ /6.5**	1.76 /69	2.16 /65	2.88 /43	**B / 8.2**	57	13
GEI	Cavanal Hill Intmdt Bond NL Inv	APFBX	**A**	(800) 762-7085	10.57	**C+ /6.5**	1.09 /60	2.24 /66	4.10 /63	**B+ / 8.6**	89	23
MUN	Vanguard Lmtd-Term Tax-Exempt	VMLTX	**A**	(800) 662-7447	11.05	**C+ /6.4**	1.57 /74	1.27 /60	1.86 /43	**A- / 9.1**	73	8
COI	Vanguard Short-Term Crp Bd Idx	VSCSX	**A**	(800) 662-7447	21.72	**C+ /6.2**	1.78 /70	1.89 /59	2.84 /43	**B+ / 8.8**	89	7
MUN	Oppenheimer Rochester Sht Term	ORSTX	**A**	(888) 470-0862	3.75	**C+ /6.1**	1.64 /75	1.82 /74	2.56 /61	**A / 9.3**	90	6
MUS	Weitz Nebraska Tax Free Income	WNTFX	**A**	(800) 232-4161	10.12	**C+ /6.1**	1.20 /70	1.22 /59	2.35 /55	**B+ / 8.9**	54	31
MUN	Pacific Capital T/F Sh-Interm Y	PTFSX	**A**	(888) 739-1390	10.25	**C+ /5.9**	1.50 /74	1.06 /55	1.35 /32	**A- / 9.0**	56	12
MUN	Vanguard Long-Term Tax-Exempt	VWLTX	**A-**	(800) 662-7447	11.87	**A+ /9.8**	4.77 /97	4.37 /97	6.39 /94	**C- / 3.9**	73	6
MUS	T Rowe Price CA Tax Free Bond	PRXCX	**A-**	(800) 638-5660	11.77	**A+ /9.8**	4.56 /97	4.39 /97	6.82 /96	**C- / 3.9**	74	13
MUS	Vanguard NY Long-Term	VNYTX	**A-**	(800) 662-7447	12.03	**A+ /9.8**	4.85 /98	4.36 /97	5.94 /92	**C / 4.3**	78	3
MUS	Vanguard PA Long-Term	VPAIX	**A-**	(800) 662-7447	11.79	**A+ /9.7**	4.31 /96	4.27 /97	5.95 /92	**C / 4.3**	75	5
MUS	Fidelity AZ Muni Income Fd	FSAZX	**A-**	(800) 544-8544	12.29	**A+ /9.6**	4.04 /94	4.05 /96	5.83 /91	**C / 4.3**	68	6
MUN	Fidelity Tax Free Bond Fd	FTABX	**A-**	(800) 544-8544	11.77	**A+ /9.6**	3.81 /93	4.04 /96	6.19 /93	**C- / 4.2**	62	7

• Denotes fund is closed to new investors

Data as of March 31, 2016

Fund Type	Fund Name (99 Pct = Best, 0 Pct = Worst)	Ticker Symbol	Overall Investment Rating	Phone	Net Asset Value As of 3/31/16	PERFORMANCE: Performance Rating/Pts	Annualized Total Return Through 3/31/16: 1Yr / Pct	3Yr / Pct	5Yr / Pct	RISK: Risk Rating/Pts	FUND MGR: Mgr. Quality Pct	Mgr. Tenure (Years)
MUS	T Rowe Price GA Tax-Free Bd	GTFBX	A-	(800) 638-5660	11.79	A /9.4	3.77 /92	3.64 /93	5.85 /91	C /4.4	53	19
MUS	Fidelity MA Muni Inc Fd	FDMMX	A-	(800) 544-8544	12.60	A /9.4	3.93 /93	3.75 /94	5.59 /89	C /4.4	55	6
MUS	Northern AZ Tax Exempt	NOAZX	A-	(800) 595-9111	10.96	A /9.4	4.06 /94	3.54 /93	5.66 /90	C /4.7	53	17
MUS	Wells Fargo CA Tax Fr A	SCTAX	A-	(800) 222-8222	12.15	A /9.4	4.19 /95	4.78 /98	7.32 /97	C /4.5	89	7
MUS	Northern CA Intermediate T/E	NCITX	A-	(800) 595-9111	11.03	A /9.4	4.02 /94	3.44 /92	5.17 /87	C /4.6	49	17
MUS	Fidelity MD Muni Income Fd	SMDMX	A-	(800) 544-8544	11.52	A- /9.2	3.94 /94	3.31 /91	4.85 /84	C /4.8	46	14
MUN	Oppenheimer Rochester Int Term	ORRWX	A-	(888) 470-0862	4.42	A- /9.1	4.74 /97	3.46 /92	4.86 /84	C /5.0	59	6
MUS	Wells Fargo CO Tax Fr A	NWCOX	A-	(800) 222-8222	11.21	A- /9.0	4.04 /94	4.21 /97	5.93 /92	C /5.0	84	11
MUS	Columbia Minnesota Tax-Exempt A	IMNTX	A-	(800) 345-6611	5.60	A- /9.0	3.86 /93	3.73 /94	5.92 /91	C /5.2	73	9
MUS	PIMCO NY Muni Bond A	PNYAX	A-	(800) 426-0107	11.43	B+ /8.9	3.56 /91	3.48 /93	4.88 /84	C /5.0	56	5
MUS	Franklin CA Interm Tax-Free A	FKCIX	A-	(800) 342-5236	12.29	B+ /8.8	3.14 /86	3.43 /92	5.48 /89	C /5.3	61	24
MUN	Thornburg Strategic Municipal Inc	TSSAX	A-	(800) 847-0200	15.38	B+ /8.6	2.85 /84	3.21 /90	6.43 /94	C /5.3	53	7
MUS	AB Municipal Income II MN A	AMNAX	A-	(800) 221-5672	10.52	B+ /8.4	3.56 /91	3.11 /89	4.75 /83	C+ /5.7	52	21
MUN	Nuveen Intmdt Duration Muni Bond	NMBAX	A-	(800) 257-8787	9.35	B+ /8.4	3.60 /91	3.09 /89	4.60 /82	C+ /5.9	53	9
MUS	Aquila Tax-Free Tr of Arizona A	AZTFX	A-	(800) 437-1020	10.95	B+ /8.4	3.20 /87	3.50 /93	5.19 /87	C+ /5.7	71	30
MUS	WA Int Maturity California Muni A	ITCAX	A-	(877) 534-4627	9.10	B+ /8.3	2.98 /85	2.98 /88	4.98 /85	C+ /5.8	51	4
MUN	Delaware Tax-Free USA Intmdt A	DMUSX	A-	(800) 523-1918	12.24	B /7.8	3.04 /85	2.47 /82	4.42 /81	C+ /6.4	38	13
MUS	Sterling Capital SC Interm TxFr A	BASCX	A-	(800) 228-1872	11.27	B /7.8	3.03 /85	2.24 /80	3.84 /76	C+ /6.5	33	16
MUS	Federated MI Interm Muni Tr	MMIFX	A-	(800) 341-7400	11.46	B /7.7	3.05 /85	2.53 /83	4.51 /81	C+ /6.8	43	18
MUS	Aquila Tax-Free Trust of Oregon A	ORTFX	A-	(800) 437-1020	11.33	B /7.7	2.91 /84	2.86 /87	4.61 /82	C+ /6.5	52	30
MUS	Sterling Capital WVA Interm TxFr A	BWVAX	A-	(800) 228-1872	10.22	B /7.6	3.06 /86	2.10 /78	3.68 /75	C+ /6.8	31	16
MUS	Columbia AMT-Fr MA Intm Muni	LMIAX	A-	(800) 345-6611	11.02	B /7.6	3.02 /85	2.39 /81	3.85 /77	C+ /6.8	39	7
MUS	Columbia AMT-Fr OR Inter Muni	COEAX	A-	(800) 345-6611	12.70	B- /7.4	2.99 /85	2.34 /81	3.96 /77	C+ /6.9	38	13
GES	GE RSP Income	GESLX	A-	(800) 242-0134	11.59	B- /7.4	1.23 /62	2.66 /73	4.14 /63	C+ /6.9	79	20
MUS	Columbia AMT-Fr MD Intm Muni	NMDMX	A-	(800) 345-6611	10.87	B- /7.3	2.75 /83	2.26 /80	3.79 /76	B- /7.2	39	5
USS	AMG Mgrs Intmd Duration Govt	MGIDX	A-	(800) 835-3879	10.95	B- /7.3	1.69 /69	2.71 /73	3.27 /49	B- /7.1	92	24
MUS	Bishop Street HI Muni Bond A	BHIAX	A-	(800) 262-9565	10.87	B- /7.3	2.88 /84	2.26 /80	3.90 /77	B- /7.0	36	9
MUS	American Century CA IT TxFr Bd A	BCIAX	A-	(800) 345-6488	12.08	B- /7.1	3.17 /87	2.54 /83	4.55 /82	B- /7.2	47	14
MUN	Nationwide HighMark Natl Int TFB	NWJOX	A-	(800) 848-0920	11.13	B- /7.0	2.25 /79	2.04 /77	3.15 /71	B /7.6	40	20
MUS	Columbia AMT-Fr NC Intm Muni Bd	NNCIX	A-	(800) 345-6611	10.66	B- /7.0	2.81 /83	2.10 /78	3.78 /76	B /7.6	38	5
GEI	Cavanal Hill Bond NL Inv	APBDX	A-	(800) 762-7085	9.67	C+ /6.8	1.91 /71	2.19 /65	3.94 /60	B /7.8	72	23
MUI	JPMorgan OH Municipal A	ONOHX	A-	(800) 480-4111	11.00	C+ /6.7	2.71 /82	2.21 /79	3.57 /75	B /7.8	46	22
GL	DFA Five Year Glbl Fixed Inc Inst	DFGBX	A-	(800) 984-9472	11.11	C+ /6.5	2.39 /74	1.95 /60	3.04 /46	B /8.2	96	17
GEI	Loomis Sayles Intm Dur Bd Inst	LSDIX	A-	(800) 633-3330	10.38	C+ /6.5	1.39 /65	2.10 /64	3.35 /51	B /8.1	77	11
USS	Federated Govt Income Trust Inst	FICMX	A-	(800) 341-7400	10.36	C+ /6.3	1.59 /67	1.99 /61	2.56 /38	B+ /8.3	85	16
MTG	Wright Current Income	WCIFX	A-	(800) 232-0013	9.41	C+ /6.2	1.57 /67	1.89 /59	2.78 /42	B+ /8.3	55	7
GL	Federated Floating Rt Str Inc Inst	FFRSX	A-	(800) 341-7400	9.65	C+ /6.2	0.64 /52	2.20 /66	3.15 /47	B+ /8.6	96	6
MUN	Thornburg Limited Term Muni A	LTMFX	A-	(800) 847-0200	14.61	C+ /6.1	1.89 /76	1.51 /68	2.88 /67	B+ /8.7	52	5
MUN	T Rowe Price Tax-Free Sh-Intmdt	PRFSX	A-	(800) 638-5660	5.65	C+ /6.0	1.36 /72	1.13 /56	2.09 /49	B+ /8.9	54	22
MUN	Wells Fargo Str Muni Bd A	VMPAX	A-	(800) 222-8222	8.99	C+ /5.9	1.96 /77	2.18 /79	3.08 /70	B+ /8.9	86	6
GEI	Vanguard Sh-Term Invest-Grade	VFSTX	A-	(800) 662-7447	10.69	C+ /5.9	1.73 /69	1.67 /55	2.25 /34	A- /9.0	86	8
MUS	Dupree NC Tax Free Sh-to-Med	NTSMX	A-	(800) 866-0614	10.99	C+ /5.9	1.42 /73	1.08 /55	2.40 /56	B+ /8.9	47	12
GL	DFA S/T Extended Quality Port Inst	DFEQX	A-	(800) 984-9472	10.87	C+ /5.7	1.80 /70	1.54 /53	2.21 /34	B+ /8.9	93	8
MUS	DFA CA Sht Trm Muni Bd Inst	DFCMX	A-	(800) 984-9472	10.35	C /5.5	1.26 /71	0.95 /51	1.21 /29	A /9.4	77	9
GES	Baird Short-Term Bond Inst	BSBIX	A-	(866) 442-2473	9.68	C /5.4	1.30 /63	1.46 /51	2.09 /32	A /9.4	88	12
MUS	Northern CA T/E Bond	NCATX	B+	(800) 595-9111	12.06	A+ /9.8	4.96 /98	4.87 /98	7.66 /98	C- /3.2	72	19
MUS	Vanguard CA Long-Term	VCITX	B+	(800) 662-7447	12.34	A+ /9.8	4.96 /98	4.79 /98	7.06 /97	C- /3.6	78	5
MUS	Nuveen CA Muni Bond A	NCAAX	B+	(800) 257-8787	11.39	A+ /9.8	5.72 /99	5.51 /99	8.39 /99	C- /3.3	91	13
MUS	Vanguard OH Long-Term	VOHIX	B+	(800) 662-7447	12.78	A+ /9.8	4.85 /98	4.47 /97	6.26 /93	C- /3.6	64	8
MUS	Fidelity OH Muni Inc	FOHFX	B+	(800) 544-8544	12.43	A+ /9.7	4.59 /97	4.30 /97	5.80 /91	C- /3.8	74	10
MUS	Vanguard MA Tax-Exempt Inv	VMATX	B+	(800) 662-7447	11.03	A+ /9.7	4.47 /97	4.10 /96	5.62 /90	C- /3.9	55	8
MUN	T Rowe Price Summit Muni Income	PRINX	B+	(800) 638-5660	12.10	A+ /9.6	4.08 /94	3.99 /96	6.59 /95	C- /3.6	46	17

• Denotes fund is closed to new investors

Fund Type	Fund Name (99 Pct = Best, 0 Pct = Worst)	Ticker Symbol	Overall Investment Rating	Phone	Net Asset Value As of 3/31/16	PERFORMANCE: Performance Rating/Pts	PERFORMANCE: Annualized Total Return Through 3/31/16: 1Yr / Pct	3Yr / Pct	5Yr / Pct	RISK: Risk Rating/Pts	FUND MGR: Mgr. Quality Pct	Mgr. Tenure (Years)
MUN	Northern Tax Exempt	NOTEX	**B+**	(800) 595-9111	10.89	**A+ /9.6**	4.28 /96	3.87 /95	6.14 /93	**C- / 3.8**	45	18
MUS	Vanguard NJ Long-Term	VNJTX	**B+**	(800) 662-7447	12.22	**A+ /9.6**	3.92 /93	3.76 /94	5.77 /91	**C- / 3.9**	44	3
MUS	Dupree MS Tax Free Income	DUMSX	**B+**	(800) 866-0614	12.35	**A /9.5**	3.85 /93	3.86 /95	5.63 /90	**C- / 4.1**	55	16
MUS	Columbia CA Tax Exempt A	CLMPX	**B+**	(800) 345-6611	7.98	**A /9.5**	4.14 /95	4.66 /98	7.62 /98	**C- / 3.7**	77	6
MUN	Dreyfus Municipal Bond	DRTAX	**B+**	(800) 645-6561	11.98	**A /9.5**	4.25 /95	3.69 /94	5.85 /91	**C- / 4.1**	47	7
MUN	USAA Tax-Exempt Long Term	USTEX	**B+**	(800) 382-8722	13.73	**A /9.5**	3.88 /93	3.81 /95	6.86 /96	**C- / 3.7**	50	N/A
MUS	T Rowe Price NY Tax Free Bd	PRNYX	**B+**	(800) 638-5660	11.90	**A /9.5**	4.10 /95	3.70 /94	5.84 /91	**C- / 4.1**	47	16
MUS	T Rowe Price NJ Tax-Free Bond	NJTFX	**B+**	(800) 638-5660	12.24	**A /9.5**	3.66 /92	3.67 /94	5.90 /91	**C / 4.3**	49	16
MUN	T Rowe Price Tax-Free Income	PRTAX	**B+**	(800) 638-5660	10.44	**A /9.4**	3.48 /90	3.63 /93	6.03 /92	**C- / 4.2**	47	9
MUS	T Rowe Price VA Tax-Free Bond	PRVAX	**B+**	(800) 638-5660	12.24	**A /9.4**	3.79 /93	3.48 /93	5.61 /90	**C- / 4.1**	41	19
MUN	Elfun Tax Exempt Income	ELFTX	**B+**	(800) 242-0134	11.95	**A /9.3**	3.83 /93	3.40 /92	5.55 /89	**C / 4.3**	42	16
MUS	Virtus California T/E Bond A	CTESX	**B+**	(800) 243-1574	12.06	**A- /9.2**	4.03 /94	4.04 /96	6.28 /94	**C / 4.3**	N/A	20
MUN	AMG GW&K Municipal Bond Inv	GWMTX	**B+**	(800) 835-3879	11.86	**A- /9.2**	3.91 /93	3.09 /89	5.18 /87	**C- / 4.2**	34	7
MUS	Columbia NY Tax-Exempt A	COLNX	**B+**	(800) 345-6611	7.61	**A- /9.1**	4.32 /96	3.83 /95	6.26 /93	**C- / 4.1**	51	6
MUN	CGCM Municipal Bd Invest	TMUUX	**B+**	(800) 444-4273	9.78	**A- /9.1**	3.32 /88	3.15 /90	4.84 /84	**C- / 4.1**	46	11
MUS	Dreyfus NY Tax Exempt Bond	DRNYX	**B+**	(800) 645-6561	15.14	**A- /9.1**	4.24 /95	2.92 /87	5.00 /85	**C / 4.5**	31	7
MUN	Eaton Vance TABS Int-Term Muni	EITAX	**B+**	(800) 262-1122	12.46	**A- /9.1**	4.26 /95	3.48 /92	5.30 /88	**C / 4.5**	50	6
MUS	American Funds Tax-Exempt of CA	TAFTX	**B+**	(800) 421-0180	17.97	**A- /9.1**	3.96 /94	4.06 /96	6.96 /96	**C / 4.5**	74	30
MUN	Madison Tax Free National Y	GTFHX	**B+**	(800) 877-6089	11.15	**A- /9.1**	3.73 /92	2.94 /88	4.49 /81	**C / 4.6**	34	19
MUS	AB Municipal Income CA A	ALCAX	**B+**	(800) 221-5672	11.50	**A- /9.0**	3.96 /94	3.79 /95	6.01 /92	**C / 4.8**	64	21
MUS	Fidelity NJ Muni Income Fd	FNJHX	**B+**	(800) 544-8544	12.00	**A- /9.0**	3.24 /87	2.99 /88	5.19 /87	**C / 4.3**	31	7
MUN	JPMorgan Tax Free Bond A	PMBAX	**B+**	(800) 480-4111	12.61	**A- /9.0**	3.91 /93	3.92 /95	5.18 /87	**C / 4.5**	N/A	11
MUN	Wells Fargo Muni Bd A	WMFAX	**B+**	(800) 222-8222	10.48	**B+ /8.9**	3.77 /92	4.12 /96	6.52 /95	**C / 4.5**	80	16
MUN	Columbia Tax-Exempt A	COLTX	**B+**	(800) 345-6611	14.00	**B+ /8.9**	3.29 /88	3.75 /94	6.45 /94	**C / 4.3**	56	14
MUS	Fidelity Adv CA Muni Inc A	FCMAX	**B+**	(800) 522-7297	13.26	**B+ /8.9**	3.64 /91	4.05 /96	6.27 /94	**C / 4.7**	75	10
MUS	RidgeWorth Seix Hi Grade Muni Bd	SFLTX	**B+**	(888) 784-3863	12.36	**B+ /8.8**	3.67 /92	4.07 /96	6.45 /94	**C / 4.5**	76	22
MUI	GuideMark Tax-Exempt Fixed Inc	GMTEX	**B+**	(888) 278-5809	11.62	**B+ /8.8**	3.18 /87	2.67 /84	4.76 /83	**C / 4.6**	26	10
MUS	AB Municipal Income II PA A	APAAX	**B+**	(800) 221-5672	10.67	**B+ /8.8**	4.16 /95	3.33 /91	5.10 /86	**C / 4.6**	44	21
MUS	SEI Tax-Exempt Tr-MA Muni Bond	SMAAX	**B+**	(800) 342-5734	10.87	**B+ /8.6**	3.46 /90	2.51 /83	4.03 /78	**C / 5.2**	32	6
MUS	Nebraska Municipal	NEMUX	**B+**	(800) 601-5593	10.67	**B+ /8.6**	3.63 /91	3.23 /90	4.55 /82	**C / 4.7**	45	20
MUN	American Funds T/E Bd of America	AFTEX	**B+**	(800) 421-0180	13.19	**B+ /8.6**	3.64 /91	3.52 /93	6.00 /92	**C / 4.9**	56	37
MUS	Oklahoma Municipal	OKMUX	**B+**	(800) 601-5593	11.92	**B+ /8.5**	3.98 /94	3.03 /88	4.75 /83	**C / 5.0**	43	20
MUS	Columbia AMT-Fr CA Intm Muni Bd	NACMX	**B+**	(800) 345-6611	10.68	**B+ /8.5**	3.58 /91	3.19 /90	5.08 /86	**C / 5.4**	53	5
MUN	Lord Abbett Interm Tax Free A	LISAX	**B+**	(888) 522-2388	10.98	**B+ /8.5**	3.30 /88	3.01 /88	5.08 /86	**C / 5.1**	42	10
MUN	Commerce National T/F Intm Bd	CFNLX	**B+**	(800) 995-6365	19.86	**B+ /8.3**	3.47 /90	2.13 /78	4.98 /85	**C / 5.1**	21	17
MUS	Franklin NY Interm Tax-Free Inc A	FKNIX	**B+**	(800) 342-5236	11.89	**B+ /8.3**	3.36 /89	2.82 /86	4.77 /83	**C / 5.2**	37	24
MUN	PNC Intermediate Tax Exempt	PTBIX	**B+**	(800) 551-2145	9.72	**B+ /8.3**	3.18 /87	3.01 /88	4.55 /82	**C+ / 5.8**	52	9
MUS	Viking Tax-Free Fund For ND Fd	VNDFX	**B+**	(800) 601-5593	10.55	**B /8.2**	3.98 /94	2.76 /86	4.40 /81	**C / 5.5**	41	17
MUN	Eaton Vance PA Muni Inc A	ETPAX	**B+**	(800) 262-1122	9.01	**B /8.2**	4.07 /94	3.41 /92	5.46 /89	**C / 5.5**	75	9
MUS	Delaware Tax Free Minnesota A	DEFFX	**B+**	(800) 523-1918	12.73	**B /8.1**	3.46 /90	3.30 /91	5.47 /89	**C / 5.3**	55	13
MUS	Aquila Tax-Free Fd of Colorado A	COTFX	**B+**	(800) 437-1020	10.83	**B /8.1**	3.20 /87	3.13 /89	4.61 /82	**C+ / 5.6**	53	29
MUS	Wells Fargo NC TF A	ENCMX	**B+**	(800) 222-8222	10.49	**B /8.0**	2.74 /83	3.30 /91	5.33 /88	**C+ / 5.7**	59	7
MUS	Viking Tax-Free Fund For MT Fd	VMTTX	**B+**	(800) 601-5593	10.31	**B /8.0**	3.35 /89	2.58 /83	4.50 /81	**C+ / 5.6**	36	17
MUN	Eaton Vance Nat Ltd Mat Muni Inc	EXNAX	**B+**	(800) 262-1122	10.16	**B /7.8**	2.78 /83	2.43 /82	4.14 /79	**C+ / 6.1**	35	2

• Denotes fund is closed to new investors

Data as of March 31, 2016

Section IV

Bottom 200 Bond Mutual Funds

A compilation of those

Fixed Income Mutual Funds

receiving the lowest TheStreet Investment Ratings.

Funds are listed in order by Overall Investment Rating.

Section IV Contents

This section contains a summary analysis of each of the bottom 200 bond mutual funds as determined by their overall TheStreet Investment Rating. Typically, these funds have invested in securities with excessive credit and/or interest rate risk. As such, these are the funds that you should generally avoid since they have historically underperformed most other mutual funds given the level of risk in their underlying investments.

In order to optimize the utility of our top and bottom fund lists, rather than listing all funds in a multi-class series, a single fund from each series is selected for display as the primary share class. Whenever possible, the selected fund is one that a retail investor would be most likely to choose. This share class may not be appropriate for every investor, so please consult with your financial advisor, the fund company, and the fund's prospectus before placing your trade.

1. Fund Type

The mutual fund's peer category based on its investment objective as stated in its prospectus.

COH	Corporate - High Yield	MMT	Money Market - Tax Free
COI	Corporate - Inv. Grade	MTG	Mortgage
EM	Emerging Market	MUH	Municipal - High Yield
GEN	General	MUI	Municipal - Insured
GEI	General - Inv. Grade	MUN	Municipal - National
GEL	General - Long Term	MUS	Municipal - Single State
GES	General - Short & Interm.	USL	U.S. Gov.- Long Term
GL	Global	USS	U.S. Gov. - Short & Interm
LP	Loan Participation	USA	U.S. Gov. - Agency
MM	Money Market	US	U.S. Gov. - Treasury

A blank fund type means that the mutual fund has not yet been categorized.

2. Fund Name

The name of the mutual fund as stated in its prospectus, which can sometimes differ slightly from the name that the company uses for advertising. If you cannot find the particular mutual fund you are interested in, or if you have any doubts regarding the precise name, verify the information with your broker or on your account statement. Also, use the fund's ticker symbol for confirmation. (See column 3.)

3. Ticker Symbol

The unique alphabetic symbol used for identifying and trading a specific mutual fund. No two funds can have the same ticker symbol, and the ticker symbol for mutual funds always ends with an "X".

A handful of funds currently show no associated ticker symbol. This means that the fund is either small or new since the NASD only assigns a ticker symbol to funds with at least $25 million in assets or 1,000 shareholders.

4. Overall Investment Rating

Our overall rating is measured on a scale from A to E based on each fund's risk-adjusted performance. Please see page 11 for specific descriptions of each letter grade. Also, refer to page 7 for information on how our ratings are derived. Most important, when using this rating, please be sure to consider the warnings beginning on page 13 regarding the ratings' limitations and the underlying assumptions.

5. Phone

The telephone number of the company managing the fund. Call this number to receive a prospectus or other information about the fund.

6. Net Asset Value (NAV)

The fund's share price as of the date indicated. A fund's NAV is computed by dividing the value of the fund's asset holdings, less accrued fees and expenses, by the number of its shares outstanding.

7. Performance Rating/Points

A letter grade rating based solely on the mutual fund's financial performance over the trailing three years, without any consideration for the amount of risk the fund poses. Like the overall Investment Rating, the Performance Rating is measured on a scale from A to E for ease of interpretation. The points score indicates where the Performance Rating falls on a scale of 0 to 10.

In the case of funds investing in municipal or other tax-free securities, this rating is based on the taxable equivalent return of the fund assuming the maximum marginal U.S. tax rate (35%).

8. 1-Year Total Return

The total return the fund has provided investors over the preceding twelve months. This total return figure is computed based on the fund's dividend distributions and share price appreciation/depreciation during the period, net of the expenses and fees it imposes on its shareholders. Although the total return figure does not reflect an adjustment for any loads the fund may carry, such adjustments have been made in deriving TheStreet Investment Ratings.

9. 1-Year Total Return Percentile

The fund's percentile rank based on its one-year performance compared to that of all other fixed income funds in existence for at least one year. A score of 99 is the highest possible, indicating that the fund outperformed 99% of the other mutual funds. Zero is the lowest possible percentile score.

In the case of funds investing in municipal or other tax-free securities, this percentile rank is based on the taxable equivalent return of the fund assuming the maximum marginal U.S. tax rate (35%).

10. 3-Year Total Return

The total annual return the fund has provided investors over the preceding three years.

11. 3-Year Total Return Percentile

The fund's percentile rank based on its three-year performance compared to that of all other fixed income funds in existence for at least three years. A score of 99 is the highest possible, indicating that the fund outperformed 99% of the other mutual funds. Zero is the lowest possible percentile score.

In the case of funds investing in municipal or other tax-free securities, this percentile rank is based on the taxable equivalent return of the fund assuming the maximum marginal U.S. tax rate (35%).

12. 5-Year Total Return

The total annual return the fund has provided investors over the preceding five years.

13. 5-Year Total Return Percentile

The fund's percentile rank based on its five-year performance compared to that of all other fixed income funds in existence for at least five years. A score of 99 is the highest possible, indicating that the fund outperformed 99% of the other mutual funds. Zero is the lowest possible percentile score.

In the case of funds investing in municipal or other tax-free securities, this percentile rank is based on the taxable equivalent return of the fund assuming the maximum marginal U.S. tax rate (35%).

14. Risk Rating/Points

A letter grade rating based solely on the mutual fund's risk as determined by its monthly performance volatility over the trailing three years and the underlying credit risk and interest rate risk of its investment portfolio. The risk rating does not take into consideration the overall financial performance the fund has achieved or the total return it has provided to its shareholders. Like the overall Investment Rating, the Risk Rating is measured on a scale from A to E for ease of interpretation. The points score indicates where the Risk Rating falls on a scale of 0 to 10.

15. Manager Quality Percentile

The manager quality percentile is based on a ranking of the fund's alpha, a statistical measure representing the difference between a fund's actual returns and its expected performance given its level of risk. Fund managers who have been able to exceed the fund's statistically expected performance receive a high percentile rank with 99 representing the highest possible score. At the other end of the spectrum, fund managers who have actually detracted from the fund's expected performance receive a low percentile rank with 0 representing the lowest possible score.

16. Manager Tenure

The number of years the current manager has been managing the fund. Since fund managers who deliver substandard returns are usually replaced, a long tenure is usually a good sign that shareholders are satisfied that the fund is achieving its stated objectives.

Fund Type	Fund Name (99 Pct = Best, 0 Pct = Worst)	Ticker Symbol	Overall Investment Rating	Phone	Net Asset Value As of 3/31/16	PERFORMANCE: Performance Rating/Pts	PERFORMANCE: Annualized Total Return Through 3/31/16: 1Yr / Pct	3Yr / Pct	5Yr / Pct	RISK: Risk Rating/Pts	FUND MGR: Mgr. Quality Pct	FUND MGR: Mgr. Tenure (Years)
GEI	Credit Suisse Cmdty Rtn Strat A	CRSAX	**E-**	(877) 927-2874	4.46	**E- /0.0**	-19.78 / 0	-17.07 / 0	-14.54 / 0	**E- / 0.0**	0	10
COH	Third Avenue Focused Credit Inv	TFCVX	**E-**	(800) 443-1021	5.21	**E- /0.0**	-33.70 / 0	-13.13 / 0	-5.44 / 0	**E- / 0.1**	0	7
GEI	Credit Suisse Commdty Ret Str	CCRSX	**E-**	(877) 927-2874	3.94	**E- /0.0**	-19.59 / 0	-17.04 / 0	-14.55 / 0	**E- / 0.0**	0	10
COH	Catalyst/SMH High Income A	HIIFX	**E-**	(866) 447-4228	3.12	**E- /0.0**	-25.42 / 0	-13.08 / 0	-6.60 / 0	**E- / 0.0**	0	8
GES	Northeast Investors Trust	NTHEX	**E-**	(800) 225-6704	3.83	**E- /0.0**	-25.81 / 0	-9.21 / 0	-2.75 / 1	**E- / 0.2**	0	N/A
USS	PIMCO StocksPLUS Short A	PSSAX	**E-**	(800) 426-0107	10.27	**E- /0.0**	-6.53 / 3	-12.27 / 0	-10.75 / 0	**E / 0.3**	0	2
GES	AB All Mkt Real Return A	AMTAX	**E-**	(800) 221-5672	7.61	**E- /0.0**	-14.66 / 0	-10.78 / 0	-7.62 / 0	**E- / 0.0**	0	1
COH	Rydex Inv High Yld Strtgy A	RYILX	**E-**	(800) 820-0888	17.92	**E- /0.0**	-6.81 / 2	-9.25 / 0	-10.94 / 0	**E+ / 0.8**	1	9
EM	Invesco Emerg Mkts Flexible Bond	IAEMX	**E-**	(800) 959-4246	6.38	**E- /0.0**	-10.75 / 0	-9.82 / 0	-4.41 / 0	**E- / 0.2**	0	3
US	Direxion Mo 7-10 Year Tr Br 2X Inv	DXKSX	**E-**	(800) 851-0511	29.47	**E- /0.0**	-9.93 / 1	-8.96 / 0	-14.53 / 0	**E- / 0.2**	11	12
COH	Access Flex Bear High Yield Inv	AFBIX	**E-**	(888) 776-3637	8.68	**E- /0.0**	-7.66 / 2	-9.52 / 0	-12.00 / 0	**E+ / 0.7**	0	11
USS	Rydex Inv Govt Lg Bd Stgy A	RYAQX	**E-**	(800) 820-0888	33.11	**E- /0.0**	-4.47 / 6	-8.17 / 1	-12.35 / 0	**E- / 0.0**	33	8
EM	Dreyfus Eme Mkts Dbt LC A	DDBAX	**E-**	(800) 782-6620	11.18	**E- /0.0**	-5.19 / 5	-8.57 / 0	-3.42 / 1	**E- / 0.1**	0	8
EM	Goldman Sachs Local Emg Mkt	GAMDX	**E-**	(800) 526-7384	6.36	**E- /0.0**	-3.57 / 9	-8.58 / 0	-3.06 / 1	**E- / 0.1**	0	8
GEI	Rydex Wekng Dlr 2x Stgry A	RYWDX	**E-**	(800) 820-0888	12.55	**E- /0.0**	6.54 /95	-9.53 / 0	-9.21 / 0	**E- / 0.0**	0	11
EM	PIMCO Emerging Local Bond A	PELAX	**E-**	(800) 426-0107	7.21	**E- /0.0**	-4.80 / 5	-8.77 / 0	-3.27 / 1	**E- / 0.1**	0	10
EM	Eaton Vance Emer Market Local	EEIAX	**E-**	(800) 262-1122	6.29	**E- /0.1**	-0.87 /23	-7.77 / 1	-3.03 / 1	**E- / 0.1**	1	8
EM	EuroPac International Bond A	EPIBX	**E-**	(888) 558-5851	8.14	**E- /0.1**	-3.34 /10	-5.75 / 1	-2.60 / 1	**E / 0.5**	2	6
MTG	ProFunds-Falling US Dollar Svc	FDPSX	**E-**	(888) 776-3637	17.27	**E- /0.1**	0.82 /56	-7.00 / 1	-6.83 / 0	**E+ / 0.8**	1	7
GL	Nuveen High Income Bond A	FJSIX	**E-**	(800) 257-8787	6.77	**E- /0.1**	-12.80 / 0	-2.70 / 3	1.74 /28	**E+ / 0.6**	8	11
GL	TCW Emg Mkts Local Currency Inc	TGWNX	**E-**	(800) 386-3829	8.53	**E- /0.2**	-3.29 /10	-6.71 / 1	-1.57 / 1	**E- / 0.2**	1	6
EM	Oppenheimer Em Mkts Local Debt	OEMAX	**E-**	(888) 470-0862	7.40	**E- /0.2**	-0.01 /31	-5.76 / 1	-1.19 / 1	**E- / 0.2**	2	1
EM	Janus Emerging Markets A	JMFAX	**E-**	(800) 295-2687	7.58	**E- /0.2**	-10.08 / 1	-2.48 / 3	-4.67 / 0	**E- / 0.0**	9	4
GL	PIMCO Emerging Markets	PLMAX	**E-**	(800) 426-0107	8.75	**E- /0.2**	-1.69 /17	-4.48 / 2	-2.75 / 1	**E+ / 0.6**	4	11
GL	Lord Abbett Emerg Mkts Currency	LDMAX	**E-**	(888) 522-2388	5.27	**E- /0.2**	-2.47 /13	-4.61 / 2	-2.68 / 1	**E / 0.5**	4	9
COH	Franklin High Income A	FHAIX	**E-**	(800) 342-5236	1.66	**E- /0.2**	-11.00 / 0	-1.74 / 5	2.56 /38	**E / 0.4**	5	25
MUS ●	Franklin Double Tax-Free Inc A	FPRTX	**E-**	(800) 342-5236	9.34	**E- /0.2**	-0.50 /26	-3.26 / 2	1.47 /34	**E / 0.5**	1	30
EM	Deutsche Enh Emg Mrkts Fxd Inc	SZEAX	**E-**	(800) 728-3337	9.04	**E- /0.2**	-2.95 /12	-2.87 / 3	0.40 /17	**E+ / 0.7**	8	5
COH	WA Global High Yield Bond A	SAHYX	**E-**	(877) 534-4627	5.83	**E /0.3**	-6.59 / 3	-1.54 / 6	2.51 /38	**E+ / 0.7**	6	10
GEI	API Efficient Frontier Income Fd A	APIUX	**E-**	(800) 544-6060	9.51	**E /0.3**	-5.80 / 3	-1.63 / 5	2.31 /35	**E / 0.3**	6	19
EM	SEI Inst Intl Emerging Mkts Debt A	SITEX	**E-**	(800) 342-5734	9.39	**E /0.3**	-1.31 /19	-3.98 / 2	1.13 /22	**E / 0.3**	6	10
COH	Direxion Dynamic HY Bond Fd	PDHYX	**E-**	(800) 851-0511	10.62	**E /0.3**	-8.56 / 1	-1.80 / 5	1.37 /24	**E / 0.5**	6	6
GL	STAAR AltCat	SITAX	**E-**	(800) 332-7738	13.10	**E /0.5**	-10.70 / 1	-0.69 /10	0.05 /12	**E- / 0.2**	39	19
EM	BlackRock Emg Mkts Flex Dyn Bd	BAEDX	**E-**	(800) 441-7762	8.82	**E /0.5**	2.27 /73	-2.09 / 4	3.51 /53	**E / 0.4**	12	8
EM	WA Emerging Markets Debt A	LWEAX	**E-**	(888) 425-6432	4.73	**E+ /0.6**	-0.16 /30	-1.65 / 5	2.35 /36	**E / 0.4**	17	3
MUS ●	Oppenheimer Rochester VA Muni	ORVAX	**E-**	(888) 470-0862	8.01	**E+ /0.6**	-0.52 /26	-0.69 /10	5.33 /88	**E / 0.3**	1	10
COI	Federated Emerging Mkt Debt A	IHIAX	**E-**	(800) 341-7400	8.20	**E+ /0.6**	0.26 /45	-1.76 / 5	3.16 /48	**E / 0.3**	3	3
GL	Templeton Hard Currency A	ICPHX	**E**	(800) 342-5236	7.77	**E- /0.0**	-6.16 / 3	-6.45 / 1	-4.14 / 0	**D / 1.6**	1	15
COH	Western Asset Short Dur High Inc	SHIAX	**E**	(877) 534-4627	4.93	**E- /0.1**	-11.38 / 0	-2.38 / 3	2.08 /32	**D- / 1.0**	5	10
GL	Templeton International Bond A	TBOAX	**E**	(800) 342-5236	10.10	**E- /0.2**	-3.65 / 9	-2.73 / 3	0.28 /16	**D / 1.6**	8	9
GL	Pioneer Global High Yield A	PGHYX	**E**	(800) 225-6292	8.23	**E /0.3**	-5.29 / 4	-1.55 / 6	1.37 /24	**D- / 1.4**	17	15
GEI	Nuveen Symphony Credit Oppty A	NCOAX	**E**	(800) 257-8787	18.41	**E /0.3**	-8.51 / 1	-0.26 /13	3.73 /57	**D- / 1.3**	14	6
GL	Templeton Global Total Return A	TGTRX	**E**	(800) 342-5236	11.40	**E /0.4**	-5.04 / 5	-1.03 / 8	2.43 /37	**E+ / 0.8**	28	8
GEI	Columbia Inflation Protected Sec A	APSAX	**E**	(800) 345-6611	8.90	**E /0.4**	-1.55 /18	-2.67 / 3	1.65 /27	**D- / 1.3**	2	4
COH	Ivy High Income A	WHIAX	**E**	(800) 777-6472	6.91	**E /0.4**	-7.85 / 1	0.38 /31	4.66 /69	**D- / 1.2**	22	3
COH	J Hancock High Yield NAV		**E**	(800) 257-3336	7.29	**E /0.4**	-8.75 / 1	-1.18 / 7	2.89 /43	**E+ / 0.7**	7	10
GEI	PIMCO Real Return A	PRTNX	**E**	(800) 426-0107	10.92	**E /0.4**	-0.70 /24	-2.04 / 4	2.24 /34	**D- / 1.1**	1	9
COH	J Hancock Core High Yld A	JYIAX	**E**	(800) 257-3336	8.91	**E /0.4**	-7.58 / 2	-0.19 /14	3.90 /60	**E+ / 0.6**	12	7
COH	WA High Yield IS	WAHSX	**E**	(888) 425-6432	7.36	**E /0.4**	-8.64 / 1	-1.00 / 8	2.97 /45	**E+ / 0.8**	8	11
COH	MainStay High Yield Opps C	MYHYX	**E**	(800) 624-6782	9.89	**E /0.5**	-7.94 / 1	-1.27 / 7	2.13 /33	**D- / 1.1**	7	9
COH	Pax High Yield Inv	PAXHX	**E**	(800) 767-1729	6.16	**E /0.5**	-7.53 / 2	-0.96 / 9	2.13 /33	**D / 1.6**	9	1
GL	Templeton Global Bond A	TPINX	**E**	(800) 342-5236	11.49	**E /0.5**	-4.31 / 7	-0.63 /11	1.93 /30	**D- / 1.1**	39	15

● Denotes fund is closed to new investors

Fund Type	Fund Name (99 Pct = Best, 0 Pct = Worst)	Ticker Symbol	Overall Investment Rating	Phone	Net Asset Value As of 3/31/16	PERFORMANCE: Performance Rating/Pts	Annualized Total Return Through 3/31/16: 1Yr / Pct	3Yr / Pct	5Yr / Pct	RISK: Risk Rating/Pts	FUND MGR: Mgr. Quality Pct	Mgr. Tenure (Years)
COH	Delaware High-Yield Opps A	DHOAX	**E**	(800) 523-1918	3.58	**E /0.5**	-6.76 / 2	-0.10 /15	3.44 /52	**E+ / 0.9**	13	4
COH	Goldman Sachs High Yield A	GSHAX	**E**	(800) 526-7384	6.02	**E /0.5**	-6.37 / 3	0.59 /35	3.70 /56	**D- / 1.3**	27	7
COH	American Funds High Income Tr A	AHITX	**E**	(800) 421-0180	9.46	**E /0.5**	-7.19 / 2	-0.21 /14	2.76 /41	**D- / 1.0**	12	27
USL	Deutsche Global Inflation A	TIPAX	**E**	(800) 728-3337	9.98	**E /0.5**	-0.25 /29	-1.80 / 5	1.78 /28	**D- / 1.3**	5	6
COH	First Eagle High Yield I	FEHIX	**E**	(800) 334-2143	8.18	**E /0.5**	-7.73 / 2	-0.74 /10	2.97 /45	**E+ / 0.7**	9	N/A
COH	Calamos High Income A	CHYDX	**E**	(800) 582-6959	8.16	**E+ /0.6**	-5.75 / 3	0.23 /29	2.91 /44	**D- / 1.3**	19	17
COH	CGCM High Yield Invest	THYUX	**E**	(800) 444-4273	3.55	**E+ /0.6**	-7.92 / 1	-0.59 /11	2.71 /40	**D- / 1.1**	10	10
COH	Natixis Loomis Sayles High Income	NEFHX	**E**	(800) 225-5478	3.84	**E+ /0.6**	-6.30 / 3	0.29 /30	3.33 /50	**E / 0.5**	14	14
MUS ●	Oppenheimer Rochester MD Muni	ORMDX	**E**	(888) 470-0862	9.44	**E+ /0.6**	0.68 /59	-0.60 /11	4.76 /83	**E / 0.4**	1	10
COH	AllianzGI High Yield Bond A	AYBAX	**E**	(800) 988-8380	8.57	**E+ /0.6**	-6.05 / 3	0.23 /29	3.45 /52	**D- / 1.2**	18	20
COH	Nationwide High Yield Bond A	GGHAX	**E**	(800) 848-0920	5.48	**E+ /0.6**	-6.10 / 3	0.49 /33	3.29 /50	**D- / 1.4**	25	6
GES	USAA Real Return Fund	USRRX	**E**	(800) 382-8722	9.47	**E+ /0.6**	-3.81 / 8	-1.85 / 5	1.16 /22	**E+ / 0.8**	5	6
COH	Touchstone High Yield A	THYAX	**E**	(800) 543-0407	7.74	**E+ /0.7**	-5.78 / 3	0.40 /31	3.57 /54	**E+ / 0.9**	20	17
COH	Waddell & Reed Adv High Income	UNHIX	**E**	(888) 923-3355	6.22	**E+ /0.7**	-6.30 / 3	1.06 /44	5.21 /73	**D- / 1.2**	40	8
COH	RidgeWorth Seix High Yield A	HYPSX	**E**	(888) 784-3863	7.61	**E+ /0.7**	-5.43 / 4	0.61 /35	3.42 /52	**D- / 1.2**	26	9
COH	RidgeWorth Seix High Income A	SAHIX	**E**	(888) 784-3863	5.92	**E+ /0.7**	-5.77 / 3	0.51 /33	3.32 /50	**E+ / 0.7**	19	5
COH	RS High Yield Fund A	GUHYX	**E**	(800) 766-3863	5.88	**E+ /0.7**	-4.77 / 5	0.22 /29	3.54 /54	**E+ / 0.9**	18	7
EM	PIMCO EM Corporate Bond Inst	PEMIX	**E**	(800) 426-0107	9.83	**E+ /0.7**	-1.95 /16	-2.03 / 4	1.88 /30	**E / 0.5**	12	N/A
GL	Wells Fargo Intl Bd A	ESIYX	**E**	(800) 222-8222	10.22	**E+ /0.8**	1.10 /60	-1.54 / 6	0.14 /15	**E+ / 0.6**	20	23
COH	PNC High Yield Bond Fund A	PAHBX	**E**	(800) 551-2145	7.10	**E+ /0.8**	-5.68 / 4	0.38 /31	3.69 /56	**D- / 1.1**	22	8
COH	Pioneer High Yield A	TAHYX	**E**	(800) 225-6292	8.80	**E+ /0.9**	-6.62 / 2	0.97 /42	2.96 /44	**E+ / 0.8**	35	9
COH	J Hancock Focused High Yield A	JHHBX	**E**	(800) 257-3336	3.22	**D- /1.0**	-5.02 / 5	0.76 /38	2.61 /39	**D- / 1.0**	30	8
EM	Columbia Emerging Markets Bond	REBAX	**E**	(800) 345-6611	10.65	**D- /1.0**	1.49 /66	-0.90 / 9	3.92 /60	**E / 0.4**	34	5
EM	PIMCO Emerging Markets Bond A	PAEMX	**E**	(800) 426-0107	9.70	**D- /1.0**	0.02 /33	-1.06 / 8	3.16 /48	**E / 0.3**	30	5
GEI	PIMCO Real Return Asset P	PRTPX	**E**	(800) 426-0107	8.22	**D- /1.0**	-1.70 /17	-2.06 / 4	4.74 /70	**E- / 0.2**	0	9
MUS ●	Oppenheimer Rochester AZ Muni	ORAZX	**E**	(888) 470-0862	10.31	**D- /1.1**	0.03 /38	0.20 /30	5.72 /90	**E+ / 0.8**	3	10
GEI	J Hancock Global Income A	JYGAX	**E**	(800) 257-3336	8.90	**D- /1.2**	-1.54 /18	-0.09 /15	2.97 /45	**E+ / 0.7**	9	7
EM	J Hancock Emerg Markets Debt A	JMKAX	**E**	(800) 257-3336	8.91	**D- /1.2**	0.02 /33	-0.86 / 9	2.67 /40	**E / 0.4**	36	3
MTG	PIMCO StkPlus Intl (DH) A	PIPAX	**E**	(800) 426-0107	6.33	**D- /1.3**	-15.26 / 0	3.56 /81	6.13 /77	**E- / 0.0**	94	1
GL	MainStay Global High Income B	MGHBX	**E**	(800) 624-6782	9.56	**D- /1.5**	3.42 /79	-2.13 / 4	2.45 /37	**E / 0.3**	11	5
LP	Driehaus Select Credit Fund	DRSLX	**E+**	(800) 560-6111	7.80	**E- /0.1**	-11.39 / 0	-3.93 / 2	-1.45 / 1	**D+ / 2.3**	3	6
US	American Century Str Inf Opp Fd A	ASIDX	**E+**	(800) 345-6488	9.17	**E- /0.1**	-4.78 / 5	-3.94 / 2	-2.91 / 1	**D+ / 2.6**	4	6
GL	Columbia Global Bond A	IGBFX	**E+**	(800) 345-6611	5.80	**E- /0.2**	-3.65 / 9	-2.90 / 3	-0.32 / 2	**D / 2.2**	8	3
GL	Forward EM Corporate Debt C	FFXCX	**E+**	(800) 999-6809	7.43	**E- /0.2**	-6.72 / 2	-3.04 / 2	-0.70 / 2	**D / 1.9**	7	5
GL	Federated Prudent DollarBear A	PSAFX	**E+**	(800) 341-7400	10.09	**E- /0.2**	3.81 /80	-4.14 / 2	-3.56 / 1	**D / 2.1**	5	16
GES	Putnam Diversified Income A	PDINX	**E+**	(800) 225-1581	6.63	**E- /0.2**	-7.23 / 2	-0.93 / 9	1.10 /21	**D / 2.1**	88	22
GL	Leader Total Return Inv	LCTRX	**E+**	(800) 711-9164	9.08	**E /0.3**	-11.20 / 0	-0.65 /10	1.82 /29	**D+ / 2.4**	39	6
GL	PIMCO Glb Advantage Strategy Bd	PGSAX	**E+**	(800) 426-0107	10.06	**E /0.3**	-1.33 /19	-2.32 / 3	0.28 /16	**D / 2.1**	10	5
GL	Aberdeen Global High Income A	BJBHX	**E+**	(866) 667-9231	8.33	**E /0.3**	-10.69 / 1	-1.10 / 8	2.01 /31	**D / 2.0**	26	14
US	Hartford Inflation Plus A	HIPAX	**E+**	(888) 843-7824	10.83	**E /0.4**	0.84 /56	-2.20 / 4	1.90 /30	**C- / 3.0**	4	1
LP	Highland Floating Rate Opps A	HFRAX	**E+**	(877) 665-1287	6.63	**E /0.4**	-10.42 / 1	0.76 /38	3.69 /56	**D / 2.1**	73	4
GES	BlackRock Inflation Prot Bond Inv	BPRAX	**E+**	(800) 441-7762	10.47	**E /0.5**	-0.37 /27	-1.63 / 5	1.99 /31	**D+ / 2.5**	3	6
GEI	Principal Infl Prot A	PITAX	**E+**	(800) 222-5852	8.44	**E /0.5**	-0.47 /26	-1.69 / 5	2.00 /31	**D+ / 2.4**	3	6
GEI	American Century Infl Adj Bd A	AIAVX	**E+**	(800) 345-6488	11.73	**E /0.5**	0.73 /54	-1.69 / 5	2.21 /34	**D / 2.2**	2	10
GL	Oppenheimer Intl Bond A	OIBAX	**E+**	(888) 470-0862	5.70	**E+ /0.6**	-0.50 /26	-1.20 / 7	1.08 /21	**D+ / 2.3**	25	3
COH	Dunham High-Yield Bond A	DAHYX	**E+**	(888) 338-6426	8.61	**E+ /0.6**	-3.93 / 8	-0.05 /15	2.47 /37	**D / 1.8**	17	11
USS	MFS Inflation Adjusted Bond A	MIAAX	**E+**	(800) 225-2606	10.48	**E+ /0.6**	0.82 /56	-1.48 / 6	2.21 /34	**D+ / 2.4**	4	13
GES	Fidelity Adv Inflation-Protect Bd A	FIPAX	**E+**	(800) 522-7297	12.03	**E+ /0.6**	0.65 /52	-1.48 / 6	2.24 /34	**D / 2.2**	2	12
GES	PIMCO Floating Income A	PFIAX	**E+**	(800) 426-0107	7.67	**E+ /0.6**	-2.82 /12	-0.73 /10	0.77 /19	**D / 2.2**	29	11
USS	AI US Infl Protected A	FNIHX	**E+**	(866) 410-2006	10.67	**E+ /0.6**	1.07 /60	-1.43 / 6	2.39 /36	**D / 2.2**	5	10
GEI	MassMutual Premier Infl-Pl A	MPSAX	**E+**	(800) 542-6767	10.30	**E+ /0.6**	0.90 /57	-1.25 / 7	2.51 /38	**D+ / 2.3**	3	13
USS	WA Inflation Indexed Plus Bond Fl	WATPX	**E+**	(888) 425-6432	11.08	**E+ /0.7**	-1.09 /21	-2.01 / 4	1.87 /30	**D+ / 2.8**	4	15

● Denotes fund is closed to new investors

Data as of March 31, 2016

Fund Type	Fund Name (99 Pct = Best, 0 Pct = Worst)	Ticker Symbol	Overall Investment Rating	Phone	Net Asset Value As of 3/31/16	PERFORMANCE: Performance Rating/Pts	Annualized Total Return Through 3/31/16: 1Yr / Pct	3Yr / Pct	5Yr / Pct	RISK: Risk Rating/Pts	FUND MGR: Mgr. Quality Pct	Mgr. Tenure (Years)
GL	Nuveen Inflation Protected Sec A	FAIPX	**E+**	(800) 257-8787	11.11	**E+ /0.7**	0.36 /47	-1.06 / 8	2.56 /39	**D+ / 2.6**	28	12
GEI	VY BlackRock Infl Pro Bond Adv	IBRAX	**E+**	(800) 992-0180	9.20	**E+ /0.7**	-0.75 /24	-2.02 / 4	1.61 /27	**D+ / 2.4**	2	6
GL	Deutsche Enhanced Global Bond A	SZGAX	**E+**	(800) 728-3337	8.98	**E+ /0.7**	0.18 /43	-0.59 /11	0.24 /16	**D+ / 2.7**	42	5
COH	Hotchkis and Wiley High Yield A	HWHAX	**E+**	(866) 493-8637	10.99	**E+ /0.7**	-5.48 / 4	1.09 /44	4.32 /66	**D- / 1.4**	42	7
GEI	Goldman Sachs Infl Prot Secs A	GSAPX	**E+**	(800) 526-7384	10.44	**E+ /0.8**	1.09 /60	-1.21 / 7	2.62 /39	**D+ / 2.6**	4	9
USS	Eaton Vance Core Plus Bond A	EBABX	**E+**	(800) 262-1122	10.95	**E+ /0.8**	-3.99 / 8	0.04 /23	5.87 /76	**D / 2.0**	21	7
COH	Wells Fargo High Inc A	SHBAX	**E+**	(800) 222-8222	6.33	**E+ /0.8**	-3.49 /10	0.13 /28	3.43 /52	**D- / 1.5**	18	18
US	Harbor Real Return Inst	HARRX	**E+**	(800) 422-1050	9.21	**E+ /0.9**	-0.26 /28	-1.88 / 5	2.21 /34	**D- / 1.3**	4	11
USS	Transamerica Prt Inflation-Prot Sec	DVIGX	**E+**	(888) 233-4339	11.14	**E+ /0.9**	-0.41 /27	-1.73 / 5	2.08 /32	**D+ / 2.5**	4	6
GEI	J Hancock Real Return Bond NAV		**E+**	(800) 257-3336	11.13	**E+ /0.9**	-0.07 /31	-1.87 / 5	2.29 /35	**D- / 1.4**	2	8
GEI	Wells Fargo Real Return A	IPBAX	**E+**	(800) 222-8222	9.93	**D- /1.0**	1.10 /60	-0.83 / 9	2.61 /39	**D / 1.9**	4	11
COH	American Century High-Yield A	AHYVX	**E+**	(800) 345-6488	5.36	**D- /1.0**	-4.55 / 6	0.57 /34	3.64 /55	**D- / 1.1**	24	8
COH	Timothy Plan High Yield A	TPHAX	**E+**	(800) 662-0201	8.57	**D- /1.1**	-3.04 /11	0.44 /32	3.20 /48	**D- / 1.0**	22	9
COH	Deutsche High Income A	KHYAX	**E+**	(800) 728-3337	4.39	**D- /1.1**	-4.00 / 8	1.42 /50	4.35 /66	**D / 1.8**	57	10
COH	USAA High Income Fund	USHYX	**E+**	(800) 382-8722	7.36	**D- /1.1**	-7.31 / 2	0.43 /32	3.80 /58	**D- / 1.4**	24	17
COH	Forward High Yield Bond Inv	AHBIX	**E+**	(800) 999-6809	8.65	**D- /1.1**	-5.79 / 3	0.15 /28	3.34 /51	**D / 1.6**	19	N/A
MUS ●	Oppenheimer Rochester MI Muni A	ORMIX	**E+**	(888) 470-0862	8.31	**D- /1.1**	0.56 /56	0.23 /31	5.16 /86	**D / 1.9**	5	10
GL	MFS Global Bond Fund A	MGBAX	**E+**	(800) 225-2606	8.86	**D- /1.1**	3.04 /77	-2.27 / 4	0.44 /17	**D- / 1.0**	11	6
GL	American Century Intl Bond A	AIBDX	**E+**	(800) 345-6488	12.80	**D- /1.1**	5.03 /88	-1.47 / 6	-0.39 / 2	**D- / 1.0**	21	7
COH	Putnam High Yield Advantage A	PHYIX	**E+**	(800) 225-1581	5.46	**D- /1.2**	-4.61 / 6	1.12 /45	4.03 /62	**D- / 1.2**	40	14
COH	Neuberger Berman High Inc Bd A	NHIAX	**E+**	(800) 877-9700	8.16	**D- /1.2**	-4.66 / 6	0.95 /42	3.56 /54	**D- / 1.2**	36	11
COH	Dreyfus High Yield A	DPLTX	**E+**	(800) 782-6620	5.85	**D- /1.2**	-4.69 / 6	1.26 /47	3.57 /54	**D- / 1.2**	45	6
COH	CNR High Yield Bond N	CHBAX	**E+**	(888) 889-0799	7.19	**D- /1.2**	-6.32 / 3	0.41 /31	3.80 /58	**D / 1.7**	25	5
COH	Fidelity Adv High Income A	FHIAX	**E+**	(800) 522-7297	7.27	**D- /1.3**	-3.63 / 9	1.19 /46	3.99 /61	**D- / 1.1**	42	15
USL	Vantagepoint Inflation Focused Inv	VPTSX	**E+**	(800) 669-7400	10.70	**D- /1.3**	0.87 /57	-1.45 / 6	2.22 /34	**D / 2.0**	6	8
GEI	Northern Multi-Mgr HY Oppty	NMHYX	**E+**	(800) 595-9111	9.01	**D- /1.4**	-5.19 / 5	0.65 /36	3.67 /56	**D / 1.9**	25	5
COH	Invesco High Yield A	AMHYX	**E+**	(800) 959-4246	3.94	**D- /1.4**	-3.95 / 8	1.24 /47	4.25 /65	**D- / 1.0**	44	11
COH	PACE High Yield Invst A	PHIAX	**E+**	(888) 793-8637	9.11	**D- /1.5**	-2.96 /11	0.93 /41	3.87 /60	**D- / 1.5**	38	1
COH	JPMorgan High Yield A	OHYAX	**E+**	(800) 480-4111	6.87	**D- /1.5**	-4.73 / 6	1.25 /47	3.82 /59	**D- / 1.5**	47	18
COH	Putnam High Yield Trust A	PHIGX	**E+**	(800) 225-1581	7.10	**D- /1.5**	-4.74 / 6	1.28 /48	3.95 /61	**D- / 1.1**	45	14
GL	PIMCO Foreign Bd Fd (Unhgd) A	PFUAX	**E+**	(800) 426-0107	9.66	**D /1.6**	1.90 /71	-0.70 /10	1.20 /22	**E+ / 0.8**	42	2
COH	Integrity High Income A	IHFAX	**E+**	(800) 601-5593	7.12	**D /1.6**	-3.77 / 8	1.30 /48	4.24 /65	**D- / 1.4**	49	8
GL	Aberdeen Asia Bond Inst Service	ABISX	**E+**	(866) 667-9231	9.95	**D /1.6**	0.10 /41	-1.23 / 7	1.16 /22	**D / 1.6**	24	7
COH	MFS Global High Yield A	MHOAX	**E+**	(800) 225-2606	5.80	**D /1.7**	-3.79 / 8	1.40 /50	3.96 /61	**D- / 1.4**	53	11
COH	AMG Mgrs High Yield Inv	MHHAX	**E+**	(800) 835-3879	7.13	**D /1.8**	-4.43 / 6	1.02 /43	4.24 /65	**D- / 1.4**	39	15
GL	UBS Fixed Income Opportunities A	FNOAX	**D-**	(888) 793-8637	8.47	**E- /0.1**	-7.52 / 2	-3.61 / 2	-1.25 / 1	**C / 4.3**	6	6
GEI	Dreyfus Opportunistic Fixed Inc A	DSTAX	**D-**	(800) 782-6620	11.02	**E- /0.1**	-10.91 / 0	-2.39 / 3	0.61 /18	**C- / 3.6**	8	6
GL	Eaton Vance Dvsfd Currency	EAIIX	**D-**	(800) 262-1122	8.95	**E- /0.2**	-1.16 /20	-2.98 / 2	-0.66 / 2	**C / 5.0**	7	8
GEI	Franklin Real Return A	FRRAX	**D-**	(800) 342-5236	9.84	**E /0.3**	-3.38 /10	-1.85 / 5	-0.65 / 2	**C- / 3.7**	7	12
GEI	Federated Real Return Bond A	RRFAX	**D-**	(800) 341-7400	10.24	**E /0.4**	-0.10 /30	-1.66 / 5	0.70 /18	**C- / 3.9**	6	10
GES	Hartford Unconstrained Bond A	HTIAX	**D-**	(888) 843-7824	9.36	**E /0.4**	-2.62 /13	-0.70 /10	2.20 /34	**C / 5.0**	10	4
GEI	J Hancock Fltng Rate Inc A	JFIAX	**D-**	(800) 257-3336	8.09	**E /0.4**	-5.73 / 4	-0.63 /11	1.65 /27	**C / 5.3**	28	9
GL	Waddell & Reed Adv Global Bond	UNHHX	**D-**	(888) 923-3355	3.55	**E /0.5**	-1.59 /18	-0.64 /11	1.14 /22	**C- / 3.3**	40	14
GL	Ivy Global Bond A	IVSAX	**D-**	(800) 777-6472	9.17	**E+ /0.6**	-1.54 /18	-0.48 /12	1.26 /23	**C- / 3.2**	45	8
GES	Oppenheimer Global Strategic Inc	OPSIX	**D-**	(888) 470-0862	3.81	**E+ /0.7**	-3.16 /11	0.06 /25	2.51 /38	**C- / 3.4**	11	7
GEN	Franklin Strategic Income A	FRSTX	**D-**	(800) 342-5236	9.19	**E+ /0.7**	-3.68 / 9	0.09 /27	2.80 /42	**C- / 3.6**	21	22
GES	Deutsche Unconstrained Income A	KSTAX	**D-**	(800) 728-3337	4.44	**E+ /0.7**	-2.99 /11	-0.27 /13	2.84 /43	**C- / 3.8**	10	10
GL	WA Global Strategic Income A	SDSAX	**D-**	(877) 534-4627	6.04	**E+ /0.8**	-3.57 / 9	0.42 /32	3.96 /61	**C- / 3.2**	82	4
COI	AB Bond Inflation Strat A	ABNAX	**D-**	(800) 221-5672	10.68	**E+ /0.8**	1.18 /61	-1.00 / 8	1.75 /28	**C- / 3.2**	6	6
GL	MainStay Unconstrained Bond B	MASBX	**D-**	(800) 624-6782	8.40	**E+ /0.8**	-4.77 / 5	-0.75 /10	2.04 /32	**C- / 3.4**	36	7
GL	Putnam Absolute Return 700 A	PDMAX	**D-**	(800) 225-1581	10.95	**E+ /0.8**	-5.06 / 5	1.48 /52	2.53 /38	**D+ / 2.7**	93	8
LP	Invesco Senior Loan A	VSLAX	**D-**	(800) 959-4246	6.02	**E+ /0.9**	-5.42 / 4	0.83 /39	3.49 /53	**C- / 3.7**	54	9

● Denotes fund is closed to new investors

Fund Type	Fund Name (99 Pct = Best, 0 Pct = Worst)	Ticker Symbol	Overall Investment Rating	Phone	Net Asset Value As of 3/31/16	PERFORMANCE: Performance Rating/Pts	Annualized Total Return Through 3/31/16: 1Yr / Pct	3Yr / Pct	5Yr / Pct	RISK: Risk Rating/Pts	FUND MGR: Mgr. Quality Pct	Mgr. Tenure (Years)
USL	• SunAmerica 2020 High Watermark	HWKAX	D-	(800) 858-8850	9.06	E+ /0.9	1.15 /61	0.14 /28	4.03 /62	C- / 3.8	13	12
MUS	Oppenheimer Ltd Term NY Muni A	LTNYX	D-	(888) 470-0862	3.00	D- /1.0	-1.39 /19	-0.29 /13	2.68 /63	C- / 3.3	6	17
GEI	Dreyfus Infl Adjusted Sec Inv	DIAVX	D-	(800) 645-6561	12.66	D- /1.0	1.13 /61	-1.69 / 5	2.10 /32	D+ / 2.9	3	11
GEI	TIAA-CREF Infltn Linkd Bd Retail	TCILX	D-	(800) 842-2252	11.25	D- /1.1	0.18 /44	-1.46 / 6	2.31 /35	D+ / 2.6	3	8
GL	Aberdeen Global Fixed Income A	CUGAX	D-	(866) 667-9231	9.72	D- /1.1	2.23 /73	-0.80 / 9	0.31 /16	D+ / 2.7	37	7
GL	GuideStone Infl Protected Bd Inv	GIPZX	D-	(888) 984-8433	10.33	D- /1.1	-0.19 /29	-1.42 / 6	2.12 /33	D+ / 2.8	20	6
GEI	SunAmerica VAL Co I Infln Prot Fd	VCTPX	D-	(800) 858-8850	10.75	D- /1.1	-0.18 /29	-1.30 / 7	2.30 /35	C- / 3.4	5	12
USL	American Century VP Infl Prot II	AIPTX	D-	(800) 345-6488	10.11	D- /1.1	-0.04 /31	-1.43 / 6	2.45 /37	D+ / 2.6	6	9
COI	Nuveen Strategic Income A	FCDDX	D-	(800) 257-8787	10.25	D- /1.2	-4.41 / 6	1.01 /43	3.80 /58	D+ / 2.5	16	16
GES	Transamerica High Yield Bond A	IHIYX	D-	(888) 233-4339	8.51	D- /1.3	-4.45 / 6	1.26 /47	4.62 /69	D / 2.1	45	10
GEI	SEI Instl Managed Tr-High Yld Bd	SHYAX	D-	(800) 342-5734	6.59	D- /1.3	-5.90 / 3	0.64 /36	4.02 /62	D+ / 2.5	31	12
GES	Federated Strategic Income Fund	STIAX	D-	(800) 341-7400	8.53	D- /1.4	-2.45 /13	0.83 /39	3.10 /47	D+ / 2.5	24	3
GL	Dreyfus Intl Bond A	DIBAX	D-	(800) 645-6561	15.34	D- /1.4	-1.16 /20	0.13 /28	1.62 /27	D+ / 2.8	75	10
GES	SunAmerica Strategic Bond A	SDIAX	D-	(800) 858-8850	3.28	D- /1.5	-2.07 /15	0.97 /42	3.26 /49	C- / 3.0	18	14
COH	Calvert High Yield Bond A	CYBAX	D-	(800) 368-2745	26.00	D- /1.5	-1.65 /17	1.32 /49	4.45 /67	D+ / 2.3	60	6
COH	First Inv Fund for Income A	FIFIX	D-	(800) 423-4026	2.37	D- /1.5	-2.25 /14	1.41 /50	4.27 /65	D / 2.0	61	7
USL	Loomis Sayles Infl Prot Sec Inst	LSGSX	D-	(800) 633-3330	10.51	D- /1.5	1.23 /62	-1.20 / 7	2.60 /39	D+ / 2.3	6	4
GES	Virtus Multi-Sec Intermediate Bd A	NAMFX	D-	(800) 243-1574	9.69	D /1.6	-1.19 /20	0.79 /39	3.51 /53	D+ / 2.8	28	22
US	T Rowe Price Infla-Protect Bond	PRIPX	D-	(800) 638-5660	11.95	D /1.7	1.20 /62	-1.01 / 8	2.54 /38	D+ / 2.4	6	14
COH	Hartford High Yield A	HAHAX	D-	(888) 843-7824	6.91	D /1.7	-3.53 /10	1.39 /50	3.78 /58	D / 1.8	56	4
GES	Morgan Stanley Gl Fxd Inc Opps A	DINAX	D-	(800) 869-6397	5.35	D /1.7	-3.54 / 9	1.72 /56	4.50 /68	D+ / 2.8	41	6
COH	Northern HY Fixed Income	NHFIX	D-	(800) 595-9111	6.42	D /2.0	-4.43 / 6	1.32 /49	4.25 /65	D- / 1.5	51	9
COI	Fidelity High Income	SPHIX	D-	(800) 544-8544	8.05	D /2.2	-4.92 / 5	0.78 /39	3.77 /58	D / 1.6	18	16
GEI	Schwab Trs Inflation Prot Sec	SWRSX	D-	(800) 407-0256	11.16	D+ /2.3	1.24 /62	-0.90 / 9	2.73 /41	D / 2.1	4	10
COH	BlackRock High Yield Bond Inv A	BHYAX	D-	(800) 441-7762	7.15	D+ /2.4	-4.67 / 6	1.88 /59	4.78 /70	D- / 1.5	77	9
COH	Federated High Income Bond A	FHIIX	D-	(800) 341-7400	7.06	D+ /2.4	-2.42 /14	1.97 /61	4.73 /70	D / 1.7	80	29
GL	GuideStone Global Bond Inv	GGBFX	D-	(888) 984-8433	9.39	D+ /2.4	-3.41 /10	0.03 /21	2.81 /42	D / 1.8	71	10
EM	• WA Global Government Bond I	WAFIX	D-	(888) 425-6432	8.18	D+ /2.5	-1.32 /19	0.10 /27	2.25 /34	D- / 1.3	73	18
COH	• Thrivent High Yield A	LBHYX	D-	(800) 847-4836	4.54	D+ /2.6	-3.21 /11	1.66 /55	4.59 /68	D / 1.6	69	19
GEI	Natixis Loomis Sayles Invst Gr Bd	LIGRX	D-	(800) 225-5478	11.18	D+ /2.6	-1.32 /19	0.95 /42	3.61 /55	D+ / 2.6	19	20
USS	Vanguard Infltn Pro Sec Inv	VIPSX	D-	(800) 662-7447	13.43	D+ /2.7	1.43 /65	-0.86 / 9	2.89 /43	D / 2.0	5	5
COH	Guggenheim High Yield A	SIHAX	D-	(800) 820-0888	10.34	D+ /2.6	-3.17 /11	2.35 /68	4.03 /62	D+ / 2.3	89	4
COH	Principal High Yield A	CPHYX	D-	(800) 222-5852	6.80	D+ /2.7	-3.85 / 8	1.67 /55	4.51 /68	D / 1.8	71	7
EM	TCW Emerging Markets Income N	TGINX	D-	(800) 386-3829	9.95	D+ /2.8	2.05 /72	-1.02 / 8	3.31 /50	E+ / 0.7	30	6
GEL	Natixis Loomis Sayles Strat Inc A	NEFZX	D-	(800) 225-5478	13.83	D+ /2.8	-5.57 / 4	2.10 /64	4.47 /67	E+ / 0.6	79	21
US	DFA Infltn Protected Sec Port Inst	DIPSX	D-	(800) 984-9472	11.95	D+ /2.8	1.88 /71	-0.84 / 9	3.24 /49	D- / 1.3	5	10
COH	Madison High Income A	MHNAX	D-	(800) 877-6089	5.76	D+ /2.9	-3.24 /11	1.59 /54	3.80 /58	D- / 1.4	61	11
COH	Virtus High Yield A	PHCHX	D-	(800) 243-1574	3.92	D+ /2.9	-2.65 /13	1.55 /53	4.59 /68	D / 1.8	63	5
COH	Deutsche Global High Income A	SGHAX	D-	(800) 728-3337	6.32	D+ /2.9	-2.33 /14	2.20 /66	4.74 /70	D / 1.8	85	10
GL	LM BW Global Opportunities Bond	GOBAX	D-	(877) 534-4627	10.64	D+ /2.9	-0.68 /24	0.19 /29	3.55 /54	E+ / 0.6	78	10
GL	Hartford Strategic Income A	HSNAX	D-	(888) 843-7824	8.42	D+ /2.9	-0.95 /22	1.30 /48	3.47 /53	D / 2.1	92	4
COH	Permanent Portfolio Versatile Bd	PRVBX	D-	(800) 531-5142	54.77	C- /3.0	-4.44 / 6	0.70 /37	1.75 /28	E+ / 0.9	36	13
EM	JPMorgan Emerg Mkt Debt A	JEDAX	D-	(800) 480-4111	7.91	C- /3.0	1.53 /67	0.35 /31	4.65 /69	E+ / 0.7	81	7
EM	Franklin Emg Mkt Debt Opportunity	FEMDX	D-	(800) 342-5236	10.08	C- /3.1	2.26 /73	-0.63 /11	3.07 /46	E+ / 0.7	41	10

• Denotes fund is closed to new investors

Section V

Performance: 100 Best and Worst Bond Mutual Funds

A compilation of those

Fixed Income Mutual Funds

receiving the highest and lowest Performance Ratings.

Funds are listed in order by Performance Rating.

Section V Contents

This section contains a summary analysis of each of the top 100 and bottom 100 bond mutual funds as determined by their TheStreet Performance Rating. Since the Performance Rating does not take into consideration the amount of risk a fund poses, the selection of funds presented here is based solely on each fund's financial performance over the past three years.

In order to optimize the utility of our top and bottom fund lists, rather than listing all funds in a multi-class series, a single fund from each series is selected for display as the primary share class. Whenever possible, the selected fund is one that a retail investor would be most likely to choose. This share class may not be appropriate for every investor, so please consult with your financial advisor, the fund company, and the fund's prospectus before placing your trade.

You can use this section to identify those funds that have historically given shareholders the highest returns on their investments. A word of caution though: past performance is not necessarily indicative of future results. While these funds have provided the highest returns, some of them may be currently overvalued and due for a correction.

1. Fund Type

The mutual fund's peer category based on its investment objective as stated in its prospectus.

COH	Corporate - High Yield	MMT	Money Market - Tax Free
COI	Corporate - Inv. Grade	MTG	Mortgage
EM	Emerging Market	MUH	Municipal - High Yield
GEN	General	MUI	Municipal - Insured
GEI	General - Inv. Grade	MUN	Municipal - National
GEL	General - Long Term	MUS	Municipal - Single State
GES	General - Short & Interm.	USL	U.S. Gov.- Long Term
GL	Global	USS	U.S. Gov. - Short & Interm
LP	Loan Participation	USA	U.S. Gov. - Agency
MM	Money Market	US	U.S. Gov. - Treasury

A blank fund type means that the mutual fund has not yet been categorized.

2. Fund Name

The name of the mutual fund as stated in its prospectus, which can sometimes differ slightly from the name that the company uses for advertising. If you cannot find the particular mutual fund you are interested in, or if you have any doubts regarding the precise name, verify the information with your broker or on your account statement. Also, use the fund's ticker symbol for confirmation. (See column 3.)

3. Ticker Symbol

The unique alphabetic symbol used for identifying and trading a specific mutual fund. No two funds can have the same ticker symbol, and the ticker symbol for mutual funds always ends with an "X".

A handful of funds currently show no associated ticker symbol. This means that the fund is either small or new since the NASD only assigns a ticker symbol to funds with at least $25 million in assets or 1,000 shareholders.

4. Overall Investment Rating	Our overall rating is measured on a scale from A to E based on each fund's risk-adjusted performance. Please see page 11 for specific descriptions of each letter grade. Also, refer to page 7 for information on how our ratings are derived. Most important, when using this rating, please be sure to consider the warnings beginning on page 13 regarding the ratings' limitations and the underlying assumptions.
5. Phone	The telephone number of the company managing the fund. Call this number to receive a prospectus or other information about the fund.
6. Net Asset Value (NAV)	The fund's share price as of the date indicated. A fund's NAV is computed by dividing the value of the fund's asset holdings, less accrued fees and expenses, by the number of its shares outstanding.
7. Performance Rating/Points	A letter grade rating based solely on the mutual fund's financial performance over the trailing three years, without any consideration for the amount of risk the fund poses. Like the overall Investment Rating, the Performance Rating is measured on a scale from A to E for ease of interpretation. The points score indicates where the Performance Rating falls on a scale of 0 to 10. In the case of funds investing in municipal or other tax-free securities, this rating is based on the taxable equivalent return of the fund assuming the maximum marginal U.S. tax rate (35%).
8. 1-Year Total Return	The total return the fund has provided investors over the preceding twelve months. This total return figure is computed based on the fund's dividend distributions and share price appreciation/depreciation during the period, net of the expenses and fees it imposes on its shareholders. Although the total return figure does not reflect an adjustment for any loads the fund may carry, such adjustments have been made in deriving TheStreet Investment Ratings.
9. 1-Year Total Return Percentile	The fund's percentile rank based on its one-year performance compared to that of all other fixed income funds in existence for at least one year. A score of 99 is the best possible, indicating that the fund outperformed 99% of the other mutual funds. Zero is the worst possible percentile score. In the case of funds investing in municipal or other tax-free securities, this percentile rank is based on the taxable equivalent return of the fund assuming the maximum marginal U.S. tax rate (35%).
10. 3-Year Total Return	The total annual return the fund has provided investors over the preceding three years.

11. 3-Year Total Return Percentile	The fund's percentile rank based on its three-year performance compared to that of all other fixed income funds in existence for at least three years. A score of 99 is the best possible, indicating that the fund outperformed 99% of the other mutual funds. Zero is the worst possible percentile score. In the case of funds investing in municipal or other tax-free securities, this percentile rank is based on the taxable equivalent return of the fund assuming the maximum marginal U.S. tax rate (35%).
12. 5-Year Total Return	The total annual return the fund has provided investors over the preceding five years.
13. 5-Year Total Return Percentile	The fund's percentile rank based on its five-year performance compared to that of all other fixed income funds in existence for at least five years. A score of 99 is the best possible, indicating that the fund outperformed 99% of the other mutual funds. Zero is the worst possible percentile score. In the case of funds investing in municipal or other tax-free securities, this percentile rank is based on the taxable equivalent return of the fund assuming the maximum marginal U.S. tax rate (35%).
14. Risk Rating/Points	A letter grade rating based solely on the mutual fund's risk as determined by its monthly performance volatility over the trailing three years and the underlying credit risk and interest rate risk of its investment portfolio. The risk rating does not take into consideration the overall financial performance the fund has achieved or the total return it has provided to its shareholders. Like the overall Investment Rating, the Risk Rating is measured on a scale from A to E for ease of interpretation. The points score indicates where the Risk Rating falls on a scale of 0 to 10.
15. Manager Quality Percentile	The manager quality percentile is based on a ranking of the fund's alpha, a statistical measure representing the difference between a fund's actual returns and its expected performance given its level of risk. Fund managers who have been able to exceed the fund's statistically expected performance receive a high percentile rank with 99 representing the highest possible score. At the other end of the spectrum, fund managers who have actually detracted from the fund's expected performance receive a low percentile rank with 0 representing the lowest possible score.
16. Manager Tenure	The number of years the current manager has been managing the fund. Since fund managers who deliver substandard returns are usually replaced, a long tenure is usually a good sign that shareholders are satisfied that the fund is achieving its stated objectives.

99 Pct = Best
0 Pct = Worst

Fund Type	Fund Name	Ticker Symbol	Overall Investment Rating	Phone	Net Asset Value As of 3/31/16	PERFORMANCE: Performance Rating/Pts	Annualized Total Return Through 3/31/16: 1Yr / Pct	3Yr / Pct	5Yr / Pct	RISK: Risk Rating/Pts	FUND MGR: Mgr. Quality Pct	Mgr. Tenure (Years)
MUH	MainStay High Yield Muni Bond C	MMHDX	**C+**	(800) 624-6782	12.35	**A+ / 9.9**	5.56 / 99	4.78 / 98	8.65 / 99	**D- / 1.3**	30	6
MUH	Nuveen High Yield Muni Bond A	NHMAX	**C**	(800) 257-8787	17.40	**A+ / 9.9**	6.17 / 99	6.24 / 99	10.93 / 99	**E+ / 0.7**	70	16
MUH	Nuveen CA High Yield Muni Bd A	NCHAX	**C**	(800) 257-8787	9.80	**A+ / 9.9**	6.23 / 99	6.89 / 99	11.74 / 99	**E+ / 0.6**	N/A	10
MUH	SEI Asset Alloc-Def Strat All A	STDAX	**C**	(800) 342-5734	14.31	**A+ / 9.9**	-0.19 / 29	7.15 / 99	8.98 / 99	**E / 0.5**	99	13
GES	Metropolitan West Alpha Trak 500	MWATX	**C**	(800) 496-8298	7.22	**A+ / 9.9**	0.53 / 50	11.58 / 99	11.75 / 98	**E- / 0.2**	99	18
US	Vanguard Extnd Durtn Trea Idx Inst	VEDTX	**C-**	(800) 662-7447	37.90	**A+ / 9.9**	1.34 / 64	8.82 / 99	15.40 / 99	**E- / 0.0**	12	3
GEI	PIMCO Extended Duration P	PEDPX	**C-**	(800) 426-0107	8.66	**A+ / 9.9**	0.63 / 52	8.61 / 99	15.16 / 99	**E- / 0.0**	4	9
MUS	Vanguard NY Long-Term	VNYTX	**A-**	(800) 662-7447	12.03	**A+ / 9.8**	4.85 / 98	4.36 / 97	5.94 / 92	**C / 4.3**	78	3
MUN	Vanguard Long-Term Tax-Exempt	VWLTX	**A-**	(800) 662-7447	11.87	**A+ / 9.8**	4.77 / 97	4.37 / 97	6.39 / 94	**C- / 3.9**	73	6
MUS	T Rowe Price CA Tax Free Bond	PRXCX	**A-**	(800) 638-5660	11.77	**A+ / 9.8**	4.56 / 97	4.39 / 97	6.82 / 96	**C- / 3.9**	74	13
MUS	Vanguard CA Long-Term	VCITX	**B+**	(800) 662-7447	12.34	**A+ / 9.8**	4.96 / 98	4.79 / 98	7.06 / 97	**C- / 3.6**	78	5
MUS	Vanguard OH Long-Term	VOHIX	**B+**	(800) 662-7447	12.78	**A+ / 9.8**	4.85 / 98	4.47 / 97	6.26 / 93	**C- / 3.6**	64	8
MUS	Nuveen CA Muni Bond A	NCAAX	**B+**	(800) 257-8787	11.39	**A+ / 9.8**	5.72 / 99	5.51 / 99	8.39 / 99	**C- / 3.3**	91	13
MUS	Northern CA T/E Bond	NCATX	**B+**	(800) 595-9111	12.06	**A+ / 9.8**	4.96 / 98	4.87 / 98	7.66 / 98	**C- / 3.2**	72	19
MUH	Vanguard High-Yield Tax-Exempt	VWAHX	**B**	(800) 662-7447	11.43	**A+ / 9.8**	4.73 / 97	4.40 / 97	6.82 / 96	**C- / 3.1**	71	6
MUH	Northern High Yield Muni	NHYMX	**B**	(800) 595-9111	9.02	**A+ / 9.8**	4.80 / 97	4.25 / 97	7.58 / 98	**C- / 3.1**	72	18
MUN	Sit Tax Free Income Fund	SNTIX	**B**	(800) 332-5580	9.80	**A+ / 9.8**	4.78 / 97	4.69 / 98	7.09 / 97	**C- / 3.0**	55	28
MUN	Dupree Taxable Muni Bd Srs	DUTMX	**B**	(800) 866-0614	10.78	**A+ / 9.8**	3.77 / 92	4.54 / 98	8.00 / 98	**D+ / 2.8**	86	6
MUH	Franklin California H/Y Muni A	FCAMX	**C+**	(800) 342-5236	10.94	**A+ / 9.8**	4.98 / 98	5.51 / 99	9.42 / 99	**D / 2.1**	82	23
MUN	Eaton Vance TABS 5to15 Yr Ldr	EALTX	**C+**	(800) 262-1122	12.26	**A+ / 9.8**	5.10 / 98	5.67 / 99	8.36 / 99	**D / 2.1**	54	6
MUH	PIMCO High Yield Muni Bond A	PYMAX	**C+**	(800) 426-0107	8.96	**A+ / 9.8**	7.10 / 99	4.55 / 98	7.59 / 98	**D / 1.9**	43	5
MUN	Eaton Vance High Yield Muni Inc A	ETHYX	**C+**	(800) 262-1122	8.99	**A+ / 9.8**	5.52 / 98	5.67 / 99	9.13 / 99	**D / 1.8**	49	12
MUH •	Invesco High Yield Municipal A	ACTHX	**C+**	(800) 959-4246	10.18	**A+ / 9.8**	5.96 / 99	5.60 / 99	8.79 / 99	**D- / 1.4**	73	14
MUH	AMG GW&K Municipal Enhcd Yld	GWMNX	**C**	(800) 835-3879	10.28	**A+ / 9.8**	4.86 / 98	4.36 / 97	8.33 / 99	**E+ / 0.6**	10	11
MUS	Vanguard PA Long-Term	VPAIX	**A-**	(800) 662-7447	11.79	**A+ / 9.7**	4.31 / 96	4.27 / 97	5.95 / 92	**C / 4.3**	75	5
MUS	Vanguard MA Tax-Exempt Inv	VMATX	**B+**	(800) 662-7447	11.03	**A+ / 9.7**	4.47 / 97	4.10 / 96	5.62 / 90	**C- / 3.9**	55	8
MUS	Fidelity OH Muni Inc	FOHFX	**B+**	(800) 544-8544	12.43	**A+ / 9.7**	4.59 / 97	4.30 / 97	5.80 / 91	**C- / 3.8**	74	10
MUS	Principal CA Municipal A	SRCMX	**B**	(800) 222-5852	10.68	**A+ / 9.7**	4.96 / 98	5.05 / 99	7.85 / 98	**C- / 3.1**	76	3
MUS	USAA California Bond Fund	USCBX	**B**	(800) 382-8722	11.29	**A+ / 9.7**	3.93 / 94	4.33 / 97	8.23 / 98	**D+ / 2.9**	59	10
MUH	American Century CA Hi-Yld Muni	CAYAX	**B-**	(800) 345-6488	10.68	**A+ / 9.7**	5.74 / 99	5.23 / 99	7.75 / 98	**D+ / 2.7**	83	29
MUH	American Funds High Inc Muni Bnd	AMHIX	**C+**	(800) 421-0180	15.81	**A+ / 9.7**	5.09 / 98	4.95 / 99	8.15 / 98	**D+ / 2.5**	78	22
MUH	T Rowe Price Tax-Free High Yield	PRFHX	**C+**	(800) 638-5660	12.09	**A+ / 9.7**	4.23 / 95	4.69 / 98	8.04 / 98	**D+ / 2.3**	49	14
MUH	AB High Income Municipal A	ABTHX	**C**	(800) 221-5672	11.51	**A+ / 9.7**	5.78 / 99	4.78 / 98	9.05 / 99	**E+ / 0.8**	18	6
USL	Rydex Govt Lg Bd 1.2x Strgy A	RYABX	**C-**	(800) 820-0888	58.50	**A+ / 9.7**	0.11 / 41	7.66 / 99	12.92 / 99	**E- / 0.0**	25	22
MUS	Fidelity AZ Muni Income Fd	FSAZX	**A-**	(800) 544-8544	12.29	**A+ / 9.6**	4.04 / 94	4.05 / 96	5.83 / 91	**C / 4.3**	68	6
MUN	Fidelity Tax Free Bond Fd	FTABX	**A-**	(800) 544-8544	11.77	**A+ / 9.6**	3.81 / 93	4.04 / 96	6.19 / 93	**C- / 4.2**	62	7
MUS	Vanguard NJ Long-Term	VNJTX	**B+**	(800) 662-7447	12.22	**A+ / 9.6**	3.92 / 93	3.76 / 94	5.77 / 91	**C- / 3.9**	44	3
MUN	Northern Tax Exempt	NOTEX	**B+**	(800) 595-9111	10.89	**A+ / 9.6**	4.28 / 96	3.87 / 95	6.14 / 93	**C- / 3.8**	45	18
MUN	T Rowe Price Summit Muni Income	PRINX	**B+**	(800) 638-5660	12.10	**A+ / 9.6**	4.08 / 94	3.99 / 96	6.59 / 95	**C- / 3.6**	46	17
MUN	MainStay Tax Free Bond Fund B	MKTBX	**B**	(800) 624-6782	10.15	**A+ / 9.6**	4.03 / 94	3.88 / 95	6.64 / 95	**C- / 3.0**	39	7
MUS	Lord Abbett Tax Free CA A	LCFIX	**B-**	(888) 522-2388	11.10	**A+ / 9.6**	4.48 / 97	4.57 / 98	7.56 / 98	**D+ / 2.9**	52	10
MUH	MFS Municipal High Income A	MMHYX	**C+**	(800) 225-2606	8.31	**A+ / 9.6**	5.72 / 99	4.79 / 98	8.16 / 98	**D / 1.8**	48	14
MUH	BlackRock High Yld Muni Inv A	MDYHX	**C**	(800) 441-7762	9.64	**A+ / 9.6**	6.17 / 99	4.82 / 98	8.66 / 99	**E+ / 0.6**	16	10
USL	Vanguard Long-Term Govt Bd Idx	VLGSX	**C-**	(800) 662-7447	26.97	**A+ / 9.6**	2.76 / 76	5.88 / 95	9.43 / 93	**E- / 0.2**	48	3
US	Vanguard Long-Term Treasury Inv	VUSTX	**C-**	(800) 662-7447	13.11	**A+ / 9.6**	2.54 / 75	5.83 / 95	9.46 / 93	**E- / 0.1**	24	15
US	Wasatch Hoisington US Treasury	WHOSX	**C-**	(800) 551-1700	18.59	**A+ / 9.6**	0.87 / 57	6.80 / 97	11.69 / 98	**E- / 0.0**	21	20
MUS	Vanguard CA Interm-Term T-E Inv	VCAIX	**A+**	(800) 662-7447	11.97	**A / 9.5**	4.04 / 94	3.73 / 94	5.54 / 89	**C+ / 5.9**	80	5
MUS	T Rowe Price NJ Tax-Free Bond	NJTFX	**B+**	(800) 638-5660	12.24	**A / 9.5**	3.66 / 92	3.67 / 94	5.90 / 91	**C / 4.3**	49	16
MUN	Dreyfus Municipal Bond	DRTAX	**B+**	(800) 645-6561	11.98	**A / 9.5**	4.25 / 95	3.69 / 94	5.85 / 91	**C- / 4.1**	47	7
MUS	T Rowe Price NY Tax Free Bd	PRNYX	**B+**	(800) 638-5660	11.90	**A / 9.5**	4.10 / 95	3.70 / 94	5.84 / 91	**C- / 4.1**	47	16
MUS	Dupree MS Tax Free Income	DUMSX	**B+**	(800) 866-0614	12.35	**A / 9.5**	3.85 / 93	3.86 / 95	5.63 / 90	**C- / 4.1**	55	16
MUN	USAA Tax-Exempt Long Term	USTEX	**B+**	(800) 382-8722	13.73	**A / 9.5**	3.88 / 93	3.81 / 95	6.86 / 96	**C- / 3.7**	50	N/A

• Denotes fund is closed to new investors

99 Pct = Best
0 Pct = Worst

Fund Type	Fund Name	Ticker Symbol	Overall Investment Rating	Phone	Net Asset Value As of 3/31/16	PERFORMANCE: Performance Rating/Pts	Annualized Total Return Through 3/31/16: 1Yr / Pct	3Yr / Pct	5Yr / Pct	RISK: Risk Rating/Pts	FUND MGR: Mgr. Quality Pct	Mgr. Tenure (Years)
MUS	Columbia CA Tax Exempt A	CLMPX	**B+**	(800) 345-6611	7.98	**A / 9.5**	4.14 / 95	4.66 / 98	7.62 / 98	**C- / 3.7**	77	6
MUH	Fidelity Municipal Inc	FHIGX	**B**	(800) 544-8544	13.55	**A / 9.5**	3.75 / 92	3.98 / 96	6.05 / 92	**C- / 3.5**	61	7
MUI	• Franklin California Ins Tx-Fr A	FRCIX	**B**	(800) 342-5236	13.27	**A / 9.5**	3.98 / 94	5.10 / 99	7.46 / 97	**C- / 3.3**	82	25
MUH	Columbia High Yield Municipal A	LHIAX	**C+**	(800) 345-6611	10.80	**A / 9.5**	4.24 / 95	4.70 / 98	7.86 / 98	**D+ / 2.6**	74	7
MUN	Oppenheimer Rochester AMT-Free	OPTAX	**C**	(888) 470-0862	6.98	**A / 9.5**	5.85 / 99	4.70 / 98	10.14 / 99	**D- / 1.3**	23	14
MUH	Oppeneheimer Rochester Hi Yld	ORNAX	**C-**	(888) 470-0862	7.10	**A / 9.5**	6.68 / 99	4.44 / 97	9.32 / 99	**E / 0.5**	11	15
US	Fidelity Spartan Lg-T Tre Bd In Inv	FLBIX	**C-**	(800) 544-8544	13.73	**A / 9.5**	2.50 / 75	5.81 / 94	9.46 / 93	**E- / 0.1**	22	2
GEI	Columbia Abs Rtn Currency & Inc	RACWX	**C-**	(800) 345-6611	10.37	**A / 9.5**	5.57 / 91	5.65 / 94	3.81 / 58	**E- / 0.1**	96	10
MUS	Fidelity MI Muni Inc	FMHTX	**A+**	(800) 544-8544	12.48	**A / 9.4**	4.11 / 95	3.62 / 93	5.20 / 87	**C+ / 5.7**	76	10
MUS	Fidelity PA Muni Inc	FPXTX	**A**	(800) 544-8544	11.39	**A / 9.4**	3.54 / 90	3.79 / 95	5.47 / 89	**C / 5.1**	74	14
MUS	Sit MN Tax Free Income	SMTFX	**A**	(800) 332-5580	10.63	**A / 9.4**	3.89 / 93	3.61 / 93	5.74 / 91	**C / 5.0**	69	23
MUS	Fidelity CT Muni Income Fd	FICNX	**A**	(800) 544-8544	11.87	**A / 9.4**	4.18 / 95	3.54 / 93	4.91 / 85	**C / 5.0**	58	14
MUS	Northern AZ Tax Exempt	NOAZX	**A-**	(800) 595-9111	10.96	**A / 9.4**	4.06 / 94	3.54 / 93	5.66 / 90	**C / 4.7**	53	17
MUS	Northern CA Intermediate T/E	NCITX	**A-**	(800) 595-9111	11.03	**A / 9.4**	4.02 / 94	3.44 / 92	5.17 / 87	**C / 4.6**	49	17
MUS	Wells Fargo CA Tax Fr A	SCTAX	**A-**	(800) 222-8222	12.15	**A / 9.4**	4.19 / 95	4.78 / 98	7.32 / 97	**C / 4.5**	89	7
MUS	Fidelity MA Muni Inc Fd	FDMMX	**A-**	(800) 544-8544	12.60	**A / 9.4**	3.93 / 93	3.75 / 94	5.59 / 89	**C / 4.4**	55	6
MUS	T Rowe Price GA Tax-Free Bd	GTFBX	**A-**	(800) 638-5660	11.79	**A / 9.4**	3.77 / 92	3.64 / 93	5.85 / 91	**C / 4.4**	53	19
MUN	T Rowe Price Tax-Free Income	PRTAX	**B+**	(800) 638-5660	10.44	**A / 9.4**	3.48 / 90	3.63 / 93	6.03 / 92	**C- / 4.2**	47	9
MUS	T Rowe Price VA Tax-Free Bond	PRVAX	**B+**	(800) 638-5660	12.24	**A / 9.4**	3.79 / 93	3.48 / 93	5.61 / 90	**C- / 4.1**	41	19
MUN	Columbia AMT-Free Tax-Exempt	INTAX	**B**	(800) 345-6611	4.09	**A / 9.4**	4.17 / 95	4.32 / 97	7.07 / 97	**C- / 3.5**	70	9
MUS	Franklin California Tx-Fr Inc A	FKTFX	**B-**	(800) 342-5236	7.59	**A / 9.4**	3.82 / 93	4.67 / 98	7.51 / 97	**C- / 3.2**	60	25
MUH	Federated Muni High Yield Advn A	FMOAX	**C+**	(800) 341-7400	9.06	**A / 9.4**	5.03 / 98	4.74 / 98	8.00 / 98	**D / 2.1**	59	7
MUH	Prudential Muni High Income A	PRHAX	**C+**	(800) 225-1852	10.39	**A / 9.4**	4.86 / 98	4.52 / 98	7.51 / 97	**D / 1.8**	39	12
MUH	Delaware Natl HY Muni Bd A	CXHYX	**C+**	(800) 523-1918	11.05	**A / 9.4**	5.06 / 98	4.59 / 98	8.43 / 99	**D / 1.8**	34	13
MUS	Schwab California Tax-Free Bond	SWCAX	**A+**	(800) 407-0256	12.15	**A / 9.3**	3.46 / 90	3.45 / 92	5.00 / 85	**C+ / 6.8**	80	8
MUS	T Rowe Price MD Tax Free Bd	MDXBX	**A**	(800) 638-5660	10.98	**A / 9.3**	3.68 / 92	3.49 / 93	5.78 / 91	**C / 4.9**	54	16
MUN	Elfun Tax Exempt Income	ELFTX	**B+**	(800) 242-0134	11.95	**A / 9.3**	3.83 / 93	3.40 / 92	5.55 / 89	**C / 4.3**	42	16
MUS	Nuveen CO Muni Bond A	FCOTX	**B**	(800) 257-8787	10.96	**A / 9.3**	4.71 / 97	4.38 / 97	6.60 / 95	**C- / 3.7**	74	5
MUN	PIMCO Municipal Bond A	PMLAX	**B**	(800) 426-0107	9.90	**A / 9.3**	4.53 / 97	3.78 / 94	6.01 / 92	**C- / 3.4**	38	5
MUS	MFS CA Municipal Bond Fund A	MCFTX	**B-**	(800) 225-2606	6.14	**A / 9.3**	5.22 / 98	4.37 / 97	7.34 / 97	**C- / 3.2**	47	17
MUS	Invesco California Tax-Free Inc A	CLFAX	**B-**	(800) 959-4246	12.40	**A / 9.3**	4.84 / 97	4.45 / 97	7.27 / 97	**C- / 3.2**	59	7
MUN	Eaton Vance CA Municipal Opptys	EACAX	**C+**	(800) 262-1122	10.53	**A / 9.3**	5.67 / 99	4.44 / 97	7.44 / 97	**D+ / 2.7**	34	2
MUN	Pioneer AMT-Free Muni A	PBMFX	**C+**	(800) 225-6292	14.77	**A / 9.3**	5.10 / 98	4.38 / 97	7.80 / 98	**D+ / 2.6**	30	10
GEI	• Vanguard Long-Term Inv Gr Inv	VWESX	**C-**	(800) 662-7447	10.43	**A / 9.3**	1.25 / 62	5.31 / 92	8.70 / 90	**E / 0.3**	23	8
US	T Rowe Price US Treas Long-Term	PRULX	**C-**	(800) 638-5660	13.52	**A / 9.3**	2.21 / 73	5.08 / 91	8.75 / 90	**E- / 0.2**	15	13
US	Dreyfus US Treasury Long Term	DRGBX	**C-**	(800) 645-6561	20.54	**A / 9.3**	2.10 / 72	5.03 / 91	8.77 / 90	**E- / 0.2**	19	8
USA	ProFunds-US Government Plus	GVPSX	**C-**	(888) 776-3637	53.63	**A / 9.3**	-2.08 / 15	5.21 / 92	10.55 / 96	**E- / 0.0**	5	7
MUS	Saturna Idaho Tax-Exempt	NITEX	**A+**	(800) 728-8762	5.53	**A- / 9.2**	3.68 / 92	3.23 / 90	4.09 / 78	**B- / 7.3**	80	21
MUN	Vanguard Interm-Term Tax-Exempt	VWITX	**A+**	(800) 662-7447	14.39	**A- / 9.2**	3.65 / 91	3.19 / 90	4.91 / 85	**C+ / 6.5**	N/A	3
MUS	Dupree TN Tax-Free Income	TNTIX	**A+**	(800) 866-0614	11.72	**A- / 9.2**	3.11 / 86	3.27 / 91	4.95 / 85	**C+ / 5.8**	61	12
MUS	Dupree AL Tax Free Income	DUALX	**A**	(800) 866-0614	12.56	**A- / 9.2**	3.13 / 86	3.41 / 92	5.50 / 89	**C+ / 5.6**	68	15
MUS	Dupree NC Tax Free Income	NTFIX	**A**	(800) 866-0614	11.78	**A- / 9.2**	3.48 / 90	3.21 / 90	5.42 / 88	**C / 5.1**	49	12
MUS	Fidelity MD Muni Income Fd	SMDMX	**A-**	(800) 544-8544	11.52	**A- / 9.2**	3.94 / 94	3.31 / 91	4.85 / 84	**C / 4.8**	46	14
MUS	Virtus California T/E Bond A	CTESX	**B+**	(800) 243-1574	12.06	**A- / 9.2**	4.03 / 94	4.04 / 96	6.28 / 94	**C / 4.3**	N/A	20
MUN	AMG GW&K Municipal Bond Inv	GWMTX	**B+**	(800) 835-3879	11.86	**A- / 9.2**	3.91 / 93	3.09 / 89	5.18 / 87	**C- / 4.2**	34	7
MUN	Nuveen All Amer Muni A	FLAAX	**C+**	(800) 257-8787	11.72	**A- / 9.2**	4.37 / 96	4.32 / 97	7.51 / 97	**D+ / 2.9**	45	6
MUH	Lord Abbett Tx Fr High Yld Muni A	HYMAX	**C-**	(888) 522-2388	11.78	**A- / 9.2**	4.47 / 97	3.59 / 93	7.23 / 97	**E+ / 0.9**	13	12
MUN	USAA Tax-Exempt Interm-Term	USATX	**A+**	(800) 382-8722	13.61	**A- / 9.1**	3.43 / 89	3.12 / 89	5.34 / 88	**B- / 7.3**	75	13

• Denotes fund is closed to new investors

						PERFORMANCE				RISK	FUND MGR	
	99 Pct = Best 0 Pct = Worst						Annualized Total Return Through 3/31/16					
Fund Type	Fund Name	Ticker Symbol	Overall Investment Rating	Phone	Net Asset Value As of 3/31/16	Performance Rating/Pts	1Yr / Pct	3Yr / Pct	5Yr / Pct	Risk Rating/Pts	Mgr. Quality Pct	Mgr. Tenure (Years)
USS	Rydex Inv Govt Lg Bd Stgy A	RYAQX	E-	(800) 820-0888	33.11	E- / 0.0	-4.47 / 6	-8.17 / 1	-12.35 / 0	E- / 0.0	33	8
GEI	Credit Suisse Cmdty Rtn Strat A	CRSAX	E-	(877) 927-2874	4.46	E- / 0.0	-19.78 / 0	-17.07 / 0	-14.54 / 0	E- / 0.0	0	10
GEI	Rydex Wekng Dlr 2x Stgry A	RYWDX	E-	(800) 820-0888	12.55	E- / 0.0	6.54 / 95	-9.53 / 0	-9.21 / 0	E- / 0.0	0	11
GEI	Credit Suisse Commdty Ret Str	CCRSX	E-	(877) 927-2874	3.94	E- / 0.0	-19.59 / 0	-17.04 / 0	-14.55 / 0	E- / 0.0	0	10
COH	Catalyst/SMH High Income A	HIIFX	E-	(866) 447-4228	3.12	E- / 0.0	-25.42 / 0	-13.08 / 0	-6.60 / 0	E- / 0.0	0	8
GES	AB All Mkt Real Return A	AMTAX	E-	(800) 221-5672	7.61	E- / 0.0	-14.66 / 0	-10.78 / 0	-7.62 / 0	E- / 0.0	0	1
EM	PIMCO Emerging Local Bond A	PELAX	E-	(800) 426-0107	7.21	E- / 0.0	-4.80 / 5	-8.77 / 0	-3.27 / 1	E- / 0.1	0	10
EM	Goldman Sachs Local Emg Mkt	GAMDX	E-	(800) 526-7384	6.36	E- / 0.0	-3.57 / 9	-8.58 / 0	-3.06 / 1	E- / 0.1	0	8
EM	Dreyfus Eme Mkts Dbt LC A	DDBAX	E-	(800) 782-6620	11.18	E- / 0.0	-5.19 / 5	-8.57 / 0	-3.42 / 1	E- / 0.1	0	8
COH	Third Avenue Focused Credit Inv	TFCVX	E-	(800) 443-1021	5.21	E- / 0.0	-33.70 / 0	-13.13 / 0	-5.44 / 0	E- / 0.1	0	7
US	Direxion Mo 7-10 Year Tr Br 2X Inv	DXKSX	E-	(800) 851-0511	29.47	E- / 0.0	-9.93 / 1	-8.96 / 0	-14.53 / 0	E- / 0.2	11	12
GES	Northeast Investors Trust	NTHEX	E-	(800) 225-6704	3.83	E- / 0.0	-25.81 / 0	-9.21 / 0	-2.75 / 1	E- / 0.2	0	N/A
EM	Invesco Emerg Mkts Flexible Bond	IAEMX	E-	(800) 959-4246	6.38	E- / 0.0	-10.75 / 0	-9.82 / 0	-4.41 / 0	E- / 0.2	0	3
USS	PIMCO StocksPLUS Short A	PSSAX	E-	(800) 426-0107	10.27	E- / 0.0	-6.53 / 3	-12.27 / 0	-10.75 / 0	E / 0.3	0	2
COH	Access Flex Bear High Yield Inv	AFBIX	E-	(888) 776-3637	8.68	E- / 0.0	-7.66 / 2	-9.52 / 0	-12.00 / 0	E+ / 0.7	0	11
COH	Rydex Inv High Yld Strtgy A	RYILX	E-	(800) 820-0888	17.92	E- / 0.0	-6.81 / 2	-9.25 / 0	-10.94 / 0	E+ / 0.8	1	9
GL	Templeton Hard Currency A	ICPHX	E	(800) 342-5236	7.77	E- / 0.0	-6.16 / 3	-6.45 / 1	-4.14 / 0	D / 1.6	1	15
EM	Eaton Vance Emer Market Local	EEIAX	E-	(800) 262-1122	6.29	E- / 0.1	-0.87 / 23	-7.77 / 1	-3.03 / 1	E- / 0.1	1	8
EM	EuroPac International Bond A	EPIBX	E-	(888) 558-5851	8.14	E- / 0.1	-3.34 / 10	-5.75 / 1	-2.60 / 1	E / 0.5	2	6
GL	Nuveen High Income Bond A	FJSIX	E-	(800) 257-8787	6.77	E- / 0.1	-12.80 / 0	-2.70 / 3	1.74 / 28	E+ / 0.6	8	11
MTG	ProFunds-Falling US Dollar Svc	FDPSX	E-	(888) 776-3637	17.27	E- / 0.1	0.82 / 56	-7.00 / 1	-6.83 / 0	E+ / 0.8	1	7
COH	Western Asset Short Dur High Inc	SHIAX	E	(877) 534-4627	4.93	E- / 0.1	-11.38 / 0	-2.38 / 3	2.08 / 32	D- / 1.0	5	10
LP	Driehaus Select Credit Fund	DRSLX	E+	(800) 560-6111	7.80	E- / 0.1	-11.39 / 0	-3.93 / 2	-1.45 / 1	D+ / 2.3	3	6
US	American Century Str Inf Opp Fd A	ASIDX	E+	(800) 345-6488	9.17	E- / 0.1	-4.78 / 5	-3.94 / 2	-2.91 / 1	D+ / 2.6	4	6
GEI	Dreyfus Opportunistic Fixed Inc A	DSTAX	D-	(800) 782-6620	11.02	E- / 0.1	-10.91 / 0	-2.39 / 3	0.61 / 18	C- / 3.6	8	6
GL	UBS Fixed Income Opportunities A	FNOAX	D-	(888) 793-8637	8.47	E- / 0.1	-7.52 / 2	-3.61 / 2	-1.25 / 1	C / 4.3	6	6
EM	Janus Emerging Markets A	JMFAX	E-	(800) 295-2687	7.58	E- / 0.2	-10.08 / 1	-2.48 / 3	-4.67 / 0	E- / 0.0	9	4
EM	Oppenheimer Em Mkts Local Debt	OEMAX	E-	(888) 470-0862	7.40	E- / 0.2	-0.01 / 31	-5.76 / 1	-1.19 / 1	E- / 0.2	2	1
GL	TCW Emg Mkts Local Currency Inc	TGWNX	E-	(800) 386-3829	8.53	E- / 0.2	-3.29 / 10	-6.71 / 1	-1.57 / 1	E- / 0.2	1	6
COH	Franklin High Income A	FHAIX	E-	(800) 342-5236	1.66	E- / 0.2	-11.00 / 0	-1.74 / 5	2.56 / 38	E / 0.4	5	25
MUS ●	Franklin Double Tax-Free Inc A	FPRTX	E-	(800) 342-5236	9.34	E- / 0.2	-0.50 / 26	-3.26 / 2	1.47 / 34	E / 0.5	1	30
GL	Lord Abbett Emerg Mkts Currency	LDMAX	E-	(888) 522-2388	5.27	E- / 0.2	-2.47 / 13	-4.61 / 2	-2.68 / 1	E / 0.5	4	9
GL	PIMCO Emerging Markets	PLMAX	E-	(800) 426-0107	8.75	E- / 0.2	-1.69 / 17	-4.48 / 2	-2.75 / 1	E+ / 0.6	4	11
EM	Deutsche Enh Emg Mrkts Fxd Inc	SZEAX	E-	(800) 728-3337	9.04	E- / 0.2	-2.95 / 12	-2.87 / 3	0.40 / 17	E+ / 0.7	8	5
GL	Templeton International Bond A	TBOAX	E	(800) 342-5236	10.10	E- / 0.2	-3.65 / 9	-2.73 / 3	0.28 / 16	D / 1.6	8	9
GL	Forward EM Corporate Debt C	FFXCX	E+	(800) 999-6809	7.43	E- / 0.2	-6.72 / 2	-3.04 / 2	-0.70 / 2	D / 1.9	7	5
GES	Putnam Diversified Income A	PDINX	E+	(800) 225-1581	6.63	E- / 0.2	-7.23 / 2	-0.93 / 9	1.10 / 21	D / 2.1	88	22
GL	Federated Prudent DollarBear A	PSAFX	E+	(800) 341-7400	10.09	E- / 0.2	3.81 / 80	-4.14 / 2	-3.56 / 1	D / 2.1	5	16
GL	Columbia Global Bond A	IGBFX	E+	(800) 345-6611	5.80	E- / 0.2	-3.65 / 9	-2.90 / 3	-0.32 / 2	D / 2.2	8	3
GL	Eaton Vance Dvsfd Currency	EAIIX	D-	(800) 262-1122	8.95	E- / 0.2	-1.16 / 20	-2.98 / 2	-0.66 / 2	C / 5.0	7	8
EM	SEI Inst Intl Emerging Mkts Debt A	SITEX	E-	(800) 342-5734	9.39	E / 0.3	-1.31 / 19	-3.98 / 2	1.13 / 22	E / 0.3	6	10
GEI	API Efficient Frontier Income Fd A	APIUX	E-	(800) 544-6060	9.51	E / 0.3	-5.80 / 3	-1.63 / 5	2.31 / 35	E / 0.3	6	19
COH	Direxion Dynamic HY Bond Fd	PDHYX	E-	(800) 851-0511	10.62	E / 0.3	-8.56 / 1	-1.80 / 5	1.37 / 24	E / 0.5	6	6
COH	WA Global High Yield Bond A	SAHYX	E-	(877) 534-4627	5.83	E / 0.3	-6.59 / 3	-1.54 / 6	2.51 / 38	E+ / 0.7	6	10
GEI	Nuveen Symphony Credit Oppty A	NCOAX	E	(800) 257-8787	18.41	E / 0.3	-8.51 / 1	-0.26 / 13	3.73 / 57	D- / 1.3	14	6
GL	Pioneer Global High Yield A	PGHYX	E	(800) 225-6292	8.23	E / 0.3	-5.29 / 4	-1.55 / 6	1.37 / 24	D- / 1.4	17	15
GL	Aberdeen Global High Income A	BJBHX	E+	(866) 667-9231	8.33	E / 0.3	-10.69 / 1	-1.10 / 8	2.01 / 31	D / 2.0	26	14
GL	PIMCO Glb Advantage Strategy Bd	PGSAX	E+	(800) 426-0107	10.06	E / 0.3	-1.33 / 19	-2.32 / 3	0.28 / 16	D / 2.1	10	5
GL	Leader Total Return Inv	LCTRX	E+	(800) 711-9164	9.08	E / 0.3	-11.20 / 0	-0.65 / 10	1.82 / 29	D+ / 2.4	39	6
GEI	Franklin Real Return A	FRRAX	D-	(800) 342-5236	9.84	E / 0.3	-3.38 / 10	-1.85 / 5	-0.65 / 2	C- / 3.7	7	12
GEI	PIMCO Unconstrained Bond A	PUBAX	D	(800) 426-0107	10.19	E / 0.3	-3.50 / 10	-1.45 / 6	0.77 / 19	C+ / 6.2	10	2
USS	Pacific Advisors Govt Secs A	PADGX	D+	(800) 282-6693	8.96	E / 0.3	-0.68 / 24	-1.08 / 8	-0.45 / 2	B+ / 8.8	20	6

● Denotes fund is closed to new investors

Fund Type	Fund Name (99 Pct = Best, 0 Pct = Worst)	Ticker Symbol	Overall Investment Rating	Phone	Net Asset Value As of 3/31/16	PERFORMANCE: Performance Rating/Pts	Annualized Total Return Through 3/31/16: 1Yr / Pct	3Yr / Pct	5Yr / Pct	RISK: Risk Rating/Pts	FUND MGR: Mgr. Quality Pct	Mgr. Tenure (Years)
COH	J Hancock Core High Yld A	JYIAX	**E**	(800) 257-3336	8.91	**E /0.4**	-7.58 / 2	-0.19 /14	3.90 /60	**E+ / 0.6**	12	7
COH	J Hancock High Yield NAV		**E**	(800) 257-3336	7.29	**E /0.4**	-8.75 / 1	-1.18 / 7	2.89 /43	**E+ / 0.7**	7	10
COH	WA High Yield IS	WAHSX	**E**	(888) 425-6432	7.36	**E /0.4**	-8.64 / 1	-1.00 / 8	2.97 /45	**E+ / 0.8**	8	11
GL	Templeton Global Total Return A	TGTRX	**E**	(800) 342-5236	11.40	**E /0.4**	-5.04 / 5	-1.03 / 8	2.43 /37	**E+ / 0.8**	28	8
GEI	PIMCO Real Return A	PRTNX	**E**	(800) 426-0107	10.92	**E /0.4**	-0.70 /24	-2.04 / 4	2.24 /34	**D- / 1.1**	1	9
COH	Ivy High Income A	WHIAX	**E**	(800) 777-6472	6.91	**E /0.4**	-7.85 / 1	0.38 /31	4.66 /69	**D- / 1.2**	22	3
GEI	Columbia Inflation Protected Sec A	APSAX	**E**	(800) 345-6611	8.90	**E /0.4**	-1.55 /18	-2.67 / 3	1.65 /27	**D- / 1.3**	2	4
LP	Highland Floating Rate Opps A	HFRAX	**E+**	(877) 665-1287	6.63	**E /0.4**	-10.42 / 1	0.76 /38	3.69 /56	**D / 2.1**	73	4
US	Hartford Inflation Plus A	HIPAX	**E+**	(888) 843-7824	10.83	**E /0.4**	0.84 /56	-2.20 / 4	1.90 /30	**C- / 3.0**	4	1
GEI	Federated Real Return Bond A	RRFAX	**D-**	(800) 341-7400	10.24	**E /0.4**	-0.10 /30	-1.66 / 5	0.70 /18	**C- / 3.9**	6	10
GES	Hartford Unconstrained Bond A	HTIAX	**D-**	(888) 843-7824	9.36	**E /0.4**	-2.62 /13	-0.70 /10	2.20 /34	**C / 5.0**	10	4
GEI	J Hancock Fltng Rate Inc A	JFIAX	**D-**	(800) 257-3336	8.09	**E /0.4**	-5.73 / 4	-0.63 /11	1.65 /27	**C / 5.3**	28	9
LP	Deutsche Floating Rate A	DFRAX	**D**	(800) 728-3337	8.29	**E /0.4**	-5.54 / 4	-0.50 /11	1.55 /26	**B- / 7.1**	31	9
GL	STAAR AltCat	SITAX	**E-**	(800) 332-7738	13.10	**E /0.5**	-10.70 / 1	-0.69 /10	0.05 /12	**E- / 0.2**	39	19
EM	BlackRock Emg Mkts Flex Dyn Bd	BAEDX	**E-**	(800) 441-7762	8.82	**E /0.5**	2.27 /73	-2.09 / 4	3.51 /53	**E / 0.4**	12	8
COH	First Eagle High Yield I	FEHIX	**E**	(800) 334-2143	8.18	**E /0.5**	-7.73 / 2	-0.74 /10	2.97 /45	**E+ / 0.7**	9	N/A
COH	Delaware High-Yield Opps A	DHOAX	**E**	(800) 523-1918	3.58	**E /0.5**	-6.76 / 2	-0.10 /15	3.44 /52	**E+ / 0.9**	13	4
COH	American Funds High Income Tr A	AHITX	**E**	(800) 421-0180	9.46	**E /0.5**	-7.19 / 2	-0.21 /14	2.76 /41	**D- / 1.0**	12	27
COH	MainStay High Yield Opps C	MYHYX	**E**	(800) 624-6782	9.89	**E /0.5**	-7.94 / 1	-1.27 / 7	2.13 /33	**D- / 1.1**	7	9
GL	Templeton Global Bond A	TPINX	**E**	(800) 342-5236	11.49	**E /0.5**	-4.31 / 7	-0.63 /11	1.93 /30	**D- / 1.1**	39	15
USL	Deutsche Global Inflation A	TIPAX	**E**	(800) 728-3337	9.98	**E /0.5**	-0.25 /29	-1.80 / 5	1.78 /28	**D- / 1.3**	5	6
COH	Goldman Sachs High Yield A	GSHAX	**E**	(800) 526-7384	6.02	**E /0.5**	-6.37 / 3	0.59 /35	3.70 /56	**D- / 1.3**	27	7
COH	Pax High Yield Inv	PAXHX	**E**	(800) 767-1729	6.16	**E /0.5**	-7.53 / 2	-0.96 / 9	2.13 /33	**D / 1.6**	9	1
GEI	American Century Infl Adj Bd A	AIAVX	**E+**	(800) 345-6488	11.73	**E /0.5**	0.73 /54	-1.69 / 5	2.21 /34	**D / 2.2**	2	10
GEI	Principal Infl Prot A	PITAX	**E+**	(800) 222-5852	8.44	**E /0.5**	-0.47 /26	-1.69 / 5	2.00 /31	**D+ / 2.4**	3	6
GES	BlackRock Inflation Prot Bond Inv	BPRAX	**E+**	(800) 441-7762	10.47	**E /0.5**	-0.37 /27	-1.63 / 5	1.99 /31	**D+ / 2.5**	3	6
GL	Waddell & Reed Adv Global Bond	UNHHX	**D-**	(888) 923-3355	3.55	**E /0.5**	-1.59 /18	-0.64 /11	1.14 /22	**C- / 3.3**	40	14
GL	Goldman Sachs Strategic Income	GSZAX	**D**	(800) 526-7384	9.41	**E /0.5**	-2.49 /13	-0.42 /12	2.14 /33	**C / 5.3**	44	6
GES	Natixis Loomis Sayles Strat Alpha	LABAX	**D**	(800) 225-5478	9.38	**E /0.5**	-3.24 /11	-0.21 /14	1.56 /26	**C+ / 6.4**	21	6
GL	Putnam Absolute Return 300 A	PTRNX	**D**	(800) 225-1581	9.39	**E /0.5**	-4.76 / 5	-0.51 /11	-0.03 / 3	**C+ / 6.7**	42	8
GES	Deutsche Ultra-Short Duration A	SDUAX	**D+**	(800) 728-3337	8.27	**E /0.5**	-2.52 /13	-0.63 /11	0.57 /18	**B / 8.1**	44	8
MUS •	Oppenheimer Rochester VA Muni	ORVAX	**E-**	(888) 470-0862	8.01	**E+ /0.6**	-0.52 /26	-0.69 /10	5.33 /88	**E / 0.3**	1	10
COI	Federated Emerging Mkt Debt A	IHIAX	**E-**	(800) 341-7400	8.20	**E+ /0.6**	0.26 /45	-1.76 / 5	3.16 /48	**E / 0.3**	3	3
MUS •	Oppenheimer Rochester MD Muni	ORMDX	**E**	(888) 470-0862	9.44	**E+ /0.6**	0.68 /59	-0.60 /11	4.76 /83	**E / 0.4**	1	10
EM	WA Emerging Markets Debt A	LWEAX	**E-**	(888) 425-6432	4.73	**E+ /0.6**	-0.16 /30	-1.65 / 5	2.35 /36	**E / 0.4**	17	3
COH	Natixis Loomis Sayles High Income	NEFHX	**E**	(800) 225-5478	3.84	**E+ /0.6**	-6.30 / 3	0.29 /30	3.33 /50	**E / 0.5**	14	14
GES	USAA Real Return Fund	USRRX	**E**	(800) 382-8722	9.47	**E+ /0.6**	-3.81 / 8	-1.85 / 5	1.16 /22	**E+ / 0.8**	5	6
COH	CGCM High Yield Invest	THYUX	**E**	(800) 444-4273	3.55	**E+ /0.6**	-7.92 / 1	-0.59 /11	2.71 /40	**D- / 1.1**	10	10
COH	AllianzGI High Yield Bond A	AYBAX	**E**	(800) 988-8380	8.57	**E+ /0.6**	-6.05 / 3	0.23 /29	3.45 /52	**D- / 1.2**	18	20
COH	Calamos High Income A	CHYDX	**E**	(800) 582-6959	8.16	**E+ /0.6**	-5.75 / 3	0.23 /29	2.91 /44	**D- / 1.3**	19	17
COH	Nationwide High Yield Bond A	GGHAX	**E**	(800) 848-0920	5.48	**E+ /0.6**	-6.10 / 3	0.49 /33	3.29 /50	**D- / 1.4**	25	6
COH	Dunham High-Yield Bond A	DAHYX	**E+**	(888) 338-6426	8.61	**E+ /0.6**	-3.93 / 8	-0.05 /15	2.47 /37	**D / 1.8**	17	11
GES	Fidelity Adv Inflation-Protect Bd A	FIPAX	**E+**	(800) 522-7297	12.03	**E+ /0.6**	0.65 /52	-1.48 / 6	2.24 /34	**D / 2.2**	2	12
GES	PIMCO Floating Income A	PFIAX	**E+**	(800) 426-0107	7.67	**E+ /0.6**	-2.82 /12	-0.73 /10	0.77 /19	**D / 2.2**	29	11
USS	AI US Infl Protected A	FNIHX	**E+**	(866) 410-2006	10.67	**E+ /0.6**	1.07 /60	-1.43 / 6	2.39 /36	**D / 2.2**	5	10
GEI	MassMutual Premier Infl-Pl A	MPSAX	**E+**	(800) 542-6767	10.30	**E+ /0.6**	0.90 /57	-1.25 / 7	2.51 /38	**D+ / 2.3**	3	13
GL	Oppenheimer Intl Bond A	OIBAX	**E+**	(888) 470-0862	5.70	**E+ /0.6**	-0.50 /26	-1.20 / 7	1.08 /21	**D+ / 2.3**	25	3
USS	MFS Inflation Adjusted Bond A	MIAAX	**E+**	(800) 225-2606	10.48	**E+ /0.6**	0.82 /56	-1.48 / 6	2.21 /34	**D+ / 2.4**	4	13

• Denotes fund is closed to new investors

Data as of March 31, 2016

Section VI

Risk:
100 Best and Worst Bond Mutual Funds

A compilation of those

Fixed Income Mutual Funds

receiving the highest and lowest Risk Ratings.

Funds are listed in order by Risk Rating.

Section VI Contents

This section contains a summary analysis of each of the top 100 and bottom 100 bond mutual funds as determined by their TheStreet Risk Rating. Since the Risk Rating does not take into consideration a fund's overall financial performance, the selection of funds presented here is based solely on each fund's level of credit risk and interest rate risk.

In order to optimize the utility of our top and bottom fund lists, rather than listing all funds in a multi-class series, a single fund from each series is selected for display as the primary share class. Whenever possible, the selected fund is one that a retail investor would be most likely to choose. This share class may not be appropriate for every investor, so please consult with your financial advisor, the fund company, and the fund's prospectus before placing your trade.

You can use this section to identify those funds that have historically given shareholders the most consistent returns on their investments. A word of caution though: consistency in the past is not necessarily indicative of future results. While these funds have provided the most stable returns, it is possible for a fund manager – especially a newly appointed fund manager – to suddenly shift the fund's investment focus which could lead to greater volatility.

1. Fund Type

The mutual fund's peer category based on its investment objective as stated in its prospectus.

COH	Corporate - High Yield	MMT	Money Market - Tax Free
COI	Corporate - Inv. Grade	MTG	Mortgage
EM	Emerging Market	MUH	Municipal - High Yield
GEN	General	MUI	Municipal - Insured
GEI	General - Inv. Grade	MUN	Municipal - National
GEL	General - Long Term	MUS	Municipal - Single State
GES	General - Short & Interm.	USL	U.S. Gov.- Long Term
GL	Global	USS	U.S. Gov. - Short & Interm
LP	Loan Participation	USA	U.S. Gov. - Agency
MM	Money Market	US	U.S. Gov. - Treasury

A blank fund type means that the mutual fund has not yet been categorized.

2. Fund Name

The name of the mutual fund as stated in its prospectus, which can sometimes differ slightly from the name that the company uses for advertising. If you cannot find the particular mutual fund you are interested in, or if you have any doubts regarding the precise name, verify the information with your broker or on your account statement. Also, use the fund's ticker symbol for confirmation. (See column 3.)

3. Ticker Symbol

The unique alphabetic symbol used for identifying and trading a specific mutual fund. No two funds can have the same ticker symbol, and the ticker symbol for mutual funds always ends with an "X".

A handful of funds currently show no associated ticker symbol. This means that the fund is either small or new since the NASD only assigns a ticker symbol to funds with at least $25 million in assets or 1,000 shareholders.

4. Overall Investment Rating	Our overall rating is measured on a scale from A to E based on each fund's risk-adjusted performance. Please see page 11 for specific descriptions of each letter grade. Also, refer to page 7 for information on how our ratings are derived. Most important, when using this rating, please be sure to consider the warnings beginning on page 13 regarding the ratings' limitations and the underlying assumptions.
5. Phone	The telephone number of the company managing the fund. Call this number to receive a prospectus or other information about the fund.
6. Net Asset Value (NAV)	The fund's share price as of the date indicated. A fund's NAV is computed by dividing the value of the fund's asset holdings, less accrued fees and expenses, by the number of its shares outstanding.
7. Performance Rating/Points	A letter grade rating based solely on the mutual fund's financial performance over the trailing three years, without any consideration for the amount of risk the fund poses. Like the overall Investment Rating, the Performance Rating is measured on a scale from A to E for ease of interpretation. The points score indicates where the Performance Rating falls on a scale of 0 to 10. In the case of funds investing in municipal or other tax-free securities, this rating is based on the taxable equivalent return of the fund assuming the maximum marginal U.S. tax rate (35%).
8. 1-Year Total Return	The total return the fund has provided investors over the preceeding twelve months. This total return figure is computed based on the fund's dividend distributions and share price appreciation/depreciation during the period, net of the expenses and fees it imposes on its shareholders. Although the total return figure does not reflect an adjustment for any loads the fund may carry, such adjustments have been made in deriving TheStreet Investment Ratings.
9. 1-Year Total Return Percentile	The fund's percentile rank based on its one-year performance compared to that of all other fixed income funds in existence for at least one year. A score of 99 is the best possible, indicating that the fund outperformed 99% of the other mutual funds. Zero is the worst possible percentile score. In the case of funds investing in municipal or other tax-free securities, this percentile rank is based on the taxable equivalent return of the fund assuming the maximum marginal U.S. tax rate (35%).
10. 3-Year Total Return	The total annual return the fund has provided investors over the preceeding three years.

11. 3-Year Total Return Percentile

The fund's percentile rank based on its three-year performance compared to that of all other fixed income funds in existence for at least three years. A score of 99 is the best possible, indicating that the fund outperformed 99% of the other mutual funds. Zero is the worst possible percentile score.

In the case of funds investing in municipal or other tax-free securities, this percentile rank is based on the taxable equivalent return of the fund assuming the maximum marginal U.S. tax rate (35%).

12. 5-Year Total Return

The total annual return the fund has provided investors over the preceeding five years.

13. 5-Year Total Return Percentile

The fund's percentile rank based on its five-year performance compared to that of all other fixed income funds in existence for at least five years. A score of 99 is the best possible, indicating that the fund outperformed 99% of the other mutual funds. Zero is the worst possible percentile score.

In the case of funds investing in municipal or other tax-free securities, this percentile rank is based on the taxable equivalent return of the fund assuming the maximum marginal U.S. tax rate (35%).

14. Risk Rating/Points

A letter grade rating based solely on the mutual fund's risk as determined by its monthly performance volatility over the trailing three years and the underlying credit risk and interest rate risk of its investment portfolio. The risk rating does not take into consideration the overall financial performance the fund has achieved or the total return it has provided to its shareholders. Like the overall Investment Rating, the Risk Rating is measured on a scale from A to E for ease of interpretation. The points score indicates where the Risk Rating falls on a scale of 0 to 10.

15. Manager Quality Percentile

The manager quality percentile is based on a ranking of the fund's alpha, a statistical measure representing the difference between a fund's actual returns and its expected performance given its level of risk. Fund managers who have been able to exceed the fund's statistically expected performance receive a high percentile rank with 99 representing the highest possible score. At the other end of the spectrum, fund managers who have actually detracted from the fund's expected performance receive a low percentile rank with 0 representing the lowest possible score.

16. Manager Tenure

The number of years the current manager has been managing the fund. Since fund managers who deliver substandard returns are usually replaced, a long tenure is usually a good sign that shareholders are satisfied that the fund is achieving its stated objectives.

						PERFORMANCE				RISK	FUND MGR	
	99 Pct = Best *0 Pct = Worst*						Annualized Total Return Through 3/31/16					
Fund Type	Fund Name	Ticker Symbol	Overall Investment Rating	Phone	Net Asset Value As of 3/31/16	Performance Rating/Pts	1Yr / Pct	3Yr / Pct	5Yr / Pct	Risk Rating/Pts	Mgr. Quality Pct	Mgr. Tenure (Years)
MUN	Alpine Ultra Short Muni Inc Inst	ATOIX	**B-**	(888) 785-5578	10.04	**C- / 3.7**	0.54 / 56	0.52 / 39	0.79 / 22	**A+ / 9.9**	82	14
USS	Touchstone Ut Sh Dr Fxd Inc Z	TSDOX	**B-**	(800) 543-0407	9.30	**C- / 3.6**	0.63 / 52	0.59 / 35	1.00 / 20	**A+ / 9.9**	81	8
MUN	BMO Ultra Sht Tax-Free Y	MUYSX	**C+**	(800) 236-3863	10.07	**C- / 3.5**	0.11 / 43	0.44 / 36	0.78 / 22	**A+ / 9.9**	75	1
GEI	RidgeWorth Seix Ultra Short Bond I	SISSX	**C+**	(888) 784-3863	9.93	**C- / 3.5**	0.41 / 48	0.58 / 35	0.89 / 20	**A+ / 9.9**	79	10
MUN	SEI Tax-Exempt Tr-Shrt Dur Muni	SUMAX	**C+**	(800) 342-5734	10.04	**C- / 3.4**	0.21 / 46	0.34 / 34	0.63 / 20	**A+ / 9.9**	72	5
MTG	Northern Tax-Advtged Ult-Sh Fxd	NTAUX	**C+**	(800) 595-9111	10.12	**C- / 3.4**	0.41 / 48	0.52 / 33	0.76 / 19	**A+ / 9.9**	76	7
GEI	Columbia CMG Ultra Short Term	CMGUX	**C+**	(800) 345-6611	9.00	**C- / 3.3**	0.48 / 49	0.46 / 32	0.64 / 18	**A+ / 9.9**	77	4
MTG	TCW Short Term Bond I	TGSMX	**C+**	(800) 386-3829	8.69	**C- / 3.3**	0.26 / 45	0.47 / 33	0.98 / 20	**A+ / 9.9**	76	6
GES	DFA One-Yr Fixed Inc Inst	DFIHX	**C+**	(800) 984-9472	10.31	**C- / 3.2**	0.51 / 50	0.40 / 31	0.54 / 17	**A+ / 9.9**	76	33
GEI	Aberdeen Ultra-Short Dur Bond	AUDIX	**C+**	(866) 667-9231	9.89	**C- / 3.1**	0.47 / 49	0.35 / 31	0.66 / 18	**A+ / 9.9**	74	6
US	RidgeWorth Seix Ltd Dur I	SAMLX	**C+**	(888) 784-3863	9.83	**D+ / 2.8**	0.25 / 45	0.21 / 29	0.46 / 17	**A+ / 9.9**	74	14
US	GMO US Treasury	GUSTX	**C+**		25.01	**D+ / 2.8**	0.26 / 45	0.15 / 28	0.13 / 15	**A+ / 9.9**	72	2
USS	RidgeWorth Seix US Gvt Sec U/S	SIGVX	**C+**	(888) 784-3863	10.03	**D+ / 2.8**	-0.13 / 30	0.26 / 30	0.73 / 19	**A+ / 9.9**	73	10
MTG	Trust for Credit UltSh Dur Gov TCU	TCUUX	**C**	(800) 342-5828	9.50	**D / 2.2**	0.01 / 32	0.04 / 23	0.24 / 16	**A+ / 9.9**	58	N/A
GES	Wells Fargo Ult ST Inc A	SADAX	**C-**	(800) 222-8222	8.45	**D / 1.7**	0.32 / 46	0.35 / 31	0.57 / 18	**A+ / 9.9**	76	14
MTG	Federated Adj Rate Sec Inst	FEUGX	**C-**	(800) 341-7400	9.69	**D / 1.6**	-0.62 / 25	-0.05 / 15	0.41 / 17	**A+ / 9.9**	53	21
GEI	PNC Ultra Short Bond A	PSBAX	**C-**	(800) 551-2145	9.95	**D- / 1.5**	0.13 / 42	-0.03 / 15	0.06 / 13	**A+ / 9.9**	57	14
MUN	Wells Fargo Ult-Sh Mun Inc A	SMAVX	**C-**	(800) 222-8222	9.61	**D- / 1.4**	0.03 / 38	0.14 / 29	0.47 / 19	**A+ / 9.9**	60	16
MTG	Wells Fargo Adj Rate Govt A	ESAAX	**C-**	(800) 222-8222	9.01	**D- / 1.3**	-0.42 / 27	0.13 / 28	0.71 / 18	**A+ / 9.9**	69	8
US	Permanent Portfolio Short-Tm	PRTBX	**C-**	(800) 531-5142	64.81	**D- / 1.2**	-0.49 / 26	-0.59 / 11	-0.59 / 2	**A+ / 9.9**	40	13
MUI	Federated Muni Ultrashrt A	FMUUX	**C-**	(800) 341-7400	9.97	**D- / 1.1**	-0.42 / 27	-0.08 / 15	0.30 / 17	**A+ / 9.9**	49	16
USS	Federated Gov Ultrashort Dur A	FGUAX	**C-**	(800) 341-7400	9.80	**E+ / 0.9**	-0.81 / 23	-0.40 / 12	-0.22 / 2	**A+ / 9.9**	46	19
MUN	USAA T/E Short Term Bond Fund	USSTX	**B+**	(800) 382-8722	10.59	**C / 4.9**	0.60 / 57	0.83 / 48	1.85 / 43	**A+ / 9.8**	76	13
MUN	Vanguard Short-Term Tax-Exempt	VWSTX	**B**	(800) 662-7447	15.82	**C- / 4.1**	0.64 / 58	0.53 / 39	0.83 / 23	**A+ / 9.8**	75	20
GEI	Northern Ultra-Short Fixed Income	NUSFX	**B-**	(800) 595-9111	10.18	**C- / 3.9**	0.69 / 53	0.74 / 38	1.06 / 21	**A+ / 9.8**	81	7
GES	SEI Daily Inc Tr-Ultra Sh Dur Bd A	SECPX	**C+**	(800) 342-5734	9.30	**C- / 3.6**	0.58 / 51	0.61 / 35	0.91 / 20	**A+ / 9.8**	80	17
GL	DFA Two Year Glbl Fixed Inc Inst	DFGFX	**C+**	(800) 984-9472	9.96	**C- / 3.5**	0.63 / 52	0.52 / 33	0.68 / 18	**A+ / 9.8**	83	17
GEI	Payden Limited Maturity Investor	PYLMX	**C+**	(888) 409-8007	9.43	**C- / 3.5**	0.33 / 46	0.55 / 34	0.72 / 19	**A+ / 9.8**	79	N/A
MUN	Wells Fargo ST Muni Bd A	WSMAX	**C+**	(800) 222-8222	9.94	**C- / 3.5**	0.79 / 62	0.87 / 49	1.59 / 37	**A+ / 9.8**	81	16
GEI	LWAS DFA Two Year Fixed	DFCFX	**C+**	(800) 984-9472	10.00	**C- / 3.4**	0.65 / 52	0.47 / 33	0.63 / 18	**A+ / 9.8**	74	N/A
USS	LWAS DFA Two Year Government	DFYGX	**C+**	(800) 984-9472	9.88	**C- / 3.4**	0.51 / 50	0.44 / 32	0.56 / 18	**A+ / 9.8**	71	N/A
MTG	PIA Short-Term Securities Adv	PIASX	**C+**	(800) 251-1970	10.01	**C- / 3.3**	0.34 / 47	0.45 / 32	0.45 / 17	**A+ / 9.8**	75	N/A
GEI	Trust for Credit Uns Sh Dur TCU	TCUDX	**C+**	(800) 342-5828	9.72	**C- / 3.2**	0.52 / 50	0.36 / 31	0.71 / 18	**A+ / 9.8**	61	21
GEI	Metropolitan West Ultra Short Bnd	MWUSX	**C+**	(800) 496-8298	4.27	**C- / 3.1**	0.17 / 43	0.44 / 32	1.31 / 23	**A+ / 9.8**	78	13
MUS	Sanford C Bernstein Sh Dur NY	SDNYX	**C+**	(212) 486-5800	12.46	**C- / 3.0**	0.27 / 48	0.16 / 29	0.72 / 21	**A+ / 9.8**	51	22
GEI	Pioneer Short Term Income A	STABX	**C+**	(800) 225-6292	9.52	**D+ / 2.9**	0.65 / 52	0.96 / 42	1.77 / 28	**A+ / 9.8**	86	10
GEI	SA US Fixed Income Fund	SAUFX	**C+**	(800) 366-7266	10.21	**D+ / 2.8**	0.35 / 47	0.10 / 27	0.20 / 16	**A+ / 9.8**	58	17
GEI	Calvert Ultra-Short Inc A	CULAX	**C**	(800) 368-2745	15.47	**D+ / 2.7**	0.17 / 43	0.49 / 33	0.78 / 19	**A+ / 9.8**	81	4
USS	Sanford C Bernstein US Govt Sh	SNGSX	**C-**	(212) 486-5800	12.47	**D / 1.7**	-0.24 / 29	-0.05 / 15	0.20 / 16	**A+ / 9.8**	49	11
COI	STAAR Inv Trust Shrt Term Bond	SITBX	**C-**	(800) 332-7738	8.93	**D / 1.6**	-0.11 / 30	-0.23 / 14	0.23 / 16	**A+ / 9.8**	45	19
GEI	Goldman Sachs Enhanced Inc A	GEIAX	**C-**	(800) 526-7384	9.41	**D- / 1.5**	0.29 / 46	-0.02 / 15	0.09 / 14	**A+ / 9.8**	58	8
GES	Federated Ultra Short Bd A	FULAX	**C-**	(800) 341-7400	9.07	**D- / 1.3**	-0.19 / 29	0.04 / 23	0.61 / 18	**A+ / 9.8**	53	18
MTG	Goldman Sachs Hi Qual Fltg R A	GSAMX	**C-**	(800) 526-7384	8.63	**D- / 1.0**	-0.81 / 23	-0.39 / 12	-0.19 / 3	**A+ / 9.8**	53	8
USS	Franklin Adjustable US Govt Sec A	FISAX	**C-**	(800) 342-5236	8.44	**E+ / 0.9**	-1.11 / 21	-0.24 / 14	0.40 / 17	**A+ / 9.8**	46	25
MUN	USAA Ultra Short-Term Bond Fund	UUSTX	**B-**	(800) 382-8722	9.94	**C- / 4.0**	-0.23 / 29	0.65 / 43	1.34 / 32	**A+ / 9.7**	80	6
USS	Vanguard Short-Term Gvt Bd Idx	VSBSX	**B-**	(800) 662-7447	20.40	**C- / 3.9**	0.89 / 57	0.68 / 37	0.80 / 19	**A+ / 9.7**	76	3
MUN	Sanford C Bernstein Sh-Dur Dvrs	SDDMX	**C+**	(212) 486-5800	12.60	**C- / 3.4**	0.45 / 53	0.28 / 32	0.75 / 22	**A+ / 9.7**	55	22
GEI	Voya Limited Maturity Bond Adv	IMBAX	**C+**	(800) 992-0180	9.90	**C- / 3.4**	0.35 / 47	0.47 / 33	0.64 / 18	**A+ / 9.7**	69	7
GL	BBH Limited Duration Class N	BBBMX	**C+**	(800) 625-5759	10.06	**C- / 3.3**	-0.01 / 31	0.57 / 34	1.13 / 22	**A+ / 9.7**	84	5
MUN	Columbia Sh-Term Muni Bd A	NSMMX	**C+**	(800) 345-6611	10.42	**C- / 3.0**	0.54 / 56	0.42 / 36	0.88 / 24	**A+ / 9.7**	59	4
GEI	PNC Ltd Maturity Bond A	PLFAX	**C**	(800) 551-2145	10.22	**D / 2.2**	0.50 / 49	0.46 / 32	0.66 / 18	**A+ / 9.7**	62	14
MUN	PIMCO Short Duration Muni Inc A	PSDAX	**C-**	(800) 426-0107	8.47	**D / 1.9**	0.63 / 58	0.51 / 39	0.56 / 19	**A+ / 9.7**	60	2

• Denotes fund is closed to new investors

99 Pct = Best
0 Pct = Worst

						PERFORMANCE				RISK	FUND MGR	
Fund Type	Fund Name	Ticker Symbol	Overall Investment Rating	Phone	Net Asset Value As of 3/31/16	Performance Rating/Pts	Annualized Total Return Through 3/31/16: 1Yr / Pct	3Yr / Pct	5Yr / Pct	Risk Rating/Pts	Mgr. Quality Pct	Mgr. Tenure (Years)
USS	Goldman Sachs Short Dur Gov A	GSSDX	C-	(800) 526-7384	10.10	D /1.8	0.44 /48	0.29 /30	0.46 /17	A+ / 9.7	62	8
GEI	Neuberger Berman Short Dur Bd A	NSHAX	C-	(800) 877-9700	7.51	D /1.7	0.45 /49	0.43 /32	1.11 /21	A+ / 9.7	62	10
GES	Federated Short Term Inc A	FTIAX	C-	(800) 341-7400	8.49	D /1.6	-0.11 /30	0.05 /24	0.82 /19	A+ / 9.7	45	21
MUN	BlackRock Short Term Muni Inv A	MELMX	C-	(800) 441-7762	10.16	D- /1.2	0.34 /50	0.12 /28	0.41 /18	A+ / 9.7	52	20
GEI	AB Short Duration A	ADPAX	C-	(800) 221-5672	11.74	D- /1.0	0.26 /45	0.17 /28	0.28 /16	A+ / 9.7	52	11
GEI	• Fidelity Short-Term Bond	FSHBX	B	(800) 544-8544	8.61	C /4.5	1.01 /59	0.97 /42	1.38 /24	A+ / 9.6	81	9
GEI	Metropolitan West Low Dur Bd M	MWLDX	B-	(800) 496-8298	8.73	C- /4.1	0.32 /46	0.96 /42	2.20 /34	A+ / 9.6	83	19
COI	TD Asset Mgmt Short-Term Bond	TDSBX	B-		10.20	C- /4.0	0.75 /54	0.71 /37	1.02 /21	A+ / 9.6	77	7
GEI	Wells Fargo Sh-Tm Bd A	SSTVX	C+	(800) 222-8222	8.74	C- /3.4	0.80 /55	1.01 /43	1.41 /25	A+ / 9.6	84	12
GEI	Fidelity Adv Short-Fixed Income A	FSFAX	C+	(800) 522-7297	9.35	C- /3.3	0.77 /55	0.76 /38	1.17 /22	A+ / 9.6	74	9
COI	Transamerica Prt High Quality	DVHQX	C+	(888) 233-4339	11.20	C- /3.2	0.54 /50	0.31 /30	0.90 /20	A+ / 9.6	58	26
USS	BNY Mellon ST US Gov Sec M	MPSUX	C+	(800) 645-6561	11.84	C- /3.2	0.59 /51	0.34 /30	0.37 /16	A+ / 9.6	56	16
GEI	JPMorgan Limited Duration Bd A	ONUAX	C+	(800) 480-4111	9.97	C- /3.1	0.19 /44	1.12 /45	2.09 /32	A+ / 9.6	87	21
MUN	Nuveen Short Term Municipal	FSHAX	C+	(800) 257-8787	10.12	C- /3.0	0.89 /64	0.79 /47	1.78 /41	A+ / 9.6	75	14
USS	Federated USG Sec:1-3yrs Y	FSGTX	C	(800) 341-7400	10.44	D+ /2.9	0.36 /47	0.15 /28	0.41 /17	A+ / 9.6	53	11
GEI	FPA New Income Inc	FPNIX	C	(800) 982-4372	10.01	D+ /2.7	0.16 /43	0.72 /37	1.24 /23	A+ / 9.6	76	12
GES	MainStay Tax Adv Sht-Tm Bd	MYTBX	C	(800) 624-6782	9.63	D+ /2.6	0.95 /58	0.18 /28	0.41 /17	A+ / 9.6	50	1
GEI	MFS Limited Maturity A	MQLFX	C-	(800) 225-2606	5.99	D /2.0	0.49 /49	0.59 /35	1.23 /23	A+ / 9.6	70	18
US	WA Short-Term Bond A	SBSTX	C-	(877) 534-4627	3.85	D /1.8	0.10 /41	0.55 /34	1.11 /21	A+ / 9.6	76	4
MTG	WA Adjustable Rate Income A	ARMZX	C-	(877) 534-4627	8.84	D /1.7	-0.05 /31	0.54 /34	1.20 /22	A+ / 9.6	77	4
GEI	JPMorgan Short Duration Bond A	OGLVX	C-	(800) 480-4111	10.86	D /1.7	0.46 /49	0.40 /31	0.78 /19	A+ / 9.6	56	10
MUS	PIMCO CA Sh Duration Muni Inc A	PCDAX	C-	(800) 426-0107	9.94	D /1.6	0.54 /56	0.34 /33	0.33 /17	A+ / 9.6	55	5
USS	Dreyfus Ultra Short Income Z	DSIGX	C-	(800) 645-6561	10.07	D /1.6	-0.75 /24	-0.08 /15	0.11 /15	A+ / 9.6	56	3
USS	American Century Sh-Term Govt A	TWAVX	C-	(800) 345-6488	9.66	D- /1.3	0.19 /44	-0.01 /15	0.29 /16	A+ / 9.6	44	14
GES	Homestead Short Term Bond	HOSBX	B	(800) 258-3030	5.20	C /4.6	0.64 /52	1.11 /45	2.06 /32	A / 9.5	84	25
MUS	T Rowe Price MD ShTm Tax-Free	PRMDX	B	(800) 638-5660	5.23	C /4.4	0.85 /63	0.59 /41	0.82 /23	A / 9.5	66	20
GEI	BMO Short-Term Income Y	MSINX	B-	(800) 236-3863	9.36	C- /4.0	0.93 /57	0.75 /38	1.52 /26	A / 9.5	73	4
GEI	Payden Low Duration Investor	PYSBX	C+	(888) 409-8007	10.05	C- /3.8	0.54 /50	0.69 /37	1.44 /25	A / 9.5	76	N/A
MUI	BNY Mellon National ST Muni Bd	MPSTX	C+	(800) 645-6561	12.81	C- /3.6	0.37 /51	0.42 /36	0.88 /24	A / 9.5	53	1
COI	Wilmington Short-Term Bd A	MVSAX	C+	(800) 336-9970	10.06	C- /3.1	0.67 /53	0.71 /37	1.10 /21	A / 9.5	76	20
MUN	WA Short Duration Muni Income A	SHDAX	C+	(877) 534-4627	5.12	C- /3.1	0.48 /54	0.80 /47	1.44 /34	A / 9.5	70	13
GEI	Columbia Short Term Bond A	NSTRX	C	(800) 345-6611	9.97	D+ /2.9	0.40 /48	0.48 /33	1.00 /20	A / 9.5	60	12
GEI	RidgeWorth Seix Sh-Term Bond A	STSBX	C-	(888) 784-3863	10.01	D /2.0	0.57 /51	0.58 /35	1.09 /21	A / 9.5	63	8
MUN	Franklin Fdrl Lmtd Trm T/F Inc A	FFTFX	C-	(800) 342-5236	10.42	D /1.8	0.50 /55	0.57 /40	1.58 /37	A / 9.5	58	13
GEI	American Century Sh Duration A	ACSQX	C-	(800) 345-6488	10.25	D /1.8	0.62 /52	0.47 /32	1.00 /20	A / 9.5	62	N/A
USS	Wells Fargo Sh Dur Gov A	MSDAX	C-	(800) 222-8222	10.00	D /1.8	0.45 /49	0.44 /32	1.00 /20	A / 9.5	59	13
GES	American Funds Sh-T Bd of Amr A	ASBAX	C-	(800) 421-0180	9.99	D /1.7	0.71 /53	0.44 /32	0.65 /18	A / 9.5	57	5
MUS	DFA CA Sht Trm Muni Bd Inst	DFCMX	A-	(800) 984-9472	10.35	C /5.5	1.26 /71	0.95 /51	1.21 /29	A / 9.4	77	9
GES	Baird Short-Term Bond Inst	BSBIX	A-	(866) 442-2473	9.68	C /5.4	1.30 /63	1.46 /51	2.09 /32	A / 9.4	88	12
GEI	Cavanal Hill Sht-Tm Inc NL Inv	APSTX	B-	(800) 762-7085	9.59	C- /4.2	0.58 /51	0.94 /41	1.99 /31	A / 9.4	77	22
GES	T Rowe Price Short Term Bond	PRWBX	C+	(800) 638-5660	4.73	C- /3.9	0.64 /52	0.70 /37	1.24 /23	A / 9.4	72	21
GEI	Principal Short-Term Income Fd A	SRHQX	C+	(800) 222-5852	12.17	C- /3.5	0.86 /56	1.06 /44	1.84 /29	A / 9.4	81	6
US	Invesco Sh Dur Infl Pro A	LMTAX	C	(800) 959-4246	10.60	C- /3.0	1.83 /70	0.53 /34	0.47 /17	A / 9.4	74	7
USS	Sterling Capital Short Dur Bd A	BSGAX	C	(800) 228-1872	8.80	C- /3.0	0.59 /51	0.77 /38	1.58 /26	A / 9.4	78	5
GEI	Nuveen Short Term Bond A	FALTX	C	(800) 257-8787	9.83	D+ /2.9	0.29 /46	0.90 /41	1.50 /26	A / 9.4	83	6
GEI	Nationwide HighMark Sht Term Bd	NWJSX	C	(800) 848-0920	9.96	D+ /2.6	0.63 /52	0.56 /34	1.13 /22	A / 9.4	60	12
USS	Oppenheimer Limited Term Govt A	OPGVX	C	(888) 470-0862	4.48	D+ /2.5	0.42 /48	0.64 /36	1.12 /21	A / 9.4	63	7
MUN	American Funds ST T/E Bnd Fd A	ASTEX	C-	(800) 421-0180	10.17	D /1.8	0.62 /58	0.58 /41	1.23 /30	A / 9.4	54	7

• Denotes fund is closed to new investors

99 Pct = Best 0 Pct = Worst						PERFORMANCE				RISK	FUND MGR	
Fund Type	Fund Name	Ticker Symbol	Overall Investment Rating	Phone	Net Asset Value As of 3/31/16	Performance Rating/Pts	Annualized Total Return Through 3/31/16 1Yr / Pct	3Yr / Pct	5Yr / Pct	Risk Rating/Pts	Mgr. Quality Pct	Mgr. Tenure (Years)
USS	Rydex Inv Govt Lg Bd Stgy A	RYAQX	**E-**	(800) 820-0888	33.11	**E- /0.0**	-4.47 / 6	-8.17 / 1	-12.35 / 0	**E- / 0.0**	33	8
GEI	Credit Suisse Cmdty Rtn Strat A	CRSAX	**E-**	(877) 927-2874	4.46	**E- /0.0**	-19.78 / 0	-17.07 / 0	-14.54 / 0	**E- / 0.0**	0	10
GEI	Rydex Wekng Dlr 2x Stgry A	RYWDX	**E-**	(800) 820-0888	12.55	**E- /0.0**	6.54 /95	-9.53 / 0	-9.21 / 0	**E- / 0.0**	0	11
GEI	Credit Suisse Commdty Ret Str	CCRSX	**E-**	(877) 927-2874	3.94	**E- /0.0**	-19.59 / 0	-17.04 / 0	-14.55 / 0	**E- / 0.0**	0	10
COH	Catalyst/SMH High Income A	HIIFX	**E-**	(866) 447-4228	3.12	**E- /0.0**	-25.42 / 0	-13.08 / 0	-6.60 / 0	**E- / 0.0**	0	8
GES	AB All Mkt Real Return A	AMTAX	**E-**	(800) 221-5672	7.61	**E- /0.0**	-14.66 / 0	-10.78 / 0	-7.62 / 0	**E- / 0.0**	0	1
EM	Janus Emerging Markets A	JMFAX	**E-**	(800) 295-2687	7.58	**E- /0.2**	-10.08 / 1	-2.48 / 3	-4.67 / 0	**E- / 0.0**	9	4
MTG	PIMCO StkPlus Intl (DH) A	PIPAX	**E**	(800) 426-0107	6.33	**D- /1.3**	-15.26 / 0	3.56 /81	6.13 /77	**E- / 0.0**	94	1
GEI	Rydex Strengthening Dlr 2x Strtgy	RYSDX	**D-**	(800) 820-0888	47.68	**C- /3.5**	-11.01 / 0	5.09 /91	4.20 /64	**E- / 0.0**	99	11
GEI	Fairholme Focused Income	FOCIX	**D+**	(866) 202-2263	9.63	**B- /7.2**	-5.74 / 4	4.87 /90	4.29 /65	**E- / 0.0**	99	7
GEN	J Hancock VIT Value I	JEVLX	**D+**	(800) 257-3336	19.99	**B /7.7**	-12.81 / 0	5.82 /94	8.02 /87	**E- / 0.0**	99	19
USA	ProFunds-US Government Plus	GVPSX	**C-**	(888) 776-3637	53.63	**A /9.3**	-2.08 /15	5.21 /92	10.55 /96	**E- / 0.0**	5	7
US	Wasatch Hoisington US Treasury	WHOSX	**C-**	(800) 551-1700	18.59	**A+ /9.6**	0.87 /57	6.80 /97	11.69 /98	**E- / 0.0**	21	20
USL	Rydex Govt Lg Bd 1.2x Strgy A	RYABX	**C-**	(800) 820-0888	58.50	**A+ /9.7**	0.11 /41	7.66 /99	12.92 /99	**E- / 0.0**	25	22
US	Vanguard Extnd Durtn Trea Idx Inst	VEDTX	**C-**	(800) 662-7447	37.90	**A+ /9.9**	1.34 /64	8.82 /99	15.40 /99	**E- / 0.0**	12	3
GEI	PIMCO Extended Duration P	PEDPX	**C-**	(800) 426-0107	8.66	**A+ /9.9**	0.63 /52	8.61 /99	15.16 /99	**E- / 0.0**	4	9
EM	PIMCO Emerging Local Bond A	PELAX	**E-**	(800) 426-0107	7.21	**E- /0.0**	-4.80 / 5	-8.77 / 0	-3.27 / 1	**E- / 0.1**	0	10
EM	Goldman Sachs Local Emg Mkt	GAMDX	**E-**	(800) 526-7384	6.36	**E- /0.0**	-3.57 / 9	-8.58 / 0	-3.06 / 1	**E- / 0.1**	0	8
EM	Dreyfus Eme Mkts Dbt LC A	DDBAX	**E-**	(800) 782-6620	11.18	**E- /0.0**	-5.19 / 5	-8.57 / 0	-3.42 / 1	**E- / 0.1**	0	8
COH	Third Avenue Focused Credit Inv	TFCVX	**E-**	(800) 443-1021	5.21	**E- /0.0**	-33.70 / 0	-13.13 / 0	-5.44 / 0	**E- / 0.1**	0	7
EM	Eaton Vance Emer Market Local	EEIAX	**E-**	(800) 262-1122	6.29	**E- /0.1**	-0.87 /23	-7.77 / 1	-3.03 / 1	**E- / 0.1**	1	8
US	Fidelity Spartan Lg-T Tre Bd In Inv	FLBIX	**C-**	(800) 544-8544	13.73	**A /9.5**	2.50 /75	5.81 /94	9.46 /93	**E- / 0.1**	22	2
GEI	Columbia Abs Rtn Currency & Inc	RACWX	**C-**	(800) 345-6611	10.37	**A /9.5**	5.57 /91	5.65 /94	3.81 /58	**E- / 0.1**	96	10
US	Vanguard Long-Term Treasury Inv	VUSTX	**C-**	(800) 662-7447	13.11	**A+ /9.6**	2.54 /75	5.83 /95	9.46 /93	**E- / 0.1**	24	15
US	Direxion Mo 7-10 Year Tr Br 2X Inv	DXKSX	**E-**	(800) 851-0511	29.47	**E- /0.0**	-9.93 / 1	-8.96 / 0	-14.53 / 0	**E- / 0.2**	11	12
GES	Northeast Investors Trust	NTHEX	**E-**	(800) 225-6704	3.83	**E- /0.0**	-25.81 / 0	-9.21 / 0	-2.75 / 1	**E- / 0.2**	0	N/A
EM	Invesco Emerg Mkts Flexible Bond	IAEMX	**E-**	(800) 959-4246	6.38	**E- /0.0**	-10.75 / 0	-9.82 / 0	-4.41 / 0	**E- / 0.2**	0	3
EM	Oppenheimer Em Mkts Local Debt	OEMAX	**E-**	(888) 470-0862	7.40	**E- /0.2**	-0.01 /31	-5.76 / 1	-1.19 / 1	**E- / 0.2**	2	1
GL	TCW Emg Mkts Local Currency Inc	TGWNX	**E-**	(800) 386-3829	8.53	**E- /0.2**	-3.29 /10	-6.71 / 1	-1.57 / 1	**E- / 0.2**	1	6
GL	STAAR AltCat	SITAX	**E-**	(800) 332-7738	13.10	**E /0.5**	-10.70 / 1	-0.69 /10	0.05 /12	**E- / 0.2**	39	19
GEI	PIMCO Real Return Asset P	PRTPX	**E**	(800) 426-0107	8.22	**D- /1.0**	-1.70 /17	-2.06 / 4	4.74 /70	**E- / 0.2**	0	9
USL	PIMCO Long Term US Govt A	PFGAX	**C-**	(800) 426-0107	6.44	**B+ /8.7**	1.53 /67	4.97 /90	8.81 /90	**E- / 0.2**	24	9
US	Direxion Mo 7-10 Year Tr Bl 2X Inv	DXKLX	**C-**	(800) 851-0511	37.17	**B+ /8.8**	4.67 /85	3.44 /79	9.02 /91	**E- / 0.2**	6	10
US	T Rowe Price US Treas Long-Term	PRULX	**C-**	(800) 638-5660	13.52	**A /9.3**	2.21 /73	5.08 /91	8.75 /90	**E- / 0.2**	15	13
US	Dreyfus US Treasury Long Term	DRGBX	**C-**	(800) 645-6561	20.54	**A /9.3**	2.10 /72	5.03 /91	8.77 /90	**E- / 0.2**	19	8
USL	Vanguard Long-Term Govt Bd Idx	VLGSX	**C-**	(800) 662-7447	26.97	**A+ /9.6**	2.76 /76	5.88 /95	9.43 /93	**E- / 0.2**	48	3
GES	Metropolitan West Alpha Trak 500	MWATX	**C**	(800) 496-8298	7.22	**A+ /9.9**	0.53 /50	11.58 /99	11.75 /98	**E- / 0.2**	99	18
USS	PIMCO StocksPLUS Short A	PSSAX	**E-**	(800) 426-0107	10.27	**E- /0.0**	-6.53 / 3	-12.27 / 0	-10.75 / 0	**E / 0.3**	0	2
EM	SEI Inst Intl Emerging Mkts Debt A	SITEX	**E-**	(800) 342-5734	9.39	**E /0.3**	-1.31 /19	-3.98 / 2	1.13 /22	**E / 0.3**	6	10
GEI	API Efficient Frontier Income Fd A	APIUX	**E-**	(800) 544-6060	9.51	**E /0.3**	-5.80 / 3	-1.63 / 5	2.31 /35	**E / 0.3**	6	19
MUS	● Oppenheimer Rochester VA Muni	ORVAX	**E-**	(888) 470-0862	8.01	**E+ /0.6**	-0.52 /26	-0.69 /10	5.33 /88	**E / 0.3**	1	10
COI	Federated Emerging Mkt Debt A	IHIAX	**E-**	(800) 341-7400	8.20	**E+ /0.6**	0.26 /45	-1.76 / 5	3.16 /48	**E / 0.3**	3	3
EM	PIMCO Emerging Markets Bond A	PAEMX	**E**	(800) 426-0107	9.70	**D- /1.0**	0.02 /33	-1.06 / 8	3.16 /48	**E / 0.3**	30	5
GL	MainStay Global High Income B	MGHBX	**E**	(800) 624-6782	9.56	**D- /1.5**	3.42 /79	-2.13 / 4	2.45 /37	**E / 0.3**	11	5
GEI	PIMCO Long Dur Total Return P	PLRPX	**C-**	(800) 426-0107	11.29	**B+ /8.6**	-0.54 /26	4.16 /85	7.79 /86	**E / 0.3**	8	9
COI	Vanguard Long-Term Corp Bd Idx	VLTCX	**C-**	(800) 662-7447	23.76	**B+ /8.7**	-1.14 /21	4.33 /86	7.89 /86	**E / 0.3**	23	7
GEI	PIMCO Long Term Credit Inst	PTCIX	**C-**	(800) 426-0107	11.40	**A- /9.0**	-1.29 /20	4.81 /89	9.24 /92	**E / 0.3**	13	7
GEL	Vanguard Long Term Bd Idx	VBLTX	**C-**	(800) 662-7447	14.04	**A- /9.0**	0.26 /45	4.64 /88	8.42 /89	**E / 0.3**	9	3
GEI	● Vanguard Long-Term Inv Gr Inv	VWESX	**C-**	(800) 662-7447	10.43	**A /9.3**	1.25 /62	5.31 /92	8.70 /90	**E / 0.3**	23	8
COH	Franklin High Income A	FHAIX	**E-**	(800) 342-5236	1.66	**E- /0.2**	-11.00 / 0	-1.74 / 5	2.56 /38	**E / 0.4**	5	25
EM	BlackRock Emg Mkts Flex Dyn Bd	BAEDX	**E-**	(800) 441-7762	8.82	**E /0.5**	2.27 /73	-2.09 / 4	3.51 /53	**E / 0.4**	12	8
MUS	● Oppenheimer Rochester MD Muni	ORMDX	**E**	(888) 470-0862	9.44	**E+ /0.6**	0.68 /59	-0.60 /11	4.76 /83	**E / 0.4**	1	10

● Denotes fund is closed to new investors

99 Pct = Best
0 Pct = Worst

Fund Type	Fund Name	Ticker Symbol	Overall Investment Rating	Phone	Net Asset Value As of 3/31/16	PERFORMANCE: Performance Rating/Pts	Annualized Total Return Through 3/31/16: 1Yr / Pct	3Yr / Pct	5Yr / Pct	RISK: Risk Rating/Pts	FUND MGR: Mgr. Quality Pct	Mgr. Tenure (Years)
EM	WA Emerging Markets Debt A	LWEAX	E-	(888) 425-6432	4.73	E+ /0.6	-0.16 /30	-1.65 / 5	2.35 /36	E /0.4	17	3
EM	Columbia Emerging Markets Bond	REBAX	E	(800) 345-6611	10.65	D- /1.0	1.49 /66	-0.90 / 9	3.92 /60	E /0.4	34	5
EM	J Hancock Emerg Markets Debt A	JMKAX	E	(800) 257-3336	8.91	D- /1.2	0.02 /33	-0.86 / 9	2.67 /40	E /0.4	36	3
COH	Loomis Sayles Inst High Income	LSHIX	D-	(800) 633-3330	6.00	C- /3.7	-8.73 / 1	1.91 /60	4.39 /66	E /0.4	51	20
EM	Fidelity Adv Emerging Mkts Inc A	FMKAX	D-	(800) 522-7297	13.16	C- /3.9	3.52 /79	0.97 /42	5.14 /73	E /0.4	90	21
GEI	J Hancock Absolute Ret Curr A	JCUAX	D	(800) 257-3336	8.85	C+ /6.1	5.86 /93	1.64 /55	1.00 /20	E /0.4	99	5
EM	Stone Harbor Emerging Debt Inst	SHMDX	D	(866) 699-8125	10.02	C+ /6.3	3.61 /79	0.52 /34	3.84 /59	E /0.4	85	9
EM	Fidelity New Markets Income	FNMIX	D	(800) 544-8544	14.96	C+ /6.5	3.99 /81	1.36 /49	5.56 /75	E /0.4	93	21
COI	Delaware Extended Duration Bd A	DEEAX	D+	(800) 523-1918	6.32	C+ /6.8	-2.85 /12	3.76 /82	8.41 /89	E /0.4	24	9
EM	● GMO Emerging Country Debt III	GMCDX	D+		9.05	B /8.0	2.53 /75	3.02 /77	7.73 /85	E /0.4	99	22
GEI	American Century Zero Cpn 2025	BTTRX	C-	(800) 345-6488	98.92	B+ /8.5	3.38 /78	3.67 /81	8.84 /91	E /0.4	8	10
EM	EuroPac International Bond A	EPIBX	E-	(888) 558-5851	8.14	E- /0.1	-3.34 /10	-5.75 / 1	-2.60 / 1	E /0.5	2	6
MUS	● Franklin Double Tax-Free Inc A	FPRTX	E-	(800) 342-5236	9.34	E- /0.2	-0.50 /26	-3.26 / 2	1.47 /34	E /0.5	1	30
GL	Lord Abbett Emerg Mkts Currency	LDMAX	E-	(888) 522-2388	5.27	E- /0.2	-2.47 /13	-4.61 / 2	-2.68 / 1	E /0.5	4	9
COH	Direxion Dynamic HY Bond Fd	PDHYX	E-	(800) 851-0511	10.62	E /0.3	-8.56 / 1	-1.80 / 5	1.37 /24	E /0.5	6	6
COH	Natixis Loomis Sayles High Income	NEFHX	E	(800) 225-5478	3.84	E+ /0.6	-6.30 / 3	0.29 /30	3.33 /50	E /0.5	14	14
EM	PIMCO EM Corporate Bond Inst	PEMIX	E	(800) 426-0107	9.83	E+ /0.7	-1.95 /16	-2.03 / 4	1.88 /30	E /0.5	12	N/A
EM	Universal Inst Emer Mrkt Debt II	UEDBX	D-	(800) 869-6397	7.75	C- /4.1	1.32 /64	-0.17 /14	3.92 /60	E /0.5	59	14
GL	LM BW International Opptys Bd IS	LMOTX	D	(877) 534-4627	11.25	C /5.1	-0.54 /26	0.15 /28	3.17 /48	E /0.5	77	7
EM	T Rowe Price Emerging Markets	PREMX	D	(800) 638-5660	11.82	C+ /5.7	4.29 /83	0.89 /41	4.31 /66	E /0.5	90	22
GEI	Calvert Long Term Income A	CLDAX	D+	(800) 368-2745	17.21	B- /7.1	-1.07 /21	3.88 /83	5.91 /76	E /0.5	13	3
MUH	Oppeneheimer Rochester Hi Yld	ORNAX	C-	(888) 470-0862	7.10	A /9.5	6.68 /99	4.44 /97	9.32 /99	E /0.5	11	15
MUH	SEI Asset Alloc-Def Strat All A	STDAX	C	(800) 342-5734	14.31	A+ /9.9	-0.19 /29	7.15 /99	8.98 /99	E /0.5	99	13
GL	Nuveen High Income Bond A	FJSIX	E-	(800) 257-8787	6.77	E- /0.1	-12.80 / 0	-2.70 / 3	1.74 /28	E+ /0.6	8	11
GL	PIMCO Emerging Markets	PLMAX	E-	(800) 426-0107	8.75	E- /0.2	-1.69 /17	-4.48 / 2	-2.75 / 1	E+ /0.6	4	11
COH	J Hancock Core High Yld A	JYIAX	E	(800) 257-3336	8.91	E /0.4	-7.58 / 2	-0.19 /14	3.90 /60	E+ /0.6	12	7
GL	Wells Fargo Intl Bd A	ESIYX	E	(800) 222-8222	10.22	E+ /0.8	1.10 /60	-1.54 / 6	0.14 /15	E+ /0.6	20	23
GEL	Natixis Loomis Sayles Strat Inc A	NEFZX	D-	(800) 225-5478	13.83	D+ /2.8	-5.57 / 4	2.10 /64	4.47 /67	E+ /0.6	79	21
GL	LM BW Global Opportunities Bond	GOBAX	D-	(877) 534-4627	10.64	D+ /2.9	-0.68 /24	0.19 /29	3.55 /54	E+ /0.6	78	10
COH	Fidelity Adv Hi Income Advantage	FAHDX	D-	(800) 522-7297	9.91	C- /3.2	-4.84 / 5	2.63 /72	4.75 /70	E+ /0.6	86	7
MUS	Oppenheimer Rochester Muni A	RMUNX	D	(888) 470-0862	14.72	C /4.3	2.03 /77	1.46 /67	6.55 /95	E+ /0.6	4	17
EM	Payden Emerging Market Bond	PYEWX	D	(888) 409-8007	13.15	C /5.0	1.42 /65	0.44 /32	4.56 /68	E+ /0.6	83	16
MUH	BlackRock High Yld Muni Inv A	MDYHX	C	(800) 441-7762	9.64	A+ /9.6	6.17 /99	4.82 /98	8.66 /99	E+ /0.6	16	10
MUH	AMG GW&K Municipal Enhcd Yld	GWMNX	C	(800) 835-3879	10.28	A+ /9.8	4.86 /98	4.36 /97	8.33 /99	E+ /0.6	10	11
MUH	Nuveen CA High Yield Muni Bd A	NCHAX	C	(800) 257-8787	9.80	A+ /9.9	6.23 /99	6.89 /99	11.74 /99	E+ /0.6	N/A	10
COH	Access Flex Bear High Yield Inv	AFBIX	E-	(888) 776-3637	8.68	E- /0.0	-7.66 / 2	-9.52 / 0	-12.00 / 0	E+ /0.7	0	11
EM	Deutsche Enh Emg Mrkts Fxd Inc	SZEAX	E-	(800) 728-3337	9.04	E- /0.2	-2.95 /12	-2.87 / 3	0.40 /17	E+ /0.7	8	5
COH	WA Global High Yield Bond A	SAHYX	E-	(877) 534-4627	5.83	E /0.3	-6.59 / 3	-1.54 / 6	2.51 /38	E+ /0.7	6	10
COH	J Hancock High Yield NAV		E	(800) 257-3336	7.29	E /0.4	-8.75 / 1	-1.18 / 7	2.89 /43	E+ /0.7	7	10
COH	First Eagle High Yield I	FEHIX	E	(800) 334-2143	8.18	E /0.5	-7.73 / 2	-0.74 /10	2.97 /45	E+ /0.7	9	N/A
COH	RidgeWorth Seix High Income A	SAHIX	E	(888) 784-3863	5.92	E+ /0.7	-5.77 / 3	0.51 /33	3.32 /50	E+ /0.7	19	5
GEI	J Hancock Global Income A	JYGAX	E	(800) 257-3336	8.90	D- /1.2	-1.54 /18	-0.09 /15	2.97 /45	E+ /0.7	9	7
EM	TCW Emerging Markets Income N	TGINX	D-	(800) 386-3829	9.95	D+ /2.8	2.05 /72	-1.02 / 8	3.31 /50	E+ /0.7	30	6
EM	JPMorgan Emerg Mkt Debt A	JEDAX	D-	(800) 480-4111	7.91	C- /3.0	1.53 /67	0.35 /31	4.65 /69	E+ /0.7	81	7
EM	Franklin Emg Mkt Debt Opportunity	FEMDX	D-	(800) 342-5236	10.08	C- /3.1	2.26 /73	-0.63 /11	3.07 /46	E+ /0.7	41	10
EM	DoubleLine Em Mkts Fxd Inc N	DLENX	D	(877) 354-6311	9.68	C /4.7	-0.73 /24	0.86 /40	3.56 /54	E+ /0.7	89	6
EM	Goldman Sachs Emg Mkts Debt A	GSDAX	D	(800) 526-7384	12.25	C+ /5.7	4.42 /84	2.35 /68	5.83 /76	E+ /0.7	97	13
MUS	Oppenheimer Rochester AMT-Fr	OPNYX	D	(888) 470-0862	11.11	C+ /6.3	3.60 /91	2.12 /78	7.33 /97	E+ /0.7	5	14

● Denotes fund is closed to new investors

Section VII

Top-Rated Bond Mutual Funds by Risk Category

A compilation of those

Fixed Income Mutual Funds

receiving the highest TheStreet Investment Ratings

within each risk grade.

Funds are listed in order by Overall Investment Rating.

Section VII Contents

This section contains a summary analysis of the top 100 rated bond and money market mutual funds within each risk grade. Based on your personal risk tolerance, each page shows those funds that have achieved the best financial performance over the past three years.

In order to optimize the utility of our top and bottom fund lists, rather than listing all funds in a multi-class series, a single fund from each series is selected for display as the primary share class. Whenever possible, the selected fund is one that a retail investor would be most likely to choose. This share class may not be appropriate for every investor, so please consult with your financial advisor, the fund company, and the fund's prospectus before placing your trade.

Take the Investor Profile Quiz in the Appendix for assistance in determining your own risk tolerance level. Then you can use this section to identify those funds that are most appropriate for your investing style.

Note that increased risk does not always mean increased performance. Most of the riskiest mutual funds in the E (Very Weak) Risk Rating category have also provided very poor returns to their shareholders. Funds in the D and E Risk Rating categories generally represent speculative ventures that should not be entered into lightly.

1. Fund Type

The mutual fund's peer category based on its investment objective as stated in its prospectus.

COH	Corporate - High Yield	MMT	Money Market - Tax Free
COI	Corporate - Inv. Grade	MTG	Mortgage
EM	Emerging Market	MUH	Municipal - High Yield
GEN	General	MUI	Municipal - Insured
GEI	General - Inv. Grade	MUN	Municipal - National
GEL	General - Long Term	MUS	Municipal - Single State
GES	General - Short & Interm.	USL	U.S. Gov.- Long Term
GL	Global	USS	U.S. Gov. - Short & Interm
LP	Loan Participation	USA	U.S. Gov. - Agency
MM	Money Market	US	U.S. Gov. - Treasury

A blank fund type means that the mutual fund has not yet been categorized.

2. Fund Name

The name of the mutual fund as stated in its prospectus, which can sometimes differ slightly from the name that the company uses for advertising. If you cannot find the particular mutual fund you are interested in, or if you have any doubts regarding the precise name, verify the information with your broker or on your account statement. Also, use the fund's ticker symbol for confirmation. (See column 3.)

3. Ticker Symbol

The unique alphabetic symbol used for identifying and trading a specific mutual fund. No two funds can have the same ticker symbol, and the ticker symbol for mutual funds always ends with an "X".

A handful of funds currently show no associated ticker symbol. This means that the fund is either small or new since the NASD only assigns a ticker symbol to funds with at least $25 million in assets or 1,000 shareholders.

4. Overall Investment Rating

Our overall rating is measured on a scale from A to E based on each fund's risk-adjusted performance. Please see page 11 for specific descriptions of each letter grade. Also, refer to page 7 for information on how our ratings are derived. Most important, when using this rating, please be sure to consider the warnings beginning on page 13 regarding the ratings' limitations and the underlying assumptions.

5. Phone

The telephone number of the company managing the fund. Call this number to receive a prospectus or other information about the fund.

6. Net Asset Value (NAV)

The fund's share price as of the date indicated. A fund's NAV is computed by dividing the value of the fund's asset holdings, less accrued fees and expenses, by the number of its shares outstanding.

7. Performance Rating/Points

A letter grade rating based solely on the mutual fund's financial performance over the trailing three years, without any consideration for the amount of risk the fund poses. Like the overall Investment Rating, the Performance Rating is measured on a scale from A to E for ease of interpretation. The points score indicates where the Performance Rating falls on a scale of 0 to 10.

In the case of funds investing in municipal or other tax-free securities, this rating is based on the taxable equivalent return of the fund assuming the maximum marginal U.S. tax rate (35%).

8. 1-Year Total Return

The total return the fund has provided investors over the preceeding twelve months. This total return figure is computed based on the fund's dividend distributions and share price appreciation/depreciation during the period, net of the expenses and fees it imposes on its shareholders. Although the total return figure does not reflect an adjustment for any loads the fund may carry, such adjustments have been made in deriving TheStreet Investment Ratings.

9. 1-Year Total Return Percentile

The fund's percentile rank based on its one-year performance compared to that of all other fixed income funds in existence for at least one year. A score of 99 is the best possible, indicating that the fund outperformed 99% of the other mutual funds. Zero is the worst possible percentile score.

In the case of funds investing in municipal or other tax-free securities, this percentile rank is based on the taxable equivalent return of the fund assuming the maximum marginal U.S. tax rate (35%).

10. 3-Year Total Return	The total annual return the fund has provided investors over the preceeding three years.
11. 3-Year Total Return Percentile	The fund's percentile rank based on its three-year performance compared to that of all other fixed income funds in existence for at least three years. A score of 99 is the best possible, indicating that the fund outperformed 99% of the other mutual funds. Zero is the worst possible percentile score. In the case of funds investing in municipal or other tax-free securities, this percentile rank is based on the taxable equivalent return of the fund assuming the maximum marginal U.S. tax rate (35%).
12. 5-Year Total Return	The total annual return the fund has provided investors over the preceeding five years.
13. 5-Year Total Return Percentile	The fund's percentile rank based on its five-year performance compared to that of all other fixed income funds in existence for at least five years. A score of 99 is the best possible, indicating that the fund outperformed 99% of the other mutual funds. Zero is the worst possible percentile score. In the case of funds investing in municipal or other tax-free securities, this percentile rank is based on the taxable equivalent return of the fund assuming the maximum marginal U.S. tax rate (35%).
14. Risk Rating/Points	A letter grade rating based solely on the mutual fund's risk as determined by its monthly performance volatility over the trailing three years and the underlying credit risk and interest rate risk of its investment portfolio. The risk rating does not take into consideration the overall financial performance the fund has achieved or the total return it has provided to its shareholders. Like the overall Investment Rating, the Risk Rating is measured on a scale from A to E for ease of interpretation. The points score indicates where the Risk Rating falls on a scale of 0 to 10.
15. Manager Quality Percentile	The manager quality percentile is based on a ranking of the fund's alpha, a statistical measure representing the difference between a fund's actual returns and its expected performance given its level of risk. Fund managers who have been able to exceed the fund's statistically expected performance receive a high percentile rank with 99 representing the highest possible score. At the other end of the spectrum, fund managers who have actually detracted from the fund's expected performance receive a low percentile rank with 0 representing the lowest possible score.
16. Manager Tenure	The number of years the current manager has been managing the fund. Since fund managers who deliver substandard returns are usually replaced, a long tenure is usually a good sign that shareholders are satisfied that the fund is achieving its stated objectives.

99 Pct = Best 0 Pct = Worst						PERFORMANCE				RISK	FUND MGR	
							Annualized Total Return Through 3/31/16					
Fund Type	Fund Name	Ticker Symbol	Overall Investment Rating	Phone	Net Asset Value As of 3/31/16	Performance Rating/Pts	1Yr / Pct	3Yr / Pct	5Yr / Pct	Risk Rating/Pts	Mgr. Quality Pct	Mgr. Tenure (Years)
MUS	Colorado Bond Shares	HICOX	A+	(800) 572-0069	9.14	B+ / 8.8	4.61 / 97	4.05 / 96	4.80 / 84	A- / 9.1	98	26
MUN	Vanguard Lmtd-Term Tax-Exempt	VMLTX	A	(800) 662-7447	11.05	C+ / 6.4	1.57 / 74	1.27 / 60	1.86 / 43	A- / 9.1	73	8
MUN	Oppenheimer Rochester Sht Term	ORSTX	A	(888) 470-0862	3.75	C+ / 6.1	1.64 / 75	1.82 / 74	2.56 / 61	A / 9.3	90	6
MUN	Pacific Capital T/F Sh-Interm Y	PTFSX	A	(888) 739-1390	10.25	C+ / 5.9	1.50 / 74	1.06 / 55	1.35 / 32	A- / 9.0	56	12
GEI	Vanguard Sh-Term Invest-Grade	VFSTX	A-	(800) 662-7447	10.69	C+ / 5.9	1.73 / 69	1.67 / 55	2.25 / 34	A- / 9.0	86	8
MUS	DFA CA Sht Trm Muni Bd Inst	DFCMX	A-	(800) 984-9472	10.35	C / 5.5	1.26 / 71	0.95 / 51	1.21 / 29	A / 9.4	77	9
GES	Baird Short-Term Bond Inst	BSBIX	A-	(866) 442-2473	9.68	C / 5.4	1.30 / 63	1.46 / 51	2.09 / 32	A / 9.4	88	12
MUN	DFA Short Term Municipal Bd Inst	DFSMX	B+	(800) 984-9472	10.23	C / 5.2	1.28 / 72	0.86 / 49	1.06 / 27	A / 9.3	77	14
MUN	USAA T/E Short Term Bond Fund	USSTX	B+	(800) 382-8722	10.59	C / 4.9	0.60 / 57	0.83 / 48	1.85 / 43	A+ / 9.8	76	13
GES	Vanguard Short-Term Bd Idx	VBISX	B	(800) 662-7447	10.56	C / 4.9	1.43 / 65	1.15 / 45	1.69 / 28	A- / 9.0	73	3
USS	Schwab Short-Term Bond Market	SWBDX	B	(800) 407-0256	9.35	C / 4.8	1.40 / 65	1.05 / 44	1.54 / 26	A- / 9.0	73	12
GEI	Weitz Short Intm Income Inst	WEFIX	B	(800) 232-4161	12.30	C / 4.7	0.83 / 56	1.09 / 44	1.97 / 31	A- / 9.0	75	20
GES	Homestead Short Term Bond	HOSBX	B	(800) 258-3030	5.20	C / 4.6	0.64 / 52	1.11 / 45	2.06 / 32	A / 9.5	84	25
GEI	• Fidelity Short-Term Bond	FSHBX	B	(800) 544-8544	8.61	C / 4.5	1.01 / 59	0.97 / 42	1.38 / 24	A+ / 9.6	81	9
USS	Sit US Government Securities	SNGVX	B	(800) 332-5580	11.07	C / 4.5	1.60 / 68	0.85 / 40	1.38 / 24	A / 9.3	79	29
MUS	T Rowe Price MD ShTm Tax-Free	PRMDX	B	(800) 638-5660	5.23	C / 4.4	0.85 / 63	0.59 / 41	0.82 / 23	A / 9.5	66	20
MUN	Vanguard Short-Term Tax-Exempt	VWSTX	B	(800) 662-7447	15.82	C- / 4.1	0.64 / 58	0.53 / 39	0.83 / 23	A+ / 9.8	75	20
US	Fidelity Spartan S/T TyBd In Inv	FSBIX	B-	(800) 544-8544	10.54	C / 4.6	1.39 / 65	0.94 / 41	1.37 / 24	A- / 9.0	70	2
USS	Vanguard Short-Term Federal Inv	VSGBX	B-	(800) 662-7447	10.82	C / 4.5	1.36 / 64	0.91 / 41	1.38 / 24	A- / 9.2	73	11
GEI	Tributary Short/Intmdt Bond Inst	FOSIX	B-	(800) 662-4203	9.38	C / 4.5	1.09 / 60	0.95 / 42	1.87 / 30	A- / 9.2	73	13
GEI	Sextant Short-Term Bond Fund	STBFX	B-	(800) 728-8762	5.04	C / 4.5	1.30 / 63	0.94 / 42	1.13 / 22	A- / 9.1	75	21
GEI	USAA Short Term Bond Retail	USSBX	B-	(800) 382-8722	9.10	C / 4.5	0.57 / 51	1.04 / 44	1.98 / 31	A- / 9.1	77	14
GES	SA Global Fixed Income Fund	SAXIX	B-	(800) 366-7266	9.73	C / 4.5	1.07 / 60	0.86 / 40	1.48 / 25	A- / 9.0	58	17
USS	Fidelity Limited Term Government	FFXSX	B-	(800) 544-8544	10.11	C / 4.4	1.09 / 60	0.90 / 41	1.36 / 24	A- / 9.0	61	8
GEI	Metropolitan West Strategic Inc M	MWSTX	B-	(800) 496-8298	7.99	C / 4.4	-0.65 / 25	1.37 / 50	3.32 / 50	A- / 9.0	88	13
GEI	Cavanal Hill Sht-Tm Inc NL Inv	APSTX	B-	(800) 762-7085	9.59	C- / 4.2	0.58 / 51	0.94 / 41	1.99 / 31	A / 9.4	77	22
GEI	Metropolitan West Low Dur Bd M	MWLDX	B-	(800) 496-8298	8.73	C- / 4.1	0.32 / 46	0.96 / 42	2.20 / 34	A+ / 9.6	83	19
US	Vanguard Short-Term Treasury Inv	VFISX	B-	(800) 662-7447	10.76	C- / 4.1	1.15 / 61	0.73 / 38	1.07 / 21	A / 9.3	74	16
MUN	USAA Ultra Short-Term Bond Fund	UUSTX	B-	(800) 382-8722	9.94	C- / 4.0	-0.23 / 29	0.65 / 43	1.34 / 32	A+ / 9.7	80	6
COI	TD Asset Mgmt Short-Term Bond	TDSBX	B-		10.20	C- / 4.0	0.75 / 54	0.71 / 37	1.02 / 21	A+ / 9.6	77	7
GEI	BMO Short-Term Income Y	MSINX	B-	(800) 236-3863	9.36	C- / 4.0	0.93 / 57	0.75 / 38	1.52 / 26	A / 9.5	73	4
GEI	Northern Ultra-Short Fixed Income	NUSFX	B-	(800) 595-9111	10.18	C- / 3.9	0.69 / 53	0.74 / 38	1.06 / 21	A+ / 9.8	81	7
USS	Vanguard Short-Term Gvt Bd Idx	VSBSX	B-	(800) 662-7447	20.40	C- / 3.9	0.89 / 57	0.68 / 37	0.80 / 19	A+ / 9.7	76	3
MUN	Alpine Ultra Short Muni Inc Inst	ATOIX	B-	(888) 785-5578	10.04	C- / 3.7	0.54 / 56	0.52 / 39	0.79 / 22	A+ / 9.9	82	14
USS	Touchstone Ut Sh Dr Fxd Inc Z	TSDOX	B-	(800) 543-0407	9.30	C- / 3.6	0.63 / 52	0.59 / 35	1.00 / 20	A+ / 9.9	81	8
GEI	• Thrivent Limited Maturity Bond A	LBLAX	C+	(800) 847-4836	12.36	C- / 4.1	0.44 / 49	0.84 / 40	1.34 / 23	A- / 9.2	72	17
GES	T Rowe Price Short Term Bond	PRWBX	C+	(800) 638-5660	4.73	C- / 3.9	0.64 / 52	0.70 / 37	1.24 / 23	A / 9.4	72	21
GEI	Vantagepoint Low Duration Bond	VPIPX	C+	(800) 669-7400	10.04	C- / 3.9	0.41 / 48	0.75 / 38	1.42 / 25	A / 9.3	72	12
MTG	AMF Ultra Short Mortgage Fund	ASARX	C+	(800) 527-3713	7.22	C- / 3.9	-0.42 / 27	1.06 / 44	1.16 / 22	A- / 9.2	86	7
USS	Homestead Short Term Govt Sec	HOSGX	C+	(800) 258-3030	5.23	C- / 3.9	0.97 / 58	0.66 / 36	1.14 / 22	A- / 9.1	58	21
MUN	JPMorgan Short Term Muni Bond	OSTAX	C+	(800) 480-4111	10.69	C- / 3.9	1.54 / 74	0.87 / 49	1.20 / 29	A- / 9.0	47	10
GEI	Payden Low Duration Investor	PYSBX	C+	(888) 409-8007	10.05	C- / 3.8	0.54 / 50	0.69 / 37	1.44 / 25	A / 9.5	76	N/A
USS	AMF Short-US Government	ASITX	C+	(800) 527-3713	9.02	C- / 3.8	0.57 / 51	0.70 / 37	1.11 / 21	A- / 9.2	N/A	7
GEI	TIAA-CREF Sh Trm Bond Retail	TCTRX	C+	(800) 842-2252	10.34	C- / 3.8	0.77 / 55	0.63 / 36	1.52 / 26	A- / 9.2	56	10
GEI	Northern Short Bond	BSBAX	C+	(800) 637-1380	18.86	C- / 3.8	0.41 / 48	0.66 / 36	1.41 / 25	A- / 9.2	63	6
USS	Commerce Short Term Govt	CFSTX	C+	(800) 995-6365	17.42	C- / 3.7	0.73 / 54	0.60 / 35	1.28 / 23	A- / 9.1	55	22
GES	SEI Daily Inc Tr-Ultra Sh Dur Bd A	SECPX	C+	(800) 342-5734	9.30	C- / 3.6	0.58 / 51	0.61 / 35	0.91 / 20	A+ / 9.8	80	17
MUI	BNY Mellon National ST Muni Bd	MPSTX	C+	(800) 645-6561	12.81	C- / 3.6	0.37 / 51	0.42 / 36	0.88 / 24	A / 9.5	53	1
GL	Payden Global Low Duration	PYGSX	C+	(888) 409-8007	9.99	C- / 3.6	0.10 / 41	0.68 / 36	1.68 / 27	A / 9.3	86	N/A
USS	SEI Daily Inc Tr-Sh Dur Gov Bd A	TCSGX	C+	(800) 342-5734	10.51	C- / 3.6	0.61 / 52	0.54 / 34	0.98 / 20	A / 9.3	59	13
USS	J Hancock Sh Tm Govt Inc NAV		C+	(800) 257-3336	9.65	C- / 3.6	0.81 / 55	0.49 / 33	1.05 / 21	A- / 9.1	52	N/A
USS	Payden US Government Adv	PYUWX	C+	(888) 409-8007	10.65	C- / 3.6	0.49 / 49	0.55 / 34	1.19 / 22	A- / 9.0	48	N/A

• Denotes fund is closed to new investors

						PERFORMANCE				RISK	FUND MGR	
99 Pct = Best *0 Pct = Worst* Fund Type	Fund Name	Ticker Symbol	Overall Investment Rating	Phone	Net Asset Value As of 3/31/16	Perform-ance Rating/Pts	Annualized Total Return Through 3/31/16 1Yr / Pct	3Yr / Pct	5Yr / Pct	Risk Rating/Pts	Mgr. Quality Pct	Mgr. Tenure (Years)
MUN	BMO Ultra Sht Tax-Free Y	MUYSX	**C+**	(800) 236-3863	10.07	**C- /3.5**	0.11 /43	0.44 /36	0.78 /22	**A+ / 9.9**	75	1
GEI	RidgeWorth Seix Ultra Short Bond I	SISSX	**C+**	(888) 784-3863	9.93	**C- /3.5**	0.41 /48	0.58 /35	0.89 /20	**A+ / 9.9**	79	10
GL	DFA Two Year Glbl Fixed Inc Inst	DFGFX	**C+**	(800) 984-9472	9.96	**C- /3.5**	0.63 /52	0.52 /33	0.68 /18	**A+ / 9.8**	83	17
GEI	Payden Limited Maturity Investor	PYLMX	**C+**	(888) 409-8007	9.43	**C- /3.5**	0.33 /46	0.55 /34	0.72 /19	**A+ / 9.8**	79	N/A
MUN	Wells Fargo ST Muni Bd A	WSMAX	**C+**	(800) 222-8222	9.94	**C- /3.5**	0.79 /62	0.87 /49	1.59 /37	**A+ / 9.8**	81	16
GEI	Principal Short-Term Income Fd A	SRHQX	**C+**	(800) 222-5852	12.17	**C- /3.5**	0.86 /56	1.06 /44	1.84 /29	**A / 9.4**	81	6
COI	Frost Low Duration Bond Inv	FADLX	**C+**	(866) 777-7818	10.24	**C- /3.5**	0.30 /46	0.54 /34	1.63 /27	**A / 9.3**	62	14
COI	Transamerica Short-Term Bond A	ITAAX	**C+**	(888) 233-4339	10.13	**C- /3.5**	0.40 /48	1.27 /48	2.35 /36	**A- / 9.2**	87	5
GEI	SEI Instl Mgd Tr-Enhanced Inc A	SEEAX	**C+**	(800) 342-5734	7.40	**C- /3.5**	-0.40 /27	0.90 /41	1.59 /26	**A- / 9.1**	83	10
COI	Hartford Short Duration A	HSDAX	**C+**	(888) 843-7824	9.80	**C- /3.5**	0.64 /52	1.03 /43	1.79 /29	**A- / 9.0**	79	4
MTG	Northern Tax-Advtged Ult-Sh Fxd	NTAUX	**C+**	(800) 595-9111	10.12	**C- /3.4**	0.41 /48	0.52 /33	0.76 /19	**A+ / 9.9**	76	7
MUN	SEI Tax-Exempt Tr-Shrt Dur Muni	SUMAX	**C+**	(800) 342-5734	10.04	**C- /3.4**	0.21 /46	0.34 /34	0.63 /20	**A+ / 9.9**	72	5
GEI	LWAS DFA Two Year Fixed	DFCFX	**C+**	(800) 984-9472	10.00	**C- /3.4**	0.65 /52	0.47 /33	0.63 /18	**A+ / 9.8**	74	N/A
USS	LWAS DFA Two Year Government	DFYGX	**C+**	(800) 984-9472	9.88	**C- /3.4**	0.51 /50	0.44 /32	0.56 /18	**A+ / 9.8**	71	N/A
MUN	Sanford C Bernstein Sh-Dur Dvrs	SDDMX	**C+**	(212) 486-5800	12.60	**C- /3.4**	0.45 /53	0.28 /32	0.75 /22	**A+ / 9.7**	55	22
GEI	Voya Limited Maturity Bond Adv	IMBAX	**C+**	(800) 992-0180	9.90	**C- /3.4**	0.35 /47	0.47 /33	0.64 /18	**A+ / 9.7**	69	7
GEI	Wells Fargo Sh-Tm Bd A	SSTVX	**C+**	(800) 222-8222	8.74	**C- /3.4**	0.80 /55	1.01 /43	1.41 /25	**A+ / 9.6**	84	12
MTG	TCW Short Term Bond I	TGSMX	**C+**	(800) 386-3829	8.69	**C- /3.3**	0.26 /45	0.47 /33	0.98 /20	**A+ / 9.9**	76	6
GEI	Columbia CMG Ultra Short Term	CMGUX	**C+**	(800) 345-6611	9.00	**C- /3.3**	0.48 /49	0.46 /32	0.64 /18	**A+ / 9.9**	77	4
MTG	PIA Short-Term Securities Adv	PIASX	**C+**	(800) 251-1970	10.01	**C- /3.3**	0.34 /47	0.45 /32	0.45 /17	**A+ / 9.8**	75	N/A
GL	BBH Limited Duration Class N	BBBMX	**C+**	(800) 625-5759	10.06	**C- /3.3**	-0.01 /31	0.57 /34	1.13 /22	**A+ / 9.7**	84	5
GEI	Fidelity Adv Short-Fixed Income A	FSFAX	**C+**	(800) 522-7297	9.35	**C- /3.3**	0.77 /55	0.76 /38	1.17 /22	**A+ / 9.6**	74	9
GEI	William Blair Low Duration N	WBLNX	**C+**	(800) 742-7272	9.17	**C- /3.3**	0.26 /45	0.39 /31	1.07 /21	**A / 9.3**	54	7
US	US Global Inv Govt Ultra-Short	UGSDX	**C+**	(800) 873-8637	2.01	**C- /3.3**	0.38 /48	0.44 /32	0.27 /16	**A- / 9.2**	64	27
GEI	Invesco Short Term Bond A	STBAX	**C+**	(800) 959-4246	8.54	**C- /3.3**	0.56 /51	1.09 /44	1.63 /27	**A- / 9.2**	82	7
GEI	Dreyfus Short Term Inc D	DSTIX	**C+**	(800) 782-6620	10.37	**C- /3.3**	-0.08 /30	0.49 /33	1.30 /23	**A- / 9.1**	52	8
GES	DFA One-Yr Fixed Inc Inst	DFIHX	**C+**	(800) 984-9472	10.31	**C- /3.2**	0.51 /50	0.40 /31	0.54 /17	**A+ / 9.9**	76	33
GEI	Trust for Credit Uns Sh Dur TCU	TCUDX	**C+**	(800) 342-5828	9.72	**C- /3.2**	0.52 /50	0.36 /31	0.71 /18	**A+ / 9.8**	61	21
COI	Transamerica Prt High Quality	DVHQX	**C+**	(888) 233-4339	11.20	**C- /3.2**	0.54 /50	0.31 /30	0.90 /20	**A+ / 9.6**	58	26
USS	BNY Mellon ST US Gov Sec M	MPSUX	**C+**	(800) 645-6561	11.84	**C- /3.2**	0.59 /51	0.34 /30	0.37 /16	**A+ / 9.6**	56	16
GEI	Aberdeen Ultra-Short Dur Bond	AUDIX	**C+**	(866) 667-9231	9.89	**C- /3.1**	0.47 /49	0.35 /31	0.66 /18	**A+ / 9.9**	74	6
GEI	Metropolitan West Ultra Short Bnd	MWUSX	**C+**	(800) 496-8298	4.27	**C- /3.1**	0.17 /43	0.44 /32	1.31 /23	**A+ / 9.8**	78	13
GEI	JPMorgan Limited Duration Bd A	ONUAX	**C+**	(800) 480-4111	9.97	**C- /3.1**	0.19 /44	1.12 /45	2.09 /32	**A+ / 9.6**	87	21
COI	Wilmington Short-Term Bd A	MVSAX	**C+**	(800) 336-9970	10.06	**C- /3.1**	0.67 /53	0.71 /37	1.10 /21	**A / 9.5**	76	20
MUN	WA Short Duration Muni Income A	SHDAX	**C+**	(877) 534-4627	5.12	**C- /3.1**	0.48 /54	0.80 /47	1.44 /34	**A / 9.5**	70	13
MUS	Sanford C Bernstein Sh Dur NY	SDNYX	**C+**	(212) 486-5800	12.46	**C- /3.0**	0.27 /48	0.16 /29	0.72 /21	**A+ / 9.8**	51	22
MUN	Columbia Sh-Term Muni Bd A	NSMMX	**C+**	(800) 345-6611	10.42	**C- /3.0**	0.54 /56	0.42 /36	0.88 /24	**A+ / 9.7**	59	4
MUN	Nuveen Short Term Municipal	FSHAX	**C+**	(800) 257-8787	10.12	**C- /3.0**	0.89 /64	0.79 /47	1.78 /41	**A+ / 9.6**	75	14
GEI	Pioneer Short Term Income A	STABX	**C+**	(800) 225-6292	9.52	**D+ /2.9**	0.65 /52	0.96 /42	1.77 /28	**A+ / 9.8**	86	10
US	GMO US Treasury	GUSTX	**C+**		25.01	**D+ /2.8**	0.26 /45	0.15 /28	0.13 /15	**A+ / 9.9**	72	2
US	RidgeWorth Seix Ltd Dur I	SAMLX	**C+**	(888) 784-3863	9.83	**D+ /2.8**	0.25 /45	0.21 /29	0.46 /17	**A+ / 9.9**	74	14
USS	RidgeWorth Seix US Gvt Sec U/S	SIGVX	**C+**	(888) 784-3863	10.03	**D+ /2.8**	-0.13 /30	0.26 /30	0.73 /19	**A+ / 9.9**	73	10
GEI	SA US Fixed Income Fund	SAUFX	**C+**	(800) 366-7266	10.21	**D+ /2.8**	0.35 /47	0.10 /27	0.20 /16	**A+ / 9.8**	58	17
MUN	Lord Abbett Shrt Duration Tax-Fr A	LSDAX	**C**	(888) 522-2388	15.76	**C- /3.2**	0.92 /65	0.76 /46	1.58 /37	**A- / 9.2**	55	8
MUN	Federated Sh Int Dur Muni A	FMTAX	**C**	(800) 341-7400	10.33	**C- /3.2**	0.24 /47	0.52 /39	1.62 /38	**A- / 9.1**	39	20
USS	Oppenheimer Limited-Term Bond A	OUSGX	**C**	(888) 470-0862	4.54	**C- /3.2**	0.10 /41	1.12 /45	2.72 /41	**A- / 9.0**	84	7
US	Invesco Sh Dur Infl Pro A	LMTAX	**C**	(800) 959-4246	10.60	**C- /3.0**	1.83 /70	0.53 /34	0.47 /17	**A / 9.4**	74	7
USS	Sterling Capital Short Dur Bd A	BSGAX	**C**	(800) 228-1872	8.80	**C- /3.0**	0.59 /51	0.77 /38	1.58 /26	**A / 9.4**	78	5

• Denotes fund is closed to new investors

Fund Type	Fund Name (99 Pct = Best; 0 Pct = Worst)	Ticker Symbol	Overall Investment Rating	Phone	Net Asset Value As of 3/31/16	PERFORMANCE: Performance Rating/Pts	PERFORMANCE: Annualized Total Return Through 3/31/16 1Yr / Pct	3Yr / Pct	5Yr / Pct	RISK: Risk Rating/Pts	FUND MGR: Mgr. Quality Pct	Mgr. Tenure (Years)
MUS	Saturna Idaho Tax-Exempt	NITEX	**A+**	(800) 728-8762	5.53	**A- /9.2**	3.68 / 92	3.23 / 90	4.09 / 78	**B- / 7.3**	80	21
MUN	USAA Tax-Exempt Interm-Term	USATX	**A+**	(800) 382-8722	13.61	**A- /9.1**	3.43 / 89	3.12 / 89	5.34 / 88	**B- / 7.3**	75	13
MUN	Federated Interm Muni Trust Y	FIMYX	**A+**	(800) 341-7400	10.31	**A- /9.1**	3.82 / 93	2.99 / 88	4.78 / 83	**B- / 7.0**	N/A	21
MUN	State Farm Muni Bond	SFBDX	**A+**	(800) 447-4930	8.88	**A- /9.1**	3.31 / 88	3.12 / 89	4.49 / 81	**B- / 7.0**	72	18
MUN	Schwab Tax-Free Bond Fund	SWNTX	**A+**	(800) 407-0256	11.99	**A- /9.0**	3.21 / 87	2.99 / 88	4.65 / 83	**B- / 7.2**	70	8
MUN	BMO Intermediate Tax Free Y	MITFX	**A+**	(800) 236-3863	11.45	**A- /9.0**	3.02 / 85	3.04 / 88	4.91 / 84	**B- / 7.0**	N/A	22
MUS	Fidelity MN Muni Inc	FIMIX	**A+**	(800) 544-8544	11.84	**B+ /8.9**	3.57 / 91	3.00 / 88	4.42 / 81	**B- / 7.1**	N/A	6
MUS	Payden CA Muni Inc Investor	PYCRX	**A+**	(888) 409-8007	10.41	**B+ /8.9**	2.86 / 84	2.94 / 88	4.42 / 81	**B- / 7.0**	63	N/A
MUS	CA Tax-Free Income Direct	CFNTX	**A+**	(800) 955-9988	11.82	**B+ /8.7**	2.67 / 82	2.73 / 85	4.71 / 83	**B / 7.6**	61	13
MUN	BNY Mellon NY Int TxEx Inv	MNYIX	**A+**	(800) 645-6561	11.46	**B+ /8.4**	3.13 / 86	2.26 / 80	4.02 / 78	**B- / 7.2**	39	9
MUI	SEI Tax-Exempt Tr-NY Muni Bond	SENYX	**A+**	(800) 342-5734	10.94	**B+ /8.3**	3.14 / 86	2.27 / 80	3.54 / 74	**B / 7.6**	48	17
MUS	Kansas Municipal	KSMUX	**A+**	(800) 601-5593	11.02	**B+ /8.3**	3.22 / 87	3.00 / 88	4.38 / 80	**B- / 7.0**	N/A	20
MUS	SEI Tax-Exempt Tr-PA Muni Bond	SEPAX	**A+**	(800) 342-5734	10.89	**B /8.1**	3.15 / 86	2.05 / 77	3.82 / 76	**B / 7.7**	42	17
MUN	Thornburg Intermediate Muni A	THIMX	**A+**	(800) 847-0200	14.38	**B /8.1**	2.75 / 83	2.62 / 84	4.64 / 82	**B / 7.7**	58	5
MUS	Victory OH Muni Bond A	SOHTX	**A+**	(800) 539-3863	11.39	**B /8.1**	2.78 / 83	2.62 / 84	3.89 / 77	**B / 7.6**	58	22
MUI	BNY Mellon PA Inter Muni Bond M	MPPIX	**A+**	(800) 645-6561	12.51	**B /8.1**	2.55 / 81	1.95 / 76	3.73 / 76	**B- / 7.1**	30	16
GEI	Ave Maria Bond	AVEFX	**A+**	(866) 283-6274	11.27	**B /8.0**	2.51 / 75	3.08 / 77	3.70 / 56	**B / 8.1**	97	13
MUN	Frost Municipal Bond Inv	FAUMX	**A+**	(866) 777-7818	10.61	**B /8.0**	2.27 / 79	2.11 / 78	3.43 / 73	**B / 8.1**	53	14
MUS	Nationwide HighMark CA Int TF Bd	NWJKX	**A+**	(800) 848-0920	10.47	**B /8.0**	2.45 / 80	2.62 / 84	3.65 / 75	**B- / 7.2**	54	3
MUN	Glenmede Intermediate Muni Port	GTCMX	**A+**	(800) 442-8299	11.10	**B /7.9**	2.42 / 80	1.87 / 75	2.81 / 66	**B / 8.2**	49	5
MUN	Russell Tax Exempt Bond A	RTEAX	**A+**	(800) 832-6688	23.53	**B /7.9**	3.30 / 88	2.81 / 86	3.81 / 76	**B / 8.0**	78	3
MUI	SEI Tax-Exempt Tr-NJ Muni Bond	SENJX	**A+**	(800) 342-5734	10.55	**B /7.9**	2.51 / 80	1.86 / 75	3.30 / 72	**B / 7.9**	42	3
MUS	PIMCO CA Interm Muni Bond A	PCMBX	**A+**	(800) 426-0107	9.97	**B /7.9**	3.33 / 88	2.36 / 81	3.76 / 76	**B- / 7.5**	46	5
MUS	Delaware Tax Free MN Intmdt A	DXCCX	**A+**	(800) 523-1918	11.33	**B /7.9**	2.90 / 84	2.65 / 84	4.29 / 80	**B- / 7.3**	52	13
MUS	Brown Advisory Maryland Bond Inv	BIAMX	**A+**	(800) 540-6807	10.80	**B /7.8**	2.66 / 82	1.70 / 72	2.72 / 64	**B+ / 8.4**	46	2
MUS	New Hampshire Municipal	NHMUX	**A+**	(800) 601-5593	10.94	**B /7.8**	2.99 / 85	2.47 / 82	3.70 / 75	**B / 8.0**	60	13
MUN	Thornburg NY Intermediate Muni A	THNYX	**A+**	(800) 847-0200	13.36	**B /7.8**	2.82 / 83	2.29 / 80	4.22 / 79	**B / 7.8**	48	5
MUN	JPMorgan Muni Income A	OTBAX	**A+**	(800) 480-4111	10.09	**B /7.8**	3.27 / 88	2.77 / 86	3.90 / 77	**B- / 7.3**	59	10
MUS	Wells Fargo WI Tax Fr A	WWTFX	**A+**	(800) 222-8222	11.03	**B /7.7**	2.76 / 83	3.00 / 88	4.21 / 79	**B / 8.0**	83	15
MUS	Thornburg NM Intermediate Muni A	THNMX	**A+**	(800) 847-0200	13.67	**B /7.6**	2.40 / 80	2.25 / 80	3.48 / 74	**B / 7.8**	48	5
GES	DoubleLine Total Return Bond N	DLTNX	**A+**	(877) 354-6311	10.87	**B /7.6**	2.20 / 73	2.93 / 76	5.11 / 72	**B / 7.7**	88	6
MUS	Wells Fargo MN Tax Free A	NMTFX	**A+**	(800) 222-8222	10.93	**B /7.6**	2.96 / 85	2.89 / 87	4.79 / 84	**B / 7.7**	74	8
MUN	Victory National Muni A	VNMAX	**A+**	(800) 539-3863	11.09	**B- /7.5**	3.00 / 85	2.05 / 78	3.68 / 75	**B / 7.9**	45	22
MUS	Fidelity CA Ltd Term Tax-Free Bd	FCSTX	**A+**	(800) 544-8544	10.76	**B- /7.4**	1.88 / 76	1.85 / 75	2.51 / 59	**B+ / 8.9**	78	10
MUS	Jamestown VA Tax Exempt	JTEVX	**A+**	(866) 738-1126	10.21	**B- /7.4**	2.37 / 80	1.53 / 68	2.48 / 59	**B+ / 8.4**	41	11
MUN	Cavanal Hill Intmdt TxFr Bd NL Inv	APTFX	**A+**	(800) 762-7085	11.25	**B- /7.4**	1.89 / 76	1.63 / 71	3.39 / 73	**B / 8.1**	35	23
MUI	CNR CA Tax-Exempt Bond N	CCTEX	**A+**	(888) 889-0799	10.78	**B- /7.3**	1.73 / 75	1.64 / 71	2.70 / 64	**B+ / 8.5**	51	7
MUS	Wells Fargo CA Ltd Tax Fr A	SFCIX	**A+**	(800) 222-8222	10.96	**B- /7.2**	1.91 / 76	2.16 / 79	3.01 / 69	**B+ / 8.9**	88	7
MTG	Vanguard Mort-Backed Secs Idx	VMBSX	**A+**	(800) 662-7447	21.35	**B- /7.2**	2.17 / 73	2.52 / 71	3.09 / 47	**B / 8.2**	69	7
MUN	Old Westbury Muni Bond	OWMBX	**A+**	(800) 607-2200	12.09	**B- /7.1**	2.35 / 80	1.37 / 64	2.60 / 61	**B+ / 8.3**	36	18
MUS	Thornburg CA Ltd Term Muni A	LTCAX	**A+**	(800) 847-0200	13.94	**B- /7.0**	1.84 / 76	1.96 / 77	3.36 / 73	**B+ / 8.6**	72	5
MUS	Dupree KY Tax Free Short-to-Med	KYSMX	**A+**	(800) 866-0614	5.41	**C+ /6.8**	2.02 / 77	1.32 / 62	2.63 / 62	**B+ / 8.8**	58	17
MUN	Wells Fargo Intm Tax/AMT Fr A	WFTAX	**A**	(800) 222-8222	11.73	**B /8.0**	2.74 / 82	2.75 / 85	4.73 / 83	**B- / 7.0**	53	15
MUS	Maine Municipal	MEMUX	**A**	(800) 601-5593	11.18	**B /7.9**	3.22 / 87	2.51 / 83	4.27 / 80	**B- / 7.1**	47	13
MUS	Columbia AMT Fr NY Intm Muni Bd	LNYAX	**A**	(800) 345-6611	12.23	**B /7.7**	3.17 / 87	2.51 / 83	4.02 / 78	**B- / 7.3**	48	18
MUS	Columbia AMT-Fr SC Intm Muni Bd	NSCIX	**A**	(800) 345-6611	10.52	**B /7.7**	3.30 / 88	2.36 / 81	4.08 / 78	**B- / 7.1**	40	5
MUS	Aquila Churchill Tax-Free of KY A	CHTFX	**A**	(800) 437-1020	10.88	**B /7.6**	2.75 / 83	2.83 / 86	4.43 / 81	**B- / 7.5**	62	7
MTG	TCW Total Return Bond N	TGMNX	**A**	(800) 386-3829	10.61	**B- /7.5**	1.59 / 67	2.84 / 75	4.93 / 71	**B / 7.7**	79	6
MUS	Columbia AMT-Fr GA Intm Muni Bd	NGIMX	**A**	(800) 345-6611	10.85	**B- /7.5**	3.02 / 85	2.36 / 81	3.83 / 76	**B- / 7.5**	47	5
MUS	AI KS Tax-Exempt Bond A	IKSTX	**A**	(866) 410-2006	11.18	**B- /7.5**	2.40 / 80	2.89 / 87	3.95 / 77	**B- / 7.2**	60	16
GES	Tributary Income Inst	FOINX	**A**	(800) 662-4203	10.41	**B- /7.3**	1.75 / 69	2.53 / 71	3.98 / 61	**B- / 7.3**	77	13
MTG	Advisors Series Trust PIA MBS	PMTGX	**A**	(800) 251-1970	9.76	**B- /7.2**	1.85 / 70	2.58 / 72	3.05 / 46	**B / 8.0**	62	10

• Denotes fund is closed to new investors

99 Pct = Best
0 Pct = Worst

Fund Type	Fund Name	Ticker Symbol	Overall Investment Rating	Phone	Net Asset Value As of 3/31/16	PERFORMANCE: Performance Rating/Pts	Annualized Total Return Through 3/31/16: 1Yr / Pct	3Yr / Pct	5Yr / Pct	RISK: Risk Rating/Pts	FUND MGR: Mgr. Quality Pct	Mgr. Tenure (Years)
GEI	WA Intermediate Bond IS	WABSX	**A**	(888) 425-6432	11.10	**B- /7.1**	2.27 /73	2.27 /67	3.63 /55	**B /8.1**	80	7
USS	Guggenheim Investment Grade Bd	SIUSX	**A**	(800) 820-0888	17.94	**B- /7.1**	0.89 /57	3.94 /83	5.04 /72	**B /8.1**	98	4
GEI	Nationwide Core Plus Bond Inst	NWCIX	**A**	(800) 848-0920	10.23	**B- /7.1**	1.76 /69	2.41 /69	4.25 /65	**B /7.7**	78	14
MUN	Dreyfus Tax Sensitive Tot Ret Bd A	DSDAX	**A**	(800) 645-6561	23.22	**B- /7.1**	2.91 /84	2.59 /84	3.84 /76	**B /7.7**	60	15
MUS	Dupree TN Tax-Free Sh-to-Med	TTSMX	**A**	(800) 866-0614	10.88	**C+ /6.8**	1.97 /77	1.37 /64	2.18 /51	**B+ /8.6**	45	12
GEI	Scout Core Bond Fund Institutional	SCCIX	**A**	(800) 996-2862	11.72	**C+ /6.8**	2.95 /76	1.87 /59	3.76 /58	**B+ /8.4**	80	15
MTG	HC Capital US Mtg/Asst Bckd FI	HCASX	**A**	(800) 242-9596	9.85	**C+ /6.8**	1.94 /71	2.23 /66	2.95 /44	**B /8.1**	51	4
GEI	Cavanal Hill Intmdt Bond NL Inv	APFBX	**A**	(800) 762-7085	10.57	**C+ /6.5**	1.09 /60	2.24 /66	4.10 /63	**B+ /8.6**	89	23
MTG	Federated Mortgage Fund Inst	FGFIX	**A**	(800) 341-7400	9.69	**C+ /6.5**	1.76 /69	2.16 /65	2.88 /43	**B /8.2**	57	13
COI	Vanguard Short-Term Crp Bd Idx	VSCSX	**A**	(800) 662-7447	21.72	**C+ /6.2**	1.78 /70	1.89 /59	2.84 /43	**B+ /8.8**	89	7
MUS	Weitz Nebraska Tax Free Income	WNTFX	**A**	(800) 232-4161	10.12	**C+ /6.1**	1.20 /70	1.22 /59	2.35 /55	**B+ /8.9**	54	31
MUS	Columbia AMT-Fr MD Intm Muni	NMDMX	**A-**	(800) 345-6611	10.87	**B- /7.3**	2.75 /83	2.26 /80	3.79 /76	**B- /7.2**	39	5
USS	AMG Mgrs Intmd Duration Govt	MGIDX	**A-**	(800) 835-3879	10.95	**B- /7.3**	1.69 /69	2.71 /73	3.27 /49	**B- /7.1**	92	24
MUS	Bishop Street HI Muni Bond A	BHIAX	**A-**	(800) 262-9565	10.87	**B- /7.3**	2.88 /84	2.26 /80	3.90 /77	**B- /7.0**	36	9
MUS	American Century CA IT TxFr Bd A	BCIAX	**A-**	(800) 345-6488	12.08	**B- /7.1**	3.17 /87	2.54 /83	4.55 /82	**B- /7.2**	47	14
MUN	Nationwide HighMark Natl Int TFB	NWJOX	**A-**	(800) 848-0920	11.13	**B- /7.0**	2.25 /79	2.04 /77	3.15 /71	**B /7.6**	40	20
MUS	Columbia AMT-Fr NC Intm Muni Bd	NNCIX	**A-**	(800) 345-6611	10.66	**B- /7.0**	2.81 /83	2.10 /78	3.78 /76	**B /7.6**	38	5
GEI	Cavanal Hill Bond NL Inv	APBDX	**A-**	(800) 762-7085	9.67	**C+ /6.8**	1.91 /71	2.19 /65	3.94 /60	**B /7.8**	72	23
MUI	JPMorgan OH Municipal A	ONOHX	**A-**	(800) 480-4111	11.00	**C+ /6.7**	2.71 /82	2.21 /79	3.57 /75	**B /7.8**	46	22
GL	DFA Five Year Glbl Fixed Inc Inst	DFGBX	**A-**	(800) 984-9472	11.11	**C+ /6.5**	2.39 /74	1.95 /60	3.04 /46	**B /8.2**	96	17
GEI	Loomis Sayles Intm Dur Bd Inst	LSDIX	**A-**	(800) 633-3330	10.38	**C+ /6.5**	1.39 /65	2.10 /64	3.35 /51	**B /8.1**	77	11
USS	Federated Govt Income Trust Inst	FICMX	**A-**	(800) 341-7400	10.36	**C+ /6.3**	1.59 /67	1.99 /61	2.56 /38	**B+ /8.3**	85	16
GL	Federated Floating Rt Str Inc Inst	FFRSX	**A-**	(800) 341-7400	9.65	**C+ /6.2**	0.64 /52	2.20 /66	3.15 /47	**B+ /8.6**	96	6
MTG	Wright Current Income	WCIFX	**A-**	(800) 232-0013	9.41	**C+ /6.2**	1.57 /67	1.89 /59	2.78 /42	**B+ /8.3**	55	7
MUN	Thornburg Limited Term Muni A	LTMFX	**A-**	(800) 847-0200	14.61	**C+ /6.1**	1.89 /76	1.51 /68	2.88 /67	**B+ /8.7**	52	5
MUN	T Rowe Price Tax-Free Sh-Intmdt	PRFSX	**A-**	(800) 638-5660	5.65	**C+ /6.0**	1.36 /72	1.13 /56	2.09 /49	**B+ /8.9**	54	22
MUS	Dupree NC Tax Free Sh-to-Med	NTSMX	**A-**	(800) 866-0614	10.99	**C+ /5.9**	1.42 /73	1.08 /55	2.40 /56	**B+ /8.9**	47	12
MUN	Wells Fargo Str Muni Bd A	VMPAX	**A-**	(800) 222-8222	8.99	**C+ /5.9**	1.96 /77	2.18 /79	3.08 /70	**B+ /8.9**	86	6
GL	DFA S/T Extended Quality Port Inst	DFEQX	**A-**	(800) 984-9472	10.87	**C+ /5.7**	1.80 /70	1.54 /53	2.21 /34	**B+ /8.9**	93	8
USA	SEI Daily Inc Tr-GNMA Bond A	SEGMX	**B+**	(800) 342-5734	10.84	**B- /7.2**	1.86 /71	2.52 /71	3.42 /52	**B- /7.0**	87	1
MUS	Columbia AMT-Fr VA Intm Muni Bd	NVAFX	**B+**	(800) 345-6611	11.14	**B- /7.2**	2.70 /82	2.24 /80	3.60 /75	**B- /7.0**	36	5
MUN	RidgeWorth Seix Inv Grade T/E Bd	SISIX	**B+**	(888) 784-3863	12.24	**B- /7.2**	2.86 /84	2.71 /85	4.60 /82	**B- /7.0**	52	24
USA	Vanguard GNMA Inv	VFIIX	**B+**	(800) 662-7447	10.79	**B- /7.1**	2.18 /73	2.45 /70	3.35 /51	**B- /7.1**	87	10
GEI	Metropolitan West Tot Ret Bond M	MWTRX	**B+**	(800) 496-8298	10.83	**B- /7.0**	0.96 /58	2.45 /70	4.63 /69	**B- /7.1**	73	19
MUS	PNC Ohio Intermediate Tax-Ex	POXAX	**B+**	(800) 551-2145	10.94	**B- /7.0**	2.76 /83	2.11 /78	3.82 /76	**B- /7.0**	35	7
GEI	Dodge & Cox Income Fund	DODIX	**B+**	(800) 621-3979	13.47	**C+ /6.9**	0.47 /49	2.42 /69	3.80 /58	**B- /7.4**	85	N/A
MUS	Eaton Vance NY Ltd Mat Muni Inc	EXNYX	**B+**	(800) 262-1122	10.09	**C+ /6.7**	2.53 /81	1.84 /75	3.27 /72	**B- /7.5**	31	2
GEI	Commerce Bond	CFBNX	**B+**	(800) 995-6365	19.98	**C+ /6.7**	0.95 /58	2.33 /68	4.05 /62	**B- /7.4**	73	22
USA	Schwab GNMA	SWGSX	**B+**	(800) 407-0256	10.21	**C+ /6.6**	2.21 /73	2.04 /62	3.00 /45	**B- /7.3**	80	13
USA	Fidelity GNMA Fund	FGMNX	**B+**	(800) 544-8544	11.64	**C+ /6.6**	1.97 /72	2.19 /65	3.40 /51	**B- /7.3**	84	12
USS	BMO Mortgage Income Y	MRGIX	**B+**	(800) 236-3863	9.36	**C+ /6.5**	1.87 /71	2.06 /63	2.91 /44	**B /7.8**	81	4
GEI	Janus Aspen Flexible Bond Inst	JAFLX	**B+**	(800) 295-2687	11.92	**C+ /6.5**	0.52 /50	2.23 /66	4.15 /64	**B- /7.4**	68	9
MUS	JPMorgan NY T/F Bond A	VANTX	**B+**	(800) 480-4111	7.09	**C+ /6.4**	2.67 /82	2.10 /78	3.65 /75	**B /7.9**	46	11
GL	Goldman Sachs Glbl Income A	GSGIX	**B+**	(800) 526-7384	12.24	**C+ /6.4**	1.67 /68	3.02 /77	4.30 /65	**B /7.6**	98	21
MUN	Fidelity Adv Interm Municipal Inc A	FZIAX	**B+**	(800) 522-7297	10.58	**C+ /6.4**	2.34 /79	2.40 /82	3.84 /76	**B /7.6**	47	10
GEI	Baird Quality Interm Muni Bd Inv	BMBSX	**B+**	(866) 442-2473	12.08	**C+ /6.4**	2.49 /75	1.90 /59	3.19 /48	**B /7.6**	61	15
MUN	Aquila Hawaiian Tax Free Trust A	HULAX	**B+**	(800) 437-1020	11.61	**C+ /6.4**	2.92 /84	2.12 /78	3.42 /73	**B- /7.5**	38	31
GEI	Baird Interm Bond Inv	BIMSX	**B+**	(866) 442-2473	11.62	**C+ /6.3**	1.69 /69	1.84 /58	3.42 /52	**B /8.1**	60	16

• Denotes fund is closed to new investors

Data as of March 31, 2016

99 Pct = Best
0 Pct = Worst

Fund Type	Fund Name	Ticker Symbol	Overall Investment Rating	Phone	Net Asset Value As of 3/31/16	PERFORMANCE: Performance Rating/Pts	Annualized Total Return Through 3/31/16: 1Yr / Pct	3Yr / Pct	5Yr / Pct	RISK: Risk Rating/Pts	FUND MGR: Mgr. Quality Pct	Mgr. Tenure (Years)
MUS	Vanguard CA Interm-Term T-E Inv	VCAIX	A+	(800) 662-7447	11.97	A /9.5	4.04 /94	3.73 /94	5.54 /89	C+ / 5.9	80	5
MUS	Fidelity MI Muni Inc	FMHTX	A+	(800) 544-8544	12.48	A /9.4	4.11 /95	3.62 /93	5.20 /87	C+ / 5.7	76	10
MUS	Schwab California Tax-Free Bond	SWCAX	A+	(800) 407-0256	12.15	A /9.3	3.46 /90	3.45 /92	5.00 /85	C+ / 6.8	80	8
MUN	Vanguard Interm-Term Tax-Exempt	VWITX	A+	(800) 662-7447	14.39	A- /9.2	3.65 /91	3.19 /90	4.91 /85	C+ / 6.5	N/A	3
MUS	Dupree TN Tax-Free Income	TNTIX	A+	(800) 866-0614	11.72	A- /9.2	3.11 /86	3.27 /91	4.95 /85	C+ / 5.8	61	12
MUN	T Rowe Price Summit Muni Intmdt	PRSMX	A+	(800) 638-5660	12.11	A- /9.1	3.55 /91	3.13 /89	4.67 /83	C+ / 6.8	68	23
MUS	Dupree KY Tax Free Income	KYTFX	A+	(800) 866-0614	7.96	A- /9.1	3.24 /87	3.17 /90	4.87 /84	C+ / 6.3	61	17
MUI	Westcore CO Tax Exempt	WTCOX	A+	(800) 392-2673	11.76	A- /9.1	3.53 /90	3.07 /89	4.49 /81	C+ / 6.0	55	11
MUI	Pacific Capital Tax-Free Secs Y	PTXFX	A+	(888) 739-1390	10.37	A- /9.1	3.68 /92	3.06 /89	4.48 /81	C+ / 5.8	52	12
MUS	Lee Fnl Hawaii-Muni Bond Inv	SURFX	A+		11.31	A- /9.0	2.83 /83	3.17 /90	4.65 /83	C+ / 6.6	70	1
MUS	SEI Tax-Exempt Tr-CA Muni Bond	SBDAX	A+	(800) 342-5734	11.03	B+ /8.9	3.36 /89	2.80 /86	4.26 /80	C+ / 6.4	53	17
MUN	SEI Tax-Exempt Tr-Intrm Term	SEIMX	A+	(800) 342-5734	11.86	B+ /8.8	3.57 /91	2.79 /86	4.51 /82	C+ / 6.3	48	17
MUI	WesMark West Virginia Muni Bond	WMKMX	A+	(800) 341-7400	10.67	B+ /8.7	2.88 /84	2.62 /84	3.77 /76	C+ / 6.9	47	10
MUN	Invesco Intm Term Municipal Inc A	VKLMX	A+	(800) 959-4246	11.32	B+ /8.6	3.45 /90	3.21 /90	4.89 /84	C+ / 6.5	69	11
MUS	Nuveen Minnesota Intmdt Muni Bd	FAMAX	A+	(800) 257-8787	10.63	B+ /8.4	3.67 /92	3.11 /89	4.67 /83	C+ / 6.7	63	22
MUS	Fidelity PA Muni Inc	FPXTX	A	(800) 544-8544	11.39	A /9.4	3.54 /90	3.79 /95	5.47 /89	C / 5.1	74	14
MUS	Sit MN Tax Free Income	SMTFX	A	(800) 332-5580	10.63	A /9.4	3.89 /93	3.61 /93	5.74 /91	C / 5.0	69	23
MUS	Fidelity CT Muni Income Fd	FICNX	A	(800) 544-8544	11.87	A /9.4	4.18 /95	3.54 /93	4.91 /85	C / 5.0	58	14
MUS	T Rowe Price MD Tax Free Bd	MDXBX	A	(800) 638-5660	10.98	A /9.3	3.68 /92	3.49 /93	5.78 /91	C / 4.9	54	16
MUS	Dupree AL Tax Free Income	DUALX	A	(800) 866-0614	12.56	A- /9.2	3.13 /86	3.41 /92	5.50 /89	C+ / 5.6	68	15
MUS	Dupree NC Tax Free Income	NTFIX	A	(800) 866-0614	11.78	A- /9.2	3.48 /90	3.21 /90	5.42 /88	C / 5.1	49	12
MUN	Dreyfus Intermediate Muni Bd	DITEX	A	(800) 645-6561	14.09	A- /9.1	3.63 /91	3.04 /88	4.75 /83	C+ / 5.8	51	5
MUN	Northern Intermed Tax Exempt	NOITX	A	(800) 595-9111	10.82	A- /9.0	3.53 /90	2.88 /87	4.61 /82	C / 5.3	41	18
MUS	AB Municipal Income II AZ A	AAZAX	A	(800) 221-5672	11.30	B+ /8.9	4.67 /97	3.45 /92	5.25 /87	C / 5.3	62	21
MUS	Aquila Tax-Free Fd for Utah A	UTAHX	A	(800) 437-1020	10.56	B+ /8.8	3.41 /89	3.87 /95	5.60 /90	C+ / 6.0	84	7
MUS	Wells Fargo PA Tax Fr A	EKVAX	A	(800) 222-8222	11.94	B+ /8.8	3.69 /92	4.05 /96	6.12 /93	C+ / 5.7	85	7
MUS	Madison Tax Free Virginia Y	GTVAX	A	(800) 877-6089	11.73	B+ /8.7	3.11 /86	2.68 /85	3.95 /77	C+ / 5.7	38	19
MUI	Commerce Kansas T/F Intm Bond	KTXIX	A	(800) 995-6365	19.64	B+ /8.4	2.72 /82	2.47 /82	4.23 /79	C+ / 6.0	34	16
MUS	Commerce Missouri T/F Intm Bd	CFMOX	A	(800) 995-6365	19.74	B+ /8.3	2.92 /84	2.22 /79	4.05 /78	C+ / 6.4	33	17
GL	SEI Inst Intl International Fx In A	SEFIX	A	(800) 342-5734	10.16	B /8.0	1.69 /69	3.47 /80	4.25 /65	C+ / 6.6	99	8
MUS	Nuveen Oregon Intmdt Muni Bd A	FOTAX	A	(800) 257-8787	10.47	B /7.8	3.27 /88	2.54 /83	4.07 /78	C+ / 6.7	42	19
MUS	Vanguard NY Long-Term	VNYTX	A-	(800) 662-7447	12.03	A+ /9.8	4.85 /98	4.36 /97	5.94 /92	C / 4.3	78	3
MUN	Vanguard Long-Term Tax-Exempt	VWLTX	A-	(800) 662-7447	11.87	A+ /9.8	4.77 /97	4.37 /97	6.39 /94	C- / 3.9	73	6
MUS	T Rowe Price CA Tax Free Bond	PRXCX	A-	(800) 638-5660	11.77	A+ /9.8	4.56 /97	4.39 /97	6.82 /96	C- / 3.9	74	13
MUS	Vanguard PA Long-Term	VPAIX	A-	(800) 662-7447	11.79	A+ /9.7	4.31 /96	4.27 /97	5.95 /92	C / 4.3	75	5
MUS	Fidelity AZ Muni Income Fd	FSAZX	A-	(800) 544-8544	12.29	A+ /9.6	4.04 /94	4.05 /96	5.83 /91	C / 4.3	68	6
MUN	Fidelity Tax Free Bond Fd	FTABX	A-	(800) 544-8544	11.77	A+ /9.6	3.81 /93	4.04 /96	6.19 /93	C- / 4.2	62	7
MUS	Northern AZ Tax Exempt	NOAZX	A-	(800) 595-9111	10.96	A /9.4	4.06 /94	3.54 /93	5.66 /90	C / 4.7	53	17
MUS	Northern CA Intermediate T/E	NCITX	A-	(800) 595-9111	11.03	A /9.4	4.02 /94	3.44 /92	5.17 /87	C / 4.6	49	17
MUS	Wells Fargo CA Tax Fr A	SCTAX	A-	(800) 222-8222	12.15	A /9.4	4.19 /95	4.78 /98	7.32 /97	C / 4.5	89	7
MUS	Fidelity MA Muni Inc Fd	FDMMX	A-	(800) 544-8544	12.60	A /9.4	3.93 /93	3.75 /94	5.59 /89	C / 4.4	55	6
MUS	T Rowe Price GA Tax-Free Bd	GTFBX	A-	(800) 638-5660	11.79	A /9.4	3.77 /92	3.64 /93	5.85 /91	C / 4.4	53	19
MUS	Fidelity MD Muni Income Fd	SMDMX	A-	(800) 544-8544	11.52	A- /9.2	3.94 /94	3.31 /91	4.85 /84	C / 4.8	46	14
MUN	Oppenheimer Rochester Int Term	ORRWX	A-	(888) 470-0862	4.42	A- /9.1	4.74 /97	3.46 /92	4.86 /84	C / 5.0	59	6
MUS	Columbia Minnesota Tax-Exempt A	IMNTX	A-	(800) 345-6611	5.60	A- /9.0	3.86 /93	3.73 /94	5.92 /91	C / 5.2	73	9
MUS	Wells Fargo CO Tax Fr A	NWCOX	A-	(800) 222-8222	11.21	A- /9.0	4.04 /94	4.21 /97	5.93 /92	C / 5.0	84	11
MUS	PIMCO NY Muni Bond A	PNYAX	A-	(800) 426-0107	11.43	B+ /8.9	3.56 /91	3.48 /93	4.88 /84	C / 5.0	56	5
MUS	Franklin CA Interm Tax-Free A	FKCIX	A-	(800) 342-5236	12.29	B+ /8.8	3.14 /86	3.43 /92	5.48 /89	C / 5.3	61	24
MUN	Thornburg Strategic Municipal Inc	TSSAX	A-	(800) 847-0200	15.38	B+ /8.6	2.85 /84	3.21 /90	6.43 /94	C / 5.3	53	7
MUN	Nuveen Intmdt Duration Muni Bond	NMBAX	A-	(800) 257-8787	9.35	B+ /8.4	3.60 /91	3.09 /89	4.60 /82	C+ / 5.9	53	9
MUS	Aquila Tax-Free Tr of Arizona A	AZTFX	A-	(800) 437-1020	10.95	B+ /8.4	3.20 /87	3.50 /93	5.19 /87	C+ / 5.7	71	30
MUS	AB Municipal Income II MN A	AMNAX	A-	(800) 221-5672	10.52	B+ /8.4	3.56 /91	3.11 /89	4.75 /83	C+ / 5.7	52	21

• Denotes fund is closed to new investors

Fund Type	Fund Name (99 Pct = Best, 0 Pct = Worst)	Ticker Symbol	Overall Investment Rating	Phone	Net Asset Value As of 3/31/16	PERFORMANCE: Performance Rating/Pts	Annualized Total Return Through 3/31/16: 1Yr / Pct	3Yr / Pct	5Yr / Pct	RISK: Risk Rating/Pts	FUND MGR: Mgr. Quality Pct	Mgr. Tenure (Years)
MUS	WA Int Maturity California Muni A	ITCAX	**A-**	(877) 534-4627	9.10	**B+ / 8.3**	2.98 / 85	2.98 / 88	4.98 / 85	**C+ / 5.8**	51	4
MUS	Sterling Capital SC Interm TxFr A	BASCX	**A-**	(800) 228-1872	11.27	**B / 7.8**	3.03 / 85	2.24 / 80	3.84 / 76	**C+ / 6.5**	33	16
MUN	Delaware Tax-Free USA Intmdt A	DMUSX	**A-**	(800) 523-1918	12.24	**B / 7.8**	3.04 / 85	2.47 / 82	4.42 / 81	**C+ / 6.4**	38	13
MUS	Federated MI Interm Muni Tr	MMIFX	**A-**	(800) 341-7400	11.46	**B / 7.7**	3.05 / 85	2.53 / 83	4.51 / 81	**C+ / 6.8**	43	18
MUS	Aquila Tax-Free Trust of Oregon A	ORTFX	**A-**	(800) 437-1020	11.33	**B / 7.7**	2.91 / 84	2.86 / 87	4.61 / 82	**C+ / 6.5**	52	30
MUS	Columbia AMT-Fr MA Intm Muni	LMIAX	**A-**	(800) 345-6611	11.02	**B / 7.6**	3.02 / 85	2.39 / 81	3.85 / 77	**C+ / 6.8**	39	7
MUS	Sterling Capital WVA Interm TxFr A	BWVAX	**A-**	(800) 228-1872	10.22	**B / 7.6**	3.06 / 86	2.10 / 78	3.68 / 75	**C+ / 6.8**	31	16
MUS	Columbia AMT-Fr OR Inter Muni	COEAX	**A-**	(800) 345-6611	12.70	**B- / 7.4**	2.99 / 85	2.34 / 81	3.96 / 77	**C+ / 6.9**	38	13
GES	GE RSP Income	GESLX	**A-**	(800) 242-0134	11.59	**B- / 7.4**	1.23 / 62	2.66 / 73	4.14 / 63	**C+ / 6.9**	79	20
MUS	Vanguard CA Long-Term	VCITX	**B+**	(800) 662-7447	12.34	**A+ / 9.8**	4.96 / 98	4.79 / 98	7.06 / 97	**C- / 3.6**	78	5
MUS	Vanguard OH Long-Term	VOHIX	**B+**	(800) 662-7447	12.78	**A+ / 9.8**	4.85 / 98	4.47 / 97	6.26 / 93	**C- / 3.6**	64	8
MUS	Nuveen CA Muni Bond A	NCAAX	**B+**	(800) 257-8787	11.39	**A+ / 9.8**	5.72 / 99	5.51 / 99	8.39 / 99	**C- / 3.3**	91	13
MUS	Northern CA T/E Bond	NCATX	**B+**	(800) 595-9111	12.06	**A+ / 9.8**	4.96 / 98	4.87 / 98	7.66 / 98	**C- / 3.2**	72	19
MUS	Vanguard MA Tax-Exempt Inv	VMATX	**B+**	(800) 662-7447	11.03	**A+ / 9.7**	4.47 / 97	4.10 / 96	5.62 / 90	**C- / 3.9**	55	8
MUS	Fidelity OH Muni Inc	FOHFX	**B+**	(800) 544-8544	12.43	**A+ / 9.7**	4.59 / 97	4.30 / 97	5.80 / 91	**C- / 3.8**	74	10
MUS	Vanguard NJ Long-Term	VNJTX	**B+**	(800) 662-7447	12.22	**A+ / 9.6**	3.92 / 93	3.76 / 94	5.77 / 91	**C- / 3.9**	44	3
MUN	Northern Tax Exempt	NOTEX	**B+**	(800) 595-9111	10.89	**A+ / 9.6**	4.28 / 96	3.87 / 95	6.14 / 93	**C- / 3.8**	45	18
MUN	T Rowe Price Summit Muni Income	PRINX	**B+**	(800) 638-5660	12.10	**A+ / 9.6**	4.08 / 94	3.99 / 96	6.59 / 95	**C- / 3.6**	46	17
MUS	T Rowe Price NJ Tax-Free Bond	NJTFX	**B+**	(800) 638-5660	12.24	**A / 9.5**	3.66 / 92	3.67 / 94	5.90 / 91	**C / 4.3**	49	16
MUN	Dreyfus Municipal Bond	DRTAX	**B+**	(800) 645-6561	11.98	**A / 9.5**	4.25 / 95	3.69 / 94	5.85 / 91	**C- / 4.1**	47	7
MUS	T Rowe Price NY Tax Free Bd	PRNYX	**B+**	(800) 638-5660	11.90	**A / 9.5**	4.10 / 95	3.70 / 94	5.84 / 91	**C- / 4.1**	47	16
MUS	Dupree MS Tax Free Income	DUMSX	**B+**	(800) 866-0614	12.35	**A / 9.5**	3.85 / 93	3.86 / 95	5.63 / 90	**C- / 4.1**	55	16
MUN	USAA Tax-Exempt Long Term	USTEX	**B+**	(800) 382-8722	13.73	**A / 9.5**	3.88 / 93	3.81 / 95	6.86 / 96	**C- / 3.7**	50	N/A
MUS	Columbia CA Tax Exempt A	CLMPX	**B+**	(800) 345-6611	7.98	**A / 9.5**	4.14 / 95	4.66 / 98	7.62 / 98	**C- / 3.7**	77	6
MUN	T Rowe Price Tax-Free Income	PRTAX	**B+**	(800) 638-5660	10.44	**A / 9.4**	3.48 / 90	3.63 / 93	6.03 / 92	**C- / 4.2**	47	9
MUS	T Rowe Price VA Tax-Free Bond	PRVAX	**B+**	(800) 638-5660	12.24	**A / 9.4**	3.79 / 93	3.48 / 93	5.61 / 90	**C- / 4.1**	41	19
MUN	Elfun Tax Exempt Income	ELFTX	**B+**	(800) 242-0134	11.95	**A / 9.3**	3.83 / 93	3.40 / 92	5.55 / 89	**C / 4.3**	42	16
MUS	Virtus California T/E Bond A	CTESX	**B+**	(800) 243-1574	12.06	**A- / 9.2**	4.03 / 94	4.04 / 96	6.28 / 94	**C / 4.3**	N/A	20
MUN	AMG GW&K Municipal Bond Inv	GWMTX	**B+**	(800) 835-3879	11.86	**A- / 9.2**	3.91 / 93	3.09 / 89	5.18 / 87	**C- / 4.2**	34	7
MUN	Madison Tax Free National Y	GTFHX	**B+**	(800) 877-6089	11.15	**A- / 9.1**	3.73 / 92	2.94 / 88	4.49 / 81	**C / 4.6**	34	19
MUS	Dreyfus NY Tax Exempt Bond	DRNYX	**B+**	(800) 645-6561	15.14	**A- / 9.1**	4.24 / 95	2.92 / 87	5.00 / 85	**C / 4.5**	31	7
MUN	Eaton Vance TABS Int-Term Muni	EITAX	**B+**	(800) 262-1122	12.46	**A- / 9.1**	4.26 / 95	3.48 / 92	5.30 / 88	**C / 4.5**	50	6
MUS	American Funds Tax-Exempt of CA	TAFTX	**B+**	(800) 421-0180	17.97	**A- / 9.1**	3.96 / 94	4.06 / 96	6.96 / 96	**C / 4.5**	74	30
MUS	Columbia NY Tax-Exempt A	COLNX	**B+**	(800) 345-6611	7.61	**A- / 9.1**	4.32 / 96	3.83 / 95	6.26 / 93	**C- / 4.1**	51	6
MUN	CGCM Municipal Bd Invest	TMUUX	**B+**	(800) 444-4273	9.78	**A- / 9.1**	3.32 / 88	3.15 / 90	4.84 / 84	**C- / 4.1**	46	11
MUS	AB Municipal Income CA A	ALCAX	**B+**	(800) 221-5672	11.50	**A- / 9.0**	3.96 / 94	3.79 / 95	6.01 / 92	**C / 4.8**	64	21
MUN	JPMorgan Tax Free Bond A	PMBAX	**B+**	(800) 480-4111	12.61	**A- / 9.0**	3.91 / 93	3.92 / 95	5.18 / 87	**C / 4.5**	N/A	11
MUS	Fidelity NJ Muni Income Fd	FNJHX	**B+**	(800) 544-8544	12.00	**A- / 9.0**	3.24 / 87	2.99 / 88	5.19 / 87	**C / 4.3**	31	7
MUS	Fidelity Adv CA Muni Inc A	FCMAX	**B+**	(800) 522-7297	13.26	**B+ / 8.9**	3.64 / 91	4.05 / 96	6.27 / 94	**C / 4.7**	75	10
MUN	Wells Fargo Muni Bd A	WMFAX	**B+**	(800) 222-8222	10.48	**B+ / 8.9**	3.77 / 92	4.12 / 96	6.52 / 95	**C / 4.5**	80	16
MUN	Columbia Tax-Exempt A	COLTX	**B+**	(800) 345-6611	14.00	**B+ / 8.9**	3.29 / 88	3.75 / 94	6.45 / 94	**C / 4.3**	56	14
MUI	GuideMark Tax-Exempt Fixed Inc	GMTEX	**B+**	(888) 278-5809	11.62	**B+ / 8.8**	3.18 / 87	2.67 / 84	4.76 / 83	**C / 4.6**	26	10
MUS	AB Municipal Income II PA A	APAAX	**B+**	(800) 221-5672	10.67	**B+ / 8.8**	4.16 / 95	3.33 / 91	5.10 / 86	**C / 4.6**	44	21
MUS	RidgeWorth Seix Hi Grade Muni Bd	SFLTX	**B+**	(888) 784-3863	12.36	**B+ / 8.8**	3.67 / 92	4.07 / 96	6.45 / 94	**C / 4.5**	76	22
MUS	SEI Tax-Exempt Tr-MA Muni Bond	SMAAX	**B+**	(800) 342-5734	10.87	**B+ / 8.6**	3.46 / 90	2.51 / 83	4.03 / 78	**C / 5.2**	32	6
MUN	American Funds T/E Bd of America	AFTEX	**B+**	(800) 421-0180	13.19	**B+ / 8.6**	3.64 / 91	3.52 / 93	6.00 / 92	**C / 4.9**	56	37
MUS	Nebraska Municipal	NEMUX	**B+**	(800) 601-5593	10.67	**B+ / 8.6**	3.63 / 91	3.23 / 90	4.55 / 82	**C / 4.7**	45	20
MUS	Columbia AMT-Fr CA Intm Muni Bd	NACMX	**B+**	(800) 345-6611	10.68	**B+ / 8.5**	3.58 / 91	3.19 / 90	5.08 / 86	**C / 5.4**	53	5

• Denotes fund is closed to new investors

Fund Type	Fund Name (99 Pct = Best, 0 Pct = Worst)	Ticker Symbol	Overall Investment Rating	Phone	Net Asset Value As of 3/31/16	PERFORMANCE: Performance Rating/Pts	Annualized Total Return Through 3/31/16: 1Yr / Pct	3Yr / Pct	5Yr / Pct	RISK: Risk Rating/Pts	FUND MGR: Mgr. Quality Pct	Mgr. Tenure (Years)
MUN	Dupree Taxable Muni Bd Srs	DUTMX	**B**	(800) 866-0614	10.78	**A+ / 9.8**	3.77 / 92	4.54 / 98	8.00 / 98	**D+ / 2.8**	86	6
MUS	USAA California Bond Fund	USCBX	**B**	(800) 382-8722	11.29	**A+ / 9.7**	3.93 / 94	4.33 / 97	8.23 / 98	**D+ / 2.9**	59	10
MUH	American Century CA Hi-Yld Muni	CAYAX	**B-**	(800) 345-6488	10.68	**A+ / 9.7**	5.74 / 99	5.23 / 99	7.75 / 98	**D+ / 2.7**	83	29
MUS	Lord Abbett Tax Free CA A	LCFIX	**B-**	(888) 522-2388	11.10	**A+ / 9.6**	4.48 / 97	4.57 / 98	7.56 / 98	**D+ / 2.9**	52	10
MUH	MainStay High Yield Muni Bond C	MMHDX	**C+**	(800) 624-6782	12.35	**A+ / 9.9**	5.56 / 99	4.78 / 98	8.65 / 99	**D- / 1.3**	30	6
MUH	Franklin California H/Y Muni A	FCAMX	**C+**	(800) 342-5236	10.94	**A+ / 9.8**	4.98 / 98	5.51 / 99	9.42 / 99	**D / 2.1**	82	23
MUN	Eaton Vance TABS 5to15 Yr Ldr	EALTX	**C+**	(800) 262-1122	12.26	**A+ / 9.8**	5.10 / 98	5.67 / 99	8.36 / 99	**D / 2.1**	54	6
MUH	PIMCO High Yield Muni Bond A	PYMAX	**C+**	(800) 426-0107	8.96	**A+ / 9.8**	7.10 / 99	4.55 / 98	7.59 / 98	**D / 1.9**	43	5
MUN	Eaton Vance High Yield Muni Inc A	ETHYX	**C+**	(800) 262-1122	8.99	**A+ / 9.8**	5.52 / 98	5.67 / 99	9.13 / 99	**D / 1.8**	49	12
MUH •	Invesco High Yield Municipal A	ACTHX	**C+**	(800) 959-4246	10.18	**A+ / 9.8**	5.96 / 99	5.60 / 99	8.79 / 99	**D- / 1.4**	73	14
MUH	American Funds High Inc Muni Bnd	AMHIX	**C+**	(800) 421-0180	15.81	**A+ / 9.7**	5.09 / 98	4.95 / 99	8.15 / 98	**D+ / 2.5**	78	22
MUH	T Rowe Price Tax-Free High Yield	PRFHX	**C+**	(800) 638-5660	12.09	**A+ / 9.7**	4.23 / 95	4.69 / 98	8.04 / 98	**D+ / 2.3**	49	14
MUH	MFS Municipal High Income A	MMHYX	**C+**	(800) 225-2606	8.31	**A+ / 9.6**	5.72 / 99	4.79 / 98	8.16 / 98	**D / 1.8**	48	14
MUH	Columbia High Yield Municipal A	LHIAX	**C+**	(800) 345-6611	10.80	**A / 9.5**	4.24 / 95	4.70 / 98	7.86 / 98	**D+ / 2.6**	74	7
MUH	Federated Muni High Yield Advn A	FMOAX	**C+**	(800) 341-7400	9.06	**A / 9.4**	5.03 / 98	4.74 / 98	8.00 / 98	**D / 2.1**	59	7
MUH	Prudential Muni High Income A	PRHAX	**C+**	(800) 225-1852	10.39	**A / 9.4**	4.86 / 98	4.52 / 98	7.51 / 97	**D / 1.8**	39	12
MUH	Delaware Natl HY Muni Bd A	CXHYX	**C+**	(800) 523-1918	11.05	**A / 9.4**	5.06 / 98	4.59 / 98	8.43 / 99	**D / 1.8**	34	13
MUN	Eaton Vance CA Municipal Opptys	EACAX	**C+**	(800) 262-1122	10.53	**A / 9.3**	5.67 / 99	4.44 / 97	7.44 / 97	**D+ / 2.7**	34	2
MUN	Pioneer AMT-Free Muni A	PBMFX	**C+**	(800) 225-6292	14.77	**A / 9.3**	5.10 / 98	4.38 / 97	7.80 / 98	**D+ / 2.6**	30	10
MUN	Nuveen All Amer Muni A	FLAAX	**C+**	(800) 257-8787	11.72	**A- / 9.2**	4.37 / 96	4.32 / 97	7.51 / 97	**D+ / 2.9**	45	6
MUH	American Century High Yld Muni A	AYMAX	**C+**	(800) 345-6488	9.61	**A- / 9.1**	5.18 / 98	3.99 / 96	7.30 / 97	**D+ / 2.8**	42	18
MUN	Lord Abbett Tax Free Natl A	LANSX	**C+**	(888) 522-2388	11.49	**A- / 9.1**	4.18 / 95	3.57 / 93	7.16 / 97	**D+ / 2.5**	16	10
GL	GMO Currency Hedged Intl Bond	GMHBX	**C+**		8.93	**A- / 9.1**	0.09 / 41	5.62 / 94	7.78 / 86	**D+ / 2.3**	99	2
MUS	Nuveen Minnesota Municipal Bond	FJMNX	**C+**	(800) 257-8787	11.94	**B+ / 8.9**	4.54 / 97	3.87 / 95	6.70 / 95	**D+ / 2.9**	39	28
MUS	BlackRock NY Muni Oppty Inv A	MENKX	**C+**	(800) 441-7762	11.21	**B+ / 8.9**	4.67 / 97	3.91 / 95	6.22 / 93	**D+ / 2.6**	22	10
MUN	Lord Abbett AMT Free Municipal	LATAX	**C+**	(888) 522-2388	16.21	**B+ / 8.8**	3.96 / 94	3.07 / 89	6.82 / 96	**D+ / 2.5**	12	6
MUS	BlackRock NJ Muni Bond Inv A	MENJX	**C+**	(800) 441-7762	11.27	**B+ / 8.7**	3.45 / 90	3.67 / 94	6.64 / 95	**D+ / 2.8**	21	10
MUS	BlackRock PA Muni Bond Inv A	MEPYX	**C+**	(800) 441-7762	11.51	**B+ / 8.7**	4.01 / 94	3.69 / 94	6.70 / 95	**D+ / 2.7**	19	10
MUS	Lord Abbett Tax Free NJ A	LANJX	**C+**	(888) 522-2388	4.99	**B+ / 8.7**	3.41 / 89	3.10 / 89	6.25 / 93	**D+ / 2.6**	12	10
MUN	Eaton Vance OH Muni Inc A	ETOHX	**C+**	(800) 262-1122	9.23	**B+ / 8.6**	4.11 / 95	3.70 / 94	6.31 / 94	**D+ / 2.8**	22	N/A
MUN	Oppenheimer Rochester AMT-Free	OPTAX	**C**	(888) 470-0862	6.98	**A / 9.5**	5.85 / 99	4.70 / 98	10.14 / 99	**D- / 1.3**	23	14
MUH	Dreyfus High Yld Muni Bd A	DHYAX	**C**	(800) 645-6561	12.08	**A- / 9.0**	6.46 / 99	4.07 / 96	7.25 / 97	**D / 1.8**	23	5
MUS	Oppeneheimer Rochester CA Muni	OPCAX	**C**	(888) 470-0862	8.39	**A- / 9.0**	4.19 / 95	4.09 / 96	9.04 / 99	**D / 1.7**	19	14
MUH	Deutsche Strat High Yield T/F A	NOTAX	**C**	(800) 728-3337	12.50	**B+ / 8.7**	4.08 / 94	3.20 / 90	6.60 / 95	**D+ / 2.5**	16	18
MUH	Franklin High Yld Tax-Free Inc A	FRHIX	**C**	(800) 342-5236	10.61	**B+ / 8.7**	3.68 / 92	3.69 / 94	6.94 / 96	**D / 2.0**	17	23
MUS	BlackRock CA Muni Opptys A	MECMX	**C**	(800) 441-7762	12.58	**B+ / 8.5**	4.18 / 95	3.60 / 93	7.23 / 97	**D+ / 2.5**	17	23
MUN	Eaton Vance AMT-Free Muni	ETMBX	**C**	(800) 262-1122	9.37	**B+ / 8.5**	4.24 / 95	3.64 / 93	7.42 / 97	**D+ / 2.5**	15	11
MUH	WA Municipal High Income A	STXAX	**C**	(877) 534-4627	14.58	**B+ / 8.4**	3.81 / 93	3.15 / 90	7.02 / 96	**D+ / 2.4**	20	10
MUS	Nuveen Nebraska Municipal Bond	FNTAX	**C**	(800) 257-8787	11.01	**B+ / 8.3**	3.72 / 92	3.34 / 91	5.42 / 88	**D+ / 2.6**	19	6
MUH	Ivy Municipal High Income A	IYIAX	**C**	(800) 777-6472	5.28	**B / 8.2**	3.53 / 90	3.35 / 91	6.77 / 96	**D+ / 2.4**	26	7
MUN	J Hancock Tax Free Bond A	TAMBX	**C**	(800) 257-3336	10.12	**B / 8.1**	3.09 / 86	3.17 / 90	5.66 / 90	**D+ / 2.9**	23	N/A
MUN	Eaton Vance MA Municipal Income	ETMAX	**C**	(800) 262-1122	9.15	**B / 8.1**	3.62 / 91	3.26 / 90	6.70 / 95	**D+ / 2.7**	14	6
COI	T Rowe Price Corporate Income	PRPIX	**C**	(800) 638-5660	9.51	**B / 7.7**	0.29 / 46	2.99 / 76	5.36 / 74	**D+ / 2.9**	62	13
MUH	Goldman Sachs High Yield Muni A	GHYAX	**C-**	(800) 526-7384	9.36	**B+ / 8.8**	4.89 / 98	4.18 / 97	8.14 / 98	**D- / 1.0**	27	16
MUH	Federated Muni & Stock	FMUAX	**C-**	(800) 341-7400	12.31	**B+ / 8.6**	1.24 / 71	4.15 / 96	6.96 / 96	**D- / 1.4**	94	13
MUH	Pioneer High Income Municipal A	PIMAX	**C-**	(800) 225-6292	7.45	**B+ / 8.5**	6.18 / 99	2.90 / 87	6.59 / 95	**D / 1.8**	16	10
MUS •	Oppenheimer Rochester Ohio Muni	OROHX	**C-**	(888) 470-0862	10.22	**B+ / 8.5**	4.02 / 94	3.46 / 92	6.85 / 96	**D- / 1.5**	10	10
COH	Access Flex High Yield Inv	FYAIX	**C-**	(888) 776-3637	32.19	**B+ / 8.5**	2.25 / 73	3.76 / 82	5.71 / 75	**D- / 1.2**	97	12
MUH	J Hancock High Yield Muni Bond A	JHTFX	**C-**	(800) 257-3336	8.25	**B+ / 8.4**	3.96 / 94	3.19 / 90	6.44 / 94	**D / 2.0**	17	N/A
MUN	Eaton Vance NC Muni Inc A	ETNCX	**C-**	(800) 262-1122	9.28	**B / 8.1**	3.35 / 89	3.25 / 90	6.09 / 92	**D / 2.0**	9	2
MUN	Eaton Vance SC Municipal Income	EASCX	**C-**	(800) 262-1122	9.44	**B / 8.1**	3.86 / 93	3.10 / 89	6.43 / 94	**D / 1.6**	7	2
COH	Putnam Tax-Free Hi-Yield A	PTHAX	**C-**	(800) 225-1581	12.69	**B / 8.0**	4.69 / 85	4.33 / 86	7.63 / 85	**D / 2.2**	99	14

• Denotes fund is closed to new investors

Fund Type	Fund Name (99 Pct = Best, 0 Pct = Worst)	Ticker Symbol	Overall Investment Rating	Phone	Net Asset Value As of 3/31/16	PERFORMANCE: Performance Rating/Pts	Annualized Total Return Through 3/31/16: 1Yr / Pct	3Yr / Pct	5Yr / Pct	RISK: Risk Rating/Pts	FUND MGR: Mgr. Quality Pct	Mgr. Tenure (Years)
GES	Wells Fargo Dvsfd Inc Bldr A	EKSAX	**C-**	(800) 222-8222	5.74	**B / 7.7**	0.17 / 43	4.34 / 86	5.81 / 76	**D- / 1.1**	96	9
GEI	Invesco Income Allocation A	ALAAX	**C-**	(800) 959-4246	10.88	**B- / 7.3**	-0.05 / 31	4.30 / 86	5.83 / 76	**D+ / 2.4**	95	N/A
COH	Westcore Flexible Income Rtl	WTLTX	**C-**	(800) 392-2673	8.43	**B- / 7.3**	-0.41 / 27	3.27 / 78	5.30 / 74	**D+ / 2.3**	95	13
GES	Pacific Advisors Inc & Eq A	PADIX	**C-**	(800) 282-6693	11.94	**B- / 7.3**	1.17 / 61	4.31 / 86	5.28 / 73	**D / 2.1**	99	15
COI	PIA BBB Bond MACS	PBBBX	**C-**	(800) 251-1970	9.13	**B- / 7.1**	-0.89 / 23	2.43 / 70	5.12 / 73	**D+ / 2.4**	32	13
COH	TCW High Yield Bond N	TGHNX	**C-**	(800) 386-3829	6.10	**C+ / 6.9**	-0.24 / 29	2.66 / 73	3.88 / 60	**D+ / 2.7**	93	5
COH	PIA High Yield Institutional	PHYSX	**C-**	(800) 251-1970	9.56	**C+ / 6.9**	-1.14 / 21	2.72 / 74	5.21 / 73	**D+ / 2.5**	92	6
COH	Vanguard High-Yield Corporate Inv	VWEHX	**C-**	(800) 662-7447	5.59	**C+ / 6.8**	-1.19 / 20	2.68 / 73	5.44 / 74	**D / 2.2**	91	8
COH	Lazard US Corporate Income Open	LZHOX	**C-**	(800) 821-6474	4.74	**C+ / 6.7**	-0.61 / 25	2.70 / 73	4.73 / 70	**D+ / 2.7**	93	13
GL	GMO Global Bond III	GMGBX	**C-**		8.77	**C+ / 6.6**	4.16 / 82	1.13 / 45	3.61 / 55	**D+ / 2.4**	92	N/A
COI	WA Corporate Bond A	SIGAX	**C-**	(877) 534-4627	11.93	**C+ / 6.3**	-0.70 / 24	3.36 / 79	5.36 / 74	**D+ / 2.8**	80	6
COI	BMO TCH Corporate Income Y	MCIYX	**C-**	(800) 236-3863	12.18	**C+ / 6.1**	-2.20 / 15	2.03 / 62	4.73 / 70	**D+ / 2.9**	38	8
GES	Putnam Ret Income Fd Lifestyle 3	PISFX	**D+**	(800) 225-1581	10.82	**C+ / 6.5**	-2.66 / 13	3.82 / 82	4.54 / 68	**D- / 1.2**	95	12
COH	Eaton Vance High Inc Opp Fund A	ETHIX	**D+**	(800) 262-1122	4.29	**C+ / 6.4**	-0.77 / 23	3.63 / 81	5.86 / 76	**D / 2.1**	96	20
COH	Federated Instl High Yld Bond	FIHBX	**D+**	(800) 341-7400	9.27	**C+ / 6.3**	-1.64 / 18	2.83 / 75	5.64 / 75	**D / 1.6**	91	14
MUS	Oppeneheimer Rochester PA Muni	OPATX	**D+**	(888) 470-0862	10.39	**C+ / 6.1**	2.17 / 78	2.50 / 83	6.41 / 94	**D- / 1.0**	7	17
GL	SunAmerica VAL Co I Intl Govt Bd	VCIFX	**D+**	(800) 858-8850	11.41	**C+ / 5.9**	3.96 / 81	0.41 / 32	2.11 / 33	**D / 1.9**	83	7
GL	J Hancock Global Bond NAV		**D+**	(800) 257-3336	12.48	**C+ / 5.8**	3.55 / 79	0.56 / 34	2.79 / 42	**D+ / 2.9**	86	1
COI	PIMCO Investment Grade Corp A	PBDAX	**D+**	(800) 426-0107	10.15	**C+ / 5.8**	0.08 / 40	2.64 / 72	5.48 / 74	**D+ / 2.8**	43	14
USS	Hussman Strategic Total Return	HSTRX	**D+**	(800) 487-7626	11.80	**C+ / 5.8**	4.43 / 84	0.66 / 36	1.05 / 21	**D- / 1.4**	16	14
COH	Payden High Income Adviser	PYHWX	**D+**	(888) 409-8007	6.25	**C+ / 5.7**	-1.38 / 19	1.85 / 59	4.34 / 66	**D / 2.0**	81	12
COH	Voya High Yield Service	IPHYX	**D+**	(800) 992-0180	9.48	**C+ / 5.6**	-1.69 / 17	1.82 / 58	4.49 / 67	**D / 1.9**	77	2
GEI	Loomis Sayles Fixed Inc Fd	LSFIX	**D+**	(800) 633-3330	12.60	**C+ / 5.6**	-2.49 / 13	1.86 / 59	4.68 / 69	**D / 1.7**	61	21
COH	Lord Abbett Bond Debenture A	LBNDX	**D+**	(888) 522-2388	7.43	**C / 5.5**	-3.45 / 10	2.94 / 76	4.89 / 71	**D / 1.8**	92	29
GEI	SunAmerica VAL Co II High Yld Bd	VCHYX	**D+**	(800) 858-8850	7.32	**C / 4.9**	-2.95 / 12	1.57 / 54	4.12 / 63	**D+ / 2.6**	55	7
MUS	Eaton Vance OR Municipal Income	ETORX	**D**	(800) 262-1122	8.82	**C+ / 5.8**	3.79 / 92	1.74 / 73	6.07 / 92	**D- / 1.0**	4	2
COH	Wells Fargo High Yld Bd Fd A	EKHAX	**D**	(800) 222-8222	3.14	**C+ / 5.7**	-0.59 / 25	2.69 / 73	4.85 / 71	**D- / 1.2**	90	3
COH	Lord Abbett High Yield A	LHYAX	**D**	(888) 522-2388	6.92	**C / 5.4**	-3.28 / 10	2.85 / 75	5.54 / 75	**D- / 1.5**	91	18
COI	Rainier High Yield Institutional	RAIHX	**D**	(800) 248-6314	10.77	**C / 5.3**	-2.82 / 12	1.96 / 61	4.82 / 70	**D / 2.0**	53	7
COH	Voya High Yield Bond A	IHYAX	**D**	(800) 992-0180	7.62	**C / 5.1**	-1.54 / 18	2.28 / 67	5.36 / 74	**D / 2.0**	87	9
MUS ●	Oppenheimer Rochester MA Muni	ORMAX	**D**	(888) 470-0862	10.38	**C / 5.0**	2.29 / 79	1.77 / 73	6.14 / 93	**D / 1.8**	7	10
COH	Columbia High Yield Bond A	INEAX	**D**	(800) 345-6611	2.80	**C / 5.0**	-1.32 / 19	2.77 / 74	5.42 / 74	**D / 1.8**	92	6
GL	Russell Glbl Opportunistic Credit Y	RGCYX	**D**	(800) 832-6688	9.16	**C / 5.0**	0.31 / 46	0.71 / 37	4.05 / 62	**D / 1.6**	87	N/A
GL	Principal Glb Divers Income A	PGBAX	**D**	(800) 222-5852	13.18	**C / 4.9**	-2.01 / 16	2.56 / 71	5.04 / 72	**D+ / 2.3**	98	6
COH	Eaton Vance Income Fd of Boston	EVIBX	**D**	(800) 262-1122	5.49	**C / 4.9**	-1.34 / 19	2.72 / 73	4.98 / 72	**D / 2.1**	91	15
COH	Fidelity Focused High Income	FHIFX	**D**	(800) 544-8544	8.10	**C / 4.9**	-2.34 / 14	1.80 / 57	4.28 / 65	**D / 1.6**	75	12
COH ●	Thrivent Diversified Inc Plus A	AAHYX	**D**	(800) 847-4836	6.79	**C / 4.8**	-1.85 / 16	2.92 / 76	5.09 / 72	**D+ / 2.4**	94	12
COH	Columbia Income Opportunities A	AIOAX	**D**	(800) 345-6611	9.41	**C / 4.8**	-1.43 / 19	2.64 / 72	5.18 / 73	**D / 1.6**	90	13
COH	Transamerica Prt High Yield Bond	DVHYX	**D**	(888) 233-4339	8.03	**C / 4.8**	-3.75 / 9	1.69 / 56	4.48 / 67	**D- / 1.4**	66	16
COH ●	SSgA High Yield Bond N	SSHYX	**D**	(800) 843-2639	7.16	**C / 4.7**	-3.14 / 11	1.64 / 55	4.34 / 66	**D- / 1.5**	N/A	5
COH ●	T Rowe Price High Yield	PRHYX	**D**	(800) 638-5660	6.25	**C / 4.7**	-3.12 / 11	2.12 / 64	4.81 / 70	**D- / 1.4**	82	20
COH	MFS High Income Fund A	MHITX	**D**	(800) 225-2606	3.20	**C / 4.5**	-3.92 / 8	1.57 / 53	4.15 / 64	**D / 1.7**	62	10
GL	PACE International Fx Inc Inve A	PWFAX	**D**	(888) 793-8637	10.39	**C / 4.4**	4.51 / 84	0.95 / 42	1.02 / 21	**D+ / 2.7**	90	21
COH ●	T Rowe Price Instl High Yield	TRHYX	**D**	(800) 638-5660	8.26	**C / 4.4**	-3.65 / 9	1.99 / 61	4.67 / 69	**D- / 1.1**	76	1
COH	RidgeWorth Seix Corporate Bond	SAINX	**D**	(888) 784-3863	8.50	**C- / 4.2**	-0.55 / 25	2.08 / 63	4.25 / 65	**D / 2.1**	91	12
COH	PIMCO High Yield A	PHDAX	**D**	(800) 426-0107	8.37	**C- / 4.2**	-2.02 / 15	2.14 / 64	4.51 / 68	**D / 1.9**	85	6
COH	Principal High Yield Fund I Inst	PYHIX	**D**	(800) 222-5852	9.24	**C- / 4.2**	-4.35 / 7	1.41 / 50	4.12 / 63	**D- / 1.3**	52	9
GL	Federated International Bond A	FTIIX	**D**	(800) 341-7400	10.45	**C- / 4.2**	7.07 / 97	0.01 / 16	-0.22 / 2	**D- / 1.3**	74	14

● Denotes fund is closed to new investors

99 Pct = Best
0 Pct = Worst

Fund Type	Fund Name	Ticker Symbol	**Overall Investment Rating**	Phone	Net Asset Value As of 3/31/16	**PERFORMANCE** **Performance Rating/Pts**	Annualized Total Return Through 3/31/16 1Yr / Pct	3Yr / Pct	5Yr / Pct	**RISK** **Risk Rating/Pts**	**FUND MGR** Mgr. Quality Pct	Mgr. Tenure (Years)
MUH	Nuveen High Yield Muni Bond A	NHMAX	**C**	(800) 257-8787	17.40	**A+ / 9.9**	6.17 / 99	6.24 / 99	10.93 / 99	**E+ / 0.7**	70	16
MUH	Nuveen CA High Yield Muni Bd A	NCHAX	**C**	(800) 257-8787	9.80	**A+ / 9.9**	6.23 / 99	6.89 / 99	11.74 / 99	**E+ / 0.6**	N/A	10
MUH	SEI Asset Alloc-Def Strat All A	STDAX	**C**	(800) 342-5734	14.31	**A+ / 9.9**	-0.19 / 29	7.15 / 99	8.98 / 99	**E / 0.5**	99	13
GES	Metropolitan West Alpha Trak 500	MWATX	**C**	(800) 496-8298	7.22	**A+ / 9.9**	0.53 / 50	11.58 / 99	11.75 / 98	**E- / 0.2**	99	18
MUH	AMG GW&K Municipal Enhcd Yld	GWMNX	**C**	(800) 835-3879	10.28	**A+ / 9.8**	4.86 / 98	4.36 / 97	8.33 / 99	**E+ / 0.6**	10	11
MUH	AB High Income Municipal A	ABTHX	**C**	(800) 221-5672	11.51	**A+ / 9.7**	5.78 / 99	4.78 / 98	9.05 / 99	**E+ / 0.8**	18	6
MUH	BlackRock High Yld Muni Inv A	MDYHX	**C**	(800) 441-7762	9.64	**A+ / 9.6**	6.17 / 99	4.82 / 98	8.66 / 99	**E+ / 0.6**	16	10
US	Vanguard Extnd Durtn Trea Idx Inst	VEDTX	**C-**	(800) 662-7447	37.90	**A+ / 9.9**	1.34 / 64	8.82 / 99	15.40 / 99	**E- / 0.0**	12	3
GEI	PIMCO Extended Duration P	PEDPX	**C-**	(800) 426-0107	8.66	**A+ / 9.9**	0.63 / 52	8.61 / 99	15.16 / 99	**E- / 0.0**	4	9
USL	Rydex Govt Lg Bd 1.2x Strgy A	RYABX	**C-**	(800) 820-0888	58.50	**A+ / 9.7**	0.11 / 41	7.66 / 99	12.92 / 99	**E- / 0.0**	25	22
USL	Vanguard Long-Term Govt Bd Idx	VLGSX	**C-**	(800) 662-7447	26.97	**A+ / 9.6**	2.76 / 76	5.88 / 95	9.43 / 93	**E- / 0.2**	48	3
US	Vanguard Long-Term Treasury Inv	VUSTX	**C-**	(800) 662-7447	13.11	**A+ / 9.6**	2.54 / 75	5.83 / 95	9.46 / 93	**E- / 0.1**	24	15
US	Wasatch Hoisington US Treasury	WHOSX	**C-**	(800) 551-1700	18.59	**A+ / 9.6**	0.87 / 57	6.80 / 97	11.69 / 98	**E- / 0.0**	21	20
MUH	Oppeneheimer Rochester Hi Yld	ORNAX	**C-**	(888) 470-0862	7.10	**A / 9.5**	6.68 / 99	4.44 / 97	9.32 / 99	**E / 0.5**	11	15
GEI	Columbia Abs Rtn Currency & Inc	RACWX	**C-**	(800) 345-6611	10.37	**A / 9.5**	5.57 / 91	5.65 / 94	3.81 / 58	**E- / 0.1**	96	10
US	Fidelity Spartan Lg-T Tre Bd In Inv	FLBIX	**C-**	(800) 544-8544	13.73	**A / 9.5**	2.50 / 75	5.81 / 94	9.46 / 93	**E- / 0.1**	22	2
GEI	• Vanguard Long-Term Inv Gr Inv	VWESX	**C-**	(800) 662-7447	10.43	**A / 9.3**	1.25 / 62	5.31 / 92	8.70 / 90	**E / 0.3**	23	8
US	T Rowe Price US Treas Long-Term	PRULX	**C-**	(800) 638-5660	13.52	**A / 9.3**	2.21 / 73	5.08 / 91	8.75 / 90	**E- / 0.2**	15	13
US	Dreyfus US Treasury Long Term	DRGBX	**C-**	(800) 645-6561	20.54	**A / 9.3**	2.10 / 72	5.03 / 91	8.77 / 90	**E- / 0.2**	19	8
USA	ProFunds-US Government Plus	GVPSX	**C-**	(888) 776-3637	53.63	**A / 9.3**	-2.08 / 15	5.21 / 92	10.55 / 96	**E- / 0.0**	5	7
MUH	Lord Abbett Tx Fr High Yld Muni A	HYMAX	**C-**	(888) 522-2388	11.78	**A- / 9.2**	4.47 / 97	3.59 / 93	7.23 / 97	**E+ / 0.9**	13	12
GEI	PIMCO Long Term Credit Inst	PTCIX	**C-**	(800) 426-0107	11.40	**A- / 9.0**	-1.29 / 20	4.81 / 89	9.24 / 92	**E / 0.3**	13	7
GEL	Vanguard Long Term Bd Idx	VBLTX	**C-**	(800) 662-7447	14.04	**A- / 9.0**	0.26 / 45	4.64 / 88	8.42 / 89	**E / 0.3**	9	3
US	Direxion Mo 7-10 Year Tr Bl 2X Inv	DXKLX	**C-**	(800) 851-0511	37.17	**B+ / 8.8**	4.67 / 85	3.44 / 79	9.02 / 91	**E- / 0.2**	6	10
COI	Vanguard Long-Term Corp Bd Idx	VLTCX	**C-**	(800) 662-7447	23.76	**B+ / 8.7**	-1.14 / 21	4.33 / 86	7.89 / 86	**E / 0.3**	23	7
USL	PIMCO Long Term US Govt A	PFGAX	**C-**	(800) 426-0107	6.44	**B+ / 8.7**	1.53 / 67	4.97 / 90	8.81 / 90	**E- / 0.2**	24	9
MUN	Eaton Vance National Muni Inc A	EANAX	**C-**	(800) 262-1122	10.00	**B+ / 8.6**	4.81 / 97	3.64 / 93	7.80 / 98	**E+ / 0.9**	7	3
GEI	PIMCO Long Dur Total Return P	PLRPX	**C-**	(800) 426-0107	11.29	**B+ / 8.6**	-0.54 / 26	4.16 / 85	7.79 / 86	**E / 0.3**	8	9
GEI	American Century Zero Cpn 2025	BTTRX	**C-**	(800) 345-6488	98.92	**B+ / 8.5**	3.38 / 78	3.67 / 81	8.84 / 91	**E / 0.4**	8	10
COH	Rydex High Yld Stratgy A	RYHDX	**C-**	(800) 820-0888	23.32	**B / 8.0**	1.66 / 68	4.39 / 86	6.54 / 79	**E+ / 0.9**	98	9
EM	• GMO Emerging Country Debt III	GMCDX	**D+**		9.05	**B / 8.0**	2.53 / 75	3.02 / 77	7.73 / 85	**E / 0.4**	99	22
GEN	J Hancock VIT Value I	JEVLX	**D+**	(800) 257-3336	19.99	**B / 7.7**	-12.81 / 0	5.82 / 94	8.02 / 87	**E- / 0.0**	99	19
MUH	Spirit of America Municipal TF Bd A	SOAMX	**D+**	(800) 452-4892	9.67	**B- / 7.5**	3.88 / 93	2.60 / 84	5.85 / 91	**E+ / 0.9**	7	7
EM	T Rowe Price Ins Emerging Mkts	TREBX	**D+**	(800) 638-5660	8.54	**B- / 7.4**	4.90 / 87	2.12 / 64	4.84 / 71	**E+ / 0.8**	97	10
GEI	Fairholme Focused Income	FOCIX	**D+**	(866) 202-2263	9.63	**B- / 7.2**	-5.74 / 4	4.87 / 90	4.29 / 65	**E- / 0.0**	99	7
GEI	Calvert Long Term Income A	CLDAX	**D+**	(800) 368-2745	17.21	**B- / 7.1**	-1.07 / 21	3.88 / 83	5.91 / 76	**E / 0.5**	13	3
COI	Delaware Extended Duration Bd A	DEEAX	**D+**	(800) 523-1918	6.32	**C+ / 6.8**	-2.85 / 12	3.76 / 82	8.41 / 89	**E / 0.4**	24	9
COH	Federated High Yield Trust Svc	FHYTX	**D+**	(800) 341-7400	6.25	**C+ / 6.4**	-3.76 / 8	3.34 / 79	6.14 / 77	**E+ / 0.8**	93	32
EM	Fidelity New Markets Income	FNMIX	**D**	(800) 544-8544	14.96	**C+ / 6.5**	3.99 / 81	1.36 / 49	5.56 / 75	**E / 0.4**	93	21
MUS	Oppenheimer Rochester AMT-Fr	OPNYX	**D**	(888) 470-0862	11.11	**C+ / 6.3**	3.60 / 91	2.12 / 78	7.33 / 97	**E+ / 0.7**	5	14
EM	Stone Harbor Emerging Debt Inst	SHMDX	**D**	(866) 699-8125	10.02	**C+ / 6.3**	3.61 / 79	0.52 / 34	3.84 / 59	**E / 0.4**	85	9
GEI	J Hancock Absolute Ret Curr A	JCUAX	**D**	(800) 257-3336	8.85	**C+ / 6.1**	5.86 / 93	1.64 / 55	1.00 / 20	**E / 0.4**	99	5
EM	Goldman Sachs Emg Mkts Debt A	GSDAX	**D**	(800) 526-7384	12.25	**C+ / 5.7**	4.42 / 84	2.35 / 68	5.83 / 76	**E+ / 0.7**	97	13
EM	T Rowe Price Emerging Markets	PREMX	**D**	(800) 638-5660	11.82	**C+ / 5.7**	4.29 / 83	0.89 / 41	4.31 / 66	**E / 0.5**	90	22
EM	MFS Emerging Markets Debt A	MEDAX	**D**	(800) 225-2606	14.24	**C / 5.5**	1.10 / 60	0.90 / 41	4.66 / 69	**E+ / 0.8**	89	18
GL	Prudential Global Total Return A	GTRAX	**D**	(800) 225-1852	6.60	**C / 5.3**	3.41 / 79	1.74 / 56	3.56 / 54	**E+ / 0.9**	95	14
GL	LM BW International Opptys Bd IS	LMOTX	**D**	(877) 534-4627	11.25	**C / 5.1**	-0.54 / 26	0.15 / 28	3.17 / 48	**E / 0.5**	77	7
EM	Payden Emerging Market Bond	PYEWX	**D**	(888) 409-8007	13.15	**C / 5.0**	1.42 / 65	0.44 / 32	4.56 / 68	**E+ / 0.6**	83	16
EM	DoubleLine Em Mkts Fxd Inc N	DLENX	**D**	(877) 354-6311	9.68	**C / 4.7**	-0.73 / 24	0.86 / 40	3.56 / 54	**E+ / 0.7**	89	6
EM	T Rowe Price Inst Intl Bd	RPIIX	**D**	(800) 638-5660	8.78	**C / 4.6**	5.79 / 92	-0.44 / 12	0.51 / 17	**E+ / 0.9**	52	9
MUS	Oppeneheimer Rochester NJ Muni	ONJAX	**D**	(888) 470-0862	9.43	**C / 4.6**	1.29 / 72	1.74 / 73	6.03 / 92	**E+ / 0.9**	6	14
MUS	Oppenheimer Rochester Muni A	RMUNX	**D**	(888) 470-0862	14.72	**C / 4.3**	2.03 / 77	1.46 / 67	6.55 / 95	**E+ / 0.6**	4	17

• Denotes fund is closed to new investors

Fund Type	Fund Name (99 Pct = Best, 0 Pct = Worst)	Ticker Symbol	Overall Investment Rating	Phone	Net Asset Value As of 3/31/16	PERFORMANCE: Performance Rating/Pts	Annualized Total Return Through 3/31/16: 1Yr / Pct	3Yr / Pct	5Yr / Pct	RISK: Risk Rating/Pts	FUND MGR: Mgr. Quality Pct	Mgr. Tenure (Years)
EM	Universal Inst Emer Mrkt Debt II	UEDBX	**D-**	(800) 869-6397	7.75	**C- /4.1**	1.32 /64	-0.17 /14	3.92 /60	**E /0.5**	59	14
GL	T Rowe Price Intl Bond	RPIBX	**D-**	(800) 638-5660	8.92	**C- /3.9**	5.61 /91	-0.77 /10	0.20 /16	**E+ /0.8**	40	4
EM	Fidelity Adv Emerging Mkts Inc A	FMKAX	**D-**	(800) 522-7297	13.16	**C- /3.9**	3.52 /79	0.97 /42	5.14 /73	**E /0.4**	90	21
MUS	• Oppenheimer Rochester NC Muni	OPNCX	**D-**	(888) 470-0862	10.93	**C- /3.8**	1.90 /76	1.30 /61	6.03 /92	**E+ /0.9**	5	10
COH	Loomis Sayles Inst High Income	LSHIX	**D-**	(800) 633-3330	6.00	**C- /3.7**	-8.73 / 1	1.91 /60	4.39 /66	**E /0.4**	51	20
GEI	Rydex Strengthening Dlr 2x Strtgy	RYSDX	**D-**	(800) 820-0888	47.68	**C- /3.5**	-11.01 / 0	5.09 /91	4.20 /64	**E- /0.0**	99	11
COH	TIAA-CREF High Yield Fund Retire	TIHRX	**D-**	(800) 842-2252	9.02	**C- /3.3**	-4.00 / 8	1.44 /51	4.50 /68	**E+ /0.9**	49	10
COH	Fidelity Adv Hi Income Advantage	FAHDX	**D-**	(800) 522-7297	9.91	**C- /3.2**	-4.84 / 5	2.63 /72	4.75 /70	**E+ /0.6**	86	7
EM	Franklin Emg Mkt Debt Opportunity	FEMDX	**D-**	(800) 342-5236	10.08	**C- /3.1**	2.26 /73	-0.63 /11	3.07 /46	**E+ /0.7**	41	10
COH	Permanent Portfolio Versatile Bd	PRVBX	**D-**	(800) 531-5142	54.77	**C- /3.0**	-4.44 / 6	0.70 /37	1.75 /28	**E+ /0.9**	36	13
EM	JPMorgan Emerg Mkt Debt A	JEDAX	**D-**	(800) 480-4111	7.91	**C- /3.0**	1.53 /67	0.35 /31	4.65 /69	**E+ /0.7**	81	7
GL	LM BW Global Opportunities Bond	GOBAX	**D-**	(877) 534-4627	10.64	**D+ /2.9**	-0.68 /24	0.19 /29	3.55 /54	**E+ /0.6**	78	10
EM	TCW Emerging Markets Income N	TGINX	**D-**	(800) 386-3829	9.95	**D+ /2.8**	2.05 /72	-1.02 / 8	3.31 /50	**E+ /0.7**	30	6
GEL	Natixis Loomis Sayles Strat Inc A	NEFZX	**D-**	(800) 225-5478	13.83	**D+ /2.8**	-5.57 / 4	2.10 /64	4.47 /67	**E+ /0.6**	79	21
GL	PIMCO Foreign Bd Fd (Unhgd) A	PFUAX	**E+**	(800) 426-0107	9.66	**D /1.6**	1.90 /71	-0.70 /10	1.20 /22	**E+ /0.8**	42	2
GL	MainStay Global High Income B	MGHBX	**E**	(800) 624-6782	9.56	**D- /1.5**	3.42 /79	-2.13 / 4	2.45 /37	**E /0.3**	11	5
MTG	PIMCO StkPlus Intl (DH) A	PIPAX	**E**	(800) 426-0107	6.33	**D- /1.3**	-15.26 / 0	3.56 /81	6.13 /77	**E- /0.0**	94	1
GEI	J Hancock Global Income A	JYGAX	**E**	(800) 257-3336	8.90	**D- /1.2**	-1.54 /18	-0.09 /15	2.97 /45	**E+ /0.7**	9	7
EM	J Hancock Emerg Markets Debt A	JMKAX	**E**	(800) 257-3336	8.91	**D- /1.2**	0.02 /33	-0.86 / 9	2.67 /40	**E /0.4**	36	3
MUS	• Oppenheimer Rochester AZ Muni	ORAZX	**E**	(888) 470-0862	10.31	**D- /1.1**	0.03 /38	0.20 /30	5.72 /90	**E+ /0.8**	3	10
EM	Columbia Emerging Markets Bond	REBAX	**E**	(800) 345-6611	10.65	**D- /1.0**	1.49 /66	-0.90 / 9	3.92 /60	**E /0.4**	34	5
EM	PIMCO Emerging Markets Bond A	PAEMX	**E**	(800) 426-0107	9.70	**D- /1.0**	0.02 /33	-1.06 / 8	3.16 /48	**E /0.3**	30	5
GEI	PIMCO Real Return Asset P	PRTPX	**E**	(800) 426-0107	8.22	**D- /1.0**	-1.70 /17	-2.06 / 4	4.74 /70	**E- /0.2**	0	9
COH	Pioneer High Yield A	TAHYX	**E**	(800) 225-6292	8.80	**E+ /0.9**	-6.62 / 2	0.97 /42	2.96 /44	**E+ /0.8**	35	9
GL	Wells Fargo Intl Bd A	ESIYX	**E**	(800) 222-8222	10.22	**E+ /0.8**	1.10 /60	-1.54 / 6	0.14 /15	**E+ /0.6**	20	23
COH	Touchstone High Yield A	THYAX	**E**	(800) 543-0407	7.74	**E+ /0.7**	-5.78 / 3	0.40 /31	3.57 /54	**E+ /0.9**	20	17
COH	RS High Yield Fund A	GUHYX	**E**	(800) 766-3863	5.88	**E+ /0.7**	-4.77 / 5	0.22 /29	3.54 /54	**E+ /0.9**	18	7
COH	RidgeWorth Seix High Income A	SAHIX	**E**	(888) 784-3863	5.92	**E+ /0.7**	-5.77 / 3	0.51 /33	3.32 /50	**E+ /0.7**	19	5
EM	PIMCO EM Corporate Bond Inst	PEMIX	**E**	(800) 426-0107	9.83	**E+ /0.7**	-1.95 /16	-2.03 / 4	1.88 /30	**E /0.5**	12	N/A
GES	USAA Real Return Fund	USRRX	**E**	(800) 382-8722	9.47	**E+ /0.6**	-3.81 / 8	-1.85 / 5	1.16 /22	**E+ /0.8**	5	6
COH	Natixis Loomis Sayles High Income	NEFHX	**E**	(800) 225-5478	3.84	**E+ /0.6**	-6.30 / 3	0.29 /30	3.33 /50	**E /0.5**	14	14
MUS	• Oppenheimer Rochester MD Muni	ORMDX	**E**	(888) 470-0862	9.44	**E+ /0.6**	0.68 /59	-0.60 /11	4.76 /83	**E /0.4**	1	10
COH	Delaware High-Yield Opps A	DHOAX	**E**	(800) 523-1918	3.58	**E /0.5**	-6.76 / 2	-0.10 /15	3.44 /52	**E+ /0.9**	13	4
COH	First Eagle High Yield I	FEHIX	**E**	(800) 334-2143	8.18	**E /0.5**	-7.73 / 2	-0.74 /10	2.97 /45	**E+ /0.7**	9	N/A
COH	WA High Yield IS	WAHSX	**E**	(888) 425-6432	7.36	**E /0.4**	-8.64 / 1	-1.00 / 8	2.97 /45	**E+ /0.8**	8	11
GL	Templeton Global Total Return A	TGTRX	**E**	(800) 342-5236	11.40	**E /0.4**	-5.04 / 5	-1.03 / 8	2.43 /37	**E+ /0.8**	28	8
COH	J Hancock High Yield NAV		**E**	(800) 257-3336	7.29	**E /0.4**	-8.75 / 1	-1.18 / 7	2.89 /43	**E+ /0.7**	7	10
COH	J Hancock Core High Yld A	JYIAX	**E**	(800) 257-3336	8.91	**E /0.4**	-7.58 / 2	-0.19 /14	3.90 /60	**E+ /0.6**	12	7
EM	WA Emerging Markets Debt A	LWEAX	**E-**	(888) 425-6432	4.73	**E+ /0.6**	-0.16 /30	-1.65 / 5	2.35 /36	**E /0.4**	17	3
MUS	• Oppenheimer Rochester VA Muni	ORVAX	**E-**	(888) 470-0862	8.01	**E+ /0.6**	-0.52 /26	-0.69 /10	5.33 /88	**E /0.3**	1	10
COI	Federated Emerging Mkt Debt A	IHIAX	**E-**	(800) 341-7400	8.20	**E+ /0.6**	0.26 /45	-1.76 / 5	3.16 /48	**E /0.3**	3	3
EM	BlackRock Emg Mkts Flex Dyn Bd	BAEDX	**E-**	(800) 441-7762	8.82	**E /0.5**	2.27 /73	-2.09 / 4	3.51 /53	**E /0.4**	12	8
GL	STAAR AltCat	SITAX	**E-**	(800) 332-7738	13.10	**E /0.5**	-10.70 / 1	-0.69 /10	0.05 /12	**E- /0.2**	39	19
COH	WA Global High Yield Bond A	SAHYX	**E-**	(877) 534-4627	5.83	**E /0.3**	-6.59 / 3	-1.54 / 6	2.51 /38	**E+ /0.7**	6	10
COH	Direxion Dynamic HY Bond Fd	PDHYX	**E-**	(800) 851-0511	10.62	**E /0.3**	-8.56 / 1	-1.80 / 5	1.37 /24	**E /0.5**	6	6
GEI	API Efficient Frontier Income Fd A	APIUX	**E-**	(800) 544-6060	9.51	**E /0.3**	-5.80 / 3	-1.63 / 5	2.31 /35	**E /0.3**	6	19
EM	SEI Inst Intl Emerging Mkts Debt A	SITEX	**E-**	(800) 342-5734	9.39	**E /0.3**	-1.31 /19	-3.98 / 2	1.13 /22	**E /0.3**	6	10
EM	Deutsche Enh Emg Mrkts Fxd Inc	SZEAX	**E-**	(800) 728-3337	9.04	**E- /0.2**	-2.95 /12	-2.87 / 3	0.40 /17	**E+ /0.7**	8	5

• Denotes fund is closed to new investors

Section VIII

Top-Rated Bond Mutual Funds by Fund Type

A compilation of those

Fixed Income Mutual Funds

receiving the highest TheStreet Investment Rating

within each type of fund.

Funds are listed in order by Overall Investment Rating.

Section VIII Contents

This section contains a summary analysis of the top rated 100 bond and money market mutual funds within each fund type. If you are looking for a particular type of mutual fund, these pages show those funds that have achieved the best combination of risk and financial performance over the past three years.

In order to optimize the utility of our top and bottom fund lists, rather than listing all funds in a multi-class series, a single fund from each series is selected for display as the primary share class. Whenever possible, the selected fund is one that a retail investor would be most likely to choose. This share class may not be appropriate for every investor, so please consult with your financial advisor, the fund company, and the fund's prospectus before placing your trade.

1. Fund Type

The mutual fund's peer category based on its investment objective as stated in its prospectus.

COH	Corporate - High Yield	MMT	Money Market - Tax Free
COI	Corporate - Inv. Grade	MTG	Mortgage
EM	Emerging Market	MUH	Municipal - High Yield
GEN	General	MUI	Municipal - Insured
GEI	General - Inv. Grade	MUN	Municipal - National
GEL	General - Long Term	MUS	Municipal - Single State
GES	General - Short & Interm.	USL	U.S. Gov.- Long Term
GL	Global	USS	U.S. Gov. - Short & Interm
LP	Loan Participation	USA	U.S. Gov. - Agency
MM	Money Market	US	U.S. Gov. - Treasury

A blank fund type means that the mutual fund has not yet been categorized.

2. Fund Name

The name of the mutual fund as stated in its prospectus, which can sometimes differ slightly from the name that the company uses for advertising. If you cannot find the particular mutual fund you are interested in, or if you have any doubts regarding the precise name, verify the information with your broker or on your account statement. Also, use the fund's ticker symbol for confirmation. (See column 3.)

3. Ticker Symbol

The unique alphabetic symbol used for identifying and trading a specific mutual fund. No two funds can have the same ticker symbol, and the ticker symbol for mutual funds always ends with an "X".

A handful of funds currently show no associated ticker symbol. This means that the fund is either small or new since the NASD only assigns a ticker symbol to funds with at least $25 million in assets or 1,000 shareholders.

4. Overall Investment Rating Our overall rating is measured on a scale from A to E based on each fund's risk-adjusted performance. Please see page 11 for specific descriptions of each letter grade. Also, refer to page 7 for information on how our ratings are derived. Most important, when using this rating, please be sure to consider the warnings beginning on page 13 regarding the ratings' limitations and the underlying assumptions.

5. Phone The telephone number of the company managing the fund. Call this number to receive a prospectus or other information about the fund.

6. Net Asset Value (NAV) The fund's share price as of the date indicated. A fund's NAV is computed by dividing the value of the fund's asset holdings, less accrued fees and expenses, by the number of its shares outstanding.

7. Performance Rating/Points A letter grade rating based solely on the mutual fund's financial performance over the trailing three years, without any consideration for the amount of risk the fund poses. Like the overall Investment Rating, the Performance Rating is measured on a scale from A to E for ease of interpretation. The points score indicates where the Performance Rating falls on a scale of 0 to 10.

In the case of funds investing in municipal or other tax-free securities, this rating is based on the taxable equivalent return of the fund assuming the maximum marginal U.S. tax rate (35%).

8. 1-Year Total Return The total return the fund has provided investors over the preceding twelve months. This total return figure is computed based on the fund's dividend distributions and share price appreciation/depreciation during the period, net of the expenses and fees it imposes on its shareholders. Although the total return figure does not reflect an adjustment for any loads the fund may carry, such adjustments have been made in deriving TheStreet Investment Ratings.

9. 1-Year Total Return Percentile The fund's percentile rank based on its one-year performance compared to that of all other fixed income funds in existence for at least one year. A score of 99 is the best possible, indicating that the fund outperformed 99% of the other mutual funds. Zero is the worst possible percentile score.

In the case of funds investing in municipal or other tax-free securities, this percentile rank is based on the taxable equivalent return of the fund assuming the maximum marginal U.S. tax rate (35%).

10. 3-Year Total Return The total annual return the fund has provided investors over the preceding three years.

11. 3-Year Total Return Percentile

The fund's percentile rank based on its three-year performance compared to that of all other fixed income funds in existence for at least three years. A score of 99 is the best possible, indicating that the fund outperformed 99% of the other mutual funds. Zero is the worst possible percentile score.

In the case of funds investing in municipal or other tax-free securities, this percentile rank is based on the taxable equivalent return of the fund assuming the maximum marginal U.S. tax rate (35%).

12. 5-Year Total Return

The total annual return the fund has provided investors over the preceding five years.

13. 5-Year Total Return Percentile

The fund's percentile rank based on its five-year performance compared to that of all other fixed income funds in existence for at least five years. A score of 99 is the best possible, indicating that the fund outperformed 99% of the other mutual funds. Zero is the worst possible percentile score.

In the case of funds investing in municipal or other tax-free securities, this percentile rank is based on the taxable equivalent return of the fund assuming the maximum marginal U.S. tax rate (35%).

14. Risk Rating/Points

A letter grade rating based solely on the mutual fund's risk as determined by its monthly performance volatility over the trailing three years and the underlying credit risk and interest rate risk of its investment portfolio. The risk rating does not take into consideration the overall financial performance the fund has achieved or the total return it has provided to its shareholders. Like the overall Investment Rating, the Risk Rating is measured on a scale from A to E for ease of interpretation. The points score indicates where the Risk Rating falls on a scale of 0 to 10.

15. Manager Quality Percentile

The manager quality percentile is based on a ranking of the fund's alpha, a statistical measure representing the difference between a fund's actual returns and its expected performance given its level of risk. Fund managers who have been able to exceed the fund's statistically expected performance receive a high percentile rank with 99 representing the highest possible score. At the other end of the spectrum, fund managers who have actually detracted from the fund's expected performance receive a low percentile rank with 0 representing the lowest possible score.

16. Manager Tenure

The number of years the current manager has been managing the fund. Since fund managers who deliver substandard returns are usually replaced, a long tenure is usually a good sign that shareholders are satisfied that the fund is achieving its stated objectives.

Fund Type	Fund Name (99 Pct = Best, 0 Pct = Worst)	Ticker Symbol	Overall Investment Rating	Phone	Net Asset Value As of 3/31/16	PERFORMANCE: Performance Rating/Pts	Annualized Total Return Through 3/31/16: 1Yr / Pct	3Yr / Pct	5Yr / Pct	RISK: Risk Rating/Pts	FUND MGR: Mgr. Quality Pct	Mgr. Tenure (Years)
COH	Advance Capital I Ret Inc Retail	ADRIX	**C+**	(800) 345-4783	8.79	**B- /7.3**	1.07 /60	2.51 /71	4.02 /62	**C /4.4**	95	21
COH	Wells Fargo Sh-Tm Hi Yld A	SSTHX	**C+**	(800) 222-8222	8.03	**C /5.2**	1.52 /67	2.16 /65	3.12 /47	**B /7.9**	94	18
COH	Aquila Three Peaks High Inc A	ATPAX	**C**	(800) 437-1020	8.41	**C+ /6.5**	2.81 /76	3.41 /79	4.45 /67	**C /4.8**	98	10
COH	Access Flex High Yield Inv	FYAIX	**C-**	(888) 776-3637	32.19	**B+ /8.5**	2.25 /73	3.76 /82	5.71 /75	**D- / 1.2**	97	12
COH	Putnam Tax-Free Hi-Yield A	PTHAX	**C-**	(800) 225-1581	12.69	**B /8.0**	4.69 /85	4.33 /86	7.63 /85	**D /2.2**	99	14
COH	Rydex High Yld Stratgy A	RYHDX	**C-**	(800) 820-0888	23.32	**B /8.0**	1.66 /68	4.39 /86	6.54 /79	**E+ / 0.9**	98	9
COH	Westcore Flexible Income Rtl	WTLTX	**C-**	(800) 392-2673	8.43	**B- /7.3**	-0.41 /27	3.27 /78	5.30 /74	**D+ / 2.3**	95	13
COH	TCW High Yield Bond N	TGHNX	**C-**	(800) 386-3829	6.10	**C+ /6.9**	-0.24 /29	2.66 /73	3.88 /60	**D+ / 2.7**	93	5
COH	PIA High Yield Institutional	PHYSX	**C-**	(800) 251-1970	9.56	**C+ /6.9**	-1.14 /21	2.72 /74	5.21 /73	**D+ / 2.5**	92	6
COH	Vanguard High-Yield Corporate Inv	VWEHX	**C-**	(800) 662-7447	5.59	**C+ /6.8**	-1.19 /20	2.68 /73	5.44 /74	**D /2.2**	91	8
COH	Buffalo High Yield Fund	BUFHX	**C-**	(800) 492-8332	11.04	**C+ /6.7**	-0.43 /27	3.38 /79	4.82 /70	**C- / 3.9**	97	13
COH	Lazard US Corporate Income Open	LZHOX	**C-**	(800) 821-6474	4.74	**C+ /6.7**	-0.61 /25	2.70 /73	4.73 /70	**D+ / 2.7**	93	13
COH	Brandes Separately Mgd Acct Res	SMARX	**C-**	(800) 237-7119	8.47	**C+ /6.5**	-1.94 /16	2.57 /72	5.00 /72	**C- / 3.8**	95	11
COH	Hundredfold Select Alternative Svc	SFHYX	**C-**	(855) 582-8006	21.55	**C+ /6.4**	-0.54 /26	2.31 /68	4.30 /65	**C- / 3.6**	92	12
COH	Value Line Core Bond Fund	VAGIX	**C-**	(800) 243-2729	15.05	**C /5.5**	1.43 /65	1.24 /47	3.38 /51	**C /4.7**	88	6
COH	Putnam Floating Rate Income A	PFLRX	**C-**	(800) 225-1581	8.33	**C- /4.2**	-1.05 /21	1.42 /51	3.09 /47	**C /5.5**	86	11
COH	Pioneer Floating Rate Fund Class	FLARX	**C-**	(800) 225-6292	6.63	**C- /3.3**	0.36 /47	1.77 /57	3.05 /46	**B /8.0**	92	9
COH	Eaton Vance High Inc Opp Fund A	ETHIX	**D+**	(800) 262-1122	4.29	**C+ /6.4**	-0.77 /23	3.63 /81	5.86 /76	**D /2.1**	96	20
COH	Federated High Yield Trust Svc	FHYTX	**D+**	(800) 341-7400	6.25	**C+ /6.4**	-3.76 / 8	3.34 /79	6.14 /77	**E+ / 0.8**	93	32
COH	Federated Instl High Yld Bond	FIHBX	**D+**	(800) 341-7400	9.27	**C+ /6.3**	-1.64 /18	2.83 /75	5.64 /75	**D /1.6**	91	14
COH	Payden High Income Adviser	PYHWX	**D+**	(888) 409-8007	6.25	**C+ /5.7**	-1.38 /19	1.85 /59	4.34 /66	**D /2.0**	81	12
COH	Voya High Yield Service	IPHYX	**D+**	(800) 992-0180	9.48	**C+ /5.6**	-1.69 /17	1.82 /58	4.49 /67	**D /1.9**	77	2
COH	Lord Abbett Bond Debenture A	LBNDX	**D+**	(888) 522-2388	7.43	**C /5.5**	-3.45 /10	2.94 /76	4.89 /71	**D /1.8**	92	29
COH	Virtus Bond Fund A	SAVAX	**D+**	(800) 243-1574	11.01	**C- /3.8**	0.18 /44	1.69 /56	3.62 /55	**C- / 3.9**	88	4
COH	Credit Suisse Floating Rate HI A	CHIAX	**D+**	(877) 927-2874	6.56	**D+ /2.9**	-0.38 /27	1.88 /59	--	**C+ / 6.1**	92	11
COH	Hennessy Core Bond Investor	HCBFX	**D+**	(800) 966-4354	7.30	**D /1.7**	-2.07 /15	0.15 /28	2.36 /36	**C+ / 6.6**	51	9
COH	Wells Fargo High Yld Bd Fd A	EKHAX	**D**	(800) 222-8222	3.14	**C+ /5.7**	-0.59 /25	2.69 /73	4.85 /71	**D- / 1.2**	90	3
COH	Lord Abbett High Yield A	LHYAX	**D**	(888) 522-2388	6.92	**C /5.4**	-3.28 /10	2.85 /75	5.54 /75	**D- / 1.5**	91	18
COH	Voya High Yield Bond A	IHYAX	**D**	(800) 992-0180	7.62	**C /5.1**	-1.54 /18	2.28 /67	5.36 /74	**D /2.0**	87	9
COH	Columbia High Yield Bond A	INEAX	**D**	(800) 345-6611	2.80	**C /5.0**	-1.32 /19	2.77 /74	5.42 /74	**D /1.8**	92	6
COH	Eaton Vance Income Fd of Boston	EVIBX	**D**	(800) 262-1122	5.49	**C /4.9**	-1.34 /19	2.72 /73	4.98 /72	**D /2.1**	91	15
COH	Fidelity Focused High Income	FHIFX	**D**	(800) 544-8544	8.10	**C /4.9**	-2.34 /14	1.80 /57	4.28 /65	**D /1.6**	75	12
COH ●	Thrivent Diversified Inc Plus A	AAHYX	**D**	(800) 847-4836	6.79	**C /4.8**	-1.85 /16	2.92 /76	5.09 /72	**D+ / 2.4**	94	12
COH	Columbia Income Opportunities A	AIOAX	**D**	(800) 345-6611	9.41	**C /4.8**	-1.43 /19	2.64 /72	5.18 /73	**D /1.6**	90	13
COH	Transamerica Prt High Yield Bond	DVHYX	**D**	(888) 233-4339	8.03	**C /4.8**	-3.75 / 9	1.69 /56	4.48 /67	**D- / 1.4**	66	16
COH ●	SSgA High Yield Bond N	SSHYX	**D**	(800) 843-2639	7.16	**C /4.7**	-3.14 /11	1.64 /55	4.34 /66	**D- / 1.5**	N/A	5
COH ●	T Rowe Price High Yield	PRHYX	**D**	(800) 638-5660	6.25	**C /4.7**	-3.12 /11	2.12 /64	4.81 /70	**D- / 1.4**	82	20
COH	MFS High Income Fund A	MHITX	**D**	(800) 225-2606	3.20	**C /4.5**	-3.92 / 8	1.57 /53	4.15 /64	**D /1.7**	62	10
COH ●	T Rowe Price Instl High Yield	TRHYX	**D**	(800) 638-5660	8.26	**C /4.4**	-3.65 / 9	1.99 /61	4.67 /69	**D- / 1.1**	76	1
COH	RidgeWorth Seix Corporate Bond	SAINX	**D**	(888) 784-3863	8.50	**C- /4.2**	-0.55 /25	2.08 /63	4.25 /65	**D /2.1**	91	12
COH	PIMCO High Yield A	PHDAX	**D**	(800) 426-0107	8.37	**C- /4.2**	-2.02 /15	2.14 /64	4.51 /68	**D /1.9**	85	6
COH	Principal High Yield Fund I Inst	PYHIX	**D**	(800) 222-5852	9.24	**C- /4.2**	-4.35 / 7	1.41 /50	4.12 /63	**D- / 1.3**	52	9
COH	Prudential High Yield A	PBHAX	**D**	(800) 225-1852	5.13	**C- /4.1**	-2.11 /15	2.32 /68	4.90 /71	**D- / 1.5**	86	17
COH	MainStay High Yield Corp Bond B	MKHCX	**D**	(800) 624-6782	5.31	**C- /3.8**	-2.49 /13	1.01 /43	3.82 /59	**D+ / 2.4**	46	16
COH	MassMutual Premier High Yield A	MPHAX	**D**	(800) 542-6767	8.32	**C- /3.6**	-2.55 /13	2.74 /74	5.82 /76	**D /1.9**	91	6
COH	J Hancock US High Yield Bd NAV		**D**	(800) 257-3336	10.29	**C- /3.6**	-4.80 / 5	1.44 /51	3.95 /61	**D /1.7**	57	11
COH	Metropolitan West High Yield Bond	MWHYX	**D**	(800) 496-8298	9.09	**C- /3.3**	-2.58 /13	0.83 /40	3.01 /45	**D+ / 2.7**	45	14
COH	SunAmerica Flexible Credit A	SHNAX	**D**	(800) 858-8850	3.29	**C- /3.1**	-1.26 /20	1.86 /59	4.18 /64	**D+ / 2.8**	85	15
COH	Loomis Sayles Inst High Income	LSHIX	**D-**	(800) 633-3330	6.00	**C- /3.7**	-8.73 / 1	1.91 /60	4.39 /66	**E /0.4**	51	20
COH	Delaware High-Yield Bond	DPHYX	**D-**	(800) 523-1918	7.23	**C- /3.5**	-4.85 / 5	1.11 /45	4.56 /68	**D- / 1.3**	42	9
COH	TIAA-CREF High Yield Fund Retire	TIHRX	**D-**	(800) 842-2252	9.02	**C- /3.3**	-4.00 / 8	1.44 /51	4.50 /68	**E+ / 0.9**	49	10
COH	Fidelity Adv Hi Income Advantage	FAHDX	**D-**	(800) 522-7297	9.91	**C- /3.2**	-4.84 / 5	2.63 /72	4.75 /70	**E+ / 0.6**	86	7

● Denotes fund is closed to new investors

99 Pct = Best
0 Pct = Worst

Fund Type	Fund Name	Ticker Symbol	Overall Investment Rating	Phone	Net Asset Value As of 3/31/16	PERFORMANCE: Performance Rating/Pts	PERFORMANCE: Annualized Total Return Through 3/31/16: 1Yr / Pct	3Yr / Pct	5Yr / Pct	RISK: Risk Rating/Pts	FUND MGR: Mgr. Quality Pct	FUND MGR: Mgr. Tenure (Years)
COI	Vanguard Short-Term Crp Bd Idx	VSCSX	**A**	(800) 662-7447	21.72	**C+ /6.2**	1.78 /70	1.89 /59	2.84 /43	**B+ / 8.8**	89	7
COI	WA Core Bond FI	WAPIX	**B+**	(888) 425-6432	12.42	**B /7.7**	1.68 /69	2.92 /76	4.12 /63	**C+ / 6.2**	89	22
COI	Scout Core Plus Bond Fund Y	SCPYX	**B+**	(800) 996-2862	32.35	**C+ /6.1**	2.59 /75	1.44 /51	4.14 /64	**B / 8.1**	75	20
COI	Baird Aggregate Bond Inv	BAGSX	**B**	(866) 442-2473	11.21	**B- /7.4**	1.47 /66	2.60 /72	4.44 /67	**C+ / 6.0**	84	16
COI	SEI Instl Managed Tr-Core Fix Inc	TRLVX	**B**	(800) 342-5734	11.46	**C+ /6.9**	1.14 /61	2.52 /71	4.31 /66	**C+ / 6.5**	84	6
COI	Federated Interm Corp Bd Instl	FIIFX	**B-**	(800) 341-7400	9.28	**C+ /6.5**	0.46 /49	2.19 /65	3.72 /57	**C+ / 6.7**	79	3
COI	Dreyfus Bond Market Index Inv	DBMIX	**B-**	(800) 645-6561	10.53	**C+ /6.5**	1.43 /65	2.00 /61	3.29 /50	**C+ / 6.6**	72	6
COI	Federated Sht-Interm Tot Ret B	FGCIX	**B-**	(800) 341-7400	10.32	**C /5.3**	1.00 /59	1.35 /49	2.61 /39	**B / 7.9**	64	3
COI	TD Asset Mgmt Short-Term Bond	TDSBX	**B-**		10.20	**C- /4.0**	0.75 /54	0.71 /37	1.02 /21	**A+ / 9.6**	77	7
COI	Payden Corporate Bond Investor	PYACX	**C+**	(888) 409-8007	10.97	**B+ /8.4**	1.66 /68	4.10 /84	5.84 /76	**C- / 3.0**	91	N/A
COI	Mutual of America Inst Bond	MABOX	**C+**	(800) 914-8716	9.98	**C+ /6.8**	1.70 /69	2.15 /64	3.47 /53	**C+ / 5.6**	75	20
COI	Payden Core Bond Adviser	PYCWX	**C+**	(888) 409-8007	10.65	**C+ /6.5**	0.94 /58	2.16 /65	3.83 /59	**C+ / 5.8**	72	19
COI	Voya Intermediate Bond A	IIBAX	**C+**	(800) 992-0180	10.09	**C+ /6.4**	1.09 /60	2.73 /74	4.71 /70	**C+ / 5.7**	85	7
COI	Nationwide Bond A	NBDAX	**C+**	(800) 848-0920	9.74	**C /5.4**	1.25 /62	1.91 /60	3.78 /58	**B- / 7.1**	71	12
COI	Domini Social Bond Inv	DSBFX	**C+**	(800) 498-1351	11.29	**C /4.9**	1.59 /67	1.44 /51	2.48 /38	**B- / 7.3**	53	11
COI	MSIF Short Duration Income A	MLDAX	**C+**	(800) 354-8185	7.88	**C- /4.2**	2.44 /74	1.49 /52	1.76 /28	**B+ / 8.5**	87	5
COI	Prudential Short-Term Corp Bond	PBSMX	**C+**	(800) 225-1852	11.11	**C- /3.8**	1.25 /62	1.42 /51	2.37 /36	**B+ / 8.9**	83	17
COI	CNR Corporate Bond N	CCBAX	**C+**	(888) 889-0799	10.41	**C- /3.7**	0.03 /35	0.65 /36	1.85 /29	**B+ / 8.9**	52	15
COI	Frost Low Duration Bond Inv	FADLX	**C+**	(866) 777-7818	10.24	**C- /3.5**	0.30 /46	0.54 /34	1.63 /27	**A / 9.3**	62	14
COI	Transamerica Short-Term Bond A	ITAAX	**C+**	(888) 233-4339	10.13	**C- /3.5**	0.40 /48	1.27 /48	2.35 /36	**A- / 9.2**	87	5
COI	Hartford Short Duration A	HSDAX	**C+**	(888) 843-7824	9.80	**C- /3.5**	0.64 /52	1.03 /43	1.79 /29	**A- / 9.0**	79	4
COI	Transamerica Prt High Quality	DVHQX	**C+**	(888) 233-4339	11.20	**C- /3.2**	0.54 /50	0.31 /30	0.90 /20	**A+ / 9.6**	58	26
COI	Wilmington Short-Term Bd A	MVSAX	**C+**	(800) 336-9970	10.06	**C- /3.1**	0.67 /53	0.71 /37	1.10 /21	**A / 9.5**	76	20
COI	Vanguard Intm-Term Corp Bd Idx	VICSX	**C**	(800) 662-7447	23.34	**B /8.1**	2.31 /74	3.31 /79	5.73 /76	**C- / 3.2**	79	7
COI	T Rowe Price Corporate Income	PRPIX	**C**	(800) 638-5660	9.51	**B /7.7**	0.29 /46	2.99 /76	5.36 /74	**D+ / 2.9**	62	13
COI	HC Capital US Corp FI Sec HC	HCXSX	**C**	(800) 242-9596	9.87	**B- /7.5**	1.07 /60	2.49 /71	4.32 /66	**C- / 3.3**	45	6
COI	Diamond Hill Corporate Credit A	DSIAX	**C**	(614) 255-3333	10.63	**C+ /6.4**	0.82 /56	3.11 /77	4.56 /68	**C / 4.7**	95	10
COI	Russell Investment Grade Bond A	RFAAX	**C**	(800) 832-6688	22.02	**C /4.8**	1.38 /65	1.99 /61	3.34 /51	**C+ / 6.5**	71	27
COI	Eaton Vance Core Bond A	EAGIX	**C**	(800) 262-1122	9.90	**C- /4.2**	0.97 /58	1.98 /61	3.38 /51	**B / 7.6**	77	6
COI	Vanguard Long-Term Corp Bd Idx	VLTCX	**C-**	(800) 662-7447	23.76	**B+ /8.7**	-1.14 /21	4.33 /86	7.89 /86	**E / 0.3**	23	7
COI	PIA BBB Bond MACS	PBBBX	**C-**	(800) 251-1970	9.13	**B- /7.1**	-0.89 /23	2.43 /70	5.12 /73	**D+ / 2.4**	32	13
COI	WA Corporate Bond A	SIGAX	**C-**	(877) 534-4627	11.93	**C+ /6.3**	-0.70 /24	3.36 /79	5.36 /74	**D+ / 2.8**	80	6
COI	BMO TCH Corporate Income Y	MCIYX	**C-**	(800) 236-3863	12.18	**C+ /6.1**	-2.20 /15	2.03 /62	4.73 /70	**D+ / 2.9**	38	8
COI	State Farm Bond A	BNSAX	**C-**	(800) 447-4930	11.45	**C+ /5.8**	2.29 /74	2.08 /63	3.50 /53	**C / 4.9**	57	16
COI	RS Investment Quality Bond A	GUIQX	**C-**	(800) 766-3863	9.79	**C /4.7**	0.52 /50	2.09 /63	3.58 /54	**C+ / 5.7**	62	12
COI	Columbia Total Return Bond A	LIBAX	**C-**	(800) 345-6611	9.11	**C /4.6**	0.96 /58	1.74 /56	3.48 /53	**C+ / 6.6**	55	11
COI	Principal Income Fd A	CMPIX	**C-**	(800) 222-5852	9.44	**C /4.6**	-0.36 /27	1.76 /57	3.79 /58	**C / 5.5**	50	11
COI	Columbia Bond A	CNDAX	**C-**	(800) 345-6611	8.67	**C- /4.1**	1.56 /67	1.72 /56	3.33 /50	**C+ / 6.3**	54	11
COI	RidgeWorth Seix Total Return Bd A	CBPSX	**C-**	(888) 784-3863	11.02	**C- /3.9**	1.00 /59	1.82 /58	3.67 /56	**C+ / 6.0**	58	14
COI	Madison Core Bond A	MBOAX	**C-**	(800) 877-6089	10.11	**C- /3.8**	1.33 /64	1.59 /54	2.64 /39	**B- / 7.5**	58	7
COI	Federated Tot Ret Bd A	TLRAX	**C-**	(800) 341-7400	10.84	**C- /3.6**	0.21 /44	1.70 /56	3.21 /48	**C+ / 6.8**	54	3
COI	Eagle Investment Grade Bond A	EGBAX	**C-**	(800) 421-4184	14.97	**C- /3.0**	1.40 /65	1.04 /43	2.40 /36	**B+ / 8.4**	57	6
COI	Transamerica Flexible Income A	IDITX	**C-**	(888) 233-4339	9.05	**C- /3.0**	-0.81 /23	1.81 /58	4.15 /64	**C+ / 6.8**	73	11
COI	STAAR Inv Trust Shrt Term Bond	SITBX	**C-**	(800) 332-7738	8.93	**D /1.6**	-0.11 /30	-0.23 /14	0.23 /16	**A+ / 9.8**	45	19
COI	Calvert Short Duration Income A	CSDAX	**C-**	(800) 368-2745	15.92	**D- /1.4**	0.41 /48	0.73 /37	1.68 /27	**B+ / 8.9**	56	7
COI	Delaware Extended Duration Bd A	DEEAX	**D+**	(800) 523-1918	6.32	**C+ /6.8**	-2.85 /12	3.76 /82	8.41 /89	**E / 0.4**	24	9
COI	PIMCO Investment Grade Corp A	PBDAX	**D+**	(800) 426-0107	10.15	**C+ /5.8**	0.08 /40	2.64 /72	5.48 /74	**D+ / 2.8**	43	14
COI	Oppenheimer Corporate Bond A	OFIAX	**D+**	(888) 470-0862	10.62	**C /5.2**	-0.94 /22	2.80 /74	5.28 /73	**C- / 3.4**	66	6
COI	Lord Abbett Income A	LAGVX	**D+**	(888) 522-2388	2.71	**C /4.8**	-1.93 /16	1.99 /61	4.76 /70	**C- / 3.0**	36	18
COI	Fidelity Advisor Corporate Bond A	FCBAX	**D+**	(800) 522-7297	11.19	**C /4.7**	-0.89 /23	2.27 /67	5.01 /72	**C- / 3.1**	35	6
COI	Federated Bond Fund A	FDBAX	**D+**	(800) 341-7400	8.93	**C /4.6**	-0.80 /23	2.31 /68	4.39 /66	**C- / 3.5**	50	3
COI	First Inv Investment Grade A	FIIGX	**D+**	(800) 423-4026	9.69	**C- /4.0**	0.55 /50	2.15 /64	4.45 /67	**C / 4.3**	50	7

• Denotes fund is closed to new investors

Data as of March 31, 2016

Fund Type	Fund Name (99 Pct = Best, 0 Pct = Worst)	Ticker Symbol	Overall Investment Rating	Phone	Net Asset Value As of 3/31/16	PERFORMANCE: Performance Rating/Pts	Annualized Total Return Through 3/31/16: 1Yr / Pct	3Yr / Pct	5Yr / Pct	RISK: Risk Rating/Pts	FUND MGR: Mgr. Quality Pct	Mgr. Tenure (Years)
EM	● GMO Emerging Country Debt III	GMCDX	**D+**		9.05	**B /8.0**	2.53 /75	3.02 /77	7.73 /85	**E /0.4**	99	22
EM	T Rowe Price Ins Emerging Mkts	TREBX	**D+**	(800) 638-5660	8.54	**B- /7.4**	4.90 /87	2.12 /64	4.84 /71	**E+ /0.8**	97	10
EM	Fidelity New Markets Income	FNMIX	**D**	(800) 544-8544	14.96	**C+ /6.5**	3.99 /81	1.36 /49	5.56 /75	**E /0.4**	93	21
EM	Stone Harbor Emerging Debt Inst	SHMDX	**D**	(866) 699-8125	10.02	**C+ /6.3**	3.61 /79	0.52 /34	3.84 /59	**E /0.4**	85	9
EM	Goldman Sachs Emg Mkts Debt A	GSDAX	**D**	(800) 526-7384	12.25	**C+ /5.7**	4.42 /84	2.35 /68	5.83 /76	**E+ /0.7**	97	13
EM	T Rowe Price Emerging Markets	PREMX	**D**	(800) 638-5660	11.82	**C+ /5.7**	4.29 /83	0.89 /41	4.31 /66	**E /0.5**	90	22
EM	MFS Emerging Markets Debt A	MEDAX	**D**	(800) 225-2606	14.24	**C /5.5**	1.10 /60	0.90 /41	4.66 /69	**E+ /0.8**	89	18
EM	Payden Emerging Market Bond	PYEWX	**D**	(888) 409-8007	13.15	**C /5.0**	1.42 /65	0.44 /32	4.56 /68	**E+ /0.6**	83	16
EM	DoubleLine Em Mkts Fxd Inc N	DLENX	**D**	(877) 354-6311	9.68	**C /4.7**	-0.73 /24	0.86 /40	3.56 /54	**E+ /0.7**	89	6
EM	T Rowe Price Inst Intl Bd	RPIIX	**D**	(800) 638-5660	8.78	**C /4.6**	5.79 /92	-0.44 /12	0.51 /17	**E+ /0.9**	52	9
EM	Universal Inst Emer Mrkt Debt II	UEDBX	**D-**	(800) 869-6397	7.75	**C- /4.1**	1.32 /64	-0.17 /14	3.92 /60	**E /0.5**	59	14
EM	Fidelity Adv Emerging Mkts Inc A	FMKAX	**D-**	(800) 522-7297	13.16	**C- /3.9**	3.52 /79	0.97 /42	5.14 /73	**E /0.4**	90	21
EM	Franklin Emg Mkt Debt Opportunity	FEMDX	**D-**	(800) 342-5236	10.08	**C- /3.1**	2.26 /73	-0.63 /11	3.07 /46	**E+ /0.7**	41	10
EM	JPMorgan Emerg Mkt Debt A	JEDAX	**D-**	(800) 480-4111	7.91	**C- /3.0**	1.53 /67	0.35 /31	4.65 /69	**E+ /0.7**	81	7
EM	TCW Emerging Markets Income N	TGINX	**D-**	(800) 386-3829	9.95	**D+ /2.8**	2.05 /72	-1.02 / 8	3.31 /50	**E+ /0.7**	30	6
EM	● WA Global Government Bond I	WAFIX	**D-**	(888) 425-6432	8.18	**D+ /2.5**	-1.32 /19	0.10 /27	2.25 /34	**D- /1.3**	73	18
EM	J Hancock Emerg Markets Debt A	JMKAX	**E**	(800) 257-3336	8.91	**D- /1.2**	0.02 /33	-0.86 / 9	2.67 /40	**E /0.4**	36	3
EM	Columbia Emerging Markets Bond	REBAX	**E**	(800) 345-6611	10.65	**D- /1.0**	1.49 /66	-0.90 / 9	3.92 /60	**E /0.4**	34	5
EM	PIMCO Emerging Markets Bond A	PAEMX	**E**	(800) 426-0107	9.70	**D- /1.0**	0.02 /33	-1.06 / 8	3.16 /48	**E /0.3**	30	5
EM	PIMCO EM Corporate Bond Inst	PEMIX	**E**	(800) 426-0107	9.83	**E+ /0.7**	-1.95 /16	-2.03 / 4	1.88 /30	**E /0.5**	12	N/A
EM	WA Emerging Markets Debt A	LWEAX	**E-**	(888) 425-6432	4.73	**E+ /0.6**	-0.16 /30	-1.65 / 5	2.35 /36	**E /0.4**	17	3
EM	BlackRock Emg Mkts Flex Dyn Bd	BAEDX	**E-**	(800) 441-7762	8.82	**E /0.5**	2.27 /73	-2.09 / 4	3.51 /53	**E /0.4**	12	8
EM	SEI Inst Intl Emerging Mkts Debt A	SITEX	**E-**	(800) 342-5734	9.39	**E /0.3**	-1.31 /19	-3.98 / 2	1.13 /22	**E /0.3**	6	10
EM	Deutsche Enh Emg Mrkts Fxd Inc	SZEAX	**E-**	(800) 728-3337	9.04	**E- /0.2**	-2.95 /12	-2.87 / 3	0.40 /17	**E+ /0.7**	8	5
EM	Oppenheimer Em Mkts Local Debt	OEMAX	**E-**	(888) 470-0862	7.40	**E- /0.2**	-0.01 /31	-5.76 / 1	-1.19 / 1	**E- /0.2**	2	1
EM	Janus Emerging Markets A	JMFAX	**E-**	(800) 295-2687	7.58	**E- /0.2**	-10.08 / 1	-2.48 / 3	-4.67 / 0	**E- /0.0**	9	4
EM	EuroPac International Bond A	EPIBX	**E-**	(888) 558-5851	8.14	**E- /0.1**	-3.34 /10	-5.75 / 1	-2.60 / 1	**E /0.5**	2	6
EM	Eaton Vance Emer Market Local	EEIAX	**E-**	(800) 262-1122	6.29	**E- /0.1**	-0.87 /23	-7.77 / 1	-3.03 / 1	**E- /0.1**	1	8
EM	Invesco Emerg Mkts Flexible Bond	IAEMX	**E-**	(800) 959-4246	6.38	**E- /0.0**	-10.75 / 0	-9.82 / 0	-4.41 / 0	**E- /0.2**	0	3
EM	Dreyfus Eme Mkts Dbt LC A	DDBAX	**E-**	(800) 782-6620	11.18	**E- /0.0**	-5.19 / 5	-8.57 / 0	-3.42 / 1	**E- /0.1**	0	8
EM	Goldman Sachs Local Emg Mkt	GAMDX	**E-**	(800) 526-7384	6.36	**E- /0.0**	-3.57 / 9	-8.58 / 0	-3.06 / 1	**E- /0.1**	0	8
EM	PIMCO Emerging Local Bond A	PELAX	**E-**	(800) 426-0107	7.21	**E- /0.0**	-4.80 / 5	-8.77 / 0	-3.27 / 1	**E- /0.1**	0	10

● Denotes fund is closed to new investors

	99 Pct = Best 0 Pct = Worst					PERFORMANCE				RISK	FUND MGR	
							Annualized Total Return Through 3/31/16					
Fund Type	Fund Name	Ticker Symbol	Overall Investment Rating	Phone	Net Asset Value As of 3/31/16	Performance Rating/Pts	1Yr / Pct	3Yr / Pct	5Yr / Pct	Risk Rating/Pts	Mgr. Quality Pct	Mgr. Tenure (Years)
GEI	Ave Maria Bond	AVEFX	**A+**	(866) 283-6274	11.27	**B /8.0**	2.51 /75	3.08 /77	3.70 /56	**B /8.1**	97	13
GEI	WA Intermediate Bond IS	WABSX	**A**	(888) 425-6432	11.10	**B- /7.1**	2.27 /73	2.27 /67	3.63 /55	**B /8.1**	80	7
GEI	Nationwide Core Plus Bond Inst	NWCIX	**A**	(800) 848-0920	10.23	**B- /7.1**	1.76 /69	2.41 /69	4.25 /65	**B /7.7**	78	14
GEI	Scout Core Bond Fund Institutional	SCCIX	**A**	(800) 996-2862	11.72	**C+ /6.8**	2.95 /76	1.87 /59	3.76 /58	**B+ /8.4**	80	15
GEI	Cavanal Hill Intmdt Bond NL Inv	APFBX	**A**	(800) 762-7085	10.57	**C+ /6.5**	1.09 /60	2.24 /66	4.10 /63	**B+ /8.6**	89	23
GEI	Cavanal Hill Bond NL Inv	APBDX	**A-**	(800) 762-7085	9.67	**C+ /6.8**	1.91 /71	2.19 /65	3.94 /60	**B /7.8**	72	23
GEI	Loomis Sayles Intm Dur Bd Inst	LSDIX	**A-**	(800) 633-3330	10.38	**C+ /6.5**	1.39 /65	2.10 /64	3.35 /51	**B /8.1**	77	11
GEI	Vanguard Sh-Term Invest-Grade	VFSTX	**A-**	(800) 662-7447	10.69	**C+ /5.9**	1.73 /69	1.67 /55	2.25 /34	**A- /9.0**	86	8
GEI	GE Institutional Income Inv	GFIIX	**B+**	(800) 242-0134	9.45	**B- /7.3**	1.20 /62	2.60 /72	4.06 /62	**C+ /6.9**	78	19
GEI	Elfun Income	EINFX	**B+**	(800) 242-0134	11.48	**B- /7.2**	1.14 /61	2.54 /71	4.07 /62	**C+ /6.9**	77	20
GEI	Metropolitan West Tot Ret Bond M	MWTRX	**B+**	(800) 496-8298	10.83	**B- /7.0**	0.96 /58	2.45 /70	4.63 /69	**B- /7.1**	73	19
GEI	Dodge & Cox Income Fund	DODIX	**B+**	(800) 621-3979	13.47	**C+ /6.9**	0.47 /49	2.42 /69	3.80 /58	**B- / 7.4**	85	N/A
GEI	Commerce Bond	CFBNX	**B+**	(800) 995-6365	19.98	**C+ /6.7**	0.95 /58	2.33 /68	4.05 /62	**B- / 7.4**	73	22
GEI	Janus Aspen Flexible Bond Inst	JAFLX	**B+**	(800) 295-2687	11.92	**C+ /6.5**	0.52 /50	2.23 /66	4.15 /64	**B- / 7.4**	68	9
GEI	Baird Quality Interm Muni Bd Inv	BMBSX	**B+**	(866) 442-2473	12.08	**C+ /6.4**	2.49 /75	1.90 /59	3.19 /48	**B /7.6**	61	15
GEI	Baird Interm Bond Inv	BIMSX	**B+**	(866) 442-2473	11.62	**C+ /6.3**	1.69 /69	1.84 /58	3.42 /52	**B /8.1**	60	16
GEI	Fidelity Intermediate Bond	FTHRX	**B+**	(800) 544-8544	10.93	**C+ /6.2**	1.62 /68	1.80 /57	3.19 /48	**B /8.1**	60	7
GEI	Parnassus Income Fd-Fixed Inc	PRFIX	**B+**	(800) 999-3505	16.74	**C+ /6.1**	1.59 /67	1.71 /56	2.74 /41	**B /7.8**	47	3
GEI	New Covenant Income	NCICX	**B+**	(877) 835-4531	23.31	**C+ /6.0**	1.61 /68	1.67 /55	2.73 /41	**B+ /8.4**	62	4
GEI	Frost Total Return Bond Inv	FATRX	**B+**	(866) 777-7818	10.27	**C+ /6.0**	-0.24 /29	2.16 /65	4.29 /65	**B /8.0**	86	14
GEI	Rainier Interm Fixed Income Orig	RIMFX	**B+**	(800) 248-6314	12.72	**C+ /5.9**	1.85 /70	1.58 /54	2.85 /43	**B+ /8.4**	58	8
GEI	Metropolitan West Interm Bond M	MWIMX	**B+**	(800) 496-8298	10.58	**C+ /5.6**	1.02 /59	1.56 /53	3.48 /53	**B+ /8.7**	74	14
GEI	Universal Inst Core Plus Fxd Inc II	UCFIX	**B**	(800) 869-6397	10.53	**B /7.6**	0.85 /56	2.87 /75	4.46 /67	**C+ /5.6**	84	5
GEI	WA Core Plus Bond FI	WACIX	**B**	(888) 425-6432	11.63	**B /7.6**	1.29 /63	2.92 /76	4.46 /67	**C /5.4**	80	3
GEI	TIAA-CREF Bond Retire	TIDRX	**B**	(800) 842-2252	10.64	**B- /7.4**	1.80 /70	2.58 /72	4.13 /63	**C+ /5.8**	63	13
GEI	Fidelity Spartan US Bond Idx F	FUBFX	**B**	(800) 544-8544	11.77	**B- /7.3**	2.02 /72	2.46 /70	3.80 /58	**C+ / 6.0**	57	2
GEI	BlackRock US Total Bond Index	WFBIX	**B**	(800) 441-7762	10.24	**B- /7.2**	1.77 /69	2.37 /69	3.58 /54	**C+ / 6.4**	56	7
GEI	Westcore Plus Bond Rtl	WTIBX	**B**	(800) 392-2673	10.78	**B- /7.2**	1.20 /62	2.46 /70	3.92 /60	**C+ / 6.3**	61	13
GEI	Vantagepoint Core Bond Index II	VPCDX	**B**	(800) 669-7400	10.36	**B- /7.0**	1.64 /68	2.24 /66	3.53 /54	**C+ / 6.7**	53	1
GEI	MFS Total Return Bond A	MRBFX	**B**	(800) 225-2606	10.74	**C+ /6.9**	0.80 /55	2.29 /67	3.90 /60	**C+ / 6.7**	59	10
GEI	T Rowe Price US Bond Enhanced	PBDIX	**B**	(800) 638-5660	11.14	**C+ /6.8**	1.60 /68	2.31 /68	3.68 /56	**C+ / 6.5**	55	16
GEI	SunAmerica VAL Co I Cap Conse	VCCCX	**B**	(800) 858-8850	9.91	**C+ /6.8**	1.45 /66	2.18 /65	3.65 /56	**C+ / 6.4**	50	14
GEI	BNY Mellon Bond M	MPBFX	**B**	(800) 645-6561	12.94	**C+ /6.6**	2.01 /72	1.92 /60	3.34 /50	**C+ / 6.7**	44	11
GEI	GE Investments Income 1	GEIMX	**B**	(800) 242-0134	11.54	**C+ /6.3**	0.49 /49	2.00 /61	3.50 /53	**B- / 7.0**	53	19
GEI	Calamos Total Return Bond A	CTRAX	**B**	(800) 582-6959	10.43	**C+ /6.1**	1.93 /71	2.65 /73	2.81 /42	**B /7.8**	87	9
GEI	CRA Qualified Investment Retail	CRATX	**B**	(877) 272-1977	10.84	**C+ /6.0**	2.15 /73	1.65 /55	3.02 /45	**B- / 7.5**	44	7
GEI	North Country Intermediate Bond	NCBDX	**B**	(888) 350-2990	10.37	**C+ /5.9**	1.85 /70	1.45 /51	2.64 /40	**B /8.0**	44	13
GEI	Madison High Quality Bond Y	MIIBX	**B**	(800) 877-6089	11.09	**C /4.9**	1.48 /66	1.07 /44	1.61 /27	**B+ /8.9**	56	16
GEI	Weitz Short Intm Income Inst	WEFIX	**B**	(800) 232-4161	12.30	**C /4.7**	0.83 /56	1.09 /44	1.97 /31	**A- /9.0**	75	20
GEI	• Fidelity Short-Term Bond	FSHBX	**B**	(800) 544-8544	8.61	**C /4.5**	1.01 /59	0.97 /42	1.38 /24	**A+ /9.6**	81	9
GEI	Cohen and Steers Pref Sec&Inc A	CPXAX	**B-**	(800) 330-7348	13.39	**A- /9.1**	2.24 /73	5.55 /93	8.01 /87	**C- / 3.4**	99	6
GEI	Vanguard Interm-Term Invst-Grd	VFICX	**B-**	(800) 662-7447	9.91	**B /8.0**	2.76 /76	3.01 /76	4.97 /71	**C /4.7**	72	8
GEI	TIAA-CREF Bond Plus Retail	TCBPX	**B-**	(800) 842-2252	10.49	**B- /7.2**	1.23 /62	2.45 /70	4.23 /65	**C+ / 5.7**	60	10
GEI	Voya Intermediate Bond Port Adv	IIBPX	**B-**	(800) 992-0180	12.73	**B- /7.1**	0.76 /54	2.50 /71	4.48 /67	**C+ / 5.8**	62	7
GEI	T Rowe Price Inst Core Plus	TICPX	**B-**	(800) 638-5660	10.37	**B- /7.0**	1.26 /63	2.33 /68	4.01 /62	**C+ / 5.7**	54	N/A
GEI	J Hancock Active Bond 1	JIADX	**B-**	(800) 257-3336	10.03	**C+ /6.9**	0.41 /48	2.55 /71	4.26 /65	**C+ / 5.9**	71	11
GEI	CGCM Core Fixed Inc Invest	TIIUX	**B-**	(800) 444-4273	8.24	**C+ /6.8**	1.42 /65	2.22 /66	4.03 /62	**C+ / 6.1**	51	2
GEI	TIAA-CREF Bond Index Retail	TBILX	**B-**	(800) 842-2252	10.98	**C+ /6.7**	1.54 /67	2.06 /63	3.29 /50	**C+ / 6.2**	43	N/A
GEI	Brown Advisory Interm Income Inv	BIAIX	**B-**	(800) 540-6807	10.67	**C /5.3**	1.42 /65	1.24 /47	2.54 /38	**B /8.2**	40	24
GEI	FCI Bond Fund	FCIZX	**B-**	(800) 408-4682	10.48	**C /5.3**	1.59 /67	1.51 /52	2.74 /41	**B /7.9**	44	11
GEI	William Blair Income N	WBRRX	**B-**	(800) 742-7272	8.99	**C /4.9**	0.86 /56	1.14 /45	2.75 /41	**B+ / 8.4**	48	14
GEI	BNY Mellon Inter Bond M	MPIBX	**B-**	(800) 645-6561	12.67	**C /4.8**	1.36 /64	0.99 /42	2.19 /33	**B+ / 8.5**	41	10

• Denotes fund is closed to new investors

Data as of March 31, 2016

Fund Type	Fund Name (99 Pct = Best, 0 Pct = Worst)	Ticker Symbol	Overall Investment Rating	Phone	Net Asset Value As of 3/31/16	PERFORMANCE: Performance Rating/Pts	Annualized Total Return Through 3/31/16: 1Yr / Pct	3Yr / Pct	5Yr / Pct	RISK: Risk Rating/Pts	FUND MGR: Mgr. Quality Pct	Mgr. Tenure (Years)
GEL	Vanguard Long Term Bd Idx	VBLTX	**C-**	(800) 662-7447	14.04	**A- /9.0**	0.26 /45	4.64 /88	8.42 /89	**E /0.3**	9	3
GEL	AMG Mgrs Bond Svc	MGFIX	**C-**	(800) 835-3879	26.76	**C+ /6.3**	0.11 /41	1.98 /61	4.56 /68	**C /4.5**	52	22
GEL	J Hancock Short Duration Opp A	JMBAX	**D**	(800) 257-3336	9.39	**D- /1.2**	-2.09 /15	0.09 /27	1.68 /27	**C /5.4**	37	7
GEL	Natixis Loomis Sayles Strat Inc A	NEFZX	**D-**	(800) 225-5478	13.83	**D+ /2.8**	-5.57 / 4	2.10 /64	4.47 /67	**E+ /0.6**	79	21

• Denotes fund is closed to new investors

99 Pct = Best
0 Pct = Worst

Fund Type	Fund Name	Ticker Symbol	Overall Investment Rating	Phone	Net Asset Value As of 3/31/16	PERFORMANCE: Performance Rating/Pts	Annualized Total Return Through 3/31/16: 1Yr / Pct	3Yr / Pct	5Yr / Pct	RISK: Risk Rating/Pts	FUND MGR: Mgr. Quality Pct	Mgr. Tenure (Years)
GES	DoubleLine Total Return Bond N	DLTNX	**A+**	(877) 354-6311	10.87	**B /7.6**	2.20 /73	2.93 /76	5.11 /72	**B /7.7**	88	6
GES	Tributary Income Inst	FOINX	**A**	(800) 662-4203	10.41	**B- /7.3**	1.75 /69	2.53 /71	3.98 /61	**B- /7.3**	77	13
GES	GE RSP Income	GESLX	**A-**	(800) 242-0134	11.59	**B- /7.4**	1.23 /62	2.66 /73	4.14 /63	**C+ /6.9**	79	20
GES	Baird Short-Term Bond Inst	BSBIX	**A-**	(866) 442-2473	9.68	**C /5.4**	1.30 /63	1.46 /51	2.09 /32	**A /9.4**	88	12
GES	J Hancock VIT Strat Inc Opps I	JESNX	**B+**	(800) 257-3336	13.31	**B- /7.5**	0.35 /47	2.99 /76	4.59 /68	**C+ /6.3**	92	12
GES	Changing Parameters	CPMPX	**B**	(866) 618-3456	9.71	**B /7.6**	1.83 /70	2.60 /72	3.02 /45	**C+ /5.6**	94	9
GES	Sanford C Bernstein II Int Dur Inst	SIIDX	**B**	(800) 221-5672	15.21	**B- /7.5**	1.64 /68	2.64 /72	3.83 /59	**C+ /5.6**	62	11
GES	Vanguard Total Bond Mrkt Index	VBMFX	**B**	(800) 662-7447	10.90	**B- /7.0**	1.69 /69	2.25 /67	3.58 /54	**C+ /6.3**	51	24
GES	Vanguard Short-Term Bd Idx	VBISX	**B**	(800) 662-7447	10.56	**C /4.9**	1.43 /65	1.15 /45	1.69 /28	**A- /9.0**	73	3
GES	Homestead Short Term Bond	HOSBX	**B**	(800) 258-3030	5.20	**C /4.6**	0.64 /52	1.11 /45	2.06 /32	**A /9.5**	84	25
GES	Sanford C Bernstein Interm	SNIDX	**B-**	(212) 486-5800	13.32	**B- /7.3**	1.58 /67	2.49 /71	3.72 /57	**C+ /5.6**	56	11
GES	Steward Select Bond Fd Inst	SEACX	**B-**	(877) 420-4440	24.76	**C+ /5.9**	1.65 /68	1.58 /54	2.44 /37	**B- /7.2**	38	6
GES	Thornburg Limited Term Income A	THIFX	**B-**	(800) 847-0200	13.35	**C /4.9**	1.02 /59	1.57 /54	3.32 /50	**B+ /8.5**	70	9
GES	SA Global Fixed Income Fund	SAXIX	**B-**	(800) 366-7266	9.73	**C /4.5**	1.07 /60	0.86 /40	1.48 /25	**A- /9.0**	58	17
GES	Berwyn Income Fund	BERIX	**C+**	(800) 992-6757	13.19	**B+ /8.7**	-0.83 /23	5.11 /91	5.45 /74	**C- /3.1**	99	11
GES	BlackRock Secured Credit Inv A	BMSAX	**C+**	(800) 441-7762	9.86	**C+ /5.7**	-0.17 /29	2.60 /72	4.38 /66	**B- /7.0**	95	6
GES	T Rowe Price Short Term Bond	PRWBX	**C+**	(800) 638-5660	4.73	**C- /3.9**	0.64 /52	0.70 /37	1.24 /23	**A /9.4**	72	21
GES	SEI Daily Inc Tr-Ultra Sh Dur Bd A	SECPX	**C+**	(800) 342-5734	9.30	**C- /3.6**	0.58 /51	0.61 /35	0.91 /20	**A+ /9.8**	80	17
GES	DFA One-Yr Fixed Inc Inst	DFIHX	**C+**	(800) 984-9472	10.31	**C- /3.2**	0.51 /50	0.40 /31	0.54 /17	**A+ /9.9**	76	33
GES	Metropolitan West Alpha Trak 500	MWATX	**C**	(800) 496-8298	7.22	**A+ /9.9**	0.53 /50	11.58 /99	11.75 /98	**E- /0.2**	99	18
GES	T Rowe Price Global MS Bd Adv	PRSAX	**C**	(800) 638-5660	11.05	**B- /7.1**	1.94 /71	2.06 /63	3.67 /56	**C- /4.0**	57	8
GES	Touchstone Flexible Income A	FFSAX	**C**	(800) 543-0407	10.58	**C /5.3**	2.13 /73	2.92 /76	4.44 /67	**C+ /6.2**	88	14
GES	Deutsche Core Fixed Income A	SFXAX	**C**	(800) 728-3337	9.93	**C /4.5**	0.76 /54	2.08 /63	3.83 /59	**B /7.6**	62	2
GES	AdvisorOne CLS Flexible Income N	CLFLX	**C**	(866) 811-0225	10.11	**C /4.5**	0.08 /40	0.90 /41	2.45 /37	**B- /7.4**	34	2
GES	Praxis Interm Income A	MIIAX	**C**	(800) 977-2947	10.52	**C- /3.8**	1.38 /65	2.03 /62	3.34 /51	**B /7.6**	56	22
GES	Semper Short Duration Inv	SEMRX	**C**	(888) 263-6443	9.88	**D+ /2.8**	1.02 /59	0.09 /27	0.82 /19	**A /9.3**	51	1
GES	MainStay Tax Adv Sht-Tm Bd	MYTBX	**C**	(800) 624-6782	9.63	**D+ /2.6**	0.95 /58	0.18 /28	0.41 /17	**A+ /9.6**	50	1
GES	Wells Fargo Dvsfd Inc Bldr A	EKSAX	**C-**	(800) 222-8222	5.74	**B /7.7**	0.17 /43	4.34 /86	5.81 /76	**D- /1.1**	96	9
GES	Pacific Advisors Inc & Eq A	PADIX	**C-**	(800) 282-6693	11.94	**B- /7.3**	1.17 /61	4.31 /86	5.28 /73	**D /2.1**	99	15
GES	T Rowe Price Spectrum Income	RPSIX	**C-**	(800) 638-5660	12.23	**B- /7.1**	0.62 /52	2.24 /66	4.06 /62	**C- /3.6**	77	18
GES	Spirit of America Income Fd A	SOAIX	**C-**	(800) 452-4892	11.91	**C+ /6.9**	0.99 /58	3.66 /81	7.21 /83	**C- /3.1**	73	7
GES	MFS Strategic Income A	MFIOX	**C-**	(800) 225-2606	6.36	**C /5.5**	-0.68 /24	1.54 /53	3.56 /54	**C /4.6**	46	11
GES	● Thrivent Income A	LUBIX	**C-**	(800) 847-4836	9.00	**C /5.2**	-0.02 /31	2.56 /71	4.46 /67	**C- /4.1**	54	7
GES	Prudential Total Return Bond A	PDBAX	**C-**	(800) 225-1852	14.36	**C /5.2**	0.49 /49	2.55 /71	4.66 /69	**C- /4.1**	44	14
GES	Wilmington Broad Market Bond A	AKIRX	**C-**	(800) 336-9970	9.91	**C /4.5**	1.10 /60	2.03 /62	3.42 /52	**C+ /5.9**	42	20
GES	Schroder Total Return Fix Inc Adv	SBBVX	**C-**	(800) 464-3108	9.89	**C /4.5**	-0.74 /24	1.11 /45	3.22 /49	**C /5.2**	20	12
GES	Nuveen Core Bond A	FAIIX	**C-**	(800) 257-8787	9.89	**C- /4.2**	-0.20 /29	1.68 /55	2.86 /43	**C+ /6.4**	37	16
GES	PNC Bond A	PAAAX	**C-**	(800) 551-2145	10.46	**C- /3.8**	0.72 /54	1.69 /56	2.96 /44	**B- /7.0**	39	14
GES	ICON Bond C	IOBCX	**C-**	(800) 764-0442	9.12	**C- /3.3**	-1.31 /19	0.75 /38	2.08 /32	**B- /7.5**	28	5
GES	Virtus Multi-Sector Short Term Bd	NARAX	**C-**	(800) 243-1574	4.65	**C- /3.1**	0.06 /39	0.94 /42	2.79 /42	**B /8.2**	59	23
GES	Ivy Limited-Term Bond A	WLTAX	**C-**	(800) 777-6472	10.87	**D+ /2.8**	0.93 /57	0.59 /35	1.53 /26	**B+ /8.7**	35	2
GES	Wells Fargo Ult ST Inc A	SADAX	**C-**	(800) 222-8222	8.45	**D /1.7**	0.32 /46	0.35 /31	0.57 /18	**A+ /9.9**	76	14
GES	American Funds Sh-T Bd of Amr A	ASBAX	**C-**	(800) 421-0180	9.99	**D /1.7**	0.71 /53	0.44 /32	0.65 /18	**A /9.5**	57	5
GES	PNC Intermediate Bond A	PBFAX	**C-**	(800) 551-2145	11.00	**D /1.7**	0.63 /52	0.86 /40	2.19 /33	**B+ /8.4**	35	14
GES	Federated Short Term Inc A	FTIAX	**C-**	(800) 341-7400	8.49	**D /1.6**	-0.11 /30	0.05 /24	0.82 /19	**A+ /9.7**	45	21
GES	Federated Ultra Short Bd A	FULAX	**C-**	(800) 341-7400	9.07	**D- /1.3**	-0.19 /29	0.04 /23	0.61 /18	**A+ /9.8**	53	18
GES	Putnam Ret Income Fd Lifestyle 3	PISFX	**D+**	(800) 225-1581	10.82	**C+ /6.5**	-2.66 /13	3.82 /82	4.54 /68	**D- /1.2**	95	12
GES	Osterweis Strategic Income	OSTIX	**D+**	(800) 700-3316	10.57	**C- /4.0**	-2.39 /14	1.45 /51	3.45 /52	**C /5.2**	89	14
GES	Pioneer Strategic Income A	PSRAX	**D+**	(800) 225-6292	10.33	**C- /3.1**	-0.70 /24	1.60 /54	3.65 /56	**C+ /5.6**	61	17
GES	Thornburg Strategic Income Fd A	TSIAX	**D+**	(800) 847-0200	11.10	**C- /3.1**	-1.23 /20	1.74 /56	4.29 /65	**C /4.8**	83	9
GES	Timothy Plan Fixed Income A	TFIAX	**D+**	(800) 662-0201	10.31	**D /1.7**	0.31 /46	0.88 /40	2.30 /35	**B- /7.0**	19	12
GES	Eaton Vance Mult-Str Absolute Rtn	EADDX	**D+**	(800) 262-1122	8.59	**D- /1.0**	-0.17 /29	0.16 /28	0.59 /18	**B+ /8.8**	34	12

● Denotes fund is closed to new investors

Data as of March 31, 2016

99 Pct = Best
0 Pct = Worst

Fund Type	Fund Name	Ticker Symbol	Overall Investment Rating	Phone	Net Asset Value As of 3/31/16	PERFORMANCE: Performance Rating/Pts	Annualized Total Return Through 3/31/16: 1Yr / Pct	3Yr / Pct	5Yr / Pct	RISK: Risk Rating/Pts	FUND MGR: Mgr. Quality Pct	Mgr. Tenure (Years)
GL	SEI Inst Intl International Fx In A	SEFIX	**A**	(800) 342-5734	10.16	**B /8.0**	1.69 /69	3.47 /80	4.25 /65	**C+ / 6.6**	99	8
GL	DFA Five Year Glbl Fixed Inc Inst	DFGBX	**A-**	(800) 984-9472	11.11	**C+ /6.5**	2.39 /74	1.95 /60	3.04 /46	**B / 8.2**	96	17
GL	Federated Floating Rt Str Inc Inst	FFRSX	**A-**	(800) 341-7400	9.65	**C+ /6.2**	0.64 /52	2.20 /66	3.15 /47	**B+ / 8.6**	96	6
GL	DFA S/T Extended Quality Port Inst	DFEQX	**A-**	(800) 984-9472	10.87	**C+ /5.7**	1.80 /70	1.54 /53	2.21 /34	**B+ / 8.9**	93	8
GL	Goldman Sachs Glbl Income A	GSGIX	**B+**	(800) 526-7384	12.24	**C+ /6.4**	1.67 /68	3.02 /77	4.30 /65	**B / 7.6**	98	21
GL	Schwab Intermediate-Term Bond	SWIIX	**B+**	(800) 407-0256	10.28	**C+ /6.1**	1.62 /68	1.76 /57	2.76 /41	**B+ / 8.3**	95	9
GL	US Global Inv Near-Term Tax Free	NEARX	**B+**	(800) 873-8637	2.25	**C /5.4**	1.43 /65	1.57 /54	2.38 /36	**B+ / 8.9**	94	26
GL	Payden Global Fixed Inc Investor	PYGFX	**B**	(888) 409-8007	8.88	**B /7.6**	1.03 /59	2.96 /76	4.15 /64	**C+ / 5.6**	98	N/A
GL	DoubleLine Core Fixed Income N	DLFNX	**B**	(877) 354-6311	10.86	**B- /7.0**	0.97 /58	2.52 /71	4.89 /71	**C+ / 6.1**	97	6
GL	GMO Currency Hedged Intl Bond	GMHBX	**C+**		8.93	**A- /9.1**	0.09 /41	5.62 /94	7.78 /86	**D+ / 2.3**	99	2
GL	PIMCO Foreign Bond (US Hedged)	PFOAX	**C+**	(800) 426-0107	10.16	**B /7.6**	0.19 /44	4.04 /84	6.09 /77	**C / 4.7**	99	2
GL	CGCM Intl Fixed Inc Invest	TIFUX	**C+**	(800) 444-4273	7.43	**B- /7.5**	0.28 /45	2.67 /73	4.66 /69	**C / 4.5**	98	2
GL	Northern Fixed Income	NOFIX	**C+**	(800) 595-9111	10.23	**C+ /6.8**	0.52 /50	2.35 /68	4.09 /63	**C / 5.2**	97	5
GL	• Brandes Core Plus Fixed Inc E	BCPEX	**C+**	(800) 237-7119	9.20	**C+ /6.0**	0.34 /47	1.79 /57	3.62 /55	**C+ / 6.9**	95	9
GL	JPMorgan Core Plus Bond A	ONIAX	**C+**	(800) 480-4111	8.22	**C+ /5.8**	0.86 /56	2.69 /73	4.10 /63	**B- / 7.1**	98	20
GL	Payden Global Low Duration	PYGSX	**C+**	(888) 409-8007	9.99	**C- /3.6**	0.10 /41	0.68 /36	1.68 /27	**A / 9.3**	86	N/A
GL	DFA Two Year Glbl Fixed Inc Inst	DFGFX	**C+**	(800) 984-9472	9.96	**C- /3.5**	0.63 /52	0.52 /33	0.68 /18	**A+ / 9.8**	83	17
GL	BBH Limited Duration Class N	BBBMX	**C+**	(800) 625-5759	10.06	**C- /3.3**	-0.01 /31	0.57 /34	1.13 /22	**A+ / 9.7**	84	5
GL	Aberdeen Total Return Bond A	BJBGX	**C**	(866) 667-9231	13.51	**C+ /5.9**	0.95 /58	1.56 /53	3.47 /52	**C / 5.2**	94	15
GL	AB Global Bond A	ANAGX	**C**	(800) 221-5672	8.36	**C /5.4**	1.70 /69	2.37 /69	3.85 /59	**C+ / 6.0**	97	24
GL	MassMutual Select Total Ret Bd	MSPGX	**C**	(800) 542-6767	10.15	**C /5.4**	1.09 /60	1.28 /48	2.77 /41	**C+ / 5.8**	92	N/A
GL	Janus Short-Term Bond A	JSHAX	**C**	(800) 295-2687	3.03	**D+ /2.9**	0.77 /55	0.83 /40	1.41 /25	**A- / 9.1**	88	9
GL	GMO Global Bond III	GMGBX	**C-**		8.77	**C+ /6.6**	4.16 /82	1.13 /45	3.61 /55	**D+ / 2.4**	92	N/A
GL	PIMCO Global Bond (US Hedged)	PAIIX	**C-**	(800) 426-0107	10.00	**C+ /5.8**	-0.44 /27	2.91 /75	5.22 /73	**C / 5.0**	98	2
GL	J Hancock Income A	JHFIX	**C-**	(800) 257-3336	6.47	**C /4.7**	0.95 /58	2.09 /63	3.71 /57	**C+ / 6.5**	96	17
GL	J Hancock Strat Income Opp A	JIPAX	**C-**	(800) 257-3336	10.48	**C /4.7**	0.01 /32	2.27 /67	3.92 /60	**C+ / 6.4**	97	10
GL	Sentinel Total Return Bond A	SATRX	**C-**	(800) 282-3863	10.35	**C /4.3**	-0.84 /23	1.75 /57	4.03 /62	**C+ / 5.9**	95	6
GL	Dreyfus/Standish Global Fixed Inc	DHGAX	**C-**	(800) 645-6561	21.37	**C- /4.2**	-1.56 /18	2.45 /70	4.02 /62	**C+ / 6.2**	97	10
GL	JPMorgan Unconstrained Debt A	JSIAX	**C-**	(800) 480-4111	9.69	**C- /3.4**	-0.32 /28	1.57 /53	2.58 /39	**B- / 7.3**	94	6
GL	WA Total Return Unconstrained FI	WARIX	**C-**	(888) 425-6432	10.03	**C- /3.0**	-1.14 /21	0.58 /35	1.99 /31	**B / 7.7**	84	10
GL	Putnam Absolute Return 100 A	PARTX	**C-**	(800) 225-1581	9.79	**D- /1.2**	-1.72 /17	0.07 /26	0.15 /15	**A- / 9.2**	68	8
GL	SunAmerica VAL Co I Intl Govt Bd	VCIFX	**D+**	(800) 858-8850	11.41	**C+ /5.9**	3.96 /81	0.41 /32	2.11 /33	**D / 1.9**	83	7
GL	Fidelity Strategic Income Fund	FSICX	**D+**	(800) 544-8544	10.36	**C+ /5.8**	-0.54 /26	1.70 /56	3.62 /55	**C- / 3.2**	95	17
GL	J Hancock Global Bond NAV		**D+**	(800) 257-3336	12.48	**C+ /5.8**	3.55 /79	0.56 /34	2.79 /42	**D+ / 2.9**	86	1
GL	Goldman Sachs Inv Gr Cdt A	GSGAX	**D+**	(800) 526-7384	9.08	**C /4.9**	-0.54 /26	2.24 /66	4.91 /71	**C- / 3.5**	97	1
GL	BlackRock Strategic Global Bd Inv	MDWIX	**D+**	(800) 441-7762	5.92	**C- /4.1**	1.67 /68	1.08 /44	2.68 /40	**C / 4.9**	91	5
GL	Eaton Vance Glb Mac Abslut Ret A	EAGMX	**D+**	(800) 262-1122	8.98	**D- /1.3**	0.58 /51	0.51 /33	1.09 /21	**B / 7.9**	82	19
GL	JPMorgan Strategic Income Opp A	JSOAX	**D+**	(800) 480-4111	11.08	**E+ /0.8**	-2.00 /16	-0.09 /15	1.35 /24	**B+ / 8.4**	58	8
GL	Prudential Global Total Return A	GTRAX	**D**	(800) 225-1852	6.60	**C /5.3**	3.41 /79	1.74 /56	3.56 /54	**E+ / 0.9**	95	14
GL	LM BW International Opptys Bd IS	LMOTX	**D**	(877) 534-4627	11.25	**C /5.1**	-0.54 /26	0.15 /28	3.17 /48	**E / 0.5**	77	7
GL	Russell Glbl Opportunistic Credit Y	RGCYX	**D**	(800) 832-6688	9.16	**C /5.0**	0.31 /46	0.71 /37	4.05 /62	**D / 1.6**	87	N/A
GL	Principal Glb Divers Income A	PGBAX	**D**	(800) 222-5852	13.18	**C /4.9**	-2.01 /16	2.56 /71	5.04 /72	**D+ / 2.3**	98	6
GL	PACE International Fx Inc Inve A	PWFAX	**D**	(888) 793-8637	10.39	**C /4.4**	4.51 /84	0.95 /42	1.02 /21	**D+ / 2.7**	90	21
GL	Federated International Bond A	FTIIX	**D**	(800) 341-7400	10.45	**C- /4.2**	7.07 /97	0.01 /16	-0.22 / 2	**D- / 1.3**	74	14
GL	PIMCO Global Bond (Unhedged) D	PGBDX	**D**	(800) 426-0107	9.18	**C- /4.1**	2.13 /73	-0.12 /15	2.22 /34	**D+ / 2.9**	62	2
GL	Invesco Intl Tot Rtn Bd A	AUBAX	**D**	(800) 959-4246	10.27	**C- /4.1**	3.49 /79	0.53 /34	1.13 /22	**D- / 1.1**	86	9
GL	PIMCO High Yield Spectrum A	PHSAX	**D**	(800) 426-0107	9.22	**C- /4.0**	-2.62 /13	2.11 /64	5.03 /72	**D / 1.9**	96	6
GL	Laudus Mondrian Intl Govt Fxd Inc	LIFNX	**D**	(800) 407-0256	9.93	**C- /3.9**	7.27 /97	-1.10 / 8	-0.86 / 2	**D- / 1.3**	30	N/A
GL	AB High Income A	AGDAX	**D**	(800) 221-5672	8.15	**C- /3.7**	-2.23 /15	1.92 /60	5.07 /72	**D / 2.2**	96	14
GL	American Funds Cap World Bond	CWBFX	**D**	(800) 421-0180	19.85	**C- /3.1**	1.60 /68	0.44 /32	1.80 /29	**C- / 3.0**	83	17
GL	Loomis Sayles Glbl Bd Ret	LSGLX	**D**	(800) 633-3330	15.42	**C- /3.1**	1.45 /66	-0.64 /11	1.15 /22	**D+ / 2.9**	42	16
GL	Janus High-Yield A	JHYAX	**D**	(800) 295-2687	8.01	**C- /3.1**	-1.91 /16	1.92 /60	4.32 /66	**D+ / 2.6**	96	13

• Denotes fund is closed to new investors

99 Pct = Best 0 Pct = Worst Fund Type	Fund Name	Ticker Symbol	Overall Investment Rating	Phone	Net Asset Value As of 3/31/16	PERFORMANCE Performance Rating/Pts	Annualized Total Return Through 3/31/16 1Yr / Pct	3Yr / Pct	5Yr / Pct	RISK Risk Rating/Pts	FUND MGR Mgr. Quality Pct	Mgr. Tenure (Years)
LP	T Rowe Price Instl Fltng Rate F	PFFRX	**B+**	(800) 638-5660	9.82	**C+ /6.1**	0.91 /57	2.56 /71	3.46 /52	**B /8.2**	96	7
LP	Lord Abbett Floating Rate A	LFRAX	**C+**	(888) 522-2388	8.85	**C /4.9**	-0.01 /31	2.08 /63	3.65 /56	**B /8.1**	94	4
LP	BlackRock Floating Rate Inc Inv A	BFRAX	**C+**	(800) 441-7762	9.91	**C /4.5**	-0.29 /28	2.03 /62	3.27 /49	**B /8.2**	95	7
LP	Voya Floating Rate A	IFRAX	**C+**	(800) 992-0180	9.70	**C /4.4**	-0.27 /28	1.92 /60	3.33 /50	**B+ /8.3**	92	N/A
LP	Columbia Floating Rate A	RFRAX	**C**	(800) 345-6611	8.64	**C- /3.8**	-0.96 /22	1.82 /58	3.22 /48	**B /7.8**	92	10
LP	Voya Senior Income A	XSIAX	**C-**	(800) 992-0180	12.24	**C /4.8**	-1.91 /16	2.47 /70	4.26 /65	**C /5.3**	93	N/A
LP	MainStay Floating Rate B	MXFBX	**C-**	(800) 624-6782	9.04	**C- /3.5**	-1.11 /21	0.71 /37	1.92 /30	**B /7.8**	73	12
LP	Virtus Senior Floating Rate Fund A	PSFRX	**C-**	(800) 243-1574	9.18	**C- /3.4**	-0.96 /22	1.47 /52	2.98 /45	**B /7.7**	91	8
LP	Eaton Vance Flt-Rate and Hi Inc A	EVFHX	**C-**	(800) 262-1122	8.88	**C- /3.3**	-1.63 /18	1.29 /48	2.97 /44	**C+ /6.9**	87	16
LP	Eaton Vance Floating Rate A	EVBLX	**C-**	(800) 262-1122	8.76	**D+ /2.5**	-1.86 /16	0.94 /41	2.52 /38	**B- /7.4**	76	15
LP	Eaton Vance Float Rate Advtage A	EAFAX	**D+**	(800) 262-1122	10.20	**C- /3.4**	-1.87 /16	1.42 /51	3.33 /50	**C /5.4**	84	20
LP	RidgeWorth Seix Fltng Rt Hg Inc A	SFRAX	**D+**	(888) 784-3863	8.33	**D+ /2.9**	-1.85 /16	1.27 /48	2.82 /42	**C+ /6.1**	85	10
LP	Franklin Floating Rate Dly-Acc A	FAFRX	**D+**	(800) 342-5236	8.35	**D /1.7**	-2.60 /13	0.89 /41	2.28 /35	**B- /7.2**	69	15
LP	Neuberger Berman Floating Rt Inc	NFIAX	**D+**	(800) 877-9700	9.64	**D /1.6**	-1.24 /20	1.22 /47	2.87 /43	**B /7.7**	86	7
LP	SunAmerica Sr Floating Rate A	SASFX	**D+**	(800) 858-8850	7.64	**D- /1.5**	-2.03 /15	1.04 /43	2.29 /35	**B- /7.3**	81	7
LP	Oppenheimer Sen-Floating Rate A	OOSAX	**D+**	(888) 470-0862	7.58	**D- /1.4**	-2.61 /13	1.11 /45	2.77 /41	**C+ /6.9**	77	17
LP	Fidelity Adv Float-Rate Hi-Inc A	FFRAX	**D+**	(800) 522-7297	9.18	**D- /1.2**	-2.06 /15	0.71 /37	1.99 /31	**B- /7.4**	71	3
LP	Delaware Diverse Floating Rate Fd	DDFAX	**D+**	(800) 523-1918	8.18	**E+ /0.9**	-1.66 /17	0.06 /25	1.06 /21	**A- /9.0**	55	6
LP	RS Floating Rate A	RSFLX	**D**	(800) 766-3863	9.19	**D- /1.5**	-2.81 /12	0.51 /33	2.46 /37	**C- /4.1**	48	7
LP	Invesco Floating Rate A	AFRAX	**D**	(800) 959-4246	7.15	**D- /1.4**	-3.45 /10	0.81 /39	2.82 /42	**C /5.5**	61	10
LP	Hartford Floating Rate A	HFLAX	**D**	(888) 843-7824	8.16	**D- /1.2**	-2.65 /13	0.60 /35	2.48 /38	**C /5.2**	55	N/A
LP	Deutsche Floating Rate A	DFRAX	**D**	(800) 728-3337	8.29	**E /0.4**	-5.54 / 4	-0.50 /11	1.55 /26	**B- /7.1**	31	9
LP	Invesco Senior Loan A	VSLAX	**D-**	(800) 959-4246	6.02	**E+ /0.9**	-5.42 / 4	0.83 /39	3.49 /53	**C- /3.7**	54	9
LP	Highland Floating Rate Opps A	HFRAX	**E+**	(877) 665-1287	6.63	**E /0.4**	-10.42 / 1	0.76 /38	3.69 /56	**D /2.1**	73	4
LP	Driehaus Select Credit Fund	DRSLX	**E+**	(800) 560-6111	7.80	**E- /0.1**	-11.39 / 0	-3.93 / 2	-1.45 / 1	**D+ /2.3**	3	6

• Denotes fund is closed to new investors

						PERFORMANCE				RISK	FUND MGR	
	99 Pct = Best *0 Pct = Worst*				Net Asset		Annualized Total Return Through 3/31/16					
Fund Type	Fund Name	Ticker Symbol	**Overall Investment Rating**	Phone	Value As of 3/31/16	**Perform-ance Rating/Pts**	1Yr / Pct	3Yr / Pct	5Yr / Pct	**Risk Rating/Pts**	Mgr. Quality Pct	Mgr. Tenure (Years)
MM	Goldman Sachs Fin Sq MM FST	FSMXX	**C**	(800) 526-7384	1.00	**D+ / 2.7**	0.20 / 44	0.11 / 27	0.13 / 15	**A+ / 9.9**	70	N/A
MM	Invesco Liquid Assets Inst	LAPXX	**C**	(800) 959-4246	1.00	**D+ / 2.7**	0.20 / 44	0.11 / 27	0.12 / 15	**A+ / 9.9**	70	N/A
MM	WA Inst Liquid Reserves Inst	CILXX	**C**	(800) 331-1792	1.00	**D+ / 2.7**	0.21 / 44	0.12 / 28	0.14 / 15	**A+ / 9.9**	70	N/A
MM	Federated Inst Money Mkt Mgt Inst	MMPXX	**C**	(800) 341-7400	1.00	**D+ / 2.7**	0.22 / 45	0.12 / 27	0.14 / 15	**A+ / 9.9**	71	N/A
MM	Harbor Money Market Inst	HARXX	**C**	(800) 422-1050	1.00	**D+ / 2.6**	0.14 / 42	0.09 / 27	0.09 / 14	**A+ / 9.9**	70	13
MM	BlackRock-Lq TempCash Instl	TMCXX	**C**	(800) 441-7762	1.00	**D+ / 2.6**	0.12 / 42	0.09 / 27	0.11 / 15	**A+ / 9.9**	70	N/A
MM	AB Exchange Reserve A	AEAXX	**C**	(800) 221-5672	1.00	**D+ / 2.6**	0.17 / 43	0.09 / 27	0.10 / 14	**A+ / 9.9**	69	N/A
MM	Dreyfus Inst Cash Advant Inst	DADXX	**C**	(800) 645-6561	1.00	**D+ / 2.6**	0.17 / 43	0.10 / 27	0.11 / 15	**A+ / 9.9**	69	N/A
MM	Federated Prime Cash Obl Wealth	PCOXX	**C**	(800) 341-7400	1.00	**D+ / 2.6**	0.16 / 43	0.08 / 26	0.10 / 15	**A+ / 9.9**	68	20
MM	Invesco STIC Prime Inst	SRIXX	**C**	(800) 959-4246	1.00	**D+ / 2.6**	0.19 / 44	0.10 / 27	0.09 / 14	**A+ / 9.9**	70	N/A
MM	Invesco Gov TaxAdvantage Inst	TSPXX	**C**	(800) 959-4246	1.00	**D+ / 2.5**	0.15 / 43	0.06 / 26	0.05 / 12	**A+ / 9.9**	69	N/A
MM	Invesco Premier Portfoilo Inst	IPPXX	**C**	(800) 959-4246	1.00	**D+ / 2.5**	0.15 / 43	0.07 / 26	0.08 / 14	**A+ / 9.9**	67	N/A
MM	Goldman Sachs Fin Sq Pr Oblg	FPOXX	**C**	(800) 526-7384	1.00	**D+ / 2.5**	0.15 / 43	0.07 / 26	0.08 / 14	**A+ / 9.9**	N/A	N/A
MM	MSILF Prime Portfolio IS	MPEXX	**C**	(800) 354-8185	1.00	**D+ / 2.5**	0.12 / 42	0.06 / 26	0.07 / 14	**A+ / 9.9**	N/A	N/A
MM	Vanguard Prime M/M Inv	VMMXX	**C**	(800) 662-7447	1.00	**D+ / 2.5**	0.13 / 42	0.05 / 25	0.05 / 13	**A+ / 9.9**	66	13
MM	Vanguard Federal M/M Inv	VMFXX	**C**	(800) 662-7447	1.00	**D+ / 2.4**	0.10 / 41	0.04 / 24	0.03 / 11	**A+ / 9.9**	66	9
MM	SEI Daily Inc Tr-Prime Obligation A	TCPXX	**C**	(800) 342-5734	1.00	**D+ / 2.4**	0.09 / 41	0.04 / 24	0.04 / 12	**A+ / 9.9**	66	N/A
MM	SEI Daily Inc Tr-Money Market A	TCMXX	**C**	(800) 342-5734	1.00	**D+ / 2.4**	0.11 / 42	0.04 / 24	0.05 / 13	**A+ / 9.9**	66	N/A
MM	Federated Inst Prime Value Obl	PVCXX	**C**	(800) 341-7400	1.00	**D+ / 2.4**	0.10 / 41	0.04 / 24	0.06 / 13	**A+ / 9.9**	65	N/A
MM	MSILF Money Mkt Cshmgt	MSHXX	**C**	(800) 354-8185	1.00	**D+ / 2.4**	0.09 / 41	0.04 / 24	0.03 / 10	**A+ / 9.9**	64	N/A
MM	BofA Government Plus Rsv Inst	CVTXX	**C**	(888) 331-0904	1.00	**D+ / 2.4**	0.07 / 40	0.05 / 24	0.03 / 10	**A+ / 9.9**	68	N/A
MM	Federated CA Muni Cash Tr Cash	CCSXX	**C**	(800) 341-7400	1.00	**D+ / 2.4**	0.08 / 40	0.05 / 25	0.04 / 11	**A+ / 9.9**	67	20
MM	MSILF Govt Portfolio Inv	MVVXX	**C**	(800) 354-8185	1.00	**D+ / 2.3**	0.06 / 39	0.05 / 25	0.04 / 12	**A+ / 9.9**	68	N/A
MM	Invesco Gov and Agency Inst	AGPXX	**C**	(800) 959-4246	1.00	**D+ / 2.3**	0.10 / 41	0.04 / 24	0.04 / 12	**A+ / 9.9**	N/A	N/A
MM	Vanguard Treas MM Inv	VUSXX	**C**	(800) 662-7447	1.00	**D+ / 2.3**	0.07 / 40	0.03 / 23	0.02 / 9	**A+ / 9.9**	66	19
MM	Wilmington Prime MM Select	VSMXX	**C**	(800) 336-9970	1.00	**D / 2.2**	0.05 / 39	0.02 / 21	0.02 / 9	**A+ / 9.9**	N/A	N/A
MM	BlackRock-Lq T-Fund Instl	TSTXX	**C**	(800) 441-7762	1.00	**D / 2.2**	0.05 / 38	0.03 / 22	0.02 / 7	**A+ / 9.9**	64	N/A
MM	PIMCO Government Money Market	AMAXX	**C**	(800) 426-0107	1.00	**D / 2.2**	0.06 / 39	0.03 / 23	0.03 / 11	**A+ / 9.9**	66	5
MM	Fidelity Spartan Money Market	SPRXX	**C**	(800) 544-8544	1.00	**D / 2.2**	0.07 / 40	0.03 / 22	0.02 / 8	**A+ / 9.9**	65	N/A
MM	Goldman Sachs Fin Sq Govt FST	FGTXX	**C**	(800) 526-7384	1.00	**D / 2.2**	0.08 / 40	0.03 / 22	0.03 / 10	**A+ / 9.9**	63	N/A
MM	Invesco Treasury Inst	TRPXX	**C**	(800) 959-4246	1.00	**D / 2.2**	0.07 / 40	0.03 / 22	0.03 / 10	**A+ / 9.9**	N/A	N/A
MM	Invesco Premier US Gv Mny Port	IUGXX	**C**	(800) 959-4246	1.00	**D / 2.2**	0.07 / 40	0.03 / 22	0.03 / 10	**A+ / 9.9**	N/A	N/A
MM	BlackRock-Money Market Prtf Inv A	PINXX	**C**	(800) 441-7762	1.00	**D / 2.2**	0.07 / 40	0.03 / 22	0.02 / 7	**A+ / 9.9**	63	8
MM	SEI Daily Inc Tr-Government A	SEOXX	**C**	(800) 342-5734	1.00	**D / 2.1**	0.04 / 38	0.03 / 23	0.03 / 11	**A+ / 9.9**	N/A	1
MM	Gabelli US Treasury Money Mkt	GABXX	**C**	(800) 422-3554	1.00	**D / 2.1**	0.05 / 38	0.02 / 20	0.02 / 8	**A+ / 9.9**	63	24
MM	PNC Government Money Market A	PGAXX	**C**	(800) 551-2145	1.00	**D / 2.1**	0.04 / 38	0.03 / 23	0.02 / 9	**A+ / 9.9**	67	N/A
MM	Fidelity US Treasury Income Port I	FSIXX	**C**	(800) 544-8544	1.00	**D / 2.1**	0.04 / 37	0.02 / 20	0.02 / 8	**A+ / 9.9**	65	5
MM	Schwab Value Adv Money Investor	SWVXX	**C**	(800) 407-0256	1.00	**D / 2.1**	0.04 / 38	0.02 / 21	0.02 / 9	**A+ / 9.9**	66	24
MM	Goldman Sachs Fin Sq Treas Sol	FEDXX	**C**	(800) 526-7384	1.00	**D / 2.1**	0.06 / 39	0.02 / 20	0.02 / 8	**A+ / 9.9**	64	N/A
MM	Goldman Sachs Fin Sq Tre Instr	FTIXX	**C**	(800) 526-7384	1.00	**D / 2.1**	0.05 / 38	0.02 / 20	0.01 / 5	**A+ / 9.9**	64	N/A
MM	Dreyfus Prime Money Market	CZAXX	**C**	(800) 645-6561	1.00	**D / 2.0**	0.06 / 39	0.02 / 19	0.02 / 7	**A+ / 9.9**	63	N/A
MM	Dreyfus Inst Pref Govt Mny Mkt	DSHXX	**C**	(800) 426-9363	1.00	**D / 2.0**	0.07 / 40	0.02 / 19	0.04 / 11	**A+ / 9.9**	65	N/A
MM	BlackRock Liqdty TempFd Dollar	TDOXX	**C**	(800) 441-7762	1.00	**D / 2.0**	0.04 / 37	0.03 / 22	0.02 / 7	**A+ / 9.9**	N/A	N/A
MM	BlackRock-Lq Federal Tr Instl	TFFXX	**C**	(800) 441-7762	1.00	**D / 2.0**	0.04 / 37	0.02 / 19	0.02 / 7	**A+ / 9.9**	64	N/A
MM	Deutsche CAT Tax-Exempt Port	CHSXX	**C**	(800) 728-3337	1.00	**D / 2.0**	0.02 / 34	0.03 / 22	0.02 / 7	**A+ / 9.9**	67	N/A
MM	PIMCO Money Market A	PYAXX	**C-**	(800) 426-0107	1.00	**D / 2.0**	0.02 / 35	0.02 / 21	0.03 / 11	**A+ / 9.9**	N/A	5
MM	Schwab Retirement Advantage	SWIXX	**C-**	(800) 407-0256	1.00	**D / 2.0**	0.03 / 37	0.02 / 21	0.01 / 6	**A+ / 9.9**	66	18
MM	Federated US Trs Csh Res Instl	UTIXX	**C-**	(800) 341-7400	1.00	**D / 1.9**	0.03 / 36	0.01 / 17	0.01 / 4	**A+ / 9.9**	63	22
MM	Federated Trust For US Trs Obl	TTOXX	**C-**	(800) 341-7400	1.00	**D / 1.9**	0.04 / 37	0.01 / 17	0.01 / 4	**A+ / 9.9**	63	N/A
MM	Dreyfus Inst Tr Agcy Cash Adv	DHLXX	**C-**	(800) 426-9363	1.00	**D / 1.9**	0.04 / 37	0.01 / 16	0.01 / 4	**A+ / 9.9**	63	N/A
MM	Fidelity Cash-MM III	FCOXX	**C-**	(800) 544-8544	1.00	**D / 1.9**	0.03 / 36	0.02 / 19	0.01 / 4	**A+ / 9.9**	65	5
MM	Fidelity Prime MM III	FCDXX	**C-**	(800) 522-7297	1.00	**D / 1.9**	0.03 / 36	0.02 / 19	0.01 / 5	**A+ / 9.9**	65	5

• Denotes fund is closed to new investors

Fund Type	Fund Name (99 Pct = Best, 0 Pct = Worst)	Ticker Symbol	Overall Investment Rating	Phone	Net Asset Value As of 3/31/16	PERFORMANCE: Performance Rating/Pts	Annualized Total Return Through 3/31/16: 1Yr / Pct	3Yr / Pct	5Yr / Pct	RISK: Risk Rating/Pts	FUND MGR: Mgr. Quality Pct	Mgr. Tenure (Years)
MTG	Vanguard Mort-Backed Secs Idx	VMBSX	**A+**	(800) 662-7447	21.35	**B- /7.2**	2.17 /73	2.52 /71	3.09 /47	**B /8.2**	69	7
MTG	TCW Total Return Bond N	TGMNX	**A**	(800) 386-3829	10.61	**B- /7.5**	1.59 /67	2.84 /75	4.93 /71	**B /7.7**	79	6
MTG	Advisors Series Trust PIA MBS	PMTGX	**A**	(800) 251-1970	9.76	**B- /7.2**	1.85 /70	2.58 /72	3.05 /46	**B /8.0**	62	10
MTG	HC Capital US Mtg/Asst Bckd FI	HCASX	**A**	(800) 242-9596	9.85	**C+ /6.8**	1.94 /71	2.23 /66	2.95 /44	**B /8.1**	51	4
MTG	Federated Mortgage Fund Inst	FGFIX	**A**	(800) 341-7400	9.69	**C+ /6.5**	1.76 /69	2.16 /65	2.88 /43	**B /8.2**	57	13
MTG	Wright Current Income	WCIFX	**A-**	(800) 232-0013	9.41	**C+ /6.2**	1.57 /67	1.89 /59	2.78 /42	**B+ /8.3**	55	7
MTG	Northern Bond Index	NOBOX	**B+**	(800) 595-9111	10.74	**B- /7.2**	1.89 /71	2.37 /69	3.66 /56	**C+ /6.7**	42	9
MTG ●	Franklin Strategic Mortgage Port	FSMIX	**B+**	(800) 342-5236	9.49	**C+ /5.8**	1.53 /67	3.01 /76	4.00 /61	**B /8.2**	87	23
MTG	RidgeWorth Seix US Mtg A	SLTMX	**B**	(888) 784-3863	11.31	**C+ /5.7**	1.70 /69	2.29 /67	3.13 /47	**B /7.8**	45	9
MTG	Goldman Sachs US Mtge A	GSUAX	**B**	(800) 526-7384	10.68	**C /5.5**	1.89 /71	2.50 /71	3.47 /52	**B+ /8.3**	73	13
MTG	JPMorgan Mortgage Backed Sec A	OMBAX	**B**	(800) 480-4111	11.66	**C /5.4**	2.45 /74	2.32 /68	3.40 /51	**B+ /8.5**	81	16
MTG	Prudential Corporate Bond Z	TGMBX	**B-**	(800) 225-1852	10.99	**B /7.8**	2.73 /75	2.46 /70	3.40 /52	**C /5.1**	45	1
MTG	Mgd Acct Srs BlackRock US Mtg	BMPAX	**B-**	(800) 441-7762	10.41	**C+ /6.0**	1.69 /69	2.97 /76	4.25 /65	**B- /7.4**	70	7
MTG	American Funds Mortgage Fund A	MFAAX	**B-**	(800) 421-0180	10.28	**C /5.5**	2.85 /76	2.32 /68	3.21 /48	**B /7.8**	49	6
MTG	Principal Govt & High Qual Bd A	CMPGX	**B-**	(800) 222-5852	10.94	**C /5.1**	1.64 /68	1.84 /58	2.97 /45	**B /8.2**	42	6
MTG	PIMCO Mortgage-Backd Sec A	PMRAX	**C+**	(800) 426-0107	10.56	**C /5.1**	2.03 /72	2.28 /67	3.23 /49	**B /8.0**	53	4
MTG	Fidelity Adv Mortgage Secs A	FMGAX	**C+**	(800) 522-7297	11.36	**C /4.8**	1.77 /69	2.17 /65	3.22 /48	**B /7.8**	40	8
MTG	AMF Ultra Short Mortgage Fund	ASARX	**C+**	(800) 527-3713	7.22	**C- /3.9**	-0.42 /27	1.06 /44	1.16 /22	**A- /9.2**	86	7
MTG	Northern Tax-Advtged Ult-Sh Fxd	NTAUX	**C+**	(800) 595-9111	10.12	**C- /3.4**	0.41 /48	0.52 /33	0.76 /19	**A+ /9.9**	76	7
MTG	TCW Short Term Bond I	TGSMX	**C+**	(800) 386-3829	8.69	**C- /3.3**	0.26 /45	0.47 /33	0.98 /20	**A+ /9.9**	76	6
MTG	PIA Short-Term Securities Adv	PIASX	**C+**	(800) 251-1970	10.01	**C- /3.3**	0.34 /47	0.45 /32	0.45 /17	**A+ /9.8**	75	N/A
MTG	Trust for Credit UltSh Dur Gov TCU	TCUUX	**C**	(800) 342-5828	9.50	**D /2.2**	0.01 /32	0.04 /23	0.24 /16	**A+ /9.9**	58	N/A
MTG	BlackRock GNMA Port Inv A	BGPAX	**C-**	(800) 441-7762	9.91	**C- /4.1**	1.72 /69	1.73 /56	3.01 /45	**B- /7.1**	24	7
MTG	WA Adjustable Rate Income A	ARMZX	**C-**	(877) 534-4627	8.84	**D /1.7**	-0.05 /31	0.54 /34	1.20 /22	**A+ /9.6**	77	4
MTG	Federated Adj Rate Sec Inst	FEUGX	**C-**	(800) 341-7400	9.69	**D /1.6**	-0.62 /25	-0.05 /15	0.41 /17	**A+ /9.9**	53	21
MTG	Wells Fargo Adj Rate Govt A	ESAAX	**C-**	(800) 222-8222	9.01	**D- /1.3**	-0.42 /27	0.13 /28	0.71 /18	**A+ /9.9**	69	8
MTG	Goldman Sachs Hi Qual Fltg R A	GSAMX	**C-**	(800) 526-7384	8.63	**D- /1.0**	-0.81 /23	-0.39 /12	-0.19 / 3	**A+ /9.8**	53	8
MTG	Pacific Financial Tactical Inv	PFTLX	**D+**	(888) 451-8734	9.31	**E+ /0.8**	-2.78 /12	-0.77 /10	0.30 /16	**B+ /8.7**	18	9
MTG	PIMCO StkPlus Intl (DH) A	PIPAX	**E**	(800) 426-0107	6.33	**D- /1.3**	-15.26 / 0	3.56 /81	6.13 /77	**E- /0.0**	94	1
MTG	ProFunds-Falling US Dollar Svc	FDPSX	**E-**	(888) 776-3637	17.27	**E- /0.1**	0.82 /56	-7.00 / 1	-6.83 / 0	**E+ /0.8**	1	7

● Denotes fund is closed to new investors

Data as of March 31, 2016

99 Pct = Best
0 Pct = Worst

Fund Type	Fund Name	Ticker Symbol	Overall Investment Rating	Phone	Net Asset Value As of 3/31/16	PERFORMANCE: Performance Rating/Pts	Annualized Total Return Through 3/31/16: 1Yr / Pct	3Yr / Pct	5Yr / Pct	RISK: Risk Rating/Pts	FUND MGR: Mgr. Quality Pct	Mgr. Tenure (Years)
MUH	Northern Short-Interm Tax-Ex	NSITX	**B+**	(800) 595-9111	10.48	**C+ / 5.8**	1.41 / 73	1.02 / 54	1.50 / 35	**B+ / 8.7**	59	9
MUH	Vanguard High-Yield Tax-Exempt	VWAHX	**B**	(800) 662-7447	11.43	**A+ / 9.8**	4.73 / 97	4.40 / 97	6.82 / 96	**C- / 3.1**	71	6
MUH	Northern High Yield Muni	NHYMX	**B**	(800) 595-9111	9.02	**A+ / 9.8**	4.80 / 97	4.25 / 97	7.58 / 98	**C- / 3.1**	72	18
MUH	Fidelity Municipal Inc	FHIGX	**B**	(800) 544-8544	13.55	**A / 9.5**	3.75 / 92	3.98 / 96	6.05 / 92	**C- / 3.5**	61	7
MUH	Columbia AMT-Fr Intm Muni Bond	LITAX	**B**	(800) 345-6611	10.81	**B / 8.1**	3.33 / 88	2.85 / 86	4.56 / 82	**C / 5.0**	51	7
MUH	JPMorgan CA Tax Free Bond A	JCBAX	**B**	(800) 480-4111	11.15	**B / 7.9**	3.17 / 87	2.86 / 87	4.60 / 82	**C / 5.2**	58	12
MUH	American Century CA Hi-Yld Muni	CAYAX	**B-**	(800) 345-6488	10.68	**A+ / 9.7**	5.74 / 99	5.23 / 99	7.75 / 98	**D+ / 2.7**	83	29
MUH	MainStay High Yield Muni Bond C	MMHDX	**C+**	(800) 624-6782	12.35	**A+ / 9.9**	5.56 / 99	4.78 / 98	8.65 / 99	**D- / 1.3**	30	6
MUH	Franklin California H/Y Muni A	FCAMX	**C+**	(800) 342-5236	10.94	**A+ / 9.8**	4.98 / 98	5.51 / 99	9.42 / 99	**D / 2.1**	82	23
MUH	PIMCO High Yield Muni Bond A	PYMAX	**C+**	(800) 426-0107	8.96	**A+ / 9.8**	7.10 / 99	4.55 / 98	7.59 / 98	**D / 1.9**	43	5
MUH ●	Invesco High Yield Municipal A	ACTHX	**C+**	(800) 959-4246	10.18	**A+ / 9.8**	5.96 / 99	5.60 / 99	8.79 / 99	**D- / 1.4**	73	14
MUH	American Funds High Inc Muni Bnd	AMHIX	**C+**	(800) 421-0180	15.81	**A+ / 9.7**	5.09 / 98	4.95 / 99	8.15 / 98	**D+ / 2.5**	78	22
MUH	T Rowe Price Tax-Free High Yield	PRFHX	**C+**	(800) 638-5660	12.09	**A+ / 9.7**	4.23 / 95	4.69 / 98	8.04 / 98	**D+ / 2.3**	49	14
MUH	MFS Municipal High Income A	MMHYX	**C+**	(800) 225-2606	8.31	**A+ / 9.6**	5.72 / 99	4.79 / 98	8.16 / 98	**D / 1.8**	48	14
MUH	Columbia High Yield Municipal A	LHIAX	**C+**	(800) 345-6611	10.80	**A / 9.5**	4.24 / 95	4.70 / 98	7.86 / 98	**D+ / 2.6**	74	7
MUH	Federated Muni High Yield Advn A	FMOAX	**C+**	(800) 341-7400	9.06	**A / 9.4**	5.03 / 98	4.74 / 98	8.00 / 98	**D / 2.1**	59	7
MUH	Prudential Muni High Income A	PRHAX	**C+**	(800) 225-1852	10.39	**A / 9.4**	4.86 / 98	4.52 / 98	7.51 / 97	**D / 1.8**	39	12
MUH	Delaware Natl HY Muni Bd A	CXHYX	**C+**	(800) 523-1918	11.05	**A / 9.4**	5.06 / 98	4.59 / 98	8.43 / 99	**D / 1.8**	34	13
MUH	American Century High Yld Muni A	AYMAX	**C+**	(800) 345-6488	9.61	**A- / 9.1**	5.18 / 98	3.99 / 96	7.30 / 97	**D+ / 2.8**	42	18
MUH	RS High Income Municipal Bond A	RSHMX	**C+**	(800) 766-3863	10.96	**B+ / 8.9**	4.17 / 95	3.76 / 94	6.82 / 96	**C- / 3.0**	48	2
MUH	Fidelity Adv Muni Income A	FAMUX	**C+**	(800) 522-7297	13.55	**B+ / 8.6**	3.24 / 87	3.69 / 94	5.82 / 91	**C- / 3.5**	51	10
MUH	State Farm Tax Advant Bond A	TANAX	**C+**	(800) 447-4930	12.05	**B+ / 8.6**	3.63 / 91	3.30 / 91	4.70 / 83	**C- / 3.2**	32	16
MUH	Value Line Tax Exempt Fund	VLHYX	**C+**	(800) 243-2729	10.12	**B+ / 8.4**	2.92 / 84	2.44 / 82	4.40 / 81	**C- / 3.7**	20	6
MUH	Waddell & Reed Adv Muni High Inc	UMUHX	**C+**	(888) 923-3355	4.90	**B+ / 8.3**	2.92 / 84	3.71 / 94	6.59 / 95	**C- / 3.3**	57	8
MUH	Delaware MN HY Muni Bond A	DVMHX	**C+**	(800) 523-1918	10.96	**B / 8.2**	3.54 / 90	3.37 / 92	5.80 / 91	**C- / 4.2**	58	13
MUH	Hartford Municipal Opportunities A	HHMAX	**C+**	(888) 843-7824	8.68	**B / 8.1**	4.03 / 94	3.07 / 89	6.11 / 93	**C- / 3.9**	41	4
MUH	Federated Ohio Municipal Inc Fund	OMIAX	**C+**	(800) 341-7400	11.37	**B / 7.9**	3.44 / 89	2.94 / 88	5.03 / 86	**C- / 4.2**	41	21
MUH	Nuveen High Yield Muni Bond A	NHMAX	**C**	(800) 257-8787	17.40	**A+ / 9.9**	6.17 / 99	6.24 / 99	10.93 / 99	**E+ / 0.7**	70	16
MUH	Nuveen CA High Yield Muni Bd A	NCHAX	**C**	(800) 257-8787	9.80	**A+ / 9.9**	6.23 / 99	6.89 / 99	11.74 / 99	**E+ / 0.6**	N/A	10
MUH	SEI Asset Alloc-Def Strat All A	STDAX	**C**	(800) 342-5734	14.31	**A+ / 9.9**	-0.19 / 29	7.15 / 99	8.98 / 99	**E / 0.5**	99	13
MUH	AMG GW&K Municipal Enhcd Yld	GWMNX	**C**	(800) 835-3879	10.28	**A+ / 9.8**	4.86 / 98	4.36 / 97	8.33 / 99	**E+ / 0.6**	10	11
MUH	AB High Income Municipal A	ABTHX	**C**	(800) 221-5672	11.51	**A+ / 9.7**	5.78 / 99	4.78 / 98	9.05 / 99	**E+ / 0.8**	18	6
MUH	BlackRock High Yld Muni Inv A	MDYHX	**C**	(800) 441-7762	9.64	**A+ / 9.6**	6.17 / 99	4.82 / 98	8.66 / 99	**E+ / 0.6**	16	10
MUH	Dreyfus High Yld Muni Bd A	DHYAX	**C**	(800) 645-6561	12.08	**A- / 9.0**	6.46 / 99	4.07 / 96	7.25 / 97	**D / 1.8**	23	5
MUH	Deutsche Strat High Yield T/F A	NOTAX	**C**	(800) 728-3337	12.50	**B+ / 8.7**	4.08 / 94	3.20 / 90	6.60 / 95	**D+ / 2.5**	16	18
MUH	Franklin High Yld Tax-Free Inc A	FRHIX	**C**	(800) 342-5236	10.61	**B+ / 8.7**	3.68 / 92	3.69 / 94	6.94 / 96	**D / 2.0**	17	23
MUH	WA Municipal High Income A	STXAX	**C**	(877) 534-4627	14.58	**B+ / 8.4**	3.81 / 93	3.15 / 90	7.02 / 96	**D+ / 2.4**	20	10
MUH	Ivy Municipal High Income A	IYIAX	**C**	(800) 777-6472	5.28	**B / 8.2**	3.53 / 90	3.35 / 91	6.77 / 96	**D+ / 2.4**	26	7
MUH	Oppeneheimer Rochester Hi Yld	ORNAX	**C-**	(888) 470-0862	7.10	**A / 9.5**	6.68 / 99	4.44 / 97	9.32 / 99	**E / 0.5**	11	15
MUH	Lord Abbett Tx Fr High Yld Muni A	HYMAX	**C-**	(888) 522-2388	11.78	**A- / 9.2**	4.47 / 97	3.59 / 93	7.23 / 97	**E+ / 0.9**	13	12
MUH	Goldman Sachs High Yield Muni A	GHYAX	**C-**	(800) 526-7384	9.36	**B+ / 8.8**	4.89 / 98	4.18 / 97	8.14 / 98	**D- / 1.0**	27	16
MUH	Federated Muni & Stock	FMUAX	**C-**	(800) 341-7400	12.31	**B+ / 8.6**	1.24 / 71	4.15 / 96	6.96 / 96	**D- / 1.4**	94	13
MUH	Pioneer High Income Municipal A	PIMAX	**C-**	(800) 225-6292	7.45	**B+ / 8.5**	6.18 / 99	2.90 / 87	6.59 / 95	**D / 1.8**	16	10
MUH	J Hancock High Yield Muni Bond A	JHTFX	**C-**	(800) 257-3336	8.25	**B+ / 8.4**	3.96 / 94	3.19 / 90	6.44 / 94	**D / 2.0**	17	N/A
MUH	Spirit of America Municipal TF Bd A	SOAMX	**D+**	(800) 452-4892	9.67	**B- / 7.5**	3.88 / 93	2.60 / 84	5.85 / 91	**E+ / 0.9**	7	7

● Denotes fund is closed to new investors

	99 Pct = Best *0 Pct = Worst*					PERFORMANCE				RISK	FUND MGR	
Fund Type	Fund Name	Ticker Symbol	**Overall Investment Rating**	Phone	Net Asset Value As of 3/31/16	**Performance Rating/Pts**	Annualized Total Return Through 3/31/16 1Yr / Pct	3Yr / Pct	5Yr / Pct	**Risk Rating/Pts**	Mgr. Quality Pct	Mgr. Tenure (Years)
MUI	Westcore CO Tax Exempt	WTCOX	**A+**	(800) 392-2673	11.76	**A- /9.1**	3.53 /90	3.07 /89	4.49 /81	**C+ / 6.0**	55	11
MUI	Pacific Capital Tax-Free Secs Y	PTXFX	**A+**	(888) 739-1390	10.37	**A- /9.1**	3.68 /92	3.06 /89	4.48 /81	**C+ / 5.8**	52	12
MUI	WesMark West Virginia Muni Bond	WMKMX	**A+**	(800) 341-7400	10.67	**B+ /8.7**	2.88 /84	2.62 /84	3.77 /76	**C+ / 6.9**	47	10
MUI	SEI Tax-Exempt Tr-NY Muni Bond	SENYX	**A+**	(800) 342-5734	10.94	**B+ /8.3**	3.14 /86	2.27 /80	3.54 /74	**B / 7.6**	48	17
MUI	BNY Mellon PA Inter Muni Bond M	MPPIX	**A+**	(800) 645-6561	12.51	**B /8.1**	2.55 /81	1.95 /76	3.73 /76	**B- / 7.1**	30	16
MUI	SEI Tax-Exempt Tr-NJ Muni Bond	SENJX	**A+**	(800) 342-5734	10.55	**B /7.9**	2.51 /80	1.86 /75	3.30 /72	**B / 7.9**	42	3
MUI	CNR CA Tax-Exempt Bond N	CCTEX	**A+**	(888) 889-0799	10.78	**B- /7.3**	1.73 /75	1.64 /71	2.70 /64	**B+ / 8.5**	51	7
MUI	Commerce Kansas T/F Intm Bond	KTXIX	**A**	(800) 995-6365	19.64	**B+ /8.4**	2.72 /82	2.47 /82	4.23 /79	**C+ / 6.0**	34	16
MUI	JPMorgan OH Municipal A	ONOHX	**A-**	(800) 480-4111	11.00	**C+ /6.7**	2.71 /82	2.21 /79	3.57 /75	**B / 7.8**	46	22
MUI	GuideMark Tax-Exempt Fixed Inc	GMTEX	**B+**	(888) 278-5809	11.62	**B+ /8.8**	3.18 /87	2.67 /84	4.76 /83	**C / 4.6**	26	10
MUI	• Franklin California Ins Tx-Fr A	FRCIX	**B**	(800) 342-5236	13.27	**A /9.5**	3.98 /94	5.10 /99	7.46 /97	**C- / 3.3**	82	25
MUI	Aquila Narragansett TxFr Income A	NITFX	**B**	(800) 437-1020	10.92	**B+ /8.5**	3.84 /93	3.51 /93	4.28 /80	**C / 4.7**	52	24
MUI	• Franklin Insured Tax-Free Inc A	FTFIX	**B**	(800) 342-5236	12.45	**B+ /8.5**	2.85 /83	3.81 /95	6.06 /92	**C / 4.5**	62	27
MUI	Putnam AMT Free Ins Mun A	PPNAX	**B**	(800) 225-1581	15.46	**B /8.2**	3.08 /86	3.31 /91	5.73 /90	**C / 4.8**	46	14
MUI	Touchstone Ohio Tax-Free Bond A	TOHAX	**B**	(800) 543-0407	11.87	**B /7.8**	3.02 /85	3.13 /89	4.92 /85	**C / 5.5**	51	30
MUI	First Inv CA Tax Exempt A	FICAX	**C+**	(800) 423-4026	13.10	**B+ /8.5**	3.89 /93	4.00 /96	6.14 /93	**C- / 3.8**	51	25
MUI	Franklin Ohio Tax-Free Inc A	FTOIX	**C+**	(800) 342-5236	12.92	**B+ /8.3**	3.47 /90	3.45 /92	5.57 /89	**C- / 3.6**	31	27
MUI	First Inv NC Tax Exempt B	FMTQX	**C+**	(800) 423-4026	13.70	**B- /7.2**	1.54 /74	1.61 /70	3.97 /77	**C / 5.1**	13	24
MUI	First Inv OH Tax Exempt A	FIOHX	**C+**	(800) 423-4026	12.79	**B- /7.1**	2.70 /82	3.02 /88	4.95 /85	**C / 4.9**	39	25
MUI	Franklin MN Tax-Free Inc A	FMINX	**C+**	(800) 342-5236	12.62	**C+ /6.9**	2.52 /81	2.53 /83	4.67 /83	**C / 5.0**	26	27
MUI	BNY Mellon National ST Muni Bd	MPSTX	**C+**	(800) 645-6561	12.81	**C- /3.6**	0.37 /51	0.42 /36	0.88 /24	**A / 9.5**	53	1
MUI	First Inv Tax Exempt Opps A	EIITX	**C**	(800) 423-4026	17.15	**B /7.9**	3.34 /88	3.44 /92	6.12 /93	**C- / 3.3**	24	25
MUI	First Inv NY Tax Exempt A	FNYFX	**C**	(800) 423-4026	14.77	**B- /7.0**	3.21 /87	2.86 /87	5.00 /85	**C / 4.6**	30	25
MUI	First Inv MI Tax Exempt A	FTMIX	**C**	(800) 423-4026	12.41	**B- /7.0**	2.81 /83	3.01 /88	5.17 /87	**C- / 4.2**	32	25
MUI	First Inv PA Tax Exempt A	FTPAX	**C**	(800) 423-4026	13.40	**C+ /6.7**	2.61 /81	2.91 /87	5.27 /87	**C / 4.4**	30	25
MUI	First Inv NJ Tax Exempt A	FINJX	**C**	(800) 423-4026	13.15	**C+ /6.6**	2.96 /85	2.63 /84	4.97 /85	**C / 4.3**	21	25
MUI	First Inv Tax Exempt Income A	FITAX	**C**	(800) 423-4026	9.88	**C+ /6.5**	2.50 /80	2.82 /86	5.17 /87	**C / 4.8**	32	25
MUI	First Inv CT Tax Exempt A	FICTX	**C**	(800) 423-4026	13.65	**C+ /6.2**	2.73 /82	2.61 /84	4.89 /84	**C / 4.8**	27	25
MUI	Dreyfus Sh-Intmd Muni Bd A	DMBAX	**C**	(800) 645-6561	13.03	**D+ /2.9**	0.95 /66	0.74 /45	1.27 /31	**A- / 9.1**	57	7
MUI	Franklin MI Tax-Free Inc A	FTTMX	**C-**	(800) 342-5236	11.80	**C+ /6.6**	1.97 /77	2.41 /82	4.47 /81	**C- / 4.1**	20	27
MUI	First Inv MA Tax Exempt A	FIMAX	**C-**	(800) 423-4026	12.13	**C+ /6.6**	2.62 /81	2.83 /86	5.14 /86	**C- / 3.7**	17	25
MUI	First Inv VA Tax Exempt A	FIVAX	**C-**	(800) 423-4026	13.34	**C+ /6.1**	2.68 /82	2.56 /83	4.53 /82	**C / 4.4**	22	25
MUI	First Inv OR Tax Exempt A	FTORX	**C-**	(800) 423-4026	13.82	**C+ /5.9**	2.80 /83	2.42 /82	4.87 /84	**C- / 3.8**	14	24
MUI	First Inv MN Tax Exempt A	FIMNX	**C-**	(800) 423-4026	12.36	**C /5.0**	2.12 /78	2.25 /80	4.59 /82	**C / 5.4**	24	25
MUI	Federated Muni Ultrashrt A	FMUUX	**C-**	(800) 341-7400	9.97	**D- /1.1**	-0.42 /27	-0.08 /15	0.30 /17	**A+ / 9.9**	49	16
MUI	JPMorgan Tax Aware Real Return	TXRAX	**D**	(800) 480-4111	9.59	**D- /1.2**	2.02 /77	-0.23 /14	1.63 /38	**C+ / 6.0**	8	11

• Denotes fund is closed to new investors

Data as of March 31, 2016

99 Pct = Best *0 Pct = Worst*						PERFORMANCE				RISK	FUND MGR	
					Net Asset Value		Annualized Total Return Through 3/31/16					
Fund Type	Fund Name	Ticker Symbol	Overall Investment Rating	Phone	As of 3/31/16	Performance Rating/Pts	1Yr / Pct	3Yr / Pct	5Yr / Pct	Risk Rating/Pts	Mgr. Quality Pct	Mgr. Tenure (Years)
MUN	Vanguard Interm-Term Tax-Exempt	VWITX	**A+**	(800) 662-7447	14.39	**A- /9.2**	3.65 /91	3.19 /90	4.91 /85	**C+ / 6.5**	N/A	3
MUN	USAA Tax-Exempt Interm-Term	USATX	**A+**	(800) 382-8722	13.61	**A- /9.1**	3.43 /89	3.12 /89	5.34 /88	**B- / 7.3**	75	13
MUN	Federated Interm Muni Trust Y	FIMYX	**A+**	(800) 341-7400	10.31	**A- /9.1**	3.82 /93	2.99 /88	4.78 /83	**B- / 7.0**	N/A	21
MUN	State Farm Muni Bond	SFBDX	**A+**	(800) 447-4930	8.88	**A- /9.1**	3.31 /88	3.12 /89	4.49 /81	**B- / 7.0**	72	18
MUN	T Rowe Price Summit Muni Intmdt	PRSMX	**A+**	(800) 638-5660	12.11	**A- /9.1**	3.55 /91	3.13 /89	4.67 /83	**C+ / 6.8**	68	23
MUN	Schwab Tax-Free Bond Fund	SWNTX	**A+**	(800) 407-0256	11.99	**A- /9.0**	3.21 /87	2.99 /88	4.65 /83	**B- / 7.2**	70	8
MUN	BMO Intermediate Tax Free Y	MITFX	**A+**	(800) 236-3863	11.45	**A- /9.0**	3.02 /85	3.04 /88	4.91 /84	**B- / 7.0**	N/A	22
MUN	SEI Tax-Exempt Tr-Intrm Term	SEIMX	**A+**	(800) 342-5734	11.86	**B+ /8.8**	3.57 /91	2.79 /86	4.51 /82	**C+ / 6.3**	48	17
MUN	Invesco Intm Term Municipal Inc A	VKLMX	**A+**	(800) 959-4246	11.32	**B+ /8.6**	3.45 /90	3.21 /90	4.89 /84	**C+ / 6.5**	69	11
MUN	BNY Mellon NY Int TxEx Inv	MNYIX	**A+**	(800) 645-6561	11.46	**B+ /8.4**	3.13 /86	2.26 /80	4.02 /78	**B- / 7.2**	39	9
MUN	Thornburg Intermediate Muni A	THIMX	**A+**	(800) 847-0200	14.38	**B /8.1**	2.75 /83	2.62 /84	4.64 /82	**B / 7.7**	58	5
MUN	Frost Municipal Bond Inv	FAUMX	**A+**	(866) 777-7818	10.61	**B /8.0**	2.27 /79	2.11 /78	3.43 /73	**B / 8.1**	53	14
MUN	Glenmede Intermediate Muni Port	GTCMX	**A+**	(800) 442-8299	11.10	**B /7.9**	2.42 /80	1.87 /75	2.81 /66	**B / 8.2**	49	5
MUN	Russell Tax Exempt Bond A	RTEAX	**A+**	(800) 832-6688	23.53	**B /7.9**	3.30 /88	2.81 /86	3.81 /76	**B / 8.0**	78	3
MUN	Thornburg NY Intermediate Muni A	THNYX	**A+**	(800) 847-0200	13.36	**B /7.8**	2.82 /83	2.29 /80	4.22 /79	**B / 7.8**	48	5
MUN	JPMorgan Muni Income A	OTBAX	**A+**	(800) 480-4111	10.09	**B /7.8**	3.27 /88	2.77 /86	3.90 /77	**B- / 7.3**	59	10
MUN	Victory National Muni A	VNMAX	**A+**	(800) 539-3863	11.09	**B- /7.5**	3.00 /85	2.05 /78	3.68 /75	**B / 7.9**	45	22
MUN	Cavanal Hill Intmdt TxFr Bd NL Inv	APTFX	**A+**	(800) 762-7085	11.25	**B- /7.4**	1.89 /76	1.63 /71	3.39 /73	**B / 8.1**	35	23
MUN	Old Westbury Muni Bond	OWMBX	**A+**	(800) 607-2200	12.09	**B- /7.1**	2.35 /80	1.37 /64	2.60 /61	**B+ / 8.3**	36	18
MUN	Dreyfus Intermediate Muni Bd	DITEX	**A**	(800) 645-6561	14.09	**A- /9.1**	3.63 /91	3.04 /88	4.75 /83	**C+ / 5.8**	51	5
MUN	Northern Intermed Tax Exempt	NOITX	**A**	(800) 595-9111	10.82	**A- /9.0**	3.53 /90	2.88 /87	4.61 /82	**C / 5.3**	41	18
MUN	Wells Fargo Intm Tax/AMT Fr A	WFTAX	**A**	(800) 222-8222	11.73	**B /8.0**	2.74 /82	2.75 /85	4.73 /83	**B- / 7.0**	53	15
MUN	Dreyfus Tax Sensitive Tot Ret Bd A	DSDAX	**A**	(800) 645-6561	23.22	**B- /7.1**	2.91 /84	2.59 /84	3.84 /76	**B / 7.7**	60	15
MUN	Vanguard Lmtd-Term Tax-Exempt	VMLTX	**A**	(800) 662-7447	11.05	**C+ /6.4**	1.57 /74	1.27 /60	1.86 /43	**A- / 9.1**	73	8
MUN	Oppenheimer Rochester Sht Term	ORSTX	**A**	(888) 470-0862	3.75	**C+ /6.1**	1.64 /75	1.82 /74	2.56 /61	**A / 9.3**	90	6
MUN	Pacific Capital T/F Sh-Interm Y	PTFSX	**A**	(888) 739-1390	10.25	**C+ /5.9**	1.50 /74	1.06 /55	1.35 /32	**A- / 9.0**	56	12
MUN	Vanguard Long-Term Tax-Exempt	VWLTX	**A-**	(800) 662-7447	11.87	**A+ /9.8**	4.77 /97	4.37 /97	6.39 /94	**C- / 3.9**	73	6
MUN	Fidelity Tax Free Bond Fd	FTABX	**A-**	(800) 544-8544	11.77	**A+ /9.6**	3.81 /93	4.04 /96	6.19 /93	**C- / 4.2**	62	7
MUN	Oppenheimer Rochester Int Term	ORRWX	**A-**	(888) 470-0862	4.42	**A- /9.1**	4.74 /97	3.46 /92	4.86 /84	**C / 5.0**	59	6
MUN	Thornburg Strategic Municipal Inc	TSSAX	**A-**	(800) 847-0200	15.38	**B+ /8.6**	2.85 /84	3.21 /90	6.43 /94	**C / 5.3**	53	7
MUN	Nuveen Intmdt Duration Muni Bond	NMBAX	**A-**	(800) 257-8787	9.35	**B+ /8.4**	3.60 /91	3.09 /89	4.60 /82	**C+ / 5.9**	53	9
MUN	Delaware Tax-Free USA Intmdt A	DMUSX	**A-**	(800) 523-1918	12.24	**B /7.8**	3.04 /85	2.47 /82	4.42 /81	**C+ / 6.4**	38	13
MUN	Nationwide HighMark Natl Int TFB	NWJOX	**A-**	(800) 848-0920	11.13	**B- /7.0**	2.25 /79	2.04 /77	3.15 /71	**B / 7.6**	40	20
MUN	Thornburg Limited Term Muni A	LTMFX	**A-**	(800) 847-0200	14.61	**C+ /6.1**	1.89 /76	1.51 /68	2.88 /67	**B+ / 8.7**	52	5
MUN	T Rowe Price Tax-Free Sh-Intmdt	PRFSX	**A-**	(800) 638-5660	5.65	**C+ /6.0**	1.36 /72	1.13 /56	2.09 /49	**B+ / 8.9**	54	22
MUN	Wells Fargo Str Muni Bd A	VMPAX	**A-**	(800) 222-8222	8.99	**C+ /5.9**	1.96 /77	2.18 /79	3.08 /70	**B+ / 8.9**	86	6
MUN	Northern Tax Exempt	NOTEX	**B+**	(800) 595-9111	10.89	**A+ /9.6**	4.28 /96	3.87 /95	6.14 /93	**C- / 3.8**	45	18
MUN	T Rowe Price Summit Muni Income	PRINX	**B+**	(800) 638-5660	12.10	**A+ /9.6**	4.08 /94	3.99 /96	6.59 /95	**C- / 3.6**	46	17
MUN	Dreyfus Municipal Bond	DRTAX	**B+**	(800) 645-6561	11.98	**A /9.5**	4.25 /95	3.69 /94	5.85 /91	**C- / 4.1**	47	7
MUN	USAA Tax-Exempt Long Term	USTEX	**B+**	(800) 382-8722	13.73	**A /9.5**	3.88 /93	3.81 /95	6.86 /96	**C- / 3.7**	50	N/A
MUN	T Rowe Price Tax-Free Income	PRTAX	**B+**	(800) 638-5660	10.44	**A /9.4**	3.48 /90	3.63 /93	6.03 /92	**C- / 4.2**	47	9
MUN	Elfun Tax Exempt Income	ELFTX	**B+**	(800) 242-0134	11.95	**A /9.3**	3.83 /93	3.40 /92	5.55 /89	**C / 4.3**	42	16
MUN	AMG GW&K Municipal Bond Inv	GWMTX	**B+**	(800) 835-3879	11.86	**A- /9.2**	3.91 /93	3.09 /89	5.18 /87	**C- / 4.2**	34	7
MUN	Madison Tax Free National Y	GTFHX	**B+**	(800) 877-6089	11.15	**A- /9.1**	3.73 /92	2.94 /88	4.49 /81	**C / 4.6**	34	19
MUN	Eaton Vance TABS Int-Term Muni	EITAX	**B+**	(800) 262-1122	12.46	**A- /9.1**	4.26 /95	3.48 /92	5.30 /88	**C / 4.5**	50	6
MUN	CGCM Municipal Bd Invest	TMUUX	**B+**	(800) 444-4273	9.78	**A- /9.1**	3.32 /88	3.15 /90	4.84 /84	**C- / 4.1**	46	11
MUN	JPMorgan Tax Free Bond A	PMBAX	**B+**	(800) 480-4111	12.61	**A- /9.0**	3.91 /93	3.92 /95	5.18 /87	**C / 4.5**	N/A	11
MUN	Wells Fargo Muni Bd A	WMFAX	**B+**	(800) 222-8222	10.48	**B+ /8.9**	3.77 /92	4.12 /96	6.52 /95	**C / 4.5**	80	16
MUN	Columbia Tax-Exempt A	COLTX	**B+**	(800) 345-6611	14.00	**B+ /8.9**	3.29 /88	3.75 /94	6.45 /94	**C / 4.3**	56	14
MUN	American Funds T/E Bd of America	AFTEX	**B+**	(800) 421-0180	13.19	**B+ /8.6**	3.64 /91	3.52 /93	6.00 /92	**C / 4.9**	56	37
MUN	Lord Abbett Interm Tax Free A	LISAX	**B+**	(888) 522-2388	10.98	**B+ /8.5**	3.30 /88	3.01 /88	5.08 /86	**C / 5.1**	42	10
MUN	PNC Intermediate Tax Exempt	PTBIX	**B+**	(800) 551-2145	9.72	**B+ /8.3**	3.18 /87	3.01 /88	4.55 /82	**C+ / 5.8**	52	9

• Denotes fund is closed to new investors

Fund Type	Fund Name (99 Pct = Best, 0 Pct = Worst)	Ticker Symbol	Overall Investment Rating	Phone	Net Asset Value As of 3/31/16	PERFORMANCE: Performance Rating/Pts	Annualized Total Return Through 3/31/16: 1Yr / Pct	3Yr / Pct	5Yr / Pct	RISK: Risk Rating/Pts	FUND MGR: Mgr. Quality Pct	Mgr. Tenure (Years)
MUS	Vanguard CA Interm-Term T-E Inv	VCAIX	**A+**	(800) 662-7447	11.97	**A /9.5**	4.04 /94	3.73 /94	5.54 /89	**C+ / 5.9**	80	5
MUS	Fidelity MI Muni Inc	FMHTX	**A+**	(800) 544-8544	12.48	**A /9.4**	4.11 /95	3.62 /93	5.20 /87	**C+ / 5.7**	76	10
MUS	Schwab California Tax-Free Bond	SWCAX	**A+**	(800) 407-0256	12.15	**A /9.3**	3.46 /90	3.45 /92	5.00 /85	**C+ / 6.8**	80	8
MUS	Saturna Idaho Tax-Exempt	NITEX	**A+**	(800) 728-8762	5.53	**A- /9.2**	3.68 /92	3.23 /90	4.09 /78	**B- / 7.3**	80	21
MUS	Dupree TN Tax-Free Income	TNTIX	**A+**	(800) 866-0614	11.72	**A- /9.2**	3.11 /86	3.27 /91	4.95 /85	**C+ / 5.8**	61	12
MUS	Dupree KY Tax Free Income	KYTFX	**A+**	(800) 866-0614	7.96	**A- /9.1**	3.24 /87	3.17 /90	4.87 /84	**C+ / 6.3**	61	17
MUS	Lee Fnl Hawaii-Muni Bond Inv	SURFX	**A+**		11.31	**A- /9.0**	2.83 /83	3.17 /90	4.65 /83	**C+ / 6.6**	70	1
MUS	Fidelity MN Muni Inc	FIMIX	**A+**	(800) 544-8544	11.84	**B+ /8.9**	3.57 /91	3.00 /88	4.42 /81	**B- / 7.1**	N/A	6
MUS	Payden CA Muni Inc Investor	PYCRX	**A+**	(888) 409-8007	10.41	**B+ /8.9**	2.86 /84	2.94 /88	4.42 /81	**B- / 7.0**	63	N/A
MUS	SEI Tax-Exempt Tr-CA Muni Bond	SBDAX	**A+**	(800) 342-5734	11.03	**B+ /8.9**	3.36 /89	2.80 /86	4.26 /80	**C+ / 6.4**	53	17
MUS	Colorado Bond Shares	HICOX	**A+**	(800) 572-0069	9.14	**B+ /8.8**	4.61 /97	4.05 /96	4.80 /84	**A- / 9.1**	98	26
MUS	CA Tax-Free Income Direct	CFNTX	**A+**	(800) 955-9988	11.82	**B+ /8.7**	2.67 /82	2.73 /85	4.71 /83	**B / 7.6**	61	13
MUS	Nuveen Minnesota Intmdt Muni Bd	FAMAX	**A+**	(800) 257-8787	10.63	**B+ /8.4**	3.67 /92	3.11 /89	4.67 /83	**C+ / 6.7**	63	22
MUS	Kansas Municipal	KSMUX	**A+**	(800) 601-5593	11.02	**B+ /8.3**	3.22 /87	3.00 /88	4.38 /80	**B- / 7.0**	N/A	20
MUS	SEI Tax-Exempt Tr-PA Muni Bond	SEPAX	**A+**	(800) 342-5734	10.89	**B /8.1**	3.15 /86	2.05 /77	3.82 /76	**B / 7.7**	42	17
MUS	Victory OH Muni Bond A	SOHTX	**A+**	(800) 539-3863	11.39	**B /8.1**	2.78 /83	2.62 /84	3.89 /77	**B / 7.6**	58	22
MUS	Nationwide HighMark CA Int TF Bd	NWJKX	**A+**	(800) 848-0920	10.47	**B /8.0**	2.45 /80	2.62 /84	3.65 /75	**B- / 7.2**	54	3
MUS	PIMCO CA Interm Muni Bond A	PCMBX	**A+**	(800) 426-0107	9.97	**B /7.9**	3.33 /88	2.36 /81	3.76 /76	**B- / 7.5**	46	5
MUS	Delaware Tax Free MN Intmdt A	DXCCX	**A+**	(800) 523-1918	11.33	**B /7.9**	2.90 /84	2.65 /84	4.29 /80	**B- / 7.3**	52	13
MUS	Brown Advisory Maryland Bond Inv	BIAMX	**A+**	(800) 540-6807	10.80	**B /7.8**	2.66 /82	1.70 /72	2.72 /64	**B+ / 8.4**	46	2
MUS	New Hampshire Municipal	NHMUX	**A+**	(800) 601-5593	10.94	**B /7.8**	2.99 /85	2.47 /82	3.70 /75	**B / 8.0**	60	13
MUS	Wells Fargo WI Tax Fr A	WWTFX	**A+**	(800) 222-8222	11.03	**B /7.7**	2.76 /83	3.00 /88	4.21 /79	**B / 8.0**	83	15
MUS	Thornburg NM Intermediate Muni A	THNMX	**A+**	(800) 847-0200	13.67	**B /7.6**	2.40 /80	2.25 /80	3.48 /74	**B / 7.8**	48	5
MUS	Wells Fargo MN Tax Free A	NMTFX	**A+**	(800) 222-8222	10.93	**B /7.6**	2.96 /85	2.89 /87	4.79 /84	**B / 7.7**	74	8
MUS	Fidelity CA Ltd Term Tax-Free Bd	FCSTX	**A+**	(800) 544-8544	10.76	**B- /7.4**	1.88 /76	1.85 /75	2.51 /59	**B+ / 8.9**	78	10
MUS	Jamestown VA Tax Exempt	JTEVX	**A+**	(866) 738-1126	10.21	**B- /7.4**	2.37 /80	1.53 /68	2.48 /59	**B+ / 8.4**	41	11
MUS	Wells Fargo CA Ltd Tax Fr A	SFCIX	**A+**	(800) 222-8222	10.96	**B- /7.2**	1.91 /76	2.16 /79	3.01 /69	**B+ / 8.9**	88	7
MUS	Thornburg CA Ltd Term Muni A	LTCAX	**A+**	(800) 847-0200	13.94	**B- /7.0**	1.84 /76	1.96 /77	3.36 /73	**B+ / 8.6**	72	5
MUS	Dupree KY Tax Free Short-to-Med	KYSMX	**A+**	(800) 866-0614	5.41	**C+ /6.8**	2.02 /77	1.32 /62	2.63 /62	**B+ / 8.8**	58	17
MUS	Fidelity PA Muni Inc	FPXTX	**A**	(800) 544-8544	11.39	**A /9.4**	3.54 /90	3.79 /95	5.47 /89	**C / 5.1**	74	14
MUS	Sit MN Tax Free Income	SMTFX	**A**	(800) 332-5580	10.63	**A /9.4**	3.89 /93	3.61 /93	5.74 /91	**C / 5.0**	69	23
MUS	Fidelity CT Muni Income Fd	FICNX	**A**	(800) 544-8544	11.87	**A /9.4**	4.18 /95	3.54 /93	4.91 /85	**C / 5.0**	58	14
MUS	T Rowe Price MD Tax Free Bd	MDXBX	**A**	(800) 638-5660	10.98	**A /9.3**	3.68 /92	3.49 /93	5.78 /91	**C / 4.9**	54	16
MUS	Dupree AL Tax Free Income	DUALX	**A**	(800) 866-0614	12.56	**A- /9.2**	3.13 /86	3.41 /92	5.50 /89	**C+ / 5.6**	68	15
MUS	Dupree NC Tax Free Income	NTFIX	**A**	(800) 866-0614	11.78	**A- /9.2**	3.48 /90	3.21 /90	5.42 /88	**C / 5.1**	49	12
MUS	AB Municipal Income II AZ A	AAZAX	**A**	(800) 221-5672	11.30	**B+ /8.9**	4.67 /97	3.45 /92	5.25 /87	**C / 5.3**	62	21
MUS	Aquila Tax-Free Fd for Utah A	UTAHX	**A**	(800) 437-1020	10.56	**B+ /8.8**	3.41 /89	3.87 /95	5.60 /90	**C+ / 6.0**	84	7
MUS	Wells Fargo PA Tax Fr A	EKVAX	**A**	(800) 222-8222	11.94	**B+ /8.8**	3.69 /92	4.05 /96	6.12 /93	**C+ / 5.7**	85	7
MUS	Madison Tax Free Virginia Y	GTVAX	**A**	(800) 877-6089	11.73	**B+ /8.7**	3.11 /86	2.68 /85	3.95 /77	**C+ / 5.7**	38	19
MUS	Commerce Missouri T/F Intm Bd	CFMOX	**A**	(800) 995-6365	19.74	**B+ /8.3**	2.92 /84	2.22 /79	4.05 /78	**C+ / 6.4**	33	17
MUS	Maine Municipal	MEMUX	**A**	(800) 601-5593	11.18	**B /7.9**	3.22 /87	2.51 /83	4.27 /80	**B- / 7.1**	47	13
MUS	Nuveen Oregon Intmdt Muni Bd A	FOTAX	**A**	(800) 257-8787	10.47	**B /7.8**	3.27 /88	2.54 /83	4.07 /78	**C+ / 6.7**	42	19
MUS	Columbia AMT Fr NY Intm Muni Bd	LNYAX	**A**	(800) 345-6611	12.23	**B /7.7**	3.17 /87	2.51 /83	4.02 /78	**B- / 7.3**	48	18
MUS	Columbia AMT-Fr SC Intm Muni Bd	NSCIX	**A**	(800) 345-6611	10.52	**B /7.7**	3.30 /88	2.36 /81	4.08 /78	**B- / 7.1**	40	5
MUS	Aquila Churchill Tax-Free of KY A	CHTFX	**A**	(800) 437-1020	10.88	**B /7.6**	2.75 /83	2.83 /86	4.43 /81	**B- / 7.5**	62	7
MUS	Columbia AMT-Fr GA Intm Muni Bd	NGIMX	**A**	(800) 345-6611	10.85	**B- /7.5**	3.02 /85	2.36 /81	3.83 /76	**B- / 7.5**	47	5
MUS	AI KS Tax-Exempt Bond A	IKSTX	**A**	(866) 410-2006	11.18	**B- /7.5**	2.40 /80	2.89 /87	3.95 /77	**B- / 7.2**	60	16
MUS	Dupree TN Tax-Free Sh-to-Med	TTSMX	**A**	(800) 866-0614	10.88	**C+ /6.8**	1.97 /77	1.37 /64	2.18 /51	**B+ / 8.6**	45	12
MUS	Weitz Nebraska Tax Free Income	WNTFX	**A**	(800) 232-4161	10.12	**C+ /6.1**	1.20 /70	1.22 /59	2.35 /55	**B+ / 8.9**	54	31
MUS	Vanguard NY Long-Term	VNYTX	**A-**	(800) 662-7447	12.03	**A+ /9.8**	4.85 /98	4.36 /97	5.94 /92	**C / 4.3**	78	3
MUS	T Rowe Price CA Tax Free Bond	PRXCX	**A-**	(800) 638-5660	11.77	**A+ /9.8**	4.56 /97	4.39 /97	6.82 /96	**C- / 3.9**	74	13
MUS	Vanguard PA Long-Term	VPAIX	**A-**	(800) 662-7447	11.79	**A+ /9.7**	4.31 /96	4.27 /97	5.95 /92	**C / 4.3**	75	5

• Denotes fund is closed to new investors

Data as of March 31, 2016

99 Pct = Best *0 Pct = Worst*						PERFORMANCE				RISK	FUND MGR	
							Annualized Total Return Through 3/31/16					
Fund Type	Fund Name	Ticker Symbol	Overall Investment Rating	Phone	Net Asset Value As of 3/31/16	Perform-ance Rating/Pts	1Yr / Pct	3Yr / Pct	5Yr / Pct	Risk Rating/Pts	Mgr. Quality Pct	Mgr. Tenure (Years)
USL	Schwab Total Bond Market Fd	SWLBX	**B**	(800) 407-0256	9.61	**C+ /6.9**	1.58 /67	2.20 /66	3.46 /52	**C+ / 6.5**	85	18
USL	HC Capital US Govt FI Sec HC	HCUSX	**B**	(800) 242-9596	10.15	**C+ /6.3**	1.98 /72	1.76 /57	2.58 /39	**B- / 7.2**	76	6
USL	WesMark Govt Bond Fund	WMBDX	**C+**	(800) 341-7400	10.12	**C /5.3**	1.81 /70	1.21 /46	2.16 /33	**B- / 7.2**	56	18
USL	Rydex Govt Lg Bd 1.2x Strgy A	RYABX	**C-**	(800) 820-0888	58.50	**A+ /9.7**	0.11 /41	7.66 /99	12.92 /99	**E- / 0.0**	25	22
USL	Vanguard Long-Term Govt Bd Idx	VLGSX	**C-**	(800) 662-7447	26.97	**A+ /9.6**	2.76 /76	5.88 /95	9.43 /93	**E- / 0.2**	48	3
USL	PIMCO Long Term US Govt A	PFGAX	**C-**	(800) 426-0107	6.44	**B+ /8.7**	1.53 /67	4.97 /90	8.81 /90	**E- / 0.2**	24	9
USL	Dupree Interm Government Bond	DPIGX	**C-**	(800) 866-0614	10.57	**B- /7.4**	2.87 /76	2.38 /69	4.44 /67	**C- / 3.1**	64	17
USL	Loomis Sayles Infl Prot Sec Inst	LSGSX	**D-**	(800) 633-3330	10.51	**D- /1.5**	1.23 /62	-1.20 / 7	2.60 /39	**D+ / 2.3**	6	4
USL	American Century VP Infl Prot II	AIPTX	**D-**	(800) 345-6488	10.11	**D- /1.1**	-0.04 /31	-1.43 / 6	2.45 /37	**D+ / 2.6**	6	9
USL	• SunAmerica 2020 High Watermark	HWKAX	**D-**	(800) 858-8850	9.06	**E+ /0.9**	1.15 /61	0.14 /28	4.03 /62	**C- / 3.8**	13	12
USL	Vantagepoint Inflation Focused Inv	VPTSX	**E+**	(800) 669-7400	10.70	**D- /1.3**	0.87 /57	-1.45 / 6	2.22 /34	**D / 2.0**	6	8
USL	Deutsche Global Inflation A	TIPAX	**E**	(800) 728-3337	9.98	**E /0.5**	-0.25 /29	-1.80 / 5	1.78 /28	**D- / 1.3**	5	6

• Denotes fund is closed to new investors

	99 Pct = Best 0 Pct = Worst					PERFORMANCE				RISK	FUND MGR	
							Annualized Total Return Through 3/31/16					
Fund Type	Fund Name	Ticker Symbol	Overall Investment Rating	Phone	Net Asset Value As of 3/31/16	Performance Rating/Pts	1Yr / Pct	3Yr / Pct	5Yr / Pct	Risk Rating/Pts	Mgr. Quality Pct	Mgr. Tenure (Years)
USS	Guggenheim Investment Grade Bd	SIUSX	A	(800) 820-0888	17.94	B- /7.1	0.89 /57	3.94 /83	5.04 /72	B /8.1	98	4
USS	AMG Mgrs Intmd Duration Govt	MGIDX	A-	(800) 835-3879	10.95	B- /7.3	1.69 /69	2.71 /73	3.27 /49	B- /7.1	92	24
USS	Federated Govt Income Trust Inst	FICMX	A-	(800) 341-7400	10.36	C+ /6.3	1.59 /67	1.99 /61	2.56 /38	B+ /8.3	85	16
USS	BMO Mortgage Income Y	MRGIX	B+	(800) 236-3863	9.36	C+ /6.5	1.87 /71	2.06 /63	2.91 /44	B /7.8	81	4
USS	WA Mortgage Backed Securities A	SGVAX	B+	(877) 534-4627	10.71	C+ /5.6	0.37 /47	3.23 /78	4.58 /68	B+ /8.4	97	N/A
USS	Glenmede Core Fixed Income Port	GTCGX	B	(800) 442-8299	11.29	C+ /6.4	1.97 /72	1.84 /58	3.19 /48	B- /7.2	62	17
USS	TCW Core Fixed Income N	TGFNX	B	(800) 386-3829	11.16	C+ /6.1	0.95 /58	1.78 /57	3.72 /57	B /7.6	68	6
USS	Morgan Stanley Mortgage Sec Tr A	MTGAX	B	(800) 869-6397	8.33	C+ /5.9	0.94 /58	3.23 /78	4.96 /71	B /8.0	96	8
USS	Hartford US Govt Sec HLS Fd IA	HAUSX	B	(888) 843-7824	10.55	C+ /5.8	1.86 /70	1.55 /53	2.66 /40	B /8.1	60	4
USS	Invesco US Mortgage A	VKMGX	B	(800) 959-4246	12.35	C+ /5.6	2.37 /74	2.61 /72	3.34 /51	B /8.2	92	N/A
USS	Fidelity Intermediate Government	FSTGX	B	(800) 544-8544	10.77	C /5.5	1.75 /69	1.38 /50	2.41 /36	B+ /8.3	57	8
USS	DFA Short-Term Government Inst	DFFGX	B	(800) 984-9472	10.77	C /4.9	1.67 /68	1.11 /45	1.67 /27	B+ /8.9	71	28
USS	Schwab Short-Term Bond Market	SWBDX	B	(800) 407-0256	9.35	C /4.8	1.40 /65	1.05 /44	1.54 /26	A- /9.0	73	12
USS	Sit US Government Securities	SNGVX	B	(800) 332-5580	11.07	C /4.5	1.60 /68	0.85 /40	1.38 /24	A /9.3	79	29
USS	Columbia US Government	AUGAX	B-	(800) 345-6611	5.46	C /4.7	1.17 /61	1.99 /61	3.92 /60	B+ /8.6	90	7
USS	Vanguard Short-Term Federal Inv	VSGBX	B-	(800) 662-7447	10.82	C /4.5	1.36 /64	0.91 /41	1.38 /24	A- /9.2	73	11
USS	Fidelity Limited Term Government	FFXSX	B-	(800) 544-8544	10.11	C /4.4	1.09 /60	0.90 /41	1.36 /24	A- /9.0	61	8
USS	Vanguard Short-Term Gvt Bd Idx	VSBSX	B-	(800) 662-7447	20.40	C- /3.9	0.89 /57	0.68 /37	0.80 /19	A+ /9.7	76	3
USS	Touchstone Ut Sh Dr Fxd Inc Z	TSDOX	B-	(800) 543-0407	9.30	C- /3.6	0.63 /52	0.59 /35	1.00 /20	A+ /9.9	81	8
USS	MSIF Trust Core Plus Fix Inc A	MFXAX	C+	(800) 354-8185	10.61	B+ /8.3	4.43 /84	4.14 /85	5.45 /74	C- /3.3	97	5
USS	Principal Preferred Sec A	PPSAX	C+	(800) 222-5852	10.03	B /7.9	1.39 /65	4.72 /89	6.45 /79	C /4.4	99	14
USS	Nuveen Preferred Securities A	NPSAX	C+	(800) 257-8787	16.61	B- /7.5	1.39 /65	4.53 /88	7.18 /83	C /4.6	99	10
USS	DFA Intmdt Govt Fx Inc Inst	DFIGX	C+	(800) 984-9472	12.86	B- /7.5	3.45 /79	2.31 /68	3.98 /61	C /4.4	51	6
USS	Vanguard Intm-Term Govt Bd Idx	VSIGX	C+	(800) 662-7447	22.35	B- /7.0	3.01 /77	2.02 /62	3.72 /57	C /5.0	45	3
USS	USAA Income Fund	USAIX	C+	(800) 382-8722	12.88	C+ /6.5	0.26 /45	2.16 /65	4.02 /62	C+ /6.1	82	4
USS	SunAmerica VAL Co I Gov Sec Fd	VCGSX	C+	(800) 858-8850	10.85	C+ /6.3	2.17 /73	1.72 /56	3.67 /56	C /5.5	44	5
USS	Federated Tot Ret Gov Bond Svc	FTGSX	C+	(800) 341-7400	11.11	C /5.4	1.54 /67	1.24 /47	2.70 /40	B- /7.3	38	13
USS	American Funds US Govt Sec A	AMUSX	C+	(800) 421-0180	14.18	C /5.0	2.61 /75	1.98 /61	3.08 /46	B- /7.0	66	6
USS	Northern US Government	NOUGX	C+	(800) 595-9111	9.87	C /4.8	1.98 /72	0.90 /41	2.16 /33	B /8.0	35	10
USS	PACE Mtg Backed Sec Fixed Inc	PFXAX	C+	(888) 793-8637	13.02	C /4.4	1.77 /70	2.02 /62	2.67 /40	B /8.0	83	3
USS	Access Cap Community Invs A	ACASX	C+	(800) 422-2766	9.25	C /4.3	1.49 /66	1.79 /57	2.70 /40	B /8.2	79	10
USS	Morgan Stanley US Govt Sec Tr A	USGAX	C+	(800) 869-6397	8.85	C /4.3	1.52 /67	1.89 /59	3.33 /50	B /8.1	81	5
USS	Victory INCORE Fund For Income	IPFIX	C+	(800) 539-3863	9.91	C- /4.2	1.34 /64	1.21 /46	2.02 /31	B+ /8.6	60	10
USS	Homestead Short Term Govt Sec	HOSGX	C+	(800) 258-3030	5.23	C- /3.9	0.97 /58	0.66 /36	1.14 /22	A- /9.1	58	21
USS	Northern Short-Int US Govt	NSIUX	C+	(800) 595-9111	9.97	C- /3.9	1.37 /64	0.51 /33	1.22 /22	B+ /8.9	42	10
USS	AMF Short-US Government	ASITX	C+	(800) 527-3713	9.02	C- /3.8	0.57 /51	0.70 /37	1.11 /21	A- /9.2	N/A	7
USS	Commerce Short Term Govt	CFSTX	C+	(800) 995-6365	17.42	C- /3.7	0.73 /54	0.60 /35	1.28 /23	A- /9.1	55	22
USS	SEI Daily Inc Tr-Sh Dur Gov Bd A	TCSGX	C+	(800) 342-5734	10.51	C- /3.6	0.61 /52	0.54 /34	0.98 /20	A /9.3	59	13
USS	J Hancock Sh Tm Govt Inc NAV		C+	(800) 257-3336	9.65	C- /3.6	0.81 /55	0.49 /33	1.05 /21	A- /9.1	52	N/A
USS	Payden US Government Adv	PYUWX	C+	(888) 409-8007	10.65	C- /3.6	0.49 /49	0.55 /34	1.19 /22	A- /9.0	48	N/A
USS	Thornburg Limited Term US Govt A	LTUSX	C+	(800) 847-0200	13.28	C- /3.6	1.17 /61	0.80 /39	1.53 /26	B+ /8.8	51	9
USS	LWAS DFA Two Year Government	DFYGX	C+	(800) 984-9472	9.88	C- /3.4	0.51 /50	0.44 /32	0.56 /18	A+ /9.8	71	N/A
USS	BNY Mellon ST US Gov Sec M	MPSUX	C+	(800) 645-6561	11.84	C- /3.2	0.59 /51	0.34 /30	0.37 /16	A+ /9.6	56	16
USS	RidgeWorth Seix US Gvt Sec U/S	SIGVX	C+	(888) 784-3863	10.03	D+ /2.8	-0.13 /30	0.26 /30	0.73 /19	A+ /9.9	73	10
USS	BlackRock US Govt Bond Inv A	CIGAX	C	(800) 441-7762	10.70	C /4.3	1.21 /62	1.81 /58	2.88 /43	B- /7.4	62	7
USS	Fidelity Adv Govt Inc A	FVIAX	C	(800) 522-7297	10.56	C- /4.2	1.59 /67	1.71 /56	2.97 /44	B- /7.1	53	9
USS	Wells Fargo Govt Secs A	SGVDX	C	(800) 222-8222	11.38	C- /4.1	1.55 /67	1.82 /58	2.89 /43	B- /7.4	60	6
USS	Goldman Sachs Govt Income A	GSGOX	C	(800) 526-7384	15.03	C- /4.0	1.66 /68	1.53 /53	2.62 /39	B /8.0	57	3
USS	Sterling Capital Interm US Govt A	BGVAX	C	(800) 228-1872	10.24	C- /3.9	1.13 /61	1.05 /44	2.17 /33	B /8.2	44	13
USS	Federated Fund for US Govt Sec A	FUSGX	C	(800) 341-7400	7.54	C- /3.8	1.30 /63	1.79 /57	2.44 /37	B /8.2	80	13
USS	J Hancock Government Inc A	JHGIX	C	(800) 257-3336	9.64	C- /3.7	1.23 /62	1.54 /53	2.94 /44	B /8.1	62	18
USS	Franklin US Government Sec A	FKUSX	C	(800) 342-5236	6.37	C- /3.4	1.05 /59	1.59 /54	2.48 /38	B+ /8.4	83	23

• Denotes fund is closed to new investors

Data as of March 31, 2016

Fund Type	Fund Name (99 Pct = Best, 0 Pct = Worst)	Ticker Symbol	Overall Investment Rating	Phone	Net Asset Value As of 3/31/16	PERFORMANCE: Performance Rating/Pts	Annualized Total Return Through 3/31/16: 1Yr / Pct	3Yr / Pct	5Yr / Pct	RISK: Risk Rating/Pts	FUND MGR: Mgr. Quality Pct	Mgr. Tenure (Years)
USA	SEI Daily Inc Tr-GNMA Bond A	SEGMX	**B+**	(800) 342-5734	10.84	**B- /7.2**	1.86 /71	2.52 /71	3.42 /52	**B- / 7.0**	87	1
USA	Vanguard GNMA Inv	VFIIX	**B+**	(800) 662-7447	10.79	**B- /7.1**	2.18 /73	2.45 /70	3.35 /51	**B- / 7.1**	87	10
USA	Fidelity GNMA Fund	FGMNX	**B+**	(800) 544-8544	11.64	**C+ /6.6**	1.97 /72	2.19 /65	3.40 /51	**B- / 7.3**	84	12
USA	Schwab GNMA	SWGSX	**B+**	(800) 407-0256	10.21	**C+ /6.6**	2.21 /73	2.04 /62	3.00 /45	**B- / 7.3**	80	13
USA	USAA Government Securities Fund	USGNX	**B+**	(800) 382-8722	10.01	**C+ /6.0**	1.52 /67	1.75 /57	2.51 /38	**B+ / 8.5**	81	4
USA	T Rowe Price GNMA	PRGMX	**B**	(800) 638-5660	9.50	**C+ /5.9**	1.53 /67	1.71 /56	2.79 /42	**B / 7.8**	77	8
USA	Voya GNMA Income A	LEXNX	**B**	(800) 992-0180	8.63	**C /5.5**	2.21 /73	2.07 /63	3.10 /47	**B+ / 8.3**	87	7
USA	Payden GNMA Adv	PYGWX	**B-**	(888) 409-8007	9.81	**C+ /5.9**	1.77 /70	1.67 /55	3.02 /45	**B- / 7.3**	71	N/A
USA	PIMCO GNMA A	PAGNX	**C**	(800) 426-0107	11.36	**C- /4.1**	1.58 /67	1.70 /56	2.99 /45	**B / 7.7**	76	4
USA	ProFunds-US Government Plus	GVPSX	**C-**	(888) 776-3637	53.63	**A /9.3**	-2.08 /15	5.21 /92	10.55 /96	**E- / 0.0**	5	7
USA	Dreyfus GNMA Fund A	GPGAX	**C-**	(800) 782-6620	15.33	**C- /3.3**	1.58 /67	1.42 /50	2.56 /38	**B / 7.9**	66	1
USA	American Century Ginnie Mae A	BGNAX	**C-**	(800) 345-6488	10.80	**C- /3.0**	1.27 /63	1.32 /49	2.53 /38	**B / 7.9**	59	10
USA	Deutsche GNMA A	GGGGX	**D+**	(800) 728-3337	14.13	**D+ /2.9**	1.02 /59	0.81 /39	2.23 /34	**C+ / 6.7**	41	14

• Denotes fund is closed to new investors

99 Pct = Best *0 Pct = Worst* Fund Type	Fund Name	Ticker Symbol	**Overall Investment Rating**	Phone	Net Asset Value As of 3/31/16	**PERFORMANCE** **Perform-ance Rating/Pts**	Annualized Total Return Through 3/31/16 1Yr / Pct	3Yr / Pct	5Yr / Pct	**RISK** **Risk Rating/Pts**	**FUND MGR** Mgr. Quality Pct	Mgr. Tenure (Years)
US	Fidelity Spartan S/T TyBd In Inv	FSBIX	**B-**	(800) 544-8544	10.54	**C /4.6**	1.39 /65	0.94 /41	1.37 /24	**A- / 9.0**	70	2
US	Vanguard Short-Term Treasury Inv	VFISX	**B-**	(800) 662-7447	10.76	**C- /4.1**	1.15 /61	0.73 /38	1.07 /21	**A / 9.3**	74	16
US	Northern US Treasury Index	BTIAX	**C+**	(800) 637-1380	22.13	**C+ /6.7**	2.25 /73	1.97 /61	3.40 /52	**C+ / 6.0**	57	7
US	Columbia US Treasury Index A	LUTAX	**C+**	(800) 345-6611	11.37	**C+ /6.2**	1.92 /71	1.68 /55	3.12 /47	**C+ / 6.2**	48	6
US	Dreyfus US Treasury Intermediate	DRGIX	**C+**	(800) 645-6561	13.46	**C /4.4**	1.56 /67	0.71 /37	1.85 /29	**B+ / 8.4**	39	8
US	US Global Inv Govt Ultra-Short	UGSDX	**C+**	(800) 873-8637	2.01	**C- /3.3**	0.38 /48	0.44 /32	0.27 /16	**A- / 9.2**	64	27
US	GMO US Treasury	GUSTX	**C+**		25.01	**D+ /2.8**	0.26 /45	0.15 /28	0.13 /15	**A+ / 9.9**	72	2
US	RidgeWorth Seix Ltd Dur I	SAMLX	**C+**	(888) 784-3863	9.83	**D+ /2.8**	0.25 /45	0.21 /29	0.46 /17	**A+ / 9.9**	74	14
US	Vanguard Interm-Term Treasury	VFITX	**C**	(800) 662-7447	11.59	**C+ /6.8**	3.06 /77	1.91 /60	3.70 /57	**C / 4.6**	46	15
US	Invesco Sh Dur Infl Pro A	LMTAX	**C**	(800) 959-4246	10.60	**C- /3.0**	1.83 /70	0.53 /34	0.47 /17	**A / 9.4**	74	7
US	Vanguard Extnd Durtn Trea Idx Inst	VEDTX	**C-**	(800) 662-7447	37.90	**A+ /9.9**	1.34 /64	8.82 /99	15.40 /99	**E- / 0.0**	12	3
US	Vanguard Long-Term Treasury Inv	VUSTX	**C-**	(800) 662-7447	13.11	**A+ /9.6**	2.54 /75	5.83 /95	9.46 /93	**E- / 0.1**	24	15
US	Wasatch Hoisington US Treasury	WHOSX	**C-**	(800) 551-1700	18.59	**A+ /9.6**	0.87 /57	6.80 /97	11.69 /98	**E- / 0.0**	21	20
US	Fidelity Spartan Lg-T Tre Bd In Inv	FLBIX	**C-**	(800) 544-8544	13.73	**A /9.5**	2.50 /75	5.81 /94	9.46 /93	**E- / 0.1**	22	2
US	T Rowe Price US Treas Long-Term	PRULX	**C-**	(800) 638-5660	13.52	**A /9.3**	2.21 /73	5.08 /91	8.75 /90	**E- / 0.2**	15	13
US	Dreyfus US Treasury Long Term	DRGBX	**C-**	(800) 645-6561	20.54	**A /9.3**	2.10 /72	5.03 /91	8.77 /90	**E- / 0.2**	19	8
US	Direxion Mo 7-10 Year Tr Bl 2X Inv	DXKLX	**C-**	(800) 851-0511	37.17	**B+ /8.8**	4.67 /85	3.44 /79	9.02 /91	**E- / 0.2**	6	10
US	Fidelity Spartan Intrm Treasury Inv	FIBIX	**C-**	(800) 544-8544	11.25	**B- /7.4**	3.39 /78	2.18 /65	4.60 /69	**C- / 3.0**	32	2
US	T Rowe Price US Treas Intmdt	PRTIX	**C-**	(800) 638-5660	5.98	**C+ /6.2**	2.87 /76	1.48 /52	3.52 /53	**C- / 4.2**	28	9
US	WA Short-Term Bond A	SBSTX	**C-**	(877) 534-4627	3.85	**D /1.8**	0.10 /41	0.55 /34	1.11 /21	**A+ / 9.6**	76	4
US	JPMorgan Treasury and Agency A	OTABX	**C-**	(800) 480-4111	9.43	**D /1.6**	0.73 /54	0.24 /29	0.56 /17	**A / 9.3**	49	11
US	Permanent Portfolio Short-Tm	PRTBX	**C-**	(800) 531-5142	64.81	**D- /1.2**	-0.49 /26	-0.59 /11	-0.59 / 2	**A+ / 9.9**	40	13
US	American Century Zero Cpn 2020	BTTTX	**D+**	(800) 345-6488	103.91	**C+ /5.7**	2.31 /74	1.27 /48	5.58 /75	**C- / 3.1**	16	10
US	Frost Kempner Treasury and Inc	FIKTX	**D**	(866) 777-7818	10.04	**D /1.6**	0.34 /47	-0.85 / 9	1.84 /29	**C- / 4.0**	7	10
US	DFA Infltn Protected Sec Port Inst	DIPSX	**D-**	(800) 984-9472	11.95	**D+ /2.8**	1.88 /71	-0.84 / 9	3.24 /49	**D- / 1.3**	5	10
US	T Rowe Price Infla-Protect Bond	PRIPX	**D-**	(800) 638-5660	11.95	**D /1.7**	1.20 /62	-1.01 / 8	2.54 /38	**D+ / 2.4**	6	14
US	Harbor Real Return Inst	HARRX	**E+**	(800) 422-1050	9.21	**E+ /0.9**	-0.26 /28	-1.88 / 5	2.21 /34	**D- / 1.3**	4	11
US	Hartford Inflation Plus A	HIPAX	**E+**	(888) 843-7824	10.83	**E /0.4**	0.84 /56	-2.20 / 4	1.90 /30	**C- / 3.0**	4	1
US	American Century Str Inf Opp Fd A	ASIDX	**E+**	(800) 345-6488	9.17	**E- /0.1**	-4.78 / 5	-3.94 / 2	-2.91 / 1	**D+ / 2.6**	4	6
US	Direxion Mo 7-10 Year Tr Br 2X Inv	DXKSX	**E-**	(800) 851-0511	29.47	**E- /0.0**	-9.93 / 1	-8.96 / 0	-14.53 / 0	**E- / 0.2**	11	12

Appendix

What is a Mutual Fund?

Picking individual stocks is difficult and buying individual bonds can be expensive. Mutual funds were introduced to allow the small investor to participate in the stock and bond market for just a small initial investment. Mutual funds are pools of stocks or bonds that are managed by investment professionals. First, an investment company organizes the fund and collects the money from investors. The company then takes that money and pays a portfolio manager to invest it in stocks, bonds, money market instruments and other types of securities.

Most funds fit within one of two main categories, open-ended funds or closed-end funds. Open-ended funds issue new shares when investors put in money and redeem shares when investors withdraw money. The price of a share is determined by dividing the total net assets of the fund by the number of shares outstanding.

On the other hand, closed-end funds issue a fixed number of shares in an initial public offering, trading thereafter in the open market like a stock. Open-end funds are the most common type of mutual fund. Investing in either class of funds means you own a share of the portfolio, so you participate in the fund's gains and losses.

There are more than 20,000 different mutual funds, each with a stated investment objective. Here are descriptions for five of the most popular types of funds:

Stock funds: A mutual fund which invests mainly in stocks. These funds are more actively traded than other more conservative funds. The stocks chosen may vary widely according to the fund's investment strategy.

Bond funds: A mutual fund which invests in bonds, in an effort to provide stable income while preserving principal as much as possible. These funds invest in medium- to long-term bonds issued by corporations and governments.

Index funds: A mutual fund that aims to match the performance of a specific index, such as the S&P 500. Index funds tend to have fewer expenses than other funds because portfolio decisions are automatic and transactions are infrequent.

Balanced funds: A mutual fund that buys a combination of stocks and bonds, in order to supply both income and capital growth while ensuring a minimal amount of risk for investors.

Money market funds: An open-end mutual fund which invests only in stable, short-term securities. The fund's value remains at a constant $1 per share, but only those administered by banks are government insured.

Investing in a mutual fund has several advantages over owning a single stock or bond. For example, funds offer instant portfolio diversification by giving you ownership of many stocks or bonds simultaneously. This diversification protects you in case a part of your investment takes a sudden downturn. You also get the benefit of having a professional handling your investment, though a management fee is charged for these services, typically 1% or 2% a year. You should be aware that the fund may also levy other fees and that you will likely have to pay a sales commission (known as a load) if you purchase the fund from a financial adviser.

The fund manager's strategy is laid out in the fund's prospectus, which is the official name for the legal document that contains financial information about the fund, including its history, its officers and its performance. Mutual fund investments are fully liquid so you can easily get in or out by just placing an order through a broker.

Investor Profile Quiz

We recognize that each person approaches his or her investment decisions from a unique perspective. A mutual fund that is perfect for someone else may be totally inappropriate for you due to factors such as:

- How much risk you are comfortable taking
- Your age and the number of years you have before retirement
- Your income level and tax rate
- Your other existing investments and personal net worth
- Preconceived expectations about investment performance

The following quiz will help you quantify your tolerance for risk based on your own personal life situation. As you read through each question, circle the letter next to the single answer that you feel most accurately describes your current position. Keep in mind that there are no "correct" answers to this quiz, only answers that are helpful in assessing your investment style. So don't worry about how your answer might be perceived by others; just try to be as honest and accurate as possible.

Then at the end of the quiz, use the point totals listed on the right side of the page to compute your test score. Once you've added up your total points, refer to the corresponding investor profile for an evaluation of your personal risk tolerance. Each profile also lists the page number where you will find the top performing mutual funds matching your risk profile.

		Points	Your Score
1.	I am currently investing to pay for:		
	a. Retirement	0 pts	
	b. College	0 pts	
	c. A house	0 pts	
2.	I expect I will need to liquidate some or all of this investment in:		
	a. 2 years or less	0 pts	
	b. 2 to 5 years	5 pts	
	c. 5 to 10 years	8 pts	
	d. 10 years or more	10 pts	
3.	My age group is		
	a. Under 30	10 pts	
	b. 30 to 44	9 pts	
	c. 45 to 60	7 pts	
	d. 60 to 74	5 pts	
	e. 75 and older	1 pts	
4.	I am currently looking to invest money through:		
	a. An IRA or other tax-deferred account	0 pts	
	b. A fully taxable account	0 pts	

5. I have a cash reserve equal to 3 to 6 months expenses.		
a. Yes	10 pts	
b. No	1 pts	
6. My primary source of income is:		
a. Salary and other earnings from my primary occupation	7 pts	
b. Earnings from my investment portfolio	5 pts	
c. Retirement pension and/or Social Security	3 pts	
7. I will need regular income from this investment now or in the near future.		
a. Yes	6 pts	
b. No	10 pts	
8. Over the long run, I expect this investment to average returns of:		
a. 8% annually or less	0 pts	
b. 8% to 12% annually	6 pts	
c. 12% to 15% annually	8 pts	
d. 15% to 20% annually	10 pts	
e. Over 20% annually	18 pts	
9. The worst loss I would be comfortable accepting on my investment is:		
a. Less than 5%. Stability of principal is very important to me.	1 pts	
b. 5% to 10%. Modest periodic declines are acceptable.	3 pts	
c. 10% to 15%. I understand that there may be losses in the short run but over the long term, higher risk investments will offer highest returns.	8 pts	
d. Over 15%. You don't get high returns without taking risk. I'm looking for maximum capital gains and understand that my funds can substantially decline.	15 pts	
10. If the bond market were to suddenly decline by 15%, which of the following would most likely be your reaction?		
a. I should have left the market long ago, at the first sign of trouble.	3 pts	
b. I should have substantially exited the bond market by now to limit my exposure.	5 pts	
c. I'm still in the bond market but I've got my finger on the trigger.	7 pts	
d. I'm staying fully invested so I'll be ready for the next bull market.	10 pts	
11. The best defense against a bear market in bonds is:		
a. A defensive market timing system that avoids large losses.	4 pts	
b. A potent offense that will make big gains in the next bond bull market.	10 pts	
12. The best strategy to employ during bear markets is:		
a. Move to cash. It's the only safe hiding place.	5 pts	
b. Short the market and try to make a profit as it declines.	10 pts	
c. Wait it out because the market will eventually recover.	8 pts	

13. I would classify myself as:				
a. A buy-and-hold investor who rides out all the peaks and valleys.			10 pts	
b. A market timer who wants to capture the major bull markets.			7 pts	
c. A market timer who wants to avoid the major bear markets.			5 pts	
14. My attitude regarding trading activity is:				
a. Active trading is costly and unproductive.			0 pts	
b. I don't mind frequent trades as long as I'm making money			2 pts	
c. Occasional trading is okay but too much activity is not good.			1 pts	
15. If the 30-year U.S. Treasury Bond advanced strongly over the last 12 months, my investment should have:				
a. Grown even more than the market.			10 pts	
b. Approximated the performance of the broad market.			5 pts	
c. Focused on reducing the risk of loss in a bond bear market, even if it meant giving up some upside potential in the bull market.			2 pts	
16. I have experience (extensive, some, or none) with the following types of investments.	Extensive	Some	None	
a. U.S. stocks or stock mutual funds	2 pts	1 pts	0 pts	
b. International stock funds	2 pts	1 pts	0 pts	
c. Bonds or bond funds	1 pts	0 pts	0 pts	
d. Futures and/or options	5 pts	3 pts	0 pts	
e. Managed futures or funds	3 pts	1 pts	0 pts	
f. Real estate	2 pts	1 pts	0 pts	
g. Private hedge funds	3 pts	1 pts	0 pts	
h. Privately managed accounts	2 pts	1 pts	0 pts	
17. Excluding my primary residence, this investment represents ___% of my investment holdings.				
a. Less than 5%			10 pts	
b. 5% to 10%			7 pts	
c. 10% to 20%			5 pts	
d. 20% to 30%			3 pts	
e. 30% or more			1 pts	
			TOTAL	

Under 58 pts	**Very Conservative.** You appear to be very risk averse with capital preservation as your primary goal. As such, most bond mutual funds may be a little too risky for your taste, especially in a turbulent market environment. We would recommend you stick to the safest bond and money market mutual funds where your income stream is predictable and more secure. To find them, turn to pages 484 - 485 listing the top performing fixed income mutual funds receiving a risk rating in the A (Excellent) range, our best risk rating.
58 to 77 pts	**Conservative.** Based on your responses, it appears that you are more concerned about minimizing the risk to your principal than you are about maximizing your returns. Don't worry, there are plenty of good mutual funds that offer strong returns with very little volatility. As a starting point, we recommend you turn to pages 486 – 487 where you will find a list of the top performing funds receiving a risk rating in the B (Good) range.
78 to 108 pts	**Moderate.** You are prepared to take on a little added risk in order to enhance your investment returns. This is probably the most common approach to mutual fund investing. To select a mutual fund matching your style, we recommend you turn to pages 488 - 489. There you can easily pick from the top performing mutual funds receiving a risk rating in the C (Fair) range.
109 to 129 pts	**Aggressive.** You appear to be ready to ride out almost any financial storm on your way toward maximizing your investment returns. You understand that the only way to make large returns on your investments is by taking on added risk, and your personal situation seems to allow for that approach. We recommend you use pages 488 - 491 as a starting point for selecting a high performing mutual fund with a risk rating in the C (Fair) or D (Weak) range.
Over 129 pts	**Very Aggressive.** Based on your responses, you appear to be leaning heavily toward speculation. Your primary concern is maximizing your investment growth, and you are prepared to take on as much risk as necessary in order to do so. To this end, turn to page 492 - 493 where you'll find the highest performing mutual funds with a risk rating in the E (Very Weak) range. These investments have historically been extremely volatile, oftentimes investing in bonds that are currently out of favor. As such, they are highly speculative investments that could provide superior results if you can stomach the volatility and uncertainty. For a list of the top performing bond mutual funds regardless of risk category, turn to page 464. Also see Section VII in *TheStreet Ratings Guide to Stock Mutual Funds* and Section VI in *TheStreet Ratings Guide to Common Stocks*.

Performance Benchmarks

The following benchmarks represent the average performance for all mutual funds within each bond or money market fund type category. Comparing an individual mutual fund's returns to these benchmarks is yet another way to assess its performance. For the top performing funds within each of the following categories, turn to Section VIII, Top-Rated Bond Mutual Funds by Fund Type, beginning on page 500. You can also use this information to compare the average performance of one category of funds to another (updated through March 31, 2016).

		3 Month Total Return %	1 Year Total Return %	Refer to page:
COH	Corporate - High Yield	2.09%	-3.86%	500
COI	Corporate - Investment Grade	2.33%	0.36%	501
EM	Emerging Market Income	5.46%	-0.63%	502
GEI	General Bd - Investment Grade	2.17%	0.16%	503
GEL	General Bd - Long	1.93%	-1.73%	504
GEN	Multi-Sector Bond	1.04%	-2.27%	
GES	General Bd - Short & Interm	1.61%	-1.33%	505
GL	Global Income	2.85%	-1.16%	506
LP	Loan Participation	1.18%	-2.01%	507
MM	Taxable Money Market	0.04%	0.06%	508
MMT	Tax Free Money Market	0.02%	0.03%	
MTG	General Mortgage	1.31%	0.91%	509
MUH	Municipal - High Yield	1.99%	4.38%	510
MUI	Municipal - Insured	1.19%	2.44%	511
MUN	Municipal - National	1.27%	2.83%	512
MUS	Municipal - Single State	1.43%	3.06%	513
US	US Treasury	3.43%	1.12%	517
USA	US Government/Agency	1.47%	1.03%	516
USL	US Government - Long	4.05%	1.06%	514
USS	US Government - Short & Interm	1.57%	0.55%	515

Fund Type Descriptions

COH - Corporate - High Yield - Seeks high current income by investing a minimum of 65% of its assets in generally low-quality corporate debt issues.

COI - Corporate - Investment Grade - Seeks current income by investing a minimum of 65% in investment grade corporate debt issues. Investment grade securities must be BBB or higher, as rated by Standard & Poor's.

EM - Emerging Market - Seeks income by investing in income producing securities from emerging market countries.

GEN - General - Seeks income by investing without geographic boundary in corporate debt, government debt or preferred securities. Investments are not tied to any specific maturity or duration.

GEI - General - Investment Grade - Seeks income by investing in investment grade domestic or foreign corporate debt, government debt and preferred securities.

GEL - General - Long Term - Seeks income by investing in corporate debt, government debt and preferred securities with maturities over 10 years or an average duration over 6 years.

GES - General - Short & Intermediate Term - Seeks income by investing in corporate debt, government debt and preferred securities with an average maturity under 10 years or an average duration under 6 years.

GL - Global - Invests a minimum of 65% in fixed income securities issued by domestic and/or foreign governments.

LP - Loan Participation - Invests a minimum of 65% of its assets in loan interests.

MM - Money Market - Seeks income and stability by investing in high-quality, short-term obligations issued by the U.S. Government, corporations, financial institutions, and other entities.

MMT - Money Market - Tax Free - Seeks tax-free income and stability by investing in high-quality, short-term obligations which are exempt from federal and the taxation of a specified state.

MTG - Mortgage - Invests a minimum of 65% of its assets in a broad range of mortgage or mortgage-related securities, including those issued by the U.S. government and by government related and private organizations.

MUH - Municipal - High Yield - Seeks tax-free income by investing a minimum of 65% of its assets in generally low-quality issues from any state municipality.

MUI - Municipal - Insured - Seeks federally tax-free income by investing a minimum of 65% of its assets in municipal debt obligations that are insured as to timely payment of principal and interest.

MUN - Municipal - National - Seeks federally tax-free income by investing at least 65% in issues from any state municipality.

MUS - Municipal - Single State - Seeks tax-free income by investing in issues which are exempt from federal and the taxation of a specified state.

USL - U.S. Government - Long Term - Invests a minimum of 65% in securities issued or guaranteed by the Government, its agencies or instrumentalities with maturities over 10 years or an average duration over 6 years.

USS - U.S. Government - Short and Intermediate Term - Invests a minimum of 65% in securities issued or guaranteed by the Government, its agencies or instrumentalities with maturities under 10 years or an average duration under 6 years.

USA - U.S. Government - Agency - Invests a minimum of 65% in securities issued or guaranteed by the Government, its agencies or instrumentalities. Investments are not tied to any specific maturity or duration.

US - U.S. Government - Treasury - Invests a minimum of 65% of its assets in securities issued and backed by the full faith and credit of the U.S. government.

Share Class Descriptions

Many mutual funds have several classes of shares, each with different fees and associated sales charges. While there is no official standardization of mutual fund classes we have compiled a list of those most frequently seen. Ultimately you must consult a fund's prospectus for particular share class designations and what they mean. Federal regulation requires that the load, or sales charge, not exceed 8.5% of the investment purchase.

Class	Description
A	**Front End Load**. Sales charge is paid at the time of purchase and is deducted from the investment amount.
B	**Back End Load**. Also known as contingent deferred sales charge (CDSC); the sales charge is imposed if the fund is sold. Class B shares usually convert to Class A shares after six to eight years from the date of purchase.
C	**Level Load**. A set sales charge paid annually for as long as the fund is held. This class is especially beneficial to the short–term investor.
D	**Flexible.** Class D shares can be anything a fund company wants. Check the fund prospectus for the details regarding a specific fund's fee structure.
I	**Institutional**. No sales charge is collected due to the size of the order. This class usually requires a minimum investment of $100,000.
M	**Mid Load**. Similar to Class A, but with a lower front end load and higher expense ratio (see page 19 for more information on expense ratios).
N	**No Load.** No sales fee is imposed.
R	**No Load**. No sales fee is imposed and fund must be held in a qualified retirement account.
T	**Mid Load**. Similar to Class A, but with a lower front end load and higher expense ratio (see page 19 for more information on expense ratios).
Y	**Institutional**. No sales charge is collected due to the size of the order. This class usually requires a minimum investment of $100,000.
Z	**No Load**. Fund is only available for purchase to employees of the mutual fund company, as an employee benefit. No sales fee is imposed.